FAMILY LEGAL GUIDE

Reader's Digest

FAMILY LEGAL GUIDE

A COMPLETE ENCYCLOPEDIA
OF LAW FOR THE LAYMAN

THE READER'S DIGEST ASSOCIATION, INC.
PLEASANTVILLE, N.Y. ▪ MONTREAL

READER'S DIGEST PROJECT STAFF

Editor: Inge N. Dobelis

Art Editor: Anita Volli

Associate Project Editor: Letitia B. Kehoe

Associate Editors: Sharon Fass, Ruth Goldeman, Robert V. Huber

Index Editor: Georgea Pace

Art Associate: Janet G. Tenenzaph

Copy Editors: Zahava Feldman, Diana Marsh, Elaine Pearlmutter

Assistant Indexer: Leslie Simmons

Editorial Assistant: Lisa B. Mevorach

Chart Typist: Grace Del Bagno

With special assistance from Associate Editor David Rattray

Contributing Editors: Robert Bahr, Maurie Sommer, Charles S. Verral, John von Hartz

Contributing Art Associate: Henrietta Stern

Contributing Copy Editors: Kathleen M. Berger, Ellane Hoose

WEST PUBLISHING COMPANY

Legal Editorial Staff for Special Projects

This work was prepared by the editors of Reader's Digest from materials supplied by the editorial staff of West Publishing Company and is based in part on existing materials copyrighted by West Publishing Company. Although great care has been exercised in the preparation of the manuscript, the West editorial staff cannot assume responsibility for its total accuracy.

Contents

How to Use This Book

FAMILY LEGAL GUIDE is arranged in alphabetical order so that you can use the book in the same way you would any dictionary or encyclopedia. Simply look up the word you want in the A–Z section of the book. The titles of all of the 2,600 articles are printed in large brown type to help you spot the one you want quickly and easily.

If the topic you are looking for is not one of these A–Z articles, it does not mean that the subject is not covered in the book—legal terms are often very different from ordinary everyday language. Turn to the special index at the back of the book, which will lead you from an everyday word or phrase to the article or articles that will give you the legal information you need.

Use of the index   There is no article in the A–Z section for the word *loan*, for example, but if you look up *loan* in the index, one of the articles to which it will send you is **secured transaction,** which is the legal term for a loan in which you pledge personal property as collateral. The index will also list all the other articles in which loans are discussed, such as **banks and banking, consumer protection,** and **credit.**

As another example, let us say you had an accident while driving a borrowed car. If you look up the word "automobile" in the index, you will find a reference to "automobile—borrowed car." This will take you to the article **bailment,** where such a situation is discussed.

Organization of articles for easy reference   As you turn through the pages of the book's A–Z section, you will notice that the longer articles have been divided by headings into short, easily identifiable sections. If the discussion under a particular section is fairly long, the topic is further broken down into two or more subheadings, each of which may have still other subheadings.

For example, the first heading in the article **consumer protection,** on page 202, is ■ **Terms of a consumer transaction.** The black square before the heading means it is a major heading. The boldface subheadings below it without the square—from **Credit** to **Refinancing**—discuss the different terms of a consumer transaction. Topics covered in even greater detail below a subheading are headed by boldface italic titles, such as *Express warranties* and *Implied warranties* under the subheading **Warranties.**

If you look at this sequence in reverse, you will see that express and implied warranties are two types of warranties, that a warranty is a term of a consumer transaction, and that the terms of a consumer transaction are a topic under the entry **consumer protection.**

After all the terms of a consumer transaction have been discussed, another general heading is introduced by a black square: ■ **Service contract.** This cycle of general headings and specific subheadings is repeated until all the topics under **consumer protection** have been covered.

If the article is a very long one, as is **consumer protection,** you should be able to spot the specific subjects you want simply by glancing through the article for the appropriate heading.

Case histories—the law in everyday life   If you now turn to the top of page 203, you will see two examples distinctively marked with a brown key: EXAMPLE O⟶✳. Hundreds of these key examples appear throughout the book to explain and dramatize how the law works in everyday, real-life situations. A key example may be an actual case whose outcome has been decided by a court, or it may be a hypothetical case created especially to illustrate or clarify a particular legal point for you.

Summary boxes—highlights of the law   You will also see on page 203 a large box entitled "Your Rights as a Consumer." Boxes such as this one summarize the key points of long articles. You may find it helpful to read the box information as a quick reference guide to the subject before reading the entry or to reread it afterward as a brief summary of the major points of the subject.

Cross-references for complete coverage   Throughout the text you will see words printed in small capital letters—for example, "See CREDIT," or "Read the terms of your contract regarding CREDIT payments." These are cross-references, and they identify additional entries that supply more information on the same topic or are related to the one you are reading.

The law in your state   At the back of the book, following the A–Z section, are 34 charts and tables outlining many of the important laws of the 50 states and the District of Columbia. Throughout FAMILY LEGAL GUIDE you will find references to these charts—for example, in **consumer protection** there is a reference to Chart 9, which covers the laws on the garnishment of wages. The charts are also indexed.

Although the charts are based on the most up-to-date law digests available, there are two reasons why you should not act in reliance on the information in them without first confirming its accuracy with a lawyer or the proper state agency. First, laws are frequently changed, and the statutes on which these charts are based may have been revised since this book went to press. Second, in order for the information to be presented in chart form, the editors have had to simplify very complicated statutes and thus could not possibly spell out all the specific details of a law, its interpretations, or its impact in a particular situation.

Special articles of unusual interest   Seventeen special articles, written by experts in the areas of law they discuss, focus on the practical aspect of common legal situations you may face some time during your life—buying a house, condominium, or co-op; planning your estate to minimize taxes; writing your will; serving on a jury; starting or defending a civil lawsuit. These special articles appear together with the encyclopedia article to which they relate—for example, "Estate Planning: How to Settle Your Affairs" is found alongside the encyclopedia article **estate and gift tax.** The special articles are self-contained—you do not need to refer to the encyclopedia article to understand and benefit from them.

Introduction

THE LAW is part of our everyday lives. Usually we are hardly aware of it, as when we automatically stop at the street corner to wait for the traffic light to change. At other times we are more conscious that the law directs our actions. If we want to buy or sell a home, we must deal with the legalities of binder, contract, mortgage, title insurance, deed, and closing. On occasion, the law reaches into our lives forcefully and unexpectedly, as when a loved one dies without a will, and we find that state law, not the deceased person's wishes, determines how his or her property will be distributed.

As society and our lives become increasingly complex, we encounter more situations with legal implications. We marry, vote, send our children to school, buy insurance, and pay taxes according to the law. It also determines our rights and obligations when we buy on credit, apply for a job, seek admission to a professional school, or plan for financial security during retirement. If we are unlucky, we may even be brushed by criminal law—we may be robbed or mugged, or one of our children may be charged with a crime. With the law ever present in our lives, it is vital to know as much about it as we can. Although FAMILY LEGAL GUIDE is not a substitute for a lawyer, it can help you avoid trouble, inform you of your rights, help protect you when trouble does arise, and save you both time and money.

Avoiding legal problems If prevention is the best kind of medicine, it is also the best kind of law. It is too late to learn *after* you have signed a contract to buy a house that the oral agreement you made with the seller to throw in his power mower and leaf shredder should have been in the written document. Or to discover, when you finally decide to sue the dealer who sold you an "antique" he knew was a fake, that the statute of limitations (the time period for starting a lawsuit) has run out. It is too late to learn when the dead tree in your backyard falls on your neighbor's automobile that he can sue you for the damage caused. As you read FAMILY LEGAL GUIDE, you will learn to spot such legal pitfalls and to avoid them.

Knowing your rights and remedies Sometimes it is impossible to avoid legal entanglements. Your landlord wants your apartment for his mother-in-law and is trying to evict you. The dog you trained to scare off trespassers bites a houseguest. You lend your car to a friend who gets into an accident with it. You find yourself hopelessly in debt and faced with bankruptcy. You slip and hurt your ankle in a department store, the store nurse tapes it up, and a company official asks you to sign a form. Your husband or wife threatens to leave you and take the children. What can you do?

In these and thousands of other common and uncommon situations, FAMILY LEGAL GUIDE, the most comprehensive encyclopedia of law ever prepared specifically for the layman, provides you with the knowledge you need both before and after you hire a lawyer to counsel you on your problem. When you have, or think you may have, a legal problem, you can consult FAMILY LEGAL GUIDE to find out, for example, your rights as a tenant; your rights and duties as an animal owner; the pros and cons of bankruptcy and the alternatives to it; or what emergency measures can be taken when a spouse threatens to run away with the children.

Getting the most out of your lawyer When you do hire a lawyer, FAMILY LEGAL GUIDE will help you make the best use of his services. One problem people often encounter with lawyers is communication. Lawyers use terms that are strange to a layman. What is a "tort" or a "cloud on a title"? Or they use everyday words that have a different meaning in the law. "Negligent" may mean one thing when you are talking about your son's failure to keep his dentist's appointment. It has an entirely different and very precise meaning when a lawyer uses it to describe a driver in an automobile accident. FAMILY LEGAL GUIDE explains the technical language called legalese. The less time your lawyer spends in explanations, the more money you save, for a lawyer usually charges by the hour.

How the law works Just as it is important to understand the language of the law, it is important to understand how the law works. One of the best ways to obtain this understanding is through case histories. This is how law students learn the law, and FAMILY LEGAL GUIDE presents hundreds of histories—both case studies from real life and hypothetical examples—to show how the law operates.

Suppose someone breaks his contract with you. You are outraged and want to sue him for all he is worth. When your lawyer says you cannot do this, you may begin to doubt him, think he is not on your side. If you consult the pages of this book, you will find that it is a basic principle in suing for breach of contract that the plaintiff (the person suing) cannot be placed in a better position than he would have been in if the contract had been fulfilled. Case studies show how and when such rules of law apply.

Why you need a lawyer FAMILY LEGAL GUIDE is not a substitute for a lawyer's advice. There are a number of reasons for this. First, the law of the United States is not one body of law: it consists partly of state laws, partly of local ordinances, and partly of federal law—all of which constantly change. No single book dealing with the number of topics discussed in FAMILY LEGAL GUIDE could state the law as it applies everywhere. What FAMILY LEGAL GUIDE does tell you is the basics of the law—which states, for example, have community-property laws and what, generally, the implications of such laws are. But only a lawyer can tell you how the law may affect you in a particular situation.

Another reason FAMILY LEGAL GUIDE cannot replace a lawyer's advice is that the law is based not only on statutes (laws passed by legislatures) but on the common law (law that has developed over the years by usage and precedent). When a judge renders a decision, he establishes or bolsters a precedent; in handing down their judgments, judges look to the decisions of other judges in previous similar cases. But these precedents, too, vary from state to state. Only your lawyer will be able to tell you how the law might apply to your case.

As you use FAMILY LEGAL GUIDE, you will find that the law has evolved and grown over the centuries to serve you and your fellow citizens in resolving disputes and righting wrongs. Because it has been extended to apply to so many new and involved circumstances, the law is extremely complex and cannot be made simple. But you will also discover that you can learn many of its complexities. Reading about the law will equip you to cope better in a society that is intricately bound up in the law.

ABA See AMERICAN BAR ASSOCIATION.

abandonment Giving up something to which one is entitled; the act of forsaking, leaving, or totally deserting one's property. This article discusses the way in which a person gives up his title to (ownership of) or interest in property and the effects of such action. For a discussion of the abandonment of a husband or wife, see DIVORCE; for abandonment of children, see PARENTS AND CHILDREN.

■ **Distinguishing characteristics** Because it is voluntary, abandonment is different from the other ways in which you may give up ownership. You are not obliged to give up your interest; you do so simply because you no longer wish to possess the property. You do not pass your title (ownership) on to anyone else. You do not care who, if anyone, becomes the next owner. You toss your blown-out umbrella in a litter basket on the street, and that is the end of it as far as you are concerned.

■ **What abandonment is** Two elements must be present for an abandonment: an intention by the owner to abandon his property and an actual giving up of possession or control over it.

Intent The intention to give up, or part with, property may be shown by an express (specific) statement by the owner, or it may be concluded from surrounding circumstances. Ordinarily, however, intention is shown by acts and conduct clearly inconsistent with any desire to retain and continue to use or own the property.

Acts and omissions A single act may be sufficient to indicate abandonment—putting the umbrella in the litter basket—but a verbal statement usually is not. In the case of personal property (as opposed to real estate), there must be an actual giving up of possession to such an extent that it is left free and open to be taken by the next comer. The act of a telephone company in placing used poles on a vacant lot, which the company did not own and which children used as a playground, and paying no further attention to the poles, amounted to an abandonment of them.

Merely not using property, even over a period of time, does not amount to an abandonment. The failure of a landowner to cultivate his land or the failure of a quarry owner to take stone from his quarry, for example, does not cause the owner to lose title to his land.

Time Time is not a necessary element of abandonment. The abandonment is complete when the intention (placing the poles on the vacant lot) and giving up of possession (paying no further attention to them) unite.

■ **Subjects of abandonment** The things most commonly abandoned are personal property. As a rule, every interest in or title to property may be lost by abandonment—except perfect or absolute title to real property (real estate), which may be lost by ADVERSE POSSESSION. Let us say that your eccentric but talented neighbor retrieves that umbrella you abandoned on the street and turns it into a work of art. You have no claim on it.

abatable nuisance An annoyance, or anything interfering with the enjoyment of life or property, that can easily be stopped or made harmless and whose continued existence is not authorized under the law—your neighbor's perpetually barking dog, for example, or objectionable odors from a nearby factory. See also NUISANCE.

abatement and revival *Abatement* is the suspension or termination of a legal action or suit when one of the parties (plaintiff or defendant) dies or when the defendant brings to the attention of the court a fact that shows the plaintiff's suit is defective in some respect. The termination of the lawsuit is usually only temporary, and the plaintiff may bring another action in a better way. *Revival* is the continuance of a pending lawsuit after the death of one of the parties. When a law provides for revival, the personal representative of the deceased party may be substituted for him as a matter of right or, in some cases, at the discretion of the court. Thus, if your father was suing one of his tenants for nonpayment of rent but died before the case came to court, you might be able to pick up the suit where he left off.

■ **Why lawsuits are abated** The purpose of abatement is twofold: (1) to save the expense of a trial when the plaintiff's suit cannot be continued in the form originally presented and (2) to give the plaintiff an opportunity to correct his errors.

■ **Grounds for abatement** A judge may grant a plaintiff's request for abatement if one of the following grounds exists: (1) a lack of jurisdiction (authority) of the court before which the case is brought, (2) the fact that an earlier case between the same plaintiff and defendant is presently in progress, (3) an error or irregularity made by the plaintiff in bringing his suit, (4) a situation in which there is some objection to the parties involved in the suit, (5) the death or disability of a party either before or after the suit has begun.

Lack of jurisdiction A lack of jurisdiction (authority) of the court may bring on an abatement of the suit when, for instance, the defendant is not served with a summons or the suit is brought in the wrong county. The case may involve a sum of money too small or too large for the particular court to hear. Fraud or misconduct by the plaintiff in his claim for DAMAGES subjects the plaintiff's case to abatement. So does the use of fraudulent means to persuade the defendant to come to a place within the jurisdiction of the court.

EXAMPLE Ted, an English literature professor, accidentally O⊶＊ discovered that Walter, the chairman of the English department, took substantial portions from Ted's copyrighted book on Shakespeare and used it in his own textbook on Shakespeare's England. Max, Ted's lawyer, started a lawsuit in state court against Walter for infringing Ted's copyright. Before the trial began, Ted learned that his case should have been brought in federal court. He fired Max and hired a new attorney, Margery, who asked the state court for an abatement of Ted's case so she could bring it in federal court. The state court agreed. It did not have the jurisdiction to hear a copyright infringement case because the matter was one of federal law. Although Ted's lawsuit was *substantively* correct because it claimed a violation of his rights under copyright law, it was *technically* defective because Ted originally asked the wrong court to give him relief.

Another case pending When an earlier case being heard within the same jurisdiction (either in the same court or another court having like jurisdiction) is based on the same legal question and involves the same parties, then good grounds exist for the abatement of the later case. A second suit, relating—but not identical—to the same legal subject matter, that arises after the first suit is brought is not a ground for abating the second suit. For instance, a suit for an overdue loan installment is not abated because the creditor has a lawsuit before the court for an earlier overdue installment of the same loan.

Defects and irregularities The plaintiff may make a mistake by suing on a contract before the time for performing its terms has elapsed. He may sue before fulfilling some necessary condition, such as providing a notice of loss to his insurance company. A difference may be discovered between two parts of the plaintiff's legal papers, such as the WRIT and DECLARATION, when the parts should be the same. These errors and irregularities are grounds for abatement.

Objection as to parties Abatement may be granted when an objection is made about the correctness of the parties to the suit in the following instances:

(1) When a plaintiff brings suit using an assumed or fictitious name that he is not entitled to use.

(2) When he is an enemy alien.

(3) When a child who has not reached the age of legal adulthood (usually 18 or 21) attempts to sue in his own name instead of using a court-appointed guardian.

(4) When the plaintiff is not the proper party to bring the case to court. You cannot sue for an injury done to your friend, for example, because your friend is the one who must bring suit.

(5) When the plaintiff does not have authority to bring suit as a representative for some other person or business association—as when a surviving partner sues on behalf of the partnership.

(6) When a necessary party—one whose rights are so involved that the case cannot be decided unless he is before the court—has not been joined (made a party) to a suit based on a contract, a tort action (involving harm to a person or his property), or a suit relating to real estate.

Death of a party Under the common law (before states adopted revival laws) any suit before the court abated if either party died when the ground for the suit—such as assault and battery—was a personal one. This rule was based on the idea that death terminates all of a person's rights and duties. Today most states have enacted statutes that determine which grounds shall survive the death of a party and which shall not. The reason for these statutes is to avoid abatements and to allow the original suit to be continued by or against the representative of the deceased person.

Examples of actions that ordinarily survive according to common law are suits for injuries to real or personal property; suits for injuries to a person's husband, wife, or child; and suits based on a contract. Thus you would probably be able to take up your father's suit against his tenant for nonpayment of rent, because a lease is a form of contract. Many actions survive only if there is a specific law or provision that says they can. These include actions for assault and battery, false imprisonment, fraud, libel and slander, negligence, personal injury, and recovery of a real-property interest.

■ **Revival distinguished from survival** Survival is a matter of right; revival is a matter of procedure. Revival operates only when a case is pending, but a suit cannot be revived unless the underlying cause of action—the ground for the suit—survives.

EXAMPLE Josh, a small retailer, sued Tim, a wholesale O⊶＊ clothing manufacturer, for breaching their contract for the delivery of 500 winter coats by August 15, 1980. After the trial began, Josh was killed in a car crash. Josh's personal representative, Bob, is entitled to revive or continue Josh's lawsuit against Tim. A lawsuit for breach of contract is a type of action that survives the death of a person who has been injured by the breach since it involves injury to property that continues to exist even after the plaintiff dies. Bob must follow the steps set out in the law if he is to be allowed to revive the suit. He might have to make a motion asking the court to permit him to revive the lawsuit or he may only have to change the original papers filed by Josh with the court and with Tim to notify them of his lawsuit. The change will state that Bob, as Josh's personal representative, is the plaintiff in the suit.

On the other hand, suppose Josh sued Tim for slanderous statements made to a credit company about Josh's credit rating. Josh died before the case came to trial, The court will not permit Bob to revive or continue the lawsuit against Tim because a lawsuit for slander does not survive the death of the injured person according to his state's law. Because in his state slander is considered a personal injury to the plaintiff, his heirs are not entitled to recover anything from the wrongdoer because they have not been injured. Today, many states permit a lawsuit for slander to be revived.

abdication The act of giving up an office, a power, the authority to act, or a right or trust.

abduction The crime of abduction is the unlawful taking of a person, including the unlawful taking of a female for marriage, sexual intercourse, prostitution, or concubinage.
■ **Nature under statutes** In its broadest legal sense abduction is the act of taking and carrying away a person, such as a child or ward, by force or fraud from one who has legal custody of him or her. Statutes that make abduction a crime usually relate, however, to unlawfully taking or detaining a female. These are designed to protect girls under a certain age and to punish persons who entice females to houses of prostitution. Although the crime of abduction generally involves only young girls, abduction and KIDNAPPING are the same in some states.
■ **Elements of the offense** The statutes in the various states do not require the same elements to establish the offense. Most statutes include at least some of the following elements: taking or detaining a female under a certain age from lawful custody by force or without her consent; a place of a particular character described in the law; an unlawful intent or purpose. In some states, the fact that the girl is under the legal age (usually 18 or 21) makes her incapable of consenting to the taking. Thus, taking an underage girl for an unlawful purpose is a crime whether or not she consents. Some states do not consider the use of force as an essential element: the abduction can be by enticement, persuasion, or other inducement.
■ **Defenses** It is no excuse that the female has been returned to her home or, if abducted for marriage, that the marriage did not take place. When the statute provides that the offended party may remove the offense by pardoning the accused, the pardon must be by the female herself, either specifically or by marriage to the accused. When marriage of the female to the accused removes criminal liability, all other persons involved in the abduction are also absolved.
■ **Persons liable** The statutes usually hold criminally liable any person who abducts a female. A husband who takes his wife to have sexual intercourse with another man is guilty of abduction if she is under the age of legal adulthood (usually 18 or 21). If she is over the legal age, her husband may not be guilty of abduction, but he may be guilty of kidnapping.

If the husband forcefully takes his wife to have sex with another man but she consents to the sex act, the law of that state will determine if the husband is guilty of abduction. For example, if adultery is not a crime in that state, the husband is not guilty because one of the elements needed for abduction is an illegal purpose or intent.

Women who take, receive, or use a minor female for illicit sexual relations with men are also held criminally liable, and aiders or abettors in the commission of the offense are frequently guilty of the crime.
EXAMPLE A man accompanied by a 15-year-old girl entered the lobby of a hotel, walked up to the reservations desk, and asked the clerk for a room. He signed the hotel register "Frank Brown and wife." The desk clerk gave the couple a room and instructed a bellhop to escort them to it. The man remained in the room for only a short period of time and then left the hotel. The desk clerk did not try to detain him. When the man was later convicted of abduction, the desk clerk was held criminally liable for aiding in the crime because he could have refused the couple the room—especially after seeing how the man signed the register. By giving the couple the keys to the bedroom, the desk clerk did "receive and harbor the female for the purpose of sexual intercourse."

In some states a female who has been taken or detained against her will for an immoral purpose may sue her abductor in a civil action for the damages she may have sustained.

abet Aid, counsel, induce, or assist in the commission of a crime. The term assumes knowledge of the wrongful purpose of the person who commits the crime.

abeyance A condition of being undetermined. The property of a bankrupt person whose case is not yet decided may be described as being in abeyance.

abide 1 Continue in a place; remain fixed or stable in some state or condition. 2 Accept or support the consequences of a thing or decision, as to abide by the terms of a contract or judgment.

ab initio (Latin) "From the beginning," or from the first act. A person may be said to be a trespasser, a contract may be void, or a marriage unlawful, *ab initio*.

abjuration A giving up, renouncing, or abandoning by an oath.

abnegation A denial or renunciation.

abolition The destruction or extinguishment of anything; often used in reference to a position or office.

abortion The destruction, expulsion, or premature delivery of the human fetus before the natural time for birth; a miscarriage induced by artificial means.
■ **Statutory provisions** Abortion laws vary from state to state, but until recently most states made it a crime to procure or attempt to procure an abortion except by medical advice in order to save the mother's life.
■ **Nature and elements in general** The elements of abortion under these laws usually include a physical act done with the intent of procuring a miscarriage. A guilty INTENT by itself is not sufficient. Thus you could not be prosecuted because you merely planned to get an abortion that you knew was illegal.

The physical act must tend to accomplish the crime but it need not actually accomplish it. For example, placing a woman upon a table in a position to be operated on and using a syringe to cleanse her in preparation for the operation has been held to be an act of abortion. If such an act were done without an intent to perform an abortion but to perform another medical purpose and the woman lost the baby, this would not be an act of abortion since there was no intent to do so.

As usually defined by statutes, the act may include the "administering" of a drug, medicine, poison, or other harmful substance, as well as the use of "instruments," and "other means."

Administering consists of providing the woman with the means to cause the miscarriage. The person who administers does not have to use force or even to be present. Sending medicine to the woman by mail, with directions given either by letter or in person for taking the medicine, constitutes administering.

The *instrument* need not be a scientific tool or surgical implement. Any physical means is sufficient. A finger inserted in the womb with the intent to produce an abortion is an instrument.

Using physical violence to cause a woman to miscarry is considered an example of some *other means* of causing an abortion—pushing her down a flight of stairs, for instance.

■ **Roe v. Wade** Until 1973, abortion statutes in most states prohibited any person from using any means to procure an abortion for a pregnant woman, with or without her consent. If the means used failed to produce the abortion, the offender was guilty of an attempt to produce an abortion when intent could be proved. If the woman died during the attempt or as a result of the abortion, the crime became murder.

In 1973 the U.S. Supreme Court decided the case of *Roe* v. *Wade.* Jane Roe, a single woman, brought suit seeking a declaration from the Court that a state abortion statute was unconstitutional. She stated that she was unmarried and pregnant and that she wanted to end her pregnancy by an abortion performed by a doctor under safe conditions. Roe stated she was unable to get a legal abortion because, under the prevailing statute, her life was not put in danger by the continuation of her pregnancy. She claimed, further, that the abortion statute was unconstitutional because it abridged her right of PRIVACY protected by the U.S. Constitution.

In deciding in favor of Jane Roe, the Court agreed that the constitutional right of privacy is broad enough to include a woman's decision to end her pregnancy. It reasoned that a statute that completely denied a woman the right to choose to end her pregnancy is harmful to her. Motherhood or additional children may force upon the woman a difficult life, both now and in the future. Her mental and physical health may be taxed by child care. An unwanted child might be brought into a family totally unable to care for its needs. In this case, and others like it, the woman might suffer the stigma of being labeled an unwed mother.

The Court thus determined that a criminal-abortion statute that excuses only an abortion procedure performed to save the mother's life, without regard to any other factors or to the stage of pregnancy, is unconstitutional. The Court decided, however, that a pregnant woman does not have an absolute constitutional right to an abortion at any time she demands it. The state has important interests in safeguard-

ing the health of its citizens, in maintaining medical standards, and in protecting future life. At some stage during pregnancy the state's interests become strong enough to permit it to regulate the abortion decision. Thus the Court concluded that the right of personal privacy includes the abortion decision but that the decision must be qualified by the interests of the state.

Status of fetus Before setting out the rights of the pregnant woman and balancing those rights against the interests of the state, the Supreme Court examined the question of whether a fetus is a person under the Constitution. The Court concluded that the word "person" has been used only postnatally—that is, after birth—and thus does not include the unborn. This conclusion and point of law have been hotly contested and have led to the proposal of a new Human Life Amendment to the federal Constitution, which would prohibit taking the life of an unborn, although it would permit medical abortion procedures to prevent the death of the mother.

In balancing the rights of a pregnant woman against the interests of the state, the Court considered the nine-month period of pregnancy in its three stages, or trimesters. Each trimester is equal to a period of 12 weeks.

First trimester During the first trimester, the abortion decision and how it is to be performed must be left up to the woman and the medical judgment of her doctor. The doctor, after consulting with his patient, is free to decide that an abortion should be performed. At this stage of the pregnancy, abortion is as safe as normal childbirth, so the state may not interfere by imposing regulations. This rule holds true, however, only when the abortion is performed by a doctor under medically safe conditions.

Second trimester During the second 12 weeks of pregnancy, the state, in promoting the mother's health, may, if it chooses, regulate the abortion procedure in ways that are reasonably related to the mother's health. It may even prohibit abortion under some circumstances, although the law has not yet been clearly established on this point. State regulations may include requirements as to the qualifications and licensing of the person who is to perform the abortion. The state may regulate the facility where the abortion is to be performed and decide whether it must be a hospital, a clinic, or like facility. Licensing of the facility may also be regulated.

Third trimester During this stage in the pregnancy the fetus becomes viable—potentially able to live outside the mother's womb with or without artificial aid. At this time the state's interest in protecting the potential new human life is very strong, and the state may step in because its regulation of the life of the viable fetus has logical and biological justification.

■ **Doe v. Bolton** In this case, decided in 1973 along with *Roe* v. *Wade*, the Supreme Court held unconstitutional three procedural conditions of a then recently enacted state abortion statute.

Hospital accreditation The first condition declared unconstitutional required that an abortion be performed in an accredited hospital. The Court found this condition to be invalid because the state failed to show that hospitals alone were able to insure the quality of the operation and the full protection of the pregnant patient. Another type of facility, such as a clinic, may possess all the necessary personnel and equipment. The Court also found the hospital requirement invalid because it failed to exclude from regulation the first trimester of pregnancy, which the state may not regulate.

Committee approval The second unconstitutional condition required the abortion procedure to be approved by the hospital's staff abortion committee. The Court concluded that the decision of a committee would be too restrictive of the patient's rights and needs. By the time the committee can reach its decision, the woman's personal doctor has already completed his diagnosis. Review by a committee once removed from diagnosis of the case is basically repetitious and unnecessary. The woman's right to medical care according to her doctor's best judgment and her doctor's right to provide it are severely limited by committee review. Moreover, the hospital does not need the committee to protect itself; it may refuse to admit a patient seeking an abortion. In addition, no other surgery was shown to be subject to committee approval under the state's criminal law.

Two-doctor agreement The third condition found unconstitutional by the Court required the approval of the abortion decision by two licensed doctors in addition to the pregnant woman's own doctor. The Court reasoned that the attending doctor's best medical judgment on the need for an abortion should be sufficient. Again, no other state statute required confirmation by two other doctors before an operation could be performed. It is usually presumed that a licensed doctor knows when to consult with other doctors. Requiring the agreement of two more doctors interferes unnecessarily with a doctor's right to practice.

■ **Other Court rulings** The constitutionality of a number of additional provisions found in state statutes has been questioned and has been decided, among them residence, the pregnant woman's written consent, her husband's consent, parental consent for minors, record keeping, the standard of medical care, and abortions performed by persons other than doctors.

Residence The Court found unconstitutional a requirement that restricted abortions to state residents, holding that a state must protect persons who enter it seeking medical services available there.

The woman's consent The Supreme Court has held constitutional one state's statutory provision requiring that before undergoing an abortion during the first trimester of pregnancy, a woman must sign a written statement that she consents to the abortion. The statement must include provisions that she has been informed about the consequences of the procedure and that her consent is freely given. The Court reasoned that the decision to undergo an abortion is of great importance and often exceedingly stressful. It must be made with full knowledge of its nature and effects. Because the woman is the person primarily concerned, she must assure the state of her awareness of the decision and its significance by giving her consent in writing before the abortion is performed.

The husband's consent Another provision of the same state statute required prior written consent by the woman's husband during the first trimester of pregnancy. The husband's consent was not needed, under the statute,

when the woman's doctor decided that an abortion was necessary to save her life. The Supreme Court held that the state may not require the consent of the spouse as a condition for any abortion during the first trimester of pregnancy. The state cannot give to the husband a power it does not have itself.

Parental consent A third provision of the statute required parental consent when the woman was under 18 years old and was unmarried. (Parental consent was not necessary if a doctor had decided an abortion was required to save the woman's life.) The Supreme Court held this provision unconstitutional. Just as in the case of a husband, the state does not have a right to give a third party, even the parents, an absolute right to stop a doctor and his patient from deciding to end her pregnancy during the first trimester. Minors are protected by the constitutional right of privacy along with adults. The Court stressed, however, that not every minor may give proper consent to an abortion. Extreme youth and immaturity may prevent the minor from giving informed consent. It seems, then, that the question of parental consent is not closed.

Record keeping Still another provision of the statute required record keeping by health facilities where abortions were performed and by the doctors performing the abortions, regardless of when the abortion was performed. The purpose of this provision was to add to existing medical knowledge. The records were to be kept confidential and to be used only for statistical purposes. They were to be retained for seven years and might be inspected by public health officials.

In holding these provisions to be constitutional, the Court stated that records and reporting requirements that tend to preserve the mother's health and properly respect her privacy and confidentiality are permitted. The records may provide useful medical information when abortion decisions must be made.

Standard of care The final statutory provision in question required a doctor to preserve the fetus's life and health just as he would if the fetus were intended to be born and not aborted. The statute provided for criminal punishment and civil liability when the doctor failed to take the steps necessary to keep the child alive. The Court held this provision unconstitutional because it did not specify that the required care had to be taken only after the fetus became viable during the third trimester of pregnancy. The statute required the doctor to preserve the life and health of the fetus regardless of the stage during which the abortion was performed.

■ **Persons qualified to perform abortions** In 1975 the Supreme Court upheld the criminal conviction of a medically unqualified person who had performed an abortion. The Court stated that its earlier decisions covered abortions performed by licensed physicians under safe, clinical conditions. Abortion prosecutions against persons who are not physicians do not violate the right of privacy secured by the Constitution against state interference. Statutes that forbid the performance of abortions by anyone other than a doctor remain constitutional.

above cited or mentioned A phrase meaning quoted before or appearing earlier in this document.

abrogation The annulment or repeal of a law by the authority of its maker—for example, the repeal of an earlier law by a legislature.

abscond Absent, withdraw, or conceal oneself secretly in order to avoid arrest or the service of PROCESS (a subpoena) in a lawsuit.

absentee One who is away from his DOMICILE or usual place of residence, or who is outside the state and has no one to represent him within the state. For instance, a corporation is an absentee when it has no legal domicile within a state and no agent upon whom PROCESS (a subpoena or arrest warrant) may be served.

absolute nuisance A NUISANCE that involves no negligent conduct.

> EXAMPLE A husband and wife owned a small farm. A manufacturer of explosives purchased the adjoining property and within a few hundred feet of the farm residence built a plant for manufacturing and storing of nitroglycerin. The farm couple sued the manufacturer for the value of their property. They alleged that the nitroglycerin plant was an absolute nuisance that made their property unsuitable for farming. The court agreed with them and had a jury determine the value of the farm.

abstention doctrine The principle that a federal court should refuse to decide certain cases even though it has the power to do so—such as a case that can be decided purely by applying state law.

abstract A summary; a complete history in a short, abbreviated form.

abstract of title A memorandum or concise history, taken from public records or documents, of the ownership of a piece of land. It includes transfers of ownership and any rights that people other than the owner might have in the land, together with a statement of all liens, charges, or liabilities to which the land may be subject and which could be important to a prospective purchaser. See TITLE.

abuse Ill use or improper treatment. In law, an *abuse of discretion* is the failure of an administrator or a judge to use sound or reasonable judgment in reaching a decision. An *abuse of process* occurs when a legal PROCESS is improperly used—for example, obtaining a warrant of arrest in order to pressure a debtor to pay his debt.

accede 1 Come into a public office. 2 Agree to.

acceleration The shortening of the time period before a scheduled future event will take place. An *acceleration clause* is a provision in a contract requiring the payment of money that makes the entire sum become immediately due because of a failure to meet some condition, such as a failure to pay an installment on time.

acceptance 1 The receipt of something with the intention of retaining it. 2 Agreeing to an offer of a CONTRACT and thereby becoming bound by its provisions. 3 The act by which a DRAWEE (a bank) agrees to pay a negotiable instrument (a CHECK), usually by writing the word "accepted" across the face of the instrument.

access The means, right, or opportunity of approaching. For example, if you own land located next to a road or highway, your right of access entitles you to go and return from your land to the road or highway without meeting a barrier or obstacle. The word also applies to the right to see and to make use of public records. It is also used in reference to the opportunity for sexual intercourse in general and between husband and wife in particular.

accession The right to all that one's property produces and to all that is added to it naturally or by the work or skill of another person. If, for example, land builds up on a riverbank, the riverbank's owner will also own the new land. If the addition made to the property by the work and skill of another is of greater value than the property itself, or if the change made is so great that the property cannot be restored to its original state, the possessor of the property may be entitled to it rather than the original owner. He must reimburse the original owner for the cost of the original property, however.

> EXAMPLE In Texas a man innocently purchased parts of a dismantled stolen car from a junkyard for $85 from which he built a truck for his business at a cost of about $800. The next year the original owner of the stolen car, recognizing a mark on the truck's hood and radiator, sued to recover it, claiming that his ownership of the car gave him the right to recover it as it was when he found it. The court held that ownership of the car had passed to the defendant by accession and awarded the plaintiff $85.
>
> On the other hand, when a man in New York willfully trespassed onto another man's farm, stole some corn, and made it into whiskey, the court held that the whiskey belonged to the owner of the corn.

accessory A person who contributes to or aids in the commission of a FELONY, a serious crime. An *accessory before the fact* is one who—although absent at the time the crime is committed—assists, counsels, encourages, or commands another to commit it. An *accessory after the fact* is one who, knowing that a crime has been committed, conceals the crime and harbors, aids, or protects the person who committed the crime or helps him escape. An *accessory during the fact* is one who stands by without interfering, or without giving whatever help he can, to prevent the commission of a crime. However, if a person cannot prevent a crime without putting himself in danger, he is not considered an accessory during the fact.

> EXAMPLE Suppose your two teenage daughters witness three knife-wielding men rob a middle-aged couple in a restaurant parking lot. The girls are not accessories during the fact because there is nothing they can do to stop the robbery without endangering themselves.

Many states recognize only accessories before and after the fact because it is difficult to determine actually when a person is an accessory during the fact. In most cases, it would not be clear whether a person had the power to prevent a crime and whether his expectation of danger was reasonable. See also CRIMINAL LAW; MISDEMEANOR.

accident An event that happens by chance or through someone's carelessness or ignorance. The word does not have a clearly defined legal meaning.

accidental-death benefit An additional insurance benefit payable when a person dies as the result of an accident; usually the same thing as DOUBLE INDEMNITY.

accommodation An arrangement made or a favor done for one person by another person who does not receive anything of value in return. It usually involves cosigning to help someone get a loan or credit.

accommodation paper A bill of exchange or a PROMISSORY NOTE signed by one person as a favor to another who wants to raise money on it. By signing the paper, the accommodating party agrees to pay it when it comes due if the borrower does not. See COMMERCIAL PAPER.

accomplice One who knowingly and voluntarily aids or assists another person in the commission of a crime.

accord and satisfaction An *accord* is a CONTRACT between two persons in which one of them undertakes to give or perform something, and the other agrees to accept it in satisfaction of his claim, even though it is different from what he thinks he should receive. A *satisfaction* is the execution, completion, or performance of the agreement.
■ **Existing controversy** An accord and satisfaction is most frequently applied in cases in which the parties have agreed upon a settlement of a disputed claim or one in which the amount has not yet been determined. There may be a valid accord and satisfaction of an undisputed claim too.
EXAMPLE Suppose you accidentally sideswipe your neighbor Sally's car while pulling out of your driveway. You tell her what has happened and offer to pay for the damage. Sally says she will let you know how much it will cost to repair the car. Two weeks later Sally slips a $100 repair bill under your door. You are aghast. You had estimated it would not cost more than $30 to fix the car. It is just before Christmas, and you cannot afford to give Sally the $100. In exchange for payment of the bill, you offer to do all the labor necessary on Sally's lawn, starting in the spring and ending after the fall leaves have been collected. Sally accepts this arrangement. Your agreement with Sally will be satisfied after you have fulfilled your part of the arrangement.
■ **Agreement** Because an accord and satisfaction is a contract, it must contain all the essential elements of a contract, including a definite offer of settlement and an unconditional acceptance of the offer. The contract must finally and definitely close the matter it covers, so that nothing is left unsettled. It need not be in writing.
■ **Subject matter** Generally, any lawful claim or demand may be the subject of an accord and satisfaction. In a case that made headlines in 1977, Christina Onassis gave her father's widow, Jacqueline, $26 million to settle Mrs.

Onassis's claim on her late husband's estate. An accord and satisfaction is also one way of discharging a duty or obligation arising from a contract or from a TORT claim—a claim based on a personal injury or injury to one's property, as illustrated in the above example.
■ **Who can make an accord** An accord and satisfaction may be made only between persons who have the legal capacity to enter into a contract. It is not binding upon a minor or upon someone who is insane or under some other legal disability.
A third person may make an accord and satisfaction on behalf of a debtor if what is offered by the third person is accepted by the creditor, and the debtor authorizes, participates in, or later agrees to the transaction.
EXAMPLE Your 23-year-old son buys a used car for $2,200 from your next-door neighbor who agrees that after $1,000 is put down, the balance could be paid in 12 monthly installments of $100. After making 9 payments, your son loses his job and catches pneumonia while he is job hunting. He misses the last 3 payments to your neighbor who tells you that if he does not get his money soon, he will take the matter to small claims court. You offer $250 to your neighbor, the most you can spare, to settle your son's debt. He accepts and your son gratefully agrees to the deal. In the eyes of the law, you are a third person. You have decided to make an accord and satisfaction on behalf of your son, even though you are not obligated to pay your son's debt since he is an adult who made a fair loan agreement on his own.
Satisfaction by one of two or more wrongdoers usually discharges the others—on the basis of the rule that there can be only a single satisfaction for an injury or wrong. If the payment is not intended or received as full satisfaction of the claim, however, a payment made by one wrongdoer does not discharge others who are jointly liable. For a full discussion of joint liability, see CONTRACTS.
■ **Method of payment** The payment of money is the usual and proper way of rendering satisfaction. The money may be paid into court, but unless the sum is accepted by the creditor, an accord and satisfaction is not reached. Payment may also be made by personal labor, a new promise, or a transfer of property. When a landlord in Arkansas accepted cotton picked and prepared for market in place of rent owed to him by a tenant, the court ruled that there had been an accord and satisfaction.

account, action on The name of a type of civil lawsuit used, for example, to recover the amount of a bank deposit that a bank refuses to deliver on request, the price of board and lodging furnished, or the cash amount due for goods sold and delivered. See ACTION.

accountant A person who specializes in keeping financial records. His duties may include setting up financial record systems, auditing these systems, and preparing financial statements. A CERTIFIED PUBLIC ACCOUNTANT holds a certificate of education and proficiency issued according to the law of the state where he practices.

accounting A common-law action to compel a person under a legal duty to render an account—a trustee or a guardian, for example—to fulfill that obligation. Accounting is a civil action based on the law of CONTRACTS, and although now generally replaced by other remedies, the action may still be used.

account render See ACCOUNTING.

accounts receivable Lists of money owed to a person or company but not yet received—such as outstanding charge-account bills and installment balances.

account stated An exact figure for money owed, calculated by a creditor and either specifically accepted as accurate by the debtor or understood as accepted by his failure to object to the figure. Your monthly charge-account and credit-card bills are accounts stated.

accredit Approve officially—as a hospital or school.

accretion The gradual growth or addition of land by natural causes, such as dirt deposited by a river on its banks after a heavy rain.

accrual basis A method of accounting that shows expenses incurred and income earned during a given time period, whether or not cash was paid out or received during the period. See also CASH BASIS; INCOME TAX.

accrue 1 Add or accumulate. 2 Become due and payable. In tax law, income accrues to a taxpayer when he has a definite right to it and there is a reasonable likelihood that the right will be converted into money or property. The estimated INCOME TAX that many of us pay four times each year is based on estimated accrued income.

accumulated-earnings tax A federal tax on corporations that pile up profits without either distributing them to stockholders in the form of dividends or reinvesting the money in the business.

accumulation trust A TRUST that keeps its income and adds it to capital during the trust period rather than paying it out regularly to the beneficiary of the trust.

accumulative sentence A criminal sentence that is imposed while a sentence from an earlier conviction is still being served and that takes effect after the first sentence is finished.

accusation A formal charge brought against a person to the effect that he is guilty of a crime.

accused The defendant in a criminal case; a person charged with a crime.

acknowledgment Admission or formal declaration, made before a proper officer of the court by a person who has executed a written document, stating that the document is his act or deed. The word also refers to the certificate or other written evidence of the officer's act of taking the acknowledgment.

■ **Purpose** Acknowledgments are used to admit the paternity of a child, to establish a document as authentic, to entitle a deed in the transfer or sale of real property to be registered or recorded, and to permit a document to be admitted as evidence in a legal proceeding.

■ **Necessity** When a statute requires a document to be acknowledged and it is not, the document is invalid. Unless an acknowledgment is required by statute, you do not need one to validate a contract.

Registration of deeds Transfers of real property, whether by sale or gift, are usually recorded in a public place often called the registry of deeds. These records are open to public inspection and are used to determine who owns the real estate located within the area served by the registry. Often the law provides that a document relating to real property cannot be recorded in the registry of deeds unless it has been properly acknowledged. Thus, if you sell your house, you may have to acknowledge the deed transferring the property to the person who bought it.

Evidence An acknowledgment may also be necessary to allow a document to be admitted as evidence in a court case or other legal proceeding when there is no other proof of the authenticity of the document. Before a will can be admitted in a PROBATE proceeding, for example, there must be proof that the deceased person's signature is authentic; this may be offered in the form of an acknowledgment by one or both of the witnesses to the signing of the will.

EXAMPLE Greg and Harry witnessed the signing of Eloise's will. After Eloise died, her executrix, Ellen, asked the court to admit the will to probate so that she could distribute Eloise's property according to its terms. The court questioned Greg and Harry about whether the signature on the will was Eloise's. Their statements that they were present when Eloise signed the will and that it was her signature were acknowledgments that the signature was authentic. The will was admitted to probate and Ellen could distribute Eloise's property.

■ **Who may acknowledge** The persons required to acknowledge a document are, in general, those who make it and those who are bound by it. Usually, if a person has the authority to complete a document, he also has the authority to acknowledge it. Some examples of persons with the authority both to complete and to acknowledge a document are: the seller and the purchaser of a house, an agent executing a contract, a corporation officer on behalf of the corporation, and a partner for a partnership.

■ **Who may take acknowledgments** Acknowledgments must be taken by the officers named by statute for that purpose or by their deputies. An officer may be disqualified if he stands to gain some benefit from or has a financial interest in the outcome of a transaction—a trustee of a trust or a stockholder of a corporation involved, for example. The officer may, however, be the agent, attorney, or even a relative of an interested party.

■ **Mode of taking** If there is no statute that prescribes the manner of taking an acknowledgment, the person who executed the document must appear before an officer of the court (such as a notary public, clerk of the court, or a county recorder) and state that he executed it. The officer taking the acknowledgment must be satisfied that the person acknowledging the document is the person described in it.

■ **Certificate**   A certificate of acknowledgment is usually necessary as evidence of a valid acknowledgment. When there is no specific requirement by statute, the certificate need only show that the document was acknowledged, the place where it was acknowledged, and the official capacity of the officer. The position of the certificate on the document is not important; it may even be attached to the document. Usually the date is not essential, and a mistake in it, or its omission, will not invalidate the certificate.

ACLU   See AMERICAN CIVIL LIBERTIES UNION.

acquiescence   Silent agreement or passive compliance; knowing about some action and remaining quietly satisfied about it.

acquisition charge   A sum charged for paying off a loan before it is due; also called a prepayment penalty.

acquit   1 Set free, release, or discharge from an obligation.   2 Determine legally that a person who has been charged with a crime is innocent.

act   1 In law, something done voluntarily and in such a way that certain legal consequences attach to it.   2 A written law passed by a legislative body, such as Congress; a STATUTE.

action   The lawful and formal demand of one's rights from another person or party made in a court of law. A *cause of action* is the set of facts on which an action is based. "Action" and "cause of action" are often used interchangeably. *He has an action* means he has a legally justifiable reason for starting a lawsuit.

Generally, the word "action" applies to any legal proceeding brought in a court. In its technical sense, action refers only to a proceeding in a court of law and not to suits in EQUITY. The word is also usually limited to civil proceedings but may be applied to a criminal trial.

■ **Elements**   The elements of an action include a right possessed by the plaintiff and a corresponding duty owed to the plaintiff by the defendant. The defendant must do a wrongful act (he smashes into his neighbor's car) or fail to act (he does not complete the installation of a swimming pool by the agreed-upon date) so that he injures a right the plaintiff has or breaches a duty he owes the plaintiff.

■ **Classification**   Actions are classified into various categories, such as public or private, real or personal, CONTRACT or TORT, civil or criminal. Generally, these categories describe the purpose of the action or distinguish one from another. An action is classified as a *civil action*, for example, to show that its purpose is to enforce a private right as well as to distinguish it from a *criminal action*, which has as its purpose the punishment of a public wrong. A *contract action* is an example of a category that is used merely to describe the purpose of the action—the recovery of damages based on a contract.

■ **Which law governs**   The subject matter of the action is governed by the law of the place where the right was acquired. For example, if you are an Arizona resident and you bring a suit on a contract made in Colorado, the rights

of the parties would be determined by Colorado law. The courtroom procedure would be determined by the law of Arizona, where the suit would take place.

In a federal court action brought on a contract between a citizen of Colorado and a citizen of Arizona, the federal court would be bound to use the law of the state where the contract was made to determine the rights of the parties. The court would use its own federal rules of civil procedure. In deciding a question of federal law, the court would use federal courtroom procedure and federal law to decide the rights of the parties.

■ **Conditions**   Sometimes you must comply with certain conditions before you may start an action.

EXAMPLE You plan to sue the county where you live because you broke the axle of your car in a pothole it failed to repair. Unless you file a notice of claim (a statement that you plan to sue that includes a brief description of the accident and your damages) with the county clerk within the time specified by law (usually 90 days or 6 months from the time you suffered harm or your property was injured), you will be barred from suing the county at all.

A buyer must give notice to a seller that the goods received do not conform to the terms of their contract, for example, and a creditor must demand payment when someone has agreed to pay a debt on request. In some cases, such as when a person claims that he has been a victim of racial or sexual discrimination in violation of federal law, he must first take all reasonable steps to get satisfaction from an ADMINISTRATIVE AGENCY before he can bring an action in court. This is known as the *exhaustion of administrative remedies*. See CIVIL RIGHTS.

■ **Persons entitled to sue and persons liable**   Usually the person entitled to sue is the one whose right has been violated. You cannot bring an action when you have no interest in the matter in dispute, and you have no right to bring an action in the name of another person without his authority. A private citizen cannot bring an action against the state to correct some public wrong unless he himself has been injured.

The person against whom the cause of action exists, and he alone, is the one liable to be sued.

A person cannot sue himself, for he cannot be both plaintiff and defendant in the same suit. For example, if you are injured on your own property you may not maintain an action against yourself in order to recover under your insurance policy.

■ **Joinder**   When provided by law, different causes of action may be joined together in the same lawsuit. The separate injuries usually must arise from the same incident or controversy. For instance, separate causes of action for personal injuries and property damage may result from an automobile accident in which the driver is injured and his automobile damaged. Other situations for joinder include injuries to character and to property and injuries to both real and personal property.

EXAMPLE Ray and Walter are out drinking at their neighborhood bar on Saturday night. After a few drinks, they begin to quarrel. Soon the argument flares up into a loud shouting match that can be heard by everyone in the bar. Ray calls Walter a thief and wife-beater and then slugs him in the jaw. Walter may later sue Ray for both slander and assault and battery in the same suit. The two causes of action are different (slander and assault and battery) but they arise from the same incident. Therefore, the two causes of action may be joined.

The purpose of joinder is to prevent many lawsuits involving the same parties when one suit might settle the entire controversy.

■ **Consolidation** Combining several actions into one, so that they lose their separate identity, is called consolidation. Consolidation is ordinarily proper when more than one action is pending at the same time between the same parties involving similar issues and subject matter.

EXAMPLE Scott White owns a two-family house. He lives in O—* one part of the house with his mother and rents the remainder to the Gray family under a two-year lease. The Grays fail to pay their rent in January and White decides to file a lawsuit against them for the money due. Subsequently, the Grays fail to pay their rent for the next three months. Each month, White files an additional suit. Now he has four separate suits against the Grays for the rent due under the same lease. The court will order White to consolidate the suits.

Suits between the same parties for the publication of the same libelous material in different newspapers would also be subject to consolidation. The purpose of consolidation is to avoid multiple lawsuits, prevent delay, clear congested courts, and save unnecessary costs or expenses. Consolidation differs from joinder: in joinder the causes of action are different; whereas in consolidation they are either the same or similar.

■ **Splitting** Splitting a cause of action means bringing an action for only part of the cause. Usually a single cause of action cannot be split, or divided. A contract action on a PROMISSORY NOTE, for example, may not be split by bringing one suit for the PRINCIPAL and another for the INTEREST due on the note. Nor may a party divide the grounds for recovery and maintain different actions on each ground. For instance, a single conversation in which slanderous words are spoken gives rise to only one action, even though the person slandered is injured both as an individual and in his business or profession. The rule limiting splitting is designed to save the defendant the expense of many lawsuits when one suit will do, and is usually strictly applied by the courts.

■ **Severance** Severance is the division of one action into a number of actions. It is proper to sever actions when separate judgments on the claims are warranted and it would be unjust to try the claims together.

EXAMPLE If you were injured in two different mishaps— O—* once when the kitchen ceiling in your apartment fell and a second time when your bathroom ceiling fell— you may not bring one action for both injuries. The two claims should be severed because the jury could be influenced by the similarity of the accidents.

If the defendant consents, claims may be severed when there are two or more plaintiffs and one of them fails to appear. The nonappearing plaintiff must bring a separate action. Severance takes place, too, when the defendant settles out of court with one of the plaintiffs and obtains a release. MISJOINDER of either the plaintiffs or defendants is

an additional ground for severance. It occurs when a party is joined who ought not to be a party.

EXAMPLE You have had your roof repaired and are not O—* satisfied with the work that has been done. You are also injured in a collision with your neighbor's car, and must bring suit to recover for your injuries. In order to save time and money, you decide to bring one suit against both the person responsible for the automobile accident and the roof repairman. In this case the two defendants have been misjoined, and severance is proper.

■ **Defenses** A defense is any fact or set of facts presented by the defendant to defeat the cause of action in whole or in part. For example, a plaintiff cannot recover for the results of an act to which he has consented, and his consent may be used as a defense by the defendant. You give your consent to your neighbor to park his car in your extra garage space. If you subsequently sue him for trespassing, you will not win the suit. An action for damages for breach of a legal duty may be defended on the basis that an ACT OF GOD has made performance of that duty impossible. If a blizzard prevents a pianist from keeping a concert engagement in Burlington, Vermont, he cannot be sued for breaking his contract to appear there. When, however, the duty arises from a specific contract that created an absolute obligation to perform, an act of God is not a defense. For instance, the company that sells you tornado insurance or earthquake insurance must compensate you for damages caused by the acts of God against which you bought insurance.

The plaintiff's motive for bringing an action is usually not important and may not be used as a defense.

EXAMPLE Owen is suing his former wife, Clementine, to O—* gain custody of their three children. Owen charges that Clementine is an unfit mother. According to him, Clementine runs around with several different men, the children are frequently left alone, their clothes are dirty, and they do not receive the proper medical care or their mother's affection. Clementine denies these charges and claims that Owen is really suing her for spite because he lost the children in the custody case. She also claims that Owen is jealous because she has an active social life and he has none. The court will disregard Clementine's claims against Owen because they are irrelevant to the issue before the court: Clementine's fitness as a mother.

■ **When an action accrues** As applied to actions, the term "to accrue" means to come into existence. A cause of action accrues when facts exist that permit one party to sue another. For example, a contract cause of action accrues when the contract is breached.

■ **How actions are started** The proper procedure necessary to begin an action is generally regulated by statute and varies from state to state. In states in which an action is begun by a WRIT or a SUMMONS, it starts at the time the writ or summons is delivered to the officer authorized to serve it. Where the filing of a DECLARATION, PETITION, or COMPLAINT is the required method, the action begins when the filing is completed in a regular and proper manner. Some states require both methods.

■ **Pendency and termination** An action is pending from the date of its beginning until its termination. It remains pending as long as it is still open to modification, appeal, or rehearing and until final JUDGMENT (the last decision of a court from which no appeals can be taken) is given. The time when an action ends differs from one state to another. In some states, an action ends when a judgment is handed down; in others it is not regarded as ended until the judgment has been satisfied—the debt has been paid, for example—or until the time for an appeal has expired. See APPEAL AND ERROR.

actionable   Providing a legal reason for a lawsuit. *Actionable words*—calling a person a liar or a thief, for example—are statements that will give grounds for a lawsuit for slander. See also ACTION; LIBEL AND SLANDER.

act of God   Any accident directly and exclusively due to natural causes, without human interference, that could not have been prevented by foresight or care. A variety of occurrences have been held to be acts of God, such as sickness or death, fire originating from lightning, cyclones, earthquakes, extraordinarily high tides, floods, droughts, and violent winds. On the other hand, freezing weather, during a season of the year when it might be expected, is not an act of God. Nor is a flood or a drought if it could have been anticipated by ordinary foresight and if the damage from it could have been prevented or reduced by diligence or skill.

> EXAMPLE In 1929 actress Helen Hayes, learning that she was pregnant, used the act-of-God clause in her contract to withdraw from a successful tour of the play she was starring in. The producer closed the show and also cited the act-of-God clause in a dispute with other members of the cast who, having run-of-the-show contracts, demanded two weeks' salary in place of notice. But the arbitration board appointed to rule on the dispute did not uphold the producer.

Although courts do not consider pregnancy as an act of God, if an actor learned he was terminally ill during the successful tour of a play in which he was starring, he could use the act-of-God clause in his contract to withdraw from the tour. If the actor decided to play out the tour but died while doing so, the producer would have no claim against the actor's estate since death is an act of God.

actual authority   In the law of AGENCY, the authority and power to act that a PRINCIPAL specifically gives to an agent or allows the agent to believe he has been given. Thus, actual authority may be either EXPRESS or IMPLIED.

actual cash value   The fair or reasonable cash price for which an item could be sold on the open market in the ordinary course of business—an automobile's Blue Book price, for example. "Fair market price" and "market value" also have the same meaning.

actual notice   Knowledge of a fact or state of affairs expressly and directly given to a person. If you tell your landlord of a loose board in the stairway, the landlord has actual NOTICE of the defect.

actuarial method   A method of accounting by which payments are first applied to interest and finance charges, then to the principal, as with mortgage payments.

actuary   A person who calculates insurance risks and premiums, such as the probability of a person's dying by a certain age and the consequent amount he should pay to insure his life.

ad damnum   (Latin) "To the damage"; the name of that part of a WRIT or DECLARATION that contains a statement of the plaintiff's money loss or damages claimed.

addict   A person who has acquired the habit of using a substance, such as a narcotic drug, and no longer has control over his intake. A person cannot be arrested just because he is an addict. He must be caught in possession of the drug or selling it. See DRUGS AND NARCOTICS.

additur   1 The power of a trial court to increase the amount of money awarded to the plaintiff by a JURY verdict.   2 An order by a COURT OF APPEALS granting a new trial—when a plaintiff requests it because the jury's award is too low—unless the defendant agrees to pay the plaintiff an additional sum of money within a certain time.

add-on   More goods bought before payment is made for goods previously purchased. Often the contract for the old goods is rewritten to include the new items.

adduce   Offer or introduce evidence at a trial.

ademption   The disposal before death of personal property (as opposed to real estate) left in a WILL so that the property no longer passes under the will. The disposition of the property may be made to anyone, including the person named to receive it under the will. If the property is given to someone else, his right to the property usually supersedes that of the person named in the will.

adhesion contract   A CONTRACT in which one side has all the bargaining power and thus can write the contract in his favor. This type of contract is often made when a buyer can locate only one seller of a particular item. Most adhesion contracts are considered unconscionable—that is, they are so unfair that a court will not enforce them because their terms "shock the conscience" of the court.

ad hoc   (Latin) "For this"; for this special purpose. For example, an *ad hoc* committee is a temporary one set up to do a particular job.

ad hominem   (Latin) "To the man." The term is used to refer to an argument made against an opponent personally instead of against his argument.

ad interim   (Latin) "For the intervening time." An officer *ad interim* is appointed to fill a temporary vacancy or to discharge the duties of the office during the absence or temporary incapacity of its regular officer. A person appointed to serve in the place of a member of Congress who has died is a representative or senator *ad interim*.

adjective law   The law that relates to legal practice and procedure; the rules that direct how proceedings are brought into court and how the court operates after they are brought in. The term is the opposite of SUBSTANTIVE LAW.

adjoining landowners Owners of connecting lands—next-door neighbors or backyard neighbors, for example. The following discussion covers the effect of excavation, buildings, trees, or plants upon an adjacent owner's right to free use and support of his property, including his right, if any, to light, air, and a clear view.

■ **Rights and duties** A landowner is responsible for damage to his neighbor caused by a negligent failure to keep his property in repair. Each landowner is expected to use his property reasonably, while considering the rights of owners of connecting land. For example, you, as a property owner, may dig on your own land for a lawful purpose. At the same time, however, you have a duty to protect your neighbor's land in its natural condition from any damage accompanying your excavation. Use of property is unreasonable, and therefore unlawful, if it amounts to undermining or taking adjoining land.

In general, a landowner has the right to grade his land or otherwise change its composition if he takes proper precautions, such as building a retaining wall to prevent dirt from spilling upon adjoining property. A landowner blasting on his own property is liable for damages caused by dirt and debris thrown onto adjoining land.

■ **Lateral support** An adjoining landowner is entitled to lateral support of his property; that is, he has the right to have his land supported by adjoining property. Therefore if you excavate close to the boundary line with your neighbor you have a duty to prevent injury arising from removal of lateral support from his property. In order to avoid liability for injury to an adjoining owner's building, a person excavating on his own land must conduct the work skillfully and prudently.

■ **Encroachments** An encroachment is an intrusion on adjoining property. No one has the right to erect buildings or other structures on his land so that any part, however small, extends beyond his boundaries and encroaches upon adjoining properties. A landowner may personally remove a neighbor's encroachment.

A landowner should not permit a tree or hedge on his property to invade the rights of adjoining landowners. For example, if you know that a tree in your yard is decayed and may fall and damage the property next door, you have a duty to have the tree cut down.

A tree on a boundary line is the property of both adjoining landowners. Each has an interest identical with the portion standing on his land and each may sever intruding tree branches or roots at the boundary line of his property, whether or not he has sustained any injury by the intrusion. The landowner cutting the branches or roots should do it in such a way that he does not kill the tree or he will be liable.

■ **Light, air, and view** A landowner does not have an unqualified right to light and air from adjoining property. Furthermore, in the absence of a law or agreement to the contrary, he has no right to the view over adjoining land. Thus, for example, by building upon his own property, your neighboring landowner may lawfully deprive you of the light, air, and view that you once enjoyed. If, however, your neighbor acts unreasonably (as measured by what the law considers a reasonable person would do under the circumstances) and substantially interferes with your use and enjoyment of your property, you may sue him for creating a NUISANCE.

EXAMPLE After accusing your children of trampling his prizewinning azaleas, your neighbor builds a six-foot fence to keep your children out of his yard. Although the fence casts a shadow upon your tomato plants, he has a right to build it. You do not have an absolute right to light or air or a view to your neighbor's property.

On the other hand, suppose your neighbor spitefully builds a 20-foot fence so that your vegetable garden will never see sunlight again. You will be able to sue him for nuisance since he has substantially deprived you of the use of your land. It is up to a jury to decide whether your neighbor's conduct is reasonable and if your right to use your property is substantially affected.

See also ANCIENT LIGHTS; BENEFICIAL USE; BOUNDARY; DRAIN; EASEMENT; FENCE; PARTY WALL.

adjournment 1 The postponement of business until another time or to another place. 2 Temporary or permanent dissolution of a court or legislative session.

adjudication The determination of a controversy; decision of a court or administrative body—such as a judge's decision that you must pay your traffic ticket.

adjudicative facts Information to be considered in a court judgment or other official decision.

adjuration A solemn oath; the swearing of a witness at a trial or hearing.

adjust Settle; bring persons to agreement, particularly about a debt or loss. The word commonly refers to the apportionment between claimant and insurer of accident or fire losses.

adjusted gross income A federal INCOME TAX term that means, in general, the money a person makes minus his deductions, such as certain travel, work, or moving expenses. The term is not used for business taxes.

adjuster One who determines or settles the amount of a claim or debt; an INSURANCE agent who settles claims.

ad litem (Latin) "For the suit"; pending the suit. A guardian *ad litem* is a person appointed to bring or defend a suit for someone, such as a child, who lacks legal capacity.

administer 1 Discharge the duties and obligations of an office. 2 Manage the affairs of a dead person. 3 Give an oath. 4 Cause drugs, medicines, or poisons to be taken. 5 Execute a court decree.

administration 1 The management of a business or government. 2 The supervision of the affairs of a dead person. See EXECUTORS AND ADMINISTRATORS. 3 Individuals running the government, particularly the President's Cabinet in Washington, D.C.

administrative agency A branch of government created to execute and enforce particular laws, such as a tax commission, public utility commission, and workmen's compensation commission. See also PUBLIC ADMINISTRATIVE AGENCY.

administrative board A broad term that sometimes means a PUBLIC ADMINISTRATIVE AGENCY and sometimes a body that holds hearings similar to court trials.

administrative discretion The professional judgment required for the exercise of official duties not precisely described by laws or rules.

administrative law See PUBLIC ADMINISTRATIVE AGENCY.

Administrative Procedure Act The law that describes how federal agencies must conduct their hearings and other business and how disputes go from these agencies into court. Some states have a similar law. See PUBLIC ADMINISTRATIVE AGENCY.

administrative remedy The means of enforcing a right by going to a PUBLIC ADMINISTRATIVE AGENCY for help or for a decision. Often you must submit your problem to the proper agency before you may take it to court.

administrator 1 Someone who is appointed by a court to supervise the disbursal of the property of a dead person. 2 Someone who conducts affairs on behalf of another. See DESCENT AND DISTRIBUTION; EXECUTORS AND ADMINISTRATORS.

admiralty A field of law concerned with maritime affairs. It deals with commerce on the seas and other waters and problems arising from their navigation by ships and other vessels. In admiralty law, the word "vessel" generally includes every kind of craft capable of being employed for transportation on waters used for commerce or of navigating any sea, channel, lake, or river used in commerce. Maritime matters, such as claims involving ocean COMMERCE and COLLISIONS between vessels, are handled by FEDERAL COURTS that have admiralty jurisdiction.

■ **Jurisdiction** A merchant ship on the high seas belongs to the country whose flag it flies. For this reason, the jurisdiction of a nation follows a ship on all its ocean voyages. This means that the law and courts of the flag nation settle all legal relations among owners, officers, crew, passengers, and cargo shippers. A country's relations with ships of other countries are controlled by international law as it is expressed in treaties and customs.

The power to legislate with respect to maritime law is given to Congress by the U.S. Constitution, which puts exclusive admiralty jurisdiction (authority) in the federal courts. If American law applies, then it is federal law that controls. Federal admiralty jurisdiction covers voyages on all the NAVIGABLE WATERS of the United States between ports within the same state, as well as on the high seas and tidewaters. Thus, if two ocean liners collided while leaving a port, any subsequent lawsuit would be brought in a federal court that has admiralty jurisdiction. All privately owned and operated vessels—of all nationalities and including pleasure craft—navigating the commercial waters of the United States are subject to the jurisdiction of the federal courts.

EXAMPLE If you were out sailing on the Great Lakes and a motorboat crashed into your sailboat, you could bring a lawsuit to recover damages in a federal court because the Great Lakes are used in commerce. However, the federal court might transfer your lawsuit to a state court because under the law of torts (injuries to a person or a property) the method of arriving at the amount of damages to be awarded to you is the same in either court. If, on the other hand, you were out sailing on Lake Minnihaha, a lake not used in commerce, you could only bring your lawsuit in a state court, not a federal court.

Vessels that are temporarily moored, laid up, aground, or in drydock are ordinarily regarded as within admiralty jurisdiction. As a general rule, however, nonmaritime property is beyond admiralty jurisdiction. This means, for example, that a controversy relating to a contract to build a ship would not be handled as an admiralty case.

Personal injuries Jurisdiction in admiralty extends to personal injuries sustained aboard a ship upon navigable waters (such as falling off an unsteady gangplank), as well as to injuries resulting from the crash of an airplane into such waters. In addition, injuries to airplane passengers traversing airspace over navigable waters are within admiralty jurisdiction, even though no contact with the water is made. For example, an air pocket causes a plane flying above the waters off the coast of Louisiana to drop precipitously, and a passenger standing in the aisle is thrown to the floor and breaks an arm. A personal injury sustained on a wharf, dock, bridge, or pier, however, is not normally within admiralty jurisdiction.

Seizure of a vessel When a U.S. marshal, under court authority, takes custody or control of a ship, the matter is brought to a court that has admiralty jurisdiction. If a ship's cargo is perishable, the court may order any portion of it sold pending a hearing. The proceeds of the sale may be distributed to those who have a claim against the property, including the owner, creditors, etc. See also MARITIME LIEN; SEAMEN; SHIPPING.

admissible evidence Testimony, documents, and exhibits that may be introduced in court; EVIDENCE that a jury may use. Eyewitness testimony, an acknowledged document, and a properly identified weapon would all be admissible evidence. Hearsay testimony, an unacknowledged document, and a weapon without the identifying mark of the officer who took possession of it would be inadmissible.

admission 1 A voluntary statement that certain facts are true; a CONFESSION, a concession, or a voluntary acknowledgment helpful to the other side in a lawsuit. 2 Introduction and acceptance of evidence by a court.

admonition 1 A reprimand given by a judge in place of a jail sentence or some other serious punishment. 2 Oral advice by a judge to a jury.

adopt **1** Accept, choose, or take as your own property, acts, or ideas. **2** Pass a law and put it into effect. **3** Take a child of another as your own, with all the rights and duties that would have existed if he or she were your own offspring. See ADOPTION OF PERSONS.

adoption of persons

The legal establishment of the relationship of parent and child between persons not related that way by birth.

■ **Who may adopt** Because the state alone has the power to determine who may adopt, you must qualify under the laws of your state in order to adopt someone. U.S. citizenship is not necessary unless required by state law.

A husband and wife may adopt a child together, and if no law prohibits it, either may adopt a child alone. An unmarried person may also adopt if no law prevents it.

EXAMPLE As far back as 1971 a bachelor schoolteacher in California was able to adopt a two-year-old boy; and an unmarried 19-year-old from the state of Washington, serving with the Navy, received the court's permission to adopt a young niece and nephew and place them in his parents' care until he completed his military service.

A guardian may adopt, but normally must meet the same standards as any other person seeking to adopt.

Although legislative policy often prefers an adoption by persons of the same religion as the child to be adopted, an interfaith adoption will be permitted when it is in the child's best interests. A New Jersey court has said that, barring special circumstances, adoption cannot be denied just because the prospective parents do not believe in a Supreme Being or are not members of any church.

■ **Who may be adopted** Whether a person is eligible for adoption depends upon state law. Children may be adopted whether their parents are living, dead, or unknown, or have abandoned them, and the fact that a minor has a legal guardian does not prevent his adoption. A parent who loses a child in a custody battle with a spouse may not adopt his legitimate child; but if there is no law against it, a parent may adopt his illegitimate child. You may adopt a child of a race other than your own: a Texas law prohibiting an interracial adoption has been declared unconstitutional.

Adoption of adults Adults may be adopted under laws that permit the adoption of any person; in some states, laws specifically permit their adoption. In a Minnesota case, it was decided that a person may be adopted by his own adult child, but in Rhode Island a judge refused to permit a 30-year-old man to adopt his 20-year-old girl friend. The purpose of adult adoption is usually to make a person eligible to inherit.

EXAMPLE In a state where adult adoptions were allowed by statute, a court held that a 56-year-old man could adopt his 45-year-old wife so that she could inherit under a trust that had been started by his mother. (Upon his death, the proceeds of the trust were supposed to go to his heirs-at-law. In that jurisdiction, an adopted child was regarded as an heir unless specifically disinherited.) Incidentally, the adoption was held not to be an incestuous relationship.

■ **Significant considerations** In this country there was a period when adoption was regarded for the most part as a means for a childless couple to "normalize" their marriage. Today it is increasingly seen primarily as a way to place a child in a better environment. When a number of states recently enacted statutes permitting adoptions to be subsidized, the procedure became a social tool to improve the circumstances of underprivileged children. The subsidy encourages adoption of children by suitable parents who could not otherwise afford it. Subsidized adoption is playing an increasingly important role in settling so-called hard-to-place children (often handicapped or nonwhite) whose sole alternative might otherwise be years in an institution. A related recent trend is the encouragement by state and private child welfare agencies of interracial adoptions. If a person is willing to adopt a hard-to-place child,

---

IF YOU ARE PLANNING TO ADOPT

■ Qualifications to adopt are set by state law. In order to adopt, you must qualify under the laws of your state. In many states an unmarried person may adopt.

■ Although interfaith adoption is often permitted if it is in the child's best interests, you will have an easier time if you adopt a child born into the same religion as yourself.

■ You may adopt a child of a race other than your own. (Laws against interracial adoption have been declared unconstitutional.)

■ If you have lost your child in a custody battle with your spouse, you may not adopt the child.

■ The free consent of the natural parents is needed for a child to be adoptable, unless their parental rights have been terminated.

■ If your prospective adopted child has reached a stated age (usually from 10 to 14, depending on your state's law), his consent is also necessary.

■ If neither of the child's parents can be found, consent of next of kin or of a guardian may be required.

■ A common way to adopt an infant rapidly is through a private adoption arranged by the mother's family or her doctor—you must usually pay the medical bills and legal expenses. Your safest way to adopt—agency placement—is also the slowest.

■ You may pay your lawyer a fee for handling the legalities of an adoption, but no more than that.

■ Do not get conned into buying a baby on the black market—it is a felony to buy and sell children.

■ Your adoptive child will receive a new birth certificate with his new name, as soon as adoption proceedings are completed.

■ Your adopted child may eventually feel he has the right to know his "roots," and that right will be recognized in several states if he chooses to exercise it.

■ Adult adoptees may sue for access to adoption records in order to receive family medical information.

■ You may usually adopt another adult in order to make him or her eligible to inherit, but carefully check your state's laws and court rulings.

some of the rules are often waived. On the other hand, strict requirements must be met if a person wants to adopt an easily placed child.

In deciding whether an adoption would be proper, a court may consider various factors bearing upon the child's welfare. Age of the adopting parents is one. The right of a natural parent to his child, though not the dominating factor, is another. Religion is a significant consideration, but not a dominating one even under state laws that require the child and adopting parents to be of the same religion whenever practicable or possible.

In some states the adopting parent must have custody of the child for a specified period of time before obtaining an adoption decree. This requirement is to prevent hasty action and to determine with as much certainty as possible whether the child's best interests will be promoted by the adoption. The best interests of the child are always the most important consideration to the court.

■ **Whose consent is required** In almost every state a child's consent to his adoption is necessary if he has reached a stated age (usually between 10 and 14 years) at the time of the adoption. See Chart 19. Consent of the natural parents is generally essential to a valid adoption, and it must be freely given. The parents' refusal to allow an adoption conclusively blocks it, even if the child would be better off with the adoptive parents.

Traditionally, the right to grant or withhold consent for adoption of an illegitimate child only extended to the mother. It was thought that the father of an illegitimate child did not have enough interest in raising the child to entitle him to decide whether the child should be placed for adoption. In 1979 the Supreme Court ruled that a law that deprived all unwed fathers of the right to veto adoption, regardless of whether they took care of their children, was an unconstitutional form of sex discrimination. The Court held that the father—who had lived with the mother for five years, during which time their children were born—had the right to block adoption of the children by a man who later married the mother. See also ILLEGITIMACY.

Consents signed before or soon after the birth of the child have been particularly susceptible to attack by the natural mother. Despite sketchy evidence, findings of involuntary consent have been handed down in these cases because of the natural mother's physical and mental condition. In determining whether a natural parent may revoke his consent, a court will consider all the circumstances, including the welfare of the child.

EXAMPLE In one famous case, Olga Scarpetta, the natural mother of an illegitimate child who came to be known as Baby Lenore, withdrew her consent for her baby's adoption. In November 1970, she sued in New York for the child's return from Nicholas and Jean De-Martino, the couple planning to adopt her. Baby Lenore had been in their home since June, and they were awaiting the end of the state's required six-month trial period. When both the lower court and the appeals court awarded the little girl to Miss Scarpetta, the DeMartinos took Baby Lenore and their other child to Florida, where they had reason to believe the courts would find in their favor. This proved to be the case. When the U.S. Supreme Court in 1972 refused to rule on the New York decision, the

DeMartinos decided to make Florida their permanent home. They cannot return to New York without giving up Baby Lenore and serving a contempt-of-court sentence for having disregarded the court order to give her up.

The case caused a stir among adopting parents and prompted efforts to enact laws that would limit the time period in which a mother may change her mind about giving up her baby for adoption. In New York it was finally legislated that a mother cannot revoke her consent after 30 days. If she revokes it before 30 days, she does not automatically get back her child, but a hearing must be held to determine the best interests of the child.

In the case of divorced parents, consent of the one who was awarded custody is required for a valid adoption of the child. Whether or not consent of the other parent is needed depends upon the state adoption law.

Consent of NEXT OF KIN or of a guardian may be required if neither parent can be found. See GUARDIAN AND WARD. Depending upon state law, consent of an agency, board, or official having custody of a child may be necessary. Consent of a parent who abandons or seriously abuses or neglects a child is not required. Abandonment means refusal to care for a child. Nonsupport is an important factor in determining whether a child has been abandoned. However, if a parent shows a continuing interest in the child's welfare and makes plans for his future, courts will generally try to keep parent and child together.

■ **Ways to adopt** Adoptions are made in several ways: through an agency, by private transfer, illegally by purchase of a child, and occasionally by contract or by deed.

Adoption through agencies State laws often provide for agencies, operated or licensed by the government, to serve as intermediaries between natural and adopting parents. When a woman turns over her child to an agency, she must sign a formal surrender agreement, which deprives her of all rights to the child and gives the agency authority to arrange for adoption by suitable applicants. When an adoption is proposed, agencies always investigate to find out whether the child is a proper subject for adoption, whether the proposed home is a good one, and whether this particular adoption is in the best interests of the child.

Private adoption Independent placement, or private adoption, takes place when a child is transferred directly from the natural mother or her representative to the adopting parents. Often, this kind of adoption is arranged by the mother's family or her doctor. Usually, the adopting parents pay the medical bills connected with the pregnancy and birth, as well as any legal expenses and fees.

EXAMPLE One New York couple, unable to have children, was called by the wife's doctor, who offered them a baby—one he had just delivered—in exchange for the natural mother's medical expenses. Three days later, consent papers were signed by the natural mother, and on payment of $710 the couple was handed the baby in the hospital parking lot.

Private adoptions are legal in most states, but if the adopting parents make payments other than those permitted by law, the adoption is illegal. Illegal adoptions are discussed later under the heading "Black-market babies."

Private versus agency placements Both private and agency placement have advantages and disadvantages.

Agency placement minimizes the risk of parents' adopting an unhealthy child, of the natural mother's discovering the identity of the adopting parents, and of the natural mother's changing her mind about the adoption. Agency adoption provides for rigorous investigation of the backgrounds of both the natural and adopting parents to insure the suitability of child and parents. In almost all cases, fees and costs are kept at a minimum when adoption is through an agency. On the negative side, agencies require adopting parents to meet strict requirements, and their investigation into the prospective parents' suitability is long. Because of the strict standards, the number of children available for adoption through agencies is limited.

Private placement is attractive because it makes adoption possible for those who might have to wait a long time or would not be eligible for an agency adoption. It provides a degree of privacy and anonymity for the natural mother. But private placement entails greater risks than does agency placement: The natural mother may not complete the adoption procedure, or she may discover the adopting parents' identity and try to claim the child. Private adoption involves the chance both that the child may not be a healthy one and that the adopting parents may not be suitable for parenthood. Finally, the line between private and black-market adoptions is thin, and there is the risk that unless proper procedures are strictly followed, the adoption will be illegal.

Black-market babies In addition to agency placement and legal private placement, there is an illegal black market in babies, which gives childless couples a chance to obtain babies. The black market is caused by the extensive delays, the complicated procedures of the agencies and courts, and the relatively small number of adoptable children for the number of individuals desiring to adopt. The black market speeds up the adoption procedure, because there is no investigation as there is in an agency adoption, and it may also offer the advantage of secrecy to the natural mother. Unfortunately, the main requirement for the adopting parents of black-market babies is the ability to pay the price—sometimes as much as $20,000—demanded by the black-market operator.

The illegality of the black-market adoption arises from the amount of money paid by the adopting parents, which by law is limited to the natural mother's delivery and confinement expenses. The prospective parents may not pay money for the infant itself, because it is a crime to buy and sell children. A Florida couple who exchanged a car for a three-month-old baby had to face FELONY charges.

In some states a lawyer may not, under any circumstances, obtain babies for clients to adopt. Usually, adopting parents may pay their lawyer a fee for handling the legalities of an adoption, but no more than that. In various cities throughout the country, there are investigations of lawyers who are believed to be guilty of crimes associated with baby selling.

Contracts or agreements As a general rule, legal adoption cannot be achieved by private contract. Nevertheless, a court may choose to treat a contract for adoption as an agreement to be enforced with all the results equivalent to a formal adoption.

EXAMPLE Marcia and Steve Macroyd, two 36-year-old college professors, tried unsuccessfully for 10 years to have a child of their own. After agreeing that adoption was their last alternative, the couple was told of a two-year waiting list for infants at the local adoption agencies. During a conference with Angela, one of her most promising premedical students, Marcia was surprised to learn that Angela was six-months pregnant. Angela had decided that she would put the baby up for adoption so that both she and the child would have better futures. Marcia and Steve asked Angela if she would be willing to allow them to adopt her baby in exchange for paying her medical expenses. Angela agreed. After the baby was born, the couple, Angela, and their attorneys met to draw up a contract based on their verbal agreements. They went to court so that a judge could witness Angela's signing of the contract and a separate consent decree in which she stated that she willingly and knowingly gave up the rights to her baby in favor of Marcia and Steve. This consent decree was required by state law in order to prevent the natural mother from later attempting to reclaim her child from the adopting parents. It would be clear that an unmarried woman entered a contract for the adoption of her baby with a full understanding of the legal consequences of her act.

Contracts between parents and orphanages have also been upheld in the courts.

An agreement for adoption can be either express (stated) or implied. Parents who give up control of their child, however, are not making an agreement that he may be adopted. Similarly, the fact that a child is received into a home, cared for, and educated does not mean that he has any other claims upon those who took him in. In such circumstances there is no implied agreement to adopt the child.

Contracts of adoption are ordinarily not thought to be injurious to public welfare, but in some states they are frowned upon, on the ground that the law should not permit a parent to trade away his child. Because the courts are hesitant to deprive a natural parent of the right to care for a child, enforcement of a contract for adoption will be refused whenever the welfare of the child requires it. Moreover, under some state laws a contract made by one parent alone, without the clear consent of the other, may not be valid.

Revocation In proper circumstances the court will permit a natural parent to withdraw from an agreement for the adoption of his child. For instance, if the parent had been forced into an adoption agreement, a court might permit him to renounce it. The court will examine the circumstances under which the parent's consent was given and, possibly, the parent's reasons for wanting to get out of the contract. Breach of promise to raise a child in the Catholic faith was not a sufficient reason to revoke an adoption agreement in Missouri.

Virtual or equitable adoption When a person agrees to adopt a child legally but fails to do so, the court may rule that there has been a virtual, or equitable, adoption.

EXAMPLE In one case, Bill and Jane Kohn (let's call them) arranged for Jane to go to Florida to bring home an infant whom they could adopt. During the 13 months that the Kohns lived together as a family, Bill supported the child and claimed her as a dependent on his federal income tax return. He even took the baby to the local synagogue so that she could be named according to the Jewish tradition. When the Kohns separated, the child stayed with Jane, and Bill stopped supporting them. Although he corresponded with the child, signing his letters "Love, Dad," she was never formally adopted.

In her divorce action, Jane asked for support for herself and the child. Bill claimed that since he had never actually adopted the baby, he could not be made to pay. He had only agreed to adopt the girl. The court rejected his argument and found him liable for the support of a child under the theory of equitable adoption. Bill had agreed to adopt the child and had supported her before the separation. Bill and Jane were the only parents the child ever knew. It was only fair that since Bill had treated her as his own, he could not refuse to support the child.

No legal relationship arises from a virtual adoption, and no relation of parent and child is created. In a few cases, however, some courts have permitted such a child to inherit from the foster parents as if the adoption had been completed. Such a ruling is fair and equitable when the child really considered these people to be his parents.

Adoption by deed In some states, adoption can be accomplished by means of a written DECLARATION or DEED, which usually must be recorded. If recording is required, the adoption is not valid until the deed has been properly recorded. See RECORD.

■ **Effects of adoption** Ordinarily, an adoption ends all legal relations between the child and his or her natural parents and creates the same relationship between the adopting parents and their adopted child as existed between the natural parents and their child. The relationship existing between a child and natural relatives other than his parents is not destroyed by the new status. An adopted child is entitled to the same rights as a natural child, except that when an adult is adopted, the adopting parent need not support him.

The name of a child may or may not be affected by adoption, depending upon applicable state law. The adoption of a minor child changes his legal residence from that of the natural parents to that of the adopting parents.

Inheritance A state legislature has the power to give or take away the adopted child's rights of INHERITANCE from his adopting parents. State laws often provide that an adopted child can inherit from the adopting parents in the same way as a natural child. Adopting parents can inherit the property of an adopted child who dies before they do.

When the adopted child has not made a will, state laws of DESCENT AND DISTRIBUTION determine whether adoptive parents have superior inheritance rights over "real" relatives (for example, a brother or aunt). However, it is important to keep in mind that an adoptive child is legally capable of making a will and can thus make any provision he wishes for his adoptive parents.

EXAMPLE Marie was adopted at the age of six months by O——＊ Bette and Mike, a young middle-class couple who had no other children. Her natural parents, Martha and Oscar, gave her up because they were extremely poor and had 15 other children. By the time she was 10, Marie was a successful child model. But her career was tragically cut

short when she was killed by a hit-and-run driver. As a result of her modeling, Marie left an estate worth $200,000. The laws of the state where she lived provided that a child's parents were entitled to two thirds of the estate with the remaining one third to be evenly divided among surviving brothers and sisters. If there were no siblings, the parents would take the entire estate. Adoption laws provided that once a child was adopted, her adoptive parents and family had superior inheritance rights to the exclusion of her natural parents and family. In this case, Bette and Mike would inherit Marie's entire estate because Martha, Oscar, and their 15 children lost whatever inheritance rights that they might have had under the law once Marie was adopted.

For state laws concerning the right of adopted children to inherit from their natural parents, see Chart 19.

■ **Revocation of adoption** An adoption decree obtained by fraud or lack of consent can be revoked. Without the consent required of *all* concerned parties stipulated by law, an order of adoption is not legal. After revocation of a decree, the child assumes the status he had before the adoption proceedings. See also PARENT AND CHILD.

■ **Summary of procedure** Formal steps in adopting a child are much the same in all states. The steps are:

Notice Notice of adoption proceedings is given to all parties legally interested in the case, with the exception of the child himself. When the child is illegitimate, the father, if he can be found, must be notified as well as the mother, although his consent may not be needed for the adoption. See ILLEGITIMACY. In some states a parent who has failed to support a child is not entitled to notice, but a parent who has been deprived of custody of a child in a divorce or separation case is. An adoption agency having custody of the child is likewise entitled to notice.

Petition The prospective parents file a petition in court, supplying information about their and the child's situation. The filing of a proper petition gives the court jurisdiction (authority) over an adoption case. To find out which court has jurisdiction in each state, see Chart 19. Either the petition or a form filed with it reveals the names and residences of the adopting parents, the child, and the natural parents, if known to the adopting parents. The child's sex and age are stated. Some states require every petition for adoption to be accompanied by a medical report on the child.

Written consent The petition for adoption is accompanied by the written consent of the adoption agency or the child's natural parents, depending upon the circumstances, as discussed earlier in this article in the section "Whose consent is required." Consent of the natural parents is not needed if a court has removed the child from their custody because of neglect.

Hearing Next, a hearing is held, during which the court examines the qualifications of the prospective parents and grants or denies the petition accordingly. At the hearing the parties must have an opportunity to present testimony and to examine or to cross-examine witnesses. Because adoption proceedings are confidential, the hearing takes place in a closed courtroom. In most cases, records of the hearing are available for examination only by court order. For example, law enforcement agencies investigating alleged sales of babies would need a court order before checking the records. The purpose of the confidentiality is to encourage the child to have a sense of security with his new family.

Probation In most states a period of PROBATION is required before the final adoption decree is issued. See Chart 19. During this time, the child lives with the adopting parents, and the appropriate state agency watches the family to see how the relationship develops. The agency is particularly interested in observing whether the new parents are able to care for the child properly. If all parties are happy with the situation, the state agency asks for a permanent adoption decree, which is a JUDGMENT of the court. If the arrangement is not satisfactory, the child either goes back to his previous home or is cared for by the state.

Birth certificate After the proceedings are completed, a new birth certificate, called a certification of adoption, is issued for the child. It gives his new family name, the date and place of his birth, and the ages of his adopting parents at the time of his birth. This certificate makes no mention of his natural parents or of the date and place of his adoption. The old birth certificate is sealed and filed away, to be opened only by a court order. If the adoption takes place when the child is too young to understand what is happening, he may never know the names of his real parents, and, unless his adopting parents choose to reveal the information, he may never even know he was adopted.

■ **Right to information about natural parents** Most states have laws denying the adoptee access to records that reveal information about his origin. Often the natural parents have required this anonymity as a condition of their consent to the adoption.

EXAMPLE Don, an adult adoptee, wants to learn the identity 0⊶✳ of his natural parents. He must ask the court to open his sealed adoption records. The court may refuse to do so unless his natural parents, who must be given notice of the action, consent and Don has shown that he has good cause for the disclosure of such information. During the time the court is making its determination, the identity of his parents remains undisclosed because notice of the action is usually given to someone other than the natural parents, named by the court, on their behalf.

With the increased public interest in tracing ethnic and family backgrounds, adoptees who have become adults are demanding the right to obtain information about their natural parents. They recognize that revealing this type of information to a minor adoptee could produce unnecessary psychological trauma but they contend that most adoption statutes do not make a distinction between minor and adult adoptees. As a result, the state, in an effort to protect minors, effectively deprives the adults of their right to know their "roots." Alabama, Kansas, South Dakota, and Virginia are among the few states that give the adult adoptee the right to see his original birth certificate or to read his adoption records.

Different approaches are being used to reach a resolution of this problem. In California, proposed legislation would require public and private adoption agencies to open their records to adult adoptees on request, with certain limitations. If the natural parents had placed the child for adoption before the effective date of the legislation, they could veto the adoptee's request to see the records. Another approach is to challenge the constitutionality of the state statutes that prevent all adoptees from having access to their records. In New York, one case has challenged the statute on the ground that it violates the 14th Amendment guarantee of EQUAL PROTECTION OF LAWS for all. The parties contend that the rights of adult adoptees have been denied because their status as adoptees prevents them from receiving family medical information, which is freely given to a nonadopted person.

The issue of the rights of the adult adoptees to obtain information about their roots is not clear-cut or isolated. There is the additional legal consideration of the right of the natural parents to privacy, which might be violated if adult adoptees have free access to court records. The competing interests of the adult adoptee and his natural parents must be balanced somehow.

adult A person who has reached the age a state has set for acquiring certain rights, among them voting in governmental elections, making a valid contract, bringing a legal action, and purchasing alcoholic beverages.

adulteration Mixing inferior, cheaper, or harmful substances with better ones in order to increase volume or lower costs of production. The term is usually applied to the act of mixing into FOOD or drink materials that lower the overall quality—frankfurters adulterated with a nonmeat product, for example. The range of laws prohibiting or regulating adulteration of products is extensive.

adultery Voluntary sexual intercourse between one person who is married and another who is not the husband or wife. The law considers adultery an offense against public morals and a violation of the MARRIAGE relationship. Statutes attempt to suppress adulterous conduct by punishing it as a crime and by permitting an innocent spouse to use it as a ground for DIVORCE.

■ **Unlawful sexual intercourse** *Fornication* differs from adultery because neither party to the unlawful sexual intercourse need be married. Under the common law a man who had sexual intercourse with a woman not his wife, whether she was married or unmarried, was guilty of fornication. Most modern statutes say that if the man and woman have sexual relations without being married to each other, both are guilty of adultery if either is married to someone else. If two unmarried people have sexual relations, both are guilty of fornication.

Rape is sexual intercourse against a woman's will, accomplished by threats or force. In a few states RAPE is also considered adultery if the man is married.

Although adultery has long been considered a legal wrong, it has not always been treated as a crime. Several states, however, make it a crime by statute. Their aim is to preserve the family and thus promote peace and order in society.

■ **State statutes** Each law defines what sexual acts are prohibited. Some laws say that both parties are guilty of a crime if either person is married to someone else, while others have said that the act is not criminal adultery unless the woman is married.

A single act of adultery is a crime under the law of some states, but in others, only an ongoing adulterous relationship is criminal. In some states the continuing relationship is considered a more serious crime than a single act, and a person who indulges in repeated acts of adultery with a lover may be punished more severely than a one-time offender. In some states more severe punishment is given for open and notorious adultery—that is, publicly living together as husband and wife.

Defenses   A person who has been accused of adultery may have a valid legal defense if the act was not consummated or if one of the parties was physically unable to achieve sexual intercourse. A woman who has been raped is not guilty of adultery. In some states it is a valid defense to prove that the accused did not know that the other person was married. Under a few statutes only a married person can be convicted of adultery. If the other party to the act is unmarried, he or she may be convicted of fornication but not of adultery.

The complaint   In some states, only the husband or wife of the accused person can commence prosecution for adultery. In states that have laws that a HUSBAND AND WIFE cannot testify against each other, however, a spouse cannot file charges. But a husband or wife can always file a complaint against his or her spouse's lover.

Evidence   The usual rules of EVIDENCE control what kinds of evidence can be offered to prove guilt or innocence. The prosecutor must show that the accused person and another named person had sexual relations and, depending on the law of the state, that one or both of them were married to someone else at the time.

Evidence that the accused woman is pregnant or has given birth to an illegitimate child may be admissible, especially if the woman is married but her husband was absent at the time she became pregnant. A judge may permit letters to be introduced into court in which the accused lovers have written about their feelings or secret meetings. Evidence showing the good or bad reputation of each party may be put before the jury. Evidence of a woman's sexual relations with men other than the accused cannot be used, but if her reputation as a common prostitute can be demonstrated that can be offered as evidence. Suspicious actions and incriminating circumstances may be used as circumstantial evidence. The state may prove, for example, that the couple spent a night together, introduced themselves as husband and wife, or frequently kept company while the husband or wife of one was out of town.

It is not necessary to have photographs or the testimony of a witness who actually saw the accused people having sexual intercourse. Usually it is enough to show that the two people had a clear liking for each other and on a certain occasion the chance to get together for sex. Evidence of *opportunity* and *inclination*—a chance and the desire—may be enough to prove guilt beyond a reasonable doubt. The rule that adultery can be assumed when there is opportunity and inclination is based on logic. Why, one judge asked, were the man and woman staying in the same hotels in six different European cities one summer if they were not meeting each other?

Judges steadfastly refuse to believe adultery has occurred unless the evidence is clear.

EXAMPLE   A judgment of divorce was reversed even though a man proved that his wife had spent three nights in the home of another man who was not married at the time. The court found that the woman was really a houseguest. She was visiting the man's married daughter, who also lived in the house. On all three occasions the wife had her three-year-old child with her. There was no evidence that this man was affectionate toward the woman accused of adultery, and the court absolutely refused to believe adultery had occurred.

Enforcement of statutes   Although adultery is criminal in a number of states, the truth is that offenders are very seldom prosecuted. This is not because the crime is difficult to prove. Our legal system is going through a period of reevaluating crimes such as adultery. Some of the questions concern the wisdom of using jail time and fines to punish adults for their voluntary sexual activities, even if these do threaten the stability of families. While the questions are debated, law enforcement officials continue their policy of nonenforcement.

■ **Excuse for a crime**   Adultery has on occasion been offered as a defense to criminal charges. It is the classic defense used by someone who is charged with murdering his or her spouse's lover. In general, courts have been unwilling to excuse murder on the ground that the accused was upset about his spouse's extramarital affair.

EXAMPLE   One criminal court in Texas was willing to take into account evidence of adultery. A man walked into a hotel room to warn another man to stay away from his family, and he found his wife in bed with the other man. He pulled out a gun and starting shooting, killing the other man and wounding his wife. The jury sentenced him to 50 years in prison for murder.

The court of criminal appeals ruled that a new trial would have to be held. It maintained that the jury should have been told that they could consider convicting the accused man of voluntary manslaughter, a much lighter charge than murder. There was evidence that the man had not planned a cold-blooded murder but had only "acted under the immediate influence of sudden passion" when he found his wife lying on the bed in the victim's hotel room. The court was not saying that the wife's adultery is a defense for the husband who murders her lover, but it did find that the adultery may have affected his mental state and, thus, the degree of the crime.

■ **Adultery and divorce**   Today adultery is mentioned more often in DIVORCE courts than in criminal courts. But recent changes in the divorce laws have made it easier for unhappy couples to end their marriages without claiming that one person committed adultery.

ad valorem   (Latin) "According to value." An *ad valorem* tax is based on the value of an item rather than on a class of items without regard to the value of each item in it. An *ad valorem* tax of say 10 percent on a $5,000 automobile would be $500, and $1,000 on a $10,000 fur coat, while a specific automobile tax might be levied on all automobiles at the rate of $250 each.

advance   1 Pay money before it is due.   2 Loan money or furnish money on credit.   3 Supply an item before it is paid for. In publishing contracts and other business transactions, money paid against expected future earnings is called an advance.

advancement   Money or property given by a parent to a child or other HEIR, the value of which is to be deducted from the child's eventual share in his estate. In some states, advancements refer to intestate property (when there is no WILL giving inheritance instructions) that is inherited according to the laws of DESCENT AND DISTRIBUTION, while in others it applies to all inherited property. Courts determine from the circumstances of the case whether or not an advancement was made.

adversary proceeding   1 A hearing or trial in which both sides of a lawsuit or criminal trial are present and generally represented by lawyers.   2 The usual form of a court trial.

adversary system   The almost universal method of American law, in which a judge acts as the decision maker between opposite sides in a hearing or trial. The contesting parties can be individuals, particular classes of individuals, partnerships, associations, corporations, the federal government, or a state government.

adverse interest   A need and a goal opposed to those of another individual; a differing legal concern or claim. Neighbors disputing a property line and drivers involved in an automobile accident have adverse interests.

adverse possession   The open and hostile possession of land to the exclusion of the true owner by a person who claims TITLE to it. If continued for the period of time set by state statute, the claim becomes an actual title. Adverse possession is simply one person's taking someone else's private property for his own use.

Title (ownership) by adverse possession comes about because the true owner has not started a lawsuit for the recovery of his land within the period set by the statute of limitations. See LIMITATIONS OF ACTIONS, and see Chart 12 for the period required by each state. Adverse possession becomes an actual title to land on the theory that the true owner abandons his rights to the property if he does not assert his rights against the occupant of the land. Adverse possession supersedes the legal principle that ownership of land cannot be abandoned because of the length of time involved and the method of possession.

Title by adverse possession to privately owned land may be acquired from any person or corporation. Consequently, every homeowner should be careful not to let others exercise possession over his land.

EXAMPLE Let us say that you are about to buy a house. You
O⸺✶ have the property surveyed and discover that the driveway of the house next door extends three feet onto the lot of the house you want to purchase. If that driveway has been in use for the period prescribed in your state's adverse possession law, that three-foot strip now belongs to the owner of the house next door.

■ **Nature of possession**   It is generally necessary that possession be actual, open, notorious, exclusive, hostile,

uninterrupted, continuous, and claimed as a right. *Notorious possession* means possession so conspicuous that it is generally known and talked of by the public or the people in the neighborhood. All of these conditions should exist. In determining whether or not they do, the courts always consider the facts of each case. In most—but not all—states, payment of taxes on the land by the nonowner is not a condition to getting title by adverse possession. Successive adverse possessions by different individuals can sometimes be added together to satisfy the requirements of the statute of limitations. For example, a landlord may add his tenant's possession to his own when they both have occupied property belonging to someone else.

It is important to remember that adverse possession requires an ouster from the property of the true owner and of any other person claiming title or possession. Adverse possession depends upon the occupant's true intention, ordinarily shown by his acts, to claim title to the property in question. Open, visible, and notorious possession is required if the true owner does not have actual knowledge of the hostile claim upon his land. Trifling acts that are doubtful in character and do not clearly indicate an intention to take over the property are insufficient.

EXAMPLE In Texas, a man who from time to time used his
O⸺✶ neighbor's land for cattle grazing and deer hunting filed a deed claiming ownership of that land, some 25 acres. He then posted no-trespassing signs and built a road in the woods to make hunting easier. His claim was denied because, the court said, the true owner could not be presumed to have known of the adverse possession.

■ **Acts of possession**   Actual possession of some part of the land claimed is an indispensable element of adverse possession. Unless prescribed by statute, there is no fixed rule as to what particular acts may or may not be actual possession. Such acts depend upon the nature, character, location, and present state of the land, as well as upon the uses to which it is put.

Excluding trespassers does not amount to actual possession, but it may be another factor supporting possession by the nonowner. Regular and seasonal cultivation of the land by the nonowner usually shows actual possession. As a rule, the use of land for pasturage must have other acts of ownership accompanying it, such as building a fence around the pasture. Taking the natural products of land, such as tapping sugar trees or quarrying stone, is taking possession of the land. Ordinarily, just cutting or mowing hay, grass, or weeds is not sufficient to constitute actual possession. Nor is surveying land or marking its boundaries. Enclosure, such as by fencing, does tend to show actual possession, and together with other acts—occupation, cultivation, use for pasturage, and the erection of buildings—is generally sufficient to constitute adverse possession.

Woodlands   There must ordinarily be a continuous and persistent cutting of timber from the property to show a claim of ownership. Marking trees, occasionally selling timber, and fencing to make a pasture are not sufficient acts to get title to woodland by adverse possession.

Vacant lots and wild land   If you claim ownership of a vacant lot and walk on it or use it for a ball field at reasonable intervals, mark its limits or corners with fences or posts, clear it of brush, grass, and weeds, and point it out as your property to your neighbors and friends, your acts could amount to adverse possession under the law.

It is generally recognized that title by adverse possession cannot be acquired to wild land that has always been open and unenclosed.

Color of title This is a title that appears valid but is not because it was given, for example, by the deed of a legally incompetent person, such as a minor. If state law permits COLOR OF TITLE for acquisition of title by adverse possession, it must be held for the full period prescribed by the statute of limitations for adverse possession.

EXAMPLE John, a senile 83-year-old man, gave his nephew O⊷⚹ Tim the deed to waterfront property. Although Mary, John's wife, knew about the transfer of the property, she did nothing. Since John was very sick and not expected to live long, Mary decided that she would let Tim improve the property and then, after John's death, have the deed declared invalid. This way she would get the benefit of Tim's improvements. Tim fenced off the land, had it landscaped, and built a house for himself and his family. Over the years, the value of the property increased. John lingered for 12 years before he died. Mary then claimed that the property belonged to John's estate (and thus ultimately to her), not to Tim, because John had been senile when he gave the deed to Tim, and thus legally incapable of transferring property.

The court rejected Mary's argument and ruled that Tim owned the land. State law provided that a person gained title to land by adverse possession if he had held color of title for 10 years. Although the deed was invalid, the length of time Tim had held color of title turned it into good (valid) title. Had Mary challenged the validity of Tim's deed anytime within 10 years from the day he received it, the court would have ruled in her favor.

■ **Public property** Generally speaking, title to property dedicated or devoted to a public use cannot be acquired by adverse possession. Accordingly, title by adverse possession cannot be acquired against a state or a county. This rule has been applied, for example, to tidelands and cemetery lands. There is a conflict, however, over whether title by adverse possession can be acquired to property held for public use by a municipality other than a county. Some courts hold that it can, others that it cannot, and the latter view has defeated acquisition of title to streets, alleys, rights-of-way, parkways, public squares, parks, fire engine lots, and public docks. Because the matter is sometimes regulated by state statute, you should find out what rules are applicable where you live.

■ **Interruption of adverse possession** Although the property owner, the adverse possessor, or even a stranger may interrupt adverse possession, usually the interruption must be by the property owner, who must either start a lawsuit or complete some unequivocal act of ownership, such as accompanying police onto the land to tell the possessor to leave. In some states, if the true owner simply enters his property with an intention to repossess it, this act will interrupt the possession of the adverse occupant. In other states, the entry must be followed by a lawsuit or by the owner's possession for a specified period of time.

Adverse possession is not interrupted by casual, occasional, or temporary entries by the true owner or by his presence upon the land with permission of the adverse occupant. Examples of casual acts that do not interrupt the period of adverse possession are occasionally using a storage shed located on the property, traveling across a path on the way to other property the owner owns, or cutting timber for firewood. A widely recognized rule is that the owner's entry must be peaceful in order to interrupt adverse possession of his property. This requirement exists to discourage dangerous and violent conduct between the people involved. The owner's payment of taxes indicates that he has not abandoned the land, but payment alone does not interrupt adverse possession unless state law so provides. Once there is any interruption the true owner is immediately repossessed of the land.

■ **Personal property** Ownership of personal property may also be lost or acquired through adverse possession. The law concerning adverse possession of personal property is similar to that for adverse possession of land, and the courts commonly use the same rules. Generally, adverse possession of personal property for the period specified by statute gives the possessor an absolute title or right to it. Everyday examples of personal property often lost in this manner include bonds, stock certificates, automobiles, jewelry, and livestock.

EXAMPLE If you ask your friend to keep your ruby ring in O⊷⚹ her safe but, instead, she wears the ring and tells people that it belongs to her, her statement may eventually become true as a result of adverse possession. If she wears the ring on occasions when you have been present and you do not challenge her claims of ownership, the ring will legally belong to your friend after a certain number of years.

Unless otherwise provided by statute, the holder's fraud or bad faith does not affect his claim to personal property by adverse possession.

See also EASEMENT; PRESCRIPTION; PROPERTY; TRESPASS.

advertising by professionals
Traditionally, advertising of services by lawyers, doctors, pharmacists, and persons in other professions was frowned upon by professional societies and the courts. In June 1977, however, the Supreme Court ruled that lawyers may advertise their services and the fees that probably would be charged; the Court maintained that a ban on advertising was a violation of the free speech guarantees of the First Amendment. The American Bar Association adopted a code of guidelines for advertising, applicable only to ABA members, but state bar associations cautioned lawyers of the dangers of advertising their services before the states established their own guidelines. There is a steadily growing trend, however, toward requiring or permitting professionals of all kinds to publicize their services, fees, and areas of specialization.

advisement
Consideration; deliberation. Case "under advisement" means the judge has heard the evidence but will delay a decision while considering the matter.

advisory jury
A jury that a federal judge can call to help decide factual questions, even though he has the right to decide the questions alone. See FACT SITUATION.

advisory opinion   A formal opinion on a question submitted to the court by the legislature or an administrative officer. At present only seven states (Colorado, Florida, Maine, Massachusetts, New Hampshire, Rhode Island, and South Dakota) have provisions for issuing advisory opinions. The court is more frequently asked for opinions on matters of PUBLIC POLICY than of property or personal rights. For example, in 1975 the justices of the Massachusetts Supreme Court gave the State House of Representatives its advisory opinion that a proposed bill on regulation of the wholesale liquor industry, although constitutional, could operate in an unconstitutional manner. Advisory opinions are not binding, and federal courts are prohibited from giving them on the ground that they would constitute judicial interference in nonjudicial affairs. See also CONSTITUTIONAL LAW.

advocacy   Forceful persuasion; arguing a position.

advocate   1 A person who speaks for another in order to persuade others to a cause.   2 A lawyer.

aeronautics and aerospace   This article discusses the operation and ownership of aircraft, the ownership and use of airspace, government regulation of aircraft and airports, as well as the duties, liabilities, and responsibilities arising from the operation of aircraft.
■ **Definitions**   Aeronautics, aerospace, and related terms have been defined by the courts and by statutes. A federal statute defines *aeronautics* as the science and art of flight. The courts have indicated that aeronautics is the science that deals with the operation of any aircraft, including balloons. *Aviation,* a more specific term, is the art or science of movement by means of heavier-than-air aircraft, such as airplanes. *Aerospace* refers to the atmosphere and the space beyond. The *aerospace industry* is concerned with the design and manufacture of vehicles, missiles, and whatever operates in aerospace. *Airspace* is the area above property. *Air transportation,* as defined by federal statute, means interstate and overseas transportation of people, freight, and mail by domestic and foreign aircraft.
■ **Rights in airspace**   The United States has sovereignty (governmental power) over airspace within its domain, and a state has jurisdiction (authority) over the airspace above the land within its boundaries except in the areas regulated by federal laws. Accordingly, an aircraft is subject both to the federal government and to the jurisdiction of a state while flying over it, but neither federal nor state sovereignty in airspace takes away from owners their lawful rights of ownership in the surface soil.

As a property owner, you have air rights above your property, but only to the extent that you can occupy the airspace and make use of it in connection with enjoyment of your land. Local ZONING laws also spell out the AIR RIGHTS above your property.

A public right of freedom of travel exists in the navigable airspace of the United States. Consequently, the entry of an aircraft into airspace over privately owned land is lawful, but an invasion of airspace that infringes on a landowner's right to possess and use his property may be the subject of a court action for TRESPASS or NUISANCE. The landowner may also be entitled to an INJUNCTION protecting him from such invasions. When, in one case for example, the noise of low-flying planes made raising chickens impossible, the landowner was entitled to damages.
■ **Regulation of air transportation**   Originally Congress gave the Civil Aeronautics Board (CAB) exclusive authority and responsibility for the economic regulation of the air transportation industry. This included the power to grant licenses to airlines, approve or disapprove rates and fares, subsidize air service to small communities, and approve or disapprove proposals for the merger or consolidation of airline companies. In 1978, however, legislation was enacted to gradually deregulate the airline business; it provided for the abolition of the CAB by 1985.

The Federal Aviation Administration (FAA) has the power to regulate air commerce in order to promote its development and safety while at the same time fulfilling the requirements of national defense. The administrator of the FAA can undertake or supervise work and testing that will lead to the creation of improved aircraft, prescribe rules and regulations for the design and servicing of airplanes, and impose strict penalties if the rules are violated. The responsibility for air-traffic control at airports lies with the FAA, which disciplines controllers.

The National Transportation Safety Board (NTSB) conducts aircraft accident investigations.
EXAMPLE Thurman Munson, former catcher of the New York Yankees, was killed in August 1979 when the twin-engine jet with which he was practicing takeoffs and landings crashed and burned at an Ohio airport. Federal investigators from the National Transportation Safety Board found that the cause of the accident was pilot error. Munson possessed a jet pilot's license and had progressed from a beginner to jet pilot status in just 14 months' time. According to investigators, this was unusually rapid progress for a part-time flier. The board concluded, however, that it was "just a case when the pilot disregarded basic procedures."
■ **Aerospace activities**   Recognizing that the general welfare and security of the United States require that adequate provision be made for space activities, Congress established the National Aeronautics and Space Administration (NASA) to coordinate research into problems of flight within and outside the earth's atmosphere, as well as the development and operation of aeronautical and space vehicles. The duties of NASA are to plan, direct, and conduct space activities; to arrange for participation by the scientific community in planning scientific observations and activities; and to acquaint the public with its activities. Activities that are primarily associated with the development of weapons systems, military operations, and the defense of the United States are directed by the Defense Department.
■ **Certification of aircraft and airmen**   It is unlawful to operate an airplane that does not have a currently valid airworthiness certificate. A plane keeps its certificate as long as it is in good repair. An inspector authorized by the FAA certifies the airworthiness of a plane, and he may not delegate his authority, nor may he substitute his own judgment for inspection procedures prescribed by the FAA administrator.

AVIATION—YOUR RIGHTS WHEN YOU FLY OR ARE FLOWN OVER

■ If, as an airline passenger, you are injured because of wrongful conduct by an airline employee, the company is liable. It is also duty bound to protect you from the misconduct of fellow passengers.

■ If you suffer injuries caused by pressure differences in the plane's cabin, the company may be held liable.

■ If your conduct or condition becomes dangerous or annoying, you may be removed from the plane when it lands.

■ An airline's liability for your baggage is limited to a declared amount, if stated on your ticket.

■ If you refuse to produce a metal object in your luggage or on your person that gave a positive reading on the magnetometer, the airline can refuse to let you board the plane.

■ You may not operate an airplane that does not have a currently valid airworthiness certificate.

■ If you own a plane and entrust it to someone whom you know to be reckless or incompetent, you may be liable for resulting injuries.

■ If you take flight training, the flying school's responsibility to you is the same as that of an airline to a passenger.

■ You have air rights above your property, but only to the extent that you occupy and use the airspace.

■ Another person has the right to fly through your airspace, so long as he does not infringe on your right to possess and use your property. You might be entitled to damages, for example, if the noise of low-flying planes made it impossible for you to raise chickens.

■ If an adjacent airport amounts to a nuisance, you as a homeowner can sue for damages; however, the court may rule that your private interests are not paramount but must give way to the interests of society as a whole.

The FAA administrator has the power to establish minimum safety standards for the operation of air carriers, and he may also regulate the inspection, maintenance, and repair of equipment.

The administrator issues airmen certificates and specifies the capacity in which certificate holders are authorized to serve—that is, their rating. "Airmen" include those who inspect, maintain, overhaul, or repair aircraft, as well as pilots and others engaged in the navigation of aircraft.

A high degree of technical ability is one prerequisite for an airline pilot rating. Medical fitness is another. Factors such as care, judgment, and emotional control are also considered. Pilots over the age set by federal regulation may be refused ratings.

The FAA administrator may suspend or revoke a pilot's certificate on the ground that the public safety requires it. The fact that the pilot is technically qualified to fly does not matter. Except in cases of emergency, a pilot or any airman is entitled to a hearing prior to losing his certificate. An appeal from an order of suspension or revocation can be taken to the National Transportation Safety Board, and further appeal may be made to a federal court of appeals.

■ **State and local regulation** A state or municipality may regulate air traffic affecting it if the regulation does not interfere with interstate commerce or conflict with federal restrictions. For example, state or local regulations on noise created by aircraft engines are valid unless they conflict with federal rules concerning noise pollution.

EXAMPLE In October 1977, when the U.S. Court of Appeals O⟵※ ended the ban imposed by the Port Authority of New York and New Jersey on flights to and from Kennedy Airport by the French and English supersonic Concorde, it was not denying the Port Authority the right to fix noise standards. The court dissolved the ban because after more than a year and a half the Port Authority had not established standards that were reasonable and nondiscriminatory, as the court had earlier asked it to do. Instead, the airport operator continued to deny landing rights to one plane—the Concorde—even though it could meet the noise standards applied to others.

■ **Operation of airports** The state can authorize a local legislature, such as that of a county or city, to regulate airports and their related facilities. A regional airport authority can be created by one or more states to operate an airport—the Tri-State Airport Authority, which operates the airports in Lawrence County, Ohio, Worthington, Kentucky, and Huntington, West Virginia, for example. A private person or corporation may build and maintain an airport, provided neighboring landowners are not deprived of the use and enjoyment of their properties.

Airports built and operated in the proper manner are not NUISANCES. If an airport does amount to a nuisance, you, as a private homeowner, can sue for damages you have suffered, and you can try to have the court restrain the operation of the airport. But note that you may have to give notice to the municipality before you can bring suit against it. In determining the need for relief against the construction and operation of airports, courts consider the conflict of interest between the concerned parties as well as current public policy. Often the interests of homeowners must give way to the interests of society as a whole.

ZONING regulations may restrict the establishment and maintenance of airports. In some jurisdictions the state authorizes a public agency to adopt zoning ordinances limiting the use of adjacent property in order to minimize interference with the airport's operation. A regional airport authority may not be precluded, however, from using land that it has acquired for purposes connected with the airport.

If an obstruction or hazard to aircraft exists on property outside the airport, the airport owner may not interfere with it except through CONDEMNATION proceedings. Future creation of obstructions may be restricted by local zoning laws and state laws providing for safe airspace.

An owner of a public airport may negotiate leases for the use of its facilities. Similarly, a municipality owning an airport may impose reasonable charges for the privilege of doing business there. The owner of a public airport may regulate its ground transportation, grant exclusive rights to carry passengers to and from the airport and to operate an automobile rental agency on the premises.

■ **Ownership and use of aircraft** The validity of the transfer or SALE of aircraft is governed by the law of the state where the document of transfer or sale is delivered.

Federal law requires the registration of aircraft and the recording of any document that affects the title to an aircraft—a mortgage, for instance—at the administration and records branch of the FAA. Federal law also requires the recording of documents creating security interests in aircraft so that future purchasers will have notice of another person's interest in the aircraft. See MORTGAGE; SECURED CREDITOR; SECURED TRANSACTION.

Generally, a buyer of an aircraft from an authorized dealer is recognized as the legal owner. He takes possession of the airplane free from any interest of the creditor financing the dealer.

Rental of an aircraft is a contract. Parties to the contract are usually bound by its terms, but the defective condition of the aircraft may give the renter a right to cancel the agreement. The party providing the aircraft has a duty to present a machine in good operating condition.

■ **Legal duties in aircraft operation** Recovery for damages or injuries arising from the operation of a plane should fairly compensate the person who is hurt.

Manufacturers Generally a manufacturer must exercise ordinary care and skill in the design and manufacture of aircraft. He may be held liable for a breach of this duty by a person injured by defects in the plane or in its component parts, even though the parts were manufactured by someone else. The law views that the manufacturer has provided an implied WARRANTY that his aircraft was properly designed and manufactured. See STRICT LIABILITY. A maker of component parts is also liable for injuries caused by his product. He must exercise a high degree of care in the design and manufacture of his components, but he need not make them accident proof. He is, however, under a continuing duty to improve his products whenever human safety is involved. See PRODUCT LIABILITY.

EXAMPLE In May 1979, 273 people were killed at Chicago's O'Hare International Airport when an American Airlines DC-10 crashed just after takeoff. It was the worst air accident in U.S. history and led to the grounding of all DC-10's pending inspection. The crash was precipitated by a 10-inch crack in the pylon (the engine mount), which caused the engine and left underwing pylon to rip away from the body of the plane, damaging the hydraulic power.

Federal Aviation Administration investigators found that there had been a major breakdown in quality control on the DC-10 production line. American Airlines accused McDonnell Douglas Corporation, the manufacturer of the plane, of faulty design, manufacture, and assemblage.

American Airlines was also found at fault—for improper maintenance of its DC-10's. Instead of following McDonnell's recommendations to remove and reinstall the engine and pylon separately, American Airlines mechanics had removed and reinstalled them as a unit, using a forklift to do so. This procedure evidently led to the formation of the 10-inch crack.

Relatives of those that were killed in the crash have sued American Airlines and McDonnell Douglas for millions of dollars. The reason for the wrongful-death suits is to compensate the survivors for the financial loss they have suffered as a result of the deaths and not to compensate them for the loss of their loved ones.

Pilots In the absence of a special law, the ordinary rules relating to NEGLIGENCE and due care govern liability growing out of the operation of aircraft. For example, the pilot of a private aircraft is required to exercise only ordinary care, and not extreme care and caution. Nevertheless, the rules of negligence when applied to aviation fix a higher degree of care than when applied to the operation of something incapable of inflicting serious injury. Let us say that a pilot does not have a rating that permits him to fly by instruments. If he is aloft when weather conditions call for instrument flight, he has not exercised the degree of care that he should, and he would be held liable for his negligence. A pilot, and not the air traffic controller, has primary responsibility for safe operation of a plane, even if the pilot is flying with air traffic clearance.

Owners Usually mere ownership of an aircraft does not impose liability upon the owner for injury or damage caused by the operator. In some states, however, the owner of a plane who entrusts it to someone, such as an employee whom he knows to be reckless or incompetent, may be held liable for resulting injuries. The federal or a state government may be held liable for injuries resulting from operation of its aircraft by government employees.

Duties of passengers As an occupant or passenger in a private aircraft you are under a duty to exercise ordinary care for your own safety. This means that you must not go on a particular flight if an ordinarily prudent man would not do so because of an obvious danger, such as a bad storm.

On regularly scheduled airlines, which are public CARRIERS, flights are usually delayed or canceled—or the airports closed—during dangerous weather conditions. Passengers on such airlines must also exercise reasonable care for their safety, such as obeying the instructions of the flight attendant to fasten their seatbelts.

Airport operators The operator of an airport and those responsible for its maintenance are required to exercise ordinary or reasonable care toward people using the airport. Failure to keep the premises in a reasonably safe condition and to use the necessary care may result in liability for injuries. In addition, the airport operator must exercise ordinary or reasonable care in protecting aircraft kept on the premises.

Air traffic control The federal government has assumed complete responsibility in the area of air traffic control. Exacting and continuously high standards must be maintained. Air traffic controllers owe a duty of care to the passengers on the planes they guide, but they do not have primary responsibility for the operation of aircraft at an airport. Their responsibility is keeping aircraft apart from one another. The United States can be held liable for the negligence of air traffic controllers. However, CONTRIBUTORY NEGLIGENCE by the person injured may bar recovery against the United States for an accident caused in part by negligence of air traffic controllers.

Airlines An airline company must exercise the highest practical degree of care for the safety of its passengers. The company is liable for injury to a passenger caused by wrongful conduct of its employees, and it has a duty to protect passengers from the misconduct of fellow travelers. Although a passenger may not be removed from a plane without good cause, anyone whose conduct or condition becomes dangerous or annoying may be put off the aircraft when it lands. An air carrier is also usually required to exercise a high degree of care to avoid injury to passengers boarding or alighting from aircraft, and it may be held liable for injuries caused by pressure differences in the cabin of the aircraft.

Air CARRIERS must use great care to preserve and deliver goods accepted for shipment. Nevertheless, liability for loss or damage of goods may be limited to a declared amount. In the case of passenger baggage, the amount must be stated on the passenger's ticket.

Flying schools   A flying school may be held liable if it interferes with the customary activities of neighboring property owners. A trainee flying with a flight instructor is a passenger, and the responsibility of the flying school to him is the same as that of a commercial airline. Nevertheless, a trainee assumes certain risks in learning how to fly. A member of a flying club may be held liable if he is an owner of a plane belonging to the club.

■ **Air piracy**   Under federal law, aircraft piracy or attempted piracy is punishable by death or imprisonment. The federal courts have recognized that it is proper to refuse a person passage on a plane if the magnetometer gives a positive reading and the traveler refuses to produce any metal object that may have activated it.

affidavit   An affidavit is a written statement of facts, confirmed by an oath and taken by an authorized officer. It is a type of EVIDENCE that can be used either in business or in legal proceedings. Because an affidavit is usually a short statement on a particular subject, it is different from a DEPOSITION, which is the record of an examination of a witness as if he were giving testimony in court. If you were the best man or maid of honor at a wedding and the record of the marriage was destroyed, you could be asked to make an affidavit stating that the ceremony did indeed take place. But a court usually has no power to force anyone to make an affidavit. See OATHS AND AFFIRMATIONS.

■ **Who may make**   In general, any person having knowledge of the facts under examination and the ability to take an oath may make an affidavit. If a good reason can be shown, an individual familiar with the matters in question may make an affidavit on behalf of another, but his authority to act must be shown in some manner. Among those who may make affidavits for others are: an authorized guardian or friend of a minor who is incapable of doing so; an attorney; a personal representative such as an executor, administrator, or guardian who is not an attorney if affidavits are necessary to the performance of his duties as a representative; an officer of a corporation on its behalf; and a partner for the partnership.

A minor who is old enough to understand the facts and the oath may make an affidavit. If there is no law to the contrary, a criminal conviction does not bar a person from making an affidavit.

■ **Who may take**   A public officer who administers the oath to a person making an affidavit must have legal authority to do so. This authority usually comes from a state

law. Various public OFFICERS or their deputies may take affidavits, including city recorders, clerks of courts, commissioners of deeds, notaries, county clerks, court commissioners, and—sometimes—magistrates and justices of the peace. Generally, officers cannot take affidavits outside the particular area in which they exercise authority.

■ **Form and content**   There is no set form for an affidavit. Officers usually indicate the source of their authority at the bottom of the document. For instance, a notary would probably show what county has commisssioned him and, possibly, when his commission expires. The residence of the maker is usually shown and is sometimes required by law. The document should give the place where the affidavit was made, but dating it is necessary only when required by statute. The affidavit should contain the maker's signature, but this is not essential if the person can be identified in another way—as the president of the Green Department Store or the sister of the defendant, for example. In some states an affirmation may be used instead of an oath if the maker's religion does not permit him to take an oath. An official seal is necessary only if required by law.

An affidavit should state the facts precisely and definitely, but it can be made on information and belief. It should then give the sources of information and the reasons for belief. Legal arguments or unnecessary words may not be part of an affidavit. The person who makes an affidavit is strictly accountable for the truth and accuracy of its contents, and an individual who makes a false statement is guilty of PERJURY. See also ACKNOWLEDGMENT; WITNESS.

affiliation proceeding   A court action to prove that a man is the father of an illegitimate child and therefore should be held responsible, at least in part, for support of that child. See also ILLEGITIMACY.

affinity   Relationship by marriage. A husband, for example, is related by affinity to his wife's sister.

affirm   1 State positively; confirm; make firm. When a higher court decides that a lower court's action was correct, it affirms the decision.   2 Repeat an agreement, as when a person who enters into a contract while he is still a minor (a child) reaccepts it upon reaching legal adulthood.

affirmance   A positive statement; a confirmation.

affirmation   See OATHS AND AFFIRMATIONS.

affirmative action   Positive steps taken by an employer, school, or organization to remedy past discriminatory practices against certain groups of people, such as blacks, Asians, or women, by giving temporary preferential treatment to individuals from these groups until they truly achieve equal opportunity to participate in American society. For example, a construction company might take affirmative action by initiating a policy of hiring larger numbers of blacks than the company has done in the past. The federal government can also order affirmative action—it can, for instance, require a medical school to accept a specified percentage of students from minority groups. See also CIVIL RIGHTS.

affirmative defense A formal ANSWER to a COMPLAINT, filed in court, which goes beyond denying the facts and arguments in the complaint. An affirmative defense presents new facts and arguments that could defeat the plaintiff's lawsuit, even though all the statements in his complaint are true. For example, when a defendant claims that the plaintiff's lawsuit must be dismissed because the time set by law for bringing it has expired, he has used the statute of limitations (see LIMITATION OF ACTIONS) as an affirmative defense. He does not even have to deny any of the plaintiff's statements.

affray Physical combat between two or more persons that occurs in a public place and causes terror among bystanders. Whether or not a deadly weapon is used, an affray is a serious disturbance of the public peace; it is an offense exclusively against the public.

An affray should not be confused with a RIOT. An affray is more private in nature than a riot. For example, if an unexpected disturbance suddenly arises between two persons meeting together for an innocent purpose, they are guilty of an affray. If they then join others and work together to demolish buildings in the area, for example, they are rioting.

To AID AND ABET an affray is also an offense—let us say you try to help a friend who is fighting by attacking his opponent. SELF-DEFENSE is an acceptable reason for committing an affray.

aforesaid Before, preceding, or already mentioned.

aforethought Planned in advance; premeditated, such as a murder that is prepared for ahead of time.

a fortiori (Latin) "With stronger reason"; an argument that because one known fact exists, another fact similar to it and more probable must also exist. For example, if a 50-pound box is too heavy to carry, then, *a fortiori*, a 60-pound box is too heavy to carry.

Afroyim v. Rusk The 1967 U.S. Supreme Court case in which it was decided that the federal government has no power to take away a person's citizenship for voting in a political election in a foreign country.

after-acquired title A legal principle that protects a purchaser who has bought land from someone who did not really own it. If the seller later becomes the actual owner, the purchaser then becomes the new owner, and the title that he acquired at the time of purchase is a good legal title. No one bargains for an after-acquired title. It is usually a remedy for a past mistake.

EXAMPLE Suppose Mr. Buck owned a house when he died O——* without leaving a will. He had two children, Susan and Julian, a fighter pilot who disappeared during the war. Susan believes that he is dead and that she has inherited the house. Susan and her husband have a nice home, so she sells Mr. Buck's house to her newly married son. Then one day Julian returns. He is entitled to a one-half interest in Mr. Buck's house as an heir with rights equal to Susan's. Susan has plenty of money and Julian does not. Susan agrees to pay Julian for his half of the house. When she does that, the deed that her son has is valid. He has an after-acquired title.

after-born child A child born after a WILL is made. Some jurisdictions have a rule that a will cannot prevent an after-born child from taking his rightful share of the parents' property.

agency A comprehensive term that, in its broadest sense, includes every situation in which one person—the agent—acts for or represents another—the principal—by the latter's authority. Agents that you deal with in everyday activities include bank cashiers, stockbrokers, attorneys, and salesclerks. This article discusses the general relationship between principal and agent and their relationships with third persons. For discussions involving specific agents, see ATTORNEY AND CLIENT; BROKER; CORPORATION; CRIMINAL LAW; FIDUCIARY; INSURANCE; PARTNERSHIP; PROPERTY; and SALES.

■ **Principles of agency law** Fundamental to the law of agency is the concept that someone acting through another is acting for himself.

Agency is a voluntary, good-faith relationship of trust: one person agrees to act for, and under the direction or control of, another. The *principal* is the person for whom another acts and from whom he derives his authority to act. The *agent* is one who, by the authority of another, undertakes to transact business or manage affairs for that person. An agent is a substitute appointed primarily to carry on business between his principal and third persons. He acts on behalf of his principal and not on behalf of himself. You can engage another person to do your housework, run your business, write an insurance policy for you, or buy and sell your goods, real estate, or shares of stock. The effect is the same as if you were present and acting in person. Agency is the means by which most business affairs are conducted, and without it business could hardly exist.

The fundamental principles of agency law—that the agent's actions are binding upon the principal and that the principal has the benefit of rights or property acquired by his agent—are widely accepted in American law. Courts have long held that common sense requires a person to be liable for acts that he has authorized.

Basic characteristics The most important feature of the agency relationship is the agent's representative function. The agent steps into the shoes of the principal. Agency is generally considered to be a FIDUCIARY relationship—that is, a personal relationship of trust and confidence. The utmost good faith is required of the principal as well as of the agent. Another basic characteristic is that the agent has power to alter legal standings between the principal and third persons. For example, if given the authority to do so, an agent can obtain a real estate mortgage from a bank for his principal. The principal is then indebted to the bank.

Test of agency The right of the principal to control the conduct of the agent in matters entrusted to him is the test of agency. There can be no agency unless the principal has some control, or right of control, over the actions of his agent, but it is not essential that the right actually be exercised or the agent's work supervised. The power of the principal to terminate the services of the agent gives him the means of controlling his agent's activities.

■ **How an agency relationship is formed** No particular method is required for the creation of an agency relationship, so long as it appears that the principal and agent have entered into an agency agreement. Creation rests in the parties' intent, which can be express (stated) or implied. Often an agency is created by a written contract, which should clearly state the principal's intention, the identity of the agent, what the agent is to do, and the matter with which he is to concern himself.

Implied agency The agency relationship may be implied from the words and conduct of the parties. Authority not expressly given to the agent may arise from the powers that the principal does expressly give to him. The express power to buy and sell land or to buy and sell personal property, for example, ordinarily implies the agent's authority to receive payment for it. An agent authorized to borrow money may ordinarily, by implication, receive payment of money loaned to his principal.

Although the agency relationship may be implied from a single transaction, it comes more readily from a series of transactions. Prior habit or dealings between two persons may imply a relationship of agency between them.

EXAMPLE Donald has been collecting rents from an apartment building once a month over a period of several years. An agency relationship between him and the landlord is implied, whether or not the landlord ever identifies Donald as the rental agent to the tenants of the building.

Approval of an agent's unauthorized act may be implied from any words or conduct by the principal that reasonably show his intent to approve. If a principal attempts to enforce rights derived from an agent's unauthorized act, he has approved it. For example, if a principal sues to enforce a contract he never authorized his agent to make, he has accepted and approved of the contract.

Requirements for principals and agents Any person who is mentally sound can appoint an agent. A principal may appoint an agent to do anything that the principal can do legally, except for some very personal acts. A person cannot, for example, delegate authority to commit a robbery, nor can a husband or wife delegate his or her sexual responsibilities.

Anyone who can act for himself can usually act as agent for another, except when there would be a CONFLICT OF INTEREST. An automobile dealer, for example, should not attempt to obtain employment as a sales representative for a competitor. On the other hand, someone whose interests are adverse to those of another may act as his agent if there is full knowledge and consent on the part of all concerned. For example, a debtor could become a collection agent for his creditor if his creditor authorized him.

EXAMPLE Quentin owes several hundred dollars to Sound System Electronics for stereo equipment he has purchased. Having lost his job, he has not been able to pay the monthly installments to Sound System for the past three months. Quentin goes to the electronics store and explains his situation, promising to resume payments just as soon as he is reemployed. Sound System's credit manager needs another collection agent and asks Quentin

if he would take the job temporarily. Quentin accepts the offer. Quentin (a debtor) is now an agent for his creditor.

■ **Kinds of agents** Agents are classified as either actual or ostensible. A person is an *actual agent* if he, expressly or by implication, is authorized to act for the principal and on his behalf. In other words, the agent must really be employed by the principal. An *ostensible agent* is one whom the principal has, intentionally or unintentionally, led others to believe is his agent, even though no authority has been conferred upon him. An illustration of an ostensible agent is a person who has been authorized to make loans for his principal but not to collect interest on those loans. People obtaining loans from the agent would normally think that he has authority to collect the interest, even though in reality this is not so.

A *universal agent* is one who is appointed to do all acts that the principal may personally do. A universal agency is extremely rare. It can be created only by clear, specific language, such as in a written contract.

EXAMPLE Jack, an attorney who is a copartner of a law firm and also owner of an antique store and a restaurant, must go to Europe to work on a lawsuit. He asks Dorothy, his law partner, to run the firm as well as the store and restaurant while he is away. In a contract they draft, Jack names Dorothy as his universal agent, specifically giving her all the powers he has in managing the law firm and in conducting the business of the store and the restaurant until he returns.

A *general agent* is someone employed to transact all business of a particular kind or to do all acts connected with a particular trade or employment. A manager of a supermarket is an example of a general agent.

A *special agent* is authorized to conduct a single transaction or a series of transactions not involving any continuity of service. He is employed for a particular purpose under limited powers. A realtor listing a house for sale is a special agent of the owner of that house. Or, if you ask a friend headed for the track to bet $50 for you on Big John in the third race, the friend is your special agent.

Agents and contractors An agent is different from an INDEPENDENT CONTRACTOR. Whether an employer controls details of the work is the usual test for determining if a relationship is that of principal and agent or of employer and independent contractor.

EXAMPLE If an employer hires a carpenter to make repairs on an office building he owns, the employer cannot control the physical activities of the carpenter so long as he accomplishes what he was hired to do. The carpenter is, therefore, an independent contractor. If, however, the employer tells a person from his building's own maintenance department to do the job, the employer can supervise and control the carpentry work and the physical actions of his employee. His employee is his agent.

■ **Results of the agency relationship** A principal's duties and liabilities to his agent depend primarily upon the terms of the agency agreement and upon an obligation to use good faith with his agent. A principal is deemed to have knowledge of all information his agent acquires in his role as agent, even though the agent does not actually inform him. If, for example, the agent buys a car for his principal, knowing that it has been driven 7,000 miles, the principal cannot claim he thought the car was completely new, whether or not the agent actually tells him about it.

When there are no contrary instructions, an agent should conform to any custom or usage applicable to his principal's particular business. He must adhere faithfully to all instructions given to him by his principal and act with the utmost good faith and loyalty to further his principal's interests. An agent may lose his right to compensation, either in whole or in part, by disloyalty toward his principal. Furthermore, the principal can sue for money he loses when his agent does not follow his instructions.

EXAMPLE Let us say that your stock in the LMNOP Company goes up five points on March 3. You tell your broker to sell your 500 shares when the market opens on March 4. He does not do so, and by March 5 the stock is down three points. You could sue your broker for the difference between the value of your stock on March 4 and what you actually realized by a sale on March 5.

A principal is liable to third persons for all wrongs that his agent commits within the scope of his employment. See RESPONDEAT SUPERIOR. The principal is not liable for acts of the agent done outside the scope of his employment.

EXAMPLE Donald drives a delivery truck for Best Bakery products. If Donald causes an accident while on his assigned route, Best Bakery is liable for any damages. If, however, Donald has an accident while using the truck to pick up some groceries on his way home, Best Bakery is not liable for any damages.

If, unknown to anyone, an agent commits fraud in negotiating a contract for his principal, the principal would probably not be liable for the agent's unauthorized deceit.

■ **Duration of the relationship** Generally, a principal has absolute power to revoke an agent's authority at any time. If a principal and agent sign a contract providing that the agency shall last one year, but the principal decides to revoke the agent's authority after six months, he may validly do so. The principal will be liable to the agent for whatever damage he causes by breaking the contract, but the agent's authority is terminated unconditionally.

Fulfillment of the purpose for which an agency is created terminates it. For example, if a principal engages an agent to negotiate a particular contract for him, the agency automatically terminates when the contract is signed.

An agency may be terminated by operation of law, as when either the agent or principal dies or becomes insane, or the principal goes into bankruptcy. An agency can also be terminated by a change in the law that makes the performance of the agent's duties illegal. For example, a liquor wholesaler's function as a sales representative would end automatically if his county enacted an ordinance prohibiting the sale of all alcoholic beverages except beer.

In general after an agency relationship ends, the rules of loyalty and good faith do not apply. A former agent may engage in the same general business as his former principal, but he may not use or disclose to others trade secrets, written lists of names, or similar confidential matters given to him only for the principal's use.

agent An individual authorized to act for another; a person entrusted with someone else's business. A company officer is an agent of the company. See AGENCY.

age of consent See INFANT.

aggravated assault A serious or dangerous attack, such as an attack with a knife. Aggravated assault is a crime in most states. See also ASSAULT AND BATTERY.

aggravation An action or occurrence that increases the seriousness of a crime but is not part of its definition. For example, use of a deadly weapon in committing a robbery is an aggravation of that offense.

aggressive collection The taking of legal steps to obtain payment of a debt. See also ATTACHMENT AND GARNISHMENT; EXECUTION; LEVY; SEIZURE.

aggrieved party The individual whose personal or property rights have been violated, usually the person who starts a lawsuit against one who has done him wrong. See also PLAINTIFF.

agreement Oral or written mutual assent to do one or more acts; a meeting of minds on one or more points; used informally to mean a CONTRACT.

agriculture In a limited sense, "agriculture" means the cultivation of grain and other field crops. In a broader sense, it refers to the production of plants and the rearing of animals useful to man. See also ANIMALS; CROPS; PROPERTY.

■ **Federal law** Congress has the power to enact legislation to promote agricultural occupations and industries throughout the nation. The President appoints the Secretary of Agriculture to coordinate and administer all national farm programs.

Since 1933 Congress has passed a number of agricultural adjustment acts to establish and maintain fair prices for farmers and, at the same time, prevent unreasonable fluctuations in supplies. The Secretary of Agriculture determines a national acreage allotment for a particular crop and apportions that allotment among the states. Committees in the states then apportion this allotment among the various counties. Finally, county committees apportion the crop allotment among local farmers.

Congress established the Farm Credit Administration in 1933 to help farmers obtain credit for the purchase of equipment, feed for livestock, and seed for crops. The Commodity Credit Corporation was established in 1933 to influence farm prices on the open market, by such means as the purchase and sale of farm products, in accordance with the Secretary of Agriculture's program of price supports.

Congress enacted the Packers and Stockyards Act in 1921 to assure fair practices in the livestock-marketing and meat-packing industries. Under the Soil Conservation and Domestic Allotment Act (1935), the Secretary of Agriculture is authorized to assist farmers and ranchers in carrying out conservation practices.

The Department of Agriculture also administers a program through which eligible households receive locally issued federal food stamps that they can use for the purchase of food. See WELFARE.

■ **State law** Many states have enacted laws concerned with the production and marketing of agricultural products. State legislation, however, must not conflict with federal agricultural laws and regulations. The inspection, grading, and storage of grain is usually controlled by state legislation. Fertilizers and plant seeds are likewise subject to state controls, and states often grant economic aid to distressed agricultural industries.

Agricultural LIENS have been created by some state laws. An agricultural lien is a claim upon a crop for supplies, services, or money advanced to aid in raising and harvesting it. After a crop is harvested, the holder of a lien can subject the crop to payment of his claim upon it. For example, a bank that has loaned money to a farmer in the spring would have an agricultural lien on the crop he harvests in the fall. The farmer's first obligation after his sale of the crop would be to pay back the bank.

■ **Societies and cooperatives** An agricultural society is an organization formed to promote agricultural interests, such as the improvement of land or of livestock. It is often not only an educational institution but also a social club for the local population.

Agricultural cooperatives, which have long been encouraged by state legislatures and courts, are groups of local farmers acting together for their mutual benefit in the cultivation, harvesting, and marketing of farm products. The cooperative may enter into contracts in which its members agree to sell their products to the cooperative, and it in turn agrees to resell them and pay the members the resale price, minus expenses.

aid and abet Intentionally help another person to commit a crime. See CRIMINAL LAW.

aid and comfort Help; support; encouragement; counsel. To give aid and comfort to enemies of the United States is TREASON under the U.S. Constitution.

air pollution See ENVIRONMENTAL LAW.

air rights The authority to build above a piece of land. For example, a state or local government may sell to a building contractor the air rights over a sunken road, so that he can put a building over it. See also PROPERTY; ZONING.

alderman An individual who has been elected to a city council or other local governing body; a local judge with limited jurisdiction.

aleatory contract A mutual agreement in which the result depends upon an event with an element of uncertainty about it. Life insurance policies are aleatory CONTRACTS, because full performance of their terms depends on when an insured's death occurs.

alia (Latin) "Others"; other things; other persons. The word is used in abbreviated form in the term *et al.*, meaning "and others"—*John Jones* et al. v. *XYZ Company*, for example, designates a class action suit brought by John Jones against the XYZ Company.

alias (Latin) Short for *alias dictus,* meaning "otherwise called"; a fictitious name used in place of one's real name.

alibi (Latin) "Elsewhere"; the defense (excuse) that an individual was somewhere else when a crime was committed and therefore could not possibly have committed the offense. See also CRIMINAL LAW.

alien A person who is born outside the jurisdiction of the United States and who has not been naturalized—admitted to U.S. citizenship—under the U.S. Constitution and federal law. This article covers the rights, duties, and disabilities of aliens; their entry to and exclusion from the United States; and their admission to citizenship.

■ **Who is considered an alien** The laws of the United States determine whether or not a person is an alien. Usually, but not always, a person born in a foreign country is an alien. For example, a child born in a foreign country to American parents is an American CITIZEN. The term "alien" includes a native-born American who has lost his citizenship by moving to a foreign country and becoming a foreign citizen.

■ **Classification** One classification of aliens is according to residence. Some laws, such as those relating to an alien's right to inherit property, distinguish between resident and nonresident aliens. Another classification deals with alien friends and enemies. An *alien friend* is a citizen of a friendly foreign country that is at peace with ours. An *enemy alien,* on the other hand, is a citizen of some hostile state. See also WAR AND NATIONAL DEFENSE. The term "alien" used alone usually refers to alien friends.

■ **Legal status** The presence of aliens in the United States is a matter of permission and tolerance, not a right. Conditions of entry and continued residence are governed by immigration laws, discussed later in this article.

Obedience to law Aliens must obey the laws of this country, and they may not avoid the consequences of their acts by claiming ignorance of the laws. While they are permitted to remain, they are protected by the U.S. Constitution and the laws of this country.

Aliens ordinarily are liable to punishment for crimes forbidden by both state and federal laws. In addition, there are criminal laws directed at aliens in particular. An alien, for instance, is subject to criminal punishment for failing to comply with the law that requires him to register each year with the Immigration and Naturalization Service. The ownership or possession of firearms may be forbidden to aliens. It is also a crime for an alien to represent himself as a citizen of the United States to a person who has some right to ask or a good reason for wanting to know his citizenship.

If an alien is accused of a crime, the criminal procedures used against him are the same as those used against a citizen. The government must prove all the elements of the crime beyond a reasonable doubt, and if he is found guilty, the sentence given him must be no different from that usually given for the crime.

General rights, duties, and disabilities Congress has exclusive power to control the rights, duties, and legal disabilities of aliens. This power includes the right to decide whether an alien may reside in the United States or in any of the individual states. The conditions of residence are also controlled by federal rather than state law.

If an alien is lawfully present in the United States, he is assured safe conduct and certain other rights, which become greater and more secure when he declares his intention to become a citizen. His duties and obligations are similar to those of a citizen. He owes his loyalty to the United States, and his services may be required for national defense in time of war. During World War II, for example, more than 125,000 aliens served in the U.S. armed forces.

The states also have the power to give rights to aliens, but a state may not discriminate against aliens in violation of federal law or the Constitution.

EXAMPLE A French student and a Canadian student challenged the New York State law that denied scholarships, tuition grants, and loans to aliens who did not apply for U.S. citizenship or sign a statement saying that they intended to apply. The Supreme Court found the law unconstitutionally discriminatory. An Arizona statute requiring a period of residency for aliens who apply for welfare was also declared unconstitutional.

Rights given by treaty The federal government may give rights to aliens by treaty, and a state may not interfere with those rights. When a state law conflicts with a treaty provision, the treaty prevails. The right to work is a treaty-given right that a state may not deny. If a treaty gives aliens of a certain country the right to conduct a business, they may form a corporation for that purpose. When treaties do not give aliens the right to be employed by a state or by a city, state laws may prevent such employment.

■ **Personal and political rights and privileges** In general, resident aliens are entitled to enjoy personal rights to the same extent as citizens. Federal law protects them from state laws that treat aliens differently simply because they are aliens. For the most part, aliens have the same rights as citizens to employment, but their right to travel temporarily outside the United States is limited by restrictions that do not apply to citizens. An alien who lawfully resides here may not, however, be prevented from leaving without first being given an opportunity for a hearing on the question of his right to leave.

Aliens may not take part in political activities, including ELECTIONS. It has been said that an alien has no right to work for the amendment of the federal Constitution.

■ **Property rights and disabilities** As a rule, an alien may acquire and own personal property in the same manner as a citizen, and his right to do so is given by state or federal law. A state has the power to decide whether an alien may own real property within its borders; it may also decide how much and under what conditions. A state constitutional provision or law may forbid an alien from owning real property. The state's power is subject to federal law, the Constitution, and treaties of the United States.

How acquired An alien may acquire real property (real estate) by buying it or by receiving it as a gift, and only the state can question his right to ownership. Private citizens cannot.

If the state does not question the alien's right, he is entitled to ownership of the property—even if there is a state law that makes a DEED to an alien void.

EXAMPLE Freda came to the United States a year ago from Freetonia. After traveling around the country, she decides to buy a condominium apartment that overlooks the ocean. She signs a deed and moves in. Her neighbors, however, are unhappy about a Freeton living in their building and they are even more unhappy about the smell of Freetonian cooking that seems to permeate the halls continuously. With a bit of research, Freda's neighbors find out that there is a state law voiding any deed made with an alien. They eagerly go to a lawyer, ready to sue to get Freda out of the building. Much to their dismay, they are informed that private citizens cannot sue an alien for his right to own property; only the state can sue. In this instance, if the state does not bring suit against Freda's ownership of the apartment, the deed will stay in force even though it is void.

States use the right to question alien ownership of land sparingly, but they always have the power to call upon it.

The state challenges an alien's right to own the property he has acquired by starting a court proceeding to decide whether he is an alien. Once the court decides the owner is an alien, the state is entitled to assume the ownership and possession of the property. Sometimes a court will excuse a person who has contracted to sell real property to an alien and let that person retain ownership, provided that the contract has not been completed and all persons have acted in good faith.

Ordinarily, if the alien becomes a citizen after he becomes the owner of real property and before the state begins proceedings against him, his ownership cannot be disturbed by any action taken by the state. Laws may entitle an alien to own real property after he takes certain steps to make his ownership valid, such as filing a statement of intention to become a citizen.

Leases Generally, a state may prohibit an alien from acquiring land under a lease when he has not declared that he intends to become a citizen or is not eligible to become a citizen. The state may sue to cancel the forbidden lease. An ordinary citizen, however, may not bring a suit to cancel the lease simply because the lease is prohibited by law.

Under its treaty-making power, the federal government may give aliens the right to lease real property. In case of a conflict with a state law, the treaty provision prevails.

Mortgages and trusts An alien may hold a MORTGAGE on real property when no state law or state constitutional provision forbids him to do so. If the mortgage payments are not made, the alien may be allowed to take title to the property and become the owner.

When state law allows an alien to own real property, a TRUST may also be set up for his benefit. The legal title to the land is held by a trustee, but any rent money and other profits earned from the land belong to the alien, and he may also live on the land. When aliens may own real property, they ordinarily may also act as trustees.

Wills and inheritance An alien may usually receive personal property by means of a will. When a person dies without making a will, his property goes to his relatives according to the laws of inheritance. See DESCENT AND DISTRIBUTION. The right to inherit personal property may exist under a state's PUBLIC POLICY or may be granted by law. When alien relatives and citizen relatives are living, the dead person's personal property is usually distributed to both according to the state's inheritance laws.

Under the common law in use in some states, real property may be left to an alien by will, and his right to own the property can be questioned only by the state. A will may leave real property to an alien with the condition that if he cannot own it, the property goes to another person. In such a case, the real property belongs to the other person and not to the state.

Some states give aliens the right by statute to receive real property under a will, while other states forbid it. In the latter case, persons other than the state may question the validity of the gift when those persons would have inherited the gift had it not been given to the alien.

EXAMPLE Suppose Freda, from the previous example, inherits an ocean-view bungalow from her great-uncle. The house is located in a state that has a law forbidding aliens to inherit real estate. Freda's cousin, who has been an American citizen for the past five years and would have inherited the bungalow had it not been given to Freda, is furious that she did not get it. She will be permitted to bring a suit against Freda for the house.

When an alien is to receive real property by will or inheritance, some states require a nonresident alien to appear and claim it within a certain period of time. Any act that makes the claim known to the person in control of the property may be sufficient, and an alien's attorney may even appear for him. If the alien fails to appear and claim the property it goes to the next person who has a right to inherit it.

Some states set a date by which an alien who inherits real property must get rid of it. If he does not, the state then becomes the owner. Other states give aliens a specified time to become citizens and take possession of the land or to sell it. In this instance, the alien becomes the owner of the real property at the time the former owner dies, but he loses ownership if he does not become a citizen or sell the property within the given time period.

Some state laws give nonresident aliens the right to receive personal or real property under a will or by inheritance only when a U.S. citizen has the same right in the alien's country. This right must be unconditionally enforceable in the courts of the alien's country. When the right to inherit property is merely a matter of permission or depends on the discretion of the foreign government, there is no similar right in the United States.

Disposition or transfer of property An alien who has become the owner of real property may usually sell or transfer his ownership to another person, but only before the state begins proceedings to end his ownership. In some states, the buyer or person who acquires the property becomes the valid owner, even against the state's interest.

EXAMPLE An alien who was ineligible for citizenship owned a plot of land. Before the state brought suit for the land, the alien executed a deed transferring the property to his minor son, who was a citizen. When the state took proceedings for the land, the court held that the transfer of the land was valid.

Some courts have decided that under the common law an alien may not leave real property under a will. Statutes and treaty provisions may, however, give aliens the right to make a will, and certain treaties have also given persons the right to inherit real property from aliens, even when they themselves are aliens.

■ **Lawsuits by and against aliens** Ordinarily, an alien may bring lawsuits in our courts. The basis of this rule is a courtesy countries extend to one another, known as the COMITY of nations.

Generally, an alien is able to maintain personal ACTIONS. For example, he may sue to recover money due under a CONTRACT or institute a TORT action to recover for personal injuries. Unless a statute expressly forbids it, an alien may be able to enforce a right given under a statute such as the WORKMEN'S COMPENSATION law.

One alien may usually sue another alien. This right applies to contracts made in foreign countries and also to torts (wrongs or injuries) committed in a foreign country or on the high seas.

EXAMPLE Jean and Claude are French aliens who live and run a business in San Diego. While in Paris on a business trip, Jean makes an insulting remark about Claude's mother, and Claude hits him in the jaw, breaking one of Jean's teeth. When they return to San Diego, Jean may sue Claude for assault and battery.

When, under state law, an alien has a right to own land, he may start a lawsuit to enforce his property rights.

An action may be brought against an alien in a court that has jurisdiction (authority) over his person or his property. In general, the alien may use any legal defense to the action that is available to a citizen defendant.

■ **Immigration** Immigration includes the admission, exclusion, detention, deportation, and expulsion of aliens. The Immigration and Nationality Act, a federal law, controls immigration. An *immigrant* is a person who comes to this country to live permanently. An *alien immigrant* is an alien who has left this country but intends to return.

Federal powers of regulation The federal government alone has the power to control immigration, and the individual states may not interfere with that power. The immigration laws are administered and enforced by the Attorney General of the United States, the Commissioner of Immigration and Naturalization, and the Immigration and Naturalization Service. Immigration officers have broad powers, including, in some instances, the right to arrest or search for aliens without a warrant. But when a search warrant to look for illegal aliens—in a house or factory, for example—is requested, there must be probable cause to believe that illegal aliens are on the premises. Immigration officers may also issue rules and regulations that have the force of law and must be obeyed.

Admission, entry, and exclusion An alien who enters the United States from a foreign port, foreign country, or outlying possession must do so lawfully, in keeping with the immigration laws. If he has not been lawfully admitted, he has no constitutional right to enter or to remain, and usually cannot establish a DOMICILE or a permanent RESIDENCE here.

Return after temporary absence A resident alien who voluntarily visits a foreign country is considered an "entering alien" when he returns to this country. He is subject to the exclusion provisions of the immigration laws. If, however, his trip was casual and brief and he did not intend to leave his permanent U.S. residence, then he does not make an "entry." For example, a return to this country after a short vacation in Canada with one's family or after a three-week trip to Israel to attend an employer's training course is not an "entry."

An alien seeking readmission must have either an unexpired immigration visa or a reentry permit. The reentry permit is given by the Attorney General if he finds that the alien has been lawfully admitted for permanent residence and wishes to return to America to resume his residency.

Visas A visa is a document of entry that the federal government requires of all aliens who want to come to the United States, whether to visit or to live. Immigration visas are a means of screening prospective immigrants, to determine whether or not individual aliens should be admitted. American consular officers stationed in foreign countries have authority to issue visas in keeping with the quota and preference provisions of the immigration laws. A visa obtained by fraud or by misrepresenting an important fact, such as the commission of a crime, is not valid.

Excludable persons Various classes of aliens are declared ineligible to receive visas and may be exluded from the country. Among them are persons afflicted with a dangerous contagious disease, a physical defect, or mental illness; those over 16 years of age, physically capable of reading, who have no reading comprehension of any language; anarchists who are opposed to all organized governments; members of the Communist Party; aliens likely to become public charges, such as those who are probably unemployable; aliens who have been deported; those seeking employment as skilled or unskilled workers, unless the Secretary of Labor certifies that there is a shortage of such workers and that employing aliens will not affect American workers; and persons convicted of a crime involving moral turpitude, such as BIGAMY, BRIBERY, BURGLARY, EMBEZZLEMENT, LARCENY, PERJURY, ROBBERY, and various sex offenses such as SEXUAL ASSAULT and RAPE.

Admission procedures Upon his arrival, immigration officers question an alien about his right to enter, and medical officers of the U.S. Public Health Service give him a physical and mental examination. Usually he is fingerprinted and registered with the Immigration and Naturalization Service. Those not registered upon entry must be registered within 30 days after their 14th birthday.

If an alien is otherwise eligible for admission, but is excluded because of a physical defect, disease, or disability that will prevent him from earning a living, he may enter after giving a BOND to the federal and state governments. The bond is used as security against his becoming a public welfare charge. When the alien leaves the country, becomes a citizen, or dies, any money held as security under the bond must be returned to the person who gave it—or to the alien's estate if he died and had posted the bond himself. A nonimmigrant alien, temporarily visiting, may have to give a bond to insure that he leaves on time.

An alien whose ability to support himself is in doubt may also be admitted on an AFFIDAVIT of support by a citizen who acts as a sponsor. The sponsor's duty is not a contractual one, however, and he cannot be made to support the alien or repay the government for any support it provides.

Exclusion proceedings Aliens seeking admission to this country are subject to exclusion proceedings by a special inquiry officer (also known as an immigration judge) to determine if they may be allowed to enter. Ordinarily, an alien who has a visa is entitled to a hearing by the immigration judge and may be excluded from the United States only for valid reasons. The question of a claim to citizenship may also be decided in such a proceeding.

An alien may appeal an order excluding him to the Board of Immigration Appeals. Thereafter, he may go to the Attorney General for a review of the board's decision. In some instances, he may obtain judicial review of a final order of exclusion. The scope of judicial review is usually limited to a determination of whether the hearings given the alien were fair and followed the requirements of the law.

How aliens qualify for immigration The admission of immigrants is controlled by a selection system and is limited to a certain number (a quota) each year. No discrimination is allowed because of race, sex, nationality, place of birth, or place of residence. The former quota system, which restricted the number of immigrants on the basis of their country of origin, has been abolished.

The immediate relatives of citizens (children, husband, wife, and parents) do not come within the quota system. Nor do certain classes of special immigrants, such as an employee or former employee of the U.S. government in a foreign country and an immigrant who was once a citizen and is eligible to regain his citizenship.

Although subject to the quota system, some other persons are given preferences, such as alien brothers and sisters of citizens. Other preferences are given to members of the professions who will help our economy, culture, or general welfare—architects and physicians, for example—and to refugees from Communist countries forced to flee because of their race, religion, or political views.

The immigration laws allow admission to certain nonimmigrant aliens in order to promote good relations among the peoples of the world. Alien crewmen on a ship or aircraft who have landed temporarily are nonimmigrants and are exempt from immigration requirements. So also are visitors on business or pleasure trips and qualified students who want to enter the country solely to study at a school approved by the Attorney General.

■ **Deportation or expulsion** Deportation involves sending the alien back to the country from which he came. Provisions for deportation apply to all aliens as well as to naturalized citizens whose naturalization has been canceled or revoked. The alien husband or wife of a citizen may be subject to deportation if, for example, he or she entered the United States without an immigration visa.

Congress establishes the grounds for deportation, and it may authorize the deportation of aliens on grounds that did not exist at the time of their entry. There are many grounds for deportation: illegal entry or presence, fraud or misrepresentation in gaining entry, entry without a required visa or passport, entry in violation of a quota provision of the immigration law, entry without inspection, breach of a condition of entry, overstaying the temporary period for which the alien was allowed to enter, becoming a public charge, suffering from a physical or mental illness at the time of entry, and membership in a subversive organization.

An alien may be deported when, before entering this country, he was convicted of a crime involving moral turpitude, or if he admits having committed it. In addition, an alien may be deported if he has been convicted in this country of any two crimes for which the prison sentence adds up to five or more years.

Proceedings for deportation Deportation proceedings are controlled by the Immigration and Nationality Act and administrative regulations. They are civil, not criminal proceedings. They are not conducted by the rules used in a court of law, but great care must be taken to be sure that they are conducted fairly.

An alien is entitled to be notified of the charges against him and to a hearing on those charges. At the hearing, conducted by a special hearing officer, the alien has the right to an attorney of his choice, to testify, to call witnesses, and to present evidence in his own behalf. The decision to deport or not to deport must be based on the charges made against the alien and must be supported by the evidence presented at the hearing.

In some cases the Board of Immigration Appeals may review a deportation decision made by a hearing officer and may make a new decision about deportation.

A deportation order is usually subject to court review. Like the Board of Immigration Appeals, the court must make its decision on the administrative record upon which the deportation order was based. When the United States tried to deport the Australian-born labor leader Harry Bridges as an undesirable alien, he carried his case to the Supreme Court, which overturned the deportation order.

■ **Naturalization** Naturalization is the proceeding by which an alien becomes a citizen. It is a privilege rather than a right and is granted only to those aliens who have all the qualifications required by law.

Qualifications A person seeking naturalization must have been lawfully admitted to this country for permanent residence and must have resided within the United States for five years. During the five years, he must have been physically present for at least half the time; a continuous absence for one year breaks the period of residence. He must have also resided for six months in the state where he makes his application for citizenship. The purpose of the residency period is to give the alien a chance to learn the principles and spirit of American government, and to give the immigration authorities a chance to observe the applicant.

The applicant for citizenship must accept the political habits and attitudes that exist in the United States and obey the laws resulting from them. The purpose of this requirement is to admit as citizens only those who are in general agreement with the basic principles of the community. This requirement is a general one, however, and must be reconciled with freedom of conscience.

EXAMPLE A member of the Mennonite faith who was an 0—➤ alien married a citizen and wished to become a citizen himself. He refused to serve in the military or to work in a plant that manufactured weapons but did agree to do work of national importance as a civilian in time of war. He was allowed to become a citizen as a person who favored the Constitution and the good order and happiness of the United States.

The alien applicant must show that he can read, write, and speak English words ordinarily used in conversation. He must also have some knowledge of American history and government.

During the required period of residence, the alien must demonstrate good moral character. It must measure up to that of the average citizen in the community where he lives—perfection is not required. Traffic violations, for example, would not be a bar to citizenship. On the other hand, citizenship has been denied when the applicant has entered into a bigamous marriage, been convicted of MANSLAUGHTER, or become addicted to narcotic drugs. Proof of ADULTERY also precludes a finding of good moral character, as does NONSUPPORT of children or family.

Proceedings Naturalization proceedings are judicial in character and are usually held in FEDERAL COURTS.

The applicant for citizenship must file a petition for naturalization with the clerk of the federal district court. The petition must be in writing, and it must contain a statement of all the important facts relating to the applicant's naturalization, which must be proved when the petition is heard. These facts include lawful entry and formal admission according to the immigration rules, intent to remain in the United States permanently, good moral character, and residence for the required period. The applicant must swear to the petition and sign it.

When the petition is heard, the applicant has the burden of proving his eligibility for citizenship in every respect. See BURDEN OF PROOF. Any evidence is admissible for the purpose of deciding if the applicant is of good moral character. The applicant's continued residence during the five-year residence period must be proved by the testimony of two witnesses who are citizens and who know about the applicant's residence.

Once the hearing is decided in favor of the applicant, an order is issued admitting the alien to citizenship. The order is a grant of citizenship, which is a final JUDGMENT.

Oath of allegiance An applicant must take an oath (or an affirmation, if his religion forbids taking an oath) by which he renounces his loyalty to his former country, swears his loyalty to the United States, and pledges to support and defend the Constitution and laws of the United States. The swearing marks the time when the assumption of duties, rights, and privileges of citizenship takes place.

If a person is opposed to bearing arms or military service because of religious training and belief, he may take a form of the oath that is in agreement with his beliefs.

Certificate A certificate of naturalization is usually given to the naturalized person as evidence of his citizenship, but if it is not, the person is still a U.S. citizen.

alienable Subject to removal or transfer. For example, real property (real estate) is said to be alienable because it may be transferred from one person to another.

alienate Transfer or convey title to real property (real estate). See also CONVEYANCE.

alienation clause A part of an INSURANCE policy that VOIDS—that is, ends—the policy if the insured property is sold or otherwise transferred.

alienation of affection Taking away the love, companionship, or aid of another person's husband or wife. In the past, alienation of affection provided grounds for a lawsuit against the person who interfered with the marriage relationship. Today, however, this is no longer the case in most states.

alimony Court-ordered payments made by a husband to his wife, and sometimes by a wife to her husband, when they are separated or divorced. Ordinarily, payments are made in money. *Temporary alimony* is an allowance made when a suit for DIVORCE is pending and may include payments for preparing the suit as well as for support. *Permanent alimony* is an order for support payments in the final judgment of divorce.

aliunde (Latin) "From another source"; from outside this document. Evidence *aliunde* may be used to explain a provision in a will.

allegation A statement in a PLEADING setting out a fact that one side expects to prove in a lawsuit. A statement that the plaintiff's personal injury was caused by the defendant's negligent act is an allegation.

allege State; charge. An alleged statement of facts is not considered a proved statement. To protect against possible libel or slander suits, a person who is suspected of, and even indicted for, a crime is called the alleged criminal until a verdict has been reached in his trial. See LIBEL AND SLANDER.

allegiance Loyalty and obedience to a country or government in return for its protection.

all fours Two cases or decisions are on "all fours" when the facts of each case are generally similar and the legal questions are decided in exactly the same way.

allocation Assignment; designation. For example, a customer has two accounts at a department store: a general charge account and a special account to pay for a television set. The customer sends the store a payment and fails to specify which account is to be credited. The store makes an allocation when it credits the entire payment to one of the two accounts.

allocution The formality in which a judge asks a defendant who has been convicted of a crime whether he has any way of showing that judgment should not be pronounced against him or if he has any last words to say before a sentence is given out.

allodial Free; describing land that is owned freely and completely.

allograph A written document or signature made by one person for another. It is the opposite of an autograph.

allonge A piece of paper attached to a negotiable instrument (such as a check or promissory note) to provide space for ENDORSEMENTS. See COMMERCIAL PAPER.

allotment 1 A share or portion. 2 The distribution of shares in a public undertaking or corporation. 3 The setting apart and dividing of property held formerly by two or more owners so that each one may hold individually his own share.

alteration The act of changing something from one thing into another, making it different from what it was without destroying its identity. For example, the front of a wooden building may be altered by bricking it over, yet the building still keeps its identity.

alteration of an instrument An *instrument* is a legal written document, such as a CONTRACT, DEED, or LEASE. An alteration of an instrument is a change in the meaning or language of the instrument—after it has been signed or completed—that one of the parties to the instrument makes without the consent of the other. A change that is made by a third person without the consent of the parties to the instrument is usually called a SPOLIATION or *mutilation*.

■ **Method** The alteration must change the face of the instrument. It may be evidenced by a difference in handwriting, a change in words or figures, an erasure, or a striking out. Since the alteration must change the meaning or language of the instrument, retracing any original writing is not an alteration, such as when a figure written in pencil is retraced in ink.

■ **Material changes** A material (substantial) alteration affects the rights of the parties involved. Usually, any material alteration releases the nonconsenting party from his obligation under the instrument. For example, if the altered instrument is a contract, the original contract is destroyed, and the nonconsenting party cannot be bound by the new contract because he never agreed to it. Even if the instrument is returned to its original form by erasing or striking out unauthorized words, the instrument does not become valid again.

Date Since the date is generally a material part of an instrument, an unauthorized change of date is a material alteration. It is easy to see how a change in date can seriously affect the right of parties when it shortens the time for payment of a loan, for instance, or lengthens the time, causing more interest to become due.

Signature When an alteration of a signature changes the legal effect of an instrument, the change is material. Adding a company or partnership name after a signature is a material change, as is erasing words that show that the signer is acting as an agent. Placing a signature in the wrong area is not material, nor is erasing a signature placed in the wrong spot.

Terms Any change in the terms of the instrument is material. For example, in a contract to sell land on commission, a change increasing the rate of commission is a material alteration.

Other alterations held to be material include a change in a deed so that it transfers a smaller piece of land, a change in the name of a purchaser in a contract, and a change in the terms of financing set forth in a land contract.

■ **Time of alteration** A change in an instrument before it is completed is not usually considered an alteration. The parties will see the instrument when they sign it and, if they sign, it is presumed that they agree upon its terms.

■ **Intention** The change must be made willfully and intentionally, but the motive prompting it is not important. A change in an instrument that is made by mistake or accident is usually not a material alteration.

EXAMPLE The Foxes are selling their house to the Neilsons. O⟶✻ Both couples are so excited about the deal that they make the signing of the papers into a champagne party for themselves, their lawyers, and the real estate agent. The next day, however, Bruce Neilson realizes that the house was put into both his name and his wife's instead of just his wife's name. He calls his lawyer who has also just discovered the mistake. The Foxes and their lawyer are notified of the error and it is properly corrected on both documents and on the one filed in the county clerk's office. This correction is not a material alteration.

■ **By whom made** No change or insertion by a third person in a written contract, deed, MORTGAGE of land, BOND, or negotiable instrument—such as a check or a promissory note—will invalidate the instrument if its original terms can be discovered. When a party to a negotiable instrument alters it materially, the instrument may be enforced against him as originally written. A change made with the consent of the parties to the instrument is binding on all the consenting parties.

EXAMPLE Let us say that an employer, an employee, and an O⟶✻ insurance company enter into a contract insuring the employee's life. Later all three parties agree to increase the amount for which the employee is insured from $25,000 to $50,000. The original contract is altered by drawing a line through the $25,000 figure and inserting above it the $50,000 figure. All three parties initial the change, and it is legally binding on all of them.

■ **Authorized alterations** An alteration made by an agent acting under the authority of a party to the instrument is binding on the party. See AGENCY. For example, a principal is liable for his agent's authorized alteration that extends the time of the due date in a promissory note.

alternative pleading A PLEADING that sets forth two or more sets of facts that cannot logically or physically exist at the same time. It is valid to use an alternative pleading in certain circumstances. For instance, in a contract action the defendant may claim both that the contract was void and that the plaintiff did not live up to his obligations and therefore the defendant cannot be under any obligation to keep his part of the bargain.

EXAMPLE Paula is suing Green Publishing Company for the O⟶✻ balance of the money owed to her for her manuscript on teaching parrots to talk. Green Publishing claims that it does not have to pay her the balance because Paula wrote mainly about taking care of parrots and very little about training the birds to speak. Green also claims that the contract was void from the beginning because the publishers never signed it. In either case, Green says that it is not obliged to pay Paula any more money.

alternative relief Asking the court, in a PLEADING, for one of two different kinds of help. For example, a person might ask for either the return of a borrowed lawn mower or for its cash value. See REMEDY.

alternative writ An order by a court commanding a person to do a particular thing or to show the court why he should not be forced to do it. For instance, a divorced husband might be ordered to pay all of his back ALIMONY or

to show the court why he should not be required to make the payments. See also SHOW CAUSE.

ambassadors and consuls An *ambassador* is the foreign diplomatic representative of a nation. His job is to conduct political negotiations between his country and the country in which he is stationed. A *consul* is the commercial agent of his country. He has authority only in business transactions and may not represent his country in political matters.

American ambassadors and consuls are appointed by the President with the consent of the Senate, while staff officers and other employees who serve under them are appointed by the Secretary of State.

■ **Powers and duties** The powers of an ambassador are defined in his credentials, or documents of introduction, which he presents to the foreign government. In addition to conducting political negotiations, an American ambassador may sue on behalf of the United States and defend suits that are brought against it. Similarly, a foreign ambassador in this country may sue and defend suits on behalf of his government.

Generally, a consul has the authority to protect the rights and property interests of the citizens of his country, to appear in court to insure that the laws of the country in which he serves are administered fairly to his countrymen. If you are in a foreign country and find yourself with a legal problem, you should seek out the U.S. consul.

Consuls also have the right and duty to protect the estates of their countrymen who die within their consular districts. This duty ends when the dead person's heirs are properly represented by an attorney.

■ **Diplomatic immunity** The purposes of diplomatic immunity are to develop friendly relations among nations and to insure against arrest, harassment, or other interferences with diplomatic representatives.

The law relating to diplomatic immunity is found in the Vienna Convention on Diplomatic Relations, which went into effect as part of our federal law in 1972. Under the provisions of the Vienna Convention the members of diplomatic missions are granted varying degrees of immunity from civil and criminal liability.

Diplomatic agents The head of a mission, such as an ambassador, and members of the mission staff who have diplomatic rank are known as diplomatic agents. A diplomatic agent is immune from criminal liability in the country in which he serves, but if he commits a crime, his country may be asked to recall him. If his country refuses, he may be expelled.

A diplomatic agent is also immune from civil lawsuits, except for (1) actions relating to real property (real estate) that is not held by him for mission purposes; (2) actions relating to estates left by deceased persons, when the agent is the executor, administrator, or a beneficiary; and (3) actions relating to any of his business or professional activities that are beyond the scope of his official duties. In addition, a diplomatic agent is not required to testify as a witness. The family members who form part of a diplomatic agent's household are also granted the same immunities.

Automobile accidents Because of the hardship diplomatic immunity imposes on the victims of motor-vehicle accidents caused by foreign diplomats serving in the United States, our federal law now requires mission members and their families to insure their personal motor vehicles, boats, and airplanes. If the mission itself owns similar means of transport, it too must obtain liability insurance. In addition, an action for damages for personal injuries, wrongful death, or property damage can be brought directly against the diplomat's insurance company. An action of this kind is tried by the court sitting without a jury.

Staff members The mission's administrative and technical staffs and their family-household members are fully immune from criminal liability. However, they are immune from civil liability only for official acts. The same is true for members of the service staff employed as domestics, but their families, and private servants employed by staff members, are not entitled to any immunity.

Status of consuls Because consuls are not diplomatic agents, they are usually subject to civil lawsuits and criminal prosecution in the country in which they are stationed. Federal law, however, grants those in the United States immunity from all suits and proceedings in state courts as a matter of policy, to prevent any embarrassment to foreign nations that might result from such proceedings.

■ **Diplomatic exemptions** Diplomatic agents in the United States and the members of their households are exempt from all federal, state, and municipal taxes. They are not exempt, however, from indirect taxes that are part of the price of goods, from taxes on any real property they own privately, from inheritance taxes on property inherited from a citizen, or from capital gains taxes on profits from private investments made in this country. Diplomatic agents are also exempt from the military service. These exemptions also apply to members of the administrative and technical staffs of the mission and their families. Members of the service staff and private servants are exempt from taxes on wages received from their employment with the mission or its members.

ambulance chaser A lawyer or a person working for a lawyer who follows up on street accidents to try to get the legal business that might arise from them. The phrase has come to mean any lawyer who improperly seeks business or tries to get people to bring lawsuits.

ambulatory Movable; revocable; subject to change. For example, a person's will is said to be ambulatory until his death.

amendment A change, usually for the better. The word may refer to a change in a bill during its passage through a LEGISLATURE, in a law that is already in existence, or in the constitutions of the states or of the federal government. The correction of an error made in any PROCESS or PLEADING in a lawsuit is also called an amendment. See also CONSTITUTIONAL LAW.

a mensa et thoro (Latin) "From table and bed"; commonly translated as "from bed and board." A separation granted by a court whereby a husband and wife, although still married, are no longer required to live together. See also DIVORCE.

American Bar Association A national voluntary organization of lawyers founded in 1878, with headquarters in Chicago. Attorneys admitted to the bar of any state are eligible. There are presently some 220,000 members—about half the country's lawyers. With a staff of 475, the ABA holds an annual convention, supervises the work of numerous committees on specialized subjects, maintains an extensive library, and on May 1 of each year sponsors Law Day to emphasize the importance of law. Each month it publishes *The American Bar Association Journal*.

American Civil Liberties Union A group founded in 1920 to protect basic constitutional rights. It provides legal counsel and AMICUS CURIAE ("friend of the court") briefs on important constitutional questions in civil liberties cases, such as those involving EQUAL PROTECTION OF LAWS, DUE PROCESS OF LAW, and the First Amendment freedoms of speech, press, religion, and assembly. Among the ACLU's famous cases are the Scopes trial (1925), the Sacco-Vanzetti case (1920), BROWN V. BOARD OF EDUCATION (1954), and MIRANDA V. ARIZONA (1966).

American Digest System A set of books containing summaries of every reported case decided in the United States since the 1600's. The cases are organized by subject according to the KEY NUMBER system.

amicable action A lawsuit that is brought by agreement of the two sides to settle a doubtful question of law. The facts of the case are agreed upon before the suit is started.

EXAMPLE In an amicable action brought by a New Jersey bank for payment of a promissory note, the bank and the defendant agreed on the date of the note, the amount, the purpose for which the money was being used, and the fact that the defendant was insane when he signed the note, although the bank did not know it then. The only point to be settled in court was whether the bank was entitled to collect. It was not, because the money was used to buy bar equipment—not considered a necessity, which is the only kind of purchase an insane person can be held to.

amicus curiae (Latin) "Friend of the court"; a person who is allowed to appear in a lawsuit and to give information to the court on a matter of law about which the court is doubtful. His appearance is a matter of discretion with the court and not a right to which he is entitled. An *amicus curiae* is not a party to the lawsuit, and he must not have a private interest in the outcome of the case.

Generally, the *amicus curiae* is an attorney, but others have been permitted to appear, including ordinary citizens, boards of education, labor unions, and hospital associations. The appearance may be made by a statement read in open court, by an AFFIDAVIT, or by a BRIEF. In the Supreme Court case of GIDEON V. WAINRIGHT, 23 states filed an *amicus curiae* brief on behalf of Gideon, a man convicted of robbery after a trial in which he had no lawyer. Test cases relating to taxation, school segregation cases, and criminal cases involving the death sentence are some other types of cases in which *amicus curiae* have been used.

The court has discretion in deciding whether it will accept the advice or suggestions of the *amicus curiae*, and the *amicus curiae* has no right to complain if the court refuses to accept his suggestions.

amnesty An exercise of the sovereign power of the government that gives a certain group of persons immunity from prosecution for a particular offense they have committed. Amnesty wipes out or abolishes the offense and forgives the accused before he ever comes to trial. A return to obedience and duty within a given time period is usually a condition of such immunity. The amnesty that President Gerald Ford granted to draft evaders in 1974, after the U.S. withdrawal from the Vietnam conflict, is an example. In contrast, a PARDON granted by a President or governor forgives a person only after he has been convicted of a crime.

The President has the power to grant amnesty if the offense is a violation of federal law. When the offense involves state or local law, the governor of the state or a local official, such as a mayor, may grant amnesty. In 1980 the mayor of New York City offered amnesty to persons who illegally possessed unregistered guns if they turned the weapons into their local police stations within the specified 30-day time limit.

amortization Paying off a debt in regular, equal payments. In amortizing a loan, the bank or other lender figures out the interest for the entire time until the loan is to be paid off, adds this interest to the amount of the loan, and divides the total by the number of payments. Most mortgage payments are calculated in this manner.

analogy Reasoning or arguing by similarities. For example, when there is no previous case on a particular subject (a PRECEDENT), lawyers argue from cases that are similar or are decided by the same general rules of law.

ancient lights Windows through which light has entered for 20 years or more. In some states, these windows may not be blocked by an adjoining landowner.

ancient writings Documents more than 30 years old that are presumed to be genuine when coming from proper custody, such as a court, a register of deeds, or a county clerk. The document must be the original and not a copy. See PRESUMPTION.

ancillary Aiding. An ancillary proceeding is a second action that helps a main one. Proceedings to enforce or change alimony or child-support payments following a divorce, for example, are ancillary to the original divorce action. Ancillary administration is a proceeding brought in a state where a dead person left property, when that state is not the one in which the person lived and in which his main estate is administered. See EXECUTORS AND ADMINISTRATORS; WILLS.

animals In law, an animal is usually defined as any living creature, other than man, that is capable of self-movement. *Domestic animals* include those tamed by long association with man, such as cats and dogs, and those man has purposely tamed, such as chickens, cows, and horses. *Wild animals* are those that man is unable to domesticate completely; force or skill is required to keep them under man's control. Not only alligators, lions, minks, otters, rats, and snakes, but bees and doves are considered wild animals.

This article covers animals as property; licensing; brands and marks; hiring; cruelty to animals; animals running at large; injuries to persons and to animals.

■ **Animals as property** All domestic animals are personal property to which the owner has the same rights as to other kinds of personal property. In the case of animals, however, his rights are subject to the state's right to pass laws and make regulations that provide for the safety,

---

WHEN YOU ARE THE OWNER OF AN ANIMAL

■ If your pet strays and is found by another person, the finder does not become the new owner—the animal is still yours.

■ If an untrained wild animal belonging to you escapes and returns to nature, you usually lose ownership.

■ Your right to use a livestock brand or mark is a property right protected by laws in several states.

■ You may kill a sick or injured animal, but you may not kill or hurt animals needlessly.

■ If you negligently let your animal stray onto a highway and it causes an accident, you can be sued by the injured parties.

■ If your dog infects a person or another animal with rabies, you usually

are not liable unless you knew your animal had rabies.

■ You have a right to keep a vicious dog for protection, but you should consult with your lawyer regarding the legal responsibilities this may entail in your state.

■ If you give your dog free run of the household while a guest is there, you are not guilty of negligence if the dog knocks down the guest—unless the dog has known vicious tendencies.

■ In some states, you are liable for bites that are inflicted by your dog, even though you did not know your dog was a biter. But even these so-called dog-bite laws do not make an owner absolutely liable under any and all circumstances.

■ If your watchdog threatens passersby, you may be sued for maintaining a nuisance, and if any injury is suffered as a result of their being startled or frightened, you can be liable.

■ If your animal is killed by someone's deliberate or negligent act, you are usually entitled to recover the cash value of the animal.

■ If your dog trespasses on a neighbor's property, he has the right to use only as much force as is necessary to drive it off. Even if your dog was tearing up the neighbor's valuable flower bed, for example, your neighbor would not have the right to kill it, except as a last resort after trying to drive it off, capture it, or inform you of its misconduct.

health, and welfare of its citizens. For example, the state may require that dogs must be vaccinated against rabies and licensed.

The owner's property rights are permanent. When an animal strays from its owner and is found by another person, the finder does not become the animal's new owner.

EXAMPLE A parrot, used by the American Society for the Prevention of Cruelty to Animals (ASPCA) in educational talks given to schoolchildren, escaped during an outdoor performance in Kings Point, New York. Some days later a parrot was found by a man in Belle Harbor. After repeated feedings, the bird came into the man's house, where he put it into a cage and called the ASPCA to ask about the care and feeding of parrots. The ASPCA sent two members to the man's house, claimed the bird as theirs, and took it away. The finder sued, claiming the parrot was now his, but the court ruled that because the bird was trained—hence not wild—the original owner was the true owner. A footnote to this story—the ASPCA assured the finder that he would be given the first parrot that came into its hands.

Generally, the person who owns the mother also owns the young animals she produces. If a stolen cow gives birth to a calf, both the cow and calf belong to the true owner.

When an animal dies, it remains the owner's property. If a steer is killed by a truck, for instance, the owner retains all rights to the carcass.

Ownership of wild animals The state owns all wild animals living within its borders as trustee for the use and benefit of its residents. The state has the power to prohibit, regulate, and control the taking of wild animals and to decide what property rights to them a person may have or acquire. Wild animals in their natural surroundings are not the property of private citizens. A person becomes the owner of a wild animal when he captures or kills it and takes it away from its natural place. A hunter does not own any of the bears in the state's forests until he kills one and takes it away with him. But if the taking is illegal—if a person removes a protected species, for example—the ownership of the animal remains with the state.

A landowner has a qualified property interest in wild animals living on his land, which becomes absolute when he captures or kills an animal. You have the exclusive right to take animals from your land, subject only to state regulation. For example, deer may live on your land, but you may kill them only during the deer-hunting season, designated by the state. If the wild animals voluntarily leave your land or are driven away, your qualified right of ownership ends.

A person who finds wild animals on another person's land does not own them. Say you find and mark a bee tree on someone else's property. Ownership of the bees remains with the landowner, but if he gives you permission to enter and capture them, then you become the owner.

Ownership of wild animals is usually lost when they escape and return to nature.

EXAMPLE An untrained sea lion, shipped from the West to the East Coast, escaped and was captured in New Jersey. The West Coast owner sued to get it back, but the court ruled that because the sea lion was a wild animal the original owner had lost his qualified right of property. And in the case above about the lost parrot, had the court

ruled that the parrot was a wild, not a trained, bird, the finder would have been entitled to keep it.

But if a wild animal escapes temporarily and is quickly chased and captured, ownership is not lost.

■ **Licenses** States often pass laws requiring the owner of a dog to pay a license fee, or a tax, for the privilege of keeping the dog. Usually, a dog must be licensed where it is kept rather than where the owner lives, if the two places are not the same. You should apply for a license for your dog at the time required by law. Failure to apply on time will not prevent you from getting a license, but you may be subject to a penalty. Many licensing laws provide a fine as a punishment for failure to license a dog. If you keep a dog owned by someone else, you are liable for payment.

Some licensing laws require a description of the dog, and the owner must be sure his dog's description is correct. A license to keep a brown dog named Dime gives the owner no right to keep a black Newfoundland named Tiny.

■ **Brands and marks** A brand is a figure or device burned on an animal by a hot iron. A mark is a change, such as splitting the ear, made in some part of the animal by a knife or other means. The brand is most commonly used today to identify horses and mules. Marks made by knife cuts in the ear are usually used to identify cattle and hogs.

The right to use a livestock brand or mark is a valuable property right. Several states have passed laws regulating branding and marking, the purpose of which is to protect the owner and prevent the theft of livestock by providing an easy means of identification. Some state laws provide for brand and mark inspection of livestock in shipment, and the inspector is given the authority to seize unbranded or unmarked animals that he believes to be stolen.

As property, brands and marks may be sold or transferred. Under some state laws, it is a crime to change a brand or mark on another person's animal without his consent and with the intent to defraud him. See FRAUD.

■ **Hiring** The hiring of an animal creates a BAILMENT, which is the word used for the delivery of personal property for some particular purpose. The person who owns the animal is the bailor, and the person who hires the animal is the bailee. A bailor must provide an animal that is fit, suitable, and safe for the purpose for which it is hired. He has a duty to tell the bailee of any vicious or dangerous habits the animal may have.

EXAMPLE A bailor knew that one of his horses had a habit of kicking with one foot in a way that made the animal more dangerous than an ordinary horse. The bailor had a duty to inform the bailee of the horse's bad habit, but he did not. When one of the bailee's horses was kicked and injured by the bailor's horse, the bailor was liable for damages.

On the other hand, the bailor has no duty to inform the bailee of habits not usually dangerous to people or property.

EXAMPLE On the first beautiful spring day, Reed hired a horse from the local stable so that he could ride around the countryside, enjoying the sights and smells of the new season. The keeper of the stable did not tell Reed that the horse was a jumper. After a short while and for no apparent reason, the horse made a sudden leap. Reed was thrown and broke both his legs. The stable keeper (the bailor) was not required to tell Reed (the bailee) that the horse was a jumper because he had no reason to believe that the horse would jump in the open countryside where there were no hurdles. Therefore the stable keeper was not liable for Reed's injuries.

A bailee who hires an animal must provide it with ordinary care. One who left a horse in a pasture on a cold rainy night was held liable for its death. The bailee, however, is not an insurer of the animal, and he may not be held responsible for an injury to the animal, or for its death, unless he is at fault. When a bailee rented a horse and agreed to return it in as good condition as when he received it, he was not found liable for damages when the horse became sick and, over his objection, was shot by the ASPCA. In another instance, a bailee was not responsible when a mule he hired was killed in a fire that was not caused by his negligence.

■ **Cruelty** Many states have laws prohibiting cruelty to animals. Under some laws, all animals are protected. Other laws are limited to domestic animals.

Cruelty to animals includes every unjustifiable act, omission, or neglect causing pain, suffering, or death. The cruelty may be in overworking, underfeeding, or not providing the animal with proper protection. The test is whether the harm done is justifiable under the circumstances. A person who kills a sick or injured animal as an act of mercy is not guilty of cruelty.

Not every act that causes pain and suffering to animals is prohibited. When the purpose is reasonable, the act that causes the pain may be justifiable. It is not cruelty, for example, to inflict pain in order to make an animal useful to man, such as in the castration of a young horse or bull to make it docile.

Methods of slaughter that cause unnecessary pain are ordinarily forbidden, as is needless killing, such as in bullfighting. Poisoning an animal has been held an act of cruelty under some statutes.

Whether killing, injuring, or abusing animals for sport amounts to cruelty depends on the circumstances and statutes involved. In some states trapshooting captive pigeons set free to act as targets is cruelty, while in others trapshooting birds is permitted. Releasing a hare and permitting it to be pursued by greyhounds that tear and mangle it is cruelty in some states but not in others.

■ **Running at large** An owner of domestic animals may, in the absence of regulation, lawfully permit them to run at large. Modern highway conditions, however, require an owner to take ordinary care to keep his animals from straying onto a heavily traveled thoroughfare. A state that prohibits animals from running at large may compel owners to keep them within enclosures, and it may provide that those found running at large may be captured and sold.

■ **Injuries to persons** The owner or keeper of domestic animals is liable for injuries caused by his animals only when he has been negligent, or when the injuries were the result of his animals' known vicious tendencies. This means that if your cocker spaniel bites the postman's leg, you will not be held liable—as long as you were not negligent and your cocker spaniel was not known to have vicious tendencies.

The most common ground of an action to recover for an injury by an animal when it does not have known vicious tendencies is NEGLIGENCE. The owner's negligent act must have been the direct or PROXIMATE CAUSE of the injury, and the injury must have been one the owner could have reasonably anticipated or foreseen. For example, if you own a pony and fail to close the gate of the pony's enclosure, you can reasonably expect the pony to escape. You can also reasonably foresee that the pony will go onto a nearby highway and cause injury to travelers and vehicles, and you are responsible if this does happen.

A *vicious tendency* is a tendency to do any act that is dangerous to another person or his property. The fact that the dangerous act was prompted by mischievousness or playfulness, rather than maliciousness or ferociousness, is immaterial. If the animal has a known tendency to do a dangerous act, the owner is liable. But if the injury results from a vicious tendency not natural or usual in the class of animals to which the animal belongs, and the owner does not know of it, the owner is not liable.

The owner's knowledge may be actual or may be implied from the circumstances. For example, animals subjected to the treatment they receive in rodeo shows become frightened, angry, and, hence, dangerous, and rodeo operators are charged with knowledge of that fact. The owner's knowledge need not be personal. If an agent or employee in charge of an animal knows of its vicious tendencies, the knowledge will be imputed, or transferred, to the owner.

EXAMPLE A riding academy employee knew that the owner's wife's dog had a tendency to rush at a certain horse. The dog's action often caused the otherwise gentle horse to rear or bolt. The employee's knowledge was imputed to the academy owner, since the employee gained his knowledge from the handling of the horse, which was a part of his duties at the academy.

The necessity for showing that an owner knew his animal had a vicious tendency usually depends upon whether or not the animal was where it belonged at the time of the injury. If the animal was where it belonged, the person injured must usually prove that the owner had the knowledge. If the animal was not where it belonged when the injury took place, then proof of the owner's knowledge may not be necessary. For example, when a horse that was being led down a sidewalk kicked and injured a pedestrian who was rightfully using the sidewalk, the owner of the horse was liable for the injury; the pedestrian did not have to prove that the owner knew of his horse's vicious tendency.

Dogs When a dog owner knows his animal has a tendency to be vicious, he has a duty to control or confine it. If he does not, he is liable.

EXAMPLE A German shepherd, confined in a yard behind a high metal fence, would lunge viciously at anyone passing by. One snowy night he badly frightened a pedestrian, and she slipped and fell. Although the dog never came through the fence, the owner was held liable for the woman's injuries because he knew about the dog's threatening behavior toward pedestrians.

Keeping a vicious animal is also thought to amount to a NUISANCE, and a person is liable for any injuries caused by a nuisance that he has maintained.

The owner of a mad dog is not liable if the dog inflicts rabies on a person or another animal, unless he knows or has reason to suspect it may have rabies.

A dog owner or keeper who is negligent in keeping or controlling his dog is, of course, liable for injuries directly resulting from his negligence. It does not matter whether or not he knew his dog had vicious tendencies.

EXAMPLE A pedestrian was injured when a dog leaped or
O───✶ fell from a window and struck her as she was passing by on a sidewalk 16 feet below. The dog had been trained as a watchdog and was free to roam about the building, which had swivel windows that could be opened with slight pressure. The court held the defendant-owner liable on the basis of negligence, even though he did not know of any prior leap by the dog.

Ordinarily, you have the right to keep a vicious dog for the protection of life and property. This right usually shields you from liability to someone who enters your premises during the night, even though the person is there for a lawful purpose. On the other hand, some courts have decided that if an owner permits his dog to run at large on his premises and a person is injured by it during the day, the owner is liable, even to a trespasser. See TRESPASS.

Some courts have held that the owner of a vicious dog kept to guard his premises does not have to give or to post notice of its vicious character to protect himself from being sued by an injured trespasser, but other courts have reached the opposite decision. In general, the courts will decide that you acted in a reasonable manner if you post signs and chain the vicious dog within the boundaries of your property.

You owe a social guest a duty of ordinary care while he is on your premises. Unless you know if your dog has some vicious tendency, giving it free run of the household does not amount to negligence. When both you and your guest know a dog is on the premises, you are not guilty of negligence because your guest was knocked down by the moving dog.

Some statutes make an owner liable for dog bites even though he did not know his dog had a tendency to bite. For example, an Illinois statute provided that if a dog, without provocation, attacks or injures any person who is peaceably conducting himself in a place where he may lawfully be, the owner of the dog is liable for damages. But these so-called dog-bite laws do not make the owner absolutely liable under any and all circumstances for injuries caused by his dog.

EXAMPLE A woman stumbled over a dog lying in her path as
O───✶ she was leaving her brother's house. In her outstretched arms she was carrying a suitcase over which some clothing was draped, and she could not see the dog. When she brought suit under the statute, the court decided that there was no "attack or injury" and that the woman could not recover damages.

A businessman, such as a storekeeper, who keeps a dog has a strong duty to protect business visitors from harm by the dog. He should post signs warning visitors that the dog is present, and he should make certain the dog is securely confined. If a business visitor is bitten by a dog of known vicious tendencies, he may recover under the principle of STRICT LIABILITY, even if the owner of the business is not negligent. There was a case in which a dog, chained by its owner who was employed in a funeral home, bit a business visitor to the home. Although the operator of the funeral home was not negligent, he was held responsible for the visitor's injury on the basis of strict liability. See TORT.

In some jurisdictions there is no longer a distinction between licensees—those who enter another's land with permission for their own purposes (postmen and meter readers, for example)—and guests who enter by invitation of the owner. Landowners and occupiers must exercise reasonable care toward all persons who enter their land, even trespassers. The movement toward a single duty of ordinary care seems to be the upcoming trend in the law in this area of negligence.

■ **Damages to property** You will be held strictly liable for damage to property caused by the animal you own if it is the kind likely to roam and do harm to neighboring property. Cattle, sheep, horses, hogs, turkeys, chickens, and pigeons are within this category, as are any kept wild animals, such as a wild boar, that are likely to escape, trespass, and damage property.

When your animal is domesticated, such as a dog or a cat, most courts will hold you absolutely responsible for the damages it causes by trespassing on another's land only if you knew or should have known about a mischievous trait it has.

EXAMPLE If your dog gets loose and repeatedly destroys
O───✶ your neighbor's garden, despite all your attempts to keep him restrained to prevent him from entering your neighbor's property, you are strictly liable to your neighbor. But if one day your normally well-behaved dog wanders over to your neighbor's yard and destroys the rosebed and the vegetable garden, you will not be liable.

You must consult the laws of your state to determine whether these general principles have been modified by statute or by decisions of the courts.

■ **Injury or death of an animal** When a domestic animal is injured or killed by someone's negligent or deliberate act, the owner is usually entitled to recover DAMAGES. Damages are limited to the cash value of the animal, however. The owner is not entitled to compensation for loss of affection caused by the animal's death.

Motor-vehicle accidents are common cases in which an owner may be entitled to damages for the injury or death of his animal. Cases involving injury or death resulting from low-flying airplanes and vehicle noises are also on record.

EXAMPLE A turkey farmer recovered damages for the death
O───✶ of his turkeys frightened by a low-flying airplane used in the aerial spraying of a neighbor's farm. The frightened turkeys ran into obstacles in their pens and were fatally injured.

The negligent use or disposal of poisons, pollutants, or waste products causing injuries to animals may also result in liability.

Trespassing animals A landowner is permitted to use only as much force as is reasonably necessary to drive off a trespassing animal, and he may kill an animal only when it is necessary to protect his person or property.

EXAMPLE For a long time a dog sucked all the eggs laid by
O───✶ the chickens on a farm. The farmer made many unsuccessful attempts to drive away the dog and to capture it. He also tried to find the owner and notify him of the dog's misconduct. As a last resort he killed the dog. When the owner of the dog sued the farmer for the value of the dog, the court decided that the farmer was not liable for killing it.

EXAMPLE Larry's dog was kept fenced in his yard, but the 0—* dog slipped out and dug up one of Paul and Dorothy's rose bushes next door. Paul was so enraged that he rigged up a spring gun to protect his shrubs. Once more Larry's dog slipped into the yard. The dog tripped the gun and was killed. Paul was liable to Larry for the value of the dog because he had no right to inflict such a severe injury. It was no defense that the dog was trespassing, because Larry had been careful in trying to keep the dog within his own fenced-in yard.

The person who kills an animal, however, must take into consideration the value of the trespassing animal in relation to the property being injured. You would not be justified in killing a valuable dog that destroys your chickens when you could have driven it away or captured it for its owner.

animus (Latin) "Mind"; "will"; "design." The form *animo* means "with intention." For example, *animo furandi* means "with intent to steal."

annex Attach. The word expresses the idea of joining something smaller with something larger. For instance, a smaller piece of land may be annexed to a larger piece, or a smaller school district may be annexed to a larger district. Annex can also mean joining a subordinate document with the main document, such as a CODICIL that adds new provisions to an existing WILL.

annotated statutes A set of books containing the laws passed by a legislature, explanations of the laws, and brief descriptions of case decisions interpreting the laws.

annotation A note or commentary on a passage in a book or document intended to explain its meaning. A legal annotation is usually an explanation of a case and a description of other similar cases. It generally follows the text of the decision in a collection of cases.

annual percentage rate The true cost of borrowing a sum of money over a one-year period. The rate is computed yearly to make it easier to understand credit terms and to shop for credit. Thus, interest of 1.5 percent a month would mean an annual percentage rate of 18 percent. The 1969 Truth in Lending Act requires that the annual percentage rate appear on all loan papers.

annuity A fixed sum of money paid to a person at fixed times for a definite period of time or for life. An annuity may be created by a gift, will, or simple contract, and a person can purchase an annuity for himself or for another person. A *continuing annuity* is one that does not end when the first person who is entitled to receive it dies. A wife, for example, might be entitled to the payments after her husband's death. On the other hand, a *life annuity* ends upon the death of the person for whom it was created. A *term annuity* is one that can be ended voluntarily—in exchange for a lump sum—by the person entitled to the payments.

The person who is entitled to payment of an annuity (the annuitant) is designated in the contract. Usually, an annuity is payable at the end of the year, although other arrangements can be made. Upon the death of an annuitant, pay-

ments may be continued or a gross sum paid to another beneficiary or to the estate of the deceased. The value of life annuities (the amount to be paid to another beneficiary or to an estate after the death of the primary beneficiary) is usually computed by consulting annuity and MORTALITY TABLES and viewing them in the light of the health and age of the person who is to receive the payments.

annulment Making something void; a declaration that something has no legal effect. If a court annuls a JUDGMENT, that judgment has no force or operation from the time it was made, not from the time it was annulled.

The *annulment of a marriage* is a judgment by a court that the MARRIAGE has never existed. It is different from a DIVORCE, which is a court order that ends a marriage, and can be obtained only when there has been a valid marriage. A divorce means that a man and woman are no longer husband and wife after the court decree. An annulment has the effect that they never were husband and wife.

Religions have different procedures for a church annulment, which affects only one's relationship to his religion and has no legal effect. It is possible to seek both a legal, or civil, annulment and a religious annulment, but one does not affect the other. This article discusses the legal annulment of a marriage. See also Chart 21.

■ **History** Unlike most American law, annulment does not have strong roots in the English common law. Until 1857 only the religious, or ecclesiastical, courts in England could annul an invalid marriage. Because of the American tradition of keeping church and state separate, there were no ecclesiastical courts here, and colonies in the Northeast passed laws permitting civil courts or legislatures to grant annulments. After independence from England, the civil courts in most states did not assume that they had power to hear annulment cases, but it was clear that people should not be held to all the obligations of marriage when the marriage was invalid. During the 19th and 20th centuries, an increasing number of states passed laws authorizing the annulment of marriages. Most states now have statutes governing annulment. In those that do not, courts have asserted their authority to declare that no marriage exists where the laws regulating marriage have not been followed.

■ **Annulment and divorce** Whether or not courts have been willing to accept someone's case for an annulment depends on the moral climate of the times and the nature of a given judge. Well into the 19th century annulment was the only way to dissolve a marriage and have the legal right to marry again. This made people seek annulments rather than divorces whenever possible.

In some states, people had to seek annulments because divorces were so difficult to obtain. Until 1966, New York, for example, would grant a divorce only on proof that a husband or wife had committed ADULTERY. If the spouse asking for the divorce had no taste for proving the other's adultery or if the marriage was dead for some other reason the marriage could be ended by annulment. The strictness of New York's divorce law encouraged judges to be very liberal in granting annulments.

As divorce has become more freely available, annulment has become much less common. States have laws that prescribe when annulment is available. Generally, if an

WHEN CIRCUMSTANCES MAY PERMIT ANNULMENT

■ Parents of underage parties to a marriage may be able to have the marriage annulled.

■ Incest may be a ground for annulment but is defined variously from state to state—some states go so far as to forbid marriage between cousins and second cousins, whereas others uphold even an uncle-niece marriage in some cases.

■ If a man conceals before marriage that he has children he does not support, the wife may obtain an annulment on the ground of fraud.

■ A man may be able to get an annulment if he later discovers that his wife was pregnant with another man's child at the time of the marriage.

■ If a person knows that he or she is unable to engage in sex for physical or emotional reasons, it is a fraud to marry without disclosing this fact, and an annulment may be granted if the other partner requests it.

■ Conditions of health that provide grounds for annulment in some states are venereal disease, incurable insanity, alcoholism, feeblemindedness, and epilepsy.

■ If a person is too drunk or too high on drugs to understand that a wedding ceremony is being performed, the marriage may be annulled.

■ If a couple marries because of pregnancy and the pregnancy turns out to be a false alarm, annulment usually will not be granted but may be in some states, especially if the couple has not lived together and neither wants to stay married.

■ Annulment may also be granted for an unexplained absence of one partner for a period of time and under circumstances indicating possible death.

■ Someone under the age of consent can ask for an annulment, but the person over the age of consent who marries him or her cannot.

■ Two elderly people who marry for companionship usually cannot later have the marriage annulled on the ground that one of them is impotent or sterile.

■ The children of a senile man who married his nurse may be able to ask to have the marriage annulled on the ground of their father's incompetence.

annulment is to be granted, the grounds listed in the law must have been present at the time the couple was married. Rather than try to prove this, it is now easier in most states to get a divorce. But in the states that still make it difficult for a divorced person to remarry, many people prefer annulment.

■ **Invalid marriages** An annulment declares that what seems to be a marriage is really not. There are two kinds of invalid marriages: void and voidable.

Void marriages A void marriage is one that was not valid from the outset and did not legally exist in any way.

What makes a marriage void depends on state law. Any attempt to marry while still married to someone else—that is, bigamy—creates a void marriage. A void marriage also results when one party is legally unable to give consent and marry voluntarily, as when a boy or girl is too young to marry even with the consent of a parent.

A marriage is said to be void on the ground of incest if the two people are already related in a way the state law forbids. Usually this means related by blood as a parent and child, brother and sister, uncle and niece, or aunt and nephew. In some cases, the prohibition extends to cousins and second cousins. In some cases, states will make exceptions to the law against marrying a relative if the marriage was valid where the ceremony was performed.

EXAMPLE In New York, where a state law prohibited uncle-niece marriages, the court approved a marriage between an uncle and a niece that had been performed in Italy. Italian law prohibited such marriages except when the people obtained permission from a public official, as this couple had done. In another marriage that took place in Italy, however, the couple had not obtained special permission to marry, so the marriage was held void. In that case, a 46-year-old aunt had married her 18-year-old nephew. Several years after they came to live in this country, the "husband" took off, and the "wife" needed a court order for support. Because there was no marriage, the court held that it could not order support.

Voidable marriages Annulment also operates to declare invalid a marriage that is voidable rather than void. Voidable means that the marriage can be declared illegal. The annulment is effective only from the time that a court gives its decision. If no one ever goes into court to seek an annulment, the marriage continues as valid. This is different from a void marriage, which is invalid whether or not the court grants an annulment.

■ **Grounds** The grounds for annulling a voidable marriage depend on the law of each state, but the underlying theory is that two people should not be bound by the obligations of marriage if there never was a real intention to be married.

Fraud The most common ground for annulment is fraud. It is necessary in most states to prove that (1) the guilty party lied to or misled the innocent party, (2) the innocent party would not have married if he or she had known the truth, and (3) a reasonable person would have been deceived under the same circumstances.

The deceit must involve something essential to a marriage relationship. Almost everyone suffers a few disappointments after the honeymoon. It is not enough that a husband is shocked to find out that his wife is not rich after all or that a wife is dismayed to learn that her husband is really bald. Even barefaced lies do not give one party the right to an annulment for fraud.

EXAMPLE A man told a wealthy woman that he had a title of nobility and a great fortune, when in fact he lived on money that other women gave him. The court said that annulment is not available just because one hoped to land a spouse with wealth or social position. It added that no reasonable person could have believed this man and would not accept the argument that the woman who married him was "blinded by love."

Courts most frequently find that fraud touches an essential of marriage if the fraud involves religion, children, or sex.

EXAMPLE One woman was granted an annulment when she
◇—✳ discovered that her husband was not an Orthodox
Jew. The court found that she had made it clear that she
could perform her duties as a wife only in an Orthodox
home and that the husband had intentionally misled her
because he was in love with her. He knew she would not
marry him otherwise.

Fraud may be proved by actual false statements or by the
failure to speak about an essential part of marriage. Having
children, for example, is recognized in law as an essential
part of marriage. If one party has a fixed intention not to
have children, or if he or she is unable to do so, the person
has an obligation to speak before the marriage. Failure to
do so is a ground for annulment. Annulment is not available, however, to someone whose partner has a change of
heart after the marriage.

EXAMPLE A wife who wished to have children was denied
◇—✳ an annulment because she had agreed before marriage to use a contraceptive for a year or so. Even though
the husband admitted that he never wanted children and
had hoped he could change her mind later, the court held
that the wife had committed herself to marriage with
contraception and could not have an annulment.

Fraud may be the ground for annulment if one party
conceals the fact that he or she already has a child—for
example, when a woman does not disclose before marriage
that she had an illegitimate child or when a man conceals
the fact that he has children he does not support.

A man can get an annulment if he later discovers that his
wife was pregnant with another man's child at the time of
the marriage. Sometimes the ground is fraud, and sometimes the court simply says the woman is incapable of
performing a wife's natural duties—that is, she is not able to
have her husband's child while pregnant with another's.

Annulment for fraud is not available if the wife told her
husband she was pregnant with his child when she was not.
If the husband had enough reason to believe that he was the
father and went ahead with marriage, then the court will
not hear his petition for an annulment.

EXAMPLE In one strange case, a young man asked the court
◇—✳ for an annulment because he said that his wife
had told him she was pregnant at the time of the marriage
and this was not true. At the same time, he claimed that he
could not have been the father and that he would not have
married her if he had known she was not pregnant. The
court said that the young man may have been stupid for
marrying a girl he thought pregnant with another man's
child but that stupidity is not a ground for annulment.

Sexual problems can give rise to an annulment action for
fraud. If a person knows that he or she is unable to engage
in sexual intercourse for physical or emotional reasons, it is
a fraud to marry without disclosing this fact. Because
sexual relations are expected by most people to be an
essential part of marriage, any condition that prevents a
normal sex life must be disclosed beforehand.

Annulments have been granted when one person had
sexual perversions that prevented him or her from having
normal sexual relations. Homosexuality has nearly always
been a legally recognized ground.

Physical and emotional conditions The purpose of
the law is to protect the right to have intercourse and to

have children. In many states the law permits annulment
without proof of fraud for an inability to engage in normal
sex or to bear children. These states protect the right of
procreation even if the person with the "physical incapacity" did not know about it before marriage.

If both partners know about such a condition from the
outset, however, it cannot later be claimed as a reason for an
annulment.

EXAMPLE Emily and Edward, two elderly people, married
◇—✳ for the comfort of a warm relationship. They
cannot later have the marriage annulled on the ground
that one of them is impotent or sterile. Because neither
person in this marriage (sometimes called a *companionate
marriage*) really expected to have children, the court will
not believe that an essential of the marriage has been
frustrated.

Other conditions of health that are grounds for annulment in some states are venereal disease, incurable insanity,
alcoholism, feeblemindedness, and epilepsy. In certain
states just the existence of one of these conditions is enough
for an annulment. In others, an annulment may be obtained
for fraud if the condition was concealed.

Lack of consent Courts consider marriage a very serious matter. They will not grant an annulment just because
someone decides after the wedding that he would rather not
be married. A party who was forced to marry at gunpoint,
however, or who suffers from extreme age or mental illness
cannot be said to have given voluntary consent.

Courts have sometimes permitted annulments when two
people married "to give a child a name" because the woman
was pregnant. The reasons behind such decisions are that
the parties never intended to live as husband and wife, so
that there was no consent to be married. In other cases,
courts have refused to grant such annulments on the principle that making children legitimate is an important purpose
of marriage. If that is what the parties have in mind, the
court reasons, they must intend the marriage to be valid.

Mistake It is rarely possible to prove a mistake of the
kind that will permit an annulment.

EXAMPLE A woman asked for an annulment after she
◇—✳ learned that her husband's real name was not
what he had told her and that he had a criminal record.
The court held that there was no mistake about identity.
She married the man she had intended to marry. She
should have gotten to know him better during a period of
courtship or engagement.

If the mistake concerns some essential part of marriage—
not just wealth or social position, for example—then it may
be a ground for annulment. A mistake about whether an
earlier marriage was really ended by divorce gives the right
to an annulment for bigamy. A mistake about whether
cousins can marry in a certain state permits annulment on
the ground of incest. A mistaken belief that impotence or
insanity has been cured may give the right to an annulment
on that ground.

Mistake means that one party entered the marriage not
really knowing what he was doing—as when someone was
too drunk or high on drugs to understand that a wedding
ceremony was being performed. There must be clear proof
that at least one of the two was completely unable to make a
rational decision. Courts will not declare a marriage invalid

simply because a bride or groom needed a few drinks in order to face matrimony.

Courts have been just as severe in cases where parties claimed to have gone through a marriage ceremony in jest.

EXAMPLE An 18-year-old college student was persuaded by 0——✻ her boyfriend to get a marriage license because "it would not hurt any and would make him feel better" and would prove she was really "his girl." Four months later the young man pressured her to go through a marriage ceremony before a minister. He had dared her to do it and argued that they each had six months to decide whether to have it annulled. They never lived together. Three months later, she and her mother asked the court for an annulment. She explained that the ceremony was "in jest," never intended to be real. She had asked him to take her back to college when they were driving to the minister's, but he would not. The court ruled that the marriage was valid. They may have intended a six-month trial period, but state law made no provision for such a thing. This young woman certainly made a mistake and may have acted half in jest, but she did not get an annulment.

Duress In many states a marriage can be annulled if one party has been forced to marry. This is called duress. A shotgun wedding is a marriage under duress. It is clear that one whose life is threatened has not voluntarily consented to be married.

The duress must be serious, however, leaving no room for choice.

EXAMPLE Thomas Thompson threatens to have Arnold 0——✻ Anders arrested for corrupting a minor unless he marries Thompson's daughter. Thompson's actions are not duress. Anders has a choice. He can marry Thompson's daughter, or he can face the charges and win if he is innocent or go to jail if he is guilty.

It is not duress when a man marries a woman because she tells him that she is pregnant. There may be fraud if the woman falsely tells him that it is his baby, but—as discussed above—a man is not entitled to an annulment if he knew that it could be his baby. The pressure to marry when a child is conceived is not legal duress. Even if the woman is not pregnant, whether she lied or was mistaken, courts generally will not permit an annulment. But some states have granted annulments when the pregnancy turned out to be a false alarm, provided the couple had not lived together and neither wanted to stay married. The general policy, however, is always to protect a marriage after it comes into existence.

Prohibition against remarriage Some states include in their divorce laws a provision that a judge may or must order one or both of the divorced parties not to remarry under certain circumstances.

EXAMPLE A woman sued her husband for divorce on the 0——✻ ground of adultery. The law in that state was that he could not remarry within one year of a divorce granted for adultery. Nevertheless, he met another woman and married her a few months later without ever disclosing his first marriage, his affair, or the divorce. When he tired of this second marriage, he went to court and asked for an annulment based on the fact that he had been prohibited from marrying at the time of the second marriage. The court agreed and declared that the marriage was invalid.

Other courts have been less accommodating for scoundrels like this man. They have held that the prohibition against remarriage can prevent a marriage but cannot be used to annul one that has already occurred.

Conditions occurring after marriage Some states permit a few exceptions to the rule that an annulment can be granted only for a condition that exists at the time of the wedding ceremony. A marriage may be annulled, for example, when one person has been insane for at least five years and appears to be incurable.

Another possibility is annulment for an unexplained absence of one partner for a period of time and under circumstances that indicate possible death. Although the court's action when one person disappears is sometimes called *dissolution of a marriage* rather than annulment, it has the same effect: freeing the remaining spouse to remarry. See "Enoch Arden" laws under DIVORCE.

■ **Consummation and cohabitation** It must always be remembered that the law of marriage rests on tradition. It does not respond to every new fad in life-styles but seeks always to protect the ancient relationship.

History has created one rule for couples who have participated in a wedding without cohabitating afterward and a different rule for people who have lived together and shared sex. Judges often say that they are much more willing to annul a marriage if it was never consummated, that is, if the parties have not had sexual intercourse. Moreover, judges are reluctant to force a "used" woman into a position where she has no legal rights to make up for the change in her status, for traditionally annulment, unlike divorce, rarely brings a woman alimony or property sharing.

It is easiest to obtain an annulment right after the marriage and before the parties cohabit. Two people change their positions—legally, financially, and socially—by living together. For this reason, courts take into account the sharing of a home and sexual relations.

This does not mean that an annulment may be had simply because a marriage has not been consummated. If one partner refuses sexual relations, this may be a ground for divorce but not for annulment, because in most cases a ground for annulment must have existed at the time of the marriage. A failure also to cohabit makes it more likely that the court will consider the ground serious enough to declare the marriage invalid.

EXAMPLE Two 24-year-olds were married in a civil ceremo-0——✻ ny. When they told their parents, the man's mother made them promise they would not live together until they had a religious ceremony. Before that was performed, the wife had a serious accident that left her paralyzed. For three years her husband was attentive, but then he fell in love with another woman. He went to court and asked for an annulment of his marriage. He explained that he and his wife had never intended to live as husband and wife until after the religious wedding and that the marriage had not been consummated.

The judge ruled that there could be no annulment. These people were married because they had done what the law required in order to create a civil marriage. The religious ceremony may be important to one's conscience, but it is not legally necessary after a civil ceremony. And while the woman might be physically incapable of a normal sex life since the accident, the law of annulment requires that the disability exist at the time of the marriage. This woman was in excellent health at that time. Sickness and misfortune, the court said, are the common lot of mankind. When they intrude on a marriage, they must be borne with courage and resignation.

■ **Defenses to annulment** If one party wishes to fight an attempt at annulment, there are several defenses he may try to prove.

Statute of limitations The most easily proved defense is statute of limitations in states that have a statute of limitations for annulments. See Chart 21. If the person seeking annulment does not start his lawsuit within the time prescribed by the law, the court will not hear his case. For example, if a state's law says that an action for annulment because of impotence must be started within two years of the date of marriage, the husband can defend solely by showing that more than two years passed between the wedding and the lawsuit.

Res judicata Another valid defense is res judicata, a Latin term meaning "the matter has been adjudicated." If the question at issue has already been decided by a court, it cannot be considered again at a later time or in a different court or state.

Antenuptial knowledge If the annulment action is based on fraud, any evidence of antenuptial knowledge—that is, knowledge of the facts before the wedding—will indicate that there was no fraud or deception.

Clean hands Another defense to an annulment action is called the CLEAN HANDS doctrine. A person cannot be said to come into court with clean hands unless he is not at fault in the situation at issue.

EXAMPLE A man seeks an annulment on the ground of a O—* fraud, claiming that his wife talked him into marrying her by saying she was pregnant when she was not. He testifies that he would not have married her if he had known the truth. The court would deny this man an annulment because of the clean hands doctrine. If he had reason to believe he had caused her to become pregnant, he cannot claim that he is an innocent victim of fraud.

Ratification Another important defense to annulment is ratification. Even if a condition exists that could make the marriage invalid, a party who stays with the marriage for a period of time has ratified or confirmed it—accepted it for what it is.

EXAMPLE A person who marries during a period of extreme O—* psychological disturbance can probably have the marriage annulled for mental incapacity or insanity. But if the mental stress is cured or disappears and this person continues to live as husband or wife for a few years, he or she has ratified the marriage.

■ **Reasons to oppose an annulment** A spouse may want to prevent an annulment because he or she either wants to stay married or prefers divorce to annulment.

In some situations an annulment is opposed because the defendant loves the plaintiff, wants to hold the relationship together, and hopes for a reconciliation. For cases that actually end up in court, this reason is relatively unusual. In other instances one person wants to stay married for the property rights a husband or wife has. Even if the two

people cannot live together, they can be legally separated, and each keeps the right to share in the other's estate if he or she dies. Some women who have spent a lifetime maintaining a home and feel they are past the age when they can start a career hold this inheritance right as an important form of financial security. A man who has planned on inheriting from his wife may be similarly motivated.

Some states still follow the rule that an annulment wipes out an invalid marriage. They have no provision for alimony payments to a woman after annulment on the theory that she was never a wife. These states may, however, make some provision for a woman who has clearly helped a man improve his financial condition, especially if they lived together for a number of years. Such decisions may find that she is entitled to payment for housekeeping services she has performed or that the man is unjustly enriched if he alone takes all the economic benefit of the relationship—the doctor whose wife worked to put him through medical school, for example. Awards like this are somewhat uncertain. That is why in states that do not provide for alimony after an annulment, women usually prefer to fight the annulment action and ask for a divorce.

In determining the economic rights of the parties, courts take into account the duration of the marriage; the age, health, and living conditions of each person; their work experience, earning capacities, financial resources; property; and children.

■ **Jurisdiction** Usually a court has the authority to make a decision if both parties live in the state where the decision is being sought. In an annulment case, however, the marriage also must be subject to the court's jurisdiction (authority), either because the wedding took place in that state or because the people once lived there as husband and wife. Even when the court does have authority to hear a case, it often decides according to the law of the state in which the wedding ceremony was performed.

■ **Who may seek an annulment** The person who is aggrieved must have *standing*, or the right to start a lawsuit for an annulment. In the case of fraud, the one who was deceived can seek an annulment, but not the other. Someone under the age of consent can ask for an annulment, but the person over the age of consent who marries him or her cannot. Someone who marries a person who is impotent or unable to have sexual intercourse can ask for an annulment; so can an impotent man or a woman incapable of intercourse if he or she was unaware of the problem before marriage.

If a marriage is void, usually either party can get an annulment, not just the innocent party, and in some cases, a person other than the husband or wife can ask the court to annul a marriage. For example, the children of an old man who has become senile and married his nurse can ask to have the marriage annulled on the ground that their father no longer has the mental capacity to understand what he is doing. They may do this to keep the new wife from receiving up to half the estate when the man dies. In another common instance, if the parties to the marriage are under the legal age to marry in their state, their parents may be able to have the marriage annulled.

■ **Consequences** The consequences of annulment depend on the law of each state. Traditionally, an annulment was a declaration by the court that no marriage had ever existed. If a marriage were ended by divorce, children of the couple were legitimate and a wife who was unable to support herself could be granted alimony. Annulment, however, made no such provisions, but most states now have laws to correct this. Children of voidable marriages, and sometimes void marriages also, are now legitimate in most states even if a court declares the marriage of their parents invalid. Some states also provide for alimony and property settlements, and many others permit their courts to fashion a fair distribution of property where necessary.

anomaly An exception to a rule.

answer The first PLEADING made by the defendant in a lawsuit. It is a response to the charges and demands of the plaintiff's COMPLAINT. The defendant usually denies the plaintiff's charges and presents new facts to defeat them.

UNITED STATES DISTRICT COURT
for the
SOUTHERN DISTRICT OF NEW YORK

Civil Action, File Number ___0101___

x JOHN DOE_____, Plaintiff

v.

x RICHARD ROE, Defendant } ANSWER

FIRST DEFENSE

1. The complaint fails to state a claim against defendant upon which relief can be granted.

SECOND DEFENSE

2. If defendant is indebted to plaintiff for the goods mentioned in the complaint, he is indebted to them jointly with Bob Spender. Bob Spender is alive, is a citizen of the State of New York and a resident of this district, is subject to the jurisdiction of this court, as to both service of process and venue, can be made a party without depriving this court of jurisdiction of the present parties, and has not been made a party.

THIRD DEFENSE

3. Defendant admits the allegations contained in paragraphs 1 and 4 of the complaint; alleges that he is without knowledge or information sufficient to form a belief as to the truth of the allegations contained in paragraph 2 of the complaint; and denies each and every other allegation contained in the complaint.

FOURTH DEFENSE

4. The right of action set forth in the complaint did not accrue within six years next before the commencement of this action.

Signed: Jane Friend

Attorney for Defendant: Richard Roe

Address: 2 Court Street

New York, N.Y.

---

ante (Latin) "Before." The word is sometimes used to refer a reader to an earlier part of a report or textbook.

antenuptial Taking place before marriage. An *antenuptial settlement* is a CONTRACT or an agreement between a man and a woman before their marriage, in which the property rights and interests of either the prospective husband or wife, or both, are determined, or in which property is guaranteed to one or both, or to their children. For a full discussion, see MARRIAGE.

anticipation The act of doing or taking a thing before its proper time. In the area of real property, anticipation is the right to pay off a mortgage before it becomes due without paying a prepayment penalty.

anticipatory breach The breaking of a contract by refusing to perform one's part of the CONTRACT before the time comes to perform it. The refusal must be unconditional and clearly made.

EXAMPLE In November 1977, when heavyweight champion Muhammad Ali announced his retirement from boxing before he fulfilled a contract to defend his title at Madison Square Garden in New York City, he committed an anticipatory breach of the contract. Actually, because Madison Square Garden Boxing, Inc., did not bring an action against Ali to enforce or reinstate the contract before the time for its performance, the court ruled that it was abandoned by mutual agreement.

antinomy A term used in law and logic to mean a real or apparent contradiction between two authorities, laws, or provisions in a law. A law is probably invalid if it is contradictory.

antitrust act A law that is designed to protect trade from MONOPOLIES.

a posteriori (Latin) "From the latter"; from the effect to the cause; a method of reasoning that begins with observations or experiments and attempts to discover general principles from them; inductive reasoning.

apparent authority In the law of AGENCY, the authority that a principal (the person whom the agent represents) knowingly allows his agent to assume, as judged by the principal's and the agent's words and actions.

appeal and error An appeal is a complaint made to a higher court calling upon it to correct an error of law made by a lower court during a trial. The person who brings the appeal is usually called the *appellant* or the *plaintiff in error*. The person against whom the appeal is brought is called the *appellee, defendant in error,* or *respondent*. This article discusses appeals of civil cases. Although the concepts are generally the same as those of criminal cases, criminal appeals are handled differently. See CRIMINAL LAW.

A party to a lawsuit does not have a natural right to an appeal to a higher court; the right is granted by constitutional or statutory provisions that prescribe the cases in which the parties are entitled to an appeal and the courts in which the appeal may be heard. Usually the proceedings are governed by the law that was in force at the time the lower court's judgment or order was handed down, even though the law may have been changed by the time the appellate court hears the case.

EXAMPLE One state had a law permitting medical malprac-
O——* tice cases to be started at any time within three years of the improper treatment. At that time, a doctor who performed abdominal surgery on a woman left a small sponge inside the woman when he stitched up the incision. The woman suffered some discomfort, but real pain did not set in for over a year. Then it was another full year until a different doctor discovered the problem and corrected it. The woman sued the first doctor and was awarded money damages. The doctor appealed the decision because the time to sue had been changed to one year before the woman started her lawsuit. The trial court decision was affirmed on appeal because the law in effect when the malpractice occurred was the law that applied to the case.

■ **Nature and grounds of jurisdiction**   If an appeal is not authorized by a constitutional or statutory provision, the appellate court may not hear the case. The existence of an actual controversy between the parties is essential for appellate jurisdiction. For example, when a lower court decides a point of law about the interpretation of a will, an appellate court cannot hear and decide the same question brought before it by "friendly" parties who want a second opinion. An appellate court may not decide a hypothetical question brought merely for the sake of argument. It may not decide a case that has become MOOT (purely abstract) because a settlement was reached between the parties while the appeal was pending. Moreover, a case that is not based on existing facts or one that seeks a decision on a pretended controversy may not be heard.

■ **Decisions that are reviewable**   The appellate court's right of review usually depends on the amount of the claim, the amount of the judgment, or the value of the property involved in the lawsuit. The purpose of fixing a minimum amount is generally to prevent appeals in trivial cases. In some jurisdictions an appellate court may grant a review,

no matter how great or small the amount at issue, when the case involves an important new question of law or one of general public concern. Cases involving constitutional questions are also usually appealable regardless of the amount at issue, as are those relating to tax questions and the interpretations of city ordinances and statutes of statewide application. A case involving title to land is another common example. In the eyes of the law, each plot of land is unique and consequently of great importance to its owner, even if its actual value is very low.

As a general rule, the amount in controversy is determined from the PLEADINGS in the lawsuit. Some jurisdictions, however, expressly make the right to appeal depend on the amount of damages awarded by the jury verdict or the judgment of the court.

Usually, for a case to be appealable, a trial court must have given a final judgment or order, which ends the lawsuit between the parties and leaves nothing further to be considered or decided. The fact that further administrative action may be necessary, such as the actual issuance of the WRIT enforcing the judgment or order, does not prevent it from being final or appealable; neither does setting aside incidental matters for further consideration, such as the computation of interest, attorneys' fees, or costs.

■ **Who may appeal**   The right to appeal is normally restricted to the parties to the lawsuit who are aggrieved by the decision made in the lower court. A party is *aggrieved* when the decision operates directly and harmfully upon his personal and property rights. Disappointment with the result or being subjected to inconvenience, annoyance, and discomfort does not make him an aggrieved party.

EXAMPLE The maternal grandparents of Sammy, a minor
O——* child, tried to appeal a court order concerning Sammy's custody. Because they were not responsible for the child's support and had no actual right to custody of the child, they were not aggrieved by an order appointing a permanent guardian for him. The grandparents were not entitled to appeal the order appointing the guardian.

Common examples of parties who may appeal include mortgagors and mortgagees, executors and administrators of estates, guardians of minors and incompetent persons, a

---

IF YOU ARE APPEALING A DECISION IN A CIVIL CASE

■ You may appeal when a decision operates directly and harmfully on your personal and property rights.

■ To appeal you must allege an error of law made by the lower court. The appeals court is not permitted to hear new evidence.

■ If you believe that the trial judge's instruction to the jury was incorrect, you may appeal. But if you claim that the sidewalk you slipped on was defective even though the court ruled otherwise, you have no ground for appeal—the appellate court does not consider findings of fact.

■ Your objections must be made in the trial court in order to raise questions for review—only questions that have been raised and properly recorded during trial in the lower court can be reviewed by the appeals court.

■ You must appeal within the time fixed by law.

■ You must often provide an appeal bond, to secure the opposing party against the costs of the appeal if he wins against you.

■ Your lawyer must file documents in your behalf, all of which must be printed at your expense in most cases.

■ If the appellate court affirms the decision of the lower court, your opponent has won his case.

■ If your appeal leads to a reversal, then you become the winning party, even though you lost in the trial court.

■ If your appeal leads the appellate court to modify the decision of the lower court—such as the amount of damages awarded—you may gain to the extent that the lower court's decision is changed.

■ If the appeals court sends the case back for trial, you and your opponent are back where you started.

partner when a decision is reached against all of the partners, an agent to protect the interest of his principal, a trustee, and the federal and state governments. On the other hand, an attorney may not appeal in his own name a decision affecting his client, even though his own rights to attorney fees and costs may be incidentally affected. A creditor cannot appeal a decision in favor of a third party against his debtor. Merely because they are married, a husband or a wife cannot appeal a decision affecting the other.

■ **Preservation of grounds for appeal**   As a rule, questions that have not been raised and properly preserved for review in the trial court cannot be raised for the first time on appeal. This rule is based on the fact that both before and during the trial in the lower court the appellant has the right to raise and preserve for review anything he wants. Thereafter, he must rest on, and be bound by, the trial record he makes. A plaintiff who appeals cannot bring a new cause of action or ground for recovery that he has not relied on in the lower court.

EXAMPLE A plaintiff was injured when a large stone fell on O—* him in an alley. He based his right to recover damages on the city's knowledge that the stone was located in a place where it was likely to fall. When he lost the case in the trial court, he could not contend on appeal that even if the city did not know of the dangerous condition of the stone, it was liable because the stone was an obstruction in the alley.

The rule is equally well established that objections must be made in the trial court in order to reserve questions for review. An *objection* is a protest that an action taken by the opposing side in a lawsuit is improper, unfair, or illegal. Objections can be made at any stage of the trial, from the pleadings that begin the suit to the instructions given to the jury by the judge. To be available for review, an objection must be made in a timely manner—that is, at the time of the act being objected to or at the earliest opportunity. The party who puts forward the objection in the appellate court must have made the objection in the trial court. When, for example, several defendants are entitled to object, each must do so if he wishes his objection heard on appeal.

An objection must include a statement of why it has been made, in order that the court may rule on it intelligently and justly.

EXAMPLE In a contract action in which the plaintiff's lawyer O—* attempts to introduce into evidence a photocopy of the contract, when his client has the actual contract, the defense attorney might object, giving the best evidence rule as the specific ground for his objection. The actual contract itself is always the best possible evidence of its existence and contents. The photocopy is secondary evidence. Because in this case the plaintiff has the original contract, he must either introduce the original or explain why he cannot.

The trial judge must rule on the objection. A mere objection without the judge's decision on it presents no question for appellate review. If, after the judge has given his decision, the lawyer who made the objection believes the judge has ruled incorrectly, the lawyer may take an exception. An *exception* is an objection to a decision of a court on a matter of law. Its purpose is to place the excepting lawyer's objection in the trial record.

EXAMPLE In the contract action mentioned earlier, if the O—* trial judge overruled the defense lawyer's objection and admitted the photocopy of the contract, the defense attorney would take exception to the judge's decision. The question of whether the photocopy should have been excluded because it was not the best evidence could then be reviewed by an appellate court.

■ **Parties**   Generally, all persons who were parties to the action in the lower court and who are affected by the judgment or order must be made parties to the appellate proceedings. When a judgment or order has been entered against several plaintiffs or defendants, and appellate review is sought only by some, their coplaintiffs or codefendants must join them as appellants in seeking review.

■ **Time limitations**   Appeals must be taken within the time fixed by statute or by the rules of the appellate court. Generally, the clock starts to run on the time allowed for taking appeals only after a final judgment or order is issued. The appeal is said to be *perfected* when the application for the appeal is made to the appellate court and notice is given to the appellee. An appeal that is not taken and perfected within the prescribed time will be disallowed or dismissed. In certain situations, an extension of time will be granted when, for example, the appellant's lawyer, by mistake or inadvertence, neglects to file the appeal, or one of the parties becomes ill, insane, or dies.

■ **Notice of appeal**   As a general rule, the opposing party must be given notice of the appeal. The notice informs him, and the appellate court, that the unsuccessful party desires a review of the case. Usually, the notice has to be a written document, addressed to the appellee or his attorney, and must describe the judgment from which the appeal is taken. If a party fails to give notice, the appeal is usually dismissed. When the appeal is made in open court at the time the judgment is handed down, however, no notice other than that given in the court and entered in the court's records is necessary because the appellee is presumed to be in court.

■ **Bonds**   The appellant must often provide an appeal BOND, which is a contract for the payment of money. Its purpose is to secure the appellee against the costs of the appeal if the appellee wins. Another purpose of the bond is to discourage frivolous appeals. If successive appeals are taken from one appellate court to a higher appellate court, a new bond is usually required. The amount of the bond may be specified by statute or fixed by the appellate court.

■ **Record on appeal**   In its review of a case, the appellate court is ordinarily limited to the record sent up from the lower court. The record must show the entry of an appealable judgment or order and the grounds for the trial judge's decision. When the trial has been by jury, the record must show the verdict. The appealing party has a duty to show clearly by the record that prejudicial error—a mistake substantial enough to have affected the decision—was committed. He must also show that the question to be reviewed was presented to, and passed on by, the trial court.

EXAMPLE Kenny drove a bakery truck. He was injured one O—* day when Sandra drove through a red light and hit his truck. When he sued Sandra, her attorney tried to show that Kenny was covered by workmen's compensation. Kenny's attorney objected on the ground that the jury might award lower damages even though the defendant was clearly responsible for the accident and should not avoid liability simply because Kenny might receive some compensation from another source. The trial judge allowed the evidence, and Kenny later appealed the amount of damages awarded. The appeals court agreed that admitting the evidence was prejudicial error, because nothing indicated that Kenny had actually received a specified amount of Workmen's Compensation benefits. The evidence surely affected the verdict adversely.

The *record proper* consists of the PROCESS (the writ issued to bring the defendant into court), PLEADINGS, verdict, and the judgment, or final order, of the court. Other matters are usually brought into the record by the bill of exceptions.

Bill of exceptions A bill of exceptions is a written statement of exceptions taken by a party to a ruling, decision, charge, or opinion of the trial judge. It sets out the trial proceedings, the acts of the judge alleged to be in error, the objections and exceptions taken to those acts, together with the grounds for the objections. Its purpose is to provide the appellate court with a history of the trial proceedings. A bill of exceptions should not include matters that belong in the record proper but should set out only those points relating to the questions of law raised by the exceptions. The appellant's lawyer prepares the bill of exceptions and presents it for settlement to the trial judge, who examines the bill to determine whether it contains a truthful account of the events of the trial. The *settlement* is an agreement between the trial judge and appellant on the contents of the bill. The judge may not arbitrarily refuse a proposed bill of exceptions that is inaccurate or defective. He should return the bill with the reasons for his refusal and suggest corrections to be made or make the corrections himself.

Ordinarily, the opposing party must be given notice of the time and place of the settlement of the bill of exceptions. Under many statutes the bill must be submitted to him or his lawyer so that he can examine it and make objections or suggest amendments before it is approved by the trial judge. The validity of the bill does not depend, however, on the opposition's approval. Once the bill of exceptions is properly settled and signed by the trial judge, it is filed as part of the record to be considered by the appellate court. The bill of exceptions then becomes part of the transcript.

Transcript A transcript is a copy of the record of the trial as it took place in the lower court. The appellant is responsible for seeing that the transcript is made, but the duty of actually preparing it usually rests on the clerk of the trial court. Unless otherwise provided by statute, cases must be submitted on appeal with a full transcript of the unabbreviated record. The transcript presents all the matters of record necessary for a decision of the questions involved in the assignment of errors (discussed below). The bill of exceptions is an essential part of a full transcript and must be included. All the evidence necessary to a review of the errors assigned must also be incorporated into the transcript, which must then be printed and filed with the appellate court. A printed copy must also be sent to the opposing party.

■ **Assignment of errors** An assignment of errors is a statement by the appellant of the errors he claims were committed in the lower court. A pleading, which performs the same function as a DECLARATION or COMPLAINT in a trial court, is the appellant's declaration or complaint against the trial judge charging harmful error. By enumerating the points of law the appellant wants reversed and limiting discussion to those points, the assignment of errors controls the scope of an appeal.

EXAMPLE McGuire was injured when the horse he had rented bolted and threw him. He sued the stable for $100,000 in damages for his pain, medical expenses, and lost wages plus another $100,000 in punitive damages because he claimed that the stable had been reckless in renting such a dangerous horse. The jury decided in his favor but awarded $5,000 only for his actual injuries. He appealed. His lawyer filed with the appeals court a bill of exceptions, approved by the trial judge, and an assignment of error, where he outlined his objection to the verdict. The error objected to by the lawyer was the refusal to award punitive damages. Later, at the appellate hearing, the lawyer also said that he was dissatisfied with the amount of actual damages awarded. The appeals court refused to let him discuss this point, however, because he was limited to the issue raised in the assignment of errors.

Under some statutes, the assignment of errors must be contained in a separate document, but usually it is set out in one of the following places: the notice of appeal, the bill of exceptions, the transcript of the record, or the brief.

■ **The brief** A brief is a printed document that presents the facts of the case, the questions at issue, and the arguments relating to those questions. Its purpose is to present the points in controversy to the court in concise form and to aid the appellate court in reaching a proper decision on the questions presented. As a general rule, both parties to an appeal must file briefs. The brief must contain a clear and accurate statement of the important facts of the case, and when questions based on evidence are raised on appeal, the brief must contain a statement of the evidence involved or a reference to where it may be found in the record. A statement in the brief of any matter in the record must be supported by an appropriate reference to the record.

The appellant's brief must specifically point out the alleged errors that entitle him to a reversal. It must also present a statement of the reasons, or argument, why each ruling of the court was wrong. Unless a point is obvious, it should be supported by the citation of authority, such as a case in which a similar point of law has been decided, or a statute that applies to the particular point at issue. The brief must not contain disrespectful, scandalous, or abusive language directed against the appellate court, the trial judge, opposing lawyers, the parties, or witnesses. When this happens, the objectionable language is stricken from the brief, and the costs of the brief, which might have been awarded by the court, are disallowed. Failure to file a brief usually leads to a dismissal of the appeal.

■ **Hearing** The clerk of the appellate court usually keeps a calendar on which he places the cases to be heard, assigning to each one a particular date. On the day of the hearing, each side is given an opportunity to present an oral argument. These arguments are intended to help the court understand the points raised and discussed in the briefs and to persuade the court to rule in favor of the arguing party. The appellant's lawyer begins by providing the court with a short history of the progress of the case through the lower court, or courts, and a statement of the facts that gave rise to the lawsuit. He then presents his arguments on behalf of the legal issues raised by his exceptions. After the conclusion of the appellant's lawyer's arguments, the appellee's lawyer presents his arguments in favor of the lower court's decision.

■ **Review** Appellate courts decide only matters before them on appeal, and no others. They will not give opinions on controversies or declare principles of law that cannot have any practical effect in settling the rights of the litigants. They do not attempt to lay down rules of guidance or precedent for fellow judges or for lawyers.

Ordinarily, only conclusions of law are reviewable; findings of fact made by the trial court usually are not. Whether a finding is a fact or a conclusion of law depends on whether it is reached by ordinary reasoning or by applying established rules of law. When a conclusion can be reached only by applying a rule of law, it is a conclusion of law. Common examples of questions of law are whether a person has marketable title to a piece of real property, whether the trial court applied the correct measure of damages, whether an instruction to the jury was correct, whether there was an error in the argument of one of the lawyers, the duty of care required of the parties in a negligence action, and the correct interpretation of a statute or municipal ordinance. Examples of findings of fact, which are not reviewable, include whether a sidewalk is defective, whether a contract had been made, whether a transaction was a sale or a gift, and whether a contract was canceled by mutual consent of the parties.

EXAMPLE Ellen was injured when she was a passenger in O⊷＊ Elliot's car and the car ran off the road. Ellen sued Elliot and at the trial introduced evidence to show that the accident occurred on a cold, clear night; that Elliot was driving about 55 miles per hour; that the car skidded when it hit a patch of ice; and that Ellen suffered cuts, internal injuries, and a broken leg. The trial judge ruled that Ellen had done nothing to cause the accident and allowed a verdict of $20,000 to compensate her. Elliot and his insurance company appealed. The appellate court accepted all the findings of fact based on the evidence presented at trial. It did not agree that all the facts added up to negligence as a matter of law. It held that Elliot could have been driving as carefully as possible and still hit an icy patch. Since there was no evidence that Elliot should have expected ice on the road that night, he could not be held liable for negligence. The appeals court reversed the decision on that point of law.

■ **Prejudicial and harmless error** In examining the errors alleged to have been made by the trial court, the appellate court must decide whether the errors are prejudicial or harmless. When the error injures one of the parties or affects the final outcome of the case, then it is prejudicial, or reversible, error. On the other hand, when the error could not or did not affect the final result of the lawsuit, then it is harmless. For instance, three witnesses were permitted without objection to give their opinions as to a man's fitness to raise his son. Allowing a fourth witness to give his opinion as to the man's fitness, after an objection was made to his testimony, was harmless error. An appellate court will not reverse or modify the decision of a trial court when the error that leads to the appeal is harmless.

After the appellate court has examined the record of the trial, heard the arguments of the lawyers on both sides, and read their briefs, it reaches its decision in the case.

■ **Determination and disposition** After reviewing and deciding the controlling questions of the case, the appellate court may affirm the decision of the lower court, modify it, reverse it, or send the case back for a new trial.

An affirmance ends the case in favor of the party who won the decision in the trial court. In effect, the appellate court states that it agrees with the decision of the lower court. When the appellate court modifies a decision, it usually agrees with part of the trial court's decision and disagrees with another part. The trial court's decision is changed accordingly. A reversal also usually ends the case, but the trial court's decision is completely changed. When a case is reversed, the party who lost the case in the trial court then becomes the winning party in the appellate court. In some instances—when, for example, the facts are disputed, not definitely settled, or obscure—the case is reversed and also sent back to the lower court for a new trial.

appear In law, to be properly before a court—for example, as a plaintiff or a defendant in a lawsuit.

appearance An appearance takes place when a person against whom a suit has been started puts himself under the JURISDICTION (authority) of the court.

■ **Voluntary or compulsory** An appearance is voluntary when it is an entirely free act, such as going to court prior to being notified legally to appear. A compulsory appearance is in response to a summons.

■ **General and special** A general appearance occurs when the party submits to the court's jurisdiction, or authority, for all purposes. The purpose of a special appearance is to object to the jurisdiction of the court. The right to appear specially is almost always recognized, except where it has been abolished by statute. A special appearance must always be made before a general one. After a general appearance, it is too late to question the court's jurisdiction.

■ **Failure to appear** A failure to appear can have serious consequences—a default judgment, for example. But if the court does not have jurisdiction over someone, it cannot penalize him for not appearing.

■ **Who may appear** The defendant may appear in person or through an authorized representative, but in most jurisdictions the plaintiff or his attorney cannot enter an appearance for the defendant even though the defendant has authorized it. If someone has an interest to protect, he may make an appearance. If a person is not a party to an action, he cannot appear unless the plaintiff agrees or the person is made a third party to the action by another legal procedure.

EXAMPLE A life insurance company, sued by the widow of a O⊷＊ policyholder for the proceeds of her husband's policy, made the decedent's daughter, who also claimed the proceeds, a third party in the suit. Similarly, a restaurant, sued by a customer for injuries caused by eating contaminated ham, obtained the court's permission to make the meat supplier a third-party defendant.

If there is more than one defendant, each one must appear.

■ **Time of appearance** Statutes or court rules usually prescribe the period in which the defendant must appear. Unless forbidden by statute, courts can generally give extensions of time to make an appearance.

■ **What constitutes appearance** Any act of the defendant that recognizes that the case is in court constitutes a general appearance—usually, participation in the proceedings or trial, either by consenting to some step or order, or by actively seeking some action or relief. Some specific examples are attacking the sufficiency of the complaint, demanding a jury trial, examining witnesses, introducing evidence, stipulating agreements between the parties, and demanding a BILL OF PARTICULARS.

■ **Effect of a general appearance** For most purposes, a general appearance, which gives the court jurisdiction over the person, is restricted to the action in which it was made; it cannot constitute an appearance in another lawsuit. If you appear in court for a breach-of-contract action brought against you by one of your customers, Mr. Smith, you are not submitting yourself to the court for a suit being brought against you by Mr. Jones.

If the court lacks jurisdiction over the subject matter—for example, a small claims court cannot hear a contest over a will—an appearance will not give the court the jurisdiction it does not have.

Once you make a general appearance, you waive the right to question the legality of any step in the start of the proceedings. For instance, general appearance usually means that a defendant cannot claim incorrect venue—i.e., that the case is being brought in the wrong place. But you do not waive any substantive rights or defenses as a defendant by making a general appearance. If, for example, an action is brought after a statute of limitations expires, you may use this fact in your defense.

■ **Effect of a special appearance** It confers no jurisdiction on the court and gives the court the right only to pass on the jurisdictional objection put before it.

■ **Withdrawal of appearance** Once having appeared, a defendant has no right to withdraw his appearance in order to destroy its legal effect. A court, however, may permit a withdrawal that it believes would be in the best interest of justice.

EXAMPLE A court in California granted a motion for withdrawal of appearance when several defendants were entered in a suit without their authority or knowledge. The attorney who appeared on their behalf had assumed they were involved in the case on the basis of a conversation he had had with the true defendant.

appellant The party who takes an appeal from one court to another. See APPEAL AND ERROR.

appellate court A court in which an appeal is taken; a reviewing court. See APPEAL AND ERROR; COURTS.

appellate jurisdiction The power and authority of a superior court to review a case after it has been decided by a lower court. See APPEAL AND ERROR.

appellee The party against whom an appeal is taken, that is, the party who is against setting aside or reversing the judgment of the lower court. See APPEAL AND ERROR.

apportionment The division or distribution of a thing, a right, or a liability among several persons in accordance with their interests. For instance, some land is owned in common by several persons who divide it into individual shares; the apportionment would take place according to the amount of the land each one owned. As another example, the U.S. Constitution requires the number of Representatives in Congress to be apportioned among the states on the basis of their populations.

appraisal A valuation or estimation of the value of property, also called an appraisement. The valuation may be set by judicial or legislative authority, but it is generally arrived at by a disinterested party. For example, the legislature may enact a schedule assigning a specific value to every model automobile. Then owners may be required to pay taxes based on the assigned value. Or if you are taking out insurance for valuables and you have no sales slip showing what you paid for them, you will need to have appraisals made to submit to your insurance company.

appreciation 1 A valuation or estimation of qualities, merit, or worth; an awareness of worth or value. 2 An increase in value. A house bought for $10,000 and sold 12 years later for $20,000 had a 100-percent appreciation.

apprehension The seizure or taking of a person on a criminal charge. The word is applied only to criminal cases. The term "arrest" is used in both criminal cases and civil cases.

apprentice In the traditional legal sense, an apprentice is a person legally bound to serve another for a specified time in order to learn some art, trade, profession, or business in which the master is obligated to instruct him. Although infrequently used today, a contract of apprenticeship is enforceable even where laws that governed apprenticeship have been repealed.

■ **Parties to apprenticeships** Both minors and adults may be bound by an apprenticeship contract, and any person with full social and civil rights may take an apprentice. Although in some states a minor may refuse to honor his contract of apprenticeship, in others the contract is considered beneficial to the minor and he cannot. Where a statute governs a minor's actions regarding apprenticeship, it must be strictly followed.

■ **The contract** An apprenticeship must be created by an agreement that has all the essentials of a valid CONTRACT. If the contract, sometimes called an *indenture,* is not to be performed within a year, it must be in writing. The contract must be signed by the apprentice, by the master, and, if the apprentice is a minor, by his father or guardian. Some states require only the father's signature, some both parents, and some require specific words of consent in addition to their signatures. Contracts should contain the provisions for the benefit of the apprentice that are prescribed by statute, such as reasonable general education, instruction in the trade or art for which the apprenticeship is created, and the care and maintenance of the apprentice. DAMAGES may be obtained for a breach of an apprenticeship contract. Except where permitted by statute, a contract of apprenticeship cannot be sold to another.

■ **Termination of apprenticeships** The apprenticeship may be ended by mutual consent, by dismissal of the apprentice, by either party for a good reason, or when no term of service is provided. It is automatically ended when the term of service expires; when the apprentice is removed against his will from the jurisdiction where the apprenticeship was created; if the apprentice enters the armed forces, even though he does so voluntarily and without the master's consent; or when either party dies. The relationship may end when an apprentice who is a minor reaches the age of legal adulthood, usually 18 or 21. Courts may end such contracts because they violate statutes, because of misbehavior by the apprentice, or because of the master's cruelty, immorality, interference with the apprentice's religion, or other misconduct.

■ **Enticing apprentices from masters** A person who persuades an apprentice to leave his master may be sued by the master, but if the master is to recover, the defendant has to have known of the apprentice relationship.

appropriation The act of setting something aside for a particular use. The appropriation of *funds* by legislative action means the designation of moneys for a particular fund, or the setting aside of specified public revenues or money in the treasury, to be applied to some governmental expenditure or to some individual purchase or expense. The appropriation of *land* means setting it aside for a particular purpose, such as for public buildings or military reservations. The appropriation of *water* means diverting it from its natural channel and applying it exclusively to the beneficial use of the appropriator. Valid land and water appropriations, whether made by a public or private party, require a beneficial use, a diversion or other physical act of taking possession and, within a reasonable time, the actual application of what was appropriated to the beneficial purpose. See PROPERTY.

approval Favorable response to a specific matter submitted for decision. Examples are the approval of a constitutional amendment by the people at a general election and the approval of a bill by its enactment into law by the legislature.

appurtenance Something annexed or attached to something of greater importance or value. In real estate transactions, appurtenances are usually defined as what is necessarily connected with the full use and enjoyment of the property. Some typical appurtenances of land are: buildings, trees, coops, fences, drainage and irrigation ditches, and outbuildings. For appurtenances that are transferred with the sale of real property, see DEEDS. Some items held not to be appurtenances are claims for trespass, automobiles, money, refrigerators placed in an apartment building, and damages incurred by the exercise of EMINENT DOMAIN. A trademark for flour was ruled not an appurtenance to a flour mill.

a priori (Latin) "From the former"; from the cause to the effect; a method of reasoning that begins with general principles and attempts to discover what particular facts or real life observations follow from them; deductive reasoning. Legal reasoning is both A POSTERIORI and *a priori*.

arbiter A person chosen to decide a controversy. He decides according to the rules of law and EQUITY in contrast to an arbitrator, who uses his own discretion.

arbitrary Willful and unreasoning; without consideration or regard for the facts and circumstances presented.

arbitration Arbitration is a contractual proceeding by which the parties to a dispute, in order to obtain a speedy and inexpensive disposition of the matters involved, voluntarily select arbitrators of their own choice to settle the dispute once and for all. Arbitration is a substitute for, and not a preliminary step toward, litigation. Its purpose is to avoid the courts, and once an award is made, it cannot be appealed in court. Most jurisdictions permit specific differences to be submitted to arbitration, but jurisdictions differ about the validity of a contract that allows all disputes arising under it to be settled only by arbitration. Generally, courts look favorably on arbitration to remove disputes from litigation.

This article covers the submission of controversies by disputing parties to persons they have chosen; the rights, powers, and duties of the arbitrators; and the requirements for and validity, operation, and effect of such submissions.

■ **Appraisal distinguished from arbitration** Appraisers act without a hearing or judicial inquiry, relying upon their own knowledge acquired independently of the evidence of witnesses. Unlike arbitrators, they usually settle only incidental matters, such as actual cash value, not the main controversy.

■ **Laws and courts** Arbitration laws are intended to discourage litigation, to provide for the enforcement of agreements, and to place the stamp of finality upon awards. Courts can suggest, but cannot impose, arbitration upon litigants. Compulsory arbitration statutes are generally invalid unless they also give the parties the further right of appeal to a court. When the state is a party, however, compulsory statutes have been held valid even without the right to further appeal.

■ **Agreement and submission** Without a binding submission—an agreement to refer the dispute to others and to be bound by the decision—there can be no arbitration. The agreement may provide for arbitration of either existing or future disputes. These agreements are subject to all laws governing CONTRACTS in general, and the burden of proving the submission is on the party claiming there was one. The scope of the agreement is left up to the parties.

■ **Parties** The general rule is that all persons or corporations with the capacity to make contracts may submit controversies growing out of their contracts to arbitration. An agent may be a party of an arbitration. See AGENCY. If one party breaches his agreement to arbitrate, the other party has the option of either insisting on the arbitration or abandoning it. There is a conflict of opinion as to whether all parties in an action—such as when there are several defendants or plaintiffs—must join in submitting the issue to arbitration. Persons not parties to an action, but interested in the subject at issue, may agree to submit to the arbitrator.

■ **Matters subject to arbitration** When there is no statute restricting the subjects that can be arbitrated, practically any kind of dispute can be submitted to arbitration. A legal CAUSE OF ACTION (ground for a lawsuit) is not necessary. An honest difference of opinion is sufficient, but the matter must be in dispute. Mere questions are not submissible. Legal as well as factual issues are arbitrable. It may be proper to arbitrate the CONSTRUCTION (interpretation) of a will or statute, a discharge in bankruptcy, property ownership, the amount of support money, and TORT liabilities, including, in some states, medical malpractice claims. Some questions, such as patent infringement, antitrust-law violations, and claims arising out of void or illegal contracts, are generally not arbitrable.

■ **Requisites** Apart from statutory requirements, an arbitration agreement or submission need not be in any particular form. It need not be in writing, and it may even be implied from the conduct of the parties.

EXAMPLE When a conductor for the Southern Pacific Railroad appealed the decision of an arbitration board to the court (the board had ruled against his claim that the railroad had unreasonably denied him a certification of physical fitness after he had undergone spinal surgery), the court ruled that the board's decision was binding. The tacit agreement to arbitrate by the conductor, the court found, could be implied by the fact that he had allowed the arbitration to take place.

A submission must name the parties to it and the subject matter of the arbitration. It may designate the time and place of the proceeding and, when required by statute, it must designate the court to which the award is to be returned.

Operation and effect An executed submission—one that has been brought to an award—waives all claims related to the controversy described in the submission. While the breach of a contract with an arbitration clause is usually remedied by arbitration, the parties may reserve the right to bring an action or agree to abandon their arbitration rights and go to court. If a lawsuit is pending and the parties decide to arbitrate, the suit is usually halted.

■ **Damages or performance** When arbitration fails because of the fault of one party, the other party may sue in court for damages. Many states permit the injured party to sue for SPECIFIC PERFORMANCE—that is, to force the other party to go to arbitration.

■ **Waiver of right** There is no set rule as to what waives your right to an arbitration. It is a matter of intention, which may be shown by REPUDIATING the contract, unjustifiably refusing to arbitrate, withdrawing from proceedings, or acting in any way inconsistent with the idea that the arbitration agreement was in effect—for instance, filing suit on an issue being arbitrated. Once you participate in an arbitration proceeding, you waive the right to object to the proceeding.

■ **Compelling arbitration** If you sue in order to compel arbitration, the court may decide only on the following issues: Is there a contract for arbitration? What is to be

arbitrated? Is there a dispute? Was there a failure to arbitrate? Other issues—the amount of damages, say—must be decided in other proceedings.

■ **Amendment, modification, and revocation** Parties may amend or modify the submission prior to an award, but a court may not do so without the consent of the parties. Generally, either party may revoke, or cancel, a submission, but this ability has been greatly affected by statutes in many jurisdictions. Note that even an agreement that a submission is irrevocable does not prevent a revocation. All the other party can do is to seek damages. Once a submission has been accepted by the court, or just before or after a final award, the right to revoke is waived. Revocation may occur as the result of some event or act that necessarily ends the proceedings, such as the death of a party, the death or refusal of the arbitrator to act, or the institution of a suit covering the same subject matter as that submitted to arbitration. Revocation makes the revoker liable for those damages that are a direct result of the revocation.

EXAMPLE Dick and Gloria both signed a separation agreement before their divorce, setting payments of $50 a week alimony and $50 a week support for their child. The agreement provided for changing those amounts in case circumstances changed substantially and for settling any disagreements by arbitration. After Gloria's employer changed her part-time position to a full-time job, Dick stopped paying alimony. Gloria started an action in court to force Dick to continue paying alimony. Dick could have submitted himself to the court, but instead he offered to continue paying the full amount if Gloria would drop the court action and add a provision to their separation agreement that the agreement to arbitrate could not be revoked.

Over the next couple of years, inflation made it very difficult for Gloria to make ends meet, while Dick's salary doubled. She started another lawsuit to have the court order increased child support. This time Dick went into court and argued that the arbitration clause could not have been revoked. The court answered that, since there was no statute in their state enforcing such a provision, the court could always protect the child's interest regardless of what amount of support the parents had set. After hearing all the evidence, the court ordered increased child support of $75 a week, but it also ordered Gloria to pay Dick $500 in damages for refusing to honor the arbitration agreement she had made.

■ **Arbitrators and umpires** An arbitrator is a person who decides the matter submitted. An umpire is a person who decides the issues when the arbitrators cannot decide. Generally, the parties to the arbitration appoint arbitrators, and arbitrators appoint an umpire by virtue of the agreement between the parties. By agreement, the parties may always substitute new arbitrators. Arbitrators must be fair and impartial and must disclose anything that may disqualify them, but the parties may waive objections to the disqualification. Statutes determine whether an oath is needed by an arbitrator and whether it can be waived. Arbitrators cannot delegate their authority, but they may consult others. An award, a revocation of a submission, or the expiration of the time in which the award must be made ends their authority. They cannot be sued for failure to exercise skill or care, but they may be criminally liable if they agree beforehand on the award they are to give.

■ **Proceedings** Arbitration is not formal like a court proceeding, but it must be fair and impartial and must follow the terms of the submission and any prevailing statutes. All regular arbitrators must have notice of meetings and participate in them. The parties receive notice from the arbitrators and are generally entitled to be present at the hearing of the EVIDENCE or the examination of witnesses and to be heard by the arbitrators. Arbitrators are not bound by rules of evidence and may use their own knowledge. They decide if evidence is admissible and what weight to give it. Subpoenas may be issued by arbitrators only where provided for by statute. Ordinarily, all arbitrators must agree in their decision unless a decision by a majority is specifically authorized.

■ **Award** This is the decision of the arbitration that the parties requested and by which they have agreed to be bound. The award is final for all matters submitted, but the parties may repudiate by mutual consent.

The award need only show the final decision and not how it was reached. A written award must usually be signed by the arbitrators or the umpire.

An award may give alternatives to the parties and still be final, but it must be so definite that it leaves no doubt about the meaning of the arbitrators. In a Pennsylvania case, for instance, the defendant was ordered either to pay $2,500 to the plaintiff or to carry out the contract, the breach of which was the subject of the arbitration.

Once an award is made, it cannot be supplemented or changed, but ambiguities may be clarified. Its validity does not depend upon confirmation by a court, but once confirmed, it becomes a JUDGMENT of the court, and every reasonable interpretation to support it will be made.

The enforcement of awards is usually governed by statute. An award can be challenged or annulled only when the award is illegal under the law or when there has been fraud, misconduct, or gross mistake or error. Claims that the arbitrators were biased, partial, or exceeded their powers may warrant setting aside the award, but newly discovered evidence will not. When an award is set aside, the parties are free to take their dispute to court. They are also free to ratify the invalid award, if they choose to do so—to avoid further litigation, for example. Returning an award to the arbitrators is governed by statute and usually done only to correct errors. The costs of arbitration, generally paid by the parties to it, may not be allowed as part of the award, either by the arbitrators or by the courts, unless permitted by statute or by the agreement.

■ **Security for submission** Although a bond for performance is not necessary to a valid arbitration, it is often used so the winner will not have to bring a court action to collect the award.

architect A person who plans or designs buildings and sometimes superintends their construction, and who may also act as contractor for their construction. The American Institute of Architects permitted its members to serve as contractors for the first time in 1978, pending a later review of its decision. A *landscape architect* arranges natural scenery for human use and pleasure by modifying the terrain, making plantings, and providing for buildings and vehicular and pedestrian traffic.

This article discusses the regulation and conduct of the business of architecture, including licensing, employment, and the rights, powers, duties, and liabilities between employer and architect.

■ **Regulation** Practicing architecture without a license is generally a criminal offense. Licensing statutes generally require applicants to be of legal age and of good moral character, to have studied prescribed courses to pass examinations, and to have had practical experience in an architect's office.

The purpose of these regulatory statutes is to protect life, health, and property. Under some statutes, a license may be revoked for cause, such as gross incompetency, recklessness, dishonest practices, or fraud in obtaining the registration. Some statutes permit partnerships between architects and nonarchitects. There is great variance among states as to whether corporations may practice architecture.

■ **Employment** An architect's employment is controlled by the general rules of the law of CONTRACTS. Statutes requiring competitive bidding are not usually applied to contracts for architectural services because such services are personal, of a professional character, and call for skill and experience. The plans the architect proposes are usually considered the property of his employer.

■ **Powers and duties** As an agent of his employer, the authority of the architect is limited to what is specifically conferred by or naturally implied from his employment. His AGENCY is limited and not general, but obviously the employer can give him any authority he wishes to. Duties depend on his contract of employment, but generally, he must perform with reasonable skill and without undue delay. Failure to perform in this manner may result in his being sued for NEGLIGENCE. He is in a FIDUCIARY capacity (one of trust) to his employer and must act in good faith.

■ **Compensation** The architect cannot be deprived of his right to compensation by minor omissions or imperfections. Generally, unlicensed architects are not entitled to compensation because they are employed in violation of statutes requiring a license. In some instances, however, persons rendering architectural services but not posing as licensed architects have been permitted to recover. The employer usually pays for the architect's plans after their delivery, and he is obligated to pay whether or not he accepts the plans. Generally, the architect may recover his fees even if the employer abandons the project. If the employer refuses payment, the architect may sue for the amount agreed to by contract or, when there was no agreement as to price, for the reasonable value of his services.

area-wide agreement A contract by a union covering more than one employer in a geographical area—for example, a union contract for building maintenance workers that covers apartment buildings in several New York City boroughs.

argument An effort to establish belief by a course of reasoning. Both the opening speech of the counsel representing one party and the answer of his opponent representing the other party are called arguments.

YOUR RIGHTS AS A MEMBER OR VETERAN OF THE ARMED SERVICES

■ If you have had to neglect your personal affairs because of entering the armed services, you may be protected by the Soldiers' and Sailors' Civil Relief Act. The statute prevents your creditors from getting a default judgment—one that is given when you cannot appear and defend yourself.

■ Enlisted men must serve out their term of enlistment. Officers may resign at any time, but the resignation must be accepted.

■ Crimes committed by military personnel in peacetime can be tried by state courts or by courts-martial.

■ A military person does not incur personal liability for obeying orders, except when an order was so unlawful that any reasonable man or woman would recognize its illegality.

■ Desertion means being absent from your unit without authority and with the intent to stay away permanently.

■ There is no time limit for an eligible veteran to apply for a home-purchase loan. You must have served more than 180 days and received any discharge but a dishonorable one, or you must have served 180 days or less and received a discharge for a service-related disability.

■ Your employer at the time you went into the service must reemploy you when you return to civilian life and must restore you to the position you formerly held or to a position of like seniority, status, and pay. You are entitled to your seniority rights as if you had been on the job continuously.

■ As a veteran you cannot be let go for one year after reemployment, as long as you adhere to reasonable standards of conduct and duty.

■ If you are denied reemployment, you may ask the court to order the employer to comply with the law and compensate you for any loss of wages or benefits.

■ All veterans with honorable discharges are entitled to be buried in a national cemetery.

---

argumentative By way of reasoning. A PLEADING is called argumentative when the premise the pleader relies on is implied rather than expressed (stated), or when, in addition to facts, it contains reasoning or arguments that should be presented at the trial.

EXAMPLE A man who had been a practicing accountant for O⟵—⁕ over 25 years brought an action to have the court declare unconstitutional the state law that set up a system of licenses for certain accountants who were able to qualify as certified public accountants. The man said in his complaint that even though the law allowed him to practice accountancy without certification, the system made him look bad compared to CPA's. He said that he was seeking "equality with certified public accountants—equality of opportunity, equality of regulation, and equality in the state's attitude." All of these words the court found to be argumentative. They failed to supply material facts. A good complaint must simply contain a plain and concise statement of material facts. The court dismissed the plaintiff's action.

armed services This article discusses the air, land, and naval forces of the federal government; MILITIA called into federal service; organization and discipline; rights, powers, and duties of individuals; aid and relief to members and their families; the relationship between military and civil authorities; criminal offenses; insurance and indemnity; and veterans' benefits. See WAR

■ **Authority of the military** The civil power is paramount over the military power. Congress has constitutional authority to raise, support, and regulate the armed services. The President, as commander in chief of the armed services, has complete authority in matters of control except as limited by law. Military law is based on the Constitution; statutes relating to military forces; regulations of the branches of the service; and orders, customs, and usages of the service and of war, provided that they do not violate the Constitution, statutes, or any written military law. Regulations have the force of law when they are consistent with existing statutes, and courts will give great weight to the interpretations of regulations by the military.

Civil courts may protect the constitutional rights of military personnel and prevent violations of statutes and regulations, but may not inquire into or supervise military determinations, such as who is fit or unfit for military duty. The regulations of the Defense Department governing speech-making activities of employees are not within the courts' jurisdiction, but a discretionary military order—one determined by the judgment of the officer issuing it—must follow the fundamental principle that no order may violate the Constitution, a federal statute, or a military regulation. The court may review such an order to determine if it violates any of those three controlling areas of law. Federal courts do not intervene until all military remedies have been exhausted, except in cases of persons who claim that they are civilians and should not be under military control or who claim they have been deprived of their livelihood by military action.

EXAMPLE A man serving as a technician in his state's Air O⟵—⁕ National Guard had several arguments with his unit commander. When his term of enlistment expired, the commander refused to let him reenlist. He sued in federal court, claiming that he had been unconstitutionally deprived of his property interest in the job. The court would consider only the question of whether his constitutional rights had been violated. The court determined that it was not a violation of due process or equal protection for the unit commander to be given authority to accept or reject an application to reenlist; therefore the commander's action was legal. The court refused to consider whether his decision was correct.

■ **Composition, organization, and facilities** The constituent parts of the armed forces are the Army, Navy, Air Force, Marine Corps, and Coast Guard. The reserves are also considered part of the armed forces. A National Guardsman is considered to have joined both the National Guard of his home state and that of the United States, a reserve component of the U.S. Army. The MILITIA of the several states may be called, in whole or in part, into the service of the United States; and when called, the militia, or National Guard, becomes a part of U.S. armed forces.

The military departments—the Army, the Navy (which includes the Marine Corps and, in wartime and at the President's directive, the Coast Guard), and the Air Force—are headed by Secretaries who are civilians. The Secretaries administer their departments under the discretion and control of the Secretary of Defense.

The service academies are established by law, and their faculties and cadets are part of the armed forces. Cadets are nominated by members of Congress and appointed by the President, but department Secretaries can dismiss cadets from the academies for cause, such as breaking the rules or failing physical or academic examinations. Dismissal for an infraction of the rules entitles the cadet to an informal hearing. He does not have the right to counsel, but he may present evidence and witnesses in his behalf.

Military facilities are controlled by the federal government. In areas open to the public, the public may enter and exercise their freedom of expression. Post exchanges and commissaries are part of the government and under military regulation.

■ **Officers, enlisted men, and civilians** The various officers, their grade and rank, promotion and authority, are governed by statute. Assignments of personnel are controlled by the military and are not subject to court review. By statute, a member of a Ready Reserve unit (see below) who has not participated satisfactorily, as by refusing to participate in drill or by failure to attend maneuvers, may be ordered to active duty. This activation is an administrative and not a punitive action. There is a military review of such calls to duty, but the courts rarely interfere. Civilian employees are not part of the armed services and not subject to the Uniform Code of Military Justice discussed later in this article.

Appointment, enlistment, or selection Officers are appointed by the President with the consent of the Senate. Enlistment is a contract to serve in a subordinate capacity for an agreed-upon period of time.

The appropriate Department Secretary may accept enlistment in the Regular Army, Navy, Air Force, Marine Corps, or Coast Guard from qualified, effective, and able-bodied persons not less than 17 or more than 35 years of age. Parental consent is necessary for persons under 18 if the parent (or guardian) is entitled to custody and control of the applicant. The term of enlistment or reenlistment is from two to six years.

An individual may enlist in or be transferred to a Reserve unit. To qualify, he must meet physical, mental, moral, professional, and age standards set by the Secretary of that branch. Persons may enlist in the Reserve of any branch for six years, serving not less than two years on active duty and the rest of the term as members of the Ready Reserve. In time of war, enlistments may be continued until six months after the end of the war or national emergency.

In addition to these provisions of federal law, there are many regulations governing enlistment in each separate branch. The regulations specify in detail how one qualifies for enlistment, with variations depending on such considerations as age and prior military service. Among other things, they specify which tests an applicant must pass, and what schools he must have attended, for various enlistment programs.

To be qualified for induction, individuals must meet minimum physical and mental standards. The normal period of service is 24 months. Under some circumstances, a draftee can transfer to a Reserve component.

Congress has the power to draft everyone, but it has provided for exemptions and deferments in recognition of military, social, and individual needs. Doctors, dentists, and allied specialists, for example, have been subject to a special call when the military had a particular need for their services. At times, doctors serving rural areas that would otherwise have no doctor have been exempted from service. Occupational deferments have been granted for other persons fulfilling special needs of society—for example, a deferment was granted to a special-education teacher who showed remarkable success with delinquent boys after five other teachers had either quit or been fired in a short period of time. Deferments and exemptions also have been granted for individuals with special needs; for example, a father with young children and a wife who was disabled. At one time, all married men with children and full-time students were granted deferments. Ministers, theological students, and surviving sons or brothers of men killed or missing in action were exempted from the draft. Conscientious objectors could be exempted from military service, subject to performing an alternative service in civilian work. Exemptions or deferments are available only as a matter of legislative grace. No one has a constitutional right to claim any one of them. When granted, they continue only so long as the conditions for which they are granted continue to exist.

The Military Selective Service Act required every male citizen and resident alien between 18 and 26 years of age to register for military service during periods of registration declared by Presidential proclamation. In 1975 registration procedures were suspended by Presidential proclamation, but they were reinstituted in 1980. From July 1, 1973, there was no compulsory draft into the armed services, and the armed services were on an all-volunteer basis.

Not everyone who registers is drafted. It is the policy of the law to select qualified persons up to the number each local draft board is notified to call. Draftees are selected without regard to race. Traditionally, draftees have been selected primarily on the basis of age, with the oldest age groups within the qualified pool being called first. There is nothing in the law to prevent selection by lottery.

Resignation, retirement, and dismissal Officers are permitted to resign, but the resignation must be accepted before it is effective. Retirement of officers may be voluntary or involuntary. Causes for involuntary retirement include physical disability or being passed over for promotion after a certain period of service. Enlisted men may retire by reason of age or physical disability.

Officers usually may not be dismissed except by sentence of a COURT-MARTIAL or, in wartime, by order of the President. If a Presidentially dismissed officer states under oath that he was wrongfully dismissed, he must be tried by court-martial on the charge cited by the President. Officers absent without leave for three months or under certain penal sentences may be dismissed by the President.

Generally, enlisted personnel are dismissed, or discharged, without court action. Unsuitability for military service or physical disability are reasons for discharge. After his term expires, an enlisted man is entitled to an honorable discharge, which results in a civilian status. An honorable discharge is considered a property right. It cannot be denied arbitrarily and without due process of law. There are military boards to review discharges and to correct errors, and judicial review is possible if regulations were not followed in the discharge.

True conscientious objection is considered a valid reason for an honorable discharge. The criteria are opposition to war in any form and a deeply held religious belief. Sincerity is the ultimate question. The military board's disbelief of the conscientious objector's sincerity is not enough to justify denying him discharge; some objective evidence is required. Judicial review is usually limited to determining if there was a good reason for the military decision.

EXAMPLE A young man registered with his Selective Service office and was granted a student deferment, which means that he was classified 2-S. That classification was renewed over a period of four years, and then he was reclassified 1-A, subject to induction. He received a notice from his draft board to report for a physical examination, and at that time he filed an application for a noncombatant classification (1-A-O) as a conscientious objector. He stated on the Selective Service form that he could not answer yes or no to the question of whether he believed in a Supreme Being, but he did not lack faith entirely. He said that he believed in and was devoted to goodness and virtue for their own sakes and had a religious faith in a purely ethical creed. He cited Plato, Aristotle, and Spinoza for support of his beliefs. His request for reclassification was denied.

On appeal the Supreme Court reversed this man's conviction for draft evasion. The law did not subject to the draft any person who, by reason of religious training and belief, was conscientiously opposed to participation in war in any form. While this did not exempt anyone for merely political, sociological, or philosophical views or solely for a personal moral code, it did extend to sincere beliefs that were like the faith in God that other people proclaim. It was not necessary for a conscientious objector to profess a specific belief in a Supreme Being.

Pay, allowances, and family benefits Congress controls all pay, allowances, and allotments to dependents. Special pay is available for hazardous duty and for reenlistment. Allowances in addition to pay may be made to provide such things as medical care, uniforms, housing, food, and transportation. Pay continues if a person in military service is captured by the enemy or is missing in action, but it may be forfeited if specified in a sentence of court-martial or on conviction of a specified military offense if the law so provides. Aid and relief are available to families and dependents of persons in military service. Retirement pay is a property right earned by years of service, not a PENSION. Certain restrictions exist as to what type of government jobs may be held while receiving retirement pay.

Civil status, rights, and liabilities Members of the military retain all the basic rights and duties of citizens, but these are conditioned by the demands of discipline and duty. They may sue in court for a contract breach or for personal injury, but they cannot be sued by other members of the military for something done within the scope of their duty. Civil remedies for abuse of authority, such as an officer assaulting a subordinate, are permitted. Persons conducting court-martial proceedings are immune from suit as long as they act within their authority.

Military persons have the same liability to civilians as do other citizens, but some immunities exist for certain actions within the scope of duty. For example, a wartime commander may seize for military use private property belonging to friendly persons, or he may destroy it to keep it from falling into enemy hands. Necessity governs such actions. A military person does not incur personal liability for obedience to lawful orders of a superior, but there is a liability if the order was so unlawful that a reasonable man would recognize its illegality. The same test is applied to criminal liability in carrying out a superior's order. See WAR CRIMES.

EXAMPLE A soldier was ordered to chauffeur his commanding officer's underage girl friend to a weekend rendezvous with the officer. The soldier could be held liable for the crime of contributing to the delinquency of a minor. He had no duty to follow this order.

The Soldiers' and Sailors' Civil Relief Act of 1940 protects the rights of persons who have had to neglect their personal affairs because of entering the armed forces. The statute does not discharge civil liabilities of military personnel but instead suspends legal proceedings temporarily and prevents default judgments (judgments entered for plaintiffs when defendants fail to appear and plead) against armed services members when they cannot appear and defend themselves.

EXAMPLE Timothy was on a tour of duty at a U.S. military station in Europe when he received a summons notifying him to appear in court in his home state to defend himself in a lawsuit brought against him by his bank for being behind on the payments on his loan. It was impossible for Timothy to get a leave from the Army at that time to defend himself in the suit. Under the Soldiers' and Sailors' Civil Relief Act, Timothy should not be subject to a default judgment and forced to pay just because he could not be in court to defend himself. This would be unfair. The court may appoint an attorney to represent him and proceed with the trial or it may postpone proceedings if he will be available within a reasonable time.

This law is superior to all state laws. It protects all armed services personnel, their dependents, and other specified persons, such as the endorser of a loan made by a person who subsequently entered the military. Some topics the law applies to are installment contracts, life insurance premiums, bail bonds, tax sales, and mortgages. A mortgage must have existed prior to the time of service, and the ability to meet the obligation must have been affected by the service. There is no help for mortgages made while in military service. Statutes of limitation are suspended during active military service. This applies to civil actions by or against persons in the armed services or their representatives. See LIMITATIONS OF ACTIONS.

EXAMPLE Garret is an enlisted man in the U.S. Navy. His
O━━➤ wife dies of a sudden heart attack. Garret is given
special leave from naval service to attend his wife's funeral, but he must return immediately for a six-month tour
of duty at sea. He does not have time to file an objection
in court against his wife's will in which she leaves most of
her assets to a man Garret knows to have been her lover.
The statute of limitations on filing such a complaint in
Garret's state is six months, but because Garret is in
active military service, the statute will be suspended until
he is able to file suit.

■ **Offenses and prosecutions** Persons in the armed
services may be guilty of criminal acts in violation of
federal or state law. By a Supreme Court decision, crimes
committed by military personnel in time of peace can be
tried only by civilian courts and not by courts-martial. In
time of war, however, all offenses committed by armed
services members may go before courts-martial or military
commissions, although the state and federal courts still
have jurisdiction (authority) over offenses against state and
federal laws.

Offenses The Uniform Code of Military Justice was
enacted by Congress to define military offenses and prescribe their punishment. For instance, it provides that
minor offenses—such as drinking while on duty or falling
asleep while at an assigned post—may be punished by the
offender's commanding officer in a specified manner.

To be charged with desertion, a most serious offense, a
member of the armed forces must be absent from his unit
without authority and with the intent to remain away
permanently. A serviceman charged with desertion is tried
by a court-martial. In time of war, a deserter may be
condemned to death or given any other punishment the
court-martial may direct. There is no death penalty for
desertion in peacetime. Soliciting or advising another to
desert is punishable as desertion if the other person actually
commits or attempts the offense. If the offense is not
committed or attempted, the punishment is as the court-
martial directs.

Offenses under general articles of the code are acts
against good order and discipline. Whether an act is against
good order and discipline is determined by the court-
martial on the basis of military custom, regulations, and
case law. Cases used as guidelines include assault with
intent to commit murder, manslaughter, rape, or robbery;
false swearing; and making disloyal statements. Officers
are under the additional stricture to act as "officers and
gentlemen." Officers have been charged with conduct unbecoming an officer and gentleman for possessing marijuana and using it in front of enlisted men, failing to pay debts,
and swearing to false statements.

The code governs the administration of military justice
and contains the procedures for the prosecution of offenses.
Self-incrimination is prohibited by the code. A court of
inquiry acts somewhat like a GRAND JURY, and its function
is to see if further proceedings are required in the matter. It
does not make judicial decisions.

Court-martial A court-martial is a military court for
trying and punishing offenses committed by members of
the armed forces. The court is temporary and once it
accomplishes its function it is dissolved. It is used for

offenses of a purely military nature, such as desertion or
assaulting a superior officer, or any other offenses made
subject to the authority of military courts by specific laws—
murder and drunken driving are two instances. Generally,
court-martial jurisdiction exists only as long as a person is
in military service. Once he leaves the service, the court-
martial loses the power to prosecute him unless it had
already started proceedings. Statutes of limitations do exist
in the code, but not for the crimes of desertion in time of
war, aiding the enemy, mutiny, or murder.

By statute, military review of all court-martial proceedings is required. The reviewing authorities must deal fully
and fairly with the constitutional contentions of a prisoner.
The first review is by the officer who convened the court-
martial. The second is by the Judge Advocate General (the
senior legal officer in each service branch) or, for certain
serious convictions, by a Court of Military Review established by him. A Court of Military Appeals, made up of
civilian judges and established by the President, is usually
the court of last resort. In addition, the President himself
must review death sentences and sentences involving a
general or flag officer (a Navy or Coast Guard officer
above the rank of captain). Although courts-martial do not
need to adhere to all the constitutional guarantees that
apply to civil courts, they must provide a fair trial, which is
in effect DUE PROCESS OF LAW.

Civil courts will not assume jurisdiction over or supervise military courts unless the defendant claims that he is
being unlawfully imprisoned or that the military court does
not have jurisdiction in his case. See HABEAS CORPUS.

Offenses by civilians Civilian offenses against the
military service include impersonating an officer, wearing
a military uniform, inciting or causing insubordination by
any member of the armed services, obstructing recruitment
activities, aiding or enticing desertion, and stealing, damaging, or trespassing on military property. Usually, civilians
cannot be tried by military courts, but Congress may provide for military courts to try civilians who accompany the
armed forces in the field in wartime, such as a civilian
mechanic working with a military unit.

■ **Insurance** Military INSURANCE policies are available
only to persons in active military service and cover the
death or the total and permanent disability of the person
insured. Some other conditions, such as length of service,
must be fulfilled. "Total and permanent disability" is difficult to define and depends on the circumstances in each
case. One general definition is an impairment making it
impossible for a person to engage with reasonable regular-
ity in any gainful employment without risk to his health.
The word "permanent" means the disability will continue
throughout the life of the insured without reasonable hope
of recovery even if properly treated.

At the death of the insured person, the policy beneficiaries will, when possible, be those designated by the insured,
but they must be within the classes of persons set by
applicable statutes. A husband or wife, parent, or child
generally fits the qualifications, but for others, even brothers and sisters, the statute must be consulted. Within the
statute's limits the insured may name anyone he wishes and
change his mind at any time. To be entitled to proceeds, a
beneficiary must survive the insured and make a written

claim for benefits. If there is a disagreement on a claim, an action may be brought against the United States.

Military term insurance is temporary, but it may be converted after the insured leaves the service into permanent forms: whole life, 20-payment or 30-payment life, 20-year endowment, endowment at age 60 or at 65.

A military insurance policy may be altered—for example, if the insured wishes to change his beneficiaries.

For the insurance to be payable, the death or disability must occur while the policy is in effect, and the cause must be as specified in the policy.

The insured may cancel his policy, and fraud by the insured authorizes the government to cancel the policy.

Nonpayment of premium will cause the insurance to lapse at the end of the three-month grace period, but in certain instances, such as total disability, the government may waive the premiums if application is made. Failure to apply for the waiver may be excused if it results from circumstances beyond the insured's control. If total disability ceases or the insured does not cooperate by permitting physical examinations, he must start paying premiums again. If the insured has any moneys due him from the government—disability payments, for example—they will be applied to the policy and it will not lapse. A lapsed policy may be reinstated upon application, but all back premiums must be paid, plus the interest on them.

■ **Veterans' benefits** As a rule, benefits to veterans and their survivors and dependents, in the form of money and privileges, have been granted by both federal and state statutes. The statutes of individual states must be consulted.

Federal veterans' benefits include compensation for disability resulting from injury or disease incurred or aggravated in the line of duty; vocational rehabilitation; pensions; educational assistance, which extends to survivors and dependents; job counseling, training, and placement service; free hospitalization and medical facilities, which in some cases may even be for a non-service-connected disability if the veteran cannot meet the expenses of necessary care; home, condominium, and mobile-home loans; and—for certain disabled veterans—automobiles and adaptive equipment. All honorably discharged veterans are also entitled to burial in a national cemetery, and benefits are provided to survivors and dependents for the death of a veteran resulting from injury or disease incurred in or aggravated by active military service in the line of duty.

Veterans' benefits are considered gifts and can be withdrawn by Congress at any time. The right to receive benefits may be lost by engaging in such activities as fraud, mutiny, treason, sabotage, and aiding the enemy. Certain discharges, such as for desertion, also bar benefits.

A veteran must apply for benefits within the time specified by statute. Generally, under federal law, no educational assistance shall be given to an eligible veteran 10 years beyond the date of his last discharge or release from active duty. An eligible veteran is under no time limit to apply for a loan to purchase a home as long as he served more than 180 days and received other than a dishonorable discharge, or served 180 days or less and was discharged for a service-connected disability. See Chart 8.

Administration and payment of benefits A claim for benefits must be filed with the Veterans Administration (VA), which manages veterans' affairs. The files of the VA are confidential and, with few exceptions, not subject to disclosure. Generally, the decisions of the Administrator of Veterans Affairs regarding benefits are conclusive, and other officers and courts may not review them. A veteran cannot sue the VA, but individual officials may be sued if they act beyond their powers. Payments are regulated by statute and may be made to a guardian or other suitable person. Improper payments, such as those made by mistake, may be recovered by the government. It is a crime for any person, other than an authorized agent or attorney, to charge fees for presenting veterans' claims.

Reemployment rights Veterans are entitled to be restored to the position they formerly held or a position of like seniority, status, and pay. This applies to all government employees, both state and federal, and to private employees as well. Enlistees—that is, volunteers—are entitled to the same benefits as draftees if the total of their service performed after August 1, 1961, does not exceed five years, with the fifth year at the request of the federal government. The employer at the time the veteran entered service must reemploy him, or that employer's successor must do so if the business changed hands. There is no duty to reemploy, however, if the business is so changed that there is no continuity between the former employer and the present employer.

EXAMPLE Herman had been in the Army for five years when he received his discharge. After a short vacation in the Caribbean, he returned to his hometown in Idaho, expecting to return to the factory work he had done before entering the Army. However, the factory had been sold during Herman's absence, and it now manufactured paper products, about which Herman knew nothing. The owner of the paper-goods factory was not required under law to hire Herman.

Returning veterans are entitled to seniority rights as if they had been in the continuous service of the employer. If wage increases were automatic, such as those based on time of service, the wages of the returning veteran must be what they would have been had he remained at his job. Increases based on management discretion, such as for job proficiency, are not a benefit the veteran is entitled to. Promotion is treated like pay: if automatic, the veteran receives the benefit; if discretionary, he does not. A veteran cannot be discharged for one year after his reemployment, but he must adhere to reasonable standards of conduct and duty. Reservists have similar benefits and should consult the VA or the statute in their state to determine their rights. If reemployment is denied, the veteran may ask the court to order the employer to comply with the statute and to compensate him for any loss of wages or benefits.

arms, right to bear   The right to bear arms is safeguarded under the Second Amendment of the U.S. Constitution, which states:

❝ A well regulated Militia, being necessary to the security of a free State, the right of the people to keep and bear Arms, shall not be infringed. ❞

The right of citizens to bear arms was not an unlimited right recognized by COMMON LAW. When the Constitution was adopted, this right was guaranteed so that the people could maintain a militia as a protection against violence. Under this amendment Congress cannot infringe upon the right to bear arms if there is a reasonable relationship between the use and possession of a firearm and the preservation of a well-regulated and efficient militia, or state national guard. Other laws include the 1934 National Firearms Act, which restricts ownership of certain WEAPONS, and the Gun Control Act of 1968, which regulates the interstate transportation of firearms.

The constitution of almost every state has a guarantee similar to that in the federal Constitution, but if it does not, the state legislature can regulate the bearing of arms. States, exercising their POLICE POWER, may prohibit the use or possession of firearms under certain conditions. See Chart 32. There is great controversy about gun-control laws. The core of the issue is whether a citizen has an absolute right as an individual to keep and bear arms or whether this right must be reasonably related to the preservation of public peace. Many states have determined that gun-control laws that do not impair the maintenance of a state militia, or national guard, are valid, and they do not violate the Second Amendment.

EXAMPLE In a New Jersey case, a group of sportsmen sued to have a state gun-control law declared unconstitutional. The statute required that all persons who wanted to buy firearms in New Jersey present a firearms-purchase permit. To obtain the permit, the person had to be investigated and fingerprinted. Permits would not be issued to habitual drunkards, narcotics addicts, or the mentally ill. Sportsmen claimed the law violated their absolute right under the Second Amendment to bear arms. The court decided, however, that gun-control laws are a proper and reasonable exercise of a state's police power as long as the maintenance of a state militia is not impaired. The state has a right to protect its citizens from the dangers of illegal firearms. "The language of the Amendment itself indicates it was not framed with individual rights in mind," the court pointed out. It refers to keeping and bearing arms in connection with a well-regulated militia. Thus, the right to bear arms must be viewed in terms of the language and purpose of the Second Amendment.

arm's length   At a distance; not on close terms. For example, a lawyer, trustee, or other person especially responsible to a person for faithfulness does not deal with that person at arm's length. Two merchants deal at arm's length with each other when buying and selling in the ordinary course of business.

arraignment   The act of bringing an accused person before a judge to answer charges against him and to enter a plea of guilty or not guilty. See CRIMINAL LAW.

array   The entire jury panel summoned to attend a court; the order in which jurors' names are ranked in the panel containing them. A *challenge to the array* is an objection to the procedures by which the panel was chosen.

arrears   **1** Money unpaid at the time due, such as back rent. **2** The remainder due after payment of part of an account. **3** Indebtedness.

arrest   Taking, seizing, or detaining someone by an act indicating an intention to put him under the control of the person making the arrest, for no matter how short a time. Detention—stopping a person for questioning or reasonable investigation—is in itself not arrest.

This article covers privilege from arrest; arrests with and without warrants; the significance of probable cause for arrest; informants and corroboration; temporary detention; what happens when a criminal arrest is made; and civil arrest. See also BAIL; CONSTITUTIONAL LAW; CRIMINAL LAW; FALSE IMPRISONMENT; HABEAS CORPUS; SEARCH AND SEIZURE.

■ **Privileged persons**   Public policy excludes some people from arrest. Congressmen may not be arrested on civil matters during their attendance at legislative sessions, but they may be for criminal reasons. Foreign ministers and ambassadors, and their households and staffs, are exempt from arrest, but consuls are not. Whether parties to lawsuits and witnesses are subject to arrest varies from state to state.

■ **Criminal arrest**   In criminal procedure, an arrest is the taking of a person into custody so that he can be held to answer for, or be prevented from committing, a crime. Anyone may be arrested to prevent him from doing harm.

Warrants   Issued by a magistrate, a warrant authorizes an officer to make an arrest and, usually, to enter a home in order to carry out the warrant. Reasonable delay in carrying out a warrant does not affect the validity of the arrest. A warrant must be served by the officer or class of officers specified in the warrant or by their authorized representatives. Private persons, not deputized, may not serve a warrant unless specifically named in it. Only the person named in the warrant may be arrested, but if the name is unknown, a fictitious name, such as "John Doe," may be used.

Arrests without warrants may be made in proper circumstances. Their validity is governed by the law of the state in which they are made, even when the arrests are for violations of federal law. Ordinarily, you as a private person may arrest without a warrant anyone who is committing or attempting to commit a FELONY in your presence. You may also arrest for a felony not made in your presence if it has actually been committed *and* you have reasonable cause to believe that the person you are arresting committed it.

EXAMPLE It is the week before Christmas and the downtown stores and streets are jammed with shoppers. As you are walking along Main Street, you see a commotion across the street. Several people are running in the same direction and a woman without a coat is shouting, "Get that man!" A few seconds later, you see a man running across the street toward you clasping a fur coat in his arms. You neatly stick out your foot, trip him, and promptly sit on him until the pursuers arrive to help you arrest him for the robbery of the fur coat.

The usual rule for a private person arresting for a MISDEMEANOR is that it must actually be committed or attempted in his presence. Private persons must arrest during or immediately after the offense; otherwise, the arrest is illegal. If you should arrest someone illegally, he or she can bring suit against you for DAMAGES.

Arrests by peace officers   Who is classified as a peace officer, such as a policeman or a sheriff, is determined by statute in most states. A peace officer has the same power as a private person and additional powers given

FACTS ABOUT ARREST FOR LAW-ABIDING CITIZENS

■ You may arrest without a warrant anyone who is committing, or attempting to commit, a felony in your presence. You may also make an arrest for a felony not committed in your presence, but you must not be making a mistake. You must arrest during or immediately after the offense—otherwise your citizen's arrest is illegal, and the person you took into your custody will have the right to sue you for damages.

■ A peace officer generally needs only a reasonable suspicion that a crime is being or is about to be committed to arrest without a warrant.

■ Under stop-and-frisk laws, peace officers may stop a person and demand an explanation of his actions. Frisking does not mean a full search but only a check for possible concealed weapons.

■ Police have the right to order a driver out of his car after stopping him for a traffic violation.

■ In making arrests police may use force, but laws vary from state to state as to when deadly force may be used.

■ A peace officer may ask a bystander to help make an arrest. The bystander has the duty to respond, even if there is danger, and he has the same protection of the law as the officer does.

■ Peace officers may break into a dwelling to prevent or suppress a breach of the peace.

■ The officer must give notice before making a forcible entry, unless such notice would endanger life, permit the suspect's escape, or result in the loss of evidence.

■ When a person is arrested, he must be advised of his rights. If arrested, you have the right to remain silent and to use the phone to obtain an attorney's help.

■ If you are suing someone for damages and discover that he plans to flee the state before the case comes to court, you can have him arrested. (To secure such an arrest, you must put up a bond, from which the defendant can be paid damages if he later wins a suit against you.)

to him by law. Under the Fourth Amendment to the Constitution, a peace officer should arrest with a warrant where reasonably possible. Usually, when circumstances prevent securing a warrant, an arrest without one is valid, as when a person is arrested in the act of committing a crime. A valid arrest by a peace officer cannot be made unlawful by subsequent events, such as an acquittal. Nor can an unlawful arrest be made lawful by subsequent events, such as finding additional evidence in a later search. State officers may generally arrest without warrants for violations of federal statutes committed in their presence, but federal officers require warrants in most cases except when they have probable cause to arrest for violations of federal law. If a peace officer is informed through official sources that a warrant exists for a person's arrest, he may make a valid arrest based on that knowledge.

As a rule, a peace officer may arrest without a warrant any person who commits a crime in his presence, when he has reasonable cause to believe a crime was committed in his presence, or when he is in "hot pursuit" of a criminal. If the officer knows of the crime by using any of his senses (he hears a shot or smells gunsmoke), it is in "his presence." An officer who sees a crime being committed and gives chase is in hot pursuit.

When a felony is committed, a peace officer may be able to arrest a suspect without a warrant in a public place. He may not, however, arrest a suspect in his home without a warrant if the crime was not in the officer's presence unless there are emergency circumstances—for example, if the officer receives an all-points bulletin on a suspect whom he spots and follows in hot pursuit to his home.

When a misdemeanor, such as a street fight, is being committed or attempted in the officer's presence, he may usually arrest without a warrant. Some jurisdictions require that the misdemeanor also be a BREACH OF THE PEACE, disturbing the public's peace and quiet. If the misdemeanor is not in the officer's presence, he needs a warrant. Some states require an actual misdemeanor for a valid arrest, but others require only a reasonable suspicion on the officer's part that a misdemeanor is taking place in his presence.

EXAMPLE Jostling can be the crime of unlawfully putting your hand close to another's pocket or purse or pushing or crowding a person while someone else puts his hand close to that person's pocket or purse. One police officer heard a woman behind him on the street cry out. She pointed to a man and said, "He tried to steal my handbag." The policeman did not see the man act, but he had sufficient reason to arrest him for jostling without an arrest warrant because jostling is a misdemeanor.

Probable cause If an officer makes an arrest for a crime not committed in his presence, he must have PROBABLE CAUSE. Probable cause—or "reasonable cause," which has the same meaning—exists if the facts the officer possessed at the time of arrest would cause an ordinary person to believe that the person to be arrested has committed or is committing an offense. Probable cause is a question of both law and fact. The jury decides if the facts exist, and the court decides if they amount to probable cause. The state must prove probable cause.

EXAMPLE Your car is disabled in a collision with another car, and the person behind the wheel of the other car drives off. You note his license number and give it to a policeman who finally arrives on the scene. The policeman can make a valid arrest of the other driver if he catches up with him and sees that his car is damaged.

On the other hand, a New York State Supreme Court justice ruled that the arrest of three men in court before him was "patently illegal" because the "gunpoint seizure of the three defendants in this case was based upon vague and unparticularized hunches at best." The men had run when they saw the policeman—not enough in itself for probable cause. The testimony of the arresting officers, the judge said, was "too implausible, too suspicious, and too incredible."

The officer's belief that an offense has been or is being committed may be based on facts within his knowledge, such as the past conduct, character, and reputation of the suspect. Probable cause has also been found when a suspect has possession of, conceals, or gives another burglary tools, narcotics, stolen property, or weapons, but the mere presence of a person on premises used for illegal activities is not sufficient probable cause.

Corroboration of informant Sometimes probable cause is based on information received from eyewitnesses, victims, or persons who have participated in the crime. In such cases the reliability of the informant must be considered. If the informant is a professional one—a so-called stool pigeon or perhaps a person convicted of a crime who is trading information for a reduction of his sentence—his reliability is judged by past experience with him, receipt of similar information from other sources, or by personal observation of the police. Citizen informers—eyewitnesses or victims—are more readily believed.

Statements from an informant require corroboration, although in some states citizen informers do not require corroboration. Corroboration may consist of such facts as duplicate data from independent sources, the suspect's conduct, or police observation. See CORROBORATE.

EXAMPLE You and your neighbor have been having a "spite war" for the past year. Just because of the bad feelings between you, he calls up the police and tells them that he saw you burying a body in your backyard. You cannot be arrested for murder on the basis of this completely uncorroborated report.

For an officer's observation to be valid, the manner of observation and his presence at the place of observation must be valid. Observation made from outside a private enclosure—by looking into an open door or window or noticing odors or sounds—are usually lawful. Observations made within a private enclosure must be preceded by a lawful entry, such as with a search warrant or while making a valid arrest. Entry to the premises with consent, given either by the party or by someone with apparent authority, such as a landlord, also validates any observation.

Temporary detention—stop and frisk A policeman does not necessarily have to have probable cause to stop you long enough to ask a question, and a valid arrest may be made if the probable cause then is revealed by the questioning.

A peace officer may in appropriate circumstances and in an appropriate manner approach a person to investigate possible criminal behavior even though there is no probable cause for an arrest. Under various statutes, popularly known as stop-and-frisk laws, peace officers may stop a person and demand an explanation of his actions if they reasonably suspect he has committed, or is going to commit, a specified offense, and they may search such a person for weapons. The detention must not amount to an arrest: it must be brief and normally without transfer to another location, such as a police station. A MIRANDA WARNING, which is the advice of the person's rights to remain silent and to have counsel, is not required.

The reasonable cause required of the officer to detain is much less than the probable cause needed to arrest, but intuition or a hunch is not enough. For example, an officer stopped a man who was barefoot, had long hair, and was shabbily dressed. A Texas court before which the accused

was brought said that this situation did not present a valid stop-and-frisk situation.

EXAMPLE On the other hand, in a California case it was decided that a Navy shore patrolman had probable cause to stop a person on the street and interrogate him for the purpose of identification, because the person fit the description of a serviceman wanted for unauthorized absence.

EXAMPLE In Illinois, police officers had been alerted that gang-related violence was expected in their area. While on patrol, officers heard shotgun blasts or revolver shots and in a matter of minutes observed a group about two blocks from where they had heard the gun reports. Since the suspects were the only persons seen by the officers in the immediate vicinity, and four of the six men wore headgear of the type worn by a gang in the area, the officers were justified in stopping the group for questioning and making a limited search.

The right to stop and frisk does not permit a search to the extent an arrest does. Frisking is justified only when a reasonably prudent man would believe that his safety or the safety of others was in danger, and it must be designed to discover objects that can be used as weapons. Its purpose is not to discover evidence of crime but to enable the officer to investigate without fear of violence.

EXAMPLE The Supreme Court ruled that an officer has the right to order a driver to step out of his car after stopping him for a traffic violation. In the case before the court, the traffic violation was an out-of-date license plate. The officer, seeing a suspicious bulge under the driver's jacket, searched him and found that he was carrying an unlicensed gun. The driver, convicted of carrying an unlicensed and concealed weapon, took his case all the way to the Supreme Court, which said that the possible danger to the officer overruled the driver's contention that the search was unconstitutional because he had been ordered out of his car.

Making a criminal arrest In making an arrest, the officer must not only indicate his intention and authority to do so, but must seize the person. Seizure involves a significant restraint of the person's movement, but touching him is not necessary if he submits to the arrest. Stopping and questioning does not amount to arrest unless there is a significant restraint of the liberty of movement of the person stopped.

When an arrest is made with a warrant, the general rule is that the warrant need not be shown. To make an arrest without a warrant, the officer usually must tell the person of his authority and why the arrest is being made, but neither statement is needed when an offense is being committed in the officer's presence or when he is met by force. After the party submits, however, the officer should state his authority and the reason for the arrest. Private persons must always notify the person being arrested of their intent to arrest and why, unless circumstances amount to sufficient notice.

EXAMPLE On your way home from the drugstore, you come upon a teenager assaulting an elderly woman in the course of stealing her purse. If you manage to overpower him and decide to make a private arrest, there is no need to announce your reason.

HOW TO CONDUCT YOURSELF DURING AN ARREST

WALTER P. CONNERY
Deputy Inspector, New York Police Department

"You are under arrest!" Will these words ever be directed at you? Will your spouse or your children someday find themselves in this situation?

In one single year 540,000 local, state, and federal law enforcement officers in the United States arrested more than 9 million individuals for various crimes and offenses, some of a serious nature and others not so serious. Many of the arrests were for the types of crime you read about in newspapers or see glamorized in police dramas on television. However, a considerable number of arrests are made to maintain public order—arrests for drunken driving, disorderly conduct, altercations between youths or adults, violations of local ordinances, and the like. It is with these types of trouble that the normally law-abiding citizen is most often involved.

If you find yourself the object of a policeman's orders, you should be aware of the policeman's latitude, as well as of your own rights and duties.

Policemen's duty and discretion

The nature of police work is a mystery to most people, and most television programs that portray various aspects of law enforcement are unrealistic. Placing a police uniform on a man does not turn him into a robot that responds automatically, with absolute uniformity, to a given situation or set of facts. Like anyone else, each officer is an individual with a unique personality. Unlike people in most other occupations, policemen have a broad range of discretionary powers on the job, especially in handling so-called "order maintenance" violations and other minor offenses. Police resolve many on-street situations and make an arrest only when their attempts to resolve these incidents are rebuffed, often because one or more of the people involved are drunk or emotionally overwrought.

The President's Commission on Law Enforcement and the Administration of Justice reports: "Policemen cannot and do not arrest all the offenders they encounter. It is doubtful that they arrest most of them." A policeman's duties compel him to exercise personal discretion many times every day, because crime does not look the same on the street as it does in the legislative chamber where the laws concerning it were passed. Taking some typical violations a policeman will see in the streets, the authors of the report posed some questions:

> How much noise and profanity make conduct disorderly within the meaning of the law? When must a quarrel be treated as a criminal assault? At the first threat, or at the first shove, or at the first blow, or after blood is drawn, or when serious injury is inflicted? How suspicious must conduct be before there is "probable cause," the constitutional basis for arrest? Every policeman, however complete or sketchy his education, is an interpreter of the law. Every policeman, too, is an arbiter of social values, for he meets situation after situation in which invoking criminal sanctions is a questionable line of action. It is obvious

that a boy throwing rocks at his school window is committing the statutory offense of vandalism or criminal mischief, but it is not at all obvious that the policeman will better serve the interest of the community or the boy by taking him home to his parents or arresting him. What of the boy's parents? Can they control him? Is he a frequent offender who has responded badly to leniency? Is vandalism so epidemic in the neighborhood that he should be made a cautionary example? With juveniles, especially, the police exercise a great deal of discretion. Finally, the manner in which a policeman works is influenced by practical matters: the legal strength of the available evidence; the willingness of victims to press charges and of witnesses to testify; the temper of the community; the amount of time and information at the policeman's disposal.

Most often, police discretion is exercised with offenses that do not require an arrest. If you commit a serious crime, you will be arrested. But if you commit one of the many minor offenses where the police might be able to exercise discretion in handling your case, it is obvious that your best course of action will be to behave in a manner that will enable them to exercise that discretion. Belligerent behavior may leave the officer no choice but to arrest you. If you have acted foolishly or intemperately, do not keep up your conduct in the officer's presence if you want to resolve the situation informally.

Modern society puts people under many stresses. And when they are subjected to a sudden additional aggravation (alcohol, a divorce, a catastrophic debt, or a frustrated romance), normally peaceful persons may behave in a manner that leads to confrontation with the police. If this happens to you, you would be best advised to *get hold of yourself, calm down, and apologize to the appropriate parties.* It may make the difference between your waking up with an aching head in your own bed and waking up in one of the rather hard institutional beds in the local lockup. Remember: If you are drinking, you may think you are right but you are probably wrong. However, if even your best behavior fails to avert arrest, let us see what will happen and what your rights are.

When and how you may be placed under arrest

What constitutes an arrest? Each state has its own definition, which varies considerably from state to state. Generally speaking, you have been arrested when a police officer or a citizen (citizens are entitled to make arrests) takes you into custody and deprives you of your freedom so that you may be held to answer for a crime or an offense that has been committed.

At this point, we ought to discuss the difference between crimes and offenses. Each state has its own criminal codes and definitions, but certain basic principles prevail nationwide. Being disorderly or drunk in public or failing to obey a local order-maintenance ordinance is an offense or violation but not a crime. Crimes are divided into felonies and misdemeanors, felonies being the more serious of the two. Murder, burglary, robbery, rape, assault with a deadly weapon, theft of large sums of money or property, and the like are considered felonies. Punishment for a felony usually involves more than one year in a state prison. Misdemeanors generally have a maximum penalty of up to a year in the local county jail or a fine. Petit larceny, shoplifting, simple assault where the victim is injured without the use of a deadly weapon, drunken driving (in many states), and some order-maintenance infractions, such as unlawful assembly, are examples of misdemeanors. Lesser offenses to public order are generally classified as violations, punishable by fines or jail sentences of no more than 30 days.

How arrests are made   There are several ways that you can be arrested. The most common is the on-the-scene arrest by a police officer for a crime or offense you have committed or are committing in his presence. You may also be arrested if the police officer has reason to believe you have committed a felony (and in some states, a misdemeanor), even though the crime was not committed in his presence. An officer may also take you into custody if you have been arrested by a private citizen and the officer believes that the arrest was proper. In none of these cases does the officer need an arrest warrant.

Anyone making an arrest without a warrant must tell you the reason for the arrest. Generally speaking, the police officer will tell you that you are under arrest for whatever the crime or offense is, so long as it is not obvious to one and all. However, if you are coming out of a bank with a gun in your hand, the officer is not going to tell you that you are under arrest for bank robbery, since it is obvious what the crime is and that you are involved. The officer will merely say: "Police! Don't move!"

Citizen's arrest   The most common arrest made by citizens is an arrest for shoplifting or for some other offense involving a merchant, where the offender is apprehended by the merchant or by one of the store's security guards. The merchant or security guard will detain you until the police arrive, then hand you over to them for transportation to the local police station and eventual arraignment in court. In these cases, the police are merely acting as escorting officers. The person who actually arrested you is the store employee who detained you.

As a private citizen you may arrest someone without a warrant if he is attempting to commit a crime in your presence. If, for example, you find someone breaking into your house, you have the right to hold him—in effect, to arrest him—for the attempted burglary of your house. When the police arrive in response to your call, you may say, "I want him arrested," but in reality you have already arrested the burglar, and the police will merely be taking him to court for you.

The significant difference between an arrest made by a private citizen and one made by the police is the liability for an improper arrest. Even though the private citizen may have had reasonable cause to believe that you committed an offense—let's say, shoplifting—if it later turns out that you did not, you can sue him for damages. However, if a policeman arrests you with reasonable cause to believe that you committed a crime and the officer was acting in an official capacity, without malice, then he is immune from a civil suit. In addition, if a citizen is attempting to arrest you for a crime and you do not believe that you did it, you may resist. But you may not resist an arrest being made by a police officer, no matter how innocent you believe you are.

Arrest warrants A police officer may also arrest you by authority of an arrest warrant—a written order issued by a judge, stating that an officer must arrest you in order to bring you before the judge to answer a complaint or charge that has been filed against you by the police, by a citizen, or by a grand jury. *You have the right to see the warrant.* However, because people sometimes try to rip up a warrant or deface it, many police officers will hold the warrant so that you can examine it but will not actually hand it to you.

Search warrants Search warrants are similar to arrest warrants in that they are issued by a judge to police officers; but instead of requiring the officer to arrest a person, they in effect require him to "arrest," or seize, the property described in the search warrant and bring it to a court. Again, the police officer will

show you the warrant if requested and will also leave you a receipt for any and all property seized.

An officer acting under the authority of a search warrant may break open a door or window if you refuse to admit him after he has given you notice. In some states, the judge who issues the search warrant is empowered to direct in writing that the officer need not give notice before breaking in. This is done when the personal property sought can too easily be destroyed (such as drugs or gambling records) or when the police would be exposed to unnecessary danger if they identified themselves before entering. In such cases, the police may break in unannounced. Anything—even something unlawful, such as stolen property—that is taken by the police without a warrant cannot later be used in evidence against you. However, anything taken under the authority of a search warrant may be used against you in court.

With the exception of the frisk situation discussed below, and when you are actually arrested, an officer who stops you on the street or who desires to enter your home must have a search warrant to search you, your personal property, or your home, unless you consent to a search.

Stop and frisk The law permits an officer to stop you in a public place if he reasonably suspects you are committing, have committed, or are about to commit a serious crime. He may demand to have your name, address, and an explanation of your actions. In addition, if the officer reasonably suspects that he is in danger, he may frisk, or pat down, your clothing or handbag for instruments or weapons that could cause injury. If the officer finds a dangerous weapon or instrument, he may keep it until he finishes questioning you. If no arrest is made, he will return the weapon to you, provided you have a permit to carry it. If, while frisking you for dangerous weapons, the officer finds something else on you that is illegal to possess (for example, drugs), he may arrest you for its possession.

The arrest is made

The officer will usually begin by telling you that you are under arrest. Since thousands of police are assaulted and many are killed while making arrests, the officer will handcuff you, probably with your hands behind your back. *Do not resist him.* If you do, he will use whatever force is necessary to overcome resistance and may also charge you with resisting arrest.

Remember, the officer is simply doing his job. If you have committed an act that requires an arrest, your guilt or innocence will be determined at a later time in court, so do not attempt to adjudicate matters in the street by resisting arrest.

Once you have been lawfully arrested, your person may legally be searched. This may include a minute examination of any personal effects on you at that time. Also, the immediate area where you are arrested may be searched. Anywhere you could easily reach for weapons, such as a nearby drawer or automobile glove compartment, may be searched by the officer.

Fingerprints If you are arrested for a violation that does not amount to a crime, you may not be fingerprinted. But if you are arrested for a crime (a felony or a serious misdemeanor), you will be fingerprinted and photographed.

If your fingerprints are taken, you will be asked to sign standard fingerprint forms. *Sign them.* Many people misunderstand this procedure, viewing it as some confession of guilt, and refuse to sign the forms. If you refuse to sign fingerprint forms, they will not be processed. Since you will not be released on bail until they are processed, cooperation is obviously your best course of action.

Besides being fingerprinted at the police station, you will have to surrender your money and personal possessions. (You will be given a receipt for them.)

Your rights when in custody If you are arrested, whether you are an adult or a juvenile, you have certain rights.

(1) *You have a right to telephone your friends, family, or lawyer in order to notify them of your arrest.* Some police agencies make these calls for you, but most dial the number for you and allow you to conduct the conversation. You have a right to speak to a lawyer at the police station house.

(2) *You have the right to remain silent—either completely silent or to answer some questions and not others.*

(3) *You cannot be made to answer any questions or sign any statement.*

Sometimes the police officer who arrested you will promise to help you in exchange for your confession or for certain other information. Such promises are binding in most states when made by the district attorney but are not always binding when made by the arresting officer. When you appear in court, you will be asked by the judge to plead guilty or not guilty. The judge may also ask you if any promises have been made to you; if such promises have been made, you should mention them before the court.

Before the police question you they must tell you of your right to remain silent and that any statements you make may be used against you. Furthermore, you must be advised that you have the right to speak with a lawyer and to have him with you when you are questioned. The police must also tell you that if you want to speak with a lawyer before being questioned and cannot afford one, one will be assigned to you without cost. If you request a lawyer, the questioning may not proceed until the attorney is present. Also note that if you allow the police to question you, you may still stop answering questions at any point and request to have a lawyer present before the questioning continues. Moreover, if you are asked to stand in a police lineup, you have the right to have a lawyer present at the lineup.

Your arrest record What about the records that are made of your arrest? Generally, unless you were arrested for a minor offense—one that does not require fingerprinting—the records of your arrest will be extensive. Copies of your fingerprints will be permanently filed with the FBI as well as with state and local repositories. A search of these files by an authorized agency 20 or 30 years after the arrest will reveal it and will, by the fingerprint classification system, positively identify you to the exclusion of all others as the individual who was arrested. Therefore, it is important to *demand the return of these fingerprints if you are acquitted of the charge.* This is generally done by filing a form with the clerk of the court.

Body cavity searches If you are arrested for a serious crime, you will be subjected to a body cavity search. Women have the right to have this search conducted by a woman.

After the booking

Once the arrest processing, or "booking," is completed, you must be taken to court without "unnecessary delay." What constitutes delay depends on where you have been arrested. If you are arrested in a suburban or rural county, you may have to remain in detention for a day or longer before you can be arraigned—that is, brought before a judge to plead guilty or not guilty. In larger cities, judges are generally available seven days a week; major cities even have night courts for the arraignment of prisoners.

Bail If you have been arrested for a misdemeanor or lesser offense, in most jurisdictions you can be released by posting a money bail. The police will not set bail for felonies.

At the arraignment (your first appearance before a judge) the judge will inform you of the charge against you, of your right to legal counsel if you appear without a lawyer, and of your right to have a lawyer assigned by the court if you cannot afford one. If the case is not a minor matter that will be settled the same day, the judge will set bail or release you on your promise to return on an appointed date. If bail is set and you do not have enough money or other security to post for the bail, you can try to hire the services of a professional bondsman. The fee for this service varies from state to state, but is usually 5 percent for the first $1,000, with smaller percentages for additional amounts. Many bondsmen will require some form of collateral or the signature guarantee of a third person.

Preliminary hearings and grand juries

If you are charged with a serious crime, you may be entitled to a preliminary hearing.

At a preliminary hearing the judge will determine whether there are sufficient grounds to hold you on the charges that have been brought against you. He will examine the person who brought the charges against you as well as other key witnesses. You have the right to make a statement on your own behalf if you wish to do so. You or your lawyer (and this should certainly be done by an attorney) also have the right to cross-examine the people who testify against you at the preliminary hearing. If the judge is satisfied that probable or reasonable cause exists for your arrest, he will direct that you be held or released on bail until such time as a formal trial can be held. "Probable or reasonable cause" means that upon analysis of the facts it is more probable than not that you committed the particular crime or offense. It is not as strict a standard as "guilty beyond a reasonable doubt," which is the standard that will be used to determine your guilt or innocence at your actual trial.

If the judge decides to hold you after the preliminary hearing, it will be for actual trial on a misdemeanor charge, or for the action of the grand jury if the charge is a felony.

A preliminary hearing is not mandatory. The prosecuting attorney may bypass it and request a grand jury to indict you. The grand jury proceeding takes the place of your preliminary hearing.

If you are charged with a minor offense for which no preliminary hearing or grand jury hearing is held, you will be asked by the arraigning judge whether you plead guilty or not guilty. Should you plead not guilty, your case may be adjourned for trial, or, in most places, you may have your trial then and there.

Awaiting trial You may proceed to have your trial without an attorney, but this is not advisable. If you wish to plead guilty to a minor offense, you can sometimes find out informally what the fine will be. However, in any case that is the least bit serious, it is advisable to have a lawyer. If you are going to be held in jail in lieu of bail, the judge must inform you of your right to use a telephone, send letters free of charge, get a lawyer, and tell family or friends about your arrest.

As you can see, the criminal justice system is complex and often confusing. It is far better to avoid this labyrinth of complexities altogether.

In making arrests, force may be used to the extent required, but it must be proportionate to the resistance offered. In felony cases, the officer or private person may ordinarily use as much force as necessary, even to the extent of killing the felon. In misdemeanor cases, deadly force cannot be used—even though the offender will otherwise escape—except in SELF-DEFENSE. Statutes vary from state to state about when deadly force may be used.

A peace officer may ask a bystander to aid him in making an arrest. The bystander is usually under a duty to respond, even if there is danger, and he has the same protection of the law as the officer has.

Time and place In most instances an arrest may be made at any time of the day or night, although some statutes forbid night or Sunday arrests except for certain cases. Generally, the arrest may take place anywhere, but an offense against the laws of one state does not justify an arrest in another state, unless the other state authorizes it, and a warrant of arrest is valid only in the state where it is issued. Some peace officers do not have statewide authority and may arrest only in their local jurisdiction. If the person being arrested does not object to an arrest outside of an officer's jurisdiction, he is considered to have waived his objection.

An officer is normally entitled to enter a dwelling peaceably to make a lawful arrest. He may enter by consent of the persons inside, or the accused himself could come to the door and be arrested on the threshold. Forcible entry with a warrant is valid to arrest a concealed offender when the crime is at least a breach of the peace, but military officers may not break into a private house to capture deserters.

In cases of felony, when a warrantless arrest is being attempted, an officer may break into the house. The statutes vary, however, in cases of lesser crimes, such as misdemeanors. Forcible entry will not be justified if there is time to get a warrant. Peace officers may also break into a dwelling to prevent or suppress a breach of the peace. But before making a forcible entry, the officer must give notice of his authority and purpose and must be refused entry. Notice is not required if it will endanger the officer or another person, permit the escape of the person sought, or result in the destruction or concealment of evidence.

EXAMPLE Patrolman Dodd was walking down the street when he heard a crying sound. He looked behind bushes and saw a whimpering teenage girl with a dirty face and torn clothing. She said that a man had attacked her and gone into a house across the street. The policeman went to the house and knocked, saying, "Open up. Police here." No one answered. Dodd looked through the window and saw a man asleep on the couch. He opened the door, went in, and shook the man, telling him that he was a policeman and the man was under arrest for rape. This arrest was valid even though Dodd had to push the door open without consent and before he could inform the accused man of his authority and purpose.

Rearrest Generally, once an arrest warrant has been used it cannot be used again, but in some cases a rearrest can be made without a warrant. This happens when the prisoner is released on a procedural technicality before his trial—such as when the INFORMATION upon which the original arrest was made did not state facts sufficient to consti-

tute a crime, or when a person escapes after trial and commitment, or is unlawfully discharged, as by a sheriff who does not have the authority to release the prisoner.

A person cannot be rearrested on the same charge after an acquittal. If repeated arrests reach the point of harassment, the victim can apply to a court to stop the prosecutor's actions on the basis of fair play.

■ **Custody and property of arrested persons** An arrested person keeps his legal rights regardless of the offense. A short delay between arrest and arraignment is all that is permitted, during which the arrested person may be questioned. The law is not clear at what point the questioning might require the presence of counsel.

When a person is arrested, he must be advised of his rights and permitted to exercise them. Some of these are the right to remain silent, to communicate with family or friends, to have visitors, although visiting hours may be restricted, and to use the telephone to obtain advice and assistance. A paramount right of an arrested person is to be permitted, without unnecessary delay, to contact an attorney and consult with him. An attorney is not required, however, until after the prisoner is booked, assuming that the questioning of the prisoner up to that point was only to determine whether or not he should be held. The prisoner may not be abused or mistreated. If he is sick or injured, medical treatment must be provided.

Putting the arrested person in a lineup for identification purposes, examining him physically for needle marks indicating drug addiction, and testing him for intoxication are all permitted. Photographing and fingerprinting are usually permitted by statute.

The officer who made the arrest must produce the person arrested before a magistrate or other judicial officer within a reasonable time. This is a statutory right existing in most jurisdictions. It does not apply to escaped prisoners, parole violators, or to prisoners who are accused of committing a crime while incarcerated. Most statutes provide that the proper magistrate is the one who issued the arrest warrant. Within a "reasonable time" means without unnecessary delay. Delay is considered necessary if the prisoner is ill or drunk or if he is arrested on a day, such as a holiday, when no magistrate is available. The delay cannot be oppressive or for the convenience of the police.

Search after arrest After a lawful arrest the prisoner may be searched without a warrant. But if the arrest is illegal, so is the accompanying search. Usually, the search follows the arrest. Some searches before arrest have, however, been held valid when the officer was justified in making the arrest and did not need the fruits of the search to justify the arrest.

EXAMPLE A report went out over the police radio that three young men had just robbed and shot a coin dealer on Sunset Highway and escaped in a red Chevrolet van. Within minutes, two police officers spotted a van with three men fitting the description speeding down the highway. They pulled the van over, ran up to it with their guns drawn, and ordered the men out. They told the men to put their hands on the side of the truck, and they searched them immediately for weapons. Only then did they feel that the situation was safe enough to place the men under arrest.

The search does not have to be made at the time of arrest but may be made later, such as after the prisoner has been taken to a station house.

To be a valid search "incident to an arrest," it must be made prior to jailing. The scope of such a search is limited to the person of the prisoner, which includes his clothing and anything he is carrying, and the area within his immediate control. It has been found lawful, too, to take samples of blood, hair, and stomach contents when this is done reasonably. For further treatment of permissible search, see SEARCH AND SEIZURE. Property of the person arrested that is unlawful or connected with the offense charged may be seized; it is put under the control of the court and ultimately returned to the proper owner. If the owner is the arrested person, it will be returned at the court's discretion.

■ **Civil arrest** An arrest in a civil action consists of taking custody of another person for the purpose of holding him to answer a civil demand. If you have such an arrest made, the wrong being sued for must have been done to you and not to a third person. Civil arrest is governed strictly by law. It has been so restricted that it is almost never used in CONTRACT actions. If it is used at all, the cases generally involve TORTS (injuries to persons or property).

EXAMPLE Let us say that a driver crashes his car into your house, wrecking your screened-in porch and greenhouse and demolishing two large trees on your property. You sue him for damages, but before the case comes to court you discover that he plans to flee the state. You can have him arrested.

Persons generally exempt from civil arrests include public and peace officers; judges; those going to, attending, or returning from court in connection with proceedings in civil suits; and witnesses. Some of the usual grounds for civil arrest are that the defendant is about to leave the state, as in the situation above, or is about to conceal or dispose of property to defraud his creditors. To make a civil arrest, you must usually put up a BOND, or security from which the defendant can be paid DAMAGES if the arrest you obtain is unlawful and he brings suit against you. An arrested person who does not give BAIL may be put in jail. It is possible to be discharged from jail if the ground for arrest does not exist, if the arrest was made by unlawful means, or if the defendant is underage or insane. Poverty is sometimes a reason for release because imprisonment might cause undue hardship for the arrested person's family. A person may also be released by putting up a bond.

arrest of judgment The act of stopping a court JUDGMENT or refusing to give one because some apparent defect in the proceedings would make it, if given, erroneous.

arrogation A claim to or appropriation of something without having any right to it.

arson Under common law, arson was the malicious burning of someone else's house. *Malicious* means burning with the intention of causing harm. This includes outrageously reckless conduct, such as pouring gasoline all over the floors in order to frighten someone. *Houseburning*—the intentional burning of one's own house in a city or near other houses—was a separate but related crime. The value

of what was burned was usually irrelevant in determining whether arson had been committed. Because of the harsh penalties for arson, defendants could be convicted only if their acts closely fitted the COMMON-LAW definition.

Today, state arson laws generally include all these traditional common-law elements of the crime and may include additional kinds of conduct. For example, burning one's own house is now arson in many states, especially if the purpose is to defraud an insurer. And most arson statutes now include the intentional burning of buildings used for commercial purposes, such as restaurants, garages, and warehouses. Although destroying a building by explosives was not considered arson under common law, the modern trend is to include it under arson statutes. Burning unfinished buildings and personal property—furnishings within a building—is not usually arson, but it may be malicious mischief. See VANDALISM.

■ **Homes** Under some arson statutes, the burned building must actually be lived in. If the occupants are temporarily away, the house, such as a cottage used only during the summer, is still considered lived in but if it is abandoned or converted to another use, burning may not be committing arson. The fact, and not the knowledge of human occupancy, is what is important. If people are living in a dwelling burned under the impression that it is not lived in, the crime is arson.

Setting fire to a house while committing another crime is usually considered arson even if the houseburning is not intentional.

EXAMPLE Three days before his marriage was to take place, a New Jersey man, having dinner at his fiancée's home, jumped up from the table, climbed to the attic, and set fire to the bride-to-be's wedding dress hanging in a closet. The flames spread to the roof, and fire damage came to more than $20,000. The man was charged with arson, and, incidentally, the engagement was ended.

■ **Penalty** Statutes frequently divide arson into degrees, depending sometimes on the value of the property, but usually on the use of the property and whether the crime was committed during the day (second degree) or at night (first degree). The most severe penalties are reserved for arson that causes a loss of life.

As with most crimes, if you conspire with, procure, aid, or advise others in the commission of the crime, you are guilty of the crime itself.

The punishment for arson—a serious crime once punishable by death—is set by statute. See also FIRES.

articles 1 The separate parts of a document, book, or set of rules. In a statute with several parts, the parts are articles. 2 A system of rules—articles of war or articles of the Navy, for example. 3 A contractual document, such as articles of partnership. 4 A naval term meaning employment contract.

articles of incorporation The document by which a private CORPORATION is set up.

articles of partnership A written agreement by which the parties enter a PARTNERSHIP and set out the terms and conditions of their association.

artificial person   A person created by law; a being or thing given some of the legal rights and duties of a human being—a corporation, for example. Under the CLAYTON ACT, municipalities and foreign nations are regarded as persons.

as is   A term describing something sold in a possibly defective condition, which the buyer takes with no promises that it is other than as seen and described.

as per   Commonly understood to mean "in accordance with," or "as by the contract authorized." For example: We will proceed as per our agreement.

asportation   The felonious removal of things from one place to another and one of the prerequisites for establishing that LARCENY has been committed. Simply putting items into a bag in which to carry them away constitutes asportation. They need not be taken from the premises.

assault and battery   Acts of violence toward another person—either with or without any actual touching—that are not connected with any other type of offense. This article covers defenses, liabilities, and remedies, both civil and criminal. Excluded, for the most part, are similar topics, such as civil liability in an assault resulting in death (see WRONGFUL-DEATH ACTION), assaults with MOTOR VEHICLES, assaults in connection with unlawful arrest (FALSE IMPRISONMENT), and assaults committed in obstructing the serving of summonses and subpoenas or in resisting an officer (OBSTRUCTING JUSTICE).

■ **Definitions**   *Assault* is a threat to do bodily harm by someone whose ability to carry out the threat is such that the victim fears he is in imminent danger. You do not have to be physically touched to be assaulted.

EXAMPLE In a Florida case, a man went to see his wife's employer—we'll call him Smith—at his home to talk to him about his wife's quitting her job. Smith told the husband to meet him at his office at 9 o'clock the next morning to discuss it. When the husband arrived he saw Smith outside his office, but since Smith looked "mad enough to cut him in two," instead of speaking to him, the husband went to his car to get a pistol. He entered the office at the appointed time and asked Smith to fire his wife because her job was breaking up their home. Smith stood up and started toward the husband, swinging his hands in a threatening manner and saying, "You damned crazy war veteran, I will beat the hell out of you." The husband, who was sickly and no match for Smith in physical combat, fired a shot to try to stop the attack and killed Smith. The Supreme Court of Florida held that the husband acted in self-defense, because he had reasonable grounds to fear great personal injury and there was imminent danger that it would be inflicted.

Battery or *assault and battery* is the touching of another by the aggressor or by something he uses such as a rock that he throws. A battery accomplishes what an assault threatens to do.

To find out the criminal liability for both offenses, you should consult the statutes in the state where the assault takes place.

■ **Assault**   To sue for assault, you must be able to prove the elements of assault described above.

EXAMPLE In an Iowa case, a former railway worker went to his previous place of employment to try to get his job back. When he entered the premises, a railroad employee holding an iron poker came toward him and ordered him to go away in a threatening manner. The court decided that the threat was an assault.

EXAMPLE In the District of Columbia, a servant sued her employer for assault when the employer locked her in a room without any explanation but thereafter released her. There was no threat of violence by the employer, and the court said that this was not an assault.

EXAMPLE In Michigan, an innocent motorist successfully sued for assault when deputy sheriffs fired at him, even though only his car was struck and he was not physically injured.

Intent   The law is not clear on whether an intention to do harm is necessary for an assault. In some states, if a defendant's actions cause reasonable fear of bodily harm, he has committed an assault even if he had no intention of doing wrong. Mere words or threats, no matter how provoking or insulting, do not amount to an assault. Intent is sometimes important, however.

EXAMPLE A salesman in Wisconsin was demonstrating a fly-repellent spray. The store owner's wife was allergic to some element in the spray and as a result suffered injuries from it. The court held that because the salesman had no intention of harming the woman, he did not commit an assault.

Force and violence   The force and violence in an assault must be unlawful and physical, but it may be of any kind or degree no matter how small.

EXAMPLE When the operators of a roller-skating rink in Wisconsin lawfully caused police to eject an unruly person, there was no assault. A policewoman in Oklahoma won an assault and battery case against a man who grabbed her wrist and kissed her while she was trying to give him a traffic ticket.

A threat resulting in mental anguish could be an assault.

EXAMPLE A driver of an automobile in Oklahoma, intending to frighten and terrorize the occupants of another car, gave chase. The chase did frighten the other people and was considered an assault. Likewise, in a Utah case, a wife whose husband's life was threatened in her presence in order to intimidate her was found to have been assaulted.

The threats must create a reasonable fear of injury. In the famous Onassis/Galella case in New York, a photographer's persistent threatening of Jacqueline Onassis by jumping from concealed locations and by following her by car at close distances was a civil assault. Although the general rule is that there must be a "present ability" to carry out a threat before an assault can occur, cases in Washington and New Hampshire have decided that a "well-grounded" fear of personal injury from a pointed firearm is sufficient for an assault even if the gun is not loaded. But in Wisconsin, when a man fired a gun for the purpose of frightening someone, the court held that fear was not "well grounded" after determining that the man had not aimed the gun nor intended to injure the other person.

■ **Battery** Execution or accomplishment of the assault is necessary to make one liable for battery. Battery is considered an intentional act.

Consent Lack of consent is essential. Acts by PHYSICIANS AND SURGEONS, such as operations, performed without informed consent and not in an emergency, are battery even though skillfully performed and beneficial to the patient. In Kentucky, it was decided that in an emergency a surgeon may operate on a child without waiting for permission from his parents, but that if no emergency exists, the operation gives the patient the right to sue.

Consent may be implied. For instance, an oral surgeon, removing an infected tooth, fractured his patient's jaw and immediately repaired it. The court held that consent to repair the jaw was implied.

Consent must be "informed." One surgeon was held liable for an operation he had performed with his patient's, consent because the patient had been given insufficient information about the operation and its probable results.

Touching and force Inflicting unauthorized force is essential to a battery. Injury is not required. The slightest wrongful touching constitutes a battery, and the touching is not restricted only to the body or clothing.

EXAMPLE In Texas, when the manager of a motor hotel O—⋇ snatched away a patron's dinner plate in a "loud and offensive manner," that was held to be enough "touching" to be a battery. In a Georgia case, when a prisoner claimed he was X-rayed without his consent and without any sound reason, he was allowed to recover for the battery of penetration by radiation.

The force can be indirect; it does not need to be aimed at the victim. In Illinois, the court decided that a person striking a glass door in the course of an argument, and breaking the glass, a piece of which flew into the eye of another person, committed a battery.

Only wrongful touching constitutes a battery, however. A New Jersey court decided that a person with the right to enter a building does not commit a battery when he removes someone who obstructs his entrance, providing no excess force is used.

Intent Generally—although there are some exceptions, as mentioned above—there is no battery unless the touching involved is done with intent to injure. Another exception is when the defendant is engaged in some unlawful act at the time of the touching. A trespasser, for example, would be responsible for any battery he caused even if he did not intend to injure—let us say he knocked someone down the stairs by accident.

■ **Persons entitled to sue** An action for assault and battery must be brought by the person whose rights have been infringed.

EXAMPLE In a New York case, a man, the plaintiff, saw O—⋇ another man, the defendant, beating the defendant's wife. The plaintiff, using reasonable force, intervened to help the wife and his clothes were torn. The court decided he could recover damages, because the injury he received while helping the woman was a battery.

■ **Persons liable for damages** Not only the actual assailant but all others who help, counsel, or encourage the wrongdoer by words, gestures, looks, or signs are equally liable. In Connecticut, a joint assault was shown when, after a conversation with the plaintiff, one defendant nodded to the other who then tore a badge from the plaintiff's coat. Mere mental approval of an assault and battery is not enough; some additional act is required before you become liable. For example, you are not responsible for a beating inflicted by another, even though you were pleased that it happened, as long as you did not help or encourage it.

You are liable if your agent uses unnecessary violence in the performance of his duties. See AGENCY. An Idaho court said that the owner of a bar could be liable for an assault on a patron by his bartender. In South Carolina, a landlord, although not personally present, was liable for the assault and battery committed by his agents on a tenant.

The legality or illegality of your actions is important also. If two persons are acting together illegally and in the

---

IF SOMEONE HURTS OR THREATENS TO HURT YOU

■ You do not need to be touched to be assaulted. The mere threat of violence is enough when it comes from someone capable of hurting you.

■ Assault becomes assault and battery when the assailant carries out the threat he has made.

■ To sue for assault, you must prove there was a threat of violence, together with imminent danger that it would be carried out.

■ The element of force and violence need not be great. If the driver of another automobile chases you in your car merely to terrorize you, his action may amount to assault.

■ If you are beaten at the instigation of a person not actually participating

in the attack, the instigator is as liable as the assailant for assault and battery.

■ If you respond violently to provocation, no matter how offensive, you may be liable for assault and battery.

■ You may use force in self-defense, but only if you reasonably fear bodily harm.

■ You do not have to retreat if attacked—you may defend yourself—but you must not kill or seriously injure the attacker if there is another way of escape.

■ To protect property, you may use force, so long as it does not endanger life or inflict great harm. (However, some states permit taking a life if it is necessary to prevent or stop a felony.)

■ You may throw out a trespasser, but only after giving him notice and reasonable time to comply. If it is useless or dangerous to give notice, then no request is needed. To know exactly how much force you may use to eject a trespasser, check your state's laws.

■ You may take back stolen property by force if you do not unreasonably hurt the wrongdoer.

■ You may use force to stop crimes being committed in your presence, but as a layman you are usually permitted to use less force than a police officer would be allowed to use. Unless you know your state's laws very thoroughly, use little or no force in such instances.

process one of them attacks a person, the other is also liable even though he did not participate in the attack.

Joint and separate liability   All persons participating in an assault or an assault and battery are both jointly and separately liable. This means that if a person helps or encourages another in an assault and battery, the assaulted person can sue both assaulters or either one of them for the total amount of his damages. Even if one had very little to do with the attack, he can be sued for all the damages.

■ **Defenses**   As a rule, in both civil and criminal actions for assault and battery, the defenses are approximately the same. Justification is one defense.

EXAMPLE A store owner attempted to get out of his store by O⊷✳ pushing a person who was blocking the entrance. After a scuffle, the owner broke away and the other person swung his fist, which went through the window, cutting him. The owner was not liable for the injuries because he was justified in pushing aside the person blocking the door.

Acting on the advice of your lawyer is *not* a defense to an action for assault and battery if your lawyer's advice to you was wrong.

The victim's negligence is also not a defense. You cannot defend yourself by saying that although you wrongfully assaulted someone, that person contributed to his own injury by being negligent.

EXAMPLE Jenkins drives through a red light and smashes O⊷✳ into Butler's brand-new car. Butler, who was listening to the World Series on his car radio, is furious both at Jenkins's negligence and at his favorite baseball team, which is trailing behind 5-0. Butler gets out of his car and hits Jenkins in the jaw. Butler cannot later defend himself by claiming that Jenkins deserved to be hit in the jaw because he had driven negligently.

Accident   It is a good defense if you unavoidably injure someone while doing a lawful act, but not otherwise. If, for example, you wrongfully strike another person, you cannot be excused because of accident, but if you had been lawfully defending yourself from an attack and you accidentally hit an innocent bystander, you could be excused because of accident.

Condition of mind   Anger, intoxication, epilepsy, or even temporary insanity are not defenses to a suit for assault and battery.

Consent   When no BREACH OF THE PEACE is involved, consent is usually a defense. If a patient knowingly consents to a course of treatment, he may not then sue for battery if the physician acts within the scope of the consent. In the case of mutual combat, consent is generally not available as a defense, and either party may sue the other. Check the law in your own state, however, because some states do not permit either party to recover damages.

Provocation   You should also check the law of your state regarding provocation, because there are some variations among the states. The general rule is that acts or words alone, no matter how offensive or exasperating (such as shaking a finger at a person from four feet away and cursing him), do not excuse an assault. In Mississippi, when a sheriff assaulted a photographer who had taken his picture without his consent, he was found liable. The taking of the picture, of course, was not an assault on the sheriff.

Self-defense   The general rule is that you may use as much force as appears necessary at the time to protect yourself from bodily harm. You do not have to retreat if you are attacked and you may defend yourself, but you should not kill or seriously injure the other person if you have another way of escape. If you were the aggressor and started the conflict, you cannot claim SELF-DEFENSE. If you started the conflict and then stopped it and the other person then attacked you, you would be entitled to defend yourself.

A trespasser cannot, ordinarily, claim self-defense, but if you lawfully enter another's property and are assaulted by the owner, you may assault him and claim self-defense.

EXAMPLE Clyde tried to recover his cattle, which Carson, O⊷✳ his neighbor, was unlawfully holding from him. When Clyde entered Carson's land, Carson and his wife assaulted him and beat him. The cattle owner correctly claimed that his part of the struggle was self-defense.

Before you may use force to defend yourself, you must reasonably fear bodily harm.

EXAMPLE Let us say someone called you names a month ago O⊷✳ and, on meeting you again, started to abuse you verbally without making any move to hurt you. It would not be reasonable for you to fear bodily harm. But if this same person had actually attacked you previously, your fear would probably then be reasonable.

When determining whether fear is reasonable, such factors as the age, size, and strength of the parties are considered. The threat to you does not have to be real as long as you reasonably think it is real.

Extent of force   Self-defense cannot be claimed when a person uses more force than appeared to be reasonably necessary for self-protection.

EXAMPLE If a slightly built woman slaps a robust man, he O⊷✳ cannot strike her with a baseball bat and expect to claim self-defense. If, on the other hand, the woman attacked the man with the bat, he would certainly be able to defend himself with more force than just his hands.

What constitutes reasonable force is affected by such factors as the relative age, size, and strength of the people involved, their reputations for violence, and whether or not weapons are being used. Reasonableness is what is important. If you are assaulted by a number of persons at the same time, you may protect yourself more promptly and more forcefully than if the assault were by a single person, but if you, a healthy adult, were attacked by a group of little children, you would have the right to use only a small amount of force.

Defense of another person   You may act the same way in defending someone else as would be justifiable while defending yourself. If you go to the defense of your brother, however, not only must you be free from fault, but so must your brother.

Defense of property   A person may use a reasonable amount of force to protect property. When a customer refused to pay the full price of some meat he had purchased, the butcher was entitled to use reasonable force to prevent him from carrying it away.

Usually, the force must not be so great that it endangers life or inflicts great harm. In some states, however, even the taking of life is permitted if it is necessary to prevent or stop a felony. See CRIMINAL LAW. In Louisiana, a burglar was shot by someone who was protecting his employer's property. The court held that the shooting was justified to stop a felony and that the thief could not recover damages.

A TRESPASS on property may be resisted by the lawful possessor of the property, such as a tenant, against everyone except the true owner. If a person in possession of the property is injured while resisting a trespass, he may sue the trespasser. An agent, servant, or employee may defend his employer's property.

Ejecting trespassers   An owner or tenant may use reasonable force to remove trespassers after giving them notice to leave, without being liable for assault and battery. The same rule applies to people who are on the property with permission and who refuse to leave upon request—store owners, for example, may remove unruly persons. A Michigan court decided that when a servant is discharged, he has a reasonable time to leave the premises, and if he continues to stay, proper force may be used to eject him.

Before using force, you should give the trespasser notice that you want him to leave and a reasonable time to do so. If it is useless or dangerous to you to give notice, such as when a trespasser forces his way in, no request is needed. If unnecessary force is used to eject an intruder, you cannot defend yourself by claiming you were defending your property. You may not use a weapon to eject a child or someone who is not dangerous, but the use of a weapon could be reasonable force if required for self-defense or to prevent a felony. To know what amount of force you are entitled to use in evicting a trespasser, check your state's laws.

Disputed property   The universal rule is that if the possession of property is in dispute you cannot settle it by force—you should resort to a court action. But you may peaceably take back property stolen from you wherever you find it, and you can use force if you do not unreasonably hurt the wrongdoer. In the state of Washington, when the manager of a store chased after a thief and took back the stolen goods by using only as much force as was necessary to recover them, he was not liable for an assault on the thief.

Although some states permit you to enter someone else's property to recover an article stolen from you, you cannot enter his property in the face of any resistance or assault him. A New York case decided that an owner of a share of a farm's products had no right to take his share forcibly from the other owner who was in possession of the products. For rights of landlords to evict tenants forcibly, see LANDLORD AND TENANT.

Exercise of duty and authority   Reasonable force may be used when a person is performing his duty, and in such cases is a defense to assault and battery.

EXAMPLE In New York, a hotel officer ordered an employee
O—* he had discharged to leave the hotel. When the man did not go voluntarily, the officer used only the necessary force to eject him and was not liable for assault.

In California, however, a private detective, who had been hired to keep order in a dance hall and bar, used a blackjack to subdue some unruly people. The court said that although he was permitted to use reasonable force to carry out his duty, he used the blackjack brutally, unnecessarily, and unjustifiably.

A peace officer may also use reasonable force in the performance of his duties without incurring liability. If he uses unnecessary violence or force, he is liable for assault and battery.

For minor crimes, such as misdemeanors, or for civil matters, an officer must not inflict great bodily harm unless it is required for self-defense. Serious crimes may justify more force, but the officer must always act in good faith. Judges, coroners, and similar officers may, without liability, have someone who interferes with their duties removed from their presence. Private citizens may use force to stop crimes being committed in their presence, but they are usually permitted to use less force than a police officer would be allowed. Unless you know the law of your state, you may be wise to use as little force as possible, or none at all, to stop a crime.

Service of summonses and subpoenas   An officer is permitted to use necessary force to overcome resistance he meets when serving summonses and subpoenas.

Relationship of parties   Some relationships carry the right to use force as long as it is not abused. Children may be physically punished without liability by parents or those authorized by them if the force used is reasonable. Generally, teachers may act as parents. Punishment of children may never be cruel or excessive.

EXAMPLE A boy was punished by a teacher for annoying
O—* small girls returning home from school. A Connecticut court ruled that even though the misconduct occurred after the pupil's departure from school, the teacher was permitted to punish him because his misconduct affected the morale and efficiency of the school.

■ **Lawsuits**   Assault and assault and battery are violations of the right of personal security, for which the law entitles the assaulted person to sue the wrongdoer for damages. In addition, the person committing the assault or the assault and battery may be subject to criminal penalties. The victim of a shooting or a knifing, for example, may sue his assailant for damages, and the assailant could also be tried by the state for his criminal act.

assembly   The meeting of a large number of persons; the lower house of many state legislatures.

assembly, right of   The right of free assembly for lawful purposes and the right to petition the government for redress of grievances are fundamental to a free government. The right of people to meet in public places to discuss openly all questions affecting their substantial welfare and to air their grievances while seeking a solution of their problems is the essence of democracy. These rights have been incorporated into the First Amendment of the U.S. Constitution as well as into various state constitutions. The due process clause of the 14th Amendment protects the rights of assembly and of petition from any state action that may deprive citizens of these rights. See DUE PROCESS OF LAW. This constitutional right of free assembly—the same thing as freedom of association—is a special form of free speech, and although not identical, the two are closely related. See SPEECH AND PRESS, FREEDOM OF.

A state law cannot limit, restrict, or impose any conditions upon the right of free assembly. For example, a state cannot constitutionally require proof from any group that they are not Communists before allowing them to exercise their right of assembly for lawful purposes. This requirement would discriminate against Communists. If, in order to prevent a meeting of a discussion group with unpopular political views, a city official enforces building regulations against the owner of the meeting hall more strictly than usual, the officer's behavior violates the guarantee of freedom of assembly.

The constitutional rights of freedom of assembly and of petition, although fundamental, are not unlimited. They may be restricted, under the CLEAR AND PRESENT DANGER rule, to prevent grave and immediate danger to interests that the state may lawfully protect under its POLICE POWER. Any attempt to restrict freedom of assembly may be justified by clear public interest against serious violence threatened in the present.

> EXAMPLE Let us say a group wishes to meet to plan bombings of all banks to demonstrate their hatred of capitalism. They would have no right of assembly for this purpose under the Constitution. The state could restrict all meetings of the group by arresting its members for conspiracy to commit a crime, since there is a clear and present danger to society. See CONSPIRACY.

The state cannot enforce measures that would deny the right of assembly to groups that have opposing political views, nor can it control a public forum by CENSORSHIP of the speakers, their ideas, or the audience. When beliefs of a certain group are censored, the state is denying that group its constitutional right of assembly to discuss its ideas publicly.

Without diminishing the right of assembly, the government may reasonably and without discrimination regulate the use of places wholly within its control—by requiring permits for public assemblies in the streets or parks, for instance. Because of the possibility of discrimination against groups who have unpopular beliefs, the requirement of a permit violates the Constitution if a public official has unlimited discretion to deny it. If a state or locality decides to open its school buildings for assemblies, it cannot arbitrarily prevent some members of the public from holding meetings there.

Shopping centers have been held to be so open to public use that they may be available for right-of-assembly activities within reasonable limits. Groups may receive permits to hold peace demonstrations in the parking lot of a shopping center but not inside a gun shop that is part of the center, because the shop is privately owned.

■ **Labor unions** The right to assemble and function through a labor union is part of the right of assembly guaranteed by the Constitution. The government may, however, reasonably regulate labor unions and their activities with a view to protecting the public interest. While picketing peacefully is a proper exercise of this right, if violence occurs the pickets lose their right to assemble and will be subject to state regulations.

■ **Public employees** Public employees enjoy the same constitutional right of free assembly as others, but forbidding their membership in subversive organizations is not a denial of this right because such groups pose a threat to the government. The Hatch Act, which restricts federal officers and employees from political activities, is not an un-constitutional denial of the freedom of assembly because of the potential for misconduct in the particular cases.

> EXAMPLE If a supervisor sells tickets to a $100-a-plate dinner for his political club, the federal employees under his supervision may feel forced to buy them in order to insure their supervisor's goodwill. By prohibiting federal employees from political activities, in this case the assembly at the dinner, the occasion for possible misconduct is avoided.

assembly, unlawful See RIOT.

assent Comply; approve of something done; agree; sometimes means the same as "authorize."

assess 1 Fix the value of. 2 Impose a monetary payment upon persons or property. 3 Make a valuation and appraisal of property for tax purposes. 4 Charge part of the cost of a public improvement to each person or property directly benefiting from it.

assessed valuation Value assigned to a property for the purpose of calculating property taxes. On each unit a prescribed amount of tax must be paid. For example, in a community with the prescribed amount of taxation at $50 per unit of $1,000, the owner of a house with an assessed valuation of $50,000 must pay $2,500.

assessment 1 Generally, the amount to be paid by each of several persons into a common fund. In taxation, assessment is (1) the valuation of property for the purpose of apportioning a tax upon it, either according to value alone or in proportion to the benefit received from it; or (2) the share of a tax to be paid by each of many persons.

> EXAMPLE A town installs a new public water system. Each one-family house is assessed $100 to pay for it. Multifamily dwellings must pay $40 per unit, and a hospital is assessed $5,000. Each type of property pays an assessment in proportion to the benefit it receives.

2 Fixing the amount of DAMAGES to which the successful party in a suit is entitled.

assets All money, property, and rights with monetary value—such as a debt owed—owned by a person or an organization. *Capital assets*, also known as *fixed assets*—land or buildings, for example—cannot be turned into cash quickly. Those that can easily be sold for cash are called *current assets, liquid assets,* or *quick assets. Frozen assets* are tied up—by a lawsuit, for instance—and cannot be used.

assign 1 Appoint or select for a particular purpose or duty. 2 Transfer or turn over formally, as in deeding land to another person. 3 Point out or set forth, such as to "assign error" by specifying the errors in a legal document.

assigned account Money owed to a business by a customer that is put up as security for a debt that the business owes to a bank.

assigned risk A type of INSURANCE, usually covering automobile accidents, that state law requires companies to provide. Persons who obtain this insurance, usually because they are poorer-than-average risks, are assigned by the state to an insurance company. Usually they pay extra for the coverage.

assignment   A transfer or turning over to another of property, usually an entire interest or property right. Sometimes the reference is to the document that is proof of the transfer rather than to the transfer itself. An *assignor* makes the assignment to another, who is called the *assignee*, and the assignment is a CONTRACT between them. The mutual agreement of parties competent to enter into a contract is required, and usually a CONSIDERATION (an exchange of something of value).

EXAMPLE Let us say that as a result of an assault you are injured and hospitalized. You are not covered by insurance and would like to turn over to the hospital, in exchange for its services, the proceeds of any court judgment paid by the person who assaulted you. If the statutes in your state permit and the hospital agrees to accept, you may assign the proceeds to it. You are the assignor; the hospital is the assignee. The hospital's cancellation of your debt is its consideration.

An assignment without valuable consideration and a gift are a great deal alike.

EXAMPLE One assignment received a certain amount of publicity in 1977, when mystery writer Agatha Christie's play *The Mousetrap* celebrated its 25th year on the London stage. The writer had assigned the royalties from the play to her grandson as a ninth-birthday gift, and speculations were that they had probably earned him more than a million dollars. Songwriter Irving Berlin assigned the royalties from at least two of his songs to others—"Always" to his wife when they were married (he had written it during their courtship) and "God Bless America" to the Boy Scouts and Girl Scouts.

assignment for benefit of creditors   A voluntary transfer by a debtor (the assignor) of his property to an assignee in TRUST, to use the property to pay his debts and to return the surplus, if any, to him. The assignment is *general* when it is of all the debtor's property for the benefit of all his creditors; *partial*, when a substantial portion of the debtor's property is not assigned; and *special*, when it is for the benefit of certain named creditors. When title to the property is assigned, the property is absolutely beyond the control of the assignor. The creation of a trust is one of its characteristics, and it should not be confused with a COMPOSITION WITH CREDITORS, PLEDGE, RECEIVERSHIP, MORTGAGE, or SALE.

EXAMPLE A company that manufactures fabrics had a bad year. The price of raw materials rose substantially, and the increase was not provided for in contracts with their customers. In addition, a number of low-cost imports flooded the market and ate into the American company's sales. Meanwhile, debts had mounted: to the suppliers of looms and dyeing machines, to a contractor who had modernized plant facilities, and to caterers who had contracts for servicing plant canteens. To extricate itself from its debts, the company decided to put two of its plants in trust, to be sold for the benefit of its creditors.

Generally, a debtor may select his own assignee, except where statutes require the sheriff to be named or allow the creditors to choose the assignee. An assignee cannot be compelled to accept the trust. If he refuses it, the court will usually appoint a new assignee. Creditors may choose to accept or refuse an assignment, but once their approval is given, they cannot withdraw it except in cases of fraud or some violation of a condition.

■ **Form**   A document establishing an assignment for the benefit of creditors—called a deed of assignment—does not require any special language, but all essential matters should be stated clearly. Although some oral assignments of personal property may be valid, as a rule statutes require that most assignments, especially those relating to real property, be written. The description of the property assigned must be adequate to identify it.

■ **Administration of trust**   The deed of assignment governs the powers and duties of the assignee. He should collect all the assets and may sue to do so in order to sell or otherwise dispose of them. The assignee may pay proper expenses out of the trust funds and has a right to be reimbursed for proper expenditures he made out of his own funds, but he is not permitted to make a personal profit from his dealings with the trust property.

A creditor may bring a lawsuit to set aside an assignment on various grounds, including fraud, but once he claims or accepts benefits under it, he cannot attack it.

Except as affected by statute, assignments for benefit of creditors are valid if made voluntarily and without fraud and are not attacked by federal BANKRUPTCY proceedings.

assigns   Assignees; those to whom property has been transferred, as in the phrase used in deeds: "heirs, administrators, and assigns." See also ASSIGNMENT.

assistance, writ of   A written order from a court authorizing enforcement of an earlier decision about who is entitled to possess a particular parcel of land. This WRIT is like an injunction in that it legally requires the occupant to give up possession of the land. It does not change ownership of the land, although the right to possess it sometimes comes from being the lawful owner.

EXAMPLE A receiver is appointed to manage all the property of someone who is insolvent. The receiver applies to the court for assistance in getting possession of a certain piece of property. As soon as the sheriff receives a writ of assistance from the court, he takes it to the premises, gives it to the person in possession—for example, a tenant—and makes him leave.

associate justice   The title of each judge in an appeals court other than the chief judge.

association   An association is an unincorporated society; a body of persons united and acting together without a charter but using methods and forms commonly used by CORPORATIONS to carry out some common enterprise. Associations may range in size from the tenants' committee in one apartment building to a nationwide organization with many thousands of members, such as the American Association of University Professors (more than 72,000 members) and the Knights of Columbus (more than 1.2 million members). If there is no statute that says otherwise, associations are usually not considered legal entities or persons. See ARTIFICIAL PERSONS. They are groups formed by contract without any grant from the state.

■ **Organization** When no specific law governs the organization of unincorporated associations, their organization ordinarily depends upon the contract of the associates, usually called the "constitution" or "articles of association." The association's objective must be a lawful one. If it is reorganized under a new name, its identity is not necessarily destroyed, but if its constitution is changed substantially, the members of the old association are not necessarily members of the new. An association may incorporate if permitted by statute or by the terms of its contract.

■ **Dissolution** An association may be dissolved under the following conditions: by the consent of its members, and unanimous consent is generally required; when the reason for its existence ends; upon the abandonment, withdrawal, or death of its members; by incorporation; by legislative action, as in the case when the existence of the association is against PUBLIC POLICY; or by a court order issued for any of these reasons. The association's net assets are usually distributed among the members at the time of dissolution. Creditors are paid before members, and non-member creditors before member creditors. A purchaser of association property ordinarily takes it free and clear of the claims of creditors.

■ **Articles, constitution, and bylaws** The articles of association or the constitution and the bylaws define the privileges and duties of the members and, if not contrary to public policy, may be of whatever the members care to adopt. These articles and bylaws are an enforceable contract between the parties. They may be amended or repealed according to the terms of the constitution or by a majority vote of a QUORUM.

■ **Rights, powers, and liabilities** These are usually determined by statute, the common law, established general procedure, or the association's articles or constitution. In most cases the body does not have corporate powers, cannot issue stock, and cannot hold property. However, property may be held by trustees for the use and benefit of the association and its members. See TRUST. Although the trustees have legal title to property holdings, courts will generally force them to follow the wishes of a unanimous vote of the society as to the disposition of the property.

Contracts, strictly speaking, cannot be entered into by an association, but they may be made in its name by its officers or members and are enforceable against them. Association members, and by statutory authority even officers or the association in its own name, have been permitted to sue on such contracts.

An association cannot commit a crime, but it may be held liable for the TORTS (civil wrongs) of its members or employees committed in the conduct of its business.

EXAMPLE A tenants' association became tired and frustrated 0—* at the landlord's broken promises to have the outside wall of their apartment building properly repaired. At a tenants' meeting, the members of the association voted to take matters into their own hands and decided to hire an engineer to fix the wall. The engineer

tore down the wall and stopped working. The tenants' association was later held liable in court for tearing down the building wall without the permission of the landlord. The member tenants were ordered to share the cost of completing repairs.

As a rule courts will not interfere in the internal management of an association unless there is evidence of fraud or a problem arises that all the remedies within the framework of the association cannot solve.

■ **Officers** The association's articles, bylaws, or established general procedure determine how officers are elected or appointed, their terms of office, and their powers and duties. An association may, however, exist without officers. When there are no officers, their functions may be performed by the individual members of the association.

Officers are ordinarily the custodians of the association's funds and records. If acting with authority, they may bind an association and all its members by CONTRACT. An unauthorized action by an officer may be ratified if the association accepts the benefits that result from it.

EXAMPLE Carla Williams retained the services of an ac-
0—* countant to audit the books and prepare whatever tax information might be necessary for the Society to Preserve Scenic McKeesport, of which she was the president. Carla had not been authorized by the members of the society to hire such a person. At the next meeting of the association, Carla reported her actions to the membership-at-large. Although the members did not condone Carla's acting without authority, they realized that the association would benefit from the accountant's services and voted to accept her action.

Officers who make unauthorized contracts may be solely and individually bound on the contracts. Officers who in the course of their duties commit torts (wrongful acts for which the injured person may sue) are usually liable for them. Officers who reap secret profits at the expense of the association may be held liable to the members.

■ **Membership** Membership in a voluntary association is not transferable unless permitted by its constitution or bylaws. Admission to membership is usually completely within the control of the association, but a person elected to membership, and then arbitrarily denied admission, may secure relief in court. A person becomes a member by any procedure that shows that a mutual membership agreement exists between himself and those in the association. Mutual intent must be shown.

If there is no statute or association law to the contrary, a member may withdraw his membership whenever he wishes, subject to whatever financial obligations he might have. The rules of the association for the suspension or expulsion of a member must be observed and the person to be expelled must receive a fair trial before an impartial group. Courts will interfere only if the expulsion is unlawful and property rights are involved. Reinstatement is possible but only when the conditions of the association are met.

Individual members, as a rule, lack power to bind the association, but the majority may bind even those who do not agree with it, if its actions are to further the association's objectives. Members are liable to the association for fraud or breach of trust and, if the articles so provide, for dues, assessments, fines, and penalties.

■ **Lawsuits**   If there is no statute allowing an association to sue in its own name, the association generally must bring the lawsuit in the names of its individual members. Or it can appoint agents to sue.

At one time it was the law that an association could not be sued unless a statute permitted it. The modern trend does permit some suits, and the law in each state needs to be carefully checked. If liability is established, each member is usually individually liable for the entire amount of any debt incurred during his period of membership.

EXAMPLE   A group of people concerned about promoting O→* the religious education of children formed an association to accomplish that purpose. They soon acquired a membership of a hundred people. One of the projects sponsored by the group was an offer of free transportation to religious services for any child in the community. The group purchased a bus and hired a bus driver. One day the bus collided with another car. No one was hurt, but the owner of the car sued for damage to his vehicle and recovered a judgment against the association for $5,000. Because the association had not purchased insurance that could have paid the damages, each member was liable for an equal share of the judgment. Some of the members protested that they did not specifically know about the details of the transportation project or approve of hiring that particular driver. The judge ruled that this made no difference, and all were equally liable for any portion of the judgment that could not be paid out of money on hand in the treasury.

association, freedom of   See ASSEMBLY, RIGHT OF; SPEECH AND PRESS, FREEDOM OF.

assumption   The act of assuming, undertaking, or adopting someone else's debt or obligation. If, when you purchase real estate, for example, you "assume" the mortgage debt existing on the property as your own, you become personally liable for its payment.

assumption of risk   A rule, existing in many states, that if you knowingly expose yourself or your property to certain kinds of known dangers, and you or your property are injured, you cannot collect damages for the injury. For example, if you break a leg while skiing and the ski-trail operators are not at fault, you cannot sue them, because you assume the risk of breaking a leg, a common danger of skiing. See NEGLIGENCE.

assured   A person who has been insured by an INSURANCE company against the losses or perils mentioned in the insurance policy. The assured may also be the person for whose benefit the policy is issued and to whom the loss is payable, not necessarily the person on whose life or property the policy is written. For example, when a wife insures her husband's life for her own benefit and he has no interest in the policy, she is the assured and he is the insured. In some instances, however, the term "assured" is used in place of "insured."

asylum   1 An institution for the relief and assistance of the unfortunate, especially INSANE PERSONS.

■ **Regulation**   The state legislatures have the power to regulate asylums, both private—those organized, conducted, and financed by private organizations—and public—those established, maintained, and financed by the state or one of its subsidiaries, such as a county. State regulation is subject only to constitutional limits and the general requirements for reasonable action. Inmates voluntarily admitted may not be retained against their will.

■ **Liability of officers**   When acting in a judicial capacity, such as deciding when to dismiss an inmate, officers cannot be held liable for mistakes.

EXAMPLE   The superintendent of a state hospital in Wash- O→* ington, who was permitted to release patients at his discretion, was not liable to a person later shot by the released person.

EXAMPLE   A Louisiana court decided that the good faith of O→* the superintendent of an asylum who exercised his discretion in releasing an inmate cannot be questioned in an action for a death caused by the inmate. This decision was handed down even though the superintendent had been charged with acting maliciously and in disregard of the rights of the public.

EXAMPLE   A Texas court decided that when there were no O→* provisions requiring inmates to be confined to an insane asylum's grounds, asylum officers who let an inmate leave under supervision were not negligent.

2 A place of refuge or shelter. *Political asylum* is the privilege of a nation to offer refuge and protection to a person fleeing his own nation for political reasons. No nation is bound to offer political asylum to an individual. Territorial asylum is giving that protection within the sheltering nation's own borders. *Diplomatic, or extraterritorial, asylum* is an offer of asylum in the sheltering nation's embassies, consulates, legations, and warships outside its borders. Asylum is generally granted only to political fugitives, not to fugitives from criminal justice. See EXTRADITION. The famous Russian ballet dancer Rudolph Nureyev was given political asylum in the United States when he defected from the Soviet Union.

International law recognizes the existence of refugees—masses of persons displaced by war, political upheaval, famine, or any other kind of disaster. Provisions are made in treaties, by the United Nations, and by international charitable organizations, to ameliorate the suffering of refugees. Individual nations may permit individuals or groups of refugees to immigrate and settle within their borders for humanitarian or political reasons. U.S. Federal immigration law strictly controls the entry of all ALIENS—including refugees—into the United States.

at issue   Whenever the parties of a lawsuit come to a point in the PLEADINGS that one party states is the truth but the other party denies, they are said to be at issue—for example, when the plaintiff in a lawsuit involving a car crash states that the defendant went through a red light but the defendant claims it was green.

at large   Unlimited; free; unrestrained; uncontrolled. An at-large election is one in which everyone votes for a choice of candidates from a political unit, such as a councilman-at-large from the whole city rather than just candidates from one area of that unit, such as a councilman from one of the city's several councilmanic units. Although at-large voting is not in itself unconstitutional, the Supreme Court has ruled that it is a violation of the Constitution if it has the effect of diluting minority voting. The Attorney General has designated areas that are underrepresentative of blacks and ordered federal monitoring of elections in those areas. See also STATUTES AT LARGE.

attachment and garnishment

Two extraordinary remedies for securing the payment of a debt or a judgment. Both measures are harsh, and courts insist that statutes controlling them be strictly followed.

■ **Meaning and purpose** *Attachment* is a temporary remedy used alongside a main lawsuit until a judgment is handed down by the court. It freezes the assets of a debtor—a boat, a bank account, or a car, for instance—so that he cannot waste them, hide them, or remove them from the state where the main lawsuit is taking place. The attached property stays in the custody of the court and is subject to orders of the court or to the final judgment in the main lawsuit. The purpose of the attachment is to force the defendant to appear in court and to put a LIEN on his property. It is a way of assuring the person bringing the lawsuit that if he wins his case, the defendant's property will be available to satisfy any judgment he might get.

Attachment seizes property while a lawsuit is in progress; *garnishment* is most often available only after a judgment in the main lawsuit has been made. As we will see later, however, this is not always the case. The purpose of garnishment is to enable a person who is owed money to lay claim to funds the debtor has coming to him from someone else. This third party is called a *garnishee*—a person who has money or property in his possession that belongs to the defendant or who owes the defendant a debt. For instance, if a loan company cannot collect a debt from a factory worker, and the loan company wins a judgment against him and garnishees his wages in order to get its money, the employer of the worker is the garnishee. The garnishee does not become a defendant himself, but under the garnishment he is responsible to answer for the money due to his employee.

■ **When the remedies may be used** Although garnishment can be used against a defendant's bank account, the most common application of the remedy is in the garnishment of wages. Pensions, however, usually cannot be garnisheed.

EXAMPLE A man was ordered to pay $125 a week as child support when he and his wife were divorced in Texas. He made the payments for a few months but then moved to Oklahoma and stopped paying. He obtained a job in Oklahoma and earned $400 a week. The woman took her judgment from the Texas divorce and filed it with other proper papers in a court in Oklahoma. The Oklahoma court entered a garnishment order in the amount of $125. Even though state law ordinarily limited the amount of garnishment to one-fourth of a defendant's earnings, garnishment of up to one-third of his earnings was permitted in some child-support cases. The effect of the garnishment was to order the man's employer to pay $125 of his wages each week to the mother rather than paying full wages.

If attachment is needed where a contract is concerned, the amount of damages must be easily arrived at.

EXAMPLE A man chartered a cargo ship for $30,000 and then failed to use the ship, causing it to sail unloaded. The shipowner was granted an attachment because his damages were easily fixed at $30,000 less what it would have cost him to load and unload the ship.

When a publisher sued a writer for $15,000—the sum advanced to him for a book he did not deliver by the agreed-upon date—the court ruled that a writ of attachment could be served on the writer.

Two other examples of easily identifiable damages are promissory notes, which promise to pay a definite amount of money on a specific day, and a contract fixing a certain amount for services, such as repairing a car. The same general rules relating to easily identifiable damages apply to garnishment.

Usually, attachment and garnishment cannot be had in actions for TORTS (civil wrongs). But there are states that now allow them in some cases.

EXAMPLE In New York, in an action involving injury to property, an attachment was granted when an occupant of the premises, having been told by the owner to leave, refused to move out his belongings. The fact that they were still on the premises was an injury to property, even though no physical harm had been done to the place.

■ **Persons entitled to the remedies** In most instances, any creditor may use the remedies if the statutes give him

---

WHAT YOU SHOULD KNOW ABOUT ATTACHMENT AND GARNISHMENT

■ Attachment is a court order bringing a debtor's assets under the control of the court—his bank account, boat, or car, for example—during a lawsuit brought by a creditor.

■ Garnishment enables the creditor to have access to property or money owed to the defendant, generally after the creditor has won his suit. If, for example, a loan company wins a judgment against you and garnishees

your wages, your employer must pay the loan company the court-ordered amounts out of your wages.

■ If you are the creditor, you have the right to resort to attachment and garnishment whether or not you live in the debtor's state.

■ Typical examples of attachable property are cars, tools, money, bank deposits, corporate stock, store merchandise, boats, properties inherited

under a will, and debts owed the defendant. Typical property exempt from attachment includes alimony, account books, and private papers.

■ Real estate may be attached if the creditor prefers, even if the debtor owns attachable personal property, such as jewelry or furniture.

■ If the defendant has a mortgage on his property, the unmortgaged amount may be attached.

grounds. Whether or not the creditor lives in the debtor's state or is a U.S. citizen usually does not matter.

■ **Persons subject to the remedies** The remedies are available against any individual or an ARTIFICIAL PERSON such as a corporation. Insane persons and children can have their property attached.

■ **Who can be made a garnishee** To be made a garnishee, the person must have property of the defendant in his possession, but states do not agree as to whether a spouse may be a garnishee. Usually, all corporations, except public corporations such as cities and villages, and all persons holding funds for legal reasons—such as trustees in BANKRUPTCY—can be garnishees. Check statutes to see who is eligible in your state.

■ **Grounds for attachment** The reason for obtaining an attachment is to protect the plaintiff if the defendant should leave the state, hide himself, conceal his property, use it all up, or do anything that will hurt the plaintiff's chances of getting his damages. If the defendant leaves the state, it must be clear that he has no intention of returning. In a case where a defendant was tricked into leaving, his property could not be attached. Any fraudulent disposition of property, no matter how small, justifies attachment if the plaintiff will be hurt by it. An attachment cannot be made on a defendant's property, however, if enough of it is still potentially available to the plaintiff.

EXAMPLE Let us say that a man owes $1,000, that he owns a O—* car worth $1,200, which he plans to give to a cousin in another state, and that he has $1,500 in a bank account. His car cannot be attached, because the money he has in the bank is more than enough to cover the debt. On the other hand, an insolvent or bankrupt person or corporation is usually not liable to attachment because nothing would be gained.

■ **Property subject to the remedies** Some examples of attachable property are cars, mechanic's tools, money, bank deposits, corporate stock, store merchandise, boats, trains, liquor, property inherited or received under a WILL, and a debt owed to the defendant.

The kinds of property exempt from attachment are alimony; account books and private papers (because their seizure would injure the defendant without benefiting the plaintiff); property in the process of being manufactured, such as disassembled minicalculators (because if attached it would be in such condition as to be practically valueless); property carried or worn by a person that could not be taken without an assault; and copyrights and literary property including unpublished manuscripts.

Nonexempt property of the defendant may be attached even if it is held by someone else, but someone else's property that the defendant is holding cannot be attached.

Real property may be attached if the plaintiff prefers, even if the defendant owns other property such as jewelry, paintings, or furniture. If the defendant has a MORTGAGE on his property, the unmortgaged amount may be attached. Property owned together with others can also be attached. See JOINT TENANCY; TENANCY IN COMMON.

Wages—a property that cannot be reached directly—are subject to garnishment rather than attachment.

■ **Writs required** Neither attachment nor garnishment can be had without a writ. A writ of attachment is issued by the court at the beginning of or during a suit. A writ of garnishment is usually issued by a court clerk.

■ **Custody and disposition of property** Attached property is controlled by the court and not the plaintiff. For example, a person who attaches land does not immediately become entitled to its possession or to the rents and profits from the land. The court holds the property to await the result of the main lawsuit and to satisfy any judgment resulting from the action. If the attached property is damaged during the period of attachment, the attaching officer, such as a sheriff or marshal, is responsible and not the plaintiff. For example, a sheriff attached a show dog and took possession of it. When the dog died because of his negligence, the sheriff was liable. The attachment of growing crops and livestock generally is different—they remain in the hands of their owner, and thus any negligence with respect to them is charged to him. The attaching officer has the right to possess the property attached and to be paid for any necessary expenses, which are usually paid by the defendant. The plaintiff, however, becomes liable for the expense of keeping the attached property if the lawsuit is dismissed, if the attachment is discharged, or if the defendant wins the main lawsuit.

The garnishee is liable for all of the defendant's property or money in his hands when the writ is served. Garnishment cannot begin before the main lawsuit starts, and it lasts until the writ is satisfied or is ended.

■ **Wrongful use of remedies** If either attachment or garnishment is not used as provided by statute, the person asking for the remedy is liable for any damages he causes the defendant.

■ **Federal law** The remedies of attachment and garnishment are harsh, and the pressure they put on a debtor or wage earner is enormous. If a storekeeper's goods are attached, he cannot conduct his business because he cannot touch, use, or sell the attached property. The same is true for a businessman's bank funds or a commuter's automobile or anyone's refrigerator, stove, or furniture.

Garnishment of wages is obviously just as harsh, if not more so. In 1969, in a case arising in California, the U.S. Supreme Court decided that except for extraordinary situations, a wage garnishment issued before the judgment in the main lawsuit is invalid unless the debtor is given notice and a hearing. It would probably be valid, however, if it excluded "necessities." Necessities are whatever is required by the defendant to live, work, support his family, or contest the lawsuit.

In addition to the protection this Supreme Court decision gives debtors against garnishment before judgment, the Federal Consumer Credit Protection Act does more. It restricts garnishment either to 25 percent of a person's disposable weekly earnings or to the amount by which his disposable weekly earnings exceed 30 times the federal minimum hourly wage then in effect, whichever is less. "Disposable earnings" are what is left over after taxes and other legally required deductions. If the minimum wage were $3 an hour, only disposable income over $90 a week ($3 × 30) could be garnisheed. If the debtor had $100 a week in disposable income, only $10 of it could be garnisheed because taking 25 percent of his disposable income would leave him with less than the $90 minimum.

Federal laws do not protect debtors against child- or wife-support orders, bankruptcy orders, or debts due for any state or federal tax. They do provide a criminal penalty for any employer who fires an employee because his earnings have been garnisheed for any one indebtedness. States can make laws that are easier on the debtor than the federal law, but they cannot pass laws that are harsher. In Chart 7 you will find the amount of income exempt from garnishment in each state. See the article PROVISIONAL REMEDY for other ways creditors can collect from consumer debtors.

attainder The extinction of civil rights that takes place when a criminal is sentenced to death. *Bills of attainder*—legislative acts that pronounce people guilty of crimes without trial or conviction according to the ordinary rules of procedure and sentence them to death and attainder—are forbidden by the U.S. Constitution.

attempt In civil matters an attempt is an intent combined with an act that goes beyond preparation but falls short of completion. In CRIMINAL LAW an attempt is an effort to commit a criminal offense that goes beyond mere preparation or planning and that will accomplish the crime if not prevented.

attest **1** Bear witness to. **2** Affirm to be true or genuine. **3** Act as a witness to. **4** Make a solemn declaration in words or writing to support a fact.

attestation The act of witnessing the signing of a document, such as a will, and, at the request of the person making the document, signing it as a witness.

attorney and client Strictly speaking, an attorney is an agent—someone who is appointed by a person to act for him—but the term is usually used to mean an attorney-at-law—someone who is appointed to act for another person in legal matters. An *attorney-at-law* is an officer of the court of justice whom you can employ to manage an ACTION (lawsuit) for you or to advise you on other legal matters, such as drawing up a will or deed. When an attorney is advising or acting for you, you are his client.

Terms that are sometimes used synonymously with "attorney" are lawyer, advocate, barrister (a term used in English law), counsel or counselor, proctor (in ADMIRALTY), and solicitor. An *attorney of record* is the attorney whose name is entered on the record of a suit as the attorney of a named party to that suit.

The *practice of law* embraces not only what an attorney does before a court but also everything else he does in connection with the case. It also includes giving legal advice and the preparation of legal documents.

A partnership may be formed between two or more attorneys, but not between an attorney and someone not authorized to practice law. This article discusses not only the office of attorney but, especially, the relationship between an attorney and his client, including their mutual rights, duties, and liabilities.

■ **Office of attorney** As an officer of the court, an attorney has an obligation to the public as well as to his client. Besides guarding his client's interests, he aids the court in seeing that proceedings before it are conducted in an orderly, impersonal, and fair manner.

Admission to the office There is no right to practice law; it is a privilege granted by the state. State legislatures decide who can practice law, and courts may also make rules for admission to the bar. Admission to the bar confers the authority, or license, to practice law. The power to admit someone to the bar belongs to the courts, which have the obligation to be reasonable and not arbitrary. For example, denial of admission to practice law for racial, religious, or political reasons would be invalid. Good moral character, especially honesty, is universally required. Citizenship used to be a requirement, but now permanent-resident aliens who meet the other qualifications may be admitted to the bar. Residency requirements, however, are generally valid. Study requirements, examinations, and possible clerkship requirements vary in, and are controlled by, the individual states, and attorneys admitted in one state may not practice law in another state without permission of the other state's authorities. Attorneys usually are required to take an oath of office.

Practicing without authority can be CONTEMPT of the court or even a crime.

EXAMPLE In Oregon, the lay author of a self-help legal O⊶✳ publication who gave legal advice to purchasers of his book when they consulted him in person was held to be unlawfully practicing law.

In New York, a law school graduate who had passed the bar examination and practiced law for more than 20 years without having appeared before a state committee on character and fitness, a prerequisite for admission to the bar, was found guilty of a misdemeanor.

A suit conducted by an unauthorized person on someone else's behalf is invalid and will be dismissed. But unless the court decides that the public welfare demands otherwise, a person who is not an attorney may represent himself in court. The wisdom of doing so has long been questionable, however. In the words of an old English proverb, "He who is his own lawyer has a fool for his client."

Disbarment Attorneys are admitted to the bar for life, but misconduct can bring suspension or disbarment as well as other appropriate punishment. As a rule, statutes regulate the courts as to when they can suspend or disbar. Generally, any conduct that would have prevented the individual's admission to the bar will be sufficient to suspend or disbar him. The criterion is whether or not the attorney is fit for the confidence and trust required in the attorney-and-client relationship. If an attorney commits a crime involving MORAL TURPITUDE he will be disbarred.

In many cases, the line to be drawn is not clear-cut and the individual facts must be carefully examined. An attorney can take a retainer fee from a person he knows is insane, but if instead of charging a normal fee he has the client turn over all his property, the attorney will be punished. An attorney usually may not represent two conflicting interests, except in some instances when both parties have full knowledge and give their consent. He may, for example, represent the buyer and the seller at a house closing or both husband and wife in an uncontested divorce action.

An attorney may not misappropriate or fail to account for the funds of his client. Conduct offensive to judges or other attorneys, such as disparaging them, or conduct that obstructs justice is punishable. Until recently, attorneys could not advertise to the public. ADVERTISING BY PROFESSIONALS is a changing area of the law, and it appears that soon there will be only minimal restrictions.

A disbarment proceeding is not the usual civil or criminal proceeding, but is rather a special legal action to protect the courts and the public from unfit attorneys. The right to bring charges against attorneys is not restricted to their clients; the courts may proceed on their own. Although disbarment of a lawyer is not necessarily final, reinstatement is difficult.

■ **Retainer and authority** A *retainer* is the act by which a client hires an attorney to manage an action for him or to advise him as counsel. The term also means the fee the client pays as a deposit on the attorney's services. Before an attorney may appear for a person, he must be employed by that person, and if he brings an action before he is hired, the client he purports to represent is not bound by the attorney's act. The contract between attorney and client is formed when the client asks the attorney for his services and the attorney accepts the request. To have an attorney-and-client relationship, the matter involved must be of a legal nature. An attorney is not a party to the lawsuits he brings on behalf of his clients. If he acts within the client's authority and wrongs a third person—makes slanderous statements about the other party in the suit, for example—the client may be liable to the third person for the wrong.

EXAMPLE Jennie Sumner was operating a bar when her liquor license was revoked because of a conviction for allowing lewd dancing on the premises. She started a lawsuit to regain the license on the ground that the lewdness statute violated her freedom of speech. When her attorney appeared in court, the judge issued an order prohibiting her from serving alcoholic beverages until the case was finished. She sold liquor anyway and, when she was cited for contempt, claimed that she had never found out about the order. The judge refused to accept this as a defense because notice to the attorney is notice to the client. Any other rule would be a hardship for the courts and other parties to lawsuits. They are entitled to rely on the attorney that a client picks for himself. If an attorney does in fact fail to pass the notice along to his client, the client can hold his attorney liable and sue him.

Information (NOTICE) given to an attorney is considered notice to the client whether or not the attorney actually passes along the information.

An attorney's authority extends to whatever he was specifically authorized to do by his client and to whatever is necessary to accomplish those purposes. Moreover, he may exercise any powers his client has told others he has. In this respect he is an agent of his client. See AGENCY. The client controls the subject matter of the suit, but the attorney controls the way in which a case is conducted. Most jurisdictions, however, recognize the client's ultimate power to discharge the attorney and to dismiss, discontinue, or settle his action even over the attorney's objections. Some examples of what an attorney can do after being retained are to make an APPEARANCE, to receive and accept papers and notices, to change the VENUE, to enter or take a dismissal or

DISCONTINUANCE that does not prevent the bringing of another suit for the same reason, to issue an attachment (see ATTACHMENT AND GARNISHMENT), and in some jurisdictions to submit a pending case to ARBITRATION.

If a client chooses to ratify an unauthorized act of his attorney, such as starting an action without his permission, he must ratify all of it. The client may ratify specifically or by failing to object to what his attorney did within a reasonable time after finding out about it.

Usually an attorney does not have to prove his authority. There is a presumption that he is authorized to act for a client he claims to represent in all matters involved in the action. He may be forced to show his authority, however, if an objection is made in court.

When the litigation for which an attorney was retained ends with a JUDGMENT (decision), most of his powers end. His only remaining authority, unless other specific authority has been given to him, is to take the necessary steps to make the judgment effective and to enforce it, or to relieve his client from its effect if it is adverse.

EXAMPLE Walter lost his case. The mortgage was foreclosed, and the judge ordered that his house be sold to pay what he still owed on it. His attorney would need new authority to appeal the case, but his present authority would continue for him to defend Walter's rights during the judicial sale.

The defeated client's attorney needs new authority from his client to appeal a court decision, but the victorious client's attorney may defend an appeal without new authority. If the suit is a claim for money, the attorney on the winning side may collect it for his client, but unless expressly authorized to do otherwise, he must collect it in full, in cash, and turn it over to his client. Usually an attorney cannot delegate his authority or employ assistants in a manner that binds the client unless he has the consent of his client.

Withdrawal by the attorney An attorney in a lawsuit cannot withdraw from a case without justifiable cause unless his client consents. Even with justifiable cause he must notify his client and receive the court's permission. Justifiable cause could be found if the client's conduct degrades or humiliates the attorney, lowers the standard of ethics, or destroys the confidence between the attorney and his client. A client's refusal to increase the attorney's fee is not justifiable cause.

Dismissal by the client The client ordinarily may change attorneys at any stage of the proceedings unless it unduly harms the other party or interferes with the administration of justice. Your opponent may enter an objection to dismissal of your attorney if that prejudices his rights. That may be unlikely during an early stage of the dispute, but it depends on the circumstances. You cannot dismiss your attorney just to cause delay and harass your adversary. He has a right to object where it will harm his case. If your opponent objects, application must be made to the court, a formal order of substitution obtained, and notice of the substitution of attorney given to the other party.

Other means of terminating The attorney-client relationship may also be ended by agreement of the parties, the attorney's disbarment, death or insanity of the attorney or client, anything that makes it impossible for the attorney to serve his client, and anything that ends the subject matter of the employment, such as the settlement of the lawsuit out of court. If the attorney is a partner in a law firm and the partnership is dissolved, this does not end the attorney-and-client relationship.

■ **Duties and liabilities of attorney to client** Not only must an attorney exercise reasonable care and diligence and possess the legal knowledge ordinarily possessed by members of the profession, but he must also conduct himself as a FIDUCIARY—a person having a position of the highest trust and confidence. In all his relations and dealings with his client it is his duty to act with the utmost honesty, good faith, fairness, integrity, and fidelity, and if he does not, he is strictly liable to his client.

Even after the relationship of attorney and client ends, the attorney cannot acquire an interest adverse to his client by breaching a confidence or using information obtained because of their former relationship.

EXAMPLE An attorney would be behaving unethically if he O— ✳ bought property worth 10 times its purchase price that he had advised his client to sell to keep it from being included in a property settlement in the client's divorce action. The former attorney for the president of the Fox Manufacturing Company is also behaving unethically if, upon becoming affiliated with the Ace Manufacturing Company, he reveals to Ace details about Fox's company that became known to him while representing Fox.

With these exceptions, an attorney is free to get an interest, title, or claim against his former client. If an attorney does have dealings with him, such transactions will be suspiciously and carefully examined for fairness and honesty. The attorney must show that no undue influence was used and that the former client received the same benefits and advantages as he would have if he were a stranger. For example, an attorney who is administering an estate cannot arrange privately to buy a house from the estate at a low price. However, an attorney who once represented a client in a divorce proceeding is not precluded from buying that client's house two years later at a tax sale because anyone can find out about a public tax sale. If the former client had independent legal advice on any transaction, that is usually enough to meet the attorney's burden to prove fairness.

Accounting Another duty of the attorney is to give the client a full, detailed, and accurate account of all money and property he handled for him. He must promptly pay over all funds or property to which the client is entitled after the deduction of the attorney's proper fees and charges. The client is also entitled to anything the attorney has acquired in violation of his duties to him, such as money the attorney took from a trust fund left for the client's benefit or any secret profit he made at the client's expense.

EXAMPLE In Delaware, an attorney for a couple hunting for O— ✳ a house suggested that they buy one from him. He then purchased a house and sold it to them, concealing from them the amount of his profit from the transaction. The court ruled that it was the attorney's duty to make full restitution of his profit to his clients.

If an attorney does not promptly pay over all funds to the client, he may have to pay him interest. The attorney is liable for fraud, unless the client caused him to commit it,

and is usually liable for any damages caused to the client by his negligence—the fine levied for the late filing of an estate-tax return, for example.

Professional advice and activities If an attorney's knowledge of the law is not equal to that ordinarily possessed by other attorneys, he is liable for any loss resulting from it. Attorneys might incur liability to their clients by giving improper advice, failing to use care and diligence in the collection of claims, improperly preparing documents, conducting the litigation carelessly, and performing any unauthorized act that injured the client. They may also be liable for losses to clients because of acts of associates, partners, or clerks.

Malpractice A client can sue his attorney for failing to perform his duty. The client may recover an amount equal to what he would have received if the attorney had not failed to perform his duty. However, the client may have to prove that he would have won his case if the attorney had not been negligent.

■ **Compensation of an attorney** Where statutes exist, they control the compensation of an attorney, and, with few exceptions, the person who hired him is responsible for payment. Unless he intended to perform his services without charge, an attorney is entitled to be paid for them if he rendered them in good faith, even though his client received little or no benefit from them.

Temporary absence from his client's trial, or acting for other parties whose interests do not conflict with the client's, does not negate an attorney's right to compensation, but fraud or misconduct, on the other hand, may. An attorney whose employment ends before he completes his task—by agreement with the client or by operation of law, such as when he becomes a judge and can no longer act as an attorney—is entitled to be paid for services rendered. Death of either the attorney or the client usually does not affect the right to payment. In some jurisdictions, if the attorney is discharged for a good reason or if he abandons his employment without good reason, he is not permitted to recover at all. When he is assigned to represent a poor person in a criminal trial, he is paid as provided by statute, and when there is no provision for payment, he must sometimes perform his services without compensation. Division of fees (fee-splitting) among attorneys is proper.

Contingent fees A contingent fee depends on the success of the services to be performed. A contingent-fee contract, which usually gives the attorney a percentage of the recovery, may not prohibit a settlement of the case by the client, but it may specify what the client is to pay the attorney if he does settle with the opposition.

EXAMPLE Andy was injured when his car was struck by a O— ✳ truck belonging to the telephone company. He retained an attorney to sue the company and agreed to pay the attorney one-third of any actual recovery. The case was complicated and the attorney worked very hard to collect evidence showing that the driver of the truck had caused the accident. Andy had been injured badly, but he recovered completely in about two years. When the case had dragged on for another two years, he became discouraged. The attorney told him to hang on because he was sure to win over $100,000. Nevertheless, Andy went to the attorney for the phone company and agreed to settle

YOU AND YOUR LAWYER

HERBERT S. DENENBERG
Former Professor of Law, Temple University;
Former Commissioner of Insurance,
Commonwealth of Pennsylvania

You do not need this advice if you already know what a lawyer does, when to use one, how to find a good one, and how to make sure the lawyer will do a good job for you for a reasonable price. Most people do not know very much about lawyers. You will wish you did if you ever have to hire one.

Contrary to popular belief, Perry Mason is not a typical lawyer. Most lawyers—or attorneys, as they are known in their own profession—rarely go to court. The practice of law usually involves giving advice, preparing legal papers, or arguing something for somebody else—all for a fee.

For most people, expense and mistrust are the biggest obstacles to getting effective legal services. And their instincts may be right. Chesterfield Smith, past president of the American Bar Association, has said that there is an incompetent "fringe" of 20 to 25 percent of the lawyers now practicing whom he "would not trust to do anything." If Mr. Smith is anywhere near right, you may have a hard time finding a lawyer you can trust. This article will tell you what to look for and what to look out for when you have to deal with a lawyer.

When should you get a lawyer?

Many people go to lawyers when they could help themselves or get help from someone else for less money. But when they really need a lawyer, many people go too late. Here are some guidelines.

Do not hire a lawyer if you do not need one. Many problems can be solved properly only with the help of a competent lawyer. Nevertheless, before running to a lawyer, you should make sure you have a problem that needs one. You should at least think about solving your problem yourself or with the help of a competent professional who is not a lawyer. For example:

■ If you think you have been cheated by a businessman, complain to your local Better Business Bureau or your local or state consumer protection agency.

■ A good insurance agent, real estate agent, stockbroker, banker, or certified public accountant may be able to provide some of the same services as a lawyer for less money or can tell you that you have the kind of problem only a lawyer can solve.

■ Marriage counselors and clergymen can often help.

■ Social welfare agencies can often help solve problems with legal aspects.

■ You may also want to sue on your own in a small claims court, which is designed to handle minor disputes without your having to employ a lawyer.

When you do need a lawyer, get one. As a general rule, you should consider consulting a lawyer regarding major life events, such as serious accidents; deaths; changes in family status, such as marriage, divorce, or adoption; substantial changes in financial status; acquisition, sale, or loss of valuable property; business transactions; criminal or civil lawsuits.

When you need a lawyer, hire one as soon as possible. A lawyer can usually help you more if you see him or her before you conclude an important deal or before you make a statement to the police or an insurance investigator. When in doubt, consult a lawyer. With legal problems, just as with medical problems, it is better to be safe than sorry. And to be safe, the sooner you see a lawyer, the better.

Types of legal services

There are many things to consider in choosing a lawyer. Are you eligible for free legal advice? Can a big firm handle your small problem? Should you go to a general practitioner or a specialist? You may have a number of options.

Public legal assistance　Because lawyers are costly, public legal assistance programs have been established to provide legal services for people who cannot afford to hire a lawyer. There are public defenders that represent criminal defendants and organizations such as Legal Aid and legal assistance offices that handle civil matters. Look in the Yellow Pages under Legal Services or contact your local bar association to find the names and locations of the free legal service organizations in your area, or call the county courthouse or the district attorney's office. Eligibility guidelines vary depending on where you live, the size of your family, and how much you earn. But if you think you cannot afford legal service, you may want to contact one of these agencies before going to a private lawyer.

Government lawyers　As a taxpayer, you are already paying for hundreds of lawyers on the payrolls of local, state, and federal governments. For example, the Commonwealth of Pennsylvania has more than 450 lawyers, assigned to such agencies as its Department of Justice, Bureau of Consumer Protection, Human Relations Commission, Department of Environmental Resources, and the Insurance Department. When you have a legal problem that involves a government service or government-regulated industry, such as insurance, take your problem first to the relevant agency before going to your own lawyer.

Nonprofit organizations　Another thing to consider before looking for a lawyer you will have to pay is the possibility that your problem may be of interest to an organization such as the Environmental Defense Fund, the National Association for the Advancement of Colored People (NAACP), or the American Civil Liberties Union. If so, you may get free representation. These organizations are listed in the telephone book.

Private lawyers　Basically, there are two types of private lawyers—individual lawyers who practice alone and group practitioners. Individual practition-

ers account for half of this country's 500,000 lawyers. Group practices are either informal arrangements in which two or more lawyers share office space to reduce operating costs or formal arrangements in which a group of lawyers is organized as a partnership or professional corporation.

The partnerships and corporations are called law firms. Approximately 30 percent of the lawyers practice as profit-sharing partners or as salaried associates of law firms. There are small firms with two or three partners and large firms with more than 100 lawyers.

As a practical matter, most small firms deal with their clients in much the same way as individual lawyers. They engage in general practice and accept employment regarding any kind of legal matter; know a lot about some areas of the law, a little about most areas, and nothing at all about others; give clients personal attention; and can handle personal matters better than complicated commercial transactions.

Large firms may provide a wide range of legal services through the firm, although each individual lawyer in the firm does not engage in general practice. The larger the firm, the more the specialization within it. Matters are assigned to the firm member with the most expertise in each field. Large firms give their clients less personal attention—the first lawyer you talk to may not be the one doing your work. They are better equipped to handle commercial matters than personal problems such as divorces, adoptions, and juvenile court cases. If handled at all by a large firm, personal matters are usually assigned to the youngest, least-experienced lawyers.

Sources for finding a lawyer

The ability, intelligence, and training of lawyers varies greatly. Picking one from the Yellow Pages of the telephone book is like playing Russian roulette with your legal rights.

In a small community, everyone usually has a pretty good idea whom he can trust and who is competent. But in larger communities, particularly in big cities, it is much more difficult to know who is dishonest or incompetent. Following these tips will improve your odds of finding a good lawyer.

(1) *Do not rely on general reference sources.* A general source cannot evaluate your specific problem; yet your problem is the most important thing to be considered when you start looking for a lawyer.

The *Martindale-Hubbell Law Directory,* found in most libraries, lists most of the lawyers in the United States and gives a rating for some of them. The ratings are based on confidential recommendations from other lawyers and judges in the area where the lawyers practice. The publishers of *Martindale-Hubbell* do not ask clients what they think of their lawyers. Moreover, most general sources do not attempt to evaluate the lawyer's scholastic achievement, the types of clients he represents, the kinds of cases he handles, or his community activities.

Legal directories such as *Martindale-Hubbell* are designed for use mainly by lawyers. In recent years, bar associations and consumer groups have started to publish detailed directories of lawyers for use by the average client. If such a directory is available in your area, it may be a useful source of information.

(2) *Do not rely on lawyer referral services.* Although most communities have lawyer referral services that can put you in touch with a lawyer, local bar associations usually compile the list of lawyers who can be contacted through the service. Because the association represents all of the local lawyers, it usually likes to list all of them, good and bad alike, although some good lawyers prefer not to be placed on the list. In addition, the referral services generally use nonlegal personnel who do not take enough information from you to send you to the appropriate lawyer. When you use a referral service, therefore, there is no guarantee that you will be sent to a good lawyer or to one qualified to handle your problem.

Some referral services do make an effort to screen lawyers who go on their lists. Ask the people at your local referral service about the criteria they use for listing lawyers. The more rigorous the criteria, the more useful the lawyer referral service can be.

(3) *Do not rely on anyone who gets a fee for referral.* Real estate agents, insurance agents, and certified public accountants sometimes fall into this category. For example, lawyer Smith will send anyone who needs an accountant to Jones (who is a certified public accountant) and vice versa. Arrangements like this are good for Smith and Jones, but can hurt you if Smith and Jones are not the right professionals for your needs. For similar reasons, especially in personal injury cases, doctors, dentists, and druggists are not always the most reliable sources.

(4) *Talk to people who are honest and knowledgeable.* If you ask a friend to give you the name of a lawyer, ask him for the name of one with whom your friend has had a good personal experience. If your friend has found a lawyer that he or she trusts, you are on the right track, especially if your legal problem is like the one the lawyer handled for your friend. Even if your problem is different, a lawyer who is trustworthy will tell you if he is not equipped to handle your problem and will send you to a good lawyer who can.

(5) *Talk to any professional person you know and trust.* A professional is a good person to ask about the right lawyer for you, provided there is no possible conflict of interest, as discussed in Point 3.

(6) *If you work for a company that retains a lawyer, try to get his name.* This lawyer may become your lawyer, or he may refer you to another lawyer. Because you are a fellow employee of the company that pays him, you are more likely to get good advice from the company lawyer than from a lawyer with whom you have no connection.

(7) *Company lawyers (house counsels) may give you objective advice on finding a lawyer.* Lawyers who are not engaged in private practice are likely to be impartial in judging lawyers who are. House counsel and lawyers employed by a local, state, or federal government agency work with lawyers who are in private practice, and usually know some good private lawyers whom they can suggest.

(8) *Shop around.* If you do not have a definite lead from a person you trust, get a few leads. Talk to a few lawyers yourself (on a free get-acquainted basis), and then decide who is the best lawyer for you.

Cross-examine your lawyer: questions every client should ask

Most lawyers will meet with you on a get-acquainted basis without charging a fee. If the first lawyer you call refuses to agree to this, call another one. One of the most important things is to find a lawyer you can trust. You want to find someone to whom you can talk and who will listen to you. Whether you go to an individual lawyer or to a law firm, do not be afraid to ask these questions:

(1) What is the history of your practice or firm?

(2) What kinds of clients do you have—mostly individuals or big businesses?

(3) Will we have a long and compatible relationship? As difficult as it is to find a lawyer you can trust, you may want to get one close to your own age. Age has impact on attitudes, and you want a lawyer whose attitudes and philosophy are similar to your own. After developing a good working relationship

of trust and confidence, you do not want you lawyer to die 30 years before you.

(4) Do you have enough experience to handle my kind of case?

(5) With whom do you consult on legal questions you are uncertain about and how often?

(6) Will you give me a full and convincing argument of the other side of my case and will you tell me how you will approach my side of the case?

(7) Will you talk to me in plain English I can understand instead of using "legalese"?

(8) Will you keep me informed in writing about all phases of my case?

(9) Do you have any conflict of interest that I should know about before I hire you?

(10) How much personal attention will I get? Are you the person in the firm who will actually be doing my legal work?

(11) Although you are a general practitioner, what is your area of specialty? Will you send me to someone else if you do not think you are capable of handling my problem?

There is a tendency in law, as in medicine, toward increasing specialization. The *Martindale-Hubbell Law Directory* notes any areas of specialization permitted by the law of the state in which the lawyer practices. Most lawyers, however, still say they are general practitioners. One of the things you must consider in choosing a lawyer is whether your problem requires the attention of a specialist. When you are evaluating a lawyer, do not assume he is a good lawyer simply because he is a specialist. Regardless of any claim or certification of specialization, you should make your own independent judgment.

Talking to your lawyer about legal problems and fees

Too few lawyer-client relationships are good ones. The essence of a good lawyer-client relationship is communication. You and your lawyer should always know where you stand on your legal problem and on fees and expenses.

Remember that you hired the lawyer and that he works for you. You are not at your lawyer's mercy. If you are not happy with the service you are getting, tell him about it. And if you are still not satisfied, consider firing him. But always keep in mind that lawyers often must say things clients do not like to hear. Sometimes the best advice is the most difficult to listen to.

Do not expect free advice. If you telephone your lawyer for his opinion or for information, be prepared to pay for it. He is giving you service, just as if you had come to his office. As Abraham Lincoln observed, "A lawyer's time is his stock in trade."

There cannot always be a black-and-white answer to a legal question, so you should not expect simple answers to complicated questions. It has been said, "Nothing in the law is certain but the expense."

Do not withhold information or slant the things you tell your lawyer. Tell the truth! Try to give him an objective statement of all the facts. It is your lawyer's job to present them in the best possible light.

If your lawyer is preparing a document such as a will or contract, give him the facts and your wishes in writing. Your written instructions will make his job easier and your bill cheaper.

Ask for copies of all correspondence and documents prepared on your behalf. This is a good way to keep abreast of what your lawyer is doing and to be sure he is doing what you want. It also tends to make your lawyer give better service.

Keep your lawyer advised of all new developments. This will help him handle your case competently and keep him from doing unnecessary work—work that you will have to pay for.

You should insist on a complete, itemized bill. If the costs seem high, ask your lawyer to show you the filing fee list from the court or agency charging the fee and ask to see a receipt. You should also be content that the expenses incurred on your behalf were necessary and reasonable. Do not be afraid to ask for an itemized list of the telephone calls made by your lawyer, if you think the charges are too high. And do not hesitate to question the amount you are asked to reimburse him for photocopying or other expenses if you think they are unreasonable.

When you go to a lawyer who cannot or will not help you but offers to refer you to another lawyer, always ask if there is a referral fee or other charge involved and inquire about the other lawyer's qualifications. Sometimes a lawyer who cannot help you will not charge you directly for the initial time spent discussing your problem, but he may get a referral fee, or similar payment otherwise described, from the lawyer he recommends, who may pass along the cost of the fee to you. To avoid this, ask the first lawyer if there will be any charge at his regular rate for the initial discussion and tell him that you are not going to permit the second lawyer to pay a referral fee. Ask each lawyer you see for an itemized bill and pay each one a reasonable fee yourself. Then remember to tell the lawyer to whom you are sent that no referral fee should be paid to the lawyer you saw first.

The American Bar Association's Code of Professional Responsibility provides that lawyers should not divide legal fees with other lawyers outside their firm, unless the other lawyers are employed with the consent of the client and unless the division of fees is based on services actually performed and responsibility assumed. In any event, the total fees paid to all lawyers may not exceed "reasonable compensation for all legal services they rendered the client."

Some states have adopted their own division-of-fee rules, but usually with similar limitations.

Handling the subject of legal fees

Before your lawyer does any work for you, reach a clear understanding about his legal fees. Some of the biggest problems between lawyers and clients arise over money; many of these problems could be avoided if they would discuss fees before any work is done. Once you have agreed on a fee, ask your lawyer for a letter that states the type of service he has agreed to provide and his actual or estimated charges. Many lawyers will do this without being asked.

The following are the different types of fee arrangements you should know about when you discuss the subject with your lawyers.

Contingent fees In some cases you may be able to arrange to pay a lawyer only if his efforts on your behalf are successful. Such an agreement is called a contingent-fee arrangement, and the fee is usually a percentage of the amount the lawyer wins for you. Since contingent fees can range as high as 60 percent of the amount recovered, you should try to negotiate the amount of the contingent fee. The bigger the potential recovery, the lower the contingent fee should be in percentage terms.

Under most contingent-fee agreements, lawyers get one-third of the recovery, whether it is obtained through negotiations out-of-court or a lawsuit argued in court. The wise client, therefore, will try to arrange a smaller contingent fee (as low as 15 percent) in the event that his claim is settled quickly by negotiation.

What many people do not realize about negligence cases (the cases that are most commonly taken by lawyers on a contingent-fee arrangement) is that most of them can be and are settled out of court—a less costly procedure than going to trial.

In a contingent agreement, insist that expenses be taken off the top before the lawyer's fee is deducted. This suggestion is somewhat complicated but can save you a lot of money. Expenses incurred by a lawyer are always paid by the client—win, lose, or draw. Under the usual one-third contingent-fee agreement, if your case is settled or won after a trial, you pay the expenses and get two-thirds of the total recovery. Your lawyer gets one-third of the recovery. In the following example, taking expenses off the top saved the client $333.

EXPENSES OFF THE TOP		EXPENSES AFTER DEDUCTION OF FEE	
Recovery	$10,000	Recovery	$10,000
Less expenses	1,000	Less ⅓ for	
Balance	9,000	lawyer	3,333
Less ⅓ for		Balance	6,667
lawyer	3,000	Less expenses	1,000
For client	6,000	For client	5,667

Retainers Be careful when you hear the word "retainer." First of all, some lawyers ask for a retainer when they really mean a down payment against whatever their total fees turn out to be. A real retainer is likely to cover most of the legal services received by a client. A down payment will not; it generally will cover only one specific service to be performed. Secondly, you cannot assume that you are entitled to certain legal services just because you pay a retainer. A retainer is based on an estimate of the time to be spent by your lawyer, the complexity of your problem, and the potential amount of money involved. If the time spent exceeds the lawyer's estimate, under most retainer arrangements you will still have to pay for all of the time he actually expended. So if you are considering a retainer relationship, find out in advance exactly what legal services are covered by it.

Hourly rates Negotiate with your lawyer regarding his hourly rate. In most cases, an agreement to pay a lawyer for his time at his regular hourly rate is most likely to produce a reasonable fee. Although they do not like to do it, most lawyers can usually predict in advance how much time they are likely to spend on your case. How much a lawyer actually asks for an hour of his time is up to him. How much his time is worth to you is up to you. Do not be afraid to negotiate with your lawyer regarding his hourly rate. And do not hesitate to shop around.

Even if you cannot predict in advance exactly how much time it is going to take a lawyer to handle your problem, it is best to discuss his fee in terms of his regular hourly billing rate, even if you later decide on another basis for computing the fee.

Always ask for a time estimate and for periodic revisions of it at various stages in your case. Many lawyers will gladly give you regular reports on how much time they have spent on your case so that you can know how much you owe them so far.

Fixed fees The most predictable fee arrangement is one in which the client agrees in advance to pay a fixed amount for certain legal services—for instance, $50 for preparation of a deed—no matter how long it takes. But fixed-amount arrangements, like contingent-fee arrangements, may bear no reasonable relationship to the amount of time actually spent by the lawyer in performing the service.

Getting what you pay for You should always find out whose time you are paying for. Make sure you are not paying a partner's hourly rate for the work of an associate (a lawyer who has less experience than a partner), a paralegal assistant (someone who is not a lawyer but who has some legal skills), or an automatic memory typewriter. A partner's time is usually worth more than an associate's because he or she can usually do more legal work better in less time. On the other hand, most uncomplicated legal matters can be handled well and for less money by less-experienced lawyers. You may be able to get four or five hours of an associate's time for $100 whereas an experienced partner can charge $100 for just one hour. A paralegal assistant may get $7.50 an hour.

Also, bcause the practice of law is repetitious, standard form documents have been devised. Many firms produce contracts and wills less expensively by using automatic memory typewriters. You are entitled to know how much of your lawyer's personal time you are actually getting for your money.

Legal insurance

Legal services can be provided for less money on a group basis rather than on an individual one. Some legal cooperatives have been formed in an attempt to provide legal services on a group basis.

In 1976 Congress passed a law that enables employers to make contributions to trust funds that can pay for legal services, just as they now do for medical services. This has increased the demand for and availability of legal insurance, and you may want to ask you employer, union, or insurance agent about it.

What to do if you are not satisfied with your lawyer

There are bound to be many unhappy clients who feel that their lawyer is incompetent, dishonest, or both. If you fall into this category, try to figure out why you are not satisfied with your lawyer. Poor attitude and poor performance are both good reasons for being unhappy with your lawyer. But do not blame your lawyer for everything. Remember, one side in a lawsuit must always lose.

If your lawyer does not pay attention to your initial complaint, complain some more. If he still does not respond satisfactorily, you should seriously consider getting another lawyer and firing yours. But first you should consult with another lawyer—to make sure your case will not be hurt in the switch. Describe your legal problem to the second lawyer before telling him of your complaint about your lawyer. If you start by complaining, you may have trouble getting another lawyer.

If you think a lawyer has been dishonest, incompetent, or has given you miserable service, you can and should complain to the bar association or to the specialized agency in your state established to handle complaints about lawyers. It may be called a Disciplinary Board of the Supreme Court (of your state) or by another similar name. Your bar association or a consumer protection agency can direct you to the best place to register your complaint. It probably will not do much good, but it will aggravate the lawyer and may make you feel better. You can also tell your friends about the miserable service you have received—and your local newspaper.

Many lawyers carry professional liability coverage known as malpractice insurance. Generally, it covers the lawyer's liability for negligent acts or omissions, but not for dishonest or criminal acts. So if your lawyer forgets to file an important paper with a court and it costs you money, think about suing him for your money or getting him to file a malpractice claim. Regarding dishonest or criminal acts, treat your lawyer as you would any other citizen—go to the police or to your local district attorney.

everything for $5,000. He had a right to do this even though it prevented his attorney from collecting a fee of perhaps more than $30,000. Andy's agreement specified that where he settled prematurely, he had to pay his attorney an hourly rate for the time spent on the case so far. Therefore, he ended up paying the attorney $4,800.

Such contracts are valid if they are reasonable and fair to the client. In a New York case the court found a contract reasonable that gave the attorney the entire recovery as a fee if his client accepted a settlement for a small sum. When a contingent-fee contract exists and the case is not successful, the attorney cannot recover the reasonable value of his services. If, however, the client dismisses the suit without receiving any recovery, the attorney may sue for damages or for the value of his services. The contingent fee must be computed on the amount of actual recovery and not on the amount of the verdict.

EXAMPLE Sylvia hired an attorney to represent her in her O—* action for divorce against her husband. Since she had no savings, she agreed to pay the attorney 20 percent of the value of any property she received as settlement in the lawsuit. The judge added up all the property that Sylvia and her husband had accumulated during their marriage and awarded her property worth $30,000, and he also ruled that Sylvia's husband was responsible for paying $10,000 worth of debts the family had. The value of this decision was $40,000, but Sylvia paid her attorney $6,000 based on the value of the property she actually received.

If the contingency the contract is based on does occur, the right to the fee is fixed even if the attorney or the client dies. If the client settles the case, and the result is substantially what the contract between the attorney and client contemplated, the attorney receives the fee agreed upon.

Lack of agreement   When there is no agreement on the fee, the attorney's fee is measured by the reasonable value of his services. When there is a disagreement, it is decided by the court. Once an attorney's fee is fixed, he may recover interest if the client delays paying him. It is the usual practice for an attorney to take the amount due him for fees from funds in his hands that belong to the client. An unpaid attorney may sue for his money.

Attorneys' liens   A lien is a claim on property for the payment of a debt, obligation, or duty. Two types of LIENS are usually available to attorneys, the retaining lien and the charging lien. The *retaining lien* is the attorney's right to keep a client's documents, money, or other property that comes into his hands because of his professional relationship with his client. The *charging lien* is his right to have moneys due him for services in a particular suit secured by the judgment or the recovery in the suit. Unless the contract between the attorney and the client provides for a charging lien, the attorney does not possess it. The term does not have to be used in the contract, but it must be clear that the attorney is to be paid out of the money from the judgment.

A retaining lien can be used not only for payments due to the attorney for a particular case but also for money the client owes him for other services. The charging lien can be used only to pay fees for the particular suit in which the judgment is obtained, and it goes into effect when the

judgment is recovered. Attorneys' liens for compensation exist until they are satisfied or released.

■ **Privileged communications**   Both at common law and under present statutes, confidential information communicated in the course of professional employment between an attorney and his client may not be divulged by the attorney without the consent of his client. As a rule, the privilege applies if (1) the person asserting the privilege is, or is seeking to become, a client, (2) the attorney is a member of the bar and acting as an attorney when receiving the communication, and (3) the communication is related for the purpose of obtaining an opinion on the law or some legal proceeding and not for the purpose of committing a crime or TORT (a civil wrong).

Purpose   This privilege—a very old one—represents an exception to the rule that every person is liable to give testimony on all facts sought in a court of justice. It exists for two reasons: to prevent the client's disclosures from being used against him in controversies with third persons and to insure freedom in communications between attorney and client so that the attorney may act with a complete understanding of the matters in which he is employed.

Existence of the relationship   The mere fact that a person is an attorney does not mean that every communication to him is privileged. In order for the privilege to apply, the relationship of attorney and client must actually exist at the time when the communication is made, or the party making the communication must believe that the relationship exists. This is the case even when the attorney is not paid a retainer or does not charge a fee for his advice. On the other hand, if someone does not recognize the lawyer as his attorney the communication is not privileged, and it does not become privileged because the person later employs the attorney in the matter to which the communication pertains. If a person consults an attorney with the thought of employing him, any information acquired by the attorney during the interview is privileged, even though employment does not result, but information given to an attorney after he has told a person he will not represent him is not privileged.

Third persons   A communication made between attorney and client in the presence of a third person is not privileged unless the third person is the agent of either party—such as a private detective. Conversations in the attorney's presence between a client and a third person, or between two clients whose legal problems are unrelated, are not privileged either. Even though the attorney and client are speaking confidentially and without intending anyone to hear, a bystander or even an eavesdropper who overhears the conversation may testify as to what passed.

On the other hand, confidential communications by the client to the attorney's clerk and communications by the attorney to an associate are privileged. Similarly, the attorney's confidential secretary and his stenographer may not testify to matters learned because of their positions, and the privilege has also been held to extend to communications between the attorney and the spouse of the client.

Matters included   A communication between attorney and client must relate to the subject matter of the employment in order to be privileged. Because the privilege pertains only to the subject matter of the case, the client's identity, the terms of the employment, and the fee to be paid are usually not privileged.

Although a client may refuse to state whether he communicated certain facts to his attorney, the fact that the attorney communicated with his client, and the date he did so, are not privileged. Neither, ordinarily, are statements made by a client to his attorney that are intended to be communicated to others—the adverse party, for example—and communications made by an attorney to his client at the request of the adverse party or his attorney.

Confidential documents such as letters, personal records, and medical reports passing between attorney and client are privileged, and neither the attorney nor the client may be compelled to disclose or produce them. If, however, documents, such as accounting records, are not privileged while in the client's possession, he cannot make them privileged by placing them with his attorney. The attorney can be compelled to produce any paper, record, or document in his possession if the client himself could be compelled to produce it. An attorney may be compelled to identify a document as one he has witnessed or prepared, but he may be protected from disclosing its contents.

The privilege of nondisclosure between attorney and client does not extend to communications concerning proposed infractions of the law, such as fraud or the future commission of a crime. The privilege is not a cloak or shield for the perpetration of a civil wrong or a crime. Communications relating to fraud or crime committed in the past, however, are privileged.

EXAMPLE When a New York attorney was told by a client O—* on trial for murder that he had committed two murders not related to the one for which he was being tried, the attorney did not pass this information on to the authorities. The New York State Bar Committee on Professional Ethics gave as its opinion that the attorney had acted properly.

Termination The termination of the attorney-client relationship does not destroy the privilege for matters that occurred while the relationship existed. Even the client's death will not destroy the privilege.

attorney general

attorney general The Attorney General of the United States is the chief law officer of the federal government. He is the head of the Department of Justice, appointed by the President, and a member of the Cabinet. "Attorney general" is also the title used to designate the chief law officer of the various state governments. The powers and duties of attorneys general are principally executive and administrative and are regulated by state constitutions and statutes.

The Attorney General of the United States supervises the conduct of all suits brought by or against the United States and advises the President and the heads of the other departments of the government.

Furnishing legal opinions to governmental officers is a duty common to all attorneys general. In some states, the officer seeking the opinion is compelled to follow it, but in many others he may treat it only as advice.

As the chief legal representative of the state, the attorney general institutes all legal proceedings to protect the public interest and defends all actions affecting it. If he has any

conflict as to what to do, he must choose whatever action is best for the public.

attorney's lien See ATTORNEY AND CLIENT.

attractive nuisance doctrine A legal principle used in some states that says a person who possesses dangerous property that might reasonably be expected to attract children must keep that property in such a way that children will not be hurt by it. The owner is liable for damages even if the children are injured while trespassing. Your backyard swimming pool is an attractive nuisance (it should be enclosed) and so is the car in your driveway if you have left your keys in it. And a car with the keys inside has been declared an attractive NUISANCE even when parked on a downtown street. It is NEGLIGENCE to create or maintain an attractive nuisance.

auctions and auctioneers An *auction* is a public sale of property to the highest bidder by a person authorized to conduct such a sale, who is the *auctioneer*. A *bid* is an offer to pay a specific price for the property being auctioned, and the *bidder* is the person who makes the offer.

■ **Regulation** Auctions are a legitimate business and cannot be prohibited, but they can be regulated by state and local authorities. If there are no statutes covering the activity, anyone may act as an auctioneer. Auctioneers may be required to procure a license to operate, which usually limits the authority of the auctioneer to a particular territory. Although licensing officers may refuse to grant an individual a license, their refusal must be reasonable, impartial, and in the public interest. In some jurisdictions auction sales are subject to a tax.

■ **Auctioneer as agent** An auctioneer is really an agent. See AGENCY. He is primarily the agent of the seller. He must act in good faith and in the interest of his principal, the seller, and the sale must be made in accordance with the seller's instructions. With the fall of the hammer, however, he becomes to some extent the agent of the buyer too. He receives the bid made by the purchaser and binds both parties by the sale.

Authority of the auctioneer An auctioneer has no authority to bind the seller by a warranty to either the title or to the quality of the goods unless the seller especially orders him to do so. His sale of the goods "as is," however, is considered to be a warranty that they are what they were advertised to be.

The particular conditions of a sale may govern the amount, kinds, and time of payment to the auctioneer. He may be authorized to accept only a deposit, in which case he cannot accept the whole price. If the seller requires that his property be sold for cash, the auctioneer cannot accept anything but cash for the property.

Private sales by an auctioneer are generally not allowed.

An auctioneer is selected because of the personal confidence and trust the seller has in him; therefore, he cannot delegate his power to sell unless he has special authority from the seller. He is allowed to delegate unimportant duties, such as using the hammer and calling out the sale, under his immediate direction and supervision. His authority usually ends when the sale is completed and the purchase price is collected. His authority can be revoked by the seller at any time before the sale.

■ **Conduct of the sale** If the owner of the property makes no special conditions, the auctioneer may conduct the sale in any manner he believes will exclude fraudulent bidders and gain the confidence of honest purchasers. He tries to get the highest possible price but may postpone the sale altogether. He may explain, but not change, printed conditions, and conditions he announces at the sale are binding on the purchaser whether or not he knew or understood them.

The auctioneer of goods advertised in a catalog may change the terms of sale at any time during the sale, as long as it is done publicly and in the hearing of all the bidders present. If the auctioneer reserves the right to resell in case of an error or a dispute, the error or dispute must be real. An important error in a description may be a sufficient reason to disallow the sale, but slight variation between the property and the description is not. The seller may withdraw his property at any time before the hammer falls and a bid is accepted.

EXAMPLE The Graysons have decided to auction off the contents of the house that had belonged to Mr. Grayson's grandparents. The auction was not without reserve because the sentiment attached to many of the items made the sale such a difficult decision. When the bidding began for the player piano, the Graysons realized that they really did not want to part with it. Just as the auctioneer shouted, "A thousand dollars once, a thousand dollars twice . . . ," Mr. Grayson interrupted him and withdrew the piano from the auction.

Generally, any act of the auctioneer, seller, or buyer that prevents a fair, free, and open sale or that diminishes competition is contrary to public policy.

Bids A bid may be made in any way that shows what the bidder is willing to pay. It may be oral or in writing or by a wink or a nod or a hand signal. Secret signs between bidder and auctioneer are not allowed, because bidders would then no longer be on equal terms. A seller is obligated only after a bid is accepted.

A bid is accepted when the auctioneer, by the fall of his hammer or by any other means that can be seen or heard, signals the bidder that he is entitled to the property upon payment of the amount of his bid. An auctioneer may reject a bid on various grounds, such as that it is below the minimum price announced by the owner.

An auctioneer cannot bid on property he is selling, but he may bid a prearranged sum for a purchaser. An agreement among prospective buyers not to bid has been held to cancel the sale to anyone who made such an agreement.

EXAMPLE Benton was a fanatic collector of rare stamps. Before one particular auction, he made a deal with some other stamp collectors, promising to pay them a certain amount of money if they agreed not to bid for certain stamps at the auction. Having eliminated his strongest competition, Benton had little trouble making the highest bid for the stamps. After the auction, however, the auctioneer learned of the deal and promptly canceled the sale of the stamps to Benton.

A *puffer* is a person who is hired by the seller to place fictitious bids in order to raise the bidding of genuine purchasers. If a purchaser at an auction can show that a puffer was used, he can usually cancel the sale if he wishes. Some jurisdictions require the buyer to have been harmed by the puffer, but others do not. Puffing and *by-bidding* are the same thing.

Deposits The deposit, a part payment of the purchase price, is usually made payable to the auctioneer, who holds it until the sale is completed.

Validity of the sale A sale by an unlicensed auctioneer may subject the auctioneer to a penalty, but it is still valid. An auction sale without the owner's authorization is invalid. Selling property belonging to one person along with property of others without notice to all may amount to fraud, and the person defrauded may cancel the sale.

■ **Rights and liabilities of the buyer and seller** Under a sale without conditions, title to the property (ownership) passes to the bidder when the auctioneer's hammer falls. If there are conditions, title passes when they are met or waived. The bidder is usually entitled to possession when he pays the amount bid. If a person bidding for someone else does not disclose that fact, he is personally liable for his bid.

A misrepresentation of an important fact on which the buyer relied or the seller's failure to give good title enables the buyer to have the sale set aside.

EXAMPLE Clarksville was holding a community auction to raise money for the local hospital. Many of the townspeople donated goods and services to be auctioned off. Francine donated the grandfather clock that had been in the family for several generations. There was much interest in the old clock at the auction and the bidding for it was lively. It was finally sold to the Mayberrys. Just after the auction was over, Francine's sister, who lived in the neighboring town, showed up, and when she discovered that Francine had donated one of the family's heirlooms, she was aghast. She went directly to the auctioneer and told him that Francine had no right to donate the grandfather clock for sale because the sisters had each inherited a half-share and thus Francine only owned half of the clock. Because Francine's sister was unwilling to sell her half-share, the Mayberrys were able to have the sale of the old clock set aside and their money refunded.

If the buyer defaults on his purchase and the seller resells to another, at a lower price, the first buyer in some states is liable for the difference between what he had agreed to pay and the resale price.

Generally, whether a deposit or partial payment for the property has to be repaid depends on whose fault it is that the sale fell through. If it's the buyer's fault, he cannot get his money back.

■ **Compensation** The auctioneer is paid a commission by the party employing him. He is entitled to his commission even if the sale is not completed, unless it is his fault that the sale falls through. If payment is not fixed by statute or by a special contract, the auctioneer is entitled to reasonable compensation.

■ **Liabilities of the auctioneer** The auctioneer is generally responsible to the seller for money paid to him by the purchasers and for losses due to his failure to obey the seller's instructions. He may be liable to the buyer for fraud, for exceeding his authority—such as giving an unauthorized warranty—and for failure to deliver the goods.

The auctioneer is liable to the buyer for his deposit in those instances when the buyer is entitled to have it returned.

audit   An official examination of an account of a person's or an organization's financial situation; weighing and deciding whether entries in books are true and correct.

authentication   An act showing that a law, record, deed, or other public document is official and correct so that it may be admitted as evidence.

authorities   References to laws, court decisions, and legal textbooks to support a legal position on a question argued by an advocate, a judge, or a scholar.

authorize   Give a right or authority to act.

automobile   See MOTOR VEHICLE.

autopsy   The dissection of a dead body to determine the cause of death. See CORONER.

autre vie   (French) "Another's life." A person who holds property for the duration of someone else's life is a tenant *pur autre vie*.

auxiliary   Aiding; attendant on; ANCILLARY.

avails   Profits, proceeds, or use. In reference to WILLS, it means what is left after the payment of the debts.

avoidance   A making void or of no effect; evading.

avowal   A declaration by an attorney made in court but out of the jury's hearing. Its purpose is to let the court know what the witness would have answered to a question objected to and sustained by the judge to avoid an appeals court's saying that the witness should have been allowed to testify before the jury.

avulsion   The sudden loss of soil or land belonging to one person, and its deposit on the land of another by the action of water. When running streams are boundaries, and the stream leaves its old bed and forms a new one by avulsion, the resulting change does not change the boundary—the original bed remains the boundary.

award   1 Grant, concede, or give by a formal process. For example: a jury awards damages; the court awards an injunction.   2 As a noun, the decision of an arbitrator or other nonjudicial person in a dispute submitted to him.

bad faith

bad faith Fraud or dishonesty in dealing with another person either by deceiving or misleading him or by refusing or neglecting to fulfill some duty or contractual obligation. If a person makes an honest mistake about his rights or duties, he is not acting in bad faith, but if he acts with a sinister motive, such conduct demonstrates bad faith. The fact that a person acted in bad faith may reduce or eliminate his legal rights in a specific situation.

EXAMPLE A health club offers a money-back guarantee that
O←—* if a customer is not satisfied with its facilities after three months, he will get back the price he paid to join the club. Shelley enrolls in the club intending to ask for her money back, regardless of her satisfaction with the facilities. She does so when the three-month trial period is up. Shelley is acting in bad faith because she never planned to honestly evaluate the services offered by the health club. She merely intended to use the services for free by abusing the terms of the offer.

When Shelley demands her money back, the club may refuse to pay and may sue her for breach of contract (violating their agreement) if it can prove that she was satisfied with its services. The health club might do this by using statements she made to her friends and club employees. A court may enforce the contract against Shelley by not ordering the club to return her money or it may decide that the club can keep an amount equal to the reasonable costs of the use Shelley made of the facilities, reimbursing her for any money paid above this amount.

Bad faith is the opposite of good faith—the general principle that requires a merchant to adhere to reasonable standards of fair dealing in trade. If you buy a 10-pound bag of potatoes from a grocery store, you can expect that the grocer has not filled the bag with 6 pounds of potatoes and 4 pounds of rocks to shortchange you. A person acting in bad faith is not viewed favorably in the eyes of the law since he has not acted fairly toward his fellowman.

"Bad faith" and "good faith" are terms that apply primarily to the law of CONTRACTS and commercial dealings such as COMMERCIAL PAPER, SALES, and SECURED TRANSACTIONS. Failure to act with good faith is not a crime nor is it, in itself, a TORT (a wrong done to a person for which he can sue), but bad faith may demonstrate that a person intended to commit a tort.

bail The release of a person from custody upon a promise that he will appear to answer the charge against him at the appointed time and place of trial. Bail usually involves the posting of a *bail bond* (a document that is a promise to pay) by a *surety* (a person who promises to be financially liable if the accused fails to appear) for a sum set by the court. The surety may be a professional bail bondsman, the accused himself, or his family or friends. If the accused fails to appear for his trial, the money specified in the bond will be forfeited to the court.

In most states, a court can release a person on his own, or personal, *recognizance*—that is, his written promise, not insured by any money, that he will appear for his trial. The accused must have steady employment, stable family ties, and lengthy residence in the community. These factors are considered as important as financial considerations that motivate the accused to appear for his trial when bail is posted. Willful violation of this promise is in itself a criminal offense.

The bail system has been criticized because it discriminates against poor defendants who cannot afford to post bail. Since the goal of bail is to give a defendant the financial incentive to appear for trial, it seems reasonable that only the likelihood of the defendant's failing to appear should determine the amount of bail to be set. This is not the case, however. Bail is usually set at an arbitrary amount governed by the seriousness of the alleged offense. Since most defendants lack the financial resources to post their own bail, they turn to the professional bail bondsman.

■ **Bail bondsmen** Bail bondsmen's offices are usually located around criminal court buildings because bail is used far more frequently in criminal than in civil cases. For a fee, usually a little more than 10 percent of the full amount of bail, the bondsman will post a surety bond with the court in the full amount of bail and obtain the release of his client. This fee is nonrefundable even if the defendant appears at trial. If the accused seems to be a poor risk, the bondsman will refuse to post bail. In most cases, the accused must provide collateral—such as jewelry, securities, or cash—or written guarantees signed by solvent relatives or friends to secure at least part of the risk. The bondsman has a common-law power to arrest his client should he fail to appear—"jump" bail. Although the bond is forfeited when the accused jumps bail, this forfeiture will normally be set aside if the bondsman brings him to court within a reasonable time.

EXAMPLE Your 20-year-old son is arrested for stealing a car. O—* He is charged with grand larceny and the judge sets his bail at $1,000, ordering him to return for trial on June 6, 1980. Your son has not saved any money, you cannot afford to put up the money yourself, and you are too proud to ask your family and neighbors to help you raise bail. On your way into the criminal courthouse, you notice a number of bail bondsman offices. You inquire inside and learn that for a fee of $100 he will post bail for your son if your son seems like a good risk and if you sign a written guarantee to pay the $1,000 to the bondsman if your son fails to return for his trial. To be considered a good risk, your son must be steadily employed, must have no prior criminal record, and must have lived in the community for at least five years. The bondsman agrees to post bail and goes to the court to do so. The court clerk notifies the police through a bail ticket or some other document that bail has been posted, and they release your son. If your son leaves the country for Mexico and refuses to return, the court will issue a warrant for his arrest for *jumping bail*. In addition, you will be liable to the bail bondsman for the $1,000 if your son does not return within a reasonable time.

On the other hand, some judges probably would have released your son on his own recognizance in light of the fact that he was a first-time offender with secure ties to the community and, more likely than not, would appear for trial.

The business of furnishing bail bonds and the activities of professional bail bondsmen are subject to regulation by legislatures. For example, a state legislature can charge bail bondsmen fees or require them to have licenses.

■ **Bail in civil and criminal actions** Bail, which in effect releases defendants from the custody of the law and places them under the custody of keepers of their own selection (their sureties), may be available to persons under ARREST in civil actions or on criminal charges.

In civil actions Under certain circumstances, which vary from state to state, a defendant in a civil lawsuit may be arrested to insure that he will appear in court to answer the claims that the plaintiff has made against him. Civil arrest prevents a defendant from leaving the state to avoid the lawsuit and from attempting to hide or give away his property so that if the plaintiff wins his case he will not be able to collect any money from the defendant. Civil arrest is considered drastic. Persons arrested in civil cases may be released on bail. The purpose of bail in a civil action is to insure that the defendant will appear for trial and pay any judgment against him. The right to release on bail is usually given by statute.

The court decides the amount of bail required. The probable amount of the defendant's liability in the case that the trial will settle is generally a determining factor. Cash may be deposited with the court in place of a bail bond when permitted by state law. Whether or not the money may be applied to pay the judgment awarded the plaintiff usually depends on the purpose of the arrest.

In criminal prosecutions The purpose of bail in criminal actions is to prevent the punishment of innocent persons—by keeping them out of jail before their trials—and at the same time to compel the presence of the defendants at trials on criminal charges.

Allowance of bail Before conviction, if you are charged with a crime, you have both state constitutional and statutory rights to bail for most offenses. Bail may be an absolute right or it may rest with the discretion of the court. Generally, all but the most serious crimes—such as murder—are bailable, but you should check the constitution and statutes of your state to determine which offenses are bailable and which are not.

The Bail Reform Act of 1966 governs the granting of bail in federal offenses. It gives the magistrate a number of alternatives that he can use to insure that the defendant will appear for trial without jailing him. The act orders a judge or magistrate to release an accused charged with a noncapital offense (one not punishable by death) on his own recognizance. If the judge believes that there is a reasonable risk that the defendant will not appear for trial, he may do one of several things: he may impose bail, either in a specified cash amount or in the form of a bail bond; he may place the accused in the custody of a designated person or organization who agrees to supervise him; or he may restrict the extent of the defendant's travel, the type of his personal associations, or where he lives. The Bail Reform Act is designed to assure that all persons, regardless of their financial status, should not be detained pending their appearance to answer charges or to testify, or pending appeal, when neither the public interest nor the ends of justice are served by keeping the defendant jailed.

ESSENTIAL FACTS ABOUT BAIL

■ Bail usually consists of posting a *bail bond*—a document that is a promise to pay a certain amount of money if a person fails to show up in court for trial. In some states, a person may be released on his own *recognizance*—a promise to appear in court—if he has steady employment, family ties, and lengthy residence in the community.

■ If you put up bail for someone and he shows up in court, or discharges the debt against him, or is arrested and imprisoned elsewhere, or dies, you will get your money back.

■ Bail may be an absolute right or it may be up to the court, according to where you are. Check the state laws.

■ Allowance of bail after conviction is usually a matter of the court's discretion and not a right. In some states, however, bail while awaiting a new trial, review, or appeal is a right in all but extraordinary cases.

■ The denial of bail is reviewable, but the higher court will interfere with the lower court only if it finds that the latter has abused its discretion.

■ Jumping bail may be a felony or a misdemeanor; it almost always causes the bail bond to be forfeited.

In exercising its discretion in the allowance of bail, the court considers the circumstances of the particular case, including the existence of doubt as to the accused's guilt and the probability of his appearing for trial. Unreasonable delay or postponement, when it is not the accused's fault, is usually a ground for bail—by absolute right in some jurisdictions, but more often at the discretion of the court. If bail is permitted by law, it will be granted when the accused has some physical disability—for instance, a heart condition—that would be aggravated by imprisonment. As a general rule, the allowance of bail after conviction is a matter of discretion and not of right.

If not forbidden by state law, bail while awaiting a motion for a new trial, a review, or an appeal is usually discretionary, although it is an absolute right in certain states. When deciding on bail, the court will consider the probability of reversal of the judgment, the nature of the crime, the possibility of escape, and the character and circumstances of the accused.

Usually, the allowance or denial of bail is reviewable. The reviewing court will interfere with the discretion of the lower court only when it finds that the discretion has been abused.

Amount of bail The amount of bail also rests with the discretion of the court, which considers the nature of the offense and of the proof, the probability of escape, and the means and circumstances of the accused. Under the Eighth Amendment of the U.S. Constitution and specific provisions of most state constitutions, bail must not be excessive.

EXAMPLE Twelve persons were charged with conspiring to violate a federal law that carried the maximum penalty of five years imprisonment and a $10,000 fine. Bail was set at $50,000 per person. The defendants asked the court to reduce bail because it was excessive. To support their motion, the defendants offered evidence of their financial resources, family relationships, health, and prior criminal records. The only reason the government gave for such high bail was that four persons who had been convicted for the same crime in the same court had jumped bail and fled. The court found this reason to be insufficient. When bail is set at an amount higher than necessary to insure that the defendant will appear at trial, it is excessive. Here the bail was higher than usually imposed in such cases. Since no evidence was offered by the government to justify the amount, the excessive bail had to be reduced.

Once bail is fixed it should not be altered, but it can be altered if good cause for doing so can be shown. For example, if the defendant can show that the amount of his bail is very high, and therefore excessive, the court may reduce it. The application for a change in bail is made to the court by a MOTION based on an AFFIDAVIT, which must state the facts that justify granting the change.

■ **Surety's liability** Once the defendant shows up in court on the appointed date or discharges the debt or judgment against him, the surety is no longer liable. Ordinarily, the surety is also free from liability if the conditions of the bond become impossible to carry out—the defendant dies, for example, or is arrested and imprisoned in another place before the date of his court appearance.

■ **Breach and forfeiture** A breach of a bail bond occurs when the defendant jumps bail—that is, when he intentionally fails to appear in court on the date specified in the bond. The act of jumping bail is usually an offense, and it may be either a MISDEMEANOR or a FELONY. The appearance required is not merely to answer the charge but also to attend the trial and receive sentence or judgment. Appearance by counsel (an attorney) in place of the defendant usually does not prevent a breach, although in some states counsel may appear for the defendant if the offense is a misdemeanor.

When there is a breach of the bond, the court enters a judgment of forfeiture of the bail. This judgment, which should contain every fact necessary to show liability, is conclusive. It can be appealed in some states if the default was excusable and the state did not lose its right to prosecute the accused.

EXAMPLE Sam was indicted for robbery and released on bail pending his trial. On the appointed day, Sam did not show up at court and no one knew his whereabouts. The court entered a judgment of forfeiture of the bail. It was later discovered that Sam had suffered a stroke and had been taken to a hospital where he remained unable to speak or identify himself. Upon his recovery Sam was able to stand trial, and so the judgment of forfeiture of his bail was appealed—because the state Sam was being tried in permitted appeals for excusable default—and the default judgment was reversed.

Final judgment generally cannot be entered on a bond without some further proceedings (usually civil) after the act that calls for forfeiture, instituted by a writ of SCIRE FACIAS or by an independent lawsuit. Review and appeals in actions on forfeited bail bonds or recognizances are ordinarily governed by the general rules of appeals in civil cases. See APPEAL AND ERROR.

bail bond See BAIL.

bailiff 1 A keeper or protector. 2 One to whom some authority, care, or jurisdiction is delivered or entrusted. 3 A person acting in an administrative capacity who manages lands or goods for the benefit of the owner or bailor and is liable to render an account to him. 4 A sheriff's deputy or low-level court official who keeps the peace in court. 5 An overseer or steward. See BAILMENT.

bailment A delivery of personal property for some particular purpose on the basis of an express (stated) or implied CONTRACT. After the purpose has been served, the property will be returned to the bailor or dealt with as he directs. A *bailor* is a person delivering personal property into the custody or temporary care of another. The person to whom such property is delivered is the *bailee*. The word "bailment" is derived from the French term *baillier*, meaning "to deliver."

Any kind of personal property in existence may be the subject of bailment, except for personal property to be acquired in the future. Personal property includes any PROPERTY that is not real property (real estate).

A great variety of transactions create bailments. The term is commonly applied to a gratuitous loan—one from which the person doing the lending derives no benefit (you let your neighbor use your power mower to cut his lawn)—or to a hiring, leasing, or renting of personal property (you rent a horse, an automobile, or glasses and china for a large party you are giving). A bailment also occurs when property is delivered to another person so that it may be repaired or other work may be performed on it—you take your coat to a tailor to have it lengthened or you take your sheets and towels to the laundry.

■ **Distinctions** Bailment is sometimes confused with the lease or sale of personal property. When personal property is deposited on the real property of another person, the relationship created between the depositor and the owner of the property may be either that of bailor and bailee or that of lessor and lessee.

> EXAMPLE When you place your car in a parking lot, you may be merely leasing a place to put the car or using the space under a license. This is often the case when you leave the car locked so that it cannot be moved by the lot attendant. A bailment relationship may be created, however, if, at the request of the attendant, you leave your car keys with him. You have thus transferred possession and control of the car to the lot attendant.

Whether a transaction is a bailment or a sale is determined by the agreement and the intention of the parties. A bailment differs from a sale in that no transfer of ownership is intended and the return of the identical thing that was delivered is required. A seller who retains property after it has been sold becomes a bailee for the buyer. When a buyer who has possession of the property cancels the sale, he holds the property as bailee of the seller.

> EXAMPLE Jack buys a washing machine from a discount dealer for $365. After the machine is delivered, Jack discovers that it is a rebuilt model worth $100. Jack calls the dealer to complain, but the dealer ignores him. Jack puts a stop order on his check so that the dealer will not be paid and demands that the dealer send someone to pick up the machine. Until the machine is picked up, Jack holds the machine as a bailee for the seller.

■ **Kinds of bailment** Bailments may be for (1) the benefit of both parties, (2) the sole benefit of the bailor, or (3) the sole benefit of the bailee.

Generally, a bailment for mutual benefit arises when it appears that both parties to a contract of bailment will receive a benefit from the transaction. For example, when you deliver your automobile to a gas station owner who will repair it for a price, a bailment for *mutual benefit* is created.

A bailment for the *sole benefit of the bailor* arises when there is a deposit of property with the bailee and a *mandate*, or a promise by the bailee to perform some act without reward—as when you check valuables in a hotel safe and no fee is charged for this service.

A bailment for the *sole benefit of the bailee* is known as a gratuitous loan—for example, when you lend your car to your neighbor.

■ **Elements of bailment** Three things are needed to create a bailment: delivery, acceptance, and consideration.

Delivery Delivery of the property to a bailee is required for a bailment. Usually, property must be taken into the bailee's actual possession so that he can exclude all other persons from the custody and control of it. Generally,

delivery that is only intended but not actual does not create a bailment.

> EXAMPLE Lola left her shoes on the sidewalk in front of her shoemaker's shop early one morning, before the shop had opened. To identify the shoes she tied a note to the shoestring of the right shoe, giving her name and address and asking the shoemaker to resole the shoes for her. But before the shoemaker arrived that morning, the neighborhood shopping-bag lady passed by, saw the shoes, put them into one of her bags, and walked away. Consequently, delivery of the property was not made to the bailee as intended and no bailment was created. The shoemaker was not responsible for Lola's shoes.

Actual delivery means that one person gives another the sole physical and legal custody and control of the designated property with the result that the recipient is the only person who possesses it. Although Lola intended the shoemaker to take delivery of the shoes, she never put the shoes into his exclusive possession. By leaving them outside his shop, she risked the possibility that someone would come along and pick them up.

Although an actual delivery must usually be made to create a bailment, a constructive delivery may be sufficient. When a person constructively delivers property to another, he gives that person the legal right to the sole custody and control of the property but does not give him the actual physical possession of the property. A third person or corporation physically holds the property.

> EXAMPLE Your attorney has taken constructive delivery of your safe-deposit box when he receives the key to it, but the bank where the box is located has actual physical possession of the box. If you had actually handed your saft-deposit box to your attorney, that would be actual delivery. In either case, a bailment is created.

Acceptance A person cannot be made a bailee without his knowledge or consent. He must have notice that the goods are in his possession and belong to the bailor. Acceptance may be either actual or implied.

> EXAMPLE Lola brought her shoes to the shoemaker while the shop was open. The shoemaker was busy with another customer, so Lola left the shoes on the counter near a pile of old shoes that the shoemaker intended to discard. Lola left without telling the shoemaker the shoes were hers or what she wanted him to do with them. Later in the day the shoemaker picked up Lola's shoes, together with the pile of shoes she had placed them near, and discarded them. When Lola came to claim her shoes a few days later, the shoemaker knew nothing about them. Since he had not been given notice that the shoes were in his possession or that they belonged to Lola, no bailment had been created and he was not responsible to Lola for having disposed of her property.

If Lola had asked the shoemaker, "Okay if I leave these here?" when she put her shoes on the counter and the shoemaker had answered, "Sure," his statement could be considered an implied acceptance of the shoes and a bailment contract for their repair. If she had waited until the other customer had left and given him the shoes directly, a bailment would have been created on the basis of an actual acceptance by the shoemaker.

YOUR PERSONAL PROPERTY AND BAILMENT

■ Bailment is a general term for putting personal property into another's temporary custody, whether by gratuitous loan, hiring out, or delivery for repair or some other service.

■ You are the *bailor* if the property is yours; the person to whom you hand it over temporarily is the *bailee*. For example, when you leave your car keys with the parking lot attendant, you are the bailor and he is the bailee.

■ A bailment for mutual benefit—for example when you deliver your car to a gas station owner who will repair it for a price—requires the bailee to exercise ordinary care.

■ A bailment for the sole benefit of the bailor—for example, when you check your valuables in a hotel's vault and you are not charged a fee—makes the bailee responsible for the property only if he acts negligently or in bad faith.

■ A bailment for the sole benefit of the bailee—for example, when you lend your car to your neighbor—requires that he exercise great care and extraordinary diligence.

■ If you lent your neighbor your car to go to the doctor and he went on a vacation with it and hit a tree, he probably will be liable to you for damages.

■ A bailee's liability may be limited by a special contract, provided the contract does not violate the law. For example, a dry cleaner may reserve the right to pay no more than $200 for a lost garment if he displays a sign to that effect conspicuously in his store.

Consideration   A contract of bailment requires consideration, which means something of value given by one party to induce the other to perform his part of the contract.

The loss that the bailor incurs by giving up his present possession or custody of the article bailed because he relies on the promise of the bailee to return the goods to him is considered sufficient consideration to support a bailment contract. The bailee's promise to return the goods is his consideration. This is not the same as the consideration required for most other contracts. In those situations, both parties must exchange something of value or suffer some detriment in order for a contract to exist.

■ **Title and right to property**   Generally, in bailments the possession of the property bailed is separated from the ownership. The bailee has possession of the property but the bailor retains ownership. The bailee has only a right to possess the property, but under the terms of bailment for a specified period of time this interest of the bailee is greater than any right of the bailor, unless the bailee violates the terms of the agreement.

EXAMPLE Let us say that you get a horse, Nelly, from a stable for two hours to ride in the park. During those two hours your right to Nelly supersedes that of the owner, unless you abuse her or, if the agreement was to ride only in the park, you take the animal onto the streets. If another rider comes to the stable as you are about to leave and offers the keeper twice the going rate for Nelly, his favorite mount, the owner could not take her away from you.

■ **Liabilities in bailments**   As a general rule, the type of bailment governs the liabilities between a bailor and his bailee. A bailee may be held liable for failure to exercise proper care for the property that is bailed. Generally, when the bailment is for the sole benefit of the bailor—you use the hotel safe, as mentioned above—the bailee is responsible only for gross NEGLIGENCE or BAD FAITH. A bailee for mutual benefit is generally bound to exercise ordinary care and is liable for ordinary negligence. When the bailment is for the sole benefit of the bailee, he is bound to exercise great care or extraordinary diligence. He may use the bailed property only as the contract stipulates and is liable for damage or loss occurring while there is unauthorized use, irrespective of negligence.

EXAMPLE You loaned your neighbor your car so that he could take his wife to the doctor. Instead, he left town with it for a week's vacation and smashed it up in a collision with another car. He is absolutely liable for the damage, even if he used the utmost care in driving the car on the trip and the collision was caused by the other driver. On the other hand, he would not have been liable if he had damaged your car while driving his wife to the doctor, as agreed upon, as long as he had exercised extraordinary care during that time.

A bailee's liability may be limited or reduced by special contract, provided the contract is not in violation of law or PUBLIC POLICY and does not relieve the bailee from the consequences of his own fraud or negligence. The terms of the contract must be clear, so that the bailor knows of the limitation. For instance, if a dry cleaner will pay no more than $200 for any garment that is lost while in his possession, a sign saying so must be posted in a conspicuous place. Similarly, a bailee may extend or enlarge his liability by special contract.

The bailor is usually not liable to a third person for damages resulting from the bailee's negligent use of bailed property. However, he may be held responsible if his own negligence directly contributed to the damage.

EXAMPLE When you loaned your car to your neighbor to take his wife to the doctor, the neighbor drove through the city at 70 miles an hour, ran a red light, and collided with another car, severely injuring his wife, a friend who was in the back seat, and the driver of the other car. Your neighbor is liable for the injuries resulting from the collision. You are not liable for them unless your state has a law making a car owner liable for damages caused by its negligent operation by someone who is driving with the owner's consent. On the other hand, if you knew the brakes were faulty when you loaned your neighbor the car, and he drove it with ordinary care but collided with another car because the brakes failed, you are responsible for the injuries suffered by anyone in that accident and the injured persons can sue you.

■ **Redelivery**   On termination of the bailment, the bailee is usually under an absolute duty to redeliver to his bailor the property bailed, in its original or altered form, or to account for the property under the terms of the contract.

Generally, loss of property, when the bailee is not at fault, will excuse nondelivery, but unjustified nondelivery may constitute a CONVERSION (an unlawful use or appropriation of the property). Loss of property results if the bailed property is damaged, destroyed, or not returned to the bailor. Conversion occurs when the bailee uses the bailed item for an unauthorized, improper purpose that causes it to be damaged or destroyed or when he does not return it to the bailor. Returning bailed property to the wrong person and refusing to redeliver property to the bailor when the term of bailment expires are examples of conversion. Selling or leasing bailed property is also conversion unless a state law or agreement gives the bailee such power.

EXAMPLE Jack sends five designer shirts to the laundry. His laundry ticket and the sign posted behind the counter state that the laundry is not responsible for losses caused by natural disasters such as floods, fires, or earthquakes. If the laundry is completely destroyed by a tornado that whips through the area, Jack cannot sue the owner for the loss of his shirts because the owner was not negligent and he had taken extra steps to guard against liability by the statements on the ticket and the sign. If the owner had committed arson by setting fire to the laundry to get insurance money, he would be liable to Jack since he directly caused the loss.

If the owner refuses to return Jack's shirts to him once they are laundered, because Jack has insulted one of the laundry workers, he will be guilty of conversion and will be forced to either return the shirts or pay for them. If the shirts are given to Jim, whose laundry mark is similar to Jack's, the laundry owner is still liable for his misdelivery even though his mistake may be understandable.

■ **Termination of bailment** The duration of a bailment contract is determined by the intent of the parties. A bailment may be ended by agreement or by the conduct of the parties (the return of the property and the payment of any fees involved), by the destruction of the property bailed, by the completion of the purpose of the bailment, or by the expiration of the time period that is specified in the bailment. A bailment for an indefinite period is usually terminable at will and on due notice to the other party. On termination, the bailor is entitled to get back his property.

bait and switch To advertise one item, usually at a reduced price, to get people to come into a store, and then persuade them to buy a different item, usually at a higher price than the product advertised. This may be illegal if the original item was in reality never available or if it was not exactly as advertised.

EXAMPLE Your neighborhood appliance shop advertises hair dryers for $9.95. You decide to buy one, but when you go to the shop, you learn that they have just run out of them. The salesman talks you into buying another hair dryer for $29.95. Later on, you overhear in your local laundromat that several women had the same experience with the shop and ended up buying the more expensive dryer. Pursuing the matter, you question an unsuspecting employee and learn that the originally advertised item was never in stock. The store is guilty of engaging in "bait and switch" practices, and you should complain to your local department of consumer affairs.

Baker v. Carr A landmark case, decided by the U.S. Supreme Court in 1962, that established the right of U.S. citizens to "one man, one vote." A Tennessee statute apportioned the number of representatives for each district to the Tennessee legislature, based on the number of qualified resident voters in each county or district, rather than on the number of residents. This plan of apportionment favored the sparsely populated rural districts, which had a greater number of qualified resident voters, over the more densely populated urban districts, where there were fewer qualified resident voters. The plaintiffs (Charles W. Baker and other voters in Nashville, Knoxville, and Chattanooga), who were from the urban districts, claimed that this plan was "discrimination based on legislative underrepresentation" and that it denied their right under the 14th Amendment of the U.S. Constitution to equal protection under the laws. They filed their suit against Joe C. Carr, then Tennessee's secretary of state. Although Tennessee voters had tried to get their legislature to apportion itself more fairly, they were unsuccessful because of the resistance offered by the overrepresented rural districts. The Supreme Court decided that the residents of the urban districts were denied equal protection of the laws because of the "unjustifiable inequality" existing between the districts.

Bakke case *(Regents of the University of California* v. *Bakke)* A case, decided by the U.S. Supreme Court in 1978, involving charges of reverse discrimination created by an AFFIRMATIVE ACTION program that gave preference to nonwhite applicants to a medical school. In the Bakke decision, the Supreme Court took its first step in dealing with the problems in implementing affirmative action programs. Allen P. Bakke, a white male, 33 years of age, applied for admission to the Medical School of the University of California at Davis in 1973 and 1974. Although he had been considered "a very desirable applicant" to the school, he was denied admission both years while minority applicants with grade-point averages, Medical College Admission Test scores, and other qualifications "significantly lower than Bakke's" were admitted under a special admissions program. The program reserved 16 of the 100 places in the class solely for blacks, Chicanos, Asians, and American Indians. In effect, white applicants could compete for only 84 of the 100 available positions while applicants belonging to the specified minority groups would be considered for all 100 places.

After his second rejection in 1974, Bakke filed a suit in the Superior Court of California alleging that the special admissions program at Davis violated his rights under the equal protection clause of the 14th Amendment; under Title VI of the Civil Rights Act of 1964, which prohibited excluding any person from a federally funded program on the basis of race; and under the California constitution. See CIVIL RIGHTS; EQUAL PROTECTION OF LAWS.

The court decided that the special program operated as a racial quota because minority applicants in the program were rated only against one another and 16 places in the class of 100 were reserved for them. The court ruled that the university could not take race into account in its admissions decisions; such a program violated both the state and federal constitutions and Title VI. But the court refused to order Bakke admitted because he had failed to show that he would have gained entrance had it not been for the special admissions program.

Bakke appealed this part of the decision in the California Supreme Court. That court ruled that it was the university's duty, not Bakke's, to show that he would have been rejected even if the special program had not been in effect. The school conceded that it could not do so and was ordered to admit Bakke. It applied to the U.S. Supreme Court for CERTIORARI (a request for review), which was granted, and the order to admit Bakke was suspended until the U.S. Supreme Court decided the case.

In 1978, in a 5-4 opinion, the U.S. Supreme Court handed down a decision that has been called "something for everyone." The Court decided that although Bakke should be admitted to medical school because he was denied admission solely on the basis of his race, the race of an applicant may be given consideration in the admissions procedure of a university in order to achieve ethnic diversity in its student body. The majority opinion represented a compromise between two opposing viewpoints.

Four justices decided that Bakke's rejection violated Title VI of the 1964 Civil Rights Act, which prohibited excluding a person from a *federally funded* program on the basis of his race and ordered that he be admitted. These justices refused to consider the question of whether the use of race as an admissions criterion was constitutional, since Bakke's problem was solved by the application of Title VI.

With a different rationale, four other justices decided that the racial classification used by the Davis Medical School did not violate Bakke's rights under the equal protection clause of the 14th Amendment or under Title VI. A state may use racial classifications "where there is a compelling government purpose to be served and . . . no less restrictive alternative is available" without violating the 14th Amendment. Racial classifications have been validly used to remedy the lingering effects of past discrimination. The admissions program at Davis was based on the conclusion that "minority underrepresentation is substantial and chronic, and that the handicap of past discrimination is impeding access of minorities to the medical school." These justices also decided that the Title VI denial of federal funds to programs that used racial classifications applied only where the racial classification violated the 14th Amendment. Since they considered the Davis program constitutional, they decided against admitting Bakke.

The majority opinion was written by Justice Lewis F. Powell, Jr. He cast the majority vote in deciding that Bakke's rejection violated Title VI's prohibition against racial discrimination because he was not allowed to compete for the 16 positions reserved for minority students. This part of the majority opinion ordered that Bakke be admitted to medical school. Powell agreed with the other justices, however, that race may be considered in the admissions procedures at universities because "the state has a substantial interest that legitimately may be served by a properly devised admissions program involving the competitive consideration of race and ethnic origin."

balloon payment The last payment in a loan that is much larger than any of the other regular payments. This

type of schedule, also called a balloon loan, gives the customer or borrower a false feeling that low payments will pay off a debt. He rarely notices the balloon payment at the end and must often refinance it, or take out another loan in order to meet the balloon payment. The Federal Truth in Lending Law requires the clear disclosure of balloon payments; many state laws prohibit them entirely.

EXAMPLE Doris buys a refrigerator for $900 on credit from a local department store. She agrees to pay off the loan over a one-year (12 month) period, with 11 monthly payments equal to $50. This means that after she has made 11 monthly payments of $50, Doris will have repaid only $550 of the $900 she owes. Her last payment to the store must equal $350, seven times her average monthly payment of $50. This last payment is called a balloon payment because it is so much larger than the average low payments. When a final payment is more than twice the size of the average monthly payment, the Federal Truth in Lending Law requires that the terms of the credit agreement clearly state the size of the balloon payment to be made.

banc (French) "Bench"; the place where a court permanently or normally does business. A court *sitting in banc* (or *en banc*) is a meeting or session of all the judges of a court together, usually for the purpose of hearing arguments on DEMURRERS or motions for a new trial.

bank 1 A commercial business or moneyed institution that is allowed by law to receive deposits, make loans, and perform other money-related functions. See BANKS AND BANKING. 2 In law, an alternate spelling of BANC.

banker's lien A bank's right to take for its own the money or property left in its care by a customer if the customer has an overdue debt to the bank and if the money or property, to the bank's knowledge, belongs fully to the customer. See LIEN.

EXAMPLE Ellen has a checking account with a balance of $50 at National City Bank and a $500 savings account at Fourth Savings Bank. One weekend, having run short of cash, and under the mistaken notion that she has $150 in her checking account, Ellen writes a check made out to herself for $100 and cashes it at Fourth Savings. Until the check clears—that is, until Fourth Savings is paid $100 by National City for the money it has paid Ellen, Fourth Savings has a banker's lien on Ellen's savings account for $100. Because there are insufficient funds in Ellen's checking account (only $50) and National City therefore refuses to pay Fourth Savings Bank, Fourth Savings can deduct $100 from Ellen's $500 account. On the other hand, if Ellen does have $150 in her checking account, so that her check clears, the banker's lien that Fourth Savings holds on Ellen's account for $100 will end once it receives payment from National City.

bankruptcy A procedure administered by federal law, benefiting both creditors and debtors and providing for relief of debtors in cases where they are unable to meet their financial obligations.

■ **The nature and purpose of the law** The Constitution gives Congress full and supreme power to establish bankruptcy laws. The only constitutional limitations on that power are that the legislation must be uniform throughout the country and that it must not deprive a person of property without DUE PROCESS OF LAW. The federal bankruptcy law is paramount to any state statute, but state laws concerned with insolvency matters outside the scope of the federal legislation are not affected by it. Commensurate with its grant of power, Congress has enacted and revised bankruptcy legislation since the beginning of the 19th century, the most recent being the Bankruptcy Reform Act of 1978. In the 1978 law a strong policy of equality among creditors prevails. The main function of the act is to provide for fair and quick distribution of the debtor's assets, if there are any, and to release the debtor from his obligations.

■ **The courts** The Bankruptcy Act provides for the establishment of bankruptcy courts in each judicial district, as a part of the U.S. DISTRICT COURT, and for the appointment by the President of bankruptcy judges, who serve for 14-year terms and may be removed only for misconduct, incompetency, disability, or neglect of duty. Bankruptcy courts have jurisdiction (authority) over all matters related to a bankruptcy case. For example, a bankruptcy court has exclusive jurisdiction over a debtor's property, wherever it may be located. Thus a bankruptcy court hearing a case in Vermont would have jurisdiction over a gambling casino the debtor owns in Nevada.

■ **Filing for bankruptcy** Bankruptcy proceedings are flexible, although somewhat formal. They are started by the filing of a *petition in bankruptcy* either by the debtor or by his creditors. (If the petition is filed by the creditors, the debtor is forced into involuntary bankruptcy.) Once the petition has been filed, the debtor is considered bankrupt and will not be able to file for a second bankruptcy for at least six years from the date the first petition is filed.

Upon filing of a petition, the court notifies all the debtor's creditors that he has filed, allowing them to file claims against the debtor. Any claims filed against the debtor should be expressed in dollar amounts. Federal law prohibits anyone from starting or continuing any kind of proceeding to recover a claim against the debtor that arose before he filed for bankruptcy, except for criminal proceedings

and lawsuits to collect alimony, maintenance, and support payments.

Soon after the petition in bankruptcy is filed, the debtor must meet with his creditors and disclose his assets in an examination under oath. If the debtor conceals his assets in an attempt to defraud his creditors, he may be prosecuted under federal law for concealment of assets. If convicted of this crime, he will face a maximum penalty of a fine of $5,000 and imprisonment for five years.

Rights of the parties The debtor and all his creditors have the right to appear and be represented by an attorney. Each is equally entitled to a speedy, full, and impartial trial of every material (important) issue in the case.

In general, the papers filed in a bankruptcy case and the dockets of the court (records of the court proceedings) are open to examination at reasonable times, without charge. Upon the request of an interested party, or on its own, the court may protect confidential research, development, and commercial information, as well as any trade secrets that arise during the case. The court may also protect an interested person from the dissemination of scandalous or defamatory matter in a paper filed in the case.

Trustee A bankrupt person's property is in the legal custody and control of the bankruptcy court from the date the petition is filed. The court may seize the debtor's property while the case is pending, in order to protect and preserve it. Or it might appoint a *trustee in bankruptcy* to assume ownership of the property and carry out the court's orders concerning it. The trustee is an officer of the court who is subject to its orders and entitled to its protection. He must reside in or have an office in or adjacent to the judicial district in which the case is pending. He is generally a competent accountant or attorney who is experienced in handling bankruptcy.

Since a trustee is the representative of the debtor's estate, he can sue and be sued. Subject to court approval, the trustee is authorized to take over or reject contracts and leases to which the debtor is a party. The 1978 Bankruptcy Act invalidates clauses that permit the automatic termination of contracts or leases in the event of bankruptcy. The tenant of a bankrupt property owner, for example, has the choice of either remaining in possession of the property or treating the lease as terminated. If the court authorizes a trustee to operate the business, he may use, sell, or lease the

IF YOU FILE FOR BANKRUPTCY

■ Bankruptcy proceedings begin with the filing of a *petition in bankruptcy* at your local bankruptcy court. You may file for yourself or your creditors may file for you, thus forcing you into involuntary bankruptcy.

■ A bankrupt debtor's property is in the custody and control of the bankruptcy court from the date the petition is filed.

■ The court may decide to appoint a trustee to administer the estate of the

debtor during the course of the bankruptcy proceedings.

■ According to federal law, exemptions from bankruptcy proceedings include a residence, up to $7,500; car, up to $1,200; household furnishings, up to $200 for any one item; and the right to receive Social Security, disability, life insurance, and alimony payments. A state may choose between these exemptions and its own list.

■ Some individual debtors may elect

a Chapter XIII repayment plan, providing for full or partial repayment of debts over a period of up to five years. Both wage earners and small businessmen are eligible.

■ Chapter XIII repayment may come from future income or a combination of future income and sale of a portion of the debtor's property.

■ The debtor has the right to set forth his own Chapter XIII plan. Creditors cannot force a plan upon the debtor.

THE INS AND OUTS OF BANKRUPTCY

JAMES H. BACKMAN
Professor of Law, J. Reuben Clark, Jr., College of Law,
Brigham Young University

Well we couldn't really afford it, but it was such a good deal we couldn't pass it up." Does that sound familiar? It could be the beginning of 202,951 true stories of bankruptcy in the United States in 1978 alone—an increase of 221 percent over the number of bankruptcies in 1958. This tremendous jump in bankruptcy was paralleled by a comparable increase in national consumer debt.

Almost everyone has some debts, and many people buy things they "can't afford," but for some overextended debtors there may be trouble ahead. The problem of indebtedness aggravates itself—through interest and fees for late payments, mental distress, health problems, divorce, and loss of work. Occasionally, as a result of unexpected problems, debtors may find themselves insolvent—that is, unable to pay debts as they come due. At this point the debtor may consider filing a voluntary petition for bankruptcy.

The Bankruptcy Reform Act of 1978 provides for two different kinds of consumer bankruptcy: (1) liquidation, or straight bankruptcy, and (2) rehabilitation. In liquidation (what most people think of as bankruptcy), the debtor's property is taken and sold by a trustee to pay off the bankrupt's creditors. Even though the sale never brings enough to reimburse the creditors in full, the debts are discharged. Legally, the debtor never has to pay them. In rehabilitation, the debtor seeks court approval to repay his debts over a period of time, usually three years.

Why people go bankrupt

Most consumer bankruptcies are brought on by unexpected occurrences. Many surveys have been taken to discover the causes of bankruptcy, and in every one of them loss of employment heads the list. Medical expenses are another leading cause, particularly when linked with loss of ability to work. Divorce is often a forerunner of bankruptcy. The legal fees and the cost of maintaining separate households may bring one or both of the former spouses to bankruptcy. A business failure, a lawsuit when an uninsured driver hurts someone, a death in the family—any of these unforeseen events may bring bankruptcy.

Overspending on installment plan purchases is another major cause.

Profile of a bankrupt

What is the typical bankrupt like? Those who have pictured him as the "deadbeat" debtor who deliberately runs up bills with no intent of paying them may be surprised at the following description. As Shirley M. Hufstedler, former judge of the U.S. Court of Appeals for the Ninth Circuit, explained:

> The average consumer bankrupt is not a lazy deadbeat. . . . He is in fact a thirty-year-old blue-collar worker, with a tenth grade education and very few marketable skills. He works hard for his annual wages. He owes on his furniture, his automobile, his household appliances, his tools, and his clothes. He also owes his landlord, he owes his small-loan company, his wife's doctor, the kids' dentist, and the vet. . . . All of his creditors want money right now, on threat of repossessing everything he has, except his wife, his kids, and the family dog, all of whom eat. Then one day something happens, indeed almost anything, such as a family illness, an accident, a plant layoff, and the inevitable financial disaster strikes.

Of course, along with the toiling worker whose financial disasters have left no alternative but bankruptcy, bankruptcy courts also provide relief to the gullible, the foolish, and the high-risk-taking wheelers and dealers.

The high cost of bankruptcy

When debtors reach the point of considering bankruptcy, they have to weigh not only their financial situations but also the personal and ethical ramifications of going bankrupt—the stigma that their families might feel, their future credit ratings, and their guilt over leaving creditors in the lurch.

First, there are many costs associated with bankruptcy. In addition to the $60 filing fee, an attorney may charge $300 to $500. The bankrupt must carefully assess whether it is worth paying this typical $500 expense. Unless bankruptcy will relieve the debtor of sufficient debts to justify the out-of-pocket costs, he ought to consider other alternatives. Experts suggest bankruptcy is inadvisable as a general rule unless the debts to be wiped away amount to at least $2,000.

Then there is the personal, ethical side of the ledger. Unfortunately, the bankruptcy will not pay off all the creditors. Perhaps the creditors will receive no payment at all. Debtors may have serious misgivings about their failure to fulfill obligations that will be legally discharged in bankruptcy. These misgivings are deeply rooted in our traditions. In Puritan times, bankruptcy was just about the most dreadful human condition imaginable, and the proverbial expression for a bankrupt was correspondingly repulsive: "He hath swallowed a spider."

The Puritan ethic has taken a beating over the years, but the great majority of Americans today still have much the same feeling when it comes to bankruptcy, as was borne out by a recent Brookings Institute survey in which people were asked how they would feel about going bankrupt. Thirty-three percent said they would go bankrupt as a last resort, 20 percent said they would rather die, and 18 percent said they would feel disgraced. People who had gone through bankruptcy were asked how they felt about their experience. Although two-thirds of them replied that they were better off financially, one-half said they would rather have paid off their debts instead of going through bankruptcy.

Changing attitudes

While the historic purpose of bankruptcy law was to protect the creditors, it is now recognized that bankruptcy also has the purpose of protecting the debtors.

In 1934 the U.S. Supreme Court commented on the bankruptcy law then in effect: "One of the primary purposes of the bankruptcy act is to relieve the honest debtor from the weight of oppressive indebtedness and permit him to start afresh."

This focus on giving the honest debtor a fresh start should be reassuring to the debtor who inadvertently got in over his head and who reluctantly decides his only alternative is to file for bankruptcy. Both the public and individual beleaguered debtors should recognize that bankruptcy is a desirable antidote to the occasional sickness that an easy-credit society inevitably produces—a necessary gesture of mercy in the impersonal business and financial world. Moreover, there is less stigma attached to bankruptcy today than there once was, as people are becoming more concerned about protecting consumers from the easy-credit, high-inflation, low-income problems that are often their downfall. In the decade 1968–78, more than 2 million Americans went bankrupt.

Nonetheless, a wise debtor will consider the effect of bankruptcy on his credit rating and on his ability to obtain credit in the future. The Brookings study showed that 35 percent of former bankrupts found it more expensive or more difficult to get credit. Some retailers are more reluctant to give credit when they know of bankruptcy, and the Fair Credit Reporting Act permits the bankruptcy to be on a bankrupt's credit report for 14 years.

Yet bankruptcy does not affect the credit rating as negatively as one might think. Credit applications are judged primarily on present and future prospects for payment. Whereas before bankruptcy a lender could obtain a credit report and find many debts, after the bankruptcy the debtor would have a cleaner slate and the creditor might think the debtor a better risk than before. Moreover, the creditor knows that the debtor cannot receive another discharge in bankruptcy for six years.

There will be individual merchants and creditors who will refuse to deal with prior bankrupts; nonetheless, credit will be available.

Are there alternatives?

If you are having trouble keeping up with payments, there are many nonbankruptcy alternatives but they decrease as your financial problems increase. The choices depend on the amount of debt, whether you have a regular income, and how willing the creditors are to help you work out solutions.

Creditor's remedies You may sit back and wait for your creditors to initiate collection. Typically, a creditor's first attempt at collecting an overdue debt is a letter asking for payment. For the first month or so he may do nothing more than add 1½ percent interest each month to the debt owing. After 60 or 90 days the letters will include an increasingly more demanding note threatening to take advantage of the arsenal of remedies available to him. When the creditor becomes concerned that he will not get his money, he may turn the bill over to a collection agency or he may bring suit himself.

If he decides to file suit, he may be able to get a prejudgment writ ordering the sheriff to attach some of your property. If property attached is personal property—that is, not land or buildings—the sheriff will seize it and keep it in his custody. If property attached is real property, the writ may be recorded in the local land records, giving notice to you and all the world that the creditor has obtained a lien on your property that will become effective if he can get a judgment against you in court.

In the normal course of events, however, the sheriff cannot seize property until the creditor gets a judgment against you. The usual collection judgment is obtained quickly—within 20 or 30 days—because it is a noncontested default judgment: The creditor files a complaint and obtains a service of process directing the debtor to answer the complaint or be subject to a judgment by default. When the debtor fails to respond, the creditor obtains his judgment.

After obtaining such a judgment, the creditor can have the sheriff seize the property and sell it to pay the debt, or he can get a court order directing your employer to pay part of your wages directly to the court for the creditor's account. This is called garnishment. There is a federal law that protects part of an employee's wages from garnishment. Under the law, no more than 25 percent of his wages (after taxes) can be garnished; or, if his wages are low enough that the alternate formula gives him greater protection, the employee must be able to keep an amount equal to 30 times the minimum hourly wage for the pay period. Garnishment restrictions also prohibit an employer from firing anyone because of a wage garnishment resulting from "any one indebtedness."

Finally, a creditor may force you into involuntary bankruptcy. Generally he will postpone this remedy as long as possible because of numerous undesirable consequences from his standpoint—such as being required to share your assets with other creditors in a bankruptcy distribution. In order to block other creditors who are also trying to grab your assets, however, he may consider using this remedy.

Some creditors keep one step ahead in the collection process. If you bought some appliances on the installment plan or borrowed money to buy the goods, the lender probably kept a security interest in the property that gives him special rights. If you should default by failing to make payments, the lender can repossess the property with or without court proceedings. Similarly, the lender for the purchase of a house can foreclose his security interest in the event of the debtor's default by causing the house to be sold to repay the debt.

Debtor's alternatives Now consider some of the positive steps available to you if you take the initiative instead of passively enduring the creditors' assaults. First, you would be best advised to face the problem back at the 30-day-overdue-notice stage. When you first find yourself unable to pay the bills, you might feel like ignoring those reminder letters. That is probably the worst thing you can do. As long as creditors have reassurances that the debtor intends to pay, they will not want to go to the expense of turning the account over to a collection agency or to the trouble of bringing suit. That is why you should contact your creditors, tell them about your problem, and ask for their cooperation. Also, try to pay something on each bill to show that you are working on a way to get your finances straightened out.

There are several different sources available for counsel and assistance in dealing with the creditors. Credit bureaus, credit unions, large retail stores that give credit, banks, labor unions, family service agencies, and consumer credit-counseling services are potential sources of help, as is a lawyer. Furthermore you can get any number of free or low-cost government booklets on bankruptcy. For information about these booklets write to Consumer Information Center, Pueblo, Colorado 81009.

A consumer credit-counseling service, a lawyer, or sometimes a credit union can help work out an informal extension plan where you can pay your debts by spreading them over a longer period of time and making smaller payments. These counselors will call the creditors and try to get them to agree to the plan.

If it seems impossible for you to pay the debts in full, the creditors may sometimes agree to accept a smaller amount. Such a plan—called a *composition with creditors*—may provide, for example, that you pay 60 percent of all debts. Creditors are sometimes willing to go along with a composition because it is less expensive than collection efforts and generally returns a greater proportion of the debt than the bankruptcy alternative.

Another solution might be to get a *consolidation loan,* pay off all the creditors, and then make payments only to one lender. This will work well if you belong to a credit union or can borrow money from relatives or someone else at a reasonable rate of interest. A consolidation loan is not a good idea if you will wind up paying just as much (or more) interest as before. For that reason avoid commercial companies that pool debts; they charge more interest than other sources, and they may keep the first several payments for their fee before they pay any creditors. Such businesses have been made illegal in many states.

In some states debtors can make an *assignment for the benefit of creditors,* turning over all their property to a trustee who will sell the property and use the money to pay creditors. Consumers rarely employ this form of relief, for it has the same disadvantage as bankruptcy—the debtor must give up his property. But unlike a bankrupt, he does not receive discharge of debts. To the extent that the debts are paid in the distribution, the debtor no longer owes them, but if the liquidated property does not cover the entire indebtedness, the debtor will remain saddled with debts. Some states provide a court-supervised process of turning part of a debtor's wages over to a trustee who will disburse it to creditors.

The new bankruptcy law

The Bankruptcy Act prior to the one enacted in 1978 was very old, dating from 1898, and was designed to liquidate businesses that had failed. In the last 30 years, however, there has been an enormous increase in personal bankruptcies. Although there are substantial arguments for treating consumer bankruptcies differently—consumers do not have many assets, and controversies are often not worth enough to adjudicate—consumer bankruptcies had to go through the same complex procedure designed for business bankruptcies. In 1978, in part to remedy this situation, Congress passed a new Bankruptcy Reform Act, which became effective on October 1, 1979.

Bankruptcy sounds a little like magic. One day the debtor owes thousands of dollars and is being harassed by creditors, and the next day he has no debts and no creditors. However, only in rare cases is it that simple. It is quite possible that the debtor will come out of bankruptcy no better off than he was. Some debtors are even worse off. So if you come to the point of considering bankruptcy, there are some very important questions that you must explore. You should probably consult a lawyer as soon as you realize that you are in over your head. Together you can decide whether bankruptcy is needed, whether it is the best solution, or whether some other alternatives might be preferable.

The Bankruptcy Act offers debtors two alternatives for seeking relief. The most frequently used bankruptcy procedure—straight bankruptcy, or "Chapter 7"—is essentially a liquidation remedy. The debtor turns over almost all of his property, which is divided among his creditors. In return he is discharged (legally forgiven) from most debts. The other procedure, provided by Chapter 13 of the Bankruptcy Act, is "rehabilitation"—in effect, a composition or extension agreement approved and supervised by the bankruptcy court. The goal of such a plan is rehabilitation of the debtor; thus it differs drastically from the liquidation objective of straight bankruptcy.

After contemplating the alternatives, you should also determine whether straight bankruptcy will really help. The most important topics to think about when considering straight bankruptcy are (1) discharge, (2) the property affected, and (3) the exemptions. Let's examine each of these in detail.

Discharge The most important question to be answered is whether a debtor will be able to get a discharge of his debts. Under the act, a discharge must be denied if during the year before filing the petition for bankruptcy the debtor has transferred or concealed property with the intent to delay or defraud creditors.

A discharge is rarely denied, but there are certain debts that can never be discharged, and there may be other debts that the debtor will feel duty-bound to pay, despite legal discharge. If too many debts fall into one of these categories, a debtor may not find bankruptcy very helpful.

Seven kinds of debts that cannot be discharged:

(1) Certain taxes, including any tax reported in a tax return within two years prior to bankruptcy.

(2) Debts the bankrupt owes a lender for money or credit that was obtained by making a false financial statement that the lender relied upon in extending credit, or debts incurred by use of a credit card for

purchases made just before bankruptcy, when the debtor had no intent to repay.

(3) Debts that the bankrupt did not include in the form identifying creditors.

(4) Debts created by fraud or embezzlement.

(5) Alimony and child support. (Courts will determine whether payments to a former spouse are part of a property settlement—which are dischargeable debts—or are nondischargeable payments for support. If the bankrupt is required to make payments on the house or other property being used by the children or former spouse, they will probably be considered payments for support and will be nondischargeable.)

(6) Liabilities for willful and malicious injuries to the person or property of another.

(7) Student loans under certain circumstances.

Secured debts Another significant class of debts, called secured debts (debts backed by collateral), is affected in a more limited manner by bankruptcy. First, judicial proceedings to enforce secured debts are automatically suspended by the filing for bankruptcy relief. (The suspension can be set aside, however, and in any event it is only for the duration of the bankruptcy.) Second, secured creditors are not allowed to seek additional recoveries against a discharged debtor beyond the value of the property (collateral) that is the security for the debt.

When you buy an item on the installment plan, the seller or lender generally keeps the right to repossess the item at any time if you fail to make the payments. What the seller or lender retains is called a purchase-money security interest in personal property. (Personal property is any property that is not real estate.) In the case of real estate what the seller or lender retains is called a mortgage. The effect in each case is pretty much the same. If you fail to make payments, the creditor may take the property and sell it, keeping the proceeds of the sale to satisfy the debt.

Even though a bankrupt's property automatically becomes the property of the bankruptcy trustee, the trustee's rights in the property are no greater than the bankrupt's. Let us say your automobile is subject to a security interest. If you file for bankruptcy, the trustee will take title to the car (assume ownership of it), but that title will still be subject to the secured creditor's interest, which gives the creditor superior rights in the car. Therefore, the creditor will be entitled to the proceeds of any sale of the car up to the amount owing to him. If the car is sold for $2,500, and the creditor has a secured claim of $2,500 or more against you, then the entire $2,500 will be turned over to the

secured creditor and there will be nothing left for the trustee to distribute to other creditors. On the other hand, if the creditor has a secured claim of $3,000 against you for the car, and the car is sold for only $2,500, the creditor will get only the $2,500 and will not be allowed to demand the additional $500.

Debtors contemplating bankruptcy may find the straight bankruptcy alternative unacceptable if the majority of their debts are secured by their property. Such debts are normally unaffected by bankruptcy because the bankruptcy discharge does not prevent creditors from ultimately repossessing and selling property of the debtor in which they have a valid security interest.

Reaffirmation One final factor detracts from the full discharge from debts that bankruptcy makes available to a debtor. You may reaffirm discharged debts, with the result that the full liability arises once again. Most reaffirmations are deliberate choices by the bankrupt. For instance, you may again need the services or supplies of a specific creditor. As a cost of renewing business with you, he may insist on having his unpaid debts reaffirmed. Or the lender may put a great deal of pressure on you to reaffirm. If another person cosigned with you for the loan or purchase, the lender may threaten to go after the cosigner unless you reaffirm the debt. This is particularly frightening if the lender has a security interest in some property of the cosigner and threatens to take that property to pay the debt.

The new Bankruptcy Reform Act of 1978 protects the bankrupt against unreasonable and oppressive reaffirmation agreements: (1) A reaffirmation must be agreed to before the debtor receives the final discharge relief. (2) The bankrupt has the right to cancel a reaffirmation agreement within 30 days after the agreement becomes binding. (3) A court hearing is held to provide clear, objective explanations of the effects of a proposed reaffirmation and to let the debtor know that he is not legally obligated to reaffirm any debt discharged in bankruptcy. (4) The court must approve the reaffirmation agreement.

Property affected The second important question to be considered is what property you will have to give up. The trustee in bankruptcy takes title to the property you hold on the date the petition is filed. If you inherit any property within six months of bankruptcy, that too will pass to the trustee.

He may also have the right to recover some property—including money—that you transferred before bankruptcy—gifts to family or friends or even a payment to a creditor. It is not very hard to understand why the law would allow the trustee to recover gifts you made on the eve of bankruptcy. Any transfer of property made by an insolvent debtor within one year of bankruptcy, for which he did not receive fair payment in exchange, is considered a fraudulent conveyance, and the trustee can void the transfer and bring the property back into the estate.

It is not quite so obvious why the trustee can void a payment you made to a creditor, but bankruptcy law is designed to treat general creditors equally. If an insolvent debtor paid a creditor within 90 days of bankruptcy because of a prior debt, and this payment allowed the creditor to receive more than he would receive under the bankruptcy proceeding, the payment is called a preference. Since bankruptcy law will not allow one creditor to be preferred, the trustee may recover the money from the preferred creditor to distribute it equally among all your creditors. The new bankruptcy provisions passed in 1978 also cancel payments to creditors closely related to the debtor if such payments are made within one year prior to bankruptcy. Certain creditors are exempt from these voidable preference provisions. For example, payments within 45 days after the debt arose will normally not be considered preferential.

Exemptions In keeping with the idea of giving the bankrupt a fresh start, bankruptcy law allows debtors to keep certain property that they and their families will need after bankruptcy and that will make it possible for them to keep their jobs or continue their trade. Property such as veterans' pensions, railroad retirement benefits, and soldiers' savings bonds are exempt from creditors' collection remedies and bankruptcy by federal law. The new Bankruptcy Act establishes a uniform federal exemption but permits a bankrupt to elect the exemptions allowed by the state if they give him greater protection. (However, states can pass laws barring their residents from taking advantage of the federal exemptions, and some have done so.) The federal exemptions include:

(1) Up to $7,500 interest in property used as a residence by the debtor or a dependent, or in a burial plot, and up to $400 (plus any unused amount of the residency exemption) in any kind of property.

(2) Up to $1,200 interest in a motor vehicle.

(3) Household and personal items not exceeding $200 value in any particular item.

(4) Up to $500 worth of jewelry.

(5) Up to $750 worth of books and tools of the trade.

(6) Alimony, support, and maintenance payments; benefits or proceeds from life insurance, pensions, annuities, Social Security, or unemployment compensation; and to some extent awards for injury, loss of future income, and wrongful death.

(7) Interests in life insurance contracts including up to $4,000 cash surrender value under a life insurance policy.

The federal exemptions are very generous in comparison with some present state exemptions. State laws may vary widely in their exemptions, but most states have exemptions for wages, insurance, and a homestead, which allows the bankrupt to keep some equity in his home. A few states and Washington, D.C., have no homestead exemption, and some states have exemptions of $1,000 or less. California allows the bankrupt to keep up to $40,000 equity in the family home (however, the amount of exemption allowed is determined by the limit at the time the debt was incurred). Some homesteads have no dollar limitation but are limited as to the number of acres. Texas allows the family to keep 200 acres. Missouri allows the family to keep 160 acres but limits the value to $10,000.

One problem with the exemption laws is that many of them are obsolete. This is apparent in exemptions of personal property. The most common personal property exemptions are for clothing, books, tools of the profession, and household furnishings. In Idaho the household furniture may not exceed a value of $300. That may only allow the bankrupt to keep the sofa. Idaho also allows debtors to keep four oxen, horses, or mules, and a motor vehicle, but their value cannot exceed $200. Texas allows the bankrupt family to keep personal property not to exceed $30,000 and lists the allowed property right down to the number of ducks, geese, and the dog and the cat. Other common exemptions are for portraits, musical instruments, insurance, jewelry, and burial sites. To find out what property is exempt in a particular state, a debtor can call the clerk at the county courthouse or the clerk of the bankruptcy court.

Just as discharge does not affect secured debts, the exemptions provide no protection if the exempt property is security for a debt. Once the bankruptcy court determines that the property is exempt and does not pass to the trustee, it has no more control over the property, and secured creditors have the ultimate right to repossess it, subject to the automatic stay (suspension) of any creditor action through the duration of the bankruptcy proceeding. The federal government also has a right to take exempt property if there is a tax lien on it, but it usually declines to do so.

Straight bankruptcy proceedings

Bankruptcy proceedings are quite different from proceedings in other courts. The following summary of the flow of a bankruptcy proceeding, from its initiation to final discharge, will serve as an introduction to the special world of the bankruptcy court.

A straight bankruptcy proceeding usually begins when you, the debtor, file a voluntary petition (or in involuntary bankruptcy, when your creditors file) with the clerk of the bankruptcy court. You pay a $60 filing fee, which may be paid in installments if necessary. Along with the petition, you file (1) a statement of affairs, (2) a schedule of your entire debts, and (3) a statement of all your property. The prescribed forms for these necessary filings are available through the clerk of the bankruptcy court. The forms are long but not hard to understand. The bankruptcy court is available to help you or your attorney if questions arise in completing the forms. It is essential that the questions on the forms be answered fully. It is also important to list *all* debts, because unlisted debts are not eligible for discharge relief.

Upon filing a voluntary petition, you are automatically adjudicated a bankrupt, and there is a stay—suspension—of any lawsuit against you on any debt. Occasionally, the creditor may persuade the judge to lift the stay and allow the suit to continue.

The court sends notices to the creditors informing them of the automatic stay and of the first meeting of creditors. The creditors are also informed that they may file claims showing what you owe them and stating their objections to any exemptions you claim or to the discharge of specific debts.

At the first meeting of creditors, you must submit to questions about your conduct, debts, and property in determining your right to a discharge. To participate in any distribution of your assets, the creditors must meet a deadline for filing proofs of claims. If a claim for taxes is not filed, you may file it. Since some taxes are not dischargeable, it is to your advantage to have at least part of owed taxes paid in the distribution, so that there is less for you to pay after the other debts are discharged.

Certain creditors, as specified by the Bankruptcy Act, elect the trustee at the first meeting. The trustee takes title to all of your nonexempt property and property that is recoverable from prebankruptcy transfers. Your property is sold, sometimes by auction. (Often the bankrupt or his relatives buy it.) The proceeds from the sale are divided according to priorities set by the Bankruptcy Act. If any secured property is sold, the secured creditor gets a share equal to the value of his security interest. Then, before any of the general creditors are paid anything, the trustee is obliged to pay, among others: (1) the costs of administration, (2) back wages and employee benefits owed by the bankrupt, (3) creditors who have prepaid for consumer sales or service contracts, and (4) certain taxes, duties, and penalties owed to government creditors. Each of these categories must be paid in full before the next group of claimants receives anything. There are often so few assets that the total sale pays only the trustee's fee, which is part of the cost of administration.

If objections to exemptions or discharge are raised, the court will hold a hearing to determine the issues. If there are no objections to discharge, the court sends all the creditors a copy of the order of discharge. Once debts are discharged, you are released from any further liability on them. Whether or not the creditors received payment, they cannot later use state law to collect the remaining debts, unless you subsequently reaffirm them.

When to file for bankruptcy

Everyone knows that tax planning can be effective in minimizing tax burdens by maximizing deductions and by postponing taxes on certain forms of income. There can also be important gains for the debtor who has done some bankruptcy planning. Proper planning before bankruptcy can affect a bankrupt's exemptions, the dischargeability of specific debts, and the property that becomes a part of the bankruptcy estate. In voluntary bankruptcies, the debtor has total control over the crucial timing date—the date of filing the bankruptcy petition. If you are faced with bankruptcy, consider timing it to make the best use of the legal protections available to you. The following is a list of significant timing decisions that may affect your net financial position after bankruptcy.

(1) Take a look at the status of your exempt assets. If there is surplus cash available, it would be wise to close the accounts and buy exempt assets with the funds. In some states you must declare a homestead before you file for bankruptcy. You may declare a

homestead, to the extent of the state homestead exemption, in the family residence simply by filing a simple form with the county recorder or other official land record office in the county where you live.

(2) Maximize the number of your dischargeable debts. For example, if a negligence complaint has been filed against you, wait until a judgment has actually been obtained by the person making the claim, because if he knows you are filing for bankruptcy he might amend his negligence complaint to a claim for willful and malicious injuries. The reason for doing so is that judgments based on willful and malicious injuries cannot be discharged by bankruptcy while those based on negligence can.

(3) Timing also affects what property is available to pass to the trustee. You must turn over to the bankruptcy trustee tax refunds, commissions, royalties, and similar income tied to your prebankruptcy past even though they are received after the bankruptcy petition was filed.

The Bankruptcy Act also stipulates that any inheritance received by the bankrupt within six months after filing for bankruptcy must go to the trustee. But you are allowed to keep assets obtained and money earned after the filing. There is a famous example of a race-car driver who filed for bankruptcy a few days before he won the Indianapolis 500 race. He was permitted to keep all his prize money and received a bankruptcy discharge for all his prior debts.

In some of these situations you will benefit if you can avoid bankruptcy until after the income tax refund, for example, or inheritance has been received and placed into assets that are exempt.

(4) You cannot get a discharge if you have had one within the last six years. Be sure to wait until the time limitation has passed before you file.

Chapter 13 bankruptcy

Chapter 13 of the Bankruptcy Act (specifically entitled "Adjustment of Debts of an Individual With Regular Income") offers an alternative to straight bankruptcy. To be eligible, you must have a regular income. You keep your property but set up a plan to reimburse the creditors from your income over an extended period of time. You work out a budget that will provide for your needs and determine what amount of your income you can afford to put into the plan each month.

A Chapter 13 plan resembles a nonbankruptcy composition or extension agreement. Under a typical plan, you will reduce your total monthly debt payments by extending the total period for repaying the debts or, in some cases, by reducing the actual amount owing. The money is usually sent directly by your employer to a trustee who will distribute payments to the creditors.

Several benefits are available under a court-supervised Chapter 13 plan that do not apply to the nonbankruptcy alternatives. First, when the court confirms the plan, it becomes binding on all the unsecured creditors, and the court will enjoin any secured creditors from taking any action to collect money from you.

The court can also be extremely flexible in administering a Chapter 13 plan. If circumstances change so that you increase your payments or you are unable to pay the amount provided for each month, the court can adjust the plan. The court may even give temporary relief from the monthly payments if necessary.

If you are buying certain property that you do not need, you can reject the contract and return the property. For example, a debtor who had been paying her creditors for about a year could not understand why her balances were not going down. The woman was making a good income. In analyzing her financial condition the trustee discovered that out of the $200 per month she was paying her creditors, $188 went for interest. So she was really only reducing her bills by $12 per month. The solution the trustee worked out was to get rid of her new car and reject a couple of other contracts.

Just as secured debts are a major obstacle to the fresh start in straight bankruptcy, they may also be obstacles to a successful Chapter 13 plan. First, the plan cannot deal with any debts secured by real property. That means debtors will have to keep up with their mortgage payments. The plan can cover debts secured by personal property, but each secured creditor must accept the plan and be assured of receiving property equal in value to his claim. Because secured creditors are in a favored position, they may demand that they be paid before the other creditors or that they receive their full payment each month. The court may intervene and help a debtor if it determines that some item is necessary to the plan. A U.S. District Court in California, for example, prevented a secured creditor from repossessing a car, even though the secured creditor did not agree to the plan, because the debtor needed the car to get to work. The court stated that when it was necessary to preserve the estate or when it was essential to the plan, the court would deny the creditor reclamation as long as the debtor had good intent and ability to pay and the creditor's security would not be impaired.

Most plans provide for paying off all debts within three years. At the end of the plan, some judges grant a discharge but many skip the formality because the debts have been paid. In any event, a discharge affects only the debts provided for in the plan. If, because of circumstances that were not the fault of the debtor, the plan has not been completed, the bankruptcy judge may nonetheless grant the debtor a discharge.

Administering the plan is somewhat costly. The initial filing fee is $15, and the fee allowed the attorney for the actual proceeding is typically $350. Further, out of the money that the employer transfers to the trustee each month, approximately 10 percent goes to the district court to pay the administrative costs, including the trustee's fee. The attorney may also seek additional fees for the time he spends getting creditors to agree to the plan. This total expense is probably close to what it would cost for a counseling service to work out a composition. An offsetting advantage of Chapter 13, which often saves enough to pay the administrative cost, is that the court may limit the interest charged by secured creditors and will not allow unsecured creditors any interest from the bankruptcy filing date. Even the precomputed interest is deducted.

One advantage of a Chapter 13 proceeding over straight bankruptcy is that there is less stigma attached. In one study on bankruptcy, half of those who filed straight bankruptcy said they felt social disapproval as compared with one-fourth of those who filed Chapter 13 plans. The debtor may also find it easier to get credit after completing a Chapter 13 plan than he would after a straight bankruptcy. Lenders are likely to think well of the debtor for having paid off his debts, and the Fair Credit Reporting Act allows reporting of a Chapter 13 plan for only 7 years, as opposed to 14 years for straight bankruptcy.

It is worth considering the Chapter 13 plan. Some attorneys fail to mention that this option exists, but if the attorney knows that you are interested he can help you decide whether the plan will work for you.

Must a bankrupt's spouse also file?

In some cases, when a married person goes bankrupt (either under straight bankruptcy or Chapter 13), it will be advisable for the spouse also to file for bankruptcy. The new Bankruptcy Act allows a married

couple to file jointly. In deciding whether to file a single or a joint petition, debtors should determine: (1) what property will pass to the trustee or be recovered as a fraudulent conveyance, (2) which debts will be discharged, and (3) what will happen to a spouse who remains liable for the debts. The answers to these questions will differ, depending on whether the property is the separate property of either spouse or is somehow held jointly by the spouses.

Let us assume that only the husband files bankruptcy. Ordinarily, property held separately by the wife will not pass to the trustee. As long as there are no joint debts, the wife will not have to worry about the effects of the bankruptcy. Only the husband's debts will be discharged, but the trustee will receive and distribute the bankrupt husband's separate property to the general creditors. The wife's separate property may be vulnerable, however, if the trustee can show that she is merely holding the property in trust for her husband or that she received the property through avoidable fraudulent conveyance from her husband prior to bankruptcy. In that case she will have to turn the property over to her husband's bankruptcy trustee. However, unless she files jointly with her husband, she will not receive any discharge for their joint debts.

The form of joint ownership may differ from state to state, depending on whether the state considers the property to be held in joint tenancy, in an estate by the entirety, or as community property. These areas are highly technical but, as a general rule, if there is considerable property that is jointly held in one form or the other, it is safest for both spouses to file jointly for bankruptcy. Otherwise joint property remaining in the hands of the nonbankrupt spouse may still be subjected to the claims of creditors who are trying to collect a debt affecting both spouses (joint debts). The bankruptcy of one spouse will result in a discharge of the debts for the bankrupt only, leaving the creditor free to pursue the nonbankrupt debtor/spouse and any property that the spouse may still hold.

Do you need an attorney to file?

There is a popular belief that it is not necessary for you to get the help of an attorney to file bankruptcy—that the money used for his fee should go to creditors who are the deserving parties. Under this view the creditors may get a little more, but you may wind up with a lot less. While the actual filing is not very complicated, there are many possible problem areas—

the timing considerations, the determination of whether bankruptcy is the answer or whether a Chapter 13 plan or some nonbankruptcy alternative would be better, and the question of converting nonexempt assets into exempt assets.

If you should decide to postpone the bankruptcy for any reason, an attorney can assist you by telling you what your rights are against creditors who are harassing you or trying to repossess goods, by helping you to keep exempt goods, and by producing some settlements. If bankruptcy ensues, the lawyer may be able to help you avoid certain liens, defend against objections to discharge, and prevent reaffirmation of debts. The court reviews attorney fees in bankruptcies to make sure they are not excessive. In addition to what the attorney saves you in assets, he will probably save you from excessive worry, fear, and unforeseen pitfalls.

How to avoid getting in too deep

Let us draw a few conclusions about how to keep from getting so far into debt.

(1) Decide how much you can spend.

(2) Keep track of how much is spent.

(3) Do not let the lenders do your budgeting. They will usually look at your monthly income and planned expenses but will not allow for any unplanned expenses, such as new tires for your car, or the continual rise in the cost of living, or the possibility of a major medical expense. Some experts have recommended guidelines to help the consumer decide what he can spend.

(4) Keep personal, nonmortgage debt below 20 percent of your take-home pay. This is the advice of the president of the Credit Union National Association International.

(5) Try to keep your house payments to no more than one-third of your take-home pay.

(6) When you buy on credit, find out how much the interest will be—not just the monthly rate but the total cost of the interest and finance charges. The Truth in Lending laws provide that in most credit transactions the finance charge and annual percentage rate must be disclosed. This allows you to do comparison shopping for financing.

(7) Shop for the lowest interest rates possible. Avoid credit cards and finance companies, which charge high interest rates. Loans from a credit union or a bank are preferable—more time is available to consider the purchase, lower interest rates are available, and these institutions will be more careful about determining how much credit you can afford.

(8) Become acquainted with consumer laws. Federal government offices have short pamphlets designed to teach the consumer his rights under the various consumer credit laws that have been passed by Congress during recent years. These include Truth in Lending, Truth in Leasing, Wage Garnishment Restrictions, Fair Credit Reporting, Fair Credit Billing, Equal Credit Opportunity, and Fair Debt Collection Practices.

debtor's property in the ordinary course of business. A utility may not discontinue service to the trustee because of a debt owed before the petition was filed. On the other hand, if the trustee does not furnish adequate assurance of payment within 20 days after the filing of the petition—by making a deposit, for example—the utility has the right to discontinue service.

The trustee may recover the amount of the debtor's interest in jointly owned property by selling it without the consent of the co-owner when dividing the property between the owners would be impractical. The rights of the co-owner are protected, however, because he has the first right to buy the debtor's share. If he refuses and the property is bought by someone else, the trustee must pay the co-owner the dollar amount of his share.

A trustee may act as his own accountant or attorney (if he is qualified to do so), or he may hire disinterested professional people, subject to court approval. A person is "disinterested" if he is not a creditor or the holder of a security (stock) of the debtor; was never the debtor's investment banker; does not have an interest that is substantially against the interest of the debtor's estate; and is not an "insider" of the debtor—such as a relative or partner of the debtor or, in the case of a bankrupt corporation, one of its directors, officers, or one of their relatives. On the other hand, a professional person cannot be prevented from working on the case just because he is employed by or represents a creditor.

The trustee in bankruptcy is not the same as the U.S. trustee, a position created by the new law in 18 federal districts to ease the administrative burdens once carried by bankruptcy judges—by examining the debtor at the meeting of his creditors, for example. The U.S. trustees are for the most part members of the U.S. Department of Justice appointed by the Attorney General, plus one Assistant Attorney General appointed by the President. In the 18 federal districts, private trustees are appointed and supervised by U.S. trustees especially in cases where the debtor has few or no assets. Sometimes a U.S. trustee may act as a private trustee. Greater supervision of bankruptcy cases is designed to achieve a more equitable treatment of a debtor's creditors. The usefulness of U.S. trustees will be evaluated during the fall of 1984 and, if considered successful, such positions will be created throughout the country.

Exemptions Interests that are exempt from bankruptcy proceedings under federal law include (1) the debtor's interest in real estate or other property (such as a mobile home) used as a residence, up to $7,500; (2) his interest in a motor vehicle, up to $1,200; (3) his interest in household furnishings, not to exceed $200 for any one item; and (4) his right to receive Social Security, disability, life insurance, and alimony payments.

The debtor is generally free to choose between these federal exemptions and those allowed by his state laws. However, the federal law permits the states to adopt legislation denying their residents the option of taking the federal exemptions.

Priorities When it is time to distribute the debtor's money and property, first priority is given to administrative expenses and expenses incurred in attempting to preserve whatever assets remain, such as the expenses incurred in collecting rent on an income-producing property. Next come creditors whose claims arose in the ordinary course of the debtor's business after the case began. Third priority is given to wages, salaries, or commissions earned within three months of the date the case started or the date the debtor's business ceased, whichever comes first, with a limit of $2,000 for each individual. The fourth goes to claims for contributions to employee-benefit plans arising from services performed within 180 days before the start of the case or after the debtor's business ceases, whichever comes first. The fifth priority is for consumers who have made deposits or partial payments on the purchase or lease of goods and services not provided by the debtor before the proceedings, with a limit of $900 for each individual. See ASSIGNMENT FOR BENEFIT OF CREDITORS; CONSUMER PROTECTION.

■ **Bankrupt businesses: Chapter XI** The Federal Bankruptcy Act also provides for the substantial reorganization of all the financial affairs of failing businesses so that a business can continue to operate, pay its creditors, and, at the same time, protect the interests of its owners. In turn, the national economy is helped because the business continues to provide jobs and goods or services.

The 1978 act combines the business reorganization chapters of the former bankruptcy law into one comprehensive Chapter XI, designed to aid debtors in reorganizing their finances and to protect creditors as well. Creditors must be properly notified of a proposed reorganization plan. An information statement approved by the bankruptcy court must be given to each creditor. In addition to the Securities and Exchange Commission, any other interested party (creditor) may be heard by the court on relevant matters in a Chapter XI case. The debtor has the right to propose a plan during the first 120 days after the case has begun. Otherwise, interested parties may file their own proposals for reorganization.

Chapter XI permits a corporate debtor company to remain in possession of its business and property. But an interested party may request that a trustee be appointed to take possession for cause, such as gross mishandling of the debtor's affairs by the current management. The amount of assets or liabilities is not a cause for the appointing of a trustee. If a request is made for a trustee, the court holds a hearing, and depending on the evidence disclosed at the hearing, it may choose to appoint one. Upon appointment, the trustee may operate the debtor's business. If the court does not appoint a trustee, it may appoint an examiner to investigate past management of the debtor's affairs.

■ **Bankrupt individuals: Chapter XIII** Under Chapter XIII of the 1978 Bankruptcy Act, individuals may develop plans for full or partial repayment of their debts. An individual "with regular income" is permitted to become a Chapter XIII debtor. This is someone whose income is sufficiently stable to enable him to make payments under a proposed plan. Both wage earners and small businessmen are eligible for relief under Chapter XIII. The debtor has an exclusive right to set forth his plan for repayment—creditors, no matter how many there are, cannot force a plan upon him. The plan may provide for repayment over a five-year period or less. Repayment may come from future income or a combination of future income and sale of a portion of the debtor's property.

banks and banking

Banking is the business of receiving on deposit money that is payable on demand, making loans, issuing negotiable notes payable on demand, and performing other money-related functions. A bank is a CORPORATION that engages in banking, although a bank does not have to exercise all the functions just named.

The banking business, because of its nature and its relation to the financial affairs of the people and the revenue of the state, is subject to regulation under the POLICE POWER of the state. A banking corporation derives its right solely from its CHARTER, which it must receive from the state (a state bank) or the federal government (a national bank). To run the everyday affairs of a bank, the stockholders or the directors may enact BYLAWS, which must be reasonable and consistent with the law in general.

A bank may be required by statute to accumulate and maintain a minimum reserve of money in order to meet its daily obligations. In some states, banks have been required to give BONDS for the security of depositors, to protect them from losing the entire amount of their deposits in case the bank can no longer remain in business. The state has the power to enact laws providing for the creation of a guaranty fund to pay depositors in case of bank failure.

A state may set up a supervisory agency over banks and may authorize the adoption of a reasonable system of inspection and reports. If the bank fails to make the required reports, it may be penalized. The federal government has the same authority over national banks, which are discussed later in this article.

■ **Kinds of banks** Technically, there are two major types of banks, banks of deposit and banks of discount. A *bank of deposit* receives money on deposit—that is, it sets up checking accounts or savings accounts. A *bank of discount* lends money on collateral (such as a home mortgage loan or a car loan) or lends money by *discounting.* A bank lends money by discounting when it collects the interest in advance or when it buys a bond, promissory note, or other COMMERCIAL PAPER that is not yet due (payable) at a price that is less than its face value, but collects the face value of the bond (as interest) when it becomes payable. The difference between the price paid and the price to be collected is the interest due on the bond.

EXAMPLE Premier Bank buys a $1,000 bond that is payable O⊷* in one year from Sweet Valley Township for $900. When the bond becomes payable, the township will receive $1,000, $100 more than it paid. This $100 is interest, which the bank earned, in effect, in advance when it gave the township $900 for a bond that was not yet payable.

Although a bank may be classified as either a bank of deposit or a bank of discount, one bank can generally perform the functions of both types.

More often, banks are classified as savings banks or commercial banks. A *commercial bank* makes discounts, issues notes, and receives deposits on which it may pay interest (savings accounts) or, in most cases, on which it may not pay interest (checking accounts). A *savings bank* is a form of bank of deposit. Some savings banks may offer checking accounts, but savings banks were originally organized to receive deposits of money that accumulated at a compound interest for the benefit of the depositors.

In addition to the various types of true banks, there are a number of other financial institutions that engage in banking activities. These include clearing houses, trust companies, and SAVINGS AND LOAN ASSOCIATIONS.

A *clearing house* is an association of banks formed for the daily adjustment of accounts and settlement of balances among themselves. Its purpose is to expedite the exchange of checks and other commercial paper among its members.

A *trust company,* or a *loan and trust company,* is a corporation that is organized to hold and administer TRUSTS rather than to carry on the ordinary functions of banking, but a trust company may be permitted some banking functions in its charter.

A *savings and loan association* is a cooperative that obtains, negotiates, and guarantees mortgages and other loans. The savings deposits it receives are invested in the mortgages and loans it transacts.

■ **Deposits** A bank may offer its customers savings accounts or checking for the customers' deposits. A deposit is a sum of money left with a bank by the depositor. The legal effect of a deposit is to create a debtor-and-creditor relationship between bank and depositor, the deposit being a debt owed by the bank to the depositor. A deposit is complete when money or a NEGOTIABLE INSTRUMENT, such as a check written on another bank, is delivered to the bank within banking hours. A passbook for a savings account or a customer's receipt for a checking account is an admission of the bank's indebtedness to the depositor.

Deposits are broadly classified as general and special. A *general deposit* passes title to (ownership of) money to the bank. The bank becomes the debtor of the creditor-depositor with the obligation to repay the money in current funds on the depositor's order or demand. A special deposit is a delivery of money or other property to a bank for safekeeping and return in kind. There is no debtor-creditor relationship in this situation, but the bank acts as bailee for the depositor-bailor. This is the case with the items you put in your safe-deposit box. See BAILMENT.

Ordinarily, a bank is strictly obligated to return the funds a customer has deposited when the customer demands them. However, a bank may have a banker's lien on the customer's deposited funds if the customer has a debt to the bank that is past due—for example, a payment due on an installment loan a month ago but not yet paid.

A *banker's lien* is the right of the bank to take for its own, money or property left in its care by a customer if he has an overdue debt to the bank and if the money or property, to the bank's knowledge, belongs fully to him. This lien will not affect the contents of safe-deposit boxes or deposits belonging to another, such as trust funds.

Deposits of trust funds If a trustee (a person entrusted with the management of trust funds) places trust funds into a bank and the bank is not aware of the trust arrangement, the deposit is regarded as a general deposit. If, however, the bank receives the funds knowing they are trust funds, the deposit is a special deposit, with the bank acting as an agent of the trustee. A bank that accepts trust funds under such conditions may be held liable to the beneficiary of the trust if it violates the contract of deposit. For example, if the bank allows a trustee to use the trust funds for his personal benefit, the bank must reimburse the

---

WHEN YOU GO TO THE BANK

■ The bank may make reasonable rules, and business customs are binding in transactions with you. For example, the bank has a right to require identification, whether you are known there or not, and to refuse payment without it.

■ You have the right to revoke a personal check by a "stop payment" order; however, if your bank has already paid out the money, your stop payment is too late.

■ Once a check is certified, it cannot be revoked under any circumstances, except when the person who wrote it dies before it is presented for payment.

■ If you endorse a check and it is lost or stolen, your bank can pay anyone who presents the check because your signature is on it. If someone forges your endorsement, however, the bank will probably have to bear the responsibility if it fails to check the validity of the signature, since a bank has a duty to know its customers' signatures.

■ If you do not report a lost or stolen checkbook, the bank will not be responsible because you were negligent.

■ If you write a check so carelessly that it is easy to alter it so as to increase the amount, the bank will not be responsible.

■ If you know or discover that your signature on a check or your endorsement was forged, notify the bank at once. Otherwise you will lose your right to recover from the bank.

■ When you are a depositor with a member bank of the Federal Deposit Insurance Corporation (FDIC), your funds are insured up to $100,000.

---

beneficiary of the trust. When, however, the bank did not know that the funds on deposit were trust funds, the bank is not liable.

Joint deposits and Totten trusts A joint deposit in a bank may be made by two or more persons. This creates a joint tenancy between the depositors, which, upon the death of one, gives the survivor or survivors the remainder of the account.

EXAMPLE Alice Ford and her favorite nephew, Eddie, had a 0—* joint bank account. The passbook read "Alice Ford and Edward Fenton." Each was permitted to deposit or withdraw as much as he or she wished. Both made deposits into the account through the years, although Aunt Alice made larger deposits than Eddie—and Eddie made larger withdrawals. When Aunt Alice died, Eddie gained possession of the entire account, and Aunt Alice's own children had no right to claim any part of the funds in the account as part of their inheritance. Had Eddie died before his aunt, then Alice would have gained possession of the entire account.

Deposits may also be made by one person in trust for another named person. An account into which such deposits are made is called a TOTTEN TRUST.

EXAMPLE Mary Smith opens a bank account for her daughter Jane, and the passbook reads, "Mary Smith in trust for Jane Smith." Mary is the only person who can deposit or withdraw money from the account. Jane has no power over it. Mary can even close the account, and Jane would get no benefit at all. When Mary dies, however, if the account is still open, it becomes Jane's property, to do with as she wishes.

Deposits for collection A deposit for collection takes place when depositor deposits a check, note, or other monetary instrument to enable the bank to act as his agent in obtaining payment of it. The collecting bank presents the check to the issuer's bank, which applies his funds to pay the check.

EXAMPLE You receive your paycheck from Whiz Company, 0—* which has its payroll money on deposit at Rich Bank. You deposit your paycheck in your savings account at First Bank, which acts as your agent for collection of payment. First Bank, the collecting bank, sends your check to Rich Bank, the drawee bank. Rich Bank deducts the amount of your check from the payroll account that Whiz Company has on deposit. This is basically the way a check is collected.

If you want to cash your check, First Bank will pay you if there are enough funds in your savings account to cover the amount of your check until it has been collected from Rich Bank.

If you owed a debt to First Bank, it would have a lien on the check you deposited for collection. When Rich Bank pays First Bank the proceeds of the check, First Bank will be entitled to a setoff (see COUNTERCLAIM), which allows it to deduct from your proceeds the amount you owe it.

■ **Interest on deposited funds** Whether or not a bank pays interest to the depositor on the funds it holds for him depends on the type of account the depositor has. Funds deposited in savings accounts accumulate compounded interest between the time they are deposited and the time they are withdrawn. Compounding interest means adding interest onto the principal, which is the money on deposit, at regular intervals and computing interest on the original sum plus the interest already earned.

EXAMPLE When you deposit $100 in a savings bank that 0—* gives you 5 percent interest per year, compounded annually, the interest earned on $100 is $5 during the first year. During the second year, 5 percent interest will be added onto the sum of $105. Basically, after the first year, you are receiving interest on interest. In actual practice most banks compute interest more frequently than once a year; some compound daily.

As a general rule, the funds that you maintain in a checking account do not earn interest. If you keep $1,000 in your checking account for one year, you will not receive any interest. The same amount kept in your savings account will receive anywhere from 5 to 8 percent interest, which will give you an additional $50 to $80 at the end of the year. (This does not include the effect of compounding interest.) In the past, federal law prohibited banks from paying interest on checking accounts, but in 1980 that law was changed, and banks everywhere could offer interest-bearing savings accounts, called NOW (*n*egotiable *o*rder of *w*ithdrawal) accounts, from which negotiable orders—

checklike instruments—can be drawn by the depositor for a charge of 10 to 15 cents for each order written.

Banks were also authorized to develop a system by which money would be automatically transferred from a customer's savings account to his checking account to cover overdrafts. This would have the same effect as an interest-bearing checking account, since the depositor would have to keep only the required minimum amount in his non-interest-bearing checking account while the rest of his money would be earning interest in his savings account. This is not to be confused with NOW accounts. Under this transfer method, once the money passes from your savings account to your checking account, the bank may penalize you with the loss of up to a quarter of the year's interest on the amount transferred.

These changes represent a trend in liberalizing banking practices concerning checking and savings accounts.

■ **Withdrawals** The possession of a passbook for a savings account or a receipt for a deposit into a checking account does not give you an automatic right to withdraw money from your account. It is a banking custom to require some proof of identification before you can withdraw money from your account. For instance, to withdraw money from your checking account, you write a check for cash, which contains your signature on the front and your endorsement on the back. The bank may also require you to show an identification card they issued you. At the savings bank you must sign a withdrawal slip. The teller compares your signature on the check or slip with your signature on file at the bank or in the passbook for proof of identification. If you try to make a withdrawal without the required identification, the bank has a right to refuse to pay you, regardless of how well you know the tellers.

■ **Periodic statements** The bank has a duty to make periodic statements, and the depositor has a duty to examine them with reasonable diligence to report any errors. For savings accounts the withdrawals, deposits, and interest earned entered in the passbook constitute this statement. Banks that offer checking accounts send their depositors statements each month, listing deposits, paid-out checks, and current balances.

■ **Checks** A check is a document by which a person, the *drawer,* tells his bank, the *drawee,* to pay a certain amount of money to another person, the *payee.* The payment authorized by a valid check must be made strictly according to its terms and properly charged to the drawer by deducting the amount from his account.

Payment of checks The bank must usually pay a check in LEGAL TENDER (money), in order of presentation, and on demand—when the payee presents the check to the drawer's bank to be cashed. Generally, payment is made to the payee when he endorses the check, but a bank need not cash a check for a payee who is not one of its depositors, because it may refuse payment to a stranger. If a bank refuses to cash a check, the payee can go to his own bank or to a check-cashing store, or ask someone who trusts him if he (the payee) can endorse the check over to that person in exchange for the amount of the check.

A bank must honor or pay a depositor's own check when he is named payee provided he has sufficient funds on deposit to cover the check. Checks that have been paid

must be returned by the bank to the drawer, who should examine them to report any errors. When a bank cashes a check made out to a depositor from a third person or company, the amount of money in the depositor's account is subject to a banker's lien until the check clears—that is, until the bank receives the money from the drawer's bank.

Lost or stolen checks A bank is protected when it pays a check that has a blank endorsement (an endorsement that does not specify to whom the check is signed over), even if it is a lost or stolen check, because the blank endorsement entitles the bank to pay anyone who presents the check for payment.

EXAMPLE Before going to the bank, you endorse your pay-
O——* check with your signature, "John Jacob Smith."
If your endorsed check is then lost or stolen, your bank has the right to pay anyone who presents this check to it, because your signature is on it.

On the other hand, a bank will be liable for paying a lost or stolen check if it ignores its duty to inquire into the validity of the signature of its customer—if, for example, someone finds your unendorsed check, forges your signature, and presents it for payment. Also, if you endorsed your check "John Smith, pay Mary Smith only" and your bank paid Joe Jones, who stole it, the bank would be liable for paying in violation of your restrictive endorsement, one that clearly specified to whom payment was to be made.

Overdrafts When a check is properly paid by the bank on which it is drawn, the transaction is closed, the check is retired, and the liabilities of the parties involved are discharged. The payment of an overdraft, which occurs when you write a check for an amount greater than what is in your checking account, amounts to a loan by the bank to you, and you are liable for the overdraft, plus interest. The bank cannot recover the money it paid on an overdraft from the payee or from anyone to whom the check was endorsed.

Wrongful payment A bank is liable to a depositor if it pays his check to someone not authorized by him or the payee. In such a case, the depositor may sue the bank to recover the amount paid. The bank is not liable, however, for payment of a check to an authorized agent of the depositor or payee.

Insolvent drawer When a person with a checking account becomes insolvent (unable to pay his debts as they come due) and a receiver is appointed to manage his property or when there is an assignment for the benefit of his creditors, the authority of the bank to pay his checks as well as the authority of the payee to collect are revoked. See ASSIGNMENT FOR BENEFIT OF CREDITORS; RECEIVER.

Out-of-state checks Since banks cash checks made out to depositors from persons who do not have accounts with them, they are often put into the position of cashing checks drawn on out-of-state banks. Ordinarily, to collect on an out-of-state check, the depositor's bank would have to mail the check to the drawer's bank and insure the cash that was to be sent back in return. However, the Federal Reserve System (discussed below) has developed a system for its member banks that is faster, safer, and less expensive, although it may seem complicated.

Banks that are members of the Federal Reserve System maintain accounts with a Federal Reserve Bank in their district (there are 12 districts in all). When a check drawn on Member Bank A in Federal Reserve District 1 is deposited in Member Bank B in Federal Reserve District 7, Bank B sends it to its Federal Reserve Bank in District 7 (its own district) for collection. The Federal Reserve Bank in District 7 sends the check to a Federal Reserve Bank in District 1. The District 1 bank debits Bank A's account and returns the check to Bank A. The District 1 Federal Reserve Bank then notifies the District 7 Federal Reserve Bank, which credits Bank B's account. Bank B, in turn, credits its depositor's account. In this way the money due on the check is transferred from bank to bank by paper work—the debiting and crediting of the banks' accounts—and no cash need be sent through the mails.

In order to facilitate the operation of this process, banks ordinarily have their depositors use printed checks that are encoded with series of numbers and symbols. The digits and symbols along the bottom of the check at the left are for routing and transit. They identify the particular Federal Reserve Bank used by the member bank, the member bank itself, and the depositor's account number. These numbers are printed in metallic ink with magnetic properties so that the checks can be processed automatically by computer. The top right-hand corner of a check usually carries a fractional number that repeats some of this information and adds the American Bankers Association transit number for the state in which the drawee bank is located.

EXAMPLE Mary's check carries the numbers 07640979 printed near its lower left-hand corner. The number "7" means that Mary's bank is in the seventh Federal Reserve District. The "6" indicates the particular Federal Reserve Bank, within the seventh district, that is used by Mary's bank. The "4" lets the Federal Reserve Bank separate the check from checks from other states in that district (as a Federal Reserve Bank may serve more than one state). The number "979" is a code for the name of Mary's bank. A little to the right of this series of numbers is another series—"300-856-8." This is Mary's account number.

The fraction "$\frac{74\text{-}979}{764}$" appears in the upper right-hand corner of Mary's printed check. The "74" in the numerator is the American Bankers Association transit number for the state in which Mary's bank is located. The bank's identifying number, "979," appears again to the right of this number. The denominator, "764," is a repetition of the Federal Reserve Bank code.

In addition to all these numbers is a final number that is added to the lower right-hand corner of a check after it has been deposited. This number is encoded at the start of the transfer process by the bank at which the customer deposited the check. It stands for the amount of the check. A check for $5.72 might be indicated as "0000000572."

Certification of checks A bank certifies a check when it marks the check in such a way as to indicate that it is guaranteed cashable by the payee or holder—for example, it stamps it "certified cashable." A certified check is the equivalent of cash. A bank is not obligated to certify a check, but once it does so, it must cash that check when it is presented for payment. If the writer of a check has it certified before he delivers it to the payee, the bank agrees to guarantee payment to the payee legally entitled to it, but the drawer still remains liable to the payee.

EXAMPLE A mechanic agrees to fix the transmission on your car only if he is to be paid $400 by certified check. You go to your bank and have your check certified. If you lose the check before you give it to the mechanic, you, the drawer, are still liable to the mechanic for $400, since he never received payment.

But if the payee or holder has the check certified after it has been delivered by the drawer, the bank becomes the absolute debtor and the drawer is released from liability.

Once a check is certified, it is guaranteed payable by the bank on which it was drawn unless the person who wrote the check dies before it is presented for payment. If the bank does pay the payee after the drawer's death, it is liable only if it had notice of the death. In some states, if the payee receives payment after the drawer's death, the payee must refund the amount to the drawer's estate and seek payment from the estate.

Stop payment When you write a check, you can revoke it unless the check has been certified or paid. Revocation is commonly known as a stop-payment order.

EXAMPLE You write a check to pay a plumber and later that day discover his repairs are faulty. You can notify your bank to stop payment on the check. This revokes your order to the bank to pay the plumber. If, however, your bank had paid him before it received your stop-payment order, your revocation is too late. If you gave the plumber a certified check for the faulty repairs, you could not revoke the check under any circumstances.

When the bank honors a check after timely notice of stop payment, it cannot recover the amount from the payee or the holder.

Forged and altered checks A bank is liable to a depositor for charging his account with a forged check, because the bank has a duty to know its customer's signature. If, however, the forgery was a result of the depositor's negligence, the bank may not be liable. If, for example, a depositor did not report a lost or stolen checkbook to his bank, he would be negligent. A bank can, however, recover the amount paid from the forger. A bank cannot recover payment from a BONA FIDE ("in good faith") holder who paid value for a forged check that he assumed was good.

EXAMPLE Smith forges Jones's signature to a check for $300 to pay Thomas for a television set. Thomas accepts the check from Smith, not knowing that it is forged, and he gives a television worth $300 to Smith, the forger. Thomas is a bona fide holder of a forged check. Jones, the person whose signature has been forged, is charged $300 against his account after Thomas has presented the check for payment. Jones may recover the $300 from his bank, which had a duty to know his signature and not pay on a forgery. Jones's bank cannot recover the $300 from Thomas because Thomas gave value in exchange for the check in good faith. The bank may recover the $300 from Smith, the forger, if it can find him.

When a bank in good faith reasonably and without negligence pays a check that has been materially altered, it can charge its customer's account for the original amount of the check before it was altered if it was completed when issued. When a check was complete when issued, the drawer (check writer) really suffers no loss when he is required to pay the amount of the original check as he intended to do. This merely prevents the check writer from getting a windfall at the expense of the bank. The bank can sue the person who has altered the check for the extra amount.

EXAMPLE Gene wrote a check on Second Bank to Larry for ○━━✱ $600 for an air conditioner. When Larry cashed the check, he had skillfully increased the amount to $700. The change was undetectable. Second Bank will be entitled to deduct $600 from Gene's checking account, the amount he originally intended to pay. Second Bank will have to recover the $100, the increase fraudulently made, by suing Larry.

Under the law, a bank that in good faith pays a check that was not completed when it was issued and that has been altered can deduct the amount of the check as it was altered or completed. If, in the example above, Gene had given Larry a blank check telling him to fill in the amount of $600 when he got the chance but Larry filled in $700 instead, Second Bank would be entitled to deduct $700 from Gene's account. When a person issues a check that is incomplete, it is fairer to require that the check writer pay more than he intended rather than making the bank responsible for the loss. Anyone signing an incomplete check should realize that he is courting trouble.

A check writer will also be responsible for a check that has been altered by increasing its amount if he was negligent—for example, if he allowed space to the left of the figures and wrote out the numbers on the check so that the amount could easily be increased. If, however, the bank knew or should have known of the alteration, the bank will be responsible to the check writer for the full amount it paid on the altered check.

EXAMPLE Jan, who runs a small jewelry shop, gave a check ○━━✱ for $4,000 to Maurice, a free-lance jewelry designer, for a number of rings and bracelets. As soon as he left Jan's shop, Maurice altered the amount of the check from $4,000 to $14,000, then cashed it and left town. Jan's bank charged the full $14,000 against her account, which almost depleted it. However, when the canceled check was returned to her, Jan saw that in altering the check Maurice had used blue ink and the check had been written in black ink. Furthermore, the added "teen" was in an obviously different handwriting from the rest of the check. Because, under these circumstances, the bank should have known of the increase, Jan was entitled to a refund of the $10,000 the bank had charged against her account in excess of the check she had written. If the bank refused to give her the refund she could sue it.

Checks to fictitious payees Sometimes a check is made out to a fictitious payee. If the check is paid on a forged endorsement, the bank will not be liable to the drawer if he intended it for a fictitious person.

EXAMPLE A dishonest treasurer of a corporation pads a ○━━✱ payroll list by including names of people who are not employees of the corporation. Checks are made out to those nonexistent employees. The treasurer then endorses the checks, forging the names of the nonexistent payees. Since the treasurer knows that the checks are being issued to fictitious payees, the bank is not liable for any payments made to them.

But if the drawer who wrote the fictitious name intended it for a real person, the bank will be liable.

EXAMPLE Let us say someone else in the corporation ○━━✱ dreamed up the fictitious-employee scheme, and the treasurer, knowing nothing about it, believed that the checks were being issued to real people who earned their pay. The bank would then be liable for payments made to the fictitious payees—under its duty to determine the genuineness of endorsements.

Duties of depositor A depositor must exercise care in examining his canceled checks and his current bank statement to see if his account has been charged with a forged check. Usually, since the bank has a duty to verify endorsements, he has a duty to examine the endorsements on his returned checks only if he has reason to believe they are forged—perhaps some checks he mailed never reached the people to whom they were sent. If the depositor knows or discovers that a check or an endorsement was forged, he must notify the bank promptly or lose his right to recovery from the bank.

Liabilities between banks If the drawee bank (drawer's bank) gave money to a collecting bank to cover a forged check deposited with the collecting bank, the drawee cannot recover its payment unless negligence can be proved. The failure of the collecting bank to check the identification of the person cashing the check would constitute negligence.

■ **Electronic banking** In recent years many banks have adopted electronic fund-transfer (EFT) systems that use computer and electronic technology instead of traditional paper checks, deposit slips, and the like for banking and payment purposes. These systems are designed to make routine banking safer and more convenient. Four major types of EFT services have been offered to consumers:

(1) Automated teller machines, popularly known as 24-hour tellers, permit customers to transact a variety of banking needs at virtually any hour of the day or night.

(2) Pay-by-phone systems let a depositor telephone his bank and order that a third person be paid from his account.

(3) Direct deposits enable a person to have his wages or Social Security benefits automatically deposited in his account. Automatic payments authorize recurring payments, such as utility bills or insurance premiums, to be automatically deducted from his account.

(4) Point-of-sale transfers permit a consumer, through the use of a computer terminal at a department store or other retail establishment, to transfer money instantly from his bank account to the merchant's.

Federal law The use of EFT systems has grown so rapidly in the past few years that they have assumed a significant role in our country's system of payments. This growth, in turn, has created important issues concerning the rights and liabilities of a person who uses an EFT system. In response to these questions, Congress enacted a law, which went into full effect in 1980.

Banks must disclose certain terms and conditions governing these types of accounts to all customers at the time they arrange for an EFT service. The information that must be disclosed includes (1) the consumer's liability if an EFT card is lost or stolen and whom to notify, (2) the type of transactions the consumer can initiate, (3) any charges for transactions, (4) the right to prompt correction of errors, and (5) what account information the bank may disclose to third persons. If any term or condition changes, the consumer must be notified in writing at least 21 days in advance if the change would increase his liability or costs.

Receipts and statements Proper receipts must be made available to customers for transactions made at automated teller machines and for point-of-sale transactions. These receipts must give the amount, date, and type of transaction; the customer's account number; the identity of any third party involved in the transaction; and the location or identification of the branch or machine involved. Receipts are not required for pay-by-phone services.

Account statements detailing EFT transactions for each month one occurs must be made, as well as quarterly statements. In addition to the information contained on a receipt, the statement must give the account's opening and closing balances, charges for transfers or for maintaining the account, and an address and telephone number customers can write or call to ask questions about their accounts or report errors. The requirement regarding statements does not apply to direct deposits of wages and benefits into passbook accounts. In those situations, the banks simply notify the customer that payment has been received.

If there is an error in an EFT account, a customer must notify the bank either orally or in writing within 60 days of receiving the mistaken statement. The bank has up to 10 days to investigate, after which the consumer's account is recredited temporarily with the amount of the alleged error. The bank can continue up to a total of 45 days after notification to investigate the claim of error. If the bank concludes that an error did not occur, it must notify the consumer in writing within three days after its investigation ends. On request, it must supply to the consumer copies of the document on which it based its decision and explain its findings. At that point, the amount of the error must be returned to the bank.

Stopping automatic payments When a consumer has arranged for the automatic payments of his bills from the account, he may notify the bank to stop payment up to three days before the payment is scheduled to be made. If the amounts of such bills vary, the bank must give reasonable advance notice to the consumer of the payment date and the amount so that there will be enough funds in his account to cover this debt.

EXAMPLE Sybil authorized her bank to make automatic
O——* payments to her insurance company and utility company. Sybil's insurance payments always remained the same, so that the bank could automatically pay the premiums for Sybil without notifying her that it was about to do so. But her utility bills varied from month to month, and so every month the bank had to notify Sybil of the amount it was about to pay to the utility company at least one week before it paid the bill to make sure that she deposited enough into her account to cover the payment and the checks she wrote.

Liability A consumer using an EFT service is liable for any unauthorized transfers that occur because his card or any other means of access to use the service is stolen, lost, or used without permission. This liability is limited to $50, however, as long as the consumer has notified the bank within two business days after discovering the loss, theft, or misuse. Failure to notify the bank promptly will extend the liability to $500. If the consumer fails to report any unauthorized charges within 60 days after he receives his monthly statement, his liability is unlimited.

The bank may be liable for any damages caused to the consumer by its failure to act according to the terms and conditions of the account, such as refusing to pay a third person when there are more than adequate funds in the customer's account.

Financial institutions are permitted to send out unsolicited cards to potential users of EFT services as long as the card is not validated. Each card must contain a consumer's identification number (validation) in order to bring about an electronic fund transfer.

The consumer has the right to sue a bank that subjects him to a violation of this law. He is entitled to money DAMAGES awarded to him by the court through his suit, a penalty of $100 to $1,000, and attorney's fees and costs.

Willful violation of the law regarding unsolicited EFT cards also carries criminal penalties consisting of a fine of up to $5,000 and imprisonment of up to a year. Conviction for the knowing, fraudulent, or unlawful use of a stolen, counterfeit, or altered EFT card or means of access (such as a private number to be given in addition to your account number) may result in a fine of up to $10,000 and imprisonment of up to 10 years.

■ **Loans and discounts** A *loan* by a bank usually involves delivering money to a person, called a borrower, upon agreement that the money will be repaid according to the terms specified. For example, you take out a car loan of $2,400 to be repaid over 24 months at 10 percent interest.

A bank has the power to charge interest at the rate permitted by state law. The interest charged usually may not exceed the legal rate before the debt matures—becomes due. In some states, however, once the debt is due, the rate may exceed the legal rate as a penalty for late payment if the loan agreement so specifies.

A *discount* is a transaction in which a bank extends credit or buys on commercial paper, such as a bond or promissory note, for less than its face value. The lower price allows for taking the interest in advance.

EXAMPLE Second Bank buys a $1,000 bond at a discount for
O——* the price of $900. The interest rate on the bond is 10 percent, and the bond is to become due for payment one year from now. Normally, a $1,000 bond with a 10 percent interest rate would yield $100 in interest for a total payment of $1,100 when the bond is cashed on its due date. The bank, however, by buying the bond at $900 instead of $1,000 is taking the interest in advance in the form of a $100 reduction, or discount. In this transaction the interest rate exceeds 11 percent, since the bank would be earning the $100 interest on a $900 investment rather than earning $100 on a $1000 investment at a 10 percent rate of interest.

A bank can also make a loan by discounting commercial paper and then sell the commercial paper to another bank.

EXAMPLE Suppose Jane wants to open a boutique but she
O——* needs $100,000 to do so. She goes to Valley Bank to negotiate the loan and is told that she must put up her $90,000 house, car, and boat as collateral. The bank also requires her to make a promissory note that she will repay the bank within one year with 10 percent interest. The

bank will deposit $90,000 into Jane's account—the borrowed sum ($100,000) minus the amount of one year's interest ($10,000). This transaction is one way a bank extends credit by discounting commercial paper.

The bank can hold the note until it becomes due or it can sell it to another bank for less than its face value. This is also discounting. If Valley Bank sells Jane's $100,000 promissory note to Hillside Bank for $95,000, it has made an immediate profit of $5,000 (it paid Jane only $90,000) without having to wait the entire year.

■ **Banks as agents** A bank can act as an agent for its customers in ordinary banking matters, but it must exercise the care required of agents generally. See AGENCY. For instance, when you tell your bank that you want to purchase some U.S. Savings Bonds, the bank, acting on your instructions, is your agent in the purchase and holds title to (the rights of ownership in) the bonds for you until it delivers them to you.

Banks can borrow money subject to restrictions imposed by statute. Acting as agents, they can transmit money or credit on specific instructions from their customers. They can issue and pay bank drafts and cashier's checks, which you might want to purchase if you needed a guaranteed check. A *bank draft* is a check or order for payment of money issued by an authorized officer of a bank either on his own bank or some other bank (known as the drawee or correspondent bank) in which his bank's funds are deposited. By issuing a draft, a bank declares that it has an account at the drawee bank sufficient to pay the draft when it is presented. A *cashier's check* is a bank draft drawn by an officer on his own bank for payment of money to someone.

A bank draft or cashier's check is often used when a creditor does not trust a debtor's check and wants to insure that he will receive payment, such as when a new retail store orders from a clothing manufacturer. The bank draft and the cashier's check differ from a certified check in that they are written by the banker. A certified check is written by a depositor and guaranteed cashable by the bank. Certified and cashier checks are more common in consumer deals; drafts in business deals.

A bank can also issue a *letter of credit*, authorizing one person to pay money or extend credit to another on the credit of the letter writer. In the days before traveler's checks, people frequently obtained letters of credit from their home bank to present to banks in the U.S. cities or foreign countries they were visiting.

■ **Dissolution and insolvency** Most states have a commissioner of banking or some other state officer whose duty it is to oversee banking practices in his state. The commissioner has the authority to take possession of an insolvent or unsafe bank. A bank is insolvent when it cannot pay its depositors and other creditors in the ordinary course of business because its liabilities exceed its assets.

Liquidation In some states the bank commissioner may LIQUIDATE an insolvent bank and wind up its affairs by paying off its debts with whatever assets remain after business is ended. Once a bank is liquidated, it can no longer transact any banking business. Generally, a bank commissioner takes complete control of all the bank's assets, which he ordinarily has the authority to sell under the direction or approval of the court. He also has the power

and duty to collect all money due the bank and to settle amicably or release any questionable debts subject to court approval. Claims of creditors against the bank must be proved and presented within the time allowed by statute.

Reorganization The reorganization of a bank occurs when the assets of an insolvent bank have been sold by the bank commissioner to a new banking corporation made up of directors and depositors of the insolvent bank, along with its creditors. A plan for reorganization must be submitted to the bank commissioner for his approval. It must treat depositors and creditors fairly. The rights of depositors, creditors, and stockholders in the reorganization are determined by statute and the reorganization agreement. A reorganized bank without a new charter is liable for the debts of the old bank. A new bank (with a new charter) is not liable for the debts of the old bank unless it has expressly assumed them.

Voluntary dissolution or liquidation A bank may go into voluntary dissolution even when it is still able to pay its debts—if, for example, it becomes apparent that its continued existence will lead it to bankruptcy. Dissolution or liquidation may be accomplished, under different statutes, either by the agreement of the stockholders, depositors, and creditors without delivering possession of the assets to the state banking department or by the directors or stockholders acting under the supervision of the bank commissioner. It may also occur when the bank, through its directors, voluntarily places itself in the hands of the commissioner. Assets in voluntary liquidation are held in trust to be distributed fairly among creditors.

■ **Consolidation and merger** A consolidation occurs when two or more existing banks are united into a single bank. The individual existence of the uniting banks is terminated. The new bank acquires the property and assets and assumes the obligations of the combining banks. A merger, on the other hand, takes place when one of the banks remains in existence, absorbing or merging the other banks into itself, acquiring their property and assets.

■ **State and national banks** The United States has both state and national banks. A state bank is chartered by the state in which it operates. A national bank is chartered and regulated by the federal government. Both state and national banks may perform the functions described above (such as receiving deposits and making loans), but national banks stand apart from state banks in some ways.

A national bank is usually regarded as a citizen of the state in which it is located and is a private corporation for private gain, much like a state bank, but it is regarded as an agency of the federal government to the extent that it promotes governmental purposes, such as providing a national currency. A national bank is subject to state laws only as long as they do not conflict with federal laws or lessen the bank's efficiency as an agency of the U.S. government.

The Comptroller of the Currency administers national banks. If a national bank is in danger of losing its assets, the Bank Conservation Act gives the Comptroller of the Currency the power to appoint a CONSERVATOR to protect and conserve the assets of that bank. The reason for appointing a conservator is to allow the bank to remain open until a receiver is appointed to supervise the payment of its debts.

■ **Federal Reserve System** The Federal Reserve System, created by the Federal Reserve Act, regulates the banking practices of member banks. The purpose of the system is to establish uniform commercial banking practices throughout the country. A national bank must become a member bank of the Federal Reserve System, and a state bank or trust company that meets the qualifications specified by the act may become a member bank in its district.

The act provides for the division of the United States into 12 federal reserve districts, under the supervision of a central Board of Governors, which is, in turn, supervised by the Secretary of the Treasury. The act authorizes the incorporation of a Federal Reserve Bank in each district. A Federal Reserve Bank, which is a federal agency, acts as a government depository of public funds (such as Postal Service Funds) and receives and maintains the legal reserves required of its member banks. This reserve is a sum of money representing a certain percent, established by statute, of the total amount of the bank's demand deposits and time deposits. This money is set aside to insure that even if the bank fails, it will still be able to pay the money it owes to its depositors and creditors.

The principal duties of the Board of Governors are to supervise the Federal Reserve Banks and their member banks and to exert influence over credit transactions. The board has the power to examine the affairs of each reserve bank and its members. It publishes a weekly report on the condition of each bank in the system as well as a general summary of conditions in all banks in the system. The board influences credit conditions through its authority under the Truth-in-Lending Act, which requires it to establish regulations to compel a meaningful disclosure of credit terms by lenders so that consumers will be able to borrow money on the best credit terms available.

■ **Federal Deposit Insurance Corporation** The Federal Deposit Insurance Corporation (FDIC) was created by Congress to promote sound banking practices and to aid the government in the performance of its financial transactions. The intent was that by insuring deposits, the FDIC would prevent runs on the bank by depositors and preserve the solvency of insured banks, thereby keeping open the channels of trade and commercial exchange. If a bank failed, the insurance paid to a depositor would restore him to the position he was in when the bank closed. Congress has the power to admit to the FDIC state banks that are not members of the Federal Reserve System.

A member bank is required to display a sign stating that it is a member of FDIC. When you are a depositor with an FDIC bank, your funds are insured up to a maximum of $100,000 in case of bank failure.

EXAMPLE Suppose you have a $10,000 savings account at your bank, which is a member of the FDIC. If the bank fails or becomes insolvent, you will recover your $10,000 and suffer no loss. If, however, your account contained $110,000 and the bank failed, you would recover only $100,000 from the FDIC. You must bear the loss of the additional $10,000 since you took the risk of depositing $10,000 more than the insured limit.

Once the FDIC pays the depositor, it has a claim for that amount against the bank. The depositor, in effect, signs over to the FDIC the right of recovery.

■ **Federal Home Loan Bank System** The Federal Home Loan Bank Board was established to encourage economical home ownership through the Federal Home Loan Bank System. The board supervises savings and loan associations, and building and loan associations, which specialize in lending money for building and buying homes. Under the act, 12 regional Federal Home Loan Banks are established. Every federal savings and loan association and every state-chartered savings and loan association insured by the Federal Savings and Loan Corporation is required to become a member of its regional Federal Home Loan Bank. Like the Federal Deposit Insurance Corporation, the Federal Savings and Loan Insurance Corporation, which was created by the National Housing Act, insures the safety of savings up to $100,000 for each qualified investor's account in an insured institution.

bar association An organization of lawyers on the local, state, or national level. Some common purposes of bar associations include the continuing education of attorneys on recent changes in the law through seminars and the publication of journals, issuing rules for professional responsibility, and monitoring the compliance of attorneys with these rules through disciplinary proceedings. In some states, an attorney is licensed to practice law by virtue of his membership in the state bar association. See also INTEGRATED BAR.

bar examination The written test that a new lawyer must pass in order to practice law. Some states use the "Multistate" exam (an examination that is given in several states); others rely entirely on their own tests.

bargain 1 Negotiate the terms of an agreement; sell for cash or on terms rather than trade or exchange; or negotiate in good faith with the intention of entering into an agreement. For example, a union bargains collectively on the proposed terms of a contract. 2 As a noun, mutual understanding, agreement, or contract of any kind, but one usually dealing with the loan, exchange, or sale of property. A contract between two parties, one of whom wants to sell goods or land and the other of whom wants to buy them, is regarded as a bargain.

bargaining agent A union that has the exclusive right to represent all the employees of a certain type at a company. For example, the Teamsters Union is the bargaining agent for truck drivers employed by a factory.

bargaining unit Those employees in a company who are best suited to be treated as one group for purposes of being represented by a union. For example, truck drivers are a bargaining unit for purposes of being represented by the teamsters union.

barratry 1 In criminal law, the offense of frequently exciting and stirring up quarrels and lawsuits. The term is usually applied to a lawyer who tries to generate a lawsuit from which he can profit. An attorney or his agent who solicits or encourages the persistent prosecution of groundless actions may be guilty of common barratry, which requires more than one act on the part of the accused. Common barratry is usually a misdemeanor punishable by fine or imprisonment or by disbarment of the attorney.

2 In admiralty law, barratry is an act committed by the master or mariners of a vessel for some unlawful or fraudulent purpose—contrary to their duty to the owners—by which the owners sustain injury. For example, if the crew mutinies and forcibly overthrows the master and other ship's officers, it commits a form of barratry.

barrister An English lawyer who argues in court trials. In England a barrister is distinguished from a solicitor, a lawyer who conducts matters out of court.

barter **1** Trade by exchanging goods or commodities for other goods, as opposed to selling or exchanging goods for money. For example, when a farmer goes to a farm machinery dealer and exchanges a cow for a tractor, he has bartered. **2** As a noun, the contract by which parties exchange goods for other goods.

basis **1** The foundation, groundwork, or support; that upon which something may rest. **2** One of the principal component parts of a thing. **3** A fundamental principle. **4** The amount that property is assumed to be worth for tax purposes at the time you receive it.

bastardy action See ILLEGITIMACY.

battery See ASSAULT AND BATTERY.

bearer A person in possession of a NEGOTIABLE INSTRUMENT (for example, a check) that is made out "payable to bearer" or of a negotiable instrument that the writer has signed without specifying the payee, so that anyone who possesses it may insert his name and cash it. See COMMERCIAL PAPER.

belief A sense of conviction about the truth of an idea that lies somewhere between "suspicion" and "knowledge." Belief has been described as being entirely a subjective condition or state of mind as a result of evidence or information received from others. It has been defined as an actual conclusion drawn from information, a conclusion arrived at from external sources after weighing various probabilities, a conviction of the truth of a given proposition, or an alleged fact based on grounds insufficient to constitute positive knowledge. The meaning of "belief" and its distinction from "fact" and "knowledge" are very important in the administration of justice.

below In a lower place, such as a lower court; inferior; of inferior jurisdiction, such as the court where a lawsuit was first started. The court from which an action is removed for review is called the "court below."

bench A seat of judgment, a court for the administration of justice; the seat occupied by judges in court. The judges regarded as a group are the bench, so that when you appear before all the judges composing a court, you are appearing "before the full bench."

bench warrant A paper issued directly by a judge to the police to permit the arrest of a person. A bench warrant is issued by the court itself, or "from the BENCH," for the attachment or arrest of a person in the case of CONTEMPT, someone who has been indicted, or a witness who does not obey a SUBPOENA.

beneficial association An organization, either voluntary or incorporated, that has been formed primarily for the protection or relief of its members or their families and not for profit; a voluntary ASSOCIATION for mutual assistance in time of need and sickness and for the care of families of deceased members. The Benevolent and Protective Order of Elks, the Grand Lodge of the Independent Order of Odd Fellows, and the Loyal Order of Moose are examples of such organizations. Beneficial associations are also known as benefit societies, benevolent associations or societies, and fraternal or friendly societies. There is, however, an essential difference between a benevolent society and a beneficial association. Unlike a beneficial association, a benevolent society—a charity, for example—gives benefits without requiring anything from the person aided.

An alleged beneficial association is illegal when its true object is opposed to the public policy. For example, when an association has as its declared object the payment of death benefits to the person named by its member as beneficiary rather than to the member's family, its purpose is against public policy. This objective is illegal because the association has taken over the function of INSURANCE companies, which are required by statute to provide payment to a designated beneficiary (not necessarily a family member of the decedent) upon the death of the insured.

■ **Incorporation** General and special statutes of the state legislatures specifically provide for the incorporation of voluntary beneficial associations. Let us say that your voluntary beneficial association has embraced a cause not covered by your state's general statute for the incorporation of associations. You find a member of your legislature who is sympathetic to its activities, and he secures passage of a special bill to permit your group to incorporate.

The state-granted CHARTER of an incorporated beneficial association determines its status and powers. A charter cannot be altered or amended by any action of the incorporators without the approval of the state legislature, unless this power is expressly granted in the charter.

Within the limitations imposed by public policy, the powers of a voluntary beneficial association and the rights and liabilities of its members are governed by the articles of association, which are its governing rules. The articles may be amended or repealed at the discretion of its members.

Incorporated associations may consolidate if permitted by law. If Friendly Association lawfully consolidates with Bountiful Association, Friendly's members become members of Bountiful Association. Bountiful Association becomes liable for the obligations of Friendly Association and is entitled to its assets. See CONSOLIDATION.

■ **Constitution and bylaws** A beneficial association, whether voluntary or incorporated, may adopt a constitution and bylaws. Bylaws are rules adopted by the corporation for the regulation of its own actions and of the rights and duties of its members. They should be adopted in the manner set by the constitution of the association. The power to enact general bylaws cannot be delegated to an inferior council or committee except by unanimous consent. In order to be valid, bylaws must apply to all members alike, and if either the constitution or the bylaws of a beneficial society are unreasonable, they are void and inoperative. For example, a bylaw authorizing the expulsion of a member without a hearing would be void. An organization's constitution and bylaws create a contract binding on its members.

■ **Rights to benefits** Benefits payable by a beneficial association are restricted to those specified in its bylaws and any controlling statutes. The contract between an association and its members determines the right to benefits.

A member failing to pay his dues may lose the right to benefits. Ordinarily, one claiming benefits from a beneficial association must exhaust all his remedies within the organization before seeking relief from the court. See EX-HAUSTION OF REMEDIES. If the association has established certain conditions to be met before its members can receive any benefits, these conditions must be satisfied.

EXAMPLE The law of Friendly Association prohibits payment to Smith, a beneficiary, unless he is a registered member. Smith, who is not registered, cannot recover any benefits. If Smith had been registered (if, for example, he had paid his annual dues and attended two meetings a year), he would be entitled to maintain an action for his benefits.

■ **Liabilities** Generally, a beneficial association may not be held responsible for the TORTS (civil wrongs) arising from the unauthorized acts of its agents or members. Nor can it be held to CONTRACTS made by agents or members without the authority to do so.

EXAMPLE Jones, the treasurer of the Policemen's Lodge, claiming to have authority to borrow money for the lodge, borrowed $25,000 from Brown. He gave Brown a note promising repayment in six months. In fact, Jones had no authority from the lodge to borrow the money or give the note. Jones failed to repay the loan in six months. The lodge cannot be held responsible for repayment of the $25,000 because it did not have knowledge or notice of the unauthorized acts of Jones.

An incorporated association may be liable for damages caused by the negligence of its employees in work of a noncharitable character.

EXAMPLE Friendly Lodge owns a building that it rents out for social functions for a profit, when it is not in use for the lodge's activities. The lodge employs a custodian to wax and polish the floors and platforms of the hall. The custodian knows that the platform is potentially dangerous because of a thick buildup of wax but neglects to warn Bella's Art Society, which has rented the hall from Friendly Lodge to hold its monthly meeting. As a member of Bella's Art Society walks across the platform, she slips on the wax, falls off the platform, and breaks her arm. Friendly Lodge will be liable for the woman's injuries.

■ **Officers** The number and kind of officers of a beneficial association, their eligibility, and their powers, duties, and liabilities are determined by its charter and bylaws. Acts of officers outside their authority are not binding on the association unless ratified. See RATIFICATION.

It is the duty of an officer to keep financial records and to account to the association for the funds entrusted to his care. He may not be held liable personally for contracts signed in behalf of the association, and when there has been no fraud or breach of duty, he may enforce a contractual obligation against the association.

EXAMPLE A member of the board of trustees of a lodge, using his own money for his own benefit, buys a mortgage that the bank holds on property belonging to the lodge. He may collect the full amount owed by the association on the mortgage. He is under no duty to purchase the mortgage for the benefit of the association, since he is clearly acting on his own behalf.

■ **Expulsion of members** A beneficial association can discipline members for violation of its rules and may suspend or expel them on just and reasonable grounds, which depend on the bylaws. Grounds may include conviction of a crime, drunkenness and other conduct unbecoming a member, and failure to pay dues. The courts have upheld the validity of bylaws requiring an expelled member of a beneficial association to exhaust his remedies within the organization before resorting to the courts for reinstatement.

As a general rule, a member is entitled to a trial or hearing of the charges against him—and always to a notice of the proceedings and charges—before he is suspended or expelled. A member cannot be tried for an offense different from the one with which he has been charged. The trial should be fairly conducted before an impartial tribunal. Reasonable proof should be presented to support the charges. The findings should show that the specific offense charged was committed, and evidence of other offenses cannot be used to support the findings. The vote or judgment should expressly find the member guilty of the charges made. A suspended or expelled member usually may appeal to some higher tribunal within the association.

■ **Property** The members of a voluntary beneficial association own its property jointly. When it is organized for a specific purpose, such as payment of sick and death benefits, the property is earmarked as a TRUST for that purpose. The interest of an individual member in the association's property ceases when his membership ends.

■ **Fines, dues, fees, and assessments** A beneficial association can discipline its members—by the imposing of fines or penalties, for example—but its power to impose fines, dues, fees, and ASSESSMENTS must be spelled out in its charter or bylaws. Unless the contract of membership provides otherwise, a member is under no legally enforceable obligation to pay dues, although he may be expelled for failure to do so. Money that a member has paid into the association's treasury cannot usually be recovered by him or his representative after his membership terminates. Before a member can be suspended or expelled for nonpayment of dues and assessments, he must usually be given written notice that he is in ARREARS.

■ **Organization** Beneficial associations often consist of a national or central body, with state organizations and local lodges. The charter of the local lodge is regarded as a contract between it and the parent organization. The rules of the association determine the respective rights of local branches and main organizations concerning funds and property. The powers and authority of the local bodies are governed by their charters of incorporation or articles of association and by their constitutions and bylaws, subject only to limitations found in the laws of the central supreme body. Usually, subordinate bodies acting within the scope of their authority may bind the main organization.

The voluntary dissolution, withdrawal, or surrender of a charter by a subordinate body must be accomplished according to statute and rules of the parent association. A unanimous vote of members is commonly required. A beneficial association may have power to suspend or expel a subordinate body, but the central body cannot terminate the legal existence of an incorporated branch. Usually, the funds and property of a subordinate branch do not pass to the main body on its involuntary dissolution, although they may if the laws of the association so provide. Illegal suspension or expulsion of a subordinate body will not deprive it of its property.

■ **Forfeiture, insolvency, and dissolution** The state may revoke a beneficial association's charter if the association has engaged in fraudulent practices. For example, when a beneficial association, in soliciting members, falsely states that they will be entitled to free dental care, the state may start a forfeiture proceeding to take away the charter of the association and prevent it from accepting new members until the proceeding has been completed. A court may dissolve a voluntary or incorporated beneficial association if it misuses or fails to exercise its powers.

A beneficial association usually may be voluntarily dissolved only by unanimous consent of its members. If a statute controls the dissolution of a beneficial association, the law must be followed strictly. A beneficial association may also be dissolved when it abandons its purpose and fails to exercise its functions for an unreasonably long time.

EXAMPLE A local chapter of an association transfers its O——※ property to trustees to be held by them until called for. If, afterward, the local chapter holds no meetings, elects no officials, nor performs any of the objectives of its charter for a long time, the central organization may go to court to have the chapter dissolved.

The occurrence of an event specified in the bylaws of the association as a cause for its disbanding does not by itself result in dissolution, but the inability of the association to accomplish the purpose for which it was organized may bring about its dissolution. Mere disagreement among the chapter members is usually not a ground for dissolution.

When a beneficial association is dissolved, its funds and property should be distributed fairly and according to the laws of the association. Usually, administrative expenses of dissolution will be paid first. Next in line will be creditors of the association. Finally, the remaining funds will be paid to the members of the association. When a branch or local lodge of an association is dissolved, its funds and property will revert or return to the main chapter or supreme body if its constitution or charter provides for this. A dissolved association may be revived when a majority of the members are interested in reforming it. See REVIVE.

A RECEIVER may be appointed for an association in INSOLVENCY or dissolution proceedings, allowing the court to assume control of the association's affairs. A receiver may also be appointed if the association has been mismanaged or if it is in danger of insolvency, but the mere reduction of receipts, such as during a period of general economic depression, is not a ground for the appointment of a receiver. Once appointed, the receiver acquires title to legal ownership of the assets of the association and has a duty to take possession of them. When appointed after insolvency, he may sue the officers of the association for mismanagement.

beneficial interest The benefit, advantage, or right to profits resulting from a CONTRACT, ESTATE, or PROPERTY, as opposed to the legal ownership of (title to) these things. The person having a beneficial interest in property takes it solely for his own use or benefit, while someone else holds the legal title. A beneficiary has a beneficial interest in a TRUST and receives income from the trust for his own use, while the trustee holds legal title to the trust.

beneficial use The right to use and enjoy property according to one's own liking or in order to derive a profit or benefit from it, including all that makes it desirable or habitable—such as light, air, and access. Beneficial use is to be distinguished from a right to occupy or possess. This right to enjoy exists when one person legally owns the property while another has the right to use it. For example, if someone builds a 10-foot concrete wall behind your backyard, cutting off the sunlight to your garden, you have been deprived of the beneficial use of your yard even though you still occupy it. You can sue the ADJOINING LANDOWNER if the law of your particular jurisdiction recognizes this as a ground for damages or if an EASEMENT has been granted to you. In some jurisdictions, you may be entitled to have the wall torn down.

beneficiary 1 A person or organization for whose benefit a TRUST is created. 2 A person to whom an INSURANCE policy is payable. 3 A person who inherits under a WILL. 4 One entitled to a BENEFICIAL INTEREST. 5 Any person who derives an advantage from the kindness of another; one who receives a benefit or advantage.

benefit of clergy The right that clergymen had in England to avoid trial by nonchurch courts. In the United States today benefit of clergy does not exist.

benevolent corporation 1 A nonprofit charitable organization. Benevolent corporations, also called benevolent associations, may receive certain tax advantages. 2 A BENEFICIAL ASSOCIATION.

bequeath Give personal property or money by will to another, as distinguished from DEVISE, which is to give real property (real estate) by will. Courts sometimes allow the misuse of the word "bequeath"—"I bequeath my house"—where the intention of the TESTATOR clearly showed he wanted the real property to pass by will, that is, by devise.

bequest A gift by will of personal property or money. See BEQUEATH. Sometimes used to mean a DEVISE of real property (real estate) when the TESTATOR clearly intended real property to pass by will.

best-evidence rule A rule of EVIDENCE requiring that the most reliable available proof of a fact must be produced. For example, if a painting is available as evidence, a photograph of the painting will not do. A written document itself is always regarded as the best possible evidence of its existence and contents; a copy or the recollection of a witness would be secondary evidence, to be received as a substitute only if the original writing cannot be produced. The best evidence of a fact is the testimony of a person who knows.

bestiality Sexual intercourse between a human and an animal—a crime in most states. See BUGGERY; SODOMY.

beyond a reasonable doubt The level of proof required to convict a person of a crime. For a jury to be convinced beyond a reasonable doubt, it must be fully satisfied that the person is guilty, not that he is probably guilty or is likely guilty. This is the highest level of proof required in any type of trial. There must be legally sufficient evidence so complete that it overcomes reasonable theories of innocence and excludes every other reasonable hypothesis.

bias 1 Preconceived opinion that makes it difficult to be impartial. 2 Preconceived opinion by the judge about one or more of the persons involved in a lawsuit, as opposed to an opinion about the subject matter. 3 A predisposition to decide an issue in a certain way, which does not leave the mind open to impartial evaluation of the evidence.

bicameral Having two chambers. A legislature with two "houses," such as the Senate and the House of Representatives in the Congress of the United States, is bicameral.

bigamy The crime of having two husbands or wives at the same time. It involves willfully and knowingly marrying a second time while being validly married to another person. In some states bigamy committed by one person gives his or her spouse a ground for divorce. See Chart 22. A bigamous marriage is always void, or without any legal effect. Bigamy is punishable by imprisonment or a fine, depending on state law.

■ **Elements** An essential element of bigamy is a valid marriage entered into by the accused bigamist before the bigamous marriage. The consent of the parties is essential to a valid prior marriage, but no particular form of ceremony is necessary. A COMMON-LAW MARRIAGE may be sufficient. The bigamist must know that his or her spouse is alive at the time of the second marriage.

A voidable marriage is sufficient to support an indictment for bigamy. For example, if both parties to the first marriage were under the legal age for marriage, the marriage is voidable, that is, it is valid unless one of the parties wants to have it annulled. If no ANNULMENT is sought by either party, however, the marriage of one of them to another person is bigamous.

If the first marriage was dissolved by annulment or divorce before the second took place, there is no bigamy, but a fraudulent or ineffective divorce is no defense to a bigamy charge.

EXAMPLE A woman goes to Nevada to obtain a divorce
O——* without her husband's knowledge and hires a man to pose as her husband during the proceedings. The resulting divorce is void, since it was obtained fraudulently. If she remarries, she commits bigamy.

Except under particular statutes, COHABITATION, or living together after the second marriage, is not essential to the offense. Bigamy is committed when the second marriage is performed.

EXAMPLE Sarah, an attractive woman of 65, met Richard, a
O——* dashing young man of 35, who swept her off her feet. Convinced that Richard really loved her and was not after her money, Sarah married him. As the happy couple was leaving the church after their wedding, Sarah's daughter-in-law rushed up to her and showed her proof that Richard already had a wife and six children, all of whom he had deserted a year earlier. Sarah was grief-stricken, but went home with her daughter-in-law and son and never saw Richard again. Even though the marriage of Sarah and Richard was never consummated, Richard was prosecuted for bigamy and found guilty.

The place where the marriage ceremony was performed has jurisdiction in prosecuting the crime. Under some statutes, however, the accused may be convicted where the bigamous cohabitation occurs, even though the marriage took place outside the state.

■ **Defenses** Certain statutes provide that remarriage after a certain time during which the former spouse was absent and thought to be dead is not bigamy. For example, when the husband disappears without any explanation from his residence for seven years, in many jurisdictions he is presumed dead. If the wife honestly does not know his whereabouts and believes him to be dead, she may legally remarry seven years after the time he disappeared if a court has declared him dead. If the wife remarries four years after the husband vanishes, however, she is guilty of bigamy in these jurisdictions, because the statutory period has not expired and her first marriage is still regarded as valid. Her remarriage is considered void and without any legal effect.

In some states an honest belief, reasonably entertained, that a divorce has been granted is a defense to bigamy; but in most it is generally held to be no defense. Erroneous legal advice that the second marriage is valid is no defense to bigamy, nor is ignorance or mistake as to the law.

EXAMPLE Mary's neighbor, a mechanic, told her that he had
O——* heard that valid mail-order divorces could be obtained from Mexico. Since Mary was no longer living with her husband, she immediately wrote for a divorce and received it. Soon after, Mary remarried. Unfortunately, the state she lived in and remarried in did not recognize mail-order Mexican divorces. Mary was guilty of bigamy even though she believed her divorce to be valid. She had the obligation to find out exactly what the law was on the subject before remarrying.

The fact that a divorce or annulment of either marriage was obtained after the second bigamous marriage is no defense either. A belief that it is not wrong to have two or more wives is not a defense, nor is the claim that a person was compelled to remarry by his religious beliefs. It is no defense that the second spouse knew of the first marriage or that the first spouse knew of the second marriage.

bilateral contract 1 A deal that involves promises, rights, and duties on both sides, imposing obligations on both parties. 2 A CONTRACT of mutual promises, such as a contract of sale, by which one party promises to deliver the thing to be sold and the other party promises to pay the price of it.

bill 1 A formal written declaration, complaint, or statement. 2 A formal written statement sent to a higher court either to inform it of certain facts or to request certain actions. For example, a bill of exceptions is a list of objections to the rulings and actions of the trial judge by one side. See APPEAL AND ERROR. 3 A draft of a law proposed to a legislature or working its way through the legislature. 4 A law passed by a legislature when it proceeds like a court, such as a bill of ATTAINDER. 5 A formal legislative declaration of popular rights and liberties, such as the BILL OF RIGHTS. See CONSTITUTIONAL LAW. 6 A list of debts, contract terms, or items, as a BILL OF LADING. 7 A type of NEGOTIABLE INSTRUMENT promising the payment of money, such as a bill of exchange, which is a written order from A to B telling B to pay C a certain amount of money. See also COMMERCIAL PAPER. 8 A statement of details in court, such as a BILL OF PARTICULARS.

bill of attainder See ATTAINDER.

bill of lading A document given by a railroad, shipping company, or other CARRIER that lists the goods accepted for transport and sometimes the terms of the shipping agreement. It is a receipt showing that goods have been delivered for transportation and may also provide written evidence of the terms of the shipping contract as well as who has title to the goods.

bill of particulars A document designed to aid the defendant in answering charges or claims by a plaintiff and in preparing for trial by giving him detailed information regarding the cause of action (ground for suing). It is neither a formal COMPLAINT nor proof of the facts contained in it. It gives the accused fair notice of what he must defend and is presented on his request.

bill of review A request, based on certain limited grounds, such as newly discovered evidence, that a court review, correct, or reverse a final decree that it has handed down. It is similar to a writ of error. See APPEAL AND ERROR.

Bill of Rights The first 10 amendments to the U.S. Constitution, which define and guarantee the fundamental rights and liberties of all persons, including freedom of religion, speech, press, and assembly, as well as guarantees of SPEEDY TRIAL by jury in criminal cases and protection against excessive BAIL, CRUEL AND UNUSUAL PUNISHMENT, unreasonable SEARCHES AND SEIZURES, and SELF-INCRIMINATION. See also ASSEMBLY, RIGHT OF; CONSTITUTIONAL LAW; DUE PROCESS OF LAW; RELIGION, FREEDOM OF; SPEECH AND PRESS, FREEDOM OF.

binder 1 A written MEMORANDUM of an agreement for INSURANCE, intended to give temporary protection awaiting the completion of an investigation of the risk involved and the issuance of a formal policy. 2 In marine insurance, an application for insurance made on behalf of the proposed insured and approved by the insurer or by his agent. 3 In real estate transactions, a written agreement between buyer and seller indicating that the buyer has paid a small sum, usually $50 or $100, for the right to purchase the property. The binder is a contract that will be replaced by the formal contract of sale, which will specify in detail the agreed-upon terms of the sale.

binding authority Sources of law that must be taken into account by a judge in deciding a case. Examples include statutes from the same state or decisions by a higher court of the same state.

binding over 1 The act by which a court requires a person to furnish BAIL or enter into a RECOGNIZANCE to assure that he will appear for trial, to attend as a witness, or to keep the peace. 2 The act by which a court transfers a defendant to another court in the same system.

Blackacre A fictitious name used by legal writers to refer to a parcel of land; often used together with Whiteacre to distinguish one piece of land from another.

blacklist A list of persons marked out for special avoidance, antagonism, or enmity on the part of the people who prepare the list or the people who consult it, such as a trade union's list of workmen who refuse to conform to its rules. The term also refers to the practice of one employer presenting to another the names of troublesome "blacklisted" employees. When used as a verb, blacklist means to intend to injure by preventing future employment. An example of this occurred when certain actors, writers, and directors were blacklisted in the 1950's in Hollywood and in the radio and television industry because they were believed to be Communists.

blackmail A crime that involves illegal pressure to extort money by threatening to expose a person's illegal act or to destroy his reputation. The term is often used interchangeably with EXTORTION. In some states, however, the threat must be in writing for the crime to be blackmail, as distinguished from extortion, when the threat is oral.

blank 1 A space left unfilled in a written document in which one or more words or marks are to be inserted to complete the sense. 2 A printed form of a legal document with empty spaces for names, dates, figures, and additional clauses. 3 As an adjective, lacking something essential to completeness; unrestricted, such as a blank check.

blank endorsement The endorsement of a bill of exchange, promissory note, or check by merely writing the name of the endorser, without specifying to whom the bill or note is to be paid. If you endorse your paycheck with just your signature, you are telling the bank to cash your check for anyone who presents it for payment, since you have not limited or restricted to whom it can be paid. See COMMERCIAL PAPER.

blasphemy   Speaking evil of the Deity for the purpose of dishonoring the Divine Majesty and alienating the minds of others from the love and reverence of God. Blasphemy is an offense at common law as well as by statute in some jurisdictions. Intent is an essential element of the offense, and the blasphemy must be published or uttered in the presence of another person. Enforcement of blasphemy statutes is virtually unheard of today.

block   **1** A square or portion of a city or town enclosed by streets, whether partially or wholly occupied by buildings or containing only vacant lots.   **2** The portion of a city surrounded by streets that is described by a map showing how a piece of land will be subdivided. It must be surrounded on at least three sides by streets or avenues.

blotter   The written record kept in each police station, in which entries are made when suspects are booked. Each entry includes facts about the person's arrest and charges, and identification (which may include fingerprints) and background information. See BOOKING.

blue book   **1** A book showing the proper form of case CITATIONS.   **2** A book that gives the organization of and lists the persons in a state government.

blue law   A state or local law that forbids selling or other business activities on Sunday. Its purpose is not to impose religious observance but to enforce one day of rest out of seven. For a full discussion of "blue laws," see SUNDAY LAW.

blue-ribbon jury   A JURY specially chosen according to procedures set by state law to try an important or complex case. This is rarely permitted.

blue-sky law   A popular name for a state law regulating and supervising investment organizations, including real estate investment companies, that sell stocks and bonds. Blue-sky laws were passed to protect people from investing in fraudulent companies that sell stocks and bonds as "worthless as the blue sky," such as visionary oil wells and distant gold mines. See also SECURITIES REGULATION.

board of directors   A group of people who make up the governing body of a CORPORATION.

body   **1** A person or an organization, such as a "body corporate" (a CORPORATION).   **2** The main, or most important, part of a document.   **3** A collection of laws.

body execution   A court order directing that the defendant be committed to jail.

boiler plate   A document form, usually sold by a stationery store. The word implies standardization or lack of tailoring to the individual legal problem. Real estate deeds are common examples.

bona fide   (Latin) "In good faith"; real; acting honestly without purpose to defraud. For example, a bona fide

purchaser is a person who purchases property for money in the belief that the seller had a right to sell and is not practicing fraud or deceit.

bond   A written promise (or obligation) binding a government, corporation, or individual, the *obligor,* to pay a sum of money to someone else, the *obligee,* on a certain date. A bond is a document that represents a debtor-creditor relationship between the obligor and the obligee. The obligor borrows money from (or sometimes promises to do something for) the obligee and gives him a bond that is evidence of his right to money (or performance of some act on a certain date). Bonds are classified as either simple or conditional.

■ **Simple bond**   A simple bond is an obligation by which the obligor binds himself or his representative to pay a certain sum to the obligee at a specified date. An example is a U.S. Savings Bond. The United States as the obligor promises to pay the amount of the bond to you, the obligee, on the date specified on the bond. When you buy a savings bond, you pay an amount less than the face amount of the bond. When the bond becomes payable and you go to the bank to cash it in, you will receive the face amount. The difference between the price you paid for the bond and the money you receive when the bond is due is the amount of interest you earned on the bond. If you cash in a U.S. Savings Bond before its maturity date (the date it becomes payable), you will not receive the face amount of the bond. Instead, you will get an amount that includes less interest than you would have earned if you held the bond until maturity.

EXAMPLE   Suppose you and your wife receive a $100 U.S. Savings Bond, Series EE, as a wedding present from your Aunt Ellen. The maturity date on the bond is 11 years from the date of your wedding. Because you have many expenses, you decide to cash in the bond after six months (the earliest date on which you can cash it). When you do so, the bank can only pay you $50, the amount Aunt Ellen paid for it, plus a small amount of interest. If, however, you keep the bond until the maturity date, you will receive $100.

Corporate bonds   A bond issued by a corporation to help raise additional capital in order to expand its operations, such as to modernize production facilities, is another type of simple bond. The corporation will offer to investors an issue of bonds that really are promises to pay a fixed sum with interest on a certain date. A corporate bond is secured (backed up) by a LIEN (a legal claim) or MORTGAGE on corporate property. This means that if the corporation should meet financial disaster, the bondholders will have the right to demand that the particular property backing up the bonds be sold to pay off their claims.

A corporate bond is often made payable to bearer (the person who has the bond in his possession) and has *interest coupons,* which reflect the obligation of the corporation to pay the interest periodically. When the interest has been earned, the bondholder clips the appropriate coupon and deposits it in a bank in order to collect the interest. Corporate bonds may also be registered in the name of a specific individual. The interest is paid directly to the registered owner and no coupons are involved.

Unlike a *stock,* which represents a share of ownership in the corporation, a bond represents a corporate debt. A bondholder is not an owner of the company, whereas a stockholder owns part of the assets and has a right to participate in the profits of the corporation. Should the corporation be dissolved, the stockholder has a right to share in the assets remaining after the debts are paid—including those owed the bondholders—according to the amount of stock he holds.

A *debenture,* in contrast to a bond, is a corporation's obligation to pay money, usually in the form of a promissory note, that is not secured or backed up by a lien or mortgage on any specific property. If the corporation has financial difficulties, investors holding debentures cannot demand that specific property be used to pay them. Although bonds and debentures differ, the term "bond" often refers to both.

Municipal bond   Another type of simple bond is a municipal bond, offered for sale by towns, cities, or other municipalities in order to finance public works projects, such as constructing sidewalks and sewers. Such bonds are usually offered for sale to investors in units of $5,000 to $10,000, payable at some future date. The interest earned on such bonds is usually exempt from income taxes.

■ **Conditional bond**   A conditional bond is one by which the obligor promises to pay the obligee only if a certain condition or event occurs. For example, when you post a BAIL bond for someone who has been arrested, you will pay (or forfeit) the amount of the bond only if the accused person fails to appear in court for his trial. In the case of an employee who is bonded—such as a messenger who delivers money, stock certificates, or bonds—the money posted becomes payable if he steals something during the course of his work. The following are some other kinds of conditional bonds:

(1) A person who has been named executor in another person's WILL may be required under state law to post a bond with the court when he asks the court's permission to distribute the dead person's property. The bond protects the heirs of the decedent against loss of the property if the executor acts dishonestly. If this occurs, the bond money will be divided among the heirs to make up for their losses. See EXECUTORS AND ADMINISTRATORS.

(2) A carnival comes to town and posts a bond with the town manager to be paid if the carnival leaves without cleaning up the grounds on which it was held.

(3) A new magazine holds a contest in order to get subscribers; it posts a bond to guarantee the prizes.

(4) A member of a church congregation offers to let the church exhibit her valuable collection of antique toys in its auditorium as part of a fund-raising drive. Since the value of the collection exceeds the church's insurance coverage, the church gives the woman a bond for the difference.

In order for a conditional bond to be valid, the condition must be clearly stated in the bond. The bond also must identify the parties involved and the amount to be paid (if the condition or event occurs); and it must be signed by both parties. An obligor may have enough financial resources to post the bond himself. Most obligors, however, obtain a bond from a surety (a person or corporation that agrees to pay the bond should the obligor become liable) for a nonrefundable fee of 10 to 20 percent of the face value of the bond. See PRINCIPAL AND SURETY.

Breach of condition   If an obligor fails to perform a condition according to the terms of the bond, the bond becomes payable on demand. This means that if someone who has been arrested leaves town in violation of the terms of his bail bond, the person who posted the bond for him will have to pay the court the face amount of the bond. Once the full amount of the bond has been paid, the bond no longer has any legal effect.

Cancellation   A conditional bond may usually be canceled by the agreement of the parties. For example, if the new magazine decides to cancel its contest, it would have to contact the surety, who in turn would notify the obligee of the bond that the obligor wanted to cancel. The obligee would have to give his assent.

booking   The process by which the police write down the facts about a person's ARREST and charges along with identification and background information. These facts are recorded on the police BLOTTER in the police station.

WHEN YOU BUY A BOND

■ A bond is a written promise to pay a sum of money to someone else on a certain date.

■ A *U.S. Savings Bond* is a *simple bond.* When you buy it, you pay less than the face value; when it becomes payable, you get the face amount; if you cash it in ahead of time, you get the purchase price plus some interest.

■ A *corporate bond* is basically a promise to pay a fixed sum with interest on a certain date; it is often made payable to "bearer"—that is, anyone who has it in his or her possession. Such a bond has attached to it coupons corresponding to interest periodically due to the bondholder—when the interest has been earned, you clip the coupon and deposit it in a bank to collect the interest.

■ The difference between stocks and bonds is clear-cut: a stock represents a share in a corporation; a bond represents a *debt* owed by the corporation. Therefore, a bondholder is a creditor of the corporation, whereas a stockholder is one of its owners.

■ Another common type of bond is the *municipal bond.* Municipal bonds are issued to finance public works projects and usually sold to investors in units of $5,000 to $10,000. The interest earned on such bonds is exempt from income taxes.

■ A *conditional bond* is payable only if a certain condition or event occurs. A bail bond, for example, must be paid if the accused person "jumps bail" and fails to appear in court. The bond on a bonded employee must be paid if that employee steals during the course of his work. In some states, the executor of a will is required to post a bond to protect heirs against loss of property if the executor acts dishonestly.

book value **1** Applied to stocks, the value per share shown by deducting LIABILITIES from ASSETS and then dividing the remaining net worth by the number of shares outstanding. For example, a corporation has 100 shares of stock issued and outstanding. Its assets equal $100,000 and its liabilities $90,000. The net worth of the corporation is $10,000. The book value of each share of stock is $100. **2** Applied to finance, the value of something shown on the company's books of account.

boundary A line or object showing the limits or farthest extent of a tract of land or territory. The phrase "land line" is synonymous with boundary. Natural and artificial monuments are often used as boundaries. Natural monuments are permanent objects found on land as they were placed by nature, such as lakes, ponds, rivers, rocks, and mountains. Artificial monuments are landmarks or signs erected by man, such as stakes, stones, or walls.

bounty A sum of money given, usually by the federal or state government, to a person for some service he has done for the public. A bounty differs from a REWARD in that a reward is usually paid only once to a person who has performed a particular service, such as providing information leading to the arrest of a criminal. On the other hand, a bounty is usually offered when the services of many persons are needed. Each person who acts is entitled to a bounty. For example, bounties are offered for destroying animals, such as rabbits, that are harmful to crops, or for those, such as wolves, that kill livestock.

boycott **1** An attempt to prevent others from doing business with a company or to harm the business of someone by threatening, coercing, or intimidating the employees of the business. **2** The refusal to do business with a company. In recent years consumers have used the boycott as a weapon to fight rising prices, refusing to buy such products as beef and coffee until the costs came down. **3** In labor law, a primary boycott occurs when an organized union of employees, through united action, stops dealing with an employer. For example, union members sometimes refuse to work in the manufacture of products not bearing the union label. A SECONDARY BOYCOTT is a tactic to put coercive pressure on customers, actual or prospective, to cause them to withhold or withdraw their patronage. For example, when union members set up a picket line in front of the entrance to a store's parking lot, this may be viewed as a secondary boycott.

breach of contract Failure, without legal excuse, to perform any promise that forms the whole or part of a contract; failure to carry out the terms of a contract. Breach of contract also takes place when one party prevents the other from discharging a duty imposed by the contract.

> EXAMPLE Smith contracts with Jones, a housepainter, to
> O⊶⚹ paint the inside of his house. After Smith has
> agreed to the estimate and the contract has been signed,
> he decides he does not want his house painted after all and
> refuses to allow Jones into his house. By this act, Smith
> has prevented Jones from discharging his duty under the
> contract. Smith is guilty of breach of contract.

You may sue for breach of contract only during a limited number of years after the breach occurs. To learn the legal limitations in your state, see Chart 7. For a full discussion of what may constitute a breach of contract, see CONTRACTS.

breach of marriage promise A right to sue for breach of MARRIAGE promise exists at common law, but this right has been abolished by many states.

■ **Agreement to marry** An agreement to marry, which can be made only between a man and a woman, is different from every other CONTRACT known to law, because its objectives as well as the relationship created between the parties are totally unlike those of any other contract. To authorize recovery for breach of promise, it must be established that there was a valid contract between the parties. This is done by showing that both parties clearly intended the agreement to be binding. If, however, the parties to the contract are incapable of making a valid contract of marriage because they are under a legal DISABILITY, such as being underage, then an action for breach of marriage promise cannot be maintained.

As a general rule, if the promisor at the time of the agreement is a minor and under the legal age to marry, it is a valid defense to a suit for breach of promise, but it is not a defense if the promisee is a minor.

> EXAMPLE If a 15-year-old boy promised to marry a 22-
> O⊶⚹ year-old woman, the woman could not bring an
> action for breach of marriage promise because the promisor, as a minor, is incapable of validly contracting marriage. If, however, a 22-year-old man promised to marry
> a 15-year-old girl, the man could not use as a defense the
> fact that the girl was under the legal age if he changed his
> mind about marrying her. Her incapacity to contract a
> marriage validly is of no consequence.

In some cases, a minor may be stopped, or prevented, from using his age as a defense in a suit for breach. This occurred when a 19-year-old man promised a 17-year-old girl he would marry her and then made her pregnant. The court decided that the defendant could not use being underage as a defense against a breach of promise action.

Someone who is incapable of making a contract because of insanity or who is so closely related to the promisor that a marriage between them would be unlawful (INCEST) cannot sue for breach of a promise to marry. If one of the parties is already married and this fact is known to the other party, a promise to marry is invalid, but if the person to whom the promise was made did not know of the marriage, DAMAGES will be allowed.

■ **Offer and acceptance** An offer and acceptance are essential to the creation of a contract to marry. The offer need not be in formal language as long as both parties understand that an offer of marriage was intended.

> EXAMPLE A man has been dating a woman for 10 years and
> O⊶⚹ has repeatedly told her that if she will "wait," he
> will "make it permanent" once he inherits the family
> fortune. If the woman agrees, it is clear that there has
> been a meeting of their minds and an offer of marriage
> was intended.

A mere statement of intention made to a third person is insufficient. When you tell your brother that you intend to marry a particular man, you cannot be liable for breach of marriage promise if you did not make the offer to the man himself. An acceptance of an offer should be communicated to the other party within a reasonable time. Acceptance may be inferred from the promisee's behavior.

Although a promise to marry must be based on a CONSIDERATION (inducement), the promise of one party is the usual and sufficient consideration for the promise of the other. Sexual intercourse is insufficient consideration.

However, the fact that there has been unlawful sexual intercourse between the parties either before or after the promise does not invalidate a promise based on lawful consideration. For instance, if a defendant promised a woman that in any event he would marry her and that he would marry her at once if he made her pregnant, the promise to marry will support an action for breach of marriage promise.

A promise to marry may be conditional. In such a case liability for a breach of promise cannot arise until after the condition has been fulfilled.

EXAMPLE A woman promises a man she will return from
O—* Europe and marry him within six months. She is not liable for breach of promise after three months. On the other hand, if a man promises a woman he will marry her if she returns from Europe within six months, he is not liable for breach of promise if she returns 18 months later and he refuses to marry her.

If no definite time is fixed for marriage, the contract will be interpreted as providing for marriage within a reasonable time as determined by circumstances of the case.

Although a contract to marry may be demonstrated by several promises made at different times, there is only a single contract and there can be only a single breach.

A promise to marry is invalid if made under DURESS or as a result of FRAUD that, if exposed, would prevent the promise from being made. If a man promises to marry a woman and then later learns that she has hidden the fact that she has an illegitimate child, he is under no liability for breach of marriage promise. Her fraud cannot impose liability on him.

A contract to marry may be abolished, RESCINDED, or released by mutual consent or by one party if there has been fraud or duress. Consenting to postpone the marriage does not show a release.

■ **Breach** A refusal to marry without a sufficient excuse is a breach of promise to marry. Postponement of the wedding does not show a breach unless there is no reasonable cause and the postponement can be regarded as a refusal to carry out the contract. When the defendant has breached his contract and the plaintiff later refuses to marry him, the plaintiff has a right to damages at least up to the time of her subsequent refusal.

EXAMPLE Annemarie and George were engaged to be mar-
O—* ried. One month before the wedding, Annemarie closed out her $15,000 savings account and she and George bought furniture and a car. The furniture was delivered to George's apartment, where the happy couple planned to live, and the car was put into George's name, because Annemarie did not yet know how to drive. Two days before the wedding, George told Annemarie that she was too boring to marry and took off in the car for Canada. Annemarie became severely depressed over her

rejection and had to undergo intensive psychotherapy. If Annemarie sues George when he returns from Canada for breach of marriage promise and wins, she may recover $15,000 (the costs of the furniture and car that she bought because of George's marriage promise) and the costs of the psychotherapy that she needed as a result of George's breach of promise.

■ **Defenses** Certain defenses to an action for breach of a contract to marry—the invalidity of the contract, the termination of the contract, and the lack of capacity of the parties—have been discussed above. There are still other defenses to breach of promise.

As a general rule, a defense to an action for breach of promise to marry cannot be based on the plaintiff's undesirable character traits or his objectionable conduct, such as drunkenness. If the conduct amounts to a FELONY, however—selling narcotics, for example—it is a valid defense.

In some states, the plaintiff's lack of love for the defendant is considered fraud in the promise to marry and is therefore a valid defense.

EXAMPLE George Greenbacks, a wealthy businessman, falls
O—* in love with Greta Goldigger and asks her to marry him. She accepts. Two weeks before the wedding is to take place, George finds out from a friend of Greta's that she is only after his money and has no intention of ever living with him. George cancels the wedding and tells Greta that he will never see her again. When Greta sues him for breach of marriage promise, George may claim Greta's lack of love for him as a defense.

The unchastity of the female plaintiff, which was unknown to the defendant at the time, affords a good defense to her suit for breach of promise, but mere rumors of unchastity do not justify a defendant's repudiating his promise. Even if the plaintiff reforms after the promise of marriage, the defendant may use the defense of unchastity at or before the time of the engagement.

Disease or physical incapacity making it unsafe or improper to marry usually is a good defense. For example, when a woman promises a man that she will marry him and later learns that she has a terminal illness, either party may repudiate the promise. No defense is available, however, when the plaintiff contracts a disease from the defendant or the defendant knows of the disability when he promises to marry the plaintiff. The disability of the defendant is not a good defense if it will not be aggravated by, or interfere with, the marital relationship. For example, a person with diabetes is capable of living a normal life. But the existence of hereditary mental defects in either party may serve as a defense.

The fact that the plaintiff was engaged to another when he or she promised to marry the defendant is not a valid defense. It is also not a defense if the plaintiff marries someone else after the defendant has breached their contract. The invalidity of the plaintiff's divorce from a prior spouse may be a defense only if the court lacked jurisdiction to grant the divorce.

EXAMPLE A plaintiff obtained a Mexican divorce from her
O—* first spouse that was invalid because the Mexican court lacked jurisdiction to render a legal divorce. If the divorce is invalid, the defendant cannot be liable for breach of marriage promise, since the plaintiff was in-

capable of validly contracting a marriage because she was still legally married to her first husband.

The plaintiff's refusal to marry the defendant is a good defense in a suit for breach of marriage promise. Once a person has breached the contract to marry, it is no defense that later he offered to go through with the marriage.

■ **Damages for breach** An action for breach of promise is similar to a lawsuit for breach of contract. Damages that may be recovered include compensation for injury to the plaintiff's feelings, health, reputation, and prospects of future marriage, as well as compensation for any financial loss incurred and for loss of advantages that would have resulted from marriage to the defendant.

breach of the peace
A comprehensive term that includes all violations of the public tranquillity and order. Generally, it is the offense of disturbing the peace and quiet of the community by any riotous, forcible, or unlawful proceeding. Some examples include resistance to lawful arrest, shooting firearms in a crowd, and TRESPASS or injury to property when accompanied by violence. Under some state laws and local ordinances, intentionally disturbing the peace of any neighborhood, family, or person by loud and unusual noises, loud and abusive or indecent conversation, or by threats and quarrels may constitute a misdemeanor. Threats of physical harm may be punishable as a breach of the peace. Under some statutes it is an offense to disturb or break the peace by tumultuous and offensive behavior, such as recklessly driving an automobile into a crowd and causing injury. One who commits a breach of the peace is guilty of DISORDERLY CONDUCT. The punishment for breach of the peace is usually fixed by statute. When there is no statute, the offense is punishable by fine and/or imprisonment.

breaking
In law, using force on and inflicting some kind of damage to property, such as picking a lock, usually to enter a building illegally. See BURGLARY.

bribery
The voluntary offering or giving of anything of value in order to influence the actions of any person who holds a position of trust or is involved in the discharge of a legal or public duty. A bribe is the gift or advantage offered to or received by such a person for the purpose of having him refrain from performing an act or to induce him to corruptly perform an act that he is under a legal duty to carry out honestly.

EXAMPLE Nick Jones, treasurer of the school district, accepts $2,500 and a free trip to Las Vegas from Seth Anderson, whose vending machine company has been awarded the contract to supply vending machines to the schools, even though his bid was not the lowest submitted. Jones, as treasurer, had sole power to award the contract. The cash and trip proffered by Anderson before the bidding deadline were the only reasons he got the contract. This is simple bribery—Jones acted corruptly when he was bound by law to award the contract to the lowest bidder.

Bribery differs from EXTORTION, which is an unlawful act of an officer in taking money or property from another by abusing his authority or by the wrongful use of force or threats by anyone. Bribery involves voluntary rather than coerced payments. Also, it may consist of either the offering or receiving of property to influence official conduct.

■ **Essential elements** An essential element of bribery is the promise, gift, or acceptance of something of value in exchange for an act by a public official that is related to his duties. The offer of, or request for, a bribe is a crime even if the accused does not directly participate in the bribery offer, if the offer is not stated in specific language, if no money is paid immediately, or if the other party does not agree to it.

EXAMPLE Let us say a third person, following the orders of the defendant in a trial, offers a bribe to a juror to find the defendant not guilty; the defendant is guilty of bribery as a result of the acts of the third person.

Or Smith, in a joking manner, asks a public officer in charge of city contracts if he would like a two-week expense-paid vacation in Las Vegas if Smith "gets a piece of the action." Smith is guilty of bribery, since the offer, although not in specific terms, clearly indicates Smith's intent. Even if the officer refuses the trip, Smith is still guilty of bribery.

When Iowa's tough new bribery law went into effect in 1978, a theater chain stopped issuing free passes to city officials, and legislators urged voters not to set up dinner meetings to discuss pending state matters unless the legislators were allowed to pay their own way. Said the governor, "If my wife cooks me a dinner and then talks about capital punishment or some other issue, we both could be in violation."

It is bribery even if the act is not specified by statute as part of the officer's duty or if the officer does not have the authority to make the final decision on a matter, as when he is a member of a committee or commission.

As a rule, an officer must be influenced on a specific matter before him and not on possible future action, although in some jurisdictions a bribe may relate to a general course of future conduct. For example, Dick, a member of the state gambling commission, accepts money from a hotel corporation to vote to grant it a gambling license after a hotel is built in 1982.

The criminality of a bribe is not dependent on whether or not the official act was proper or improper.

Suppose Patsy is arrested for speeding even though she has not exceeded the speed limit. Too upset to think clearly, she offers a bribe to the officer. He accepts the bribe and lets her go free. Both are guilty of bribery. It makes no difference whether the arrest was valid to begin with.

It is not essential that the act for which the bribe was given be accomplished, but it must be an act capable of being done. If Dick, in the above example, accepted the bribe but then the corporation went bankrupt before it could seek a license, Dick would still be guilty of bribery.

Corrupt intent Unless a statute says otherwise, the bribe must be offered or accepted with a corrupt intent by one person to influence another's actions. Only one of the parties to the bribe have to have the corrupt intent. An official who accepts a gift after he has completed an official act is not guilty of bribery if he did not know beforehand that the gift was intended to influence him. The gift giver, of course, would be guilty of bribery if his intent was to influence the official.

WHEN MONEY CHANGES HANDS—BEWARE OF BRIBERY

■ If you offer a politician a campaign contribution to induce him to vote against a bill you would like to see not passed, you are attempting to bribe him. If the politician accepts the money after having voted for the bill, he may be found not guilty of bribery, but you may still be prosecuted.

■ If you are a contractor and offer the official in charge of city contracts an expense-paid vacation in exchange for "a piece of the action," you are guilty of bribery, even if the official refuses the trip.

■ Under the bribery laws of some states, what might seem to be a harmless little gift can get you into serious trouble with the law.

■ If you are arrested and offer the officer a bribe, which he accepts, both the offer and the acceptance are criminal. It makes no difference whether or not you were legally arrested.

■ It is unlawful for officials to induce citizens to commit bribery in order to prosecute them. If, for example, an examiner for the Internal Revenue suggested that the payment of a bribe would lessen your tax, you paid the bribe, and he then reported your act to the police, you may have a right to plead entrapment. If, on the other hand, you yourself offered the IRS examiner a bribe, then a trap could be lawfully arranged to catch you in the act of giving him the money.

EXAMPLE Patsy offered the judge at her hearing two tickets to the Super Bowl to insure that the charges against her would be dismissed. The judge had already decided that there was insufficient evidence to justify her arrest and dismissed the charges. The judge would not be guilty of bribery if he did not know that Patsy meant to bribe him. Patsy, however, would be guilty since she had a corrupt intent.

■ **Persons subject to bribery** When a person offers a bribe to another, who accepts it, each person is separately guilty of bribery. A failure to convict one party does not prevent the prosecution of the other.

EXAMPLE Smith offers a public officer $500 as a campaign contribution with the intent that the officer will vote against a housing bill. If the officer accepts the money after he has already voted for the bill, he may be found not guilty of bribery if he did not know of or understand the dishonest condition attached to the contribution. This, however, does not bar the prosecution of Smith for bribery.

Among the classes of persons who may be bribed are those whose official conduct is in any way connected with the administration of justice or governmental affairs at the time the bribe is given. Specific examples of persons who may be bribed include municipal officers, sheriffs and other peace officers, jurors, witnesses, school officers, officers of any public or private institution or corporation, and delegates to political conventions, committees, or gatherings.

If the person bribed is an officer of the United States or a person acting in an official function under authority of any department, the crime is bribery under federal law. Some examples are federal narcotics agents, U.S. attorneys and the Attorney General, as well as income tax inspectors. However, this does not apply to all persons employed by the United States, such as secretaries or clerks. The test in each case is whether the person performs an official function.

Anyone exercising the functions of an office in fact, but not entitled by law to do so, is also subject to bribery statutes. See DE FACTO. In a prosecution for bribery it is no defense that the accused, who pretended to be an officer acting within his authority, had no right to act as such.

■ **Defenses** It is a valid defense that the accused was unlawfully induced to commit bribery. See also ENTRAPMENT.

EXAMPLE An examiner for the Internal Revenue Service suggests to Tad Taxpayer, whose federal income tax return he is auditing, that the payment of a bribe would reduce the amount of tax he owes. Tad pays the bribe to the examiner. The entrapment of Tad in this situation is unlawful. If, however, Tad is the one who suggests paying the bribe, a trap may be lawfully arranged to catch him in the act of bribing a federal agent. In this instance, the entrapment is lawful and Tad cannot defend himself by claiming that he was entrapped.

Failure of the prosecution to establish any essential element of the crime constitutes a defense. An example of this is when the accused was intoxicated at the time he offered a bribe to a juror. If the accused was incapable of knowing what he was doing, it is a defense to bribery, since the prosecution cannot prove the existence of a corrupt intent.

One who solicits or receives a bribe to influence his official acts cannot assert as a defense that he intended to do the act anyway. When money is offered and accepted with intent to influence official conduct, it is no defense that the money was given as a campaign contribution; what matters is not the use to which the money was put but the purpose for which it is paid. In a prosecution for accepting a bribe, the identity of the bribe giver is not important.

■ **Related offenses** There are a number of offenses related to the actual giving or receiving of a bribe.

Aiding and abetting A person who aids and abets another, the principal, to bribe an officer may be held equally guilty with his principal. See CRIMINAL LAW.

Attempted bribery An attempt to commit bribery is an offense. Attempt consists of either an unsuccessful offer of a bribe or acts falling short of a bribe offer. For example, a person offers $500 to a juror to find a defendant not guilty. The juror refuses. The person who offered the bribe is guilty of attempted bribery.

Solicitation Solicitation of a bribe by an officer is a criminal offense, even though no agreement to give the bribe is reached and the official act promised is not performed. Generally, solicitation by a person who promises to influence a public officer is also an offense, even if the accused made no attempt to bring influence or was not authorized by the officer to solicit the bribe. But a jury in New York acquitted two men of conspiracy to bribe a public official because the so-called bribe was never paid nor had the men ever intended to pay it. (They had collected $100,000 from podiatrists who wanted a public official to kill legislation that would have made podiatry treatments ineligible for Medicaid.)

■ **Punishment** The severity of the sentence rests with the discretion of the trial court. When there is no state statute making the crime of bribery a FELONY, it is punishable at common law as a MISDEMEANOR by fine and imprisonment. Bribery of an officer covered by statute must be prosecuted according to the statute.

bridge A structure erected over a river, railroad, or other obstruction in a highway, so as to make a continuous roadway from one side of the obstruction to the other. A public bridge spans an obstruction in a public highway and is considered part of the highway with which it connects. Generally, a private bridge is privately erected and used.

■ **Establishment and construction** The construction of public bridges is almost exclusively regulated by state statute. The state's power is limited only by the Constitution or contract. When, for example, a bridge is to be built across international waters, the right to build the bridge originates with the state, but under federal law the state must secure congressional consent. The state may exercise its power directly or may delegate it to a government agency, such as a state highway commission.

Counties and municipalities get their authority to build bridges from the state. One subdivision of a state usually cannot compel another to assist it in building bridges over their common boundaries.

The general location of a bridge may be determined by the state or by citizen vote. The kind of bridge to be built and the method and time of erection are within the discretion of the county or officials in charge of the matter. Generally, the duty to build a bridge includes the duty to build the approaches to it.

■ **Expenses** Construction costs may be shared by the whole state or divided among or between political subdivisions at the discretion of the legislature. The cost does not have to be divided on a joint or equal basis. For example, the state may require one county to bear the whole expense of an intercounty bridge. Funds may be raised by APPROPRIATION, bond issue, taxation, or ASSESSMENT.

■ **Bridge companies** The state legislature may grant FRANCHISES for the construction of public bridges, such as toll bridges, by private capital, and it may delegate this power to counties or municipalities. A bridge company may thus be either a private or public corporation.

■ **Maintenance and repair** Public officials may use their discretion in maintaining and repairing bridges. Private individuals or corporations may be obligated by contract to maintain and repair bridges on public roads. A toll-bridge company is usually under a duty to keep the bridge in repair.

Guardrails on bridges and their approaches are required by statute so that drivers may be prevented from driving off the bridge or approach. Bridges should have lights at night as well as other customary safeguards, such as guard gates at a drawbridge. Insufficient barriers or warnings on a defective bridge may constitute a ground for liability for resulting damage. Bridge proprietors, however, may not be held responsible for injuries caused by a lack of sufficiently strong guardrails to withstand extraordinary and unanticipated strain—for example, a vehicle driven at a speed well over the legal limit. Intentional neglect or failure to maintain bridges properly may result in criminal liability for the government or private company that was responsible.

■ **Injuries to adjoining landowners** A private person or corporation may usually be held responsible for damage to adjoining property caused by NEGLIGENCE or other default in the construction or maintenance of a bridge, but a state, town, or county may not be held liable for such injuries unless a statute so provides.

■ **Tolls** Bridge tolls are charges authorized by statute and subject to legislative regulation. The regulation may be given to commissions created by the legislature. Tolls should be reasonable and based on the fair value of the bridge and the cost of maintaining it.

brief **1** A written summary or condensed statement of a series of ideas or of a document. **2** A written statement prepared by the parties in a lawsuit to explain their respective cases to the judge. It usually contains a summary of the facts, a discussion of the relevant law, and an argument about how the law applies to the facts, as well as the relief sought by each party.

bring an action Start a lawsuit, usually by filing the first papers; sue. See ACTION.

broker A person hired to arrange sales for other people, often by negotiating a contract, such as a real estate broker or a stockbroker. You might hire a real estate broker to sell your house and a stockbroker to buy an interest in a company for you. Or you might turn to an INSURANCE broker when you are in the market for life, fire, or automobile insurance.

It is important to distinguish between an insurance agent and an insurance broker. An insurance agent is a representative of the company. An insurance broker represents you, the person who is insured. During his employment, an insurance agent has a fixed and permanent relationship with the company he represents, and owes an allegiance to it. On the other hand, an insurance broker does not owe allegiance to any particular company.

Because the broker-client situation is one form of the AGENCY relationship, general rules of agency law apply to almost all transactions affecting brokers. The client is the principal, the broker his agent.

"Agent," however, is a broader and more comprehensive term than "broker." Even though a broker is an agent, his powers are limited. For example, when you engage a real estate broker to sell your house, his authority ordinarily is only to find a purchaser to buy on the terms fixed by you. He can make a binding contract of sale only when you specifically authorize him to do so. Since he has no control over the property, he has very little authority as an agent. It is always a good idea if you are buying through a broker to find out the extent of his authority before dealing with him.

The chief feature that distinguishes a broker from other agents is that he is a middleman. In arranging a sale he acts, in a sense, as the agent of both parties to the transaction. He conducts negotiations that bring people together to form their own contract.

■ **Good faith** It is a broker's duty to act with utmost good faith and loyalty in the interest of his client. The broker is obligated to make a full disclosure to his client of all facts affecting the client's interests. He is expected to exercise reasonable care in carrying on the business entrusted to him. Accordingly, he is accountable for all funds or property coming into his hands during the course of the business relationship with his client. For example, stocks purchased by a broker for a client should be delivered to the client soon after he pays the broker for them, unless the client arranges for them to remain with the brokerage firm.

■ **Regulation** The state has the power to regulate the business of a broker, and under authority granted by the state, a municipality (such as a city or town) may also regulate the practices of a broker working within its boundaries. A broker usually has to acquire a license and pay a fee for the privilege of engaging in his business. State licensing authorities have the power to fine a broker for conducting business without a license. In some states it is illegal to pay any person other than a licensed broker for services in connection with real estate transactions. A license takes effect from the date it is issued, and it cannot be made retroactive in order to validate transactions conducted before that time.

Anyone who regularly acts as a middleman or negotiates business transactions on behalf of clients is usually deemed a broker for purposes of a license tax. A federal court has held, however, that a law requiring a broker to obtain a license applies only to someone whose occupation or vocation is brokerage, not to a person who arranges only one or two sales.

Sometimes the power to revoke a license is given to a particular commission whose function is to hear complaints of brokers' fraudulent practices. The proceedings of the commission are usually informal and free from the technical rules of procedure observed in courts of law. A broker's license may be revoked if the evidence shows that he has been dishonest in dealing with the public.

State regulations generally require a broker, particularly in the real estate business, to give a BOND insuring faithful performance of his duties. The liability of the SURETY (the person guaranteeing the bond) extends only to acts arising in the course of the broker's business and intended to be included in the bond.

> EXAMPLE If a customer pays more money for a home O—★ because of a broker's false representations concerning the quality and value of materials used in its construction, the surety on the bond is liable for the customer's financial harm. If, on the other hand, the broker causes an automobile accident on his way home from his office when he stops to buy a quart of milk, the surety on the bond is not liable for damage resulting from the accident. The broker's trip to the grocery store had nothing to do with his business.

■ **Commissions** A broker's commission for his services is usually a percentage of the sale price of the property. In most cases he earns it when the buyer and seller come to an agreement. It is common practice for a broker to withhold his commission from the money he collects for his client.

To be entitled to a commission, the broker must bring the buyer and the seller into communication to negotiate the sale. Unless the broker and his client agree otherwise, the broker is entitled to a commission if he produces the customer, even though final arrangements are made by the client. The broker's compensation depends upon his presentation of a customer who is able, ready, and willing to buy. Naturally, the terms of the deal must be satisfactory to his client (the seller). Above all, the prospective buyer must be able to produce the necessary funds at the proper time. If, however, the broker has faithfully performed his duties, he should not be deprived of his commission because the parties fail to complete the transaction.

A broker is not entitled to receive compensation if he has volunteered his services to a client who has not agreed to employ him.

> EXAMPLE You are planning to sell your house. A neighbor- O—★ hood real estate broker knows this. On his own accord, he produces a person ready, willing, and financially able to buy the house at your asking price. You and the prospect make a deal. You owe the broker no commission, unless you and he signed an agreement making him your agent before the sale.

A broker is not entitled to a commission on a sale made by the owner after their relationship has terminated, such as after the LISTING of real estate has expired. The rule against the payment of a commission is firm, even though the sale is made to a person originally produced by the broker, if the broker was given a fair opportunity to make a sale but failed to do so.

> EXAMPLE The Dawsons' real estate broker made a valiant O—★ attempt to sell their house for them at the price they were asking for it. The problem with the house, however, was that it needed quite a bit of repair work and most of the prospective buyers were unwilling to pay the Dawsons' price and also invest a large chunk of money into repairing the house. After three months, the Dawsons ended their relationship with the broker but continued to try to sell the house on their own. The Laughlins, who had originally been introduced to the Dawson house by the Dawsons' broker, decided to take another look at it and finally decided to buy. The Dawsons do not have to pay a commission to their broker because the sale was arranged after their relationship had terminated.

Of course, the broker is entitled to a commission if his client cancels their relationship in the midst of negotiations and completes the deal himself.

Clearly, a broker who fraudulently misrepresents facts will forfeit his right to compensation for his services, but negligence in performance of his duties when there is no BAD FAITH will not necessarily cost him his commission. If, for example, a real estate broker innocently tells the prospective buyer of a house that the seller will accept less money than he said he would, the broker is entitled to a commisson if the seller actually does take a lesser sum.

Brown v. Board of Education In this 1954 landmark case, the U.S. Supreme Court ruled that racially segregated public education facilities are illegal. Chief Justice Earl Warren, speaking for the Court, indicated that the doctrine of SEPARATE BUT EQUAL has no place in public education. Separate educational facilities are inherently unequal.

In the 1896 case of *Plessy* v. *Ferguson,* the Supreme Court had upheld racial segregation of passengers on public trains in "separate but equal" facilities. In the 1954 case the Court specifically overruled its previous holding. *Brown* v. *Board of Education* has been the law of the land ever since. See also EQUAL PROTECTION OF LAWS; CIVIL RIGHTS.

buggery Sexual activity against nature. Copulation by a man or a woman with an animal, or a man with a man, or a man unnaturally with a woman. See SODOMY.

building and loan association See SAVINGS AND LOAN ASSOCIATION.

building line A certain distance inside the boundary of a piece of land, beyond which no building may extend. The purpose of a building line is to maintain a uniform appearance along city streets. See ZONING.

bulk transfer A sale of a major part of the materials or supplies of a business; a sale of inventory that does not arise in the ordinary course of the business. Laws regulating a bulk transfer are to protect people who have loaned money to a merchant. If there were no such restrictions, a merchant could sell all, or most, of the goods that he has promised as security for his loans. See SECURED CREDITOR.

bulletin An officially published NOTICE or announcement of the progress of matters of public importance. For instance, a weekly or monthly tax bulletin makes accountants and lawyers aware of the latest governmental rulings concerning the payment of their clients' income taxes.

burden of going forward The obligation to provide EVIDENCE on a particular question in a lawsuit rather than wait for the other side to do so. Also called the "burden of proceeding."

EXAMPLE Suppose you are suing someone because of the injuries you received in an automobile accident. It is up to your lawyer, not the opposing lawyer, to show the court that you suffered a broken leg. Your lawyer has the burden of showing that your leg was in fact broken, such as by producing the doctor who can testify to the treatment he gave your leg.

burden of proof The obligation to demonstrate to the court that the weight of EVIDENCE in the entire lawsuit is not evenly balanced but favors your side rather than the other side. Let us say that you are suing another driver because of injuries you received in an automobile accident that you claim was his fault. You and your lawyer have the burden of proving that your injuries resulted from the NEGLIGENCE of the other driver.

bureaucracy An organization with (1) a chain of command with fewer people at the top than at the bottom; (2) well-defined positions and responsibilities; (3) inflexible rules and procedures; (4) a lot of red tape; (5) many forms to be filled out; (6) authority delegated downward

from level to level. The U.S. Army and the various governmental agencies are examples of bureaucracies.

burglary In its general sense, burglary means breaking into and entering the house of another with an intent to commit a crime or breaking into and entering any kind of building with an intent to steal. Burglary is a separate crime from LARCENY or ROBBERY. See also CRIMINAL LAW.

Burglary, as defined at common law, was the breaking and entering of the dwelling house of another, during the night, with the intent to commit a FELONY (usually THEFT), whether or not the felony was actually committed. This definition has been variously modified by the states. For example, burglary has been defined to include entering any building (not only a dwelling) with an intent to commit larceny or breaking and entering a building at any time with an intent to steal, if any valuable thing is kept or deposited there. As in common law, to amount to a burglary, the breaking and entering must be with the intent to commit some crime, whether or not that crime is ever committed.

EXAMPLE While a family was away on vacation the police were called to their home by a silent alarm system. They found two back doors that had been forced open and a man undressed down to his shorts sound asleep in the master bedroom. Safecracking tools were found with his clothes. He was charged with burglary.

In most states, a person may be held guilty when his part in the burglary consists of acting as a lookout, aiding the escape of his companions, or hauling away the loot.

Sometimes a law punishing burglary does not define it. When this happens, the common-law definition applies.

■ **Breaking** Some kind of breaking is usually essential to the crime of burglary. The breaking required must ordinarily involve force, no matter how slight (such as picking a lock), and usually some part of the building must be broken. Breaking an inner door or window may be burglary, even when entrance to the building itself was made without a breaking. Entering through a fully open door or window is not a breaking. Except in some states, neither is pushing farther open a door or window already partially open. In most states, entering without breaking, and then breaking out to escape, is not burglary. Depending, however, on the law of the particular state, this act might well be the lesser offense of HOUSEBREAKING.

■ **Entering** Entry is an essential element of burglary. The entry must be into some part of the building. Entry of a chimney or attic, for example, would be sufficient. Under some state statutes, shooting firearms into a building is regarded as an entry.

Entering a place where one has a right to be, although with an intent to commit a crime, is not burglary. Anyone with a general right to be in a building, however, may be guilty of burglary if he enters at a time when he is not authorized to do so—when a store is closed, for example.

■ **Nighttime** The common law required breaking and entering to be at night in order to be burglary. Nighttime meant the period between sunset and sunrise during which there is not enough daylight to discern a man's face. At common law, it was not essential for the breaking and entering to take place at the same time, and they could occur on different nights. Under modern statutes changing the common-law rule, nighttime is not an element of burglary. As a general rule, breaking and entering still must occur at the same time, but state laws vary on this point.

■ **Dwellings and other structures** At common law, burglary could be committed only against the dwelling place of another person. The temporary absence of the occupant—if he is away on vacation, for example—does not deprive the house of its character as a dwelling. In the case of an apartment building, each individual unit is regarded as the dwelling of its occupant. The owner of an apartment building can be guilty of burglary if he breaks and enters an apartment while it is occupied by his tenant.

> EXAMPLE Ned and Karen live in a garden apartment. They O— ✷ have fought with their landlord over the continuous lack of hot water. One day, while Ned and Karen are gone, the landlord uses his passkey to enter the apartment. If the landlord steals something—for example, a color television—he is guilty of trespass and larceny. His actions would not be considered burglary because no force was involved. On the other hand, suppose Ned and Karen anticipate some kind of trouble with the landlord and add an extra lock to their front door. When the landlord uses his passkey, he cannot get into the apartment, so he picks the second lock. This use of force is breaking into the apartment, so that if he takes the television he will be guilty of burglary.

Under modern state laws, burglary can be committed against buildings that are not dwellings, such as shops, stores, warehouses, factories, and offices. It is burglary to break and enter a church with an intent to commit a felony. Even the breaking and entering of a railroad car is burglary under some state laws.

■ **Attempted burglary** An attempt to commit burglary, whether successful or not, is a criminal offense. To demonstrate an attempt, there must be an act indicating an intent to commit burglary. Mere preparation to commit burglary is not enough. For example, merely rattling a window is not attempted burglary because this does not demonstrate an intent to break and enter to commit burglary—the intent could be simply to attract the attention of someone inside. However, turning a knob and trying to open a door by pushing could be attempted burglary.

■ **Punishment** Burglary is punishable by a fine and/or a term of imprisonment. The laws of your state must be consulted to determine the maximum penalties.

business judgment rule
The principle that if persons running a CORPORATION make honest, careful decisions within the scope of their knowledge, they will not be held liable for injuries to the corporation resulting from those decisions.

> EXAMPLE Suppose the officers of a company that sells pic- O— ✷ ture posters of famous people decide to market a poster of a popular television actress. Several months later she leaves her television series and is no longer in the public eye. The company is stuck with her posters, because no one is interested in buying them now. The officers cannot be held liable for the company's losses on the poster. They made an honest business decision, within the scope of their responsibilities, which, at the time,

seemed to pave the way for phenomenal sales of the company's product.

business record exception
A rule that permits original, routine records (usually those of a business) to be used as EVIDENCE in a TRIAL. It is an exception to the "HEARSAY rule," which bars evidence that is not from the personal knowledge of the witness. According to the business record exception, records of a finance company may be used in a trial concerning a borrower's default in payments to the company.

business trust
An organization whose property is held by trustees for the use of beneficiaries whose interests consist of shares in the business. It is often referred to as a Massachusetts Trust or a Common-Law Trust. The early business TRUSTS developed most extensively in Massachusetts, growing out of the desire of investors to benefit from being organized like a CORPORATION without being restricted by the accompanying regulations. Business trusts are recognized in some states.

The essential characteristic of a business trust is the placing of property into the hands of trustees who manage it for the good of the beneficiaries, but who are free from their control. The trustees hold the title to (ownership of) the trust's property. If the beneficiaries retain control of the trust, the organization is treated as a PARTNERSHIP.

Unless there is a law against it, a business trust may engage in any business in which either individuals or corporations may engage. It may, for instance, develop land, purchase, manage, and sell properties, deal in securities or other personal property, or sell commodities.

Unlike other trusts, these trusts do not have a fixed duration and may last as long as the trust agreement provides. If a shareholder dies, the trust is not affected. The object of business trusts is to provide a medium for conducting a business and for sharing its gains.

Because business trusts have so many corporate powers, and a U.S. Supreme Court decision held that Congress intended to tax these trusts in the same manner as a corporation, how then are they any different? A trust does not receive a corporate franchise. Its members do not need to comply with a general corporation law. They do not receive approval from the state but instead derive whatever power and authority they have from the voluntary action of the individuals forming the trust.

but-for rule
A principle of NEGLIGENCE law. Negligence alone will not cause responsibility for damage unless that damage would not have occurred except for *(but for)* the negligence. Failure to signal a turn while driving is negligent behavior. If, however, the other driver involved in the accident was looking the other way, failure to use a turn signal did not cause the accident.

bylaws
Rules or regulations adopted by an organization. For instance, a CORPORATION, ASSOCIATION, club, or TOWN can adopt bylaws. The bylaws of a corporation usually set forth the way the company will carry out its purposes. The bylaws of a town might tell how changes in the present structure of local government can be achieved.

Cabinet   The principal advisory body to the President of the United States. Each member heads a major executive department, of which there are currently 13: State, Treasury, Defense, Justice, Interior, Agriculture, Commerce, Labor, Health and Human Services, Education, Housing and Urban Development, Transportation, and Energy. The head of the Department of Justice is the ATTORNEY GENERAL. The heads of the other departments are called Secretaries—such as the Secretary of State. A state governor may also have a cabinet.

calendar   A list, or DOCKET, of lawsuits ready for the court to hear.

call   **1** Summon or demand by public announcement, such as to call an election.   **2** As a noun, a demand for the presence and participation of a number of persons by calling aloud their names—as a call of names of members of the House of Representatives.   **3** A formal demand for payment according to the terms of a contract, such as a financing agreement.

camera   (Latin) "Room"; a judge's chambers. See IN CAMERA.

canal   An artificial channel for the conveyance of water, ordinarily used for the purpose of transportation. The construction and operation of canals by private canal companies are usually under state supervision. A company can locate its canal only where the state authorizes.

A canal company may occupy only as much land as is reasonably necessary to carry out its functions. In case of a dispute, the courts decide what is reasonably necessary. Property used for building and maintaining canals must be acquired in the way provided by state law—that is, by condemnation or APPROPRIATION, DEDICATION (as a gift), CONTRACT or GRANT, and, occasionally for maintenance, by ACCRETION. See CONDEMN.

The power to exact tolls for use of a canal depends upon the state statutes. Rates must not be discriminatory, and they cannot exceed the amount fixed by law. The state can authorize and supervise the construction of BRIDGES over public canals, and a city may construct bridges over canals in the city, but it cannot interfere with a state bridge on state property within the city.

cancellation of instruments   A judicial remedy of setting aside CONTRACTS or DEEDS (instruments) after they have been made final by the parties. The court will decide to set aside or cancel an instrument, such as a contract or a deed, only if it appears that no injustice will be done by placing both parties in the positions they occupied before the instrument was created.

Generally speaking, a court will not cancel a contract or deed if there is another way of solving the problem. Certainly, it will not deliberately interfere with a valid contract before being asked to do so. If requested, however, a court might cancel a contract or deed that has been based upon fraud or that resulted from duress or undue influence exercised by one party upon the other.

In most instances, instruments will not be canceled on the ground of fraud unless the fraud is definitely proved and unless the complaining party has been injured financially. Forgery is one type of fraud for which the courts will cancel an instrument. False representation is another. An insurance company has the right to sue to cancel an insurance contract if the applicant made false representations to the company—lied about his age, for example, or did not report that he had had a heart attack.

Duress and undue influence—usually involving some sort of threat against a person entering into an agreement—are often grounds for cancellation of instruments. So is the mental incompetence of one of the parties, especially if the other knew of the condition.

canon law   Ecclesiastical law; the constitutional law of a church; rules and regulations that govern a church or some part of the church.

canons of construction   The system of fundamental rules and maxims that governs the interpretation, or CONSTRUCTION, of written documents in order to decide their legal effect. See STATUTE.

capacity   In law, the legal right to do something. If you are an adult of sound mind, for example, you have the capacity to enter into a contract with someone else. If you are below a certain age, you lack the capacity to do many things, such as voting, making out a will, or being legally able to purchase or drink alcoholic beverages.

capital 1 Head; chief; major. Capital crimes are those punishable by death. Capital punishment is the death penalty. 2 Assets or worth relating to wealth. For example, capital stock is the stock issued by a corporation in exchange for money invested in the company.

capital asset In tax law, almost all property that can be owned, other than what is ordinarily held for sale. Examples include a company-owned building or trademark; land, jewelry, or stock owned by an individual.

capital gains tax A tax on the profit you make when you sell a CAPITAL ASSET that has increased in value since you acquired it. Under federal tax law, capital gains are taxed at a lower rate than is regular income, and you must have owned the asset a specified period of time before your profit is considered a capital gain.

capitalize 1 Treat the cost of an improvement or other expenditure as a CAPITAL ASSET for income tax purposes. For instance, the owner of a business might capitalize the cost of remodeling a work area for his employees. 2 Figure out the net worth upon which an investment is based. You might, for example, want to figure out the net worth of your shares of stock in order to treat them as capital assets for income tax purposes. 3 Issue company stocks or BONDS to cover an investment. This kind of capitalization is a basic method of obtaining financing for CORPORATIONS.

capitation tax (From the Latin *caput*, meaning "head.") An imposition or tax on a person at a fixed rate, regardless of his income or worth; often called a head tax. A POLL TAX is a common illustration of a capitation tax.

caption The heading or introductory section of a legal paper that gives the names of the parties, the court, and the case number.

care 1 Custody or safekeeping. 2 Attention, heed, or caution. There are various kinds of care that apply to different situations in law. For example, in a normal driving situation, a person is expected to act with "reasonable care," meaning the ordinary or due care that may be expected from a normal person under the circumstances. See NEGLIGENCE. Another kind of care is that which you are expected to exercise if someone trusts you with a car, a watch, or some other valuable. See BAILMENT.

carnal knowledge Sexual intercourse; traditionally, the act of a man in having sexual bodily connection with a woman. See ADULTERY; RAPE; RAVISHMENT.

carrier A person or organization for hire that transports property or people. There are two classes of carrier: common carriers and private carriers.

A *common carrier* is one that, as a regular business, transports personal property or people from place to place for a charge. To qualify as a common carrier, its services must be for hire and it must hold itself out as engaged in public service for everyone who wishes to hire it—it is liable for damages if it refuses its services to anyone without any justifiable excuse.

A *private carrier* undertakes by special agreement in a particular instance to transport property or people without being bound to serve every person who applies to it. The terms of its contracts with the shipper or passenger are what determine its duties and liabilities.

Railroads, truckers, and express companies are ordinarily common carriers of goods received for transportation, but a chartered cargo plane is a private carrier of goods. Public passenger trains, buses, taxis, and scheduled airlines are common carriers of passengers, but chartered buses and chartered airlines are private carriers of passengers. The duties and liabilities of common carriers and private carriers differ, as do the duties and liabilities of carriers of freight and carriers of passengers. For specific applications of the concepts discussed in this article, see AERONAUTICS AND AEROSPACE; MOTOR VEHICLE; RAILROAD; SHIPPING.

■ **Regulation and control** The business of all common carriers is subject to government regulation. A state has powers to regulate and control the operation and management of common carriers within the state, and those engaged in interstate transportation are subject to regulation by the federal government under the COMMERCE CLAUSE of the U.S. Constitution. A state may regulate common carriers through a public commission, whose regulations must be authorized by state law.

■ **Carriers of freight** A common carrier may make reasonable rules for the conduct of its business and may change them on reasonable notice. It may fix the times, places, methods, and forms in which goods shall be delivered to it, as well as the mode of packing, loading, and transporting.

Charges A state has the power to regulate the rates for transportation of property by common carrier within its borders, and under the Interstate Commerce Act, the federal government regulates rates charged in interstate shipment. Under the Interstate Commerce Act, common carriers can establish interstate rates and put them into effect only by filing a proper schedule with the Interstate Commerce Commission and then making the schedule public. State laws often require that the schedule of intrastate rates be filed with a state regulatory commission and made public.

Usually the consignor—the person who delivers the goods to the carrier—implicitly assumes an obligation to pay the freight charges. Unless there is a specific or implied agreement to the contrary, the consignee—the person to whom the goods are shipped—is generally not liable for freight charges. A carrier may demand payment of its charges in advance.

Unless a law provides otherwise, the private carrier has the primary right to fix its own rates.

Liens Generally, a common carrier has a LIEN on the goods transported for the freight charges and other charges or expenses lawfully incurred in connection with a particular shipment. If the party responsible for paying the shipping charges does not pay them, the carrier may hold the merchandise being shipped.

EXAMPLE Makeshift Clothiers buys and pays for a new
0—* computer to handle its extensive billing. The computer is shipped by railroad. Without bothering to find out how much the freight charges are, Makeshift agrees to pay them upon delivery. The railroad charges Makeshift its standard freight rate for such a shipment, but Makeshift is horrified at the amount of the bill and refuses to pay it. The railroad does not have to hand the computer over to Makeshift until it pays the freight bill. If Makeshift never pays the bill, the railroad can sell the computer, keep what is owed the carrier, and return the rest to Makeshift.

The lien of a carrier is usually limited to the property for which the unpaid charges were incurred. If a carrier makes several shipments for the same party and the party pays the charges on all but one shipment, the carrier has a lien on that shipment only and may not hold other merchandise belonging to the offending party. A private carrier is generally held to have no right to a lien for his services unless this right is given by a state law or by special agreement between the carrier and its customer.

The carrier is bound to exercise ordinary care for the protection of goods retained under its lien for charges and is responsible for any loss or injury that such care might have prevented.

EXAMPLE If a shipment consists of parts a manufacturer of
0—* snowplows has ordered and if the parts rust because of a leaky roof in the warehouse where the carrier has stored them, the carrier would be liable for damages. It cannot be held responsible, however, for loss over which it had no control. If the snowplow manufacturer fails to meet a contract date for the delivery of his plows because he does not have the necessary parts, he cannot sue the carrier.

Duties A common carrier has the duty to furnish reasonable and necessary facilities to handle the volume of freight it can reasonably anticipate—including refrigerator or ventilated cars for perishables and cars suitable for shipping livestock—and to use the care necessary for safe transportation of the goods. It is under an obligation to follow the shipper's specific instructions to which it has agreed, whether the contract to that effect is express or implied. If the directions are not clear, the carrier must hold the goods until it receives further directions. The shipper has the right to specify the route and manner of shipment, but if he does not do so, the carrier may choose any convenient one that is not to the shipper's disadvantage.

A common carrier is not liable, as a general rule, for loss resulting from defects in cars furnished by the shipper if the defects are not discoverable by the exercise of due care or if the shipper himself voluntarily selects the cars in circumstances where he has full knowledge of all defects and relies on his own rather than on the carrier's judgment.

WHAT DO YOU KNOW ABOUT CARRIERS?

■ Common carriers include railroads, express companies, public buses, taxis, and scheduled airlines. Private carriers include chartered cargo or passenger planes and chartered buses.

■ A common carrier's services are for hire for anyone who wants them. It can be sued for damages if it refuses to serve anyone without justification.

■ A private carrier is free to make individual contracts without being bound to serve everyone.

■ A common carrier has a lien on goods for charges. For example, if a piece of equipment is shipped by railroad to the purchaser, who had agreed to pay the freight charges, and he refuses to pay, the railroad may hold the goods until the charges are paid.

■ A common carrier must furnish reasonable and necessary facilities to handle the freight anticipated, and it must handle the goods with care.

■ If the goods are perishable and the recipient refuses them, the carrier must sell them to prevent loss to the shipper, but first it must notify the shipper that it is about to do so.

■ A common carrier is absolutely responsible for loss or injury to goods received for shipment, with some exceptions. One exception is an "act of God," an event not caused by man or preventable by due diligence, such as an earthquake.

■ A common carrier is responsible for loss due to acts of mobs, even if the carrier was not negligent. If, for example, a truck carrying a load of television sets is stopped and looted during a riot, the carrier is liable.

■ If the shipper packs the goods improperly, the carrier is not responsible.

■ A private carrier is not responsible for insuring the safety of goods unless it is bound to do so under contract; it is usually liable only when damage results from its negligence.

■ If the common carrier delivers goods to the wrong person, it will be responsible for the value of the goods unless it is the fault of the shipper who gives the wrong address.

■ A carrier is liable for injuries to passengers only if the carrier has been negligent.

■ A common carrier of passengers must exercise the highest degree of care, skill, and diligence.

■ A private carrier is usually required to exercise only ordinary care and diligence—except in some states where a private carrier is required to exercise the same degree of skill and care as a common carrier.

■ A carrier must exercise great care to guard passengers from harm threatened by fellow passengers but, as a rule, is not liable for unexpected injuries caused by them.

■ However, if a plane is hijacked, the carrier is liable.

■ Without negligence, a carrier is not liable for injuries due to natural causes beyond its control—such as pneumonia caught on board a bus trapped by an avalanche.

■ A carrier must exercise reasonable care in keeping its premises safe for passengers. For example, if you hurt yourself on a rotten wooden ramp leading to a railroad platform, you are probably entitled to damages from the railroad company.

A common carrier usually does not have the right to sell the goods that it transports. If goods are perishable and the consignee refuses to accept them, however, the carrier has both the right and the duty to sell them to prevent loss to the shipper. It must notify the shipper of the arrival of goods at their destination and of its intent to sell them. If the carrier fails to notify the shipper, it becomes liable for the value of the goods. After the sale, the carrier gives the shipper the proceeds minus the cost of transportation.

EXAMPLE Shipper Greenthumb delivers 5,000 heads of lettuce to Carrier Icebox, which ships them to Store Greengrocer. Greengrocer refuses to accept the shipment, and the carrier, Icebox, notifies the shipper Greenthumb. If Greenthumb consents, Icebox has the duty to sell the lettuce to prevent loss to Greenthumb. If the proceeds from the sale are $500 and the shipping charge was $100, the carrier would return $400 to the shipper. If Greenthumb was not notified of the sale, Icebox would be liable to him for $500, the value of the goods.

If the goods are not perishable the carrier may hold the goods subject to a lien or he can return them to the owner and sue for damages.

Duty of loading and unloading The common carrier ordinarily has the duty to load and unload freight, except that it is not required to unload bulky freight shipped in carload lots or in cars to be delivered off its premises. In this case, the carrier may deliver the car in a safe and convenient position for unloading at the place designated by the contract. For instance, when a man who owns timberland and a lumber mill contracts with a carrier for a carload of timber to be delivered to his mill, which is next to the railroad depot, the carrier is not required to unload the timber at the mill.

If the shipper or recipient assumes the duty of loading or unloading, the carrier will not be liable for loss as a result of defective performance. An example of this occurs when a shipper's employees load machines on a truck to be shipped to the buyer but fail to secure the goods properly. The shipper, not the carrier, is liable to the buyer for any damage to the goods resulting from improper loading. The carrier must give the shipper or recipient a reasonable amount of time to load or unload the goods. But after this reasonable time, the carrier may claim demurrage.

Demurrage is a claim for damages for unreasonable delay in unloading the property that was transported. It is usually made by a railroad carrier or a shipowner against the person responsible for unloading the railroad cars or vessel. Very often this is the consignee, or recipient. *Reciprocal demurrage* is a claim by a shipper for a carrier's delay in furnishing cars or a vessel. Payment is generally excused if the delay was caused by a natural disaster. Unless it is authorized by law, contract, or custom, there is usually no right to a lien for demurrage charges.

Bills of lading and shipping receipts When a carrier transports goods, he usually issues a bill of lading to the consignee, or recipient, and a shipping receipt to the consignor, or shipper.

A bill of lading is both a receipt and a contract. It is a receipt, signed by the carrier or his agent, giving the quantity and description of the goods shipped, and a contract to transport and deliver them to the designated person on the

terms specified. A bill of lading serves as documentary evidence of ownership or possession. There are two types: a *straight bill,* in which the goods are consigned directly to a specified person, and an *order bill,* in which the goods are consigned "to the order of" the person or company named in the bill, so that the goods are released only when he makes payment.

EXAMPLE If you, John Jones, order furniture directly from Pinetree Company, a furniture manufacturer in North Carolina, Pinetree will ship it to you by common carrier, to be picked up at the carrier's depot or warehouse. If you have not paid for the furniture, the manufacturer will instruct the carrier to issue an order bill of lading "to the order of Pinetree Company." This is to insure the manufacturer of payment before you take possession of the furniture. You have no legal rights to it until you pay the manufacturer and he orders the carrier to release the furniture to you. On the other hand, if you pay Pinetree in full before it ships your goods, it will tell the carrier to issue a straight bill of lading. The bill will read "To John Jones." As soon as the furniture arrives at the carrier's depot, you are legally entitled to pick it up.

In the commercial world, possession of goods symbolized by a bill of lading is the same as actual possession—in other words, possession of a bill of lading has the same legal effect as possession of the goods it represents. When the shipper puts the bill of lading in the name of the consignee (the person receiving the goods), he is in effect transferring ownership to him.

A shipping receipt given by the carrier to the shipper may be either simply a receipt for the goods or a contract of the terms of carriage between the carrier and shipper. The Bill of Lading Act imposes on the common carrier of goods in interstate commerce the duty to issue either a bill of lading or a shipping receipt. Failure to do so, however, does not relieve the carrier of the obligation to deliver the goods to the consignee at the address shown on the shipment within a reasonable time.

Liability of common carriers The liabilities of a common carrier are fixed by federal and state statutes, the terms of the bill of lading, and the rules of common law. A common carrier is absolutely liable for loss or injury to goods received for shipment, subject to certain exceptions. One of these exceptions is an ACT OF GOD—that is, an event of such a nature that it could not be caused by man or prevented by the exercise of due diligence on the part of the carrier. A loss by fire is not considered an act of God and is chargeable against the common carrier, even though the fire started outside of the premises it controlled and was not due to any act or fault on its part. When the fire was caused by lightning, however, and the carrier was not guilty of negligence after the fire was discovered, the carrier is not liable. A flood of such extraordinary character that the carrier could neither have foreseen nor made provisions for is an act of God.

The common carrier is liable for loss of goods due to the acts of mobs, rioters, or strikers even though it was not negligent. If a truck carrying a load of color television sets is overturned and looted during a riot, the carrier is liable to the shipper even though it took all possible precautions to protect the goods. A carrier is not responsible for damages resulting from the negligence or wrongful act of the shipper. When a shipper ships fruit during freezing weather, the carrier is not liable for loss if the shipper did not ask the carrier to heat the cars while in transit.

As a general rule, when the shipper either by his acts or his omissions fraudulently conceals the nature or the value of the goods shipped, the carrier is released from its liability as an insurer for loss.

EXAMPLE Harry had a large number of diamond bracelets he wanted shipped to Louis, but he did not want to pay the high shipping rate charged for diamond jewelry. Consequently, he placed each bracelet into the spine of a book, and packed the books into wooden crates. Harry shipped the crates with Fly-by-Night, an airfreight company that specialized in overnight deliveries. But Harry told Fly-by-Night that the crates contained only books. Fly-by-Night lost Harry's shipment, but was liable only for the price of the books, and not for the diamonds, because Harry had misled the carrier.

Failure to give notice that the contents of a package are perishable or easily broken exempts the carrier from liability for the consequences of such failure. If the shipper packs his goods improperly and the carrier is unaware of this fact, the carrier is not liable for loss resulting from the packing. If, however, the carrier's negligence is the main cause of the damage (if it knew the goods were improperly packed, for example, or could have noticed this by exercising reasonable care), then it is liable. A carrier may reject defectively packed goods for shipment, but once it accepts them, knowing they are poorly packed, it becomes liable for loss or damage on its premises or in transit.

As a general rule, when a carrier deviates from its ordinary route without any reason, it will be liable for loss occurring during the deviation. If the loss or injury to goods results from an act of God or other cause that is an exception to the rule and the carrier neglects to avoid or lessen the damages, it is liable. For example, if cattle in transit are caught in a blizzard and the carrier fails to shelter the animals properly, it would be liable.

Liability of private carriers A private carrier is not responsible for insuring the safety of goods entrusted to it for transportation. Usually it is liable only when damage results from its negligence or its failure to use ordinary care, unless the terms of contract provide otherwise.

Limitation on liability A common carrier's liability may be limited by the clear and unambiguous terms of its contract with the shipper. The validity of the contract will be determined by state law in shipments within the state and by federal law when an interstate shipment is involved. When a shipper of goods signs a shipping receipt or accepts a bill of lading that contains terms limiting the carrier's liability, he cannot later claim ignorance of the limitations. The limitations of liability found in bills of lading are governed by statute.

To be binding as part of the contract of shipment, a stipulation relieving the carrier from its liability must generally be contained in the contract made at the time the goods are shipped. The stipulation must be reasonable; supported by sufficient CONSIDERATION, such as the lowering of shipping charges; and not contrary to public policy. For instance, if a provision exempted a carrier from liability for loss from any cause whatever, this would be against public policy and void, because the carrier is attempting to relieve itself from its public duties and from the consequences of its negligence. Restrictions exempting the carrier from liability for loss resulting from leakage, a strike, a mob, or a riot are permissible and, unless prohibited by statute, a carrier may stipulate against liability for loss or damage by fire not due to its negligence. If the carrier deviates from the stipulated or customary method of shipment, it ordinarily may not claim the benefit of contractual limitations of liability.

The liability of a carrier may usually be extended by statute or by contract, as when the shipper pays a higher rate to insure complete recovery in case of loss.

Delivery of goods The duties and obligations of a common carrier begin when it receives and unconditionally accepts the goods. If, however, the goods are delivered with directions to hold them until further orders are sent by the shipper, the carrier is responsible for injury to the goods only as a WAREHOUSEMAN, not as a carrier.

Notice of arrival of the goods at their destination must be given to the party receiving them (the consignee) and a reasonable time must be allowed for their removal before the carrier's liability terminates. Unless there is a contract provision that specifies a place of delivery, the carrier's duty is to bring the property to his usual place for making deliveries, such as a station, freight depot, or warehouse. Once the goods reach there, the carrier has a duty to deliver them according to instructions, and the consignee has the duty to accept delivery. If the consignee requests that the goods be held by the carrier, the liability of the carrier as an insurer is altered to that of a warehouseman.

If the common carrier delivers the goods to the wrong person, it will be liable for the value of the goods, unless misdelivery was caused by the negligence of the shipper, such as when he improperly addressed the goods. Delivery of goods to the consignee without payment of a draft attached to the bill of lading makes the carrier liable, since the draft constitutes positive instructions to the carrier to collect payment before delivering goods. See COMMERCIAL PAPER. When goods are taken from a common carrier under a legal order, such as by attachment, the carrier is excused from further liability if it acts in good faith and without negligence in surrendering the goods. See ATTACHMENT AND GARNISHMENT.

■ **Carriers of passengers** A carrier of passengers—whether a private or common carrier—undertakes the transportation of persons from place to place. It is distinguishable from a carrier of goods not only by the extent of its liability but also by the nature of the contract. Carrying goods is a BAILMENT, and liability for injuries to the goods arises from the contract between the shipper (the bailor) and the carrier (the bailee). Carrying passengers is not a bailment, and liability for injuries arises only if the carrier is negligent.

Regulations The general public has such an interest in the business of a common carrier of passengers that it is properly the subject of state regulation when it involves transportation within the state and of federal regulation when transportation is interstate. Thus a state may require yearly inspections of common carriers to protect the general public from riding in vehicles that are in poor condition. The carrier itself may make reasonable rules and regulations that will protect its interest and the interest of the traveling public, and the passengers are bound to obey them. An example is a regulation of a railroad allowing only 120 passengers in a car and refusing admittance to others once all the seats are taken.

Fares A fare is the price paid to the carrier for transporting a passenger. A ticket becomes a fare when it is accepted by the conductor. A state has the power to regulate passenger rates of common carriers within the state, and the Interstate Commerce Commission establishes rates to be charged for interstate transportation. The rates must be reasonable as well as nondiscriminatory—if there are special fares for schoolchildren or senior citizens, they must be extended to all schoolchildren and all senior citizens.

Liability A carrier of passengers, unlike a carrier of goods, is liable only for injuries to the passengers caused by its negligence. A common carrier must exercise the highest degree of care, skill, and diligence for the safety of its passengers as required by the nature and risk of the type of transportation used, but a private carrier is usually required to exercise only ordinary care and diligence, unless the contract of carriage provides otherwise. In some places, however, a private carrier is required to exercise the same degree of skill and care as a common carrier.

A carrier has a duty to exercise great care and vigilance in preserving order and in guarding passengers from annoyance, violence, insult, or other misconduct threatened by fellow passengers. If an airplane is hijacked, however, the carrier will be responsible to its passengers for any resulting injuries, as required by the Federal Air Transportation Security Act of 1974. Without negligence, a carrier is not liable to a passenger when the only injury is due to natural causes that are beyond its control.

EXAMPLE A public bus was taking passengers through a
O⊷✳ mountainous region in a northern state when an avalanche occurred. The driver, hearing the falling snow as it rushed down the mountainside, bringing down giant trees as it fell, managed to pull the bus close to the edge of an overhanging cliff. The bus was buried by several feet of snow, but the road on each side of the bus was heaped with mounds of snow, logs, and debris that were up to 20 feet high. It was two days before rescue teams could reach the bus and dig it out. Several of the passengers died of pneumonia as a result of the accident. But since the driver was not negligent (he had, in fact, saved the lives of most of the passengers), the bus company was not liable to the families of the passengers who died.

Limitation of liability In some places, a carrier may, for a sufficient consideration to the passenger in the form of reduced fares, limit its liability for its negligence. This limitation will be invalid, however, unless the passenger is given the option of purchasing a full-price ticket under which the liability of the carrier is unlimited. In many jurisdictions, when a passenger rides under a free pass that exempts the carrier from liability for injuries caused by its negligence, the limitation on liability is valid and binding on the passenger up to the amount specified on the ticket.

Baggage A carrier, on assuming the care and custody of baggage, is liable, generally, as an insurer—but only up to

the amount specified on the ticket. When a passenger voluntarily retains possession and control of his baggage, the carrier is liable only for its negligence.

Care of the premises A carrier is generally required to exercise only reasonable and ordinary care in keeping its premises safe for its passengers. Its duty extends to only those parts of the premises where the public and passengers are expected to be, such as waiting rooms, and where they necessarily or ordinarily go to board the carrier, such as platforms and ramps. The carrier must provide and maintain safe and adequate approaches to its stations, platforms, or vehicles. If, for instance, the wooden ramp leading to the railroad platform is rotten, the railroad company is liable for injuries to its passengers or the public if it fails to repair the ramp or warn of the existing dangerous condition.

carrier's lien See CARRIER.

carry-back A tax rule—also known as "carry-over" —that allows a person or a company to reduce income taxes by spreading losses over a period of years prior to, or following, the loss. See INCOME TAX.

carrying charges 1 The costs of owning property, such as taxes and mortgages. 2 INTEREST payments.

cartel 1 A combination of producers of any product joined together to control its production, sale, and price and to obtain a monopoly in the particular industry or commodity. 2 A close association of companies carrying on the same business or similar businesses formed for the purpose of preventing extreme or unfair competition by promoting the interchange of knowledge resulting from scientific and technical research. 3 In war, an agreement between two hostile powers for the exchange of prisoners or deserters or authorizing certain nonhostile intercourse between each other that would otherwise be prevented by the state of war—for example, agreements for intercommunication by mail, telegraph, and telephone.

case 1 All the facts or evidence assembled by one party to prove his version of a controversy in court. 2 In general usage, an entire legal action, or lawsuit.

casebook A collection of written legal opinions, all of which concern a particular subject of law, such as divorce or income taxes. Casebooks are used for teaching or studying the law.

case law The legal principles established by written opinions of judges in individual cases. Case law is a constantly developing source of law because, in our COMMON LAW system, the decisions of higher courts are binding on lower courts. This rule is called STARE DECISIS. It means that the decisions actually are law in the same sense that STATUTES are law.

case method A system of teaching or studying law by reading and discussing individual cases instead of consulting textbooks written on various subjects. Professor Christopher Langdell introduced the method at Harvard

Law School in 1869. Most law schools use it now because it relies on a primary source of law, the cases themselves, and it encourages students to reason from particular facts to general principles of law.

cash surrender value   The amount of money a life INSURANCE policy will bring if it is cashed in with the company that issued it. Generally, a small surrender charge will be subtracted from the value of the policy.

casual   Accidental, unforeseen, occasional. *Casual employment,* for example, might include occasional bartending done to supplement one's income.

casualty   An accident, a sudden unexpected event, or the loss or destruction resulting from such misfortune. *Casualty insurance* is purchased to protect in the case of certain accidents specified in the policy.

categorical   1 Unconditional or without qualification, restriction, or limit, as in a categorical statement or answer. 2 For a particular group. Some social welfare programs are called "categorical assistance" because they are intended to benefit only one category of people, a particular group. Aid to Families with Dependent Children and aid to the blind are examples of such programs.

causa mortis   (Latin) "On account of death"; in contemplation of death. For example, a GIFT *causa mortis* is a gift from someone who believes he will die soon. This can be important for getting the gift back or paying taxes on it.

EXAMPLE A young man is injured in a flaming motorcycle 0———* accident and believes he is going to die. Grateful to the stranger who pulls him out of the fire and believing that he will no longer need the things of this world, he gives the stranger all of the IBM stock he has inherited from his grandfather. When the young man unexpectedly recovers, he wants to get back his stock to pay for college. He may recover it because a gift *causa mortis* is effective only if the person giving it does in fact die.

EXAMPLE During his lifetime an 89-year-old man manages 0———* to put aside half a million dollars. Knowing that he will not live much longer, he gives the money to his two grandchildren, thinking that in this way he can avoid estate taxes. Unfortunately, he is wrong. Gifts given by one who expects to die soon may be taxed the same as gifts given by will.

cause   1 Reason. Sometimes "cause" is used in the sense of "just cause." For example, if an employee is dismissed or a claim for public assistance denied "for cause," this means that the action taken is reasonable and justified.

Sometimes the law will permit a person to act for "no cause" but not for "bad cause." A landlord may refuse to rent to an individual for no reason at all, for instance, but he may *not* refuse to rent because the individual is black.

In criminal law, probable cause must exist before a policeman may search or arrest someone without a warrant. The officer must be able to show specific facts that caused a reasonable suspicion of wrongdoing in his mind before he

stopped, searched, or arrested someone. These facts must all have existed *before* he acted and cannot depend on anything dicovered later or as a result of the search or arrest. Facts indicating probable cause must also be shown to a judge before he can sign a warrant for search or arrest. See SEARCH AND SEIZURE.

2 In civil law, each separate event that brings about a given result, or effect. It is necessary to prove causality in civil cases. If you are harmed in some way and want the court to hold someone else responsible for your injury, you must show how his conduct led to it. Whether the defendant is held liable and to what extent will depend on how his conduct caused the injury and whether an injury could have been expected to result from such conduct.

The defendant's act can be the actual cause, immediate cause, PROXIMATE CAUSE, INTERVENING CAUSE, unforeseeable cause, or remote cause of injury to the plaintiff. The *actual cause* is the one that really did the harm. An *immediate cause* is one that came directly before the injury, with nothing happening between it and the injury. A *proximate cause* is one that produced an injury that would not otherwise have occurred. Sometimes an *intervening cause* comes between the proximate cause and the injury. An *unforeseeable cause* is one that could not have been predicted to result from the proximate cause. A *remote cause* comes from a person or event that is separate from the proximate cause. Sometimes one act can be called more than one kind of cause. These labels determine the kind of legal responsibility that flows from the act. See also NEGLIGENCE.

EXAMPLE George and Cathy are having dinner at a restau- 0———* rant when Cathy tells George that she has decided not to marry him because he is a bully. Then she stands up and walks over to the bar. The waiter, who has overheard the conversation, brings George a stiff drink and says: "I wouldn't let any woman talk to me like that. Why don't you smack her around a little?" Fortified, George charges over to the bar, grabs Cathy, and throws her through a plate-glass window.

When Cathy is treated for her cuts at the hospital, Dr. Clark discovers that she also suffers from anemia. He gives her the wrong injection to treat her condition, and she needs medical treatment for an extra month.

In this case Cathy can sue George for all her injuries. In proving her case she can show that George's throwing her through the window is the actual and immediate cause of her being injured. The waiter's meddling is an intervening cause. The preexisting condition of anemia is an unforeseeable cause of harm to her, and the doctor's mistake is a remote cause that aggravates her injury. As long as Cathy can show that George's throwing her through the window was the proximate cause of her injury, the other contributing factors will not relieve him of liability to her.

cause of action   Facts that give rise to a right to seek relief in court. Every type of lawsuit has specific elements that must be claimed or the plaintiff has no case. There is no cause of action for battery, for example, unless facts proving intentional, unwanted physical contact are alleged. If a man accidentally bumps a newsboy on a station platform and makes him fall onto the train tracks, the boy may have a cause of action for negligence—but not for battery, because the contact was not intentional.

caveat emptor   (Latin) "Let the buyer beware." A rule of law that, when it applies, means that a buyer accepts what he purchases "as is." He assumes the risk that the product might be defective or unsuitable for his needs. Of course, this rule was never intended to protect a seller who makes false or misleading representations about quality or condition. That kind of conduct is a FRAUD.

For the most part, *caveat emptor* is no longer the rule of the marketplace. The buyer is still responsible for inspecting goods before he buys them and cannot later complain about obvious defects, but now a seller also has responsibilities. Usually the law assumes that the seller made certain WARRANTIES unless he and the buyer agreed otherwise.

If the seller specializes in selling the type of goods in question and the buyer is an average consumer, the seller may be held to a high standard of fair dealing. See SALES. If you buy a painting from an art dealer, for example, you are entitled to rely on the seller's expertise more than if you buy from a youth on a street corner. The law might also presume that if both the buyer and the seller were art dealers, they bargained as equals. In that case, *caveat emptor*.

cease and desist order   A command from a PUBLIC ADMINISTRATIVE AGENCY prohibiting some action that has been found to be unfair competition or an unfair labor practice. It is similar to a court INJUNCTION. See FEDERAL TRADE COMMISSION; LABOR RELATIONS; TRADE-MARKS AND TRADE NAMES.

celebration   A formal ceremony. Some states require that a marriage ceremony be "celebrated" in order to make the marriage legal. The type of celebration required is governed by state law and religious custom.

cemetery   Land used for burial of the dead. Public cemeteries are open to every member of a particular church or community regardless of who owns them, while private burial grounds serve only a family or small group. Because of the special needs and public purpose served in managing these lands, they are usually governed by laws that apply specifically to cemeteries. Often the size of cemeteries is limited by law. Zoning laws usually determine where a cemetery may be located and restrict the use of that land to burial and related cemetery activities. The land may be exempted from real property taxes or subject to a reduced rate. Local laws control the kind of organizations that may own cemetery land and whether it may be operated at a profit.

The owner of cemetery land keeps the right to sell the whole cemetery to another person or group, but only for continued use as a cemetery. The purchasers of individual lots obtain an EASEMENT, a right to use their own plots for burial and the roads and paths for access, subject to the rules of the association owning the cemetery or to the restrictions in the contract of sale.

The owner of the cemetery cannot prevent lot holders from erecting markers (of the type specified by the cemetery owner), entering the land, or burying family members in the plots they own. These rights pass to the heirs of the lot holders in the same way that personal property passes when there is no will. See DESCENT AND DISTRIBUTION. A headstone or marker is considered the personal property of whoever places it, and ownership of it, too, passes to the persons who inherit his property.

Use of the land as a cemetery may cease only when the cemetery is abandoned under the law—when all the DEAD BODIES are removed or when the property is so neglected that it completely loses its identity as a cemetery. Public authorities may order the removal of all the bodies, for instance, when a dam is to be built that will flood the cemetery lands. A cemetery owner may decide not to continue selling lots, but he may first need permission from a local government official or a special board.

The cemetery owner or a cemetery association must care for the property. Because of strong public interest in maintaining burial grounds, there may be many local regulations.

Although trespassing on public cemetery land generally is not an offense, vandalism and the destruction of headstones are criminal acts. In addition, owners of the cemetery or of individual lots may sue anyone who interferes with the cemetery or destroys property. Because feelings are very strong in this matter and the greatest injury is the indignity of the act, most jurisdictions permit the recovery of not only compensatory DAMAGES for the destroyed property but also an extra amount of money called punitive damages to discourage acts of desecration.

censorship   An act or system that denies free speech or freedom of the press. Censorship comes *before* something is publicly said or written and prevents communication or publication. See SPEECH AND PRESS, FREEDOM OF.

census   An official tally of the people in a state, nation, or district based not on estimates but on an actual counting. The U.S. Constitution requires that a national census be taken once every 10 years. Direct taxes, the number of representatives each state sends to Congress, and the distribution of electoral districts are based on census figures.

Congress alone has the power to decide where someone will be counted. It does not matter whether a state considers someone a resident for voting purposes, workmen's compensation, divorce statutes, or anything else. Congress has decided that everyone will be counted where he usually eats, sleeps, and works. This means that people in institutions will be counted where their institutions are, college students at their colleges, and military personnel at their bases. If members of the armed services are stationed outside the country, they are counted in the state that is their "home of record" but not within any particular electoral district in that state.

No personal information given in a federal census may be used for any purpose other than producing the census result. It is a crime to refuse to give required information or to falsify any answers given.

certificate   An official document; a paper prepared by an official as a regular part of his duties. A certificate, such as a birth or death certificate, is generally acceptable as evidence in a court case because officials prepare them and have no interest in falsifying them. If you objected to a certificate as evidence, you would have to show either that it was not filled out by the official having authority to make it or that it was not prepared in the normal way. See also Chart 3, "Where Records Are Kept."

certification proceeding   The legal action taken by the National Labor Relations Board to find out whether employees of a company want to be represented by a particular union.

certified check   A check that a bank guarantees can be cashed. The bank may use a special printed cashier's check or a teller may sign and write across the face of the check a statement that the check is good when properly endorsed. When you ask for a certified check, the bank deducts the amount of the check from your account when it certifies it, rather than waiting until the check is presented for payment. See COMMERCIAL PAPER.

certified public accountant   An accountant who is licensed (certified) by the state after passing a national examination given by the American Institute of Certified Public Accountants. A certified public accountant (CPA) may not only do all types of accounting work but may also examine the books or accounts of corporations, other businesses, and individuals, and report on them as provided by law.

Under the institute's Code of Professional Ethics, a CPA must keep his client's business affairs in strict confidence and must maintain high professional standards. For instance, he is obligated to report any important omissions or misleading facts in financial statements, and he cannot give an opinion on a financial statement unless he or a member of his firm has examined it. If a CPA violates the code, he may be suspended or expelled from the institute, and the state may suspend or revoke his license. A CPA has a FIDUCIARY relationship (position of trust) with his clients.

certiorari   (Latin) "To be informed." Certiorari is a proceeding in which an appeals court "certifies a question" of law and orders the lower court to send up the record of a case for review. It is not a right. A dissatisfied party may ask the appeals court to certify a question decided against him, or a lower court may certify and send up the record when it cannot decide a case until some important question of law is settled by the higher court. After looking over the record and the written opinion sent up, the appeals court will rule "cert granted" or "cert denied," meaning that it either will or will not rule on the question.

Most jurisdictions provide that in some situations the possibility of appellate review is automatic. Certiorari, therefore, is a request for review when the party is *not* otherwise entitled to it. For certiorari to be granted, the petitioner seeking it would have to show what he believed to be a serious mistake of fact or error of law or procedure by the trial court. The procedure to be followed by one seeking a writ of certiorari—an order granting review by an appellate court—is determined by the rules of practice for each jurisdiction. See APPEAL AND ERROR.

cf.   (Latin) An abbreviation of *confer,* "compare." This signal directs the reader's attention to another work or another part of the same work—another volume, case, or the like—where contrasting, analogous, or explanatory views can be found. *"Cf. Black's"* means "look at *Black's Law Dictionary* for a comparison with, or explanation of, what is being discussed."

CFI   An abbreviation for cost, freight, and insurance. The price fixed in a contract may include not only *cost,* but *freight* and *insurance* to be paid by the seller. Also abbreviated as CF&I.

CFR   See CODE OF FEDERAL REGULATIONS.

chain of title   The series of owners of a piece of land from the original owner down to the present one. For title (rights of ownership) to be good and marketable, the seller should be able to show who owned the land at any given time and how that person came into the chain of title. See MARKETABLE TITLE.

chain referral   A marketing scheme that persuades a consumer to buy something on the promise that the amount of money he owes will be reduced for each additional buyer he can recommend. Chain referral plans are illegal or strictly controlled because they make impossible promises to people. See PYRAMID SALES SCHEME.

challenge   1 Dispute or object, as to question the validity of a document or the fitness of someone for a public office.   2 As a noun, an OBJECTION.

When a jury is being selected, several types of challenges may be made. A *challenge for cause* is an objection to a possible jury member for a stated and justifiable reason. In criminal law, each side is generally permitted to make a certain number of *peremptory challenges* to particular prospective jurors without giving any reason. A *challenge to the poll* is an objection to a particular juror, and a *challenge to the panel* or *array* is a claim that the whole process of selecting the jury was unfair. A *challenge to the favor* is based on the suspicion that a juror could not be impartial, perhaps because he is related to one party, employed by him, or a shareholder of a corporation involved in the case.

chambers   The private office of a judge. A judge may hear motions, sign orders, or write opinions "in chambers" but a trial must be held in a public session of court.

champerty and maintenance   *Champerty* is the illegal purchase of a share in someone else's lawsuit. *Maintenance* is the illegal financing of someone else's lawsuit for personal gain. Both offenses have been illegal since the early days of common law because they stir up litigation and bring profit to someone who was not originally harmed. An attorney found guilty of either will lose his license to practice law.

Champerty and maintenance occur only when the *stranger,* or third party, makes his profit out of a recovery in a lawsuit. It is not champerty, for example, for a collection agency to buy a batch of "bad" accounts from a department store. The agency does not buy a lawsuit but rather a right to try to collect on the accounts. And it is not maintenance to loan money to a poor person who is involved in a lawsuit unless the loan is intended to make the lawsuit possible and repayment of the loan is to be a share of the recovery.

EXAMPLE A woman owes her attorney $500 for past legal services, which she cannot afford to pay. Knowing that her former husband owes her $4,000 in back alimony and child support, her attorney offers to represent her in a suit against her ex-husband in order to get his $500 in addition to the fee for the new suit. This is maintenance.

A contingent-fee arrangement (in which an attorney takes a percentage of his client's recovery as his fee) generally does not violate rules against champerty and maintenance. The attorney does not own any share of the lawsuit or pay the costs of maintaining it. Often contingent-fee arrangements are permitted only in certain types of lawsuits—personal injury actions, for example—and they are closely supervised by the courts. They serve the purpose of permitting a poor person to sue for injuries he suffered when he could not otherwise afford an attorney.

It has been suggested that selling shares in a legal action is a good way to finance a public interest lawsuit. Since no one can afford by himself to sue a big oil company for oil spilled on a beach, a corporation could be formed and shares sold to raise money for legal expenses in a particular case. Unlike a class-action suit, however, the parties in such an action would not have to prove they were actually harmed by the oil spill. While the idea may have merit as a social reform or as a business venture, it is still unclear whether it is legal. Champerty and maintenance were intended to prevent speculating on the injuries of others.

chancery See EQUITY.

character evidence In a trial, proof or testimony about someone's traits or habits. It may be based on the opinions of close friends or on a person's general reputation in the community. See EVIDENCE.

charge 1 An obligation, debt, burden, or lien. 2 The formal accusation of a crime. 3 A judge's final summary of the case and instruction to the jury.

charge-off A write-off; the removal of something from a company's records, such as a debt that has become too difficult to collect.

charitable trust Property—such as a sum of money or shares of stock—that is set aside to be managed by one person for the accomplishment of some public purpose, such as to benefit a church or the Society for the Prevention of Cruelty to Animals. Generally, a trust is not valid unless the property held in it is to be paid out within 21 years after the death of someone alive and named in the trust when it was created. This is called the RULE AGAINST PERPETUITIES. Its purpose is to prevent the tying up of large fortunes over a long period of time because that is harmful to business and commerce. Charities serve such an important public purpose, however, that the law in most jurisdictions does

not apply the rule to a charitable trust, and the trust may continue as long as the charity functions. See also TRUST.

charity A group organized not to make a profit but to provide some benefit to society. Its purpose may be humanitarian, religious, educational, or moral. Because charities promote the public good and lessen the burdens of government, they are favored by the law. They generally are not required to pay business or property taxes or assessments for municipal improvements.

Under the old common law, a charitable organization could not be sued for injuries caused by it or its employees. The theory was that society as a whole was better off if the charity did not use up its resources paying off parties to lawsuits. The effect of this rule, however, was to put the whole burden of an injury on the victim even if the charity clearly was at fault. Now most states have adopted the policy that charities, like everyone else, are responsible for negligence. As a result, each charity diverts a small amount of its money to buy liability insurance.

Charities may charge a fee for some of their services and still be considered charitable organizations. For example, a church-sponsored hospital will charge for its services, and the Red Cross may sell its doughnuts, but these organizations are still charities because they serve a public purpose and make no profit.

Charities generally are supported by gifts from donors. See SUBSCRIPTION. In order to prevent the abuse of the public's generosity, most states control the way in which funds are solicited and require charities to disclose their financial structure and condition. To prevent charities from using high-pressure tactics to obtain bequests or donations from the old or the seriously ill, some states will not recognize gifts made to charity within a certain period of time before death. Other states permit relatives to protest if the gift is more than a certain percentage of the estate.

It is possible to make a gift by will that is effective only as long as the charity continues a particular purpose.

EXAMPLE Peter left all his property to his son, James, except for 100 acres of forest land, which he left to the Boy Scouts "only as long as the land is used as a camp." When the Scouts leased the land to a farmer one year later, James was entitled to take the land away from them.

charter 1 Lease a form of transportation. For example, a junior high school charters a bus to take children to a museum or an exporter charters a ship to deliver machinery to a foreign port. 2 As a noun, a deed from the sovereign ruler giving land and the right to govern it. To develop colonies in America, kings of England granted charters to joint stock companies, such as the Virginia Company of London (in 1606); and to individuals, such as James E. Oglethorpe (in 1732), whose territory included what is now the state of Georgia. 3 The basic document of law for a city, granted by the state. 4 A grant of authority from the legislature or the paper by which the grant is given. For example, a legislature passes laws that permit corporations to be created by charters.

chattel An item of personal PROPERTY; something that can be moved. Chattel is a broad general term that includes everything that can be owned except real property (real estate). A truck, a wristwatch, a racehorse, a stock certificate, money, are all chattels.

chattel mortgage A loan for which repayment is guaranteed by a pledge of personal property. Because the property pledged as collateral can be sold to pay off the loan, the loan is secured.

The rights of the lender are good only against those who *knew* or *should have known* of his security interest in the pledged property. Since the borrower keeps possession of the property, a potential buyer cannot know whether a chattel mortgage on it exists unless there is some way to look it up. Therefore, each state has a system for filing papers showing the existence of chattel mortgages on property.

For example, a buyer of a piece of heavy construction equipment should first find out whether some lender holds a mortgage on the machine. If so, the buyer might find after he pays for the equipment that he has to pay off the mortgage or lose his equipment to the holder of the mortgage. A smart buyer always checks the files in the county clerk's office before he agrees to buy an item on which there might be a chattel mortgage, such as an automobile. If there is a mortgage, he bargains for a lower price.

If a buyer *can* know about a mortgage, because it is properly filed, the law will presume that he *does* know. Therefore the buyer purchases the debt along with the property even when he does not inspect the records.

In the past businessmen often ran into difficulties because the laws on chattel mortgages and the filing requirements differed in each state. By 1952, however, a Uniform Commercial Code was developed to apply the same law to all kinds of agreements to secure loans. Now, every state except Louisiana has adopted the code at least in part. Article 9 of the code establishes the law for loans guaranteed by a pledge of personal property and calls all such agreements SECURED TRANSACTIONS.

chattel paper A paper that shows a debt is owed and its payment is guaranteed by a pledge of certain personal property.

check A written order directing a bank to pay a specified amount of money on demand from the account of the person who writes it. A check is payable only to the person named on it or, when it is made out to "bearer" or to "cash," to the person holding it. See BANKS AND BANKING; COMMERCIAL PAPER.

A check is different from a DRAFT; a check is always drawn on a bank, while a *draft* is an order for payment drawn on anyone, including an individual, a bank, or a trading account with a company.

A *certified check* is marked "payment guaranteed" by the bank. When you have a check certified, the bank will immediately subtract the amount of the check from your account rather than when it is cashed. A *cashier's check* is written by the bank rather than by you as a depositor. You must pay the bank the amount of the check plus a service charge when the check is issued. Sometimes the person you are paying will insist on a cashier's check because the bank guarantees payment on it. Certified and cashiers' checks are

generally used for large transactions, such as the purchase of a home or business. A *traveler's check* is made out by a bank or other financial institution. The purchaser must sign the check when he buys it and again when he cashes it. This procedure provides some protection against forgery to the businessman who accepts the check.

checkoff A system in which an employer deducts the amount of an employee's labor-union dues from his paycheck and sends the dues directly to the union. Unions like the automatic checkoff because then they receive dues without fail, but employers do not relish the extra work.

children See INFANT; PARENT AND CHILD.

choate Complete; the opposite of INCHOATE, which is more frequently used. When a right is choate, it is certain. Everything needed to make it valid has occurred. No later claims can take away the right.

chose in action A right that can be enforced by a lawsuit. It may be a right to recover money owed on a debt, for example, or damages for an injury or for failure to do what was promised in a contract. *Chose* is French for "thing." Chose in action literally means the thing that someone is entitled to possess but can get back only by bringing a lawsuit.

circuit One of the judicial territories into which the nation, a state, or a county is divided. A particular COURT has legal power to hold sessions in each of the circuits. See FEDERAL COURTS.

circuit court A COURT that has legal power to hold sessions within a specified geographical area. Generally, it is a trial-level court; appeals from it go to some kind of superior court. The name of these courts dates back to the time when one judge "rode circuit" to conduct trials by turn in each county of his territory. Even today, in sparsely populated areas, a circuit court is more economical than having a different judge for every small town.

circuit court of appeals A court that reviews decisions made at trials in lower-level courts within its geographical area (circuit) when any of the parties to those trials choose to appeal. See APPEAL AND ERROR. A circuit court of appeals may have the power to hold sessions at different places within its circuit. In the United States, the FEDERAL COURT system is divided into 12 circuits. Appeals for cases that started in the district courts are taken to the U.S. Court of Appeals in each circuit.

circumstantial evidence Facts that tend indirectly to establish a main issue in question. The facts themselves are shown directly, but they are used to prove something else that is really the main issue.

EXAMPLE One of the main issues to be proved if a will is contested might be whether or not the dead person was of sound mind when she wrote the document. The fact that she was mentally incompetent at the time could be proved by the report of a doctor or by a court that appointed someone to manage her property because she was no longer able to do it herself.

When no such direct proof is available, the court relies on circumstantial evidence. If friends can testify that she was a happily married woman who began to accuse her husband of adultery when they were both in their eighties, that she told everyone he kept her locked in the cellar, and that she refused to eat anything but oranges because the devil was trying to poison her, these circumstances might be enough to prove unsound mind without direct evidence of insanity.

Circumstantial evidence is no less useful in court than direct EVIDENCE and in fact may be more persuasive.

EXAMPLE Testimony by a driver that his speed was "about 0⊶⊷ 30 miles per hour" when he ran into a van carrying senior citizens is direct evidence. When a policeman testifies, however, that the van was pushed 100 feet down the road, all of its passengers were seriously injured, and the car broke off a telephone pole, these circumstances prove the real speed much better than the direct evidence.

The strength of circumstantial evidence is logic. If all the circumstances surrounding an event lead to a certain conclusion, it will be difficult to convince a jury otherwise.

citation   1 The practice of referring to specific statutes or cases to prove a point. A lawyer knows he must quote specific examples to illustrate his interpretation of the law. He will very carefully choose citations to cases that are most like the question he is arguing. The reference to the case, constitution, or statute, or to an article or book that explains the law is also called a citation. Lawyers and judges discover the law on a subject by research, and citations lead them to the information they need.   2 A paper that notifies someone that he must appear in court. A *traffic citation*, for example, is issued for a violation of the traffic laws.

citator   A set of books that keeps track of cases or statutes. Lawyers always check a citator before they quote a case in order to make sure it has not been overruled by a later case or reversed on appeal. A citator is published periodically with columns of CITATIONS noting any new decisions made on each case or any other decisions that refer to it. If a lawyer finds that the case has been quoted with approval in another very recent case, he can safely rely on it as good law. If he finds that the case has been "distinguished"—that is, a judge has ruled differently in another, similar case—he will read the newer case to find out how it limits the effect of the original decision.

The most frequently used citator is *Shepard's Citations*. It covers cases and statutes for every part of the country and the federal government. It is so commonly consulted that lawyers say "shepardizing a case" for "using a citator."

cite   Quote or refer to some legal authority to support a view of the law on some issue. See CITATION.

citizen   A member of a particular country; a person who is protected by his country and in turn is faithful to it or owes it his allegiance. Living in a particular country does not usually determine citizenship.

People who live in this country but are not U.S. citizens are considered resident aliens. They do not enjoy all the rights that citizens have, but they are entitled to DUE PROCESS OF LAW (the opportunity to defend themselves in court), and they owe a temporary allegiance to the United States whenever they are here. The rights of resident and nonresident aliens are discussed in the article ALIEN.

Corporations are often treated like persons in law; the people involved in them lose their separateness and become components of the corporation. A corporation then has citizenship for purposes of law. It is a citizen of the country and of the state in which it was first organized. But it can apply in any other state to do business there. See DOING BUSINESS.

■ **International law**   Under INTERNATIONAL LAW, each country decides who qualifies for its citizenship. Questions about a person's citizenship are generally solved by treaties between the countries concerned. If countries rely on different facts for citizenship, then one person may qualify for citizenship in more than one country, depending on treaties and the laws of the countries concerned. The result is dual nationality.

Dual nationality   A person with dual nationality usually has the right to elect the country of which he wishes to be a citizen.

EXAMPLE Sven was born in Minneapolis and therefore was 0⊶⊷ a U.S. citizen. When Sven was only six months old, his parents, who were Swedish immigrants, took him to Sweden to live. Whether or not Swedish law could consider the child a Swedish citizen, it could not take away his U.S. citizenship. When Sven grows up he will be able to choose between his two nationalities. If he returns to the United States within a short period of time after he becomes an adult he may elect to preserve his U.S. citizenship. If he lives in this country and announces his allegiance to it, he will continue to be a native-born American. If he continues to live in Sweden until he is 28 years old, he will lose his right under U.S. law to choose to be a U.S. citizen.

Someone who has connections with two countries does not always have dual nationality. West Germany, for example, might usually consider everyone born in that country to be a West German citizen, but it could still sign a treaty with the United States that makes an exception for the children of U.S. citizens. Then a child born in West Germany of American parents would be an American only. The only way to determine an individual's status is by asking an embassy or consulate about treaties on the subject of citizenship.

Law of the flag   The citizenship of persons born on ships is fixed by the law of the flag, which holds that a child born on a ship becomes a citizen of the country under whose flag the ship is sailing. However, this rule is constantly bent as citizenship laws of different countries and treaties between countries are rewritten to meet new political conditions. In general, a child born of American parents on a U.S. or foreign vessel anywhere in the world is a U.S. citizen. A child born of foreign parents in U.S. waters on a ship from a foreign country is a citizen of that foreign country if his parents are from the same country. If the child's parents are from another foreign country his citizenship depends on existing treaties between the countries concerned.

■ **Constitutional provisions** The 14th Amendment of the U.S. Constitution begins with a guarantee:

" *All persons born or naturalized in the United States, and subject to the jurisdiction thereof, are citizens of the United States and of the State wherein they reside.*"

This means that the important right of citizenship, whether for native-born or naturalized citizens, cannot be taken away. It cannot be withdrawn as punishment for a crime or for any other reason. A naturalized citizen, however, may have his citizenship revoked if he has gained it through illegal or fraudulent means.

In 1868, when the 14th Amendment was added to the Constitution, the words "all persons" were intended to confer citizenship on former slaves. Since 1924 the amendment has been extended to include American Indians as well. U.S. citizenship does not negate an Indian's tribal citizenship—the two exist alongside each other. The 14th Amendment does not apply to the children of foreign AMBASSADORS AND CONSULS and foreign military officers. They take the citizenship of their parents and are not subject to the laws of the United States.

Even though the 14th Amendment provides that U.S. citizens are also citizens "of the State wherein they reside," it is not necessary to be a resident of a state to be a U.S. citizen. Americans living abroad, for example, are citizens of the United States but not of any state. But being without citizenship in a state creates one serious legal disadvantage. The Constitution says that our federal courts may hear "controversies . . . between citizens of different States." The phrase "citizens of different States" includes citizens of Washington, D.C., Puerto Rico, the U.S. Virgin Islands, and Guam, but if you do not live in one of these places or in one of the 50 states, even if you are a U.S. citizen, you cannot initiate this kind of lawsuit in federal court.

■ **How American citizenship is acquired** One becomes a U.S. citizen either by birth or by naturalization, a legal process that a qualified person may follow.

Citizenship by birth Federal law explains exactly what is meant in the 14th Amendment by "born . . . in the United States, and subject to the jurisdiction thereof." People who are born in any of the 50 states, the District of Columbia, Puerto Rico, the U.S. Virgin Islands, Guam, and the former Panama Canal Zone are all native-born citizens. A person born outside the United States or its territorial possessions is a native-born citizen if one or both of his parents is a citizen who has lived in this country for certain periods of time.

Persons born in outlying possessions of the United States, such as Wake Island or Midway Island, and their children are called *nationals*. They owe allegiance to the United States and enjoy some of the rights of citizens.

An illegitimate child born outside the United States and its territories takes his citizenship from his mother. He is an American if she was a U.S. citizen at his birth and had at some time lived in this country for at least one year.

Citizenship by naturalization Aliens may become U.S. citizens by complying with certain federal laws, which describe the qualifications and the steps to be followed. This process of *naturalization* is discussed in detail in the article ALIEN.

Derivative citizenship It is possible for a child born in a foreign country to become an American citizen just because his parents become naturalized citizens. If you were brought to the United States before you were 18 years

---

CITIZENSHIP—HOW IT IS ACQUIRED, HOW IT MAY BE LOST

■ People born in any of the 50 states, Puerto Rico, the Panama Canal Zone, the U.S. Virgin Islands, and Guam are native-born citizens.

■ If you were born outside the United States, you are still a native-born American if one of your parents is a citizen who has lived in the United States for certain periods of time.

■ Persons born in outlying possessions, such as Wake Island, and their children are called nationals. They enjoy some citizenship rights.

■ An illegitimate child born outside the United States and its territories takes his citizenship from his mother. He is an American if she was a U.S. citizen at his birth and had at some time lived in the United States for at least one year.

■ A child born of American parents on an American or foreign vessel anywhere in the world is an American.

■ U.S. citizenship does not negate an Indian's tribal citizenship—the two exist alongside each other. The children of foreign ambassadors, consuls, and military officers born in the United States take their parents' citizenship and are not subject to citizenship laws of the United States.

■ Your U.S. citizenship cannot be taken away from you as punishment for a crime. You may, however, do something voluntarily that amounts to giving it up.

■ Acts that may trigger a loss of U.S. citizenship include serving in the armed forces of a foreign country, holding public office in a foreign nation and taking an oath of allegiance to that country, being convicted for an attempt to overthrow the U.S. government, and becoming a naturalized citizen of a foreign country.

■ Unless a treaty between two countries requires a person with dual citizenship to make a choice, he does not have to give up his rights to either nationality.

■ You do not have to be a resident of a state in order to be a U.S. citizen. Americans living abroad are citizens of the United States but they are not citizens of any state.

■ You have the right to travel in and out of the United States, and wherever you go you are entitled to receive U.S. protection.

■ If you left the country without bothering to get a passport, even though you knew you should have one, you must be allowed to enter when you return.

■ A naturalized citizen has rights that are equal to those of a native-born American in every respect except one: he can never be President of the United States.

old and your parents became citizens, you can claim citizenship when you reach 18. Since your birth certificate shows that you are foreign born, you should apply to the Secretary of State for a certificate of nationality. If your U.S. citizenship is denied by a government agency or official, you may start a lawsuit to prove that you are an American.

■ **Rights of citizens**   Everyone within the jurisdiction of the United States is protected by most of the guarantees and safeguards of the Constitution. A U.S. citizen has all of those rights and a few more. Wherever a U.S. citizen goes, he is entitled to the protection of the United States. When a U.S. merchant ship is seized by a hostile force and its crewmen are taken prisoner, the U.S. Marines can be sent in to rescue them. If a businessman has all his property stolen while he is in a foreign country, the U.S. consul may lend him money to get home. Americans, of course, do not have the right to break the laws of other countries they are visiting. But if an American is arrested while in a foreign country, someone from the U.S. Ambassador's office may see him, and officials will remind the foreign nation that the United States is watching closely to see how the American is treated.

American citizens also have the important right to travel into and out of the United States. Many countries do not guarantee this to their citizens. A U.S. citizen, however, is entitled to a passport, which certifies to foreign nations that he is under the protection of the U.S. government. The right to enter and leave the United States is so fundamental that a citizen cannot be prevented from entering the United States merely because he has no passport. If you left the country without bothering to obtain a valid passport, even though you knew you should have one, you must be allowed to enter when you return. You may use documents such as your birth certificate or an expired passport as evidence of your citizenship, or you may swear an oath. But it is a crime for a U.S. citizen to enter or leave the country without a valid passport.

The U.S. government does have the power to deny you the right to travel in certain named countries because they are hostile to the United States and dangerous for its citizens. If you ignore these restrictions, you cannot count on U.S. protection, and your passport can be revoked. During war or national emergency travel to such countries is a crime.

A naturalized citizen has rights equal to those of a native-born American in every way except one: He can never be President of the United States.

■ **Duties of citizens**   A judge once wrote in an opinion that the 14th Amendment is not a suicide pact. It guarantees that the government will protect the rights of citizens, but it does not prevent the government from requiring certain duties of its citizens.

Most fundamental among the obligations of a U.S. citizen is loyalty to his country. At the very least, he owes allegiance to its people because they are the source of the American form of government. Allegiance is not a blind acceptance of every statute or officeholder; it is rather a general faith in the American system and goals.

In times of national danger, citizens may be called upon to defend the country. Military service may be required, or

an alternative service, such as work in a hospital. The government also has the authority to ration essential items, such as food, oil, steel, and rubber.

■ **Loss of citizenship**   Taking away someone's citizenship has been called the harshest punishment known to man. After a country withdraws the rights and protections of one of its citizens, it has no power to grant him citizenship in another country. A man without a country has no refuge, no place where he can claim a right to live. Today the ancient penalty of banishment, driving the convicted person away from his home and into exile, is considered primitive and barbarous all over the world. This is why citizenship occupies the special place of a constitutional right in our law.

Once you have U.S. citizenship, it may be taken away only if you have used illegal or fraudulent methods to gain it, such as hiding the fact that you had an extensive criminal record in your native land. You may act in such a way that the government considers you have given up your citizenship by choice. This is called EXPATRIATION, and it can come about in two ways: An American may declare that he no longer wishes to be a citizen or owe allegiance to the United States. Or he may do something voluntarily that amounts to giving up U.S. citizenship.

In the past women who married aliens automatically lost their citizenship; so did draft-age men who left the country to avoid military service. Those laws were held to be unconstitutional, however, because it cannot be assumed that people doing either of those things intended voluntary expatriation.

Voluntary acts   The test of whether a person voluntarily abandoned citizenship does not depend on his *intention* to give up his citizenship. The issue is whether his acts were of his own choice and whether they affected his allegiance to the United States. If such is the case, then federal law says that he has voluntarily given up his right to citizenship.

Acts that will trigger a loss of U.S. citizenship include (1) serving in the armed forces of a foreign country, (2) holding a post as a public official in a foreign nation and taking an oath of allegiance to that country, (3) being convicted for an attempt to overthrow the U.S. government, and (4) becoming a naturalized citizen of a foreign country.

Acts that might seem to be a renunciation of citizenship do not always constitute voluntary expatriation.

EXAMPLE   Anthony's parents came to the United States before he was born. He was born here, and when he was only six weeks old his parents moved back to Italy with him. Just before World War II, Anthony was drafted into the Italian Army at the age of 17 and took an oath of allegiance to the king of Italy. After serving throughout the war, even after he reached the age of majority, Anthony claimed his U.S. citizenship.

In this case, Anthony never gave up his constitutional right to citizenship as a native-born American. Even if he had *willingly* joined the Italian Army at age 17 and had *wanted* to swear allegiance to Italy, the decisions of someone below the age of majority are of no effect. Although he became an adult while he was in the army, he certainly could not choose to quit at that time. As long as he claimed his U.S. citizenship within a reasonable time after he became an adult, it could not be kept from him.

Unless a treaty between two countries requires someone with dual citizenship to make a choice, he does not have to give up his rights to either nationality. Just because a person benefited from the services of another country and exercised legal rights there does not mean that he chooses to surrender his U.S. citizenship.

EXAMPLE A young woman has dual citizenship because she O⊶✳ was born in California and her parents are British. When she is 22 years old, she moves to Britain for a year. During the year she accepts free medical care, starts a lawsuit after she trips on a broken stair, and registers for reduced-rent housing. Has she abandoned her rights as an American? No.

The Supreme Court has held that Congress has the power to list actions considered acts of expatriation. The right to citizenship is so important, however, that these acts must be closely related to a very clear shift of allegiance away from the United States.

Criminals' loss of rights A person convicted of a crime may sometimes be deprived of some of his rights of citizenship. Long ago, such a person actually lost his citizenship. This was sometimes called *civil death*. Now, however, only some of his rights are taken away, even if the particular law is called *loss of citizenship*. A state has the authority, for example, to refuse to allow someone to vote after he has been convicted of a felony or an "infamous crime," such as bribery or perjury. This punishment may continue until the time of the sentence is finished, including periods of parole, or it may be permanent. Generally, full rights can be restored to a citizen by a pardon from the President or a governor. Some states permit a judge to restore rights to a former prisoner who is rehabilitated.

civil action Every kind of lawsuit except a criminal proceeding; a lawsuit brought by one person or group against another to enforce a legal right or to recover money as payment for an injury or loss. See ACTION.

civilian 1 Someone who is not a member of a uniformed service, such as the military, police, or fire department. 2 One who has studied and knows the civil law.

civil law 1 A legal system based on the one the Romans used. 2 A system of law based on a CODE rather than on CASE LAW and statutes. Most English-speaking nations follow the the latter, COMMON LAW system, but other countries generally use civil law. Louisiana has a civil law system because of its strong French and Spanish heritage, but all the other states and the federal government are entirely common law in approach. 3 Government run by civilians instead of military officers; not martial law.

civil rights Rights that belong to each person because he is a member of the community or country. They are areas in each person's relations with the community where no one else may interfere. Where a right exists for one person, a duty is always created for someone else.

Many of our laws protect individuals from discriminatory acts that interfere with their civil rights. Not every kind of discrimination is illegal. In fact, most personal prejudices are protected by each person's freedom to choose his own associates, express himself, and maintain his privacy. Civil rights laws resolve the controversy, however, when one person's exercise of his own preferences and prejudices interferes with certain protected rights of another. The laws settle the conflict in a way that best promotes the interests of society as a whole.

This article discusses which civil rights are recognized by law. It gives some history, explains what kinds of discrimination are illegal, and explores in detail the major civil rights laws of recent years. These laws prohibit certain kinds of discrimination in public accommodations, public facilities, public education, employment, housing, and federal programs.

■ **Related fundamental rights** In addition to civil rights, the law sometimes speaks of the *natural rights* of each human being. Life is a natural right that creates the duty in everyone not to kill. Natural rights grow out of moral obligations related to physical existence. See NATURAL LAW.

People also have *political rights* that depend on their relationship with their government. These include the power to establish a government, vote, hold office, and petition to change or improve the law. You may have to be a citizen in order to exercise political rights.

Personal rights are also fundamental to law and, especially in our legal system, are carefully guarded. Personal rights protect each person's life, body, health, reputation, and freedom. See CONSTITUTIONAL LAW.

These definitions are only guides, because rights are not kept neatly in legal categories. Civil rights are social rights, the privileges of being part of society. In ordinary usage, the term can include natural, political, and personal rights.

In law, civil rights are those that are legally enforceable. All adults in the United States, even those incapable of managing their own affairs, are entitled to have their civil rights protected by the law if they have not lost those rights through a criminal conviction.

Constitutions, laws, and all the cases explaining them make up the list of what can be claimed as civil rights. A license to drive a car is *not* a civil right, for example. Nor do you have a right to prevent a newspaper from publishing your picture if you are arrested. You have no right to join a private club that insists on denying you membership.

People often speak of children's rights or PRISONERS' RIGHTS, but these are not legal terms. In practice, however, laws that affect each person individually usually affect small groups too, and therefore this article brings together those parts of the law that affect groups of people. It is important to remember, however, that the law may vary greatly from state to state, and local laws must be checked.

■ **History** Rights reserved for the people were the foundation of the new government created after the Revolutionary War. The first words of the Constitution are "We the People of the United States. . . ." And Article IV states: "The Citizens of each State shall be entitled to all Privileges and Immunities of Citizens in the several States." These privileges and immunities include all the rights of free people recognized under the common law even before the writing of the Constitution. They are the legal rights

CIVIL RIGHTS—YOUR PROTECTION AGAINST DISCRIMINATION

■ It is illegal to discriminate against people using places of public accommodation such as a hotel or restaurant because of their race, color, religion, or national origin. But private clubs may discriminate in any way they choose. A so-called club that sells one-day memberships is not a legitimate private club, however, and cannot discriminate.

■ No state or local government can pass a law that aids illegal discrimination, nor can anyone acting in an official capacity assist it.

■ Discriminatory acts by private people are not illegal, but when a public official acts, even without authority, he is not a private person.

■ Schools may not penalize or otherwise discriminate against students who observe religious holidays. They must excuse a child's absence on such days and let him make up his work.

■ Schools may not keep a handicapped child out of school without notice to his parents and a hearing. If it is decided that the child cannot attend regular classes, some kind of "free, appropriate" public education must be made available to him.

■ An employer may discriminate in hiring if he has a very good reason related to the job itself—a French restaurant can take on only a French cook, a religious bookstore can hire only members of a particular faith as clerks, and so forth. This is commonly known as a BFOQ (bona fide occupational qualification).

■ If you are discriminated against while on the job or in seeking a job and wish to take action, you must file with your state civil rights or human rights agency—if there is none, send a written and sworn-to complaint to the federal Equal Employment Opportunity Commission (EEOC).

■ File promptly after the discriminatory act because time limitations are short—as brief as 30 days—and unless you file, no action can be taken.

■ If you are a federal employee, first consult your Equal Employment Opportunity Counselor and then file with the EEOC.

■ If you win, the courts may enforce your rights by such methods as ordering back pay or retroactive seniority or assessing damages for you.

■ It is illegal to use racial quotas in renting public housing or low-income apartments.

■ Some types of sex discrimination have been held unlawful. It is a violation of constitutional rights, for example, to require a father to support a son to age 21 but a daughter only to 18 or to permit a man in military service to receive additional allowances if he has a wife while denying the same benefits to a married female naval officer.

■ The Supreme Court has said, on the other hand, that a state may require women to take their husband's last name when they marry and may refuse to pay disability benefits to women workers who are unable to work for a time because of pregnancy.

■ Because the problem of equal rights regardless of sex is not yet settled, the Equal Rights Amendment to the U.S. Constitution (the ERA) was proposed. If ratified, the ERA will be the 27th Amendment to the Constitution and will guarantee that "Equality of rights under the law shall not be denied or abridged by the United States or by any State on account of sex."

■ At least 15 states already have equal rights provisions in their state constitutions—Wyoming has constitutionally prohibited sex discrimination since 1890.

relating to persons, places, and property. *Privileges* are the advantages of living in this country, such as the right to start a business, sell land, write a will, or get a divorce. *Immunities* are the protections that keep the government or other people from interfering in one's life. They include such legal rights as freedom from illegal searches, freedom from arrest for publishing a newspaper, and the freedom to continue a lawful business. The privileges and immunities clause prevents each state from discriminating against citizens of other states.

The first 10 amendments to the Constitution, the Bill of Rights, describe very specific rights reserved for "the People." See CONSTITUTIONAL LAW. These rights, however, were not really for all the people—in fact, adult white men were the only ones granted protection. In 1857 the Supreme Court held that the Constitution did not apply to a black man named Dred Scott because, when the Constitution was written, Negroes were regarded as an "inferior class of being." Constitutional changes were necessary to extend civil rights to all people.

Constitutional amendments   The changes began in the wake of the Civil War. First, the 13th Amendment to the Constitution outlawed slavery and every form of involuntary servitude in 1865 and gave Congress the power to pass laws to enforce the amendment.

In 1868 the 14th Amendment was added to the Constitution. It makes each person born or naturalized in the United States and subject to its legal authority a citizen. Then it guarantees that no state will frustrate the civil rights of a citizen or deny him DUE PROCESS OF LAW (the right to defend himself in court, among other things) and EQUAL PROTECTION OF LAWS. Again, and very importantly, Congress is given the power to pass laws to enforce these rights. The effect of the 14th Amendment is to put upon states the responsibility of protecting the civil rights guaranteed by the federal Constitution. It was clearly black people who were intended to benefit, but it is significant that Congress chose the phrase "all Persons" rather than "all Negroes."

Nineteenth-century civil rights laws   In the years just following the Civil War, Congress enacted five federal civil rights laws.

The first of these guarantees equal rights under the law for "all persons within the jurisdiction of the United States."

The second assures every citizen of an equal right to own, inherit, rent, buy, and sell real and personal property.

A third was the Ku Klux Klan Act of 1871—an attempt to stop the wave of murder and assault of blacks and Union sympathizers in the South when the war ended. It gives citizens the right to sue in a civil action for violation of protected rights.

A fourth made it a crime to use "force, intimidation or threat" to deny anyone equal protection of the laws.

The fifth of the civil rights laws included a provision that no one could be denied service at a *public accommodation*—any business open to serve the public—for an illegally discriminating reason. This law was struck down, however, because the Supreme Court determined that there was no state or public involvement at that time in the operation of local accommodations like hotels and restaurants. The 14th Amendment guaranteeing equal protection of the laws applies only when a state action is involved.

Twentieth-century civil rights laws For 82 years, from 1875 to 1957, there was no major civil rights legislation. In 1957 Congress established the Civil Rights Commission to investigate and analyze race relations for Congress and the President. Then the Civil Rights Act of 1960 guaranteed that qualified voters would not be denied their right to register in any state. Voters were given the right to sue anyone who kept them from registering, whether he was a state official or was merely acting as one.

The most far-reaching civil rights legislation in our history became law in the Civil Rights Act of 1964. It includes provisions for equality in the use of public accommodations, public facilities, public education, employment, and federally assisted programs. The most recent major law on the subject is the 1968 Civil Rights Act, which prohibits discrimination in housing.

The Civil Rights Acts of 1964 and 1968 guarantee equal opportunities in accommodations open to the public, public facilities, public education, federally assisted programs and benefits, employment, and housing. They prohibit discrimination on account of race, color, religion, national origin, and, in education and employment, on account of sex. They provide criminal penalties for some violations. They create the right to sue and collect money damages from anyone who interferes with your civil rights, conspires to deny them, or uses government authority or public office to deprive you of them.

■ **Public accommodations** The Public Accommodations Act of 1964 made it illegal to prevent anyone from using places of public accommodation. The Supreme Court has said that the purpose of the act is to stop unfairness, humiliation, and insult to customers of places serving the general public. Courts give this act the widest possible application. The places covered are those that provide lodging, food to be eaten at the place where it is served, restrooms of gasoline stations, and places of entertainment. Courts have found that taverns, nightclubs, trailer parks, movie theaters, snack bars, beach houses, motels, skating rinks, and YMCAs fall within this definition.

The test is whether the establishment affects interstate commerce, which Congress has a duty to regulate under the COMMERCE CLAUSE of the Constitution. This has been held to be the case, regardless of the owner's intention, when the business is located near an interstate highway, uses products made in another state, or has hired a person from out of state. Specific examples include a sports club that purchased footballs made in another state, a casino that featured an entertainer from another state, a restaurant that bought beef raised and packed in a different state, and a privately owned beach resort in Florida that advertised in newspapers in northern states.

EXAMPLE A corporation owned and operated a golf course seven miles from Richmond, Virginia, that was open to all members of the public except Negroes. Four black men sued the golf course for violation of their right to use public accommodations. The golf course claimed that it was a purely local business that did not have to comply with the Civil Rights Law of 1964. The federal court held, however, that the golf course was an "establishment affecting interstate commerce" because it had a lunch counter that served the general public, including interstate travelers. Furthermore, the golf course was a "place of exhibition or entertainment" within the terms of the statute because it regularly hosted a golf team from outside the state. The golf course had to serve all members of the public, regardless of race.

Private places Private clubs may discriminate in any way they choose. If a club is not operated for profit, is genuinely selective in its membership, and is supported entirely by private funds, it may refuse to admit certain people for any reason. Simply having a state liquor license does not make a club public. However, a bar that permits every white customer to buy a one-day membership, but no black person, is not a legitimate private club.

Constitutionality When the Public Accommodations Act was enacted, its constitutionality was challenged in every possible way. The Supreme Court answered most questions in December 1964 when it decided the *Heart of Atlanta Motel* v. *United States* case. The Court found that a law requiring that the owner of a public accommodation serve all customers does not interfere with his personal liberty or take his property without just compensation. Nor does it make him in any way a slave to the government or certain customers, in violation of the 13th Amendment to the Constitution.

Government activity The statute that prevents discrimination by the owner of a public accommodation also prohibits discrimination by the government. No state or local government can pass a law that aids illegal discrimination. Nor can anyone acting in an official capacity assist illegal discrimination. A police chief, for example, cannot arrest black people who are peacefully sitting in a hospital lobby even though the receptionist is frightened and intimidated because black people have never sat there before.

Color of law The discriminatory acts of private people are not illegal in most cases. When a public official acts without authority, however, he is not a private person. He is said to be acting under *color of law,* even if he misuses his authority. If his actions are discriminatory, they violate the Civil Rights Acts.

■ **Public facilities** It is illegal to bar someone's access to public facilities because of his race, color, religion, or national origin. Facilities are public if they are owned, operated, or managed by or for a state or local government. Examples include a county jail, a state hospital for the mentally ill, a public park, and a municipal auditorium.

A state or local government cannot avoid civil rights requirements by turning over or selling cheaply public facilities to a private group. Nor is it legal to operate separate facilities for blacks and whites. But there is no requirement that a local government provide certain public facilities. This is true even if the problems of integration or civil rights laws are the reasons for not operating them.

EXAMPLE Suppose that a man who died in 1975 left his large O━━* house in a major city to be run by the city as a refuge for young people who have run away from home. His will said, though, that ownership of the house would return to his heirs if the city ever permitted "Jesus freaks, Moonies or Hare Krishnas to set foot in this house."

The Public Facilities section of the 1964 Civil Rights Act makes discrimination on account of religion illegal. Since the city is not required to operate this or any other house as a public facility, it may decline to accept the gift in order to avoid discriminating.

Nor can a city be required to continue operating a public facility. A city operating segregated swimming pools in 1964, when the Civil Rights Act was enacted, could decide that desegregated pools would lead to racial disturbances and that attendance would therefore decline. City officials could then close down the pools.

Governmental officials need not deny the use of public facilities to groups that discriminate in their memberships. A private church, for example, has the right to refuse membership to everyone of a particular race or color. That it does so is not a valid reason for city officials to prevent the church youth group from using a public playground.

■ **Public education** You have no fundamental legal right to be educated. When public education is provided, however, it is illegal to offer less than equal opportunity to all students. See also SCHOOLS.

Separate but equal In 1896 the Supreme Court held that a Louisiana law that required railroad passengers to be separated by race was not unconstitutional. The Court wrote that the 14th Amendment to the Constitution, even though it guaranteed equal rights to all citizens, was never intended to prohibit "separate but equal" accommodations. To support its decision, the Court pointed to the custom of requiring black children and white children to attend different schools. See PLESSY V. FERGUSON.

In 1954 the Court first considered directly whether separate but equal public schools violated the constitutional rights of children. The answer was a sharp yes. The nine judges agreed that separate schools were not in fact equal. States were ordered to reorganize their school systems "with all deliberate speed" to admit students to public schools without regard to race or color. See BROWN V. BOARD OF EDUCATION.

A single school system It is illegal for a state to be involved in an educational system that denies children an education because of their race. The requirement is that each school district operate one system without creating racially identifiable schools. The guarantee of equality is there for *every group*, whether black, Hispanic, Chicano, white, Indian, or Asian.

EXAMPLE The Board of Supervisors of Prince Edward O━━* County, Virginia, decided that they would have no public schools if the races could not be separated; so white parents formed an organization that established private schools for their children. The county gave these parents a sum of money for tuition. Moreover, if this amount was not enough, the county also reduced the parents' property taxes. The federal court ruled that although Virginia was not constitutionally required to provide public schools, it could not use tax money to help maintain segregated private schools.

De facto and de jure segregation Racial segregation can be either de facto or de jure. *De jure* means "in law," and *de facto* means "in fact," or in actuality. Every kind of state-supported—that is, de jure—segregation is prohibited by federal law. The state has a further obligation to minimize the effects of de facto segregation—the kind that develops from factors other than government action, such things as patterns of segregation in neighborhoods, which lead to segregation in the schools.

Affirmative steps It is not the responsibility of the schoolchildren or their parents to ask for desegregation. The school boards must take affirmative steps to bring it about and without delay, because education must be provided within a few years or students will miss the opportunity just by growing older. It is not enough for an individual black or Chicano that, in general, educational opportunities for his race have been improved.

Lawsuits Federal district courts have the power to hear cases brought by persons denied their rights to equal education or by the Attorney General's office suing on their behalf. Neither public displeasure nor threats of violence will excuse judicial delay.

Integration plans An integration plan permitted in a district should consider local conditions, but barriers that never stopped segregation, such as traffic hazards, cannot be allowed to delay integration. Black students cannot be asked to travel farther to school than white students. And no student can be transported a long distance from home in order to prove that integration will not work. It is not necessary that the number of each race in a school reflect the racial balance in the community, nor is it necessary to meet quotas in each school.

Antibusing The antibusing provision of the 1964 Civil Rights Act states that the courts lack the power to order bus transportation from one school or district to another to achieve racial balance. This law does not deny a court's authority to use busing in a comprehensive plan for desegregation. A school district may use busing as a step to eliminate segregation, but there is no authority for using it to insure a complete balance.

Employees Desegregation applies not only to students in public schools but also to faculty and staff. Teachers and employees cannot be hired, fired, promoted, or assigned to schools because of race. However, a school board may be permitted to reassign a black teacher to correct an earlier pattern of segregation in a school. School officials should encourage voluntary transfers of teachers to end segregation.

Sex discrimination In 1972 Congress outlawed sex-based discrimination in public schools. The law includes activities incidental to education itself. But courts have been less vigorous in protecting rights to participate in sports and extracurricular activities when a factor other than race is involved. Sometimes these rights have been called privileges, and sometimes the courts simply require very little justification for discriminating on the basis of sex.

EXAMPLE One court found that a girl was not deprived of
0⊷＊ equal educational opportunities when she was
refused admission to a public high school for boys in
Philadelphia. The court said that the boys' school was an
especially good academic school, but there is a girls' high
school that is nearly as good. The judges were not willing,
on appeal, to say that the city could not offer these two
single-sex schools as alternatives to the many coeducational schools in Philadelphia.

Girls must be given the opportunity to participate in
sports, but strict equality is often not required. At least one
federal judge has ruled that girls must be offered a chance
to try out for teams even in such contact sports as football,
basketball, and wrestling. Some educators believe it is
unfair to have girls and boys compete, because boys will
nearly always win. Others say that girls should nevertheless
be given the opportunity if they are physically qualified,
because not every boy is able to outplay every girl.

Hair On at least one issue—hair—boys have consistently claimed to have been mistreated in public schools. A
number of lawsuits were started when boys were suspended
because their hair was long, but no longer than that of girls.
Federal courts have become annoyed when students bothered them with hair-length questions. At least as many
courts have decided to leave the problem to school admin-
istrations as have struck down short-hair rules. One court
has stated that long hair on boys in public schools does "not
rise to the dignity of a protectable constitutional right."

Clothing styles Dress codes have been found to be
illegal restrictions, but schools have the right to exclude
persons whose clothing is unsanitary, obscene, or too
scanty. Federal courts in the districts covering 22 states
have held that hair and dress styles are *personal rights* under
the Constitution. The states are Maine, New Hampshire,
Massachusetts, Rhode Island, Vermont, Connecticut, New
York, Maryland, Virginia, West Virginia, North and
South Carolina, Indiana, Illinois, Wisconsin, Minnesota,
North and South Dakota, Iowa, Missouri, Nebraska, and
Arkansas.

Students with special needs Until recently, handicapped and disturbed children were completely excluded
from public education. Children who were mentally retarded, emotionally disturbed, or physically handicapped
were seldom permitted to attend school at all. The result
was that many simply grew up as wards of the state,
supported completely at taxpayers' expense. The greater
tragedy was that some of these children were either misdi-
agnosed or never professionally evaluated at all.

EXAMPLE One young man was labeled mentally retarded
0⊷＊ for more than 14 years. He was termed uneducable, was refused schooling, and was eventually put into an
institution for the severely retarded. Only when civil
rights leaders began investigating the treatment of mental
patients was it discovered that this young man was not
retarded at all. He had a physical illness that, while
incurable, could have been controlled if he had received
treatment, training, and therapy.

Federal courts have ruled that handicapped children
cannot be kept out of school without notice to their parents
and a hearing, and in 1975 Congress passed the Education
for All Handicapped Children Act. See HANDICAPPED PER-
SONS. A "free appropriate public education" must be available to children of the ages for which the state usually
provides schools. They must be kept in regular public
schools as much as possible, with attention given to their
special needs. Private or separate schools can be established
where appropriate, but children with widely different
needs cannot be simply dumped into the same program.

Other children with special needs are those who do not
speak English. Cities with large Spanish-speaking populations often try to help by offering bilingual classes. Parents
have the legal right to insist, however, that their children be
taught English. A federal court in California has ruled that
San Francisco's 1,800 Chinese-speaking children are being
cheated by a system that fails to recognize their inability to
speak English. The court did not tell San Francisco which
language should be used, but it did insist that the children
must be educated somehow.

Religion The right to be educated at public schools
without religious discrimination exists alongside the constitutional guarantee of freedom to practice one's religion.
For example, a state's compulsory education laws may not
require children to attend public schools. Parents have the
right to send their children to private or parochial schools if
they choose. State law also must make an exception in the
case of Amish parents, whose religious and cultural values
are violated if their children are required to attend school
until age 16.

A public school may not discriminate against students
who celebrate religious holidays. The school need not close
on every holiday observed by a small number of students,
but the school must excuse a child's absence on his religious
holidays and permit him to make up work. See also RELI-
GION, FREEDOM OF.

■ **Federal programs** No one can be kept out of any
federally assisted program, be denied its benefits, or be
subjected to discrimination under it. This section of the
Civil Rights Act of 1964 applies to programs directly
administered by the federal government as well as to state
agencies and private companies that accept federal money
or benefits.

EXAMPLE A city police department was not permitted to
0⊷＊ refuse to hire black policemen if it accepted funds
through the Law Enforcement Assistance Act. Farm
workers were able to stop discrimination by the Department of Labor office that was supposed to help them find
employment. Black physicians were granted staff privileges at a publicly supported hospital. It was established
that welfare programs must be administered so that they
serve all racial, religious, and ethnic groups equally.

The term "benefit" need not be an outright grant of
money from the federal government. A private college was
not permitted to discriminate when it was shown that the
school received almost $400,000 a year through federal
assistance to student veterans. Any tax advantages enjoyed
by private organizations are also considered benefits. On
behalf of black citizens, federal courts have denied tax-
exempt status to nonprofit, segregated academies started by
people who wanted to avoid school desegregation.

Under the federal Civil Rights Act of 1964, state officials
may specify how contractors receiving federal money will
comply with the statute. They have, for example, required

that a certain number of minority trainees be hired for work on a highway construction project and that a fixed percentage of moneys appropriated under a public works act be reserved for minority group contractors.

The federal civil rights law does not forbid organizations that have federally assisted programs from discriminating on the basis of sex. The Chamber of Commerce, for example, administers federal programs and spends federal money, but it does not have to accept women as members.

■ **Employment**   Today it is unlawful to discriminate in employment on the basis of race, color, religion, sex, or national origin.

Government employees   Since 1972 state and local governments have been prohibited by federal law from discriminating among their employees on the basis of race, color, religion, sex, or national origin. Most government employees are further protected by CIVIL SERVICE systems that prohibit arbitrary or discriminatory personnel policies.

Civil rights statutes do not protect elected officials or their appointees. For example, a district attorney, an elected official, may arbitrarily fire an assistant district attorney, even on the basis of race or sex.

Title VII   The most comprehensive source of employment rights is Title VII of the 1964 Civil Rights Act. It prohibits discrimination by all employers who have 15 or more employees. Included are state and local governments and labor unions, but not the federal government, Indian tribes, certain agencies in the District of Columbia, clubs, and religious organizations. These rights, however, were extended to federal employment by EXECUTIVE ORDERS from Presidents Lyndon B. Johnson and Richard M. Nixon.

The 1964 Civil Rights Act was written for everyone, not just traditional minorities. It protects black, white, Chinese, and Spanish-surnamed Americans. One exception in the statute permits an employer near an Indian reservation to give employment preference to Indians. Another permits employers to favor U.S. citizens over ALIENS. An employer can hire only American citizens if he treats all citizens equally. He cannot refuse to hire all Italians, whether naturalized or not, while hiring persons of other national origins.

Employment agencies   Agencies that secure employees for companies with at least 15 employees are also restrained from discriminating. A newspaper that publishes notices of jobs, if it exercises any editorial judgment, is covered by Title VII. For example, it is illegal for a newspaper to use "Help Wanted: Male" and "Help Wanted: Female" headings in its classified advertising.

Professionals   Title VII does not apply to professional licensing by states, such as for doctors or teachers.

EXAMPLE Black law school graduates sued the Georgia
O⊷—※ State Board of Law Examiners because every black person who took the bar exam in Georgia in July 1972 failed it and was refused a license to practice law. The federal court said that Title VII would permit the court to presume that an employer was discriminating if he never hired a black person, but Title VII does not apply to state licensing or certification procedures. In the case of the Georgia bar exam, it was up to the plaintiffs to prove that the bar examiners failed them because they were black. None were able to prove this.

Sex discrimination   The law prohibits discrimination in employment on the basis of sex, but this means gender, not sexual preference or conduct. An employer is not prevented from firing a man because he discovers he is homosexual, promiscuous, or living with a woman who is not his wife—as long as male and female employees are treated alike.

Sex discrimination means refusing to hire or promote someone simply because he is a man or she is a woman. A bank is discriminating, for example, if all of its tellers have always been women and all its head tellers men.

It is no excuse to say that customers have a preference. A law firm cannot say, for example, that its insurance company clients do not like to deal with women attorneys. Nor is it permissible to fall back on traditional stereotypes, as did the airline that unsuccessfully argued that women make better flight attendants because they are more compassionate than men and better able to calm passengers' fears and anxieties.

Conditions of employment   In 1963 Congress enacted the Equal Pay Act, which requires that men and women be given the same wages when the work they do is similar. It is also illegal to treat employees differently on the job. Women cannot be given longer coffee breaks than men or the right to decline overtime work when men are not. Facilities for the two sexes must be equal. Even if there is only one woman employee, a rest room must be convenient for her.

Hiring   Tests or qualifications required of job applicants must be related to the work to be done.

EXAMPLE One young woman was hired as a temporary
O⊷—※ employee by a community college to operate audiovisual equipment. She was the first woman ever hired to do this work, and she did the job well for more than a year. When she was offered permanent status, she was told that to qualify she would first have to pass a weight-lifting test by raising 25 pounds over her head with one arm held straight out in front of her. She could not do so. The test was found invalid because the job had never required that kind of weight lifting.

Requirements that job applicants be a certain weight or height have been thrown out when they are not necessary to performance on the job. Women, Puerto Ricans, and Asian Americans have complained that they are usually too small to meet such requirements and, as a group, are consequently blocked from jobs they are able to do. In one case, a power company was ordered to stop using a written test that black job applicants nearly always failed, because the knowledge needed to pass the test was not needed for the job.

Sex-plus   Another barrier to equal opportunities in employment has been the use of "sex-plus" classifications. In this case, employers are treating certain employees differently because of their sex plus some other factor. One company refused to hire women with preschool-age children. It argued that it was not discriminating *against* women but only *among* women. The Supreme Court said that the rule was unfair because it was applied to women but not to men with young children. In another case, an airline was told to stop firing female flight crew members who married unless it did the same to males.

Another sex-plus problem concerns pregnancy. It is not permissible to discriminate against women of childbearing age because they might get pregnant. Nor may a company force a woman out of her job because she is pregnant unless she is unable to do her work. The automatic suspension of airline stewardesses who become pregnant was held non-discriminatory by the Supreme Court, however, on the ground that pregnancy "could incapacitate a stewardess in ways that might threaten the safe operation of aircraft." States do not have to provide disability benefits for women when they cannot work because of pregnancy, even when state disability insurance does cover medical problems that affect only men (such as prostate surgery) or certain elective treatments, such as cosmetic plastic surgery. Some states have chosen, however, to provide disability benefits for pregnancy-related medical problems.

Grooming An employer need not have identical grooming standards for employees of different sexes. He can refuse to permit women to wear pants even though men do or to let men wear long hair even though women do. The courts will be much stricter, however, if an employer interferes with a Jew's preference for facial hair or a black's decision to wear an Afro. This does not mean that an employer must tolerate outrageous clothing or hairstyles that offend his customers. In such a case, he can properly claim the business necessity of requiring a neat appearance.

Although the general public may have a special image of what makes a person attractive, courts have held that it is arbitrary to require women but not men to meet that image. Women cannot be required to wear contact lenses or keep down their weight when men are not. This point was established in a case brought by airline hostesses.

Bona fide occupational qualifications An employer accused of illegal discrimination can defend himself if he is classifying job applicants according to a *bona fide occupational qualification*, called a BFOQ. It means that an employer can choose to discriminate in hiring if he has a very good reason related to the job itself. A BFOQ can be based on sex, religion, or national origin, but not on race. A French restaurant can take on a French cook, and a religious bookstore can hire only members of a particular faith as clerks. A movie producer can consider only women for the role of Juliet in *Romeo and Juliet*.

The Equal Employment Opportunity Commission (EEOC), which is charged with settling differences between employers and employees who claim discrimination (see below), has decided to treat BFOQ as a very narrow exception applicable in only rare cases, as when the employer wants a wet nurse or a sperm donor. The EEOC—whose capacity is only advisory, however—maintains that traditional notions that men should do dirty, dangerous, and uncomfortable work and women should have jobs that require attention to detail but no supervisory responsibilities should no longer be permitted. The fact that certain people could not perform a job is no reason to refuse similar people a chance for the job. For example, all Spanish-Americans cannot be excluded from a job requiring excellent language skills in English. Males should not be prevented from applying for typing jobs, and women cannot be rejected for jobs that require the strength to lift a certain amount of weight, if they have that capacity.

Religion If an employee has special religious needs, an employer must make efforts to accommodate him, un-

less the employee accepted the job knowing that the employer could not oblige him. The employee does not have to profess the Judeo-Christian beliefs most common in our country, but his religion must involve some sincere discipline. It cannot be something concocted as a shield for antisocial conduct.

An employer does not have to disrupt his entire business at great cost for an employee who refuses to work on his Sabbath. Other employees can, however, be required to substitute for someone absent from work because he is practicing his religion.

The lack of a religious belief is protected, too. One federal court ruled that an atheist cannot be required to attend daily religious services conducted by an employer.

EEOC The Equal Employment Opportunity Commission (EEOC), a federal agency, considers complaints based on employment discrimination. It cannot force settlements but it does try to negotiate compromises. It also publishes guidelines that explain or define the law, but these guidelines are only advisory opinions and do not have the force of law. Many states have agencies or human rights commissions like the EEOC. See also Chart 30.

Procedure If you are discriminated against, you must first file a complaint with your state agency. If there is none, send a written and sworn complaint to the EEOC. It is important to do this promptly after the discriminatory act because time limitations are as short as 30 days. Unless you file, no action can be taken.

If the complaint has merit and the controversy cannot be settled, a legal action can be started against your employer. In one case, an insurance company was obliged to pay $1.5 million in back pay to women and blacks who had been discriminated against. The company also agreed to promote minorities and hire them in greater numbers to make up for past discrimination. CLASS ACTIONS also have been very effective in the area of employment discrimination.

A federal employee follows a different procedure. He must first consult his Equal Employment Opportunity counselor. Then he can file a formal complaint with the EEOC, which rules on the validity of the grievance. This decision can be appealed to the Civil Service Commission. Any decision it makes can be reconsidered by the Appeals Review Board of the commission. Only then can a federal employee start a lawsuit.

Lawsuits Judges enforce equal-employment rights by issuing INJUNCTIONS to stop discriminatory practices, by ordering back pay or retroactive seniority or by awarding court-assessed attorneys' fees and money damages to the injured party. If both a union and an employer have been involved in the discrimination, the court can apportion damages between them. The courts are more severe when the discrimination is willful. They order additional penalties for an employer who retaliates against anyone who files a complaint.

■ **Housing** The Civil Rights Act of 1866 is still in effect today. It provides that all citizens of the United States have the same rights as whites to inherit, buy, lease, sell, own, hold, and transfer title to any real property (real estate) or personal property. The act has been held to protect only against discrimination on account of race. Landlords who did not consider race have been allowed to refuse to rent to someone, for example, because of his credit standing, assets, reputation in the community, age, children, appearance, or for no reason at all.

Race cannot be used to prevent someone from visiting a home or apartment when he or she is invited by a person who has a right to be on the property. Cemetery lots offered to the public cannot be refused to a potential buyer because of race, and insurance policies must be offered to everyone regardless of race.

It is also illegal for government officials to help private people discriminate.

EXAMPLE A white man owned a house in a development O⊶—✳ where all the deeds contained an agreement, called a racially restrictive covenant, that the owner would not sell his house except to another white. When this man decided to sell his house, a black man offered to buy it. The neighbors sued to prevent the sale, but the Supreme Court held in 1948 that the neighbors could not use the courts, police, or any official machinery to enforce a racially restrictive covenant.

Open housing The 1968 Civil Rights Act prohibits discrimination in the sale or rental of 80 percent of the housing in this country. The law covers all housing built with federal financial assistance, multiple dwellings with more than four units, single-family homes sold in real estate developments that are not owned by private individuals, and any private housing sold or rented by a real estate agent. Not only owners but brokers and people involved in financing arrangements are required to comply.

Suits based on this law, the Fair Housing Chapter of the 1968 Civil Rights Act, can be started in federal district court regardless of the amount of money the plaintiff claims as damages. This is an exception to the usual rule that federal cases must involve at least $10,000.

These statutes constitute very broad open-housing legislation. Although they were enacted principally to create fair opportunities for blacks who were restricted to racial ghettos, cases have been won by would-be renters or purchasers who were turned away because they were Japanese, Puerto Rican, or Jewish. The courts have said that race and religion must not be factors in the transfer of dwellings.

EXAMPLE In one recent case, however, a divorced black O⊶—✳ woman with children wanted a particular apartment. The landlord refused to rent to her. She sued, complaining of discrimination on account of race, sex, and her status as a single parent. The landlord replied that he had other tenants who were black, many who were women, and a few who had children. He turned this woman away, he said, because she was an attorney. He was afraid she would be a pain in the neck, constantly demanding her rights. The landlord won. It is not illegal, the court said, to discriminate against lawyers. The only factors that cannot justify a refusal to rent are those stated in the civil rights law.

Public housing Government officials must be fair when they deal with housing. It is illegal to use racial quotas in renting public housing or low-income apartments. In one case, a local housing authority had to stop giving Jewish applicants priority in a project that was near a synagogue. The Department of Housing and Urban Development cannot approve federal money for local projects unless it is clear

that there will be no discrimination in the program. This includes no preferential treatment for any group.

Zoning Local government officials are also prohibited from enacting ZONING laws to prevent integrated housing. But it may not be illegal to zone only for very large housing lots in a community if the purpose is to preserve an uncrowded neighborhood. Even four-acre minimum lots have been approved. A number of individuals and organizations are challenging this kind of zoning because it keeps low- and moderate-income people out of large areas in the most populous states and particularly hurts racial minorities. Some of these cases are working their way through the courts now. It is unclear how the Supreme Court will finally balance environmental and open-housing needs.

Blockbusting and redlining Both federal and state laws have been directed at two harmful business practices—blockbusting and redlining. A blockbuster is usually a real estate agent or other person with a financial interest in breaking up a neighborhood. *Blockbusting* consists of frightening homeowners into moving by telling them that people of a certain race, religion, or national origin are moving into their neighborhood. The homeowners worry that property values are going to drop, and they sell out at a low price. The unscrupulous agent then sells to members of minority groups at an inflated price and makes a fat profit. In blockbusting, both buyer and seller lose money. The laws making it illegal to induce panic selling are designed to protect the large investments of homeowners.

Redlining makes fair-housing opportunities unavailable to certain groups by limiting financing arrangements. If a bank or mortgage company thinks a neighborhood is on a downhill slide, it can draw a red line around the area and refuse to make mortgages on homes there. A neighborhood is sure to deteriorate if homeowners are thus stopped from selling or from borrowing for home improvements. The Fair Housing Act does not make redlining illegal, however. As long as a bank's refusal to lend money is not based on the applicant's race, color, religion, or national origin, there is no violation of the statute. Some states are trying to control redlining, but it is difficult to write laws for this purpose. It is useless to demand a loan if the bank believes it would be a poor risk. See CREDIT.

■ **Prisoners** The 13th Amendment to the Constitution was the first of the Civil War amendments. It abolished slavery, but with an important exception. It says:

❝ *Neither slavery nor involuntary servitude, except as a punishment for crime whereof the party shall have been duly convicted, shall exist within the United States, or any place subject to their jurisdiction.*❞

It is not illegal to put people in jail if they have been convicted by DUE PROCESS OF LAW, nor is it illegal to ARREST and hold someone if the policeman has a reason for thinking he has committed a crime. See PROBABLE CAUSE. It *is* illegal, however, to treat prisoners differently on account of their race. The only time the races may be separated is to reduce tension if there is an immediate danger of a violent racial confrontation.

It is a denial of civil rights to confine prisoners in overcrowded, filthy, dark, airless, or damp jails with poor food or no exercise or recreation. It is also a violation of civil rights laws to refuse to give necessary medical treatment, to deny religious materials to members of some faiths but not of others, and to censor civil rights complaints that prisoners wish to mail to government officials. Solitary confinement is not illegal unless inhumane treatment is part of the punishment.

Some states have laws or constitutional provisions that make contracts for the sale of prison labor illegal.

The sentence or punishment given a convicted person must be administered evenly for all groups. Parole is not a right that any prisoner can claim after a certain time, but parole boards must not treat prisoners differently because of race. See PRISONERS' RIGHTS; SENTENCE.

■ **Affirmative action** Race and sex classifications are clearly suspect, but courts can use them when correcting patterns of discrimination. Even though this creates a double standard, the courts say that it is not necessary to be color blind when civil rights have been abused.

Quotas Even though the law requests the use of race and sex classifications in enforcing civil rights, it says that quotas are not required. If the population of a county where a candy factory is located is 51 percent women and 23 percent black, this does not mean that employees must reflect the same proportions.

There are times, however, when quotas may be appropriate. If all the employees at this factory are white men, some blacks and some women could well sue for the opportunity to work. When a court orders the factory to stop discriminating in its employment practices, the owners of the company will want clear guidelines. These guidelines will be goals and timetables that are related to the purpose of fair employment.

The court can also order *affirmative action,* a positive effort on the part of an employer or labor union to recruit minorities that have always been discouraged from seeking work. The theory behind affirmative action is that if such recruitment did not take place, the effects of discrimination would continue throughout the lifetimes of more people. Under affirmative action, temporary preferential treatment for minorities is permitted.

Reverse discrimination in education Affirmative-action programs in education have been under severe attack. Professional schools that train doctors and lawyers have been in a particularly difficult position. They can accept only a certain number of students, and only those they take can enter the professions. In the past, most students were white males. When schools tried to change this pattern by making special efforts to recruit minority students or by using different standards to judge their qualifications, persons denied admission filed lawsuits.

EXAMPLE In 1978 the Supreme Court decided its first case questioning the constitutionality of affirmative action college admissions programs. In that case, the Court held that Allen Bakke had been refused admission to the medical school of the University of California at Davis solely because he was white. The school had set aside 16 of 100 places in the entering class for persons who were black, Chicano, Asian, or American Indian. Since Bakke was white, he could compete only for the other 84 places in the class. Applicants who fitted one of the minority-group categories had a better chance of being admitted because they could be considered for all

100 places. The Supreme Court found that this particular affirmative action program violated the law, and it ordered that Bakke be admitted to the September class.

This first decision on reverse discrimination did not outlaw all affirmative action programs, however. None of the judges wrote that it is illegal to consider race as one factor in evaluating a candidate's application, and a majority pointed out that considering race is not necessarily illegal. See also BAKKE CASE.

Other courts have said that applicants must be judged on the basis of *all* their qualifications. A student who overcame an impoverished background to get good grades might make a better doctor or lawyer than a student with slightly better grades who never had to work during college, for example. One judge commented that the United States really has a class system that is based more on intelligence than on race or sex. He said he was not certain that this is best for society. For one thing, such a system does not take into consideration the importance of values and morality.

Reverse discrimination in employment Employers and unions argue that affirmative action programs discriminate against people who are already working. The counterargument goes that the programs do not require a preference but rather a correction of an illegal system. White male workers contend that they are being denied equality when their seniority rights are threatened by a program requiring blacks or women to be promoted. The opposing argument is that these men enjoyed a great advantage when they were hired, since they did not have to compete with blacks or women for their jobs.

In 1979 the Supreme Court first ruled on the constitutionality of an employment practice that was claimed to cause reverse discrimination.

EXAMPLE A Kaiser Aluminum and Chemical plant in Louisiana voluntarily adopted an affirmative action plan to open up opportunities for blacks. Kaiser started the job-training program when only 5 of its 273 skilled craft employees were black. Under the plan only half of the employees accepted for the training program could be white until blacks had been promoted in a proportion roughly equal to the percentage of blacks in the local labor force. In order to reach enough blacks to make up half the number of trainees, Kaiser had to select blacks who had less seniority than some of the white production workers whose applications were turned down. One of those white workers, Brian Weber, sued Kaiser. He claimed that he had been discriminated against in violation of the civil rights law prohibiting discrimination based on race in employment.

The Supreme Court held that the plan did not violate Title VII of the Civil Rights Act of 1964. The Court noted that the plan did not remove any white workers from their jobs and replace them with blacks. Nor did it block white workers from certain jobs as the old system had nearly done to blacks. Finally, the plan was a temporary measure intended only to break the cycle of giving good opportunities only to workers with experience that blacks were never able to get.

See also WEBER CASE.

■ **Sex discrimination in general** The fight to end discrimination against blacks goes back to the era of the

Civil War. So does the fight for women's rights. Women who got caught up in the fight to end slavery suddenly began to realize that many of their own rights were being squashed and they soon began to fight for themselves. Nevertheless, the fight to end discrimination between the sexes has progressed more slowly than that against racial discrimination because it extends deeper into our everyday lives. It is a matter that deeply affects our traditional view of family life. Although sex discrimination has been aimed mainly against women, it has also been used against men.

Discrimination against women   The U.S. Supreme Court has repeatedly said that it will continue to recognize differences between men and women that the law has always acknowledged unless there is no reasonable basis for them. It was not until 1971 that the Court struck down a state law that automatically preferred men over women.

EXAMPLE The mother and father of a child who died without a will both individually applied for letters of administration of the child's estate. In Idaho the law provided that men were to be given preference over women when they were equally entitled to administer. When the father was appointed, the mother appealed on the ground that the law unfairly discriminated against her. The Supreme Court found that giving a preference to men in this situation was arbitrary, had no reasonable basis, and therefore the Idaho statute was unconstitutional.

In recent years the Court has also ruled that it is a violation of constitutional rights to require a father to support a son to age 21 but a daughter only to 18. Similarly, it is unconstitutional to permit a man in military service to receive additional allowances if he has a wife, when a woman naval officer is not entitled to the same benefits if she has a husband.

For a while it seemed that the Supreme Court would rule against sex discrimination as often as against race discrimination. But it specifically uses a less stringent test for sex discrimination. The Court has said that a state may require women to take their husband's last names when they marry and that a state can reduce the cost of a disability-insurance program by refusing to pay benefits to women workers who are unable to work for a time because of pregnancy.

Discrimination against men   Many sex discrimination cases have been brought by men, and decisions do not seem consistent. In one case, the Supreme Court said that a father was entitled to raise the children he had always lived with and supported after their mother died, even though he and the mother were never married. In 1974, however, the Court ruled that Florida could legally refuse to give a property-tax exemption to widowed men that it gave widowed women if it thought women needed it more. In 1975 the Court told the Social Security Administration that it would have to start giving the same type of benefits to a father whose wife had died as it gave to widowed mothers.

The ERA   Because the problem of equal rights regardless of sex is not yet settled, the Equal Rights Amendment to the Constitution was proposed. It reads: "Equality of rights under the law shall not be denied or abridged by the United States or by any State on account of sex."

If the ERA were to become the 27th Amendment to the Constitution, it would control action by federal, state, and local governments. They would be prevented from passing discriminatory laws or from enforcing laws in an unequal way. The kind of discrimination prohibited is that based on gender, male and female. It has nothing to do with one's sex life or with homosexuality, marriage, or abortion. It simply means that being male or female must not be the factor that triggers application of a law. It would require that laws be written so that they apply to the people they are intended to affect, and it would eliminate the use of words that mean male or female when that is not the intent of the law. For example, a law could say that alimony is possible after a divorce for a spouse who has kept house and raised children for a certain number of years. Of course, this would often be the wife, but the law would use words related to its purpose instead of assuming that the dependent spouse will *always* be a woman.

At least 15 states have equal rights provisions in their state constitutions. Wyoming, for example, has constitutionally prohibited sex discrimination since 1890.

■ **Other civil rights**   Many different groups have begun agitating for civil rights. For more information, see the following articles:

Age discrimination	— See INFANT; RETIREMENT.
Children's rights	— See INFANT; GAULT, IN RE.
Citizens' rights	— See ALIEN; CITIZEN.
Consumers' rights	— See CONSUMER PROTECTION.
Credit discrimination	— See CREDIT.
Jury duty	— See JURY.
Parents' rights	— See PARENT AND CHILD.
Patients' rights	— See HOSPITAL; PATIENTS' RIGHTS.
Soldiers' rights	— See ARMED SERVICES.
Voting rights	— See ELECTION.
Welfare rights	— See WELFARE PROGRAMS.

civil service   **1** Government employment in general.   **2** A system of hiring and promoting government employees other than elected officials and military personnel. Under civil service systems, employees are hired, fired, and promoted according to professional standards. People who want government jobs compete by taking examinations, and only those who score highest can be considered for appointment. Once a civil service system becomes law, politicians cannot replace people on the public payroll with their supporters after each election. The system gives employees the right to keep their jobs as long as they do the work, and it provides all applicants a fair chance to be hired. These rights can be enforced by applying to a civil service commission or to a court.

C.J.   Chief Justice; circuit judge.

claim   All the facts that make up one party's case in a lawsuit; an application for relief that the petitioner believes is just, such as a claim for workmen's compensation benefits or a claim for the proceeds of a life insurance policy.

claim for relief   The main part of a COMPLAINT in a civil lawsuit. The complaint is the first paper served—it starts the suit. The person who wants relief in the form of money damages or a court order draws up a complaint through his attorney. Its purpose is to warn the defendant that a legal action is started. The claim for relief is a short, clear statement of the specific relief to which the plaintiff feels he is entitled.

class action A lawsuit that the court permits one plaintiff or a small number of plaintiffs to maintain on behalf of everyone who has been harmed as a result of what the defendant did. A class action is an exception to the usual rule in lawsuits. Normally, everyone who will be affected by a decision must be notified that an action has been started and given an opportunity to appear and present his side of the case. This basic right is very important because everything decided in a legal action is binding on all parties. Once the appeals are over, any issue brought up in the case is settled. The parties involved cannot reargue one of the questions in future lawsuits.

If the court agrees to consider the plaintiff "as a class," then the entire group is bound by the decision. The court decides who is in the class, and everyone who fits that description must accept the final decision whether or not he appears in the lawsuit. Even if he did not know about the lawsuit, he is bound by it. There is a very important reason for this exception to the general rule. A class action protects the rights of people who otherwise have no legal remedy, especially when a large number of persons each have a small claim against the same defendant.

EXAMPLE A public official decides before an election to tell the voters that he has reduced the number of people on welfare. To do this, he orders the county welfare department to delay all new applications for assistance as long as possible. An elderly man who has just applied for welfare and cannot survive if his application is delayed goes for help to a neighbor who has just become a lawyer. The lawyer calls the welfare department and gets the impression that, if he complains loud enough, his neighbor's case will get quick attention. But that does not solve the real problem. So the lawyer files a class-action suit in the local court asking that this one old man represent everyone who is being unfairly treated in this situation for political reasons.

If the court finds that it would be difficult or impractical to make everyone whose welfare application is delayed a party in the lawsuit, it may permit a class action. In this case, some of the people may not understand their legal rights. Others may be afraid that if they get involved in a lawsuit their applications for assistance will be denied. Most will probably throw away any notice they get in the mail, because they cannot afford to hire lawyers individually.

This is a good case for a class action. The same legal question is the issue for everyone whose welfare application is delayed, and the one case of the old man is typical. His lawyer should be able to represent the interests of everyone in the class. In this situation, the unfair practice will probably continue if the old man wins a case just for himself, but everyone is protected if he is permitted to represent the entire class.

It is not always the person starting the lawsuit who represents a class. Defendants can also be treated as a class.

EXAMPLE Suppose that John Barley has invented a new corn seed by treating normal seeds with a certain process. This new seed is totally resistant to disease. Because the process is so valuable, Barley has it patented. When a seed company begins to use Barley's process without buying his permission, he promptly sues for patent infringement. Now, however, his secret process has been exposed, and 400 companies in 42 states begin to produce and sell seeds treated by Barley's process. Suing each of these companies in courts all over the country would be impossibly expensive. The solution is for Barley to bring a class action in federal court against all seed companies that have stolen his process.

clause One paragraph, sentence, or phrase in a document. Clauses can be numbered for easy reference, as in a will, statute, or constitution.

Clayton Act A federal antitrust law in effect since 1914. In 1890 the SHERMAN ACT provided penalties for MONOPOLIES and business practices that discriminated among customers to make them cooperate in unfair schemes. The Clayton Act was added to prevent concentrations of economic power—to stop monopolies before they began. Both acts are intended to protect free competition.

clean hands With honesty in relation to the situation in question. A person who starts a legal action with clean hands has acted fairly and honestly in all matters connected with his lawsuit. Otherwise, the suit will be dismissed. The rule is that "he who seeks EQUITY must come into court with clean hands." Judges often say that this rule does not require the plaintiff to have led a blameless life but only that he has been reasonable in this particular situation with the defendant.

The clean hands doctrine applies only to actions seeking fair treatment. If the suit is for money damages the rule does not apply, because the court can reduce the amount recovered by the plaintiff to penalize him for his misconduct.

clear Plain, obvious, or free from doubt. *Clear title* means that there is no doubt about who owns the property. A check is *cleared* when the bank on which it is drawn makes final payment on it. At this point, there is no more doubt that it is a good check.

clear and convincing proof The amount of EVIDENCE sometimes needed in civil cases to prove a fact. In a criminal case, it takes a great deal of evidence to convict someone, because there must be enough evidence to establish the defendant's guilt BEYOND A REASONABLE DOUBT. But in a civil action, it is usually necessary only for the evidence to weigh more on one side than on the other. Anything more than 50 percent is enough to support the verdict. This amount of proof is called a mere PREPONDERANCE OF EVIDENCE or the weight of evidence. Clear and convincing proof is a presentation of evidence that goes beyond a mere preponderance but that does not necessarily establish the fact beyond a reasonable doubt.

Clear and convincing proof may be necessary to prove a fact in a civil case if the fact will have a great effect. For example, if the court finds that one of the parties is a FIDUCIARY (someone in a position of trust) to the other, such as a guardian or trustee, then he has a strong duty to take care of the other person's interest. A fiduciary has liabilities, or legal obligations, he would not otherwise have. Therefore, there must be clear and convincing proof to show that a fiduciary relationship exists.

Clear and convincing proof is also needed to overcome a presumption or to prove the exception to a rule. For example, it is good public policy to presume that every marriage is valid. If you wanted to prove that a certain marriage was not valid so that you could inherit some property, you would have the almost impossible task of showing that the two people in question never were married. As another example, it is a rule in many states that a written contract must generally be accepted the way it stands. If one party wants to show that the price stated in the contract was changed during a face-to-face conversation, he must give clear and convincing proof that there was such a discussion and that the price change was agreed to.

clear and present danger　An immediate threat of actual violence. The phrase was first used by Oliver Wendell Holmes in 1919 in *Schenck* v. *United States*. In that case, the U.S. Supreme Court decided unanimously to uphold convictions for persons who printed circulars that encouraged draft dodging and desertion during World War I. The Court said that every crime depends on the circumstances surrounding it:

❝ We admit that in many places and in ordinary times the defendants in saying all that was said in the circular would have been within their constitutional rights. But the character of every act depends upon the circumstances in which it is done. The most stringent protection of free speech would not protect a man in falsely shouting fire in a theater and causing a panic. It does not even protect a man from an injunction against uttering words that may have all the effect of force. The question in every case is whether the words are used in such circumstances and are of such a nature as to create a clear and present danger that they will bring about the substantive evils that Congress has a right to prevent.❞

See SPEECH AND PRESS, FREEDOM OF.

clear title　Legal ownership that is free from restrictions or doubt; good title. Sometimes clear title is called marketable title. This means the property can be easily sold because a buyer has no reason to worry about whether the seller does in fact own it.

clemency　Mercy. When an executive such as the President or a governor has the power to grant clemency to a convicted criminal, he can reduce the punishment. Clemency is not a right. It is granted because our system of law includes the capacity to forgive.

clerical error　A mistake made by someone in copying or writing or typing. A mistake in an official document, such as a judgment, can be corrected and no one can object to the correction. If a court reporter mistakenly writes down that the defendant owes the plaintiff $40,000 rather than $40 for a broken lamp, for example, plaintiff cannot demand that the defendant pay the higher amount.

clerk of the court　The official employed to keep the records and files for a court. In some states, he is appointed after scoring well on a competitive examination; in others, he is selected by the court. His pay is determined by state laws. He may receive a salary, or he may be permitted to receive fees for certain services, such as making a certified copy of a judgment or holding money that has been deposited with the court. A clerk may be required to post a certain amount of money as a BOND when he takes office. If he does not perform his duties properly—either inadvertently, as when he loses the file for a case, or intentionally, as when he illegally charges a fee for filing a plaintiff's papers—the bond will be given up as a penalty.

client　A regular customer of a businessman; someone who uses the services of a professional person, such as an attorney. A client has a relationship that entitles him to more concern for his situation than if he were only a one-time customer. See ATTORNEY AND CLIENT.

Clifford Trust　A tax savings device by which a taxpayer in a high income bracket sets aside some of his money or income-producing property, such as stocks or bonds, in a trust for the benefit of another person (the beneficiary), usually a child, who is in a lower income tax bracket. The property is managed by an independent person (the trustee), whom the taxpayer has named. The trustee pays the income earned from the property (such as interest) to the beneficiary, but does not pay out any of the principal (the original property). The income from the trust property must be paid to the beneficiary for at least 10 years.

Although the taxpayer does not give up his ownership of the property, he cannot receive any benefit from it or exert any control over it for 10 years. This means that his taxable income will be less, because the income paid by the trust will be included in the taxable income of the beneficiary. The lower a person's taxable income, the less income tax he will have to pay each year. This income tax advantage will be lost if the taxpayer receives any income from the trust or if he tells the trustee how to manage the property within the 10-year period. If the advantage is lost, the income that is earned by the trust will be included in the taxpayer's taxable income for every year that the trust continues in existence.

In order, then, for such an arrangement to be treated as a Clifford Trust, the taxpayer must do two basic things: (1) He must give up all control over the property, including the right to tell the trustee how to manage the property for at least 10 years, and (2) he must give up the right to revoke the trust and to receive income from it for 10 years.

The Clifford Trust is often used by a taxpayer who can afford to divert income until he retires and falls into a lower tax bracket.

People who want to accumulate funds for their children's college education often make use of Clifford Trusts. If a parent opens a savings account to set aside funds for his son's or daughter's college tuition, the interest earned by the account will be included in the parent's taxable income, thus increasing the amount of income taxes he will owe. If the parent puts the savings account in the child's name alone, the parent gives up total ownership of the money. With a Clifford Trust, the parent keeps the property, while the interest or income earned by it is paid to the child. Income tax is not due on the interest, because the child does not usually have any other source of income.

The Internal Revenue Service sets out detailed requirements that a Clifford Trust must follow in order to qualify for favorable tax treatment. A tax attorney should be consulted in setting up a Clifford Trust.

A Clifford Trust differs from a traditional private TRUST governed by the law of trusts. Although a person gives up his right to control the property or revoke the trust for at least 10 years under a Clifford Trust, he is still considered the owner of the property held in trust (but not the income, which belongs to the beneficiary). In contrast, once a person gives up the right to revoke a private trust (an irrevocable trust), he no longer owns the trust property.

close   Finish; shut. A lawyer closes his case when he makes the last speech to the court. The contract for a sale of land is closed by giving money for the deed. See CLOSING. To close a courtroom, a judge orders that all reporters and the public must stay out. This cannot be done without good reason because the U.S. system of law calls for public trials.

closed corporation   A CORPORATION in which all the shares of stock are held by a limited number of people, who generally manage and operate the business. Closed corporations—also called close corporations—usually agree not to sell any stock to outsiders. In many ways, closed corporations operate like partnerships, but the people involved have limited liability, as in any corporation. This means that only the property of the business can be used to pay its debts, and none of the personal property of the owners can be taken.

closed shop   A company that will not employ anyone who does not belong to a certain union. A closed shop agreement makes a union very strong. Some workers believe, however, that they should not be forced to join a union, even if it is to their benefit, and in some states closed shops are illegal. See RIGHT-TO-WORK LAW.

closing   The final meeting between the buyer and the seller of real property (real estate). After negotiations are completed and the contract of sale is signed, these two parties and their attorneys meet to exchange money for the deed to the property. If MORTGAGE money is used as part of the purchase price, the bank or savings and loan association lending the money usually sends an attorney to the closing too. The buyer has to pay this attorney, his own attorney, and the closing costs.

The costs may include all the charges for transfer taxes, mortgage fees, a credit report or title search, and title insurance. All of these expenses should be written down on a closing statement called the settlement sheet.

cloture   The formal ending of debate on a particular topic or issue in a meeting or legislature.

cloud on title   Some outstanding claim that makes it uncertain whether ownership of property is free and clear. A break in the CHAIN OF TITLE is a cloud, and so is a lien for unpaid taxes or a judgment that has been docketed against the owner. In the case of land, a cloud on the title makes the property worth less money and more difficult to sell. See QUIETING TITLE.

club   An association whose members come together for a common purpose—often at regular meetings. Club is also a general term that includes every kind of group that has members. A chess club, health club, country club, Greek letter fraternity, the Women's Christian Temperance Union, and Diners Club are all examples of clubs.

Clubs can be organized for any legal purpose. But states have the right to regulate them under their POLICE POWER. See ASSEMBLY, RIGHT OF. Incorporated clubs are governed by the CORPORATION law of the state. If the clubs are not incorporated, they may be controlled by a group of state laws covering unincorporated ASSOCIATIONS or membership societies. Different laws may apply to profit-making clubs and to charitable or nonprofit organizations. See CHARITY.

co-   A prefix that means together, or with. A co-owner is one who owns something jointly with another. Codefendants are all the persons being sued together in a civil case or tried together in a criminal case.

code   1 A set of rules or laws.   2 An organized collection of laws that a legislature passes—usually on a particular subject, such as commerce or bankruptcy. A *code* is a new law in itself. It is different from a *digest*, which is a collection of all the existing laws on a subject. A digest of banking laws, for example, is useful for anyone researching laws covering banking in all 50 states.

Code of Federal Regulations   A publication in which all federal administrative rules are collected.

Code of Hammurabi   One of the first complete sets of laws, handed down by King Hammurabi of Babylon 4,000 years ago. It was remarkably complete, and many of its provisions are surprisingly humanitarian. On the other hand, the code contained the theory of punishment known as "an eye for an eye," the concept of fitting the punishment to the crime.

Code of Judicial Conduct   A set of rules governing the professional behavior of judges. For example, Canon 3 of the code says that "a Judge should perform the duties of his office impartially and diligently." Thus, a judge who spends more time playing golf than deciding cases can be disciplined or removed from the bench. The Code of Judicial Conduct is now law in many states and has been adopted by the American Bar Association.

Code of Professional Responsibility   A set of rules governing the conduct of lawyers. The code was adopted by the American Bar Association in 1969 and has since been enacted in the states. It consists of the following nine canons, or principles:

Canon 1. A lawyer should assist in maintaining the integrity and competence of the legal profession.

Canon 2. A lawyer should assist the legal profession in fulfilling its duty to make legal counsel available.

Canon 3. A lawyer should assist in preventing the unauthorized practice of law.

Canon 4. A lawyer should preserve the confidences and secrets of a client.

Canon 5. A lawyer should exercise independent professional judgment on behalf of a client.

Canon 6. A lawyer should represent a client competently.

Canon 7. A lawyer should represent a client zealously within the bounds of the law.

Canon 8. A lawyer should assist in improving the legal system.

Canon 9. A lawyer should avoid even the appearance of professional impropriety.

Excerpted from the Model Code of Professional Responsibility
as amended 1980, copyright American Bar Association

Each of the canons is broken down into ethical considerations and disciplinary rules. The ethical considerations describe goals for the lawyer to keep in mind when he faces a moral dilemma in his practice. Disciplinary rules, on the other hand, are requirements of the profession. An attorney who violates such a rule may be fined, suspended, or disbarred. See also ATTORNEY AND CLIENT.

codicil A paper that adds to a WILL or changes it. It must be made with the same formality as the will itself.

EXAMPLE A man writes a will in 1975 leaving "$10,000 each
O➤—※ to Stephen and Patrick, my loving sons." Then he has another child. Rather than rewrite the entire will, he can write a codicil, sign it, and have it properly witnessed. Without changing any provisions of his will, he can also leave $10,000 to his youngest child, Mary.

A codicil usually changes one or more provisions of a will without completely revoking or canceling the earlier will.

codification The process of collecting and arranging all the laws on a particular subject into a system to be enacted by the legislature as one CODE. Legislatures also codify when they set up categories into which new laws will be organized.

coercion Unfair or illegal force compelling someone to act against his will. Violence is not necessarily a part of coercion. Threats are enough if they force the victim to do something he should not legally be obliged to do or prevent him from doing something he is legally entitled to do.

It is coercion to keep employees from joining a union by threatening to fire them, because discharging someone who engages in legitimate union activity is illegal. It is not coercion to threaten to foreclose on a mortgage if payment is overdue. Foreclosure in that case is a proper remedy.

In some states, coercion is a crime. Forcing another person to commit perjury by threatening his family, for example, is an act of criminal coercion. Someone accused of criminal coercion can defend himself by showing that the harm he threatened was not illegal or the act he forced another person to do was something that should have been done anyway.

cognizance Jurisdiction; the choice by a judge to take notice of a matter and give a decision on it. Cognizance suggests not only that the judge will try and determine the case but also that he has the authority to do so.

cognovit note A paper by which a debtor admits that he owes someone money.

cohabitation Living together as husband and wife. Cohabitation does not *always* mean that two people have a sexual relationship, but it does indicate that they share the same home. If a man wishes to divorce his wife on the ground that she has abandoned him, he usually must testify not only that she left him but also that they have not cohabited for a certain period of time. See MARRIAGE.

coinsurance A division of risk between an insurance company and the insured, the person who bought the insurance. While insurance spreads the risk of any loss among everyone who buys it, coinsurance allocates the risk fairly according to the amount of insurance paid for by each person. For example, fire damage generally results in less than a total loss. If everyone could collect for the entire value of small losses, purchasers of full coverage would be cheated. With coinsurance clauses, owners of buildings who want to pay small premiums must accept a greater share of risk than owners who pay to insure their property for its full value.

One state, for example, permits the owner to collect for the full amount of any loss up to the figure written in the policy if he has insured the property for at least 80 percent of its replacement value. (You may, of course, insure for up to 100 percent of replacement value.) If the amount of the policy is less than 80 percent of the replacement value, then the recovery is proportionately reduced.

EXAMPLE A woman owns a $100,000 house, but she insures
O➤—※ it against fire loss for only $40,000. To collect the full amount of her loss under the coinsurance clause, she should have insured the property for at least $80,000. If her house burns and she suffers a $30,000 loss, she will be permitted to recover only $15,000. The reason for this is that for full compensation she was required to have a minimum of $80,000 fire insurance and she carried only $40,000, or one-half the required minimum. The amount she can recover is therefore also reduced to one half the amount of the loss she actually incurred.

collateral On the side; attached on one side; indirect. For example, *collateral facts* may prove surrounding circumstances in a lawsuit, but they do not settle the main issue. Uncles and aunts are *collateral ancestors,* but parents and grandparents are direct ancestors. A car may be pledged as *collateral security* that can be seized to satisfy an unpaid debt. Sometimes the property pledged to guarantee payment on a debt is itself called collateral: it stands beside the original debt. See also SECURED TRANSACTION.

collateral attack An attempt to avoid or defeat a judgment or a judicial proceeding. It is collateral, or indirect, because the attempt is made in some action other than the original proceeding.

EXAMPLE A Maryland man leaves his wife and children and moves to Virginia. There he goes to court and wins a divorce that makes no provision for him to help support his family. His wife can attack the judgment directly by appealing the decision in Virginia, or she can attack it collaterally by starting her own matrimonial action in Maryland. In the latter case, she will try to prove that the Virginia judgment was based on wrong facts or should never have been in that court.

A judicial proceeding can be attacked collaterally in one's own state. This is a good approach, for example, if a state agency is abusing its authority.

EXAMPLE Suppose a local zoning board refuses to consider an application for a variance for political reasons that have nothing to do with the property. If the board refuses to act on the application, it would do no good to follow an appeal procedure that involves the board. It might be better to attack the case collaterally by starting an action in a state court.

collateral estoppel

The conclusiveness and finality of a judgment or a finding by a court. In law there is a principle called res judicata, a rule that once something has been decided, it is finished. An appeal can be taken, but the same question cannot be argued again in a different court or in a later lawsuit. Collateral estoppel is a part of this rule. It means that anyone who tries in a later action to argue a point already decided is "stopped from the side." The other party does not even have to answer. He can just claim collateral estoppel.

EXAMPLE Suppose that a husband and wife go to Nevada for a quickie divorce. They win the divorce by lying to the court about how long they lived in Nevada. When the wife returns home, she regrets that she cooperated in the scheme because now she wants more alimony. She starts a lawsuit in her own state, claiming that the Nevada divorce is invalid because of fraud and the failure to meet residency requirements.

The husband can stop his wife's legal action by claiming collateral estoppel. The judge will not even ask whether the Nevada divorce was fair or legally proper. He will cite Article IV of the Constitution, which says, "Full Faith and Credit shall be given in each State to the public Acts, Records and judicial Proceedings of every other State." The judge here must rule that the wife is collaterally estopped, and he must dismiss her action.

collective bargaining

Negotiation between an employer and people from the union representing employees. Collective bargaining is exclusively regulated by the National Labor Relations Act. It protects the right of employees to choose their own bargaining representative and requires both the union and the employer to bargain in good faith. See LABOR RELATIONS. The purpose of collective bargaining is to help both sides reach agreement concerning such issues as wages, hours, and conditions of employment. The law does not require that an agreement be concluded, but sets up standards for fair and open dealing.

colleges and universities

Educational institutions offering instruction beyond high school. The word "college" is broadly used to refer to many different kinds of schools, including ones offering vocational training, such as a barber college. Correspondence schools, however, have been held not to be colleges. College also means a school that offers academic degree programs, such as in the arts, sciences, or business administration. When a group of such colleges join together, usually with graduate or professional schools, they comprise a university.

A *land-grant college* is a school that was founded when the government gave the state land to establish a college for the study of agriculture and the mechanical arts (for example, engineering). A *branch college* or *university extension* is a part of the school that holds classes somewhere other than at the main campus.

A *junior college* offers only the first two years of a liberal-arts college education and sometimes technical training as well. *Community colleges* are junior colleges, usually publicly owned or supported, that do not provide housing but serve students who live nearby.

A college may be publicly owned or operated by a private company, person, or religious group. Private colleges are usually financed by income from investments and contributions from alumni, charities, and businesses.

■ **Authority from the state** States have the power to prohibit use of the word "college" or "university" by any institution that does not meet certain educational standards. A state may also require a college to have a charter before it can operate. The charter is a grant of authority from the state that lists the college's powers. It may, for example, give the school the right to build dormitories, create new colleges within a university, or maintain a student health clinic. Most colleges are incorporated. See CORPORATION.

Colleges receive from the state the power to give each student a degree when he successfully completes a program of study. A diploma, given as proof of the degree, is a formal paper imprinted with the college or university seal.

A *diploma mill* is a school that passes out degrees without strictly enforcing academic attendance requirements, or one that has no authority to give degrees at all.

■ **Legal powers and liabilities of a college** A university has the same power to make contracts as other similarly organized businesses. It can negotiate contracts with its employees. It can agree to buy books or land and engage in building construction. It can contract to sell such things as agricultural products, medical services, or electricity to housing units on campus.

Another kind of contract colleges make is an agreement by which a private donor promises to give money to a university. If the school does something relying on the agreement, such as contracting to build a stadium with the money, then the promise to donate can be enforced in court. See SUBSCRIPTION.

The law once was that charities and government agencies could not be sued for accidents caused by their employees. This is no longer true in most states, but to sue a public university you must follow the special procedure required for a lawsuit against a government agency. See MUNICIPAL CORPORATION.

A university generally can be sued for injuries caused by either the NEGLIGENCE or the intentional acts of its employees. See RESPONDEAT SUPERIOR. It also has the capacity to sue for harm done to itself. For example, if a school hires an architect who improperly designs a 10-story classroom building so that its windows keep popping out, the school can sue the architect.

Trustees, officers, and staff   Colleges may be governed by a board of trustees or directors, or by state officers, such as regents. The trustees, directors, or regents usually choose the president or other high officers of the college. The president hires the staff and faculty and runs the school within the guidelines established by the board and state law. The nonprofessional staff may have union representation, and in a public college they can be civil service employees. The teaching staff is usually protected by tenure rights and may be represented by a professional association.

■ **College students' rights**   There is no right to higher education in this country. States are not required to provide institutions of higher education, nor do parents have to pay for their children's college education even in those states that require them to support their dependent children up to the age of 21.

Admissions   Only students who meet certain conditions can enter college. Schools have the right to demand a record of good grades, attendance, physical fitness, high moral standards, and residence within the state. Public schools cannot arbitrarily refuse to accept a student who meets these conditions, but private schools can. A school does not have to explain its decision in individual cases. A student who is denied admission probably cannot get a court to order the school to admit him unless the rejection is illegal. It is illegal, for example, to deny admission to a public college on the basis of race. See CIVIL RIGHTS.

Due process   Once admitted, students do not leave their constitutional rights at the campus gate. They may be disciplined or dismissed for violating the rules, such as failing to attend classes, cheating on examinations, or parking illegally. But they are entitled to some DUE PROCESS OF LAW when the charges are serious. They must be told what charges have been made against them and given an opportunity to explain. They can present evidence and witnesses and appeal a dismissal decision in a court. Students cannot be expelled for printing unpopular opinions in a campus newspaper or gathering peacefully to protest cafeteria food. The courts have not entirely struck down dress codes, but beards, long hair, and casual clothes are generally acceptable if they do not disrupt the educational process.

Students cannot be expelled automatically for being arrested, but a conviction based on the arrest might justify dismissal. In the case of large-scale disobedience, such as a sit-in or demonstration, a court may issue an injunction that applies to everyone who is described in the order and receives NOTICE of it. Anyone who remains in the area after the order to disperse is guilty of CONTEMPT of court. The school may choose to punish these students on its own, but it must give them due process.

Campus police   Some universities have expanded into full-fledged towns. Most of them have campus security officers with the powers of a local police force. They may control traffic, give tickets, and investigate minor crimes. In some cases, they are authorized to carry guns.

In loco parentis   Most colleges no longer act *in loco parentis,* "in the place of a parent." Far fewer rules regulate the student's private conduct—he must now be responsible for himself.

Campus activities   The constitutional right of free expression guarantees that students can form organizations for any lawful purpose. But colleges have the right to regulate extracurricular activities so that they do not interfere with classes and to set standards to decide which groups may be formally recognized. An activity fee may be collected from each student and distributed to student organizations as the college sees fit.

Right to privacy   A student is entitled to a certain amount of privacy. Not even a private school can claim the right to search his room without a search warrant or his permission. The student also has the right to inspect his school records and to prevent the release of this information without his permission. See PRIVACY, RIGHT OF.

Nonstudents   Outsiders have some rights in a college because of the school's public purpose. The grounds of a campus have been compared to a neighborhood park. As in the case of a park, nonstudents are not trespassers if they are behaving lawfully. Outsiders also have the right to speak to peacefully assembled students.

A nonstudent does not, however, have a right to live in student housing on campus.

EXAMPLE   In a recent case, a man started a legal action to force a university to call him a student. He had moved into a student apartment on campus when he entered graduate school 17 years earlier, took only an occasional course, and never completed requirements for a degree. When the university tried to evict him, he claimed he was a student and could not be forced to leave. The court ordered him out to make room for someone who was serious about earning a degree. It held that the school has the right to decide who is a student.

■ **Tuition**   Tuition rates, the amount charged for attending courses at a college, vary tremendously among the different schools. Public universities funded primarily by state tax money generally charge much higher fees for out-of-state students than for residents.

Scholarships   Scholarships are grants to help some students pay their tuition, and sometimes their other expenses, such as room and board and textbooks. Courts have viewed scholarships as contracts between the student and the donor. If the student relies on the contract, as when he enrolls in school and becomes indebted for tuition, then he can enforce payment of the scholarship money in court. The person giving the scholarship also has the right to enforce conditions that were part of it. For example, a basketball player who accepts an athletic scholarship is obligated to attend practice sessions and play in games.

Student loans   Another way to finance a college education is through student loans. The student is given a favorable rate of interest and can delay repayment until he is able to earn money with his new education. The bad faith of some students who never intended to repay their loans and the bad luck of others who were unable to find jobs after graduation have cast a shadow on student loan programs. One state's highest court has held that payments due on student loans cannot be discharged in bankruptcy.

collision   In the strict nautical sense, collision means the striking together of two moving ships including pleasure craft. But the term generally includes the hitting, running afoul, or any violent contact of one vessel by another. Collision as it relates to motor vehicle insurance is discussed under INSURANCE.

■ **Negligence**   Liability for injury or damage from a collision is based on the fault of the party through negligence or misconduct. Once a mariner realizes there is a danger of a collision, he must use all his care and skill. For instance, when a mariner sees that his ship is on a collision course with another, he must give a danger signal—several rapid blasts of the ship's whistle.

Fault need not be intentionally wrongful. It may consist of an error in judgment in navigation. The question to be answered in establishing fault is whether there was a lack of good seamanship or of prudent navigation. Negligence may be a lack of diligence in correcting a defect in the ship that led to the collision.

Both ships may be at fault for a collision between them. The initial fault of one vessel, however, does not exempt the other from taking precautions to avoid a collision. It is a well-settled rule of maritime law that if one properly navigated vessel becomes aware of a dangerous condition on a mismanaged vessel, it must use all available means to prevent the collision.

■ **Rules of navigation**   The Inland Rules and the International Regulations, which are enactments of Congress, are the "rules of the road" for ships. They are designed to prevent collisions and are binding on privately owned U.S. vessels, whether navigated for profit or pleasure, and on publicly owned American vessels in times of peace. The Inland Rules govern the navigation of all harbors, rivers, and inland waters of the United States except the Great Lakes and their tributaries and connecting waters as far east as Montreal, the Red River of the North, and rivers emptying into the Gulf of Mexico, which are covered by their own rules. Foreign vessels as well as all ships on the high seas are bound by the International Regulations. For an extended discussion of the rules and regulations of navigation, consult the publications of the U.S. Coast Guard Auxiliary on the Inland Rules and International Regulations. See also ADMIRALTY.

One vessel has the right to assume that another will comply with the rules, unless it has some special knowledge to the contrary. If circumstances indicate that compliance with the rules of navigation will lead to a collision, the navigator must break the rules to avoid the disaster. When a navigator suddenly realizes that a collision is about to happen through no fault of his own and he does something that further contributes to the collision, his act is excusable because of the emergency situation.

■ **Liability**   A vessel whose negligence caused a collision may be liable for all resulting damage. The owner is personally liable for injuries if his ship's master (captain) and crew are negligent in navigation. When a vessel is chartered, the liability for a collision depends on whether or not the ship's master and crew are the employees of the owner or the charterer. If the crew is under the control of the owner, he will be liable for collision. If the crew is directly employed by the charterer, he is liable. If the master is in actual command at the time of collision, he shares responsibility for resulting damage.

The liability of seamen for loss of or injury to cargo in collision is limited to cases of willful misconduct. If the crew gets drunk, ties up the master, and takes over the ship and the ship then collides with another, the crew is liable for loss of cargo. Neither the vessel nor the owner is exempt from responsibility for the act of a pilot voluntarily hired by the owner to bring a vessel into port. But when a collision is caused by a pilot whom the owner was required to hire by law, the owner is not liable.

■ **Inevitable accident**   A collision is regarded as an inevitable accident when it is not caused by the negligence of either vessel. Neither party is liable, and each bears his own loss. Freedom from fault is generally determined by the precautions taken. There are three major types of inevitable accidents: (1) sea peril (such as dense fog) causing the collision, (2) a sudden gale making the vessel unmanageable, and (3) maneuvers of a third vessel that force one ship to collide with another. Inevitable accidents can also be brought on by hidden defects in a vessel. A collision in dense fog is considered inevitable, however, only when the rules of navigation and good seamanship were followed—ships going at an excessive speed on a dark, foggy night cannot claim the inevitability of a collision.

collusion   A secret agreement between two or more persons to cheat another, to commit fraud, or to obtain an object forbidden by law.

A classic case of collusion to defraud occurs when two persons agree that one should sue the other because the second person is covered by insurance. They then split the proceeds of any court award from the insurance company. Another example is when the low bidder on a construction contract withdraws from the bidding in return for the promise of a subcontract from the second-lowest bidder.

In DIVORCE proceedings, collusion is any agreement between husband and wife that one of them will commit acts that would justify a divorce. It is also used to mean conspiracy in starting or prosecuting the divorce suit, such as when the parties agree to help each other in carrying the action through to a final decree. Collusion in divorce actions would bar the divorce and parties could be held in contempt. With the enactment of no-fault divorce statutes by most states, agreements or acts of collusion are no longer necessary.

color   Appearance or semblance; a disguise or pretext. *Color of authority* or *color of office* is a presumption by public officers to justify actions for which they have no authority. For example, if a policeman in uniform stops a person on the street and searches him without probable cause, he is acting under the color of his authority. See SEARCH AND SEIZURE.

Acting under *color of law* is taking an action that looks lawful but is not. When civil rights demonstrations were planned in the South, the leaders of the demonstrations were often arrested by the local police on suspicion of violation of the law and jailed until the time for the planned action had passed. In fact, the leaders had not violated any law. The local police acted under color of law by arresting them on groundless suspicion to make the demonstration less effective.

color of title
1 An appearance of title to (ownership of) property based on a written document, such as a deed or a court decree, that in reality is not title. **2** A document that professes to pass title but does not, either because the grantor does not own the property or because the document transferring title is defective. A deed not signed by the grantor would be an example of a defective document. See CONVEYANCE.

comaker
A second (or third or more) person who signs a type of COMMERCIAL PAPER, such as a promissory note, and thus promises to pay it in full if the borrower defaults. It is common in a loan for a lender to require that a borrower find a comaker to sign the agreement.

combination
1 An alliance of persons working together for a common purpose. Under the Sherman Anti-Trust Act, an illegal combination in restraint of trade occurs when there is an agreement that the participants will abandon their freedom to trade at will—or help one another take away trade freedom from others—by the use of such devices as price-fixing agreements and boycotts. For example, when a group of mattress manufacturers refuses to supply their bedding to discount department stores that sell the product at less than the list price, this is an illegal combination in restraint of trade. **2** In PATENT law, a combination is the putting together of several inventions. Each of these might be already patented, but all of them working together produce a new result. This new combination might be granted a patent.

comity
1 Courtesy and respect. **2** A willingness to do something official, not as a matter of right, but out of goodwill and tradition.

Comity of nations is a body of rules that nations observe toward one another from courtesy or mutual convenience, although the rules do not form part of international law.

Judicial comity is the principle by which courts of one jurisdiction will observe the laws and judicial decisions of another. They do this not as a matter of obligation but out of deference and respect. State and federal courts depend on comity to keep many of their results in line with one another. Comity is not a rule of law; it is a rule of practice, convenience, and expediency. It is not just courtesy, which would be simply deferring to the opinions of others. It has a real value in securing uniformity of decisions and in discouraging repeated litigation of the same question.

Comity of states is the practice by which the courts of one state follow the decision of another on a like question, although not bound to do so.

commerce
1 The exchange of goods, production, or property of any kind. **2** Intercourse by way of trade and traffic between different peoples or states. This includes the purchase, sale, and exchange of commodities, the agencies by which the exchange is promoted, the means by which it is carried on, and the transportation of persons as well as goods. **3** The exchange of merchandise on a large scale between different places. Although commerce and trade are often used interchangeably, commerce is usually restricted to large-scale activity while trade describes traffic within a state or community.

commerce clause
The part of the U.S. Constitution that gives Congress the power to regulate interstate and foreign commerce. The U.S. Constitution under Article I, Section 8, Clause 3, gives Congress the power "To regulate Commerce with foreign Nations, and among the several States, and with the Indian Tribes." Commerce among the states is business in all forms between citizens of different states. It may include communication by telegraph, telephone, or radio, or the movement of persons from one state to another for any reason, including pleasure. Commerce with foreign nations is business between U.S. citizens and subjects of foreign governments that occurs outside this country. Intrastate, or "domestic" commerce, does not move across state lines. It is exclusively controlled by the state.

■ **Power to regulate** The purpose of this congressional power is to safeguard the free flow of interstate commerce and to protect it from local restraint. Congress may constitutionally provide the point at which subjects of interstate commerce shall fall under state regulation. Although no state is deprived of its constitutionally guaranteed right to regulate its local domestic and internal commerce, this right must not interfere with interstate commerce. But even though a state may not govern foreign and interstate commerce, it may indirectly affect it by a bona fide exercise of its POLICE POWER. For instance, it may enforce its own controls on food, such as fish, coming in from another state. A state cannot control commerce with Indian tribes.

The nature of the subject determines whether Congress has the exclusive power to regulate. If the subject to be regulated is national in character, the power of Congress is exclusive. Courts determine the character of the subject by balancing the national interest against that of the state.

EXAMPLE The U.S. Supreme Court declared invalid an Arizona statute that prohibited railroads within the state from having more than 70 cars in a freight train or 14 cars in a passenger train. This law was designed as a safety measure to prevent accidents by reducing the length of trains passing through the state. Its real effect was to place an unreasonable burden on interstate commerce by requiring railroads at each border of the state to break up 100-car freight trains into two trains and to put on additional crews, at great expense to the railway companies. The desired safety effect was not achieved. In fact, the increase in the number of trains and train operations actually increased the possibility of accidents. The Court held that the operation of a uniform, efficient railway system was more important than a state safety law of dubious effect.

If there is a compelling interest to protect, however, state regulations may be valid. For example, a state may prescribe the weight load of motor vehicles using its highways. Highways can withstand only so much stress from the weight of the motor vehicles that constantly pass over them. To compensate for additional wear and tear on the road, a state may impose a gross-weight registration tax.

This tax is computed on the gross weight at which the truck has been operated in excess of the maximum weight allowed on the highway.

In those fields of commerce where national uniformity is not essential, either the state or federal government may act. For instance, a state may pass statutes governing the local moving business. If Congress passes legislation concerning the local intrastate moving business, clearly demonstrating its intent to regulate the entire field, the state cannot pass subsequent laws—even if there is no conflict between the state and federal law. This is known as federal PREEMPTION of the field.

■ **Acts of commerce**   The courts look to practical considerations and the established course of business to decide whether an act constitutes interstate commerce. Although activities may be intrastate in character, if they have a substantial effect on interstate commerce, Congress has the authority to control them.

EXAMPLE In an interesting case, a federal court decided that O—* the movement of air pollution across state lines from Maryland to Delaware was interstate commerce. Under the Federal Clean Air Act, the plaintiff, the United States, sought a court order to prevent the continued operation of a fat-rendering plant until it installed devices to eliminate its noxious odors. The defendants, the plant owners, contended that the plant operation was a purely intrastate activity, which Congress had no power to regulate. The court decided that foul-smelling air pollution that adversely affects business conditions and property values also impedes industrial development and would clearly interfere with interstate commerce. Therefore, it was subject to congressional regulation.

In another case, the U.S. Supreme Court upheld the right of Congress, in the Consumer Credit Protection Act, to forbid "extortionate extensions of credit" in strictly local activities. The justification was that nationally organized crime draws much of its revenue from loan-sharking—unlawful threats or use of violence to collect a debt advanced at an illegally high rate of interest. Racketeering, though illegal, is still a business in interstate commerce.

The operation of a hotel or motel, when its activities have an effect on interstate commerce, is subject to congressional supervision under the commerce clause. Racial discrimination by a hotel or motel affects interstate commerce by impeding interstate travel and is prohibited by the Civil Rights Act of 1964.

EXAMPLE The constitutionality or validity of the act was O—* challenged in a case that involved a local motel's refusal to accept black guests. The motel owner contended that Congress had no power over his motel since its operation was purely local. The Supreme Court held that the power of Congress to promote interstate commerce also includes the authority to regulate local activities, in the states of both origin and destination, that might have a harmful effect on that commerce. Congress may prohibit racial discrimination by motels serving travelers since it would obstruct interstate travel by blacks.

Private contracts   The regulatory power of Congress extends to private contracts that relate to interstate or foreign commerce. Although labor contracts are not commercial transactions, congressional authority extends to

acts growing out of labor disputes that block interstate or foreign business.

EXAMPLE One of the nation's largest producers of steel O—* discharged some employees and was charged with unfair labor practices under the National Labor Relations Act of 1935. It was alleged that the company was trying, by intimidation and coercion, to prevent its employees from freely organizing unions. The company charged that the act was unconstitutional because labor relations and the hiring and firing of employees were strictly local problems. The Supreme Court decided that the act was constitutional. The company's nationwide transportation system was interstate commerce and any disruption of peaceful relations between management and labor was bound to affect it.

Insurance   Insurance business conducted across state lines is within the jurisdiction of Congress, if the activities affect interstate commerce.

EXAMPLE Insurance employees in the main office in Hart- O—* ford, Connecticut, solicit sales, process applications, and prepare or type policies for out-of-state offices. The main office also receives policy forms and other materials and communications from out-of-state offices. These activities are interstate commerce, which means that Congress can regulate the insurance business under its commerce clause power. The insurance employees are subject to federal law on minimum wages. On the other hand, an insurance contract between an insurance company located in one state and the insured in another state is not interstate commerce, because under the law a contract itself is neither an article of commerce nor a commercial transaction.

Transportation   Transportation across state lines is within the constitutional control of the federal government. The transportation may be of persons or property, by land, water, or air. But, no matter what its purpose, it must be conducted for others as an independent business, not as a private or personal act. The act of sending an article from one state to another is interstate commerce. So is the means through which transportation is furnished. Intrastate commerce becomes interstate as soon as a state boundary is crossed, and federal law holds sway over state law. Interstate commerce cannot be established by trickery, however.

EXAMPLE A company that did not have authority from the O—* Maryland Public Service Commission to handle intrastate shipments sent its trucks across the nearby Delaware state line and back to qualify as an interstate shipper. The court decided that the trucking company could not avoid the Maryland law merely by routing small shipments through Delaware.

Commerce begins with the actual movement of the product or person and ends with arrival at its destination. Every link of a continuous passage from one state to another is a transaction of interstate commerce. A temporary break does not necessarily rob a shipment of its interstate character.

Goods shipped between states are in interstate commerce as long as they remain in the original package. This is known as the *original package doctrine.* An original package is the same one in which the goods were delivered by the consignor (shipper of the goods) to the CARRIER. Articles become subject to state regulation when they are taken from their original package. Goods are no longer in the original package when they are sold or offered for retail sale. Opening a package for the sole purpose of inspection does not destroy its original character.

EXAMPLE A shipment of stereos from California, which is stored in Ohio until it can be sent on to be sold in Pennsylvania, is not subject to any Ohio regulations as long as the stereos remain in their original cartons and are not used or offered for sale there. Once they arrive in Pennsylvania and are put on the market, they are no longer in interstate commerce. They become subject to legislation enacted by Pennsylvania even though they may still be in their original packages. For example, they may become subject to a state sales tax when sold by a department store to customers.

Fishing The state may regulate coastal fisheries and fishing within its territorial waters if there is no conflicting federal law. If, however, the catch from a commercial fishing fleet is shipped to another state, it is subject to the commerce clause. State power to regulate fishing is subordinate to congressional authority. See FISH.

Navigation The states cannot enact laws that will hinder navigation. The business of ferrying across a navigable stream between two states is interstate commerce. Navigation on the high seas is subject to the supervision of Congress. See ADMIRALTY.

Highways Congress can legislate business on interstate highways. A state may not discriminate against interstate commerce on highways, but it may construct highways and set rules for their use. Nondiscriminatory state regulations that restrict the size and weight of motor vehicles, require their registration and the licensing of their drivers, or impose other requirements to promote public safety are lawful under the commerce clause.

Communications The interstate transmission of information by telephone, telegraph, radio, television, or mail is regulated by Congress. But local authorities govern the sending of messages within a state.

Businesses affecting commerce Not every private enterprise that involves interstate shipments comes under the control of Congress. For example, the construction of a factory is not interstate commerce, even though the building is for the manufacture of goods for sale in many states. This is true even though the construction material will cross state lines as it is transported to the site.

Various businesses, however, such as advertising, hotels and restaurants, and the entertainment and sports industries, may be subject to federal regulation. Even a business that operates strictly intrastate activities, such as local sporting events or theatrical exhibits, may make such wide use of regional channels that the business assumes an interstate character.

EXAMPLE The business of producing, booking, and presenting legitimate stage attractions on a multistate basis is interstate commerce, although the actual performance of a legitimate stage attraction is a local affair. Readying a musical comedy for a New York production through road tryouts from New Haven to Boston to Philadelphia involves interstate commerce, although the New York performance does not.

Production or manufacture of commodities is not commerce; therefore, it is not subject to the commerce clause even when the commodities are sold outside the state. Coal mining is not interstate commerce even though practically all the coal is shipped out of the state or consumed by a railroad company doing business between states. Some manufacture or production may, however, be regulated.

EXAMPLE The Agricultural Adjustment Act of 1938 expressly authorizes the measurement of wheat acreage on farmlands. Although the wheat is grown for home consumption, and the farmer never intends to sell it, the fact that all wheat farmers must measure their acreage brings wheat into interstate commerce. From the information gained, the government can regulate wheat production nationwide and prevent either shortages or surpluses.

Other operations subject to federal regulation are the canning and packing industry, the production of dairy products, the manufacture of clothing, lumber mills, and the operations of steel and mining companies.

Instrumentalities of commerce The instrumentalities of commerce are the means by which business is conducted. They include private and common carriers, bridges over navigable waters and the waters themselves, railroads, tracks, terminals, switches, cars, engines, vessels, wharves, automobiles, roads, canals, the U.S. mails, pipelines, aircraft, stockyards, warehouses, grain elevators and other storage facilities, and offices of businesses engaged in commerce. All are regulated by Congress if they participate in business between states.

■ **Means of regulation** Congressional sway over commerce also encompasses the means to promote and protect it by enacting statutes that have the force of police regulations. But federal rules must have some real connection with the business being regulated. Congress may pass inspection laws, for example, that pertain to foreign or interstate commerce. But in the absence of federal legislation, states may enact nondiscriminatory inspection laws that only incidentally affect foreign or interstate commerce. Federal quarantine and sanitary laws are valid if limited to foreign and interstate commerce. State health, sanitary, and quarantine laws are also legal if they do not conflict with federal regulations.

Congress may enact prohibitory legislation to prevent interstate commerce from spreading harm. For example, actions either by Congress or the states concerning food that is mislabeled, adulterated, or unfit for human consumption may be legal.

A state cannot go beyond what is necessary for self-protection when it interferes with transportation through its territory. A state regulation enacted solely to curtail interstate commerce cannot be upheld as a health measure, for example. A state could not ban lower-priced milk from an out-of-state source by claiming it wanted to insure a wholesome supply of the product when its real purpose was to keep the other state's lower-priced milk from competing with its own dairies' products.

There is no requirement that the regulation of interstate commerce be uniform throughout the United States. Congress may devise a national policy with due regard for the interests of different regions. The Sugar Act of 1948, for example, defines five domestic sugar-producing areas and allots annual marketing quotas to each and partial exemption to some.

A state may not ban a foreign corporation from entering its territory to engage in interstate commerce. Nor may it restrict interstate business. A state may, however, regulate a corporation engaging solely in intrastate business.

■ **Taxation**   The power to tax interstate and foreign commerce is vested in Congress, and the states may not interfere with it by exercising their taxing powers. Congress may prohibit the imposition of a state tax if it finds that it adversely affects the free flow of business.

Property tax   A state may tax the property of persons engaged in interstate commerce when there is a taxable SITUS (location) within the state. For example, the property of a railroad company within a state, such as a depot, is subject to a property tax. Goods in transit are not taxable by the state of origin, the state of destination, or intermediate states. This rule is not changed by the fact that the owner of the property is a citizen of any of these states. A state cannot tax goods transported into the state until they lose their character as imports by being used or offered for sale. Nor can a state levy a tax on exports to foreign countries or to other states.

License and privilege tax   For the privilege of engaging in interstate commerce, the state may require a LICENSE, provided it does not impose a burden on interstate commerce. A trucking company based in your state must have licenses for its trucks there even though they are used in interstate commerce.

Property formerly in interstate commerce is liable to state taxes, and provisions of state cigarette-tax acts are generally held to be legal. A state may not tax the gross receipts and earnings derived from interstate or foreign commerce, but it may tax receipts from intrastate business or use the gross receipts as the basis for computing a tax.

Radio and television stations broadcasting within a state may have to pay local taxes. The sale of gasoline or other motor fuels shipped from another state are taxable by the state. This duty may be placed on dealers or distributors, such as gas-station owners. A state may tax interstate trucking companies to help pay for the construction, maintenance, and regulation of its highways.

In 1978 the U.S. Supreme Court decided that a state may levy a business tax on the loading and unloading of cargo from ships occupied in interstate and foreign transactions without infringing on the right of Congress.

EXAMPLE   In 1974 the state of Washington levied a tax of 1 0◄—✳ percent on the cargo-loading business. The right of the state to levy the tax was challenged, and ultimately went to the Supreme Court. The Court reasoned that a state tax is unconstitutional "only when it unfairly burdens commerce by exacting more than a just share from the interstate activity," which this tax did not. This decision was a significant development toward allowing states to tax goods and services involved in interstate commerce.

■ **Offenses against commerce**   Congress may declare punishable a number of offenses under its authority to regulate interstate and foreign commerce. The federal statute known as the Mann Act, or the White Slave Act, makes it a criminal offense to transport across state or national boundaries any woman for prostitution or other immoral purposes. This is a constitutional exercise of the power of Congress to regulate commerce.

Under federal statutes it is an offense to use a common carrier for the interstate transportation of obscene materials in order to sell or distribute them. Congress may also prohibit the importation of obscene matter. Racketeering involving robbery and personal violence that affects interstate commerce is within federal legislative control under the Anti-Racketeering Act. Under the provisions of the National Stolen Property Act, anyone who transports over state lines or foreign boundaries stolen goods worth $5,000 or more is guilty of a criminal offense.

■ **Interstate Commerce Commission**   The Interstate Commerce Commission was created by Congress in 1887 to promote commerce by assuring just dealing between CARRIERS and the public. It does so by adopting rules and regulations to carry out the policies of the Interstate Commerce Act. The commission has jurisdiction over carriers and transportation, such as railroad lines, sleeping-car companies, and express companies (which transport parcels or personal property for speedy delivery of small but valuable packages of goods and money). Transportation by motor carrier is vested in the commission by the Motor Carrier Act—part of the Interstate Commerce Act. The Interstate Commerce Act also regulates and licenses motor-transportation brokers in order to protect carriers and the public from dishonest and financially unstable middlemen.

The duties of the commission with respect to rates, fares, and charges are prescribed by the act. Proceedings before the commission are usually instituted by a complaint by the person affected or on the motion of the commission.

commercial paper   Written documents that represent the promise or obligation of one person to pay money to another. They are used in everyday business transactions. Checks, drafts, promissory notes, and certificates of deposit are types of commercial paper. Commercial paper is a sure and convenient method of handling usually large amounts of money that lessens the risk of theft accompanying the use of cash. This is achieved as a result of the most important feature of commercial paper—its negotiability. A writing is *negotiable* if it meets certain requirements discussed below that enable it to be freely transferred from one person to another by means of *endorsement* (a writing that authorizes its transfer) or by *delivery* (giving the document to someone else). A negotiable instrument is another name for commercial paper.

Commercial paper is personal property, and so it may be transferred by sale or gift, loaned, lost, stolen, and taxed. But it is a special form of personal property and as such is subject to laws that do not apply to other forms of property. The law of commercial paper contained in the UNIFORM COMMERCIAL CODE has been adopted by all 50 states, the District of Columbia, and the Virgin Islands.

■ **Four kinds of paper**   The Uniform Commercial Code lists four types of commercial paper: promissory notes, drafts, checks, and certificates of deposit.

Promissory notes   The simplest form of commercial paper is the promissory note, a written promise to pay money. It is a two-party instrument (paper). The party who makes the promise to pay is called the *maker,* and the party to whom the promise is made is the *payee.* The payee may be a particular person or simply the bearer of the note. When an instrument is payable to "bearer," its contents may be given to anyone who presents it for payment.

A note may be payable on demand or at a specified time. When the note is *payable on demand,* the holder (the payee) may redeem it any time. When the instrument is a *time note* (when a date for payment is indicated on the face of the note), it is good only after the date indicated, and the holder must wait until then to collect.

The promissory note is generally used to borrow money. Credit or loan agreements are not promissory notes, however. The agreements describe the terms of the transactions but the actual notes are separate pieces of paper.

EXAMPLE An inventor who holds a patent on an item wants to manufacture and sell it. He needs cash to start his business. He goes to the loan department of First Bank, which agrees to lend him $100,000. As evidence of the loan, First Bank requires the inventor-businessman to make a promissory note payable in one year's time with interest. First Bank then deposits the borrowed sum,

---

COMMERCIAL PAPER: NEGOTIABLE DOCUMENTS OF PAYMENT

■ Commercial paper is a document that represents the obligation of one person to pay money to another. The most important thing about commercial paper is that it is negotiable. A document is negotiable if it can be transferred freely from one person to another by endorsing it or by simply giving it to someone else. Under the law, there are four types of commercial paper: promissory notes, drafts, checks, and certificates of deposit.

■ A *promissory note* is a promise written by one person to pay money to another. Promissory notes are often used to borrow money. If you get a loan from a bank, the bank may ask you to sign a promissory note for the amount borrowed plus interest. The bank may keep the note until you have paid off the loan, or it may sell the note to another bank and the bank that buys it can collect from you the money you owe on the loan.

■ A negotiable bond, such as a U.S. Savings Bond, is a promissory note.

■ A *draft* is a written order by one party to another, such as a bank, to pay a third party. A cashier's check is a draft. Businessmen often use drafts to pay for goods that must be shipped over a long distance.

■ A *check* is a special type of draft drawn on a bank and payable on demand.

■ A *certificate of deposit* (CD) is an acknowledgment written by a bank that you have a certain amount of money deposited in the bank and a promise by the bank to repay you the money with interest. CD's generally come in specified denominations and are usually for large amounts, such as $10,000 or more. They bear interest at a higher rate than ordinary savings

accounts, but they must be left on deposit for a definite period of time. If necessary, you can quickly convert a CD into cash before the end of that period, but if you do, you will forfeit some of the interest.

■ Commercial paper must be payable in money. A paper that is payable in anything else, such as land, beaver pelts, or gold dust, is not negotiable and is therefore not commercial paper.

■ Commercial paper can be antedated, postdated, or undated and still be negotiable.

■ *Endorsement* is the act of signing the back of a paper in order to transfer its rights to someone else—for example, when you sign the back of your paycheck to cash it.

■ A special endorsement is one that names the person to be paid—for example, if you wrote "pay John Smith" above your signature. A paper with a special endorsement can be cashed or further transferred only by the person named in the special endorsement.

■ A blank endorsement is one that is not made to anyone in particular; it is merely your signature. A check with a blank endorsement can be cashed by anyone who has it.

■ A qualified endorsement is one that disclaims liability for paying the check. If you endorse a check you get from someone else with the words "without recourse" above your name, the person you give it to cannot make you pay it if it later bounces, nor can anyone else make you pay it.

■ A restrictive endorsement is a conditional endorsement that tries to prohibit further transfer of the paper. If you endorse a check "for deposit only," you have used a restrictive endorsement.

■ Any person who signs or endorses a commercial paper is liable to you for payment unless he specifically waived that liability in his endorsement. If you present a paper for payment when it is due and you are refused payment, you may sue anyone who signed or endorsed the paper. You need not sue the first or last person who endorsed it; you can sue any of the endorsers. You should sue the person from whom you will be most likely to recover.

■ A minor or a person who is not mentally competent under the law cannot be held liable for a paper he has signed or endorsed. If you are tricked into signing a commercial paper, you are not liable to pay it. On the other hand, if you give a check to a roofer for repairing your roof, but when it rains the next day the roof leaks and you stop payment on the check, you may still be liable to pay the check.

■ When any major change has been made to a commercial paper, you will probably not be liable to pay it in its changed form. If you wrote a check for $9 and someone changed the amount to $90, you would be liable for only the $9 unless you had written the check so carelessly that it was easy to change the amount.

■ If a bank cashes an altered check, it will not be liable to you if the forgery was imperceptible, but if the check is an obvious forgery and the bank cashed it anyway, the bank would have to pay you back the money you lost.

■ If a bank pays someone from your account on a check that contains your forged signature, the bank is responsible, because a bank should know the signatures of its customers.

$90,000–$100,000 minus $10,000, the amount of the one year's interest—in the inventor's account. First Bank could then hold the note until it became due. It could also endorse the note and discount it (sell it for less then its face value) at another bank, Second Bank.

Second Bank becomes the *holder* of the note. If First Bank, after paying the inventor $90,000 on the note, immediately sells the note to Second Bank for $95,000, First Bank makes an immediate profit of $5,000 without having to wait a full year. Once First Bank has endorsed the note, however, it becomes secondarily liable. This means that if the inventor-businessman (who is primarily liable) fails to repay the $100,000 to Second Bank at the end of the one-year period, First Bank must pay the full amount—$100,000—to Second Bank.

When used for buying an item on credit, such as an automobile, a promissory note is evidence of the debt. Just as in the example above, the note may be endorsed and negotiated (sold) at a discount. Each party who endorses the note becomes secondarily liable for the total amount. Many consumer-credit transactions are financed by means of promissory notes. See CONSUMER PROTECTION.

A note is also used as evidence of a preexisting debt. A retail store owner who is unable to pay his supplier for merchandise within the customary 30-day period might ask for an extension of credit. To protect himself, the supplier will ask the store owner to make a promissory note. The supplier might then negotiate the note to pay his own debts.

Negotiable bonds, such as U.S. Savings Bonds and corporation bonds, are forms of promissory notes that are sold at a discount—that is, they are sold for less than their face value but cashable at a specified later date for the full amount. The difference between the price paid and the price received when the bond is cashed constitutes the interest earned by the holder of the bond. Bonds generally come in standard denominations—such as $100, $500, and $1,000—and have maturity dates of 10 years or more in the future. In some cases, bonds that are not cashed when they are due accumulate interest after the due date and are, consequently, worth more than their face value when they are cashed at a later date.

Drafts A draft (sometimes called a bill of exchange) is a three-party instrument that orders the payment of money. The party who issues the order is called the *drawer,* and the one to whom the order is given is the *drawee.* Just as with a promissory note, the party to whom the draft is payable is the *payee.* Again like a promissory note, the draft may be payable to a particular payee or the bearer, and on demand or at a given date. A cashier's check is a form of draft.

The draft is frequently used by businessmen as a means of obtaining payment for goods that must be shipped over long distances. The buyer may wish to inspect the goods before paying for them, or he may not have the necessary cash on hand at the time of the sale. The seller, not sure that the buyer's credit is good, wants payment as soon as possible. This is how he goes about getting his money:

When the seller ships the goods, he receives a bill of lading from his CARRIER, such as a trucking company. The *bill of lading* is both a contract to carry the goods and a certificate of title to (ownership of) the goods themselves. The title is usually in the seller's name. At the time the goods are shipped, the seller may draw a draft against the buyer. The buyer is the drawee, who must pay the draft. The seller's bank is made the payee. The seller endorses the bill of lading over to his bank and attaches the bill to the draft. He may either sell these documents to his bank at a discount or use them as collateral for a loan. The seller's bank endorses the documents and sends them to a correspondent bank in the buyer's area. The correspondent bank brings the draft to the buyer for payment. When the buyer pays the draft, the correspondent bank endorses the bill of lading over to the buyer. The endorsed bill of lading transfers title to (ownership of) the goods to the buyer, who can then collect the goods from the carrier.

Checks A check is a special type of draft. It is a draft drawn on a bank, payable on demand. Like a promissory note and a draft, the check may be payable to a particular person or to the bearer. Checks payable to the bearer may be written to "cash."

When you open a checking account, you enter into a contract with your bank. You agree to deposit your money with the bank, and the bank agrees that it is indebted to you for the sum on deposit in your checking account. The bank also pledges to honor the checks you write for payment against your account. See BANKS AND BANKING.

Certificates of deposit A certificate of deposit—often referred to as a CD—is a written acknowledgment by a bank of the receipt of a sum of money and a promise to repay the sum. Since the certificate is issued by the bank, the bank is the maker. The bank is also the drawee. The person who makes the deposit is usually the payee.

Certificates of deposit generally come in certain denominations and are generally only for large amounts of money, such as $10,000 or more. They are used primarily as savings devices by corporations and individuals. They usually bear interest at a higher rate than an ordinary savings account, but they must be left on deposit for a definite period of time. Generally, they may be converted into cash before the time elapses, but in most instances at the loss of some interest.

■ **Negotiability** In order for commercial paper to be negotiable, the instrument must (1) be in writing, (2) signed by the person who promises to pay the document (the maker or the drawer), (3) contain an unconditional promise (such as a promissory note) or order (a check or draft) to pay a sum certain (a specific amount) of money, (4) be payable on demand or at a definite time, and (5) be payable to order or to bearer.

Writing The writing requirement is satisfied in any number of ways. The instrument may be printed, typed, engraved, or written in longhand in ink, pencil, or both. Usually the various types of commercial paper are available on printed forms from banks and stationery stores.

Properly signed The SIGNATURE may be made in many different ways, including a simple mark—such as an X—made by a person who is unable to write his name. Initials, a symbol, a business or trade name, or an assumed name are also permitted. The signature may be handwritten, printed, typed, or stamped by machine. Even a thumbprint is legal.

Unconditional promise The promise or order to pay must be unconditional. A negotiable instrument usually passes through the hands of many persons. If it is to be used as a substitute for money and as a means of obtaining credit, the person who takes the instrument must be certain that it will be paid.

Additional facts When the instrument contains an unconditional promise or order, it may also mention additional facts that do not destroy its negotiability. For example, the instrument may note the business transaction that brought about its creation. It may state that it arises out of a separate agreement or that it is secured by a mortgage. The paper may indicate a particular account or fund from which payment is *expected* (but not required) to be made. This is usually done for accounting purposes and does not make a promise or order to pay conditional. Payment may also be limited to the entire assets of a partnership, an unincorporated association, or a trust by which the instrument is issued.

On the other hand, when an instrument states that it is *subject to* or *governed by* another agreement, the promise to pay *is* conditional. For example, language such as "subject to the terms of the contract between ABC Corporation (the maker) and XYZ Corporation (the payee)" would destroy negotiability and consequently the instrument would not be commercial paper. The holder would be forced to look beyond the paper's face to discover the terms of payment. Also, the instrument is *not* negotiable when it pays *only* out of a *particular* fund. An exception occurs when the paper is issued by a government or governmental unit.

Strength of terms In a promissory note, almost any language that sets out a definite promise, such as "I promise to pay," is sufficient. A simple IOU (short for "I owe you"), however, is not considered a definite promise. Thus an IOU cannot be a negotiable instrument.

The order to pay in a draft or check must not be merely a request. Language such as "I wish you would pay" is not strong enough. But expressions of courtesy such as "please pay" or "kindly pay" do not destroy the order. Examples of proper instructions for payment are "pay to the order of John Doe" or "pay to John Doe or his order."

A sum certain The *sum certain* requirement means that the holder must be able to know the exact value of the paper from its face. In some cases the computation of interest may be necessary—a promissory note, for example, bears interest at a certain rate per year. The interest provision does not, however, destroy the certainty of the sum. Similarly, the fact that the interest rate may differ before or after default or before or after a specific date does not change the sum's certainty. Moreover, the sum payable is a sum certain even when paid by installments or allowed to be discounted if made good before a fixed date or increased after the payment date. A provision for collection costs and attorneys' fees does not affect the certainty.

EXAMPLE Tim Hanley needed $5,000 to add an extension to O⊶✳ his home. He went to National Bank and asked for a loan. The loan officer told Tim that he had to execute a promissory note for $6,600 in order for him to receive $5,000 in cash from the bank. Part of the interest on the loan in the form of a discount, $1,600, had already been calculated in determining the face amount of the note. The note stated that Tim would pay off the note in 60 monthly installments of $110 a month. It also included

a provision that in case Tim defaulted on the loan, the bank would be entitled to counsel fees in the amount of 20 percent of what was due at the time the matter was referred to an attorney for collection. These provisions did not affect the certainty of the sum owed to National Bank as evidenced by the face value of the note.

The payment must be made in money. Money is a medium of exchange adopted by governments. A paper payable in something other than money, such as beaver pelts or gold dust, is not negotiable.

Payable on demand or at a definite time To be negotiable, an instrument must be payable on demand or at a definite time. Instruments payable on demand include those that are payable on presentation and those in which no time for payment is stated. Most checks fall into this category because they are payable on demand.

A note or draft is negotiable at a definite time when its face bears notice that the paper is payable on or before a stated date or for a fixed period after that date. *Payable on or before* means that it *must* be paid by the date specified but *may* be paid before that time. In like manner, an instrument that is payable at a fixed period *after sight* is also payable at a definite time. "After sight" means that when the holder presents the instrument to the maker, payment will be made after the length of time specified on the note. For example, if you are the payee of a note that is due one month after sight, the maker of that note must pay you within a month of the day you present it to him for payment. He need not pay you as soon as you present it to him, as a bank must pay a check, which is payable on demand.

A note may also provide that the time for payment be *accelerated* on the occurrence of a certain event or at the option of one of the parties.

EXAMPLE Say a man borrows $5,000 from a loan company. O⊶✳ In return he writes a numbered series of promissory notes. Each note, due on a specific day of the month, contains a provision that if payment is not made within 15 days after the due date, then all the later notes in the series must be paid right away. Acceleration clauses do not destroy an instrument's negotiability so long as the time for payment is definitely stated.

Extensions of the time for payment are also quite common. The extension may be at the option of the holder, the maker, or the acceptor or automatically upon the occurrence of a specified act.

EXAMPLE Suppose that the same loan company (as in the O⊶✳ example above) allowed the man to include in his promissory notes a provision that, in the case of illness, he would have an additional 15 days to pay his loan without the acceleration clause going into effect. This extension of time, in addition to the original 15-day grace periods in the notes, gives him 30 days after the due date to pay without having all his later notes come due automatically on the 16th day.

An instrument that is payable only upon an act of indeterminate timing is not negotiable, even though the event is certain, such as death. This rule eliminates papers that anticipate inheritances.

Whether an instrument is undated, antedated, or postdated, its negotiability is not hurt. A paper without a date becomes effective when delivered to the payee. An antedated instrument is given a date that is already past. For example, a check written on December 14, 1980, but dated December 4, 1980, is antedated. A postdated instrument is one that is given a future date. A check written on December 4, 1980, but dated December 14, 1980, is postdated. When an instrument is antedated or postdated, the date on which it is valid depends on the date on its face and on whether it is payable on demand or at a definite time. For example, a promissory note payable on demand is issued on December 10; the note is dated December 15, the day the note is due. A note issued on December 15, but dated December 10 and stated to be payable five days after date, would be due when issued. Even though a check is ordinarily payable on demand, a postdated check cannot be cashed before the date on its face.

EXAMPLE On March 15, Hilda was suddenly called out of town on an emergency, which would keep her away for at least a month. Hilda's rent was due on April 1, but she did not have enough money in her checking account to pay it at that time. Hilda arranged to have her employer deposit her pay into her checking account on March 30, and she gave her landlord a check dated April 1 to cover the rent. Even though the landlord had the check two weeks before the date on its face, he could not cash it before April 1, and if he tried to cash it early the bank would refuse to pay him.

Payable to the order or to bearer The *order* requirement is satisfied when the instrument is payable to the bearer or to a person named on the paper or to his order—to "John Doe or his order." It may be made out to two or more payees, together or in the alternative (any one of them)—for example, to "John and Mary Kelly" or to "John or Mary Kelly." If it is made out to two or more payees together (John and Mary) all the payees must endorse the instrument to cash it. If it is made out in the alternative (John or Mary) only one payee need endorse it. Or it may be payable to an estate, trust, corporate officer, partnership, or unincorporated association.

Drafts and checks are usually written on printed forms that are often payable both to order and to bearer. A blank space is left between "pay to the order of" and "or bearer." When the drawer fills in the name of the payee, the instrument is considered to be an order instrument even though the words "or bearer" are not struck out. In this case, the drawer is presumed to have neglected to strike the words "or bearer." When, however, the instrument is payable to the order of a particular payee and the words "or bearer" are handwritten or typewritten on the instrument, then it is bearer paper.

Bearer paper is payable to the holder, to a particular person or bearer (for example "Mary Doe or bearer"), or to cash. Frequently it is payable to the "order of bearer." This happens when a printed form is used and the word "bearer" is inserted after "pay to the order of." In this case the word "bearer" makes the instrument bearer paper. Bearer instruments are like cash and may be negotiated from person to person without an endorsement. For this reason they are riskier then order instruments because they can be easily stolen and must be paid to whoever has it in his possession. Many banks, however, do require customers to endorse bearer paper before payment. This gives both the

drawer and the bank the name of the person to whom payment is made.

■ **Endorsements** Endorsement is the act of signing the back of an instrument so that its rights are transferred to another person. There are four main types: special, blank, qualified, and restrictive.

Special endorsement This names a person to whom the instrument is payable.

EXAMPLE Gary Gunn owes Malcolm Mix some money. Rather than pay cash, he endorses a promissory note due him to Malcolm Mix. On the back of the note, Gary writes "Pay to the order of Malcolm Mix, Gary Gunn." This is a special endorsement. Gary Gunn is the endorser, and Malcolm Mix is the endorsee. The endorsement need not contain the word "order." "Pay Malcolm Mix, Gary Gunn" would be sufficient for transfer. After Malcolm in his turn endorses the instrument, it can be negotiated again. There is no limit to the number of times a paper may be endorsed.

Blank endorsement The signature of the payee made without naming an endorsee is a blank endorsement. A check made payable to the order of Gary Gunn, for example, is endorsed by the signature of "Gary Gunn." As soon as an instrument has such an endorsement, it becomes bearer paper, which is almost as negotiable as cash. In the example above, if Malcolm Mix endorses the check only with his name, without making the check payable to a specific third person, the check becomes bearer paper and can be cashed by anyone who has it. For this reason it is a very poor practice to endorse an instrument, such as a check, until you are ready to cash it. If you lose your endorsed check, the finder may cash it. A blank endorsement is converted into a special endorsement by writing a clarifying note above the signature of the endorsee.

EXAMPLE If Gary Gunn endorses the check in blank and gives it to Malcolm Mix, Mix can write "Pay Malcolm Mix" or "Pay to the order of Malcolm Mix" above Gary Gunn's signature. Since Mix's endorsement is now necessary to transfer the instrument, he is protected if it is lost or stolen.

Qualified endorsement This is one in which the endorser disclaims liability as an endorser. Anyone who endorses a paper becomes obligated to pay if the maker or drawer fails to do so. But if, for example, the endorsement is written "Without recourse, Malcolm Mix," Mix disclaims any liability for payment of the instrument. He is never obliged to pay it. A qualified endorsement has no negative effect on the instrument—it remains negotiable.

EXAMPLE Suppose Malcolm Mix owes Arthur Auger, the local plumber, the same amount as the amount of the check he received from Gary Gunn. Arthur agrees to accept the check and Malcolm endorses it with the words "Without recourse, Malcolm Mix. " When Arthur tries to cash the check, the bank refuses to pay on the order of Gary. If this happens, Arthur cannot sue Malcolm for the money since Malcolm has disclaimed any responsibility for payment by his qualified endorsement of the check. Arthur may sue Gary, however.

Qualified endorsements are often used by lawyers who receive checks in settlement of their clients' claims. They are usually made payable jointly to the lawyer and to the client. The lawyer endorses it without recourse and transfers it to his client. If the client does not receive the money, he cannot sue his lawyer for it.

Restrictive endorsement This type of endorsement (1) is conditional; (2) attempts to prohibit further transfer; (3) includes words that indicate the paper is meant for limited use, such as "for deposit only" or "for collection"; or (4) states that the instrument is meant for the benefit of the endorser or another person, such as "Pay Joy Jones in trust for Ben Smith."

A conditional endorsement simply imposes a condition. For example, a check payable to Malcolm Mix might be endorsed "Pay Gary Gunn when he has completed repairs on my truck." In this case Mix is attempting to be certain that Gunn fixes the truck before he receives payment. This does not affect the negotiability of the check because it does not put a condition on the order to pay the check. Gary can cash the check even if he does not complete the repairs on Malcolm's truck. But if he does so, Malcolm can sue Gary for the amount of the check for violating their agreement.

An endorsement that attempts to prohibit further transfer, such as "Pay Gary Gunn only," is of no effect. An instrument containing such an endorsement is still fully negotiable.

An endorsement that indicates the instrument is for deposit or collection is often used by a bank depositor to be certain that the money is credited to his account.

EXAMPLE A check endorsed "for deposit only in account No. 123 of Malcolm Mix" is lost or stolen. But depositor Mix is protected. If his bank cashes the check for another person instead of crediting it to his account, the bank is liable for the amount of the check, because it disregarded Mix's restrictive endorsement.

■ **Liability of parties** When you look at an instrument, you should be able to tell who is liable to you for payment. Any person who signs an instrument is liable. But a person's signature or name need not appear on the paper for him to sue. For example, the holder of a promissory note that is payable to bearer may sue the maker or any endorser for the money. *Any endorser* means that if there is more than one, you do not have to sue the last. You can sue any endorser along the line. You should choose the one from whom you would most likely be able to recover.

A person who signs an instrument is either primarily or secondarily liable. The primary liability goes to the one who is expected to pay first. The person accountable when the primary party fails to pay is secondarily liable.

Maker The maker of a promissory note is primarily liable. He is the one who has promised to pay. Unless he has been discharged of his debt or has some defense, he must make good on the note when it becomes due.

Drawer The drawer of a draft or check (the person who writes it) is only secondarily liable. He does not promise unconditionally to pay the instrument. He expects the drawee (for example, the bank) to pay. The drawer in effect promises that he will pay the amount of the paper if he is notified that the drawee has dishonored it (refused to pay it because of insufficient funds, a stop-payment order, or some other reason).

Drawee The drawee (such as a bank) of a draft or check is primarily liable to the holder when the drawee accepts the paper. A draft is accepted when the drawee so writes on the face of the draft. A check is accepted by a bank, for example, when it certifies the check. If the drawee refuses to pay a properly written draft or check, he is liable to the drawer. Such a refusal would be a breach of his contractual duty to the drawer.

Endorsers Anyone who puts his unqualified endorsement on the instrument becomes secondarily liable for paying it. His liability arises only after he receives notice that the person primarily liable refuses to honor the note, check, or draft.

An endorsement by any person using the name of the payee holds the maker or drawer liable for payment in any of the following three situations:

(1) When an imposter causes the maker or drawer to issue the instrument to him.

EXAMPLE Green is an imposter who uses the mails to defraud the public. He advertises in rural newspapers, calling himself Nino, the leading designer of fashionable jeans. In his ad, he offers his "Nino" jeans for $20, a lower price than other designer jeans offered in local shops. When enough customers send him checks made payable to Nino, he cashes them at a local bank where he has established an account under the name "Nino." He then closes the account and leaves town. His customers never receive any merchandise. Jones sends Green a $20 check, which Green endorses as Nino and then endorses it to Brown, a local dentist, for treatment of a toothache. Brown is an innocent endorsee, who knows nothing of Green's impersonation of Nino or his fraudulent use of the mails. Brown then seeks payment from Jones's bank—the drawee bank. The bank pays the check, charging Jones's account. If Jones discovers the ruse and sues to get his money back, the courts will regard endorsee Brown as more innocent than Jones in this situation. Jones will have to bear the loss or try to recover from Green.

(2) When a person signing on behalf of the maker or drawer intends the payee to have no interest in the instrument. This situation concerns a fictitious payee.

EXAMPLE Hart, a trusted employee, is given the authority to write checks to pay company bills. Hart needs money, so he writes a check for $1,000 payable to Greer, a fictitious person. Hart then endorses Greer's name and cashes the check at the bank upon which the check is drawn. The employer discovers Hart's treachery and demands that the bank credit his account for the $1,000. The bank refuses, and the employer sues the bank. The employer is the loser.

(3) When an agent or employee of the maker or drawer has supplied him with the name of the payee, intending the payee to have no such interest in the instrument. This situation is a variation of the fictitious payee.

EXAMPLE Hart prepares a padded payroll for the company's treasurer, which includes the name of the fictitious Greer. The treasurer does not know that Greer does not exist. He draws a check payable to Greer, and Hart cashes it. Again the employer must bear the loss.

In both situations involving fictitious payees, the employer failed to exercise the necessary care in selecting and supervising his employee. An employer can avoid losses resulting from such oversights by insuring himself against them. He can write off the cost of the insurance as a business expense.

Conditions for secondary liability Parties who are secondarily liable on an instrument are not required to pay unless the instrument has been presented for payment and dishonored and the parties have been given notice of dishonor.

The paper must first be presented to the person who is primarily liable for payment—a note is given to its maker, a draft to the drawee, and a check to the drawee bank. When an instrument states a day on which it is payable, it must be presented on that date. If the person with primary liability dishonors the paper (refuses to pay it because of insufficient funds, a stop-payment order, or some other reason), it must be presented to a secondary party within a reasonable time. Just what is reasonable depends on the instrument.

In the case of a check, the drawer is primarily liable for 30 days after the date of the check or the date it was issued (given or sent to the payee), whichever is later. An endorser is accountable secondarily for seven days after he endorses the check. When presentment is not made within these periods, either the drawer or the endorser may be excused from liability.

Once a paper is dishonored by a refusal to pay, those who are secondarily liable must be given notice of dishonor. Otherwise, they may not be held responsible. A bank must give notice before midnight on the day after the instrument was dishonored.

EXAMPLE A bank refuses to honor a depositor's check on January 3. But it must notify the depositor of its refusal before midnight of January 4. If the bank mails the notice, it must be in the mail before midnight of the fourth. Any other person must give notice before midnight of the third business day after dishonoring the instrument.

Notice may be written or oral. Any words that identify the instrument and state that it has been dishonored are sufficient. If two or more persons are eligible to receive payment, only one of them has to give notice to those secondarily liable.

■ **Defenses** When a holder of a negotiable paper is refused payment on it even though payment is due him, he may sue the person or persons who are liable to pay him. When a person is sued on a negotiable instrument, he will usually attempt to defend his right to refuse to pay it. Some defenses, called *real defenses*, are good both against ordinary holders and holders in due course. Others, called *personal defenses*, are good only against ordinary holders.

A holder is a person in possession of a paper that is either payable to him as the payee, endorsed to him, or payable to the bearer. Persons who take instruments after the payee are holders if the paper is payable to the bearer or properly endorsed to the order of the person. When a necessary endorsement has been forged, the person in possession can never be a holder.

EXAMPLE Malcolm Mix writes a promissory note payable to the order of Peter Piper. Piper endorses the note payable to the order of Brian Boland. The note is stolen from Boland by Frank Foxy, who forges Boland's endorsement and negotiates it to Jake Jervis. In this case

Jervis can never be a holder because Boland's valid endorsement was necessary to negotiate the instrument. And Boland never endorsed it; his signature was forged.

Under the law, a holder may be an ordinary holder or a holder in due course. Any holder who is not a holder in due course is an ordinary holder. A holder in due course has firmer rights to payment than an ordinary holder.

Holder in due course In general terms, a holder becomes a holder in due course when he takes an instrument in the belief that it will be paid to him and knows of no reason why it should not be paid to him. Technically, to be a holder in due course, a person must take the instrument (1) for value, (2) in good faith, (3) without having notice that it is overdue, (4) without having notice that it has been dishonored, and (5) without having notice that there is a claim against it. You have NOTICE of something if you are told about it or have reason to believe it exists.

For value A holder receives a paper for value when the CONSIDERATION agreed upon has been performed—that is, when the holder has given something of value (property or services) in return for the value of the instrument, as agreed upon. He becomes the holder in due course for value.

EXAMPLE Bill White, a painter, agrees to paint your house for $500. He completes the job, and you give him a check for the full amount. Bill White is a holder in due course *for value* because in return for your check he has given you consideration by painting your house.

If you take a paper in payment of, or as security for, a debt, you take it for value. This is true even though the debt is not due when you take the instrument. Similarly, if you exchange one negotiable instrument for another, you have given value for the one received.

Anyone who receives a check or other negotiable instrument as a gift is not a holder in due course since no value has been exchanged by both parties. He is an ordinary holder, however. This is an important distinction. A person who takes an instrument as a holder in due course is better protected to enforce its payment than an ordinary holder.

EXAMPLE Sam, a local restaurateur, gives Alice a $200 check for her freshly baked pies that he wants to serve to his customers. She is a holder in due course because value has been exchanged—pies for money. Alice endorses the check to Eddie, her nephew, for his birthday. When Eddie tries to cash the check, Sam's bank refuses to do so according to Sam's order. Sam was not satisfied with Alice's pies and had received complaints from his customers. Eddie sues Sam, claiming that since his aunt supplied the pies, Sam had no right to refuse to pay his $200 debt. Sam's only defense to Eddie's lawsuit is that since Alice did not receive anything of value from Eddie when she gave him the check, Eddie is not a holder in due course. This means he does not have the legal right to challenge the contract between Sam and Alice, which was the basis of the check. If Eddie had exchanged something of value with Alice, such as giving up smoking for one month, he would be a holder in due course. Sam's defense against Eddie's lawsuit would be worthless. The court would order Sam to pay Eddie.

In good faith The paper must be taken in *good faith*, that is, with honesty in the transaction. Good faith is entirely subjective—good faith in a naive person may not be good faith in a highly sophisticated person. The fact that you later suspect something is wrong is of no importance.

Overdue notice A due date is often written on the face of an instrument. If, for example, a note is payable on January 15 of this year, and you are given the note on January 20, you are considered to know it is overdue. With a demand instrument such as a check, you have notice that it is overdue when you are taking it after you have been told that a demand for payment has already been made or if a reasonable time has passed since it was issued. Thirty days after the date on a check—its issue date—is a reasonable period within which it should be presented to the bank for payment. If you accept a check that is more than 30 days old, it is assumed that you know it is overdue.

Notice of dishonor A dishonored instrument usually has some suitable notation on its face, such as "insufficient funds," "account closed," or "payment stopped." If you accept such a paper, you are thought to have knowledge of the dishonor and you can never be a holder in due course.

Notice of claim When you receive an instrument with notice that there is a claim against it, you cannot be a holder in due course. A person has a claim on a paper when it was stolen from him or if he was induced by fraud to transfer it.

Specific defenses Generally, any defense that might be used as a defense to a lawsuit over a CONTRACT may also be used to defend a suit on a negotiable instrument. Such defenses include the legal incapacity of the maker, drawer, or endorser; a signature made under duress; fraud; and alteration of the instrument.

Legal incapacities A primary real defense is *infancy.* Under the law, minors are INFANTS. The law protects minors by allowing them to avoid their contractual duties, in some cases even though they have enjoyed their benefits. In many states the holder is prohibited from recovering anything on a note from a minor.

EXAMPLE Jamie, a 17-year-old motorcycle enthusiast, signed a promissory note with Wildermann's Bike Shop to finance a motorcycle for himself. Later, Wildermann's sold the promissory note to Never Sleep Collection Agency, who demanded payment from Jamie. But Jamie's state did not allow a holder to collect on notes from minors, so Never Sleep could not force Jamie to pay.

If the person has been legally declared insane or incompetent, he is not liable for any contracts he makes. Consequently, his insanity or incompetency can be used as a defense. If he signs or endorses a commercial paper, the transaction is void; it is as if his name never appeared on the paper. On the other hand, intoxication, although an incapacity, is not a real defense.

Duress When the person being sued can prove he was under *great pressure* at the time he signed the instrument, duress is a good defense. If the person sued had been forced to sign the instrument at gunpoint or under some other threat of death, his signature is of no effect and his obligation nonexistent. However, some duress that causes a person to sign—a threat to bring a civil lawsuit or to report some wrongdoing to the police—is not a good defense against a holder in due course, although it can be a good personal defense.

Illegality In some states, an instrument that has been negotiated to pay a gambling debt or a usurious loan—one made at a higher rate of interest than allowed under the laws of the state—is void. In such a case, a person can defend himself against paying the instrument to a holder in due course on the ground of the illegality of the debt it was intended to pay.

Fraud There are two types of fraud: fraud in the essence and fraud in the inducement. Fraud in the *essence* is committed when a person is deceived as to the nature of the instrument or its terms. It is a real defense—one that is good against any holder.

EXAMPLE An old man with poor eyesight is tricked into signing a check by someone who tells him he is signing a rent receipt. Or the man is told he was signing a check for $10 when, in fact, it was for $1,000. If the man can prove that he was unable to learn the true nature of the instrument or its terms (the amount), he can defend himself against a holder in due course.

Fraud in the *inducement* is committed when the person who signs the instrument is aware of its nature and terms but is led to believe that the reasons for his writing it have been fulfilled when in fact they have not. For example, Bailey is induced to issue his check for $500 to Jones, who claims he repaired Bailey's leaky roof. But the roof was never repaired, as Bailey discovers during the next rainstorm. In this case fraud is a personal defense, good only against an ordinary holder.

Alterations The material alteration of a commercial paper is often a good defense against paying it. An alteration is an addition or deletion made to an instrument. When the alteration changes the obligations of any party, it is *material.* Examples of material alterations include a change in the amount to be paid or the date when payment is to be made. Any person whose negligence contributes to a material alteration of a commercial paper may not claim it as a defense against a party who pays the instrument in good faith or against a holder in due course.

EXAMPLE Ralph met Alvin on the street, and Alvin sold him a diamond ring for $99. Ralph gave Alvin a check for the $99, but wrote it so sloppily that there was plenty of room at the left of the figure and the written amount. Alvin changed the amount to $599 and induced Veronica, another innocent customer, to cash the check for him for the altered amount. Veronica was entitled to recover the $599 from Ralph because Ralph had been negligent in writing the check. If Ralph had not been negligent, then Veronica, although she was a holder in due course, could have recovered only $99, the amount of the check as it was originally written.

When an alteration is made by a holder and is both material and fraudulent, all those whose contracts are changed can use the alteration as a defense against paying on the instrument. If the alteration is not made by the holder or if it is not both material and fraudulent, the instrument may be enforced according to the way it was originally written. None of the parties can use the alteration as a defense against paying the original amount of the instrument.

A holder in due course who acquires the instrument after it has been altered fraudulently by the previous holder has the right to payment according to the original terms. None of the persons liable to pay it can use the alteration as a defense. They may use it as a defense, however, against an ordinary holder.

EXAMPLE Ryan writes a note for $4,000 and delivers it to O⟶✳ Kelly in exchange for a sailboat. Kelly, in turn, negotiates the note to Field, who changes the amount payable from $4,000 to $14,000. Field then sells the note to Blore for $14,000. If Blore is a holder in due course, he may enforce the note for $4,000, the amount for which it was originally written, against either Ryan or Kelly, and he may try to recover the remainder of his $14,000 from Field. If Blore is an ordinary holder, he may try to recover from Field, but he may not recover from Ryan or Kelly. They were discharged from their obligation to pay when the contract to pay $4,000 was changed to $14,000.

■ **Discharge from liability** More than 99 percent of the negotiable instruments written in the United States each year are paid promptly and without difficulty. *Payment* is thus the most common way of being discharged from liability. Intentional *cancellation* by the holder of the instrument by marking it paid or by destroying it discharges any person liable on it. *Renunciation* by the holder also discharges liability. It may be done by a document signed and delivered by the holder or by the surrender of the instrument to the person being discharged. Finally, a stop-payment order may be put on a check by its drawer. This discharges the bank from liability for dishonoring (refusing to pay) the check but it may not discharge the drawer from his liability if he was bound to pay the payee under a contract or other agreement.

commingling Mixing together in one mass. For example, a lawyer receives a sum of money belonging to a client. He should deposit the money in a separate bank account in the client's name. Instead, the lawyer deposits it in his personal account and mixes it with his own money. A lawyer who commingles funds in this way may be censured or disbarred.

commission 1 A written grant of authority issued by the government, a department of the government, or a court, giving a person power to perform certain acts or duties—a military officer's commission, for example. 2 The person or persons given the grant of authority, such as a trustee in BANKRUPTCY or the Federal Trade Commission. 3 In business, a payment based on a percentage of sales or profits. A salesman, for example, may be paid a commission—a percentage of the total value of his sales. 4 In criminal law, the doing of a criminal act.

commissioner 1 A member of a commission. 2 An officer who is charged with the administration of the laws relating to a particular subject, such as the commissioner of motor vehicles, or with the management of some government bureau or agency, such as the commissioner of education.

commitment 1 The act of sending a person convicted of a crime to prison; the authority for holding the person in prison. 2 The formal process of putting a mentally ill person into the official care of another person, such as the head of a psychiatric hospital.

committee 1 Persons whom a larger group has delegated to do specialized work, such as the Senate Committee on Energy and Natural Resources. 2 Those appointed by a court as guardians of an INCOMPETENT person and his property. See GUARDIAN AND WARD; INSANE PERSONS.

commodity Goods, wares, merchandise, and other forms of movable personal property that may be bought and sold. Raw or partially processed materials are included, as are farm products, such as wheat and corn.

common carrier See CARRIER.

common council A form of local government, such as a town or city legislature.

common count See COUNT.

common land A piece of ground left open for common, or public, use by the community. Common lands may be created by government grant, by government appropriation of land for common purposes (see EMINENT DOMAIN), or by private deed. These lands were originally used for growing crops, pasturing animals, collecting firewood, or as diggings for stones and other building materials. Today most common lands are public recreation areas.

common law The common law in the United States is based on the common, or unwritten, law of England as the law existed in 1607, when the first English colonists settled here. It also includes English statutes, enacted before the American Revolution, that applied to life in the Colonies. The common law may be thought of as the embodiment of principles and rules dictated by natural reason and by man's sense of justice, voluntarily adopted by men to govern themselves in social relations.

Unlike statutory law, which consists of fixed and absolute rules, the common law is a flexible body of principles designed to accommodate new conditions, public policies, trade, commerce, inventions, and knowledge. The principles of the common law are developed by, and found in, the decisions of the courts, which establish precedents. The common law, then, is the accumulated expressions of the courts in their efforts to determine what is right and just between individuals in their private disputes.

Today in the United States both the law of CONTRACTS and the law of TORTS (injuries to persons or property) are based on the common law. With minor exceptions, the states have not enacted statutes that pertain to these topics. When, however, a state has modified or replaced the common law with a statute, the statute prevails.

Automobile accident cases, for example, are decided not only by the common-law rules of torts but also by state statutes that replace or augment the common law. Originally, the courts treated automobile accident cases the same way as other accident cases. The prevailing rule of torts is that a person who was negligent and thereby caused harm to another person or to someone else's property can be made to pay money damages to compensate the injured person. This rule proved unsatisfactory in automobile cases because the person found to be at fault frequently had no money to pay his victims. Plaintiffs began to sue not only the careless driver but also the automobile owner in the hope that a person who could afford to own a car would be more able to pay a money judgment. This approach was successful, however, only when the victim could show that the owner himself was negligent in lending the car to someone who turned out to be careless.

Today, states generally have statutes that enable innocent victims of automobile accidents to be compensated. Many states have "consent" statutes, which allow a court to hold the owner of an automobile liable for any injuries caused by the negligent operation of his vehicle. These statutes usually presume that the owner has consented to the use made of his car unless the owner clearly proves that he has not given consent, as when a car is stolen. State legislatures also have enacted compulsory insurance laws, which require owners of automobiles to purchase a certain amount of insurance to cover their potential liability.

EXAMPLE Alice, an unemployed teacher, borrows Matthew's car to drive to a job interview when her own car will not start. Since she is a half hour late, Alice speeds, exceeding the speed limit by 25 miles per hours. She collides with the rear of Randy's station wagon, which is stopped at a traffic light. Luckily Randy escapes injury but his car suffers $1,500 worth of damages.

Under common law, Alice would be liable to Randy for the property damage caused by her negligence. Because Alice has been out of work for over a year, however, she has no money to pay him. Randy could sue Matthew, the car owner, for his damages but he would win only if he could prove that Matthew was negligent in lending his car to Alice. This could not be done since Alice had never been involved in a car accident before.

Fortunately for Randy, his state has a consent statute that makes Matthew, the car owner, financially responsible for the damages caused by Alice's careless operation of his car. Matthew could avoid liability only if he could prove that Alice stole his car. In addition, the state has compulsory insurance laws, which require Matthew to have enough automobile insurance to cover liability in case of accident. Once Randy has proved his case, he will be able to recover his losses.

While the criminal law is also derived from the common law, it has been collected, amended, and passed in statutory form by the various legislatures. Now it can no longer be considered a body of common law.

common-law action A civil lawsuit, such as an ACTION on a contract, between private individuals or organizations in which the relief (help) sought generally is money DAMAGES.

common-law marriage A MARRIAGE that is not solemnized by a wedding ceremony. It is created when a couple agree to marry, publicly present themselves as married, and live together as married for a period of time sufficient to create a legal marriage. The common-law marriage is recognized as a valid marriage in some states. See Chart 20.

common-law trust See BUSINESS TRUST.

common pleas The name given to some courts of general jurisdiction that handle civil trials according to the principles of common law.

common scheme 1 Two or more different crimes planned together. 2 A plan for dividing a piece of land into lots with identical restrictions on land use.

common stock Shares, in the form of printed certificates, indicating the ownership in a CORPORATION. The shares are personal property. Each share is a contract between the shareholder and the corporation. A share of common stock ordinarily entitles its owner to participate in and to vote at stockholders' meetings. When the corporation earns a profit, it usually declares a dividend (a part of the profit) on each share. Dividends are usually paid on common stock only after the payment of dividends on PREFERRED STOCK. See SECURITIES REGULATION.

communism A political theory that supports the belief that the ownership and control of property and the means of production should belong to the working class. The opposite of the system of capitalism.

community property Property owned in common by a HUSBAND AND WIFE. In some states almost all property acquired by a husband and wife during marriage becomes the property of both, even if some property was acquired in only one name.

commutation The change in a criminal punishment from a greater to a lesser one. For example, a death SENTENCE might be commuted to life imprisonment.

compact An agreement or contract. The word is usually applied to agreements between nations, but the most famous compact in American history, the Mayflower Compact, was an agreement among individuals. An agreement to establish self-government for the Plymouth Colony, the compact was signed by most of the men who sailed to America in 1620 on the *Mayflower*.

company A number of persons organized for the purpose of doing business. The term is comprehensive and may refer to individuals, a PARTNERSHIP, or a CORPORATION.

comparative negligence A rule in the law of NEGLIGENCE by which the degree of fault of the plaintiff is compared with the degree of fault of the defendant. Without this rule, the defendant may use as a complete defense that the plaintiff contributed to his own injury by his own negligence. Even though the negligence of the plaintiff is slight, he must bear the entire loss, and the defendant is freed from any liability for DAMAGES. To eliminate the injustice created by the rule of contributory negligence, many states have passed comparative-negligence statutes. Under these statutes, when both the plaintiff and the defendant are negligent, the plaintiff is not barred from recovering damages—such as money to compensate him for his injury—but his damages are reduced according to the degree he is found to be at fault. However, the plaintiff may recover only when his fault is less than that of the defendant.

comparative rectitude   A rule whereby a DIVORCE was granted to the spouse who was least at fault when both husband and wife showed grounds for divorce. This kind of divorce—now rarely if ever granted—is also called a least-fault divorce. The spouse whose fault was the least might have rights that are denied to the other—such as, in some states, the right to remarry.

compelling state interest   A reason for a state law, regulation, policy, or action that is strong enough to limit a person's constitutional rights. For example, a state may regulate the time, place, and manner in which you may distribute religious leaflets but, before banning the distribution, it must show a compelling state interest—such as the fact that the literature advocated violent overthrow of the government.

compensation   **1** Payment of DAMAGES.   **2** Something given to restore an injured person to his former position or to make up for the loss he has suffered.   **3** The wages paid to an employee or the salaries paid to a company's executive officers.

compensatory damages   The DAMAGES awarded in a lawsuit to replace the loss suffered by the plaintiff as a result of the defendant's wrongdoing.

competent   Duly qualified; having sufficient ability or authority; possessing all the requirements of law. For example, a testator (person who makes a WILL) is competent when he understands what it means to make a will, when he knows what kinds of and how much property he owns, and when he understands how making the will affects his relatives and anyone else named in it. A defendant is competent to stand trial for a crime when he is found to be sane enough to take part in his own defense. He need not have been sane at the time of the crime for which he is on trial. See also INCOMPETENT.

competent evidence   Any EVIDENCE that tends to prove a point in question and is the proper kind to prove that point. For example, when the contents of a written contract are in question, the contract itself is competent evidence.

complainant   Generally, a person who applies to the courts for legal redress. The term is the proper designation for a person who brings a suit in EQUITY. In CRIMINAL LAW, the state is usually the complainant.

complaint   The complaint is the first PLEADING brought by a plaintiff in a civil lawsuit. Its purpose is to give the defendant facts on which the plaintiff is relying to support his lawsuit. The complaint usually contains (1) the names of the plaintiff and defendant, (2) the name of the court, (3) the name of the county in which the trial is to be heard, (4) a statement of the facts that make up the grounds for the suit, and (5) a demand for the legal remedy to which the plaintiff thinks he is entitled. When the demand is for the recovery of money, the amount must be stated. Here is a sample of a complaint in a simple legal action:

UNITED STATES DISTRICT COURT
for the
SOUTHERN DISTRICT OF NEW YORK

Civil Action File Number _____0101_____

X   JOHN DOE_____, Plaintiff
                v.   } *Complaint*
X   RICHARD ROE_, Defendant

    1. Jurisdiction is founded on diversity of citizenship and amount. Plaintiff is a corporation incorporated under the laws of the State of Connecticut and having its principal place of business in the State of Connecticut and defendant is a corporation incorporated under the laws of the State of New York and having its principal place of business in a State other than the State of Connecticut. The matter in controversy exceeds, exclusive of interest and costs, the sum of ten thousand dollars.

    2. Defendant owes plaintiff twenty thousand dollars for goods sold and delivered by plaintiff to defendant between June 1, 1978, and June 1, 1979.

    WHEREFORE plaintiff demands judgment against defendant for the sum of twenty thousand dollars plus interest and costs.

Signed:_____

Barry Barrister_____, *Attorney for Plaintiff*
Address:_____100 Bench Street_____

---

compliance   Obedience; conformance; acting in a manner that does not violate a law. For instance, a state that receives federal money for highways must act in compliance with the federal law regulating the maximum speed at which motor vehicles may travel. The state must post signs that read "Speed Limit 55 MPH," and then must also enforce that speed limit.

composition with creditors   An agreement made by a debtor with his creditors by which the creditors agree to accept a certain percentage of their claims as a settlement. A composition debtor need not be insolvent (unable to pay his debts when they become due), but he must be in financially embarrassed circumstances.

As with any other contract, a meeting of the minds must take place between the debtor and the creditors before a valid composition can be reached. An offer by the creditors to settle for a percentage of their claims is not binding until the debtor accepts. In addition, a composition must show a meeting of the minds among the creditors who participate in it, having made individual concessions for their common purpose.

Generally, it is not necessary for all or even the majority of the creditors to join in a composition. It is binding on all those who join it and the debtor himself.

A series of separate and independent compromises with individual creditors is not a composition. But if the common purpose is present, the fact that the debtor agrees with each creditor separately means the arrangement may be considered a composition.

EXAMPLE Saul, a dressmaker, could not afford to pay his ⊙—※ bills that were due in one month. Another businessman offered to buy the business from Saul. As part of the deal, he offered to pay Saul's creditors 40 cents on the dollar. One of Saul's creditors did not find out about the offer, but the others were notified and accepted the offer. Later, one of the creditors who had accepted the offer tried to sue the business for the full amount owed to him. The court refused to allow him full recovery because he was bound by the composition agreement. The creditor who learned about the composition after it was made, and had no chance to accept or refuse it, could try to collect the full amount owed to him by the business or he could ask to be included in the composition.

■ **Form** The composition contract may be written or oral, but very often it is in the form of a DEED. In the deed, the debtor agrees to pay each participating creditor a fixed sum or a certain percentage of the debt. Payment may be due at once or at a specified future time and may be either in a lump sum or in installments. Security for the debtor's performance, such as a mortgage on a piece of land he owns, may or may not be included. The deed will also contain a condition that the creditors will accept what is offered as complete satisfaction of their claims.

■ **Consideration** A composition must rest on consideration. The promise of each creditor is consideration for that of the other creditors and the debtor. This means that each creditor surrenders his legal right to the full amount of the debt owed him, accepts settlement, and shares proportionately in the debtor's funds. The debtor's consideration is the surrender of his right to pay any one creditor more than the amount or percentage agreed upon for all, and the abdication of his right to file for BANKRUPTCY.

■ **Performance** The composition must be performed strictly according to its terms. For instance, the composition money must be paid on time. If the debtor fails to perform any of the terms of the agreement (called a breach of performance), the creditors can start a lawsuit against him to recover the total amount of the original debt. A creditor who commits a breach of the composition will be liable to his fellow creditors for any damages he causes. For example, a creditor who attaches the debtor's property (takes legal steps that bring it under court control) before the debtor's payment is due, has breached the composition contract. See ATTACHMENT AND GARNISHMENT.

The debtor is released only when he performs the promises he has made. A creditor who has joined a composition cannot revoke his assent or withdraw without the consent of the other parties. Once completed, a composition settles the claims and extinguishes all the debts included in it.

compounding an offense
The crime of perverting justice by bargaining to allow a criminal to escape conviction or showing him some favor for that purpose. The necessary elements for the offense are (1) the commission of a crime, (2) an agreement not to prosecute the person who has committed the crime, and (3) the receipt of CONSIDERATION (something of value) for the agreement.

The person who committed the crime need not have been tried or convicted, but in most states there must have been a crime committed.

An agreement not to prosecute the crime or to withhold evidence of it is the second essential element. A person who merely takes back his own stolen property, who accepts a return of embezzled funds or receives some security for the return of those funds does not compound the crime unless he also agrees to shield the thief or to refrain from prosecution.

The last element is consideration for the agreement. It may be anything of value or the promise of something valuable, such as money or a promissory note, given by the criminal to the person who allows him to get away with his crime. This shows that the agreement was made for the sake of gain and not from weak or compassionate motives.

It is no defense that the person charged with the crime was acquitted.

EXAMPLE Paul knew that his brother Jack had bribed the ⊙—※ local officials in order to get his liquor license. In return for Paul's silence about the bribery, Jack paid him $1,000. When stories about widespread corruption among local officials appeared in the newspapers, an investigation ensued, and Jack was implicated and later formally accused. At his trial, it was discovered that he had also paid off his brother to keep him quiet. Although Jack was acquitted, for lack of proper evidence, Paul was still liable for compounding the offense.

Nor is it a defense for a policeman who has agreed not to prosecute in exchange for a sum of cash, that he acted under the direction of a superior officer and gave him all the money. Others who may be guilty of compounding an offense include a person who accepts money for encouraging the absence of a witness and someone who delays the trial of a criminal prosecution, such as a sheriff who deliberately fails to arrest the defendant.

compound interest
Interest on interest. The sum of $1,000 is deposited in a savings bank, for example. Interest is paid on the $1,000 at a rate of 5 percent per year. At the end of the first year the $1,000 has earned $50 in interest. The $50 is then added to the $1,000 for a total of $1,050. If the money is left on deposit the following year, interest at the 5-percent rate would then be paid on the $1,050. Many banks compound interest on savings accounts at each quarter of the year; some compound interest daily.

compromise and settlement
A compromise is an agreement between persons who, in order to prevent or end a lawsuit, adjust their differences by mutual consent. Many out-of-court settlements are the result of compromises. Compromises and settlements are encouraged by the courts, since the state favors ending litigation as soon as possible. If the compromise is made fairly, the court will sustain it. A valid compromise agreement is as binding on the parties as a court ruling.

The words "compromise" and "settlement" are often used interchangeably, but "settlement" has a broader meaning. While a settlement may be the result of a compromise, it can also be reached where there is no dispute or lawsuit between the parties. A settlement may take place,

SETTLING FOR LESS: THE LAW OF COMPROMISE AND SETTLEMENT

■ The essence of compromise is that you agree to settle for less than you think is your due, in order to avoid the expense and risk of total loss that would be the price of a court action.

■ From your point of view as the debtor in a case where you feel the other party has no right to demand so much, compromise and settlement can represent the best available out—you offer what you think you owe, and even more, by way of a compromise. The other person may accept your compromise as a settlement of the disputed amount.

■ Typical subjects for compromise include a disagreement between you and your doctor on his fee, for which you have an implied contract to pay; or an award for $5,000 in damages that has been made to you, and you, knowing the defendant is broke, accept his pledge to pay you $3,000; or an auto accident for which the parties involved reach a compromise on the cost of car repairs but leave the amount to be received for bodily injuries to be assessed by the court.

■ A compromise agreement must be mutually binding on both parties;

therefore, a lawsuit to enforce it may be brought by either party.

■ You may withdraw an offer of compromise before acceptance but not afterward.

■ You are free to settle your differences for any consideration (something of value), however great or small. A court will not ordinarily question the adequacy of the consideration unless it grossly shocks the moral sense.

■ A compromise agreement need not be in writing unless required by state law or a court rule.

---

for example, when the parties agree to an accounting to decide how much one owes the other.

■ **Subjects for compromise** Any disputed right or claim made in good faith generally may be the subject of compromise. The dispute may arise, for example, out of a contract. You and your doctor disagree on his fee, for which you have an implied contract to pay. Or a contest might stem from a TORT. Someone publicly called you a liar and you say you will take him to court for DAMAGES. In each case you and the person with whom you have the dispute can arrive at the amount owed out of court.

A civil judgment may also be compromised. The court awards you $5,000 in damages, and knowing the defendant is broke, you accept his pledge to pay you $3,000.

The parties to a dispute may even settle part of it between themselves and leave the rest for a lawsuit: The driver of a car in an accident is sued for damages for the harm he did to the other car and for personal injuries he caused its driver. Both parties reach a satisfactory compromise on the car-damage figure, but they decide to leave the amount of personal injury damages up to the court.

Family difficulties may be compromised and settled. In fact, courts usually encourage family settlements as long as they are free from fraud and the rights of minor children are not violated. For example, parents cannot reach a settlement that modifies a divorce judgment in such a way that it deprives children of the support to which they are entitled.

■ **Necessary elements** The required elements for a compromise and settlement are a controversy between the parties and their agreement to mutual concessions. A debtor's agreement simply to pay an amount he owes is not a compromise. Because compromises and settlements are contractual in nature, they must have the elements of other CONTRACTS.

A compromise and settlement of disputed claims may be made at any time—for example, right after a contract has been breached, when a lawsuit on the breach is started, during the lawsuit, or after a judgment has been given by a court. Usually, the parties themselves agree on the terms of the compromise. It does not matter that one party gets the better of the bargain or that the agreement does not resolve

the dispute in the same way a court might have. When the aid of the court has been requested, however, the settlement may require court approval or permission. A compromise agreement should be complete and certain in its terms and must be mutually binding on both parties. This means that a lawsuit to enforce it may be started by either party.

Parties involved A compromise may be made by any parties legally competent to enter into a contract. Agents and attorneys, acting with the authority of the parties, for example, may make compromise agreements. Frequently, however, the parties may settle their differences without the aid of attorneys.

Offer and acceptance There must be a meeting of the minds—an actual offer of compromise and an acceptance. The offer can be made by either party. If you make an offer, it must be definite enough to show your willingness to assume liability for the amount of money you suggest. But if you offer to pay a debt in property instead of money, that is not a compromise if the land is worth what you owe, nor is your offer to settle a promissory note by giving your creditor another note.

You may communicate the offer or acceptance verbally or in writing. Making an acceptance with complaints or under protest does not invalidate it because you can still accept a bargain that you do not like. But when the acceptance is dependent on a condition that proves impossible to perform, there is no settlement. For example, a compromise to accept part payment of the agreed price of corporate stock in the form of a loan from a certain bank would be ineffective if the bank refused to make the loan.

You may withdraw an offer of compromise before acceptance but not afterward. When an agreement is to be put in writing and signed, either party may withdraw before signing. If court approval is necessary, one party may repudiate the agreement before the court validates it.

Consideration Anything of benefit to one party or at the expense of the other, including money or property, is consideration for a compromise.

Disputed claim Settling a dispute by paying more than the amount you admit is due is a sufficient consideration. In other words, there must be a dispute between the parties concerning the subject of the claim, and one of them—say someone who owes you money or the person you are about to sue for libel—must pay something he does not admit he owes.

EXAMPLE You have loaned money to a friend, who is paying 0—* you back gradually. One day he hands you a check and announces that this squares things between you. You remind him, however, that in addition to the original loan of $500, he borrowed another $100 that day in May when you went to the track together. Your friend claims that the original loan was only $400 and that he made a note of it, and you say that your records show $500. After talking it over, the two of you finally agree that if he pays you another $50, this will settle things.

A refusal to pay an undisputed claim does not create a dispute, and an agreement by a creditor to accept less than the amount due is not sufficient consideration. There must be an honest disagreement, and the amount of the claim must be fairly in dispute.

The person who advances the claim must make it in good faith. But good faith alone is not enough to sustain a compromise. If you make a claim but have no facts to back you up, you are not acting in good faith. But when you make a claim in good faith, the compromise is valid, even though the other party assents believing that your claim is without right.

EXAMPLE Art believes that the automobile accident in 0—* which he was involved was really the other driver's fault. In order to avoid the time and expense of a lawsuit to prove this point, however, he settles out of court with the other driver for an agreed-upon sum. He has acted in good faith and the compromise is valid.

Family controversies The termination of family controversies is consideration for a family settlement. This principle extends to cases in which the aim is to restore peace in the family or to preserve family property—for example, an out-of-court settlement on the amount of alimony and child support payments.

Illegal claims The settlement of an illegal claim cannot support a compromise agreement because the person making the illegal claim cannot bring a lawsuit based on it. An example would be the settlement of a claim that is against public morals—a disputed bill between a wholesaler and a retailer of obscene films. Another is a disagreement over a contract between a nightclub owner and the person he has hired to run the club's unlawful gambling operation.

Adequacy of consideration The parties may settle their differences for whatever consideration they have agreed on. Ordinarily, a court will not inquire into the adequacy of the consideration, however small or slight it might be, unless it grossly shocks the moral sense.

■ **Form and execution** No form of agreement is essential to make a compromise valid. The agreement need not be in writing unless required by a statute or a court rule. If the parties want to withhold assent until the compromise is in writing, then their oral agreement holds until the written agreement is drawn up later.

When the agreement is in writing, technical language is not demanded so long as the agreement shows its purpose clearly. As a rule, a written agreement is not binding until it is signed.

■ **Operation and effect** Compromises and settlements are not admissions that the claims are valid. The compromise merely admits that there is a dispute and that an amount of money is to be paid to end the controversy.

When the parties to a pending lawsuit compromise the case and the terms are fulfilled, the lawsuit is ended.

comptroller 1 A public officer of a state or municipal corporation who has certain financial duties, such as examining the accounts of collectors of the public moneys, keeping records, and reporting the financial situation. A principal duty of a state comptroller is the final auditing and settling of all claims against the state. 2 The chief financial officer of a private corporation.

compulsory process The method used to force the attendance in court of a person wanted, for example, as a witness. Compulsory process includes not only the ordinary SUBPOENA but also a WARRANT of arrest.

con 1 A slang abbreviation for confidence, as in *con* man or *con* game for a person or scheme that takes advantage of a victim after winning his confidence. 2 Also used as an abbreviation for the word *contra*, which means "against."

concealment of birth or death The concealment of the birth or the death or body of a newborn child is a statutory criminal offense, and the laws vary from state to state. The gist of the offense under some statutes is the concealment of birth, while under others it is the concealment of death. When the facts of a case show that the disposal of the baby's body was not intended to be a concealment, there can be no conviction. Failure to give notice of the birth of an infant who subsequently dies does not by itself constitute a concealment.

In most states the dead child must have been born illegitimate, since concealment is usually attempted only by an unwed mother.

The act must be done in such a way that it cannot be determined if the child was born dead or alive or whether he was murdered. The concealment need not be from everyone, and the act is still punishable when another person participates in it.

It is usually essential to show the birth of a child to the woman charged with the crime. But evidence that the child was born dead has brought acquittal under some statutes. In some states, a person may be convicted of concealment whether the child was born alive or dead.

conciliation The process of bringing together two sides to make a compromise agreement.

conclusion of law An argument or answer arrived at by applying law to the conclusion drawn from facts. For instance, it is a conclusion of fact to say that a man hit a pedestrian with a car, but it is a conclusion of law to say that the accident was the driver's fault. See PLEADING.

conclusive Beyond dispute; final. For example, *conclusive* EVIDENCE is evidence that cannot be contradicted, either because the law does not permit it or because it is so convincing that it establishes a point in question beyond any reasonable doubt.

concur   Agree; act together; consent. In the practice of appellate courts, a *concurring opinion* is an opinion filed by one of the judges. In it he agrees with the conclusions of another opinion registered in the case but wishes to state separately his reasons for reaching the same result.

concurrent   Running together; having the same authority or joint and equal authority. In criminal law, *concurrent* SENTENCES are prison terms that are served at the same time.

concurrent jurisdiction   The jurisdiction of several different COURTS, each of which has the authority to deal with the same subject matter, such as a personal injury action. The person who is bringing the lawsuit selects the court in which he will file.

condemn   **1** Find a person guilty of a crime. **2** Declare a penalty or punishment.

condemnation   See EMINENT DOMAIN.

condition   A future and uncertain event that creates, destroys, or changes rights or obligations when it does happen. Conditions are either express (stated) or implied. An *express condition* is incorporated in definite terms in a deed, contract, or lease. It is intended and created by the parties. When a building contract states that if the building is completed before a certain date, the builder must be paid an additional sum, there is an express condition.

An *implied condition* is an invention of the courts, created by the law in an attempt to do justice to the parties. It is a condition that the law presumes—from the nature of the transaction or the conduct of the parties—was understood between the parties as part of their agreement, even though it was not stated.

EXAMPLE   Before Prohibition became the law of the land, a ○━━✳ saloon owner purchased a bar, bar mirrors, and beer pumps with taps. The saloon owner promised to pay the supplier for the items in installments, and he did so until Prohibition forced him to close his saloon. The supplier sued the saloon owner for the balance due. The court decided that when it became impossible to use the saloon because of Prohibition, the law implied a condition excusing the saloon owner from making the rest of the payments.

Conditions may also be precedent or subsequent. A *condition precedent* is performed before an agreement becomes effective. It calls for some event to occur or some act to be performed before a contract is binding on the parties. For instance, two parties sign an agreement and send it to a third party with the understanding that it will not become effective until he signs it. The agreement becomes a contract when his signature is added.

A *condition subsequent* is part of a contract already in existence. For example, under an alimony agreement a divorced husband is obligated to pay his former wife $500 per month for the rest of her life, on the condition that she

does not later (subsequently) remarry. A condition subsequent may also be applied to a gift. In some states, an engagement ring is considered conditioned on the subsequent marriage of the engaged couple. The ring must be returned if the wedding is called off.

conditional   Dependent upon or granted subject to a CONDITION, such as a conditional sale.

condominium   A multiple-unit dwelling, such as an apartment house or a group of townhouses, in which there is separate ownership of the individual units and shared ownership of the land and common areas. *Common areas* are parts of the building and surrounding land that can be used by any or all of the individual owners, such as common entrances, laundry rooms, elevators, and hallways. The owners of the individual units form an association, which elects officers and a board of directors. The condominium association manages the building and land directly or hires professional managers. The owners of the individual units share the costs of maintaining the building and common areas but pay all the costs of maintaining their particular units.

■ **Ownership**   When you buy a unit in a condominium, you receive title to (ownership of) the unit in FEE SIMPLE—that is, you own it outright and have all the legal rights of ownership, including the right to sell the unit to whomever you please at whatever price you please unless you sign a COVENANT that restricts you from using the unit in some way. It is just like owning a single-family house. Unlike owning a house, however, your title includes ownership with all the other unit owners of the land and the common areas. This shared ownership means that you have certain rights, such as use of the common areas, and certain obligations, such as paying your share of the expenses incurred for maintenance or improvements of the common areas. You will even have to help pay for improvements you disapprove of or cannot afford. For example, if the unit owners in your building vote to construct tennis courts on the grounds, you will have to pay your proportionate share in the cost of building and maintaining the courts even if you had voted not to build them.

The size of your share in the costs of maintaining and improving the building and common areas depends on the size of your unit and is established as a certain *percentage share*. For example, a building that has a total of 100 rooms (not counting common rooms) might count each room as a 1-percent share. In that case, if you owned a three-room unit you would be responsible for a 3-percent share of the building's expenses in addition to anything you spend on your own unit. If a swimming pool was built you would have to pay 3 percent of the cost of building and maintaining it as well as 3 percent of the taxes on the building and 3 percent of the cost of heating the building, keeping up the grounds, repairing the roof of the building, and keeping the hallways clean.

■ **Documents**   There are three documents involved in the purchase of a condominium: a DEED to the individual unit, a declaration of condominium, and the bylaws of the particular condominium association, the members of which consist of the owners of the individual units.

Deed When you purchase a condominium, you will receive a deed, which is recorded in the county records office. The deed will usually include a description of the individual unit, the building in which the unit is located, and the land on which the building is constructed. It will also include any restrictions that may have been put on the use of the unit, the percentage share in the common areas that is assigned to the unit, and any other details that the buyer or seller of the unit agree on. No deed may contain provisions that are against the rules of the condominium or that contradict the declaration of condominium.

Declaration of condominium The declaration of condominium is the official record of the rights and obligations of the owners and a statement of exactly what parts of the condominium the owner of a unit actually owns and is responsible for. State law dictates what must be included in the declaration of condominium, and the requirements vary from state to state, but generally a declaration of condominium must include the following information:

(1) A legal description of the condominium's land and buildings. This is the same information that is included in the deed for the unit.

(2) A description of each individual unit in the condominium. The description should include the unit's address and apartment number (if any), its size, the number of rooms it has, and its exact location—for example, east building, sixth floor, northwest corridor, first unit west of the elevator.

(3) A description of the common areas and facilities and a statement of the conditions under which their use may be restricted. For example, a gymnasium in an apartment building may only be used during the day or a swimming pool may be available only to owners of large units.

(4) The monetary value of each individual unit, the entire condominium, and the land under it, and the percentage of shares in the common areas that is assigned to each individual unit owner.

(5) The number of votes assigned to each unit and the procedure for deciding on repairs, improvements, and other costs, and provisions for amending the declaration or terminating the condominium arrangement. The number of votes assigned to each unit owner is generally proportional to his percentage share.

(6) The procedures for paying maintenance fees and other costs, and the penalties for failing to pay them.

Bylaws The bylaws of a condominium building contain the rules and regulations by which the condominium association governs itself. The bylaws are usually drawn up by the original developers of the condominium, but they may also be created by the initial purchasers of the individual units. The bylaws generally include the procedures for electing the officers or board members of the condominium association, conducting meetings, and handling routine building maintenance and insurance for the common areas. They also set any restrictions that may be placed on the sale of individual units and penalties for nonadherence to the rules. The owner of a condominium unit is bound to follow the regulations established by the bylaws.

■ **Financing** A condominium unit may be purchased for cash, or more commonly, a MORTGAGE may be obtained for it. Since each unit is individually owned, no other condominium owner may be made liable for another's default on his mortgage payments or property taxes.

condonation The voluntary forgiveness and pardon of a past offense committed by a husband or wife, upon the condition that the offense will not be repeated. For example, a wife learns that her husband has committed adultery. She forgives him and continues to have sexual relations with him on the condition that thereafter he remain faithful to her. If the wife later sues for divorce on the ground of that act of ADULTERY, the husband can fight the DIVORCE on the basis of his wife's condonation of the offense.

confederacy **1** The banding together of persons for the purpose of committing an act forbidden by law. CONSPIRACY is another word for this offense. **2** In international law, the term means an agreement between nations, in which they unite for their mutual welfare.

confession A voluntary statement made by a person charged with a crime, in which he acknowledges himself to be guilty of the offense and also discloses the circumstances of the act or the share he had in it. Confessions may be judicial or extrajudicial. A *judicial confession* is made before a magistrate or court during a criminal proceeding. An *extrajudicial confession* is delivered out of court to any official or other person.

An *implied confession* occurs when the defendant does not expressly plead guilty but indirectly admits his guilt by placing himself at the court's mercy and asking for a light sentence. An *involuntary confession* is brought about by hope, fear, promise, violence, torture, or threat. When a confession is not supported by evidence of the commission of a crime, it is a *naked confession*. See CRIMINAL LAW.

confession and avoidance An answer from a defendant to a statement of fact by a plaintiff in his COMPLAINT. See PLEADING. Confession and avoidance is considered an AFFIRMATIVE DEFENSE. The answer admits the truth of the plaintiff's statement but brings to light some new matter that may deprive the facts of their legal effect or even cancel them. For example, in his lawsuit the plaintiff states that the defendant owes him $1,000. In his answer, the defendant confesses (admits) that he borrowed the money but he avoids the legal effect of his confession by stating that he repaid the $1,000.

confession of judgment The act of a debtor in permitting a JUDGMENT for a sum of money to be entered against him by his creditors without a lawsuit. The debtor usually gives his creditor written permission for this. For example, he may give his creditor a promissory note containing a phrase authorizing a confession of judgment if the note is not paid by a certain date. Confessions of judgment are illegal or severely limited in many states.

confidentiality See PRIVILEGED COMMUNICATION.

confidential relationship Any relationship between two persons in which one of them has a duty to act with the utmost good faith for the benefit of the other. A

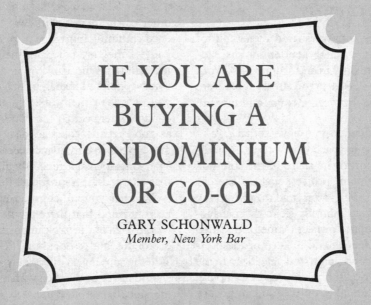

IF YOU ARE BUYING A CONDOMINIUM OR CO-OP

GARY SCHONWALD
Member, New York Bar

Congratulations! You have decided to become a homeowner. The home you envision buying, however, is not a dream house in a quiet tree-lined city or suburban neighborhood. This home is an apartment you own—either as a condominium (a condo) or as a cooperative (a co-op). These words were not in most people's vocabulary until recently, but because a home purchase may be the largest single expenditure you incur in your lifetime, these words are of great consequence to you.

Why are families buying homes that are a part of larger complexes? The reasons are varied but all are basic. The buyer of a condo or a co-op is looking for one or more of the following advantages:

Lower price per room. There are more dwelling units in an apartment building on five acres than there would be if there were four houses per acre. Hence, land cost is reduced in the cost of the home.

Ease of maintenance and sharing of costs. When the burden of spending endless weekend hours repairing an individual home is placed on a group, it is easier to handle the responsibilities of home ownership. Perhaps more important, a homeowner must be able to reduce heating and maintenance costs. Because of the compactness of apartment buildings, for example, heating an apartment may cost less per room than heating a house. Furthermore, spreading maintenance costs among many people reduces the impact on the homeowner's monthly budget.

Security. Many people believe in the old principle of "safety in numbers." Living in a cluster of apartments may make a woman feel safer when her husband is away than living in a house that is out of sight or sound of neighbors.

Tax and investment benefits. In these days of inflation many people are looking at their homes both as a means to get certain tax advantages and as an investment. If you own your home, you can deduct on your income tax return the interest and taxes paid. Moreover, if you own a home and have lived there for any length of time, chances are that you would be able to sell the home and make a profit because of a price rise resulting from inflation. The fact is that in order to protect your financial position, it is becoming necessary in many suburban and metropolitan areas to consider investing in buying housing.

Conversions. Finally, many people are looking at condominiums and cooperatives because they have to. Landlords have discovered that an apartment is worth a lot more to them when sold for cash as a condo or co-op than it is when kept as a rental unit. As a result, there has been a wave of conversions of rental-apartment buildings into condos and co-ops. If you are a tenant in such a building, you may have no choice but to buy the unit you are living in, because satisfactory rental units are no longer available in your area. As more buildings convert, there are fewer rental buildings for everyone.

Condo versus co-op

In most places in the country shared ownership of housing is principally through condominiums. Cooperatives are found mainly in and around New York City and some other large urban areas. There are some basic differences between a condominium and a cooperative.

As the owner of a condo you have actual *title* to (ownership of) the living space you occupy. In addition, you own a proportionate share of the common areas in the condominium project, such as the entrance to the project, the elevators, and the swimming pool, if there is one. Your monthly fee to the management of the condominium project (sometimes called *maintenance)* covers the general upkeep of the project. When you buy a condo unit, you get a deed to the property, just as you would if you purchased a house, and you pay real estate taxes on it. You can finance your purchase with a mortgage from a bank, using the unit itself as security for the loan and paying off the mortgage in monthly installments.

As the owner of a co-op, you do not have actual title to your living space. Rather, you get shares of stock in the cooperative corporation that owns the entire property. The cooperative corporation then joins in a cooperative lease with you (known as a *proprietary lease).* When you buy or sell a co-op unit, the documents of ownership that are exchanged are the shares of stock and the proprietary lease assigned to your particular co-op unit. If you finance your purchase of a co-op, you must find a lender, such as a bank, that is willing to accept the shares of stock as security for your loan (sometimes referred to as a *mortgage* even though it is a personal loan). You will be paying off this loan in monthly installments, just as you would if you mortgaged your condo unit. Like the condo owner, you also own a proportionate share of the common areas.

Most often the cooperative corporation will have a mortgage on the entire property (sometimes referred to as the *building mortgage),* which will not only affect the price of your co-op's shares but also your monthly fee to the co-op corporation. Your monthly charges cover the upkeep of the property, your share of the corporation's mortgage payments, and your share of the corporation's taxes on the entire property.

A major difference between owning a condo and a co-op is that the liability of a co-op owner is potentially much greater because his fate is financially linked to that of his neighbors. If your neighbor in a co-op fails to pay his maintenance, you and the other co-op owners will have to make up the difference—building mortgage payments and taxes must be paid. If they are not paid, the building will fall into the hands of the bank or under the authority of a court-appointed manager. In a condo the only risk to you of nonpayment of maintenance by your fellow condo owners is that the building will not be kept in as good repair. You may also find that the co-op is more expensive to finance because you must take out a personal loan at a generally higher interest rate than that charged for a mortgage loan.

Whether you are considering a condo or a co-op, keep in mind that there are two kinds of complexes within each of the two categories: (1) older complexes of condos and co-ops and (2) newly created ones. Whether buying an old or new apartment or unit, you should never be satisfied with a proposed sale until all the documents and the necessary information are made available to you. You should consult a lawyer, even though the documents in these transactions may appear routine. The dollar amount of the transaction mandates that you get the best legal protection you can before you put your name on the dotted line, not after. So, bearing in mind that the following cannot be expected to substitute for sound legal counsel, please read on.

Buying an existing condo

If you do not live in the New York City area or some other large urban area where cooperative ownership exists, chances are the apartment you buy will be a condominium. Unless the existing condo has been recently converted from a rental building (or is a brand-new one), a *prospectus* (offering plan) describing the condo will not usually be available. If you can obtain the prospectus, you will find that it contains much of the information you must have. With or without a prospectus, you should obtain and review the following information with your lawyer:

(1) *Financial statements* for the condominium that cover at least the past few years, and have been audited by a certified public accountant, plus unaudited interim statements for the current year. You should have the statements examined by an accountant or your attorney to determine whether the building is well managed. For example, if the monthly maintenance charge is constant and the net income of the building is decreasing, you know that maintenance costs are rising. If you find that there is no

special building fund for major repairs, you know you will have to pay your share of their cost.

(2) *The purchase and sales contract.* You should read this document as soon as possible, but sign it only after you have all the other information discussed in this section and only if you are satisfied that you are getting a fair deal. In most states a preprinted form of a condo contract will be available. You should go over the contract carefully with your attorney and make sure that every aspect of your purchase is covered by the form contract.

When completed, the contract must describe the condo unit in detail and state your share of the common condominium property that goes with your particular unit. The document will mention you as the buyer and specifically state who the seller is; specify the purchase price, including the amount of the down payment; and specify the maintenance fees. It should also state the amount of real estate taxes on your unit. The contract will also set a *closing date*—the date when you and your lawyer sit down to complete the real estate transaction. In addition, it should contain representations and warranties by the seller stating, for example, that the title is free and clear of any claims and that the physical condition of the unit is as promised by the owner. If you are being given a mortgage by the seller, the contract should state the amount of the monthly mortgage payments. There should also be warranties about previous special assessments, if there have been any, as well as a disclosure about the finances of the condo project, such as the cash reserves for repair of the common areas.

There are other things to watch out for. Make sure that there is no misunderstanding between you and the seller about which items are personal property that the seller intends to take with him and which are fixtures that stay with the apartment. Does the contract clearly provide that you are buying certain fixtures—the dishwasher? the windowshades? the walnut bookshelves? You should know whether you are excused from closing (and therefore entitled to get your deposit back) if you cannot get financing.

(3) *The enabling declaration,* or *master deed.* This document describes the physical location and size of the condominium's land, buildings, each individual condo unit, and the common areas. It declares the monetary value of each unit and the percent share each unit has in the common areas and the number of votes in the condo association that this percent share represents. It contains the conditions and restrictions of condominium ownership and provides for the establishment of a condominium association, composed of the owners of condo units. The board of directors of the association has the power to administer the condominium complex, including the right to set rules and regulations and the penalties for breaking them. For example, the board determines what will happen to you if you fail to pay a special assessment or your monthly maintenance fee. The master deed should also cover such necessities as hiring a management company to run the complex and keep it in good repair, insurance costs, and the maintenance budget for the common areas.

(4) *The association bylaws and house rules.* These contain all the rules and regulations of the condo, including specific guidelines for the condo board of directors. The bylaws will be explicit about the requirements for election to the condo board, for meetings of both the board of directors and the association, and for voting at the meetings. The bylaws also provide for dues and special assessments, use and maintenance of the common property, and provisions for professional management.

(5) *A mortgage* (or, in California, a *deed of trust*) and related documents. If you are borrowing money to buy your condo unit, these documents will show the amount of your personal obligation to the lender and the pledge of the condominium association to the lender to secure the loan if you have used the condo unit as security for the mortgage.

(6) *A list of special assessments* that have been paid by the building's condo owners during the past three years and any proposed special assessments. A special assessment is a charge for unanticipated expenses, such as a jump in fuel prices or the cost of replacing a collapsed roof or worn-out elevators. If the cost of fuel oil rose 15 percent in the past year, you should know the effect these price jumps had on the condo's maintenance charges or special assessments.

(7) *The current contract with building employees.* Escalations projected under that contract (and the effect they will have on maintenance) and the contract's renewal date are important to know.

(8) *A summary of the physical and structural condition* of the building, including any projected major repairs. From this you can assess how realistic the current maintenance charges are and what the prospect is for a future special assessment.

(9) *A copy of the management agreement.* If a management company operates the building, are the rates fair? When does the agreement expire?

(10) *A title search.* This is something your attorney must do to make sure that the seller is selling you the condo free and clear. If available, you should buy title insurance from a reputable title company.

Buying an existing co-op

If you are thinking of buying an existing co-op, you should review the following information and documents with your lawyer, much of which is similar to what you must look at if purchasing a condo:

(1) *Financial statements,* as discussed above.

(2) *A copy of the proprietary lease used by the corporation.* (All tenants should be given the same lease.) The proprietary lease is the major declaration of your rights in the cooperative corporation. It states that you have an obligation to pay a monthly maintenance charge (the amount of which is based on the number of shares of stock you hold in the corporation) and that the corporation has the obligation to provide you with your apartment and, under the authority of the board of directors, to keep the building and its grounds in good shape. You are responsible for the care and general repair of the interior of your apartment, but the cooperative board has the authority to require you to correct any problem in your apartment (such as carpeting or soundproofing your apartment) or to limit the kind of appliances you have. Further, if you do not respond properly, the board can undertake to remedy such a problem or change the appliance and charge you for its action. This is the price you pay for the benefits of shared ownership.

(3) *Bylaws and house rules.* These will probably contain the rules specifying the percentage amount you must put down in cash for the co-op. The bylaws also provide the procedures for voting and state what constitutes a quorum at meetings of shareholders and directors, the size of the board of directors, what officers the co-op has, the form of the proprietary lease, the number of corporate shares, and routine corporate matters.

(4) *A list of special assessments* made during the past years, as discussed above in the section on condos.

(5) *The current contract with building employees.*

(6) *A summary of the physical and structural condition of the building,* including any projected major repairs, also as discussed in the condo section.

(7) *A copy of any management agreement* with a building management company, as discussed above.

(8) *Profiles of the members of the co-op's board of directors.* Ask your real estate agent to get this information for you. Insist that he be candid about the board's history of accepting applications. Your application for board approval is going to take time and effort. You may not want to go through this procedure if the board tends to be arbitrary in its decisions. Furthermore, some boards will not approve the sale unless you intend to pay for the unit fully in cash. Before you make an offer to buy a cooperative apartment, make sure that you understand what the board will approve with respect to financing.

(9) *Contract of sale.* After you have examined all of the above documents, you are ready to sign a contract of sale. As in the case of condos, in most states a preprinted form of the co-op contract will be available. Go over the contract carefully with your attorney, and make sure that every aspect of the transaction you are entering is covered.

In addition to the list of standard concerns already listed in the description of a condo sale or contract, you should check that the contract faithfully sets forth the number of shares you are buying, the percentage voting interest in the co-op corporation that these shares represent, the current maintenance, and any current or projected special assessments. Make sure that you will be able to get your deposit back if the board does not approve you. Do not neglect to find out what the cooperative apartment will charge for closing costs. It is traditionally the buyer's obligation to pay attorneys' fees incurred by the cooperative corporation for issuing a new proprietary lease and a new stock certificate.

(10) *Stock certificate.* This document is proof of your status as a shareholder in the cooperative corporation. When the stock is issued to you, you have the right to receive a lease for the apartment specified in your purchase agreement. Through your stock ownership, you have a voice in the operation of the building. You have a right to vote, and you may seek election to the building's board of directors.

(11) *A title search.* This search will differ somewhat from one done for a condo, but your lawyer will know how to handle it.

Buying a newly built or converted condo or co-op

Almost every state has laws governing the sale of real estate through new condominium or cooperative ventures, and these statutes dictate the specific documents required. If you are buying a unit in a new building, you will receive a prospectus (offering plan) that should disclose all the financial costs of shared ownership—for the present and for the near future. The prospectus will also include most of the documentation discussed above, but instead of a purchase agreement it will have a subscription agreement for you to sign.

If you live in one of the cities where conversions of rental buildings into condos or co-ops have become popular, you may face the prospect of being an involuntary buyer. In a conversion, the landlord of a rental building sells each apartment individually. Conversions are regulated by the state government.

If you are a tenant in a building that is being converted, you may wish to oppose the conversion or see that it goes through on terms that are fair to the tenants. In either case, the tenants as a group should hire an attorney who is experienced in condo or co-op conversions to advise all of you. Conversions can be advantageous to existing tenants, but to secure the benefits of conversion you need skilled professional guidance. By banding together and forming a tenants' committee, pooling the costs, and following your lawyer's advice, you may get the housing bargain of your life.

When a landlord is converting a building into a condo or co-op, the first question you may ask is, What is he trying to get away with? Clearly the landlord thinks he is going to make a lot more money from selling the apartments individually than if you were to keep paying him rent. You should assume that the landlord may do the following:

(1) Charge you more than the apartment is worth.

(2) Not fully disclose the physical condition of the building and therefore offer a repair fund that is wholly inadequate.

(3) Attempt to divide and conquer the tenants, who may prefer to keep the building as a rental.

As a tenant you have certain basic rights that are set forth in your state's laws. You will have a period of time before conversion during which your tenants' committee and your group lawyer should bargain for, demand, cajole, and otherwise solicit the following information on your behalf:

(1) A report of the condition of the building by an independent engineer. An apartment building involves considerably more maintenance problems than a single-family house. The cost of repairing a 20-year-old apartment building, for example, may be far beyond anything you might imagine.

(2) An estimate of fuel and electrical costs for the building by an independent engineer.

(3) If the building is being converted to a co-op, an analysis of the building mortgage.

(4) An examination of the warranties (guarantees) given by the landlord concerning the physical and financial condition of the building.

(5) The market value per room of the building on the open market versus the price asked by the landlord.

It is not unusual for tenants to get, through negotiations with their landlord, a substantial reduction of price per room, a substantial increase in the reserve or repair fund, and full disclosure of actual fuel and electrical costs.

If you are a prospective buyer of a unit being offered in a conversion of an existing building and are not a tenant, you should examine the information being offered just as closely as a tenant would. Every item listed above adds up to major dollars and cents for any buyer.

A word about lenders

If you are buying a newly converted or built co-op or condo, the best place to look for financing is to the owner or developer, because he often offers attractive financing with a low down payment as an inducement to buy. If you are buying from an individual seller, you should first see if his mortgage can be transferred to you and if its terms are better than those currently available. For example, the interest rate on his five-year-old mortgage may be lower than what you can presently obtain at a bank. If neither of these options is available, you will have to go to a financial institution, such as a bank.

Do not think that all lenders are alike. Their charges for fees for legal services and lending fees (that is, *points*) can vary greatly. You should know that the Federal Real Estate Settlement Procedures Act will help protect you. When you fill out a loan application, the lender is required to give you a good-faith estimate of each settlement charge you may incur plus a statement of the total cost of settlement. Among the fees that settlements may include are a survey fee to determine the exact location of the unit and a fee for termite or pest inspection. Some lenders require you to prepay certain items at the time of settlement, such as part of the interest on your mortgage or loan. Finally, some banks may require you to make a reserve deposit, known as an escrow account, from which future payments of recurring charges, such as real estate taxes, may be paid.

confidential relationship involves two elements, secrecy and trust. The relationship need not be a legal one. It may be moral, social, domestic, or personal. Some common examples are the trustee and the beneficiary of a TRUST, GUARDIAN AND WARD, ATTORNEY AND CLIENT, PARENT AND CHILD, and HUSBAND AND WIFE. Also included are principal and agent (see AGENCY), MASTER AND SERVANT, physician and patient (see PATIENTS' RIGHTS; PHYSICIANS AND SURGEONS) and, generally, all persons who are associated by a relationship of trust and confidence. These relationships are also known as FIDUCIARY relationships.

confiscation   Condemnation and seizure of private property without payment. Transporting untaxed cigarettes or alcoholic beverages, for example, or breaking the narcotics laws by being found with a trunkful of marijuana are typical violations of the internal-revenue laws that can incur confiscation. See also FORFEITURE.

conflict of interest   A conflict between a person's private interest and his responsibilities to others. It occurs when a person's own needs and wishes could lead him to violate his duty toward others who rightfully depend on him. For instance, when a lawyer has to decide whether to sue his own client or when a judge who is a shareholder in a corporation presides over a lawsuit concerning it, there is a conflict of interest. Government agencies and officials are particularly sensitive to charges of conflict of interest. They try to avoid even the appearance of such a conflict.

conflict of laws   The body of rules that directs the choice a court makes when the court must decide whether to apply the law of one state (or nation) or another to settle an issue in a case. When there is a conflict between the laws, principles called *choice of law* rules are applied to settle the question.

The COURTS of more than one state may have the authority to hear a lawsuit. When this happens the plaintiff can decide where to initiate his lawsuit. But because letting the plaintiff shop around for a friendly forum would be unfair to the defendant and inconvenient for the courts, courts try to be consistent in deciding which law to apply in various types of cases. Nevertheless, shopping around cannot be entirely prevented.

EXAMPLE Ted Jones, who lives in a big city in State A, rents O—* a cottage and spends the summer in State B with his gentle dog Tooth. While he is there, the dog bites a six-year-old neighbor named Frank Roberts. The next day, Jones returns to his home in State A. Mr. Roberts, Frank's father, wants to sue Jones for the expensive plastic surgery Frank needs. His lawyer tells him that the courts of State B have the power to hear cases involving injuries that occur within the state, but the courts in State A have the power to hear lawsuits against people who live in that state. Therefore, Roberts can sue in either state. His lawyer also tells him that the laws are different in the two states. State A has a law that will not allow recovery of money damages for injuries caused by dogs unless the owner knew before the injury that the dog had vicious tendencies. In State B, a statute makes owners liable for every injury their dogs cause. Roberts cannot be sure that

State B is the best place to start his lawsuit, however, until his lawyer checks the conflict of law rules in both states.

In this case, both State A and State B follow the rule in tort actions that they will apply the law in effect in the state where the injury occurred. Therefore, Roberts has a good chance of winning in either state because both will follow the law that holds owners strictly liable for injuries caused by their dogs. Roberts thinks that juries in the big city are likely to award a larger amount of money damages, so he finally decides to sue in State A rather than in rural State B despite its distance from his home.

There are several principles that may guide the court in the place where a case is being heard (called the *forum*) in deciding which law to apply to the case. When there is a statute that requires the application of the law of a particular place, then the statute must generally be followed. For example, a statute may say that no court in the state can enforce a contract requiring a debtor to pay more than 18 percent interest on a consumer loan. In this situation, no court in that state would enter judgment against a debtor for 20 percent interest even if the contract was legal in the state where it was made.

Another principle that courts may observe is called *false conflicts,* which means that, if the result will be the same regardless of which law the court applies, the court will generally apply the law of its own state.

When there is a genuine conflict among the laws of the states connected to a case, the forum court usually applies the law of the place where the event occurred for a case involving injuries to persons or property (tort) or for a criminal case. A breach of contract action is generally governed by the law of the place where the contract was made. These rules are not followed religiously, however. In recent years, courts have been more willing to apply the law of the place that has the most connection to the case if the traditional rules would cause an unjust result. This approach is called a *grouping of contacts,* or *finding the center of gravity.* Courts continue to apply the law of the place where the property is situated in almost all cases involving real property.

EXAMPLE Howard and his wife lived in State A. Their car O—* was registered and insured in State A, and Howard had a driver's license from that state. While they were driving through State B, their car collided with Amanda's car. Amanda was from State C, had her driver's license from that state, and registered and insured her car there. Howard died after the accident, and his wife sued Amanda in federal court in State A.

The first question that faced the court was which law to apply. In this case, State B limited the amount of damages recoverable in a wrongful-death action to $20,000, but State A set no limit. In State A, damages were calculated according to the amount of income that the deceased person could have been expected to earn in the remainder of a normal lifetime. Howard's expected earnings were an average of $50,000 each year for another 10 years. The traditional rule in tort cases was to apply the law of the place where the accident occurred, but the court applied the law of State A, allowing Howard's wife to collect $500,000. The court found that State B had almost no connection to the case. The law that limited liability in

State B was intended to protect residents of that state. People living there knew that they needed insurance only in that amount and could expect to collect only that amount if they were killed in an accident there. Amanda did not have those expectations. The state with the most significant contacts with the case was State A. It had a strong interest in providing for the widow so that she would not become a public charge.

Some states recognize a rule of conflicts called RENVOI, from the French word *renvoyer*, which means "to send back." This rule says that the forum court will, when it applies the law of another place, apply all the law of that place (called the "whole law"), including that jurisdiction's conflicts law. It may be that the other jurisdiction's conflicts law will say to apply the original forum's law, in effect sending the forum court's search back to where it started. Some American courts refuse to apply the doctrine of renvoi because it quickly becomes unnecessarily complicated.

There are some cases when a court will refuse to apply the law of another place because to do so would violate strong PUBLIC POLICY of the state where the lawsuit has been brought or of the country as a whole. For example, a court may refuse to apply a law that would give an inheritance to a person in a communist country where the government would probably confiscate the money.

conformed copy An exact copy of a document that contains written explanations of things that could not be copied. For example, the handwritten signature and date might be replaced on the typewritten copy of the document by the notation "signed by John Jones on March 3, 1980."

confrontation In criminal law, placing a witness face-to-face with a defendant. Then the witness may identify the defendant or the defendant may make any objection he has directly to the witness and cross-examine him.

confusion of goods A mixing together of the property of different persons so that it is not possible to tell what belongs to whom. Ordinarily, if someone fraudulently mixes his goods with another's so that they cannot be distinguished, he forfeits all his interest in the mixture to the other person. Oil is a common example of a substance to which the principle of confusion of goods might apply.

conglomerate A corporation that owns or is made up of companies in many different industries.

Congress The lawmaking branch of the federal government. This article is a general overview of the organization and function of Congress and the APPORTIONMENT of its members among the states, as well as the methods for their election and the regulation of their conduct. It also discusses the powers and functions of congressional committees. The HOUSE OF REPRESENTATIVES and the SENATE are also discussed under those headings, and the process of lawmaking is found under LEGISLATION.

The U.S. Constitution, Article I, Section 1, provides that
“ *All legislative Powers herein granted shall be vested in a Congress of the United States, which shall consist of a Senate and House of Representatives.* "

The two houses of Congress separately possess not only the powers granted to them by the Constitution but also any additional ones necessary to make effective use of these powers. Each house of Congress may determine the rules of its proceedings and appoint officers to assist in discharging its duties. See CONSTITUTIONAL LAW.

■ **Members** A member of Congress must take the oath of office as a senator or representative. Although he represents a state, he is a federal officer.

Election and qualifications Members of the House of Representatives and the Senate are chosen by the people of each state at elections prescribed by the legislatures of the state, subject only to changes dictated by Congress. The qualifications of members of Congress are limited to those regarding age, citizenship, and residence stated in the Constitution under Article I, Sections 2 and 3:

“ *No Person shall be a Representative who shall not have attained to the age of twenty five Years, and been seven Years a Citizen of the United States, and who shall not, when elected, be an Inhabitant of that State in which he shall be chosen.*"

“ *No Person shall be a Senator who shall not have attained to the Age of thirty Years, and been nine Years a Citizen of the United States, and who shall not, when elected, be an Inhabitant of that State for which he shall be chosen.*"

Apportionment By the dictates of the Constitution, representatives are apportioned among the states according to their populations, which are determined by the national census conducted every 10 years. No state receives less than one member. Each state is represented by two senators.

Division of state into districts Although not required by the Constitution, each state—except for those having only one representative—may be divided by its legislature into congressional districts. But states may not apportion congressional districts on a discriminatory basis. There must be equal representation for equal numbers, as discussed in the case of BAKER V. CARR. Any abuse of the power of the state legislature to apportion representatives among its districts is subject to intensive examination by the federal courts.

Primary elections and corrupt practices The states have a constitutional grant to regulate the nomination of members of Congress and may enact primary laws governing political-party nominations. Congress, however, may also make or alter such regulations. For example, Congress has enacted a Corrupt Practices Act, which limits how much candidates for the Senate and House may spend in primary elections.

Filling vacancies Under the authority of the Constitution and federal statutes, the state governor issues a writ of (a call for) election to fill vacancies in the Senate or the House of Representatives. He may also be permitted by the state legislature to make temporary appointments to the Senate until the vacancy is filled by an election. The dates for such elections are fixed by the states.

Ruling on elections Under Article I, Section 5, of the Constitution, each house of Congress is the judge of the elections, returns, and qualifications of its members. But neither the Senate nor the House of Representatives has the authority to exclude a duly elected person who meets the requirements of age, residency, and citizenship.

EXAMPLE In a case involving the late New York congressman Adam Clayton Powell, Powell sued the House of Representatives for refusing to seat him at the opening session of Congress. The House resolution to exclude Powell was based on misconduct that occurred before he was elected to that session. Powell claimed "that the House could exclude him only if it found he failed to meet the standing requirements of age, citizenship, and residence contained in Article I, Section 2, of the Constitution"—requirements the House found Powell met—and thus it had excluded him unconstitutionally. The U.S. Supreme Court agreed with Powell. He had been duly elected by voters of his district and was not ineligible to serve under any provision of the Constitution.

Salaries The compensation of members of Congress is fixed by federal statute.

Privileges and immunities Senators and representatives are privileged (exempt) from arrest while going to and from and during their attendance at sessions of their houses, in all cases except for TREASON, FELONY, or BREACH OF THE PEACE. They are not exempt from arrest, however, while Congress is in recess, nor are they exempt from the operation of ordinary criminal laws.

Article I, Section 6, of the Constitution provides that for "any Speech or Debate in either House, they [members of Congress] shall not be questioned in any other Place." The purpose of this clause is to promote free expression on the floor by relieving congressmen from fear of judicial proceedings. When a former congressman was convicted of conflict of interest and conspiracy to defraud the United States under federal statutes, the Supreme Court ordered a new trial because the evidence was based on the defendant's speech on the floor of Congress.

Probably the greatest benefit this right confers on members is that they may say what they wish during legislative deliberations without fear of being sued for slander or libel. The immunity provision applies to conduct at legislative committee hearings as well. But the protection does not extend to activities that are not part of the legislative process. A congressman, for example, is not protected for what he says in a newsletter to his constituents.

Expulsion Article I, Section 5, Clause 2, authorizes each house of Congress to punish its own members for disorderly behavior. Punishment may be censure, expulsion, or even imprisonment.

Criminal responsibility To insure integrity in government, various statutes make specific conduct by members of Congress a criminal offense. For instance, it is a crime for a member of Congress to receive money from someone in exchange for procuring a government contract. See BRIBERY. The statutes were enacted to keep a member from using his position for his own profit.

■ **Sessions** The 20th Amendment to the Constitution provides that Congress shall assemble at least once a year. Article II, Section 3, states that the President

❝ may, on extraordinary Occasions, convene both Houses, or either of them, and in Case of Disagreement between them, with Respect to the Time of Adjournment, he may adjourn them to such Time as he shall think proper.❞

■ **Administrative agencies** In the exercise of its legislative power, Congress may make use of PUBLIC ADMINIS-TRATIVE AGENCIES and boards for the enforcement of its policies and the determination of facts. Two examples are the National Highway Traffic Safety Administration and the National Mediation Board.

■ **Congressional committees** Either house, or both acting together, may investigate or form investigative committees to secure information for the exercise of their constitutional powers. The scope of the committee's authority is set at the time the information is sought, and it cannot be enlarged by subsequent action of Congress. The procedure may be informal, but there must be due regard for rights of witnesses. Congress may compel the attendance of witnesses or the production of evidence before it or its committees. Federal statutes assist investigations by requiring the attendance of witnesses, their full response to questions, and the production of records.

Subjects of investigation In determining the subject matter, scope, and extent of an inquiry, Congress has broad discretion. For example, to regulate interstate commerce, Congress has power to investigate all matters affecting commerce between the states, including nationwide organized crime. It may also secure information bearing solely on some aspects of intrastate commerce (commerce within a single state). See COMMERCE CLAUSE. Or an investigation may, for example, center on lobbying—activity intended to influence legislation by persuading a congressman to vote a certain way or to introduce a new bill.

Congress and its committees, however, cannot examine private citizens indiscriminately in the hope of stumbling on valuable information. The inquiry is limited to representations made directly to Congress, its members, or its committees. The fact that a person registers under the Federal Lobbying Act does not entitle a committee to investigate all his affairs.

Congress can investigate potential threats to itself and the country and may inquire into SEDITION, disloyalty, and espionage. In such an investigation, Congress is not limited to an appraisal of an organization's propaganda, but it may also look into the group's finances and personnel.

Compliance by witnesses Persons properly summoned by Congress by a SUBPOENA have the duty to comply. A witness before a congressional committee is not deprived of his legal rights or his constitutional privileges. He is not required to testify when he is physically or mentally unable to do so or if doing so would impair his health. He may rightfully refuse to answer questions if they exceed the power of the investigating committee or are not pertinent. If a witness has not been given a grant of IMMUNITY from prosecution, he may refuse to answer questions that tend to incriminate him. Millions of Americans became familiar with the phrase "taking the Fifth," when the Senate Crime Investigating Committee hearings were televised in the early 1950's. Witness after witness pleaded the Fifth Amendment of the Constitution and refused to answer questions that tended to incriminate them. See SELF-INCRIMINATION.

Congress has the power to punish those who thwart its investigations. The intentional failure of a witness to produce evidence or appear or give testimony before a congressional committee is the criminal offense of CONTEMPT of Congress, which is punishable by fine and imprisonment. Perjury (false testimony) committed by a witness is also a punishable crime.

Congressional Record

A printed daily record of the proceedings in Congress. The *Congressional Record* tells which bills were sent to and from committee and how each bill was voted on. The record also contains a substantially verbatim transcript of all speeches made on the floors of both houses.

conjugal

Belonging to or having to do with marriage. For example, conjugal rights are a husband's and wife's rights to mutual companionship, love, and sex.

connivance

The secret or indirect consent of one person to the commission of an unlawful act by another. For example, a husband might secretly hire a man to seduce his wife in order to bring a DIVORCE suit against her on the ground of adultery. Usually, however, the wife could use the connivance as a defense to the divorce suit.

consanguinity

The relationship of persons descended from the same stock or a common ancestor; kinship; blood relationship. *Lineal consanguinity* exists among persons who are descended from one another in a direct line such as a grandfather, father, and son. *Collateral consanguinity* is the relationship between persons who have the same ancestors but who do not directly descend one from another, such as uncle and nephew.

conscientious objector

A person who by reason of his religious training and belief is opposed to participation in war of any form. There are two classes of conscientious objectors. One group consists of persons opposed to both combatant and noncombatant military service. When compulsory military service is in effect, members of this group are exempt from being drafted but are compelled to serve in civilian work that contributes to the national welfare, such as the Goodwill Industries. The second group objects only to combatant military service. They are inducted into the military for noncombatant assignments, such as serving in the medical corps. See ARMED SERVICES.

A person's objection must be founded on deeply held moral, ethical, or religious beliefs. A religious belief need not be based on traditional concepts if it stems from moral, ethical, or religious convictions about what is right or wrong. Lastly, these beliefs must be sincerely held. The test of sincerity is subjective—that is, the important factor is what the *individual* believes. The objective (actual) truth of the beliefs does not bear on sincerity.

People serving in the armed services may obtain a release on the ground of conscientious objection, but they must satisfy certain tests established by the federal courts. They have to be opposed to war in any form and also to any type of service in the armed forces. Opposition to a particular war is not sufficient. A person does not have to be a total pacifist, however. He may, for example, be willing to use force to protect himself and his family. His objection to participation in war in any form must have become fixed after he had entered the service. An application for a discharge may not be denied on the basis that enlistment is inconsistent with a claim of conscientious objection.

consecutive sentence

See CUMULATIVE SENTENCE; SENTENCE.

consent

Voluntary and active agreement. If the parties to a lawsuit want to settle their disputes and end the case, they may do so by agreeing on a *consent judgment,* which is approved and recorded by the court. Another way of settling legal actions by consent is the *consent order.*

EXAMPLE Bert Lance, a former federal budget director, was accused by two federal agencies of civil fraud in violation of banking and securities laws. Two banks of which he had been a director were also named as defendants. The case did not go to trial. Lance, the banks, and the federal agencies agreed to a consent order whereby the court issued an injunction restraining Lance and the banks from future violations of those laws.

For other applications of the concept of consent, see ABORTION; ASSAULT AND BATTERY; PATIENTS' RIGHTS; and RAPE.

consequential damage

A loss or injury that does not follow directly from an act but only from its results. Let us say that a company failed to complete the installation of an elevator in an apartment house within the time provided by the contract. The plaintiff suing the company for the resulting loss of rents (the consequential damage) might be awarded compensatory DAMAGES.

conservator

A guardian of property, usually appointed by a court, for a person found to be legally incapable of managing his affairs. See GUARDIAN AND WARD.

consideration

The reason or main cause that induces a person to enter into a CONTRACT; a thing given or done, now or later, or abstained from, by one party to a contract, which is accepted by the other party as an inducement to perform his part of the agreement. Consideration is something of value that is transferred from one person to another. For example, two persons enter into a purchase-and-sale agreement for a $50,000 house. The buyer's agreement to pay $50,000 is consideration for the seller's promise to deed the house over to the buyer. The seller's pledge to deed the house is consideration for the buyer's promise to pay him $50,000.

consignment

The act of sending goods to a merchant or agent for sale. The consignor (shipper) usually retains ownership of the goods. For example, the owner of a painting might send it to a gallery on consignment.

consolidation

1 The act of uniting two or more lawsuits into one trial, when they are between the same parties, before the same court, and involve substantially the same subject matter, issues, and defenses. For example, when a mother brings two separate lawsuits against the same defendant for the deaths of her two minor daughters in the same automobile accident, the court will consolidate the two suits.

2 The uniting of two or more CORPORATIONS to form an entirely new corporation. The former corporations are completely extinguished, and the new one has the combined capital, franchises, and powers of the original. A consolidation is different from a MERGER, in which one corporation absorbs another and remains in existence while the other is dissolved.

consortium The conjugal fellowship of husband and wife and the right of each to the company, cooperation, affection, and aid of the other. Loss of consortium makes up part of the damages a husband suffers when, for example, his wife is injured or killed in a bus accident and he temporarily or permanently loses her services. He may include the value of the lost consortium in a lawsuit to recover for his wife's injury. For further discussion, see HUSBAND AND WIFE.

conspiracy The combination (joining together) of persons who make an agreement to commit an unlawful act or some act, innocent in itself, that becomes unlawful when done by the concerted effort of the conspirators.

■ **What a combination is** The essence of a criminal conspiracy is the combination. The crime of conspiracy is complete when the combination is formed—no overt act is necessary unless a statute says otherwise. The reason for this rule is that the joining together of persons to commit a crime presents a greater danger to society than does one person's criminal activity.

Number of persons Two or more persons must combine—a person cannot conspire with himself. One person also may be found guilty of conspiracy, however, if his coconspirator dies before indictment or is dead at the time of trial. Formerly a husband and wife could not be found guilty of conspiring with each other because the law considered them one person. Today a wife has a legal identity of her own, and a husband and wife can now be guilty of conspiracy.

A corporation may be one of the members of a conspiracy, and two corporations may form a conspiracy, but a conspiracy cannot be formed by the acts of one person who is an agent for two corporations.

When one of two persons merely pretends to agree to an unlawful enterprise—as a joke, to get the other person into trouble, or to entrap him—there is no conspiracy. But if three or more persons conspire to commit a crime, the fact that one of them only pretended to conspire or intended to stop the conspiracy will not prevent the other two from being convicted.

Necessity for an agreement The parties to a conspiracy must agree among themselves to commit an unlawful act, and they must enter into this agreement willingly. The conspiracy is brought about by the agreement.

Associating with conspirators does not make one a conspirator. If a person knows about or even approves of a conspiracy but does not agree to cooperate, he is not a coconspirator. He must deliberately commit himself to the conspiracy and be determined to further the common purpose.

Character of the agreement No written, formal, or definite agreement is necessary to make a conspiracy. It is enough if there is a meeting of the minds—a mutual, implied understanding of all parties working together with a single design. The crime of conspiracy may be committed whether or not the parties understand its entire scope, whether they act separately or together, and whether or not the parties are known to each other—as long as their actions lead to the same unlawful deed. The law does not set a particular length of time that the combination has to be formed before the unlawful deed. A time need not be set for the completion of the design. The agreement may result from hours of planning or may arise on the spur of the moment.

■ **Unlawful end or means** Either the object of the conspiracy or the means of accomplishing it must be illegal. There can be no conspiracy to do a lawful act in a lawful way. For example, persons who in good faith collaborate in a lawful effort to convict a person of a crime are not conspirators.

Some statutes require that the purpose must be to commit a crime. Under other statutes it is sufficient if the act agreed to is a civil wrong—that is, the planned act is corrupt, fraudulent, or immoral, and in that sense illegal. Not all acts for which there may be civil liability are the subject of criminal conspiracy—the unlawful act must be serious enough to be harmful to the general public. For example, if two real estate brokers, one representing a buyer and the other representing a seller, agree to split the commission the seller's broker receives, this is a breach of duty, not a conspiracy. While wrong in itself, the act is not serious enough to justify prosecuting the brokers for criminal conspiracy. However, the buyer and seller may sue the brokers, and the brokers may lose their licenses.

Among the indictable conspiracies are those to commit the following offenses: alteration of ballots, arson, assault, bribery, burglary, transferring land to an alien, embezzlement, false advertising, kidnapping, larceny or robbery, perjury, operating a lottery, or procuring an illegal abortion.

■ **Overt act** In states where the common-law rule concerning conspiracy is in effect, no overt act is needed to commit criminal conspiracy. The offense is done when the agreement is made and the combination formed. Some states have passed laws, however, that say an overt act must be attempted to complete the offense. The purpose of these statutes is to give the conspirators an opportunity to abandon the conspiracy and avoid the penalty before any decisive action is taken. Committing an overt act shows the continued existence of the agreement.

The overt act must follow the conspiracy agreement and be intended to carry out the purpose of the conspiracy—even if it fails to do so. Unless required by the conspiracy statute, it is not necessary that all the conspirators take part; an act by one of them is sufficient.

EXAMPLE Three men agree to kidnap a wealthy woman. One of the three stations himself near the woman's house so he can become familiar with her schedule. This is an overt act. All three can be convicted of conspiracy even though none of them are guilty yet of kidnapping or even an attempt to kidnap. The police can arrest them without waiting to see whether harm will be done.

Moreover, the overt act does not have to be the crime that is the purpose of the conspiracy. For example, three men are planning to rob a bank. One of them buys guns to use. That is an overt act, and it completes the conspiracy. They can be convicted even if arrested before they actually attempt the robbery.

Conspirators can be found guilty even if they did not profit from the crime, or if the purpose of their conspiracy was impossible to accomplish. Two or more persons who conspired to forge endorsements on federal bonds, for example, could be prosecuted although the forgeries were improperly done and the forger could never have obtained money for them from the government.

■ **Criminal intent**   There must be a corrupt motive or specific criminal intent to do either an unlawful act or a lawful act in an unlawful manner. A dual mental state is said to exist: the intent of the parties to act together and the intent to commit the unlawful act. The fact that the motive of a person was not corrupt when he joined a conspiracy does not free him from guilt if he remains a member after learning of its illegality.

EXAMPLE Ivan goes into partnership with two friends, Boris
O•——* and Bill, who are opening an employment agency to provide domestic help. One day, Ivan discovers that the work force is made up of illegal aliens whom Boris and Bill are smuggling into the country. Ivan wants no part of this enterprise. But it is his duty to quit the partnership or take some definite step to withdraw from the venture. Otherwise, he remains part of the conspiracy.

Guilty knowledge of the act done by the conspirators is a necessary element of the offense. For example, in order to convict the employees of an operator of a numbers game for conspiracy to evade payment of federal taxes, the government has to prove the employees knew their employer was liable for taxes on the profits from the gambling operation.

A person does not become criminally involved by providing services to the conspirators if he is unaware that the conspiracy exists. Acts done innocently and without criminal means, even though they tend to accomplish the conspiracy, do not make a person a coconspirator.

Sales to conspirators   In making sales to conspirators, the rule is let the seller beware. In one case the court held that a person who does not know about a conspiracy does not join it through the sale of materials or supplies to the conspirators—even if he realizes that the goods are for an illegal purpose. The defendants had sold yeast and other supplies to a person, knowing that he was going to manufacture liquor illegally. But they did not participate in the manufacture of the liquor, so, the court said, they could not be convicted of conspiracy to operate illegal stills.

A similar case, however, was decided differently.

EXAMPLE A drug manufacturer supplied a physician who
O•——* practiced in a community of 2,000 people with large quantities of morphine. Although all business was transacted by mail, and the manufacturer and physician had never met face-to-face nor had any personal communication except the mail-order business of drugs, the court found them guilty of conspiracy to violate a federal narcotics statute. The manufacturer knew from the large quantities purchased and the small town in which the physician lived that he must have been dispensing the drug illegally. Because the manufacturer continued to supply the drugs to make profits from the sales, the court

concluded that he had a stake in the physician's illegal activities, and that his continued sales to the physician constituted a conspiracy.

■ **Merger in other offenses**   In some states, when the objective of the conspiracy is a felony, the misdemeanor of conspiracy is merged into the felony and is no longer punishable. In most states, a conspiracy to commit a crime is a separate offense and is not merged into the crime itself. This means that a person can be convicted for both the crime and the conspiracy, even though the conspiracy is usually a misdemeanor and the crime a felony.

EXAMPLE Three men were found guilty of conspiring to
O•——* defraud the government by concealing the racetrack winnings of two of them. The third man cashed the winning ticket, worth more than $120,000, in his name in return for a percentage of the payoff. The two winners were then tried for income-tax evasion.

■ **Defenses**   In states where an overt act is essential to a conspiracy, a conspirator may avoid liability by showing that he voluntarily withdrew from the conspiracy before the act was committed. But he must have performed some act in good faith that demonstrated to his coconspirators that he was quitting. When no overt act is required to complete the offense of conspiracy, its subsequent abandonment by one or all of the conspirators does not relieve any of them from criminal responsibility.

The fact that an accused person neither derived nor expected to derive a monetary benefit is no defense to a charge of conspiracy. It is no defense, for example, that a person accused of conspiracy to commit an abortion was paid nothing for his participation.

constable   See SHERIFFS AND CONSTABLES.

constitute   Compose or make up. *Duly constituted* means properly put together, formally valid and correct.

constitutional law   A constitution is the basic law by which a system of government is created and from which it derives its power and authority. The essential difference between a constitution and a statute or ordinance is that a constitution generally states principles and establishes a foundation of law and government; a statute or ordinance must provide details of the subject it treats. A constitution, unlike a law, is intended not merely to meet existing conditions but to govern future contingencies. The term "constitutional law" designates the area of jurisprudence that deals with the nature, formation, amendment, operation, and interpretation of constitutions.

The purpose of a constitutional government is to secure for people certain unchangeable rights and remedies, and to shape and fix the limits of governmental activity. A constitution is not primarily designed to protect majorities, which are usually able to protect themselves, but to preserve and protect the rights of individuals and minorities against the arbitrary actions of those in authority. The U.S. Constitution, with its 26 amendments, is the supreme law of the land, which federal and state judges, legislators, and executives are bound by oath to enforce. The "supreme Law of the Land" as declared in Article 6, Section 2, of the Constitution, includes the Constitution, laws of the United

States made in accordance with it, and treaties made under the authority of the United States.

The constitution of a state, like that of the nation, is the supreme law within the realm of its authority. It is a limitation on the power of the state's legislature, binding on the several departments of state government, and on the people themselves, subject only to the restraints that result from the federal Constitution.

■ **U.S. Constitution** The Articles of Confederation were the fundamental body of national law established after the American Revolution by the 13 original states because of their need for unity. The Articles gave all federal power to the Continental Congress. The national government that was established, however, was weak and ineffective because the Articles required that all 13 states consent before the Continental Congress could take any action. One state could block a measure that the other 12 desired. The failure of the Articles to establish an effective centralized government led to the adoption of the U.S. Constitution. A convention of delegates representing 12 of the original states (Rhode Island did not take part) framed the Constitution in 1787. It was submitted to and then ratified by the states according to its provision for ratification.

Separation of powers To assuage the lingering fears about the powers of a centralized government, Articles I, II, and III, respectively, of the federal Constitution provide for the separation of governmental powers into legislative, executive, and judicial branches. It is an established and fundamental principle of the Constitution that one governmental branch cannot interfere with or encroach upon another unless expressly authorized by the Constitution. This prevents the concentration of the fundamental powers of government in the hands of a single person or group and protects the populace from possible arbitrary and oppressive acts of those who have political power. The tripartite division of government also creates a system of "checks and balances," which permits each branch to check on the others while having its own power balanced by the power of the others.

The legislative branch determines what the law shall be; the executive branch executes or administers the law; and the judicial branch interprets and applies the law. In theory, no branch can act in a capacity that has been solely confined by the Constitution to another branch. In actual practice, each of the three branches normally exercises powers that are not strictly within its province. The power of IMPEACHMENT, for example, is expressly vested by the Constitution in the legislature, and yet it is a judicial function, as it involves a trial of the President or other high public official to determine whether he should be removed from office.

Legislative branch Legislative power includes authority to investigate, conduct hearings, and do whatever is necessary and proper in making laws. Article I of the Constitution vests federal legislative power in CONGRESS. This power consists of express, or enumerated, powers specifically set forth in Article I, Section 8; implied powers, which are derived from those express powers; and certain sovereign or inherent powers, which are not created by the Constitution, but which all branches of the federal government possess as a government, such as the power to expel

undesirable aliens. Among its enumerated powers Congress has the authority to regulate interstate and foreign commerce under the COMMERCE CLAUSE, to establish and maintain a national currency, to tax and collect duties on imports, to establish and maintain post offices, and to declare WAR and maintain ARMED SERVICES. See also CUSTOMS; POST OFFICE; TAXATION.

Article I, Section 8, Clause 18, of the U.S. Constitution empowers Congress

❝ To make all Laws which shall be necessary and proper for carrying into Execution the foregoing Powers, and all other Powers vested by this Constitution in the Government of the United States, or in any Department or Officer thereof.❞

This clause, known as the necessary and proper clause, is the basis of the doctrine of implied powers. It gives Congress the appropriate means to accomplish its express powers. For example, Congress has the express power to establish post offices. From this is implied the power to acquire land on which to build post offices. The power to investigate, to hold hearings, to compel witnesses to attend, and to enforce this power by the punishment of contempt are all given to Congress by the necessary and proper clause.

Although Congress may make laws, it is expressly forbidden by Article I, Section 9, of the Constitution to enact any bills of attainder or ex post facto laws. A *bill of attainder* is a legislative act that inflicts punishment without a judicial trial. A law that deports a citizen on the ground of his country of origin alone, for instance, is a bill of attainder. An *ex post facto* law is one that (1) makes punishable as a crime an act that was committed before the law was passed and that was lawful at the time it was committed, (2) makes a crime a greater offense than it was when it was committed, or (3) alters the legal rules of EVIDENCE required for conviction of the crime.

EXAMPLE John is charged with criminal assault for beating O—※ his wife with a baseball bat. The maximum sentence he can receive under the statute is three months in jail. John pleads guilty because he feels that a three-month separation might improve the marriage. While he is waiting to be sentenced, the state legislature, citing the increased number of assaults, changes the statute so that the maximum sentence is increased to five years, to be applied retroactively to all cases in which a sentence has not yet been determined. The new statute drastically alters John's situation, because the court will not allow him to change his guilty plea to not guilty. He would not have pleaded guilty if he had known he might be in jail for five years. But the new statute must be ruled unconstitutional as far as John is concerned, because it is an ex post facto law. His sentence will not be affected. The law will be valid, however, for criminal assaults committed after its effective date.

If a new statute authorized a shorter prison sentence than the former statute—in other words, if there is a change that benefits the individual who broke the law—in most jurisdictions the new statute may be applied retroactively.

The constitutional prohibition of ex post facto laws applies only to criminal matters, not to civil matters. The purpose of the prohibition is to insure substantial personal rights against arbitrary and oppressive legislation, because laws that make an innocent act criminal after it has been

SOME POINTS OF CONSTITUTIONAL LAW

■ The Constitution gives Congress the power to make laws but forbids Congress to enact bills of attainder or ex post facto laws. A *bill of attainder* is a legislative act that inflicts punishment without a trial. An *ex post facto law* punishes an act committed before the law was passed or puts a greater penalty on a crime than was legal when the crime was done.

■ A court cannot annul a law or declare it void unless the law contradicts the Constitution.

■ Anyone (even a noncitizen) can argue that a statute is unconstitutional if he personally will be injured by it.

■ Persons who do not belong to the class alleged to be discriminated against by a statute cannot attack its validity—for example, a man cannot challenge a statute that discriminates against women.

■ A person who has tried unsuccessfully to use a statute in a proceeding for his own benefit cannot later attack its constitutionality in an appeal from the decision or in a subsequent case involving the same law.

■ An accused person may waive any constitutional right that does not affect the rights of others and the jurisdiction (authority) of the court. If, for example, an accused and his lawyer decide not to challenge a jury from which blacks have been unlawfully excluded, that objection is waived and cannot be raised in a later proceeding. A waiver of a constitutional right must be voluntarily made, with the accused fully aware of his rights. The waiver must not be the result of duress or misrepresentation.

■ To protect the accused from an unwilling or an unintentional waiver, courts presume that his fundamental constitutional rights have not been waived unless the evidence clearly shows otherwise.

■ If a person is serving a prison sentence after being convicted of a crime under a statute that is subsequently declared unconstitutional, he can apply in court for a writ of habeas corpus in order to be released.

performed or that aggravate an offense are harsh and oppressive.

Executive branch The function of the executive branch is to administer and enforce the laws as written by the legislature and interpreted by the courts. Article II of the U.S. Constitution vests the executive power in the PRESIDENT. It confers on him the authority to carry out the laws passed by Congress and requires him to report to Congress on the state of the union and to recommend appropriate action. Executive power over domestic matters includes the power to commute or PARDON offenses against the United States but not against the individual states; the power to VETO bills passed by Congress; the control of executive employees by appointment and removal; the power to issue proclamations and orders; and the responsibility for directing the administration of laws.

All power over international matters rests with the President, except that TREATIES must be ratified by the Senate, and the President may not deprive persons of their constitutional rights. As Chief Executive and Commander in Chief of the armed forces, under Section 2 of Article II, the President can seize property under the war powers, govern any captured territory until Congress establishes a civil government, declare martial law when and where there is an actual and present danger that civil administration is about to cease functioning, and end a war by treaty or presidential proclamation. But the President may not declare war; this power is given to Congress under Article I, Section 8.

Judicial branch The judicial branch has the power to hear and determine those matters that affect life, liberty, or property. It is charged with interpreting and applying the law. The judicial power of the federal government is, by Article III of the federal Constitution, vested in the SUPREME COURT and lower tribunals established by Congress. The judiciary must accept the law as it is enacted by the legislature, unless a law is plainly contrary to the Constitution.

The courts may declare the meaning and the effect of statutes, but they cannot legislate under the guise of statutory interpretation and construction. If a statute is plain and unambiguous, the court must enforce it as it is written. Courts determine what the rules of common law are, and adapt and apply them to new situations, but only the legislature may make changes in the common law. See also COURTS; FEDERAL COURTS.

Relations among the states Article IV of the U.S. Constitution sets forth certain relationships among the states and between the states and the federal government. The major provisions of Article IV are

(1) FULL FAITH AND CREDIT clause, which is the basis upon which one state will recognize the public acts, records, and judicial proceedings of another state.

(2) PRIVILEGES AND IMMUNITIES clause, which prohibits a state from discriminating against citizens of another state.

(3) EXTRADITION clause, which provides for the return of a fugitive from justice who flees to another state.

(4) Property clause, which gives Congress sole discretion to deal with property it owns, such as a military base, even though it is within a state (called a federal enclave).

(5) Guaranty clause, by which the federal government guarantees each state a republican form of government.

In addition to these provisions in Article IV, which deals exclusively with the states, Article I, Section 10, forbids the states to exercise certain powers. These powers include the power to enter into treaties, coin money, impair CONTRACTS, or pass bills of attainder or ex post facto laws.

Finally, the equal protection clause of the 14th Amendment to the Constitution prohibits any state from denying to any person within its jurisdiction the EQUAL PROTECTION OF LAWS. This means that, under similar circumstances and conditions, all persons subject to state legislation shall be treated alike, both in privileges conferred and liabilities imposed. The clause is intended to secure equality of rights and to safeguard against intentional and arbitrary discrimination. As long as they are physically present in the state, all persons—including aliens and citizens of other states—are entitled to the equal protection of the laws of that state. This protection extends to private corporations, either domestic or foreign, when they are within the jurisdiction of that state. Not every discrimination between foreign and domestic corporations or between corporations and natural persons is a denial of equal protection, if there is a rational basis for the difference in treatment.

Amending the U.S. Constitution Under Article V the federal Constitution specifically provides the manner by which it can be amended. Amendments may be proposed by a vote of two-thirds of both houses of Congress or by a convention called by the legislatures of two-thirds of the states. An amendment does not become a part of the Constitution unless it is "ratified by the Legislatures of three fourths of the several States, or by Conventions in three fourths thereof." If a state votes to reject an amendment, it can reconsider and adopt it later. It is unclear at the moment whether a state that has ratified an amendment may subsequently rescind or nullify the ratification prior to the adoption of the amendment. Three states—Idaho, Nebraska, and Tennessee—have rejected the Equal Rights Amendment after having ratified it. Which are valid—the rejections or the ratifications—is a political question for Congress to determine.

■ **Rights of the people** The U.S. Constitution not only dictates how the government shall be set up, it also prohibits the government from interfering with certain fundamental rights of the people, including both political rights and CIVIL RIGHTS. *Political rights* are those that entitle a citizen to participate—directly or indirectly—in the government. The right to vote and the right to petition the government are political rights guaranteed by the Constitution. *Civil rights* are those belonging to a person by virtue of his citizenship, including the right to life, liberty, and property. Most of the civil rights guaranteed by the Constitution are listed in the Bill of Rights, and the government is prohibited from doing anything that will unjustly violate those rights.

The Bill of Rights is enumerated in the first 10 amendments to the U.S. Constitution, which provide for

(1) Freedom of speech, religion, press, assembly, and the right to petition the government. See ASSEMBLY, RIGHT OF; RELIGION, FREEDOM OF; SPEECH AND PRESS, FREEDOM OF.

(2) The right to bear arms. See ARMS, RIGHT TO BEAR.

(3) Freedom from being forced to give room or board to soldiers, except during time of war as prescribed by law.

(4) Freedom from unreasonable SEARCH AND SEIZURE, and the requirement that no warrants for search or seizure be issued without probable cause.

(5) The requirement that a person cannot be tried for a crime without an INDICTMENT; the prohibition against DOUBLE JEOPARDY; the freedom from SELF-INCRIMINATION (testifying against yourself in a criminal trial); and the requirement that no rights be taken away without DUE PROCESS OF LAW, and that no property be taken by the government by EMINENT DOMAIN without just compensation.

(6) In all criminal prosecutions, the right to a speedy trial, counsel (see COUNSEL, RIGHT TO), an impartial JURY, knowledge of the CHARGES, CONFRONTATION of adverse witnesses, and the compulsory attendance of WITNESSES in court. See COMPULSORY PROCESS.

(7) In all civil lawsuits, the right to a jury trial, "when the value in controversy shall exceed \$20."

(8) The prohibition against excessive BAIL, excessive fines, and CRUEL AND UNUSUAL PUNISHMENT.

(9) The fact that some rights are spelled out in the Constitution does not mean that these are all the rights that people have.

(10) Reserving for the states and the people any powers not belonging solely to the federal government.

Originally the Bill of Rights was a limitation on the power of the federal government only. If a state or local authority deprived you of a right, the federal Bill of Rights did not protect you. The 14th Amendment, through its due process of law and equal protection clauses, is used by the courts to meet this problem. It is construed (interpreted) to make most of the guarantees of the Bill of Rights applicable to the states by selective incorporation. This means the Supreme Court incorporates rights from the Bill of Rights into the 14th Amendment in lawsuits contesting the deprivation of particular rights. The Court traditionally incorporates fundamental rights, which are "principles of justice so rooted in the traditions and conscience of our people as to be ranked fundamental."

Although it is not listed specifically in the Constitution, the right of privacy is also held to be a constitutional right because many of the other provisions of the Bill of Rights imply it. See PRIVACY, RIGHT OF.

The right to travel is another implied fundamental right given by the Constitution.

In addition to these rights, there is the right to freedom. The 13th Amendment to the Constitution, enacted after the Civil War, abolished involuntary servitude—that is, compelling a person by force, coercion, or imprisonment and against his will to work for another, whether or not he is paid. The amendment does not, however, forbid enforcement of those duties that individuals owe to the state (such as jury service) or to the country (such as service in the armed forces).

■ **State constitutions** Eleven of the original 13 states had adopted constitutions upon their separation from the mother country, England, and these became the first constitutions of the states' independent existence. These constitutions—promulgated by conventions without submission to the people, except in Massachusetts—all antedate the U.S. Constitution. (Connecticut and Rhode Island were among the original 13 states, but they continued to govern themselves under the provisions of their colonial charters and did not adopt constitutions until 1818 and 1842 respectively—although they declared their independence.) Through the power the federal Constitution gives Congress over the admission of new states to the union, Congress has been able to control the formation and the subject matter of the constitutions of all states admitted into the union after the original 13.

Like the federal Constitution, the various state constitutions have their own bills of rights for the protection of their citizens. They also incorporate provisions that dictate how the state governments are to be set up, allowing for the separation of powers. The governor as chief magistrate of the state is vested with the executive power of the state. He is confined to exercising the powers conferred on him by the state's constitution and its laws. The legislature is empowered to pass state laws. Unless prohibited by the particular state constitution, the legislature may delegate to local governmental agencies the power to legislate local affairs—for example, to pass regulations concerning streets, highways, and sewers. Within constitutional limits the legislature may also delegate power to levy taxes for local purposes. A state judiciary system hears cases brought on state laws. State courts cannot hear federal cases.

Police power   State constitutions also regulate how the state's police power is to be exercised. *Police power* is the state's right to make laws and regulations to protect the health, safety, morals and well-being of its people—such as requiring all physicians to be licensed to practice in the state in order to protect the citizens from incompetence.

The United States has no police power, since none has been given to it by the federal Constitution or by the states. The police power rests with the individual states and is primarily vested in the state legislatures. The power may be exercised by subordinate government divisions, such as cities, towns, and villages, to the extent that a state has delegated them police power. Although it is difficult to fix bounds definitely, as a general rule the possession and enjoyment of all rights are subject to a reasonable exercise of the police power. Each state must determine for itself, subject to fundamental rights and liberties guaranteed by the federal Constitution, how it shall exercise the power.

Securing the general welfare, comfort, and convenience of the people is the real object of the police power. It is the right and duty of a state to pass laws for the preservation of public health. For instance, a state requirement that all school-age children be vaccinated against diphtheria is a valid exercise of the police power, as are actions in the interest of the public safety. Public nightclubs and theaters must comply with state and local fire codes requiring reasonable fire escapes and other precautions to protect the public in case of fire. In the exercise of the police power, legislatures may enact laws to maintain public peace and good order. Thus, drunk and disorderly conduct in public places can be punished. The police power can be exerted to preserve and protect the public morals by making prostitution a punishable crime. It may also extend to the regulation of cigarettes, billboards, dance halls, and racetracks. The police power may also be validly exercised to provide relief in emergency situations such as setting up sleeping facilities in a local high school gym for victims of a fire.

Businesses and occupations are subject to regulation under the police power, but the regulations must not be unreasonable or arbitrary. Occupations that are regulated include, among others, accounting, barbering, plumbing, and the sale of securities, as well as the professions of law, medicine, and optometry, which if practiced by persons without specialized training would present a danger to public health and welfare.

The police power has its limitations. It must be exercised only under conditions that are reasonable and for the public good, and always with scrupulous regard for constitutionally guaranteed rights. The government may not use the police power arbitrarily to invade the liberty of an individual—the limitation must have some relationship to the safety of the state.

EXAMPLE The Supreme Court has held that a woman has
O—*   the fundamental right to choose whether to bear children and that the constitutional right to life, liberty, and privacy includes the right to terminate a pregnancy by abortion. A state requirement that refused a woman a therapeutic abortion unless she had been a resident of the state for a certain length of time was ruled to violate the constitutionally protected right to travel.
See ABORTION.

The state constitution may limit the scope of the police power. Courts have the duty to pass on the validity of police regulations and to enforce those passed by the legislature in good faith and with reasonable regard for the protection that the state owes to its citizens.

Amending a state constitution   Generally, the people of a state are supreme in determining what their constitution shall be. Subject to the limitations of the federal Constitution, they may amend their constitution only by the method prescribed in it. An amendment is any addition, deletion, or rewriting that effects a change in any of the constitution's provisions. The power to amend a constitution includes the power to repeal a provision or even to replace the entire constitution with a new one. Before it can become effective an amendment must generally be ratified by the people and it remains in effect until it is voted out by the people.

Some state constitutions authorize the state legislature to frame and submit constitutional amendments to the people. Others call for amendment by a constitutional convention. A state legislature can call a constitutional convention and provide for the election of delegates to the convention even when its constitution does not specifically provide for this.

Authorities are divided on the question of the powers of a constitutional convention. Under the *strict view,* a constitutional convention has only the powers expressly conferred on it by the act of the legislature that assembled it, together with the implied powers necessary to carry out its purpose. According to this view, the power of the convention is limited to the framing of proposals for changes in the constitution for submission to the people; the convention has no power to promulgate amendments to the existing constitution.

According to the *liberal view,* the members of a constitutional convention are the direct representatives of the people and may exercise all sovereign powers that are vested in the people of the state. Some state constitutions have been proclaimed by the conventions without submission to the people, and in no case have the actions of the conventions been judicially declared illegal. Generally, however, when the law does not give the convention the power of independent legislation, convention ordinances must be ratified (approved) by the people.

Ratification by the people is a vital element in amending constitutions, but the people cannot modify a proposed amendment submitted to the popular vote—they must accept or reject it as submitted. The number of votes required to ratify a constitutional amendment is usually specified in the constitution or in the act submitting the amendment.

■ **Operation and effect of constitutions**   A constitution usually takes effect when it is ratified. In the case of the admission of a TERRITORY to statehood, provisions of the act admitting it may fix the effective date of its constitution. An amendment to the constitution may take effect either on the day it becomes law or at a later date fixed by the constitution or the amendment.

Provisions added   A constitutional provision is not retroactive unless its language or purpose clearly indicates otherwise. As a general rule, a right or claim is not denied by the subsequent enactment of a constitutional provision regulating or affecting its subject matter. For example, the right of an employee who was injured on his job to sue his employer would not be affected by a constitutional provision for WORKMEN'S COMPENSATION adopted after his injury. On the other hand, liability for penalties and forfeitures incurred under statutes made invalid by the repeal of a constitutional provision cannot be enforced after repeal, nor can prosecutions for offenses committed under repealed statutes be continued or begun. When the 18th Amendment to the federal Constitution (which prohibited the manufacture, sale, and transportation of alcohol) was repealed by the ratification of the 21st Amendment, pending federal prosecutions for traffic in intoxicating liquors were not continued. See PROHIBITION.

Provisions of a constitution that are not continued in force by a new constitution are superseded when the new constitution is adopted. But a new constitution does not necessarily supersede the entire body of statutory law. If existing statutes are not expressly or implicitly repealed by the constitution or its amendments, they remain in full force and effect. A saving clause—a clause that excepts, or "saves," specified matters from the consequences of constitutional provisions—may continue statutes in force. The COMMON LAW, where it is not in conflict with the constitution, remains in effect on the adoption of a constitution. Statutes enacted in anticipation of new constitutional provisions have been upheld, even though at the time they were enacted the constitution prohibited the legislation. For instance, a state legislature may pass a law creating a joint city-county board of tax assessors in anticipation of a constitutional amendment authorizing the board to levy property taxes. But certain nonlegislative acts in anticipation of constitutional changes are invalid and ineffective—for example, executive appointments made in anticipation of vacancies pending constitutional changes.

Self-executing provisions   A constitutional provision is self-executing when it is complete in itself and is effective without the aid of supplemental or enabling legislation. For example, a constitutional provision that forbids the manufacture or sale of intoxicating liquors or their transportation is self-executing. On the other hand, provisions declaring that the state shall control the manufacture and sale of intoxicating liquors under laws to be enacted by the legislature cannot be carried out until the supplementary legislation is passed.

The provisions in the bills of rights of the federal and state constitutions and provisions conferring privileges or imposing liabilities are generally self-executing, and so is the right to vote granted by the U.S. Constitution to persons having specified qualifications. A constitutional provision for free ELECTIONS, however, is not self-executing but requires the legislature to provide for the conduct of elections and the method of selecting nominees.

■ **Constitutionality of statutes**   A constitution is the supreme written will of the people who have adopted it as a framework or basis for their government. The validity of an act of Congress depends primarily on whether or not power to enact it has been granted by the U.S. Constitution, either expressly or by implication. The validity or constitutionality of a state statute depends on whether or not it violates the limitations or prohibitions of the state or federal constitution. A statute will not be held unconstitutional merely because it violates the natural, social, or political rights of citizens unless it can be shown that these rights are guaranteed and protected by the U.S. Constitution, or, where appropriate, by the state constitution. In general, a court cannot annul an act or declare it void unless it contradicts the U.S. or applicable state constitution.

Persons entitled to raise constitutional questions Anyone, including ALIENS, can argue that a statute is unconstitutional if he personally will be harmfully affected by it. Its operation must deprive him of a constitutional right, thereby giving him what is known as STANDING. A person who has merely a public interest in the constitutionality of a statute does not have standing. The federal government can assert that a statute is inconsistent with the federal Constitution. A state (represented by its governor or attorney general, for example) or any of its subdivisions may question the validity of an enactment of its own legislature when the state is adversely affected by the statute. Generally the interest of a public official, as such, is not sufficient to entitle him to question the validity of a law. Like a private citizen, he may do so only if he can show that it affects his personal rights.

The question of the constitutionality of a law on which the court bases a decision may be raised only by parties to a lawsuit whose rights are affected by the law. In criminal prosecutions, the accused can assert the invalidity of the law, regulation, or rule under which he is being prosecuted, because, clearly, he is personally and adversely affected.

Persons not belonging to the class alleged to be discriminated against cannot attack the validity of a statute on the ground that it discriminates between persons or classes of persons. Thus, a man cannot challenge a statute that discriminates against women.

Waiver or estoppel   In general, the right to assert a constitutional right or to challenge the constitutionality of a statute may be lost by WAIVER or ESTOPPEL. Once a person waives (gives up) a constitutional right, he is estopped (prevented) from alleging that someone has violated that right. In such a case, waiver results from estoppel, which in turn may be created by conduct that is inconsistent with the exercise of the right.

EXAMPLE   The right to picket—a private, individual right protected by provisions of the Constitution relating to freedom of speech—was waived (relinquished) by members of a local union who entered into collective bargaining with the management of their plant. Once the union signed the new contract, which prohibited strikes, its members were estopped (barred) from exercising their constitutional right to strike. They had, by contract, waived their constitutional right to strike.

Estoppel may also result from a person's unsuccessful challenge of an allegedly unconstitutional law. If a person participates, without any objections, in judicial or quasi-judicial civil proceedings based upon a statute that is unconstitutional, he by fair inference acknowledges the validity of the statute and cannot attack it. For example, a person who has tried unsuccessfully to use a statute in a proceeding for his own benefit cannot later attack its constitutionality in an appeal from the decision or in a subsequent proceeding involving the same statute.

Waiving rights of accused Whether an accused in a criminal case can waive constitutional rights depends on the nature of the particular rights. In general, he may waive any constitutional right that does not affect the rights of others and the jurisdiction (authority) of the court. If an accused and his counsel decide not to challenge a jury from which blacks have been unlawfully excluded, that objection is waived and cannot be raised in a later proceeding. In order to be valid, the waiver must be made voluntarily and with understanding, with the accused fully aware of his rights. It must not be the result of duress or misrepresentation.

In recent years the validity of a waiver of constitutional rights by a person accused of a crime has been a hotbed of controversy. Beginning with the MIRANDA V. ARIZONA case in 1966, both the federal and state courts have tried to define clearly what is acceptable as a valid, intelligent waiver of constitutional rights under the Fifth and Sixth Amendments. To protect the accused from an unwilling or unintentional waiver, courts presume that fundamental constitutional rights have not been waived unless the evidence clearly shows otherwise. See COUNSEL, RIGHT TO; FIFTH AMENDMENT.

Determination of constitutional questions The final authority in determining whether or not the legislature, in enacting a statute, acted within its constitutional authority, is vested in the judiciary. In a JUSTICIABLE case (one proper to be examined in court), it is the duty of the courts to declare an unconstitutional statute void, even if in the past it has been treated as constitutional. This power, however, must be exercised with caution, and a statute should be upheld as constitutional if it is reasonably possible to do so.

The federal courts determine whether state and federal legislation violates the U.S. Constitution, but usually state courts are the final arbiters as to whether state laws conflict with the state constitution. State courts may also declare state statutes to be in violation of the federal Constitution.

Generally courts will rule on the constitutionality of a statute only if, and to the extent that, it is directly and necessarily involved in a real controversy subject to court action. The decision regarding constitutionality must be essential to the protection of the parties concerned. General or vague attacks on a statute will not be considered. In order to warrant determination by the court, constitutional questions must be duly raised and insisted upon at the earliest time possible in the trial, usually in the PLEADINGS. Determining the constitutionality of a statute, which is a question of law, generally involves what is called a CONSTRUCTION of the statute—deciding its sense or real meaning, including its terms, objects, purposes, practical operation, and effect as a whole.

A statute is presumed to be valid and constitutional. Therefore, the party attacking a statute has, first of all, the burden of overcoming this presumption by rebutting every reasonable basis that might support its classification as a valid statute. Secondly, he must show clearly or beyond a reasonable doubt that the statute is unjustly discriminatory or that its classification is arbitrary or unreasonable, at least when applied to him; or that it is in violation of the EQUAL PROTECTION OF LAWS guaranteed by the 14th Amendment of the federal Constitution.

Declaring unconstitutionality A statute declared unconstitutional generally becomes null and void as of the date of its enactment. It then binds no one, confers no rights, affords no protection, and imposes no duties. If a person, for example, is serving a prison sentence after being convicted of a crime under a statute that is declared unconstitutional, he can apply in court for a writ of HABEAS CORPUS in order to be released from custody. The courts have the power to grant additional relief, such as erasing the record, if appropriate under the facts of the case. When only a particular part of a challenged statute is found to be unconstitutional, that part will be declared void and of no legal effect, but the rest of the statute will remain in effect.

construction A decision, usually by a judge, of the meaning and legal effect of ambiguous or doubtful words, terms, or provisions in a statute, a written document (such as a contract), or an oral agreement. The court arrives at a construction by looking not only at the words themselves but also at surrounding circumstances and relevant laws and writings. By taking into consideration all these factors, the court determines the probable aims of the doubtful provision. Construction can be used only to discover the true intent and meaning of an ambiguous statement; it cannot be used to change the meaning. When the language is plain and obvious, the provision must be applied as stated. For a full discussion of how laws are construed, or interpreted, see STATUTE. See also CONSTITUTIONAL LAW.

A *strict, or literal, construction* of ambiguous words in a document or agreement takes the language used in its exact and technical meaning and does not recognize any considerations that were not expressed.

A *liberal construction* of ambiguous words in a document or agreement allows a fair and reasonable consideration of the words in order to attain the purpose for which the whole document or agreement was designed. Liberal construction does not mean that the words may be forced out of their natural meanings.

When an oral or written CONTRACT or other agreement contains ambiguous provisions, many courts apply the *parol evidence rule*. This rule is a legal doctrine by which a court considers the circumstances surrounding the completion of a deal or the signing of a document to help it construe unclear terms. Evidence other than the actual agreement itself is used to determine what the parties meant by the writing.

EXAMPLE A cotton broker enters a contract with a manufacturer to sell 125 bales of cotton to arrive in May 1980 on a ship, the *Queen of the Sea,* sailing from Bombay, India. If two ships of the same name are scheduled to arrive from Bombay during the same month of the year, a court would use parol evidence to clarify which *Queen of the Sea* the parties intended.

constructive   True legally even if not factually; established by a legal interpretation; inferred or implied.

    EXAMPLE   The rents in your apartment building are comparatively low. Your landlord would like to see you move out so that he could lease your apartment for more money. But you have 2½ years to go in your lease and are a model tenant. There is nothing he can do to evict you. So when he fails to provide heat in the winter without good reason, the court might interpret the lack of heat as a sign that he is trying to force you out of your apartment. His action would be constructive eviction and it might give you the right to withhold your rent.

    Constructive knowledge is knowledge (NOTICE) of circumstances that a reasonable and prudent person is considered to have about the fact in question or that he might have acquired by diligence. A storeowner is charged with constructive knowledge of a pothole in his parking lot and is liable for injuries resulting from it if he could have discovered it by reasonable inspection and within a reasonable time before an injury occurred. See NEGLIGENCE.

constructive desertion   Constructive desertion occurs when the deliberate conduct of a guilty husband or wife ends their living together, forcing the innocent spouse to leave. In many states after the husband and wife are no longer living together the innocent spouse is entitled, for a certain length of time fixed by statute, to sue for DIVORCE or separation based on the misconduct of the guilty spouse. The misconduct must be of such a nature that it makes the continuance of marital relations unbearable, forcing the innocent spouse to leave the marital home.

    EXAMPLE   When a husband by his continued cruelty forces his wife to leave their home, she is not a deserter, but he is a constructive deserter. When there is justification for leaving home, the departure by the innocent spouse is not considered a desertion, which could be a ground for divorce.

A husband's communicating a venereal disease to his wife (or vice versa) may constitute constructive desertion if it causes the innocent spouse to leave home. In some states, an unjustified refusal to have sexual intercourse with your spouse for a certain period of time is constructive desertion, but not if you refuse because of health reasons. Constant nagging or drunkenness is not considered justification for a divorce or separation based on constructive desertion.

constructive trust   A remedy used by the courts to compel someone who unfairly holds money or property to transfer it to the person to whom it justly belongs. It is applied when one person has legal title to (ownership of) property that should, in fairness, belong to someone else because the title was gained (usually) by fraud. The courts may treat the property as if the legal owner holds it in a beneficial TRUST for the enjoyment of the real owner.

    EXAMPLE   In one case a woman wrote a will leaving the bulk of her estate to the leader of a religious cult. When the woman learned that the leader had lied to her, she told him and others that she was going to change her will and leave her estate to a relative. Before she could do so, the cult leader and his followers used undue influence and restrained her physically to keep her from changing her will. When the woman died, the court held that the leader could not inherit her estate because he had stopped her by force from changing her will. The court instead imposed a constructive trust on her estate, under which the leader could not touch any part of the woman's property for his own benefit and enjoyment, but had to hold the proceeds of the estate for the beneficial enjoyment of the relative.

consul   See AMBASSADORS AND CONSULS.

consular court   A court held by a consul (a representative of a country) in a foreign country, under authority given by TREATY, for settling civil cases between citizens of the consul's country or between sailors on ships flying the consul's flag. See AMBASSADORS AND CONSULS. When a consular court also has criminal jurisdiction, its decisions are subject to review by the courts of the home government.

consumer protection   Consumer transactions are business deals all of us make for personal, family, or household purposes. Both buying and borrowing are included. Because consumers are generally not as wise about business transactions as businessmen, some federal and state laws have been enacted in recent years to protect consumers from dishonest practices and to strengthen the consumer's position in relation to the businessman's.

The law traditionally assumed that business deals of every kind were made by two people who negotiated until they reached terms agreeable to both. This is hardly ever the case in consumer transactions. A merchant puts his goods out on shelves with price tags on them. His lawyer draws up a short contract with all the terms in the merchant's favor, and the merchant has this printed up to use as a bill of sale. The consumer can take it or leave it. Even if he asks what the terms are, he probably will not understand all their legal effects. People do not take lawyers with them when they go to buy refrigerators and use credit cards to pay for them.

■ **Terms of a consumer transaction**   Every commercial transaction requires agreement on a number of terms. The typical sales transaction between a merchant and a consumer is so standardized that there is little or no negotiating over terms. Nevertheless, you can shop around for the best terms. In all transactions, you will get the best possible deal by knowing your rights and by understanding the legal effect of various terms.

    Credit   Credit is probably the most important term in a consumer transaction. Much recent legislation intended to protect consumers regulates the granting of credit. For a complete discussion of consumer credit, credit bureaus, discrimination, and the disclosure of terms, see CREDIT.

    Price   A price may be so unfair that it is shocking to an average person's conscience, or *unconscionable*. Courts will usually not enforce such purchase agreements but they will also look at all the circumstances. The relative bargaining power of each of the parties is important. Because businessmen and merchants generally know more about the deals they are making than their customers do, a court will be more careful to protect the customer. However, an unconscionable price is not found very often.

EXAMPLE One court refused to enforce an agreement by a
0———* student that he would pay a trade school $2,400 tuition when he enrolled and that, even if he canceled, the school could keep $600, plus $7 for each class hour. In another case, a price of $1,550 plus sales tax was found to be unconscionable for catering a party because the full amount was due even if the consumer canceled.

There is a whole line of "freezer cases" in which courts have refused to make customers pay the full contract price on freezers because the agreements obligated the unsuspecting purchasers to pay $1,500 or more for freezers that cost $300.

An exorbitantly high price by itself does not necessarily make a price illegal. Consumers have the right to make bad deals as well as good ones as long as there is no fraud or unfair surprise.

EXAMPLE In one case, a group of poor people sued to
0———* prevent an appliance store in their neighborhood from collecting the money they all owed. They said that this store was charging much higher prices than stores in

better areas. The owner of the store came into court with proof that the cost of running a business in that neighborhood was unusually high. Insurance, when he could get it, was very expensive. More customers than in other locations failed to pay their bills, and losses from theft and vandalism were almost routine. The court found that in view of these special expenses the prices charged by the merchant were not unfair. Higher prices are the only way stores can survive in some neighborhoods, and residents can shop elsewhere.

In other cases, additional factors tipped the scales toward the consumer to make a high price illegal: the consumer was not fluent in English; he had no means of shopping elsewhere; or the contract had unfair terms buried in the fine print. High-pressure tactics in making the sale can also affect the fairness of a price.

Another consideration in connection with price is the possibility of *cash discounts*. A merchant who accepts a credit card when he makes a sale receives 3 to 5 percent less than the full price from the credit card company. This is his

YOUR RIGHTS AS A CONSUMER

■ Everytime that you buy something, two implied warranties are promised to you by law: that the product is fit to be sold and used for its ordinary purpose, and that it is fit to be used for the particular purpose you told the merchant you had in mind. If the seller made a disclaimer, of course, you will not be covered.

■ Federal law requires every seller and manufacturer to explain in simple language the terms and conditions of any warranty he makes—this applies to written sales contracts for products costing more than $5.

■ The manufacturer or dealer must repair a product that is defective, and if repeated repairs fail to fix it, the consumer must get the choice of a refund or a free replacement.

■ About 40 states require that consumers be given a cooling-off period, usually 72 hours, after they obligate themselves to buy from a door-to-door salesman. This means generally that you can cancel the sale within that time. You do not have to give a reason if you change your mind, but in some states you may have to pay a small fee or the seller may keep part of your down payment.

■ If you are the victim of a billing error, send the creditor a written complaint including your name and account number, the amount of the error, and an explanation of why you

think there is a mistake. The law requires the creditor to acknowledge such a complaint within 30 days and send you a response within 90 days. If he believes there is no mistake, he must send a written explanation plus copies of substantiating documents upon your request.

■ If, because of a disputed bill, a creditor reports the consumer to a credit bureau or anyone else, the law requires him to give the consumer the name and address of the bureau or person notified. When the dispute is settled, the creditor must notify the credit bureau.

■ If the creditor does not follow these requirements, he cannot collect the disputed amount even if the consumer was wrong.

■ If a creditor provides a time period in which there is no finance charge, the law requires him to send out bills early enough so that consumers can take advantage of the free-credit period.

■ The law limits the property a creditor can claim to pay a debt owed him. For example, a family home, life insurance policy, and Social Security benefits are property that is protected from creditors. Moreover, no creditor can leave a debtor with a weekly income equal to less than the minimum hourly wage times 30.

■ A seller is prohibited from including a provision in his sales contract

allowing him to seize anything the debtor owns if he misses a payment.

■ You have the right to sue a seller for deceit or fraud if you can prove (1) that the seller falsely represented a *fact* about the product, (2) that the seller knew the advertisement was false, (3) that you relied on the advertising when you bought the product, and (4) that you suffered because you bought this product from the seller—you lost money because of the transaction.

■ The Federal Trade Commission (FTC) can stop false advertising by ordering the advertiser to withdraw his false ads and to make new ones that correct any misconceptions.

■ Under the federal Truth in Lending Act, terms must be fully explained in consumer credit transactions. The Truth in Lending Act sets up three rules: (1) A lender may not advertise a terrific deal unless it is available to any average customer. (2) Ads must include all the terms or none of them. (3) If there are more than four payments, the agreement must state conspicuously that "The cost of credit is included in the price quoted for the goods and services."

■ Small-claims courts are quick and inexpensive for consumers because they use informal procedures. However, they will hear only cases involving money below a certain amount. Check your state.

payment for the credit card company's service. Smart shoppers can see that credit card purchasers are getting, in effect, the value of a discount, because the merchant is paying for their use of the credit card. Customers who understand this, and can pay cash, have asked to be given the same 3 to 5 percent off the purchase price, which they can pocket when they pay cash.

Until recently, there were barriers to these discounts. First, credit card companies usually made merchants agree *not* to give cash customers a break, but the new Fair Credit Billing Act prohibits such an agreement. It says that merchants do have the option of offering cash discounts if they like, but fews merchants do. Second, merchants had been required by the Truth in Lending Act to disclose all financing terms when a customer paid a "finance charge." The small percentage difference between the cost to a credit card purchaser and a cash purchaser is really a finance charge. But now the Fair Credit Billing Act does not require a merchant to disclose all the financing terms when he gives the cash discount of 5 percent or less.

Warranties The Uniform Commercial Code governs sales transactions in every state except Louisiana. The code covers two types of warranties—or promises by the seller or manufacturer—that are most important to the consumer: the express WARRANTY and the implied warranty.

Express warranties An express warranty is a clear promise, usually written right into the contract of sale. It can also be a promise made during talks closing the deal, but spoken promises are not of much value because they are difficult to prove.

An express warranty deals with fact, not opinion. Consumers do not have the legal right to rely on broad, general claims such as "mint condition" and "will last a lifetime," which are merely examples of normal "puffing" by sellers.

An express warranty can be created by a description or sample. For instance, the words under a picture in a catalog are a description. If the shirts are said to be "100 percent cotton" or "a perfect match with these slacks," then they had better be. A floor model or demonstrator is a sample. The consumer has the right to assume that the vacuum cleaner he orders will be the same model as the one he was shown in the store. In these cases, the express warranty must be a "basis of the bargain." If the seller can prove that the buyer did not rely on an express warranty made by a description or sample, then the buyer cannot complain.

Implied warranties There are two implied warranties promised by the law, which the consumer may assume are part of every sales contract unless the seller specifically disclaims them. The first is a *warranty of merchantability*—an assurance by every merchant that a product is fit to be sold and used for the purpose ordinarily expected of such a product. For example, there is an implied warranty that shampoo will not make your hair fall out. If it does, the shampoo should never have been sold.

The second assurance a consumer can count on is the implied *warranty of fitness for a particular purpose.* This warranty can be relied on whenever the seller, whether he is a merchant or a friend selling you something, has reason to know (1) that the buyer has a particular use in mind for the goods and (2) that the buyer is relying on the seller's judgment and skill in selecting goods suitable for that use.

If a carpet salesman, for instance, knows that his customer wants carpeting for his restaurant rather than for a guest room in his home, the customer has a right to expect that he will be sold commercial-quality carpet that can stand up to heavy traffic.

To recover on the basis of an implied warranty, the consumer must prove not only that (1) there was a warranty but also that (2) there was a breach of that warranty, (3) the breach caused some harm, (4) the consumer dealt directly with the person responsible for the warranty, and (5) the consumer notified the seller within a reasonable time after he discovered or should have discovered the problem.

If the consumer proves these things, he can cancel the contract and recover any down payment he has made. If the seller refuses to return the down payment, the consumer can sue for money damages. The amount of damages is the difference between the value of the goods he received and the value they would have had if they had been merchantable or fit for his particular purpose. The consumer has a certain time within which to sue. See Chart 7.

If the consumer decides to sue for damages, he can also recover for any financial loss he has suffered or for injury to people or property caused by the breach.

The consumer should remember that a seller can make a written disclaimer of these two implied warranties. But the words must be conspicuous—that is, set apart or in large type so that a reasonable person would notice them. To exclude an implied warranty of merchantability, the word "merchantability" must be used. For example: "SELLER MAKES NO WARRANTY OF MERCHANTABILITY WITH RESPECT TO GOODS SOLD UNDER THIS AGREEMENT."

The Magnuson-Moss Warranty Act, a recent federal law, requires every seller and manufacturer to explain the terms and conditions of written warranties in simple language. This law applies to written sales contracts for products that cost more than $5. The law requires a manufacturer or dealer to repair a product that is defective or fails to fit the warranty. It also has what is called an *antilemon provision,* which says that if repeated repairs fail to fix the product, the consumer must be given the choice of a refund or a replacement without charge. For a further discussion of warranties, see PRODUCT LIABILITY.

Credit insurance There are other terms that are not in every sales or lending agreement, but a consumer should know about them because they can be used unfairly. One term that appears frequently is credit insurance, in which the consumer pays a fee to an insurance company so that his debt will be paid if he dies or is disabled. By the beginning of 1978, the amount of credit life insurance in force was $139 billion.

There are several problems with credit insurance. One is overinsurance. The consumer pays a rate that is based on the size of his debt rather than the size of the risk. For instance, a young person in good health pays more than he should. The insurance may be for the full amount of the debt until it is completely repaid; thus if the consumer repays the debt in installments, he pays for insurance coverage on a part of the debt that no longer exists. In other instances, a consumer who wants to extend the time to repay or to refinance, will be required to buy a second policy to cover the same debt. This is called "pyramiding."

Some lenders refuse to extend credit without the protection of consumer-paid credit insurance. This kind of coercion is especially unfair to an established, responsible borrower. It is even more unfair when the creditor has an agreement to funnel all its insurance business to one company for a fee. In some cases, the creditor does not ask for a fee but receives compensation indirectly. For example, if a bank is the creditor, it might require the insurance company to leave large sums of money in interest-free accounts.

Credit-insurance abuses are a big problem. In a single year, witnesses told a Senate investigating committee, consumers were being overcharged more than $200 million. The basic problem is "reverse competition." The insurance companies are competing for the business of the creditors, not the consumer-borrowers. The creditors have no interest in keeping rates low. The larger the premium, the larger the insurance company's fee to the creditor.

Balloon payment   Another term in a sales contract that can cause trouble for consumers is the BALLOON PAYMENT—a final payment that is considerably larger than any of the other payments. For example, an agreement may provide for 11 monthly payments of $100 and a final payment of $1,000. A balloon payment arrangement can be useful for people with seasonal or irregular incomes, but it is not a wise arrangement for most consumers.

EXAMPLE Pearl bought a diamond bracelet for $5,000. She made a down payment of $1,000 and agreed to pay only the interest for a year and the balance of the price at the end of the year. If Pearl cannot pay the required $4,000 at the end of the year, she will be forced to give up the bracelet and will have nothing to show for her down payment and her interest payments unless she refinances, usually at a much higher rate of interest.

Prepayment   A prepayment clause in a loan requires the borrower to pay the interest on the loan before he gets the money. If he does not have enough money to do that, he can borrow a larger amount and use the difference to pay the interest. The result is that he will be borrowing and paying interest on a larger sum than he needed for the purpose of the loan.

Refinancing   A very high percentage of consumer loans, especially those made by small finance companies, are refinanced—the borrower borrows more money before the balance is due. Critics of refinancing loans call this *flipping*. Flipping can lead to interest rates that are above the amount allowed by law.

EXAMPLE In a case in Tennessee, a porter borrowed $72 from a finance company, payable in several installments. He received only $60 because the rest was applied to prepaid interest, investigation of his credit worthiness, and credit insurance. One month later the loan was flipped. The porter signed a note for an additional $378 loan, part of which he used to pay off the original $72 loan. But none of the prepaid interest on the $72 loan was refunded. The highest legal rate of interest that could then be charged in Tennessee would have amounted to 36 cents on this $72 loan.

Most states now require that prepaid interest be returned to borrowers (but not with interest). Flipping consumer loans is not in itself illegal, but it is certainly a trap that careful consumers should avoid if they can.

■ **Service contract**   A service contract is a business transaction with someone who performs a service instead of delivering a product. A service contract is personal and nontransferable—that is, only the person who was hired can do the work. A person hired to baby-sit cannot substitute a friend without the employer's permission, nor can a barber stop in the middle of a haircut and let another barber finish. The rule governing service contracts differs from the one covering a sale of goods in that an entire store can be sold to a new owner who replaces the previous owner in every sales contract. If four people are waiting for their new furniture to be delivered when the store changes hands, the new storeowner must deliver what was ordered.

Only one type of service is held to the same warranty standards as goods, and that is the serving of food and drink. The law says that a restaurant must serve food fit to be sold and fit to be eaten, just as a grocery store must. This is not a guarantee that you will like the way the food is prepared, only a warranty (promise) that it is pure and safe.

Contracts for service can be especially annoying for a consumer because of the uncertainty about how much he may have to pay and whether he will be satisfied with the result. When you buy a coat, you look at the coat, read the label, and try it on before paying for it. But if you hire someone to put aluminum siding on your house, you have to rely on the contractor's reputation for doing a satisfactory job. If you hire a plumber, you may get only an estimate of what the work will cost. You will not know the total price until the service has been performed. Unfortunately, the law offers little protection for consumers in service contracts.

Licensing   Some protection is afforded by state licensing of certain kinds of workers. States may require a LICENSE before anyone can offer his services as a plumber, beautician, electrician, pharmacist, optometrist, or liquor-store owner. Some licenses, such as one for a taxi driver, may be granted on proof of good moral character. However, this may mean no more than proof that the applicant has never been arrested. Other licenses may require years of education and passing a comprehensive state examination, as in the case of lawyers, veterinarians, and teachers.

Even if the state routinely issues licenses to almost all applicants, the consumer is protected by the fact that a license can be taken away from a dishonest practitioner. It may take a number of complaints to get the state to act, but a dissatisfied consumer can always add his letter to the files the state collects on dishonest license holders.

Consumers must recognize that the results of a service cannot always be guaranteed. A doctor, for example, cannot be expected to guarantee results, even for a simple operation. A guarantee, under the law, is a contract. If anything should go wrong, even if it was something beyond the doctor's control, he could then be sued for breach of contract. See PATIENTS' RIGHTS.

Reasonable performance   Although results cannot be guaranteed, the law requires that services be performed in a reasonable way. A consumer must be warned of possible difficulties and given a chance to decide whether or not to proceed. In medical matters this permission is called *informed consent*, but your right to know the facts extends to other service contracts, too. The excavator hired to put in a new sewer line is obligated to refill holes and replace plants, but he should warn a homeowner that a particular tree may not survive. The homeowner then has the option of laying the line somewhere else. The concept of reasonableness applies to more than the actual service itself. Certainly a housepainter must paint the house properly, but he must also pay for any damage to shrubs or windows caused by his carelessness.

■ **Sales schemes** The federal and state governments regulate certain methods of selling merchandise.

Door-to-door sales Most states specifically regulate door-to-door or home-solicitation sales for a number of reasons. One is that the door-to-door salesman has a captive audience. A customer can always walk out of a department store, but an aggressive salesman may not leave your home until you throw him out. Moreover, people who are homebound and lonely are often the most vulnerable: invalids, the elderly, mothers with young children. Then, too, customer relations are less important to a door-to-door sales company than they are to a store. What is more, the salesmen do not have supervisors watching them. And while a consumer can pick which store to patronize, honest and dishonest salesmen alike can knock on the door of any home. Finally, a consumer at home has no chance to compare products or prices and is therefore more likely to buy something at an unfair price.

About 40 states now require that consumers be given a cooling-off period after they obligate themselves to buy something from a door-to-door salesman. Generally, this means that a consumer can cancel the sale within 72 hours. The salesman gives him a printed form that tells him he has the right to cancel. The consumer is not required to give a reason for changing his mind, but in some states he may have to pay a small fee or the seller may keep part of the down payment.

Most of these laws make an exception if the buyer asks the salesman to provide the goods or services without delay and the seller has done so. Then the buyer cannot cancel the contract or return what he has bought, and the salesman does not have to provide the right-to-cancel notice.

The Federal Trade Commission also has rules covering home-solicitation sales. It says that the door-to-door salesman must follow the FTC rule or the state law, whichever is stricter. The FTC requires, for example, that the right-to-cancel notice be in Spanish if the sale was made in that language. The FTC regulations apply to both cash sales and credit transactions.

Referral sales Referral sales involve two agreements: (1) that the consumer will buy something (usually at an outrageously high price) and (2) that the seller will give the consumer a credit, discount, commission, or rebate for other customers he refers to the seller.

The basic idea of referral sales is unfeasible, because the success of the arrangement depends on an unending supply of customers. For example, if each buyer supplies the seller with 25 names and each of these people buys under the same arrangement, it would take 6.1 *trillion* persons to finish the seventh round of referrals.

Referral sales have also been tied in with other dishonest schemes. For example, the promise that the consumer can earn or save money by merely talking a few of his friends into buying the same product may induce him to buy the product at a price that would horrify him in other circumstances. Moreover, knowing that a buyer cannot enforce an unwritten agreement in court, the seller usually does not put his promise to pay these commissions in writing.

EXAMPLE Clark Fenton, owner of a small-appliance store,
O——※ uses a written contract with an "integration clause" that says all the terms of the entire agreement are integrated, or included, in the written contract. It looks official, so customer Chuck does not notice that the referral clause has been left out. Later, Fenton sues for the amount due on the price of the product, and Chuck has no evidence that he is entitled to a discount for the seven friends he talked into buying the same article from Fenton.

If the buyer does notice that the referral agreement is not mentioned in the sales contract, the salesman may hand him a second, separate contract. Both parties sign it, and it is then legally enforceable. But the problem is that the second contract is not a part of the agreement to pay the purchase price. The seller who wants his money immediately can sell the sales contract to a finance company. The finance company then is a HOLDER IN DUE COURSE. It "holds" the consumer's debt without any connection to the terms of the sale. Even though the consumer has an enforceable contract to reduce the price for referrals he makes, he can enforce it only against the seller—if he can find him. Meanwhile, the finance company has a right to collect the full price written in the sales contract.

Both courts and legislatures have disapproved of referral-sales schemes. Courts have applied laws that prohibit sales of lottery tickets to referral sales. In those cases, the sellers were found guilty of crimes and permanently enjoined (stopped) from using their illegal schemes. Some states prohibit any rebate plan that depends on something that occurs after the consumer has agreed to buy or lease. Under these laws, a seller can offer an agreement promising the consumer something for giving the seller names of potential customers, but the seller cannot say he will discount the price *only* if those people referred actually buy from him. If the person selling or leasing the product violates this law, the consumer can keep the goods without paying for them.

A number of recent consumer-protection statutes have reduced the usual problems of a lawsuit by enabling a successful plaintiff to recover "reasonable" attorney's fees. Of course, the consumer cannot collect unless he wins.

■ **When the seller transfers the debt** Generally, a merchant who sells on credit *assigns* (transfers) the debt to a bank or finance company. A storeowner will say: "I'm not in the credit business. I'm in the paint and wallpaper business." There is no law obliging those who sell on credit to collect their own accounts, and for most of them it is not practical. They are not collection specialists, and they cannot afford to tie up their capital for any period of time. Less than 15 percent of installment debts remain outstanding in the hands of the original seller or lender.

EXAMPLE Tom buys a trash compactor from Johnson
O——※ Brothers at $8 a month for 36 months. Before the first payment is due, Johnson sells the debt to Grand Bank for cash at a discounted rate—$238. If Grand Bank

collects the full debt, it will have $288, but it must wait three years for the money.

The law says that Grand Bank must give Tom notice that the debt has been assigned—that the right to collect has been transferred. If Tom asks, Grand Bank must furnish proof that it is entitled to receive the payments.

Now the trash compactor stops compacting, and Grand Bank wants its money anyway. What can Tom do? Grand Bank is called a "holder in due course," that is, it has a right to collect regardless of a problem with the original seller. Tom must keep making payments while his garbage stacks up unless he can prove that (1) he never agreed to the sales contract, or he thought it was another agreement, or he does not understand English or cannot read; or (2) the seller and the bank are so closely connected that they should be treated by the court as if they were one company rather than two.

A dishonest seller can always get his money by working with a dishonest finance company that claims to be a holder in due course. Arrangements for assignment of debt were never intended, however, to protect a company that routinely cheats customers. In one case, a finance company set up a series of companies that declared bankruptcy and thus could not be sued for all the shoddy merchandise they sold. The finance company, of course, tried to keep on collecting the installment payments.

Some states are beginning to limit by statute the degree to which a holder in due course can insulate himself from claims that the buyer would be able to prove against the seller. The FTC has also proposed some regulations.

The seller can also include in the sales contract a provision that says: "The buyer hereby *waives* against any *assignee* any claim or defense he may have against the seller." This is a *waiver of defense*. It is smart for the seller to include this provision because then it enables him to sell the debt to an assignee for a better price. It is not smart for a consumer to overlook the waiver or to sign the contract in spite of it. Some state courts and legislatures have begun to restrict its use in consumer transactions, but the seller and assignee are certainly not going to tell that to the consumer.

A consumer probably cannot recover any money he has paid to the assignee even if he can prove that he should not have been made to pay. The common-law rule is that the consumer cannot get back anything he has already paid. Most consumer legislation that regulates the holder-in-due-course and waiver-of-defense provisions follows the same rule. The consumer's only remedy is to stop making payments to the assignee. This does not relieve the debtor of his obligation to pay what he owes. If he stops making payments he is legally obligated to pay, he will still have to pay. The common-law rule means only that he cannot get back money that he did not have to pay to the assignee.

Credit cards   If Tom uses a credit card to pay for his trash compactor, he may run into a problem similar to the one in which the seller assigns the debt.

EXAMPLE   If Tom buys from Sears and uses his Sears credit card, he can certainly argue against Sears if the machine is defective and he is sued for the balance due. But if Tom uses a bank's credit card at Sharp Appliance Store, there are at least three parties involved—Tom, Sharp, and the bank—and three contracts. Tom can com-

plain about the defective machine to Sharp, but Sharp has already received its money from the bank. The bank paid off the store and wants its money. It neither made nor sold the trash compactor. It has never even seen it.

Under the Truth in Lending Act, the consumer can argue against the credit card company only if (1) the seller is closely associated in business with the credit card company, or (2) the sale was for more than $50, and the seller is in the same state or within 100 miles of the consumer's billing address (his home or office), or (3) the item was purchased from the seller's advertisement sent with the credit card's monthly statement.

■ **The Fair Credit Billing Act**   A number of consumer-credit problems are regulated by the Fair Credit Billing Act of 1975. Among other things, this federal law prohibits banks from requiring people to keep money in accounts at the bank or to pay for other bank services in order to get a credit card. The law also restricts how a bank may take money out of a depositor's account to settle his credit card bill. And it regulates two other areas that frequently cause consumer headaches: billing errors and the billing period.

Consumers who find a billing error in a monthly credit statement or who question an item are usually prompt in writing to the company for an explanation or a correction. But months or even years may go by without resolving the problem. Meanwhile, a computer somewhere continues to send nasty letters threatening the consumer with legal action or a bad credit rating. Some people write to the president of the company or to their senator, and eventually they may hire a lawyer. Occasionally, the error is corrected, but often people give up and pay the disputed amount out of sheer frustration.

Complaint procedures   The Fair Credit Billing Act establishes procedures for consumer complaints, and it requires the creditor to explain or correct a mistake. First, the consumer needs to know where to complain. Look on a recent bill. An address must be printed on it. Next, write out the complaint. Do not write on the payment stub because your message may easily be overlooked and it will not go to the right person. The company does not even have to accept a notation on a stub as a complaint if the original agreement so states.

There are six requirements for the complaint: (1) it must be written; (2) it must be received at the address the creditor gives; (3) he must be able to identify the name and account number (if any) of the consumer; (4) the complaint must say that the consumer believes there is a billing error; (5) it must give the amount of the error; and (6) it must explain why the consumer thinks there is a mistake.

If the complaint is properly presented, the creditor must acknowledge within 30 days that he received it and send a response within 90 days. The response can be an agreement to correct the mistake or an explanation if the creditor disagrees on the amount. The consumer can request copies of documents that the creditor relies on. If the creditor believes there is no mistake, he must send a written explanation and, if the consumer requests, copies of documents.

Until at least 10 days after the response is sent, the creditor cannot (1) take any action to collect the disputed amount, (2) restrict the consumer's credit because of it, or (3) report the consumer to a credit bureau. If after 10 days the creditor reports the consumer to a credit bureau or anyone else as delinquent, he must report that the bill is in dispute and must give the consumer the name and address of the bureau or person notified. When the dispute is settled, the creditor must notify the credit bureau. If the creditor fails to follow these procedures, he cannot collect the disputed amount or any finance charges up to $50— even if the consumer was wrong.

Billing periods The Fair Credit Billing Act also regulates billing periods. If a creditor provides a period during which consumers pay no finance charge, the law requires him to tell consumers about it and to send out bills early enough for consumers to take advantage of the period of free credit.

Several different kinds of billing systems are currently in use. The amount of the finance charge depends on the system used. For example, the finance charge for the same pattern of purchases can vary from 75 cents with the "adjusted balance system" to $3.75 for the "ending balance system," even when both systems use the standard charge of 1.5 percent a month on the unpaid balance. The various systems are so complicated that most consumers do not even try to figure them out. Some states have begun to outlaw systems that charge interest on a part of the bill that has been paid, but the only real protection for consumers is in legislation that requires companies to explain the cost of their credit. Such information would enable consumers to shop around for credit.

■ **Collection of debts** Creditors have a right, called *judicial collection,* to collect debts by going to court. All attempts to collect without going to court are called *extrajudicial collection,* discussed below. Courts are presently improving the balance between the creditor's right to collect and the debtor's right to DUE PROCESS OF LAW.

Property exempt from judicial collection All states have laws that limit the property a creditor can claim to satisfy a debt. See EXECUTION. These laws try to protect some of the debtor's property from creditors so that the debtor can support himself and his family and not become a burden to the public. Creditors must keep these limits in mind when they decide whether to lend money or extend credit. See Charts 9 and 10.

State laws may protect the family home, tools necessary to earn a living, life insurance policies, wages to some extent, and the family Bible. Sometimes even these exempt items of property can be claimed for certain types of debts, such as federal income taxes, alimony, and child support.

U.S. statutes protect some of the benefits of federal social legislation, including Social Security and veterans' benefits. A federal law prevents state law or state courts from ordering payment of more than 25 percent of a debtor's disposable earnings to a creditor or leaving the debtor with less weekly income than the minimum wage times 30 hours a week.

Provisional remedies A creditor's right to enforce payment of a debt in court is of little help if the property the debtor owes money on is going to be used up or taken out of state or if the debtor is outside the court's jurisdiction, threatens to flee, or is about to go bankrupt. By the time the creditor wins his case, the judgment may be worth no more than the paper it is written on. To protect lenders and

sellers in their legitimate attempts to recover what is owed to them, the law allows for PROVISIONAL REMEDIES, court orders that temporarily protect the status quo until the legal controversy can be resolved.

EXAMPLE A seller who had not received regular payments o—* on a color television set decided to sue the buyer. His lawyer drew up a summons, and a process server went to the buyer's home to serve it. He found the buyer packing household items into boxes and preparing to move. "I'm going back to Oklahoma," the buyer told the process server. "You can keep that piece of paper you have there."

The process server called the seller, who immediately went to a judge and asked for an order of attachment. The judge granted the order, directing the sheriff to pick up the color television and hold it until the lawsuit over the debt was finished.

Court judgments Creditors like to get a judgment as quickly and inexpensively as possible. Then they can use all the means the state provides to enforce it. But court judgments can sometimes be unfair to consumers.

A creditor can get a *default judgment,* by which he wins his case automatically, if a debtor does not show up in court. In the absence of the debtor from court, a creditor may lie about the debtor's receiving notice of the lawsuit. Dishonest process servers may submit false affidavits claiming that they personally served summonses on the debtor. The debtor first learns about the lawsuit when the sheriff arrives to cart off his possessions in satisfaction of the judgment. In such cases, the debtor can ask the court to cancel the judgment or to reopen the default suit.

Another judgment problem for consumers is the cognovit note or CONFESSION OF JUDGMENT. The cognovit note is an agreement in the sales or loan contract that the creditor has the right to appear in court for the debtor and enter a confession of judgment against him. In effect, the debtor consents to a judgment without a trial. The Supreme Court has said that this agreement is not illegal, but that it violates due process if the parties do not have equal bargaining power, if the debtor has no real opportunity to negotiate the cognovit provision, or if he receives nothing of value for giving up the important right to contest a lawsuit. Many states have outlawed or severely limited confessions of judgment.

Extrajudicial collection Some creditors not only have collection rights enforceable by statute or in court, but they also hold LIENS against the debtor's property. A *lien* is a security interest in a particular item of property (such as something that was pledged as security, or collateral, for a loan) that gives the lienholder some rights in it.

Wage assignments A wage assignment is an agreement signed by the consumer by which a consumer's employer subtracts payments from the consumer's paycheck and sends them to the creditor. If the employer refuses to honor the agreement, the creditor can force him to do so in a lawsuit. Sometimes a consumer may not even realize he has signed a contract with such a provision until he receives a smaller paycheck!

A wage assignment is similar to a garnishment in that the creditor gets his money from the consumer's earnings. Garnishment, however, is by order of a court while a wage assignment is agreed to by contract. See ATTACHMENT AND GARNISHMENT and Chart 9.

In every state except Georgia, wage assignments are regulated by statute, but there is little uniformity among the states. Ten states prohibit wage assignments. Four prohibit the assignment of future wages. Most other states make a certain dollar amount or percentage of wages exempt and thus beyond the reach of wage-assignment agreements.

Security   The requirement of security can be very much abused. The seller may have a provision in his sales contract that he can seize anything the debtor owns if the debtor misses a payment. Or when a seller knows that the value of his goods, such as an automobile or a refrigerator, decreases rapidly after they are used, he may want the buyer to pledge additional property as security. The seller may even include property the buyer does not own when he signs the agreement. The Uniform Commercial Code prevents a creditor from including in the contract anything the consumer buys more than 10 days after he agrees to this kind of security provision.

Another problem for the consumer in security arrangements is that he can use credit to buy a number of items from the same seller, but no one item is considered paid for until the last installment payment is made. For a detailed discussion of security arrangements, see SECURED TRANSACTIONS.

EXAMPLE   In one classic case, the consumer bought 16 items worth a total of $1,500 from a furniture and appliance dealer over a five-year period. When the consumer failed to keep up payments on the last item purchased, the seller repossessed everything. The court said that this kind of agreement can be "unconscionable" and unenforceable.

Repossession and resale   A lienholder may repossess or foreclose without starting a lawsuit in court. See EXECUTION; FORECLOSURE. The remedy of REPOSSESSION is called a "self-help" remedy because the lienholder legally helps himself to the property involved. What is the debtor going to do? He may be able to outfox the collection agent by hiding, but he certainly will not get a court to make the creditor return the repossessed property to him.

If the agent forces himself into the debtor's home or tries to repossess the property when the debtor is present and likely to put up a fight, the creditor or his agent may be charged with "breach of the peace." While breach of the peace laws do not limit the creditor's right to repossess, they do warn him to be discreet.

After the creditor repossesses the property, he may keep it, thus canceling the rest of the debt, or he may resell it and hold the debtor liable for any amount still due. Most creditors resell. Although forced sales (where the debtor does not voluntarily sell) do not usually bring in more money than the debtor owes, any extra money must go to the debtor.

Resale is subject to abuses that are not really controlled by present laws.

EXAMPLE   A man bought a $35 battery for his car. He paid all the installments on it except the last, which amounted to $11.75. The creditor repossessed the car, because the man had pledged it to guarantee payment for the battery, and resold it. The creditor also went to court for a judgment to recover his expenses. The debtor was left with no car, no battery, and a bill for $128 to meet the creditor's expenses.

The law says that the creditor must give the debtor "reasonable notice" of the resale and the sale must be "commercially reasonable." When the debtor receives notice that his property will be sold, he can redeem it by paying the entire debt (not just a missed installment) and all the expenses the creditor incurred by repossessing his property. Instead of a $20 installment payment, the debtor might have to come up with several hundred dollars in order to stop the resale. The sale will be judged commercially reasonable unless the debtor can prove that the creditor cheated in reselling the property—by letting his son have the repossessed car for $40, for example.

Collection abuses   Some people have been subjected to much abuse when they could not to keep up payments.

EXAMPLE   One court described how a debt collector harassed a man and his wife in Texas. The abuse included: "Daily phone calls to both Mr. and Mrs. Duty that extended to great length; threatening to blacklist them with the Merchants' Retail Credit Association; accusing them of being deadbeats; talking to them in a harsh, insinuating, loud voice; stating to their neighbors and employers that they were deadbeats; asking Mrs. Duty what she was doing with her money; accusing her of spending money in other ways than in payments on the loan transaction; threatening to cause both plaintiffs to lose their jobs unless they made the payments demanded; calling each of the plaintiffs at the respective places of their employment several times daily; threatening to garnishee their wages; berating plaintiffs to their fellow employees; requesting their employers to require them to pay; calling on them at their work; flooding them with a barrage of demand letters, dun cards, special delivery letters, and telegrams both at their home and their places of work; sending them cards bearing this opening statement: 'Dear Customer: We made you a loan because we thought that you were honest.'; sending telegrams and special delivery letters to them at approximately midnight, causing them to be awakened from their sleep; calling a neighbor in the disguise of a sick brother of one of the plaintiffs, and on another occasion as a stepson; calling Mr. Duty's mother at her place of employment in Wichita Falls long distance, collect; leaving red cards in their door, with insulting notes on the back and thinly veiled threats; calling Mr. Duty's brother long distance, collect, in Albuquerque, New Mexico, at his residence, at a cost to him in excess of $11, and haranguing him about the alleged balance owed by plaintiffs."

The court held that Mr. and Mrs. Duty could sue the finance company for injuries intentionally caused by its harassment. The harm suffered included extreme mental anguish, nervousness, dangerous weight loss, and the dismissal of Mrs. Duty from her job. The court held that no creditor has the right to disrupt debtors' lives so completely and expressed the belief that no honest businessman would ever resort to such outrageous tactics.

Legal remedies for collection abuses   There are a number of statutes that can curb collection abuses. Federal regulations that control use of the telephone or the mails have been used to prosecute creditors. In every state (except Louisiana) the Uniform Commercial Code prohibits "fraudulent or unconscionable conduct in the collection of debts." This provision may be used by the consumer as a defense in a lawsuit by the creditor. In addition, the Federal Trade Commission has proposed a rule that in most cases the creditor cannot contact anyone except the debtor, the debtor's spouse, and his attorney in most cases.

It is difficult, however, for a consumer to maintain a lawsuit for injuries suffered as a result of overzealous debt collection. How many phone calls make up harassment, for example, or how late at night is too late to bother a debtor?

Furthermore, many courts will not hear a case for mental distress unless some physical injury was also inflicted. It must be proved that the mental strain was severe, and that the creditor caused harm intentionally. Even if the debtor can prove these elements, a court may still refuse to find that damages have been proved in any dollar amount.

Individual's right to privacy   It is sometimes possible to base a complaint against a collection agent in terms of injury to one's *privacy*. See PRIVACY, RIGHT OF. Publicly disclosing private facts is an invasion of privacy. A creditor who notifies a debtor's employer that the debtor is slipping into financial difficulties is disclosing a detail of the debtor's personal life, but this disclosure may not be sufficient to create a right to sue. Because the employer has an interest in his employee's debts, the information is considered a "privileged communication." Some courts have permitted recovery of money against a creditor who does more than simply notify the employer that a debt is past due—for example, calling the employer repeatedly or visiting the workplace and disrupting business.

Courts have permitted suits against a creditor who called a debtor's neighbors, published the debtor's name and the amount of the debt in the newspaper, and posted notice of the debt at the creditor's store.

In balancing the right of the creditor to collect what is owed him against the debtor's right of privacy, courts consider whether the creditor's conduct was reasonable—how and where the debtor was contacted, how often, and at what time of day or night. For example, it is unreasonable to pressure the debtor through relatives or neighbors or to threaten anything except the legal action that the creditor has a right to take.

Debtors may also sue creditors for defamation, which is a false statement that injures one's reputation. However, recovery of money damages is rare. A creditor can say or write that a debt is due, owing, and unpaid. As long as a statement is true, there is no basis for a lawsuit for defamation. A debtor might be able to recover if he can show that the creditor falsely accused him of a general unwillingness to pay his bills, provided that he can also prove that the accusation harmed him in a way measurable in money.

■ **Protection against false advertising**   Besides the complexities of dealing with merchants and buying on credit, consumers face another hazard when they make purchases. The truism "They couldn't say it if it weren't true" is accurate only to the extent that honest advertising can be enforced by law. Consumers receive protection against false advertising from the common law, state law, FTC regulations, and the Truth in Lending Act, which is part of the 1968 Consumer Credit Protection Act.

The common law   Under the common law, you as a consumer have the right to sue a seller for *deceit* or *fraud*. You must prove (1) that the seller falsely represented a fact about the product; (2) that the seller knew that the advertisement was false, or did not bother finding out when he should have, and that he intended to influence buyers with the false statements; (3) that you relied on the advertising when you bought the product; and (4) that you suffered because you bought this product from the seller. The sum of these conditions most often means that you lost money because of the transaction and that you would not have if the seller had been honest.

You should notice in particular that the misrepresentation must concern a *fact*. You cannot sue just because you disagree with the seller's opinion. The law calls most of a merchant's claims for his product "puffing"—broad, general statements about quality—and considers puffing normal. You have no legal right to make a seller prove the accuracy of such a claim as "My apples are the reddest and crunchiest on the market today."

A second common-law remedy for false advertising is a lawsuit for *breach of warranty*, but it is available only to people who deal directly with each other and is therefore of limited usefulness.

EXAMPLE A consumer is extremely upset after paying Crazy Cheap Appliance Center $600 for a new "Gyp" color television and discovering that it becomes dangerously hot every time he turns it on. He bought a "Gyp" because he had seen commercials for it on network television saying that it was completely safe. "Gyp" Corporation falsely advertised and is responsible for manufacturing the set improperly. But the consumer cannot sue "Gyp" for common-law breach of warranty because he bought his set from Crazy Cheap and did not deal directly with the manufacturer. The law calls this lack of direct contact a *lack of privity*.

For more discussion on warranties, see PRODUCT LIABILITY.

State laws   A consumer is more likely to be protected by state laws than by the unwritten common law. Many states control advertising of specific products, such as food or drugs. Sometimes false advertising is dealt with in broader legislation regulating particular businesses or professions. Often these laws are enforced by agencies that have the authority to revoke or suspend licenses for violations. Other statutes single out certain deceptive practices, such as the bait-and-switch scheme—advertising an article at a low price, having it available in a small quantity, and then trying to sell the customer a higher-priced item. This shows an intent not to sell what was advertised.

In 1911, *Printer's Ink*, a trade journal for the advertising industry, published a proposed law that made false advertising a crime. This model statute was later enacted in some form by 44 states to make "untrue, deceptive or misleading" representations in advertising a misdemeanor. But the *Printer's Ink* statutes have not been effective. Like the common-law remedies, they prohibit only false *facts*. Thus prosecutors are very reluctant to start criminal actions against advertisers because it is difficult to prove the kind of dishonesty necessary to convict.

The FTC and advertising   The Federal Trade Commission can stop false advertising by issuing a cease-

and-desist order. Sometimes the FTC not only makes a company withdraw its false advertisements but also orders affirmative disclosure, or corrective advertising. This requires the company to make new advertisements that tell how the earlier ads were misleading and then correct any remaining misconceptions from the earlier advertisements.

EXAMPLE Listerine commercials claimed that the product 0━━✳ prevented, treated, and cured colds and sore throats. An FTC administrative judge said, "Prove it." When Warner-Lambert, the manufacturer, could not show that its claims were true, all Listerine advertising for two years had to include the disclosure: "Contrary to prior advertising, Listerine will not prevent or cure colds or sore throats, and Listerine will not be beneficial in the treatment of cold symptoms or sore throats."

The FTC also has the authority to make sure that the punishment fits the crime—that the remedy fits the abuse.

EXAMPLE The FTC capped a two-year investigation of 0━━✳ STP, a motor-oil additive, by ordering the corporation to pay a $500,000 fine and to spend an additional $200,000 to publicize the government finding that its advertisements were false. The company agreed to buy advertising space in *The New York Times, The Wall Street Journal, The Washington Post, Time, Newsweek,* and other publications to correct earlier claims that STP reduced oil use by 20 percent, made motor oil "slipperier and made tune-ups unnecessary." In its detailed order, the FTC told STP Corporation to cease and desist from any further advertising that "reliable scientific tests" or "objective data" proved the effectiveness of the gasoline treatment, oil additive, and oil filters made by the company.

Truth in Lending Act   The Consumer Credit Protection Act of 1968 was the first general federal consumer-protection legislation. Title I of that law is called the Truth in Lending Act. It requires that terms be fully explained in consumer credit transactions. Advertisements covered by the act include written statements—such as newspaper or magazine advertisements—window displays, price tags, and television or radio commercials. A statement made by a clerk or salesperson trying to make a sale is *not* an advertisement subject to this law.

Basically, the Truth in Lending Act sets up three rules:

(1) A lender cannot advertise a terrific deal that in fact is rarely available to anyone except a preferred borrower. If an advertisement says credit is available up to $10,000 or a $200 down payment is enough, for example, then that must be "usually and customarily" true.

(2) Advertisements must include all the terms or none of them. If a car dealer advertises "48 months to pay," he must also include the cash price, the amount of the down payment, the size of each payment, and the annual percentage rate of interest. Either that or the ad must be vague, with such phrases as "easy credit" and "liberal terms."

(3) Finally, if the goods or services are to be paid for in more than four installments, the agreement must state in "clear and conspicuous" print that "The cost of credit is included in the price quoted for the goods and services."

This law controls only the advertiser, not the advertising medium, such as the newspaper, television station, or radio announcer. Furthermore, it does not allow individuals to file suits against advertisers who violate its terms. However-

er, the act does allow the government to bring a criminal prosecution against advertisers who willfully and knowingly violate it. Several federal agencies have the authority to enforce the act; the FTC, for example, can investigate false advertising and order a company to cease and desist.

■ **Lawsuits**   The right to sue has never widely appealed to consumers. Not only are people afraid that legal action will cost too much, but they also know that it will take a lot of time. Often the amount of money involved is not large enough to justify a lawsuit.

A number of recent consumer-protection statutes have reduced the usual problems of a lawsuit by enabling a successful plaintiff to recover "reasonable" attorney's fees. Of course the consumer cannot collect unless he wins.

A consumer who wins his lawsuit will not be permitted to recover attorney's fees and other legal costs unless a law expressly authorizes it. One case did establish that if attorney's fees are appropriate, they should be awarded even when the plaintiff is a Legal Aid client who does not have to pay his lawyer. The purpose of this rule is to encourage consumers to stand up for their rights and to punish merchants who violate the law.

Small claims courts make legal action more available to consumers in many states. They are quick and inexpensive because procedures are more informal than in other courts—some states do not permit either party to bring an attorney. Small claims courts will hear only cases involving sums of money below a certain amount and generally are restricted to ordering money damages for relief, but they have proved to be very satisfactory forums for consumers. So when, for example, the gas station does not replace the water pump for which it charged you, the restaurant loses your coat, or the appliance store wants to keep repairing your new television set every other week instead of replacing it, consider taking your case to a small claims court. For a discussion of the procedure to follow, see SMALL CLAIMS.

Class actions are lawsuits brought by one person or a few people, who represent everyone who has suffered the same harm. They are especially useful when an unfair or illegal practice by a business has affected a large number of consumers, but the amount of money each of them can recover is rather small. Because of the many restrictions on when federal class action suits can be brought, however, they are of only limited usefulness to consumers. Now a number of states also have laws permitting CLASS ACTIONS.

■ **Administrative agencies**   Public agencies have assumed a major responsibility for enforcing consumer protection, because bringing a lawsuit is too large a burden for most people. A wide variety of federal and state agencies investigate and resolve different kinds of consumer complaints. See PUBLIC ADMINISTRATIVE AGENCIES.

The FEDERAL TRADE COMMISSION (FTC), the largest of these administrative agencies, is responsible for policing the consumer marketplace by controlling false advertising and unfair or deceptive trade practices that, although locally operated, have a harmful effect on interstate commerce. The FTC has championed the cause of consumers in many ways. It ordered the Adolph Coors Company to stop restricting the territory where its beer could be sold and required the Dollar-a-Day car-rental service to change its name to fit its rates.

EXAMPLE Around income-tax time one finance company advertised "Instant Tax Refunds." The FTC ordered an explanation of the term. It heard a number of witnesses testify that they did not understand that the advertisements referred to normal loans, not to some type of advance on anticipated tax refunds, and that borrowers still had to meet the usual standards of creditworthiness. It was no excuse, the commission said, if these witnesses were especially thickheaded; they were part of the audience at whom the commercials were aimed.

In recent years the FTC has permitted and encouraged comparative advertising. Formerly an advertiser could not legally mention a competitor by name because he was thereby using the competitor's protected trademark for his own commercial benefit. Radio, television, and the print media observed a policy of comparing an advertiser's product only with "another leading brand." Brand X became the most widely advertised product in the country.

Then in 1971 the National Broadcasting Company announced that it would accept commercials that named competitors by brand. The FTC permitted a tryout of this policy and then persuaded other communications media to adopt it. Believing that the consumer is best served by receiving the most accurate information possible, the FTC found that the use of Brand X is not necessary.

In the early 1960's Ralph Nader, a consumer activist, studied the FTC and concluded that it was ineffective in protecting consumers and policing antitrust violations. In the 1970's the FTC took a more vigorous position and strongly supported the cause of consumer protection. For instance, it encouraged advertisement of prices for eyeglasses and regulated the sales pitches made by trade and vocational schools. New requirements that appliances be labeled with energy-efficiency information recognize another consumer concern.

■ **Conclusion** The best consumer protection is education. If you understand your rights as a consumer and use credit wisely, you are going to stay ahead.

consummate Finish; complete what was intended. For example, to consummate a deal means to complete it after all the terms have been agreed upon and met. To consummate a marriage means to complete the union by sexual intercourse.

contemner A person who commits CONTEMPT of court.

contemplation of death A term in statutes that means an apprehension of death from some *present disease* or *impending danger*. It does not refer to the expectation of eventual death that all of us have. When applied to transferring of property, the phrase means that the driving cause of the transfer, which is called a gift CAUSA MORTIS, is the thought of imminent death.

EXAMPLE If you tell your daughter that you want her to have your diamond bracelet in case you do not survive the heart surgery scheduled for tomorrow, this gift is made in contemplation of death. If you die during the heart surgery, the bracelet belongs to her. If, however, you survive the surgery but are killed one month later in a car crash, the bracelet does not belong to your daughter because your death did not result from the heart surgery, which was the motive for the gift.

A GIFT made in contemplation of death does not avoid estate or inheritance taxes. See ESTATE TAX AND GIFT TAX.

contempt A willful disregard or disobedience of a public authority. It may be a disregard or disobedience of the rules of order of a judicial or legislative body; or it may be disorderly behavior or insolent language in the presence of the court or legislature or so near it as to disturb its proceedings or to impair the respect due it.

This article discusses contempt of Congress, acts that constitute contempt, the power of the courts to punish contempt, contempt proceedings, and types of punishment.

■ **Contempt of Congress** Congress has the power to punish anyone other than its members for contempt of its authority in cases over which it has authority. The power given Congress to legislate implies that Congress also has the right to preserve itself by dealing with direct obstructions of its legislative duties. This power extends only to acts that prevent it from discharging its duties. In conducting an investigation by a committee, for example, Congress may compel a witness to disclose relevant facts. If the witness refuses to answer a pertinent question, he may be in contempt of Congress. He will not be held in contempt if he refuses to answer a question that would incriminate him. Congress has no power, however, to expose a person's associations or beliefs to public view only for the sake of exposure.

In the 1950's, during the so-called McCarthy era when fear of Communist infiltration was at its height, the House Committee on Un-American Activities held numerous sessions to inquire into the extent of Communist Party influence in America. The committee adopted rules that said that a witness could request a closed-door executive hearing, which would be granted if a majority of the committee found "that the interrogation of a witness in a public hearing might endanger national security or unjustly injure his reputation or the reputation of other individuals." If the request was denied, the witness would be questioned in a public hearing.

EXAMPLE In one case, a witness, upon receiving a subpoena to appear before the committee, sent a telegram requesting an executive (or closed) session. The request was denied by a staff director who lacked the authority to do so. When the witness appeared before the committee in a public session, he refused to answer certain questions and was held in contempt of Congress. The Supreme Court decided the witness was not guilty because the committee had not complied with its own rules regarding the choice between executive and public sessions.

Congress can find a person in contempt and punish him by a fine or imprisonment only if the refusal to cooperate obstructs Congress's legislative duties. In reviewing contempt of Congress cases, courts try to balance public and private interests in order to determine the propriety and pertinence of questions asked of witnesses.

■ **Contempt of court** A contempt of court may be defined as a disobedience that undermines the court's authority, justice, and dignity and thus obstructs justice.

WHAT IS CONTEMPT OF COURT?

- Contempt of court is any disobedience of the court that undermines its authority or obstructs justice.
- Examples of contempt of court include altering a court order after it is signed or deliberately destroying it; opening a package that the court has ordered sealed; suing the same person on the same complaint on which you have already lost a previous case or filing a complaint unsupported by facts; and obtaining the opinion of the court when no real controversy exists or obtaining a postponement on the ground of feigned illness.

- You will not be held in contempt for acts done by your attorney without your direction or knowledge or for mistakes in procedure.
- If an attorney is constantly late for the trial session, he may be found in contempt of court.
- Civil contempt infringes on the rights of individuals, as when a person disobeys a court order to produce his tax records. The punishment imposed by the court is coercive—for example, imprisoning him until he produces the records—rather than punitive, as in cases of criminal contempt.

- Criminal contempt subverts the court's dignity and authority and may be punished by fine or imprisonment as an offense against society.
- Criminal contempt is wide ranging, including, for example, (1) a defendant screaming obscenities in the courtroom and refusing to stop when ordered to by the judge; (2) trying to bribe a juror in the hallway of the courthouse; (3) swearing at the attorney; (4) being armed with a deadly weapon in the courtroom; and (5) a court officer accepting a bribe to fix a traffic arrest.

A *direct contempt* is committed in the presence of the court while it is in session. Direct contempt consists of any conduct that tends to embarrass or obstruct the court in the administration of justice or brings the administration of the law into disrepute. If a defendant refuses to stop screaming obscenities during his trial, for example, he may be held in direct contempt of court.

A *constructive, indirect,* or *consequential contempt* is committed outside the presence of the court. It is an act done at a distance, which tends to belittle, degrade, obstruct, interrupt, or embarrass the court in the administration of justice. For example, trying to bribe a juror in the hallway of a courthouse may be constructive contempt, as well as the crime of BRIBERY.

A *criminal contempt* is conduct directed against the dignity and authority of the court, and a *civil contempt* consists of failing to do something the court has ordered in a civil lawsuit for the benefit of the opposing party in the lawsuit. A criminal contempt is an offense against society; a civil contempt is an infringement on the rights of private persons. Civil and criminal contempt proceedings are discussed later in this article.

- **Conduct constituting contempt** Conduct that constitutes contempt is usually defined by both federal and state laws. In essence, it is misbehavior that hinders the fair and efficient administration of justice. Not all acts that impede the course of justice, however, are considered contempt—only behavior that clearly disobeys any of the court's direct orders or that directly tends to bring the court in disrepute. For example, if a court officer accepts money in exchange for a promise to fix a traffic arrest, it is a clear case of constructive contempt of the court in which the traffic prosecution is pending.

Unlawfully delaying or interfering with the proper execution of the legal process usually constitutes contempt. A court is justified in punishing an attorney for contempt when he has aided and abetted the accused in evading a trial, as by sending his client on a prolonged vacation to Mexico. If a person conceals books, papers, and documents that he has been ordered to produce in court, he is guilty of contempt.

Unless a statute provides otherwise, whether or not an act constitutes contempt usually depends on its nature and not on the actual intent of the act. But when the act is one that a person may rightfully do if he is acting in good faith, the intent may determine whether the conduct is contemptuous. For example, if you moved for the postponement of a trial because of illness you would not be acting in contempt. But if you moved for a postponement knowing that an extended delay will mean that the only witness to the lawsuit may die, you would be acting in contempt. Inconvenience alone does not justify a finding of contempt. There must be an attempt to block justice.

The manner in which an act is done, or words are spoken, may be an important element in determining contempt. Courts look not only to the words but also to the surrounding circumstances, the connection in which they were used, the tone, the look, the manner, and the emphasis.

EXAMPLE In a New Jersey case, a defendant disrupted a hearing that sought to determine the extent of his wealth. He deliberately and continually interrupted the witnesses and told the opposing counsel, "It takes a pig to represent a pig." The court decided that his intentional misconduct was aimed at obstructing justice and held the defendant in criminal contempt.

An attempt to do something that constitutes contempt may be treated as contempt. For example, John, the defendant in an income-tax case, tries to bribe a juror by offering him money, but the juror refuses it and reports John to the court. John may be held in contempt of court even though his bribery attempt failed. On the other hand, some courts have decided under federal law that a CONSPIRACY to commit a contempt of court, without any overt act, is not a contempt.

EXAMPLE John and his friend Arthur decide that at John's income-tax evasion trial they are going to scream obscenities at every witness who takes the stand. On the day of the trial, Arthur has the flu and John wakes up with laryngitis. Their plan to disrupt the trial was never consummated, although they did conspire to commit a contempt of court. If their scheme comes to the attention of the court, neither John nor Arthur will be held in contempt because their plans, without any overt act, had no effect on the administration of justice.

Abuse of legal process If you sue a person on the same complaint on which you lost in a previous lawsuit or if you file a complaint unsupported by facts, you are willfully abusing the legal process—an act of contempt. A person who obtains court orders by fraud or deceit—such as a parent who falsely charges that the other parent is a drug addict in order to secure temporary custody of their child—will be held in contempt because false information hinders justice. If you obtain the opinion of the court when no real controversy exists or gain the CONTINUANCE (postponement) of a case on the ground of feigned sickness, your conduct is contemptuous. Numerous postponements with the court's approval, however, are not grounds for a contempt action.

A direct contempt of court is committed if, upon the death of a wealthy uncle, greedy relatives file a fraudulent will knowing that it is false and seek to have it admitted to probate so that it will be recognized by the court as valid.

If you lie in an affidavit and justice is hindered, you may be punished for contempt. (You could also be brought to trial for PERJURY.) A client will not be held in contempt for acts done by his attorney without his direction or knowledge, or for mistakes in procedure, or if the action is based on the wrong legal theory.

Filing papers and destroying records Filing papers in court in a contemptuous manner constitutes contempt. So does filing papers that show disrespect for the dignity or authority of the court or tend to interfere with the administration of justice. Two examples are using abusive, violent, and improper language in an affidavit and filing a forged affidavit or a motion falsely charging the court with dishonesty without a proper investigation.

As a rule, when a person refuses or neglects to return papers taken from court files, he may be held in contempt. If a court order is altered after it is signed, or deliberately destroyed, this conduct clearly shows an intent to obstruct justice and is punishable as contempt. If a person opens a package that the court has ordered sealed—as when a newspaper reporter obtains the sealed record of a scandalous divorce proceeding between a politician and his wife and publishes it verbatim—he will be held in contempt.

Destruction of the subject matter Generally, it is a contempt of court to dispose of, conceal, destroy, or remove the subject matter of litigation from the court's jurisdiction. This applies to persons as well as to property.

EXAMPLE When foster parents remove their foster child O——* from the state while awaiting the outcome of a custody proceeding brought by the child's natural mother, they may be held in contempt of court if they refuse to tell where the child is or return him to the jurisdiction.

EXAMPLE Albert, the defendant in a lawsuit resulting from O——* his drunken driving, expects to have to pay substantial damages to the party he injured. He wants to avoid payment, so he puts all his property and bank accounts in his brother's name. Albert will be held in contempt because his behavior impedes the administration of justice.

As a general rule, it is also contempt to interfere with persons or property in the custody of the law. For example,

a person in custody who escapes or lets himself be rescued is guilty of contempt, as is a sheriff who makes no effort to protect a prisoner in his custody from mob violence.

Disobedience of an order Resisting, disobeying, or trying to prevent the performance of a lawful, specific, and clearly expressed order, decree, or mandate of a court constitutes contempt. Disobedience may be either civil or criminal contempt or both. If the defendant has been ordered to transfer land to the plaintiff but instead he transfers it to another person, this disobedience constitutes both a civil and a criminal contempt. It is a civil contempt because the defendant failed to perform an act for the benefit of the opposing party in a civil suit. It is a criminal contempt because the defendant blatantly disregarded the court's authority.

In order to be held in contempt for not complying with an order or decree of the court, you must have actual knowledge of the order or have been given a copy of it. Failure to obey an order of the court is not contempt if the person under the order is unable to comply, unless he cannot comply because of his own wrongful act.

EXAMPLE If Jake's Trucking Company has gone out of O——* business, Jake will not be held in contempt for not reinstating an employee who was discharged because of his union activities. If, however, Jake closes down his business and immediately reopens it under a different name to avoid obeying the order, he will be held in contempt of court for refusal to comply with the order.

To be held in contempt for disobeying a court order to pay money, you must be able to comply with the order. Unless there is a law that states otherwise, your inability to pay because of poverty, insolvency, or some other reason that is not your fault will generally be accepted as a valid excuse. When the inability results from your wrongful act—for example, you misappropriated funds you held as a trustee or FIDUCIARY and now you are expected to pay them—you would be held in contempt.

A proper demand for performance must be made before you can be found in contempt of an order for the payment of money or the delivery of property. What is a sufficient demand depends upon the nature of the order, but if the demand is made before the time specified by the order, refusal to comply with it is not contempt. You are required to perform only by the date specified. For example, a court decree that orders you to turn over an expensive painting to the county sheriff on August 8, 1980, is a demand for performance on that date.

Misconduct by jurors, witnesses Any misconduct by a juror that prevents a fair and impartial consideration of the case constitutes contempt: refusing to serve, defying the orders of the court, refusing to carry out the instructions of the trial judge, acquiring information out of the courtroom regarding a pending trial, disclosing grand jury proceedings to an outsider, separating yourself from the other jurors in violation of the court's order, improperly talking with the parties in the suit or trial, and determining a verdict by lot or chance. If a potential juror conceals or misstates an important fact during a VOIR DIRE (preliminary) examination to select a jury, he may be guilty of contempt. All willful attempts to influence jurors improperly constitute contempt. Approaching a juror to find out how he stands on a case or sounding out a juror to find out whether he can be corruptly influenced constitutes contempt.

If the misconduct of a witness has a direct tendency to obstruct justice, it is contempt. A witness may be punished for contempt for refusing to obey a proper order of a court—as by remaining in the courtroom after the court has ordered him to leave. Generally, PERJURY (false swearing by a witness) is contempt if it obstructs the court in performance of a judicial duty. For instance, when a court recognizes false affidavits as false, the perjured testimony is not an obstruction of justice—but is an offense in itself. Trying to induce witnesses to testify falsely, to change their testimony, or not to testify or attend the proceedings constitutes contempt. It is contempt to try to bribe a witness or to use persuasive or threatening language to get him to testify falsely or not to testify.

Misconduct under the eye of the court If a deputy sheriff in charge of jurors secretly buys liquor for them and they all become drunk, both the jurors and the sheriff may be held in criminal contempt because the misconduct was committed under the eye of the court. Other examples of contemptuous misbehavior committed in the presence of the court are disorderly conduct; carrying a deadly weapon in the courtroom; using threatening or insulting language to the court, its officers, witnesses, or opposing counsel; and picketing or demonstrating at the judge's home.

Federal statutes speak of contempt "in the presence of the court or so near thereto" that it obstructs the administration of justice. Any contempt committed in any place set apart for the court while it is in session, including the judge's chambers, is generally viewed as having been committed "in the presence of the court." The words "so near thereto" are, at least in the federal courts, interpreted geographically. Acts that are committed at a substantial distance from the court do not come within the federal statute, even though they obstruct the administration of justice or tend to do so.

EXAMPLE In one case, the federal court did not have the power to punish as contempt acts of persons responsible for a television broadcast that claimed to be a reenactment by members of the jury of their deliberations in a criminal case. Under the statute, the court could not punish those who participated in the program or its preparation, even though the broadcast interfered with the orderly processes of justice. It was not performed "in the presence of the courtroom" or "so near thereto."

Misconduct by attorneys Misconduct by an attorney that insults the dignity or authority of the court or hinders the administration of justice is contempt. An attorney's refusal or failure to heed a proper order or warning of the court, such as repeating objections or asking a witness improper questions, constitutes contempt. If an attorney is constantly late for the trial session, he may be found in contempt of court. In some courts, statements that are not contemptuous in themselves may be contempt if an attorney makes them in a rude and disrespectful manner.

Disturbing the order of the court A person who disturbs the peace and good order of the court is guilty of contempt. For example, a newspaper photographer who takes pictures in the courthouse contrary to the court's order is guilty of contempt. An interruption in itself does not necessarily constitute contempt. An attorney is not guilty of contempt if he interrupts a trial to present an emergency motion when justice would otherwise be defeated or irreparable injury would result to his client.

EXAMPLE In Illinois an order finding an attorney guilty of direct contempt was overturned because the reviewing court found that he had acted in the interests of justice. During the course of a criminal trial, the judge had refused the request of the state's prosecutor that exhibits used by the defense attorney be turned over to the state. After the defense attorney left the courtroom, the prosecutor, without notifying the defense attorney, repeated his request, which the judge granted. Upon learning of this, the defense attorney went to the courtroom where the judge was hearing another case and interrupted the proceedings to make an emergency motion preventing the state from obtaining the exhibits. He believed that his client would be irreparably harmed once the exhibits had been turned over. The judge refused to allow the attorney even to address the court, and when he persisted, held him in contempt and sentenced him to two days in the county jail. The reviewing court found that the attorney was unjustly denied a reasonable opportunity to explain why he was interrupting the judge. A trial judge has no right to refuse to hear an emergency motion just because he is hearing a different case.

Criticism of the court Criticism of a court's rulings or decisions is not improper and may not be restricted after a case has been finally settled. Criticism of the court while a case is being adjudicated may be contempt if it is aimed at obstructing justice. For example, criticism to the press about a case that is being tried is not contemptuous unless it severely prejudices the case, resulting in the case being dismissed. Neither libel nor slander of a judge is contempt unless the attack on his character or on his acts interferes with his administration of justice.

EXAMPLE A minister commented in his sermon on the final decision in a case involving the rights of federal employees to hold county office and how the interests of the local political clubhouse coincided with the judge's decision. There was no interference with the administration of justice because the case had already been decided. Therefore, the minister could not be held in contempt.

Publications Irrespective of truth, falsity, or intent, any publication in newspapers or radio or television broadcasts that relates to judicial action is contemptuous when it tends to intimidate, influence, impede, embarrass, or obstruct the court and constitutes a clear and present danger to the administration of justice in matters pending before the court. But not all forms of newspaper comment or criticism regarding a pending case are contemptuous. If a newspaper article severely criticizes the court for appointing a receiver who is the son-in-law of the judge in a proceeding pending before it, the court cannot punish the publisher for contempt.

Any publication that interferes with the functions of a sitting grand jury constitutes contempt. Publication of news articles reporting judicial decisions or proceedings that could interfere with the trial of a criminal case, misrepresent the decision of a court, or divulge court secrets may constitute contempt.

■ **Rights of parties**   A person should not be permitted to use criminal contempt proceedings in order to achieve a private result. Under some statutes, however, acts that tend to defeat or impair a person's rights or remedies constitute contempt, especially when no other adequate remedy exists except to require the guilty person to do something he has already refused to do.

EXAMPLE   Under the terms of an agreement, Harper is to transfer the deed to farmlands to Carson. But when the time comes, he refuses. The most adequate remedy for Carson is to have the court compel Harper to transfer the deed to him. If he still refuses, he will be guilty of both civil contempt, for refusing to remedy a private wrong to Carson, and criminal contempt, for refusing to obey a court order and impeding the administration of justice.

■ **Persons liable for contempt**   A person may be punished for contempt for violating a court order even though he is not a party to the lawsuit or proceeding that gave rise to the order. This situation can occur if he has notice (knowledge) of the order and is within the category of persons whose conduct is to be governed by it or if he acts jointly with a party under the order and knowingly violates it.

EXAMPLE   During the student riots of the late 1960's injunctions (court orders) were issued against the leaders of radical student groups to prohibit demonstrations. Students, whether members of the groups or not, were guilty of contempt if they joined with the groups and continued to demonstrate despite the injunctions.

Corporations   Corporations and their members, officers, and agents may be liable for contempt.

Court officers   Court officers—such as clerks, bailiffs, sheriffs, and marshals—are subject to punishment for contempts they commit, as are judges, magistrates, and attorneys. Persons occupying FIDUCIARY positions (positions of trust) may be punished for contempt for failing or refusing to perform the trust imposed on them.

■ **Proceedings for contempt**   There are two classes of contempt proceedings: criminal and civil. Ordinarily, proceedings are criminal when the purpose is primarily punishment and civil when the purpose is primarily remedial or compensatory. The aim of a criminal contempt proceeding is to vindicate the authority and dignity of the court. It is an independent and separate proceeding apart from the case in which it arose. The public is on one side and the person held in contempt is on the other. A civil contempt proceeding is instituted to preserve and enforce the rights of a private party in a legal action and to compel obedience to a judgment or decree intended to benefit him. Proceedings in civil contempt are between the original parties and are tried as part of the main case.

In general, civil contempt proceedings are started by a person who has a legitimate right to be protected. In criminal contempt proceedings, the state is usually the prosecutor. The court may, on its own motion, start proceedings to punish offenses against its dignity and authority.

EXAMPLE   If during the course of a trial a newspaper publishes sensational articles about the private life of the accused, the court may begin contempt proceedings against the paper for attempting to prevent a fair trial or trying to influence the jury or court.

Ending contempt proceedings   A civil contempt proceeding is usually abated (ended) when the suit in which the contempt arose is finally settled. Once those rights have been settled, there is no longer any need for contempt proceedings. Proceedings for civil contempt do not abate if the person charged with contempt dies. The innocent party can continue to try to enforce his private rights against the estate of the deceased. See ABATEMENT AND REVIVAL.

Criminal contempt proceedings are not usually ended when the main case ends. The contempt itself still remains to be punished. Violations of an order are punishable as criminal contempt even though the order is set aside on appeal if the violation occurred while the appeal was pending (unless the order is found to be absolutely void) or if the main case becomes MOOT (the issues of the case have been resolved without court action).

Requirements for a hearing   Usually, a direct contempt committed in the presence of the court may be summarily or immediately punished by it. A formal entry in the court record that shows the facts of the contempt is essential to enable the contempt order to be reviewed, and in many states, failure to provide one may justify the reversal of a contempt conviction.

Proceedings to punish contempts committed out of the court's presence (indirect contempt) must ordinarily be started by filing an accusation, pleading, or affidavit. The court, however, may make an accusation on its own motion. Contempt proceedings whether for civil or criminal contempt, do not require the presence of a jury unless specified by statute.

■ **Power to punish**   The power of the courts to punish for contempt is essential to the administration of justice. When the courts hold a person in contempt, they exercise a drastic and extraordinary power. It should not be used when other adequate statutory proceedings are available.

Punishment   A court may punish contempt either by a fine or imprisonment or both. Imprisonment must generally be for a definite term.

EXAMPLE   When a witness who was offered immunity refused to testify before the grand jury about a series of bombings in New York City committed by members of a radical political group, she was found guilty of criminal contempt for obstructing justice. She was ordered imprisoned until she would testify or until the term of the grand jury expired. At that point, the grand jury had 18 months to run.

In a civil contempt proceeding, the punishment usually must be coercive or remedial in nature, rather than a punitive sentence, as in criminal contempt. An example of coercive punishment would be imprisoning an employer when he disobeys a subpoena to produce the tax records of his business. An example of a remedial punishment would be fining a manufacturer when he continues to use another's trademark in violation of a court order prohibiting him from using it. If imprisonment is imposed for civil contempt, it is usually not for a definite term but rather until the person who committed the contempt performs the act required by the order of the court. If a reporter refuses a defense attorney's request and a court's order to reveal the source of his information that has led to the prosecution of a doctor for murder, the defense attorney may ask the court to hold the reporter in civil contempt and imprison him until he discloses his source.

When the acts of contempt infringe on the injured party's rights or remedies, fines to compensate him for loss or expenses are authorized by statute in some states.

Because punishment for contempt usually rests with the discretion of the trial court, it is generally not reviewable unless the court appears to have abused its discretion. A reviewing court may determine whether the punishment was so excessive and disproportionate to the gravity of the offense that it was arbitrary and vindictive.

contest **1** Oppose or defend against a lawsuit or other legal action or challenge the validity of a WILL. **2** As a noun, a legal action begun or a defense raised in a controversy before the courts.

context The context of a particular sentence or clause in a statute, contract, will, or other legal document is that part of the text that immediately precedes and follows it. The context may sometimes be examined to aid in the interpretation of an ambiguous passage.

contingent Depending on some future events or actions that may or may not happen. For example, you give a contingent estate to your unmarried grandson, which is to take effect at the birth of his first son. The right of your grandson to use the property depends on an uncertain future happening, the birth of his first son.

contingent fee A fee agreed to be paid to an attorney for his services in conducting a civil lawsuit only if he is successful. The fee is based on a certain percentage of the amount recovered in the suit. An attorney is not entitled to a contingent fee unless a contract specifically says so. A contingent-fee contract that prohibits the client from settling the case is void because it is against PUBLIC POLICY—which in this case is to encourage people to settle their differences out of court.

Contingent-fee agreements are generally used when the person seeking recovery cannot afford to hire an attorney in advance and thus would be unable to prosecute his claim effectively. Personal injury cases are the most common type of lawsuit in which these arrangements are used.

EXAMPLE You become paralyzed after taking a particular brand of sleeping pill. The drug manufacturer admits that it knew of this potential side effect but did not reveal the information to the Food and Drug Administration because it thought the chances of paralysis happening were very slight. You cannot afford to hire an attorney, but you learn of one who specializes in this type of case. You approach him and he offers to represent you on a contingent-fee basis of 25 percent of what he can recover for you. You agree. The trial takes 18 months, but the jury returns a $1 million verdict in your favor. Under your agreement with the attorney, you will collect $750,000, or 75 percent of the proceeds, while he collects 25 percent, or $250,000. You would not have recovered any money at all except for the contingent-fee arrangement.

■ **When permitted** Contingent-fee agreements are valid only if they are fair to the client. For example, an agreement in which an attorney received 95 percent of the amount recovered and the client received only 5 percent would be declared invalid. Contingent-fee agreements are not permitted for performing minor legal services. For example, a contingent fee of one-third of the benefits collected under an insurance policy was held by a court to be unreasonable and UNCONSCIONABLE because the insurance company was not contesting the claim and the legal services performed consisted only of filing the proper claim forms with the company. Contingent fees are also not permitted in criminal cases because there are no monetary proceeds from which the attorney can take a percentage as his fee. Contingent-fee arrangements are strongly discouraged in divorce actions on public policy grounds. Contingent-fee arrangements are closely scrutinized by the courts.

When an attorney employed on a contingent-fee basis dies, his estate is not entitled to any fee unless he fully performed his contract. If the client dies after the contract has been performed, the attorney may be entitled to recover his share of the proceeds. If the client dies while the jury is deciding a verdict, the attorney is entitled to his fee from the proceeds if the verdict is in favor of the deceased. If the suit is dismissed or settled by the deceased client's representatives, the attorney may not be entitled to a fee unless the contract provided for an agreed fee in case of settlement. But the lawyer may be entitled to recover reasonable costs of the services he rendered.

continuance Postponement of a court action to a later day of the same TERM or to another term; the entry of a postponement on the court record in order to provide formal evidence of it. A continuance is part of court TRIAL procedure. Once a trial has begun or while motions are awaiting court decisions, the court has discretion to grant continuances if proper cause is shown. Courts have inherent power, subject to limits imposed by statutues, to grant or refuse continuances.

■ **Right to continuance** Courts are generally liberal in granting continuances when they are necessary to prevent the miscarriage of justice. Continuances are not favored, however, if their only purpose is delay. The parties to a legal action are entitled to a prompt trial, unless a good cause for a postponement is shown.

■ **Continuance by operation of law** When a case has not been tried or otherwise disposed of during a term of a court, it is continued by operation of law. If the case was not heard during the term because of unforeseen circumstances, such as delays in the cases preceding it, the case will automatically be postponed, or continued, until the next term. The rights of the parties in the continued cases are not adversely affected or terminated but only delayed. A continuance by operation of law may also occur when a term of court is not held at the regular time or when the judge is disqualified—for example, if he is a stockholder of a corporation that is the defendant in the case.

■ **Grounds for continuance** In deciding on a motion for a continuance, the court will consider all the facts and circumstances of the case—in particular, the applicant's good faith, his purpose for delay, the necessity of granting a continuance, the probable advantage that would result from it, and whether the interests of the other parties would be harmed. When the circumstances for granting a continuance are debatable, courts usually tend to continue the case upon the defendant's request but not usually upon the plaintiff's, because the plaintiff should have been adequately prepared before starting his suit.

Multiple defendants   When there are several defendants in a case, a continuance granted to one defendant operates as a continuance of the entire case. A trial court may order a continuance if some or all of the parties fail to appear on the day set for the hearing, but it is not obligated to do so. A court may also, in its discretion, postpone a case when both parties or their attorneys consent or stipulate. See STIPULATION. Some of the more common grounds are discussed below.

Inadequate notice of case   A lawsuit normally begins when the plaintiff notifies the defendant of the existence of a lawsuit against him by serving him with a writ or a subpoena. If the SERVICE is defective or does not give adequate notice of the case, the court may grant a continuance to the plaintiff to complete the service so that he will not lose his opportunity to have his suit tried. If the plaintiff does not act diligently in obtaining proper service, such as not correcting errors promptly, he is not entitled to a continuance.

A delay in filing PLEADINGS (written statements that present each side of the case) by one side usually entitles the other side to a continuance if the delay affects the issues in the case. He must be given time to prepare his response before the trial or his rights will be severely injured. A party whose pleadings fail to disclose a worthy cause of action or defense is not entitled to a continuance. If, after review by an appellate court, a case is remanded (sent back for a new trial), a continuance should be granted if sufficient time has not been allowed to prepare for the new trial. Usually, the parties must be ready for trial by the next term after the appellate decision.

Loss of papers   If papers in the case—such as the pleadings, are accidentally lost or destroyed, a continuance may be granted to the party if he has not been at fault and the papers cannot easily be replaced.

Lack of preparation   Generally a request for continuance due to a lack of preparation will be refused, especially when the party is guilty of inexcusable ignorance, delay, or negligence in preparing his case. To be entitled to a continuance on this ground, an applicant must show a specific, legal reason for his lack of preparation and must also show that he was reasonably diligent in trying to be prepared for the suit.

EXAMPLE When the sole witness to a gangland execution
0⊷—⊛ mysteriously disappears 24 hours before the trial, the court may properly grant the state prosecutor a continuance until the whereabouts of this key witness is discovered. On the other hand, a continuance to allow a party to obtain better proof is unwarranted.

Change of counsel   Lack of preparation that results from the withdrawal of counsel or the engagement of new counsel just before the trial date is not necessarily a ground for continuance. If it appears that a defendant has employed a series of lawyers in a case just to obtain continuances by constantly hiring and firing them as the trial date approaches, and the defendant has used this same DILATORY,

or delaying, tactic in another case before the same judge, his motion for a continuance will most likely be denied.

Outcome of another case   Usually, a continuance should be granted when justice requires the suit to await the trial and conclusion of another proceeding affecting the same parties. Even if the parties are not identical, there may still be a continuance as long as their interests in the case are closely related.

EXAMPLE Smith, your employee, while driving your truck
0⊷—⊛ during business hours, collides with a car driven by Jones. Jones is injured. Jones sues you, claiming the accident was Smith's fault. He knows that you, as an employer, are responsible for the acts of your employees done for business purposes during business hours. He also realizes that because you are a wealthy businessman he will probably be able to recover more money from you if he is successful in his case than from your employee. Smith, however, has already brought a suit against Jones, claiming Jones caused the collision by running a red light. This suit is already being tried.

The basic issue of both suits is determining who was responsible for the accident. Both you and your employee have closely related interests—if the accident was his fault, both of you will be liable. Because this issue will be decided in the Smith suit, you may move for a continuance in the Jones suit against you, pending the outcome of Smith's suit. If Jones is found to be responsible for the collision in the Smith suit, then he will not be able to sue you, because the accident was his fault. If the continuance is granted, the trial court would dismiss the entire case against you after the verdict went against Jones.

When the pending action has no possible bearing on the issues in the action sought to be continued, it is proper to deny the continuance.

EXAMPLE If you had moved for a continuance in the Jones
0⊷—⊛ suit against you on the basis of the Smith suit, but that suit instead involved Smith's suing Jones for breach of contract for failing to paint Smith's house, then the court would properly deny the continuance. The breach-of-contract suit would not affect any of the issues in the personal-injury suit.

Illness   The illness of a party is not automatically a ground for continuance. If injustice is as likely to follow from granting a continuance as from its refusal, a court may refuse the motion.

EXAMPLE In one New York case, a defendant with connec-
0⊷—⊛ tions to organized crime, on trial for arson and murder, had been granted 64 continuances because of a heart condition. During this time, the key witness for the prosecution died. The court properly refused to grant the defendant's request for still another continuance, particularly when it was discovered that the defendant had not been hospitalized for the last month.

If, however, a party's illness makes his presence at the trial impossible, a continuance will be granted, but only if (1) he has immediately notified the court and the other party that he is sick rather than waiting until the actual date of the hearing before telling anyone of the delay or (2) the sickness is not feigned or the result of a deliberate act to delay the trial. The fact of illness should be established by a sworn statement, such as a physician's affidavit.

■ **Hearing and determination**   Every application for a continuance should be heard by and determined by the court after all the circumstances of the case have been put into evidence by a formal written statement or affidavit. If the continuance is granted, the trial court will fix a reasonable length of time for it, with regard for the rights of both parties. During the continuance, the trial court may revoke or modify the order for reasonable cause. It can attach any limitations or conditions that seem necessary and proper.

Second or subsequent continuances are usually denied unless the applicant has demonstrated that he acted diligently to achieve the results that are now the ground of the second continuance. For example, if the ground for the second continuance is newly discovered evidence—such as a gun found buried in the woods only after a highway crew began to dig up the woods to build a new road—the court may deny it if the applicant could have discovered the evidence sooner by exercising reasonable diligence.

After the reason for granting a continuance has ceased to exist, the court may properly revoke the continuance and require the case to proceed.

■ **Waiver**   A person waives his right to a continuance if he lets the trial start without requesting one, if he does not object after his motion for a continuance has been ignored or overruled, or if he withdraws his pleadings.

contra   (Latin) "Against"; confronting, on the contrary, in opposition to. For example, *contra bonos mores* means "against good morals."

contraband   1 Goods exported from or imported into a country against its laws; articles that cannot be owned or possessed legally, such as stolen property, counterfeit money, or drugs.   2 As an adjective, against law or treaty; prohibited.

contracts   The law of contracts affects your everyday life. Contracts include every kind of oral or written agreement—such as a lease, a sales contract, or an employment contract—that has legal consequences for the parties involved. In all these agreements a person either expressly or implicitly binds himself, in exchange for something of value, to pay a sum of money or to perform or refrain from a certain act. For example, when you sign an apartment lease you agree, among other things, to pay a certain sum in exchange for the use of living quarters, which is valuable real estate belonging to the landlord.

Your right to make contracts is a natural and inalienable right, which is protected by federal and state constitutions. You are free to make whatever contracts you please, so long as no fraud or deception is practiced and the contracts are legal in all respects.

This article presents an overview of the law of contracts, identifies the essential elements of a valid contract, describes the different types of contracts, discusses performance of the terms of a contract, and points out the legal consequences of a breach of contract. See also Charts 6 and 7.

The law of the sale of goods between merchants, such as between wholesalers and retailers, is based upon general principles of contract law. The Uniform Commercial Code governs those transactions and they are fully discussed in the article SALES. For a discussion of the law of sales as it applies to consumers, see CONSUMER PROTECTION.

■ **Contracts in general**   The purpose of a contract is to establish the conditions to which the parties agree and their rights and duties under those conditions. A valid contract must be enforced by the courts according to its terms.

In general to be enforceable in court a contract (1) must be made by legally competent parties; (2) must not have as its purpose something that is illegal to do or have; (3) must include a valuable consideration—an inducement for each party to carry out his part of the bargain; (4) must impose a mutual obligation on the parties; (5) must be the result of mutual agreement between the parties; and (6) must be in writing if a written document is required under the STATUTE OF FRAUDS, as for a contract involving the sale of land. If any of these essential elements are missing, the contract cannot be enforced.

Not every agreement results in a binding, legally enforceable contract. When a contract affects the general public, legislation may prescribe and limit its terms. For example, the terms of an insurance contract to protect a bus company in the event of accidents may be set by statute so that the public will be assured of adequate recovery of claims against the company.

If the parties have not agreed on the essential terms of an agreement, a court will not supply them. A court's function is to enforce existing agreements, not to create them by imposing terms it considers reasonable.

Contracts by competent persons, fairly made, are usually valid and enforceable. The parties are bound by the terms to which they have agreed as long as they have not been swayed by fraud, violence, or undue influence. This is true even if the contract causes a hardship or appears to be foolish, oppressive, or a bad bargain. However, the court will consider the fairness of the transaction and its freedom from any taint of oppression when weighing the right of a party to the court's aid in enforcing a contract.

A contract shows a meeting of the minds of two parties acting in good faith. Once formed, it may not be rejected merely at the whim of one party or the other. Usually the time when you can change your mind without penalty ends when you complete the agreement. An exception is the cooling-off period available in many states for purchases from door-to-door salesmen.

■ **Kinds of contracts**   The many different kinds of contracts include contracts under seal and express, implied, executed, executory, bilateral, unilateral, aleatory, adhesion, conditional, void, and voidable contracts.

Contracts under seal   A contract under SEAL is a formal contract. In the past, all contracts had to be stamped with an official seal in order to be valid. The seal demonstrated that the parties had seriously entered into the agreement. But the seal has lost either some or all of its effect in many states through legislation and through recognition by the courts of informal contracts, which can be both express (specific) or implied.

Express contracts   An express contract is one in which the terms are specifically declared by the parties, either orally or in writing, at the time it is made. One party makes a definite offer that the other accepts in a manner that expressly shows assent.

EXAMPLE Daniel asks Rosalie to sell him her stereo for $400. She agrees and he picks up the stereo at her apartment after handing her $400. Daniel and Rosalie have made an express contract for the sale of the stereo.

Implied contracts   Implied contracts are classified as contracts *implied in fact* and contracts *implied in law*.

Implied in fact   A contract does not have to be put into words. It can be implied from facts and circumstances that show the mutual intention of the parties to make a contract. An implied contract is as firmly binding as an express contract.

EXAMPLE When your father dies and you select a casket and make the funeral arrangements, there is a contract implied in fact to pay the undertaker. The implication of a mutual agreement can be reasonably deduced from the circumstances and from the relationship between you and the undertaker.

When the relationship between the parties indicates that they were not making a contract, there can be no implied promise.

EXAMPLE Your daughter asks you for a loan of $25,000 to attend medical school. You give her the money and after she graduates and establishes a successful practice, you ask her to repay the loan. She refuses and you threaten to sue her. Her failure to fulfill her implied promise to repay the loan would not be considered a breach of contract because the family relationship negates the inference that she intended a contract with you.

When an agreement expires by its own terms, but the parties continue to perform according to it, an implication arises that they have mutually agreed to a new contract containing the same provisions as the old one.

EXAMPLE I hire you to work as a cashier for $100 a week for three months. We sign a contract. At the end of three months, I continue to pay you $100 a week and you keep on working. There is an implied contract. Usually, the existence of such a new contract is determined by the test of whether or not a reasonable man would think the parties intended to make such a new binding agreement.

Implied in law   A contract implied in law, on the other hand, is not a true contract but a QUASI contract. It is a duty imposed by law and is treated as a contract only for the purposes of a remedy for a situation. In a contract implied in fact, the contract defines the duty—such as, in the example above, to work as a cashier and be paid $100 a week. In a quasi contract, the duty defines the contract.

EXAMPLE John's wife, Selma, separates from John for justifiable reasons. In order to get necessary clothing for herself and their son, Selma buys them from Klein's store, charging them to John. John is quasi-contractually bound to pay for them, because he has a legal duty to support his family. This legal duty defines his contract to pay Klein's.

Contracts implied in law are based on (1) a presumption of performance of duty, regardless of whether the parties agreed, and (2) the principle prohibiting UNJUST ENRICHMENT, which says that if one person obtains property from another without authority and unjustly, the law will compel restitution (repayment). Similarly if one person confers a benefit on another, who accepts and keeps it, it is unjust for the recipient to keep the benefit without payment.

EXAMPLE Spark pays taxes and makes certain improvements on land that he mistakenly believes he owns, without the knowledge or assent of Flint, the actual owner of the land. Flint has a quasi-contractual duty to reimburse Spark for the taxes, because it was Flint's legal duty to pay them. If he refuses to reimburse Spark, he would be taking advantage of Spark's mistake and acting in bad faith. As for the improvements, Flint may have to pay Spark for them, depending upon the law of the state in which he lives.

According to the common-law measure of DAMAGES (compensation) for unjust enrichment, the reasonable value of the defendant's (Flint's) unjust enrichment is determined by the benefit he received, according to the use for which he held the land. Today, however, most states measure the damages for unjust enrichment by the reasonable costs of the goods or services to the plaintiff (Spark), rather than the actual enrichment of the defendant.

EXAMPLE Suppose the improvements cost Spark $5,000 but only contributed to Flint's use of the property to the extent of $2,500. Under the common-law measure, Spark would be reimbursed only for $2,500. His mistaken belief that he owned the property would have cost him $2,500. Under modern law, however, Spark would recover the entire $5,000 and thus would not be punished for his mistake.

Executed and executory contracts   An executed contract is one that has been carried out by both parties. It is no longer a contract because it has been completed. A housepainter agrees to paint your house for $1,000, completes the job, and is paid. That is an executed contract. Nothing remains to be done by either party. An executory contract is one that is not yet completed. For example, a written and signed promise to pay money at a future time is an executory contract. Most contracts are executory until they are executed, or completed.

Bilateral and unilateral contracts   A bilateral contract is one of reciprocal (mutual) promises. The promise that one person makes is sufficient inducement (consideration) for the promise made by the other. If I promise to pay you $10 because you promise to repair my broken window, a bilateral contract results. Mutual obligations arise from mutual promises.

A unilateral contract is one in which there is a promise on one side only. It is a promise by one party, the *offeror*, to do a certain thing if the other person, the *offeree*, performs a requested act. The performance of that act is the acceptance of the offer, and the contract is then executed, or completed. This type of contract is unilateral because only the offeror, the person who makes the promise, will be legally bound. The offeree may or may not act as requested, as he wishes. He cannot be sued for failing to perform, or for abandoning performance once he begins, because he has not made any promises. A REWARD is an example of a unilateral contract. Offer and acceptance of bilateral and unilateral contracts are discussed in greater detail under "Essentials of Contracts."

EXAMPLE I promise to pay you $10 for driving me home at the end of the day. You say nothing but when the time comes you take me home. I am obligated to pay you. If I refuse to pay you, you can sue me for the $10, because

I made a promise by which I became legally bound once you performed the act. On the other hand, if you refuse to drive me when I first ask you, I have no right to sue you, because you did not make any promises.

Aleatory contracts An aleatory contract involves a mutual agreement, the effects of which depend on an uncertain event. There must be risk—either on one side or on both sides—and the risk must be assumed by the parties. A fire INSURANCE policy is one type of aleatory contract. A person will not receive the proceeds of the policy unless a fire occurs, an event that is uncertain. Similarly, the proceeds of a life insurance policy cannot be paid until the insured's death—an event that is bound to occur but whose timing is uncertain.

Contracts of adhesion A contract of adhesion is a contract between a party of superior bargaining strength, a party who can only accept or reject the contract. This type of contract occurs when buyers have no real choice among the sellers of a particular item. For example, when you want to buy the latest model of a certain automobile, you really do not have much choice among car dealers. The dealer has the superior bargaining position, and you either accept his price or refuse to buy the car. Our society uses many adhesion contracts. Most businesses would never

THE BASICS OF CONTRACTS

■ To be enforceable, a contract must meet these six requirements: (1) The parties to the contract must be legally competent. (2) The contract cannot be for something illegal. (3) There must be something of value in it for both sides, an inducement or consideration for each party to carry out his side of the bargain. (4) It must be mutually binding on the parties. (5) It must be the result of a mutual agreement between the parties. (6) It must be in writing if a written document is required for that kind of contract.

■ Contracts can be express or implied. An express contract is one whose terms are specifically stated and agreed upon. An implied contract is one that is implied from facts and circumstances. For example, there is an implied contract to pay your doctor for treating you.

■ A void contract has no legal effect—no rights or duties—and is unenforceable. A contract made by a minor or an insane or intoxicated person can be made void.

■ A contract is formed when an offer is accepted. An offer consists of an expression of your intent to enter a contract, definite and certain terms, and your communication of the offer to the other person.

■ An offer of a prize in a contest may become a binding contract for a successful contestant who complies with the terms of the offer.

■ An offer made and accepted as a joke cannot be the basis of a contract.

■ A general advertisement is not an offer—it is only an invitation for an offer to make a binding contract.

■ If you make an offer (or an acceptance) through an intermediary, such

as the telegraph company, and there is a mistake, you may be bound by it unless the mistake is obvious and the other person should have realized it. For example, if you sent a telegram offering your car for $500 and the message was mistakenly transmitted as $400, you may lose $100 because of the error. (In some states, the courts would hold the contract invalid because of the error in transmission.) If the telegram read $50,000, you would not be held to it because the mistake was obvious.

■ You may reject an offer by (1) refusing to accept it, (2) making a counteroffer, or (3) accepting it on some condition. Once you reject an offer, you cannot turn around and accept it without getting the offeror's renewed consent.

■ To accept an offer, you must (1) know of the offer, (2) show your intention to accept it, (3) accept it unequivocally and unconditionally, and (4) accept it by the method stated in the offer.

■ A contract is formed when the acceptance is sent—this is known as the mailbox rule.

■ If a response to an offer seems to accept but adds qualifications or conditions, it is a counteroffer, not an acceptance.

■ In some states, unsolicited merchandise received in the mail may be considered an unconditional gift and you may use it for free. In other states, if you use the goods, a contract is formed and you must pay for them.

■ If goods are sent to you by mistake and you know about it, you must pay for them if you do not return them.

■ A contract is unenforceable if a

mistake, fraud, innocent misrepresentation, duress, or undue influence is involved.

■ A *mistake* is a clerical or computation error, not a mistake in judgment.

■ *Duress* may be blackmail, violence or the threat of it, or oppressive threats to start legal proceedings.

■ An example of *undue influence* is a salesman's bulldozing a frail octogenarian into a 20-year installment contract to buy an encyclopedia.

■ The basic remedies for a breach of contract are reformation, damages, rescission, restitution, and specific performance.

■ *Reformation* means the correction of a contract by a court, to make it correspond to the real intentions of the parties. Reformation may be sought when a written agreement does not correspond to the intended contract, as a result of fraud or mutual misunderstanding.

■ *Damages* is the amount of money that is to compensate you for your loss when the other party failed to meet the terms of your agreement.

■ *Rescission* means the contract is put to an end, and all parties are left in the position of never having made a contract.

■ *Restitution* means restoring the injured party to the position he was in before entering into the contract.

■ *Specific performance* requires the actual promise to be carried out as nearly as practicable. This remedy is applied to contracts involving parcels of land and other one-of-a-kind things. Specific performance cannot be applied to a personal service or employment contract because the Constitution prohibits slavery.

achieve their volume of transactions if it were necessary to negotiate all the terms of every consumer-credit contract, for example. Courts, however, sometimes refuse to enforce contracts of adhesion. They hold that there was never a true meeting of the minds of the parties or a true acceptance of the offer because the buyer really had no choice in the bargain. In such cases, the contract is considered unconscionable—that is, it is so unfair that it shocks the court and will not be enforced.

Conditional contracts A conditional contract is one whose existence depends upon a certain condition happening. Gail promises to pay her friend Joann $100 if she stops smoking cigarettes so that Gail may use the experience as material for a magazine article. This is a conditional contract dependent upon Joann's quitting smoking.

Void and voidable contracts Contracts may be classified as void or voidable. A void contract has no legal effect: no legal rights, duties, or obligations are imposed upon either party by it. A void contract is neither valid nor enforceable.

EXAMPLE Bob verbally agrees with Ted to buy his house for $45,000 and gives him $15,000 as a down payment. While waiting for Ted to move out, Bob learns that Ted has signed a written contract with Nicholas to sell the house for $48,000. Bob sues Ted to make him honor his oral contract. A court cannot enforce their agreement because a contract to buy real estate must be in writing in virtually every state. Therefore it is a void contract. Since they did not comply with the law, neither Bob nor Ted can have the court enforce the contract against the other. Ted can be made to return Bob's $15,000, however.

A voidable contract is an agreement that is valid and enforceable unless one of the parties chooses to treat it as void because he lacked some legal capacity to make a contract in the first place (such as being a minor, insane, or intoxicated) or was a victim of fraud. But the contract is void only when he chooses to treat it as such.

EXAMPLE Your 17-year-old daughter signs a contract to buy a color television from a discount appliance dealer. The contract is voidable because she is underage and does not yet have the legal capacity to enter into a legally binding contract. She may treat the contract as void, so that it would have no legal effect on her (disaffirmance), or she may choose to ratify (treat the contract as legally binding) and pay the dealer for the television.

A voidable contract may be ratified by express or implied conduct. An express ratification occurs when the party (who has, say, come of age or regained his sanity) states that he ratifies or accepts the contract. An implied ratification occurs when the party's conduct shows his intent to ratify a contract, such as by performing its terms. Ratification of a contract involves some of the same elements as the making of a new contract. There must be an intent to ratify and a full knowledge of all the important facts and circumstances. Oral acknowledgment of a contract, accompanied by a promise to perform, is considered sufficient ratification. Remember, however, that ratification by a minor is not legally binding until the child reaches the age of legal adulthood. Thus, if the 17-year-old in the above example tells the appliance dealer that she will pay for the color television, she will not be liable unless she ratifies

the contract after she becomes an adult under the law, usually at the age of 18 or 21. Once a contract is ratified, the power to avoid (disaffirm) its terms is lost forever.

Joint and several contracts Sometimes contracts are made that involve promises by more than one person to accomplish a single act. These are called joint and several contracts. Two or more parties who promise the same promisee (or group of promisees) that a particular performance shall be given may bind themselves jointly, severally, or jointly and severally.

Joint liability Promises impose joint liability only when promisors promise as a unit. Tom, Dick, and Harry write: "We promise to pay Charles $100." Tom, Dick, and Harry as a unit owe the debt to Charles. It is not promised by each of them individually but as a group. If Tom and Dick default, Harry will have to pay the whole $100, but he can then sue Tom and Dick for their proportionate shares. They are all thus jointly liable to Charles.

Several liability Promises impose several liability only when each individually promises to pay or act. Charles is owed $100. If the fellows had written, "Each of us, Tom, Dick, and Harry, singly and not jointly, promises to pay Charles a total of $100," it is as though there are three distinct and individual contracts, except that Charles is to receive a total of only $100. The three men do not promise together. They each singly, or severally, assume to pay the entire sum. If Tom and Dick default, Harry himself is liable for the whole $100 and he cannot collect from Tom and Dick.

Joint and several liability Promises impose joint and several liability when the promisors promise, both as a unit and individually, to pay or perform according to the terms of the contract. Tom, Dick, and Harry write: "We promise, and each of us promises, to pay Charles $100." The three of them, as a unit and individually, promise Charles. They are jointly and severally liable. If Tom and Dick default and Harry pays the $100 to Charles, Harry is then entitled to collect from Tom and Dick. However, unlike joint liability where Harry would have to sue both Tom and Dick, Harry need only sue one of them to get back two-thirds of the amount. If Harry sues Tom for the two-thirds, Tom may then sue Dick for his one-third.

Frequently when a husband and wife enter a contract, such as for a lease of an apartment, a mortgage on a house, or a retail installment contract, they sign as "William Smith and/or Mary Smith." They become jointly and severally liable for the payment of the contract. If either spouse dies, the duties under the contract are not discharged and the remaining spouse is still liable.

If a promisor who is jointly or jointly and severally liable on a contract performs or pays the promisee in full, the other promisors are thereby discharged from their obligations on the contract. The promisor who performed, however—the OBLIGOR—has a right of CONTRIBUTION against his copromisors. This entitles him to receive from the other copromisors their fair share of the debt.

■ **Essentials of a contract** The essential elements of a contract are (1) legal capacity to enter into a contract, (2) proper subject matter, (3) mutual agreement, (4) offer and acceptance, (5) valuable consideration, and (6) a written document if required by law.

Legal capacity   A person who agrees to a contract must have full legal capacity to become liable for duties under the contract. A minor (an INFANT), an INSANE PERSON, or someone who is intoxicated does not have this capacity. The legal capacity of the parties to enter into a contract may determine whether or not a contract is valid and thus enforceable.

Minors   Legally, a minor (infant) is a person under the age of 18 or 21, depending on the state. A contract made by a minor is valid and enforceable unless he chooses to disaffirm it (treat it as void). He may do this without being penalized for breach of contract. The basis for this treatment of minors rests in PUBLIC POLICY, which is to protect an immature and naive young person from being liable for an unfair contract. He is considered too inexperienced to negotiate on an equal footing with another party.

Once a minor reaches his majority (the age at which he is legally considered an adult), he must choose either to disaffirm the contract or ratify it. If he fails to disaffirm it within a reasonable time, determined by the circumstances of the particular case, the contract is considered ratified and he becomes bound to perform its terms. If he disaffirms the contract, he must return any benefits he received under it that are still in his possession. If he has used up or destroyed the benefits he received, he usually cannot be compelled to make restitution to the other party. However, he will have to pay to prevent his being unjustly enriched by the benefits needed for his health, comfort, or education. See NECESSARIES.

EXAMPLE Charlie, a 15-year-old high school sophomore, must attend summer school because of his failing grades in biology and French. The courses, including books and lab fees, cost $100 and are to be paid for on the day the student registers. Due to a clerical error, Charlie is allowed to complete the courses before it is discovered that only Charlie's signature, not his mother's, is on the registration card and the $100 has not yet been paid. The school sues Charlie for its money. It will be able to recover the reasonable value of the courses, books, and fees—in this case, $100. Such education is considered a necessary for which a minor is financially responsible.

If a minor willfully misrepresents his age, the courts hold that he may still disaffirm the contract. Generally, however, he must place the adult party in the *status quo ante*, meaning the situation he was in before the transaction took place. See STATUS QUO. The party who makes the contract with the minor can disaffirm a contract he entered into on the basis of a minor's fraudulent misrepresentation of his age or other important facts.

EXAMPLE Floyd, your 16-year-old neighbor, buys a motorcycle from Mrs. Green, an elderly widow who has just taken over her husband's business. Floyd tells her he is 22 and plans to use the motorcycle to commute to medical school. Mrs. Green is so impressed with Floyd that she lowers the price and lets him give her one-half of the price immediately, with the balance to be paid in two days. On his way home Floyd wrecks the motorcycle. Mrs. Green sues Floyd for the balance. Floyd will be allowed to disaffirm his contract. He need not return anything to Mrs. Green, because the motorcyle was completely destroyed.

Suppose Floyd does not wreck the motorcycle, and before he pays the balance Mrs. Green learns that he is only 16. On the ground of fraud she may then disaffirm the contract by returning his money.

Mental incapacity   Mental incapacity exists when a party does not understand the nature and consequences of the contract. If a party to a contract is mentally incompetent a distinction must be made between a person who has been judged incompetent by a court and has had a guardian appointed and a mentally incompetent person who has not been so judged.

A person who has been declared mentally incompetent in a court proceeding generally does not have the legal capacity to contract. He is unable to give the necessary consent because the court has determined that he does not understand the obligations and effects of the contract. Any contract he makes is void and unenforceable. Thus neither party is under a legal duty to perform or comply with the terms of the contract.

If there has been no formal declaration of insanity, the contract usually is voidable by the incompetent party. However, if the contract is inherently fair to both parties and has been executed to such a point that the competent party cannot be restored to the position he was in before the contract, the contract cannot be made voidable.

EXAMPLE Jackson, who appears and acts normal but is insane, although not judicially declared insane, borrows $2,000 from Brown. He gives Brown a promissory note and a mortgage on his property as security for the loan. Jackson spends the money and then tries to have the note and mortgage set aside as a voidable contract, claiming incapacity. Jackson will not succeed, because the contract was fair to both parties and he received full value in cash for his promise and security. Because Jackson has spent the money, he cannot return it to put Brown in the same position as he was before the contract. Brown, therefore, can enforce the contract against Jackson, because it was inherently fair to both parties and Brown has no other adequate remedy.

Many rules that apply to minors also apply to mentally incompetent persons. For example, when a voidable contract is disaffirmed, the incompetent person still has the duty of restitution and an obligation to pay for the reasonable value of necessary goods or services he reserved. The incompetent, his personal representative after death, or his guardian has the right to disaffirm the contract. The other party does not have the right to disaffirm it. A voidable contract can be ratified by the incompetent only if he recovers his mental health and thereby his capacity to contract.

Intoxicated persons   A contract made by an intoxicated person is voidable. If, when he is sober, he promises to perform the contract, or if he fails to disaffirm the contract within a reasonable time, he is considered to have ratified the contract and is legally bound to it. The same is true for a person under the influence of DRUGS.

Subject matter   Anything not forbidden by law may be the subject of a contract, such as leasing an apartment, buying a house, selling a car, or obtaining life insurance.

Any contract that is based on an illegal objective is void and without any legal effect. If your father-in-law offers to pay you $10,000 to divorce your wife and you accept, this contract will not be enforceable in court because it is against the law and public policy to foster a divorce. If a woman offers a professional killer $10,000 to kill her husband, this contract is illegal and will never be enforced in court. Contracts made in restraint of trade are also not enforceable in court.

EXAMPLE Chip Corporation owns Yum Yum, a brand name of ice cream. Chip requires its distributors to buy from it, at inflated prices, all ingredients for making Yum Yum ice cream. This type of contract is not enforceable because it deprives the distributor of his right to seek the best purchase price on the market for his supplies.

The subject matter of contracts may include future rights and liabilities, the performing or refraining from some specified act, or the assumption of certain risks or obligations. If I promise to pay you $1,000 if you promise to paint my house next week, and you agree, this contract gives you a future right to $1,000 when you paint my house and imposes a future liability on me to pay you when you finish the job.

A valuable idea may be the subject of a contract. If you invent a toy that consists of a flat board secured to the top of a roller skate, you may enter into a contract with a toy manufacturer to produce your idea in exchange for a share of the profits. But an idea that never takes concrete form at the time it is disclosed, even though it is new and unusual, is not the subject of a contract.

EXAMPLE You send your idea for a love story set in outer space to a book publisher. The publisher contracts with you to expand the idea into a detailed outline within a month, but you fail to do so. You have no enforceable contract rights against the publisher. If he later publishes a novel by another writer based on the same idea, you have no right to sue him for violating or breaching the contract because your idea had not taken a definite form when you revealed it.

A person cannot legally contract to others a right he does not have himself.

EXAMPLE When you buy a house a title search, which traces the ownership of the house back to its original owners, is usually required by the bank that gives you a mortgage. This assures the bank and the buyer that the seller owns the house free and clear of any debts or obligations to any other persons. If obligations do exist, the seller cannot enter a valid contract to sell the house free and clear of all debts, because he himself does not own the house free and clear.

Other situations when a contract may not be legal are discussed later in this article under "Illegal contracts."

Mutual agreement Agreement between the parties, or mutual assent, is essential to a contract. The parties must have a common intention—what the law calls a meeting of the minds—on the terms of the contract. They must both agree to the same bargain. Generally, if any portion of the proposed terms remains unresolved, there is no agreement.

The parties may settle one term at a time, but their contract becomes complete only when the last essential term is agreed upon.

Mutual agreement comes about through an offer by one party and its acceptance by another.

Offer An offer is a demonstration of willingness to enter into a bargain. It lets another person know that his assent to the bargain is invited and will conclude it.

The essential elements of an offer are (1) an expression of a present intent to enter a contract, (2) definite and certain terms, and (3) the communication of the offer. The presence of these three elements creates in the *offeree* (the recipient of the offer) the power to accept it and thereby create a contract.

EXAMPLE If I tell you that I will sell you my car for $500, I have made an offer because I indicated that I intend to make a contract. I was definite and certain in my terms, and I communicated my offer to you. You now may accept the offer and, if you do, you create a contract.

When an offer is made, merely performing the act does not form the contract. The act must be performed with knowledge of the offer. For example, the state offers a REWARD for the capture of an escaped convict. Jones captures the convict, not knowing of the reward. Jones is not entitled to the reward because he did not perform the act with knowledge of the offer.

Expressing present intent The person who makes an offer (and the person who accepts it) must show an intention to enter into a contract and thus affect the legal relationship between them. Mere statements of intention, promises, or proposals to make a deal, such as advertisements, requests for bids and jokes, are not sufficient.

Advertisements An advertisement, price quotation, or catalog is usually considered only an invitation to a customer to make an offer and not an offer itself. One reason is that a store may not have enough articles on sale to meet potential demand. A customer could not reasonably expect his acceptance of the offer to create a binding contract with the advertiser.

EXAMPLE An antique dealer sends out a circular that reads: "I have a set of pewter candlesticks dating back to the Revolutionary War, which I will sell for $150." In the mail he receives three checks from three people, each for $150, each stating, "I accept your offer." No contract is formed between the dealer and any of the customers, because the dealer's letter was, in effect, an invitation or a request for an offer from potential buyers. It was not an offer *to a particular person,* and so it did not express a present intent to contract.

Another reason why an advertisement is not a binding offer is that it can be revoked at the will of the offeror. For a discussion of false advertising, see CONSUMER PROTECTION.

EXAMPLE An advertisement offered for sale, as a one-day special, an electric sewing machine at a named price. A customer mailed the store a check for the purchase price, but the store refused to sell her the machine. The court said that the advertisement was "not an offer made to any specific person but was made to the public generally. Therefore, it . . . could be withdrawn at will and without notice." The customer could not require the store to sell the sewing machine under the terms of its ad.

There is, however, an exception to this general rule on advertisements. If the ad specifies the quantity offered and contains words of promise, such as "first come, first served," or "one color television set for $50 to the first person in the store on December 10," courts have allowed recovery for breach of contract when the customer offered the money and the store refused to sell the product.

EXAMPLE A store owner placed an ad in a newspaper reading: "1 Ranch Mink Stole, Beautiful, Worth $500—$10. First Come, First Served on Tuesday, March 15." George Smith was the first customer at the store that Tuesday. He offered $10 for the stole, but the store owner refused to sell the stole, stating that by the "house rule" the offer was intended for women only. Smith sued the store owner, contending that the newspaper ad was an offer he accepted and that the store owner violated the contract by refusing to sell him the stole. The store owner claimed that the ad was an invitation to an offer that could be withdrawn at any time before the sale without notice.

The court said that when the offer is clear, definite, and explicit, and leaves nothing open for negotiation, it is an offer that, if accepted, will complete the contract. In this case, the offer of the sale of the stole was clear, definite, and explicit and left nothing open for negotiation. Smith was the first person to appear at the store to be served, as required by the ad. He offered the stated purchase price and was entitled to the stole. The store's house rule had no effect on Smith. The ad did not restrict the offerees to women, and the store owner could not impose new conditions on the offer after Smith accepted it.

Request for bids A request or advertisement for bids for the sale of property or for construction work is only an invitation for offers. A county that has certain road repairs to be done, publishes an invitation in the local newspaper to bid for this public contract. Several construction companies submit bids, stating the lowest price they would charge to make the repairs. The invitation to bid is not an offer. If it were, the bids submitted would be acceptances, and the county would be placed in the impossible position of having formed numerous contracts to complete a single job. A contract is formed only when a particular bid is accepted.

Prizes An offer of a prize in a contest may become a binding contract for a successful contestant who complies with the terms of the offer. See REWARD.

EXAMPLE You enter a contest that offers you $10,000 for submitting the most creative poem about peanuts, to be judged by a panel of English professors. You comply with the terms of the contest, which are that you enclose the labels from 3 jars of your favorite peanut butter, submit 14 copies of your poem, and have your entry postmarked by midnight on February 1. If your poem is chosen by the panel, you have accepted the offer of $10,000 and a contract will be formed. If, however, you submitted only 13 copies of your poem and 2 labels, even though your poem is selected by the panel, no contract will be formed because you did not comply with the terms of the offer.

Jokes An offer made and accepted as a joke cannot be the foundation of a contract. If I offer to sell you my $50,000 house for $25, you cannot claim that you accepted my offer and a valid contract was formed, because it would never appear to a reasonable man that my offer was anything but a joke.

Definite and certain terms To determine whether the terms of an offer are definite and certain, you must find out if the following elements have been specified: (1) the identity of the offeree and subject matter; (2) the price to be paid; (3) the time of payment, delivery, or performance; (4) the quantity involved; and (5) the nature of the work to be performed.

Communicating the offer If there is a mistake in the transmission of an offer (or acceptance) by an intermediary, such as a telegraph company, most courts hold that the party who sent the message is bound by it. A minority of courts hold that if there is an error in transmission, no contract comes into existence.

EXAMPLE If I telegraph an offer to sell you my car for $500 but the telegram states $400, then most courts would allow you to accept my offer at $400. I would lose $100 because of the telegraph company's error. A minority of courts would decide that no contract was formed and I would not be penalized for the error.

If, however, the offeree (recipient) knows or should know of the mistake in the transmission of an offer, he may not take advantage of the known mistake by accepting the offer. If the telegram had read $50 instead of $500, a court will expect you to have realized that there was a mistake in the transmission of the offer. You cannot take advantage of an obvious mistake by accepting the offer. No contract would be formed.

When an offer becomes irrevocable An offer made for a consideration (something given or done by the offeree, such as paying money) is a binding contractual obligation, and it is irrevocable during the time specified in its terms. This offer, which lapses after the specified time, is called an *option*. Because an option is paid for, it cannot be revoked by the person who makes it. The person who has the option, however, is free to reject the offer until the option time lapses.

EXAMPLE A man has offered to sell you a Cadillac for $2,500 in cash. You ask him if he will take $25 to keep the offer open for three days until you are sure you can raise the money to pay for the car. He agrees. You do not have to accept his offer because you have paid only for the right to keep it open for three days. You would not be entitled to the return of your $25, because that is the fee you paid for the privilege of keeping the offer open.

This option payment differs from a deposit, which is a part of the purchase price you put down on a product after you accept the seller's offer to buy. If you accept his offer to buy the Cadillac and put $25 down as a deposit, you cannot later reject the deal, because a contract has already been formed. If you refuse to go through with the contract you will be liable for breach of contract.

Most courts hold that an offer for a unilateral contract (a promise by one person if another performs a requested act, such as my promise to pay you $10 for driving me across the bridge) becomes irrevocable as soon as the offeree starts to perform the requested act. For example, if I offer you $500 to swim across Lake Erie and you begin to swim, I cannot cancel my offer after you dive in the water and head for the opposite shore. If an offer for a unilateral contract calls for several acts, completion of the first act indicates acceptance.

Termination of an offer An offer continues and is binding on the offeror until the time specified for its continuance has expired or, if there is no time limit, until a reasonable period of time has passed. For instance, I offer to sell you my car for $1,000 and you make no response to my offer. If I sell my car to my neighbor three months later, you cannot claim that you intended to accept the offer. A reasonable time is determined by what a reasonable person would consider sufficient time to accept the offer under the circumstances of the case.

An offer lapses if either party dies or becomes insane before acceptance is communicated. But once the offer has been accepted, the contract is binding even if one of the parties dies or becomes insane after acceptance.

An offer ends if an essential element of the contract is destroyed—say a house offered for sale burns down—or if events occur that make the contract impossible to perform—say I offer to pay you $500 to fly a private plane to Vermont on a certain day, and on that day a blizzard grounds all planes.

The intervening illegality of a proposed contract may also put an end to an offer. I offer to sell you a particular brand of imported caviar, but before you accept my offer, the Food and Drug Administration bans it from being sold in the United States.

Revocation of the offer by the offeror, either by words or conduct that clearly shows that the offer is not open, becomes effective when the offeree learns of it. If the offeree has relied on the offer and suffers a loss as a result of the offer being withdrawn, the offeror may be bound by the offer because there is no other way to compensate the offeree for his loss. See PROMISSORY ESTOPPEL.

EXAMPLE Roger offers Eileen $6,000 to buy a new car so that she can use the $4,000 she has already saved to remodel her kitchen. She immediately signs a contract with a car dealer, putting $1,000 down as the deposit until she receives the money from Roger. She also signs a $4,000 contract with a builder to do her kitchen. Roger changes his mind, however, and tells her to forget his offer. Because she relied on Roger's offer, Eileen is legally committed to pay two different contracts worth $9,000, or $6,000 more than she has. A court can make Roger honor his offer because Eileen will otherwise incur a substantial financial loss.

Rejection of an offer   An offer may be rejected in three ways: (1) by stated refusal to accept it; (2) by a counteroffer, which rejects the offer by implication; or (3) by a conditional acceptance, which is really a counteroffer and thus a rejection by implication.

EXAMPLE Vince offers to sell Paula his bicycle for $100. Paula replies that she will give Vince $85 for it. Paula's response is a counteroffer that rejects Vince's offer by implying that she will not give the offered price of $100, but will give only $85. If Paula had merely asked Vince, "Will you take $85 for the bike?" her inquiry would not operate as a rejection. It would mean that she was still considering it while hoping to settle for $85, and therefore the offer was still binding on Vince.

Suppose Vince had also said that his original offer would remain open beyond any counteroffers. Paula makes the counteroffer of $85, which Vince rejects. If Paula then accepts the offer at $100, a contract is formed. The offer may also continue if the offeree specifically states that his counteroffer is not a rejection of the offer.

Once an offer is rejected, the offeror is relieved from liability. The party who rejected it cannot afterward decide to accept it without getting the offeror's renewed consent.

Acceptance   The essential elements of an acceptance are that (1) the offeree (recipient) must know of the offer; (2) the offeree must show an intention to accept; (3) the acceptance must be unconditional; and (4) the acceptance must be made according to the terms of the offer.

To determine whether there has been a valid acceptance, you must establish whether some act or promise was required of the offeree. When an offer is made that requires an act to complete the agreement, a *unilateral contract* is formed, and the offeree does not have to give notice of intended performance unless the offeror requests it or unless the offeree has reason to believe that the offeror will not learn of his acceptance with reasonable promptness.

EXAMPLE John promises to pay Tony $500 for sodding his lawn. Before Tony starts the job, John leaves on an extended trip to Europe for the summer. Tony knows that unless he notifies John when he completes the job, he may not be paid until John returns home three months later. In this situation, Tony's notifying John of his performance is a good idea. John could have required Tony to notify him of his intent to perform so that if Tony rejected John's offer, John could make the offer to someone else before he left the country.

In contracts requiring an exchange of promises *(bilateral contracts)* the offeree can accept by any means authorized by the offeror, either specifically or by implication. The acceptance becomes effective when it leaves the possession of the offeree, regardless of whether it reaches the offeror, unless the offer specifies otherwise.

EXAMPLE I mail you an offer promising to pay you $2,500 if you promise to paint my house during the second week of April. You mail me your acceptance—after that, if I go out and find another painter, I have breached the contract. A contract is formed when you drop your acceptance into the mailbox. This is known as the "mailbox rule." If your acceptance is lost in the mail and I never receive it, the contract is still formed, unless in my offer I specified that its acceptance is valid only when received. This mailbox rule usually does not apply to an option contract, whose acceptance becomes effective only when received by the offeror.

Acceptance of an offer by a means not authorized by the offeror is effective upon receipt as long as the offer is still open. Rejection of the offer is also effective upon receipt. A late acceptance is treated as a counteroffer and must be accepted by the offeror to create a contract.

An acceptance must comply exactly with the requirements of the offer. It must omit nothing from the promise or performance requested. If a response to an offer seems to accept it but adds qualifications or conditions, it is a counteroffer, not an acceptance.

Acceptance of an offer may be inferred from the offeree's acts or conduct.

EXAMPLE Adolph, a retired concert pianist, advertises in local newspapers offering to give piano lessons. The first lesson is free, but after that the student must take a 20-lesson course for $300. Nancy, a housewife who dropped out of music school to get married, calls Adolph for the trial lesson. She is so satisfied that she and Adolph agree to meet every Thursday afternoon for lessons. Nancy has accepted Adolph's offer by her conduct. They have a valid contract.

Acceptance may also be deduced from silence only if both parties intended it to be a method of acceptance, but silence alone can never constitute acceptance.

EXAMPLE Lana offers to sell to Duncan for $250 a horse that
O—* Duncan already has in his possession, saying: "I am so sure that you will accept that you need not trouble to write me. Your silence alone will operate as acceptance." Duncan does not reply, but neither does he intend to accept. There is no contract because Lana and Duncan did not intend silence to have the same meaning.

The meaning of ambiguous silence (silence that may or may not be treated as an acceptance) must be determined from the circumstances in the case. Previous dealings between parties may create a duty to act, and silence under such circumstances constitutes acceptance.

EXAMPLE From time to time Mr. Trapper has sent mink
O—* skins to Mr. Tanner, who is in the business of tanning hides. On each occasion, Tanner has simply sent Trapper a check in payment for the skins. Trapper sends five more skins to Tanner. An unreasonable time elapses, during which Trapper hears nothing. When Trapper demands payment, Tanner claims the skins were never accepted. The court would find that Tanner's silence and his keeping the skins constitute acceptance, in view of the previous dealings between the men. If Tanner did not intend to accept the skins, he had a duty to tell Trapper. Similarly, if the offeree exercises rights of ownership over an item, acceptance can be concluded. If Tanner tans the hides, it is clear he has accepted them.

Accepting unsolicited goods Under the COMMON LAW, when unsolicited goods are sent in the mail, the recipient is not obligated to accept or return them. If you receive a radio in the mail that you did not order, you do not have to accept or return it. If you use the goods, however, a contract results and you are obligated to pay.

Some states have changed the common-law rule by enacting statutes to protect the public from unwanted solicitations. Statutes provide that when unsolicited merchandise is received as part of an offer to sell, it may be considered as an unconditional gift. The recipient may use the merchandise as he wants, and he has no obligation to return or pay for it.

EXAMPLE A health-food distributor sends you a book on
O—* nutrition, along with order forms for his products. You did not request the forms or the book. Under the statutes concerning unsolicited goods, you may keep the book and treat it as a gift from the distributor without any obligation on your part to return or pay for it.

If, however, goods are sent to you by mistake and you know about the mistake, you are obligated for their value if you use them.

EXAMPLE Suppose you ordered a food processor through
O—* the mail. You cancel your order 30 days later because you receive one as a gift. One week after you mail your cancellation, the processor is delivered by mail. You know that the delivery is a mistake, so you must either return the processor to the manufacturer or pay for it.

Writing of a contract and other formalities No particular formalities or language are essential in making contracts unless specified by statute. (For the kinds of contracts that must be in writing, see STATUTE OF FRAUDS and Chart 6.) If an agreement is required by statute to be in writing (such as a contract for the sale of real estate), then no legal action can be maintained against it unless there is a written note or memorandum of its subject matter, terms, and conditions, and the identity of the parties. One essential part of a written contract is its signing by the parties or their agents. Statutes may require that the SIGNATURES on a written contract be AUTHENTICATED or that a contract be FILED or RECORDED. The purpose of the statute is to prevent the possibility of a nonexistent agreement being "proved" by FRAUD or PERJURY.

Otherwise, a contract may be made in various ways, including by the conversation of the parties, their conduct, or both. The language of a contract must be sufficiently clear and definite to enable a court to ascertain the terms by which the parties intended to bind themselves.

Consideration CONSIDERATION is something of value requested by the offeror in exchange for his promise to the offeree. It is an inducement to get a person to perform his part of the bargain, or contract, such as by paying him money. A valid contract requires consideration by both parties. As a general rule, in a bilateral contract one promise is a valid consideration for another promise. Bob promises to pay Jake $500 in exchange for Jake's promise to cater a cocktail party in Bob's office. Bob's consideration is the promise to pay $500 while Jack's consideration is his promise to cater. In a unilateral contract, the agreed performance by the offeree is the necessary consideration as well as the acceptance of the offer. Mary offers Ann $25 to make her a quilt. The $25 is Mary's consideration and the quilt, once started by Ann, is her consideration.

Consideration may be in the form of a FORBEARANCE, such as refraining from suing or from doing something that you are legally entitled to do. This applies to both unilateral and bilateral contracts.

EXAMPLE In one case, an uncle told his nephew that if he
O—* would refrain from drinking, smoking, and gambling until he became 21, he would pay him $5,000. The nephew fulfilled his part of the agreement, having refrained for six years, and wrote to his uncle informing him of this fact. When the uncle replied that he had deposited the money in the bank for him, the nephew agreed to this arrangement. Twelve years later the uncle died, without having paid any money to his nephew. The nephew presented his claim to the executor of his uncle's estate, who refused to pay. The nephew sued for the $5,000, plus interest, contending that he had fully performed a unilateral contract with his uncle. The executor contended that there was no enforceable contract, because there was no consideration for the uncle's promise.

The court found that the contract was enforceable. A forbearance, detriment, loss, or responsibility given or undertaken by the promisee is sufficient consideration for a promise. "Consideration means not so much that one party is profiting as that the other abandons some legal right in the present, or limits his legal freedom of action in the future, as an inducement for the promise of the first." The nephew gave up his legal right to smoke, drink, and gamble. This constituted a legal detriment, which was bargained for, and thus the nephew was entitled to the money promised by his uncle.

The consideration required for a contract must be a "valuable" one. Love and affection do not constitute a valuable consideration in the eyes of the law. In a promise to make a gift there is no valuable consideration on the part of the expectant recipient, and thus the promise may not be enforced.

EXAMPLE A man gave his daughter a deed to certain property. He promised to pay off two mortgages on the property when they became due. He told her that the deed and his promise were Christmas presents. He never paid off the mortgages and he never recorded the deed to show that he had given the property to his daughter. After his death, the daughter tried to have the mortgages paid off by the estate according to his promise. The court held that the father's transfer of title and promise constituted a gift that was not supported by consideration. The daughter could not enforce her father's promise to pay off the mortgages because she had not given a valuable consideration for the promise.

Enforcing the promise of a gift Because a promise to give a gift is freely given by the promisor, who is not under any legal duty to do so, the promise is not enforceable unless there is PROMISSORY ESTOPPEL.

EXAMPLE Let us say that the daughter, relying on her father's promise to pay off the two mortgages as Christmas presents, completely renovates the property for $25,000, and has paid for the renovation before her father's death. She has changed her position substantially by paying $25,000 in reliance upon her father's gratuitous promise. She will be able to enforce the promise to pay off the mortgages under the theory of promissory estoppel.

The elements of promissory estoppel are (1) a promisor makes a gratuitous promise, which he reasonably expects will cause some definite action or forbearance by the promisee; (2) the promisee justifiably relies on the promise; (3) the promisee is caused a substantial detriment, such as financial loss, by his action or forbearance; and (4) injustice can be avoided only by enforcing the promise. Most states apply this doctrine if all these elements are present. A minority of courts, however, limit the application of this doctrine to specific situations, such as gift promises to transfer real property, gratuitous BAILMENTS, and charitable SUBSCRIPTION agreements.

Mutual obligation When the consideration in a contract consists of mutual promises, they must be mutually binding—that is, create mutual obligations. If one party does not actually obligate himself to some performance or forbearance, he has made an ILLUSORY PROMISE and there is no enforceable contract. If one party has an absolute and unlimited right to cancel the contract, for example, the promise is illusory and the contract fails for lack of consideration. If I promise to cut your lawn for $5 "if I feel like it," it is obvious that by reserving this absolute right to cancel, I have promised nothing at all. No mutual obligation exists. On the other hand, if the power to cancel the contract is limited in any way, the contract is usually considered binding.

EXAMPLE A drug manufacturer offers to a hospital a particular type of drug, of which it has a surplus, at a substantial discount, but reserves the right to cancel the contract if a shortage of supply develops. If the hospital accepts the offer, a binding contract is formed because the power to cancel the contract is restricted to a particular situation—if a shortage occurs.

Fulfillment of a void contract When one party fully performs a promise under a bilateral contract that is unenforceable, this may make the other promise legally binding even though initially there was no mutual obligation.

EXAMPLE Suppose John orally promises to sell land to Susan, for which Susan orally promises to pay John $1,000. In all states an oral contract to sell land is not merely unenforceable but is absolutely void. However, John transfers his land to Susan anyway. Now, the void part of the agreement has been performed and the purchaser, Susan, has received the title. Susan is therefore bound to perform her promise to pay John $1,000.

Promise to perform legal duty A promise to do an act that one is legally bound to do does not constitute consideration for another promise. A police officer who performs only his legal duty, such as arresting a criminal while on duty, has given no consideration to support a claim for a reward. If, however, he has performed an act beyond his legally imposed duty, such as arresting a criminal while off duty, he has given consideration that will support a claim.

Promise to perform moral duty A moral obligation is not recognized in most states as a valid consideration, because no adequate test exists to define the limits of moral duty.

EXAMPLE In one case, right after Frank returned from a voyage at sea, he suddenly became ill. Because Frank was poor, his friend Sarah took care of him for about two weeks. Frank had not lived with his father, Edward, for many years, but when Edward learned of Sarah's actions, he promised to reimburse her for her expenses. Edward's written promise proved to be no more than a transient feeling of gratitude, however, and Sarah sued Edward. Edward contended that there was no consideration for his promise and, therefore, it should not be enforced. The court decided that Sarah could not recover. Although there was a moral consideration for Edward's promise, that by itself did not create a legal obligation. "It is only when the party making the promise gains something, or he to whom it is made loses something, that the law gives the promise validity." Here Edward did not receive any benefit nor did Sarah lose anything by his promise because it was made after Sarah had finished caring for Frank.

A minority of courts will enforce a moral obligation where there has been a benefit conferred on the promisor. If, instead of Edward, Frank himself had made the promise to reimburse Sarah, some courts would allow Sarah to recover.

Mutual assent Before a legal contract can be created the parties must mutually assent to its proposed objectives and terms. To determine whether a contract exists, courts examine the acts or words of the parties in light of whether a reasonable person could conclude that they did intend a contract. For instance, I offer to sell you my 1975 car for $1,000, which you agree to pay. Clearly you and I have demonstrated our common intent to contract, and any reasonable person could decide that we have.

The secret intention of one party, whose conduct appears to indicate agreement, has no bearing usually on whether the parties mutually assented to a contract. But the subjective intention of the parties may be taken into account when there is no outward expression—no acts or words—to show their common intent.

EXAMPLE Smith owns two cows, a brown one and a white one. He offers to sell Jones "a cow for $100." Jones eagerly accepts the offer. There is no outward expression of their common intent concerning the identity of the cow. Their subjective intentions will establish an enforceable contract if both were thinking that the same cow was for sale. Jones, however, actually believed he was buying the brown one for $100, while Smith intended to sell the white one; therefore, there was no contract.

When there is no real assent between the parties, there can be no binding contract. Apparent assent may not be valid for a number of reasons—mistake, fraud, innocent misrepresentation, duress, or undue influence—which may prevent the enforcement of a contract.

Mutual mistake   When there is a mutual mistake of an important fact that affects the substance of the contract, no contract is formed.

EXAMPLE Suppose Smith agrees to sell Jones a cow, which both of them believe cannot breed. The contract price for this cow is much lower than for one that can breed. But before the cow is delivered to Jones, Smith learns that it is with calf and therefore is worth 10 times the amount he will receive under the contract. Smith tries to cancel the contract, but Jones refuses, so Smith brings the issue to court. The court finds that the mutual mistake goes to the subject matter of the contract, and therefore there is no contract. The cow that was bargained for and intended to be sold was substantially different from the cow that was to be delivered.

If, however, the difference in the subject matter concerned some minor quality, which did not affect the value of the subject of the contract, the contract would have been binding. This holds true even when the mistake was the motivation for the purchaser, the seller, or both.

Unilateral mistake   When a contract contains a mistake in the terms, such as one caused by a typographical error, it may be corrected. Generally such a unilateral mistake affords no ground for disaffirming a contract, unless it (1) results in a great difference in value in what is to be exchanged or (2) is caused by or known to the other party. The mistake must be a clerical error or a mistake in computation, not a mistake in judgment.

Unilateral mistakes frequently occur when a contractor submits an erroneous bid for a municipal project—to install county sewers, for example, or to pave a highway. If the bid is accepted, the contractor will be allowed to disaffirm the contract provided that the agreement is still to be carried out or the other party can be placed in the position he was in before the contract.

Illiteracy   A person's illiteracy does not mean that he cannot learn the contents of a written contract and there-fore give his valid assent. He can get someone to read the contract to him and explain it if necessary. Illiteracy may, however, be a ground for invalidating a contract if the person who reads the contract to the illiterate misrepresents its terms and acts in COLLUSION with the other party to the contract.

Fraud   Fraud is the deliberate misrepresentation or concealment of an important fact of the contract in order to induce or persuade another person to enter into it. When there is fraud there can be no mutual assent. If A contracts with B knowing that B is entering the contract under an important mistake of fact, B cannot be held to the contract. B can, if he wishes, stick to the contract. In the past, courts often held that fraudulent concealment could not be based on mere silence of the guilty party, but now the trend is toward finding a duty to disclose.

EXAMPLE Suppose Bob sells his house to Cal, knowing it is infested with termites. Bob does not disclose this fact and Cal could not readily discover it. Cal sees the termites after he moves in and sues Bob for knowingly concealing the fact. Under previous court decisions, Cal could not recover for fraud. Now, many jurisdictions allow Cal to recover, because Bob had special knowledge of a material fact that he had a duty to disclose.

Because there can be no meeting of the parties' minds when there is fraud, a contract brought about by fraud is either void or is voidable and unenforceable. If the fraud occurs in the execution of the contract, such as A persuading B to sign a document that B does not understand and therefore cannot intend to execute, then the contract is void from the very beginning—void *ab initio*. Nor will the signing of a contract obligate the signer if, by trickery, a different contract has been substituted for the one he intended to execute.

EXAMPLE You go to your lawyer's office to sign a contract to buy a house. You read the contract thoroughly and agree with all the terms. The telephone rings and your lawyer answers it. He excuses himself, your contract in hand, to go out to check a particular file with his secretary. When he returns he hands you the contract, which you eagerly sign. The contract signed is not the one you just read, but one that, in addition to being a contract for sale of the house, gives the lawyer complete control over all your affairs. It will not be enforced by the courts, because you were tricked into signing it. If, however, when you went to your lawyer's office, you told him that you just wanted to sign the contract and did not want to be bothered reading it, you could not later claim that the contract was unenforceable because of fraud. Because you were negligent in refusing to read the contract you could not claim that you were deceived.

If, because of fraud, a contract fails to express the agreement that the parties intended, the defrauded party may seek a decree of REFORMATION, by which the court will rewrite a written agreement to conform with the original intent of the persons making the deal. See FRAUD for a full discussion.

Misrepresentation without fraud   An innocent misrepresentation on which a person rightly relies may invalidate a contract for lack of mutual assent if it relates to an important matter.

EXAMPLE I sell my refrigerator to you for $100, assuring you it is in good condition. Two days after you get it home, it breaks down. Although I had no knowledge of the structural defect that caused the breakdown, my innocent misrepresentation related to a material matter—the working condition of the refrigerator. You will be able to have the contract invalidated.

Duress   Duress is a wrongful act or threat that compels another person to do some act, such as sign a contract, that he would not have done voluntarily. There is no true meeting of the minds of the parties.

EXAMPLE Jeff has contracted to deliver a restaurant-size freezer to Ray, which Ray desperately needs for his new cafeteria. Jeff threatens to withhold delivery unless Ray agrees to sell him his house for a low price. Ray would not enter this contract without Jeff's threat.

A contract signed under duress is voidable and the innocent party may have it declared unenforceable. The duress must cause fear that prevents the person from freely choosing whether or not to sign.

EXAMPLE Sam threatens Julia that unless she gives him the contract to repair the typewriters in her office he will tell her husband of the affair she is having. Julia is deprived of her right to contract freely. Under duress, she signs the contract with Sam. Later, Julia may go to court to have the contract declared unenforceable, or she may allow it to remain in effect.

Duress may be in the form of blackmail, threats of physical violence, or abusive or oppressive threats to start legal proceedings. A threat to bring a lawsuit is a legitimate form of coercion protected by law and the Constitution, but most jurisdictions agree with the rule that the threat to start legal proceedings becomes wrongful if it is "made with the corrupt intent to coerce a transaction grossly unfair to the victim and not related to the subject of such proceedings."

EXAMPLE If a husband threatens his philandering wife with a suit demanding custody of their children on the ground of her adultery unless she transfers certain securities to him, the jury must decide whether the transfer is the result of duress. Because the purpose of the husband's threatened custody action was to obtain the wife's securities, not the best interests of his children, most juries would find that the transfer was the result of duress.

Undue influence   Undue influence is unlawful control exercised by one person over another in order to substitute his will for that of his victim. It involves the question of whether the party's assent to the contract was made by his own free choice. Legitimate persuasion and suggestion that does not destroy a person's free will does not destroy the validity of a contract. See CONSUMER PROTECTION.

There are two types of situations in which undue influence operates. In one, a person takes advantage of the mental, physical, or psychological weakness of another to influence him to agree to a contract to which he normally would not consent.

EXAMPLE A door-to-door salesman takes advantage of a frail and enfeebled 83-year-old man by influencing him, through high-pressure sales tactics, to enter into a 20-year installment contract for the purchase of an encyclopedia. It becomes clear that the victim has been subjected to undue influence, particularly when it is learned that this is the third set he has bought from the same salesman in the past month. The man may seek relief from the court by having the contract declared unenforceable because of undue influence.

The second situation involves undue influence based on a FIDUCIARY relationship that exists between the parties—when one party occupies a position of trust and confidence in relation to the other, such as in family or professional-client relationships.

Most undue-influence cases are started by relatives after the death of the person who was the victim of undue influence. Contracts that are claimed to be voidable because of undue influence must be clearly one-sided or unfair before the courts will declare them unenforceable.

■ **Illegal contracts**   As stated earlier in this article, the subject matter of a contract cannot be anything that is forbidden by law. An illegal agreement will not be enforced and is not a contract. As a general rule, all contracts are illegal that involve, or have as their objective, violating a law, committing a crime, or perpetrating a fraud on another person or on the public.

Agreement against public policy   If an agreement binds one or both parties to do something that is against the PUBLIC POLICY of the state or nation, it is illegal and absolutely void. Constitutions, statutes, judicial decisions, the continued practices of government officials, and the general customs of the people determine public policy. For example, a contract between a common CARRIER, such as a bus, and its passengers that releases the carrier from all liability for injuries resulting from its negligent operation is void because it is against public policy.

Agreement by unlicensed persons   A common problem is the delivery of goods or performance of services by someone who does not possess the required license. Some licensing statutes specifically provide that persons contracting without a license may not enforce those contracts, but often many laws are silent on this matter.

Courts then try to distinguish between licenses that are designed to raise revenue for the government and those designed to protect the public from unethical or incompetent persons. To practice law in a given city, a person may be required to obtain a state license, which involves passing a test to demonstrate competency, and a city license, which simply involves paying a fee. Contracts for legal services made by a lawyer who does not have the city license could be enforceable, because that licensing requirement is designed solely to produce revenue for the city. If, however, the lawyer does not have a state license, the contract would not be enforceable.

Partially illegal agreement   If an agreement is illegal in part only, the lawful portion is sometimes enforceable if the legal and illegal parts can be separated.

EXAMPLE Ned promises to paint Wendy's house in exchange for Wendy's promise to pay $1,000 and drive a carload of untaxed whiskey from Florida to Connecticut. Ned paints the house. Wendy's promise to pay $1,000 will be enforceable in many jurisdictions. When one legal performance, the painting of a house, is given for two promises, one lawful—the payment of $1,000—and the other unlawful—transporting untaxed whiskey—the general rule is that the lawful promise is enforceable.

An exception to this rule occurs when the illegal promise is immoral or extremely dangerous to public safety. If Wendy had promised to pay $1,000 and shoot Jean, even if Ned had painted the house he could not enforce Wendy's promise to pay $1,000.

Unconscionable contracts A contract that is unfair or too partial toward the person with greater bargaining power is considered UNCONSCIONABLE. The term is defined as "affronting the sense of decency." No one in his right senses would consent to an unconscionable contract, no fair and honest person would accept it, and the courts refuse to enforce such a contract.

Typically, unconscionability is found in CONSUMER PROTECTION cases involving the extreme one-sidedness of a term that disclaims a WARRANTY, limits damages, or restricts the rights of the purchaser to seek court relief against the seller.

EXAMPLE Martha was supporting herself and her seven children on monthly welfare payments of $200. She purchased a stereo set for $500 from Parker, a retail furniture dealer, on an installment credit agreement. Parker knew of her situation and had sold her furniture in the past. When Martha failed to make a payment, Parker sued her in an effort to take back all of the furniture Martha had purchased over the years, as was provided for in the installment obligation. The court agreed with Martha that the installment contract was unconscionable and refused to enforce it.

Unconscionability is determined by examining the circumstances of the parties when the contract was made. It is usually used by the courts to protect uneducated and poor people, who are often victims of such contracts.

■ **Discharge of contracts** The discharge of a contractual obligation is a legally binding termination of the duty. Performance is the usual way parties discharge their contractual obligations. But it may also occur by some other voluntary act of the parties (discussed below) or by OPERATION OF LAW.

EXAMPLE Kurt promises to sell land to Lamar. Lamar promises to pay Kurt $5,000. Kurt delivers his deed to the land to Lamar, who accepts it, and Lamar pays $5,000 to Kurt, who accepts it. Both parties have performed their respective duties. They are discharged from further liability on the contract. The contract ceases to exist by operation of law.

The discharge of a contractual duty may occur by operation of law through objective impossibility (discussed below), illegality (discussed earlier), merger, and statutory release, such as a discharge in BANKRUPTCY. Discharge of a contractual obligation by merger occurs when one contract is extinguished because it is absorbed into another. It usually occurs between debts of different degrees. The smaller debt is merged or absorbed into the larger one by operation of law.

EXAMPLE A customer is sued by a department store under a contract for failing to pay the $400 purchase price of a couch that was delivered to her according to the terms of the contract. The court finds that she did breach the contract and renders a $400 judgment against her to be paid to the store. Her duty to perform under the contract with the store has been merged into the judgment and is discharged. If she fails to pay, she cannot be sued again for breach of contract, but she can be sued to have the judgment enforced.

■ **Impossibility of performance** IMPOSSIBILITY of performance of a contractual obligation falls into one of two categories. *Subjective impossibility* is due to the inability of the promisor as an individual to perform, as by illness or death. *Objective impossibility* is due to the inability of anyone to perform the act. A contractor cannot repair a building if it burns down. The term "impossibility" includes not only literal impossibility but also impracticability because of extreme and unreasonable difficulty, expense, injury, or loss involved.

Voluntary discharge The most important methods of voluntary discharge in the absence of performance of the original contract are (1) ACCORD AND SATISFACTION and (2) novation. An *accord* is an agreement to accept or settle for something other than what was due under an earlier contract. Satisfaction is the performance of that accord.

EXAMPLE Abby owes Stanton $1,000 for farm equipment but they have disagreed on the price for six months. Finally Stanton agrees to accept from Abby four specific cows as full payment of the obligation. Abby agrees and delivers the four cows to Stanton and he accepts them for the debt. The agreement was the accord. The delivery by Abby and acceptance of the cows by Stanton constituted the satisfaction of the accord. This transaction discharges Abby of her duty on the contract and terminates Stanton's rights under it.

A *novation* substitutes a new party and discharges one of the original parties to a contract by agreement of all three parties. A new contract is created, with the same terms as the original one. Only the parties are changed. To be effective as a discharge, there must be (1) a previous valid obligation, (2) a mutual agreement of at least three parties to the new contract, (3) a new agreement that must expressly and immediately extinguish duties under the original contract, and (4) the new agreement must be a valid contract that is supported by a consideration.

EXAMPLE Suppose Rudy, a builder, is under a contractual obligation to build a house for Babette, for which Babette has agreed to pay $20,000 upon completion. If Rudy goes to Seth, another builder, and offers him the job and Seth accepts, there has *not* been a novation. All that has occurred is an assignment (transfer) of the right to payment from Babette and the delegation to Seth of the duty to build. Rudy remains liable on the contract, and Babette could argue that the duty to build was too personal to delegate. For a novation to take place, Babette would have to agree to release Rudy from his duty to build in exchange for receiving a promise from Seth to build; also Babette would have to promise to pay the $20,000 to Seth upon completion. A novation immediately discharges the previous contractual duty of the promisor.

Other methods of voluntary discharge include agreement by the parties, ESTOPPEL, avoidance of voidable duties—for example, a minor disaffirming a contract—and the cancellation, intentional destruction, or surrender of a contract under seal, with the intent to discharge the duty.

■ **Breach of contract** A breach of contract is an unjustifiable failure to perform all or part of the contract. It may occur by anticipatory repudiation, by one party's hindering or preventing performance by the other party, or by failure to perform a duty under the contract. Anticipatory repudiation (or ANTICIPATORY BREACH) occurs, for example, when a promisor declares, *before* it is time for him to perform, that he will not go through with his part of the contract. You promise to pay me $50 if I promise to paint your garage on September 20. On September 19, you tell me you have changed your mind and will not pay me. You have committed an anticipatory repudiation of our contract.

Any voluntary act by the promisor that makes it impossible or apparently impossible for him to perform his contract is also anticipatory breach.

EXAMPLE Archie contracts to sell certain land to Clem, the deal to be closed on December 1, 1980. On August 20, 1980, Archie sells the land to Ed, who knows nothing of the contract with Clem. Archie has made it impossible to convey to Clem on the day for performance.

When one party hinders or prevents the performance of the other party, he has breached his contract.

EXAMPLE Della promises to pay Joan $100 if Joan will build Della a desk, using some Mexican mahogany Della has in her possession. Joan agrees. Della changes her mind and does not give the wood to Joan. Joan sues Della for breach of contract. Joan will win because Della's failure to provide the wood breaches her contract with Joan.

When a party who has a duty of immediate performance fails to perform, he has breached his contract. If you agree to pay me $100 if I sew you a set of slipcovers, and I complete the job, your refusal to pay me constitutes a breach of contract.

A breach may be a *total* (or *major, material,* or *substantial)* breach; that is, a failure to perform properly an important part of the contract. Your refusal to pay me in the above example would be a total breach of contract. A breach may also be *partial* (or *minor)*. This is only a small deviation from the required performance. If, in the above example, you paid me $99, claiming that I owed you $1 for breaking a needle on your sewing machine, which I had used to make the slipcovers, you would be guilty of a partial breach of our contract. The differences in the types of breach are important in determining the kinds of remedies and damages a victim of a breached contract may seek.

■ **Remedies for breach of contract** Among the basic REMEDIES for breach of contract are REFORMATION, DAMAGES, RESCIND, RESTITUTION, and SPECIFIC PERFORMANCE.

Reformation The equitable remedy of *reformation* may be applicable when the written agreement does not correspond to the contract actually made by the parties as a result of either fraud or mutual mistake. The court, after investigating the intentions of the contracting parties, decrees that the contract does not express these intentions and a new, correct contract is made.

Damages *Damages* means a sum of money awarded as a compensation for injury caused by a breach of contract. Whether a breach is material or partial determines the extent of damages awarded. In the case of total breach of contract, the wronged party may receive full damages. If the breach is partial, damages are restricted to the difference between the performance given and the one called for by the contract. The contract may provide for a specific amount of damages for breach. This is known as *liquidated damages.*

Rescission *Rescission* puts an end to the contract. When this remedy is applied, the parties are left in the position of never having made the contract.

Restitution The purpose of RESTITUTION is to restore the injured party to the position he was in before he entered into the contract.

Specific performance The remedy of SPECIFIC PERFORMANCE is one by which a person is required to carry out, as nearly as practicable, the actual promise, because money damages would not compensate for the breach. For instance, a contract to sell a parcel of land is specifically enforceable—you are entitled to have the specific parcel of land you contracted for—because each parcel of land is considered unique and money damages or a different parcel of land are inadequate substitutes. The same is true of antiques, heirlooms, property of sentimental value, and one-of-a-kind items. If someone contracts to sell you a chair in which Abraham Lincoln was sitting when he signed the Emancipation Proclamation and then decides to accept a higher offer for it, you would want the remedy of specific performance—that particular chair and no other.

A personal-service contract or an employment contract that requires a person to do something, however, cannot be specifically enforced, because the 13th Amendment of the federal Constitution prohibits slavery.

EXAMPLE If I hire you to cater my parents' 50th anniversary party for $500 and you refuse, after having accepted my offer, I cannot ask a court to force you to cater the party. On the other hand, if the contract prohibits a person from doing something, breach of this "negative covenant" *can* be specifically enforced. For example, you are hired as a research chemist at Bowler Drug Company to develop a new type of cold tablet. Your contract includes a negative covenant in which you promise not to work in the research department of any competitor drug companies for two years after you leave Bowler. Six months later, you get a fabulous offer to be the head of the research department at Zorba Drug Company, Bowler's fiercest rival. If you accept the new job, Bowler will go to court to ask for specific performance of your negative covenant. If the negative covenant is valid, the court will grant Bowler specific performance of it by prohibiting you from taking the job at Zorba's.

■ **Conditions and promises of performance** Many contract promises do not create a duty to carry out the terms of the contract unless and until some condition, express (stated) or implied, occurs. On the other hand, an unconditional promise creates a duty of immediate performance.

EXAMPLE If I promise to pay you $1,500 for your car on August 8, I must pay you when August 8 arrives. But if I promise to pay you $1,500 for your car on August 8 if I win the state lottery, my promise does not create an immediate duty to pay you unless I win the lottery. The promise is conditional. The condition is express because you and I have specifically mentioned the event of winning the lottery as being a condition of payment.

An implied condition is one that the parties should have reasonably understood to be part of the contract because of its presence by implication.

EXAMPLE Joel asks Pat to build a desk from mahogany ○──✱ wood, which Joel promises to supply. Pat agrees. Pat cannot perform until Joel supplies the wood. Although it is not expressly stated in the contract, the condition is implied that Joel will furnish the wood before Pat's obligation to build the desk arises.

Types of condition   There are three important types of condition in the performance of contracts: condition precedent, condition concurrent, and condition subsequent.

A *condition precedent* is one that must exist as a fact before the promisor has any liability. Milt tells Dan that if Dan enters and wins the 100-yard dash this afternoon, Milt will give him $100. The entering and winning of the race must exist as a fact before there is any liability on Milt. As soon as that fact occurs, Milt is liable to pay Dan $100.

A *condition concurrent* is one that must exist as a fact when both parties to a contract are to perform at the same time. Concurrent conditions usually occur in contracts for the sale of goods and for the conveyance (transfer) of land. For example, the seller of the land is obligated to deliver a deed and the buyer to pay money. Although neither party has a duty to perform until the other has performed, as a practical matter, the party who wants to complete the transaction must take steps that give the other party the duty to take steps. The performances are concurrently conditional upon each other.

A *condition subsequent* terminates the obligation to perform the contract or to pay for its breach.

EXAMPLE An insurance contract provides that a lawsuit ○──✱ against it for a loss covered by the policy must be started within one year of the insured's loss. If the destruction of Bennett's house by fire is a risk covered by the policy, and Bennett has a fire, he must file suit against the insurer within one year or the company's liability will be ended by the condition subsequent.

Substantial performance   A person's failure to comply strictly with the terms of a condition will not prevent him from getting his due if he has carried out a substantial part of the contract. This doctrine was developed by the courts as an instrument of justice to prevent FORFEITURES. However, DAMAGES are awarded for any injuries caused by the failure to give complete performance.

EXAMPLE Forsyth, a contractor, built a house for Dawson at ○──✱ a contract price of $77,000. All of the price had been paid except $3,500. The contract specified that a particular brand "X" of pipe be used in the building and that a certificate from Armstrong, the architect, would be a condition precedent to the last payment of $3,500. An architect's certificate demonstrates that the construction has been completed to the architect's satisfaction and the terms of the contract. Armstrong refused to give the certificate unless the "X" pipe was used. Forsyth had accidentally overlooked the description of the pipe to be used and instead had installed a pipe that was the same kind, quality, and price as "X" pipe. If Forsyth is required to remove the installed pipe, some parts of the building would be substantially destroyed and the cost would be way over the balance due on the contract.

Forsyth sues Dawson for the $3,500 balance, which he will be able to recover. Although the general rule in building contracts is that a certificate of an architect is a condition precedent to recovery of the contract price, Forsyth has substantially complied with his contract with Dawson. The pipe that was installed was substantially the same as "X" pipe. To make Forsyth tear down the walls to install "X" pipe would be inequitable and would result in no greater value to Dawson.

To determine whether a contract has been breached or substantially complied with, courts consider the purpose to be served, the desire to be gratified, the excuse for deviation from the letter, and the cruelty of enforced adherence to the contract. If the deviation was accidental and resulted only in a trivial difference between what was called for by contract and what was performed, as in the above example, the courts will usually award the injured party only NOMINAL (insignificant) damages.

Conditions of satisfaction   When a contract is conditioned on satisfying of a person's opinion, taste, or fancy, this option may be exercised without any particular reason. Most courts, however, will apply a good-faith test.

EXAMPLE Kenneth contracts with a portrait painter to sit for ○──✱ a portrait. He agrees to pay him $500 if the portrait captures the real Kenneth. Before the painting is finished, Kenneth bets $500 on the wrong horse in the Kentucky Derby. The portrait turns out to be an almost perfect likeness, but because Kenneth does not have the money to pay for it, he tells the painter that the portrait makes him look like his grandfather on a bad day and he refuses to pay. The painter sues him for the $500. Although the contract was conditioned on Kenneth's approval of the portrait, the court will examine Kenneth's reason for rejecting it and will examine the portrait as well. In this case there is a clear example of bad faith, so the court will allow the painter to enforce the contract.

If it is apparent, however, that the question of satisfaction relates to the commercial value or quality of the subject matter of the contract, then the deficiency must be shown and the dissatisfaction must be reasonable and well founded. The test is: What would satisfy a reasonable person?

EXAMPLE Valerie purchases a used car from a dealer who ○──✱ tells her he will return her money if she is not completely satisfied with how it performs. After driving the car for a week, Valerie discovers a squeak in the windshield wipers and decides to return the car. The dealer refuses to take back the car, and Valerie sues him for breach of contract. The question of satisfaction has to do with the subject matter of the contract—the car's performance. Valerie's demand is unreasonable because the defect in the car's performance is such a minor one. The court will not allow her to return it.

Divisible contracts   If the entire performance of a contract is the condition for one party's duty to perform, the contract is an *entire contract*. The party who is first required to perform must give full performance before being entitled to payment from the other contracting party.

Sometimes a contract is treated for practical purposes as if it were several contracts. It is then said to be legally divisible. A contract is legally divisible when (1) the performance of each party is divided into two or more parts; (2) the number of parts due from each party is the same; and (3) the performance of each part by one party is the agreed exchange for a corresponding part by the other party.

EXAMPLE If Anderson and Barnes agree that Anderson will
O⊷⚹ act as Barnes's secretary for one year at a salary of
$150 per week, the contract is said to be divisible. Each
week's performance on Anderson's part is an implied
condition precedent to his right to a week's salary. His
right to the salary is not conditioned on performance of
his obligation to work for one year.

In most employment contracts, the courts permit the
employee to recover for the service rendered on the theory
that such a contract is divisible.

A lease of an apartment for 12 months may be viewed as
a divisible contract actually consisting of 12 separate contracts. If you breach your lease by moving before its entire
term has expired, you will be liable for the remaining
months' rent as each month occurs but not before that time.
In effect, the court treats the lease as a contract for each
month, with rent due on the first of each month. See
LANDLORD AND TENANT.

A retail installment-credit contract may also be viewed
as a divisible contract consisting of a certain number of
contracts.

Breach of conditions Noncompliance with a condition may be permitted in certain circumstances. Sometimes
if a condition is not met, the court can find that no contract
existed, and thus there can be no lawsuit for breach of
contract (discussed earlier in this article). At other times a
condition that is not met is considered waived and a contract is said to exist, however.

EXAMPLE Suppose Louise hires an architect, Gabriel, to
O⊷⚹ design a home that can be built for $30,000.
Louise and Gabriel meet to review the preliminary plans,
which show that owing to rising construction costs, the
price for the house will be $39,000. Louise agrees to the
plans and tells Gabriel to proceed. When the plans are
completed, Louise decides that the house is too expensive
to build after all and refuses to pay Gabriel for his work.
Gabriel sues her. Although originally he was bound by
the condition of the $30,000 cost limitation, when Louise
approved the preliminary plans and told Gabriel to proceed, she waived the cost as a condition.

Other excuses for nonperformance, or breach, of a condition are created when one party prevents or hinders the
other from carrying out his part of the contract or when
death or illness makes it impossible for someone to perform
personal services.

If an unintentional failure to perform a condition would
result in a substantial financial loss to the innocent party
who, through no fault of his own, could not perform, a
court may permit noncompliance to prevent injustice.

EXAMPLE Jack was exploring for oil on land leased from
O⊷⚹ Bill. Jack became seriously ill and was unable to
pay the rent when it came due. Time was of the essence in
the agreement (that is, any delay in performance violated
the entire contract), which is customary in oil leases. Jack
paid the rent 13 days late with interest. Bill refused to
accept it. Jack had already spent $250,000 exploring for
oil before he became ill. The court excused Jack's failure
to pay the rent on time because the breach of condition
was not willful and the condition, if enforced, would have
resulted in a substantial forfeiture. The condition was to
pay the rent only on the due date or lose the lease.

If compliance with a condition is excused by either the
other party or the court, the duty of performance by the
other party is the same as if the condition had been fulfilled.

■ **Transferring contract rights** The transfer to another person of the rights of performance is called an
assignment of contract.

EXAMPLE Sally contracts to sell a bicycle to Lou for $100.
O⊷⚹ Lou is to take possession of the bicycle immediately and pay the money in 30 days. Sally delivers the bike
to Lou and has the legal right to receive $100 from him
within 30 days. Sally transfers this right to Elfreda. Elfreda, who notifies Lou of the transfer, now has the right
to receive $100 from Lou within the 30-day period. Sally
has made an assignment of the contract to Elfreda.

Most contracts are assignable unless the contract or its
terms shows that the parties intended to make it personal to
themselves and therefore unassignable.

■ **Third-party beneficiaries** An ordinary contract involves only two principal parties. One party is bound to
provide some specified benefit to the other in return for a
benefit from him. In some instances, however, contracts
are arranged so that one party receives only a partial benefit
and the major benefit is conferred on a third person. In
effect, a person who is not a party to the contract is given a
legal right to enforce it.

Creditor beneficiary When a promise is made for
payment of a real or supposed legal duty, the third party is a
creditor beneficiary.

EXAMPLE Janet lends $300 to Steve, which Steve promises
O⊷⚹ to repay on the following day by paying off Janet's $300 debt to Dustin. Steve is the promisor, the person
who makes the promise to be enforced. Janet is the
promisee, the one to whom the promise is made. The
contract is between Janet and Steve; the consideration for
the promise by Steve is Janet's $300 loan to him. Dustin is
the third-party beneficiary, a creditor beneficiary because
Steve owes Dustin a duty to pay him Janet's $300 debt.
The next day, Steve refuses to pay Dustin. Dustin can sue
Steve for the $300, or Janet can sue Steve to compel him
to pay Dustin. Either way the money will be ordered to be
paid to Dustin, as Janet and Steve intended by the terms
of their contract. Of course, Dustin can sue Janet for the
$300, because she owed him a legal duty to repay his loan.
Janet can then sue Steve for breach of his contract with
her to pay Dustin.

Donee beneficiary When a promise is obtained to
make a gift to a third party, this third person is a *donee
beneficiary* of the contract.

EXAMPLE Elaine wishes to give Nick $100 as a birthday
O⊷⚹ present. She also plans to sell her horse to Pearl
for $100. Elaine does sell her horse to Pearl, and Pearl
promises Elaine to pay Nick the $100 directly. Nick is a
donee beneficiary of Pearl's promise for $100, and he can
enforce his claim against her, the promisor, for $100.
Nick has no claim against Elaine, the promisee, because
Elaine had no legal duty to Nick but was simply giving
him a gift. Elaine would, however, be able to sue Pearl for
refusing to pay Nick, which would be a breach of the
terms of the contract of sale between Elaine and Pearl.

■ **Parol evidence rule** A contract made by the parties
supersedes all tentative terms discussed in earlier negotia-

tions. The parol (oral) evidence rule comes into play when a dispute arises over a written contract. Under this rule, when parties put their agreement in writing, all *previous* and current oral agreements merge in the writing. The contract as written cannot be changed by parol evidence when it has been legally executed by a person intending it to be the final and complete expression of his intention, unless there has been some mistake or fraud in the preparation of the writing.

The purpose of the parol evidence rule is to carry out the presumed intention of the parties, to achieve certainty and finality concerning the rights and duties of the contracting parties, and to prevent fraudulent and perjured claims.

■ **Interpretation of ambiguous contracts** Ambiguity means that after using the rules or tools of interpretation, the court is not able, with certainty, to attach a meaning to the language used. Some courts apply the PLAIN MEANING RULE to determine whether a contract is ambiguous. Under this rule, if the contract appears to the trial judge to be clear and unambiguous on its face, no parol evidence is admissible. Once a writing is shown to be ambiguous, however, parol evidence is always admissible to clarify terms. Parol evidence admitted to explain the meaning of a writing does not attempt to change but only to clarify the contract as it is written, and does not offend the parol evidence rule.

Other means have been used to resolve ambiguous terms. If the parties give an ambiguous expression the same meaning, a contract is formed, but if each gives it a different meaning, there is no contract, at least if the ambiguity relates to an important term. When one party knows or has reason to know of the ambiguity and the other does not and thinks the meaning is clear, the contract bears the meaning given to it by the latter. In other words, the contract is based upon the meaning of the party who is without fault.

Under the Constitution a person has the right to make contracts without governmental interference. This right is not absolute and may be reasonably restricted by the federal or state government in the interest and welfare of its people. For example, contracts in RESTRAINT OF TRADE are properly prohibited by government.

■ **Which law governs** Although there is a general body of contract law, some aspects of it, such as the interpretation of ambiguous terms, vary among the different states. When courts must choose which law should govern a contract, they consider several factors: the intention of the parties about which law should govern, the place where the contract was made, and the place where the contract is to be performed. Under the modern doctrine of the "grouping of contacts" the law of the jurisdiction (state) having the closest or most significant relationship with the subject in dispute applies.

EXAMPLE You, a Vermont resident, while at a sales convention for restaurateurs, in New York, contract with a Vermont manufacturer for the purchase and delivery of Vermont maple syrup to your chain of pancake restaurants in Vermont. The manufacturer violates a term of the contract, and the contract did not specify which law was to apply if there was a contract dispute. Although the contract was made in New York, the jurisdiction having the most significant relationship with the disputed contract is Vermont. The parties are Vermont residents, the

subject matter is Vermont maple syrup, and the place of performance is Vermont. Clearly, under the "grouping of contacts" doctrine, Vermont law should apply.

In many cases, the courts will apply the law that the parties expressly or presumably intended to govern the contract, so long as it is reasonably related to the transaction and the parties acted in good faith. Other courts apply the law of the place where the contract was made or was to be performed, unless the parties clearly intended to have some other law govern. See also CONFLICT OF LAWS.

Contracts governed by foreign law may be recognized and enforced under the doctrine of COMITY.

contravention Conduct that violates a legal obligation. For example, speeding in a crowded downtown area is usually in contravention of the traffic laws.

contribution The right of a party who has paid an obligation that he had in common with another person to get back his fair share from that person. He need not have paid the entire debt, but he must have paid more than his agreed-upon share. He must have been under a legal obligation to make the payment, either because the liability was joint (shared by two or more debtors) or joint and several (assumed by the debtors as a group and individually). But when the parties are severally (individually) liable for a specific portion of a debt and one person pays more than he is liable for, he is not entitled to contribution from the others for the excess. See CONTRACTS.

EXAMPLE Jason and Mario agree that together they will pay Lyle $100 to drive them to California. They are jointly liable to Lyle. Jason pays Lyle the entire $100. Jason has a right of contribution that entitles him to receive $50 from Mario, which is Mario's proportionate share of the liability. Jason would also have a right of contribution if he and Mario, acting both together and as individuals (jointly and severally), had made a contract promising to pay Lyle $100. But if Jason and Mario acted individually, with Jason promising to pay Lyle $60 and Mario promising to pay $40, Jason has no right of contribution against Mario for $40 if Jason decides to pay Lyle the entire $100.

Transactions involving contracts may result in a common liability or debt that is owed, such as when Jason and Mario hired Lyle to drive them to California. But the common-law rule in TORTS (wrongful acts to persons or property that justify lawsuits) is that joint tort-feasors (wrongdoers who have acted together) have no right of contribution because the court will not be a party to a dispute between wrongdoers. As a result of the injustices created by this rule, however, many states have changed it by statute to allow contribution between joint defendants in certain situations—for example, when the tort-feasors are equally guilty of a tort.

EXAMPLE Earl and John together beat up Norman, who sues them for assault and battery. Norman is awarded $1,000 in damages, which Earl pays. In states that allow contribution in this type of situation, Earl is entitled to contribution from John in the amount of $500.

The right of contribution is usually enforced by a separate lawsuit. Sometimes, however, the trial court may order contribution to be paid to a defendant who is entitled to it in the same case in which his common liability with another defendant is established.

contributory negligence   A careless act or failure to act by the injured or complaining party in a lawsuit that, together with the defendant's NEGLIGENCE, is the PROXIMATE CAUSE (direct cause) of injury. The law imposes a duty on persons to protect themselves from injury. Lack of ordinary care by the injured party is a breach or violation of that duty, because it contributes to his injury. Without his carelessness the injury might not have occurred or might not have been as serious.

> EXAMPLE If you are hit by a speeding car while you are
> O⟶＊ crossing the street against the traffic light, you are
> guilty of contributory negligence. Your injuries might not have occurred without your careless behavior, even though the driver was negligently operating his car by speeding. In some states, the concept of contributory negligence has been replaced by comparative negligence.

controller   The top financial officer of a CORPORATION. See also COMPTROLLER.

controversy   A civil lawsuit. The word "controversy" is more restrictive than the word "case." "Controversy" refers only to civil cases, while "case" includes all suits, criminal as well as civil. See CIVIL ACTION.

controvert   Dispute; deny; oppose or contest; take issue. If you, the defendant, controvert the plaintiff's testimony, you deny its truthfulness.

contumacy   **1** The refusal of a person who has been duly cited before a court to appear and defend the CHARGE laid against him. **2** The refusal of a person who is duly before the court to obey some lawful order or direction. See CONTEMPT.

contumely   Rudeness that shows haughtiness and CONTEMPT. For example, a defendant who calls the judge a pig during the trial is guilty of contumely and would probably be held in contempt of court.

convention   **1** As a legislative term, a meeting of delegates or representatives chosen by the people for special and extraordinary legislative purposes, such as the framing or revision of a state constitution. See CONSTITUTIONAL LAW. **2** An assembly of delegates chosen by a political party or by the party organization to nominate candidates for an approaching ELECTION, such as the Democratic or Republican convention to select a Presidential candidate. **3** A pact or agreement between states or nations in the nature of a TREATY. The word usually refers to agreements or arrangements preliminary to a formal treaty or to international agreements for the regulation of matters outside the sphere of politics or commerce, such as the protection of submarine cables.

conventional   **1** Usual or ordinary. **2** Created by an agreement between persons rather than by the effect of a law. For example, a home MORTGAGE is conventional (usual) when the individual or bank making the loan assumes the full risk, as opposed to being guaranteed by the Federal Housing Administration (FHA mortgage) or Veterans Administration (VA mortgage). A mortgage is also called conventional if the mortgage agreement allows the borrower to keep the house in his possession, as opposed to one that requires the borrower to give up possession of his mortgaged property until he pays off the loan.

conversion   Any act that deprives an owner of his personal property without his permission or without just cause. Personal property is any property that is not real property (real estate). Conversion generally involves the unauthorized use or misuse of someone else's personal property.

■ **What constitutes a conversion**   When someone, without justification, intentionally interferes with a person's possession of his personal property in any way, he is guilty of conversion and can be sued by the owner for the value of the property. He can interfere with the possession of property by (1) keeping the property away from its rightful owner or aiding and abetting someone else in doing so, (2) selling the property or changing it in some way without the owner's permission, or (3) using the property in a way he should not use it.

> EXAMPLE If you refuse to return a book you borrowed from
> O⟶＊ your neighbor when he asks for it, you are guilty
> of a conversion. Your neighbor, as owner of the converted property, is deprived of his property for an indefinite period of time—or even permanently. If your son helps you hide the book after your neighbor asks you to return it, he is also guilty of conversion because he is aiding and abetting you in keeping the property.

The owner's lack of consent to possession of the property by the wrongdoer is essential to a conversion, however.

> EXAMPLE If your neighbor willingly lends you the book and
> O⟶＊ does not ask you to return it, you are not guilty of
> a conversion if you keep it indefinitely. A conversion results only if you refuse to return the book after your neighbor asks you to return it.

An unauthorized sale of another's personal property is a conversion. For example, if you borrowed your neighbor's lawnmower and later sold it without his permission, you would be guilty of a conversion. The mistaken delivery of the proceeds of an authorized sale to someone other than the owner of the goods is also ordinarily a conversion.

> EXAMPLE Dennis was bringing some old tools to a second-
> O⟶＊ hand dealer to sell them. His two neighbors, Al-
> bert and Sasha, heard about this and asked Dennis to sell something of theirs, too. Albert gave Dennis a used power drill to sell and Sasha gave him a coffee maker. Dennis sold Albert's power drill but could not sell Sasha's coffee maker because there was a leak in its base.
>
> When Dennis returned home, he got confused about who had given him what, and he gave Sasha the money he had received for Albert's power drill and then tried to give Albert Sasha's defective coffee maker. When Dennis tried to straighten out the mess he had created, Sasha refused to refund the money Dennis had mistakingly given him and Albert became furious and threatened to

sue Dennis for conversion. If Albert went through with his suit, he would win it. Albert could also successfully sue Sasha, who has kept property (money) rightfully belonging to him.

Any unjustified act that changes the nature of someone else's property is a conversion. If you borrow your neighbor's automobile and trade it in for a different model without his consent, you are guilty of conversion. You are also guilty of conversion if you take the car apart and use the parts in a new machine you have invented or if you have the car reduced to scrap metal. Misuse of someone else's property is also a conversion.

EXAMPLE Paul lends his horse, Strider, to Dave to ride to 0——* the foot of White Mountain. He tells Dave not to ride Strider up the path that climbs the slopes of the mountain. Nevertheless, after he reaches the foot of White Mountain, Dave decides to disregard Paul's instruction, thinking that Paul will never know the difference. About halfway up the path Strider drops dead from the strain of hard climbing at a high altitude. Dave's misuse of Strider (Paul's personal property), exceeding Paul's permission, is a conversion causing the death of the horse. Paul can sue Dave to recover damages for the value of his horse.

■ **Suing for conversion**   Since early times in England, the law has protected an owner's rights in his personal property by permitting him to file a suit, called an *action in trover*, against anyone who is responsible for a conversion of his property. When a person sues another for conversion of his property, he will be awarded money damages equal to the value of the goods at the time of the conversion. In other words, if the converted property has been changed enough to affect its value, the owner is entitled to the value of the property before it was changed. In the above example, Paul would be entitled to enough money to cover the value of Strider when he was alive and not after he had been killed by Dave's misuse of him. If a neighbor wrongfully takes apart your car, you are entitled to the value of the car before it was dismantled.

A person guilty of conversion cannot force an owner to accept the return of the converted property in hopes of barring a lawsuit or reducing the amount for which he will be liable. But if an owner willingly accepts the return of his property—let us say your neighbor made a better car from the parts of the old one he took apart—the damages that the defendant is liable for will be reduced accordingly.

conveyance   1 Under real-property law, a transfer of legal TITLE to (ownership of) real estate. See PROPERTY. In its popular sense and as generally used by lawyers, conveyance can include the transfer of EQUITABLE title as well as legal title. Equitable title is title that in all fairness is deserved by a party but that under the strict letter of the law does not belong to him.

EXAMPLE Jake murders his brother Leroy during a fight 0——* over whether to sell farmlands that they had inherited from their late father. Although Jake legally owns the land once Leroy dies, some courts will rule that Jake has only legal title to the land but the equitable title to the farm belongs to Leroy's only survivor, his daughter, Natalie. Natalie would be entitled to do anything she

wants with the land since, in fairness, it belongs to her. The ownership is split into legal and equitable titles because it would be unjust to allow Jake to profit from his wrongdoing. Natalie would be able to transfer her equitable title in the land to anyone she wants since in justice she owns the land. Jake will eventually be forced to transfer his legal title by conveyance to Natalie. Conveyance also refers to any written document, such as a DEED or a MORTGAGE, by which property or any right to property is transferred.

2 In laws concerning transportation, anything that serves as a means of transportation. A city bus is a public conveyance. See CARRIER.

convict   1 Condemn after judicial investigation; find a person guilty of a criminal charge.   2 As a noun, a person who is condemned by a competent court for a crime and sentenced to prison. See PRISONERS' RIGHTS.

cooling-off period   1 A period of time during which no action of a certain kind may be taken by either side in a dispute. For example, in a labor dispute, there may be a cooling-off period of one month after a union files a grievance against a company, or vice versa. During this period, the union may not strike and the company may not lock out the employees. See GRIEVANCE PROCEDURE; LOCKOUT.   2 A period of time in which a buyer may cancel a purchase. Many states require a three-day cooling-off period for door-to-door sales. See CONSUMER PROTECTION.   3 An automatic delay in some states between the filing of DIVORCE papers and the divorce hearing.

cooperative   A corporation organized for the purpose of performing an economic service to the shareholders who own and control it. For example, a cooperative apartment house is owned and managed by a corporation, from which each tenant leases his apartment. The size of the apartment a tenant wishes to lease determines the number of shares of stock he must purchase in the corporation. For instance, a tenant who leases a three-room apartment might be required to purchase 20 shares of stock, while a tenant who leases a four-room apartment might be required to purchase 30 shares. Each tenant must pay a monthly assessment based on the number of his shares of stock. The assessment includes the principal and interest on the apartment mortgage, taxes, and building-maintenance expenses. See also CONDOMINIUM.

A farmer's cooperative is an organization composed of neighboring farmers to market their combined crops, produce, and livestock. The cooperative attempts to sell crops and livestock at the optimum price. For example, it might store grain so that the price of grain will rise as a result of its shortage on the market.

A food-buying cooperative is an association of local families who join forces to buy fresh fruit, vegetables, and meat as well as other staples for the best possible prices from food wholesale distributors. By buying in bulk quantities and by eliminating the need for the middlemen retail grocery stores, whose higher prices include advertising and packing the items, members of the cooperative usually save substantially on the cost of groceries.

copyright

The exclusive right of a creator or an owner of an intellectual work such as a book, play, painting, movie, or piece of music to control the copying, publication, sale, and distribution of his work. He alone can say whether or not it may be copied, performed, reprinted, reproduced, or distributed by anyone else.

The owner of a copyright has the exclusive rights to do or to authorize any of the following: (1) to reproduce the copyrighted work; (2) to prepare derivative works based upon it; (3) to distribute copies of the copyrighted work to the public by sale, rental, lease, or lending; (4) to publicly perform copyrighted literary, musical, dramatic, and choreographic works, pantomimes, and motion pictures and other audiovisual works; and (5) to publicly display copyrighted literary, musical, dramatic, and choreographic works, pantomimes, and pictorial, graphic, or sculptural works, including the individual images of a motion picture or other audiovisual work. These exclusive rights constitute the bundle of rights that make up a copyright. Each one may be separately owned and enforced.

EXAMPLE If you write a play, you can sell one person the exclusive right to reprint the play in his theater magazine and another the exclusive right to include the play in an anthology his publishing company is preparing. Even though you have given away the magazine and book rights to your copyrighted work you still own the exclusive rights to have it performed publicly and used as the basis for the preparation of derivative works, such as movies, ballets, or operas. People who wish to use your work must in most instances get permission to do so. If they fail to seek your consent, they will be liable for damages for copyright infringement.

■ **Background** Article I, Section 8, of the U.S. Constitution gives Congress the power to enact copyright and patent laws that offer protection to works for a limited period of time:

" The Congress shall have Power . . . To promote the Progress of Science and useful Arts, by securing for limited Times to Authors and Inventors the exclusive Right to their respective Writings and Discoveries."

Until 1978 there was a dual system of copyright in the United States. Published works were protected by federal law and unpublished works were protected by common law. In 1978 a new federal law was passed that abolished the old dual system.

Old copyright system In the early years of the nation federal laws were enacted to protect published books and other printed works. Later, published musical compositions, fine arts, and other types of works were given federal protection. From 1909 to 1977 published works could be protected for a period of 28 years and that period of protection could be renewed in the final year of protection for another 28 years. For a work to receive protection under the old federal law it had to be published with a notice of copyright and registered with the Copyright Office in Washington, D.C. If a person's rights under the federal copyright law were violated, he could sue the violator, or *infringer,* in federal court.

At the same time, common-law copyright afforded protection to unpublished literary, artistic, dramatic, and musical works, and was enforced by state law. Common law prohibited any kind of interference with, or unauthorized use of, an unpublished work by someone other than its creator or proprietor (anyone to whom the creator had legally transferred the right). A common-law copyright was of indefinite or perpetual duration, continuing with the owner until he abandoned it by allowing someone else to publish his work or forfeited it by presenting the work to the public or offering it for sale. The owner of an unpublished intellectual composition had an absolute and exclusive right to do whatever he wanted with his work—have it published, circulate it among friends, or keep it private and seek redress in court against unauthorized publication.

During the 19th century, publication of a work could serve as a practical dividing line between common-law and federal copyright protection, because works were then circulated almost exclusively through printed copies. With the 20th-century revolution in communications technology—including the development of sound recordings, films, and videotape—the concept of just what constitutes publication became more obscure and uncertain. Courts interpreted publication differently, resulting in unfair and unpredictable application of the law to individuals. A new law was needed to fit the times, and that new law was ultimately enacted. It became effective on January 1, 1978.

The 1978 law Under the 1978 law all forms of communication that can be recorded in any tangible medium are protected for a limited period of time. The period of protection begins with the creation of the work, when it is fixed in a copy for the first time. The copy may be a visual record, such as a book or diagram, or an aural record, such as a sound recording. The copy must contain a notice of copyright but it need not be registered with the Copyright Office for protection to begin. However, registration must be made within five years to adequately protect an author's rights—obviously, the sooner the better.

Published works and unpublished works are treated the same. Under the old system, unpublished works were given common-law protection of infinite duration while published works were given limited statutory protection. The 1978 federal law includes protection for both published and unpublished works and so must limit the period of protection for both in response to the Constitutional provision for securing rights for "limited times."

The new federal law specifically preempts and abolishes any rights under common or state law that are equivalent to copyright and that cover works within the scope of the federal copyright law. The federal law prevents the states from protecting a tangibly expressed work of authorship even if, failing federal criteria, it is denied federal copyright. The 1978 law retains common-law copyright protection for only one important class of works: those that have not been fixed in any tangible medium of expression, such as an impromptu speech or an improvised dramatic sketch.

If someone videotapes an improvised skit, that recording falls under state rather than federal law if the person recording the show is not connected with performers. Once the sketch is videotaped on the performer's orders it becomes protected by federal law.

Works eligible for copyright Under the 1978 law, copyright protection covers "original works of authorship fixed in any tangible means of expression, now known or later developed, from which they can be perceived, reproduced or otherwise communicated, either directly or indirectly with the aid of a machine or device." More specifically, protection is offered for the following categories of works:

Literary works These are works "expressed in words, numbers, or other verbal or numerical symbols . . . regardless of the nature of the material objects, such as books, periodicals, manuscripts, phonorecords, film, tapes, disks or cards in which they are embodied." This category covers books, poems, articles, catalogs, directories, and compilations of data as well as computer-data bases and computer programs.

Musical works When the work has lyrics, both the lyrics and the melody receive protection.

Dramatic works These include any accompanying music, such as the scores of musical comedies.

Pantomimes and choreographic works A dance that is choreographed and fixed in a tangible medium of expression (such as notations or a videotape by a ballet choreographer) can be copyrighted, but simple dance steps or routines, such as the hustle, cannot.

Pictorial, graphic, and sculptural works This category includes not only "works of art" in the traditional sense but also graphic art, illustrations, art reproductions, plans and drawings, photographs and reproductions of them, maps, charts, globes, and any such works made for advertising and commerce—for instance, lithographic reproductions of the works of Rembrandt that are sold as postcards.

Motion pictures and other audiovisual works These include films, videotapes, video disks, and filmstrips.

Sound recordings These include the sum total of musical, spoken, or other sounds that have been fixed in tangible form on phonograph records, magnetic tape, and the like.

In addition, the language of the 1978 law is deliberately broad enough to cover future scientific discoveries and technological developments, such as electronic music and computer programs, that will make possible new forms of creative expression.

Originality To be entitled to copyright protection, the work of authorship must be original—that is, its author must have created the work by his own skill, labor, or judgment, without either directly copying someone else's work or imitating it with the purpose of evading copyright law. The court does not presume to measure the artistic merit or literary skill of the work before copyright protection. If you write an original short story that earns you a D in your creative writing course, you may still get copyright protection as long as you comply with the requirements of the statute and the Copyright Office.

Similar works may each receive copyright protection if each is the result of independent work and judgment.

HOW COPYRIGHT LAW WORKS

■ A copyright is your exclusive right to control the publication, sale, and distribution of a book, play, painting, movie, piece of music, or the like that was created by you or belongs to you.

■ To be entitled to copyright protection, your work must be original. A compilation of nonoriginal materials may be copyrighted if the selection, arrangement, and combination of the materials show more than a trivial variation from the old work and result from your original and creative effort.

■ Copyright does not prevent others from using ideas or information revealed in your work.

■ No work can be copyrighted that is indecent, immoral, passed off as someone else's, or otherwise illegal.

■ Copyright in a protected work is initially owned by the author or authors of the work. However, if you are doing "work for hire"—say you are a free-lancer hired to write the biography entries for a desk encyclopedia—the publisher who hires you is considered the author of the work for which you are paid, and he holds the copyright, unless there has been a written agreement stating otherwise.

■ Under the law, copyright lasts as long as you, the author, live and for another 50 years after your death. The law requires that you publish a copyright notice in all publicly distributed copies of any work for which you claim protection.

■ The notice must contain the symbol © or the word "Copyright" or the abbreviation "Copr."; the year of the work's first publication; and the name of the owner of the copyright.

■ Once a work has been publicly distributed, copies must be registered and deposited with the Copyright Office in Washington, D.C.

■ Application for copyright registration and a fee of $10 must accompany the copies.

■ A copyright owner who has not registered his work may still sue someone who has infringed his work, but he cannot enforce his rights unless he registers the work during the course of the trial or before he sues.

■ To establish an infringement of your copyright you must prove that the alleged infringer has copied your work and there is a substantial similarity between it and the copy.

■ If someone infringes your copyright, you may sue him, but you must start your suit within three years of the infringement.

■ The distinction between infringement and fair use is sometimes a fine one, but you are not infringing if you quote excerpts from a novel in a book review for purposes of illustration or comment or if you reproduce a small part of a work for classroom use—that sort of thing is fair use.

■ Once a person is found guilty of infringement, the court may issue an order to prevent further infringement and it may also grant money damages.

■ Anyone of the following is criminal infringement: (1) fraudulent use of a copyright notice; (2) fraudulent removal of a notice; (3) false representation in making a copyright application; and (4) willful infringement for profit.

■ A common type of criminal infringement is record piracy—making cheap copies of a successful, copyrighted sound recording—on disk or tape—for discount sale to the general public. A person can get a $25,000 fine or a year in jail or both for record piracy on his first offense.

Historical, scientific, statistical, and other facts are part of the public domain—that is, they may be freely copied and reproduced by the general public. But if two historians, one in New York and one in Oregon, each working separately, write articles presenting similar analyses of the causes of the stock market crash of 1929, based on the same statistics and other data, each article will be entitled to copyright protection.

A compilation of nonoriginal material may be copyrighted if the selection, modification, arrangement, and combination of these materials show more than a trivial variation from the old work and result from original and creative work by the author.

EXAMPLE If you decide to publish a collection of sonnets by Shakespeare, you will be protected by statutory copyright for your compilation if it is arranged or annotated in any original way that shows your independent creation. The copyright will only cover and protect your compilation; the sonnets themselves remain available for others to use.

Works not eligible Copyright protection does not extend to any idea, procedure, process, system, method of operation, concept, principle, or discovery, regardless of the form in which it is described, explained, or illustrated. However, these may be protected under PATENT laws. Copyright does not prevent others from using the ideas or information revealed by an author's work.

EXAMPLE After reading an article based on your experiences as a medical student, I decide to write an article about my experiences as a medical student. You cannot claim that I have violated your copyright, because ideas are not copyrightable. But if I actually use your article, making only minor changes in the people's names and the identity of the school, I will be liable for copyright infringement or violation because your copyright bars me from copying your expression of an idea.

No copyright can be acquired for a work that is indecent or immoral in character, is deceptive in its authorship or contents, or is otherwise illegal. Because these works are not protected by copyright, they become part of the public domain, and anyone may copy or distribute them.

EXAMPLE If Sloan publishes a book that is so indecent and immoral that it has been refused a copyright by the Copyright Office, the novel becomes part of the public domain. If Wolf takes the book, copies it for use as a script for a pornographic film, and distributes the script under his name, Sloan cannot sue Wolf for infringement of his copyright, but Wolf may be subject to criminal prosecution for violating obscenity laws.

Vulgarity and coarseness of language alone are not sufficient to deny a copyright to a work, and the courts have denied copyright protection on the basis of immorality in only a few cases—because this would be a violation of freedom of speech. See SPEECH AND PRESS, FREEDOM OF.

Other examples of works not subject to copyright are

(1) Words and short phrases, including names, titles, and slogans; familiar symbols or designs; slight variations in typography or ornamentation; lists of ingredients, or tables of contents.

(2) Blank printed forms for recording information, such as time cards, graph paper, account books, diaries, bank checks, scorecards, address books, report forms, and salesmen's order forms.

(3) Works consisting entirely of information that is common property and containing no original authorship, such as standard calendars, height and weight charts, tape measures, schedules of sporting events, and lists taken from public documents or other common sources.

(4) Works produced for the U.S. Government by its officers and employees, such as the FEDERAL REGISTER.

■ **Persons entitled to a copyright** Copyright in a protected work is initially owned by the author or authors of the work. If you write a poem, you own its copyright. In the case of what is called a "work for hire," the employer is considered the author of the work and is regarded as the initial owner or proprietor of the copyright unless there has been a written agreement stating otherwise.

EXAMPLE If you are a free-lance writer hired by the publisher of a national magazine to write an article on the latest winter fashions, the copyright belongs to the publisher, unless your contract specifies that you will own the copyright on your article. If a different publisher reprints your article, only your publisher—not you—can sue for copyright infringement. And if your publisher later uses your article in a regional magazine he owns, you cannot sue him.

The ownership of a copyright, or any part of it, may be transferred by any means of CONVEYANCE or by OPERATION OF LAW, say, when a person dies without leaving a will. See ASSIGN; DESCENT AND DISTRIBUTION. A copyright is treated as personal PROPERTY when the owner dies. Copyright ownership and ownership of the material object in which the copyrighted work is embodied are entirely separate things. Transfer of the material object, such as an original manuscript, a negative of a photograph, or a master tape recording, does not in itself also transfer any rights under the copyright. When a person buys a copyrighted novel in a bookstore he does not acquire the copyright on it. Transfer of a copyright does not necessarily require the conveyance of any material object. If you are a sculptor, for instance, and plan to give your son the copyright on one of your statues, it is not necessary to give him the statue itself.

■ **Duration of copyright** Congress has no power, under the Constitution, to grant perpetual copyrights. Copyright of a work created on or after January 1, 1978, is effective from the time of its creation to 50 years after the author's death.

For example, Jessica Candle writes a novel in 1981. She dies in 2001. Her manuscript is protected by copyright from 1981 until 2051—that is, 50 years after her death. Before the 1978 law, the term of a copyright was divided into two parts—a first or original term and a renewal or extended term, each of which ran for 28 years.

EXAMPLE Under the old law, if a 20-year-old playwright published a play and received a statutory copyright, the first term of his copyright would have ended 28 years from the date of publication, when the playwright was 48 years old. If he had renewed his copyright for the additional 28-year term, his copyright would have expired when he was 76 years old.

Copyrights that were in their first term under the old law when the new law took effect—on January 1, 1978—will be allowed to complete their first 28-year term. If the copyright owners apply to the Copyright Office for renewal within one year before the first term runs out, they will be granted an additional 47 years of copyright protection. Posthumous works, those that were first published after the author's death, are also included in this category. If a renewal is not applied for, the copyright will expire at the end of the first term, or 28 years after it was granted.

EXAMPLE If you had published a novel in 1970 and had registered it with the Copyright Office, the old law would have been applied to it and the copyright would remain in effect for 28 years from the date it was originally secured. Your copyright would expire in 1998. If you apply to the Copyright Office for an extension of the copyright in 1997, which is within one year prior to the expiration of the original term, your copyright will probably be extended an additional 47 years, finally terminating in 2045.

The duration of any copyright that was in its renewal term between December 31, 1976, and December 31, 1977, inclusive, or for which renewal registration was made at that time is extended for 75 years from the date the copyright was originally secured. This provision extends an already renewed copyright from 56 years to 75 years.

When the final term of copyright expires, the work falls into the public domain and anyone may use it for any purpose. The copyright owner loses all rights in the work.

When a copyright is owned by a publishing house, the copyright will expire 75 years from the year in which it was first published or 100 years from the date the copyrighted work was created, whichever is shorter. For example, a writer wrote a poem and sold it to a literary magazine in 1978. The poem was not published until 1980. The copyright owned by the magazine publisher would expire in 2055, 75 years after publication, which is less time than 2078, 100 years after the poem was created. This rule also applies to anonymous or pseudonymous works. If, however, the identity of an author is revealed in special records in the Copyright Office, the term of his copyright in the anonymous or pseudonymous work is converted into the ordinary life-plus-50-years term. If two or more authors were responsible for the creation of such a work and the identity of only one author is disclosed, the term of the copyright is based on the life of the identified author.

■ **How to copyright a work** It is very easy to get a copyright. First, you must put a notice of copyright on every copy of the work that will reach the public. This will protect your rights to the work for a period of five years. To secure your rights more firmly, you must register your copyright with the U.S. Copyright Office within five years after the work is made public. The earlier you register, the better it may be for you, because your rights are more firmly established after registration than before and you will be more likely to be able to prove that you own a copyright in a court of law if you have registered it.

Notice of copyright There is a statutory requirement that the public be given formal notice of every work in which a copyright is claimed. The purpose is to prevent someone from violating the copyright inadvertently. The notice informs the public that the work is copyrighted and that unauthorized copying or sale of it will constitute an infringement of the owner's rights, which will result in a penalty for the infringer.

The notice of copyright must be placed on all copies that will reach the public. It must contain (1) the symbol ©, the word "Copyright," or the abbreviation "Copr."; (2) the year of the first publication of the work; and (3) the name of the owner of the copyright, an abbreviation by which the name can be recognized, or some other generally known designation of the owner. For example, a notice might read "Copr. 1981 Arthur Penmann" or "Copyright © 1981 The Book Writers' Press, Inc." In the case of compilations or derivative works incorporating previously published material, giving the year of first publication of the compilation or derivative work is sufficient. In other words, if in 1981 someone published a collection of the best short stories of the 1970's, he would use the year 1981 in his notice of copyright even though the individual stories had been published in the 1970's. The year may be omitted from a notice if the copyrighted work is reproduced in or on greeting cards, postcards, stationery, jewelry, dolls, toys, or any useful articles.

To be legally effective, the notice of copyright must be in a position to be easily seen by the public. In a musical work, for example, it must appear on either the title page or the first page of music, and it must be legible to the naked eye. If the notice is so blurred that it is impossible to determine the name of the owner and the year of publication, it is ineffective, and the courts will probably treat it as an omission.

The outright omission of a copyright notice does not automatically forfeit protection and throw the work into the public domain, as happened under the former law. Under the present law, omission of the notice, whether intentional or not, does not invalidate the copyright if (1) only a relatively small number of copies have been publicly distributed without notice, or (2) if registration for the work has already been made or is made within five years after the publication without notice and a reasonable effort is made to add notice to copies publicly distributed in the United States after the omission is discovered.

The purpose of this major change in the law is to prevent unfair or unjustifiable loss of copyright on technical grounds. The 1978 law also shields an innocent infringer from unreasonable liability, which may result from his copying a copyrighted work that lacked the required notice of copyright. In order to benefit from this protection, however, the innocent infringer must prove to the court that he (1) was misled by the omission of the copyright notice, (2) was completely unaware that the work was copyrighted, and (3) honestly believed that it was part of the public domain.

If a person knows that the copyright notice is missing from a work, he cannot take advantage of the law to infringe a copyright wrongfully. The court may allow the owner to recover from a willful infringer any profits that can be shown to have resulted from the infringement—an increase in magazine sales because of the unauthorized publication of excerpts of a novel, for instance. The court may also prevent any continued infringement by granting an injunction to restrain the wrongful conduct, and finally, if the owner agrees to let the infringer continue to use his work, the court may order the infringer to pay the owner a reasonable license fee.

Registration Once a work has been made available to the public with proper notice, copies must be deposited with the Copyright Office in Washington, D.C., for registration purposes. It is not necessary that they be deposited promptly for the work to be protected by statutory copyright. Deposit absolutely insures that the owner will have all the legal remedies available to him in case of infringement. An application for copyright registration in the form required by statute and a fee of $10 must accompany the copies. Statutory provisions and rules of the Copyright Office about affidavits accompanying the application must be observed. However, an unimportant mistake—in the date of completion of the printing of a book, for example—will not invalidate the copyright. The application may be corrected. After receiving the copies of the work and the appropriate papers, the Register of Copyrights will decide whether or not the work is something that can be copyrighted. If he finds that it can, he will register the claim and issue a certificate of registration to the applicant. If he finds that the work is something that cannot be copyrighted or that the claim is invalid for any other reason, he will refuse to register it and will notify the applicant.

EXAMPLE Suppose you want to register a poem with the O⟶✷ Copyright Office. First, you would make sure that a copyright notice appears legibly on the back of the title page and contains the proper symbol for copyright, the date of the poem's first publication or completion, and your name. If your poem has not been published, you would deposit one copy with the copyright office. If it has been published, you would deposit with the Copyright Office two complete copies of the best edition of the work within five years after the date of its publication. Along with your poem, you would have to submit an application for copyright registration, which would include your name, the title of the work, the year you completed it, the date it was published (if it was), and other detailed information. You would also have to include the $10 fee to cover the costs of registration. Once the Register of Copyrights has determined that your work can be copyrighted and that the statutory requirements have been met, he will register the claim and issue to you a certificate of registration under the seal of the Copyright Office.

A certificate of registration must be given PRIMA FACIE weight (must be presumed to be true) in any judicial proceedings if the registration was made "before or within 5 years after first publication of the work." The five-year limit recognizes the fact that the longer the lapse of time between publication and registration the greater the possibility of inaccuracy in the facts stated in the certificate and the greater the opportunity for innocent infringement of the work.

A copyright owner who has not registered his claim may sue someone who has infringed his claim, but he cannot enforce his rights until he has registered the work, either before filing suit or during the trial but before a judgment will be given.

■ **Infringement** To establish a copyright infringement, the owner of the copyright must prove that the alleged infringer has copied the protected work and that there is a substantial similarity between it and the copy. He must start his suit against the defendant within three years of the alleged infringement.

Copying Copying is the exact or substantial reproduction of an original that uses the original as a model. There can be no infringement without copying. Similarity or even identity does not constitute infringement when both works are original and there is, in fact, no copying. Infringement may take the form of literal reproduction, copying with no substantial change, or indirect copying or reproduction from memory. Acknowledgment of the source or the creator of the work does not protect the infringer from legal liability, because he is still violating the exclusive rights of the creator by using the material without his permission.

EXAMPLE You write a best-selling novel about the Civil O⟶✷ War, which has a very dramatic and touching death scene involving two brothers. You have complied with statutory requirements and registered your novel with the Copyright Office in Washington. Jones writes a play about World War I. It contains the same dramatic death scene involving two brothers, which he copied from you. He has added some psychological dimensions viewed by some critics as an improvement on the death scene in your novel. Nevertheless, Jones has infringed your copyrighted work. He would be unsuccessful if he argued that there are different audiences for a best-seller and a play. It is not necessary that there be any competition between the original and the infringing work.

Fair and unfair use The question of fair or unfair use arises when a copyrighted work is copied. Under the 1978 copyright law the fair use of a copyrighted work, including the copying of parts of the work for such purposes as criticism, comment, news reporting, scholarship, or research is not an infringement of copyright. Nor is a teacher's multiple copies of a work for classroom use. The courts' criteria for determining fair use are (1) the purpose and character of the use, including whether such use is of a commercial nature or is for nonprofit educational purposes; (2) the nature of the copyrighted work; (3) the amount and substantiality of the portion used in relation to the copyrighted work as a whole; and (4) the effect of the use upon the potential market for or value of the copyrighted work.

Some activities that might be regarded as fair use are quoting excerpts of a novel in a book review or work of criticism for purposes of illustration or comment; and quoting short passages in a scholarly work to illustrate and explain the author's observations. It is legal for a person to tape commercial recordings from radio or movies from TV for his own use. A student who photocopied an entire work—such as a play or an article—that was no longer in print would not be in violation of a copyright that was still in effect if he was using it only for scholarly purposes and not commercial purposes. There is no violation if the copy (1) was made for educational purposes and (2) does not affect potential market for the work since the work is no longer in print. These two points outweigh the fact that the entire work was copied, which, under other circumstances, could justify a finding of infringement.

Under the doctrine of fair use, a public or nonprofit-making library or archive has the right to reproduce or distribute one copy of a work, as long as it is not done for any direct or indirect commercial advantage. Such material must be available to the public and must include a notice of the copyright.

Systematic reproductions of single or multiple copies of copyrighted works, intended as substitutes for subscriptions or purchases, are prohibited. Problems have arisen in determining when systematic reproduction of a copyrighted work violates the law. For example, libraries frequently make more than one photocopy of a copyrighted work solely to meet the demands of their patrons, although according to the words of the statute, this violates the law. The court must determine how this section of the law will be enforced.

Violation of a license   A person who has received the permission of a copyright owner to copy, reprint, reproduce, sell, or distribute the copyrighted work has been given a LICENSE. The violation of any restrictions that the owner has placed on the license is a form of copyright infringement.

EXAMPLE Delbert, a movie star, writes his autobiography, 0—* which promises to be a sensational exposé of the Hollywood scene. He complies with all the statutory requirements and the book is registered with the Copyright Office. He hires an agent, Rodney, and gives him an exclusive license to sell the book to the movie company making the highest bid, but he imposes a condition on Rodney's license. Rodney must secure a promise by the movie company to star Delbert's girl friend, Tanya, in any filmed production of the book. The agent negotiates a multimillion-dollar deal with Colossal Pictures, Inc., and concludes the sale, but without being able to secure Colossal's promise to use Tanya in the film. Delbert can sue Rodney for copyright infringement, because his sale was actually unauthorized.

■ **Remedies for infringement**   Copyright infringement deprives a copyright owner of his exclusive right to copy, reprint, sell, or distribute his work. Once a person is found guilty of having infringed another's copyright, the court may grant a temporary or final INJUNCTION (a court order) to prevent or restrain infringement.

EXAMPLE A screenwriter copies entire chapters from an 0—* author's copyrighted novel built around the history of the automobile industry. His script is made into a film, which is now ready for worldwide distribution. The novelist sues the screenwriter for copyright infringement. The court may grant a preliminary injunction to prevent the distribution and exhibition of the infringing film. This is the most effective means of preventing the continued infringement of the author's copyright while awaiting the court's determination of whether there is infringement. Once the court decides that the film does infringe the author's novel, it may grant a permanent injunction to the author, should it appear that money damages would be difficult to compute if the film were released.

If the copyright owner seeks money DAMAGES, he may recover *actual damages,* which compensate him for the losses that result from the infringement, plus any additional profits the infringer makes, to prevent him from unfairly benefiting from his wrongful act.

EXAMPLE The copyright of a Pulitzer prize-winning author 0—* is infringed by the unauthorized publication of one of his short stories in a pornographic magazine. The author may be able to recover damages if, because of the resulting bad publicity, he loses a contract for the exclusive publication of the same story in a religious magazine. He may also be allowed to recover the profits realized by the pornographic magazine from the increased sale of the magazine issue in which his story appears if he can show that it resulted from the alleged infringement.

The copyright owner may choose, instead, to receive *statutory damages,* or damages prescribed by law. They range from a minimum of $250 to a maximum of $10,000, as the court deems just. Sometimes, the court is permitted to reduce the damages to $100 or increase the maximum to $50,000. Statutory damages can be asked for at any time during the trial before the court has made a final judgment.

■ **Criminal offenses**   There are four types of criminal offenses involving infringement of a copyright: (1) fraudulent use of a copyright notice, (2) fraudulent removal of a notice, (3) false representation in connection with a copyright application, and (4) willful infringement for profit. The first three are all punishable by fines not exceeding $2,500. Conviction for willful infringement brings a maximum fine of $10,000 and imprisonment for one year.

A special penalty is provided when a person willfully infringes a copyrighted sound recording or a motion picture for commercial advantage. The maximum fine for the initial offense is $25,000 and one year's imprisonment. For subsequent offenses, the maximum fine is $50,000 and the maximum imprisonment is two years. An example of this occurs when someone reproduces a copyrighted, highly successful record album on a tape cassette, which he plans to sell to the general public at a discount price. This is record PIRACY. When a person is convicted, the court, in addition to imposing the described penalties, will order the forfeiture and destruction, or other disposition, of all infringing copies and all equipment used to manufacture them.

corespondent   The "other man" or "other woman" in a DIVORCE suit based on ADULTERY.

corner   A not necessarily illegal COMBINATION among investors or dealers in a specific commodity, such as wheat, for the purpose of buying up a large portion of that commodity and holding it back from sale until the demand is so much greater than the limited supply that the market price increases abnormally.

coroner   A public officer of a county or city charged with certain public duties, such as ordering autopsies when needed, conducting inquiries into the cause of any violent or suspicious death within his territory, and having any unclaimed bodies of strangers or paupers buried at the expense of the county or city. He may also act as a substitute for the sheriff in the case of the sheriff's incapacity to act. Although the coroner is a very ancient COMMON LAW office, many states have passed their own laws to control the procedure and terms of the office.

■ **Autopsies**   The coroner has the right to order an autopsy when he thinks it an appropriate means of discovering the cause of death. Generally, a coroner may authorize an autopsy without the consent of the deceased's NEXT OF KIN. The coroner may employ a physician or medical examiner to conduct the postmortem examination and may decide who is permitted to attend it.

■ **Inquests**   Holding inquests is a coroner's principal duty. An *inquest* is an investigation by a coroner and jury into the cause of a violent or suspicious death to obtain evidence to be used by the police in the detection and prosecution of a crime. Although an inquest is essentially a criminal proceeding (at least from the time when it is established that death was caused by a criminal act), it is not a trial involving the merits of a case but is rather a preliminary investigation. An inquest is not part of a criminal prosecution, even though it may discover facts that may lead to one.

When an inquest is needed   State laws require an inquest to be held whenever there is reasonable ground to believe that a death was from unknown causes or the result of violence or other unlawful means. No inquest is necessary when death results from disease, an act of God, negligence of the deceased, natural causes, accident, or suicide, unless required by statute.

The decision to hold an inquest belongs to the coroner. It is presumed that he acts in good faith and for sufficient cause. Under most statutes he must make some inquiry into the cause of death before summoning a jury, but he should not be regarded as having acted outside his authority just because the inquest jury decides that the deceased died a natural death.

Procedures   An inquest should be public. The coroner and jurors, having had a view of the body, may retire to take testimony and make up the report. A coroner can compel witnesses to attend and testify at the inquest, and if they refuse to do so, he may punish them for CONTEMPT. The coroner may summon a physician as a witness to give his professional opinion of the cause of death. A person suspected of a crime has no constitutional right to be confronted by the witnesses or to produce his own witnesses, and generally, neither the suspect nor the witnesses are entitled to representation by counsel.

A view of the body by the coroner and jury, including a careful examination to determine the circumstances surrounding the death, is an essential part of an inquest. For this purpose, a body may be exhumed (removed from a grave) if necessary.

Findings   It is the coroner's duty to receive the jury's verdict, which should state who the deceased was (or that his identity is unknown), and how, when, and where he died. The coroner then prepares a *return of inquest,* also called an *inquisition,* which is the record of the jury's findings. Under some statutes, after the inquest the coroner must make out a certificate of death showing the cause and probable manner of death. When there is no jury for an inquest—this is permitted when someone is already under arrest for the killing—the coroner alone makes the decision on the cause of death.

Where common law is being followed, the finding of a coroner's jury is the equivalent of a finding by a GRAND JURY. It is a sufficient basis for prosecution for murder or MANSLAUGHTER. Under various state laws, the coroner's

verdict serves only as probable cause to arrest a person suspected of causing the death of the victim.

As evidence in civil actions   Evidence given at an inquest has usually not been allowed to be used against parties in a civil lawsuit. Some courts, however, will allow the witness's testimony before a coroner to be used to show contradictions in his testimony in a civil action in which he is a witness or a party.

EXAMPLE Calvin dies of gunshot wounds of the head, but it O✺═✳ is not clear whether his death was an accident or suicide. His wife, Trixie, testifies at the coroner's inquest that Calvin had been severely depressed about his unemployment and had often told her that she would be better off if he were dead. The coroner's verdict, based partly on the wife's testimony, is that the death was suicide. Subsequently, Trixie sues the insurance company when it refuses to pay her the proceeds of her husband's life insurance policy because, according to its terms, if the policyholder commits suicide the company is relieved of its duties to pay the beneficiary. Trixie testifies at the civil action that her husband was a cheerful, happy-go-lucky man who had everything to live for. The attorney for the insurance company may use Trixie's statements at the inquest to impeach or contradict her testimony in the civil action.

In a few states the coroner's verdict or findings may be used in a civil action to show the cause of death, but most states will allow the verdict only to indicate that the deceased is in fact dead. The reason for the latter rule is that a person is not entitled to have a lawyer at an inquest. If the coroner's verdict were used as evidence of the cause of death, it could easily become the most significant piece of evidence in the action. It would most likely be formally adopted as the verdict in the lawsuit, thus depriving a defendant of his right to his "day in court" to dispute the evidence against him.

As evidence in criminal prosecutions   The proceedings of a coroner's inquest generally cannot be used as evidence at a trial for HOMICIDE, because the main function of an inquest is to furnish information and evidence to be used by law officers in the detection and investigation of a crime. There are some exceptions, however. Inquest testimony given by a person under arrest may be used against him in a subsequent trial if he gave the testimony voluntarily after he was advised of his rights. If you testify of your own free will as a witness at an inquest and are later indicted and tried, your inquest testimony may be used against you, because you testified voluntarily. The testimony of a witness at a coroner's inquest may be used against a defendant in his trial for homicide if the witness dies or is not available for some other reason.

■ **Arrest**   The coroner has the power and duty to order the arrest of persons who are implicated in the death of the victim by the findings of the inquest. A person committed to jail by a coroner for the crime of murder is not entitled to a preliminary examination before a MAGISTRATE unless this is required by statute.

■ **Liability of coroner**   When determining whether an inquest should be held, a coroner acting under authority has not been held liable in a legal action for his mistake, error, or, in some states, even his misconduct. Under some statutes, it is an indictable criminal offense for a coroner knowingly to hold an inquest that, under the circumstances, he has no right to hold.

Some courts hold that although an autopsy may be properly authorized by the coroner because of the violent or suspicious circumstances surrounding the death, this does not justify the removal and unreasonable detention of any organs of the deceased by the coroner's physician, particularly after a proper demand for the return of the body has been made by the next of kin. If the coroner, without the consent of the next of kin, orders an autopsy in a case in which he lacks the authority to do so—say when a person dies of a terminal disease after many months of hospitalization and there is no possibility that death was caused by violence or resulted from suspicious circumstances—the next of kin may sue the coroner for damages in a civil action.

corporal punishment
Punishment inflicted on the body, such as whipping or beating, rather than punishment *of* the body, such as imprisonment. In some contexts, however, the term may include imprisonment. Corporal punishment may refer to any kind of physical deprivation or suffering, as distinguished from pecuniary punishment, such as a fine or award of punitive DAMAGES, that is inflicted by the court to penalize an offender.

See also CRUEL AND UNUSUAL PUNISHMENT; PRISONERS' RIGHTS; SCHOOLS.

corporate
Belonging to a CORPORATION. For instance, a corporate name belongs to a corporation. Any action taken by a corporation, such as entering into a business contract, is a corporate action.

corporate veil
The legal assumption that actions taken by CORPORATIONS are not the personal actions of the corporation's owners. This means that the owners are not usually held individually responsible for the actions of their corporations. In other words, they can hide behind the corporate veil.

Sometimes, however, courts will pierce the corporate veil if the owners commit illegal acts through the corporation. If, for example, the owners of a steamship company are using its ships to carry illegal drugs in from Central America, the courts, piercing the corporate veil, will hold the owners personally responsible for their actions.

corporation
A corporation is an artificial being created by law to accomplish some particular purpose, such as finding a cure for cancer or governing a city, or to engage in some particular business, such as manufacturing automobiles or running a restaurant. Even though it is composed of individual persons, a corporation has a legal identity entirely separate and distinct from those individuals and has the capacity of continuous existence or succession, even after there are changes in its membership. Like a natural person, however, a corporation can take, hold, and convey property; enter into contracts; sue and be sued; and exercise any other powers and privileges granted to it by the law that created it. A corporation is defined by statute or by the state constitution.

The following definition of a corporation was given by John Marshall, Chief Justice of the United States from 1801 to 1835:

"A corporation is an artificial being, invisible, intangible, and existing only in contemplation of law. Being the mere creature of law, it possesses only those properties which the charter of its creation confers upon it, either expressly or as incidental to its very existence. These are such as are supposed best calculated to effect the object for which it was created. Among the most important are immortality, and, if the expression may be allowed, individuality; properties by which a perpetual succession of many persons are considered as the same, and may act as a single individual."

■ **History** Basic corporate concepts were developed early in recorded history. Corporate personality was recognized, to some extent, as early as the Code of Hammurabi, formulated more than 3,000 years ago in Babylonia. Roman law recognized that the corporate personality could exist with permission of the state. The Romans established corporations in Britain after they conquered it, and subsequently, these bodies were recognized by English law.

English kings and Parliament created corporations in the American colonies. After the American Revolution, state legislatures assumed the powers to grant CHARTERS to corporations. For many years, this power was limited for the most part to public ventures, such as the construction of roads and bridges.

Industrialization and the growth of large businesses during the 19th century made the corporation an ideal vehicle for big-business development. It combined centralized direction with limited financial commitment by a theoretically limitless number of investors. At first, corporations could be formed only for certain purposes—usually those that required a relatively large amount of financing, such as transportation, banking, insurance, mining, and manufacturing enterprises—and were found mainly in heavily industrialized states. The duration of corporate existence was generally limited to a period of 20, 30, or 50 years. All, or at least a majority, of the incorporators were required to be residents of the state of incorporation. The powers of the corporation were sparingly granted and strictly interpreted, and the amount of indebtedness was severely limited.

Soon, however, the nonindustrial states, eager to attract the revenue from new corporations, removed most of the restraints from their laws. In response, the great industrial states also removed their limitations on corporations in order not to lose their revenue and power.

■ **Corporations today** Today the corporation is the dominant business enterprise in America. One reason for this is its feature of limited liability: the corporation, and not the investors, is liable on business contracts it makes (at least in ordinary circumstances) because the corporation is a separate entity from the people involved in it. And because a corporation is a separate entity, it is the only form of business enterprise that theoretically has perpetual existence. No matter who dies, the corporation can go on.

Besides the advantages of limited liability and perpetual existence, the corporate form provides (1) centralized management, (2) easily transferable interests, (3) a body of rules to guide its actions, (4) tax advantages, and (5) ease in acquiring financing through the sale of STOCK.

HOW CORPORATIONS ARE SET UP

- A corporation exists separate and distinct from the individuals comprising it, and it continues to exist even when its members change.
- A corporation, like a person, can take, hold, buy, and sell property. It can make contracts, sue, and be sued.
- In most states, a corporation comes into being when *articles of incorporation* are filed with the secretary of state. Contents of the document vary from state to state, but in general they must give the name of the corporation, its intended duration, its purposes, its address, the number and names of the initial board of directors, and the names and addresses of the incorporators.
- Traditionally, at least three adults were required to incorporate, but an increasing number of states now permit one person to incorporate.
- All states require the incorporators to sign the articles of incorporation, and some verification of their signatures is usually required.

- The rules and regulations a corporation adopts to govern its own actions are known as *bylaws.*
- Bylaws do not have to be filed, but they do have to be consistent with the articles of incorporation and with any relevant state laws.
- The finances needed to launch a corporation are obtained from investors who become shareholders, and subsequent funding is commonly obtained from a variety of sources, such as short-term loans, installment purchasing, depreciation deductions, and government loans.
- Shareholders traditionally elect from their ranks a board of directors. Until recently a board of directors had to have a minimum of three directors. Nowadays, in many states, corporations with only one or two shareholders are permitted to operate with a minimum of one or two directors.
- The board of directors selects the officers—though in a growing number of states, shareholders may elect offi-

cers. Directors and officers are not barred from engaging in other businesses, but they may not further their competing outside interests at the expense of the corporation. For example, they may not use corporate personnel, facilities, or funds for other businesses; nor may they disclose trade secrets. If at a board meeting a director hears about a good investment for the corporation, he may not take advantage of it personally at the expense of the corporation.
- All states require the articles of incorporation to give the number of shares of stock the corporation is authorized to issue.
- Registered shareholders may inspect corporate books and records in order to protect their investment.
- Each share entitles its owner to one vote at shareholder meetings. Voting may be accomplished either in person or by proxy—authorizing someone else to vote for you.
- Stock certificates are transferable.

On the other hand, a corporation is subject to greater formalities, publicity, and governmental regulation (both state and federal) than other forms of business enterprise. For example, in order to do business in a particular state, a corporation is usually subject to minimum capital requirements. Federal laws govern the sale of shares in the corporation. See SECURITIES REGULATION.

Kinds of organizations The most important forms of corporate organization are (1) *private corporations,* formed for the purpose of engaging in business for profit; (2) *municipal corporations,* such as cities and towns, formed to assist the state in carrying on the processes of government; and (3) *nonprofit corporations,* usually formed to carry on activities benefiting the general public rather than to produce profit for their members.

Corporations that have been held to be private include a state historical society, organized and controlled by private persons; a corporation for the purpose of operating a racetrack and offering purses and prizes; a corporation for establishing and maintaining a private park; and a corporation for the purpose of operating a general storage and elevator business.

Corporations that you might normally think of as private may be classified as quasi-public (similar to public) corporations when their business is devoted to a public use. Because of the public nature of their functions, quasi-public corporations usually have the power of EMINENT DOMAIN. This means that they can take property under the authority of the government in order to carry out their purposes. They must, however, pay just compensation to

the owner of the land they take. Examples of quasi-public corporations are most private corporations that maintain or operate a toll bridge, a railroad, a canal, or a turnpike, as well as those that supply a municipality with water, gas, electricity, or heat. Other corporations that have been held to be quasi-public are levee, drainage, reclamation, and irrigation corporations; steamboat companies; telegraph and telephone companies; and cemetery companies.

A special kind of private corporation is a *closed corporation,* one whose stock is held by a single individual or a closely knit group of individuals. It is usually a relatively small enterprise, sometimes owned by one family. The few stockholders, who are active in the conduct and management of the business, want to keep outsiders out. The emphasis is on informal procedures. A closed corporation is formed to achieve the tax advantages and limited liability of a corporation while at the same time preserving the simpler procedures of a partnership. Closed corporations with legitimate purposes will be recognized and approved by taxing authorities if the business is conducted on a corporate, not a personal, basis and if it has an adequate financial base. Salaries to officers are subject to close scrutiny by state and federal taxing authorities.

- **Creation of a corporation** The original method of creating a corporation was by a special act of the state legislature. Today the states enact general laws authorizing persons to form corporate bodies.

Corporations may be formed for any lawful business purposes. The purposes must be clearly stated and recorded at the time of incorporation. The statement of purposes defines and limits the nature of the corporation's business for the protection of management, shareholders, and third parties. Corporations generally have implied powers to do all reasonably necessary things to carry out their purposes, such as to (1) acquire and hold property, (2) borrow money and mortgage property, (3) loan corporate funds, (4) acquire and hold shares in other corporations, and (5) contribute to charities.

Promoters A corporation results from the preliminary planning and arrangements of promoters, the people who plan the creation of the corporation and who often continue in control after incorporation. Promotion activities include discovery of the business opportunity, investigating its economic feasibility, and assembling the necessary resources, property, and personnel to set the business in motion. To get the corporation under way, the promoters usually hold organization meetings at which the people who form the corporation, its owners, the stockholders, approve the corporate seal, adopt preincorporation agreements, elect corporate officers, and select a bank as a depository for the corporation's funds.

Articles of incorporation The basic instrument that usually creates the corporation is called the "articles of incorporation" or "certificate of incorporation." In most states, corporate existence begins when the articles of incorporation are filed with the secretary of state. Unless the corporation is being formed for a particular time period or until it achieves a particular goal, it is generally considered to be perpetual, although some states impose limitations on corporate duration that must always be followed.

The contents of the articles of incorporation vary according to the state's incorporation laws but, in general, they must

(1) Give the name of the corporation, which must then always be used to identify the corporation, as in advertisements and on letterheads.

(2) State the duration of the corporation, at least when state law imposes limitations on duration or the corporation is not intended to be perpetual.

(3) Set forth the corporate purposes. Most states require the statement to be reasonably definite. In contrast, corporate powers usually need not be spelled out. A frequent practice, however, is to commingle powers clauses with purposes clauses. Most states expressly permit regulations for the internal affairs of the corporation.

(4) State the address of the corporate office or place of business.

(5) Give the number or the names of the initial board of directors. Boards of directors are further discussed below.

(6) State the names and addresses of the incorporators. Traditionally, at least three adults were required, but a growing number of states now permit only one incorporator. All states require the incorporators to sign the articles of incorporation, and verification of the signatures is usually required. Some states require the filing of duplicate originals of the articles of incorporation.

Bylaws Bylaws are the rules and regulations enacted by the corporation to govern its own actions and concerns. Bylaws also control the conduct of directors, officers, and shareholders. Unlike the articles of incorporation, bylaws are usually not filed in any public office, but they must be consistent with the articles of incorporation and the state laws that govern them. In practice, bylaws range from brief statements of rules to comprehensive manuals.

Financing The finances necessary to launch and operate the corporation, at least initially, are obtained principally from investors who receive securities, or shares, issued by the corporation. These shares (also called stocks) are evidence of the holders' rights in the corporation. After the corporation is launched, funds are obtained from various other sources. Short-term borrowing, installment purchasing, depreciation deductions, and government loans are common sources of corporate financing.

■ **Directors and officers** Shareholders traditionally elect from their ranks a board of directors who manage the corporation. Until recently, nearly all states required at least three directors. Many statutes now permit a minimum of one or two directors in corporations with only one or two shareholders. A few statutes prescribe a maximum. The number of directors is usually stated in the articles of incorporation or the bylaws.

The board of directors generally selects the officers of the corporation, although a growing number of states permit shareholders to elect officers. Usually selected are a president, one or more vice presidents, a secretary, and a treasurer. The board of directors delegates to the officers the authority to execute and administer its policies. Officers may be removed by the board of directors. Because officers are agents of the corporation, their conduct is measured according to the principles of AGENCY law.

Salaries The directors' and officers' compensation for management is determined by a combination of practical matters: a fair division of corporate earnings among labor, management, and shareholders, and tax factors. Management compensation is also based on two sets of legal considerations: those of corporation law and those of taxation law, especially federal income tax laws. Executive compensation must be reasonable in amount and based on services actually performed for the corporation. The amount is usually determined before the services are performed.

Fiduciary relationship A growing number of statutes restate in general terms the rule that directors and officers have a FIDUCIARY relationship to their corporation: they hold positions of trust. Increasingly, directors and officers are being required to give undivided loyalty to the corporation and to show good faith and fair dealing in corporate matters. Competing with the corporation, usurping a corporate opportunity, and having some interest that conflicts with the best interests of the corporation all run counter to the fiduciary concept.

Directors and officers are not necessarily barred from engaging in other businesses, but they may not take advantage of their office to prevent the corporation from competing with their outside interests. They may not use corporate personnel, facilities, or funds for other businesses. Neither may they disclose corporate trade secrets or lure away corporate business and personnel. The "corporate opportunity" doctrine, another aspect of the undivided loyalty rule, bars corporate personnel from diverting to themselves business opportunities that, in fairness, belong to the corporation. For example, if, at a board meeting, a director hears about a good investment for the corporation, he may not take advantage of it personally at the expense of the corporation. The undivided loyalty rule is also applied when a director or officer has an interest in a transaction that conflicts with that of the corporation. This conflicting interest might be personal—for example, when a corporation officer sells property to the corporation—or it might involve a business relationship—for example, when a person is an officer in two corporations and there is a transaction between them.

■ **Shareholders** Anyone with the legal capacity to own property can own an interest in a corporation. The interest consists of a share of stock, usually represented by a stock certificate. The interest of a shareholder in a corporation is in proportion to the number of shares he owns out of the total number of shares issued. All states require the articles of incorporation to state the number of shares of stock the corporation is authorized to issue.

Any deception in the sale of corporate stock is illegal, especially under federal rules and regulations.

EXAMPLE Let us assume that certain insiders, perhaps officers of a corporation, know that it is going broke. They withhold that fact from the public. Meanwhile, having just retired, you invest your life's savings in the company's stock. Why not? You were led to believe the corporation was on sound financial ground. The company then goes under. You can sue the officers for whatever losses you suffered because of their fraud in withholding information about the company's true financial state. So could any other shareholder who suffered losses because he had been misled by the insiders.

The registered owners of stock shares have the right to inspect the corporate books and records in order to protect their investment. They traditionally assert their rights by voting at shareholder meetings. Each share entitles the owner to one vote, unless there is a provision to the contrary. Shareholder approval is required for various extraordinary corporate matters, such as the amendment of the articles of incorporation. Shareholders routinely vote on (1) election and removal of directors; (2) adoption, amendment, and repeal of bylaws; and (3) ratification of those actions by the board of directors specified in the bylaws as requiring stockholder approval, such as the election of corporate officers. Many state laws provide that voting at shareholders' meetings may be accomplished either in person or by PROXY. The term "proxy" sometimes causes confusion because it has various meanings: (1) the authority to vote, given by the shareholder to his agent; (2) the written instrument showing this authority; (3) the agent (called the proxy holder); and (4) the exercise of authority by the agent (voting by proxy).

Share certificates are usually freely transferable. In other words, if you own an interest in a company, you may transfer your stock certificate to someone else. Shares may be sold directly to another person, but they are usually sold through an intermediary, called a stockbroker. See BROKER.

Dividends The term "dividend" means the distribution to shareholders of corporate earnings and profits. Dividends are usually paid at the discretion of the board of directors. Only when the directors abuse that discretion will the courts step in and order a distribution of dividends.

The principal kinds of dividends are cash dividends—cash from available funds—and STOCK DIVIDENDS—additional shares in the corporation (usually a fraction of a share for each whole share the stockholder owns). The distribution is generally expressed as a ratio. A 10-percent distribution means that the stockholder receives one additional share for each 10 shares already held. If he owns only one share, he receives an additional one-tenth of one share. Stock dividends result in more shares representing the same total worth of the company, but each share's value is diluted accordingly. The principal purpose of stock dividends is to keep profits in the business while at the same time distributing them to shareholders.

EXAMPLE When you buy a particular stock, the amount of cash dividends it will pay per share of stock you own is usually stated. Let us say Blackout Utility Corporation sells for $25 a share and pays a dividend of $2.50 a share. If you own $25,000 worth of Blackout stock, you will earn $2,500 in cash dividends a year unless its board of directors decides not to pay out dividends.

On the other hand, suppose Lightning Electric Corporation does not pay cash dividends but instead provides stock dividends. You own 10 percent, or 10,000 shares, of Lightning out of 100,000 total shares it has issued to the public. It has an extremely profitable year and issues a 5-percent stock dividend to all its stockholders. This means you will receive another 500 shares of stock for the 10,000 shares you presently hold. Lightning can afford to do this because it has added more money (undistributed profits) to its capital. You still own the same percentage of Lightning, 10 percent, as you did before the stock dividend was issued, because everyone received the same percentage, 5 percent of dividends. Stock dividends differ from cash dividends in that they are not paid in money. They are usually issued by corporations that are interested in growth or development of new technologies as opposed to an immediate return of profits offered in the form of cash dividends by corporations.

Derivative actions Through the years, the courts and legislatures have developed a type of lawsuit called a "derivative action," so that a shareholder can enforce a corporate right or claim. In this kind of court case, the shareholder also indirectly protects his investment. A derivative action is used only when the people in control of the corporation refuse to sue in the corporate name. Before a shareholder may sue derivatively, there must be proof of an unsuccessful demand upon the corporation to take steps to remedy the alleged wrong. Any funds that are recovered from a derivative action go into the corporate treasury to protect the whole community of corporate interests—shareholders and creditors alike. In this way, the derivative action is unique, because the plaintiff-shareholder does not sue in his own right for his own direct benefit but as a guardian of the corporation's interests.

The need for a derivative action is best illustrated when those in control of the corporation are known to be lining their pockets with corporate funds.

EXAMPLE Suppose the Explorer Corporation is formed to search for crude oil, and after a few months oil is discovered. Ted Greene, a director of the corporation and thus an insider, is told exactly where the oil is located.

Instead of allowing Explorer Corporation to profit by selling this information to another company that wants to drill for oil, Greene sells it to a business acquaintance and pockets the money. Because Greene would not vote to have the corporation bring a court action against himself, a shareholder could start a derivative action on behalf of the corporation, in order to recover the money Explorer Corporation should have made.

One of the values of the derivative action is that it allows a single lawsuit to be brought by one shareholder on behalf of other shareholders, thus avoiding much unnecessary litigation by each individual shareholder. Derivative actions are sometimes referred to as actions "in the right of a corporation," "secondary actions by shareholders," or "actions to enforce a secondary right on the part of shareholders."

■ **Affiliated corporations** Large corporations sometimes own the controllng number of shares in one or more subsidiary companies. The parent corporation, together with its affiliates, remains a single taxable entity for most federal and state tax purposes. Separate identities of affiliated corporations have been recognized by the courts when (1) their respective business transactions, accounts, and records were not intermingled; (2) the formalities of separate corporate procedures were observed; (3) each corporation was adequately financed as a separate unit for its future obligations; and (4) the businesses were presented to the public as separate enterprises.

corporeal   Having a body or material existence. Anything that can be seen or touched is said to be corporeal. *Corporeal hereditaments* are tangible, substantial items of property that can be inherited—land, for example. *Incorporeal hereditaments* are legal rights that can be passed on to heirs. They may grow out of or concern something corporeal, but they are not the thing itself. The copyright of a work of art is an example. In feudal society, titles of nobility and offices were among the most important incorporeal hereditaments.

Corporeal is different from *corporal*, which means "relating to the body." Spanking, for example, is a form of CORPORAL PUNISHMENT.

corpus   (Latin) "Body," mass, sum, aggregate. The corpus of an estate is the total sum of property left when someone dies. The corpus of a TRUST is the amount of money, stocks, or other property set aside to produce income for a beneficiary.

corpus delicti   (Latin) "Body of a crime"; the thing upon which a crime has been committed, such as a dead body or a safe that has been broken into; the facts that prove a crime has been committed. The *corpus delicti* is the first thing that must be established in order to convict a defendant of a crime. The second thing that must be established is that the defendant is the person who committed the crime.

corpus juris   (Latin) "Body of law." A comprehensive collection of the law of a given country, especially Roman or civil law. *Corpus Juris Secundum* is the name of the second edition of the standard corpus of American law.

Corpus Juris Civilis   (Latin) "The Body of the Civil Law"; the comprehensive code of Roman law compiled by the Emperor Justinian in the sixth century. The name *Corpus Juris Civilis* was first applied to this system of law early in the 17th century.

correctional institution   See PRISON; PRISONERS' RIGHTS.

correspondent   1 Something that matches or compares closely.   2 One who has regular business relations with another.   3 A person who communicates with another by letter.   4 In banking, a financial institution that collects mortgage payments for the lender.

The word "correspondent" should not be confused with "corespondent," the "other man" or "other woman" in a divorce suit based on adultery.

corroborate   Strengthen a legal case or add weight to the EVIDENCE of some fact by showing additional or related facts, thereby making proof more certain. The law sometimes requires that certain kinds of evidence, such as the testimony of a small child or of an accomplice, be corroborated, or no conviction can result.

cosigner   A person who signs a document along with another person. Depending on state law and the circumstances of the agreement, the cosigner may be equally liable for the debt or he may have to pay the debt only if the other person does not. If the document concerns property, both the law and agreement between the parties will determine whether the cosigner has any rights in the property.

costs   A sum of money allowed to cover the expenses of a lawsuit. In a given case, a judge may order the losing party to pay costs to the successful party if such payment is fair and the law permits costs for that situation.
■ **Items included in costs**   Costs include court fees for starting the lawsuit, filing papers, or having papers served by a public officer. If the judge appoints a commissioner from outside the state to hear testimony, a referee to hear highly technical or detailed evidence, or a receiver to hold a defendant's property during the trial, then the fees of these people can be included in costs. Court expenses involved in interviewing parties or witnesses before a trial and the fees paid to witnesses who testify are costs. Expenses for the printing of necessary papers or the preparation of maps or copies of documents may also be included.

Attorney's fees   The cost of an attorney is not properly included in costs. Court-ordered costs are expenses between two parties in a suit, not between a client and his attorney. Attorney's fees may be awarded in addition to costs but only when a statute specifically allows it—in actions for copyright infringement, for example. There have been cases in which judges ruled that circumstances required attorney's fees to be included in costs, but these are the exception rather than the rule.
■ **Who pays costs**   The costs of maintaining a lawsuit are the responsibility of the person who incurs them. Each party must ask the court for costs. The court usually waits until judgment (decision) is given and then decides whether

the successful party is entitled to costs. The rule is that costs are generally granted in a lawsuit for money damages, but in a suit for other types of relief, such as an INJUNCTION or an ACCOUNTING among partners, the court decides whether it is fair to award costs to the winning party in each particular case. Costs are not considered a penalty.

Security Sometimes, while a trial is going on, one of the parties involved may be ordered to post a security to insure that he will pay costs if he loses. For security the court will accept (1) the promise of a financially responsible person to pay for the party, (2) the party's signed statement that he will pay, or (3) the deposit of an adequate amount of money with the court.

Parties may agree about who will pay costs. The court will enforce a stipulation (a formal agreement reached in court) or a provision in a contract, such as a paragraph in a lease. Sometimes a lease provides that a tenant will pay the landlord's costs if he has to sue the tenant to collect the rent. Even if the parties have an agreement, however, the court will allow costs only for necessary expenses, not for a frivolous or premature action.

Prevailing party Costs are awarded to the winning, or prevailing, party in a civil lawsuit even if he does not win on every point or fails to win the full amount of money he sought. If the case is a draw neither receives costs. If an action is dismissed, costs may be granted to the defendant.

The prevailing party who deserves costs can be a person who originally lost in court. For example, costs may be granted to the losing party who is able to convince an appeals court to set aside a jury verdict against him. In one case, costs were finally awarded to a plaintiff who was not successful until the third trial, after the juries could not agree in the first two trials.

Other factors Because costs are not a penalty, they cannot be ordered against a party just because he is stubborn or fights to the bitter end. But no costs will be allowed to a party who is offered a sum of money to settle and rejects it, unless he finally wins more than what was offered. A difficult case might require higher than usual costs and justify a larger award.

■ **Denial of costs** Federal courts and higher state courts usually accept only cases that involve large amounts of money. If a plaintiff manages to bring a small case to a higher court, he will not get costs unless he recovers more than the minimum amount that the court usually accepts. This practice encourages the use of the lower courts and reduces the demand on higher courts, which always have overcrowded calendars.

If a party chooses a more expensive remedy than is necessary, he may be denied costs.

EXAMPLE Let us say that the plaintiff pays the sheriff a fee O⊶⚹ to seize the defendant's property on the ground that the defendant is about to leave the state with it. Later it turns out that the seizure was inappropriate because the defendant, a friendless recluse, had broken his back and was hospitalized, probably for months. In such a case, the plaintiff cannot recover the sheriff's fee as part of his costs.

Costs may also be refused for misconduct. In one alimony case, the husband was ultimately able to defeat his former wife's action to increase the amount of payments, but the court denied him costs because he had tried to conceal his true financial condition.

Finally, costs may be refused for the inadequate preparation of a case.

EXAMPLE Sam sued his neighbor to stop the noise created O⊶⚹ when he left a refrigerator truck running all night to keep its cargo cold. Sam won, but the court refused to award costs because his attorney was so inadequately prepared that the court incurred extra expenses. The court might also have ordered Sam's attorney to pay his client's costs.

■ **Amount** Sometimes a statute fixes the amount of costs. When that is the case, a party who wins costs would receive only the amount allowed by law for each expense, such as for printing, fees, and witnesses.

■ **Multiple parties** When cases involve more than one plaintiff or more than one defendant, a court may divide responsibility for costs among the losing parties. If the defendant causes great inconvenience in the lawsuit—for example, if he brings a motion for the sole purpose of causing a delay—he may have to pay the costs resulting from the delay for every other party, including his codefendants.

If one party is a stakeholder, he generally gets costs either from all the other parties or from the "stake." A typical stakeholder case involves an insurance company that does not know who is entitled to benefit.

EXAMPLE Brian was married to Bertha for several years. He O⊶⚹ then got a Mexican divorce and married Lottie. A few weeks later he died. The beneficiary on his life insurance policy is not specifically named, but is instead referred to as "my wife." Bertha claims that Brian's divorce was not valid and that she is his wife and beneficiary. Lottie claims that the divorce was legal and that she is Brian's wife and beneficiary. The proceeds for the policy are paid into the court. The insurance company takes its costs for this procedure out of that sum and withdraws from the case. Bertha and Lottie must battle it out in court for the rest of the money.

council An assembly of persons who make up a local legislature, usually for a city. A member of a council may be called a *councillor*. Sometimes a legislative body is called the *common council*. It is called the *select council* if it is the upper house of two branches in the legislature.

counsel 1 Give advice. 2 As a noun, often the advice a professional gives his client regarding a particular course of conduct. 3 The one who gives advice; an attorney. "Of counsel" is the label given to an attorney who only assists on a case and is not the primary lawyer. "Of counsel" after an attorney's name on a letterhead or office sign means that he or she is associated with the law firm but is not primarily employed by it.

counsel, right to A person's constitutional right to be aided by an attorney in any criminal prosecution that is directed against him. The Sixth Amendment to the U.S. Constitution provides, in part, that in all federal criminal proceedings the accused shall enjoy the right to have the assistance of counsel (an attorney) for his defense. This right was fully applied to the states through the due process clause of the 14th Amendment. See DUE PROCESS OF LAW. Therefore, no person may be imprisoned for any federal or state criminal offense—whether a petty offense, a MISDE-MEANOR, or a FELONY—if he was not represented by counsel at his trial, unless he intelligently and knowingly waived this right. If the accused cannot afford to hire an attorney, the court will appoint one. In a landmark case, GIDEON V. WAINWRIGHT, the Supreme Court required the state to make appointed counsel available to poor defendants in all criminal cases. The assistance of counsel insures that the accused is fully aware of the nature of the proceeding against him and of the possibility of imprisonment and that he will be fairly treated by the prosecution.

This article discusses the application of the right to counsel in police investigations, grand jury proceedings, preliminary hearings, pretrial procedures, trials, and appeals. It also deals with the requirements of a valid waiver of this right, the right of a defendant to be his own lawyer, and the right to effective assistance of counsel.

■ **When you are entitled to counsel** The right to counsel is limited to criminal prosecutions. It applies not only to the trial but also to all critical stages of the proceedings—that is, whenever "substantial rights of the accused may be affected."

Police investigations When a person has been arrested, taken to a police station for questioning, or otherwise significantly deprived of his freedom of action, he has a right to counsel. Before the police ask a single question, the suspect must receive the MIRANDA WARNINGS that tell him what his rights are while he is in custody, including his right to consult an attorney. If the person says he wants to see a lawyer, he cannot be questioned until he has spoken with one. When the police are gathering information about a crime, however, the witnesses interviewed have no right to counsel, because they have not been accused of any crime. However, if the police question someone as a witness, without letting him consult an attorney, and later discover he is a prime suspect, what he had said as a witness can later be admitted as evidence in his trial.

Police lineups Police lineups conducted before formal charges or indictments have been brought are not considered critical, and counsel is not required for a suspect. But police lineups after formal charges have been made do constitute a critical stage of criminal adversary proceedings, and the accused must have counsel.

Preliminary hearings A preliminary hearing is held to determine whether there is probable cause to hold the accused for possible prosecution. The final decision to prosecute ordinarily rests with the prosecutor or grand jury. In some states, however, a preliminary hearing is held instead of convening a grand jury. A preliminary hearing is a critical stage requiring the right of counsel when it is held to determine whether there is enough evidence to prosecute a person after a formal charge has been made against him. During this hearing the suspect may confront and cross-examine witnesses. But when the purpose of the preliminary hearing is only to decide if there is a probable cause to charge the suspect with a crime or hold him for trial, the prosecution is not required to produce witnesses for cross-examination. This is a nonadversary proceeding and therefore not a critical stage. See also CRIMINAL LAW.

Grand jury proceedings When a GRAND JURY is considering charges against a person, he has no constitutional right to present his case, either by himself or by counsel. Grand jury sessions are protected by requirements of secrecy, and the target of the investigation need not even be informed of the ongoing proceedings.

In most states a person who is the subject of a grand jury investigation can be called to testify. He keeps his constitutional right to refuse to answer questions—under his privilege against SELF-INCRIMINATION—but courts traditionally have held that representation by counsel is not necessary to protect the exercise of that right. Some states have rejected this traditional position on the ground that the target of the grand jury investigation is in a situation similar to that of being questioned while in custody and is therefore entitled to the help of counsel while testifying. The attorney is not allowed in the grand jury room, but before a person testifying before a grand jury answers a question that might be self-incriminating, he may consult with his attorney in an adjoining room. In some states, however, when a person testifying before a grand jury has waived immunity from prosecution for the crime being investigated, he may have an attorney at his side. The Supreme Court has not yet considered the question of whether there is a constitutional right to counsel in grand jury proceedings.

Arraignments An arraignment is a critical stage in which the defendant is required to enter a plea. Thus he has a right to counsel. The failure to appoint counsel at arraignment may be a harmless error if the defendant is later permitted to withdraw a guilty plea and his rights have not been damaged by the denial of counsel. Likewise, if the defendant who is without counsel pleads not guilty at an arraignment and is not damaged by the failure to have the advice of counsel, the denial is a harmless error.

Pretrial procedures Certain pretrial procedures do not require the assistance of counsel. Handwriting samples may be taken from an accused before indictment without the assistance of counsel. When photographs are shown to witnesses before trial for indentification purposes in a criminal case, there is no need for advice of counsel because there is no trial-type confrontation.

A motorist accused of driving while intoxicated may not call his lawyer for advice on whether or not to submit to a physical test that will provide evidence of the amount of alcohol he consumed.

Trials and posttrial procedures The right of counsel in a criminal trial is the most important of the "assistance of counsel" rights under the Sixth Amendment. In addition, the U.S. Supreme Court has ruled that the following posttrial proceedings are "critical stages" at which the defendant is entitled to be represented by counsel:

(1) When the sentence is imposed.

(2) When a determination is made whether or not to revoke PROBATION and impose a new sentence. If the revocation of probation is the only subject to be considered, the right to counsel is determined by the court on a case-by-case basis and depends on the complexity of the issues and how well the accused is able to present them.

(3) When an indigent wishes to appeal his conviction and the state provides for appeal of a criminal conviction as a right. In one case, a California law that provided for

counsel to be appointed for appeals only after appeals on FRIVOLOUS grounds had been screened out was held to be unconstitutional. It violated the equal protection clause because defendants who could afford to hire their own counsel could appeal a conviction even if the appeal was frivolous.

■ **Waivers** The Supreme Court has frequently stated that a defendant may waive his constitutional right to assistance of counsel as long as he does so "knowingly and intelligently." At the same time, the prosecution must show that the defendant was specifically told of his right to the aid of appointed or employed counsel and that he has clearly refused such assistance. The standard "knowingly and intelligently" means that the waiver was the result of a reasoned and deliberate choice based upon adequate knowledge of what the assistance of counsel, or lack of it, would involve. In determining whether the defendant's rejection was made in this manner, the courts rely on an analysis of the particular facts of the case, including the defendant's age, mental condition, and experience; the particular setting in which the offer of counsel was made; and the manner in which it was explained.

A valid waiver at one stage of the proceedings (such as the preliminary hearing) does not necessarily indicate an intent to waive at a later stage (such as the trial). The prosecution must show that the defendant was given the opportunity to exercise his right to counsel at each stage of the proceedings.

If a defendant at an arraignment seeks to waive counsel and enter a plea of guilty, the court must make certain that he understands the nature of the charge made against him and is fully aware of the significance of his decision.

■ **Acting as your own lawyer** The Supreme Court has ruled that the Sixth Amendment guarantees to the defendant the right to appear *pro se* ("for himself")—that is, to act as his own lawyer. The Court stated that while the Sixth Amendment does not specifically refer to the right of self-representation, that right is "necessarily implied" in the amendment. The Sixth Amendment also provides that the accused must be informed of the accusation against him, be confronted with the witnesses against him, and be given power of SUBPOENA to compel the appearance of witnesses who may provide valuable information in his defense. The right to counsel only enhances these rights. A defendant may choose to represent himself as long as he is aware of the dangers and disadvantages of appearing *pro se* and has made an intelligent and knowing waiver of his right to counsel.

■ **Inadequate assistance** In its interpretations of the Sixth Amendment the Supreme Court has assumed that the constitutional right to counsel is based on the premise that counsel will effectively assist the defendant—because if the assistance need not be effective, the Sixth Amendment would be a sham. If the lawyer does not provide a good defense, the defendant's constitutional right will have been denied, and thus his conviction must be reversed. Although the Supreme Court has only rarely examined the effective-counsel requirement, lower courts have frequently dealt with it but have varied considerably both in their definition and application of this standard.

Perhaps the most frequent reason for challenging counsel's effectiveness is his performance at the trial itself, such as his failure to object to inadmissible evidence, to vigorously cross-examine witnesses, or to introduce favorable evidence.

EXAMPLE In 1978 a California district court of appeals ordered a new trial for a man convicted of the murders of 25 farm workers, maintaining that his attorney had "failed to raise the obvious alternative defenses of mental incompetence and/or diminished capacity and/or legal insanity. Still worse, trial counsel failed to present any meaningful defense at all." In fact, he had resisted the request of the court and the prosecution for further psychiatric examination of the defendant.

Many courts tend to assume that alleged trial errors or omissions reflect trial strategy and hold that mistakes in strategy do not reach the level of constitutional incompetency unless the alleged mistakes were the products of the attorney's inexcusable ignorance of legal rules.

Another common ground for attacking counsel's effectiveness is that he was appointed too late to prepare a competent defense. Competent assistance of counsel requires appropriate investigation, both legal and factual, of all possible defenses, and investigation takes time.

The Supreme Court has ruled that if the same attorney represents two defendants in the same case and the interests of the two are clearly in conflict, he cannot provide an effective defense for either. Conflicts of interest exist when co-defendants have factually inconsistent ALIBIS, when one defendant makes a statement that puts the entire blame on the other, and when the WEIGHT OF EVIDENCE is significantly greater against one of the defendants.

counselor Lawyer, attorney, ADVOCATE, BARRISTER. In a few states, "counselor" and "attorney" refer to lawyers of different rank, and no one can become a counselor until he has practiced as an attorney for a certain period of time and passed an additional examination. In most states, however, "counselor" and "attorney" are used interchangeably to mean all lawyers, or "counselor" is not used officially at all. See ATTORNEY AND CLIENT for a discussion of a lawyer's qualifications, duties, rights, and liabilities.

count 1 Declare each fact that makes up the plaintiff's cause of action (facts that give a person a reason for seeking relief in court); plead. 2 State or argue a case. 3 As a noun, each fact or element that makes up a case.

In a civil COMPLAINT a plaintiff sets out each part of his case as a separate statement or paragraph. Each part is made up of counts—the facts or elements required to make a case, or cause of action. Every law specifies elements that must be proved in order to win a suit on the grounds provided for in that law. Usually each count is numbered for easy reference. If a plaintiff claims the elements required to win his case, he is said to have stated a prima facie case, a claim sufficient to win the case unless the defendant disproves it.

EXAMPLE If you lend your neighbor $100 and he promises to repay it on July 1, but does not, you can sue him for breach of contract. If you do, your complaint should list all the elements necessary to establish a breach of contract under the law. This means that it would have to state (1) the fact that you lent him the money, (2) the amount of money you lent him, (3) the date you lent him the money, (4) the fact that he promised to pay you back, (5) the date on which he promised to pay you back, and (6) the fact that he had not paid you back. If you list all these counts, you have a prima facie case, which you will win unless your neighbor can prove that the claims you have made in the complaint are not true.

In a criminal action, each count in the indictment, or formal accusation, charges the defendant with a specific crime. A count will be dismissed if it fails to list exactly the elements required by law to make up a particular crime.

EXAMPLE If a state defines robbery as the taking of money, personal property, or any other thing of value that is in the possession of another person, from his body or immediate presence, against his will, and by means of force or fear, then a criminal count must allege all of these circumstances or it will be dismissed. Bill was charged under such a statute with "removing complainant's fur coat from her person under the guise of checking it for her but instead threatening to hit her and walking out of the restaurant door with the coat." The court dismissed this count of the indictment because it failed to allege that the taking was against the complainant's will.

Common counts are general forms that can be declared by a plaintiff who wants to be sure that his complaint is not dismissed for being insufficient. For example, a lawsuit over a debt may include counts claiming that goods were sold, that the buyer had promised to pay on a certain date, and that he has not paid.

A *special count* differs from a common count by stating an actual fact in the particular case. It is specific rather than general—for example, "Bulk Warehouse failed to redeliver air conditioners stored in its building after plaintiff presented proper documents of title on April 12."

A *money count* is a claim that refers to a sum loaned, not received, or due—for example, "Defendant owes plaintiff twenty thousand dollars for goods sold and delivered by plaintiff to defendant between June 1, 1980, and February 1, 1981."

An *omnibus count* is a count that includes all the money counts in a case, plus the facts relating to them—for example, that certain goods were sold and delivered or that a variety of work was ordered and done.

When a defendant replies to the complaint of the plaintiff, his answer will also contain separate counts, which he may number to correspond with the counts to which they reply. In addition to counts that reply to the counts of the plaintiff, the defendant may include COUNTERCLAIMS—counts that specify claims he has against the plaintiff.

See also ANSWER; COMPLAINT.

counterclaim Three types of claims by which a defendant in a civil lawsuit can try to have the amount of DAMAGES sought by a plaintiff reduced because the plaintiff has wronged him. The term "counterclaim" is also used to include setoffs and recoupments.

■ **Setoff** A claim for a setoff (often called an offset) is a demand by a defendant for money from a plaintiff that is independent of the plaintiff's lawsuit against the defendant. The money damages to which a plaintiff is entitled will be reduced by the amount of any legitimate claim that the defendant has against the plaintiff. Generally, a contract claim is asserted as a setoff in a contract lawsuit but many states permit TORT claims (claims for harm done a person or his property) to be used.

EXAMPLE Mary Smith sues Dave Thomas, owner of Dave's Department Store, for keeping her locked in a room for three hours before determining that she had not shoplifted a pair of slippers. Dave files a claim against Mary for breach of contract, stating that she failed to pay five $20 installments on her television set. Dave's lawsuit against Mary is a setoff; it is independent of Mary's claim against him. If Mary wins her lawsuit, the amount of damages she is awarded will be reduced by $100, the amount of money she owes Dave under the contract—if he succeeds in his setoff action.

■ **Recoupment** Recoupment is the recovery of damages by a defendant from the plaintiff in the same action. It can be awarded if the plaintiff has violated a contract provision that is the basis of his own lawsuit. Recoupment of damages is usually allowed a defendant when the plaintiff who has only partially performed his portion of a contract comes into court asking compensation for his partial performance.

EXAMPLE Jones agreed to construct a garage for Stanton. Jones was to be paid as he completed parts of the garage and received certificates approving them from the architect. Jones completed one part and obtained a certificate, entitling him to $25,300. Soon after, he abandoned the project. Stanton suffered $15,000 worth of damages because of this breach. Jones sued Stanton for the $25,300 already due. Stanton claimed that he was entitled to deduct his $15,000 in damages from the $25,300 he owed Jones. The court allowed this recoupment, and Jones received only $10,300.

In a lawsuit for work, labor, and services, if it appears that the work was not performed in a skillful, workmanlike manner, defendant may recoup the amount of his damages.

EXAMPLE Suppose you have to notify 30 people of an emergency meeting the following day. You do not have enough time to contact each of them by phone, so you send them all telegrams. Most of the telegrams are delivered later that day, but two of them are not delivered until the following evening—after the meeting is over. In anger, you write the telegraph company, complaining bitterly about the delayed telegrams and refusing to pay the bill for any of the telegrams. Subsequently the telegraph company sues you to recover these tolls. You would in all likelihood be able to recoup money for damages arising from the delay in delivering the telegrams that caused two people to miss a vitally important meeting. If, however, you either expressed or implied acceptance of the service rendered by the telegraph company as a full performance of their contract with you, you would not recoup anything for improper performance. The court might decide that you gave your implied acceptance of the service if, for example, you failed to complain about the service to the telegraph company and simply ignored the bill when you received it, without giving any reason for refusing to pay it.

■ **Counterclaim** A counterclaim is a claim by the defendant against the plaintiff that arises from or is otherwise connected with the same controversy that is the basis of the plaintiff's complaint. It represents the defendant's right to have the claims of both parties counterbalanced in whole or in part.

EXAMPLE Jake sues Ned for injuries he received in an automobile accident that occurred when Ned negligently ran a red light and crashed into Jake's car. In the same lawsuit Ned makes a counterclaim for assault and battery on the ground that he was injured when Jake pulled him out of his car and hit him with a wrench.

■ **Differences** Although a counterclaim is usually considered to include both setoffs and recoupments, all three are distinguishable. In a counterclaim or setoff the amount the defendant can recover can be in excess of the plaintiff's demand, while a recoupment is usually limited to the amount of the plaintiff's demand. A counterclaim arises from or is otherwise connected with the same controversy as that described in the plaintiff's complaint, whereas a recoupment arises from a contract or transaction that is the cause of the lawsuit, and a setoff arises from an independent transaction.

All three types of claim serve to prevent the courts from being swamped with multiple lawsuits by allowing an entire controversy between parties to be settled in one action. A person cannot initiate a setoff, counterclaim, or recoupment unless the matter would support an independent action. State law determines which type of claim can be used for which types of cases.

counterfeiting   Making a counterfeit. A counterfeit is a false or fraudulent copy or imitation of something (often a FORGERY) or an unauthorized alteration that the counterfeiter tries to pass off as genuine. Counterfeiting is a criminal offense.

Counterfeiting most often refers to illegal changes in currency to increase its value or the illegal printing of currency. It is a crime to make coins out of base metals or to print copies of paper currency, either foreign or domestic. The question is not whether an alteration enhances the face value of the money but whether there is an intent to defraud. Ordinary coins that were sold as rare collectors' items have been held to be counterfeit.

To be a counterfeit, the copy must be enough like the original so that it could be mistaken for it, but it is no defense that the imitation is not perfect. The counterfeiter can be convicted if he intended to deceive and if an unsuspecting person would have been deceived because he thought he was dealing with an honest person.

It is illegal to make a new counterfeit item, such as to print copies of paper money or stamps. It is also illegal to alter existing things, such as to change the number on a bond or to shave down and coat pennies for use as dimes.

Whether or not an intent to defraud must be proved depends on the particular law that the defendant is charged with breaking. It may be illegal to print pictures of money or stamps that could be used as the real thing even without an intent to deceive.

EXAMPLE A stamp dealer was charged with counterfeiting when he reproduced stamps in full size and color in a catalog. It was not necessary under the law to prove that he was trying to defraud the government or a person. If he had printed the stamps in black and white rather

than in color, or made his illustrations larger or smaller than the originals, he would not have been charged. Under the circumstances, however, the dealer faced conviction under the statute.

It may be unlawful to buy, import, obtain, or possess counterfeits. To *pass* something counterfeit means to give it as money or as something of value that can be used as money. To *utter* a counterfeit means to offer to deliver it or to declare it to be good with an intent to pass it. Putting counterfeit money on a gaming table in a gambling casino is an *uttering;* losing it is a *passing.* A statute may make uttering, passing, selling, and publishing counterfeit items all separate crimes.

Ignorance is no defense. If a forgery is so sloppy that an average person should have detected it, one cannot claim that he did not know a bill was counterfeit. Nor does offering to take back a counterfeit bill absolve a person from guilt for passing it.

Usually the law does require an intent to deceive in order for the act to be a crime. Someone too drunk to see clearly cannot be proved to have "intended" to pass a bogus $20 bill. Also, a small businessman who makes rubber stamps to order cannot be convicted of counterfeiting if he unknowingly makes it possible for someone to print an illegal tax stamp on smuggled cigarettes. Counterfeit money will always be confiscated and the person who held it will suffer the loss. If you give a well-made counterfeit $100 bill to a bank teller without knowing it is counterfeit and without intending to pass a counterfeit, the bank will keep the bill and give you nothing in return. If you intended to defraud the bank you would probably be charged with a crime.

EXAMPLE Gary was on trial for using a phony $50 bill to purchase a pair of shoes. He was charged under a statute forbidding any attempt to pass, utter, publish, or sell any counterfeit obligation of the United States with an intent to defraud. He defended himself with the claim that he did not know the bill was counterfeit. The prosecutor conceded that Gary could not be convicted if he really did not intend to defraud. In such a case, Gary would simply have to give up the bill and bear the loss of the $50. However, evidence of an earlier conviction for possession of plates used for making counterfeit bills was introduced, and the jury convicted Gary. He was sentenced to seven years in prison.

If a bank unknowingly accepts counterfeit money and then passes it on to a customer, the bank should exchange the counterfeit for good money when the customer discovers that the original money was counterfeit.

counteroffer   A proposal made in response to an original offer. In the law of CONTRACTS, a counteroffer operates as a rejection of the original offer, which means the original offer cannot be accepted later on.

EXAMPLE Joe's Bicycle Shop offers to buy 100 bicycles from Winston Manufacturing for $45 apiece. Winston can accept the offer and create a binding contract, but instead it answers Joe's letter with a counteroffer. It will sell the bicycles for $50 each. Joe decides to buy Salem Company's bicycles for $45 instead, so he rejects the counteroffer. When Winston sees the deal slipping out of its hands, it no longer has the right to accept Joe's original offer. The original offer has ceased to exist because of the counteroffer.

countersign An extra signature that is added to a document to certify that the principal signature on that document is genuine. For example, an ordinance passed by a local zoning board may not be valid until a certain official signs it and the county clerk countersigns it. An insurance policy might provide that it is not in force until the agent who sold the policy countersigns it after the insured signs it.

Sometimes it is necessary for the same person to sign twice. Then the signatures can be compared to prove the identity of the person signing. For example, if you buy travelers' checks you must usually sign each check at the bank when you make the purchase. When you cash one of those checks you must countersign it in front of the person accepting the check.

county A political subdivision of a state. The state divides its area into counties for its convenience in managing the business of the state. Counties are considered in law to be agencies of the state and have only the authority granted to them by the state. Often they are also the judicial districts in the state court system.

A county government is not affected by the presence of a city within it. See MUNICIPAL CORPORATION. A county can even be wholly within a city and continue to perform its function. There are five counties completely within New York City, for instance.

In Louisiana a political subdivision of the state is called a *parish*. Like counties, parishes have no existence separate from the state.

■ **Historical importance of county government** The county unit of government dates back further than either the town or the state. In England the county has always been the principal subdivision of the kingdom. It was originally a portion of land not too large for public officials to manage by riding circuit. County was the same as "shire." The governor of the shire was called "shirereeve," or sheriff.

In the United States emphasis on the county in local government is pronounced in the South and many midwestern, western, and northwestern states. The simple form of government organized around the town in small New England communities was less suitable in the early South Atlantic colonies, where large plantations were the equivalent of small kingdoms, with great numbers of servants and dependents. Consequently, the county system provided government on just the right scale.

As states and territories were organized farther west, townships in 36-square-mile blocks were laid out before many of them had a single inhabitant. There, too, the county was the only practical level of government to reach the average citizen.

In the Middle Atlantic states the two systems—town and county—have always clashed somewhat. There is often a certain overlap of services—and taxes—and some ambiguity in the relative authority of TOWNS, villages, counties, and the state.

■ **Status of a county** In the United States, counties are created by the state according to the procedure required by its constitution. Some states require a minimum size, population, or property value for the creation of a county. A county government may be abolished if it proves to be too small, or it may be reorganized under a consolidation plan to combine urban and rural areas. If it becomes too populous or too diverse after a long period of development, a state can break off an area to create a new county. Cities are generally considered corporations, but whether or not a county is treated like a corporation when it makes contracts or becomes party to a lawsuit depends upon state law.

States are entitled to refuse to let anyone sue them. This principle, called SOVEREIGN IMMUNITY, extends to the counties. In other words, states and counties can be sued only in situations where state law specifically permits.

■ **Boundaries** The state legislature generally has the right to fix the boundaries of a county. State law determines how boundaries can be altered and how counties can be combined or divided. Citizens cannot prevent the state legislature from changing county lines, but the legislature cannot juggle boundaries to affect the voting power of some of its citizens. See ELECTION. Some state laws prohibit the drawing of a new county line too near to an existing county seat or the creation of a county in anything but a fairly regular and compact shape. Usually voters have the right to petition for the enlargement of a county or for the division of an existing county into two counties. They can also counterpetition against such proposals.

The state can create special districts for irrigation, flood control, fire protection, library services, and other similar services. This has no effect on existing counties.

■ **County government** A county's government is prescribed by state law. The government is located at the *county seat*—the town or city in which court sessions are held and county officers perform their duties. The *county board* is the governing body of the county. It is made up of public officials who either are elected to serve on it or are elected or appointed to some other post that gives them a place on the board. Other county officials are the sheriff, clerk, surveyor, treasurer, comptroller, and commissioners with responsibilities in special areas such as welfare, highways, consumer affairs, and human rights.

Counties are given the authority from the state to buy and sell property; raise money from taxes, licenses, or bond issues; and provide for public health, safety, welfare, and morals. They regulate building, zoning, traffic and parking, public parks and recreation, and public improvements such as roads, bridges, airports, and mass-transit systems. They may establish water, power, and sanitation districts. The state may choose to establish courts on the county level or to use counties to mark judicial districts within the state.

course of dealing The pattern of prior conduct between parties to a business transaction. This pattern is important in determining what the parties meant when they made a CONTRACT. It must be assumed that the contract was hammered out in accordance with the way business was conducted *before* it was signed. Courts will take into account evidence of the course of dealing when they try to interpret a provision in a breach-of-contract action. For example, if a dry cleaner had always covered clean clothes with a plastic garment bag this would establish a course of dealing and he could not start charging extra for the bag without warning the customer.

Courts may also consider the *course of performance*—the pattern of conduct between the parties *after* the contract is made—as a good indication of what the parties intended the agreement to mean. If a supplier had a contract to sell syrup to a bakery and had been delivering the syrup ordered under this contract in five-gallon cans that were very convenient for the bakery, he could not switch to 50-gallon drums. The conduct of the parties before and after the contract may sometimes be considered together, and courts may refer to the entire history of the parties' business relationship as the course of dealing.

Other circumstances outside the actual contract that the court will consider are custom and trade usage. The rule is that CUSTOM AND USAGE are part of the contract without being written into it because both parties must have known about common practices. If neither party objected or insisted that the agreement exclude them, they are part of the contract and part of the course of dealing. For example, if fishermen in a particular bay use distinctive floats to mark their lobster pots, no one has the right to take lobsters from another's traps on the ground that they did not belong to anyone. The custom led to a rule of local usage. *Trade usage* is the general pattern observed by nearly everyone in a particular business. Certain ways of doing things or special meanings for words in the trade can be so common that a court assumes both parties had them in mind when the contract was drawn up. As the business community reacts to new circumstances and creates new solutions to problems, new customs and courses of dealing also develop to which the law extends its protection.

Testimony concerning course of dealing does not change or contradict the meaning of the contract; it only explains the meaning of the contract. A term that may have seemed clear when the agreement was signed may later prove to be a point of strong disagreement.

EXAMPLE Suppose a businessman rents a factory for three O↠✳ years. At the end of that time, the businessman and the landlord renew the lease for three more years at a slightly higher rent. The businessman's busy season is the two months before Christmas, when he has three shifts working around the clock.

The second year into the new lease, fuel prices double. The landlord reduces the heat to 45° after 5:00 P.M. every day, including the two months before Christmas. The shivering factory workers threaten to walk out, and the businessman stands to lose his best season. The landlord maintains that the lease obligates him to provide heat but does not require him to provide heat through the night for two months a year. From now on, he says, that will cost extra. The businessman sues the landlord.

The landlord will lose. The prior course of dealing between these two parties included heat around the clock for two months each year. The businessman was entitled to rely on this practice. If the landlord had wanted to protect himself from a big jump in the price of fuel oil, he could have bargained for a provision to cover that possibility at the time the lease was renewed.

course of employment   Within the time, place, and circumstances of one's job; directly related to employment, during working hours, or at the place of work.

It is important to determine whether an employee has done something in the *course of his employment* anytime an injury occurs. If the employee hurts someone else during the course of his employment, the employer is liable. If a deliveryman for a dairy runs over a child, for example, a suit on behalf of the child can be brought against both the driver and his company. See RESPONDEAT SUPERIOR.

If the employee himself is hurt during the course of employment, WORKMEN'S COMPENSATION laws require the employer to pay him benefits, according to a schedule for his particular type of injury. The course of employment has been held to include not only actual work time but also recreation time provided by the employer. An employee cannot, however, receive benefits for injuries that occur during the time he is at home preparing for work or on his way to or from his place of employment. These situations are not considered within the course of employment.

course of performance   The pattern of conduct between two parties to a business transaction after a contract has been signed. In a dispute over the terms of a contract, a court may consider the course of performance as an indication of what the parties intended the agreement to mean when they signed the contract. See COURSE OF DEALING.

court commissioners   Officials elected or appointed by a judge to hear particular controversies, certain types of cases, or some of the evidence in one case. The court commissioner may be another judge, a retired judge, an attorney, or someone with the training or experience necessary to understand a complicated or special issue. The decisions of a court commissioner are generally reviewed only by the court he serves, and his powers are determined by the law in each state.

Commissioners may take testimony in the following kinds of proceedings: (1) depositions for a court in a different state or foreign country, (2) pretrial hearings in criminal cases, (3) hearings to determine whether a will is genuine and should be used to distribute property to heirs, (4) boards of inquiry in labor disputes, (5) examinations of witnesses who cannot appear in court, (6) family-court hearings for petitions to change the amount of alimony or child support, and (7) entries of default JUDGMENTS or STIPULATIONS.

court-martial   A military court that tries and punishes offenses committed by members of the ARMED SERVICES. It is created by military law (the Uniform Code of Military Justice), and a commanding officer gives it authority to act in each instance. A court-martial cannot punish civilians or try military personnel for nonmilitary offenses.

court of appeals   A court with authority to review decisions made by lower courts, in order to correct any errors. There are state and federal courts of appeals.

Court of Appeals is the name of the highest state court in Kentucky, Maryland, New York, and the District of Columbia. In Virginia and West Virginia the court of last resort is called the *Supreme Court of Appeals*. In Connecticut it is the *Supreme Court of Errors*, and in Massachusetts and Maine, the *Supreme Judicial Court*. In other states the highest court is named the *Supreme Court*. The *Courts of Civil Appeals* in Texas are below the state Supreme Court.

In the FEDERAL COURT system there are 12 judicial circuits. In each of these a *U.S. Court of Appeals* reviews decisions on appeal from the *district courts* in the circuit. For an explanation of court systems, see COURTS; Chart 1. See also APPEAL AND ERROR.

court of claims
A FEDERAL COURT established in 1855 to hear lawsuits against the United States. It decides only cases for money damages based on government contracts or federal laws and cases brought by public officials who need approval for money paid out. The court, which consists of a chief justice and six associate justices, holds an annual term in Washington. Its decisions can be reviewed by appeal to the Supreme Court.

Some states also have either a special court called a court of claims or an ordinary court that sits as a court of claims at a particular session. These courts determine whether claims against a county or the state are valid and how much money should be awarded. They may approve expenses incurred by the county and provide for payment out of certain taxes. For an explanation of court systems, see COURTS; Chart 1.

court of probate
A COURT that administers the estates of persons who have died and the estates of persons who have, by legal process, been declared incompetent to manage their own property, such as INSANE PERSONS, alcoholics, or SPENDTHRIFTS. In some states courts of PROBATE have limited civil and criminal authority in estate matters. They may also be called *orphans' courts* or *surrogate's courts*. See also Chart 1.

courts
Judicial assemblies that administer justice. They do not represent the public or the government, but rather stand between parties and decide how to resolve their controversies. Even though courts do not represent the government, they are created by the government by law or by constitution. The duty of the courts is to enforce the law for the good of society. Courts are available equally to anyone who has a reason to sue and to anyone formally accused of a crime.

Courts are open to the public. Anyone may attend trials as a spectator unless a judge must close the courtroom to maintain order, assure due process, or protect a witness's identity. In law, the terms "court" and "judge" are often used interchangeably.

■ **Court systems** Two court systems operate in the United States—the state and the federal. See Chart 1.

State courts State courts are organized in layers. The lowest level of state courts consists of the courts of *limited jurisdiction* (authority to hear cases). These include justice-of-the-peace court (justice court), magistrate's court, police court, city court, traffic court, and small claims court. Their powers may be limited by the amount of money involved in cases or the severity of the crimes charged. Generally, no record is made of their proceedings, and it is not possible to have a jury in cases before them. An appeal from the lower courts is usually made by starting a new trial from scratch in the court of general jurisdiction, discussed below.

In courts of limited jurisdiction a case is nearly always tried before one judge. All the judges in a particular court take cases in turn as they come up. One judge hears a case from beginning to end and then gives his decision.

Each state has a court of *general* (or *unlimited*) *jurisdiction*. It is sometimes called county court, circuit court, superior court, district court, or court of common pleas. Below it are *special courts*, such as juvenile courts, criminal courts, and probate (or surrogate's) courts. These special courts have as much power as the court of general jurisdiction, but only within their own subject area. Sometimes appeals from a special court go to a court of general jurisdiction, and sometimes they go to a higher court.

Sixteen states have intermediate appellate courts to review the decisions of the general and special courts. When there is an intermediate court, appeals generally must be made to it first. In some cases, an appeal to the highest state court can be made only if the judges of the intermediate court disagree in their decision—that is, if their decision is not unanimous. For a discussion of the process of making an appeal in a civil case, see APPEAL AND ERROR; for appeal of criminal cases, see CRIMINAL LAW.

If a party decides to appeal to a higher court, any of the judges on that higher court can be assigned to hear the appeal unless the law says otherwise. Generally, the highest court in each state hears appeals *en banc* ("on the bench"). This means that all the judges of that court, or at least a certain number, sit "on the bench" together and hear the appeals collectively. Decisions are made by majority vote, as is done in the U.S. Supreme Court. The number of judges on each appellate court is fixed by the law or constitutional provision that created the court.

Federal courts The FEDERAL COURTS are also organized on levels, with appeals spiraling up to the higher courts. There are 12 judicial districts, with each state, the District of Columbia, Puerto Rico, Guam, the Northern Mariana Islands, and the Virgin Islands wholly within a district. These judicial districts are called *circuits*. In each circuit there are *district courts*, and a *U.S. court of appeals* that hears appeals from them. There is at least one district court in each state.

In addition to the district courts and the court of appeals in each circuit, there are certain specialized federal courts. The *Tax Court* and the *Court of International Trade*, formerly the *Customs Court*, hear cases concerning tax and customs *matters*. The *U.S. Court of Customs and Patent Appeals* reviews cases involving import-export duties and patent infringement, and the *Court of Claims* hears lawsuits against the United States arising from a federal law or any contract with the government. The U.S. Court of Military Appeals hears appeals from military tribunals. Bankruptcy courts have jurisdiction over BANKRUPTCY cases.

The *U.S. Supreme Court* is the highest court in the land. It has the power to review any court decisions that involve either the Constitution or a federal law. Appeals from a court of appeals are taken to the SUPREME COURT. The nine justices on the Supreme Court decide whether or not to take particular cases. If decisions on a given subject have been contradictory in different circuits, they will usually take a case to settle that point of law. When the Supreme Court decides not to review a decision, the parties must accept that decision as final.

When federal courts hear a case, they always follow federal rules of procedure or practice. The rights involved are determined by federal law if a federal question is involved; otherwise, by state law.

■ **Jurisdiction** Jurisdiction is the court's authority to hear and determine cases. The jurisdiction of each court is spelled out in the statute or constitution that created it. Questions of jurisdiction may involve choices between federal or state courts or among the various federal and state courts.

Whether or not a federal court has authority to exercise jurisdiction depends on the kind of controversy and the character of the parties—whether, for example, a state is suing another state or a resident of one state is suing a resident of another. In some cases, federal jurisdiction is *concurrent*, meaning either federal or state courts may hear the case, and in other cases the federal court has *exclusive jurisdiction*.

If a question of federal law is involved, the federal courts will hear cases involving at least $10,000. This is called *federal-question jurisdiction*. Cases that are less than $10,000 should be brought in state court.

Federal courts will hear cases that involve only state law if the amount in dispute is at least $10,000 and if the parties are citizens of different states or if one party is a citizen of another country. This is called *diversity jurisdiction* because the people who are parties are from diverse places.

Only federal courts can hear BANKRUPTCY, ADMIRALTY, and PRIZE cases. Admiralty cases involve maritime affairs, such as ocean COMMERCE and ship COLLISIONS. Prize cases determine rights in ships and cargo captured at sea.

Once it is determined which court system—federal or state—has jurisdiction, it must be decided which court within that system has jurisdiction over a case. Jurisdiction can be based on a variety of different factors.

Civil and criminal jurisdiction It is not unusual for a state to have some courts with jurisdiction only over civil cases and others with jurisdiction only over criminal cases.

Territory Jurisdiction may also be limited geographically. Courts may hear only cases concerning events that took place within their territory or between parties who live there. A state can exercise jurisdiction only within its boundaries, and it may limit the jurisdiction of some of its courts to certain areas, as is often done with county courts.

Jurisdictional amount One jurisdictional factor, usually in civil cases, is called the *amount in controversy*. This is the dollar amount that a plaintiff is likely to win from the defendant if he is successful. Small claims courts, for example, will not accept cases that involve more than a certain amount, usually a few hundred dollars. A wildly exaggerated claim that has no basis in the facts alleged by the plaintiff will not be accepted by a court as fulfilling a required jurisdictional amount.

Original and appellate jurisdiction Courts with *original jurisdiction* are trial courts in which actions of all kinds are first started. An appeal to a higher court to correct an error by a lower court must be addressed to a court that has *appellate* jurisdiction—authority to review lower court cases and to reverse, affirm, or modify their decisions. Appellate courts can only determine whether there was a mistake in applying the law or in procedure. They cannot review the trial courts' findings of fact.

Personal jurisdiction No matter what kind of case is before the court, the court must have the authority to give orders to the parties involved. This is called *in personam jurisdiction*, or *personal jurisdiction*. There must be certain kinds of connections between a defendant and a court before the court can force a defendant to appear and submit to its power. The fact that the defendant is a resident of the court's state or judicial district is a sufficient connection, for example. Sometimes personal jurisdiction is created when the defendant committed the act complained of within the state or signed the disputed contract within the state. A court has personal jurisdiction over a corporation that is chartered (organized) in its state or authorized to do business there.

In rem jurisdiction A court can also hear cases concerning a "thing" that is within its power. This is called *in rem jurisdiction*, or authority over the thing. The "thing" could be a parcel of land, an antique weather vane, or the contents of a safe-deposit box. Or it could be something intangible, such as a debt, a bank account, or the proceeds from an insurance policy. If the thing is before the court, anyone with an interest in it must be notified of the case and given the opportunity to appear. If, after being notified, a person fails to make an appearance, he may never reargue the case in another court or at a different time.

Subject-matter jurisdiction Apart from *in personam* and *in rem* jurisdiction, all of the limits on a court's power to hear a particular case establish the court's *subject-matter jurisdiction*, sometimes called *competence*. The competence of a court to hear a case depends on the facts of the controversy: the court's geographical limits, the dollar value of the cases the court can hear, and the separation of civil and criminal matters. Every state, however, has a court of general jurisdiction that can hear cases which do not fall within any other court's competence. But no court can hear a case without personal jurisdiction—as when the defendant cannot be found.

Special courts are often set up to handle particular parties, such as juveniles, or particular subjects, such as patents and trademarks. These are some of the courts in the United States that have limited subject-matter jurisdiction:

tax courts	Indian tribal courts
bankruptcy courts	juvenile courts
circuit courts	probate courts
civil courts	small claims courts
criminal courts	surrogate's courts
family courts	traffic courts

When a court finds that there is a justifiable controversy and there are facts to support subject-matter jurisdiction plus *in rem* or *in personam* jurisdiction, then that court may hear the case. It may order the parties to appear, and it may punish them for contempt if they disobey its orders. Its decision is final and binding on the parties unless and until a higher court changes the decision on appeal.

Inconvenient forum Once a court has jurisdiction of a matter, it may still decline to do so on the ground that it is located in an inconvenient place for the trial. This is the doctrine of *forum non conveniens* ("inconvenient forum"). For example, attorneys for plaintiffs in accident cases prefer to start their lawsuits in New York City if possible, because New York juries have a history of giving verdicts for huge sums of money.

EXAMPLE Suppose a New York resident is riding in his O▬➤ friend's car in Philadelphia when there is a collision. Both cars are registered in Pennsylvania and both drivers are Pennsylvania residents. The driver of the second car makes a trip to New York one month later to attend a medical convention, and the New York resident serves him with a summons to start a lawsuit in the New York state court.

The New York court has jurisdiction. It is authorized to hear auto accident cases, and service of papers within the state gives the court *in personam* jurisdiction. But the court should decline to hear this case. The plaintiff is a New Yorker, but the accident occurred in Pennsylvania—all the witnesses are in Pennsylvania, the defendant lives in Pennsylvania, and New York courts are very overcrowded. New York is clearly an inconvenient forum.

Change of venue Courts can also change the place of a trial within a judicial district. This is called a *change of venue*, or of place. The change may be for the convenience of the parties, the witnesses, or the court. Often a change is not necessary in law but is ordered based on the court's good judgment.

The effect of jurisdiction The FULL FAITH AND CREDIT clause of the U.S. Constitution requires every state to recognize and enforce the final decisions of courts in other states, but this does not apply to decisions that were made by courts without jurisdiction. If a court mistakenly hears a case without the necessary authority, its decision is void.

A decision made in a foreign country is void if the court there lacked jurisdiction. When a foreign court does have jurisdiction, its decision will generally be enforced here as a matter of respect, but our courts are not required to accept a foreign decision that is contrary to American public policy. See COMITY.

■ **Organization** The way a particular court is organized is determined by the statute or constitution that created it. The organization of a court involves the duties of its personnel, the fixing of its terms and sessions, and its procedures.

Personnel The papers for each lawsuit are received by the *clerk* of that court. The clerk and his staff hold and file all the records for the *judges* assigned to that court. In addition, each judge may have a *law secretary* or *law clerk* who does legal research and writing for him. *Court officers, attendants,* or *bailiffs* keep order in the courtroom or courthouse. They often wear uniforms and sometimes carry guns. *Interpreters* may be available to translate for witnesses or parties who do not speak English well. The court *stenographer* takes down in shorthand a word-for-word record of proceedings. A *sheriff* or *federal marshal* may be responsible for taking action to enforce a court's orders.

Probation officers, usually civilian employees, assist the court by administering the PROBATION system for criminal offenders and supervising court-ordered custody or payments of money, especially for children.

Attorneys are called officers of the court because they have a duty to protect the legal system while pursuing their clients' claims. They may practice only in the courts where they have been admitted to the bar. For example, an attorney who has been admitted to the bar in one state is entitled by that state to practice in its courts but not in the courts of other states or in the federal courts.

Terms and sessions Particular terms and sessions may be fixed by law for courts. If none are fixed, the court is open for all kinds of business at all times. A *term* is the period of time prescribed for a court to hear cases, and a *session* is the time that a judge actually hears cases. A *regular term* is one called for by law, and a *special term* is assembled by a judge or other official for a particular purpose. It is possible to have one's case heard by a jury during the *jury term* or to argue motions at the *motion term.* See MOTIONS AND ORDERS. A *general term* may designate the time when all the judges of a court sit together, or en BANC; or designate the time when one judge hears all the cases on a particular subject—such as divorce.

Procedure *Practice* and *procedure* refer to the system of rules prescribing how a legal right is enforced. Each of the state courts and the federal courts has its own procedure that must be followed. Without strict observance of the rules of practice—for example, the rules of EVIDENCE, methods of SERVICE of process, time to file papers—it would be impossible for courts to carry on their business. The rules are calculated to bring out the truth, insure equal treatment of all parties, and protect constitutional rights. In addition, a good system of rules promotes efficiency as well as justice. Rules come from the legislature and from the courts themselves.

■ **Decision making** The purpose of the courts is to furnish decisions on disputes. A defendant is summoned and made to appear. In a civil case he faces the plaintiff, and in a criminal case he faces the district attorney or prosecutor, who speaks for the people of the state. The plaintiff or the prosecutor presents evidence, including the testimony of witnesses, to establish a case; and the defendant has a chance to disprove those facts, explain them, or prove a case against the plaintiff. If there is a jury, it decides which among all the facts are true. This is its *verdict.* If there is no jury, the judge decides which facts are true. In either case, the judge decides how the *law* applies to the case and gives a *judgment.* He may write down his thoughts, and they may be published as a *reported decision.*

If the same controversy has been at issue (in dispute) in a separate, earlier case involving the same two parties, the judge, after hearing the case, is required to make the same decision regarding that controversy as was made in the earlier case—according to the rule that controversies must at some point come to an end. Argument and litigation must finally stop, and the issue must be settled. This rule is called ESTOPPEL.

■ **Which law the court applies** Generally a state court applies the laws and rules of practice of its own state, but sometimes it applies the laws of the place where the event in question took place or where a disputed contract was signed. See CONFLICT OF LAWS. Federal courts enforce federal law, of course, but they also apply the laws of the state in which they sit.

Article VI, Clause 2, of the U.S. Constitution says:
" This Constitution, and the Laws of the United States which shall be made in Pursuance thereof; and all Treaties made, or which shall be made, under the Authority of the United States, shall be the supreme Law of the Land; and the Judges in every State shall be bound thereby, any Thing in the Constitution or Laws of any State to the Contrary notwithstanding."

This statement is sometimes called the supremacy clause. It says that federal law and treaties made by the United States and the Constitution are supreme. State courts *must* apply them. Every citizen enjoys the rights guaranteed by the Constitution, and no state may enforce a law contrary to it. Because the supremacy clause includes treaties made with other countries, all the courts in this country have an obligation to respect the international law embodied in treaties. Thus the Constitution makes international law a part of U.S. law.

Another rule that affects which law a court will apply is the doctrine of *preemption.* The Constitution requires states to step aside whenever there is a federal law covering a particular subject. One reason for this is the responsibility Congress has to promote business and commerce among the states. A different law in every state concerning the maximum size of trucks, for example, would create an intolerable burden on shipping. Therefore, courts cannot apply any state law that contradicts a federal law.

covenant　A written promise or agreement. Often a covenant restricts one party in order to protect the other. In law, the word most frequently refers to an agreement to use or not to use land in a particular way.

Take the case of a farmer who wants to sell off part of his property to a developer. He may have to agree that he will never use the specific fields next to the homesites to raise farm animals. That land is now said to be *burdened,* or *encumbered,* by a *restrictive covenant* because the way it can be used is specifically limited. This type of agreement is called a *covenant in gross* because it binds the owner and not the land itself. A new owner is not bound by it. The farmer might be able to get an even higher price for the homesites if he promises not to sell the burdened land unless the buyer also agrees to keep farm animals off the property. In this case, the covenant is said to *run with the land* because it remains with the land regardless of who owns it. Naturally, a covenant of this kind makes the homesites, called the *dominant property,* more valuable.

Expensive new neighborhoods are often created by covenants. A housing developer buys up undeveloped land for a low price, lays out building plots, and sells the plots, each of which is burdened with a long list of restrictive covenants. He may put into the contract of sale a requirement that the owner will keep the original size of his lot, never selling off a smaller piece. He can require owners to agree that houses will all meet minimum-size standards, include garage space for two cars, be of conventional rather than prefabricated construction, and have a full basement and a fireplace.

It may seem that the property would be more difficult to sell with so many restrictions on what the new owner can do with it. In fact, the opposite is true. The property will bring premium prices because the covenants assure new owners of minimum standards for the entire neighborhood. The covenants in this case are part of a *neighborhood plan,* which courts will enforce as long as the restrictions benefit and burden all the property owners in a neighborhood equally. Covenants have no effect, however, if they are intended to accomplish an illegal purpose.

EXAMPLE In the case of *Shelley* v. *Kraemer* (1948), a group of neighbors sued to prevent a property owner from selling his home to blacks because of a restrictive covenant that burdened the land where he bought the house. The neighbors argued that the owner had bought the restrictive covenant along with the property and he could not later break his promise. The U.S. Supreme Court ruled that the covenant was unenforceable because no court or state official can take any action to enforce a racial covenant. The Court's decision was based on laws providing for equal opportunity in housing.

In recent years there has been much argument that the effect of neighborhood plans is to keep people of low and even moderate incomes out of certain areas. The plans have not been held to be illegal, however.

cover　1 Make good or provide for, as to cover a check by putting cash into a bank account. 2 Protect. For example, fire insurance covers, or protects, the insured against the loss of his home by fire.

coverage　Amount and type of INSURANCE. An insurance policy is said to provide coverage for particular losses.

coverture　A term from English common law referring to the legal position of a married woman. By marrying, a woman was said to come under both the protection and the control of her husband. This created legal rights as well as legal disabilities. *During coverture* means while the marriage lasts. For example, in some jurisdictions a woman has a legal interest in all land her husband buys "during coverture."

CPA　See CERTIFIED PUBLIC ACCOUNTANT.

craft union　A labor union whose members practice a particular craft. A *craft* is a mechanical skill or trade, an occupation that relies on use of the hands. Plumbers and electricians are craftsmen. Craft union members perform their work in different industries for a variety of employers.

credibility　The quality of being worthy of credit or belief. For example, the testimony of a witness must be both competent and credible. It is *competent* if it is admissible under the law that determines what kinds of EVIDENCE can be presented and if it is related to the issue. Testimony is *credible* if it is logical enough to be trusted or believable.

credit　The ability to borrow; an arrangement that permits repayment of a debt to be delayed. The term "credit" can be applied to borrowing transactions in several different ways. First, it may mean the ability to postpone payment. For example, Mrs. Donald can have credit with her neighborhood butcher. She sends her son Joshua to pick up meat for dinner three or four times a week. Then she settles the account by paying the full amount due every couple of weeks when she happens to be passing by the shop. Credit in this sense can also be a very formal arrangement called a *line of credit.*

EXAMPLE Suppose that Mr. Celantano is in the business ○┅─＊ of constructing one-family homes. His banker knows him to be a highly respected builder, so the bank extends a line of credit to him. This is a definite agreement to make a series of loans to Mr. Celantano as he needs them in his business, up to a specific, maximum limit. Because of this fixed limit, Mr. Celantano must make payments to reduce the amount he owes anytime he approaches his maximum. This is how he keeps his line of credit open, insuring that he will have money to buy materials whenever he contracts to build another house.

A *bill of credit* is used extensively by merchants and bankers. It gives the person to whom it is issued the authority to collect money owed to the merchant or bank. Governments also issue bills of credit, which can be circulated as money and redeemed for their cash value at some date in the future. These bills are accepted only because the people have faith in their government.

A *letter of credit* is a sealed or open letter written by a merchant or bank asking anyone or some particular person to advance money or goods on credit to the person who holds the letter or is named in it. The merchant or bank issuing the letter guarantees repayment of the debt. Letters of credit were frequently used by wealthy world travelers before the advent of credit cards and traveler's checks.

Personal credit means that the credit is extended to an individual on the basis of his character, reputation, and business standing. *Consumer credit* is credit that permits a person to borrow money or purchase goods on time for personal, family, or household purposes. Access to credit generally increases one's opportunities for home ownership, education, investment, business ventures, and a higher standard of living.

■ **Classifying consumer-credit transactions** There are a number of ways to classify consumer-credit transactions: according to whether or not they are installment credit agreements, according to who receives payment, or according to who extends the credit.

Installment or noninstallment Installment credit means credit that is repaid by more than one payment. Loans repaid in a lump sum are classified as noninstallment credit. People who delay payment to dentists or who pay a service charge for bounced checks are using noninstallment credit. Installment credit has grown rapidly. More and more consumers are purchasing durable goods on credit and spreading payment over a series of installments. Between 1950 and 1978 the amount of outstanding consumer credit rose from $14.7 billion to $227.5 billion.

Originator or holder Credit can also be classified according to the status of the person who receives repayment. This can be the *originator,* the person who originally extended the credit, or some other *holder* who "bought" the debt at a discounted price in order to collect payments at a later time. For example, a great deal of automobile credit is originated by dealers at the time of sale. They subsequently assign the loans to commercial banks or sales-finance com-

panies, who then *hold* the loans. See SECURED TRANSACTION.

Commercial banks also originate loans themselves for all kinds of purposes, and the widespread use of bank credit cards has contributed to the tremendous growth of the banks' share of the consumer-credit market.

Sales-finance companies, like banks, buy and hold consumer installment debts connected with the sale of durable goods. *Finance companies* called *small-loan companies* make loans directly to consumers and thus are originators. The distinction is becoming less important, however, because small-loan companies now conduct business on both levels.

Vendor or lender In some instances the law views credit differently, depending on who extends it, a vendor or a lender. A furniture store gives credit to customers when it lets them take its sofas and chairs home and pay for them over a period of time. This is *vendor credit.* If the consumer borrows money from Friendly Finance Company and then uses that money to pay for his furniture, this is called *lender credit.* The finance company lends, but it does not sell.

Either vendor or lender can charge the consumer interest for using the borrowed money for a period of time. Traditionally, usury statutes that limit the legal rate of interest have been applied only to lender credit. The law assumed that a seller, or vendor, could adjust his price to allow for the time he waits for payment and that a consumer had a choice. If the vendor's *time price* was too high—if it included a high interest rate for credit—the consumer could choose to pay the *cash price.* The courts relied on competition to keep sellers from charging too much when they extended credit. They let the seller decide how much extra money he was willing to give up for cash in hand.

Although this seems to contradict state usury laws, which limit the rate of interest charged by lenders, the doctrine has stood firm for more than 100 years. Since 1970, however, some courts have found that it should not apply to *revolving charge accounts.* They note that department stores do not offer customers a different price for cash or time. Finance charges are computed on the cash price. Furthermore, department stores are applying the vendor-credit exception to the usury laws not to one sale, which is the traditional basis for the rule, but to a revolving charge account, which involves numbers of sales and is computed on the balance due, rather than the payment of a single item. This dilutes the effect competition can have in controlling the time price.

When courts have said that state usury laws must be applied to vendor credit extended to revolving charge account customers, state legislatures have passed laws to raise the legal rate of interest they may charge because most consumer credit cannot exist within the limits of usury law.

■ **Licensing creditors** Under state or federal law, many lenders must be licensed—banks, savings and loan associations, and finance companies, for example. Some states license credit companies that buy retail installment debts from sellers who own them. The debts are assigned to the credit companies for collection.

The primary purpose of licensing creditors is not to protect the borrowers but to raise money for the state. Often, all a creditor has to do to get a license is to file an application and pay a fee. Even when an applicant is required by law to have good character or sound business experience, the public is protected only if these requirements are energetically enforced.

■ **How to get credit** Financial institutions need proof of creditworthiness before they will take a chance on an individual. They want to know whether he has both the ability and the willingness to repay. A person who wants to use credit must have sufficient income and must carefully build up a reliable credit history.

Income The ability to repay must be demonstrated by an income large enough to pay living expenses, existing debts, and the loan for which the consumer is applying. Income usually means salary, but it can also be investment income from stocks or a trust. Alimony and child-support payments do not have to be disclosed on a credit application if a woman does not want to reveal that she is divorced, but they do have to be shown if she needs them as proof that she has enough income to repay the loan.

Establishing a legal name The first decision every credit seeker must make is what name to use. A person may legally use any name he wants, as long as he uses it consistently and has no intention of cheating creditors.

In order to build a good credit history, you must use the same legal name all the time. Whether you decide to use your full name, initials, or a nickname, plan to use it every

---

HOW MUCH DO YOU KNOW ABOUT CREDIT?

■ *Credit* means a reputation of trustworthiness in money matters that enables you to get money or goods now and pay later.

■ A *line of credit* is an agreement by a lender to make loans up to a specified amount. To keep your line of credit open, you make periodic payments to reduce the amount you owe whenever you approach your maximum.

■ Banks and merchants extend *personal credit* on the basis of an individual's character, reputation, and business standing.

■ To get credit you must carefully build up a reliable credit history. Your ability to repay must be demonstrated by an income large enough to pay living expenses, existing debts, and the loan for which you are applying.

■ You must use the same legal name all the time. Whether you prefer your full name, initials, or a nickname, settle on one form and use it every time you sign a check, credit application, or any legal document.

■ A woman should always use her first name after marriage—"Mrs. Mary Doe," *never* "Mrs. Richard Doe." She is also free to use either her maiden or married surname. A woman who establishes her legal identity will have credit available to her if she is divorced or widowed.

■ Husbands and wives should build credit separately. This guarantees that one spouse will not lose his or her good credit rating if the other abuses a line of credit, dies, or moves away.

■ If you have no credit, begin to build it by applying for a local credit card. Use that card for four to six months, then apply for a second card at another local store. After a couple of months, go for a third. When all has gone smoothly for a year or so, apply for a national credit card. You will probably get it.

■ If it is impossible to pay on time, notify the credit manager.

■ If you want credit, you must have a credit history—no credit history is just as bad as a poor credit record. In practice, your *credit history* consists of a detailed file on your finances, debts, bill-paying habits, occupation, marital status, and lawsuits. Unfortunately, the files are often inaccurate, and they are not kept private. One of the largest credit bureaus in the country admits to a 30-percent error rate.

■ You have the right not to have false information in your files.

■ You can file a statement correcting wrong information. The credit bureau must include that statement in your file and, if you request, send copies to all recent users of the report.

■ Persons using credit reports must file statements certifying the purpose for which the reports will be used; it is against the law to use them for any other purpose.

■ You do not have the right to see your file, but if you have been denied credit because of the report, you have the right to know the "nature and substance" of all information except medical information in the file. You also have the right to learn the name of anyone who has received the report for employment purposes during the last two years or for any other purpose during the last six months.

■ The foregoing rights and restrictions are embodied in current federal law. If you suffer financial or personal harm as a result of violations by a credit bureau, you can sue for damages. If the credit bureau's violations are willful and intentional, those responsible are subject to criminal prosecution, fines, or imprisonment.

■ More than half the states now prohibit credit discrimination on the basis of sex or marital status. According to the federal Equal Credit Opportunity Act, creditors may not (1) assign a value to gender or marital status in a credit evaluation; (2) assign a value to having a telephone in the applicant's name; (3) inquire about plans to have children; (4) change terms of credit when marital status changes; (5) refuse to count a spouse's full income; (6) tell an applicant what name to use—that is, direct a married woman not to use her maiden name when in fact this is her legal right; (7) delay action on an application or refuse to consider it; or (8) discourage someone from applying for credit.

■ If you are refused credit, ask for the reason to be given you in writing. If the grounds are discriminatory, you have a right to complain.

■ If you think you are paying an illegally high interest rate on a loan, you should check your state law—most states impose penalties for usurious loans. In many states, the lender cannot get any interest at all when the agreement provided for an illegal rate. In some states, he must give up several times the amount of interest he charged, while in others, he forfeits only the excess above the legal rate. Several states permit the borrower to keep all the interest and repay only a percentage of the amount borrowed. Quite a few states cancel a usurious loan and let you keep the principal.

time you sign a check, a credit application, or any legal document. If you are a "Jr." or "III," do not forget to include that.

Married women may use a maiden or married last name, but they should always use their own first name, even after marriage. A name such as "Mrs. Richard Doe" is not considered a legal name but a social one, which could be used by a succession of wives. A woman who firmly establishes her own legal identity will have credit available to her after divorce or widowhood.

Establishing a credit history   To build a good credit history, you should first apply for a credit card in a local department store. Be prepared to pay promptly the full balance due. Keep in mind that the Fair Credit Billing Act does not require the store to send out the bill more than 14 days before it is due. People sometimes assume they have 30 days to pay, but this may not be true.

Always try to notify the credit manager if it is impossible for you to pay on time, especially if you have just started to build a credit history. Otherwise, the store will not know whether you intend to pay at all.

A husband and wife should build credit separately. Apply for some loans or credit cards and pay some utility bills in each name. Under federal law, credit accounts may be maintained in one name only. This guarantees that one spouse will not lose his or her good credit rating if the other starts abusing a line of credit, dies, or moves away.

Use your credit card periodically to create a history of borrowing. A card that you keep in the safe-deposit box is not going to show how financially responsible you are.

Apply for credit at only one place at a time. Use your first local credit card for four to six months, then apply at another local store. Wait at least two months more, and then apply for credit at a third local store. Then try for a national credit card.

If your history of using these cards is good, you will probably get national credit. Most national companies require consumers to have minimum annual incomes and to have held the same job for two years or show clear advancement in their employment over that period of time. They prefer applicants who have lived in the same area for years; own some kind of valuable property, especially a home; and can show a history of paying bills. No credit history at all is considered as bad as an unsatisfactory credit history.

If your credit card is lost or stolen, you must immediately notify the credit card company. The credit card company cannot recover charges made on the lost or stolen card above the amount of $50 or any charges at all that were made after you notified the company. The company must warn the consumer what his liability is, give him a postcard he can mail to it if the card is lost or stolen, and provide some way to identify the person using the charge card (such as a signature on the card).

When borrowing from a bank, you can get a passbook loan, where your savings account is pledged as collateral, or even a small signature loan, which has nothing but your signed name to back it up. A string of these loans can build a credit history to the point where a large amount of money may be borrowed for a good purpose. You may, just to establish a good credit history, borrow money, put it in a savings account, and pay it all back when the loan is due.

■ **Credit reports**   When a consumer applies for credit, most creditors routinely order a credit report on the applicant to see whether he is worth the risk. Files are kept by agencies known as credit bureaus and credit-reporting bureaus. Credit reports are used chiefly by merchants who need to decide whether to let customers buy on time. The reports generally disclose only financial information. They may give the location and size of an individual's bank accounts, his charge accounts and other debts, his bill-paying habits, income, occupation, marital status, and any lawsuits he is or has been involved in. Evidence of marital problems is sometimes included because divorce often causes financial havoc. Credit reports have been known to include nonfinancial information such as an applicant's IQ, high school attendance record, or sexual habits on the ground that this information reveals his character.

Credit agencies make this information available to subscribers who, in turn, supply them with additional information for their records. All information received is filed. Nonsubscribers can obtain the same information as subscribers by paying a higher fee.

Financial reports on individuals for purposes other than obtaining credit are prepared by credit-reporting bureaus. These reports are used by employers to evaluate job applicants, by insurance companies calculating the risk of someone who wants to buy a policy, and by landlords who want to avoid renting to tenants who will damage property, annoy neighbors, or carry on illegal activities. These bureaus collect information and file it away until it is requested.

Problems with credit reports   A congressional investigation found in 1967 that credit agencies maintained files on half the individuals in the country. Unfortunately, these files often contain inaccurate, misleading, or irrelevant information, and they are not kept private. One of the largest credit bureaus in the country admits to a 30-percent error rate. It is not unusual for credit bureaus to file information that is irrelevant to creditworthiness, such as filing the fact that someone is having an affair under the category "medical." The most common error is to confuse two people with the same or a similar name.

State laws   A number of states have tried to regulate credit agencies by statute, but the size of these bureaus makes federal regulation more appropriate. The Retail Credit Company of Atlanta, Georgia, for example, has more than 1,000 branch offices throughout the country.

Fair Credit Reporting Act   In 1970 Congress enacted the Fair Credit Reporting Act, which is Title VI of the Consumer Credit Protection Act. This law applies to businesses that regularly collect consumer credit information for other businesses, whether for a fee or as part of a cooperative exchange. Any report by a credit bureau (or credit-reporting bureau) is covered by this law if it concerns a consumer's "credit worthiness, credit standing, credit capacity, character, general reputation, personal characteristics, or mode of living," and if it is to be used to evaluate a consumer for (1) credit or insurance for personal, family, or household purposes; (2) employment; (3) licenses to operate certain businesses or to practice a profession; or (4) any other "legitimate business need."

Credit bureau regulations   Credit and credit-reporting bureaus must have standard procedures for checking the accuracy of information in their files and keeping it up to date. Information must not be more than seven years old unless it concerns bankruptcy; then the limit is 14 years. Any personal information concerning character, reputation, or life-style that is obtained through interviews with the consumer's friends or neighbors cannot be used unless it is rechecked every three months.

The most serious complaint against credit agencies is their uncontrolled invasion of individual privacy. The Fair Credit Act does not correct this problem. Nonfinancial information such as hair length, political beliefs, and sexual preference and behavior can be included as long as the information is accurate and up to date.

Those who use the credit reports must file a statement with the bureaus that certifies the purposes for which the reports will be used and that states they will not be used for any other purposes. It is illegal to use credit reports to satisfy your curiosity about a neighbor, investigate your daughter's fiancé, or embarrass an enemy.

Consumers' rights A consumer has the right not to have inaccurate or obsolete information kept in his or her files, to be notified each time a creditor relies on a credit report, to learn what kind of information is in the report, and, sometimes, to correct information in it.

A consumer does not have the right to see his file. But if he has been denied credit because of a report, he can find out the "nature and substance" of all information (except medical information) in the file, the source of the information (except interviews with neighbors and associates), and the name of anyone who has received the report for employment purposes during the last two years or for any other purpose during the last six months.

If the consumer finds inaccurate or misleading information in the report, he can ask the agency to reinvestigate. He can also file a brief statement, correcting wrong information or explaining the circumstances surrounding damaging information. The agency has the right to reduce this statement to 100 words but only if it provides trained personnel to work with the consumer. The agency must include the statement in the consumer's file and, if the consumer requests, send copies to all recent users of the report.

Enforcement Federal agencies such as the Federal Trade Commission can issue orders to enforce this law. Willful, intentional violations subject officers and employees of the credit or credit-reporting bureau to criminal prosecution, fines up to $1,000, and imprisonment up to one year. A consumer may sue a credit agency if it has failed to treat him according to the law. He must show that the agency or the business using the report failed to maintain reasonable procedures in order to obey the law, that this failure was negligent or careless, and that he suffered financial or personal harm as a result.

■ **Credit discrimination** The Equal Credit Opportunity Act, enacted in 1974 and amended in 1976, prohibits discrimination on the basis of the applicant's race, color, religion, national origin, sex, or marital status in any credit transaction.

Discrimination against women Hearings held by Congress in the 1970's showed that women were systematically denied credit, regardless of their ability to repay loans. There were five areas of particular difficulty:

(1) Single women had more trouble obtaining credit than single men, especially for home mortgages.

EXAMPLE One woman who earned a good income doing free-lance writing at home was shocked to find that creditors did not consider her a serious wage earner. Another professional woman who decided to buy a house when she was 42 years old had to get her 80-year-old father to cosign for the mortgage.

(2) Creditors generally required women (but not men) to reapply for credit when they married.

(3) Creditors were unwilling to extend credit to a married woman in her own name. Single women who had credit cards in their own names were told that when they married they could not use them until they transferred the accounts to their husband's name. This discrimination occurred even though marriage does not change the fact that a woman is as legally responsible for her debts as is a man.

(4) Women had great difficulty reestablishing credit when they were divorced or widowed. Women separated from their spouses found that only the husband got credit for a good history of paying bills. And he got to keep the charge accounts they had both used in his name.

Because credit is equivalent to opportunity, women and also their families were denied access to an improved standard of living.

(5) Creditors did not count all of a woman's income when figuring the creditworthiness of a married couple. Bankers refused to consider a married woman's income when a couple applied for a loan. Before a bank would grant a mortgage based on a couple's combined income, it often demanded a "baby letter" from a doctor, swearing that either the husband or wife was sterile. The assumption was that a working wife who became pregnant would quit her job and permit a foreclosure on her home rather than continuing to work after she gave birth.

More than half the states now have some sort of law prohibiting discrimination on the basis of sex or marital status, and the federal Equal Credit Opportunity Act is very specific in its prohibitions. Creditors may not (1) assign a value to gender or marital status in evaluating the creditworthiness of an applicant; (2) assign a value to having a telephone in the applicant's name (creditors used to think people with telephones were more stable, but they also were usually male); (3) inquire about a couple's plans to have children; (4) change the terms of credit when someone's marital status changes, or require a reapplication; (5) refuse to count the full income of an applicant or his spouse; (6) tell an applicant what name to use (a married woman may use her maiden name); (7) delay action on an application or refuse to consider it; (8) discourage someone from applying for credit.

Race and age discrimination Although sex discrimination was the original focus of the federal law, recent amendments have added race and age discrimination. The act says that a creditor can consider an applicant's age only when older people receive a preference or when a particular kind of credit is given to someone because he is elderly. The law also requires creditors to count public-assistance benefits as part of the applicant's income. A bank cannot refuse a mortgage on a house in a changing or black neighborhood because race is then the reason for the refusal.

■ **When credit is denied**   Never just shrug your shoulders if you are denied credit. Remember your rights under recent laws regulating credit bureaus and prohibiting discrimination. The decision to turn you down could have been based on mistaken or illegal information or on discriminatory criteria. If you are refused credit, always ask for a written reason. If the grounds are fair, you will know how to improve your credit history. If the grounds are illegally discriminatory, you have the right to complain or take other action. Sometimes you may find that what appears to be discrimination is, in fact, not.

EXAMPLE One professional woman in Washington was told 0⸺※ by a loan officer that his bank always required married women to have their husband cosign for loans. She pressed the bank for an explanation and found that all married borrowers, men and women, had to have their spouse's signature on auto loans if they had only the car itself to put up as collateral.

Federal agencies such as the Federal Trade Commission can prevent violations of the Equal Credit Opportunity Act by issuing restraining orders. The consumer cannot initiate the proceedings—the FTC must act. Consumers can, however, sue creditors who have refused them an equal opportunity to obtain credit. If a state law also prohibits discrimination, the consumer may choose to sue in either the state or the federal court.

■ **Usury**   Once you have been extended credit you should make sure that the interest that is to be charged for your use of credit is not above the amount allowed by law. Charging interest that is higher than the law allows is USURY. Laws prohibiting usury govern most consumer-credit transactions. Three things must be shown to prove usury: (1) a loan or a willingness to wait for payment that is due; (2) charging more than the maximum amount of interest the law allows on such a loan; and (3) an intent to do this in spite of the law.

Intent   Whether or not an intent of usury exists depends on the evidence. If it is clear from the agreement that the amount of interest to be paid is more than the legal rate, the law will assume that the lender intended to take advantage of the borrower's need for cash. However, some courts have refused to punish a lender who intended to charge the high rate but who did not intend to violate the law—say he made an honest mistake in computing the interest—especially if he caused only slight harm to the borrower or if he refunded the excess as soon as the problem was discovered.

The legal rate   There are a number of different ways to compute interest, and lenders naturally look for the most profitable. For example, 8 percent interest on $100 is clearly $8 if the loan is repaid in one payment at the end of the year. But if the creditor subtracts his interest at the beginning and gives the borrower $92 when the loan is made, the interest is 8.70 percent and not 8 percent. This is so because although only $8 was paid in interest, the borrower is really paying the $8 on a $92 loan. If the interest is deducted at the beginning and the loan is repaid in 12 monthly installments, the interest actually paid is 15.68 percent. This is because by paying the full $8 interest at the beginning, receiving only $92 as in the previous example, plus paying back part of the loan each month, the borrower does not even get a year's use out of the $92 he borrowed!

Another problem in figuring the legal rate of interest is determining which expenses are part of the interest or the finance charges, which could include the interest on the unpaid balance, plus a fixed charge of say 50 cents per month. Usually the following are not considered part of the finance charges: (1) fees for filing or recording a document, for an appraisal, or for the cost of preparing documents; (2) closing costs in home purchases; (3) penalties for paying off the loan sooner than the lender expected when he figured interest over the whole term.

Borrowers must look to state law for relief from a usurious loan, unless the lender is a national bank. The penalties vary greatly from state to state. In many states the lender cannot receive any interest at all when the agreement provided for an illegal rate. In some he must give up several times the amount of interest he had tried to collect, but in others he forfeits only the excess above the legal rate. Several states permit the borrower to repay only a percentage of the amount borrowed and to pay no interest. Finally, quite a few states cancel the loan and allow the borrower to keep the principal.

Federal law controls usury by national banks. It enforces the rates set by the law of the state in which the bank is located but applies penalties provided by the National Banking Act, which requires the bank to give up all future interest on a usurious loan and to return to the borrower twice as much interest as it has collected.

credit bureau   A private business that collects information on the CREDIT history of individuals. It makes reports, based on this information, to stores and lending institutions that ask about the financial reliability of people.

credit line   The maximum amount of CREDIT given to a borrower, who draws on the funds as he needs them.

creditor   **1** One to whom a debt is owed because of a business or financial transaction.   **2** A person who has a legal right to demand and receive money, whether by contract or on account of some injury suffered because of another's careless or intentional wrong.   **3** One who is in the business of lending money or selling goods without demanding immediate payment.

A *judgment creditor* is one who has gone to court and won a JUDGMENT against the debtor. He can have the debtor's property seized and sold in order to pay the amount of the judgment. An *attachment creditor* is one who has secured a court order of attachment, which empowers the sheriff to seize the debtor's property pending the final judgment. See ATTACHMENT AND GARNISHMENT and Chart 9. A *secured creditor* is one who holds a special legal right in the debtor's property that helps assure, or secure, repayment. A creditor protected by a LIEN on an automobile or a MORTGAGE on a house, for example, is secured. See also SECURED TRANSACTION. A *single creditor* is one who has a lien on only one fund or account owned by the debtor. A *general creditor* or *creditor-at-large* is one who has neither a lien on nor a security interest in the debtor's property. He has a right to collect the debt but not a special right to recover through a particular item of property.

A *junior creditor* is one whose right to collect is secondary to someone else's right to collect from the same debtor. The one whose right is superior is called a *senior creditor*. It is important for creditors to fix priorities in case the debtor does not have enough assets to pay everyone. A *principal creditor* is one whose claim against the debtor is much larger than the debt owed to any other creditor.

Petitioning creditors are all the creditors of one debtor who petition the BANKRUPTCY court to collect the debtor's property and distribute it among them fairly. Together they authorize the payment of one attorney's fee.

A sale *in fraud of creditors* is an attempt to put the debtor's property beyond the reach of creditors.

EXAMPLE Debbie owes Susan $5,000. If Debbie does not O—* pay, Susan can by legal action seize enough of Debbie's property to satisfy the debt. If Debbie sells her property and puts the money in the bank, the money is still available to pay off the debt. But if she sells all of her property to her son-in-law for $12 and puts that in the bank, Susan has been cheated. The law says that this is no sale at all, and Susan can reach the property even though Debbie claims it is no longer hers.

creditor's suit   A lawsuit brought against a debtor who has not paid what he owes. It is a request to the court to order ways of satisfying a debt when normal procedures are not adequate.

EXAMPLE Brown, an actor who rents an apartment in O—* Green's house, maliciously cuts down a 200-year-old oak tree in the front yard, which is Green's pride and joy, because it is keeping the sunlight from his rented rooms. Green sues Brown and wins. Brown is ordered to pay Green $5,000 in damages. Brown does not pay promptly, so Green pays the sheriff a fee to seize Brown's property, sell it, and use the money to pay him. But it turns out that Brown has only $1,000 worth of property, so Green starts a creditor's suit, asking the court to authorize a way to reach money owed Brown from other people, such as royalties from television commercials.

Retirement annuity checks, corporate stock, growing crops, and a debt that someone else owes the defendant can all be subjected to creditors' suits. But a creditor's suit cannot be used to take away a liquor license, property in another state, or salary that is not yet earned.

credit union   An organization that collects money deposited by its members in order to make small, low-interest loans to members. Members must be part of a closed group—retired civil service employees, for instance, or teachers in a certain group of schools.

crime   An act or omission that is prohibited by law because it is harmful to the public. A crime is punished by the state, in its own name or in the name of the people, after the person who performed the offense is found guilty in a criminal proceeding. Crime, which implies serious wrongdoing, usually means either a FELONY or a MISDEMEANOR. A traffic violation, for example, is generally not a crime. See also CRIMINAL LAW.

criminal   1 A person who has committed a crime.   2 Something that has the character of a crime or pertains to or is connected with the law of crimes or the administration of penal justice.

criminal action   The procedure by which a person charged with a crime is accused, brought to trial, and judged. See CRIMINAL LAW.

criminal conversation   The tort (civil wrong) of seducing a wife, for which a husband can sue the seducer for money damages. Not every state allows such an action.

criminal forfeiture   The loss of property to the government because it was involved in a crime. For example, an automobile used in violation of the internal revenue laws to transport a bookmaker and his gambling records is subject to criminal forfeiture.

criminal law   The branch of the law that defines crimes and provides for their punishment. A *crime* is any act or omission that is prohibited by law because it is harmful to the public and that is punished by the state in a proceeding in its own name or in the name of the people. The words "crime," "offense," and "criminal offense" are used interchangeably.

The first half of this article discusses the basics of criminal law: the classification of crimes, powers of the state and federal governments, amendment and repeal of criminal statutes, the elements of a crime, attempt to commit a crime, parties to a crime, jurisdiction (authority) of criminal courts, venue (the place where a crime can be tried), time limits for prosecution, and double jeopardy. The second half of the article describes the procedures and rights involved in a criminal prosecution, including steps to be taken before a person can be brought to trial; the trial itself; and procedures that may follow the trial, including sentencing, parole, and appeals. For discussions of specific crimes, such as MURDER, RAPE, and ROBBERY, see those entries. For a discussion of the role of bail in criminal law, see BAIL.

■ **Classification**   Crimes are usually classified as either felonies or misdemeanors. The law also recognizes lesser offenses below the grade of misdemeanor, such as littering, which do not amount to crime, and which are punishable by minor penalties. Such lesser offenses are often called violations.

Crimes punishable by death or by imprisonment in a state penitentiary, with or without hard labor, are *felonies*. The maximum punishment that may be imposed is usually the decisive factor in determining whether a crime is a felony or a misdemeanor. This is true even though the court or jury may have the discretion to reduce the punishment for a felony to imprisonment in a local jail or to a fine.

Crimes that are not felonies are misdemeanors. Under most state statutes, misdemeanors include all offenses for which a punishment other than death or imprisonment in the state prison is prescribed by law. Misdemeanors are usually punishable by fines or imprisonment in a county jail, or both.

Mala in se and mala prohibita   Offenses *mala in se* are acts that are in themselves immoral or wrong—such as murder, rape, arson, and burglary. Offenses *mala prohibita*

SOME BASIC FACTS ABOUT CRIMINAL LAW AND PROCEDURE

■ Crimes are grouped under two classifications: felonies and misdemeanors. Misdemeanors include all offenses for which a punishment other than death or a term in the state prison is prescribed by law.

■ Misdemeanors are punishable by fines, by short terms of imprisonment in the county jail, or by both.

■ In order to be a crime, the act must usually be accompanied by general criminal intent—willfully and knowingly doing something that is wrong.

■ The accused must be shown to have the mental capacity to form a criminal intent—otherwise he cannot be held responsible.

■ Most states have juvenile court systems that handle cases involving children under 18. In these courts, juveniles are tried as delinquent children rather than as criminal defendants.

■ A person who is legally insane cannot be criminally responsible.

■ Generally, voluntary intoxication from drugs or alcohol is no defense, but involuntary intoxication is.

■ Protection against double jeopardy—being prosecuted twice for the same crime—is a constitutional guarantee, but there are situations in which a person may legally be put in jeopardy twice. For example, if a person appeals his conviction and the appellate court sets it aside, he could then be prosecuted a second time for the same crime. Also, if a trial court grants a motion for a new trial, a convicted person may be tried again. Finally, if the court discharges the jury because it cannot reach a verdict or because a juror becomes ill, leaves without permission, or acts inappropriately, the accused may be tried a second time.

■ The first step in a criminal prosecution is a *complaint,* or *pleading,* which shows the charge. The complaint serves to advise the accused of the charge and enables the magistrate to decide whether or not the accused should stand trial.

■ Generally a warrant is necessary to arrest a person who is accused of a crime. It must give the accused's name—or, if unknown, it must describe him—and state the charge. A policeman can make a warrantless arrest for certain misdemeanors not committed in his presence when there is probable cause to believe the person arrested committed the crime—shoplifting, for example. He can make such an arrest in a public place—in a store or on the street—but he must obtain a warrant to arrest a person in his home.

■ A police officer may legally stop any person on foot or in a vehicle for investigation when he believes that a crime may be or has been committed.

■ Any person taken into custody must be warned, before questioning begins, (1) that he has a right to remain silent; (2) that any statement may be used against him; (3) that he has a right to the presence of an attorney; and (4) that if he cannot afford a lawyer, one will be appointed for him before any questioning takes place, if he so desires. (The foregoing is known as the Miranda rule.)

■ After the person accused of the crime is arrested, he is given a preliminary hearing before a judge or magistrate or brought before a grand jury or both. The main purpose of these proceedings is to determine whether an offense was committed and whether there is probable cause to believe the person accused committed it.

■ If probable cause is discovered, the accused person will be indicted and arraigned.

■ The accused person is arraigned when he is called to the bar of the court to answer the accusation and plead either guilty, nolo contendere (no contest), or not guilty.

■ If a defendant pleads guilty, he waives his right to a trial and submits himself to sentencing by the judge.

■ The plea of nolo contendere (no contest) is an implied confession of guilt and the equivalent of a guilty plea. However, it leaves the defendant free to deny his guilt at any subsequent proceedings; the plea cannot be used against him.

■ When a defendant pleads not guilty to a criminal charge, the judge will set a date for the trial.

■ The right to a speedy trial is guaranteed by the Constitution. When the court decides that that right has been denied, the charges against the defendant will be completely dismissed.

■ The defendant has the constitutional right to a public trial.

■ The right to trial by jury applies only to serious crimes, not to petty offenses. At the trial, the prosecution must establish the guilt of the accused person beyond a reasonable doubt. It does so by presenting evidence—that is, by presenting documents and exhibits and examining witnesses.

■ The accused person, in turn, presents evidence to refute the prosecution and to show his innocence. He also cross-examines the witnesses for the prosecution.

■ Besides denying that he committed the act, the accused person may also claim certain defenses that free him from blame in committing it. For example, self-defense is a good defense against a charge of murder.

■ Once all the evidence has been submitted and the prosecuting and defense attorneys have made final statements summing up their cases, the jury deliberates and gives its verdict.

■ If the jury's verdict is guilty, the defendant is convicted and the judge will sentence him. In some states the jury may recommend or even determine punishment, but the judge always pronounces the sentence.

■ A motion may be brought to set aside the judgment—this may happen if important facts were kept out of the trial by fraud, duress, or mistake. These must be facts that would either have changed the outcome of the trial or have cast the defendant in a better light. If the motion is granted, a new trial is usually ordered.

■ There is no constitutional right to appeal every criminal conviction. A prisoner who believes he is being illegally held can always test the legality of his detention by petitioning for a writ of habeas corpus—the most basic right guaranteed by the Constitution—which orders the person holding the prisoner to produce him in court and justify depriving him of his liberty.

are acts that are wrong only because they are prohibited by law because they infringe on the rights of others—speeding and parking violations, for example.

Merger of offenses   At COMMON LAW—the law that exists, in the absence of written statutes, in the form of custom and court decisions—when the same criminal act includes both a misdemeanor and a felony, the misdemeanor is merged into the felony, and only the felony is punishable. For example, the lesser crime of assault with intent to commit rape is a necessary element of the greater crime of rape, and the two crimes merge when a conviction for rape is reached. In many states the common-law rule of merger has been greatly modified by statute, and in some it has been abolished.

■ **Power to define and punish**   Congress derives its powers to define and punish crimes from the U.S. Constitution, but it may exercise these powers only to accomplish the objectives of the government. It cannot, therefore, pass laws that make an act criminal unless that act harms the public. Congress is generally limited to defining as crimes only acts that affect more than one state or that affect federal property or the federal government itself. For example, it can make laws forbidding certain acts in interstate commerce, such as the transportation of pornography across state lines or gambling or loan sharking that crosses state borders, or it can prohibit bribes to federal government officials or destruction of federal government property.

State legislatures also have the power to define and punish crimes, providing they do not violate the restrictions of the federal constitution or their own respective constitutions. Generally, state legislatures are limited to defining as crimes only acts that affect the particular state and not those that affect other states or the nation as a whole. For example, a state may make the sale of alcoholic beverages illegal within its own borders, but it cannot make it illegal in a neighboring state. In addition to defining crimes, a legislature may declare an act to be a crime that previously was not a crime. A criminal statute passed by a legislature must have some relationship to the welfare and safety of society and must be based on reasonable grounds. Like Congress, a legislature cannot make criminal an act that is by nature innocent. For example, although idleness may be a source of crime, it is not proper for a legislature to make it a crime without some qualifications. Loitering in itself is not an offense, but loitering by a school without a legitimate reason may be made illegal.

Municipalities may define and punish crimes and violations only to the extent that the power is given to them by the legislature. When, for example, a municipality has been given the authority to prohibit disorderly conduct, it can define what constitutes disorderly conduct.

■ **Prohibition by law**   Unless an act or omission is prohibited and punishable under the common law, a federal or state statute, or a municipal ordinance, it cannot be punished as a crime.

Certainty and clarity   Statutes creating criminal offenses should be clear and unambiguous so that both citizens and the courts have a similar understanding of their requirements. A penal statute should also explicitly establish the elements of the crime and provide some reasonable standards for establishing guilt.

The statute must show what the legislature intended to prohibit and punish; otherwise it will be void for uncertainty. The measuring stick in deciding whether a statute is sufficiently certain, or definite, is the person of ordinary intelligence—that is, if a statute fails to give a person of ordinary intelligence fair notice that his intended conduct is forbidden, the law is indefinite and void. This principle is based on the belief that no person should be held criminally responsible for conduct he could not reasonably understand to be forbidden.

Amendment of statutes   In the past, the amendment of a criminal statute usually did not affect the prosecution or punishment of a crime committed before the amendment became effective; the original statute remained in force. In modern practice, however, if a criminal statute is made less harsh than it was when the crime was committed, the courts have in many instances applied the newer and less harsh provisions. For instance, in many states laws making the use of marijuana a lesser crime have been applied to persons who violated the harsher, earlier laws. If an amendment to a statute makes the penalties harsher than they were when the crime was committed, the court must apply the lighter penalties. Applying harsher provisions that did not exist at the time of the crime is considered to be the same as punishing a person for actions that were not criminal when they were committed—a violation of the Constitution's provision barring EX POST FACTO laws.

Repeal of statutes   A criminal statute remains in effect until the legislature passes a law repealing it, even though the authorities fail to prosecute and convict those who violate the statute.

When a statute is repealed, the punishment provided under it cannot be enforced nor can a pending proceeding be prosecuted further, even when the accused pleads guilty, because a court cannot inflict punishment under a nonexisting statute. The repeal of a criminal statute after a conviction, or while an appeal from the conviction is pending, requires that the conviction be set aside. But a repeal after a final judgment of conviction on appeal does not require a reversal of the judgment.

■ **Elements of a crime**   A crime cannot be committed unless all of its elements have been fulfilled. Elements are the conditions that make an act a crime. Every law is made up of certain elements. For example, ROBBERY is generally defined by state laws as the taking of goods or money from someone's person by force or intimidation. The elements of robbery, then, include (1) the taking of goods from someone's person, (2) the use of force, and (3) the lack of consent of the person from whom the goods or money is taken. If someone picks your pocket without your knowing it, he has not committed the crime of robbery because he did not use force or intimidation, which is one of the elements of robbery. He is probably guilty of LARCENY, however, as the elements of larceny do not include the use of force or intimidation. Similarly, the crime of RAPE is unlawful sexual intercourse with a woman without her consent. Lack of consent is one of the elements of rape. Consequently, if the woman consents, even though she does so reluctantly, the act cannot be rape.

Committing a wrongful act is not necessarily a crime in itself, even when all the elements specified in a criminal statute are fulfilled. According to the law, a crime consists not only of the overt act—pointing a gun at someone to force him to give you his money—but also of an intent to commit a crime. Criminal intent is an element of most crimes, even when it is not specifically indicated in the statute defining the crime. Furthermore, a person cannot be convicted of a crime if he does not have the legal capacity to do so—for example, because he is a child or is insane.

Criminal intent   In order to be a crime, the act must usually be accompanied by a criminal intent—that is, an intent to do, knowingly and willfully, an act prohibited by law on pain of punishment. Such an intent is called a *general criminal intent.* Under the law, negligent or reckless conduct is equivalent to a general criminal intent.

Guilty knowledge   The term "knowingly" implies that the accused person was aware that he could not lawfully do the act with which he is charged. To act knowingly means to act voluntarily and purposely and not because of mistake, inadvertence, or some other innocent reason. Without such guilty knowledge, general criminal intent cannot exist.

Intent and knowledge eliminated by statute   A legislature may make an act a crime without regard to the intent or knowledge of the person doing the act. If the statute is silent on the subject, knowledge and criminal intent are generally essential if the crime is inherently immoral, as are murder or arson. On the other hand, if the offense is wrong only because a law prohibits it, intent and knowledge are not elements of the crime. Statutes not requiring knowledge and intent are generally those having to do with illegal sales of liquor, violations of antinarcotic acts, criminal nuisances, motor-vehicle laws, and violations of regulations passed for the safety, health, or well-being of the community.

Motive   Motive is the cause that induced a person to commit a crime. It should not be confused with intent. Motive is not an essential element of a crime. The most praiseworthy motive is no defense when a crime is committed, nor does an evil motive in itself make an act criminal.

Proof of a motive is not essential to a conviction. Motive is unimportant when the guilt of the accused person is clearly established, but proof of a motive may be relevant when guilt is not clearly established, and in such cases may be of great importance in determining whether the accused committed the crime. The existence of a motive tends to prove guilt, while the absence of proof of a motive indicates innocence. When reliance is placed entirely on circumstantial evidence to establish a crime and the evidence establishes a strong lack of a motive, this is considered a powerful circumstance tending to clear an accused person.

Malice   Malice is a state of mind that prompts a person to do great bodily harm to another person without just cause. "Malice" is a word commonly used in connection with murder and is synonymous with criminal intent.

Presumption of intention   The intent to commit a crime may be inferred from established facts. For example, if a person is friendly with known criminals, accepts employment from them, aids them in their plans, secretly receives stolen money from them, and offers no reasonable explanation of his conduct, then guilty knowledge may be inferred from his actions.

A general criminal intent may be presumed from the commission of a criminal act. For instance, proof that the owner of a mortgaged automobile sold the car without paying off the mortgage creates a presumption that the automobile owner intended to defraud the lender or mortgagee. He can rebut this presumption by introducing evidence showing that he did not have a criminal intent.

The accused person, if sane, is presumed to have intended the natural and probable consequences of his unlawful acts. For example, if a person maliciously puts poison into a sack of flour expecting the flour to be baked into bread and eaten, he is conclusively presumed to have intended the death of anyone who eats the bread.

The rule of consequences holds true in all criminal cases. Moreover, a person may also be criminally liable for the natural consequences of his unlawful acts, even though the consequences were unintended. When done with criminal intent, an act directed against one person is equally criminal when it affects another.

EXAMPLE A bank robber unintentionally shoots and kills a teller instead of the bank guard who is shooting at him. In the eyes of the law, the death of the teller followed as a natural consequence of the unlawful act of shooting at the guard, and the robber is criminally responsible for it.

Specific intent   A specific criminal intent is a required element of some crimes. A specific criminal intent, unlike a general criminal intent, cannot be presumed from an unlawful act. It must be proved as an independent fact. The specific intent must exist at the time the crime is committed.

EXAMPLE In most states burglary is the crime of breaking and entering into another person's home with the specific intent of committing a felony—such as murder, rape, or robbery—while in the house. This means that the burglar must have intended to commit the felony at the time of breaking and entering in order to be convicted.

Capacity to commit a crime   The mental and legal capacity to commit a crime is an essential element of responsibility for it. There is no crime without a criminal intent and there can be no criminal intent without the mental capacity for it.

Age   A child under a certain age (called an INFANT in lawyers' language) cannot be held criminally responsible for his actions until he is old enough and sufficiently intelligent to form the necessary criminal intent. The child must be able to understand what he is doing and whether it is right or wrong. For example, a child who takes money from his teacher's desk must know that he is taking someone else's money and that taking the money is wrong.

At common law a child under seven years is conclusively presumed to be incapable of committing a crime. Between the ages of 7 and 14 a child is also presumed to be incapable of committing a crime, but the presumption is rebuttable. The state must overcome the presumption by introducing evidence to prove that the child knew what he was doing and knew that what he was doing was wrong.

EXAMPLE Jimmy, a 13-year-old, has been accused in the mugging and brutal beating of an 84-year-old woman. From the time he was nine, Jimmy had been in various juvenile detention centers for such acts as assault, robbery, and possession of a deadly weapon. Psychiatrists who examined and tested the child over the years agreed that Jimmy was an extremely bright child who knew that what he was doing was wrong but was also smart enough to realize that, as a minor, the legal consequences of his acts would be minimal. The state may use the testimony of such psychiatrists to rebut the presumption that Jimmy is incapable of committing a crime.

A child beyond the age of 14 is presumed to be capable of committing a crime, and if accused he has the burden of overcoming this presumption by showing either mental or physical incapacity.

These common-law rules remain the law in most states today, but they are not as important as they once were because of JUVENILE COURT systems. Practically all states now have courts with the authority to hear criminal matters involving juveniles under 18. Most juveniles are tried in these courts as delinquent children rather than criminal defendants, thereby making the defense of infancy (under-age) irrelevant in most cases.

Insanity A person suffering from insanity in the legal sense of the word cannot form criminal intent and cannot be held criminally responsible for his acts. See INSANE PERSONS. When a particularly brutal murder occurs, the ordinary person often concludes that the murderer is insane because a sane person does not commit such acts. Although this may be true psychologically, insanity in criminal law is a concept used to identify guilty persons for whom criminal punishments are inappropriate. If the law were otherwise, a murderer could use insanity as a successful defense simply by acting in a brutal or senseless manner.

There are a number of legal tests used to determine the sanity of a criminal defendant. The one used most often is the M'Naghten Right-Wrong Test, established in 1843 by an English court in the M'Naghten case.

EXAMPLE Daniel M'Naghten had an insane delusion that the prime minister was trying to kill him. Believing the prime minister's private secretary to be the prime minister, M'Naghten murdered the secretary. He was tried on a charge of murder and acquitted because of insanity.

Under the test of insanity established in the M'Naghten case, a defendant must be affected by a disease, such as insane delusions of the mind, at the time he commits the act. The disease must cause his ability to reason to become so defective that either he does not know the nature and quality of his act or, if he knows the nature and quality of the act, he does not know the act is wrong. The term "nature and quality" has been interpreted as the physical consequences of the act. For example, a man who squeezes his wife's neck believing he is squeezing lemons does not know the nature and quality of his act.

An *insane delusion* is a belief that something is true or exists that a sane person would not believe. When the M'Naghten rule is applied, a defendant who was suffering from an insane delusion at the time of the crime is treated as though things were just as he perceived them. For example, Bruce is under the delusion that Edwin is attempting to kill him, and Bruce kills Edwin. Bruce believes he is acting in self-defense and would be exempt from punishment under the M'Naghten rule.

A number of states that use the M'Naghten rule supplement it with the *irresistible-impulse* test, which provides that if the defendant is suffering from a mental disease that prevents him from controlling his conduct—even though he knows the difference between right and wrong—he may be found not guilty by reason of insanity.

EXAMPLE Rudy was charged with the murder of his daughter. During the trial expert testimony showed that although at the time of the murder Rudy could appreciate the difference between right and wrong, he had an irresistible impulse to kill his daughter because she had been convicted of prostitution. Rudy was acquitted of the crime, the reasoning being that a defendant cannot be found guilty of an act that he was impelled to do by an irresistible impulse.

Still another test was provided in 1962 by the American Law Institute's *Modern Penal Code* (MPC), which has been adopted by almost all the federal courts and by a few states. Under the MPC the test of insanity is as follows: (1) A person is not responsible for criminal conduct "if at the time of such conduct as a result of mental disease or defect he lacks substantial capacity either to appreciate the wrongfulness [criminality] of his conduct or to conform his conduct to the requirements of law. (2) The terms 'mental disease or defect' do not include an abnormality manifested only by repeated criminal or otherwise antisocial conduct."

The phrase "lacks substantial capacity" modifies M'Naghten and the irresistible-impulse test, both of which require a total lack of capacity. The MPC test also has a requirement of causality between the mental disease and the commission of the crime. A defense of insanity can be established not merely by proving the existence of a mental disease, but only by proving that as a result of the disease the defendant cannot be held responsible for the crime he is charged with. For example, kleptomania may be a defense to larceny, but not to rape.

Intoxication Generally, voluntary intoxication from drugs or alcohol is no defense to a criminal act, especially when a specific intent is not a necessary element, as in second-degree murder. Similarly, voluntary intoxication may prevent someone from forming a specific intent to kill with premeditation—a necessary element of first-degree murder in most states—so that a first-degree murder conviction might be reduced to second-degree murder.

EXAMPLE Hall was given a pill by a friend, who told him it would make him feel "groovy." When Hall later took the pill, it caused him to have hallucinations. He reported that a friend who had given him a ride home turned into a rabid dog, and so Hall shot him dead. The pill was discovered to be LSD. Hall was tried for first-degree murder, which in his state had to be premeditated. At the trial, Hall defended his case on the basis of temporary insanity caused by drug intoxication. The prosecution claimed that Hall had intended to kill the man for weeks because he had not repaid a $1,000 loan Hall had made to him. The court rejected Hall's defense, stating that the temporary mental condition caused by voluntarily taking alcohol or drugs does not constitute a complete defense. Hall's mental condition could have affected his intent and could be used as a ground for reducing the crime from first-degree murder to second-degree murder (for which premeditation is not a requirement), but it could not be used as a ground for acquittal. Hall's testimony showed that he intended to kill his victim. He did not take the pill by mistake, thinking it was candy. He chose to experiment by taking the pill and, therefore, he must accept the consequences.

When the offense must be combined with a specific intent, then evidence of intoxication, even though voluntary, may be introduced as a defense.

EXAMPLE Michael is charged with larceny, which requires a specific intent to steal. If at the time of the alleged act he was so drunk that he could not have had or could not have formed a specific intent to steal, Michael is not guilty of larceny because a necessary element of the crime does not exist.

Involuntary intoxication, on the other hand, may be used as a defense to the same extent as insanity. If the defendant's intoxicated condition caused the criminal act, the defendant will not be found guilty if an insane person would also be excused under the insanity test used in the jurisdiction. A person becomes involuntarily intoxicated when he is forced to take an intoxicating substance against his will or when he takes it by mistake, not realizing how the substance will affect him.

EXAMPLE Suppose Oscar drinks a glass of beer and becomes intoxicated because of a blood disease that he does not know he has and that causes one beer to make him thoroughly drunk. Thinking his wife, Hilda, is attacking him, Oscar cuts her throat and she bleeds to death. Because of his intoxication Oscar could not appreciate the criminality of his conduct or conform his conduct to the requirements of law when he committed the crime. If that is a valid defense for insanity in the jurisdiction, Oscar has a valid defense of involuntary intoxication.

■ **Attempt to commit a crime**   An attempt to commit a crime is an act done with intent to commit a crime—beyond mere preparation, but falling short of its actual commission. The law recognizes a distinction between an "intention" to commit a crime and an "attempt" to commit a crime. Intent is a mental quality that implies a purpose, while an attempt implies an effort to carry out that purpose.

As a general rule, an attempt to commit a crime is an offense that is separate and distinct from the crime itself. Ordinarily, it is a misdemeanor, whether the crime attempted is a felony or a misdemeanor. In some cases, however, the law may classify an attempt to commit a crime as a felony. For example, in some states attempted murder is a felony.

Elements   An attempt to commit a crime is made up of the following elements: (1) the specific intent to commit the crime, (2) the performance of some overt act toward the commission of the crime, and (3) the failure to consummate its commission.

The specific intent required is the intention to commit the particular crime that was attempted.

EXAMPLE A burglar enters a home and attempts to steal the coin collection of the owner, Calhoun. Awakened by the clink of coins, Calhoun gets his shotgun and starts downstairs. The burglar hears him coming, drops the coins, and rushes for the window by which he had entered. He and Calhoun meet at the window. Seeing the shotgun, the burglar becomes frightened, pushes Calhoun aside, and dives out the window. Calhoun loses his balance, trips over a chair, and the shotgun discharges and a pellet grazes his head. Later the burglar is captured and charged with attempted murder, among other crimes. Evidence shows that he was unarmed and did not intend to hurt anyone. The burglar cannot be convicted of attempted murder. He did not possess the specific intent to kill Calhoun, only the intent to steal the coin collection.

Similarly, negligent or reckless conduct may not be used to convict a person for an *attempt* to commit a crime, although it may be an element of an actual offense.

EXAMPLE You are hurrying to catch a plane and drive your car at 50 miles an hour through a stop sign. You did not intend to harm anyone by your reckless driving. Nevertheless, you strike a pedestrian, knocking him 30 feet in the air and almost killing him. Are you guilty of the attempted murder of the pedestrian? No. You did not intend to kill the pedestrian, so you cannot be guilty of attempted murder. If the pedestrian later dies from his injuries, however, you might be found guilty of reckless homicide.

The overt act must be more than mere preparation and move directly toward commission of the crime.

EXAMPLE Let us say that Leon is planning to burglarize his local savings bank. He rents the building next to the bank and begins to drill through the adjoining wall. Before he is able to break through, a passing policeman hears the noise, investigates, and arrests him. Leon is charged with attempted burglary and found guilty. His acts went beyond mere preparation to commit the crime. He rented the building and began to drill.

When the circumstances or the means used are absurd and totally insufficient to accomplish the intended crime, no attempt exists. For instance, a person purchases a soft rubber dagger at a toy store and then stabs someone in the back. Under the law, this act cannot be attempted murder. The person who bought the toy dagger could not have the necessary intent to kill.

Impossibility   The impossibility of committing the attempted crime is a defense in some instances. Impossibility may be either factual or legal. Factual impossibility occurs when some circumstance, unknown to the defendant or beyond his control, prevents him from committing the intended crime. Ordinarily, it is not a strong defense.

EXAMPLE Mitchell went to the window of the bedroom where he thought his intended victim, Warren, was sleeping. It was dark, and Mitchell fired his gun at Warren's bed, intending to murder him. Warren was not in bed, and no one was hurt. Mitchell was tried and convicted of attempted murder. Mitchell appealed his conviction on the ground that it was factually impossible to have killed Warren because he was not in his bed. Mitchell's conviction was affirmed. The court reasoned that Mitchell intended to murder Warren and did everything necessary to complete the crime. The fact that Warren was not in his bed did not make Mitchell's attack anything less than an attempt.

On the other hand, legal impossibility is usually a strong defense. Legal impossibility occurs when the intended act would not be a crime, even if it had been completed. In this situation the person thinks he is committing a criminal act, but the act is really lawful.

EXAMPLE Suppose a man plans to have forcible sexual relations with his sister-in-law. He sneaks into her dark bedroom to carry out his plan. In the process of completing the act, he discovers the woman he is raping is his wife. In this case everything the man was attempting to do was allowed by law. In most states, he would not be found guilty of raping his own wife.

■ **Parties to offenses** A person who commits a criminal offense or is involved in one in some affirmative way is a party to the offense. When the offense is a misdemeanor, all the parties are considered to be principals. When the offense is a felony, the participants are grouped into two general classes: principals and accessories. These classes are in turn subdivided into principals in the first and second degree and accessories before and after the fact.

Principals in the first degree A principal in the first degree is the person who commits the crime, whether a felony or misdemeanor. When two people are the perpetrators (doers) of a crime, each is a principal in the first degree. Someone can commit a crime as a principal without actually being present—for example, when he leaves poison in a sugar bowl for another person to take in his absence or when he obtains money under false pretenses by sending a letter through the mail.

Similarly, several persons may act together with a common intent and design to commit a crime. When each performs some part of the crime, each is guilty as a principal, even though all of them are not actually present when the act is finally completed. This rule has been applied, for instance, when several persons joined together to forge a document. Each person carried out a distinct part of the forgery, but they were not together when the document was completed.

Principals in the second degree A principal in the second degree is a person who is present when the crime is committed by another person. The principal in the second degree aids and abets in its commission, but he himself takes no part in it. He is also frequently called an aider and abettor. Aiding and abetting means to assist the perpetrator of the crime by acts or words of encouragement, incitement, or support.

EXAMPLE A businessman and his secretary are eating in a restaurant when a woman at a nearby table upsets the secretary by making an insulting remark about her dress. Unknown to the secretary, the woman is the businessman's ex-wife. He has been making large alimony payments to her for a number of years, and he would like to stop. During the meal the businessman encourages his secretary to use her steak knife on the insulting woman. After finishing her meal, the secretary gets up and stabs the ex-wife to death as the businessman calmly looks on. The businessman is a principal in the second degree.

A person's presence at the time and place may be actual or CONSTRUCTIVE—that is, interpreted by law as being present. A common example of constructive presence is the lookout who keeps watch at a distance from a felony in order to warn his friends of anyone coming.

Accessories before the fact An accessory before the fact is a person who has counseled, procured, or commanded the commission of a felony by another person, but who is absent at the time it is committed.

EXAMPLE Clara, who hates her wealthy husband, Jim, advises and urges Robert, Jim's hunting companion and Clara's lover, to shoot her husband on a hunting trip. She tells Robert that since accidents frequently occur on hunting trips he will never be charged with murder. The two men go hunting, and Robert shoots and kills Jim. A game warden witnesses the shooting and arrests Robert, who is charged with murder. Claiming that Clara planned the murder and urged him to do it, Robert confesses and is convicted. He is a principal in the first degree. Clara is an accessory before the fact.

Accessories after the fact An accessory after the fact is a person who, knowing that a felony has been committed, assists the felon. Knowledge that a felony has been committed is essential, as is the intent to help the felon escape detection and arrest.

EXAMPLE Phil drowns his wife in the bathtub. He then tells John, his neighbor and good friend, of the murder, about which John knew nothing until Phil told him. Phil wants the murder to look as if it were an accident and plans to put his wife's body in his swimming pool. He needs John's help to carry the body to the pool. John agrees to assist, and the two men drop the body into the pool. A neighbor sees them and calls the police. Phil is convicted of murder, and John is found guilty as an accessory after the fact.

■ **Jurisdiction of criminal courts** When applied to criminal courts, jurisdiction means the authority to inquire into facts, apply the law, and declare punishment for an offense in the regular course of a judicial proceeding. Criminal jurisdiction extends only to criminal matters.

Jurisdiction over the subject matter of the offense and over the person of the accused is necessary for a valid conviction.

EXAMPLE Fred lived and worked in Louisiana but failed to support his wife and children. After years of neglecting them, he took his family to Mississippi to live with his mother-in-law. He himself traveled around the country, working in various states. Later, while Fred was passing through Louisiana, a prosecution was filed against him for failure to support his minor children while he was working in Louisiana. Because Fred was in Louisiana when the prosecution was filed, the Louisiana court had jurisdiction over his person. The court also had jurisdiction over the offense because he failed to support his children while they were living in Louisiana.

Generally, when several courts have concurrent jurisdiction (jurisdiction over the same offense), the court that first obtains jurisdiction to prosecute retains it to the exclusion of the other courts. A person accused of a crime has no right to choose where he will be tried; this is usually a decision for the prosecuting authorities. Once the trial court has been designated, a prosecution for the same offense brought in another court should be dismissed. When, however, the first court that has jurisdiction voluntarily dismisses or abandons the prosecution, the second court regains its right to jurisdiction. A court's exclusive jurisdiction over the offense does not begin until jurisdiction over the person has been obtained—as by his arrest.

When someone is accused either of several offenses that can be tried by different courts within the same state or of offenses against the laws of different states, the court that first acquires jurisdiction over the offender is entitled to retain it exclusively until its duty is fully performed. This is a rule of *comity* (courtesy), necessary to prevent an undignified struggle for the person of the accused.

The court or state first acquiring jurisdiction may, however, waive its priority and surrender, or lend, the offender to another court or state. This situation occurs, for instance, when a person charged with a relatively minor crime in one state is wanted for a murder prosecution in another. Because the offender has no right to choose the jurisdiction in which he should be tried, he cannot complain or prevent the waiver. Generally, a court or state may lend an offender for trial without losing the right to have him returned for trial or punishment after judgment has been handed down by another tribunal.

Constitutional and statutory provisions   The jurisdiction of the criminal courts in all 50 states comes from state constitutions or statutes and must be exercised in accordance with them, as well as with existing and consistent common-law rules. The U.S. district courts have jurisdiction over all offenses against federal laws. Because the federal courts do not use the common law as a source of criminal jurisdiction, they can try and punish only those crimes specifically designated by Congress.

Federal and state offenses   Federal courts have exclusive jurisdiction over federal offenses, and state courts have exclusive jurisdiction over state offenses, but the same act may be a violation of both state and federal law. A state cannot punish crimes against the United States: The federal courts have exclusive jurisdiction in matters over which Congress has the exclusive power to legislate, such as the federal banking laws and the internal revenue laws.

Both state and federal courts may have concurrent jurisdiction over matters that are not within the exclusive powers of Congress. For example, the federal courts do not have exclusive jurisdiction over a prosecution for unlawful possession of opium. When the person charged appears to have obtained the opium from a local source who has no connection with importation from a foreign country, the offense can be dealt with under state narcotics statutes.

When a defendant has been brought before a state court, it may decide whether the offense violates state or federal law. This decision is subject to review by the U.S. Supreme Court. The rule of comity (courtesy) exists between federal and state courts, and when either can take jurisdiction, the one that first acquires it holds it exclusively.

Locality of offense   The courts of one state have no jurisdiction to enforce the criminal laws of another state, nor can one state punish crimes committed by its residents in another state or in a foreign country.

Generally, unless there is a statute to the contrary, a crime committed partly in one jurisdiction and partly in another is punishable only in the jurisdiction where the crime is completed. The exception to this rule occurs when the crime is a continuing one.

A felon may be *constructively present* in a jurisdiction if he is beyond the limits of a state but puts into operation a force that results in a crime within those state limits. If jurisdiction can be obtained over his person, he is liable to prosecution and punishment just as though he had been within the limits of the state when the crime was committed. When, for example, a person in state A causes a drug to be delivered within state B for the purpose of procuring an abortion, he may be prosecuted in state B for procuring an abortion. The court in state A, where the offense was started, may, however, have concurrent jurisdiction.

On the other hand, when a person shoots someone or commits some other act in state A that takes effect and causes death in state B, the general rule is that only the courts of state A have jurisdiction. The shot that caused the victim to die constitutes the offense; the place where the victim dies is not important. The law in regard to these situations is not uniform. When a statute in the state where the death occurs gives that state's courts jurisdiction over the homicide, the statute is decisive and its courts may take jurisdiction.

Mode   A court acquires jurisdiction to bring a person to trial by following the mode prescribed by law. Jurisdiction over the offense is acquired when the appropriate charge is filed in the court. Jurisdiction over the person is acquired when the person is arrested or voluntarily appears in court and submits himself to its authority.

A person accused of a crime against the laws of state Y may be in the custody of state Z, or out on bail for an offense against Z's laws, or an escapee from one of Z's prisons. None of these facts affects the courts of state Y when the accused is surrendered to its courts for trial of an offense over which it has jurisdiction.

Loss   Generally, once a court obtains jurisdiction over the person accused and over the offense, it retains it until the final disposition of the case. Some cases hold that the jurisdiction of a court continues until the judgment is satisfied—that is, until the person has served his sentence. After a person has served his full sentence and has been discharged, the court cannot recommit him. Any criminal action against the accused person ends when he dies.

■ **Venue**   Venue is defined as the locality, usually the county, where the offense can be tried. When the act is done in different counties, the general rule is that the offense is considered to be committed in the county in which it is completed.

A person accused of a crime against the United States is entitled to be tried in the state and federal district where the offense was committed. A federal offense committed in more than one district may be tried in any district in which it was begun, continued, or completed.

Change   Usually, only the person accused may obtain a change of venue, but a state may apply for it if that state has a law that authorizes it to do so. Unless a state constitutional provision or a statute provides otherwise, the person accused in a criminal case has no absolute right to a change of venue, which can be granted or refused at the court's discretion.

The general ground for a change of venue is the fact that a fair and impartial trial cannot be conducted in that county, perhaps because of local prejudice. The prejudice must be personally directed against the accused and extend throughout the county. Newspaper articles and other forms of publicity, such as television and radio broadcasts, are considered prejudicial only when they so arouse public hostility that they preclude a fair trial.

Threats of mob violence against the accused or his witnesses may be sufficient for a change of venue.

EXAMPLE When public sentiment against a black man 0⟶ charged with the rape of a young white girl was so great that the police considered it necessary to keep him in jail 90 miles away and to keep the courtroom heavily guarded during his trial, the court deemed that a change of venue was necessary.

When permitted by statute, the trial court may change the venue of a prosecution.

EXAMPLE A person was prosecuted for being an accessory 0⟶ to robbery. His case had been tried twice previously in the same county. The principal in the robbery had also been tried in that county. The trial court found that many people had attended the trials and that the wide publicity given to the cases prevented either side from receiving a fair trial in that county. State law permitted the trial court to change the venue in such a situation and the trial was moved to another county.

■ **Time limits for prosecutions** Time limitations on criminal actions are prescribed by statute and are considered a surrender of a state's right to prosecute. If there is no statute on the subject, there is no limitation on the time within which a particular criminal offense may be prosecuted. The purpose of time limitations is to bar prosecution on old and untrustworthy evidence and to end prosecutions for crimes after a reasonable time has elapsed and no further danger to society could be foreseen from the criminal activity. Statutes of limitations are liberally interpreted in favor of the person accused and against the prosecution. Courts do not look kindly upon prosecutions that have been long delayed.

States may have both general statutes of limitations and special limitation periods for particular crimes. When the two periods of limitation conflict, the special limitation period for a particular crime will be used.

EXAMPLE Say that a state had a general statute of limitations 0⟶ of five years for felonies and a special limitation of four years for daytime burglaries. If a prosecution is brought against a person for a daytime burglary that took place four and one-half years before the date of the start of the prosecution, the four-year limitation period would apply, rather than the longer five-year period, and the prosecution would be barred.

Generally, a statute of limitations begins from the time the offense is committed and not from the time the offense is discovered or the identity of the suspected offender becomes known. In homicide cases, the period of limitation runs from the victim's death, not from his wounding. In bigamy cases, the period runs from the date of the bigamous marriage, not from the subsequent cohabitation.

When the crime is a continuous one, it is the termination date or the date of the occurrence of the most recent act that governs the statute of limitations, and not the starting date.

EXAMPLE A building collapsed on one of its occupants, 0⟶ resulting in his death. The building was improperly designed, and in addition, it had been constructed in violation of the building code. A manslaughter prosecution based on the death of the occupant was brought against the architect. The architect claimed that because the prosecution had not been brought within two years

after the building was erected or the plans drawn, it was barred by a two-year statute of limitations. The court disagreed. The court reasoned that the building constituted a "public nuisance" that continued until the collapse occurred and the death resulted.

Usually, the running of a statute of limitations for criminal offenses may not be interrupted. Under various statutes, however, definite exceptions or conditions are provided that will toll (stop) their operation.

EXAMPLE A statute provided that all prosecutions for willful neglect to support a child born out of wedlock 0⟶ were to be brought within two years of the birth of the child. The statute also contained an exception. When the reputed father voluntarily contributed to the child's support or acknowledged his paternity in writing, the prosecution might be brought at any time within two years of the contribution or acknowledgment. A case was brought under the statute in which the child was four years old. The reputed father claimed that the prosecution was barred by the two-year statute of limitations. Evidence revealed, however, that he had visited the child when she was sick and in the hospital and had contributed $25 toward her expenses. The prosecution was brought within 10 months of the date of the contribution. The court held that the voluntary contribution brought the case within the exception contained in the statute and found the man guilty of willful neglect to support the child.

■ **Double jeopardy** The doctrine of double jeopardy holds that a person may not be tried or prosecuted a second time for the same offense. The word "jeopardy" means the danger of conviction and punishment faced by an accused person in a criminal action. Double jeopardy is considered to be a sacred principle of the criminal law—it does not apply to civil suits—and also a part of the universal law of reason, justice, and conscience.

The idea underlying the doctrine is that the state, with all its power and resources, should not be allowed to make repeated attempts to convict a person. No one should be subjected to the embarrassment, expense, and ordeal of repeated prosecutions. Nor should he be compelled to live in a continuing state of anxiety and insecurity over the possibility of repeated prosecutions. Moreover, repeated prosecutions increase the possibility that an innocent person may be found guilty.

Protection against double jeopardy is a constitutional guarantee. It is part of the Fifth Amendment to the U.S. Constitution, which states that no person shall "be subject for the same offense to be twice put in jeopardy of life or limb." This protection has been extended to the states through the due process clause of the 14th Amendment. See DUE PROCESS OF LAW.

When a person raises the defense of former jeopardy, it is necessary to determine if he has, in fact, been in jeopardy at a previous prosecution. This is not always easy to determine. In criminal proceedings, appearances in court may be classified into three categories: a preliminary hearing, an arraignment, and a trial. Jeopardy does not begin at a preliminary hearing. It ordinarily begins at an arraignment when the accused person pleads guilty or not guilty to a GRAND JURY indictment or an information (a formal, written accusation made by an authorized public official). On the other hand, a person is not placed in jeopardy when an indictment or information is so defective that it will not support a conviction or when the court does not have jurisdiction to try the case. For example, when some of the members of a grand jury are incompetent and its indictment is therefore declared invalid by the court, the indictment will not put the person accused in jeopardy and bar another prosecution. Also, when a court lacks jurisdiction because of improper venue or because it does not have the constitutional or statutory authority to try the case, its judgment is not a bar to another prosecution.

There are situations in which a person may legally be put in jeopardy twice. For example, someone who is convicted of a crime appeals his conviction, and the appellate court sets it aside. He could then be prosecuted a second time for the same crime. Similarly, if a trial court grants a motion for a new trial, a convicted person may be tried again. In a third situation, if the court discharges the jury because it cannot reach a verdict or because a juror becomes ill, leaves without permission, or acts inappropriately, the person accused may be tried a second time.

Determining the same offense   Several principles are used to decide whether the offense being tried is indeed the same as one for which the defendant was previously indicted. If under the first indictment the person accused could have been convicted of the same crime charged in the second indictment, then former jeopardy is available as a defense against the second indictment.

EXAMPLE   Green was tried for arson and murder. Under the
O⊶＊ court's instructions to the jury, Green could have been found guilty of first- or second-degree murder. He was found guilty of second-degree murder. He appealed and was given a new trial. Green, once again charged with first-degree murder, claimed that the double jeopardy rule barred another first-degree murder prosecution. The court agreed because the jury verdict had implicitly acquitted him of first-degree murder when it convicted him for second-degree murder. A second trial for first-degree murder would be a second jeopardy for the same offense.

If, however, all the facts are not in existence when the accused person is convicted of the lesser offense, then that conviction is not a prohibition against a later conviction of the greater offense.

EXAMPLE   Martin has an argument with his automobile me-
O⊶＊ chanic over the amount of his repair bill. The argument becomes heated, and Martin assaults and beats him. While the mechanic is still living, Martin is convicted of assaulting and battering him. Thereafter, as a result of the assault and battery, the mechanic dies. Martin is then charged with the murder of the mechanic. His conviction for assault and battery is no defense.

When the state has a choice of prosecuting either for a higher or lesser offense and it chooses to prosecute the lesser and the accused person is convicted, the conviction bars a later prosecution based on the higher offense.

EXAMPLE   A wife stabs her husband with a paring knife. The
O⊶＊ crime is complete and all the facts exist when the district attorney decides to prosecute the wife for assault and battery. He could have chosen to prosecute for assault and battery with a dangerous weapon or assault and battery with intent to kill. The wife is convicted. Later,

and on the basis of the same facts, the wife is charged with assault and battery with intent to kill. In this case, the trial on the lesser offense of assault and battery, which is included within the higher offense of assault and battery with intent to kill, places the wife in double jeopardy and bars a prosecution on the higher offense.

Dual sovereignty doctrine   An act denounced as a crime by both federal and state sovereignties is an offense against the peace and dignity of both and may be punished by each. A state prosecution that follows a federal prosecution for the same offense (and vice versa) does not violate the guarantee against double jeopardy. This is known as the dual sovereignty doctrine.

EXAMPLE   In 1968 a defendant was tried in a federal district
O⊶＊ court and found guilty of robbing a Tennessee bank in violation of federal law. In May 1969 he was indicted for the same robbery in a state court in violation of the criminal law of Tennessee. The defendant filed a motion to dismiss the state prosecution on the basis of double jeopardy. The motion was denied, and he was found guilty and sentenced to 30 years in prison.

Many states, however, have enacted laws prohibiting prosecution for the same criminal act that the federal government has already prosecuted. In addition, it has been the policy of the federal government since 1959 not to prosecute a person for the same criminal act for which he has been previously tried in a state court.

EXAMPLE   The doctrine of dual sovereignty was applied in
O⊶＊ April 1978 in the case of a New York City policeman who was acquitted under state law of the murder of a black college student. Despite the federal policy of not prosecuting a person for a crime for which a state court has already tried him, the policeman was subsequently charged under federal law with violating the civil rights of the dead student—a different offense but one arising from the same criminal act.

The dual sovereignty doctrine does not apply to state and municipal prosecutions because they are not separate sovereigns. Counties, cities, and other municipalities are political subdivisions of the state, which assist the state in carrying out its governmental functions. The same act, therefore, cannot constitute a crime against both a state and a city within that state. In one case, a defendant's conviction in a municipal court for drunken driving was a bar to subsequent prosecution on a state felony charge for the same action under the doctrine of double jeopardy.

Collateral estoppel doctrine   The defense of double jeopardy includes the doctrine of collateral estoppel. *Collateral estoppel* means that when a factual issue comes before the court and is resolved, the issue cannot come up again in another trial between the same parties. (In a criminal matter, the parties are the state or a subdivision of the state and the defendant.) A party claiming an estoppel has the burden of proving what issues were decided in his favor at his earlier trial. The doctrine is usually applied in favor of the defendant.

EXAMPLE   In one Missouri case, three or four armed men
O⊶＊ robbed six poker players in the home of one of the victims. The defendant was charged in separate counts with robbery of the six poker players. He was tried on one count and was acquitted because there was insufficient

evidence to identify him as one of the robbers. When he was brought to trial a second time for the robbery of another victim of the same crime, he filed a motion to dismiss based on his previous acquittal. The motion was overruled. This time, the identification evidence was stronger and the defendant was found guilty and sentenced to a 35-year term in the state penitentiary. He petitioned for a writ of habeas corpus. The U.S. Supreme Court, which finally agreed to hear the case, applied the federal rule of collateral estoppel, which is embodied in the Fifth Amendment guarantee against double jeopardy. Because the jury in the first trial could not find that the defendant was one of the robbers, he could not be retried for the same robbery of a different victim.

The concept of collateral estoppel does not apply in cases of dual sovereignty (when an offense violates both state and federal laws) because there are two different parties involved—the federal government and the state government.

Collateral estoppel may be used by the government in a civil proceeding that follows a criminal conviction, if the civil proceeding concerns matters distinctly put in issue and directly determined in the criminal prosecution.

EXAMPLE Lyman was found guilty of the crime of making O⊶⚹ false vouchers and conspiring to defraud the U.S. government. The government filed a civil suit against Lyman to recover damages for money paid to him under the false claims that were the subject of the criminal prosecution. Lyman denied submitting any false claims to the government. The government contended that Lyman was conclusively estopped from asserting the same defense he used in the criminal action. The court held that the conviction in the criminal case conclusively established the issues both in that case and in the subsequent civil action.

■ **Steps leading to a criminal trial** Before a person can be brought to trial on a criminal charge, certain steps must be taken to establish whether the crime charged has been committed and, if so, whether there is probable cause to believe that the person accused committed it. The steps leading to a criminal trial vary from state to state but they generally include the complaint, warrant, arrest, a preliminary hearing or grand jury hearing or both, and arraignment, at which time the accused person gives his plea.

Complaint After a crime has been committed there is usually an investigation by the police. The investigation eventually leads to a *complaint,* or *pleading,* a legal paper that shows the charge against the person accused. The purpose of a complaint is to advise the accused of the charge and to enable the magistrate to decide whether or not the accused should stand trial for the offense charged.

Generally, the complaint is necessary in order for the court to take jurisdiction and for the examining magistrate to hold a preliminary hearing. The complaint is made under oath before a magistrate or judge. The complainant may be a witness to the crime, a victim, or the police who are investigating the case, but must be a person who is competent to testify about the facts involved in the violation of the criminal law.

A complaint is not merely a formality but a safeguard of the rights of the accused. It must state facts showing probable cause for believing that the alleged offense has been committed by the person accused. *Probable cause* means that the facts would lead a reasonably prudent man to believe that the offense charged was committed by the accused. The complaint must state the essential elements of the offense so that a person of average intelligence could understand the nature of the charge against him. The name of the person accused of the alleged crime must appear in the complaint, if it is known. If it is not known, a fictitious name, such as John Doe, can be used, but the person charged with the offense must be described.

Warrant A warrant is a written order issued by the court in the name of the state. It is based on a complaint and is addressed to a police officer, sheriff, or constable, commanding him to arrest and return before the court the person named in it. Generally, a warrant is necessary to start a criminal prosecution. Like a complaint, a warrant must give the name of the person accused of the alleged crime or, if his name is unknown, it must describe him. It must also state the offense by name or describe it sufficiently to inform the person of the charge against him. The warrant must be signed by an authorized officer.

In some states in the case of minor offenses, such as assault and battery, a summons may be issued instead of a warrant. A summons notifies a person to appear in court on a certain day to answer a complaint that has been made against him.

When a complaint is given to a magistrate, he must examine under oath the informant or prosecutor and any witnesses who are produced in an effort to determine whether grounds for a warrant exist. A warrant should not be issued on mere suspicion or on evidence that does not show probable cause. The evidence, however, does not have to be so clear and convincing that it would be sufficient for a conviction.

Arrest An arrest is the taking of a person into custody for the purpose of detaining him to answer a criminal charge. The arrest may be made with or without a warrant. When an arrest is made with a warrant, the warrant must be properly authorized and the person making the arrest must have authority to act under the warrant.

Under the common law, a police officer may arrest any person described in a warrant, whether the crime is a felony or misdemeanor. Without a warrant, he may arrest anyone who he has probable cause to believe committed a felony. However, he must get a warrant to arrest a person in his home unless the felony was committed in his presence or there is some emergency situation justifying a warrantless arrest—such as the officer's spotting and chasing a suspect wanted on an all-points bulletin. He may arrest a person for a misdemeanor without a warrant only when the offense amounts to a BREACH OF THE PEACE and is committed in the officer's presence.

Under the common law, a private citizen may make an arrest only when a felony is committed and there is probable cause to believe the person arrested committed it or when a misdemeanor amounting to a breach of the peace is committed in his presence by the person arrested.

Most states have passed statutes that modify the common-law rules of arrest. Generally, a police officer is now permitted to make a warrantless arrest for certain misdemeanors not committed in his presence when there is probable cause—for shoplifting, for example, as long as the arrest is made in a street or public place. Similarly, most states have statutes that permit private citizens to make an arrest for any offense committed in their presence.

Use of force Generally, either a police officer or a private citizen is permitted to use reasonable force in making an arrest. Under the common law, deadly force was not to be used to arrest a person fleeing from an arrest for a misdemeanor. It was permissible, however, to kill a fleeing felon, because all felonies were punishable by death. Today most felonies are not punishable by death, and the common-law rule permitting the use of deadly force against a fleeing felon is undergoing change. For further discussion on the use of force, see ARREST; ASSAULT AND BATTERY.

Resistance At common law a person was permitted to use reasonable—that is, nondeadly—force to resist an unlawful arrest by a police officer. Today, however, many courts have decided to the contrary.

Stop and frisk A person may be detained by the police without being arrested. A police officer may legally stop any person on foot or in a vehicle for investigation when he believes that a crime may be or has been committed. The officer must believe that the person he stops has committed or will commit a crime or has information relating to a crime committed by another person. He must have reasonable ground for his belief, and there must be an absolute necessity for immediate investigatory action.

A person stopped for such an investigation may be patted down, or frisked, in order to expose concealed weapons. The purpose of the "stop and frisk" procedure is to insure that the investigation can be completed without risk of harm to the police or nearby citizens. See also ARREST; SEARCH AND SEIZURE.

Miranda rule After a person is taken into custody or deprived of his freedom in any significant way, and before any questioning by law-enforcement officers begins, the person must be warned that (1) he has a right to remain silent; (2) any statement he does make may be used as evidence against him; (3) he has a right to the presence of an attorney; and (4) if he cannot afford an attorney, one will be appointed for him before any questioning takes place, if he so desires.

These warnings—called the MIRANDA WARNINGS because they were formulated in the case of *Miranda* v. *Arizona*—are designed to protect the privilege against SELF-INCRIMINATION. In order for evidence obtained during the interrogation to be used against the person accused, it must be demonstrated at the trial that the Miranda warnings were given to the defendant or that he waived the right to use them. His waiver must have been made voluntarily and knowingly. The prosecution has the burden of proving the waiver beyond a reasonable doubt.

Preliminary hearing and grand jury Before a person who has been accused of a serious crime can be brought to trial, he must first be given a preliminary hearing or be brought before a grand jury or both. A *preliminary hearing* is provided to a person accused of a felony or arrested without a warrant for a misdemeanor. The hearing is usually held before a magistrate or municipal court judge and serves as a screening process to prevent hasty, malicious, and oppressive prosecutions. It also protects the person

charged from a formal accusation of a crime and in many cases saves the time and expense of an unnecessary trial. A person charged with a crime has the right to have an attorney at a preliminary hearing and to cross-examine the witnesses.

The preliminary hearing may serve as an informal DISCOVERY device by which the defense can find out the extent of the evidence and the witnesses that the prosecution has. Its main purpose, however, is not discovery but to determine whether an offense was committed and whether there is probable cause to believe the accused committed it.

EXAMPLE A man named Rideout and others were accused of transporting marijuana. At the preliminary hearing a police officer, the state's only witness, testified that while making a legal search of a car he found a "crutch" on the floor in front of the back seat. (A crutch is a device used to hold marijuana cigarettes.) The officer then found marijuana in an ordinary cigarette package behind the back seat. Rideout filed a petition with the court to prohibit the prosecution on the ground that there was no probable cause to support the accusation. The magistrate found probable cause and held the defendants to answer for the crime.

Rideout and the other occupants of the back seat claimed the evidence was insufficient to find probable cause that they unlawfully transported marijuana, and they appealed the magistrate's finding. The appellate court agreed with the magistrate, pointing out that evidence in a preliminary hearing does not have to be sufficient to support a conviction. Probable cause is shown when a man of ordinary prudence believes or strongly suspects that the person accused may be guilty.

If the magistrate or judge finds that there is no probable cause for believing that the accused person has committed a crime, the charge is dismissed, although it can be brought again at a later date, as a preliminary hearing is not a trial and does not put the accused person in double jeopardy. If the magistrate or judge finds that there is probable cause for believing that the accused person has committed a crime, the case will probably be presented to a GRAND JURY.

A *grand jury* is a group of people summoned by a court to hear preliminary evidence and decide whether or not formal charges (an indictment) should be made against the accused person. The U.S. Constitution guarantees a grand jury hearing to all persons accused of a federal crime. In addition, many states use grand juries for felony cases. A grand jury hears evidence and examines evidence, but the accused person generally has no right to have an attorney present or to cross-examine witnesses. If a grand jury finds that there is enough evidence to warrant a trial, the accused person is indicted and will ultimately be brought to trial. If the grand jury decides that there is not enough evidence to warrant a trial, the case is dismissed, but the person can later be brought before another grand jury for the same crime if new evidence is discovered.

In some states a case can be brought before a grand jury without a preliminary hearing. A preliminary hearing is not required after a grand jury has returned an indictment, which is the equivalent of probable cause. In states that have no grand jury system, a person can be brought to trial on the finding of a preliminary hearing alone. In other states, both a preliminary hearing and a grand jury indictment may be necessary.

In most states, neither a grand jury nor a preliminary hearing is required in misdemeanor cases because the penalties involved are minor.

When a defendant enters a plea of guilty, grand jury and preliminary hearings are automatically waived because there is no need to determine probable cause.

Arraignment and plea An accused person is arraigned when he is called to the bar of the court to answer the accusation in the indictment. The objective of the arraignment is to establish the identity of the accused person, inform him of the charge, and obtain his plea. The person accused must be arraigned promptly after the indictment has been filed against him. Arraignment is a critical stage of a criminal proceeding, and the defendant is entitled to be represented by counsel (a lawyer). Before a plea is entered, the court must inform the defendant of his right to counsel. See COUNSEL, RIGHT TO. The three pleas available to a defendant are: guilty, *nolo contendere* (no contest), and not guilty.

Guilty pleas A guilty plea must be made voluntarily and knowingly, and the court record must specifically show this. The defendant must understand the meaning of the charge, the elements of the crime, and the consequences of pleading guilty. When a defendant pleads guilty, he waives his right to a jury trial and submits himself to sentencing by the judge. The judge will either give the sentence immediately or set a date for sentencing.

EXAMPLE A defendant named Brady was charged with kidnapping under a federal statute, which provided that when a defendant decided on a jury trial, he faced the death penalty if the jury recommended it. The statute called for a lesser penalty, however, after a trial before a judge without a jury or after a plea of guilty. Brady originally pleaded not guilty. After learning his codefendant had confessed and could testify against him, Brady changed his plea to guilty and was imprisoned. While he was imprisoned, the kidnapping statute was held unconstitutional because the constitutional right to a jury trial cannot carry with it the possibility of a death sentence when a trial without a jury does not.

When Brady learned that the kidnapping statute had been held unconstitutional, he sought his release. He claimed his guilty plea was not voluntary because the possibility of a death sentence after a jury trial forced him to plead guilty. The court disagreed. The court stated that Brady's plea of guilty waived his rights to a jury trial.

A defendant is not entitled to withdraw his plea at a later time because he was mistaken about a relevant fact, the strength of the case against him, or the probable penalties resulting from different courses of action. For example, a guilty plea, as in Brady's case, is not invalid just because a defendant accepts the probability of a lesser punishment rather than face a possible higher penalty.

Before a guilty plea is entered by the defendant, his attorney will usually meet with the prosecuting attorney in order to strike some bargain concerning the plea. Ordinarily, the plea-bargaining process results in a guilty plea to a lesser included offense. For example, robbery (the crime of taking goods or money by force or intimidation) includes the offense of larceny (taking personal property with intent to steal). A defendant accused of robbery might agree to plead guilty to larceny rather than stand trial for the more serious crime of robbery. The process of plea bargaining has been criticized both because serious offenses are often treated with inappropriate leniency and because an innocent person might be induced by an offer of leniency to plead guilty to a crime he did not commit.

The approval and supervision of a judge are necessary to avoid abuse and injustice in the plea-bargaining process. The court is duty bound to address the defendant personally to be sure that he has made the plea voluntarily and understands the charge and the consequence of the plea.

Nolo contendere A plea of *nolo contendere* is not, strictly speaking, a plea, but a formal declaration by the accused that he will not contest the charge against him. It must be entered knowingly, voluntarily, and intelligently, and the person accused should be represented by counsel. The plea of *nolo contendere* is not available to the accused as a matter of right. It is allowed only at the court's discretion. The court may ask the accused why he wishes to plead *nolo contendere* and may ask the prosecutor if he has any information the court should have in deciding to accept the plea.

The plea of *nolo contendere* is an implied confession of guilt and the equivalent of a guilty plea. But unlike a guilty plea, it has no effect beyond the particular case. The defendant can deny his guilt at a later proceeding, and the plea cannot be used against him as an admission of liability (responsibility) in a civil suit for the same act. Similarly, the plea may not be used to affect civil rights or to bring about civil disqualification.

EXAMPLE Swift was accused of driving a car under the influence of intoxicating liquors. He entered a plea of *nolo contendere* based on an agreement that the prosecutor would recommend that he be permitted to pay a fine. The court allowed the plea, ordered Swift to pay a fine of $300, and suspended his license for 60 days. When Swift appealed the suspension of his license, the appellate court held that the suspension of the driver's license was a civil disqualification and it reversed the decision of the trial court to suspend Swift's license.

The fact that the court accepts the plea of *nolo contendere* does not reduce its power to impose the maximum penalty for the offense. The court may hear evidence for the sole purpose of fixing punishment. If, after taking the evidence, it appears the defendant is not guilty, the court should advise him to withdraw his plea and to stand trial.

The plea of *nolo contendere* has been accepted by federal and state courts for most types of crimes, even when the offense is punishable by mandatory imprisonment. It cannot be used, however, in the case of capital crimes, such as murder or kidnapping.

Not guilty When a defendant pleads not guilty to a criminal charge, the judge will set a date for the defendant's trial. If only a minor offense is involved in the case, the judge may hear the case immediately if he so chooses.

As a general rule, the court, not the person accused, sets the time for a criminal trial. In some jurisdictions, the district attorney sets the schedule for criminal trials, but this does not limit the power of the court to advance or postpone cases.

■ **The right to a trial** Every person accused of a crime has a right to a speedy, public trial. He also has a right to trial by jury if he is charged with a major crime. When a person is tried by a jury, that jury must be impartial and must be chosen in a way that is not discriminatory.

Speedy trial The right of a person accused of a criminal offense to a SPEEDY TRIAL is guaranteed by the Constitution. A person does not have to be in jail in order to assert the right. An accused who has been released on bail is protected, as is a person paroled in the custody of counsel and one who has been indicted but not arrested. Even someone serving a sentence in the penitentiary is entitled to a speedy trial of other crimes with which he is charged.

No general principle fixes the exact time within which a trial must begin, but the federal—and often state—constitutional provisions protect against arbitrary and oppressive delays. Whether or not a defendant has been deprived of a speedy trial is determined by balancing four factors: the length of the delay, the government's reason for the delay, the defendant's assertion of his right, and prejudice (harm) to the defendant from the delay.

Some delay presumed to be prejudicial to the defendant is permissible. The amount of delay permitted depends on the circumstances of the case. The delay that could be tolerated in a simple assault-and-battery case, for instance, is shorter than for a complicated murder case. In the case of *Barker* v. *Wingo*, the U.S. Supreme Court said:

❝ Closely related to length of delay is the reason the government assigns to justify the delay. Here, too, different weights should be assigned to different reasons. A deliberate attempt to delay the trial in order to hamper the defense should be weighted heavily against the government. A more neutral reason such as negligence or over-crowded courts should be weighted less heavily but nevertheless should be considered since the ultimate responsibility for such circumstances must rest with the government rather than with the defendant. Finally, a valid reason, such as a missing witness, should serve to justify appropriate delay.❞

When the court decides that the right to a speedy trial has been denied, the charges against the defendant will be completely dismissed. Merely giving a defendant credit toward his sentence for the time of the unreasonable delay is not a remedy.

Public trial A defendant also has the constitutional right to a public trial, the purpose of which is to guarantee that a defendant will be fairly treated and not unjustly condemned. A public trial means that members of the general public ordinarily may not be excluded from a courtroom.

EXAMPLE When Jelke was on trial for the crime of inducing 0⊷✳ women to become prostitutes, his trial received wide publicity. Shortly after the trial began, the judge excluded all but Jelke's relatives and friends from the courtroom until the trial was completed. The judge based his ruling on the fact that obscene evidence would be introduced and on his belief that justice and the interests of good morals would be better served by excluding the public. The jury found Jelke guilty and he appealed.

The appellate court held that people may be excluded to preserve order or to protect the rights of parties or witnesses, but that the denial of the right to a public trial is not justified because of general considerations of public decency and morality. Jelke was awarded a new trial.

Jury trial Under the Sixth Amendment to the Constitution, a person is entitled to trial by JURY in certain circumstances. This right also applies to the states under the 14th Amendment to the Constitution. This means that if a defendant in a federal prosecution is entitled to a jury trial, then a defendant in a similar state prosecution is also entitled to one. Even when a defendant has a right to a jury trial, however, he may waive that right and be tried before a judge only. A defendant might do this if he felt that a judge would be more likely to decide for him than a jury would.

The right to trial by jury applies only to serious crimes—those punishable by prison sentences of more than six months—and not to petty offenses.

EXAMPLE Duncan, a black, was driving along a Louisiana 0⊷✳ highway when he saw his two younger cousins talking with four white boys by the roadside. The cousins, recently transferred to a previously all-white school, had experienced racial difficulties at the school. Duncan attempted to get his cousins into his car and away from the situation. According to the testimony of the white boys, just before he got back into his car Duncan slapped one of the white boys on the elbow. According to the black boys, Duncan merely touched one of the white boys on the elbow. Duncan was charged with simple battery and convicted. The offense was classified as a misdemeanor, punishable by a maximum of two years in jail and a $300 fine.

The Louisiana constitution provides for a jury trial only in capital cases and in cases in which imprisonment at hard labor may be imposed. Duncan was sentenced to 60 days and fined $150. He appealed, contending that it was unconstitutional to deny him a jury trial. The state contended that even if it were required to grant jury trials in serious cases, Duncan's conviction was valid, because the sentence was for only 60 days. The court reversed Duncan's conviction. A crime punishable by two years in prison is not a "petty" offense and would have entitled Duncan to a jury trial in a federal court. Therefore, Duncan must be given a jury trial in the state court.

Although most people think of a jury as having 12 members, many juries are smaller. A 12-member jury is not required in either state or federal prosecutions.

EXAMPLE Before his trial a defendant, who was charged 0⊷✳ with robbery, requested a trial by a 12-member jury. Under the law of his state only a six-member jury was provided in noncapital cases. His request was denied and he was convicted. The defendant appealed, contending his right to a 12-member jury was guaranteed by the Sixth Amendment. The court disagreed and affirmed his conviction. It stated that the number "12" is nothing more than a historical accident.

This particular court did not decide exactly how few jurors would satisfy the constitutional guarantee of a jury trial, but in 1978 the Supreme Court, overturning a conviction in Georgia by a five-member jury, ruled that a jury in a criminal case must have at least six members.

Impartial jury An impartial jury is one that is not prejudiced and is chosen in a way that does not discriminate on account of race, creed, color, or sex.

EXAMPLE In one instance, the defendant, a black man, was indicted by an all-white grand jury for murdering a white man, convicted by an all-white petit jury, and sentenced to death. In the county where the trial took place, not a single black had served on either a grand jury or a regular jury in more than 30 years, although blacks made up more than one-third of the adult population. The defendant contended that any plan that excluded black persons from jury duty over such a long period of time was discriminatory and unconstitutional. The court agreed that a jury chosen under any method that results in the systematic and complete exclusion of black persons cannot be impartial.

In another case, where state law excluded women from jury duty unless they filed a written declaration stating that they wished to serve, the appellate court reversed the conviction of a defendant whose jury was not selected from a representative cross-section of the community as guaranteed by the Sixth Amendment.

■ **The criminal trial by jury** A criminal trial begins with the selection of the jury in a process known as *voir dire*. Prospective jurors are brought in and questioned by the judge or by the prosecuting and defense attorneys. The prosecuting and defense attorneys may challenge jurors and have them disqualified *for cause*—if there is reason to believe that they will be unfair. For example, a witness may be challenged for cause if he is extremely prejudiced against the defendant or if he is related to the defendant, the victim, or one of the attorneys handling the case. The attorneys for both sides can also make *peremptory challenges*—that is, they may disqualify a certain number of jurors without giving a reason. Once the full jury has been accepted by both sides, it is sworn in by the judge.

The trial then proceeds with an opening statement by the prosecuting attorney, which outlines the charges against the defendant and the EVIDENCE that the prosecution will present against him. The defense attorney then makes his opening statement, refuting the charges. Following these opening statements, the prosecution produces his evidence in order to prove his case. He does this by presenting documents, exhibits, and WITNESSES whom the defense attorney may cross-examine to challenge their testimony. The defendant then offers his evidence in opposition and the prosecuting attorney has the same right to cross-examine the defendant's witnesses and rebut the evidence. Numerous types of evidence are allowed or prohibited and various defenses are available to the defendant, as explained below. Once all the evidence has been presented, the defense attorney and the prosecuting attorney make their closing statements, summing up their cases.

Evidence Evidence is the means by which the truth of a matter may be established. The term includes any matter of fact introduced by either side in the trial that tends to substantiate or contradict the existence of some other fact. The purpose of evidence is to present a fact favorable to the cause of the party introducing it or to contradict a fact the opposing party has attempted to establish. The trend in U.S. law is to be very liberal in the admission of evidence. Evidence should not be barred unless clearly prohibited by statute or in the interest of a well-known public policy. Certain types of evidence are generally admissible, while certain other types are generally inadmissible. There are also numerous rules governing the admissibility of evidence in a criminal trial.

Judicial notice Judicial notice means that courts accept, without proof, matters that are known to all well-informed persons. The doctrine of judicial notice avoids the necessity of the formal introduction of evidence when there is no need for proof.

Courts judicially notice not only facts within the common experience and knowledge of every person of ordinary understanding and intelligence but also matters that are known within their respective jurisdictions. For example, courts have taken judicial notice of commonly known facts relating to the prevalence of crime or to the commission of particular crimes. For example, it is commonly known that those who commit robbery use pistols, ammunition, blackjacks, masks, and the like.

Courts take judicial notice of the ordinary properties of matter—that fire will burn, that gas will illuminate, and that more than two highballs will intoxicate the average moderate drinker.

Courts take judicial notice of well-known scientific facts and natural laws, including facts printed in encyclopedias, dictionaries, and other standard publications. Notice is not taken of facts in a work that is not a recognized standard authority. Furthermore, judicial notice is not taken of scientific facts that are not generally known to ordinary persons or are not matters of general knowledge.

Other facts commonly judicially recognized include physiological facts, such as that the discoloration produced by a blow is the blood showing through the outer skin; geographical facts, such as a state's boundaries or the location of a lake or river; historical facts, such as the dates of World War II; time, days, and dates, such as the fact that in California the sun set at 5:35 P.M. on February 13, and consequently a burglary committed at approximately 7:30 P.M. on that date was committed at night.

The federal Constitution and the public laws passed by Congress must be judicially noticed by all state and federal courts. The constitution and public statutes of a state are likewise noticed judicially by all courts of the state and by the federal courts, particularly those located in the state.

Burden of proof The burden of proof is the duty of positively proving guilt with sufficient evidence. In general, the burden of proof to establish the guilt of the accused beyond a reasonable doubt is on the prosecution. The prosecution must prove every essential element of the crime charged. The burden rests on the prosecution from the beginning of the trial until the moment of conviction or acquittal.

For example, the prosecution first has the burden of proving that a crime has in fact been committed. Next, it must prove that the crime was committed within the territorial jurisdiction of the court trying the case. If the defendant claims the prosecution is barred by the statute of limitations, the prosecution must prove otherwise.

Presumptions A presumption is an inference that one fact exists because another fact does. It has also been defined as a deduction that the law specifically directs to be made from particular facts. For example, a person who has been missing for several years (usually seven) is presumed by law to be dead. Some courts distinguish between an INFERENCE and a presumption by holding that an *inference* is nothing more than a permissible deduction from the evidence, while a *presumption* is compulsory and cannot be disregarded by the jury.

A distinction also is made between a presumption of fact and a presumption of law. A *presumption of fact* is considered to be merely a strong inference, subject to rebuttal by contrary testimony. For example, a person who consumes three whiskey sours in an hour may be presumed to be intoxicated but this may be rebutted by the fact that the drinks contained exceptionally small amounts of liquor. A *presumption of law* is a rule or conclusion of law.

Presumptions of law are frequently classified as conclusive and rebuttable. A *conclusive presumption of law* is an inference that must be drawn from proof of given facts, which no evidence can overthrow so that it is actually a rule of law. An example of this type of presumption is the rule that a child under seven years is presumed to be incapable of committing a crime. A *rebuttable presumption of law* is an inference that remains true until proven otherwise. The presumption that a child between the ages of 7 and 14 is incapable of committing a crime may be rebutted.

For the most part, presumptions in criminal prosecutions are in favor of the person accused. For example, a person accused of a crime is presumed to be innocent until his guilt is proved beyond a reasonable doubt by legal evidence in a fair trial. The presumption of innocence exists in every criminal case, and it applies to every element of the crime charged. It continues to exist even though the person accused fails to testify, or to deny his guilt, or to offer any evidence. The presumption may be rebutted by the prosecution's introduction of evidence of guilt beyond a reasonable doubt. The presumption of innocence is a rebuttable presumption that is intended to prevent the conviction of an innocent person, not to protect the guilty.

Another rebuttable presumption is that an accused person was sane at the time the crime was committed. This presumption exists until contrary evidence is introduced and insanity is established.

Similarly, there is a general presumption that the accused is a person of common understanding and ordinary intelligence, capable of committing a crime. For example, a person over the age of 14 is presumed to be of sufficient mental capacity to form a criminal intent.

Relevancy Relevancy is the principal test of the admissibility of evidence in a criminal prosecution: Does the evidence prove or disprove, or tend to prove or disprove, the crime charged? For instance, evidence showing that the accused person owned, possessed, or had access to tools, weapons, or any articles with which the particular crime might have been committed is relevant. Similarly, fingerprint evidence and evidence of tracks, footprints, or shoe marks are relevant and admissible to prove the identity of the accused.

On the other hand, evidence offered on matters that have no bearing on the points at issue in the case are ordinarily excluded. For example, in a prosecution for blackmail, evidence of commendatory medals and citations received by the defendant is irrelevant, because bravery has nothing to do with the tendency of one person to blackmail another.

Competency Competent evidence is pertinent evidence that tends to prove the issue and to show that the accused is guilty of the crime charged. For example, narcotics legally seized by the police from the defendant at the time of his arrest is competent evidence to prove that the defendant is guilty of a charge of narcotics violations.

Res gestae The rule of *res gestae* means that, in general, everything said and done at the time and place of the crime is admissible in evidence. The things said and done are so spontaneous and so contemporaneous with the event they concern that they could not have been the result of deliberation or fabrication. The facts and events speak for themselves through the words and acts of the participants. For example, in a murder prosecution, testimony of the dying words of the victim given by the police officer to whom they were spoken was admissible as part of the *res gestae,* without proof that the victim was competent and in full possession of his faculties at the time he made the statement. Similarly, the acts and statements of the accused are admissible in evidence when they are part of the *res gestae.* In a prosecution against a father for the murder of his infant child, for instance, evidence that the father was found with his wrist cut near the body of the dead child in an apparent suicide attempt was admissible.

Character and reputation The defendant is generally entitled to introduce evidence of his good character as proof of his innocence. But when he does so, he puts his character in issue, which permits the prosecution to introduce any evidence it has in rebuttal. As one judge said, "the price a defendant must pay for attempting to prove his good name is to throw open the entire subject which the law has kept closed for his benefit and to make himself vulnerable where the law otherwise shields him."

Evidence of character, both good and bad, usually must be confined to proof of character or reputation around the time the offense was committed and to the community where the accused lives or formerly lived.

Evidence of other offenses Evidence that the person accused has committed another crime unconnected with the one for which he is on trial is as a rule inadmissible. The person accused is entitled to be tried for the crime charged and not for being a criminal generally.

This general rule is subject to a number of exceptions, however. Usually the evidence that the accused committed a previous crime is admissible if it proves the accused's identity as the perpetrator of the crime he is accused of. But the prosecution must show some connection between the two offenses.

EXAMPLE A defendant was charged with larceny. A theater patron identified him as the thief who stole her purse and testified that he had changed from the seat in front of her to the seat behind her, all the while looking at her and not at the show. The testimony of a detective as to similar actions by the defendant in the same theater in reference to other women spectators of the show a few days later, when the defendant was arrested, was admissible for the limited purpose of establishing the identity of the thief.

Evidence of other offenses committed or attempted by the accused is usually admissible to show his criminal intent to commit the offense charged. In a prosecution for abortion, for instance, evidence of other such offenses is admissible to show intent, knowledge, or practice of criminal abortions, but it is not admissible to prove that the accused committed the act charged. Similarly, in a prosecution for arson, evidence of other fires or attempts at other fires is admissible if relevant to an issue in the case.

Best and secondary The best-evidence rule requires the production of the best evidence the nature of the case permits. This means that no evidence can be received by the court as a substitute for original evidence when the original evidence can be obtained. The rule generally applies to written documents.

When there is written evidence of a fact, the writing itself is usually the best evidence of it. For example, a forged check must be put in evidence before the forgery will be admitted, unless the failure to produce the forged check is justified—as it would be if the check was destroyed by a fire.

When the contents of a writing cannot be proved by the primary evidence—the writing itself—the secondary evidence will be admitted only after it is proved that the primary evidence cannot be produced. If, for instance, a trial attorney seeks to introduce a photocopy of a check as secondary evidence because the original check is lost, he must be able to prove that a diligent but unsuccessful search was made for the original. Secondary evidence may consist of oral testamony about the contents of the writing or exact copies or summaries of the writings that cannot be produced. Even a copy of a copy has been held to be admissible.

Demonstrative Demonstrative, or real, evidence is addressed directly to the court or jury without the intervention of testimony by witnesses. As a general rule, demonstrative evidence is relevant and admissible if it shows that the crime was committed or throws light on the way it was committed. For instance, articles and objects that form part of the criminal action are admissible as demonstrative evidence for inspection by the jury. Examples include bloodstained money, a bullet-riddled door, scrapings taken from the accused's fingernails, objects with fingerprints, weights attached to a body taken from water, and weapons or other instruments used in the crime.

Hearsay Hearsay is evidence that is what the witness says he heard another person say out of court. Hearsay evidence is inadmissible when used to prove the truth of a matter asserted in the statement.

EXAMPLE In a narcotics prosecution, a customs agent who arrested the defendant and the defendant's girl friend is called to testify as a witness. The agent states that the girl told him that she and the defendant went to Mexico to get him a fix and that the portion of heroin found in his possession was the remainder of that fix. In this case, if the agent's testimony about what he heard the girl say is offered as proof of the truth of her statements in court, it is inadmissible hearsay.

Hearsay is admissible, however, when used for some other purpose. It is admissible when it is an admission against interest (discussed below) or when it is a dying declaration, a statement by the victim of a crime who knows he is about to die that implicates or accuses the defendant.

EXAMPLE Dan received serious wounds after being shot during a holdup of his gas station. Before he died, he told police that his nephews Tom and John were the robbers. Dan's statement to the police would be admissible in the criminal prosecutions of Tom and John.

The rule excluding hearsay is designed to have the parties who made the statements in question brought into court, where they are forced to testify under oath. As witnesses they can be observed by the judge and the jury, and they may also be subject to cross-examination by the opposing party.

The rule excluding hearsay is not confined to oral statements. It also includes written, printed, or typewritten evidence.

EXAMPLE In a robbery prosecution, a newspaper article containing an account of the robbery is inadmissible as hearsay if it is introduced to prove how the victim described the robbers immediately after the robbery. But if the victim himself gave the description in court, it would be admissible.

Other examples of writings inadmissible as hearsay include letters, postcards, and telegrams.

Admissions An admission is something less than a confession. It is an acknowledgment by the accused of a fact or of circumstances from which, together with other facts, guilt may be inferred. An *admission against interest* (a damaging admission) is admissible because of the strong probability that a person would not make an untrue statement harmful to himself. Such a statement may be repeated by another person on the witness stand in a criminal prosecution, even though it is hearsay. Because an accused person can admit the whole case against him by pleading guilty, he can admit any part of it. A voluntary admission does not violate the constitutional provision against self-incrimination.

EXAMPLE One evening, Jack meets Harry the Count, a mobster to whom he owes money, and Harry demands payment. Jack refuses to pay and a fight ensues. During the fight Harry stabs Jack, who retaliates by shooting Harry. Badly wounded, Jack flees from the scene and makes his way to a friend's apartment. Before losing consciousness from loss of blood, he tells his friend that he was in a fight with Harry. The friend calls the police, who take Jack to a hospital for treatment of the stab wound. They also question the friend about how Jack was injured, and he tells them what Jack told him. The police find Harry's dead body and charge Jack with his murder. At the trial, the friend would be permitted to testify about what Jack told him when he arrived at the apartment. Jack's statement that he had a fight with Harry would be admissible in evidence, not as a confession but as an admission against interest. This is a permissible exception to the hearsay rule because Jack himself could take the witness stand and give an explanation to refute the statement he made to his friend.

Confessions A confession is an acknowledgment by the person accused that he is guilty of the crime charged against him. When the prosecution attempts to introduce a confession as evidence against the person accused, an objection may be made on the ground that it violates the privilege against SELF-INCRIMINATION, guaranteed under the Fifth Amendment of the U.S. Constitution, which provides in part that no person "shall be compelled in any criminal case to be a witness against himself." If the confession was involuntary—one that a person has been compelled to make by coercion, brutality, violence, or mental torture—it is inadmissible in evidence. It is also inadmissible if it was made voluntarily but in violation of the defendant's constitutional rights. It can be used in evidence, however, if it was given voluntarily and without any violation of the defendant's constitutional rights.

Defenses Every person accused of a crime has the right to avail himself of all the defenses the law permits. The fact that a person commits a crime on the advice, direction, or authority of another is not a defense. For instance, an employee cannot escape the consequences of driving while intoxicated by claiming that he was acting within the scope of his employment.

Alibi An alibi is the defense that the person accused was at a different place at the time the alleged crime was committed. An alibi is not established merely by showing that the person accused was not at the scene of the crime. It must appear that he was at some other specified place at the time the crime was committed. When proof establishing the alibi is accepted by the court or jury, it is a complete defense and precludes the possibility of guilt. The defense is of no use, however, when the theory of the prosecution is that the person accused acted through an agent.

Condonation and settlement The status of a crime is fixed when the crime is completed. It cannot be changed by later acts of the criminal or a third person. The fact that a person injured by a crime condones the offense or makes a compromise or settlement with the accused or with a third person in his behalf does not relieve the accused of responsibility or bar a prosecution by the state. While the law encourages the COMPROMISE AND SETTLEMENT of civil cases, it discourages them in criminal cases.

In a number of jurisdictions, however, misdemeanors may be compromised according to statute in cases where the public will not suffer any damage. Obtaining unemployment benefits while earning wages is an example of a crime that may be compromised in some states. If the accused made restitution by returning the money he got illegally, he might be charged with a lesser offense. Under the common law, some cases, such as assault and battery, may also be compromised.

Self-defense Generally, a defendant may claim SELF-DEFENSE when the use of force was reasonably necessary to protect himself from injury by another. Deadly force—force that causes death or serious bodily harm—is excusable only when the defendant was protecting himself from immediate death or serious injury. Some states require a person who is protecting himself from another to retreat instead of using deadly force, except when he is being robbed, defending his life or home, or legally arresting his attacker.

Duress or compulsion A criminal act may be excused if it is committed under duress or compulsion strong enough to cause a well-grounded fear of death or serious bodily harm. There must be no reasonable opportunity for the person to escape without committing the crime. A threat of future injury is not enough.

EXAMPLE Let us say that you are standing at the window of a jewelry store looking in at a large diamond ring. Suddenly a stranger walks up behind you, puts a pistol to your head, and orders you to break the glass and steal the ring. He warns you that you must act quickly or he will blow your head to pieces. You comply, and the alarm begins to ring. You and the stranger are arrested and charged with burglary. The defense of duress would be available to you at your trial.

The rule has no application in homicide cases. Compulsion cannot be used as an excuse for taking the life of an innocent person. Nor can it apply when the accused claims he acted on the orders of someone who has authority over him, such as a parent, school principal, employer, or superior officer. A child old enough to be responsible for his own acts, for example, cannot claim as a defense that his parents compelled him to commit a crime.

Entrapment Entrapment is the act of a law-enforcement officer who conceives and plans a crime and induces its commission by a person who would not have perpetrated the crime except for the trickery, persuasion, or fraud of the officer. The criminal intent or design originates in the mind of the officer, who seeks to lure and to entrap the person into committing the crime solely for the purpose of arresting and prosecuting him.

EXAMPLE Sherman was receiving medical treatment for narcotic addiction. During one of his visits to his doctor's office, he met Kalchinian, who claimed that he was having the same treatment. After a number of similar meetings the two men became friendly. Eventually, Kalchinian told Sherman that he was not responding to the treatment and asked Sherman if he could supply him with drugs. When Sherman refused, Kalchinian persisted, and after several requests Sherman finally agreed. Kalchinian was a government informer, and after Sherman sold him the narcotics, Sherman was arrested by officers of the Bureau of Narcotics and convicted of unlawfully selling narcotics. His conviction was reversed on appeal because he had been entrapped.

Entrapment can be used as a defense because the function of law enforcement is the prevention of crime and the apprehension of criminals, not the manufacture of crime.

Ignorance or mistake of fact As a general rule, ignorance or mistake of fact exempts a person from criminal responsibility, unless the mistake is caused by negligence. Most crimes require the element of criminal intent. When a person does an act that would be innocent if the facts were actually as he mistakenly believes them to be, he does not have the necessary criminal intent and the law does not hold him responsible.

EXAMPLE The classic case of mistake of fact is a person who honestly, and on reasonable grounds, believes a burglar has broken into his home. He shoots and kills the "burglar," who is in fact his servant. The law treats the person as though he had killed a burglar instead of his servant. His mistake eliminates the necessary criminal intent and provides him with a good defense.

Mistake of fact is not an excuse, however, for violating a statute that punishes a prohibited act regardless of criminal intent, such as statutes forbidding the sale of liquor to minors or the sale of adulterated foods.

Mistake of law   A mistake of law occurs when someone acts with knowledge of the facts but is mistaken about the legal consequences of his act. The rule that ignorance of the law is no excuse is deeply rooted in the U.S. legal system. Everyone is presumed to know the law. If this rule were not in effect, anyone who wished to commit a crime might do so and later defend himself by saying that he did not know his conduct was against the law.

The general rule does not apply, however, when a specific intent (discussed earlier in this article) is an essential element of the crime. Ignorance of the law negates the existence of a specific intent, and it is a good defense.

EXAMPLE A man moved from Delaware to Arkansas, where 0—* he filed for divorce. Notice of the divorce proceeding was published in a Delaware newspaper. The wife did not appear at the Arkansas divorce proceeding and later denied actual notice of it. The man returned to Delaware and married another woman, having been told by an attorney that the second marriage would be lawful. Later the man was charged with bigamy and convicted. He appealed and his conviction was reversed, because the appellate court held that the absence of a criminal intent is a good defense to bigamy. The man relied in good faith on the advice of his attorney, and the man's mistake of law negates the specific criminal intent required for bigamy.

The verdict   After all the evidence is presented and the prosecutor and the defense attorney have given their summations to the jury, the judge instructs the jury about the laws that are involved in the case. The jury must apply these laws when considering its verdict.

Federal courts require the jury to reach a unanimous verdict in order to convict a defendant of a criminal offense, but a unanimous jury verdict is not required in all criminal cases in state courts.

EXAMPLE A person was convicted of robbery by a vote of 0—* nine to three in a state where a unanimous verdict was not required. He appealed, claiming the jury's vote showed that the state failed to prove his guilt beyond a reasonable doubt. The court found that there was no evidence that the jurors who voted to convict were not convinced of the defendant's guilt beyond a reasonable doubt. The verdict reached by the majority was not invalidated by the fact that three jurors voted to acquit.

If the verdict is not guilty, the case is dismissed. If the verdict is guilty and the defendant is convicted of the crime, the judge will sentence him and other post-conviction procedures may follow.

■ **Post-conviction procedures**   There are several post-conviction procedures that may follow a judgment in a criminal case. The trial court imposes a SENTENCE, which may involve PROBATION or PAROLE. It may also hear and decide a motion to set aside the judgment. A higher court may hear an appeal based on the defendant's claim that errors of law were made at his trial. At any time a prisoner who believes he is unlawfully imprisoned may petition a federal or state court for a writ of HABEAS CORPUS. Each of these procedures is regulated by different legal rules and, at each stage, the rights of the defendant vary.

Sentencing, parole, and probation   Sentencing follows a guilty plea or a conviction by a judge or a jury. Because it is a critical stage in the proceeding, the defendant is entitled to be represented by an attorney. In most jurisdictions the trial judge may use discretion in determining an appropriate sentence. He is usually aided by a presentence report made by probation or parole investigators. They check on the defendant's background, prior criminal record, family, educational and employment record, and other circumstances of his life. The judge can consider all of this evidence, including information based on hearsay and crimes for which the defendant was not actually convicted. In some states the jury has authority to recommend or even to determine punishment, but the judge always pronounces the sentence.

Sentencing may include probation or parole—a period of time in which the defendant is allowed to live in the community rather than being imprisoned. The defendant is subject to certain conditions and his activities are supervised by a probation or parole officer. The decision to grant probation or parole is usually within the discretion of the judge, and his decision can seldom be appealed. A defendant who violates the conditions of his probation or parole can be imprisoned for a specified time. He is entitled to a hearing and, when necessary, he may have an attorney.

Motion to set aside a judgment   A writ of *coram nobis* is an ancient remedy for setting aside a judgment that never should have been pronounced. Its purpose is to bring to the court's attention facts that were kept out of the trial, usually because of fraud, duress, or an excusable mistake. These must be facts that either would have changed the outcome of the trial or would have cast the defendant in a more favorable light. It must not be the defendant's fault that the facts were not brought out at trial, because he is not entitled to litigate the same issues all over again. However, when it appears that a witness was bribed or lied on the stand, it is a matter of justice for the court to set aside a conviction based on that testimony.

Many states have replaced the writ of *coram nobis* with statutes that set modern procedures for bringing new facts to a court's attention, but the new statutes so closely adhere to the writ's principles that they are informally called *coram nobis*. The new statutes usually give the defendant a right to make a motion in the court that convicted him, to vacate, or set aside, the judgment. Such motions may be based on (1) a lack of evidence to sustain the conviction; (2) newly discovered evidence; (3) erroneous instructions to the jury; (4) prejudicial comments or conduct by the prosecutor during the trial; or (5) incorrect rulings by the judge. If the motion is granted, a new trial is usually ordered.

Appeals   Under the common law, a convicted defendant could test what he considered to be mistakes made during his trial by filing a writ of errors in a higher court. The writ pointed out mistakes in the written record of the proceedings, such as an insufficient indictment or a sentence not authorized by law. Defendants usually had the right to file writs of error after any conviction. Some states have incorporated the idea of writs of error into their statutes, but some hold that the right to file such a writ exists even when a statute provides for another appeal procedure. When a different adequate remedy is available to a defendant, the writ of error will be denied.

Unlike a *coram nobis,* or motion to set aside a judgment, an appeal procedure opens up for review all the questions of law that arose during a trial. The appeal is made to a higher court, asking it to review certain points of law that are claimed to have been incorrectly ruled on by the trial judge. For example, convicted defendants frequently challenge the use of confessions or evidence that they claim was illegally obtained.

There is no constitutional right to appeal every criminal conviction. The right to appeal is created by statute, available only when and for whom federal and state criminal laws allow. Congress first enacted a law permitting an appeal as a right in criminal cases in 1889. That law gave a right of appeal to everyone convicted of a crime that was punishable by death. A general right of appeal in federal criminal cases was not created until 1911.

The states have been somewhat less concerned about creating a right of appeal for convicted criminals. In 1965 the Supreme Court decided that states must have some procedure by which prisoners can show that they have been convicted in violation of their constitutional rights. However, a full right to appeal is not required in every case.

The Sixth Amendment guarantee of a right to counsel does not necessarily extend to every step of the appeals process. An attorney may be appointed after the initial stages of an appeal procedure when it is clear that serious issues are at stake. If a prisoner cannot afford the costs of an appeals proceeding, the state must waive the court fees and provide a free transcript of the prisoner's trial when required. See also the general discussion of appellate procedure in APPEAL AND ERROR.

Habeas corpus   A prisoner who believes that he is being illegally held can always test the legality of his detention by petitioning for a writ of HABEAS CORPUS. Called the most basic right guaranteed by the Constitution, a writ of habeas corpus orders the person holding the prisoner to produce him in court and to justify depriving him of his liberty. The writ may be available when the court that ordered the petitioner to be imprisoned lacked the authority to do so or when the prisoner's constitutional rights were violated. One federal judge remarked that the writ is so fundamental to our system of law that he would treat a handwritten note from a prisoner as a formal petition for a writ of habeas corpus. He would order the prisoner to be brought into his court and given a chance to be heard.

The Constitution provides that the "Privilege of the Writ of Habeas Corpus shall not be suspended, unless when in Cases of Rebellion or Invasion the public Safety may require it." Every state, either by statute or constitutional provision, provides for the writ of habeas corpus to be issued in a proper case.

Habeas corpus is usually considered an extraordinary remedy, available only when there is no other adequate procedure to protect the petitioner's rights. It is not intended as a second chance to try a case or as a substitute for normal appeal procedures. It will not be granted, for example, to find out whether the evidence was strong enough to justify a conviction or to bring up an alibi that could have been used as a defense at the trial. Habeas corpus is available, however, for a prisoner who has been denied his right to have a lawyer or who has been unlawfully denied a release on bail while he appeals. Federal courts will accept habeas corpus applications from the state prisoners whose rights under the Constitution or the laws and treaties of the United States have been violated, if there are no state remedies to protect them. See PRISONERS' RIGHTS.

criminology   The scientific study of crimes and their prevention and punishment.

crops   The law defines crops as all products of the soil that are grown and raised annually and gathered in a single season. Crops are divided into two groups. *Fructus naturales* are crops that grow without the necessary aid of human labor, such as uncultivated trees that produce fruit, hay that spontaneously grows from perennial roots, and wild blackberries that grow on bushes. Such crops are a part of the soil and, while unharvested, are considered real property, or land. When harvested, they are personal property and would not be included as part of the sale of the land. *Fructus industriales* are crops obtained by yearly labor and cultivation, such as wheat, corn, and vegetables.

As a general rule, crops are the property of the owner of the land. The owner may harvest and sell them without selling the land on which they are grown. But it is also possible for the land to belong to one person and the crops to another: A person living on the land by contract with the owner is entitled to the crops he has raised and harvested.

Crops attached to land when it is sold pass to the purchaser of the land unless the owner imposes a condition that title to the crops does not pass with the land. Under some laws, a trespasser who sows crops does not acquire title to them; they belong to the person who is lawfully entitled to possession of the land. Under others, unharvested crops grown by a trespasser are the property of the landowner, but harvested crops belong to the trespasser—provided he remains in possession of the land until the harvest.

cross claim   A claim usually brought by one party against a coparty in a lawsuit, such as one defendant against a codefendant. The cross claim must arise from the same occurrence as the subject of the main lawsuit.

   EXAMPLE   A father sues an airline, charging that his son's
   O⊶⊶*   death was caused by the operation of an airplane that needed repairs. He also sues the manufacturer because the airplane was negligently constructed. The airline believes the defects in the airplane were caused by the manufacturer's failure to fulfill its contractual duty to keep the plane in good repair. The airline is entitled to bring a cross claim against the manufacturer for breach of its contract to repair the airplane.

cross complaint   See COUNTERCLAIM; CROSS CLAIM.

cross demand   See COUNTERCLAIM; CROSS CLAIM.

cross-examination   The examination of a WITNESS during a trial or hearing by the party opposed to the one who called the witness.

   EXAMPLE   Paul is driving his friend Norman home when a
   O⊶⊶*   truck veers around a corner and smashes into the right side of the car, severely injuring Norman. The truck was being driven by Mack, who had been drinking.

Norman sues Mack. During the trial, Norman calls Paul as his witness. After Paul has finished his testimony on behalf of Norman, he may then be cross-examined by Mack's attorney, who will attempt to discredit Paul's testimony.

cruel and unusual punishment Punishment that is torture or barbarity; any punishment that is so disproportionate to the offense as to shock the moral sense of the community. It is prohibited by the Eighth Amendment to the U.S. Constitution.

This article defines the constitutional prohibition of cruel and unusual punishment and discusses its relation to the death penalty, excessive prison sentences, solitary confinement, physical abuse, prison conditions, and school discipline.

■ **Prohibition** The Eighth Amendment prohibition of cruel and unusual punishment applies to the federal government and, by virtue of the due process clause of the 14th Amendment, to the states as well. See DUE PROCESS OF LAW. This means that crimes in violation of either federal or state statutes cannot be punished in a way that is considered inhuman, barbarous, or shocking to the moral sense of the community. The interpretation of the prohibition against cruel and unusual punishment has developed on a case by case basis, and its scope has not been conclusively defined.

■ **Death penalty** It was not until the 1972 case of *Furman* v. *Georgia* that the U.S. Supreme Court considered the constitutionality of the DEATH PENALTY by reviewing a case in which three black defendants were sentenced to death, one for committing murder and two for committing rape. The defendants claimed that the death penalty was applied in an arbitrary and discriminatory manner that constituted cruel and unusual punishment. The Court agreed that the death penalty had not been uniformly applied but had been imposed more often on poor and black defendants. The Court decided that when the death penalty is ordered at the discretion of the judge or jury, without fixed standards to guide them, it constitutes cruel and unusual punishment in violation of the 8th and 14th Amendments. Each Supreme Court justice in the five-to-four decision wrote his own opinion, and no clear rule of law can be derived from them. Three justices stated that the infrequent use of the death penalty, combined with the fact that its imposition in this case was entirely at the discretion of the jury, constituted cruel and unusual punishment. Two justices stated that the death penalty itself was degrading to human dignity and violated the Eighth Amendment. The four dissenting justices concluded that the death penalty was not "cruel and unusual" because 41 states and the District of Columbia provided for such punishment and Congress had, on four occasions in the past 11 years, added certain acts, such as aircraft hijacking, to federal crimes punishable by death. Two points that are clear from this opinion are (1) that the imposition of the death penalty cannot be left to the unguided discretion of the jury and (2) that the penalty is cruel and unusual in the sense that being struck by lightning is cruel and unusual, so rare and random is its occurrence.

■ **Excessive sentences** On a few occasions the relative harshness of sentences other than the death penalty have also been challenged on Eighth Amendment grounds. For example, to divest a person of citizenship may constitute cruel and unusual punishment.

EXAMPLE A man court-martialed for deserting his post during wartime was stripped of his citizenship. He had been absent from his post for less than a day and had voluntarily surrendered to the authorities. He appealed, contending that the punishment was cruel and unusual. The Supreme Court said that the punishment must be considered "in light of the basic prohibitions against inhuman treatment" and held that loss of citizenship was unconstitutional, particularly when it was so disproportionate to the offense committed.

Although the Court has been reluctant to find that specific sentences constitute cruel and unusual punishment, it has overturned some particularly harsh sentences.

■ **Personal condition as a crime** To punish a person simply for being what he is, without his having committed some criminal act or having been involved in criminal circumstances is cruel and unusual punishment under the Eighth Amendment.

EXAMPLE When a California statute that carried a mandatory prison term of at least 90 days for being "addicted to the use of narcotics" was appealed, the law was found to be unconstitutional because it made the status of being addicted to narcotics a criminal offense. The Court reasoned that such a law was akin to declaring mental illness a crime.

In Texas the conviction of a chronic alcoholic for being intoxicated in a public place was upheld, however. Unlike the California case the Texan was not convicted because of his status as an alcoholic but for the specific offense of being intoxicated in a public place. The statute did not attempt to regulate the man's activities in his home, only in public.

■ **Solitary confinement** To many prison officials, the best way to deal with troublesome or offending prisoners is to segregate them from the general prison population. Many critics consider placing prisoners in solitary confinement for indefinite periods of time as a cruel and unusual punishment. They base their arguments on three points: (1) solitary confinement constitutes psychological torture more severe than whipping and violates standards of decency; (2) solitary confinement is inconsistent with a recognition of the humanity of the inmate and thus constitutes excessive cruelty and inhumane treatment; (3) solitary confinement constitutes unnecessary cruelty if a less severe form of punishment would achieve the same purpose.

The Supreme Court has never decided whether solitary confinement is by its nature an unconstitutional form of punishment. Nearly all lower courts considering the issue, however, have held that it is not. Courts, in general, believe that solitary confinement may be necessary to protect the general prison population, staff, or the prisoner himself; to discipline the prisoner for disobedience of orders; and to prevent a prisoner from escaping. Although courts have been unwilling to rule out solitary confinement per se, they have intervened in individual cases, depending on the duration and conditions of solitary confinement.

There is no uniformity on the issue of the proper duration of solitary confinement or agreement on an appropriate test to be applied.

EXAMPLE In one Pennsylvania case, the court upheld punishment of 400 days segregation for participation in a religiously motivated disturbance. But a federal court decided that segregation for some 480 days for participation in an Illinois prison work stoppage was cruel and unusual punishment. In Indiana the court decided that indefinite segregation is permissible as long as periodic reviews are conducted in accordance with minimal requirements of due process of law.

Many courts, however, attempt to determine whether the duration is reasonably related to the offense. In one case, a two-year confinement for participation in an illegal religious service was judged invalid because it was not reasonably related to the offense committed.

Courts have ordered prisoners released from solitary confinement because conditions were "shocking," "barbarous," or "debasing" and thus constituted cruel and unusual punishment. Civilized standards of decency were violated, for example, when a prisoner was confined to a bare cell, stripped, exposed to the winter cold, and deprived of the basic elements of hygiene, such as soap and toilet paper.

■ **Physical abuse** It was not until 1968 that a court specifically ruled that whipping a prisoner with a leather strap as a disciplinary measure constituted cruel and unusual punishment. An earlier case decided by a federal district court in 1965 stated that if whipping was to be done, it had to be carefully controlled. In the 1968 case, however, the court decided that the use of a leather strap, "irrespective of any precautionary conditions which may be imposed, offends contemporary concepts of decency and human dignity." This reasoning has since been applied to prevent the use of physical force on juveniles, such as "beating, slapping, kicking and otherwise physically abusing" them, except when the circumstances, such as a riot, require this treatment.

A prison's use of tranquilizing drugs without adequate medical guidance has also been regarded as cruel and unusual punishment.

To date, most courts have been reluctant to consider isolated assaults on inmates by prison guards as cruel and unusual punishment or as grounds for lawsuits under the federal Civil Rights Act. See PRISONERS' RIGHTS. Courts have been even more hesitant to apply the Eighth Amendment to circumstances where force was used to quell disturbances or other problems, even if the force was excessive. A California court avoided applying the Eighth Amendment by deciding that "the amount of force used cannot be measured by a micrometer, nor can it be considered separate and apart from the circumstances at hand."

Courts have also been reluctant to impose liability on prison officials for failing to protect inmates from assaults by other inmates. Several decisions, however, have stated that there is a constitutional right of inmates to be afforded some degree of protection from attacks. The test that has been applied in these cases is that "there must be a showing either of a pattern of undisputed and unchecked violence or, on a different level, of an egregious [flagrant] failure to provide security to a particular inmate, before a deprivation of constitutional right is stated."

■ **Conditions of prison** A fundamental issue that several courts have addressed since 1970 is whether the conditions of certain institutions as a whole, aside from individual incidents, are so shocking that they constitute cruel and unusual punishment. In a landmark case, *Holt* v. *Sarver,* the federal circuit court decided that the whole Arkansas prison system violated the Eighth Amendment prohibition against cruel and unusual punishment. The court found, among other things, that (1) the prison was largely run by inmate trusty guards who stirred up hate and mistrust; (2) the open barracks within the prison invited widespread physical and sexual assaults; (3) the isolation cells were overcrowded, filthy, and unsanitary; and (4) there were no rehabilitation or training programs.

■ **In schools** The U.S. Supreme Court decided in a 1977 case that the Eighth Amendment prohibition against cruel and unusual punishment did not apply to paddling children as a means of maintaining discipline in public schools. Rather, it is the function of the state court, with its particular expertise in TORT (personal injury) and CRIMINAL LAW questions, to examine the proper use of corporal punishment in public schools. See SCHOOLS.

cruelty An act that inflicts unnecessary pain. In DIVORCE law, cruelty (used in such phrases as "cruel and abusive treatment" and "cruel and inhuman treatment") may sometimes be available as a ground for divorce.

culpable Blamable; censurable. In law, the word implies that a particular act or course of conduct is wrong but not criminal. For example, you are driving to the hospital to visit your favorite aunt, who has just had a heart attack. Your mind is not on your driving, and you accidentally strike a parked automobile. Your conduct is culpable but not criminal.

culprit A person charged with a criminal offense but not yet convicted. The word is not a legal term and, as it is commonly used, implies only a light degree of censure.

cum testamento annexo (Latin) "With the will attached." The term is used in regard to an administrator who is appointed by a court to supervise the distribution of the property of a deceased person. Ordinarily, a WILL names a person, called an executor, to distribute the deceased person's property. If that person dies or refuses to act as executor, the court appoints someone else, an administrator *de bonis non cum testamento annexo* ("of the goods not [already administered upon] with the will attached"). See also EXECUTORS AND ADMINISTRATORS.

cumulative evidence Any EVIDENCE from the same witness or a different witness that repeats or adds to what has been testified to previously.

EXAMPLE A wife brings a divorce action against her husband. The suit is based on the ground of cruelty. The first witness on the wife's behalf testifies that on July 4, 1980, he gave a party, which both spouses attended. During the party the couple began to quarrel, and the husband slapped his wife three times. A second witness on the wife's behalf testifies that she also saw the husband slap his wife three times. The testimonial evidence given by the second witness is cumulative.

cumulative sentence Separate SENTENCES, each additional to the others, imposed on a defendant who has been convicted of two or more crimes.

> EXAMPLE Gus robs a bank. During the robbery he shoots 0⊷✶ and wounds a bank guard. Later he is arrested, brought to trial, and convicted of the attempted murder of the guard. He is also convicted of the bank robbery. Gus is sentenced to 25 years for attempted murder and 20 years for robbery, to be served one after the other. The robbery sentence will begin when the 25-year sentence for attempted murder expires.

cumulative voting A system of voting frequently used to elect the directors of a corporation. Every shareholder has one vote for each share he owns multiplied by the number of directors to be elected. The purpose of cumulative voting is to help holders of small numbers of shares to be represented on the board.

> EXAMPLE Five directors are to be elected. There are three 0⊷✶ electors: Ames, Bolton, and Clay. Ames owns 25 shares, Bolton owns 30 shares, and Clay owns 45 shares. Ames is entitled to cast his entire 125 votes (25 shares × 5 directors) for one director, if he wishes.

cunnilingus Oral stimulation of the female sexual organ. Under the common law the act was not considered a crime, but today it is a criminal offense in many states. The act is usually classified under the general crime of SODOMY.

cure The act of healing or restoring to soundness. For example, a seller delivers goods, which the buyer rejects because of some defect; if the seller then delivers the proper goods his act is considered a cure. When applied to a default in payments of money due, the word means the payment of all amounts in default.

curfew A regulation that prohibits certain or all pedestrians and vehicles from being out on the streets of a designated area after a designated hour of the evening. Curfews are often imposed during a natural disaster, a catastrophe, or similar public emergency.

The custom dates back at least to King Alfred (871–899) of England who ordered the inhabitants of Oxford to cover up their fires and go to bed at the ringing of a bell. The word "curfew" is related to the French *couvrefeu*—literally "cover the fire"—a practice that also prevailed in other countries of Europe, doubtless as a precaution against fires.

curtesy At common law, a husband was entitled to a life estate (ownership during his lifetime) in all the land that his wife owned at any time during their marriage, provided there were children born who could inherit the land. This kind of estate was known as curtesy. For example, John and Joan are husband and wife who have a child named Mark. Joan owns Greenacre Farm. Joan dies, and John and Mark survive her death. John now owns a life estate in all of Greenacre Farm under common-law curtesy. Curtesy has been abolished in a majority of states. Instead, the husband is given a distributive share in his wife's estate. See Chart 17. See also DESCENT AND DISTRIBUTION; WILL.

custody Possession and control. A valuable painting turned over to a court clerk for care and keeping during a lawsuit to determine who owns it is in the custody of the court. A prisoner is in custody when police officers detain or arrest him. Custody of children includes all aspects of their care and guardianship.

This article will discuss the law of custody of children, the factors that a court considers when deciding custody between parents after a DIVORCE or separation, and the results of custody disputes that involve someone who is not a parent. See also INFANT; PARENT AND CHILD.

■ **Custody in an ongoing family** Custody in its broadest sense refers to the rights and obligations of parents and children in an ongoing family. Usually parents and a child live together, but even if the child is away at boarding school his parents' residence remains his home. The parent has an obligation to care for, educate, and supervise the child, and the child has a right to receive this care. The parent must support the child, but he has a right to the child's earnings. Generally, the law does not interfere with this type of custody unless the child is neglected or abused.

The law will not interfere with a parent's care of his child unless custody is in dispute or the child is in danger. Moreover, one parent may not impose his opinions on another by court order unless there is danger to the health, education, or morals of the child.

> EXAMPLE In one New York case in 1936, an invalid mother 0⊷✶ was awarded sole custody of her 10-year-old daughter to the exclusion of the father, even though the family lived together very pleasantly except for a disagreement over religion. The mother wanted to prevent the father from teaching the child the beliefs of an obscure religious cult. The higher court reversed this order, however, on the ground that courts must not interfere with an intact family.

> EXAMPLE In a more recent Alabama case, a father won an 0⊷✶ injunction to prevent his wife from interfering with his right to enroll their seven-year-old daughter in a parochial school rather than a public school. Again the higher court overruled this order. When parents live together, they must settle their child-rearing differences without resorting to a court.

■ **When the family breaks up** The law will determine custody when a family breaks up. When more than one person wants custody, the court can investigate everyone involved and decide who will care for the child and to what extent each party may supervise the child.

A child becomes a legal adult when he reaches the age of majority (usually at 18 or 21), marries, or becomes self-supporting. When he is underage but is self-supporting or married (emancipated is the legal word), questions of custody may arise in spite of the child's legal status as an adult. He may still have claims against his parents for certain kinds of care—in a medical emergency, for example. An absent parent of an underage emancipated child may have some enforceable rights to visit the child or supervise his care.

■ **Background** Every judge's goal is to arrive at a solution that approaches the wisdom shown by King Solomon in the Bible. In that ancient case two poor women shared a bed and slept with their infant sons. One night one of the women rolled over on her baby and suffocated him. Each woman claimed the surviving child as her own. When Solomon announced that he would cut the baby in half with a sword and give half to each mother, only one woman cried that she would give up the child rather than have him die. Solomon decided that she was the baby's real mother.

English courts first asserted their jurisdiction (authority) in determining the custody of children in the 17th century. In American courts, jurisdiction to control the fate of children has been recognized from earliest days. The government has an obligation to protect children who are severely abused or neglected. If there is an argument over who will care for a child, the courts must decide who is to have custody and must see that someone will care for the child properly. The fact that a child lives or is simply present in the state or in the territory where the court has jurisdiction gives the court the authority to settle a custody dispute.

Under the old common law, a patriarchal law was written for landowning families, which passed wealth and position from father to son. All children were possessions of their fathers. If two parents separated, the child was delivered to the father. The harshness of the patriarchal rule, which permitted even suckling infants to be torn from their mothers and delivered to fathers, eventually led to the *tender-years doctrine,* a theory that small children are best nurtured by their mothers. The younger the child, the more likely a court was to award custody to the mother.

The tender-years doctrine became so entrenched that courts assumed that mothers were better custodial parents than fathers unless there was clear proof to the contrary. In

HOW CHILD CUSTODY DECISIONS ARE DETERMINED

■ The law determines custody when a family breaks up, and if more than one person wants custody the court can investigate everyone involved and decide who will care for the child.

■ Under the so-called tender-years doctrine, courts in the first half of the 20th century tended to assume that mothers were better custodial parents than fathers unless there was clear proof to the contrary. Since the 1960's the tender-years doctrine has lost ground, and some states now have laws requiring courts to give no weight to the sex of the parent claiming custody.

■ When neither parent wants the child, the court can place him or her with foster parents or, in extreme cases, terminate the natural parents' rights and free the child for adoption.

■ Parents can settle the question of who gets custody by a written separation agreement, subject to the court's supervision. The court looks out for the child's interests because the child has no voice in the negotiations.

■ The goal in custody cases is to determine the best interests of the child. Courts consider such things as the child's physical condition and general health, together with evidence of how well either or both parents have been contributing to these. They also consider the child's education, whether the child will be separated from brothers or sisters, the child's preference (this may be accorded great weight or ignored, according to the case), who has cared for the child in the past, and the parent's educational

background, living arrangements, religion, and general health—although a handicap may not prevent a parent from winning custody.

■ Courts prefer to give custody to the parent who continues to live in the family home.

■ The courts will want to know what plans the parent has to care for a child and provide for his education.

■ Children deriving their citizenship from an American parent must live in this country for a certain number of years in order not to lose their U.S. citizenship. Because American citizenship is a valuable right, courts often award custody to the parent intending to keep his or her children in this country.

■ The morals of parents determine many custody decisions, and women have traditionally been held to a stricter standard of conduct—in at least two states it still may be impossible for a mother to win custody if she has been guilty of adultery.

■ In the case of illegitimate children, the mother generally has the primary right to custody and loses it only if it is proved that she has abandoned the child or is otherwise seriously unfit.

■ An unwed father usually has more right to custody than any other relative except the mother, but he may lost this right if he fails to support the child, visit him, or show any interest in him for a period of time.

■ Six states have laws granting fathers visitation rights with illegitimate children, and courts in nearly every other state have granted the right.

■ An unwed father may also be able to prevent the adoption of his child.

■ Courts are reluctant to change custody. Solid proof of a serious change in circumstances is usually necessary.

■ If one parent objects to custody being given to the other parent because of a fear that the child will be taken a great distance away, the court can require the custodial parent to live within a certain geographical area unless he or she has a good reason to move.

■ Visitation rights protect the child's right to continue his relationship with the noncustodial parent, but under important restrictions. For example, babies often cannot be taken out of the house they live in, while teenagers may decide for themselves whether they will visit the absent parent.

■ If the parent who has custody refuses to allow visitation, courts often suspend the obligation of the absent parent to pay child support for as long as visitation is denied.

■ Some courts have permitted parents to experiment with dual custody; although this has worked well in some cases, most courts still regard it as an unusual solution for child care and will not order it unless both parents agree to the plan.

■ A custody case can be started by filing a writ of habeas corpus, asking the court to decide whether one who has possession of another person is entitled to have custody.

■ "Snatching" one's own child is not kidnapping, but it may be punishable as contempt of court or as the crime of interfering with custody.

the first half of this century, most divorces permitted under the law were based on adultery by husbands. It is not surprising, therefore, that courts developed a tradition of giving preference in custody disputes to women who were forced into divorces by guilty husbands.

By the 1960's pressure grew to swing back to a more balanced position. As a result, judges have increasingly declared the preference for mothers to be basically unfair. Some states now have laws that specifically require courts to give no weight to the fact that the parent seeking custody is the mother or the father.

■ **Children of divorce** Many judges admit to sleepless nights when they must decide custody cases in which the children are the victims. It has been said that there are four possibile situations for children when parents separate. The luckiest of these children have two parents who love and want them but at least one who is willing not to fight for custody. Somewhat less fortunate are those children who have one parent who loves and cares for them and one parent who is indifferent and will not fight for their custody. Very unfortunate are the children who have two parents who love them and will battle over custody at any cost. Saddest of all are the children who have two parents, neither of whom loves them enough to care for them.

Neither parent Sometimes neither parent really wants the children.

EXAMPLE A mother turned her six children over to their 0—* father so that she could prepare herself for employment. The father agreed to let the children live with him for a while. The mother decided that her best opportunity lay in joining the army. Before she was accepted, the army required her to present a court judgment naming the father as custodian of the children. The woman petitioned the court for such an order, but the father opposed it and the court refused to award custody to either parent.

Fortunately, children who have two completely irresponsible parents can usually be protected by the law. Courts can place them with trained foster parents or, in extreme cases, completely terminate the natural parents' rights and free the children for adoption.

EXAMPLE The parents of three young children had a history 0—* of serious and continuous use of drugs. The court provided foster care for the youngsters while the parents were given time to break their drug habits and establish a home for their children. When the parents failed even to show interest in the children (they visited the oldest only three times in 4½ years and the two younger ones only once in 20 months), the court found that the children were "permanently neglected." This freed them for adoption.

One parent In cases where one parent willingly provides care for the child and another parent backs off—either because he is indifferent or because he wisely spares the child a custody battle—courts are not called upon to protect the interests of the child.

Parents can settle the question of custody by a written separation agreement, which frequently provides that one parent has custody of the children and the other does not object. The court will supervise such an agreement to protect a child who has had no voice in the negotiations.

Dispute between two parents When a court must decide a custody case between two parents who have separated, it will investigate the child and the parents. It will consider the child, the living arrangements and psychological fitness of each parent, and sometimes the reasons for the divorce or separation. Courts can usually impose conditions on the custody arrangement and allow visitation rights for the noncustodial parent.

Custody decisions are not easily made. Often neither parent is an ideal custodian. So custody decisions try to do what is in the best interests of the child. While this seems obvious, it is a distinct change from the ancient principle of parents' rights. In general, in determining the child's best interests courts consider all the circumstances of both parents' homes, as discussed in the following sections.

■ **The child** It is very important for the court to investigate the child. If one parent had custody for a while or if one parent took primary responsibility for his care while the parents lived together, the child's physical, mental, and emotional condition will indicate the workability of the existing relationship.

Physical condition The physical condition of a child may show how much attention he is receiving.

EXAMPLE A baby girl found at a bar where the mother was a 0—* dancer was wrapped in a soiled blanket with no other clothing on. The court held that she was not receiving proper care. A man in another case tried to get custody of his eight-year-old son because the boy sometimes had a dirty face and messy clothes when his father picked him up for visitation. The court recognized that keeping a small boy clean at all times is impossible. Custody remained with the mother.

The court must consider all the circumstances when evaluating the physical condition of a child.

EXAMPLE In the case of a 16-year-old boy, the court 0—* changed custody not only because he was grossly overweight but also because it found that he spent most of his time watching television and snacking. He did not get along well with other young people, so he generally stayed home. His mother worked afternoons and evenings and seemed unable to help the boy learn to handle his personal problems. The court hoped that the father could present a worthy role model for the boy and spend more time with him as the custodial parent.

Health The health of a child is always considered. Custody can be changed if the parent who has the child fails to provide routine dental care or the usual vaccinations to prevent childhood diseases, if the child is unusually pale or thin, or if he often suffers from illness or accidents.

Education and social adjustment The education and social adjustment of a child are good indicators of the care he receives. If a child is frequently absent from school or becomes a discipline problem for his teachers, a court may properly ask about the positive efforts by his custodial parent to help him adjust.

Brothers and sisters Most courts try to keep brothers and sisters together.

Preference of the child If the child is old enough to understand the situation, the court will often ask him whether he prefers to live with his mother or his father. Often, though, the child's preference is not an important factor in the judge's decision because a child may prefer the parent who gives him everything he wants. While the case winds its way through the courts, a parent may take better care of the child to show the court what a good parent he is. This does not mean that the child will be well cared for after custody is awarded.

In deciding how much weight to give a child's preference, the court will take into account his age, the reasons for his preference, and the strength of his preference for one parent or his dislike of the other. Generally the court interviews the child in a room other than the courtroom, especially if the child is young. In some states the parents and their attorneys cannot be present, and usually no record is made of the conversation so that the child will talk freely. But he must not be forced to express an opinion about his parents if he does not want to, nor be made to feel that he is responsible for the final decision concerning custody.

If a child is old enough, the court may refuse to make any decision concerning custody. It may be better for a 17-year-old, for example, to work out living arrangements with his parents by himself. If both parents agree to living arrangements for an older child—as in the case of a student away at college—a rigid court order may get in the way of cooperation concerning his vacation time.

Who has cared for the child in the past The court may take into account the history of care the child has received. If only one parent has prepared meals or provided clothes for the child, tended him when he was sick, helped him with his homework, and gone to his Little League games, these facts may be taken into account. But present circumstances can defeat the importance of earlier attention. The fact that a parent provided good care for many years is not important if that parent now drinks heavily and disappears for days at a time. On the other hand, a court may not be impressed by a show of great concern for the child's welfare if the parent seems only to have discovered his child after a divorce.

■ **The parents** The rule is that, all things being equal, both parents have a right to custody of a child. The court will investigate each parent.

Sex Occasionally, the sex of a parent affects a judge's decision. Mothers are still more often given custody of small children because mothers more often have been caring for them. When the custody of a teenager is at issue, some judges choose the parent of the same sex as the child.

Health The parent's health may be important. A parent should not lose custody, however, solely on the basis of a handicap. In fact, it can be an inspiration for children to live in a home that is well run despite a parent's deafness or arthritis, for example.

EXAMPLE One divorced mother became paralyzed after suffering a rare reaction to medication. She sent her two children to live with their father during the months she needed to recover. When the father refused to return the children, a court found that even though the mother would always need a cane to walk and sometimes slurred words when she talked, she had made a remarkable recovery and was able to care for the children properly again. She should not lose custody of her children just because she made temporary arrangements for their care while she was disabled.

A parent who is addicted to drugs or alcohol, on the other hand, certainly is in no condition to care for children. Mental problems that make it difficult for a parent to provide a stable home, handle stress, and make firm decisions will nearly always lead the court to deny custody. But a mental or physical problem that has been cured should not be held against a parent seeking custody. In fact, overcoming a problem may have made the parent a better custodian. The court will look for positive signs of recovery, such as a settled home life or a steady job.

The parent's home Courts prefer to give custody to the parent who continues to live in the family's home, where the child can remain in his own room, rather than to the parent who remarries and wants the child to live with stepchildren in a crowded apartment.

The wealth or poverty of a parent should be given very little weight in deciding custody. A parent who claims that he can give the child more material benefits can do so whether or not he has custody.

EXAMPLE A nine-year-old boy, whose father was remarried to a wealthy woman and lived with her on her family's estate, said he preferred to live in his father's "castle." But the court refused to take the child away from his mother. The judge said that if the father now had so much money and the mother barely enough, the answer was to increase the child-support payments.

Plans for the child Most courts want to know what plans a parent has to care for a child. If, for example, the father owns a luncheonette and works 12 hours a day, seven days a week, the court needs to know what arrangements he can make for the care of the child.

EXAMPLE One woman who worked full time and attended college four nights a week lost custody because she thought her 11-year-old daughter was old enough to be left alone all the time. The court emphasized that while neither father nor mother can be penalized for seeking an education, because this usually will benefit the child, adequate provision must still be made for the child.

Education The level of education achieved by a parent should not determine custody. A warm and loving person is able to raise a child regardless of his or her formal education. A court will be interested, however, in the plans a parent has for his child's education. Sometimes courts expect parents to plan for their child to be educated at least as much as they are. If both father and mother have postgraduate degrees and professional careers, the court may question the fitness of a parent who does not insist that the child attend school regularly or who says that planning for the child's college education is not important.

Race There have been instances in which the race of a parent has been the deciding factor in a custody case. Children of a white and a black parent, for example, have been given to the black parent because courts thought they might suffer less from prejudice in the black community than among whites. Many courts have now ruled that race must be completely disregarded in a custody case because of equal rights guarantees in the Constitution.

EXAMPLE Two white parents were divorced, and the mother remarried a black man. The court ruled that this was not reason enough by itself to refuse the mother custody. The judge recognized that racial tensions exist in this country but pointed out that in the mother's home the children might learn tolerance.

Religion   Religion has historically been treated with great respect in custody cases. Courts sometimes question parents about their religious views and church attendance. Although it can be argued that religious observance does not guarantee a good relationship between parent and child, a parent who goes to church every week often wins custody over a parent who is indifferent to religion.

When parents practice different religions, courts generally try to avoid judging the correctness of either religion unless there seems to be a danger to the child. When a parent's religion forbids surgery or blood transfusions, a court may grant custody only if the parent agrees to permit normal medical care should the child need it.

Antenuptial agreements—contracts made before the parents were married—sometimes state that children will be raised in a particular religion. If the parents separate and one strays from religion, adopts a new religion, or practices a religion different from the one named in the agreement, the other parent may ask for custody on that ground. Usually, however, courts will not enforce such antenuptial agreements.

Citizenship   Children who are not born in the United States but derive their citizenship through an American parent must live in this country for a certain number of years in order not to lose their U.S. citizenship. Courts often award custody to a parent who intends to keep his or her children in this country, because American citizenship is a valuable right.

EXAMPLE One court refused to give a mother permission to take her five-year-old daughter to Australia, because, it said, "Nowhere in the world today is the right of citizenship of greater worth to an individual than it is in this country. It would be difficult to exaggerate its value and importance." In another case, however, the question was whether the custody of two girls should be given to an aunt in France after their father had murdered their mother. The Supreme Court of Oklahoma permitted them to go to France after a French official testified that in France the children would have free medical care, free education to the Ph.D. level, a family, and an orphan's allocation of about $150 a month per child.

Sex and morals   The sex life and morals of parents have determined the outcome of many custody battles. Although more men than women have been denied custody, women have traditionally been held to a stricter standard of conduct than men. In some states it still may be impossible for a mother to win custody if she has been guilty of adultery.

The possibility of taking custody of a child away from a parent by proving that the parent was engaging in sexual activity outside of marriage has encouraged both spying and litigation. But now an increasing number of states require proof that a custodian's activities directly harm the children before they will change a previous custody decision.

EXAMPLE In an Iowa case, the court concluded that a mother's illicit relations with a man were so open that the children were being harmed. Her 15-year-old daughter suffered embarrassment among her friends, and a 9-year-old daughter described an incident in which she was sleeping with her mother when the man crawled into bed with them. Custody was awarded to the children's father.

EXAMPLE In a New York case, a father won custody of six- and nine-year-old children from their mother when he proved that she continued to keep company with a man after she discovered that the man was married, that she and the man had answered "swinger" ads in a pornographic magazine, and that she had a copy of the magazine in her home. On appeal, the change of custody was reversed. The court found no evidence that the children had ever been exposed to pornography or had been neglected or harmed because of their mother's affair. To find parents unfit just because they indulge in "free sex," the court said, would justify the state in putting the children of all "swinging" parents in foster homes or orphanages.

EXAMPLE In 1973 a Nevada court had to decide custody in a bizarre case. Four daughters were living with their mother when she underwent a sex-change operation. The mother began sporting sideburns and a mustache and appeared to all to be a strong and healthy male. She, now he, entered a marriage ceremony with a woman, and together they made a home for the children.

The court specifically considered the relationship the girls had with each parent. It found that the natural father had obtained a court order for their custody, but they had run away. After being reported missing, they were picked up and held in jail, where their mother was not permitted to visit them. Throughout the trial, the court observed, the father never spoke to the girls except to say "hello," and there was obvious affection between the children and the sex-changed mother. One daughter testified that the children understood their mother's change of sex and appreciated it for what it was. The court awarded custody to the mother.

Homosexuality   It is only in recent years that a homosexual parent has been able to enforce the right even to visit his or her children. Generally, visitation has been restricted by conditions that the children not be exposed to any of the parent's homosexual friends or spend the night at the parent's home if the parent is living with anyone but a lawful spouse.

In a few cases, homosexual parents have been permitted to retain custody if they agreed not to flaunt their life-style or entangle the children in publicity.

EXAMPLE One father in Oregon was charged in a custody dispute with being homosexual because he lived with a male business partner. The court refused to change custody to the mother because she had had almost no contact with her two sons for 11 years. The court noted that the father was not openly homosexual and that the boys had not been exposed to deviant sexual acts or adversely affected in any way.

Unwed parents   The illegitimacy of a child will influence a judge's decision. Many courts have said the mother should have custody unless she is unfit, and others find that it is usually in the child's best interest to stay with his mother. But a mother loses her right to custody in most states if it is proved that she has abandoned the child.

A father usually may not win custody from the mother unless she is unfit, but he may have more right to custody than another relative, a foster parent, or a stranger who wishes to adopt the child. A father may lose this right if he fails to support a child, visit him, or show any interest in him for a period of time.

EXAMPLE A father and mother had lived together for many years but never married. When the mother died, the father sought custody from the foster parents who had been caring for his children during the mother's illness and after her death. The court held that a father who has lived with his children and supported them cannot be denied custody just because he was not married to their mother. He must at least be given a hearing where he has the chance to prove that he is fit to have custody.

Alabama, California, Massachusetts, New York, Pennsylvania, and Wisconsin have laws granting fathers visitation rights with their illegitimate children, and courts in nearly every other state have granted the right as well. An unwed father can also prevent the adoption of his child. For further discussion of the custody of illegitimate children, see ILLEGITIMACY.

■ **Doctors' opinions** The use of psychiatric reports and examinations to determine the mental state of the children and adults in custody cases is widely accepted. Judges do not presume to understand all the subtleties of psychology and are happy to turn to experts for their opinions, but they should always require a psychologist or psychiatrist to explain the facts on which he relies.

In any case in which psychiatrists are called to testify or submit reports, the testimony of any doctor, including the family physician, who regularly treats a person is acceptable, but the court may give it less weight than a report from an impartial, court-appointed psychiatrist.

In most states, a court has the authority to order psychiatric examination of the people involved in a custody case. The court may require the person who started the case to pay for these examinations. They can be rather expensive and thus may discourage legal action by someone who does not seriously seek custody but wants only to harass the person presently caring for the children.

■ **Dual custody** Some courts have permitted parents to experiment with dual (joint) custody, an arrangement in which each parent takes full responsibility for the care and supervision of the child about half the time. Dual custody has not been particularly favored, because parents who cannot cooperate enough to stay married usually do not work together well enough to share custody.

EXAMPLE Two parents were allowed to split custody in a complicated arrangement by which each week was divided between them. Their son, a preschooler, kept clothes and toys at each apartment—they were only a few blocks apart—and alternated between the parents. The plan was approved because it had worked out well for the few months before the custody hearing.

EXAMPLE In another case, two other parents, both professionals, had been married nearly 20 years. They decided to share custody of both home and children. Instead of shuttling the children between them, the children stayed at home and the parents alternated visits.

Dual custody sometimes works, but most courts still regard it as an unusual solution for child care. Courts will not order it unless both parents agree to the plan.

■ **Parent v. nonparent** Custody battles between a parent and another relative of the child or a "stranger"—someone not related to the child—are decided much the same as disputes between parents. The difference is that a parent is usually given preference unless he or she has long neglected the child. Such cases often arise when the child's parents are divorced, the custodial parent remarries and later dies, and the stepparent refuses to give the child to the natural parent.

EXAMPLE In Mississippi the parents of three children, aged 15, 13, and 11, had been divorced for eight years. During that time the mother had custody and the father had contributed less than $500 for the children's support. The father said that the mother agreed to let him skip support payments if he stayed away from the children. He visited them "several times" in eight years.

The mother had remarried. When she died, the children continued to live with their stepfather, and the father sought custody. The court decided that the father had a superior right to custody over anyone who was not a natural parent. The judges on appeal were not concerned that the father drank beer and did not go to church or that he had sold his visitation rights in exchange for the mother's agreement not to demand support. The judges condemned the stepfather for breaking up the marriage of the children's parents and on that basis found that he should not have custody.

At no time did the court discuss where the children wanted to live. They had lived in the stepfather's home for eight years, but there was no consideration of their growth or condition. Nothing was said about their education, maturity, or physical fitness. Neither the father nor the stepfather was asked about plans for the children's futures. The court disapproved of the stepfather's "amorous proclivities" but overlooked evidence of the father's drunkenness. The court strongly protected the parent's right to custody over the nonparent. Although the court's decision in this case has been criticized as extreme, the decision is nevertheless the law.

Sometimes the fight for custody is between a parent and grandparents.

EXAMPLE In a famous Iowa case decided in 1966, a natural father lost custody of his seven-year-old son. After the boy's mother died, his father sent him from California to live with his wife's parents on a farm in Iowa. After the father remarried, he asked to have his son back, and the grandparents refused. The boy, Mark, had lived with them from age three to age seven.

The court discussed the father's irregular employment record and failure to establish a home or make plans for Mark's care, in contrast with the education, community standing, and church ties of the grandparents. They found that the child knew who his father was but really saw his grandfather in the role of father. The decision created a stir all over the country when the court wrote:

"The [grandparents'] home provides Mark with a stable, dependable, conventional, middle-class, middle-west background and an opportunity for a college education and profession, if he desires it. It provides a solid foundation and secure atmosphere. In the [father's] home, Mark would have more freedom of conduct and thought with an opportunity to develop his individual talents. It would be more exciting and challenging in many respects, but romantic, impractical and unstable."

In 1969, however, Mark's grandparents allowed him to visit his father in California. When Mark wanted to stay with him, his grandparents did not oppose a temporary order changing custody to his father.

■ **Conditions imposed on custody and visitation** Courts have the authority to grant custody with whatever conditions seem necessary to protect the child. It is not unusual to require that certain other persons be kept out of the child's presence—perhaps a lover who contributed to the breakup of the parents' marriage. If one parent objects to custody being given to the other parent because of a fear that the child will be taken a great distance away, the court can require the custodial parent to live within a certain geographical area unless he or she has a good reason to move.

EXAMPLE A father was afraid the mother would take O—* the children back to her native Morocco and he would never see them again. The judge ordered the mother to post a $50,000 bond whenever she took the children to North Africa to visit their grandparents. The money would be forfeited if the children did not return within six weeks. In another case, the mother was protected because the father, a French national, was required to leave his passport with her when the children visited him during their summer vacation.

Conditions can also be attached to visitation, which is really a kind of temporary custody. Visitation rights protect the child's right to continue his relationship with the noncustodial parent. Sometimes a court will restrict the distance a child can be taken while he visits the noncustodial parent or require suitable sleeping arrangements before the child can be taken overnight. Babies often cannot be taken out of the house they live in, while teenagers may decide for themselves whether or not they will visit the absent parent. If the parent who has custody refuses to allow visitation, courts often suspend the obligation of the absent parent to pay child support for as long as visitation is denied.

■ **Change of custody** Although it is a basic rule of law that litigation must finally come to an end, and the parties must live with the decision, society has such a strong interest in protecting children that courts will continue to supervise their custody when necessary. It is in everyone's interest, however, to consider custody a settled, long-term arrangement. A judge in Oregon once remarked that he found that the chances of a child growing up with emotional problems increase in direct proportion to the thickness of his file in a custody case.

Solid proof of a serious change in circumstances since the original decision was made is usually necessary to change custody. The fact that a parent who lost custody now has a pleasant home, more money, or greater maturity is not enough justification to change a custody decision. It must be shown that the child is suffering from some new, different, or more serious problem in the home where he is presently living.

■ **Procedure** Usually the issue of custody arises because of a matrimonial action—that is, a suit for separation or divorce. In most states, custody can be decided even if the divorce or legal separation is not granted.

A custody case can also be started by filing a writ of HABEAS CORPUS, which asks a court to decide whether someone who has custody of another person is entitled to it. In addition, custody may be determined during child-abuse or neglect proceedings, in guardianship proceedings, or by bringing a petition in EQUITY in some states that still use special equity courts for custody cases.

Generally, a custody action may be started in any state in which the child is located, even if a custody order has already been entered in another state, on the theory that custody decisions are never final to the extent that courts will not change them if necessary to protect a child.

Parental kidnapping Because a new custody case can be started if a child is moved to a different state, parents sometimes "kidnap" their own children, take them to a different state, and try their luck at winning custody in a court there. A mother who lost custody might take her child to a state that applies the "tender-years doctrine," which gives preference to mothers. "Kidnapping" one's own child is not generally a crime, but it may be punishable as a CONTEMPT of court if the parent goes back to the first state.

EXAMPLE Ian and Joan Macklinson were separated when O—* Joan started a lawsuit against him for divorce. One weekend, Ian took their son Mark for a visit and refused to return him. When the divorce case came up in court three weeks later, the judge ordered Ian to produce the child in court three days hence. Ian arrived without Mark. He said that he did not bring the boy to court because he thought Joan would take him and refuse to let him ever see Mark again. The judge found Ian guilty of contempt for willfully disobeying the court order and sentenced him to 10 days in the county jail, sentence to be suspended if he appeared with the child at the courthouse within 24 hours.

The federal Uniform Child Custody Jurisdiction Act proposes a law for the states to enact. See UNIFORM ACT. This law requires that the court having the "closest connection" to the child and the most evidence concerning circumstances of his "care, protection, training, and personal relationships" will decide the issue of custody. A number of states have in fact adopted the law. Then other courts decline to hear the case and suggest that parties return to that state with the closer connection to the case.

custom and usage The regular practice or normal way of doing things within a geographical area or a certain type of business. Custom and usage can have the force of unwritten law because a court looks at the usual routine when it must interpret the words of a contract, apply a particular law, or decide ownership of something.

EXAMPLE A general rule of law is that no one can own a wild O—* animal unless he has actual possession of it. It was once the usual practice in a particular village for every whale hunter to put an identifying mark on his harpoon. When a whale was hit by a harpoon, the whaler would wait for his catch to die and float to shore. The custom and usage in this village was never to cut up the carcass of a whale killed by another hunter's harpoon. Because it is difficult to hold onto a whale after it is speared, this custom was necessary to the whalers. If someone discovered a whale on the beach and took possession of it, a court would certainly apply the local custom rather than the general rule of law. The hunter who harpooned the whale would have the greater right to it.

Trade usage refers to the customary practice within a particular business or industry.

EXAMPLE One famous case, decided by a federal court in 0→—＊ 1960, began with the words, "What is a chicken?" The case grew out of the rapidly expanding business of selling frozen American chickens abroad after World War II. The court had to decide what was meant in a contract by the word "chicken."

A Swiss importer had agreed to buy 175,000 pounds of frozen chicken from a New York sales company. The court noted that the parties had used the English word "chicken" rather than the German word *Huhn,* even though the two contracts were mostly in German. The Americans sent different grades of chicken, including young broilers and older fowl, and the Swiss protested that they thought "chicken" meant only "young chicken." They sued for damages, claiming money for the difference in value of broilers and fowl.

The court looked at the language of the cables the two parties had sent to each other, the grades used by the U.S. Department of Agriculture, and the custom and usage of the trade. It found that people in the chicken business use the word "chicken" to mean "everything except a goose, a duck and a turkey." If the plaintiff had wanted a better grade of chicken, he should have bargained for it specifically.

customs Duties, tariffs, or taxes on merchandise imported from, or exported to, a foreign country. To be an import within the customs laws, goods must be brought into a proper port of entry (there are about 300 such ports in the United States) with an intent to unload them.

The main purpose of customs laws is to impose duties on certain articles that enter the country's commerce, with the object of protecting American industries against unfair competition from foreign countries. Other purposes are to make customs duties uniform with those imposed by other countries and to provide revenue for the government.

The U.S. Court of International Trade, formerly the Customs Court, and the U.S. Court of Customs and Patent Appeals have been created by Congress to hear cases regarding customs duties. See FEDERAL COURTS.

Congress has the exclusive power to decide how the right to import may be exercised and the exclusive power to levy duties that discriminate between nations.

■ **Goods and articles subject to duty** Whether particular goods or articles are subject to an import duty depends upon the federal *tariff schedules,* which list the articles on which a duty is imposed and the rates at which they are taxed.

Exemptions A resident of the United States returning from a trip abroad is exempt from paying duty on certain articles. In order to qualify for the exemption, the person must stay abroad for a minimum of 48 hours. The exemption is based on the reasonable retail value of each article in the country where the item is purchased. The total amount of the exemption is $300 per person; children are entitled to the same sum. The items must be obtained for your own personal or household use or as gifts. Cigarettes, cigars, and alcoholic beverages are included within the exemption but limited to 200 cigarettes, 100 cigars, and one liter of alcoholic beverages. There is a $600 exemption for persons returning from insular possessions, such as American Samoa, Guam, and the Virgin Islands. One gallon of alcoholic beverages may be brought back from these places duty free.

Vehicles, such as automobiles, taken abroad for a non-business purpose may be sent back without payment of a duty. Proof that the vehicle was shipped from the United States is necessary. Proof may be in the form of a state motor vehicle registration certificate or a customs-registration certificate that is obtained when the automobile is registered before shipment. If repairs are made on the automobile while it is abroad, then the value of the repairs must be declared and a duty paid on that value.

Draperies, rugs, furniture, and other household goods obtained abroad and used there for one year may be imported without paying a duty, provided they are not imported for sale or for use by some other person. Articles such as cameras, hi-fi equipment, and watches are not included in the category of household goods, and duty must be paid on such articles. When household goods are shipped abroad from the United States, they may be returned duty free. Similarly, personal items such as cameras and watches originally manufactured in a foreign country but purchased in the United States may be returned duty free if they were identified and registered with customs before being taken abroad.

Gifts Gifts received abroad must be included within a person's $300 exemption, as must gifts brought home for oneself or others. Gifts valued at $25 or less in the country of shipment can be accepted by the recipient in the United States duty free. The same person may not receive more than one $25 gift on any single day. If he does, a duty (and tax, if applicable) must be paid on all items—even the first $25 item. Gifts of liquor or tobacco are not included within the $25 exemption.

Additional items When the total value of the imported items exceeds the $300 exemption, a written declaration listing all items must be prepared. Duty must be paid on the excess amount. The duty on the additional items is based on their fair retail value. Those items that are assessed at the highest duty rates are included within the $300 exemption. The items assessed at lower rates are placed in the excess category.

EXAMPLE You have purchased a bone china figurine worth 0→—＊ $300 and a chess set that is also worth $300. The duty rate for bone china is 17½ percent, but the duty rate for chess sets is only 10 percent. The bone china figurine would be placed under your $300 exemption. The chess set would be considered an item in excess of your customs exemption, and you would pay $30 in duty.

Payment of the duty on the items in excess of the $300 exemption may be made in American money, personal check, government check, traveler's checks, or money orders. Personal checks must be drawn on a national or state bank or trust company of the United States.

Restricted items Certain items are restricted because they are harmful to the general welfare of the United States or to a particular area of our society. Plants and plant products, for example, may have harmful insects or other pests that could cause extensive damage to crops or forest areas. Permits are required before restricted plants can be imported. Common examples of plants or plant products that require permits include cotton plants, corn, and fresh berries. Permits are also required for live animals, such as horses, goats, sheep, and zoo animals. Pets must be inspected by veterinarians of the U.S. Department of Agriculture, and they must frequently be quarantined for a period before entry.

Permits must be obtained when firearms, such as rifles and shotguns, and ammunition are imported. Weapons taken abroad for use on a hunting trip may be returned without a permit by the same person who took them abroad. Ordinarily, firearms are registered with customs prior to departure, but no more than three firearms and 1,000 cartridges can be registered.

■ **Prohibited items** The importing of narcotic drugs is strictly prohibited. Medication containing narcotic substances must be properly identified, and a prescription or statement by a physician relating to such medication should be carried by the traveler. Other prohibited items include plants in soil; citrus peels; coffeeberries; hay, straw, and grass; fresh dairy products; and seeds from a variety of plants. All items exported from certain countries, including Cuba, North Korea, and Vietnam, are also prohibited. Photographic film is prohibited when it contains obscene or treasonable material or when it advocates the overthrow of the government or forcible resistance to our laws.

■ **Penalties** Items brought home from abroad must be declared. When an item is not declared, or its value is understated, it is subject to seizure and forfeiture. In addition, the traveler must pay a penalty equal to the item's value in the United States, not in the country where it was purchased. A criminal action may be brought against a person who fails to declare an item. See also SEARCH AND SEIZURE; SMUGGLING.

cy pres (Anglo-French) "As near as possible"; a rule used in interpretating documents such as charitable TRUSTS and WILLS. Under cy pres the intention of the person who wrote a document is carried out as nearly as possible, when it is impossible or illegal to carry it out literally.

EXAMPLE A provision in a will makes a gift of money to a hospital to be used for the construction of a new building or to be used to dedicate an existing building. The gift is not large enough to construct a new building, and the existing building named in the will has already been dedicated. The court applies the cy pres rule and allows the hospital to build a new structure on the roof of one of its existing buildings. The new structure is devoted to medical research and laboratory use, and on it is placed an appropriate tablet stating the origin of the gift.

Two elements are required in the use of cy pres. There must be a general charitable intent, and the property must be applied to a purpose similar to the one designated in the trust or will. If the property given in trust is to be applied to a specific charitable purpose, and the trust provides that if that purpose fails the entire trust is to terminate, cy pres will not be used.

The modern trend is to expand the ability of the court to choose among several schemes and not be limited to the one most like that designated in the will. Some common situations in trusts and wills that might bring cy pres into use are when the amount of property is insufficient for the purpose; when the purpose is already accomplished; when the consent of a third person is not obtainable (for example, a historical house is left as a gift to be open to the public if the town consents to maintain it, and the town refuses consent); when the purpose is useless (such as the funding of large centers for the treatment of smallpox, a disease that has been virtually eliminated); when the purpose is illegal (such as maintaining a public park for whites); and when the circumstances have changed (such as a gift to orphans in a town where there are no orphans).

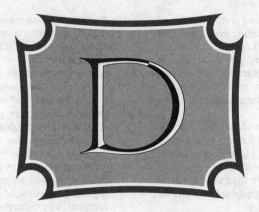

damages The COMPENSATION in money that a court will award in a lawsuit to make up for a loss or injury sustained by a person because of someone else's wrongful conduct. Damages express the injury in dollars and cents. They differ from COSTS, which are the expenses of the lawsuit that a judge orders a losing party to pay, and from the VERDICT, which is the final decision of the jury.

This article explains the major classes of damages—compensatory, nominal, punitive—and when they may be awarded in actions arising from violations of CIVIL RIGHTS, CONTRACTS, and TORTS (wrongful conduct that arises from something other than a contract). It also defines liquidated damages and distinguishes them from penalty provisions found in contracts. Finally, it discusses the procedure to correct an excessive or inadequate award of damages.

■ **How damages operate** Damages are based on the principles of just compensation, indemnity, or reparation for a loss or injury. The object of awarding damages is to help the injured party regain as nearly as possible his position or condition before the injury. The injured party usually receives no more than just compensation for the loss or injury sustained.

Ordinarily, damages are calculated on the basis of the injured party's loss and not on the wrongdoer's gain, but there are exceptions to this—in COPYRIGHT infringement, for example. Damages are usually considered remedial—that is, their purpose is to right a wrong rather than punish or prevent wrongful actions. Punitive (or exemplary) damages are sometimes awarded, however.

There are various methods of assessing damages, but responsibility for the wrongful conduct must first be established in a civil TRIAL. The trial, which may be before a judge and jury or before a judge alone, determines whether or not the plaintiff (the complaining party) has, in fact, sustained an injury that was caused by the defendant (the party being sued), and if so, the nature and extent of that injury. In a jury trial, the judge decides the measure, or type, of damages available; how much to award the injured person under that measure is left to the jury. If there is no jury, the judge decides both matters.

The process of assessment in each of the three main categories of damages—compensatory, nominal, and punitive—is discussed below.

■ **Compensatory damages** Compensatory damages are awarded to replace the loss or injury to the plaintiff that is caused by the defendant's wrongful acts. A wrongdoer is liable (legally responsible) for all the natural and direct consequences of his acts, but there is a limit to the extent of liability—remote consequences of a defendant's act are not a proper basis for an award.

EXAMPLE I am speeding in my car and hit a taxicab. I am liable for the taxi driver's injuries (such as a broken leg) or losses (the cost of the demolished cab). But I am not liable for the remote consequences of my speeding.

EXAMPLE The taxi driver claims that his possible future career as a neurosurgeon is ended as a result of the accident; he has lost some mobility in his leg and cannot stand for the long periods of time required of a surgeon performing operations. He will not be awarded damages for this loss. The end of this imagined career is at best remotely related to the accident. It is not a natural result of my act, particularly if the taxi driver had never shown the inclination or intellectual ability to become a neurosurgeon before he was injured.

Compensatory damages for a further loss or injury resulting from the consequences of the defendant's wrongful act but not directly from the act itself are called *consequential damages*.

EXAMPLE Suppose the taxi driver in the example above developed gangrene in his broken leg. The gangrene is an injury that is consequential to my car's hitting him, and I will be liable. Another consequential damage is the loss of business the taxi driver suffers because his cab was demolished.

Cause for recovery A person is entitled to recover compensatory damages only when he can show that his injuries or losses were proximately caused by the defendant. The *proximate cause* is the direct cause of the injury, with no broken connection between the act and the resulting damage.

EXAMPLE If I push you and you fall, breaking your arm, my act is the proximate cause of your injury. But suppose, while you are in the hospital having your arm set, your doctor neglects to administer an antibiotic so that you develop a blood infection that requires an added six weeks' hospitalization. Although the proximate cause of your broken arm was my pushing you, your blood poisoning was caused by the intervening negligence (the intervening cause, discussed below) of your doctor.

Concurring causes There may be more than one proximate cause of injury. When several proximate causes contribute to an accident, the injury may be attributed to any or all such causes. These simultaneous acts are known as concurring causes of injury.

EXAMPLE Charles stabs Floyd in the chest with a knife, O—* while Peter crushes Floyd's skull with a rock. Either wound would be fatal and Floyd dies from the effects of both. Charles and Peter will not be relieved of liability because Floyd would have died as a result of either act alone. Each cause has played a substantial role in producing the result.

Intervening cause An intervening cause is an independent act or omission that breaks the chain between the proximate cause and the injury or loss to the plaintiff. It produces the injury or loss after the original wrongful act of the defendant. If the intervening cause can reasonably be anticipated, the defendant may be liable because he was negligent and failed to guard against the injury.

EXAMPLE John is installing some wires and leaves them O—* unattended (the original wrongful act). A curious passerby inspects them (the intervening cause) and is electrocuted. John could have anticipated that people might touch the wires and become injured. Although the plaintiff's act (touching the wires) has intervened between the defendant's wrong (leaving the wires in a public place) and the plaintiff's injury (electrocution), the defendant is not excused if the intervening act was the result of his earlier wrong. John's failure to guard against foreseeable intervening events is considered NEGLIGENCE.

Preexisting conditions A tort-feasor (wrongdoer) takes the person he injures as he finds him—he is liable even if his victim is more susceptible than most to injury.

EXAMPLE In one case, the plaintiff's physical condition O—* made him peculiarly susceptible to nausea and to injury from vomiting. This did not excuse the defendant, a bottling company, from negligence in processing a bottled beverage that contained a dead mouse.

The injured person may also recover damages that result from the activation of a dormant disease or condition.

EXAMPLE If a hemophiliac child is hit by a speeding truck, O—* the driver will be liable for the child's injuries, including the additional costs of numerous blood transfusions. The truck driver cannot disclaim liability for the transfusions on the ground that the need for them did not directly result from the wrongful act.

On the other hand, if a preexisting disease is aggravated by the wrongful act of another person, the victim's recovery in damages is limited to the additional injury caused by the aggravation.

EXAMPLE Let us say that you are suffering from a heart O—* ailment and are hit by a car, which breaks your leg. The driver of the car will be liable for the expenses of your broken leg, but only for those treatments relating to your heart disorder that were needed because of the accident and not for all treatments given to you for your heart condition for the rest of your life.

Breach of contract Compensatory damages for breach of contract (failure of one party to keep his side of the bargain) are awarded for injury or loss that results from the breach itself.

EXAMPLE Carol signs a contract with Specialty Favor Com-O—* pany for monogrammed napkins, specially printed matchbooks, and other favors for her parents' 50th wedding anniversary party. The contract specifies that the favors are to be delivered by June 1, one week before the party. When they do not arrive on time, Carol calls Specialty Company, which tells her that it has lost the order and cannot now fill it on time. Carol gets Custom Favor Company to provide the favors but at a much higher cost because of the rush. Carol will be entitled to compensatory damages for her injury—the difference in price between the two orders—which in this case arose directly from Specialty's breach of contract.

Compensatory damages may also be awarded for injury or loss arising from a situation that both parties should have known about and considered when they made the contract. To determine what should have been considered, the court looks at the nature and purpose of the contract and the attending circumstances known to each of the parties when the contract was executed. A party who breaches a contract is not required to compensate for injuries he had no reason to foresee would result from his breach.

EXAMPLE Hal sends a part from his malfunctioning com-O—* puter to Compufix, Inc., which contracts with Hal to repair it within two weeks. Hal does not mention the fact that his business must close down until the part is fixed. When Compufix breaches its contract with Hal by failing to repair the part within the two weeks specified, Hal cannot recover the profits he lost when he was forced to close his business as a result of Compufix's delay. If, however, Hal had mentioned this special circumstance to Compufix when the contract was made, he would be entitled to these damages.

Notice given after the contract is made is not sufficient. But notice may be implied from circumstances and the COURSE OF DEALING (pattern of former business deals) between the parties. From this the parties know that special damages could be the expected result of any contract breach. In the above example, if Hal had been sending his computer parts to Compufix for repair for years and had repeatedly made it known in the past that he had to shut down his business while his computer was under repair, notice of his forced closing would be implied in the present case and would not have to be specified.

Torts A tort-feasor is responsible for injuries that are the natural and probable consequence of his wrong.

EXAMPLE Suppose a man who lives in the apartment above O—* you lets his bathtub overflow and the water drips through the ceiling and damages your apartment. This is a natural and probable consequence of his negligent act in not keeping a close watch on his tub. It is a foreseeable result and he will be liable to you for the amount of money it takes you to return your apartment to the condition it was in before his negligent act.

Nature of the consequences Consequences must be reasonably foreseeable in order to recover compensatory damages. It is not sufficient that the consequences are merely *possible.* Consequences should also be unavoidable. A plaintiff will generally not be awarded damages for injuries he could have taken steps to avoid.

Speculative consequences In actions based on torts or contracts, there can be no compensation for damages that are uncertain or contingent on speculative events.

EXAMPLE If a 12-year-old girl suffers a concussion that is not considered permanent, the impairment of her prospects of becoming a doctor is too uncertain to enable her to recover damages. But suppose the girl is 23 years old. The weekend before beginning medical school she is blinded in an explosion of a hot-water heater negligently maintained by her landlord. Then the recovery of damages for the impairment of her career would not be speculative.

The amount of damages must be established with reasonable certainty. But uncertainty does not completely bar recovery, because the plaintiff may be entitled to nominal damages, discussed below. This is true in both contract and tort cases, especially those resulting in personal injuries.

When compensatory damages are sought, there must be evidence of their nature and extent of the injury and some data from which the damages may be computed. No substantial recovery may be based on guesswork or inference. If there is evidence of injury from various causes but none that implicates the defendant exclusively, the proof is too uncertain to permit the arbitrary award of damages.

Avoidable consequences The rule of avoidable consequences imposes a duty on an injured person to minimize damages. Generally, there can be no recovery for losses

WHEN YOU ARE ENTITLED TO DAMAGES

■ Damages are the money compensation awarded to make up for a loss or injury sustained as a result of another's wrongful conduct. There are three classes of damages: compensatory, nominal, and punitive.

■ *Compensatory damages* are awarded to replace loss or injury caused by the defendant's wrongful acts. A wrongdoer is liable for all the consequences of his wrongful act. If, for instance, you are speeding in your car and hit a cabdriver, you are liable for injuries (such as a broken leg) and losses (wages the driver does not collect while he is recuperating). If you only smashed up his cab, you are liable for the loss of business he suffers.

■ An injured person must exercise reasonable care to bring about a cure, both in his selection of a doctor and in his own conduct. If, for example, after sustaining injury from someone else's wrongful act, you ignore the doctor's orders to stay in bed for a week and thereby aggravate your injury, the defendant is not liable for the additional injury.

■ There can be no recovery for losses that might have been prevented by the injured person.

■ If you treat what you reasonably believe to be a minor injury with home remedies and then call in a doctor when you find that it is not healing, you are not barred from recovery, even though the general rule is that you should seek medical attention if the injury requires it.

■ Compensatory damages may be sought for physical and mental pain

caused by a wrongful act—the two kinds of suffering are computed separately in most cases.

■ You can get compensatory damages for a variety of losses involving earnings and time. For example, the commissions a salesman loses as a result of injury are recoverable if he can prove what he has been making on commissions in the recent past. If you had to turn down a promotion because of an injury, that loss of future earnings would be a proper element in your lawsuit. Even if you are unemployed or retired when injured, you still have the right to recover damages for loss of earning capacity.

■ Loss of profits from the destruction or interruption of an established business may be recovered if the amount is reasonably certain.

■ If you incur increased living costs as a result of a wrongful injury, you may usually recover damages. Any expense resulting from loss or damage to property can usually be recovered—for example, the cost of repairing a damaged car and of renting a replacement while repairs are being made.

■ A person injured by the breach of a contract must make reasonable efforts to mitigate the damages—for example, when a tenant moves out before his lease is up, the landlord has a duty to minimize his damages by trying to find a new tenant immediately.

■ If a person fails to pay money owed under a contract on the date it is due, interest will be allowed as damages, especially if the money is wrongfully withheld.

■ The measure of damages for permanent injury to real estate is usually the difference between the fair value of the property just before and just after the injury.

■ *Nominal damages* are awarded in cases where a technical or actual wrong has been suffered that cannot be translated into terms of dollars and cents—when you are deprived of your right to vote, when your property rights are violated, or when your good name is called into question. By awarding you a symbolic, nominal sum—in many cases $1—the court is, in effect, ruling that you *were* in the right. In some states, the party you sued may also have to pay the costs of the lawsuit.

■ *Punitive damages* are awarded to punish the offender and serve as a warning to him and others. They are awarded when the defendant's conduct was willful, wanton, reckless, or malicious.

■ Generally, the amount awarded for punitive damages rests with the discretion of the jury or the judge. Some states refuse to award punitive damages in any action.

■ Punitive damages may be awarded in civil rights actions when the defendant acted with malice or reckless disregard of the plaintiff's civil rights. The plaintiff does not have to have suffered actual loss to recover.

■ Punitive damages are personal to the injured party—if he dies while the case is in court, damages cannot be awarded to his beneficiary, except in certain states.

that might have been prevented by the injured person, especially if the act that caused the original loss was not willful, intentional, or done in bad faith.

The efforts the injured party must make to avoid the consequences of the wrongful act need only be reasonable.

EXAMPLE In one case, a research engineer for a government O——＊ contractor sued the United States for loss of wages between the time security clearance was withdrawn and the time it was restored. The engineer was not required to take a menial job merely to prove that he had looked for work.

Failure of the plaintiff to mitigate (lessen) damages will not bar him entirely from a recovery, but it will prevent him from recovering the amount of damages that he could have avoided had he taken reasonable care. When it is necessary to spend money to guard against the wrongdoer's act, for example, the injured person need not make extraordinary expenditures. His lack of funds may excuse him from making costly efforts to lessen the injury.

Breach of contract A person injured by the breach of a contract ordinarily must make reasonable efforts to mitigate the damages.

EXAMPLE A contract between an advertising agency and an O——＊ advertiser calls for the rental of a particular space in a train or bus. If the advertiser breaks the contract, the agency is bound to use reasonable diligence to rent the space to another advertiser.

When a tenant abandons the premises and defaults in the payment of rent, the landlord must minimize his damages by trying to rent the premises to someone else.

This obligation to mitigate damages does not apply, however, in an action on a contract for a compensation that has been agreed upon.

EXAMPLE Suppose the tenant and the landlord had agreed O——＊ that in case the tenant broke his lease, the landlord would be entitled to keep the two months' rent that he received as security at the time the lease was signed to compensate him for his loss. The tenant could not claim that the landlord had a duty to rent the apartment immediately after his departure to reduce the damages that he owed, because he and the landlord had agreed to a fixed compensation in case of breach.

Property damage from torts Ordinarily, a person whose property is endangered or injured must use reasonable care and moderate expense to mitigate the damages.

EXAMPLE Some neighborhood children break into your O——＊ weekend home while you are away. You are notified of the fact but make no attempt to repair a water pipe they have broken. You cannot recover for water damages after the time when you could have repaired the pipe.

This obligation to mitigate damages is especially true when the party seeking to recover them has been notified of the wrong or injury and has not taken any steps to protect himself from further loss. If the property is merely damaged and not wholly destroyed, the owner cannot make the person who caused the injury liable for the entire value of the property by abandoning it.

When injury to property prevents the owner from pursuing his usual employment, he is not entitled to recover for the loss of income occasioned by the injury if he made no effort to find other employment.

EXAMPLE Hank, a self-employed taxi driver, loses the use of O——＊ his cab when Burt hits the cab with his car while speeding through a school district. Hank sues Burt for the damages to his cab and for damages resulting from his inability to pursue his usual employment—driving a cab. But Hank does not try to get a job driving for a taxi-fleet company, and so he is allowed to recover for the damage done to his cab but not for his loss of employment.

Personal injury from torts A person who sustains personal injury must use ordinary care to get well and lessen the damages. An injured person should seek medical attention if his injury requires it. He need not, however, submit to unduly painful treatment or treatment that involves hazard of death or injury or offers only a possibility of a cure. Pain involved in the treatment helps determine whether the plaintiff acted reasonably in failing to seek medical or surgical attention. Submitting to treatment is not a condition to the recovery of damages, but increased damages resulting from the failure to obtain medical attention will not be allowed.

On the other hand, the fact that medical aid was not sought immediately, or at all, will not necessarily defeat a recovery. For example, if a person treats what he believes to be a minor injury with home remedies and then consults a physician when he discovers that it is not healing, he is not barred from recovery. An injured person is under no absolute obligation to follow the advice of his physician to minimize his damages. He may be under a duty to use ordinary care, however, in following such advice.

Compensation for personal injuries When someone suffers personal injuries as a result of another's wrongful conduct, he may be entitled to compensatory damages for physical or mental impairment and for physical or mental pain and suffering.

Physical impairment Damages may be awarded for disease or physical impairment directly resulting from an injury. They are not given for minor injuries or the unforeseeable consequences of the injury.

EXAMPLE If a person in a car crash is thrown through the O——＊ windshield, which results in large scars on his face, he may be entitled to recover damages for his physical impairment. Because the jury considers both the future and present effects of the injury, disfigurement is a proper element of damages. The injured person does not have to prove with absolute certainty that the disfigurement will be permanent. It need only be established by a preponderance of the evidence.

Mental impairment Harm to mental faculties, such as loss of memory or intellectual capacity, constitutes an element of damages; so does nervousness resulting from physical injuries.

Physical pain and suffering Damages may be sought for the physical pain and suffering resulting from an injury to a person as a result of a wrongful act. The plaintiff is entitled also to recover for pain that is reasonably certain to occur in the future—for example, a leg injury that involves irreparable damage to a nerve and is likely to cause pain in coming years. There is, of course, no exact measure by which to determine how much money will compensate for physical pain and suffering. The amount awarded is decided by the jury, or where there is no jury, by the judge.

Mental pain and suffering Mental pain and suffering includes fright, nervousness, grief, anxiety, worry, shock, humiliation, and indignity. Impotence resulting from an injury is classified as mental and physical suffering.

Mental pain and suffering as a direct consequence of a physical injury is a distinct cause for recovery of damages. Often, so is mental pain in contemplation of a permanent disfigurement. Some states, however, will allow recovery for disfigurement only; they consider mental pain caused by the contemplation of disfigurement too remote.

Distress caused by sympathy for another's suffering and fright due to a wrong against a third person usually are not compensable. There are exceptions to this rule if the injury to the third person is willful or malicious.

EXAMPLE The defendant maliciously beat the plaintiff's
O—* father in the plaintiff's presence. The plaintiff was so greatly frightened by the attack that she had a nervous breakdown and had to be placed in a mental institution for care. The defendant was liable to the plaintiff for all damages that could be directly traced to his conduct, even though he was not aware of her presence.

Sometimes damages may be recovered for emotional trauma and physical injury that result when the plaintiff witnesses an accident in which a closely related person is injured or killed by a negligent act of the defendant. Usually this happens only if the plaintiff was within the "zone of danger" or could reasonably fear for his own safety.

EXAMPLE A person drives a speeding car through a play
O—* street that is closed to all traffic. If he hits your son as you watch, you may recover damages not only for your child's injuries but also for your emotional trauma.

Usually, there can be no recovery for mental anguish suffered by the plaintiff because of harm done to his property. But when the act causing the property damage is inspired by fraud or malice, mental suffering may be considered. For instance, the owner of a dog that was maliciously mutilated and killed by the defendant may be entitled to recover for the mental suffering that aggravated his nervous condition.

As a general rule, no damages for mental suffering are allowed for breach of contract. The breach does not by itself cause the injury, and the parties to the contract did not consider the injury as a legal possibility when the contract was drawn.

EXAMPLE Rose hired Dirk to cater a party, and the food
O—* Dirk served made all the guests ill. Rose sued Dirk for mental anguish she suffered as the result of his breach of contract to furnish food fit for consumption. The court refused to allow Rose to recover damages for mental anguish, but she could have sued for the value of the contract—the price of the food and service.

Lost pay A person may be compensated for the loss of earnings resulting from personal injury. The measure of damages is the amount of money the injured person might reasonably have earned during the time he was incapacitated if he were engaged in his usual occupation. This amount may be established by considering the wages or earnings actually lost by the injured party or by figuring his average earnings in his particular business. For example, the commissions a salesman loses as a result of injury are recoverable if he can prove what his earnings were in the past.

The loss of earnings, wages, or salary may not be speculative. A person who buys his first farm three months before he is injured cannot recover for the loss of his own services. That would involve speculation as to his probable earnings, because he has had no prior experience in farming. But loss of earnings from having to turn down a promotion because of an injury is a proper element in a personal-injury action.

In making an award for permanent disability, future loss of earnings is taken into consideration. If you are permanently disabled from a smashed kneecap and forced to give up your career as a dancer, future loss of earnings is an important element in an award for damages. Injuries need not be permanent, however, to justify an award for loss of future earnings. Say you break your leg as a result of a wrongful action and will be out of work for three months. You will be entitled to an award for the loss of your future earnings even though your injuries are not permanent.

Inability to earn a living Impaired or decreased earning capacity that results directly from a permanent disabling injury is measured by the difference between the amount the plaintiff could earn before his injury and what he is capable of earning afterward, in view of his life expectancy. Damages should be based on the injured person's ability to earn money rather than on what he actually made before he was hurt. Even if he is unemployed or retired when he is injured, a person still has the right to recover damages for loss of earning capacity measured by the activities he has performed while unemployed or retired.

EXAMPLE Howard, a retired microbiologist, lost his eye-
O—* sight in an accident. Until the accident, Harold had taken over the household and child care responsibilities from his wife, Clarice, so that she could go back to college. As a result of the accident, Howard and Clarice had to hire a housekeeper for $200 a week to do what had been Howard's job. A jury may use the salary paid to the housekeeper as a yardstick to decide what damages it should award Howard for his impaired earning capacity. On the other hand, if Howard had been unemployed, rather than retired, at the time of the accident and had been looking for another job as a microbiologist, his damages would be determined by reference to what he had previously earned as a microbiologist; for example, the average salary he earned over his career or the average of the last five years he worked.

Compensation for loss of profits A plaintiff may recover for loss of profits if he can prove that it stems from the defendant's wrongful act or omission. Anticipated profits cannot be recovered when they depend on uncertain and changing conditions, such as market fluctuations, or when there is no evidence from which they may be intelligently estimated. Loss of profits from the destruction or interruption of an established business may be recovered if the amount is reasonably certain. This rule does not apply to a new or contemplated business, although in such a case damages may be assessed by some other measuring stick.

EXAMPLE Peterson agreed to clear and grade a site for
O—* Hartman's drive-in movie theater by June 1. Peterson did not complete the work until the middle of August. Hartman sued Peterson for lost profits for the time of delay. He contended that the lost profits could be

measured by profits earned by other drive-in theaters during the same period the previous year, when the weather conditions were about the same. The court rejected this argument. "Loss of profits from a business which has not begun operations may not be recovered because they are too speculative and incapable of being ascertained with the required degree of certainty. Where there is insufficient basis to determine lost profits, damages may be measured by the rental value of the property."

Breach of contract   When the terms of a contract are breached, the injured party may generally recover profits he would have made if the contract had been performed. This applies as long as the loss can be stated with reasonable certainty and it results from the breach.

EXAMPLE In one case, the plaintiff contracted to manufacture a number of specially designed automobile bodies. The defendant repudiated the contract after production had begun and about one-quarter of the bodies had been delivered. Because there was no market yet for auto bodies of this special design, the plaintiff could not reduce his damages by completing the remaining bodies and selling them on the market. The court decided that the plaintiff could recover the profits he would have made if the contract had been fully performed. In addition, the plaintiff was permitted to recover other losses he sustained, including his payment for labor and materials.

The profits claimed cannot be speculative or conjectural; rather they must have been considered by the parties when the contract was made. In the case of a breach of contract to pay money, such as an employment contract to pay a salary, the actual amount of the last salary may be recovered but profits anticipated from the use of the salary (by investing it in the stock market, for example) are usually too speculative to be allowed.

Torts   Loss of profits because of a tort (accidental or intentional injury to a person or property) may be recovered if the amount is certain. There must be a satisfactory basis, however, for estimating what the probable profits would have been if there had been no tort.

When loss of anticipated profits results from injury to property, recovery is limited to the sum necessary to restore the property to its condition immediately before the injury. If the property was completely destroyed, the measure of damages is the full value of the property.

Compensation for expenses   All expenses that are the result of the defendant's wrongful act may be recovered by the injured party.

Breach of contract   When a contract is breached, the injured party may recover any expenses he incurred.

EXAMPLE Smith contracts with Jones to buy 100 pianos for $80,000. But Smith refuses to pay when they are delivered to his music store. Jones will be entitled to recover as an element of damages the necessary and reasonable expenses he incurred in shipping and storing the pianos.

For further discussion of expenses recoverable in the breach of a contract for the sale of goods, see SALES.

Torts that cause personal injuries   Such expenses as increased living costs incurred as a result of a wrong that causes personal injury are usually recovered as damages. Necessary and reasonable expenses for medical attention, nursing, and medicine—including those needed for future treatment—may be awarded to the injured party. The fact that the plaintiff has been reimbursed for medical or hospital expenses under the terms of an insurance policy or a welfare fund does not prevent him from also recovering these expenses from the defendant. This is known as the collateral source rule.

Damage to property   Any expense that results from loss of or damage to property, even if the property has not been fully paid for, can usually be recovered. The cost of repairing a damaged motor vehicle and the money spent to hire another vehicle while the repairs are being made may be awarded as damages.

As a rule, a party is entitled to all legitimate expenses he incurred while attempting to reduce damages caused by the defendant's wrongful conduct. For example, if the defendant has injured the plaintiff's pet collie, the plaintiff may recover the money he paid a veterinarian. A recovery for expenses reasonably incurred in an attempt to mitigate or avoid damages may still be granted, even though the attempt was unsuccessful and increased or aggravated the loss. The plaintiff need only believe he was avoiding or reducing damages.

Lawyer's fees and costs   Generally the expenses of litigation and attorney's fees in tort or breach of contract actions cannot be recovered as damages unless authorized by statute or as a term of the contract. See also COSTS.

Award of interest   The purpose of awarding interest as damages is to compensate the aggrieved party for the defendant's having kept money rightfully due him. As a general rule, compound interest (interest on interest) is not allowable as damages.

Breach of contract   When a contract to pay money is breached, the damages awarded may include interest on the money from the time of default, which may be specified in the contract. If no time of default is given in the contract, interest is awarded from the time the plaintiff makes a demand or begins a suit. See DEFAULT; DEMAND.

Torts   Interest may be permitted as an element of damages in tort actions, depending on the nature of the tort. Interest is usually not allowed in personal injury or WRONGFUL DEATH ACTIONS (lawsuits for death wrongfully caused by another) because the damages cannot be computed with certainty. In an action for injuries to property, however, the owner may recover interest on the damages if the damages can be determined by known standards of value.

EXAMPLE The Whitmans dug a ditch that encroached on the Emerson's property. The Emersons sued the Whitmans for trespass. They were awarded $5,000 in actual damages, which were determined by the difference in the value of the property before and after the ditch was dug, plus the interest on the $5,000 for the period between the digging of the ditch and the time the jury found for the Emersons.

Measuring the compensation   The measure of compensatory damages is the sum that will both fairly compensate the injured person for his loss and impose the least burden on the wrongdoer. Since the only compensation the law can compel is in the form of money, the injury must be measured by something real and tangible that will gauge the pecuniary loss. The determination of the pecuniary loss by the court or jury calls for the exercise of good judgment, experience in the affairs of life, and knowledge of social and economic conditions. The amount the plaintiff demanded in attempting to negotiate an out-of-court settlement before bringing his case to court does not limit what he can recover. The financial condition of the parties involved should have no bearing on the amount to be awarded as compensatory damages.

When there are several ways of estimating damages, the most definite one should be adopted. If either of two measures will fully compensate the injured party, the one least expensive to the wrongdoer must be adopted.

The sections below tell how damages are measured in various types of contract and tort cases.

Contracts In breach of contract, the measure of damages is the amount that will, as far as possible, place the injured person in the position he would have been in had the contract been honored. He is entitled to the "benefit of his bargain," which is the net gain he would have made under the contract. On the other hand, he is not to be put into a better position than he would have been in if the contract had been performed.

When a contract is to be performed in installments, as in the lease of an apartment, the damages for breach must be measured as of the time at which each installment is due, not when the entire performance is completed.

EXAMPLE You sign a one-year lease to rent an apartment O⟶⁕ beginning in November. You decide in January that the apartment is too small, so you move out without paying the January rent. You have breached your lease. Your landlord sues you in May for breach of contract and for payment of the rent that you owe. If he has made reasonable efforts to relet your apartment but was unsuccessful, he will be awarded damages for the rent from January, February, March, April, and May, the installments that have already become due. He cannot recover for the remaining months of June through October until each installment has become due, at which time he must sue again.

A party to a contract with a "no damage" clause cannot be deprived of the benefit unless he acts in BAD FAITH or shows other tortious (wrongful) intent. Parties may agree to a "no damage" clause in a contract when the goods contracted for are in great demand and are being obtained at a good price. In order to give the buyer such a good deal, the seller may require a "no damage" clause releasing him from liability if, for example, the shipment does not arrive by the specified time. The seller may, however, be liable for damages if he acted in bad faith.

Part performance When a contract has been only partially performed, the reasonable cost of completing the work is usually the measure of damages, but it is not necessarily the sole measure. If a contractor abandons an unfinished building that was to be a hotel or an apartment, for instance, a judgment for the owner may include the loss of income.

If a contractor has substantially performed the job when he stops work on it—if the work has been done but not strictly according to the terms of the contract—he may be entitled to recover damages if the owner refuses to pay him for the work he has done. The contractor will be awarded the reasonable value of his labor and the value of the materials he furnished, using the contract price as a guide. The amount of damages awarded may not exceed the benefit received by the owner; furthermore, it will be reduced by the amount of damages the owner suffered from the contractor's failure to complete the job. But if the value of the work done is greater than the contract price, the contractor is not entitled to recover the excess.

Defective performance The measure of damages for defective performance of a contract is generally the difference in value between what is tendered and what was required. But if the party for whom the work was done or to whom the goods were delivered, for example, accepts the performance as complete, the other party can recover the full contract price.

In the case of defective performance of a construction contract, the measure is the sum that will compensate for any losses the owner suffers as a result of the defects. If there has been substantial performance, the measure of damages will be the difference between the value of the property with the work as it is and what it would have been had there been strict compliance with the contract.

EXAMPLE You sign an agreement with a contractor to purO⟶⁕ chase a home to be built according to your specifications. The contractor mistakenly installs pipes in the plumbing system that are not the brand you specify. There is only a trivial difference between the two brands. To replace the pipes would be costly and involve an unreasonable waste of time. You will receive as damages the difference between the value of the property with the work as done and what it would have been if the contractor had strictly adhered to your specifications.

The cost of repairing the defects or making the building or structure conform to the specifications may be recovered if the work can be done at a reasonable cost.

If a contractor intentionally departs from the contract *without* substantial performance, the measure of damages is the actual cost of reconstructing the building according to the contract. If a contractor substitutes inferior materials that fail to meet safety regulations or result in weak or flammable structures and people are hurt in an accident or fire because the contractor did not use the materials he had contracted to use, he may be sued for the torts of fraud and negligence or prosecuted criminally if violation of safety regulations is defined as a crime in his state.

Delay in performance The loss resulting from the defendant's wrongful delay in performing a building contract is the measure of damages. This loss may be determined by considering the rental value of the property, the value of the use of the property, interest on the value of the property, or—if the contract specifically provides—the loss resulting from increased material and labor costs.

Torts Compensation for torts falls into three broad categories: personal injury, damage to personal property (any PROPERTY that is not real estate), and damage to real property (real estate).

Personal injury The measure of damages for personal injury is a sum that will compensate the plaintiff for any losses he has sustained as a result of the injury. These include compensation for his pain and suffering, for his loss of income during recuperation, for medical attendance and support during the period of his disability, for impairment of his earning capacity, and for any permanent injury and continuing disability, all of which have been discussed above in the section "Compensation for personal injuries." The amount of the award in this type of case rests largely with the discretion of the jury or the court.

Personal property The measure of damages for an injury to or loss of personal property by a tort is compensation for the actual loss sustained. Usually this is the property's reasonable value at the time of loss. For instance, when equipment in very poor condition is destroyed, the cost of replacing it with new equipment is *not* the proper measure of damages. When animals are lost, the owner is entitled to recover their value at that time, together with the expenses reasonably and prudently incurred in searching for them.

When personal property is harmed but not destroyed, the measure is the difference between the property's value immediately before and after the injury or the reasonable cost to restore the property to its previous condition. If repair or replacement does not appear economically feasible, the measure of damages is the full value of the property at the time of the tort, minus its salvage value—that is, what it would bring as junk.

The measure of damages for depriving someone of the temporary use of his or her personal property is also the value of its use. This value cannot be recovered if the property was destroyed and if full worth was awarded. In such cases damages are measured by the amount of injury to the property plus the value of its use while it is being repaired.

EXAMPLE When a tractor-trailer was damaged, the cost of 0—* renting a replacement was allowed as an element of damages because the expense to the owner was caused by the damage to his tractor-trailer. The owner also recovered the costs of repairing the tractor-trailer.

Real property Examples of torts that cause damage to real property include digging a ditch that undermines the foundation of a neighbor's house or inground swimming pool, putting up an unauthorized structure, removing or destroying valuable plants, allowing ANIMALS to destroy plants, and wrongfully flooding cropland. The measure of damages for a permanent injury to real property is usually the difference between the fair value of the property immediately before and just after the injury.

Damages that arise from temporary injury to the land may be measured according to the circumstances of each case. If it is practical to repair the property, the measure of damages should include the cost of restoration. This cost will not be awarded, however, if it exceeds the value of the property in its original condition, or the depreciation in its value, or the actual damage sustained by the plaintiff. If the land is usually rented, the diminution in rental value from the time of the injury is a proper measure of damages. The measure of damages for temporary injury to the real property may also include recovery for the loss or decrease in value of the premises during the time that the injury exists or during the period for which the action is brought. Damages for the loss of the use of property are to be measured by the injury actually sustained and not by the value of the property if it were used for another purpose. For example, if property you used as farmland was flooded

through your neighbor's negligence, you could not recover damages for the value of the property as if it was the grounds of a resort hotel.

■ **Multiple damages** Although a double recovery of compensatory damages is generally not permitted, in certain types of cases the amount recoverable may be a multiple of the actual loss sustained. This is usually two or three times the amount. For example, federal law calls for triple damages in antitrust suits. See MONOPOLY.

EXAMPLE ABC Corporation has monopolized the market on 0—* computers for years. XY Company, a young struggling firm, has started making dents into ABC's midwestern market. It must, however, buy certain computer parts from ABC. ABC refuses to sell to XY, thereby forcing it out of the computer market. XY sues ABC under the federal antitrust laws. It proves that the refusal of ABC to sell essential computer parts to it has cost XY $7 million in business in one year. The jury finds that ABC has monopolized the market and awards XY $7 million in damages. The judge then trebles the award so that XY Company will be awarded $21 million in damages. Treble damages are intended not only to redress private wrongs but to protect public interest in the free enterprise system by deterring violations of antitrust laws.

Multiple damages may be recovered only if they are permitted by statute.

■ **Nominal damages** Nominal damages are awarded when the plaintiff suffers no actual injury or loss but only a technical injury to his legal rights. For example, if a person is wrongfully deprived of his right to vote, he will be awarded nominal damages. He has not been injured but a legally protected right has been denied him. As the name indicates, nominal damages are small—they can be a trifling 10 cents or $1.

A plaintiff may recover nominal damages if he establishes that he has sustained losses or injuries—even severe physical injuries—as the result of the defendant's misconduct but fails to submit proof of the injury. For example, if you were injured by an automobile that ran a red light, you may be awarded only nominal damages if you sue the driver but fail to submit medical reports or X-rays to prove you were injured.

A plaintiff cannot recover both nominal and compensatory damages. If the legal wrong and its resulting damages are established, the plaintiff can recover compensatory damages. An additional award of nominal damages would be superfluous.

Breach of contract Nominal damages have been awarded in contract lawsuits started for either of two purposes. First, the plaintiff may attempt to obtain nominal damages to establish a PRECEDENT in a TEST CASE or in a dispute that is likely to occur again. Under modern statutes, however, he is more likely to seek a DECLARATORY JUDGMENT to establish his legal rights under the contract. Second, and more frequently, the plaintiff may start his lawsuit in the belief that he is entitled to substantial damages. At trial, he may establish that the contract was breached, but fail to prove he has suffered actual damages and thus be entitled only to a judgment for nominal damages.

Nominal damages may be awarded even if the wrong has resulted in a benefit to the plaintiff.

EXAMPLE Under terms of a contract, Andy agrees to sell
O→——* Craig 10 bushels of wheat for $1 per bushel.
Andy breaches the contract by refusing to sell to Craig.
Craig can buy the same type of wheat in the open market
for 80 cents per bushel. Under the contract, Craig would
have to pay Andy $10, but now he can buy the same
wheat in the market for $8. Andy's breach has not caused
any damage to Craig. But Craig still has a legal right to
have the contract performed. The law will permit Craig
to sue for breach of contract, but he will be entitled to
recover only nominal damages against Andy.

Torts Nominal damages awarded in tort actions (lawsuits) for ASSAULT AND BATTERY, FALSE IMPRISONMENT, LI-
BEL AND SLANDER, CONVERSION, and TRESPASS symbolize
judicial recognition that the defendant has violated a legally
protected interest of the plaintiff. The plaintiff does not
have to allege or prove any loss.

EXAMPLE If a driver refuses to stop his car so that someone
O→——* riding inside can leave, he has committed the tort
of false imprisonment. Although the plaintiff may not be
able to prove that he has suffered actual injury or loss, he
will be entitled to recover nominal damages because the
defendant has wrongfully interfered with his legal right
to freedom of movement. If the plaintiff can prove actual
injuries, he will be awarded compensatory, not nominal,
damages. He may also receive punitive damages if he can
show malice, willfulness, or wantonness in the defendant's wrongful act.

An award of nominal damages in tort actions may serve
to (1) determine disputed property rights of the plaintiff, as
in an action for trespass; or (2) vindicate the plaintiff's
reputation, as in an action for libel or slander. See LIBEL
AND SLANDER.

■ **Punitive damages** The theory behind punitive, or
exemplary, damages—"smart money," as they are sometimes called—is based on both the interests of society and
those of the injured individuals. The purpose of these
damages, which are awarded only in certain types of cases, is
to punish the offender rather than to compensate the victim.
They serve as a warning to him and others that wrongful
conduct will not be tolerated by the community. A few
states refuse to award punitive damages in any action; some
actually have statutes forbidding such damages. When a
state forbids punitive damages, the judge and jury are
powerless to award them. Even in states where they are
allowed, a judge or jury may decline to award them.

Contract and tort actions Punitive damages are generally not recoverable in actions for breach of contract
unless specifically authorized by statute. They may be
allowed in tort cases that incidentally involve a contract if
the requisite aggravating circumstances, such as spite or
malice, are present.

EXAMPLE If Cary maliciously influences Hal to breach his
O→——* contract with Mike in an attempt to drive Mike
out of business, Cary has committed the tort of interference with advantageous relationships. Mike will be able
to recover punitive damages from Cary since his wrongful act was intentional. Cary acted solely out of spite and
not to protect a legitimate business interest.

In tort actions not involving contracts, punitive damages
will not be awarded for mere negligence unless the defen-

dant's conduct was willful, wanton, reckless, or malicious.
Willfulness means that there must be an intent to do wrong
and inflict injury. If you slap someone, you have willfully
committed the tort of battery. Conduct is *wanton* if the
person doing the act is conscious of his behavior and,
although he does not intend to injure anyone, knows that
his action will naturally and probably result in injury. For
instance, firing a shotgun into a crowded bus is acting
wantonly. Even if there was no intent to harm anyone, it is
probable that someone on the bus will be injured. *Recklessness* is similar to wantonness. It is acting with complete
disregard of injurious consequences, which are clearly
foreseeable. A *malicious* act is one with an evil intent or a
wrong and unlawful motive.

An award of punitive damages may be based on the
exercise of a legal right in an improper manner—for example, the tort of abuse of process, which is the intentional
wrongful use of the legal process for an improper purpose.
If Gloria prosecutes Bob for writing a bad check simply to
pressure him into selling her his $5,000 car for $1,000, she
is using the legal process for a purpose for which it was not
designed.

The tort of FRAUD may be a basis for awarding punitive
damages.

EXAMPLE Suppose you are considering investing in shares
O→——* of stock in a hotel corporation and you read its
prospectus to help you to decide. The prospectus includes
an untrue statement about the financial condition of the
hotel. On the basis of this intentional misrepresentation,
you invest $25,000. Although the federal laws dealing
with securities regulation permit no punitive damages,
you could receive an award under state law in a tort action
for fraud. The state's logic is that the fraud was intentionally aimed to influence the public to buy stock on the
basis of lies.

See SECURITIES REGULATION.

Civil rights actions Under federal law, any person
who wrongfully uses his office to deprive another of his
civil rights will be liable for nominal or compensatory
damages, plus punitive damages.

EXAMPLE In a recent case, a man who operated a food-
O→——* vending truck outside a courthouse was brought
before a judge in handcuffs. His crime was selling "pu-
trid" coffee to the judge. In the judge's chambers, he
remained handcuffed while the judge interrogated and
berated him and threatened his livelihood. As a result of
this scene, the vendor began to stutter, was unable to
sleep, and suffered other physical and psychological
problems. He brought an action under the civil rights law
against the judge and was awarded $80,000 compensatory
damages and $60,000 punitive damages—awards that
were upheld on appeal.

Punitive damages are properly awarded in civil rights
actions when the defendant acted with malice or blatant or
reckless disregard of the plaintiff's civil rights. In such a
case the plaintiff does not have to suffer actual loss in order
for punitive damages to be awarded.

Who may recover Punitive damages are personal to
the injured party. Once he dies, the right to sue for punitive
damages dies with him. If he dies while his case is in court,
damages will not be awarded to his BENEFICIARY unless

state law permits. If he dies after the judgment is rendered but before the money is paid him, the damages become part of his ESTATE.

Persons liable Punitive damages are awarded against a person who has participated in or contributed to the wrongful conduct that resulted in the plaintiff's injury or loss. They will not be awarded if the defendant dies before or during trial; their purpose is to punish the wrongdoer and this is thwarted by his death. Once a plaintiff receives a final judgment in his favor, he can collect his punitive damages from the defendant's ESTATE if the defendant dies after the award was made.

Establishing the awards There is no fixed standard for the measurement of punitive damages. The amount of the award is largely a matter resting with the discretion of the judge or jury who considers the nature of the defendant's conduct, the seriousness of the harm done to the plaintiff, and the extent to which the wrongful conduct offends the public sense of justice and propriety. In some jurisdictions, the social position and financial condition of the parties may be taken into account.

■ **Liquidated damages** The term "liquidated damages" means the sum to be paid if a contract is breached—a sum the parties agree on when they sign the contract. The sum is an estimate of the extent of the injury a breach of the contract would cause. The parties to a contract may fix this sum only if the actual damages that can be expected to result from a breach of the contract are uncertain in nature or amount or difficult to establish. Liquidated damages clauses are often found in employment contracts or contracts that restrain another person from practicing a profession in the same area.

EXAMPLE Suppose you buy a beauty salon from Mr. Rick. O⟶＊ The contract provides that you can call your salon Mr. Rick's, hoping to retain his clientele. Rick agrees that he will not open a beauty salon in the same town for 18 months or else he must pay you $5,000. This is a liquidated damages clause. It would be difficult for a court to determine how much financial damage you would suffer if Mr. Rick opened his own place during this time.

A provision for liquidated damages for failure to pay an installment of rent is usually invalid. The damages resulting from this type of breach can be accurately measured—the amount of rent owed, plus interest—and therefore is not the proper subject of liquidated damages.

The amount agreed upon must not be extravagant or unreasonably disproportionate to the damages that would actually occur. Otherwise fraud, error, or oppression in the making of the contract may be implied, which would make the agreement unenforceable. The agreement must not violate some principle of law or public policy.

Not as a penalty Liquidated damages must reflect the amount of damages that would probably result from a breach of contract. A penalty secures performance of the contract, while liquidated damages constitute a sum paid in lieu of performance. Unless there are good grounds for it, the court will not declare a provision for liquidated damages to be in the nature of a penalty.

Whether a sum named in a contract to be paid on its breach is regarded as liquidated damages or as a penalty is generally a question of law for the courts to determine. The court considers the situation of the parties and all the facts and circumstances under which the contract was drawn. If the provision was inserted to deter the defendant from breaching his contract by penalizing him for doing so, and was not intended to specify damages that would ensue from a breach, the provision is regarded as a penalty and is unenforceable. The law of damages is based on compensating a person for his losses, *not* punishing a person for failing to perform a duty. The only exceptions are cases in which punitive damages are authorized by statute. Only the state, not private individuals, can impose a penalty in matters of criminal law or to serve the public interest. For example, a provision by which money or property would be forfeited without regard to the actual damage suffered from a breach of contract is an unenforceable penalty and the successful plaintiff would, instead, be awarded his actual damages.

To be considered valid as liquidated damages, the amount agreed upon must result from an honest attempt by the parties to estimate a fair compensation for any loss sustained because of a breach. And it must bear a reasonable relation to the probable damage. The greater the difficulty of estimating damages, the greater the range of estimates the court will uphold as reasonable.

Delay in performance Stipulations for stated amounts to be paid as damages for delay in performance are usually construed as liquidated damages. They are common in building and construction contracts. (In everyday language, liquidated damages clauses in construction contracts are often referred to as penalties, but this use of the term is legally inaccurate.)

EXAMPLE In one case, the plaintiff had contracted with the O⟶＊ state to construct a highway, valued at $531,000. It was completed 67 working days after the date fixed by the contract. The state withheld $14,000 liquidated damages, which it computed on a per diem basis as provided in the contract. The plaintiff sued for the money withheld, claiming that the liquidated damages were an unenforceable penalty. The state court did not allow the plaintiff to recover. An unexcused delay in performing is a breach of contract for which damages are allowable. In this case, damages for delay could not be measured, so the provision tried to fix fair compensation for the loss, inconvenience, and deprivation of the use of the highway.

The role of reasonableness If the amount stated is reasonably related to the probable damages resulting from a breach, it will be treated as liquidated damages. When the amount is clearly out of all proportion to the probable loss, it will be considered a penalty and is thus unenforceable. For instance, a provision for forfeiture of $10,000 for nonperformance of a contract valued at only $5,000 is obviously a penalty. But if you contract with an automobile dealer to buy a car for $4,000 and put down a $100 deposit, which he will keep if you later decide to cancel your purchase, the $100 may be viewed as liquidated damages. The amount is reasonable, and damages for the breach would be difficult to determine.

Contracts for money only The courts will read a provision for the payment of a stipulated sum of money on default of a loan payment as a penalty, regardless of the intention of the parties or the language by which it is expressed. The law provides for the determination of damages in the event of a breach of this type of contract; therefore, the parties cannot determine their own remedy. A provision in a MORTGAGE that in case of FORECLOSURE the mortgagor (borrower) shall, in addition to the debt and its interest, pay the costs and a stated amount as liquidated damages is legally unenforceable.

A stipulation on the rate of interest after default may be accepted as the measure of damages. But it must compensate the loss arising from the breach of contract and can exceed neither the permissible legal rate nor the rate charged before default. For example, failure to pay a car loan on time may result in an additional 2-percent interest charge to cover the lender's expense of hiring a collection agency to obtain your delinquent payments. This would not be considered a penalty.

Contracts of personal property Provisions for amounts to be paid as liquidated damages for the breach of contracts for the sale of personal property (property other than real estate) will be regarded generally as a penalty, because actual damages are usually easy to determine. But in certain instances—where damages are difficult to estimate—such provisions may be valid.

EXAMPLE A wealthy tycoon agrees to buy 20 gold bars from O—* a gold dealer for the going price on the market on the day of delivery of the bars. Because of the substantial fluctuations in the price of gold, the parties agree to a liquidated damages clause for 10 percent of the market price on the day of the breach should either break the contract. This is a valid liquidated damages clause.

Usually, when the amount involved is 10 percent or less of the contract price, the provision will be regarded as one for liquidated damages. If the sum exceeds 10 percent, it will usually be considered a penalty.

Employment contracts Reasonable amounts called for in contracts as damages for the breach of employment contracts are usually regarded as liquidated damages. A provision for payment to an employee on his discharge will more readily be upheld as liquidated damages if the sum is graduated according to the length of time the employment contract has to run. If the discharged employee's compensation is based on commissions for sales, the difficulty in determining damages may support a provision for liquidated damages.

■ **Excessive or inadequate damages** In jury trials, the amount of an award of damages is a matter resting with the discretion of the jury. The verdict, however, is subject to supervision by the court (judge) if it is either grossly excessive or inadequate. If the court finds the verdict to be completely unreasonable in light of the circumstances, it may grant a motion for a new trial. It may also order the plaintiff either to release the defendant from that part of the jury's award of damages the court finds excessive or to submit to a new trial. This is known as REMITTITUR. If a jury has assessed punitive damages in a case where the evidence fails to show any malice, willfulness, or wantonness, the court may correct the award by *remittitur*. If the award is totally inadequate, the court may order the defendant to pay a greater sum than was specified by the jury or else submit to a new trial. This is known as ADDITUR.

The purpose of *remittitur* and *additur* is to correct a clearly erroneous award of damages by the jury without the necessity of a new trial or an appeal. Both are discretionary with the trial judge. The denial of *remittitur* or *additur* by the trial court is a ground for an appeal, so that an appellate court can grant *remittitur* or *additur*. *Remittitur* occurs most commonly when the defendant asks for a new trial because of what he considers an excessive verdict for the plaintiff.

EXAMPLE In one case, a plaintiff sued for alleged police O—* brutality after his civil rights were violated when he was wrongfully beaten by police after his arrest for drunken driving. His actual damages were $95 worth of medical bills and one month's lost wages, about $650. He had no permanent injuries and no punitive damages had been pleaded. The jury awarded him $17,500. The defendant moved for a *remittitur* or a new trial on the issue of damages. The jury's verdict, considering the circumstances of the case and the actual damages proved, "shocked the conscience of the court" and the court ordered a *remittitur* of $11,500 or a new trial. In determining the amount of the *remittitur*, the court considered jury awards in two similar cases, in which $5,000 had been awarded in one and $5,100 in the other.

damnum (Latin) "Damage." The loss someone causes to another person or his property either with the intention of injuring him or through negligence and carelessness. The word is used in a number of legal terms. For example, *damnum fatale* means damage caused by a chance event or an unavoidable accident, such as lightning or a shipwreck. See also AD DAMNUM.

dangerous instrumentality An object that is dangerous either in itself or because its use is intended to be harmful. Common examples include gas heaters, hunting rifles, and wires charged with electricity. On the other hand, courts have held that such objects as a cement mixer and an overhead garage door are not dangerous instrumentalities.

day certain A fixed or appointed day. For example, a contract specifies payment for March 1, 1985. That means March 1, 1985, is a day certain.

day in court A person has his day in court when he is given a date to appear before the bench to be heard in his own behalf. In popular usage, the phrase refers to the *opportunity* to present one's claims or rights in a court hearing rather than the *time* appointed for a hearing.

days of grace A number of days allowed, as a matter of favor or grace, after the time originally set for performing an act or making a payment has elapsed. If your mortgage is due on the first of the month, your bank may give you an additional seven days of grace before you are charged an interest penalty for making a late payment.

dead body The body of a human being recently deprived of life. The word "body" does not include the remains of a human corpse that has long since decomposed.

■ **Rights of property** A dead body is considered property or QUASI property only as far as is necessary to protect the legal rights of the surviving spouse and next of kin with respect to the body. There is no property right in a body in the common meaning of "property." After burial the body becomes part of the ground to which it is committed. Articles that could be buried with the body, such as jewelry, may be taken by the person who inherits them.

EXAMPLE When a woman in Maryland had the funeral director place her daughter's "jewelry, diamond rings, mink coat, mink stole, and other items of personal property" in the coffin with her daughter's body, the lawyer representing the daughter's estate obtained a court order to have the articles removed from the coffin.

Once buried, a corpse is no longer the subject of property ownership for most purposes. The coffin is the property of the person who buried the deceased and therefore may be the subject of LARCENY (theft) under the criminal law.

■ **Rights of burial** There is no universal legal rule about who has the right to bury a body. Each case must be considered individually. The right to bury a body is a sacred trust for the benefit of all those who have an interest in the remains.

The right of burial includes the right to determine the time, manner, and place of interment and the monument that will mark the grave.

Unless the deceased has expressed a wish about the disposition of his remains, the right of burial belongs to the surviving spouse or the next of kin. The surviving spouse has the paramount right unless he or she is absent or neglects or refuses to act or if the spouses were separated at the time of death. If there is no surviving spouse, the right of burial rests with the next of kin of legal age, in order of relationship to the deceased—for example, children, parents, brothers and sisters, and more distant kin. If a person is survived by both a parent and a child and the right of burial is in dispute, the court makes the decision, based on who has the closer relationship with the deceased. When a child of divorced parents dies, the parent to whom custody has been awarded has the paramount right of burial.

Carrying out individual wishes Every person has the right to determine what shall happen to his body after death. In some states this right is given by statute. No particular formality is required in order to direct the disposition of one's own remains. Directions may be given verbally. The deceased's wishes are not absolute, but they are paramount and a court will usually honor them, even over the objections of the surviving spouse or next of kin. When the deceased's directions cannot be carried out, the surviving spouse, next of kin, or executor of the deceased's will may seek the court's guidance if there is a dispute about the burial. The court may then decide what disposition should be made of the body according to the wishes of the surviving spouse or next of kin.

EXAMPLE In his will the deceased directed that no funeral be held and that his body be donated to a certain institution for scientific use. His wish could not be honored because the institution refused to accept the body. The surviving spouse and children wanted a simple funeral service, but the executor of the deceased person's will objected. The court honored the family's wishes.

Death at sea When death takes place at sea, the captain of the ship has absolute discretion over the disposition of the body. The custom of burial at sea has long been sanctioned by common usage. A passenger on an ocean-going ship has agreed to be bound by the custom of the sea if he dies during the voyage.

■ **Burial duties** There is a duty to society and the deceased that the body be decently buried without unnecessary delay. Under the common law, the duty of providing a decent burial is imposed on the person under whose roof death took place. For example, a daughter whose widowed father was living with her at the time of his death has the obligation of burying him, even though he left no estate with which she could pay the necessary expenses.

Statutes in some states specify those persons charged with the duty of burial. These statutes are enacted in the interests of public health, to protect the general welfare, and to relieve the anxiety people might have that they be properly buried when they die.

Who pays for funeral or burial expenses Although funeral expenses are usually deducted from the decedent's estate, a person may be liable for funeral or burial expenses by reason of his relationship to the deceased, such as a husband for his deceased wife, parents for a deceased child, or an adult child for his parents. Some statutes that designate who shall be charged with disposal of a body do not impose financial responsibility for funeral or burial expenses. Other statutes do but only on the one who is first in order of responsibility. Those who are later in order have the duty of burial without the financial liability. When relatives are not required to pay for funeral expenses, the municipality will assume the cost.

Ordinarily, liability for funeral or burial expenses is not imposed on a person just because he has benefited financially as a result of the death. For example, just because the deceased's niece is the named beneficiary of his life insurance policy, this does not mean she is liable for his funeral expenses. Similarly, a tenant may not be charged with the burial expenses of his fellow tenant because he jointly owned property with the deceased that he will now inherit. See JOINT TENANCY.

A person may obligate himself by contract to pay for funeral expenses. This agreement to assume liability must be spelled out very clearly. Simply placing an order for funeral services does not create a contract to pay for those services when it is clear that the person doing the ordering does not intend to assume liability for payment.

EXAMPLE Victoria was so stunned by the sudden death of her husband, Albert, that she fell into a temporary state of shock and was unable to make any of the necessary arrangements for his funeral. So her longtime neighbor Lolly took over the task of notifying friends and relatives and making arrangements with the local funeral parlor, which included the type of casket and the amount of flowers for the funeral. It is clear that Lolly does not intend to pay for the funeral. She is not obligated to pay just because she is the person who ordered the funeral.

■ **Disinterment** After burial a body is considered to be in the custody of the law. Disinterment of a body (removal from a tomb or grave) is not a right that belongs to an individual; rather, it is under the control of a court. Except in certain instances, discussed below, the law honors the sanctity of the grave, and a body once suitably buried will remain undisturbed.

A change of burial place is frequently permitted, however, to enable those who were close in life to be together in death. The courts will usually authorize disinterment so that a body may be reburied in a family plot acquired at a later date.

Disinterment may also be allowed for the following reasons: when the cemetery is needed for a public improvement; when it is abandoned as a burial place; or when it is about to become unsightly. In deciding whether to grant permission to disinter a body, the courts give consideration to the wishes of the deceased, although such wishes do not always prevail.

EXAMPLE Dorothy, who had built a mausoleum in New York, in which she was placed, intended that her son and two daughters also be buried there. But the two daughters moved to another state and the son did not want to be buried in the mausoleum. He requested that the mother's body be removed and buried in a nearby plot. The cemetery corporation objected, but the court granted the son's request.

A body cannot be disturbed against the will of those persons who have a right to object, except when events after the burial show that removal is reasonable.

EXAMPLE A widow allowed her husband to be buried in a plot owned by her husband's father. After the burial, it became practically impossible for the widow to visit the grave. Her husband's family was extremely hostile toward her, and she could not visit the cemetery without being harassed by them. The court ruled that the widow was entitled to remove her husband's remains to a burial place of her choice.

Financial benefit is usually not a sufficient reason for disinterment.

EXAMPLE During his lifetime William built a substantial mausoleum at considerable expense. His wife and daughter petitioned the court for permission to disinter his body and remove it to another cemetery because the mausoleum was expensive to maintain. They claimed a change in their financial circumstances made it necessary to sell the mausoleum and the plot on which it was built. The court refused permission.

When a body is buried in a plot belonging to someone else, without that person's consent, it is not properly buried and the court will order it removed and reburied.

If a landowner consents to a burial on his property, he cannot later remove the body against the wishes of the surviving spouse or next of kin. If the landowner does not consent to the burial but fails to object for a long time, he may not claim that the burial lacked his consent in order to have the body removed. A landowner is, however, entitled to object to the removal of a corpse that is buried on his land.

Disinterment for evidence Courts will allow a body to be exhumed and an autopsy performed for the purpose of discovering the truth and promoting justice. However, the law will allow disinterment only when there is justification for an autopsy and when there is reasonable probabil-

---

RIGHTS AND DUTIES RELATING TO BURIAL

■ There is no universal legal rule about who has the right to bury a body—that is a sacred trust for those who have an interest in the remains. But unless the deceased has expressed a wish about his burial, the right usually belongs to the surviving spouse or next of kin—children, parents, brothers, or sisters.

■ When a child of divorced parents dies, the parent to whom custody has been awarded has the paramount privilege of burial.

■ Every person has the right to determine what shall happen to his body after death, and some states guarantee this right by law. Although the deceased's wishes are paramount, they are not absolute. However, a court will usually honor those wishes, even against opposition by the surviving spouse or next of kin.

■ Articles that could be buried with the body, such as jewelry, may be taken by the person who inherits them.

■ After interment the body is in the custody of the law, and disinterment is subject to court control.

■ The law honors the sanctity of the grave and will not permit a suitably buried body to be disturbed except in cases of necessity or for praiseworthy purposes.

■ A change of burial place is often allowed to enable those who were close in life to be together in death.

■ Disinterment may be allowed if the cemetery is needed for a public improvement, when it is abandoned as a burial place, or when it is about to become unsightly.

■ If a landowner consents to a burial on his property, he cannot later remove the body against the wishes of the surviving spouse or next of kin.

■ A body may be exhumed and an autopsy may be performed on it for the purpose of discovering truth and promoting justice.

■ When a person agrees to bury a body properly, a lawsuit may be brought against him if he negligently allows the body to be taken from his custody or gives it an improper burial.

■ A person may be liable for funeral or burial expenses by reason of his relationship to the deceased. State laws designate who shall be charged with the disposal of a body. In some states they impose financial responsibility and in others they impose the duty of burial but not the liability of paying for it.

■ A person can be brought to court for breaching any duty or violating any right associated with a dead body, and survivors have the right to sue. A typical example is that of the hospital that negligently mixed up the bodies of two patients who had died at the same time and sent them off to the wrong undertakers. In that case both families sued and were awarded damages.

■ Unauthorized embalming or unauthorized autopsy may form the basis for a lawsuit when it was done in violation of the law.

■ Wrongful disturbance, disinterment, or destruction of a dead body entitles survivors to sue for compensatory money damages, and if the injury is malicious or the result of gross negligence, then punitive damages may also be awarded.

ity that violating the grave will establish what is sought. For a discussion of autopsies, see CORONER.

Civil liabilities The breach of any duty or violation of any right associated with a dead body is a TORT (civil wrong) for which a lawsuit for DAMAGES may be brought. When a person agrees to bury a corpse, he may be sued if he negligently allows the body to be taken from his custody or gives it an improper burial. A lawsuit may also be brought for violating the right to custody of a body, for interfering with the right to embalm and bury a body, or for treating the body with disrespect and indignity.

EXAMPLE Two patients at a hospital died during the same O⊶⊷ hour. One patient was Jewish and the other Roman Catholic. A tag bearing the name of the deceased was attached to each body. The families were notified and the bodies removed by the undertakers. One body was prepared for an Orthodox Jewish burial. When the family was permitted to view the body, they found the wrong one had been readied. Similarly, the other body had been embalmed and placed in a coffin with a crucifix and rosary beads in its hands in accordance with the customs of the Roman Catholic faith. The hospital asked the undertakers to return both bodies. In the presence of both families the bodies were identified and exchanged.

Both families sued the hospital. The court awarded each family damages for deprivation of the right to the bodies and the resultant mental sufferings. The court held that the surviving kin have a right to the immediate possession of the body for purposes of preservation and burial. Anyone who interferes with that right or deals improperly with the body will have to pay damages. The court further stated that it was primarily concerned not with the mishandling of the dead body but with how the actions affected the feelings of the surviving kin.

Mutilation, embalmment, and autopsies The right to give a corpse a decent burial includes the right to receive the body in the condition in which death left it. A lawsuit for damages may be brought for the unauthorized mutilation of a dead body. No separate recovery is allowed, however, for mutilation caused by the same event that caused the death, such as a train accident.

The unauthorized embalming of a body does not usually form the basis for a lawsuit except when other factors are involved—for example, if embalming is against the deceased's religious beliefs. In such a case, a legal wrong has occurred for which damages will be awarded.

An unauthorized autopsy is a TORT (civil wrong) for which a lawsuit for damages may be brought. There is no liability, however, when the autopsy is performed with the consent of the person who has the right of burial. A coroner who orders or performs an autopsy when he lacks the authority may be liable to the next of kin for damages, but when the coroner is acting within his authority and the autopsy is properly performed, the coroner is not liable. An undertaker is liable for an unauthorized autopsy performed in his establishment only when he permits it knowing that consent was not given.

Damages for disturbance Substantial compensatory damages may be recovered for the wrongful disturbance, disinterment, or destruction of a dead body. When the deceased, mistakenly buried in the wrong plot, was removed to another plot, failure to notify the deceased's father authorized an award of compensatory damages, even though the move was made in an orderly manner. If the injury to the plaintiff is malicious or the result of gross negligence, then punitive damages may be awarded in addition to compensatory damages and may even be greater.

EXAMPLE A man collapsed in a subway station on his way O⊶⊷ home from work. He was taken to the city hospital and pronounced dead on arrival. After his identity was determined, he was taken to the city morgue. The death was not reported to the police, who usually notify the next of kin. The body lay in the city morgue for eight days before the deceased's widow was notified. She brought suit against the city for mental anguish, suffering, and distress for wrongfully withholding from her the report of her husband's death and also for the fact that his body lay unclaimed in the morgue for eight days. A jury awarded the widow $5,000 in damages against the city.

dead man's statutes Laws designed to protect the estate of a deceased person against fraudulent claims made by someone who had transactions with him. Under these laws a person is not allowed to testify in a civil lawsuit brought against the deceased's estate about any transaction he had with the deceased because a dead person cannot defend himself.

EXAMPLE A physician made a claim for $3,500 against the O⊶⊷ estate of a deceased man named Turner. Turner's executor rejected the claim and the physician brought suit. During the trial the physician testified about the medical treatment he provided for Turner and gave his opinion of its value. The trial court backed the doctor and awarded what he asked—$3,500. The executor appealed. The appellate court reversed the decision and ordered a new trial. It ruled that the physician's testimony was about a transaction with a deceased person and should have been barred under the state's dead man's statute.

death The end of life. Under the law, *natural death* means dying of causes that occur without the assistance or interference of any person or thing. A heart attack and cancer are natural causes. A *violent death* is death caused or hastened by the application of extreme force.

A person is *legally dead* when the law presumes his death has occurred because he has been absent for a specified number of years and no other reason is known for his disappearance.

Civil death, in some states, is the condition of someone sentenced to life imprisonment. It means that his civil rights, such as the capacity to marry or to own property, have been lost as a result of the sentence.

■ **Determining when death has occurred** The law does not have a medical definition as to when the exact moment of death occurs. Determining whether someone has died and the exact cause of death is a medical, not a legal, decision, and judges will accept the opinion of qualified doctors. In most instances, if circulation has completely stopped, and heartbeat, breathing, and brain waves have ceased, the person is dead.

Because of recent technological advances, however, the question of medical death can create a legal question.

Sophisticated life-support systems can maintain a human body at a level that is less than life but is not death.

EXAMPLE The case of Karen Quinlan brought this issue into O⊷✳ sharp focus. When the 20-year-old woman went into a coma, her parents authorized the doctors to do everything they could to help her. After months of testing and treatment, the doctors had to admit that they could not improve Karen's condition. She could not breathe without a mechanical respirator. No doctor would call the case hopeless, but all agreed that the chances of Karen's regaining consciousness were remote.

Mr. and Mrs. Quinlan gradually gave up hope. They sought advice from their parish priest, who said their church would not condemn removal of the mechanical equipment that supported Karen's life. He and the Quinlans agreed that it would be wrong to stop Karen's breathing, but it would not be wrong to turn off a machine that did the breathing for her. They said they wished to leave to God's will whether she should continue breathing. The parents signed a document authorizing the hospital to turn off the respirator and promising not to hold the hospital or the doctors responsible. But the doctor caring for Karen refused to turn off the machine. To do so, he said, would violate his professional oath.

Mr. Quinlan started a lawsuit asking the court to prevent the doctors and the hospital from interfering with the family's decision. He declared that no one would be criminally liable for homicide if Karen died after removal of the respirator.

The highest court in New Jersey ruled that Karen Quinlan had a right of privacy that could be protected by her legal guardian. Although current medical opinion held that a respirator should not be removed in a case like this, the court stated that this opinion should not interfere with the private decision of Karen's family. If a hospital ethics committee agreed that the prospect of recovery was very small, the respirator could be turned off without criminal liability. The respirator was removed and Karen continued to live in a coma.

The decision in this case confirmed the legal principle that death is defined by medicine and not law. Courts are not authorized to ask how hopeless a case is or to determine when efforts to preserve life should stop. These decisions must be made by doctors.

■ **Right to die** Controversy over the Quinlan case raised another important legal question: whether a person has a right to die. The New Jersey decision entitled residents to decide whether life-support apparatus can be disconnected from someone who will never regain consciousness. It was not at all clear how often that rule would be applied or whether other states would follow New Jersey's decision.

Several states have enacted right-to-die statutes. These laws give patients the power to tell their doctors to cut off life-support systems when death is at hand. In at least one state the directive is only advisory, not binding, on the physician. Most states restrict the law in some way by requiring that the patient be certified by a physician as terminally ill before he can sign a right-to-die order. Other restrictions exclude pregnant women or require that a witness also sign the order. At least two states permit a right-to-die order to be signed on behalf of a minor. Very few

patients have used their authority to stop extraordinary medical treatment when death was near. It has been suggested that healthy people should be able to sign right-to-die statements that could be withdrawn any time they change their minds.

■ **Missing persons** The law considers a person who has disappeared to be alive until there is a reason to believe that he is dead. For example, if the missing person was last seen boarding an airplane that vanished somewhere in the Bermuda Triangle, this would be a reason for believing that he had died.

When there is no evidence that the missing person was exposed to a specific danger, the law will presume that he is dead after seven years. This seven-year absence is a common-law rule. Some states have enacted laws shortening the seven-year requirement. For example, some states permit a MARRIAGE to be dissolved or an estate to be distributed among the proper heirs after an unexplained disappearance that lasts less than seven years. See Chart 15.

Most states will not assume that a missing person is dead if there is a good reason for him *not* to return. A man who tells his wife he is running off with another woman before he disappears is not presumed dead; nor is a person who is wanted for armed robbery and drops out of sight.

A special problem arises when someone disappears after a threat is made on his life. On the one hand, he has a good reason for fleeing and hiding. On the other hand, the plot may have succeeded and he may in fact be dead. A court looks carefully at the facts of each case.

Some states hold that death will not be presumed until a serious search is made for the absent person. Public records must be checked wherever he might have lived—for evidence of marriage, death, payment of taxes, or an application for such public benefits as Social Security. Inquiry must be made among friends or relatives who might have heard from him.

Missing persons and inheritance In matters of inheritance, it is always necessary to locate all family members and other beneficiaries. Anyone who has long since disappeared must be searched for. If he cannot be found he may be presumed to be alive—and therefore entitled to his share of the inheritance. But if he has been absent for seven years, he may be considered legally dead and therefore not entitled to inherit.

■ **Survivorship** When people are victims of a *common disaster*, courts frequently must determine who died first in order to administer estates.

EXAMPLE Let us say a man and his adult son, an only child, O⊷✳ die when their fishing boat sinks. Who died first has real legal significance. The law of their state says that the property of a person who left no will goes to his spouse, if he has no children, or, if there are children, one-half to the spouse and one-half to the children. Both father and son were married. The son has no children. Neither father nor son left a will.

If the father died first, one-half of his property goes to the mother and one-half to the son, because the son outlived him. Since the son is now dead, all his property goes to his wife, including his half of his father's property.

If the son died first, all of his property goes to his wife because he has no children. All of the father's property

DEATH AND THE LAW

■ Under the law, *natural death* means dying of natural causes—such as cancer or a heart attack—without the assistance or interference of any person or thing. Death caused or hastened by application of force is known as *violent death*.

■ If a person is absent for a specified number of years and no reason is known for his disappearance, he may be found legally dead.

■ Civil death, in some states, is the condition of someone sentenced to life imprisonment. The death is civil because his civil rights have been lost.

■ The law does not have a medical definition of death. Determining whether someone has died and the cause of death are medical decisions.

■ Several states have enacted right-to-die statutes giving patients the power to tell their doctors to "pull the plug" when death is at hand.

■ Right-to-die orders from patients—where they are allowed—have many restrictions. For example, in at least one state the directive is only advisory, not binding, on the physician. In most states the patient must be certified as terminally ill before he can sign a right-to-die order, and a witness must be present at the signing.

■ A person who has been missing for no reason for seven years may be presumed dead. Some states now permit a marriage to be dissolved or an estate to be distributed among the proper heirs after an unexplained disappearance lasting less than seven years.

■ Most states will not assume a missing person is dead if there is good reason for him *not* to return—for example, a man who runs out on his wife with another woman or a man wanted for armed robbery.

■ The death of a missing person will not be presumed until a serious search for him has been made.

■ In every state the cause of death must be determined and noted on the death certificate.

goes to the mother because no child was alive when he died. In this example, the disposition of one-half of the father's estate depends on who died first.

Courts will consider *any* evidence that one person lived longer than the other, even for a fraction of a second. In the example above, there may be proof that the son was in excellent health and was an experienced swimmer while the father had recently suffered a heart attack. Perhaps when the bodies were recovered it was found that the father had suffered from burns when the boat's engine exploded but the son had not. Perhaps the son's lungs were filled with water, indicating that he had drowned; but the father's lungs were not, indicating that he was already dead when the boat sank.

When there is *no* proof that one person lived longer than the other, as when a husband and wife die in an airplane crash, many states distribute the property of each as if each one had lived longer. This avoids paying death taxes twice on the same property (and thus saves assets) as it passes from one deceased person's estate into another deceased person's estate and then to a living person. See also the discussion of simultaneous death in WILLS.

■ **Death certificates** In every state the cause of death must be determined and noted on a death certificate. This requirement is for purposes of record keeping; it is not intended to establish whether someone can be legally blamed for causing the death. That is determined by CRIMINAL LAW if someone is charged with homicide or by the law of TORTS (injury to persons or property) if the death is the subject of a civil lawsuit for DAMAGES. See CORONER.

death penalty
A sentence requiring that a convicted criminal forfeit his life. A sentence of death is not in itself unconstitutional.

Challenges to state laws permitting execution of criminals have been based on the Eighth Amendment to the Constitution, which prohibits CRUEL AND UNUSUAL PUNISHMENT. Early cases applied this prohibition to torture, unnecessary cruelty, and methods of execution that caused a lingering death. In a 1947 decision, the Supreme Court held that it was not cruel to attempt execution by the electric chair a second time after an unforeseeable mechanical problem made the first attempt a failure. More recent challenges have focused on death itself as a cruel and unusual punishment.

■ **Standards for penalty** In the 1972 case of *Furman* v. *Georgia*, the Supreme Court held that the conviction of William Henry Furman, a black man, for killing a white householder while trying to break in at night, was unconstitutional because it was authorized by a statute that permitted a judge or jury to impose the death penalty without any standards to guide them. The court found that such a law almost always exposed only poor, black, uneducated, unpopular, or unstable defendants to the death penalty.

Other rulings have held that any law that automatically imposes the death penalty for a particular crime is unconstitutional; that the circumstances of the individual offender must be considered in each case; that the law must also allow for court review of the sentence so that arbitrary or capricious sentences will not be imposed; and that time for this review must be allowed between sentencing and execution, but a delay of many years should not be permitted.

■ **The Gilmore case** In January 1977 Gary Gilmore became the first person to be executed in the United States since 1967. It had taken a jury only three days to convict him of shooting a motel clerk in the back of the head at point-blank range. Gilmore was sentenced to death. He fought the delay that has followed most death sentences in modern times and ordered his lawyers not to appeal. When they ignored him and won a short stay of execution, he hired another lawyer, who pressed his case for a quick execution. In the meantime Gilmore swallowed enough pills to require hospitalization but too few to kill. After two days, he was back on Death Row. Finally, after a second reprieve by the governor and a short delay by a federal judge, the death sentence was carried out.

Numerous religious and civil rights groups had opposed Gilmore's execution. They cited several grounds: (1) moral, because states have no right deliberately to kill; (2) practical, because the death penalty does not deter psychopathic killers like Gilmore; and (3) legal, because a sentence of death is impermissibly cruel. Some also shared Gilmore's belief that life imprisonment is a crueler punishment than death. None of these arguments prevented Gilmore's execution. And they have failed to remove the death penalty from our criminal law.

debenture Any document that formally acknowledges a debt and promises payment, including any written BOND or PROMISSORY NOTE. A debenture may be secured or unsecured—that is, it may or may not be backed up by collateral, property pledged by the debtor to protect the creditor's interest. In finance, the term "debenture" is usually restricted to a corporate bond that is not secured by specific property.

debit 1 A charge or sum that is owed or due. 2 As a verb, to debit means to charge a person or an account with all that is supplied to him or paid out for him. See CREDIT.

de bonis non (Latin) "Of goods not [administered]." When an administrator is appointed to succeed another administrator who has left a dead person's estate partially undistributed, he is said to be granted "administration *de bonis non*." See EXECUTORS AND ADMINSTRATORS.

debt Money owed by one person to another. See CREDIT; CREDITOR'S SUIT.

debtor An individual who owes money; one who is expected to pay a CLAIM. See CREDITOR.

debt pooler A person or organization that accepts a debtor's money and then pays it in small monthly payments to people the debtor owes; also known as a *debt adjuster* or *consolidator*. Unless this kind of service is provided by a nonprofit credit-counseling organization, you will probably end up paying much more money in interest than if you yourself make the monthly payments.

debt service A term that includes regular payments of principal, interest, and other costs, such as insurance, made to pay off a MORTGAGE loan.

decedent A person who has died, especially one who has died recently. See DEAD BODY; DESCENT AND DISTRIBUTION; WILL.

deceit An intentionally false statement that misleads another person and causes him some kind of harm.
> EXAMPLE Suppose your friend borrows money and says he
> 0—* will pay you back on payday. In fact, he lost his job last month, although he has not told anyone yet. He used deceit to get the loan. He made an intentionally false statement that tricked you into lending him your hard-earned cash. If he attempted to deceive a bank or a loan company his deceit would probably have more serious consequences, because a lending institution is quicker to file suit than an individual.

decision The formal determination of a dispute. In law, the term usually refers to the resolution of a legal controversy by a court. See JUDGMENT.

decision on the merits Final determination of all ISSUES involved in a case. After a decision on the merits, the plaintiff is forever barred from bringing another lawsuit based on the same grounds against the same defendant.

declaration 1 A formal statement of fact. A person who wants to become a United States citizen, for example, has to make a preliminary declaration of his intention to do so. A deathbed statement revealing who fired the fatal shots is called a *dying declaration*. A statement that is detrimental to the best interests of the person speaking is called a *declaration against interest*. A dying declaration and a declaration against interest are illustrations of out-of-court statements that are often used as EVIDENCE in court. 2 A public proclamation, such as the Declaration of Independence.

declaration of trust A written statement by a person owning property that he or someone else, called a trustee, is holding it for the benefit of someone else. This is an informal way of setting up a TRUST. It is much better, however, to set up a trust with sound legal advice.

declaratory judgment A court action that clarifies the rights of the parties (the plaintiff and defendant) or expresses the opinion of the court on some legal controversy without ordering anything to be done. The purpose of a declaratory JUDGMENT is to provide a speedy way of determining the legal rights of the parties before any wrongs can be committed.

decree A court JUDGMENT that sets forth the legal consequences of the facts in a case and orders the court's decision to be carried out. For example, a DIVORCE decree gives the court's conclusions concerning the facts given as grounds for the divorce and orders that the marriage be dissolved. A *consent decree,* often issued in divorce cases, is one agreed to by the parties.

dedication The giving of land to the government for a specific public use. The land is then accepted by the government on behalf of the public for that use. Land is sometimes dedicated for the construction of streets and for the construction of telephone or telegraph lines. A dedication may be made for school or other public-educational purposes as well as for public cemeteries.

Land for parks or for other recreational facilities is often dedicated by subdividers when they develop new residential areas. Communities near sprawling cities are beginning to require some form of recreational dedication before they will allow further development. The theory is that suburban fringe areas should not be built up without adequate parks and recreation areas.

deductible 1 Capable of being taken away or subtracted; something allowed to be subtracted from your income for tax purposes. For example, interest that you pay on a loan, such as a MORTGAGE on your house, is deductible on your federal INCOME TAX form.   **2** Describing a clause in an INSURANCE policy making the insured responsible for a certain amount of money before the insurance company will pay for a loss. Deductible clauses are common in automobile and medical insurance policies.

deduction   **1** An item subtracted from income for tax purposes. INCOME TAX regulations must be carefully checked to find out what your permissible deductions are. Those most commonly permitted are for charitable contributions, medical and dental expenses that exceed a certain percentage of your income, certain local taxes, casualty losses, and business expenses.   **2** A conclusion drawn from proven principles or facts. Sometimes a deduction can be drawn from testimony that a witness gives in court. If the witness testifies that he heard a shot and saw the accused person leaving the room with a smoking pistol in his right hand, a jury could logically draw the deduction that the accused fired the shots. See EVIDENCE.

deed   A written document that transfers TITLE to (ownership of) land and the buildings or other structures located on it. In law, transferring land is called *conveying land,* a deed is called an *instrument of conveyance,* and transferring land by deed is called *conveyancing.* The person who transfers the land is called the *grantor.* The person who receives it is called the *grantee.*

Land can be transferred from one person to another only in the way prescribed by law. Under the Spanish law in effect at an early date in western areas now a part of the United States, a written deed was not necessary to convey title to land. The transaction could be accomplished by a verbal grant of land, accompanied by a transfer of possession—for example, by the owner's moving off the land and allowing someone else to assume or exert control over it. The propriety of verbal grants of land made under the Spanish law in force at the time, such as those in Texas, has been recognized in U.S. courts.

In most parts of the United States, however, land has traditionally been transferred by a written deed. A deed must describe the property and clearly indicate that it is being conveyed. Technical terms need not be used. The deed must identify both the grantor and the grantee and in some states must also give their residences by town, city, county, and state.

■ **Executing a deed**   The signature of the grantor in the proper place on the document is an essential element for the proper execution of a deed, but the signature of the grantee (the recipient) is not necessary. States usually require the grantor to sign a deed in the presence of witnesses. The execution of a deed also involves delivery, acceptance, and recording.

Delivery   A delivery of the deed from the grantor to the grantee is essential to the legality of the transaction. No particular act, method, ceremony, or active physical delivery of the document by the grantor to the grantee is required. For example, depositing a deed, addressed to the grantee, in the post office is sufficient delivery. So is delivery by an attorney who has drawn up the deed for the grantor. The fact that the grantee has obtained possession of the deed does not establish delivery—the grantor must

have intended to deliver the document. Unless a state law provides otherwise, a deed takes effect from the date of its delivery.

Acceptance   Acceptance of a deed by the grantee usually does not have to be in writing or expressed in any other particular way. All that is needed is some act or words showing an intention to accept. A grantee usually accepts by keeping the deed or mortgaging the property.

Recording   The policy of the law is that deeds to property should be a matter of public record. Thus, after a deed has been delivered to and accepted by the grantee, it should be recorded in the proper place.

The deed is first taken to the recorder's office in the county where the property is located. The recorder's office photocopies the document and inserts the copy into the current book of official records. These record books consist solely of copies of deeds and are labeled in numerical order. The deed is then returned to the owner; the copy is all the recorder's office needs.

A properly recorded deed gives constructive NOTICE of its contents. This means that all people concerned with the transaction are considered to have knowledge of it whether or not they actually see it. Most states put the burden on home buyers to learn whatever information would be disclosed through an appropriate inquiry. References in the records to other deeds for that particular property, for example, alert a home buyer to find out whether those documents give rights in the property to other individuals.

A map referred to in a recorded deed and describing the land conveyed becomes part of the deed. For example, Smith, being the owner of a city lot, conveys "to Jones, my property, being Lot 2, Block 3, of the Erieview Addition to the City of Kingsville, according to that certain map on page 66 of Book V of Maps and Plats [Plots] in the Office of the County Recorder of Onondaga County, State of Nebraska." For the purpose of identifying Smith's lot, the map on page 66 of Book V becomes part of the deed from Smith to Jones.

■ **Indexes**   In addition to the official book of deeds, the recorder's office maintains a set of indexes to facilitate a search for a deed. Most states have a *grantor-grantee index*—a set of books listing all recorded deeds by the grantor's name in alphabetical order. The index will show the name of the grantor, then the name of the grantee, then probably a description of the document and perhaps of the property, and finally a reference to the volume and page in the official record book where the copy of the document is kept. A *grantee-grantor index* contains the same information but it is organized according to an alphabetical list of grantees. A *tract index* organizes all of the entries according to the location of the property.

Indexes are often filed by dates. There may be one set of indexes covering all documents recorded between 1920 and 1950, another set covering 1950 to 1980, separate sets for each of the months of the current year, and, finally, a weekly and/or daily index for the current year.

Here is the way an index works: A deed for Morningside Gardens from Quinn to Hahn, recorded in 1965, will be placed in the grantor-grantee index for the decade 1960 under the name of Quinn. It will be listed in the grantee-grantor index for the same decade under the name of Hahn.

It will be put in a tract index under Morningside Gardens.

If a deed cannot be located through the indexes, a very real problem can result.

EXAMPLE Anthony deeds his property to Rosenberg, who 0⟶※ has it recorded. The recorder erroneously indexes the deed under the name of "Palmer," rather than "Anthony," in the grantor column. Knowing about the mistake, Anthony decides to take advantage of it and deeds the property to Myers. Because of the misindexing, Myers will not find the deed to Rosenberg (since he will search only for the name "Anthony" in the grantor-grantee index). The courts in many states will hold that the deed to Rosenberg was not recorded because it was not indexed to give notice to someone checking Anthony's title to the property and that the land therefore belongs to Myers. In other states, where the law provides that a deed is deemed recorded when deposited in the proper office, Rosenberg will prevail because his deed is technically recorded even though it cannot be found. In states ruling in favor of Myers, it is the duty of all grantees (in this case Rosenberg) to return to the recorder's office at a later date to protect themselves by checking the indexing of their documents. In states holding for Rosenberg, however, there are no practical steps for subsequent purchasers such as Myers to take to avoid this hazard.

You will want to check on your own state's law, or check with your attorney, when the deed to your house is recorded. It is a good idea anyway to go to the recorder's office to make sure your deed is properly recorded and indexed. See also REGISTRATION OF LAND TITLES.

■ **Your deed** When you were given the deed to your house, you probably received what is known in the law as a FEE-SIMPLE estate in the land. This means that as an owner of the ESTATE, you have four basic rights in the land: (1) you may use the land; (2) you may take the fruits of the land, such as crops grown on it; (3) you may abuse the land, if you wish; (4) you may transfer the land by deed or by WILL whenever you want to.

A person selling a house is generally required to disclose any important defect known to him and not known to the buyer. If the seller does not disclose such a defect, the buyer may cancel the deed, sue for money DAMAGES, or possibly recover for personal injuries suffered as a result of the defect. If you are, or will be, a homeowner, you should know what the law in your state says about this.

Types of deeds There are three basic types of deeds: the quitclaim deed, the grant deed, and the warranty deed.

In the *quitclaim deed* the grantor says, "I quitclaim [release] the property to you." By these words, the grantor does not claim that he owns the property to be conveyed—only that if it is proven that he owns the property described, or any interest in it, it is to be transferred to the grantee. This type of deed is used when ownership of property (TITLE) is in dispute or uncertain.

EXAMPLE Myra neglected to pay real estate taxes on her 0⟶※ house for two years, and owed the state $2,000. The state filed a lien against Myra's land so that the land might eventually be sold by the state to satisfy the tax debt. Myra sold the house to David and gave him a quitclaim deed in which she transferred her interest in the property

to him. By doing so, Myra only sold the interest she had, which was the value of the land subject to its possible tax sale by the state because of Myra's overdue taxes.

In the *grant deed* the grantor says, "I grant [or convey] the property to you." These words usually imply that the grantor does own the property being transferred.

In the *warranty deed* the grantor can make various promises about his title to the land and his transfer of it. These promises could be that his title was in fee simple; that the premises are free from encumbrances, such as financial claims, debts, or COVENANTS, except those specified; or that he will provide any further necessary assurance of the title.

■ **Validity** A deed must be made voluntarily in order to be valid. The test of whether a person has the capacity to execute a valid deed lies in his ability to understand the consequences of the act.

EXAMPLE Suppose you have an 87-year-old uncle who is 0⟶※ starting to get feeble. He can no longer walk to the store or go to the bank, but his mind is as keen as ever. Your uncle's lawyer comes to his house and they draw up a deed making you the owner of that property. Since your uncle still has the mental capacity to dispose of his own property, the deed is valid and will stand up to any of your relatives' objections to it.

Fraud committed by either the grantor or the grantee can cause a deed to be declared invalid. A forged deed, for example, is a fraud and completely ineffective.

Exercise of undue influence will invalidate a deed. The test of undue influence is whether or not the grantor acted voluntarily in executing the deed. To invalidate a deed, ordinary influence is not enough; the influence must confuse the judgment or control the will of the grantor.

Deeds between persons having a confidential relationship will be closely scrutinized by the courts for undue influence. Broadly speaking, "confidential relationship" refers to all instances in which one person places trust in another and is under his influence. For instance, the courts will take a good look at a deed given to the grantor's business agent, attorney, priest, or physician. In doing so, they may at times discover undue influence. The fact that the grantor drinks to excess, for example, is a circumstance to be considered when a court determines whether undue influence was exercised upon him.

deed of trust A document used in some states to serve the purpose of a MORTGAGE on real estate. It transfers the ownership of land to TRUSTEES, who, in turn, hold the land as security to assure the payment of a debt. If for any reason the debt is not paid, the trustees sell the land and pay the debt with the proceeds.

deem Treat as if; hold. If a fact is deemed true, it is treated as true. If a law deems an act a crime, it is held to be a crime.

de facto (Latin) "In fact"; actually. The phrase is used to describe an officer, a government, or a state of affairs that must be accepted for all practical purposes but that is illegal or illegitimate. The phrase "de facto" is distinguished from DE JURE, which means rightful, legitimate, just, or constitutional.

EXAMPLE An officer, king, or governor de facto is one who is in actual possession of the office or power without having lawful title. An officer, king, or governor de jure is one who has just claim and rightful title to the office or power but who has never had complete possession or is not in actual possession of it. De facto segregation means segregation that is actually taking place, regardless of the laws against it.

defalcation Failure to account for money in one's care. The word usually implies that the money was misused. A company treasurer's use of corporate funds for his private purposes is a defalcation.

defamation Injuring someone's character or reputation by making false and malicious statements about him to other people. The law recognizes a difference between defamation and mere criticism of an individual. Criticism deals only with matters that legitimately invite public attention or call for public comment. In contrast, defamation usually involves a person's private life and domestic affairs. Calling a woman a prostitute or a banker an embezzler on a television or radio program are examples of defamation. The term "defamation" includes both LIBEL AND SLANDER.

default Failure to perform a legal duty, take care of an obligation, or observe a promise. Failure to pay a debt when it comes due is a default on the debt. Failure to take a required step in a lawsuit can be a default. For example, if you fail to file a required paper in court on time, the person opposing you in a lawsuit may obtain a default JUDGMENT against you, which means you automatically lose your case. Courts do not favor default judgments because controversies should be settled on their merits, not on default.

defeasance clause The part of a MORTGAGE that says the agreement is ended when all of the payments have been made.

defeasible Subject to being defeated, ended, or undone by a future event or action. This term is most often used regarding interests in land. For instance, the interest of the person or institution that holds a MORTGAGE on land is defeasible when all the payments have been made.

defective Lacking something needed to be legally sufficient or binding. A defective WILL, for example, is one that is improperly drawn up, fails to comply with a law, or is obtained by illegal means.

defendant The person against whom a civil lawsuit or criminal proceeding is brought. If a landlord sues his tenant for the rent, the tenant is a defendant in a civil action. If the state prosecutes a murder case, the accused person is the defendant in a criminal action. See CRIMINAL LAW.

defense The sum of the facts, law, and arguments presented by the side against whom a legal action, either civil or criminal, is brought. If the only response of an accused murderer is that he was in another place at the time of the killing, that ALIBI is his defense. See CRIMINAL LAW.

deficiency A lack or shortage. A deficiency in a legal paper means that it lacks some element necessary to make it legally effective. The difference between a tax that is owed and a tax that is actually paid is another example of a deficiency.

deficiency judgment The court's decision, or JUDGMENT, that a person must pay more money than has been obtained through the sale of his property that he promised to guarantee payment of a debt.
EXAMPLE Let us say Mike, an automobile dealer, has taken back a car from Susan for her failure to make the regular payments on it. Although the debt owed is $1,000, Mike's sales representative gets only $800 when he resells the car. Some states will allow Mike to sue Susan for a $200 deficiency judgment.
See also SECURED TRANSACTION.

deficit Less than what should be; a minus balance. If a city takes in less money than it must pay out during the same time period, the situation is called "deficit financing" or "deficit spending."

definitive Capable of completely settling a legal question or a lawsuit. The Supreme Court, for example, gave a definitive opinion on the illegality of racial segregation in public schools.

defraud Cheat or trick; deprive someone of money or property by deceit. Advertising that you are collecting money for a charity and then using the donations to buy yourself a new car is an example of defrauding the public. See FRAUD.

degree A division or grade; the division of a crime into different levels of severity. For example, first-degree MURDER carries a more severe maximum punishment than second-degree murder. See CRIMINAL LAW.
Relatives are sometimes spoken of as related in degrees. Accordingly, a brother and sister are related in the first degree while a parent and child are related in the second degree.

de jure (Latin) "By right"; legitimate; lawful; the opposite of DE FACTO. For example, a government that has been established according to a country's constitution and is legally entitled to govern is a de jure government. Even if revolutionaries seize power, the original government would still be the de jure government but the revolutionaries would be the de facto government.

del credere (Italian) "Of trust." Roughly equivalent to GUARANTY. A *del credere* agent, for example, is someone who sells goods for another and guarantees the seller that the buyer will pay in full. He is paid an additional commission for this guaranty of payment and if the buyer defaults, the *del credere* agent must pay the seller what is owed.

delectus personae (Latin) "Choice of person"; the right of a partner to choose, approve, and disapprove of other partners. See PARTNERSHIP.

delegate   A person who is chosen to represent others. Your representative in the state legislature is the delegate from your district.

deliberate   **1** Consider carefully, discuss, work toward making a decision. A jury deliberates before giving its verdict.   **2** As an adjective, intentional; planned in advance. Killing a person by inserting small amounts of poison into his food over a six-month period is an illustration of a deliberate act.

delinquency   An omission or violation of duty; misconduct. Falling behind on payments to your debtors is a form of delinquency. For a discussion of juvenile delinquency, see INFANT.

delinquent   **1** A person who commits an offense or crime. A minor (a child under the legal age of adulthood, usually 18 or 21) who commits an offense is called a juvenile delinquent. This topic is discussed under the heading INFANT.   **2** As an adjective, failing to meet an obligation, such as a payment on a debt.

delivery   The transfer of an object or a legal document from one person to another; an act having the legal effect of a transfer even though the object has not been physically handed over. A delivery can take place, for example, when goods are placed in a warehouse while the person scheduled to receive them is notified that he can pick them up.

demand   An assertion of a legal right; a forceful claim that presupposes no doubt of its validity. A NEGOTIABLE INSTRUMENT (a legal document that can be exchanged for money, such as a bank check) is often made *payable on demand.* This means that the money represented by the instrument must be paid immediately upon request. See COMMERCIAL PAPER.

de minimis   (Latin) An abbreviation of the legal maxim *De minimis non curat lex:* "The law does not care about trifling matters."

demise   **1** A transfer of property, usually a transfer of an interest in land. A lease is a common example of a demise.   **2** A person's DEATH.

demonstrative evidence   EVIDENCE besides oral or written testimony, such as a gun shown to a jury.

demonstrative legacy   A gift in a WILL that is to be paid from a specifically named part of the dead person's property. For example, a demonstrative LEGACY could provide that $1,000 is to be paid to the oldest niece from the money hidden in a box in the basement.

demur   Take an exception to a legal PLEADING or an allegation of facts. See DEMURRER.

demurrage   Money paid to a shipowner by someone who holds the ship beyond the agreed-upon time. Demurrage is a compensation for the earnings a vessel loses as a result of such a delay. See SHIPPING.

demurrer   A legal PLEADING filed in court that says, in effect: "Even if, for the sake of argument, the allegations presented by the people on the other side are true, those facts do not give them an argument that can stand up in court." A demurrer is a legal way of saying, "So what?" In many courts, the use of a motion to dismiss a case has replaced the demurrer. See MOTIONS AND ORDERS.

denial   **1** A deprivation or withholding, such as denial of a legal right.   **2** A refusal or rejection, such as the denial of welfare benefits to a family that earns too much money to qualify.   **3** That part of a legal PLEADING that refutes the facts claimed by the other side in a lawsuit or criminal trial; also called "answer" in a civil trial.

de novo   (Latin) "Anew"; again. The phrase is usually used in reference to a trial. For example, if a jury is unable to agree on a verdict, the court may order a trial *de novo,* which is an entirely new trial.

dependent   **1** A person supported primarily by another, such as a young son or daughter. See INCOME TAX; PARENT AND CHILD.   **2** As an adjective, conditional. A dependent, or conditional, CONTRACT is an agreement in which one party does not have to perform the terms of the contract until the other party does what is required.

dependent relative revocation   The legal principle, recognized in some states, that if a person cancels a WILL with the intention of making a new one, which is never made or is DEFECTIVE, it is assumed that he would have preferred the old will to none at all.

depletion allowance   A reduction of taxes given to developers of oil, minerals, and other natural resources because of their nonreplaceable nature. The depletion allowance provided by the federal tax laws has been modified to give smaller allowances to big companies.

deponent   A person who gives sworn out-of-court testimony in a DEPOSITION.

deportation   See ALIEN.

depose   Give sworn testimony out of court, rather than on a witness stand. See DEPOSITION.

deposit in court   Property or funds placed in the charge of an officer of the court, such as the court clerk, for safekeeping during a lawsuit. A bankbook might be deposited, for example, until the court can decide who is entitled to the money in the account.

deposition   **1** The out-of-court recording of a witness's sworn TESTIMONY, which can be used as EVIDENCE in a civil lawsuit or a criminal trial. A deposition is usually taken by the lawyer who wants the witness's testimony, with the attorney for the other side having a chance to ask his own questions. It is especially important for a deposition to be taken if a witness cannot attend a trial. **2** The written record of a deposition proceeding. See also DISCOVERY.

depository A place where deposits of money, legal documents, or other valuables are kept; a person with whom the deposits are left. U.S. Depositories are banks selected to receive deposits from the public funds of the United States.

depreciation A marked decrease in value or a noticeable reduction in the worth of an item that produces income—such as office equipment, a two-family home, or business machinery—due to its use, deterioration, or the passage of time. Depreciation is usually measured by a formula that takes the original cost of the item minus its salvage value, measures its worth at the end of its usefulness against its estimated useful life, and estimates the period of time over which the item may reasonably be expected to be useful to its owner in his trade, business, or in the production of income. The amount of depreciation claimed each year is then subtracted from the amount of income earned by that item to arrive at the taxable income of the item's owner.

If the same amount of depreciation is taken for each year of an item's projected useful life, it is called STRAIGHT-LINE DEPRECIATION.

EXAMPLE Henry buys a brand-new apartment building for
O—* $100,000. (This figure does not include the cost of the land, which cannot be depreciated since it has an unlimited useful life.) The building has a useful life of 40 years and a salvage value of $20,000 at the end of 40 years. Henry will be entitled to depreciation allowances totalling $80,000 (original cost minus salvage value) over 40 years or $2,000 per year. Henry's yearly income from renting the apartment building will be reduced by $2,000 a year for tax purposes.

On the other hand, if a greater amount of depreciation is taken earlier during an item's useful life, it is called *accelerated depreciation*. Hal owns a rent-a-car business. Since his automobiles decrease in value more rapidly than cars used in other businesses, Hal may take accelerated depreciation on his tax return. One way of taking accelerated depreciation is the sum of the years' digits method. According to this formula, the cost of the item minus the salvage value multiplied by a constantly decreasing fraction, the numerator of which is the remaining years of useful life of the asset at the beginning of each year, and the denominator is the sum of the years' digits of useful life at the time of the acquisition.

EXAMPLE Hal paid $200,000 for his fleet of 500 auto-
O—* mobiles. The useful life of the fleet is five years, at the end of which it will be worth $50,000. The first year, Hal can deduct $60,000 from the income produced by the fleet. The cost, $200,000, reduced by the salvage value, $50,000, is $150,000 multiplied by the fraction of 4/10, 4 being the remaining years of useful life while 10 is the sum of the years' digits (1 + 2 + 3 + 4) of the fleet's five-year useful life at the time the asset is acquired. The second year, Hal will only be able to take a $45,000 deduction because the fraction will be 3/10, since there

are only three remaining years of useful life. The third year, the depreciation will be only $30,000 because the fraction will be 2/10, reflecting only two years of usefulness remaining; while the fourth year, only $15,000 can be deducted from the fleet's yearly income as there is only one year of useful life left to the fleet.

Whatever method is used to take depreciation, the total amount taken over the useful life of an item cannot exceed the original cost of the item minus its salvage value.

deputy A substitute; someone appointed to act on behalf of another person and in his name; a person authorized by an officer to exercise some or all functions of the office—a deputy sheriff, for instance. See SHERIFFS AND CONSTABLES.

derivative action A lawsuit by a stockholder of a CORPORATION against another individual (usually an officer of the company) to enforce claims the stockholder thinks the corporation has against that person. He is suing a guardian of the corporation's interests.

derivative evidence Information collected by following up on EVIDENCE that was illegally obtained. Derivative evidence may not be used in a trial. The theory is that the court will not accept "fruit of the poisonous tree." See also SEARCH AND SEIZURE.

EXAMPLE Suppose the police search a house to find a knife.
O—* But they neglect to obtain a search warrant, even though they have ample time to do so. While the police are looking for the knife, the homeowner confesses to stabbing his girl friend. Because the confession was derived from a warrantless search, it cannot be used as evidence in court.

derogation The partial abolition of a law by a later enactment that limits its effectiveness. Let us say a state has prohibited the sale of all alcoholic beverages. Then, without formally repealing its law, the state legislature passes another statute prohibiting the sale of all alcoholic beverages except what is called "3.2 beer." The second law is in derogation of the first. See REPEAL.

descent and distribution The way a person's real property (real estate) and personal property are distributed by law to his descendents when he dies without leaving a will. *Descent* refers to the right to inherit or share in the property of a person who has died intestate, that is, without disposing of his property (estate) by will. In general, descent is based on an individual's blood relationship to the intestate.

Distribution is the division, under the authority of a court, of an intestate's property among those entitled to a share of it. This occurs only after the payment of the intestate's debts and charges, such as estate taxes. Strictly speaking, distribution refers only to personal property, but it is commonly applied also to the division of real property. A *distributee* is a person entitled to share in the distribution of an intestate's estate. He receives a distributive share. *Succession* is the transfer of title to (ownership of) property to an intestate's heirs under the laws of descent and distribution. It is also called hereditary succession, intestate succession, or succession by law.

The laws of descent and distribution do not apply when a deceased person has disposed of all his property in a valid will. They do apply, however, if part of the decedent's property has not been disposed of in his will or if a will is declared invalid—for example, when it was not properly witnessed. This article explains the nature of the right to inherit or share in the division of the estate of a person who died intestate (without leaving a will). Some of the concepts—such as the rights of the surviving spouse, advancements, and release of inheritance rights—also apply to property that is given by a will. The distribution of real and personal property by a person who has left a will is discussed in WILL.

■ **The right of succession** The law confers the right of succession and determines who shall take intestate property. Statutes in every state set the order in which persons succeed to a decedent's property if he dies intestate. (See Chart 16.) The aim of the statutes is to carry out the distribution that most intestates would have specified if they had made wills. The law assumes that most persons prefer to have their nearest relatives inherit property rather than those who are only remotely related. A typical order of preference is wife, children, parents, brothers and sisters and their lineal descendants, grandparents and their lineal descendants; if there are none, then next of kin (nearest blood relatives) inherit; if none, then ESCHEAT (reversion) to the state. Lineal descendants are persons directly descended from the same ancestor; father and son are lineal descendants of the father's father and grandfather, for example.

■ **Which law governs** When the property of the intestate is located in the state of his DOMICILE (permanent residence) at the time of his death, the law of that state will govern its descent and distribution. The law of the place where real property is located, however, supersedes the law of the deceased's domicile and thus usually determines the distribution of land, houses, and farms.

Since the privilege of receiving property by inheritance is not a natural right but one created by law, the legislature of a state has complete power over the descent and distribution of property within its borders, subject to restrictions

WHO WILL INHERIT IF YOU DIE WITHOUT A WILL?

■ *Descent and distribution* is the term for the way state laws prescribe how your property will be distributed when you die without a valid will.

■ An *intestate* is a person who dies without leaving a valid will.

■ *Descent* is your right to inherit or share in the property or estate of a person who died intestate. In general, it is based on your blood relationship to the deceased.

■ State laws specify the order in which succession (right of inheritance) is conferred when there is no will. A typical pattern of succession is: spouse, children, parents, brothers and sisters and their lineal descendants, grandparents and their lineal descendants; if none, then next of kin (nearest blood relatives); if none, then the property goes to the state.

■ *Lineal descendants* are directly descended from the same ancestor: father, son, and grandson, for example. Some states consider an adopted child to be a lineal descendant.

■ Stepchildren do not inherit from a stepparent except in a few states.

■ Brothers and sisters inherit only when there are no other survivors with priority—for example, the intestate's spouse, children, or grandchildren.

■ Nephews and nieces inherit only if their parent who would have inherited from the intestate is deceased.

■ In some states one or both parents inherit when their child dies childless and without a will. The laws vary, however, as to whether the parents must share with the brothers and sisters of the intestate.

■ If you die without a will and have children from different marriages, your property will be divided equally among them, after your surviving spouse has taken his or her legal share. But some states prohibit this method of distribution when your property was inherited from a deceased spouse of a former marriage.

■ Usually a widow may choose the larger of one-third (or one-half, depending on the state) of her husband's property and what he left her in his will. This is called her *right of election*. In the few states that still have dower (a fixed interest in all the land owned by the husband), a widow may choose between that and a specified share.

■ A widower's rights of inheritance are regulated by state law unless the state still adheres to the common-law principle of curtesy (the husband obtained absolute ownership of all his wife's real property, or real estate, when she died). Where curtesy exists, the widower may choose between that and a specified distributive share.

■ A surviving spouse's rights of inheritance are not affected by his or her remarriage unless state laws provide otherwise.

■ A spouse may waive his or her right to inherit from the other spouse by an antenuptial (prewedding) agreement. This is sometimes done to protect the inheritance rights of children from earlier marriages.

■ If a spouse dies before a marital separation or divorce becomes final, the surviving spouse is still entitled to his or her rightful share.

■ A man or woman who is divorced has no claim to the former spouse's property, unless so provided by a will.

■ No one is an heir to a living person. Therefore, you cannot sue your elderly father, who has never drawn up a will, for transferring his land to your sister, his favorite child.

■ A person usually has the right to dispose of the property as he sees fit. Heirs and others entitled to inherit cannot attack gifts and other transfers of property made by the deceased when he was alive, even when they may be unfair.

■ The law of descent and distribution that is applied when a person dies without a valid will is the law of the state where the deceased had his permanent residence. If he or she owned real property in another state, then the law of that state governs the distribution of that property.

found in constitutions or treaties. The disposition of the property of an intestate is governed by the statutes in force at the time of his death.

■ **Property subject to descent and distribution**   Property subject to descent and distribution includes all vested (absolute) rights and interests owned by the deceased at the time of his or her death. For example, the property rights granted absolutely to a woman by a final divorce decree passed, on her death, to her heirs. On the other hand, rights or interests that are personal to the deceased and not of an inheritable nature—such as a lifetime right to use a piece of land or to receive money from a trust fund—are not subject to descent and distribution.

If a landowner had entered into a contract to sell his land but died before the transaction was completed, his heirs are obligated to transfer the land to the purchaser according to the contract.

In some states the property of an intestate is distributed among different persons based on whether it is real estate or personal property but in others such a distinction is not recognized.

■ **Persons entitled to inherit**   Statutes generally confer rights of inheritance only on blood relatives, adopted children, adoptive parents, and a surviving husband or wife. After the spouse has been provided for according to the law (see the section "Surviving spouse" below), direct *descendants* usually have first preference; followed by *ascendants,* such as parents; and, lastly, *collaterals,* those who have a common ancestor but who are not in a direct line of descent, such as cousins and brothers and sisters. Persons who have descended one directly from the other or all from a common ancestor are placed in a *line of descent* showing the connection of all the blood relatives in the order of their birth. Each generation is called a *degree* that determines the blood relationship (consanguinity) of one or more persons to an intestate. When the next of kin are equal in degree of kinship to the intestate, such as children, they share equally in his estate. For example, the father of two sons, who are his only living relations, dies intestate, leaving $50,000. The two sons are in the same nearness of blood relationship to their father and therefore each inherits $25,000.

Descendants   The word "descendants" generally means children or children's children to the remotest degree, such as great-great-grandchildren. It does not include collaterals, ascendants, or a surviving spouse. *Issue* is defined as all persons in the line of descent without regard to the degree of nearness to the source. Both children and great-grandchildren are issue.

Children   Subject to the rights of the surviving spouse, children inherit by descent to the exclusion of other blood relatives. Often this is true for adopted children of the intestate as well. Once the debts of the estate have been paid and the surviving spouse has taken his or her legal share (depending on the law of the state), the remainder of the estate is apportioned in equal shares among the children of the decedent. The decedent's children inherit to the exclusion not only of his brothers and sisters, nephews and nieces, and other collateral kindred, but also his parents.

Posthumous children   A posthumous child is one born after the death of its father or mother (say by Caesar-

ean section). A posthumous child inherits as long as it is born within nine months after the death of the intestate father. Some statutes require that a child born within 10 months after the death of the intestate father also be regarded as a posthumous child.

Children of successive marriages   On the death of an intestate who had children by different marriages, his estate descends equally to all the children. Some states prohibit this method of distribution when the property of the intestate was derived from a deceased spouse. In that instance, only children of the marriage with that spouse can inherit that property. See HUSBAND AND WIFE.

Issue of children who predecease the intestate   The share of a child who dies before the intestate is inherited by his children or other descendants by the right of representation (discussed below). Such grandchildren inherit to the exclusion of the intestate's brothers and sisters and their children. Note, however, that they do not participate in the estate unless their parent, the child of the intestate, is dead.

Illegitimate children   At common law, an illegitimate child was a child of no one *(filius nullus)* and had no right to inherit. This has universally been changed by statutes, which vary from state to state. The general rule is that an illegitimate child is treated as the child of the mother and may inherit from her and her relatives and they from him.

In some states, the illegitimate child is treated as the child of both its natural parents. Usually, however, an illegitimate child is not regarded as a child of the father unless he is made legitimate by the subsequent marriage of his parents or acknowledged by the father as his child. A legitimated child is treated the same for inheritance purposes as any other child of the parent. The trend is toward liberalizing the rights of illegitimate children to inherit from their fathers. In 1977 the Supreme Court decided that it was unconstitutional for states to deprive an illegitimate child of the right to inherit from his intestate father, especially when paternity had already been established in state court proceedings before the father's death. For further discussion of the rights of illegitimate children, see ILLEGITIMACY.

Parents   In some states one or both parents inherit the property of a child who dies intestate, leaving no issue or descendants. Statutory provisions vary considerably as to whether one or both parents inherit and whether they must share the property with their remaining children—the intestate's brothers and sisters.

Stepchildren and stepparents   The term "kindred of the half blood" means a half-blood relationship to the intestate. Stepchildren who share the same parent biologically are related by blood and are of the half blood. They inherit equally with kindred of the whole blood unless prohibited by statute.

> EXAMPLE Arthur and Bonnie shared the same father with
> O———✳ Cassie and Doris but had a different mother.
> Suppose Arthur dies intestate, having never married or
> had children. His parents do not survive him. In these
> circumstances, Cassie and Doris would share equally
> with Bonnie in Arthur's estate.

Usually, a stepparent does not inherit from a stepchild. Stepchildren may inherit from their stepparents depending on state law.

Brothers and sisters If an intestate dies without issue, parents, or a spouse, the estate usually goes to his brothers and sisters and to the children of deceased brothers and sisters. Brothers and sisters inherit when and only when there are no other surviving persons having priority.

Nephews and nieces Nephews and nieces usually inherit only if their parent (the brother or sister of the intestate) is deceased and would have inherited if he or she had outlived the intestate.

Grandparents Grandparents of the intestate who are related to him by blood share equally in his estate. Where the estate descended to the intestate from his father, it will go to a paternal grandparent to the exclusion of a maternal grandparent, according to some state laws. Various state laws differ as to whether the grandparents inherit all, or, when there are surviving aunts and uncles, as to whether they are excluded by the grandparents. There is a similar division of authority as to whether great-grandparents exclude or share with surviving great-uncles and great-aunts.

Surviving spouse The right to share in the estate of a deceased spouse arises automatically from his or her marital status. See Chart 17. Statutes conferring rights of inheritance on a surviving spouse make him or her a statutory heir. Some statutes distinguish between property acquired by the deceased spouse before and during the marriage. Usually, however, the surviving spouse is entitled to share in the property that the deceased spouse received as a gift or through inheritance.

A widow At common law, the wife was entitled to DOWER—a fixed interest in all the land her husband owned during their marriage. However, she had to survive her husband before she could take possession of her interest in the property.

Most states have abolished common-law dower and replaced it with laws allowing the widow to take either an elective share (usually one-third or one-half, depending on the state—that is, what would have gone to her by intestacy) or what is provided in her husband's will. This is called her right of election. The method of computing the widow's share depends on the laws of each state. Ordinarily, her rights apply only to property that her husband fully owned at the time of his death.

A widower At common law, a surviving husband had by CURTESY absolute title to (ownership of) his wife's real property when she died. Curtesy has been abolished by many states, and today a husband's rights of inheritance are regulated by statute. Where curtesy does exist, a widower usually can inherit only property that his intestate wife fully owned at the time she died.

Election between distributive share and dower or curtesy In the few states that have not abolished dower, a widow has the right to elect, or choose, between it and a certain distributive share. A right of election between curtesy and a widower's distributive share is also given to the surviving husband in a few states. In these states the dower and curtesy shares are equal by law. The right of election usually must be exercised by the surviving spouse during his or her lifetime and thus cannot be conferred on someone else by a will.

If as a surviving spouse, you choose to exercise this right of election, you must follow exactly the requirements set out by your state statute. A number of states have only a few or no formal requirements other than that the election be made within a specified time after the spouse has died. Generally, once an election is made, it is conclusive on the survivor and will not be set aside by a court unless there is good and sufficient cause—such as undue influence on the surviving spouse by another heir.

Second marriages A surviving spouse's rights of inheritance are not affected by his or her second marriage, unless a statute provides otherwise.

If you are the second or subsequent spouse of the deceased, your rights of an inheritance are the same as if you were the surviving spouse of the first marriage. In a number of states, the rights of a surviving spouse of a second or subsequent marriage of the deceased or of a surviving spouse who subsequently remarries are, or have been, governed by specific statutes.

The immediate remarriage of a surviving spouse after the death of the former spouse has no effect on his or her right to inherit the deceased spouse's estate.

EXAMPLE Doug and Dana were married for 25 years. Doug repeatedly told his family that, should he die first, he did not want Dana to remarry and if she should, he did not want her to have any of his property. One week after Doug's death, Dana marries the gardener, Francesco. Dana's remarriage has absolutely no effect on her right to inherit Doug's property under the laws of intestacy.

Spouse's release of inheritance right A spouse may waive his or her right of inheritance in the estate of the other spouse by an antenuptial agreement (one made before the marriage). Antenuptial agreements are frequently made by couples who have children by earlier marriages and who wish to protect the children's inheritance rights.

EXAMPLE John, a wealthy 65-year-old attorney, marries Matilda, an equally wealthy 62-year-old psychiatrist. They sign an antenuptial agreement by which they both agree to give up their inheritance rights in each other's estates. In addition to insuring the inheritance rights of their children, the estates are not reduced by the share given to the surviving spouse under the laws of intestacy and rights of dower and curtesy.

A husband or wife usually may waive, release, or be prevented from claiming inheritance rights in the estate of the other by certain acts during the marriage, such as an express postnuptial agreement.

In some jurisdictions, a separation agreement may mutually release the rights of each spouse in the other's property. A property settlement agreement that is part of a DIVORCE may not bar a spouse's statutory share in the estate of the husband or wife if he or she should die before the divorce becomes final.

If the surviving spouse made an agreement with the deceased spouse through ignorance or mistake as to his legal rights, he or she will not be prevented from claiming his rights in the estate. For a full discussion of antenuptial and postnuptial agreements, see MARRIAGE.

Inheriting by representation Representation is the rule of law by which the children (or their descendants) inherit the property of a deceased person who, if he had lived, would have inherited the property of an intestate. The children thus stand in the deceased person's place and collectively take his share of the property. Inheriting by representation is termed taking *per stirpes,* from the Latin meaning "by stock" or "by roots."

EXAMPLE John, who has two children—Mary and Sue—dies O——⚹ intestate, leaving an estate of $200,000 after the payment of debts and charges. Under a typical state law, John's daughters would each receive $100,000. But daughter Mary has died before her father, leaving two sons, Steve and Jeff. Since Mary cannot take her share, there would be a *per stirpes* division of John's estate.

This means Mary's share of $100,000 would be divided equally between Steve and Jeff (her children). Sue's share of her father's estate remains unaffected. Since Steve and Jeff are brothers, the degree of consanguinity (blood relationship) between them is equal, and therefore they take *per capita* (or equal) parts of Mary's share. They have, however, taken *per stirpes* shares of John's estate.

If Jeff, in this hypothetical family, also died before his grandfather, leaving two daughters, Diane and Kathy, and Steve were still alive, Steve would still take $50,000 but Diane and Kathy would equally share $50,000. Sue, who is still alive, would, of course, still be entitled to her $100,000 share of John's estate. The degrees of consanguinity among Steve and Diane and Kathy are unequal, since Steve was John's grandchild while Diane and Kathy are his great-grandchildren. Steve and Diane and Kathy share Mary's portion of John's estate *per stirpes.* Steve takes 50 percent, or $50,000, whereas Diane and Kathy each take 25 percent, or $25,000, because of their unequal degrees of blood relationship to Mary. This example can be pictured in the following chart:

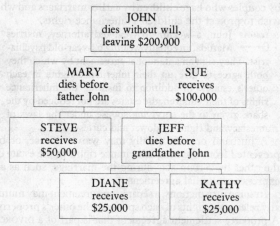

Forced heirs Under the law called forced heirship, certain relatives (besides a husband or wife) had an absolute legal right to a certain portion of the decedent's estate. Neither a will nor a gift could deprive them of it. Now, except in Louisiana, a person generally cannot prevent another from disposing of his property by will or gift to someone else. In Louisiana the law restricts the amount of property that a person can donate or give away so long as he has parents or legitimate children or their descendants who would inherit upon his death. These persons are expressly declared to be forced heirs. They cannot be deprived of their portion of an estate reserved to them by law unless the one who wills the estate has a just cause to disinherit them.

The person who unjustly received the property may be required to return it or compensate the forced heirs for it.

■ **Forfeiture of spouse's rights** Misconduct by a surviving spouse usually will not bar his rights of inheritance, unless the law makes an exception of misconduct.

Desertion A spouse who has deserted or abandoned his or her spouse is not necessarily barred from his or her rights of inheritance in the estate. See DESERTION. Specific laws in some places do not permit a surviving wife to succeed to her husband's estate if she has left him to live in adultery. Similarly, a surviving husband is barred from access to his wife's estate if he deserted her or if he refused to support her for a period of time specified by law. If there is a separation agreement, adulterous conduct by one spouse does not deny him or her the right to share in the decedent's estate.

Murder of intestate The states differ about whether a person who murders his spouse is entitled to succeed to the estate as surviving spouse. Some states refuse to recognize the convicted murderer as a surviving spouse. Other states make no exception for criminal conduct, thus entitling a person to inherit from the spouse he murdered. Still other states have laws that preclude any person who has caused or procured the death of another from inheriting his property if the cause comes within the provisions of the law, such as when one spouse's negligence caused the other's death. There would not be a criminal conviction in this case, however.

Illegal second marriage A spouse who is guilty of BIGAMY may be denied any rights of inheritance in the estate of his lawful spouse in some states. This is true even if the bigamous marriage was ended long before the lawful spouse died.

Divorce Generally, a man or woman who is divorced cannot claim a distributive share in the estate of the former spouse. Under some statutes a DIVORCE from bed or board (a separation) may cancel any right of the spouse's intestate inheritance, even though the couple was lawfully married when the decedent died.

■ **Rights and liabilities of heirs** No one is an heir to a living person. Any prospective interest or right to inherit as an heir is just an expectancy or possibility, not a vested interest or a right. For example, you cannot, simply because you expect to inherit from your elderly father who has never drawn up a will, sue him for transferring his house to your sister, his favorite child. Nor can you, before his death, sue him to enforce or determine your anticipated right in his property.

Advancement If an heir freely releases his expected share in his relative's estate for an advancement or some other valuable consideration, the heir usually is excluded from sharing in the relative's estate. An advancement is an absolute or irrevocable gift of money or land or personal property to a child by his parent in anticipation of what the child's intestate share will be when the parent dies. The gift enables the child to anticipate his inheritance (discussed below). To be enforceable, a release of inheritance rights must be made by a person who is legally competent to enter into a CONTRACT; it must not be obtained by fraud or undue influence; and the document should clearly state that it is a release or contract barring inheritance.

EXAMPLE A daughter gave her father a receipt acknowledging payment of money that she accepted as her "partial" share of all real estate owned by him. The court decided that she was not barred from sharing in the remainder of the real estate left upon the death of her father. The word "partial" indicated that the money received was only an advancement for a portion, not all, of her share in his property.

An advancement differs from a gift in that an advancement will reduce the child's distributive share of his parent's estate by the amount of the advancement. A gift, of course, would reduce the entire estate and not only the distributive share of the person receiving the gift. The doctrine of advancements is based on the theory that a parent intends to have all his children share equally in his estate. They share not only in what may remain at his death, but equally in all that came from him.

An advancement is not limited to a gift to a child by his parent. Grandparents and, where statutes permit, spouses and collateral relatives may also make advancements. Several statutes provide that no gift or grant of land may be deemed an advancement unless it was expressed in writing by the donor or acknowledged in writing by the recipient. A gift based on love and affection or given in exchange for something of nominal value may be an advancement.

Gifts and transfers in fraud of heirs A person usually has the right to dispose of his property as he sees fit. His heirs, whether under a will or under the laws of descent and distribution, cannot attack transfers or distributions the deceased made during his life on the ground that they were made without consideration (that the giver got nothing in return) or on the ground that a gift was made in fraud of their rights. For example, a parent during his life may unequally distribute his property among his children, with or without reason. Those discriminated against have no standing to complain.

One spouse may deprive the other of statutory rights of inheritance by transferring ownership of his property during his life to someone else. However, transfers made by one spouse solely to deprive the other of a distributive share are invalid in some places. Whether a transfer was real or was made to deprive the other spouse is determined by whether or not the person actually gave up complete ownership of the property.

EXAMPLE When a husband transfers all his property to a trustee, the transfer is void as far as the rights of his surviving wife are concerned if he reserves to himself the income of the property for life, the power to revoke and modify the trust, and a substantial measure of control over its management. It is clear that the husband never intended in good faith to give up ownership of his property until he died.

Gifts to children, including children by a former marriage, that were not made with an intent to defraud a spouse, give that spouse no ground for complaint. Good faith is shown when the other spouse knew of the gifts to the children. If a spouse gives all or most of his property to the children without the other spouse's knowledge, there is a PRESUMPTION of fraud.

Acceptance or renunciation of rights An heir may accept his inheritance either by an express or implied act. Under most statutes, once a person accepts his intestate share he cannot subsequently renounce it.

An heir may give up his rights to an estate by an express (specific) waiver or release, which may require a formal document. A person may be barred (estopped) from accepting his rights to an estate by a lapse of time as specified in local statutes. An heir cannot revoke an announced renunciation unless the other heirs have not yet accepted ownership of their share of the estate.

Title of heirs and distributees Rights of heirship or inheritance vest immediately on the death of an intestate. His heirs are ordinarily determined as of that time. The title to real estate vests in the heirs immediately, subject to certain burdens, such as the rights of the surviving spouse, the debts of the intestate, funeral and estate expenses, and debts against the real estate itself.

The title to personal property of a deceased person does not usually vest in his heirs, next of kin, or distributees immediately on his death. Legal title to personal property is suspended between the time of the intestate's death and the granting of the letters of administration to the administrator of the deceased's estate. See EXECUTORS AND ADMINISTRATORS. When the administrator distributes the property to the distributees, title to the property reverts to the date of the intestate's death. Although the title to (ownership of) personal property does not immediately pass to the heirs, their interest in it does, subject to the rights of creditors and to charges and expenses of the estate. The personal estate of an intestate goes ultimately to those who are his next of kin at the time of his death, not to those who are his next of kin at the time of distribution. If a person who is entitled as a distributee dies after the death of the intestate and before distribution, his share goes to his estate, not to the other persons entitled as distributees.

desertion 1 Abandoning a military post and duty without permission and with no intention of returning. See ARMED SERVICES. 2 Abandoning wife, husband, or child with no intention of either returning or resuming the financial obligations and other duties of marriage or parenthood. See DIVORCE.

destroy Annul the effectiveness of a legal document. Destruction does not necessarily mean total physical annihilation of a WILL, CONTRACT, or other legal document. You can destroy a document's legal effect by tearing it in half or by writing over it.

detainer 1 The unlawful keeping of another person's property, even if your possession of the property was originally lawful—for example, you borrow your neighbor's power mower with his consent and never return it. See CONVERSION. 2 Holding a person against his will. See FORCIBLE ENTRY AND DETAINER.

detective One whose business it is to watch alleged wrongdoers and furnish information concerning them and their habits; someone who discovers secret matters in order to protect the public. As portrayed by the entertainment media, a detective may be either a "private eye" or a public police officer.

detention Holding a person ___ nst his will. *Detention for questioning* is the holding c ___ person by a policeman or similar public official withou ___ formal ARREST. See SEARCH AND SEIZURE.

determinable Subject to being ended when a certain event occurs. If the death of a particular person can cancel a lease, the parties have a determinable interest in the lease.

determination A final decision. A determination is usually made by a court or other formal decision maker, such as a hearing officer.

detinue A type of lawsuit to get back property that is unlawfully held by another person and to recover damages for the wrongful withholding. See CONVERSION.

detriment Any harm or loss, as of a right, a benefit, or some kind of property.

devest See DIVEST.

deviance A noticeable difference from average or normal behavior. The word is usually applied to activities that society does not condone, such as the illegal use of drugs or unusual sexual behavior.

devise A gift by WILL, usually of land.

devolution The transfer from one person to another of a right, a liability, a TITLE (ownership), an office, or some kind of property by process of law. Devolution is usually used to mean the transfer of an individual's property upon his death. See DESCENT AND DISTRIBUTION; WILL.

devolve Transfer by DEVOLUTION.

dictum (Latin) Short for *obiter dictum*—"something said in passing." In law, a remark or statement made by a judge about some side issue not essential to the decision of the court. In ordinary usage it is also a formal authoritative pronouncement of a principle, proposition, or opinion.

dilatory Tending to cause delay or to gain time. Lawyers are sometimes accused of using dilatory tactics when a case is supposed to go to trial.

diligence Carefulness; prudence. The law recognizes three degrees of diligence: (1) common or ordinary, the care that people generally practice with respect to their own concerns; (2) high or great, which is more than that care; and (3) low or slight, which is less. A reasonably prudent person is not the average person but a composite of the community's judgment on how an average person ought to behave in certain kinds of situations. The concept of diligence is applied in NEGLIGENCE and in FIDUCIARY relationships (those involving trust).

diminution A reduction; an incompleteness. In law, diminution signifies that the record of a case sent up for review from a lower court to a higher one is incomplete, possibly because it has not been fully certified by the proper officer. The superior court might state that there is a diminution in the record.

directed verdict A legal procedure by which a judge takes the decision out of the hands of the JURY and tells the jurors what they must decide.

EXAMPLE A man was charged with robbery in a state where a conviction could not be based solely on the unsworn testimony of a child. The victim of the crime had not seen the robber, and the only witness to the crime was a six-year-old boy. The prosecutor called the boy to the witness stand, but the judge asked him questions before he would allow him to give testimony. The judge concluded that the boy did not sufficiently understand the difference between truth and falsity, so he would not allow the boy to be sworn in as a witness. When the prosecutor was unable to offer other evidence sufficient to indicate the guilt of the defendant, the judge entered a directed verdict of acquittal.

direct evidence Proof of a fact without the need for other facts leading up to it. If James testifies that he saw Donald walking in the rain, for instance, the court has been given direct EVIDENCE that Donald did in fact walk in the rain. Another example of direct evidence is bringing a live dodo bird into court to prove that dodo birds are not extinct. See also CIRCUMSTANTIAL EVIDENCE.

direct examination The first questioning of a WITNESS by the side (defense or prosecution) that called him or her to the trial. Questioning of a witness by the opposing side in a trial is called cross-examination.

director The head of an organization, group, or project. One of a group of men and women elected by the owners of a CORPORATION to make important decisions.

directory Advisory. In a statute, for example, directory language might instruct an official on how he should carry out the functions of his office. These instructions are not mandatory and if he does not follow the directory language, his actions are still valid. In a statute, directory language uses the verb "may," while mandatory language uses "must," "is required to," and so forth.

direct tax A tax paid straight to the government by the person taxed. An income tax is direct, but a manufacturing tax is not, because it is passed on to the buyer in the form of higher prices. See TAXATION.

disability 1 The absence of adequate physical or mental powers; a reduction in earning ability due to this deficiency. 2 The lack of legal capacity to accomplish an act. For example, a minor (a child below the age of legal adulthood, usually 18 or 21) has an age disability that prevents him from entering into a formal CONTRACT with another person. A married person has a disability that prevents any remarriage until the present union is ended, either by divorce or by death. Under which circumstances a person is incapable and what he is prevented from doing depends on the reason for his incapacity. The disability of being a minor is discussed in INFANT; mental incapacity is in INSANE PERSONS; and there are references to legal disability in GUARDIAN AND WARD, CIVIL RIGHTS, and CITIZEN.

disaffirm   Repudiate; take back consent; refuse to stand by former acts. The term is usually used when someone may have a right to cancel a previous agreement. For instance, if your new home is not finished by the date you and the builder have previously agreed upon, you may disaffirm your promise to pay him in full by that date. See CONTRACTS.

disallow   Refuse; deny; reject. If your insurance company declines to pay for repairing the fender you bent in an auto accident, it is disallowing your claim for damages.

disbar   Take away a lawyer's license to practice law. This action is usually taken because of the lawyer's unethical conduct, such as stealing his clients' funds. See ATTORNEY AND CLIENT.

discharge   1 Release; remove; free; dismiss. To discharge a CONTRACT is to end the obligation by agreement or by carrying out the terms of the contract. To discharge a prisoner is to free him. To discharge a court order is to dismiss or revoke it. To discharge a person in bankruptcy is to absolve him from his debts. To discharge an individual from the army is to release him from the military service. 2 As a noun, the document showing that a person has been released from military service. See ARMED SERVICES. 3 The performance of a duty. Lawyers speak, for example, of discharging a legal obligation.

disciplinary rules   The list of actions a lawyer is prohibited from taking, such as not keeping complete records of all funds and securities belonging to a client that come into the lawyer's possession. If he violates the rules, he can be disbarred or deprived of his license to practice. See also CODE OF PROFESSIONAL RESPONSIBILITY.

disclaimer   A refusal or renunciation of a power; a refusal to accept a particular responsibility. A disclaimer clause in a contract might say, "We give you, the purchaser, all the above promises but disclaim all other promises or responsibilities."

discontinuance   Another term for the DISMISSAL of a lawsuit.

discount   1 Collect interest in advance. When a bank discounts, it lends money on a promissory note (see COMMERCIAL PAPER) and deducts the interest in advance. See BANKS AND BANKING. 2 As a noun, a reduction. A lower price for merchandise is an example of a discount.

discovery   A procedural device used before a trial to find out pertinent information in civil and criminal cases. The concept of discovery in relation to scientific inventions is discussed in PATENT.

Discovery is used (1) to establish grounds for a lawsuit before filing, (2) to help the defendant establish facts for his defense, and (3) to help the plaintiff establish facts to bolster or strengthen his case. Discovery is a method of making an opponent in a lawsuit reveal facts, deeds, documents, or other things that are in his exclusive knowledge or possession and are needed to prepare or prove the case.

■ **Right of discovery in civil cases**   Discovery procedures used today are determined by the Federal Rules of Civil Procedure, which regulate discovery in federal cases, and state laws that govern civil procedure for local lawsuits. See FEDERAL CIVIL PROCEDURE. Discovery is usually obtained either by a SUBPOENA (an order of the court) or by the applicant's attorney serving a NOTICE on the other party in the suit.

The modern policy in civil cases is to permit full disclosure—to give the parties to a lawsuit access to all material (important) facts not protected by PRIVILEGE. See "Privileged matters," below. This includes facts and information needed to prepare a party's PLEADINGS and to frame the issues of the case. A plaintiff may use discovery to obtain facts to frame his COMPLAINT; a defendant may use it to learn facts to draft his ANSWER to the plaintiff's allegations.

EXAMPLE John Jones broke his ankle when he tripped over a raised and jagged piece of concrete in the parking lot of Green's Grocery. He hired a lawyer to sue Green. A summons was served on Green, notifying him of the lawsuit. In order to establish his case, John needs to find out if Green knew or should have known about the dangerous condition. If he did know, Green's failure to make the necessary repairs would make him liable to John. John's attorney may ask the court to order Green to submit to questioning about his prior knowledge of the condition so that John may prepare his complaint. Usually, when discovery is used in this way, the plaintiff's attorney must also request the court to extend the time limits for serving a complaint on the defendant.

Discovery procedures are used before a trial primarily to narrow the issues of a lawsuit, to obtain evidence, and to secure information about evidence that may be used at trial. They may also persuade the parties to settle their dispute out of court.

The plaintiff must believe he has a valid ground for a lawsuit before discovery will be granted. Discovery is legitimate when it is specifically addressed to the disclosure of information that pertains to the issues of a lawsuit.

EXAMPLE On her way home from work, Madge is hit by Fred's car. She claims that Fred was speeding, but he denies this and says he has eyewitnesses who will testify that Madge was drunk and staggered into the middle of the street against the light. Madge has a legitimate right to discover the names and addresses of those witnesses whose testimony would destroy her case.

Discovery will not be given to enable a plaintiff to engage in a "fishing expedition" to obtain information that he can then use to start a lawsuit or to enable a defendant to develop his defense or to enable either to pry into the case of his adversary. This means if you think you may have a right to sue but are not sure, you cannot have a complete investigation of the defendant under the guise of discovery to save yourself the work of developing and investigating facts that are easily available to you. The court has a duty to protect a person against undue or unreasonable investigation into his affairs. Discovery and investigation cannot be used in bad faith or to annoy, embarrass, oppress, or injure the parties or the witnesses.

EXAMPLE Suppose a giant corporation is being sued by the federal government for monopolizing the computer industry for the last 25 years. The government has worked on its case for five years, preparing thousands of different documents. The attorneys for the corporation know that discovery of all the government documents, totaling 100 million pages, would require the lawsuit to be delayed at least four years—the time needed to index and analyze the documents for discovery purposes. In such a case, a court would deny the request for discovery since it is apparent that the indiscriminate request for all documents was merely aimed at delaying the action.

Who may be examined Those who may be examined are the plaintiff and defendant and other persons, such as witnesses, specified by statute or the rules of civil practice. When the law permits, a corporation may be examined before a trial through its officers, agents, or employees but usually not through former employees.

Matters disclosed Courts permit pretrial discovery to learn the identity of persons who have information relevant to the lawsuit. In some states, discovery may be used to determine the proper person to sue. A plaintiff or a defendant in a lawsuit may be required by statute or the Federal Rules of Civil Procedure to disclose to his adversary the names and addresses of witnesses.

If an applicant for pretrial discovery already has knowledge of the matters that are the subject of the examination, he may be denied discovery. He may also be denied discovery if he can readily learn the facts in other ways—such as by searching public records. These rules are to prevent an applicant from asking for discovery just to cause delay and expense to his opponent.

The questioning must relate to the issues at hand and to matters within the personal knowledge of the person being interrogated. Questioning is usually limited to factual information and may not call for opinions, conclusions, or inferences.

■ **Privileged matters** In either civil or criminal proceedings, a person called on to give discovery may decline to disclose matters that are privileged. For instance, a person cannot be compelled to reveal confidential communications between himself and his attorney concerning professional business or contemplated or pending litigation. The rule of PRIVILEGED COMMUNICATION is often applied to deny an applicant the right to examine material prepared by the opposing party for use in the trial, such as an accident report of an insurance company or material and research prepared by an attorney involving trial strategy. See WORK-PRODUCT RULE.

Because of the constitutional privilege against SELF-INCRIMINATION, a person cannot be made to reveal any matter that would tend to subject him to a criminal prosecution or a FINE, penalty, or forfeiture. In one case, a defendant, on examination before trial, could not be required to answer questions that would tend to prove him guilty of larceny. A claim of privilege against self-incrimi-

nation may not, however, preclude a pretrial examination if the examined party has been granted IMMUNITY from prosecution. If the defendant just mentioned had been granted immunity from prosecution for larceny, he would have been obliged to answer the questions about larceny.

A person who refuses to answer questions on the ground of privilege must make his claim under oath at the time of the examination. Neither his attorney nor the court may do this for him. A protective order may be granted to a party who can show that the matters properly sought to be discovered should not be disclosed, such as the name of a witness whose life might be in danger.

■ **Objections** An objection to the validity of a pretrial examination generally must be brought to the attention of the court before trial. It is, however, only at the trial itself that the court will determine whether the witness and the testimony he gave at a pretrial examination is competent (legally qualified) and should be allowed into evidence.

Failure to appear or answer A person who fails to appear or to answer questions at a proper examination may be punished for CONTEMPT, particularly if he has disregarded a subpoena. If a party to a civil lawsuit refuses to comply with discovery proceedings, the court may order that the matters that were questioned be admitted in favor of his adversary. This is known as an *order of preclusion*—the party is precluded from denying or contradicting matters admitted because he willfully failed to comply with a discovery order.

Costs A party in a civil action who asks for discovery proceedings may be required to pay for costs, such as expenses for taking depositions. If he wins the lawsuit, he may be entitled to recover his costs from the losing party.

Methods of discovery There are several means by which discovery may be obtained in a civil lawsuit: depositions, interrogatories, production and inspection of writings and other materials, requests for admissions of facts, and physical examinations.

Depositions Generally, a party to a civil action may arrange a pretrial, oral examination of an adverse party or witness. This is known as a deposition. The testimony of the party or witness (the deponent) is given under oath in response to questions asked him by the adversary's attorney. It may be offered in evidence at the trial, usually only if the witness cannot appear in court, but it may also be used to impeach the credibility of a testifying witness. The questions should be limited to the particulars specified in the notice or order of examination that was sent to the deponent; but the scope of the examination rests largely with the discretion of the court. Under some statutes, the production of books and documents may be required to refresh the memory of the deponent in his testimony. See REFRESHING MEMORY. The inspection of books and documents is limited to what is relevant to the inquiry and may be used only in connection with the examination of the person producing them. This is different from the discovery device of production and inspection, discussed later.

Interrogatories Interrogatories are written questions asked by the applicant and given to his adversary, who must supply written answers under oath. They are designed to obtain facts that may be admitted into evidence at trial. Interrogatories must be specific and relate to relevant matters. Also they must be phrased so that a responsive answer will be material to the issues. For example, if a plaintiff claims a loss of earnings in a personal injury suit, the defendant may give him interrogatories requesting itemization of the wages lost. Like all discovery methods, interrogatories are improper if used in bad faith to harass the other party, to fish for information, or to pry into an adversary's case.

Production and inspection By statute, the plaintiff and defendant in civil suits usually have the right to procure the production and inspection, and even the copying and photographing, of writings or other objects in the possession or control of an adversary. All pertinent books, papers, and documents that will serve to aid those involved in the suit are discoverable. Under particular statutes, physical objects—such as automobiles, photographs, and X-rays—may be discoverable.

EXAMPLE In a suit against the manufacturer of pajamas that burst into flames while a child was wearing them, the manufacturer may be granted the right to examine the remaining parts of the pajamas to determine whether the fire was a result of some defect in the fabric.

A mere suspicion that books or objects might contain pertinent evidence will not justify an order to produce them. This situation differs from a deposition, in which a party is compelled to produce books or materials to refresh his memory. Under the production and inspection method of discovery, the applicant is interested in examining an actual object; in a deposition he seeks oral testimony.

Requests for admissions of facts One side in a lawsuit may call on the other to admit any important facts or verify the genuineness of any paper or document he intends to use at the trial. This form of discovery is known as a request for admissions of facts. It is used to eliminate facts that are not in dispute from those that are at issue at the trial. It relieves the parties of the cost and inconvenience of proving irrelevant facts and expedites the trial.

EXAMPLE A defendant's request for a plaintiff in a negligence suit to admit that he was guilty of contributory negligence by making a left turn into oncoming traffic against the light does not fall within the recognized scope of request for admissions of facts. Such an admission would be one of the major issues at the trial. On the other hand, the defendant's request for the plaintiff to admit that he was in the left lane of traffic waiting to make a left turn into the intersection on the day of the accident would be proper—it is an important fact that neither party disputes.

See CONTRIBUTORY NEGLIGENCE; NEGLIGENCE.

The party requesting an admission does not have to get the court's permission to make the demand. But he must comply with the requirements of statute or rule of procedure. The request must specifically set forth the matters that the party wants admitted. It should describe any document for which an admission of genuineness is requested. The party making the request must fix a time limit for the response.

The response should be candid and not evasive. It should contain an admission or denial of the request, and it should state the reason for denying the request. If, for example, the request calls for a matter of opinion, the court should deny the request, stating that an opinion, not a fact, had been asked for. A matter will be considered admitted if the party of whom the request was made actually affirms the truth of the request or if he fails to respond in the manner required by law. If the party fails to follow the required procedure, the matter may be admitted against his interest if permitted by statute. The party who was subject to the request cannot later contest these admitted matters at trial.

Physical examination A court may authorize a physical or mental examination of a party whose condition is important to the issues involved, as in a personal injury suit. Such an order usually rests with the discretion of the trial court.

Right of discovery in criminal cases Under traditional common-law rules there was no discovery in a criminal case. Today, at least limited discovery is permitted in federal and state courts. This discussion is a general description of how discovery operates in criminal proceedings, but detailed aspects may vary, and you must consult the Federal Rules of Criminal Procedure as well as procedural provisions of state penal laws to find out exactly how they apply in a particular situation.

Discovery may occur before the trial, at the trial, or after the trial when the presentence report is demanded by the defendant. See SENTENCE. Most courts deny full disclosure of documents in the possession of the prosecution because it may lead to the intimidation of witnesses for the prosecution or to PERJURY.

EXAMPLE Rufus, who has connections with organized crime, is charged with the murder of Angus. Bobby, an eyewitness to the killing, is a witness for the prosecution. Rufus seeks to discover the identity of Bobby as well as his eyewitness account of the murder. A court may refuse to disclose that information. Rufus will be entitled to Bobby's statement when Bobby testifies. Then Rufus's attorney can prepare his cross-examination of the witness.

In federal and state courts, discovery is provided for both the prosecution and the defendant. The defendant is usually entitled to inspect and copy or photograph the following: (1) statements made by him that are in the government's possession, including grand jury testimony relating to the offense charged; (2) his own criminal record; (3) books, papers, or other tangible materials in the government's possession that are important to the preparation of his defense, that are intended to be used against him as evidence, and that are obtained from or belonging to him; and (4) results or reports of physical and medical examinations, such as autopsies, and scientific tests, such as blood tests matching the blood of the accused with that discovered at the scene of the crime.

Reciprocal discovery rights If the defendant requests and receives certain items from the government, the government is entitled to similar items from the defendant. The defendant must disclose documents and tangible objects as well as reports of examinations and tests in his possession if requested by the government.

There is a limitation on discovery under this rule. Neither the government nor the defendant is entitled to any reports or witnesses' statements that are made in connection with the investigation of the case. Furthermore, the prosecution's right to discovery is limited by the defendant's Fifth Amendment privilege against self-incrimination and his Sixth Amendment right to COUNSEL and the resulting attorney-client privilege. Total discovery of a defendant's case could violate his constitutional rights.

The prosecution, however, has a duty of disclosure, which is violated if the prosecutor suppresses evidence beneficial to the defense. Such actions would be a denial of the defendant's right to DUE PROCESS OF LAW. See also SUPPRESSION.

The Jencks Act In a federal criminal proceeding, the defendant is entitled under the Jencks Act to have access to certain government documents after the government's witness has completed his testimony on DIRECT EXAMINATION. These documents—only those relating to the witnesses' testimony—can help in the cross-examination of prosecution witnesses if they show that the witness made earlier statements out of court that contradict his present contentions. In practice, the government often makes the statements available in advance of its direct examination. The states are not bound by the requirements of the Jencks Act, but most have adopted a disclosure procedure similar to it.

discretion In law, an act of a judicial character that requires judgment and a consideration of the facts and circumstances necessary to make a fair determination of the situation. In a broad sense, *judicial discretion* is the option a judge may legally exercise to determine between two or more courses of action. It is the exercise of his judgment, within the law, to apply the law of the land to the facts of each case so that the rights of the parties may be declared and enforced. Judicial discretion is not to be exercised arbitrarily or irrationally. Discretion is needed in the absence of any hard-and-fast rule or mandatory procedure.

With respect to public officials or FIDUCIARIES (persons in positions of trust, such as TRUSTEES), discretion means their right or power to act solely according to their own judgment and conscience. This power, however, is to be exercised under the terms and procedure prescribed by the law—for example, the statutes that define a trustee's duties.

discretionary trust A TRUST that directs the TRUSTEE to pay a BENEFICIARY only as much of the income as the trustee decides. The beneficiary has no vested, or absolute, interest in the body of the trust (principal). A discretionary trust is used when the person who sets up the trust does not want the beneficiary to have access to the principal or to control the amount of income he or she receives, such as when the beneficiary is a young child or an elderly person who is senile.

discrimination Unfairly, injuriously, and prejudicially distinguishing between persons and objects when no actual distinction exists; the failure to treat equals equally; the setting up of arbitrary standards to justify treating persons unfairly; illegally unequal treatment based on race, religion, sex, or age. See CIVIL RIGHTS; EQUAL PROTECTION OF LAWS; PRIVILEGES AND IMMUNITIES.

disfranchise Take away the rights of a CITIZEN, usually the right to vote.

dishonor To refuse to accept or to pay COMMERCIAL PAPER, such as a promissory note, when it comes due. See ACCEPTANCE.

disinherit The act by which a person deprives a person, who in all likelihood would otherwise be his heir, of the right to inherit. A father disinherits his only child, Paul, for example. He specifically states in his WILL that he is disinheriting Paul for all the trouble he has caused the family and is leaving his entire estate to his wife. A person can be disinherited only by a valid will.

disinterested Not having any interest in a matter or controversy; impartial; not affected personally or financially by the outcome of a lawsuit. A *disinterested witness* is one who has nothing to gain or lose in the matter at issue and who is therefore lawfully COMPETENT to testify.

dismissal A court order (JUDGMENT) ending a civil lawsuit or criminal prosecution either before a trial or during a trial but before a verdict is reached.
■ **Civil suits** There are two types of dismissals in civil lawsuits—dismissals with prejudice and dismissals without prejudice—each having different legal ramifications. Dismissals are granted by the court's exercising its discretion after evaluating the particular case. Because state statutes or rules of civil procedure and the Federal Rules of Civil Procedure determine how and when dismissals may be granted in state and federal cases, respectively, you should consult these rules if you require a more detailed knowledge of this area of the law.

Dismissal with prejudice A dismissal with prejudice is a judgment on the merits of the lawsuit that prevents the plaintiff from bringing the same lawsuit against the same defendant in the future. It may be granted after a defendant has made a motion (request) to the court, or, in some instances, the court may *sua sponte* (on its own will) decide to dismiss the action with prejudice.

Dismissal on defendant's motion A defendant's motion to the court for a dismissal of the plaintiff's lawsuit with prejudice is usually based on the plaintiff's failure to appear in court and prosecute a lawsuit that he has started. This is known as a failure to prosecute.

EXAMPLE Mary sued Giorgio, a restaurant owner, for personal injuries she allegedly received when, on the way to her table, she tripped over a dessert cart that she claimed had been left blocking the aisle. She filed her complaint against Giorgio on the last day of the year following her injury, the latest time set by law for filing such a suit. She did not, however, serve Giorgio with a copy of the complaint until almost a year thereafter. Mary had no reasons to justify such an unnecessary delay. In the two years from the time of the accident, Giorgio's staff changed so that he lost track of many witnesses to the accident, thereby prejudicing (injuring) his defense against Mary's lawsuit. Giorgio asked the court to dismiss the case with prejudice because of Mary's failure to prosecute. The court agreed and granted the dismissal with prejudice.

It is the duty of a plaintiff to prosecute his case with due diligence. Failure to do so within a reasonable time may justify dismissal with prejudice when the defendant is hurt by the passage of time. A suit will not be dismissed, however, if its prosecution is impossible, as when the delay is caused by the death of the plaintiff and a personal representative has not yet been appointed. If a delay is caused by the parties during their attempts to reach a settlement, a dismissal for failure to prosecute will not be granted. But a plaintiff may not use the possibility of a settlement as an excuse for delaying prosecution.

To obtain the dismissal of a suit for failure to prosecute, the defendant must not do anything to prevent the plaintiff from bringing the suit for trial. If the defendant has actively caused or acquiesced in the delay—for example, if he left the state to avoid trial—the case should not be dismissed.

Dismissal by court sua sponte   Courts have inherent power *(sua sponte)* to dismiss with prejudice lawsuits that are vexatious (without good cause), when it is clear that there is no real controversy, when the lawsuit was brought in BAD FAITH (in fraud of justice), or when the plaintiff has failed to prosecute it. A court also has the power to dismiss a suit with prejudice if the plaintiff disobeys a court order. For example, if the plaintiff refuses to submit to a physical examination ordered by the court in a personal injury suit against an insurance company, his refusal may justify dismissal with prejudice.

Dismissal with prejudice is a harsh remedy that is used sparingly by the courts. It disposes of the case so completely that the controversy can never be brought to court again. Dismissal with prejudice is meant to deter a plaintiff from unjustifiably delaying a properly filed lawsuit so that the case of the defendant will be hurt by the lapse of time. It is also used to prevent court calendars from becoming congested as a result of unnecessary delays in pending cases.

Dismissal without prejudice   A dismissal without prejudice is the termination of a lawsuit that is not based on its merits so that the plaintiff may at a later date sue the same defendant again on the same issues. This leaves the situation as if the lawsuit had never been brought in the first place. For example, there are certain requirements set by law for serving a SUMMONS and COMPLAINT on a defendant to notify him that a plaintiff is planning to sue him. If a plaintiff fails to fulfill any of these requirements, the defendant can claim that he is not subject to the court's jurisdiction (authority) to determine the case. The plaintiff can ask the court to dismiss his case without prejudice so that he may properly serve the defendant for a determination of the case.

Notice and stipulations   Sometimes a plaintiff will decide after he has served a complaint on a defendant that it would be wiser not to pursue the matter at the present time because, for example, some witnesses have unexpectedly become unavailable. If the defendant has not yet answered the plaintiff's complaint, the plaintiff may serve a notice of dismissal on the defendant and file it with a clerk of the court. This preserves the right of the plaintiff to bring the same action at a later date.

If the defendant has already responded to the plaintiff's complaint by serving him with an answer, the plaintiff may have the suit dismissed by signing a formal agreement, known as a STIPULATION, with the defendant. It, too, must be filed with the clerk of the court, and it is the duty of the court to put the agreement into effect. The court order enforcing the stipulation by dismissing the suit as agreed upon by the parties is called a *dismissal agreed*. It is a declaration that the subject matter of the suit has been settled by the parties themselves.

Court order   If a plaintiff is unable to serve a notice of dismissal or to obtain a stipulation, he must ask the court to dismiss his action without prejudice. A dismissal will not be granted to a plaintiff if it would adversely affect the rights of anyone else who has a legal interest in the lawsuit.

EXAMPLE Ted and Nellie sign a lease as joint tenants in an apartment. They sue their landlord because they have not had heat or hot water for the last nine months. After the landlord has served his answer to their complaint, Ted decides that they should withdraw their case so that they can get more evidence. Nellie disagrees. Without Nellie's consent, Ted will not be able to have the case dismissed without prejudice if the court determines that such a dismissal would adversely affect her legal rights in the matter.

■ **Criminal prosecutions**   In criminal law, a dismissal is a decision by the court before the trial begins, or before a verdict is reached, that the proceedings against the defendant must be terminated—usually because the prosecution has unnecessarily delayed the action. The states' rules of criminal procedure and the Federal Rules of Criminal Procedure that govern dismissals are designed to serve the public interest by insuring the prompt prosecution of those persons believed to be guilty of criminal conduct. As in civil actions, dismissals in criminal prosecutions may be with or without prejudice and are granted by a court that has exercised its discretion in evaluating the particular case.

Dismissal with prejudice   When a prosecution is dismissed with prejudice, the state or federal government is barred from trying the accused on the same charge at a later date. Such dismissals are granted after the accused has made a motion to the court for dismissal or are made by the court *sua sponte,* usually after it has determined that some constitutional right of the accused—such as his right to a speedy trial—has been violated by the unnecessary delay in trying him. In determining whether a delay is unnecessary, the court must consider the length of the delay, the reason for the delay, the prejudice to the defendant, and the acquiescence of the defendant in the delay.

EXAMPLE In one case, a defendant was indicted for stock fraud, but more than 10 years had passed before the case was brought for trial. The federal district court on its own motion dismissed the action with prejudice since no reason for the delay appeared in the record, a number of prospective witnesses had died during the delay, and the defendant was not responsible for the delay because the prosecutor had indicated during another trial on a similar offense that a trial on this particular charge might not be brought.

A defendant who has had the charges against him dismissed with prejudice cannot be indicted again at a later date on those same charges as this would violate his constitutional right to be protected against DOUBLE JEOPARDY.

Dismissal without prejudice   A dismissal without prejudice may be made after the prosecuting attorney has made a motion to the court to do so, or the court may do so *sua sponte* (on its own motion). Such a dismissal is based on a ground that is not prejudicial to the accused.

> EXAMPLE Hank was indicted for robbery five weeks after O⟵─✳ the crime occurred. Seven months later, after numerous delays caused mostly by Hank's defense attorney, the prosecutor asked the court to dismiss the action without prejudice so that if missing evidence were found, Hank could be reindicted. The court granted the motion since it did not prejudice Hank's rights.

disorderly conduct   A broad term usually referring to certain minor OFFENSES, below the grade of MISDEMEANOR, which are QUASI criminal in nature. Words and acts that tend to disturb the peace or endanger the morals, safety, or health of the community are punishable as disorderly conduct. If a man in your town gets drunk and wanders naked into a trailer park screaming obscenities, he may be guilty of disorderly conduct. The punishment for disorderly conduct is usually fixed by a state law or local ordinance. Various acts—such as the use of vulgar and obscene language in a public place, VAGRANCY, loitering, causing a crowd to gather in a public place, or annoying passengers on a vehicle of public transportation—may be prohibited by law as disorderly conduct.

disorderly house   A place where people live or which they visit for purposes that are injurious to public morals, health, convenience, or safety and which constitutes a NUISANCE in the neighborhood. Disorderly house is a broad term that includes houses of prostitution and places for illegal gambling or drug activities. A beer-and-billiard parlor that attracts motorcycle gangs may also be judged to be a disorderly house. In some states, the illegal sale of alcohol may make the place a disorderly house. Maintaining a disorderly house is an OFFENSE. This means you are guilty even if you are not the owner of the disorderly house. It is enough if you are part of the management of the premises and know of its improper use. Disorderly houses are prohibited by the state and its subdivisions under the exercise of its POLICE POWER to protect the public health, welfare, and morals.

By law, a disorderly house must be a public place where persons are admitted for illegal purposes. In some states, however, it is sufficient if the place creates a nuisance to the neighborhood and poses a threat to the public welfare. The fact that the place is also used for other purposes is not important. Thus, a house of prostitution also used as a boardinghouse is a disorderly house nonetheless. The improper use of the house must be frequent, customary, common, or habitual. A single instance is usually not sufficient to constitute disorderly use. The punishment for keeping a disorderly house is regulated by statute. It is often an offense for someone to frequent, patronize, or occupy a disorderly house.

disparagement   1 An untrue or misleading statement about a competitor's goods that is made to influence the public not to buy. 2 Printed matter intended by its publisher to cast doubt upon the existence, extent, or quality of another's property. See LIBEL AND SLANDER.

disposable earnings   Total pay minus the deductions required by law, such as those for INCOME TAXES and SOCIAL SECURITY contributions. This is not the same as *take-home pay,* which is disposable earnings minus any deductions for health insurance or contributions to PENSION plans.

disposition   1 The final settlement or ultimate determination of a matter—for example, a court's disposition of a lawsuit by a judgment in favor of the plaintiff or defendant. 2 The giving up of property—the disposition of a farm by WILL, for instance.

dispositive fact   A fact that clearly settles a legal question in court. For example, the fact that the plaintiff was crossing a street against the traffic light when he was hit by a car clearly settles the question of his CONTRIBUTORY NEGLIGENCE in a personal injury suit.

dispossession   Ouster; wrongfully taking another person's property by force, trick, or misuse of the law; putting a person off his property without his consent.

dispute   1 Argue, debate, question. 2 As a noun, a disagreement between persons about their rights and legal obligations to each other.

disqualify   Deprive of qualifications; make ineligible or unfit. For example, a judge may be disqualified from hearing a lawsuit involving a company in which he owns stock because of his personal interest in the case. A juror may be disqualified if he holds a preconceived opinion about the defendant's guilt. A candidate for public office may be disqualified because he does not live in the district.

dissent   In law, the explicit disagreement of one or more judges of a court with the decision passed by the majority. A dissent may or may not be accompanied by a written dissenting opinion.

dissolution   1 The termination or destruction of a union. The dissolution of a CONTRACT occurs when both parties agree to terminate the agreement. The legally binding force of the contract is destroyed and each party is restored to the position he was in before making the contract. A PARTNERSHIP or CORPORATION may be dissolved when it ceases all business activity and ends its existence. 2 The act of pronouncing a legal proceeding or order NULL and VOID. For instance, the effect of a dissolution of an injunction (court order) by a court is as though the injunction never existed. 3 The act of terminating a marriage by DIVORCE (but not by ANNULMENT).

distinguish   Point out an essential difference. To distinguish a case being used as a PRECEDENT, for example, is to show why the decision previously reached by the court does not apply to the lawsuit currently being decided.

distrain   See DISTRESS.

distress   1 The process whereby personal property, such as furniture or a car, is taken from a person to enforce the performance of something due from him, such as the payment of rent or taxes. The public sale of personal property seized to enforce the payment of taxes is known as a *distress sale,* which is discussed in EXECUTION. Distress has replaced the term "distrain" in legal usage. **2** A situation of misfortune or danger. It includes anguish or suffering of both mind and body, such as emotional distress caused by wrongful conduct. See TORT.

distributee   A person who is entitled under state statutes of DESCENT AND DISTRIBUTION to share in the estate of a person who died intestate (without leaving a will).

district   A subdivision of many different types of areas (such as states, counties, or villages) for judicial, political, or administrative purposes. Some common types of districts are school districts and sanitation districts. The United States is divided into judicial districts, each of which has a district COURT.

Districting is the process of drawing boundary lines for the purposes of APPORTIONMENT for the election of government representatives.

district attorney   An officer who represents his district, such as a state or county, in criminal proceedings. District attorneys, also called prosecuting attorneys, are either appointed or elected to office, depending on the law in the particular jurisdiction. Their term is determined by statute. As a general rule, a district attorney must be an attorney-at-law licensed to practice in his state. He may be required to reside in his district, to meet a certain minimum age requirement, or to have practiced in his state for a certain number of years. See ATTORNEY AND CLIENT for a discussion of attorneys in general.

■ **The job**   It is the duty of the district attorney to see that wrongs suffered by the public are righted by prosecuting those responsible. He is given wide discretion in deciding how to carry out these duties, but he must be fair and impartial to insure that the defendant is not deprived of any constitutional or statutory right. The legislature may regulate the functions of a district attorney.

For criminal offenses, it is the district attorney's job to decide when to begin a prosecution and how to conduct the prosecution in court. He may not, however, prevent the GRAND JURY from considering criminal charges by declaring that the government will not prosecute. Nor can he dismiss a criminal charge pending before a grand jury.

The duties of the prosecuting attorney in civil proceedings are defined by statute.

The powers of the district attorney are not the same as those of the state ATTORNEY GENERAL, who is the chief legal representative of the state. The district attorney may not encroach on powers reserved exclusively to the attorney general, nor may the attorney general increase or diminish the powers reserved to the district attorney.

A district attorney acting within the scope of his official duties cannot be held liable for DAMAGES.

The compensation of district attorneys is set by statute.

■ **Removal or suspension**   A district attorney can be removed or suspended from office only for the grounds specified by statute. These include official misconduct or

neglect of duty when he improperly refuses to undertake criminal investigations or prosecutions or when he conducts them inefficiently. For example, if a district attorney fails to start an investigation into the murder of a prostitute because the last person to see her alive was the governor of the state, he may be removed from office. Other types of official misconduct are refusing to disclose to an accused person evidence that would clear him of the crime or awarding jobs in the attorney's office to his friends regardless of their qualifications.

Misbehavior while in office, such as habitual drinking, is not necessarily sufficient ground to remove a prosecuting attorney. The private conduct of a prosecuting attorney, wholly outside his judicial duties, however, may reveal character defects that make him subject to removal. For example, if a district attorney supplies marijuana to his guests at parties, he may be removed from his office because his conduct shows a double standard in his selective enforcement of drug laws.

The procedure for removing a prosecuting attorney from office is prescribed by state law. In some states, the district attorney may be removed by the court by IMPEACHMENT or in proceedings brought by interested persons.

■ **Assistants**   Assistant district attorneys may be appointed for the district attorney as provided by statute. Also, courts have long exercised discretionary power to appoint attorneys to aid the prosecuting attorney in individual criminal cases. The qualifications, salary, tenure, powers, and process for removal of assistant district attorneys are largely controlled by statute.

■ **U.S. attorney**   The U.S. attorney represents the United States and government officials and employees in the prosecution or defense of criminal and civil actions in his district. The U.S. attorney, also called the U.S. district attorney, is authorized to prosecute violations of federal law that occur in his district. He also defends civil and criminal actions against government officials, employees, and military personnel for acts done in the performance of their official duties.

The ATTORNEY GENERAL of the United States is the chief law officer of the federal government.

district court   A federal trial COURT. Each U.S. district court is in a federal district that may be a whole state or a part of one. District court is a low-level state court in some states. For a comprehensive treatment of U.S. district courts, see FEDERAL COURTS.

District of Columbia   The formation and status of the District of Columbia, its government, and the rights of its residents are discussed here.

■ **How it was formed**   Established under the authority of the Constitution as a symbol of the federal union of states, the District of Columbia was created to be free from the control of any one state. Maryland and Virginia originally ceded to Congress portions of their lands, including the cities of Georgetown and Alexandria. On December 1, 1800, the District became the capital and permanent seat of the federal government. The portion of land granted by Virginia, including Alexandria, was returned to that state in 1846 at the request of its citizens.

■ **Is it a state?** Legally the District of Columbia is neither a state nor a territory—it is subject to the authority of Congress. For a discussion of the District of Columbia court system, see FEDERAL COURTS.

■ **Government** The District of Columbia's form of government has varied during different periods of history. From its inception up until 1874, the District had a municipal government run by officials elected by its residents. In 1874 Congress revoked the right of District residents to vote for their local officials. Instead, the President appointed a three-man board of commissioners to exercise administrative and quasi-legislative powers. In 1967 President Lyndon B. Johnson signed an order that reorganized the structure of the District government by replacing the board of commissioners with a presidentially appointed District of Columbia Council supervised by a mayor. Finally, in 1973, Congress passed the District of Columbia Home Rule Act, which restored to residents the right to elect their own officials. In the general election of November 1974, a mayor and a 13-member council, including a chairman, were elected by the newly enfranchised voters.

The Home Rule Act The 1973 congressional act gave legislative power to the District Council and executive power to the mayor, subject to the limitations specified under the act. Neighborhood commissions are elected by the residents to advise the council on matters of public policy, such as health, safety, sanitation, and local social service programs. Congress, however, still retains ultimate legislative authority over the District and may veto locally passed legislation.

■ **Residents' rights** Although District residents have always been subject to federal income taxes and to military service, they did not have the right to vote in Presidential elections. With the ratification of the 23rd Amendment in 1961, the District was given a number of votes in the ELECTORAL COLLEGE based on the number of congressmen it would be entitled to if it were a state, but not more than the number given to the least-populated state.

In 1970 the President approved the passage of the District of Columbia Delegate Act, which authorized the election of a nonvoting representative from the District to Congress. Although the purpose was to give the District a link to Congress, the nonvoting delegate has no decision-making power. A constitutional amendment is necessary to give the District full representation in national government because the constitutional provisions for the election of Congressmen are restricted to states. The amendment currently proposed would neither make the District a state nor take away the plenary powers of Congress to legislate for the District. It would, however, permit District residents to vote for both senators and representatives of Congress; to be fully represented in the Electoral College on the basis of its population rather than its present limited representation; and to participate in ratifying new constitutional amendments.

disturbance of a public meeting

An action that unlawfully interrupts or disturbs a gathering of people who are assembled together for any lawful purpose. It is ordinarily an OFFENSE to disturb a public meeting from the time the people have begun to assemble until the proceed-ings are over and the crowd has left the meeting area. Disturbance of a public meeting is now largely regulated and defined by state and local law.

The defendant's conduct must be the cause of the disturbance, but under some laws the defendant need not have intended to cause the disturbance.

A disturbance may be accomplished by carrying a weapon into the meeting, by acts of violence, or by indecent language or conduct. For example, if a parent brings a rifle into a parent-teacher meeting, his act may constitute a disturbance of a public meeting. The exercise of a legal right in a lawful manner, however—such as the peaceful picketing of a lecture—is not a disturbing act.

The punishment should conform to the requirements of the statutes and tend to prevent a recurrence. The nature and extent of civil liability—that is, whether or not a person can be sued by another person or group for such a disturbance—has not been clearly defined but sometimes is based on NUISANCE theory.

disturbing the peace

A broad term that describes the conduct of a person who maliciously and willfully disturbs the peace and quiet of any neighborhood, family, or person by loud or unusual noise or by offensive, abusive, or violent acts. Disturbance of the peace is synonymous with BREACH OF THE PEACE, which includes all violations of the public peace and order. A person who engages in such conduct may be guilty of a crime, depending on the local statutes. Examples of conduct that may disturb the peace are the loud playing of a stereo after midnight; a drunken brawl outside a bar; and drag races through the streets of a residential neighborhood in the early hours of the morning.

The punishment for disturbing the peace, usually a fine and/or imprisonment, is set by statute.

diversion

1 A turning aside or altering the natural course of a thing, such as a diversion of a stream. See PROPERTY. 2 The use of particular funds for an unauthorized purpose or in an unauthorized manner, such as the diversion of TRUST funds by the trustee for his own personal use in violation of his FIDUCIARY duty to the BENEFICIARY of the trust.

diversity of citizenship

Having citizenship in different states. Diversity of citizenship—when the opposing parties come from different states—is one basis on which FEDERAL COURTS may hear a case. This basis for federal COURT action, which is authorized by the Constitution, is called *diversity jurisdiction*. For instance, if Lance, a Florida resident, breaches a contract with Duane, a resident of Alaska, there is diversity of citizenship. Duane may be able to sue Lance in a federal court for breach of CONTRACT if the matter in controversy is more than $10,000.

divest

Deprive; withdraw. Usually used in relation to authority, power, PROPERTY, or TITLE (ownership). For example, a traitor may be divested of his citizenship.

dividend

The part allotted to each person entitled to share in profits or property. It usually denotes a fund set apart by a CORPORATION out of its profits to be divided among the shareholders. It is also the proportional amount paid to each.

divorce A judgment from a court that legally ends a marriage. It prescribes the new relationship between the former husband and wife and their rights and responsibilities concerning property, money to support one or both of them, and arrangements for their children. Divorce ends all the legal rights gained by marriage. A divorced spouse no longer has the right to sex, support (except for alimony that may be awarded by the court), or a share of the other's estate when he or she dies.

The aim of divorce laws is to provide legal solutions for problems a couple cannot solve on their own. Because stable family relationships are a cornerstone of society, the law has an overriding interest in regulating responsibility and protecting the interests of all parties when a family breaks up. The authority of the courts to decide whether and under what conditions to grant a divorce comes from the court's role in PUBLIC POLICY, the aim of which is to preserve a stable society.

■ **Divorce, separation, and annulment** There are several types of divorce, some of which are not total divorces, but mere legal separations. In addition, a marriage can be annulled—declared never to have been valid.

Divorce *a vinculo,* or *a vinculo matrimonii*—divorce from the bonds of matrimony—is a complete and final divorce. It frees a husband and wife to remarry.

Divorce *a mensa et thoro*—divorce from bed and board—is a *legal separation,* or limited divorce. It gives husband and wife the legal right to live apart but does not end the marriage. The parties cannot remarry. Some states permit parties to live this way under a court decree or by agreement.

Foreign divorce is a divorce granted by a court outside the home state of the parties, either in a different state or in a foreign country. A foreign divorce is not always valid.

Annulment is a decree that a marriage was never valid. Most states have laws specifying the conditions under which their courts may grant an ANNULMENT. A Roman Catholic can obtain an annulment through the church, but such an annulment has no legal validity.

A *Get* is a legal paper of divorce among Jews. Like an annulment granted by the Catholic Church, it does not dissolve a marriage legally.

■ **Origins of divorce law** In ancient times, there were few laws relating to marriage. For the most part, acceptable behavior was obtained not by law but by social pressure. In many societies a man's power over his family included the right to kill unwanted children, usually infant girls, and to cast out a wife at will.

Unlike most other ancient peoples, the Jews consistently condemned sex outside of marriage, as the laws in the books of Leviticus and Deuteronomy demonstrate. On the other hand, Jewish law permitted a husband to cast out his wife whenever he wished. In the Sermon on the Mount, Jesus seemed to be criticizing this harsh rule, and biblical scholars interpreted this and other statements in the Gospels to mean that Jesus condemned divorce.

Among the Greeks and the Romans, divorce was obtained by an act between husband and wife, called *repudi-*

ation, but when the Roman Empire became Christian, the emperors, who enforced both civil and religious law, tried to control the practice of repudiation by a husband. Generally, however, repudiation was justified if there was good reason to believe the wife had committed adultery, tried to kill her husband, or committed a serious crime. A woman could also repudiate her husband, but if she did so she was usually prohibited from remarrying for five years, to prove she had not acted out of greed or lust.

Christian law The early Christian Church developed the doctrine that marriage is a sacrament, a sacred union that cannot be dissolved. The church permitted husband and wife to live apart if they obtained a religious divorce *a mensa et thoro* (divorce from bed and board), but they were still married for life and could not take another spouse. Even this kind of limited divorce was granted only after careful investigation of each case. Eventually, the church developed its own court system to handle such matters. Spain and many South American countries still leave most matrimonial questions to church courts.

Protestant reforms The absolute divorce, which completely ends a marriage, accompanied other changes demanded by those who separated from the Catholic Church in the 16th century during the Reformation. The leaders of the Reformation believed that marriage is a matter of earthly concern and should be regulated by the civil government, not the church. Martin Luther believed that divorce should be available to a man whose wife committed adultery or permanently abandoned him. John Calvin believed that a husband's adultery was equally damaging to family life and that wives as well as husbands should be allowed to divorce for adultery. Other grounds were recognized as time went on. Gradually, the law in the Western world moved to a civil procedure of presenting grounds for divorce to a judge or magistrate. The adversary system was applied, setting husband and wife against each other, and an innocent spouse had to prove fault on the part of the other before a divorce could be granted.

English and colonial law When the pope refused to declare Henry VIII's first marriage invalid so that he could marry Anne Boleyn, Henry broke away from the Catholic Church and in 1534 declared himself head of the Church of England. The Anglican Church did not fully adopt all Protestant teachings, however, and for the common people marriages still could not be dissolved.

In the American Colonies, civil magistrates had the power to perform marriage ceremonies and to grant divorces, but very few marriages were ever dissolved. Although a few divorces were granted late in the colonial period by legislative acts, officers of the British crown declared the divorces invalid.

United States law After the Revolutionary War the American states were free to write their own laws. They ended up with a hodgepodge. Wealthy and prominent people could still get divorced by legislative act, but there were no legal safeguards to protect the person being divorced. The grounds for court-granted divorce varied tremendously from state to state, and most states granted only divorce *a mensa et thoro* (legal separation). No clear policy of law developed during this period because in fact divorces continued to be rare.

WHEN YOU ARE INVOLVED IN A DIVORCE SUIT

■ Divorce ends all the rights gained by marriage. A divorced spouse no longer has the right to sex, support, or a share of the other's estate when he or she dies.

■ Divorce laws vary from state to state. In many states you must show that either the husband or wife was responsible—at fault—for the breakup of the marriage because he or she was guilty of something the state regards as a ground for divorce. In other states you may get a no-fault divorce—that is, you need not show that either party was at fault but only that there has been an "irretrievable breakdown" of the marriage. Some states allow either type of divorce.

■ Grounds for divorce may include adultery, bigamy, imprisonment for longer than a specified period, abandonment, nonsupport, denying one's spouse the comforts and benefits of marriage without actually leaving the home (technically termed "constructive abandonment"), physical or mental cruelty, personal indignities, sexual misconduct amounting to cruelty, insanity, venereal disease, alcoholism, drug addiction, maliciously locking out the spouse, and an invalid divorce obtained in another state.

■ Bear in mind that *grounds* such as the foregoing may not be the same as the *reasons* for a divorce; they are simply the legal basis for granting it. You may want a divorce for many reasons—incompatibility, constant arguments over money or in-laws, drinking, desertion, nonsupport, conflicting personalities and values—all of which may be real enough—but to get the divorce, you must prove whatever grounds your state requires.

■ Depending on the state, divorce may be granted on demand if both parties agree that the marriage cannot be salvaged, if one party asserts that the marriage is dead and he or she wants out, or if one person asks for a divorce after certain events, such as a voluntary separation, have occurred.

■ A state may have a law permitting divorces for couples who have voluntarily separated and lived apart for a specified length of time.

■ When a divorce case comes to court, the spouse who is sued has the right to various types of defense. A classic defense is *recrimination:* "Yes, I'm guilty, but so are you." Another defense is *provocation:* "You drove me to it." Yet another long-recognized defense is *condonation:* "You forgave me at the time—why are you suing me now?" Another is *connivance:* "You had a share in causing or promoting my misconduct; you just stood by and let it happen, so you have no right to complain now." Still another is *collusion:* "You talked me into helping you trick the court so we'd be granted a divorce—now I've changed my mind!"

■ At present, some states still cling to the fault concept and will not grant divorce without fault. Others have swung to the other extreme and require only proof of irretrievable breakdown. Most have chosen a middle-of-the-road approach, retaining the traditional list of grounds and completing it with "incompatibility" and "living separate and apart."

■ To start a divorce action, you should bring suit in the state where you and your spouse maintain a permanent legal home, and your action must be based on a ground legally recognized in that state.

■ If neither you nor your spouse lives where the divorce is granted, the decree may not hold up later in court.

■ If you evade your home divorce laws by flying to Haiti, Mexico, or the like for a divorce, you will have no protection if the foreign divorce is later attacked.

■ Most divorce cases are uncontested. The husband and wife negotiate a settlement concerning alimony, child custody and support, and division of property, and the defendant agrees not to contest. When the husband and wife cannot agree upon a settlement, the court decides the issue.

■ Alimony is actually uncommon—most divorces are granted without alimony orders. Once they have been ordered, alimony payments must be continued until modified by court order, or one of the parties dies, or the spouse receiving them remarries.

■ Sometimes a husband is required to maintain a life insurance policy for the benefit of his former wife to give her some added security if he dies before she does, particularly if she has little work experience that would enable her to earn her own living.

■ The divorce decree gives custody of children to one of the parents, but all parents can be required by law to support their children. Considerations on which courts base the amount of the parents' child-support obligation include the child's needs, the parents' living standard, financial condition, and earning ability, the child's educational plans, the child's age and earning ability, the responsibility of each parent for the support of other people, and the value of the care given by the custodial parent.

■ Property settlements are governed by either of two sets of rules, according to the state where you live: separate property or community property. Most states consider everything in marriage as separate property—each spouse retains ownership of everything he or she held before the marriage and acquired during the marriage. This has led to many injustices in the past, and a number of separate-property states are treating marriage as a partnership in an effort to attain economic justice in individual cases.

■ Eight states use the community-property system—property acquired during marriage is considered to be community property to which each partner has an equal claim. Community-property states return to each partner what he or she owned before the marriage and property acquired in certain ways (as by inheritance) during the marriage, and they divide the rest equally at divorce.

■ If you are thinking about getting a divorce, keep in mind that two people probably do not have any idea how much property and income is actually available when they divorce until they have explored options, considering especially the financial consequences of taxes. Your wisest course is to negotiate and compromise.

When a divorce case was being heard, it seemed appropriate to take evidence concerning the married life of the couple and to judge whether one of them had destroyed the relationship. In this way, fault was established as a basis for granting divorce. Often the same circumstances that gave one party the right to divorce could convict the other of a crime—adultery, bigamy, incest, or failure to support, for example.

The theory that a marriage is alive until one person is guilty of conduct that destroys it has persisted until today. The concept of fault has produced the twin evils of lying to the court (when both parties want the divorce) and of destroying any hope of future cooperation (when each party is convinced the other is wholly to blame).

In recent years, some state legislatures have begun to reform divorce laws. They have asked their judges to find out *whether* a marriage is dead rather than *why*. Some states specify only one ground for divorce: irretrievable breakdown. If the marriage cannot be put back together, the state will grant the divorce.

■ **Divorce and the Constitution** The U.S. Constitution does not specifically mention divorce, but several constitutional requirements have been applied to limit the ways states can apply divorce law.

There is no constitutional right to a divorce, but all the states have enacted laws that specify whether divorce is available and under what circumstances. Because the only way to get a divorce is through the state, the state must make divorce available to everyone. A plaintiff who can prove that he has no money may file his lawsuit for divorce without paying court costs, filing fees, or the cost of having legal papers served or published.

States can and do limit divorce cases to state residents. The shortest residency requirement is six weeks, but most states require one year and some two years. Some states require the plaintiff to have lived within one county for a period of months. The reason for these residency requirements is that the state considers the status of being married a thing, or *res*. The marriage itself must be present in some sense in order for it to be before the court. Otherwise the court does not have JURISDICTION, or authority, to determine the matter.

If the court in one state has jurisdiction, then a divorce it grants cannot be challenged in the court of another state because the Constitution says that the laws of each state are entitled to "full faith and credit," or final effect, throughout the country.

■ **Grounds for divorce** The grounds for divorce are specified in the laws of each state, and they vary from state to state. Keep in mind that the *grounds* for divorce are not the same as the *reasons* for divorce. The grounds are the legal bases for granting the divorce. A person may have many reasons for wanting a divorce, such as sexual incompatibility, arguments over money or relatives, alcoholism, desertion, nonsupport, a love affair, cruel or authoritarian treatment, no real home life, or conflicting personalities or values. But laws that permit divorce only for fault do not always consider such reasons as legal grounds. If you want a divorce, you must be prepared to prove whatever grounds the court requires for a divorce. See Chart 22 for permissible grounds for divorce in each state.

Adultery The oldest ground for divorce dates back to the Old Testament, when a husband could cast out an adulterous wife at will. In states where adultery is a ground, either husband or wife can plead it against the other. Proof must show that the other spouse has had voluntary sexual intercourse outside the marriage. A husband may not divorce his wife because she has been raped, because her sexual act was not voluntary, but if a man rapes a woman other than his wife, he has committed adultery as well as rape, and his wife has a ground for divorce. Some states grant divorces based on adultery for sex acts other than intercourse. For example, a man can divorce his wife if she has had a lesbian experience.

The difficulty of granting divorces for adultery is that the act is usually committed in private. For 200 years, until 1966, New York allowed divorce only on the ground of adultery, with the result that its courtrooms were subjected to a parade of indignities.

EXAMPLE The typical case involved a couple who had come to the conclusion that they could not continue to live as husband and wife. The woman hired a detective out of the Yellow Pages who made his living from this law. The husband agreed to meet a young woman in a particular hotel room at a certain time, strip to his shorts, and pose for a photograph taken by the detective. The young woman always wore a negligee. When the detective appeared at the trial, he showed the court his photographs and testified to the husband's "adultery." The divorce was granted, and everyone who had helped was paid his fee.

Courts often suspected deceit in cases involving adultery (in New York and elsewhere), but because judges could not easily establish who was lying or how much, most of them required evidence from another source to corroborate the detective's testimony. If it was discovered that attorneys were promoting the fraud, they were disbarred.

EXAMPLE In one case where witnesses to the adultery were missing, the court accepted evidence that a wife and her suspected lover had a record of visiting cities all over the world on the same dates. In nearly every city they had checked into the same hotel. The court said that the evidence proved the woman had both the opportunity and the inclination to commit adultery. The court assumed the act had been done unless the wife could prove otherwise.

Some state laws have required evidence of more than a single act of adultery. One state held that a wife could not divorce her husband unless his adultery brought her public scandal and disgrace—even when he contracted venereal disease from the adulterous intercourse and infected her. Other states deemed adultery too difficult to prove. Consequently, they permitted a husband to divorce his wife simply for lewd and lascivious behavior, without establishing that she had engaged in sexual intercourse with another man. But these states did not permit a wife to obtain a divorce on similar grounds. Such provisions, like most other grounds that could be used only by a husband or a wife, have been abolished.

Bigamy In theory, a bigamous marriage is no marriage at all because a person who is married cannot marry again. States that follow this reasoning generally permit either party to a bigamous marriage to obtain an annulment. Other states prefer instead to grant a divorce, because an annulment can mean that a wife may not get alimony or child support and that her children may be regarded illegitimate.

EXAMPLE The typical situation in which bigamy is a ground
O⊷—⚹ for divorce involves a man who leaves his wife, obtains an invalid divorce in another state or county, and then marries a second wife. When the second wife learns of the invalid divorce, she asks the court for a divorce—and alimony—on the ground of bigamy. The first wife can then prove adultery and also obtain a divorce—and alimony—from the man.

Several states now require proof that the person suing for divorce on the ground of bigamy had no reason to believe that his or her spouse was still married.

Imprisonment   Some states will grant a divorce to someone whose spouse has been convicted of a crime and sentenced to prison for a certain minimum period of time, usually one, two, or three years. Generally, a divorce may be granted if the sentence is long enough and some time is spent in prison, regardless of subsequent parole or pardon.

Abandonment   Desertion—the intentional abandonment of one's spouse without a valid legal reason—is a ground for divorce in nearly every state. Most states require proof that the guilty spouse has been away from the marital home without the consent of the other for at least one year before the divorce action can be started.

Proof of abandonment is usually a factual matter. Courts require evidence that the absence was voluntary and that the abandoned spouse neither provoked nor agreed to a separation. If a husband leaves his wife, for example, it is not necessary to prove that he hated her or wished her harm, but only that he intended to leave the marriage and not to return. The law will not find his departure justified because he was subjected to small annoyances. His leaving may be an abandonment even though his wife nagged him, occasionally drank too much, or refused to starch his shirts. In order for his leaving not to be an abandonment, he may have to show that his wife committed acts that would give him grounds for a divorce. Then he can divorce her for those acts.

A marital separation is not abandonment if both parties agree not to live together. Furthermore, there is no abandonment when two people live apart but routinely meet for sexual intercourse. Whether one or two acts of intercourse can interrupt the time required for an abandonment depends on state law.

Willful desertion is not always clear-cut, however. It can be proved in cases other than those in which one spouse packs up and leaves. For example, a man has traditionally had the right to decide where the family will live, especially if he chooses to move to get another job. His wife must follow; if she refuses, he can divorce her for abandonment. This is true in most states, although challenges based on sex discrimination laws or the constitutional right to equal protection have begun.

EXAMPLE A woman whose husband was suing her for di-
O⊷—⚹ vorce because she refused to move with him pleaded that she was near the end of a nurse's training program, preferred to live near her family, and hated the Sun Belt desert area where her husband chose to relocate. She said that he had never discussed moving and had set out without a job waiting for him in the new state. The court granted the husband a divorce nevertheless. It said that he, not the wife, was obligated to support the family. Even though he did not have a job when he left, it was reasonable for him to believe that more opportunities awaited him in the Sun Belt.

A husband must not be too unreasonable in forcing his wife to move with him. He must provide a home in the new location, give her enough time to prepare for the move, and furnish transportation for her and their household goods. Otherwise the wife is justified in refusing to go. No divorce will be granted if it appears that the man is trying to provoke a divorce by moving to an area that is unsafe or unsuitable for his wife. For example, a man cannot require his wife to move to a damp climate if she has a serious asthma condition.

If one party abandons the other but later offers to reconcile, the other party has a legal obligation to accept the offer. Failure to cooperate in a reconciliation attempt, whether required or not, is itself an abandonment, and the party who is willing to try again may secure a divorce against the other. But an offer to reconcile that is made only to defeat the other's divorce action on the ground of abandonment will not be successful.

Sometimes a state requires the complaining spouse to show that he or she has tried to reconcile with the partner who has left home.

Enoch Arden laws   An unintentional desertion is not abandonment. Let us say a young sailor marries, sires children, and then signs up for an extended voyage. His ship is later reported sunk, he fails to return, and his wife must struggle to support the children. Can she remarry?

The wife cannot have a divorce for abandonment in such a situation because her husband did not intend to desert his family and escape the marriage. After seven years, the common law would permit her to presume that he was dead, but if he ever returned, she would still be married to him.

This is exactly what happens in Alfred Lord Tennyson's narrative poem "Enoch Arden." A sailor shipwrecked on a desert island returns after 10 years to find that his wife has remarried. Heroically, he does not declare himself, but follows the progress of the new family from a distance. Later he dies of a broken heart.

Modern Enoch Arden laws permit a divorce on proof that one's spouse has disappeared. This is possible after a certain number of years have passed. For each state's law concerning the number of years that must pass, see Chart 22. If circumstances indicating the DEATH of the missing husband or wife can be shown, the time requirement may be reduced.

EXAMPLE A man who was depressed because of illness and
O⊷—⚹ mounting debt left for work one morning as usual and was seen boarding a ferry. His shoes were later found washed ashore, but he was never seen again. The court granted the wife an Enoch Arden decree on the ground that the husband was presumed dead.

In states with strict divorce laws, an Enoch Arden decree may be called a dissolution of the marriage instead of a

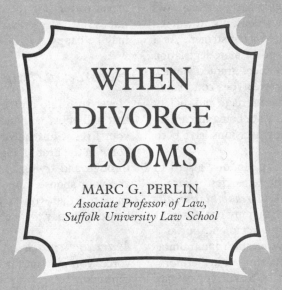

WHEN DIVORCE LOOMS

MARC G. PERLIN
*Associate Professor of Law,
Suffolk University Law School*

Marriage is forever. Or at least it should be. Almost every man and woman who marry believe that their love for each other will last forever. But sometimes the harsh realities of everyday living grind away at a couple's love and compatibility, and life together finally becomes intolerable. At such a time, a man and wife may consider ending their marriage—divorce looms over them.

In the recent past, most states required one of the spouses to be guilty of adultery, extreme cruelty, or some other ugly fault before they would grant a couple a divorce. Consequently, in order to get a divorce, a couple had to subject themselves to nasty accusations in public courtroom scenes. Furthermore, the man often suffered because of the court's traditional views of the role of the sexes in marriage— the woman was generally awarded alimony and custody of the children whether she deserved them or not. Finally, decisions about custody and other matters that would profoundly affect the lives of those involved were being made by judges who were strangers to them and who knew little about the social and psychological problems involved in dividing up a family. But times have changed, and divorce laws have begun to change with the times.

Recent trends in divorce law

The decade of the 1970's witnessed major changes in the laws that regulate marriage and divorce and in society's attitudes toward the institution of marriage. These dramatic changes make it vitally important for married persons to understand their legal rights and to know what to do if their marriage breaks down.

No-fault divorce and its effects Perhaps the major reform during the 1970's was the adoption in most states of no-fault divorce grounds (legally referred to as incompatibility or irretrievable or irremediable breakdown of a marriage). In a no-fault state, a spouse no longer must prove that the other committed a marital wrong, such as adultery or extreme cruelty, in order to obtain a divorce. Rather, the husband or wife seeking a divorce has only to show that the marriage has completely broken down and that there is no likelihood of reconciliation. Therefore, the other spouse typically can no longer prevent a divorce, since a judge is likely to find that a marriage is in fact over if one partner indicates that it is over, even when the other may disagree. In a few states another type of no-fault divorce ground is available, which is based on the parties' living apart for a specified period of time, commonly one year.

With the issues in a divorce no longer focused on which spouse is at fault, a major task for couples seeking divorce, their lawyers, and judges is to address and resolve the economic problems that accompany divorce. Questions of alimony, child support, and property division are now the major issues in divorce negotiations and courtroom processes.

Equality of sexes A second trend of the 1970's was the movement toward equality of the sexes in the resolution of marital disputes. The 1979 Supreme

Court case of *Orr* v. *Orr* held that Alabama laws that allowed alimony to be awarded only to women unconstitutionally discriminated against men. As a result, both of the *Orr* case and of state legislation modifying the preferential treatment granted women in marriage and divorce, old stereotypes concerning the roles of men and women in marriage and society are being reexamined, and many are being discarded. Both alimony and child custody decisions have been affected.

The traditional notion that an alimony award to the wife will continue until she remarries or dies is being replaced by the concept of *rehabilitative alimony*. This concept recognizes alimony not as a pension that lasts for the life of the recipient, but as a means for a wife to acquire the education and training necessary to become self-supporting. Furthermore, under appropriate circumstances, a wife today may be ordered to pay alimony to her husband.

In the past, the mother was almost always awarded custody of her child when her marriage ended in divorce. Now the father may be awarded custody if that is in the child's best interests.

New methods for resolving disputes

A third consideration, and one that may revolutionize divorce procedure, is the growing dissatisfaction with the current legal system and the methods used to resolve marital disputes. Some critics of the system feel that domestic disputes involve issues requiring training in psychology or psychiatry for their proper resolution. Skills in these areas are often needed if a judge is to decide custody or visitation disputes, for example. In addition, a busy judge may not have the time to consider each case thoroughly. Critics also feel that a judge whom the divorcing couple do not know should not be the person to decide crucial issues in their lives and in those of their children, particularly when the life-style of one or both spouses differs from the judge's view of what a suitable home life for a child should be.

New methods are evolving to handle some of the domestic problems currently resolved in the courtroom. For example, some divorcing couples are beginning to use the skills of trained and neutral mediators to explain the laws and the options available, so that amicable agreement can be reached on all issues. Others use arbitration procedures, agreeing to accept the decisions of a neutral arbitrator. And increasingly, the attorneys representing husband and wife now negotiate and resolve disputes rather than leave matters for the decision of a judge who may impose an order with which neither husband nor wife may be happy.

Before starting a divorce action

Never rush into a divorce. Divorce is a serious step that will affect you and your children for the rest of your lives. Consequently, you should not seek a divorce in the heat of anger or without thinking things through and trying to reconcile differences. If you and your spouse cannot amicably settle your differences together, you may contemplate seeking outside help or you may try a separation rather than a divorce.

Marriage counselor

If you are thinking of divorce, you may find it helpful to consult a marriage counselor before making a firm decision to begin legal proceedings. The counseling may give you the opportunity to explore the reasons behind your existing marital problems and to determine if further counseling, either alone or with your spouse, may help save your marriage.

Of course, not everyone has the luxury of such an option, especially when conditions in the home may pose a danger to the safety of the spouse or a child. In such cases, legal proceedings may have to be started immediately and counseling pursued later.

Voluntary and judicial separation

Sometimes a husband and wife simply need time to consider the future, and in such cases a separation rather than a divorce may be advisable. This separation may be a voluntary one—both spouses simply agree to live apart. Many couples who agree to separate have their attorneys draw up a formal separation agreement, which sets forth in writing their understanding as to alimony, child custody and support, the division of their mutually owned property, and their continuing rights and duties toward each other. Once such a separation agreement has been signed by both husband and wife, it becomes a contract that binds both spouses for as long as they live or until both agree to change or end it, or it may be adopted by the court and become an enforceable court order.

Often, however, one spouse refuses the other's request to leave home voluntarily, or one spouse leaves with the agreement of the other, who may nevertheless fear that support money will not be paid. In such cases a judicial, or court-ordered, separation may be advisable.

In a judicial separation, the court may order the defendant to pay support; it may restrain the defendant from abusing or interfering with the liberty of his or her spouse; or it may issue orders regarding the custody and safety of children. The grounds for a judicial separation vary but usually involve such matters as the failure of one spouse to support the family or the existence of such circumstances as physical abuse that justify living apart.

The legal effect of a separation, whether voluntary or judicial, is to suspend the marital relationship, allowing the parties to live separate and apart. Because they legally remain husband and wife, however, neither may remarry. In fact, in some states a separated spouse may inherit from the other spouse if the latter dies without leaving a will. A separation may be the best solution for incompatible couples who object to divorce for religious or other reasons.

Finding the right legal assistance

If you feel that you have no choice but to seek a divorce (or separation), your next step should be the selection of an attorney who is familiar with divorce law and who is prepared to represent you vigorously and protect your legal rights. Often, the best way to find such an attorney is through friends who have been well represented in their own divorces.

If an attorney's services are beyond your financial reach, you may be entitled to government-funded legal services if you meet specified income guidelines. You may find office locations in a telephone book or government listing or from local bar associations, state public assistance offices or, perhaps, the clerk's office of your local family court.

Finding the right attorney is often difficult. The temptation may be to answer an advertisement or resort to self-representation. Both are fraught with pitfalls.

Low-cost uncontested divorces View with caution advertisements that offer low-cost divorce services. The fee may cover only routine divorces, in which there is no dispute over money, property, alimony, or child support, custody, or visitation rights. Routine divorces are rare. A client who initially believes that his or her divorce will be a simple, dispute-free event may not anticipate the various disagreements that often arise. For example, income tax can become an issue if one spouse will benefit more than the other by filing a joint return. A couple must also decide who will claim their child as a dependent for income tax purposes (only one of the parents may claim the dependency exemption) and who will pay the mortgage on the family home and thus be able to deduct the interest on his or her income tax return. An advertised flat fee for an "uncontested" divorce probably does not include negotiations concerning these and many other issues that may arise.

"Do-it-yourself" divorces Be wary of the "do-it-yourself" divorce kits and books. No kit or book can anticipate all the problems that may occur in any particular divorce action. An advantage of competent legal help is that an attorney's advice is based on personal knowledge of the facts of each individual case and is fashioned to fit each client's needs. In addition, an attorney should know how the laws are actually applied in the local family court. Finally, problems created by self-representation may cause costly litigation at some time in the future. An ambiguous provision in a self-written separation agreement may later result in a lawsuit to determine the meaning of that provision.

"Quickie" divorces Another note of caution. The "quickie" divorce is often advertised by lawyers as being available in countries whose laws allow a divorce to be granted without residency requirements and without a waiting period. Such a divorce may not be recognized as valid in the home state of the spouse who obtained it, even if the other spouse participates in the divorce proceeding. Anyone contemplating "quickie" action should do so only after having made certain that such a divorce will be valid.

Attorneys' fees Once the proper attorney is chosen, he or she should explain the procedures applicable in the case and be candid about the legal fees and expenses. A client who hires an attorney is entitled to know what the divorce will cost him. In many instances, a lawyer may not be able to give a precise figure in advance, since the amount of the fee depends on the length of the procedure and the complexity of the negotiations and court hearings. However, some attorneys do charge a flat fee plus such expenses as court and sheriff fees. An attorney who charges an hourly rate should tell you what it is. Many attorneys periodically send a letter to their clients indicating the number of hours spent and a breakdown of what work was done during those hours.

Immediate considerations

Divorce proceedings may take a long time, and there are certain matters you should consider and act upon immediately, without waiting for the divorce to become final. What you do now may affect you later. For example, remaining in your marital home and keeping your children with you may affect the decision of the court regarding custody.

Court orders

In some of the circumstances discussed below, you may want to get a court order to solve immediate problems or to avoid possible trouble in the future.

You may obtain a court order by applying directly to the court in person or through your attorney. Generally, your spouse will be notified that you are applying for an order before it is issued so that he or she may appear before the court and give reasons why it should not be issued. Sometimes orders may be issued *ex parte* (that is, without notice to the other side), but only if there is an urgent need for them—to keep your spouse from beating your children, for example. If you are requesting an *ex parte* court order, you must file a *motion* (a written request to the court for the order) and an *affidavit* (a statement under oath setting out the factual basis for your request).

Protection against violence and abuse

Over the past few years a number of states have enacted family abuse statutes because of growing concern over the staggering number of cases of child abuse and battered wives and husbands. These laws allow a spouse to obtain promptly from the court a restraining order that directs an offending spouse to stop his abusive acts. Often, police must be notified of the order and must enforce it. It may also be possible to obtain money compensation ("damages") for injuries sustained as a result of the spouse's abuse.

Evicting a spouse

If your marriage is so intolerable that you feel you must separate immediately from your spouse and he or she refuses to leave your marital home, you may have to obtain a court order requiring him or her to vacate the premises even before you are granted a divorce or judicial separation. However, you will be granted such an order only if sufficient grounds are presented to the court.

If your spouse refuses to move out, but you prefer not to resort to a court order to force him or her out, it would probably be better if you both remained in the house until the divorce proceedings are over. It may not be advisable to move out of your marital home. If you walk out, you assume the risk that your spouse may change the locks and not allow you back in even to pick up your personal belongings. If this happens, you will have to start a court action, usually in connection with a divorce or legal separation, either to force your spouse out of the home or to gain access to it yourself.

Keeping the children

It may be particularly unwise to move out and to leave the children in the care of your spouse if a custody dispute is in the offing. If you do, you may later be faced with the argument that you abandoned the children and that their welfare was not a primary concern to you, thus demonstrating that you would not be a fit person to be awarded custody. In addition, the longer the children remain in the custody of one parent and in a stable home environment, the less likely it is that a court will disrupt the status quo and order a change in custody. Should you be forced to move out, however, take the children with you, if at all possible, if you want to have custody of them after the divorce.

Although matters such as the ultimate disposition or sale of the home and the permanent custody of the children may be subject to negotiation or litigation between you and your spouse, you should be aware that a court will usually grant exclusive use of the home to the spouse who has temporary custody so that the lives of the children will be disrupted as little as possible.

Protecting financial interests

Joint bank accounts often lead to problems for couples who are getting a divorce. When the divorce action reaches the court, the judge may order a joint bank account to be divided evenly between the husband and wife, especially when both contributed to the account or when one worked while the other provided household services. In some states (called equitable distribution states), a court may divide all property acquired during the marriage, including bank accounts, in a fair and equitable manner. In other states (called community property states), marital property must be divided evenly.

If you are getting a divorce and fail to get a court order dividing a bank account for many months—perhaps not until the case is finally resolved—you may find that the money has long been dissipated or transferred out of the joint account by your spouse.

For that reason, it may be advisable to close your joint account immediately and to open a different account (preferably in another bank) with the proceeds from the joint account, especially if you need immediate funds for ongoing living expenses.

Note well, however, that if you close out a joint bank account and spend the entire contents, a court may later order you to pay a portion of it to your spouse. You would be wise, therefore, to avoid spending the money until its disposition has been settled. If you need the family car for work or other important purposes, you may be able to get a court order granting you the use of the car.

Temporary support and custody Once a couple has decided to seek a divorce or legal separation, it is customary to obtain court orders to preserve the status quo during the litigation process, especially when minor children are involved. Such orders insure both that the other spouse will pay his or her share of the support obligation and that temporary custody of the children will be legally settled. Usually, a court will not enter a temporary alimony or child support order without prior notice to the affected spouse and without an opportunity for that spouse to appear before the court to be heard on the amount of the order.

If a temporary alimony or support order is to be handed down in your case, however, it is important that your attorney secure an order that is in your best interest. Although the order will be effective only until the divorce is final, the amount of a temporary alimony or support order may be used as a guideline by the court when it has to make a permanent order, and the temporary order might serve as a negotiating tool by either you or your spouse in reaching a final support order.

Basic divorce process

The general court-related procedures involved in obtaining a divorce, as well as legal terminology, vary from state to state, but the process is basically similar throughout the country.

In most states, the plaintiff (the party seeking the divorce) must live in the state and have resided there for a certain period of time (commonly one year or less) prior to filing for divorce. A divorce must be sought in a court that is designated as having the power to dissolve marriages—a domestic relations, family, or probate court—in a county or district where one of the parties resides. In addition, some state laws require that a husband and wife live apart for a period of time (for example, 30 days) before filing for divorce.

The divorce complaint The first step in the judicial process is usually the filing of the divorce complaint (also called a petition or libel), which typically states the names and addresses of the parties, the date of their marriage, and the names and birth dates of any children they may have. In the complaint, the plaintiff requests that a divorce be granted on a particular ground—such as adultery, cruelty, or incompatibility—and may also request alimony, child support, property division, custody, or permission to resume a maiden name. Although there is usually a filing fee, it may be waived if the party cannot afford it. The couple's marriage certificate must be filed.

The next step is for the plaintiff to serve the defendant (the party being sued for divorce) with a summons and a copy of the divorce complaint. The summons is a court document formally notifying the defendant that a court action has been started. The method of service differs from state to state. The summons and complaint may be delivered to the defendant by a sheriff or other official or by some other neutral person; in some cases, certified mail or publication of the complaint in a local newspaper may be used. When the separation has been amicable or the parties are negotiating a divorce agreement, the defendant may save the plaintiff the expense of formal service by "accepting" service, usually by signing the summons in acknowledgment that he or she has received the papers.

Within a specified number of days after service, the defendant must file an answer or other response to the complaint, admitting or denying the statements made in it. If a defendant fails to respond, the divorce may proceed uncontested, and only the plaintiff will be heard at the trial. If a defendant files an answer that denies or objects to facts or demands in the complaint—thus contesting the divorce—those matters will be resolved in court unless the parties settle them prior to the trial.

Pretrial court actions Sometimes, after a case has been filed, it is referred for conciliation or counseling to determine whether the parties may be reconciled, or it may be referred to a mediator in order to narrow the areas of disagreement. When there is a dispute over child custody, a court usually has the power to appoint a psychiatrist or social service agency to investigate the parents, and he may appoint an independent attorney or guardian to represent the interests of the child. Often, some type of discovery procedure takes place, typically where one spouse is seeking to learn more about the finances and property of the other. *Discovery* is a court-monitored exchange of relevant information between the parties, using written questions and answers or oral testimony. Both parties must also file sworn financial statements with the court showing assets, liabilities, and income, particularly when alimony or child support is an issue. These statements aid the court in making a fair and appropriate order for alimony or child support.

Meanwhile, the parties, through their attorneys, may be attempting to negotiate a divorce agreement. If they do not reach an agreement, the court may require them to attend a conference with a judge or court official who will try to help them reach a compromise in order to avoid litigation.

The court hearing A court hearing of the divorce complaint then occurs. If the case is uncontested or if the parties have reached an agreement, the hearing is usually perfunctory. If a divorce agreement has been reached, it is presented to the court, which approves the agreement if it is fair and reasonable.

If there is no agreement, the plaintiff may be required to testify regarding the grounds for the divorce and any other matter to be resolved by the court. The defendant will also be heard, if the case is contested. The court will then decide whether or not to grant the divorce and will then enter appropriate orders regarding alimony, child support, property division, or custody, when these are in issue.

Occasionally, after a contested hearing, a dissatisfied party may appeal to a higher court, claiming that the judge wrongly applied the law or that the facts on which the judge based an order were without any support in the evidence presented.

In some states, a judgment or decree of divorce does not become operative immediately. There is often a waiting period during which remarriage may be illegal. Once the judgment or decree becomes final, it is advisable for the parties to obtain certified copies of the decree in case either party desires to remarry.

divorce, although the effect is the same. In either event the marriage is ended once the decree has been granted, even if the absent one returns.

The court usually requires the plaintiff to show that an effort has been made to locate the spouse who disappeared. This may include asking the missing person's friends or relatives whether they have heard from him and checking public records for a marriage license, death certificate, tax payment, or application for Social Security in places where he is known to have lived.

Constructive abandonment If one partner denies the other the comforts and benefits of marriage without actually leaving the home, he may be providing grounds for divorce for constructive abandonment. Denial of sexual relations is not always enough to prove constructive abandonment, especially if the complaining spouse has permitted the situation to continue for years or if the offending spouse suffers from ill health.

Often it is a combination of factors that is so destructive of the marital character of a relationship as to warrant a divorce—as in one case in which a wife refused to do her husband's laundry, prepare his meals, or help out in his small store.

Constructive abandonment was also found when a wife's relatives visited every evening and stayed overnight on weekends despite the husband's protests, when a husband contracted venereal disease, and when a woman had the locks on the doors changed one day after her husband left for work.

In some cases, a spouse who leaves home may get a divorce from the spouse who stays at home on the ground of constructive abandonment.

EXAMPLE In New Jersey, a man beat his wife and carried on an adulterous relationship with a servant girl, whom he refused to put out of the house. In desperation the wife left home. Even though the wife was the one who refused to live with the husband, the court held that the husband had already abandoned her by beating her and denying her all marital relations. The wife was found justified in leaving her husband.

Unhappiness in a marriage does not legally justify moving out of the home. One court held that a woman who had been severely beaten by her husband had no right to leave him, and the judge denied her a divorce or alimony, but granted her a legal separation. In this case, the court found that an isolated assault, no matter how severe, was not a good reason for deserting the marital relationship.

Courts require proof of willful desertion over a period of time because time seems to show that the abandonment is meant to be permanent. If constructive abandonment has lasted many years, however, a court may assume that both parties had agreed to it and that it is therefore not really abandonment.

EXAMPLE Alfred was a farmer who enjoyed solitude. His wife, Virginia, was a schoolteacher who had always been outgoing. After their three children were born in rapid succession early in their marriage, they drifted apart because of their personality differences. Virginia took an active interest in her students and frequently stayed after school to work with them. Alfred learned to cook for himself and grew more and more reclusive.

Through most of their 30-year marriage, they had no sexual relationship. Then Virginia ran for the school board. Neighbors began coming by every day. The telephone rang all the time, and campaign headquarters were set up in the kitchen. Alfred had had it. He sued for divorce, claiming the only ground possible from their marriage, constructive abandonment. The court denied the divorce, reasoning that these people had lived for many years with a marriage that had no companionship. One partner could not now say that that amounted to an abandonment.

In cases of constructive abandonment, as in cases of willful desertion, the abandoned party is obligated to accept an offer of reconciliation.

Gross neglect of duty If a husband or wife fails to do what the marriage relationship requires of him or her, a divorce may be granted for *gross neglect of duty*. Traditionally, the husband's primary duty has been to support and the wife's primary duty has been to serve. Gross neglect is a serious failure to fulfill one's duty. The combination of factors sufficient to constitute gross neglect depends on the case. For a wife, it could be sloppy housekeeping, frequent refusal to prepare dinner, keeping unsanitary animals in the home without the husband's consent, failure to keep his clothes clean and repaired, failure to keep adequate nutritious foods on hand or obstinately preparing foods he does not like, failure to care for him when he is ill, and refusal of companionship or sex.

Nonsupport, usually by a husband, is one form of gross neglect. In some states, nonsupport is a ground for divorce against a husband only. In other states, either spouse may charge the other with gross neglect of duty, which may include nonsupport by a husband. States do not generally allow a man to divorce his wife for nonsupport.

The things that must happen in a marriage before a court will grant a divorce for gross neglect of duty must be severe. A wife's poor housekeeping is generally not enough by itself, nor are a husband's stinginess and coldness, but these things in combination with other things might justify a divorce for gross neglect.

If a husband is accused of nonsupport, he may defend himself by showing that he is unable to support his wife. In the past, it made no difference if a woman could support herself. She could still require her husband to support her and divorce him if he did not. Now, where equal rights laws are in effect, husbands and wives may both have the right to claim support from a spouse.

Cruelty Mental and physical cruelty are grounds for divorce in most states. Although states use different words to describe cruelty, the words apply to the same kinds of behavior.

Physical cruelty has long been recognized as a legal reason for ending a marriage. The law does not require two people to live together when one threatens or commits violence that endangers the other. It must be shown that the violence was more than a single isolated act and that the safety of the mistreated spouse is at stake.

Some states that strictly limited divorce to cases in which one spouse was at fault vastly increased the opportunity for divorce by allowing mental cruelty as a ground. Whereas physical cruelty can be proved only by actual incidents of violence, mental cruelty depends on individual circumstances and the condition of the parties involved.

EXAMPLE In one case, a woman showed how her husband's
O—* drug addiction amounted to cruelty that made her life wretched. The husband admitted to the court that he loved heroin more then he loved his wife. Testimony showed that he was unable and unwilling to engage in sexual relations. The judge found that the man's total failure to fulfill human and social needs in his marriage entitled his wife to a divorce for cruelty.

Courts have counted behavior as cruelty when one spouse falsely accused the other publicly of adultery, afflicted his or her partner with venereal disease, forced the spouse to engage in unconventional sex acts, or had a homosexual relationship.

When a single act is not serious enough to constitute cruelty, a series of acts may accumulate to give grounds for a divorce.

EXAMPLE A doctor required his wife to take full responsi-
O—* bility for the house and yard, handle a move to a new house when she was recovering from a painful back injury, take all of his night telephone calls, move her car if he went out at night, and bring him drinks of water or anything else on command. When he began falsely accusing her of paranoia, the court granted her a divorce. The full effect of the husband's selfish behavior constituted cruelty.

In some instances when a wife sued for divorce on the ground of her husband's cruelty but failed to make a case, judgment was given to the husband if he wanted a divorce. Those courts said that if the claim of cruelty cannot be proved to be true, the false accusation is cruelty to a husband, and he should be granted the divorce and relieved of responsibility for the wife.

Personal indignities A few states have permitted divorce for personal indignities, which are a form of mental or physical cruelty combined with insult or hatred that cannot be relieved by any efforts of the injured spouse. There are no set rules explaining the behavior covered by such a law, but the situation must have become intolerable. Acts of rudeness, ridicule, disdain, contempt, and vulgarity that are neither trivial nor occasional can be assaults on the dignity of a husband or wife.

A husband's running around with other women, especially if he also neglects his wife, is an indignity to the wife even when adultery cannot be proved. A man may complain of indignities if his wife refuses to have sexual intercourse or perform housekeeping services unless she is paid for them. It is an indignity for a woman to tell her husband's employer about his extramarital affair or drinking problem if she is only trying to hurt his reputation. Threats and violence against a wife are indignities. Where these can be proved, a court in a state that grants divorces for indignities may grant the injured spouse a divorce.

Disagreements over religion can lead to indignities, but the conduct must be unbearable.

EXAMPLE When a wife only allowed use of the radio in the
O—* home for religious programs, constantly criticized the religion of her husband, his family, and his friends, and attempted to convert everyone who visited their home, the husband was granted a divorce for indignities.

EXAMPLE In another case, however, a wife's refusal to use
O—* makeup or have her hair styled, and her disapproval of movies, dancing, drinking, smoking, and card playing were not enough to warrant granting her husband a divorce for indignities.

In states where personal indignities are not grounds for divorce, the abusive behavior may qualify as another ground, such as cruelty, abandonment, or nonsupport.

Insanity A number of states permit divorce on the ground of a spouse's insanity—that is, when there is a mental condition that makes normal married life impossible. Many states require some evidence that the mental illness cannot be cured. Almost all states require evidence that the illness has continued for a specified period of time—in many states, five years. In some states, that period of time need not be continuous and uninterrupted; it may be made up of shorter periods of insanity that total the required amount. Some statutes specify that the insane spouse must have been confined in a hospital—presumably as an indication that the illness is real and substantial. Often the spouse who gets the divorce must pay support for the insane spouse. For a discussion of how the law views mental illness and mental incompetence, see INSANE PERSONS.

Alcoholism and drug addition Several states permit divorce for alcoholism. Sometimes it must be shown that the drunkenness has continued for a specified period of time, usually one year. Anyone seeking a divorce on this ground must show that the drinking goes on most of the time, that the drinker consumes enough to become intoxicated, and that a normal married life with the drinker is nearly impossible. In some states, alcoholism is not a ground if it existed when the marriage took place because it is assumed the innocent spouse knew about the condition and agreed to live with it.

Some states have broadened their alcoholism statute to include addiction to drugs. Some other states have a separate law that makes drug addiction a ground for divorce.

Other personal infirmities Most states follow the policy that marriage is "for better or for worse." Except for venereal disease and insanity, most personal infirmities arising after the marriage, even those that make sexual intercourse impossible, must be borne with courage.

EXAMPLE In two cases in which the wives said that their
O—* husbands were so careless about personal hygiene that it was impossible to live with them, the court refused to grant the divorces, holding that the wives were not entirely blameless. The judges agreed with the wives that the men were not easy to live with, but maintained that this was not enough justification for divorce.

Other grounds A variety of other grounds for divorce are recognized in some states:

(1) Pregnancy of the wife by another man at the time of the marriage, unknown to the husband.

(2) An attempt by one spouse on the life of the other.

(3) Conviction of a serious crime before marriage, unknown to the spouse.

(4) Repeated false statements about the character of one's husband or wife, intended to injure his or her reputation.

(5) Maliciously locking out the spouse.

Some states will grant a divorce or an annulment when the marriage is invalid because one person was tricked or forced into marrying, was underage or insane at the time of the marriage, or knew but withheld the fact that he or she was incapable of a normal sex life or of having children.

Incompatibility, the no-fault divorce All the grounds discussed so far have required one marriage partner to prove that the other was at fault in destroying the relationship. But fixing blame has proved to be most unsatisfactory, because in marriage usually neither party is entirely blameless. Instead of making the guilt of one spouse the issue, some states focus on the condition of the marriage itself and whether the two people can continue to be married. These states grant divorces on the ground of incompatibility, irreconcilable differences, or an irretrievable breakdown of the marriage relationship.

The first U.S. jurisdiction to permit divorce on the ground of incompatibility was the American Virgin Islands, in 1921, followed by New Mexico in 1933, Alaska in 1935, and Oklahoma in 1953. Some judges have, however, continued to require proof of some fault before granting divorces for incompatibility. In 1965 the federal court in the Virgin Islands reversed a decree based on incompatibility, because no proof of serious fault by either party had been shown. The court refused to believe the proof offered that the couple were hopelessly incompatible.

Some states have tried to minimize fault. These states do not require the person seeking divorce (the plaintiff) to show that he or she is entirely blameless or is the only one who has been injured. In other words, it takes two to be incompatible. Most courts will deny a divorce for incompatibility if the plaintiff seems to be seriously at fault. They will not, for example, listen to a man who complains that he and his wife are incompatible because she is constantly nagging him, when the subject of her nagging is his girl friend. Furthermore, courts require clear proof that the personality conflict is so deep that it destroys all the legitimate ends of matrimony and makes reconciliation hopeless. It is the duty of the court to test every petition for divorce against these standards.

Divorce on demand Although divorce for incompatibility is said to be no-fault, it is not the same as divorce on demand, which truly does not require that either partner or both partners be blamed for the failure of the marriage. Some states now permit divorce on demand in certain situations: if both parties agree that the marriage cannot be salvaged; if one party asserts that the marriage is dead and he or she wants to get out of it; or if one person asks for divorce after certain events, such as voluntary separation, have occurred.

A state may permit divorces for couples who have voluntarily lived apart for a specified length of time. The theory behind such a law is that marriages that have ceased to exist in fact should be allowed to be terminated in law. The requirement that the separation be accepted by each marriage partner is intended to protect the person who does not wish to give up on the marriage. If one person still wants to try to reconcile, this law does not prevent it, but a sincere effort at reconciliation must be shown.

EXAMPLE A wife sued for divorce on the ground of voluntary separation. The parties had lived apart for more than five years, with his home in Florida and hers in the District of Columbia. The husband argued against the divorce, claiming that the separation was not voluntary on his part. He said that he had sent gifts and letters asking his wife to join him and once sent a check to cover part of the expense of a trip to Florida for her. The court found that these few gestures by the husband were not enough to defeat the wife's action for divorce.

Conversion divorces Some states permit divorce when the parties have lived apart for a certain period of time either after both have signed a separation agreement or after one of them has obtained a court-ordered separation decree. The divorce decree is legal recognition of the fact that a particular marriage cannot be saved—even though one partner may not want separation or divorce. Such divorces are sometimes called conversion divorces because the separation decree is converted into a divorce after a certain time has passed.

Conversion divorces were intended to eliminate the need to prove fault in the courtroom. In addition, the required wait offered the advantage of preventing hasty divorces. But fault is not always irrrelevant to a conversion divorce. If a husband (or wife) who wants a legal separation has given his spouse any grounds for a fault divorce—for example, because of infidelity—he may find himself at a disadvantage because of his guilty behavior. He may have to give up more when the terms of the separation are negotiated. If he does not make generous concessions regarding property, custody, and support payments, he may find himself before a judge who grants a divorce against him for fault and imposes punishing conditions of settlement.

The lengthy separations required in most cases for conversion divorces did not satisfy the public, and in states calling for long periods of separation—some as much as five years—people continued to seek divorces on grounds of fault because such divorces were quicker to obtain. New York reduced the period of separation from two years to one shortly after the conversion divorce became possible. In Massachusetts less than 10 percent of the divorces have been granted under a recent conversion law. There the separation must last two years if it is not agreed to by both parties—but only 10 months if it is—and 6 months must pass before the divorce decree becomes final.

Some attorneys routinely advise their clients to seek an immediate divorce on the ground of a spouse's misconduct even when a divorce based on separation can be obtained more easily. The reason is that during the period of separation an innocent spouse may give his or her partner grounds for divorce and thereby risk losing all the economic rights he or she has from the marriage and, in some states, custody of the children.

EXAMPLE Suppose a man comes home one evening and tells his faithful and loving wife that he is tired of being married. They had married young, and he now believes he has missed too much excitement in life. He assures her that he is finished with their marriage and will never live with her again. He packs his bags and moves out, telling her to speak to his attorney.

The woman is shocked. In a few days she sees an attorney who advises her to start an action for divorce on the ground of desertion. This seems too drastic for her, so instead she goes to court and obtains a decree of separation, hoping that she and her husband will get back together. If they do not, she can convert this decree to a judgment of divorce in her state after one year.

Then she joins a women's group. She is counseled to find a job and to start a new life. Finally, she accepts a date and eventually sees the man in her home in the evening so she will not have to go out and leave her children. One month later she receives a paper informing her that her husband is suing her for divorce on the ground of adultery. If he can prove that she had the "opportunity and inclination" to carry on sexual relations with another man, she may lose her right to alimony and other economic rights she has from the marriage and she might even lose custody of her children.

Irreparable, or irretrievable, breakdown There is a serious problem with irretrievable breakdown divorce laws that permit one party to have the marriage dissolved solely on his or her testimony that the relationship cannot be retrieved and that the differences cannot be reconciled. The law attaches certain rights and duties to marriage. If one partner can end his or her obligations without regard for the condition of the other, then the other is losing rights to which he or she is entitled. At least when the parties agree to negotiate a settlement, they have an opportunity to bargain for whatever is important to them. Irretrievable breakdown laws permit one person to refuse to cooperate in the marriage and then to win a divorce on the ground that the marriage will not work. When such a situation occurs, judges can minimize its unfairness by ordering alimony or deciding how to divide property owned by the couple.

■ **Defenses against divorce** A spouse who is sued for divorce because of fault or misconduct has the right to defend himself or herself. The defenses, like the original grounds for divorce, were developed when the Catholic Church and the Church of England had complete authority in marital matters. Because remarriage was not permitted and sexual relations outside of marriage were forbidden, the churches tested every petition for divorce by requiring the grounds to be fully proved and every possible defense to be raised against them. Very seldom would the ecclesiastical courts permit an accused spouse to confess his fault or keep silent. The marriage was to be preserved whether the husband and wife wanted it or not.

Recrimination In the past, the fault concept was carried to an extreme with the defense of recrimination. Recrimination allows the accused spouse to stop the divorce action by saying, "Yes, I am guilty, but so are you." The theory was that divorce could be granted only to an innocent spouse against a guilty spouse. If neither spouse was innocent, the court left the marriage intact.

Ironically, increasing the grounds for divorce made recrimination easier to prove. When the only ground for divorce was adultery, it was difficult for the accused party to establish the defense that the accusing spouse was also guilty of adultery. But when mental cruelty became a ground, almost any evidence could be offered to show that the defendant had suffered as much as the plaintiff.

Some states have limited or abolished recrimination as a defense to divorce. Some permit it only to allow the defendant to prove that the spouse complaining of adultery has committed the same offense. Other states have tried to balance the plaintiff's accusation and the defendant's defense by allowing only grounds of equal magnitude to be offset in recrimination.

EXAMPLE Alice sued Jerome for a divorce, charging him
O—＊ with abandonment. Jerome counterclaimed, asking the court to grant him a divorce on the ground of Alice's cruelty to him. The court found that each of them had proved facts sufficient to warrant a divorce, but it did not grant a divorce to either of them. In their state, recrimination barred divorce for grounds that were considered equally bad. Under the divorce law of that state, only the ground of adultery was considered worse than all other permissible grounds. All other grounds were equal and resulted in recrimination if both parties proved a case. If Alice had shown Jerome to be guilty of adultery rather than abandonment, the court would have granted her a divorce in spite of Jerome's evidence that Alice was guilty of marital cruelty.

Several states that permit divorce on the ground that the relationship is irretrievably broken may hear a defense based on serious misconduct of the one asking for the divorce.

Provocation If the plaintiff provoked the behavior presented as a ground for divorce, the divorce action will fail. Provocation is more than small annoyances, and the retaliation cannot be greater than the provocation.

EXAMPLE One woman sought a divorce because her hus-
O—＊ band was frequently drunk, slept on the front lawn, vomited all through the house, and picked fights with her. He even threatened her life with a gun. The husband's defense was that his wife had provoked his bad behavior by an affair she had had several years earlier. The court found that the man must have forgiven his wife, because he had continued to live with her for years after the affair had ended. Her one mistake could not justify a whole course of serious misconduct by him.

Condonation Another long-recognized defense is condonation, or an earlier forgiveness of the offense. Condonation is most often used to excuse sexual misconduct and in some states is expressly limited to a defense against the charge of adultery.

EXAMPLE A wife permits herself to be flattered into a brief
O—＊ affair. Her husband discovers her adultery and confronts her with his suspicions. When she promises never to repeat the mistake, he tells her he forgives her. If he later tries to secure a divorce based on this adultery, the wife can defend herself by showing condonation. The matter is closed.

Condonation is hard to prove, as in the case described above, because it is usually a matter of one person's word against the other's. But most states have resolved this difficulty. If the aggrieved spouse resumes marital relations voluntarily and with full knowledge of the offense, the court will presume condonation.

Many courts hold the traditional view that condonation is conditional—forgiveness on the condition that the offense not be repeated. Some courts go further and hold that a generous husband or wife who forgives is entitled to "conjugal kindness" in return. Under the law, conjugal kindness may mean that the one who has made a mistake stands to lose a spouse's forgiveness if he or she does not jump to every marital demand, whether it is for sex, personal services, or more spending money. A refusal to be especially nice often leads to angry accusations that the offender is not really trying. Eventually, arguments ripen into full-fledged battles, and the original adultery comes back to legal life as a ground for divorce, when the spouse who once forgave can go to court for a divorce. Some states do not consider condonation to be conditional because of these problems. Once marital relations are resumed, the forgiveness extinguishes the prior misconduct as a ground for divorce in those states.

Connivance If the spouse suing for divorce had a share in causing or promoting the misconduct that he complains about, the defense available is connivance. Connivance means that the innocent spouse must have either participated in the wrong or stood idly by in order to accumulate grounds for a divorce.

EXAMPLE A married couple were drinking with a male friend. About 1:00 A.M., the friend said, "I have no wife tonight. Why don't you come home with me?" The husband said nothing, so the wife replied, "Why not?" She testified that earlier in the evening her husband had said she was undersexed and should find herself a man and learn something.

The husband asked for a divorce for his wife's adultery, saying he had thought the two were joking. The court would not accept his statement. The husband had waited 20 minutes before following them to the other man's house. The friend's car was parked in the driveway and the lights were out. Instead of bursting into the house, the husband called a friend, who could later testify as a witness, and a police officer, who could later identify the wife and the friend. The court dismissed the man's action to divorce his wife because of his connivance in the course of events.

Collusion A defense based on the claim that the plaintiff cooperated with his or her spouse in doing something wrong is called collusion. It means that the husband and wife have secretly agreed to trick the court into granting a divorce. They may act together to convince the court that one party is at fault when he is not, or they may agree that the defendant will not use any defenses even though he is legally entitled to do so. Collusion goes against the state's policy of preserving marriage because it allows those who are willing to lie to win a divorce. Sometimes the court discovers the fraud, and sometimes one person will regret his part in the collusion and will admit the scheme to the court, offering it as a defense. In either event the court will deny the divorce, and all who were involved will be subject to criminal penalties for lying in court.

Invalid marriage It is possible to defend against a divorce action by proving that no marriage exists. This defense was not unusual when divorce was difficult to obtain in some states and easy in others.

EXAMPLE A man who cannot get a divorce in his home state leaves his wife and establishes a home in a state that permits divorce actions after a very short period of residence. Before his wife can do anything, he goes into court and obtains a divorce judgment. Then the wife starts an action for divorce in the home state where she hopes to prove the husband's misconduct during the

marriage in order to win a good economic settlement. The husband answers that there can be no divorce because now there is no marriage. If he has followed all the necessary procedures to get a valid divorce in the other state, the wife's action is dismissed.

Sometimes a defense can be based on the invalidity of the marriage because the parties were legally incapable of marrying when and where they did or because they failed to follow the state requirements for a valid wedding ceremony. For example, a woman may wish to get a divorce from her husband and get alimony. If her husband can show that the marriage was invalid, the court may refuse both the divorce and alimony. For a discussion of marriage requirements, see MARRIAGE and Chart 20. See also ANNULMENT.

Lack of intent In some states, a defendant can admit to the marital offense he or she is charged with and be excused because of lack of intent. If the accused spouse was insane and so could not understand the nature of the act or if he did not commit the offense voluntarily, he cannot be blamed for destroying the marriage. For example, a man who beat his wife because of insane delusions may defend on the ground of insanity, and a woman who has been raped cannot be divorced for adultery.

Statute of limitations The divorce law of some states includes a provision called a statute of limitations, which means that a divorce action based on a particular ground must be started within the time allowed by law. See LIMITATIONS OF ACTIONS.

Laches The general rule called LACHES is similar to a statute of limitations. Laches does not specifically limit the time when a lawsuit can start. Rather it is a principle that says courts should throw out cases that are long delayed, because as time goes on a defendant may be less able to answer the charges or he may have believed that no legal action would be started. The authority to apply the laches principle rests within the discretion of judges. Some states do not permit laches to be pleaded in a divorce action.

Clean hands Another general legal principle that may provide a defense to a divorce action is called clean hands: someone who has been unfair or at fault himself may not ask the court to grant him relief. Like laches, clean hands is a matter of fairness left to a judge's discretion.

EXAMPLE Sue and Tom were married in 1949. In 1971 Sue told Tom that she was having an affair. She continued that relationship for another year, and then Tom and Sue invited the other man to move into their home. Sue and her friend shared a bedroom. About a year and a half later, Tom got a job in another state and started a divorce action on the ground of adultery. Sue defended on the ground of clean hands: Tom should not have invited her lover to move in. The court granted Tom a divorce because that state had abolished clean hands as a defense on the theory that it is useless to preserve a dead marriage. A marriage is no less dead because the plaintiff has also done wrong.

Abolishing defenses Most of the defenses explained above were developed as answers to divorce actions based on fault. When states began liberalizing their divorce laws, many of them did so by eliminating some of the defenses. This helped to end the practice of bouncing blame back and forth between husband and wife.

■ **Divorce procedure** Only a few states still refuse to grant divorce without fault. Several others have swung to the other extreme, requiring only proof of irretrievable breakdown. Most have chosen a middle-of-the-road approach, adding "incompatibility" or "living separate and apart" to their traditional set of fault grounds. Fault is still important because it offers a quick divorce for people in states that attach waiting periods to no-fault grounds, and because in most cases relative fault influences custody and property settlements.

Where to bring the action The plaintiff must start the divorce suit in the state where the husband or wife maintains a permanent legal home. The action must be based on a ground legally recognized in that state. If the defendant does not answer the charges, the court sometimes has no authority to make binding orders concerning alimony, division of property, and other issues.

If neither party lives where the divorce is granted, the decree is called a *migratory divorce*. It may be possible to get a migratory divorce if both parties agree to submit to a court's jurisdiction, duping the court into believing they live in its jurisdiction. The court does not actually have authority to act, however, because the marriage itself is not before the court (as the law requires), only the parties. Neither party can later claim that the divorce is invalid, because they both participated in it. Other people who are affected by it may be able to attack it later, however, because the court that granted the divorce did not have the authority to act.

EXAMPLE Hilda and Wayne live in Pleasantville, New York, where they own their own home. Wayne works in New York City. After 15 years of married life in New York State, Wayne and Hilda drive to Atlantic City, New Jersey, for a weekend, leaving their children with Hilda's mother in upstate New York. Hilda and Wayne rent a cottage in Atlantic City and apply to the local court for a divorce, giving the address of the rented cottage as their residence. As soon as the divorce has been filed they return to New York, going back to New Jersey only when they must appear in court to get the divorce. As soon as they have their New Jersey divorce, they get rid of the cottage in Atlantic City and return to New York. Hilda and the children move in with Hilda's mother and Wayne lives in the Pleasantville house he and Hilda had lived in during their marriage.

New Jersey did not have jurisdiction over Hilda's and Wayne's marriage and had no power to grant them a divorce. The divorce is, in effect, invalid, but neither Hilda nor Wayne can claim that it is. If Hilda later decides that she did not want the divorce after all, she can do nothing about it. But if Wayne remarried and the New York District Attorney discovered the circumstances of Wayne's "divorce" and remarriage, he could prosecute Wayne for bigamy because his divorce from Hilda was not valid in the eyes of the law.

The U.S. Constitution does not require state courts to recognize any legal judgments, including divorces, granted in other countries. Americans who evade state divorce laws by flying to Haiti, Mexico, or the Dominican Republic for an overnight divorce have no protection if the judgment is later attacked.

In the courtroom If a divorce is contested—opposed by the defendant—the court will order a trial of the suit, which is a civil ACTION. Each side presents evidence to prove his case, and the judge makes his decision, which in a few cases is based on the verdict of a jury. A decision for divorce may include provisions concerning alimony, child custody and support, and division of property. It is written down as a judgment, signed by the judge, and filed. Each party gets a copy. If, in the future, any provisions regarding money, property, or children are not honored, they can be enforced by court order.

Most divorce cases are uncontested. The parties negotiate a settlement concerning alimony, child custody and support, and division of property. The plaintiff appears in court on the appointed day, and a hearing is held at which he or she answers questions in order to establish a legal case on a ground recognized in that state. As long as the settlement reached by the parties seems fair and reasonable, the judge usually accepts it as written. Judgment for divorce is granted, signed, and filed, and a copy given to each party. Again, orders concerning the settlement can later be enforced if necessary.

A discussion of alimony, child support, and division of property appears below. For a full discussion of child custody in divorce cases, see CUSTODY.

Conciliation Some courts have the authority to order or to recommend marriage counseling, or conciliation sessions, in an effort to save the marriage. There are constitutional questions, however, about whether a court has the right to invade the privacy of a person's married life. Another consideration is the high cost of counseling sessions. By the time most people reach the divorce court, the chances for a reconciliation are usually not good.

■ **The economic consequences of divorce** Because a family usually functions as a single economic unit, divorce has serious economic consequences. As long as the relationship between husbands and wives followed a standard pattern, it was not too difficult for the law to make rules to resolve the economic problems caused by divorce. As patterns of family responsibility have changed, however, inflexible rules governing property settlements and support payments have resulted in more hardships.

The economic rights and duties of a divorcing husband and wife involve alimony, child support, and division of property. These items in turn raise questions of inheritance, pensions, and tax liabilities.

Alimony Alimony is an amount of money a husband pays to a wife for her support after they separate or divorce. Occasionally, the wife makes payments to the husband, but this is still rare. Alimony dates back to the time when a woman could not support herself. Her father supported her until she married; then her husband supported her for life and, if he died first, she was usually permitted to use one-third of his property for her lifetime. Divorce as we know it was not possible, but if the parties separated, the husband's responsibility to support the wife continued. When he died, she kept her right to inherit the use of part of his land during her lifetime.

When divorce became possible, blame for breaking up the marriage rested on one person. If the husband was at fault, it seemed only fair to preserve the wife's right to support. A woman who was found to be at fault was denied alimony, but most divorces were, in fact, granted to women against men.

The reality of alimony   Public indignation sometimes arises over extravagant awards of alimony.

EXAMPLE The wife of San Francisco's former mayor Jo-
O—* seph Alioto sought $9,019 a month in alimony to cover her normal expenses, including $2,090 for clothing, $200 for the telephone bill, $250 for beauty shop and cosmetic expenses, and $1,050 for a maid and other costs of running the household. In addition, she wanted $2 million worth of personal assets, possession of the marital home, and title to some valuable real estate. The court granted her $5,500 a month for her temporary support while litigation was in progress, based on the mayor's net worth of approximately $8.5 million.

The truth is that not many divorced women live in luxury while their former husbands support them for life. People who read about the chorus girl who grabs a million dollars in alimony after a brief marriage may never hear about the typical case, in which there is too little money to make any kind of provision for alimony. As a practical matter, alimony is uncommon. Most divorces—probably about 90 percent—are granted without it.

Most states provide by law that a judge may order alimony when it seems fair to do so. In other areas of law, a consensus about what is "fair," has generally been developed over a period of time. Alimony, however, is a comparatively new concept and no widespread agreement has developed concerning it. One belief is that a woman is entitled to live at the same economic level she enjoyed during the marriage. Obviously, this solution is impossible for most couples because two households have to be maintained on the same number of dollars that formerly supported one.

Another view of alimony is based on the assumption that men and women are financially equal. But the assumption is wrong. Most women who work are still clustered in job categories that produce the least income. Furthermore, it is unrealistic to assume that a woman with children is always free to work once the youngest starts school, because schoolchildren are out of school much of the time. In addition, the responsibilities of a mother toward her children often limit her freedom to seek a better job.

EXAMPLE In a 1975 New York case, a husband argued that
O—* his state courts traditionally did not order alimony if a woman was capable of supporting herself. His wife could expect to earn $10,000 a year as an executive secretary. Her husband had graduated from law school and begun a meteoric rise in a prominent Wall Street law firm. The court's decision was based on the fact that the wife had supported her husband while he was in law school. The judge awarded her $200 a week to support herself and her child while she earned her medical degree, a career she had always wanted. He did not require her to stay in her secretarial job.

Factors courts consider   When courts are deciding whether to award alimony and how much, they generally consider all the circumstances affecting the financial conditions of both husband and wife. The Uniform Marriage and Divorce Act is a law that states can use as a model in writing their own laws. It suggests that a court take into account (1) the financial resources of the party asking for maintenance payments; (2) the time necessary to acquire education or training for appropriate employment; (3) the standard of living during the marriage; (4) the length of time the couple were married; (5) the age, physical fitness, and emotional condition of the one who seeks support; and (6) the ability of the other to meet his own needs and still contribute to his former spouse's support.

The model law recommends that support not be ordered unless the one asking for it has too little property to provide for his or her needs and is unable to earn sufficient income, or unless he or she has custody of a young child and should not be forced to work outside the home.

Fault   The Uniform Act specifically states that support should be ordered when appropriate "without regard to marital misconduct." Many states, however, still grant or withhold alimony on the basis of fault. Some states absolutely prohibit granting alimony to the person against whom the divorce judgment is granted. Others bar it only in the case of a wife who has been divorced for adultery, and still others consider evidence of any misconduct during the marriage in settling the amount of alimony.

EXAMPLE One state that denies alimony to wives who are
O—* divorced for fault made an exception in the case of a woman who was divorced for her habitual drunkenness. The court ordered her former husband, who earned $34,000 a year, to pay back to a social services agency the welfare payments his ex-wife received. The court ruled, however, that this was not alimony for the wife, but a debt that this well-paid man owed to society.

States that permit no-fault divorce have had to decide whether to allow alimony regardless of fault. The Uniform Marriage and Divorce Act recommends and some states fully adopt the view that fault should not be considered in determining alimony in a no-fault divorce. Other states hold that in a no-fault divorce, evidence of marital misconduct should be taken into account when a court decides whether to award alimony.

When payments change or end   Alimony payments usually continue until they are modified by court order, one of the parties dies, or the spouse receiving them remarries.

The amount of alimony can usually be changed at a later date by the same court that awarded it. Courts have no patience with someone who runs to court every month for a modification of payments, but a significant change in circumstances—such as a much smaller income for a man who has retired or a higher salary for a woman who has finished college—will be heard. Some states follow the rule that alimony can be increased to keep pace with inflation in order to maintain a woman's income at the same level—as long as the man can afford it. If a woman's former husband becomes more prosperous after the divorce, however, she has no right to a share in his wealth.

Whether or not alimony can be awarded later if it is not ordered in the judgment of divorce depends on state law. If the judgment specifically bars alimony, no award can be made later no matter how much circumstances change.

Usually a divorced wife has no right to any share in her former husband's estate when he dies. There have been cases, however, where alimony was ordered for a wife "until she dies or remarries." Some courts have interpreted this to create a right for the wife to collect money from the husband's estate when he dies in order to furnish her support for life. Sometimes a husband is required to maintain a life insurance policy for the benefit of an ex-wife who is completely dependent on alimony for support. This gives her some security if he dies before she does, particularly if she has little work experience.

Many states allow an automatic end to alimony payments when the person receiving them remarries. In a few states the person who pays the alimony must apply to the court to end it when his or her former spouse remarries.

Living with another person When a divorced woman remarries, her new husband assumes the legal obligation to support her. But what happens if she lives with a man without benefit of marriage?

The law calls this *cohabitation,* which is discussed under MARRIAGE. Originally, many laws said that alimony could be terminated if the new couple led people to believe that they were married. A man should not be forced to support an ex-wife everyone thinks is another man's wife, even though the couple are not married. In recent years, women have been able to continue to enforce alimony obligations in such circumstances. As long as a woman neither remarries nor presents herself as another man's wife, the former husband must mail out the checks. Some courts, however, have reduced the amount of alimony to guarantee that none of the money helps support the man with whom the former wife is living.

EXAMPLE An Ohio court cut off alimony payments on the theory that the relationship of the ex-wife and the man with whom she was living in Florida would be a valid common-law marriage in Ohio even though it was not a marriage in Florida. The woman admitted that she had stopped short of the wedding ceremony in order to continue collecting her $400-a-month alimony.

There may be constitutional problems if a court interferes with a former wife's private life. The court cannot require a person receiving alimony not to have sexual contacts when it cannot restrict the person paying alimony in the same manner. On the other hand, a former husband should not be supporting another man who moves in with his ex-wife on a permanent basis.

EXAMPLE When Marlon Brando and his wife, Movita, separated, they agreed that alimony could be terminated by her remarriage, including her "appearing to maintain a marital relationship with any person."

When the issue came to court, evidence showed that Movita and another man had "enjoyed a relationship of substantial duration, which bore the objective indicia of marriage." He kept his clothes in her home, often purchased groceries on her account, cooked and ate with her, and used her cars and a department store credit card. He gave her address on his driver's license and in reporting to his probation officer.

The court agreed with Brando that the other man enjoyed "the usual rewards of marriage without assuming the obligations which flow from a ceremony of marriage." The court rejected Movita's argument that they did not give the *appearance* of being married because they told everyone that they only lived together. "This inter-

pretation," the judge wrote, "would place a premium on the persistence with which [the wife] publicized the illicit nature of the relationship."

Some states have tried to solve the problem of deciding at what point a person's private life will cancel his former partner's obligation to pay alimony. They have passed laws that specify exactly when alimony can be terminated—for example, after 30 days of cohabitation, which must be consecutive in some states and need not be consecutive in others. The best solution may be for both parties to negotiate such terms in a separation agreement, which is later incorporated into the divorce judgment.

Alimony after an annulment Many alimony cases have involved an ex-wife's second marriage that is void or voidable. If a woman believes she is married but the marriage is later declared invalid in an annulment proceeding, must the ex-husband start paying alimony again? Most states will reinstate the support order after the annulment of a *void* marriage on the theory that the marriage never existed. If the marriage was only *voidable* at the option of the wife, most courts will not reinstate alimony payments by the first husband.

■ **Child support** All parents are required by law to support their children. Conversely, a child has a right to be supported by his parents—even if the parents are divorced. A parent does not have the right to burden society with the support of his child.

A divorce decree generally gives custody of minor children to one of the parents. Often an order directing support payments from the noncustodial to the custodial parent will be part of the agreement that settles economic relations between the parties. Occasionally, a parent will be ordered to pay support directly to the child—for example, when he lives at college—or to a guardian who manages the property of a (usually wealthy) child. It is possible for a court to order payments to be made directly into a fund, such as a TRUST, to be held for the child's use at some future time.

Many states have now lowered the age of majority (legal adulthood) for most purposes to 18, but they have reserved the right to order a parent to support a child beyond that age. See INFANT. Therefore, a child-support provision in a judgment of divorce may order payments until the child is 21 or as long as he attends school full time. In some states, support payments may be stopped before 18 if the child marries, obtains full-time employment, or willfully refuses to accept a parent's discipline or guidance.

Generally, support obligations end when the supporting parent dies. He may provide for his child by carrying a life insurance policy for the child's benefit or by leaving the child property in his will. In some cases, a court will order a supporting parent (usually the father) to carry life insurance naming the child or the custodial parent (usually the mother) as beneficiary. Unless the custodial parent has sufficient means of support, it is better to name her rather than the child on the policy, unless she is completely irresponsible. Otherwise, the money can be tied up in court after the death of the supporting parent and will not be readily available to the child.

Amount of payments In fixing the amount of child support, courts balance all the factors affecting the child's maintenance. The Uniform Parentage Act, a statute that states can follow as a model when enacting their support laws, suggests a reasonable list of considerations: (1) the needs of the child, (2) the standard of living and circumstances of the parents, (3) the financial condition of the parents, (4) the earning ability of each parent, (5) the child's educational plans, (6) the age of the child, (7) the financial resources and earning ability of the child, (8) the responsibility of each parent for the support of other people, and (9) the value of the care given by the parent who has custody.

Parents may provide for the amount of child support in a separation agreement, but the amount is always reviewable by a court, because neither parent may bargain away the child's rights. A settlement that is fair in light of all the economic circumstances of the case is generally acceptable.

Changing the amount An award for child support can be changed. Courts insist that a significant change of circumstances be shown, however, before they will consider modifying the amount of a child-support order.

Fathers frequently argue that their circumstances are significantly changed when they remarry and start new families. In the past, courts uniformly ruled against such pleas, holding that a father takes on new responsibilities at his own risk and not the child's. Recently, however, they have begun to give some consideration to the needs of the father's new family.

A father's decision to change jobs may alter the amount of child-support payments. Sometimes the support payments are reduced to encourage a man to start in a new field that is low paying at first but offers a better future. Reductions in child-support payments have been granted a salaried construction worker whose income was cut in half when he started to practice law, a physician who undertook training to become a psychiatrist, and a police officer who wanted to become a pilot. A physician who gave up his practice and his income to write a book about divorce, however, was jailed for contempt when he failed to keep up his support payments. A machinist who changed his name to Krishna Venta and founded a religious society that paid all of his expenses, including child support, had to comply with an order for increased support payments.

Division of property When a marriage breaks up, the property must be divided between husband and wife. There are two different systems that set the rules for property settlements. One is called separate property; the other, community property. These systems influence negotiations for separation agreements and establish approaches of judges in settling controversies.

Separate-property states All but eight states consider everything in marriage as separate property. Each spouse retains ownership of everything he or she held before the marriage and acquired during the marriage through gift, inheritance, or income from earnings or investments. The only way one spouse has a legal right to property owned by the other is to receive it as a gift or, where permitted, through a business venture.

EXAMPLE One decision in New York strictly followed the principles of separate property, with disastrous results for one of the parties. During a marriage that lasted several decades, the couple had pursued a strict savings plan in order to provide for their retirement. For many years the family lived primarily on the wife's earn-

ings while most of the husband's income went into savings and investment. Title to everything was in his name. When they divorced, the court refused to make the husband share anything with the wife. The fact that the husband had promised to set aside the money "for the two of us" did not, the court said, create a legal obligation.

This "title rule," which gives property according to the name on the title, also preserves ownership of property that each partner had before the marriage.

Today separate-property jurisdictions are increasingly treating marriage as a partnership. As of 1979, only 15 states adhered to the strict rule of separate property, and at least 25 states were finding ways to attain economic justice in individual cases. The problem with this situation is that changes are made piecemeal rather than through comprehensive legislation. When current law creates a startlingly unfair result, one case is widely publicized, and the legislature rushes to amend one portion of a statute. The result is that it is practically impossible for people to order their lives according to a reasonable divorce law.

Community-property states Eight states consider the property acquired during marriage to be community property to which each partner has an equal claim. Those states are Arizona, California, Idaho, Louisiana, New Mexico, Nevada, Texas, and Washington.

Community-property states return to each partner what he owned before the marriage and property acquired in certain ways (such as inheritance) during the marriage and divide the rest equally at divorce. Generally, the courts reserve the right to determine what is an equitable distribution. The advantage of the community-property approach is that it gives economic recognition to the contributions made to the marriage by a spouse who was not a wage earner. It avoids the unrealistic assumptions of the separate-property laws: that a man puts property in his wife's name only because he wants to give her a gift (when instead he is thinking about taxes) or that the names on titles to property should be honored because the couple has carefully made an overall plan of property ownership, which is seldom the case.

EXAMPLE In one community-property case, the court equally divided all the assets accumulated during three years of marriage, and then assigned responsibility for the debts of the parties. The wife received property worth $3,500 and was told to pay $1,000 worth of debts. The husband also received $3,500 in property and was ordered to pay $5,450 worth of debts. The man appealed, claiming that his wife came out $2,500 ahead, while he had a deficit of $1,950. The court rejected his argument because his earning capacity was much greater than his wife's. There is nothing fair or equal, the court held, in ordering a spouse who earns $500 a month to pay as much indebtedness as a spouse who makes $1,000 a month.

The court in the above case made the point that it is entirely proper, even in community-property states, to consider all the financial factors of a case. This means that community-property settlements are not entirely predictable. Furthermore, most marriages in which one spouse has been dependent on the other for support do not have property to provide for the economic needs of both parties by a strict division of community property.

The differences In most states, the differences between alimony, child support, and property settlements are

(1) Alimony and child support may be enforced by wage garnishment (deducting an amount from one's salary) and jail for contempt; property settlements are enforced by civil lawsuits. See ATTACHMENT AND GARNISHMENT; TRIAL.

(2) The person who pays alimony may deduct it from his income when computing his taxes, and the person who receives alimony must add it to his or her income. Child-support payments cannot be deducted from one's income and are not income to the parent who receives them. See INCOME TAX.

(3) The amounts of alimony and child support can be altered if circumstances change substantially, but property settlements cannot.

(4) The divorcing couple may settle alimony and property agreements between themselves, but the court always supervises child-support agreements.

(5) Alimony ends when the receiving spouse remarries; installment payments in a property settlement continue until the total is paid up; child support usually continues until the child reaches the age of majority.

(6) Alimony and child support generally terminate when either the person paying or the person receiving dies; property settlements can be enforced either by or against the estate of someone who has died.

(7) Alimony and child-support obligations continue despite BANKRUPTCY, but a property settlement may be discharged in bankruptcy.

Alimony, child support, and division of property should be considered together in assessing the fairness of an economic settlement between divorcing spouses. Depending on the circumstances of the case, one benefit may be compromised while another is increased.

Other economic factors A multitude of economic factors must be considered in addition to alimony, child support, and property settlement, including pension rights and taxes. A dependent wife may want to postpone the divorce for a few months when she learns that she can collect Social Security on her husband's account, even though divorced, if they were married at least 10 years. Both parties should know what pension rights they have, whether in their own right or derived through the spouse.

Tax consequences should be worked out in detail for various options. A man who thinks he cannot afford to pay child support on his salary may find that calling part of the payments alimony will change his tax liability enough to give the effect of a higher income. Or he can keep title to the marital home while his ex-wife and children live there, make payments on the mortgage, and deduct the interest on the mortgage from his tax bill. Such an arrangement is worth more to him than to his former wife if he is in the higher tax bracket. The parties can discuss who will take the children as dependents for tax-exemption purposes.

Responsibility for capital-gains taxes must be considered in connection with property settlements, depending on whether the divorce is in a separate- or a community-property state. Gift taxes are assessed when property is given by one spouse to the other during the marriage but not on divorce. For a discussion of gift taxes, see ESTATE AND GIFT TAX.

Two people do not know how much property and income is available when they divorce until they have explored options, considering especially the financial consequences of taxes. The wisest course is negotiation and compromise before a case comes before a court.

■ **Do-it-yourself kits** The law concerning divorce seems unnecessarily complicated to many people. In some states, do-it-yourself divorce kits sell for less than $100. But unless the marriage has been very short and there are no children and little property, people should be very careful in proceeding without a lawyer. An inexperienced person, distraught over the strains of a divorce, may mistakenly insist on one small point in a settlement without realizing the overall consequences of a provision that could disrupt his or her life for many years after the divorce.

docket A record book listing cases to be tried in a court; the schedule or calendar of cases that will appear before the court. *To docket* means to make a brief entry of any proceeding of a court in the docket.

document A paper containing information—such as a letter, map, photograph, will, deed, or record of account. An *ancient document* is a paper that the court assumes is genuine because it is over a certain age and has been produced from "lawful custody"—that is, from safekeeping in a place where it would logically be found. A deed to land that had been kept in a safe-deposit box for 40 years would be considered an ancient document. A *public document* is one that is, or should be, open to public inspection, such as a document issued by Congress.

documentary evidence Written information that can be offered during a trial to prove a fact. A telegram, for example, could be introduced as documentary EVIDENCE to show what quantity of goods had been ordered under a contract.

document of title A paper used by businessmen to show who is entitled to possession or ownership of goods. Bills of lading and WAREHOUSE RECEIPTS are documents of title. For more information on the law relating to documents of title, see the discussion of bills of lading under CARRIER.

doing business Carrying on business for profit within a particular state.

A company is *doing business* in a state if in that state it sells its product, has an office, signs contracts, owns and uses property, pays employees to represent it, or owns a subsidiary company. Sometimes an out-of-state company must obtain a license to do business in a state. The company need not be headquartered in the state or carry on most of its activities there.

If a company does business in a state, the laws of the state regulate the company's relations with its customers and other people. It is considered as being present in the state, with the result that the courts there have authority (jurisdiction) over the company and can insist that it appear in a lawsuit started against it. If the company is sued in the state, the court has authority to issue orders to the company or award a JUDGMENT against it. For more information about jurisdiction, see the discussion in COURTS.

domain The ownership and control of property. *In the public domain* means available to the public. National forests, for example, are in the public domain because the federal government owns and manages them for the good of the country. A book is in the public domain when the COPYRIGHT, which gives the author ownership and control for a period of years, has expired. Once books, articles, or movies are in the public domain, anyone may copy or distribute them for his own profit. EMINENT DOMAIN is the government's right to take private property when necessary, provided the government pays a fair price for it.

domicile A permanent home; legal home; main place of residence. A person's permanent domicile is different from his present residence in that the domicile is his actual home, whether or not he is currently living in it, while his residence can be temporary. If you live half the year in one house and half the year in another, the house that you treat as your permanent home is your legal domicile. The address that you use when you register to vote in political elections also establishes your legal domicile.

domiciliary Relating to a person's permanent home. For instance, the term *domiciliary administration* means the administration of a dead person's property in the state where he last had his permanent home.

dominant Having rights that prevail over those of others. For example, a person who owns a majority interest in a corporation would probably be the dominant party in a management dispute. A person owns a dominant parcel of land when he has some right to another's servient piece of property, such as the right to cross over the servient property to get to the street. See EASEMENT.

dominant cause The real source of an accident or other injury, regardless of when it occurred. See CAUSE; NEGLIGENCE; PROXIMATE CAUSE.

dominion Ownership or power. For example, a state has dominion over lands within its borders.

donative In the nature of a gift. A donative TRUST, for instance, is set up as a gift to another person.

donee 1 A person to whom a gift is given. 2 An individual to whom a POWER OF APPOINTMENT is given.

donor 1 A person making a gift to another. 2 An individual who gives a POWER OF APPOINTMENT to someone.

doom A word formerly used for a court's JUDGMENT. In modern usage, some criminal sentences still end with the words: ". . . which is pronounced for doom."

dormant Inactive; silent; concealed; sleeping. For example, a dormant partner has a financial interest in a business but takes no active role in it.

double indemnity A double INSURANCE payment that is made if an event happens in a specified way. For example, if a woman dies, the ordinary payment on her life insurance might be $10,000, but if her death is caused by an accident, the payment might be $20,000. In such cases, the double-indemnity payment is called an *accidental-death benefit*.

double insurance Duplicate coverage by different INSURANCE companies for the same purpose. When a husband buys medical insurance to cover himself and his wife, and she does likewise, the couple have double insurance. Although it is rarely possible to collect twice in such a situation (because most insurance contracts prohibit it), a couple often carry double insurance when one policy covers treatment or care that the other does not.

double jeopardy A second prosecution of a person for the same crime once the first prosecution has been completed and the defendant has been acquitted or convicted of the crime. Both the federal and state constitutions prohibit double jeopardy. See CRIMINAL LAW.

doubt Uncertainty. In law, the word is used in regard to proof offered in a trial. For instance, guilty beyond a reasonable doubt is the standard of proof required to convict an accused person of a crime. This is the highest standard of proof required in any kind of case, but it does not mean beyond all doubt. See EVIDENCE.

dower A widow's right to part of the property her husband owned during his lifetime; the interest a wife has in the estate of her deceased husband. Recognized very early in English common law, dower is a right still provided by a few states to insure the continuing welfare of a wife who survives her husband. Even if a husband leaves nothing to his wife in his WILL or dies without making a will, she is nonetheless entitled to some property as provided by state law. See also DESCENT AND DISTRIBUTION.

down payment Money that must be paid initially when an item is bought on CREDIT and the balance is to be paid later in installments. See CONSUMER PROTECTION.

draconian law Especially severe law. The term had its origin in a harsh code of laws prepared by Draco, the celebrated lawgiver of Athens in the seventh century B.C.

draft An order for the payment of money drawn by one person on another; a common term for a bill of exchange. Broadly speaking, the term "draft" includes a bank cashier's check. See COMMERCIAL PAPER.

draftsman In law, one who writes a legal document—a person who writes a contract, for example.

drainage district A drain is an artificial channel through which water flows. In the interest of the public welfare, a state may provide for the construction of drains for emptying swampy, marshy, and flooded areas. Many states have elaborate laws governing the reclamation of swamp, marsh, and flooded lands. Provision is usually made for the creation and organization of reclamation or drainage districts, which might include the territory of a village or a city or lands in two or more counties. Land that will be benefited by drainage improvements may be included within a district. For instance, the property of adjoining landowners who are outside the drainage district but have made connection with a ditch within the district may be added to that district.

Drainage districts have been held liable, in some cases, for a failure to maintain existing drains. To help alleviate this problem, landowners are sometimes allotted a certain portion of a drain to clean out and keep in good repair. Whether or not a landowner is responsible for maintenance, he may not close or obstruct a drain without the consent of his neighbors. As a matter of fact, if your land is harmed because your neighbor is obstructing a public drain, you can sue him for DAMAGES.

Within constitutional limitations, a state legislature can authorize drainage districts to impose special assessments to pay the cost of drainage improvements. Ordinarily, only the lands located within a drainage district are subject to assessment, and some states exempt school lands. Objections to drainage assessments are heard by review boards or by the courts. As a property owner, you can go to court to challenge what you think is an unjust assessment against your property. A court challenge to a drainage assessment can be a long and expensive undertaking, however, and a penalty can be imposed for nonpayment of a valid drainage assessment.

draw Prepare a legal document, such as a will or a deed to land; write out and sign a CHECK. See COMMERCIAL PAPER.

drawee The bank upon which a check is drawn and which is requested to pay the amount of it. Payment by the bank is called acceptance of the check. A drawee can also mean a bank that has a deposit withdrawn from it. See BANKS AND BANKING; COMMERCIAL PAPER.

drawer The person who writes out and signs a CHECK. See BANKS AND BANKING; COMMERCIAL PAPER.

Dred Scott decision The Supreme Court case, decided before the Civil War and prior to passage of the 14th Amendment to the U.S. Constitution. The Court held that (1) a Negro did not become free when taken into a free state; (2) a Negro born in the United States, even of free parents, was not a United States citizen; and (3) Congress had no right, under the Constitution, to make a Negro a United States citizen. After the Civil War, the Constitution was changed by the 14th Amendment to grant citizenship to Negroes. See CONSTITUTIONAL LAW.

druggist One whose business is to sell drugs and medicines. In strict usage, the term is distinguished from "apothecary" and "pharmacist." A druggist deals in uncompounded medical substances. The business of an apothecary and a pharmacist is to mix and compound them. Because the same persons usually do both, however, the two words are used interchangeably. A druggist is also the

name for someone who simply owns a drugstore. See DRUGS AND NARCOTICS.

drugs and narcotics This article discusses the manufacture, sale, and control of drugs, including narcotics, medicines, and devices used to treat disease or to affect any structure or function of the human body. It covers the duties of those authorized to handle drugs as well as criminal laws restricting drug use. For a discussion of alcoholic beverages, see INTOXICATING LIQUOR. See also POISON.

■ **Definitions** The law regulating *drugs* can cover medicines and articles, such as a hypodermic needle, that are used either in or on the body to treat disease or to affect some bodily function.

Narcotics are drugs that, when used in moderation, induce sleep, relieve pain, and blunt the senses, but when taken in larger doses, can produce stupor, coma, convulsions, or death. The word "narcotics," as it is used in statutes, is a legal, not a scientific, term. Some laws spell out specifically which drugs are meant by the word. Unless the law says otherwise, coca leaves, opium, cannabis, and anything chemically or physically like them are narcotics.

Medicines are drugs that can cure or relieve the symptoms of diseases. *Patent medicines* are made from someone's individual formula, put up in his original package, and sold bearing the name he has given the formula. Sometimes the process is the exclusive property of the owner, and it may be secret. Patent medicines, also called *proprietary medicines,* do not contain narcotics. They are not covered under the laws requiring that they be sold only by a licensed pharmacist.

A *prescription* is a written order for a drug. State law determines who may write a prescription. The practice of *pharmacy* involves compounding, dispensing, and retailing drugs, medicines, and poisons. One must be licensed by the state to practice pharmacy.

A *pharmacist* (or *apothecary*) is a licensed person who prepares and sells drugs and medicines. A druggist may be a pharmacist or someone who employs a pharmacist in his drugstore, if state law permits.

Courts have decided that some related activities do not amount to the practice of pharmacy and do not require a license—for example, preparing medicines or teas from a package of herbs or adding inorganic chemicals, such as fluoride, to a public water supply.

■ **State regulation of drugs** State legislatures have the authority to regulate the manufacture, sale, and dispensing of drugs through their general power to impose reasonable restrictions to protect the public welfare. Among other measures, a state may prohibit the dispensing of certain drugs without a prescription, prohibit traveling salesmen from selling drugs or patent medicines, and regulate manufacturers and wholesalers of medicines and medical devices. Most states have enacted pure drug acts that outlaw the sale of impure or improperly labeled drugs.

■ **The Food, Drug, and Cosmetic Act** The federal government, through the Food, Drug, and Cosmetic Act, controls drugs in interstate commerce. The basic purpose of the act is to protect public health by making sure that drugs are pure, safe, and effective when used as intended. The act also protects consumers from dangerous drugs,

DRUGS AND THEIR USE

■ Federal law regulates "articles intended for use in the diagnosis, cure, mitigation, treatment, or prevention of disease in man or other animals; and articles (other than food) intended to affect the structure or any function of the body of man or other animals." This extremely broad coverage brings under federal control a much wider variety of items than the medications we ordinarily think of as "drugs."

■ For example, not only are such things as herb tonics, cold sore salves, laxatives, and vitamin pills regulated under the law but also toothbrushes, phonograph records sold to treat insomnia, and just about anything else that can be sold for use in treating any medical or quasimedical problem you may have.

■ The states also have the authority to regulate the manufacture, sale, and dispensing of drugs. A state may, for example, prohibit the dispensing of certain drugs without a prescription, prohibit traveling salesmen from selling drugs or patent medicines, and outlaw the sale of impure or improperly labeled drugs.

■ Under the federal Food, Drug, and Cosmetic Act, consumers are protected from dangerous drugs, misleading labels, and fraud.

■ A drug or device is misbranded if its label does not accurately describe the product in standard terms or if it does not provide adequate directions for use and warnings against uses that can be dangerous. Labeling includes all printed matter related to the sale of the product, such as a reprint of an article enclosed in the package and instructions pasted on a treatment machine. Anyone who does not read the label is said to have assumed the risk of being harmed.

■ Drugs sold only on a doctor's prescription do not have to be labeled with all the information usually required. But prescription drugs dispensed in the manufacturer's package rather than the pharmacist's bottle must be fully labeled.

■ Drugs sold in the manufacturer's package must have the drug's generic name (its chemical name) on every label in letters at least half as big as the manufacturer's name for the drug.

■ Some states let consumers buy generic prescription drugs, which are cheaper, unless the doctor insists on a brand name.

■ States can prohibit the sale of certain drugs without a prescription and can mandate procedures for handling drugs and keeping pharmacy records.

■ Generally, it is not illegal for a pharmacist to fill a prescription when a doctor gives him instructions by phone, even though the doctor fails to send a written authorization later.

■ A pharmacist is not obligated to fill every prescription, but if he refuses to fill a prescription, he generally must return it to the customer. A pharmacist is liable for his own negligence and that of his employees, but generally he cannot be held responsible for injuries caused by patent medicines sold in their original packages.

■ The law attempts to strictly control the sale and use of opiates, barbiturates, stimulants, hallucinogens, and marijuana. The nonmedicinal use of these controlled substances is generally prohibited by law because their abuse can be dangerous to the user and a threat to the community. Misuse of these drugs can lead to injury or death, and their continued use might lead to addiction, which—in turn—can lead the addict to resort to any means, including criminal ones, to obtain the drugs his body needs.

■ The simplest drug crime is possession of a controlled substance.

■ *Possession with intent* to sell is a more serious crime than simple possession. In some states, a jury may presume that quantities of a drug greater than a certain amount would not be in the defendant's possession unless he intended to sell.

■ Almost all states make the sale of illegal drugs to a child a degree worse than a sale to an adult.

■ Some states have tried to outlaw drug *paraphernalia*—the equipment or accessories associated with drug use, such as hypodermic needles and hashish pipes.

■ In some states, drug addicts may avoid prosecution or imprisonment by qualifying for one of the following alternatives: probation, parole, diversion, or civil commitment. (*Diversion* is being assigned to a long-term rehabilitation program instead of being put on trial. *Civil commitment* is being placed in a locked treatment center.)

---

misleading labels, and fraud. This exercise of federal authority does not affect the power of each state to control drugs within its own territory, provided its laws are consistent with federal law.

The Food, Drug, and Cosmetic Act includes in the term "drugs" a wide variety of products that are promoted for use in treating the physical problems of humans and animals. Courts will look at printed matter distributed either with a drug item or separately to see if it promotes the product for therapeutic use. Labels, advertising, and broadcast commercials are all considered. The following items have been held to be drugs subject to regulation by the Food, Drug, and Cosmetic Act: herb tonics, cold sore salves, laxatives, weight-reducing cigarettes containing tartaric acid, suppositories, minerals used to treat bloated cattle and sheep, and vitamins.

Donated blood has been considered a drug, and sometimes honey is considered a drug when it is advertised as a panacea for various ailments. The fact that a product is labeled "nutritional" rather than "medicinal" does not guarantee that it will not be considered a drug.

Cosmetics are covered by special sections of the Food, Drug, and Cosmetic Act, but a product can be covered by either the drug sections or the cosmetic sections or both, depending on its nature. The drug provisions are more stringent than the cosmetic because they apply to products that are intended to produce actual changes in the body. Because cosmetics are usually meant simply to help make people look better, the law intends only to prevent dangerous or harmful products from being sold as cosmetics. Manufacturers need not prove that their cosmetic products are effective in any dramatic way.

Devices also can be considered drugs when they are intended to diagnose, treat, cure, or prevent disease. A variety of devices have been so classified: toothbrushes; machines to treat eye disease; phonograph records sold to treat insomnia; manuals of facial exercises; galvanometers, which treat ailments with ultrasound; and surgical pins, which frequently remain in the patient's body for months.

Adulteration The federal Food, Drug, and Cosmetic Act prohibits the movement across state lines of drugs that are adulterated. A drug that is listed in the *United States Pharmacopoeia* or some other standardized book describing drugs and medical preparations but does not fit the description given is considered adulterated. If the drug differs from the standard strength, quality, or purity described in an official pharmacopoeia, it is considered adulterated. This rule also applies to devices listed in pharmacopoeias.

A cosmetic is adulterated if it contains a poison or any substance that causes injury, even when the product is used in the normal way or as directed. Any drug or device that is not manufactured according to current good practices is assumed to be adulterated. This rule requires manufacturers to keep their premises sanitary and to keep records showing all the details of their manufacturing process.

Misbranding The act also bans misbranded drugs, devices, and cosmetics. An article is misbranded if its label does not accurately describe the product in recognized standard terms, or if the article has no label. The purpose of this provision is to protect a consumer from false or misleading labels and from the risk of confusing different products. Regulations prescribe how a product must be identified—on the label, container, or package liner—and in some cases require that specific warnings be included. For example, it may be necessary to date products that deteriorate rapidly or to print a warning on items that can be habit-forming.

Misbranding provisions prohibit false or misleading labeling and require special treatment of prescription drugs. Labeling includes all printed matter that relates to the sale of the product—such as reprints of a scientific article enclosed in the package, instructions pasted on a treatment machine, and leaflets handed out by a religious group making medical claims for its health products.

A drug or device is misbranded if its label does not provide adequate directions for use and warnings against uses that can be dangerous. Directions should state the purposes, conditions, or diseases for which the drug is intended, the recommended dosage, and how often, when, and how the drug should be taken. The directions must make it possible for the consumer to take the drug safely by himself. It is illegal to print minimal instructions on a bottle and expect the druggist to tell the consumer everything else he needs to know.

Drugs and devices that can be used only by licensed physicians must also be properly labeled, but the label does not have to be clear to the average consumer. If the drug can be used safely only under a physician's supervision, the product must contain a warning stating that fact. Free samples from drug companies that physicians can give away to patients must be labeled as not for sale.

Misbranding provisions prohibit not only false claims but also ambiguities that can mislead the public. The label must not only not lie; it must tell the truth. A fine-print disclaimer that an item "contains no known therapeutic ingredients" does not overcome the effect of exaggerated claims all over the package and on the store display.

Drugs are mislabeled if the strength or quality is less than that stated on the label. Whether a product is effective at all is a question of fact, which, if challenged, must be proved by evidence at a trial. A wide variety of products have been taken off the market because they could not live up to the claims made for them—diet candy, vitamin capsules, electric stimulators, and laxatives are examples.

Prescription drugs Certain categories of drugs are required by law to be dispensed only on the prescription of a licensed physician. If any of these drugs are not labeled with a statement that federal law prohibits dispensing them without a prescription, they are misbranded and penalties can be imposed.

Prescriptions have several purposes. They protect the public from uncontrolled use of dangerous drugs, relieve retail pharmacists and the public of unnecessary restrictions on drugs by having a physician supervise their use, and (when renewals are limited or prohibited) encourage users to check back with a doctor.

Drugs sold only on prescription do not have to be labeled with all the information normally required on drugs. This applies only when they are dispensed to a consumer. However, they must still be properly labeled by a manufacturer for the physician or pharmacist who may handle them. Prescription drugs dispensed in a manufacturer's package rather than a bottle supplied by the pharmacist must be fully labeled.

Generic-name drugs The established chemical name of a drug, the *generic name,* must be printed on every label in letters at least half as large as the manufacturer's name for the drug. This is intended to alert doctors and patients to the fact that drugs sold under their generic names are actually identical to those sold by brand names. Some states are beginning to require that consumers be given the opportunity to buy generic prescription drugs, because they usually cost much less than brand-name prescription drugs. No federal law prevents a company from giving its own brand name to a generic drug that it develops.

New drugs New drugs cannot be put on the market until they have been approved under the provisions of the Food, Drug, and Cosmetic Act. A *new drug* is any that is not already "generally recognized as safe" among experts who are qualified by training and experience to evaluate drugs. Drugs that have been "generally recognized as safe" are designated GRAS by the FOOD AND DRUG ADMINISTRATION.

In determining whether a new drug should be approved as safe and effective, the Commissioner of Food and Drugs may question whether the drug has any toxic effect on the body, whether it is effective, and how carefully the manufacturing process is controlled. A drug that is already generally recognized as safe may need new approval when it is marketed for new uses. A new combination drug must be approved even though each of its ingredients is generally recognized as safe.

The Food and Drug Administration will refuse to approve any new drug that is not proved safe and effective by substantial evidence submitted by the manufacturer. The agency also has an obligation to withdraw approval if it later finds the drug to be unsafe or ineffective.

A special provision in the Food, Drug, and Cosmetic Act, called a GRANDFATHER CLAUSE, says that the manufacturer of any drug commonly sold before the law was passed does not have to demonstrate its *effectiveness* as long as the drug is marketed for use exactly as the label intended. These drugs are all entitled to be called GRAS.

New drugs used by qualified experts for testing and scientific investigation do not have to be approved.

Most people who manufacture, prepare, or process drugs must be registered under the Food, Drug, and Cosmetic Act. Federal drug-abuse laws also require a special registration for anyone who handles "controlled substances," which are discussed later in this article.

■ **Authority to prepare and dispense drugs** States have authority to regulate the preparation and dispensing of drugs as a public health measure. They can prohibit the sale of certain drugs without a prescription, specify who may deal in prescription drugs, and require all drugstores to be registered. Statutes may establish procedures for handling drugs and provide for inspection of drugstores and pharmacy records by state officials. They may also ban any kind of improper competition that tends to lower the standards of service. They may, for example, prohibit advertising of drug prices or names.

Pharmacists Only a pharmacist may dispense prescription drugs, and in some states, the person in charge of a drugstore must be a pharmacist. States may and do require pharmacists to be licensed, but the qualifications may not be unreasonable. For example, a state may require pharmacists to be college graduates, but it may not require them to be native-born American citizens. Generally, a pharmacist must be a graduate of an accredited school and be of good moral character. He may have to pass a written examination. Someone who meets all the qualifications cannot ordinarily be denied a license.

A pharmacist licensed in state A has no authority to dispense drugs in state B unless state B agrees to recognize the license issued by state A. A license may have to be renewed periodically. It can be revoked or suspended for misconduct—the sale of even a single unlabeled drug, the substitution of cheaper drugs, or a sale to someone who does not have a valid prescription. Any decision by a state board to grant, revoke, or suspend a pharmacy license may be reviewed in court.

It is not necessary for a pharmacist to know everything about drugs, but he must be as skilled as most members of his profession in his area. He owes his customers a high degree of care in his service to them. They are entitled to assume that the drugs he sells are suitable to use for the purpose the pharmacist recommends, and they may rely on any specific claims he makes for the drugs.

Pharmacy laws generally do not interfere with a physician's right to sell drugs to his patients. However, a physician cannot make a practice of filling prescriptions sent to him by other doctors.

Pharmacists must keep written records of the drugs they sell and must permit the proper officials to inspect these records. Generally, it is not illegal for a pharmacist to fill a prescription on the authority of a doctor who telephones, even though the doctor fails to send a written authorization later. The pharmacist, however, must make a written record at the time he fills the prescription.

A pharmacist has no obligation to fill every prescription presented to him. In fact, he may not fill a prescription that looks like a fake. If a pharmacist refuses to fill a prescription, he must give it back to the customer.

Liability for injuries A licensed pharmacist is liable for his own negligence and that of his employees. A consumer may sue a pharmacist or the druggist who employs him if the consumer is injured because either failed to meet his legal responsibilities. Generally, however, a druggist or pharmacist cannot be held responsible for injuries caused by patent medicines he sells in their original packages.

Government agencies have been held liable to individuals injured by drugs distributed by the government. For example, a husband and wife recovered damages from the United States when the wife contracted polio from an improperly tested vaccine. If a drug administered to military personnel is later found to cause injury, the government is responsible for notifying all those involved.

Consumers can sue manufacturers or wholesalers of drugs that are unsanitary, mislabeled, or not marked with appropriate warnings. In some states, the rule of strict liability has been applied to drug manufacturers. See PRODUCT LIABILITY. A manufacturer has an obligation to the public to test a drug extensively and to alert the consumer to any dangers connected with it. A manufacturer is not, however, liable for unusual reactions in very sensitive people.

A court can order money DAMAGES damages to compensate a consumer injured by a drug manufacturer's negligence, and it can also prohibit further sales of a dangerous product. If a stock of misbranded or dangerous drugs remains in the hands of a manufacturer or druggist, the supply can be seized or condemned. Manufacturers and pharmacists can also be punished under various federal and state criminal statutes.

The label on a patent medicine or prescription drug is supposed to give a consumer all the information he needs to take the drug safely. Anyone who does not read the label is said to have assumed the risk of being harmed. He cannot blame the manufacturer or pharmacist if he uses a drug improperly and is injured. He is said to be contributorily negligent. See CONTRIBUTORY NEGLIGENCE.

■ **Drug abuse** The federal government and the states control the manufacture and sale of most drugs because of the hazards to the public if they are handled carelessly. Some drugs are considered so dangerous that they are either illegal or very strictly controlled. Federal law defines drugs as

❝Articles intended for use in the diagnosis, cure, mitigation, treatment, or prevention of disease in man or other animals; and . . . articles (other than food) intended to affect the structure or any function of the body of man or other animals. . . .❞

Drug abuse means using drugs in a way that is not approved by society. As social acceptance of certain ways of using drugs changes, there is pressure to change laws until they conform with the way most people feel about drugs. Alcohol is a drug that is an ingredient in numerous medicines as well as in beverages. Social disapproval of drinking in this country was once so widespread that a constitutional amendment prohibiting the sale of alcohol was passed. When enough voters became convinced either that the evils of drinking had been exaggerated or that prohibition was a poor way to control it, another amendment was passed repealing the earlier one. As in all areas of law, society's values are eventually reflected in statutes.

The question of what is a drug also varies according to public opinion. Most people agree that heroin, amphetamines, and barbiturates are drugs. Fewer people recognize the druglike effects of alcohol and tobacco. The fact is that substances are drugs because they act according to certain general principles. Their effects are different for different doses. For each drug there is an *effective dose* that produces the desired effect, a *toxic dose* that harms the body, and a *lethal dose* that kills. Almost every drug is dangerous for some people, even in small doses, and all can be dangerous when taken in large doses.

Despite these principles, no state has a set of drug laws based on the policy of treating all drugs as drugs. Instead, laws reflect prevailing notions of what constitutes abuse. Generally, laws forbid the use of drugs (other than tobacco or alcohol) for recreational or nonmedical purposes, and they classify the drugs into various groups.

Classifying drugs The classification of drugs is no easy task. A drug can be identified by its source or by its chemistry. Morphine, for example, is both an opiate, because it comes from the opium poppy, and an alkaloid, because of its chemical structure.

Another way to classify drugs is by their effect on the body. Morphine, by this system, is a narcotic, or sedative; an analgesic, which relieves pain; an antitussive, which suppresses coughs; an emetic, which induces vomiting; and more. It would be misleading to identify a drug by only one of its functions. Doctors prescribe a drug for an intended effect, knowing that there may also be side effects. Also, what may be a side effect for one person is the intended effect for another.

Drug laws vary tremendously from state to state. A drug-related crime that might result in a one-year suspended sentence in one state could bring life imprisonment somewhere else. Moreover, some items have mild, druglike qualities but are so commonly used that the law classifies them as food—for example, coffee, tea, cocoa, and cola drinks. The druglike effect of nicotine is clear to anyone who has ever tried to quit smoking. Yet the law omits tobacco from the drug laws. Alcohol is regulated somewhat more than tobacco, but it is not treated as an illegal drug. For more about the legal control of alcoholic beverages, see INTOXICATING LIQUOR; PROHIBITION.

Controlled substances The law attempts to control very strictly the sale and use of opiates, barbiturates, stimulants, hallucinogens, and marijuana.

Opiates Opium is a natural substance that comes from the opium poppy. It contains more than 20 different alkaloids, which together make up about 25 percent of its weight. Morphine is one of these alkaloids. So is codeine, which is milder than morphine and especially useful as a cough suppressant. Heroin is made from morphine and has a similar effect except that its pain-relieving effect is about three times greater than that of morphine.

Methadone is a synthetic opiate, manufactured in the laboratory, of about the same strength as morphine. The synthetic meperidine is about 10 to 20 percent as strong as morphine—most people know it by its trade name, Demerol.

Barbiturates and other tranquilizers Tranquilizers are used to depress the central nervous system. Among the drugs that most frequently cause harm are *barbiturates* (derivatives of barbituric acid), *methaqualone* (Quaalude), and *meprobamate* (Equanil, Miltown), *glutethimide* (Doriden), *chlordiazepoxide* (Librium), and *diazepam* (Valium)—drugs from different chemical families, prescribed to relieve anxiety. More than 2,500 kinds of barbiturates have been compounded in laboratories, at least 12 of which are commonly used, including secobarbital (Seconal) and pentobarbital. A number of other "sleeping pills" and tranquilizers that are not barbiturates are also used to treat mental disturbances. Barbiturates and other depressants are important medical drugs, but they have a dangerous potential for abuse. Large quantities of barbiturates are deadly.

Stimulants Stimulants arouse physical and mental activity in the user. They include (1) *amphetamines* (Benzedrine, or "speed")—synthetic drugs that stimulate the central nervous system; (2) *methamphetamines*—drugs closely related to amphetamines; (3) *phenmetrazine*—almost indistinguishable from amphetamines in effect; (4) *cocaine*—an alkaloid made from the coca plant, which, after an initial stimulation, has a narcotic effect; and (5) *methylphenidate* (Ritalin)—a mild stimulant.

Amphetamines Doctors use amphetamines to treat narcolepsy, a rare disease that makes it impossible to stay awake; to control hyperkinetic children who have trouble concentrating, developing motor skills, or dealing with frustration; and to suppress the appetite of overweight patients, although the results here have not been impressive. Many people buy amphetamines illegally when they need extra energy—students, athletes, and long-distance truck drivers, for example. Some who have become dependent on amphetamines need them just to bring their functioning back up to normal.

Cocaine South American Indians have been chewing on coca leaves for the effect of the cocaine in them since time immemorial. The Incas considered it a divine drug. When the Spaniards arrived, they were amazed at the endurance of Andean Indians in their harsh mountain environment. The Indians were able to undertake prolonged and difficult marches with little but coca leaves to sustain them.

Cocaine, the alkaloid that is the chief active ingredient in coca leaves, was first isolated in 1844. In 1883 a German army physician reported that it improved the ability of soldiers to endure fatigue. Soon various researchers began to publish warnings, and one scientist attacked cocaine as addictive.

Hallucinogens Hallucinogens distort perception. They produce visual delusions, but not classic hallucinations in which users see things that are not there. The best-known hallucinogen is LSD (lysergic acid diethylamide), or "acid," a synthetic drug discovered in 1938. Hallucinogens appear naturally as *mescaline*, an alkaloid of the peyote cactus, and *psilocybin* and *psilocin*, which are active alkaloids of a Mexican mushroom.

Phencyclidine, or PCP, is the notorious "angel dust." It was developed as an anesthetic to be used during surgery but was later made illegal because of its unpleasant side effects. Illegal PCP is often mixed with other drugs, such as LSD and marijuana, and a user may buy it without knowing. The drug gives the user a feeling of apathy, emptiness, and depersonalization; it causes distorted vision and sometimes hallucinations.

Marijuana A kind of hemp plant, marijuana is a tall weed that grows wild all over the world. The most potent plants grow in hot, dry climates. The dried leaves and stems can be chopped up, rolled into cigarettes, and smoked for a mild intoxicating effect. The chemical name for marijuana is *cannabis sativa. Hashish* is a pure resin scraped from the flowering tops of the female marijuana plant. It produces a stronger intoxicating effect than marijuana. It is smoked in a pipe, chewed, or made into a drink.

Drug addiction The nonmedicinal use of the controlled drugs discussed above is generally prohibited by law because their abuse can be a danger to the user and a threat to the community. Misuse of these drugs can result in injury or death, and the continued use of some of them can lead to addiction. An addict, in turn, may resort to any means—even criminal ones—to obtain the drugs his body needs, and therefore constitutes a threat to his community.

The World Health Organization of the United Nations defines drug addiction as

&& *a state of periodic or chronic intoxication detrimental to the individual and to society, produced by the repeated consumption of a drug (natural or synthetic). Its characteristics include: (A) an overpowering desire or need (compulsion) to continue taking the drug and to obtain it by any means; (B) a tendency to increase the dose; (C) a psychic (psychological) and sometimes a physical dependence on the effects of the drug."*

Legal control of dangerous drugs To control drugs, the law classifies them in groups. Forty-eight states began regulating dangerous drugs by adopting the Uniform Narcotic Drug Act (first proposed in 1932), which made illegal the possession or sale of any drug classified as narcotic. The act originally said that narcotic included "coca leaves, opium, and every other substance neither chemically nor physically distinguishable from them; and any other drugs the importation, exportation, or possession of which is prohibited, regulated, or limited under the Federal Narcotics Law." In 1942 the act was amended to include cannabis, and most states adopted the amendment.

In the 1970's all but a few states repealed laws based on the Uniform Narcotic Drug Act and instead enacted laws based on the Uniform Controlled Substances Act of 1970. This law classifies drugs by placing each of them on one of five schedules and prescribing controls and penalties for each schedule.

Heroin, hallucinogens, and marijuana were placed on Schedule I because they were believed to have a high potential for harm and no real medical use. Other opiates and cocaine were put on Schedule II. Most depressants and stimulants were placed on Schedule III, but some, such as secobarbital and amphetamine, were later shifted to Schedule II when their high potential for abuse became clear. Some of the mild tranquilizers were placed on Schedule IV,

and Schedule V was reserved for such drugs as cough syrup mixtures that contain codeine. Schedule V drugs are considered medically useful and not as dangerous as the drugs on the other schedules, but they can cause limited physical or psychological dependence.

Penalties are highest for narcotic drugs on Schedules I and II—that is, opium, coca leaves, opiates, and compounds that are chemically indistinguishable from them. A person convicted of making or selling one of these can get 15 years in prison and a $25,000 fine (or 30 years and $50,000 for a second conviction). Nonnarcotics on Schedule I or II and drugs on Schedule III can merit sentences of 5 years and fines of $15,000 (or 10 years and $30,000 the second time). Simple possession of *any* controlled substance is good for a sentence of one year and a fine of $5,000. The penalty can be doubled if the offender has been convicted before.

The U.S. Attorney General has the authority to consult with the Secretary of Health, Education, and Welfare to make changes in the drug categories.

Constitutional restraints on drug laws There are constitutional limits to the ways drugs may be controlled by law. One limitation arises out of the First Amendment right to freedom of religion. The Supreme Court of California found that this right prevented the state from prosecuting Indians who, according to a long-established tradition, used peyote during their religious ceremonies. But the First Amendment does not protect "religions" concocted to dodge the law. People who wanted to use marijuana in services of the Universal Life Church of Christ Light were held to be outside that protection because their real purpose was to avoid criminal penalties.

The constitutional right of privacy also sets limits to how much the state can interfere in an individual's life. In 1975 the Alaska Supreme Court held that citizens in that state have a constitutional right to use marijuana in the privacy of their homes. The court's decision was based on protections in the federal and state constitutions. Other states—even those, such as California and Hawaii, that specifically recognize a right to privacy in their state constitutions—have steadfastly refused to follow Alaska's lead.

The Supreme Court of the United States has said that any criminal law that attempts to punish someone simply for being an addict is unconstitutional. Criminal laws may only forbid doing certain acts. Thus it is unconstitutional to sentence someone for his *status as an addict,* but it is not illegal to convict an addict for the criminal act of possession. Possession laws may have the effect of causing an addict to seek treatment, and they help law-enforcement officials to control illegal traffic in drugs.

A sentence may be so severe that it violates the constitutional provision against CRUEL AND UNUSUAL PUNISHMENT.

EXAMPLE In 1972 the Supreme Court of Michigan found 0⊷* unconstitutional a law that required a minimum 20-year sentence for anyone convicted of selling marijuana. In this case, a 23-year-old man who lived with his parents and was employed full time at General Motors was sentenced to 20 to 21 years under the statute. The court noted that no minimum sentence was prescribed for someone convicted of second-degree murder, kidnapping, or rape. The court found that minimum sentence so excessive that it "shocks the conscience."

A number of other constitutional questions arise during trials on drug charges. Defendants generally try to show that they are put in DOUBLE JEOPARDY if both the federal government and the state try them. If they are charged with selling drugs to an undercover agent, they often try to prove that they are victims of ENTRAPMENT. Frequently, they try to show that the drugs have been discovered by an illegal SEARCH AND SEIZURE. Several judges, however, have ruled that dogs who sniff out drugs are not part of an illegal search.

Drug crimes Possession and sale of drugs are major areas of drug crime.

Possession The simplest drug crime is possession of a controlled substance. In order to convict, a prosecutor must show that the accused did more than just touch the drug. One conviction was reversed when the defendant said that he had touched the heroin only long enough to throw it away. He had found it in a friend's pocket before taking him for emergency medical treatment.

Sometimes it is difficult to determine who has possession. Generally, police arrest everyone present in a room or automobile if illegal drugs are in plain sight. Decisions depend somewhat on the circumstances of each case.

EXAMPLE Ten people at a party where a large quantity of marijuana is being smoked would probably all be convicted of possession. A court would presume that anyone who disapproved of the drug could have walked out. On the other hand, a woman who could prove she never used drugs probably would not be convicted if she was in the car with her husband when he was arrested for having a packet of heroin on the seat beside him. It is not reasonable for the law to say that a husband and wife should not be in a room or car together unless both of them intend to possess a drug.

A person arrested for possession of drugs may defend himself by showing that he had *no knowledge* of the drug or *intent* to possess it. A hitchhiker, for example, is not guilty of possession if he did not know that there were four bags of marijuana in the trunk of a car he was riding in. But it is no defense that the defendant had illegal phenobarbital when he thought he had illegal secobarbital, or that he had mescaline when he thought he had LSD. It also is no defense to avoid knowledge deliberately.

EXAMPLE A Los Angeles man who accepted $100 from a stranger in Tijuana, Mexico, to drive a car across the U.S. border was convicted of possessing 110 pounds of marijuana hidden between the rear seat and the trunk. The court could not believe that he had no knowledge. "Knowledge," the court said, "includes a mental state where the defendant knows that a fact is highly probable and he consciously avoids learning the truth."

Possession convictions may also depend on the amount of the drug involved. Some courts require more than a trace of the illegal drug. A little crust on a heroin spoon (a spoon used to hold the drug while it is being cooked over a flame) or the residue scraped from a marijuana pipe may not support a conviction unless there is a "usable amount."

The way in which the amount of a drug is measured depends on the law in each case. Some states measure the entire weight of whatever is seized. This is called the *aggregate weight*. For example, a drug pusher often buys one ounce of heroin and turns it into two ounces by "cutting," or diluting, it. Even though diluted by half, the aggregate weight is still two ounces. *Pure weight* is the total amount of the drug alone, excluding anything mixed with it. A pure-weight law is highly unsatisfactory from a law-enforcement point of view. If a quarter-ounce of marijuana is baked into a pan of brownies, a chemist may be able to pick out all the marijuana bits, but when he weighs them, his measurement might be no more meaningful than an aggregate weight. Will the marijuana weigh more because it has absorbed moisture from the brownies? Should this be subtracted? How much? Is it possible that the cocoa and flour have absorbed some of the chemicals from the marijuana? Should that be subtracted from the weight of the marijuana? How much? It is of little help to suggest that only the THC, the chief psychoactive ingredient in marijuana, be weighed. THC is difficult and expensive to isolate.

An obvious solution is to forget amount in drug offenses and to make possession of a controlled substance illegal in any amount. But making penalties based on amount was a response to public sentiment that if a small amount of the drug can do harm, a large amount can do more harm to more people. The community wanted sellers punished more harshly than users.

Sale Possession with intent to sell is usually a more serious crime than simple possession. A court or jury may find that the defendant intended to sell because of what he did or said to possible customers. In some states a jury may presume that quantities greater than a certain amount would not be in the defendant's possession unless he intended to sell—he can defend himself only by giving a satisfactory explanation for having a large amount of the drug. In other states possession of huge amounts may be in itself a serious crime.

Depending on the law concerned, *selling* may include distributing a controlled substance in any of a variety of ways without a lawful prescription. It may not be necessary for money to change hands. The federal law prohibits distribution or delivery by anyone except an authorized person. The 1973 New York drug law says that "sell" means "to sell, exchange, give or dispose of to another, or to offer or agree to do the same." Under that law, every person sitting on the floor in a circle "sells" when he passes a hash pipe to the person next to him.

Many parents are frightened by the possibility that drugs may fall into the hands of young people who often lack the good judgment not to use them. Almost all states make the sale of illegal drugs to a minor a degree worse than the same offense would be otherwise—for example, from criminal sale in the third degree to criminal sale in the second degree. "Minors" usually means those under 21, but sometimes it means persons under 18. Sometimes selling to minors is criminal only if the seller is more than a certain number of years older than the buyer. In such a case, a 14-year-old who sold drugs to another 14-year-old would not be guilty of selling to a minor, although he might be guilty of a simple sale of narcotics.

Another selling offense is concerned with convicting big-time drug dealers. The federal act provides penalties of 25 years to life imprisonment for anyone who "engages in a continuing criminal enterprise."

A fairly frequent problem in enforcing criminal drug-sale laws occurs when there is a mistake about the kind of drug sold. An undercover police officer may negotiate a purchase of thousands of dollars worth of heroin or cocaine, only to learn from the police lab that he has purchased crushed aspirin. If the seller believed that he was selling an illegal drug, he can still be convicted of an attempted sale. If he knew what he was selling was not an illegal drug and was just deceiving the undercover agent, he probably cannot be convicted, even for the attempt to sell. This situation is called a *counterfeit sale,* and some states have solved the problem by making counterfeit sales a separate crime.

Lesser included offenses   Another illegal sale problem is how much to prosecute. A person cannot be convicted of both possessing with intent to sell and selling the same batch of drugs. Possession is a *lesser included offense* in sale. This means that the larger crime of sale includes the lesser crime of possession.

Sometimes a person can be convicted of more than one crime for the same act. In deciding whether the defendant can be convicted of the different crimes, courts may look at the purpose of each law.

EXAMPLE   A man was convicted of selling a drug without a
O⊷—⊷ lawful prescription and of selling the same drug
not in its original package. The court found that Congress had enacted these two laws in order to control different problems, and that each of them should be enforced separately. Consequently the man was found guilty of two crimes for making a single sale.

Other crimes   A variety of laws in addition to those concerned with possession and sale have been enacted to control dangerous drugs. State and federal laws punish such actions as illegally importing drugs into the country, transporting drugs, distributing drugs on a forged prescription, and unprofessional conduct by a doctor in prescribing drugs. These laws are intended to catch those people contributing to the national drug problem who might otherwise slip through the enforcement net. Sometimes the person who is the target of an investigation has committed the crimes of possession or sale, but the prosecutor cannot make a good case. Then it may be effective to convict for one of his other roles in the distribution of drugs.

Paraphernalia laws   Some states have tried to control drug abuse by outlawing not only the drugs but also the *paraphernalia*—equipment or accessories—associated with their use. Law-enforcement officials were often frustrated to find paraphernalia in a drug user's possession but no drugs. No arrest could be made for possession of a drug that had already been used because the Supreme Court had said that this type of arrest punished a person for *being* a drug user, rather than for *doing* something illegal. To make an arrest possible in a situation where the police were sure there had been illegal drugs, some states made possession of paraphernalia illegal.

Because criminal laws must be very specific, the paraphernalia statutes often list the illegal items—hypodermic needles, cigarette papers, hash pipes, coke spoons, glassine envelopes, and so on. Enforcement of paraphernalia laws has been difficult, however. For one thing, most of these items could have a nondrug use, and secondly, users can often find a substitute for any item on an illegal paraphernalia list. A number of these laws have been declared unconstitutional.

Even so, many people believe that paraphernalia laws are useful. When everything except the drugs themselves can be sold openly, specialized stores—"head shops"—appear. Many parents believe they glamorize drug use and pander to young people.

One drug rehabilitation agency in New York sent four children through the city to see whether they could buy drug paraphernalia. Although they were obviously underage, the children returned with imitation marijuana cigarettes, a child-sized cocaine cutting kit, pipes, and inhalants with intoxicating butyl nitrate and nitrous oxide.

Alternatives to criminal laws   The control of dangerous drugs through the criminal law process has not been entirely satisfactory. Alternatives have been tried with varying degrees of success.

Dispensing drugs to addicts   In England it is possible for heroin addicts to obtain the drug at clinics from authorized physicians, and smuggling and trafficking in drugs are subject to stiff penalties. It has been suggested that the same system be tried in the United States, but the American drug problem is quite different from the British. For one thing, the British narcotics problem involves very small numbers of addicts compared to the numbers concentrated in some cities in the United States.

This country's equivalent of the British system has been *methadone maintenance centers.* Heroin addicts are given methadone, the same class of drug as heroin, which cuts off their craving for heroin but does not give them a high. This enables an addict to hold a job and take care of his family in spite of his habit. He usually goes to his treatment center at least twice a week and takes his dose of methadone in a glass of orange juice.

Methadone has been criticized because it simply substitutes one drug for another. It does not end an already established drug habit. Efforts to taper off the amount until an addict is weaned have generally been unsuccessful. Furthermore, larger doses of methadone can get a person high, so an illegal market has developed.

On the other hand, methadone maintenance programs have brought tens of thousands of addicts into contact with treatment personnel. Although only small numbers have actually stopped using drugs, large numbers have stayed out of jail and out of the hard-drug scene. Methadone has helped them reenter the mainstream of society.

Therapeutic communities   Another way of treating addicts is in the therapeutic community. The first voluntary center was Synanon House, founded in California in 1958, where former addicts helped persons dependent on drugs to give them up. Other group homes followed the Synanon model. As time went on, each developed its own variations. Daytop Village was established as a halfway house for drug offenders on probation. Odyssey House added psychiatrists to their staff of former addicts.

Most of the therapeutic community houses eventually gave up the idea of "curing" addicts. People who responded well to the pressure and support of the community usually went back on hard drugs when they left. Nevertheless, therapeutic communities have helped some addicts.

A choice other than prison In some states drug addicts who come to the attention of law-enforcement officials may avoid prosecution or imprisonment by following one of several alternatives. These alternatives include diversion, civil commitment, probation, and parole.

Diversion is a system that "diverts" a defendant away from the criminal-justice system after charges have been brought against him. In many states an accused person may ask the court to consider assigning him to a drug treatment or rehabilitation program instead of putting him on trial. Diversion has the advantage of avoiding the risk of conviction and a criminal record, but the defendant is often supervised for a much longer period of time than if he had been sentenced.

State diversion programs for drug addicts usually follow the same pattern. Only those who meet the state's requirements are accepted. They may be disqualified if they have prior convictions, have already participated in a treatment program, or are poorly motivated. Some states require consent from the prosecutor. Supervision may include regular professional counseling and treatment in a drug program. Generally, if the defendant completes treatment and is not arrested for any other reason, charges are dropped after the prescribed period of time.

Civil commitment is a system of putting addicts into a treatment center they cannot leave. In some states addicts may volunteer for civil commitment in order to get treatment. In others, a judge may commit a convicted addict instead of assigning him to a prison. The advantage of civil commitment is that the addict can no longer cause trouble to society, use drugs, or associate with drug-using friends.
EXAMPLE In a famous case in 1966, the Supreme Court of
0⊷—∗ California found that evidence showed that comedian Lenny Bruce had possessed heroin but that did not prove he was an addict. The court said that the state had no right to order civil commitment of anyone who was not already an addict or about to become one. Bruce was released, but died within months from an overdose.

Probation is a sentence given after conviction, usually for a minor crime, that permits the defendant to stay out of jail as long as he remains on good behavior for the duration of the sentence. *Parole* is the same privilege given to someone who has been serving his sentence in prison. The value of probation and parole is that they encourage an offender to be a responsible member of society while a law enforcement officer supervises his behavior. It is lawful to attach certain conditions to a period of probation or parole. Of course, a drug offender must not use illegal drugs. He may have to participate in a treatment program, permit searches of his home at any time, and submit to periodic urine tests to prove that he is not using drugs.

The question of legalizing marijuana A growing number of people have become dissatisfied with the current marijuana laws. They claim that laws controlling marijuana are generally as stringent as those governing opiates and hallucinogens; yet marijuana is not nearly as dangerous. Tests have shown that heavy use of marijuana can be harmful to health, but probably no more so than alcohol. Many people believe that the marijuana laws should be relaxed. Some feel that use of the drug should be legalized.

In 1973 Oregon reduced possession of an ounce or less of marijuana to an offense similar to a traffic violation. Users could be given a citation by a policeman and fined up to $100. The typical fine was $25. There was no criminal record, and the penalty was not increased after the first offense. However, it was still a crime to sell, buy, transfer, or grow marijuana. Studies found that use of marijuana did not substantially increase and that the state did not become a haven for pushers.

After Oregon's action, Alaska, Maine, Colorado, Ohio, California, and South Dakota decriminalized marijuana. The trend continues. In states where possession of marijuana is still a criminal offense, 90 to 95 percent of the arrests are for simple possession, not sale. Two-thirds of the possession arrests involve an ounce or less of marijuana. It has been estimated that half a billion dollars a year has been spent in this country enforcing marijuana laws, but with very little effect.

drunkard A person with whom drunkenness has become a habit. Occasional periods of drunkenness do not make a person a drunkard. On the other hand, one need not constantly be under the influence of alcohol in order to be a drunkard. The test is whether an individual has a fixed habit of drinking to excess. The law relating to drunkards is discussed extensively in the article INTOXICATING LIQUOR.

dual nationality The situation in which two countries have an equal claim at the same time to the allegiance of an individual. For example, a girl born in the United States of European parents could be claimed as a citizen both by her parents' country and by the United States. Under law, the child would be an American citizen because she was born in this country. For further discussion, see CITIZEN.

duces tecum (Latin) "Bring with you"; the name for a type of legal WRIT that requires a party summoned to appear in court to bring with him documents, such as business records or some other kind of physical EVIDENCE, to be used or inspected by the court. It is usually called a *subpoena duces tecum.*

due **1** Owing; payable. A debt is often said to be due from an individual when he is the person who owes it and who is therefore expected to pay it. **2** Just, proper, lawful, sufficient, or reasonable. For example, exercising due care in crossing a street means using proper or reasonable care, considering the traffic at the time.

due date The day by which a tax or debt must be paid. For example, the annual due date of your federal income tax is April 15th.

dueling Fighting between two persons, with deadly weapons and at an appointed time and place, to settle a quarrel. It is usually a crime under state law. Fighting with weapons that are not hazardous to life is not dueling. Dueling is different from an AFFRAY. A duel is always planned in advance; an affray occurs over a sudden quarrel.

due notice   Adequate, reasonable, and timely notification of facts or circumstances to the proper person. Because the facts and circumstances of each case are different, there is no fixed rule that clearly states what due NOTICE is. Let us say your state law requires notice of a divorce proceeding to be given to a spouse within 10 days after the first papers are filed in court. If you have the sheriff serve the notice on your spouse eight days after filing, you have given due notice.

due process of law   The constitutional guarantee protecting an individual from arbitrary and unreasonable actions by the government that would deprive him of his basic rights to life, liberty, and property. Due process is guaranteed by the 5th and 14th Amendments to the Constitution and is limited only by the valid exercise of the states' POLICE POWER for the protection of the community. When the government takes an action that may interfere with an individual's interests it must observe due process of law, except on those occasions when the interests of the community far outweigh those of the individual.

In this article due process is discussed in terms of its application in civil lawsuits; administrative proceedings (for example, when you may or may not have a right to a hearing before a government agency); rights and property that are protected by due process; students' rights to due process; and due process in criminal proceedings.

■ **Background**   Constitutional guarantees of due process are rooted in the principles expressed in the MAGNA CHARTA, adopted in England in 1215. This historic document provided that every free man was protected in the enjoyment of his natural rights of life, liberty, and property unless deprived of them by the "judgment of his peers or the law of the land."

The Fifth Amendment to the U.S. Constitution provides that no person shall "be deprived of life, liberty, or property, without due process of law." This amendment is a limitation on the federal government and its powers over the individual. The 14th Amendment to the Constitution provides ". . . nor shall any State deprive any person of life, liberty, or property, without due process of law." This amendment limits the power of the states over the citizen. Together, these amendments protect the right of every person to due process from encroachment by government at any level. The provisions in state constitutions regarding due process are usually considered identical in scope and purpose with those of the federal Constitution.

Meaning of due process   These constitutional mandates mean that no governmental body, agency, or officer may deprive a citizen of his life, liberty, or property without observing the elementary principles of fair play. The guarantees apply only when the government takes action against an individual. If a police officer, for example, arrests a person without probable cause or reason, his conduct is a government action that violates due process. But when one person acts against another in an individual capacity, due process is not violated, even though some other right may be.

Two different forms   Due process has two distinct aspects: procedural and substantive. *Procedural due process* is the method by which government power is exercised.

Under procedural due process a citizen is entitled to (1) notice of the proceedings, such as a civil or criminal lawsuit; (2) the opportunity to prepare for a hearing; (3) the chance to be heard both in presenting his own claim and in combating the claim of his opponent; (4) a fair hearing; and (5) an impartial tribunal before which the hearing is to be held.

Substantive due process is a curb on the government's authority to make laws to cover a particular situation. In deciding whether or not a law provides substantive due process, a court considers the following: (1) Does the statute have a proper and reasonable purpose? (2) Has there been any substantial impairment of constitutional rights? (3) Are the provisions of the statute related to the objective of the statute? (4) Is a criminal statute so clear that a person will know what is required of him? A law that violates substantive due process is unconstitutional. A person's liberty cannot be restricted except when regulations and prohibitions are imposed in the interests of the community.

EXAMPLE A case brought in a federal district court questioned the validity of a Department of the Interior regulation banning nude bathing at Cape Cod National Seashore, where the increasing numbers of bathers were causing a serious environmental problem. Although the court recognized that nude bathing at a remote piece of federal land rarely frequented by the general public was entitled to constitutional protection as a personal-liberty right under the due process clause of the Fifth Amendment, it decided that the liberty involved—nude bathing— was far outweighed by the legitimate governmental concern in minimizing damage to the environment.

Even when a law does not violate substantive due process, the method used by the government in enforcing it may violate procedural due process.

EXAMPLE The government may not take a parcel of land from you because it wants to build a highway without first giving you notice of its plans. This provides an opportunity for hearings on whether the use for which the land is taken benefits the public and whether the compensation you receive is the fair market value of the land. The sovereign power of the state to claim private land for public use is known as eminent domain and is constitutional. Taking your land without giving you a chance to be heard is unconstitutional, however, because it violates the requirements of procedural due process. If you are given adequate notice and an opportunity to present your case, you have not been denied due process.

Both the substantive and the procedural aspects of due process are liberally applied by the courts in order to give people an opportunity to challenge any government action that may deprive them of their constitutional rights. The true test of due process is essentially one of reasonableness. Is the government—including the executive and judicial as well as the legislative branches—exercising its power in a reasonable manner to accomplish an objective within the scope of its authority? Has the person been given adequate notice and a reasonable opportunity to present his side of the story in a legal dispute? If the answers to these questions are yes, due process of law has not been violated.

Persons who are protected   The due process clauses of the federal Constitution protect all persons within the jurisdiction of the United States, including Indians, ALIENS, inhabitants of U.S. territories, members of the armed forces, students, and prisoners. Corporations are also entitled to due process protection.

Property protected Every kind of property right or property over which a person has exclusive control is constitutionally protected and cannot be taken from him without due process. However, a person's right to the property must be complete and absolute before his interests will be constitutionally protected.

EXAMPLE A union employee sued his former employer and
O— ✷ his union on the ground that they violated his constitutionally recognized property right in his job. The employer violated and the union failed to protect this

right when the job was terminated. The 55-year-old employee had worked at the same job for 30 years when the employer moved to a city hundreds of miles away. The employee was given the choice of moving and starting again as a new employee, without either his accumulated seniority or pension rights, or signing a complete release of all rights arising from his job for $1,500. The federal district court ruled that even though an employee has worked for an employer for 30 years, he has no property right in his job—he does not own it—under the due process guarantees of the Constitution. The court noted that unemployment insurance and Social Security give workers some financial protection in such cases.

HOW DUE PROCESS PROTECTS YOUR RIGHTS

■ Due process is a constitutional mandate based on the Fifth Amendment, which provides that no person shall "be deprived of life, liberty, or property, without due process of law," and on the 14th Amendment, which prohibits state governments from encroaching on the individual's rights without due process of law.

■ Due process protects you from having your basic rights violated by government officials at any level—federal, state, or local.

■ In order for a government to exercise its power over you, due process requires that you be given (1) notice of the proceedings, (2) an opportunity to prepare for the proceedings, (3) the chance to be heard both in presenting your own claim and in combating the government's claim, and (4) a fair hearing before an impartial tribunal.

■ Due process also refers to the government's power to make laws so long as it observes the following criteria: (1) The law in question must have a proper purpose. (2) Constitutional rights cannot be violated. (3) The means used must actually be related to the desired end. (4) A criminal law must be so clear that a person will know what is required of him or her. If the foregoing criteria are not met, the law is unconstitutional. For example, if a law is so vague that persons of common intelligence must guess at its meaning, the law violates due process.

■ The true test of due process is reasonableness: Is the government exercising its power in a reasonable manner to accomplish an objective within the scope of its authority?

■ All persons under authority of United States law are protected by due process, including Indians, aliens, residents of the territories, members of the armed forces, students, and prisoners.

■ The government may treat different classes of people differently as long as there is a rational or compelling reason for this treatment—but arbitrary discrimination violates due process. For example, a provision of the Social Security Act was found unconstitutional because it unfairly denied insurance benefits to fathers whose wives had died. The Supreme Court ruled that the different treatment of surviving fathers and surviving mothers violated the guarantee of due process. On the other hand, a state does not violate due process by charging out-of-state students higher tuition at the state university than residents because out-of-state families are not local taxpayers.

■ The government may restrict individual rights, but in order not to violate the constitutional guarantee of due process the restrictions, such as traffic laws and laws regulating the sale of liquor, must be for a public purpose and apply to everyone. But a law requiring children to attend only public schools would be unconstitutional because it would interfere with the freedom of parents to supervise the education of their children.

■ The Supreme Court has ruled that municipally owned utilities cannot cut off service without giving the customer due process—that is, an opportunity to challenge the action. (This protection does not apply to customers of private utilities, however.)

■ Four constitutional amendments (the Fourth, Fifth, Sixth, and Eighth) guarantee due process in criminal cases. The Fourth Amendment prohibits the unreasonable search and seizure of a person or his property. The Fifth Amendment guarantees against double jeopardy (being tried twice for the same crime) and compulsory self-incrimination. It does not prevent the accused person from being fingerprinted, photographed, or appearing in a lineup. The Sixth Amendment provides for a speedy and public trial, confrontation with adverse witnesses, the right to compel the presence of witnesses for the defense, and the right to the assistance of counsel for one's defense. The Eighth Amendment prohibits cruel and unusual punishment. The Eighth Amendment also guarantees that bail shall not be excessive, but this right has not specifically been made applicable to the states by the due process clause of the Fourteenth Amendment.

■ In all criminal cases, due process guarantees that a defendant be presumed innocent until proved guilty beyond a reasonable doubt.

■ No one in custody may be interrogated without the Miranda warnings—a set of procedural safeguards to prevent an accused from being convicted by a statement made without a lawyer's advice. They also deter police from going for confessions by third-degree methods.

■ An indictment must inform the accused of the specific charge.

■ Inflammatory publicity before or during a trial that is likely to prejudice a jury is a denial of due process.

■ **Substantive due process** Due process demands that any legislation conform to these fundamental principles, which are derived from the common law of fairness: (1) a law must be definite and directed toward its purpose; (2) the legislature must have the power to act on the subject matter; and (3) the law must apply equally to all persons.

Definite and direct If a law is so vague that persons of common intelligence must guess at its meaning, then the law violates due process. Statutes that define crimes or otherwise penalize individuals must be clear and unambiguous, so that a person will know what conduct is required or prohibited. Otherwise the statute will be VOID.

EXAMPLE A law that makes it a crime for a person to loiter, O—* remain, or wander about a place for no apparent reason and under circumstances that justify suspicion that he might be about to engage in crime is unconstitutional because of vagueness and indefiniteness. There are no definite standards to determine what would be a sufficient reason for remaining in a place, or what circumstances would justify suspicion that a crime might take place. Under the broad language of this statute, a person who pauses to look at the display in a jeweler's window may be as guilty of loitering as the person standing near the same shop waiting for the right moment to rob it. This law would violate due process because reasonable people could disagree about what type of conduct was outlawed and against whom the law should be enforced.

Legitimate government interest Under the 5th and 14th Amendments, substantive due process has been applied to a wide range of laws and government actions to insure that neither the federal nor state governments arbitrarily or unfairly deprive a person of life, liberty, or property. If a disputed law action restricts a person's constitutional rights, the courts will determine whether the law was necessitated by a legitimate government interest. The law will be declared unconstitutional if it is an arbitrary one enacted for no good purpose.

Both the federal and the state governments can enact statutes and issue regulations that are meant to protect the health, welfare, and safety of the public. The law or regulation must bear a reasonable relation to its purpose, however, and it may not be arbitrary or discriminatory. For example, the Food and Drug Administration's regulations, which protect the public health by forbidding the interstate shipment of known poisons and impure food, do not deny a person's rights to life, liberty, or property without due process; nor does the Securities and Exchange Commission's regulation of the stock market to protect investors from fraudulent business practices.

Equal protection The guarantee of due process does not prohibit placing people into classifications for the purpose of legislation. There must be a natural and reasonable basis for the classification, however, and a significant difference between those to whom it does and does not apply. The law must be framed to extend equally to all who are or may be in similar circumstances. A state does not violate due process by charging out-of-state students higher tuition at the state university than it charges residents, for example. There is a logical basis for this difference in treatment because state residents support the university through state income or real estate taxes.

If a law unjustly discriminates between persons in similar circumstances, relief may be sought under the due process clauses of the federal or state constitutions, depending on whether the law is a federal or state one. The Supreme Court has consistently interpreted the due process clause of the Fifth Amendment as providing for EQUAL PROTECTION OF LAWS in federal courts in cases involving unjust discrimination by the federal government.

EXAMPLE A man whose wife died in childbirth brought an O—* action challenging the provisions of the Social Security Act that govern the payment of "mother's insurance benefits." He maintained that the provisions violated the concept of equal protection implicit in the Fifth Amendment. Benefits based on the earnings of a deceased husband and father were payable both to the widow and to the couple's minor children. When a wife and mother died, however, the benefits were payable only to the minor children, not to the widower. In this case the man had stayed home to care for his minor children before his wife's death and he wanted to continue to do so. The Court decided that this gender-based discrimination violated the right to equal protection secured by the due process clause. It unjustifiably discriminated against female wage earners by giving less protection to their survivors than to those of male wage earners.

Arbitrary discrimination without any reasonable basis or governmental interest is contrary to the due process clause of the Fifth Amendment. In determining whether a particular classification of persons violates due process, federal courts use one of two standards, the *rational basis test* or the *compelling governmental interest test*.

Rational basis test Congress, for example, enacted the Social Security laws to protect people from financial hardship caused by the disability or death of the family wage earner. This legislation applies only to the segment of the population that falls within a particular classification. A provision of the Social Security Act was found unconstitutional, as we have seen above, because it unfairly denied insurance benefits to certain widowers. The court used the rational basis test to determine that the difference in treatment of widows and widowers in similar circumstances was totally without justification.

When the federal or state government decides that it has a serious need (compelling interest) that must be protected, it can take measures that might otherwise be unconstitutional.

EXAMPLE During World War II, curfew regulations created O—* under the authority of an executive order were imposed upon all persons of Japanese ancestry in military areas on the West Coast. Japanese-Americans claimed that such regulations discriminated against them because of their race and brought their case to the Supreme Court. The Court ruled that the federal government had a compelling interest to protect—to prevent espionage and sabotage of U.S. military installations as well as a possible Japanese invasion. The regulations were upheld as serving this serious need.

In only a few instances have statutes qualified as protecting a compelling interest.

■ **Police power** Under the 14th Amendment, the states are required to observe due process before interfering with a person's rights to life, liberty, and property. Under its

POLICE POWER, however, a state may impose reasonable regulations and restrictions on a person's liberty or property when it is essential for the general welfare, health, or safety of the public. Such regulations and restrictions, however, must be related to a public purpose and apply to everyone. For example, public safety statutes may limit the speed of automobiles on highways and require large gasoline storage tanks to be built underground. State laws that protect public morals by suppressing houses of prostitution and prohibiting the sale of alcohol to minors do not violate due process. A state that requires all school-age children to be vaccinated against smallpox or polio is validly exercising its police power in the promotion of public health. But a state statute that requires all children between the ages of 8 and 16 to attend only public schools is unconstitutional because it interferes with the freedom of parents to supervise the education of their children.

The federal government, although it does not have the police power of the states, may also enact legislation to protect legitimate government interests without violating due process. Federal laws requiring that antipollution devices be installed in automobiles are valid because the government has a legitimate interest in protecting the environment. If, however, the government arbitrarily exercises its power by enacting a law not reasonably related to its purpose, due process has been violated. The statute will be declared unconstitutional when challenged in court.

Although a person does not own his job—as discussed earlier, it is not his property—he has the constitutional right to contract his labor or personal services. He is free to take any job that is offered to him unless it violates the law. This right has been recognized as a liberty and property right under the 5th and 14th Amendments. It is not absolute, however, and an individual's right to accept any job may be subject to government regulations in the public interest.

State laws limiting working hours to eight per day or requiring overtime pay at the rate of 1½ times the usual wage have been considered a valid exercise of the state's police power, for example. They do not arbitrarily infringe upon a person's liberty to contract, because they aim to promote the public health and welfare. Actions that might otherwise violate due process are constitutional if done as an exercise of police power. Similarly, state laws forbidding the employment of children under 16 years of age in hazardous occupations, and laws requiring the payment of minimum wages, are valid.

■ **Procedural due process** The purpose of procedural due process as it relates to judicial procedure is to insure that the courts administer laws in a uniform fashion. Due process is no guarantee against unjust or erroneous decisions, however, and it does not assure uniformity of judicial decision or guarantee any particular decision. But procedural due process does provide certain fundamental guarantees: A person must be given notice of any legal action taken against him that threatens to deprive him of his constitutional rights. He must have an opportunity to present his side of the story before a tribunal authorized by law, and to be confronted by those who have complained against him and to cross-examine those who testify against him. These guarantees apply to all types of legal actions—civil, administrative, and criminal.

EXAMPLE In one case, the Supreme Court declared unconstitutional a state statute that provided for merchandise purchased under an installment sales contract to be repossessed without any type of court participation. A writ of replevin (a document ordering repossession) was issued by the court on the bare assertion by the creditor that he was entitled to it. The statute merely provided for a hearing at some future time. Clearly, the state law deprived the debtor of his property without giving him an opportunity to present his side of the dispute.

If you are a party to a lawsuit, you have a right to DISCOVERY proceedings. This enables you to obtain knowledge that only your opponent possesses and that you need to prove your case properly. Discovery proceedings are a procedural safeguard mandated by due process in both civil and criminal cases.

EXAMPLE Suppose Sheila brings a product-liability suit for injuries she received from an electric hair dryer manufactured by Gabriel. Gabriel has a right under discovery to demand that Sheila allow him to inspect the hair dryer to determine whether there is, in fact, a defect that could have caused the injury. This discovery safeguard gives Gabriel an opportunity to prepare his defense adequately.

On the other hand, these safeguards are not required under due process if a government body is merely investigating, studying, and reporting facts and has no authority to decide on persons' rights.

EXAMPLE Congress established the Commission on Civil Rights to investigate facts, make findings, and report to Congress concerning the denial of voting rights to blacks in Louisiana. The commission, authorized to make its own rules, decided that the identity of persons making complaints to the commission need not be disclosed and that there was no right to cross-examine any witness either by other witnesses or by those against whom complaints had been made. When the registrar of voters was called to testify, he challenged the constitutionality of the rules under the due process clause of the Fifth Amendment. The Supreme Court decided that the purposes of the commission were simply to investigate, make findings, and report to Congress. Since it had no power to determine rights, its procedural rules were not a violation of due process.

Civil proceedings In civil suits, procedural due process requires that a federal or state court must have proper jurisdiction (authority) over a person, land, or other property in order to decide legal interests. A comprehensive discussion of jurisdiction is found in COURTS. If you want to use the federal courts to resolve a legal dispute, you must meet the conditions imposed by the Constitution and other federal laws. Your lawsuit must involve a federal question—has one of your constitutional rights been violated, for example? Or your lawsuit must be against a person from a different state and must involve an amount over $10,000.

EXAMPLE Suppose you want to use the federal courts to sue someone who lives in your state for failing to meet a contract commitment to deliver a diamond worth $20,000. The federal court has no power to decide the parties' legal rights, since it does not have jurisdiction over them: There is no federal question involved and the parties are not from different states. A state court would have to decide the matter.

The requirements that must be met before a person may use a state court vary from state to state. Usually, the parties must be within the geographical area in which a court has the right and power to operate. The subject matter of the suit and the remedy sought must be within the power of the court to give. A state court cannot constitutionally exercise its powers over a person or land or other property outside the area of its authority. Any judgment the court may give is not legally binding because the court never had the power to make a judgment on the matter in the first place.

EXAMPLE Henry, a Vermont resident, wants to sue Eli, a O—* Hawaiian, in state court for stealing Henry's patent on a food processor. Should the Vermont court accept the lawsuit and make a judgment in Henry's favor, it has acted unconstitutionally and violated due process. A state court does not have the power to decide matters of patent law. Only federal courts have such jurisdiction.

Administrative proceedings Minimum requirements of due process must be met in any administrative proceeding that could result in a person being deprived of his constitutionally protected interests.

EXAMPLE Suppose state law provides that, before unem- O—* ployment compensation payments could be discontinued, notice had to be given to the recipient. If the recipient wants his case reviewed, he has to submit a written statement as to why he should continue to receive payments. He can obtain a trial-type hearing only if payments are terminated. This system would be unconstitutional under the due process clause of the 14th Amendment because it lacks procedural safeguards. The decision to terminate benefits is an action that determines important rights. If benefits are terminated while a controversy is being resolved, a recipient may have nothing to live on. He must be given adequate notice detailing the reasons for the proposed termination, an opportunity to confront and cross-examine the witnesses against him, and the right to present evidence and to argue orally. The agency must give the recipient a statement of the reasons and the evidence it relies on in reaching the decision. This procedure would allow unemployment compensation recipients accused of being ineligible to continue to receive benefits until they can present their side of the story at a hearing.

Substantive due process requires that an administrative agency set precise standards for performing its legislative tasks. If an agency does not follow its own regulations, which have the force and effect of statutes, it has violated procedural due process.

Rights that are protected If the federal government or a state is accused of violating a person's right to procedural due process, the courts must first determine whether the person's property or liberty is at stake. If not, the concept of due process may not be used.

EXAMPLE An assistant professor at a state university who O—* did not have tenure rights to continued employment was told he would not be rehired after his first academic year. He sued in federal court, alleging that he had been deprived of his constitutionally protected prop-

erty right—his job—without due process because he was not given an opportunity to present his side in a hearing before university authorities. The case reached the Supreme Court, which decided that the plaintiff's job was not a property interest protected by the 14th Amendment. Thus, the university authorities were not required to give him a hearing when they declined to renew his contract, and he was not deprived of a constitutionally protected liberty when he was not rehired.

If your protected interests *are* implicated, your right to some kind of prior hearing is paramount.

Property interests Your protected property interests encompass much more than, say, your home or automobile. As the cases below illustrate, in some situations the rent or utility bills you pay may qualify as property interests.

EXAMPLE Tenants in low rent farm-labor housing projects, O—* operated by a county housing authority and funded through the federal Farmers Home Administration, sued in federal court to have rent increases declared unconstitutional as a violation of procedural due process under the Fifth Amendment. The county housing authority had increased the rents without giving the tenants notice. The federal district court found that the tenants had a constitutionally recognizable property interest in not paying higher rents. They were entitled by statute to benefits under a government program and could expect to continue to receive low-cost housing. As a result of the increases, the plaintiffs had lost property (money) without having an opportunity to present their side of the case.

The court decided that the federal agency, to meet procedural due process requirements, should have provided the tenants with (1) an impartial decision maker, (2) notice of the proposed increases, (3) an opportunity to present written objections, (4) a review of the written evidence, and (5) a concise statement of reasons for the increase.

Some claims to continued utility service (such as water, gas, or electricity) have been recognized by the Supreme Court as a property interest with due process protection. In one case the Court decided that when a municipally owned utility cut off service to its customers without giving them an opportunity to challenge the action, the utility had violated procedural due process. When a customer failed to pay his bills, he would receive a final notice saying only that failure to pay the amount due would result in service being cut off. The notice failed to inform the customer that "a dispute concerning the amount due might be resolved through discussion with the representatives of the company" or that "credit counselors are available to clear up any questions, to discuss disputed bills, or to make any adjustments."

The Court found that this action by a government agency clearly deprived customers of property without due process of law. "Utility service is a necessity of modern life. . . . Indeed, the discontinuance of water or heating for even short periods of time may threaten health or safety." This protection does not apply to customers of private utilities, however, because there is no government action involved that would bring it within the scope of the 14th Amendment.

Liberty rights   The liberties protected by due process include the right to pursue one's chosen occupation. When an action by the government threatens to take away a person's opportunity to continue his career, due process is violated if the person is not given a chance to show that the action is unfair.

EXAMPLE A registered nurse who had worked in a federal O—* Public Health Service hospital was fired two months before she was to complete her one-year probationary period. The letter of termination contained a list of alleged job deficiencies, including a charge of "irregularities in the inventory of controlled drugs"—an extremely serious accusation. Probationary employees have limited administrative appeal rights under Civil Service Commission regulations. The grounds for the nurse's dismissal did not come within the regulations, and her request for a hearing on the merits of the charges was denied. She looked for another job but was unsuccessful because her former employers released the detrimental information. The nurse, as plaintiff, charged that the Public Health Service had violated her rights to procedural due process under the Fifth Amendment by denying her the opportunity to refute the charges against her. The charges were so serious that they deprived her of her liberty to pursue her occupation. The federal district court decided that due process required that she be given the chance to defend her good name and reputation at an appropriate administrative proceeding. She had, in effect, been deprived of her constitutionally protected right to engage in her occupation.

Rights of students   The procedural safeguards of due process are not usually required in administrative proceedings involving the dismissal of students from school for academic reasons. Courts usually defer to the broad discretion vested in public school officials under state and local laws. They will rarely review the decision of an educational institution concerning the academic performance of a student. A hearing to assess scholarship is regarded as useless or even harmful.

EXAMPLE In 1978 the Supreme Court reaffirmed this posi-O—* tion. It rejected the claim of a former medical student who challenged her dismissal from a state medical school. She had been dismissed for failing to meet academic standards as well as for lateness and poor personal hygiene. She claimed that she had been denied due process and that she was being deprived of her liberty rights because her dismissal substantially impaired her opportunity to continue her medical education or to obtain employment in a medically related field.

The Court found that she had been given sufficient notice of faculty dissatisfaction with her clinical progress. She had been given warning that her performance was below that of her peers and had been advanced to her final year on a probationary basis. In the middle of that year, when she continued to perform poorly, she was told she would not be allowed to graduate unless her performance radically improved. She was given the opportunity to appeal the decision by taking examinations before seven impartial physicians, who were to recommend whether she should be allowed to graduate. The Court decided that the student had been given more than sufficient

notice and opportunity to defend the charges against her. The matter at issue was clearly an academic dismissal.

Although the courts are reluctant to intervene in matters involving the academic policy of a school, procedural safeguards of due process are required when a student's good name, reputation, honor, or integrity is at stake. In such cases, a school has gone beyond a factual evaluation of a student's academic performance.

EXAMPLE A violation of procedural due process was found O—* in a case in which a medical student was dismissed from school. The student was informed that he was being dismissed because of poor academic performance. On a form available to any medical school to which he might apply, the school included a statement that his dismissal was due to "poor academic standing apparently resulting from lack of intellectual ability or insufficient preparation." The student was never notified of the comment or given an opportunity to rebut the charges. A federal district court reasoned that the comment attacking the intellectual capability of the student imposed on him a stigma that would prevent his being admitted to other medical schools. He was effectively deprived of his constitutionally protected liberty of engaging in his chosen career. The court decided that the student was entitled to notice in writing of the alleged deficiency in his intellectual ability. He was also entitled to an informal hearing before the administrative body that had dismissed him, to give him a chance to clear his name.

Disciplinary proceedings   Proceedings in which a student faces possible suspension or expulsion from school are subject to more stringent requirements of procedural due process.

EXAMPLE The Supreme Court decided that students who O—* were facing temporary suspension from a public high school were entitled to due process protection. The students were suspended for up to 10 days for participating in demonstrations in which a police officer was attacked, classes disrupted, and school property damaged. Under state law, the students were not entitled to a hearing. The Court reasoned, however, that if the charges were included on the school's records, the students could later be deprived of their constitutionally protected liberty to continue their education and pursue careers.

A student is entitled to either oral or written notice of the charges against him. If he denies the charges, he should be given an explanation of the evidence the authorities have and an opportunity to present his side of the story in an informal hearing, preferably before he is suspended. When prior notice and a hearing are not feasible (such as when there is an immediate threat of violence), the suspended student should be given notice of the charges and an opportunity to give his side of the story as soon as practicable. If there is a serious dispute about the facts that led to the charges, a more formal type of hearing may be necessary. Suspensions for more than 10 days and permanent expulsion may also require more formal procedures.

■ **Criminal law and due process**   Due process of law is satisfied when an accused is convicted of a crime after having been fairly notified of the charges against him and following a fair trial according to constitutional procedural safeguards. The first 10 amendments to the Constitution, known as the Bill of Rights, apply to the federal government and most of the rights guaranteed thereunder have been applied against the states through the due process clause of the 14th Amendment. Four of these amendments guarantee the defendant due process in criminal proceedings.

The Fourth Amendment prohibits the federal government from making a SEARCH AND SEIZURE of a person or his property without probable cause. Furthermore, illegally obtained EVIDENCE cannot be used against an accused person. This is known as the *exclusionary rule,* whose purpose is to deprive authorities who illegally seize evidence of the chance to use the evidence to achieve their goal—conviction of the accused.

The Fifth Amendment guarantees against double jeopardy and compulsory SELF-INCRIMINATION. The double jeopardy ban insures that once an accused person is either acquitted or convicted, he cannot be tried again for the same crime. The guarantee against self-incrimination means that no person can be compelled to give testimony that might be used against him in a criminal case. For a full discussion of double jeopardy, see CRIMINAL LAW.

The Sixth Amendment provides that in all criminal prosecutions the accused shall enjoy the following rights: to have a speedy and public trial by an impartial jury in the state and district where the crime was committed; to be informed of the nature and cause of the accusation; to be confronted with the witnesses against him; to be able to compel the appearance in court of witnesses in his favor; and to have the assistance of counsel for his defense. These rights constitute the minimum procedural safeguards required in criminal prosecutions and they must be observed at every stage of a criminal proceeding, from the arrest through a trial in a courtroom presided over by an impartial judge.

The Eighth Amendment prohibits the infliction of CRUEL AND UNUSUAL PUNISHMENT, which includes imposing excessive bail or fines on the individual.

Presumption of innocence   In a criminal case, due process of law includes the presumption of innocence. It places the burden on the prosecution to prove the guilt of the accused beyond a reasonable doubt by evidence it offers and inferences that may reasonably be drawn. If the prosecution proves facts that imply the accused's guilt, the defendant need only present enough evidence to raise a reasonable doubt as to the validity of the inference.

Notice   The criminal process begins once a person has been accused of violating a criminal statute. In certain circumstances, due process may require that a person have actual NOTICE of a law in order to be convicted under its provisions. Notice is knowledge that a law exists. In some cases, a lawbreaker is absolved of his crime because he had no notice of a law.

EXAMPLE A city ordinance required convicted felons to register if they were in the city for more than five days or visited it for five days during a 30-day period. Dan, a convicted felon, was charged with failure to register. He did not know of the law and contended that it violated the notice requirement of the due process clause of the 14th Amendment. He was convicted and appealed. The Supreme Court reversed his conviction.

Pretrial procedures   The right of the accused to due process may be violated by pretrial identification procedures, such as a lineup, if they can lead to mistaken identity. It is the likelihood of misidentification that violates a defendant's right to due process. In determining whether such a likelihood exists, the courts apply the "totality of circumstances" test. This includes several basic considerations: whether the witness or victim had an opportunity to see the criminal at the time of the crime; the accuracy of the witness's prior description of the criminal; the level of certainty demonstrated by him at the pretrial confrontation; and the length of time that elapsed between the crime and the pretrial confrontation.

EXAMPLE Suppose a woman is mugged on a rainy night on a dark street by a man of average height, weight, and build, wearing a ski mask and gloves. The mugging takes approximately one minute. Three months later the police pick up for questioning a man named Wendell, who matches that general description. They place him in a lineup with two midgets and a seven-foot-tall basketball player. All wear ski masks and gloves. The victim swears that Wendell is the mugger. Obviously, this lineup has violated Wendell's constitutional right to due process. Applying the totality of circumstances test, the victim had little time and opportunity to get a good look at the assailant; her general description of the assailant would fit a large portion of the population; and three months have elapsed since the crime was committed. In addition, the lineup in which Wendell was placed was unduly suggestive—he was the only person who bore the slightest resemblance to the described assailant. Because there was a substantial likelihood of misidentification in this confrontation, Wendell was deprived of due process.

On the other hand, if the totality of circumstances indicates that there is little likelihood of mistaken identification, a lineup is considered trustworthy by the court.

EXAMPLE After Helen had been raped, she gave the police a detailed description of her assailant. Several times during the next seven months, she viewed a number of suspects but could not identify any of them. The police then conducted a one-man showup of a suspect, Paul, because they could not find other persons with similar characteristics for a lineup. Two detectives walked Paul past Helen. At Helen's request, the police directed Paul to say "Shut up or I'll kill you"—words the rapist uttered during the attack. Helen identified Paul and he was charged with rape. Paul was convicted partly on the basis of Helen's identification. His conviction was affirmed on appeal. He then sought a writ of habeas corpus on the ground that his identification at the showup was so suggestive that it violated due process and made the subsequent in-court identification inadmissible.

The Supreme Court disagreed and denied Paul's petition. Applying the totality of circumstances test, the court considered Helen's detailed description immediately after the rape, the length of time she was with Paul, the opportunity she had to see him, and the fact that she had made no previous identification. The Court concluded that Helen's identification was reliable. Since there was "no substantial likelihood of misidentification," the pretrial confrontation did not violate due process.

Arrest A formal complaint against the accused, charging him and stating the facts that make up his crime, is essential to meet the Sixth Amendment's requirement of notice of charges.

The constitutional guarantee of due process encompasses the Fourth Amendment right to freedom from AR-REST unless probable cause exists. Once a suspect has been lawfully arrested, requiring him to submit to fingerprinting, photographing, or measurements, to write or to speak for identification, to appear in court, to stand, to assume a stance, to walk, or to make a particular gesture is not a violation of due process. These procedures result in evidence that identifies the physical characteristics of the accused and do not violate an accused's right to be tried on legally obtained evidence.

Any police questioning of an accused person in custody, either as a suspect or after arrest, must be examined by the court to insure that it has not violated due process, such as his Fifth Amendment right against self-incrimination. The accused must be given the MIRANDA WARNINGS before he makes any statements that may be used against him in the criminal prosecution. The Miranda warnings are a set of procedural safeguards to prevent an accused from being convicted by the statements he makes without the advice of counsel. They also deter illegal police conduct by removing any benefits the police could expect to derive from coerced confessions.

Once a person is arrested and charged with a crime, it is not an improper invasion of his personal liberty to detain him until the time of his trial. He may be released on BAIL if, in light of the nature of the charge and other significant factors, the court is satisfied that he will appear for trial and submit to sentence if convicted.

EXAMPLE Sam was charged with assault with a dangerous weapon. The government sought to have him imprisoned without bail because he had threatened the victim and other witnesses. Sam had prior felony convictions and was on parole when the present crime was committed. The court found that under these conditions Sam's pretrial detention was proper because his release on bail might endanger the safety of the community.

The right to be protected against excessive bail is granted by the Eighth Amendment in federal cases, but this right has not been extended to apply to persons arrested for state crimes. The constitutional guarantee against excessive bail does not mean that everyone has a right to be free on bail. In federal cases, the federal Bail Reform Act regulates when bail will be granted, while state laws establish this right for state crimes.

When a state authorizes bail, the accused must be given an opportunity to apply for it. An arbitrary denial is a deprivation of the accused's constitutional right to liberty without due process.

Indictment and information After the accused has been brought before a magistrate for a preliminary hearing and it is determined that there is probable cause to prosecute him, his case may go before a grand jury, which will decide whether to indict him. Or the prosecutor may swear an information (accusation) on his oath. An INDICTMENT or INFORMATION must fairly inform the accused of the specific charge against him. It must state the acts that constitute the

offense so that the accused will have a reasonable opportunity to prepare his defense. He will then be arraigned, at which time he enters his plea. The requirements of due process are met when the accused has been clearly informed of the charges and enters his plea. He has been denied due process if he pleads guilty and it is discovered that the plea was (1) induced by coercion, (2) made while under the influence of drugs, (3) made without advice of counsel or without Miranda warnings, or (4) entered under any other unfair circumstances.

Trial The Sixth Amendment insures that the accused be given the fundamental right to a speedy and public trial by an impartial JURY. The 14th Amendment extends the right of jury trial to all criminal cases tried by the states.

Due process is denied when unfairness prevents a fair trial. Due process requires an unbiased, impartial judge, free from any personal interest in the verdict.

EXAMPLE The mayor of a city received as his compensation whatever costs he assessed in mayor's court. He could assess costs only when he found the defendant guilty. The Supreme Court stated that where a trial judge has a direct and substantial pecuniary interest in rendering a verdict against a defendant, the defendant's rights are violated under the due process mandate of the 14th Amendment.

Due process requires an impartial tribunal.

EXAMPLE A mob marched on a jail determined to lynch the defendants. The mob was turned away only after a promise of a speedy trial. But the defendants' counsel had no time to prepare for trial or to consult with his clients, and they were convicted in state court. On a habeas corpus petition, the Supreme Court reversed the conviction and ordered a new hearing in a federal court. It stated that whenever a judge and a jury are dominated by a mob there is not an impartial tribunal.

The jury must be selected without the intentional exclusion of any group.

EXAMPLE A black man was indicted by an all-white grand jury for murdering a white man. He was then convicted by an all-white jury, which sentenced him to death. Evidence disclosed that not a single black person had served in the county on either a grand or a trial jury in more than 30 years although more than one-third of the adult population in the county was black. The defendant contended that the exclusion of black persons from jury duty over such a long period of time was discriminatory and unconstitutional. The Supreme Court agreed.

Not all economic, social, religious, and other groups need be represented on every jury, since such a requirement would be impossible to meet. Moreover, a prosecutor may deliberately exclude certain groups from juries by using his PEREMPTORY CHALLENGES—his right to reject without cause a certain number of potential jurors.

Sometimes jurors opposed to the death penalty are automatically excluded and are not asked whether they could consider the question impartially. The Supreme Court has found that this interferes with the right to a fair trial.

EXAMPLE A man was convicted of murder and sentenced to death. The Court decided that the death sentence could not be carried out because the jury had been chosen by excluding potential jurors simply because they voiced general objections to the death penalty or expressed conscientious or religious scruples against it. The Court stated, "In its quest for a jury capable of imposing the death penalty, the state produced a jury uncommonly willing to condemn a man to die." No one can constitutionally be put to death by a tribunal so selected.

Jurors must reflect "the conscience of the community." The jury is given broad discretion to decide whether or not death *is* the proper penalty in a given case. A juror's views about capital punishment play a major role in his decision.

Prejudicial publicity   Inflammatory publicity before or during a trial that is likely to prejudice a jury is a denial of due process.

EXAMPLE A man was convicted of murder following intensive and hostile news coverage. The trial judge had granted a change of venue, and the trial was moved to a different place, supposedly with an impartial atmosphere. But the new court was in an adjacent county, which had been exposed to essentially the same news coverage. At trial, 430 persons were called for jury service and 268 were excused because they had fixed opinions about the guilt of the defendant. Eight of the 12 jurors thought the defendant was guilty, but said that they could render an impartial verdict. On review, the court ordered a new trial, stating that "with his life at stake, it is not requiring too much that the petitioner be tried in an atmosphere undisturbed by so huge a wave of public passion."

The right to a jury trial guarantees the accused a fair trial by a panel of impartial, "indifferent" jurors.

The Sam Sheppard case   In the famous case of Dr. Samuel Sheppard, who was convicted of murdering his wife in the 1950's, the Supreme Court provided guidelines for a trial court on the issue of news coverage in criminal prosecutions. The failure of the trial court hearing Sheppard's case to take any safeguards against massive and pervasive publicity in order to shield the jury and the courtroom from its disruptive forces was a clear infringement of due process. It necessitated a reversal of Dr. Sheppard's murder conviction. From the day of the victim's funeral until after the defendant's conviction, Sam Sheppard was virtually tried in the press. The newspapers repeatedly emphasized alleged evidence (which was never presented at the trial) that tended to incriminate Sheppard. Reporters pointed out inconsistencies in his statements to authorities. Sheppard himself made many statements to the press and wrote feature articles asserting his innocence. "Throughout the preindictment investigation, the subsequent legal skirmishes, and the nine-week trial, circulation-conscious editors catered to the insatiable interest of the American public in the bizarre," the Court said. "In this atmosphere of a 'Roman holiday' for the news media, Sam Sheppard stood trial for his life."

During the course of the proceedings, the names, addresses, and pictures of the jurors frequently appeared in the news. The judge allowed the press to have a table inside the bar (an area traditionally reserved for the parties, counsel, and jury) within close proximity of the defense table, thus depriving the defendant of his right to confer with his counsel in privacy. The Supreme Court decided that the state trial judge clearly failed to exercise his power to control the prejudicial publicity.

The Court held that the state court should have tried to insulate the jurors and witnesses from the media and to control the release of "leads, information, and gossip" to the press by both parties. Reporters who wrote or broadcast inflammatory stories should have been warned of the impropriety of publishing material not introduced in the proceedings. In addition, the court should have sequestered the jury when they were not in the court. Then they would not have been subjected to newspaper, radio, and television coverage of the trial. See SEQUESTRATION. The Court said:

❝ *Given the pervasiveness of modern communications and the difficulty of effacing prejudicial publicity from the minds of the jurors, the trial court must take strong measures to ensure that the balance is never weighted against the accused.*❞

Due process requires the accused to receive a fair trial by an impartial jury free from outside influences. The Court decided that Sheppard was deprived of such a trial.

Familiarity and prejudice   Pretrial publicity itself does not necessarily lead to an unfair trial. The Supreme Court examines all the circumstances surrounding a case to see if massive pretrial publicity made a fair trial impossible. The Court distinguishes between a jury's "mere familiarity" with a defendant and "an actual pre-disposition against him." Only when the jurors have a "potential for prejudice" is a fair trial impossible.

EXAMPLE In one case, the Court decided that a defendant was not denied due process because members of a jury had learned from the newspapers about his prior felony conviction for a famous jewel robbery and certain facts about the present crime with which he was charged. The Court reasoned that although due process requires a fair trial by impartial jurors, "qualified jurors need not . . . be totally ignorant of the facts and issues involved. . . . It is sufficient if the juror can lay aside his impression or opinion and render a verdict based on the evidence presented in court."

Attempts by the courts to limit pretrial publicity in connection with procedural due process must be balanced against the right of freedom of the press guaranteed by the First Amendment. See SPEECH AND PRESS, FREEDOM OF.

Sentencing   Once an accused is convicted of a crime or pleads guilty to the charges, he will be sentenced by the court. See SENTENCE. Here, as during judgment, the Sixth Amendment guarantees the right to counsel.

The trial judge generally has discretion in determining the appropriate sentence. Usually a presentence report is requested. It is made by probation or parole investigators on the defendant's background, prior record, education, employment, and other circumstances. In determining a sentence, a judge may consider all relevant information, including HEARSAY evidence contained in the presentence report and evidence of previous crimes to which the defendant had confessed or of which he was identified as the perpetrator even though there was no conviction. In the trial itself such evidence would violate due process.

EXAMPLE In a 1949 case, the defendant was convicted of first-degree murder. The jury recommended a sentence of life imprisonment, but the judge imposed the death sentence. In giving his reasons, the judge discussed in open court not only the evidence upon which the jury had convicted but also additional information obtained through the court's probation department and other sources. The consideration of the additional report was permitted by state statute. The defendant appealed, contending that the statute violated the due process clause of the 14th Amendment "in that the sentence of death was based upon information supplied by witnesses with whom the accused had not been confronted and as to whom he had no opportunity for cross-examination or rebuttal."

The Supreme Court decided that it was proper for the judge to consider the probation report before passing sentence. A sentencing judge needs as much information as he can get about the defendant's background and character in order to select the appropriate sentence. Much of the information gathered by probation workers would be unavailable if it was restricted to that given in open court by witnesses subject to cross-examination. In this case, the contents of the probation report were disclosed in open court at the time of sentencing. The defendant had adequate opportunity to challenge the report, but failed to do so. The sentence was affirmed.

Defendant's interests It has become clear that under due process the defendant has a legitimate interest in the procedure that leads to sentencing, even though he may have no right to object to a particular result of the sentencing process. In every case, the reasons for which the court has imposed the death sentence must be clearly stated so that, on appeal, the reviewing court will have adequate information. Without full disclosure of the basis for imposing the death sentence, the state death-sentencing procedures would be subject to the defects that resulted in the ruling of unconstitutionality in *Furman* v. *Georgia*. See CRUEL AND UNUSUAL PUNISHMENT; DEATH PENALTY.

Probation and parole revocation When a person who has been convicted of a crime is threatened with having his PROBATION or PAROLE revoked, procedural due process safeguards must be observed. *Probation* following a conviction returns the criminal to society under judicial supervision instead of sending him to jail. He is subject to certain restraints and conditions imposed by the court for a prescribed period of time. The decision to place a convicted person on probation instead of sending him to prison is usually within the discretion of the trial judge and is seldom subject to review.

Parole is the conditional release of a prisoner from confinement before his sentence expires. If a defendant violates a condition of his probation or parole, he may be jailed. The courts do not treat probation and parole revocation hearings as a stage in criminal prosecution but as an administrative procedure. At the hearing a probation officer or similar government official tries to determine whether or not the convicted criminal should be imprisoned. Although probation and parole are not considered protected liberty or property interests, a probationer or parolee is entitled to many of the basic rights granted to everyone. Therefore, proceedings to revoke probation or parole must meet minimum procedural due process requirements—notice of the charges and an opportunity for defense. For a full discussion of procedural requirements, see PAROLE.

dummy 1 Make-believe; sham; pretended. 2 An imitation; a person set up as a front; a mere figurehead, who discharges no duties. For example, dummy incorporators set up a corporation to meet the formal requirements of a state's corporation laws and then drop out.

duress Unlawful pressure put upon a person to make him do what he otherwise would not. Duress includes force, threats of violence, and physical restraint put upon either an individual or members of his family. If a neighbor threatens to beat up your children unless you vote against school busing, he is guilty of duress. See also CONTRACT; WILL.

duty 1 Any obligation that one person owes another. Whenever one person has a right, another person has a corresponding duty to preserve that right—or at least not to interfere with it. If a divorced woman has a right to receive alimony payments, for instance, her ex-husband has a duty to make the payments. 2 A tax on imported goods. See CUSTOMS.

duty of tonnage A charge upon a vessel for entering, lying in, or leaving a port, imposed for the privilege of doing business in the port.

Dyer Act The popular name for a former federal law that punished a person who transported a stolen motor vehicle across a state line. Current laws on the crime provide for a maximum $5,000 fine and/or a maximum five-year prison term for a violation.

dying declaration A deathbed statement. It is a statement made by an individual who is conscious that death is certain and imminent, after he has lost all hope of recovery. If it can be shown that the person making the declaration has the *slightest* hope of recovery, no matter how unreasonable, the declaration is of no value. Since the general belief is that people who know they are about to die do not lie, these declarations are given a high degree of credibility.

After the person dies, his deathbed statement can be used as evidence in court. Testimony of a person who heard the dying declaration is used to confirm it. The declaration may, of course, be written, in which case it would in itself be admissible as evidence as long as its authenticity could be proved.

The person who makes the declaration must have been competent; the same standards of competency apply to a dying man as apply to a person in good health. For a discussion of standards of competence, see WILL.

Dying declarations are not restricted to such dramatic situations as the naming of killers in unsolved murder cases. A son's deathbed admission that he had forged his father's will might be accepted as evidence by a court examining that will. The dying declaration of a property owner revealing the truth about the sale of his land was accepted by a Kansas court.

It is permissible to discredit a dying declaration. If the person who made the dying statement was a notorious liar, this could be used to diminish or destroy its value as evidence.

earned income Money or other compensation, salaries, fees, or wages received for work. As the term implies, some kind of labor or effort must be made before the income you receive can be considered earned. Consequently, even though you worked hard to buy a house, the money you get from renting it is not earned income in the eyes of the law. Other examples of unearned income are interest and stock dividends. See TAXABLE INCOME.

earnest money A deposit. Money paid by a buyer to hold a seller to a transaction and to show the buyer's good faith. When you decided which car you wanted to buy, you left a deposit of earnest money with the salesman. Now the salesman will hold the car for you until all the papers are signed and the financial arrangements made.

easement The right of a nonowner to use a specific part of your land for a particular purpose. This right is usually granted to a next-door neighbor, the government, or the general public. It will probably remain with the land, if and when you sell it. Typical easements include the right of a property owner with no access to the street to use a strip of his neighbor's land to reach the road, and the right of a city to run a sewer line across an owner's land (often called a right-of-way).

An easement entitles the holder to use someone else's land. It does not give him the right to remove anything such as soil, crops, or timber. The right to remove things is called a *profit* and should not be confused with easement. See PROFIT À PRENDRE.

■ **Types of easements** An *appurtenant* easement is one that is attached to a piece of land and benefits the owner. Carl Porter owns property that has no access to the street. He buys the right to cross his neighbor's land (a right-of-way). This right-of-way is appurtenant to Porter's land.

An *affirmative* easement gives the owner of the easement the right to do something on the land of another, such as Porter's right to cross his neighbor's land in the example above. A *negative* easement takes away a landowner's right to do something on his own property. For example, Brady makes an agreement with his adjoining landholder, Ross, that Brady will not build any structures on his land that will block the light and air going onto Ross's property.

The land that gives up an easement is called *servient*. The property that benefits from an easement is called *dominant*. An easement *in gross* occurs when there is a servient piece of land without a dominant piece being affected.

EXAMPLE Martin owns vast timberlands. Hawkins does not own any land, but by contract with Martin he may enter Martin's land and remove timber. Therefore, Hawkins has an easement in gross (and a profit) in Martin's servient land even though there is no dominant land.

Easements may be transferred from one person to another by DEED or by WILL and may be inherited under the laws of DESCENT AND DISTRIBUTION when there is no valid will.

■ **How easements are made and ended** Easements may be created in many ways. An *express* easement is stated in a contract, deed, or will and must meet the requirements of the STATUTE OF FRAUDS. An easement *by implication* can arise when an owner divides a piece of land into smaller pieces and then sells one of these pieces.

EXAMPLE Platt sells part of his land to Kramer, forgetting to mention to him that a common sewer pipe serving both parts runs under Kramer's land. Kramer finds the pipe and plugs it. Platt may sue Kramer to unplug the pipe because Platt is considered to have an implied easement to use the sewer pipe.

Another common way of creating an easement is by *prescription,* which is created when someone simply uses another's land without getting the right to use it by a deed or some other legal means. An easement will be recognized if the use is (1) adverse (against the interests and without the permission of the landowner), (2) open and notorious, (3) continuous and without interruption, and (4) for the period of time prescribed by state law.

EXAMPLE Farmer Parsons creates and uses a path across farmer Welby's land without Welby's permission, in the open for all to see, continually and for longer than the period prescribed by the state law. An easement by prescription will come into being, and Welby will not be able to prevent Parsons from using the path.

Easements are ended when their term expires or when one of a number of possible events occurs: (1) The person who has an appurtenant easement becomes the owner of both the dominant and the servient land. (2) The owner of an easement in gross becomes the owner of the servient land. (3) The owner of the dominant property executes a deed or a will releasing the easement in favor of the owner of the servient land. (4) The holder of the easement abandons it, by not using the right for a period of time with the intent never to use it again.

EBT The abbreviation for "examination before trial" of a person involved in a lawsuit, especially a witness. In some states, EBT is another name for a DEPOSITION, which is testimony taken out of court and put in writing. See DISCOVERY; WITNESS.

edict A major law proclaimed by a head of state. An edict enacts a new statute; a public proclamation is a declaration of a law before it has actually been enacted.

EEOC The abbreviation for EQUAL EMPLOYMENT OPPORTUNITY COMMISSION.

effective rate 1 The true rate of interest that is paid on a loan. It takes many factors into account besides the stated annual rate of interest—such as the rate of repayment of principal, and the portion of the loan on which the stated annual rate is applied. It therefore provides a more accurate indication of the true interest rate. See CREDIT; REVOLVING CHARGE. 2 The rate of tax that you pay, especially for federal INCOME TAX purposes.

effects The personal property of a dead person or of someone who makes a WILL. If your father in his will leaves you all his effects, it means that you will inherit all of his personal property.

efficient cause The actual CAUSE of an accident or other injury. When or where the efficient cause occurs does not matter. There could be an efficient cause long before an accident—as when a car that is manufactured and sold with a faulty transmission later causes a collision. See also PROXIMATE CAUSE.

ejectment A lawsuit for recovering possession of real property (real estate) by the person rightfully entitled to it. The plaintiff claims ownership of the property even though someone else (the defendant) currently possesses it. The plaintiff cannot win his suit for ejectment unless he can show that he has rightful TITLE to (ownership of) the property—or at least that he had possession of it before the person he is suing.

Sometimes a property owner stays away for a number of years, and someone else uses his land. When the owner returns, he can bring a suit for ejectment to recover possession of the land. Or if there is a controversy over whether a landlord or his tenant is entitled to possession of property, the landlord may file an action for ejectment against the tenant. Ejection is similar to EVICTION. Eviction may occur when the landlord actually reenters the property and changes the lock or when he brings a legal proceeding, called an ejectment proceeding in some states, to regain the apartment. Statutes authorizing eviction are modifications of common-law ejectment.

Possession has always been an important concept in our legal system. A possessor has a recognized status in the law, even when he is not an owner. Property rights are attached to possession of land. For instance, the possessor of farmland has the right to harvest the crops growing on it.

Even if a possessor is subject to ejectment by the rightful owner, he is nevertheless entitled to maintain his possession against the rest of the world. This means that if a stranger tries to dispossess him, he may bring a lawsuit for ejectment against that stranger. It is no defense for the stranger to show that the possessor is not the owner.

EXAMPLE Michael purchases and moves onto lot No. 1 ○—→ under a deed he believes to be valid. Michael goes away for three months and is ousted from possession by Loraine (a stranger). He brings a suit for ejectment against her. At the trial, Michael discovers that his deed is defective. It did not transfer ownership to him. Nevertheless, he will win the suit against Loraine since he was in peaceful possession of lot No. 1 before her entry.

Actions for ejectment are regulated by state law. See also ADVERSE POSSESSION; FORCIBLE ENTRY AND DETAINER; PROPERTY.

ejusdem generis (Latin) "Of the same kind." The term is generally used to place a limitation on some concept in the law—in other words, to narrow it down. Let us say that a city ordinance permits the building of public secondary schools and other educational institutions in a section of town otherwise restricted to one-family homes. The words "other educational institutions" would be understood to mean only schools similar to public secondary schools. Private secondary schools would be permitted in the neighborhood but not a large university. Private secondary schools would be recognized as *ejusdem generis* with respect to public secondary schools.

election The power to confer and to regulate the privilege of voting is inherent in the state and federal governments. Since the right to vote within the states comes from the states, they have the authority to regulate that right. But state election laws must be within constitutional limitations. They must not unduly restrain the right of suffrage, the right to vote in an election.

■ **Who votes** During the nation's first century only free white males were eligible to vote. The 15th Amendment to the U.S. Constitution (ratified in 1870) states that the right of citizens to vote may not be denied or abridged by the United States or the states on account of race, color, or previous condition of servitude (slavery). Federal law authorizes the U.S. Attorney General to institute proceedings to protect and enforce the rights guaranteed under the 15th Amendment. But even this amendment did not extend suffrage to women, who for the most part were disfranchised until ratification of the 19th Amendment to the Constitution in 1920. Under the 26th Amendment to the Constitution, citizens who are 18 years of age or older cannot be denied the right to vote on account of age.

The right of citizens to vote in any Presidential election for electors for President and Vice President or to vote for members of Congress cannot, under the 24th Amendment, be denied or abridged by their failure to pay a poll tax or

ELECTION REGULATIONS

■ In most states, a *general election* is any election of state and county officers, Congressional Representatives, or U.S. Senators. A *special election* arises from an urgent need—to supply a vacancy in office before expiration of the full term, to raise money for a public improvement, or the like. A *primary election* is one at which members of a political party choose their candidates.

■ A *registered voter* is one whose name is in the record books of duly qualified voters. Citizenship is generally a prerequisite to the right to vote. Residence in the locality is usually a requirement—however, college students are now getting the right to vote in the college town where they reside.

■ Persons convicted of such serious crimes as treason, robbery, murder, rape, and arson are generally not entitled to vote.

■ A voter may at any time have his registration transferred elsewhere by following the required procedure.

■ Although states have the right to prescribe qualifications for voters in both state and federal elections, they may not discriminate racially. Federal law guarantees the registration of persons who have been wrongfully denied. The right to register can be enforced in federal court.

■ The official state register of qualified voters may be inspected, copied, or photographed by the public.

■ Unauthorized persons are excluded from the polling place and their admission can result in rejection of the entire vote from that polling place.

■ A candidate is usually not allowed to be present in a voting place while the polls are open except to cast his own ballot.

■ In most states, erasures and obliterations are not permitted—so if you make a mistake on your ballot, ask for a clean one.

■ Absentee voting is a privilege, not a right; the local board of elections can decide what circumstances justify issuing absentee ballots—for example, if you are a member of the armed services stationed abroad.

■ Political parties may be permitted to have "watchers" at the polls to be sure there are no irregularities that would hurt their candidate. Parties are also entitled to have "challengers," who may question the eligibility of prospective voters.

■ Financial contributions to campaign funds have been a traditional method of buying influence with elected officials. To eliminate this, Congress has enacted legislation placing a $1,000 limitation per election on any individual or nonpolitical group contributions made to a single candidate for federal office. Contributions by a political committee are limited to $5,000 per election. There is an annual ceiling of $25,000 on all contributions by any individual.

■ The federal government now provides for the public financing of Presidential nominating conventions and both primary and general election campaigns for President. The money is collected in the form of a dollar contribution that taxpayers check off on their federal income-tax returns. A person's income tax is not increased by a dollar because he has checked this contribution box. Similarly, a taxpayer's liability is not reduced by a dollar if he refuses to have his dollar go to this fund.

■ Promising to appoint a particular person to an office or position in exchange for his support is illegal in some states.

---

any other tax. In accordance with the federal Constitution, the time, place, and manner of holding elections for U.S. Senators and Representatives are to be prescribed in each state by its own legislature. Congress may at any time, however, make or alter the regulations, except those concerning the place for choosing Senators.

■ **What is an election?** Courts have defined election as the embodiment of the popular will and the expression of the sovereign power of the people. In a narrower sense, election means the choice of persons for political offices by a vote of the people. Ballots are cast and counted, and the results are announced. Election also refers to a choice made by an electoral body, such as the ELECTORAL COLLEGE, that chooses the U.S. President and Vice President.

Usually a *general election* is one that is held throughout the state to elect government officers who will serve after the terms of the current officers expire. A general election can be for electing state and county officers, Congressional Representatives, U.S. Senators, and President and Vice President of the United States. A general election is held for a definite purpose and recurs at fixed intervals without any requirement other than the passage of time.

A *special election* is one provided for by law under particular circumstances, such as to fill a vacancy in office. Or it can be an election in which some question or proposition is submitted to the vote of the people. A special election arises from some urgent need, to raise money for a public improvement, for instance. If an election is confined to an area less than the whole state, it is usually a special election.

A *primary election* is one in which members of a political party choose their candidates for public offices.

■ **Voter registration and qualification** Voter registration records the individual as having the necessary qualifications to vote in elections. The term also refers to any list, registry, or schedule on which the names of eligible persons must appear as a prerequisite to their right to vote. A *registered voter* is one whose name is placed in the record books of duly qualified voters. The term "legally qualified voter" is used interchangeably in some states with the term "registered voter." A *voter* is a person who, after registering in compliance with his state's requirements, casts a ballot in an election.

The word ELECTOR is a technical term that describes a citizen who has the constitutional and statutory qualifications to vote. It includes not only citizens who do vote, but also those who are qualified yet fail to exercise their right of franchise.

The U.S. Supreme Court has indicated that the states are entitled to a reasonable period of time in which to investigate the qualifications of prospective voters.

Registration procedure   State legislatures have the authority to require that all prospective voters register. Laws of this nature are generally valid when they are reasonable, impartial, and uniform in operation.

Registration laws are a way of giving citizens the fullest opportunity to vote while protecting them and society against fraud. In many states, registration officials sit publicly as a board to register all qualified voters. A voter must register for an election at the time and place prescribed for his residence—unless he can show that it would be impossible or extremely inconvenient. In about one-third of the states, citizens may register by mail. See Chart 34.

State law may require that an official register of qualified voters be ready for use at an election. Subject to reasonable regulations, the list may be inspected or copied by the public. At any time, a voter may have his registration transferred to correspond with a change of residence, provided he follows the procedure required by his state.

Qualifications   The states have the right to set qualifications for voters in both state and federal elections—as long as the qualifications are within constitutional limits. Discrimination by barring or hindering citizens of a particular race from registration is prohibited by the 15th Amendment. Congressional legislation to enforce the amendment guarantees the registration of persons who may have been wrongfully denied it under state laws. It does this by automatically suspending literacy tests in areas with less than 50-percent registration of eligible voters. The right to register can be enforced in federal court.

Citizenship   The states make citizenship a prerequisite to the right to vote. A voter must be a citizen of the United States and a resident of the state in which he votes. An ALIEN who has filed a declaration of intention to become a U.S. citizen is not entitled to vote until he receives a certificate of naturalization.

Residence   Residence in the locality is usually required as a qualification for voting. Traditionally, the question of whether a student had a voting residence at the place where his school was located depended on the particular case. Now the courts are beginning to say that all bona fide resident students have the right to register and vote in the college or university community in which they reside.

Criminal conviction   A person convicted of such serious crimes as treason, robbery, murder, rape, and arson is generally not entitled to vote.

■ **Right to an election**   In all popular forms of government, the power of a majority to bind the minority by a vote of the people depends on the elections being held under some legal authority. There is no inherent right or power in the people to hold an election. It arises from federal and state constitutions and laws, which designate the officer or agency empowered to fix the time for holding an election. Similarly, the place for holding an election (the polling place) must be fixed (and changed) by the proper authorities. Moreover, the public must receive reasonable advance notice of the time and place for holding the election in order to give voters sufficient time to consider the issues and deliberate on how they wish to vote.

Voting places   State laws governing polling places are usually strictly enforced. Each voting place usually serves a single geographic area, with every voter living within that area casting his ballot there. Unauthorized persons are excluded from the polls, and admission of unauthorized persons to the polls can result in rejection of the entire vote. A candidate is usually not allowed to be present in a voting place while the polls are open except to cast his own ballot.

■ **Election districts**   The voting territory is commonly divided into separate election districts, each of which is under the authority of election officers. A district usually coincides with the boundaries of a subdivision of the state or of a large city—a county, city, town, or borough. If no election district has been designated, the citizens vote on an at-large basis—that is, for candidates running statewide or citywide, rather than in a particular district. The Supreme Court has upheld the constitutionality of at-large elections.

■ **Party organization**   A political party is a group of persons associated for the purpose of promoting certain views, opinions, or principles on the subject of government. In the United States, political parties are a necessary part of the republican form of government. Although the people have an inherent right to form and operate political parties, that right may be reasonably regulated by the state legislature. In the absence of legislative regulation, parties have broad powers over their internal affairs. For example, a political party is usually the proper judge of its own membership qualifications. The privilege of membership in a party is not, nor should it be, a concern of the state. A voter is free to join a particular party with whose principles he agrees. A party may not deny membership on the basis of race, creed, or ethnic origin, but it can throw out a member who fails to attend meetings, make contributions, distribute literature, and the like.

Officers and committees of political parties are not usually regarded as public officials. Nevertheless, a party committee must conform to state law. For example, reasonable notice must be given of party committee meetings. Candidates for committees or other offices may be nominated or designated by a petition of the party members. The name and emblems used by a political party can be protected from infringement, and candidates have the exclusive right to the use of their party's name and symbol.

■ **Nomination of candidates**   A political party is entitled to nominate candidates for public office, subject to state regulation, but it can name only one candidate for each office sought. Candidates are usually nominated at party conventions. Proper notice is essential if these conventions, and therefore the nominations made at them, are to be valid. The time and place for holding party conventions can be determined by party rules, laws, or simply the convenience of the members. Delegates to party conventions are usually chosen by a party caucus. Candidates are nominated by a majority of delegates attending the convention.

Persons not members of a political party may nominate by a petition signed by voters, when permitted by state law. But they cannot name a candidate who already has a spot on the ballot. To sign a nominating petition, a person must be a qualified voter in his geographic area. The state legislature determines the number of petitioners required for a nominating petition to be valid.

Primaries   Primary election laws allow the people to choose their candidates directly, rather than having them chosen by party functionaries. Primaries are separate elections—state laws prohibit the consolidation of other elections with them. Whether or not a primary is the exclusive method for party nominations depends on the state constitution and statutes, but once a primary is called, it cannot be canceled by a party committee.

A candidate who wants to run in a primary is usually required to file, within a certain period of time, papers containing his declaration of candidacy and statements showing his qualifications or party affiliation. A party committee cannot impose requirements in addition to those dictated by statute.

A voter in a primary must live in the district in which his vote is cast. He may be required to have lived in the area for a specified period of time before the election. Rules safeguarding vote secrecy and the manner of marking primary ballots are very important. For example, a ballot that has any distinguishing mark, such as a code symbol, will not be counted. When permitted by statute, a voter may write in the name of a candidate not on the primary ballot.

■ **Balloting** The state legislature may regulate the casting of ballots. Voting booths should be provided in compliance with statutory regulations. States usually have laws prescribing the number, location, and the manner of locking ballot boxes and voting machines.

The form and content of an official ballot—which may be either a paper ballot or a voting machine—are generally regulated by state law. The right of a political party to have its name printed on the official ballot is also governed by state law. Usually, only candidates nominated by a political party are entitled to have their names on the official ballot in the proper party column, under the appropriate party designation.

The manner in which questions or propositions are placed on the official ballot must conform to state law. Two or more questions or propositions may appear on the same ballot, provided the voter can indicate his choice on each. The full question or proposition need not appear if enough is printed to identify it. The state legislatures often require official ballots to bear the signatures, names, or initials of specified election officials.

A ballot mutilated by a voter is not usually counted, but if the mutilation was accidentally done by election officials the ballot counts. Small irregularities, such as the order and arrangement of names on the ballot, will not invalidate an election. But a serious mistake, such as the wrong name of the office to be filled, will cancel the election. The procedure to correct an irregularity or error on the ballot is governed by state law. An election that has been completed will not be overturned unless there was an irregularity that interfered with the full and free expression of the popular will of the people. Such a situation might arise if there was an intentional omission of a proposition from the ballot in certain districts in the state.

Voting machines and ballot boxes Voting machines are used in the balloting process. After a person signs the registration book, he enters the voting booth and pulls the large lever at the base of the machine from right to left to close the curtain behind him. The names of the candidates, their political parties, and the offices they are running for are all shown on the face of the machine. Next to each name is a small lever to be pulled to cast a vote for the candidate.

Once the lever has been pulled, a small X will appear in the box next to it to show that a vote has been cast. If a voter wishes to change his vote, he can return the lever to its original position and select another candidate. After a voter has finished selecting candidates, he must pull the large lever at the base of the machine from left to right to register his vote on the machine's tabulator and to open the curtain so he may leave the booth. Once he has pulled the lever, his vote cannot be changed.

In some elections, a ballot box is used. After a person signs the register book, he is handed a ballot. The nature of the mark used by a voter to indicate his choice on the ballot is governed by state law. If a law requires the voter to indicate his choice by a certain mark, an X, a ballot lacking the X will not be counted. But an imperfect mark made in good faith does not prevent the vote from being counted.

Write-in votes for persons whose names are not on a voting machine are usually permitted if the voters place them in the proper slot. In most states, erasures and obliterations are not permitted—so if you make a mistake on your ballot, ask the election officials for a clean ballot.

Secrecy Every voter is entitled to cast his ballot in secrecy, usually inside a voting booth. Depositing the ballot in the proper box by an election official or by the voter himself is normally essential to completing the secret ballot.

Absentee Most states now have laws permitting a person to vote when he has to be absent from the polls. Absentee voting is regarded as a privilege, not an absolute right. Most states require the voter's absence to be truly unavoidable—arising from military service or other occupational duties. The local board of elections has the power to determine what circumstances will justify absentee ballots.

EXAMPLE In Arkansas, workers who would be away from their county of residence on election day because they were harvesting peaches in another county were found to be unavoidably absent and therefore entitled to vote. So was a New York State student who would be away at school.

A board of elections will not issue a ballot to a voter who is absent for reasons of pleasure. If no facts are stated in a voter's application for an absentee ballot, the board of elections has no authority to issue one. Absentee voting laws have been held valid against objections based on lack of secrecy and violation of residency requirements.

■ **Watchers and challengers** Political parties may be permitted to have *watchers* present at polling places. Watchers are not election officials or public officers. They watch over the election to be sure no irregularities occur that would hurt their party's candidate. Refusal of the election officers to admit a watcher to the polls is not a reason for throwing out the votes unless there is some indication of injustice.

As a rule, political parties are also entitled to have *challengers* present at the polls while they are open. A challenger questions the eligibility of a prospective voter. A challenge generally must be made prior to the casting of the ballot. Once a ballot has been cast, its identity is lost and thus may not be challenged later.

■ **Canvass of returns** The purpose of elections is to see which candidate received the most votes. It is the duty of election officers to count correctly all the votes cast. The *canvass* of the election is the gathering and examining of returns. The canvassers determine if the papers transmitted to them are genuine election returns and then declare the election results, as shown by the face of the returns. The declaration is binding on everyone. It is the duty of the canvassers to issue a certificate of election to the person who is declared the winner.

■ **Limits on contributions** In the past, large financial contributions to a political candidate often led later on to his granting special favors to his contributors, such as procuring government contracts for private business. In an attempt to eliminate this influence-buying on Capitol Hill, Congress enacted legislation placing a $1,000 limitation per election on any individual or group contribution made to a single candidate for federal elective office. Contributions made by a political committee to any single candidate for federal elective office are limited to $5,000 per election. The overall annual limitation on contributions to all candidates made by an individual is $25,000.

Political committees must keep detailed records of contributions and expenditures, including the name and address of each individual contributing more than $10, and his occupation and principal place of business when the contribution exceeds $100. Political committees are also required to file quarterly reports with the Federal Election Commission, in which they must disclose the source of every contribution exceeding $100, plus the recipient and purpose of every expenditure over $100.

■ **Funding elections** The federal government has provided for public financing of Presidential nominating conventions and primary and general election campaigns. A federal tax law allocates funding by establishing three categories of parties: (1) *Major parties* are those whose candidates received 25 percent or more of the vote in the most recent election. They are entitled to receive public funding in amounts matching contributions from their supporters. (2) *Minor parties* are those whose candidates received at least 5 percent but less than 25 percent of the votes at the last election. They receive a percentage of the funds to which the major parties are entitled. (3) *New parties* (all other parties) are limited to receipt of funds after the election, based on the number of votes they receive. If their candidate receives less than 5 percent of the vote, they are not eligible for funds.

To be eligible for matching public funds, a candidate in a Presidential primary must receive more than $5,000 from private sources (counting only the first $250 of each contribution) in each of at least 20 states.

You may recall that in filling out your federal income-tax return, you indicated whether or not you wanted a dollar to go toward public financing of the next Presidential election without increasing your tax or reducing your refund. This contribution is called the Presidential Election Campaign Fund check-off.

■ **Corrupt-practice acts** Since questionable election practices can cast doubt on the results of an election, most states have enacted corrupt-practice acts. The purpose of these acts is (1) to preserve the purity of elections, (2) to require an aspirant for office to rely on honest means to obtain it, and (3) to prevent voters from improperly influencing candidates.

Most corrupt-practice acts require a candidate to make his campaign contributions and expenditures public. A candidate for public office generally must file a statement of his receipts and expenditures in the campaign, and laws regulating the expenditure of money in elections are usually strictly enforced. Expenses connected with maintaining a permanent party headquarters, however, are not charged against the candidates of any particular election.

Under a corrupt-practice act a candidate is forbidden to make false statements of fact. The act does not forbid criticism, even though unfair and unjust, if the criticism is based on known facts. Furnishing free transportation to voters to get to the polls is not a corrupt practice.

Offenses Any votes obtained through BRIBERY—for example, giving or promising a government job in exchange for votes—are invalid. Promising to appoint a particular person to an office or position in exchange for his support is illegal in some states. Paying people to distribute campaign literature is not a prohibited activity, unless it appears that the number of persons employed or the compensation paid to them is disproportionate to the service performed. The pledge or offer of a candidate to serve in office without compensation, or for less than the regular compensation, has been held as a corrupt practice under some statutes. But when the candidate advocates a lower salary without promising to serve for less than the amount fixed by law, there is no violation.

It is not a corrupt practice for a candidate to claim that he will obtain a greater share of federal funds and services for his constituents.

Some of the other numerous election-law offenses are obstruction of and interference with election officers or qualified voters; tampering with ballots and falsifying election returns; and injuring, threatening, intimidating, and oppressing voters. Courts sometimes impound ballots, registration books, returns, and other election records to preserve them against loss or destruction pending any investigation of irregularities. See also CIVIL RIGHTS; EQUAL PROTECTION OF LAWS; INITIATIVE; REFERENDUM.

election of remedies The right to choose or the act of choosing one of several legal means—called remedies—afforded by law for the redress of an injury. When one remedy is chosen, another cannot later be invoked. Suppose a bottle of soda explodes and injures you. You will have to decide whether to sue the soft-drink company for NEGLIGENCE in bottling the drink (a TORT action) or for violating its implied WARRANTY that the product is fit for human use (a CONTRACT action). The remedy you select becomes important when the law has different limitations on the number of years within which a suit may be started. See LIMITATIONS OF ACTIONS.

EXAMPLE Let us say that a lawsuit for a breach of contract must be started within six years of the controversy. But a tort action must be brought within three years after the alleged wrong. It would therefore be in your best interest to make an election of remedies within three years. In this case, you would have to elect your remedy within the shortest time-limitation period imposed by the law in order to retain a choice between contract and tort actions.

elector A person who is qualified to vote; one who has a voice in choosing public officers and voting on the adoption of measures submitted to the electorate for decisions. Registration is not a prerequisite for being an elector. Although the terms "elector" and "voter" are usually used interchangeably, technically an elector is an individual who is entitled to vote, whether or not he ever exercises that right. A voter is one who exercises this right.

Electoral College

The body of electors, from each state and the District of Columbia, that chooses the President and Vice President of the United States every four years. Citizens do not vote directly for Presidential and Vice Presidential candidates. Rather they cast ballots for members of the Electoral College, each of whom in turn votes for a Presidential and Vice Presidential candidate. The electors usually vote for their party's candidates, but it is an important and little realized fact that they need not follow their party's wishes or the vote of the people. They may vote for whomever they please.

The irony is that a President may win the popular vote but lose the election in the Electoral College. Twice, in fact, Presidents elected by the Electoral College ran behind in the popular vote: Rutherford B. Hayes in 1876 and Benjamin Harrison in 1888.

Congress determines the time for choosing the electors and the day on which they must cast their votes.

The number of electors appointed by each state is equal to the combined total of the state's U.S. Senators and Representatives. (The District of Columbia appoints three, the number given to the least populous state—two Senators and one Representative.) No Senator, Representative, or person holding a federal office of trust or profit can be appointed an elector. The electors meet in their respective states and vote by ballot for President and Vice President. They make separate lists of all persons who received votes as President and Vice President and of the number of votes cast for each. They then sign, seal, and certify the lists and send them to the President of the Senate in Washington, D.C. In the presence of both houses of Congress, he opens all the certificates and the votes are counted.

If no candidate has a majority of the electoral votes for President, the House of Representatives immediately chooses the President by ballot from the three persons having the highest numbers on the list. The votes are taken by state, with each state having just one vote, regardless of its population. A majority of all the states is necessary for a choice. Only twice in U.S. history has the House selected the President—in 1800 when it chose Thomas Jefferson over Aaron Burr and in 1824 when it chose John Quincy Adams over Andrew Jackson and William H. Crawford.

If the House does not choose a President before the fourth day of the March following Election Day, the Vice President must act as President. (Note: Although Inauguration Day has been advanced from March 4 to January 20, this procedure has not been amended.)

The person having the greatest number of votes for Vice President becomes the Vice President if he receives a majority of the electors' votes. If no person has a majority, the Senate must choose the Vice President from the two highest numbers on the list.

electricity Although electricity is not a material substance, it is considered by law to be personal property—with highly dangerous characteristics—which may be owned, bartered, or sold.

■ **Regulations for sale** The right to produce and sell electricity is open to everyone. But because it is so dangerous a commodity, persons engaged in manufacturing and handling it are subject to regulations and restrictions imposed by the states in the exercise of their POLICE POWER.

When the electricity is supplied to the public, it is also subject to regulation as a public service. But when the sale is incidental to some other business—such as a paper mill that produces its own electricity and sells its excess to nearby farmers—it is not subject to such regulation.

Public service commissions The authority to regulate and control electric companies is generally vested by statute in a public service commission. The rules and regulations of the commission have the power of law and must be observed by the power companies.

Licenses and taxes The selling, buying, using, or distributing of electricity is usually a proper subject of taxation. A reasonable license fee may be imposed by a municipality on electric companies for poles and wires maintained in the streets for the supply of electricity to private consumers. Some tax provisions may apply to all persons or corporations providing electrical energy. For instance, the tax may be applicable to a landlord submetering electricity to tenants.

■ **Government ownership and operation** A state legislature may create agencies to engage in the business of manufacturing and selling electric power for the benefit of its people. Whether a municipality may own and operate a power plant or distribution system must be decided by a popular vote under some statutes. Once the voters have agreed, equipment or facilities may be purchased or erected without further voter approval.

■ **Supply to consumers** A public service electric company must supply electricity safely and conveniently. The company must exercise reasonable care in operating its system in order to avoid risks of harm to the lives and property of its customers. It may not refuse electricity to a customer in the territory it covers on the ground that to do so would be too expensive. The company may, however, refuse to supply a competitor with electricity.

A company that delivers electricity to the public must furnish continuous service—but it cannot insure constant service. Uncontrollable conditions, such as fire or a fallen wire, may give the company the right to cut the wires or shut off the current to certain property. This protects the company's interests and the public's safety. The danger must be immediate, however, and the act must not be arbitrary.

Meters and power failures Service may be discontinued when a customer has tampered with his meter, but not when the meter fails because of a defect for which the company is responsible. If a company removes your meter without establishing that you tampered with it, the company must replace it immediately.

An electric company is not required to give notice to its customers of a power failure, unless the company knows of the particular needs of a customer.

EXAMPLE A power company was aware that one of its customers depended on a continuous supply of electricity to provide fresh water for its fish hatchery. A power failure occurred, for which the company was not responsible but which it knew about. The company could have notified the customer in time for him to take proper precautions, but it did not. The customer brought suit for damages for the death of his fish. The court found that the power company did not exercise reasonable care when it failed to notify the customer, and it held the company liable for damages.

Payments and discontinuing service To be entitled to service, you must fulfill certain conditions beforehand, such as payment of a deposit, which may be prescribed by the company or by law. The duty to furnish light or power may also depend on a request or an application for service.

Service may be discontinued if you do not pay for electricity you have received, but it cannot be shut off to force you to pay an incorrect or unfair bill or a bill you are justifiably disputing. The company may be liable for damages resulting from the disconnection of the current if the bill is unjust or incorrect.

A dangerous condition found on the customer's premises, such as defective wiring or a defective appliance, may call for the discontinuance of service without notice. But when a company regulation imposes the duty of giving notice, the regulation is binding and notice must be given. In some instances, laws establish the time required for notice. The notice may be sent by regular mail.

All customers are equal An electric company or a municipality providing electricity may not discriminate among its customers. All customers who comply with proper conditions must be treated impartially and uniformly. A company cannot, for example, require a deposit or bond from one consumer and not from another. Those supplying electricity to the public are liable for damages to any person injured as the direct result of unlawful discrimination.

A utility furnishing electric current must properly calculate the bills submitted to its customers, but when an error has been made in the customer's favor, the company may present a bill for the balance.

■ **Rates and charges** The rates and charges for electrical service supplied as a public utility are subject to regulation under a state's police power. The legislature may exercise this power directly or delegate it to municipal corporations, commissions, or agencies. When the authority to fix rates is delegated, the legislature must provide standards to be followed. The power to regulate prices includes the right to fix definite maximum and minimum rates; to regulate or prohibit charges for the use of meters; to determine which one of several rates is applicable to a purchaser; and, under most statutes, to direct the company to make refunds to consumers who have been overcharged. Provisions for a discount for prompt payment may be proper.

When a customer is eligible for one of several optional rates, the utility must give him the choice of the most favorable rate, but the company has no legal duty to select the most favorable classification for him. A consumer who believes he is entitled to a more favorable rate classification may seek relief from the regulatory commission.

Combined or conjunctive billing may be authorized by statute or regulation. This means, for example, that a utility may send the landlord of an apartment building one electric bill for the entire building rather than separate billings for each apartment.

Proceedings to establish rates Rates for electricity are ordinarily initiated by the public utility when it files a schedule with a regulatory commission. The rates become automatically effective if the commission takes no action. While in force, they are the only lawful rates.

On an application for a rate increase, the commission has the power not only to deny the increase but to order a decrease in the rates. The commission may even reject a rate schedule without determining what is a proper rate.

The commission may be authorized to order temporary rates pending an investigation of the proposed schedule of rates. The commission may also be authorized to order an emergency rate adjustment without holding a hearing.

In a proceeding by a customer attacking his rate classification, the hearing need not be broadened to include a discussion on the fairness of the company's overall rates.

Charging a fair fee The rates levied for electricity must be reasonable and not confiscatory (extremely unfair). This is true whether the rates are fixed by a municipal ordinance, ordered by a state public utilities commission, or set by the utility. The courts can decide whether or not a particular rate is confiscatory. A reasonable rate is one that produces enough—but not more—gross earnings to cover operating costs and expenses, taxes, and annual depreciation, plus a fair return on the capital investment.

eleemosynary Relating to the distribution of alms, bounty, or CHARITY. The word usually denotes the goal of promoting the welfare of mankind by works of charity. An incorporated society for the prevention of cruelty to children, for example, is an eleemosynary corporation.

element A basic part or component that unites with other basic parts to form a whole. The word is often used in law to refer to the parts of a civil lawsuit or a crime. For example, the crime of rape is unlawful sexual intercourse with a woman without her consent. Lack of consent is one of the elements of the crime. If the woman consents, although reluctantly, the act cannot be rape in the eyes of the law.

eligibility 1 The capacity or qualification to hold office. 2 Satisfying all legal requirements. Eligibility for Social Security benefits, for example, means meeting all the legal requirements.

emancipation The act by which a person who has been under the power and control of another is set free. The term is frequently used to refer to the emancipation of a minor child by his parents. It involves surrender of the right to the care, CUSTODY, and earnings of the child, as well as a renunciation of parental duties. For example, a child who has married before reaching the age of majority (the age at which a person is legally entitled to manage his own affairs, usually 18 or 21) is often called an *emancipated minor*. See PARENT AND CHILD.

embargo A proclamation or order of a nation, usually issued in time of hostilities, prohibiting the departure of ships or goods from the country's ports. When placed on ships belonging to citizens of the nation imposing the embargo, it is called a *civil embargo*. When put on ships belonging to the enemy, as more commonly happens, it is called a *hostile embargo*.

embezzlement The fraudulent appropriation of property by a person to whom it has been entrusted. Embezzled property is taken from the victim without his consent. Embezzling is not to be confused with the crime of swindling—obtaining money by false pretenses—in which the victim voluntarily transfers the property to the wrongdoer. State laws governing embezzlement vary widely. To determine what constitutes embezzlement you must consult the laws of your state.

■ **Elements of the crime** To prove embezzlement, it is generally necessary to show the following elements: (1) The property appropriated is protected by statute. (2) The property belongs to someone other than the person accused. (3) It was in the possession of the accused at the time it was converted (taken) and thus no trespass was committed in taking it. (4) The accused occupied a position of trust—the property was placed in his possession and was held by virtue of his employment or office. (5) His handling of the property constituted an appropriation of it. (6) The accused had a fraudulent intent to deprive the owner of his property.

Protected property Property protected against embezzlement includes money, goods, chattels (movable, personal property), evidence of debt, and anything else of value. Accordingly, promissory notes, checks, drafts, shares of stock in a corporation, and municipal bonds may be embezzled. Under some statutes anything that is the subject of LARCENY (theft) may be embezzled.

Ordinarily, the value of the property converted is not an element of the crime, but the property must have some value. For example, a stockbroker who was accused of embezzling stock certificates could not be found guilty when the certificates turned out to be void and valueless.

Property ownership The property embezzled by an employee or agent must usually be owned by the employer or principal at the time of the offense. But a special interest in property is sufficient to sustain the charge. For example, a corporation controlled a special fund, even though it lacked the right to spend the money. A corporate officer's personal use of the money constituted embezzlement from the corporation, regardless of the exact manner in which the corporation held the fund.

A person cannot steal his own property. Therefore, the embezzled property cannot be owned by the person accused, even in part. A co-owner of an automobile, for example, cannot be found guilty of embezzling it when each co-owner has an equal right to its possession.

The courts have held at times that a husband can embezzle funds belonging to his wife.

EXAMPLE Martin received money from his wife, Sheila, for
O——* the specific purpose of buying them a home. He mingled her money with his own and then used it for his own purposes. Martin was convicted of embezzlement.

The court reasoned that he had held his wife's money in trust. The money did not cease to be Sheila's separate property merely because Martin mingled it with his. In some states, however, a husband cannot be convicted of embezzling funds belonging to his wife.

An officer of an unincorporated ASSOCIATION cannot be exempted from prosecution for embezzling its funds on the ground that as a member of the association he is part owner of the funds.

EXAMPLE The bylaws of an unincorporated theatrical club
O——* provided that the members were not to receive compensation or profit from the organization. The club decided to put on a show and the secretary, who was given exclusive charge of selling tickets, used the money from the ticket sales for his own purposes. When he was charged with embezzlement, he attempted to defend on the ground that as an officer and member of the club, he was one of its owners and as such could not embezzle from himself. The court held that in selling the tickets the secretary acted as agent for the club. In view of the by-law, he was guilty of embezzlement.

Possession of property Although the person accused must have lawful possession of the embezzled property, it is not necessary for him to have actual physical or even exclusive possession of the property. CONSTRUCTIVE possession (implied possession—that is, the power to control the property) is sufficient.

EXAMPLE An attorney needed money. One of his clients
O——* owned municipal bearer bonds. The client authorized the attorney to deposit the bonds with a bank as security for loans made by the bank to the client. The attorney later ordered the bank to sell the bonds in satisfaction of the loans. A surplus of cash was left from the bond sales, which the attorney used for his own purposes. Although the attorney had the implied power to order the bank to sell the bonds to pay off his client's loans, he was not entitled to pocket the surplus after the sale. He was charged with embezzlement and found guilty. The court reasoned that even though the bonds were in the physical possession of the bank, the attorney continued to have control over their disposition and was in constructive possession of them.

Possession of the property must be more than simple custody of it. If a servant or an employee merely has custody, his wrongful appropriation of the property for his own use would be larceny rather than embezzlement.

EXAMPLE A truck driver was employed to deliver whiskey
O——* for his employer, who owned the whiskey. Instead of delivering the liquor, the truck driver sold it. The court found that the employer had legal possession of the whiskey, so when the driver sold it he committed larceny, not embezzlement.

Relationship of trust Embezzlement statutes are limited to cases in which there is a relationship of trust or confidence. The statutes were designed for those cases in which a person converts property for his own use when the property is lawfully in his possession. The crime of embezzlement has not been committed when the relationship between the prosecutor (the person from whom the property was stolen) and the accused is merely that of debtor and creditor, such as when a borrower fails to repay a loan.

Similarly, embezzlement is not committed when a person who is employed as an agent or broker is authorized to mix money he has received with his own money. Nor is it embezzlement when a seller fails to deliver property for which he has been paid under a CONTRACT of sale, but it would be a breach of contract.

Appropriation of property The word "conversion" as used with respect to embezzlement means to take money or property for one's own use or to assume the right of ownership of property in defiance of the true owner's rights. Embezzlement is complete the moment the money or property is converted or misappropriated.

EXAMPLE A trustee of a union welfare fund withdrew an 0——* unauthorized sum in the form of a cashier's check, but he did not endorse or cash the check. The check was, however, still outstanding at the time prosecution for embezzlement was brought. The court held that the embezzlement was complete at the time the check was drawn, even though the trustee claimed that he intended to return the check to the trust fund.

However, the mere failure to return property or account for a fund, while evidence of conversion, does not necessarily prove embezzlement. There must also be an intent to embezzle.

EXAMPLE John, a bank teller, is owed $10 by another teller, 0——* Mary. A few minutes after asking her to return his money, John sees a $10 bill near his cash drawer and pockets it, thinking it was his money returned by Mary. The $10 bill was bank money and John converted it when he took it, but since no criminal intent existed, no embezzlement took place.

When a statute imposes an absolute duty to return property or to pay over money on demand, however, the failure to do so is embezzlement. For example, a man rented an automobile and failed to return it as agreed. Later, he was prosecuted and found guilty under a statute that said a person who converts property delivered to him in a situation like this, called a BAILMENT, is guilty of embezzlement.

Ordinarily, no demand for return of the property has to be shown when the accused has fled or when the time for payment of the money or the return of property is definitely fixed. When the time for payment or return of property is indefinite or when a conversion is not established by other proof, the prosecution must prove that a demand was made. The demand should be clear and specific, but the word "demand" need not be used.

Intent There must be a fraudulent intent to deprive the owner of his property. Fraudulent intent is the intent to willfully misapply a principal's or employer's property for a purpose other than its proper use. It need not exist at the time the accused is entrusted with possession, but it must exist at the time the property is wrongfully appropriated. The motive (the reason for committing the crime) is not important.

■ **Defenses and no defenses** Many commonly attempted defenses to prosecution for embezzlement have been ruled invalid. For example, it is no defense if the accused delivered the money or property to another person who converted or lost it. Nor is it a defense by the person who took corporate money for an unlawful purpose that he appropriated it under the direction of a corporate officer. A

subsequent approval of the fraudulent act, the fact that the owner of the property has not complained, or the fact that the accused did not benefit from the appropriation will not constitute a defense.

If property is converted without concealment and in good faith, the conversion is not an embezzlement, however unfounded the defendant's claim to it may be. In such a case the rights of the parties should be decided in a civil suit and not in a criminal embezzlement prosecution. If there is a fraudulent intent, the fact that there was no concealment or secrecy is no defense. The validity of a defense depends on whether the accused believed in good faith that he had the right to withhold the property or devote it to his own use. The circumstances must show he acted in good faith. A mere claim by the accused that he did so is not sufficient.

If an embezzler offers to or does return what he fraudulently converted, he is not barred from prosecution for embezzlement. The offense is complete at the time of the conversion.

■ **Persons liable** When embezzlement is committed by several conspirators, each of them is liable for the acts of the others.

EXAMPLE Three labor union officers sold 16 automobiles 0——* belonging to the union, but they paid the union only part of the proceeds they received. Although a check for the purchase price of each car was made out to just one of the three officers, each was liable for all of the thefts.

A principal is responsible for embezzlements by his agents. For example, a stockbroker who received a customer's money that had been misappropriated through the fraudulent acts of his agents was guilty of embezzlement, even though he did not know of the fraudulent transaction. See AGENCY.

A person may also be guilty as an accessory before the fact, although he does not have a FIDUCIARY position (one of trust and confidence). For example, a depositor who persuades an assistant cashier of a bank to misappropriate funds and falsely credit the depositor's account is as punishable as the assistant cashier for the crime of grand theft by embezzlement.

emblement A CROP produced annually by a person's labor and cultivation, such as corn, wheat, and oats. The term also denotes a tenant's rights to harvest and use the annual crops that he has grown, even if his tenancy has ended before time of harvest. See also PROPERTY.

embracery The crime of attempting to corrupt a juror, regardless of whether he acquiesces. A corrupt intent or purpose is essential. Someone whose words are likely to influence a juror's verdict, but who speaks while unaware of the juror's presence, is not guilty of embracery.

The mere intent to influence a juror is not enough. The attempt must be, by word or conduct, to use *improper* influence on him. Improper influence is the use of bribes, threats, blackmail, or psychological coercion to reach a biased verdict. In contrast, proper influence is the use of logic or philosophical discussions to fairly determine guilt. An attempt to use improper influence on a juror is the only overt act necessary because the crime of embracery is only an attempt. (If the attempt is successful and a juror is influenced, the one who exerted the influence may be guilty of BRIBERY, CONTEMPT, or OBSTRUCTING JUSTICE.) For embracery to take place, it is not important whether the juror is approached personally or through an agent. Words need not be spoken directly to the juror; they may be spoken in a manner intended to be overheard by him.

Embracery can be committed when the person solicited has been summoned as a juror or grand juror. He need not have been impaneled (selected) and sworn in; it is sufficient that his name has been drawn and published as a juror. It is a crime to solicit another person to commit embracery.

eminent domain The right or power of the nation or an individual state to condemn and appropriate private property for public use. Eminent domain is a necessary attribute of governmental sovereignty and is in force independently of constitutional provisions. Constitutional provisions do exist, however, to restrict the power. The Fifth Amendment to the U.S. Constitution provides: ". . . nor shall private property be taken for public use, without just compensation." State constitutions contain similar clauses.

When the government exercises the right of eminent domain, it is, in effect, forcing an owner to sell his interest in the property to the government. The individual's rights yield to considerations of public welfare. The owner's consent to the sale is not required—the power of eminent domain is superior to all property rights. For example, all contracts for the sale of land are made subject to the governmental power of eminent domain, which cannot be surrendered, diminished, or bargained away. A government cannot bind itself to refrain from exercising this power.

■ **Who may exercise the power** The federal and state governments are the prime users of the power of eminent domain. It may be delegated, however, to municipal or private corporations engaged in public activities such as providing natural gas, electrical power, and other energy to a community. Eminent domain may be exercised by numerous local governmental agencies, including these authorities: drainage, levee, or flood control districts; highway districts; turnpike authorities; port authorities or commissions; public works or building authorities; and river authorities.

■ **Land for public use** In the law of eminent domain, a public use may be broadly defined as a utilization of land affecting the public at large, as distinguished from particular individuals. The courts have held the following activities to be public uses of property: maintaining roads, highways, and bridges; maintaining railroads or rapid transit subways; maintaining telegraph or telephone lines; furnishing water to a community; maintaining canals, harbor ports, and wharves; constructing ditches or drains for the purpose of reclaiming large areas of land; maintaining city sewers; constructing and repairing levees and dikes; maintaining city cemeteries; maintaining parks and game reservations; slum clearance and community redevelopment projects; flood control and soil conservation projects; distributing electricity to a community; and maintaining municipal parking lots.

■ **What is "taking?"** Taking property—for which compensation must be paid—does not always require physical possession. In the law of eminent domain, property is taken if its value to the owner is diminished.

EXAMPLE Peter operated a small dairy and chicken farm O⊶—⚡ near an airport that was leased to the U.S. government. Planes taking off and landing flew at low altitudes over the farm. As a result of the noise and vibrations from the planes, Peter's cows gave less milk than before and his chickens failed to lay eggs. Peter sued the government. He claimed that his property had been taken and that he was therefore entitled to compensation. The court agreed. It held that the flights were so low and frequent that there was a direct and immediate interference with the use of the land. It awarded Peter just compensation.

Compensation must be paid when the use of an individual's property becomes so restricted that it amounts to an appropriation. If government authorities flood land with water or heap sand or earth or put a building on it, there has been a taking of property requiring compensation. Interfering with a landowner's right of entry to his property is also a taking that must be paid for. A court held this so in Wisconsin when a county, while raising the grade of a highway, placed gravel and sand 20 feet into the abutting land, preventing use of a private walk and driveway to the owner's house and garage.

Compensation must be paid for the appropriation of land for widening of a street or highway. Money must also be paid for the taking of such property as dirt, timber, or rock from a private owner's land for construction of a highway. A private way cannot be changed into a public road without compensation being paid to the landowner.

Covering of land Burying lands under mud, silt, and salt water as a result of the government's dredging of a harbor has been held by a federal court to be a taking of the property. The owners recovered DAMAGES from the U.S. government. In the state of Washington, when a county built a roadway up a steep hillside, the property of an owner downhill was hit by a landslide. The court held the county liable for damages.

Loss of waterfront Water rights are usually a property interest. If land is changed from waterfront to inland property by construction of a highway on the shoreline, owners of the affected properties are entitled to compensation for their lost waterfront privileges. Flooding land by backing water onto it from downstream can also be a taking of property. For example, when the federal government built a dam that destroyed all use of the land because of flooding, it was considered a taking.

Other takings Situations held by the courts to be takings include using farm property for construction and maintenance of a toll bridge; closing a paved highway on two sides of privately owned property, leaving, as the only means of access, two circuitous and practically impassable dirt roads; the passing of turboprop and jet aircraft over private homes several times a day, at altitudes of less than 500 feet, while flying into and out of a city-owned airport; and the operation of a dam by a utility company, resulting in the flooding of neighboring property during a period of severe rainfall.

Anticipation is not taking Planning by the government or one of its authorized agencies in anticipation of a public improvement is not a taking of property. Nor is the publicizing of plans, even though the publicity hinders the sale of your land. When local authorities plot, locate, or lay out streets, highways, or other public works, they are not taking. In Texas tenants learned of a planned condemnation of the land underneath their building and chose to vacate the property. The owner of their building tried to recover damages from the state, but the court felt that there had not yet been any interference with the property.

EXAMPLE In New Jersey, under a slum clearance and urban
0•—❋ redevelopment statute, a particular section of a city was designated as a "blighted area." This was held by the court not to be a taking of private property. The court reasoned that although a foundation was being laid for a subsequent appropriation, the actual taking occurs only when the condemnor obtains possession of the property.

■ **Compensation** No exact formula exists to evaluate just compensation for taking private property. The amount awarded should be measured by the owner's loss, not by the taker's gain. The owner is entitled to be paid the market value of the property taken.

Market value and other considerations The market value of the property is defined as the price the property will bring when offered for sale on the free and open market. It is not the amount the owner paid for the property. It is not panic value, auction value, or a value fixed by depressed or inflated prices. It is not what might be realized from a campaign of high-powered salesmanship.

But market value is only one element—although an important one—in the compensation formula. Every element that can fairly enter into the question of value may be considered: the original cost of the property; the cost of replacing the property, minus depreciation; and the effect of the appropriation on the land that is left to the owner.

The value of property is estimated in the light of all the uses for which it is reasonably adaptable. The history and general character of the area, and the adaptability of land for future building may be important. The use to which the property is devoted at the time that it is taken is considered in determining its value and is often the best yardstick because economic demands usually cause an owner to put his land to its best use.

The fact that the condemnor does not propose to put land to its best use should not deprive the owner of that valuation. Rental income that existing buildings are likely to produce in the future and the value of crops, grass, trees, and minerals on condemned land may be taken into account in awarding compensation.

Payment A property owner is generally entitled to have compensation fixed, determined, and paid at the earliest time possible. If there are several owners, the compensation should be divided among them according to their respective interests. Laws authorizing eminent domain usually make provision for a fund out of which compensation is drawn. Prepayment is generally not a prerequisite to taking, although provision is sometimes made for partial payment in advance of appropriation. When full payment does not accompany the taking of property, the owner is usually entitled to an additional sum to compensate him for the delay; it is usually awarded as interest or as damages.

■ **Condemnation proceedings** Condemnation proceedings vary according to state and federal laws, but they should occur without needless delay. A court trial is not required as long as an impartial body considers and awards the damages.

Condemnation proceedings may consist of two distinct phases: (1) proceedings relating to the right of the condemnor to take, and (2) proceedings to fix the amount of compensation to be paid for the land taken. Statutes prescribe special procedures for different types of cases.

The classifications are based either on the reason for which the property is sought or on the character of the party seeking to take it. For instance, procedures vary according to whether a property is sought for a street or highway; a park; a drain, levee, or sewer; a waterway; a wharf or dock; an irrigation or water supply; a dam; a railroad; a turnpike; a telegraph or telephone line; or an electric light and power supply. Classifications according to the character of the party seeking condemnation are based on whether the condemnor is a state or state board; a city, county, or town; a municipal officer or board; a drainage, levee, or irrigation district; a waterworks company; a railroad company; a turnpike company; a telegraph or telephone company; or an electric light and power company.

The start of condemnation proceedings should not prevent ordinary use of the property being sought, but the owner cannot make substantial changes in its condition if they would seriously injure its value. A court may authorize the condemnor, after giving security, to take possession of the property while awaiting the proceedings.

An attempt to agree to the purchase price with the owner before the proceedings is usually not essential, but when the law calls for it, the attempt must be made in good faith. Negotiations can generally be ended when they indicate the impossibility of agreement. In the event that the condemnor and landowner do reach an agreement and enter into a CONTRACT for the taking of the property, there is no necessity for condemnation proceedings.

Under some statutes, the filing of maps, plans, or the like is a prerequisite to the condemnation and taking of property. A map or survey can limit the extent of condemnation.

Due process of law The owner of the condemned property is entitled to ample notice of the proceedings and an opportunity to protect his rights. The notice should fairly define the nature, location, and extent of the proposed improvement and describe accurately the property to be taken. The notice should contain the names of all the owners whose lands are affected. To receive DUE PROCESS OF LAW, the person whose property is taken must have an opportunity to be heard on the issues of whether the use for which the property is to be taken is public and whether the compensation is just. Due process requires an opportunity to present evidence and confront or cross-examine witnesses.

Due process does not require trial by jury. There are, however, various constitutional and statutory provisions for a jury to assess the compensation for property taken in condemnation proceedings. A court often has the power to grant or refuse a motion for a view of the premises by a jury. A condemnation JUDGMENT or order must be recorded.

■ **Everyday effect** Eminent domain is not just a legal concept that you read about in a book. Owners of private property are affected by it daily as their homes are taken to make way for government construction of roads, highways, and other public improvements. If it looks as if this is going to happen to you, by all means consult a lawyer. In many states you may sue to protect your rights. In some states you may petition the court to compel proper condemnation proceedings when the party seeking to appropriate your land has not taken the necessary steps to provide for payment of compensation. If a condemnor has wrongfully attempted to appropriate your property, you may protect your property from injury by an INJUNCTION (a court order). Property may not be taken in some places unless payment of compensation has first been made or at least provided for by a stipulated fund. See also POLICE POWER; ZONING.

emolument The compensation or profit from holding an office or being employed; a salary for services performed as part of the duties of an office or position. Emoluments may be in the form of money or special privileges, such as the use of a chauffeured car.

empirical Based on experience; able to be proved by an experiment or observable facts. For example, an art dealer, asked to give empirical data about the value of a painting, may point to the artist's reputation, the age and quality of the painting, and the price last paid for it.

employer and employee See MASTER AND SERVANT.

employers' liability acts The laws that require employers to pay benefits to employees who are injured on the job. These laws replaced the old common-law rule that prevented most employees from receiving compensation for work-related injuries. The old rule made an injured employee prove that neither he nor any of his fellow workers had been careless. Employers' liability acts provide for benefits without any proof of NEGLIGENCE. Generally, employers buy WORKMEN'S COMPENSATION insurance to cover this responsiblity.

enabling clause The part of a statute that gives officials the power to enforce it. For example, the 24th Amendment to the U.S. Constitution guarantees to every citizen the right to vote in federal elections without paying a poll tax. Section 2 of the amendment is the enabling clause. It says: "The Congress shall have the power to enforce this article by appropriate legislation."

enabling statute A law that grants new powers, usually to a public official or to corporations. A law that gives a state attorney general the power to sue a dishonest businessman on behalf of the consumers the businessman has cheated is one example. Another is a state law that prescribes how a corporation may be formed in the state.

enact Pass a law and cause it to go into effect. New laws often begin with the words, "Be it enacted . . ."

encroachment An illegal intrusion onto property. A fence or wall or other fixture that extends onto land set aside for a highway is an encroachment, whether it interferes with traffic or not. Sometimes a homeowner is or-

dered by a court to remove a wall or fence if it encroaches on his neighbor's property. See ADJOINING LANDOWNERS; EASEMENT; NUISANCE.

encumbrance Anything that lessens the value of property or hinders its sale. Any claim that someone other than the owner has on the property is said to *encumber,* or burden, the property. A LIEN or MORTGAGE is an encumbrance because anyone who buys the property will have to pay off the lien or mortgage. A lease that gives a tenant the right to possess the property for a period of time is an encumbrance because a new owner will have to honor it. An EASEMENT that gives a utility company the right to erect poles and wires on the property is also an encumbrance. The right of a store to the merchandise it is selling on an installment plan (as a SECURED TRANSACTION) is also an encumbrance, as in a chattel mortgage on a car.

endorsement A signature on a paper or document. An endorsement on a negotiable instrument, such as a check, makes it possible for all the rights represented by the instrument to pass to another person. Usually, a person endorses a check by signing on the back of it. An endorsement is valid, however, even if the signature is placed elsewhere. It can even be on a separate, attached piece of paper called an *allonge.* See COMMERCIAL PAPER.

endowment A fund set up as a gift to benefit another person or institution. For example, in his will a wealthy man may endow the college he attended with a million dollars. This money can be held in a fund that is invested so that it earns a regular amount of income for the school. Sometimes an endowment is set up to support a specific activity, such as a hospital facility, a library, or a scholarship fund. A group of donors may enable a hospital to add a new wing by each donor's setting up an endowment fund that will earn enough income to pay the expenses of a single room.

An endowment is sometimes used for setting aside the amount of property a wife is legally entitled to inherit from her husband. Under the common law, when a woman was married she was "endowed at the church door." This meant that she acquired the right to use one-third of her husband's land after his death for as long as she lived. This is the wife's right to *dower.* The same kind of right for a man is called *curtesy.* Dower rights are now regulated by state law. The rights of a husband and wife to inherit are discussed in WILL and in DESCENT AND DISTRIBUTION (the laws that apply when there is no valid will).

enfranchise 1 Free from slavery. 2 Grant full citizenship rights, especially the right to vote and hold office.

engage 1 Take part in, or do, usually more than once and perhaps regularly. You may be said to engage in farming, for example.   2 Bind someone to do something. You may engage someone by agreement or CONTRACT. To engage a taxi, for example, is to bargain for service in exchange for money, even though the agreement is informal. A man and woman become engaged when they bind themselves to an agreement to marry. See MARRIAGE.

engagement A coming together of minds, as in a bargain, CONTRACT, or agreement to assume an obligation. An engagement of two people to be married is based on their pledges to each other. A contract that says "any engagement or transaction respecting the real property (land)" refers to any agreement that binds or affects use or ownership of the property. An *engagement of the partnership* is a contract that creates obligations that the partners as a group must meet. An *engagement letter* spells out the agreement covering a particular employment or project. An attorney might ask his client to sign an engagement letter that says the attorney has been hired to do specified work for a certain fee.

engross Make a final copy of a document. For example, the terms of a DEED or CONTRACT were worked out originally in a rough draft. Then someone engrossed it on parchment—that is, carefully copied it out in large, legible writing. Today, the word "engross" includes modern forms of copying, such as engraving or any other form of printing that will give a good final copy.

In the legislative process, bills are debated, read, and amended until they are voted on in a final form. Once an act is passed, it may be ordered engrossed. This means that it is printed up in a final form and enrolled in the statutes. See LEGISLATION for a more detailed discussion.

enhancement An improvement or an increase in market value based on an improvement. A manufacturer may enhance the value of seashells, for example, by making them into expensive buttons.

enjoin Require or command. A court may enjoin one party in a lawsuit to do, or not to do, something in order to prevent permanent loss to the other. This order is called an INJUNCTION.

enjoyment In law, the possession of something and the legal right to use or occupy it. It is the right of enjoyment that gives property its value.

EXAMPLE A tenant who rents an apartment infested with
O⊶⊷ rats cannot live in it. If the landlord sues to make him pay rent according to the lease, the tenant can claim that he has been denied the use and enjoyment of the apartment. He should not have to pay rent until the rats are exterminated.

enlarge As used in law, the word means to set free, as to release a person held in custody.

enrolled bill A proposed law that has gone through all the necessary steps in a legislature to become a statute; the final printed form of a law that has been enacted by a legislature. For a detailed discussion of how a bill becomes a law, see LEGISLATION.

entail Property that is limited in the way it can be inherited. Usually, property can be given by a WILL to anyone named or can be shared by all the heirs, including a wife, brother, parents, children, uncles, and so on. See DESCENT AND DISTRIBUTION. When the owner of an entail

dies, however, this property can pass only to the heirs of his body, meaning children, grandchildren, great-grandchildren, and so on. In the United States the system has been generally abolished by statute. See ESTATE; FEE TAIL.

enter 1 Go onto property in order to take possession. 2 Place formally on the record, as to *enter evidence* at a trial. A court's JUDGMENT—its decision and the orders based on it—is usually not effective until it is entered in the official records, such as those kept by the county clerk. An attorney or a party to a lawsuit *enters an appearance* by submitting a paper to the court that says he is formally taking part in the case.

enticement An alluring trick; an attempt to delude or persuade someone against his better judgment. It is often associated with sex crimes, such as statutory rape (having sexual intercourse with a minor girl). Sometimes it is used to mean ENTRAPMENT.

entirety A whole; something not divided into parts. A TENANCY BY THE ENTIRETY (or entireties) is a form of PROPERTY ownership shared by a husband and wife.

Lawsuits based on CONTRACTS often involve the question of whether the contract must be treated as an *entirety* or whether different provisions are *severable* (divisible).

EXAMPLE Matthew agreed to buy 25 bushels of apples from
O⊶⊷ Mark's produce farm every week for 10 weeks. The first week, the price of apples in the stores was down, so Matthew accepted only 15 bushels and sent back 10. Over the next few days the price went up rapidly. Matthew called Mark to say that he would take the full 25 bushels for the second week. The price by then was so high that Mark knew he would get more for his apples on the open market than if he gave them to Matthew at the contract price. He told Matthew that the *entire* contract was at an end, not just the part referring to the delivery the week before. If he is right, Mark can sue Matthew for the price of the 10 bushels he did not accept. If the provisions of the contract are severable, however, Matthew can sue Mark for all the profits he loses over the next nine weeks. The answer will depend on how the contract was written.

entitlement The right to receive something for which one is legally qualified. For example, entitlement to Social Security benefits may require the applicant to be retired, over a certain age, and to have paid money into the program while he was working. Entitlement to federal disaster relief funds may depend on whether the applicant lives within a certain area and suffered damage from a specified disaster.

entity Anything that has a separate legal existence of its own. A CORPORATION, for example, is a legal entity in the law. It can sue or be sued. But often a business PARTNERSHIP is not considered an entity; the partners must sue or be sued as individuals.

entrapment The act of an officer or the government in inducing a person to commit a crime he had not contemplated so that the person may be prosecuted for the offense. Entrapment is a defense to criminal charges. When a defendant can show that a law enforcement official lured him into an illegal act, he establishes the defense of entrapment. The defendant then maintains that he should not be convicted. The entrapment defense is a check on governmental misconduct. Entrapment is not an excuse, however, if the crime is promoted by a private person who has no connection with government. Someone who is set up by a friend to sell drugs, for example, has no legal excuse when the friend, for his own reasons, tips off the police.

Entrapment is a delicate issue, particularly in cases involving undercover police work. An undercover agent's role in a crime can be small or great. An officer in a drug case may do no more than ask if he can buy drugs from someone who has a reputation as a pusher. Or he may establish a friendship with someone he wants to arrest and then play on the friendship to persuade this person to sell him some drugs. In general, the first situation is not entrapment but the second one is. Courts will let a policeman discover who is actually willing to sell illegal drugs, but they do not want policemen looking for ways to arrest people who were not willing to commit the crime.

■ **The view of the court** There are two ways that courts test whether the defendant willingly committed a crime or was entrapped. Some states look at the conduct of the law enforcement official. If he had offered the defendant an irresistible reason for violating the law, the court will find that any ordinary person would have been entrapped, and the defendant will not be convicted. In the second view, held by most states, the defendant is required to show that he never had any intention of committing the crime. If the defendant was disposed to become involved in the kind of criminal activity he is charged with, the court will say he had a *predisposition* to break this law and was therefore not entrapped. To find out whether the defendant had such a predisposition, the court will ask about his past criminal record and about the way he was acting preceding the crime.

EXAMPLE Suppose a policeman says to a woman who is standing on a street corner, "Will you come to my hotel room for an hour? I'll give you $1,000."

The woman answers, "Sure thing, honey. And for another $100, I'll spend the whole night."

Then the policeman arrests the woman for prostitution. Has she been entrapped?

A state that looks only at the conduct of the undercover officer may find that he has offered so much money that many young women who had never considered prostitution could be led astray. It would not convict this woman on the ground that she had been entrapped.

Most states, however, would study the conduct of the arrested person. This woman's answer suggests that she was not an innocent lured into crime by a scheming police officer. The court could convict her on the ground that she had a predisposition towards prostitution. The policeman did no more than discover her criminal bent by asking the right question.

Sometimes a defendant will claim he was entrapped when an undercover agent offered to supply an illegal article the accused needed to commit the crime.

EXAMPLE An agent for the Bureau of Narcotics was trying to find out where methamphetamine—"speed"— was being manufactured illegally. The agent offered to supply a suspected manufacturer with a necessary ingredient, phenyl-2-propanone, that was difficult to obtain. The manufacturer agreed to give him half of the drug produced in return for the ingredient. When the illegal drug was made, the manufacturer was arrested. He screamed, "Entrapment!"

No, the court found, this defendant was not entrapped. The law will not let policemen trap gullible, innocent people, but they can trap careless criminals. In this case, the government agent did not plant the criminal idea in the defendant's mind because it was already there. The defendant was already making "speed" in his secret laboratory when he agreed to buy an additional supply of one ingredient from the agent.

■ **Not a guaranteed defense** Entrapment is not a constitutionally guaranteed defense. It may be pleaded only in states that recognize that the defense helps to make the criminal justice system fair and more efficient. Tennessee has totally rejected it, reasoning that anyone who can be talked into a crime is guilty.

Other constitutional protections may be available to a defendant when the circumstances look like entrapment. A person who is tricked into incriminating himself can claim a violation of the Fifth Amendment, which provides that no person shall be compelled to testify against himself. See SELF-INCRIMINATION. If the government illegally searches him or seizes his property, he can plead that his protection against unlawful SEARCH AND SEIZURE, guaranteed by the Fourth Amendment, was infringed.

The Model Penal Code recommends that states not allow entrapment as a defense to crimes that involve bodily harm to someone else. It is no defense if a hired assassin proves that an undercover officer paid him $100,000 to kill someone—even though the payment was a trick that prompted the killer to reveal his profession.

entry 1 The act of going into a building. An essential element of the crime of BURGLARY is illegal entry. 2 The recording of a legal document, such as a deed, judgment, or lien. 3 A notation in the records of a business. If an entry was made in the regular course of business, it is usually admissible into EVIDENCE at a trial when it tends to prove a particular fact. 4 In property law, the act of going onto a piece of land, especially for the purpose of claiming a right to possess or own the property. Even a person who has a right of entry may go onto land only if he can do so peaceably. If he is likely to be met with force or violence, he must instead go to court and ask for a court order permitting his entry. See ENTRY, WRIT OF; REENTRY.

entry, writ of An order issued by a judge to recover possession of real property (real estate). The order is issued on behalf of the person who shows he is entitled to hold and use the land. A writ of entry does not establish or recognize who *owns* the land, but merely fixes who is entitled to *possess* it (hold and use it). Therefore the defendant in possession of the land cannot use the defense that the person who obtained the writ of entry is not the true owner.

The sole question is which of the two parties has the greater right to hold and use the property at the time of the lawsuit. The greater right might be based on ownership, but this is not always the case. For example, a case might involve a tenant who has a lease on the property. The court must ask how and when each party acquired ownership or possession in order to determine the priority of their rights.

In recent times, only Massachusetts, Maine, and New Hampshire have recognized the writ of entry as a legal remedy to recover possession of land. The trend is to call such a lawsuit an "action to recover possession of real property."

enumerated   Numbered, listed, or mentioned specifically. For example, enumerated items on a tariff schedule are specific articles to be taxed at a stated rate; other kinds of merchandise are listed in general categories. The U.S. Constitution lists specific enumerated powers that belong to the federal government.

environmental law   A wide-ranging body of laws designed to protect human health from excessive noise and pollutants of the soil, air, and water and to maintain wildlife and vegetation, the cleanness of atmosphere and water, and the scenic beauty of the environment.

Although laws affecting the environment were passed in the second half of the 19th century (including those establishing the first national parks) and during the first half of the 20th century, the great need for such legislation did not become apparent to the public as a whole until fairly recently. Environmental protection became a popular cause in the 1960's, and today it still remains of serious concern, with long lists of cases awaiting hearing in the federal courts alone. The federal environmental laws of the 1970's have had great impact, best compared to the striking changes created by the civil rights laws of the 1960's or the securities regulations of the 1930's. Environmental law is expanding into so many areas of modern life and is developing into such a comprehensive body of law that it will probably become one of the nation's most important legal reforms.

When the need to protect the environment became obvious in the 1960's, the federal government did not at first create new laws but applied existing ones to the newly recognized need. For example, federal laws aimed at accurate labeling of pesticides were extended to limit the use of pesticides in order to protect the environment. Several federal agencies, such as the Bureau of Mines and the National Oceanic and Atmospheric Administration, had their responsibilities increased to help assure a clean and safe environment.

■ **National Environmental Policy Act**   The National Environmental Policy Act (NEPA) of 1969 is the cornerstone of today's environmental law. So far reaching and fundamental are the changes NEPA has stimulated in environmental law and its administration that it has been considered as important to the country as a Constitutional amendment.

NEPA is a government commitment to give a high national priority to environmental factors when planning major federal projects. Its purpose is to monitor, discover, and disclose the impact of federal projects on our environment. The statute reads in part:

&& *The Congress . . . declares that it is the continuing policy of the Federal Government, in cooperation with State and local governments, and other concerned public and private organizations to use all practicable means and measures, including financial and technical assistance, in a manner calculated to foster and promote the general welfare, to create and maintain conditions under which man and nature can exist in productive harmony, and fulfill the social, economic, and other requirements of present and future generations of Americans."*

Council on Environmental Quality   NEPA established the Council on Environmental Quality (CEQ), which reports directly to the President. Its most important responsibilities are:

(1) To prepare an annual report on environmental quality and on existing and proposed federal efforts to improve it.

(2) To evaluate the programs and activities of the federal government in light of the national policy to preserve the environment. Every federal agency and government department must comply with NEPA in several broad *"action-forcing"* provisions. The agencies are required to recognize and respect environmental qualities that cannot be scientifically measured—beauty, serenity, and peacefulness, for example—and not merely economical and technical factors.

(3) To develop and recommend specific policies that protect the environment in ways consistent with the conservation, social and economic, health, and other needs and goals of the country.

(4) To gather and analyze environmental information, survey and monitor trends, and document changes in our natural environment.

The NEPA requires all government agencies to assist the CEQ in fulfilling its responsibilities.

Environmental Protection Agency   The NEPA also paved the way for an executive order that President Richard Nixon submitted to Congress in July 1970. The order reorganized the nation's environmental efforts under the new and powerful Environmental Protection Agency (EPA). Today the EPA administers CEQ policies and most federal environmental statutes. The exceptions: the Agriculture Department administers parts of some laws governing pesticide use and the Interior Department handles some conservation measures related to environmental law. Thus, with virtually all environmental laws under the ultimate control of the EPA, the agency can take a comprehensive and coordinated approach to complex environmental matters.

Environmental impact statements   The EPA is charged with enforcing the CEQ's policy of a clean, healthful, and beautiful environment, and one way it fulfills that responsibility is to require any government agency planning a major federal project to submit an environmental impact statement—that is, a statement showing the impact the project can reasonably be expected to have on our environment. The EPA has the job of reviewing those statements and approving or rejecting the project.

A "major" project is one that requires much planning and a great use of time, money, and natural resources. But

SOME LAWS THAT PROTECT THE ENVIRONMENT

■ Federal environmental law aims to protect public health, safeguard the use of land and natural resources, and preserve interesting or scenic sites. Specifically, it deals with regulation of technological advances, energy, government lands, wildlife, air and water, and related matters.

■ The cornerstone of present-day environmental law is the National Environmental Policy Act (NEPA) of 1969, which requires every federal agency to consider how its actions will affect the environment. The Environmental Protection Agency (EPA) administers most federal environmental statutes and policies.

■ Agencies are now required to submit, along with every proposal for a major federal action project that might affect the environment, a so-called environmental-impact statement—that is, a statement providing a rigorous analysis of the impact the action can reasonably be expected to have on our environment.

■ Federal actions are those involving the U.S. government. They include projects for building or financing highways, dams, or buildings; initiating programs for managing national parks; leasing the right to cut timber on federal lands; and urban renewal and federal housing programs.

■ Agencies must make their statements available to the public and to other agencies, and they must hold public hearings for large or controversial projects.

■ The Federal Water Pollution Control Act regulates discharge of wastes, especially from industry, municipal sewage plants, and agricultural feedlots (where animals are fattened before butchering); it also has authority over spills of oil and other hazardous substances. An amendment to this law, known as the Clean Water Act, aims to protect fish, shellfish, and wildlife; to stop the discharge of pollutants or toxins into water; and to promote cooperation among all levels of government and with other countries.

■ The Clean Air Act sponsors research and technical programs to clean up the air, and it regulates pollution by establishing and enforcing standards.

■ The EPA sets standards for air quality and legal limits for specific pollutants. Violations are punishable by fines of $25,000 per day and jail sentences of up to a year.

■ The Noise Control Act aims to free the environment from noise that jeopardizes health and welfare. It concentrates on controlling noise from industrial machinery, appliances, and vehicles, including aircraft, trains, and trucks. The EPA sets the standards, with violations punishable by fines of up to $25,000 a day and prison sentences of up to a year. Citizens may sue violators, including government agencies, the federal government, and even the EPA itself to force compliance with the Noise Control Act.

■ The Marine Protection, Research, and Sanctuary Act of 1972 outlaws the dumping of wastes into the oceans without a special permit.

■ The regulation of nuclear power is under the Nuclear Regulatory Commission, which reports all nuclear accidents or abnormal occurrences to Congress and evaluates plans for new nuclear plants.

■ Other federal laws control the quality of our drinking water, the disposal of hazardous wastes, and the use of pesticides and other toxic substances.

■ The federal government is the biggest landowner in the country—it owns 750 million acres of land. Three categories of federally owned land are earmarked for preservation: the National Park System, the National Wilderness Preservation System, and the National Wildlife Refuge System. Other public lands owned by the government may be used and developed—the ocean floor for oil and mineral deposits, for example, and lands that may someday serve as hydroelectric power-plant sites—but these are all subject to very strict controls under environmental law.

■ Under the Endangered Species Act, a list of endangered and threatened species of fish, plants, and wild animals is being kept by the federal government. ("Endangered" means on the brink of extinction; "threatened" means that protective measures must be taken.) It is illegal to import or export an endangered species, to hunt it within the United States or on the high seas, or to possess, sell, offer to sell, or transport it.

■ The states help to implement the policies established by federal environmental law. In addition, more than half the states have their own environmental laws. Most state programs are financed at least in part by the federal government.

even a small project is considered major if it has a large impact on the environment—a project that gives off even a small amount of radiation, for example.

A "federal" project is one involving the U.S. government, whether or not a city or state is also involved. A program for managing a national park is a federal action. Granting federal money to a state for building highways and leasing the right to cut timber or graze livestock on federal lands are federal actions.

EXAMPLE A citizens' group called Natural Resources Defense Council (NRDC) became concerned that federal lands were being overgrazed by livestock, thus endangering the natural habitats for wildlife. In October 1974 the NRDC sued the Federal Bureau of Land Management. The citizens argued that, as a federal agency, the bureau should require local environmental impact statements whenever it permits government lands to be used for grazing. In that way, a balance could be struck between the need for grazing land and the protection of such wildlife as big horned sheep and salmon, both endangered by the excessive erosion grazing can cause. In December 1975 a federal court ruled in favor of the citizens, and by the following fall the Supreme Court had upheld the decision.

Federal actions also include activities related to lawmaking—agencies recommending new laws or changes in any existing federal rules, regulations, procedures, or policies must take into account the environmental impact the legislation will have. Any project undertaken by a state or local government, a utility company, or any other business that requires approval, a license, or a permit from a federal regulatory agency is a federal project.

EXAMPLE When the state of Texas was required to meet O⊷⊶ complicated NEPA requirements in building a highway, state authorities returned all the federal funds it had received and vowed to build the entire highway with "100 percent state money if necessary." Of course, the state admitted, it intended to make up the same amount by applying for federal funds to finance other eligible projects. The federal court held that Texas could not avoid the requirements of NEPA "by a mere change in bookkeeping or by shifting funds from one project to another."

The trend has been to consider all projects involving oil refineries, offshore oil drilling, highways, water resources, sewage treatment plants, and the generation of electricity as having an important impact on the environment, requiring submission of environmental impact statements before they may be undertaken. The same is true for urban renewal and federal housing programs.

An agency may have to prepare several statements for a single ongoing project. An extensive highway-building program, for example, may require separate statements for the different locations affected. A project whose construction extends over a long period of time also requires a series of environmental impact statements.

In general, a statement must analyze the risks of a proposed project thoroughly and rigorously. It is not necessary to speculate about far-fetched possibilities, but foreseeable effects must be considered. It is not enough to list facts or statistics—their effects on the environment must be analyzed and the agency must explain where its information came from and how it arrived at its conclusions.

Enforcement of the NEPA During the early years following NEPA's creation, regulations growing out of the act were enforced primarily in the courts, and those court decisions shaped new policies of law and government. For example, the courts decided that citizens were entitled to sue government agencies that did not fulfill their obligations under NEPA, and then they applied tough standards in the flood of litigation that poured into federal courts—suits started by manufacturers and associations of businessmen, by such conservation groups as the Environmental Defense Fund and the Sierra Club, and by private individuals whose lives or property were affected by such projects as federally approved dams, highways, and nuclear power plants. Agencies that claimed the law did not apply to them were told that the law says "all agencies," and that is what it means. Agencies submitting superficial environmental impact statements were informed that the reports must be complete and precise. Others were told to go back and write about the alternatives to their projects and to give reasons why the alternatives were not chosen. Agencies were made to keep complete records of their actions on each project so that courts could review their decisions to see if they were fair. Finally, courts issued injunctions to stop projects until proper environmental impact statements were filed.

■ **Federal antipollution laws** In addition to the National Environmental Policy Act, the federal government

has passed a number of important laws to deal with environmental problems caused by the private sector. Two of these laws, the Federal Water Pollution Control Act and the Clean Air Act, were passed even before the nation as a whole became concerned with environmental quality, and both of these laws were later amended and strengthened. Other laws were passed in the 1970's when concern over the environment was at a peak.

Federal Water Pollution Control Act First enacted in 1948 and amended in the 1950's and 1960's and again in 1972 and 1977, the Federal Water Pollution Control Act regulates the discharge of wastes, especially from industrial plants, municipal sewage treatment plants, and agricultural feedlots. It also regulates the cleaning up of oil spills and other hazardous substances. Furthermore, the law provides federal money to help build sewage-treatment plants and provides money to be given as grants for research or as scholarships for college students preparing for careers in the prevention and control of water pollution.

The Clean Water Act, the name of the 1977 amendments to the Federal Water Pollution Control Act, creates a new goal for environmental legislation. The goal is to clean up the water; protect fish, shellfish, and wildlife; stop the discharge of pollutants and toxic substances; and promote cooperation among all levels of government and with other countries.

Clean Air Act The Clean Air Act was enacted in 1955, but significantly amended on several occasions. The most notable amendments to this act were made in 1977.

The 1977 amendments to the Clean Air Act went to great lengths to protect air quality. They confirmed that the primary responsibility for preventing and controlling air pollution at its source rests with state and local governments, but they provided federal financial assistance and leadership to develop programs of cooperation among all levels of government. One aspect of the 1977 amendments directs the Environmental Protection Agency to help federal, state, and local agencies set up programs to inspect and regulate motor vehicle emission, to control on-street parking in order to discourage the use of automobiles in congested areas, to regulate vehicle idling, to set up bicycle storage facilities and cycle lanes on roads, and to encourage employer-sponsored car pooling. The EPA has also set air quality standards for various regions of the country and legal limits for specific pollutants.

The EPA has the authority to enforce its standards stringently. In certain areas where the levels of the most dangerous pollutants are above EPA standards, EPA requires those areas to bring pollution levels within required limits before permitting any further industrial expansion. The EPA monitors sulfur dioxide, particulates, carbon monoxide, hydrocarbons, nitrogen dioxide, and photochemical oxidants. Of these, only sulfur dioxide is not related to automobile emissions. Therefore the effect of limiting those pollutants is to encourage a number of states to introduce laws requiring auto-exhaust emissions to be tested and tuned regularly, and repaired if they fail the inspection.

The Clean Air Act also has a provision allowing citizens to sue anyone who violates the law and causes air pollution. Citizens may even sue the government in such a case.

EXAMPLE The District of Columbia's entire battery of solid-waste incinerators was found to produce excessive air pollution in violation of the Clean Air Act. In an implementation plan filed with the EPA, the District agreed to close all the incinerators but one, which would continue in operation until July 4, 1973, at which time the other incinerators, modified to keep air pollution within legal limits, would take over.

On May 31, 1973, however, the District's city council amended the plan to close the incinerator, postponing the move until September 4. Again on September 4, the council voted to enact a second postponement, this time until July 30, 1974.

Following the second postponement, a citizens' environmental group, the Metropolitan Washington Coalition for Clean Air, acting under the citizen suit provision of the Clean Air Act, sued the District to force the closing of the incinerator. A lower court ruled in favor of the city council, but the citizens appealed to the U.S. Court of Appeals, which ruled that a city council's decision to postpone any aspect of an implementation plan must be expressly approved by the administrator of the Environmental Protection Agency. As a result, the lower court ruling was reversed, and the District was compelled to expedite the closing of the incinerator.

If the EPA fails to be sufficiently stringent in its regulation of air pollution, citizens may use the citizen suit provision to sue the EPA itself.

EXAMPLE In May 1972 the Sierra Club and other private environmental protection groups took the Administrator of the Environmental Protection Agency to court to stop him from approving certain state implementation plans. EPA regulations pertaining to the Clean Air Act required that a state's overall pollution levels remain below specific ceilings—but a state with particularly clean air was free to pollute it up to that ceiling. The Sierra Club's attorneys argued that a major purpose of the Clean Air Act was to "protect and enhance the quality of the Nation's air resources," and that meant both cleaning up dirty air and maintaining what was already clean.

In a landmark decision, the courts enjoined the EPA administrator from approving any state plan "unless he approves the state plan subject to subsequent review by him to insure that it does not permit significant deterioration of existing air quality in any portion of the state where the existing air quality is better than one or more of the secondary dirtier standards propagated by the Administrator." The case was appealed to the Supreme Court, which upheld the lower court's decision.

Federal Pesticide Act The most important, although not the first, federal law regulating pesticides is the Federal Environmental Pesticide Control Act of 1972. That law and its subsequent amendments requires that all pesticides be registered before sale in order to identify unreasonable hazards to humans or the environment. Pesticides must be classified according to general or restricted use, and the users of restricted pesticides must be certified. Labels must be informative and accurate.

Noise Control Act Under the common law, one neighbor could sue another if he was constantly disturbed by ongoing, obnoxious noises under what is called a NUI-SANCE action. Modern industry, however, has the potential to create such an onslaught of noise that private nuisance actions are inadequate to cope with the problem. For that reason, the Noise Control Act of 1972 was created. Its purpose is to reduce or eliminate noise that jeopardizes health and welfare. It concentrates on controlling noise from industrial machinery, appliances, and vehicles, including aircraft, trains, and trucks. The Environmental Protection Agency analyzes the sources of noise and sets standards for noise emission. Violations are punishable by fines and prison sentences, with substantial increases in the penalties for repeating violators. In addition, citizens may sue violators, including government agencies (even the Environmental Protection Agency) or the United States itself, to force compliance with the Noise Control Act. This act also requires that the federal government buy quiet motors, engines, transportation, and electrical equipment.

Marine Protection, Research, and Sanctuary Act "Unregulated dumping of material into ocean waters endangers human health, welfare, and amenities, and the marine environment, ecological systems, and economic potentialities," said Congress in formulating the Marine Protection, Research, and Sanctuary Act of 1972. The act outlaws the dumping of wastes into the ocean, without a special permit from the EPA, and empowers the EPA to designate certain areas where dumping is permitted and others where it is banned. The law also authorizes research programs on ocean pollution, and bars all ocean dumping of radioactive wastes and poisons formulated for chemical or biological warfare.

Energy Reorganization Act The Energy Reorganization Act of 1974 abolished the Atomic Energy Commission, transferring its regulatory responsibilities to the Nuclear Regulatory Commission (NRC). The NRC licenses and regulates the uses of nuclear energy to protect the public health and safety and the environment. It makes rules and sets standards for obtaining licenses, and carefully inspects the activities of the persons and companies licensed to insure that they do not violate the safety rules of the commission. The major share of the commission's effort is focused on the use of nuclear energy to generate electric power.

EXAMPLE The NRC was at the center of controversy when in March 1979 the most serious nuclear power plant accident to date occurred near Harrisburg, Pennsylvania. A series of valve failures at the Three Mile Island nuclear power plant on the Susquehanna River led to the escape of radioactive steam into the environment and a partial meltdown of the reactor's core. The potential for a catastrophe remained high for several days, and thousands of people were urged by Pennsylvania's Governor Richard Thornburgh to evacuate the area. In reaction to the Three Mile Island incident, the NRC dramatically tightened its surveillance and standards, and several nuclear power plants built on the order of the one at Three Mile Island were closed until the likelihood of a similar failure could be eliminated.

Safe Drinking Water Act Passed in 1974 and amended in 1977, the Safe Drinking Water Act sets standards for maximum allowable levels of certain chemicals and bacteriological pollutants in public drinking water.

Resource Conservation and Recovery Act The major federal law governing the disposal of solid wastes is the Resource Conservation and Recovery Act of 1976, which amended and strengthened the Solid Waste Disposal Act of 1965 and the Resource Recovery Act of 1970. The new law charged the EPA with proposing regulations for the handling and storage of hazardous wastes, including hundreds of named chemicals and other substances and any other wastes that are ignitable, corrosive, toxic, or reactive—that is, liable to explode. The regulations went into effect in 1980. Anyone wishing to operate storage or disposal facilities for hazardous wastes or to treat them must first acquire a permit from the EPA. The agency also makes grants to states for hazardous waste treatment programs under this law.

Toxic Substances Control Act In the early 1970's, it became obvious that at least some of the estimated two million chemical compounds present in the environment were dangerous. Vinyl chloride, for example, commonly used in plastics, was found to have caused the deaths of workers who were exposed to it. Asbestos caused cancer when inhaled, and mercury was also dangerous to those exposed to it regularly. Polychlorinated biphenyls, or PCB's, which are both toxic and persistent, were discovered in the human body and in milk. In 1976, after years of procrastination, Congress finally passed the Toxic Substances Control Act to deal with dangerous chemicals before they cause widespread and irreversible harm.

The 1976 law authorizes the EPA to require manufacturers to test chemical mixtures that could present an unreasonable risk of injury to health or to the environment. The agency was given the authority to seek a court injunction halting the sale and distribution of any chemical that presented an imminent hazard and to ban or restrict the use of any chemical presenting a serious risk of cancer, gene mutations, or birth defects. PCB's and related chemicals were specifically banned by the act.

■ **Technology Assessment Act** Aware of the impact technology can make on the environment, Congress passed the Technology Assessment Act in 1972. This act creates an Office of Technology Assistance (OTA), consisting of six senators, six representatives, and an appointed director, whose basic responsibility is to provide Congress with "early indications of the probable beneficial and adverse impacts of the applications of technology."

Support for OTA grew out of frustrations the senators and representatives felt when they had to rely on others for their information. Agencies from the executive branch of the federal government might present a biased argument for the President's latest program, and expert witnesses at congressional hearings often addressed themselves to narrow aspects of a question without trying to harmonize the splintered reports or reconcile differing opinions. During debates on the supersonic transport (SST) that ended in 1971, for example, many congressmen complained that they were never given a reliable analysis of the costs versus the benefits of developing the plane. OTA supplies a better source of information on professional advice than was previously available—one that is more responsive to the needs of congressional committees in their efforts to assess the impact of new technologies on the environment.

■ **Federal wilderness and wildlife legislation** Since the federal government now owns more than 770 million acres of this nation's land, it is obvious that the environment cannot possibly be preserved and enhanced unless federal lands are managed according to principles of environmental protection. Congress itself recognized the need to preserve the American wilderness heritage as long ago as 1872, when it set aside a tract of land in what became the states of Montana, Wyoming, and Idaho to create Yellowstone National Park. The commitment to federal conservation of land was continued and enhanced by the Forest Reserve Act of 1891 and by subsequent laws that allowed private developers and ranchers to use federal land only after obtaining licenses or permits. In the 1960's, Congress created the Public Land Law Review Commission, declaring that public land should be kept and managed or disposed of only in ways that benefit the public at large.

Federal land preservation Under current legislation, the federal government requires three categories of land to be preserved. These categories are specified under three separate systems: The National Park System, the National Wilderness Preservation System, and the National Wildlife Refuge System.

The National Park System is made up of more than 25 million acres of land, including natural, historical, archeological, and recreation areas. The recreational areas include national seashores, lakeshores, scenic parkways, scenic riverways, and wild rivers. More commercial uses are permitted in the recreation areas than in natural and historical areas, but Congress has authorized only uses that fit into the basic plan of each area.

The National Wilderness Preservation System was established by Congress to save some part of the U.S. wilderness heritage for future generations. The areas it preserves, ranging from the Bering Sea Wilderness in Alaska to the Passage Key Wilderness in the Florida Keys, are marked by solitude and are not intended to be used by man.

The National Wildlife Refuge System is dedicated to the preservation of fish and wild game. It sets aside areas in which the wildlife cannot be disturbed.

Other public lands retained by the government may be used and developed, but are subject to strict controls. For example, the Multiple-Use–Sustained-Yield Act of 1960 and the National Forest Management Act of 1976 are efforts to reform the management of national forests that had been leased out to commercial companies and had been unwisely timbered. In some cases, the land was left barren, offering no shelter to wildlife, no attractive forests, and sometimes permitting serious erosion.

Endangered Species Act Congress has been equally persistent in protecting the nation's wildlife. The move has come none too soon, for toward the end of the 19th century, industrial expansion and unrestricted hunting almost annihilated the American bison and did cause the extinction of one of the most common birds in the country, the passenger pigeon.

The strongest wildlife legislation is the Endangered Species Act of 1973. This law authorizes the Secretary of the Interior to draw up a list of endangered and threatened species of fish, plants, and wild animals. *Endangered* means that the wildlife is in immediate danger of becoming extinct throughout all or a significant part of its range. *Threatened* means that a species is likely to become endangered if protective measures are not taken. The law recognizes that species can become endangered because of loss of habitat, overuse by commercial or sporting interests, disease or predatory animals, inadequate conservation regulations, and other causes. It is illegal for any person to import or export an endangered species, to hunt it within the United States or on the high seas, or to possess, sell, offer to sell, or transport it. The secretary is directed to cooperate with other government agencies, states, and foreign nations in protecting endangered species.

EXAMPLE   The Endangered Species Act led to a highly controversial Supreme Court decision in 1978. As the Tennessee Valley Authority approached completion of its $120 million Tellico Dam, the Secretary of the Interior learned that completion of the project would destroy the habitat of the snail darter, a fish that grows to a length of two or three inches and requires shallow, fast-flowing water to live and spawn. At the time, authorities believed that the only place in the world where snail darters existed was along a 17-mile stretch of the Little Tennessee River, where the dam was to be located.

The case went to the Supreme Court, which heard arguments that the dam was necessary for flood control, water storage, and the generation of electric power—values that, according to supporters of the dam, clearly outweighed the preservation of a small, useless fish. But the Court ruled that the project could not be finished. It held that the Endangered Species Act clearly states that in weighing different interests, endangered species must be given the highest priority. If the dam was to be completed, Congress would have to change the law.

That is what Congress set about doing. It voted to set up a Cabinet-level board empowered to study such conflicts between endangered species and projects such as Tellico and to grant exemptions when called for. At the board's first meeting, however, its members voted unanimously not to exempt Tellico.

In the summer of 1979, the House of Representatives quietly included in an appropriation bill an amendment that exempted the Tellico from any law that might hinder its construction. After some resistance, the Senate finally voted for the bill and it became law.

Happily, while the dam was being completed, two other snail darter populations were discovered in Tennessee. The dam did not make the species extinct after all.

■ **State laws**   The federal government is in a better position to solve many environmental problems than the individual states are. It is the biggest landowner (it owns more than one-third of the country), the biggest purchaser of goods, and the biggest user of services in the nation. The federal government also provides one-third of the nation's commercial timber and owns half the nation's oil and gas reserves. Furthermore, it owns or regulates all the electricity generated from hydroelectric and nuclear sources. Without national policies effectuated by federal action, the environment simply could not be adequately protected.

Without the help and the initiative of the states, however, the federal government would be incapable of fulfilling the goals of the National Environmental Policy Act. By the beginning of 1979, 26 states had passed their own environmental laws—and 2 states, New York and California, had laws even tougher and more stringent than those of the federal government. The programs established by those laws were funded at least in part by the federal government.

Many states require their own environmental impact statements before they will permit industrial growth, and many have developed their own provisions for monitoring air quality and conforming to the 1977 amendments to the Clean Air Act. For the names and addresses of state environmental agencies, see Chart 33.

■ **Worldwide impact**   The environmental laws of the United States have had a significant influence in other countries. The European Economic Community, for example, is instituting its own version of the environmental impact statement, and toward that end the United States Senate in 1978 adopted a resolution calling for an international use of environmental impact statements. The United States also cooperates with other countries, both near and far, in their efforts to protect wildlife, preserve natural resources, and help clean up the world.

Environmental Protection Agency   The federal agency that enforces pollution control and does research on the environment. Established in 1970 to coordinate the functions and activities of a number of government bureaus, the EPA is concerned with many different kinds of environmental problems: air, water, and noise pollution; solid-waste disposal (garbage); radiation control; environmental damage from pesticides; and protection of endangered species. The agency's most common contact with the general public is in its efforts to control the air pollution that comes from automobile exhausts. See ENVIRONMENTAL LAW.

Equal Employment Opportunity Commission   A federal agency that attempts to end job discrimination by employers by setting goals for hiring and monitoring internal promotions. The commission investigates unlawful employment practices, such as discrimination against a job applicant because of race or sex. It is authorized to file lawsuits against offending employers. See CIVIL RIGHTS.

equal protection of laws   Your constitutional right to receive the same protection under state law as any other person. The 14th Amendment to the U.S. Constitution prohibits any state from denying to any person within its jurisdiction the legal rights it grants to others. This constitutional provision, which is generally referred to as the equal protection clause, reads:

❝ No State shall . . . deny to any person within its jurisdiction the equal protection of the laws.❞

The equal protection clause was meant to prevent the states' governments from favoring or preferring particular groups of people at the expense of other groups. Originally, a principal purpose of the clause and of the entire 14th Amendment (which was enacted by Congress shortly after the Civil War) was to assure newly emancipated blacks all the civil rights under the law that white persons enjoyed. The equal protection clause guarantees that all persons

WHEN A STATE MUST GRANT EQUAL PROTECTION

■ Equal protection is a basic principle of justice under the law—it is your constitutional right to receive the same protection under state law as any other person. Equal protection is guaranteed by the 14th Amendment to the U.S. Constitution. You are guaranteed equal protection under federal law by the Fifth Amendment. State constitutions also contain equal protection clauses.

■ The 14th Amendment applies only to actions taken by a state government or its agencies—not to discriminatory actions committed by private individuals or corporations. However, if the state is significantly involved in a private action that deprives someone of equal rights or equal treatment, the courts may determine that the action constitutes state action. Typical of this were the preprimary elections conducted by a white voters' association in Texas—although the organization, without black voter participation, actually chose public officials it claimed to be private. The Supreme Court ruled that since the group was performing a government function, it had to afford everyone the right to vote in its elections.

■ A state is also involved if its actions help discrimination. A provision of California's constitution that gave a person the right to refuse to sell, lease, or rent real estate to anyone he chose encouraged private discrimination against nonwhites and therefore denied equal protection of the laws to all people within California's borders.

■ All persons physically present in the state are entitled to equal protection—including the poor, children, prisoners, minorities, aliens (noncitizens), and nonresidents.

■ Legal classifications made solely on the basis of noncitizenship are strictly scrutinized by the courts and upheld only if there is a compelling state interest to be served. State welfare laws that made benefits dependent on citizenship and imposed residency requirements on aliens were declared violations of the equal protection clause of the 14th Amendment by the U.S. Supreme Court.

■ Discrimination based on sex has only recently been held unconstitutional. The Supreme Court struck down one state law that established a different age of majority for girls than for boys, for example.

■ If a sex classification is reasonably related to a proper government objective, it will be upheld, however. For example, the Supreme Court has decided that giving widows (but not widowers) a certain exemption from property taxation was valid because it had a fair and substantial relation to the object of the law, which was to reduce the disparity between the economic capabilities of a man and a woman.

■ The Supreme Court has declared that a state law requiring husbands, but not wives, to pay alimony upon divorce violated the constitutional guarantee of equal protection.

■ Equal protection applies to the right of any person to engage in a legitimate business or occupation—but the state may *reasonably* regulate a business concerned with a public interest or a trade, occupation, or profession that affects the public welfare—hence, licensing requirements for doctors, lawyers, and the like.

■ The equal protection clause does not forbid states from establishing relevant qualifications for jurors or from providing exemptions as long as jury panels are representative of the community. It forbids only the systematic and deliberate exclusion of any definable class of qualified persons, such as blacks.

■ Unequal administration of a state statute offends the equal protection clause only when intentional discrimination is shown. For example, a city cannot prosecute one businessman for violating Sunday closing laws while others openly violate the same law with impunity. The plaintiff in such a case must, however, demonstrate that the city is purposely discriminating against him.

■ States and cities are required to extend to all races and nationalities equal treatment in all public facilities. Closing a public facility rather than operating it without race discrimination is not, however, a denial of equal protection.

■ Convicts do not lose all civil rights, and the equal protection clause follows them into prison. Troublemakers may legitimately be segregated from their fellow inmates, but officials cannot segregate prisoners solely on the basis of race.

■ Under the present interpretation of the 14th Amendment, each voter's vote has equal weight—therefore, a legislative apportionment plan that does not guarantee this equality in representation is unconstitutional. When a Congressman from one state district represents two or three times as many voters as Congressmen from other state districts, voters are denied equal protection.

■ Legislative gerrymandering for the purpose of disenfranchising black voters violates both the equal protection clause and the 15th Amendment.

■ The 14th Amendment has been interpreted by the courts as permitting the correction of historical discriminations against minorities, and courts have imposed affirmative action programs that prescribe racial goals and timetables.

■ But what about reverse discrimination? If a minority applicant gets admitted to a college ahead of a nonminority candidate with stronger academic qualifications, does this policy deny equal protection of the law to the nonminority candidate? Courts have been reluctant to issue any sweeping decisions on this matter, but they have decided that in proper circumstances reverse discrimination is constitutional.

■ If preferential policies of reverse discrimination really accomplish their purpose, the period and extent of their use should be temporary and limited. They should then be phased out as soon as goals are achieved. If they do not work, they should be discontinued. The Supreme Court's present position is a middle-of-the-road one, with some concessions both to advocates and to opponents of affirmative action programs.

subjected to state laws shall be treated alike both in privileges conferred and liabilities imposed. Neither the government nor any of its branches or agencies can set up unreasonable categories to justify unfair or unequal treatment to a person on the basis of his sex, race, religion, or nationality. The clause also prohibits the states from taking away anyone's life, liberty, or property, except by proper state action.

Equal protection clauses are also found in the constitutions of various states. They are interpreted by the courts as having the same force and effect as the equal protection clause of the 14th Amendment.

This article discusses how the principle of equal protection operates and who is guaranteed equal protection. It looks at equal protection in terms of its prohibitions—the making of discriminatory laws and the unequal and unfair administration of fair laws. Also considered is the application of equal protection to voting rights and reverse discrimination.

■ **Only for state actions** The 14th Amendment applies solely to actions taken by a state government, its political subdivisions, or its agencies. Thus the amendment is in effect for the actions taken by the state's legislative, judicial, or administrative branches; its towns, counties, or cities; and such agencies as its schools, police, or licensing commissions. Relief for discriminatory actions committed by private individuals or corporations may be obtained through other federal and state statutes. See CIVIL RIGHTS. The federal government is not bound by the 14th Amendment, but it is prohibited from denying a person equal protection of the law under the due process clause of the Fifth Amendment, because even though the Fifth Amendment lacks a specific equal protection clause the courts have interpreted its due process clause to include the guarantee of equal protection of the laws. See DUE PROCESS OF LAW.

For the equal protection clause to apply to a case, a state must be significantly involved in the action by which a person is being denied equal rights or equal treatment. For that reason constitutional problems, especially those involving racial segregation and voting rights, frequently require the courts to determine whether the conduct of private individuals constitutes state action.

Organizations doing state work To evade the law, private individuals or organizations often conduct what is essentially a public or governmental function.

EXAMPLE Blacks were excluded from preprimary elections O——* of the Jaybird Democratic Association, an organization of all the white voters in a Texas county. It operated like a regular political party, and since 1887 its candidates had nearly always run unopposed and won in the regular Democratic primary and the general election. This procedure was challenged as a violation of the 15th Amendment (which prohibits a state or the federal government from infringing upon a person's right to vote based on his race or color or the fact that he had been a slave) and of the equal protection clause of the 14th Amendment.

The Jaybird Association claimed it was a private social club whose actions were not within the scope of the protection of the 14th and 15th Amendments. The U.S. Supreme Court, however, decided that the organization performed a government function by running what was, for all practical purposes, the only electoral apparatus in the county and thus took on the attributes of government. Therefore, the association had to give the individual the same constitutional rights as the state would be required to do.

When the state helps discrimination State action may be found when the state, by its conduct, officially encourages discriminatory behavior by private parties.

EXAMPLE A provision of the state constitution of California O——* gave a person the constitutional right to refuse to sell, lease, or rent his real property (real estate) to anyone he chose. The Supreme Court decided that this provision involved the state in private racial discriminations to an unconstitutional degree. A person could refuse to sell his property to a black, secure in the knowledge that the court of California would support his position. The Court held that through this provision the state had officially encouraged private discrimination by making it legally permissible. This denied equal protection of the laws to all people within the borders of California.

State action may be found when the state or its agency enters into a contract or a lease with a private individual or corporation that engages in discriminatory conduct.

EXAMPLE A coffee shop owner who leased part of a building O——* owned and operated by the Wilmington Parking Authority, an agency of the State of Delaware, refused to serve black customers. A suit was brought against the authority for violating the equal protection clause. The authority claimed that the shop was acting in a purely private capacity under its lease and that therefore there was no state involvement. The U.S. Supreme Court rejected this argument. It reasoned that since the building was publicly owned and was maintained by public funds, it was dedicated to public uses. The Court decided that there was significant state participation to qualify the discriminatory action of the state's lessee.

State as nondiscriminatory If the state has not significantly participated in the discriminatory action, courts will refuse to find a violation of equal protection.

EXAMPLE A private club refused to serve a black guest of a O——* member at its bar. This discrimination was challenged as unconstitutional because the club was required to have a state license to serve alcoholic beverages. The plaintiff argued that the discrimination was state action and therefore unconstitutional. The Court concluded that the mere licensing of the club by the state did not implicate the state in the club's discriminatory practices. Although the state can regulate its liquor licensees, this does not make the state a venturer in the enterprises. The licensing relationship here does not approach "the symbiotic relationship between lessor and lessee," as it did in the case of the coffee shop. Therefore, there was no denial by the state of equal protection of laws to blacks. In this case the state was not significantly involved in the discriminatory action of a private club.

■ **Persons protected** All persons physically present in the state are entitled to the equal protection of its laws, including the poor, children, prisoners, and minorities. The fact that a person is an ALIEN or a nonresident of the state does not exclude him while he is within its borders.

EXAMPLE In 1886 the Supreme Court decided that Chinese
◦—∗ aliens were entitled to equal protection of the
laws of California. A San Francisco ordinance made it
unlawful to operate a laundry except in a store or brick
building and with the consent of supervisory authorities.
This consent was withheld from Chinese aliens. Some 80
other people, not Chinese subjects, were granted permission to operate the same business under similar conditions. The Court held that discrimination in the
administration of an ordinance based solely on race and
nationality is illegal. This, however, does not mean that
aliens have all the rights and privileges citizens have.

Coverage for corporations Equal protection of the
laws of a state extends to a private corporation, domestic or
foreign (from another state), when it is within the jurisdiction of that state—that is, when it has met the requirements
imposed by state law. A foreign corporation may be treated
differently from a domestic corporation before it is permitted to do business in the state. But once it has been licensed,
it has the benefit of protection under the equal protection
clause of the 14th Amendment.

EXAMPLE When a state charged a domestic corporation a
◦—∗ license fee of $10 per year and a foreign corpora-
tion a license fee of $25, it did not violate the equal
protection clause. After the foreign corporation was licensed to do business in the state, however, its net receipts were assessed 100 percent of their value, while the
domestic corporation's net receipts were assessed 30 percent of their value. Now both corporations were "within
the jurisdiction" of the state. The higher assessment on
the receipts of the foreign corporation denied it equal
treatment and equal protection of the state's laws.

Corporate uniqueness under the law In extending
equal protection to corporations, however, courts take into
account the distinct advantage a corporation has over individuals or partnerships in the same business.

EXAMPLE An Illinois law provided for the taxation of per-
◦—∗ sonal property owned by corporations but not by
individuals. The Court upheld the law. "Where taxation
is concerned, and no specific federal right, apart from
equal protection, is imperiled, the states have large leeway in making classifications and drawing lines which in
their judgment produce reasonable systems of taxation."
Courts will overturn such statutes only where it is clearly
shown that the corporation is being unjustly and unfairly
treated. Corporations have special advantages in business,
such as the absence of individual liability and infinite
duration, which do not exist when the same business is
conducted by private individuals or partnerships. "It is this
distinctive privilege [of incorporation] which is the subject
of taxation."

■ **Prohibition on legislative action** The equal protection clause prohibits states from making laws that discriminate against persons who are in similar circumstances and
from applying fair laws in a discriminatory manner.

A state or its political subdivisions cannot pass laws that
make *unreasonable distinctions* between persons similarly
situated and treat one more favorably than another. This
does not mean, however, that a state or municipality cannot
enact legislation that recognizes different situations and
discriminates accordingly. But the discrimination or dis-

tinction must have a rational basis and cannot be arbitrary.
For example, a state law that prohibits red-haired people
from driving cars because they are believed to have reckless
personalities is clearly an arbitrary distinction.

Laws passed by state or local legislative bodies are presumed to be constitutional and courts will not lightly
assume legislative arbitrariness. In determining whether
the law is arbitrary or rational in its distinctions, the courts
will see if any facts may be reasonably conceived to justify
the difference in treatment.

Statutes may establish different sets of rules for different
categories, or classes, of persons. In the eyes of the court,
these classifications are either suspect or nonsuspect. A
classification is *suspect* if it isolates a particular class of
persons because of their race or alienage (noncitizenship). A
classification is *inherently suspect* if it deprives a person of
a fundamental right, such as the right to travel or to vote. A
classification is *nonsuspect* when it treats a certain category
of persons differently on a rational ground—such as requiring stringent educational and training experience before
granting a license to a surgeon to practice his profession.

The courts will examine statutes to see if there has been a
violation of the equal protection guarantee only if a person
claims he is being subjected to intentional or invidious
discrimination by the state or its agencies. The traditional
test employed by the courts involves first determining the
type of classification at issue. If the court determines that
classification is suspect or involves fundamental rights, it
has traditionally applied a *strict scrutiny test*. This test
requires that unless the purpose of the law is a state interest
so compelling and substantial that it justifies the classification used, the law is unconstitutional.

Most classifications by statute, however, are nonsuspect—that is, they are reasonably related to some legitimate legislative objective. This is known as the *rational
basis test,* which is usually passed with ease. Recently,
however, there has been a movement away from these
traditional tests toward a middle ground of review. According to the Supreme Court, this approach concentrates on
"the character [of the classification] in question, the relative
importance to individuals in the class discriminated against
of the governmental benefits that they do not receive, and
the asserted state interests in support of the classification."
Although the Supreme Court has not expressly discarded
the traditional tests, this new approach—sometimes called
the factual rationality test—has been applied.

■ **Suspect classification—strict scrutiny test** After
the court determines that a classification is suspect because
it discriminates on the basis of race or nationality or affects
fundamental rights, the government must establish that the
classification is necessary to achieve a compelling state
interest.

Race A Virginia law was designed to prevent interracial marriages. The classification of persons under that law
was of course based solely on race.

EXAMPLE A black woman and a white man were married in
◦—∗ the District of Columbia and returned to reside in
Virginia. They were convicted under the state antimiscegenation statute, which prohibited marriages between
white and "colored" persons or Indians. The state asserted that the statute served a compelling state interest by

preserving the racial integrity of its citizens. The Court rejected this claim. "The fact that Virginia only prohibits interracial marriages involving white persons demonstrates that the racial classifications must stand . . . as measures designed to maintain white supremacy." There was no legitimate state interest in this discrimination.

In only a few cases has the government succeeded in establishing compelling governmental interest to justify the use of racial classifications. One case involved action taken by the federal government against Americans of Japanese ancestry during World War II, which involved equal protection claims under the Fifth Amendment.

EXAMPLE Japanese-Americans were required to leave their 0——* homes on the West Coast if they lived within certain designated military areas. They were sent to "relocation centers" run by military authorities. The Supreme Court decided that the relocation order, although discriminatory against Americans of Japanese ancestry, was essential to protect against espionage and sabotage of war materials and utilities thought to be in danger of Japanese invasion and air attack.

Noncitizenship Any classifications made solely on the basis of noncitizenship will be strictly scrutinized and upheld only if it serves a compelling state interest.

State welfare laws that made benefits dependent on citizenship and imposed residency requirements on aliens were declared by the Supreme Court to be violations of the equal protection clause of the 14th Amendment.

EXAMPLE An Arizona statute required a person to be a 0——* citizen or to reside in the United States for a total of 15 years in order to qualify for welfare benefits. A Pennsylvania welfare statute completely excluded resident aliens from receiving assistance. The Supreme Court held that when the Constitution prohibited a state from denying to "any person within its jurisdiction the equal protection of the laws," the word "person" entitled legal resident aliens as well as citizens to equal protection of the laws of the state in which they reside.

Arizona and Pennsylvania claimed that their restrictions on the eligibility of aliens for public assistance were justified. The state had a "special public interest" in favoring its citizens over aliens in distributing limited resources. The Court rejected this argument because aliens paid taxes on an equal basis with citizens and should be entitled to share in the revenues.

EXAMPLE A New York law provided that only U.S. citizens 0——* could hold permanent positions in the competitive class of the state civil service. Four legal resident aliens were discharged from their jobs solely because they were not citizens. The Supreme Court decided that New York's flat statutory prohibition against the employment of aliens was invalid as a violation of the equal protection clause. The classification could be upheld as serving a legitimate state interest if New York had restricted the employment of noncitizens as civil servants in areas where they would make or execute government policy. This would avoid the possibility of competing obligations to another sovereignty. But since the citizenship restriction applied to a wide range of positions from sanitation men to typists to policymakers, the classification could not withstand strict judicial scrutiny.

Fundamental rights Any classification affecting a fundamental right must serve a compelling governmental interest in order to be valid. A fundamental right is one guaranteed explicitly or implicitly in the Constitution. For example, a person has the right to life, liberty, and the pursuit of happiness as explicitly granted in the BILL OF RIGHTS. He also has the right to privacy that is implied from the prohibition against unreasonable SEARCH AND SEIZURE and from other amendments. See PRIVACY, RIGHT OF.

The social importance of the right, however, does not determine whether it is covered by the equal protection clause. The right to an education, for instance, is not a fundamental right since it is not guaranteed either expressly or by implication by the Constitution.

Right to liberty A person has a fundamental right to liberty, which cannot be taken away from him without due process of law. A state law that treats a poor person convicted of a crime differently from a wealthy person is unconstitutional—it deprives the poor person of his right to equal protection of the laws.

EXAMPLE A poor man in Texas was convicted of traffic 0——* offenses and fined a total of $425. Texas law provided only fines for such offenses. If a person was unable to pay, he was jailed for a sufficient time to satisfy the fines at the rate of $5 per day. The man was committed to the municipal prison farm. His application for a writ of habeas corpus to obtain his release was denied. The Supreme Court decided that limiting punishment to payment of a fine was a denial of equal protection to those unable to pay. The equal protection clause of the Constitution requires that the maximum imprisonment for any substantive offense be the same for all defendants, regardless of economic status. The Court recognized, however, that it was not a violation of equal protection to imprison a person who refused to pay the fine.

Right to travel Many residency laws—including those that make state residence a requirement for welfare assistance—have been held unconstitutional because they violate a person's right to travel. See RESIDENCY LAWS.

Right of privacy The Supreme Court has recognized the right of personal privacy as a fundamental right created implicitly by the Constitution. The Court has held as fundamental the right to marry and have children.

EXAMPLE A public school policy required that a teacher be 0——* dismissed from her job at the end of her sixth month of pregnancy. This policy was challenged as an unconstitutional denial of equal protection to women teachers. Since the school system did not demonstrate any compelling governmental interest to justify the policy, the classification (teachers at the end of the sixth month of pregnancy) infringed on the fundamental right to bear children. It made a woman teacher choose between having children and continuing her job.

The government cannot interfere with basic matters of procreation, marriage, and family unless there are compelling governmental interests that cannot be served by less restrictive alternatives.

EXAMPLE A man named Griswold operated a Planned Par-0——* enthood Center where information and instruction in the use of contraceptives was distributed to married couples. State laws, however, made the giving of birth control information as well as the use of such information and devices a misdemeanor. Griswold was convicted of a misdemeanor under the "giving" law and fined. He appealed, claiming that the law was unconstitutional. The Court agreed because the law infringed on the exercise of a fundamental right without demonstrating a compelling state interest to be served. The right of privacy in marital relationships is implicitly granted by the Constitution.

The constitutional right of privacy also encompasses a woman's decision to terminate her pregnancy. This right, however, is not absolute. The state may properly assert important interests in safeguarding health, maintaining medical standards, and protecting potential life. At some point in the pregnancy, the state's interests become sufficiently compelling to sustain regulation of factors that govern ABORTION. For example, the decision of a woman to have an abortion in the first three months of pregnancy is protected by the equal protection clause. During that time, the state can have no compelling reason that might override a woman's right to an abortion.

■ **Nonsuspect classifications—rational basis test**
Most nonsuspect classifications are subject to the standard of rationality, which tests whether they bear a reasonable relationship to some legitimate legislative purpose.

Economic and social legislation The rational basis test has been leniently applied in the areas of economics and social welfare, where the Supreme Court has decided that "if the classification has some 'reasonable basis,' it does not offend the Constitution simply because it is not made with mathematical nicety or because it results in some inequality."

EXAMPLE An out-of-state applicant for admission to a state
O—* university sued the school officials, claiming that more stringent standards were employed for out-of-state applicants than for those who resided within the state. She claimed this violated her right to equal protection and equal treatment under the law. The federal district court applied the rational basis test to the school's policy. The classification was not suspect or inherently suspect. It did not involve fundamental rights because a person does not have a fundamental right to a university education. The Court decided that the state university's program of preferential admissions of in-state students was reasonable and did not violate the equal protection clause. The state had a legitimate interest in giving its residents preference in admission. The state could also charge an out-of-state student higher tuition under the same reasoning without violating the equal protection guarantee.

As long as there is no invidious discrimination against a particular class of persons—as is the case with residence requirements for welfare applicants—state officials usually have broad leeway concerning the allocation of welfare funds.

EXAMPLE In Maryland, a "standard of need" was set for
O—* each family receiving public welfare. Families received benefits sufficient to meet their needs up to a certain limit. Recipients with large families sued because the amount they got was far below their requirements. They contended that the maximum grant limitation discriminated against them merely because of their large families, thereby violating the equal protection clause.

Maryland argued that the maximum limitation was valid because, among other things, it encouraged employment and allocated public funds to meet the needs of the largest number of families. The Court held that the "Equal Protection Clause does not require that a state must choose between attacking every aspect of a problem or not attacking the problem at all. It is enough that the state's action be rationally based and free from invidious discrimination." The suit was dismissed.

Illegitimacy A statute that classifies persons according to the status of their birth is constitutional only when the classification is reasonably related to what the statute is seeking to accomplish.

EXAMPLE A Louisiana statute denied equal recovery rights
O—* to a dependent illegitimate child under workmen's compensation laws for the death of his natural father if the father had not recognized the child as his. Legitimate and illegitimate children who were acknowledged by their father shared any recovery equally. Unacknowledged children could inherit only if there were any benefits left after all other surviving dependents had taken their share. The state claimed that the statute was designed to protect the family as a unit and to prevent fraudulent claims by persons who were not actually related to the dead man.

The Supreme Court rejected the arguments. "No child is responsible for his birth, and penalizing the illegitimate child is an ineffectual—as well as an unjust—way of deterring the parent." As for the greater potential for fraudulent claims, the Court reasoned that since a person would not be entitled to recover unless he could show his dependence on the dead man, this greatly reduced the possibility of fraud. The inferior treatment of dependent, unacknowledged illegitimate children was not reasonably related to the purposes of workmen's compensation statutes, nor did it serve any legitimate state interest.

■ **Sex discrimination—a special case** Discrimination based on sex is prohibited to the federal government by the due process clause of the Fifth Amendment. The Supreme Court has never explicitly decided that sex is a suspect classification, and until 1971 it had never held any discrimination against women to be in violation of equal protection of laws.

EXAMPLE One of the first cases concerning sexual discrimi-
O—* nation decided by the Supreme Court involved a law governing the administration of wills. An Idaho statute that regulated the choice of persons qualified to act as administrator when someone dies without a will provided that males be preferred to females. The Supreme Court found that the unequal treatment of women was completely unrelated to the purpose of the statute, which was for administrative convenience and quick distribution of the assets of an estate. The arbitrary and irrational preference of males over females, when both were equal under the eyes of the law, violated the guarantee of equal protection of laws to women.

A federal district court used the rational basis test to determine whether barring girls from an interscholastic athletic program on the basis of their sex denied them equal protection.

EXAMPLE In an interscholastic athletic program authorized by state law, two public high school girls were prohibited from participating with boys in the noncontact sports of tennis, cross-country skiing, and running. The girls were fully qualified to compete with the boys in these sports and their high schools did not provide teams for girls. The girls claimed that the prohibition was arbitrary and unreasonable as a violation of their right to equal protection of laws.

The court decided the purpose of the athletic program was to allow persons with similar qualifications to compete with each other. This program barred girls from competing with boys on the basis of "an outdated image of women as peculiarly delicate and impressionable creatures in need of protection from the rough and tumble of unvarnished humanity." The prohibition of girls from the program because of their sex clearly deprived them of equal protection of the laws as guaranteed by the 14th Amendment.

The mandate of equality of opportunity does not dictate a disregard of differences in talents and abilities among individuals, however. There is no right to a position on a school athletic team, but only a right to compete for it on equal terms.

In 1975 the Supreme Court found that a Utah law establishing a different age of majority for girls and boys had no rational basis and was a violation of equal protection of laws.

In the late 1970's the Supreme Court moved one step beyond the rational basis test in sex discrimination cases. It favored an approach that examined the relative importance of the individual interest compared with the government objective.

EXAMPLE A Florida statute gave widows a $500 exemption from property taxation. Its constitutionality was challenged as a violation of the equal protection clause because it denied the same exemption to widowers. The Supreme Court decided that the classification "widow" was valid because it has a "fair and substantial relation to the object of legislation," which is to reduce "the disparity between the economic capabilities of a man and a woman." The Court said: "There can be no dispute that the financial difficulties confronting the lone woman in Florida, or in any other state, exceed those facing the man . . . the job market is inhospitable to the woman seeking any but the lowest-paid jobs." The law is reasonably designed to further the state policy of cushioning the financial impact of the death of a spouse for whom the loss imposes a disproportionately heavy burden.

Sometimes a law, although written in sex-neutral terms, unintentionally discriminates against the members of one sex. This does not necessarily mean that the equal protection clause has been violated.

EXAMPLE A Massachusetts law gave all veterans who qualified for state civil service jobs an absolute lifetime preference over nonveterans. In order to get a civil service job, a person had to take a competitive examination, the score of which, in addition to his training and experience, would be used to arrive at his grade. The job applicants would then be ranked in order of their scores on an "eligible list." Veterans were ranked according to their respective ratings above all other job applicants, even though many nonveterans had higher ratings. Female civil service workers and, in particular, one woman who repeatedly lost job promotions because of the preference challenged the law, claiming that it unfairly discriminated against women in violation of the equal protection clause.

The district court agreed. Although the aim of the preference was legitimate and the law was not designed to discriminate against women, its impact severely limited a woman's civil service opportunities. The case reached the Supreme Court, which found the preference law valid. The preference was "designed to reward veterans for the sacrifice of military service, to ease the transition from military to civilian life, to encourage patriotic service, and to attract loyal and well-disciplined people to civil service occupations." The disproportionate preference given to men (98 percent male veterans in Massachusetts) was not intentional—it was due largely to "the simple fact that women have never been subjected to a military draft." In this case, the law was written to help any person who was a veteran, not to discriminate against women.

■ **Police power** The equal protection clause was not intended to deprive a state or its political subdivisions of its POLICE POWER. This includes the power to pass laws that protect public health, safety, and morals and promote the general welfare of its residents. These laws, however, must apply equally and uniformly to all persons. Any classification contained in them must be based on some legitimate distinction and have substantial relation to the object of the legislation. For example, fluoridation of the water by a city is a valid exercise of its police power to protect public health. It is not unconstitutionally discriminatory because it benefits children only. The long-range benefits of fluoridation extend into adulthood and thus ultimately aid all citizens.

Gambling and business The state can validly exercise its police power to outlaw certain forms of gambling that are considered to be injurious to the public.

EXAMPLE In one Maryland case, the constitutionality of a statute that prohibited slot machines was challenged. The plaintiff claimed that the state was discriminating against poor people, who would use slot machines, because gambling at racetracks, where the rich dropped their money, was permitted. The state court rejected this claim. The law was designed to protect public morals, a proper exercise of the police power.

The guarantee of equal protection of the law applies to the right of any person to engage in a legitimate business or occupation. The state may, however, reasonably regulate a business concerned with a public interest or a trade, occupation, or profession that affects the welfare of the public. In order to protect people against incompetent persons and harmful practices, states may establish mandatory qualifications for persons seeking to practice a profession requiring special knowledge or skill—doctor, lawyer, optometrist, or dentist. The state regulates the practice of these professions by setting licensing requirements that aim to produce both honest and competent professionals.

The state may prohibit persons within its borders from engaging in occupations or businesses that are detrimental to the public welfare—itinerant peddlers of fraudulent cure-alls, for example. The legislature may generally classify businesses and occupations for the purposes of regulation and limit a regulation to a particular kind of business.

EXAMPLE A Detroit ordinance that forced topless go-go dancers to obtain identification cards and prohibited them from being waitresses did not deny them equal protection. The state court recognized that the operation of a topless go-go bar is a business that affects the public health, morals, and welfare to such an extent as to warrant its regulation and licensing.

But a state may not use its police power to interfere arbitrarily with a private business or occupation or impose unreasonable or unnecessary restrictions.

EXAMPLE A city ordinance prevented the plaintiff company from operating its windshield-replacement business at customers' homes or other places convenient to them, which was the plaintiff's major selling point. A state court declared this statute unconstitutional because it did not serve a legitimate public interest and so could not justify the city's exercise of its police power.

Proper powers Various statutes have been upheld as valid exercises of a state's police power. A town may enact Sunday closing laws, for instance, that prohibit the sale of such commodities as alcohol and services, in order to afford employees a day of rest and recreation. A county whose economy is dependent on apples may enact an ordinance requiring the destruction of cedar trees to protect orchards from cedar rust.

A state law may be limited in its operation to a particular part of the state or it may prescribe different rules for different areas. But there must be a reasonable basis for the limitation or distinction with all persons similarly situated being treated alike. For example, ZONING ordinances that exclude commercial buildings from a residential district do not violate equal protection laws. Zoning laws are intended to promote the public health, safety, welfare, convenience, morals, or prosperity of the community. They limit the use of land in the interest of public welfare by preserving and stabilizing the character of the community. As long as classifications under zoning ordinances serve the interests of the community, they will not be considered as violating the equal protection clause.

Similarly, a city's approach to the elimination of slums and blight on a designated-area basis is a valid exercise of its police power. It accomplishes the objectives of the legislation authorizing such action. The city has a vital interest and public purpose in the prevention of slums and blight. The ordinance that sets more stringent requirements for maintenance of the buildings within the designated urban renewal areas is another constitutional application of the police power of the city.

The state under its police power can establish requirements for marriage that must be observed to safeguard public morals.

EXAMPLE In a proceeding to review the denial of a marriage license, a state court decided that a law prohibiting same-sex marriages did not violate the equal protection clause of the 14th Amendment. The court applied the rational basis test. It held that marriage is a private relationship between a man and a woman that involves

interests of basic importance to society. Although the state cannot require all married persons to have children, marriage is needed to afford a favorable environment for bringing up children. Therefore there can be no doubt that there is a rational basis for the state to limit the protection of its marriage laws to unions between men and women and to exclude same-sex marriages.

■ **Discriminatory application of the law** The equal protection clause prohibits the discriminatory administration of laws that by their language are fair. Sometimes this comes about when a rule or classification that in itself is nonsuspect (treats one class of person differently from others on rational grounds) has a demonstrable impact on a historically suspect class (isolates a class of persons because of race or citizenship). The word "demonstrable" is important here, because not every minor difference in the application of laws is a violation of equal protection—exact equality is not a prerequisite. Moreover, the unequal application of a state law against suspect groups does not deny equal protection unless it is intentional or deliberate discrimination.

EXAMPLE A classic case of the discriminatory administration of a law that appears to be fair occurred in Alabama. The law required that the jury rolls be made up of the names of all males over the age of 21 who were considered respectable citizens. As the law operated, however, blacks were systematically barred from serving on juries. The Supreme Court ruled that a state that deliberately excludes blacks from participating as jurors in the administration of justice violates the equal protection clause. If no black has served on a jury for a number of years even when qualified blacks were available, the state must show that the exclusion was caused by some reason other than racial discrimination. The case against the state is not destroyed by the token inclusion of a few blacks on the jury panel.

The equal protection clause does not forbid states from establishing relevant qualifications for jurors or from providing exemptions as long as jury panels are representative of the community. It forbids only the systematic and deliberate exclusion of any definable class of qualified persons from juries that is inconsistent with the principle of a fair trial by an impartial jury. The Supreme Court has recognized, however, that a prosecutor who uses his PEREMPTORY CHALLENGES to strike all blacks from the jury does not violate the equal protection clause. These challenges are designed to permit the rejection of any juror for "real or imaginary partiality that is less easily designated or demonstrable."

Deliberate discrimination Conscious selectivity in enforcing state criminal laws violates equal protection only if selectivity is "deliberately based upon an unjustifiable standard such as race, religion, or other arbitrary classification." The plaintiff must show more than a mere failure to prosecute other offenders. Unequal administration of a state statute offends the equal protection clause only when intentional discrimination is shown. In one case, the police enforced a state's antiobscenity law against bookstores that specialized in pornography in an attempt to drive all such stores out of business. At the same time, no action was taken against movie theaters that violated the law by showing pornographic films. The selectivity in enforcement of this law amounted to intentional discrimination. In another case, a court decided that a city could not continually prosecute one businessman for violation of Sunday-closing laws while other persons openly violated the same law with impunity.

The plaintiff, however, must demonstrate that the city is intentionally discriminating against him. There must be sufficient proof of deliberate discrimination in the administration of a neutral law before a court will declare the action a violation of equal protection.

EXAMPLE In 1971 a suit charged that the mayor of Philadelphia had racially discriminated in his appointments to the city's Nominating Panel, whose function was to nominate members of the school board. Under the city charter, the panel was composed of 13 persons: the highest-ranking officer of the nine designated categories of citywide organizations—a labor union council, commerce group, parent-teacher association—and four from the citizenry at large. Approximately "34% of the population of Philadelphia and approximately 60% of the students attending the city's various schools were Negroes," but "the 1971 Panel had 11 whites and 2 Negroes." The Supreme Court held the proof "too fragmentary and speculative" to establish "a prima facie case of racial discrimination." Because of the designated qualifications for panel members, it could not be shown that any "members of a particular class have been unlawfully excluded."

Job qualifications Mental and physical employment qualifications may have an adverse impact on a particular race or nationality. This neutral classification is not normally judged by strict scrutiny or by the compelling state interest test. Rather, the courts analyze the employment qualifications to determine their factual rationality to the job requirements.

EXAMPLE Some black and Spanish-surnamed residents of a city claimed that police recruiting and hiring practices, although apparently neutral, discriminated against them under the Civil Rights Act of 1964 and denied them equal protection of the law. They contended that minimum height requirements of five foot seven inches, a swimming test, and a high school diploma were used to exclude them from applying for the job of policeman. The criteria, they claimed, were wholly unrelated to job performance. A federal court of appeals decided the requirements were not wholly unrelated to job performance. The plaintiffs failed to demonstrate that the height requirement or the swim test had a disproportionate impact on blacks and Spanish-surnamed applicants as a group. The educational requirement was viewed by the court as "a bare minimum for successful performance of the policeman's responsibilities."

Punishing crimes In the exercise of its police power to promote public safety, a state may enact statutes that define and establish punishments for criminal conduct. Both the equal protection and the due process clauses emphasize that the central aim of the U.S. judicial system is that all people charged with a crime stand equally before the bar of justice. No state can deprive persons or groups of persons of equal and impartial justice under the law, nor can a state legislature prescribe different punishments for the same crimes committed under identical circumstances.

There is no requirement, however, that two persons convicted of the same offense receive identical sentences.

EXAMPLE A 35-year-old man who has a string of felony convictions may be sentenced to life imprisonment upon conviction for armed robbery. Meanwhile an 18-year-old who has never before committed a crime may receive a five-year sentence for the same crime committed under identical circumstances. Equal protection does not require that all persons be dealt with identically. But it does require that distinctions in classifications for the purpose of sentencing have some relevance to the purpose.

The fact that the prosecution, when faced with charging a defendant under different statutes, chooses to prosecute him for the offense carrying the more serious penalty does not deny equal protection. The exercise of this "prosecutorial discretion" is unconstitutional discrimination only if deliberately based upon an unjustifiable standard, such as race, religion, or some other arbitrary classification.

EXAMPLE If a county prosecutor always prosecutes poor blacks for burglary while on the same set of facts he always tries whites for breaking and entering, a lesser offense, there is a denial of equal protection of law. The difference in treatment is based solely on race.

Discipline and treatment of prisoners Although convicts may lose many of the rights and privileges of law-abiding citizens, such as the right to vote or to engage in certain occupations, they do not lose all civil rights and the equal protection clause follows them into prison. When disciplinary measures are reasonably maintained in state prisons, however, the state's action will not be declared unconstitutional under this clause. Prison authorities may classify and segregate prisoners who pose a serious threat to the maintenance of discipline and security without violating equal protection. There is a compelling and legitimate state interest to be served by isolating troublemakers from the general prison population. But officials cannot segregate prisoners solely on the basis of their race.

EXAMPLE County prison officials habitually place young black prisoners in solitary confinement for a minor infraction, such as refusal to make their bunks. White prisoners are denied exercise-yard privileges for one day for the same acts. Equal protection has been denied the black prisoners.

■ **Segregation** There are laws segregating or otherwise classifying on a racial basis that, in a literal sense, treat all races identically. If the administration of these laws, however, results in segregation in public schools, public facilities, or public housing, they deny equal treatment under the law as guaranteed by the equal protection clause.

Education Segregation in education has been considered "inherently unequal" since the 1954 Supreme Court decision of *Brown* v. *Board of Education*. Up until that time, segregation in public education rested on the doctrine of "separate but equal," which the Court had announced in the case of *Plessy* v. *Ferguson* in 1896. In *Plessy,* the Supreme Court found that the racial segregation of passengers on public trains in separate but equal facilities complied with the requirement of the equal protection clause. States applied this doctrine to education and established a separate system of schools, curricula, teachers' qualifications, and salaries.

The separate educational facilities established for blacks, however, were *not* equal to those set up for whites. In 1954 black children sought the aid of the courts in obtaining admission to local public elementary and high schools on a nonsegregated basis. They claimed that state laws, which denied them admission to the public schools on the same basis as white children, denied them equal protection of the laws. Compelling them to attend schools that were separate but equal did not comply with the requirements of the 14th Amendment. The lower courts held that the separate but equal facilities provided by the states complied with the Constitution. The Supreme Court set aside the lower courts' decisions, stating: "Segregation with the sanction of the law has a tendency to retard the educational and mental development of Negro children and to deprive them of some of the benefits they would receive in a racially integrated system." See also CIVIL RIGHTS.

Public facilities A state or municipality is required by the equal protection clause to extend to members of all races and nationalities equal treatment in all facilities or privileges provided from public funds—transportation, parks, hospitals, libraries, auditoriums, homes for the aged, as well as recreational, artistic, cultural, or entertainment facilities.

The equal protection clause prohibits state discriminatory action of every kind, including state participation through any arrangement, management, funds, or property. Even though a city may not own the land upon which parks are located, for example, its activities in landscaping the grounds, providing personnel, and operating the facilities as city parks is state action—blacks cannot be excluded from these parks. If the city leases a public golf course to a private individual to operate on its former segregated basis, this does not remove the course from "state action" and it violates this clause.

Closing a public recreational facility, rather than operating it without racial discrimination, is not a denial of equal protection. A municipality was ordered by the Court to desegregate its swimming pools. It closed the pools instead. The Court decided that the closing was constitutional. There was no official encouragement of discrimination because both black and white students were deprived of the use of the pools.

Housing Discrimination based upon race or color in housing provided by branches or agencies of the state violates the equal protection clause.

EXAMPLE A privately owned apartment complex was built O⊶⊷∗ as part of an urban renewal project with planning, administrative, and financial assistance from the state and federal governments. Its owners cannot refuse to supply application forms to people on welfare solely on the basis of their race or economic status without depriving them of their constitutional right to equal protection.

Discrimination in private housing is prohibited by specific federal statutes concerning CIVIL RIGHTS.

■ **Voting rights** The 15th Amendment provides for equality of voting rights for all citizens. This right is guaranteed against infringment by the state and federal governments on the basis of race, color, or previous condition of SERVITUDE. The equal protection clause of the 14th Amendment also protects this fundamental right to vote. A state may impose reasonable restrictions on the right to vote only as long as they serve a compelling state interest and do not discriminate against any class of persons.

Qualifications for voting State standards for the qualifications of voters must be administered equally. A statute requiring the payment of a poll tax before a person will be allowed to vote in an election violates the guarantee of equal protection of laws because it deprives poor people of their fundamental right to vote.

Residence requirements, previous criminal record, and age are other factors a state may consider in determining the qualifications of voters.

EXAMPLE A Texas constitutional provision denied armed O⊶⊷∗ services personnel, who were not originally residents, the right to vote even after they had established permanent residence in the state. The Supreme Court declared this provision a violation of the equal protection guarantee when the state could offer no compelling state interest to justify this denial of a fundamental right.

Residency requirements A state may require a person to be a resident for a reasonable period of time in order to vote in state ELECTIONS.

EXAMPLE The Supreme Court decided that Tennessee's O⊶⊷∗ voting registration requirements of residence in the state for one year and in the county for three months violated equal protection. It divided residents into two classes, old and new, and discriminated against the latter. These laws restricted two fundamental rights—the right to vote and the right to travel. Although a state can impose qualifications on its voters, it cannot restrict the right to vote beyond preserving a compelling state interest. Tennessee made two claims: that the residency requirement prevented fraud in elections and insured that a person would vote knowledgeably, as he would be more familiar with the issues. The Court rejected both arguments. It stated that 30 days' residence in the county before an election would give both the state and the voter sufficient time to prepare for the election.

Literacy tests The ability to read and write has some relation to standards designed to promote the intelligent use of the ballot box. Literacy and illiteracy are nondiscriminatory classifications as far as race, creed, and sex are concerned. But their application can be discriminatory.

EXAMPLE To register as a voter one applicant had to under- O⊶⊷∗ stand and give an interpretation of any section of the state or federal Constitution read to him. This requirement violated the 14th and 15th Amendments. "The cherished right of people to vote cannot be obliterated by the use of laws which leave the voting fate of citizens to the passing whim or impulse of the individual registrar." The evidence showed that the literacy test, although neutral in its language, was administered in a discriminatory manner to disenfranchise blacks.

Congress, which is authorized to enforce the equal protection clause by appropriate legislation, passed the Voting Rights Act of 1965, which specifically permits voting based on Spanish literacy.

EXAMPLE New York City's practice of preparing and dis- O⊶⊷∗ tributing ballots, voting instructions, and other election materials only in English constituted a condition on the right to vote by basing it on the ability to read and understand English. This practice deprived Puerto Ricans of their constitutional and statutory right to vote. They spoke, read, wrote, and understood Spanish, but had little or no ability with English.

Special elections A state may not exclude qualified voters from voting in a limited or special purpose election unless it is necessary to promote a compelling state interest.

EXAMPLE New York law limited the right to vote in school 0—* district elections to persons who owned or leased taxable real estate, to the spouses of these persons, and to parents or guardians of schoolchildren. Paul was a bachelor who lived with his parents and did not lease or own property and was therefore not eligible to vote under the statute. Paul challenged the law's constitutionality. The Supreme Court ruled that even if the state was allowed to limit voters to those "primarily interested in school affairs," the statute did not accomplish that purpose with sufficient precision to justify denying Paul the right to vote. Other people with only a remote interest in school affairs—such as the mere fact of property ownership or tenancy—were permitted to vote. Therefore, Paul was denied equal protection under the 14th Amendment.

The state sometimes has the requisite compelling state interest to exclude qualified voters in a special election.

EXAMPLE A California statute permitted only landowners 0—* to vote in "water-storage districts" elections. These elections dealt with water acquisition, storage, and distribution, plus the setting of charges for these services. Votes were apportioned according to the assessed valuation of the land. The Supreme Court upheld this voting system because of the special limited purpose of the water-storage districts and its great effect on landowners as a group. Lessees could be excluded because their interest in the land was short term.

■ **Legislative apportionment** Legislative apportionment refers to the division of a state, county, or municipality into defined areas, such as wards, precincts, and districts for the purpose of representation in Congress or in state or local legislative bodies. Only since 1962, with the case of *Baker* v. *Carr*, has the Supreme Court considered state legislative apportionment plans subject to judicial inquiry to protect the franchise and to assure the equal protection guarantee. In *Baker*, the Court announced that the 14th Amendment gave equal weight to each voter. Therefore, a legislative apportionment plan that does not guarantee that each voter's ballot will have the same force as one in another district may be declared unconstitutional. See BAKER V. CARR.

In another case the Supreme Court invalidated the Georgia county unit system for nominating primary candidates. In this system, a combination of units from counties having the smallest populations gave one third of the total state population a clear majority of county units. This case and *Baker* established the basis for the one man, one vote decision. Under this rule, there can be no significant difference in the population of districts in state and congressional elections. When one elected Congressman represents two or three times as many voters as other Congressmen from other state districts, voters are denied equal protection of laws. One man's vote in a congressional election must be worth as much as another man's vote.

States have the power to reapportion districts for representation in Congress and in state and local legislatures. When a statute reapportions for congressional elections, the courts examine the plan. They insure that the population shifts that caused the reapportionment were significant, that good-faith efforts were made to achieve absolute equality, and that such factors as distinct interest groups, integrity of county lines, and population trends justified the change.

The redistricting for a state or local legislature is judged by the equal protection test. This requires that districts in state reapportionments be "as nearly of equal population as is practicable." But some deviations from the equal population principle are permissible as long as they have a legitimate purpose. Legislative gerrymandering (manipulation) of city and state electoral boundaries for the purpose of disenfranchising black voters violates both the equal protection clause and the 15th Amendment. See GERRYMANDER.

■ **Reverse discrimination** Reverse, or benign, discrimination may be defined as a classification designed to assist groups of persons presumed to be disadvantaged. (In a somewhat broader sense, the term "affirmative action" is used.) Although race classifications are clearly suspect, lower courts use them to remedy past racial discriminations. The 14th Amendment has been interpreted by the courts as permitting, if in fact not requiring, the correction of historical discriminations.

If a government employer has illegally discriminated against a racial minority in the past—such as by the use of criteria wholly unrelated to job performance—the courts will impose remedies that require racial preference in hiring. For example, a written multiple-choice test for firefighters, on which minorities typically performed poorly, is found not to be job related. The court orders a preference for minorities in future hiring to remedy past discrimination. Similarly, a government employer may use double-standard employment qualifications, such as a typing speed of 30 words per minute for minority applicants and 50 words per minute for all others. Even when there has not been illegal conduct in the past, the courts have upheld governmentally imposed affirmative action programs that impose racial goals and timetables. The principle is that they are related to the legitimate state interest of insuring full utilization of minority workers.

An edge in college admissions The controversy about reverse discrimination is largely centered on the preferential treatment of minorities in gaining admission to colleges, universities, and professional schools for law and medicine. This is a special advantage since competition for a small number of positions is especially keen. Reverse discrimination boils down to this—a minority applicant is given admission preference over a nonminority applicant with stronger academic qualifications. The crucial question asked is: Does this policy deny equal protection of laws to the nonminority applicant?

Courts have been reluctant to find reverse discrimination unconstitutional.

EXAMPLE In one case, a nonminority applicant sued in state 0—* court to compel a state medical school to provide him with a place in its 1974–75 class. He held he was denied admission because minority students, presenting inferior academic credentials, were accepted. He claimed that the school's refusal to accept him was arbitrary and capricious and its preferential treatment of minorities was in violation of law. The court decided that in proper circumstances reverse discrimination is constitutional.

As expected, there must be a substantial state interest underlying the preferential-treatment policy. The school must show that a nonracial classification or a less objectionable alternative would not accomplish the same purpose. This does not mean, however, that courts give wholehearted approval to admissions policies based on reverse discrimination. Such policies have detrimental side effects that make them undesirable. Among these are polarization of the races, the elimination of incentive to attain higher academic standards, and the attitude among the public that minority professionals are less qualified than their non-minority colleagues. See CIVIL RIGHTS.

Limits to preferential treatment If preferential policies really work, the period and extent of their use should be temporary and limited. As goals are achieved, the use of these policies should diminish. But if no improvement is noted, consideration should be given to the discontinuation of the practice. The court concluded that in the case of the applicant denied admission to medical school in 1974 it did not have to determine whether less objectionable standards existed. He would not be entitled to admission even if the entire minority program were eliminated. Even without the minority students, 114 students would have priority over him.

EXAMPLE In the *De Funis* case, an unsuccessful white applicant to the University of Washington law school brought an action against state and university officials challenging the constitutionality of his rejection. He claimed that the admissions committee discriminated against him on the basis of his race, in violation of the equal protection clause. Minority applicants with inferior academic qualifications were admitted while he was rejected. The state trial court agreed with his claim and ordered the law school to admit him. The school appealed to the highest state court, which set aside the lower court's decision. It found that the law school admissions policy did not violate equal protection. By this time the plaintiff was in his second year. He petitioned the Supreme Court, which agreed to hear the case and suspended the effect of the state court judgment that would require the plaintiff to leave school until it gave its decision. By the time the Supreme Court got around to hearing the *De Funis* case, in 1976, the plaintiff was in his last quarter of the final year in law school. The Supreme Court used this fact to avoid deciding the constitutionality of reverse-discrimination policies of admissions. It stated that since the plaintiff was in his final quarter, he was entitled to complete his studies and receive his degree. It concluded that the determination of the legal issues was unnecessary since the case was moot—that is, the controversy no longer existed. This refusal of the Supreme Court to address the issue of reverse discrimination left the area of preferential treatment of minorities in admissions and hiring up in the air.

The Bakke case In June 1978, when it handed down its decision in the BAKKE CASE, the Supreme Court took the initial step in evaluating the constitutionality of racial classifications used in admissions procedures in universities.

EXAMPLE Bakke, a white male, was rejected twice from the medical school at the University of California at Davis. Meanwhile, minority applicants with academic credentials "significantly lower than Bakke's" were admitted under a special admissions program. The program set aside 16 of the 100 places available in the class exclusively for blacks, Chicanos, Asians, and American Indians.

Allen P. Bakke challenged the constitutionality of the program. He asserted that he was denied equal protection of the laws as he could not compete for those 16 places solely because of his race. After being ordered to admit Bakke, the university appealed to the Supreme Court. The Court agreed that Bakke should be admitted. He was denied a chance to compete for those 16 positions solely on the basis of his race in violation of Title VI of the Civil Rights Act of 1964. However, the Court said race could be given consideration as a factor in the admissions policies of universities. This 5–4 decision has been called an opinion with "something for everyone," since it has been claimed as a victory by both advocates and opponents of affirmative-action programs.

equal rights See CIVIL RIGHTS.

equitable Fair, right, and just. Conforming to the principles of justice and fairness. What is equitable is decided by considering the rules of EQUITY and the circumstances of the individual case, not by statutes and normal legal procedure.

Equitable estoppel, for example, is a rule that a person may not take advantage of his own wrongful act. Someone who claims he was injured in an automobile accident, but will not submit to a medical examination, is stopped from suing another driver. This is a simple rule of fairness, an equitable rule. See ESTOPPEL.

Equitable recoupment means that a person who no longer has a legal right to pursue a claim against another person (say, the statute of limitations ran out) can defend himself to the extent of that claim if the other person sues him. This prevents someone who is suing from recovering money owed him—for instance, from collecting the full amount if he is unfairly holding something that belongs to the debtor.

EXAMPLE The Brown Company incorrectly figures its taxes and pays too much to the state over a period of years. The company is entitled to recover the excess it paid for whatever years are within the statute of limitations, the time limit allowed. But it cannot start a lawsuit to recover the excess taxes if paid for the years beyond the legal time limit. If the state government later sues the Brown Company for paying too little in taxes, however, the company can ask for a recoupment, a credit for the excess taxes paid years ago and now beyond its reach.

equity 1 Fairness and justice. 2 A set of legal rules that developed over the centuries to do justice when money damages could not repay the party to a lawsuit. The principles of equity are said to be founded on conscience and a sense of fair play, not burdened by technicalities that would produce an unfair result. **3** The value of property that is not subject to LIENS, MORTGAGES, or claims by anyone other than the owner. Equity is the amount the owner would have left after selling his property and paying off all of the charges against it with part of the purchase money.

Equity is explored here as that part of our legal system based on historical ideas of justice. The article gives a brief history of equity, examines the rules expressed in the maxims of equity, and discusses the kinds of equitable actions.

■ **When equity applies** An *equitable right* is a legal right that should be enforced because of fairness or a right that is enforced by a court order for relief other than money damages. *Equity jurisdiction* is the power of a particular court to hear equity cases—the authority of a court to order relief other than common-law DAMAGES.

Equitable remedies are ways to enforce rights, prevent violation of rights, or pay for harm caused other than by payment of money damages. Remedies such as an accounting, constructive trust, partition, specific performance, injunction, declaratory relief, interpleader, restitution, rescission, and reformation are discussed later in this article.

■ **Equity and English common law** When William the Conqueror seized the British crown in 1066, he found a well-organized system of local courts. Generally content to let them function on their own, he nevertheless intervened by dispatching his officers to hear special local cases or sometimes by sending a writ to the local baron or sheriff. An English monarch was above the law. He could follow his conscience—or whim—instead of the laws. In 1215 the barons forced King John to sign the Magna Charta. The king promised to stop issuing writs that deprived freemen of the right to have their cases heard in local courts.

By the end of the 13th century the phrase "the common law" was being used to mean the collection of laws that prevailed in the courts—the law common to all Englishmen. It included all the rules and principles arrived at by judges from previous cases. And it existed along with local customs, statutes, and the king's sovereign right to hold himself above the law.

Role of the chancellor By the early 13th century, three royal courts had developed—the King's Bench, the Court of Common Pleas, and the Exchequer, which also served as an administrative office. One of the Exchequer's departments was the Chancery, headed by the chancellor, the king's secretary or secretary of state. The chancellor, who was usually a bishop of the Church, was the king's personal representative in matters of law. He kept the great seal and supervised all writing done in the king's name. One of his duties was to draw up the writs—orders from the king and in the king's name. Writs were needed to start any lawsuit. No one, however, could bring a suit against the king.

Another of the chancellor's duties was to listen to petitioners who could not get justice in the law courts and were imploring the king for justice "for the love of God and in the way of charity." The strict rules of the common law often left the litigants' problems unrelieved. Occasionally, the rules produced a harsh or unfair result.

Fairness from conscience The chancellors tended to settle a controversy according to general notions of right and wrong, regardless of the rules. They added a special element of conscience bred from their ties to the Church and the king. Although they began by hearing cases that fell between the cracks of the common law, the chancellors actually developed an entire system of law, called equity. By now, equity has existed for hundreds of years alongside the common law.

If the common law was the mind of the law, equity was its heart. Just as the common law promoted social order, equity gave justice to the individual. The tension between these two goals has refined the law as it continues to grow.

A famous 17th-century judge compared the fairness of equity to the chancellor's foot. A rule of law gave an individual a measure by which to calculate justice, he said. It was a thing to be trusted. Equity was governed only by the conscience of the chancellor. Since one chancellor might have a long foot and another a short one, the same could be said for the chancellor's conscience.

By 1660 the chancellors' opinions had become consistent enough to be written down. Decisions referred to earlier opinions, and principles of equity—called *maxims*—developed. Eventually, textbooks were published. Equity took its place alongside the common law as the law of the land.

■ **Equity in the United States** At the time of the American Revolution, the growth of equity was constricted by a general distaste for all things English. Some states did not grant equity powers to their courts. Some, like Pennsylvania, found that individuals who would have petitioned the king in England for relief were instead petitioning the state legislatures. As a result, they had to pass a variety of private bills to give equitable relief to individuals. In time, however, almost every state incorporated equity into its judicial system.

Some states had two different court systems, one for equity and the other for law. In other states the same courts could sit in equity or in law, but the cases and procedures were kept separate. As time passed, however, more states abolished the distinction between law and equity.

Now courts of general jurisdiction—those that have the authority to hear all kinds of cases—may apply rules of law or equity. Rather than labeling a case "law" or "equity," these courts recognize only one kind of lawsuit, usually called a *civil action*. In 1938 the Federal Rules of Civil Procedure also established one system for processing both law and equity cases in the federal courts. These are also called civil actions.

A great advantage of this merged system is efficiency. One set of rules is followed in both kinds of cases, as well as in mixed cases where both legal and equitable elements are involved. At the outset there need be no dispute whether legal or equitable relief will be appropriate. Nor is it necessary to dismiss an incorrectly categorized case, forcing a party to start all over again in another court. One judge may order complete relief to an injured party, even if this requires a mixture of legal and equitable remedies. For example, if the foundation of a house is being eroded because of a mining operation just beyond the homeowner's property line, he may recover money damages (a legal remedy) and an injunction against future mining (an equitable remedy). All can be ordered in one lawsuit.

■ **Right to a jury trial** The major practical difference between law and equity today is the right to demand a jury in actions at law. From the earliest times, juries were selected to determine *questions of fact*—they heard the evidence and decided how things had happened. When damages were appropriate, juries decided the dollar amount. In courts of equity, however, the chancellor or judge heard both sides and decreed the settlement.

Constitutional guarantees   The Sixth Amendment to the U.S. Constitution guarantees the right to a trial by jury "in all criminal prosecutions." The Seventh Amendment guarantees the right to demand a jury "in Suits at common law, where the value in controversy shall exceed twenty dollars." These provisions apply to federal courts. Many states also guarantee a jury trial in all criminal cases, in any cases involving a recovery of money, and in all cases where this right has already existed.

When a plaintiff starts a legal suit, the defendant generally has the right to demand a jury trial. But if the plaintiff is suing in equity, the defendant usually does not have this right. Defendants often prefer a jury because the plaintiff's case can be defeated on technical rules. If the plaintiff is suing only in equity, a defendant may be able to add a legal cause of action against the plaintiff just to get a jury. This is a COUNTERCLAIM. The court, however, will look beyond the language used in the papers to see whether either party has an argument that is *really* legal or equitable. A plaintiff cannot deprive a defendant of his right to a jury, for example, simply by asking for an injunction, which is an equitable remedy. If it appears from the plaintiff's papers that this kind of dispute is usually settled by money damages, the defendant should be entitled to a jury.

Rules for each action   In the case of mixed actions, where the parties ask for both legal and equitable remedies, states settle the jury question in different ways. Sometimes the right to a jury is controlled by the character of the most important issue—the first one the court must decide and the one on which other issues depend. Sometimes the plaintiff is considered to have *waived,* or given up, his right to have a jury if he joins legal and equitable claims. It is not unusual for a party entitled to a jury to waive that right. This is frequently done by businesses that are parties to very technical lawsuits. When the facts are likely to be complicated—when they are scientific or mechanical information, for example—parties may not wish to risk a verdict based on possible misunderstandings by jurors. Unlike a jury, a judge can keep asking questions until he has a grasp of each party's arguments.

THAT JUSTICE MAY BE DONE—HOW EQUITY WORKS

■ The rules of equity are designed to do justice when money damages cannot repay a party to a lawsuit. *Equitable remedies* enforce rights, prevent violations of rights, and provide forms of relief other than money damages. They also make it possible to enforce what is just and fair even when doing so does not follow the letter of the law.

There are several types of equitable remedies that the court may order to give relief.

■ The first of these remedies is an *accounting.* If the person who has been handling your money for you turns out to have been wasting it or spending it on himself, the court may require him to file a report of all transactions with the money and to make up your losses.

■ Another remedy is the creation of a *constructive trust.* Let us say a son talks an aged parent into putting all of the parent's money into a joint checking account as a precaution against a sudden illness, and then the son uses all the money for himself. A court using the rules of equity can treat all the money in the account as a trust and stop the son from taking advantage in this way. "At law," the court could assume that at least half the money was intended as a gift, but since in this case such an assumption based on a legal technicality would lead to an unfair result for the parent, the court handles the matter in equity.

■ A *partition* is a lawsuit to divide up real estate owned by two or more persons when there is no written agreement about the respective rights of the owners. Since the court cannot merely apply technical rules and award money damages in such a case, but must look at all the circumstances to make a fair decision, a partition is an equitable remedy.

■ When the subject of a contract is unique and money value does not apply, the court may enforce *specific performance* as an equitable remedy. For example, if you sign a contract to buy a particular land site and the seller breaks the contract, the court may compel the seller to sell you that site and not substitute another site. Another equitable remedy is an *injunction*—a court order telling someone to do or not to do something. Injunctions are hard to get, but you may obtain one if you can show that you will suffer a harm that cannot be undone unless the injunction is issued—if, for example, someone is about to start building a factory in a residential area and you want to challenge his right to do so.

■ *Declaratory relief* is a court judgment that declares the rights of the parties involved. It lets the parties carry on, secure in the knowledge that the question central to the lawsuit has been given a final answer. In one case a woman had to go to court to prove she was her husband's wife. Her husband had left her, got an invalid Mexican divorce, and remarried someone else, leaving his original wife in trouble when she applied for credit and for Social Security benefits. With the declaratory judgment in hand, the woman no longer had to prove her status.

■ When one person has money or goods that several people are claiming, he can start an *interpleader* action, in which he deposits the property at stake with the court and lets the court decide who is entitled to it.

■ The court may simply make one party give back something that in fairness he should not be allowed to keep—this is called *restitution.*

■ A court sitting in equity may correct a mistake or misunderstanding in a contract so as to make it express the original intentions of the parties. This is called *reformation* because the court *reforms* the contract. When a contract is clearly unfair, the court may *rescind,* or cancel, it.

Even when parties are not entitled to demand a jury, judges in federal and many state courts have the authority to call for an *advisory jury*. A judge sitting in equity must still make a final decision on both the facts and the law, but there are times when an advisory jury's opinion of the facts is helpful.

■ **Maxims as principles** The rules of equity are expressed in *maxims*—broad statements of principle whose reasonableness and truth are self-evident. They were originally quoted in Latin, and many of the Latin phrases are still familiar to lawyers today. The maxims were not written down in a code or enacted by a legislature, but they have been handed down through generations of judges. Because of this, the wording of the same maxim can vary from case to case.

The principles of equity and justice are universal and apply with equal force in all the common-law courts of the world. They are flexible, seeking justice for both sides in each individual case. No maxim is ever absolute, but all the principles must be weighed and fitted to the facts of the case. A rule does not apply where it will produce an unfair result. A party can never legally complain that a strict technicality that favored his cause was not enforced, because, above all, equity demands justice. After balancing the interests of the parties, the court must also consider the conveniences of the public.

Equity is predicated on a number of maxims, each of which is discussed below.

"Equity will not suffer an injustice." "Equity acts in personam." These two maxims form the basic foundations of equity. The first explains the whole purpose of equity. The second highlights its personal nature. Unless a statute expands the powers of an equity court, it can make decrees concerning property only indirectly, phrasing them as decrees against the person. In both, however, equity looks at the circumstances of the individuals and fashions a remedy directed at the defendant. It is said that these are the oldest maxims of equity. All others are consistent with them.

"He who seeks equity must do equity." This maxim is not a moral persuasion but an enforceable rule of law. It does not require every plaintiff to have an unblemished background, but the court will refuse to help anyone whose action is founded on his own misconduct toward the other party.

EXAMPLE A finance company loaned Billy money to buy a stereo system. He was old enough to be legally responsible for the debt but young enough for a slick loan officer to have talked him into a big commitment he clearly could not afford. The finance company repossessed the stereo after six months and, after selling it, sued Billy for the amount of the debt still outstanding as well as for a long list of "collection expenses." Because of the unfairness of the finance company's tactics, a court could in equity refuse to award all of the company's claims.

"He who comes into equity must come with clean hands." This maxim bars relief for anyone who is himself guilty of improper conduct in the matter under dispute. It operates to prevent any recovery for the person with "unclean hands," no matter how unfairly his adversary has

treated him. Its purpose is to protect the court's integrity. The court not only disapproves of illegal acts but will also deny relief for any bad conduct that, as a matter of public policy, should be discouraged. A court will ask, however, whether the bad conduct was intentional—clean hands doctrine is not meant to punish carelessness or a mistake.

It is possible that the bad conduct is not an act but a failure to act. For example, someone sits silently while his hired agent misleads another party in negotiations for the sale of an automobile. The agent's employer is as much responsible for the false statements as if he had made them himself. Similarly, a husband hires a private investigator not to discover evidence of his wife's adultery but because he wants the detective to seduce her. The husband should be denied a divorce for unclean hands. Likewise, a used car salesman who sells a car knowing that it has serious mechanical defects should be denied judgment when he sues for payments due.

The bad conduct condemned by the *clean hands doctrine* must be a part of the subject of the lawsuit. But it is not necessary that this conduct actually hurt the other party. For instance, equity will not help someone, even if he has been cheated by the other party, if he had been trying to evade taxes or defraud his creditors in the same transaction of which he is complaining.

EXAMPLE After a fire in their restaurant, Homer sued his business partner, James, for half the insurance money. During the trial, the court discovered that the partners had set the fire themselves in order to collect the insurance. The court refused to order a sharing of the insurance proceeds. It referred the matter to the district attorney for a criminal investigation.

In one classic case, called *The Highwayman*, a robber filed a bill in equity for an accounting against his partner in crime. When the real nature of the bill was discovered, it was promptly dismissed. The lawyers were held in contempt for bringing it into court. Judges have since said that they will not sit to take a reckoning between two robbers. Equity also will decline relief when both parties have schemed to circumvent the law.

"Equity aids the vigilant, not those who slumber on their rights." This principle recognizes that an adversary can lose evidence, witnesses, and a fair chance to prove his case after time has passed. The law encourages a speedy resolution of every dispute. It does not favor the cause of someone who suddenly "wakes up" and starts to enforce his rights long after he has discovered that they exist. If a party can show that he would be disadvantaged because he relied on the fact that no lawsuit against him would be started, the case should be dismissed. See LACHES; LIMITATIONS OF ACTIONS.

"Equity acts specifically." This means that a party who sues in equity can recover the precise thing that he seeks rather than money damages as a substitute for it. This is the remedy of *specific performance*.

"Equity follows the law." When the procedures at law are inadequate, equity finds a way of reaching a fair result. Equity does not replace or violate the law, but supplements it. Equity also follows appropriate rules of law, such as those of EVIDENCE and DISCOVERY.

"Equity delights to do justice and not by halves." It is the purpose of equity to find a complete answer to the problems involved in a lawsuit. It will bring all necessary parties into the case, balance their rights, and give a decree that should protect all of them against future litigation on the subject. Whenever necessary, equity will retain the authority to oversee the carrying out of relief. For example, a lawsuit will remain open as long as an injunction is in force. Either party can come back into the courtroom and ask the court to reconsider its decree if circumstances change. In the same way, courts retain jurisdiction when child-support payments are ordered. The amount can be changed if, for example, the child's needs require an increase or if the supporting parent becomes unemployed, ill, or retired.

"Equity will not suffer a wrong to be without a remedy." It is the traditional purpose of equity to find solutions in lawsuits. When money will not pay for the injury, equity has the authority to find a remedy. This maxim restates a broader legal principle—*Ubi jus ibi remedium* ("Where there is a right there is a remedy"). It calls forth recognized remedies for well-established wrongs. Here, a wrong is an act such as an invasion of property rights or civil rights that the law considers serious enough for legal action. A wrong is not every little annoyance or immoral act.

"Equity regards substance rather than form." Equity will not permit justice to be withheld because of a mere technicality. Formalities that frustrate justice will be disregarded for a more suitable approach based on the individual case. Equity enforces the spirit more than the letter of the law.

EXAMPLE A husband and wife purchased a house shortly after they were married, intending to take title in both their names. Twenty-one years later, when they were involved in a divorce action, they discovered that the title had only the husband's name on it. No one knew how this had happened. There was no evidence that the husband had intentionally tried to trick his wife when they bought the house, but now he claimed that she was not half owner. The court agreed that the law considered the person whose name was on the title to be the owner, but it would not allow the husband to take advantage of the mistake. In equity, it found that each party was entitled to half the money when the house was sold.

"Equality is equity." This is equivalent to saying that equity will not play favorites. But the maxim applies only to parties who are on the same footing. For example, if a woman is killed in an auto accident and is survived by her three adult children, the three should each share equally in any money recovered in a lawsuit against the driver. If the woman died leaving three minor children, however, the amount each would receive might depend on the difference in their ages. A younger child will have lost his mother for more childhood years than an older brother or sister.

"Between equal equities the law will prevail." When two parties want the same thing and the court cannot in good conscience say that one has a better right to it than the other, equity will leave ownership with the party that currently has it under the law.

EXAMPLE A manufacturer of campers had been collecting a certain tax from his purchases and turning it over to the federal government. When the government later admitted that the tax was a mistake, the manufacturer sued for a refund. The court refused to refund the money. It found that the customers, not the manufacturer, had paid the tax. Although the customers had a right to seek a refund, they were not parties to the suit. The manufacturer admitted that he had no way of tracking them down to pass along the refund. The manufacturer and the government were each less entitled to the money than the customers, but the government was presently the rightful owner. The government was permitted to keep the money mistakenly collected.

"Between equal equities the first in order of time shall prevail." When two parties each have the same right in equity to own or possess something, then the one who acquired his interest first should succeed in his claim.

EXAMPLE Let us say that Franklin puts this advertisement in the local newspaper: "Twelve-foot sailboat for sale—$200." Charles answers the ad, looks the boat over, and offers $180. Franklin accepts the offer. Charles pays Franklin and says he will pick up the boat on Saturday. Later on Joan stops by to look at the boat, says she will take it, and hands over $200 to Franklin. Who owns the boat? Contract law and equity agree that the first buyer gets the boat and the second buyer gets her money back.

"Equity abhors a forfeiture." A forfeiture is a total loss of a right or a thing because the person has failed to do or not do something that is required. A total loss is generally a stiff penalty. Unless the loss is reasonable in relation to the seriousness of the required action, forfeiture is too harsh. In fairness and good conscience, a court of equity will refuse to enforce an unreasonable forfeiture. For example, the law shows great respect for ownership of land. It should never be lost for a trivial reason. This issue has come up in many cases where real estate has been sold and the purchaser has failed to do one small thing required in the contract of sale.

EXAMPLE The contract said that the agreement was at an end and ownership of the land returned to the seller if the buyer defaulted on *any* of his obligations. This was a forfeiture clause. When the buyer's payment check arrived two days late one month, the seller demanded that he return the property. The court refused to take away the land for such a small mistake. If the seller could show how he was harmed, he might be able to recover damages at law for the amount of his loss.

Equity generally will not interfere with a forfeiture required by law. The maxim "Equity abhors a forfeiture" does not supersede the maxim "Equity follows the law."

Neither will equity disregard a fair contract provision. It is assumed that someone who does most of what is required in a business contract should not suffer for violation of a minor technicality. For example, a contractor who completes work on a bridge one day late should not be treated as though he had completely broken the contract. If the parties agree, however, to a provision in the contract stating that "time is of the essence," both understand that the entire contract requires things to be done at the time stated. If a television sportscaster is hired to cover the Kentucky

Derby, he cannot show up a couple of weeks late and offer to cover the Indianapolis 500. The court will refuse to apply the maxim, and the sportscaster will forfeit all his rights under the employment contract.

■ **Judicial discretion** Discretion is the use of good judgment rather than specific rules. Judicial discretion is the authority that a court in equity possesses to decide questions according to fairness rather than statutes. Whether or not to apply the rules of equity, to grant relief, or to choose a particular remedy are all matters of judicial discretion. A judge in equity has no right, however, to favor a personal whim. He cannot be arbitrary or make decisions without explanation. He must weigh the value of legal traditions and the needs of the parties before him. He must ascertain what the law declares for a certain set of facts and decide accordingly. For instance, it is a matter of discretion whether or not a case should be heard in equity. A judge may find that the plaintiff can be adequately compensated in an action at law. No one has an absolute right to start an equity action.

■ **Equitable remedies** Equity cases can be distinguished from law cases by the type of remedy sought. Broadly speaking, law cases involve a problem that can be solved by payment of money damages—even when money obviously cannot fully compensate for the harm done to the plaintiff. The value of a person's life, for example, can never be figured in dollars. But since a judge cannot restore a loved one to his family after someone has caused his death, a judgment is given for money damages.

Money damages are, in fact, favored in all kinds of cases. Courts will refuse to exercise equity jurisdiction—that is, to grant relief other than money damages—unless there is no adequate remedy at law. It is said that equity is extraordinary. It is appropriate only under special circumstances when the court must go beyond the common law and statutes to give relief. The rules of equity are traditionally applied in certain types of cases, many of which involve the violation of a trust or some kind of bad faith.

Accounting An accounting is a detailed written statement of money owed and paid. A plaintiff may bring an action for an accounting against someone who has been handling money that belongs to the plaintiff or to both of them. A person who handles someone else's money is said to be a *fiduciary*. He is required to be scrupulously honest in protecting the assets that do not belong to him—even more careful than he would be with his own money.

EXAMPLE A guardian who holds money that a child has inherited is a fiduciary. He must take care of that money until the owner becomes an adult. If it appears that the guardian is violating his fiduciary duty by wasting the assets or spending part of the money on himself, an action can be brought to make him account. First he must file a written report of all transactions with the money. If the court decides he is guilty of misusing the fund, he can be required to pay back any losses, plus additional penalties. If he is a professional person, such as a lawyer, he can also lose his license.

Trust or constructive trust A breach or violation of fiduciary duty may also be involved in a TRUST case.

EXAMPLE A mother who has always cared for a retarded child might wish to leave all her property in a trust when she dies. She can ask a bank to hold and manage the property, sending the income it earns to the special home where her retarded adult child lives. She expects the bank to be very careful with the child's inheritance because the child cannot protect his own interests. If the bank carelessly invests the money, it can be summoned to court to give account.

Sometimes a court will treat an informal agreement the same way it treats a formal trust. If it appears that the two parties had a close personal relationship, a court may in equity prevent one from taking advantage of the other.

EXAMPLE A daughter may talk her elderly mother into putting all of the mother's money into a joint checking account. In this way she can take care of her mother if she gets sick. At law, a court can assume that at least half of the money put into a joint bank account was intended to be a gift. But in equity, it can treat the money as a trust—it is called a constructive trust—and stop the daughter from using for herself money that was meant to pay for her mother's needs.

Partition A lawsuit asking the court to divide up real estate owned by more than one person is called a partition. Since the court is not merely applying technical rules of law and awarding money damages, it is sitting in equity and must look at all the circumstances to make a fair decision.

EXAMPLE If a ranch has been operating under a partnership of three people, a court cannot just divide the land into three equal parcels when the partnership breaks up. Land with road frontage, a flowing stream, or buildings will be worth more than uncleared or marshy land. A fair division must take into account the circumstances of each partner and the character of the land.

The situation here would be different if the partners had a written agreement that spelled out each partner's rights when the partnership dissolved. The court would then simply enforce the contract and award damages for a breach of contract—an action at law.

Specific performance A court order to compel the actual carrying out of an agreement that has been made is called a SPECIFIC PERFORMANCE. It is used when the subject of the contract is unique—when money value cannot be assessed or compensate for what is lost. For instance, someone who signs a contract to buy a particular land site is entitled to that site—not a substitute one or money damages—if the seller breaks the contract. Similarly, let us say that the three ranchers in the example above had developed a new strain of beef cattle and one partner took all the animals when the partnership dissolved. If a partnership contract said the other two should get half the cattle, they would be entitled to their share of those unique animals. No amount of money could replace them.

This remedy also applies to things of sentimental value.

EXAMPLE Suppose Ruth sells her old family house to the Pearson clan but tells them she wants to keep the bell that has always hung outside the front door. The Pearsons take the bell anyway. When Ruth sues to recover it, the Pearsons claim the bell had little value but are willing to pay Ruth for it. Ruth, though, is entitled to specific performance—to recover the family heirloom that is worth more to her than its dollar value.

Injunction An injunction is a court order telling a party to do or not to do something. Courts grant injunctions reluctantly, when nothing else will solve the problem. Often the plaintiff must show that he will suffer a harm that cannot be undone unless the injunction is issued.

An injunction can be granted to prevent a threatened act. If the act has huge consequences, the person threatening to do it should be stopped until he can demonstrate a clear legal right.

EXAMPLE A company that wishes to build a paint factory on a lot it recently purchased plans first to clear the land. The lot is right next to a residential neighborhood. Children play among the trees, and the woods act as a buffer between the houses and an interstate highway. Everyone is certain that the builders did not get a proper zoning variance that would allow them to construct a factory. By the time a lawsuit winds its way through the courts, the trees will have been cut down and construction begun. The first thing the neighbors must do is ask the court for an injunction, an order stopping all work on the project until the controversy is resolved. They must show that they are directly affected by the question before the court and that the harm in cutting down all the trees cannot be undone if the builders are in the wrong. Because a delay will seriously inconvenience the builders, each day costing them more money, the people will have to show evidence that the zoning laws have been violated. They will also have to convince the court that they are likely to win in the lawsuit. An injunction may then be issued.

An injunction may also be granted to put an end to an ongoing harm.

EXAMPLE A factory is flushing chemicals into a creek upstream from a farm. Suing the factory for damages to pay for all the harm done up to the time of his lawsuit will not give the farmer the relief he needs. He wants the factory to stop poisoning his animals. The factory, however, may be making so much money that it is willing to let the farmer sue periodically and to pay him whatever damages are awarded. The only practical solution is to order the factory to stop polluting the stream.

In equity, hardships must be balanced. A court must compare the harm done to the farmer with the hardship an injunction inflicts on the factory. If the farmer has one cow that can easily be watered at a trough, money damages may be adequate. If the factory is a major employer in the county and no practical way of treating its pollutants has been developed, it may be unreasonable to close down operations suddenly.

An injunction usually orders a party *not* to do something. Traditionally, judges word injunctions in terms of a prohibition even if the real object is to make the party *do* something. For example, a judge who wanted a person to remove a fence that illegally extended onto his neighbor's property would order him not to permit the fence to continue encroaching on the adjoining property. Today, however, many states permit an injunction to be affirmative as well as negative. An example of an affirmative injunction in one that orders SPECIFIC PERFORMANCE of a contract for the sale of a rare antique.

Declaratory relief Courts sitting in equity are often asked to do no more than declare the rights of the two parties. Unlike other forms of remedies, nothing has to be done to put a decree into effect if the plaintiff asks only for declaratory relief. Declaratory relief uses the important legal rule *res judicata*—that any question settled by a court is settled forever between the parties involved. Declaratory judgments let the parties carry on, certain and secure in the knowledge that the question central to the lawsuit has been given a final answer.

EXAMPLE Helena had to go to court to prove that she was Floyd's legal wife. Floyd had abandoned her, obtained an invalid Mexican divorce, and remarried someone else. With a declaratory judgment in hand, Helena will not have to prove her status again in the future, as when she applies for credit or for Social Security benefits.

Declaratory judgments can state that title ownership of an item of property cannot be challenged in the future. They can settle an argument over the meaning of a contract provision before either party misinterprets it and breaches the contract. They can also resolve disputes about taxes before tax returns are filed and declare contracts and notes (promises to pay money) rescinded (canceled).

Interpleader When one person has money or goods that several people are claiming, he can start an interpleader action, naming all of them defendants. He deposits the money or property, called the *stake*, with the court and lets the court decide who is entitled to it. This way he is not sued by different claimants and is spared the risk of having conflicting decisions telling him to pay over the stake to more than one person.

Restitution An order making one party give back something that in fairness he should not be allowed to keep is called restitution. This remedy does not depend on the existence of a contract, but it is granted as if there were a contract in order to be fair to the parties.

EXAMPLE The All-Fizz Beverage Company, owner of Lot 47, built a soft-drink bottling plant on Lot 46. It was an honest mistake. The owners of Lot 46, Globe, Inc., did not discover the building until it was completed and in operation. Globe claimed ownership because the building was on their property. Lot 46 was worth $2,000 and the building was worth $17,500. The court ordered restitution: Globe could not keep the building without paying what it cost to build. If they chose not to do that, Globe would have to sell the property to All-Fizz. The court recognized this as the fairest solution.

Reformation This is a court's correction of a mistake or a misunderstanding in a contract—a typographical error in the date of delivery or different interpretations of the same terms by the parties to a contract. The court reforms the contract so that it expresses the original intentions of the parties.

Rescission When a contract is clearly unfair, a court may rescind, or cancel, it. This means the contract is no longer a legal obligation.

EXAMPLE Jonathan asks a real estate broker to sell a store that he owns. The broker mails a sales contract to Jonathan, who signs it. Afterward, the broker and the buyer learn that Jonathan is insane and unable to manage his own affairs. They want to enforce the contract because of the attractive price. But Jonathan's family does not want to sell even though the other parties acted honestly. The court should order rescission because Jonathan was legally incapable of making a contract.

■ **Equitable defenses** A number of arguments can be used against the plaintiff's case that will appeal to the conscience of the law.

The clean hands doctrine The rule that the plaintiff must have acted fairly and honestly toward the defendant in the transaction in dispute can be used as a defense in equity cases. If the plaintiff's hands are not clean, the court should not give him equitable relief. (See Maxim 4 above: "He who comes into equity must come with clean hands.")

Laches If a person delays in enforcing his rights until the other party has been disadvantaged by the passage of time, the defense is called laches. Laches is a doctrine applied by the court for reasons of fairness. It does not suggest a specific period of time (as does the statute of limitations) but depends on the facts of the particular case. See LIMITATIONS OF ACTIONS.

EXAMPLE A homeowner sat back and watched while a new neighbor built an expensive addition to his house—an addition that extended beyond their common boundary line. The homeowner is barred by laches from asking a court to order the neighbor to tear down the part of the addition that extends onto his land.

■ **Enforcement of equitable decrees** Equitable decrees are not enforced the same way as money judgments. Courts have the authority to order a defendant's property seized to satisfy an uncollected money judgment. Equity traditionally deals not with money but with the defendant himself.

Contempt In the early days of English law, the chancellor could enforce his decrees only by holding a stubborn defendant in contempt. Generally, this meant that the defendant was thrown into jail and left there until he agreed to do as the chancellor ordered. Some took more time than others, but most eventually obeyed the decree. Modern opinion is very strongly against imprisonment for private wrongs. Judges are reluctant to throw someone in jail simply because he refuses to obey an order to remove a fence that is set six inches into his neighbor's property, for example. If jailing on contempt were the only remedy, defendants would often go unpunished.

Another problem with contempt is that it is often ineffective in enforcing court decrees. Take the case of the embittered husband who would rather go to jail than make court-ordered alimony payments. A primary purpose of jailing someone for contempt is to force him to comply with a court order. Here, putting the husband in prison will still not make him pay the alimony. In some cases, judges will release a person because he or she cannot be forced to do something and further imprisonment is considered cruelty. Usually, the threat of contempt is enough to encourage people to accept and live with a court decision.

Validating a deed If a defendant refuses to sign a deed giving over property to its rightful owner, the court may authorize an official to sign a valid deed. This is sometimes done to transfer property awarded as part of a divorce decree. U.S. marshals can execute deeds for property seized and sold for failure to pay taxes.

Receivers In cases where none of the joint owners can be trusted to hold or manage property during litigation, the court may appoint a receiver. A receiver is an impartial person who can be trusted to care for property that might otherwise be wasted or lost. Courts also appoint receivers to care for the property of an incompetent or underage person who cannot manage his own affairs.

References A reference is a court order that the case, or certain issues in the case, be sent to a court-appointed referee. A judge may refer a highly technical case to an expert. If the case requires the analysis of a long account— that is, many separate bookkeeping entries—a referee can be appointed to hear proof that each entry is accurate.

Bonds Judges in some cases require a party to post a bond, a sum of money that is forfeited if he fails to obey the decree. The bond may be posted by paying the money to the court. The party loses his money only if he does not live up to the conditions of the decree. Some state laws require a plaintiff to post a bond whenever he is granted an injunction (a writ forbidding or ordering a defendant to perform some act). If a later decision finds that the plaintiff never should have inconvenienced the defendant with the injunction, the defendant can be given money—up to the amount of the bond—to pay for the harm done to him.

EXAMPLE A manufacturer was granted a temporary injunction that prevented a store from selling the manufacturer's stereos at less than the price agreed upon in the sales contract. The injunction was granted only on condition that the manufacturer post a bond of $5,000. At the hearing held on enforcement of the contract between the store and the manufacturer, the store was able to prove that setting a minimum price for the stereos violated state antitrust laws. Because the store was able to show that it had lost business while the injunction prevented it from selling the stereos at the lower price, the court awarded the store the $5,000 bond as damages.

Sequestration Courts in equity may order the defendant's property collected and held (sequestered) until the defendant does what the court requires him to do. Sequestration has been especially useful in matrimonial cases where a man has left the state so that he cannot be served with legal papers or ordered to make alimony payments. In such a case, the court can sequester bank accounts, real estate, or any other assets within the state. The court can decree that the sequestered property be released if the defendant returns to the state to appear in the lawsuit.

Writs A variety of special writs were developed early in the history of equity to grant authority to enforce decrees. A *writ of delivery* commanded the sheriff to take possession of specific items of property and give them to the person entitled to have them. If the property could not be found, the sheriff was to take the person responsible for hiding them into custody.

A *writ of assistance* commanded the sheriff to assist someone entitled to recover possession of land. If the person to be ousted put up a fight, the sheriff could summon anyone in the county over the age of 15 to assist him. This authority was called the *posse comitatus*, or the "power of the county." The sheriff's posse of the Old West is a descendant of this English tradition. Most of the authority expressed in the old writs still rests in our modern courts, but procedure has been simplified so that the formal writs are often no longer used.

equity of redemption The right of someone who owes money on a MORTGAGE to prevent foreclosure after he has failed to make payments when they were due. He may do this by paying off the amount of the mortgage debt plus interest and costs. This rule is applicable to any mortgage up until the time of a sale after foreclosure. It is only right that a property owner be given one last chance to hold on to his property even though he is in default for missing one or more payments. The property is bound to be sold in any case, and equity of redemption gives the owner the first right over any other buyers. See also STRICT FORECLOSURE.

ergo (Latin) "Therefore."

Erie v. Tompkins A case decided by the U.S. Supreme Court in 1938 that limited the power of federal courts to apply their own rules of law. The federal courts must apply federal statutes, if appropriate, in cases in which the parties are from different states. When there are no federal laws to answer the question in a lawsuit, they must follow the law of the state that is involved. That includes both state statutes and controlling decisions (decisions followed by other courts) made by the state's highest court.

One dark night a man named Tompkins was walking on a frequently used footpath alongside the railroad tracks. The footpath was on land owned by the Erie Railroad Company. A passing train struck and injured Tompkins. He thought he had been hit by a door sticking out from one of the freight cars and claimed that the railroad was careless in operating or maintaining the train.

Tompkins wanted to sue the railroad and recover money DAMAGES for his injuries. He was a citizen of Pennsylvania and the Erie was a New York corporation. He brought an action in a federal court because the parties were from diverse, or different, states. This federal authority is called *diversity jurisdiction.*

■ **Applying the proper law** The problem before the federal court was what law to apply in deciding the case. There was no federal statute to decide whether Tompkins was entitled to receive damages. Neither was there a Pennsylvania statute that was applicable. But the highest court of Pennsylvania did have a rule to be followed in state courts whenever a case like this came up. The Pennsylvania rule was that people who use pathways alongside of railroad rights-of-way are trespassers and railroads are not liable to them unless the trespassers were injured by reckless or wanton acts.

The federal judge in Tompkins's case refused to apply the Pennsylvania rule. He found that *Swift* v. *Tyson,* a case decided by the Supreme Court in 1842, gave federal judges the right to ignore state rules not enacted as statutes by their state legislatures. He held that it was more important for federal courts all over the country to follow a uniform rule when there was no statute to settle the case, rather than to make each federal court apply local state rules. He let the jury decide whether the railroad company was negligent. The jury returned a verdict of $30,000 for Tompkins.

The U.S. Supreme Court reversed the decision. The 1842 rule that allowed federal judges to ignore state court decisions in diversity cases was struck down. According to this rule, Tompkins could get his money damages if he sued in federal court, but he could not get them if he sued a few blocks away in Pennsylvania state court. Because the plaintiff and defendant were citizens of different states, the plaintiff could take advantage of the right to sue in federal court. There he might win even though he had been trespassing on railroad property. If the plaintiff and defendant were both citizens of Pennsylvania, the plaintiff could *not* sue in federal court. Pennsylvania courts would all be bound to follow the rule that prevented recoveries for people who used paths alongside railroad tracks. It was unfair, the Supreme Court held, for the plaintiff's chances of winning to depend on whether the railroad was a Pennsylvania corporation.

■ **Uniformity of federal courts** One result of this case is that the decisions of federal courts all over the country are now truly uniform only when a question of *federal* law is involved. Otherwise, the states are free to have their own laws applied to state questions that come into federal court when the parties are from different states. It was the Supreme Court's opinion that the Constitution requires exactly that. The Constitution carefully saves for the states all the powers that are not specifically given to the federal government.

erratum (Latin) "Error"; mistake. When a case is reviewed by a judge, he might reply, *"In nollo est erratum"*—There was no error.

error See APPEAL AND ERROR.

escalator clause A provision, usually in a contract or lease, that allows for an increase in the money to be paid. For example, a lease for a rent-controlled apartment frequently contains an escalator clause that obligates the tenant to pay a higher rent any time regulations authorize an increase. Business contracts often contain escalator clauses to increase prices if the cost of labor or materials is more than anticipated.

escape The crime of leaving or allowing someone else to leave lawful custody without permission or right. A prisoner who breaks out of a city jail or a state penitentiary is guilty of escape. A man who manages to slip away from a large group of gamblers who have been arrested and are waiting for the police to take them to jail has also committed an escape. If a police officer helps the man get away—for example, because the officer knows his father—then the policeman also is guilty of escape.

The crime of escape may be committed either by a prisoner or by a person responsible for keeping him in custody. The custodian of the prisoner is not the prison warden, however, but rather the guard immediately responsible for watching the prisoner. Some states now choose to punish careless guards administratively, perhaps taking away rank or seniority or firing them. Criminal punishment is saved for guards who actually cooperate in helping a prisoner to escape.

■ **When it happens** An escape occurs when the prisoner manages to get outside the control of an authorized custodian. A prisoner may be guilty of escape if he hides outside his exercise area or cell block but still remains inside the prison walls. One man was convicted when he went fishing on a prison farm without permission.

A prisoner can be guilty of escape even though he never should have been arrested to begin with—for example, because he was illegally arrested in his home without a search warrant. One cannot be guilty of escape, however, if the arrest was totally illegal—as by a store security guard who had no power to arrest a shoplifter.

To prove a criminal escape, it is usually not necessary to show that the accused was confined within prison walls. Once an arrest has taken place, the prisoner has no right to leave. Frequently, the seriousness of the crime of escape is worse when the escape is made from a certain type of confinement. For example, the law may deal more harshly with someone who escapes from a chain gang than with one who walks away while an arresting officer is questioning witnesses. The degree of criminal escape may depend on the gravity of the crime that put the prisoner in jail.

It usually must be proved that the escaped prisoner was trying to evade lawful custody. If he mistakenly went to the wrong place or was unable to think clearly at the time, he probably did not commit escape.

■ **Related crimes** There are crimes related to escape. A person other than a policeman or guard who helps a prisoner escape may be guilty of *aiding escape*. This is the crime committed by someone who smuggles a weapon into prison, for example, or knowingly carries a prisoner out of jail in a truck delivering food. In one case, a prisoner who helped a convicted murderer escape was found guilty of aiding escape and given the same sentence that the murderer was then serving—199 years. Usually, however, the length of a sentence for aiding escape depends on the number of years specified in the criminal statute.

Harboring or concealing an escaped prisoner is a separate crime in some states. It must be shown that the accused person believed he was helping an escaped prisoner and intended to help him evade lawful custody. As with all escape crimes, it is no defense that the prisoner should not have been arrested.

A prisoner may be charged with *prison breach* if he uses force to make his escape. This is more serious than escape accomplished by a strategy or trick. If prison breach is not a separate crime, the state may consider a violent escape to be a more serious degree of criminal escape.

An attempt to commit a criminal escape, or any of the related crimes, may be punishable even though the attempt failed.

escheat
The right of a state to take property for which there is no owner. The taking is called *an escheat,* the sum of the property may be called *the escheat,* and it can be said that the property *escheats*. Escheat is not favored in the law, and courts will energetically seek to avoid it.

■ **Grounds for escheat** The most common reason for an escheat is that a person dies without a will and without having any surviving relatives who would be entitled to inherit his property under the laws of DESCENT AND DISTRIBUTION. States have the power to enact escheat statutes defining this power. Unclaimed or abandoned property in some cases is subject to escheat.

■ **Escheat and forfeiture** Escheat and FORFEITURE are different, although their effect is often the same. *Forfeiture* includes the loss of any kind of interest in property, such as possession, the right to inherit, or the right to a REVERSION (return of property) if the present owners violate a specific condition. *Escheat* means complete loss of ownership. Another difference is that forfeiture operates against the one having an interest in the forfeited property. An escheat occurs for lack of a person with a proper interest in the property. Today, a forfeiture is frequently a penalty for an illegal act, while escheat is not tied to any illegality.

■ **Property liable to escheat** All the property of the owner that is within the state when he dies without heirs or a will is subject to escheat. The doctrine originally applied only to real property (real estate), but it has been extended to include personal property (all other kinds of property), including such intangibles as shares of stock and bank accounts. Statutes in each state determine when a deceased person's property is subject to that state's laws.

Federal law provides that the property of veterans who die without heirs or a will can escheat to the United States, but usually escheated property goes to the state in which it is located. Even land that was granted to its owner by the federal government becomes the property of the state if it is subject to escheat. Occasionally, a state law gives escheated property to a county or town.

Unclaimed or abandoned property escheats to the state under some statutes. Laws like this must function within constitutional limits, of course. The state cannot simply declare property abandoned and appropriate it. DUE PROCESS OF LAW must be observed. It must have a routine procedure for notifying the public and must give possible claimants an opportunity to argue that the property may belong to them. The state may lawfully hold the property for a period of time so that claims can be asserted.

A state is not required to take over unclaimed property—it may choose to exercise the power to escheat only when legal proceedings are not too expensive in relation to the value of the property. In such cases, other persons may assert their claims to ownership.

Common subjects The following are often subject to escheat: unclaimed bank accounts; deposits left with utility companies; stock or dividends whose owners cannot be found; unpaid wages; unclaimed legacies from a relative's estate; insurance money owed to unknown beneficiaries; unclaimed money held by employers or public officials.

The law of some states specifies that the property of charitable or religious institutions escheats when they are dissolved. This applies only to property that donors do not have a right to recover when it is no longer used for the religious or charitable purpose. Some states require escheat of property belonging to religious societies that have failed to incorporate as required or have promoted illegal acts.

The property of inmates who die in a state institution—such as a prison, a mental hospital, or a veterans' home—may also be subject to escheat.

At common law, any property belonging to ALIENS was subject to escheat. Aliens could not inherit property or sometimes just land. Any such property left to them when someone else died went to the state. State laws that preserve this rule have been held not to violate the U.S. Constitution.

■ **The steps in an escheat** The escheat statutes establish a procedure for trying to find the rightful owner. If the effort to find the rightful owner fails, then the property is subject to escheat. If the state takes it over, the property presumably should benefit everyone. Without escheat, the property would go to the one who just happens to be holding it.

The procedure for escheat varies for different states, different kinds of owners, and different kinds of property. The only necessary parts for the procedure are NOTICE (usually by a summons) and an opportunity for possible claimants to be heard.

In some states, title to property automatically passes to the state when it escheats for lack of a proper claimant. In others, a certain period of time must pass after the death of the owner, and then the state may start escheat proceedings. Claimants usually must assert their rights within a given period of time or lose them. Often persons handling estates must notify the state government of property that could be subject to escheat. If the state is not notified, there is no limit to the time within which it can start an escheat action.

The state has the primary burden of proving that there is no proper person entitled to the property. The rules regarding what kind of EVIDENCE is admissible in court apply. Rules of presumption may support the state's case. For example, the state may ask the court to presume that a missing heir is dead after he has disappeared without explanation for seven years. This is the common-law presumption of death. Once the state has proved a legally sufficient case, anyone who claims a right to the property may argue against the state's evidence.

Paid informers Some states offer money to informers who report property subject to escheat. Informers may have to provide evidence and pursue the case to a conclusion in order to earn their fee. Other states provide compensation for an *escheater,* a person appointed by the court to manage the state's claim for escheat. An escheater is entitled to be paid even if he does not succeed in recovering the property for the state.

escrow A document or sum of money deposited, usually with an impartial party, until a promised act is done or an event occurs. The instructions given to the person who accepts delivery of the document are called the *escrow agreement.* This agreement is between the person who promises and the person to whom the promise is made. The document or money is held *in escrow* by a third person until the purpose of the agreement is accomplished. When the specified condition is fulfilled, the person holding the document or the money gives it to the party entitled to receive it. This is called the *second delivery.*

Any written document that is made with all the necessary legal formalities may be deposited in escrow. This can be a deed, mortgage, promise to pay money, bond, check, life-insurance policy, license, patent, or even a contract for the sale of property.

The escrow agreement is a CONTRACT. Parties to the agreement decide before the deposit takes place when it should be released. Once the escrow agreement has been made, the terms for holding and releasing the document or money cannot be changed unless all the parties agree.

The custodian of the deposit—the person holding it—is called a *depositary.* He is not a party to the escrow agreement. He does not have the right to alter its terms or to prevent the parties from making a change. The depositary must only agree to hold the deposit according to the terms and conditions of the escrow agreement. Usually he has nothing to do with the agreement, but in a few states an interested person may be selected as a depositary if all the parties consent. In any case, a depositary must live up to the trust placed in him. If he delivers to the wrong person or at the wrong time, the depositor can get his property back.

The document or money is not in escrow until it is actually delivered to the depositary. Courts are generally strict in requiring that terms of the escrow agreement be fully performed before the deposit is released. Usually a reasonable amount of time must be allowed for doing what must be done. Parties may agree, however, to the legal restriction that "time is of the essence." Then any delay beyond the time specified in the agreement makes the person who is obligated to act lose all his rights in the property in escrow.

■ **Escrow and mortgages** Mortgage companies frequently require that with each month's mortgage payment homeowners pay an extra amount of money to be used for paying taxes at the end of the year. This amount is held in escrow. If taxes on the mortgaged home are $1,200, for instance, the homeowner may pay an extra $100 per month into escrow. Since this money does not belong to the mortgage company, the company cannot use it. The money must be kept in a special bank account, separate from money used by the company in its usual business. Similarly, the security tenants pay to their landlords when they sign a lease must be kept in a separate escrow account. This security is held until the tenant moves out and the landlord assays the damage, if any, that the tenant did to the premises. The landlord then uses whatever part of the security is needed to pay for repairs.

Esq. The abbreviation for the word *esquire,* a title used by lawyers—for example, Michael Alexander, Esq.

establishment clause See RELIGION, FREEDOM OF.

estate The degree, quality, and extent of a person's ownership of real or personal PROPERTY, from absolute ownership down to naked (unconfirmed) possession. Real property is land and anything that is a part of the land or attached to it, including houses and other structures. Personal property is any property that is not real property.

■ **Fee simple** A fee simple estate is the greatest estate and the most extensive interest that a person can possess in real property.

EXAMPLE Suppose you are John Jones. You purchase a 10-acre plot, and the owner deeds the 10 acres to you. The deed states that the owner grants the property "to John Jones." The words "to John Jones" have the legal effect of giving you a fee simple estate in the land. You are now the owner of the 10-acre plot in fee simple. You have the right to immediate and exclusive possession of the land and you may do anything you wish with it. In the eyes of the law your estate is to last forever. If you still own the land when you die and you have not made a will, the land is inherited by your nearest relatives. They become the owners of the 10 acres in fee simple, exactly as you were.

■ **Fee tail** A fee tail is an estate in land with restrictions on who may inherit it. It is created by deed or by will.

EXAMPLE Charles Gold owns Goldacres in fee simple. He
○━━✻ deeds Goldacres "to my son, Harry Gold, and the heirs of his body." The words "and the heirs of his body" have the legal effect of creating the fee tail. During his lifetime Harry Gold may use the land as he wishes. He may use it himself or lease it to a tenant. If he does lease to a tenant, the lease terminates upon Harry's death. Harry may not, however, sell the land or bequeath it by will because the deed says the land is to go only to the heirs of his body—that is, his children and through them to his grandchildren in a direct line. Harry Gold's issue take the land from Harry's father, Charles, the person who created the fee tail, and not from Harry.

Fee tail estates have been either entirely abolished or greatly modified in most states. An attempt to create a fee tail often converts the estate to one in fee simple in the hands of the first taker (Harry). In other states, the first taker has only a life estate in the land. Upon the death of the first taker, the land is inherited by his children in fee simple or by those to whom the land would pass according to the laws of DESCENT AND DISTRIBUTION.

■ **Life estate** A life estate in land is held for the life of a particular person. A life estate is ordinarily created by a deed or lease. No special language is required; it need only be free of ambiguity and clearly show an intent to create a life estate. The person to whom the life estate is granted is called the *life tenant*. The estate may be given to the life tenant for the duration of his own life. For example, Bill Green, who owns Greenacre in fee simple, grants or leases Greenacre "to John Marsh for and during John Marsh's natural life."

The life estate may also be given to the tenant for the life of some other person. This is called an *estate pur autre vie*. Sam Black, who owns Blackacre in fee simple, grants or leases Blackacre "to my son-in-law Will Waters for the lifetime of my daughter Jane Black Waters."

A life estate may be *determinable*—that is, it may end automatically upon the occurrence of some event.

EXAMPLE Anna Hawthorn owns Thornacre in fee simple.
○━━✻ She grants Thornacre "to my son Paul for life as long as no alcoholic beverage is sold on Thornacre." Paul's determinable life estate ends automatically if and when an alcoholic beverage is sold on Thornacre.

A similar situation is a life estate that is *subject to a condition subsequent.*

EXAMPLE Ralph Rancher owns Corral Ranch in fee simple
○━━✻ absolute. He grants Corral Ranch "to my grandson Tom Rancher for life. But if Corral Ranch is used to raise sheep, then I, Ralph Rancher, have the right to enter and terminate the life estate." Tom Rancher has a life estate that continues until he begins to raise sheep on Corral Ranch *and* his grandfather Ralph acts to exercise his right to terminate the life estate. Since Tom Rancher may never raise sheep and his grandfather may never terminate the grant, Tom has a life estate.

■ **Remainders** A remainder is what "remains" after a particular earlier estate has ended. It is created at the same time and by the same deed or will that created the earlier estate. It must be designed to take effect immediately upon the termination of the earlier estate. Land is frequently granted to a life tenant and thereafter to some other person in fee simple.

EXAMPLE Ed White owns Whiteacre and he deeds it "to my
○━━✻ son, Bob White, for his lifetime, then to my grandson, David White, and his heirs." David White has a remainder interest in Whiteacre and he is called a *remainderman*. When Bob White dies, David White immediately becomes the owner of Whiteacre in fee simple.

Remainder interests are either vested (absolute) or contingent. A *vested remainder* is one in which a present interest passes to a specific person, to be enjoyed in the future. The remainder is vested even though the actual time of enjoyment is postponed or uncertain. In the previous example, David White has a vested remainder in Whiteacre. David is a specific person who has a present, absolute interest, which passed to him when his grandfather deeded Whiteacre to David's father, Bob, for life.

A *contingent remainder* is one in which the estate in remainder is granted provided a dubious and uncertain event occurs. A contingent remainder cannot vest until some condition has been satisfied.

EXAMPLE Morris Redman owns Redacre. He deeds Red-
○━━✻ acre "to Nick Frank for life, remainder to Jay Hable, if and when Jay Hable pays me $10,000." Hable's remainder is contingent upon the condition that Hable pays $10,000 to Redman. The payment is an uncertain event that may never take place.

EXAMPLE Colonel Patrick owns Plantation Acres. His only
○━━✻ child, a son named Major, has been married for many years, but Major and his wife are childless. The colonel has promised Major that he will give Plantation Acres to Major's son. Major's wife becomes pregnant. The colonel is excited about the prospect of a grandchild, and deeds Plantation Acres "to my son, Major, for life, remainder to my grandson and his heirs." In this example, the condition is the birth of a male grandchild. The child might be a girl, or Major's wife might miscarry, or the child might be born dead, and the contingency would not be satisfied. The plantation would eventually go back to the colonel or his estate if the grandson dies without heirs before Major.

■ **Reversions** Reversion has two meanings: (1) the estate left in the grantor for the duration of a particular estate, and (2) the return of the land to the grantor or his heirs after the grant is over. A reversion differs from a remainder in that it occurs by law (automatically), while a remainder is an act of the parties through the terms of a deed or will.

EXAMPLE Adam Troy owns Aegean Farms. Adam's son,
○━━✻ Sidney, has tried a number of different occupations and now wishes to become a farmer. Adam does not believe his son's interest in farming will last very long, but he loves his son and thinks Sidney should have the opportunity to try farming. Adam grants Aegean Farms "to my son, Sidney, for five (5) years." Adam Troy thus retains a reversionary interest in Aegean Farms. Adam has granted to his son an estate that is shorter in duration

than the one that Adam owns. There is a residue that remains in Adam. When the five-year term expires, Adam is again entitled to possession and control of the property. Adam might have granted his son a life estate instead. In that case, Adam would still have had a reversionary interest because even a life estate is less than Adam's interest in Aegean Farms. Adam owns Aegean Farms in fee simple, and his ownership continues until he decides how to dispose of his entire interest.

■ **Merger** Whenever a greater and a lesser estate meet in the same person, the lesser estate is immediately absorbed into the greater estate.

EXAMPLE A tenant leases a farm for 10 years. He is so 0——※ successful with his crops that he purchases the farm from his landlord in the fourth year. The tenant's leasehold estate is merged into the greater fee simple estate he obtained when he purchased the farm.

■ **Personal property** The greatest estate in personal property is called the *absolute title* in it. Estates in personal property may be less than absolute, however. There can be an estate for life or an interest for a term of years in one person, with a remainder over to another. The most important point about estates in personal property is that they are governed by the same general principles that rule similar estates in real property.

estate and gift tax
Estates and gifts are usually subject to both federal and state taxes. Because the 50 states have widely different systems for taxing estates and gifts, this entry deals only with federal law. Inheritance taxes are also defined.

■ **The nature of the taxes** An *estate tax* is a tax on the privilege of transferring property at death. The tax is imposed on the value of the entire estate, after it has been reduced by certain expenses and deductions and before its assets have been distributed to the decedent's heirs. An *inheritance tax* is levied on the privilege of receiving property from a decedent. It is usually based on the amount of property received by each individual heir and by his or her relationship to the decedent.

Both estate and inheritance taxes use a graduated rate scale—the larger the estate or inheritance, the higher the tax rate. In the past, a person could sometimes avoid certain estate taxes by making gifts during his lifetime (called *inter vivos* or lifetime gifts) that reduced the size of the estate. Now, however, there is a federal gift tax on such gifts when they exceed $3,000 per person per year. In 1976 a new law provided for a $47,000 unified tax credit (against taxes on both estate and taxable lifetime gifts), which permits a person to leave the equivalent of a $175,625 estate to his heirs tax-free.

■ **The 1976 Tax Reform Act** The Tax Reform Act of 1976 was the first sweeping revision of federal estate and gift taxes since 1948. The act reduced taxes on medium-sized estates left by the average person by increasing the amount of the gross estate (see below) subject to federal estate tax from $60,000 to the equivalent of $175,625, effective January 1, 1981. The $60,000 estate-tax exemption was enacted in 1942 when very few people left estates worth that much. Today, if you own your own home, an automobile, and a color television set and have a bank account of $10,000, the value of your estate may easily exceed $60,000. By increasing the amount of the estate that is tax-exempt, the tax burden has been lifted from modest-sized estates.

■ **The unified tax credit (unitax)** The Tax Reform Act ended the separate federal tax rates for estates and lifetime gifts and applied a single unified estate tax (unitax) to both. It replaced the $60,000 estate-tax exemption and the $30,000 lifetime exemption for taxes on gifts made before January 1, 1977, and gradually phased in the unitax system to be fully effective on January 1, 1981. Under that system a person's estate is entitled to a $47,000 tax credit, to cover both his estate taxes and gifts he made in excess of $3,000 annually. Under the new law, a donor can make each year as many tax-free gifts of less than $3,000 to any number of persons he wishes.

The equivalent exemption column below, which shows how the new tax credit was phased in, indicates the maximum amounts (in addition to the $3,000 annual exclusion per person) that became free from federal gift and estate taxes in the year indicated.

YEAR	UNITAX CREDIT	EQUIVALENT EXEMPTION
1977	$30,000	$120,667
1978	34,000	134,000
1979	38,000	147,333
1980	42,500	161,563
1981 and after	47,000	175,625

This is how it works. Suppose that Peter makes outright gifts to Barbara of $175,625 in the early part of 1981. By use of the unitax, there will be no gift tax:

Gross amount of 1981 gifts	$175,625
Less the $3,000 annual exclusion	3,000
Total taxable gifts	$172,625
Tentative gift tax	46,040
Less the available unitax credit	47,000
Gift tax	− 0 −

If Peter dies in 1982, the total amount of his gift to Barbara ($175,625) would be included in his gross estate because the gift was more than $3,000 and was made less than three years before his death. (See "Lifetime gifts," later in this article.)

Gifts are subject to the unitax at the time they are given, and will be taken into account when estate taxes are computed.

■ **Gross estate** The gross estate of a decedent is "the value (at the time of his death) of all his property, real or personal, tangible or intangible, wherever situated." The gross estate includes such items as real estate, houses, stocks and bonds, furniture, jewelry, works of art, cars, bank accounts, as well as salaries and debts that are owed to the decedent.

Life insurance policies payable on a person's death are included in the gross estate if the policy is to be paid to the estate or if the decedent kept "incidents of ownership."

EXAMPLE If, at the time of his death, John still had the 0——※ power to change beneficiaries or to borrow against the cash value of his policy, the proceeds of the policy would be included in his gross estate. This is regardless of the fact that the policy was to be paid to his

THE BASICS OF ESTATE AND GIFT TAXES

■ An *estate tax* is a tax on transferring property at death and is charged against the value of the entire estate. An *inheritance tax* is what you pay for the privilege of receiving property in this manner—it is based on the amount you receive and on your relationship to the deceased. The bigger the inheritance, generally the higher the tax you will pay.

■ There is a federal tax on gifts exceeding $3,000, and many states also impose a gift tax.

If your estate amounts to less than $175,625, it will be exempt from federal estate tax.

■ You cannot exclude the value of a gift from the estate of the donor when the gift has been made in the last three years of his life and is more than $3,000.

■ You can make tax-free gifts of up to $3,000 to any number of individuals each year, but larger gifts made within three years of death will be automatically included in the gross estate.

■ For federal estate-tax purposes, the gross estate—all property of any kind owned by the decedent at his death—may be valued at the date of death or within six months after—this is intended to give the heirs a break if the gross estate loses value.

■ To appraise the estate, "fair market value" is the yardstick—this means the price at which the property would change hands in a free and open market; it is *not* a dealer's price but the price for which it could be bought by an ordinary member of the public.

■ Family farms and businesses are protected from ruin by estate taxes by being assessed at the value of their actual use as long as they remain in the family. But if the property is sold to someone outside or is no longer used for farming or other small-business purposes within 15 years after the decedent's death, the tax saved by the special valuation will have to be paid.

■ The taxable estate is found by taking the value of the gross estate and

reducing it by the amount of deductions authorized by law.

■ Property passing from decedent to surviving spouse is allowed a special marital deduction. The maximum deduction is $250,000 or one-half the adjusted gross estate of the decedent, whichever is greater.

■ A person can now give up to $100,000 tax free to his spouse (in addition to the $3,000 annual exclusion).

■ A federal estate-tax return must be filed for the estate of every citizen or resident of the United States whose gross estate at death is greater than $175,625.

■ The return must be filed by the executor or administrator, together with tax payment, within nine months after the death date. Extensions are granted if there is a good reason for the delay.

■ The estate tax is paid before the assets are distributed. Otherwise the beneficiaries may be liable for the unpaid tax.

wife or mother. If, however, John had signed all control of the policy over to his wife four years before his death, the proceeds would not be included in his gross estate.

If the decedent owned property jointly with another person (see JOINT TENANCY) or owned some community property with a spouse (see TENANCY BY THE ENTIRETY), only the value of his individual share (and not the total value of the property) will be included in his gross estate. This is important because the less the value of the gross estate, the lower will be the estate tax.

Lifetime gifts A person can make tax-free gifts of up to $3,000 per person to any number of individuals each year, even if the gifts are made one day before the giver dies. This is the *$3,000 annual exclusion* for gifts. For example, Jim makes gifts of $3,000 each to Jane, Kate, and Mary in 1977 before he dies. The $9,000 total will be excluded from his gross estate because each gift did not exceed $3,000.

Gifts of more than $3,000, however, made within three years of a person's death, are automatically included in the gross estate. This applies to gifts made after December 31, 1976. If, for example, Jim gave Jane, Kate, and Mary $4,000 each in 1977 and died the following year, the total of $12,000 (and not just the excess of each gift over $3,000) would be included in Jim's estate. Previously, such gifts were excluded from the estate, unless it was proved that the gift was made by the donor in contemplation of his death primarily to avoid estate taxes. See GIFT.

Any taxes paid by the decedent or the estate on gifts made in the last three years of the donor's life are also

included in the gross estate. This is called *gross-up of gift taxes.* They will later be subtracted from the tentative tax of the gross estate. The value of such gifts as shares of stock is measured by the market price on the date of death, not the date of the gift.

A gift-tax return must be filed by the giver on a quarterly basis when the taxable gifts made in those three months exceed $25,000 (over and above the $3,000 annual exclusion), or when the total amount of gifts made during a calendar year reaches $25,000 at the end of a particular quarter. When gifts total less than $25,000, they do not have to be reported until the end of the year.

Valuation of property For federal estate-tax purposes, the gross estate may be valued at the date of death or within six months after the decedent's death. This is called the *alternate valuation method.* Its purpose is to reduce the tax on an estate that has decreased in value since the decedent's death.

EXAMPLE Suppose that at the time of his death John owned 10,000 shares of stock in XYZ Company worth $50 per share, for a total value of $500,000. Two months later, XYZ is investigated by the Securities Exchange Commission and the value of the stock in John's estate suddenly drops to $10,000 (or $1 per share). The executor or administrator of John's estate can choose to assess the estate at $10,000, its value two months after John's death, rather than its value at the date of his death. By using the alternate valuation method, the executor will not have to pay estate tax on John's estate. It is actually worth only $10,000, well within the $175,625 exemption figure for

1981. Without the alternate valuation method, it would be financially impossible for John's executor to pay the estate taxes—the tax on a $500,000 estate would exceed the actual value of the estate, $10,000.

When the executor or the administrator chooses to value the estate on an alternate valuation date, he must value all of the property in the gross estate on that date.

EXAMPLE Suppose that in addition to his stock in XYZ Company, worth $500,000, John also owned stock in ABC Company (10,000 shares at $2.50 per share), worth $25,000 on the date of his death. Two months later, the actual value of the stock in XYZ Company drops to $10,000. The value of the ABC stock, however, dramatically increases from $25,000 to $750,000. The executor cannot value the XYZ stock as of the date two months after John's death while valuing the ABC stock on the date of John's death. In order to decide which date to use, the executor computes the date on which the *total value* of all the estate assets will result in the lowest amount. In this example, John's executor should use the date of death to value the gross estate.

Fair market value Whatever date is used for appraising the estate, its fair market value is what must be calculated. Fair market value is the price at which the property would change hands between a buyer and a seller in a free and open market. For example, the fair market value of an automobile is the price for which a car of the same (or similar) description, make, model, age, and condition could be purchased by a member of the public. It is *not* the price a used car dealer would pay for it.

Farms and family businesses The 1976 act allows farms and other types of family businesses that are the major assets of estates to be valued according to the use they were put to during the decedent's lifetime—when they remain in the family. In the past they were valued, like other assets, at their "highest and best use," which often posed a severe hardship. Suppose that the owner of a 2,000-acre farm dies. Although the land was used for farming, its worth would have tripled if it had been converted to commercial purposes, such as for a shopping center. Under the old law, the land would be taxed on its commercial value, its highest and best use, even though it had never been used for that purpose. In such cases family members often had to sell their farms and small businesses in order to pay the estate taxes.

Now family farms and businesses can be saved by being assessed for estate-tax purposes at the value of their actual use as long as they remain in the family. If the property is sold by an heir to someone outside the family or if its use for farming or other small-business purpose is discontinued within 15 years after the decedent's death or on the heir's death (whichever is sooner), the tax saved by the special valuation will have to be paid.

■ **Taxable estate** Once the total gross estate has been valued at its fair market value, the taxable estate must be determined. The taxable estate is found by taking the value of the gross estate and reducing it by the amount of deductions authorized by law. These deductions include funeral expenses; administration expenses such as attorney's fees, court costs, or executor's or administrator's commissions; any mortgages or debts that the decedent owed at his death;

any losses to the estate during its administration, such as by theft, vandalism, or fire; the marital deduction or the orphan's exclusion (if there are surviving children but no surviving parent); and the amount of charitable gifts made by the decedent.

To the taxable estate is added the total amount of taxable gifts made after December 31, 1976. Already in the gross estate are those gifts of more than $3,000 made within the three years prior to the decedent's death plus the amount of gift tax that had been paid on those gifts. But suppose John made gifts of $6,000 to each of his three children, Sally, Susan, and Shirley, in 1980, five years before his death in 1985. The $18,000 total in gifts will be added to his taxable estate. It is this figure on which the *tentative tax* will be based. Once computed, the tentative tax is reduced by the amount of gift tax John has already paid. This remainder is the figure to which John's heirs apply the unified credit against estate tax. The resulting figure is the tax that John's estate owes—unless it can be further reduced by various credits authorized by law, such as one for death taxes the estate paid to the state.

■ **Marital estate-tax deduction** There is, in addition to the unified tax credit, a maximum marital deduction for property passing from the decedent to a surviving spouse. The deduction is $250,000 or one-half of the decedent's adjusted gross estate, whichever is greater. This will be reduced in certain cases; see the discussion on "The marital gift-tax deduction" below. The *adjusted gross estate* is the total gross estate less some of the deductions described above. A married person with an adjusted gross estate of less than $500,000 can pass $250,000 tax-free to his surviving spouse.

EXAMPLE Richard dies in 1981, leaving an adjusted gross estate of $300,000. Mary, his wife, is entitled to the maximum marital deduction of $250,000. The remaining balance is the taxable estate, $50,000. The tentative tax on a $50,000 estate is $10,600. The unified credit in 1981 is $47,000, which wipes out any estate tax on Richard's estate.

Tax-free estates for spouse In estates of less than $500,000 the marital deduction, when combined with the unified tax credit, permits a spouse to pass the following estates (the adjusted gross figures in the last column) tax-free to the surviving spouse:

YEAR OF DEATH	UNIFIED CREDIT	EXEMPTION EQUIV-ALENT*	MARITAL + DEDUCTION	ADJUSTED = GROSS ESTATE
1977	$30,000	$120,667	+ $250,000	= $370,667
1978	34,000	134,000	+ 250,000	= 384,000
1979	38,000	147,333	+ 250,000	= 397,333
1980	42,500	161,563	+ 250,000	= 411,563
1981 and after	47,000	175,625	+ 250,000	= 425,625

*The amount of the adjusted gross estate that will pass to a person's heirs tax-free by use of the unified credit.

Not claiming the marital deduction For some estates under $500,000 it might be better *not* to take the maximum marital deduction. This is done with an eye toward reducing the estate tax for the heirs. Property that the surviving spouse inherits tax-free under the marital deduction will be subject to estate tax paid by the heirs

ESTATE PLANNING: HOW TO SETTLE YOUR AFFAIRS

E. LISK WYCKOFF, JR., Consultant
Member, New York Bar

Estate planning is really planning for the family. Its main purpose is to provide for your family and other loved ones and to protect the property you have worked so hard to amass from being whittled away by taxes or from going to a "laughing heir"—a relative you may dislike or one you have never even heard of but who is legally your heir. Estate planning can also benefit you during your lifetime by giving you tax advantages as well as a feeling of security.

Decisions about estates involve what happens not only to your property after death but also to property arrangements during your lifetime. For example, what kind of life insurance should you buy? Who should own it? How much property should husband and wife own jointly? What about individual ownership? Should you place some of your assets in a trust during your life, one paying income with no tax liability? Or should you provide in your will for a trust that takes effect after your death? What are the benefits of giving gifts during your lifetime as opposed to giving them by will after your death?

If you do not leave a will or an estate plan, the law of your state will decide who gets your property. Sometimes the state itself will get it. The problem with most state plans is that you probably would not like the way they distribute your property. So it is best to make your own distribution. Being poor is no excuse for not having an estate plan. If a poor man is killed in an accident, for example, proper arrangements could entitle his family to claim valuable damages.

The major part of any estate plan is usually a will. But a will is only one way of transferring your property to someone else. You can also use gifts, life insurance, trusts, employee death benefits, estate marital deductions, and jointly owned property. As you will see, some of the methods have tax advantages that a will does not have. For example, instead of leaving your child $5,000 in your will, which will be taxed as part of your estate, it might be better to leave the $5,000 to the child in a living trust, which will not be taxed as part of your estate and which also permits the principal to earn tax-free interest.

Usually the family lawyer is called upon to make up the estate plan. However, it is a good idea to have the help and advice of an accountant, insurance agent, banker, investment counselor, or even all these specialists. Although the use of so many advisers may seem staggering, the truth is that no estate plan is ever simple. No single formula can be followed for estates. Each person's and each family's needs and priorities are different. Moreover, the tax laws are so complicated that it is virtually impossible to have a simple solution, even for a modest-size estate.

When considering an estate plan, it is important to look at the total picture. While one facet of your plan may save you $20,000 in taxes, its effect may end up costing you more somewhere else. Weighing the advantages and disadvantages of each option and seeing how the parts fit into the whole will enable you to set up an estate plan that will truly benefit you and your family. The following are just two examples of what can happen if you fail to plan ahead.

Sam took a new job in another state where the income taxes are less than in his former state of residence. Although Sam bought a new home and moved his family to the new state, he kept his old home and rented it out, continued to vote in his former state, and kept other contacts with the state, including his bank account. Sam's new job required him to be physically present in the former state not more than three months a year. A year and a half after Sam left his former state, the state's tax commission assessed an income tax on Sam because he had never given up his resident status in the state. Sam died six months later and his former state claimed that because Sam never lost his domicile status in the state, his estate was liable for inheritance taxes on all of his assets. Sam could have avoided this by changing his resident and domicile status to the new state.

Mrs. Eastworth is 64 years old. Her husband died five years ago, leaving her property now worth about $500,000, which consists mostly of stocks and bonds. Mrs. Eastworth has been very careful to keep her will current, realizing that recent tax changes could affect how much income and property she will have and how much she can pass along to her children and grandchildren. Suddenly, she is struck with a debilitating illness that prevents her from managing her property. None of her beneficiaries has a durable power of attorney, nor is there a trustee who can manage her property for her. Six months after the onset of the illness, most of Mrs. Eastworth's securities have declined by 20 percent because she has sole power to handle those securities and nothing can be done because she is incapacitated.

Information you need to plan your estate

To plan your estate, begin by making two lists, one containing pertinent personal information and the other your assets and those of your spouse.

Personal information   The statement of personal information should include the following:

(1) *Your place of domicile.* This should be the place you consider to be your home. If you have a home in two different states, you must be careful not to be domiciled in both states because each state might determine that you were domiciled in it, thus permitting each to levy estate and inheritance taxes.

(2) *Your residence.* The residence rule for income-tax purposes usually requires you to be in the state for a certain period of time each year. This becomes significant if you live in one state and work in another or even in several states.

(3) *Your marital status.* This includes not only your current status but also any previous marriages and the terms of the separation and/or divorce decrees. If you are contemplating marriage, you may want to consider an antenuptial agreement concerning the division of property under certain circumstances—for example, if you have children by a previous marriage and want to be sure they inherit the bulk of your estate.

(4) *The complete name, address, and birth date of each beneficiary.* This includes spouse, children, grandchildren, other relatives, and nonrelatives. A statement about the mental and physical health of a beneficiary should be included when necessary, as when your aged mother is not legally competent to manage her own affairs. The adoptive or illegitimate status of beneficiaries must also be noted, because in some states they do not automatically qualify to share in your estate.

(5) *The location of assets.* List the location of your safe-deposit boxes and the names of those people who have access to them. Also state where such important documents as wills, deeds, insurance policies, mortgages, and separation agreements are kept.

(6) *Your power of attorney.* If you have given anyone the power of attorney to act as an agent in your place, give the name of the person and the location of the document giving him or her this authority.

Net worth statement   The following is a sample net worth statement, which includes a listing of your assets and liabilities. People are often surprised to learn that they are worth more than they realized.

ASSETS
1. Cash in banks .... $_____
2. Stocks .... _____
3. Bonds .... _____
4. Closely held business interests (family business) .... _____
5. Real estate .... _____
6. Life insurance .... _____
7. Employee-benefit plans .... _____
8. Tangible personal property (such as household furnishings, jewelry, vehicles) .... _____
9. Notes and mortgages owed by others _____
10. Other property .... _____

Total: $_____

LIABILITIES
1. Mortgages .... $_____
2. Notes owed to others .... _____
3. Other indebtedness .... _____
                              Total: $_____

NET WORTH .... $_____

In addition to listing the above information, you must know how title to (ownership of) the assets is held: individually, joint ownership with right of survivorship, tenancy in common or tenancy by the entirety, community property, or partnership. The owner and beneficiary of life insurance policies should also be shown. If you are an employee of a company that has benefit plans in which you share (such as pension, group life insurance, profit sharing), you must know what the provisions are and whether the plans are contributory or noncontributory. Frequently, small corporations have agreements restricting the transfers of stock at death either to other shareholders or to the corporation. Such agreements must also be considered in the estate plan.

Methods of transferring property at death

Wills, jointly held property, trusts, and life insurance policies are the most common ways of transferring property at death.

Wills A will is the most widely used method of transferring property at death from one person to another. Property given by will is subject to taxes and probate, a sometimes lengthy and costly court procedure that proves the will is valid and can be put into effect. A will cannot transfer all kinds of property. It does not include jointly owned property, life insurance proceeds paid directly to beneficiaries, and property held in trusts, although a will may establish a trust. If a substantial amount of your property is held outside your will, your estate may suffer a needlessly high tax bill, as in the case of the survivor in jointly held property. Therefore, it is important to analyze how title to all property is held.

Jointly held property Many married couples share the ownership of their property. There are a number of different ways to do this, each with a different impact on the estate.

The most popular method is *joint tenancy with right of survivorship*, probably because when one spouse dies, the other automatically inherits the property. This eliminates the need for a will and probate on that property and insures that the surviving spouse will inherit it—even if there is a will saying that the spouse cannot have it! In addition, in most states each party has total control over the whole property—in the case of joint bank accounts, for example, either spouse can withdraw money without the consent of the other.

It is common for husbands and wives to hold title to real estate, such as the family home, in *tenancy by the entirety*. While tenancy by the entirety insures that the surviving spouse will get title to the property, neither can sell it without the consent of the other. In *tenancy in common*, on the other hand, each person totally owns his or her share of the property, which can be sold or given away without the other's consent. And only each person's share of the property goes into his or her estate, not the whole property. However, if minors or incompetent persons are tenants in common, selling the property can be a problem.

Eight states (Arizona, California, Idaho, Louisiana, Nevada, New Mexico, Texas, and Washington) have *community-property ownership*. This means that any property acquired during the marriage belongs to both husband and wife in equal shares. Each has a right only to his or her half of the property, and each can dispose of the half in a will. Property each spouse owned before marriage or inherited after marriage is not included in community property.

Contrary to popular belief, joint ownership, while eliminating the need for a will and probate proceedings, does not also eliminate taxes. Often it means more taxes. For instance, the law presumes that the spouse who dies first owned *all* of the property held jointly, with the result that the whole property is taxed, not just part of it.

Joint property can also be subject to double taxation—first, when one owner dies and then again when the surviving owner dies. This, of course, leaves less for the heirs. However, because small estates (currently those under $175,625) are exempt from federal estate taxes and because probate costs can be high, jointly held property is an advantage to many people. But in estates over the $175,625 exemption, joint ownership may not be beneficial for the estate tax bill.

It is usually a good idea to keep at least one bank account in joint names, in case of emergency, plus your home and automobile. Beyond that, you probably should consider other forms of ownership and ways to transfer ownership. Finally, joint property may thwart the original estate plan. For example, if the surviving spouse remarries and puts his or her property from the first marriage in joint ownership with the new wife or husband, all of the property may go to the new spouse rather than to the children of the first marriage. Property left in trust for the children would prevent this.

Trusts "Put not your trust in money," advised Oliver Wendell Holmes, "but put your money in trust." A *trust* is a legal arrangement whereby property is held and managed by a *trustee*—a person or a financial institution, such as a bank—for the benefit of someone else, called a *beneficiary*. The amount of property can be great or small. The beneficiary can be one or more persons and usually is a spouse, child, parent, or the person who set up the trust, called a *settlor* or *grantor*. The settlor can have some control over the property by giving the trustee certain instructions at the outset, such as paying the beneficiary from either the income or the principal or both. Trusts can be *revocable*, amended or canceled at any time, or *irrevocable*, not amended or canceled. All trust arrangements (except those that have a charity as a beneficiary) have termination dates—for example, when the beneficiary dies or, in the case of a minor, when he or she reaches legal age. The property is then distributed according to the instructions by which the settlor set up the trust.

A settlor can set up a trust in his will to take effect upon his death. This is called a *testamentary trust*. Or he can set up an *inter vivos trust*, a trust between living persons, which is effective during the settlor's lifetime and is distributed upon his death according to his instructions in the trust. For example, a husband can set up a living trust for his wife, who then receives interest or dividends from the property. The husband can instruct the trustee to dip into the principal when the wife has need of it, such as for medical or educational expenses. The trust can be operative during the husband's lifetime or thereafter, or both. When the wife dies, the children usually inherit the principal. In this way, the family can be provided for on a long-term basis and their immediate needs taken care of as well.

A *revocable inter vivos trust* is widely used as a substitute for a will because it has many advantages and few disadvantages. In order to set up a revocable *inter vivos* trust, a settlor transfers his cash, securities, and other property to a trustee or trustees. The trustees manage the property held in the trust during the lifetime of the settlor, paying him income and principal as desired. When the settlor dies, the trustees hold or dispose of the trust property according to the provisions of the trust. Such a trust may be amended or canceled at any time during the settlor's lifetime.

A revocable *inter vivos* trust is particularly useful in situations involving (1) young adults or minors who have substantial assets, (2) older persons who may not be able to handle the day-to-day management of their assets, (3) persons who are incapacitated, (4) persons who intend to live outside the country but who do not want their assets administered by a foreign country upon death, (5) payment of insurance proceeds and employee benefits, and (6) certain business situations, such as family businesses, copyrights, and patents.

A revocable *inter vivos* trust permits the settlor to enjoy the use and control of his property while (1) permitting the trustee to manage the property if the settlor becomes unable to do so, (2) avoiding probate and thus the publicity that comes with a will, (3) permitting the selection of a place of administration other than the settlor's domicile, which cannot be done with a will, (4) using the law of trusts to minimize unfavorable local laws, such as laws prohibiting excessive charitable gifts, and (5) helping the settlor to protect himself against loss of property by rash or impulsive investments.

There is no tax advantage to the settlor in a revocable trust because he must still pay the income taxes on the income of his estate while he lives and the assets of the trust will be subject to estate taxes upon his death. However, taxes can be saved when certain trusts pass from one generation to the next, as when a husband's trust for his wife passes to the children upon the wife's death. Her estate will not have to pay taxes on it.

A *long-term irrevocable trust*, in which property is likely to appreciate over a long time, can also be used for the well-being of one's family and to save taxes too. Prior to the 1976 Tax Reform Act, individuals with high incomes frequently established a type of trust known as the Clifford Trust. This is an irrevocable trust that pays income to the beneficiary (other than the spouse of the individual) for a period of more than 10 years. At the end of the period, the property either reverts back to the individual or passes to a beneficiary other than the one who had received the income.

Such a trust reduces an individual's income tax by having the income paid to a beneficiary in a lower tax bracket. Because of the unified estate tax credit enacted in 1976, however, the income tax saved on such a trust may be less than the estate tax later charged on the property. The effect of such a trust therefore should be carefully evaluated.

A drawback of establishing an irrevocable or a revocable trust is that fees are usually involved in trusts, such as the one for the trustee's services or for transferring stock to the trust.

Life insurance   Life insurance is the principal asset of the estates of many Americans. In fact, for many families, estate planning is solely life insurance planning. Its importance, therefore, cannot be overemphasized. All the various possibilities in purchasing and owning life insurance should be considered. Also, many states give total or partial inheritance tax exemptions for life insurance proceeds. The laws in your own state should help you decide what kind of insurance plan to have.

In addition to increasing the size of one's estate, life insurance can be a way of providing immediate funds upon death to pay taxes, debts, funeral expenses, and to keep a business going. Life insurance, if paid to an insurance trust, also permits professional management of such funds if a large sum of money is involved rather than having a beneficiary receive the proceeds directly.

Generally, the proceeds of life insurance are taxable under federal estate tax laws (1) if the insured owns his or her own policy or the proceeds are received by the insured's estate or executor, (2) if the insured had "incidents of ownership" in the policy (kept some control over it), and (3) if a transfer concerning the policy was made within three years of the insured's date of death.

It is possible through careful planning, however, to escape federal estate taxes on life insurance. Some of the methods are (1) assigning all of the rights under the policy to someone else, such as a spouse or a child; (2) having someone other than the insured, such as a spouse or child, own the policy from the start; (3) assigning the policy to an irrevocable insurance trust with a trustee who pays the policy's premiums and who, upon the death of the insured, receives the proceeds of the policy for distribution to the beneficiaries; and (4) having the trustee purchase the insurance for the insured.

The method of avoiding gift estate taxation of life insurance also involves the matter of whether the policy is a straight life policy, a term policy, an endowment policy, or a limited-payment life policy.

Each type of policy should be evaluated for both protection and taxation benefits. How the proceeds ought to be paid out is another consideration. Should the beneficiary receive the proceeds outright, for example, or through a trust? Or should the proceeds be held by the insurance company to be paid out under an optional plan, such as an annuity?

The use of an *irrevocable inter vivos life insurance trust* (a trust between living persons that cannot be amended or canceled) is often desirable because it provides management of a large sum of money on behalf of the beneficiary and may avoid or minimize estate and gift taxation. Such a trust is very useful when the premiums can be paid from a funded trust (one in which the insured has given the trustee enough assets to pay the premiums) or when premiums are paid through annual gifts made by the insured. In another type of trust, known as the Crummey Trust, beneficiaries have the right—for a limited time—to withdraw part or all of the premiums paid into it, thus allowing the insured to make use of the annual $3,000 gift tax exemption. (See "Lifetime gifts," below.)

If life insurance is assigned by the insured spouse to the beneficiary spouse or is purchased by the insured spouse for the other, it is most important to provide in the policy or in the owner-spouse's will for the possibility of the owner-spouse's dying before the insured. Usually the insured spouse assumes that he will die first. But frequently the other spouse is the first to die, and the ownership of the policy reverts to the insured. This, of course, defeats the original purpose of eliminating the tax. To avoid this, (1) the life insurance policy can provide for the transfer of ownership if the owner-spouse dies before the insured spouse, or (2) the owner-spouse's will can transfer ownership of the policies to someone other than the insured, such as the children, or provide for the creation of a testamentary trust to receive the proceeds of the policy, or (3) if the insured spouse is also an executor or trustee of the owner-spouse's will, the will can prohibit him or her from exercising any powers over life insurance policies on his or her own life that were owned by the spouse.

Federal estate and gift taxes and the marital deduction

The 1976 Tax Reform Act made sweeping changes in the estate and gift taxation for all U.S. citizens and residents. The act substituted a single unified rate in place of the former separate estate and gift tax rates.

The new rate enables a person dying in 1981 or thereafter to leave an estate of up to $175,625 without having to pay any federal estate taxes. There will usually be, however, state death or inheritance taxes.

If one spouse leaves all of his property, say $175,625, to the other spouse, who happens to have $175,000 in her own name, then her estate will be $350,625 ($175,625 + $175,000). Without an adequate estate plan, the federal tax on such an estate will be more than $43,000. State taxes will further enlarge the tax bill. Although the unified tax system results in less tax on the death of the first spouse, the ultimate tax on both estates (when the second spouse dies) will be costly unless there is an effective estate plan.

The federal estate tax law provides that a spouse may leave to a surviving spouse tax-free either one-half of his or her adjusted gross estate or $250,000, whichever is greater. This marital deduction can be left outright or in a trust. It is unavailable, however, to couples in community-property states because the surviving spouse automatically receives half their property free of taxes. Such couples might be eligible for this deduction for property they acquired prior to their being in a community-property arrangement, however.

When the unified tax credit and the $250,000 marital deduction are taken together, it is possible for a spouse to transfer $425,625 tax-free to the surviving spouse.

In addition, a spouse can give $100,000 to the other spouse without incurring a gift tax. For example, assume the husband has all of the assets, which amount to $275,000, and that when he dies he leaves a gift of $100,000 to his wife. This results in no tax on the husband's estate because it has been reduced to $175,000, qualifying it for the tax exemption allowed to estates of less then $175,625. Furthermore, if the husband left the rest of the property in trust for the wife, it escapes tax on her death. And because her estate (the $100,000 gift) is less than $175,625, that too passes free of tax. This plan results in a tax savings of more than $25,000. A gift of up to $200,000 is taxed only on the amount above $100,000, and gifts over $200,000 are taxed on one-half their amount, minus the $100,000 deduction. This gift tax marital deduction should not be used randomly but with the total estate plan in mind, because once the $100,000 gift tax marital deduction is used, the full $250,000 marital deduction cannot also be taken. The amount then deductible is restricted by a legal formula.

The particular circumstances of each spouse must always be carefully evaluated to find out whether the ultimate estate tax payable on both estates will be increased or decreased by combining the unified tax credit, the maximum marital deduction, and the gift tax marital deduction. For instance, the $250,000 marital deduction is practical only for estates under $500,000 because larger estates will benefit more by leaving the surviving spouse half of the adjusted gross estate.

The following example illustrates how use of the $250,000 marital deduction in an estate of less then $500,000 can affect the ultimate tax bill. Assume that the husband, Harry, dies in 1981, before his wife, Wilma, leaving a marital deduction bequest to Wilma, who has no assets of her own. The balance of Harry's property is left in a residuary trust, which is not taxable to Wilma's estate and through which she receives income or principal at the discretion of the trustee appointed by her husband.

(1) Harry leaves a marital deduction formula bequest of one-half of the adjusted gross estate:

Harry's estate	$300,000
Marital deduction	150,000
Balance in residuary trust	$150,000
Harry's estate tax	-0-
Wilma's estate tax on $150,000	-0-
Combined	$ -0-

(2) Harry leaves the maximum marital deduction bequest to Wilma. By not reducing the marital deduction, he can increase the unified tax credits available to the estate, but look at the result:

Harry's estate	$300,000
Maximum marital deduction	250,000
Balance in residuary trust	$ 50,000
Harry's estate tax	-0-
Wilma's estate tax on $250,000	23,800
Combined	$ 23,800

(3) If, however, Harry reduces the marital deduction bequest to the amount that will also take advantage of the unified tax credits, see what happens:

Harry's estate	$300,000
Marital deduction reduced	121,700
Balance in residuary trust	$178,300
Harry's estate tax	-0-
Wilma's estate tax on $121,700	-0-
Combined	$ -0-

Despite the tax savings that are available by using a residuary trust and the maximum credits, family circumstances may dictate that the tax saving is outweighed by the financial needs of the surviving spouse or other family members. Or if the surviving spouse has separate assets, then a decision has to be made about whether to use a maximum marital deduction bequest, which may increase the ultimate estate tax. This leaves less for the heirs and more for the tax collector. These are just some of the reasons why it is important that all of the factors in an estate plan be evaluated.

Lifetime gifts

Mention of lifetime gifts may create the false impression that such gifts are useful only to persons of great wealth. Actually, the sensible making of lifetime gifts can be of value to most people, such as by using the $3,000 gift tax exclusion. This means that a person can give to as many individuals as he desires up to $3,000 per year per individual tax-free. For example, if a man has two children, he can, by making gifts of $3,000 per year to each child, give $60,000 to them over a 10-year period without the money being subject later to the estate tax. This money can be used for the children's education or other expenses. Gifts to minors can be made under the special Uniform Gifts to Minors Act, which allows minors to hold property as long as their parent or other adult acts as custodian or trustee of the fund. When the children come of age, the money then belongs to them. In the meantime, any income earned by the trust is not taxed at all because children are not usually liable for income taxes and because the parent has removed the money from his estate. Thus even small gifts can be used to avoid estate and income taxes. The $3,000 annual gift exclusion can be made outright as well as in trust, such as by giving $3,000 per year to an aging parent for his or her immediate needs.

Under the unified estate and gift tax system, a person can give away up to $175,625 (over and above the $3,000 per person, per year exemption) without incurring a gift tax. However, the property is still included in the estate of the donor at his death for tax purposes. The tax value of such large lifetime gifts is that the unified estate and gift tax is postponed until the donor's death and if the gift consists of property that is likely to appreciate in value, then the increase will not be taxed at all if death occurs more than three years after the date of the gift. For example, if the donor is 40 years old, no tax is likely to be levied on a gift for a considerable period of time. A gift of cash or property could also be used to buy substantial life insurance for the donor, thus enhancing the value of the gift.

If the gift was made *more than three years before* the donor's death, it is valued as of the date it was given. If the gift was made *during the three years before* the donor's death, it is valued as of the date of death. (The $3,000 annual gift exclusion is exempt from this rule.) The different valuation dates are important when considering any increase, or appreciation, in the value of the gift. For instance, suppose Bruce gave Felicia 100 shares of stock two years before he died. At the time of his death, the stock had doubled in value. Bruce's estate will have to pay a tax based on the appreciated value of the stock, even if Felicia had already sold the stock to pay for medical costs. However, if Bruce had given the stock to Felicia four years before his death, then Bruce's estate would be liable only for the value of the stock as of the date that he made the gift.

By making gifts sooner rather than later, a donor may avoid both income and estate taxes on the increased value of a gift. Gifts of stock, closely held stock (such as family businesses), art objects (such as paintings), and real estate interests are a few examples of the kinds of property that can be given with beneficial tax results. Because of the way the gift and estate tax credits work, once the credit is used for gifts, it is not available to protect the estate from taxes. Therefore, some balance needs to be worked out for the whole estate.

For people whose estates consist of family business interests, lifetime gifts may be used to qualify the estate for favorable estate tax deferrals. If, for example, Randolph owns a business that has a value in excess of 65 percent of his adjusted gross estate (the net estate after funeral and administrative expenses and debts have been paid), the estate can choose to pay part or all of the estate tax over a 15-year period, with interest at the rate of only 4 percent for the first 5 years on the first $324,000 of tax. If Randolph's estate has other interests that reduce the percentage below the 65-percent level, lifetime gifts may adjust the balance to enable the estate to qualify for the favorable deferral provisions.

Lifetime gifts can also be used to qualify the estate for another estate tax deferral plan. This one permits a 10-year payout of federal estate taxes if either 35 percent of the value of the gross estate or 50 percent of the taxable estate consists of a closely held trade or business.

Lifetime gifts are thus a good way to transfer property that would otherwise be subject to estate tax and, in some instances, income tax as well.

Charitable gifts

Another way in which the federal estate tax can be reduced is by making gifts to qualified charities. These can be outright gifts or gifts in trust. But any charitable gift involving a trust must be given very careful attention because of the special rules governing private foundations. A person can make a gift in a split-interest trust. This is a gift in trust to an individual beneficiary for his or her lifetime with the remainder passing to charity upon the death of the beneficiary. A person can also create a *charitable lead trust,* which gives the income interest to the charity with the remainder passing to family members after a specified number of years. A person may place his or her residence or farm in trust with a life interest in it and the remainder passing to a qualified charity on the death of the life tenant. Thus a person may obtain a charitable deduction by deeding his residence or farm to charity on his death. Anyone considering a charitable gift should review the appropriate laws of his state. Some states, such as New York, allow parents and children to challenge testamentary charitable gifts that are more than half of the person's net estate. Charitable gifts are frequently reviewed by the state's attorney general's office, which supervises and regulates charitable organizations.

It is usually a good idea to discuss a contemplated charitable gift beforehand with the beneficiary. This will enable the donor and beneficiary to work out a mutually beneficial arrangement.

Employee benefits

Many people have estates made up of substantial interests in profit-sharing plans, pension plans, deferred-compensation plans, and other employee-benefit plans. An annual review should be made by the employee on the nature and extent of such benefits. It is sometimes surprising how little an employee knows about his or her benefits even though most employers provide good explanations of them. Your lawyer or tax adviser may want to get in touch with the company employee handling such benefits when your estate plan is being formulated, because of the complexity of the laws involved. For instance, if the employer contributes part or all of the benefits and if the employee dies before retirement, there is an employer-contribution tax exclusion that will apply only if the benefits are paid in two or more annuity or deferred payments and not in one lump sum. However, each method has effects on income tax and the marital deduction; so again, each choice must be evaluated with the total picture in mind.

when he or she dies. By reducing the marital deduction and using all the other credits available (such as the unified tax credit and the state death-tax credit), the tax liability of the estate will be reduced.

Suppose Richard dies in 1981 and leaves property that qualifies for the marital deduction to Mary, his wife, who has no assets of her own. The balance of Richard's property is to be left in a trust, which will produce income for Mary but will not be taxable in her estate. Richard provides in his will a marital-deduction formula gift (a formula using less than a $250,000 marital deduction) in the amount equal to one-half of his adjusted gross estate:

Richard's estate	$300,000
Marital deduction	$150,000
Balance left in tax-free-type trust	$150,000
Tax on Richard's estate (to be paid by Mary)	– 0 –
Mary's estate upon her death (the amount she received under the marital deduction)	$150,000
Tentative tax on $150,000 estate	$ 29,800
Unified credit in 1981	$ 47,000
Estate tax to be paid by Mary's heirs	– 0 –
Combined estate taxes on the estates of Richard and Mary	– 0 –

If, however, Richard chooses to use his maximum marital deduction:

Richard's estate	$300,000
Maximum marital deduction	$250,000
Balance in tax-free-type trust	$ 50,000
Tax on Richard's estate	– 0 –
Mary's estate on her death (the amount she received under the marital deduction)	$250,000
Tentative tax on $250,000 estate	$ 70,800
Unified credit in 1981	$ 47,000
Estate tax to be paid by Mary's heirs*	$ 23,800
Combined estate taxes on the estates of Richard and Mary	$ 23,800

*This amount may be further reduced by the state death-taxes credit if applicable.

These examples illustrate the benefits of using a marital-deduction bequest to take advantage of other credits available and to provide a tax savings on the death of the surviving spouse. The personal needs of the surviving spouse or other family members, however, may outweigh the need for a tax savings. The goal of any estate planning is to minimize the tax burden left on the heirs, particularly in estates of less than $500,000.

■ **The marital gift-tax deduction** The Tax Reform Act also revised the marital deduction for gifts made after December 31, 1976. A person can now give up to $100,000 tax-free to his spouse (in addition to the $3,000 annual exclusion). For gifts between $100,000 and $200,000, the first $100,000 remains tax-free while the amount above $100,000 is taxable.

EXAMPLE Suppose Sam, who had never made any gifts before, gave his wife $130,000 as a gift in 1981. The $3,000 annual exclusion is deducted from the gift. The next $100,000 will be tax-free under the marital gift-tax deduction. The remaining $27,000 will be taxed at a much lower rate than the $130,000 amount. (Since gifts are taxed on a graduated scale, the lower the amount of the taxable gift, the lower the gift tax to be paid.) In fact, Sam will not pay any gift tax because the unified credit ($47,000) is greater than the tentative tax on the $27,000 gift ($5,500). Sam's $47,000 unified credit will be decreased by the $5,500 tentative tax. The remaining credit of $41,500 can be used against future gift taxes.

If the gift is greater than $200,000, a marital deduction of one-half the value of the property given to the other spouse can still be taken.

Once a spouse has taken a marital gift-tax deduction, he or she cannot also take the maximum marital deduction in the estate. The full marital deduction ($250,000) will be decreased by the difference between the marital gift-tax deduction and 50 percent of the gift. This is done because the giver has already enjoyed a tax advantage by using the marital gift-tax deduction.

EXAMPLE Jeff gives $150,000 in total lifetime gifts (excluding gifts that qualify for the $3,000 annual exclusion) to his wife, Ellen, and takes the maximum gift-tax deduction, $100,000. When Jeff dies, Ellen will not be entitled to take the full marital deduction, $250,000, because the full marital gift-tax deduction, $100,000, has already been taken. The $250,000 will be reduced by $25,000—the difference between the maximum marital gift-tax deduction ($100,000) and 50 percent of the gift (one-half of $150,000, or $75,000). Jeff's estate can take only a $225,000 marital deduction.

■ **Orphan's exclusion** This provision permits a limited deduction from the adjusted gross estate for property passing from a decedent who does not have a living spouse to his minor child who does not have a known living parent. A minor child is less than 21 years old at the decedent's death and can be an adopted child of the decedent. This deduction is $5,000 multiplied by the number of years by which 21 exceeds the child's age at the decedent's death.

EXAMPLE Six-year-old Joyce is the sole survivor of Ralph, her father, who dies in 1981 leaving a gross estate of $250,000. Funeral costs, along with other expenses and deductions, reduce the estate to $225,000. The formula for Joyce's orphan exclusion is $5,000 × 15 (21 – 6, Joyce's age) = $75,000. The orphan's exclusion reduces the taxable estate to $150,000 ($225,000 – $75,000), which under the 1981 tax-free $175,625 estate exemption will not be subject to estate tax.

■ **Generation-skipping trusts** The 1976 Reform Act corrected a tax inequality by imposing a tax on generation-skipping trusts—trusts that have beneficiaries in two or more generations younger than the person who created the trust. This applies to trusts created after April 30, 1976. When property is bequeathed from a parent to a child, then from the child to a grandchild, and finally from the grandchild to a great-grandchild, an estate tax is imposed three times. Under the old law, if the parent had placed the property in a trust from which the child and the grandchild received only the income and the great-grandchild received the principal, he would have skipped two generations of estate tax. Here the principal would be included only in the great-grandchild's gross estate. In this way estate taxes were sometimes avoided for 100 years. The 1976 act generally treats property passing in trust from one generation to following generations in substantially the same manner as property that is transferred outright from one generation to the next. There are exceptions to this general rule, however. If the trust is revocable, that is, if you keep the right to revoke it, then the principal will be included in your gross estate. If it is irrevocable, it will not be included but the value of its principal will be included in the gross estate of the person who is entitled to it once the trust terminates, but the tax will be paid from the principal of the trust.

■ **Filing estate-tax returns**   A federal estate-tax return must be filed for the estate of every citizen or resident of the United States whose gross estate at the date of death is greater than $161,563 in 1980 or $175,625 thereafter.

The executor or administrator of the estate must file the return with the U.S. Internal Revenue Service, along with payment of the tax due, *within nine months* after the date of the decedent's death.

An extension of time to file the return may be granted if there is a good reason for a delay—if, for example, the executor is stationed with the Navy in the Arctic and will not be back in the country for another 10 months. An extension cannot be granted for more than six months after the due date of the tax return, unless the executor or administrator is abroad. An extension for paying the tax must be asked for separately from an extension for filing, and again a good reason must be given. Extensions may be granted annually for a period up to 10 years after the original due date of the tax payment.

■ **Obligation to pay tax**   The estate tax is usually paid by the executor or administrator from the estate before the assets are distributed to the heirs. If the executor distributes the assets before the tax is paid, the heir or beneficiary may be liable for the unpaid tax up to the amount of the share that he has received.

EXAMPLE The executor of Thomas Brown's estate distrib- O⟶＊ uted the entire taxable estate to the beneficiaries before having paid the estate's $4,000 tax. Brown's brother, James, received $5,500 as his share. Because the amount he received from the estate is more than the tax on the estate, James could be assessed for the entire tax. On the other hand, if the unpaid tax was $15,000, James could not be assessed for more than the share he received, $5,500. James can seek to be reimbursed for the tax that he paid from the other heirs, who did not contribute their share. The beneficiaries can sue the executor or administrator for failing to fulfill his fiduciary duties. See EXECUTORS AND ADMINISTRATORS.

estimated tax

estimated tax   The tax an individual calculates will be imposed on his income. If you are self-employed, this is your estimated income tax for the year. If you are employed by someone else, it is the tax that you estimate you will owe over and above what has been withheld from your pay. When your gross income (income from all sources) that is not subject to payroll withholding is more than $500 and your estimated tax is $100 or more, you must file a declaration of estimated tax. This often happens when you have a second job that does not withhold payroll taxes or when you receive income, such as dividends, from which taxes are not withheld.

You must file a declaration of estimated tax if you are (1) a surviving spouse, a head of household, or a single person with an estimated gross income in excess of $20,000; (2) a married person entitled to file jointly, whose spouse receives no wages and whose estimated gross income is more than $20,000; (3) a married person entitled to file jointly, with both spouses receiving wages, whose estimated individual gross income exceeds $10,000; (4) a married person who is not entitled to file jointly and whose estimated gross income exceeds $5,000; or (5) an alien.

These are the official regulations. However, if you do not file an estimated tax because you are employed and your employer withheld federal taxes, the Internal Revenue Service will not penalize you if your total tax liability at tax time (April 15) is less than 20 percent of your annual tax. Many people who might exceed this 20 percent liability limit avoid it by voluntarily increasing their withholdings.

A trustee of a trust, an executor of an estate, or any other fiduciary does not have to file a declaration of estimated tax on the trust or estate.

Declarations of estimated tax must be filed on or before April 15, just like income-tax returns. The full amount of the estimated tax may be paid when the declaration is filed or it may be paid in quarterly installments: by April 15, June 15, September 15, and January 15 of the following year. If you file your form 1040 by January 15, however, the fourth installment need not be paid until January 31 of the following year. Anyone who should file a declaration of estimated tax and does not or who does not pay the full amount due on a quarterly installment may be subject to a penalty.

estoppel   A prohibition that prevents a person from denying the truth of a fact already settled by judicial proceedings or by an act of the person himself. The purpose of estoppel is to prevent injustice through inconsistency or fraud.

■ **The truth of court records**   Estoppel by record prohibits a person from denying the truth of matter contained in a judicial or a legislative record. Court records represent absolute truth. No one may challenge them in a related proceeding by offering evidence that denies the facts on record.

The rule of estoppel by record bars a second suit between the same parties on an issue raised and decided in the first suit. The issue raised in the second lawsuit must be identical with the issue—or one of the issues—raised and determined in the first lawsuit.

EXAMPLE When Maxwell sued his wife, Agnes, for divorce, O⟶＊ he stated in his complaint that he and Agnes did not own any community property, and the court found Maxwell's statement to be true. The court granted him a divorce. Maxwell later remarried and changed the beneficiary of two insurance policies, which he had purchased during his first marriage, from his divorced wife to his second wife. Maxwell died. Agnes sued to recover the proceeds of the policies, but the court ruled that she was not entitled to them. The divorce decree was a final decision that Maxwell's insurance policies were not community property. Agnes was estopped from litigating the issue again upon Maxwell's death.

■ **The truth of property deeds** Estoppel by deed prohibits a person from denying the truth of his deed to property. It is used to compel parties to fulfill their contracts. In order for an estoppel to arise, the deed must contain representations (statements of fact) or promises. In addition, an estoppel by deed may be used only in a lawsuit based on the deed or in a lawsuit relating to a right arising out of the deed. It cannot be used in a lawsuit in which the deed is unimportant.

An estoppel by deed is usually enforceable only when one of the parties changes his situation as a result of statements in the deed. The party who wants the estoppel must show that he relied on the statements and that he will suffer some loss or disadvantage if the statements are now changed.

EXAMPLE The Petrol Corporation owned a gasoline service
O•—＊ station, which it sold to the Filler-Up Company. The deed of sale contained covenants (agreements) that Petrol's products, such as gas and oil, would be used at the gasoline station for a 15-year period. The covenants were to "run with the land" (the gasoline station) and thus be binding on anyone to whom Filler-Up sold the gasoline station. Filler-Up later sold the gasoline station to the Drive-Us Corporation and agreed, for an extra bonus, to try to get the binding covenants removed. Filler-Up brought a suit to have the court cancel the covenants so that Drive-Us could own the gas station free from the covenants. The court refused. It held that the Petrol Corporation had relied on the agreement when it changed its position from owner of the gasoline station to a seller with covenants.

After-acquired title A person who acquires a title to (ownership of) or interest in real property that he previously conveyed (transferred) to another by mistake cannot deny that his AFTER-ACQUIRED TITLE was given along with the conveyance.

EXAMPLE Suppose Corrigan believes he has inherited a 10-
O•—＊ acre plot from his grandfather when, in fact, he has inherited only a half interest. His sister has inherited the other half. Corrigan deeds the 10-acre plot to his neighbor. After his sister dies, Corrigan inherits her one-half interest. The doctrine of estoppel applies here, and Corrigan's after-acquired title passes to his neighbor through the doctrine of estoppel by deed.

But let us say that Corrigan, unsure of his exact interest, deeds "all the interest I presently own in my 10-acre plot" to his neighbor. This turns out to be five acres. When he inherits the remaining five acres from his sister, estoppel by deed does not apply to his after-acquired interest.

Recitals All parties to a deed, and those who claim through them, are bound by its recitals (detailed statements). They are estopped from denying them. Recitals must be clear and relate to a particular fact—the existence and value of the property mentioned in the deed, the identity of the grantee (the person to whom the land is transferred), and the extent of the estate transferred.

EXAMPLE A husband accepted a deed conveying title to a
O•—＊ plot of land to him and to his wife as "tenants in common." This meant that each tenant held a share of the land, which could be inherited by the tenant's heirs. After the wife died and her son by a previous marriage sued to receive his share of the property, the husband claimed that he and his wife had owned the property as "tenants by the entirety." This meant that the surviving spouse was the sole owner of the property. The court declared that the husband was estopped from claiming that the title was held as tenants by the entirety by the recital in the deed that said he and his deceased wife had held the property as tenants in common.

■ **Equitable estoppel** Equitable estoppel, or estoppel by misrepresentation, is a rule preventing a person from taking advantage of his own wrongful act. It arises when someone intentionally or negligently leads another to believe that certain facts exist. This may be caused by a person's acts, representations, admissions, or even his silence when it is his duty to speak. The second person rightfully relies and acts on the belief that the facts exist. He will be disadvantaged if the first person is permitted to deny the existence of such facts.

EXAMPLE A doctor had been insured for his life for many
O•—＊ years by the Acme Insurance Company. Acme was taken over by the Providence Insurance Company. Providence notified the doctor of the takeover and sent him a new policy and a transfer form for the insured to sign. The form contained a provision stating "the insured warrants himself to be in good health." The new policy was not to take effect until the form was signed and returned with an additional sum of money. Since the doctor was not in good health, he did not sign or return the form.

A Providence agent called upon the doctor and was informed that the doctor was not in good health. The agent told the doctor that Providence had sent him the wrong form and that, in taking over Acme, Providence had to insure both good and bad risks. The doctor then signed another form, which did not contain a warranty relating to his health, and gave the agent a check, which Providence cashed. A short while later, the company discovered that its agent had given the doctor the wrong form to sign. The doctor was notified of the error and asked to sign the correct form. The doctor did not do so, but Providence retained his money and did not cancel his policy. Thereafter the doctor died and his wife brought suit to recover the proceeds of her husband's policy. When Providence attempted to defend the lawsuit by denying the existence of the policy, the wife contended that it was estopped from denying the existence of the policy, and the court agreed. The court held that the doctor acted honestly and in good faith. The agent made false representations, either intentionally or unintentionally, and the doctor acted upon those representations by signing the form and making out his check to Providence. Because the agent had been acting within the scope of his authority, he bound his principal, the Providence Company.

estoppel certificate A document drawn up by a mortgagor (the person whose property is mortgaged). It states that the MORTGAGE is valid, declares the amount of principal and interest due on the date the document is signed, and affirms that there are no defenses or offsets (counteractions) to the mortgage. The estoppel certificate is usually requested by someone who is purchasing the mortgage, often at a discount, from the original mortgagee (the party that loaned the money for the purchase of the property). The estoppel certificate prevents the mortgagor from later denying the validity of the mortgage and the amount of the principal and interest due.

et al. (Latin) An abbreviation for *et alii,* "and others." The singular is *et alius,* which means "and another." For example, when the words "Robert Jones et al." are used in a judgment against several defendants, the quoted words include all the defendants.

et cetera (Latin) "And other things"; and others of like character; and the rest; and so on. In its abbreviated form (etc.) this phrase is often added onto a series of items or names to show that others are intended to follow or are understood to be included.

ethical considerations General guidelines for proper behavior as a lawyer. These guidelines appear in the CODE OF PROFESSIONAL RESPONSIBILITY.

ethics 1 Principles, values, and customs among members of a profession. The ethics of members of the legal profession involve their moral and professional conduct toward one another, their clients, and the courts. 2 The branch of philosophy that deals with the principles of conduct and the moral responsibilities owed to others.

et seq. (Latin) An abbreviation for *et sequentes,* meaning "and the following." For example, "p.1, *et seq.*" means "page one and the following pages."

et ux. (Latin) An abbreviation for *et uxor,* meaning "and wife." For example, when the wife of a seller—call him Mark Fitch—joins him in conveying (transferring) a title to real property, the deed might refer to "Mark Fitch, *et ux.*"

et vir (Latin) "And husband."

eviction The process by which a landlord puts a tenant out of possession of real property. An eviction may be actual or CONSTRUCTIVE. *Actual* eviction is a physical ouster or dispossession from the property, or some substantial part of it, by the landlord.

EXAMPLE Let us say that Willis was living in a furnished O⟶✳ house that he had rented for two years. After eight months in the house he went on a two-week vacation, without paying the three months' rent he owed. When Willis returned, he found that the landlord had boarded up the house and changed the locks. Willis had been evicted.

Ordinarily, a landlord covenants (agrees) in his lease with his tenant that the tenant is entitled to quiet enjoyment of the premises. A *constructive* eviction occurs when a landlord violates his covenant of quiet enjoyment.

EXAMPLE Suppose when you rented your apartment you O⟶✳ were unaware that it was infested with cockroaches. After you moved in you told your landlord about the roaches both by telephone and by letter. He is well aware of the condition, but he refuses to remedy it. Your enjoyment of the apartment is greatly impaired, and you may consider yourself to be constructively evicted. Apparently the landlord, by not acting, is telling you that he would like you to leave.

See LANDLORD AND TENANT.

evidence Any kind of proof offered to persuade or induce belief. Evidence includes testimony (oral evidence given by a WITNESS under oath), writings, physical objects, and other things presented to show the existence of a fact. It is the means by which a fact is proved. It can be used to identify a person or thing, to show that something did or did not happen, or to establish a person's character or reputation. This article discusses evidence and its use in civil cases (lawsuits). For a discussion of evidence in criminal actions, see CRIMINAL LAW.

■ **Direct and circumstantial evidence** All evidence is either direct or circumstantial. Both may be used in court. *Direct evidence* is anything that proves a fact without the need for other facts leading up to it. If a witness testifies that he saw a man throw a rock through the window of a supermarket, the court has direct evidence that a man did in fact throw a rock through the window of a supermarket. If a two-headed cow is shown to the court, the court has direct evidence that two-headed cows can exist. *Circumstantial evidence* is indirect evidence. It tends to prove circumstances surrounding the fact in dispute rather than the fact itself. Once these circumstances surrounding the disputed fact are established, the jury may infer that the disputed fact did occur. If the relationship between the fact and the circumstance is too tenuous, the circumstantial evidence will not be admitted at trial. It must be closely related to the issue involved in order to have value as proof.

EXAMPLE Mrs. March sued an insurance company because O⟶✳ it refused to pay her on her husband's accident policy when he fell to his death from the roof of their home. The insurance company defended itself by trying to prove that Mr. March had committed suicide. To disprove the idea of suicide, Mrs. March's attorney introduced photographs of a smiling March family as circumstantial evidence of her husband's happy home life shortly before the accident. The court allowed the evidence to be used.

■ **Forms of evidence** In addition to statements made by witnesses about what they observed, evidence can take a number of different forms, ranging from the opinions of witnesses to the exhibition of X-rays that show the extent of an injury or of contracts in dispute to the opinions of experts. Technically, these forms of evidence are classified as demonstrative, real, documentary, or opinion.

Demonstrative and real evidence Demonstrative evidence and real evidence are addressed directly to the senses, without the intervention of witnesses. Demonstrative evidence includes such objects as models, photographs, or X-ray pictures, which serve as visual aids to help the jury and the court understand the verbal testimony of a witness. Real evidence is the display of an object that had a direct part in the incident at issue. Relevant objects may be introduced for inspection if they are identified and in the same condition as at the time in controversy.

DETERMINING THE FACTS—EVIDENCE IN CIVIL LAWSUITS

■ Evidence comprises anything that may prove the existence of a fact, including writings, objects, and the testimony of witnesses.

■ Evidence may be direct or circumstantial. *Direct evidence* is anything that proves a fact without needing other evidence to back it up. If a witness testifies that she saw a man throw a rock through a window, she has given direct evidence of the fact that the man threw the rock. *Circumstantial evidence* is indirect evidence. It tends to prove the circumstances surrounding a fact rather than the fact itself. A picture of a man happily playing with his children may be used as circumstantial evidence to show that the man was happy and was not likely to commit suicide the day after the picture was taken.

■ Evidence may be demonstrative, real, or documentary, as well as in the form of verbal testimony.

■ *Demonstrative evidence* consists of models, photographs, X-ray pictures, or any other objects that serve as visual aids to help understand a witness's verbal testimony.

■ *Real evidence* is anything that had a direct part in the incident in issue—for example, a forged document in a forgery suit or a twisted arm in a malpractice suit.

■ *Documentary evidence* includes every form of writing, public and private. *Public documents* record facts for the benefit of the public, such as birth certificates and marriage licenses. *Private documents* include deeds, wills, contracts, and business letters.

■ A witness's conclusions, opinions, and inferences are usually irrelevant and not admissible.

■ A competent witness may give an estimate or opinion about a person's identity, age, race, temperament, state of drunkenness, and the like. A licensed driver may testify as to the distance within which a moving vehicle could be stopped. He can also testify that a driver was going too fast for road conditions, or give his estimate of the apparent speed of a car.

■ Experts, on the other hand, may testify about matters in their field of specialization but not about matters of common knowledge. The expert's opinion is admitted only when it is clear that lay persons, such as the jurors, are not capable of drawing correct conclusions from the facts.

■ The duty of proving a fact in dispute is known as the burden of proof. More specifically, *burden of proof* refers both to the duty of presenting evidence as a case progresses and to the duty of producing evidence that has greater credibility than the opponent's.

■ Sometimes a fact can be proved by an inference or a presumption. An *inference* is a deduction that one may logically make from facts in the case. A *presumption* is a recognition of a fact drawn from other proved facts. For example, when a man vanishes for seven years, without reason and without a word, he is presumed to be dead.

■ Certain matters of common knowledge may be accepted without evidence—this is known as *judicial notice*. Courts take judicial notice of matters concerning general custom and usage, geographical or historical facts, and the familiar laws of nature and facts of life.

■ Evidence must be relevant and material. It is *relevant* if it helps to prove or disprove a disputed fact and moves the inquiry forward. Evidence is considered to be *material* when it is not only relevant but has substantial importance—enough to influence the outcome of the case.

■ Under the *best-evidence rule*, a party representing evidence must produce the highest degree, or best possible, evidence that is available—for example, signed originals of a document (primary evidence) must be produced if they are available; the unsigned carbon copies (secondary evidence) are admitted only if the originals cannot be produced.

■ *Parol evidence* is verbal evidence. Under the parol evidence rule, when parties put their agreement in writing, all previous oral agreements merge in the writing. Any oral agreement made before the agreement is written is unenforceable unless it appears in the written document. This rule does not apply to changes made after the agreement is signed. If you are bringing suit because the other party has violated an oral promise that you agreed upon subsequent to signing the contract, you will be allowed to testify to that promise without violating the parol evidence rule.

■ Evidence of a person's character is generally not admissible as a substitute for proof of a fact. It may be admissible, however, if character is in issue because of the nature of the suit—for example, in a child custody case the character of the contending parties is a proper subject of proof.

■ Evidence is *hearsay* when it does not come from the personal knowledge of the witness. Hearsay is usually inadmissible as proof of the fact asserted in the overheard statement. Exceptions to the hearsay rule are daily increasing, however—based on necessity, common sense, and the trustworthiness of past experience.

■ One exception to hearsay is *res gestae*—a rule that is often used to admit unsworn statements of fact made out of court. The statements must occur virtually simultaneously with the event and be so spontaneous that they could not have been deliberated upon or fabricated.

■ Another exception to the hearsay rule is *previously recorded testimony*. Even though a witness may not appear to testify, a court record of testimony he gave in another judicial proceeding can be introduced into a later proceeding without being subject to the hearsay rule.

■ Admissions are also exceptions to the hearsay rule. An *admission* is a concession made by a party to a civil suit of facts relevant to his adversary's cause. Any admission against your own interest and relating to a material fact is admissible against you. An admission must be a statement of fact, not an opinion or conclusion. However, statements by a person that he was at fault or that his adversary is free from fault are usually admissible, even though they may be regarded as opinions.

EXAMPLE A debtor brought suit against moneylenders to recover compensatory and punitive damages for using unreasonable collection methods that injured his health. At the trial, empty medicine bottles were admissible. They supported testimony by the debtor that he had purchased and used several different medicines on the advice of his doctors.

The court may permit an injured person to exhibit his injuries as real evidence, as long as the evidence is not calculated to prejudice the jury. Courts have permitted the exhibition of an ankle, knee, foot, leg, hand, and various other parts of the body. Similarly, a plaintiff may be permitted to remove an artificial eye in the jury's presence and display the empty eye socket.

The court and jury are allowed to judge the age, color, credibility, intelligence, identity, race, and sex of persons in the courtroom simply by observation—but they cannot make a judgment about a person's previous weight or appearance simply by looking at him in court. The court or jury may decide whether a man is the father of a child if the question can be determined by comparing the race or color of the man and the child. In some states, however, exhibiting a child is not permissible when the purpose is to prove a resemblance to its alleged father.

Documentary evidence Documentary evidence includes every form of writing, both public and private. Private documents include deeds, wills, and contracts. Public documents record facts for the benefit of the public; they include registers of birth, baptisms, marriages, deaths, citizenship, elections, and licenses.

Private writings Generally, the genuineness of a private writing must be established before it may be admitted in evidence. Private documents are usually authenticated by facts apart from the documents themselves. The writer or the signer of the writing may say that he did indeed write or sign it. Or a witness may be called to testify that he saw the author actually write the document or that the handwriting is in fact that of the author.

Proof of authenticity may also be shown indirectly by circumstantial evidence. Old documents are often difficult to authenticate because the author may be dead or witnesses may be unavailable. The rule of authenticating so-called ancient writings requires proof that at least 30 years have passed since the writing. The old writing must appear to be genuine on its face. It must have come from a place where such a writing would have been kept or from a person who would ordinarily have had possession of it. When the writing is a deed to real estate, some courts also require that possession of the property must have been taken under the deed.

EXAMPLE John Wilson died and under his will he gave his land to his wife, Adelaide; upon her death, their children were to inherit it. Wilson's will also empowered Adelaide to sell the land if necessary. In 1865 Adelaide deeded the land to Hester Huyck. Afterwards, the land changed ownership eight times, but the deeds were not recorded. In 1905 it was sold to Chester Snow. The following year, Adelaide Wilson died and the children brought a suit against Chester Snow to evict him from the land. The children claimed that the last valid owner was the owner whose deed had been recorded, that is, Ad-

elaide. Chester Snow had to prove that his deed was valid even though the public records showed no chain of title from Adelaide to him. He did this by offering the deed as an ancient document. The court admitted the deed into evidence because it was more than 30 years old and it was in the possession of Chester Snow, a person who would ordinarily be expected to have it, since he was in possession of the land. Chester Snow's ownership of the land was affirmed by the court.

Other common examples of private documents include business records, letters, telegrams, photographs, photographic copies, X-rays, books of science, mortality tables, stock market quotations, newspapers, hospital and doctors' reports, hotel registers, maps, and diagrams.

Public records The test of admissibility of a public record or document is its public character. It must be a record that a public officer is required to keep and one that is open for public inspection. It must have been made by a public official for the benefit of all persons and must contain facts, not conclusions or opinions.

Among the public documents that may be admissible are applications for licenses, ballots and election returns, bank examiners' reports, previous judicial proceedings, census returns, foresters' reports, passports, public school reports and records, sheriffs' deeds, police reports of motor vehicle accidents, surveyors' reports, tax receipts and records, and public land-office records, including official maps of public lands.

Public records are often "self-proving." This means they are executed in a way that shows them to be genuine on their face. Documents of this kind include certified copies of a recorded document and statute books published under public authority. A certified copy is one that is signed and declared to be a true copy by the public officer to whose custody the original is entrusted. Statute books contain the official state law and are ordinarily published under authorization of the legislature.

Opinions as evidence Great efforts are made during a trial to confine the testimony of witnesses to what they actually saw or heard and to differentiate this from opinions derived from their observations. When a person testifies about what he perceives—sees, hears, feels, smells, or tastes—it is a statement of fact. When he offers an opinion that is an interpretation of what he perceives, it is a conclusion, and not a statement of fact. Generally, opinions are not accepted by the courts as evidence.

EXAMPLE Bernard saw a truck and an automobile collide at a busy intersection. The driver of the car sued the truck driver and Bernard was called as a witness. When asked by the examining attorney to describe what happened, Bernard said that the truck had run a red light and the truck driver was at fault. Bernard's observation that the truck had run a red light was a matter of fact and could be used as evidence, but his comment that the truck was at fault was an opinion and the court refused to let it be used as evidence.

In many cases, however, it is impossible to draw a distinction between perception and opinion. Even a simple statement of fact involves a conclusion or inference. Facts and inferences are often so blended that they cannot be separated. The court tends to place more importance on getting at the truth than quibbling over impracticable distinctions. Thus a witness is permitted to state a fact within his knowledge or an observation even though the statement involves some inference. In addition, the opinions of expert witnesses may be actually sought by the court.

Ordinary witnesses' opinions An ordinary witness (as opposed to an expert) may give his estimate of distances. For example, a witness who heard thunder "within half a minute" after a lightning flash could express his opinion that the lightning struck close by. A licensed driver may testify about the distance within which a moving vehicle could be stopped.

A competent ordinary witness may also give his estimate or opinion about the age of human beings—whether they are adults or minors. If the person whose age is in question is in the courtroom, however, the estimate is unnecessary and should be rejected.

Handwriting Witnesses familiar with a person's handwriting may state their opinion about whether a particular writing was made by the person. The witness may be qualified (although less convincing) even if he saw the person write just once. The ordinary witness may testify about a person's handwriting from a judgment formed by the receipt of letters or other documents from the person, even though he never has seen the person. Grandchildren, for instance, who never met their grandmother but know her handwriting from reading the letters she sent to their mother are qualified to give opinions about the genuineness of their grandmother's signature.

Drunkenness A witness may state that a person was intoxicated at a particular time or place, provided the witness had opportunities for observation. If he testifies that the person was drunk, he may give his opinion as to the extent of the drunkenness. Although a witness may state whether a person had been drinking or was just recovering from a state of drunkenness, testimony that a person was sober at a certain time has been held to be a conclusion and inadmissible.

Vehicular accidents In motor vehicle actions, a witness may testify about the motion of the car and the driver's control over it. He can also testify that a driver was driving too fast for the road conditions, that a vehicle stopped suddenly, that the brakes were no good, or that the brakes failed. On the other hand, statements that one vehicle struck another with great violence and that the driver of an approaching vehicle had swerved in an attempt to avoid hitting a dog have been excluded as opinions or conclusions.

Speed A witness may state his estimate of the apparent speed of a moving object, such as flowing water, the wind, an animal, a boat, an automobile, or a train, but he should also give the facts on which he bases his estimate.

EXAMPLE A husband brought suit to recover damages O——* against a railroad company for causing the death of his wife when their car collided with a train at a crossing. One of the issues was the speed of the train. The husband testified that on previous occasions he had driven down the highway at speeds between 50 and 55 miles per hour and that the train later involved in the collision would pass him by. He stated that from these experiences he formed an opinion that on the morning of the accident the train was going around 70 or 75 miles per hour. The

husband's testimony was admissible, because it revealed the basis for his opinion about the train's speed on the day of the accident.

A witness does not have to state his opinion in miles per hour. Courts have admitted descriptions of a rate of speed such as "going like mad," "like a bat out of hell," "just running," "rapid," or "terrific."

Other kinds of opinions by ordinary witnesses The opinions of ordinary witnesses are also admissible to prove a person's identity, the temperament of animals, the state of the weather, a person's race, and even a person's emotions.

Expert opinion Although ordinary witnesses are discouraged from giving opinions, experts are invited to present theirs. Expert testimony is the opinion of a witness who has special knowledge, skill, or information about a subject that is under consideration. His expertise may have been acquired by academic study, investigation, observation, practice, or experience. The opinion of an expert witness should never be admitted unless it is clear that the jurors, because of their lack of experience or knowledge, are not capable of drawing correct conclusions from the facts. In other words, experts may not testify about matters of common knowledge.

An expert witness must be properly qualified in order to testify. He will be examined and cross-examined to establish evidence of his qualifications. A plaintiff is entitled to have evidence of his expert's qualifications heard by the jury even when the defendant concedes that the witness is well qualified.

The opinion of an expert witness should be based on facts in evidence—not on the opinions or conclusions of others—but it may be based on facts related by other witnesses. An expert witness may be asked to assume the facts in the form of a hypothetical question.

EXAMPLE ATTORNEY: Dr. Examiner, let's assume that the O——* jury should find from the evidence that Mrs. Quiet was found dead in her kitchen at about 11 o'clock A.M. on May 31, 1972. Her body was taken to a funeral home and embalmed and buried on June 1, 1972. Then on June 30, 1972, her body was removed and a postmortem examination was made by you. Let's further assume that the jury should find that there was gas in the room where the deceased was found at the time of her death, that the odor of gas could be detected when entering the house, and that at the time the body was discovered it had the appearance of a cherry-red color. From your autopsy and postmortem examination, do you have an opinion satisfactory to yourself as to the cause of the death of Mrs. Quiet?

DOCTOR: Yes, sir, I have an opinion.

ATTORNEY: What is your opinion?

DOCTOR: It is my opinion that Mrs. Quiet died of carbon-monoxide poisoning.

■ **How much evidence is enough** The primary purpose of evidence is to lead to the truth. The law cannot be applied to a situation until the true facts of the situation are determined. The amount of evidence needed by a party depends on (1) the legal standard of proof for cases of the type being argued and (2) the burden of proof established by a law for the issue at hand. Evidence is measured not by how many items or witnesses are offered but by how persuasive they are. One authentic document could outweigh the testimony of 10 witnesses whose testimony is implausible.

The *standard of proof* is the degree of persuasiveness needed to win a point or the entire lawsuit.

In criminal cases, the standard of proof necessary to support a conviction is very high. It is called "proof beyond a reasonable doubt." This is just short of absolute certainty. Because civil actions usually involve money rather than liberty, the standard of proof is lower. Most civil cases can be won with a "mere preponderance of the evidence." This means that one party's version of the facts is more persuasive than the other party's, though ever so slightly. Some types of cases can be won only with "clear and convincing evidence," which is more than a mere preponderance but less than beyond a reasonable doubt. For example, a man seeking to win a divorce by proving his wife's adultery may be required by state law to come up with clear and convincing evidence because of the serious consequences of divorce. There are various other standards of proof, and statutes and developments in case law help to pinpoint how much evidence each of them requires.

The *burden of proof* is the responsibility of one or another of the parties to a lawsuit to offer evidence tending to establish the existence of a fact. Which party has the burden of proof is fixed by law and depends on the type of case at hand. For example, if you were hurt in an automobile accident and sued the driver of the other car for your injuries, you and your lawyer would have the burden of proving that your injuries resulted from the NEGLIGENCE of the other driver. The party who has the burden of proof must offer evidence that will win his case if not refuted. If he fails to do this, the other party wins without offering any evidence at all. If he does offer enough evidence to establish a legally sufficient case, then the other party has the *burden of going forward*. This means that he must answer with his own evidence at that point or he loses. The burden of going forward may shift from party to party during the trial, but the ultimate burden of proof does not change. The party who started the case with the obligation to convince the judge or jury of his version of the facts must do so by the end of the trial if he is to win.

EXAMPLE Peterson sues Davidson to force him to repay a
O—* loan. Davidson answers the charge by making a general denial—he says that he did not borrow anything from Peterson. At the trial Peterson produces a promissory note that acknowledges the loan and has Davidson's signature on it. He also testifies that Davidson has never repaid the loan. By introducing the promissory note, Peterson establishes his *prima facie case*—that is, the evidence is strong enough to compel the opposition to rebut it. This shifts the burden of going forward to Davidson, who then presents evidence that the signature on the note is a forgery—shifting the burden of going forward back to Peterson. Peterson next introduces testimony of the genuineness of Davidson's signature. During the entire trial the burden of proof rests on Peterson even though the burden of going forward shifts back and forth between him and Davidson. If Peterson does not sustain the ultimate burden of proof on his claim that Davidson owes him money, he will lose his case.

■ **Evidentiary shortcuts** Sometimes a fact can be proved without any offer of evidence. The legal mechanisms for such proof are inferences, presumptions, and judicial notice. Inferences and presumptions establish unknown facts by making conclusions on the basis of known facts. Judicial notice accepts as fact certain matters that are generally accepted as true.

Inferences An inference is a conclusion that may be made in the courtroom on the basis of logic and reasoning. For example, a man who is accused of injuring the left eye of another man by striking him with his fist may offer evidence in court that he is left-handed. He is asking the jury to draw the commonsense conclusion that he did not cause the injury because it is more likely that he would strike out with his left hand and land a blow on the victim's right side. The jury is entitled to make this inference whether or not the accused offers any other evidence of his innocence.

EXAMPLE While drinking a bottle of cola, a woman finds
O—* that part of the carcass of a dead mouse has sloshed into her mouth. She becomes violently ill and sues the bottling company. The accident was one that does not ordinarily happen without negligence. The woman was not at fault in any way. When it is time for the jury to reach a decision, the jury is free to infer, or refuse to infer, negligence on the part of the defendant bottling company. If the jury draws an inference of negligence, it will find a verdict for the woman. If the jury refuses to draw the inference of negligence, it will find for the defendant bottling company.

Presumptions A presumption is a conclusion directed by the law. A presumption may be conclusive or rebuttable. If it is a conclusive, or irrebuttable, presumption, the law requires that conclusion and no evidence to the contrary may be offered. For example, a simultaneous death statute says that when two deceased people (such as husband and wife) stand to inherit from each other and it is impossible to tell who died first, each will be presumed to have died first. This saves taxes that would otherwise be due twice, as the property passes from husband to wife and from wife to husband before it finally goes to a living person. Because the presumption called for is conclusive, the law requires the property to be distributed as though each person died before the other. See DEATH.

Many legal presumptions are rebuttable rather than conclusive. This means that the law requires that a certain conclusion be drawn from known facts unless it can be disproved. For example, there is a common-law presumption that a person who has disappeared without explanation and remained absent for seven years or more is dead. This presumption allows the property in his estate to be distributed and the benefits of his life insurance policy to be paid. The presumption can be defeated by persuasive evidence, however. The insurance company may be able to show that the man was having marital difficulties and was keeping company with another woman who disappeared at the same time as the man. This evidence may convince a jury that the man is not dead in spite of the presumption.

A person once shown to be insane is presumed by law to continue to be insane. This presumption is rebuttable by satisfactory evidence that the person has recovered.

EXAMPLE In a lawsuit contesting a will, the contestants
○—* claimed that the testator was insane at the time he
made his will. The evidence showed that 28 years before
his death he was discharged from an insane asylum.
During the 28 years, he had successfully carried on a
business. The will was executed some 26 years after his
discharge. The court ruled that any presumption of continued insanity was rebutted by the evidence.

Judicial notice Judicial notice is the act of a court
(judge) in recognizing the existence of a fact without requiring it to be put into evidence at the trial. Courts will
take judicial notice of facts that are universally accepted—
for example, that the moon is a satellite of the earth. They
will also take judicial notice of matters of general custom
and usage—for instance, the customary interval between
death and burial is usually no longer than three days,
Sunday has a special significance as a day of rest, airmail is
widely used in international business communications, and
the date of a postmark commonly coincides with the day of
mailing or the day after.

Geographical and historical facts may be judicially noticed. Among the geographical facts are the existence and
location of prominent lakes, rivers, and streams; the boundaries of nations, states, and territories; and the location of
cities and public buildings—the state prison and city
schools, for example. Historically, the events in the state or
territory may be noticed as may facts about war and national defense—for example, a court may take judicial notice of
the fact that unsettled economic conditions and fears prevail in a country at war.

The list of things covered by judicial notice is constantly
growing, and no exact limit can be placed on it. Judicial
notice has been taken of facts relating to businesses as
diverse as bakeries, barbershops, and cigar stands.

The familiar laws of nature are judicially noticed—the
ebb and flow of the tides and the fact that wind currents can
change at any moment. Recognition is given to the laws of
physics, the expansion and contraction of metals in heat
and cold, and the qualities and properties of matter—gases,
petroleum products, intoxicating liquors. The calendar and
its division of time are noticed, including the day of the
week on which any date has fallen; the exact moment of
sunrises and sunsets; and the duration of twilight.

Well-known facts relating to the phenomena of human
life are also subject to judicial notice. These include the
anatomy, physiology, and diseases of humans, the nine-
month period of human gestation, and even a person's
general habits and inclinations.

■ **Admissibility** Not every kind of evidence offered at
trial is admissible. A judge may rule that certain testimony
or items of evidence must be excluded for any one of a large
number of reasons. These reasons have been developed
over the years in order to keep out evidence that might
cause confusion, prejudice, or the violation of a right. The
general rule is that evidence is admissible when it is pertinent to the issue in the case and properly should be considered. The rules of evidence that govern admissibility are
embodied in statutes and controlling decisions in other,
similar cases.

Relevancy and materiality Evidence will not be admitted unless it is relevant and material. Evidence is rel-

evant if it helps to prove or disprove a disputed fact and
moves the inquiry forward. Logic is the determining factor
in the modern law of evidence. When a party offers to
prove a fact, he is saying that there is a logical relationship
between the fact offered and the fact in dispute. The fact
offered makes probable (or improbable) the fact in dispute.
The relationship between the two is termed "relevancy."

Practical considerations, however, do not always permit
the court to hear *all* the relevant facts. Therefore, facts
received in evidence must have the greatest value in proving the disputed fact. They must be material, or substantially important enough to influence the result of the trial.
Materiality is usually determined at the discretion of the
trial judge. A fact that is relevant, but has only a little value
in proving the disputed fact, tends to confuse matters and
may properly be excluded as immaterial.

■ **Similar acts and occurrences** Evidence of similar
acts may be relevant and material to issues or evidence
already received, and therefore admissible. Similar acts
may indicate that the act in issue has been committed, or
they may show the state of mind of a person.

EXAMPLE While a man named Radencic was sleeping in a
○—* freight train, he was awakened by Evans, a special
railroad police officer. Evans forced Radencic out of the
freight car and held him while another officer beat Radencic with a blackjack. Later, Radencic sued the railroad
company for damages of $2,500 in compensation for his
injuries and $500 in punitive damages for the assault and
battery. Under the law of the state, punitive damages
could be awarded in civil actions involving malicious
acts. The jury awarded Radencic punitive damages. The
railroad appealed the decision because the trial court had
admitted as evidence the fact that Evans had committed
other similar assaults. The appellate court affirmed the
trial court's judgment. It stated that evidence of similar
prior assaults was admissible to show the existence of
malice. The railroad had retained Evans even though it
knew of his tendency to use excessive force and violence.

The occurrence of a fact, condition, or event may be
proved by evidence about the occurrence of similar ones
under the same circumstances.

EXAMPLE A suit was brought to recover under a windstorm
○—* insurance policy. Testimony was offered about
hurricane damage to other buildings located on the same
island as the insured property. The testimony helped to
show that the island was hit by the hurricane on the date
the damage was done to the insured property.

Competence In order to be admissible, evidence
must be not only relevant and material but competent.

Evidence is competent if its presentation is capable of
establishing the fact that it seeks to prove. For example, a
written lease is competent evidence when it is presented to
show the terms to which a tenant and landlord agreed and
which are the issue in an eviction proceeding. On the other
hand, the lease for an apartment may not be competent to
show that the landlord has always provided a doorman for
the building and that the tenant had relied on having a
doorman as a security measure. If the tenant sues to force
the landlord to continue providing a doorman even though
the lease does not cover that point, the tenant will have to
use other evidence that is competent, such as testimony

from the management company or from other tenants in the building.

Testimony about the identity of a voice, the calculations of an adding machine, documents affecting the ownership of real estate, and even evidence of a person's weight shown on a card obtained from a commercial scale are competent if they can prove or disprove a disputed fact—a person's identity, a money matter, the ownership of land, or a person's health, for example.

Evidence is competent even if it is weak. The fact that a witness was 1,150 feet from the scene of an accident, for example, may affect his persuasiveness, but it does not make his testimony incompetent. Similarly, unexplained contradictory statements may affect how much weight a jury gives a witness's testimony, but the testimony still may be competent as evidence.

Rules of evidence also require that a witness be competent before he can give any testimony as evidence. This means that there must be no reason why the law will not let the witness answer questions under oath. In general, a witness is competent if he is able to observe, to remember, and to narrate and if he feels an obligation to be truthful. Insane persons and children are usually ruled incompetent because of their limited understanding. People in certain confidential relationships—such as a priest, spouse, or attorney—are generally not allowed to testify about privileged communications. Most states also forbid testimony from someone who stands to gain by telling about conversations he had with someone now dead. These laws are called dead man's statutes, and their coverage varies from state to state. For a full discussion of the competence of witnesses, see WITNESS.

Best evidence rule Another requirement affecting admissibility of evidence is the best evidence rule. Under this rule, the highest degree of proof available must be produced. No evidence is to be received when the party can obtain better evidence. All evidence that is not best, or primary, evidence is called secondary evidence. The best evidence rule usually applies only to documentary evidence.

Primary evidence includes both original writings and duplicate originals—carbon copies or photocopies of the original. Each one has the same legal effect as the original, and each is admissible to prove its contents.

EXAMPLE A manufacturer of sporting equipment, Hi-Fun, O—* and a retail seller, Sports Days, agree to a contract, which is typed with two carbon copies. Both Hi-Fun and Sports Days sign each of the three documents. The two carbon copies are duplicate originals. Each of the contracts is equally admissible. If the two carbon copies had not been signed or if photostatic copies of the typed, unsigned contract had been made, these would be considered secondary evidence. Similarly, if the contract had been tape-recorded, microfilmed, or copied by hand, any of these records would be secondary evidence.

Before secondary evidence can be introduced, the party who seeks to do so must explain why he cannot produce the original.

EXAMPLE The Athletico Manufacturing Company enters O—* into a contract to supply 500 leather-covered baseballs with red stitching to Sportsland, a retail store. The contract is typed and signed by both parties. The retailer keeps the original, and an unsigned photocopy is given to the manufacturer. When the baseballs arrive at Sportsland, they are covered in a synthetic material with black stitching. Sportsland's manager calls the manufacturer and informs him that the baseballs do not conform to the terms of the contract. Athletico claims they do. Sportsland sues Athletico for breach of contract but cannot produce the original contract because it was destroyed in a fire.

At the trial, Athletico attempts to testify orally about the terms of the contract. Sportsland objects because the testimony of the manufacturer is not admissible unless he produces the photocopy of the contract or explains why it is not available. In this situation the court would sustain Sportsland's objection. The best evidence was the original contract signed by both parties, but it was destroyed in the fire. Both the manufacturer's oral testimony and his photocopy are secondary evidence, but the photocopy is more reliable than his testimony.

Before the manufacturer may testify about the contract, he must produce the photocopy or explain why he is unable to do so. If he refuses to produce it, he cannot testify about it. If he does produce the photocopy, then it will be admitted without oral testimony. Finally, if the manufacturer shows that the photocopy is not available and why it is not, then he will be permitted to testify.

Some states, however, do not recognize degrees of secondary evidence. Instead, they would judge the photocopy and the manufacturer's oral testimony to be equally admissible.

Parol evidence rule The parol evidence rule also determines the admissibility of some evidence. Parol evidence is verbal evidence. Under the parol evidence rule, when parties put their agreement into writing all previous oral agreements merge in the writing. From then on, verbal evidence is not admissible to change the written agreement. The rule is founded on long years of experience that written evidence is much more accurate than evidence that rests in memory. The written agreement must be an *integration*—the parties must have intended it to be both complete and final. It must include all the prior and current negotiations, understandings, and terms that the parties intended.

The parol evidence rule applies to CONTRACTS.

EXAMPLE Your neighbor wants to sell her automobile, and O—* you and she agree on a price. In addition, she verbally promises to pay for the repair of any defect for the next three months. The two of you then sign a written agreement for the purchase and sale of the automobile, which does not mention the promise to repair the automobile. The agreement does state, however, "The buyer and seller agree that this is the entire contract and there are no promises or representations which do not appear herein." Within one week after you take possession of the automobile, the engine breaks down. You have it repaired at a cost of $600. When your neighbor refuses to reimburse you, you bring suit against her. At the trial, you attempt to testify that your neighbor verbally promised to pay for any necessary repairs. Her attorney objects, citing the parol evidence rule. His objection is sustained. The agreement specifically states that the contract is complete and that all previous negotiations are included. The parol evidence rule prevents you from testifying about your neighbor's earlier promises.

The rule does not apply to subsequent oral changes to a contract—changes made after the contract is signed.

EXAMPLE You purchase the automobile from your neighbor. The contract contains exactly the same terms as in the example above. The engine breaks down within a week and you complain to your neighbor. She tells you that you paid a fair price for the automobile and that in further consideration of your agreement she will pay for the engine repairs. When you have the automobile repaired, she refuses to reimburse you. You bring suit against her. In this situation, your neighbor's promise is a subsequent oral modification of the contract. You would be allowed to testify to the promise without violating the parol evidence rule.

Character and reputation Evidence of a party's character is generally not admissible as a substitute for factual proof or primary evidence. Evidence of character may be admissible, however, when character is in issue because of the nature of the suit. For example, in a fight for custody of a young child, the character of the contesting parties becomes a matter in issue and is a proper subject of proof. Similarly, evidence of the good character of a party may be admissible when his character has been challenged by the opposing party.

EXAMPLE Selena was suing to recover the $250 that she had lent to Bart. Bart denied the loan and then accused Selena of embezzling his money. Selena's reputation for honesty was thus put in issue. Evidence that she had the character trait of honesty was admissible.

Evidence of character traits, however, is not admissible to prove or disprove conduct.

EXAMPLE Fred sued for personal injuries he received when he was hit by a car driven by Nicky. Evidence that Nicky had the reputation of being a reckless driver was not admissible on Fred's behalf. The question at issue was not Nicky's reputation as a driver but whether or not he had been reckless when he injured Fred.

Hearsay rule and its exceptions The hearsay rule is a broad requirement that witnesses should testify about what they know rather than about what someone else told them he knows. The rule insists that the other person, who directly witnessed the event in question, should give testimony himself. Many other rules of evidence stand as exceptions to the hearsay rule. They have been developed because there is reason to believe that in some instances the truth is best discovered when hearsay is not barred from the courtroom.

Evidence is hearsay when it does not come from the personal knowledge of the witness. Literally, it is what the witness says he heard another person say. Hearsay evidence is usually inadmissible as proof of the fact asserted. For example, testimony of statements made to a witness by a child about her mistreatment by her mother and stepfather was held to be hearsay and inadmissible.

The right to cross-examine witnesses, which guards against false and inaccurate testimony, is protected by the rule that excludes hearsay evidence. If hearsay were allowed, it would be used to relate what persons who are not testifying in the case had said, because there is no need to introduce hearsay to prove the facts related by parties and witnesses who take the stand and testify. If overheard statements made by persons who are not able to take the stand were admitted as evidence, there would be no opportunity to test their truth through cross-examination. On the other hand, hearsay may be used in the cross-examination of a witness in order to discredit or impeach that witness's testimony.

EXAMPLE Gladys was suing her next-door neighbor, George, for cutting down her prize oak tree, even though George denied doing so. Before the tree had been cut down, however, Bob, another neighbor, overheard George tell his wife that the tree was a mess and a nuisance because it dropped acorns and leaves into his backyard and blocked his light. During the trial, George testified that he had always admired the tree and enjoyed the shade it cast into his yard. Gladys's attorney asked him if he had ever said anything derogatory about the tree, and George insisted that he had not. The attorney then asked George if he ever told anyone that the tree was a mess and a nuisance. George denied ever saying anything of the sort. Gladys's attorney then called Bob to the stand to tell the court what he overheard George tell his wife. Although Bob's testimony was hearsay, it could be used in this instance to impeach George's testimony.

The hearsay rule applies *only* when out-of-court remarks are offered as evidence of the facts they relate. But when the hearsay remarks are offered for some other purpose, they are admissible.

EXAMPLE While driving home, you see a man lying by a crosswalk. Thinking that the man is injured, you stop your car and jump out to help him. The man is badly hurt and bleeding but still conscious. He tells you that he was struck by an oil truck bearing the name of a particular company. Before the man can tell you anything else, he loses consciousness. The man dies three days later without regaining consciousness. His executor brings suit against the oil company and the truck driver for causing the man's wrongful death. The executor is also seeking money damages for any conscious pain or suffering the man may have endured prior to his death. As a witness, you are asked to testify about what the man told you before he lost consciousness. Your testimony is hearsay. It is, however, admissible—not to prove that the oil truck hit the man but to prove that he was conscious right after the accident.

Exceptions to the hearsay rule are increasing in such numbers that they have virtually swallowed the rule. The exceptions are based on necessity, common sense, and the trustworthiness of past experience. Some common exceptions to the hearsay rule include *res gestae*, previously recorded testimony, admissions, and declarations against interest.

Res gestae *Res gestae* ("things done") are circumstances, facts, and statements that grow out of and illustrate the main event leading to the lawsuit. The *res gestae* rule is an exception to the hearsay rule. It says that a comment made spontaneously and in the middle of an event is likely to be truthful. Therefore someone who heard the comment can later repeat it in court even though it is hearsay for him to testify about what the other person said.

In order to be admissible as testimony under the *res gestae* rule, the statement must possess the following elements: (1) It must tell of an event and explain or characterize it. (2) It must be a natural statement growing out of the event. (3) It must be a statement of fact and not an opinion. (4) It must be a spontaneous thought, prompted by the event itself, and not the result of premeditation, reflection, or design. (5) It must be made at a time and under circumstances that demonstrate that it is not the result of deliberation—though it need not be made at the time the event takes place. (6) It must be made by a person who witnessed or participated in the event.

EXAMPLE Bill was riding his bicycle after work one afternoon when he was struck by the car that Dolores was driving. Dolores jumped out of the car and exclaimed over and over, "I didn't see you. I don't know how I could have missed seeing you." Later, when Bill sued Dolores, he called Michelle, who had been a bystander at the scene of the accident, to testify about what had happened. Michelle was allowed to repeat what Dolores said in her outburst because it was so closely connected to the collision that it was a part of the entire event. The court concluded that it probably was not fabricated because Dolores had had no time to think. The court said that the outburst was part of the *res gestae* and an exception to the hearsay rule.

Previously recorded testimony In order to be admissible as an exception to the hearsay rule, previously recorded testimony—testimony given in an earlier case—must have been given under oath, and the opposing party must have had the opportunity to cross-examine the witness who gave the testimony. The issue on which the testimony is being offered in the later case must be the same as the one in the earlier case, and the witness must be unavailable to testify personally because of absence from the state, illness, insanity, or death.

EXAMPLE While alighting from a bus, a woman fell and injured her knee. Her husband sued the bus company for the loss of her services due to the injury, and she also sued the company for her injury. Her husband's suit was the first to come to trial. In it he alleged that just as his wife was alighting, the bus lurched forward, causing her to fall. A witness for the bus company testified that the bus did not move until after the woman had fallen from the lowest step. In both the husband's and the wife's suits the issue was whether or not the bus company (through its driver) was negligent in its handling of the bus. By the time of the wife's suit, the witness who had testified for the bus company had moved out of state and was unable to appear in court. When the defendant bus company offered to introduce a transcript of the witness's earlier testimony, the wife's attorney objected on the ground that it was hearsay evidence. He was overruled, however, and the testimony was admitted. The issue to which it pertained—the company's negligent operation of the bus—was the same in both cases.

Admissions Admissions are out-of-court statements made by a party to a civil suit that concede facts relevant to his adversary's cause. (They should not be confused with CONFESSIONS, which are used only in criminal cases and apply to acknowledgment of guilt.) Any admission that relates to any material fact and is against a party's own interest is competent evidence and admissible against him. It is not important to whom the admission is made. Evidence of an admission, therefore, is yet another exclusion to the hearsay rule.

To be accepted as evidence, an admission must be a statement of fact, not an opinion or conclusion about a fact or about the law. The reason that courts do not admit such conclusions and opinions about the law is that an individual should not be affected by statements based on a misunderstanding of his legal rights. Even so, statements by a person that he was at fault (a conclusion of law) or that his adversary is free from fault are usually admissible.

EXAMPLE A woman named Davis was injured when a passing vehicle sideswiped her car, causing it to strike a tree. After the collision, a witness to the accident overheard the driver of the other vehicle, a Dr. Strickland, state that the accident was all his fault. Mrs. Davis sued Dr. Strickland for damages. At the trial, Mrs. Davis's attorney offered in evidence the statement made by Dr. Strickland, whose attorney objected on the grounds that it was an opinion and a legal conclusion, not a statement of fact. The court overruled the objection and admitted Dr. Strickland's statement. It held that the statement was a mixture of law and fact. It was the opinion of Dr. Strickland that he was at fault. His opinion implicitly applied an assumed legal standard of conduct to his actions. The statement was admissible for consideration by the jury along with all the other facts. But it was not conclusive of his legal liability.

Admissions that appear in the records of court proceedings are called judicial admissions and are also exceptions to the hearsay rule. Like admissions made out of court, judicial admissions may be used to attack a party's credibility or as proof against him. The admission may have been made in the case at hand or in an earlier one. The record of the former case is admissible into evidence to establish the admission. For instance, statements that are made in a PLEADING (the pretrial accusation by the plaintiff or the reply by the defendant) are generally admissible against the party making them.

EXAMPLE Dora sues Jesse for failing to repay $1,000 he had borrowed from her. Dora claims that Jesse had signed a note promising to repay the $1,000, but then refused to honor the promissory note. Jesse admits in his pleading that the note contains his signature but claims that he never received the loan the note was meant to cover. Afterwards, Jesse changes his answer and claims that the signature on the note is a forgery. During the trial Dora's attorney offers in evidence the original answer as an admission by Jesse that he had signed the note. Jesse's answer should be admitted for consideration by the jury.

An offer to compromise usually cannot be entered into evidence as an admission because the law favors settling controversies out of court. See COMPROMISE AND SETTLEMENT. A compromise, then, is *not* an exception to the hearsay rule. A person is entitled to attempt to "buy his peace" without being disadvantaged should his effort fail. A true offer of compromise does not indicate an admission by the defendant that he is at fault or by the plaintiff that his case is groundless or even doubtful. A true offer of compromise is made tentatively, hypothetically, and in expectation of mutual concessions.

Declarations against interest Declarations against interest are statements that conflict with the pecuniary (financial) interest of the person making them. They are admissible as hearsay only when the declarant (the person who made the statement) is unavailable as a witness. Some states hold that a declaration is admissible only when the declarant is dead.

The declaration must be against an obvious and existing pecuniary interest of the declarant—an acknowledgment that the declarant owes a debt to another person, for example, or that nothing is due to the declarant on a particular account.

EXAMPLE Two farmers were neighbors and close friends. Their relationship was almost that of father and son since one was nearly 30 years older than the other. The younger man needed money to expand his farm and so mortgaged his property to his older friend. When the older man died, his executor brought suit to foreclose the mortgage. At the trial, the younger friend claimed that the mortgage had already been paid off and that the older farmer had acknowledged the fact in a conversation. He attempted to introduce his deceased friend's notebook—which had entries of the mortgage payments—as proof of what the older man had said. The court held that the notebook entries were admissible as declarations against the interest of the deceased friend. The old farmer would not have made entries showing that money owed him had been paid unless it had.

evidentiary fact
A fact giving evidence that some other fact exists. Examples include photographs, correspondence, plats (land maps), deeds, and leases. Evidentiary facts are necessary to prove ultimate facts, such as whether or not a crime has been committed or whether or not a contract has been broken (breached).

examination
1 In criminal law, the preliminary hearing that determines whether the person charged with having committed a crime should be held for trial. 2 In trial practice, the interrogation of a witness. This consists of a series of questions put to him by the attorney of a party to the lawsuit to elicit the witness's knowledge of the facts in dispute. 3 In bankruptcy proceedings, the interrogation of the debtor. 4 In property law, the investigation of a TITLE to real estate to reveal to the person intending to buy the property the history and present condition of the title to (ownership of) the land and what liens or other incumbrances it may have.

examiner
The name given to an officer at a hearing, an administrative judge, or an officer of the patent office who determines the patentability of inventions.

exception
A formal objection made during a trial when the court refuses a request or overrules an objection made by an attorney. It implies that the attorney taking the exception does not agree with the court's decision and will appeal it to a higher court. The attorney's exception saves his objection for review by the higher court.

EXAMPLE Mrs. Doe brings a divorce suit based on cruelty. She alleges that her husband severely beat her on a number of occasions. Her attorney calls Mrs. Neighbor as a corroborating (supporting) witness. Mrs. Neighbor testifies that although she never saw Mr. Doe strike his wife, her son, Junior Neighbor, once saw the Does fighting. The following dialogue takes place:

MRS. DOE's ATTORNEY: Did you ask Junior any questions concerning the fight?

MRS. NEIGHBOR: Yes, I did.

MRS. DOE's ATTORNEY: What did he say about it?

MR. DOE's ATTORNEY: I object. Any testimony this witness might give concerning what her son told her is hearsay.

THE JUDGE: Objection overruled. I want to hear what Junior said he saw.

MR. DOE's ATTORNEY: I take an exception.

THE JUDGE: Your exception is noted.

The judge later grants Mrs. Doe the divorce. Mr. Doe wishes to appeal the court's decision. Since Mr. Doe's attorney has saved his objection to the admission of the hearsay testimony by taking exception to the judge's ruling, the appellate court may review that ruling. See APPEAL AND ERROR.

exchange
An association of persons engaged in the same type of business. It provides facilities for its members' transactions and maintains standards of fair business practice. The New York Stock Exchange and the American Stock Exchange are familiar examples of these associations.

excise
A tax on the privilege of pursuing certain occupations; on manufacturing, selling, or using a specific type of commodity; on licenses; or on corporate privileges. Excise taxes are a kind of sales tax. Some states impose an annual excise tax, for example, on the privilege of owning an automobile. The tax is assessed at a fixed percentage of the automobile's value, such as 5 percent. The federal government levies excise taxes on certain items, such as liquor, tobacco, and motor fuel. Duties collected by the U.S. Customs Service are also considered excises.

exclusionary clause
A CONTRACT provision that attempts to restrict the legal remedies available to one of the parties if the contract is broken.

EXAMPLE André agrees to buy Susan's house on March 1, but Susan is worried that her plans to buy Philip's house in February may fall through. Usually, once a person has a contract to buy real estate he has the right to force the seller to hand over the property. But Susan asks André for an exclusionary clause in the contract to sell her house, and André agrees. As a result, if Susan fails to get Philip's house for herself, and she refuses to let André have her house, she will have to pay André only the money he lost because the sale did not go through.

exclusionary rule
The principle that illegally gathered evidence may not be used in a criminal trial. For example, articles seized by police who break into a home and search it without a warrant usually may not be used as evidence in a criminal trial. See SEARCH AND SEIZURE.

exclusive agency   An agreement that prohibits the principal (someone who employs an agent) from appointing another agent to represent him. For example, if a salesman has an exclusive AGENCY to sell a wholesaler's products, this usually bars a competing agent from selling the same products in the territory.

exculpate   Free from blame. Exculpatory evidence, for instance, is evidence that tends to clear a person from fault or guilt.

exculpatory clause   A clause that expressly relieves a trustee from personal liability for any losses that result from his management of TRUST property, provided he acts in good faith. The clauses are very often found in wills that create trusts.

excuse   A matter alleged in court as a reason for exemption from guilt. *Excusable assault,* for instance, is an accidental assault by someone who was otherwise acting lawfully, with ordinary caution, and without unlawful intent. A police officer who fires his revolver to summon help but accidently injures an innocent passerby has committed an excusable assault.

execute   Complete; perform. For example, the execution of a CONTRACT includes doing everything that is necessary to carry out its terms. A TRUST does not become fully executed until its property has been properly paid to its beneficiaries. A WILL is executed when all its terms are written down and it is signed.

execution   A judicial writ (order) issued from the court that handed down a JUDGMENT. It is the means by which the judgment is enforced—the final process, the act of carrying into effect the judgment or decree of a court. The execution is directed to an officer of the court and can be against a person or property.

When a creditor sues a debtor and wins the suit, the judge will hand down a judgment—that is, the court will order the debtor to pay the creditor a certain amount of money. Once the creditor has received the judgment he will ask the court to issue a writ of execution, which will be delivered to the sheriff or other authorized officer, directing him to seize the debtor's property to satisfy the debt. Executions are authorized in any lawsuit or proceeding in which a money judgment is handed down or when dictated by statute.

Executions against persons are called body executions; they are discussed at the end of this article.

■ **The basis of an execution**   An execution cannot be lawfully issued unless a judgment, which determines the rights and liabilities of the parties, is handed down by a court. An execution issued without a judgment is void. The courts adhere strictly to this rule. A court cannot issue an execution for a debt not included in a judgment. A jury's verdict for damages is not sufficient.

When there are two or more plaintiffs, and a judgment decrees a distinct and separate amount for each of them, a separate execution may be issued to each plaintiff. But when there is one plaintiff, only one execution is issued—even though there were several COUNTS in the complaint on which the lawsuit was based, and there were separate awards on each count. For example, in a suit based on an automobile mishap, one sum of money is awarded for property damage and another for pain and suffering. Only one execution is issued, stating the total of the two sums awarded.

A single execution cannot be issued on two or more separate judgments, even when they are all in favor of the same plaintiff or against the same defendant.

The person against whom a judgment is issued is called the judgment debtor; the person in whose favor it is handed down is the judgment creditor.

■ **For whom is it issued?**   The judgment creditor or someone acting for him has the exclusive right to have the execution issued. An execution may be assigned (transferred) by the person who received the judgment to someone else. The execution may then be issued at the request of the assignee (the one to whom it is transferred) in the name of the assignor. See ASSIGNMENT.

One of several creditors who jointly receive a judgment may take out an execution without consulting the others. If one of two joint plaintiffs dies, the execution should be issued in favor of the survivor.

■ **Against whom is it issued?**   An execution may be issued against anyone against whom a judgment has been handed down. If a party to a lawsuit has appeared in a representative capacity, such as a guardian on behalf of his ward or a parent for a child, the execution must be issued against him in that same capacity.

■ **Agreement not to issue**   An agreement not to issue an execution may be made for a valid consideration— something of value that would induce the person who received the judgment not to enforce it.

EXAMPLE The watchdog that Gilbert kept at his service 0⊷* station bit Kathleen, and she recovered a judgment for her injuries in the amount of $10,000. Kathleen's attorney wanted to execute the judgment by having Gilbert's assets seized and sold. Gilbert rented his station, so the only property he owned was his truck and tools. He pointed out to the attorney that a forced sale of the truck and tools would not bring in enough money to satisfy the judgment, and it would put him out of business. If Kathleen would agree not to execute, Gilbert could continue his business and pay off the judgment in installments over a period of time.

Upon any breach of an agreement not to issue an execution, an execution may be immediately issued. In the above example, if Gilbert failed to make his promised installment payments, Kathleen could have an execution issued. If an execution is issued in violation of the agreement (if Kathleen had an execution issued even though Gilbert was making his payments), it will be set aside at the demand of the defendant, or the defendant may sue for any damages that result from its issuance.

■ **Property subject to execution**   Most types of property are subject to seizure under an execution. In most states the real estate of a judgment debtor is subject to seizure and sale on execution. In other states it is not primarily liable—that is, the debtor's other property must be exchanged before his real estate can be seized. State law determines what property can be seized and what cannot. Certain property is exempt from seizure and sale, but these exemptions vary from state to state. Most states have homestead laws that exempt family homes from seizure. Many states exempt property and food that is needed to support the debtor's family. For a full discussion of the types of property that can be exempted from seizure, see EXEMPTION. See also Chart 10.

In order to be seized and sold, property must be in existence at the time. For example, beer in a state of fermentation has been held not to be subject to execution because the sheriff could not actually seize it without destroying its value.

■ **Issuance of the writ** An execution on a judgment is usually issued by the clerk or deputy clerk of the court in which the judgment was handed down. The clerk can issue a writ of execution only when (1) he is directed to do so by the judgment creditor or his attorney and (2) the judgment is unsatisfied (remains unpaid). When a clerk wrongfully refuses to issue the writ, the usual remedy is MANDAMUS, a court order commanding him to do so.

The time within which an execution must be issued varies. Some courts hold that the time runs from the rendition (announcement) of judgment and others from the point it is entered in the court records. On a judgment payable in installments, the period runs from the time when each installment falls due. In computing the time period, the time during which an execution is stayed—say by agreement of the parties or by an appeal—should be excluded.

A writ of execution is not considered issued until it has been delivered to the sheriff or other authorized officer or his deputy by the judgment creditor. Often, the officer to whom the writ is directed must endorse it with the day, hour, and minute he received it. Executions are directed to the sheriff or other officer in the name of the state or the people, not in the name of the court. The officer gets his authority from the direction in the writ.

The writ should command the sheriff or some other officer to make a levy of the execution (seize the property). When a money judgment is being recovered, the writ should not specify any particular property to be seized. The writ should state the return day—the day when the sheriff must bring the writ back to the court with an account of the time and method of its execution—or his failure to accomplish it.

■ **Levy and custody of the property** The levy of the execution is the officer's act of seizing the judgment debtor's property to satisfy the command of the writ. Its purpose is (1) to take property into the custody of the law so that it can be sold to satisfy the judgment and (2) to prevent the judgment debtor from diverting the property to any other use. When the officer receiving the writ is given instructions by the judgment creditor on how and when to carry it out, the officer must follow reasonable orders.

Importance of a levy In order for the sheriff to sell the property and give the purchaser a valid title, there must be a levy on the property sold—the officer must have officially seized it. A judgment debtor may, however, waive a levy on his property—that is, give the sheriff the right to take his property. When he does, the sale passes title (ownership) as effectively as if a levy had been made.

Who makes a levy A levy of execution must be made by an officer, such as a sheriff, who is qualified to act under the terms of the writ. It cannot be made by a private person. An officer generally has no authority to make a levy on and to sell property located beyond the boundaries of his district. When a tract of land is divided by a county line, the officer is sometimes authorized by statute to act outside his county. If he is not, the sale is valid only for the part within his county.

Its time limit A levy cannot be made until the officer has received the writ of execution, but then it must be made within the time fixed by statute—by the return day.

Method of the levy When the method of making a levy is set by law, the officer is to follow it strictly. For instance, some states require the officer to demand payment from the judgment debtor before making the levy in order to give the debtor an opportunity to pay the execution without incurring further costs.

The judgment debtor usually has the right to select the property on which he wants the levy to be made. But the judgment creditor may disregard the debtor's selection, if there is a good reason to do so—if the property is mortgaged, has a lien on it, or is otherwise encumbered. The debtor, of course, has no right to designate property that he does not own outright.

The officer is permitted by law to enter the debtor's premises to make a levy on his personal property. He must take possession of the property or bring it within his control by actual or constructive seizure. *Actual seizure* is taking physical possession of the property. *Constructive seizure* occurs when the officer has control of the property but not physical possession of it. For example, an officer who makes an inventory of the debtor's property and then files it with the court when he returns the writ is in constructive possession of the property.

The officer must have the property in view at the time of making the levy. Sometimes it is not necessary for the officer to see the property if he has an inventory and the debtor acknowledges the officer's control of the property. The officer should act openly and clearly in making a levy. He should have one or more witnesses to his levy and should note this on the writ of execution. An unwitnessed levy is usually held invalid if other creditors claim the property.

■ **An execution sale** After the sheriff has made the levy, it is his duty to sell the seized property in an execution sale. He cannot, for instance, deliver the property to the plaintiff in satisfaction of the claim, except in the case of a levy on money. If the debtor or any other responsible person offers to pay the debt, the sheriff must accept the offer and withdraw the property from sale. When only part of the judgment has been paid, a sale to obtain the balance is valid.

Conduct of the sale An execution sale should be conducted in a manner that promotes competition and obtains the best price. Although the officer who sells the property should be sensitive to directions given by the execution creditors, he is not their servant. He is the agent or trustee of the debtor as well as the creditor, and he has the duty to protect them both. If necessary, he may make an auctioneer his agent in order to get the most favorable price. An officer should not sell more of the debtor's property than is necessary to satisfy the judgment. When a part can be conveniently separated from the whole, it should be sold separately.

A cardinal rule in an execution sale of real estate is that the property should be identified with absolute certainty. A sale is void if it involves an unspecified part of a large tract of land, when the portion sold cannot be distinguished from the remainder. Personal property to be sold should be on hand so that the bidders can examine it.

The sale usually must be made at public auction at the place specified in the notice of sale, but if all the parties agree, the property may be sold privately.

Posting notice To publicize the sale to obtain the best price for the property, notice of the sale is usually required. Posting announcements in one or more public places in the county where the property is located and advertising in a local newspaper are the usual methods. If the place of sale is omitted from the notice, then no notice has been given.

Bids A bid may be made in person or through an agent. It may be done in writing or by telephone, provided it is publicly announced before the property is given to such a bidder. The officer making the sale cannot bid for the property, either for himself or as an agent for another person. The sale should be made to the highest bidder, but a sale is valid even if there was only one bidder.

■ **Redemption** Generally, an execution debtor may redeem (buy back) property sold on an execution against him, but most states limit the time period when property can be redeemed—check the laws in your state and see Chart 13. Some statutes require the debtor to meet the price paid at the execution sale. Other states require him to pay also such additional items as taxes paid by the purchaser, the value of improvements and repairs, interest on the purchase price, or compensation for the care of the property. An amount may also be fixed by an agreement between the parties. When the agreement is made at the time of the sale, a fair allowance should be paid for the purchaser's time, trouble, and expenses, in addition to the price agreed on.

■ **Body executions** An execution may also be against the person himself—that is, the sheriff may arrest and imprison the defendant until he satisfies the judgment or is released by the order of the creditor. A body execution is an extraordinary remedy that is used only if the amount of the judgment cannot be obtained by an ordinary execution. In fact, most states prohibit imprisonment for debt or restrict the right to imprison debtors. The laws permit imprisonment only for the purpose of compelling a debtor who is able to pay but refuses to reveal property that he has fraudulently withheld and from which the judgment may be satisfied. Laws that prohibit imprisonment for debt do not prevent the arrest of a judgment debtor who is about to leave the state, however. See ARREST.

Who is exempt? Various classes of persons are exempt from arrest and imprisonment on body execution. They include INFANTS (minors); INSANE PERSONS; SPENDTHRIFTS under guardianship; witnesses going to, attending, or leaving court; parties in court during their lawsuits; and members of the legislatures while performing their duties.

Arrest and custody The arrest must be made by a proper officer within his jurisdiction. Although authorized

to use such force as is necessary to accomplish the arrest, he is not usually permitted to break and enter the debtor's home. If an arrest has been made, however, and the debtor escapes to take refuge in his home, the officer may break and enter in pursuit—but only after he has announced his business, demanded entry, and been refused admission.

For the debtor to be in lawful custody, he must be delivered to the jail, where he will remain until he finally agrees to satisfy the debt.

Discharge from jail A debtor can be released from jail when he has paid the amount of the execution and fees. The settlement must be in money, unless another form of payment is authorized by statute or agreed to by the creditor. The creditor may at any time order the release of a debtor, but first the creditor must make an agreement with the debtor or accept some other form of security.

executive The administrative branch of the U.S. government, which is charged with the duty of carrying out or enforcing the laws. Its head and chief executive is the PRESIDENT of the United States. The executive is distinguished from the legislative branch (Congress), which passes the laws, and from the judicial branch (the courts), which rules on the laws. See CONSTITUTIONAL LAW.

executive order An order issued by the President of the United States, or by a state governor, that has the force and effect of law.

executors and administrators Persons who settle the estate (property) of a deceased person. When a person dies leaving property, his estate is usually set apart to be administered, or settled, under the immediate supervision of a special county court known as a probate, surrogate, or orphans' court, depending on the state. Since this area of the law is regulated by the states, the laws may differ from state to state. In every state, however, the main objectives of the administration are to collect, preserve, and account for the assets of the estate; to pay the decedent's debts out of the assets; and to distribute whatever remains to his heirs.

This article discusses the rights, powers, duties, and liabilities of executors and administrators in collecting, managing, and distributing the estate of a decedent.

■ **Personal representatives** The personal representatives of the deceased—a term that applies to both executors and administrators—have the duty of settling and distributing estates under court supervision.

An *executor* is a man named in a WILL to administer the estate. A woman designated to perform these functions is an *executrix*.

An *administrator* or *administratrix* is appointed by the court to administer the property of a person who died without leaving a will or whose will has been declared invalid. When an executor cannot or will not serve—if he is seriously ill or has serious differences with the decedent's family, for example—or when the will fails to name an executor, the court will appoint an administrator. He is known as an *administrator c.t.a.* (in Latin, *cum testamento annexo*, meaning "with the will annexed"). The court may appoint an administrator for an estate that a prior executor or administrator has failed to completely settle. He is called an *administrator de bonis non* or an *administrator d.b.n.,* which means "administrator of goods not administered."

Because executors and administrators are court appointed, they serve as officers of the court. They act in a *representative capacity* and bear a FIDUCIARY relation (position of trust) toward all parties having an interest in the estate. As a fiduciary, the executor or administrator owes absolute loyalty to the beneficiaries of the estate and must administer it solely in their interest.

Special administrator   A special administrator is a person named by the court to watch over the assets of an estate until its proper legal representative is appointed. He is usually given the authority to administer some particular property of the decedent but not the whole estate.

EXAMPLE David Miller owned a grocery store at the time of his death. The court immediately appointed a special administrator to sell the perishable goods in the store. If the court had delayed the sale until the assignment of the regular personal representative, the goods would have been totally wasted and an asset of the estate would have been lost.

A special administrator may also be appointed to collect the proceeds of a decedent's life insurance policy until the outcome of a contest over a will is decided. The authority of a special administrator usually ends automatically when a regular personal representative is appointed.

■ **Estate and probate**   The estate of a deceased person is the sum total of his assets and liabilities. An estate is *testate* if it is to be distributed according to the directions in a valid will. In this case, the dead person is called the *testator.* If a person dies without leaving a will or if his will is declared invalid by a court, both he and his estate are known as *intestate.* The estate will be distributed according to the applicable laws of DESCENT AND DISTRIBUTION.

PROBATE proceedings insure the orderly transfer of assets, the protection of creditors, and the identification of the rightful heirs of the estate. Specifically, probate is the process by which the court establishes that a document is the last will of a competent testator. The first step in the probate process is filing the will in the appropriate court. With the will is a petition to admit it to probate and to grant letters testamentary to the person designated as executor. A petition to admit a will to probate may be filed by the

ADMINISTERING ESTATES—THE DUTIES OF EXECUTORS AND ADMINISTRATORS

■ Executors and administrators (both are also known as representatives) are persons representing someone who has died, to administer his estate—that is, to collect, preserve, and account for its assets, pay its debts, and distribute what is left to the heirs.

■ If the person designated to perform these functions was appointed for the job and named in the decedent's will, he is called an executor. (A woman so named is called an executrix.) If the decedent died without a will and the court must appoint someone to administer the estate, that person is called an administrator or administratrix.

■ Usually a representative does not administer property outside the state or county of his appointment. If a legal resident of Idaho dies and leaves property there and in Iowa, for example, separate administration is usually necessary in each state.

■ Before naming someone as your executor, you should ask the person if he or she will accept the position. If the person named as executor refuses the appointment when your will is brought to probate, the court must appoint another representative; this will delay settlement and cost more in legal fees.

■ Anyone who is competent to make a will is also competent to be an ex-

ecutor. A person cannot be rejected as an executor just because he may inherit part of the estate.

■ When a court must appoint an administrator, preference is usually given to the surviving spouse or, if there is no spouse, the next of kin.

■ An executor or administrator is generally required to take an oath. He may also be required to post a bond.

■ A representative is not required to perform every single act involved in the job—he may hire an accountant and an attorney.

■ The first step a representative must take is to find out the extent and value of the estate and make up an inventory, which must be filed with the court. He must take custody of assets, books, and papers and keep accounts to make sure the assets are properly handled.

■ The estate bank account should be in the representative's name, but with identification that he is the executor or administrator.

■ The representative must wind up the decedent's business, unless given authority by the court to continue its operation.

■ A representative is personally answerable for the waste (mismanagement), conversion (using the estate assets for oneself), or embezzlement of the assets of an estate.

■ The real estate of the deceased may be sold only if the representative needs the proceeds to pay estate debts.

■ The surviving spouse and minor children are often entitled to an immediate allowance from the estate. There can be no valid final distribution of the estate until all taxes have been paid.

■ Debts that become due after the person has died, such as payments on a stereo bought on the installment plan, are payable from the estate.

■ In many states, laws require that claims against the estate be presented to the personal representative, the probate court, or a court-appointed commissioner. The validity of a claim must be established by the court or by the executor or administrator before payment may be made.

■ Estate debts are paid in order of priority—administration costs and family allowance come first, together with taxes. The order of other claims varies from state to state; check the laws of your state.

■ A representative should retain from a legacy the amount of any debt that the beneficiary owes the estate.

■ Personal representatives are, as a rule, allowed by law to have compensation, the amount of which varies from state to state.

executor or by any interested person, such as a relative or business associate. Once the court finds the will authentic, it usually approves the appointment of the executor named in the document and issues letters testamentary to him. These letters are the formal documents of appointment and authority given to an executor.

If the executor is unable or refuses to serve, the court will appoint an administrator c.t.a. If the court refuses to admit the will to probate because it is false or the person who wrote it was incompetent at the time, the estate is treated as if the person had died intestate, and the court appoints an administrator to handle the estate. *Letters of administration* are the court papers authorizing a person to serve as an administrator of an intestate estate.

■ **Necessity for administration** To preserve the assets of the estate and to protect the rights of creditors and heirs, all property left at the time of a person's death is subject to administration. If a person dies penniless—having no assets but owing no debts—there is no need for administration. When an estate is left and there are no known living heirs, the state usually receives the property under the doctrine of ESCHEAT. Such an estate is not administered unless there are debts to be paid before the state takes its interest.

■ **Nature of proceedings** The administration of a decedent's estate is under the exclusive jurisdiction (authority) of the states and is controlled by state law. The probate court determines whether the facts essential to the administration of an estate exist. For example, it is absolutely necessary that a person be considered legally dead before the court can authorize the administration of his estate. Although this appears to be an obvious point, it is extremely important when dealing with the estates of persons who are missing and presumed dead.

Courts determine whether the person may be legally presumed to be dead. See DEATH. If the person was, in fact, alive when the administration of his estate was granted, many courts will declare the administration void. Statutes may authorize the courts to administer the estate of such a person under a reasonable procedure to protect his property rights if he should turn out to be alive. This procedure, dictated by the concept of DUE PROCESS OF LAW, guarantees that no person shall be deprived of his property without notice and a hearing to defend his rights. Should the deceased later be found to be alive, the court simply returns everything to him.

Probate jurisdiction The place of the decedent's last DOMICILE (legal residence) determines the probate jurisdiction (the state) that will supervise the settlement of his estate. This is known as the *administration-in-chief*. This jurisdiction gives letters testamentary or letters of administration. But these documents do not authorize the representative to administer property outside the state or county of his appointment.

EXAMPLE If a legal resident of New York dies and leaves property there and in Iowa, a separate administration is usually necessary in each state. The administration in New York, the state of domicile, is the *primary* or *domiciliary administration*. The one in Iowa is the *ancillary* (subsidiary) *administration*.

By law, many states permit the domiciliary representative to act also as ancillary administrator. Other states require that the ancillary administrator be a resident, which automatically disqualifies the domiciliary administrator.

The principal purpose of ancillary administration is to insure the payment of the decedent's debts to local creditors. The ancillary administrator collects the decedent's assets, pays the local creditors, and distributes the remainder to the domiciliary representative, who then distributes the estate to the heirs.

■ **Appointment of executors** A testator has the right to name in his will a person who will administer his estate. Many people choose their surviving spouse—he or she is usually familiar with the decedent's financial affairs and family situation. Before you name someone as executor in your will, however, you should ask him (or her) if he will accept the position. This small but practical courtesy may ultimately save time and money for the heirs. If the person named as executor refuses the appointment when the will is brought to probate, the court must appoint another representative. This means a delay in the settlement as well as additional legal fees. It is also a good idea to name an alternate in case the designated executor cannot serve.

Some people name several persons as coexecutors to insure that the estate will be administered fairly. A frequent combination is a family member or close friend who knows the family situation and a professional—an attorney or a TRUST COMPANY—to handle the more complex duties. You may cancel your designation of an executor either by making another will or by writing a CODICIL (a document changing the provisions of a will).

Suitable capabilities Generally, any person who is capable of making a will is held by the court to be competent as an executor. The court will disqualify anyone who is legally incompetent (such as a senile person or a minor) or unsuitable. The probate court usually approves the testator's choice of executor unless the case involves outrageous circumstances—say the executor murdered the testator to gain control of the estate. A person cannot be rejected as an executor merely because he will inherit part of the estate or because he is poor.

EXAMPLE John died owing Jim, his old Army buddy, $2,000. John had designated Jim as executor of his estate. The $2,000 debt does not automatically disqualify Jim from acting as executor. His claim against the estate should be paid off—along with any others—before he distributes the estate to John's heirs.

A corporation with the required charter power may qualify as an executor. This right is usually restricted to corporations of a fiduciary nature, however, such as trust companies or banks.

A person named as executor is free to accept or reject the position. Any acts that show his intention to take the position, such as filing a bond with the court or applying for letters testamentary, are considered an acceptance of the position.

■ **Appointment of administrators** The probate court appoints an administrator when a person has died intestate, that is, without leaving a will. State laws determine who is entitled to be an administrator, and this person must file a petition for the grant of letters of administration. Nonresidence in the state, lack of mental capacity, infancy (being below the legal age of adulthood), and conviction of a crime are among the reasons that would disqualify a person from acting as an administrator.

The law usually grants preference to a surviving husband or wife to be an administrator. The right of a spouse to be an administrator may be given up by an agreement made between the spouses before or during the marriage, and in such a case, the next qualified person under the law will be appointed. An alimony agreement that is made before a divorce becomes final does not bar the right of the surviving spouse to administer the deceased spouse's estate.

When the rights of a surviving spouse are not involved, letters of administration will usually be issued to the next of kin of an intestate. The next of kin is determined by the state laws of descent and distribution, and usually means those relatives—parents, children, brothers and sisters, nieces and nephews, or cousins—whose relationship to the intestate entitle them to share in his estate.

The guardian or trustee of a minor child or other legal incompetent (such as an INSANE PERSON) may qualify as administrator in place of the incompetent. See GUARDIAN AND WARD.

EXAMPLE Three children under the age of six are orphaned
O—※ when their widowed mother is killed in a car crash. She has not left a will. According to the laws of descent and distribution of that state, her children would be considered her next of kin, entitling them to serve as the administrators of her estate. Because of their young age, however, they are disqualified. Their guardian, if legally qualified, may be entitled to be appointed administrator of the mother's estate.

A creditor may be named administrator in cases when the surviving spouse and next of kin fail to apply for appointment or are disqualified. When there is more than one creditor, the selection of an administrator is regulated by statute. The usual determining factors include the different amounts of the creditors' claims and whoever applied first.

Before appointing a person as an administrator the court must inquire into his character, integrity, soundness of judgment, and general capacity.

Public administrators Some statutes provide for the appointment or election of a public administrator, who administers estates when no relatives living within the state are competent or willing to take out letters of administration. He has the same rights, duties, and liabilities as a private administrator.

■ **Requirements for executors and administrators** An executor or administrator generally is required to take an oath, the swearing of which is an acceptance of the office. Informalities in taking the oath, however, are regarded with lenience. A person who takes charge of an estate does not escape liability by failing to take the oath.

The executor must file a BOND with the court for the protection of those interested in the estate. Although many states allow the testator to waive the bond from the executor he names in his will, the court still has the authority to require one. An administrator always must post a bond, even when the decedent's estate is insignificant in value. The amount of the bond is usually determined by the estimated value of the estate. When a bond is filed, the court issues letters testamentary to the executor or letters of administration to the administrator—evidence that the personal representative is an authorized officer of the court.

■ **Duration of authority** The authority of an executor or administrator continues until the estate has been completely administered; until he dies, resigns, or is removed; until his letters are revoked (canceled); or until a temporary order of suspension is made. His authority also ends when a will is declared invalid—but not when a will is contested.

Discharge of representative The court usually has no legal authority to discharge an executor or administrator before the estate is settled. An executor or administrator must apply to the court for discharge after he submits his final accounting to the court. If property belonging to the estate is found after the final accounting and discharge, the court will usually reappoint the representative.

Resignation An executor or administrator has the right to resign but this right is not absolute. The matter is sometimes decided at the discretion of the probate court. A representative who wants to resign should petition the court and notify the interested parties. The court's acceptance of a resignation ends the representative's duties. It has the same effect as a revocation (cancellation) of his letters testamentary or of administration.

Revocation of letters The courts can revoke letters testamentary or of administration when it is found that the letters should never have been issued in the first place—for example, when a will is found naming an executor after an administrator has been appointed or when, under the law, another person should have been appointed. Letters may also be revoked if the personal representative becomes incapacitated or fails to administer the estate properly.

The letters of an executor or administrator may also be revoked on account of mismanagement; wasting assets; disloyalty; improper administration; negligence; failure to file proper inventories, accounts, or tax returns within the required time; failure to comply with a court order to give or increase the amount of a bond; or the representative's becoming bankrupt or insolvent (unable to pay his debts). The representative should be removed when his personal interests conflict with his official duties. If he has a hostile attitude toward the beneficiaries, he may be removed only if it prevents him from properly managing the estate.

Any interested person may ask the court to revoke letters of authority. Before the court may revoke the representative's letters, he is entitled to a hearing, particularly when there are charges of misconduct. The application to revoke may be denied because of practical reasons, as when the estate is ready for a final decree of distribution and the rights of all the parties can be protected in an accounting proceeding (discussed toward the end of this article, under "Accounting and settlement").

■ **General duties** The duties of an executor or administrator are to administer the estate to the best advantage of all concerned and to distribute the assets of the estate as quickly as possible. A person who knows that he has been designated executor in another's will has an obligation to see that it is submitted to probate and to carry out its terms once it has been declared valid.

Delegation of powers A personal representative usually cannot delegate his authority to another person to avoid liability or to escape his obligations.

EXAMPLE A wealthy elderly man named his young wife O⸻❋ executrix of his estate in his will. The probate court approved her appointment. The wife, claiming that she "didn't have a good business head," asked her husband's stockbroker to take charge of the administration of the estate. She told him she would sign any papers or forms he prepared because her husband always had absolute confidence in his integrity. The woman never asked the probate court to approve this arrangement. The stockbroker was, in fact, acting as the executor of the estate, although he had not been appointed by a court. He hated the wife and managed to swindle the estate by getting her to sign the various forms without reading them. Once this situation was discovered, the wife became liable to the other heirs for her gross mismanagement of the estate. The wife abused her duty as an officer of the court by giving her power away without court approval. She failed to fulfill her fiduciary duty to those persons who had an interest in the estate.

A representative is not required to perform every single act needed to carry out his job, however. He may hire skilled professionals, such as accountants or attorneys, to handle any tax problems or litigation that may arise in connection with the administration of the estate. But he must use utmost care in hiring people to help him, and he alone must decide how best to administer the estate.

Supervision An executor or administrator is technically under the supervision of the court until he is discharged. Although the court has the right to see that he performs his duty in accordance with the law and that there is no loss or destruction of the estate, it rarely exercises its supervisory powers.

The representative may apply to the court for guidance when he is unsure about how to proceed. Instructions in matters of administrative judgment are given only if unusual circumstances exist. For example, in one case, a representative consulted the court about the distribution of an estate when the assets included 51 percent of the stock in a corporation that had gone bankrupt just before the death of the decedent.

If there is no doubt about the meaning of a will, the court will not interfere. The court will not (1) take the place of a general legal adviser to the administrator, (2) consider theoretical questions, or (3) give instructions merely because an interested person requests them.

■ **Assets of an estate** The property owned by the decedent makes up the assets of the estate. Generally, the assets administered by an executor or administrator are limited to the real and personal property within the state or county granting administration. If outside assets come into a representative's hands, however, they will be considered part of the estate's assets. Real property includes lands and the buildings on it. Personal property includes cars, bank accounts, furniture, jewelry, and stocks and bonds. Whether a person dies with or without a will, the TITLE to (ownership of) his personal property vests in (passes to) the personal representative, who transfers it to the lawful heir when the administration of the estate is completed. This is the case even if the property—a mink coat, let us say, or a piece of jewelry that a decedent loaned to a friend—was in the possession of a third person at the time of death.

If a person is legally entitled to property but dies before he takes possession, it goes to his executor or administrator. All debts owed to the decedent are treated as assets of the estate, including any that the executor or administrator may personally have owed him.

When a person dies, title to any real property (real estate) he owns immediately vests in those named in his will or in those eligible through descent and distribution. It does not go through the hands of the personal representative unless the property is needed to pay estate debts.

No rents, profits, and income of real estate that were due before the death of the owner are assets in the hands of his personal representative. Those that become due after his death ordinarily are not assets of the estate and go to the person who received title to that property.

The question of whether the proceeds of an insurance policy are assets in the hands of a personal representative is determined largely by the type of policy and the law that applies to it.

Property that a decedent held as a fiduciary (trustee) does not become part of the assets of his estate. See TRUST.

EXAMPLE John was appointed by the court to serve as the O⸻❋ administrator of the estate of his sister Mary, who had died without leaving a will. Shortly thereafter, John died. The property that John held as the administrator of Mary's estate is not an asset in John's estate. But if John shared in Mary's estate under the laws of descent and distribution, his share of Mary's estate would be treated as an asset of his estate.

Obviously, any property that a person has legally transferred, sold, or given away during his lifetime is not part of his estate. If George sold you his car under a valid contract three days before his death, the car is yours and not part of his estate.

A *gift causa mortis* is a GIFT made by someone who anticipates his death from a particular cause and so states to another person. It is effective only when the giver dies from that cause. Such a gift may be retrieved for the decedent's estate only for the payment of his debts or estate taxes.

EXAMPLE Mathilda, on her deathbed, tells Bessie that she O⸻❋ wants her to have her diamond bracelet if "her ticker gives out." She hands the bracelet to Bessie. Five minutes later, Mathilda's ticker gives out. The *gift causa mortis* to Bessie has taken effect. But if Mathilda has not paid any of her bills in the last 12 months and the proceeds from the sale of the bracelet are needed to pay off her debts, the diamond bracelet may be included in Mathilda's estate.

If Mathilda had died three days later from injuries when a fire swept her apartment, Bessie would not be entitled to the bracelet because Mathilda's death was not caused by her bad heart. The diamond bracelet, in this situation, would be treated as an asset of the estate.

Inventory and appraisal One of the first steps a personal representative must take is to learn the extent and value of the decedent's estate. He must track down all the belongings of the decedent. This means going through the safe-deposit box, safe, desk drawers, locked cabinets, closets, and anywhere else he thinks the decedent might have kept his property—even if it means looking in a mattress for hidden valuables. A representative must do a thorough job.

The discovery of any assets after the completed administration will mean additional legal expense. If the omission was clearly the fault of the representative—if he failed to check a desk drawer or a safe—he may be personally charged for the expense of administering the newly discovered property.

An executor or administrator must file with the court an inventory and appraisal of the estate's assets. This serves as the basis for his accounting and liability. The inventory usually itemizes all the property that the decedent owned. It is considered PRIMA FACIE evidence (evidence that establishes the truth, unless it can be disproved or contradicted) of the assets of the estate.

The court also appoints impartial appraisers who place values on the inventory items. These valuations are assumed to be correct. The property should be appraised at its market value at the time the representative received it.

The court has the discretion to dispense with an inventory but only for good cause—as when no assets have come within the representative's possession. A provision in a will saying that an inventory does not have to be filed should be disregarded. Although the failure to file an inventory is a breach of the representative's duty, it does not ordinarily make him liable unless there has been a loss to the estate.

Collection of assets   The personal representative collects all of the assets of the estate. He has the right to sue for debts that are due and to begin lawsuits or settle claims when there is a fair chance that the estate will gain financially. The representative also must substitute himself in all pending legal actions to which the decedent was a party.

EXAMPLE Suppose Jack sued an automobile dealer for 0⟶✳ breach of contract because the dealer had failed to deliver a car with an AM/FM radio and power brakes as specified in the sales contract. Shortly after the lawsuit started, Jack died. Jack's personal representative continues the suit by having himself substituted as a party by the court.

The executor and administrator must recover possession of assets for the payment of debts—such as gifts *causa mortis* or real estate. The representative is entitled to reimburse himself from the assets of the estate for reasonable expenditures—payment for the decedent's funeral, preservation of estate assets, attorney's fees, and other administration costs.

If any debts or assets are not collected, the liability of the personal representative for the loss depends on his conduct. If he acted in good faith without mismanagement of the estate, he is not liable. If the opposite is the case, he is liable for the amounts lost, plus interest.

A representative must file and pay all the federal and state taxes due on the estate. He is responsible for any charges incurred by late filing and payment.

When an estate is insolvent (its debts exceed its assets), the executor or administrator must inform the probate court so that the existing assets may be administered for the benefit of the creditors. They will then be paid according to the prevailing statutes.

■ **Management of the estate**   An executor or administrator must preserve and protect the estate for distribution to the heirs. He should take custody of the assets, books, and papers, and he must keep accounts to make sure the assets are properly handled. Usually, he deposits the funds in a reputable bank, to be withdrawn only to pay estate expenses and later to be distributed to the heirs.

The bank account should be in the representative's name, but with identification that he is the executor or administrator of the estate—"John Thomas, as executor of the estate of Bessie Brown," for example. If the account is in the representative's name only, he is liable for any loss from the disposition of the funds—such as the confusion that might arise if he had two accounts under his name, one for himself and one for the estate. This is true whether or not he was negligent or intended to use the funds as his own.

When a bank is named as executor or administrator, it may deposit the funds with itself, unless a local law states otherwise.

Gifts   The executor or administrator has no right to give away any assets of the estate, regardless of their value. When an unauthorized gift is made, it may be recovered either from the person to whom it was given or from the executor.

EXAMPLE Rose, the executrix of her brother Rex's estate, 0⟶✳ gives her husband Rex's Silver Cloud Rolls-Royce, which is standing idle in the garage. The probate court will demand that Rose return the car to the estate. The court may even hold Rose liable for a breach of her fiduciary duty. Her improper gift shows she is not managing the estate in the best interests of the heirs.

Obligations of the decedent   The personal representative is legally bound to perform impersonal obligations of the decedent, such as the repayment of a loan. Personal property must be sold by the representative to pay estate obligations. This can usually be done without court authority. Real estate generally passes directly to those who inherit it. But the representative may sell land if he is given authority by will or if the personal assets are insufficient to pay the debts and the court orders the sale. When real estate or personal property is sold by court order, the representative usually is required to report the sale to the court.

Personal obligations   A personal representative is not obliged to fulfill personal contracts. If the person whose estate he is administering was a lawyer, for example, he would not have to fulfill the lawyer's commitment to defend a client in a lawsuit. Personal obligations, by their very nature, are terminated by the decedent's death.

Decedent's business   The representative must wind up a decedent's business—unless he is given authority to continue its operation by the court, the will, or the consent of all interested parties. As a general rule, if an executor or administrator carries on the business with the funds of the estate, he is personally liable for all losses incurred and must pay any profits made to the estate. When he is authorized to carry on the business of the decedent, debts incurred may be charged against the estate.

The representative of a deceased partner has no right to continue in partnership business unless authorized to do so by will or a contract of PARTNERSHIP.

Investment and loans   Unless authorized by statute, the will, or the necessities of the situation, an executor or administrator usually cannot invest funds belonging to the estate. As a trustee, he is liable for all losses from unauthorized investments. If an unauthorized investment results in a profit, the beneficiaries may either charge the representative with only the funds used or accept the investment plus the profit.

The representative is bound by provisions in the will that dictate the investments he is to make, even if he doubts their wisdom. Because he must follow these directions, he is protected against liability for the results.

States have various laws governing authorized investments by administrators and executives. Some hold the representative to the "prudent person" standard. If he has exercised prudence in investing the funds, he is not responsible for a loss. He is liable, however, for losses resulting from lack of prudence. For example, an executor invests estate money in municipal bonds that promise 10 percent interest, but there is a 50 percent chance that the municipality will declare bankruptcy any day. In states with the "prudent person" standard, the executor may be liable for jeopardizing the safety of the principal and for any losses.

Some state laws, called *legal list statutes,* say that the representative must put funds in stable investments that produce a moderate amount of income—blue chip stocks, for example. A legal list statute sometimes allows the trustee to invest money outside the list, but he must justify all investments that are not on it.

The representative has no inherent authority to borrow money. Loans to him that are not authorized by the will, a statute, or a court order are not binding on the estate. An executor or administrator who lends estate money without authority is liable for any loss.

Interest on estate funds   Beneficiaries are entitled to interest on estate funds—bank interest from money deposited in an estate account and the interest from approved investments. If the personal representative fails to invest or deposit estate funds to make them income producing within a certain time, he may be charged interest.

A personal representative will not be penalized for depositing estate funds in a bank in which he is financially interested. This is true even when the executor is a bank and deposits the estate moneys with itself.

An unreasonable postponement in settling an estate or a delay that extends beyond the period for settlement allowed by statute may make the representative liable for interest, especially if the delay is the result of his neglect or misconduct. But he is not liable when the delay is caused by prolonged litigation between relatives or by problems in tracing and notifying all the heirs.

An executor or administrator does not have to pay interest on a sum he keeps on hand or on deposit to meet estate expenses.

The representative may be charged interest on estate funds lost through improper or unauthorized investments or disbursements or from failure to collect debts and interest owed to the estate.

The rate of interest depends on the amount the estate funds earned or should have earned. The interest rate paid by banks is frequently considered proper. The time from which an executor or administrator is charged interest depends on the case. When the court orders the representative to pay over certain moneys, interest starts from the date specified in the order. A representative is rarely charged compound interest unless he has acted with willful or gross delinquency.

Expenses   An executor or administrator pays the expenses of administration, such as funeral costs, attorneys' fees, and debts of the estate. If he pays expenses out of his own funds he is entitled to be reimbursed for them.

Self-interest   When the personal interests of an executor or administrator conflict with those of the estate, he is obliged to protect the estate—even to his own loss or disadvantage. He cannot promote interests that are against the benefit of the estate or make a personal profit from his dealings with the property. He should not speculate with estate property for his own benefit, divert the funds into business or investment, for his gain, or sell his own property to the estate.

EXAMPLE   On the morning of the Kentucky Derby, an executor gets a "hot tip" about a horse running in the race. He needs $10,000 in quick cash, but his bank is closed. Fortunately, the bank having the estate account is open, and he withdraws the $10,000 from that account. He plans to replace the money first thing Monday morning when his bank opens. When this unauthorized loan is discovered, the executor can be removed from his position by order of the probate court. He will be made to account to the estate for the original $10,000 "borrowed," and if his horse wins, he will have to pay his winnings to the estate.

When a representative, acting for his own benefit, makes a deal with a third person involving estate assets, the deal may not be canceled if the third person did not know that the representative was using funds that were not his own. But the beneficiaries can sue the representative for breach of his fiduciary duty. On the other hand, a third person who knows that the representative is violating his trusted position will not be protected by the law. The transaction will be set aside by the probate court, and the representative will be liable to the beneficiaries. The law is clear: personal representatives are not allowed to use estate assets for their private advantage.

EXAMPLE   New York resident Mark Rothko, a renowned abstract expressionist painter, died in 1970. In his will he named three coexecutors to handle his estate, the principal assets of which were 798 paintings of tremendous value. One coexecutor was the director, treasurer, and secretary of a corporation that owned two art galleries to which the paintings were sold; another was an artist; and the third was a university professor and friend of Rothko. The 798 paintings were sold at a low price to the art galleries with which the first coexecutor was associated. Rothko's children sued the coexecutors, seeking their removal and damages (money), as well as restitution (the return) of the paintings. The children claimed that the coexecutors breached their fiduciary duties.

The Court of Appeals, New York State's highest court, affirmed the Surrogate Court's original decision that the three executors had committed breaches of trust that justified their removal. Two of the coexecutors were clearly in the position of serving conflicting interests and should have asked the court for guidance or resigned as executors. The first coexecutor, the corporate director of the galleries that bought the paintings, had them appraised "for a fraction of their wholesale value" by a biased appraiser who had previously worked for the galleries. This enabled the executor to make an excellent deal for the galleries and enhance his prestige and status in the art world. The second coexecutor, the artist, approved and signed the contract for the sale of the Rothko paintings because he wanted to get into the good graces of one of the art galleries. Within months after signing the estate contracts, he entered a favorable contract with the gallery for the sale of his own paintings.

The third coexecutor, the professor and friend of Rothko, knew that the other coexecutors were involved in advancing their own personal interests at the expense of the estate. Although he was not actually involved, he knew the other executors were violating their duty, and he failed to take positive action to avert an obvious loss to the estate.

The court ordered that the executors be charged for their breach of duty and that restitution for the paintings be made to the estate. An executor who sells trust property when it is in the best interests of the estate to keep it is financially responsible for appreciation damages—that is, any subsequent rise in the value of the property from the time it was sold up until the time the court decree for damages is issued.

One of the galleries had sold 140 paintings to unsuspecting purchasers. The court did not require these works to be returned, but said the galleries, along with two of the executors, had to pay appreciation damages of $9.3 million. It also ordered that the remaining 658 paintings be returned to the estate.

The third executor, the professor, was held liable only for the actual value of the paintings on their dates of sale ($6.4 million) because he did not have a conflict of interest, nor did he act in his own self-interest. He was guilty only of having negligently performed his duties.

Waste of assets   An executor or administrator is personally answerable for the waste, CONVERSION, or EMBEZZLEMENT of the estate's assets. *Waste* is any mismanagement of the assets. It consists of any act that causes the estate to suffer a loss—for example, investing estate funds in speculative shares of gold mines in Australia; selling estate property for a price lower than can be obtained on the market; failing to deposit estate funds in banks giving the usual rate of interest; paying claims that the representative should have known were illegal.

An executor or administrator may be guilty of *conversion* when he uses the estate assets for himself, has them transferred to his own name, or otherwise disposes of them for an unauthorized purpose. A representative who withdraws $15,000 from estate funds to buy himself a foreign sports car, for example, has converted the estate assets for an unauthorized use. An executor or administrator has committed a conversion when he combines his own or other property with that of the estate—by depositing estate funds in his personal checking account, for example.

The liability of a representative for waste or conversion is usually for the value of the property at the time of the misconduct, plus interest. The beneficiaries may sue the representative personally for waste or conversion and they can sue to have his bond made payable to them. The representative may also be subject to criminal penalties for conversion, embezzlement, and related offenses.

EXAMPLE An attorney, Harry, is serving as an executor of O——* your friend's estate. He embezzles $5,000 from the estate to pay his malpractice insurance premiums and records the $5,000 as payment for legal services to the estate. Harry is liable to the estate for $5,000 plus interest. He can also be prosecuted for embezzlement. He will face disciplinary proceedings by the state or local bar association, which could start court proceedings to disbar him.

Loss or depreciation of assets   A personal representative who acts in good faith is not personally liable for loss caused by theft, war, fire, or the misconduct or negligence of his agents. An executor or administrator who decides to keep property, securities, or other assets instead of selling them is not liable for their loss if he acted properly. Only when a loss or depreciation of assets is caused by the representative's bad faith or lack of due care will he be held personally responsible.

The sale of real estate   The real estate of the decedent may be sold only if the representative needs the proceeds to pay the estate debts. Such a sale is also permitted if the will, a court order, or a statute authorizes it. An unauthorized sale is not binding, but if the beneficiaries approve a sale they cannot later claim it was invalid.

The power of an executor to sell real estate is *discretionary* when the will allows the executor freedom to sell the property if he believes it to be in the best interests of the estate. A power of sale is *mandatory* when the will imposes upon the executor an absolute duty to sell. A power of sale usually does not include the right to exchange the property for other property.

A person who buys real estate from an executor under a testamentary power of sale takes all the interest and title (ownership) the testator had in the property, free of any claims of beneficiaries and creditors. In some instances, however, a sale of realty by the executor under a power conferred by the will may be set aside.

EXAMPLE An executor, Bill, is given the power in a will to O——* sell Jim's summer home. The house is deemed worth $65,000 because similar houses in the area have sold for that amount. Bill, however, sells the house to his own real estate firm for $35,000. The sale is set aside by the probate court because Bill apparently took unfair advantage of his position of trust. He served his own interests and those of his firm at the expense of the beneficiaries of Jim's estate.

Lease and mortgage of real estate   An executor or administrator has no authority to lease or mortgage the decedent's realty, unless he is so instructed by the will, a statutory provision, or a court order. When authorized, real estate leases should be for short terms, but the heirs may subsequently approve a lease for an unauthorized term. Should the estate be settled before the lease expires, the lease does not end.

Personal property   The legal title to (ownership of) the personal property of the decedent usually vests in (passes to) his representative. In most cases, he takes title only as a trustee for the benefit of the heirs and creditors. His hold on the property is regarded as the possession of the court. He acquires only such title as the decedent had at the time of his death, subject to any and all valid LIENS. For example, at the time of Alan's death, Alan still owed $2,000 on a loan for which he put up his late-model foreign sports car as collateral. The representative of Alan's estate takes the car subject to this $2,000 lien.

When it is necessary to raise money to pay estate debts, a representative usually may sell the personal property as he sees fit, but in some states he may need a court order to do so. When a power of sale is given to an executor by the will, a court order is not required. If an executor or administrator must sell or dispose of personal property, he must seek the best price. Only a gross inadequacy in price, however, is a sufficient ground for invalidating a sale.

Anyone may buy the property of the estate, even the representative himself if he pays full value.

The liability of a representative selling personal property depends on whether he acted with good faith, due diligence, and sound judgment. If he acted improperly and the sale is not invalidated, he will be charged with the amount by which the value of the property exceeded the sale price.

■ **Family allowance** The surviving spouse and minor children are often entitled to an allowance for their support from the estate immediately upon the spouse's death. Some laws limit family allowance only to those in need.

In fixing the amount of the allowance given to a widow, various factors are considered—her usual standard of living, her private worth, and the size of her husband's estate. When the value of the estate is less than a certain amount, the whole estate is sometimes set aside for the widow or minor children. A widow is often entitled to specific articles, such as household furniture or clothes, which become hers absolutely and are not included as part of her share of the estate. These items are known as *personal exemptions*.

If no widow survives, the allowance usually goes to the dependent children who lived with the decedent. For example, a married 17-year-old daughter usually would not be entitled to the allowance, because her husband has the legal duty of supporting her. Some states exclude stepchildren from the allowance, while others include illegitimate children. A surviving husband may be entitled to an allowance from his wife's estate under some laws.

Usually the family allowance is an administration expense. As a *preferred claim* against the estate, it will be paid to the family ahead of any creditors.

■ **Taxes** There can be no valid final distribution of an estate until all of the taxes against it have been paid. The personal representative must see that federal estate taxes are filed and paid within nine months after the person's death, unless an extension of time has been granted by the Internal Revenue Service. Estate taxes—and indeed all taxes—are considered preferred claims and must be paid before other creditors. The representative may be held liable if he fails to pay estate taxes. If the estate has already been distributed to the heirs, the Internal Revenue Service may seek payment from the beneficiaries. But each is liable only to the extent of his inherited share of the estate. If this happens, the beneficiaries may sue the representative for failure to perform his duties. See ESTATE AND GIFT TAX for a full discussion of federal estate taxes.

The Tax Reform Act of 1976 requires the representative to provide both the heir and the Internal Revenue Service with written information on the value of each inherited asset. This information is called the *carryover basis*, and it is needed to calculate the capital gains tax if the heir sells the assets. If an executor or administrator fails to submit the information to the heir or to the Internal Revenue Service, he may be penalized for each failure.

The representative is also responsible for the final federal income tax return of the decedent, due by April 15 of the year following his death. Generally, the executor or administrator will file a joint return for the decedent and surviving spouse. If no representative has been appointed by the time the return is due, the surviving spouse alone may file it. The representative should also pay assessed taxes that have become a LIEN (a legal claim) on the decedent's real estate before his death.

■ **Claims** Before the estate is distributed to the heirs, the executor must settle all debts and other claims against it. A claim against the estate of a deceased person must be based on some valid obligation, but the obligation need not have been put in writing.

EXAMPLE A painter spent one week painting the outside of
O—* John Jones's house. Everyone in the neighborhood admired the job. Two weeks after the job was completed, John Jones was killed. The painter, who had not yet been paid, became a creditor of Jones's estate. Although he did not have a written contract with Jones, he still had a legally enforceable claim against the estate for the value of his services.

EXAMPLE Suppose, on the other hand, that after Jones's
O—* obituary appeared in the local paper, Roberto Thomas came forward and claimed that he and Jones had verbally agreed that Jones would pay Thomas $50 per hour for boxing lessons every Saturday morning. Thomas claimed that Jones had taken five lessons before his untimely death and that Jones did not pay for those lessons. Thomas submitted a $250 claim against the estate as a creditor. Everyone who knew Jones was flabbergasted at Thomas's claim because Jones's dislike of fighting was well known. In addition, at the time the supposed lessons took place, Jones was umpiring weekly Little League baseball games. Clearly, Thomas's claim against the estate was not legally enforceable.

If the claim is for services that were performed voluntarily and for free, compensation will not be allowed from the decedent's estate.

EXAMPLE Suppose you have a wealthy great-aunt Lolly,
O—* whose house you offer to clean once a week, in the hope of inheriting her fortune. You do Lolly's housekeeping chores for five years before she dies. Lolly leaves her $1.8 million to her male nurse. You cannot make a claim against the estate, because you had freely offered your services to her.

The courts usually presume that services by members of a family to each other were given freely and voluntarily. Therefore, to establish claims made by relatives for personal services to the decedent stronger proof is needed than for claims by strangers. This presumption may be disproved by evidence that shows payment was intended, as when there was a contract.

EXAMPLE Sam's son-in-law, Mark, spends his weekends
O—* helping Sam build a backyard patio. The job is completed in a month. Shortly thereafter, Sam dies. Mark brings a claim of $1,500 against Sam's estate for his

services in building the patio. Unless he can clearly show that there was a specific or implied contract for those services, Mark will not be paid from the estate. In some states, however, Mark may be entitled to be paid as long as he and Sam did not live in the same house.

Loans or advances to a decedent can be recovered from the estate if a debtor and creditor relationship had existed and if the decedent had a legal obligation to make repayment, enforceable by a court.

Fixed claims that become due in the future are payable from the estate if the amount owed can be determined. For instance, Marilyn buys a color television on an installment plan with 12 monthly payments of $50. After she makes her sixth payment, Marilyn dies. A claim for the remaining installments is recoverable from Marilyn's estate.

There is no obligation for the executor or administrator to pay claims that are barred because the statutes of limitations (legal time limits) ran out or the doctrine of LACHES (unreasonable delays) was applied before the death of the decedent. See LIMITATIONS OF ACTIONS.

Presentation of claims   In many states, specific laws require that claims against the estate be presented to the personal representative, the probate court, or a commissioner appointed by the court to examine all claims. Usually, the presentation should be within a specified time after the death of the person, the appointment of a personal representative, or the publication of a notice calling for claims. Some laws require that the claim be in writing. Generally, even when a representative knows about a claim against the estate, a presentation is still required. Presentation laws usually apply only to those claims that existed during the decedent's lifetime—not to claims, such as funeral expenses, that come into existence following his death.

A secured creditor (one who holds a mortgage or a lien) usually need not present his claim in order to preserve his right to the property. The claim of a secured creditor is the right to specific property that has been set aside for payment of the debt (collateral). This property does not belong to the estate unless its value is greater than the debt owed.

The presentation of a claim against the estate is a demand for payment. Failure to present a claim on time may have one of the following consequences: (1) the representative may be relieved from liability, and the creditor will have to try to get his money from the heirs if the law allows him to do so; (2) the claim may not be paid until presented debts are paid; or (3) the claim may be barred against both the estate and the heirs.

Once a claim is filed and presented, its validity must be established by the court or the representative before payment may be made.

Priorities and payment   One of the most important duties of the personal representative is the payment of debts against the estate in their order of priority. Before he can do this, however, he must remember that administration expenses, such as a family allowance, are given priority. Federal law also provides that debts due the government, such as income and estate taxes, must be paid before any other debts of the decedent. Funeral costs and expenses incurred in the course of the administration of the estate are not considered debts.

An executor or administrator must then look to state law to determine in what order he should pay off the claims. Ordinarily, he must pay claims as speedily as possible. The failure to pay may make him personally liable to the creditor; if he honors an improper claim he may not charge it to the estate. Executors and administrators are generally required to reserve a portion of the assets to pay contingent claims, pending lawsuits, or claims that have not yet come due. Payments to creditors that were made improperly or through mistake of fact are usually recoverable.

■ **Accounting and settlement**   A personal representative's account is a brief statement of the conduct of the administration, with the receipts and expenditures of the estate itemized. *Settlement* means the adjustment of claims in favor of and against the estate but does not include the distribution of the estate. The purpose of an accounting is for the probate court to evaluate the type of job the representative is doing as well as to insure equality in the distribution of the estate's assets.

The representative must file a first account within a certain time from the date of his appointment. Thereafter, he gives accounts at stated intervals, and upon completion of the settlement, he must present a final account and settlement. The legal penalties for a representative's failure to supply accounts include suing on the personal representative's bond (to make it payable to the estate and ultimately the beneficiaries) and revoking his letters testamentary or letters of administration.

An executor or administrator must account for all the assets, debts, and expenses of the decedent's estate. The inventory of the estate, which the representative must make, is the basis for the accounting. It is not, however, conclusive concerning the assets for which he is accountable or for their value. He may be required to account for assets that he did not inventory or credit—if $25,000 worth of diamonds are discovered hidden in the decedent's mattress three months after the representative has filed his inventory, he is still accountable for them.

Upon final settlement of the estate, the court then gives a decree of final distribution for the persons entitled to share under the terms of the will or, if there is no will, under the laws of descent and distribution. The decree of final distribution is a JUDGMENT. It is conclusive and binding—on the legatees (heirs of personal property), devisees (heirs of real property), and other heirs—and is subject only to appeal or relief for fraud.

■ **Distribution of the estate**   The distribution of the estate should take place as soon as practicable, unless a particular method of paying an heir is expressly stated in the will or by law. A *specific legacy* is a gift by will of a particular thing, such as a dog, a piece of furniture, or a painting. A *money legacy* or *bequest* should be paid in cash. A distribution in kind is generally authorized when the parties involved do not insist on converting the property into money.

EXAMPLE   Bob is left $25,000 in John's will. The assets of
O↖—⁎   John's estate include not only $15,000 in cash but also shares of IBM stock worth $400,000 and a home worth $85,000. John's executor makes a distribution in kind of shares of IBM stock worth $25,000 after Bob consents to it.

An executor or administrator should retain from a legacy the amount of any debt that the heir may owe the estate. The indebtedness must be either admitted by the heir or determined by the court. This is known as the *right of retainer.*

Payment of a legacy (from a will) or distributive share (from the estate of a person who died without a will) should be made to the person entitled to it or to his authorized representative, unless he or the court orders that payment be made to a third person. Generally, the share of a minor should be paid to his properly qualified guardian or, if there is none, into the court. The legacy or distributive share of a person who has been declared insane by a court is paid to the committee (guardian) of his property.

The share of a deceased person is generally payable to his executor or administrator. If a legatee or distributee is unknown, or is absent and not heard from, his share should be invested or paid into the court for the benefit of whoever may later claim a legal right to it. Sometimes this rule also applies to an heir who lives in a foreign country.

Effect of distribution Unless there is fraud or a mistake, a payment or distribution properly made is binding on the representative. It is also binding on the heir who accepts it and it gives him complete title to (ownership of) the property he has received. Following distribution, the representative is entitled to a discharge, whereby his authority is terminated. Generally, he is released from liability to heirs and creditors.

A personal representative who pays assets to the wrong person or forgets someone entitled to share may be held liable for the amount wrongfully given out. He may be compelled to pay the rightful person from his own funds. A payment is usually not wrongful, however, if it is made in good faith under a will that is later declared invalid. If an administrator of an intestate estate pays the distributees before receiving the authorization of the probate court, he does so at his own peril because these payments, although not favored by the court, are usually considered legal. If he pays out more than the estate is worth, he may not be reimbursed.

A beneficiary is liable to refund any amount that has been overpaid, under a mistake of fact, on his share.

EXAMPLE Let us say that there are two cousins named James Barker. The middle initial of one is S, the other's is F. It would be a mistake in fact if the representative paid a larger share meant for James S. to James F. The liability of James F. may be enforced by the personal representative or, if he refuses to act, by a proceeding brought in probate court by the other beneficiaries.

When a decree of distribution is reversed by a court, the representative can recover all the property, or its value, that was distributed.

An executor or administrator may be held liable for any loss that occurs through his unreasonable delay or failure to make payment—unless he is excused by the court. When he unreasonably holds the amount of a legacy without a good reason, he is usually held liable to the heir for the amount plus interest, from the date when the payment should have been made.

■ **Compensation** Personal representatives are, as a rule, allowed by law to have compensation for performing their services. In some cases, the decedent has specifically allocated in his will the amount that the executor should receive. Commissions are the most common form of compensation. Laws about the computation of commissions differ from state to state. Extra or special compensation is sometimes allowed when the administration of the estate has imposed unusual burdens on the representative—if he was a lawyer and had to defend the estate in numerous lawsuits brought by relatives, for example, or if he continued to run the decedent's business. In general, probate fees are expensive. They are imposed as a percentage of the value of the estate, thus reducing its worth. See Chart 18.

executory Something that is yet to be performed or carried into effect. For example, a CONTRACT is executory until all its terms are completed.

exemplary damages DAMAGES awarded to the plaintiff in a lawsuit over and above the compensation for his personal injury or property loss—when the wrong done to him was aggravated by the defendant's violence, malice, or fraud. Also known as *punitive damages,* they are designed to punish the defendant for his bad behavior or make an example of him.

exemplification A copy or transcript of a document, such as a death certificate, taken from public records and authenticated by the seal of the official who has custody of the original.

exemption A right given to a debtor to keep a portion of his property even though it is legally subject to seizure and sale for the payment of his debts in the EXECUTION of a JUDGMENT rendered in a lawsuit.

EXAMPLE Let us say you lent an old friend $2,500 and when the time came for him to pay you according to your agreement, he refused. He claimed he had fallen on hard times. He was in danger of losing his job because his company was moving out of town, his wife was recovering from an operation, and his three children all needed braces on their teeth. Since lending him the $2,500, you have learned he was given to exaggeration about his pitiful financial condition. You sue him and get a judgment for the $2,500. He still refuses to pay. Along with the judgment comes the right of execution—that is the right to have the sheriff seize your former friend's property, which if sold, might bring $2,500. If your friend still does not pay up, the property can be auctioned and $2,500 of the proceeds used to pay you. But your friend has certain rights. One of these is the right to keep certain kinds of property from the sheriff—even if this property is all he owns and its sales would be your only means of recovering your money. This is the right of exemption.

The right of exemption rests entirely on provisions created by law; therefore, the types of property that can be claimed as exemptions vary from state to state. The types of property that are most commonly exempted include the debtor's home, food, household goods, and furniture. (These exemptions are not related to tax exemptions, which are discussed under INCOME TAX.) Exemption laws are designed to protect the family, not creditors. Their purpose is to insure that the unfortunate debtor has the means to support himself and his family. This article discusses under what circumstances a person is entitled to an exemption and what types of property are exempt.

■ **Who is entitled**   State exemption laws apply to anyone in the state who has a judgment and execution against him and who comes within the terms of the statutes that create the specific exemptions. Many states, for example, require a person to be a resident of the state and/or the head of a family to claim an exemption. Under such a law, any state resident or any head of a family may claim the exemptions allowed by that law if he is sued and a judgment and writ of execution are handed down against him. A person whose assets are about to be seized should consult his state laws to see if he is entitled to an exemption.

Residence requirements   When the statute expressly requires residence, nonresidents—even those living temporarily in the state—cannot claim its benefit. But when residence is required, the person need not have been a resident at the time he incurred the debt. He need only be a resident at the time the levy (seizure) is made on the property.

EXAMPLE   In the above example, your friend—let's call him O⊷✶ Harry—would qualify because he is a resident of your state and you obtained the judgment in your state. Even if his company had sent him to another state for a year of training, he would still be a resident of your state and entitled to an exemption.

A person who moves into the state with his family and personal property is considered a resident under the exemption laws even before he finds a permanent home. He becomes a resident as soon as he enters the state with the intention of making it his home. When residence is necessary, a debtor loses his benefit of the exemption laws by running away or moving from the state. None of the property he leaves behind is exempt.

Moving from place to place within the state does not affect the debtor's claim to exemptions, nor, generally, does a temporary absence from the state, of whatever duration. As long as the debtor maintains his residence and intends to return to the state, he is entitled to his exemption.

Who is entitled to an exemption depends on what the statute says. Usually statutes say resident, head of household, wage earner, or some combination of these. Statutes do not include or exclude married or unmarried persons. To claim an exemption, you must come within a category defined by a particular statute. States may have different statutes covering different types of debtors.

Family exemptions   Laws giving exemptions "for the use of a family" or "to a family member," are intended only for the benefit of debtors who have families. A family means two or more persons who live together in one home and whose relationship is a permanent and domestic one. One person alone does not constitute a family—that is, the debtor himself cannot be the family. A group that lives together temporarily for convenience and to whom the debtor has no obligations of financial support—such as roommates who share the household expenses—is not a family. Neither is a group bound together by a contractual relationship, such as a rooming house landlady and her boarders—even though they are related.

Head of family   Some laws limit family exemptions "to the head of a family." The head must have a legal or moral obligation to support the other members, who are dependent on him. The head-of-the-family exemption does not require that the members live in the same house.

Rulings concerning separated couples vary as to who is head of the house. Some courts have held that if a wife has custody of the children but the husband-debtor supports them, he retains his head-of-the-family exemption.

When a statute specifically gives the exemption "to the family," a divorced husband who does not have custody of his children and lives as a single man is not entitled to the exemption from execution of a judgment against him, even if he contributes to his family's support. A debtor who has deserted his family and contributes nothing to its support forfeits his right to an exemption.

Unmarried persons   An unmarried person who has no dependents is not the head of a family, although he may keep a house and servants. But an unmarried person who has children or relatives who live with him and are dependent on him for support may be the head of a family. An unmarried debtor who contributes to the support of relatives not living with him is not the head of the family, the courts have held.

■ **Property that is exempt**   The property that a debtor may claim as exempt is determined by state law. Generally, these exemption laws limit the value of the property a debtor may exempt to a certain sum. They may also restrict the number of articles the debtor may claim. If the value of all the debtor's property does not exceed the amount of the exemption allowed, nothing may be seized or sold.

The debtor must have title to (legally own) the property he claims as exempt. If he sells his property he loses his right to claim it, of course, but if he has contracted to sell or exchange it but has not yet actually done so, he may claim it as exempt. If he broke the contract, he could be sued by the other party to the contract; but if he went through with the sale, the creditor would take the money he got from the sale (unless that money was exempt for some reason).

Most states have passed homestead laws that exempt the debtor's home from seizure. These laws are based on the theory that preservation of the homestead (the family residence and the land on which it is situated) is of greater importance than the payment of debts. These laws allow the exemption up to a certain dollar value or a certain size of the property or both.

Individual state laws may exempt real property, personal property, or both. *Real property* is property that is generally referred to as real estate (land and whatever is attached to it, including houses and other structures); *personal property* is any property that is not real property, including money. When the law refers only to "property," the debtor may select either real or personal property for exemption from seizure. He may choose to claim his entire exemption from real property, even though he owns personal property. When the law exempts personal property only, however, a debtor cannot claim real property, but he can usually select which personal property he wants exempt, such as wages or income from a TRUST.

Personal property ordinarily includes even property that is not yet in the debtor's possession, such as money due to be received from an insurance policy, a debt due from another person, or a judgment in favor of the debtor. An heir under a will may claim his exemption out of his share of the property left to him.

EXAMPLE Horace borrowed $15,000 (including interest) O—* from Benevolent Finance Company to be paid back in monthly installments. After Horace paid back only $5,000 of the loan, his mother became seriously ill and he was forced to quit his job to take care of her. Unfortunately, Horace had no property except for a few hundred dollars for food and rent, and he was unable to keep up his loan payments. Benevolent sued him and won a judgment against him for $10,000. During the trial Horace's mother died, leaving him $2,000 in her will and a $5,000 life insurance benefit. Although Horace did not yet have the $7,000 in hand, it was subject to seizure under the judgment. However, the state Horace lived in allowed him an exemption of $6,000 in personal property. Consequently, Horace could keep the $6,000 of the money due from the insurance company and under the will, and the finance company could lay claim to only $1,000 of that money.

Exemption laws usually list specific items. They are often based on a rural life-style, and many are illogical. Some laws have limits regarding the value of the property claimed as an exemption, but most simply list items.

Food   Only the food and provisions necessary to sustain the debtor and his family are exempt. This does not include provisions for servants and other hired help, food prepared by a restaurant owner for his customers, or provisions for sale in a debtor's store. If the debtor owns livestock he may be allowed an exemption for food for the livestock only if there is a specific provision for it in the law, and then only those crops that are suitable for fodder or were planted for that purpose are exempt. The fact that the animals may be exempt does not automatically exempt the fodder.

Household goods   Household goods and furniture are usually exempt by laws liberally interpreted in favor of the debtor. The exemption is ordinarily limited to necessary articles, but they may include what is needed for comfort and convenience. The fact that a household item, such as a rug, is also ornamental does not exclude it from being exempt where one rug is allowed an exemption. Nor does the furniture have to be in actual use at the time of the seizure under a statute that exempts furniture. It is exempt if it is stored and the debtor intends to use it again. Household furniture does not include furniture in the debtor's shop or office or in an apartment that the debtor has sublet to a tenant. Property may be exempt as household furniture even though the debtor is living alone.

Beds, bedding, and cooking stoves may be exempt as household furniture. A "family library" that includes all the books used by the family may be exempt by law. The following, however, have been held not to be exempt: a television set, a rifle, a cabinet box, and an automobile not in use and kept on the debtor's driveway. Most states do allow an exemption for the family auto if it is not worth more than a certain amount.

Professional library or instruments   The library or instruments of a professional are exempt in several states.

As with any exemption statute that sets a ceiling on the value of an exemption, only books and instruments within the legal limit are exempt. The profession in which the instruments are used need not be the debtor's only occupation. Some examples of items that have been exempt are a minister's gospel books, surgical instruments, a lawyer's law library, and a music teacher's musical instruments.

Wages, salary, and earnings   Wages and salary (payment for personal services) are exempt under some laws. They are distinguished from the profits made in running a business or other commercial dealings, returns from investments of capital, or from the labor of others.

The earning of wages or salary implies an employer-employee relationship. Generally, only wages earned for manual labor are exempt, but some states exempt the wages and salary of both manual workers and those whose service calls for special skill or intellectual training, such as a stenographer or an architect.

For commissions to be exempt there must be an employer-employee relationship. For example, renewal commissions due a life insurance salesman as payments for personal services given to his company are exempt as wages and salary. But commissions earned by an independent broker or sales agent are not.

The compensation of an independent contractor who is not an employee is not exempt as wages.

EXAMPLE A salesman, Hank, sold oil-field tanks for State O—* Oil Company on a commission basis. He sent orders to State Oil, which sent him his commission. State Oil did not tell the salesman where to work or whom to see. In this case, the court held that the salesman was not a corporate agent or employee but an independent contractor whose commissions were not exempt.

A number of states allow exemptions for earnings. The term "earnings" is broader than the terms "wages" and "salary." Earnings are the reward of labor or the price for professional services and include the earnings of artists, photographers, professionals, and those selling independently on commission.

Under some statutes, the exemption of wages, salary, or earnings is restricted to the amount needed for the debtor's family or sometimes for the debtor himself. What is necessary under such a statute may depend on the circumstances of the family and the discretion of the court. If all the debtor's earnings are required, he may hold all of them. These laws give the debtor a fair chance to remain productive and to protect his family from want. See ATTACHMENT AND GARNISHMENT; Chart 9.

Property used by tradesmen and businessmen   Some states give persons engaged in certain trades and businesses exemptions for property they use in their work. Seizure in these cases would prevent the debtor from gaining a livelihood. Some courts restrict the meaning of the word "trade" to mechanical pursuits. Others take it to be the same as occupation, employment, or business. It has been held to include the occupation of baker, carpenter, insurance agent, school bus operator, or motion picture theater owner-operator. But most courts exclude the professions, such as medicine, dentistry, and optometry.

When the term "mechanic" is used in such laws, it usually includes persons who work with tools and machines. Again, persons engaged in the professions are not mechanics. Nor are those in occupations such as writing, photography, and architectural drafting. Owners of factories and machinery are not mechanics, except when the owner himself works with the machinery or tools. A debtor loses his right to claim an occupational exemption if he permanently abandons the trade or business. A temporary suspension of work in order to move from one location to another, however, is not considered abandonment.

■ **Making a claim** To have the benefit of an exemption, a debtor must claim his right to keep an exempt item. If, however, the debtor has no property except what is exempt by law, it may not be necessary to make a claim.

The laws usually require the exemption claim be made within a specified time after the notice of the execution is sent to the debtor or the property is seized by the sheriff. If there is no express provision, the time period is decided by the courts.

If the debtor does not make his claim in the manner set by law, it is the same as not making a claim at all. The claim often must be made in writing, but under some laws an oral demand is sufficient. Whether it is written or oral, the claim should enable the court to determine whether the property seized is exempt.

Property list A schedule (list) of the property claimed as exempt must be made by the debtor when required by statute. It should enable the appraisers to identify each article and fix its value. When the debtor owns only money and the exemption claim is for the full amount, a sworn statement that the sum is all of the claimant's property is a sufficient inventory.

Appraisal Under some statutes, property claimed as exempt must be appraised at its fair market value—the price upon which a willing seller and buyer might agree. Appraisal establishes whether the property has greater or less value than the allowable exemption. If the law requires appraisal, the debtor must hold the property in readiness for it. An appraisal is not required when the debtor takes his exemption in money or wages.

The duty of having the property appraised belongs to the sheriff, who must insure that the appraisers are legally appointed. They should not be appointed by the debtor. The appraisal should be made in public, and the debtor, creditor, and their attorneys are entitled to be present.

exequatur A certificate issued by the foreign department of a country to a consul or commercial agent of another country. It recognizes the official character of the consul or agent and authorizes him to fulfill his duties.

exhaustion of remedies The taking of all reasonable steps to settle a dispute through a PUBLIC ADMINISTRATIVE AGENCY, when possible, before taking the problem to court. Whenever a dispute has an administrative remedy, a person must exhaust all such remedies before applying to the court.

EXAMPLE Suppose your income-tax return is audited by the Internal Revenue Service, and the examiner disagrees with one of your deductions. If you wish to appeal his decision, you take it first to the District Conference Staff of the Internal Revenue Service. If you do not agree

with their decision, you must then appeal to the Appellate Division in the office of the Regional Commissioner. If after a hearing with the Regional Commissioner's office you are still in disagreement, you may then appeal to the U.S. Tax Court. The court receives your appeal because you have legitimately exhausted your remedies.

exhibit An object or document shown and offered as evidence to a court during a trial or hearing, to a commissioner taking depositions, to an auditor, or to an arbitrator. When accepted, the exhibit is marked for identification and made part of the case.

EXAMPLE You break your tooth on a piece of steel mixed in the hamburger you ordered in a restaurant. You sue the restaurant owner. Both the piece of steel and the remains of your broken tooth would be offered in court as exhibits in your lawsuit.

ex officio (Latin) "From office"; by virtue of office; officially. The term describes the authority derived from an office. The authority is not expressly conferred on the person in office but is instead attached to the official position. For example, a judge has *ex officio* the powers of conservator (preserver) of the public peace. *Ex officio* also refers to an act done in an official capacity or as a result of the office—without any other authority than that given by the office itself.

exoneration 1 The removal of a burden, charge, or duty. For instance, land acquired from a state by the federal government for building a post office is said to be "exonerated" from all state taxes. 2 In criminal law, an acquittal or pardon of a crime.

ex parte (Latin) "On behalf." *Ex parte* implies the presence of one of the parties and the absence of the other. For example, an *ex parte* order is often made in a divorce action when the husband or wife who is being sued for divorce fails to appear to contest the suit. The term is also used to describe proceedings in which there is no adverse party, such as a citizenship naturalization proceeding. When the term is used in the heading of a reported case, such as *"Ex parte* Smith," Smith is the party who has brought the case to be heard.

expectancy Something that is only hoped for. For example, an inheritance under a will is an expectancy because the person who made the will might change his mind and leave his property to another person. Expectancy also refers to the interest of a beneficiary in a life insurance policy when the insured person reserves the right to change the beneficiary or when the policy requires the beneficiary to outlive the insured.

expert witness A person who is skilled in a science, profession, art, trade, or other specialized activity and who appears in court to explain and testify about matters relating to his expertise. See EVIDENCE.

explosive A substance that blows up upon rapid decomposition or combustion. This explosion may result in substantial personal injury or property damage. Gasoline, oil, dynamite, and nitroglycerin are common types of explosives. The regulation of the manufacture, sale, and use of explosives and the liabilities for injuries and damages that result from them are discussed here.

■ **Regulations for safety** Laws that regulate explosives are intended to minimize the dangers to persons and property that might result from their improper handling. The laws governing the storing, handling, transporting, and use of inflammable and explosive substances are enacted under the POLICE POWER of the states and municipalities—that is, their authority to protect the health, safety, and general welfare of the public. For example, the regulation of the use and sale of fireworks in a city is a legitimate exercise of its police power. The state legislature also may require that a person or business obtain a permit to detonate blasting explosives, and it may strictly control the distribution and sale of gasoline.

Suppose you want to uproot some tree stumps with dynamite that you keep in a wooden shed on your property. Are you allowed to keep the explosives on your land? May you use dynamite to blast the stumps? It depends on local laws. Check with your local government—there may be laws against your plan. There are almost certainly rules and regulations that you must observe.

Municipalities are usually given the power by state legislatures to protect themselves against the hazards of explosion and fire arising from the storage of all explosive or combustible materials. Laws may require that explosives and their storage places be inspected. Ordinances may limit the maximum amounts of gunpowder, dynamite, nitroglycerin, gasoline, or other explosive material that may be stored in one place or transported in one vehicle. Storage tanks for kerosene and gasoline are usually required to be underground.

■ **Civil liability** A person who suffers injuries or property damage from an accident involving explosives may be able to bring a TORT action—a lawsuit for injury to person or property. The suit must be based on either a NUISANCE claim or on the existence of negligence. An example of a nuisance claim is when a restaurant owner is deprived of the use of his property because the recently built dynamite plant next door threatens the lives of his customers. Negligence occurs, for example, when a manufacturer does not tell a truck driver that his cargo is nitroglycerin.

To prove that the defendant was negligent, the injured party must show that his injuries and losses were proximately (directly) caused by the defendant's failure to observe standards of care and safety. See PROXIMATE CAUSE. The more dangerous the explosive, the greater the standard of care. For example, a person handling nitroglycerin will be held to a higher standard of care than a person handling gasoline—nitroglycerin is a more highly volatile explosive. If a law or an ordinance regulating the handling or storing of explosives was violated and the alleged action resulted in an injury, the breaking of the law may itself be considered negligence and the grounds for a lawsuit.

Manufacture A maker or seller of an article that is dangerous to human life is liable (financially responsible) to any innocent person who suffers an injury as a direct result of negligence in its manufacture or sale. When the manufacture of an explosive constitutes a nuisance, anyone injured can recover damages (money) without having to show negligence. This would be the case if the restaurant owner mentioned above sustained a broken arm when one wing of the neighborhood dynamite plant exploded. In all other instances, a person injured in an accident involving explosives must show that the manufacturer was negligent before damages will be awarded.

Storage A person who stores gunpowder, nitroglycerin, dynamite, or other explosives under circumstances that make him guilty of maintaining a nuisance is liable for all damages resulting from their exploding, whether or not he was negligent.

EXAMPLE Suppose Max keeps a large amount of nitroglycerin in his apartment. He has warned his next-door neighbor, a drummer in a rock band, not to practice at home because the slightest vibration might set off the nitroglycerin. Max is creating a nuisance, which is interfering with the drummer's use and enjoyment of his property. If there is an explosion, Max will be liable for any damages.

When storing explosives is not a nuisance or a violation of the law, there is no automatic liability for damages resulting from an explosion. If the person failed to maintain the required standard of care, however, he will be held liable. A person who stores explosives must use the utmost caution and highest degree of care, particularly when children have access to the storage place. Anyone who leaves dynamite caps in an unlocked, abandoned shed within 300 feet of a school, for example, is negligent. He will be responsible for any injuries resulting from his careless conduct. Because disastrous results from negligence in the care of dangerous explosives may be anticipated, the courts will usually hold an owner responsible for his failure to exercise care.

Sale A person who sells explosives is liable for injuries resulting from his negligence. A manufacturer-seller can be held to a higher degree of care than a dealer because he knows the formula by which a compound is made and therefore the nature of the danger. If the article is not inherently dangerous, the manufacturer and the dealer will be held to the same standard of care.

The seller of an explosive substance must notify the purchaser of its dangerous character, by label or otherwise, or he will be liable for any resulting injuries.

EXAMPLE Clint at the gas station sells you gasoline in a container labeled "kerosene for outdoor lamps." You go home, pour it into your lamp and light it. The resulting explosion burns both arms badly. Clint is liable for your injuries. You used the substance according to the instructions on the label and were hurt as a result.

Similarly, a person who sells an explosive or highly flammable stove polish with no warning on the label is liable for any injuries resulting from his negligence.

Use A person whose business requires the use of explosives must exercise the highest degree of care and utmost caution. Since blasting is usually considered intrinsically dangerous, a person lawfully engaged in it is responsible for damage caused by the explosions themselves and their vibrations, whether or not he has been negligent. This is known as the rule of *absolute liability,* or STRICT LIABILITY.

EXAMPLE In one case, XYZ company was enlarging a river channel, which required considerable blasting with dynamite. Vibrations broke many water and heating pipes and caused other damage in a hotel 230 feet away. The court applied the rule of strict liability. Because the blasting was inherently dangerous to others, the defendant was strictly liable. The hotel was entitled to recover the costs of repairing all the damage caused by the blast even if the company was not negligent. If any guests in the hotel suffered injuries they too would be able to sue the defendant for their injuries.

Where strict liability for damages from blasting is not the law, liability will be imposed only when there has been negligence. Failure to comply with blasting regulations is taken as evidence of negligence. To avoid liability, a person engaged in blasting must have the most cautious regard for his neighbors' rights. For instance, it is his duty to give timely notice to everyone expected to be within the range of an explosion.

Transportation Railroads, trucks, and other carriers that transport explosives must use care equal to the danger. They are liable to those injured through their negligence. They are also liable when the shipment becomes a nuisance, as when it is unnecessarily held in a populated area. Federal laws regulate the transportation of explosives across state lines.

Discharge of fireworks A person who sets off fireworks unlawfully or in a way that creates a nuisance is liable for causing injury, whether or not he is negligent. When, however, the fireworks are not unlawful and do not create a nuisance, liability is based on negligence. This means there can be no recovery unless the negligent handling of the fireworks was the proximate (direct) cause of the injuries.

■ **Defenses** In lawsuits for injuries from explosives, CONTRIBUTORY NEGLIGENCE may be a defense when the suit is based on the negligence of the defendant.

EXAMPLE Suppose Smith stores dynamite caps in a metal shed in an isolated field behind his barn. One night he accidentally leaves a box of the caps outside the shed. Sid, who is over 18, sees the caps and, knowing what they are, takes a handful. He throws a few caps into a fire. When the caps do not explode immediately, he goes closer to the fire to see what happened. At that point the caps explode and Sid is blinded in one eye.

Sid sues Smith for his injuries. He alleges that the accident would never had happened if Smith had not negligently left the box outside the door. Smith will be able to claim that Sid's own negligent act—looking into a fire into which he had just thrown dynamite caps—was a significant factor in bringing about his injury. This is the defense of contributory negligence—the plaintiff's own negligence contributed to his injury, which in turn was brought about by the defendant's negligence. This defense will bar the recovery of money damages. Many states have replaced this defense with the rule of comparative negligence, which allows Sid to recover damages reduced by the proportion of fault that is his if he is less than 50 percent responsible.

If Sid had been under 18, the ATTRACTIVE NUISANCE DOCTRINE might have come into play. Then the owner of the dynamite could have been held totally liable because the owner created a temptation that a young person could not be expected to resist. However, if the lawsuit is based on strict liability, as in the case of using explosives, contributory negligence is not a defense.

If a person knowingly exposes himself or his property to the dangers of an explosion, then sues when he is hurt or his property is damaged, the party responsible for the explosion may use the defense of *assumption of risk*.

EXAMPLE Suppose Jones blasts on his own land, showering Brown's house with rocks. Brown, hearing the rocks hit against the outer walls, sticks his head out the window to see what is happening and is injured by a rock. Jones cannot use contributory negligence as a defense because blasting is an ultrahazardous activity, which a person does at his own peril.

Suppose, however, that after Brown knows that there is to be another blast, which will bring about another hail of rocks, he again puts his head out the window. This time he is severely injured by the flying fragments. Brown's conduct may be considered an assumption of risk, which Jones can use as a defense in Brown's lawsuit. This defense means that the plaintiff understood the risk he was taking and decided to take it. Brown exposed himself to the known dangers of Jones's blasting and therefore some states will not allow him to collect any damages from Jones.

■ **Criminal responsibility** Some laws make it a criminal offense to use, keep, sell, or transport explosives without legal authorization. Explosives that are unlawfully kept may be forfeited and the owner penalized. Federal laws have made it a federal offense to import, manufacture, distribute, or store explosive materials in interstate or foreign commerce without a license. The penalties for violation of the federal law include a fine of not more than $10,000, imprisonment of not more than 10 years, and seizure and FORFEITURE of the explosives.

expository statute A law that is enacted to explain the true meaning and intent of a previous law.

ex post facto (Latin) "After the fact." For example, an ex post facto law is one that makes an act punishable as a crime after the act has been committed, or increases the punishment for crimes already committed. Ex post facto laws are forbidden by the U.S. Constitution. See CONSTITUTIONAL LAW.

express Specific; clearly stated or written in words; unambiguous; the opposite of implied.

EXAMPLE Suppose you purchase a new automobile. You receive a written warranty from the manufacturer that any part found to be defective during the first 12 months or 12,000 miles, whichever occurs first, will be replaced free of charge to the purchaser. The manufacturer's warranty is an express warranty.

An implied warranty, conversely, is not expressly stated.

EXAMPLE You buy a vacuum cleaner from Sam, a merchant whose store stocks many reputable brands. There is implied in the sales contract a warranty that the vacuum cleaner is fit for its intended purposes. This warranty is not written, nor is it based on any oral statement made to you by Sam. This type of warranty is known as an implied warranty of merchantability.

expressio unius est exclusio alterius

(Latin) "The expression of one thing is the exclusion of another"—a rule used by judges in interpreting laws or documents. When certain persons are specified in a statute, for example, an intention to exclude all others from the law may be inferred.

> EXAMPLE Suppose a civil service statute specifically excludes the assistant superintendent of schools, assistant town clerk, assistant city attorney, and assistant city engineer from the classified service. But it does not mention the assistant tax collector. Diana, the assistant tax collector for the past 15 years, receives a dismissal notice from the tax collector. She appeals her dismissal to the civil service commission, which refuses to hear her appeal on the ground that she did not hold a position in the classified service. Diana then sues the commission to force them to hear her appeal. The court holds that because the civil service law defined the exclusions so specifically, the rule of *expressio unius est exclusio alterius* applies. Since it was not expressly excluded, the position of assistant tax collector is within the classified civil service. The court ordered the commission to hear Diana's appeal from her dismissal.

expropriation

The taking of private property for public use, such as for a park, railroad, or public work. Expropriation is synonymous with the exercise of the power of EMINENT DOMAIN.

ex rel.

(Latin) Abbreviation for the Latin *ex relatione*, "on relation"; on information. Legal proceedings started by the attorney general in the name of the state but on the information and at the insistence of a person who has an interest in the matter are said to be taken ex rel. (on the relation of) such a person, who is called the relator.

> EXAMPLE Donna Jones is called to testify as a witness at a coroner's inquest, but she refuses to answer questions asked by Smith, the coroner. Coroner Smith then informs the attorney general that witness Jones refuses to testify and requests him to bring contempt proceedings against her. The attorney general agrees, and the contempt proceedings against Jones are entitled "*State ex rel. Smith v. Jones.*"

extenuating circumstances

Facts surrounding a crime that make it less serious, evil, or reprehensible. These facts do not lower the degree of the crime from first to second degree, but they do tend to decrease the punishment imposed after a conviction. Before sentencing a defendant, for example, a judge may consider these extenuating circumstances: the defendant's probation report, age, mental and physical condition, reputation in his community, family status, and ability to earn a living.

extinguishment

The destruction or cancellation of a right, power, contract, or property interest. For instance, a debt is extinguished when it is paid. A tenant's obligation to pay rent is extinguished when the tenant purchases the rented property from the landlord.

extortion

The crime committed by a public officer when he misuses his office to compel another person to give him money or something else of value. Under some statutes it is also the crime committed by anyone who obtains money or other property through the use of threats or by instilling fear. Some statutes make extortion a misdemeanor; others make it a felony.

■ **Public officers** Under the common law and statutes based on the common law, only a public officer can commit the crime of extortion. Generally, public officers include any federal, state, municipal, or judicial officer and any person occupying an official position, such as a city fire marshal or an inspector in a city department of health. A public officer is not responsible for extortion practiced by his official agent, but if an officer authorizes his agent to extort, both are guilty.

Types of extortion by officials The following ways by which an officer may obtain money illegally are classified as extortion:

Fees not allowed by law An officer who demands unlawful fees is guilty of extortion.

> EXAMPLE Jay, a special agent of the Department of Justice, gave false information to Pierre when he applied for a visa to visit the United States. To get the visa promptly, Jay told Pierre that a courier had to make a special trip to Washington, which would cost $300. After the application for the visa was returned from Washington, Jay required Pierre to pay the $300. Jay's actions were discovered and he was found guilty of extortion.

If an officer accepts money for performing official duties, he commits extortion even though the transaction is disguised as a gratuity. It does not matter when the money is paid.

Fees greater than allowed by law It is also criminal for an officer to take a larger fee for his services than the one fixed by law. The fee must be demanded of a person who believes himself legally obligated to pay some amount.

Fees exacted before due A third way a public officer can commit extortion is to receive a fee before it is due, even if no extra amount of money is taken. As a rule, a fee becomes due when an officer completes his official service—when the sheriff, for example, has seized a debtor's property for the creditor. Courts have held, however, that receiving fees before they are due at the request and convenience of the person paying them is not criminal.

Fees for services not performed A fourth way in which an officer can commit extortion is by taking fees for official services he has not performed. For example, a fire inspector who was entitled to collect from a developer $10 for approving the installation of an oil tank at each new house the developer built would be guilty of extortion if he did not actually check each installation. An officer, however, cannot be guilty of extortion if he takes a fee for omitting to do some service or act that is outside his official capacity. In that case, he could be guilty of larceny or obtaining property by false pretenses.

Color of office Finally, an officer may commit extortion by accepting money or other property under color of office. Color of office means that the officer claims or assumes powers because of the office he holds, when, in fact, the office does not entitle him to such powers.

EXAMPLE When an officer of a highway department took excess money from a tax-delinquent automobile owner on the pretense of collecting a fine and costs, he was extorting under color of office. The person paid not voluntarily, but because he believed he had to yield to official authority.

Corrupt intent Generally, to be guilty of extortion, a public officer must act with corrupt intent. In order to demonstrate that he did not have a corrupt intent, an officer accused of extortion may show that the money was not for his own use, that the total fee was less than the amount he had a right to demand, or that the payment was made voluntarily. Under some statutes an officer who takes money that is not due him commits the crime of extortion even without a specific intent.

Money or thing of value Money or some other thing of value must be received for extortion to exist, but a promise or agreement to pay does not amount to extortion. It does not matter whether the person pays the unlawful fee or has someone else pay it on his behalf. Nor is it material whether the officer collected the fee for himself or for another person.

■ **Extortion by threat** Many statutes provide that any person who obtains money or other property through the use of threats or by instilling fear is an extortionist. This applies to anyone, public official or not. Under these laws the threat may be to cause bodily injury to another person, then or at some future time. For example, a person who makes another give him money by threatening, "Get me $5,000 by next Tuesday or I'll bust your nose," is guilty of extortion in some states. The threat may be to accuse the other person of a crime or to expose some secret that would subject the other person to contempt, ridicule, or hatred.

The threatened act need not even be unlawful. If a person threatens to tell one spouse of the other's infidelity—such as, "John, give me $500 or I'll tell your wife you have been seeing Joan"—the threat to tell John's wife of his infidelity is not in itself unlawful but the demand for money to keep quiet is extortion. Also ordinarily included in extortion laws are threats to start a strike or boycott that will injure another's business, as well as threats to testify against someone or to withhold testimony necessary to his defense or claim if the threat is made only in order to obtain money illegally for the extortioner. Extortion statutes usually contain a catchall provision that any threat to harm another person in his business, calling, career, or reputation is extortion, even though the person making the threat does not benefit from it.

■ **Punishment** Extortion is punishable by fine, imprisonment, and, when an officer is involved, removal from office. The extortioner may also have to pay a penalty to the victim if the victim sues him. The same penalties may be imposed for attempted extortion but to a lesser degree.

extradition Giving up a prisoner to the state or country that wants him for a criminal trial. The state or country that has accused or convicted the prisoner has no

authority to reach into another state or country to snatch the person who is wanted. The orderly way to gain custody of someone in such a situation is by extradition.

■ **Extradition from one state to another** The U.S. Constitution gives state governors the right to demand that people who have committed crimes and then left the state be returned by the states in which they are found. Extradition is intended to protect the public from criminals who might otherwise escape punishment simply by crossing a state line. It helps the criminal courts do their job, but it is not a judicial operation. It is a function of the executive branch of the government and is by order of the governor.

According to the Constitution, anyone charged with "Treason, Felony, or other crime" must be turned over to the state demanding him. *Treason* is the crime of doing things to overthrow the United States government, such as making war against it or helping foreign enemies. A *felony* is any serious crime—it usually carries a prison sentence of at least one year. *Crime* as used here means that a person charged with a misdemeanor can be extradited. A *misdemeanor* is a crime less serious than a felony but more than a simple infraction, such as a traffic violation.

Only persons who have been charged with a crime can be extradited. The charge must be specific. It must refer to criminal conduct in the state where the charge is made—whether or not the act is a crime in the state where the person is found. A person is still charged after he has been convicted. He remains charged until he has completed his sentence, probation, or parole or has paid his fine.

When a prisoner breaks parole and escapes to another state, he can be extradited for the original crime rather than for violating parole, which might not be a crime at all.

Fugitive from justice A person is subject to extradition if he is a *fugitive from justice*—that is, if he leaves the state after being charged with a crime. He is a fugitive regardless of the reason for which he left the state and even if state authorities knew that he was leaving. Thus a person is a fugitive if he left the state for good business reasons, was returning to his home in a different state, or was tricked into entering the other state. The state where the fugitive is found is called the *asylum state.*

The fugitive generally does not have to be handed over to a state demanding him if he has already been arrested on charges made by the asylum state. The asylum state may try the fugitive, convict him, and keep him in jail for the duration of his sentence before handing him over to the state demanding extradition.

A fugitive may be arrested and held in custody if there is information that he has been charged with a crime in another state. He can be held until papers demanding extradition are prepared. Even someone who has been illegally arrested can be extradited. If an unreasonably long period of time passes and no papers are delivered, however, the asylum state assumes that the state charging the fugitive has abandoned its extradition effort. Then the asylum state may release him.

What a demand must say A demand for extradition must show that a crime has been charged, that prosecution has begun, or that the person sought has been convicted of a crime. In the case of conviction, the demand must state that the person broke his parole, escaped from jail, or violated the terms of his bail or probation. It must also say that he is a fugitive from justice. But the facts of the crime do not have to be explained. Sometimes it is not even necessary for the fugitive to have been in the state demanding him. For example, a parent is charged with abandoning a child. He need not have been in the state with the child to have committed the crime. He can be in a different state and still be guilty of criminal nonsupport.

Decision and consent The governor of the asylum state must decide whether the person is charged with a crime and whether he is a fugitive from justice. If the governor so decides, he has a legal duty to sign extradition papers. A governor cannot, however, be forced to grant extradition. He may wish to hold the fugitive to answer for charges made in his own state or because he fears the fugitive would be in danger if he was returned.

EXAMPLE The governor of California refused to extradite the leader of the American Indian Movement to South Dakota, where he had jumped bail after having been convicted of assault and riot. The California governor felt that the Indian leader would not be safe if he were returned to South Dakota. In 1978 the California Supreme Court upheld the governor's decision.

Most people faced with extradition consent to being transferred to the demanding state without formal proceedings. But a person who wishes to fight extradition can usually do so by HABEAS CORPUS. He files a writ in the asylum state, asking a judge to find out whether it is right for him to be held in custody. At the habeas corpus hearing, the judge will not hear evidence about the underlying crime but will decide only whether the prisoner is lawfully held.

■ **Extradition from one country to another** The right of one country to ask another to surrender a fugitive from justice exists by treaty, or by agreement between the countries. In extradition treaties, *asylum* means a place where the person charged may not be tried.

The United States will not extradite fugitives without the authority of a treaty. It may refuse to surrender American citizens for crimes committed in a foreign country unless that is part of the treaty. Extradition of U.S. citizens may also depend on the language of the treaty or the laws in the two countries.

EXAMPLE An American citizen claimed that he should not be handed over to a foreign government that had once refused to extradite one of its citizens. The treaty between the two countries had no provision about either one surrendering its citizens. The court found that, in the earlier case, the foreign country had the power to convict its citizens for crimes committed in the United States. The fugitive did not escape prosecution just because he was not extradited to the United States. American law was different. The American citizen could not be prosecuted here for a crime he committed in the foreign country. Therefore, the court ruled to extradite him.

During time of war, extradition treaties are usually considered suspended but not completely ended. For an alleged crime committed by an American in Germany during World War II, however, the United States refused to consider an extradition treaty merely suspended—it felt the treaty did not apply during wartime, and would not extradite the American citizen even after the war.

Some treaties provide for extradition only for certain crimes. A treaty often specifies very serious crimes and may include acts that are criminal in one country but not in the other. In some treaties, only acts that are criminal in both countries give the right to demand extradition. It is U.S. policy to negotiate treaties that provide a right of extradition only for conduct that is generally recognized as criminal all over the world.

Countries will not extradite fugitives for political crimes. A political crime may be a real crime, such as a murder, but international law recognizes it as political if it is part of political disturbances.

EXAMPLE The United States was able to gain custody of one of Lincoln's assassins who fled the country. John H. Surratt was charged with having assisted John Wilkes Booth in his plot to kill President Lincoln. Surratt was discovered in April 1866, working in the military guard serving the Pope. The U.S. government requested extradition, and the papal government complied. Surratt was arrested, but he escaped. When he was finally found in Alexandria, Egypt, he was rearrested and returned to the United States, where he was tried but not convicted because the jury could not reach a verdict.

Criminal flight International relations have become very strained at times over the flight of criminals from one country to another. Demands that terrorists or airline hijackers be returned to face trial are not always met. Sometimes extradition procedures are not even attempted—the accused is kidnapped and carried away by force to the nation that has charged him.

The position of the United States is that a fugitive cannot avoid trial by claiming that he was illegally brought into the country. His remedy is to sue his abductors for money damages. Once he is within reach, the court has the authority to try him on the criminal charges.

EXAMPLE In one Supreme Court case, decided in 1886, a man claimed that he could not be convicted for larceny and embezzlement committed in Illinois because he had been kidnapped in Peru and brought back to the United States. The defendant had fled to Peru. Once this was discovered, an official request had been sent by the United States asking that he be extradited. When an official was sent to Peru to pick up the man, he made no demand to the local authorities. Instead the official seized the accused and forcibly transported him to California. The governor of California then surrendered the prisoner to the governor of Illinois. The Supreme Court held that the right of Peru to grant a fugitive asylum in its country did not give the fugitive any claim to a right to stay there, unmolested and secure.

EXAMPLE This same reasoning was applied to a very famous case in 1957. Morton Sobell, who was accused of spying for the Soviet Union, had gone to Mexico in 1950. While he was there, the Mexican Security Police seized him, took him to the Texas border, and turned him over to U.S. authorities. When Sobell claimed that the Mexican police had assaulted and kidnapped him and violated lawful extradition procedures, the court cited the earlier case involving Peru. It held that once Sobell was in custody in the United States it was perfectly proper to try him with his codefendants, Julius and Ethel Rosenberg.

extrajudicial   Something that is not founded on, or not connected with, the action of a court of law. For example, an extrajudicial oath is taken formally before a proper person, such as a notary public, but it is not taken during courtroom proceedings.

extraordinary remedy   A method of enforcing a right (a REMEDY) used by a court only when absolutely necessary. The writs of MANDAMUS, QUO WARRANTO, HABEAS CORPUS, and some others are sometimes called extraordinary remedies to distinguish them from the ordinary remedy or recourse offered by an action at law (lawsuit).

extraterritoriality   The act by which a country extends its jurisdiction into the territory of another nation and exercises its power over its citizens located there. It is usually based on a treaty of extraterritoriality. Modern nations are loath to grant extraterritorial rights, but the concept has survived in those instances where, by treaty, the United States has retained civil and criminal jurisdiction over its armed forces stationed abroad.

extrinsic evidence   Evidence that is not contained in the body of a contract, will, trust, or other written agreement.

EXAMPLE A woman died and left a will in which she bequeathed property to her grandniece Alicia. Two grandnieces, each named Alicia, survived her. At the time the will was made, one was 17 years old, the other 20. Because the name used in the will could be applied equally to both girls, the court held that extrinsic evidence was admissible to help in deciding which one was meant. After hearing the testimony, the court decided that the will referred to the older grandniece.

eyewitness   A person who has firsthand knowledge of an act, event, or transaction by having seen it occur.

EXAMPLE Suppose you are waiting to cash a check at your bank when two men armed with shotguns push you away from the cashier's window. One of the men hands the cashier a sack and orders him to fill it with money. The cashier fills the sack, and the two men flee from the bank. You are an eyewitness to a bank robbery.

face   **1** Outward appearance; the surface of anything, especially the front, upper, or outer part.   **2** In business law, the face of an agreement or other document means only the words contained in it and nothing else. For example, a person could have been forced to sign a contract at gunpoint and it would look valid on its face, but no court would uphold it.   **3** When applied to a house, the face contains the main entrance, which is usually the most attractive side of the house.

face value   The amount of money that can be determined from the words of a written document, without having to refer to any other source and excluding any interest that might have accrued on it. The face value is the amount upon which interest is computed. For example, the face value of a $5,000 promissory note means the amount of money written on it, excluding 8 percent interest (for example) and other fees that the lender has charged the borrower.

fact   Something done; an event or circumstance. The word "fact" is often contrasted with the word "law." Law is a principle; fact is an event. Law is a rule of obligation or duty; fact is what has actually been done.

A *question of fact* concerns what actually happened and is decided by a jury or, in a criminal case, by a judge when the defendant requests a trial without a jury. A *question of law* deals with the legal principles that affect the facts and is decided by a judge. For example, a frequent question of fact is whether a particular vehicle struck a pedestrian; while a question of law is whether the driver's statement to a witness to the accident that he was speeding is admissible as EVIDENCE in the trial.

factor   An agent who, in the course of his business and for compensation, sells goods or merchandise that the owner has entrusted to him. The principal is the person who owns the merchandise or goods; the factor is the person who sells them for him. Fuller Brush men and Avon ladies are factors. (For a discussion of the relationship between a principal and his agent, see AGENCY.) A factor is sometimes called a commission merchant or consignee. He usually makes a commission on his sales, and the goods he receives for sale are called a consignment. He is called a *home factor* when he lives in the same state or country as his principal, and a *foreign factor* if he lives in a different state or country.

The main difference between a factor and other types of agent is that a factor must have possession of his principal's property while other agents do not. The following are the essential elements of being a factor: (1) a factor has possession of the goods; (2) he is directed to sell the goods; (3) he is in the business of selling; and (4) he receives compensation for his services. The relationship of principal and factor is usually created by a CONTRACT between the parties. In most cases either party may terminate the agreement, or it may be terminated by operation of law—for instance, if either factor or principal dies or if the product is declared illegal, the law says the relationship is ended.

Most states regulate the business of factors to protect the people who transact business with them. In some states a factor must obtain a license and pay a tax or fee, and in some states he must be bonded. See BOND.

■ **Relationship between factor and principal**   Since a factor has the power to sell the consigned goods in his possession, he also has power to do everything reasonably necessary to accomplish this. Consequently, he may sell in his own name, and he may give a warranty about the quality of the goods. But he cannot exchange the goods for other goods, mix the goods with those of others, or cancel a completed sale.

A factor must exercise reasonable care, skill, and diligence in transactions for his principal and is responsible for losses resulting from his failure to do so. For example, if a factor fails to lock the warehouse where he is storing the consigned merchandise, he will be liable (financially responsible) if the goods are stolen. But if he protects the goods consigned to him, he is not responsible. A factor may not use the goods for his own benefit—by selling the goods at a higher price than he indicates to his principal and pocketing the difference, for example.

A factor must follow the instructions of his principal or be liable for any resulting loss, provided the instructions were clear. But he is not liable for failing to carry out his principal's instructions if circumstances beyond his control make it impossible for him to do so. If, for example, a principal tells his factor to sell the goods on January 15, but because of a severe blizzard no business can be transacted that day, the factor is not liable for failing to follow instructions. A factor must inform his principal of any adverse facts or circumstances so that the principal can protect his interests.

A factor must sell at the highest price available in the current market. If he agrees, or is instructed, to sell at a specified price, he must sell at that price unless particular circumstances make this impossible.

Payments Usually, the factor takes payment in cash when he delivers the goods. If he is authorized to sell on credit, he usually has the authority (whether or not it has been stated) to sell on whatever credit terms are customary. He must exercise reasonable care to verify the financial standing of a purchaser and should inform his principal of the purchaser's ability to pay, but he is not responsible for nonpayment unless his contract makes him liable.

A factor should exercise proper care in collecting payments. He need not remit the payments immediately, unless he has agreed to do so, but he should not mix them with his own funds or those of another. He must keep regular and accurate accounts of all his transactions and let his principal inspect them.

The principal usually pays the freight charges on a consignment sent to his factor. If the factor advances money for the freight charges (depending on the arrangement between him and the principal), he usually has the right to sell as much of the goods as he needs to reimburse himself, if the principal fails to repay him.

Compensation A factor's right to compensation is based on his contract with his principal. Unless the contract provides otherwise, he is entitled only to commissions on his sales and on funds he has advanced for the principal's benefit. He is also entitled to be reimbursed for all necessary expenses he incurs for the principal's benefit, but he may forfeit this right if his NEGLIGENCE, fraud, or misconduct causes the loss.

Lien A factor has a general LIEN (a legal claim) on the goods consigned to him for all commissions due him and for all his expenditures, but only if he has complied with all the requirements of his contract and the applicable laws. For example, the lien can exist only when the factor has possession of the goods, regardless of whether his possession is actual or constructive. *Constructive possession* means that he has control of the property but does not hold it—for instance, when the property is kept in a warehouse. As a rule, a factor may enforce his lien by holding the principal's property (money or goods) until commissions and expenditures are paid. When the principal pays the factor the amount due, he discharges the lien. If the principal fails to satisfy the lien within a reasonable time, the factor may sell enough of the principal's property to satisfy his claim.

■ **Controversies** If a factor violates his principal's instructions or otherwise breaches his duty, the principal may recover for whatever damage he sustains. If the factor delays in remitting payment for the goods after the sale, the principal may recover interest. If the factor delays in selling the goods, he is liable for any loss incurred through a decline in the market price. If he sells before the time authorized, he is liable for any increase in price he could have obtained. If a factor makes a warranty without authority or without disclosing his principal, he is bound by it.

fact situation The summary of all the events, or circumstances, of a case, without any comments or legal conclusions. The fact situation of one case is seldom exactly the same as that of another.

failure of issue Dying without children. In law, children are often referred to as the *issue of a marriage.* Failure of issue becomes important when there are no children to inherit the deceased's property.

fair comment A privilege granted to the news media protecting them against libel actions for opinions and criticisms on matters that substantially affect public interests, such as political and artistic criticism. Criticizing an actor's performance in a movie is an example of a fair comment, if it is made without MALICE (knowingly or recklessly publicizing falsehoods). Sarcastic and even vicious comments, if justified by the facts, are permitted under the fair comment doctrine.

As a result of the Supreme Court's decision in the 1964 case of *New York Times* v. *Sullivan,* fair comment is a constitutional privilege when it concerns the official conduct of an elected or appointed official. In that case, the Court held that a public official may not recover damages for libel unless he can prove that the attacks on his character or reputation were made with malice. Thus a public official will not be able to recover damages for untrue statements about his official conduct, unless the statements were made with knowledge or reckless disregard of their falseness. Such a privilege has also been applied to criticism of public figures, such as celebrities. See LIBEL AND SLANDER; SPEECH AND PRESS, FREEDOM OF.

fair hearing A legal proceeding that is conducted according to the principles of DUE PROCESS OF LAW but does not follow the formalities, such as the rules of EVIDENCE or procedure, of a regular court proceeding. In a fair hearing, a person has the right to be informed of the evidence against him, to cross-examine opposing witnesses, to present evidence in his own favor, and to speak, at least briefly, in his own defense. For example, a police officer charged with misconduct is entitled to a fair hearing before he is disciplined, and a person seeking Social Security disability payments can ask for a fair hearing if his application is denied. If a person is dissatisfied with the ruling at a fair hearing, he can seek review of the decision in a court. Other examples of fair hearings are those disputing the revocation of welfare benefits or the firing of public employees. Administrative agency hearings are also fair hearings.

fair market value The price at which real estate or personal property would change hands in a transaction between a willing buyer and a willing seller.

In real estate transactions, the traditional test of fair market value is the amount that a purchaser, who is willing but not obligated to buy, would pay to an owner, who is willing but not obligated to sell. Many factors can affect the fair market value of real estate, including (1) the demand for similar property, (2) recent sales of land of comparable location and description, (3) the uses to which the property is put, and (4) rental income produced by the property.

When a government authority takes over private property in an EMINENT DOMAIN proceeding, it must pay the owner the fair market value of the land.

fair-trade law

A form of legalized price-fixing that allows a manufacturer to set a minimum price at which retailers may sell his goods. Fair-trade laws are now illegal, except for those regulating the price of liquor that is sold within a state.

California was the first state to enact such laws in 1931, and others soon followed. When fair-trade laws began affecting interstate commerce, however, they violated federal antitrust laws; therefore in 1937 Congress exempted them from the antitrust laws. Some manufacturers tried to set resale prices not only for retailers who had signed fair-trade contracts with them but also for those who had not. In 1951 the Supreme Court, in *Schwegmann Bros.* v. *Calvert Distillers Corp.*, ruled this practice illegal, but the following year, in response to the Schwegmann case, Congress enacted provisions that permitted states to pass fair-trade laws with *nonsigner* clauses that permitted retailers to choose whether or not to sign a fair-trade agreement with the manufacturer. As long as one retailer signed the agreement, the manufacturer would be able to set fixed resale prices for *all* retailers. Finally, in 1975, the federal law was amended, and the provisions exempting fair-trade laws from federal antitrust laws and permitting states to enact nonsigner provisions were eliminated. Thus, a fair-trade law would now violate federal antitrust laws and would be declared invalid. Suggested prices by manufacturers are not affected and are still legal.

Liquor is not affected by the amendment of the fair-trade laws because the 21st Amendment to the Constitution gives the states broad powers over the sale of alcoholic beverages. Therefore, liquor manufacturers in states that have passed price-fixing statutes under the 21st Amendment may enforce resale prices.

fair use

The limited use of copyrighted material, such as quoting a few lines from a novel in a review of it. In another sense, fair use means that only the underlying idea of the material is used, not the material itself. A theme or an idea cannot be copyrighted. Therefore, it is not a COPYRIGHT infringement if you write a novel with the same theme as one that has already been published or a new book on a popular subject, such as how to gain confidence or how to grow better vegetables.

false

1 Intentionally, knowingly, or negligently untrue. 2 Untrue by mistake, by accident, or honestly after the exercise of reasonable care. The meaning of the term must often be determined by the context in which it is used. In law as well as in popular use, false usually means something more than a mere untruth. It implies an intent to deceive or to commit some treachery or fraud.

EXAMPLE A salesman makes false claims about the low mileage on a used car in order to convince you to buy it at a much higher price than it is worth. The salesman knows that his boss had the odometer turned back in violation of the law. His statements are intentionally false.

false arrest

False ARREST is an unlawful detention or restraint on a person's liberty and freedom of movement, whether in prison or elsewhere. It is a TORT—a harm that one person does to another, willfully or through negligence, and for which he can be sued. The term "false arrest" is sometimes used interchangeably with FALSE IMPRISONMENT, but actually a false arrest is committed by any law enforcement officer or person claiming to have legal authority who arrests and detains a person without legally sufficient grounds, while a false imprisonment is any unlawful confinement of another committed by a person without any claim of legal authority.

EXAMPLE If a sheriff arrests and jails a person without any probable cause or reasonable basis, he has committed false arrest. He has acted under the guise of legal authority to unlawfully deprive a person of his liberty of movement.

EXAMPLE But suppose a man drives his secretary home after the office Christmas party and then refuses to let her out of his car after she rejects his advances. He is not making a false arrest, because he is not claiming to act under legal authority, but he is committing the tort of false imprisonment; he is unlawfully depriving her of her liberty of movement.

A police officer is not liable for false arrest in three situations involving felonies: (1) He may arrest a person who has actually committed a felony, such as armed robbery, in his presence. (2) If a felony has been committed and there are reasonable grounds for believing a certain person committed it, the officer may arrest him. (3) If no felony has been committed but there are reasonable grounds to believe one will be, the officer may arrest the person he suspects. The law grants these privileges to its peace officers to shield them from liability in cases where there is a reasonable presumption of serious crime.

A person who has been falsely arrested may sue in a civil court for the damages he incurred—attorney's fees, loss of salary while imprisoned, or mental suffering. If a person knowingly gives false information to the police in order to have someone arrested, he has committed the tort of MALICIOUS PROSECUTION.

false imprisonment

The unlawful confinement of one person by another against the former's will by depriving him of his freedom of movement. A restraint of a person's liberty by any law enforcement officer without proper legal cause is a FALSE ARREST. No such claim of authority is necessary for false imprisonment.

Although the term "imprisonment" conjures up pictures of stone walls and barred cells, a person may be falsely imprisoned if his freedom is restrained in any way, such as when a man is surrounded on the street by a gang of hoodlums or a woman is trapped in a speeding automobile by a rejected and angry suitor.

Like false arrest, false imprisonment is a TORT—a harm that is done by one person to another, for which the doer can be sued. It is also punishable as a crime with penalties set by state law.

■ **Elements** Two elements—restraint and the intent to restrain—are necessary for an act to constitute false imprisonment.

Restraint The restraint used must be total—the mere obstruction of a person's right to go where he pleases, as by blocking his passage in one direction, is not considered false imprisonment. A person's freedom of movement must be actually and completely restrained, even if only for a few minutes. The use or threat of physical force is not essential. Fear of force that can be reasonably inferred from the circumstances is enough.

EXAMPLE Suppose a man pointing a butcher knife at your throat tells you very politely to accompany him past the police barricade set up outside the bank he has just robbed. Although no actual force has been used or threatened, it is clear from the circumstances that you are being unlawfully detained against your will. The bank robber has committed false imprisonment in addition to his criminal acts.

When a person is arrested by an officer who does not have the legal authority, such as a warrant, or the grounds, such as PROBABLE CAUSE for believing the person committed an offense, a false arrest results. The illegal restraint imposed creates a false imprisonment.

If a person claims to be obeying a law while detaining someone against his will and such a law does not exist, a false imprisonment has occurred.

EXAMPLE Suppose a passenger on an express bus becomes ill and tries to get off the bus as it approaches a hospital. The bus driver, claiming that a municipal ordinance forbids discharging passengers except at designated stops even in an emergency, refuses to open the doors until he reaches the next scheduled stop, half an hour away. If there is no municipal ordinance, as he claimed, and it is normal procedure to allow sick passengers to leave the bus, the driver has falsely imprisoned the sick passenger.

If a policeman stops a person to question him, no unlawful restraint occurs. But should the police officer point a gun at him and warn him that if he makes a move he will shoot him, the tort of false imprisonment may be reasonably inferred. The tort is false imprisonment, because no arrest has yet been made.

The restraint must be against a person's will and without legal justification. If someone freely chooses to surrender his freedom of movement, such as by voluntarily remaining in a room, there is no imprisonment. A person who has been detained because there is probable cause to believe that he has committed a crime is not entitled to bring an action for false imprisonment, because there is legal justification for his confinement.

Intent Intent to restrain a person is an essential element of false imprisonment. A restraint that is purely accidental cannot constitute a false imprisonment.

EXAMPLE Your 15-year-old son gets locked in a department store overnight because, as a prank, he and his friends hid in the furniture section. As your son's legal representative, you cannot successfully sue the store for false imprisonment, because it is clear that there was no intent on the store's part to detain your son unlawfully.

EXAMPLE On the other hand, suppose your son is locked in a department store overnight because the night watchman wants to teach him a lesson for lurking around the store at closing time. The night watchman's intent to

restrain your son is sufficient to support a lawsuit if you decide to sue for false imprisonment.

■ **Shoplifting and employee theft** In the past—under the COMMON LAW—the tort of false imprisonment was found in cases against storekeepers who detained innocent persons for an unreasonable time or in an unreasonable manner while they investigated whether the customer had paid for his purchases. But in recent years, because shoplifting has reached epidemic proportions, many states have enacted statutes that permit a storekeeper to detain a customer long enough to find out whether he has taken something, even if it turns out he has not.

False imprisonment occurs when an employer detains an employee for an unreasonable time or in an unreasonable manner to investigate whether the employee has stolen or misappropriated the employer's property. Force is the clearest kind of unreasonableness.

EXAMPLE Suppose an employer calls an employee to his office, locks the door, and questions him several hours without calling the police or letting the employee call a lawyer. That is false imprisonment. But suppose the employer calls the employee into the office to question him about a theft. The employee asks permission to leave, and the employer answers that he wants the employee to stay. There is no false imprisonment. The interview was lawful as long as no force was used to detain the employee.

■ **Persons liable** As a general rule, in order for a person to be liable for false imprisonment, he must have personally participated in the wrongful detention of another.

■ **Damages** False imprisonment is a civil wrong that entitles a person to bring a lawsuit to recover DAMAGES for interference with his personal right of liberty of movement. If a person has not suffered any actual harm from his unlawful restraint, he will be given nominal (token) damages. If he was harmed, he is entitled to compensation for any injuries or expenses caused by his false imprisonment, such as physical injuries, mental suffering, attorney's fees, or loss of salary or business. Punitive damages (to punish the offender) may be awarded in addition to compensatory damages if the unlawful detention was malicious or involved unnecessary and extreme violence.

false personation The criminal offense of falsely representing oneself as another person in order to deceive others and thereby gain a profit or enjoy a right belonging to the person impersonated or subject him to an expense, charge, or liability. *Personate* and *impersonate* have the same meaning: to pretend to be a particular person.

EXAMPLE Suppose you go to your doctor's office to pay in cash an overdue bill for $200. The regular receptionist is not there. Another woman, who tells you she is substituting for the vacationing receptionist, graciously accepts the money. The following week you receive another bill for $200. You call the office and learn that the receptionist has not taken a vacation in six months; she was just on her coffee break when you came by. The woman who accepted your cash is guilty of false personation of the receptionist.

The offense and punishment of false personation are usually defined by state and federal statutes, which vary one from the other. In Utah, for example, a young man who ran up bills when he represented himself as the son of the governor of Missouri was held for questioning on a possible theft-by-personation charge.

Federal law makes it an offense to falsely pretend to be a U.S. citizen; a federal officer, such as a Congressman; a federal employee, such as a Central Intelligence Agency agent; a diplomat or official of a foreign government; a member, agent, or representative of the 4-H clubs; or an American National Red Cross member or agent soliciting or receiving money.

The offense consists of an untrue or false personation of the officer or person designated in the statute, usually with an intent to defraud. The false personation may be accomplished by verbal declarations or simply by showing a badge or certificate. To complete the crime, something beyond the false personation is required. As a general rule, the impersonator must receive some type of financial benefit or advantage from his pretense.

EXAMPLE Suppose a man flashes a fake police badge at a tollbooth attendant so that he can cross the bridge without paying the toll. Depending on the law in his state, this man may be guilty of false personation, because he is falsely representing himself as a policeman. The offense, however, would not have been completed if, after showing the badge, the man decided to pay the toll after all, because he would not have derived any benefit from his act.

false pretense The crime of falsely representing a past or existing fact to defraud a victim into parting with his property without receiving adequate compensation. This is commonly known as the crime of obtaining property by false pretenses. States have enacted false pretenses statutes to protect cautious and prudent people as well as those who are ignorant, credulous, or foolish. False pretense and false representation are synonymous and can be used interchangeably. They are a type of FRAUD.

■ **What constitutes false pretense** For the crime of false pretense to be committed, the following elements must be present: (1) a specific intent to defraud, (2) a false statement of fact, and (3) inducing someone to part with his property.

Intent A specific intent to cheat and defraud is essential to the commission of the crime of false pretense. An innocent or inadvertent misrepresentation of a fact is not a crime, because there is no intent to cheat anyone. The intent to defraud does not have to be directed against any particular person—against the public in general will suffice.

Misrepresentation of fact Unless the law provides otherwise, the pretense must be a representation about an existing fact or past event, not about a future event.

EXAMPLE If John tells Mark that he intends to pay Mark next week for the motorcycle he is buying today, but John does not intend to pay him at all, some states would find John guilty of obtaining property by false pretenses because his statement was false about his present intention. But other states would consider John's statement merely an expression of future intention, not based on an existing fact, and, therefore, would refuse to prosecute him for obtaining property by false pretenses. He might, however, be prosecuted on other charges.

A false statement of expectation, desire, or a prediction does not qualify as a false pretense. Nor do statements of opinion, judgments, or salesmen's spiels that "puff up" the quality of their products, because PUFFING is considered part of salesmanship. Whether or not statements about the value, quality, quantity, nature, or conditions of property are false pretenses depends largely on whether they are statements of fact or opinion. For example, it is opinion when a real estate agent says she thinks a particular house is 100 years old, but a fact when she states it is 100 years old.

Inducement to part with property In order to commit the crime, there must be something more than a false statement. The misrepresentation must be an important factor in persuading the owner to part with his property, although it need not be the only factor.

EXAMPLE A jeweler tells you that the diamond bracelet you are interested in buying is worth $15,000 because of the fine quality of the stones. In fact, it is worth only $3,000. The jeweler has intentionally made a false statement about an existing important fact in order to induce you to buy the bracelet at an exorbitant price. If you purchase the bracelet, the jeweler is guilty of obtaining property by false pretenses.

False representations about your financial condition usually come under false pretenses statutes.

EXAMPLE Peter walks into his friendly neighborhood finance company to borrow $3,000 for a cruise to the Mediterranean. Unfortunately, Peter has been unemployed for the past six months and, afraid that the company might not consider him a good credit risk, states on the loan application that he is currently employed as an attorney, making $40,000 a year. If he obtains the loan on the basis of his alleged occupation, he may be guilty of using false pretenses to defraud the finance company.

It is essential that the pretense be false when it is made *and* that the property is obtained. If the statement is not false, the crime is not committed, even though the accused believed the statement to be false when he made it. Suppose, in the case of the jeweler who tried to sell the diamond bracelet for $15,000 when he believed its real value was $3,000, that the bracelet was in fact worth $15,000. The jeweler would not be guilty of false pretenses, because his statements were true. Also, if the pretense or statement is false when made but by the time the property is obtained it becomes true, the crime is not committed. The person who parted with his property got what he was told he was getting in exchange.

■ **Form of pretense** A false pretense may be made by any method that communicates ideas from one person to another, such as any act, word, symbol, or token intended to deceive.

EXAMPLE Bill Jones knowingly forges an endorsement on a check and presents that check to a bank for payment. Jones is guilty of false pretenses because by his act and writing he has falsely represented that he is legally entitled to be paid. He is also guilty of forgery.

When a person knowingly gives another a worthless check, his action is regarded as a false pretense. Depending on the "bad check" laws of the state, it may be a crime to draw, pass, or deliver, with knowledge or fraudulent intent, a check for which there are insufficient funds on deposit in the bank to cover it or without reasonable grounds for believing that it would be paid.

EXAMPLE Jim gave Susan his personal check for $1,700 for her car and immediately left the state. One reason for Jim's hasty departure was that he had closed out his checking account two weeks earlier. Jim is guilty of obtaining Susan's car by false pretenses. By giving Susan his check, he was falsely representing that he had a checking account with sufficient funds to pay her. Susan had relied on his bogus check and thus parted with her property.

In most states, the crime of false pretenses is not committed unless the person from whom the property is obtained is defrauded. But he does not have to suffer an actual money loss as long as he does not receive what was promised to him.

Other provisions cover cheating or defrauding a person in or by a *confidence game*—a scheme by which a swindler wins the confidence of his victim and then cheats him out of his money or property. The confidence must be won by a trick, device, false representation, or swindling operation, and the property must be obtained by a betrayal of the confidence won.

EXAMPLE You receive a brochure in the mail offering you a "once-in-a-lifetime" opportunity to buy waterfront lots in Florida for the amazing price of $250 per acre. The brochure assures you that the actual value of these lots is $2,500 per acre. The land company explains that it can make this offer because it had the "savvy" to buy the lots before the current real estate boom. The brochure lists the names of famous people—including several movie stars and Congressmen, as well as your local mayor, minister, and PTA president—who have already "scored big" with this offer. On the basis of the statements in the brochure, you purchase four acres, sight unseen. One month later, you go to Florida to inspect your holdings and learn that they are in the swamplands of the Everglades National Park. You have bought land belonging to the government. In short, you have been swindled. Your mayor, minister, and the PTA president have never heard of the company. The land company is guilty of obtaining your $1,000 by false pretenses.

Defense and punishment As a general rule, it is no defense that the accused made, offered to make, or intended to make restitution to the victim or that the victim was himself guilty of a wrong or was negligent, because a crime is an injury to society.

The sentence and punishment for the crime of obtaining property by false pretenses are fixed by statute.

family 1 Parents and children. 2 People related by blood or marriage. 3 A group of persons living together as a single group, sharing living space and housekeeping. Because "family" does not have a precise meaning, most laws include a definition of the term when they use it.

■ **What constitutes a family** In its most restricted sense, family means only people who are related by blood or marriage and live together. Most often this means parents and children. In a larger sense, a family also includes such relatives as grandparents, uncles, aunts, and cousins, who may or may not live in the same household, city, or

even country. Family can refer to all the people descended from a common ancestor.

Another way that a family can be distinguished is by its permanent and domestic nature. Members of a family stay committed to one another for an unlimited period of time. Their relationship is considered domestic because they share a home and responsibilities for financial support and household duties. Traditionally, household servants were included in the term "family," but this meaning is dying out. However, a family can also include lodgers, boarders, or an unmarried cohabitant.

By contrast, a group of college students who agree to share expenses and chores in an apartment is not a family because the students' arrangement lasts only as long as they are in school or it is convenient and their legal responsibilities to each other are limited. The law does not expect from them the same obligations as it does from family members.

No specific number of persons is necessary to make up a family. The law may treat one child as a family by himself, such as a child who lives with foster parents to whom he is not related. For example, federally subsidized school lunches may be provided for the children of low-income families. Income level is calculated on the number of people in the family and, in this case, the foster child might be considered a family of one.

Zoning laws Sometimes a group of unrelated people are treated like a family for certain purposes. This issue has become especially important to people challenging the restrictions of ZONING laws. Since 1926 the Supreme Court has permitted towns to restrict the use of land in some areas to "single-family homes." Zoning ordinances that set aside certain residential areas for single-family homes have defined family in a number of ways. A typical law says that a group of persons may live together in a single-family house if they constitute "a single housekeeping unit made up of persons who are related by blood, marriage, or adoption, plus no more than two unrelated persons."

When this is the law, a group that does not fit the definition may not live in a single-family house. In 1974 the Supreme Court upheld such a statute.

EXAMPLE The owners of a large house in a wealthy village on the north shore of Long Island, New York, rented their house to six unrelated college students. The students were not a family within the meaning of the zoning ordinance. The Supreme Court found not only that the village had a right to use zoning laws to keep out noise and congestion but also that a law based on the definition of family is fair.

Many zoning laws that allow only families to live in certain residential areas make exceptions for special groups, such as religious orders and fraternities. In some states, group homes for foster children are permitted because they function like families and lack only biological ties.

■ **Suing a family member** The law sometimes permits and sometimes prohibits a civil lawsuit solely because the two parties are members of the same family.

Originally, the common-law doctrine merged all the members of a family into one person for legal purposes and the husband was that person. Anyone who wanted to sue the wife, for example, had to sue the husband because the wife could not legally be sued. The husband could not sue his wife because that was the same as suing himself, and the wife could not sue her husband because she did not have the right to sue anyone. Starting in the 1800's states began giving women the right to sue, but many new laws prohibited suits for injuries caused by one's spouse. The trend has been to abolish this exception, and about half the states have eliminated or restricted the immunity from lawsuits for injuries by one's spouse.

The theory of making a person immune from lawsuits by a member of his family was based on the idea that litigation destroys harmony within a household. There also seemed little sense in awarding money DAMAGES that would simply shift the family cash out of the left pocket and into the right. As more people began taking out insurance, a question arose as to whether one family member might claim serious injury caused by another family member in order to collect on a policy. On the other hand, peace in the family is better preserved when there is insurance to repay the costs of injuries. The opportunity for cheating an insurance company may be no greater for two family members than for two good friends. This debate is still going on in state courts and legislatures.

■ **Crimes between family members** Some states treat crimes that occur within a family differently from crimes between persons who are not related. New York and the District of Columbia have been in the forefront of a reform movement that has decriminalized certain acts that would be criminal if they were committed by people not related to each other. By not pushing family members into the extreme antagonism created by a criminal court action, the family unit has a better chance to survive. Civil remedies, such as an INJUNCTION (a court order to refrain from doing something), are flexible enough to meet temporary and special emergencies while deeper problems are worked out. For example, recent studies suggest that there may be up to one million cases a year of wife beating. In the District of Columbia alone about 10,000 such cases a year are diverted from the criminal courts to the family division.

Sex offenses Prosecution for committing certain sex offenses is affected by a family relationship.

By definition, INCEST is a family offense. Criminal incest is sexual intercourse between a man and a woman who are not married to each other but who, according to state law, are too closely related by blood or by marriage. The penalties are usually much more severe if one person is a child: a man and his 13-year-old daughter, for example.

In most states RAPE is not a crime if the man is married to his victim. The man may, however, be guilty of assault and battery if he uses a great deal of force.

ADULTERY is voluntary sexual intercourse between a man and a woman who are not married to each other but at least one of whom is married to someone else. This is considered a crime in some states because it is an offense against marriage. In many states an act of adultery gives the spouse of the adulterer a ground for a DIVORCE. See Chart 22.

■ **Family law** Family law is not one set of laws. It consists of all the statutes enacted by legislatures, all the decisions made in courts, and all the rights guaranteed by the federal and state constitutions. An attorney who practices family law must know how the law from each of these sources affects family relationships, rights, duties, and finances. He must understand how the family can be protected from intrusions from the outside and how the interests of individuals within the family must be balanced against the interests of the family as a whole.

American family life and family law have changed in fundamental ways in recent years. Many ideas that seemed strange in the 1960's were absorbed into our culture in the 1970's. For the first time, illegitimate children have some rights equal to those of children whose parents have married. See ILLEGITIMACY. Women have more equality. See EQUAL PROTECTION OF LAWS. Children are no longer treated as the possessions of their parents. See PARENT AND CHILD. Since 1973 ABORTION has become legal if performed according to the law and thus has become more common. Divorce and remarriage occur with greater frequency, and many different life-styles are now tolerated.

State law Each of the 50 states has its own family laws. For example, state homestead laws allow the family to keep its home despite creditors' claims against it as payment for debts. See EXEMPTION and Chart 10. Laws affecting families range from town ordinances to state constitutional provisions, including equal rights amendments.

Uniform laws Few states have reviewed all of their laws that affect families in order to form a comprehensive, modern family law. The National Conference of Commissioners on Uniform State Laws, a group that draws up model laws for state legislatures, has prepared several statutes in the area of family law, including the Uniform Marriage and Divorce Act, the Uniform Parentage Act, the Uniform Probate Code, the Uniform Reciprocal Enforcement of Support Act, and the Uniform Child Custody Jurisdiction Act.

The value of a uniform act, a law that is basically the same in different states, is well illustrated by the Uniform Child Custody Jurisdiction Act. One purpose of this proposed model law was to curb interstate "kidnapping" by a parent who had lost custody of his child and who would snatch the child from the custodial parent and move from state to state until a sympathetic court was found. As a result, each parent sometimes had a court order giving him custody of the child in a different state. The Uniform Child Custody Jurisdiction Act encourages cooperation among states so that the state best able to judge the situation is the one that decides who shall have custody. By 1980 more than 75 percent of the states had enacted the Uniform Child Custody Jurisdiction Act.

Another example is the Uniform Reciprocal Enforcement of Support Act (URESA), which is in effect in one form or another in all states. It permits a person entitled to receive support payments from someone living out of the state to sue for those payments in his own state. This avoids the expense and inconvenience of traveling to the other state to sue.

Federal laws Important family policy issues are affected by a great variety of federal social assistance laws. Laws concerning equal employment rights, public housing, and subsidized day care, and information and assistance programs for birth control, abortion, and medical care all come under "family law." Even the tax and Social Security laws are "family law" because they affect the taxpayer's family and dependents.

Specific areas of family law More detailed information about specific areas of family law can be found in several other articles indicated below.

MARRIAGE discusses the relationship between a married couple and society. It explains who can marry, what they must do to become married, the different kinds of marriages, and the legal consequences of cohabitation, or living together without being married.

HUSBAND AND WIFE defines the rights and responsibilities each person has in relation to his or her spouse. The changes brought about by the equal rights movement are discussed there, as well as the ways the law now handles cases of spouse abuse. The entry contains information about each spouse's right to sue the other, to enter into legal agreements, to testify against the other, and to own property, either separately or jointly.

ANNULMENT explains the grounds on which a court can declare a marriage invalid and the effects of having a marriage annulled. DIVORCE discusses the grounds for having a marriage legally ended, legal defenses that will prevent a divorce even if grounds are proved, new changes in divorce law, and the consequences of divorce, including alimony, child support, property settlements, and taxes.

The subject of children is covered under the legal term INFANT. PARENT AND CHILD discusses the rights and obligations of parents and children. ILLEGITIMACY explains the more limited rights of children born to parents who are not married. GUARDIAN AND WARD describes the duties of a person appointed by a court to care for a child or his property. ADOPTION OF PERSONS explains the change in legal rights when a person is adopted. GIFTS TO MINORS discusses property given to persons under the age of majority (usually 18 or 21). CUSTODY explains in detail the rights of an adult entitled to control and care for a child.

Property can be passed from one generation to another in two ways. WILLS explains how a person may leave his property to certain people after his death. DESCENT AND DISTRIBUTION tells which family members are entitled to inherit property when a person dies without a will.

The article on NAMES tells how to use a name, when the law may require use of a certain name, and how to change a name legally.

EXEMPTION discusses what type of property is beyond the reach of creditors when a family member has fallen so deeply in debt that a court has permitted the creditor to seize the debtor's property.

family car doctrine In NEGLIGENCE law, this rule, also called the family purpose doctrine, makes the owner of an automobile liable (financially responsible), in most cases, for damage caused by a family member while driving the car. See Chart 28. The basis of the doctrine is that the automobile is furnished by the head of the family for family use and that the operator is the owner's agent. A wife, for example, can be her husband's agent when she drives the children to school. The person liable under the doctrine must own, provide, or maintain an automobile for general family use. It must be shown that the automobile is a family car used for pleasure. However, an automobile used for business may also come within the doctrine when it is used for family driving.

Fannie Mae For a discussion of this federal housing subsidy program, see FEDERAL NATIONAL MORTGAGE ASSOCIATION.

fatal Causing death; deadly; destructive; disastrous. A mistake in legal procedure is fatal if it unfairly hurts the person who complains about it. A fatal error can warrant a new trial. For instance, if an accused criminal has no chance to present his side of the story, there is a fatal error in his trial.

fault Lack of care; NEGLIGENCE; error; mistake of judgment or of conduct; mismanagement; neglect of duty. However the word is used, it always connotes an act to which blame, censure, impropriety, shortcoming, or culpability can be attached. An automobile driver who runs through a red light and hits a pedestrian in the crosswalk is at fault.

FBI See FEDERAL BUREAU OF INVESTIGATION.

FCC See FEDERAL COMMUNICATIONS COMMISSION.

FDA See FOOD AND DRUG ADMINISTRATION.

FDIC Federal Deposit Insurance Corporation. See BANKS AND BANKING.

feasance The performance of an act. For example, the creation of a statute is a feasance. See MALFEASANCE; MISFEASANCE; NONFEASANCE.

federal Belonging to the government or union of the states; founded on or organized under the laws of the Constitution of the UNITED STATES. In political and judicial writings, "federal" is used to describe the form of government of the United States. The term "national" is sometimes substituted for "federal." "Federal" is more appropriate when referring to the government of the union of the states. "National" is preferable when making a distinction between levels of government—state or national.

In a broader sense, "federal" is commonly applied to a compact (agreement) between two or more states (or provinces), uniting them under one central government. The Dominion of Canada is an example of such a federal union. See CONSTITUTIONAL LAW.

Federal Bureau of Investigation A branch of the Department of Justice that discovers and prosecutes crimes committed against the United States; assists in protecting the President; and, under the direction of the U.S. Attorney General, conducts investigations of matters controlled by the Justice and State departments. The FBI's directors, inspectors, and agents may carry firearms, serve warrants and subpoenas, and make arrests. The Director of the FBI is appointed by the President, with the advice and consent of the Senate, for one 10-year term of office. He reports directly to the President.

federal civil procedure The rules that regulate the handling of civil (noncriminal) actions in federal courts. They are set forth in the Federal Rules of Civil Procedure.

Federal Communications Commission

The U.S. agency established to regulate interstate and foreign commerce in wire and radio communication in order to provide national and international communication services at reasonable rates, to serve national defense, and to promote the safety of life and property. Its powers and duties include the licensing and regulation of private and public communication facilities, including radio and television stations—but as with other aspects of government, there is a trend toward deregulation.

The Federal Communications Commission (FCC) is a PUBLIC ADMINISTRATIVE AGENCY. It has seven members, not more than four of whom can belong to the same political party; all are appointed by the President.

■ **Background** Government regulation of radio began in 1910, when radio was considered primarily a safety device in maritime operations and potentially useful to the military. Anyone wanting to use radio frequencies had to register with the Department of Commerce, which assigned the frequency.

During World War I, radio's commercial possibilities were recognized, and by the mid-1920's hundreds of commercial radio stations were in operation. The Secretary of Commerce still assigned the frequencies, but his authority to regulate broadcasting was not clear. In 1927 the Federal Radio Commission was established to assign frequencies to applicants who met specific engineering standards and to establish and enforce certain rules for broadcasters in exchange for the privilege of using the airwaves. As a result of the Communications Act of 1934, this commission developed into what is today the FCC.

■ **Functions** The FCC sets the ground rules by which commercial and educational radio and television stations can be licensed. It chooses between applicants for the same frequency and sets up a framework that attempts to promote competition. It allows the free market to determine such matters as advertising costs, expenses, cost of equipment, and choice of programming by broadcasters.

The FCC does not regulate commercial advertising; this is done by the FEDERAL TRADE COMMISSION (FTC), which, for example, determines whether commercials are or are not false or misleading. The FCC would, however, act if a licensee continued to broadcast an advertisement that the FTC had determined to be false or misleading. The FCC has not attempted to set rates for pay television or cablevision.

In addition to commercial and educational broadcasting, the FCC regulates nonbroadcast use of communications facilities such as interstate telephone and telegraph services; carrier communications systems used in interstate

HOW GOVERNMENT CONTROLS THE AIRWAVES

■ The Federal Communications Commission (FCC) is a creation of the 1930's New Deal administration; however, government regulation of broadcasting dates back to 1910, when radio was considered primarily a safety device for ships—at that time a person had to register with the Department of Commerce to use the airwaves.

■ FCC regulation covers commercial and educational broadcasting, interstate telephone and telegraph services, interstate carrier communications systems, industrial radio systems, marine radio, aviation frequencies, citizens band (CB) radio, ham communications, police and fire networks, computer-to-computer communications, and cable and pay TV.

■ The FCC grants three-year licenses to all radio and television broadcasters, subject to their ability to meet eight FCC-set qualifications: U.S. citizenship, character (criminals are disqualified), financial capability, technical capacity, diversity of media ownership (to prevent monopoly situations), familiarity with the needs of the community they propose to serve), proposals for programming, and adoption of equal-employment-opportunity policies.

■ If other stations, or members of the general public in significant numbers, protest an impending grant, the FCC must schedule a hearing. For example, if the only classical music station in town is sold to a new owner who plans a hard-rock format and there is a public uproar, there will have to be a hearing.

■ Federal law requires that legally qualified candidates during an election campaign be granted equal opportunity to use broadcasting facilities. This law does not apply to broadcasts or advertisements in which the candidate does not appear. Broadcasters who sell time to political candidates must charge them the lowest unit rate during the 45 days before a general election. Appearances by spokesmen on behalf of candidates are not entitled to this rate, however.

■ No broadcaster may censor a political broadcast. A legally qualified candidate is free to say anything at all, even if it is scandalous or obscene.

■ If you are subjected to a personal attack impugning your honesty, character, or integrity on the airwaves, you have the right to appear in your own defense. The station must inform you of the attack, give you a script or tape of it, and offer you an opportunity to respond.

■ Broadcasters are free to refuse commercials they consider unsuitable to go on the air.

■ The FCC has no limit on the ratio of commercials to programs, but the National Association of Broadcasters has: radio, no more than 18 minutes per hour; TV, no more then 16 minutes per hour; children's programs no more than 9½ minutes per hour on weekends and no more than 12 minutes per hour during the week.

■ Cable TV is not really broadcasting (because it does not use the airwaves for transmission), but the FCC nonetheless regulates it, with a dual-licensing scheme whereby the state and/or local government issues the license and imposes whatever obligations it thinks necessary, subject to certain FCC standards. After a hearing, the cable system gets a certificate of compliance from the FCC.

■ To use a CB radio, you must apply to the FCC for a license, for which you must be at least 18 years old.

commerce; radio systems for industrial use, such as truck-to-truck communications, taxicab networks, and communications between a central plant and its repairmen or servicemen; communications between hospital and doctor; marine and ship radio; aviation frequencies; citizens band radio; ham (amateur radio operator) communications; police and fire communications networks; computer-to-computer communications; and cable and pay television.

Government regulation of broadcasting seems to conflict with the constitutional protection given to the print media. See SPEECH AND PRESS, FREEDOM OF. It is often justified because of the scarcity of broadcast frequencies, but there are far more radio and television stations than there are daily newspapers in the United States. Two newspapers can physically operate in the same community at the same time, however, while usually only one radio and perhaps one television frequency is available in a particular community. Two stations cannot operate on one frequency; if they did, neither would be heard. Therefore, the government must make the choice. Even when there is only one applicant for a particular open frequency, the government determines whether the applicant has the proper qualifications and will operate in the public interest.

■ **Licensing** Broadcasters are granted an exclusive right, or license, to operate a station over a particular frequency for a limited time, usually a maximum of three years. One set of frequencies is set aside for standard (AM) broadcast stations, another for frequency modulation (FM) stations, and a third for television stations. The FCC grants licenses only if public convenience, interest, or necessity is served and the applicant is properly qualified.

Qualifications Before granting a license to operate a radio or television station, the FCC considers eight points:

Citizenship A commercial broadcasting license may not be held by a noncitizen, a foreign government, or a corporation in which any officer or director is an alien or more than one fifth of the stock is voted by aliens or representatives of foreign governments.

Character The FCC evaluates applicants to determine whether they fulfill the agency's standards of character, relying primarily on the truth of the information provided by the applicants themselves. Any deliberate misrepresentation of a fact, even though insignificant, will seriously jeopardize a license application regardless of any positive qualities the applicant can demonstrate.

Violations of criminal law, especially those involving moral turpitude, such as rape or murder, usually result in a denial of a license. Misdemeanors and traffic violations are usually ignored.

Financial qualifications An applicant must show that he is financially capable of constructing and operating the proposed facility for one year, even if the station should earn no revenue. If the applicant intends to rely upon anticipated revenues, he must file evidence that these revenues will, in fact, be earned, by providing affidavits stating the intentions of prospective advertisers.

An applicant who wants to purchase an existing profit-making station must show only that the station is financially able to operate without revenues for the first three months after the purchase. An applicant who wants to buy a

station in financial difficulty must show that the station will be able to overcome the seller's deficits in the first year of operation.

Technical showing Applicants must meet all of the technical requirements specified in the FCC's rules, such as using approved transmitting equipment and operating during appropriate hours.

Diversity of media ownership The FCC has enacted multiple-ownership rules to restrict persons or companies from dominating the airwaves. A single company may not own more than one station offering the same service, such as more than one AM station in the same community, or even in nearby communities if their signals would overlap. (Noncommercial stations are exempt from these rules.) A single company may own an AM and an FM station in the same community, but not an AM station and a television station or an FM station and a television station. In those instances when a single company is allowed to own an AM, FM, and television station, the owner had to acquire them before the passage of the present rules. When stations are sold, the multiple-ownership rules have to be met.

A single company may own no more than seven AM, seven FM, and seven television stations anywhere in the United States. Only five of those seven television stations may be VHF (very high frequency) television stations.

Because television facilities are quite limited—there were only 516 VHF and 211 UHF (ultrahigh frequency) stations in the United States as of January 31, 1978—the FCC has restricted ownership of VHF stations in the country's 50 largest markets. If an owner wants more than three VHF stations in one of these markets, he must demonstrate how the public interest would be served by the acquisition.

Until 1975, there was no prohibition against a newspaper's owning a radio or TV station in the same community. The FCC now prohibits such ownership. The FCC has ordered some newspaper-broadcaster owners to get rid of their dual interests because they were the only source of information in the community, thus creating a MONOPOLY.

Community studies A broadcast applicant must demonstrate a familiarity with the needs of the community it will serve. It must interview community leaders and survey the general public to help determine the problems and needs of the community and develop a responsible program schedule.

Programming Applicants must indicate the type of programming they plan to broadcast, and identify the nonentertainment programs that are intended to meet the specific problems and needs of the community. The applicant must specify the percentage of total programming to be presented in a typical week in such nonentertainment categories as news and public affairs. The FCC has no official minimums for any programming category, but generally applicants propose some public affairs or news programming.

Equal employment showing Since 1967, the FCC has required all applicants to adopt and file an affirmative action, equal opportunity policy to insure nondiscrimination against minority groups.

Processing A license may be granted without a hearing unless there is a substantial and material (important) question of fact—for example, whether the applicant has sufficient funds to cover estimated construction costs and first-year operating expenses—or the FCC is unable to verify that the grant would be in the public interest. For example, if the only classical music station in a community is to be sold to someone who plans a hard-rock format and there is much public protest, the FCC will schedule a hearing to determine whether the change should be allowed.

Representatives of the public may participate in the licensing process if granting the application sought would affect upon them. A black group in a southern community, for example, might protest a renewal grant to a broadcaster who had repeatedly disregarded the needs or interests of the black community. Any such group that suffers a particular injury can file a *petition to deny* the license with the FCC. If the group raises a substantial question of fact or a policy issue that the FCC cannot resolve on the basis of the information in the application, a hearing will be held.

Renewal and revocation   A broadcaster must file for license renewal every three years. There is no guarantee that a license will be renewed.

Although a license may be revoked during its term, the FCC can do so only after giving the broadcaster notice and a full opportunity to be heard. The FCC must explain its decisions through written findings on a public record containing a full explanation of its rationale and actions. These decisions may be appealed to the U.S. Court of Appeals.

■ **Standards**   Although the FCC's primary function is to grant licenses, it has also been involved with the manner in which stations are operated. Certain areas of program content may be controlled by the commission.

Political broadcasting   From the start of broadcast legislation, Congress has recognized the enormous potential of radio as a political tool. A major concern of lawmakers is that a broadcasting facility may be able to influence an election improperly by giving only one candidate access to its audience. To prevent this, Congress passed a law requiring that if a licensed broadcaster permits a legally qualified candidate for public office to broadcast during his election campaign, that broadcaster must give all other candidates for that office equal opportunity to use his station. Criminal penalties are imposed for willful violations of the statute.

Use   This equal opportunities provision does not apply to broadcasts or advertisements on behalf of the candidate in which he does not appear. The candidate's appearance is considered a use whenever his identity can be reasonably presumed known to the audience and the appearance is an integral part of the program.

EXAMPLE Suppose a candidate gives a five-second introduction to a half-hour program devoted to appearances by his supporters. The introduction would be so integral to the program that the entire program would constitute a use. Therefore, an opponent would be entitled to a half-hour of time.

A candidate's appearance will be considered a use even if he is appearing for a completely unrelated purpose and never mentions his candidacy.

EXAMPLE A station's weather reporter is also a candidate for local office. An appearance in his normal role of weatherman would be considered a use entitling his opponent to equal time, even if he never mentions his candidacy. His appearance is considered a benefit because of the "identification factor" in politics. People are more likely to vote for candidates they recognize.

As a practical matter, on-air staff personnel who become candidates are usually taken off by the station in order to avoid equal time problems.

Exemptions   Certain exemptions to the equal time doctrine exist. When a candidate appears on a bona fide newscast, news interview, news documentary, or on-the-spot coverage of a bona fide news event, the equal time doctrine does not apply. The reason for such exceptions is to avoid the situation in which an incumbent appears on a news program at a ribbon-cutting ceremony, for example, and all his opponents demand equal time.

Newscasts, interviews, and documentaries are essentially under the control of the station, not the candidate, so the candidate cannot misuse his appearance to gain an improper advantage. If the intent of the station is to favor one candidate over another, the appearance would not be bona fide and the equal time requirement would apply.

As to on-the-spot coverage of a bona fide news event, questions have arisen about how a bona fide news event should be defined. Should it be based on the subjective determination of the broadcaster or on an objective determination by the FCC? Suppose two gubernatorial candidates have been invited by a local professional group to debate important issues. The debate is considered a bona fide news event by a local station, which desires to carry it live as a matter of interest to its audience. Would the debate be an exempt program, so that the station need not offer equal time to other candidates for the same office who were not invited to the debate? In recent years the FCC has held that, at least with respect to debates and press conferences by candidates, the subjective judgment of the station, not of the FCC, determines exemptability. If the station in good faith believes the debate or conference is newsworthy, it can cover it without being subject to the equal time rule for opposing candidates.

Reasonable access   A broadcaster could avoid the equal time requirement entirely simply by refusing to allow any candidate to appear on his station. In doing so, however, he would violate later additions to the Communications Act of 1934, which requires a broadcaster to allow a legally qualified candidate for federal elective office to have "reasonable access" to his station or to permit the candidate to buy "reasonable" amounts of time on the air. Although state and local candidates are not specifically mentioned, broadcasters are prohibited from refusing to allow these candidates on the air merely in order to avoid the equal time requirement.

What represents reasonable access has not been precisely defined, but the FCC has established certain guidelines. It has never required that every candidate for every nonfederal office be given access. A broadcaster can prune out the minor contests and allocate time only for the major ones.

A broadcaster's discretion is much more limited with respect to federal offices. He cannot, for example, emphasize only the presidential race and refuse time for congressional or senatorial races. All federal candidates must be given reasonable access, but the broadcaster has some discretion in determining the manner of access. It is not required to sell programming or advertising time to candidates. Some broadcasters choose to meet their obligation to give reasonable access to all candidates by presenting, for example, a forum-type debate, inviting all of the candidates to participate on an equal basis, and doing so twice or three times in the campaign.

If, however, a broadcaster decides to sell time, he must sell the time at rates comparable to those offered commercial clients. This means that if a broadcaster sells 60- or 30- or 5-second spots during prime time to commercial advertisers, he cannot refuse them to federal candidates. Similarly, he cannot restrict federal candidates to hours outside of prime time. Broadcasters who choose to sell time to political candidates must charge them the "lowest unit rate" during the 45 days before a general election, but appearances by spokesmen on behalf of candidates are not entitled to this rate.

Legally qualified candidates　Equal time obligations apply only to "legally qualified candidates for public office." A candidate is legally qualified if he meets the requirements of the law of the state in which the election is to be held. Not all elections are for public office. For example, the position of delegate to a party convention is not a public office, even though the name of the delegate may appear on an election ballot. A candidate who is the subject of a bona fide write-in campaign can be legally qualified.

A person must publicly announce his candidacy. An incumbent president, for example, is not a candidate for reelection unless he announces his candidacy. Until he does, none of his appearances can be considered a use triggering equal time requirements.

Censorship　The law prohibits any broadcaster from censoring the material broadcast on a political program. When a legally qualified candidate for public office appears on a program, he is free to say anything, whether or not it relates to the candidacy, even if it is scandalous, obscene, or in any other way unsuitable for broadcast. (The station cannot be sued for defamation when it is used by a candidate in this manner.) This freedom from censorship applies only to a candidate, not to any person speaking on his behalf or to appearances by noncandidates under the fairness doctrine (discussed below).

Timely demand　Equal time rights can be lost through delay. A candidate must request equal time within one week of the day of the first use by his opponent. If someone was not a candidate at the time of the first use, he is entitled to match any uses made by his opponents during the week before the new candidate announced. A broadcaster does not have to inform all other candidates that a particular candidate is appearing on his station; the candidates must be viligant on their own behalf. There is one exception to this rule. When the candidate is the licensee of the station involved, he must inform his opponent of the specific days he will be using the station for his candidacy.

Political editorializing　When a broadcaster either endorses or opposes a legally qualified candidate in an editorial, he must, within 24 hours after the broadcast, notify the other candidate of the date and time of the editorial, give him a script or tape of it, and offer a reasonable opportunity for the candidate or a representative to respond. If the editorial is aired within 72 hours of the election, the broadcaster must do this far enough in advance of the broadcast so that a candidate has time to prepare a reply. This duty arises only when a station endorses a candidate. It does not apply to editorials on subjects not involving candidates, such as, for example, municipal bond issues.

Candidates' spokesmen　The FCC has created a *quasi-equal opportunity doctrine* that relates specifically to appearances by spokesmen for candidates, which are not covered by the equal time doctrine. When a station sells time to supporters or spokesmen of a candidate during an election campaign, it must offer comparable time to the opponent's spokesmen, but it need not provide fringe candidates or minor parties with broadcast time under this quasi-equal opportunity.

Fairness doctrine　The fairness doctrine established by the FCC obligates a broadcaster "to operate in the public interest and to afford reasonable opportunity for the discussion of conflicting views on issues of public importance." A broadcaster must devote a reasonable amount of air time to the discussion of controversial issues, and must do so fairly by affording reasonable opportunity for the presentation of opposing viewpoints. Without this dual requirement of access plus fairness, a broadcaster might decide to be fair by never presenting any controversial material.

Fairness　Fairness means that a broadcaster cannot use his facilities to present only one point of view on a major issue. But he is required to be fair only with respect to important issues of public controversy.

EXAMPLE　Mr. A, an avid television viewer, is firm in his conviction that there is no God. He is extremely upset with one station because it presents many religious programs affirming the existence of God. Mr. A writes many agitated letters to the station demanding that it schedule a program for atheists or take the religious programs off the air. Under the fairness doctrine, however, the station does not have to present an agnostic or atheistic point of view unless the existence of God is currently a matter of major public controversy.

A broadcaster has a great deal of discretion as to how much time to give to a particular controversy, what issues to cover, and whom to invite to present them. Only when the broadcaster has clearly abused his discretionary powers can the FCC step in and order a particular course of action.

Certain limits are imposed upon the broadcaster's discretion. As part of his obligation to operate in the public interest, he must encourage the presentation of opposing views. He cannot defend his failure to present different views on the ground that no one asked to respond. If a broadcaster has reason to believe that a group or person would speak out on an issue if informed of the broadcast, he must seek out that group or person. If one side of a controversial issue is presented on a sponsored (paid) basis, the broadcaster must air contrasting views even if those with such views cannot afford to purchase the time.

Unless a person or group filing a complaint with the FCC can show that a broadcaster has violated the fairness doctrine by failing to present varying views on the point at issue, the FCC will not require the broadcaster to respond. Otherwise, too great a burden would be placed upon broadcasters, and they might give up covering controversial issues entirely. Although the FCC receives thousands of complaints of unfairness each year, very few are ever followed up with demands for further information from broadcasters. The FCC has only rarely ruled that the broadcaster in fact breached his responsibilities under the fairness doctrine. A more vigorous enforcement might have an improper chilling effect on broadcasters' freedom of speech.

EXAMPLE When the question of whether cigarette smoking ○━━✳ was dangerous to health was under investigation by the Surgeon General, cigarette companies continued to advertise their product over radio and television. In response to a complaint, the commission decided that the mere presentation of product advertising was itself a statement of a point of view on the controversial issue of whether cigarettes were damaging. Stations running cigarette advertising were under an obligation to present "anticigarette advertising" in some reasonable proportion to the amount of cigarette ads. This decision created many problems. Environmentalists demanded opportunities to respond to advertisements for automobiles, gasoline engines, and public utilities on the ground that these ads were statements on the controversial issue of pollution. Eventually, the FCC reversed its decision and decided that product advertising in itself is not a statement on a controversial issue so long as the advertising merely extols the virtues of the product and takes no stand on matters of public controversy.

News programs are often charged with being slanted, but the FCC responds cautiously. It recognizes that direct intervention into the thought processes of reporters (by demanding to see their files, for example) could well have an extremely repressive effect in an area explicitly protected by the First Amendment. The agency therefore requires some additional evidence that the news is being slanted before it will hear complaints concerning the fairness of news presentation—for example, statements of persons present during an interview that was alleged to be biased when aired.

Personal attack rule Arising from the fairness doctrine is the personal attack rule, which gives a person who has been attacked on radio or television the right to defend himself. When a station airs a controversial issue of public importance and an attack is made on the honesty, character, or integrity of an identified person or group, the station must, within one week of the attack, notify the person of the broadcast, give him a script or tape of it, and offer him a reasonable opportunity to respond.

The personal attack rule applies only to broadcasts presenting views on a controversial issue of public importance. A person attacked on some other type of program must look to the law of LIBEL AND SLANDER for remedy. The rule does not apply to attacks on foreign groups or foreign public figures; personal attacks made by legally qualified candidates for public office or persons associated with them; and bona fide newscasts, interviews, or on-the-spot coverage of bona fide news events.

Prime time access rule Networks are, generally speaking, organizations set up to create and distribute programs to individual television stations. They also act as advertising clearance centers for all network-affiliated sta-

tions. Although most networks assume many of the same responsibilities as individual stations, the networks themselves are not directly regulated by the FCC. Instead, the FCC regulates the networks indirectly through its power over the individual stations. For instance, individual stations are prohibited from entering into contracts with networks that contain provisions the FCC finds offensive to the public interest, such as clauses preventing the station from broadcasting the programs of any other network.

Among the most important of FCC's so-called network rules is the prime time access rule, which reflects a concern over local programming among network affiliates. Television stations owned by, or affiliated with, a national television network in the 50 largest television markets may present only three hours of network programs (including reruns) during the four hours of prime time (7–11 P.M. Eastern and Pacific Time, 6–10 P.M. Central and Mountain Time). Certain types of programs are not counted in the three-hour limitation: children's shows; public affairs or documentary programs; special news programs and political broadcasts; regular network news broadcasts up to one-half hour in length when immediately preceded or followed by a full hour of locally produced news; and national sports events or other special programs.

■ **Commercials** A broadcaster determines what programs and commercials his station will broadcast. As long as he adheres to the FCC standards discussed above, he can use his own discretion regarding programming. He is also free to refuse to broadcast commercials he considers unsuitable. Commercials that have been refused air time include those for computer dating services that offer cash bonuses for attractive women, schools for croupiers, and baby-selling agencies geared to unwed teenagers.

The FCC has no formal limits on how many minutes of commercials may be broadcast per hour of programming, but broadcasters themselves observe unofficial limits suggested by the National Association of Broadcasters. Those limits are: for full-time AM and FM stations, 18 minutes of commercial time per hour; for television stations, 16 minutes per hour; for children's programs, 9½ minutes per hour on weekends and 12 minutes per hour during the week.

■ **Public broadcasting** Public broadcasting systems are noncommercial radio and television stations that are supported by public and private contributions along with federal, state, and local governments. Their purpose is to offer an alternative to the programming aired by commercial channels. About half of the U.S. public television licenses are held by states.

Since 1962, Congress has given public broadcasters matching grants (certain amounts of money based on a proportionate share of private contributions) to encourage the expansion of noncommercial broadcasting. The Corporation of Public Broadcasting, a private, independent, nonprofit corporation established in 1967 by the Public Broadcasting Act, also helps to establish and develop public stations, and in November 1978 Congress enacted the Public Telecommunications Financing Act to continue and increase the amount of federal financing for public broadcasting channels. A total of $180 million will go to public broadcasting in 1981, $200 million in 1982, and $220 million in 1983. Stations receiving the money must make their financial reports available to the public and allow the public to attend board meetings at which programming and major policies are decided upon. In the past, all public broadcasters were prohibited from editorializing on issues of public importance. Now only broadcasters on stations licensed to state and local governments are prevented from editorializing.

■ **Cable television**   A television signal can travel only a certain distance through the airwaves. This fact, coupled with the FCC's policy of limiting the number of frequencies assigned to particular cities, creates a significant reception problem in rural areas and the fringe areas of big cities. Some mountain towns get poor reception even from their local stations. Many communities solved this problem through the Community-Antenna Television (CATV) system by which extremely tall receiving towers at the highest point in the area pick up the signals from the airwaves and retransmit them over cables run from the tower to the homes of subscribers. The subscriber pays a one-time installation fee and a monthly service fee.

Although the original CATV systems were intended mainly to fill in the blanks within normal coverage areas, CATV also brings in service from distant cities that, under the FCC's plan, were never intended to serve that particular community.

EXAMPLE Kingston, New York, which is 90 miles from O←—※ New York City, was never intended to receive transmissions from New York City TV stations. Kingston was to be served by the closer Albany, New York, facilities. Cable television, however, can bring in all the New York stations, a benefit to Kingston residents but a possible economic detriment to the Albany station, which may lose some of its "natural audience"—and hence, revenue-producing advertisers—in Kingston.

CATV-system operators can offer other communication services. Originally these were no more than weather and time checks, but later CATV began to offer full-fledged programming. Consequently CATV became more competitive with regular broadcasting.

Regulating CATV   Although cable television is not broadcasting in the traditional sense, the FCC has stepped in to regulate it. Under a dual-licensing scheme, the state and/or local government issues the license to the cable operator and imposes whatever obligations it thinks necessary, subject to certain FCC standards. Before a license is granted there must be a public hearing and an evaluation of the applicant's character and his financial and technical qualifications. Each cable system must then get from the FCC a certificate of compliance in which the cable operator demonstrates that it will comply with FCC rules and that its local authorization meets FCC's franchise standards.

Transmitting over the airwaves without a license, sometimes called air piracy, is a federal offense punishable by a fine of up to $10,000, one year in jail, or both.

EXAMPLE In one of the first instances of airwave piracy, an O←—※ unused channel in the Syracuse, New York, area started broadcasting such movies as *Deep Throat* and *Rocky*, as well as episodes of *Star Trek* and *Twilight Zone*. The pirates were students at a local university that had broadcasting facilities.

Pay-cable regulation   Home box office (HBO), as it is called in some parts of the country, broadcasts films, sports events, and a few special programs, on the unused channels of a cable system, for which the subscriber pays an extra fee. Since the return to producers from cable exhibition might be greater than that which regular television stations or networks could pay, the FCC feared that producers would withhold their product from commercial television and make it available only to cable television subscribers. To prevent this, the FCC tries to prohibit pay-cable showings of feature films or sports events that traditionally have been broadcast on so-called free television. The rules are also aimed at making it difficult, if not impossible, for pay-cable systems to carry events traditionally shown on commercial television—for example, the World Series, the Super Bowl, and the Olympics.

■ **Citizens band radios**   In recent years citizens band radios, or CB's, have become increasingly popular. They are used by motorists and travelers to check road and weather conditions as well as to report emergencies. People who wish to use a CB must apply to the FCC for a license. An applicant must be 18 years old or over.

■ **Violence on television**   With the increase in violence portrayed on television, serious problems have developed as to what type of programming is inappropriate.

EXAMPLE A major network and its local affiliate were sued O←—※ for $11 million in damages by the mother of a young girl who was sexually attacked in an alleged reenactment of a scene from a television movie. The movie, shown early in the evening, depicted a girl being held down and sexually abused with a broom handle. Three days later, the plaintiff's daughter suffered a similar attack with a bottle. When caught, the children who took part in the attack allegedly told police that they were imitating the scene in the movie. The girl's mother sued the network for "wanton, careless and negligent acts," with "willfully and intentionally" showing the movie at a time when impressionable children could see it, and with acting "maliciously and in reckless disregard of its possible results." The lower court dismissed the suit because of the potential conflict with freedom of expression guaranteed by the First Amendment.

The state appellate court reversed the decision of the lower court and sent the case back for retrial, saying that the mother should not be prevented from convincing a jury that the broadcaster, by his choice of programming, should be responsible for her daughter's injuries. At the new trial, the judge dismissed the claim of negligence and held that the plaintiff would have to prove that the network intended to incite its viewers to imitate the violence in the movie in order to win her case. This test indicated that the court viewed the controversy strictly as a First Amendment problem. The plaintiff could not prove intent, and the case was dismissed.

Although this case was dismissed, it still poses significant problems in broadcast law. Broadcasters have a duty to present programming in the public interest. But by depicting sordid events in an exciting way, they may inadvertently move impressionable viewers, particularly children, to action. Should broadcasters be liable for programming decisions that lead to imitation of criminal scenes, or must they have actually intended to incite violence by their choice of programming? The legal-incitement theory, which is virtually impossible to prove, has rarely been used. In one case, when a 15-year-old boy did use it as a defense to a murder charge, claiming that he was "involuntarily intoxicated" by all his years of watching television violence, the jury rejected his defense and found him guilty.

Freedom of expression has always been guaranteed by the Constitution. If a broadcaster is to be held responsible for the possible consequences of his programming, this will have the effect of hindering artistic creativity and be in conflict with the First Amendment.

federal courts   U.S. courts. They have the power to hear and determine ADMIRALTY and maritime cases; cases arising under the Constitution, laws, or treaties of the United States; and certain other kinds of cases. The Constitution establishes the SUPREME COURT and gives Congress the authority to create other federal courts below it. The federal courts are entirely separate from the state court systems. The authority of the federal courts comes from the federal laws that create them.

This article discusses the different kinds of federal courts and their jurisdiction (authority). See also Chart 1. *District courts* are the general trial-level courts in the federal judicial system. An appeal from a district court decision must be taken to the appropriate *court of appeals*. Three special courts are also discussed—the Court of Claims, Court of International Trade, and Court of Customs and Patent Appeals—as is the judicial system of the District of Columbia. For a discussion of the U.S. Tax Court, see TAX COURT. For information about appealing the decision of a lower court to a higher court in a civil (noncriminal) case, see APPEAL AND ERROR. Appeals of criminal cases are discussed in CRIMINAL LAW. The U.S. Court of Military Appeals hears appeals from court-martial decisions.

■ **Jurisdiction** The source of the Supreme Court's authority to decide cases is the U.S. Constitution. The powers of other federal courts are fixed by statutes passed by Congress. Each court can hear only cases that it is empowered to hear. This authority is called jurisdiction.

Federal courts have jurisdiction in federal criminal cases and both at law (where money damages are sought) and in EQUITY (where the court does justice). The primary responsibility of the courts is to enforce federal law, and they may determine all issues raised by a case, issue WRITS, and order provisional REMEDIES as necessary. They do not hear matrimonial cases or cases involving the PROBATE of wills. Generally, federal courts in one state will not enforce a criminal or tax law in effect in another state. State laws relating to WRONGFUL-DEATH ACTIONS (lawsuits in which money damages are sought by the survivors of a person killed by another person) or authorizing business corporations usually may not be enforced in federal courts. For a detailed discussion of jurisdiction, see COURTS.

The geographical jurisdiction of each federal court is generally limited to a particular area. (The Supreme Court and special federal courts, such as the Court of Claims, can hear cases originating anywhere in the United States or its territories.) The territory of the United States, Puerto Rico, Guam, the Northern Mariana Islands, and the Virgin Is-

lands is divided into 12 *judicial circuits.* The 12 circuits are

District of
Columbia   Washington, D.C.
First .... Maine, Massachusetts, New Hampshire, Rhode Island, and Puerto Rico
Second ...... Connecticut, New York, and Vermont
Third .... Delaware, New Jersey, Pennsylvania, and the Virgin Islands
Fourth ...... Maryland, North Carolina, South Carolina, Virginia, and West Virginia
Fifth .... Louisiana, Mississippi, and Texas
Sixth .... Kentucky, Michigan, Ohio, and Tennessee
Seventh .... Illinois, Indiana, and Wisconsin
Eighth ...... Arkansas, Iowa, Minnesota, Missouri, Nebraska, North Dakota, and South Dakota
Ninth .... Alaska, Arizona, California, Hawaii, Idaho, Montana, Nevada, Oregon, Washington, Northern Mariana Islands, and Guam
Tenth .... Colorado, Kansas, New Mexico, Oklahoma, Utah, and Wyoming
Eleventh .... Alabama, Florida, and Georgia

These circuits are made up of *judicial districts,* the number of which depends on the size and the population of the area. Every state has at least one judicial district, and the largest—California, New York, and Texas—have four.

Judicial districts covering very large areas are separated into divisions. Indiana, for example, has two judicial districts, the Northern District and the Southern District. The Northern District has three divisions. Court for one division is held at Fort Wayne, for another at South Bend, and for the third at Hammond and Lafayette. The Southern District has four divisions, with district courts sitting at Indianapolis, Terre Haute, Evansville, and New Albany. Federal judges in these courts are appointed for life by the President, with the consent of the Senate.

■ **District courts**   U.S. district courts have original and general jurisdiction. Most federal cases start (originate) in district courts, which hear civil actions at common law and in equity. District courts can hear only cases within the jurisdiction granted them by federal law. They have original jurisdiction to hear any case that arises under the Constitution or the laws and treaties of the United States and involves more than $10,000. This is called *federal-question jurisdiction.* If the amount in dispute is less than $10,000, the action must be started in a state court.

Any civil case between citizens of different states or between an American citizen and a foreign citizen or government can be started in federal district court, provided at least $10,000 is at stake. This is called *diversity jurisdiction* because the parties in the case are from diverse, or different, places. In a diversity case, the federal court has the authority to apply state laws.

The federal district courts have original and exclusive jurisdiction of ADMIRALTY, BANKRUPTCY, and PRIZE cases. Admiralty cases concern ocean commerce, collisions between vessels, and other controversies related to the sea. Prize cases determine rights in ships and cargo captured at sea.

In addition to the above, federal district courts have the authority to hear a variety of other matters relating to federal law, with differing limitations on the exercise of this authority:

(1) INTERPLEADER actions, in which money or other property is given to the court to determine who has the right to receive it. The stake paid into court must be worth at least $500, and claimants must be citizens of different states.

(2) Postal matters.

(3) Federal tax cases, except those handled by the U.S. Court of Claims or the U.S. TAX COURT.

(4) PATENT, COPYRIGHT, and TRADEMARK AND TRADE NAME cases based on federal law or an unfair-competition case in one of these areas. The U.S. Court of Customs and Patent Appeals can also hear some of these cases.

(5) Federal CIVIL RIGHTS cases.

(6) ELECTION disputes involving constitutional rights but not controversies that arise over the election of a President, Vice President, U.S. Senator or Representative, or a member of a state legislature.

(7) Actions in which the United States or a federal agency is a plaintiff and most actions in which the United States is a defendant. The U.S. Court of Claims also has jurisdiction in some of the cases where the United States is a defendant.

(8) PARTITION actions to divide property owned by the United States and someone else.

(9) Many lawsuits by the federal government against national banks.

(10) Many actions involving INTERNATIONAL LAW as it affects ALIENS or diplomats.

(11) Lawsuits that involve Indian lands or rights, including water rights.

(12) EMINENT DOMAIN proceedings for the U.S. government to take private land for a public purpose.

(13) An action to force a federal officer to do his duty. Every judicial district has at least one district court judge. Most districts have from one to three judges sharing the case load, but heavily populated areas that are also centers of business and government activity have more— the Southern District for New York, for example, has 27. The number of judges can be changed by Congress. Each judge may preside alone, and where there are two or more judges in a district, all may hold sessions of court at the same time.

Bankruptcy courts Congress has established new bankruptcy courts as adjuncts to the district courts in each judicial district. A single bankruptcy judge may hear a case arising under the federal bankruptcy laws. Three bankruptcy judges may be required to hear appeals from the bankruptcy courts in a judicial circuit. Where three bankruptcy judges have not been appointed to hear appeals, the appeal may be taken to a federal district court. Bankruptcy decisions may also be appealed to the U.S. Courts of Appeals. Each bankruptcy judge is appointed by the President, with the advice and consent of the Senate, and holds office for 14 years.

■ **Courts of appeals** The decisions made in federal district courts may be reviewed by a court of appeals in each circuit. The number of circuit judges and the place where court is held in each circuit are fixed by federal law,

which can be changed at any time by Congress. As of October 1981, the number of judges in each circuit and the places where U.S. Courts of Appeals hold sessions are

District of		
Columbia	11	Washington, D.C.
First	4	Boston
Second	11	New York City
Third	10	Philadelphia
Fourth	10	Richmond and Asheville
Fifth	14	New Orleans, Fort Worth, and Jackson
Sixth	11	Cincinnati
Seventh	9	Chicago
Eighth	9	St. Louis, Kansas City, Omaha, and St. Paul
Ninth	23	San Francisco, Los Angeles, Portland, and Seattle
Tenth	8	Denver, Wichita, and Oklahoma City
Eleventh	12	Atlanta, Jacksonville, Montgomery

The rules of court in each circuit may provide for sessions to be held in other places when appropriate.

Appeals cases are usually heard by three judges, but each circuit arranges to hear some cases *en banc*—that is, with all its circuit judges sitting together and ruling by majority vote. A majority of the circuit judges in regular active service in the circuit may order a case heard *en banc* at any time. This is usually done if the decision in the case is likely to affect issues in many other cases, especially when an important question of constitutionality or jurisdiction or when the right to appeal is involved. For more information about appeals, see APPEAL AND ERROR.

■ **Court of Claims** As a rule, governments cannot be sued. This privilege of the government is called *sovereign immunity*. Its purpose is to protect governmental stability by barring a multitude of claims that would bankrupt the public treasury. From the early days of the United States, however, persons whose rights were violated by the federal government could ask Congress to pass a *private bill* authorizing a payment of money to compensate them for their loss. Eventually, so many of these bills were introduced that they slowed down the work of the legislature. So, in 1855, Congress created the Court of Claims, which was organized as an administrative agency or advisory body with the authority to hear claims against the government and report its findings to Congress, along with proposals for solving the problem in each case.

By the end of 1861, Congress was still overburdened by the necessity of reexamining claims that had first been submitted to the Court of Claims. In his State of the Union message that year, President Abraham Lincoln recommended that judgments made by the Court of Claims be considered final without any further action by Congress, and on March 3, 1863, Congress agreed. Appeals, when permitted, were made directly to the Supreme Court. Over the years, Supreme Court decisions have firmly established the Court of Claims as a court, not merely a congressional agency. The court has earned a reputation for fairness and independence from both the legislative and executive branches of government.

The Court of Claims hears lawsuits against the United States based on the Constitution, federal laws, or contracts.

It may hear cases on salaries of public officers or agents, damages for someone unjustly convicted and imprisoned for a federal crime, and some Indian claims.

The President, with the advice and consent of the Senate, appoints a chief judge and six associate judges to sit on the Court of Claims, which holds an annual term in Washington. The judges are appointed for life. Either two or three judges hear a case, unless the chief judge decides that a case is important enough to require a hearing *en banc*, for which four judges are necessary.

■ **Customs and patent appeals courts** Congress has also created the U.S. Court of International Trade (formerly the Customs Court) and the U.S. Court of Customs and Patent Appeals. Like the Court of Claims, these courts can hear only cases in their own special area of the law. The Court of International Trade has exclusive jurisdiction when a person protests the amount of duties charged by CUSTOMS officials. The court can reconsider tariff rates, the category into which merchandise is put for tax purposes, and the refusal by Treasury Department officials to make a refund that is claimed. The Court of Customs and Patent Appeals has the power to review certain decisions made by the U.S. Patent Office, the U.S. International Trade Commission (formerly Tariff Commission), and the Secretary of Commerce.

The Court of International Trade has nine judges, appointed by the President, who designates one of them chief judge. The judges hold office for life if they meet the constitutional requirement of "good Behaviour." One judge may hear any case, but a panel of three may hear an important case. The Court of International Trade is located in New York City, but the chief judge has the authority to send judges to other ports to hear cases.

The Court of Customs and Patent Appeals is made up of a chief judge and four associates, also appointed by the President for life on the condition of good behavior. Court may be held at times and places fixed by the rules of the court. At least three judges must sit to hear a case, and the agreement of three judges is needed for a decision.

■ **Courts in the District of Columbia** The DISTRICT OF COLUMBIA has a special place in the U.S. legal system. Its courts can be established only by an act of Congress, and until 1970 legal matters in the District were handled by federal courts. Then Congress enacted the District of Columbia Court Reform and Criminal Procedure Act of 1970, which established for the District a court system similar to those of the states.

The District of Columbia Superior Court is a trial court, consisting of 44 judges, that hears cases concerning both federal and District of Columbia laws, including prosecutions for crimes, lawsuits for money damages up to $10,000, and cases involving taxes, juveniles, domestic relations, and landlords and tenants.

The District of Columbia Court of Appeals has the authority to review decisions of the Superior Court as well as actions taken by local government agencies and by the Commissioner and the Council for the District of Columbia. The court has nine judges and, most importantly, it is the court of last resort for local cases. For all practical purposes, the District of Columbia Court of Appeals functions like a state supreme court.

Federal Deposit Insurance Corporation
See BANKS AND BANKING.

Federal Insurance Contributions Act
The act establishing the SOCIAL SECURITY tax imposed on income from employment. The tax is collected by the employer, who deducts it from the employee's wages. The law provides for matching payments by employers. The revenue from FICA taxes is used to pay old age, survivors, disability, and hospital insurance benefits under the Social Security system.

federalism A system of government, such as that in the United States, by which sovereign power is divided between the national and state governments.

Federal National Mortgage Association
A privately owned purchaser of home MORTGAGES, created to stop, or at least retard, a decline in mortgage lending and home building. The association, popularly known as Fannie Mae, is sponsored by the federal government. It finances home mortgages for people who are unable to obtain housing under established home financing programs.

Fannie Mae differs from the federal housing authority (FHA), which guarantees loans made by banks to individual home buyers. Fannie Mae purchases mortgages that have already been made by lenders, such as commercial banks and savings and loan associations. In this way it encourages these organizations to extend mortgages. Fannie Mae also liquidates mortgages for the federal government—such as those acquired by the FHA through its guarantee program—by selling the mortgages to investors.

federal question A legal question that directly involves the U.S. Constitution, federal statutes, or treaties between the United States and a foreign country. Cases involving federal law are called federal question cases. The authority to hear lawsuits that turn on a point of federal law is called federal question jurisdiction. FEDERAL COURTS can hear federal question cases only if the dispute involves more than $10,000. Actions for less than $10,000 must be started in a state court.

Federal Register
A daily publication issued by the National Archives and Records Service, which makes available to the public regulations and legal notices issued by federal agencies. These include (1) presidential proclamations, (2) executive orders and federal agency documents having general applicability and legal effect, (3) documents required to be published by an act of Congress, and (4) federal agency documents of particular public interest. Documents are placed on file for public inspection at the Office of the Federal Register in Washington, D.C., the day before they are published. There are no copyright restrictions on material appearing in the *Federal Register*.

Federal Trade Commission
An agency of the U.S. government whose purpose is to keep the nation's business enterprises both free and fair. Established in 1915, the Federal Trade Commission (FTC) is a PUBLIC ADMINISTRATIVE AGENCY. It has five commissioners who are ap-

HOW THE FTC REGULATES BUSINESSES

■ The Federal Trade Commission (FTC) has five commissioners who are appointed by the President for seven-year terms; not more than three of the commissioners can be members of the same political party.

■ The FTC regulates businesses that are involved in or affect interstate commerce. It enforces consumer protection laws as well as laws and regulations against false advertising and all other kinds of unfair or deceptive practices in commerce, whether these practices affect competitive businesses or consumers.

■ In its efforts to curb unfair business practices, the FTC issues *industry guidelines* describing in layman's language the practices in a particular industry that should be avoided. It also issues *trade regulation rules* that have the force of law. For example, the FTC might issue a guideline saying that in its opinion the failure to include the statement "All aspirin is alike" in aspirin advertisements is a deceptive act or practice. It could also issue a trade regulation rule requiring that all aspirin advertisements include the statement. In the first instance, if a company omitted the suggested statement, the FTC could not bring action against the company merely for failing to do so—the FTC must prove that the advertising misled or deceived the public. In the second instance, however, the FTC need only show that the company had violated the rule by omitting the statement.

■ When the FTC steps in to protect the public interest against a given instance of unfair or deceptive practice, the business involved is given a chance to stop, either by informal agreement or by signing a consent to a written cease-and-desist order.

■ If the case is not settled by agreement or consent, the FTC will issue a complaint with a notice of hearing. The hearing is held before an administrative law judge of the FTC. The judge hears testimony and then draws up an opinion, on which the commission bases a decision. If that decision results in a cease-and-desist order, the business involved can obey the order or appeal the decision.

■ To appeal, the business must file a petition asking the local U.S. Court of Appeals to review the decision within 60 days. If it does not appeal, the order becomes final after 60 days. If it does appeal, the order cannot be enforced until the appeal is finished.

■ The FTC can sue in state and federal court for money damages on behalf of persons, partnerships, or corporations that have been injured by unfair or deceptive acts or practices.

pointed by the President for seven-year terms. Not more than three can be members of the same political party. It is the responsibility of the FTC to enforce a number of CONSUMER PROTECTION laws. The act that created the commission outlawed unfair methods of competition in commerce, but in 1938 this section was amended to give the FTC additional authority over all kinds of unfair or deceptive acts or practices in commerce, including those that deceive even if they do not interfere with competition.

■ **Unfair methods of competition** Unfair competition is any act that attempts to pass off goods as those of another, hinder healthy competition, or take business away from competitors by dishonest means. Infringement of TRADEMARKS AND TRADE NAMES, the wrongful taking of trade secrets, and price fixing in violation of federal and state laws are all forms of unfair competition. More elusive kinds of unfairness are also included, as a case decided in 1934 illustrates.

EXAMPLE In *Federal Trade Commission* v. *R. F. Keppel & Bro.*, the Supreme Court held that the FTC had properly ordered a candy company to stop marketing its product in an unfair way. The company was earning a substantial profit in various states in the penny candy trade. The unfair practice was the sale of candy in break-and-take packages, which gave Keppel a great advantage over competitors who sold candy in straight goods packages. Break-and-take packages injected the element of chance into candy buying. The manufacturer would deliver to the store an assortment containing, for example, 120 pieces of one-cent candy, four of which had a penny wrapped inside. The purchasers—usually children—who got those pieces would in effect get their candy free. In another assortment a few of the candies had colored centers rather than white, which entitled the purchaser to a prize. The manufacturers gave store owners colorful displays for each batch of break-and-take candy they bought. All the break-and-take candies were either smaller or of poorer quality than straight package candy sold at the same price.

The FTC found that children, attracted by the chance to gamble, were spending much more money on those candies than on the straight goods packages. The commission further found that lotteries and gambling devices were illegal in some states. The Supreme Court agreed that the FTC had the authority to order this manufacturer to stop using break-and-take packages.

Another penny candy case helped establish the limits of the FTC's authority. After the Supreme Court decided *Federal Trade Commission* v. *Bunte Bros, Inc.,* in 1941, the Federal Trade Commission was limited to prohibiting unfair competition only in *interstate commerce.*

EXAMPLE Bunte Bros. was selling penny candy in Illinois in break-and-take packages. The FTC ordered the company to stop because the practice was affecting interstate commerce. As a federal agency, the FTC has authority over business only on the national level. Bunte Bros. was operating only within Illinois. Candy companies from other states could not cross state lines with break-and-take packages because the FTC had already prohibited that in the *Keppel* case. The FTC said that it was unfair for Bunte Bros. to market the candy even within a single state because this gave the company an advantage that affected the flow of interstate commerce.

The Supreme Court ruled against the FTC and for Bunte Bros. It said that the FTC had the power to prohibit unfair competition by a business operating in more than one state but not if the business stayed completely within one state. It was up to the state, not the FTC, to regulate business wholly within its borders.

In 1975, however, the Federal Trade Commission Act was amended, and Congress gave the FTC authority to regulate not only businesses *involved in* interstate commerce but those *affecting* interstate commerce.

■ **Unfair or deceptive acts or practices** The FTC issues guidelines, called *industry guides,* or *trade practice rules,* that describe in layman's language those acts or practices in a particular industry that the FTC wishes to prohibit. The guides are not laws but warnings that certain kinds of activities are likely to be considered illegal.

Since 1962 the FTC has also issued *trade regulation rules* that do have the force of law. A violation of a trade regulation rule is a violation of the statute from which the rule is derived. The following illustrates the difference between industry guides and trade regulation rules:

EXAMPLE Suppose the FTC issues a trade regulation rule
O⊶—※ that aspirin advertisements must include the statement "All aspirin is alike." (It has not, of course.) If one company violates this rule, the FTC can prosecute the violation by issuing a complaint. The complaint does not allege a deceptive practice; it simply charges the company with a failure to include the required statement. The FTC does not have to prove that the absence of the statement deceives or misleads the public. All the FTC must show is that a rule required the company to include the statement in its advertising and that the company failed to do so.

Suppose, instead, that the FTC issues an industry guide saying that, in its opinion, failure to include the statement "All aspirin is alike" in aspirin advertisements is a deceptive act or practice. The FTC must then show that the aspirin company has violated the statute prohibiting unfair or deceptive acts or practices. It is not enough to show that the company omitted the statement in its advertising. The FTC must prove that advertisements without the statement mislead or deceive the public.

The FTC can decide for itself whether to issue a guide or a rule. The power of the commission to issue rules that have the force of law was challenged by the National Petroleum Refiners Association.

EXAMPLE In 1962 the FTC issued a rule that failing to post
O⊶—※ octane-rating numbers on gasoline pumps at service stations was "an unfair method of competition and an unfair or deceptive act or practice." Two trade associations and 34 refiners attacked the rule. The U.S. District Court agreed with the refiners, holding that the FTC had no power to make broad rules binding on everyone in an industry. The FTC could stop an individual company only after the company had done something unfair to consumers.

The U.S. Court of Appeals for the District of Columbia reversed the decision. The court noted that it is fairer to have rules apply equally to all companies. Business, industry, and the public have an opportunity to comment on a proposed rule and to recommend changes before it actually goes into effect. In addition, business people should know what the rules require of them. It is difficult for executives to plan when they cannot be sure how

strictly industry guides will be applied, but a published set of rules can be very clear.

■ **Enforcement of rules** The FTC is charged with protecting the public interest, and it may issue a complaint in order to protect that interest. Generally, before the complaint is issued, the party involved is given a chance to stop the unfair or deceptive practice. He may agree informally to discontinue the practice, or he may sign a consent to a formal cease-and-desist order. A *consent* is an agreement not to do the prohibited act in the future. It does not mean that the party admits to any past violations.

If a case is not settled by an informal agreement or a consent order, a complaint with a notice of hearing is issued. The complaint details the charges being made, and the notice announces that a hearing will be held before an administrative law judge of the FTC. The hearing is a full trial, with all legal rights provided for the parties. The judge hears testimony and then draws up an opinion for the FTC. The commission makes a decision based on this opinion and the facts that were shown in the hearing. If the FTC believes that the act or practice violates the law, it issues a cease-and-desist order, which directs the party to stop that act or practice.

A person named in a cease-and-desist order can obey the order or appeal the decision. To appeal, he must file a petition asking the local U.S. Court of Appeals to review the decision within 60 days. If he does not appeal, the order becomes final after 60 days. If he does appeal, the order cannot be enforced until the appeal is finished. Appeals may go all the way to the Supreme Court, and some cases have dragged on for years.

Until recently, only the violation of a cease-and-desist order could be punished. There was no penalty for the first violation—the conduct that gave rise to the order. Moreover, the penalty for the second violation—disobeying a cease-and-desist order—was only a $5,000 fine.

A more effective FTC In 1969 an energetic group of consumer advocates published a report severely criticizing the FTC for failing to protect the public interest. Shortly after that, an American Bar Association report reached the same conclusions. The FTC needed more power if it was to do its job of protecting consumers.

The agency was given the authority to stop actual or threatened violations of the laws it enforces by means of temporary restraining orders and preliminary INJUNC-TIONS. The penalty for disobeying a cease-and-desist order was doubled, and the FTC was authorized to send its own attorneys into court if the U.S. Attorney General failed to take proper action.

In 1975 the FTC's enforcement powers were made even broader. First violations (before a cease-and-desist order) can now be punished in two situations: if someone knowingly violates a trade regulation rule and if someone knowingly violates a cease-and-desist order issued against someone else.

EXAMPLE Suppose the FTC issues a trade regulation rule
O⊶—※ barring auto companies from advertising fantastic mileage that only expert test drivers can achieve under excellent driving conditions. If Ford uses these mileage figures, it has violated the rule even though no cease-and-desist order has been issued.

Suppose, on the other hand, there is no trade regulation rule on this subject. General Motors advertises the results of mileage tests performed by professional drivers without stating that the drivers were professionals. The FTC finds that this misleads the public and issues a cease-and-desist order. If American Motors then uses the same kind of deceptive advertising, the FTC can seek a civil penalty against it. The cease-and-desist order issued in response to a deceptive trade practice devised by General Motors has the force of a rule that applies to all auto manufacturers.

Recent amendments to the law authorize the FTC to sue in state or federal court for money damages on behalf of persons, partnerships, or corporations that have been injured by unfair or deceptive acts or practices.

Protection of consumers The modernized FTC showed great vigor in protecting consumers. It ordered an air-conditioning manufacturer to stop advertising that its units were "unique" and had "reserve cooling power," when this was not so. It required a finance company to explain in advertisements that "instant tax refund" borrowers would have to meet the usual standards of creditworthiness. It ordered the company that makes Listerine to run corrective advertising, forced the manufacturer of Geritol and FemIron to stop claiming that the products could cure tiredness, and found that the maker of Wonder bread and Hostess Snack Cakes was misleading the public with its nutritional claims.

In 1978 the American Society of Anesthesiologists signed an FTC consent order allowing anesthesiologists to work under contract to hospitals rather than always billing patients individually. The FTC had found that the society prohibited or discouraged competition by limiting the ability of hospitals to negotiate freely and contract for services with society members. This was the FTC's first significant attack on anticompetitive practices of a profession.

federation A formal group of persons, organizations, or governments loosely united for a common purpose. The term is synonymous with "league" and "union." The European Common Market is a federation.

fee 1 A charge for services, such as a lawyer's fee for representing his client in court. 2 An interest in land, which is called an ESTATE. See FEE SIMPLE; FEE TAIL.

fee simple An interest in land that entitles the owner to all rights in the property. A fee simple ESTATE is the greatest possible interest an owner can have in land. He is entitled to exclusive possession of the land. He may use the land and the fruits of the land (such as crops). He may abuse it, if he chooses, and may dispose of it, either by deed or by will. If he dies without a will, the land is inherited by his rightful heirs. The word "fee," used alone, is sufficient to describe this kind of estate. The word "simple" is added in order to clearly distinguish this estate from any other kind of estate, such as a FEE TAIL.

fee tail An interest in land that restricts who may inherit it. The typical words creating the fee tail ESTATE are "to A and the heirs of his body." The fee tail can be special (limited to the children of a particular spouse) and can also be limited to male or female heirs (fee tail male or fee tail female). This estate passes, by inheritance, from generation to generation (to the heirs of the body of the original heir and to the heirs of their bodies). It cannot be inherited by other (collateral) heirs, such as nieces and nephews.

The holder of a fee tail estate (the fee tail tenant) has limited power. He can use the land during his lifetime but cannot prevent its descent to his children, if he has any. If the holder of a fee tail dies without any surviving children, the property goes back to the original owner (the person who created the fee tail estate in the first place). If the original owner is dead, the property goes to his estate.

EXAMPLE Alphonse Schmidt willed his mansion to his "eldest son, Alphonse Schmidt, Jr., and the male heirs of his body." When Alphonse, Sr., died, the mansion passed to Alphonse, Jr., who lived in the mansion and rented out some of the rooms. Although Alphonse, Jr., could rent the mansion throughout his own lifetime or use it in any other way he wished, he could not sell the mansion, destroy it, or will it to anyone. When Alphonse, Jr., died, the mansion went to Alphonse III, the only son of Alphonse, Jr. Alphonse III was also able to use the mansion as he wished but, when he died, the mansion passed to his own son. Unfortunately, Alphonse III had no sons, only 13 daughters. Because he held the mansion in fee tail, his daughters could not inherit the mansion from him. The mansion went back to the estate of Alphonse, Sr., to be disposed of to the relatives who would have been entitled to inherit his property if he had died without leaving a will—in this case, Alphonse, Sr.'s younger son and daughter. At this point, the fee tail was extinguished.

Because the fee tail restricts the freedom to transfer property, most states have altered or abolished it. Some states transform a fee tail into a FEE SIMPLE (absolute ownership) for the first heir. Other states give the children of the first heir a fee simple interest in the property.

fellatio The criminal offense committed when a man places his penis in the mouth of another person, male or female. The crime can be victimless, with both parties acting as willing accomplices, or it can involve an innocent person who is forced to participate in the act. If two adults engage in the act willingly, both are guilty of the offense. If an adult and a minor engage in the act, the minor is considered by the law to be too young to grant consent, and so only the adult is guilty.

Traditionally, heavy jail sentences and fines were imposed for fellatio and other deviate sexual conduct. Some state legislatures have been considering revising their statutes to make deviate sexual conduct punishable only if force or young people are involved. A few states have reclassified such deviate acts as misdemeanors, except when force or children are involved. See SODOMY.

fellow servant rule A traditional common-law rule that holds that a master (employer) is not liable for injuries to his servant (employee) caused by the negligence of a fellow servant. A servant is an AGENT employed by a principal (the employer, or master) to perform services for him. The servant's physical conduct is subject to the control of the master. Although the concept of master and servant is outdated, the terms are still used in court opinions for cases involving employers and employees.

EXAMPLE In a Mississippi case, an employee was injured 0↦—* when he was hit by a truck that a group of his coworkers were vigorously rocking back and forth in order to get it out of a mudhole in which it was stuck. The employer was not held liable for the injury.

The fellow servant doctrine is an exception to the general rule that a master is responsible for injuries caused to a third person by any negligence or misconduct of his servant acting within the scope of his employment. See RESPONDEAT SUPERIOR. The ground most often cited for the fellow servant doctrine is that a fellow servant's negligence is a risk that goes with a job and is assumed by a servant. The risk is considered an implied term of an employment contract. Another ground given for the fellow servant doctrine is that co-workers can promote safety on the job better than their employer can. If the conduct of a fellow servant is so negligent that it is likely to cause injury to a fellow worker, the endangered worker can notify the employer.

The fellow servant doctrine ordinarily frees the master from liability for injuries caused by his servant's negligence even when the injured servant is a minor, if the minor had the capacity to take care of himself and understood the risks involved in his job. The rule also applies after the official day's work is over—for example, if an employee is injured while putting away his tools, changing his clothes, preparing to leave, or working overtime—as long as, at the time of the injury, he was doing something he had a right or obligation to do in the course of his job.

■ **Liability of master** The master has a duty to hire enough people to do a particular job. If a servant requests additional help but is refused by his employer or foreman, the master is liable if the servant is injured because of the lack of help. A master also owes his servant a duty to hire only competent fellow servants and is liable if he carelessly hires incompetent workers. For example, it is a construction contractor's duty to hire men who, when felling trees to clear a site, will not endanger their fellow employees. To be competent, a servant must be both capable and reasonably careful. Youthfulness, a physical disability, and lack of experience do not necessarily make a servant incompetent, although they may be contributing factors. But a disability may result in incompetence, as in the case of a telephone operator who becomes deaf and is unable to do his work properly. Carelessness and drunkenness may also make a servant incompetent.

A master is responsible for knowing that his servant is incompetent if he could reasonably have found it out. A master is also responsible for knowledge that has or should have been obtained by a supervisor who represents him in hiring and keeping competent employees.

EXAMPLE Suppose that Frank, a foreman at Slag Steel Mills, 0↦—* knows that a certain employee, Kurt, is belligerent and often violent. The owner of the mill can be held liable if Kurt assaults a co-worker, because the owner has a duty to select and retain workers who will not endanger other employees. Frank, as foreman, should have told the owner about Kurt's irascibility; but even if Frank did not, the owner is responsible for knowing it. He has a duty to hire a foreman who gives him such information.

A master is also expected to provide enough general supervision to make the conduct of his business reasonably safe. He cannot avoid liability by designating someone else to be responsible for the safe conduct of the business.

■ **Who is a fellow servant** There is no single definition of a fellow servant applicable in all states. In general, fellow servants are employees who are (1) serving a common employer, (2) working under the same control, (3) deriving authority and compensation from the same source, and (4) engaged in the same general business. In order to fall within the fellow servant rule, coemployees should be doing work that brings them into necessary and frequent contact with each other—in the same department, some laws say. If employees are working independently of each other, they are not engaged in common employment.

It is not necessary that fellow servants be hired or discharged by the same person or that they be paid the same way. The relationship does not depend on personal acquaintance, previous association, or the length of time the employees have worked together. A general manager or a supervisor of a department is not usually considered to be a fellow servant of the employees under him. In most cases, an employee who represents the master in hiring and firing other employees is not a fellow servant.

Many states have greatly modified or eliminated the common-law fellow servant doctrine so that an employer can no longer advance the rule as a defense to a suit brought against him by an employee. See WORKMEN'S COMPENSATION.

felon A person who commits a felony, which is a major crime, such as robbery or murder.

felonious Done with the intent to commit a major crime; malicious; unlawful.

felony A crime more serious than a misdemeanor; generally, an offense punishable by imprisonment of a year or more in a state or federal penitentiary or by death. Under various state laws, such crimes as arson, burglary, rape, robbery, and murder are usually classified as felonies. See CRIMINAL LAW.

felony-murder rule The law in some states that a killing that occurs during the commission of a major crime (felony) is classified as a murder, whether or not the suspect had any intention to kill. An arsonist who sets fire to a building, believing it empty, can be charged with murder if someone dies in the fire. Similarly, if a passerby is killed by a stray bullet fired during a bank holdup, the robbers can be charged with murder, even if the bullet was fired by a policeman attempting to subdue the robbers. Some states restrict the felony-murder rule to specific violent felonies, such as robbery, burglary, kidnapping, arson, and rape.

Although in most states the rule is rigidly applied to all participants in a felony, some statutes allow a defendant to claim as a defense that he was unarmed and had no idea that any of his companions were armed or had any intent to endanger anyone's life.

fence **1** Colloquial term for a person who knowingly receives stolen property. **2** An enclosure around a field, yard, or other piece of land, intended to prevent intrusions from the outside. A landowner has the right to build a fence along the boundary of his property, but state laws sometimes regulate the construction and maintenance of fences.

As a general rule, a landowner has the right to build a partition fence on the boundary of lands adjoining his. ADJOINING LANDOWNERS may make agreements about their rights and liabilities concerning the building, upkeep, and repair of partition fences. When these obligations are not regulated by state statutes, the duty of maintaining a partition fence usually rests equally on both parties. Under most statutes, if your neighbor fails to build or maintain his share of a fence that you both agreed to build and maintain, you may do all the work and sue him for half the cost. Under some statutes, you can get a LIEN (legal claim) on his land for the amount you win in the suit. In theory, a partition fence should be located along the boundary line between adjacent lands, but an equal and reasonable amount of each party's land may be used.

Because a partition fence is the joint property of adjoining owners, neither of them may remove it without the consent of the other. If a fence has been improperly removed or destroyed, an adjoining landowner may sue for whatever damages he suffers.

An owner may remove a fence that was built on his land by a person who had no authority to do so. Unlawfully fencing another person's land is a crime in several states. See NUISANCE.

ferry **1** A necessary service by a specially constructed boat to carry passengers and property across bodies of water from one shore to the opposite shore for a reasonable charge. The service connects with a thoroughfare on each side. **2** Technically, a continuation of a highway from one side of the water to the other. **3** Sometimes the landing place for the boat is called a ferry.

The privilege of operating a ferry is a FRANCHISE granted by the state and is a contract between the ferry owner and the state. Usually, the grant of a ferry franchise implies the power to collect tolls. Either by law or by contract with the operator, the state has power to regulate and control all ferries operating within its borders. It may impose a license fee or tax and regulate the carrying of dangerous articles, the character and frequency of service, and the location of terminals.

fiat (Latin) "Let it be done"; a command. An order or warrant of a judge or magistrate directing an act to be done.

FICA See FEDERAL INSURANCE CONTRIBUTIONS ACT.

fiction Something that is created by imagination and not true. A *legal fiction* is something that is assumed to be true when in fact it is known not to be true or as likely to be false as true. Legal fictions are invented or assumed for the purpose of promoting justice. An example of a legal fiction is the rule of *vicarious liability* in the law of TORTS—injuries to a person or his property for which he may sue the person who caused the harm. Under this rule, an employer is responsible for any tort his employee commits during the course of his employment.

EXAMPLE Suppose that while driving the company truck to make a delivery, an employee negligently runs down a pedestrian, seriously injuring him. Through the legal fiction that the employer is assumed to be in control of his employee's actions, the employer may be successfully sued by the pedestrian for damages (money).

fictitious Founded on a fiction; pretended; counterfeit. For example, a fictitious action is a lawsuit undertaken to get a court's opinion on a point of law, not to settle an actual controversy between the parties. If a court discovers that an action is fictitious, it will refuse to hear the case.

fidelity bond An insurance contract against losses caused by dishonest employees or other persons holding positions of trust. For example, a bank or trust company might purchase fidelity bonds covering its officers and staff, or an armored car service that delivers cash payrolls might insure its drivers.

fiduciary **1** A person who manages money or property for another person and in whom the other has the legal right to place great trust and confidence. **2** Any relationship in which one person is under a duty to act for the benefit of another. Fiduciary relationships can be formal or technical, such as that of banker and investor or guardian and ward, or informal, such as that of an aged parent and his adult child or of a husband and wife.

As a general rule, a fiduciary relationship is established only when the confidence placed by one person is actually accepted by the other. Respecting another's judgment or trusting his character is usually not enough to create the relationship.

Courts deliberately avoided defining the circumstances for fiduciary relationships in order not to exclude any new situations. There are, however, certain relationships that are readily recognized as fiduciary, including that of ATTORNEY AND CLIENT; BROKER and principal; executor or administrator and heir (see EXECUTORS AND ADMINISTRATORS); GUARDIAN AND WARD; HUSBAND AND WIFE; partners; priest and communicant; principal and agent (see AGENCY); and trustee and beneficiary of a TRUST.

Fiduciary relationships may be moral, social, domestic, or purely personal. In fact, they extend to every possible case in which confidence is placed on one side and accepted on the other, with a resulting dependence by the one party and influence by the other, such as a psychiatrist's relationship to his patient. On the other hand, the fact that two people are blood relatives—parent and child, say, or brother and sister—does not automatically make one the fiduciary of the other.

A person acting as a fiduciary is not permitted to make use of the relationship for his own personal benefit, except with the full knowledge and consent of the other person, and the other person must be mentally competent before the courts will consider him bound by that knowledge or consent. The courts carefully scrutinize any transaction between persons in fiduciary relationships, particularly if the dominant person profits at the expense of the person under his influence. Such a transaction is presumed to be fraudulent and void, and the court will strike it down unless the person who asserts that it is valid can clearly establish its fairness.

FIFO   First in, first out. A method of identifying and valuing inventories. It assumes that the first goods purchased are the first ones sold and that the goods left in the inventory at the end of the year are purchased last. FIFO contrasts with LIFO, last in, first out.

Fifth Amendment   The amendment to the U.S. Constitution that protects personal rights. It prohibits the federal government from (1) charging a person with a capital or infamous crime unless he is indicted by a GRAND JURY; (2) subjecting any person to DOUBLE JEOPARDY for the same offense (see CRIMINAL LAW); (3) compelling any person to be a witness against himself in a criminal case (see SELF-INCRIMINATION); (4) depriving any person of life, liberty, or property without DUE PROCESS OF LAW; and (5) taking private property for public use without just compensation (see EMINENT DOMAIN).

When a person says he is "taking the Fifth Amendment," he is exercising his privilege against self-incrimination by refusing to answer a question because it might implicate him in a crime.

file   **1** A law office folder containing all the papers relating to a particular client's case or business records.   **2** The complete court record of a case, including the original subpoenas and all subsequent papers. A legal document is filed with a court clerk when it is placed in his official custody and deposited in the place where official records and papers are usually kept. A document is also filed by a clerk when he stamps the date he received it on the document and holds it in his office for inspection by any interested person.

filiation proceeding   A court action to prove that a man is the father of an illegitimate child and therefore should be held responsible, at least in part, for support of that child. The action is sometimes called an affiliation proceeding or paternity suit. See ILLEGITIMACY.

final argument   The last statement made by each attorney to the jury during a TRIAL. It summarizes the evidence admitted during the trial in order to focus the jury's attention on the pertinent points. See CRIMINAL LAW.

final decision   A decision by a court or a series of courts that leaves nothing open to further dispute and conclusively settles the lawsuit between the parties. A final decision cannot be appealed. An example is a decision by the Supreme Court on a question of constitutional law—for example, its decision that segregating minority children in public schools deprives them of the equal protection of the laws guaranteed by the 14th Amendment.

The term "final decision" is also used to mean the last act by a lower court that ends a lawsuit, such as handing down a final judgment. After such a final decision, an appeal to a higher court can be made.

finding   A decision about a question of fact based on an examinaton, investigation, or deliberation by a court, jury, referee, coroner, or other lawful authority.

finding lost goods   The finding of personal property that the owner has involuntarily and unknowingly parted with and does not know where it is. (Personal property is any property that is not real estate.) The law must determine what property is lost and who has rights to property that is lost. Lost property should not be confused with mislaid or abandoned property. Property is *mislaid* when an owner intentionally places it where he can find it again but then forgets where he put it. Property is abandoned when the owner leaves it somewhere with no intention of reclaiming it. See ABANDONMENT.

A person's right to possess property he has found depends on whether the property is lost by definition of the law. This is decided according to the particular facts and circumstances of the case. The place where the property is found is an important factor. Under the law of lost property, if the article is in the possession and protection of the owner of the place where it is discovered, it is not lost in the legal sense.

EXAMPLE   A man who rented a safe-deposit box from a trust company found a bond on the floor of the private room where the boxes were kept, a room to which only vault customers were admitted. The trust company was unable to learn who owned the bond, and a lawsuit developed between the finder and the trust company over who had the right to it. The court held that the trust company's right to custody was superior to the finder's, because the trust company was its customer's agent, even when the customer-owner of the bond was unknown.

The situation changes, however, if the property is discovered in a public or semipublic place where the public is invited and expected to be.

EXAMPLE   Money was found in a bank lobby leading to the safe-deposit department and other offices. Since the lobby was used by persons who were not safe-deposit box holders, the bank was not an agent of the owner of the money that was found, and so the money was held to be lost property.

■ **Treasure trove**   Under the common law lost property was distinguished from treasure trove. Treasure trove is any money, gold or silver in coin, plate, or bullion found concealed in the earth or in a house or some other private place. The owner must be unknown or the treasure hidden for so long that its owner is probably dead. If the original owner is known, the property is not treasure trove.

EXAMPLE   Three boys found $2,180 in paper currency in a pond located on property owned by a man who had recently died. The money was wrapped in waxed paper and sealed in a fruit jar, which was sealed in a wooden box. The box was sealed in an inner tube, which was secured to the bottom of the pond with ropes. The boys gave the money to their parents, who in turn presented the money to the local sheriff. The sheriff and the administrator of the deceased man's property brought suit to determine who owned the money. The court held that the currency was too new to be treasure trove, and, because such care had been taken to preserve and conceal the money, it was not lost or abandoned property. The money was the property of the owner of the pond, and, because he was dead, it became the property of his estate.

EXAMPLE In 1971 the wreck of a Spanish galleon that went ○—✷ down in 1622 was found off the Florida Keys after a six-year search that cost $2 million. The federal government argued that the ship and its treasure, which was worth some $6 million, were public property because the ship was within its territorial waters; therefore, by virtue of various laws, it owned the vessel. The U.S. Court of Appeals for the Fifth Circuit found that the ship lay just beyond U.S. territorial waters. The court therefore ruled that the finders could keep the treasure.

■ **Rights of the finder** A person who finds lost property does not obtain absolute title to it—that is, he does not own it outright. However, he does have some rights in connection with the property.

Rights v. those of true owner The finder is only the apparent owner of what he has found. His title (ownership) is contingent and may be lost if the true owner turns up. The true owner's title is not affected by the fact that he lost his property.

Because the finder does not acquire title to the property he has found, he cannot transfer title to someone else—that is, he cannot sell it or give it away. If the true owner is dead, his administrator has the same right to the lost article as he has to other property of the deceased owner. Similarly, a person who inherits a specific item of lost property under a will has the same right and title to it as the deceased person.

When there is a dispute between the finder of treasure trove and its true owner, the true owner is entitled to it. But it has been held that the finder of treasure trove is entitled to it rather than the heirs of the person who concealed it.

Right to compensation and reward The finder of lost property is entitled to recover the necessary and reasonable expenses incurred in recovering and preserving the property. For example, the finder of a lost automobile who takes possession of it is entitled to a reasonable storage fee. The true owner is responsible for paying the expenses. The finder may even be entitled to a small sum for his time and trouble, but he does not obtain a LIEN (a legal claim on property to pay a debt) against the property. He cannot use the property to reimburse himself for his expenses and time, nor is he entitled to a reward if none has been offered.

Some statutes, however, do provide that in addition to expenses, the finder is entitled to a reward for holding the property. These statutes are not inconsistent with others providing that the finder must restore the property to its true owner and that a finder who knows the identity of the true owner is guilty of larceny if he keeps the property. In effect, these statutes make it the public policy of the state to reward the finder of lost property, repay him for his expenses, and fix a reasonable value for his services.

Claim by third persons Generally, a person who finds and takes possession of lost property acquires title to it and the right to possess it against everyone except the true owner. Under some statutes, however, if the true owner fails to claim the property within a certain period of time after the finding of the article is announced in a local newspaper, the finder is entitled to only part of the property or part of its value. The state gets the remaining portion.

fine A sum of money imposed on a person convicted of a crime or a lesser offense. It may be imposed instead of a term of imprisonment or in addition to imprisonment.

Fines should be distinguished from FORFEITURES. Fines are payable in money, while forfeitures are PENALTIES that cause loss of ownership of property. Sometimes, when the word "forfeit" or "forfeiture" is used in a criminal statute it is equivalent to "fine," while other times a fine imposed for a criminal offense may be in addition to a forfeiture of property. For example, a person convicted of smuggling marijuana hidden in his clothes into the U.S. can be fined and imprisoned, and the marijuana will be forfeited.

■ **Imposing a fine** Fines make up part or all of the punishment for many offenses. They are usually intended to punish the guilty person for the offense he has committed and to discourage others who may be tempted to commit similar offenses.

If a statute does not specify whether its violation is civil or criminal but provides that the party convicted of violating the statute shall be fined or imprisoned or both, the statute is interpreted as requiring a criminal proceeding against the accused violator.

Usually, imposing a fine is a JUDGMENT of the court. It is just as much a sentence as a term of imprisonment is. Under the common law the jury determined a defendant's guilt or innocence, and if they found him guilty, the judge determined the amount of the fine. Some states still follow this rule, while others have statutes that say the jury must also determine the amount of the fine.

■ **Payment of fines** A judgment that imposes a fine is satisfied when the fine is paid. Usually, a court officer has no authority to accept anything other than money for payment of the fine—he cannot, for example, accept a mortgage on the defendant's land. On the other hand, some statutes provide that fines may be paid in coupons from state bonds, by the defendant's promissory note, or with some other security.

When the sentence is either a fine or imprisonment and a statute does not set the time within which the defendant must pay his fine, some courts have ordered him to pay immediately or face imprisonment. Others fix a reasonable time for payment, based on the circumstances of the case. When a person who is fined dies before making payment, the fine cannot be enforced as a claim against his estate.

■ **Enforcement of payment** Under some statutes a judgment imposing a fine is the equivalent of a civil money judgment, and thus the fine becomes a LIEN (a claim on property to satisfy a debt). It is regarded as a debt owed to the state, and it may be enforced by EXECUTION (an order to seize and sell property for payment of a debt) against the defendant's property.

Generally, a court that has the authority to impose a fine also has the authority to imprison the person for failure to pay the fine. This imprisonment is not part of the penalty for the offense; it is a means of enforcing the judgment of the court. If the defendant refuses to pay and is imprisoned, he is not sentenced to a specific term in prison. The time he spends in prison depends on when he pays the fine and the amount of the fine.

In most states the length of the imprisonment for nonpayment is specifically regulated by statutes. Usually, the court provides in the judgment for the defendant to be imprisoned until the fine has been paid or settled in accordance with the law. A common provision for satisfaction is a credit in a dollar amount—such as $3 a day—for each day of imprisonment served by the defendant. When he has paid the fine in full or remained in custody for the length of time required to satisfy the judgment, he is entitled to a discharge.

When a person is fined and also sentenced to prison as an additional punishment, the term of imprisonment to enforce the fine begins after the term of imprisonment as punishment expires. Consequently, when a statute limits the period of imprisonment for nonpayment of a fine, time served as punishment for the offense is not counted.

Many states have provisions for discharging those who are imprisoned for nonpayment of fines before the fine is satisfied. Such provisions usually contain conditions that must be fulfilled. A common one is that the prisoner must have served a minimum time before he is entitled to a discharge. The minimum time may be satisfied by serving the additional time on parole, rather than in jail.

In most places, serving time for nonpayment of a fine does not relieve the defendant of his liability to pay the fine. A release from imprisonment is not a release from the fine, except when the fine is satisfied by the credit system described above.

When money is deposited in the court instead of BAIL or when money is found on a prisoner who is arrested for drunkenness and searched by the police, it may be used to pay any fine imposed on him. A third person may also pay the defendant's fine.

fire   The burning of property. Under the common law and a number of statutes, it is a crime to burn or set fire to various kinds of property under certain circumstances. Some of these offenses are treated as ARSON, but arson is usually limited to the burning of buildings and their contents.

The act of willfully and maliciously burning another person's property—such as stacks of hay or grain, grasses, fences, and woods—is usually a criminal offense. *Willfully* means with an evil intent. The *malice* must be directed against a person, usually the owner of the property, and not the property itself. In some states the offense is a misdemeanor—an offense punishable by less than a year in a local jail. In other states, however, the offense is ranked as a felony—an offense punishable by a year or more in a state penitentiary.

Under some statutes, a person who willfully or negligently sets fire to his own woods, prairie land, or other specified area may be guilty of a misdemeanor. It is also a misdemeanor to burn these areas without giving advance notice to adjoining landowners or to permit a fire kindled on one's own land to spread to a neighbor's property. Statutes that make it a crime to burn cultivated ground do not apply to ordinary, lawful acts of husbandry, such as burning a section of land to prepare it for planting.

Some of the laws prohibiting or regulating the setting of fires impose fines for violations. Depending on the law in your state, you might be subject to a fine if you permit a fire to spread from your own land, whether deliberately or not.

A person who willfully and intentionally sets a fire can usually be held liable for DAMAGES. Some statutes that provide criminal liability for setting certain types of fires provide that the person whose property is harmed may also bring a civil lawsuit to recover his loss. As a general rule, damages are limited to the loss actually caused by the fire, but under some laws double or triple damages may be recovered. The fact that the destroyed property was insured does not affect the amount of damages that may be awarded, but an insurance company will be entitled to be refunded for the amount it paid the plaintiff.

firm offer   A written proposal (offer) to enter into a CONTRACT. The proposal usually states that it will be held open for a fixed period of time, usually not to exceed three months, during which the proposal is irrevocable. Firm offers are often made by merchants who wish to buy or sell goods. The following is an example:

EXAMPLE I, Seymour Seller, offer to sell to you, Bruce
O—* Buyer, 10,000 Gadgets at 50 cents per Gadget. You may have until August 1, 1983, in which to act on this offer.

June 1, 1983   *Seymour Seller*

first impression   In law, a *case of the first impression* is a case of a kind that has not been encountered before. It presents an entirely new question of law for the court to consider. The question cannot be decided by any existing precedent, such as an earlier case involving a similar question of law or similar facts.

first instance   In law, a *court of first instance* is the original trial court where the parties bring their lawsuit, as opposed to an appellate court, which is a *court of last instance,* where the parties submit their suit for final resolution.

fiscal   Financial. A fiscal year is a 12-month period, not necessarily coinciding with the calendar year, during which appropriations are made and expenditures authorized. The beginning of a fiscal year is often the first of April, July, or October. At the end of the fiscal year, the accounts of a business or an individual are drawn up and the books are balanced.

fish   In its broadest sense, the word means almost any exclusively aquatic animal, including shellfish. Because of their migratory characteristics and lack of a fixed habitat, fish are legally classified as wild ANIMALS. A fishery is a place for catching fish as well as the right to take fish at a certain place or in particular waters.

■ **Property**   As long as fish remain in their natural habitat, they belong to the state for the benefit of all its people. Even if you own land on which there is a stream filled with fish, you still do not own the fish as long as they are in the water. Similarly, the fact that you earn your living by fishing does not give you any property rights in the fish until you have caught them.

Once you catch a fish, it belongs to you, if you took it in accordance with the law. But if you trespass on private land, the fish you catch belongs to the owner of the land.

■ **Fishing rights in private waters** Generally, the right to fish in waters located on private land belongs exclusively to the landowner. Because this is a property right, he may grant the right to others.

The owner's rights If you own land along the bank of a nonnavigable stream (one not used by boats), your exclusive fishing rights usually extend from the bank to the middle of the stream. If you own land on both sides of the stream, you have the exclusive right to fish in the whole stream for as far as your land runs along its banks. But your fishing rights as a landowner are subject to the state's right to regulate and preserve the fish for the good of the public. Even when the state has not passed a regulatory statute, you must not exercise your rights in a way that will injure other landowners who are downstream or upstream from you. For example, you have no right to wantonly injure or destroy the fish that pass through the stream on your land, nor may you dam the stream to prevent the fish from passing through.

When several persons own an inland lake, each owner may use the whole lake for fishing as long as he does not interfere with the reasonable use of the waters by the others. If you own land that encloses a small lake or pond, the right to fish in it belongs exclusively to you. A person whose land is adjacent to yours may not take fish from the lake unless the right was reserved when he purchased the property. The right to fish in a lake or pond is also subject to the state's right to regulate and preserve the fish for the public good.

The rights of others If you sell your land, you may, by deed, reserve fishing privileges in the water on that land for yourself and your HEIRS and assigns (others whom you designate)—provided the purchaser agrees. A fishing right reserved in this way is considered an interest in land that is inheritable when granted in FEE SIMPLE (with full rights of ownership). When the words "heirs and assigns" are not used in the deed transferring the fishing privileges, the privileges are not inheritable. See ESTATE.

A grant or lease of land on the banks of a nonnavigable stream usually includes fishing rights. Similarly, a grant of land on which there is a landlocked lake implies exclusive fishing rights in the waters of that lake.

Fishing rights may be acquired by ADVERSE POSSESSION. This means that someone completely takes over a fishery in such a way that it appears he is the owner.

Because fishing rights and licenses can be validly granted only to individuals, the public at large cannot acquire either. Consequently, without permission from the owner, the public has no right to fish in the waters of a nonnavigable stream or lake for any purpose. The courts have also held that the fact that a state stocks a private pond or stream with fish does not give the public any right to fish in it.

■ **Fishing rights in public waters** As a rule, all members of the public have common fishing rights in public waters, such as the sea and other NAVIGABLE WATERS. The right to fish on the high seas, outside the territorial limits of any nation, is common to all mankind and cannot be granted or restricted by any particular nation.

Great ponds and lakes The right to fish in a navigable lake is a public right. Under some statutes the right to fish in a "great pond" of a size specified by the law is also a public right. An owner of land bordering one of these lakes or ponds has no greater rights than anyone else to fish in front of his land, unless there is a local law that gives him special rights. But if a pond is leased to private individuals for the purpose of cultivating fish, they have the exclusive right to fish in it. Fishing rights in the Great Lakes and in their nonnavigable bays is a public right.

Extent of the rights Fishing rights in navigable waters must be used by each person without interfering with the rights of others. Consequently, when you establish yourself at a particular fishing place, you have a right to fish there without being disturbed until you choose to leave. The right to fish in navigable waters does not give you the right to build a hut on the shore.

A waterfront-property owner may dig a ditch to prevent his lands from being flooded, even though this might result in the destruction of fish. If he artificially raises the level of the waters on a navigable lake, river, or stream in order to flood his own land, the public's right to fish is correspondingly extended to the flooded land.

The public's right to fish in navigable waters must give way to the public right of navigation, as long as it is necessary or reasonable.

Anyone may fish from a boat in navigable streams. You may also fish from the edge of a bridge or a section of a state highway, directly into the stream below, without committing a trespass, as long as you do not go on the uplands of a waterfront owner's property. The right to fish in navigable waters does not give you the right to trespass on privately owned land to reach the water or to occupy land above the high-water mark, which ordinarily belongs to the owner of the shorefront property.

■ **Rights to shellfish** As a rule, the right to take oysters, clams, and other shellfish from land under public waters, below the high-water mark, belongs to the public, but shellfish grown in beds located on private property belong to the property owner.

In most places the right to cultivate oysters, clams, and other shellfish is now regulated by state or local laws, which generally provide that a person may be allotted or leased a limited area of public lands that have not already been cultivated. The planter must usually give notice of his intention to lease or locate an oyster bed and mark it properly to distinguish it from water where the public has fishing rights. He must have the location recorded and pay a rental fee.

■ **Protection and regulation** Public policy is aimed at protecting and conserving fish for present and future generations. The state's power to regulate fishing extends to fisheries in private or nonnavigable waters that are connected with other waters in which the public has fishing rights. A state may regulate how and when fish may be caught and make it an offense to violate its regulations. In a number of states, it is an offense to take, sell, or buy certain kinds of fish during a particular season of the year, commonly called the closed season. In many states it is an offense to catch fish in certain waters or at certain times by any means other than hook and line. In some states it is an offense to take fish by draining a pond.

The state may protect the purity of its streams, lakes, and ponds in order to preserve the fish in those waters and to assure that the fish will continue to breed. Accordingly, it is often an offense to place any harmful substance in a stream or other body of water.

■ **Licenses** A license may be required in order to fish. If so, you are committing an offense if you fish without one. You may also be required to get a license to fish by certain methods, such as nets, traps, baskets, or manufactured fishing tackle; to fish for profit; or to ship certain kinds of fish, such as lobster, to other states.

Some statutes require a fisherman to wear his license button on his outer clothing while fishing. Others say he must carry his license with him and display it when requested to do so by a fish warden. Failure to obey these rules may be a separate offense from the offense of fishing without a license.

States usually charge a fee for a fishing license, and may charge nonresidents a higher fee than residents. A license to fish may be revoked by the state without notice at any time.

fishing trip The questioning of a witness in a lawsuit in a vague and unrestricted way or about something that is not relevant to the facts at issue in the lawsuit. Such questioning is not permissible in court. For example, if the real purpose of examining a witness's records is to use them in another lawsuit, the examination is a fishing trip.

fixed asset Property that is held for the purpose of conducting a business. Such property includes land, buildings, and machinery.

fixture An article of movable personal property (property that is not real estate) that has been attached to real property (real estate) in such a way that it is considered part of the real property. In a few states, a fixture is an article of personal property that, even though attached to real property, can be removed by the person who attached it. In these states a fixture is not part of the real estate.

■ **Classification and requirements** Fixtures that are classified as domestic, ornamental, or trade usually are not considered part of the real estate when placed by a tenant on the landlord's premises. Domestic and ornamental fixtures are articles that a tenant might attach to his rented premises in order to make it more comfortable and convenient. Stoves, cupboards, shelves, bells, and lighting equipment are domestic fixtures. Ornamental fixtures include curtains, window blinds, and chimney grates. A tenant can remove new domestic ornamental fixtures he purchases for his house or apartment when he moves as long as he replaces them with the original fixtures he found when he first moved in.

EXAMPLE Fred's landlord refused to replace an old refrigerator and ancient Venetian blinds in Fred's apartment. Fred buys new items, placing the old ones in storage. When Fred moves, he can take the new refrigerator and blinds with him provided he returns the original ones to the kitchen. If Fred had thrown them out, he would have to leave the new refrigerator and blinds behind or pay the landlord for their replacement.

Trade fixtures are articles that merchants attach to rented buildings in order to store, handle, and display their wares

for sale—booths, display cases, lights, freezers, and soda fountains, for example.

To become a fixture the article must meet three requirements. (1) It must be physically attached to the real property. For example, an in-ground swimming pool built in your backyard becomes a fixture of the real estate. (2) The attached item must be used for a purpose for which the real property is devoted—for instance, an elevator installed in a 10-story office building. (3) The person who attaches the article must intend it to be a fixture. The person need not express his intent in words; his intent has only to be apparent.

The court will decide whether or not there was intent on the basis of all the facts and circumstances relating to the attachment of the article.

EXAMPLE A man buys land and builds a home for himself and his family. He installs plumbing, wiring, and lights in an ordinary way. After living in the house for a number of years, he sells it. After the buyer has moved in, the former owner declares that the plumbing, wiring, and lights belong to him and he is going to remove them. The buyer refuses to allow the removal and a lawsuit results. In this case, the builder owned both the articles and the property to which they were attached. When plumbing, wiring, and lights are installed in a home, they merge into the building. They are affixed to the property in such a way that their removal would cause serious damage. The facts and circumstances in this case imply that the builder's apparent intent was to permanently install the plumbing, wiring, and lights as fixtures, and he would not be permitted to remove them.

■ **Agreement of the parties** As a general rule, the owner of real estate may enter into an agreement about a fixture with a party who wishes to buy or rent the real estate. When this right is provided by statute and the rights of third persons are not harmed, the law will enforce such an agreement.

Domestic and ornamental fixtures Rights between a landlord and tenant concerning domestic and ornamental fixtures are frequently included in the lease. For example, a lease might state that the tenant of an apartment can install a chandelier in the living room and can remove it and take it with him when he moves away. Or a lease may provide that anything a tenant adds to the apartment that is nailed or screwed into the building—such as built-in bookcases or cabinets and chandeliers—become a part of the building and belong to the landlord. If a stipulation in a lease clearly gives a tenant the right to remove particular articles, the fact that their removal damages the premises is immaterial.

Generally, when there is no agreement about the fixtures between the landlord and tenant, the tenant, at the time he leaves, may remove articles he attached, providing they can be removed without injuring the premises. The law is extremely indulgent toward the tenant, favoring his claim to have particular articles considered personal property rather than part of the real estate, but you should check your lease or the law in your state to be sure of your rights.

Trade fixtures A tenant who has attached articles to real estate in order to conduct a trade or business can usually remove them when he leaves. This right is usually safeguarded by a provision in the lease signed by the tenant.

It exists even if there is no provision in the lease, however, to encourage trade and industry. However, he has no right to remove a trade fixture if its removal would substantially injure the real estate. But in order to prevent a removal, the injury must be substantial.

EXAMPLE Jim Michaels installed a steam boiler for a dry-cleaning business. When he decided to move after his lease expired, he was entitled to remove the boiler—even though it was necessary to tear down and replace a small part of one of the brick walls in the building. The damage to the wall was not considered substantial enough to prevent the boiler's removal.

■ **Time of removal** If a fixture is not removed from the premises during the term of the lease or within the time specified in the lease after the tenant leaves, it becomes part of the real estate and belongs to the landlord. The tenant is presumed to have abandoned the fixture by failing to remove it.

If the landlord prevents the tenant from rightfully removing a fixture, the time for removal is extended until removal becomes possible. Similarly, if the landlord wrongfully ousts the tenant—as when the landlord terminates the lease before it expires—the tenant has a reasonable time in which to remove his fixtures.

After a lease has expired, a landlord can require the tenant to remove unwanted fixtures. If the tenant fails to do so, the landlord can have the fixtures removed and charge the cost to the tenant.

flag A light, flexible, rectangular cloth, bearing a design or symbol to indicate the organization or the nation it represents. It is commonly attached to a staff or pole.

Desecration or mutilation of the American flag or a state flag is a criminal offense under various statutes, which have been upheld on the grounds of preventing breaches of the peace and contributing to the dignity of a flag.

EXAMPLE In a case decided during the Vietnam conflict, a federal court held that a man who tore an American flag while standing in a crowd was guilty of publicly mutilating the flag and knowingly casting contempt upon it. During the same era, a university student in Ohio was fined for wearing a pair of blue jeans with a U.S. flag sewn on the seat.

The federal government has the power to reasonably regulate how the American flag should be displayed and used. For example, it should not be displayed during inclement weather; other flags should not be placed above it; it should never touch the ground or the floor beneath it; it should never be used as apparel; and when it becomes so tattered that it is no longer a fitting emblem for display, it should be destroyed in a dignified way, preferably by burning.

Some state laws prohibit displaying or carrying a red flag in any public assembly, parade, or demonstration, even if it bears an inscription or symbol in another color. The red flag has long been viewed as the emblem of anarchy, and it has been commonly accepted as a challenge to law and order and a threat to use force.

The term "law of the flag" means that a seafaring vessel is part of the territory of the nation whose flag she flies. Thus, a shipowner who sends his vessel into a foreign port gives notice that the law of his flag will regulate his business contracts.

flagrante delicto (Latin) "While the crime is blazing." In the very act of committing the crime.

floating lien An arrangement between a debtor and creditor in which collateral offered by the debtor as security for a loan will also secure any future loans from the creditor to the debtor. For example, a loan company may lend $1,000 to a customer on the condition that the customer puts up his furniture as collateral for the $1,000 loan and any future loans. If the customer agrees, borrows the money and pays it back, then gets a second loan, the furniture will be collateral for the second loan without any new agreement being signed. If the customer defaults on paying back the second loan, the finance company can have the furniture seized and sold to pay off the loan.

flotsam The wreckage of a ship and the goods that float upon the sea when cast overboard for the safety of the ship or that rise to the surface when a ship is sunk.

FOB An abbreviation for "free on board," which means that the seller or consignor of goods will deliver them onto a railroad car, truck, vessel, or other transporter without expense to the buyer or consignee.

EXAMPLE A buyer in Boston purchases a car from a manufacturer in Detroit, "FOB Detroit." The manufacturer must pay for loading the automobile onto the train or truck in Detroit. If the automobile is damaged during loading, the manufacturer is responsible. But once it is on board, his responsibility ends. The buyer pays the freight charges from Detroit to Boston. He is also responsible for any damage to the car while in transit.

food The things we eat and drink. The quality, safety, and cleanliness of the foods we eat and drink are stringently regulated by federal, state, and local law.

Food laws have existed since the ancient Hebrews and Egyptians regulated the handling of meat and the Greeks and Romans outlawed the watering down of wine. In 1202 King John of England prohibited the adulteration of bread with such ingredients as ground peas or beans. Many of our current food laws deal with that same matter of adulteration—mixing defective, cheaper, unsafe, or impure substances with better ones in order to increase volume or lower costs of production.

The first general law against food adulteration in the United States was enacted by Massachusetts in 1785. The federal government was much less quick to respond to the need for food standards. In 1880 a U.S. Department of Agriculture chemist, Peter Collier, recommended a national food adulteration law. During the next quarter century more than 100 food and drug bills reached Congress, which enacted a series of special-interest laws concerning such commodities as oleomargarine, tea, meat exports, and opium imports. An 1891 law called for the inspection of meat animals before they were slaughtered, and in 1902 the Virus, Serum, Toxin Act set up licensing control to insure the safety and potency of drugs for humans. Finally, in

1906 Congress—prompted by the public outcry over unsanitary conditions in meat-packing plants and the use of poisonous preservatives and dyes in foods—passed the Federal Meat Inspection Act and the Food and Drugs Act. The latter, which was intended to prohibit interstate commerce in misbranded and adulterated foods, beverages, and drugs, was replaced in 1938 by the Federal Food, Drug, and Cosmetic Act, which was intended to assure that foods are pure and wholesome, safe to eat, and produced under sanitary conditions. In 1957 Congress passed the Poultry Products Inspection Act. Through the years various amendments have been made to these laws in an effort to set and enforce standards that will insure the health of all Americans.

■ **Meat and poultry inspection acts** The federal Meat Inspection Act, and its companion law, the Poultry Products Inspection Act, require that about 85 percent of all the meat and poultry sold in the United States be inspected before it reaches the market. The laws, which are administered by the Department of Agriculture, now require that all meat and poultry—whether shipped interstate or intrastate—meet rigid requirements for wholesomeness and sanitation. The animals must be examined both before and after they are slaughtered in order to identify and eliminate all diseased or injured stock. All plants in which such operations are conducted must meet approved standards of cleanliness and sanitary working conditions.

■ **Food, Drug, and Cosmetic Act** The FOOD AND DRUG ADMINISTRATION (FDA) is charged with enforcing the federal Food, Drug, and Cosmetic Act and federal laws.

The federal Food, Drug, and Cosmetic Act is enormously detailed and comprehensive, regulating virtually every aspect of food manufacturing, packaging, and sale. Some of the more important areas of the act controls are labeling, dietary foods, sanitation, and additives.

Labeling The law states that the required label information must be conspicuously displayed and written in terms that ordinary people can understand. The product's common name must be used on the label with an accurate statement of the net amount of food in the package. In addition, all the ingredients in a food must be listed by their common names and in descending order of their weight in the food. For example, in a can of tomato soup, the water would be listed first, followed by tomato paste, corn syrup, wheat flour, salt, partially hydrogenated vegetable oils (soybean, palm, or cottonseed oil), natural flavoring, ascorbic acid (Vitamin C), and citric acid. In some standardized foods, such as milk chocolate, in which the major ingredients are generally recognized, they need not be listed on the label, but optional ingredients must be listed.

Dietary foods Foods for special dietary use include those supplying (1) a special dietary need that exists by reason of a physical condition, including but not limited to the conditions of disease, convalescence, pregnancy, infancy, food allergy, overweight, and the need to control the intake of sodium; (2) a vitamin, mineral, or other ingredient for use by man to supplement his diet by increasing the total dietary intake; and (3) a special dietary need because a particular food is used as the sole item in the diet.

Foods claiming to provide special dietary needs must include label information detailing the claims. For example, labels for low-sodium-diet foods must explain the precise amount of sodium in the foods, and those claiming to have higher than average nutritional value must detail the nutritional content. Special regulations spell out the required composition and labeling of many dietary foods.

If a food claims to provide disease prevention, treatment, mitigation, cure, or diagnosis, it ceases to be considered food and instead falls under the jurisdiction of the drug regulations of the act. See DRUGS AND NARCOTICS.

Sanitation One of the functions of the FDA prescribed by the Food, Drug, and Cosmetic Act is to inspect facilities where food is produced, processed, or packaged for interstate shipment to assure that food is produced under sanitary conditions. For example, the FDA will look at ventilation, toilet and washing facilities, cleaning of equipment, handling of materials, and vermin control to make sure that the plant is operating in a sanitary manner. The FDA sets and enforces its rigorous standards for sanitation, but the standards do not demand the impossible. To rid every insect from a crop would require such an extravagant use of pesticides that the chemicals themselves might become more dangerous to human health than the insects are. To condemn a shipment of carrots because some of the earth in which they grew still clung to them would not prove beneficial to anyone. The agency has therefore established Food Defect Action Levels, which permit certain levels of harmless contamination.

Additives The FDA has issued regulations detailing the conditions under which food additives can be used, and new food additives cannot be used until their safety is established. Manufacturers wishing to include food additives are responsible for proving to the FDA's satisfaction that they are safe.

Any substance used in producing, manufacturing, packing, processing, preparing, treating, or transporting food—even including radiation—is considered a food additive if it thereby becomes a part of the food itself either directly or indirectly. Generally, all food additives must conform to FDA regulations. There are, however, substances excluded from the regulations. They include

(1) Additives on the *Generally Recognized As Safe* (GRAS) list, which has been drawn up by qualified experts. Such substances include commonly used flavoring ingredients and preservatives.

(2) Substances that gained previous approval under the Food, Drug, and Cosmetic Act, the Poultry Products Inspection Act, or the Meat Inspection Act and have been in use since gaining that approval.

(3) Pesticide chemicals in or on raw agricultural products. Although not considered food additives, pesticides are strictly regulated by the Environmental Protection Agency. Pesticides may be considered food additives, however, when the agricultural products are processed. In that case, certain specific food additive regulations might permit trace amounts of particular pesticides.

Color additives are not included under ordinary food additive regulations but they are controlled in a similar manner. The FDA maintains a list of color additives permitted in foods and even stipulates limits on the amount of certain ones. The agency also tests and certifies each batch of synthetic colors before they are shipped for use in foods, drugs, diagnostic devices, and cosmetics except in some specifically exempted cases.

Standards of quality   The U.S. Department of Agriculture establishes grades for meat and other agricultural products, including eggs. The U.S. Department of the Interior establishes its own voluntary quality standards for fishery products.

The FDA sets minimum standards on products not covered by these agencies. If a food falls below that minimum standard it must be labeled: "Below Standard in Quality, Good Food Not High Grade."

FDA standards of identity and quality have been drawn for a great many classes of food and also specific foods. There are regulations that apply to canned fruits and fruit juices, vegetables, dried fruits and vegetables, jams, jellies, marmalades, candy, seasonings and seafood, bottled water, and nonalcoholic beverages. The FDA has some jurisdiction over alcoholic beverages, but they are also regulated by the Federal Alcohol Administration Act, administered by the Bureau of Alcohol, Tobacco and Firearms in the U.S. Treasury Department.

■ **Other federal regulations**   The federal government has many departments that are concerned, as part of their overall responsibility, with the quality of food. In addition to those mentioned, the Environmental Protection Agency sets minimum standards for drinking water. The Department of Defense regulates the quality of foods used by the armed forces. Additional food standards are set by the Department of Commerce, the Federal Trade Commission, the Veterans Administration, and the General Services Administration.

The responsibilities of these agencies sometimes overlap. For example, while the Department of Agriculture regulates the quality and purity of meat and poultry before it is shipped to market, both the Department of Agriculture and the FDA assume responsibility for it after it leaves the slaughterhouse or processing plant.

■ **State and local regulation**   The right of a state to regulate food in the public interest is inherent in the state's POLICE POWER. State regulations concern the production, manufacture, sale, marketing, and transportation of food. Among the more common are rules (1) requiring food producers or dealers to obtain a license, (2) prohibiting the sale of food that is adulterated or unfit for human consumption, (3) forbidding the sale of food products below a minimum standard of quality, (4) requiring that eggs be sold according to established grades, (5) prohibiting the sale of inedible eggs, (6) confiscating substandard poultry, (7) prohibiting the sale of meat falsely represented to be kosher, (8) prohibiting the sale for food of meat from a dead animal that has not been slaughtered, and (9) regulating the manufacture and sale of soft drinks.

Most states have enacted food inspection laws, and in practice they are usually patterned after the federal laws, since, with some exceptions, the federal laws apply only to foods shipped from one state to another. Because much food is grown or manufactured in the same state in which it is sold, state food laws play a vital part in maintaining the quality, cleanliness, and safety of foods. States often share some of their authority in matters of food regulation with local health departments.

■ **How to get help**   The various governmental agencies and departments charged with protecting the quality of food have several ways of fulfilling that task. They can revoke the violator's license or they can bring violators to court, and the court can order the violator to stop manufacturing and distributing a food product that does not meet government standards. The agencies can also ask violators to take all remaining stocks of the food off the market and, when possible, to notify all those who have purchased it that the product is harmful. Violators can also be ordered to pay a fine, and they can even be imprisoned.

If you feel that a particular food does not meet government standards, you may report that fact to the proper agency. If you have complaints about the following, these are the agencies to inform:

(1) False advertising—FEDERAL TRADE COMMISSION.
(2) Meat and poultry—Department of Agriculture.
(3) Sanitation of restaurants—local health authorities.
(4) Products made and sold exclusively within the boundaries of one state—local or state health department or similar law enforcement agency.

Food and Drug Administration   The agency of the U.S. Department of Health and Human Services that is concerned with the purity and safety of foods, drugs, and cosmetics. It is a PUBLIC ADMINISTRATIVE AGENCY. Congress has given the Food and Drug Administration (FDA) the responsibility of making sure that (1) foods are pure, wholesome, safe, and produced under sanitary conditions; (2) labels are accurate and informative; (3) drugs, medical devices, and biologic products—such as vaccines, serums, and blood—are safe and effective when used according to directions; (4) drug labels include warnings when necessary; (5) drugs that are too dangerous for over-the-counter sale are restricted to prescription marketing; (6) every drug plant in the country is inspected at least once every two years; (7) samples of antibiotics, insulin drugs, and colorings used in foods, drugs, and cosmetics are tested in the FDA's own laboratories before they are marketed; (8) chemicals used in foods are proven safe before being added to foods; and (9) cosmetics are safe.

The FDA goes even further to protect consumers, inspecting plants where foods, drugs, medical devices and equipment, cosmetics, and even television sets are made in order to assure adequate manufacturing or processing procedures. The agency also sets safety standards for radiation-emitting products, including diagnostic X-ray equipment and such household appliances as microwave ovens and television sets.

■ **Laws enforced by the FDA**   As the watchdog of the food, cosmetic, drug, and medical devices industries, the FDA is charged with enforcing all or significant parts of five federal laws: the Tea Importation Act; the Public Health Service Act; the Federal Food, Drug, and Cosmetic Act; the Fair Packaging and Labeling Act; and the Radiation Control for Health and Safety Act. The agency also has limited authority under other statutes, including the Federal Meat Inspection Act, the Federal Caustic Poison Act, and the Import Milk Act.

Tea Importation Act   The oldest law for which the FDA is responsible is the Tea Importation Act of 1897.

The agency examines samples of all imported tea to make sure that they meet the standards of quality set by the U.S. Board of Tea Experts before the shipments are allowed on the U.S. market.

Food, Drug, and Cosmetic Act Enacted in 1938, and amended several times thereafter, the Federal Food, Drug, and Cosmetic Act is the cornerstone of consumer protection in the United States. The act is intended to assure that all foods, drugs, cosmetics, and medical devices are pure, safe, effective, and correctly labeled.

In 1962 the drug safety aspects of the act were amended under dramatic circumstances. In late 1961 the world learned that the drug thalidomide, widely marketed throughout the world, had caused thousands of babies to be born deformed when their mothers used it during their pregnancies. It had not been approved for use in the United States, but that fact was more to the credit of one FDA medical officer, Dr. Frances Kelsey, who had insisted on delaying approval for the drug long beyond the usual time period, than to any FDA policy or to legislative guidelines. Until then, the agency had required a drug company applying for a "new drug" approval simply to present evidence that it had tested the drug and found it safe. The agency sometimes relied on the company's report and could give its approval within 60 days, although it was usually longer.

As a direct result of the thalidomide scare, Congress passed the Drug Amendments of 1962. In most cases, these amendments allow the agency to study new drug applications for at least 180 days—instead of 60 days as generally provided in the 1938 law. They also empower the Secretary of Health and Human Services to withdraw any new drug from the market, even before giving the manufacturer a hearing, when he or she believes it presents an "imminent hazard" to the public health.

The 1962 amendments also require that drugs be proven effective as well as safe before they can be marketed. They also give the FDA the authority to regulate prescription drug advertising. (In general, the FEDERAL TRADE COMMISSION oversees advertising, including advertising for over-the-counter drugs.)

Public Health Service Act The FDA enforces two sections of the Public Health Service Act of 1944. It assures that biologic products—such as vaccines, serums, and blood—are safe, pure, and potent before they can be sold in interstate commerce. The agency also assures the safety of pasteurized milk and shellfish; the sanitation of food services; and the safety of the food, water, and sanitary facilities for travelers on trains, planes, and buses.

Fair Packaging and Labeling Act Enacted in 1966, the Fair Packaging and Labeling Act strengthens the Federal Food, Drug, and Cosmetic Act by requiring that the net weight of foods and drugs, and medical devices and cosmetics when applicable, be accurately stated in a uniform location on the product's label. In areas other than those under the FDA's jurisdiction, it is the Federal Trade Commission that enforces labeling information under the Fair Packaging and Labeling Act.

Radiation Control for Health and Safety Act Intended to protect the public from unnecessary exposure to radiation from electronic products such as television sets, microwave ovens, and X-ray machines, the Radiation Control for Health and Safety Act was passed in 1968. It authorizes the FDA to set performance standards for such products and to enforce them.

■ **Structure of the agency** The FDA is divided into six bureaus: Foods, Drugs, Veterinary Medicine, Radiological Health, Biologics, and Medical Devices. Each bureau carries out its own research, does its own testing, reviews industrial testing of products, and makes recommendations for methods of enforcement. The Bureau of Drugs has a national network of poison control centers and a nationwide Adverse Drug Reaction Reporting System.

■ **Enforcement** The FDA's six bureaus make every effort to bring the industries it regulates into conformity with the law through a cooperative and nonbelligerent approach. The bureaus write many letters, hold conferences, give speeches, publish bulletins, offer exhibits, and provide individual counseling so that manufacturers and shippers will be well informed about what the law requires and what they must do to comply with it. A product may be recalled by a manufacturer on his own volition or at the request of the FDA. On occasion, however, a company is found in violation of the law. If its executives refuse to destroy or recall a product or make it comply with FDA regulations, the FDA has three means of dealing with the situation. It may ask the U.S. Attorney to seize the product, prosecute the violator, or obtain an injunction against further shipment.

Seizure When the FDA learns through inspection or laboratory analysis that a product that has been transported from one state to another fails to meet the standards the law requires, the agency may ask the U.S. Attorney's Office to file a *libel* with a federal court. Then, acting on a warrant issued by the court, a U.S. marshal is empowered to seize the product.

The purpose of the seizure is not to punish but to prevent consumption or use of the product—"stopping the bullet in its flight," in the words of the Supreme Court. The owner then has the opportunity to contest the FDA's charges. If he fails to appear or to persuade the court that the seizure was unjustified, the court will order that the products either be destroyed or disposed of in some other way. If the seized item is a food that is simply mislabeled, for example, it might be given to a charity.

The owner might also appear in court or file papers admitting the violation and request an opportunity to recondition the product and make it comply with the law—for example, by applying new, accurate labels to the product. If the court agrees, it will issue a *consent decree of condemnation* and order the owner to put up a bond, which is generally more than twice the cash value of the goods. The court will then order the goods released and, under the supervision of an FDA inspector, whose time is paid for by the owner, the goods will be reconditioned. The results of the procedure must then be reported to the court and, if acceptable, the owner will be given the right to sell the merchandise and his bond will be returned.

Criminal prosecution Even an unintentional violation of the Federal Food, Drug, and Cosmetic Act can lead to fines and imprisonment if the FDA chooses to prosecute. When the violation occurs without intention to defraud or mislead the public, the violator can be fined up to $1,000 or imprisoned up to a year for each illegal shipment he made or for each illegal act he committed, or both penalties can be levied. If the violation was intentional, or if it was a second or further offense, the maximum fine is $10,000 and the maximum prison term is three years for each violation.

Injunction proceeding When a person or a firm has a record of repeated violations, the FDA need not wait until a product is shipped interstate and then seize it or begin criminal prosecution. The agency can obtain an injunction to prevent an existing product, or any products produced at the same plant, from being shipped until the company meets the standards of the law. If the company acts in violation of the injunction, it is guilty of CONTEMPT and, at the judge's discretion, may be punished severely.

The injunction is used when inspectors discover that food is being produced under unsanitary conditions, which allow it to become contaminated. To obtain an injunction, the FDA must show that, if an injunction is not issued, another violation will probably occur.

■ **Limitations** The FDA can act only within the scope of the powers granted to it by congressional acts. It cannot, for example, require premarket approval for the safety of cosmetics. If a cosmetic is adulterated or mislabeled, or if people are harmed by a cosmetic after it is marketed, the FDA can take legal action to prevent its continuing sale. In general, the agency cannot prevent marketing of a product that is manufactured and sold within the same state, although there are many exceptions to this rule. Nor can it control the price of a product.

The agency is not involved in regulating the advertising of any product except prescription drugs and certain medical devices. Even blatantly false advertising for foods and cosmetics is not under the jurisdiction of the FDA unless it claims FDA approval. It is, however, under the jurisdiction of the Federal Trade Commission.

■ **Reporting a violation** If you believe that a food, cosmetic, drug, or medical device does not conform to FDA regulations, the agency encourages you to report it and will promptly investigate your complaint. You can give your complaint in writing or by phone to the nearest FDA field office. There are more than 150 of them throughout the United States, located mainly in large cities. Check your telephone directory under "United States Government, Department of Health and Human Services, Food and Drug Administration." Or you may write directly to FDA headquarters, 5600 Fishers Lane, Rockville, Maryland 20857.

force Unlawful or wrongful violence. Taking a person's money at gunpoint is threatening force to rob him. If your neighbor shoots you for picking a rose from her bush while you are walking along the public sidewalk, the force she uses is excessive and unlawful.

forced sale A sale ordered by a court to pay off a judgment—a sale of what is left of a bankrupt person's property, for example. See EXECUTION.

forcible detainer A situation in which a person who rightfully possesses real property (real estate) refuses to surrender it when his right to possession ends. A tenant who bolts himself inside his apartment when his lease expires is creating a forcible detainer. A landlord in this situation would bring a proceeding for FORCIBLE ENTRY AND DETAINER to get the apartment back.

forcible entry and detainer A civil proceeding brought by the rightful possessor of real property (real estate) against a person who has forcibly invaded it. The objectives of the court action are to prevent a disturbance of the public peace and to prevent people from violently taking matters into their own hands. In most cases, the immediate right to possession of real estate is all that is involved in the action.

A plaintiff's right to bring an action for forcible entry and detainer exists only under certain circumstances, which vary from state to state. Broadly speaking, the plaintiff must have had possession of the property and the defendant must have forcibly intruded upon it and must be in possession of the property when the lawsuit is started.

To be forcible, the entry must be accompanied either by actual violence or by circumstances that terrify the person in possession into surrendering his rights. For example, threatening violence or breaking into a building are both acts amounting to forcible entry. See EJECTMENT.

A person cannot sue for forcible entry and detainer if, before the entry, he abandoned possession of the property and had no intention of returning.

foreclosure An action by a party holding a MORTGAGE (such as a bank) to take the property away from the mortgagor (often a homeowner), to end the mortgagor's (homeowner's) rights in the property, and to sell the property to pay off the mortgage debt. Both the process (which is usually a lawsuit) and the result are called foreclosure. See Chart 13.

foreign 1 Belonging to another nation or country. See ALIEN 2 Legally attached to another jurisdiction, such as a state or county. 3 Subject to the laws of another state. A Maine court would call a Delaware-based company a foreign corporation.

foreman The presiding member of a jury. The foreman speaks for the jury, asks questions for it, and answers questions directed to it.

forensic Concerned with courts and the law. For example, forensic medicine is the science that applies every branch of medical knowledge to the purposes of the law. An expert in forensic medicine can help a court decide a contested question that affects life or property, such as whether a person died of natural causes or from poison.

forest A large group of trees and the land on which the trees stand. Standing and growing timber form a part of the land, and they belong to the owner of the land as much as the soil itself. The public officer administering and enforcing the laws relating to forests and the protection of trees is called a *forester*.

■ **State powers** The state has the right to compel and encourage private owners to participate in programs for the reforestation of land. It can require private property owners engaged in commercial lumbering operations to provide for reforesting by leaving a certain number of trees for reseeding purposes or by restocking the area with seedlings. The property owner's logging permit can be conditioned on his participation in the reforestation program.

In order to promote public safety on the highways, the state can give a forestry department the authority to plant roadside trees and to regulate the cutting and trimming of trees along the highways. Various statutes have also been passed for the nurture and protection of shade and ornamental trees on public streets and highways.

Many statutes require that precautions be taken against forest fires. The state can prohibit property owners from setting fires during the summer without permission and it can authorize a state forester to determine whether an owner of forest land has provided sufficient protection against fire. During a period of drought, when the danger of fire is great, the public can be prohibited from entering forests and woodlands.

Finally, a state can ordinarily create forest reserves, or state forests, when reasonably necessary to promote the public welfare. A state can also appropriate taxes for the support of such forests.

■ **National forests** The federal government has established national forests for the public welfare. Congress has the power to provide for the establishment and maintenance of national forests and to acquire land for such purposes. Congressionally mandated regulations relating to national forests and their protection supersede state laws.

In 1979 there were 154 national forests located in 41 states and Puerto Rico. National forests are managed and regulated by the Forest Service, a branch of the Department of Agriculture. The creation of a national forest removes the reserved land from the public domain. The land is no longer subject to use for private purposes, except according to applicable statutes and regulations.

A percentage of the proceeds from the use of a national forest is allocated to the state in which the forest is located. The money is to be spent for the benefit of public schools and roads in the counties encompassing the forest.

forfeit Lose the right to something because of a neglect of duty, an offense, or a breach of contract. For instance, if a defendant who is free on bail fails to show up for his trial, he forfeits the amount of his bail bond. A buyer who refuses to buy a house after signing the contract of sale forfeits his down payment—usually 10 percent of the purchase price—for his breach of contract to the seller.

forfeiture The loss of specific property without compensation as a penalty for neglect of duty, an offense, or a breach of contract. A forfeiture can apply to any kind of property a person owns or in which he has a right. Forfeitures are usually not favored by the courts because they have been traditionally considered harsh penalties.

At the present time, many statutes allow the forfeiture of specific property that has been used in, or in connection with, violating particular federal and state laws once a person has been convicted of the crime. Suppose the police found 100 cartons of untaxed cigarettes in a car and later

refused to release either the cigarettes or the car. This is a valid forfeiture of specific property used in a crime—the evasion of taxes; it is authorized both by federal law and by many state laws. Forfeiture of both a vehicle and all the narcotics hidden in it would also result if the authorities caught the driver SMUGGLING drugs into the country and the driver was convicted.

The owner of forfeited property must be given a hearing. If he fails to appear at the hearing, the court may approve the forfeiture when the facts justifying it are apparent from the record, unless a hearing is required by statute. Items that are forfeited are usually sold at "public sales" and the proceeds are used for various government purposes.

Forfeited property or its proceeds are disposed of according to the laws of the state or federal government. Some laws specifically provide that a person entitled to part of the proceeds from the forfeited property may start a forfeiture action or he may join with the government in an action to recover the property.

EXAMPLE Suppose a boat used to transport illegal drugs into
O——* the country is forfeited to the government upon its owner's conviction. The owner had bought the boat on credit, giving the seller the right to repossess the boat if he should fall behind on payments. At the time of his conviction, the owner is $10,000 behind in payments and will still owe $20,000 in the future. The seller may be entitled to a proportionate share of the proceeds from the sale of the boat.

A person whose property has been forfeited may challenge the forfeiture, but as long as the court determines that the act or event causing the forfeiture did, in fact, occur, the forfeiture will be upheld.

forgery The crime of intentionally making a false document or substantially altering a genuine one with an intent to defraud someone. The false or altered document itself is also called a forgery. Forgery is now classified by statute as a FELONY.

The essential elements of forgery are (1) a fraudulent intent and (2) a written document capable of carrying out a fraud. A *false making* occurs when the entire document is forged. Suppose someone steals your checkbook and writes a check for $1,500 to a department store for a stereo, signing your name. He has falsely made the check. On the other hand, a *false altering* occurs when the document itself is genuine, but part of it has been changed in a substantial way. Suppose Steve Brown improperly adds words to his father's will, which he found under the mattress of his father's bed. This is a forgery if the court finds that the added words substantially change the will.

Filling in a blank in a legal document without authorization and for a fraudulent purpose is also an alteration.
EXAMPLE Your neighbor gives her car mechanic a signed
O——* blank check and he promises her that he will fill in the amount for $150, the cost of replacing the car windshield. Instead, he completes the check for $1,500, cashes it, and leaves town for a weekend in Las Vegas. He has committed forgery because he falsely completed a blank check with an intent to cheat your neighbor of $1,350.

■ **Intent** An intent to defraud is the essence of the crime of forgery. If a person makes or alters a document in good faith and honestly believes he is authorized to do so, he is not guilty of forgery.

EXAMPLE The first number on a note (a promise to pay) O—✳ from someone who owes you money is illegible. You think it is a "5" and go over it with a pen. It really is a "3," but you are not guilty of forgery because you thought you would just make the number clearer.

A person who signs his own name to a document with the intent that it be mistaken for the document of another person with an identical name is guilty of forgery.

EXAMPLE Suppose your neighbor Calvin Carruthers has the O—✳ same name as the wealthiest man in town. Your neighbor Calvin has been unemployed for the last 28 months and desperately needs a new suit for job hunting. So he goes into a large department store and charges a suit to the account of the other man by signing the name they share. Your neighbor is guilty of forgery.

To be a forgery, the forged name need not be a real person's, nor must a forged signature resemble that of the person whose writing it pretends to be. No one has to be actually injured or defrauded by the forgery. It is sufficient that the false or altered document was made with the intent to defraud and *could* hurt the rights of a person who accepts it as genuine.

■ **Documents subject to forgery** Unless otherwise provided by statute, a forged writing may be handwritten, printed, typewritten, or engraved. Any writing that may defraud or jeopardize another's rights or that, if accepted as genuine, would result in another person's liability—such as checks, promissory notes, deeds, mortgages, wills, and public records and documents—may be the subject of forgery. A letter of introduction or an unsigned document cannot be the subject of forgery because it has no legal significance—it does not create a legal right or liability.

Publishing, or uttering, a forged document (offering it as genuine) is a different offense from forgery. *Publishing* occurs when a person knowingly offers a forgery to someone else, pretending either in words or actions that the writing is genuine and intending to defraud. It does not matter whether or not the offer is accepted. The person publishing the forgery need not have participated in the forgery, and no one has to be actually harmed by it.

EXAMPLE Suppose John Smith was given a check for O—✳ $2,000, which he learned was a forgery. Smith owes $2,000 to his son's orthodontist for braces. He signs the forged check over to the orthodontist and catches the next flight to Brazil for an extended holiday. Smith has committed the crime of uttering, or publishing, a forged document, but not the crime of forgery. But if he himself had forged the check and then passed it on to the orthodontist, he would be guilty of both forgery and uttering a forged document.

A person is guilty of forgery if he knowingly participates with another in falsely making or altering a document with an intent to defraud. Forgery is generally punishable by a fine, imprisonment, or both.

■ **Civil liability** When a legal document has been falsely altered, the person who made the change is criminally liable. But the civil liability for the forged document depends on the circumstances of the case. The person who originally made or wrote the document is responsible only for the amount of the document before it was altered—provided he was free from fault or negligence.

EXAMPLE Suppose a person writes a check for $5.00. He O—✳ places the word "five" to the extreme left on the line where the amount is written out in words and fails to indicate either by drawing a line or adding "and ⁰⁰/₁₀₀" that the amount is to be five dollars. On the line where the amount is entered in numbers he puts "5," without adding ".00" to indicate $5.00. If the person who receives the check adds the word "hundred" to the word line and "00" to the number line, the check will read $500. The person who originally wrote the check may be held liable for the entire amount of $500, rather than $5.00, since the check could be substantially altered because of the careless way he wrote it.

When a person intentionally leaves a blank on his check, he may be liable for the whole amount to anyone who accepts the check in good faith, believing it is genuine.

EXAMPLE In the example cited earlier, the bank that cashed O—✳ the $1,500 check for the car mechanic may hold your neighbor liable for the entire amount. Her remedy is to have the mechanic criminally prosecuted and also to sue him in order to get her money back.

formal party A party to a lawsuit who has nothing to gain or lose by the outcome, but who has an interest in the subject matter because when the present suit is settled, he may be spared future litigation.

EXAMPLE Noreen opened a bank account in her name and in O—✳ the name of Thomas Adams. She added sums to the account regularly and occasionally made withdrawals. When she died, the bank wanted to turn all the money in the account over to Thomas. It found that Noreen had two relatives with the name Thomas Adams, and they both claimed the money. The bank started a lawsuit against both Thomases and paid the money into court. The bank (the plaintiff in the action) was only a formal party. It could not keep the money no matter what the court decided. Its interest in the outcome of the suit was that the final decision would give the money to one Thomas and prevent the other from ever making an additional claim for the money.

form of action This procedural term is the general description of the ways each different type of lawsuit once had to be presented in court. If a legal problem did not fit into one of the existing categories, such as DEBT or REPLEVIN, it could not be presented in many courts. Today, in federal and most state courts, there is only one form of action, a civil ACTION, which allows a person to present all his claims against another in one lawsuit instead of having separate suits for each different form of action.

fornication The criminal offense under the common law of illicit sexual intercourse between an unmarried woman and a married or unmarried man. (If the woman was married, the crime was ADULTERY, regardless of the marital status of the man.) Modern statutes often define fornication as sexual intercourse between unmarried persons. When one of the persons is married, some statutes make the crime fornication by the unmarried person and adultery by the other, while other statutes make the crime adultery for both. Fornication is an element of various sex offenses, such as RAPE, INCEST, and SEDUCTION.

Many states do not enforce the laws against fornication on the theory that it is a "victimless" crime. Where the laws are enforced, the crime of fornication may be punished by a fine, imprisonment, or both.

forswear In criminal law, to swear to a statement that a person knows to be untrue. This term is broader than PERJURY, which is lying under oath before a court about an important issue.

fortuitous Happening by chance or accident. For example, payment of benefits on a fire insurance policy is based on a fortuitous event—the unexpected destruction of a building by a fire.

forum In Roman times, the marketplace or paved public court in the city of Rome, where assemblies of the people, judicial trials, elections, and other public business were transacted. From this use, the word has come to mean a COURT of justice, judicial tribunal, or place of litigation. The proper forum for a lawsuit depends on which court has JURISDICTION (authority) over the parties and the subject in dispute. When people make a contract, they may specify the forum (court) that will determine any disputes that may arise under the contract, as long as the forum has the proper jurisdiction. This is often called a *forum selection clause*.

Forum shopping occurs when there is more than one court with the power to give the plaintiff the relief he seeks, and the plaintiff chooses the one that is to his greatest advantage. Sometimes this imposes an extreme hardship on the defendant. For example, a plaintiff may choose to start his suit in a forum so remote from the defendant's residence that the defendant cannot afford to bring himself or his witnesses to that court. If the defendant fails to appear for trial, the plaintiff may win the case by default. Federal and state rules, however, restrict a plaintiff's choice of forum to locations that are reasonably convenient for both parties. See CONFLICT OF LAWS; VENUE.

forum non conveniens (Latin) "Forum not convenient"; a doctrine that allows a forum (COURT) to refuse to hear a case over which it has jurisdiction (authority) if, in the interests of justice, the lawsuit should be heard in another forum. The application of this doctrine depends on the court's discretion.

forwarding fee Money paid to an attorney who refers a client to another attorney. It is paid by the lawyer who receives the client. The CODE OF PROFESSIONAL RESPONSIBILITY established for attorneys by the American Bar Association—and subsequently adopted by many state bar associations—prohibits forwarding fees (also called referral fees) paid to an attorney who has merely brought about the employment of another attorney without providing any service or assuming any responsibility to the client. A division of reasonable fees between lawyers is proper only if the client consents. The division should be proportionate to the work done by each attorney.

foundation 1 Basis. For example, the foundation of a trial is the group of issues in dispute between the parties as stated in their PLEADINGS—what the plaintiff claims and the defendant denies. 2 The establishment of a charity; the incorporation or endowment of a college or hospital. 3 An institution, such as the Ford Foundation, that supports publicly oriented projects, such as scientific research and cultural activities.

franchise A special privilege conferred by the government on an individual or CORPORATION. The term is also used to describe some agreements between private companies and individuals.

■ **Government franchises** The primary objective of franchise grants is to benefit the public, making the interests of the grantee (franchisee) secondary. In exchange for the franchise privilege, a person or company may agree to pay money to the government, bear some burden, or perform a public duty. All corporations are franchises as are the various powers given to them—the power of an insurance corporation to issue an insurance policy, for example. Public-utility companies, bridge and tunnel authorities, and taxi companies all operate under franchises. The term has also been popularly used to describe the various rights of citizens, such as the right to vote, called the elective franchise. For an extended discussion of the right to vote, see ELECTION.

The charter of a corporation is its *general franchise*. The franchise authorizing its formation and existence is sometimes called a *personal* or *primary franchise*. *Secondary* or *special franchises* are the special rights, privileges, or grants that the corporation receives under its charter or from a MUNICIPAL CORPORATION, such as the rights to use the public streets, exact tolls, or collect fares. A *property franchise* authorizes a corporation to use its property for a particular purpose, such as constructing and operating a railroad. A *franchise tax* is a tax imposed by the state on the right and privilege of carrying on business as a corporation. See TAXATION.

Power to grant franchises The power to grant franchises is vested in the state legislature, subject to limitations imposed by the state constitution. A franchise may be obtained indirectly from the state through the appropriate agency. A franchise frequently contains specific conditions and stipulations that the grantee, or holder of the franchise, must perform.

EXAMPLE Let us say you want to start an express bus service
O—* between a city and its suburbs. You would have to apply for a franchise either to the state or to the local transportation agency if the state has delegated its powers to that agency. Once you have been granted a franchise to start your bus service, your buses may be restricted to certain routes convenient to the public, or you may be allowed to operate it only if you provide service during hours that best serve the riders.

Regulation The state or its political subdivisions may regulate the grant or exercise of franchises.

Right to compete A franchise may be exclusive or nonexclusive. An exclusive franchise means that no one else can be granted a similar franchise in your territory. A nonexclusive franchise does not prevent the grant of a similar one to a lawful competitor, but it does prevent competition from someone who does not have a franchise.

EXAMPLE Suppose you have been granted the franchise for O⸱——⸱＊ your bus service, and suddenly an unfranchised company begins taking your best route, which helps pay for the service you have to provide on less traveled routes. Its lower fares and better schedules on that route prove devastating to your overall service. You may bring a lawsuit for an injunction (a court order halting the company's service on your route) and money damages for the unlawful invasion of your franchise.

Time limits The legislature may fix the length of time of a franchise. Whether or not the state's political subdivisions (such as a county or municipality) may do so depends on the state's statutes or the limitations of the state's constitution. A franchise may be terminated by a mutual agreement between the state and the grantee. A change in the organization of a state's political subdivision does not end a previously acquired franchise, and the legislature or proper agency may not arbitrarily revoke a franchise unless it has reserved that power.

Forfeiture The state may order the forfeiture of a franchise if it is not used—for instance, if you stop running your buses for three months during the winter because you cannot afford to equip them with snow tires. Misuse or failure to provide adequate services under the franchise may also result in its forfeiture.

Transfer of franchises When a state's constitution or statute permits, franchises may be sold or transferred, (such as a medallion that gives its owner the right to operate a taxi in New York City); but when they involve public service (such as bus transportation), state authorization is generally needed. The person or corporation who buys a franchise must accept the franchise with its limitations, such as having authorization to run buses only along a certain route.

■ **Nongovernment franchises** In recent years certain contracts granted by private individuals or companies have become loosely referred to as franchises. The franchise system, or method of operation, has had a phenomenal growth in particular industries, such as automobile sales, fast foods, and ice cream. This use of the franchise has enabled individuals with little capital to become entrepreneurs. The cornerstone of the franchise system is the trademark or trade name of a product. See TRADEMARKS AND TRADE NAMES.

Used in this manner, a franchise is a license from an owner of a trademark or trade name permitting another to sell a product or service under that name or mark. Under an elaborate agreement a franchisee, for a fee paid to the franchisor, is permitted to conduct a business or sell a product or service according to the methods and procedures established by the franchisor. The franchisee is usually granted an exclusive territory in which he is the only distributor of the particular goods or services. The franchisor is usually obligated by contract to assist the franchisee through advertising, promotion, research and development, quality purchasing, training and education, and other management resources.

Deceptive practices As rapidly as the franchise business developed, so did the number of unscrupulous franchisors. Advertisements claiming that potential investors needed no business experience attracted people who, on the whole, had little or no business acumen. Many signed contracts and made large down payments without verifying the facts. Most failed to obtain the advice of an attorney or accountant to explain the legal consequences of complicated contract provisions or to present a realistic financial picture of their potential investment.

Unfulfilled contracts After a contract was signed, a franchisee frequently encountered problems in having the franchisor fulfill his part of the contract. Delays of several months between signing the contract and selecting the location—usually made by the franchisor—were not uncommon. During this time, the franchisee would receive inventory and supplies and would have to rent storage space, at his own expense, until the franchise site was selected. Sometimes inventory, such as foods, would spoil because of the long delay, but the franchisee was still contractually bound to pay for the goods even though their destruction was the franchisor's fault. Sometimes the site selected had little profit potential. In addition, a franchisee was often duped about the exclusive nature of his territory. It was not rare to discover that someone else had the same "exclusive" territory.

Other abuses Other abuses included misrepresented earning potential of the franchise, unsalable or poor-quality supplies, inadequate or worthless advertising programs for which the franchisee paid dearly, and unsatisfactory training programs.

Financial disclosure laws Before 1979, less than 20 states had enacted laws to protect prospective franchisees from being cheated by dishonest franchisors. These laws required that anyone offering franchises for sale in the state had to disclose the facts that play a crucial role in deciding to buy a franchise, including the true costs of running a franchise, any recurring expenses, and substantiated reports of profits. In states without these laws, the investor remained at the mercy of the franchisor. A franchisee could, of course, sue a franchisor for breach of contract, but this was expensive and frequently unsuccessful—unscrupulous franchisors often declared bankruptcy, preventing the franchisee from recovering his money.

FTC regulations Late in 1978, the FEDERAL TRADE COMMISSION (FTC), having received numerous complaints about unfair and deceptive practices in the sale of all types of franchises, issued regulations that became effective in July 1979. In addition to requiring franchisors and their representatives to disclose the necessary facts for an informed decision about buying a franchise, the FTC regulations established certain practices to be followed in the franchisor-franchisee relationship:

(1) A franchisor must now reveal the history of the company for its previous five years. He must say whether any of the company's executives have, within the last seven years, been convicted of or pleaded NOLO CONTENDERE to FRAUD; held liable in a civil lawsuit for fraud; subject to a court order or administrative agency ruling concerning the franchise business or fraud; or involved in any proceedings for bankruptcy or corporate reorganization for insolvency.

(2) A factual description of the franchise must be provided as well as a clear statement of the total funds to be

paid, such as initial franchise fees, deposits, down payments, prepaid rent on the location and equipment, and inventory purchases.

(3) The conditions and time limits to obtain a refund, as well as its amount, must be specified.

(4) The amount of recurring costs—such as royalties, rents, advertising fees, and sign-rental fees—must be included.

(5) Any restrictions imposed must be discussed—such as on the amount of goods or services to be sold; the types of customers with which the franchisee may deal (for example, the franchisor may reserve all government groups as its own customers); the geographical territory and whether the franchisee is entitled to protection of his territory by the franchisor.

(6) The length of time the franchisee may hold the franchise, in addition to the reasons for terminating or not renewing the franchisee's license when it expires, must be explained.

(7) The number of franchises voluntarily terminated by franchisees or by the franchisor must be reported.

(8) The franchisor must disclose the number of franchises operating at the end of the previous year as well as the number of company-owned outlets.

(9) The franchisee must also be supplied with the names, addresses, and telephone numbers of the franchisees of the 10 outlets nearest the prospective franchisee's location, so that he can check out the day-to-day operations of a franchise.

(10) If the franchisor makes any claims about the actual or projected sales of his franchises or their actual or potential profits, he must be able to substantiate them.

These facts must be incorporated into an accurate, clear, and concise document and must be given to the prospective franchisee at least 10 days before any contractual relationship is entered or a deposit is made, whichever comes first. The purposes of this disclosure statement are to give the potential investor a realistic picture of the proposed business venture and to eliminate unscrupulous franchisors from the field. Failure to comply with FTC regulations can result in a fine of up to $10,000 for each violation.

Termination Another area of controversy is the right of a franchisor to terminate the franchisee's license. Only a few states have enacted laws that prohibit a franchisor from terminating a franchise without good cause. Good cause usually means that the franchisee has breached his contract. The franchisor is then entitled to reacquire the outlet, usually by repurchasing the franchisee's assets, such as inventory and equipment. In states without termination laws, franchisees claim that they are victimized by franchisors who want to reclaim outlets that have proved highly profitable. (Company-owned outlets yield a greater profit to the franchisor than royalty payments received from franchisees.) Some franchisees allege that, to harass them into selling their stores back to the franchisors at a fraction of their worth, the franchisor imposes impossible or ridiculous demands. Other franchisees claim that their licenses have been revoked or not renewed because they complained to various state and federal agencies about how the franchisors operate. Many cases are presently being litigated in the courts to determine what circumstances justify a

franchisor's termination of a franchisee's license. In addition, Congress has been asked to enact legislation to prohibit franchisors from terminating franchises without good cause.

fraud A comprehensive term describing all the ways that human ingenuity can devise to gain an advantage over another person by false suggestions or by concealing the truth. It has been used interchangeably with the words "misrepresentation" and "deceit." This article discusses the essential elements of fraud, the remedies for relief for victims of fraud, and criminal responsibility.

■ **Actual and constructive** Fraud may be classified as actual or constructive. *Actual fraud* consists of deception intentionally and successfully practiced to induce a person to part with property or to surrender some legal right. For example, a man comes to your door saying he is collecting for a local charity. You give him $50 and later learn that the charity does not exist. You have been the victim of an actual fraud.

Constructive fraud is a breach of a duty that becomes legally fraudulent because of its tendency to deceive, violate confidence, or injure public interests. There does not have to be an intent to deceive or a dishonest purpose. Constructive fraud is most frequently found when there has been a breach of a duty arising from a fiduciary relationship—a relationship of trust and confidence.

EXAMPLE Frances, the wife of the deceased and the executrix of his estate, tells John, the only other beneficiary, that there are few or no assets remaining to pay John his share. Accepting her word, he assigns his interest in the estate to her for a small consideration. Later, $300,000 worth of bankbooks and stock certificates in the decedent's name are discovered in the decedent's safe-deposit box, which Frances had forgotten to search. This is constructive fraud because Frances had breached her duty as executrix to make a thorough search for her husband's assets. As a result of her breach of duty, John was defrauded of his rightful share in the estate.

The term "fraud" as it is popularly used refers to actual fraud, which is the subject of the remainder of this article.

■ **What constitutes fraud** Fraud occurs when one person suffers some harm because of his reliance on the fraudulent actions or statements of another. In order for a person to sue for fraud, all of the following elements must be present: (1) A statement of a material (substantial) fact is made. (2) The statement is false, and the defendant knows it is false. (3) The defendant intends to deceive the plaintiff. (4) The plaintiff justifiably relies on the statement. (5) The plaintiff suffers some harm as a result.

Materiality A material fact is one that substantially affects a person's decision to enter into a contract or pursue a particular course of action. A misstatement of an immaterial fact—one that is trivial or unrelated to anything of real importance in the transaction—will not support a lawsuit for fraud.

EXAMPLE Peter bought a leather jacket from Don because Don stated that he was a good and loyal alumnus of the college Peter had attended. The jacket was exactly as Don had claimed it to be, but Don was not an alumnus of Peter's college—he had intentionally lied. Peter sued

BEWARE! YOU MAY BE A VICTIM OF FRAUD

■ *Actual fraud* is deception intentionally and successfully practiced to induce a person to part with property or surrender some legal right.

■ The law also recognizes *constructive fraud*, which may have been committed without dishonesty or intent to deceive—for example, the executor of a will who failed to make a thorough search of the decedent's assets and thereby defrauded beneficiaries of property due them.

■ Actual fraud can be proved only when the following five elements are present: (1) a statement of a material (important) fact is made; (2) the person who makes it knows it is false; (3) he makes it to deceive the other person; (4) the person to whom the statement is made justifiably relies on it and (5) suffers harm as a result.

■ Typical fraudulent statements are ones about the financial condition of a person or a business or about the quality or quantity of goods.

■ If you are a seller, and the buyer seeks information on the thing you are selling, you must either tell the whole truth about it or nothing. A misleading half-truth is ground for an action for fraudulent misrepresentation.

■ The intent to deceive lies at the heart of fraud. Be very careful when you make a representation concerning something you are not altogether sure about. It is better to qualify a representation by saying it is merely your opinion based on information you have received but cannot vouch for.

■ A person cannot win a lawsuit for fraud unless he was really deceived. The fact that misrepresentations were made to him is not enough if he could have discovered through ordinary diligence and prudence that it was unreasonable to rely on those statements.

■ A person can win a lawsuit for fraud only when he has suffered some harm that puts him in a worse position than before the fraud.

■ The amount of damages awarded follows the loss-of-the-bargain rule in some states and the out-of-pocket rule in others. The *loss of the bargain* rule means that you recover the difference between the actual value of the property you got and the value of the property as it was represented. The *out of pocket* rule means that you recover only the money you actually lost—the difference between the actual value of the property and the amount you paid for it.

■ If you entered a contract based on fraudulent misrepresentations, you may sue to have the contract canceled and be restored to your original position—with all the money paid under the contract returned to you.

Don for fraud. But because the fact that was misrepresented was not important in the transaction, it was not a sufficient basis for an action for fraud.

EXAMPLE Suppose, however, that Don had stated that the jacket was made of "genuine cowhide exactly as it came from the cow" when he knew that the original leather had been split. This misrepresentation of a material fact would support an action for fraud.

Statements about the financial condition of a person or a business or about the quality and quantity of goods are typical misrepresentations that may be material in an action for fraud.

False statement There can be no fraud without a misrepresentation, which is a false statement or lie about a past or existing fact. Neither a prediction of things to come nor a promise can give rise to an action for fraud.

EXAMPLE Dave Brown sells stock in the Xyletol Corporation to Pat Smith, making two representations to Smith. He tells Smith that these stocks will surely increase in value and that he will find a job for Smith. The stocks go down in value, and Brown does not even attempt to find Smith a job. Smith sues Brown for damages for fraud, but there is no ground for the suit because neither representation is a statement of fact, past or present. One is a prediction and the other is a promise.

A misrepresentation may be expressed by acts as well as by words—keeping an insolvent bank open for business, for example, or selling unregistered or stolen securities, or turning back an odometer on a car offered for sale.

As a general rule, the expression of an opinion or a belief is not a statement of fact upon which a person can justifiably rely. Whether a particular statement is one of opinion or fact depends on the circumstances of the case.

EXAMPLE Jones is a salesman of new cars. He tells Thomas, a prospective purchaser, "This is the finest car on the market; it is the most economical one you can buy; you can't beat it for safety." Thomas buys the car and finds it is not the "finest," not "economical," and not "safe." If he sues Jones for fraud, the action would be dismissed. All these are statements of opinion, seller's talk, or *puffing*, a common sales technique. They are not intended as statements of facts, and Thomas was not justified in relying on them. If, however, Jones told Thomas that the car was equipped with power steering and brakes when, in fact, it was not, Thomas would be able to sue for fraud.

When the person expressing the opinion has or professes to have superior knowledge of the subject in question, a statement that under other circumstances would be an opinion may constitute fraud.

EXAMPLE A statement to a prospective buyer by the builder of a house that there would be no water in the basement was not a mere expression of opinion as to the dryness of the basement. It would be reasonable for the purchaser to assume that the house was designed and built in a way that would prevent the flooding of the basement. The buyer could sue the builder for fraud if the basement flooded, since the builder had superior knowledge about the construction of the house, which he misrepresented.

When the particular circumstances impose a duty to speak on a person and he deliberately remains silent, his silence is equivalent to a false representation. If one person knows a fact that the other person is justified in assuming does not exist, a duty of disclosure exists; but if the information is equally available to both, there is no such duty.

EXAMPLE In one case, a man—let's call him Harper—sold ○—✱ his house, which was infested with termites, to an unsuspecting buyer. Harper did not disclose the fact, and reasonable inspection of the house by the buyer did not reveal the insects. After moving in, the buyer discovered them and sued Harper for knowingly concealing this material fact. Harper lost.

If a prospective purchaser seeks information from a seller, the seller can either refuse to give any information or make a full and truthful disclosure. He must tell the whole truth or nothing. An answer that is a misleading half-truth is ground for an action for fraudulent misrepresentation.

When a relationship of trust and confidence exists between the parties—a fiduciary relationship—there is a duty to disclose all material facts, and failure to do so constitutes fraud. Among particular relationships considered fiduciary are those involving attorney and client, physician and patient, partners, and officers and stockholders of a corporation, as well as persons making insurance contracts. For instance, if a person applying for a life insurance policy is under treatment for a terminal illness, he must disclose that fact or be liable for fraud.

As long as people continue to rely on a statement, new information that makes it untrue or misleading must be disclosed.

EXAMPLE Miller, an independent public accountant, audit-○—✱ ed the financial statements of a company. He certified that the information sent to stockholders in the company's annual report and filed with the Securities and Exchange Commission was correct. When Miller learned that the financial statements were incorrect, he failed to disclose that fact publicly. In a subsequent suit against him by the stockholders and bondholders for losses they sustained by Miller's nondisclosure, the court decided that even though Miller did not profit from the nondisclosure, he had a duty to correct his original representation, because he knew that people were relying on it.

If a person making an immaterial representation later discovers that it has become material and that the other person is about to act on it in a business transaction with him, he has a duty to disclose it.

Intent One person's intent to deceive another lies at the very heart of fraud. This kind of intent is known as *scienter*, or knowledge that an act will cause injury. An intent to deceive may exist when someone makes a statement that he knows is untrue—for example, a man, knowing that the dog he is selling is not pedigreed, tells the purchaser it is registered with the American Kennel Club. An unqualified and positive claim that a person has knowledge he does not have is a false representation. A person who doubts the truth of his representations or speaks with deliberate ignorance or reckless indifference about their truth is also guilty of fraud.

EXAMPLE Your neighbor Howard takes his car to Jiffy ○—✱ Carfix, a local auto repair shop, to get new brakes installed. When Howard returns to pick up his car, the shop's owner tells him "everything's been taken care of" when, actually, the owner has no idea what his mechanic did. The owner's statement would make him liable for fraud, because he was indifferent to its truth and because faulty brakes could cause an accident.

A person who qualifies his representation by indicating that it is merely his opinion or belief based on information he received is not liable for its falsity.

Reliance A person cannot obtain relief for fraud unless he was deceived by the misrepresentation of a material fact he believed to be true. The plaintiff's reliance on the misrepresentation must be justifiable. When deciding justification, the court considers the intelligence, experience, and capacity of the plaintiff and the means available to him for observing—without having to make an investigation—the truth or falsity of the defendant's representation. A plaintiff of average intelligence, for example, may not justifiably rely on the absolutely absurd statement of his optometrist that eyeglasses would automatically adjust themselves to the defective condition of his eyes. People who are illiterate or exceptionally gullible, superstitious, or ignorant have been awarded money damages for fraud when the defendant knew and took advantage of their condition.

When the parties deal on equal terms, misrepresentations will not support an action for fraud if the plaintiff, through ordinary diligence and prudence, could have discovered it was unreasonable to rely on those statements.

EXAMPLE Paul tells Dave that he will buy a car from him ○—✱ only if it has air conditioning. Dave says, "Okay, take this one." Paul test-drives the car and buys it without checking to see if it is air conditioned. When Paul later discovers that the knob labeled "Air" is for ventilation only, he will be denied compensation in a fraud action. Ordinary care is a subjective standard, determined by the intelligence and experience of the misled individual. In this example, Paul could easily have determined whether the car had air conditioning, and he was not justified in relying on Dave's representation.

Harm A person may recover for fraud only when he has suffered some harm that puts him in a worse position than before the fraud.

■ **Remedies for fraud** A person may bring a civil action for DAMAGES for fraud. The amount of money he will receive is determined by the rule of damages used in his state. Most states follow the *loss-of-the-bargain* rule, which allows a plaintiff to recover the benefit of his bargain. This means that he can recover the difference between the actual value of the property he got and the value of the property as it was represented.

EXAMPLE You buy a painting for $1,500 after an art dealer ○—✱ tells you it is actually worth $2,500 on the open market. You later discover that it is worth only $100 because the dealer painted it himself three days before he sold it to you. Under the loss-of-the-bargain rule, you may recover $2,400 in damages, the difference between what you were told the value of the painting was ($2,500) and what its actual value is ($100).

Some states follow the *out-of-pocket* rule, which allows a plaintiff to recover only the money he has actually lost—the difference between the actual value of the property and the amount paid for the property. This rule reimburses the plaintiff but denies him the benefit of his bargain. In the example of the painting, your out-of-pocket damages would be $1,400, the difference between $100 and $1,500.

Regardless of which rule the court chooses to apply, the plaintiff may also be entitled to recover additional expenses he has incurred as a result of the fraudulent transaction. If you had purchased an insurance policy on your painting that cost $250, you would be entitled to recover that amount in addition to your loss-of-the-bargain or out-of-pocket damages.

The court may also decide to award a plaintiff punitive damages when the fraud was commited with MALICE (knowledge that harm would result).

EXAMPLE A woman tells an art dealer that she is recently widowed and to preserve her meager finances she has decided to invest in art. Because she seems particularly gullible in her aggrieved state, the art dealer intentionally defrauds her. When she learns of the fraud and sues the dealer, she may receive punitive damages, in addition to all the other damages she is entitled to, because of the malicious nature of the fraud.

When a person has entered a contract based on fraudulent misrepresentations, he may sue to have the contract rescinded (canceled) and be restored to his original position—that is, have all the money he paid under the contract returned to him. A person who seeks this remedy must return any benefits he has received from the other party.

■ **Criminal responsibility** Various acts and transactions of a fraudulent nature have been made criminal, including false and misleading advertising. See CONSUMER PROTECTION. Punishment for criminal offenses involving fraud are set by statute.

fraudulent conveyance
A debtor's transfer of his property to someone else in order to cheat his creditors, who would have a right to it in payment of the debts due.

EXAMPLE Your neighbor owes $500 to one creditor and $2,500 to another. He has $5,000 in a bank account, which he transfers to an account in his brother's name. He tells his brother that the money still belongs to him—he just wants to keep it out of the reach of his creditors who are "hounding him" for the money he owes them. This is a fraudulent conveyance, which may be set aside (canceled) by the court at the request of the defrauded creditors.

Every kind of property that can be used for the payment of debts may be the subject of a fraudulent conveyance and may be reclaimed by creditors. Many states, however, exempt personal items such as clothing, kitchen appliances, and household furniture from being reached by creditors. See EXEMPTION.

Any creditor who can show that a debtor owed him a valid and enforceable debt at the time a conveyance was made has a proper case, and he can seek to have the conveyance set aside. Generally, a creditor must have a LIEN (legal claim) on a particular item of property or acquire a JUDGMENT for a certain sum enforceable against the property. A judgment shows that a valid and enforceable debt exists. In many states, if the debtor can pay off the debt with property other than the property that was fraudulently conveyed, the court will not set aside the conveyance.

■ **Fraudulent intent** For a conveyance to be fraudulent, the intent to defraud must exist at the time the transfer of property was made. Suspicious circumstances surrounding the transfer of property by a debtor may justify an inference of fraud. Some examples: a sale or transfer carried out in great secrecy and haste; the failure to record a conveyance, such as a deed to land, together with other questionable conduct; or not releasing personal property after it has been "sold."

■ **Valuable consideration** If a debtor transfers his property for a valuable consideration (an appropriate price), the conveyance is not fraudulent. The reasoning behind this is that the debtor then has received money (or other assets) that his creditors can reach. But if he conceals the proceeds to cheat his creditors the conveyance is fraudulent.

Paying money or giving up a legal right—such as the right to bring a lawsuit for enforcement of a court order, for example—is usually regarded as a valuable consideration. To defend against an attack by creditors, a debtor must show that he received a valuable consideration for the property he conveyed. Even when a debtor intends to defraud his creditors by transferring property, if a valuable consideration is paid to him by someone who does not know of his fraudulent intent, the creditors cannot have that transfer set aside. In either event, the debtor still has something his creditors can go after. But if a voluntary conveyance leaves a debtor without the means to pay debts that existed at the time of the conveyance, it is fraudulent regardless of his intent.

EXAMPLE Carl borrowed $25,000 from a bank to support his family while he tried to build up his own business as a management consultant for small manufacturers. Unfortunately, the economy took a nose dive, and Carl was never able to get his business off the ground. After six months, he took a salaried position with a large company that paid enough to meet his household expenses but not enough to pay off the large loan. The bank threatened to force a sale of his home in order to collect the debt. Carl decided that, if he were going to lose the house anyway, someone might as well get a good deal. He sold the house to a young couple for a mere $10,000. When the bank sued Carl and the new owners, the court set aside the sale as a fraudulent conveyance because it left Carl with neither the house nor its value in money. If Carl had sold the house for $50,000, its true value, the couple could have kept the house because the bank could have collected the debt out of the proceeds of the sale.

■ **Family relationships** A conveyance by one spouse to the other, based on a fictitious or nominal consideration, is generally viewed as fraudulent.

EXAMPLE Your neighbor sells his Jaguar to his wife for $50 because he knows that his creditors are trying to have the court order its sale to pay off his debts. This is a fraudulent conveyance because $50 is clearly only a nominal consideration. But if your neighbor's wife paid her husband the market value of the car, the transfer would not be set aside.

When a conveyance between spouses is made in consideration of love and affection, it is fraudulent if it leaves the debtor spouse unable to pay his existing debts. If property is purchased in the name of the wife but is paid for with the funds of the husband, this is a conveyance without valuable consideration and may be challenged by his creditors. A bona fide debt owed by one spouse to the other—which may be established by showing that the spouses dealt with each other as debtor and creditor—may be considered property, and its transfer can serve as sufficient consideration for payment of a debt to a third person. The amount of the debt, however, must be proportionate to the value of the property conveyed.

EXAMPLE Martha owes her husband, George, $200 for the O➛✱ bill he paid for the repair of her car. George owes Benjamin $200 for a rifle he bought from him. George can assign Martha's debt to Benjamin. If Martha's creditors got a judgment on her property, the transfer of her debt would not be a fraudulent conveyance.

A conveyance by a parent to his child (or between any family members) for a consideration will generally be upheld against the parent's creditors, unless it is for a grossly inadequate consideration and the circumstances indicate fraud—if it leaves the debtor unable to meet his obligations to his creditors, for example.

■ **Preferences** A debtor may prefer one or more of his creditors by paying them off first, as long as he does not intend to cheat his other creditors. A debtor has this right because as absolute owner of his property he may do with it as he pleases as long as the law is not violated. His motives for a preference are unimportant. The property transferred to a preferred creditor must not unreasonably exceed the amount of the claim, however, because this would unfairly deprive the other creditors of their claims. In addition, the transaction must not offer special benefits to the preferred creditor—for example, giving him rapidly appreciating shares of stock. The fact that a family relationship, such as husband and wife, exists between the debtor and preferred creditor does not of itself affect the validity of a preference. However, a transaction involving family members will be more closely examined than one between strangers.

There are exceptions to the privilege of the debtor: certain debts that are given a preference by statute (such as those owed to the United States) and secured debts, both of which must be paid before any creditors to whom the debtor may give a preference. See SECURED TRANSACTION.

■ **Remedies** When declaring a conveyance void, the court may order a sale of the property under its own direction. The proceeds are used to pay the costs of the suit and the complaining creditors. A debtor who has fraudulently transferred his property to cheat his creditors may also be subject to statutory penalties and criminal prosecution, depending upon the law in his state.

freehold An interest in land, called an ESTATE. Fee simple, fee tail, and a life estate are all freehold estates.

friendly fire A fire burning in a place where it was intended to burn. For example, a fire in an incinerator or a fireplace is considered a friendly fire, even though it may cause extensive smoke damage. A fire insurance policy usually does not cover damages caused by a friendly fire; it covers only those caused by an uncontrollable HOSTILE FIRE.

friendly suit Any proceeding instituted by agreement between the parties to obtain the opinion of the court on a disputed or ambiguous issue. It is not to be confused with a FRIVOLOUS SUIT.

friend of the court See AMICUS CURIAE.

frisk In criminal law, the rapid, superficial running of the hands over a person's body by a law enforcement official in order to determine whether or not that person is carrying an illegal object, such as a concealed weapon or drugs. See SEARCH AND SEIZURE.

frivolous Legally worthless. A frivolous suit is one that has no legal merit. If it is begun in bad faith to harass the defendant, the plaintiff may be liable for damages in a subsequent suit brought by the defendant for MALICIOUS PROSECUTION. An ANSWER to a COMPLAINT in a legal case is frivolous when it is insufficient or irrelevant and when, in view of the facts pleaded, it does not present a defense. An appeal that presents no legal question or is so lacking in substance that it could not possibly succeed is frivolous.

fruit In its legal use, fruit is considered synonymous with "product" and "revenue." For example, rental income is the "fruit of renting out land," and stolen money is the "fruit of crime." Evidence illegally obtained by police in the investigation of a crime is called "fruit of the poisonous tree" and will be excluded from a criminal prosecution. See SEARCH AND SEIZURE.

frustration In contract law, the doctrine of frustration applies when the value of what has been bargained for by a person (the promisor) is destroyed by an event that the parties did not take into consideration when they made their contract. The promisor's duty to perform the contract is discharged or ended even though literal performance by the promisee is possible.

EXAMPLE In the classic case, Henry rented a room from O➛✱ Krell to view the processions to be held in connection with the coronation of Edward VII of England. The rental for two days, excluding nights, was £75. The processions did not take place, however, because of the illness of the king. When Henry refused to pay because the value of the contract was destroyed by the cancellation, Krell sued him for the amount of the rental. The court decided that Krell was not entitled to the rent due under the contract. At the time the contract was made, both parties expected that there would be a procession, and the rental was fixed accordingly. The illness of the king and cancellation of the processions were unexpected events that destroyed the value of the contract.

FTC See FEDERAL TRADE COMMISSION.

full faith and credit Article IV, Section 1, of the U.S. Constitution requires that "Full Faith and Credit shall be given in each State to the public Acts, Records, and judicial Proceedings of every other State." The aim of this clause is to end litigation. When a court in one state makes a final decision in a case, it should not be brought to trial again in another state. A marriage performed and valid in New York will be recognized as a valid marriage in Oregon. A final JUDGMENT rendered by a court having JURISDICTION (authority) in Kansas will be recognized as binding on the parties in New Hampshire.

Although this clause dictates a uniform policy of recognizing and enforcing judgments throughout the United

States, enforceability is not automatic. A lawsuit must be filed in the second state requesting it to give formal full faith and credit to the judgment from the first state. In contrast, a judgment from a federal court may be directly registered in a federal court in another jurisdiction and enforced without filing an additional suit.

Child CUSTODY judgments are not subject to full faith and credit, because these decrees are not final judgments. They may be modified at any time to protect the best interests of the child. Child support orders may be given full faith and credit only if the delinquent installments have been reduced to a money judgment or if the accrued payments cannot be modified in the original state. If an amount can be modified, no full faith and credit can be given because there is no sum certain (specified amount) to enforce. If a parent is sued for arrears in his support payments and has no valid defense (such as unemployment), then a judgment is entered for a sum certain that can be enforced in any state where the debtor or his property can later be found.

The full faith and credit clause does not apply to the judgments of foreign nations. They are sometimes said to be enforced only as a matter of COMITY, which is not constitutional mandate.

fundamental law   The basic law and principles that are embodied in constitutions (both federal and state), which prescribe and regulate the manner of the exercise of government. See CONSTITUTIONAL LAW.

fungible   Things or goods that are interchangeable or easily replaced with each other. Pounds of rice are fungible because one pound may be substituted for another, but horses are nonfungible because

they differ individually and are not interchangeable.

future-acquired property   See AFTER-ACQUIRED TITLE.

future earnings   A convenient way of designating earnings a person could have made in the future if he had not been injured. See DAMAGES.

future interest   An interest or right that does not entitle the holder to currently possess an asset but that may or will entitle him later. For example, if you give property "to my son Jim Jones for his lifetime, then to my granddaughter, Millie Jones, and her heirs," Millie has a future interest in the property. She is not entitled to possession of the property until Jim Jones dies. This type of future interest is known as a REMAINDER.

Another type of future interest is a REVERSION, which occurs when a person who owns land transfers it to someone else for a limited period of time while reserving the right of ownership and possession of the land after the time has expired. This right is known as a *reversionary interest* to future possession of the land. For example, suppose your neighbor, Steve Brown, owns some valuable lakefront property. He gives the property to his son Jeff for 10 years. Steve Brown has retained a future interest that entitles him to repossession of the property after the 10 years have lapsed. See ESTATE.

futures   Contracts promising to buy or sell standard commodities, such as rice or soybeans, at a future date and at a set price. These highly speculative transactions are "paper" deals and involve profit and loss on promises to deliver, not on possession of the actual commodities.

game Wild and undomesticated animals. Each state owns the game within its borders—even the game on private property—for the benefit of all its people. You can acquire ownership of game only by hunting and killing it under a license. As a general rule, you have the right to hunt game on public property, provided you do not infringe on the rights of others or violate any laws, and you can sue anyone who interferes with that right. You have no right to hunt on private land without the owner's permission.

A landowner's property rights are subject to the state's right to regulate and preserve game for public use.

A law prohibiting the hunting of game without a license is a proper exercise of the state's POLICE POWER. Game laws are enforced by game wardens, who usually have the power to arrest violators and to seize illegally hunted game. A hunter must show his license when requested or be held in violation of the law. Under many laws, you can be punished for killing or taking certain kinds of game during certain seasons.

When you legally capture game animals alive and care for them as domestic animals, you are allowed to kill them. You may be justified in killing game illegally in order to protect persons or property—for example, killing a bear that is attacking your companion. Sometimes it is an offense to carry game outside the county or state in which you kill it or to ship it for sale without proper packaging or information on the carton.

The federal government has established game refuges for the protection of game and migratory birds and has prohibited hunting in those areas. It has also made treaties with other countries—including Canada, Great Britain, and Mexico—to protect migratory birds and game mammals. See also ANIMALS; FISH.

gaming An agreement between two or more persons to play a game of chance; gambling. At stake in the game—blackjack, craps, poker, baccarat—is usually a money wager. All players contribute through bets, the money gathered going to the winner. State legislatures may, within their POLICE POWER, pass laws that either outlaw or legalize gambling.

Most gaming contracts and transactions are illegal and therefore cannot be enforced. But the law of the state where the contract is made determines its validity—for example, in many states betting on races is allowed. When a wager is legal, the winner may enlist the courts to recover the stake.

■ **Penalties** The courts help enforce laws against gaming, such as those providing for FORFEITURES of wagers or property used in gambling. A court may authorize the seizure of roulette wheels and crap tables when there is PROBABLE CAUSE to believe that the premises are being used for illegal gambling. See SEARCH AND SEIZURE. Some laws allow a loser to sue the winner to recover the amount he lost in an illegal gaming transaction.

Criminal liability Gaming is usually a criminal offense. Some states prohibit all types of gambling, including bingo, while others outlaw only certain forms. A change in the name of a game or how it is played will not alter its legal status as long as its principle remains the same. Generally, gaming in your own home is legal—thus, your weekly poker game may be perfectly within the law. But local laws do make it a criminal offense to place bets in taverns, hotels, restaurants, gaming houses, or other public places.

It is best to check your local laws before setting up even a temporary gaming house for charitable causes.

A LOTTERY is considered a form of gaming and is legal in some states. Selling tickets for a raffle is a lottery and is not legal in those states that do not permit lotteries.

The punishment for gaming and related offenses depends on the laws where the gambling occurs.

GAO See GENERAL ACCOUNTING OFFICE.

garnishee A person who holds money or property belonging to a debtor who is subject to a garnishment proceeding by a creditor. This topic is discussed more fully in ATTACHMENT AND GARNISHMENT.

EXAMPLE Suppose your neighbor Bill has no other income except his salary from AB Company and he owes a large debt to Smith. Smith gets a judgment on the debt from the court and brings a garnishment proceeding. This means he can collect his debt directly from the salary that AB Company owes Bill. AB Company is the garnishee.

garnishment See ATTACHMENT AND GARNISHMENT.

gas company This article discusses the use and distribution of fluid gas for light, cooking, and heat. Natural gas is regulated by the law of MINES AND MINERALS.

Supplying gas is not a municipal duty, but if a city assumes this function, it acts as a public authority or public service corporation. The charter of a gas company is a FRANCHISE, or special privilege, granted by the state. A private gas company may be organized as a PUBLIC UTILITY. Because the manufacture of gas and its distribution through pipes placed under streets affect the public, the state may regulate gas companies to protect the public or delegate the regulatory power to a public service commission or similar agency. The commission usually establishes rates and sets rules and regulations for the conduct of the business.

■ **Supply to consumers** A gas company must serve all persons within its area who desire service and comply with the rules. It may make reasonable regulations to insure the payment of bills, such as cutting off service to a nonpaying customer. If, however, there is a genuine dispute over the amount owed or if the company has not demanded payment from the customer, it may not discontinue service. It has no right to require the owner or occupant of a building to make good on the unpaid bills of a former owner or tenant before it will continue service.

A gas company can be sued for money DAMAGES if it wrongfully refuses to supply a consumer with gas. Some states have statutes that prescribe penalties for this type of violation.

If a customer tampers with a meter that the company has installed for registering the amount of gas used, the company may discontinue service until the customer pays for the unmetered gas he used.

■ **Rates** One purpose of regulation is to fix reasonable prices for gas sold to the public. Rate increases are allowed only after an impartial investigation that considers the needs of both the company and the public. When the gas rates are unreasonable, the public may ask the courts to decide whether the rate-making group acted beyond its authority. The courts can overturn a decision because it is beyond the authority of the agency or against the weight of the evidence and send the case back for a new decision. The courts cannot, however, say what prices are reasonable and put them into effect.

■ **Injuries** A gas company must use ordinary care and prudence in the conduct of its business and in the construction of its works, so that it does not endanger life and property. Gas company employees entering premises on business—to check on a reported gas leak, for instance—must use care to avoid injuring the property and the occupants. The gas company will be held liable (responsible) if it fails to exercise this care—if one of its employees lights a match after having found a gas leak and an explosion results, for example.

When a gas company uses a street in constructing, repairing, or operating its plant or equipment, it is responsible for any injuries received by a person on the street.

EXAMPLE Suppose the Urban Gas Company failed to
O━━* mount lighted barriers at night around a trench it
had dug to lay pipes, and Jean is injured when she drives
her car into it. The company is liable for injuries Jean

receives and for damage to her car. If, however, Jean drives her car into the open trench in daylight while speeding at 100 miles per hour, she may not recover money damages.

A gas company is liable when its negligence allows escaping or exploding gas to cause injuries. If breaks or defects are caused by faulty construction or maintenance, the company is responsible for resulting injuries even though it did not know about the problem. But when a defect or break in the pipe occurs through natural causes, such as an earthquake, or the act of a third person, the company must be given time to repair the break before it will be held liable. After it has had notice of gas escaping, service must be shut off until repairs have been made.

When there is unauthorized interference with its mains, pipes, and other equipment, the company is entitled to damages and an INJUNCTION (a court order). For example, if the construction of sewers by the county harms gas pipes, the company may obtain an injunction to stop construction and collect money damages for the harm already inflicted.

Gault, in re A landmark decision by the Supreme Court in the area of children's rights.

On February 25, 1964, 15-year-old Gerald Francis Gault of Arizona was put on probation for six months because he had been with another boy who stole a wallet from a woman's purse. On June 8, while still on probation, Gerald was picked up by the police after a neighbor complained that he had made an obscene phone call to her. He was taken into custody at home while both his parents were at work. When his mother returned and found he was not there, she sent his older brother to look for him. The brother learned that Gerald was being held at the local detention home. There a deputy named Flagg told Gerald's mother and brother that a hearing would be held at Juvenile Court the next day, June 9.

■ **No formal complaint** On June 9, Gerald, his mother, his older brother, and two probation officers—one of them Flagg—appeared before the judge. No formal complaint had been drawn up to state what crime Gerald was charged with committing. The woman who had complained was not there. No one swore to tell the truth. At the end of the hearing, the judge said he would "think about it." Without explanation, Gerald was taken back to the detention home for a couple of days and then released, still with no explanation. No record of the hearing had been taken, and later there was disagreement about what Gerald had said when the judge asked him about the obscene phone call.

Another hearing was held on Monday, June 15. Gerald's mother asked to have the woman who had complained come in and testify, but the judge said "she didn't have to be present at that hearing." The judge never talked to the woman or asked her any questions. Officer Flagg had spoken to her only once—over the telephone on June 9. At the end of this hearing, the judge sentenced Gerald to the State Industrial School "for the period of his minority [until he reached age 21], unless sooner discharged by due process of law." The judge said he believed the boy was a "delinquent child" who was "habitually involved in immoral matters." In addition to the charge that had subjected him to probation in February, Gerald had been reported to the police when he was 13. Another boy had accused him of stealing a baseball glove, but there was no evidence. Arizona law did not allow a juvenile case to be appealed.

■ **A child's rights** Gerald's parents brought a HABEAS CORPUS proceeding (a proceeding for release from unlawful imprisonment) that finally went to the U.S. Supreme Court. The Court noted at once that Arizona punished adults in similar circumstances with a fine of only $5 to $50 or imprisonment for not more than two months. It ruled that Gerald's conviction was unconstitutional and Gerald was released. The Court said that in any case in which a child may lose his liberty—whether he is sent to a jail, a home, a training school, or any other state facility—the child has the following rights:

(1) Written notice must be given to him and to his parents describing the kind of proceedings that have been started and the acts that he is accused of committing.

(2) Before a hearing begins, the child must be told that he is entitled to have an attorney. If his family cannot afford to hire one, the child can ask the court to provide one.

(3) A written record should be made of the proceedings, which can be used in an appeal or any other proceeding.

(4) The child must be told that he has a constitutional privilege not to confess. Some children are easily pressured into saying what they think the police officers want to hear. This is not reliable evidence.

(5) The child must be given the right to confront a person who charges him or complains about his conduct. That person must appear at the hearing and state his charges in the presence of the child.

(6) The child, generally through his attorney, must be given a chance to cross-examine anyone who testifies against him. This questioning makes it more likely that the truth will come out.

By establishing the legal rights of children accused of crimes, this Supreme Court decision initiated guidelines in an area where there were few. It made the dispensation of justice to juveniles accused of crimes clearer and fairer. See INFANT; JUVENILE COURT.

General Accounting Office
A federal agency that assists Congress in financial matters, audits and investigates federal programs, and settles claims by and against the United States involving individuals, businesses, and other governments.

General Assembly
1 The entire legislature, in many states. For example, the Senate and House of Representatives make up Missouri's General Assembly. **2** In other states, only the House of Representatives. **3** The large policymaking body of the United Nations. Each member nation can send from one to five delegates to the General Assembly, but each nation has only one vote.

general creditor One to whom money is owed but whose debt is not secured—that is, no property has been pledged to back up the debt in case payment is not made; a creditor-at-large. See CREDITOR; SECURED TRANSACTION.

general execution A court order directing a sheriff or other official to seize personal property (generally, any property that is not real estate) belonging to a defendant in order to pay off a judgment. See EXECUTION.

general jurisdiction The power of a COURT to hear all cases that come up in the geographical area over which it has authority.

general lien An agreement between parties that one of them can hold property belonging to the other until he has been paid money the other owes him. See LIEN.

General National Mortgage Association
A federal organization, nicknamed *Ginnie Mae,* that operates special programs in which housing MORTGAGES are bought and sold to encourage private lending in certain types of housing. It does not lend money to homebuyers.

General Services Administration
The federal agency that manages all U.S. government property. The GSA supervises construction and the operation of federal buildings, the procurement and distribution of supplies, disposal of surplus government property, administration of traffic and communications facilities, the stockpiling of strategic and critical materials, and the management of automatic data processing resources.

gerrymander Manipulate the boundaries of election districts in order to give one party a great advantage. For example, it may be possible to set up 10 election districts so that all of the strength of the opposition party is concentrated in 3 districts. Although that party may win those 3 districts by a wide margin, it will lose the other 7 districts by a slim difference. This political trick was first made famous by a 19th-century Massachusetts governor named Elbridge Gerry, who drew up an election district that defied natural boundaries. A drawing of the new district that appeared in the local papers so resembled a salamander that political wags immediately dubbed it a gerrymander.

Gideon v. Wainwright
An important case decided by the Supreme Court in 1963, guaranteeing the right of criminal defendants who are too poor to hire a lawyer to have court-appointed attorneys in state courts. This right had already been guaranteed in federal courts.

Clarence Earl Gideon was charged in Florida with breaking and entering a poolroom with the intent to commit a misdemeanor. Gideon, who appeared in court without funds or a lawyer, was denied his request to have an attorney appointed for him. He conducted his defense as well as a layman could and was convicted and sentenced to prison for five years. The Supreme Court reversed the conviction and sent the case back to the Florida courts with instructions to provide an attorney for Gideon. In his new trial Gideon was acquitted.

gift A voluntary transfer of property at no cost to the one receiving it. The person who gives a gift is called a *donor,* and the person who receives it is called a *donee.*

The law of gifts, which varies very little from state to state, dictates the circumstances under which a donee is

IF YOU ARE THINKING OF MAKING A GIFT

■ There are two basic kinds of gifts: gifts *inter vivos* (between living persons) and gifts *causa mortis* (prompted by impending death).

■ Whether or not an *inter vivos* gift has been made depends on intent, delivery, and acceptance. Because intent must exist, a gift mistakenly given to the wrong person is invalid. The giver must also be able to form an intent—a senile person or a child cannot legally give away the family home, for example.

■ Delivery may be actual, implied, or symbolic, but some affirmative act must have occurred. A man who changes title to his house from his name alone to his and his wife's names together is making an implied delivery of a gift of half the value of the house. Handing over a set of car keys can be a symbolic delivery of the car as a gift. Until the donor actually gives

up the gift, it does not belong to the recipient.

■ Canceling a debt is a gift and delivery can be accomplished by destroying the promissory note or by returning it to the debtor.

■ Gifts of land can be made only by putting the transfer down on paper. Ordinarily a court will assume that a gift has been accepted unless something shows it was not.

■ Regret and disappointment after the gift has been made are not enough reason for a court to restore the donor's property to him.

■ A donor can limit his gift *inter vivos* in some ways, such as by time. He might, for example, give a loyal employee a life interest in a farm, which would revert to the donor upon the employee's death.

■ However, if the donor reserves the right to revoke his gift or if the gift is

not to be made until some future time, there is no gift at all. For example, if a man says he is giving his house and furniture to his fiancée, but the gift is to take effect only after their marriage, the gift is void.

■ A gift *causa mortis* is made because the donor thinks he is about to die. If he lives, the gift must be returned.

■ A gift *causa mortis* can be only personal property, not real estate.

■ The law will permit the recipient to keep the gift only if the donor clearly meant for the gift to take effect at the time it was made—for example, if a hospitalized woman puts her rings in her son's hands moments before she dies. If the gift was made in writing, to take effect only after the donor died, then the writing must meet the legal requirements for a will.

■ Most courts will not recognize a gift made in contemplation of suicide.

---

entitled to keep a gift. The law that applies is the one in force on the date and in the place where the gift was made. Gifts are not enforceable in the way CONTRACTS are because there is no *consideration*—nothing of value is promised or given in return for them. Special rules determine whether a legal gift has been made. Different rules are applied to gifts made during the life of a donor and gifts made when he expects to die.

■ **Gifts inter vivos**   *Inter vivos* is a Latin phrase meaning "during one's life." A gift *inter vivos* is a voluntary transfer of property at no cost during the donor's life. It is not prompted by thoughts of impending death or a desire to wrap up one's estate just before death. It is a gift from one living person to another, and it is intended to be completed at the time it is made.

A gift *inter vivos* is different from a sale, a loan, or barter because in those transactions something is exchanged for the benefit of the person making the transfer. Whether the value given in exchange is money, a percentage interest, an item of property, or a promise to repay, that element of exchange makes the transfer different from a gift. Even a bonus, such as an extra $100 from the boss at Christmas, is not a gift. It is extra compensation—a sum paid for services already performed.

■ **How gifts inter vivos are made**   During his lifetime a person can give away just about anything—jewelry, color television sets, or an interest in real estate. But he can give only what he himself owns. A woman who has the right when her mother dies to take money that has been held in trust can write out a document giving that same right to someone else. One partner can give to another partner all his interest in their business. This will transfer legal rights in addition to physical possessions.

Whether or not an *inter vivos* gift has been made depends on intent, delivery, and acceptance.

Intent   An intent to make a gift must actually exist. Certainly a used car salesman who lets a customer try out a car does not intend to make a gift. A gift to the wrong person is not valid. If a man mistakenly gives shares of stock to an imposter whom he thinks is his nephew, the gift is invalid because he had no intention of benefiting anyone but his nephew.

The donor must legally be able to make a gift—this is essential to prove that a gift has been made. A person who is legally INCOMPETENT is considered unable to form an intent. For example, a person who has become senile cannot make a gift of his family's house; nor can a child.

The intent to give must exist at the time the donee claims the gift was made. Suppose a rich man promises to give a beach house to a young artist "someday." A court will not enforce the promise because no gift was intended to take effect at the time the promise was made. The expectation that something will someday be given does not create a legal gift.

Delivery   A delivery may be actual, implied, or symbolic, but some affirmative act must occur. A man who gives his granddaughter a horse makes an actual delivery when the animal is brought to her farm. A man who changes TITLE to his house from his name alone to his and his wife's names together is assumed to have made a gift of half the value of the house. Recording the new DEED is an implied, or constructive, delivery of the gift to his wife. A father presenting his daughter with a set of car keys can be a symbolic delivery of the car as a gift.

Delivery has not occurred unless the donor surrenders control of the gift. Until the giver actually gives up the gift, it does not legally belong to the recipient. For example, a woman who opens a bank account in both her and her brother's names and who makes deposits and withdrawals whenever she likes has not given up complete control of the money in the account. The brother cannot claim that all the money in the account is a gift from his sister.

Delivery requirements   Most states are fairly practical about the requirements of a delivery. When the donor and the donee live in the same house, it is usually not necessary to remove the gift to prove that a delivery was made. As a rule, if the donee has possession of the property at the time that the donor also gives him ownership, the property need not be passed back and forth to make a legal delivery. Ordinarily, any proof that the donor gave up all claim and recognized the donee's right to control shows that a gift was made. For example, a share of stock in a corporation may usually be given to someone else by having ownership transferred on the corporation's books or by issuing a new stock certificate in his name. Canceling a debt is considered a gift of the money owed, and delivery can be accomplished by destroying the promissory note or by returning it to the debtor. Generally, a life INSURANCE policy can be given by delivering the document to someone. But you should make a written statement that all interest in the policy is transferred to the donee and notify the insurance company. Some states may require these formalities because insurance is strictly controlled by state law. Gifts of land can only be made by putting the transfer down on paper.

When transfer to the donee is impossible—say he is on vacation—delivery can be made to someone else who agrees to accept the property on his behalf. But if the person accepting delivery works for the donor, the court will assume that delivery has not really been made because the donor still has control of the property. The person accepting delivery must be holding the property for the recipient and not for the donor. In cases when the donee is not legally capable of accepting delivery—for example, a child—delivery can be made to someone, such as a parent or guardian, who will hold the gift for him.

Acceptance   This final essential element of a legally valid gift means that the person receiving the gift unconditionally agrees to take it. Ordinarily, a court will assume that a gift has been accepted unless something shows that it was not. The recipient does not have to agree to accept when delivery is made.

The donor can revoke the gift at any time before it is accepted.

EXAMPLE A man wants to buy a bigger and newer boat. He
O⊷※ tells his son that he may have the boat the father presently owns. The son says he would love to have it but since he is struggling to support a young family, he is not sure he can afford the maintenance, dock fees, and insurance. When the father begins shopping for a new boat, he finds that inflation has pushed prices much higher than he expected. He signs an agreement to buy a new boat, trading in the old one as part of his down payment. Now who owns the old boat? The answer is that the father still owns it because his son did not accept it without condition. Until the son accepted, the father had the right to sell the boat to someone else.

Because gifts are often made in an informal manner with no disinterested witnesses who can later describe the transaction, courts require proof of intent, delivery, and acceptance. Even then, they will set aside an otherwise valid gift if it appears that the donor was actually cheated by lies of the donee, forced against his will to make the gift, or strongly influenced in an unfair way.

The law favors enforcing gifts because every person has the right to dispose of his property as he likes. This includes the right to be silly, unreasonable, or unfair in making gifts. Regret and disappointment after the gift has been made are not enough reason for a court to restore the donor's property to him.

Limitations   A donor can limit his gift *inter vivos* in some ways, such as by time. He might, for example, give an especially loyal employee a life interest in a farm. This means the donee can have the farm as long as he lives and then the farm returns to the donor.

But a donor cannot use certain limits because they make the gift invalid. If the donor reserves the right to revoke his gift, for example, there is no gift at all. If he says that he gives the jewelry in his safe-deposit box to his fiancée, but the gift is to take effect only after their marriage, the gift is void. A gift must go into effect at the time it is made.

If the property offered as a gift has a LIEN (a legal claim) or MORTGAGE on it, the donee receives the debt along with the property.

EXAMPLE A mother gives the family farm to her son when
O⊷※ she retires. The son becomes owner of the land and responsible for any money owed on a mortgage.

If a brother gives his motorcycle to his sister before it is fully paid for, she owns the motorcycle but must continue making payments on it as long as they are due.

■ **Gifts causa mortis**   *Causa mortis* is a Latin term meaning "on contemplation of death." A gift *causa mortis* is made because the donor thinks he is about to die. It takes effect immediately but if the donor does not die, the gift must be returned. A bequest in a will is effective only after the death of the donor. Unlike gifts *inter vivos*, gifts *causa mortis* can only be personal property, not real estate.

The donor of a gift *causa mortis* does not have to die immediately, but he must die without recovering from the condition that existed when the gift was made. If the donor changes his mind and revokes the gift, or if he recovers or survives, the gift is invalid. A donor can require that debts or funeral expenses be paid out of the value of the gift.

Gifts *causa mortis* are usually made informally. Often the reason for the gift is that a dying person wants to be certain that his dearest possessions go to someone he loves. In a hospital room a mother hands her wedding and engagement rings to her son and says, "Take these. I want you to have them."

A donor approaching death may make gifts by writing down his intention. This is likely to be done when the donee is in another state or when delivery is impractical. People making a gift *causa mortis* almost never have the law of gifts in mind. But a court, in looking back to judge the validity of the gift, will permit the donee to keep the gift only if the donor clearly meant for it to take effect at the time it was made. If the gift is in writing and is meant to take effect only after the donor dies, then the writing must be a will. However, the law in each state is *very strict* about the features that make a will valid—for example, witnesses must sign a will. If the donor writes down that he is making a gift but what the donor has written qualifies neither as a gift nor a witnessed will, then the donee cannot keep the gift.

Intent, delivery, and acceptance As with a gift *inter vivos*, a gift *causa mortis* is not valid unless there has been intent, delivery, and acceptance. The intent here is to make an immediate gift because of a belief that death is imminent. The belief must be a specific apprehension of death from some existing disease or known danger, such as surgery to be performed the next morning. It is not necessary to prove that the donor really expected to die but only that he was making plans in case he did. A general depression or melancholy is not the same as apprehension of a specific danger. Most courts will not recognize a gift made in contemplation of suicide.

The requirement of delivery is sometimes relaxed. A donor is unlikely to be able to make an actual delivery as he gets closer to death. At least some effort at delivery must be apparent, however. A symbolic delivery, like handing over a key to a jewel box, is enough to indicate that the gift was made. It is the overt act that helps a court sort out all the claims made after someone's death.

EXAMPLE A woman who had brought food to her elderly neighbor insisted that he had given her all his possessions as a gift just before he died. He had no close relatives. She said that he told her he could not last more than a couple of days, so she should take the bankbooks on his table and a key from the pocket of his pants hanging in the bedroom. The woman said that she did not touch any of these things because she was afraid of the contagious disease her neighbor had.

The court held that she could not have the property because there was no delivery of the gift. The woman's story might very well be true, but the court could not accept it as long as she did not take any part of the gift into her possession.

A court will assume that there has been acceptance of a gift *causa mortis* of substantial value unless there is evidence to disprove it. Another person may accept a gift for the donee. For example, shares of stock can be given by mailing them to the donee's attorney.

gifts to minors Every state has enacted a law based, with only small variations, on the Uniform Gifts to Minors Act. (See UNIFORM ACT.) A state's Gifts to Minors Act permits a person who wants to give property to a child to select the custodian who will have authority over the property. This spares the donor the expense and inconvenience of a court-supervised guardianship of the property. The custodian must manage it wisely—depositing money in an interest-bearing account at a federally insured bank, for example, rather than investing it in speculative stock. He must keep accurate records of all transactions and give the property to the child when he becomes an adult. If necessary, he may pay out money for the child's support. But he may not use any of the property for himself or for anyone except the child, nor can he mix the property with his own, such as by depositing it in his own bank account.

If a professional custodian, such as a trust company or a lawyer is chosen, he is usually paid a fee from the child's property and is held to a higher standard of care in managing the property. See GUARDIAN AND WARD.

When a custodian resigns, dies, or is removed from his position by a court order, a successor can be appointed, either by the departing custodian or by the court, as the circumstances dictate. A petition to appoint a new custodian can be filed in court by the person who originally made the gift, by an adult member of the child's family, a guardian, or usually by the child himself if he is over 14.

The age when a child becomes an adult is not the same in all states. Therefore, if you want to give property to someone you think is a child, you should check the Gift to Minors Act in the state where the child lives.

gift tax See ESTATE AND GIFT TAX.

Ginnie Mae See GENERAL NATIONAL MORTGAGE ASSOCIATION.

going public Changing the ownership of a CORPORATION from a small, closed group of people (a closely held corporation) to the general public (a publicly held corporation) by selling shares to anyone who wants to buy them.

good behavior Orderly and lawful conduct that is proper for a peaceable and law-abiding citizen. Exactly what is required for good behavior depends on how the phrase is used. Good behavior for an elected official, for example, is different from that expected of a prisoner who is trying to earn privileges. Sometimes a criminal's SENTENCE is suspended for good behavior. That is, he does not have to go to jail during his sentence as long as he does not break any more laws. Federal judges, says the U.S. Constitution, "shall hold their Offices during good Behaviour." This means that they cannot be fired arbitrarily and are independent of politics. They can be impeached for misconduct, but otherwise they serve for life.

good cause Legally sufficient grounds; not an arbitrary reason. An employee who is discharged for good cause has been fired for reasons that are directly related to his work. A person in a lawsuit who wants more time to file an answer to a complaint than allowed under the rules of civil procedure must show good cause. For example, if the person was in the hospital during the time he was to appear in court to answer the complaint, this may be good cause, justifying an extension of time.

good faith Honesty in fact. For a merchant, the law requires good faith according to the reasonable commercial standards of fair dealing in the trade.

good will The reputation and customers of an established business. The value of good will can usually be calculated as the amount a buyer will pay for a business above the worth of its physical property and the money that is owed to it.

Good will may exist even though the business is not making a profit. It is considered a property interest in itself, but it exists only in connection with other property, such as the business's name or location. Some courts will not recognize good will that rests only in the personal qualities of the owner. For example, a lawyer cannot sell good will in addition to his office, furniture, and books, because his reputation is based only on his own professional skills.

Good will can be transferred to another person or business by a sale or a bequest in a will. Generally, a sale of property to which good will is attached also transfers the good will to the buyer. Of course, the seller and buyer may change this or spell out details in their contract of sale.

A former owner is not entitled to interfere with the new owner's enjoyment of good will after a sale—even if the contract does not specify that such interference is prohibited. He is barred from soliciting his old customers or leading them to think he is still carrying on the same business, because such behavior weakens the value of the good will that was purchased. If the buyer does not want the seller to start a new business competing with him in the same vicinity, he should bargain for that in their agreement. An agreement not to compete is different from good will.

grace period   The brief period of time after payment of an INSURANCE premium is due in which the company will not cancel coverage.

graduated tax   A schedule of TAXATION that places a heavier burden on those who have more money and property. Federal INCOME TAX is a graduated tax. A person with an income of $10,000 might pay a 10 percent tax, while another person with an income of $20,000 might pay taxes at the rate of 25 percent.

grandfather clause   A part of a law stating that the law does not apply in circumstances where certain previous conditions exist. For example, a new law that requires dietitians to be licensed may have a grandfather clause exempting practicing dietitians from taking a LICENSE test. It is presumed they are qualified by experience.

Grandfather clauses were originally named for amendments to some state constitutions that were intended to, and did, prevent blacks from registering to vote. These amendments—later declared unconstitutional—made it difficult to qualify as a voter, requiring, for example, ownership of a large amount of land. Exceptions to such qualifications were always made for veterans of the Civil War, men who were qualified to vote before 1866, and their descendants. Thus, if your grandfather could vote, you could vote. See CIVIL RIGHTS; EQUAL PROTECTION OF LAWS.

grand jury   A group of people summoned by a court to hear complaints of crimes, to consider preliminary evidence, and to decide whether formal accusations should be made against individuals. It is called a grand ("large") jury because traditionally more people serve on it than on a trial jury, known as a petit ("little") jury.

Under the common law, a grand jury had from 12 to 23 members, and this is still the rule in some states. Federal grand juries have from 16 to 23 members, and at least 12 must agree in order to return an INDICTMENT, which is a formal accusation.

Jurors are selected from lists of local residents. Those who are qualified are called by the court and sworn in. They hear evidence that the prosecutor, such as the district attorney, has gathered and decide whether crimes have been committed. As long as the members of a grand jury act in good faith and as one group, they may largely decide for themselves how they will proceed. They have the right to call witnesses and can usually force them to appear or produce documents by having them served with a SUBPOENA. A witness's refusal to answer questions can be punished as a CONTEMPT. The grand jury can listen to HEARSAY and other evidence that would not be admissible in court.

Before an indictment is prepared, a grand jury may draw up a set of charges called a *presentment*. In some states, the presentment is an informal statement given by the grand jury to the prosecutor, telling the prosecutor to draw up an indictment. It is not a formal charge, or accusation, and a prosecution cannot be started on it alone.

If enough members of a grand jury agree that a crime has occurred, they ask the prosecutor to draw up formal papers against the accused. This is the indictment. It must be a plain and concise statement of all the facts of the crime charged, and it should be signed by the jury foreman and the prosecutor.

■ **Right to grand jury proceedings**   An individual's right to grand jury proceedings in federal cases outside of military law is guaranteed in the Fifth Amendment to the Constitution. Because the charge of a crime is a serious situation for the accused, the Founding Fathers thought it was not enough to say that he can be acquitted at his trial—because by that time publicity would have invaded his life, and his family and career would have suffered. It seemed better that no one be brought into court on a serious criminal charge unless a group of local people could first be convinced that the prosecutor had a case.

As a rule, courts can call special grand juries to investigate unusually important or complicated cases. One was convened by a circuit judge in Illinois after a federal grand jury voted no indictments for the killing of two Black Panthers during a police raid in Chicago in 1969. This incident aroused national controversy as the police and local officials were charged with a cover-up.

■ **Rights of those charged**   A person against whom charges are being considered has no constitutional right to present his side of the case to the grand jury, either by himself or through his attorney. In fact, the target of a grand jury probe may not even know the investigation is going on. If the grand jury orders him to appear, he can refuse to answer questions that might incriminate him. But he is not constitutionally entitled to have a lawyer along to warn him when not to answer. Some states, however, do allow a witness to leave the room and consult with his attorney outside the door if he fears SELF-INCRIMINATION in answering a question.

■ **Private proceedings**   Proceedings of a grand jury are not usually made public. The reasons are (1) to prevent the accused from escaping before arrest or tampering with witnesses, (2) to protect people who are not indicted but about whom disreputable things have been revealed to the grand jury, (3) to encourage witnesses to speak freely without fear of retaliation, and (4) to enable the grand jurors themselves to deliberate openly without fear that their comments or votes will become public.

Under some laws, disclosure of grand jury secrets can be punished as a CONTEMPT of court. Interfering with the grand jury, bribing jurors, or threatening witnesses may be a contempt or a crime, depending on your state laws.

grand larceny   See LARCENY.

grant   1 Bestow, give, or confer. "Grant" is a broad term that includes more specific words of transfer—ASSIGN, BARGAIN, or DEVISE, for example.   2 As a noun, a GIFT of property or legal rights to property, such as a life estate.
See also LAND GRANT.

gratuitous licensee   A social guest. A LICENSEE is someone who is permitted to visit, and gratuitous suggests that he is not coming for business reasons.

gravamen   The material, or significant, part of a criminal charge or civil complaint; the basis for or gist of the complaint; the essence of a grievance.

grievance procedure   An orderly, regular way of handling problems, particularly those that arise between workers and employers; a system by which workers' complaints are transmitted to management, often through their union, for consideration. See LABOR RELATIONS.

gross   1 Great or large, such as in the term "gross NEGLIGENCE."   2 Shameful or flagrant, as in "gross immorality" or a "gross injustice."   3 Complete or total, such as in "gross weight" or "gross earnings."
In gross means existing in its own right and not as part of something else, before any deduction is taken away. For example, a *sum in gross* is one amount rather than several separate payments. A debtor who owes $5,000, $7,000, and $10,000 may be able to make an arrangement to settle for a sum in gross of $20,000, even though this sum is $2,000 less than what he actually owes.

gross estate   See ESTATE AND GIFT TAX.

gross income   See INCOME TAX.

ground   Basis; foundation; legal point relied on. Grounds must be sufficient to support a lawsuit. For example, a couple may want to divorce because they have a terrible sex life or frequently battle about money. A court may not grant a DIVORCE, however, unless one of them pleads a ground that is acceptable under the law of their state—adultery or cruelty, for example.

ground rent   A long-term agreement by which rent is paid to a landowner and his descendants or to someone to whom he transfers his interest in the land. A LEASE with a ground rent agreement may last for 99 years. Since most of these agreements are automatically renewable, almost every ground rent can last forever.

Pennsylvania and Maryland are the only states in which the ground rent system has been used to any extent for residential property. These agreements became popular as a way of encouraging renters to improve the property because they could own the buildings while paying rent on the land. They were also favored by investors who bought and sold shares in ground rent agreements. In Pennsylvania a ground rent ends if no payment or demand for payment has been made in 21 years, and in Maryland after 20 years of nonpayment. Maryland also outlaws ground rent agreements that do not permit the renter to buy his way out of the agreement.

Today, ground leases are used extensively for commercial leases for land on which the tenant erects a building for business purposes. The landlord continues to hold the land, but the tenant owns all of his buildings and pays rent only for the ground. This is really a financing arrangement for the development of land. It offers significant tax advantages for both parties to the lease.

GSA   See GENERAL SERVICES ADMINISTRATION.

guaranty   A promise by one person to answer for the debt of another if that person fails to meet his obligations. The one who makes this promise is the *guarantor,* and he gives the promise to the *guarantee,* or creditor. The person whose debt, conduct, or contract is guaranteed is called the *principal* or *principal debtor.* The guaranty is a contract that exists only in addition to the original transaction or agreement. It does not exist apart from it.

The words "warranty" and "guaranty" both come from the French word *garantis.* Originally, they had the same interpretation in law, and today some people still use them interchangeably. In fact, warranty and guaranty now have different meanings: a guaranty is made by a person who is not a party to the underlying contract, whereas a WARRANTY is given by the same person who makes the contract.

EXAMPLE   Aaron decides to pursue a full-time career in rock music. He goes to his local bank and applies for a loan of $5,000 to buy musical instruments, electronic amplifiers, tape recorders, and other equipment. The loan officer at the bank knows Aaron, feels that he is talented, and is willing to give him a break, but he needs a guaranty on the loan. Aaron's mother agrees to repay the loan if her son defaults. This is a contract of guaranty.

The loan agreement is between Aaron and the bank, and the guaranty agreement is between Aaron's mother and the bank. If Aaron does not repay the loan, the bank has the right to insist that his mother pay the balance. The bank must formally notify her that Aaron has defaulted and demand a specific sum. Depending on the guaranty agreement, she may have to pay the balance due, interest, and legal or collecting costs. If the bank ever changes its agreement with Aaron, however—by giving him more time to pay, for example—his mother is relieved of her obligation because she agreed to guarantee only the original agreement.

By contrast, the typical warranty is an agreement between a seller and a buyer. It is an extra promise about the quality or quantity of the subject of the contract. The seller says, for example, "I warrant that the frozen chickens I am selling you are all tender and young and weigh between two and four pounds each."

guardian and ward   A guardian is a person who has the responsibility for someone legally unable to care for himself and manage his affairs; a ward is a person who is cared for by a guardian. Guardianship is the relationship between guardian and ward and the authority and responsibilities of a guardian under the law. The role of guardians and the kinds of legal proceedings that involve them are the subject of this article. For more information about people who do not have the legal power to handle their own affairs, see INFANT (minors); INSANE PERSONS.

■ **Types of guardians**   The term "guardian" is most often applied to someone caring for a *minor,* anyone under the legal age of adulthood. The word is also used for a person charged with the care of idiots, lunatics, habitual drunkards, and spendthrifts. However, the term "committee" is often used for this kind of guardianship, even if the responsibility is given to only one person. Some states use the word "conservator" for a person designated to manage the property of a person who is frail and confused by age, disease, or disability.

A *general guardian* is someone charged with the care of both the child and his property. A *special guardian* has specific limited authority. One might be appointed, for example, to manage a lawsuit for a child, in which case he is a *guardian ad litem.* A *guardian of the person* has custody of the child and responsibility for his daily care. A *guardian of the estate* or *guardian of the property* manages all property belonging to the child.

The *natural guardian* of the child is his parent, who needs no appointment by a court. Some states still call the father the natural guardian, but if the father is dead, the mother holds that title. Each parent has the same rights, duties, and powers when the child is legitimate. If parents are divorced, the one granted custody of the child is his natural guardian. A stepparent is a natural guardian only if

he adopts the child. Should both parents die, grandparents may be the natural guardians. See PARENT AND CHILD.

A *guardian in socage* is an ancient relationship still recognized in the law of a few states. Under the common law, he was the guardian who cared for a child under 14 and certain land the child inherited. It was supposed to be the child's nearest relative who had no chance of inheriting the property if the child died.

A *guardian ad litem* is someone appointed by the court to handle a lawsuit for or against a person who is considered unable to manage it. He has no right to the property or to take custody of the person he represents. His authority ends when the lawsuit is settled.

■ **Persons for whom a guardian may be appointed** A guardian cannot be appointed unless there is a person whose needs must be supervised by a court. A guardian can be named for an unborn child because the common law recognizes life from the time the child is able to stir in the mother's womb. The legal rights of that child do not become absolute until he is born alive, but a guardian can manage property for him before his birth.

A court has no power to pick a guardian for a person who is of legal age and able to manage his own affairs, nor can such a person make himself a ward. Once married, an individual is considered an adult even if he or she is below the age of majority. A guardian cannot be appointed for a married 17-year-old girl, for example. This does not change if the girl is divorced or widowed before reaching full legal age. She is still an adult before the law.

A guardian can be appointed for an adult who lacks the mental capacity to take charge of his own affairs, who becomes unfit because of old age, who is imprisoned, or who squanders his money because of a drinking or gambling problem. Guardians can also serve in medical emergencies. When parents refuse to permit necessary

---

YOUR RESPONSIBILITIES IF YOU ARE APPOINTED A GUARDIAN

■ A *guardian* is a person who is responsible for someone legally unable to care for himself and manage his affairs. A *ward* is a person cared for by a guardian.

■ A guardian can be appointed for an adult who lacks the mental capacity to take care of his own affairs or becomes unfit because of senility, imprisonment, alcoholism, or gambling. Guardians can also serve in medical emergencies. When parents refuse to permit necessary medical treatment, a court may name a temporary guardian who has the authority to give consent.

■ A parent may name a guardian in his will. Most states allow a child to choose his own guardian if the child is over 14 years of age.

■ A guardian may be required to take an oath of office and post a bond.

■ If you are a child's guardian, your authority generally continues until the child legally becomes an adult, usually at age 18 or 21.

■ If the child marries while still a minor, the guardianship ends.

■ You have a right to move to a different state with your ward, but you usually need to notify the court concerning your move.

■ Most courts prefer to appoint a guardian who will raise the child in the parents' religion.

■ You are expected to use your own money before touching the child's resources. You will generally be permitted to use income and interest from the ward's property to pay for his or her needs, but courts will be reluctant to let you spend the principal or use up the assets.

■ A dishonest guardian can be removed by court order and another one appointed.

■ After the child becomes an adult, he can sue you if you have wasted his assets, converted them to your own use, or embezzled his funds.

■ At the end of the guardianship, you must account to the court for all transactions involving your ward's property.

■ A guardian who participates in a lawsuit for his ward sues or is sued only as the child's representative. For example, if the guardian sues a doctor on behalf of his ward for malpractice and recovers money damages, the money does not belong to the guardian. Similarly, if someone wins damages against the ward, the money must come from the ward's property.

treatment, such as a blood transfusion or vaccination for a child, a court can name a temporary guardian who has the authority to give consent. An adult has the right to refuse medical treatment, even when his life is in immediate danger, but if there is evidence that he is not thinking clearly or is not making his decision voluntarily, a guardian can be assigned to make the decision for him.

■ **Who picks the guardian** Guardianship appointments can be made by COURTS of general jurisdiction (authority) in most states. In addition, courts that hear cases involving juveniles or wills and the property of people who have died usually have the power to appoint guardians. Generally, a court names a guardian who lives where the minor lives. A guardian may also be named by a parent in his will; he is called a *testamentary guardian.*

Some states allow a child to choose his own guardian, sometimes called a *guardian by election,* if he is over a certain age, usually 14. Ordinarily, a court will approve this choice if the proposed guardian is suitable, even if the court thinks that someone else would be better. The court must be sure that the minor is able to understand the effect of his choice and that it is not detrimental to the child's interests or against the law.

Any person listed in the state's guardianship law—such as a brother, grandparent, or child welfare agency—has the right to ask a court to choose a guardian for a child, and laws specifically permit an application to be filed by such a person. The court will decide whether the person asking for a guardian really has the child's interests at heart.

■ **Who the guardian should be** The choice of a guardian is guided by the child's needs. Courts prefer to leave a child with a competent person who has been caring for him, especially if the child has affection for him, rather than disrupt a stable home. The court will look at the financial condition, age, health, education, judgment, morals, and character of a person being considered for guardianship. Although age alone does not decide the issue, it may bear on the individual's ability to fulfill his duties for the full period of guardianship. And although wealth does not make one person a better guardian than another, a guardian must be reasonably secure financially. As a rule, courts prefer someone with the same religious background as the child. A person being considered as a guardian must not have interests that are antagonistic to the child's, but a close family member who stands to inherit the child's property will not be automatically disqualified.

A divorced parent can be a guardian of a child's property even if the other parent has custody. For example, if the mother has custody but no experience with business, the father may be appointed to manage an inheritance or large DAMAGES award for the child. The court will almost always favor a parent over anyone else, unless there is reason to believe the parent is not fit.

A parent can be disqualified as a guardian for, in the phrases of state laws, "notoriously bad conduct," for "willfully and knowingly abandoning the child," or for "failing to maintain the child" when he is financially able to do so. A parent may forfeit his right to be a guardian if he abandons, neglects, or abuses his child. If a parent gives up custody of his child (such as when a father gives custody of his three children to his sister because he cannot both care

for them and hold down two jobs), that is not considered abandonment, but if he fails to contribute the support he is required to give, that *is* abandonment.

■ **How the guardian is appointed** Once a guardian has been selected, he may be required to take an oath of office and to post a bond—a sum of money paid into court from which a ward can be repaid if the guardian fails to perform his duties. Some laws allow a judge to waive a bond if the child's property is of little value or if the guardian managing the property is a financial corporation, such as a bank.

The formal appointment of a guardian occurs only when the court issues a certificate called *letters of guardianship.* A guardian named in the will is only nominated. He still needs letters of guardianship to give him authority to act.

■ **How long a guardian serves** The authority of a guardian generally continues for as long as the ward is below the legal age of adulthood. If the child marries while still a minor, the guardianship ends. (In some states, guardianship of the property continues after the ward's marriage until he or she reaches the legal age of adulthood—except when a female ward marries an adult.) See PARENT AND CHILD; MARRIAGE.

A guardian may be stripped of his authority if a court becomes convinced that he has neglected his duties or mismanaged property.

■ **Guardianship of the ward's person and estate** It is more efficient for just one guardian to care for a child and manage his property. But sometimes the responsibilities of guardianship are divided between two people. One person will have custody of the child himself and another will have custody of his property. For example, one mother continued to have custody of her children after their father's death, but the court refused to appoint her guardian of the children's estates because she was a spendthrift.

Let us suppose you have been appointed guardian of the person and property of a 15-year-old girl named Alice Carrol. What would be your duties?

Custody and care of the ward As guardian of Alice's person you have the right to prevent certain people from seeing her, but a court will not allow unreasonable restrictions. You also have the right to move to a different state with Alice, but you may need to assure the court regarding her care. You must provide for her support, education, and religious training, probably in the religion of her parents. Courts generally will permit you to use income and interest from her assets to pay for her needs, but they will be reluctant to let you spend the principal. (A parent is expected to use his own money before touching the child's resources.) Alice has a right to receive all of her property when she reaches the age of adulthood.

Custody and care of the ward's estate As guardian of Alice's property, you are a FIDUCIARY (trustee). You are therefore legally obligated to protect her interests as if they were your own. You do not have the right to invest her property in risky ventures; to agree not to sue someone who owes her money; or to neglect legal proceedings, tax bills, or maintenance of land, crops, and buildings that may be part of her estate. You may not make gifts from Alice's estate. You must sell a business that she has inherited. You cannot let anyone else hold onto her property without supervising its care. You must earn income from Alice's property by investing it in a sound way—such as by depositing life-insurance proceeds and all money in a federally insured, interest-bearing bank account separate from your own money. If she owns real estate, you must lease it to a responsible tenant.

You must take inventory and collect all of Alice's assets. When permitted by law, you take title (ownership) in her name. Otherwise, you own the property "as guardian for Alice Carrol." This shows that you have the right to hold or sell the property but no authority to use it for your own benefit. You must determine the value of each asset and file a list with the court. If you do not collect the assets promptly, you will owe her estate if any value is lost. For example, if you fail to collect a debt owed to her estate because you were not diligent, you must make good the loss.

As a guardian you do not have authority, in general, to make contracts for Alice without permission from the court. If she is a party to a lawsuit, you cannot compromise it without first submitting the terms of the settlement to the court for approval.

Handling of money   You may not tie up Alice's money by purchasing real estate, but you can lend her money to someone else buying real estate if the property is good security for the loan. You cannot lend Alice's money to yourself—not even if you guarantee the loan by a pledge of real estate. You can lease land Alice owns but usually the lease cannot extend beyond the time when she reaches the age of adulthood. You cannot mortgage her real estate or permit her personal property to be held as security against payment of a debt. You will need permission from the court to sell any real estate she owns, but you can sell items of personal property at a fair price without court approval.

Dishonest guardian   A ward is not liable (financially responsible) for acts of his guardian that are not authorized by law or the courts. After Alice becomes an adult, she can sue if you have wasted her assets, converted them to your own use, or embezzled her funds. Before a ward is old enough to sue for herself, a dishonest guardian can be removed by court order and another one appointed.

Accounting   At the end of your guardianship, you must account for all transactions involving Alice's estate. Usually, you already will have submitted interim reports with the court. Your final report must also be filed, and all property turned over to the proper person—a new guardian if Alice is still a minor or Alice herself if she has reached the age of adulthood. You are entitled to be paid from the ward's estate for managing her assets. If you are responsible for losses, you must repay the ward.

Guardianship by parents   Two parents are generally entitled to share the rights and responsibilities of caring for their child. If the child is illegitimate, the father may have less right to be a guardian than the mother. See ILLEGITIMACY. If the child is legitimate and one parent dies, the other parent must continue caring for the child and managing his property. Any parent who fails to care for an offspring as required by law can lose his rights in the child.

EXAMPLE Susan, who is divorced and has custody of her two children, ages 10 and 12, wants to prepare a will. She cannot appoint a guardian who will take custody of the children after her death, because their father will have more right to care for them than anyone else. But in case the children's father cannot or does not assume responsibility for their daily care after Susan dies, Susan can name her brother guardian of the person for the children. A court will give great consideration to Susan's choice of her brother.

Next, Susan can name a guardian of the property for the children. She knows that if she dies before the children are grown, their father must support them. By naming a guardian of their property, she is able to set aside some money for their adult years, when their father will no longer be legally obligated to support them. If the property is managed well, it can help pay for a college education, special job training, starting a business, or buying a first home. Of course, a parent-guardian is supposed to leave his children's property intact, but the court often gives more discretion to a parent than to an outsider.

■ **Legal actions**   A guardian can sue someone else on behalf of his ward. But if the ward wants to sue his guardian, another guardian must handle the legal action for him. Anytime there is a conflict between the interests of a guardian and those of his ward, a separate guardian—a *guardian ad litem*—is appointed to manage the lawsuit.

A guardian participating in a lawsuit for his ward sues or is sued only as the child's representative, not personally. For example, if the child sues a doctor for malpractice and recovers money damages of $5,000, the money does not belong to the guardian even though he started the lawsuit. In the same way, if someone else wins money damages against the ward, the money must come from the ward's property. If both the guardian and ward are parties in one lawsuit, the guardian is treated as two different people. He appears both as guardian and as an individual in the action.

guest   Legally, someone who is on premises owned by another, such as a person riding in someone else's car or staying at a hotel. The term "guest" is used to determine legal liability. See INNKEEPER; TORT.

A *guest statute* is a law that prevents passengers in automobiles from suing their drivers in certain cases. If the passenger is a guest—not paying for the ride or carrying on business with or for the driver—the driver is responsible for injuries to the passenger only if he is reckless. Not all states have guest statutes. See NEGLIGENCE and Chart 28.

guilty   Having committed a crime; not innocent. A prisoner who is willing to accept legal responsiblity for having committed a crime answers "Guilty" when the judge asks how he wishes to plead. For a full discussion of criminal procedures, see CRIMINAL LAW.

A JURY that finds a defendant has committed a crime returns a verdict of *guilty*. A jury that is not convinced that the prisoner is guilty can return a verdict of *not guilty*. This does not necessarily mean that the jurors think the defendant is innocent but only that they do not believe enough evidence has been presented to prove him guilty.

In civil cases, the word "guilty" is occasionally used without implying criminal responsibility. For example, a disbarred attorney may be *guilty of professional misconduct* without having committed a crime.

gun control   See ARMS, RIGHT TO BEAR; WEAPON.

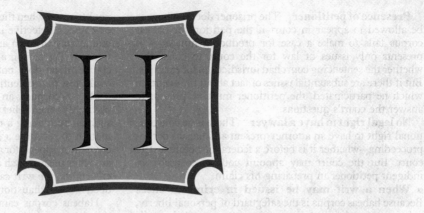

habeas corpus (Latin) "You should have the body." Habeas corpus is one of the most sacred rights in the English common law. Sometimes called the Great Writ, the writ of habeas corpus is a court order directed usually to a government official, such as a warden, who has restrained someone, commanding that the prisoner be produced at a designated time and place so that the court may determine the legality of his custody. If he is being detained illegally, the court will order his release. The writ of habeas corpus, which was available at common law in England to protect a person against unlawful imprisonment, was brought to the United States by the colonists. When the colonies became independent states, the right of a citizen to the remedy of habeas corpus was recognized and preserved by federal and state constitutions and statutes. In fact, it was considered so important by the framers of the Constitution that Article I, Section 9, Clause 2, provides:

" *The Privilege of the Writ of Habeas Corpus shall not be suspended, unless when in cases of Rebellion or Invasion the public Safety may require it.* "

This provision did not convey authority to federal courts to issue habeas corpus, but the Judiciary Act of 1789 authorized federal courts to grant writs of habeas corpus where a "prisoner . . . is in custody under the authority of the United States," and in 1867 the writ was made applicable to any person "restrained of his . . . liberty in violation of the Constitution," including state prisoners. Although the U.S. Constitution does not require a state to provide any habeas corpus procedure, every state, either by its statutes or its constitution, provides for a writ of habeas corpus virtually the same as the federal writ, although minor variations may be found from state to state. All mention of habeas corpus in this article refers to federal habeas corpus unless state habeas corpus is specifically designated.

Although originally used to test the legality of the imprisonment of someone convicted of a crime, habeas corpus has also been used in civil cases by ALIENS resisting deportation, by persons challenging the authority of the armed services to force continued service, and by persons seeking to obtain child CUSTODY.

■ **Jurisdiction** The question of jurisdiction (authority) is perhaps the most important element involved in the writ of habeas corpus. First of all, the purpose of the writ is to challenge defects in jurisdiction. This means the writ allows a court to investigate whether a prisoner has been illegally detained by a court that did not have the authority to detain him and thus order his release. A state court does not have the jurisdiction to issue a writ of habeas corpus for a person being held in custody by federal officers under the authority of the United States—only a federal court can do so. A state court issuing a writ of habeas corpus must have jurisdiction in the county in which the prisoner either was sentenced or is confined.

■ **Application for habeas corpus** A person who believes his detention is illegal—or someone acting on his behalf—may apply for a writ of habeas corpus to the court authorized to issue the writ. He presents a petition, which details why the court should investigate his detention. The petition is usually directed against the person (the respondent) who has custody of the petitioner (the prisoner) and has the power to produce him physically. If the petition fails to disclose grounds justifying the writ, the court will dismiss the application. If the court decides that there are sufficient grounds, it will order the respondent to produce the prisoner and show by what authority he detains him.

There is no fixed time for an application. The right to habeas corpus is not lost by delay that is sufficiently explained. But if the respondent has been harmed by an unreasonable delay, the writ will not be issued.

EXAMPLE John Smith voluntarily pleaded guilty to a charge
○→─✷ of manslaughter after shooting his wife's lover. He was informed of his constitutional rights and had consulted with two well-known, competent attorneys before submitting his guilty plea to the court. He was sentenced to 15 years in prison. Eight years later, after the deaths of his two attorneys and all the witnesses to the shooting, including his wife, Smith applied for a writ of habeas corpus. He alleged he was denied effective assistance of counsel because his attorneys had conspired with his wife to have him sent to prison. The court would be justified in denying his petition, because his unreasonable delay in asserting his claim injured the state. The state would be unable to question the wife or the attorneys to determine whether the petitioner's contentions—completely unsupported by the facts of the case—would warrant his release.

Presence of petitioner The prisoner does not have to be allowed to appear in court if the petition for habeas corpus fails to make a case for producing him or if it presents only issues of law for the court to consider—whether the sentencing court had jurisdiction, for example. But if there are substantial issues of fact about the events in which he participated, the petitioner must be present to answer the court's questions.

No legal right to have a lawyer There is no constitutional right to have an attorney present at a habeas corpus proceeding—whether it is before a federal or before a state court. But the court may appoint counsel to assist an indigent petitioner in preparing his claim.

■ **When a writ may be issued in criminal cases** Because habeas corpus is the safeguard of personal liberty, prisoners must have access to courts to present their applications. The right of a person to the writ depends solely on the legality of his detention and not on his guilt or innocence. If the court in which he was convicted lacked the authority to try him, his constitutional rights have been violated.

A petitioner must be under some form of custody to justify the issuance of the writ. Although actual physical confinement in prison is not necessary, a restraint on his liberty must exist. A writ of habeas corpus generally will not be issued when the petitioner has agreed to be held. For example, a detective investigating a crime may ask someone to stay in town and be available for additional questions. If the person agrees, he cannot challenge this. Of course, if he does not agree, he may be arrested and he could test *that* detention by habeas corpus.

Habeas corpus is an extraordinary remedy that should be used only when relief cannot be obtained by other means, such as by making a motion for a new trial, by making a motion to set aside a judgment, or by obtaining a writ of error or of appeal (for a trial by a higher court). When there are other means, such as appeal, of preserving the petitioner's rights, the writ cannot be used. This is known as the doctrine of exhaustion of remedies.

Habeas corpus cannot be used to postpone a trial, to prevent prosecution for an offense, or to retry issues that have already been decided against the petitioner.

State prisoners The right of a state prisoner to federal habeas corpus relief is available only for violations of the laws, treaties, or Constitution of the United States. Even if he has been convicted of a crime under a state law, he has rights guaranteed to him by the U.S. Constitution and federal laws. Violations of these rights are what entitle him to seek a federal habeas corpus. Usually, however, he can apply for a federal habeas corpus writ only after he has tried

---

HABEAS CORPUS—YOUR PROTECTION AGAINST ILLEGAL DETENTION

■ *Habeas corpus* is Latin for "You should have the body," an order commanding a government official to produce a prisoner at a designated time and place so that the court may determine the legality of his custody. Habeas corpus gives a prisoner an immediate hearing on the legality of his detention.

■ A person who believes his detention is illegal may apply to the court for a writ of habeas corpus. The petition must disclose grounds justifying the writ.

■ The right of a person to the writ depends solely on the legality of his detention, not on his innocence.

■ While actual physical confinement in prison is not necessary, there must be some restraint on the petitioner's liberty.

■ Habeas corpus and an appeal of a case cannot be sought simultaneously. As long as there is a possibility of appeal, habeas corpus cannot be used.

■ The right of a state prisoner to federal habeas corpus relief is available for violations of the laws, treaties, or Constitution of the United States. He can apply for a federal writ after trying all available state remedies. A federal prisoner can apply for a writ after trying all the remedies available under federal law.

■ Someone who has been denied bail in a state or federal case may use the writ to obtain his release on bail. Excessive bail is considered the same as denial of bail—in such cases, habeas corpus is available for a discharge on less bail.

■ Courts will not issue writs to review the conditions of a prisoner's lawful confinement unless the conditions constitute a form of cruel and unusual punishment.

■ Habeas corpus will not be given a prisoner who claims he has been denied medical treatment unless the situation is cruel and unusual—say, if the prison doctor plans a lobotomy on a troublesome prisoner who is complaining of a sinus condition.

■ The writ may also be granted if probation is improperly revoked—when the probationer has not been given notice of the claimed violations or a hearing or written report on the reasons for revocation.

■ Habeas corpus can be a remedy for detention of aliens, men and women in the armed services, children in custody cases, insane persons, drug addicts, and people quarantined for public health reasons.

■ An alien can use habeas corpus to review the legality of a decision to keep him out of the country.

■ A member of the armed services who claims to be unlawfully retained in military service may obtain habeas corpus.

■ A court will not allow a parent to use habeas corpus as a way to obtain custody of a child while a permanent custody proceeding is pending, unless the court feels the child faces serious harm to his health or morals.

■ Habeas corpus can also challenge the legality of the detention of children in reformatories.

■ When a person is committed to an institution because of mental illness, habeas corpus may be granted to review his confinement.

■ Habeas corpus can question the detention of a person under quarantine for a contagious disease.

■ Under habeas corpus a person who has been committed as a drug abuser can contest whether he is in fact an addict and if the commitment proceedings were proper.

all the available state remedies. The purpose of the federal relief is to assure that a state prisoner will have an independent decision by a federal court about the legality of his detention.

Federal intrusion is justified only when circumstances indicate the unfairness of the trial or the infringement of constitutional rights. For example, a prisoner accused or convicted of a crime may be deprived of his federal constitutional rights if the police fail to give him the MIRANDA WARNINGS. This denies him his privilege against SELF-INCRIMINATION and his right to obtain the advice of counsel. See COUNSEL, RIGHT TO. His constitutional rights can also be violated by the use of evidence obtained from an illegal SEARCH AND SEIZURE.

A state prisoner is free to seek federal habeas corpus if he claims that, contrary to a state court's judgment, his confession was involuntary and inadmissible.

EXAMPLE A man is arrested by the police on suspicion of O←─* murder. He is subjected to intensive questioning for long periods of time and threatened with physical harm if he does not tell everything he knows about the murder. He is never informed of his constitutional rights by the Miranda Warnings and is given nothing to eat for four days. He confesses to the murder because he is scared and hungry. The confession is the most significant piece of evidence in the case. At his trial, his attorney argues that his client's confession should not be used as evidence since it was obtained in violation of his federal constitutional rights. The man is convicted of murder after the court refuses to find that his confession is involuntary. At that point, the prisoner may petition the federal court to make an independent examination into the constitutional question of the voluntariness of the confession.

In all other circumstances, federal courts normally will not interfere by granting habeas corpus until the prisoner has gone through the course of state court procedure. If he fails to use available state remedies, he will not be barred from petitioning for federal habeas corpus relief, but a federal court may deny it because he has deliberately forfeited state remedies. The federal court decides whether the petitioner *understandingly and knowingly* gave up his right to challenge his confinement in the state courts. For example, suppose an accused is told before his case is tried that he has the right to appeal a state conviction. His failure to file an appeal in state court after his conviction is a knowing waiver of that right.

Federal prisoners A federal prisoner may apply for a writ of habeas corpus in another federal court to test the legality of his detention only if he cannot obtain adequate relief in the court that imposed sentence. Congress has passed a law enabling a federal prisoner to appear in the court that sentenced him and move to have his sentence *vacated* (set aside) or corrected because it (1) was imposed in violation of the Constitution or laws of the United States, such as a sentence imposed on a woman for obtaining an abortion during her second month of pregnancy; (2) was more than the maximum time authorized by law, such as one imposed for 12 years when the maximum was 10 years; or (3) is subject to attack in a later proceeding other than an appeal, such as when a new trial is needed because evidence that could not be discovered earlier has turned up.

As long as this remedy of vacating or correcting a sentence—or any of those mentioned earlier—is available, habeas corpus is inapplicable. When no other methods are available to the prisoner, he may apply for a federal writ of habeas corpus in the district where he is confined. See FEDERAL COURTS.

Bail BAIL is the release of a person from custody upon his posting of a bond, the amount of which is set by the court. If he fails to appear in court when required, he forfeits the amount of his bond, and a warrant will be issued for his arrest. A writ of habeas corpus will not be granted to release a person who has been properly imprisoned just because he cannot furnish bail, but someone who has been denied bail may use the writ to obtain his release on bail. Bail may be granted to release a person from federal or state custody. State habeas corpus proceedings may be instituted to free a state prisoner who has wrongfully been denied bail.

After a person has been convicted of a crime, he cannot raise the question of the denial of his petition for bail before his trial.

EXAMPLE Rhoda is arrested for trafficking in illegal drugs. O←─* She is denied bail because the judge strongly suspects she will use her underground contacts to skip town and will not appear in court to be tried. Rhoda remains in prison until her trial and does not petition the court to release her on habeas corpus. She is tried and convicted. It is now too late for her to test the denial of bail by petitioning for habeas corpus.

Excessive bail is equivalent to a denial of bail. In such cases habeas corpus is available for a release on less bail. Usually, the petitioner must show that he applied for a reduction of bail and was denied it.

The use of federal habeas corpus to review BAIL set in state proceedings is restricted. The federal court will inquire only whether the bail is arbitrary or discriminatory, in violation of the U.S. Constitution, or results in a denial of counsel or of a fair trial.

Extradition Habeas corpus can secure the release of a person illegally detained for EXTRADITION as a fugitive from justice in another state. The writ tests only the lawfulness of the arrest by the authorities of the asylum state.

EXAMPLE Willy Fox was arrested in state X at the request of O←─* state Y, which wanted to prosecute Willy on charges of armed robbery and rape. State Y informed officials of state X of the charges against Willy, and the governor filed the proper papers. State Y described Willy—white, 6½ feet tall, 250 pounds, with a tattoo of a poodle on his right hand. When the police in state X arrested Willy, it was obvious that he fit the description. If Willy can prove that he was in state Z when the crime in state Y was committed, he will be granted a release on habeas corpus because state X has unlawfully arrested him. But because he cannot prove that he was not in state Y when the robbery and rape were committed, his petition for a writ of habeas corpus will be denied.

Prison conditions Courts ordinarily will not issue a writ of habeas corpus to review the nature and conditions of a prisoner's lawful confinement. Unfit or unsanitary PRISONS are not grounds for habeas corpus relief unless the conditions are so outrageous that they are a form of cruel and unusual punishment. For example, a state prisoner was kept completely nude in a cell stripped of all furnishings simply because he did not return a book to the prison library on time. The court held that his punishment was cruel and unusual.

Habeas corpus will not be given to a prisoner who claims he has been denied necessary medical treatment unless exceptional circumstances exist—obvious neglect or intentional mistreatment, for example. If the prison doctor plans a lobotomy on a troublesome prisoner who complains of a sinus condition, the prisoner would be entitled to habeas corpus. In cases such as these, a state prisoner could apply for both state and federal habeas corpus because, in all likelihood, his rights under the federal constitution as well as the state constitution have been violated. See also PRISONERS' RIGHTS.

Probation   A person convicted of a criminal offense is on probation when his sentence is suspended. He is allowed then to stay out of jail under conditions supervised by his probation officer. A writ of habeas corpus—state or federal, depending on the situation—may be sought to test the legality of the proposed conditions, to enforce continued probation, and to secure the reconsideration of probation that has been refused. The writ will also be granted if probation is improperly revoked—for example, without giving the probationer notice of the claimed violations or without a hearing or written report on the reasons for revocation.

Parole   PAROLE is the conditional release of a prisoner before he has served his entire sentence. If the parolee fulfills the conditions of his parole, he will receive an absolute discharge from the balance of his sentence. But if he violates the conditions of his parole, he will be returned to jail to serve the unexpired time. Habeas corpus will not be awarded to challenge the decisions of a parole board. But it is available to insure that a prisoner's application for parole is considered. It is also there to enforce the right of a paroled convict to remain on parole, unless he has violated its conditions, as by carrying a weapon.

Pardon   A PARDON releases a person convicted of a crime from all of his punishment and from all the penalties that go with conviction—loss of the right to vote, for example. The validity of the conditions imposed in a conditional pardon may be tested in either a state or a federal habeas corpus proceeding. A federal court cannot, however, review the pardoning power of a state governor.

■ **Others who may benefit**   Habeas corpus can be a proper remedy for the detention of ALIENS, men and women in the armed services, persons held for contempt, minors in custody cases, insane persons, drug addicts, and people quarantined for health reasons.

In most cases, the writ proceedings determine (1) whether the administrative body was legally constituted and its findings were proper, (2) whether it had jurisdiction, and (3) whether there was a fair hearing with the constitutional rights of the petitioner duly recognized. The writ may only be sought after all administrative avenues have been tried and failed.

Aliens   An alien can use habeas corpus to review the legality of a decision to keep him out of the United States—even when he is not in the physical custody of the immigra-

tion authorities. An alien may be denied entry to this country if he is likely to become a public charge or has been convicted of a crime involving MORAL TURPITUDE.

Habeas corpus is usually the correct remedy to review proceedings for deportation or to gain the release of an alien who has been unlawfully detained for deportation. For instance, holding an alien incommunicado for six days without a warrant of arrest, on suspicion that he was not telling the truth about how he entered the country, justified his release on habeas corpus.

Armed services   The writ is applicable to members of the armed services who claim to be unlawfully retained in service or wrongfully held under military arrest. The federal courts will review the decisions of military officials to insure that the rights guaranteed by the Constitution or by military regulations are protected. Unless there are extraordinary circumstances, however, the courts will not review discretionary decisions by military officials.

EXAMPLE A habeas corpus proceeding was brought by Al, a
O—* Marine who had been denied his request for a hardship discharge. The district court had to decide not whether Al was entitled to a discharge but only if there was substantial evidence to support the Marine Corps in refusing it.

Habeas corpus may be used to secure the release of a person in the armed services who has not actually enlisted or who has signed up illegally.

EXAMPLE Habeas corpus served in one case in which a
O—* National Guardsman contended that a medical condition prior to his enlistment made his induction void. He asserted that his continued involuntary membership in the Guard violated his rights. The court agreed and granted him a release from further service.

A writ will not secure a release, however, if an enlistee is awaiting trial or undergoing punishment for an armed services offense. As a rule, habeas corpus can test the legality of restraint after a court-martial.

Contempt   Habeas corpus usually will not be granted to obtain the release of a person imprisoned for CONTEMPT. An exception is when the contempt proceedings are void because the body that brought them—whether legislative, judicial, or executive—had no authority to act. For instance, habeas corpus may compel the release of a person jailed for his refusal to testify before a legislative committee investigating election frauds when the committee was not given the authority to punish.

Relief by writ is possible when the petitioner is being held while awaiting contempt prosecution for disobeying an unconstitutional or illegal court order or when a contempt has not been committed and the judgment of contempt is clearly arbitrary and capricious.

Child-custody cases   Any person with a legal right to the CUSTODY of a minor child—a parent or guardian, for example—usually may obtain a writ of habeas corpus in a state court to win that custody. (Normally, federal courts do not have jurisdiction in child custody contests.) The writ will be granted even if the child is not held by actual force but remains voluntarily with the person (the *respondent*). The writ will not be allowed until the petitioner can show that he has demanded custody of the child from the respondent and has been refused.

EXAMPLE Bob and Betty are divorced, and custody of their
daughter Carol is awarded to Betty. Bob, however, has visitation rights with Carol for one weekend a
month and one month in the summer. Betty drops Carol
off at Bob's apartment for the summer month. At the end
of that time, Bob refuses to return Carol despite Betty's
persistent demands. Betty may be entitled to bring a
habeas corpus proceeding directed against Bob to compel
Carol's return.

A habeas corpus proceeding decides only the right to
immediate possession of a child. It is not the proper proceeding to settle the question of permanent custody. Courts
will not allow habeas corpus for the custody of a child while
a permanent custody proceeding is pending, unless it feels
the child faces serious harm to his health or morals.

EXAMPLE Sam and Donna decide to divorce. Custody of
their 10-year-old son Peter is awarded to Donna,
but Sam is awarded visitation rights of one weekend a
month. After one of these weekends, Sam refuses to
return Peter to Donna, because she is living with her
hairdresser, Mr. Raymond. Donna brings a habeas corpus
proceeding to have the court order Sam to return Peter.
The court may require that Mr. Raymond move out of
her home before ordering Sam to return Peter to her
custody if the court feels that Mr. Raymond's presence is
detrimental to Peter's welfare. Ordinarily, in an award of
custody, the court favors the party having the legal right
of custody. If Donna becomes a heroin addict after her
divorce is granted, however, the court may refuse to order
the return of Peter. Another proceeding would take place,
however, to reconsider and decide again whether Sam
should be awarded permanent custody in light of Donna's
drug addiction.

Habeas corpus can also challenge the legality of the
detention of children in juvenile asylums, training schools,
reformatories, and other institutions to which they have
been assigned.

Insane persons When a person is committed to an
institution because of mental illness, habeas corpus may be
granted to review his confinement. The court must consider whether the person is likely to menace his own safety or
that of others if he is released. The writ may also be used to
test an accused's right to a sanity hearing.

After exhausting the remedies provided by state law, a
patient in a state mental hospital may test the validity of his
commitment in a federal court when he can show that his
federal constitutional rights—such as the rights of notice
and of a hearing of the charges against him—were violated.
See INSANE PERSONS.

Quarantine and health Habeas corpus can question
the detention of a person under quarantine or health regulations because he may have a contagious disease or has
been exposed to contagion. The hearing on the writ determines the authority of the health statute and whether the
quarantine was humanely conducted.

Drug addicts Under habeas corpus a person committed as a drug abuser can contest whether he is, indeed, an
addict and if the commitment proceedings were proper.
Because the purpose of a narcotic-addict commitment program is to treat, cure, and rehabilitate, a person who has
been released from institutional confinement and placed on

aftercare at a rehabilitation center is not considered restrained in his liberty. He is not entitled to habeas corpus.

habendum (Latin) The part of a DEED to real property (real estate) that begins with the words "To have and to
hold." It describes the ownership rights of the person to
whom the property is being transferred. The part may
explain, reduce, enlarge, or qualify the estate that is being
granted in the land. A common example is "To have and to
hold the premises herein granted unto the party of the
second part, the heirs or successors, and assigns of the party
of the second part forever." See ESTATE.

habitability The requirement that a rented house or
apartment be fit to live in with reasonable comfort. See
LANDLORD AND TENANT.

habitual Customary or regular. Under the laws of
some states, a person who has been convicted of two
crimes, one of which is a felony, is a "habitual criminal,"
and he may receive a longer SENTENCE than a person who
has never been convicted.

habitual drunkenness The custom or habit of
getting drunk, in many states a ground for DIVORCE. It may
also be called habitual intemperance or intoxication. See
INTOXICATING LIQUOR.

handicapped persons People with a mental or
physical disability that makes major life activities such as
taking care of one's self, walking, seeing, hearing, speaking,
breathing, learning, and working more difficult than for
persons who are not disabled. If a person has a history of
such a condition, or if his disability does not limit major life
activities but is erroneously considered to do so by others,
he is considered handicapped. Cancer and diabetes are such
disabilities, as are alcoholism and drug addiction when they
significantly interfere with life activities. Handicapped
persons are specifically recognized in laws that prohibit
unnecessary discrimination or require consideration of
their special needs. These statutes are fairly recent and have
not always been widely enforced.

■ **Employment** Broad civil rights legislation has not
required employers to hire handicapped individuals. The
federal Civil Rights Act of 1964, for example, prohibits
employment discrimination on the basis of race, religion,
sex, or national origin, but it offers no protection for
handicapped job applicants. The federal Rehabilitation Act
of 1973 addresses this kind of discrimination. The purposes
of the law are to evaluate the problems of handicapped
individuals and to assist in the development of programs
that meet their needs.

The act directed the Department of Health, Education
and Welfare (now the Department of Health and Human
Services and the Department of Education) to draw up
regulations for any person, group, or company receiving
federal benefits. These rules bar discrimination in recruitment, hiring, compensation, job assignment or classification, and fringe benefits. For example, they require
employers who test job applicants to use procedures that do
not unfairly screen out handicapped persons. This means,

for instance, that an employer must give a written rather than an oral typing test to a deaf person applying for a job as a typist. An employer can require a medical exam after the handicapped individual receives a job offer if it is the normal requirement for other prospective employees. If the exam reveals a condition that makes the person unsuitable for the job, the offer may be withdrawn.

A prospective employer cannot ask whether a person has a handicap, but he may inquire whether the person can handle the job. For example, an epileptic applicant cannot be asked about his condition, but he may be asked if he has a driver's license if he is applying for a delivery job.

The rules also require an employer to make reasonable efforts to adapt to workers with handicaps. Often relatively slight architectural changes can make it easier for people on crutches or in wheelchairs to get around in a building. Similarly, tasks on an assembly line can be divided so that some jobs can be done by mentally retarded individuals.

Another important provision of these regulations is program accessibility. The rules state that handicapped persons cannot be turned away by any program receiving federal money or any business with a federal contract simply because they cannot get into the facilities. Ironically, a large city that held hearings on special parking rights for handicapped people did so in a room that many of those most concerned were unable to reach.

The law recognizes that not all buildings can be redesigned immediately, but it demands consideration of handicapped people anyway. If, for example, a Medicare office must be at the top of an old narrow stairway, then interviewers must go to the homes of handicapped people who call for appointments. Meanwhile, old buildings must be improved as time and money permit, and new buildings must always be designed with the handicapped in mind.

■ **Education** Until recently, millions of handicapped children in the United States were excluded from public schools because they were labeled uneducable.

EXAMPLE The first case to determine that all children can benefit from appropriate education was decided in Pennsylvania in 1972. The parents of 13 retarded children and the Pennsylvania Association for Retarded Children challenged a state law that kept children out of school if school psychologists certified them as "uneducable and untrainable." The court decided that the state may not refuse to educate retarded children and noted that labeling a child as retarded and placing him in a special class for the retarded was itself a handicap.

EXAMPLE In another case, a federal court in Washington, D.C., then held that *all* handicapped children are entitled to an education. The court estimated that as many as 18,000 "exceptional" children in the capital were not being reached in 1972. This included children who were mentally retarded, emotionally disturbed, physically disabled, hyperactive, and those with behavioral problems. The court said that these children are entitled to equal protection under the education laws and that their parents are entitled to be informed of and involved in school decisions about how to handle them. It added that tight budgets are no excuse for cutting off exceptional children. Whatever money is available must be spent fairly on all the children.

The most significant federal law is the Education for All Handicapped Children Act of 1975. It requires states to provide a free and adequate public education to handicapped children of the same ages as other public school children and makes federal money available to the states for the extra cost of educating a handicapped child. Regardless of the severity of a child's handicap, he must be educated in the least restrictive environment possible. This means that a regular school classroom is better than a special class but that any kind of teaching is better than no education at all. Approved private schools are acceptable when no public facilities are available.

An individualized written plan must be worked out for each handicapped child and reviewed annually. This is usually done by a committee of the local school district with input from the child's parents and former teachers along with some opinions from experts in that area of education. School districts must keep these records confidential, but parents must be able to see them and must always be given notice before any change is made in a child's placement or program. If a parent is not satisfied, he may demand a hearing before the local school district and be represented by a lawyer or a person trained in the problems of handicapped children. Any decisions made may be reviewed by the state commissioner of education. From there, the decision can be appealed in state or federal court, but it is better to challenge the decision in federal court.

Federal law also makes money available for states and local districts to remove architectural barriers from educational facilities, to pay for designing new buildings, and to purchase special equipment.

■ **Accessibility** It is not the handicap but the lack of accessibility—to important information, for example, or to public buildings or places of employment—that isolates many people with special needs and puts them at a disadvantage.

Emergency information is of immediate importance to everyone, but when it is not available to a handicapped person, the result can be disastrous. For example, a landlord who called to a boy to leave his building fired a shot when the boy did not respond to his warning. The boy, who was killed, was deaf and mute.

The Federal Communications Commission (FCC) has tried to make disaster warnings more accessible to handicapped persons. It ordered television broadcasters to present warnings of such threats as hurricanes, tornadoes, or flash floods both as spoken announcements and written displays. The FCC has also suggested that television stations be equipped to broadcast written subtitles to viewers who order the service and attach a small adapter to their television sets. This is available only from stations that volunteer it.

Proper building designs The Architectural Barriers Act of 1968 requires the Secretary of Housing and Urban Development to prescribe rules for the design, construction, and alteration of residential structures built for or financed by the federal government. The Administrator of General Services and the Secretary of Health and Human Services must do the same for public buildings.

For example, if a federal courthouse is being renovated and the work will involve improving existing elevators, stairs, rest rooms, drinking fountains, and telephone locations, the proposed new design must accommodate physically handicapped persons whenever possible.

Another example is the East Building of the National Gallery of Art in Washington, D.C. People who are impressed by the long, elegant walk that goes up to the building may not realize that it was designed for access by people in wheelchairs.

The conflicting needs of people with different handicaps can create seemingly unsolvable problems for those trying to comply with federal regulations. For example, people who use wheelchairs, crutches, or canes need curb cuts—gentle ramps at intersections. Blind people who use canes, however, need curbs to warn them where the sidewalk ends and the street begins. The conflict was settled in many cities by installing curb cuts with a surface different from that of the sidewalk and street. Thus, wheelchairs can cross easily and yet blind people are warned.

Mass transit   The Urban Mass Transportation Act requires any mass-transit system that receives federal money to plan for use by handicapped persons. It includes a provision that special efforts must be made in the planning and design of mass transportation facilities and services. Also, any state or local community applying for mass transit funds must give assurances that handicapped and elderly people will be able to buy tickets during off-peak hours at no more than half the usual cost.

harbor   Shelter, conceal, or protect a person for an illegal purpose, such as taking in a criminal fleeing from the police. See CRIMINAL LAW.

Hatch Act   A federal law prohibiting federal employees from holding public office, influencing elections, and taking part in political management or in political campaigns. It also applies to persons employed by state agencies, such as a city housing authority, which are either partly or wholly financed by federal grants and loans. This law does not prevent such employees from voting or from expressing their opinions on politics and candidates for political offices.

have and hold   See HABENDUM.

hawkers and peddlers   A *hawker* is a traveling trader who carries his goods with him for sale, attracting attention by crying out in public; by using placards, labels, or signs; or by displaying his goods in a public place. A *peddler* is a traveling retail dealer who also carries his merchandise with him but makes his sales by going from house to house to display his goods. The terms "hawker" and "peddler" are frequently defined by state statutes or city ordinances.

■ **Who is a peddler?**   To be considered a peddler in the eyes of the law, the person cannot have a fixed place of business. He must carry his wares with him, offer them for immediate sale, and deliver them then and there—a person selling homemade candies, for example.

A person who goes from house to house, selling goods to different persons in small quantities, such as a person selling designer jeans bought wholesale, is a peddler. This is true even if he or she makes daily sales to regular customers—an ice-cream-truck driver, for example, who announces his coming by ringing bells and makes sales wherever he can.

A peddler is different from a FACTOR. A factor sells goods entrusted to him by his principal. A peddler usually buys the goods from a wholesaler and then sells them at a retail price he fixes.

Those who sell articles from house to house, for a limited time, and use the profits for educational and religious purposes are not peddlers. Girl Scouts raising funds for their national organization by selling cookies fall into this category. So do high-schoolers selling goods door to door in order to raise funds for the class trip.

Generally, a person is not a peddler if he solicits orders but does not deliver the articles at the time of the sale—for example, an Avon Lady and a Fuller Brush man. Thus, a traveling salesman, an encyclopedia seller, or a merchant who has a store and solicits orders is not a peddler.

■ **Licensing**   A municipality may regulate hawking and peddling within its boundaries. When a license is required, a hawker or peddler must obtain one before he begins his selling. The license must be issued to the person who is actually doing the peddling and is not transferable.

An applicant must sometimes establish certain facts, such as good moral character. He may have to take an oath, give a bond, or make a deposit.

Licensing statutes and ordinances frequently exempt certain persons—those selling goods or articles they have made themselves, honorably discharged or disabled veterans, poor or disabled persons generally, and clergymen selling religious publications. The exemption is a personal one and does not extend to their agents or employees.

H.B.   The abbreviation for *House Bill,* a proposed congressional law introduced in the House of Representatives. See LEGISLATION for a description of how a bill becomes a law.

head of family   A person who actually supports and maintains in one household one or more people who are closely related to him by blood, MARRIAGE, or adoption (see ADOPTION OF PERSONS). The head has a right to exercise FAMILY control and to provide for the dependent members based on a legal or moral obligation. See HUSBAND AND WIFE; PARENT AND CHILD.

head of household   A filing status for federal income tax payers. A person who qualifies as head of household pays taxes at a rate higher than that paid by a married couple filing a joint return and at a rate lower than a single person filing an individual return. To qualify, the taxpayer must be single on the last day of his tax year. He must contribute more than one half the cost of maintaining a household, which must also be the principal residence of one relative for the entire year. His relatives include his mother and father, child, grandchild, stepchild, brother or sister, half brother or half sister, stepbrother or stepsister, and so on. Unlike other relatives, however, a parent does not need to be in the same residence as the taxpayer for him to claim head of household status as long as he meets the support requirements.

hearing 1 A proceeding in which EVIDENCE is taken to decide a question of fact or law. A hearing ordinarily takes place between adversary (opposing) parties who are before a court or a federal or state administrative agency. See PAROLE; PUBLIC ADMINISTRATIVE AGENCY. Reasonable notice must be given of when and where the hearing will be held and of the charges or claims that will be presented. Each party has the right to have a lawyer at the hearing. Each side may offer and refute evidence and present arguments about the strengths and weaknesses of the evidence and the applicable law. An administrative or legislative hearing is usually less formal than a TRIAL; for example, standards for the admissibility of evidence are not as stringent. In contrast, a judicial hearing usually must meet the same requirements as those imposed in a trial. A judicial hearing usually decides a preliminary aspect of the lawsuit, whereas a trial is a determination of the merits of the lawsuit as presented by the issues in the case.

2 A meeting of a legislative committee, such as the Senate Select Committee on Indian Affairs, appointed to gather information.

hearing examiner An official who presides over a HEARING held by an administrative agency and whose duties are essentially the same as those of a judge presiding over a courtroom without a jury—to hear and decide on questions of law and fact.

hearsay Evidence that does not come from a witness's own personal knowledge. Literally, it is what the witness says he heard another person say. For a more extensive treatment, see CRIMINAL LAW; EVIDENCE.

heart-balm act A law limiting or abolishing lawsuits, called *heart-balm actions*, brought by plaintiffs who seek money damages to soothe their broken hearts. Heart-balm suits are based on the principle that the law frowns on any interference with the status of MARRIAGE or with family relations. They include actions for BREACH OF MARRIAGE PROMISE, alienation of affections, criminal conversation, and seduction.

■ **Breach-of-promise suits** The theory that underlies breach-of-marriage-promise suits is that a promise made should be kept even though following this principle frustrates a primary purpose of the engagement period—finding out whether the parties are well enough suited to go forward with the marriage. There are times, however, when one person takes advantage of another. Breach-of-promise suits may compensate the injured party.

EXAMPLE In 1953 a 48-year-old widow answered an advertisement to work as a farmhand for a 55-year-old man in Minnesota. He called on her a few times and then asked her to marry him. She accepted and agreed to move in with him with the understanding that they would be married within a year. Thereafter, he became evasive. After a serious illness in 1959, he promised to marry her "before school was out" but he failed to honor this commitment. Finally, in 1963, she sued him for breach of promise to marry and won a jury verdict of $20,000.

Many states have abolished breach-of-promise suits. When Indiana did so in 1935, an estimated $15 million had been awarded in breach-of-promise damages in that state during the preceding 10 years.

■ **Alienation of affections and criminal conversation** A lawsuit can also be brought against someone who interferes with a marital relationship. *Alienation of affections* means winning away a spouse's love. *Criminal conversation* is adultery. *Conversation* in this context means sexual intercourse; it is criminal because it violates the law.

Originally, only a husband could bring these suits, because a wife had no legal capacity to sue. The law sought to preserve the integrity of the family by guaranteeing the husband exclusive rights to his wife.

EXAMPLE A Texas case decided in 1972 illustrates this attitude. The plaintiff—let's call him Tex—complained that the defendant, Bob, began staying around Tex's cocktail lounge, where his wife Lil tended bar. He said that Bob deliberately set out to win Lil's affections and finally accomplished this purpose when he took her to a lakeside house and kept her there until 6:30 in the morning.

The trial judge dismissed the suit, but the case was sent back after appeal. The appeals court said that as long as Tex claimed he could prove that Bob had had sexual intercourse with Lil during their marriage, Tex was entitled to sue Bob for criminal conversation.

It is not always a lover who is responsible for alienation of affections. Mothers-in-law have often been accused, and sometimes even a religious institution is blamed.

EXAMPLE In Ohio a man sued the Radio Church of God, its local minister, and the founder of a theological school associated with it. The man and his wife had married after he was divorced. The wife tuned in to broadcasts by the Radio Church of God, sent for literature, and became converted. The church taught that the words of the Bible should be accepted literally, and that if a divorced man remarries he is committing adultery. The woman left her husband and sued him for divorce. He sued the church for alienation of affections, and a jury awarded him $30,000 in damages. But the verdict was overturned on appeal because the church had "the right to advocate and to disseminate any religious faith no matter how offensive . . . to others."

Judges nearly always criticize suits for alienation of affections and criminal conversation, and they frequently urge legislatures to outlaw them. One court reversed an award of $5,000 in PUNITIVE DAMAGES because the state's criminal-adultery statute provided for punishment of not more than $200 or three months in jail. Some of the verdicts do indeed look like prizes. A man in Oregon won $10,000 for his wife's straying, and in 1974 a North Carolina husband got $70,000.

■ **Lawsuits for seduction** A seduction suit is a heart-balm suit brought by a father against a man who has had sexual intercourse with his daughter. Under the common law, the daughter generally had no right to sue for her own seduction. If she was seduced by a promise of marriage, she could sue for breach of promise, and if she submitted to sexual intercourse because of force or duress, she could perhaps bring charges of rape or assault. Usually, however, whether the woman was an adult or a minor child, seduction was considered an injury to her father.

Early cases permitted a father to recover money damages only for services he lost as a result of the seducer's interference—if, for example, the girl became listless and neglected her chores around the house or farm. Later, fathers were also permitted to recover damages for medical expenses, such as those occasioned by pregnancy or venereal disease, and for the father's own distress and sorrow. There are very few suits for seduction today, chiefly because they only serve to publicize the daughter's humiliation. At least nine states have abolished them altogether.

■ **Laws limiting heart-balm suits** Most judges and legal scholars agree that all lawsuits for breach of promise to marry, alienation of affections, criminal conversation, and seduction should be abolished. A number of states have passed heart-balm acts, some of which attempt to limit the amount of money damages an aggrieved plaintiff can recover.

For example, Illinois passed a law that prohibited recovery for anything except an *actual* loss. The law said that no jury should even consider the wealth or position or prospects of the defendant; the mental anguish suffered by the plaintiff; any shame, humiliation, sorrow, or mortification felt by the plaintiff; or any dishonor or damage to the reputation of the plaintiff or his or her family.

New York's legislature went even further and absolutely barred any lawsuit based on heart-balm actions. Because the legislature believed that these suits provided a blank check for blackmailers, the law went so far as to make it a criminal act in New York to start, threaten to start, or settle or compromise a lawsuit based on one of these claims. Violation of this law is a felony, punishable by a fine of up to $5,000 and a prison sentence of one to five years.

A judge in Pennsylvania wrote: "If the plaintiff's wife has a constitutional right to secure contraceptive devices, to undergo an abortion, to undergo a hysterectomy . . . all without the consent of her spouse, it stands to reason that she likewise has the right to engage in voluntary, natural sexual relations with a person of her choice."

Even after states have outlawed heart-balm suits, however, there remains the question of exactly which lawsuits are prohibited. For example, New York judges have said that its very strong heart-balm act was not intended to prohibit every kind of lawsuit based on sexual misconduct. A court will look at the actual nature of the case and not at what one party or the other calls it.

EXAMPLE A young woman was permitted to sue her psychiatrist after he aggravated her mental problems when he "treated" her by having sexual relations with her. The doctor claimed that all lawsuits based on injured feelings resulting from a sexual relationship had been abolished. The court answered that the doctor could be guilty of medical malpractice, and that had not been abolished by the heart-balm act.

EXAMPLE In another case, a man had arranged a sham marriage ceremony. The woman proceeded to live with him as his lawful wife until she discovered the truth. When she sued for money damages, he answered that breach-of-promise suits had been abolished. The court held that this woman had a valid cause of action for fraud and that it was not the purpose of the heart-balm act to promote exploitation by a sham marriage.

EXAMPLE A highly sensational New York case turned out to be much less satisfactory for the plaintiff. In 1961 an 18-year-old girl sued the estate of film star Errol Flynn for his injuries to her before his death. She claimed that he had first seduced her in Los Angeles in 1957, taking advantage of her immaturity and her "longing to be a star." Her complaint stated in lurid detail how he "led her along the byways of immorality . . . deprived her of the God-given opportunity of coming into bloom as a normal woman."

The judge granted that the young woman had been victimized but dismissed the complaint, contending that the state's heart-balm act "erected an insuperable barrier" to her suit. The girl claimed that her suit was based not on the old form of seduction prohibited by the law but on "debauchery," which her attorney called a more persistent form of sexual immorality. Nevertheless, the judge found that injuries of this sort could no longer be redressed by the recovery of money damages in a court of law.

Recovery of gifts Heart-balm acts created one other legal problem: Did they prevent the recovery of gifts given during courtship or the engagement? In the interest of fairness, New York passed a law saying that the heart-balm act does not prevent either party from recovering courtship or engagement gifts. Rings and other jewelry, bank accounts, and real estate can all be restored to the original owner regardless of who breaks the engagement. Courts in some other states—including California, New Hampshire, New Jersey, and Pennsylvania—have ruled in individual cases that these gifts must be returned if the marriage does not take place.

heat of passion The state of mind that exists when overpowering emotions—such as anger, rage, hatred, furious resentment, or terror—obscure reason and produce impulsive rather than voluntary actions. In the CRIMINAL LAW, a homicide committed in the heat of passion may be reduced from MURDER to MANSLAUGHTER.

heir Someone who inherits property under the laws of DESCENT AND DISTRIBUTION from an ancestor who has died without executing a will. For example, you have two living relatives, your sister and your uncle. Your uncle, who has never married, dies and does not leave a will. Under your state's laws of descent and distribution, you and your sister are your uncle's heirs and will inherit all his property.

Technically, a person who is left real property (real estate) in a will is called a *devisee;* one who is left personal property (any property other than real estate) by a WILL is called a LEGATEE. Often, however, such persons are also referred to as heirs.

held When referring to the decision of a court, the word means decided, as in "the court held that the plaintiff could recover damages." See HOLDING.

henceforth In legal documents, "from the present time forward." It excludes the past. See HEREAFTER.

hereafter In legal documents, a word that always indicates a future time, excluding the present and the past.

hereditament Anything that can be inherited. There are two kinds of hereditaments, corporeal and incorporeal. *Corporeal hereditaments* are permanent, physical objects that can be seen and handled, such as a house, coal, or stone. *Incorporeal hereditaments* are invisible, intangible rights, such as an EASEMENT.

hierarchy A chain of power linking persons together. For example, officers in a church or government form an ascending series of ranks of power. Each rank is subject to the authority of the one immediately above—in most cases, the higher the level, the smaller the number of people. A typical hierarchy is an army, with many privates at the bottom, a number of majors farther up, and only a few generals at the top.

high crimes and misdemeanors The traditional basis for impeaching public officials. The phrase can include felonies or other offenses that have serious governmental or political consequences. Opinions about its exact meaning have differed over the years. See IMPEACHMENT; PRESIDENT.

highway A road or thoroughfare—such as a street, boulevard, or parkway—that is open to public transportation. The character of a public highway must be determined from its origin, the intention and plans of the authorities, and the use to which it has been put. The fact that a road is designated as private does not change its character if it is, in fact, a public road or highway. A PRIVATE ROAD is not intended for the public.

This article covers the ways a highway may be established, the power of public authorities to create and maintain roads, the title and rights to land used as a highway, the removal and responsibility for obstructions, and the role of federal agencies in promoting highway safety.

■ **Establishing highways** Highways may be established in three ways: (1) by PRESCRIPTION, or long use; (2) by the DEDICATION of land to the public by the owner, with the consent of public authorities; and (3) by statute. Prescription and dedication were COMMON LAW methods, not requiring passage of a law; today most highways are established by statute.

Prescription Prescription is public use of a piece of property over a long period of time without the consent of the owner.

EXAMPLE For the past 25 years people have been using a
O—⚹ path through Simon's property, without his permission, as a shortcut to the town swimming pool. This spring Simon decides to put a compost heap in that section of his land to cut down the number of persons using the shortcut. Depending upon the law in his state, Simon may have lost the right to use his property as he wishes if the shortcut has been legally recognized as a highway because of its long use as a thoroughfare. He may even be held liable for obstructing a highway if he decides to go ahead with his plans for the compost heap.

The number of persons actually taking the road or the frequency or extent of the use is unimportant as long as the land is openly and continuously traveled without any restrictions. If the state recognized a prescriptive right after 20 years of public use and Simon put up his compost heap in the 19th year of its use as a shortcut, the highway would not be recognized. But mere verbal objections by the owner or unsuccessful attempts to block the shortcut—such as by posting a "keep out" sign—usually will not prevent recognition.

The right to the land as a highway is an EASEMENT on the owners' property, given to the public. The area covered by an easement is the width and length actually employed for highway purposes.

Any land that becomes a road by long use must meet the conditions set forth in the state's highway statutes.

Statute The establishment of highways is a function of government, and the power to appropriate property for them is by right of EMINENT DOMAIN. The legislature determines what highways are necessary, and it then provides for their establishment by local boards or courts. In determining whether a highway is necessary, a legislature considers such factors as topography, soil character, population, the location of highways already existing or proposed, and the probable extent of the new road's use. Some laws prohibit highways from being laid out through gardens, orchards, dwellings, or commercial buildings.

The legislature creates boards and commissions to construct, improve, and maintain highways. It also forms highway and road districts as subdivisions of the state to aid in the administration of highways.

■ **Alteration, vacation, and abandonment** An alteration of a highway is a change in its course. The state may make an alteration in the public interest.

A highway is vacated when state officials take the proper action to end its existence. Some statutes provide that town highways may be vacated by a vote of the townspeople. As a rule, highways cannot be vacated unless they are useless, inconvenient, or burdensome. Construction of a highway that has been laid out but not built may be discontinued if a change of circumstances—the pattern of traffic, for example—makes it unnecessary.

Nonuse of a highway is regarded as abandonment under some statutory provisions.

EXAMPLE For a number of years, a county fails to repair a
O—⚹ highway. Finally, driving conditions become so hazardous that the public stops using it. If the law in that state contains a nonuse provision, the highway will be considered abandoned.

Delay in opening a highway or failure to repair it will be considered an abandonment only when provided by statute.

■ **Title to land** Generally, the public acquires only a right to use the highway. The owner retains title to his land, and if the highway is discontinued or abandoned, ownership reverts to him. If, however, his land was taken by eminent domain, he is no longer considered the owner of the land because he has received just compensation for it.

■ **Funding for construction and maintenance** Money raised from motor vehicle taxes, gasoline taxes, property taxes, or the sale of bonds may go for the construction and repair of public roads. The power to impose highway taxes is vested in the legislature. The U.S. government administers a federal aid program that assists states in the construction of highways. Under the National System of Interstate and Defense Highways, the federal government provides

90 percent of the funds for the development of highways selected by the state as the primary road system. The improvement of secondary roads is financed on a 70 percent federal and 30 percent state basis.

Duties of highway authorities   The state highway authorities decide whether the construction and maintenance of a highway will be carried out by the state, local communities, or a special agency. The legislature determines the routes of the highways in its state, but the location of a federally aided state highway must be designated according to both federal and state statutes. If the highway has a significant effect on the environment, the project must be approved by the federal Environmental Protection Agency. See ENVIRONMENTAL LAW.

■ **Obstruction**   Officials have a right to obstruct highways to make improvements or repairs, but all unauthorized obstructions that interfere with the use of highways—such as fences, gates, or ditches—are unlawful and are considered under the law to be NUISANCES. Anyone who causes or permits an obstruction to be placed on a public highway may be compelled to remove it.

> EXAMPLE Jim, a local landowner, hires Jake to cut timber on his property. Jake lets a few logs fall onto the highway and obstruct traffic. He makes no attempt to remove them. Alice, driving her car home from work, slams into a log on the highway. She sues Jim for property damage to her car and personal damages for her injuries. Jim is ruled liable. He is also accountable when it is discovered the logs cut off access to a neighbor's property.

■ **Use of the highway**   The state controls the public highways as long as its regulations do not interfere with the right of travel or impede interstate commerce. See COMMERCE CLAUSE. The state may determine what kind of vehicles are allowed on its highways and may exclude those that weigh more than the maximum allowed by law or impose a tax on them based on their excess weight. This is done to compensate for the additional costs of maintaining the highway as a result of severe wear and tear.

To safeguard public health, the state may exclude trucks carrying dangerous chemicals or explosives from passing through populated areas within its borders. In interstate commerce, however, the U.S. Secretary of Transportation regulates the safety performance of all commercial motor carriers of explosives or other dangerous articles, such as flammable or radioactive materials.

The state may also limit the speed of vehicles, outlaw parking on highways except in emergency conditions, and impose restrictions on bicycles on highways—such as requiring them to be equipped with lights at night.

The *law of the road* is a system of rules based on the traditional practices governing safe travel on highways. These rules are frequently embodied in statutes or other government regulations. For example, when two cars approach a highway intersection, the first to reach it has the right of way. If they reach the intersection at about the same time, the car approaching from the right usually has the right of way. These rules are so well established that the law presumes everyone knows them and will comply with them. Anyone who fails to observe the law of the road will be responsible for the damages caused by his NEGLIGENCE. Special circumstances may justify a violation, however—

when, for instance, a person acts to avoid colliding with another car or hitting a pedestrian.

■ **Injuries from badly maintained highways**   Highway authorities—state, county, or municipal—must keep public highways in a safe condition for travel. A failure to do so may impose liability on the authorities for damage to a motor vehicle or injury to its occupants. To hold the highway authority liable, the road must be open for travel. There is ordinarily no liability for injuries on a highway that has been closed for repairs. If you drive on a road closed to traffic, you do so at your own risk. The authority may not be held liable for a private road or one that has not been dedicated as a public highway.

Highway authorities are responsibile if they fail to maintain a safe and convenient highway. The authority is not liable for conditions over which it has no control. When, however, a defect appears on a highway or the danger from a defect is increased by the action of the elements, a highway authority can become liable when it fails to make repairs and a motorist is injured. To be liable, however, the authority must have had sufficient time to make repairs.

> EXAMPLE A county received notice of a defective condition only a few hours before a truck driver was injured and his truck damaged. Extensive repairs were necessary to correct the defect, and men were not immediately available. At least an hour before the accident the county had sent out an employee who put up flare pots and warning signs. When the driver sued the county for damages, the court held that under the circumstances the county was not liable for his injury.

The duty of the authorities is to provide safe streets for prudent drivers. They are not responsible for insuring the safety of drunken persons, or reckless or careless drivers. Nor must they guard against an operator's gross negligence.

Highway authorities are not automatically liable if a motorist or his vehicle is harmed on an unpaved, unimproved street. Nor is it necessarily negligence for authorities to construct a road with a hard-paved surface down the center and a softer surface at the side, to cover the roadbed with a layer of sand or gravel, or to place loose gravel along the shoulders of a macadam surface to level them with the road surface.

Slippery road conditions may be caused by a fresh application of oil, tar, or some other surfacing substance. When the surface is extremely slippery and causes an accident, the person injured can recover damages, as long as he was operating his vehicle carefully. A municipality also may be liable when the slippery condition of the resurfacing material is caused by rain. On the other hand, an accumulation of oil spilled and tracked over a period of time by vehicles belonging to a refining company is not a defect for the purpose of recovering damages.

There is no liability for injury or damage caused by icy or slippery highways when the condition is not due to any negligence on the part of the highway authority. Thus the fact that ice exists on a highway does not by itself make it defective, but liability may be based on negligence in permitting the condition to remain. When, for example, the state had notice that water frequently ran over a road, the state was negligent in allowing water to collect and ice to form and create a hazard to travelers.

The duty of the highway authorities to act against the danger of icy roads is greater in thickly settled areas than in open country. When ice has formed only on a portion of the highway, authorities are bound to take precautions to warn motorists of the dangerous conditions.

A hole, rut, or uneven surface may amount to a defect. In order to impose liability, the rut must make the street unsafe for motorists driving with ordinary care. Liability may not be assumed because of trivial defects. Ruts or uneven surfaces do not make a street unsafe when a great majority of motorists use it without injury. The visibility of the rut or uneven surface is an important factor in deciding whether the defect is one upon which liability can be based.

The highway authorities may be liable for damage to a vehicle or its occupants resulting from an obstruction in the highway if they were negligent in placing—or failing to remove—barriers or warning signals. They are within their rights in closing off any part of the highway they find unsafe for travel.

■ **Federal agencies** In response to the increasing number of deaths and injuries from traffic accidents on the nation's highways, the National Highway Traffic Safety Administration came into being under the Highway Safety Act as part of the Department of Transportation. It sets safety standards and tests vehicles and equipment to see if they comply.

EXAMPLE Recently the National Highway Traffic Safety
0———* Administration tested a well-known manufacturer's automobiles, which were labeled unacceptable by a leading consumer group. The manufacturer claimed that the tests by the group were unrelated to normal highway driving. After its own tests were completed, the administration announced there was no evidence of problems in handling that would pose a threat to the safety of drivers in normal highway driving.

The administration also investigates reports of safety-related defects not covered by any of its standards and can require a manufacturer to take certain action, such as recalling defective vehicles. In recent years the administration has forced manufacturers to recall cars and trucks for defects in such parts as gas tanks, steering mechanisms, brakes, and windshield wipers. An agency recall order may be enforced by court action.

holder A person who legally possesses a negotiable paper, such as a check or a promissory note, and is entitled to payment on it unless there is someone with a greater claim to payment, such as a holder in due course. See COMMERCIAL PAPER.

holder in due course A person who takes a negotiable paper—a check or a promissory note, for example—in good faith, believing it to be valid, and having no knowledge that anything is wrong with it. He is the person with the greatest claim to be paid under the terms stated on the paper. See COMMERCIAL PAPER.

hold harmless Agree to pay any claims that might come up against someone else. For example, the employment contract of a physical education teacher might contain a hold-harmless clause in which the school district

agrees to pay money damages awarded by a court or jury if the teacher is sued by a student who was injured during gym class.

holding The core of a judge's decision; the part of the judge's written opinion that applies the law to the facts of the case. When courts follow the decision of a previous case as established precedent, they rely on the holding only, ignoring any broad generalizations the judge may have made. See DICTUM.

holding company A corporation that, by owning sufficient stock in another company, can dictate that company's policy.

holdover 1 A tenant's possession of real property after his lease has expired without the landlord's consent. 2 An officeholder's continuation in office and exercise of its functions after his term is up.

holiday A consecrated day, day of recreation, or day of cessation from work. A *legal holiday* is a day established by legislative action to commemorate some important historical event. Both public and private businesses usually close on legal holidays; however, private businesses may remain open if they wish. Consult the law of your state to determine the effect of a legal holiday, because it varies from state to state.

holograph A WILL or a DEED to real estate written entirely by the signer with his own hand.

home rule Self-government granted by the state to its local subdivisions, such as cities, towns, and villages.

homestead A FAMILY residence, including the land on which it is situated. As used in various homestead EXEMPTION statutes, the term means the right to have the family home protected from the owner's creditors. The homestead exemption prevents the court from ordering that the property be sold for payment of the owner's debts. On the theory that preservation of the homestead is of greater importance than payment of debts, nearly all the states have enacted homestead exemption laws. Most of them also consider the surviving spouse's right to keep the family home to be superior to any claim by a creditor. See Chart 10.

In some states homesteads are exempt from taxation in whole or in part, particularly from estate taxes. It should be noted, however, that a state law eliminating homesteads from all state tax rolls does not keep them from paying local real estate and school taxes.

homicide The killing of a human being. Homicide is frequently defined as the killing of one human being by another. Homicide may be unlawful or lawful (felonious or nonfelonious), intentional or unintentional. Felonious homicide is killing a human being without legal justification. It is a killing committed with intention, MALICE, or NEGLIGENCE and is either MANSLAUGHTER or MURDER, which are discussed in their respective entries in this encyclopedia. This article discusses nonfelonious homicide, also called justifiable homicide.

Any human being, including an infant, can be a homicide victim. Under the common law, a child had to have been born and have an existence independent of his mother before his death could be considered a homicide. As abortion becomes legalized, however, this distinction in the law is coming under closer judicial scrutiny. For example, abortion during the first trimester is legal because the fetus is not considered to have an independent existence, while it is legal in the third trimester only if the mother's life is in danger, because the fetus is viewed to be a viable human being.

■ **When is a person not responsible?** A person who did not know what he was doing when he committed a homicide (such as a person who was under the influence of angel dust and thought he killed a menacing bear instead of his friend) is not criminally responsible for his act, nor is someone who is insane. The ability of a person to distinguish right from wrong and to know the nature of his act when he did it has been the most frequently applied test of sanity. Some courts hold that a person who acts under an irresistible impulse produced by a disease of the mind is not criminally responsible for a homicide. Anger, jealousy, or an emotional frenzy not associated with mental disease does not excuse a person from responsibility for his actions. See CRIMINAL LAW.

A person who participates in a plan to commit an unlawful act involving danger to life—assault or robbery, for example—is responsible for a homicide committed during the crime, even when he is not the actual slayer and the plan did not originally involve the taking of a life. Such a homicide is called felony murder.

■ **When is homicide justifiable?** A homicide is justifiable when the killer has a legal right to kill, as when he is acting in self-defense. Homicide committed by a policeman when it is the only reasonable way for him to perform his official duties is generally justifiable, but only then. He cannot, for instance, justify taking a life during the course of an argument with his neighbor.

A homicide is justifiable when committed to prevent a serious crime (FELONY) attempted by force, but not to stop a MISDEMEANOR. For example, a person has no right to kill a trespasser when there is no imminent danger of great bodily harm. Killing a felon while trying to ARREST him is usually justifiable if it is the only way to prevent his escape.

Homicide in defense of one's home can be justifiable if it is apparent that the person is making a forcible entry to commit a felony, such as robbery, or to inflict great bodily harm. Before resorting to homicide it is the occupant's duty to try to prevent entry by peaceful means—warning or wounding the assailant, for example—if he can do so without endangering his own safety.

EXAMPLE Arlene and Bill Cleary and their two children O—* were sound asleep when Bill was awakened by footsteps on the first floor of their house and heard the clinking of silver being dropped into a pouch. After awakening his wife and telling her to call the police, Bill took his hunting rifle out of the closet, loaded it, and silently crept down the stairs.

Upon finding the burglar, Bill turned on the lights, telling him to drop everything, that the police would be there in a few minutes. The burglar shot the lights out and nicked Bill's shoulder with a bullet. Bill fired the rifle and hit the burglar between the eyes, killing him. This would be considered justifiable homicide because Bill acted in self-defense in returning the burglar's fire after first trying to handle the situation without the use of deadly force.

If Bill found the burglar in the dark with the intruder's back facing him and proceeded to empty the bullets from his rifle into the burglar without saying anything, Bill's act would not be viewed as justifiable homicide because he made no attempt to deal with the problem without using deadly force. Deadly force may be used to stop a crime only when there is no reasonable alternative available. To justify a homicide committed in SELF-DEFENSE, a person must have had to defend himself against death or severe bodily harm. In most cases, mere threats do not justify a slaying. The courts in some states have said that no words, however offensive, can condone a killing. To invoke the right of self-defense, the slayer must have been free from all fault in provoking the killing. If his acts or words show a willingness to enter the conflict, he cannot plead self-defense. And if he armed himself with a weapon, that may be a significant factor in denying him this defense.

homosexuals, rights of A homosexual is someone whose sexual inclination is toward those of his or her own gender. To date, there is no well-defined body of law on the rights of homosexuals. A financially eligible homosexual couple who are denied a mortgage may sue the bank for discrimination, for example. See CUSTODY; MARRIAGE; PRISONERS' RIGHTS.

honor Pay a negotiable instrument (such as a check) when it is presented. The bank honors your paycheck by cashing it after you endorse it. See COMMERCIAL PAPER.

hornbook A study book summarizing the basic principles of one area of the law—contracts, for instance.

hospital An institution for the care of sick, wounded, infirm, or aged persons. The state has the power to regulate the establishment and maintenance of hospitals, but it usually delegates this authority to its municipalities. Often municipalities also maintain their own facilities.

The rights of patients, particularly mental patients, is a relatively new concern of the law. See PATIENTS' RIGHTS. Among the rights that are becoming widely recognized are (1) admission to a proper facility, (2) release at the right time, and (3) effective orientation of a mental patient on release.

hostile fire A FIRE that becomes uncontrollable or that escapes from where it started and was confined; a fire that was not intended. See also FRIENDLY FIRE.

hostile witness A WITNESS who shows so much prejudice against the party who called him that he can be cross-examined as though he were called by the other side.

housebreaking Breaking and entering a dwelling with the intent to commit a felony inside. If done at night, it is BURGLARY. Housebreaking may also be escaping from a house after illegal access was gained either with or without forcible entry. See ROBBERY.

household A FAMILY living together under one domestic head. Sometimes the word includes servants.

House of Representatives

The chamber of the U.S. CONGRESS, whose members are chosen every second year by the people of the states they represent. The District of Columbia also sends a representative to the House. No one can be a member unless he is 25 years old, has been a U.S. citizen for seven years, and is a resident of the state in which he or she is chosen.

Representatives are apportioned among the states according to their populations, determined by the national census taken every decade in the year ending with zero. The number of representatives may not exceed one for every 30,000 people, but each state must have at least one.

Each state legislature prescribes the time, place, and manner of holding elections for its representatives, but Congress may make or alter those regulations at any time. The House determines the rules of its own proceedings. It may punish or expel members for disorderly behavior.

Most of the legislative work in the House is accomplished by committees. There are 22 regular or "standing" committees, each composed of 30 to 40 members; some 130 subcommittees; joint committees with the Senate; and various other special committees. Committee chairmen are members of the political party that holds a majority in the House. They obtain their posts through seniority and wield much power and influence. See LEGISLATION for an explanation of how a bill gets through the committee system to become a law.

The House has the responsibility of electing a President should no candidate receive a majority of votes from the ELECTORAL COLLEGE. Each state then casts a single vote. Presidents Thomas Jefferson and John Quincy Adams were chosen this way. Only the House of Representatives can initiate IMPEACHMENT proceedings against a President or other federal official (the Senate conducts the trial) and only the House can originate tax bills.

Unlike members of the SENATE, representatives cannot be appointed to fill unexpired terms. When a vacancy occurs in the representation from any state, the governor issues a writ for a special ELECTION to be held to fill it.

Housing and Urban Development, Department of

The department in the President's CABINET that is primarily responsible for developing national policies on housing and land use. The Secretary of Housing and Urban Development (HUD), who heads the agency, is appointed by the President.

HUD See HOUSING AND URBAN DEVELOPMENT, DEPARTMENT OF.

hung jury A JURY so completely divided in opinion that it cannot reach a verdict about a defendant's innocence or guilt. When a hung jury makes a retrial a "manifest necessity," the new trial is not a violation of the constitutional guarantee against DOUBLE JEOPARDY—that is, a second trial for the same offense. The jury is discharged by the court because it cannot reach a verdict. Since no judgment has been made on the defendant's innocence, a new trial is not giving the government a second chance to convict him. It never had a full first chance. See also CRIMINAL LAW.

husband and wife This article discusses the relationship of husband and wife and the legal rights and duties that grow out of it. For information about the relationship between the married couple and society, see MARRIAGE. To see how a marriage is ended legally, see the articles on ANNULMENT and DIVORCE.

A *husband* and *wife* are a man and a woman who are married to each other and thus endowed by law with certain rights and obligations. They are *legal correlatives*, that is, each acquires a status from the relationship with the other. A *spouse* is either a husband or a wife.

Coverture is the period of a marriage. A woman under coverture is a married woman. Sometimes the term *feme covert* is used to mean married woman. *Feme sole* is an unmarried woman.

■ **The English common law of husband and wife** Under the common law, a grown woman had some rights before she married. She could own property, make contracts, and sue or be sued. On the other hand, she had only limited rights of inheritance, and she could not vote, hold public office, or serve on a jury. Those restrictions were removed in the first quarter of the 20th century.

Upon marriage, however, a woman gave up her legal identity as an independent person. A husband and wife were one, and that one was the husband. A wife's personal possessions became the property of her husband, and he had the right to use the land she owned upon marriage or inherited afterward and to keep the rents and profits from it. He could sell these rights, but he could not sell the land. If the marriage produced a child, and the wife died, the husband was entitled to the rents and profits of the land as long as he lived. When he died, the land passed to his wife's heirs. If the marriage was childless and the wife predeceased her husband, the property immediately passed to her heirs.

The law regarding interests other than property rights was equally restrictive for a married woman. She was not allowed to make contracts, either with her husband or anyone else, and she could not sue or be sued without her husband's being joined in the suit. Since a husband could hardly be expected to sue himself, a wife could not in effect sue her husband. She had only the right to bring a matrimonial action in the ecclesiastical (church) courts.

A wife's responsibilities A wife was forbidden from making a will and from testifying for or against her husband, either in civil or criminal lawsuits. The wife was fully responsible for crimes she committed under the common law, but strangely enough, the law presumed that her husband had forced her to do any act she committed in his presence. Novelist Charles Dickens evaluated this rule in *Oliver Twist*:

❝ '*If the law supposes that,' said Mr. Bumble, 'the law is a ass—a idiot. If that's the eye of the law, the law is a bachelor; and the worst I wish the law is, that his eye may be opened by experience—by experience.'* ❞

A husband was liable for his wife's responsibility for causing injuries (torts), whether accidental or intentional.

Under the common law a married woman generally depended on the benevolence of her husband. A wife was entitled to support, but her husband was free to decide the standard of living he would provide. A husband had to pay debts incurred by his wife before their marriage.

Rights of each spouse   The common law preserved certain inheritance rights for husband and wife. The man's right is called CURTESY, and the woman's DOWER.

Under *curtesy,* the husband inherited land that his wife owned during their marriage. He acquired this right only if they had a lawful child born alive, and he had ownership only during his lifetime.

A woman's *dower* was the right to own and use for life one-third of the lands that her husband owned at any time during the marriage. Of course, a husband could write a WILL leaving more to his spouse, but he could not leave less. For a full discussion of modern inheritance rights, see DESCENT AND DISTRIBUTION.

The worst features of the treatment of married women's property rights by the common law were softened in courts of EQUITY, which were specially charged with dispensing fairness in spite of technical rules of law. During the 18th century they allowed a married woman to own her personal property and the income earned on her real estate. The theory was that a husband, because of his obligation to support and protect his wife, really held her property in trust. This meant that he could not waste all of it during their marriage. This also meant that if a daughter married a spendthrift, her father could leave property to her in his will with clear orders that her husband could not take it. The courts also permitted a married woman to do things with the separate property she acquired. She could give it away or sell it, make contracts in connection with it, sue or be sued, and money she owed could be paid out of this separate property.

■ **American law**   The right of a married woman to own property was accepted in this country from the very beginning, but it did not get written into American law until the 19th century. In 1839 Mississippi enacted the first of what were called Married Women's Property Acts. The act permitted husbands to let their wives own property separately. In 1844 Maine—the first northern state to enact such a law—passed a statute requiring husbands to keep their hands off property owned by their wife. Finally, every state gave married women the right to own property free of control by their husband. Gradually, wives won the right to enter contracts; to sell land; to write wills; to sue and be sued; and eventually, in some states, to sue for injuries their husband caused them.

■ **The duties of husband and wife**   A husband and wife are unique in society and in law. Their management of a family unit is more than a business, and their mutual trust and interdependence make them more than a partnership. Because marriage is so important to society, a husband and wife are not free to define their own rights and responsibilities toward each other. Special rules of law determine the limits within which each husband and wife may act.

The obligation to support and to serve   The basic rule of law is that a husband must support and a wife must serve. Traditionally, this has meant that the man must provide a safe house; pay for furniture, utensils, food, clothing, and other necessities; and live in the home. A wife is obliged to keep the home clean and decently furnished, cook and do laundry, live in the home, and have sexual relations with her husband when he desires them.

In law, rights are only as good as remedies. It is small comfort to have a right and no way of enforcing it. Generally, a court will not interfere with an ongoing marriage. If a man decides, for example, to make his wife live on a very small allowance while he pursues education or special training, this is viewed as his decision to invest in the future. As a practical matter, most couples make this kind of decision together. If there is disagreement, however, a court will not hear the wife's lawsuit and then substitute its judgment for that of the husband. This rule is sometimes carried to extremes.

EXAMPLE   In 1953 a Nebraska wife started an action to force her husband to provide her with suitable maintenance and support money. The facts were not in dispute. The husband owned 400 acres of land worth $84,000 and with a rental value of at least $6,000 a year. He owned $104,500 worth of U.S. government bonds and had bank deposits of $12,768.31. The parties had been married in 1919, and at the time of the trial she was 66 years old and he was 79.

From the beginning of their married life the husband supplied only the barest necessities. He did not even pay for groceries until the last three or four years. The only clothing he ever bought his wife was a coat in 1950. He had not taken her to a movie for the past 12 years. They had no social life in the community. The house had no bathing facilities, inside toilet, or kitchen sink. It was heated by an old pipeless coal furnace. The wife had only her chicken-and-egg money until age and poor health stopped this income.

The trial court ruled that the wife was legally entitled to use her husband's credit to pay for repairs, improvements, furniture, and appliances up to several thousand dollars. It ordered the husband to buy a new car, to pay for trips for his wife to visit her married daughters at least once a year, to let her use his credit to buy necessary items, and to give her an allowance of $50 a month. As an alternative to restoring the house, he was permitted to buy a new one if his wife agreed.

The Supreme Court of Nebraska reversed the ruling. It held that as long as the parties were not separated or living apart from each other, the wife could not sue her husband for support and maintenance.

The wife's right to spend her husband's money   A wife does not, simply by marriage, acquire the right to spend her husband's money. If she goes to a store and buys a $50 dress, promising that her husband will pay for it on Friday, he is not obliged to do so. The store may sue the wife, not the husband, for the cost of the dress.

A husband may give his wife the right to spend his money, however. If he supplies her with a credit card, for example, he must pay the bills charged on that account. He may also give her the right to charge things in his name just by letting her do so for a period of time. If a woman buys all her clothes from a special shop and her husband sends a check for whatever is owed at the end of each month, the store may rely on this pattern of doing business. Legally, the wife is an agent for her husband. See AGENCY.

If the husband decides for any reason to cut off the wife's line of credit, he must notify the appropriate people. The wisest plan is for him to send a letter to all the merchants likely to extend her credit, paying whatever balance is owed and directing them to deal only with him in the future. An open announcement in the classified advertising section of the local newspaper may warn merchants who have never dealt with this woman that her husband is no longer assuming responsibility for her debts.

Even without express authority, a wife may always purchase necessaries on her husband's credit. *Necessaries* are food, clothing, and shelter at some humane level. Judges sometimes say the term includes any item required to maintain the standard of living a husband has already established. This has led to decisions ordering husbands to pay for legal fees, medical bills, fur coats, jewelry, and even cases of champagne.

Criminal nonsupport laws   Some states enforce the husband's duty to support the wife with the threat of jail. Criminal nonsupport statutes are intended to keep a man's wife from becoming a public charge. In fact, these laws seldom apply to an ongoing marriage. A man is charged with criminal neglect only after he leaves his wife or locks her out of the house and she then applies for welfare. A man can be convicted only if he can afford to support his wife and refuses to do so.

Money earned by husband or wife   Earnings coming into the family generally belong to the person who earned them. Under the common law, a man must use part of his earnings to support his wife, but a wife need not contribute to her husband's upkeep. A wife who does use her earnings to help support the family is usually presumed to have made a gift. She cannot win back the money later even if the husband is solely responsible under state law for maintaining the family.

A wife cannot earn wages for performing homemaking duties—this is her marital obligation under the law. A woman who voluntarily helps in her husband's business outside the home cannot later collect wages, because any amount of work done is considered her contribution to the family. Most statutes permit a wife to be reimbursed for work done outside the home if her husband expressly agrees to pay her. In the same way, a wife can be her husband's business partner and share in the profits, but there must be clear proof of a partnership agreement.

Support and equal rights   Some recent statutes and cases have moved away from rigid common-law rules and toward greater equality of the sexes. Many states still do not believe a wife should be financially responsible for her husband, or they ask it only when he cannot support himself and is in danger of becoming a public charge.

EXAMPLE In 1975 a man in Louisiana complained that he O——* should not be convicted of criminal neglect of his wife because a Louisiana constitutional provision prohibited any law that "arbitrarily, capriciously or unreasonably" discriminated on the basis of sex. The court held that, because "the husband is invariably the means of support for the couple," the law imposing criminal penal-

ties for husbands who do not provide support for their wives was not unreasonable.

Next, the man argued that the Louisiana law violated the 14th Amendment guarantee of equal protection for all citizens. Again the court answered that the law was valid. That amendment has never been interpreted to mean that men and women are always equal under the law.

Some states have enacted state versions of the proposed federal Equal Rights Amendment. Generally, dependent mates are still given some financial security with their wage-earning spouses. Other states are beginning to make gradual changes in their laws. For example, the word "spouse" is used instead of "husband" and "wife." Laws written to protect the spouse who stays out of the job market in order to care for home and children are still in effect, but they use the term "dependent spouse" rather than "wife," so that in the rare case where a man assumes the dependent role, he receives protection too.

■ **Ownership of property**   The question of who in the marriage owns their property is settled under one of two systems in the United States. Forty-two states recognize separate property, while community property laws apply to the remaining eight—Arizona, California, Idaho, Louisiana, Nevada, New Mexico, Texas, and Washington. Tradition, court decisions, and statutes provide some variations from state to state.

Separate-property states   Each party in separate-property states (also called common-law jurisdictions) usually owns whatever property is in his or her name. This is usually easy to ascertain for such personal items as clothing and jewelry or for possessions that have the name of an owner recorded somewhere, such as homes, automobiles, corporation stock certificates, and bank accounts. It may be more difficult with other types of property, and there are exceptions to the rule.

EXAMPLE Mr. and Mrs. Hardy lived well from 1948 to O——* 1958. He gave her about $125 a week for household expenses, and out of that she paid a maid $35 a week. With whatever money Mrs. Hardy saved, she bought securities. Then she discharged the maid and did the housework herself. She testified in a divorce action that her husband agreed to let her keep what she saved by doing her own housework. She continued to buy stocks. Mr. Hardy claimed that he had made no such agreement and that he did not know about the stocks until 1961.

The court held that the stocks belonged to Mr. Hardy. He was obligated to provide some kind of allowance for his wife's personal needs—such as clothing, entertainment, and transportation—but not a stock portfolio. Mrs. Hardy was entitled to no consideration for doing the housework, because wives are required to do that anyway. Mr. Hardy did not owe the money to Mrs. Hardy, and she could not prove that it was a gift from him.

Separate-property states recognize certain forms of joint ownership by spouses. One kind is called a *tenancy by the entirety.* This means that both husband and wife own the entire property (usually real estate) together. Neither can sell the property or his interest in it alone, and if one dies the other automatically takes full ownership as the survivor. If the husband provided all the money to pay for the property—say a house—the law generally presumes that he intended to give a one-half interest to his wife as a gift. No such presumption arises, however, if the wife buys a house. One state, Pennsylvania, has come to the obvious conclusion that this is discriminatory under the state's Equal Rights Amendment.

Questions of who owns what do not generally come into court during an ongoing marriage. Courts are reluctant to settle disputes over property ownership when a couple is living together. For an explanation of how a court supervises the division of marital property, see DIVORCE.

Community-property states   The laws in community-property states give each husband and wife a one-half interest in what is defined as *community property,* which is everything the couple owns except the separate property of one of them. *Separate property* is whatever each brought to the marriage as well as anything that either inherits during the marriage. What is considered separate property depends on the specific definitions used in each state, however.

EXAMPLE   Carolyn owns stock that brings her about $1,000 a year at the time that she and John are married. After their marriage, John inherits a small apartment building from his mother. Carolyn's stock and John's apartment building are considered separate property in the community-property states. The income earned from both these assets is community property in Texas and Louisiana, but in the other states John is the legal owner of the rental income from his building and Carolyn is the owner of the earnings from her stocks.

Most of the property acquired by husband and wife during marriage is community property in the community-property states, but the laws differ as to how this property is managed. Texas, for example, permits each spouse to manage his or her own earnings, income from separate property, and money DAMAGES recovered for personal injuries. For instance, a wife who inherits an interest in a family business can use the income from it to buy herself a new car every year. Separate property can be subject to joint control by both spouses provided it is actually combined with the couple's community property and they have not agreed to manage it separately. For example, both husband and wife would have joint control of the proceeds from the sale of the house the wife inherited from her mother if the wife pooled the proceeds with the rest of their investment portfolio. In Texas, a couple that has only one wage-earning spouse is in much the same legal position as a couple in a separate-property state; a nonearning spouse really has few property rights during marriage.

Arizona, on the other hand, adheres more closely to the pure community-property theory. In that state, "the spouses have equal management, control, and disposition rights over their community property, and have equal power to bind the community." For a discussion of how community property is divided upon divorce, see DIVORCE.

■ **Inheritance laws for husband and wife**   In separate-property states, modern statutes provide for a surviving spouse to receive a specified share of the deceased spouse's property when he or she does not leave a will. A typical statute directs that a surviving spouse may take one-third or one-half of the estate (or sometimes more), with the size of the share often depending on whether there are also children who survive.

Most states have now abolished the common-law rights of DOWER and CURTESY. See DESCENT AND DISTRIBUTION. Instead, when one spouse leaves a will disinheriting the other, the survivor generally has a right to take an *elective share* (usually one-third) of the deceased spouse's estate. Some of these laws give this right only to a surviving wife. However, the elective-share statutes do not prevent the estate from being dissipated before the spouse dies. A man can, for example, give everything to his children or his mistress during his lifetime and leave little to make up his widow's one-third share. Some states have begun to enact laws that return certain kinds of gifts into a husband's estate in order to enlarge the widow's share.

In addition to giving widows or widowers the right to take a share of a spouse's estate regardless of terms in a will, many states also say that a surviving spouse is entitled to keep certain personal property, called the family exemptions. Included may be the family Bible, car, or kitchen utensils. The right to use the family home after the death of one spouse may be provided for in state HOMESTEAD laws.

In the eight community-property states, each spouse owns one-half of the couple's property. When one of them dies, only half of the marital property is at issue. The law does not force the deceased spouse to leave a particular share of his half to his spouse. This is considered unnecessary. The survivor has already been provided for by his own half interest in the community property.

■ **Sexual relations**   The most distinguishing characteristic of the husband-wife relationship is the legality of the sexual relationship. For example, many states will grant a DIVORCE to a husband or wife who is denied sex by his or her spouse. An ANNULMENT might be granted if the spouse is physically unable to engage in sex or if the spouse committed fraud by concealing the fact that he or she is unable to have children.

The right to marital privacy   The Constitution protects the sexual relationship in marriage by limiting the rights of states to interfere with it. In 1965 the U.S. Supreme Court held in *Griswold* v. *Connecticut* that state laws cannot unreasonably intrude into the marital bedroom. In this case, the Court ruled that Connecticut could not enforce a law making it a crime for doctors to counsel married couples on the subject of birth control. The Court stressed the importance and constitutional dimensions of privacy in marriage. Justice William O. Douglas wrote:

❝ *We deal with a right of privacy older than the Bill of Rights—older than our political parties, older than our school system. Marriage is a coming together for better or for worse, hopefully enduring, and intimate to the degree of being sacred.* ❞

But other states have decided that the amount of privacy to which a husband and wife are entitled is not absolute.

EXAMPLE   In 1976 Arizona held that a man could properly be sentenced to two to four years in prison for violation of state laws prohibiting sodomy and fellatio. The convicted man appealed to a Supreme Court judge on the ground that a state statute cannot prevent married couples from voluntarily performing sodomy or fellatio. But his appeal was rejected because the jury found that his wife had not consented and the state does have the right to protect wives from forcible unnatural sex acts.

Sex crimes It is no defense to criminal charges for any violent sex crime that the accused and the victim were married. But the crime of RAPE does not include forcible natural sexual intercourse between a husband and his wife. This attitude has been frequently criticized because rape is more violent than normal sex acts, but only a few states have changed their laws. Violent assaults on one's spouse are not legal in any state, however, so a vicious rape attack by one's husband may be punishable as assault or even attempted murder.

Abortion and birth control ABORTION is another limitation on the sexual rights of a married couple. A husband has no right to prevent his wife from having a legal abortion, and he cannot force her to have one. A married couple has the right to buy and use contraceptive devices, although a prescription from a licensed physician may be needed to obtain some of them. A person who uses contraceptives or obtains sterilization against the will of a spouse may give grounds for ANNULMENT or DIVORCE.

■ **Tort law for husband and wife** The law of TORTS (injuries to persons or property) has always had special rules for husbands and wives. These rules concern cases against outsiders for harm to the family relationship, the responsibility of one spouse for harm the other causes a third person, and lawsuits between husband and wife.

Loss of consortium An action for loss of consortium is a lawsuit demanding money damages for the inconvenience of having an injured spouse. Lawsuits have been won for injuries resulting from medical malpractice, assault and battery, train and automobile accidents, the sale of habit-forming drugs, injury by vicious animals, and even false imprisonment, malicious prosecution, or libel and slander, if they have a debilitating effect.

Consortium is the right to services performed by a spouse. Under the old common law, a wife could not sue for her injuries because she had no legal right to sue. A husband was believed to have suffered real legal damages, however, if his wife was temporarily incapacitated. His claim was that someone had harmed his wife so that she could not provide him with her companionship, sexual relations, and regular services, which included cooking, cleaning, industry, and frugality. As time went on, even if a man's wife was not responsible for housekeeping in their home—for example, if they had a maid—he was still able to recover damages just for the loss of fellowship, affection, and sexual intercourse. Originally, the right to sue for loss of consortium belonged only to a husband. Today, however, a wife as well as a husband can sue for loss of consortium. But it was not until 1950 that a court gave a woman that right, and for a time the decision faced strong opposition.

EXAMPLE A man was seriously injured while working, and O—* his wife sued the employer for loss of consortium. The District of Columbia court that heard the case rejected the rule that only husbands could sue for loss of consortium as being arbitrary.

The person suing for loss of consortium must often assert his or her claim in the same lawsuit in which the other spouse is suing the third party to recover damages for injuries. The purpose of this is to prevent double recoveries. Some states recognize that there may be times when it is inconvenient or impossible to join both claims. Then the judges try to supervise whichever suit is second, to make sure that juries do not get carried away in determining the amount of damages.

Interference with the marital relationship At one time a husband could sue a person who induced or compelled his wife to live away from him. He acted under the law that entitled him to sue for damages anyone who deprived him of a servant.

Today other types of lawsuits can be brought against a person who interferes with a marriage. They are called "heart-balm" actions. The plaintiff claims that a recovery of money damages will soothe his broken heart. See HEART-BALM ACT.

A husband can sue another man for interfering with his marital rights through lawsuits for alienation of affections and criminal conversation. *Alienation of affections* means winning away the heart of another man's wife. *Criminal conversation* is a euphemism for adultery.

An injured husband can file suit for criminal conversation if his wife was raped, consented to adultery, or actually sought it.

EXAMPLE When one defendant, Harry, was charged with O—* criminal conversation, he claimed his innocence. Harry insisted he should not have to pay because the woman had actively seduced him. The judge snapped that "that old cowardly excuse" had not saved Adam and it would not save him.

Criminal conversation is said to interfere with the husband's exclusive right to his wife's sexual services, but cases have been won by men who were admittedly impotent. The real basis of recovery is the preservation of the integrity of the family by guaranteeing the husband's exclusive rights to his wife. England abolished the action for criminal conversation in 1857, but only a few states have done that in this country.

Alienation of affections requires proof that the husband has been deprived of the love, companionship, and comfort of his wife. There must be some noticeable difference in her conduct toward him, but it is not necessary to show that she has committed adultery, abandoned their home, or neglected her housekeeping. In truth, these actions have been brought at least as often against a meddling mother-in-law as against a lover.

■ **Responsibility for injuries** At common law, a husband was liable for all the torts committed by his wife because she could not be sued alone. In every state in this country, however, specific statutes or the Married Women's Property Acts make women fully responsible for accidental and intentional injuries they cause others.

Either spouse can be directly liable for injuries caused by the other if he himself is also negligent. This is a common rule of torts that has nothing to do with the husband-wife relationship. For example, a wife may be guilty of negligence for accidentally poisoning a guest, but her husband may also be responsible if he recklessly stored the poison in a sugar bowl.

A husband or wife can also be responsible for his or her spouse's actions when acting on behalf of the family. For example, many states hold a husband liable for injuries caused by his wife when she is driving his car if she is on family business, such as food shopping. See FAMILY CAR

DOCTRINE; RESPONDEAT SUPERIOR. A person who employs a spouse in business is responsible for the spouse's torts just as he is for those committed by any employee. See AGENCY.

The right to sue one's spouse Special rules have always applied to lawsuits between a husband and wife. Originally, they could not sue each other, because in law they were one. Today about one-half of the states have eliminated this *tort immunity* or at least permit lawsuits in cases of NEGLIGENCE. The greatest benefit of this change is to allow a person to recover insurance money after an auto accident caused by a spouse. See TORT.

The question of allowing lawsuits based on a spouse's intentional violation of property rights is a different matter. Courts have generally held that the Married Women's Property Acts gave wives the right to sue their husband for violating their property rights. Thus a wife may, for example, sue for CONVERSION (wrongfully appropriating someone else's property) if her husband uses her shares of stock for himself, or for waste if he cuts timber on her property in a way that ruins the land, or for FRAUD if he talks her into signing over the house by lying to her. Of course, the same laws allow a husband to sue his wife.

Most states do not allow lawsuits between a husband and wife for personal injuries intentionally caused, such as assault and battery, false imprisonment, malicious prosecution, or defamation. The reasoning of the courts generally is that each spouse has enough remedy in the criminal and divorce laws. To permit lawsuits for money damages to compensate for personal injuries would destroy the harmony of the home.

■ **Abuse by husband or wife** Today it is illegal to assault your spouse, but wife-beating and assaults on husbands still occur. Until recently, victims of domestic violence did not talk about it. But as the women's rights movement gained momentum, wives were encouraged to speak up and seek help if their husband abused them, and legal authorities became aware of the scope and severity of the problem. State laws that attempt to cope with the special nature of abuse by a husband or wife (spousal abuse) are still developing.

Basically, the law is clear. It is illegal to beat someone, even one's husband or wife. If the aggressor and the victim live together, enforcement of this law is difficult. Wives frequently say that they do not want to divorce their husband or send him to jail; these women simply do not want to be beaten. Many women have complained that police are not helpful.

EXAMPLE Roxanne Gay, wife of professional football player Blenda Gay, said that on one occasion when she called for assistance, police officers ended up talking football with her husband. Mrs. Gay claimed that her husband, a 255-pound defensive lineman for the Philadelphia Eagles, beat her regularly throughout their marriage. In 1976 she stabbed him to death. She was acquitted by reason of insanity and committed to a psychiatric hospital for treatment of paranoid schizophrenia. The judge found that there had been playful "roughhousing," but Mrs. Gay had built these incidents up in her mind as beatings.

Sometimes the victim endures years of torment, and the law gets involved only after he or she finally strikes back.

EXAMPLE One Jackson, Michigan, housewife said that her husband had beaten her for 15 years whenever he was displeased with her cooking or clothes. Finally, she poured gasoline around his bed one night and set it ablaze. The jury acquitted her of murder on grounds of temporary insanity.

Attorneys who have defended battered women warn that it is just as illegal to murder a bad husband as a good one. A jury may sympathize but still convict because killing is not an acceptable way to solve the problem.

Defenses against abuse Wives have been acquitted of homicide for acting in SELF-DEFENSE. Their lawyers point out that a small woman with a weapon may be no more than an even match for a bigger man.

EXAMPLE One defendant in Fort Lauderdale, Florida, emptied a gun into her husband's body after he attacked her with a rusty kitchen knife. She was acquitted. But deadly force can be used only to stop an immediate threat of deadly force. A woman who waited for her drunken husband to pass out and then sewed him up in the bedsheet before attacking him could not use a plea of self-defense to earn acquittal.

One obvious remedy for spousal abuse is to seek a divorce or a legal separation. If the parties are legally separated, the abusive spouse has no right to enter the home of the separated spouse. It may be possible to have an order included in the separation decree prohibiting the abusive spouse from harming or molesting the other. A violation of such an order could be punishable as a CONTEMPT of court.

An abused spouse who wishes to keep the marriage together must try to deal with all the serious psychological problems accompanying domestic violence. Some states provide counseling services; the abusive spouse is sometimes ordered by the court to seek counseling. Domestic violence cases must be sent to special family courts in some states, especially if the marriage can be saved.

Many professionals in the field of family relations believe that prompt enforcement of existing criminal laws would go far to deter spousal abuse. Policemen are reluctant to walk into family disturbances, however, because they are injured more often in these than in any other kind of situation and because they have trouble judging the seriousness of each individual case.

EXAMPLE In 1976, 71 women sued the New York City Police Department claiming that it had unlawfully denied them assistance when they reported beatings. After two years, the city's attorneys entered into an out-of-court settlement with the women on behalf of the Police Department. Without admitting guilt, the Police Department obligated itself to arrest any husband who seriously batters his wife or assaults her with a deadly weapon. They agreed that a suspect would not be released simply because he was married to the victim, nor would they let him go free just because he had already left the scene. In other words, as one lawyer said, battered women in New York City "are now officially entitled to the same police protection as other victims of crimes."

■ **Husband-and-wife conspiracies** A husband and his wife could not be convicted of conspiracy under the common law, because it was legally impossible for them to plot together since they were considered one person. More recently, almost every state that has had occasion to reconsider the common-law rule has rejected it. Noting that the "oneness" of husband and wife is no longer recognized in other areas of the law, courts have decided that criminal plots hatched by a husband and wife are just as dangerous to society as conspiracies by other people.

■ **Love-triangle murders** Some states actually enacted laws that permitted a husband to kill his wife's lover. In fact, Utah, New Mexico, and Texas, which called the act justifiable HOMICIDE, have only recently repealed them. In a number of states, a person who kills a spouse or paramour upon discovering them in adultery can be convicted of voluntary manslaughter, a lesser charge than murder, simply because the provocation is so serious. Many an enraged husband has not been convicted at all because he found a sympathetic jury.

■ **Husband or wife as a witness** The law of evidence includes a special privilege for husbands and wives. The common-law rule originally prohibited one spouse from testifying either for or against the other, but each state has a variety of exceptions. The purpose of the rule was to protect family harmony and privacy and to encourage marital communication by absolutely forbidding either spouse to reveal statements made in confidence.

Generally, a husband or wife may testify against a spouse accused of injuring him or her or their child. Various courts also allow one spouse to testify against another accused of certain crimes against the family relationship—such as bigamy, adultery, rape—and during abandonment or support proceedings.

In 1980 the Supreme Court decided that one spouse could *voluntarily* testify against another in a federal criminal prosecution. In state criminal prosecutions, 24 states permit a spouse to testify against the other only if the accused spouse consents. In the other states, the husband or wife of an accused is considered an ordinary witness who can be compelled to testify against his or her spouse.

EXAMPLE In one case, a man shot his wife in the arm and it
O——* had to be amputated. The court held that the woman was entitled to testify against her husband, but she could not be compelled to do so. By contrast, another wife was compelled to testify against her husband when he was accused of transporting her across a state line for prostitution.

Divorce generally destroys the privilege of not testifying against a spouse.

■ **A married woman's name** For centuries women traditionally took their husband's surname when they married. It was only when a substantial number of women began to claim a freedom of choice between their maiden and married names that the law became involved.

EXAMPLE In 1971 a married woman sued to force the state
O——* of Alabama to issue her driver's license in her maiden name. Alabama claimed its common-law rule was that every woman's legal name was her husband's surname and that for accurate record keeping it was more efficient to require everyone to use a specified legal name on drivers' licenses. The U.S. Supreme Court affirmed the decision.

Many other states hold that each person may be called by whatever name he likes as long as he uses it consistently and without any purpose to defraud someone else. A number of states have specifically held that a married woman need not use her husband's surname or that she may use her married name in her personal life and her maiden name in her professional life. In 1975 the Supreme Court of Wisconsin said that a woman's married name is not her legal name except as "the result of usage and her holding out to the world that the surname is the same as the husband's."

Laws that create procedures for changing one's name, which many states have, do not interfere with a woman's right to take her husband's surname when she marries him.

■ **Equality under the law** The equal protection clause of the Constitution says that no state shall "deny to any person within its jurisdiction the equal protection of the laws." But the Supreme Court has never said that this means states cannot write laws that treat husbands and wives differently. In a number of cases, the Court has considered whether particular laws go beyond what is reasonable and are, therefore, unconstitutional. It is not always easy to predict how a decision will go.

EXAMPLE In 1971 the Supreme Court invalidated an Idaho
O——* statute that favored males over females as administrators of estates. The statute provided for the appointment of a deceased person's father rather than his mother to administer his estate after his death without any hearing to determine who was better qualified.

EXAMPLE In 1973 the Court held unconstitutional a law that
O——* always gave dependent's benefits to the wife of a soldier but permitted the husband of a servicewoman to receive the same benefits only if his wife provided more than half of his support.

EXAMPLE In 1974 the Court permitted Florida to give a
O——* property-tax exemption to women who were widowed but not to men. The majority held that it was reasonable to give elderly women a break because most women are not in fact financially equal to men.

EXAMPLE In 1975 the Court ruled that it was unfair to
O——* convict someone with a jury picked by a system that excluded women. The Court said that "states are free to grant exemptions from jury service to individuals in case of special hardships or incapacity," but it is not reasonable to excuse all women on the ground that they cannot be spared from household duties. In the same year, the Court said that widowed fathers with low incomes must, like widowed mothers, be permitted to receive Social Security benefits when they care for children.

Laws that treat husbands and wives differently are constitutional. The rights, responsibilities, and privileges described in this article continue to depend largely on the sex of a spouse. If the Equal Rights Amendment to the U.S. Constitution is ratified, many of the existing principles of law, which impose specific rights and obligations on one sex or the other, would be changed by constitutional mandate. See also EQUAL PROTECTION OF LAWS.

hypothetical question A question directed to an expert WITNESS in a lawsuit. A hypothetical question is framed to include all the facts in EVIDENCE that are necessary to form an opinion. Then, assuming the facts to be true, the witness is asked if he has been able to form an opinion and if so to state it.

ICC Interstate Commerce Commission. See COMMERCE CLAUSE.

illegal   Against the law, but not necessarily immoral.

illegitimacy   The state of being born out of wedlock or unlawfully conceived. This article explains the presumption of legitimacy; how an illegitimate child may become legitimate; the rights and duties of unmarried parents to their children; paternity suits; and the legal rights of illegitimate children, whose number has increased more than five times in recent years. The term *nonmarital child* is beginning to replace *illegitimate child* in legal usage.

■ **Who is illegitimate**   At common law, a child born of a married woman was presumed legitimate, but when circumstances made it physically impossible for the mother's husband to be the father—as when he was impotent or had been away from his wife at the time of conception—the child was traditionally labeled a bastard. At common law, the children born of a void (illegal) marriage were illegitimate. For instance, if a man took a second wife while he was still married to the first, any children born of this bigamous marriage would be considered illegitimate.

Illegitimate and legitimate children were treated differently under the common law, partly because of the Judeo-Christian belief in the sanctity of marriage and partly because blood relationships determined property rights. The legal rights and obligations of a person born to married parents could be established with greater certainty than those of a person born out of wedlock. Finally, society's wish to maintain a stable family structure also contributed to a preference for a legitimate child.

The distinction between legitimate and illegitimate children still remains, but not to the same extent that it existed under the common law. Most states have agreed for some time that the child of almost any union that resembles a formal marriage is entitled to legitimate status. This may include children of parents whose marriage was voidable (without legal effect if one of the parties chose to get out of it) because they failed to comply with formal requirements, such as not meeting the age requirements. It may also include children whose parents' marriage was void—perhaps because one parent was already married.

A common-law MARRIAGE occurs when a man and a woman live together for a long time and present themselves to others as husband and wife without having formalized their union according to the laws of the state. In the states that recognize common-law marriages as valid, the resulting children are legitimate.

■ **Presumptions of legitimacy**   It is the policy of the law to favor the legitimacy of children for the sake of stable family relationships and society. This PRESUMPTION of legitimacy is one of the strongest presumptions known to law. It can be rebutted or destroyed only by facts that clearly establish that the child is illegitimate. A child born in wedlock is presumed to be the legitimate child of the husband unless facts clearly show that it would be impossible for the husband to be the father—for example, if he had had a vasectomy or was not with his wife when the child was conceived. Blood tests that exclude a husband as the father may or may not be sufficient to destroy this presumption, depending on the particular state's attitude.

A child born during a valid marriage is presumed legitimate even if the birth occurred so soon after the wedding that it is certain he was conceived before the marriage. A child conceived during marriage but born after the marriage is ended by ANNULMENT or DIVORCE is also legitimate.

These presumptions are important in a number of lawsuits in which the legitimacy of a child is challenged, including proceedings to determine the right to inherit or share in property and a suit by a mother seeking child support from a man other than her husband.

Rebutting and supporting the presumption   Some states permit a husband to deny or contest the legitimacy of a child born in wedlock in a divorce suit based on adultery. In this case, however, the issue of legitimacy is subordinate to the main issue of adultery. If the court finds that the facts do not sufficiently establish adultery, it cannot decide the question of legitimacy.

Once a parent acknowledges a child, the child is presumed legitimate, and the presumption cannot be rebutted when it has been established for a long period of time.

EXAMPLE   A couple—call them Lowell and Karen—had been
O—✳ married for 21 years, during which time four children were born. When Karen filed for divorce, she requested support and custody of three of the children;

the husband kept one. The divorce was granted. But in order to escape responsibility for some of the child support, Lowell denied paternity of their 15-year-old twins, whom he had acknowledged as his own since their birth. When Lowell asked the New Hampshire court to consider the results of blood tests that proved he was not their father, the court refused, saying that blood tests could not be used to rebut the presumption of legitimacy when the man had acknowledged the children as his own without challenge for 15 years.

When a person uses the presumption of legitimacy to support a claim, he may have to prove certain facts. If, for example, someone challenges your right to share in the property of your deceased father, you may have to establish both that your mother and father were lawfully married and that the date of your birth indicates you were conceived during or in the nine months before their marriage.

Infidelity of the mother of a child conceived or born in wedlock cannot be used to rebut the presumption if the adulterous acts were committed before the marriage or after the birth of the child. But evidence of adultery at or about the time the child was conceived may be used to rebut the presumption when it supports proof that the husband was incapable of fathering the child, because he was sterile or impotent or was not near his wife. Sometimes physical characteristics or resemblance in appearance between the child and the alleged father has been allowed to establish legitimacy.

■ **Legitimation** Legitimation is the act of changing the status of a child from illegitimate to legitimate. Under some laws, a child may be legitimated when the father openly acknowledges that the child is his. Oral admissions of paternity to friends and acquaintances are enough unless state law requires a written statement. If the statement must be in writing, any document with an admission in it will serve as acknowledgment of paternity—even a letter written to the child by his father that reads, "Dear Son . . . Love, Father." Some states require that the acknowledgment be signed in the presence of witnesses. A motel registration card, for instance, signed by the father for himself and for his daughter in the presence of the night clerk was considered sufficient. So was a father's employment application listing his illegitimate son as his dependent signed before the personnel supervisor.

Most laws, however, require an act in addition to acknowledgment before a child can be declared legitimate. For instance, some states recognize a child born out of wedlock as legitimate if the child is acknowledged by the father and taken into his family with the consent of his wife. Some states will accept the subsequent marriage of an illegitimate child's natural parents. A few states provide that all children are the legitimate children of their natural parents—and thus do not classify any child as illegitimate, even if born out of wedlock.

The law of the state in which the father lives determines whether or not his acts have legitimated the child in all the other states.

EXAMPLE The father of an illegitimate child resided in state O—* R. The child lived with his mother in state M. Under the law of state R, a written acknowledgment of paternity by a natural father legitimates the child. This was not true under the law in state M. The father wrote a letter in state R in which he addressed his child as "Dear Son" and sent the letter to the child in state M. The father subsequently died and did not leave a will. The son claimed to be his father's heir under a law that permitted only legitimate children to inherit from their fathers. (Today this law would be unconstitutional.) The son was entitled to inherit as an heir of his father, because the act by which the father acknowledged that the boy was his son satisfied the requirements for legitimization in state R, the father's domicile.

Once a child is deemed legitimate, he receives the same rights and protection as a child whose legitimacy has never been questioned.

Birth records In nearly all states, the illegitimate (nonmarital) child has the right, upon legitimation, to have any reference to his former illegitimate status removed from all birth records. Some states permit birth certificates to be amended or new ones to be issued when paternity is established in a court proceeding or by a legally sufficient acknowledgment, even though the child may not be legitimized by these actions. Often there is the provision that the new certificate cannot show that it is not the original. Similarly, to prevent the information that a child was born out of wedlock from becoming generally available, many statutes require that all official proceedings relating to a child's parentage—including those for ADOPTION—be confidential.

■ **Right to custody** The natural parent of an illegitimate child is entitled above all others to custody of the child if the parent is a fit and proper person who will not jeopardize the child's welfare. The mother is usually given first priority over the father, but this right is not absolute and must yield to the best interests of the child as determined by the court. The father of an illegitimate child has, in general, the right to custody against all persons except the mother.

Rights of unmarried fathers In the past, the laws governing illegitimate children were based on the belief that fathers of illegitimate children were irresponsible and unconcerned about the welfare of their children. Recent decisions, however, have shown a shift in the attitude toward unmarried fathers who have assumed some kind of responsibility for their children.

EXAMPLE In 1972, in *Stanley* v. *Illinois,* the Supreme Court O—* struck down an Illinois law that denied only unwed fathers (unlike all other parents) a hearing to determine whether they were fit to take custody of their children upon the death of the mother. Stanley, the father, had lived with a woman for 18 years without marrying her. They had had three children whom they had both raised as a family. When the mother died, the children were declared wards of the state and placed by the court with guardians. The father was not even given a hearing to determine whether he was an unfit parent before his children were removed from his custody. He claimed that since married fathers and unwed mothers could not be deprived of their children without a hearing, unwed fathers were being denied equal protection of laws guaranteed by the federal Constitution. The Court agreed.

Consent for adoption The *Stanley* decision has had an impact in cases where the unwed mother has later married and her husband wants to adopt her illegitimate child. When a child is legitimate, the consent of both parents is required for adoption unless one parent has given up his rights to the child, as by abandoning him. In the past, if the child was illegitimate, many states required only the consent of the natural mother for adoption. An unwed father, regardless of his involvement with his child, had no right to prevent his child's adoption. This is no longer the case. A new rule was established in a case in which Georgia's adoption laws were challenged as an unconstitutional violation of the equal protection guarantee. These laws did not deny all unwed fathers the authority to prevent the adoption of their illegitimate children, but only those who had never assumed responsibility for their children.

EXAMPLE An illegitimate child had remained in the custody O—* of his mother. His father contributed to his support, but irregularly. The mother later married and her husband wanted to adopt the child. The natural father had notice of the adoption proceedings and tried to prevent the adoption. He did not want custody, he merely sought visitation rights. Under Georgia law, an unwed father acquires the power to veto the adoption of his child only if he legitimates his child. The unwed father in this case had never attempted to legitimate his child. The trial court decided it was in the best interests of the child to remain in his existing family and granted the adoption.

The father appealed, alleging that the adoption laws violated his right to equal protection of the laws. He claimed that his interests in the adoption were no different from those of a married father who was divorced from the mother and living apart from the child so that the different treatment was not justified. The U.S. Supreme Court disagreed. The unwed father in this case "never exercised legal or actual custody of his child, and thus had never shouldered any significant responsibility with respect to the daily supervision, education, protection, or care of the child. . . . In contrast . . . even a father whose marriage has broken apart will have borne full responsibility for the rearing of his children during the period of the marriage." The difference in treatment of unwed fathers who had never assumed responsibility for their children and all other fathers was justified.

In 1979 the U.S. Supreme Court decided that a New York law that permitted an unwed mother, but not an unwed father, to block the adoption of their child by withholding her consent was unconstitutional as a violation of the equal protection clause. See EQUAL PROTECTION OF LAWS.

EXAMPLE During the five years a man and woman had lived O—* together, two children were born. The man, named as father on each child's birth certificate, lived with the mother and children until the woman left him,

HOW THE LAW VIEWS THE ILLEGITIMATE CHILD AND HIS PARENTS

■ The presumption of legitimacy is one of the strongest presumptions in law—a child born in wedlock is presumed to be the husband's legitimate child unless facts prove it to be impossible—for example, the father was away at the time of conception.

■ A child born during a marriage is presumed legitimate even if birth occurred so soon after the wedding that it is certain the child was conceived before marriage.

■ A child conceived during a marriage but born after a divorce or annulment is also legitimate.

■ In states that recognize common-law marriages as valid, the resulting children are legitimate.

■ *Legitimation* means changing the status of a child from illegitimate to legitimate. This may be accomplished by the father's acknowledging the child as his (in some states, an oral admission suffices) or by an act in addition to the acknowledgment, such as the subsequent marriage of the child's natural parents.

■ In a few states, *all* children are considered the legitimate children of their natural parents.

■ In nearly all states, when an illegitimate child has been legitimated, any reference to his former illegitimate status is removed from all records, including his birth certificate.

■ When custody of an illegitimate child is at issue, the mother has first priority over the father, but this right must yield to the child's best interests as determined by the court. The father generally has the right of custody against everyone but the mother.

■ Fathers now have visitation rights in all states unless the court decides in an individual case that it is against the child's best interests to have his natural father see him.

■ An unmarried mother is responsible for supporting her child, but she may bring a paternity suit to compel the natural father to provide support. If she does not start the suit within the time limit specified by law, she loses her right to establish the father's paternity and his obligation of support.

■ Under some state laws, the sole testimony of the mother may be enough to determine that the defendant is the father. Other laws require corroboration or additional evidence.

■ Some states give great weight to blood tests proving nonpaternity of the alleged father. Others give blood tests no more weight than any other evidence because they believe that slipshod testing often causes errors. Unless required by state law, a court cannot compel the parties to take blood tests in paternity suits.

■ The states disagree about whether it is proper to bring the child into the courtroom so that the jury can consider his or her resemblance to the alleged father. In some states, the child is not brought before the jury, but racial characteristics may be compared by photographs.

■ In some states, failure to support one's illegitimate child is a crime.

■ In almost all states, an illegitimate child has the same right to inherit from his mother as a child born in wedlock. An illegitimate child has the right to inherit from his natural father when he dies without leaving a will, but his rights are not equal to those of a legitimate child.

■ The best way to protect an illegitimate child's inheritance rights is by legitimation.

taking the children with her. The father kept in touch with the children. After her marriage, the woman and her new husband petitioned the court to adopt the children. Their father also sought to adopt the children.

A court granted the mother's petition. State law only gave the unwed father, regardless of any responsibilities he had assumed toward his child, the right to be heard in opposition to a proposed adoption proceeding, not the right to veto it. Such an adoption could only be stopped if it were shown that it was not in the children's best interests.

On appeal in state court, the father unsuccessfully argued that the state law was unconstitutional because the difference in treatment between unwed mothers and fathers was based solely on their sex. The U.S. Supreme Court, however, agreed with his argument and reversed the appellate court's decision. An unwed father could not be deprived of the right to consent to his child's adoption solely because he was a man.

The Court held that treating unwed mothers and fathers differently was not substantially related to the state's interest in providing illegitimate children with adoptive homes. This does not mean, however, that the consent of an unwed father must be obtained in every adoption proceeding. "In those cases where the father has never come forward to participate in the rearing of his child, nothing in the equal protection clause precludes the state from withholding from him the privilege of vetoing the adoption of the child." The Court also noted that, under the laws of that state, adoption proceedings may take place without the father's consent if the father has abandoned the child.

The state law challenged in this case was unconstitutional because it deprived *all* unwed fathers, whether or not they demonstrated a significant paternal interest in the child, of the right to veto the adoption of their children.

Visitation rights   Although at common law an unwed father was entitled to visit his child, many statutes in the past categorically denied him visiting rights. Today the fit though unwed father has been specifically granted visitation rights in many states, including Alabama, California, Massachusetts, New York, Pennsylvania, and Wisconsin, and may be considered to have visitation rights in all other states. Courts may refuse to grant visitation rights, however, when they decide that it is against the child's best interests to allow his natural father to see him. For instance, if the child goes into a severe depression and refuses to eat for a week after his natural father visits him, or if the father uses his visitation rights as a tactic to disrupt the lives of the mother and child, the court may stop the visits.

■ **Paternity suits**   An unmarried mother has the basic responsibility for supporting her child, but she can bring a civil action called a paternity suit or affiliation proceeding against the natural father to compel him to provide support—and also, in many instances, to pay her pregnancy expenses. In some states she can initiate proceedings that can result in criminal penalties.

The action must be brought in a court that has personal jurisdiction (authority) over the alleged father—that is, a court in the state where he lives. The mother or child does not have to live in that state, nor need the child to have been born or conceived there unless required by statute. The state in which the suit is taken to court will apply its own laws in determining the rights of the parties. Such a suit must be started within the time specified by state law. When bastardy proceedings are criminal actions, however, they must be brought in the state where the crime (fathering the illegitimate child) occurred.

Parties   Paternity suits are usually started by the mother of the child. If the mother is a minor (under the age of legal adulthood), some states require that the proceedings be initiated on her behalf by her guardian or legal representative, such as her parent. Some laws provide that public authorities, such as the local social services department, may bring a paternity suit if the mother refuses to do so or if she ends her lawsuit after accepting an inadequate settlement of her claim against the child's father. If proceedings are not started within the time limit specified by law, the mother loses her right to establish the father's paternity and his obligation of support.

Evidence   The purpose of a paternity suit is to establish that the man is the father of the child so that the duty of support can be imposed upon him.

Blood tests   Unless required by law, a court cannot compel the parties to submit to blood tests in paternity actions. Blood tests are useful because if the blood types of a mother and father are known, it is possible to predict by the laws of genetics that their children will have one of several blood types and definitely will not have others. In paternity suits, blood tests are evidence only to establish that the defendant could *not* be the child's father. If the test shows nonpaternity, its reliability is high.

EXAMPLE   Suppose both the mother and the alleged father, the defendant, have blood type A and the child has blood type B. It is genetically impossible for the defendant to be the father. At least one parent of the child has to have type B blood because everyone inherits his blood type from his parents. Because the mother does not have type B, it would have to be inherited from the father. Therefore, the defendant, who has type A, cannot be the child's father.

A number of states authorize and give great weight to blood tests establishing nonpaternity. Others give blood tests only the same weight as other evidence, because they believe that slipshod and inadequate testing often causes errors in the results. When the scientific evidence and the human testimony conflict, a jury must determine which is the more believable.

EXAMPLE   In a 1946 case, a California jury disregarded blood tests that established the nonpaternity of Charlie Chaplin in an affiliation proceeding and decided that he was the father of an illegitimate child, legally liable for her support. As recently as 1974, the North Carolina Supreme Court upheld a jury's decision to disregard blood test results that excluded the defendant as father.

Other evidence   The issue of paternity is determined from all the evidence that can help the jury reach a judgment. Under some laws, the sole testimony of the mother may be enough to determine that the defendant is the father. Other laws require corroboration, or additional evidence. The mother's general reputation for chastity or the lack of it usually cannot be offered as evidence. In some states, however, this evidence is allowed when it is for the time period within which the child was conceived—for example, if the mother had sexual relations with other men about nine months before the baby's birth. Statements, declarations, and admissions of the defendant tending to show paternity can be used. Intimacy between the parties may be shown. Acts of intercourse before the alleged act that resulted in conception may indicate the probability of intercourse at the time stated in the complaint. The states disagree about whether it is proper to bring the child into court so the jury can consider his resemblance to the alleged father. It may be allowed if the child is old enough to have well-defined features. In some states the child is not brought before the jury but racial characteristics may be compared on the basis of photographs.

In a civil proceeding, the issue of paternity must be proved by a PREPONDERANCE OF EVIDENCE. This means that the facts presented—such as the testimony of the mother or testimony of witnesses who state that the mother and alleged father lived together until the child was born—must be more convincing that the defendant is the father than the evidence offered that he is not the father. When the proceedings are criminal (in states that allow them), the facts must show BEYOND A REASONABLE DOUBT that the defendant is the father of the child. The evidence must show that the mother had sexual intercourse with only the defendant during the period when the child was conceived.

Defenses   Any matter that shows the defendant's innocence or that bars the right to proceed against him in a paternity suit may be used as a defense. For example, if the defendant can show that he was stationed with the U.S. Army in Alaska at the time of the child's conception, the suit will be dismissed. It is no defense to show that the mother of the child already has another illegitimate child. Once a paternity suit has been decided by the court, the issue of paternity cannot be tried again.

Settlements   A settlement of the paternity obligation by contract between the mother and father may also serve as a valid defense to a paternity suit. Statutes often require, however, that a COMPROMISE AND SETTLEMENT meet a prescribed minimum and be officially approved, either by a court or by the state's attorney. When a mother of an illegitimate child releases the reputed father from support for a settlement in an amount less than the minimum set by statute, she may bring a paternity action against him unless the court had approved the settlement. The law will not allow a child's right to support to be bargained away or defeated by an inadequate settlement.

EXAMPLE A wealthy politician seduces a young girl who later bears him an illegitimate child. The politician offers the girl a color television and $1,000 in exchange for signing a release that relieves him from his duty of child support. The girl, unaware of her legal rights, accepts the offer. When the $1,000 runs out, she applies for public assistance and reports the meager settlement she accepted. She can bring a paternity action to enforce the politician's duty to support his child, if the time limit set by state law has not expired.

When the mother and father marry, a settlement of sorts occurs because the paternity claim is extinguished by their marriage. The child's right to support by his father may,

however, be jeopardized in states that require more than the marriage of the parents to make the child legitimate. To protect the child's interests in this situation, a declaration of legitimacy by a court should be obtained or any other conditions that are required by law for legitimation should be satisfied—for example, the husband should acknowledge his paternity.

A release or settlement may be made before the start of a paternity action or may occur any time before final judgment. The court will then dismiss the proceedings, and this dismissal prevents any further proceedings. If there has been FRAUD, mistake, or DURESS (compulsion) by either party, the court may cancel the settlement and permit a new paternity action.

End of proceedings   Anything that defeats the purpose of a paternity suit or bastardy proceeding (criminal prosecution) will end, or abate, it—a release or a settlement, for example, or the marriage of the mother and the alleged father. If the mother marries another man, however, she may continue the proceedings against the defendant. The adoption of the child, which makes the adopting parents responsible for his support, usually ends the proceedings but the mother may still seek to recover her pregnancy expenses. In states where the establishment of paternity makes the man responsible for the woman's pregnancy expenses, the fact that the child is born dead or the mother had an abortion will not end the proceeding. Whether the death of any of the parties ends, or abates, the suit depends on the law in each state. See ABATEMENT AND REVIVAL. Once a paternity suit abates, there can be no future proceedings.

Award for support and expenses   When a jury decides in favor of the mother, a judgment is given containing an award for support of the child and, usually, for the expenses of the legal proceedings. The maximum amount the defendant may be made to pay for the support of the child is often set by law, but the exact amount of the award and the frequency of the payments are matters within the discretion of the court. Periodic support payments are the rule, but lump sum settlements are sometimes permissible. Reasonable expenses resulting from pregnancy and the birth of the child may also be recovered. The judgment often specifies to whom the payments should be made—usually the mother.

■ **Contracts for support**   When an alleged father accepts responsibility for an illegitimate child as his own, he may be financially liable to a person other than the mother—a boarding school, perhaps, or a housekeeper or babysitter he hires to care for the child. In a settlement, for example, a man does not have to admit that he is the father, but he enters into a contract with the mother or someone else (such as a grandparent who gained legal custody of the child) to support or to contribute to the support of the child. The mother or other person may sue on the contract if he fails to make payments. In some states, the right of the child to enforce a contract between the mother and the alleged father has been recognized, while in others this right has been denied.

■ **Neglect of support**   In general, the obligation of a father to support his illegitimate child, as established in a paternity suit, must be enforced in the manner specified by law. Under some statutes, the mother may sue in her own name, on behalf of the child, to compel the father to fulfill his duty. In states where the failure of a parent to support an illegitimate child is a criminal offense, the district attorney can prosecute. These criminal laws are supplementary to bastardy laws.

■ **Inheritance rights**   Most state legislatures have given illegitimate children the right to inherit when there is no will. Because the child's relationship to the mother is usually beyond doubt, almost all the states provide that the nonmarital child has the same right to inherit property from his mother and from his mother's relatives as a child born in wedlock.

In the past, many states did not permit an illegitimate child to inherit from his father unless he was named in his father's will. Some states made an exception to this rule when the father had legitimated the child. An Illinois law that gave illegitimate children the right to inherit only from their mothers when there is no will while legitimate children could inherit from both parents was declared unconstitutional by the U.S. Supreme Court. This decision invalidated similar laws of more than 20 other states.

While the Supreme Court's decision gives illegitimate children the right to inherit, it does not make their inheritance rights equal with those of legitimate children. Nevertheless, it gives them some inheritance rights—particularly when there has been a court order establishing the paternity of the alleged father during his life.

EXAMPLE   The Court also upheld a Louisiana law that permitted a nonmarital child who had been acknowledged by her father but not legitimated to file a claim for support against his estate after he died without leaving a will. She received the support; but she was denied a share of the estate because her father had failed to formally legitimate her.

Clearly, the most effective way to protect an illegitimate child's inheritance rights is by legitimation.

At common law, a bastard had no heirs except his children and grandchildren. Most state laws now allow the mother of an illegitimate child and her family to inherit from him if he dies without leaving a will, provided that he is not survived by a spouse or children of his own. But the common law (where it applies) and many state laws still deny the natural father the right to inherit from his nonmarital child. If the right is given by state law, illegitimate children of the same parent and combinations of legitimate and illegitimate children of the same parent may inherit from each other.

■ **Property rights**   In 1968 the Supreme Court used the equal protection clause of the Constitution to establish the principle that the nonmarital child is entitled to legal equality with legitimate children in most areas of the law. Numerous state laws on the subject were then declared unconstitutional.

If a state law gives only legitimate children the right to support from their fathers, it will be declared unconstitutional because it denies equal protection to illegitimate children. Similarly, the Supreme Court struck down a New Jersey welfare law that provided benefits only to legitimate children.

The Court also declared unconstitutional a provision of the Social Security Act, which discriminated between two kinds of illegitimate children—those who are acknowledged by their fathers and those who are not—in awarding benefits under a program for their father's disability. In 1976, however, the Court upheld a section of the Social Security Act that required only illegitimate children who have not been legitimated or acknowledged by their father to prove their dependency on their fathers before benefits would be awarded. The Court believed that this difference was justified to facilitate the handling of the claims.

In addition, a Louisiana law that did not allow nonmarital children to recover for the wrongful death of their mother and another that denied a mother recovery for the wrongful death of her nonmarital child were declared unconstitutional. In both situations, recoveries had been allowed when legitimate children were involved. See WRONGFUL-DEATH ACTION.

■ **Artificial insemination**   Questions have been raised about the legitimacy of children conceived by artificial insemination—the impregnating of a woman with the semen of a donor, either her husband or a third party (usually unknown), by a method other than sexual intercourse. Many states have not passed laws to establish the legal status of these children. Children conceived when the donor is the husband obviously have natural fathers who are married to their natural mothers and, therefore, are treated as legitimate. But the legitimacy of children conceived when the donor is a third party is another matter.

In states with traditional viewpoints, a child conceived in this way, even with the husband's consent, is considered illegitimate. The husband, however, may be responsible for child support.

EXAMPLE   In one case, a husband and wife agreed in writing during marriage that the wife would be artificially inseminated by a donor. Later, the husband sued for annulment and in his suit claimed that the child was not his, and he therefore was under no duty to support it. The court decided, however, that even though the child was illegitimate according to state law, the husband had a duty to support the child because his conduct and consent to the artificial insemination of his wife implied a promise to support any offspring born from this procedure.

Many courts are now taking a more enlightened view and are declaring legitimate those children born by means of artificial insemination to which the husband consented.

EXAMPLE   The second husband of a woman wanted to adopt her child, born as a result of artificial insemination while she was married to her first husband. Both the separation agreement and the divorce proceeding ending the first marriage declared the child to be the "daughter" and "child" of the couple. When the first husband refused to consent to the adoption, the court—which had in an earlier case declared that a child born as a result of consensual artificial insemination was illegitimate—decided that "a child born of consensual artificial insemination during a valid marriage is a legitimate child entitled to all the rights and privileges of a naturally conceived child of the same marriage." Therefore, the consent of the first husband was required for adoption.

Although some courts treat children born by artificial insemination of the wife by a third-party donor as the legitimate child of the married couple, only a few states have gone so far as to enact laws giving legitimate status to these children. In all the others, the status of each child is determined in court on a case by case basis.

Sometimes the presumption of legitimacy will protect the child if the artificial insemination procedure is carried out matching the husband's blood group with that of the donor and mingling his semen with the donor's. It then becomes very difficult for a husband to rebut the presumption that the child is his.

When an unmarried woman is artificially inseminated, the child will in all probability be labeled as illegitimate because of the mother's marital status. The identity of the father is usually unknown, because most third-party donors remain anonymous.

illicit Not allowed; forbidden by law, such as illicit intercourse or an illicit trade.

illusory promise A statement that appears to be the basis for a CONTRACT, but when closely examined promises nothing absolute or legally binding. When a promise is illusory, no contract exists. For example, a promise in an agreement between a railroad and an iron producer in which the railroad promised to purchase as much iron as its board of directors might advise was held to be illusory.

immaterial Not important; unnecessary. For instance, immaterial EVIDENCE is any fact not essential either to the prosecution or defense of a lawsuit.

immediate cause The last cause in a chain of causes, which in itself and without any further cause directly produces the result or event. See PROXIMATE CAUSE.

immediate issue Children. In law, a couple's children constitute the immediate issue of their MARRIAGE.

immigration See ALIEN.

immunity An exemption from any charge, duty, office, tax, or penalty. A person testifying before a GRAND JURY investigating a crime is often granted immunity from a prosecution based on any self-incriminating statements he might make. The principle that the government cannot be sued without its consent is SOVEREIGN IMMUNITY.

impanel Make up the list of jurors selected for a particular trial, a job assigned to the clerk of the court. The final JURY will be selected from this list.

impeachment A criminal proceeding against a public officer, such as a federal judge, before a court consisting of other public officers. The proceeding is started by a written accusation called articles of impeachment. Article II, Section 4, of the Constitution provides: "The President, Vice President and all civil Officers of the United States, shall be removed from Office on Impeachment for, and Conviction of, Treason, Bribery, or other high Crimes and Misdemeanors." The House of Representatives writes the articles of impeachment—the charges—and sends them to the Senate, which has the power to try all

such impeachments. The Chief Justice of the United States presides over the Senate when the President is tried. In order to convict and remove a person from office, two-thirds of the Senate must vote for it. See CONGRESS.

State constitutions may also have provisions that permit the impeachment of various officials, such as the governor, for crimes or misconduct committed during their terms.

impediment A disability or hindrance that prevents a person from making a CONTRACT. For example, an impediment to a marriage could be a still valid earlier marriage. The fact that a person is insane is an impediment to his making any valid contract. See INSANE PERSONS.

implead Bring into a lawsuit. *Impleader* is a procedural device by which a defendant in a lawsuit brings in a third person who will ultimately be liable, either wholly or in part, for the claim made against the defendant. Impleader laws help avoid delay by disposing of two or more trials in one.

EXAMPLE A man named Conte drove his automobile over a log that was used as a backstop in a parking lot. Part of the automobile landed in a ditch and part remained in the parking lot. Conte asked a man named Musco to help him get the automobile out of the ditch and back into the lot. Musco tried to help, but he badly injured his hand while doing so. He was taken to a hospital, given an anesthetic, and operated on. The anesthetic was negligently administered and Musco died. Musco's wife sued Conte for damages for causing Musco's wrongful death. Conte, in turn, impleaded the hospital and Phillips—a hospital attendant whose negligence contributed to Musco's death—to force the hospital and Phillips to pay their share of the damages awarded to Musco's widow. The court agreed that both the hospital and its attendant could be held liable and that they could be impleaded.

implied Expressed indirectly; suggested by surrounding circumstances, such as by the words or actions of the persons involved. For example, if you take a shortcut across your neighbor's property each day without his complaining about it, his failure to object can be considered implied permission for you to cut across the property.

implied warranty A warranty imposed by law. An *implied warranty of merchantability* is a promise the law imposes on a merchant guaranteeing that any article he sells is fit for normal use. If you purchase a washing machine, you should be able to wash clothes with it. If you cannot, you may sue the merchant for the breach of his implied warranty. For extended discussions relating to warranties, see CONSUMER PROTECTION; PRODUCT LIABILITY.

impossibility Something that cannot be done. In law the word is usually used in the term "impossibility of performance," a defense raised by a party to a CONTRACT who is sued for breach of contract. There are two types of impossibility: objective and subjective. Objective impossibility is something that would prevent anyone from performing his part of a contract.

EXAMPLE A pianist rents a concert hall for a series of recitals. The pianist advertises and sells tickets, but before the first recital takes place the concert hall burns down. Neither the pianist nor the owner of the hall expected it to burn down, and the fire was not caused by the owner's negligence. The pianist sues the owner of the hall to recover the money he lost in advertising the recitals. He will not collect. The subject of the contract, the concert hall, was destroyed without either party being at fault, so both parties are excused from the contract.

Subjective impossibility occurs when one of the parties to the contract becomes unable to carry out his part of the agreement, but someone else can.

EXAMPLE Suppose the pianist rents the hall and advertises the recitals. This time, however, the concert hall is mortgaged and the owner has failed to make several mortgage payments. The mortgage is foreclosed, the concert hall is sold, and the new owner refuses to allow the pianist to give his recitals. The pianist sues the former owner to recover his lost advertising expenses. The former owner is not relieved of his duty to fulfill his part of the contract and the pianist could recover his advertising expenses. The former owner should have anticipated the foreclosure and its effect on the contract. He should have notified the pianist so that he could arrange for another concert hall to hold the recitals.

impound 1 Take into the custody of the law or a court. For example, after records have been produced in obedience to a subpoena, the court may impound them for safekeeping. 2 Keep stray animals in a pound.

imprisonment See PRISONERS' RIGHTS.

imputed knowledge Knowledge attributed to a person because the facts in question were available to him and it was his duty to inform himself of them. For example, if a customer is injured on a defective stairway leading to a retail store, the store owner cannot avoid responsibility for his customer's injury by claiming that he did not know the stairway was defective. Knowledge of the defect is imputed to him. See NEGLIGENCE; NOTICE.

imputed negligence Charging one person with the responsibility for another person's NEGLIGENCE because of some relationship that exists between the two persons. Let us say that a department store deliveryman carelessly drops an air conditioner on a customer's toe. His negligence can be imputed to the department store, because the store is liable for the injuries caused by its employees during the course of their employment.

imputed notice Holding one person responsible for information given to another person. For instance, NOTICE of a lawsuit given to an attorney is imputed to his client.

inadmissible evidence Facts, physical objects, or testimony that, under established rules of law, cannot be received in EVIDENCE in a trial. Hearsay testimony is an example of inadmissible evidence.

inalienable Unable to be bought, sold, or transferred from one person to another. Rivers, public highways, and the personal rights to life and liberty guaranteed under the U.S. Constitution are all inalienable. See CONSTITUTIONAL LAW.

in blank Without restriction. The term refers to the endorsement of a negotiable instrument, such as a check or promissory note, without making it payable to anyone in particular. When you sign your name on the back of a check without any instructions such as "for deposit only," you are endorsing the check in blank. See COMMERCIAL PAPER.

in camera (Latin) "In [the judge's] chamber"; in private. A case is heard in camera when the hearing is before a judge in his private room or when all spectators are excluded from the courtroom.

incapacity 1 Lack of legal ability or qualifications. For example, a person incapacitated by insanity lacks the legal ability to enter into a contract or to bring a lawsuit. 2 Under WORKMEN'S COMPENSATION laws, the inability to find and keep employment because of an injury or a disease that prevents a person from performing the usual tasks of an employee.

incest Sexual intercourse or marriage between a man and woman who are so closely related by blood—or, in some states, by affinity (marriage)—that marriage between them is prohibited by state law. See Chart 20. Incest is a crime—usually a felony or a serious misdemeanor. The purpose of incest laws is to prohibit sexual intercourse between certain related individuals in order to promote domestic peace and prevent genetic deficiencies such as imbecility.

Incest and RAPE are separate offenses. In most states mutual consent is required in incest but not in rape. Consequently, if a man forced his daughter or sister to have intercourse with him, the man would be tried for rape, not incest. If the female consented, he would be tried for incest but only if she was legally capable of giving consent. If the female was a minor, the man would be prosecuted for statutory rape, regardless of whether force was used. In states that define incest as not requiring mutual consent of the parties, the man could be prosecuted for either rape or incest, regardless of the age of his daughter or sister. If no force was involved, however, he could be prosecuted only for incest.

Under the various laws, intermarriage and sexual intercourse are prohibited between parent and child, brother and sister, uncle and niece, aunt and nephew, and half bloods, such as brothers and sisters who have one parent in common. Legally, half bloods are usually regarded as whole bloods. Some laws include first cousins; others do not.

States that extend incest laws specifically to relatives by marriage prohibit sexual intercourse between a stepfather and his stepdaughter, a stepmother and her stepson, or a brother-in-law and sister-in-law. The relationship of affinity must exist at the time the sexual intercourse occurs. If the relationship has ended before the act takes place, then the act of sexual intercourse or intermarrying is not incest, no matter how offensive it may be to others. Usually affinity ends by the divorce or death of the blood relative through whom the relationship was created. For example, after a man is divorced or after his wife dies it is not incestuous for him to marry or have intercourse with his former wife's sister or daughter by another husband.

A person charged with incest cannot claim as a defense the fact that he was drunk, if his drunkeness was voluntary, or that he had an uncontrollable impulse. The fact that the woman previously had sexual relations with other men or has a reputation for unchastity is also not a defense. In some states, not knowing the relationship was incestuous is a defense. But when statutes require the accused person to have known that the relationship was incestuous, it is not necessary for both persons to have known this in order to convict the one who was aware of the incest. The crime of incest may be punishable by a prison sentence.

inchoate   Begun but not completed. For example, an inventor has an inchoate property right to his invention while his application for a PATENT is pending. It matures into a full property right when the patent is issued.

incidental   Depending on or relating to something else that is more important. For example, a risk is incidental to employment under Workmen's Compensation laws when it is associated with whatever an employee has to do to fulfill his employment contract. If a person is employed as a truck driver, for instance, a collision with another vehicle is a risk that is incidental to the truck driver's employment so that the truck driver cannot sue his employer for his injuries as long as his truck was in good condition. He can only sue the driver of the vehicle that caused the accident. The risk of motor accidents was assumed by the truck driver since the nature of his job exposed him to a greater possibility of involvement in such accidents.

incite   Arouse; stir up something, such as a RIOT.

income tax   A levy placed by the government on the income of taxpayers under its jurisdiction. In the United States the federal government imposes an income tax and some states and even cities impose income taxes on all those who live or earn money in those states or cities. This article explains the purpose of the federal income tax; who must pay it; and such various topics as gross income, personal and dependency exemptions, adjustments to income, itemized deductions, capital gains and losses, and credits. Discussions of estimated tax, refunds, and an income tax audit are also included. This article deals only with the federal income tax imposed on individual taxpayers. If you live or work in a state or city that also imposes income taxes, consult the laws of your state or city.

■ **Why an income tax**   The federal income tax, established in 1913 by the 16th Amendment to the U.S. Constitution, is the largest source of revenue in the budget of the federal government. In addition, it encourages certain kinds of economic and social behavior, such as buying on credit and contributing to charities (by allowing deductions for interest and contributions), redistributes wealth, and stimulates or stabilizes economic growth. The Internal Revenue Service (IRS) is the federal agency that enforces the regulations of the Internal Revenue Code.

■ **Who must file**   The federal income tax applies to all residents and citizens of the United States. Your gross income, marital status, and age determine whether you must file a return. *Gross income* includes all taxable income you receive in the form of money, property, and services. (An example of taxable income in the form of property and services would be the value of a car you received as a gift or maid service you won in a contest.) Your marital status is determined as of the last day of your tax year, which is December 31 for most taxpayers. You are considered age 65 on the day before your 65th birthday.

In 1980, for example, a single individual had to file a return if his gross income was $3,300 or more. If that person was 65 or older, his gross income had to be $4,300 or more before he had to file a return. Married persons had to have a combined gross income of $5,400 or more, be filing a joint return and be still living together at the end of the tax year before a return had to be filed. A married person who did not live with his spouse at the end of the tax year or who filed a separate return needed only a gross income of $1,000 to be required to file a return. If one spouse was 65 or older, the amount of gross income increased to $6,400 and if both were 65 or older, a return was necessary only if their gross income was $7,400 or more.

For many people much of the tax is collected in advance. When a person is hired for a job, he completes a W-4 form, which authorizes his employer to withhold a specified amount from his salary or wages and to turn it over to the government as prepayment of his income tax. This is called a *withholding tax.* If you are self-employed, you must file a return when your net earnings from self-employment are above a certain amount (in 1980, $400). Even though you may not owe any income tax, you have to file an income tax return in order to pay your self-employment tax (equivalent to the SOCIAL SECURITY tax withheld from an employee's wages). Self-employed taxpayers make quarterly prepayments based on an estimate of their income.

If a person must file a return because he meets the income requirements because of salary or income from property, he must also include his net self-employment income regardless of its amount.

The tax return, filed on or before April 15 by most individual taxpayers, makes a final report and reconciles earlier withholding or estimated tax payments with the actual liability. Taxpayers may receive a refund or have to make an additional payment with the final return.

A final income tax return must be filed for any person who died during the year. The executor, administrator, legal representative, or survivor must file the final return and any other return still due for the decedent. The return is usually due on April 15 of the year following the death.

■ **Progressive tax**   The federal income tax uses a graduated rate structure. This means that the percentage of tax a person pays increases as his income increases. For example, suppose a person pays tax at a rate of 20 percent on $3,000. A man with a taxable income of $30,000 would be taxed 20 percent on his first $3,000, then 23 percent on his next $5,000, and then 27 percent on the next $7,000, and so on. Rates differ depending upon the marital status of taxpayers. Long-term capital gains, profit realized on the sale of stocks or bonds held longer than 12 months, are taxed at lower rates than ordinary income, and the tax on them is not graduated.

■ **Annual tax periods and accounting** The federal income tax is based on a yearly system of reporting. A taxpayer's income may be determined on either a calendar year basis, which ends on the last day of December, or on a fiscal year basis, which ends on the last day of any month other than December. Generally, a taxpayer may choose between the two, and most individuals select the calendar year basis.

A taxpayer determines what income is to be included and what deductions are to be taken by using either the cash or accrual method of accounting. Under the *cash method,* income and expenses are reported in the year they are actually received or spent. The *accrual method* requires income to be included for taxation in the year the right to receive it becomes fixed, and deductions for expenses are taken when the obligation to pay has become unconditional.

EXAMPLE A surgeon performed a tonsillectomy in October 0—* 1978. He did not receive payment until the following January. If he is a cash-method taxpayer, he did not have to report his fee as income until he actually received it in January 1979. This fee was included as income taxed for the calendar year ending December 31, 1979. If the surgeon is an accrual-method taxpayer, he had to treat his fee as income for tax purposes for the year ending December 31, 1978, even though he did not actually receive payment until January 1979.

Suppose that the same surgeon bought a new examining table for his office in November 1978 but did not pay the bill until the following February. If he is a cash-method taxpayer, he could not deduct the business expense until he actually paid for it in 1979. As an accrual-method taxpayer, however, he had to take the deduction for the 1978 tax year when he incurred the expense.

■ **Estimated tax** Whether a person will be required to file a declaration of ESTIMATED TAX depends on how much he estimates his taxable income will be for that year and how much of it will be withheld by his employer for the payment of his income tax. The estimated tax is the amount by which the total expected income tax and self-employment tax exceeds the amount of tax you anticipate will be withheld from your pay. Estimated tax payments are generally required of self-employed persons and of employees who have income from which not enough tax is being withheld or income that is not subject to withholding, such as annuities, interest, dividends, rent, or capital gains. The full amount of the estimated tax may be paid when the declaration is filed or it may be paid in quarterly installments during the year it is meant to cover (the year in which the declaration is filed).

■ **Gross income** Gross income is the starting point in determining what is to be taxed. It has been defined as "all income from whatever source derived." Income is generally regarded as any gain produced by personal services, business activities, or capital assets, such as stocks.

Income from employment All types of compensation received for personal services are part of gross income. This includes many fringe benefits as well as wages, sala-ries, commissions, tips, and fees for professional services. Money withheld from your pay for income and Social Security taxes or savings bonds is treated as if it had been received by you and must be included in your income in the year it was withheld. If your wages are attached or garnisheed (a creditor got a court to order your employer to give the creditor a part of your wages to pay your debts), their full amount must still be included in your gross income. See ATTACHMENT AND GARNISHMENT.

Company-paid insurance Hospitalization premiums paid by your employer are not income if they are not withheld from your pay, nor are employer-paid amounts that entitle you to use a group legal-services plan.

Premiums paid by your employer on your behalf for group life INSURANCE may or may not be counted as income depending to some extent on whether the insurance is permanent life insurance or term life insurance. *Permanent life insurance* is life insurance that is usually for 20 years or life, may be borrowed against, and has a cash surrender value. *Term life insurance* is life insurance that is only for a fixed period and has no borrowing or cash surrender rights. Premiums paid on permanent life insurance are income to you unless the policy states that you lose your right to the insurance when you leave your job. The cost of coverage for group term life insurance in excess of a specified amount ($50,000 in 1979) provided to you under a policy carried by your employer is income to you. Your employer will note this as additional compensation on your W-2 form—the form you receive early in the year stating your income and taxes withheld during the previous year. Any part of the cost of the insurance that you pay will reduce, dollar for dollar, the amount you would otherwise include in your income.

The cost of group term life insurance protection in excess of the stated amount will not be taxed to you if (1) the coverage continues after you have terminated your employment and you have either reached retirement age or become disabled; (2) your employer is directly or indirectly the beneficiary of the policy for the entire period the insurance is in effect during the tax year; or (3) the sole beneficiary of the excess over $50,000 is a qualified charitable organization for the entire period the insurance is in effect during the tax year. In this instance, you cannot take a charitable deduction for naming a charity as the beneficiary of your policy.

Rewards and bonuses Any rewards or bonuses paid to you for outstanding work are income.

EXAMPLE Rose, a sales representative for a business ma-0—* chine company, has made a record number of sales in her district for the month of October. Her company gives her a trip to Hawaii for two as a reward. She must include the fair market value (cash value) of her reward in her gross income.

If the bonus or prize is payable some time in the future at the option of your employer, it is not taxable until you receive it. When your employer, to promote goodwill, gives away turkeys, hams, or similar items, to all employees at Christmas or other holidays, the cash value of those gifts is not income. Cash or gift certificates distributed by your employer will, however, be treated as additional salary or wages. If your employer sells you property, such as stock in

BASIC FACTS ABOUT FEDERAL INCOME TAX

■ Federal income tax law applies to all U.S residents and citizens. Gross income is the starting point from which you figure what is to be taxed. *Gross income* means all income from whatever source, be it personal services, business, or capital assets such as stocks and bonds. Income also includes all types of compensation, including fringe benefits and bonuses.

■ Severance pay is treated as income in the tax year it is received.

■ Any interest that you receive is gross income, unless it is specifically exempt from tax.

■ Stockholders' dividends above the first $200 are taxable as income.

■ Rents that you receive must be included in gross income.

■ A *capital asset* is any property you use and own for personal purposes, pleasure, or investment. A *capital gain* is the profit you get from a sale or exchange of a capital asset; a *capital loss* is the loss you incur in a sale or exchange. In general, your capital gains are taxable and your capital losses are deductible—the rules vary from case to case.

■ Short-term gains on assets held for 12 months or less are taxable as ordinary income.

■ Long-term gains on assets held more than a year get a tax break—only 40 percent is taxed. For example, if you make a profit of $10,000 on the sale of an asset you have held longer than a year, you will be required to pay taxes on only $4,000 of it; the rest is tax-free.

■ When you sell your house at a profit, income tax on a portion or all of the gain may be deferred—this is what is known as a *rollover*.

■ Personal bad debts may be treated as short-term capital losses. Business bad debts can be fully deducted from ordinary income. Bad debts are deductible in the year they are incurred.

■ Alimony payments you receive are counted as income, but child-support payments are not. Compensation for personal injuries or damages won in lawsuits is not taxable, but punitive damages and compensation for lost profits are considered income. Dam-ages won for property damage must be included only to the extent the amount was deducted from your income tax as a casualty loss.

■ Gifts, bequests, or inheritances you receive are not income, but if they later produce interest, dividends, or rentals, that income will be taxable to you.

■ You are entitled to claim yourself as a personal exemption, even if you are financially dependent on another taxpayer.

■ If you and your spouse file jointly, you may claim an exemption for your spouse; if you file separately, you may claim an exemption for your spouse only if he or she has no gross income.

■ You may get an exemption for each person qualifying as a dependent—the IRS uses the following tests to determine which persons may be claimed as dependents: (1) support test (you must provide more than half the dependent's total support); (2) gross-income test (your dependent cannot have made more than $1,000 that year, unless he or she is your child; up to age 19, a dependent child may have any amount of income so long as the other tests are satisfied); (3) member-of-household or relationship test; (4) citizenship test (for some part of the tax year your dependent must be a U.S. citizen, resident, or national, or a resident of Canada or Mexico); and (5) joint-return test (you cannot get an exemption for a married dependent who files a joint return with his or her spouse).

■ If you are one of two or more persons contributing to the support of a dependent, you may claim the exemption only if the others agree in writing not to claim it on their tax returns.

■ If you moved because you changed your job or became self-employed, you are entitled to deduct the expenses of the move from your gross income, subject to a number of rules that you will need to study in order to discover which ones apply to you.

■ If you are divorced or separated, you may deduct alimony or similar payments, provided such payments are (1) required by court order; (2) based on the marital relationship; (3) paid after the decree; and (4) periodic—that is, either a fixed amount for an indefinite period or an indefinite amount (such as 15 percent of a fluctuating income) for a fixed or indefinite period.

■ If a taxpayer is under 65 and retired on disability or is permanently and totally disabled, he may exclude up to $5,200 a year from his gross income.

■ Once the adjustments applying to you have been deducted from your gross income, the remaining figure is your *adjusted gross income.* Subtract the deductions you are allowed (for example, for medical expenses) from the adjusted gross income, and the remainder is your taxable income.

■ Whether or not you choose to itemize your deductions, you will be given a so-called *zero-bracket amount.* This is a specific amount, determined by your filing status, that has been built into the tax tables and rate schedules, and it shows just how much you owe, given your income, your filing status, and exemptions. If your itemized deductions exceed the zero-bracket deduction, the excess is subtracted from the adjusted gross income, and from the remaining sum you can find the amount of tax in the table that applies to you. Besides medical expenses, deductible expenses include dental expenses, taxes, interest expenses, charitable contributions, losses resulting from casualty or theft, and other miscellaneous deductions.

■ Once you have determined the amount of tax you owe, you should check to see if you can reduce the amount by applying any of the available tax credits. You may, for example, take half of your contributions to candidates for political office as a direct credit against your tax, up to $50 on a separate return or $100 on a joint return. If you are a working mother, you can write off the day-care center and babysitter expenses for child-care credits on your tax return.

■ For most taxpayers, the deadline for filing and paying taxes is April 15. Late filing and payment will subject you to a penalty.

the company, at a reduced price, the difference between what you paid and its fair market value is income to you.

When an employer pays for the use of an athletic club or health spa for its executives, the expense is considered additional compensation. Property such as stock, which is received for a job well done, is usually included in gross income at its fair market value in the year it is received. If, however, the property is not freely transferred (if a restriction is made on it—such as that it cannot be sold for three years) or there is a substantial risk that it may be forfeited, it is not taxed until these restrictions no longer exist.

EXAMPLE Let us say that you receive stock from your employer for work you performed. There is a provision, however, that the stock will be forfeited unless you complete three years of service. The value of the stock will not be taxable until you have completed three years of service.

Meals and lodgings The value of meals and lodgings that are provided to you for free by your employer is not income to you if certain conditions are met. They must be furnished on the business premises of your employer for his convenience. Generally, a taxpayer does not have to report the value of meals furnished to him during working hours because he must be on hand to answer emergency calls or because the nature of the employer's business restricts him to a short meal period (30 to 45 minutes). However, when you receive a cash allowance from your employer for meals or lodging, it must be included as income if it is compensation. For instance, a state police officer who receives a cash allowance to pay for meals while on duty must consider it additional compensation to be taxed. In the case of lodging, it is tax-free only if you must accept the lodging on your employer's premises in order to do your job. For example, a forest ranger or a fireman is required to live in his station while on duty so that he will be available at all times during his working hours.

Pension and profit-sharing plans Contributions to a pension plan through payroll deductions are included in your gross income if they are voluntary or if they are compulsory but nonforfeitable. Your contributions are nonforfeitable if, for example, the plan has a refund provision that upon termination of your employment, you may exchange your interest in the annuity for cash or take over payments for the annuity. When your employer contributes to a qualified stock-bonus, pension, profit-sharing, annuity, or bond-purchase plan in which you participate, the amount is not taxable to you at the time the contributions are made but you will be taxed when payment is received.

Other job-related income Severance pay as well as a lump-sum payment for cancellation of an employment contract is treated as income in the tax year it is received. When a prospective employer pays you an allowance to cover transportation and other travel expenses for a job interview, you must report the amount received as income only to the extent that it exceeds your actual expenses.

In the past, unless you were required to take educational courses in order to keep your job, any course expenses paid by your employer had to be reported as income. For a five-year period that started on January 1, 1979, this is no longer true. Courses involving sports, games, or hobbies, however, are not included in this provision.

When money is withheld from your pay for union dues, assessments, or contributions, it is treated as if you received it and is income. Unemployment benefit payments you receive from a fund to which you voluntarily contribute are income only to the extent that they exceed your payments into the fund. Strike and lockout benefits, including both cash and the fair market value of other property, paid by a union from its dues, are income unless the facts show that they were intended as a gift.

Military pay—such as pay for active duty or reserve training, reenlistment bonus, armed services academy pay, or military retirement—is taxable. Veterans' benefits for education, disability, or pension payments are not taxed as gross income. Veterans' insurance proceeds and dividends are not taxable either to veterans or to their beneficiaries.

Interest income Interest that you receive or that is credited to your account is included in your gross income, except for an exempt amount, as indicated in "Dividends," below. Interest received from bank accounts, bonds, loans, notes, U.S. Savings Bonds, and credit-union accounts is fully taxable. The interest received on obligations of the United States, such as treasury notes and bonds, is fully taxable. If you receive a tax refund that includes interest on the amount refunded, the interest must be included in your gross income. The fair market value of automobiles, boats, color television sets, or other property or services received for making long-term deposits or for opening accounts in saving institutions is interest and must be reported as income in the year received.

Interest on obligations of a state (an Ohio state bond, for example) or its political subdivision (a city of Cleveland bond), the District of Columbia, or Puerto Rico is exempt from federal tax.

Dividends A dividend is a distribution from the earnings and profits of a CORPORATION to a stockholder. It is usually taxable as income to the stockholder. The first $200 of dividends or interest is not taxed. A husband and wife, filing either jointly or separately, may each use the $200 exclusion on dividends or interest that each received during the tax year. Neither can include any part of the dividends or interest received by the other in computing the exclusion.

EXAMPLE Suppose a wife receives $250 in dividends or interest while her husband receives only $150. She will exclude $200 and he will exclude $150 or a total of $350 on a joint return. The husband may not exclude the $50 balance his wife was unable to exclude.

Taxpayers who are residents of community property states will need additional information on the taxability of dividends.

Rents Rents that you receive must be included in gross income. Rents are payments received for the use and occupancy of a private house or rooms or other space in a boardinghouse, apartment, motel, or trailer court.

A security deposit of one or two months' rent that a landlord receives is usually not treated as income when received, but if he keeps part or all of it because the tenant violates the lease, then it is treated as income.

Expenses for DEPRECIATION, repairs, and maintenance reduce the amount of rent that is taxed as income. *Depreciation* is the reduction in value of a building due to the passing of time. The owner is allowed to use the drop in value as a deduction. Repairs and maintenance must not greatly increase the value or useful life of the property; if they do, no deduction will be permitted. For instance, the expense of replacing a broken window is deductible as a rental expense. On the other hand, the cost of replacing all the living room windows with ceiling-to-floor windows to increase the value of the house does not reduce the rental income. It is considered a *capital expenditure,* which is an investment of money made (1) to acquire property having a useful life of more than one year, (2) to increase the value of the property, or (3) to prolong its life. A capital expenditure is usually recovered by deductions for depreciation over the useful life of the property.

Other expenses that reduce the amount of taxable rental income include advertising, janitor and maid service, utilities, fire and liability insurance, taxes, and commissions for the collection of rent.

Capital gains and losses   A *capital asset* is any property you use and own for personal purposes, pleasure, or investment. Stocks or bonds held in your personal account, the home you owned, household furnishings, and an automobile used for pleasure or commuting are some examples of capital assets.

A *capital gain* is the profit or gain you realize from a sale of a capital asset; a *capital loss* is the loss you incur in selling a capital asset. Long-term capital gains are earned on property held by the taxpayer for more than 12 months before its transfer. Sixty percent of these gains are excluded from gross income; therefore if you have made a profit of $10,000, only $4,000 (or 40 percent of it) will be taxed. Because of this exclusion, long-term capital gains are often said to be taxed at lower rates than ordinary income. Short-term capital gains on assets held 12 months or less are taxable as ordinary income. Long-term capital losses must first be balanced against long-term capital gains, while short-term losses must be balanced against short-term gains. If there are any capital gains existing after this point, any remaining capital losses will be offset against them. The gains or losses remaining after this calculation will be taxed according to their original character. For example, if long-term capital gains remain after being offset by short-term losses, they are still taxed as long-term gains.

EXAMPLE Suppose Don received a salary of $20,000. He also realized a long-term capital gain of $8,000 by selling stock he had owned for several years and a long-term capital loss of $4,000 on other stocks. On selling some land he had just bought three months before, he enjoyed a short-term capital gain of $1,000, and he suffered a short-term capital loss of $500 on selling a bond. Assuming all his gains are includable in his gross income and that all his losses are deductible, he should go about computing his tax as follows: By netting his long-term transactions in stock, he sees that he has a net long-term capital gain of $4,000 ($8,000 minus $4,000). By netting his short-term transactions in land and the bond, he has a net short-term capital gain of $500 ($1,000 minus $500). His net short-term capital gain of $500 must be added to his $20,000 salary in computing taxable income, since it is to be taxed at the same rate as his salary (ordinary income). Only 40 percent of his net long-term capital gain ($4,000), or $1,600, must be included in his gross income.

After all the capital gains have been eliminated, only up to $3,000 of any remaining capital losses may be deducted from ordinary income. Additional losses may be carried forward to future tax years and deducted until they are eventually used.

There is a method to determine the amount of remaining capital losses. Net short-term capital losses can be used to reduce income dollar for dollar subject to certain limitations, but only 50 percent of net long-term capital losses can be used this way.

EXAMPLE John's ordinary income was $30,000. He suffered short-term losses of $400 and long-term losses of $6,300. The maximum amount of capital losses he could use to reduce his income was $3,000. Because short-term losses could be deducted dollar for dollar from income, his $400 short-term loss reduced his ordinary income to $29,600. This $400 had to be deducted also from the $3,000 limit on the use of capital losses in one year, leaving John with $2,600 more of capital losses to be used to reduce his income. John also had a long-term loss of $6,300. Only 50 percent of long-term losses could be used to reduce ordinary income and there was also a $3,000 limit on the use of losses, $400 of which had been taken already. The remaining $2,600 that can be deducted from John's income ($29,600 minus $2,600, giving John $27,000 ordinary income) is equal to $5,200 of John's long-term capital loss (because only 50 percent of long-term capital losses can be used). John, however, had $6,300 of this type of loss. The $1,100 of capital loss remaining after $5,200 has been subtracted from $6,300 will be carried over to the next tax year for use to reduce John's ordinary income for that year.

Sale and purchase of residence   When a taxpayer sells his home at a profit, income tax on a portion or all of the gain may be deferred. This is commonly referred to as a rollover of the capital gain. The entire gain realized on the sale of your home is not taxed at the time of the sale if within 18 months before or 18 months after the sale, you buy and occupy another home that costs the same or more than your old one. (If you are having your new home built, more time is allowed.) If the purchase price of the new home is less than the sale price of the old, the gain that will be taxed in the year of the sale will be the lesser of the profit on the sale of the old house or the excess of the sale price of the old house over the purchase price of the new home. The tax on the remaining gain (the difference between the profit on the sale of the old house and the excess of the sale price of the old home over the purchase price of the new one) is postponed, but it is not canceled. Any gain not taxed in the year you sell your home is subtracted from the cost of your new home, giving your new home a tax basis lower than its actual price. (The tax basis is the figure from which you calculate capital gains when selling an asset.) This means that when you later sell your new home at a profit, the amount to be taxed will be greater than if the tax basis of your new home was its purchase price.

EXAMPLE Suppose you sell your home and realize a $5,000 gain. (Your house originally cost you $35,000 and you added a new bedroom that increased its value to $40,000. You sold your house for $45,000.) Within 18 months you buy another home for $55,000, which is more than you received for the old one. The gain will not be taxed in the year of the sale. The $5,000 gain will be subtracted from $55,000, making the tax basis of your new home $50,000. If you later sell the new home for $56,000 and do not buy another home within the required time, you will be taxed on the $6,000 gain in the year of the sale. If you sold the second home for $53,000, you would be taxed on $3,000—the difference between the sale price, $53,000, and the basis of your home, $50,000.

Taxpayers 55 years old or older at the time of the sale of their home may choose to exclude from their gross income for that year up to $100,000 on the sale, even when the taxpayer has previously used the rollover provision to defer capital gain realized on the sale of his home within the 18-month period. The taxpayer must meet certain conditions, however. He must have owned and used the property for at least three years within the five-year period ending on the date of the sale, and the $100,000 exclusion may be used only once during his lifetime. If only part of the exclusion is used, the rest of it is lost. A taxpayer who makes an $84,000 capital gain on the sale of his home and uses this provision cannot exclude the remaining $16,000 on a subsequent sale. When the property is owned jointly by the taxpayer and his spouse, as community property, or as tenants in the entirety (the names of both husband and wife appear on the deed), only one of them must be over 55.

Bad debts Bad debts not originally created or acquired in your trade or business are nonbusiness or personal bad debts and must be treated as short-term capital losses. Business bad debts, on the other hand, can be fully deducted from ordinary income. Gifts are not bad debts, nor are loans made by parents to their minor children. A debt is bad or worthless when you take reasonable steps to collect it but cannot do so. Bad debts are usually deductible in the year they become worthless. Any bad debt recovered after it was claimed as a deduction must be included in income to the extent it previously reduced your tax liability.

Other income Other types of income that are taxable are fees received for serving as a corporation director, an executor or administrator of an estate, a notary public, a member of a jury, or an election precinct official. Alimony payments that you receive must be included as income, but child-support payments you receive are not income. Royalties from copyrights, patents, and oil, gas, and mineral properties are taxable as ordinary income, and a canceled debt or one paid by another person is generally income to the debtor unless it was intended as a gift.

Compensation received from lawsuits for DAMAGES to your character or for personal injury or illness is not taxable, but punitive damages and compensation for lost profits are considered income. Damages for injuries to property are taxable income to the extent that you have previously used such expenses as deductions for casualty loss from your taxable income of prior years. Compensatory damages received for patent or copyright infringement, breach of contract, or interference with business operations replace lost profits and are taxable.

Although a PARTNERSHIP pays no income taxes, it must file an information return showing the results of the partnership's operation for the tax year and showing how the items of income, gain, loss, deduction, or credit affected the partners' individual income tax return. Unlike partnerships, TRUSTS may be required to pay federal income tax, and a beneficiary must pay tax on his share of the income from the trust.

■ **Items not taxed** Gifts, bequests, or inheritances you receive are not income, but if they later produce taxable income, such as interest, dividends, or rentals, that income is taxable to you. Life insurance proceeds paid to you because of the death of the insured person are not taxable unless you paid the policyholder to transfer ownership of the policy to you.

Unemployment benefits paid by a state are not taxable unless a person's income exceeds a certain level, which depends upon his filing status. For example, in 1980, a single taxpayer making more than $20,000 a year, including his unemployment benefits, was taxed on part of them. The amount taxed was one half the excess of gross income over $20,000.

EXAMPLE Suppose that Ned earned $20,000 in 1979 from
O⊷✶ interest he received from a trust fund, stock dividends, and rental income from the apartment house he owns. That same year, he lost his job and received $1,000 in unemployment benefits, bringing his gross income to $21,000. He would have been taxed on $500 of the $1,000 of benefits received.

State employees entitled to benefits similar to unemployment compensation under a collective-bargaining agreement must include the benefits as income.

Social Security benefits received monthly or in a lump sum are not taxable, nor are basic railroad retirement benefits, but a supplemental annuity received under the Railroad Retirement Act is. Public assistance payments, such as welfare or disability payments; payments from a state compensation fund for the victims of crime if they are in the nature of welfare payments; and federal grants to assist victims of natural disasters are not considered income. Usually scholarships and fellowships are also excluded from gross income as long as the payment is made primarily to further the recipient's education and training. Pulitzer, Nobel, and other prizes awarded in recognition of past accomplishments are not taxable if the recipients are selected without action on their part and are not expected to perform any future services.

■ **Personal exemptions and dependents** Generally, the taxpayer's gross income is reduced by a certain amount of money for every person he fully supports, including himself. These amounts are called exemptions. The value of each exemption is $1,000. Every taxpayer can claim himself as a personal exemption, even if he is the dependent—an individual who is financially supported by another—of another taxpayer. A taxpayer is allowed an additional exemption if he is 65 or older on the last day of the year, and he is entitled to another exemption if he was blind on the last day of the year, but he must attach to his return a corroborating statement from an ophthalmologist or optometrist.

The reduction for exemptions is built in to the tax tables unless you fill out Schedule TC. Most taxpayers use the short form and therefore do not subtract their exemptions. They turn to the tax tables where it is done for them.

Exemptions for spouse A taxpayer who files a joint return may claim an exemption for his spouse because of the

IF THE IRS AUDITS YOUR TAX RETURN

HAROLD DUBROFF

*Professor of Law, Albany Law School
of Union University*

Each year more than 2 million taxpayers receive the unwelcome news that their tax returns are to be examined by the Internal Revenue Service (IRS). These examinations, known as audits, are the principal means by which the federal government tries to insure that its income tax laws are obeyed.

Notification of an audit usually comes in a form letter from the local district director of Internal Revenue. If you receive one of these letters, do not panic. The selection of your return for audit does not mean that the Internal Revenue Service has concluded that you are guilty of some wrongdoing or even that you owe more tax. Many examinations result in no additional tax. Occasionally, facts come to light showing that an overpayment was made, and the excess payment is refunded.

How the IRS selects returns for audit

In most cases, a taxpayer is selected for audit by a sophisticated computer program operated by the IRS. The computer scans returns for items that indicate a likelihood of error, such as claiming large interest deductions in proportion to the amount of income. Generally, taxpayers in higher income brackets are more likely to be audited than those with moderate incomes, and some returns are randomly selected under a research program to measure and evaluate characteristics of taxpayers. Sometimes the computer will repeatedly select a return for an audit that has the same disputed items year after year. If a

tax return was examined in either of the two previous years for the same items and the audit resulted in no change in tax liability, the taxpayer should contact the IRS. The audit will be suspended pending a review of IRS files. If, however, the return was selected randomly, it will not be exempt from audit.

Naturally, the specific criteria used by the computer are kept as confidential as possible by the IRS. If they were made public, tax evaders could simply fashion their returns to escape selection for audit.

Although computers play an important role in the audit process, the final decision to audit is made by Internal Revenue employees who review each return selected by the computer. If it is apparent that there is no error on the return, the reviewer will override the computer decision to audit. Thus many taxpayers whose returns are selected by the computer never even know about it.

It is good to bear in mind this method of audit selection when preparing your tax return. For example, if you take unusually large deductions for charitable contributions, you run a greater risk that the computer will select your return for audit. However, if you include adequate proof of the deductions with your return, such as receipts from the charities, the reviewing agent will probably decide that no further examination is necessary.

Some audits do not require a personal meeting with an IRS examiner. These audits, called correspondence audits, may be entirely resolved by mail, with the taxpayer supplying the information requested. In most cases, however, notification of an audit will request that the taxpayer or a representative meet with an Internal Revenue agent. Do not be misled by the word "request." The tax laws give broad powers to the IRS, and if you refuse its "invitation," a court order may compel you to accept.

A personal audit can be either an *office audit,* made at an Internal Revenue office, or a *field audit,* in which an Internal Revenue agent visits the taxpayer's home or office. The field audit is generally limited to the larger and more complicated returns and to homebound taxpayers, such as invalids. You will find the IRS is willing to make reasonable accommodations for the taxpayer's convenience. For instance, if the date or time of an examination is not convenient for you, the interview may be rescheduled. Or if you have moved to a different part of the country since filing the return, you may have the audit transferred to a nearby IRS office.

Preparing for an audit

If you are notified that you will be audited, one of your first decisions must be whether to seek the advice of a lawyer or an accountant. An important factor to consider is cost. Taxpayers are understandably reluctant to incur additional expenses in connection with paying taxes. In fact, many handle the audit themselves—a course of action that is not necessarily ill-advised. The IRS has stated repeatedly that the purpose of a tax audit is not to collect additional taxes but rather to arrive at an accurate figure of tax liability—whether it be the same as, less than, or more than the figure reported on the return. Thus the IRS auditor should be viewed as an impartial expert, not an adversary.

If you decide not to seek professional assistance, you should try to understand as fully as possible the applicable laws and regulations governing the issues involved. Many publications, written for people not trained in tax matters, are available to assist you. One of the best is published annually by the IRS itself and is entitled *Your Federal Income Tax.* This document, also referred to as Publication 17, is one of many fine IRS publications that explain various aspects of the tax laws and that are free of charge. These government publications reflect only the IRS's interpretations of the law, but they are usually, though not always, accepted by the courts if you decide to take your case that far.

Although you will save professional fees by handling your audit yourself, there are good reasons for being represented by an attorney or accountant. The issues involved in your return may be too complex for someone not trained in tax law. Also, professionals are accustomed to dealing with IRS agents and are more familiar with the strategies to adopt during an audit. Moreover, if you suspect that the IRS may be contemplating a charge of tax fraud against you, you should consult an attorney at once. In such a situation, the questions are so complex and there is so much to lose that representing yourself is not worth the risk.

In the notification of an audit, the IRS usually requests that the taxpayer bring records concerning the specific items on the tax return that the computer has selected as having a likelihood of error. It is usually a good idea to go over these records before the meeting so that you will be able to clear up questions with the least difficulty. As a rule, you should bring only the records specifically requested.

Although most audits initially focus on specific issues, there is nothing to prevent the examiner from pursuing other matters while the audit is in progress. This may cost you more tax. Therefore, it is generally a mistake for the taxpayer himself to raise new issues during an audit. The only time a taxpayer should bring up new items is if they indicate an overpayment of tax. For example, if a return included tax-exempt income or if allowable deductions were not claimed, these points may be raised to offset unfavorable items or to entitle the taxpayer to a refund. Remember, however, that if you do not have professional advice, introducing new items may lead to the exploration of areas you have not considered, and the result may be more, rather than less, tax due.

The examination

If you are audited, you will find that IRS examinations are informal. The examiner will typically spend time both reviewing your records and discussing with you certain questions of fact and points of law. It is important to realize that examiners are just people trying to do a good job. Occasionally, a bad apple may be encountered, but in most cases examiners are not out to get the taxpayer. Therefore, be friendly and cooperative but not to the extent of volunteering information. If you think an examiner is acting improperly, ask to see his or her supervisor.

An audit may involve more than one conference with the examiner, or sometimes the taxpayer will be asked to submit additional information by mail. Once the examination is completed, the taxpayer will be informed of the auditor's findings. If your return is accepted as originally filed, no further action is necessary. If, on the other hand, the agent concludes that an additional tax is due—and this happens in about 75 percent of the cases—you will have to consider whether to pay the additional amount (called a *deficiency*) or to appeal the decision.

If you disagree with the IRS decision

Your strategy when you are asked to pay a deficiency will depend on whether you think it is unjustified, and if so, whether you think that an appeal to the IRS will be successful or whether you prefer to fight the deficiency in court. Evaluating the accuracy of a deficiency depends on the facts of the individual case. The examiner will probably have explained the legal reasons for concluding that a deficiency exists, and this will give you some basis for reaching your own conclusion. At this point, you may want to consult a lawyer if you have not already done so.

If you conclude that an appeal will be useless, the IRS will give you a form to sign that states that you agree with the deficiency. This agreement stops the running of interest on the deficiency 30 days after you have filed it, provided that you pay the bill for the additional tax that the IRS sends to you. The law requires you to pay interest on underpayments of tax starting from the time the tax payment was due. On the other hand, if tax is overpaid, the government must generally pay you interest from the time of overpayment, unless it is refunded within 45 days after the tax return was due or was actually filed, whichever is later.

If you disagree with the decision and the examination was an office audit, you may request an immediate meeting with the examiner's supervisor. If you are still unable to reach an agreement (or if the audit took place outside the office), the IRS will send you a transmittal letter—called a *30-day letter*—informing you of the amount of the proposed deficiency and of your right to an administrative appeal within the IRS if you act within 30 days.

Appeal within the IRS At your conferences with the IRS appeals office the original agent generally will not be present, so you should feel free to discuss the original examination frankly. If you are successful in convincing the appeals office that no

deficiency exists, you will not have to pay additional taxes. A fact to take into account in your decision to appeal within the IRS is that the appeals office is permitted to compromise a case on the basis of "hazards of litigation." Therefore, even if the appeals office does not completely agree with your position, it may conclude the case on terms that are favorable to you in order to eliminate further controversy.

Many taxpayers do take their cases to the appeals office. These appeals, which do not require a lawyer, are held in local IRS offices, and they offer inexpensive and speedy resolutions to tax disputes. They have possible disadvantages, however.

First, by pursuing appellate remedies within the IRS, you will be extending the time that interest will accrue on any deficiency ultimately found.

Second, if the proposed deficiency exceeds $2,500 and results from a field audit, you must file a written protest explaining your reasons for disagreeing with it. The protest need not be an involved document but should include a statement that you want to appeal the findings; the tax years involved; a list of the disputed items; a statement of facts supporting your position in any contested factual issue; and a statement outlining the law or other authority, such as a previous ruling on a similar case, upon which you rely. The protest must be signed with the declaration that it is true under penalty of perjury.

Finally, by appealing within the IRS you run the risk that the IRS will bring new issues against you. As a matter of policy, the IRS usually will not raise new issues at the appellate level unless there are substantial grounds that will have a potential material effect on your tax liability. However, if new grounds are raised, an even larger deficiency may be found. Ordinarily, the taxpayer has the burden of proof as to any issue raised before the case is brought to court. If you take the case to court, the IRS still has the right to raise new issues, but it will also have the burden of proof. So if you think you will not be able to reach agreement with the appeals office, consider bypassing it and taking your case straight to court.

Appeal to the courts You may challenge an unfavorable IRS decision in one of three courts: the U.S. Tax Court, the U.S. district court for the district in which you live, or the U.S. Court of Claims.

U.S. Tax Court Two attributes of the Tax Court make it the most popular choice of taxpayers. First, the Tax Court is the only court in which you may contest a tax dispute without first paying the disputed amount in full. Second, the Tax Court has a special procedure for cases involving not more than $5,000 in disputed taxes for any one taxable year. This procedure was specifically designed to let the average taxpayer challenge unfavorable IRS decisions quickly and inexpensively. It dispenses with various formalities, such as rules of evidence and the filing of legal briefs, which generally require an attorney. Small tax cases are heard by special trial judges of the Tax Court, who are usually familiar with and sympathetic to the average taxpayer not represented by an attorney. A hearing by one of these judges is informal and permits the taxpayer to recite the facts and get an independent review of the IRS's findings. Decisions of the Tax Court in small tax cases are final and may not be appealed to a higher court.

You may, if you wish, petition the Tax Court without electing the small tax case procedure even if your case involves $5,000 or less; but if you do, the regular Tax Court procedures and rules of evidence will apply. Although many taxpayers do not use lawyers in regular Tax Court proceedings, this is usually not a good idea and only increases the IRS's chances of success. The benefit of the regular procedure is that you may appeal to a higher court if the Tax Court finds against you.

Although the Tax Court is a national court with headquarters in Washington, D.C., it holds regular hearings in more than 50 cities and small tax hearings in 85 cities. Information about the Tax Court and the small tax case procedure can be obtained by writing to the U.S. Tax Court, Washington, D.C. 20217.

A Tax Court proceeding begins when the taxpayer files a petition with the court to review a deficiency asserted by the IRS. The petition may not be filed until the IRS has mailed a *deficiency notice* to the taxpayer. The deficiency notice states that additional taxes are due and that administrative proceedings with the IRS have been concluded. It is different from the 30-day letter, which only proposes a deficiency and informs the taxpayer of further appeal rights within the IRS. A deficiency notice is also called a *90-day letter* because the IRS may not assess or collect the deficiency for 90 days after the letter is mailed, during which period the taxpayer may file a petition with the Tax Court.

If the taxpayer petitions the Tax Court, the IRS may not assess or collect additional taxes while the lawsuit is in progress. It is critical that the petition be filed within the 90-day period. A petition filed either earlier or later will be invalid. At any time after the

initial examination, the IRS will honor a taxpayer's request to end further administrative proceedings and send a deficiency notice. By asking for an end to the proceedings, a taxpayer can accelerate the settlement of the dispute and thereby reduce the interest on any deficiency ultimately found.

District courts and Court of Claims   The other two courts with jurisdiction over federal tax disputes, the district courts and the Court of Claims, may be petitioned only after the disputed tax has been paid and a claim for refund denied by the IRS. The taxpayer is well advised to be represented by an attorney in these courts. A principal difference between the two is that only the district courts permit jury trials. Neither the Court of Claims nor the Tax Court has provision for jury trials. Also, like the Tax Court, the Court of Claims is national, with headquarters in Washington, D.C. District courts, on the other hand, are permanently located in the various federal judicial districts throughout the country. As with appeals to the Tax Court, the taxpayer may terminate the administrative process after the initial audit and take the case directly to the district court or the Court of Claims. If you choose to do this, you simply request immediate assessment of the proposed deficiency, which you then pay. Following payment, you must submit a claim for refund to the IRS. When the service denies the refund claim, or six months after the claim is filed, whichever comes sooner, you may start a lawsuit for refund in either the district court or the Court of Claims.

Further appeals   Adverse decisions of the district courts and the Tax Court (except in small tax cases) may be appealed by either the government or the taxpayer in one of the federal courts of appeal. Further appeal may be taken to the U.S. Supreme Court. Appeals of decisions of the Court of Claims may be taken only to the Supreme Court. It should be noted, however, that the Supreme Court agrees to hear only a handful of tax cases each year.

Be prepared, not alarmed

Tax audits, like taxes themselves, are an unpleasant but inevitable fact of life. There is nothing mysterious about the process, and taxpayers should not be alarmed because their returns are selected for examination. Ample opportunity exists for full hearings on tax disputes both within the IRS and in the courts. Although much can be said for seeking professional representation, it may not really be necessary.

marital relationship. A married taxpayer who files a separate return may claim an exemption for his spouse only when the spouse has no gross income and is not the dependent of another taxpayer—for example, a person who receives more support from his parent than from his spouse. (Your spouse is never considered your dependent.) An exemption is allowed for a spouse even if he or she is a nonresident alien. If your spouse has gross income, you may claim exemptions for both of you only if you file jointly.

A spouse who has died during the year and had no gross income may still be claimed as an exemption on a joint return. The additional exemptions for age and blindness may also be claimed for the deceased spouse. A taxpayer who has remarried in the same year may not claim an exemption for his deceased spouse. In the year of one spouse's death, the surviving spouse without gross income may be claimed as an exemption on both the final separate return of the deceased spouse and the separate return of the new spouse. If the surviving spouse files a joint return with the new spouse, the surviving spouse may be claimed as an exemption only on that return.

A taxpayer who was divorced or legally separated at the end of the year cannot claim his former spouse as an exemption even if he fully supported his former spouse.

Exemptions for dependents Every taxpayer is entitled to an exemption for each person who qualifies as his dependent. The exemptions for age and blindness cannot be claimed by a taxpayer for his dependents. Any child who was born alive, even if he lived only momentarily, may be claimed as a dependent, but there is no exemption for a stillborn child. If a dependent died during the year, a taxpayer may be entitled to claim the full exemption if the dependency tests are met for the part of the year the dependent lived.

Dependency tests The Internal Revenue Service (IRS) uses a certain group of tests to determine which persons may be claimed by a taxpayer as a dependent.

Support test A taxpayer must provide more than half the dependent's total support during the calendar year. This is determined by comparing the taxpayer's contribution to the dependent's support with the entire amount of support received by the dependent from all sources, including that provided from the dependent's own funds, such as wages from a summer job. Total support includes expenses for food, shelter, clothing, education, medical and dental care, recreation, transportation, and other necessities. Tax-exempt income, such as Social Security benefits, welfare benefits, nontaxable pensions or armed forces family allotments, savings, and borrowed amounts used for the support of a dependent, must be included in figuring total support.

EXAMPLE You contributed $1,500 to your mother's support for the year. She had taxable income of $800, Social Security benefits of $1,200, and tax-free interest on municipal bonds of $200, all of which were used for her support. You may not claim your mother as a dependent, since your contribution of $1,500 was not more than half of her total support of $3,700. On the other hand, suppose your son borrowed $2,500 as a student loan to pay his college tuition. He is personally liable for the loan. You borrow $3,000 from a bank to pay the rest of his school expenses and contribute $2,500 more toward his support.

You may claim your son as a dependent, since the $5,500 you provided is more than half his total support of $8,000.

Benefits received by veterans under the GI Bill for tuition payments and allowances while attending school are used to determine support, but scholarships received by your dependent child are not included.

EXAMPLE Suppose your son received $1,750 from the government under the GI Bill, which he used for his education. You furnish $1,500, the balance of his support. You cannot claim your son as a dependent because you provided less than half his total support. On the other hand, your daughter is awarded a $4,000 scholarship. In the same year you provided $1,000 as her only other support. You can claim her as a dependent.

Gross-income test As a general rule, a taxpayer may not claim a person as a dependent who had a gross income over a certain amount for the year. In 1980 the amount was $1,000. But a taxpayer's child who is less than 19 years of age at the end of the tax year may have any amount of income and still be claimed as a dependent as long as the other tests are satisfied. When the child is a student, age is not a factor. To qualify as a student, the child must be a full-time student at any primary or secondary school, college, university, normal school, technical school, medical school, law school, mechanical school, or similar organization. Correspondence schools, on-the-job training, night schools, or noneducational organizations will not qualify the child as a student.

Relationship and member-of-household tests Related dependents include children, grandchildren, stepchildren, brothers, sisters, step and half brothers and sisters, parents, grandparents, stepparents, aunts, uncles, and in-laws. A related dependent need not live with you or be a member of your household to entitle you to an exemption so long as he meets the other dependency tests.

A child who was legally adopted by the taxpayer is considered the taxpayer's child. Before legal adoption, the taxpayer may claim an exemption for the child if he or she was placed with the taxpayer for adoption by an authorized adoption agency and was a member of his household.

When the taxpayer files a joint return, he does not have to show that the dependent is related to both persons. A husband may, for example, claim an exemption for his wife's grandfather who receives more than half his support from him. When married taxpayers file separate returns, however, the unrelated taxpayer cannot claim an exemption for his spouse's grandfather unless the grandfather meets the member-of-the-household test.

A person who is a member of a taxpayer's household and lives with him for an entire year—a foster child, for example—does not have to be related to him in order to be a dependent if he meets the other tests. When the taxpayer is paid to be a foster parent by a child-placing agency, however, he cannot claim the child because any reimbursed expenses are incurred on behalf of the agency and any other expenses may be deducted either as a charitable contribution or as a business expense.

The taxpayer is entitled to an exemption even if the dependent is temporarily absent from the home for such reasons as vacation or school. Confinement in a nursing home for constant medical care is a temporary absence.

Citizenship test The dependent must be a U.S. citizen, resident, or national, or a resident of Canada or Mexico for some part of the tax year. Children are usually citizens or residents of the country of their parents. If the taxpayer was a U.S. citizen living abroad when his child was born there to a nonresident alien, the child may have dual citizenship and be recognized as a U.S. citizen—and an exemption—for tax purposes, even though the child lives abroad with the alien parent. A taxpayer living abroad who legally adopts an alien child may claim him as a dependent if the child is a member of the taxpayer's household for the entire tax year.

Joint-return test No exemption is allowed for a married dependent—such as a child in college for whom you provide more than half the support—who files a joint return with his or her spouse. A taxpayer may claim an exemption, however, if neither the dependent nor the spouse is required to file a return because each had less than $1,000 gross income for the year.

Multiple-support agreement Sometimes no one person contributes more than half the support of a dependent. Instead, two or more persons together provide it. In these cases, only one of the persons—if he contributed more than 10 percent—may claim the exemption. This applies only to persons who could have claimed the individual—for example, on the basis of kinship—as a dependent if it were not for the support test. Written statements in which the other contributors agree not to claim the exemption for that year must accompany the tax return of the person who is taking the exemption.

EXAMPLE Suppose you, your sister, and your two brothers 0⟶⚹ provide the entire support for your father. You contribute 45 percent; your sister, 35 percent; and each brother, 10 percent. Either you or your sister may claim an exemption for your father for the year, as long as the other files a written statement disclaiming an exemption for him. Since neither of your brothers qualifies for the exemption, they do not have to file any written statements. If each member of the family contributes only 10 percent toward your father's support, and the remaining 60 percent is provided by persons not related to him or with whom he does not live, the exemption cannot be taken by anyone because more than half his support is furnished by persons who cannot claim him as a dependent.

Support by divorced or separated parents The divorced or separated parent who has custody of the child for the greater part of the year is usually treated as the parent who furnishes more than half the child's support, whether or not this is the case. Custody is normally determined by the terms of the most recent decree of divorce or separate maintenance (financial support), a subsequent custody decree, or a written separation agreement. When the custodian of the child is not clearly established, the parent with physical custody of the child for the greater portion of the year will be treated as having custody of the child for the tax year.

The parent who does not have custody of the child is not always prevented from claiming an exemption, however. If he or she contributes $600 or more toward each child's support during the tax year and the decree or written agreement between the parties specifies that this parent is entitled to the exemption, he may claim it. The written agreement must be attached to the return of the parent claiming the exemption. The parent who does not have custody of the child may also claim an exemption if he provides $1,200 or more of support for each child for the tax year and it is not clearly established that the parent having custody provided more support.

EXAMPLE Suppose under the terms of Val's divorce, his 0⟶⚹ former wife received custody of his two children. Val provided $1,800 in support for each child during the calendar year. His ex-wife can prove she paid only $800. Val is entitled to the exemptions, but if he had provided only $1,000 for each child, he would not be.

Child support furnished by a third party, such as a grandparent, on behalf of a divorced or separated parent does not count as support furnished by that parent. If a divorced parent who has custody of a child remarries, any support furnished by the new spouse will be treated as provided by the remarried parent.

■ **Adjustments to income** After you have listed all your gross income, you can deduct certain expenses. These deductions are called adjustments to income.

Moving expenses If you moved to a new residence during the tax year because you changed your job or became self-employed, you may be entitled to deduct the reasonable expenses of your move from your gross income, even if you do not itemize your deductions. To qualify for the deduction, the new place of work must be at least 35 miles farther than your old residence was from your former place of work. For example, if your former place of work was 10 miles from your old home, your new place of work must be at least 45 miles from your old residence. You must be employed or self-employed for at least 39 weeks of the 12 months immediately following the move. In general, the moving expenses must be reasonable and must have occurred within one year from the time you began your new job. If you can show circumstances that prevented you from moving at that time, you may be able to deduct moving expenses incurred after that first year. Among the moving expenses that are deductible are travel expenses, such as meals and lodgings for yourself and your family while en route from your old to your new home; the costs of moving household goods and personal effects; expenses such as transportation, meals, and lodging incurred in house-hunting trips; and the costs of selling your old home, such as real estate commissions and attorney's fees. The maximum deduction for house-hunting trips, temporary quarters, and selling and purchasing expenses is $3,000.

Nondeductible moving expenses include a loss on the sale of your home, prepayment of rent, money spent on fixing up your home to assist in its sale, or any part of the purchase price of the new home. If, as a result of your move, you lose your security deposit because you have broken your lease, this amount will be allowed as a deduction. No deduction can be claimed if the deposit is forfeited because your old residence needed cleaning or redecorating.

Employees' business expenses "Outside" salespersons, such as traveling salesmen who do their selling away from their employer's place of business, may deduct travel, entertainment, and gift expenses incurred in connection with their employment. If these salespersons are partly reimbursed by their employers, the amount of the deduction is reduced unless the reimbursement is treated as additional income to the salespersons. Salespersons who are required to sell at the employer's place of business as a regular part of their employment, even if only for a specified period of time each week, are not considered outside salespersons entitled to this deduction, nor are employees who make sales but whose principal duties are service or delivery—milkmen, for example. Incidental activities, such as writing up and transmitting orders or spending short periods of time to make or to receive telephone calls at the employer's place of business, do not disqualify a person as an outside salesperson. A corporate officer who claims a deduction for travel, entertainment, or gift expenses incurred on behalf of the corporation must be able to show that they were necessary expenses of the office, and if the expenses are lavish or extravagant under the circumstances or were incurred for personal or vacation purposes, they may not be deducted.

Certain expenses incurred for entertainment facilities used in business—such as yachts, hunting lodges, swimming pools, tennis courts, hotel suites, or vacation homes—are no longer deductible, but dues paid for country clubs are, since they are used primarily as informal settings for business discussions.

Payments to individual retirement plans   The Individual Retirement Savings Program is designed for employees who are not covered under a qualified retirement plan at their job. A taxpayer who is eligible for an Individual Retirement Account (IRA) and decides to establish one at a participating bank or savings institution will be entitled to deduct his yearly payments to the account from his gross income. The deduction to be taken is the smallest of: the actual amount of the payment, or $1,500, or 15 percent of his compensation.

Instead of setting up a pension plan, an employer may contribute to an employee's IRA. If he does so, the maximum contribution he can make is $7,500 or 15 percent of the employee's salary, whichever is less. If the employer contributes less than $1,500 or 15 percent of the salary, the employee may make tax-deductible additions to his account until those limits are met. A tax will be imposed on any contribution over these limits.

Self-employed persons can enjoy similar benefits under Keogh plans, in which the amount of the contribution and resulting deduction may be greater than those allowed under the IRA.

When a husband and wife are each eligible and have their own separate IRA or Keogh programs, they will each be entitled to the deduction, regardless of whether or not they file a joint tax return.

Contributions to an IRA or Keogh plan become taxable as gross income during the taxpayer's working years if he violates a term of the arrangement, as by withdrawing funds from the account. Usually, however, the contributions and accumulated earnings become taxable only when they are distributed to the taxpayer after his retirement, at which time he will probably be in a much lower tax bracket than he was while working. Generally, the earliest age at which distributions may be made is 59½ unless the taxpayer has become disabled. If it is made earlier, the amount

received will be included in the taxpayer's gross income for that tax year, and his income tax will be increased by 10 percent of the amount paid. Distributions must begin before the end of the year in which the taxpayer reaches 70½; if it does not begin then, he will be liable for a 50 percent tax on the minimum payout requirement for the tax year in question. See PENSION.

Forfeited-interest penalty   A taxpayer may deduct from his gross income any interest forfeited to a bank or savings institution by his early withdrawal of funds from a time savings account or a certificate of deposit. These accounts offer higher rates of interest on savings, but they must be kept on deposit for a certain period of time.

Alimony   A taxpayer may deduct alimony, separate maintenance (a money allowance for support), or similar payments made to his current or former spouse. Child support is not deductible, but the taxpayer may be entitled to claim the dependency exemption for the child, as discussed above. To qualify for a deduction, alimony payments must be (1) required under a divorce and separation decree or a written agreement attached to the decree; (2) based on the marital or family relationship; (3) paid after the decree; and (4) periodic, which means that they must be of a fixed amount (such as $200 a month) for an indefinite period or of an indefinite amount (such as 15 percent of a fluctuating income) for either a fixed or an indefinite period. If the decree or agreement does not specify an amount as child support, the entire payment is alimony. It is deductible by the person who pays it and is income to the former spouse who receives it.

Disability-income exclusion   If a taxpayer is under 65 and retired on disability or is permanently and totally disabled and not yet at the mandatory retirement age, he may exclude up to $5,200 a year (or $100 a week). The amount he can exclude will be reduced by one dollar for every dollar that his adjusted gross income exceeds $15,000. The total amount of disability payments received must be reported before the exclusion can be taken. After age 65, these individuals may be eligible for the credit for the elderly (discussed below). Whether a disability pension is subject to this exclusion depends on how the pension plan was financed.

■ **Deductions from adjusted gross income**   Once these total adjustments have been deducted from total income, the remaining figure is the taxpayer's *adjusted gross income*. In order to establish his taxable income, the taxpayer subtracts the deductions he is allowed from his adjusted gross income. Until 1978 a taxpayer who did not choose to itemize his deductions was given a standard deduction. Since that year, however, the standard deduction has been replaced by the *zero-bracket amount*. This is a specific amount, determined by the taxpayer's filing status, which has been built into the tax tables and rate schedules. The zero-bracket amount applies to all taxpayers, whether or not they itemize their deductions. Upon arriving at his adjusted gross income, a taxpayer who does not itemize his deductions will consult the appropriate tax table (for single people, married couples filing jointly, etc.). Under the column with the total number of exemptions claimed, he will find the amount of tax he owes. For a taxpayer to itemize his deductions, the deductions must exceed the value of the zero-bracket deduction. This excess is then subtracted from the adjusted gross income. Once this amount is determined, the taxpayer will find the amount of tax he owes in the table that applies to him. Expenses that make up the itemized deductions include medical and dental expenses, taxes, interest paid out, contributions, and losses resulting from casualty or theft.

Medical and dental expenses Certain medical and dental expenses for yourself, your spouse, and dependents may be taken as itemized deductions. Medical expenses must have been paid to diagnose, cure, relieve, treat, or prevent disease; to affect a structure or function of the body; or to provide insurance that covers medical care for you, your spouse, or dependents. Medical care includes hospital, nursing, medical, laboratory, surgical, dental, diagnostic, and healing services, X-rays, medicines, drugs, artificial teeth or limbs, and ambulance service. The costs of acupuncture, vasectomies, cosmetic surgery, abortions, and psychiatric treatment are deductible as medical expenses, as are prescribed and nonprescribed medicines and drugs, special goods and beverages prescribed solely for the treatment of an illness and not as a substitute for normal consumption, birth-control pills or devices prescribed by your doctor, and vitamins or iron supplements prescribed or recommended by your doctor. A guide dog for a blind person is deductible. A wig for a daughter who lost her hair due to disease, and clarinet lessons recommended by an orthodontist to help correct your son's malocclusion are allowed to be deducted. Vitamins for your general health are not, nor are diaper services, health club dues, or maternity clothes. One half of the amount you paid for medical insurance premiums is deductible up to $150. The balance is added to your other medical expenses, which are deductible only if the total exceeds 3 percent of your adjusted gross income. The cost of medicine and prescription drugs must exceed 1 percent of the taxpayer's adjusted gross income *before* it can be included as part of the 3 percent needed to take the deduction. For instance, if the taxpayer has an adjusted gross income of $8,000, the first $240 (3 percent) of unreimbursed medical expenses cannot be deducted. The medical expenses must actually be paid by the taxpayer before a deduction can be claimed. If your insurance company reimburses you for a medical expense in the taxable year in which you paid it, you cannot take a deduction for that expense. Payment during the year for services performed in prior years can be deducted, but advance payments for future services cannot be.

Taxes If you itemize deductions, certain taxes that you have paid during the tax year may be deducted: state, local, or foreign income taxes; real estate taxes; state or local personal property taxes; general sales taxes; and taxes on gasoline used for business. (Foreign income tax may be taken as a credit, instead.) You may not deduct taxes that are imposed by the federal government, such as federal income taxes and Social Security taxes withheld from your pay; federal excise taxes on gasoline, tires, telephone service, and air transportation; customs duties; federal estate and gift taxes; and state and local taxes on inheritance, gifts, cigarettes, tobacco, and alcohol.

Interest deductions Interest is defined as compensation for using or not using money. To be deductible, interest must be paid on a debt for which you are legally responsible. No deduction is allowed for payments made on behalf of someone else if you were not legally liable to make them. Items that may be deducted as interest include the interest portion of your mortgage payment as well as a mortgage prepayment penalty, finance charges separately stated, interest on credit-card debts; note-discount interest, installment-plan interest, and interest on a personal or business loan. Interest paid on a personal loan that was made to buy a color television set or take a vacation trip to Europe is just as deductible as interest on a debt that was incurred to provide working capital or to purchase a factory. But service charges, credit-investigation fees, loan fees, and interest relating to tax-exempt income (interest you pay on money borrowed to buy tax-exempt bonds, for instance) are among items not deductible as interest.

Charitable contributions Any taxpayer may deduct a contribution to a qualified charity paid within the tax year. Payment may be made in money or property, such as by donating a color television set to an orphanage. A pledge made to donate money to charity is not deductible until the money is actually paid. The face amount of the contribution is reduced or eliminated for tax purposes if the taxpayer receives anything of value in return. For example, tuition paid to a parochial school cannot be deducted as a charitable contribution. If a taxpayer buys a dinner ticket to a charity ball for $100, he will not be allowed to deduct the $100, whether or not he uses the ticket. If, however, he can show that the dinner had a value less than the price of the ticket, the difference between them is deductible. Thus, if the dinner was worth $25, the taxpayer would be entitled to a $75 ($100 minus $25) deduction. This deduction—when the contribution exceeds the value received—is called the excess value rule.

When you volunteer your services to a charity, such as collecting donations for the United Way, you may not deduct the value of your time or services, but any out-of-pocket expenses that you pay while giving your services to an eligible charity are deductible as contributions. These include amounts you pay for transportation from your home to the place where you serve. If you use your car, you may deduct the costs of gas and oil used or seven cents per mile, plus parking fees and tolls. When you pay for meals and lodging while you are away from home overnight donating services, these expenses are deductible as long as they are reasonable.

A donation of property other than money, such as clothing or furniture, may be deductible as a contribution to the extent of its fair market value at the time of the gift. Fair market value is defined as the price that a willing buyer would pay a willing seller. The fair market value of used clothing or furniture is substantially less than its original cost because a buyer will not pay full price for used items.

When you donate such property as stock or real estate, whose fair market value is greater than what you paid, you have to reduce the fair market value by the amount the property has appreciated. If the property would result in ordinary income or short-term capital gain if it were sold on the date it was contributed, your deduction is limited to the fair market value less the amount that would be ordinary income or short-term capital gain.

EXAMPLE In January, Rosemary bought some stock in an up 0⊶❋ and coming company for $700. Four months later, in April, she donated the stock to her church, at which time the stock had increased in value to $1,200. Because $500 of appreciation would have been a short-term gain if Rosemary had sold the stock in April instead of giving it to charity, her deduction was limited to the $700 she had paid for it originally.

A gift of capital-gains property, which would result in long-term capital gain if it were sold at its fair market value on the date it was contributed, usually may be deducted at its fair market value. The contribution will be reduced by 50 percent of the amount of gain in certain instances, however—for example, when the property will not be used by the charity for its exempt purpose. If a minister takes flat silver given to the community house of his church and uses the silver in his home, the gift is not deductible by the donor.

Contributions to civic leagues, social clubs, international or Communist organizations, and chambers of commerce and other business leagues or organizations are not deductible as charitable contributions. Blood donated to the Red Cross or to other blood banks is not deductible. Contributions made directly to needy or worthy individuals are not deductible because they are not eligible charities under the law. Amounts you pay to purchase raffle or lottery tickets, to play bingo, or to engage in other games of chance are not deductible.

In general, your deductions for charitable contributions cannot exceed 50 percent of your adjusted gross income for the year. There is a 20 percent limitation on contributions to certain organizations, such as war veterans' groups, domestic fraternal societies (the Elks, for example), and nonprofit cemeteries. You must keep records, receipts, canceled checks, and other evidence to establish your deductions. For each gift of property for which you have deducted more than $200, you must attach to your return a detailed statement about the nature and extent of the property and donation.

Losses resulting from casualty and theft   A casualty is the complete or partial destruction or loss of property resulting from an identifiable event that is sudden, unexpected, or unusual. Some examples of losses resulting from casualties are damage from hurricanes, tornadoes, floods, storms, fires, accidents, sonic booms, or vandalism. These losses may be taken as itemized deductions on your federal income tax return, and so can losses resulting from the theft of personal and business property. A taxpayer must be able to prove that he suffered a loss due to casualty or theft and the amount of the loss. A loss of personal property resulting from casualty or theft is deductible only to the extent that the loss was greater than $100 for each casualty or theft. If the stolen or damaged property was used for business or to produce income, the loss is fully deductible. Insurance proceeds or other compensation received or expected to be received for the damage or loss must be used to reduce the amount of the loss.

Other itemized deductions   Certain miscellaneous expenses may be deductible. Additional employee expenses that may be deductible include uniforms and special equipment required of ballplayers, firemen, police officers, letter carriers, nurses, and jockeys; musicians' and entertainers' theatrical clothing and accessories; and protective gear, such as safety shoes, hard hats, work gloves, and rubber boots. Employment agency fees and other expenses you incur in seeking new employment are deductible only if you are looking for a job in the same business or trade. If you are currently unemployed, your trade or business consists of services performed for previous employers. When you have been out of work for a substantial period of time, however, or are seeking employment for the first time, your expenses in finding a job are not deductible. Any reimbursement for agency fees that you receive from your employer must be included in your gross income. Dues paid to professional organizations, subscriptions to trade and professional magazines related to your work, and malpractice insurance premiums paid by a physician who is an employee are also deductible.

Educational expenses incurred as a result of your employment, trade, or business are usually deductible if your employer does not provide financial assistance. This would be the case if your employer changes the minimum educational requirements for your job and you must return to school in order to keep it or if you have to take refresher courses to improve skills needed in your occupation. In a recent case, the tax court permitted a nursing educator to deduct the cost of a full-time, three-year Ph.D. program in nursing education. If, however, the courses qualify you for a new trade or business or even a new job with the same company, no deduction will be allowed. If the nursing educator had earned a Ph.D. in history, her educational expenses would not be deductible. Any reimbursement received from an employer after the deduction has been taken must be reported as additional income.

If you use a portion of your home regularly and exclusively for certain business purposes (this has been interpreted to mean a room), you may deduct a pro rata portion of the operating and depreciation expense on your home. If you use part of your home for both personal and business purposes, the expenses generally are not deductible unless your home is used as a day-care facility. Using your den as an office for preparing tax returns or writing magazine articles or monthly office reports will not entitle you to a deduction. Your deductions for expenses incurred by the business use of your home may not be greater than the amount of gross income you earned for this use—reduced by taxes, interest, and casualty losses arising from this use.

Certain expenses that produce taxable income may be taken as itemized deductions. You may, for instance, deduct investment counsel fees paid to care for your investments, and expenses incurred in hiring an attorney to help you collect taxable alimony.

■ **Credits**   Once a taxpayer has determined the amount of tax he owes, he should check to see if he can reduce the amount by applying any of the available tax credits. The most important of the various allowable credits are those for contributions to candidates running for public office, credit available to the elderly, credits for child- and dependent-care expenses, and credits for earned income.

Contributions to public candidates   A taxpayer may take half of his contributions to candidates running for political office and to a national, state, or local committee of a national political party as a direct credit against his tax. The credit, however, cannot exceed $50 on a separate return or $100 on a joint return.

Credit for the elderly   Under the Tax Reform Act of 1976 a taxpayer who is 65 or older or one who is under 65 and receives a taxable pension or an annuity (pension) from a government retirement plan may claim this credit. The amount of the credit must be computed separately for each individual. To compute the credit for the elderly, you must begin with the amount of income for credit computation allowed for you. This amount is listed in your tax forms and depends on your age and marital status. If you are married, the age of your spouse and whether you file jointly or separately will also affect the figure you use. For example, in 1980 the amount of income for credit computation was $2,500 if you were single or if you were married and filed a joint return and you or your spouse was 65 or older. The amount was different if your circumstances were different. If both spouses were 65 or older and filing a joint return, the initial amount is $3,750, while for a married individual filing a separate return, the amount is $1,875. Once you have established the proper figure for yourself, you must subtract from it the sum of certain nontaxable pensions and annuities, such as Social Security retirement benefits, and one half of your adjusted gross income that exceeds $7,500 if you are single, $10,000 if you are married and filing a joint return, or $5,000 if you are married and filing a separate return. The credit for the elderly is 15 percent of the balance.

EXAMPLE You are 66 years old and single. The amount of income for credit computation is $2,500 for single persons. Your adjusted gross income is $7,400 and you receive $1,900 from Social Security. Your credit would be:

Initial amount of income for credit computation	$2,500
Social Security pension	–1,900
Balance	$ 600
Credit for the elderly (15 percent of $600)	$ 90

You do not deduct any of your adjusted gross income from the initial amount of income for credit computation because it is less than $7,500. Your credit is $90, which is deducted directly from the tax you owe. The credit can never exceed the tax you owe.

Child- and dependent-care expenses   A taxpayer who is employed and pays expenses for household services and care of a child, a disabled dependent, or a disabled spouse may be entitled to a tax credit of 20 percent of his payments for such services. The credit cannot exceed $2,000 for one child under 15 or one dependent or $4,000 for two or more qualifying dependents. To be eligible for the credit, you must be employed or looking for a job during the time the expenses are incurred; your household must include one or more of the qualifying individuals; the expenses must be necessary to help you keep your job; and payments must be to other than dependent relatives. Payments made to grandparents for care of their grandchildren may qualify for this credit.

Earned-income credit   A low-income taxpayer who meets certain requirements may be entitled to a tax credit if his earned income or adjusted gross income, whichever is larger, is less than $10,000. Among other requirements, he must live in the United States with a child who qualifies as a dependent and file a joint return if married. The credit is $500 for the first $5,000 of income. If the taxpayer's income is more than $5,000, the credit is reduced by 10 percent of the amount over $5,000.

EXAMPLE In 1980 Marsha received wages of $6,500 and interest income of $1,500. She filed a joint return with her husband (who had no income) and claimed her child as a dependent. Marsha's earned income credit would be $200. This is computed by subtracting 10 percent of the amount by which Marsha's adjusted gross income of $8,000 exceeds the $5,000 limitation (10 percent of $3,000, or $300) from the $500 maximum credit.

■ **Maximum tax**   There is a maximum tax rate of 50 percent on an individual's personal-service income, which includes pension and annuity income resulting from past personal services as well as earned income (salary or wages). This limit applies if you are single or the head of a household and have a personal-service taxable income of more than $40,200 or if you are married and filing jointly and have a personal-service taxable income of more than $55,200. The maximum tax-rate limit does not apply to taxpayers who are eligible to file a joint return but choose to file separately or who use income averaging.

■ **Income averaging**   If a taxpayer's income has increased substantially in a tax year, it may be to his advantage to compute his tax under the income-averaging method. This permits a part of an unusually large amount of taxable income to be taxed in lower brackets and results in a reduction of the amount of tax due. For such taxpayers as authors, actors, and athletes who have fluctuating or bunched income, and who face graduated tax rates that apply on an annual basis, income averaging can be most important. To use income averaging, a taxpayer must have been either a citizen or resident of the United States throughout the computation year (the current tax year) and the base-period years (the four immediately preceding tax years). He must also have provided 50 percent or more of his own support during each of the four base-period years. Individuals who have been full-time students during the base-period years cannot use income averaging. A taxpayer's averageable income must be more than $3,000. Averageable income is the amount by which your adjusted taxable income for the current year exceeds 30 percent of your total income for the four preceding tax years.

■ **Payment**   For most taxpayers, a tax return along with payment of any tax owed is due on April 15. Late filing and payment will subject the taxpayer to a penalty, which is interest charged on the tax due. If the taxpayer intentionally lies or misrepresents the information on his return to reduce his tax liability, he may be subject to prosecution for TAX EVASION in addition to interest and penalties. When a taxpayer has made an honest mistake, he will be subject to interest on his late payment but if he can show that his nonpayment resulted from reasonable cause (a question of fact) he may not have to pay penalties.

■ **Refunds**   Once you have paid your tax, you have the right to file a claim for a refund if you think you have paid too much. The claim should be filed with the same IRS office where you filed your original return, and it must be filed within three years from the date the return was filed or the due date, or within two years from the date the tax was paid, whichever is later.

■ **An income tax audit** Although most taxpayers are honest in completing their returns, one of their greatest dreads is an audit of their tax returns by the IRS. The audit verifies that the taxpayer has correctly reported his income, exemptions, and deductions. Such an examination does not necessarily mean that the government suspects a person of being dishonest or criminally liable for intentionally lying on his return. Most returns are selected for an audit by a computer that identifies the returns with the greatest probability of error. Once a return has been selected by the computer, an IRS agent reviews it to confirm that it has a high-error potential before an audit will take place. Some returns, however, are audited because the taxpayer has been under investigation for tax evasion or has been involved in an area under investigation by the IRS, such as tax shelters.

Being audited does not necessarily mean a taxpayer will have to pay more tax. Sometimes, taxpayers have received unexpected refunds for overpayment.

In the late 1970's the IRS audited a little more than 2 percent of the returns filed, or about 1.7 million out of 82.5 million. Taxpayers in higher income brackets are more likely to be audited than those with moderate incomes.

in common Ownership shared by two or more persons for their equal advantage, use, or enjoyment without dividing the whole into individual parts. If four persons own one lot of land in common, each one owns and has the right to use the entire lot. See PROPERTY.

incompatibility The impossibility of two or more things logically, physically, or legally existing together; the inability of a husband and wife to live together harmoniously in marriage. In some states incompatibility is a ground for DIVORCE, which can be granted without either party being at fault. See Chart 22.

incompetent Lacking the capacity or legal right to act. An incompetent person is one who lacks the mental ability to handle his own affairs, such as a child or senile person, and who must have someone appointed by the state to manage his finances. See INFANT; INSANE PERSONS.

incompetent evidence EVIDENCE not permitted by law to be used in a legal proceeding. Offering proof that an accused murderer is not a U.S. citizen is an example of incompetent evidence. It has nothing to do with the case.

inconsistent Mutually incompatible or contradictory. Inconsistent defenses to a crime contradict each other. If an accused robber first says he was in California at the time of the robbery, but later says he was in Florida, he has offered inconsistent defenses.

inconvenience rule The rule that says that laws should be interpreted to avoid inconvenience. When applied to the public, this means avoiding a sacrifice of important public interests, such as hampering the activities of government and business. When applied to individuals, the rule means that a law should not cause serious hardship or injustice.

incorporate Formally and legally create a CORPORATION. The persons who form the corporation are called the incorporators.

incorporate by reference Declare that one document is part of another document without having to write it out in its entirety. For instance, you say in Contract A that Agreement B is part of Contract A, just as if Agreement B were actually written out in Contract A. This is a technique used by legal writers to save space, particularly in lengthy documents, such as insurance contracts.

incorporeal Without body; not of a substantial nature. For example, if you have an idea for a novel in your head, it is an incorporeal concept. You cannot obtain a copyright until you actually write down the idea.

incriminate Charge with a crime; involve oneself or another in a criminal prosecution. A witness is not required to offer testimony or other evidence that would tend to incriminate him. See SELF-INCRIMINATION.

indefeasible That which cannot be revoked or made void. The term is usually applied to a right that cannot be defeated. An interest in land, for instance, is indefeasible if the owner was given an estate in FEE SIMPLE (absolute and unconditional ownership).

indefinite term A jail or prison SENTENCE for a length of time that is left open except that it specifies a certain maximum. For example, a convicted criminal could be sentenced to prison for up to 25 years. When indefinite terms are given it is up to correction officials to decide exactly when the prisoner is to be released.

indemnity Compensation for loss, damage, or injuries; reimbursement. Indemnity is the obligation of one person to make good any loss or damage another person has incurred or may incur. The right to indemnity and the obligation to indemnify almost always spring from a contract. The contract is usually either against liability or against loss or damage. Suppose your father-in-law agrees to reimburse you for any damage caused by his employee's use of your driveway to park his car. He has made an indemnity contract with you. All INSURANCE policies are indemnity contracts.

indenture A DEED to which two or more persons are parties and in which they enter into reciprocal and mutual obligations toward each other. A deed in which a seller promises to transfer ownership of land to a buyer, who promises to pay for it, is an indenture.

independent contractor Someone who contracts to do a piece of work according to his own methods and without being subject to his employer, except for the results of the work. An independent contractor, such as one in the construction industry, has the right to employ and direct his workers independently of his employer.

indeterminate Uncertain; not specified or designated. For instance, an indeterminate SENTENCE is a criminal prison sentence for which a minimum sentence must be served but no maximum time is set (although the term may not exceed the maximum penalty set by law for the crime involved). A sentence of from 25 years to life is an indeterminate sentence. Some states allow judges to give only indeterminate sentences and have special boards decide the exact time period later.

Indians The name given by the European discoverers of America to its native inhabitants. They are entitled to all the rights, privileges, and immunities of other Americans. Indians born in the United States are U.S. citizens. They are entitled to vote and may sue in federal and state courts. Persons of mixed blood are classified as Indians according to the applicable laws or treaties.

A *tribe* is a group of Indians united under one leadership, who live in a designated, although sometimes loosely defined, territory. A *band* is a smaller and less permanent group than a tribe. A *nation* of Indians is a large tribe, or a group of affiliated tribes, acting together for the time being. Indian tribes and nations are recognized by the federal government. They have, in their local affairs, certain legal and political powers that sovereign nations have. For example, two or more tribes may consolidate or one tribe may divide into separate bands. In addition, an Indian tribe may impose taxes and require licenses within the limits of its territory. An Indian tribe also has SOVEREIGN IMMUNITY— that is, the tribe's government cannot be sued without its consent. When there are no conflicting federal laws, Indian laws and customs control the internal affairs of the tribes. In 1968, Congress enacted the Indian Civil Rights Act, which requires that the self-governing Indian tribes protect the civil liberties and rights of their members. This act, based partly on the Bill of Rights, is designed to insure the fair administration of justice by tribal authorities.

EXAMPLE In one case, a female member of the Santa Clara Pueblo sued in federal court for relief against the enforcement of a tribal ordinance that denied membership in the tribe to children of female members who married outside the tribe. Children of male members who married outside the tribe were given membership. When the case reached the Supreme Court, a majority of justices held that (1) suits against the tribe, under the Indian Civil Rights Act, are barred by its sovereign immunity; and (2) the Indian Civil Rights Act does not authorize private actions for relief against the tribe's officers.

The court's reasoning was that tribal courts are available to vindicate rights created by the Indian Civil Rights Act. Moreover, the issues in these cases frequently depend upon questions of Indian tradition and custom, which tribal forums can evaluate better than federal courts.

A *reservation* is a part of the public domain designated for the use and occupation of a tribe, or tribes, of Indians. Only the federal government can deprive Indians of their rights on a reservation, and even the federal government should not do so without compensating the Indians. Under special acts of Congress, various Indian tribes are now able to recover from the United States for the wrongful taking of their lands.

indicia (Latin) "Signs"; indications; circumstances that make a certain fact probable, but not certain. For instance, "indicia of partnership" are facts that lead you to believe a person is a partner in a business, even if he does not claim to be. If he supervises and gives directions to employees, that fact could help you form your belief.

indictment A written accusation of a crime. Traditionally, there can be no trial, conviction, or punishment for a crime without a formal accusation. When no formal accusation exists, the courts have no JURISDICTION (authority). If a court does assume jurisdiction, any resulting trial or conviction is nullified. In most, if not all, states a person charged with committing a felony can be prosecuted when a GRAND JURY has issued an indictment. After a crime has been committed and reported to the authorities, the prosecuting attorney draws up a bill of indictment. This is submitted to the grand jury. If the grand jury finds there are sufficient reasons for believing that a crime has been committed and that the accused committed it, the grand jury will present the indictment as a *true bill*. The purposes of an indictment are to inform an accused person of the charge against him so that he can prepare his defense and to make sure that the prosecutor is justified in conducting a criminal trial against the accused. See CRIMINAL LAW.

indirect evidence Something that only tends to establish a theory by showing consistent facts. Assume, for instance, a witness testifies that every day for the past 20 years she has seen a certain man come into her store at noon and buy a newspaper. Although she was not in the store on the day in question, her testimony could be accepted by some courts as indirect EVIDENCE that he was there.

indispensable party A person who has such an interest in the subject matter of a lawsuit that a final decree made without his participation in the legal proceedings would affect his interest or would be wholly against good conscience. For example, both drivers of the two automobiles involved in a crash in which a third person was killed would be indispensable parties to a resulting lawsuit.

individual retirement account Popularly known as an IRA. See PENSION.

industrial union A labor union whose members may have different skills but who work in the same type of industry, such as clothing manufacture, printing, or an automobile assembly.

in extremis (Latin) "In extreme circumstances"; at the point of death.

infant The term used in law to mean every person who has not yet reached the age of legal adulthood. The age of 21 became the age of adulthood, or majority, for knights in medieval times, apparently because at 21 men were thought to be strong enough to wear their heavy armor. Eventually it became the age of majority in common law. Today, the age of majority varies from state to state and differs for various purposes. Although this may seem confusing and illogical, it really is an acknowledgment that maturity is acquired over a period of years. In the state of Georgia, for example, the legal age for marrying without parental consent is 16, while the legal age for making a will is 14.

A *child* is an infant, but the term is not generally used in law because it does not have an exact legal meaning. *Minor* is another word for infant, and *minority* is the period of time during which a person is an infant. *Majority* is the time of adulthood, and the *age of majority* is the age at which one becomes an adult. Although the common-law age of majority is 21, legislatures can change the age of majority by statute. An infant reaches full legal age on the first moment of the day before his 21st birthday. For example, a person born on January 15, 1975, would become 21 for legal purposes at 12:01 A.M. on January 14, 1996.

An unborn child is not an infant because he has no legal existence. An infant has legal rights from the time of his conception or from the time he first stirs in his mother's womb; for example, he has a right to share in an estate or in a trust. But these rights do not develop into full legal existence until after the child is born. For example, a child who is born after his father's death is called a *posthumous child*. He can inherit property from his father after his birth. See DESCENT AND DISTRIBUTION.

This article discusses the legal status of persons who are not of adult age, including their special rights, legal disabilities, and judicial control.

■ **Child welfare** A state has both the right and the duty to protect the welfare of the children within its borders. This authority can be traced to the ancient concept of *parens patriae*—a Latin phrase meaning "the father of his country"—which refers to a king's relationship with his subjects. Today it is recognized that the public has an interest in making sure that children receive proper care. The state may assume this responsibility when necessary.

The power of the state as *parens patriae* is limited. A delicate balance exists between the state's necessity to act when a child's welfare is threatened and the legitimate right of parents to be left alone. Certainly it is proper for the state to assume responsibility for a child who has no one to give him parental care. But in cases where a parent is not fulfilling his responsibility, the state's intrusion should be as small as possible.

In general, courts have complete authority to provide for the CUSTODY, care, and control of children who are in the geographical area of their jurisdiction. In many states, particular courts are designated to hear cases involving infants—juvenile courts, family courts, probate courts, or surrogates' courts, for example.

Every state permits corporations, societies, or agencies to be established to care for needy or neglected children or to help prevent cruelty to children. These organizations, which are bound by state laws and must be licensed in some states, are supervised by the courts when dependent children are committed to their care. They can be appointed as guardians for children. See GUARDIAN AND WARD.

A child does not have a constitutional right to a safe home, a permanent and stable family, or even to adequate care. But because our society believes that all children should be provided for, federal and state laws try to insure that they will have not only food, clothing, and shelter but also such other basic needs as medical and dental care. The money that the states set aside to provide for the support of needy children must be dispensed fairly to all children entitled to receive it. See SOCIAL SECURITY; WELFARE PROGRAMS. When a parent is able to support a child but refuses or neglects to do so, the state has a right to recover from him whatever public money is spent on behalf of his child.

■ **Privileges and disabilities of infancy** From early times the common law imposed *disabilities* on persons under legal age; this meant that certain acts of minors had no legal effect. Today laws that set the varying legal ages of majority establish the *privileges and disabilities* of infancy. They are intended to protect children from the consequences of their own lack of judgment and to prevent them from doing things they are too immature to undertake carefully. For example, the rule that infants may not be held to contracts they make protects them from unwise transactions.

Voting rights Congress fixed the voting age at 18 for all state and federal elections in the Voting Rights Act of 1970. When that law was challenged, the Supreme Court ruled that although it was perfectly proper for Congress to set the voting age for federal elections, it was unconstitutional for Congress to set the age for state and local elections. Congress then proposed a constitutional amendment for that purpose, and the states ratified it. It became effective on July 5, 1971. This 26th Amendment says:

❝ The right of citizens of the United States, who are 18 years of age or older, to vote shall not be denied or abridged by the United States or any State on account of age."

Generally, a minor becomes eligible to hold public office when he is old enough to vote, but the Constitution makes exceptions for the highest federal offices. A member of the U.S. House of Representatives must be at least 25 years old, a Senator at least 30, and the President and Vice President at least 35 years of age.

Ownership of property A person under the legal age is capable of acquiring and owning property. Although he can transfer ownership of his property by gift or by sale, he can change his mind up to the time he reaches the age of majority or soon afterward. Because no one wants to make agreements with a person who is not bound by them, it is customary to appoint a guardian to manage an infant's property. See GUARDIAN AND WARD. To avoid the expense and inconvenience of a court-supervised guardianship when making certain kinds of GIFTS TO MINORS, the giver (donor) can simply name an adult to take custody of the gift and manage it for the infant.

Contracts An infant can make a CONTRACT with an adult and enforce that contract against the adult, but the adult cannot necessarily enforce the contract against the infant. An infant can disaffirm, or negate, a contract at any time up to the age of majority or within a reasonable time thereafter. If both parties are infants, either may disaffirm the contract. The right of an infant to disaffirm a transaction is not affected even if his parent let him enter the

MINORS—THEIR RIGHTS, OBLIGATIONS, AND PROTECTIONS

■ *Infant* is the term used in law for a person who is underage—a minor.

■ The age for majority (legal adulthood) is 21 at common law and remains so in many states, but quite a few states have lowered the legal age for certain activities, such as making contracts or driving, and the 26th Amendment to the U.S. Constitution has lowered the voting age to 18 throughout the United States.

■ A minor can make a contract with an adult and enforce that contract against him, but the adult cannot necessarily enforce the contract against the minor.

■ Under some laws, however, all contracts involving a minor's business are binding on him. This gives minors an opportunity to go into business on their own.

■ A minor is legally responsible and can be sued for injuries he or she causes others.

■ A minor can sue or be sued in his or her own name, but when a minor sues someone a legal representative must initiate the suit.

■ When minors violate criminal laws, they are called *delinquents*. When they commit illegal but noncriminal acts, they are called *status offenders*. Status offenses include truancy, running away from home, and refusing to obey parents, teachers, or legal authorities.

■ About 75 percent of the states place minors under court supervision when there is more evidence than not that the child needs supervision.

■ Some constitutional rights of due process of law are available to juveniles accused of crimes, although not all the rights afforded an accused adult. An accused juvenile is entitled to (1) the right to be given notice of the charges against him; (2) the privilege not to incriminate himself; (3) the right to have an attorney and to have one appointed if he cannot afford one; and (4) the right to confront and cross-examine witnesses who give evidence against him.

■ State laws often protect minors from abuse or negligent care. It is a crime in some states for physicians, teachers, and certain other professionals not to report a case of suspected child abuse.

■ *A dependent child* is one who does not have parental care (or parents willing and capable of taking care of him). A dependency proceeding is conducted by the state to determine what is to be done with such a child—for example, whether he is to be placed in the custody of another relative or in a foster home.

■ A state may declare a child dependent, or a ward of the state, so that the state can give its consent for lifesaving medical treatment when the parent refuses consent (typically on religious grounds). Courts have ruled time and again that transfusions and other medical treatment ordered to save a child's life under such circumstances in no way interfere with the parent's freedom of religion.

---

contract or gave approval for it. The rule is meant to protect young people, even from parents.

Because children, and especially teenagers, have their own money to spend, the right to disaffirm a purchase agreement could seriously interfere with the flow of business. Therefore, many current laws limit the child's absolute right to disaffirm contracts.

Many states have lowered the legal age to make contracts, generally from 21 to 18. Frequently, they authorize children to make certain kinds of contracts, such as for making purchases and establishing credit. States now generally require minors to pay the bills for any "necessaries" furnished to them—food, clothing, shelter, medical care, and so on. This makes it possible for someone under age to acquire on credit the items he needs to survive and then pay for them when he has the money. Statutes often permit children to transact business with banks; for the protection of the banks these transactions are legally binding on the child as well as the bank.

Child performers in New York and California can make binding employment contracts as actors or athletes, although a court may check to be sure the contract is reasonable. In New York, for example, the court may require that part of the money earned be held for the infant's future.

Under some laws, all contracts involving an infant's business are binding. This gives minors an opportunity to go into business on their own because others can rely on their contracts.

Disaffirming a contract   In general, a minor does not have to take any legal action to disaffirm a contract as long

as neither party has begun to do what the contract requires. Once one person begins to carry out the contract, however, the minor must make it clear that he does not intend to be bound by the contract.

EXAMPLE   Suppose a 15-year-old goes into an expensive ○━━✳ shoe store and selects a pair of boots. He gives his name and address to the clerk and says, "I'll be back Friday. I definitely want those boots." That is a valid, enforceable contract except for the buyer's infancy. This boy can simply wait until the shoe store sues him, assert his infancy, and be free of the obligation.

If, however, the boy went to a shoemaker, ordered a pair of handmade boots, and waited until the craftsman had cut the leather, he would have to do something to make it clear that he disaffirmed the contract. He could send the shoemaker a letter or visit him personally and absolutely repudiate the contract.

It is no good for a merchant in the first situation to claim that he thought the infant was an adult. Because the rule is intended to protect minors, the adult has the burden of finding out his customer's age. In fact, most courts will permit an infant to disaffirm a contract even if he lied about his age and showed false identifications as proof. This puts business people in a tough spot, so some courts will permit the adult to recover money damages from the infant to the extent that he has been harmed by the deceit.

EXAMPLE   Vic, two months shy of his 18th birthday, talks a ○━━✳ used-car dealer into selling him a car by lying about his age. While driving home, Vic misses a turn and hits a tree. He walks to the nearest phone booth and calls the dealer to disaffirm the contract. Some courts will let Vic recover his purchase price, but they will permit the dealer to keep enough money to pay for the car's loss in value. Most states also require an infant to return anything he gained from the bargain that is still in his possession. In this case Vic would have to give back the remains of the car.

Settling out of court   Agreements to settle out of court with an adult who has caused some injury to a child, sometimes called *infants' compromises* or *infants' settlements,* are special kinds of contracts that courts usually supervise for children. Ordinarily, a guardian (usually the parent) is appointed for the child, and he settles the child's claim for money damages without demanding a trial. In exchange, the guardian gives the person who would be sued a *release,* a written statement that the infant will not sue at a later time. Generally, a court must look over the facts of the case and approve the amount of the settlement. This insures that a parent in need of money will not quickly settle for an amount sufficient only to pay immediate medical expenses when it is likely that the child will continue to need care, perhaps even for permanent injuries.

Consent to medical treatment   A consent to allow a doctor to perform surgery is considered similar to a contract because it is an agreement. Because a child does not have the legal capacity to consent to medical treatment, the consent must come from his parent or guardian.

Making a will   Every state has a law setting the age at which a person becomes qualified to make a WILL. This age was 21, but many states have now lowered it. See Chart 14.

Other legal responsibilities   A minor can act as an agent—that is, a person who is authorized to act or do business for someone else (a principal). See AGENCY. A minor can also be a principal and designate someone else to act as his legal agent, but he does not lose his right to disaffirm contracts made for him by his agent. This means that an infant can be a member of a PARTNERSHIP, because partners are principals and agents for one another. State law varies on a child's right to recover money he invests in a partnership when he disaffirms the partnership agreement.

Minors cannot qualify as executors of wills, administrators of estates, or trustees (administrators) of TRUSTS because they do not have the authority to make binding legal contracts. See EXECUTORS AND ADMINISTRATORS. In most states minors cannot form or be directors of CORPORATIONS.

Liability for injuries to others   Unlike the law of contracts, the law of TORTS, which allows you to sue anyone who has injured you or damaged your property, is more concerned with compensating an injured party than it is with protecting a young person. Therefore, a minor is legally liable for injuries he causes others and most states have laws making a parent responsible for certain torts of his child up to a certain amount. See Chart 5. Minors have been ordered to pay money damages for assault and battery, trespass, converting another person's property to their own use, defamation, seduction of another minor, fraud and deceit, and negligence. Sometimes, however, it is difficult to prove that a young child is capable of a particular state of mind that the law says must exist if one is to be held responsible for a certain action. For example, in order to show that a person committed battery, it must be proved

that he specifically intended to cause physical contact. It may be impossible to show that a young child really understood the nature and consequences of what he did.

People who have been cheated on a contract by an infant who has lied about his age have tried to sue the infant for the tort of deceit. Some courts have permitted this, but others have not. When they do not permit it, the rule that was intended as a shield for innocent young people becomes a sword for young con artists.

Right to sue   At common law, a minor could only be a party in a lawsuit if he was joined with his guardian or a "next friend"—an adult willing to start the action for him. It is still necessary to have an adult involved to see that the child's interests are properly represented, but the precise procedure varies from state to state. Sometimes an infant can sue (or be sued) in his own name, but sometimes the name of his legal representative must be used—either alone or with the infant's name. See GUARDIAN AND WARD.

Serving as a witness   Whether a child can be a witness at a trial depends on his ability to recall and communicate facts that he is asked about and to understand the meaning of truth. The child's maturity is evaluated by the judge. If a child is not able to understand and take the oath, his unsworn testimony may sometimes be used, but it does not have the same weight as sworn testimony.

Employment   Under the common law, a child was obligated to work for his parents, and if he earned money it belonged to his father. A father could sue for money damages to pay for loss of services if his child was hurt by someone else and unable to work. Today, as a general rule, the parent having legal control and custody of a minor child (not necessarily the father) has the right to his services and earnings.

The employment of children is regulated by the Fair Labor Standards Act and by various state child labor laws. These statutes set minimum ages below which certain kinds of employment are prohibited. They generally prohibit a minor from working with dangerous machines or serving or selling alcoholic beverages. State laws also restrict the number of hours a child may work per day and set minimum wages and the minimum amount minors must be paid for overtime. See Chart 31. The purpose of child labor laws is to protect the child from risk of injury, overwork, and exposure to dangerous, immoral, or unhealthful conditions and to protect the public from the consequences of exposing children to such conditions.

An employer is usually responsible for discovering whether a job applicant is under age. He can therefore be subject to criminal penalties for hiring a child for a job that is prohibited to minors even if he did not know the person he hired was a minor.

■ **Emancipation**   Emancipation means the legal release of a child from the custody and control of his parents. If a child is self-supporting, he then has the legal right and responsibility to supervise his own conduct. He is generally held to be able to keep his own earnings and choose where he will live. On the other hand, once he is emancipated, he usually has no further right to insist that his parents support him. Emancipation, along with other facts of a situation, may show that the child is mature enough to make binding contracts and be a party to a lawsuit. A parent cannot emancipate a child by abandoning him. Most states hold that a minor is emancipated by a valid marriage whether or not he or she is self-supporting.

■ **Juvenile delinquents and offenders** When children violate criminal laws, they are called *delinquents*. When they commit illegal but noncriminal acts, they are called *status offenders*. They may also be *traffic offenders*.

Delinquency Children have been judged delinquent for a variety of acts, including possession of alcoholic beverages, possession or sale of narcotic drugs, possession of a weapon, assault and battery, truancy, or refusal to obey a court order or the reasonable orders of a parent or legal guardian. Some kinds of conduct by a child may irritate parents or legal authorities but are not acts of juvenile delinquency—refusing to salute the flag, accidentally discharging a gun, using loud and offensive language, marrying without a parent's consent at an age when consent is required by law, or having an illegitimate child.

As a general rule, a child may be judged delinquent if he violates state or local criminal laws. Several states also include violation of federal laws, and some even include violation of another state's laws. This is an exception to the general rule that a state does not enforce another state's criminal laws. Children are also delinquent when they violate laws that apply only to children, such as a law forbidding anyone under the age of 16 to possess air guns or those under 21 to buy alcoholic beverages.

Violations of curfew laws that require children under a certain age to be off the streets by a specified hour, are sometimes handled in delinquency proceedings. Some of these laws allow a judge to put a curfew violator on probation or send him to a reform school, but this is rarely done unless the child is a habitual offender. Parents can sometimes be fined for permitting their children to violate curfew laws.

Juvenile courts The judicial system for juveniles is separate and distinct from the adult CRIMINAL LAW system. In some states, however, when a child has committed a serious offense—such as murder or rape or a crime that is punishable by death or life imprisonment for adults—he is treated as an adult, not as a delinquent, and is brought to the regular criminal court.

Because it was believed that children could be rescued from a life of crime if they were properly rehabilitated, a court system for juveniles was developed that was different from the one for adults. Thus the category of delinquent child was introduced. A child who ran afoul of the law was ushered into the presence of a judge, often a specialist in such matters, who determined whether the child was delinquent. If the judge, without a jury, found that the child was delinquent, the judge could give him a stern lecture and send him home or he could assign him to a reform school. This reform movement was part of a larger one aimed at protecting children, expressed also in laws dealing with child labor and cruelty to children. Instead of punishment a child received rehabilitation. But as authorities subsequently began to realize that reform schools seemed like prisons to the children who were locked up in them, it became clear that children had to be given constitutional rights.

Constitutional rights The U.S. Supreme Court ruled in 1967 that juveniles are entitled to some constitutional rights of DUE PROCESS OF LAW guaranteed by the U.S. Constitution. See GAULT, IN RE. Not every right afforded an accused adult must be extended to juveniles, the Court held. For example, a juvenile is not entitled to BAIL, to INDICTMENT by a grand jury, to a public trial, or to trial by jury. But a child today is entitled to (1) the right to be given notice of the charges against him; (2) the privilege not to incriminate himself, which includes the right to remain silent; (3) the right to have an attorney and to have one appointed if he cannot afford one; and (4) the right to confront and cross-examine witnesses who give evidence against him. Juveniles are entitled to these rights whenever they face possible confinement in a state institution. They cannot be convicted unless there is proof "beyond reasonable doubt of every fact necessary to constitute the crime."

Status offenses In addition to criminal cases, state courts can hear cases of noncriminal misbehavior by juveniles, such as truancy from school; running away from home; refusing to obey parents, teachers, or legal authorities; or endangering the health or morals of themselves or others. These are called *status offenses,* and they account for at least one-third of the cases in juvenile courts.

In most states, status offenses are included in the definition of delinquency. But increasingly, states are channeling children accused of status offenses into a different procedure, not calling them delinquents, but rather *persons* or *minors* or *children in need of supervision*—PINS, MINS, or CHINS. About 75 percent of the states place children under court supervision on the basis of a simple criterion: that there is more evidence than not that the child needs supervision. Paradoxically, this standard is much less strict than the criminal standard of proof beyond a reasonable doubt required in delinquency proceedings.

A child in a status-offense proceeding has no right to have a lawyer provided by the court, and as a rule evidence that would be inadmissible at a delinquency hearing—a child's coerced confession to police, for example—can be admitted. Sometimes a child is charged with a status offense when his conduct falls just short of criminal behavior. For instance, making threats with a toy gun is not a crime, but a 15-year-old who does this to intimidate younger children could be held for the offense of endangering the morals, health, or general welfare of another child.

Charging juveniles with status offenses has been strongly criticized. Does it make sense, for example, to bring a PINS proceeding against runaways who are trying to escape an intolerable home life? Should a runaway child be sent to the same courtroom and reform school as someone who has committed crimes? The basic question is whether the juvenile justice system is appropriate for dealing with children who are troubled but have not committed crimes.

Some authorities defend the PINS system because it is, at least, a way of helping troubled children. For example, San Francisco police say that they used to enforce a curfew law to pick up youngsters loitering in the notorious Tenderloin District, where both sexes solicited for prostitution. When status crimes were eliminated in California, the police lost a way of pulling those children off the streets.

Traffic offenses The established procedure of handling minors separately from other offenders has been generally disappearing when the offense is a MOTOR VEHI-

CLE violation. This is the largest exception to the rule of keeping juveniles out of the adult criminal system.

Many states recognize that the sheer volume of traffic cases is enough reason to keep them out of juvenile courts, especially since regular traffic courts are better equipped to handle the necessary assembly-line processing. Some states reserve serious traffic offenses for juvenile courts. The theory is that a minor charged with such offenses as driving under the influence of liquor or narcotics, driving without a license, or reckless homicide has a better chance of rehabilitation if he is treated as a juvenile delinquent rather than as an adult offender.

■ **Laws protecting children** The state has the power to enact legislation protecting the health and morals of minors. These laws generally prohibit conduct likely to harm children as well as conditions that directly endanger their moral or physical well-being. Laws intended to protect the morals of minors, for instance, forbid selling or furnishing narcotics, tobacco, or intoxicating liquors to children; displaying obscene pictures or magazines in public places; loitering near schools; publishing the name of a child brought into court; betting with a child; or buying junk or used goods from a child (on the theory that this encourages children to steal). Owners of certain establishments—poolrooms, dance halls, houses of prostitution, or bars—can be convicted for allowing minors to enter their premises.

Every state has laws to punish an adult for contributing to the delinquency of a minor, taking indecent liberties with a child, or sexually molesting or abusing a child. These statutes are intentionally broad and are interpreted to protect children. In order to convict an adult of contributing to the delinquency of a minor, it is not necessary to show his behavior had that effect.

EXAMPLE A man who gave a lewd note to a little girl, asking O⊶✳ her to meet him in a secluded spot that night, was convicted even though the girl did not meet him. Another man was convicted of indecent exposure even though the children turned their heads and did not look.

Even if the child cooperates, the adult can be convicted because a child's consent is no consent at all in law. For example, an adult is guilty of statutory RAPE when he has sexual intercourse with a girl under legal age, even if the girl agreed or actively solicited him.

Adults can be held responsible for contributing to the delinquency of a child when they help the child do something illegal. For example, a father was convicted for allowing his daughter to sit at a table while a group of adults passed around a marijuana cigarette, allowing her to take an occasional puff. A doctor was convicted for giving prescriptions for huge quantities of amphetamines and barbiturates to minors without making the slightest effort to discover how old the minors were.

EXAMPLE A Detroit man met a girl who told him she was 18 O⊶✳ years old, was tired of living at home, and had written a song she wanted to sell to Motown Records. He told her that if she ever got to Detroit, she could call him and he would help her find a place to stay. She did call and he paid for a motel room for her until she was picked up as a runaway. It turned out that she was only 16, and he was convicted of contributing to the delinquency of a minor. The man protested that he was only trying to be a good Samaritan, but the court said that the law was intended to prevent people from encouraging children to run away from home and seek glamour in the big city.

Child abuse It is a crime for anyone to be cruel or physically abusive to a child. But only in the past 20 years have legislatures tackled the problem of abuse by parents or other adults entrusted with the care and supervision of children. See PARENT AND CHILD. A 1977 study for the U.S. Department of Health, Education, and Welfare revealed more than 500,000 reported cases of child abuse annually. Unfortunately, not all cases are reported, and situations in which a child's health and welfare are threatened are frequently not discovered until the child is permanently injured—or dead.

The laws punishing assault and battery can be enforced against anyone who intentionally strikes or injures a child—except a parent, who has the right to punish a child "moderately." But moderately does not mean unreasonably. Parents and other adults have been sent to jail for whipping a boy with a cat-o'-nine-tails; dressing a 12-year-old boy in girl's clothing and shaving his head; having an older brother practice karate on a two-year-old girl; and chaining, tying, or locking up children as punishment.

Some states have made it a criminal offense for physicians, teachers, or certain other professionals not to report a case of suspected child abuse to the proper authorities. In at least one case, a child was permitted to sue a doctor for malpractice through a guardian when the doctor did not report a clear case of child abuse. He had sent the child home from the hospital with her parents, who then injured her even more seriously.

Special laws now apply in many states to cases of child abuse by parents or others who are responsible for the care of a child. These laws apply not only to a person who has legal custody of the child but also to a babysitter, another adult family member, or even a parent's friend. Some of these cases are handled in the state's family court or juvenile court, but the most serious cases—those involving death or permanent injuries—are often processed in the regular criminal court.

Child neglect Child abuse in some states is considered an aggravated, or more serious, form of neglect. Neglect laws set criminal penalties for a parent or other custodian who fails to provide proper food, clothing, shelter, and medical treatment for a child; to supervise the child; and to plan for his needs and his future. A mother who left a baby in the car on a hot day with the windows rolled up was charged with neglect. A parent who fails to send a child to school regularly may be guilty of neglect. See PARENT AND CHILD.

Dependent children A dependent child is one who is under legal age and does not have parental care or does not have parents who are willing and capable of exercising control and care of him. A dependency proceeding, conducted by the state, determines what is to be done with the child. A child is not dependent just because his parents are poor and need welfare assistance to provide for him, but he may be dependent if his parents do not bother to apply for assistance if they need it.

Children whose father had killed their mother and grandmother were found dependent, and so was a child whose only parent was permanently bedridden. Any child who is being cared for by a person who is not legally responsible for him is dependent.

EXAMPLE A 13-year-old girl, whose father had disappeared ⚬—✱ when she was a baby, was declared dependent when her mother died in an accident, even though the girl moved in with an older sister. The court did not necessarily consider the older sister unfit to raise the girl, but finding the girl to be dependent was the first step toward determining who should have custody.

A state may declare a child dependent, or a ward of the state, so that the state can give its consent for life-saving medical treatment when a parent refuses to give consent.

EXAMPLE A child afflicted with erythroblastic anemia was ⚬—✱ about to die because his father refused to permit a blood transfusion on religious grounds. The court ruled that ordering the life-saving transfusion for the child did not interfere with the parent's freedom of religion.

Although a needy child has no constitutional claim to a decent or permanent home, the law recognizes that he should be provided with food, clothing, shelter, and medical care. To accomplish this, states have set legal standards for orphanages, group homes, foster parent systems, and social welfare programs. See PUBLIC WELFARE; SOCIAL SECURITY. States may authorize courts to commit dependent children to the care and custody of appropriate agencies or to a legally appointed guardian.

inference A truth or proposition drawn from another, which is supposed or admitted to be true; the process of reasoning by which a fact or proposition sought to be established is deduced from other facts already proven or admitted. For instance, if the first four books in a set of five have green covers, it is a logical inference that the fifth book also has a green cover. In a trial, the judge or jury may make inferences based on the EVIDENCE placed before them.

inferior court 1 Any court but the highest in a particular judicial system. For example, any federal court is inferior to the U.S. Supreme Court. 2 A court with special, limited responsibilities, such as a probate court.

infirmity 1 A defect. If the papers transferring ownership of a car are incomplete, there is an infirmity in the transaction. 2 A physical weakness.

in forma pauperis (Latin) "In the character or manner of a pauper." The phrase is used to describe permission given to a poor person to bring and continue a suit without paying any court costs. The person is then said to "proceed *in forma pauperis.*"

information A formal, written accusation of a crime made by a proper public official, such as a prosecuting attorney. An information differs from an INDICTMENT in that it is presented by a public officer on his oath, instead of by a GRAND JURY. In the American legal system, there can be no trial, conviction, or punishment for a crime without a formal accusation. Its purpose is to inform the accused person of the charge against him, so that he and his lawyer can prepare his defense.

informed consent Permission given to perform some act after a person has been made aware of all the facts and fully understands the surrounding circumstances. For instance, informed consent in medical procedure is giving your permission for surgery after you have been told (and fully understand) exactly what your condition is, all the hazards involved in the operation, and the chances for success. See ABORTION; PATIENTS' RIGHTS.

infraction A breach, violation, or infringement, such as of a law, a contract, or a duty. The term is often used to refer to minor violations, such as parking infractions.

infringement A breach or violation of a right. For example, the unauthorized copying of an item protected by a copyright is an infringement of the copyright.

inherent Belonging to the basic character of something. For example, an object that is inherently dangerous is dangerous merely by existing. A homemade bomb is inherently dangerous; a pipe wrench is not.

inherent vice A basic defect. An automobile manufactured and sold with a loose steering assembly has an inherent vice.

inheritance Property received from a dead person, either by WILL or, if the person dies without making a will, according to state laws of DESCENT AND DISTRIBUTION. See Chart 16. Generally, a child or adult who is legally adopted can receive an inheritance the same as anyone else. See ADOPTION OF PERSONS. A current problem concerns exactly how an illegitimate child can inherit if his father dies without leaving a will. See ILLEGITIMACY.

initiative The power of the people, in some states, to propose laws and to enact or reject them at the polls, independently of the legislature. An initiative is a kind of election, started by collecting enough signatures to put a particular issue on the ballot for a vote by the people. It can be used to enact a measure the legislature failed to pass.

injunction A judicial order by which a person is required to do or refrain from doing certain acts.

■ **Reasons for granting** Injunctions are extraordinary remedies, reserved for extraordinary cases. The most common purpose of an injunction is to temporarily preserve the status quo (the existing situation), although, under certain circumstances, it may be a permanent remedy. An injunction is usually obtained in aid of other legal proceedings.

EXAMPLE Suppose your neighbor announces plans to build ⚬—✱ a garage on a part of your land, on which you have cultivated a bed of rare roses. Claiming that the land is his, he prepares to dig out the roses and start construction. You go to your attorney, who starts a court action in which the right to ownership and possession of the land is the issue. You and your attorney can immediately apply to the court for an injunction against your neighbor to restrain him from digging up the roses. You are seeking the injunction as a supplementary remedy in your lawsuit against the neighbor.

The propriety of granting an injunction varies with each case. It is generally issued only when irreparable injury to the rights of an individual would otherwise result. An injury is irreparable when it cannot be adequately compensated in money. If a loss can be ascertained in money damages, no irreparable injury is shown, and a court's refusal to grant an injunction is proper.

EXAMPLE Your neighbor promises to sell you an air conditioner for $150. He reneges on his promise by selling the item to someone else for $200. A court will refuse to grant you an injunction to stop your neighbor from delivering the air conditioner to the purchaser, because you can easily be compensated by money damages. You will recover the difference in price that it will cost you to buy a comparable air conditioner in the open market as opposed to the $150 contract price.

Loss of profits alone is not sufficient to establish irreparable injury as a basis for an injunction, but potential destruction of property is.

■ **Types of injunctions** The various types of injunctions, which are explained below, are applied according to the particular situation.

Restraining order A restraining order of short duration is granted without a hearing in court in order to maintain the status quo until a hearing for a temporary injunction can be held. Such an order merely suspends activities until there is an opportunity to inquire whether or not an injunction should be granted.

EXAMPLE A restraining order could be issued to stop the planned bulldozing of a state nature preserve by a private company, scheduled two hours from the time the application for the order was made by a local environmental group. In such an emergency situation, disastrous consequences would follow if no action was taken until a court could determine whether or not the environmentalists had a legal basis for their protest.

Preliminary injunction A preliminary, or temporary, injunction (the terms are used interchangeably) is used to prevent the destruction of the plaintiff's rights. The key reason for the use of a preliminary injunction is the need for speedy relief. A preliminary injunction seeks to prevent a threatened wrong, further injury, and irreparable harm or injustice, until the rights of the parties can be finally settled. It guards against a change of circumstances that would hinder or prevent the granting of proper relief after the completion of a trial.

EXAMPLE Suppose a rock group, the Funky Fuzz, made a contract to appear at a certain theater for a series of concerts and to appear nowhere else during that period. They then announce that they are going to appear during the same period at a local nightclub, claiming that the clause in their theater contract preventing them from taking on other engagements was added by fraud. In such circumstances, a preliminary injunction might be granted to prevent them from appearing at the nightclub. The injunction would be effective only until a court could decide whether or not the contract provision prohibiting other engagements was binding on the group.

Preventive injunction An injunction that directs a person to refrain from doing an act is described as preventive, prohibitive, or negative. Such an injunction prevents a threatened injury, preserves the status quo, or restrains an ongoing wrong. In the above examples, both stopping the bulldozing and keeping the rock group from appearing at the nightclub are preventive actions.

Mandatory injunction An injunction that directs a person to do a specific thing or to perform a positive act is described as mandatory. Mandatory injunctions are not favored by the courts. A mandatory injunction can be issued for the removal of a building wrongfully placed on someone else's land.

Permanent injunction A permanent injunction is granted by the judgment that settles the injunction suit. This type of injunction must always be a final relief. Permanent injunctions have been granted to (1) prevent blasting on neighboring premises; (2) prevent interference with planting, cultivating, and harvesting crops; (3) enjoin (prohibit) the dumping of earth or other material on someone else's land; (4) prevent pollution of the water supply; (5) prevent picketing strikers from physically interfering with workers who are trying to enter their place of work; (6) protect a trade secret; and (7) restrain the unauthorized use of a celebrity's name or picture for advertising purposes.

■ **Violating an injunction** Violation of an injunction is punishable as a CONTEMPT of court. In general, a person charged with contempt for violating an injunction is entitled to a trial or a hearing. The punishment imposed may be a fine, imprisonment, or both.

injurious falsehood An untrue statement that is intended to harm someone's reputation. See DEFAMATION; LIBEL AND SLANDER.

injury Any wrong or damage done to another person's body, rights, reputation, or property. In theory, the law provides a remedy for every injury. See TORT.

in kind Of the same class or group. A loan of an article is returned in kind when a similar but not identical article is returned to the lender. For example, your neighbor borrows your brand-new lawn mower and ruins it. He buys a new one of the same make and model and gives it to you. Your lawn mower has been returned in kind.

in loco parentis (Latin) "In the place of a parent." **1** The relationship that a person assumes toward a child who is not his own but whom he presents to the community as a member of his family and to whom he owes the duty of care and supervision. **2** The term also refers to the authority to discipline a child as a parent can. Teachers and summer-camp counselors are often empowered to act *in loco parentis.*

innkeeper Someone whose business is to provide accommodations for all transients who are in fit condition and willing to pay an adequate price. A *guest* is a transient who receives accommodations at an inn. His transient character is the essential difference between him and a boarder or roomer in a boarding or rooming house who agrees to take a room for a certain period of time. The relationship between a roomer or boarder and the owner is that of LANDLORD AND TENANT.

Proper grounds for an innkeeper's refusal to receive a proposed guest are generally limited either to lack of accommodations or unsuitability of the guest. After a guest has been assigned to a room, he is entitled to its exclusive occupancy for all lawful purposes. His occupancy, however, is subject to the right of the innkeeper to enter the room at proper times for proper purposes. For example, an innkeeper who knows of an intruder in a guest's room might be justified in entering it in order to assist the police.

■ **Fee** An innkeeper can charge only a reasonable fee, and he must usually perform his whole obligation before being entitled to it. If the guest does not pay, the innkeeper is entitled to a LIEN on his property—traditionally, his luggage—which continues until the guest pays his bill. The innkeeper may remove a guest who refuses to pay his bill, but he must not use excessive force.

■ **Liability** An innkeeper has a duty to take reasonable care of his guests. For instance, he must protect his guests from injury by other guests and from assaults and negligent acts of his own employees. He must warn guests of any hidden dangers that he can reasonably foresee. His duty includes inspecting the premises, furnishings, and equipment to make sure they are safe. He is liable if a guest gets food poisoning from meals when provided as part of the service of the inn, contracts a fungus or other medical problem from using unlaundered linens, or is injured because fire regulations were not observed.

The prevailing common-law view is that an innkeeper should pay for any goods of the guest's that are lost at the inn. Statutes usually modify the common law by limiting the innkeeper's liability for a guest's belongings to a specified amount and by requiring guests to deposit valuables in a safe. Guests must be notified of any limitations of the innkeeper's liability. Generally signs are placed on the inside of motel or hotel doors and statements are printed on the guest registration forms. No liability is incurred when the guest has the entire control over his property—if he parks his automobile in a lot or garage provided by the innkeeper but keeps the keys, for example.

innocent Free from guilt; acting in good faith and without knowledge of any incriminating circumstances, defects, or objections.

innocent purchaser A person who, by an honest agreement, purchases property without knowing that there may be an infirmity (something wrong) in the transaction.

inoperative Void; producing no effect. The commonly understood meaning of the word is that something, such as a law or a contract, is not currently in effect.

in pari delicto (Latin) "In a similar offense." When the parties to a lawsuit are *in pari delicto,* neither one can obtain relief from a court.

EXAMPLE Andrews sued Evans for not paying off a loan
O•—* Andrews had made him. The court held both parties *in pari delicto* when it discovered that Andrews had charged Evans 40 percent interest on the loan (which is unlawful), and it dismissed the suit. Andrews was later prosecuted for the crime of usury.

in pari materia (Latin) "On the same subject matter." The phrase applies to laws that were enacted at different times but relate to the same subject matter. Laws *in pari materia* must be interpreted together.

in perpetuity Of endless duration; forever. See RULE AGAINST PERPETUITIES.

in personam (Latin) "Against the person." The phrase refers to a lawsuit that is directed against a specific person or persons.

EXAMPLE You have entered into a contract with a house
O•—* painter who agrees to apply two coats of white paint to your house. Instead, he applies one coat of red paint. You sue him for money damages for breach of contract. Your lawsuit is an action in personam, and if you win your suit, the court will give you an in personam judgment against him.

An action in personam is the opposite of an action IN REM, which is brought to enforce a person's rights in a thing.

inquest An investigation by a CORONER into the cause of death of anyone who is found dead or dies suddenly, violently, or in prison.

inquisitorial system The method of legal practice in which the judge digs out facts while at the same time representing the state's interests in a trial. It is the opposite of the Anglo-American system, in which each side, whether an individual or the state, represents its own interests through its attorney, while the court is impartial.

in re (Latin) "In the matter of"; concerning. This is the usual beginning of a title for an IN REM lawsuit—a judicial proceeding in which there are technically no adversary parties, but there is some *res* ("thing") on which judicial action needs to be taken. For example, a proceeding to distribute the property of a deceased person might be entitled *"In re* Smith's Estate."

in rem (Latin) "Against the thing." The phrase refers to a lawsuit brought to enforce rights in a *res* ("thing"). Actions in rem are the opposite of actions IN PERSONAM, which are directed against a specific person. Although, strictly speaking, an action in rem is brought directly against a res, it is usually brought between parties to decide the ownership of property or the status of a person. One common example is an action to establish ownership of a parcel of land—the res. Once the court decides who owns the land, it hands down an in rem judgment that is binding on everyone. Similarly, in the law of domestic relations, a suit for an annulment or a divorce is an action in rem because the court's decree affects the *status* of the parties, which is the res in the suit, not the parties themselves.

insane persons Human beings of unsound or disordered mind; deranged or mad persons. In law, *insanity* means unsoundness of mind, madness, or derangement—resulting from a defect or disease that involves a person's intellect, emotions, will, or moral sense. Insanity may be characterized by delusions, inability to reason or judge, or uncontrollable impulses. The Latin phrase *non compos mentis* ("not having control of one's own mind") is used to describe a person of unsound mind.

In law, insanity generally does not include temporary mental disturbances such as trances, epileptic seizures, hysteria, or an alcoholic stupor. Temporary insanity is a legally defined defense to a criminal prosecution meaning that at the time the crime was committed, the accused did not know or understand the nature or consequence of his action. The insanity is temporary because after the crime is committed, the accused realizes what he has done, thereby regaining his sanity. An example of this is a crime committed in the heat of passion.

Insane persons constitute a legal class of people who, like INFANTS (minors), are considered unable to manage their own affairs. This legal disability prevents them from making decisions that are legally binding on them. When insane persons do act, the law does not give legal effect to their actions.

Medical and legal insanity are not necessarily the same. Feeblemindedness and mental retardation of various degrees are recognized as medically different from insanity. Legally, however, these conditions can be treated the same as insanity because they prevent individuals from managing their affairs. Habitual drunkards and narcotics addicts may also be treated in court as legal incompetents. The term "incompetent" refers to anyone lacking sufficient mental capacity to manage his affairs, whether the cause be mental or physical disease, mental retardation, or senility.

■ **The legal effects of insanity** There are many areas of law in which the insanity of a person is an important factor. These include crimes; the making of wills or contracts; marriage; damage suits; and the ability to exercise a citizen's rights to vote, take an oath, or be a witness.

Crimes In CRIMINAL LAW, insanity may be pleaded as a defense. A person who is accused of committing a crime states, through his attorney, that he is suffering from a deranged mental condition that makes him incapable of distinguishing between right and wrong, that he cannot understand the nature of his act, or that his free will has been destroyed. Generally, the law says that an insane person cannot be guilty of intentional crimes because he is unable to form a criminal intent in his mind.

An insane delusion may excuse the accused person if the facts would have excused his conduct had they been true. For example, a defendant who killed someone he imagined was trying to kill him may be acquitted because self-defense would have been a valid defense had he been right. A person who was insane, even temporarily, when he committed a crime is generally held not to be responsible for his act. In most jurisdictions, there are three possible verdicts—guilty, innocent, not guilty by reason of insanity. This last verdict results in automatic commitment to a mental institution in a number of states, while in others, the judge or jury exercises its discretion, sometimes in a separate hearing, to determine commitment of the accused.

A person who is insane when his case comes up in court generally will not be tried because he is unable to understand the charges against him or to work with his defense attorney. When a person is incapable of standing trial, he may be committed until he is capable of doing so.

Wills Insanity may become an issue in proceedings to prove the validity of a WILL. If the person writing a will does not have *testamentary capacity,* the will is invalid. A person has testamentary capacity if he is capable of understanding the general nature and extent of his property, the purpose of distributing it by will, and the types of persons—for example, relatives, people who have helped him, and charities in need of funds—to whom possessions would normally be given. Showing that a deceased person was eccentric or had odd personal habits does not prove that he lacked testamentary capacity.

Contracts Insane people cannot be bound by CONTRACTS they have signed because they cannot understand their promises and obligations. The insanity need not extend to a total loss of reason but only a defect of memory, judgment, or reason that calls into question the person's understanding of the nature and consequences of the agreement.

EXAMPLE Suppose your senile 89-year-old grandmother signed a long-term contract with a health spa to use its facilities, but she thinks she had merely agreed to get a beauty treatment. Because she did not understand what she was signing, your grandmother is not bound by law to perform the contract.

Marriage Insanity in a husband or wife may justify the dissolution of a MARRIAGE. For example, some states will give an ANNULMENT—declare that a marriage was void from the beginning—when one person is shown to have been insane and therefore unable to give genuine consent at the wedding. Some states will grant a DIVORCE to a person who proves that his or her spouse has been insane for a certain number of years and that the condition is incurable. Courts have refused annulments and divorces when one spouse was shown to be only retarded or a compulsive thief.

Damage suits In a lawsuit against someone who has caused injury to another, insanity is not a defense but it may defeat an argument that the harm was intentional. When the defendant is proved to be insane, the money DAMAGES may be limited to an amount appropriate to compensate the injured person without any additional punitive damages.

EXAMPLE John, who had been certified as insane but was considered harmless, lived with his guardian, his older sister Lois. One day he got into his neighbor Anna's car and drove it right through her newly planted nursery-grown hedge. John was liable only for the cost of replacing the hedge. A sane person, acting equally recklessly, might have had to pay an additional amount as punishment.

When an insane person is a party to a lawsuit, a court will appoint a representative to protect his interests. A judgment against an insane person is as binding on him as on any of the other parties.

Because an insane person cannot be expected to understand his legal rights, states generally do not count periods of insanity when calculating the time within which a lawsuit must be started. See LIMITATIONS OF ACTIONS.

Citizens' rights Insanity may affect a citizen's ability to vote, take an oath, or be a witness. The test is whether a person is generally able to understand the nature of what he is doing and has enough intelligence and memory to exercise judgment. It is not required that a person be able to remember everything clearly in order to testify as a witness.

Eccentricity, crankiness, and feeblemindedness do not disqualify a person, nor do insane delusions that do not affect the matter at hand.

Suicide and life insurance   People frequently try to prove that their insured relatives who committed suicide were insane, because life insurance companies, in some states, are not required to pay benefits on someone who has deliberately taken his own life unless he was insane and did not know what he was doing. If, because of insanity or delusions, a person does not realize that his actions will cause his death, the death is considered accidental or unintentional. It is up to the beneficiary, however, to prove the insanity. Most life insurance policies stipulate that no proceeds will be paid if the insured person commits suicide within two years from the date the policy was issued. Such a provision releases the insurance company from paying under such circumstances, whether the insured person was insane or not.

■ **Support of an insane person**   In many states, when an insane person is institutionalized at public expense, the hospital or the mental health commissioner is authorized to collect support money from the patient's relatives. Which relatives are financially responsible depends on state law. A husband can always be required to help pay the expenses of his insane wife, and some states now impose the same obligation on a wife for her insane husband. Only a few states require parents to pay support for an adult child, but all hold parents financially responsible for their minor children. If an insane adult has money or other property, his guardian can be required to use it for the patient's support, and if an institutionalized insane person receives an inheritance, the state can sue to collect money for his support.

■ **Supervision**   States have special procedures for handling people who are legally insane. For example, a court may select someone to take custody of the insane person in order to provide daily care and supervision. Sometimes such a person is called a *guardian*. A person or group of persons appointed by a court to manage the person or property, or both, of an insane person is often called a *committee;* a person who has the guardianship of a mentally incompetent person, such as a senile or sick person, is often called a *conservator*.

If an insane person is a threat to the community, the court can order *civil commitment* (discussed below), which is the confinement of persons not accused of a crime. For example, if a patient tells his psychiatrist that he plans to blow up the local police station and he brings the makings of a bomb and a floor plan of the police station to his next session with the psychiatrist, he may be committed al-

HOW THE STATE TREATS INSANE PERSONS

■ The law views insane persons as a class of persons who, like children, are unable to manage their own affairs or make legally binding decisions. In law, insanity refers not only to madness and derangement but to feeblemindedness.

■ In criminal law, insanity may be pleaded as a defense. A person may claim that he is suffering from a deranged mental condition that makes him incapable of distinguishing between right and wrong.

■ Insane delusion may excuse an accused person if the facts would have excused his conduct had they been true—for example, if a woman, under the delusion that a man was attacking her with a knife to kill her, shot him dead in "self-defense."

■ A person who was insane, even temporarily, when he committed a crime is generally held not to be responsible for his act.

■ A person who is insane when his case comes up in court generally will not be tried, because he is unable to understand the charges against him or work with his defense attorney.

■ Insane persons cannot be bound by contracts they have signed, because they cannot understand their promises and obligations.

■ Some states will grant an annulment of a marriage when one person is shown to have been insane at the time of the wedding. Some states will grant a divorce when a spouse is incurably insane.

■ If an insane person is a party to a lawsuit, the court appoints a representative to protect his interests.

■ In many states, the authorities may collect support money from relatives when an insane person is institutionalized at public expense.

■ A husband can be required to help pay for an insane wife, and in some states the same obligation is imposed on the wife for an insane husband. Only a few states require parents to pay support for an adult child. All states hold parents financially responsible for minor children.

■ If an insane adult has money or other property, his guardian can be made to use it for the patient's support.

■ If an institutionalized insane person receives an inheritance, the state can sue to collect money for his support.

■ If an insane person is a threat to the community, the court can order civil commitment—the confinement of persons not accused of a crime. However, the state has no right to lock up a person against his will and keep him indefinitely without treatment just because it finds that he is "mentally ill."

■ A person who can survive safely in freedom by himself or with the willing help of family or friends cannot be confined against his will unless he poses a serious threat to the safety of the community.

■ The current rule of thumb set forth by the Supreme Court is that it is proper for a state to provide facilities for insane persons who prefer them and for those who may injure others, but the state cannot institutionalize harmless persons simply because they do not conform to the community's norm of behavior.

■ In the case of children who are presented for commitment, when the medical staff of the hospital independently reaches the same conclusion as did the parent who wants to commit the child, the child has no right to a formal hearing.

■ Some 27 states have laws providing for sterilization of mentally deficient or feebleminded persons.

though he has not yet violated any law. The patient's parent or spouse may bring the proceeding. The psychiatrist usually will not, because of the patient-physician privilege, but this has become a hotly contested issue. In some states a psychiatrist has been held liable for failing to warn a potential victim of the criminal plans of his patient. In a civil commitment, the court will appoint an institution, such as a private mental hospital, or an official, such as a state director of mental health, to supervise the insane person. These court proceedings are variously called *inquisitions of lunacy, inquests of lunacy, lunacy proceedings, insanity proceedings, commitment proceedings,* or *incompetency proceedings.*

■ **Commitment to an institution**   States are not required to take control of insane persons. Until well into the 19th century, states frequently left insane persons to whatever care—or lack of care—their families or others provided. Those who were scooped up by the authorities were usually deposited in poorhouses, almshouses, or jails, simply to isolate them from the community. But as the demand for reform grew, states began to establish institutions, or asylums, for insane persons for the purpose of providing more humane living conditions and treatment.

Although troubled individuals may voluntarily go to mental institutions, most patients are involuntarily committed. In 1975, ruling on the *Donaldson* case, the Supreme Court finally set up some ground rules for patients who are civilly, not criminally, committed against their will.

EXAMPLE Kenneth Donaldson had been a self-supporting adult for 14 years until his father presented him for commitment to a state mental hospital because he was suffering from "delusions." A judge heard evidence that Donaldson suffered from "paranoid schizophrenia" and sent him to the hospital in January 1957. No one had suggested that Donaldson was dangerous to himself or others, but he was kept at the hospital against his will for nearly 15 years. Both a halfway house for former mental patients and a college classmate and longtime family friend repeatedly offered to take responsibility for him. The hospital refused to release Donaldson in spite of his repeated requests.

The Supreme Court held that a state has no right to lock up a person against his will and keep him there indefinitely without treatment just because it finds that he is "mentally ill." A person who can survive safely in freedom by himself or with the willing help of family or friends cannot be confined against his will.

It is entirely proper for a state to provide facilities for people who prefer them and for people who may injure others, but a state cannot institutionalize harmless people simply because they do not conform to the community's norm of behavior.

In 1979 the Supreme Court announced the amount of EVIDENCE required to commit someone to an institution against his will. Most civil cases are won by whichever side has more than half (a preponderance) of the evidence on its side. If one side proves its case better than the other, no matter how slightly, that is enough. But this is not enough, said the Court, when the question is whether a person is so insane that he should be involuntarily committed. The Court noted that everyone does something a little strange

once in a while and that psychiatric diagnosis is largely based on "medical 'impressions' drawn from subjective analysis and filtered through the experience" of the doctor. Therefore, in order to commit an unwilling person to a mental institution, the evidence must be "clear, unequivocal and convincing" to a jury.

Insane children   Children do not have the same rights involving confinement as adults. The National Institute for Mental Health has estimated that over 80,000 minors (usually a person under 18 or 21, depending on the state) are admitted to mental institutions and the psychiatric units of general hospitals each year. Most of these children are turned over by their parents or guardians, and children—whether sane or insane—are not legally capable of giving consent themselves. In 1979 the Supreme Court held that parents must be presumed to be acting in the best interests of their children. If the hospital's medical staff independently reaches the same conclusion as the parent who committed a child, then the child has no right to demand a formal hearing or "convincing" evidence of his insanity.

Criminal sexual psychopaths   Many states have special provisions for handling cases involving sex offenders who suffer from mental disorders. These persons, often called *criminal sexual psychopaths*, are not considered insane in a general way, but because they cannot handle sex in a normal manner they are a threat to society. By enacting a special law for sex offenders, the state does not have to prove general insanity.

Frequently, these laws do not require a prior conviction, either for a sex crime or any other crime. In fact, persons charged with being criminal sexual psychopaths may have been accused of serious crimes and then found not guilty by reason of insanity. These laws are constitutionally valid when the necessary elements of DUE PROCESS OF LAW are present—for example, notice of the charges, an opportunity for a hearing, and the chance to cross-examine witnesses.

■ **Sterilization of insane persons**   The first compulsory sexual sterilization law was enacted in 1907 by Indiana. It made the sterilization of confirmed criminals, idiots, imbeciles, and rapists mandatory in state institutions when a board of experts recommended it. By 1968, 27 states sterilized mentally deficient or feebleminded persons. The Supreme Court first considered the validity of a compulsory sterilization law in 1927.

EXAMPLE In *Buck* v. *Bell,* the Court wrote that Carrie Buck was "a feebleminded white woman who was committed to the State Colony for Epileptics and Feeble Minded." She was 18 years old when the case for her sterilization came to trial, and was the daughter of a feebleminded woman in the same institution and the mother of an illegitimate feebleminded child. Her attorney argued that sterilization could not be justified.

The Court disagreed. It held that sterilization was appropriate for mentally defective persons who could be safely discharged into the community to become self-supporting if they were incapable of procreating. Justice Oliver Wendell Holmes wrote: "The public welfare may call upon the best citizens for their lives. It would be strange if it could not call upon those who already sap the strength of the State for these lesser sacrifices, often felt not to be such by those concerned, in order to prevent being swamped by incompetence. It is better for all the world, if instead of waiting to execute degenerate off-spring for crime or to let them starve for their imbecility, society can prevent those who are manifestly unfit from continuing their kind. The principle that sustains compulsory vaccination is broad enough to cover cutting the Fallopian tubes." Holmes summed up with: "Three generations of imbeciles are enough."

Sterilization laws won popular support through the 1920's and 1930's, but in the 1940's, Hitler's racial policies made forced sterilization repugnant to many people. Now it seems that this was just a swing of the pendulum. State laws still authorize compulsory sterilization, and courts continue to uphold them.

EXAMPLE In 1968 the Nebraska Supreme Court upheld a ○─── sterilization order against a 35-year-old mentally deficient mother of eight illegitimate children. In this case, the woman could refuse the operation but if she did she could not be released from the mental institution in which she was confined. The court found the order reasonable and fair. The woman would not be harmed except for losing the ability to have more children, and the legal process leading to the order was constitutional.

In 1976 the Supreme Court of North Carolina approved a sterilization order entered against a minor with his consent and that of his mother and specifically stated that sterilization is not cruel and unusual punishment.

insecurity clause An acceleration clause. See ACCELERATION.

insolvency The inability to pay debts as they become due; the state of someone whose entire property and assets are insufficient to pay his debts. See ASSIGNMENT FOR BENEFIT OF CREDITORS; ATTACHMENT AND GARNISHMENT; BANKRUPTCY; COMPOSITION WITH CREDITORS.

in specie (Latin) "In kind"; in the identical form; without alteration; specifically. The term is used by the courts to refer to decrees requiring SPECIFIC PERFORMANCE.

inspection The right of a plaintiff and a defendant to see and copy documents, enter upon land, and conduct other examinations in order to gather evidence. See DISCOVERY.

installment A regular, partial payment on a debt, such as on an automobile loan. See CONSUMER PROTECTION.

instance An earnest and urgent request. An act is often performed at a person's special instance.

instant Present or current, such as the instant case before the court.

instigate Stimulate to an action, especially a bad action; push into a situation, such as a crime; abet.

instructions Directions given by the judge to the JURY, including a statement of the factual questions to be decided by the jury and a statement of the laws that apply to the facts of the case. See TRIAL.

instrument A formal or legal document in writing, such as a contract, deed, lease, will, bond, or check.

instrumentality A subordinate or auxiliary agency. A subsidiary corporation's separate existence will usually be disregarded when the company is only an arm, or instrumentality, of the parent corporation. The parent corporation is responsible for the debts and other obligations of the subsidiary under what is known as the "instrumentality rule."

insurance A contract between two parties in which one party, in return for regular payments of certain sums of money by the other, promises to pay for specified losses, liabilities, or damages incurred by the second party while the contract is in effect. The party who makes the regular payments is the *insured party,* or *policyholder,* and may be an individual, group, or organization. The payments he makes are the *premiums.* The other party is the *underwriter*—usually an insurance company, although an individual may also underwrite insurance. The contract between the two parties is the *policy;* and the specific losses, liabilities, and damages the insurance company promises to pay under a given policy constitute that policy's *coverage.*

Generally, when an insured party incurs losses, the insurance company reimburses him for his losses directly, but when the life of the insured party is covered, the company must pay the beneficiary when the insured party dies. A *beneficiary* is the party named in a policy as the one the insurance company must pay when the insured person dies.

Insurance is generally sold by either agents or brokers. An *insurance agent* is a person employed by an insurance company to solicit and write insurance for that company. An *insurance broker* is a person who works for himself and acts as a middleman between the insured party and the insurance company he selects.

The purpose of insurance is to protect persons from losses resulting from risks, or perils. In return for the policyholder's payment of regular premiums, the insurance company pays losses resulting from the policyholder's covered risks. Such coverage is known as *indemnity insurance* because it is intended simply to indemnify, or reimburse, the insured party for his losses. Indemnity insurance is the only legal insurance, for, according to law, no person is allowed to profit by collecting insurance—otherwise, people would be more likely than ever to destroy lives and property to collect the money.

The types of risks generally covered by insurance fall into three major categories: personal risks, property risks, and liability risks. *Personal risks* are those that affect the insured party's person, including his life, health, and well-being. *Property risks* are those involved with losses of or damage to property by such things as fire, theft, or storm. *Liability risks* are those involving the insured party's responsibility for the injury of another person or the damage or destruction of another person's property.

Some types of insurance fall under one of these general categories, while others fall under two of the categories or all three. This article discusses some of the more important forms of insurance, including life insurance, health insurance, group insurance, fire insurance (as a representative of the various types of property insurance), personal liability insurance, and automobile insurance. This article also shows how the law affects insurance applications, cancellations of policies, and the payments of claims. It closes with a discussion of state regulatory agencies.

■ **Life insurance**   A life insurance policy promises basically that, if the insured party dies during the period covered by the policy, an agreed-upon sum of money will be paid to the beneficiary—the person or persons named in the policy to receive the payment.

Insurable interest   The purchaser of the policy—the one who makes the premium payments—need not be the insured person, although, of course, he often is. A husband, for example, takes out a life insurance policy on himself so that, at his death, his wife and family will still be provided for although his income ceases. In fact, anyone may purchase a policy insuring the life of another, providing the purchaser has an *insurable interest* in that person; that is, providing he stands to benefit by the fact that the insured person remains alive, and he will suffer real loss should he die. Such a loss is easy to identify when it is economic, but the courts will also honor ties of affection, blood, or marriage as insurable interests. These are some insurable interests the courts uphold:

(1) A creditor has an interest in keeping you alive until you pay back the money you owe him, and may insure your life for that amount.

(2) You may insure a business partner's life if his death would throw an economic burden upon you.

(3) Key executives are difficult to replace, and corporations can insure the lives of their executives to absorb the expense of finding another person for the position.

(4) Husbands and wives have an insurable interest in each other as well as in their children, but because some people have murdered their children for insurance gains, state laws strictly limit the amount for which parents can insure their minor children.

Some such insurable interest is required at the time you take out a life insurance policy on another person. You may not, for example, take out a policy on a racing car driver you do not know in the hope he will be killed during the Indianapolis 500. However, if the driver once owed you money and you insured his life, then you may maintain the policy after the interest has expired with the paying of the debt, and you may collect if he dies. With the exception of your spouse and children, anyone whose life you intend to insure must agree. You may not legally insure someone without his knowledge and cooperation.

Types of life insurance   Some people make the error of thinking that all life insurance is the same. And when they find out otherwise it is too late, for courts will not intervene when a person, through his own carelessness, signed one valid insurance contract when he wanted another kind of coverage. The most common types of life insurance are whole life insurance, endowment life insurance, various types of term life insurance, military life insurance, and flight insurance.

Whole life insurance provides coverage for the insured person's entire life and is payable only when he dies. One big advantage of whole life insurance is that, over the years, the policy may earn dividends, which are either paid to the

policyholder or allowed to accumulate as a part of the cash value of the whole life policy. *(Cash value, or cash surrender value,* is what the policy will pay you if you decide to end it before its term expires.) If you have a whole life policy, you can borrow money from the insurance company against the policy's cash value. If you decide to give the policy up after many years, the insurance company must pay you the cash value of the policy.

There are two types of payment plans for whole life insurance—limited payment and ordinary. Under *limited payment,* or *paid-up,* insurance, you pay for only a specified number of years, at which point the policy is paid up. Under *ordinary* insurance, you continue to make payments throughout your life (or to a considerably advanced age, such as 85).

Endowment life insurance allows the insured person, who is also the beneficiary, to collect the insurance money if he lives until the policy matures—usually 20 years. If he dies before the policy matures, the money is paid to the secondary beneficiary, named in the policy. You will pay higher premiums for an endowment policy than for other life insurance, because the company has fewer years in which to collect from you all the money it must pay back when the policy matures.

Term life insurance pays money only if the insured person dies within the limited period specified in the policy. Term insurance is less expensive than others, and it has some important benefits.

EXAMPLE   Suppose you want to borrow money from a relative for an investment. At the end of five years, you will have saved enough to pay back the loan in full, but should you die before then, your family would be unable to carry on and still pay back the money. A five-year term life policy would guarantee the money to pay off the debt at little cost.

Convertible term insurance gives the purchaser the option of converting his term insurance to a permanent plan, such as whole life insurance, before the term expires. Under a convertible term policy, the insurance company cannot legally deny exercise of the conversion option because the insured person is in poor, or even critical, health.

Renewable term insurance allows an insured person to renew his policy for another term of the same length without taking a medical examination. Usually, the policy can be continually renewed until the insured person reaches a certain age. In some policies, the number of allowable renewals is specified.

Decreasing term insurance is an effective and inexpensive way to protect the family with children should the breadwinner die. While the coverage is high in the beginning—when the children are farther from maturity and the ability to support themselves—it decreases year by year until, by the end of the term, it is reduced to nothing. The premiums remain the same throughout, but are the lowest of any form of life insurance.

Military life insurance is issued by the federal government on the lives of U.S. military personnel. Since it would be an obviously bad risk for an insurance company to issue a policy on the life of a soldier in combat, and any that did so would necessarily charge extremely high premiums, the government offers low-priced life insurance to all those

SOME THINGS YOU SHOULD KNOW ABOUT INSURANCE

■ When you insure your own life, you should name at least two beneficiaries—a primary and secondary one. If the primary beneficiary dies before you, the insurance money will go to the secondary beneficiary.

■ If you name a minor as a beneficiary of an insurance policy, be sure to appoint a guardian to handle the money for him. Minors are legally incapable of handling their own assets. If you do not appoint a guardian, the court will, and that may prove more costly and less satisfactory for the child.

■ Separating from or divorcing your spouse does not automatically affect his or her position as a beneficiary. If your former spouse remains named as a beneficiary of your life insurance policy, the courts will grant him or her the money. The only way to change your beneficiary is to notify the insurance company.

■ An insurance company can cancel your policy if it discovers that, in filling out your application, you committed fraud or hid or misrepresented facts—if you concealed your heart disease when you applied for health insurance, for example. However, if an insurance company discovers that you lied about your age in order to lower your premium, it can merely lower the amount of the coverage to accord with the lower premiums you are paying.

■ If a company does cancel a policy, it must do so within a specified period of time after it takes effect—usually two years. Beyond that period, you are protected by the *incontestability clause,* which is required by law for most types of policies. The incontestability clause prevents companies from allowing people to pay premiums for years and then canceling the policy when benefits become due.

■ A person who buys insurance and pays the premiums must generally have an *insurable interest* in that person or property being insured. To buy life insurance, he must stand to benefit if the insured person lives and to suffer a loss if he dies. A spouse or blood relative has an insurable interest in a person's life. So might a creditor or business partner. A person has an insurable interest in property if he owns it. A mortgagor—someone who has lent money on the collateral of property—has an insurable interest in the property, but he loses it when the mortgage is paid up.

■ In order to collect on fire insurance, the fire that damaged the property must be a *hostile* fire—unintended and out of control. If a valuable manuscript is hidden in a fireplace and burned by a log fire, it is not covered—it was burned by a *friendly* fire.

■ No insurance company is legally required to sell automobile insurance to a particular applicant. In states that have an *assigned risk plan,* in which the state orders every insurance company to give policies to a certain quota of high-risk drivers, an impartial agency makes the assignment of insurance companies.

■ You should report an automobile accident promptly. If you fail to report it within a reasonable time (usually 20 days), your insurance company may refuse to pay your claim.

■ Your automobile insurance company has the right to challenge any repair bill you submit. Typically, the company will have its own claims adjuster estimate the cost of the damages or require you to submit two estimates from recognized professionals.

who serve in the armed forces. The Servicemen's Group Life Insurance (SGLI) provides automatic coverage of $20,000 for all military personnel including cadets and midshipmen, and premiums are automatically deducted from each person's pay, unless he states in writing that he does not wish to participate or that he prefers a lesser amount of insurance. Another military insurance company, the Veterans Group Life Insurance (VGLI), covers everyone released from active duty on or after August 1, 1974. It also provides insurance for reservists who, while on active duty or inactive duty for training, suffer an injury that makes them uninsurable at standard premium rates. Today, anyone discharged from military service can convert his SGLI policy to a five-year nonrenewable VGLI term policy, and when that expires, more than 600 participating commercial companies will convert it to a standard insurance policy.

Flight insurance is commonly available at airports, through both over-the-counter sales and vending machines. These policies provide a substantial face amount of coverage for a single premium of usually no more than a few dollars. They cover accidental death (and dismemberment) during the flight that is being insured, and they also cover accidents at the airport or in vehicles controlled by the airport or airline. They can cover a round-trip flight if the return is made within a one-year period. Flight insurance policies often impose limitations—for example, on the types of flights covered, such as scheduled flights, or on the amount to be paid to a single beneficiary. These limitations should appear on the policies and on any vending machines that sell them, but legal problems have arisen because passengers have misunderstood pertinent details in vending machine policies.

EXAMPLE In one case, a court denied payment on three of eight $5,000 policies—totaling $40,000—because of a $25,000 total limitation clause, clearly displayed on the vending machines and on the policies. The court did order payment, however, for a trip on a nonscheduled flight, for, although it was stated both on the vending machine and in the policy that coverage was limited to scheduled flights, the statement was in fine print. Also, the vending machine was located in front of a counter used by all nonscheduled airlines, which led passengers to believe that the policies applied to nonscheduled flights.

Exclusion clauses   Most life insurance policies exclude death resulting from certain activities (such as piloting private planes) or from certain professions (particularly those of the armed forces). The insurance companies have the right to make these exclusions, unless specifically forbidden by statute, and the courts have upheld their refusal to pay beneficiaries when those insured have died under circumstances excluded in such clauses.

Double indemnity Many life insurance policies carry a double indemnity clause, promising to pay twice the policy's face value if the insured person dies as a result of an accident. In collecting double indemnity, it is the beneficiary's responsibility to prove accidental death.

Beneficiaries of life insurance policies Upon the death of a person who has life insurance, his beneficiary will be entitled to the proceeds after any debts outstanding against the policy have been deducted. A person otherwise entitled to receive the proceeds of a life insurance policy may be disqualified if he helped bring about the death of the person whose life was insured. This disqualification applies chiefly to cases of intentional, unlawful killing, not to negligently or recklessly causing death.

Both primary and secondary beneficiaries can be named in a policy. When the insured person dies, the proceeds of the policy are paid to the primary beneficiary if he is alive. If the primary beneficiary is dead, the proceeds go to the secondary beneficiary. If two or more primary beneficiaries are named in a policy, the proceeds are distributed in equal shares among them. If the primary beneficiary is dead and there are two or more secondary beneficiaries, the proceeds are divided equally among the living secondary beneficiaries. If all the beneficiaries are dead, the money is paid to the insured person's estate, and divided among his heirs, according to the laws of DESCENT AND DISTRIBUTION. In general, it is wise to name both a primary beneficiary and a secondary one.

EXAMPLE Assume that, as most husbands do, Lenny names his wife as the primary beneficiary in his life insurance policy, and designates no secondary beneficiaries. Unfortunately, both Lenny and his wife are killed in an auto accident. Eventually, the money will be passed on to Lenny's children, but not until it has gone through all the red tape of estate settling, and all the taxes, probate costs, and expenses involved have been deducted. Had Lenny named his children as secondary beneficiaries in the first place, the money would have been paid to them promptly and in full.

Minor children as beneficiaries According to law, minor children are not legally capable of handling their own assets, and if you name them as beneficiaries of an insurance policy without appointing a guardian, the court will appoint one for you if you die and the money goes to them before they reach adulthood. The court's choice may not be one you would have made, and it might be more expensive. The time to appoint a guardian for your children is when you draw up your will—and it is wise to name an alternate in case the first guardian is unable to take the responsiblity. See GUARDIAN AND WARD.

Changing a beneficiary It is usually very easy to change the name of the beneficiary of your own life insurance. The procedure is generally spelled out on the policy itself. Whenever circumstances warrant, you should change your beneficiary in order to avoid legal problems later.

Separating from or divorcing your spouse does not automatically affect his or her position as a beneficiary. If, for example, you allow your former wife to remain listed as the beneficiary of your life insurance policy, the courts will grant her the money even if in your will you indicated that your current wife should receive it. Therefore, it is essential that, if your marital status changes, you review any life insurance policies that you have in order to decide whether the beneficiary designated must be changed.

Cancellation Once an insurance contract is issued, the purchaser pays premiums on a time schedule—monthly, quarterly, semiannually, or yearly. If the policy is silent on the question, failure to pay a premium when due usually will terminate the coverage, thereby canceling the policy. Most policies, however, contain explicit provisions for termination.

Life insurance contracts commonly extend coverage during a grace period immediately following the due date, giving a later due date for paying the premium. For example, if your life insurance policy gives you a grace period of 30 days, you can pay your premium up to 30 days after it is due without any consequences. Policies usually terminate automatically if payment is not received by the end of the grace period, but the cash surrender value of the policy or any dividends earned by it may be applied to continue the policy until these funds run out.

The insurance company can also cancel your policy if it can show that, in filling out your application, you committed fraud, concealment, or misrepresentation of facts. The insurer cannot avoid liability, however, if an applicant for life insurance deliberately lies about his age in order to lower his premium, because there is a standard provision in most policies that anticipates this type of deception. When this particular misrepresentation is discovered, the insured person will be insured not for the face amount of the policy but only for the amount his premium would have entitled him to if he had correctly stated his age.

If a company cancels a policy, it must do so within a specified time period after it takes effect—usually one or two years. Beyond that period, you are protected by the *incontestability clause,* which is required by law for most types of policies. The incontestability clause prevents insurance companies from permitting people to pay premiums for several decades, then canceling the policies when benefits become due.

Life insurance policies often contain a clause declaring that the insurance company can cancel the policy if the person insured is not "in good health" on the date the policy is issued or delivered. Here again, the incontestability clause comes into play; the courts have ruled in favor of the insurance companies when they have shown that people have taken out life insurance policies while knowing they were seriously ill—but only if the policy is canceled within the specified time.

The requirement that the applicant be in good health is met as long as the applicant *believes* he is in good health, even though his physician and family may know he is incurably ill. Some policies sidestep the whole problem by including a provision that declares that the insurance company is not liable for death resulting from a disease existing on the date the policy becomes effective. The provision avoids any question of the insured person's knowledge of his illness and avoids application of the incontestability clause. Courts will generally uphold such a provision many years after the policy has taken effect.

If a person has committed suicide, the insurance company may, in some states, be released from its obligation to pay the proceeds to the beneficiary. But if the decedent was insane and did not know what he was doing at the time of death, the company may not refuse to pay the proceeds to the beneficiary since the death is considered accidental or unintentional. This must be proved by the beneficiary. If the suicide occurs within two years of the date coverage begins, no proceeds will be awarded, if the policy clearly specifies that no proceeds be awarded in cases of suicide committed within two years of the date that the policy was issued. The apparent conflict between suicide as intentional killing and, therefore, not covered by the policy as opposed to suicide as unintentional because it was committed by an insane person who did not know what he was doing and, therefore, covered by the policy, can be resolved only by consulting state law and the terms of the policy in question.

■ **Health insurance** One of the most essential types of insurance protection offered today is health insurance, designed to defray the exorbitant expenses involved in the treatment of a prolonged illness. The majority of Americans are protected by some form of health insurance, whether it is government-sponsored Medicaid (see WELFARE PROGRAMS) or Medicare (see SOCIAL SECURITY) or whether it is offered as a group plan or as an individual policy. There are as many kinds of health insurance as there are contracts providing differing degrees of coverage. You should check the protection you have under your policy to learn how you are protected because no two policies of health insurance are alike.

Coverage and limitations Although the type of coverage provided by health insurance varies according to the terms of each policy, a traditional comprehensive medical insurance policy usually offers three types of coverage—hospitalization, general medical, and major medical.

Hospitalization Virtually every kind of health insurance covers some or all the costs of hospitalization up to a certain number of days. Should you be hospitalized for a particular illness, your insurance company will pay the per diem cost of your room. Most policies limit payment to a semiprivate room. If you insist upon a private room, your policy may state that you must pay the difference in cost of a private room over a semiprivate room.

The amount of coverage for hospitalization is limited up to a certain number of days per year. For example, one health insurance plan will cover the cost of 240 days in the hospital but specify that if the confinement is for tuberculosis, nervous disorders, or mental illness, coverage is for only 70 days.

Under coverage for hospitalization, many policies include expenses incurred while hospitalized, such as the operating room, surgical dressings and plaster casts, serums, intravenous solutions, physical and oxygen therapy, electrocardiograms, X-rays, and clinical and pathological laboratory services, for example. A patient must pay his own telephone bill or television rental fee, however.

General medical Although policies differ, the general, or basic, medical protection afforded by health insurance covers fees of physicians, surgeons, and anesthesiologists who perform services for a patient, whether hospitalized or not, as well as diagnostic, X-ray, and laboratory services required to treat an illness in a doctor's office, the patient's

home, or an outpatient department of a hospital. General medical coverage pays only a certain amount of the covered charges, based upon what the insurer considers a reasonable fee for the particular service rendered. The amount payable for combined diagnostic, X-ray, and laboratory services per year may also be limited by the terms of a policy. Some policies include prescription drugs used to treat an illness as a covered expense. The differences between what a person collects under his general medical policy and what he has paid his doctor is used to determine what he will recover under his major medical policy.

Major medical In addition to hospitalization and general medical care, a traditional health insurance policy provides major medical coverage. This reimburses the policyholder for a certain percentage (usually 80 percent) of an amount approved by the insurer of his expenses for general medical care only after he has paid a certain amount (usually $100), called a deductible, out of his pocket. He is financially responsible for his remaining medical expenses. The deductible must be met each year before a policyholder can begin to collect under major medical.

Depending upon the terms of his policy, a person's coverage under major medical may be limited to a lifetime amount, such as $250,000. If his medical expenses exceed the lifetime limit, he will be responsible for the excess.

A new concept in health protection In the 1970's a new type of health insurance emerged to meet the medical needs of the public. The Health Maintenance Organization (HMO) plan provides to its members, for a fixed monthly premium, comprehensive medical care. Medical charges for in-hospital care, doctor's office visits, surgery, X-rays, laboratory work, ear and eye examinations, and physical therapy are completely paid by the insurer as long as the members agree to go to doctors and hospitals that are part of the HMO. The member usually must pay a minimal amount for emergency room services, prescriptions, and maternity charges. There are no approved charges and no deductibles to be met in order to be covered.

HMOs are usually offered as group plans, which have the provision that if you are not satisfied with your coverage, you may have the opportunity to return to the traditional comprehensive health plan. Some HMO plans provide that when a group member reaches 65 his coverage ends, but that he must be given the opportunity to return to group insurance coverage if he likes.

Cancellation Like other types of insurance, a person's medical insurance may be canceled for failure to pay the premium promptly. If a policyholder should conceal or misrepresent his true medical condition on his application for insurance, such as refusing to disclose that he has a rare terminal disease that, in its final stages, will require hospitalization, his insurance company is entitled to cancel his policy upon discovery of the truth.

■ **Group insurance plans** The most economical way to purchase insurance is through group plans, which are offered to large groups of people, such as employees of a particular employer, members of labor unions, or professional associations. As with the marketing of any product or service, the high-volume dealings involved in group plans reduce administrative and sales expenses so that the premiums to be paid for such plans are lower than premiums for individual plans. If the employer pays the entire premium for group coverage, the plan is called *noncontributory,* but if the individual member pays some of it directly or through deductions from his paycheck, the plan is called a *contributory plan.* Health and life insurance are the most common types of insurance offered as group plans, although many group plans now provide accident and dental insurance to their members.

The terms under which an insurer agrees to make contracts available to individual members of the plan are stated in a master policy between the insurer and the group representative. Each participant receives a certificate that specifies the principal terms of coverage, but usually refers to the master policy for various details, such as whether the consent of policyholders is needed for any future modification of coverage.

Health and life insurance risks   Some persons who would be considered by the insurer to be bad risks for health and life insurance, and who would thus be charged high premiums for protection, benefit greatly from inclusion in the group. If the group is large, the presence of a small percentage of these "bad risks" is not enough to increase the group rates as long as the vast majority of the group is viewed as a good risk by the insurer. Should the group contain a significant percentage of bad risks, the group premium would be adjusted accordingly but still would be lower than if each member purchased an individual policy.

Cancellation   A member of a group plan may have his coverage canceled for a variety of reasons. If a person leaves the group because he has changed jobs or retires, his policy will be canceled. Special provisions of a group policy may, however, give a retired individual the right to retain some protection. When the group plan is financed partly by the individual members, failure to pay the premium may terminate an individual's coverage. If the individual member has acted fraudulently by concealing or misrepresenting an important fact on his application for the group policy, the policy may be canceled upon the discovery of the truth, except in life insurance policies where the time specified under the incontestability clause has expired.

■ **Fire insurance**   Fire insurance is a contract against loss of or damage to property by fire or lightning. It offers the property owner a way of recovering at least part of his losses when his property is partially or completely burned.

Insurable interest   As with life insurance, a person must have an insurable interest in a property before he is entitled to take out a fire insurance policy on it. A person usually has an insurable interest if he would either receive financial benefit or advantage from the preservation of the property or would suffer monetary loss or damage if it was damaged or destroyed. Different people may have separate insurable interests in the same property—for example, the owner of a house and the company that holds a mortgage on the house both have an insurable interest in it, but the *mortgagor* (lender) will lose his interest once the mortgage is paid off. The *mortgagee* (borrower), because of the amount he has paid toward ownership of the property in addition to the amount he owes on the mortgage, has an insurable interest equal to the entire purchase price of the property. The mortgagor has an insurable interest only to the extent of the money he has lent the mortgagee. A *vendor*

(owner), who has contracted to sell the property but still legally owns it or has a lien on the property until the purchase price is paid, also has an insurable interest.

In life insurance, an insurable interest must exist at the time one person takes out a life insurance policy on another, but it need not exist when the insured person dies. On the other hand, an insurable interest in property must exist both when the policy for fire or other property insurance is obtained and when the property is damaged or destroyed.

EXAMPLE Smith takes out a fire insurance policy on his men's clothing store. He sells the store, but forgets to cancel the policy and continues to pay the premiums. When the store burns down two weeks later, Smith has no right to recover the insurance proceeds because he had no insurable interest in the property at the time of the loss. He may, however, recover the premiums he paid during the time he no longer owned the store. If an insurable interest were not required at the time of loss, Smith might be tempted to burn down the buildings he no longer owned in order to collect the insurance money.

Coverage   There is considerable variation among the types of coverage offered by fire insurance policies, and you must read your own policy carefully to determine what coverage it provides. In general, fire insurance covers damage of which the fire is the proximate, or immediate, cause.

EXAMPLE If your neighbor's garage bursts into flame, burns the base of a nearby telephone pole and the pole falls, crashing through the roof of your house, your fire insurance policy will probably not cover the damage to the house, for that sort of damage was not what you and the company had in mind when the two of you signed the fire insurance contract. However, if the fire engulfs the telephone pole, and when the burning pole falls it sets fire to the house, that destruction would be covered.

The fire must also be *hostile*—one out of control and therefore unintended. To discover too late that your wife has been hiding a valuable medieval manuscript in the fireplace chimney is to suffer a loss for which the insurance company will not reimburse you—the fire you built in the fireplace is a *friendly fire.*

Property need not be damaged by the fire itself. You are covered for damage done by smoke, charring, and blistering. You are even covered for any destruction caused by the firemen in attempting to fight the blaze, including water damage and broken windows.

Limitations   Certain kinds of property—money, deeds, and securities, for example—are excluded from coverage under all fire policies. Anything you do that increases the chance of a fire, such as storing explosives on the insured premises, will discharge the insurer from liability. Unless your policy has special provisions for homes occupied only part of the year, leaving an insured house unoccupied for 60 consecutive days or more will also discharge the insurer from liability.

Coinsurance   Fire insurance policies generally contain a COINSURANCE clause, which says you must keep your property insured for at least 80 percent of its actual cash value (what a similar house would cost in a similar neighborhood) in order to be fully reimbursed for its partial or total destruction by fire—up to the face amount of the policy. Otherwise, you are responsible for a proportionate share of the loss, thus becoming a coinsurer of your property. For example, if your house is worth $100,000 you should insure it for at least $80,000. If you insure it for only $40,000—half the amount in the coinsurance clause—and a fire causes damage of $20,000, you will collect only $10,000, or half the amount of damages, from the insurance company.

Claim investigation When you report fire damage to your insurer, do not be surprised if the claim is investigated. According to recent statistics, more than one in every three fires is deliberately caused, frequently by owners who cannot sell the property for nearly the amount of money that it is insured for. Although arson is difficult to prove, investigation is worth the company's efforts, for no insurance company will be required to pay damages the owner deliberately causes. In fact, the policy states that you must take all reasonable precautions to avoid a fire, and when one occurs, you must do your best to protect the property from further damage. You must not, for example, refuse to call the fire department until you are convinced that the property will be a total loss.

Cancellation As a general rule, when a person seeking fire insurance intentionally misrepresents the ownership of the property being insured, its value, description, location, or use, the insurance company may cancel the policy. It may also cancel the policy if the policyholder does not pay his premiums promptly unless his policy provides for a grace period that extends his time to pay a fixed number of days. When an insurance company cancels a policy it must notify the insured person that it has done so.

■ **Personal liability insurance** Liability insurance is designed to pay for injuries or damage that the insured party caused to other people or their property. Personal liability insurance covers homes and families. If you have a personal liability policy and you or someone else in your immediate family causes bodily injury to another person, or damages or destroys another person's property, your insurance company will defend you in court if you are sued by the injured party and will pay the damages awarded in the suit up to the maximum amount indicated in your policy. If the damage or injury has been intentionally caused by you or your family, the insurance company will be discharged from liability, however.

Most personal liability policies require the insurance company to defend any civil suit that alleges that the policyholder committed bodily injury or property damage covered by the policy even if the basis of the suit is groundless, false, or fraudulent. The obligation to defend is determined by the nature of the claim, regardless of its merit. If a company wrongfully refuses to defend a policyholder, it must fully reimburse him for any reasonable expenses he incurs in providing his own defense.

Coverage Most homeowners have liability insurance to cover guests and workmen who might be injured on the premises. If your dog bites the mailman, your comprehensive personal liability insurance will probably cover it.

Limitations Personal liability does not cover accidents that occur to you or members of your household. Coverage extending to accidents in swimming pools is not generally included in standard policies, but such coverage can be added for higher premiums. Automobile accidents are also excluded from coverage, but a separate automobile liability insurance may be available as discussed below.

If you own more than one home, the standard personal liability policy does not cover the second home. To cover both, the policy must be extended and an additional premium paid. A personal policy usually excludes using your home for business purposes. If you have an in-house part-time office, you must bring that fact to your agent's attention. Separate policies are available for places of business and rented property, such as apartment buildings.

Cancellation Like other kinds of insurance policies, coverage under liability insurance can be canceled if the policyholder fails to pay his premium promptly or if he has committed fraud by concealing or misrepresenting facts that, if disclosed to the insurance company, would result in the denial of the policy to the applicant.

EXAMPLE Otto, the owner of a dairy, has a liability policy to protect him against financial responsibility for accidents caused by his drivers while delivering milk. As a favor to his sister, Otto hires his nephew, Nick, as a driver, although Nick has had his license suspended twice for drunken driving. The policy specifically prohibits the use of anyone who has been convicted of driving while intoxicated. Otto fails to notify the insurer of Nick's driving record. The company can cancel the policy should it discover Nick's past.

■ **Automobile insurance** There are numerous types of automobile insurance, including liability insurance and no-fault insurance, which are discussed below. In addition, there is *collision insurance,* which provides for an additional premium to the basic policy and stipulates that the insurance company will repair or replace a covered car if it is involved in an accident, and *comprehensive coverage,* which pays for damage caused not only by accidents, but also by fire, theft, and vandalism. If you are financing a new car, the company lending you the money may require that you buy collision or comprehensive coverage. Without such coverage, the car—your creditor's collateral for the loan—could be destroyed in an accident or stolen, and the company would have no simple way of recouping its money should you then default on your payments.

Standard automobile liability insurance Some states require a standard automobile liability policy. Under such a policy the insurance company must pay any money that the insured party is legally obligated to pay because of any bodily injury, illness, death, or property damage caused by accidents and arising out of the ownership, maintenance, or use of the insured automobile.

Coverage When a policy promises to cover accidents "arising out of the ownership" of a vehicle, the insurance company is responsible when the car is operated by someone other than the owner, as long as that other person has the owner's permission to drive it. Depending upon the terms of the policy, any newly acquired autos belonging to the policyholder may be automatically covered if reported to the company within 30 days. Coverage under automobile liability insurance is generally broad.

EXAMPLE In one case, a court held that an automobile liability policy covered a man who, in approaching a car's open gas tank with a lighted cigarette, was injured in the resulting explosion. In another case, when oil leaked from a car engine onto a highway and other cars skidded on it and crashed, the damage was covered by the company insuring the car with the leaking engine.

Limitations   If an automobile is insured strictly for private use or pleasure, it is not covered if it is involved in an accident while being used for business purposes. Insurance companies are also wary of possible collusion between the person insured and his family, friends, and business associates in staging an "accident" in order to collect benefits. Therefore, some policies specifically deny liability for (1) the insured person if he is injured in his own car while someone else is driving, (2) the insured person's spouse and other members of his household if they are injured while the insured person is driving, or (3) any occupants in the insured person's automobile.

If you are being sued after an automobile accident, you should obtain your own lawyer when your policy does not cover the entire amount the plaintiff is seeking. You should also have a lawyer if you choose to file a COUNTERCLAIM against the plaintiff. And you will certainly need a lawyer if your insurance company, by settling the claim against you, leaves you open to a criminal charge, such as driving while intoxicated.

Uninsured motorist coverage   In some types of policies the insurance company agrees to pay the policyholder's damages when he has an accident involving another person's uninsured vehicle. Thus, if a policyholder or a member of his household is injured by a financially irresponsible motorist or a hit-and-run driver, he is given the same protection he would have received in an accident involving an insured automobile.

In many states, claims up to a given amount are paid by a state fund or state corporation. Certain victims, such as the operator of an uninsured vehicle or someone driving with a revoked or suspended license, are usually excluded from receiving benefits. The right to claim benefits may also be confined to residents of the state.

No-fault automobile insurance   In no-fault automobile insurance each driver's insurance company pays for his injury or damage up to a certain limit no matter who is responsible for the accident. Now required by many states, no-fault insurance resulted from widespread dissatisfaction with the traditional system for compensation of losses—in particular, the sometimes years-long delay between the accident and the trial to settle claims. In 1970, Massachusetts became the first state to enact a no-fault automobile insurance law. Other states quickly followed with their own no-fault laws.

According to the various state laws, if you have no-fault coverage you may not sue someone who causes an accident and injures you or damages your property if the policy covers it. But you may sue if your no-fault policy does not cover the particular injury or damage. If the damage exceeds the amount covered by no-fault insurance, most states allow you to sue for the difference.

Under some statutes, a person who does not have the required coverage at the time of the accident becomes personally liable for the payment of no-fault benefits. Other statutes make him liable only in certain circumstances, such as when the harm was intentionally caused, when the injured person dies or suffers serious injuries, or when the

cost of his medical expenses exceeds a certain amount.

Some statutes allow a person to sue for pain and suffering, but only if his medical expenses exceed a specified amount. Others allow such suits regardless of the medical expense incurred. Under these laws, damages for pain and suffering may be sought in all cases involving specified types of injuries, such as those causing death or resulting in a fracture, loss of body member, or permanent or serious disfigurement.

Coverage   Under some no-fault statutes, the insurance company will pay for personal injuries suffered by the insured person, members of his household, authorized operators or passengers in his automobile, and pedestrians struck by him. No-fault insurance statutes generally provide for payment of reasonable expenses incurred for medical, hospital, surgical, nursing, dental, ambulance, X-ray, and prescription drug services, and other specified benefits. Some states require that these expenses must be incurred, or the need for them be determined, within a specified time after the accident. The expenses of rehabilitation training or treatment have been included under some statutes. Other laws provide for limited funeral, burial, or cremation expenses.

In many no-fault states, your insurance company is also responsible for accidental damage to tangible property arising out of the ownership, operation, maintenance, or use of a motor vehicle. If, for example, you back into your neighbor's valuable bonsai garden, your company would pay damages.

Limitations   Motorcycles are often specifically excluded from coverage under no-fault automobile insurance policies. Some statutes also exclude from benefits anyone who is injured while (1) driving under the influence of alcohol or narcotics, (2) committing a felony or trying to avoid arrest, (3) intentionally trying to injure himself or others, (4) operating a motor vehicle in a race, (5) operating or occupying a vehicle he knows is stolen, (6) or driving the insured vehicle without the consent of its owner.

Alternatives   Not all states have enacted no-fault insurance statutes. Some require automobile drivers to take out a liability policy or post a bond as security to insure that people or property injured or damaged by their faulty operation of a vehicle will be compensated. Other states require that a driver who has already been involved in an accident give security to cover the resulting losses to others and may require him to furnish future proof of security or lose the right to drive. See Chart 26.

Dealing with your automobile insurance company Everyone who has automobile insurance should be aware of some basic laws regarding his relationship to the company that insures him—particularly those having to do with the company's rights to cancel the policy and the policyholder's responsibilities regarding claims.

Cancellation   No insurance company is required to sell a particular applicant automobile insurance. In those states with an *assigned risk* plan, in which the state orders every insurance company to give policies to a certain quota of high-risk drivers, an impartial agency makes the assignment and the applicant has no choice of companies.

When a company does grant auto coverage, it can cancel the policy for any reason within 60 days after it takes effect if its provisions so permit. Thereafter, however, it may cancel for only three reasons: (1) If you fail to pay the premiums when due; (2) if your driver's license is revoked or suspended; or (3) if the insurance company discovers that, in applying for the insurance, you lied about important information, such as your prior accident record.

In many states, the insurance company is not required to renew your policy when it expires—and the reason need not have anything to do with you or your driving. You may simply live in an area where there is a particularly high accident ratio or where the company feels the premiums the law allows it to charge are too low. Some states, however, do not let companies refuse to renew policies without substantial reasons, which must be explained to the policyholder.

Denying payment Even though you are insured, the courts have ruled that under certain circumstances the company does not have to pay your claim. You can forfeit coverage, for example, if you fail to report a minor accident in the hope that, by not calling it to the company's attention, you will avoid higher premiums or a policy cancellation. Not only must you report all accidents, but you must report promptly—if you delay beyond what the courts consider a reasonable time (often 20 days), your insurance company may have grounds for refusal to pay claims.

The company has the legal right to challenge any repair bill you submit to it if you have the car fixed before the company authorizes it. Typically, the company will have its own claims adjuster estimate the cost of damages or require that you submit at least two estimates from recognized professionals. Then the company will write you a check for repairs or replacement, and if necessary you and the company can haggle about the amount paid while the damaged car is still available as evidence.

■ **Other types of insurance** The types of insurance discussed above are simply some of the more common types. There are a great many others, including credit life insurance (to pay off a car or mortgage in case the buyer dies while payments are still owed), homeowner's insurance (usually incorporating fire, personal liability, theft, and other coverage into one policy), and title insurance (which protects you against claims made on the land you own). You can take out a policy to protect your television service, your plateglass windows, your property against strike and riot, hail, and use and occupancy. Lloyd's of London has insured Jimmy Durante's nose and a racehorse's fertility.

What is more, you can attach *floaters* for added protection to most policies. For example, a personal property floater is an all-risk policy that protects property, other than real estate and merchandise, against loss or damage, regardless of where the property is when the loss occurs. Thus, a fire insurance policy that would protect an antique chair in the home might carry a floater to protect the same chair from fire damage no matter where it might be moved to.

Finally, there are a number of government-sponsored insurances. The most notable of these are Medicare and Old-age, Survivors, and Disability Insurance (which are part of SOCIAL SECURITY); UNEMPLOYMENT COMPENSATION; and WORKMEN'S COMPENSATION.

■ **The insurance application and policy** An application for insurance consists of two parts: a request for insurance and the information necessary for the company to make an informed decision. Unless a statute or the insurance company itself requires a written application, an oral one is sufficient. A written application is signed by the applicant to bind him to the truth of his statements, and he may have to make a separate application for each policy he wants, depending on the company. An application is not a contract, but merely a request for insurance. The applicant has the right to withdraw his application any time before it is accepted.

An applicant for life insurance must usually submit to a medical examination so that the insurer can determine whether or not it wants to insure the individual. The company is free to accept or reject an application, but it must notify an applicant when he is rejected so that he may seek insurance elsewhere.

Frequently, there is a substantial interval between when a person applies for insurance and when he is issued the policy. In some cases, the agent does not have authority to issue the policy immediately, and often either the agent or the company investigates the statements made on the application before undertaking to insure the risk. During that period the applicant is responsible for any loss that may occur—as well as any change in circumstances that may make him uninsurable, such as coming down with a sudden serious illness just after he has applied for life insurance or health insurance. On the other hand, the company runs the risk that the applicant may change his mind and buy from a competitor or may decide against buying insurance altogether. The insurer would lose the considerable expense of investigating and processing the application and often paying for the medical examination in the case of life and health insurance.

The solution in both cases is a *binder*—a temporary contract by a written memorandum of vital terms, such as a description of the person or property to be insured, the types of risks, and the duration of coverage. In life insurance, such binders are usually issued only after payment of the first premium, and they are called binding receipts. For most other types of insurance, binders are often issued before any premium is paid.

The courts do not usually consider mere delay in deciding on an application as acceptance by the company, even if a premium accompanied the application and is being held by the company. But if the applicant was led to believe and did believe that his application was accepted, the company may not deny it. When, for instance, an agent has told an applicant that "everything is taken care of," the company cannot disclaim responsibility.

An unconditional acceptance of the application by the insurer completes the contract and makes it binding on both the applicant and the company unless the application states otherwise—for example, if it states "this policy is to take effect at 12:01 A.M., July 1, 1982" it does not take effect until that time even if it is accepted much earlier. Unless the law or the policy states otherwise, an applicant who has been accepted for insurance need not actually receive the policy in order to be insured.

If the company, instead of accepting the application, makes a counteroffer, the applicant is free to accept it or reject it. A counteroffer may be a policy different from the one applied for. It does not become a contract until it is accepted by the applicant. A contract of insurance is a voluntary commercial contract subject to the same rules that govern all contracts. See CONTRACTS. The elements of an insurance contract are (1) a subject matter, such as a car; (2) a risk or contingency that is insured against, such as the theft of the car; (3) a promise to indemnify for a particular amount and for a specific period of time; (4) a premium and its period of payment; and (5) an agreement of the parties on all the essential elements. A binder is a preliminary contract. The policy itself is the final contract.

■ **Responsibilities of the insured party** Whatever type of insurance you have, your policy spells out certain responsibilities that you must meet. If you fail to carry out these responsibilities, the insurance company can cancel the policy or refuse to pay a claim. Other steps are not required, but are wise ones to take. Here, in summary, are your major responsibilities, some of which were discussed earlier in relation to the various types of insurance in which they are particularly important:

Notice and proof of loss Most accident and fire insurance policies require the policyholder to file a notice and proof of loss within the time specified in the policy before a claim will be paid. Proof of loss is the formal evidence that enables the insurer to determine its liability.

If in a fire policy the insured person lies in his notice or proof of loss in order to cheat the insurance company, he usually forfeits any right of recovery. Courts generally require that the false statement be material (important), however. For example, if the owner of a house states that it had been occupied at the time a fire broke out when, in fact, it had been deserted for five months, the insurer is discharged from its liability to the owner.

All state laws require that you notify your insurance company promptly—usually within 20 days—of any claims you or others make against your policy. Failure to serve notice or proof of loss may be excused, however, if the circumstances make it impossible or unreasonable to do so. For example, if you have a personal liability policy you may assert that the incident leading to a lawsuit was so trivial that you believed no claim for damages would arise. Many companies would consider this a reasonable excuse for delay.

Policyholders may also be excused for delayed notice because they did not realize that the policy covered the type of incident involved.

EXAMPLE Marvin's unruly stepson, Butch, stole the family O——* car even though he did not have a driver's license. Butch drove wildly through the city streets and collided with another car. Marvin had automobile liability insurance, but he did not know that his policy covered such an accident. Consequently, he did not notify the insurance company of the collision. Months later, the driver of the other car involved in the collision sued Marvin, and Marvin hired a lawyer to handle the suit. The lawyer examined Marvin's insurance policy and discovered that the accident was covered. Marvin then notified the insurance company of the collision. Even though the policy required Marvin to notify the insurance company of an accident with 20 days, the delay was held not to violate the notice requirement because Marvin had not known he was covered in this case.

Cooperation in defending or settling claims Your policy obligates you to cooperate with your insurance company in defending a claim the company decides to fight in court; that is, you must be willing to appear at hearings as a witness and supply all the information you have. Except in some malpractice cases, you must also allow the company to handle the case in any way it sees fit. If you try to settle the case by yourself, you will do so at your own expense, and the company will be free from responsibility for the claim. If the company wants to make a settlement and you refuse, your conduct may entitle the company to wash its hands of the case.

■ **Collecting from the insurance company** Insurance companies are not likely to prolong small claims settlements. The agent who sold you the policy may act as the adjuster (also called the investigator or examiner), file a report on the value of the loss, and then negotiate the settlement with you. But if you have suffered a personal injury or a substantial loss, negotiations can sometimes be lengthy, and many people prefer to have an attorney represent their interests, even to the extent of negotiating with the adjuster. Should you wish to handle your claim yourself, here are some details you should know:

Adjustments An adjustment is a settling of the amount of money that the insured party is entitled to receive after all proper allowances and deductions have been made. Any authorized officer or agent may bind the company by adjusting with the insured party the amount to be paid for the loss under the terms of the policy. Once an adjustment is made, it is valid unless there has been fraud or mistake in the matter.

EXAMPLE Your neighbor's car has been sideswiped in an O——* accident. His insurance company tells him to send estimates of the damage, so he takes the car to a body shop owned by his nephew, Bruno. Bruno inflates the cost of a repair that would normally be $150 to $450. The company sends its adjuster to examine the car. He is a friend of Bruno's and agrees to his estimate because Bruno will give him $100. But the adjustment may be set aside if the insurance company learns of this fraud—and, of course, your neighbor, Bruno, and the adjuster all risk imprisonment.

The company may dispute a claim and make a counteroffer for settlement. In the example above, rather than sending an adjuster, the insurance company may offer your neighbor $300; if he accepts, the claim is settled.

Appraisal and arbitration Some policies, including standard fire insurance forms, provide that if the company and the policyholder fail to agree upon the value of the property or the amount of loss, either may demand an appraisal by two appraisers, one appointed by each party. When two appraisers are used, an umpire is also appointed to resolve the difference.

Making settlement Once you sign a release and accept a settlement, you have discharged your insurance company from any additional obligation regarding the claim. Should you later find that an injury requires additional medical treatment, for example, you will not be able to collect any more money. The courts will take you at your word—you have released the company from any additional liability on the claim.

Most companies are fair about settling claims, but a few will try to save money by rushing you into hasty and minimal settlements. Prepare yourself with complete knowledge and documentation of the value of your property losses and injuries before making a settlement and signing a release, which it will be almost impossible for you to contest in court.

Nonpayment and late payment of claims Some states have laws providing special remedies to the policyholder for the insurance company's nonpayment or late payment of a valid claim. In addition to paying the claim, the law usually requires the company to pay the claimant's attorney's fee plus an additional penalty. When there is no such statute, the insurer is generally not responsible for either an attorney's fee or a penalty.

Wrongful cancellations If your insurance policy is wrongfully canceled, you or your beneficiary may legally treat it as though it were still in force and recover on it all the benefits that are payable under its terms. You may also sue the insurance company in court to have the policy restored or to receive money DAMAGES as compensation. A cancellation is invalid if it is obtained by fraud, by mutual mistakes, or without the full knowledge and understanding of the insured person.

> EXAMPLE A computer printout indicated that a policyholder had more accidents during a three-year period than the company permitted, so the company canceled the policy. In fact, however, the insured driver had not had the accidents, and was able to prove it through the state motor vehicle records. The policyholder presented his evidence, and was promptly reinstated.

■ **State regulatory agencies** Although the federal government has little control of the insurance industry (except for those companies that advertise and sell policies through the mail), every state has stringent laws controlling the insurance industry and an insurance supervisor or commissioner whose department enforces them. Through these departments, the state legislatures regulate rates and require standard forms for policies. They require that companies have sufficient assets to pay valid claims, and make certain they do so.

When an insurance company has violated the state's regulations, the insurance commissioner may impose either civil or criminal penalties on the company, its agents, or brokers, and even revoke the company's license to do business within the state.

intangible Personal property in the form of a right, rather than a physical object. For example, such assets of a business as GOOD WILL, TRADEMARKS, COPYRIGHTS, and FRANCHISES are intangibles.

integrated agreement In the law of CONTRACTS, a contract is integrated when the parties adopt a document as the final and complete expression of their agreement. This document is called an *integration*.

integrated bar A system by which all the attorneys in a state are organized into an association, called a BAR ASSOCIATION, which they must join in order to practice law in their area.

integration 1 The act or process of making something complete, such as an INTEGRATED AGREEMENT. 2 The conversion of a segregated public school system to a nonracial, nondiscriminatory system of students, faculty, staff, facilities, and activities. See CIVIL RIGHTS.

intent A resolution to use a particular means to reach a certain end; a design; an aim. Since intent is a state of mind, it usually cannot be proved directly but must be inferred from the facts of a situation, especially in interpreting a person's behavior. Although intent and motive are often used interchangeably, they are not the same thing. Motive is the desire for a particular goal that moves a person to achieve it; intent is the decision to use a particular means to achieve the goal. For example, one man may want another man's money and kill him in order to get it. The motive for the murder is the money, but the intent is the decision to kill the other person in order to obtain the money. For further discussion of intent, see CRIMINAL LAW.

intention In law, a decision (to act in a certain way or to do a certain thing) that can be demonstrated by words or conduct. This is in contrast to an INTENT formed in a person's mind without his necessarily doing or saying anything about it. For example, in interpreting WILLS and CONTRACTS, intention can be derived from the words used by the maker of the document.

inter alia (Latin) "Among other things." The term is often used when a few items are selected from a larger list. For example, "Found alongside the victim's body were, *inter alia*, credit cards, a checkbook, and a laundry ticket."

interest 1 The most general term for any right that a person has in real property (real estate) or personal property (any property that is not real property). For example, a landlord and the tenant who leases his house for several years both have an interest in the real estate, although the interests are not identical—the landlord's being one of ownership and the tenant's one of possession. 2 Compensation for the use of borrowed money. There are two kinds of interest, conventional and legal. *Conventional interest* is interest at the rate agreed upon by the parties themselves. *Legal interest* is the rate of interest prescribed by state law as the highest that may be lawfully charged. See CONSUMER PROTECTION; CREDIT; USURY.

interference In PATENT law, a declaration by the patent office that two pending applications, or an existing patent and a pending application, cover the same invention. An investigation is then made to determine which invention has priority.

interlineation The act of writing between the lines of a document; words written between the lines of a document. Suppose that two people enter into a CONTRACT, and after it is typed and signed, they decide that a sentence must be inserted between the lines to clarify one of the provisions. The new sentence is an interlineation, which should be initialed and dated by both parties to show that they know it is there and agree to it.

interlocutory   Provisional; not final. Something intervening between the beginning and the end of a lawsuit that decides some point or matter but is not a final decision of the whole lawsuit. For example, a court order requiring a husband to pay his wife a certain amount of money per week for her support pending a divorce trial is an interlocutory order.

Internal Revenue Code

The federal law—Title 26 of the United States Code—on the payment and collection of taxes. See ESTATE AND GIFT TAX; INCOME TAX.

Internal Revenue Service

The federal agency that collects taxes. See INCOME TAX.

International Court of Justice

The principal judicial tribunal of the United Nations, which functions according to a statute annexed to the United Nations Charter. The court consists of 15 judges, no two of whom may be citizens of the same country. The court's permanent home is at The Hague, Netherlands.

The court has authority to hear only those questions of INTERNATIONAL LAW that parties choose to lay before it. Representatives of nations submit a written request to the court, stating exactly the question upon which the court is asked to rule. The court then notifies all nations entitled to appear before it and sets a time within which written statements and oral arguments may be presented.

The court delivers an advisory opinion in open court after notifying the Secretary General, member nations, and any other states or international organizations concerned with the question. The opinion is called *advisory* because the court cannot force the parties to abide by its decision.

international law

The law that different nations agree to be bound by in their dealings with one another. It is different from the *internal* or *municipal law* that is in force within a nation. In this country, international law is part of the Constitution (Article VI):

> " *This Constitution, and the Laws of the United States which shall be made in Pursuance thereof; and all Treaties made, or which shall be made, under the Authority of the United States, shall be the supreme Law of the Land; and the Judges in every State shall be bound thereby, any Thing in the Constitution or Laws of any State to the Contrary notwithstanding.* "

This part of the Constitution makes every treaty part of the law, enforceable by every state and federal court. Because the Constitution is the supreme law of the land, no state legislature may pass a law that violates a treaty to which the United States is a party. A *treaty*—which can also be called a *compact, accord,* or *agreement*—is like a contract between nations.

In international law, a *state* is an entire country, made up of citizens, a defined territory, and an organized government. Only states can be parties to treaties, and they frequently refer to themselves as *high contracting parties.* A state's authority to deal with other states comes from the fact that it has a permanent system of government. A territory ruled by an occupying army does not have a permanent government, for example, but a state that periodically picks new leaders by orderly elections does. Even when a part of the country is in armed revolt, the government of that country is lawful as long as it functions. If the rebels set up their own lasting government, as happened during the U.S. Civil War, their territory may become a state. Sometimes a government is said to be *de facto,* which means that it exists in fact, even though unlawfully. A government maintained by an active military power against the authority of the established lawful government may, for example, be imposing order in fact.

The authority that states have in international law is called *sovereignty,* which is the supreme, absolute, and unquestioned power that an independent state possesses, including the political right and power to regulate its internal affairs without foreign interference.

A state has full legal status in international law when it is recognized by other states. *Recognition* is a formal declaration by a nation that another nation exists. Thus, recognition is a matter of policy, not of law. A state may negotiate with representatives of a de facto or provisional government to work out conditions of recognition. The United States may refuse to recognize a new government, for example, unless it agrees to let both blacks and whites vote. Once recognized, a government has the right to exchange diplomats and to participate in international agreements.

■ **Written and unwritten laws**   Much of international law is unwritten. It is based on custom, which is nevertheless just as binding as a written treaty. When a nation wants to discover what the law is on a particular subject, it studies treaties, diplomatic papers, history, and the opinions of legal writers. The international community accepts the existence of international law in both its written and unwritten forms. International law regulates refugees; oil, mineral, and water rights; fishing rights; the protection of wildlife; international aviation; outer space; piracy; slavery; the acquisition of new territories; and armed conflict by armies, terrorists, brigands, and guerrillas.

■ **Enforcement**   States do not routinely ignore the rules of international law because it is not in their self-interest to do so and because world opinion, economic reprisals, and the threat of war are usually enough to prevent a nation from violating an international law.

There are sanctions that can be imposed on a state, however, when it does violate an international law. If part of a treaty is violated, another party can declare the entire treaty void. A state can submit the dispute to the INTERNATIONAL COURT OF JUSTICE for an advisory opinion, or the United Nations General Assembly can discuss it and make recommendations for a peaceful settlement.

If the General Assembly cannot defuse the situation, the United Nations Security Council may call for appropriate measures, including "complete or partial interruption of economic relations and of rail, sea, air, postal, telegraphic, radio and other means of communication, and the severance of diplomatic relations." If that proves inadequate, the Security Council can send in a peacekeeping force.

When peaceful sanctions are not successful, states may resort to armed conflict. War itself is not a violation of international law; it is a recognized instrument of foreign policy. One function of international law, however, is to regulate the conduct of warring nations.

■ **Law of war** The law of war sets up limits on a state's right to use force in pursuing its political objectives. It establishes the point at which an armed conflict can be considered war; how a conflict may be ended, for example, the procedure for negotiations, truces, declarations of peace, and settlements; the right of victors to occupy a defeated nation; and the rights of neutral nations, noncombatants, and refugees. The law of war regulates the hostile measures that can be taken without causing a full-scale war, such as retaliation, reprisals, blockades, or embargoes. Both custom and treaties regulate the way warring armies must treat the wounded, the dead, and prisoners of war.

The law of war is not codified—that is, written up in one system of statutes. It has changed as methods of war have changed, and nations do not always agree on some points. It has always been a rule, for example, that armies should fight armies, not civilian noncombatants. When German planes were sent to Spain in April 1937 to aid insurgents in the Spanish civil war, their indiscriminate bombing of women and children at Guernica outraged the world and became a symbol of fascist brutality. In more recent wars, strategic bombing became routine, regardless of the presence of civilians in the target area. The direct, intentional killing of noncombatants is still clearly illegal, however. The United States convicted one of its own officers for shooting women and children in a small village in Vietnam. American soldiers are all taught the law of war and instructed that it is no defense to claim that a superior officer ordered them to do an illegal act. See also WAR.

interpleader A procedure for deciding the rights of rival claimants to money or property held by a third person, called a *stakeholder,* who has no personal interest in the money or property. The purpose of interpleader is to protect the stakeholder by permitting multiple claims to be settled in one lawsuit.

EXAMPLE The owner of an automobile brings it to a mechanic for repairs. While the automobile is in the repair shop, before being repaired, a finance company employee comes to the shop and tells the mechanic that he must repossess the automobile because the owner is four months behind in his payments. The finance company employee demands both the keys and the automobile and threatens to sue if the mechanic does not give them to him. The mechanic calls the automobile owner and explains the situation. The automobile owner also threatens to sue the mechanic if he gives the automobile to the finance company. In this situation, the mechanic is the stakeholder. He may bring an interpleader proceeding that will force the autombile owner and finance company into court to settle their claims. Once the rival claimants are in court, the mechanic can ask the court to discharge him from any liability to either claimant.

Interpol International Criminal Police Organization. Its purpose is to facilitate cooperation and assistance among the criminal police forces of its member nations and "to effectively prevent and suppress crime."

There are 126 member countries, each of which maintains and staffs its own national central bureau. The U.S. bureau, located in Washington, D.C., is directed and staffed by the Justice and Treasury departments. The General Secretariat, the international headquarters in Paris, coordinates the organization's worldwide activities.

Interpol assists American law enforcement agencies by locating suspects, fugitives, and witnesses. It investigates criminal activities connected with counterfeiting; fraud; theft; traffic in weapons, explosives, and narcotics; terrorism; murder; and rape. It provides criminal history checks on applicants for visa and import permits and traces vehicle registration and ownership. It does not deal with political crimes, such as espionage.

EXAMPLE When a hit-and-run accident occurred in Washington, D.C., in which a mentally retarded girl was critically injured, a car with foreign license plates was believed to be involved. The U.S. requested the assistance of countries in Western Europe and Canada to check vehicle registration records. As a result, the registered owner, an embassy employee, was apprehended.

Interpol also performs humanitarian services, such as tracing missing tourists or notifying their families of serious illness or death.

interpretation The process of discovering the meaning of a STATUTE, WILL, CONTRACT, or other written document. When the writer's intention is determined only from the words in the document, and not from the surrounding facts and circumstances, the interpretation is called *literal.* Suppose John's will provides that Betty, his only niece, is to inherit his house located at 25 Maple Avenue, Star, Iowa. This will would be interpreted exactly as the words appear in the document. The term *mixed interpretation* is applied when the meaning of the words is doubtful and conjecture is necessary to find out the sense in which the words are used.

EXAMPLE If Jim enters a contract with Bob to sell Bob "my car" for $1,500 but Jim owns two cars, a mixed interpretation of this contract would be necessary to decide which car was sold. A court would need to know the circumstances surrounding the contract, such as which car had been advertised for sale in the local newspapers, and the value of each car so that it could decide whether it would be more reasonable that the parties intended, for example, a five-year-old compact in good condition as opposed to a brand-new sportscar worth $25,000.

When the words do not express at all what the writer wants, his intention must be determined from probable or rational conjectures, and the process is called *rational interpretation.*

EXAMPLE Your elderly uncle specifies in his will that you are the sole heir to his meager life savings. At his death, you learn that your uncle was worth $12.5 million, with holdings in real estate and a bulging investment portfolio as well as a savings account of $225,000 that he had squirreled away since his childhood. Your envious brother, Cain, brings a construction (interpretation) proceeding in probate court, claiming that your uncle only gave you the savings account of $225,000 and that the rest of the estate must pass according to the laws of descent and distribution, with a share going to him. A court may apply a rational interpretation to the will, holding that it is reasonable to believe that your uncle intended you to be the only heir of his vast fortune.

interrogatory   A written question sent from one party in a lawsuit to the opposing party in order to get a written answer to a factual question relating to the lawsuit. Interrogatories must be answered under oath. The following interrogatory might be asked of a defendant in a lawsuit that involved a car accident: What are the names and addresses of all persons you know or believe witnessed the collision that is the subject of this action? See DISCOVERY.

Interstate Commerce Commission   See COMMERCE CLAUSE.

interstate compact   An agreement between two or more states that becomes a part of the law of each state.
EXAMPLE A number of states have entered into "Driver's
0⸺⸺* License Compacts" for license reciprocity. When a resident of party state A moves to party state B, he can exchange his driver's license for a new one issued by state B without taking another road test. Cooperating states also send reports of convictions of motor vehicle violations to a nonresident's home state. If a resident of state A is convicted in state B of drunk driving, notice is sent to state A, where the conviction is given the same effect as if it had occurred there. If the penalty for conviction is revoking the driver's license, his license will be revoked.
Other areas of law that are the subject of interstate compacts include flood control, port regulation, EXTRADITION and conservation.

intervening cause   In the law of TORTS (covering injuries to a person or property), a new and independent CAUSE that comes between an original wrongful act and an injury. It changes the natural sequence of events, producing a result that could not reasonably have been anticipated. An intervening cause therefore always relieves the original wrongdoer from responsibility. See NEGLIGENCE.
EXAMPLE An airplane crashed into an automobile, killing
0⸺⸺* the driver. At the time of the accident the driver was using a detour that ran close to an airplane landing field maintained by a town. The detour had existed for more than eight months. The administrator of the deceased driver's estate brought suit against both the town and the pilot, alleging that the town's negligence in not maintaining its streets made it necessary for the driver to use the detour, thereby causing his death. The court held that the accident was not a natural consequence of the town's negligence. The town could not have anticipated or foreseen the type of injury that occurred. A new and independent cause, the airplane, intervened between the town's negligence and the driver's death.

intervention   A method by which the court permits a third person to make himself a party to the lawsuit, by joining either the plaintiff or the defendant. The third party is called an *intervenor*.
A person has the right to intervene when he may be bound by the judgment of the lawsuit and when his interests are not adequately represented by the existing parties. Intervention is also allowed when, in the discretion of the court, the intervenor's claim and the main lawsuit have a question of law or fact in common.

EXAMPLE After a buyer entered into a contract to purchase
0⸺⸺* 15 acres of land on the condition that it could be used for industrial purposes, the town in which the land was located changed it from a residential to an industrial zone. Four residents who owned adjacent property brought suit against the town and the seller of the 15 acres to have the zoning change declared unconstitutional and void. When the buyer tried to cancel his contract, the seller sued to have the contract carried out. The buyer believed the claims of the adjacent residents were correct. If the court upheld their claim, the contract would be declared void and the buyer would be released from it. The buyer therefore brought a motion for permission to intervene and join the plaintiffs. The court held the buyer had an interest in the land that could be affected by the judgment and permitted him to intervene.

inter vivos   (Latin) "Between living persons." Ordinary GIFTS, such as graduation or Christmas presents, are gifts *inter vivos*. See CAUSA MORTIS; TRUST.

intestate   1 Without making a WILL. 2 As a noun, a person who dies without having made a will. A person is said to die intestate when he dies without having made a will or without having left any instructions about the disposal of his property. The inheritance of an intestate's property, determined by state laws of DESCENT AND DISTRIBUTION, is called intestate succession. See Chart 16.

intolerable cruelty   Extreme cruelty, which is a ground for DIVORCE.

intoxicating liquor   An alcoholic beverage capable of producing a state of inebriation. A huge variety of intoxicating liquors have been defined by courts and statutes struggling to separate legal from illegal drinks. Some laws specify that liquors containing more than a certain percentage amount of alcohol—such as brandy, whiskey, rum, gin, beer, wine, and bitters—are subject to state regulations. These are called *controlled liquors*. Sometimes the term "malt liquor" is used for beer, ale, porter, and stout.
■ **The nature and effect of alcohol**   An intoxicating liquor is generally conceded to be a drug. See DRUGS AND NARCOTICS. As with other mind-altering drugs, the effect alcohol has on a particular person depends on other drugs he may be using and on his personality and physical condition.
Doctors can measure the amount of alcohol in the blood, and that level is closely associated with the effects a person will experience. For example, a blood alcohol level of 0.20 percent generally impairs one's senses and motor control. At 0.50 percent, drunkenness usually occurs; at 0.60 percent, unconsciousness; and at 0.70 percent, death.
Heavy use of alcohol invites a variety of social and psychological problems. Heavy drinkers suffer a high frequency of certain diseases, and have high accident rates. Society suffers the tragedy of auto accidents, suicides, murders, and other crimes associated with chronic drinkers.
■ **The history of legal controls**   Since their early history, most modern nations have regulated the production and distribution of alcohol. The American colonies specified closing hours for taverns, prohibited the sale of alcohol to

Indians, and punished drunkenness. In 1777 the Continental Congress adopted a resolution that "recommended to the several legislatures of the United States immediately to pass laws the most effectual for putting an immediate stop to the pernicious practice of distilling grain, by which the most extensive evils are likely to be derived, if not quickly prevented."

The Congress of the United States, at its first session under the Constitution, placed a tax on the importation of ale, beer, porter, cider, malt, molasses, spirits, and wines—primarily to raise revenue and to protect domestic trade. In 1791 it approved an act raising the duties on imported liquors and placing an excise tax on all spirits distilled within the United States. Opposition to this tax at the grass roots level was swift and strong, because distilled liquor was a "cash crop" for many farmers. In western Pennsylvania opposition was so violent that it was called the Whiskey Rebellion.

In 1862 a comprehensive act was adopted, imposing federal taxes on the sale of liquor and providing for the issuance of federal licenses. From 1862 until World War I every brewery and distillery in this country operated under a federal license. When the United States entered the war, however, there was a consensus that the manufacture and sale of liquor should be stopped to aid the war effort. Accordingly, in May of 1917, Congress prohibited the sale of liquor to soldiers and in September prohibited the manufacture and importation of distilled liquor for beverage purposes. It authorized the President to reduce the alcoholic content of beer and wine and to limit or prohibit their manufacture. In 1919 the manufacture of beer and wine and the sale of all intoxicating liquors were prohibited.

During this period a movement began to eliminate intoxicating liquors by constitutional amendment. A joint resolution was introduced in the Senate on April 4, 1917, to prohibit the manufacture, sale, and transportation (not just possession) of intoxicating beverages within—or the importation of them into—the United States or any territory under its jurisdiction. The resolution led to the enactment of the 18th Amendment, which brought on national Prohibition, one year after its ratification, on January 29, 1919.

In the end, Prohibition proved unworkable. On December 5, 1933, the 21st Amendment repealed the 18th, prohibiting only the delivery of liquor into a state where it is illegal under that state's laws.

■ **Regulation of intoxicating liquors** State legislatures may regulate the sale of liquor to protect public safety, health, and morals. This authority is generally exercised through an agency known as a state liquor authority or an alcoholic beverage control board or commission.

Local laws States also regulate the local use and distribution of alcohol, except on U.S. military bases, on airplanes, and on Amtrak trains. Through its zoning powers, a town may restrict the type of building where liquor can be sold, but a local government has only the authority that the state gives it by law to regulate liquor sale and use. A municipality cannot prohibit sales unless the state permits a *local option*—that is, the state allows all or some of its subdivisions to regulate or prohibit liquor, usually by a vote on a specific liquor ordinance in a popular referendum. The results of such an election must apply uniformly to the entire district. Kensington township in Cougar county voted overwhelmingly to permit retail sales of liquor. But Cougar county itself voted to stay "dry." If the local option in the state applies to counties and not townships, then Kensington township cannot permit liquor to be sold.

A state may give local governments the authority to enact some liquor ordinances, but a local law cannot conflict with state law. Sometimes, a local law that is stricter than state law but does not conflict with state law is valid. For example, a state law may prohibit drinking by anyone under age 19, but a county may set the minimum at 21 years of age. Or a municipality may require bars to close at 1:00 A.M. when state law allows them to be open until 3:00 A.M.

Liquor laws and constitutional rights State or local laws regulating alcoholic beverages are valid if they are reasonably related to the purpose of controlling intoxicating liquors without violating anyone's constitutional rights. For instance, it is not a denial of EQUAL PROTECTION OF LAWS to prohibit the sale of alcoholic beverages to minors, but it is unconstitutional to distinguish between male and female minors.

EXAMPLE In 1976 the Supreme Court reversed an Oklahoma decision permitting the state to allow females but not males between 18 and 21 years of age to buy beer that is no more than 3.2 percent alcohol. The federal court in Oklahoma said that the law was valid because males in that age group were far more likely to drink beer, drive cars, and cause auto accidents. The Supreme Court refused to accept this reasoning, saying that treating males and females differently under the law must serve an important governmental purpose and be substantially related to that objective. Basing such a distinction on broad social statistics is not justifiable. The Court noted that more men than women are arrested in every age group, and that only 2 percent of the total number of young men between 18 and 21 had been arrested for drinking and driving.

Sex discrimination in liquor laws has been challenged in other areas. Various courts have struck down laws that prohibit employing women as bartenders, serving drinks to women in bars "likely to be rough places," serving drinks purchased by a man for a woman, or serving a woman at the bar rather than at a table. Many of these laws were originally intended to reduce prostitution, but courts found that they were not closely enough related to that purpose.

Vice laws Prostitution, gambling, and corruption have always flourished around the liquor industry. Therefore, regulations that would be unreasonable for other businesses are valid to control vice associated with intoxicating liquors. For example, it has been held illegal for the holder of a liquor license to keep coin-operated pinball machines or jukeboxes as gambling devices, and state authorities may revoke the liquor license of a retailer who permits prostitutes to operate in his bar or allows homosexual activities there.

Many cases in recent years have concerned the right of bar owners to feature nude entertainers in their establishments. The claim has often been made that strippers, nude dancers, and "topless" waitresses are protected by the constitutional guaranty of free speech because they are expressing themselves artistically. The question comes into

HOW THE LAW REGULATES LIQUOR

■ Liquor is the subject of laws at federal, state, and local levels. Federal regulation is limited to the collection of liquor taxes; the issuance of permits to manufacturers, wholesalers, and importers; the regulation of wholesale trade practices; customs regulation of imports; and a program to enforce standards of quality and safety.

■ Regulation of liquor use and distribution is a prerogative of the individual states, whose laws differ widely.

■ Liquor laws at the city or county level may not conflict with state law. Those that are stricter than state law but do not conflict with it are valid.

■ Some states have local option laws that permit localities to regulate liquor sales—whether to allow it to be sold at all or whether to permit it to be sold in liquor stores but not in restaurants or bars.

■ Sex discrimination in liquor laws is currently under attack in many states. Courts have struck down laws that prohibit employing female bartenders, serving drinks purchased by a man for a woman, or serving a woman at the bar rather than at a table.

■ Prostitution and gambling are recognized as problems connected with liquor sales, and many regulations that would be unreasonable for other businesses have been upheld to control vice associated with drinking—hence the ban on pinball machines in bars in many localities, for example. Similarly, in many places, a bar owner may lose his liquor license for allowing prostitutes to pick up men at the bar.

■ The right of nude dancers or waitresses to express themselves "artistically" in a bar cannot be abridged; however, the state can revoke the privilege of selling liquor for what it deems good cause.

■ In many places, it is illegal for a bar to let a patron run up a credit tab.

■ Many states have laws that permit someone injured by a drunken person to sue the bar owner. Such laws are known as *dramshop acts*. People who have recovered damages under such laws include a child whose father killed his mother in a drunken rage and persons injured by drunken drivers. In each of the cases, the bartender who continued to serve an already-drunken customer was held liable (financially responsible).

court when entertainers and owners are arrested for violation of laws prohibiting public nudity, indecency, or lewdness. If the laws are specific about the kind of conduct that is prohibited, the courts will generally uphold them. When a bar owner successfully wins his stand on the First Amendment, however, and is permitted to continue featuring nude dancers, he may instead lose his privilege to sell liquor. Although a state law cannot abridge the freedom of expression, it can revoke the privilege of selling liquor for what it deems good cause.

Many laws have been specifically designed to keep the old-style saloon from reappearing. Some states prohibit a retail establishment from using "saloon" in its name. Frequently, states prohibit or restrict the number of bars that can serve drinks to patrons who are standing up, or they allow alcohol to be served only in a place that also prepares and serves food. Another type of law intended to prevent the freewheeling atmosphere of the old saloon days makes it illegal to sell liquor on credit.

Price laws Laws that regulate the prices that every liquor dealer must charge prevent large discount stores from squeezing independent owners out of the market.

■ **Liquor licenses or permits** States have established liquor licensing to keep criminals out of the business and to enforce high standards of business conduct among those who deal in intoxicating liquors.

A *liquor license* is a privilege to traffic in intoxicating liquors, granted by the state for a specific period of time. The privilege is not an item of property that can be owned or sold. If the licensee violates a state liquor law, he loses his license.

Regulations generally limit the number of liquor licenses one person can hold, and they do not permit one person to hold licenses for more than one purpose, such as wholesale and retail sales licenses. A state may also limit the number of liquor stores or bars in certain areas.

Different kinds of licenses are available. A liquor permit may give the holder a right to manufacture, dispense, or sell liquor at the wholesale or retail level. Separate permits may cover beer, wine, and distilled spirits. A permit may allow beverages to be sold only in their original containers (sometimes in containers no less than one pint or one-half pint) or only by the glass, to be consumed at the place where it is sold. Sometimes drinks can be sold only in a restaurant where food is served or only to members of a licensed club.

A license is valid only for the place for which it is issued. Licenses generally will not be issued for sites too close to churches, schools, and other public buildings, or an existing liquor store.

Depending on local law, an individual, a partnership, or a corporation may apply for a liquor license. An individual may have to show what financial interests he holds in other liquor businesses. He may be disqualified if he has been convicted of certain crimes or had a liquor license revoked in the past. When a partnership or a corporation applies for a license, each person in the organization may be scrutinized on an individual basis.

Sometimes an applicant must publish notice of his intention to open a liquor store or tavern. In some states, the community may be allowed to file written objections, sign petitions, or testify at a hearing against the application. A liquor board, however, may not grant or withhold a license simply because that is the wish of the majority. The decision must be based on clearly established rules, and the applicant is entitled to know why he is turned down. Moreover, a liquor license cannot be revoked without good cause.

■ **Penalties for violating liquor laws** There are various penalties for violating state or federal liquor laws. Transporting liquor for which taxes have not been paid or for which a vehicle permit for shipping alcoholic beverages has not been obtained can cause the owner to forfeit his car or truck as well as the liquor in it. If an owner permits his place of business to become disorderly or a public NUI-SANCE or if he sells liquor during prohibited hours, an order of abatement or an INJUNCTION can be issued ordering him to stop or else, in some cases, be closed down. Criminal law violations like making moonshine whiskey, selling liquor in a "dry" county, or providing minors with liquor are punishable with jail sentences and fines.

One of the most common violations is a morals charge. A liquor license holder who permits gambling, prostitution, lewdness, or violence in his bar is held responsible, and can have his license revoked—even if he claims he did not know about the illegal activities because he was not present. The rule of law is that the owner "knew or should have known." See NOTICE. The purpose of this rule is to force licensees to keep close watch on their businesses because immoral activities are frequently associated with liquor. The threat of losing a valuable liquor license is usually enough to make most bar owners vigilant. Generally, an isolated incident will not result in the loss of a liquor license unless the license holder himself is somehow responsible. For example, in one case a woman who had a liquor license for her bowling alley was not held responsible when her husband enticed an eight-year-old boy into an upstairs rest room and sexually molested him.

■ **Dramshop acts** Dramshop laws permit someone injured by an intoxicated person to sue the bar owner. The purpose of dramshop laws is to put the burden on the person who derives a profit from selling intoxicating liquors, not on the innocent victim. It is not necessary to show that the bar owner was negligent but only that he sold liquor to a habitual drunk or to a person already drunk—a sale that is generally illegal in itself. If the intoxicated person is injured, he cannot sue, nor can a companion who actively participated in the drinking. People who have recovered money damages under a dramshop act include a child whose father killed his mother in a drunken rage, a pedestrian and a motorcyclist struck by drunk drivers, and a wife who lost support because her intoxicated husband dived into a sandbar and suffered permanent brain damage. In each case, the liquor seller who continued to serve drinks to a customer who was already drunk was held liable.

intrinsic evidence EVIDENCE learned from a document itself, without reference to any other source.

inure To be of use or benefit to a person; to take effect. For example, when a will provides that all real property (real estate) is to inure to the benefit of a certain person, then that person receives title to (ownership of) all the real estate owned by the deceased. Similarly, the proceeds of a life insurance policy inure to the beneficiary of the policy.

invalid Having no force or effect; null; void. For example, a will that is not properly witnessed is invalid.

invention See PATENT.

inventory 1 A detailed list of property, such as an annual stocktaking in a business. 2 The list made by an executor or administrator of a deceased person's estate. See EXECUTORS AND ADMINISTRATORS.

investment credit A sum of money that is subtracted from the amount of tax a taxpayer owes. The credit is a certain percentage of the purchase price of tangible personal property (as opposed to real estate), such as machinery and equipment, that a taxpayer has bought to use in his trade or business. The property must have a useful life for a length of time specified in Internal Revenue Service regulations. It must also be obtained and used within a certain period. Such a credit is given to stimulate investment and the modernization and expansion of industries.

EXAMPLE After filling out his tax return, a furniture upholsterer determines that his corporate tax liability for a certain year is $4,000. In February of that year he invested $2,000 in a new sewing machine. He can subtract 10 percent (or whatever percentage is allowed that year) of the value of his new machine ($200) from his tax liability so that his tax bill is $3,800.

invitation In the law of TORTS (injuries to persons or property), the act by which a landowner or an occupant of property persuades or attracts others to enter, remain in, or make use of his property. For example, a store or theater owner, simply by being open for business, is inviting the public to come onto his premises and make use of his facilities. Such a landowner or occupant must use reasonable care to make certain his property is safe for the use of those who are invited. He owes a higher duty of care to persons who enter by invitation than he does to those who TRESPASS or to LICENSEES (such as a meter reader) who enter his property for their own purposes. See INNKEEPER.

invitee A person who goes onto another's premises by the specific or implied INVITATION of the owner or occupant for their mutual benefit.

invoice A written account or itemized statement of merchandise sent to a buyer stating the quantity and price of each item shipped.

ipse dixit (Latin) "He himself [she herself, the court itself] said it." A statement that rests entirely on the authority of the person making it. For example, a court decision that is contrary to a statute is said to have no legal support "save the arbitrary *ipse dixit*" of the court.

ipso facto (Latin) "By the fact itself." For instance, if a man with a smoking gun in his hand is found in the same house as the person who was shot, this does not ipso facto prove him guilty of murder.

IRA Individual Retirement Account. See PENSION.

irregularity In a lawsuit or other legal proceeding, a departure from the regular way of doing things or from a prescribed rule or regulation. Although an irregularity is not an illegal act, in some cases it may be serious enough to invalidate a lawsuit. For example, in many states, when an orphaned child is sued, a guardian must be appointed to represent his interests. The failure to appoint a guardian is an irregularity that can be used as a ground for setting aside a judgment entered against the child.

On the other hand, the defect or failure that constitutes the irregularity may be a simple mistake that is easily corrected. In such a case it does not invalidate the proceeding. A judgment of conviction in a criminal trial, for instance, is not void just because the judge fails to sign it.

irrelevant Not relating or applicable to the matter at issue. In a lawsuit or criminal case, EVIDENCE is irrelevant when it has no tendency to prove or disprove an issue in dispute. For instance, a witness in a slander suit, called to testify about the plaintiff's general reputation for honesty, might state that he knew the plaintiff's father well and that the father was an honest man. This testimony would be irrelevant because it would not relate to the issue of the plaintiff's honesty.

irreparable injury An injury that cannot be repaired, restored, or adequately compensated by money DAMAGES and that is serious enough to cause the court to issue an INJUNCTION (a court order to do or not do a certain thing). For example, a person buys a house in a residential neighborhood and uses it to store explosives used in his construction business. This causes an irreparable injury to the other landowners that justifies the court's issuing an injunction on their behalf against the purchaser, ordering him to remove the hazardous materials.

irresistible impulse Used chiefly in CRIMINAL LAW, the phrase means a compulsion to commit a criminal act that the defendant cannot resist or overcome because insanity or mental disease has destroyed his free will and power of self-control.

IRS The Internal Revenue Service. See INCOME TAX.

issue **1** In its most general sense, to send out or promulgate—an officer issues orders and a court issues a subpoena.

2 In finance, when applied to notes or bonds of a series, "date of issue" usually means the date fixed as the start of the term for which they run.

3 In a lawsuit, the issues arise from the PLEADINGS. Issues are disputed questions of fact or points of law that are affirmed by one side and denied by the other. An *issue of fact* exists when the judge or jury must weigh conflicting EVIDENCE in order to reach a decision. In a personal injury suit for damages resulting from an automobile accident, for example, an issue of fact might be whether or not the defendant had fallen asleep at the wheel. An *issue of law* arises when the evidence is undisputed and only one conclusion can be drawn from it. Judges decide issues of law. For example, in a malpractice suit, the issue of whether the statute of limitations begins to run from the time the malpractice occurred or from the time it is actually discovered is an issue of law that must be resolved by the judge.

4 Descendants. In DEEDS to real estate, issue means all those descended from a common ancestor. In this sense, the word includes not only a child or children, but all descendants of whatever relation.

When used in a WILL, issue must be given the meaning intended by the deceased, as determined from his will, rather than its technical meaning. Thus, issue may be restricted to children or to the descendants on one side of the family. Some courts hold that this does not include illegitimate issue when it is the father's will and he has not acknowledged the child as his own. See ILLEGITIMACY.

jactitation A false boasting or claim; at common law, a defamation of another person's title to (claim to ownership of) real estate, also known as slander of title.

jail A building for the confinement of persons who have been convicted of minor crimes or who are under arrest awaiting trial but unable to get out on bail. A jail is more than a temporary place of detention, such as a police station or a lockup, but less permanent than a large PRISON.

jailhouse lawyer The name given to a prisoner who uses his knowledge of and research in the law to deal with his own legal problems or those of his fellow prisoners.

J.D. See JURIS DOCTOR.

jeopardy Danger; hazard; peril; the danger of conviction and punishment faced by a defendant in a criminal prosecution. Jeopardy begins when a jury has been sworn to try a criminal charge. See DOUBLE JEOPARDY.

jetsam Cargo and other goods cast overboard to lighten a ship in a storm or other emergency.

jobber A merchant who buys and sells goods from a manufacturer in entire lots; a wholesaler or middleman. The jobber relieves the manufacturer from dealing directly with retailers. See HAWKERS AND PEDDLERS.

John Doe In legal proceedings, a fictitious name given to a party until his real name can be established.

joinder A coming together of parties to a suit, grounds for suit, or issues in a suit. A *joinder of the parties* is the joining of several parties as coplaintiffs or codefendants in one lawsuit. The court allows a joinder of parties when there are common questions of law and fact that can be settled in one case.

EXAMPLE While stopped for a red light at an intersection, a truck is struck from behind by an automobile. After exchanging information with the driver of the automobile, the truck driver climbs back into his vehicle to move it out of the way. Before he can do so, a second automobile hits the truck from behind. In this situation there are common questions of law and fact. It would be proper for the truck driver as plaintiff to request the joinder of the two automobile drivers as codefendants in one lawsuit.

In some cases a lawsuit cannot be continued unless all parties who have a similar interest in the controversy are joined as either codefendants or coplaintiffs. This occurs in an ACTION brought to revoke a TRUST. All the beneficiaries as well as all the trustees must be joined as codefendants before the suit can proceed.

A *joinder of actions* means uniting different causes of action (grounds for a suit) in one lawsuit.

EXAMPLE A tree surgeon buys a new chain saw. The first time he uses it, the chain breaks, flies off, and badly injures his arm. The tree surgeon has two separate causes of action against the manufacturer—one for negligence in the production of the saw and another for breach of the warranty that was implicit when the tree surgeon bought the saw. Because both causes arose from the same injury, they can be joined and resolved in one lawsuit.

A *joinder of issues* takes place when the parties to a lawsuit (the defendant and plaintiff) reach the point in their PLEADINGS where one party asserts a fact to be true and the other denies it. At this point, the suit begins.

joint United; combined; shared by or between two or more persons. For example, joint debtors are two or more persons who are liable for the same debt. See CONTRACTS.

joint adventure An association of persons to carry out a business enterprise for profit, sometimes called a joint enterprise or a joint venture. As a legal concept, it is of comparatively recent origin and is still in the process of development.

Unlike a partnership, which is an ongoing, continuous business, a joint adventure is limited to a single transaction. In it, there must be a desire to accomplish a common goal, a shared proprietary interest in the subject matter, a joint obligation to control, a right to share in the profits, and a duty to assume equally any losses. A joint adventure is founded entirely upon a contract between the parties.

Transactions that have been held to be joint adventures have included agreements (1) to purchase and develop land; (2) to buy or sell a large amount of corporate stock; (3) to acquire government contracts; (4) to construct a building; (5) to manage a racehorse.

A contract of joint adventure may be terminated by the consent of all the parties or by the accomplishment of its purpose. If a disagreement among members is so serious that it jeopardizes the enterprise, a court will decree a dissolution.

Joint adventurers usually buy property with each contributing a proportionate share of the purchase price. When they sell the property, they split the profits accordingly.

joint and several Liability either together or individually. For instance, a debt is joint and several if the creditor may sue the debtors as a group (each debtor would have to contribute toward the loss) or individually (one debtor might have to pay the entire amount). Liability is established by the kind of CONTRACT you sign.

joint stock company An association of individuals who have organized to make a profit. The members contribute capital, which is divided into transferable shares (stock). A joint stock company is a form of PARTNERSHIP, but it has some of the characteristics of a CORPORATION. It is usually formed when a group of persons want to avoid the state supervision that is applied to corporations.

A partnership is made up of a few persons bound together by mutual confidence. One partner may act as agent for the firm, but he cannot retire and name a substitute without the consent of all the other partners. If one partner dies, the partnership is dissolved. A joint stock company consists of a large number of people not usually acquainted with each other. Changes in members are not an important matter and the death of a member does not cause a dissolution. Unlike partners, individual members cannot speak and act as agents for the company.

A corporation and an unincorporated joint stock company resemble each other in several ways. They both enjoy perpetual succession: a transfer of shares by any member has no effect upon the life of the organization. Both corporations and joint stock companies act through their boards of directors, trustees, or governors. No individual member can act for the aggregate body.

There are differences between the two, however. Although a corporation can exist only under the authority of the state, a joint stock company does not depend on a grant of such authority. It is wholly the product of the mutual agreement of the stockholders.

In a corporation, individual rights and liabilities of the members are merged into the corporation. Its members are usually not responsible for debts of the organization. In contrast, the members of a joint stock company are liable as partners. A corporation generally brings and defends lawsuits in its corporate name. A joint stock company sues and defends in the name of a designated officer.

joint tenancy The single ownership of property by two or more persons. In some states, if the joint tenants are HUSBAND AND WIFE, they have a *tenancy in the entirety*.

Survivorship is the distinctive characteristic of joint tenancy. When a joint tenant dies, the property is inherited by the surviving tenants, and, at length, by the last one. Survivors take the whole estate free from the ownership claims of anyone else. A surviving tenant of a bank account held in joint tenancy takes the entire account, regardless of who contributed to it, but that amount may be subject to the claims of the decedent's creditors. For estate tax purposes, however, the survivor will have to show the amount he contributed so that the entire account will not be taxed as part of the decedent's estate but only that part which the decedent actually contributed. Jointly owned property will not, however, have to pass through probate, thus saving the estate PROBATE costs. The right of survivorship terminates only when the property comes into the hands of the last survivor. For all practical purposes, joint tenancy is the same as joint estate.

Joint tenancy was originally applicable only to land. Now, however, any property that can be owned by an individual can be held in joint tenancy. For a joint tenancy to be created, the following four elements are needed:

(1) *Unity of time.* Each joint tenant must receive his interest at the same time—that is, at the time when the deed to or contract (as in the case of a bank account) for the property is delivered.

(2) *Unity of title.* Each tenant must receive his title from the same grantor.

(3) *Unity of interest.* Each tenant must own not a section of the property but an undivided interest in the entire property.

(4) *Unity of possession.* Each tenant must have the right of possession of every part of the whole property, not merely a portion of it.

See also TENANCY IN COMMON.

Jones Act The federal law that governs actions for a seaman's injuries or death. Under the statute, a seaman who is injured during his employment may sue for damages, with the right of trial by jury. If a seaman dies as a result of the injury, his personal representative may bring suit.

journal In legislative bodies, a daily record of the actions of committees and the introduction of bills.

J.P. See JUSTICE OF THE PEACE.

judge 1 Make a decision, as in a court case, or come to a conclusion after examining all the facts. 2 As a noun, a public officer selected to preside over and administer law in COURT. The method of selecting state judges varies—it may be through appointment by the governor, joint ballot of the two houses of the state legislature, or election by the people. In the FEDERAL COURT system, all judges from the Supreme Court down are appointed by the President, with the advice and consent of the Senate.

■ **Who can be a judge** The qualifications needed to become a judge are usually set by state constitution or statute. Provisions often declare that no person shall be eligible unless he is learned in the law. This has been construed to mean that he must have been admitted to the bar. Some states mandate that a judge must have been a practicing attorney for a stated period. Citizenship, age, and residence qualifications are common. Length of judicial terms depends on the state and the particular office. Federal judges are appointed for life, subject to their continued good behavior.

■ **Function of judges** The state legislatures usually prescribe the judges' function. Broadly speaking, it is to hear and decide on controversies between opposing parties without personal bias. Judges need not pretend to believe that all policies, or even all laws, are wise and just. Nevertheless, they must read, interpret, and apply the laws as written. They also have the power to take proper action to promote justice by correcting abuses in the administration of justice. For example, an attorney who continuously harasses and badgers a witness may be found by a judge to be in CONTEMPT of court.

■ **When judges can be disqualified** A judge will be disqualified from hearing any case in which he is not wholly free, impartial, and independent. He may, for instance, be disqualified because he has a financial stake in the outcome of the lawsuit, is a member of a religious or educational group involved in the litigation, or has been connected with a bank that is a party to the lawsuit. A judge must not have an interest in any transaction that conflicts with his official duties. Under some state laws, he is forbidden from carrying on any business. A judge cannot act as counsel in a case pending before him or before the court of which he is a member. Nor can he hear a case in which he acted as counsel in the past.

judge advocate The officer of a court-martial, whose duty is to swear in the other members of the court, advise the court, and act both as prosecutor and as counsel for the prisoner. He keeps the prisoner from answering incriminating questions and objects to unacceptable questions asked of other witnesses. For a discussion of court-martial, see ARMED SERVICES.

judgment A decision by a COURT or other tribunal, based on EVIDENCE that has been presented. In most instances, the judgment is the final determination of all the issues in a case and the parties can never again bring the same issues to court in a different case. A judgment binds the parties. Unless it is changed on appeal, they must obey its terms—even if they think the terms are unfair—or risk legal penalties, such as a fine or imprisonment. In a civil lawsuit, an award of money DAMAGES by the court is part of a judgment; in a criminal case, the SENTENCE is part of the judgment.

■ **What makes a judgment valid** A judgment is valid only if the court had proper JURISDICTION (authority) over the parties and the issues of the case. It must be in writing and state the names of the parties involved in the case and the date. It must show that the issues have been decided according to the evidence presented in the case. It cannot be based on speculation, surmise, or suspicion. A judgment must be definitive—it must specifically grant or deny the relief sought by the plaintiff or prosecutor. For example, if a wife brings suit against her husband for divorce, the judgment must either grant or deny her a divorce. It cannot avoid a decision, say, by recommending that she take a

month's vacation away from her husband. The amount of a money judgment, such as in an automobile accident suit, must be stated precisely in both words and figures, and it must be in American dollars and cents, not in a foreign currency. When land or buildings are involved, the judgment must clearly identify the property.

A valid judgment may be rendered against a defendant only when he has had NOTICE of the proceedings. If proper steps were not taken to notify him, the judgment will be declared void. A judgment is final when signed by the judge.

In most states the clerk of the court is required to docket the judgment. He does this by making the proper entries in a docket book, alphabetically arranged, so that interested third persons may have official notice of the judgment. Usually the court also keeps an index of judgments. The docket and index are particularly important when you are buying a house because you need to know whether there are any outstanding claims or LIENS against the property that you may have to assume. See DEED.

■ **Satisfaction** Payment to satisfy a judgment should be made by the judgment debtor to the plaintiff. If there are several judgment creditors, payment usually may be made to any one of them. Payment is generally noted on the judgment docket. Such an entry is not, however, essential to satisfaction of the judgment. Payment itself is the satisfaction.

The court rendering the judgment has the power to see that it is enforced. The usual method, when the judgment is for a sum of money, is by writ of EXECUTION. Other remedies, such as ATTACHMENT AND GARNISHMENT, are also recognized.

■ **Res judicata** Res judicata is a rule of law that says that once something is decided judicially, it is settled forever and cannot again be litigated between the same parties. Under this doctrine, a judgment that is upheld throughout the system of appeals is regarded as the final word in the dispute. A losing party cannot bring the suit again hoping for a different outcome.

Under the FULL FAITH AND CREDIT clause of the Constitution, a judgment rendered by the court of one state must be recognized and respected by every other state. Thus, a judgment in one is conclusive in the other. Similarly, federal courts are required to give full faith and credit to judgments of other federal courts.

■ **Other types of judgment** Besides the type of judgment that gives relief to one party after a trial, there are other types of judgment: consent, default, summary, and declaratory judgments.

Consent judgment A consent judgment contains provisions and terms that have been agreed to by the parties. It is, in effect, a contract between the parties, acknowledged and recorded in open court. Consent judgments are common in domestic relations cases, after a husband and wife have agreed to a property and support settlement.

Default judgment A default judgment is given to a party either because the other party did not appear in court or because he failed to follow the proper procedure. Traditionally, a default judgment was rendered against a defendant who, after having been appropriately summoned, failed to show up in court for the start of the suit. Now, it is also applied when a party does not appear in court when he is required to do so after he has made an initial appearance—if he fails to return after the first day of trial, for example. A default judgment can also be rendered for failure to follow procedure, such as not filing a particular paper in court. Because the policy of the law is to try every case on its merits, judgments based on default are not favored by the courts.

Summary judgment A SUMMARY judgment is a final decision in a case that does not require a trial with a lengthy presentation of EVIDENCE. It is considered an extreme measure and should be granted only when it is clear that there is no material (important) issue of fact. It completely avoids the necessity of a trial because the issues are clear. Here is the way it works:

A party to a lawsuit will request the court to render a judgment based on the papers already before it. The requesting party is usually confident that he will win his case because there is no genuine issue of fact and he feels the law is on his side. The court must evaluate the affidavits and other documents submitted to determine whether there is a legitimate question of fact in the case. Once the court decides to rule on a motion for summary judgment, it examines the entire record of the case and may, on its own motion, award a summary judgment in favor of either the defendant or the plaintiff if the evidence justifies it. If a factual question does exist, the motion for summary judgment will be denied and the case will be resolved by a trial.

Declaratory judgment A declatory judgment clarifies the rights of the parties or expresses the opinion of the court on some legal question without ordering anything to be done. Its purpose is to provide a speedy way of determining the legal rights of the parties before any wrongs are committed. A declaratory judgment differs from other judgments in that no party to the suit is seeking to recover rights, money, or other property.

EXAMPLE In one case, the Wyoming attorney general interpreted a section of the state constitution as prohibiting state senators from running for another elective office during the period of their terms. An incumbent state senator wanted to run for governor. The attorney general asked the court to declare what rights the state senator had under the constitution. The state senator requested the same relief. The court entered a declaratory judgment holding that the section only prohibited a state senator or representative from being appointed, not from being elected, to state office while serving his term, so that the senator could run for office.

The court will exercise its authority to hear a declaratory judgment case only when there is an actual legal controversy between the parties. If the case involves a hypothetical question, the court will not hear it. Similarly, the court will not use a declaratory judgment to anticipate the trial of an issue in another legal proceeding.

Some examples of controversies decided through declaratory-judgment procedure are an employee's rights under WORKMEN'S COMPENSATON laws; a dispute between a local union and its international parent; the legitimacy or ILLEGITIMACY of a child; the validity or invalidity in the United States of a DIVORCE obtained in a foreign country; the meaning of the language in a business CONTRACT, a separation agreement, or a WILL; the extent of coverage by an automobile INSURANCE policy; and the extent of the taxing powers of a municipality.

The validity or constitutionality of a law is sometimes tested in a declaratory judgment proceeding. There have been declaratory judgments on laws concerned with such matters as abandoned property, city charters, public housing, neighborhood zoning, rent control, voter registration, and school busing.

■ **Amendment of judgment** A court has a right to correct any errors or omissions in its judgment so that the judgment will express what was actually intended. Parties who were not before the court may not be brought in. Clerical errors such as the misspelling of the parties' names or an error in court costs are the most common grounds for amending a judgment.

■ **Effect of a judgment** A judgment creates a LIEN (a claim for payment of a debt) on the property of the party who loses his case in a lawsuit. He is called the judgment debtor. The lien entitles the winning party (the judgment creditor) to collect the amount owed to him in the judgment and to seize property should the judgment debtor fail to pay up. Generally the lien is held against all of the judgment debtor's property and not against specific property—unless specific property was the subject of the suit. For example, if a man sued to recover an heirloom wrongfully taken from the house he was selling, the judgment would give him exactly that item rather than its value in money damages.

■ **Relief from a judgment** Relief from a judgment, although not favored by the courts, may nevertheless be obtained if circumstances warrant. You may get relief if a judgment was rendered against you without proper notice of the suit, if the court did not have jurisdiction over that type of case, or if the judgment was fraudulently altered to increase the amount granted or to include a person not originally a party named in the suit. Some authorities will not grant relief because of newly discovered evidence; others will. The authorities are agreed, however, that relief on the grounds of new evidence will not be granted if the complaining party failed to make every effort to produce the evidence for the original action.

judgment creditor A person who has obtained a judgment against another person in court and is entitled to use court processes to collect it. The party who owes the money is called a *judgment debtor*. See EXECUTION.

judgment note A promissory note authorizing an attorney, the holder of the note, or the clerk of court to appear in court and allow a judgment to be entered against the note maker because he failed to pay the sum when due. See CONFESSION OF JUDGMENT; COMMERCIAL PAPER.

judgment-proof Said of a person against whom a money JUDGMENT will have no effect, because he has no money or is sheltered—for example, by a law that protects his wages from garnishment up to a specified amount.

judicial 1 Connected with the COURTS; involved with JUDGES. 2 The branch of government that interprets the law and decides legal questions. See CONSTITUTIONAL LAW.

judicial notice Acceptance by a court of the truth of a fact without a party's having to prove it or offer EVIDENCE of it in a trial. For example, judicial notice is taken when facts are undisputed common knowledge, such as that Canada is in North America, or when they cannot be disputed, such as the texts of the U.S. Constitution or of the criminal statutes in a state.

judicial question An issue for a court to decide, as opposed to a question that falls within the province of either the legislative or the executive branch of government. See POLITICAL QUESTION. A typical judicial question is the interpretation of a statute.

judicial review The power of a COURT to look over the decision of a public administrative agency; a sort of appeal from the decision of an agency.

judicial sale A sale made under a court order by a person appointed to sell. The court itself is the seller, acting through its appointed agent. A judicial sale is usually conducted to raise an amount of money necessary to pay off an amount found due in an order or judgment of the court. Judicial sales often arise in MORTGAGE foreclosure and bankruptcy cases. See ATTACHMENT AND GARNISHMENT; EXECUTION; LEVY.

judiciary The branch of government charged with interpreting and applying the law; the system of COURTS in a country; a body of JUDGES; the BENCH. The FEDERAL COURT system of the United States—made up of District Courts, Circuit Courts of Appeal, the Supreme Court, and some special courts—is an example of a judiciary.

junior Younger; later born; later in rank. For example, a junior mortgage is subordinate in rank to another mortgage that took effect before it.

The word "junior" or its abbreviation, "Jr.," following a person's NAME is a description of the individual, not part of his legal name. If, for example, a person receives a summons to appear in court, the fact that "Jr." is omitted after his name is not a good reason for his failing to show up.

jural Relating to natural rights recognized by law. For example, the *moral sphere* includes the entire discipline of ethics, but the *jural sphere* includes only those areas of morality that have been made the subject of legal protection or legal sanctions.

jurat The certificate of an administering officer that a written document was sworn to by the person who signed it. The jurat is not part of an oath. See OATHS AND AFFIRMATIONS. It is evidence that an oath was properly taken before a duly authorized officer. For example, the clause at the end of an affidavit, stating when, where, and before whom it was sworn, is a jurat.

juridical 1 Relating to the administration of justice or the office of a JUDGE. A juridical day is a day on which the COURTS are in session. 2 Done in conformity with the laws and the practices of the courts.

jurisdiction The authority of the courts and judicial officers to hear and decide legal proceedings. For a detailed explanation, see COURTS.

jurisdictional Pertaining to jurisdiction. For example, jurisdictional facts—such as that the defendant has been served with a summons and other necessary legal papers—must be proved to exist to show that a court has jurisdiction (authority) over the case. Similarly, some courts cannot hear cases unless the amount in dispute between the parties exceeds a sum of money, called the *jurisdictional amount*. For a discussion of jurisdiction, see COURTS.

jurisdictional dispute A controversy involving two labor unions. Two different kinds of conflict are possible. There can be a dispute over whether certain work should be performed by employees of one union or another. An example is whether employees in the carpenters' union or the glaziers' union should install wood-framed glass windows.

Another kind of dispute can be over which union should represent employees doing a particular kind of work. An example is whether the longshoremen's union or the truck loaders' union should represent employees who transfer containers of cargo from a ship to a truck parked at the dock. See LABOR RELATIONS.

juris doctor Doctor of Jurisprudence. The basic degree awarded to a law school graduate. It replaced the LL.B. (Bachelor of Laws degree) in the late 1960's.

jurisprudence The philosophy of law or the science dealing with the principles of law adopted for the government of an organized society.

jurist A JUDGE; one skilled in the law. The term is now usually reserved for persons who have distinguished themselves by their writings on legal subjects.

juristic act 1 An act designed to have a legal effect, such as the act of a court when it hands down a JUDGMENT. 2 An individual act that is intended to begin, end, or change a legal right, such as entering into a CONTRACT, canceling it, or changing its terms.

juristic person A person for purposes of the law. The term includes "natural persons" (men, women, and children) and "artificial persons," such as CORPORATIONS.

juror 1 A person selected for JURY service. 2 A member of a jury who has been accepted and sworn to try a case.

jury A jury is a body of persons legally summoned, sworn, and impaneled (listed by the court clerk) for a trial. In a civil lawsuit the trial settles a dispute between two parties while in criminal cases it determines the facts that prove or disprove the guilt of the accused based on evidence offered in court. The word "jury" usually refers to a petit jury, or trial jury, as distinguished from a GRAND JURY, which receives COMPLAINTS in criminal cases, hears evidence presented by the state, and finds INDICTMENTS. It is

THE RIGHT TO TRIAL BY JURY—WHAT IT MEANS TO YOU

- A jury is a group of persons summoned, sworn, and impaneled (listed by the court clerk) to hear and decide civil or criminal suits.
- *Jury* used by itself usually means a trial jury. A *grand jury* is a larger group that sits to receive complaints in criminal cases, hear evidence presented by the state, and return indictments.
- State laws set the qualifications for being a juror. Generally, you must be a citizen of the United States, a resident of the state or county, a certain age (usually between 18 and 72), and able to understand English.
- Serving on a jury is a duty of citizenship. If you are called, you must answer the notice or risk being arrested, fined, or imprisoned for contempt. If you have an excuse for not serving that is valid under your state's law, you may apply for an exemption.

- Jurors are generally paid a fee for each day of service. Unless bound by an employment contract or union agreement, your employer is not obligated to pay you for the time you spend on jury duty.
- Your right to a trial by jury is a basic constitutional right. However, the right to a jury does not include trials for petty offenses.
- An impartial jury must be selected in a way that does not discriminate as to race, color, creed, or sex.
- Most people associate a jury with the number 12. In many states, however, juries may be made up of fewer persons. The Supreme Court has ruled that six members is the minimum acceptable in a state criminal trial. The parties in federal criminal cases may stipulate that there be fewer than 12 jurors.

- You can request a jury trial in federal civil cases. Federal law provides that the parties can agree to a jury of less than 12.
- The states set their own laws on jury trials in civil cases. Many, however, provide for less than 12 jurors in civil suits.
- A unanimous verdict is necessary to convict a criminal defendant in federal courts. It is not necessary in state courts.
- Several states allow for less than unanimous verdicts in civil suits. Sometimes the number of jurors needed for a majority vote is set by law.
- In federal civil cases the parties can stipulate that the verdict of a stated majority will be accepted. In the absence of such a stipulation federal courts have traditionally required unanimous verdicts in civil cases.

called a grand jury because it is generally composed of more jurors than a petit jury (*petit* is the French word for "small").

The word "jury" also describes other groups chosen to decide on certain facts; a CORONER's jury, for example, helps a coroner investigate the cause of a death. A *special jury,* or blue ribbon jury, is one ordered by the court at the request of either party to try an important or complicated case. It is still authorized by statute in some states but it is rarely used today.

- **How a jury is selected**   State law usually directs a specific public official, often called a jury commissioner, to draw up from time to time a *jury list,* which contains the names of persons called for jury service. The law may require the list to be made up from the rolls of taxpayers, property owners, voters, motor vehicle operators, or even from lists of those living in the county and using public utilities. The names chosen from the list must be randomly selected, and the selection system must in no way exclude women or minority groups in the community. The official in charge of the system sends notices to enough names on the list to satisfy the projected needs of the courts for the prospective jurors. Those who do not have a legitimate reason for avoiding jury service must appear and wait to be called for a particular jury.

Impartiality   An impartial jury must be selected in a way that does not discriminate against any group because of race, color, creed, or sex. This principle has been restated by the Supreme Court many times.

EXAMPLE   When a black man named Patton was charged O—* and convicted of murdering a white man, he was sentenced to die in the electric chair. Both the grand jury that indicted Patton and the petit jury that convicted him were all white. Patton moved to quash (cancel) his indict-

ment because the lists from which the grand and petit jurors were selected did not contain the name of a single black person, although there were many blacks qualified to serve. He alleged that the practice of not selecting blacks as jurors was deliberate and had continued for many years. Patton contended that this practice resulted in denying him equal protection of the laws under the 14th Amendment. Evidence showed that in the county where Patton was convicted not a single black person had served on a jury in more than 30 years; yet census figures showed that blacks made up more than one-third of the county's adult population. The Supreme Court agreed with Patton and reversed his conviction.

The Court held that whenever a jury selection program results in the total and long-term exclusion of even one member from a large group of blacks, or any racial group, indictments or verdicts handed down against one of that group by juries so selected must be overturned. See EQUAL PROTECTION OF LAWS.

To be considered impartial, the jury must be chosen from a representative cross section of the community, including women.

EXAMPLE   A Louisiana man named Taylor was convicted of O—* kidnapping by a petit jury selected from a list composed entirely of men. State law provided that a woman could not be selected for jury duty unless she had filed a written request with the clerk of the court. Although women made up 53 percent of the population of the parish (county), very few had served as jurors. Not one of the 175 persons drawn for jury service at the time of Taylor's trial was a woman. Taylor appealed his conviction, claiming that he was denied his right to an impartial jury trial guaranteed under the Sixth Amendment because the jury was not selected from a representative cross section of his community. The court found the Louisiana law unconstitutional and reversed Taylor's conviction.

In a later case, the Supreme Court has held that ". . . systematic exclusion of women that results in jury venires [lists] averaging less than 15 percent female violates the Constitution's fair cross-section requirement."

Qualifications to be a juror   Every state prescribes by law who can serve as a juror. To qualify as a juror, a person generally must be a citizen of the United States and a resident of the state or county, of the proper age, not suffering from a physical or mental disability that would prevent jury service, and able to understand the English language. The age requirement usually means that the person be at least the legal age of an adult, and it may disqualify persons over a certain age, such as 72, or it may allow older citizens to be excused on request. Various states also require jurors to be taxpayers or qualified to vote. States generally have eliminated the requirements of loyalty oaths and avowals of religious belief.

Certain persons may be automatically disqualified from serving on a jury, such as public officials, judges, and convicted felons. Other persons may apply for an exemption if they are called for jury service, on the general ground of undue hardship to the individual or his family. A state may allow exemptions for persons in the armed services, for doctors and lawyers, firemen and policemen, parents responsible for the care of small children, clergymen, small businessmen, or those who have served on a jury in the recent past.

Selection for specific trial   From the list of persons who have been called to the courthouse on a particular day, some are selected for a specific trial. Many states still put all the names into a ballot box, mix them thoroughly, and draw out by hand the necessary number. These persons are called into the courtroom for the VOIR DIRE, the selection process for the actual jury. The judge or the attorneys in the case may question each prospective juror to discover facts in that person's background that would make it difficult for him to make an unbiased decision in the case. Those persons who are not selected may be discharged or sent back to the central jury room to await another call. Enough persons are chosen to make up the jury plus one or more alternates who will substitute for a juror if he cannot continue to serve.

■ **Duty to serve**   A person called to jury duty cannot ignore the notice or refuse to answer it. Serving on a jury is one of the obligations of citizenship. A person who has an excuse valid under the law of his state generally must answer the notice by applying for an exemption. Persons who fail to appear as ordered can be arrested and brought before the court and may be fined or imprisoned or cited for CONTEMPT.

■ **Fees to jurors**   Individuals called for jury duty generally are paid a fee set by the law for each day of service, and they may also receive an allowance for travel to and from the courthouse. Some states specifically provide that an employer may not discharge an employee because of jury service if the employer has been notified in advance of the reason for the employee's absence from work. Unless an employment contract or agreement with a union provides otherwise, an employee generally has no right to collect his wages while he is away from work for jury service.

■ **Right to trial by jury**   The right to trial by jury was introduced to America by the English colonists. It remains today the cornerstone of America's legal system. The right to a jury trial is expressly guaranteed in the federal and state constitutions. For a step-by-step description of a civil trial, see TRIAL; for a criminal trial, see CRIMINAL LAW.

Criminal cases   The Sixth Amendment to the Constitution says that in all criminal prosecutions the accused shall enjoy the right to a speedy and public trial, by an impartial jury of the state and district in which the crime was committed. These provisions have been held by the Supreme Court to apply to the states through the DUE PROCESS OF LAW clause of the 14th Amendment.

Petty offenses   The right to a jury trial, however, does not include trials for petty criminal offenses.

EXAMPLE A man named Baldwin was convicted of "jostling," bumping another person in order to pick his pocket. The crime was a misdemeanor punishable by a maximum sentence of one year's imprisonment, which Baldwin was given. Prior to his trial and conviction before a judge, Baldwin had asked for a jury trial. His motion was denied because a rule of the court provided that such trials were to be without a jury. Baldwin appealed, claiming that the court rule was unconstitutional because it denied him his right to a jury trial under the Sixth Amendment. The Supreme Court held in this 1970 case that no offense is petty when a sentence of more than six months' imprisonment may be imposed and reversed Baldwin's conviction.

Number of jurors   Most people associate a trial jury with the number 12. Yet many states have laws providing that juries may be composed of fewer persons. These laws have been held to be constitutional.

EXAMPLE A Florida man named Williams was indicted for robbery. A Florida statute called for a six-man jury in all noncapital cases. Williams' request for a trial by a 12-man jury was denied. The six-man jury convicted him and he was given a life sentence. Williams appealed his conviction, claiming he was denied his right to be tried by a 12-man jury guaranteed by the Sixth Amendment. But the Supreme Court affirmed his conviction.

When the Court examined the development of the jury, it concluded that the number 12 was a historical accident. As a result of the Georgia case described just below, the Supreme Court has held that at least six jurors are required to satisfy the constitutional requirement of a jury trial.

EXAMPLE The defendant, named Ballew, was charged with knowingly distributing obscene material, a misdemeanor. The Georgia court refused to impanel the 12-member jury asked for by Ballew, and a jury of five members convicted him on two counts.

Ballew appealed, and after reviewing scholarly reports relating to jury size, the Supreme Court agreed with him. The reports showed that smaller juries were less likely to encourage effective deliberation. The studies also cast doubts on the accuracy of verdicts reached by smaller juries. The risk of convicting an innocent defendant was found to increase as jury size decreased. In reversing Ballew's conviction, the Court concluded ". . . the pur-

WHEN YOU ARE CALLED FOR JURY DUTY

RICHARD L. ROE AND EDWARD L. O'BRIEN
National Street Law Institute, Washington, D.C.

Imagine that you have been called for jury duty and are serving on a jury in an automobile accident case. Mrs. Ames, who was injured in a collision, is the plaintiff bringing the suit. At the trial, her lawyer claims that Mr. Baker, the driver of the car that hit Mrs. Ames's car, was speeding and went through a red light. The lawyer for Mr. Baker responds by explaining that Mr. Baker was within the speed limit and that it was Mrs. Ames who went through the red light. Both sides present witnesses who testify and are cross-examined in turn. The lawyers make their closing arguments, and the judge gives the jury instructions. You retire to the jury room to review the evidence and to reach a verdict.

If you are like most jurors, you are serving on a jury for the first time. This article will answer some of your questions about jury service, such as: What are my responsibilities as a juror? How did I get selected? Do I have to serve and for how long?

Reasons for trial by jury

A *jury* is a group of ordinary citizens that is given the power and public authority to pass judgment on the actions of others according to the standards established by law. This means that a jury listens to the evidence, determines the facts, and decides whether a person should be convicted of a crime or whether a claim in a civil case should be granted.

The Sixth Amendment to the U.S. Constitution gives the defendant in a criminal case the right to trial "by an impartial jury" in all but the most minor criminal cases. The Seventh Amendment gives parties the right to a jury trial in certain civil cases "where the value in controversy shall exceed twenty dollars." The courts of the United States have decided that in certain types of cases—such as those having to do with juvenile delinquency, families, and taxes—juries need not be provided.

The major reason for having juries centers on the idea that persons charged with crimes or involved in lawsuits should get a fair trial, or what is termed "due process of law." Many persons feel that the judgment of a jury of ordinary citizens is a fairer instrument of justice than that of a judge, who, despite his legal training, is only one person. In addition, juries are designed to protect citizens against the possible arbitrariness and power of the prosecutors and judges, who are either elected or appointed, whereas juries are accountable only to themselves and to their consciences. Juries also give the community a voice in the administration of justice.

Selection of potential jurors

The selection of a jury from a representative cross section of the local population is an essential component of the Sixth Amendment right to trial by an impartial jury. Juries are intended to speak for all segments of the community. There are two steps in the selection process: (1) choosing potential jurors from the population at large and (2) choosing jurors at the courthouse to serve on an actual jury.

Potential jurors are selected in a process usually conducted in three stages: (1) setting up a master list,

(2) establishing a qualified list from those on the master list, and (3) summoning those qualified persons.

The master list, which should include every person eligible for jury service, is usually compiled from the voter registration list. The use of that list alone, however, often underrepresents minorities and poor and young people, because these groups do not register to vote in proportion to their numbers. To make the list more representative, some courts take names from city directories and other such sources. When master lists can be shown to have been set up in such a way as to exclude, for example, blacks or women on a regular basis, the courts will act to correct this.

This master list process is considered fairer than the traditional *key man* system. In the older system, jury commissioners nominate a group of men, called key men, to name potential jurors. Although in theory the purpose has been for these men to appoint qualified jurors, in practice the jurors selected often have not been representative of the community. Although the key man, or key person, system continues to be used in some places today, the entire group of key persons must be reasonably representative of the community at large.

Qualifications to serve   After a list of potential jurors is set up by either method discussed above, many people on the list are sent qualification questionnaires, which seek to obtain information helpful in determining who is qualified to serve. Not everyone on the list receives these questionnaires, and many who fill out and return the questionnaires will never be called.

Courts have different rules regarding who is qualified to serve on juries. Generally, there is a minimum-age requirement of 18 or 21 and an upper limit such as 70 or 75. A juror must be in adequate mental and physical health, have a sufficient command of the English language, and in most states, must not have been convicted of certain listed crimes. Some methods of testing jury qualifications (such as reading ability) have been criticized because they tend to exclude minorities and low-income people.

Periodically, names are selected randomly from the qualified list. The persons selected are mailed a summons that notifies them that they have been called for jury service and where and when to report.

Getting excused   If you are called for jury duty and there are important reasons why you should not serve, you may make a special request to be excused permanently or to have your term of service postponed. If the summons does not explain how to make such a request, contact the clerk of the court's office and ask if this should be done in writing or in person. In some places, persons with jobs that are considered important public services—such as government officials, doctors, military personnel, policemen, and journalists—are routinely excused. Special obligations, such as running a small business or taking care of children at home, may also be a valid excuse. Note, however, that the American Bar Association recommends that no qualified citizen be exempted from jury duty and that excuses be granted sparingly, and this is now the practice in many courts.

Any person who cannot or does not get excused or obtain a postponement must serve at the time designated on the summons. Willful disobedience of a summons may be criminal contempt of court, which is punishable by a fine or imprisonment or both.

What happens when you report for jury duty?

When you arrive at the courthouse for your first day of jury duty, bring your summons with you and check in with the court clerk or the jury office. Many courts provide an orientation session, which may consist of a welcoming lecture by a judge or court clerk, or the distribution of a jury handbook.

As you wait to be selected for a particular trial, you should remain in the jury lounge. The jurors in the lounge make up the *jury pool* and are called when needed. Despite a court calendar, trials often do not occur on schedule because of settlement before trial, guilty pleas, postponements, or other unpredictable occurrences. As a juror, you should expect to spend much of your time waiting to be called.

Selection of juries   A judge will call for a *panel*, chosen at random from the pool, when he needs to select a jury. From this panel, jurors are picked to try the particular case. Those remaining return to the pool. The trial jury itself need not reflect the makeup of the community; a jury is considered impartial as long as the pool and panel from which it is selected represent a cross section of the community.

Part of the selection process is the examination of the prospective jurors, called *voir dire*. Usually, the judge or the attorneys or both will question you to determine if there are any reasons why you should not serve on the case at hand.

Lawyers may *challenge for cause* jurors who possibly have a bias. For example, you may be challenged for cause if you are related to the defendant or if you work for an insurance company and the case is a suit against an insurance company.

Lawyers may also exercise a limited number of *peremptory challenges,* by which they exclude jurors without giving a reason. Jurors should not take the exercise of this safeguard personally. Lawyers use a variety of techniques to help them determine which prospective jurors they think will be more or less favorable to their clients, including psychological profiles, public opinion surveys, and the opinions of body-language experts. The effectiveness of these techniques is unproved, and some lawyers disregard all of them and base their choices on pure instinct.

The use of peremptory challenges has been criticized because it may result in eliminating all members of a certain race or other types of people from a jury in a particular trial. For example, in a well-publicized 1980 trial, in which Miami police officers were being prosecuted for alleged police brutality against a black citizen, attorneys for the defense were able to remove all blacks from the jury through the use of their peremptory challenges. Some critics claim that this appearance of unfairness contributed to the anger of blacks over the not-guilty verdict at the trial and the riots that took place in Miami following the trial.

The process of selection continues until a full jury has been picked. Although most states require 12 members on certain kinds of juries, many have switched to a smaller number of jurors, such as six or eight, for specific types of cases in order to modernize procedures, speed up the trial process, and reduce costs. In many trials, alternate jurors are added to the jury to hear evidence in the event that the court has to replace a regular juror because of sickness or some other emergency. Alternate jurors hear all the evidence but do not participate in the deliberations unless a regular juror is dismissed.

Because it is hard to predict how many prospective jurors will be eliminated in *voir dire,* the panel is always larger than the jury. It may take as few as 24 or as many as 120 people to provide a full jury.

Length of service Length of jury service varies from court to court. The average time is two weeks, but many courts now use terms of one week or less, making it possible for more people to participate as jurors and to serve with a minimum of personal hardship. Once you are selected to serve on a particular trial, however, you must continue to do so until it is completed. Jurors are rarely *sequestered,* that is, kept overnight and isolated, but you may be sequestered while deliberating on a criminal verdict or during a highly publicized trial.

Some courts have successfully used the one-day/one-trial method of service, in which jurors report for one day only. Even if they are not picked to hear a case on that day, they have fulfilled their jury obligation for a year. If they are picked to serve on a trial, then they continue to serve for the duration of the trial, which is usually no more than a few days. Courts are also setting up call-in systems that let jurors telephone the court the night before they are scheduled to serve to see if they are needed the following morning. If they are not needed, they do not have to report that day. Not only do these changes make the jury system work better, but they often save money because jurors must be paid for the time they spend in the jury pool.

Payment to jurors Payment for jury service varies from as little as $5 a day to as much as $25 a day. Many employers continue to pay employees while they are on jury duty or make up the difference between jury payment and salary lost. Like short terms of service, higher payments for jury duty allow more persons to serve without hardship.

You will usually be reimbursed for travel to and from the courthouse, but you should keep accurate records of your mileage or the expenses you incur for public transportation. As a rule, child-care expenses are not allowed. Meals are ordinarily not provided, but if you are deliberating during mealtimes, the judge may send out for food.

During the trial

The trial begins as soon as all the jurors and alternates have been selected and are seated. You will be asked always to sit in the same seat in the jury box. Most courts do not allow you to take notes in the belief that note taking will place undue emphasis on certain facts.

Your most important job is to listen closely to the evidence with an open mind. Wait until all the evidence is in before starting to make up your mind. You must not discuss the case, even with other jurors, before the trial is over and you retire to the jury room to deliberate. The reason for this rule is that any conversation about the case, even if only to clarify a point, may start you on the process of weighing the evidence, and favoring one side over the other before you have heard the entire case. What is more, you should never talk to anyone involved in the case—party, witness, or lawyer—even if it is a friendly conversation not concerning the case. If any person insists on talking to you about the case or tries to influence you, immediately report this to the judge.

You may not read newspaper articles or watch television news reports on the case before it is over. These could influence you unfairly.

Jurors should never make an independent investigation or inspect the scene of an accident or other event connected with the case. If it is proper and necessary for the jury to inspect a place involved in a case, the judge will order it.

Because evidence that may mislead the jury is not allowed, lawyers will sometimes object to certain testimony or exhibits. Occasionally, they will also have conferences with the judge outside the jury's hearing on points of law or on issues such as relevance. Delays resulting from this and other developments are necessary and regular parts of the trial.

It is not important that you understand the technicalities of the rules of evidence, but you should understand the result of the judge's rulings. If the judge considers evidence to be proper, he or she will *overrule* an objection to it and you may consider the evidence. If the evidence is inadmissible, the judge will *sustain* the objection and ask you to disregard the evidence. When this occurs, even though to do so may be difficult, try not to let the evidence have any influence on your decision. Whether or not a judge admits evidence is no indication that he favors one side over the other. Even if a judge decided every objection in favor of one side, you should not conclude that that side is entitled to win the case.

As you listen to the proceedings, you may have questions you want to ask the witnesses or judge. The role of the jurors, however, is to listen to what is presented, not to participate directly in the trial. Many of your questions will be answered in the course of the trial. If you must ask a question, write it out and send it by way of the court attendant to the judge. The judge will rule on what to do about your question and give you an appropriate response. However, you should raise your hand and tell the judge if you cannot hear a witness, an attorney, or the judge.

After the opening statements by the attorneys on both sides, the examination and cross-examination of witnesses, the introduction of physical evidence, and the closing statements by the attorney for each side, the jury receives its instructions. The judge explains the rules of law the jurors are to consider in weighing the evidence and reminds the jurors that the lawyers' opening statements are not evidence. Sometimes these instructions are legalistic and difficult to understand. Some courts have revised their rules to make them clearer to nonlawyers.

Deliberation in the jury room

After the judge's instructions, the jury retires to the jury room to attempt to agree on the verdict. One of the jurors must act as the foreman (or forewoman or foreperson) to preside over the deliberations. It is his or her duty to see that the jury is run democratically and that each juror gets a fair opportunity to express his or her views. In some courts, the first juror selected is the foreman; in others, the jurors elect one when they retire to deliberate; and in still other courts, the foreman is chosen by the judge.

The jury has complete freedom in reaching its decision and is rarely instructed as to how it should go about the process. However you go about deliberating, you should keep in mind certain principles.

You should feel free to express your opinion openly and honestly. You should also listen carefully to the views of the other jurors. As you review the facts, you may persuade others to your point of view or you may be persuaded by theirs. You can expect differences of opinion and different interpretations of the evidence—it is natural for a number of persons to observe the same events differently.

You should try to work out the differences among yourselves. If you have any questions or need to review certain testimony, you may communicate with the judge in writing, but you should do this only after you have made every effort to resolve the differences yourselves. You should do your best to reach an agreement as to guilt or innocence. You should not hesitate to change your mind as you come to accept reasons put forth by others, but your final vote should represent your own opinion.

The federal courts and most states require a jury's decision to be unanimous in many kinds of trials—that is, all members must agree to the verdict. Many states, however, permit verdicts that are less than unanimous in civil cases or noncapital criminal cases.

When a jury cannot agree, the judge may declare a *hung jury,* which ends the trial in favor of neither party. When this occurs, a new trial can be ordered or the case can be dropped. Even though a hung jury may mean that the trial must be repeated, you should not change your mind on a verdict unless you are firmly convinced of the other point of view.

Grand juries

The juries described above are trial juries, or petit (small) juries. There are also grand juries, and you may be called to serve on one. Grand juries, which are used only in criminal cases, decide if persons should be charged with a crime and stand trial.

A *grand jury* is composed of ordinary citizens who listen to evidence presented by a prosecutor and decide whether or not to *indict* the defendant—charge him with a crime. The number of grand jurors may vary in different jurisdictions, anywhere from 5 to 23 members. A majority vote is usually sufficient to indict. As a grand juror, you do not decide the defendant's guilt or innocence but decide instead if a crime has been committed and if the defendant may have committed it. Grand juries are required by the Fifth Amendment to the U.S. Constitution for "a capital, or otherwise infamous crime" and, consequently, are used in all federal felony cases and in all states for certain crimes. Some grand juries also meet to conduct investigations of government affairs and possible criminal activity even when no definite defendant is named.

To illustrate the grand jury's role, suppose that while driving her car, Mrs. Ames was involved in a collision and died from her injuries. The local district attorney wants to indict Mr. Baker, the driver of the other car, on the count of manslaughter and brings the case before a grand jury that you are sitting on. The prosecutor calls as witnesses a passenger in Mrs. Ames's car and the policeman who investigated the accident. They testify that Mr. Baker was speeding, ran a red light, and, in addition, appeared drunk. You are free to ask any pertinent questions the prosecutor does not ask, although you should do this by calling the prosecutor to you quietly and asking him to direct the question to the witness. The prosecutor also reads the pertinent law on manslaughter to you and explains it in layman's terms. On the basis of this testimony and information, you would vote whether or not to indict Mr. Baker for manslaughter. If you believe that there is enough evidence to justify having Mr. Baker put on trial for manslaughter, you should vote to indict him. If a majority of your grand jury votes for indictment, Mr. Baker will be brought to trial. Otherwise he will not.

Grand juries have come under increased criticism in recent years because when the prosecutor gives the state's side of the case, the defendant usually is not present and cannot question the prosecutor's witnesses, present his own witnesses, or tell his side of the story. If the defendant does appear, he must testify without the presence of his lawyer, because defense attorneys are usually barred from grand jury proceedings. However, the defendant may consult his lawyer outside the courtroom before answering any questions, and he may decline to appear without jeopardizing his position. Some states have eliminated grand juries in many cases or modified the procedure to allow defense attorneys to be present.

Grand jurors are selected in the same way as trial jurors. If you are called to serve on a grand jury, you may be required to serve for only one particular case or for a specific length of time—30 days, for example—depending on how the process works in your area. The most important thing to remember is that as a grand juror you are an independent arm of the court and have the power to ask questions. Before voting to indict, be certain that there is enough evidence to warrant that the defendant stand trial.

Why you should willingly accept jury duty

As you have seen, a juror's role is not an easy one. Whether you are sitting on a trial jury or a grand jury, you may be away from your job and other responsibilities for an extended period, and you may receive only small fees or actually lose income. You may spend long hours waiting in a jury lounge and only a few hours listening to cases.

Despite these drawbacks, you should willingly accept jury duty and not ask to be excused or seek endless postponements without good reason. Jury service is one of the few opportunities you will have to participate directly in the administration of justice. As a juror, you will be called on not only to resolve disputes between other citizens and to determine the guilt or innocence of alleged criminals but also to protect people's rights and liberties. Citizens who serve on juries also become better informed about the problems in our legal system and are better able to propose reforms when they are needed. It is not surprising, then, that most people who have served on a jury view their experience as a positive one.

pose and function of the jury in a criminal trial is seriously impaired, and to a constitutional degree, by a reduction in size to below six members."

In federal criminal cases, however, the rule is that juries must be composed of 12 members—although there are exceptions. The prosecution and defendant can enter into a written agreement that the jury can consist of fewer than 12 members or that if the court finds it must excuse some jurors after the start of the trial, a valid verdict can be returned by a jury of fewer than 12.

Unanimous verdicts   In federal court a unanimous verdict is needed to sustain the conviction of a criminal defendant. In state courts, a unanimous verdict is not necessarily required in criminal cases. In Louisiana, for example, a statute authorizes nonunanimous verdicts by 12-man juries in serious but noncapital cases.

EXAMPLE   When a defendant named Johnson was charged ○─┅─✳ with robbery and convicted by a vote of 9 to 3, he appealed to the Supreme Court. He argued that since three jurors voted to acquit him, the standard of proof of his guilt beyond a reasonable doubt as required by the due process clause of the 14th Amendment was not satisfied. Therefore, his conviction should be overturned. The Court held that a unanimous verdict is not required by due process of law, nor does the lack of unanimity among jurors mean that a reasonable doubt exists. If it did, a hung jury would amount to an acquittal, and it does not.

In a companion case, the Supreme Court heard appeals by three Oregon defendants, convicted by nonunanimous verdicts. They argued that majority verdicts would permit defendants to be convicted without the assent of minority factions within the community. This, they contended, would be contrary to the 14th Amendment, which says jury panels must be representative of a cross section of the community. The Court found fault with this argument and upheld the use of less than unanimous verdicts.

❝ *One [fault] is petitioners' [defendants'] assumption that every distinct voice in the community has a right to be represented on every jury and a right to prevent conviction of a defendant in any case. All that the Constitution forbids, however, is systematic exclusion of identifiable segments of the community from jury panels and from the juries ultimately drawn from those panels; a defendant may not, for example, challenge the makeup of a jury merely because no members of his race are on the jury, but must prove that his race has been systematically excluded . . ."*

Civil cases   The Seventh Amendment to the Constitution applies only to jury trials in federal civil cases. It states: "In Suits at common law, where the value in controversy shall exceed twenty dollars, the right of trial by jury shall be preserved . . ." In state civil suits, the state legislatures can enact their own laws regarding the procedures for jury trials. For example, one state may permit a jury in one type of case while in another state, only a judge will hear the same kind of case. States also differ as to the requirements for the number of jurors in civil suits and for verdicts.

Number of jurors   Many states call for juries of fewer than 12 members in civil cases. Federal law grants federal district court judges in civil cases the power to set the size of juries. Federal law also provides that the parties can agree to a jury of fewer than 12 persons.

Unanimous verdicts   A number of states allow less than unanimous verdicts in civil suits. Sometimes the exact number of jurors needed for a (nonunanimous) vote to be valid is specified by state statute. If a specified majority, such as five-sixths, of the jurors agree on a verdict, it is valid provided all of them take part in the deliberations.

Federal law says that the parties can stipulate that a verdict of a stated majority will be accepted as the jury's verdict. In the absence of such a stipulation, federal courts in the past required unanimous verdicts in civil cases.

jury box   The enclosed place in the courtroom where the jury sits during a trial.

jury commission   A group of officers who select the names of prospective jurors or draw the list of jurors for a court term. In some states these officers are elected; in others they are appointed by the governor or by judges. They decide who is fit to serve as a juror as prescribed by the statutes. The list must be selected without discrimination from the pool of qualified persons.

jury list   1 A paper containing the names of all the persons qualified to serve as jurors within a geographic area, such as a county or city.   2 The names of all persons summoned to serve as jurors during a court term or the names of the jurors selected to try a case.

jus   (Latin)   1 Law in the abstract, considered as a science or branch of learning. In this sense it may be used to specify a system or body of law, such as *jus civile,* the civil law.   2 A legal right. For example, a *jus in re* is a property right that a person has in an item, implying complete ownership and valid possession.

just   Conforming to what is legally right or lawful. For example, just compensation for property taken by a municipality for public use means a settlement that leaves the owner no better or worse off financially than he was before his property was taken. See EMINENT DOMAIN.

jus tertii   (Latin) "The right of a third party." For example, a landlord sues a tenant for possession of leased property. The tenant defends the suit by answering that the title to the property belongs to someone other than the landlord—a third party. The tenant's answer is known as a *jus tertii* defense.

justice   1 The fair and equal treatment of all persons under the law. Providing justice is the goal of the law.   2 The word is sometimes used to refer to a JUDGE—for example, Justice Smith.

justice of the peace   A state judicial officer of lesser rank with limited jurisdiction (authority). His powers include conserving the peace, presiding over minor civil and criminal cases, and committing offenders. Depending on the law of each state, the authority of a justice of the peace may be limited to a county, township, precinct or city—or extend to the whole state. As a rule, the office is an elective one, but some justices are appointed.

■ **Duties** A justice of the peace has only those powers that are expressly granted by law. Under statutes in some states, he may not be involved in any other business or profession. This does not bar him from investing money or receiving a salary from a business, so long as he does not devote any of his time to it.

Conserving the peace As a keeper of the peace, a justice of the peace has the power to arrest and commit criminal offenders or INSANE PERSONS, require persons to post bonds, order the removal of disorderly persons from public meetings, and order the return of stolen property to its rightful owner.

Criminal matters Justices of the peace have limited authority in criminal matters. Generally they preside over the trial of misdemeanors or minor offenses but not FELO-NIES. They have jurisdiction over ASSAULT AND BATTERY when no serious injury results and no deadly weapon is used; disorderly persons; cruelty to ANIMALS; disturbing a lawful assembly, religious meeting, or public school (see DISORDERLY CONDUCT); FORGERY; gambling (see GAMING); indecent exposure; malicious destruction of property; VA-GRANCY; and violations of liquor laws (see INTOXICATING LIQUOR), MOTOR VEHICLE, and FISH and GAME laws.

Offenses beyond the authority of justices of the peace include assault with intent to inflict great bodily harm or to MURDER; assault and battery with a weapon; maiming; RAPE; and ROBBERY.

Civil cases Just as in criminal matters, justice of the peace courts, or justice courts, are restricted in the kinds of civil cases they may hear. They may usually preside over cases involving money claims only up to a specified amount. This amount varies, however, not only from state to state but also in the same state, according to the type of suit, such as a CONTRACT suit or TORT suit (one for injury to a person or property). The amount claimed by the plaintiff in his PLEADINGS determines whether the case will be heard by the justice court or a different court.

The most extensive civil jurisdiction of the justices is over contracts, including suits for breaches of warranty. Actions for such torts as injuries to personal property resulting from an automobile accident are sometimes heard. Some statutes allow actions for injuries to the person, such as FALSE IMPRISONMENT, MALICIOUS PROSECUTION, or LIBEL AND SLANDER.

Generally, justices of the peace have no authority over suits involving titles to rights of way across lands or EASE-MENTS. Since disputes concerning boundaries and division fences usually include the question of title to land, justices may not be involved in such disputes. When the relationship of LANDLORD AND TENANT is established, a justice can hear an action for rent.

■ **Civil liability** A justice of the peace is not civilly liable (financially responsible) for any error or irregularity in performing judicial acts. Judicial acts include issuing ARREST or search warrants (see SEARCH AND SEIZURE), granting adjournments, issuing writs of ATTACHMENT AND GAR-NISHMENT, rendering JUDGMENTS, and imposing fines.

■ **Qualifying steps** Before entering office, a justice of the peace is required to take an oath of office, and he must give an official bond that is approved before he can serve. Under some statutes, he must also file an affidavit that he

has never been convicted of a misdemeanor or a more serious crime.

■ **Term** The term of office depends on the provisions of the state's constitution or statute under which the position is created. A vacancy is usually filled by the governor or some other public body, such as the county commissioners or supervisors, but under some statutes a special election may be held. A person filling a vacancy generally holds the office only for the unexpired term or until the next regular election of a successor.

■ **Removal and resignation** A justice of the peace may be removed or suspended by the state legislature, the governor, a proper court, or by the body designated by statute to do so. Usually, he must first be informed of the charges against him and given an opportunity to respond.

Conviction of a crime, such as conspiracy to prevent and obstruct justice, is ground for removal or suspension. So is misconduct in office—being drunk, for instance, while performing official duties. The acts with which a justice of the peace is charged must have been done with improper motives and with the knowledge that they were wrong.

The resignation of a justice of the peace must be presented to the proper official, such as the county court or judge. Once accepted, it cannot be withdrawn.

justiciable Proper to be decided by a COURT. A matter is justiciable if it can be acted on by a court, as distinguished from a debate or disagreement that cannot be resolved by a JUDGMENT or decree.

The U.S. Constitution and in general the state constitutions limit the jurisdiction (authority) of courts to cases and controversies that are justiciable. This means there must be an actual dispute between persons whose interests are opposed. There can be no friendly lawsuits. The plaintiff must have a legally protectable interest at stake, and the question must be RIPE for judgment, for no decision will be reached on some future issue.

justification A reason that is acceptable in court for an action that would otherwise be unlawful. For example, SELF-DEFENSE is sometimes offered as justification for a killing.

juvenile court A special court that has the authority to hear and decide cases involving delinquent or neglected INFANTS—children under the legal age of adulthood, usually under 18 or 21. See Chart 2. The authority of a juvenile court is spelled out in state laws and generally covers criminal acts by juveniles and may also cover noncriminal misbehavior such as truancy. Juvenile courts handle matters relating to the care, control, and custody of delinquent, abused, and neglected children.

■ **Delinquency proceedings** A juvenile court may be empowered to hear any case in which a child is accused of an act that would be a crime if he were an adult. However, juvenile court is not an ordinary trial court with a JURY. A judge hears the case, decides whether the child is delinquent and whether to send him to a state institution (such as a reform school) for a specified period of time. Although the proceedings are not considered criminal, the judge must use the standard of proof required in criminal trials—

proof beyond a reasonable doubt that the child before him committed the act charged. The objective of delinquency proceedings is not to punish children for crimes but rather to promote their welfare through rehabilitation.

In some states, a child accused of a serious crime—such as murder, rape, or a crime that is punishable by death or life imprisonment for adults—is treated as an adult and is brought to the regular criminal court. Sometimes a local court instead of juvenile court may hear a case involving the violation of a local law.

■ **Noncriminal misbehavior** Noncriminal misbehavior by juveniles—such as truancy from school; running away from home; refusing to obey parents, teachers, or legal authorities; or endangering themselves or others—is called a *status offense*. It may be handled by a juvenile court in a proceeding that differs from delinquency proceedings. First, the standard of proof required is different. In status offense proceedings, a court may place a child under its supervision when there is more evidence than not that a child needs it. In delinquency proceedings, proof beyond a

reasonable doubt is needed. Second, evidence inadmissible in a delinquency hearing may be admitted in a status offense hearing. Third, a child in a status offense hearing does not have the right to have a lawyer provided by the court. One question that has been raised about status offense proceedings is whether the juvenile court is the appropriate place to help children who are troubled but who have not committed crimes.

Rights of accused child The Supreme Court ruled in 1967 that in any case in which a child might lose his liberty by being sent to a home, a jail, a training school, or other state facility, the child has the following constitutional rights: the right to prior written notice of the court proceedings and the accusations against him; the right to have an attorney, appointed by the court when necessary; the right to remain silent and not to incriminate himself; and the right to cross-examine his accuser and witnesses who testify against him. See GAULT, IN RE.

juvenile delinquent See INFANT.

kangaroo court The popular expression for an unofficial court that has no legal powers. When used as a derogatory term, the word usually refers to a court that seems to be weighted against a particular individual.

Keogh Plan See PENSION.

key number A reference system that classifies legal subjects by specific topics and subtopics, with one or more digits assigned to each classification. Any point of law can be traced through different law books—such as those in the AMERICAN DIGEST SYSTEM and the NATIONAL REPORTER SYSTEM—by following the cases listed under a particular key number in each series.

kidnapping Generally, the criminal offense of carrying away a person, against his will, through the use of unlawful force. The precise definition of kidnapping depends upon the applicable common law, state statutes, or federal statutes. Kidnapping can mean seizing and holding a person for the purpose of carrying him away later, for example. In California, taking a motorist at knife point from his car and holding him a mere 50 feet away against his will was held to be kidnapping.

■ **Essential elements** Restraint of liberty against the will of the victim is essential to the crime of kidnapping; so is unlawful detention of the victim or at least an intention to detain him. A demand for ransom is not an essential element. If a third person prevents the kidnapper and his victim from reaching their destination, the kidnapper is still considered to have committed the crime.

The kidnapper does not have to use actual physical force; a threat of physical harm to the victim is sufficient. When a man induces a girl into his car for a legitimate purpose, such as driving her home from a babysitting job, but then takes her elsewhere, he is guilty of kidnapping accomplished by fraud.

■ **The Lindbergh Act** The Federal Kidnapping Act, known as the LINDBERGH ACT, makes interstate transportation of the victim a federal crime. The kidnapper must knowingly set the interstate trip in motion, intentionally go to the place he has selected, and cross the state line with the victim in his custody.

■ **Defenses to kidnapping** If the accused believed, in good faith, that he was acting within the law, that may be a defense to the crime of kidnapping.

EXAMPLE A private detective who asked Gary to assist him in capturing Louis, a suspected robber, appointed Gary a "special deputy." Gary "arrested" Louis and confined him. The private detective, however, had neither the authority to arrest Louis nor to deputize Gary to do so. When Gary was tried for kidnapping, he had a valid defense.

Another defense to kidnapping is that the alleged kidnapper did not intend to detain the victim.

EXAMPLE While driving along an interstate highway, Jake sees a disabled vehicle on the shoulder of the road. He stops and finds the driver, who appears to be under the influence of drugs. Jake offers to take the driver to the nearest hospital across the state line two miles away, but the man refuses. As Jake is about to leave, the driver lapses into unconsciousness. Jake puts him in his car and takes him to the hospital. When the driver regains consciousness, he tries to have the U.S. Attorney charge Jake with kidnapping under the Lindbergh Act. The U.S. Attorney will refuse to bring charges because it is clear that Jake had no intent to kidnap but merely acted reasonably under the circumstances.

■ **Stealing children from custody** Statutes in many states have created the crime of interference with the custody of children, or child stealing. This crime is the taking of a child under a certain age, such as 18, from one who has lawful custody. The offense is a misdemeanor. It often involves the taking of a child by a parent who was denied CUSTODY in a divorce case. The accused person has a defense to child stealing if he reasonably believed that his conduct was necessary to preserve the child's health or welfare. Suppose you see your neighbor beating his child. If you take the child to protect him, you have committed no crime. See ABDUCTION; FALSE IMPRISONMENT.

kin Relationship by birth; relatives by blood or sometimes by marriage.

kiting Writing checks against a bank account when funds are insufficient to cover them. See OVERDRAFT.

labor relations

labor relations The relationship between management and labor as it pertains to terms of employment. The basic purpose of labor relations laws is to settle labor disputes promptly. The term *labor dispute* includes any controversy about the terms, tenure, or conditions of employment. It also covers the representation of employees in negotiations with their employer, usually by a labor organization (union).

■ **History** The history of labor relations in America goes back to the early 1800's when workers who joined together to STRIKE for better working conditions were treated as criminals. This attitude gradually changed to government recognition that employees have the right to organize and bargain collectively with their employers. From 1842 to 1932, employers used INJUNCTIONS (court orders to do or not to do something) to quash the union movement. But in 1932 Congress enacted the *Norris-LaGuardia Act,* which exempted certain types of union activities from injunctions. Employers could no longer use the federal courts as a weapon against unions.

The National Labor Relations Act of 1935, popularly known as the *Wagner Act,* clearly set forth the right of employees "to form, join, or assist labor organizations, to bargain collectively through representatives of their own choosing, and to engage in concerted activities for the purpose of collectively bargaining or other mutual aid or protection." Unfair labor practices and discriminatory conduct by employers that intimidate employees from joining a union are prohibited by this act. (See "Unfair labor practices" below.) Once employees vote to join a particular union or bargaining unit and have it serve as their representative, their employer is legally required to bargain with it. The Wagner Act also established the National Labor Relations Board (NLRB), a government agency that administers and interprets its provisions. The board has the power to order employers or unions to cease and desist from unfair labor practices. The board may, for instance, demand that an employer or union that will not engage in collective bargaining cease and desist from its refusal. Since 1935, the NLRB has had the paramount authority to develop federal law relating to collective bargaining.

As unions grew in strength and number, Congress recognized the need to outlaw certain union "bad practices." In 1947, the *Labor Management Relations Act,* familiar to most as the *Taft-Hartley Act,* was passed to prohibit certain union practices, such as charging excessive initiation fees and dues, and to make collective bargaining agreements enforceable in court. *The Labor-Management Reporting and Disclosure Act,* better known as the *Landrum-Griffin Act,* was passed in 1959 to correct abuses in handling union funds and to provide union members with a bill of rights. Financial information has to be disclosed and if financial abuses are discovered union officers may be subject to civil and criminal penalties.

Federal laws apply to businesses involved in interstate commerce. States are empowered to enact their own labor laws to control those businesses that are strictly engaged in intrastate commerce.

■ **Unions** A *labor union* is an organization of employees for the purpose of securing by united action the most favorable working conditions, pay, and benefits for its members. A group of employees is not considered a union unless it exists to negotiate or bargain with employers. The right of employees to form unions is derived from their constitutional rights of assembly and freedom of expression, in addition to their fundamental right to liberty and property. Employees also have a right to band together to persuade fellow workers to unionize.

Formation When employees decide that they want to be represented by a union, the local division or parent association of a national union, such as the Teamsters, is contacted for guidance and assistance. The union can campaign for members by distributing leaflets and holding meetings on how it can improve working conditions.

The employees, union, or even the employer can file a petition with the NLRB to hold an election to determine whether the union should be the representative for collective bargaining. When a petition is filed, it must be supported by at least 30 percent of the employees in the bargaining unit named in the petition. Such support is demonstrated by signed, dated authorization cards that are issued by the NLRB regional director once interest in unionizing is shown. The employer is not allowed to see the cards.

An employer can file a petition only if one or more unions claim to be the exclusive representative of his employees, if a union claims to represent the majority of employees, or if a union wants the employer to bargain with it. If a union is merely encouraging people to unionize, an employer will not be permitted to file a petition because a premature election can set back unionization attempts.

After a petition has been filed, the National Labor Relations Board must decide if there are any obstacles to holding the election. For example, if an employer does not have at least $50,000 worth of business crossing state lines, he is exempt from NLRB (federal) jurisdiction. If there are no obstacles, the NLRB will try to have the union and employer agree to an election. If no agreement is reached, the NLRB will hold an administrative hearing to determine which employees are to vote for the union so that it can be designated an appropriate bargaining unit of a certain category of employees. An NLRB representative conducts the election by secret ballot. A majority of employees must vote for the union in order for it to be certified as their bargaining agent. If a losing party claims that there was some error in the election process or misconduct by the winner, it may seek to have the election set aside. The NLRB regional director decides whether the election results are valid. His decision may be reversed by a court. Once a union is recognized by the NLRB as the representative of employees, it has the exclusive right to represent them.

Membership Employees are generally free to choose whether or not to join unions. A union may solicit members and establish rules under which it will accept new members, but it must not discriminate on the basis of sex, race, creed, or national origin. Membership in a union is not a right, however, and courts are reluctant to order that an individual be admitted to membership. Supervisory personnel, such as foremen, can be excluded because of their close ties to management.

Whether a person must join a union in order to get or keep his job depends upon the type of job he has and the state in which he works. The Taft-Hartley Act prohibits a *closed shop*—that is, an agreement between a union and an employer that obligates the employer to hire only union members and to fire anyone who is not a member. Only businesses that deal in interstate commerce are affected.

In contrast, a person can be required to join a union if he is to keep his job. This arrangement is called a *union shop*. Union membership is not necessary in order to be hired, but the new employee must join the union within a certain period of time or be fired. A number of states have enacted RIGHT-TO-WORK LAWS that make it illegal to mandate union membership as a condition of employment, even though the employer has agreed with the union to do so. See Chart 30.

Once a person joins a union, he is bound by the rights and duties contained in its constitution. Under federal law, every member in good standing is eligible to participate fully in union affairs and is entitled to participate in regular membership meetings. Seniority rights (such as preference in job openings and vacation time); health, strike, and pension benefits; and the payment of dues are a few of the items determined by the constitution and bylaws of the union.

Penalties for breaking rules A member's violation of union rules may subject him to disciplinary proceedings and his being fined, suspended, or expelled by the union. For example, a member may be fined for not attending a certain number of union meetings a year or suspended or expelled for not paying his dues. Disciplinary action is administered by a board of union officials. A member must be informed of the charges against him and in most cases (except for the nonpayment of dues) must be given a hearing to refute the charges. It is unlawful for a union to fine, suspend, expel, or otherwise discipline members for exercising their rights, which include freedom of assembly, freedom of speech, freedom from arbitrary increases in dues or assessments, and equal rights in nominating candidates or voting in union elections. Courts are loath to interfere with union affairs, but if a union member is wrongfully suspended or expelled, as for criticizing the management of union funds, a court can order his reinstatement. Money DAMAGES to compensate the member for money he actually lost as a result of his illegal suspension or expulsion can be awarded by a court.

■ **Collective bargaining** Collective bargaining is the process of negotiating an agreement between an employer and the authorized representative of his employees on wages, hours, and other conditions of employment. The rules for collective bargaining were established by the federal National Labor Relations Act of 1935. The main objective is to promote industrial peace between employers and employees. The end product of the bargaining process is the agreement, which is an enforceable contract between an employer and a union that sets forth the terms and conditions of employment.

Employees have the right to bargain collectively through their union, while an employer is duty bound to enter negotiations when the employees' representative requests it. The duty to bargain, however, does not mean that the parties must reach an agreement. Both sides may stick to their positions until negotiations reach an impasse.

Under federal law the parties are required to negotiate in good faith. Legal pressures, such as filing unfair labor practice charges or calling a strike, are not inconsistent with this policy. Neither party is relieved of its mandate to bargain because of the other's legal pressures. There are three major kinds of pressure to reach a labor agreement: the boycott, the strike, and the lockout.

Boycott A union on strike will often call for a BOYCOTT—a refusal to purchase or handle an employer's products. By this tactic, a union seeks to keep the public from patronizing a business. Employees may lawfully participate in a boycott, if they act peacefully and honestly.

Strike A *strike* is a collective refusal of employees to perform assigned work. Its purpose is to force the employer to grant concessions that the employees have demanded. Employees' right to strike is vigorously guarded in the courts, but a strike should be conducted in an orderly manner; intimidation and coercion by either side is unlawful. Striking employees have the right to peacefully carry signs and banners that publicize a labor dispute and to picket—post members at the site of the strike or boycott to interfere with the business or influence the public against patronizing the employer. The use of force on a picket line is illegal, and striking workers do not have the right to seize any part of the employer's property.

Lockout A *lockout* occurs when an employer closes the door of his business to employees. He thus withholds work to gain a concession from them. The lockout is the employer's weapon, just as a strike is the sword of the union.

■ **Unfair labor practices** Neither employers nor unions may commit unfair labor practices. The National Labor Relations Act prohibits such practices by employers, while employees are forbidden from similar actions by the Taft-Hartley Act.

By an employer Any conduct or statement by an employer that interferes with the right of employees to organize and to bargain collectively is an unfair labor practice. This interference may take the form of threats, promises, or offers to employees.

Labor relations laws are not meant to obstruct an employer's power to hire and fire. An employer retains the right to hire on the basis of individual merit, without regard to union affiliation. Refusal to take on an applicant solely because of his affiliation with a labor union, however, is an unfair labor practice. Other such illegal acts are firing an employee for union activities or membership, dismissal for filing unfair labor-practice charges or for giving testimony in such a case. An employer's motive may determine whether the firing is an unfair labor practice, and a history of antiunion bias is a highly significant factor. It is not an unfair labor practice, however, to fire an employee for misconduct, illegal activity, disloyalty, insubordination, inefficiency, disobedience, or failure of the business.

It is an unfair labor practice for an employer to contribute financial or other support to a union, to favor one union over another, or to interfere with union administration. An employer may not refuse to bargain about conditions of employment after a request to do so has been made, nor may he refuse to sign a written contract embodying the terms of an agreement reached with a union.

It is not unlawful for an employer to terminate his business, regardless of his motive. But partial termination is illegal if it is motivated by antiunion considerations rather than economic necessity. For example, an employer may not close down a branch office because employees in it are seeking to unionize.

By a union A union commits an unfair labor practice when it causes or attempts to cause an employer to hire, discharge, or discriminate against an employee in any way in order to influence union activity. It is also illegal for a union to block the rights of employees to (1) form, join, or assist other labor organizations; (2) bargain collectively; or (3) refrain from any of these activities. A union may not refuse either to bargain collectively or to sign a formal document of agreement with an employer.

■ **The steps to arbitration** The grievance provisions of a collective-bargaining agreement set the procedure by which on-the-job disputes may be settled. Grievance procedures usually have at least three steps: (1) an employee and his union steward voice their complaint to the foreman, who may settle it; (2) if the matter is not resolved, the complaint is put in writing, and the steward and union officers confer with management; and (3) if no agreement is reached, the aggrieved employee may submit the matter to ARBITRATION, which is binding on all parties.

Arbitration of grievances is favored by the law, and the courts can compel it in accordance with clauses in the collective-bargaining agreement. Typical grievances settled under arbitration clauses include disputes over seniority rights, employee discipline, pension or welfare benefits, rates of pay, and hours of work. As a rule, the question of whether a strike or lockout is legal is also a proper subject for arbitration.

■ **Injunctions** The authority of the courts today does not usually include the restraint of conduct in economic conflicts. Consequently, INJUNCTIONS—court orders to do or not do certain acts—are extraordinary remedies in labor relations. Nevertheless, injunctions are sought by both employers and employees.

The courts, particularly those in the federal system, do not hand down an injunction in labor disputes unless there is no other way to end the unlawful conduct. The purpose of an injunction is not to punish past conduct but to provide protection for the future. For example, a court will rarely issue an injunction to stop peaceful picketing, but it might grant one if the picketing is accompanied by violence or intimidation. Isolated incidents of unlawful activity, however, do not justify an injunction against picketing.

■ **Wages and hours laws** Both Congress and the states have enacted various laws that govern the minimum wages and the maximum hours of workers. The federal laws apply to those who work in a business that does interstate commerce, while the state laws apply to employees of intrastate businesses. For example, if you are a billing clerk in a factory that manufactures goods that will be shipped out of your state, you are protected by the federal law. But if the goods never leave town, you must look to your state laws for protection. See Chart 31.

State laws apply to all employees in the state. There are exceptions to the federal laws, however. For example, executives, administrative employees, and some employees of certain transportation companies are not subject to the federal Fair Labor Standards Act. Some employees, such as handicapped workers and students, may be paid a lower minimum rate. And some employees of the airlines, service stations, railroads, shipping lines, and other industries may be excluded from the federal provision on overtime, which says that if you work more than 40 hours a week, your employer must pay you at least one and a half times your regular hourly wage for the extra hours.

If an employee is not paid the legal minimum, he may sue for the wages owed him and, in addition, may request an equal amount as DAMAGES. He is also entitled to his court costs and his attorney's fee. His suit must be filed within two years of the employer's failure to pay. It is illegal to discharge an employee if he files a suit or lodges a complaint.

Complaints for violations of the federal laws are handled by the Wage and Hour Division of the U.S. Department of Labor, which maintains field offices in most of the states. Violations of state laws are handled by the state Department of Labor. The Department of Labor may sue to compel an employer to pay back wages or get a court order to stop him from violating the law. Serious offenders are subject to fines and imprisonment.

■ **Safety and health** In 1970 Congress passed the Occupational Safety and Health Act that created the Occupational Safety and Health Administration (OSHA) to deal with the problems of health and safety conditions in places of employment. OSHA develops and promulgates health and safety standards that employers must meet, conducts inspections to determine whether employers are complying with these standards, and issues citations and proposes penalties for violating the standards.

EXAMPLE Suppose the ceiling in your office is flaking large 0•——*· chips of asbestos, a cancer-causing substance. You report the situation to your company, which owns the building, but the company fails to do anything about it. You can write OSHA and request that an inspector be sent to determine whether the asbestos level in your office poses a health threat. If it does, your company can be ordered to replace the asbestos or be subject to a fine.

States have similar laws designed to reduce the number of injuries, illnesses, and deaths among workers. State health and safety laws and codes cover seven major areas: (1) buildings and their appurtenances, (2) construction, (3) equipment and machinery, (4) fire safety, (5) health, (6) industry safety, and (7) licensing and qualifications for various occupations.

laches   A defense to a suit in EQUITY that bars the plaintiff from receiving relief from the court. Equity is justice based on fairness rather than on formulated laws. The principle of laches says that if a plaintiff delays his suit for so long that the defendant loses his opportunity to defend himself, a court of equity will, in effect, dismiss the case. The concept is reflected in the maxim, "The laws serve the vigilant and not those who sleep on their rights."

land grant   A donation of public lands from one level of government to a subordinate level of government or a corporation. For example, the United States may give a parcel of land to a state for a park or to a railroad company to allow it to construct tracks. In 1862 the federal government granted to several states 30,000 acres of land for each of its senators and representatives serving in Congress. The lands were then sold by the states with the proceeds used to establish and maintain colleges primarily devoted to teaching agriculture and engineering. These institutions are known as land-grant colleges.

landlord and tenant   A relationship that arises from a CONTRACT by which one person occupies the property of another with his permission. The occupant is the *tenant*. The owner of the property and the person to whom the tenant pays rent is the *landlord*.

The terms *lessor* and *lessee* are used almost interchangeably with *landlord* and *tenant*, although, strictly speaking, they refer only to those named in a formal lease. A *subtenant* is one who leases all or part of the rented premises from the original tenant for a term (period of time) less than that held by the tenant.

■ **Essentials of the relationship**   Generally the following elements must be present for the landlord-tenant relationship to exist: (1) the landlord must consent to the tenant's occupancy; (2) the tenant must have a legal INTEREST in the property; (3) possession and control of the premises must be transferred to the tenant; (4) the landlord must have the right to take back the property after the tenant's legal interest ends; and (5), usually, a contract between the parties must have been made.

■ **Creating the relationship**   The rights and duties of the landlord and tenant are established by their contract.

YOUR RIGHTS AND DUTIES AS LANDLORD OR TENANT

■ The rights and duties of landlord and tenant are established by the terms of their contract, usually a lease.

■ Many states require that the lease be in writing, but others accept an oral agreement. The lease should contain the names of the landlord and tenant, a description of the property, the date the lease takes effect, and the length of time the lease is to cover. If the starting date is not stated, the date that the lease is signed is often used instead.

■ A person whose name is not mentioned in the lease cannot be bound by it—even if he has signed the lease.

■ If a tenant has a written lease that has not been signed by the landlord and the tenant is allowed to move in, the lease will be upheld. Most leases that extend over three years must be recorded in the local county or risk being considered void.

■ A tenant has the right of entrance and exit and the right to use steps, stairways, porches, and halls when they give access to the property.

■ A landlord is not obligated to furnish services of any kind to a tenant, except those mandated by law or the terms of the lease. Under a tenant's warranty of habitability, for example, a landlord is obligated to provide hot and cold running water, a certain amount of heat, and adequate plumbing and lighting. In addition, the building must not be in violation of local building and sanitary codes.

■ If the landlord fails to maintain this standard, the tenant may sue him for money damages or get a court to order him to restore the living quarters to habitable conditions.

■ Most leases allow a landlord to enter the premises to maintain and repair the property, in cases of emergency, such as fire, and in order to comply with health department or police regulations. Of course, the landlord may also enter with the consent of the tenant.

■ If the landlord wrongfully enters the tenant's premises, it is considered a trespass and the tenant can sue.

■ A landlord can sue his tenant for causing permanent property damage. A tenant is not usually liable for fire, unless caused by his negligence.

■ A landlord may recover his property from a tenant by eviction proceedings. Grounds for eviction include breaching the terms of a lease, nonpayment of rent, and remaining on the premises after the lease has expired. Laws permitting eviction are interpreted in favor of the tenant.

■ A tenant can defend himself with proof of his lease, an extension or renewal of his lease, a new agreement, or a timely payment of rent due. Under some laws, a tenant will not be evicted if the tenant pays the court while eviction proceedings are pending.

Express contract   The express contract that forms the landlord-tenant relationship is called a *lease.* No particular words are necessary in the lease to create the relationship. Use of the words "lease," "landlord," and "tenant" shows an intent to form the relationship, but it does not fulfill all the requirements of valid lease. (See "Leases" below.)

Implied contract   The relationship may also be created by an implied agreement between the parties or by circumstances. Usually the relationship is implied when you occupy another person's land with his permission. Although occupancy alone is not sufficient to establish the relationship, it is strong evidence of it.

In some states, if you have a written agreement to lease and move onto the premises with the landlord's consent, the relationship is established even though the owner later refuses to sign the lease. Similarly, if you are permitted to enter the property and the lease later turns out to be invalid, the relationship is established. In both these circumstances the relationship arises from occupancy of the property.

The relationship may also be implied if you agree to pay rent. The amount need not be settled, as long as you occupy the land with the owner's permission and realize that rent will be demanded.

■ **Leases**   A lease is a contract for the possession of land. A *leasehold* is the tenant's legal interest in the property under the lease. The law considers it to be intangible personal property, called *chattel real.*

Types of leases   Traditionally, there are four basic types of leases: (1) *a term for years*—a lease for a definite period of time that ends automatically when the time is up; (2) *a periodic tenancy*—a lease for a recurring term, such as a month-to-month lease; (3) *a tenancy at will*—which either party can end at any time as long as the other is properly notified of the termination; and (4) *a tenancy at sufferance*—a situation in which a tenant, who originally had rightful possession of the premises, remains on the premises after his right ends, with the consent of the landlord. He can, however, be ejected anytime the landlord desires.

Today, however, statutes simply speak of express and implied leases because it is the intention of the landlord and the tenant, as specified or implied in their contract, that determines the duration of the lease.

What makes a lease   Because a lease is a contract, all the rules governing contracts must be observed. For example, there must be an offer and acceptance of the offer. There must be CONSIDERATION (the exchange of something of value), which in leases is usually the payment of rent for the use of the property, but can be something else, such as a percentage of the tenant's business.

Many states require the lease to be in writing; in some instances, it may be oral. See Chart 6. It may be prepared by either the landlord or the tenant. It must contain the names of the landlord and tenant. A person whose name is not in the lease is not a party to it and cannot be bound either as a tenant or a landlord—even if he has signed the lease.

The lease usually contains a description of the property accurate enough to show just what property is covered. Any part of the property, such as trees, minerals, or a wall, may be the subject of a lease as well as the land itself.

The date the lease goes into effect and the length of the term should be included, but these facts are not essential. If the time when the lease begins is not mentioned, the date that the lease is signed is often regarded as the starting date.

The lease must be executed (signed), delivered, and accepted according to the principles of the contract law. For example, physical transfer (delivery) of the lease to the tenant is not necessary. If the tenant moves in and acts as though he holds the lease, delivery of the lease will be presumed.

Recording a lease   Every lease that lasts longer than a stated period—often three years—usually must be recorded in the local county or district. The failure to record voids the lease, and, under certain conditions, the property will be available to another.

EXAMPLE A landlord owns a building that he has renovated as a retail store. His advertisement for the building is answered by Sawyer, the manager of a newly formed business. On June 15, Sawyer and the landlord execute a five-year lease, and the landlord accepts two months' rent in advance. The lease is to begin on July 1. Sawyer, unaware of the recording requirement, fails to record his lease. On June 17, a friend tells the landlord that the newly formed business is not properly funded and may not be able to meet the rent. On the same day, the landlord is approached by Hawkins, the owner of an established retail business, who asks to rent the building. The landlord agrees, and he and Hawkins execute a lease, also to begin on July 1. Again the landlord accepts two months' rent in advance.

Hawkins records his lease the following day. Before signing the lease, he checked the recording office to be certain that the building had not been rented previously. Between the two lessees, Hawkins is entitled to possession of the building. He rented it without knowledge of the previous lease, paid a valuable consideration of two months' rent, and recorded his lease first. Sawyer can sue the landlord only for damages resulting from breach of the first lease.

However, if Hawkins had actual notice of Sawyer's lease, Sawyer could move into the building, even though his lease was not recorded.

Between two unrecorded leases on the same property, the first lease takes precedence and the first tenant is entitled to possession. Under some statutes, an unrecorded lease is void altogether.

If the premises are rented and then sold, a lease properly recorded before the deed of sale has priority over the deed.

■ **Right of a tenant under a lease**   A lease gives the tenant a valuable right in property that is owned by someone else. This right is legally called the use and enjoyment of the premises.

Use and enjoyment of the premises   A tenant is entitled to everything for which he has contracted in the lease. A lease of land generally includes all the buildings on it, and a lease of an entire building usually includes the land under and adjacent to it that is necessary for its use and enjoyment.

The outside walls are usually considered part of the whole structure. Thus, when a portion of a building bounded by an outside wall is leased, then that part of the wall is included. A roof, however, is ordinarily included as part of a lease on a whole structure. A common roof over a build-

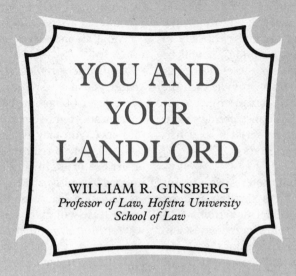

YOU AND YOUR LANDLORD

WILLIAM R. GINSBERG
*Professor of Law, Hofstra University
School of Law*

The use of a summer cottage, a house, or an apartment owned by someone else involves what has been referred to as the second most passionate relationship a person can have—that which exists between a landlord and his tenant. Centuries ago the obligations of a tenant included bearing arms to fight and perhaps to die for his landlord, a practice that fortunately has been abandoned.

A *landlord* is an owner of real estate who for a price (rent) permits another person (a tenant) to occupy his property (the premises) for a period of time (the term). A *tenant* is a person who occupies the real estate owned by someone else in exchange for the payment of rent.

The rental of different types of property—industrial, commercial, agricultural, or residential—involves different kinds of owner-tenant relationships. All have some elements in common, but this article will concentrate on the relationship between the owner and the tenant of residential property. A few communities have laws that limit the rent an owner may charge or regulate the owner-tenant relationship in some other way. Because they vary from locality to locality and are the exception rather than the rule, such laws are beyond the scope of this discussion.

Signing a lease

When occupancy is for a short term, as in a hotel, a motel, or a rooming house, it is not customary to have a written agreement. A rental, or *rate,* is agreed upon orally, and major problems rarely develop. A longer term relationship, however, presents a greater risk. Oral agreements that exist only in the minds of the owner and tenant may be remembered differently. It is desirable for the owner and tenant to have a lease, which sets forth their rights and obligations. In most states, an agreement to rent real estate for more than one year is void if it is not in writing. In some states, the period is three years.

A lease must contain certain basic information, including the name and address of the owner and the tenant, a description of the property being rented, the amount of the rent, and the length of time the tenant will occupy the property. It will also contain other information: when the rent is to be paid; what furniture or equipment, if any, is included; the amount, if any, of a security deposit; whether or not the tenant can sublease; and who pays for such utilities as electricity, gas, or oil.

The rent When you rent property, you are buying the right to occupy space from an owner who is selling that right. The price, or rent, will depend on many factors: the size, age, and location of the property; its condition; whether it is rented with or without furniture; and, of course, the bargaining position of the parties. Are there similar premises available so that you have a wide choice, or is space scarce? The time of year may affect the rent—a cottage near a beach may go for a premium price in the summer and be a bargain in the winter. A tenant is entitled to a house or apartment that is clean and in good condition. An apartment is quite often freshly painted for a new tenant. An owner may rent for less if the tenant is willing to do the painting or make the repairs. If the rent includes such utilities as gas and electricity (a practice that is becoming less common), it will be higher than if the tenant pays for these charges. A long-term lease of a house may provide that the tenant will pay the real estate taxes or keep the property insured and pay the insurance premiums. In this situation, the rent should be set at a level that takes these payments into consideration.

The term   It is usually in your interest as a tenant to have a residential lease for a three-year term, assuming there is a right to sublet or terminate. A long-term lease protects you from rent increases during the term (unless the lease provides for them), and you are spared the expense and inconvenience of perhaps having to find a new home at the end of one or two years. The owner will usually like the idea of a steady tenancy without the loss of income and additional expense that tenant turnover brings. However, he may want the opportunity to negotiate a higher rent or select a new tenant—opportunities that usually arise only when a lease expires. It is unusual to have an apartment lease run for more than three years. In a period of rising costs, owners want their rental income to keep pace with inflation.

Long-term leases usually have escalation clauses allowing for periodic rent increases. These leases often provide that the tenant is to pay a share of increases in major expenses, such as real estate tax. In a long-term lease of a house, the tenant is often responsible for repairs. This is less common in short-term leases, such as those for a beach house or a ski lodge, because it would be unreasonable to expect a tenant to spend substantial sums on a house he will leave in a few months or even a year.

Provisions for renewing the lease   If you expect to remain in an area for a long time and have found a desirable apartment or house, you may want a long-term lease or the right to renew a short-term lease for a second term. In such a situation, the owner often wants an increase in rent when the lease is renewed, for he will worry about being "locked in" while the costs of ownership continue to rise. Arrangements can be made to satisfy both your desire for stability and the owner's desire for increased income. The rent can be tied to the cost-of-living index published by the U.S. Bureau of Labor Statistics, or you may agree to a specified percentage increase if you decide to

exercise your right to renew the lease. A provision for renewal at a rental "to be agreed upon" is no agreement at all and serves no purpose in a lease.

Provisions for moving out early   On the other hand, you may be reluctant to assume a two- or three-year lease obligation because you suspect that you may want to move out before the lease expires. For instance, you may be expecting that your employer will ask you to relocate. Or you may be anticipating marriage or a growing family, which will make the rented premises inadequate. In such a situation, a termination clause or the right to sublet or assign your lease will give you the necessary protection.

Termination   If you expect to have to move from the rented premises before the term is over, you should try to have a termination provision put into the lease. Typically, such a clause requires the tenant to give written notice of his desire to vacate two or three months before he wishes to have the lease terminated. In addition, the owner will probably require an extra charge (one or two months' rent) to cover the expenses connected with rerenting and the risk that the premises may be vacant before a new tenant can be found. If there are many vacancies in the area, an owner will be reluctant to have a termination clause because he may end up without a tenant. The length of notice the owner requires and the amount of the surcharge depend on the length of the lease, how long it has left to run (a termination clause may provide that it cannot be exercised for a specified period of time at the start of the lease), and local rental market conditions.

Sublet and assignment   One of the most important safety valves that you can have is the right to sublet or assign your lease to someone else if you no longer wish to occupy the property yourself. An assignment means that you may turn over the entire premises to another person (the *assignee)*, who takes over your lease for the remainder of the term.

A sublet occurs when you, as the tenant, rent out part of the premises (for example, one or two rooms in a larger house) to another person, who is called a *sublessee.* It also occurs when you rent out the entire premises for part of the remaining term of your lease. In a sublet arrangement, you become a landlord with respect to the sublessee but remain a tenant under your lease and are still responsible for carrying out your obligations as spelled out in it.

Many form leases prohibit assigning or subletting without the owner's consent. If you want the right to assign or sublet, you should demand the elimination of the clause prohibiting these activities. Without a right to terminate, assign, or sublet, you could be forced to continue to pay rent even though you no longer occupy the house or apartment.

An owner may be reluctant to give you the right to assign or sublet because that puts the choice of the assignee or sublessee entirely in your hands. It is therefore fairly common to provide that the assignment or sublease will require the owner's consent and that the consent "will not be unreasonably withheld." This raises the question of what is unreasonable. In most instances, the owner's concern should be limited to the ability of the assignee or sublessee to pay the rent, the number of people who will occupy the rented property, and the use to which the property will be put. If the proposed assignee or sublessee intends to use the rented premises in a manner similar to your use of them and is at least as financially responsible as you are, the owner must consent. The selection of an assignee or sublessee who is able to pay the rent is important to you because you will remain responsible to the owner if the assignee or sublessee does not pay the rent or if he damages the premises. The owner can, of course, release you from this obligation but may be reluctant to do so.

Some owners will prefer to enter into a new lease with the proposed assignee or sublessee, thus creating a new landlord-tenant relationship and releasing the old tenant from any responsibility. This will occur only when the owner is satisfied that the new tenant is desirable. The prospective assignee may want a longer term than that remaining on the existing lease, and he may be willing to pay a higher rent to obtain it. It will then be to the owner's advantage to enter into a new lease; otherwise an assignee is obligated to pay the owner only the rent agreed to in the existing lease for the remainder of the lease term.

Security deposit   Leases generally provide that the tenant will deposit a sum of money with the owner (usually one month's rent) and that the owner will hold this money during the term of the lease. This is called a security deposit. If you have paid the rent, have not damaged the premises, and have otherwise performed your obligations, the deposit should be returned by the owner when you move out. The money continues to belong to you while it is held by the owner and should be deposited in a separate account, apart from funds belonging to the owner. In many states, the owner must inform his tenants of the

name and branch of the bank in which their deposits are held and the name of the account. Many states also require that interest on the funds be paid to the tenant. As with other aspects of the landlord-tenant relationship, you should check the laws in your state and community on this subject.

The amount of the deposit required by the owner may be higher if the premises are rented furnished and the possibility of damage is greater. Security may also reflect the financial ability of the prospective tenant; if a tenant does not have steady employment or other dependable sources of income with which to pay the rent, the owner may want more security. (If a prospective tenant appears to have insufficient income to pay the rent, the owner may also require that some other person, such as a parent or friend, guarantee the tenant's obligation to pay.) If a landlord asks you for additional security, you should request that it be returned before the end of the lease—perhaps by being applied to rent due. For instance, if he requires a security deposit equal to three months' rent on a lease with a three-year term, you might ask that the lease provide for one-third of the deposit to be applied in payment of the first month's rent for the second year of the term, one-third to be applied in payment for the first month's rent for the third year of the term, and the balance to be returned at the end of the term.

Your security deposit should be returned to you at the end of the term or, if you renew the lease, when you finally vacate the premises, provided you paid the rent and did not cause substantial damage to the premises. Ordinary wear and tear, scratched paint, or holes from picture hooks are not sufficient reasons for an owner to refuse to return the security deposit. If you fail to pay rent and are evicted or if you leave before the lease expired, the owner has the right to keep as much of the security deposit as is necessary to compensate him for the loss of income and cost of rerenting the property.

Your rights and obligations as a tenant

A tenant may use rented property essentially as if he owned it, subject only to the terms of the lease. Activities that would be lawful in property owned by the occupant would also be lawful in property rented by the occupant, but an owner has the right to alter or destroy the structure and a tenant usually does not. If you want to make structural changes, install equipment, or attach large cabinets to the walls, you should first obtain the owner's consent in writing. Note, too, that such improvements become part of the real estate and must be left when you move out unless the owner has consented to their removal. Minor additions, such as curtain rods or a few shelves, will cause little harm, can easily be removed, and should not require written consent. You are responsible for damage to the rented property, including equipment, such as a refrigerator or stove, but you are not responsible for ordinary wear as a result of reasonable use.

Promptly notify your landlord of any problems, such as broken windows, a leaking pipe or roof, or cracking plaster, so that he can make repairs and avoid further damage.

Your landlord has no right to enter rented premises without your permission except in emergencies or to make required repairs. Owners usually retain keys for rented apartments and in some localities are required to do so. This enables an owner to enter in the tenant's absence if a pipe breaks, a sink overflows, or a fire starts. Except in such circumstances, however, the owner must not interfere with your privacy, and you may use the property in any manner not prohibited by law or by the lease.

The tenant, his family, and his guests may make reasonable use of common areas in apartment buildings, such as halls, elevators, lobbies, and stairs. They may not, however, interfere with the use of these areas by other tenants. Fire laws usually prohibit the use of hallways for storing bicycles, baby carriages, or other household items. Many apartment buildings provide storage rooms for such purposes.

Maintenance and repairs

When the roof leaks or the furnace breaks down, who is responsible for repairs? Unfortunately, the answer is not an easy one. It depends on the nature of the rented premises (apartment or single-family house), the provisions of the lease, and the laws of the state and community in which the property is located.

Historically, tenants were responsible for all repairs and maintenance. The assumption was that a tenant should know the condition of the property he was renting, and if he made a mistake, it was his misfortune. However, this was at a time when most tenancies concerned the occupancy and use of farms and were for long terms. In recent years, with increasing urbanization and modern residential leasing arrangements, responsiblity for repairs and maintenance has shifted by law and custom to the owner.

For apartment rentals Today tenancies are usually for short periods. Tenants often lack the skill necessary to make major repairs and cannot reasonably be expected to pay for having them made. With dwelling units stacked one on top of the other, the failure or inability of one resident to make a repair may cause damage to other apartments. Moreover, most apartment houses have heating and water systems and elevators that serve the entire building. It would be unfair and impractical to expect tenants to be responsible for such equipment. Owners of apartment houses are therefore responsible for the maintenance of the building structure, mechanical systems, and common areas.

Difficult questions arise, however, concerning repairs within apartments. If the lease makes no provision for repairs, local law or custom will apply. The owner will usually be responsible for major repairs and replacement of equipment. Tenants will often be expected to take care of minor problems, such as leaky faucets and other routine maintenance work.

Many large communities have laws that set standards for the condition of all dwellings, including apartment buildings. Building or health codes usually require the owner to provide heat and hot and cold water for each apartment and to maintain the building in a safe condition. Garbage left uncollected in a building may be a violation of city, health, or sanitation laws. Fire laws may limit the kinds of material that may be stored in the basement of a building or require that such combustible items as books and clothing be stored in fire-resistant containers. These laws apply to both owners and tenants. Under some circumstances, serious violations of these laws may be grounds for eviction.

For house rentals Tenants of houses have greater responsibilites than do apartment dwellers. Unless the lease provides otherwise, house tenants are usually required to repair and maintain the building and surrounding grounds. When a house lease is entered into, the parties should spell out in detail their mutual understanding concerning repairs. Ordinarily, the owner will be responsible for major structural work and for the replacement of equipment, such as stoves, refrigerators, or pumps, that cannot be repaired. The tenant must usually make minor repairs to the house and its equipment. This could include fixing the furnace or repairing a leak. It is obvious that even in a carefully written lease, words such as "major" or "minor" leave room for argument. While short-term rental rarely requires a tenant to make substantial repairs, he will remain responsible for any damage he causes and should notify the owner promptly when repairs are needed.

The tenant of a house is usually responsible for shoveling snow from the sidewalk and mowing the lawn. He is also responsible for fuel and utilities unless the lease provides to the contrary.

The owner and tenant should agree on who is responsible for losses resulting from fire, flood, or storm, so that the necessary insurance can be obtained. Except for very long term leases, this will usually be the owner's responsibility.

Personal injury   If you, a member of your family, or a guest is injured in your rented house or apartment because of a hidden defect in the structure, which the owner knew about, the owner will be responsible for the damages. In many states, this will be true even if the owner was not aware of the defect. The law assumes that the owner is in a better position than the tenant to know of hidden dangers or should find out about them. If, however, you know of a dangerous condition and do not inform the owner or repair it yourself, you also will be responsible for any resulting injury.

The owner of an apartment house must keep common areas in a safe and usable condition. If he does not, and a tenant, a member of a tenant's family, or a guest is injured as a result, the owner will be responsible. The tenant of a house is reponsible for injuries suffered because of his failure to make repairs or shovel snow from the walk.

Resolving differences

The tenant and landlord are often pictured in controversy. Typically, the landlord plays the role of the villain, attempting to evict an aged and infirm tenant. Such stereotypes tend to obscure the nature of most landlord-tenant relationships, which usually do not end up in court. Ruptures occur only when one party or the other is unable or unwilling to meet agreed-upon responsibilities.

What are the owner's reasonable expectations? The owner expects the tenant to pay the rent when due, to avoid causing physical damage to the house or apartment, and not to disturb other tenants.

A tenant expects the rented premises to be in good condition at the beginning of the term, except for any defective conditions that he has seen and is willing to accept. In an apartment house, the tenant expects heat, hot water, and other services, such as keeping the common hallways clean and the structure in good repair. In addition, a tenant wants a reasonable degree of peace and privacy. This includes not only freedom from unnecessary intrusions by the owner but also from disturbances by other tenants, such as noisy parties late at night or dogs that bark continually. The tenant will want the owner's cooperation in stopping such nuisances. The owner will want the tenant's cooperation in avoiding them.

Notification   Whenever a problem exists between an owner and a tenant, the first course of action should be for one party to notify the other. If the rent is unpaid, the owner should contact the tenant before beginning an eviction proceeding. Such a notification is often required by law. Similarly, if the tenant has a problem the owner should be notified before legal proceedings are begun. A telephone call, followed if necessary by a letter, is all that is required to solve most landlord-tenant problems. It is polite and inexpensive and maintains a reasonably businesslike relationship Legal action should not be threatened or started unless it is clear that other efforts have failed. A tenant's rent check may have been lost in the mail. An owner may be unaware that a repair is needed. To err is human, even for landlords and tenants.

Sometimes a landlord or tenant will fail to fulfill his obligations even after notification and friendly prodding. In such cases, both the landlord and the tenant have legal remedies at their disposal.

The tenant's remedies   Although the tenant's obligations do not vary greatly in most communities, there is considerable variation in the obligations of owners in different states and localities. Some communities, particularly large cities, have laws and describe an owner's duties in considerable detail. These can range from the temperatures that must be maintained in the building at different times of the day to the wattage of the light bulbs that must be used in the hallways. Such responsibilities can be found in health codes, building maintenance codes, and laws concerning fire safety and sanitation. If you, as a tenant, believe that such a law is being violated and the owner ignores your request to correct the violation, the usual remedy is to complain to the government agency in charge of enforcing the law—for example, the health department, the fire department, or the building department. The agency should send an inspector in response to your complaint, and if he confirms that the condition exists, the agency will issue a summons or file a *violation* against the building. The owner then has a period of time in which to correct the condition. If he fails to do so, he may be fined. In a few areas, if the violation is serious, the city may have the necessary work done and charge the owner for the cost.

A complaint to a government agency does not cost you anything and will, in some circumstances, achieve the desired result. It is, however, often a slow procedure and sometimes ineffective. In most circumstances, even if a local law has been violated, you must continue to pay rent in the amount agreed upon or face eviction.

The remedy for lack of services and repairs is usually to sue the owner for damages, but this is slow and expensive. A few communities permit the tenant to have necessary work done (or to purchase needed fuel) and deduct the cost from the rent. In all states, if conditions deteriorate to the point where the premises are unlivable or unsafe (including unsafe to health because of rodents, vermin, or lack of heat), the tenant may move out and stop paying rent. Such a situation is referred to as *constructive eviction*. But simply moving out may be difficult in areas where rental housing is scarce.

Courts and legislatures in several states have required owners to provide residential rental property that is reasonably safe and fit to live in. This requirement is called an *implied warranty of habitability*. If the owner fails to maintain the property in proper condition, the tenant may raise this as a defense in a lawsuit against him for nonpayment of rent. The tenant need not move out in order to claim the defense. The court may then order the owner to do the necessary repairs or other work and may reduce the rent until the work is done.

Although the implied warranty of habitability is the current trend, it has not been adopted in many states. In these states, a tenant should obtain a provision in the lease stating that the premises are suitable for residential use, that they comply with local building and health codes, and that they will be maintained in such condition during the term of the lease. In the absence of this type of agreement in states without an implied warranty of habitability, the tenant must continue to pay the agreed-on rent regardless of the condition of the premises.

The landlord's remedies There are two major remedies that a landlord may seek when a tenant does not fulfill his obligations: eviction and payment of rent. The owner's main objective is to obtain his rent on time. If it is not being paid, however, or if the term of the lease has expired and the nonpaying tenant fails to move out, the owner will want to remove him so that a new tenant can be found. The specific procedures involved in a court proceeding differ from one locality to another, but everywhere the tenant must be served with a summons and given written notice. Legal proceedings concerning the occupancy of real estate are specialized. They usually take less time than other legal proceedings because the longer the tenant remains without paying rent the greater the benefit to the tenant and the greater the loss of revenue to the owner.

Courts are reluctant to evict tenants for minor matters, but the remedy may be granted for the violation of major lease provisions or for a use of the premises that is against the law.

Ending the relationship

Most owner-tenant relationships end peacefully. The term of the lease expires and the tenant leaves. If the premises being leased are in demand, it is quite possible that another tenant has signed a lease and is waiting to move in. Therefore, it is polite as well as legally desirable for the tenant to let the owner know as soon as possible if his departure is going to be delayed. If no agreement has been reached, the owner has two choices when the tenant remains after the expiration of the lease. He can bring an eviction proceeding or permit the tenant to remain on a week-to-week or month-to-month basis, depending on their prior arrangement and local custom or law. A tenant who stays after the lease expires is called a *holdover*. If the owner allows the holdover to remain, the rent and other conditions of occupancy continue as they were under the expired lease.

In order to avoid a misunderstanding, the owner should notify the tenant before the lease expires. He may also indicate the basis on which he is willing to renew the lease. But in the absence of a local law to the contrary, the owner is under no obligation to renew. The tenant is responsible for moving out, taking his belongings, and leaving the premises in good condition. The owner should then return the security deposit with interest, if required by law. Under most circumstances, the tenant's rights end on the final day of the lease term, whether or not the owner has sent a notice.

ing occupied by a landlord and tenants, or by different tenants, remains in the landlord's control.

A lease of a house or building gives the tenant the right of entrance and exit and the right to use steps, stairways, porches, walks, and halls when they give access to the property. Tenants who lease space in a building do not obtain implied EASEMENTS (rights) or parking privileges in an adjacent area simply because it is convenient. On the other hand, space needed for parking a motor vehicle may have been a condition of the lease. An easement for parking may be implied, as when a tenant rents commercial space in a drive-in shopping center.

A landlord is not obligated to furnish services of any kind to a tenant, except those mandated by statute or by provision in the lease. In buildings occupied by several tenants, a landlord usually must light and maintain well-traveled areas, such as halls and stairways.

Warranty of habitability Integral to the use and enjoyment of the premises is the tenant's right to have the premises he has leased for residential use in habitable (livable) condition during the term of his lease. This is known as the *warranty of habitability*. Hot and cold running water, heat when the temperature is below that set by law, adequate plumbing and lighting are basic services that anyone renting an apartment would have reason to expect from the landlord-tenant relationship.

Such a warranty means that the premises are free from violations of local building and sanitary codes, so that it is a fit place to live. Most states, either by statute or court decision, treat this warranty as being implied by a landlord when he rents the apartment for residential use. If, after a tenant moves in, the landlord fails to maintain and repair an apartment so that it becomes uninhabitable during the lease, the tenant may (1) bring a lawsuit against the landlord for breaching his lease to recover money DAMAGES or to obtain an injunction (a court order) to restore the apartment to a habitable condition or (2) terminate the lease and his duty to pay rent, if the conditions are so intolerable as to be considered a constructive (implied) EVICTION of the tenant.

Entry by landlord A landlord has no right to enter the premises if the tenant does not consent or the lease does not dictate it. Most leases provide that a landlord may enter the premises if necessary to maintain and repair the property in keeping with the warranty of habitability or in case of an emergency, such as a fire. The tenant's right to possession is presumed to be exclusive.

The landlord may, of course, enter with the consent of the tenant. The landlord usually has the right to show the leased property to prospective purchasers at reasonable times. He may also be allowed in to comply with health department or police regulations.

A wrongful invasion of the tenant's right of possession by the landlord, including unauthorized entry, is a TRESPASS. Ordinarily, the landlord has no right to interfere with the means of entering or exiting, such as a driveway that existed when the lease was signed. Nor can the landlord hinder the tenant's use of electricity or water.

A tenant, under his right to sue the landlord for wrongful interference, has a choice of remedies: he can bring suit to prohibit illegal interference with his possession, to recover damages, or to recover possession if he has been evicted.

■ **Rights of landlord under lease** Rented property belongs to the landlord even though he has given up his right of present enjoyment. When a lease is made for a specific period of time, the only right remaining to the landlord is called the *right of reversion*—that is, the right to the enjoyment of the property after the lease has expired.

Transfer of landlord's right in the property The landlord may transfer his right to the property to someone else, including the tenant. Suppose that during the term of your lease, you purchase the rented property from your landlord. The sale means a MERGER of your leasehold right and the landlord's reversion right into one right in the property now owned by you. In another instance, suppose the landlord sells the property you rent to someone else. You cannot prevent him from selling or resist a change of landlords unless you have a lease prohibiting a sale. The sale ordinarily transfers the landlord's interest in your unexpired lease, and you then become the buyer's tenant.

The purchaser is bound by the terms of the lease if he had actual NOTICE of it, even if the lease is unrecorded. If he does not have notice of the lease and it is unrecorded, then he is not obligated by it. If the tenant is occupying the property, however, the purchaser is bound by the lease, even if he has no knowledge of it.

Generally, the rights and liabilities existing between the tenant and purchaser are the same as those between the tenant and his former landlord, once the tenant is notified of the transfer. Thus a purchaser is bound by previous agreements made by the former owner, such as a waiver of a restriction against subletting, or by interpretations of the lease by the former owner and tenant. A purchaser is not bound, however, by an oral agreement about a minor issue made by the former owner, by a personal arrangement between the former owner and tenant, or by an agreement about personal property. When a landlord sells leased property and his deed provides that possession goes to the purchaser on the day the existing lease expires, he is not responsible to the buyer if the tenant wrongfully remains in the place after the expiration date.

Injury to the landlord's right The landlord usually can sue for an injury to his right of reversion—that is, he can sue the tenant for damages to his future interest in the property. The suit can be brought while a tenant is in possession. Such injuries include destroying a fence; removing a wall between two rooms; flooding the land; diverting or obstructing a natural watercourse; removing timber, stone, gravel, or valuable topsoil; and similar acts.

When property is leased, there is an implied agreement that the tenant will use it without injuring it. A tenant who wrongfully causes a permanent injury to the premises is liable to his landlord.

EXAMPLE Abe rents a building on the highway from Jack. He tells Jack, who so stipulates in the lease, that the building will house an ice cream parlor. After moving in, Abe instead sets up a storage area for flammable materials. Abe does this at his own risk. If the building is destroyed through Abe's unlawful use, he is liable to Jack—even if Abe was not negligent.

A tenant must care for the leased premises in the same way that a prudent person would use his own property. Thus a tenant is not liable for ordinary wear and tear.

Unless he has agreed to assume liability, a tenant is not liable when the property is injured by fire. On the the other hand, he is liable for a fire caused by his NEGLIGENCE, and he may also be responsible for one caused by the mistakes of his servants or employees. See RESPONDEAT SUPERIOR.

■ **Termination of lease** A lease generally terminates at the end of the term fixed by the lease. Sometimes the term may depend on a particular event stated in the lease, such as the dissolution of a partnership or the failure to obtain a liquor license. A lease may also be terminated before it expires if both parties agree. A tenant may be entitled to end a lease before the term is up if the landlord has breached his implied warranty of habitability (discussed above).

Death of landlord or tenant As a general rule, a lease is not ended when either the landlord or tenant dies. This rule may be altered by statute, such as one that limits long-term leases to a period of 12 months upon the death of the tenant. The lease may provide for its own termination if either party dies.

■ **Reentry and possession by landlord** A landlord may reenter and take possesson without legal proceedings when he can do so without force—for example, on the date the lease expires. Similarly, the landlord may reenter and take possession when the tenant has surrendered the lease or abandoned the premises.

Ordinarily, the landlord may not reenter if the tenant has breached a provision of the lease. Exceptions are when the lease specifies that the landlord gains the right of reentry or that the tenant forfeits his interest when the tenant commits a breach. Generally, the landlord may reenter for nonpayment of rent, provided the lease gives him the right and he has properly demanded the money.

A landlord who is entitled to repossession of the leased premises may sue for eviction, a writ of entry, or for trespass. A landlord usually cannot start a repossession suit unless he first gives the tenant a notice to quit or a demand for possession. On recovering possession, the landlord may be eligible for damages—usually the fair and reasonable value of the premises during the time possession was wrongfully withheld.

■ **Eviction proceedings** A landlord may recover his property from a delinquent tenant under statutes permitting SUMMARY (short and simple) proceedings, popularly known as eviction proceedings. (The proceedings may also be called ejectment or summary ejectment, justice ejectment, dispossessory warrant proceedings, summary process, unlawful detainer, forcible detainer or detention, forcible entry and detainer, or landlord-and-tenant proceedings.) These statutes are designed to bring about recovery simply, quickly, and inexpensively and to prevent landlords from taking the law into their own hands by throwing out tenants by violence. The statutes are interpreted in favor of the tenant.

Generally, a relationship of landlord and tenant must exist between the parties to sustain an eviction proceeding. It cannot be used when the relationship is that of donor and donee, mortgagor and mortgagee, or seller and buyer. This rule holds true even though a landlord-tenant relationship formerly existed between them.

The proceeding is purely to recover possession. The primary issues are whether the relationship of landlord and tenant exists and whether the tenant is or is not to be dispossessed. Other issues, such as money damages to the tenant from a breach of lease, may not be decided during the proceeding. Nor may the landlord ordinarily be awarded rent or money damages for the leased premises, although some statutes do make provision for their recovery in the eviction proceeding.

Grounds The statutes generally authorize eviction proceedings to oust a tenant who remains after his lease expires. A landlord can also evict if the tenant has breached the terms of the lease. Nonpayment of rent, failure to pay taxes when required by the lease, and use of the premises for an unlawful purpose are grounds for summary dispossession.

Conditions to be met To sue for eviction, the landlord must comply with all conditions precedent (the steps that must precede bringing the proceedings). Some statutes, for example, specifically require as a condition precedent a demand for the rent or a written notice to the tenant to pay the rent or face eviction. The demand or notice must conform to statutory requirements, such as stating the amount of rent due or the amount demanded. The amount of the demand can include interest.

Defense against eviction Because eviction involves only the present right to possession, the defenses to it are very limited—as a rule, only those that prove rightful occupancy are permitted.

Any agreement with a landlord authorizing the tenant to keep possession is a good defense against eviction. The tenant may show, for example, that he is occupying the premises under a valid and unexpired lease, under an extension or renewal of the original lease, or under a new agreement.

A timely payment is a good defense to an eviction for nonpayment of rent. An offer to pay after the due date, however, is not the equivalent to payment and is no defense. Under some statutes, if the tenant pays the court while the proceedings are pending, he will not be evicted. An offer to pay is no defense when made after the lease has expired, particularly if the proceeding is on the ground of holding over (occupying the premises after the lease has expired) rather than for nonpayment of rent.

landmark 1 A rock, stake, or other marker set up to fix the boundary lines between adjoining plots of land. 2 A historical site protected by law from radical change or destruction. Each of the states and more than 500 municipalities have enacted landmark laws intended to preserve park sites, buildings, and other monuments that have special architectural, cultural, or historical significance. Congress has also passed the National Historic Preservation Act, along with other measures to preserve the history and culture of America. Landmark laws have been upheld by the Supreme Court.

EXAMPLE The Penn Central Transportation Company leased its Grand Central Terminal in New York City to a tenant who planned to construct a 20-story office tower over the station. Under its landmarks law, the city designated the terminal as a historic landmark and prohibited the office building from being erected. Penn Central appealed, complaining that the law was unconstitutional because it caused the company's property to be taken from it without just compensation. The Supreme Court disagreed with Penn Central. It found the landmark law constitutional and upheld the ban on construction of the tower.

Landmark laws are considered akin to ZONING laws as a valid exercise of a government's POLICE POWER to promote the general welfare of the public. Such laws usually restrict the uses to which these structures can be put. Owners of designated properties have claimed, however, that they have been deprived of their properties by the government without just compensation, a violation of the EMINENT DOMAIN power of both federal and state governments granted by the U.S. Constitution. Courts have upheld landmark laws because they do not necessarily amount to a "taking" that must be compensated by the government as long as they serve a substantial public purpose that does not significantly interfere with the present or planned uses of the structures by their owners.

Landrum-Griffin Act A federal law designed to curb abuses in labor-management relations. It requires full reporting and public disclosure of internal union activities and financial operations. It also provides criminal penalties for failing to file these reports or for producing false ones. See LABOR RELATIONS.

lapse In law, the failure to perform some required act within a specified time that results in the termination of a right. For example, in INSURANCE law a lapsed policy is one on which the premiums have not been paid. In the law of WILLS, a legacy lapses when the person to whom the property is left dies before the one who made the will.

larceny Taking and carrying away a person's personal property without his consent, by another who is not entitled to it and who intends to deprive the owner of it permanently. Larceny is regarded as a crime against the right of possession.

ROBBERY is a form of larceny that involves violence or intimidation against the victim. Thus, robbery is a forcible larceny from the victim. An easy way to distinguish between the two is to remember that larceny is an offense against possession while robbery is against the person. Because robbery includes larceny, once robbery is established no additional proof is required to prove larceny.

In some states, larceny also includes the crimes of EMBEZZLEMENT and obtaining property by FALSE PRETENSES.

■ **Property that qualifies** To be the subject of larceny, the item taken must be personal property (not real estate, or land) of some worth, but it need not have any special or market value or be valuable to anyone except the owner. The amount of value relates only to the penalty that can be imposed for taking it.

Specific property All forms of personal property, including domestic and foreign coins and paper money, can be the subject of larceny. Water and heating gas located in mains and service pipes that supply customers belong to the municipality or corporation owning the pipes. A person who steals gas or water from a service pipe is guilty of larceny. Taking electricity is also larcenous in some states.

Because it is not considered property, the body of a dead person cannot be the subject of larceny. See DEAD BODY. But the coffin, the shroud, the clothing or jewelry on the body, or the wreaths on the grave can be, because they are the property of the person who supplied them.

Taking domestic animals that are valuable for work purposes or for food, such as horses, cattle, hogs, and barnyard fowl, has always been an act of larceny. Stealing a dog, cat, or other inedible domestic animal is larceny in most places.

Things considered part of the land, such as minerals in the soil, a house, or such structural parts of a building as doors, piping, or a copper roof become the subject of larceny when they are severed from the real estate by the person taking them. Similarly, so do things growing out of the soil, such as trees and unharvested crops, when they are detached from the ground.

Other items of personal property that can be the subject of larceny include stock certificates, bills of lading, railroad tickets, postage stamps, intoxicating liquors, and motor vehicles or accessories.

■ **Elements of the crime** Six elements usually must be proved to establish that larceny has been committed.

Taking The item must be taken out of the owner's possession into that of the thief. If possession and control are not complete and absolute, the act is only an attempt.

> EXAMPLE A pen on display at a counter in a stationery store is attached by a cord for safekeeping. Harold, the would-be thief, tries to steal the pen but fails to break the cord. There is no taking, even though the pen is in Harold's grasp when he is detected and stopped. Similarly, if Harold lifts a watch from a man's pocket, the act does not amount to a taking unless the watch chain that attaches it to the victim is broken.

Once possession becomes absolute, the length of time the thief has control is unimportant. The taking is complete, even if the thief immediately abandons or returns the item or never even takes it from the owner's presence or premises.

Although the taking must be without the owner's consent, its precise manner is not important. It may even be accomplished by using an innocent agent. A person who induces a child to remove an article from a strange house, for example, is as guilty as if he had taken it himself.

Unless a statute provides otherwise, the taking is of equal seriousness whether committed in the daytime or at night. Similarly, the place from which the property is stolen is not an element of the offense.

Asportation Asportation means carrying goods away. It is the second element of larceny. The act is complete whether or not the goods are removed from the building in which they are kept. The thief's act of putting an article into his pocket is an asportation even though he does not leave the owner's premises. So is moving an article from its original position with a wrongful intent, as when a person puts his hand in a drawer stuffed with cash, grasps the money, and changes its position, even if the person is seized before he removes any money from the drawer.

Ownership The property taken and carried away must be owned by another person. It is not larceny if you take your own property back from another person who has no legal right to it. As an element of larceny, ownership and possession are considered synonymous. Anyone who has a right to possess an article is considered the owner of it—at least as far as the thief is concerned. Thus, it is no defense for a thief to say that the property belonged to someone other than the person from whom it was taken. So the thief who took your gold watch from the repair shop where you had left it has committed larceny.

Possession and custody The article need not be in the actual physical possession or custody of anyone at the time it is stolen. Articles left on a sidewalk in front of a store at dawn for the store owner to take in when he arrives can be the subject of larceny, even though no one has physical possession when they are taken. In the eyes of the law, the person last holding an article has CONSTRUCTIVE (implied) posssession until he abandons it.

Taking lost property from either the loser or the finder is considered larceny.

The fact that the person from whom the property was stolen had himself acquired it illegally is not a defense. This rule is applied, for example, to the theft of property acquired by illegal gambling or the illegal sale of intoxicating liquors.

EXAMPLE Perry had always admired Guy's well-stocked O—➤ wine cellar. One night, Perry allowed his admiration to become greed and stole every bottle in the place. During the investigation that followed Perry's arrest, it came to light that Guy was part of a ring of international wine smugglers. The wine Perry had taken had been stolen from another country and secretly slipped into the United States to avoid import duties. Perry is guilty of larceny even though he stole already-stolen goods.

Nonconsent of owner The taking must be against the owner's will or without his consent. The owner's failure to resist is not consent. For example, if the taking is so sudden that the owner does not have time to resist, consent cannot be implied.

Limited consent to use property for a special purpose does not excuse a person who takes the property to use for a different purpose.

EXAMPLE A city program provides free antitoxin to Dr. O—➤ Smith so that he can treat patients who are too poor to pay for the treatments. Dr. Smith uses some of the city's free antitoxin, however, to treat some of his paying patients. Dr. Smith is guilty of larceny.

Intent Felonious intent, or knowledge that the act is wrong, is also an essential element of larceny. Taking something from someone else merely as a practical joke, in the spirit of mischief, or by mistake is not larceny, especially when done openly in the presence of witnesses.

EXAMPLE After lunch in a restaurant, Mel inadvertently O—➤ carried away another man's hat, thinking it was his own. Although Mel took the hat, he was not guilty of larceny. If, however, Percy stole a coat that had a watch in one of the pockets, Percy would be guilty of larceny of both. This is true even though Percy did not know that the watch was inside the coat.

The intent to steal, which means to deprive the owner of his property permanently, is an indispensable part of larceny. However, the taking without permission of a horse, an automobile, a bicycle, or a boat by a person who wants to use it temporarily and then return it to its owner, is not larceny in many states but is the offense of joyriding, a less serious offense, punishable as a misdemeanor. But it is larceny when an automobile is taken with the intent to steal the engine, the radio, other parts, or the car itself.

Generally, the intent to steal must exist at the time the property is taken. If the property was originally removed with the owner's consent, and the taker later decides to keep it, the offense committed is not larceny.

EXAMPLE Farmer Kent is given lawful possession of a herd O—➤ of milk cows under a pasturing agreement. Some time after Kent takes possession of the animals, he decides to sell them and use the money to buy a new tractor. Because he had not formed the intent to steal the cows at the time he took possession of them, he has not committed larceny. However, the owner of the herd can sue Kent for the tort of conversion.

See also BAILMENT; CONVERSION.

Under a general theft statute that combines larceny with other similar offenses, such as embezzlement and false pretenses, it does not matter whether the fraudulent intent was formed before or after the offender obtained possession of the property. Thus, Farmer Kent could be prosecuted for theft under this type of law.

An intoxicated person who is incapable of forming an intent to steal is not guilty of larceny if the stolen property is recovered from him before he becomes sober, if he abandons it, or if he tries to return it when he sobers up. If, however, when sober, he forms an intent to keep the property taken, and does keep it, he has committed larceny.

■ **Degrees of seriousness** Larceny is usually divided into two grades, grand and petit, based on the value of the property taken. The value of a stolen article is its fair market value at the time and place the crime was committed. Grand larceny is usually punishable as a FELONY; petit larceny is a misdemeanor.

last-clear-chance rule

A principle in the law of TORTS (injuries to persons or property) that says a plaintiff's own NEGLIGENCE does not prevent his recovering damages when it appears that the defendant could have avoided injury to the plaintiff. This rule is an attempt by the courts to avoid the harsh rule that a plaintiff's CONTRIBUTORY NEGLIGENCE bars his recovery.

EXAMPLE Late one night, while walking along a railroad O—➤ track in the dark, a woman slipped and caught her foot under a rail. Just when she realized she could not free herself she noticed the lights of an approaching train. Raising herself to one knee, she took out her handkerchief and began to signal the engineer to halt the train. Evidence showed that the train's headlight illuminated the track for a distance of 2,000 feet—a light bright enough to enable anyone riding in the engine to see a rabbit cross the tracks 1,500 feet ahead. Evidence also showed that the engineer blew the train whistle a few times when the train was approximately 1,500 feet from the woman, thus indicating that he saw her. The woman managed to free her foot just as the train was almost upon her, but her left arm was crushed under the wheels. She sued the railroad.

The railroad contended that the woman's contributory negligence barred her recovery. The court found that the woman was spotted far enough away for the train to have stopped before striking her. The engineer had the last clear chance to avoid injuring the woman. But since he did not stop or even slow down the train, the railroad, as his employer, was guilty of negligence under the last-clear-chance rule.

last resort Used to describe a COURT from which there is no appeal. The U.S. Supreme Court is a court of last resort.

latent Hidden or concealed. A latent defect in the TITLE to land is one that is not discoverable by a careful inspection of the title. Similarly, a latent defect in an article of merchandise is one that could not be revealed by a customary inspection or test.

lateral support See ADJOINING LANDOWNERS.

law 1 Generally, those rules by which a nation governs itself and which every citizen of the state is bound to obey. For example, the law of the United States is found in its Constitution, acts of Congress, and in its treaties, all as interpreted by its courts. 2 In a more particular sense, a statute passed by Congress or a state legislature, and approved by the President or a state governor. 3 The statutes, regulations, and case decisions that make up a particular branch of the law, such as CONTRACT law.

law date 1 Regarding foreclosure proceedings on real estate, the last day set by the court on which the mortgagee can pay off the mortgage debt, redeem the real estate, and prevent it from being sold. 2 In CONTRACT law, the day specified for paying money due under a contract.

law merchant The system of rules, customs, and usages generally recognized by merchants and traders as regulating transactions and resolving controversies. The law merchant is now found in the Uniform Commercial Code, which has been adopted in part by all the states except Louisiana. See SALES.

law of nations See INTERNATIONAL LAW.

law of the case The rule that the final JUDGMENT of the highest court of appeal is the final determination of the parties' rights.

law of the land The U.S. Constitution; general public laws equally binding on all members of the community. The law of the land has been interpreted by various tribunals and the Supreme Court to mean the guarantees of DUE PROCESS OF LAW. It includes all rules of law and equity defining human rights and duties. The law of the land provides for the protection and enforcement of these rights, so that neither the state nor any of its citizens can infringe upon them.

law report Any of numerous published volumes containing written reports of cases argued and adjudged in the courts.

law review A law school publication containing scholarly articles on legislation and case decisions.

Law School Admission Test The test used by most American law schools to determine whether an applicant has the potential needed to complete the studies leading to a law degree.

lawsuit An ACTION (proceeding) in a civil court begun by one party to compel another to do him justice. The word refers to civil, not to criminal, proceedings.

lawyer A person learned in the law, whose business is giving legal advice and who is licensed to prosecute or defend lawsuits and criminal cases in federal and state courts. The term is synonymous with attorney or counsel. See ATTORNEY AND CLIENT.

leading case A case that settles a previously unresolved question of law or overturns existing law and establishes legal principles that serve as guidelines for later decisions. For example, MIRANDA V. ARIZONA—which imposed restrictions on an interrogation of a suspect by police—is a leading case, and the principles set forth by the court are known as the Miranda rule.

leading question A question that is phrased by an attorney in a way that suggests how a witness should answer it; words put into the witness's mouth that he is to echo back. Leading questions during direct examination of a witness generally are improper and should be excluded. This rule, enforced in both criminal and civil cases, applies to someone testifying in his own behalf as well as to other witnesses. For example, in a suit to recover DAMAGES for ASSAULT AND BATTERY, the defendant appeared as a witness in his own behalf. The question "Did you try to disengage him from his hold on you?" asked by the defense attorney was held to be leading and improper. The question put words into the defendant's mouth. A better question would have been, "Under what circumstances did you hit the plaintiff?"—allowing the defendant to speak for himself.

lease A CONTRACT that creates the relationship of LANDLORD AND TENANT. When land is sold and then leased by the seller back from the buyer, the transaction is known as a *leaseback agreement*.

leasehold A legal interest in land held under a lease. See LANDLORD AND TENANT.

leave 1 Give by a WILL. 2 As a noun, permission. For example, "leave of court" is permission from the judge to take some action in a lawsuit that requires absence or delay, such as an attorney's leave to file an amended PLEADING.

legacy A gift by a WILL. Formerly, the word referred only to a gift of personal property, as distinguished from real estate. Now a legacy can mean any gift left by a will.

legal 1 Required or permitted by law; not forbidden by law. 2 Concerning the law.

legal age　The age at which a person acquires the legal capacity to make his own CONTRACTS and DEEDS, to transact business generally, and to enter into particular relationships, such as MARRIAGE. The legal age, also called the age of consent, is different for different purposes and in each state. See INFANT.

legal aid　An office that provides free legal help to those who cannot afford to pay for it. Often, such offices are sponsored and financed by local governments.

legal assistant　See PARALEGAL.

legal cause　A substantial factor in bringing about harm. See PROXIMATE CAUSE.

legal detriment　The assumption of liabilities or change in financial position that results from entering into a CONTRACT.

legalese　Lawyer talk; unnecessary jargon. Most states are enacting plain-English laws to permit consumers to understand their own INSURANCE policies, DEEDS, MORTGAGES, leases, and other legal documents.

legal ethics　Usages and customs among members of the legal profession, involving their moral and professional duties toward one another, their clients, the public, and the courts. See CODE OF JUDICIAL CONDUCT; CODE OF PROFESSIONAL RESPONSIBILITY.

legal fiction　An assumption that something false or nonexistent is true or real. To bring about justice, the law will sometimes permit or invent a legal fiction. For example, to sue or be sued, a CORPORATION is regarded as a legal person. Otherwise, a corporation could avoid all liability for its wrongful conduct, such as selling a product that it knows to be defective, since it could not be sued. This would be unjust, so a corporation's status as a person was invented.

legal proceeding　**1** A case heard in court or another tribunal.　**2** An ACTION connected with a lawsuit, such as evicting tenants when the landlord's mortgage is being foreclosed.

legal representative　A person who handles another's business involving the courts, especially EXECUTORS AND ADMINISTRATORS of wills and estates.

legal residence　The place in which a person actually lives and intends to stay. It is important to have a legal residence, for example, to vote in elections. See DOMICILE.

legal right　An interest that the law protects; an enforceable claim; a right created by law or by contract. The rights to just compensation for property taken from you by the government, to protect yourself against self-incrimination, to a jury trial, to vote, and to be regarded equal to a person of a different race are all legal rights. See CIVIL RIGHTS; CONSTITUTIONAL LAW.

legal tender　Official money, such as coins and bills for dollar amounts. On the face of each bill, there is a statement that the money is legal tender.

legatee　A person who receives either personal property or real estate through a WILL.

legislation　Lawmaking; the process by which statutes are enacted; the laws themselves, such as municipal ordinances. This article explains what legislation is, where the ideas for it originate, how a bill becomes law, and the workings of legislatures on every level of government. For a discussion of statutes, see STATUTE. For information about the legislative branch of the federal government, see CONGRESS, HOUSE OF REPRESENTATIVES, and SENATE.

■ **"A bill for an act"**　A *bill* is a draft, a tentative version of what may become the written law, called an *act* or *statute*. The formal work of a legislature begins with the submission of "A bill for an act," referring to the legislative procedure that starts with the bill's first version and continues to the point when it becomes law. Before a bill is voted on, it may be changed and polished by *amendment*. This process accommodates interested and affected groups and eliminates any technical defects. More legislative attention is devoted to decisions on amendments than to the passage of a bill. Many important provisions that become law are added by amendments.

■ **The structure of a legislature**　A legislature can be *bicameral,* with two chambers, or *unicameral,* with one. The U.S. Congress and 49 state legislatures are organized as bicameral bodies. The Nebraska state legislature and most county and city legislative councils are unicameral. Each of the bicameral legislative houses has its own procedures and leadership. Getting a bill passed involves two battles, one in each chamber.

Elected members make up only part of the legislative institution. The staffs of the legislators, reporters, lobbyists, and other interested citizens also actively participate. A *lobbyist* is someone who is hired, usually by a company, a civic group, or an agency, to advocate a particular cause and to persuade legislators to vote for it. Although the lobbyist often supplies factual information, he nevertheless remains partial to the political constituency he represents.

Committees　Legislatures function through the *committee* system that divides the work load and amends bills until they satisfy a majority. Nearly every legislative action in this country is the result of a committee recommendation, which is reported to the floor of the house and confirmed by a vote. Not all bills are reported to the floor, however. In most states a committee can shelve (put aside) a bill by not putting it on the agenda.

The amount of freedom a committee has in making its decisions varies, but no matter how strong and independent it becomes, it is still subject to the consensus of the legislative body. If a committee is seriously out of step with majority opinion in a house, its decisions will be attacked and reversed.

Generally, the majority party in a legislature has a steering group that sets the structure of the committee system. The system for the U.S. Congress and some state and local legislatures, however, is prescribed by statute.

The work of a legislature is further apportioned to *subcommittees*. There are standing (permanent) subcommittees that deal with recurring subjects and ad hoc (temporary) subcommittees that deal with special problems. Subcommittees do much of the legislature's groundwork—taking testimony, rewriting bills, and developing necessary compromises before a bill can be submitted to the full committee or to the floor.

The speaker of the assembly is usually the dominant legislator in that house. He and the leader of the majority party often work as a team, overseeing the committee work and giving directions on key issues. The leadership of the senate is generally a group of committee chairmen.

Seniority One of the most universal characteristics of a legislature is the seniority system. Newcomers serve an apprenticeship during which they learn the rules and customs and develop some expertise through committee assignments. With reelection, they are likely to win more prestigious assignments or at least remain with the ones they previously had. Thus, the longer a member serves, the better his assignments and the more entrenched he becomes in powerful committees. Most legislative bodies have found the seniority system useful. It recognizes the value of experience and maturity and reduces fierce political and personal competition within the legislature. Other methods of assigning committee memberships and chairmanships are more open to factionalism, political maneuvering, vote-trading, resentment, and a disintegration of order.

■ **The origins of legislation** Ideas for legislation are frequently copied. An idea that works well in one state is often useful to others. Legislators also receive a steady supply of proposals from the National Conference of Commissioners on Uniform State Laws. The 250 commissioners are all lawyers—practitioners, judges, and professors—appointed by governors to represent the states. The UNIFORM ACTS that they propose generally have a scholarly quality beyond the capabilities of a state legislature working on its own; therefore, uniform acts have been widely enacted. The Council of State Governments, the American Law Institute, the American Bar Association, and numerous other organizations produce MODEL ACTS for legislatures. Even if a uniform or model act or a law used in a neighboring state is not totally applicable, legislatures find it infinitely easier to revise an existing bill than to draft a new one.

HOW LAWMAKERS WORK FOR YOU

■ The U.S. Congress and all the state legislatures except one are organized as bicameral—two chamber—bodies with upper and lower houses. The exception is Nebraska, whose state legislature, like legislatures of most county and city councils, is unicameral—one chamber. Getting a law passed therefore involves two battles—one in each house of the legislature.

Proposed laws (known as bills) are parceled out to various legislative committees, which may either recommend them to the house or shelve them by omitting them from the agenda.

■ Legislatures often divide up further into subcommittees—standing subcommittees to deal with recurring subjects and ad hoc (temporary) subcommittees to handle special problems. Much of the groundwork is done by the subcommittees—taking testimony, rewriting bills, developing compromises, and the like.

■ Where do new laws come from? Lawmakers draw on a variety of sources, frequently the laws of other states—if an idea works well in one state, it may in another. State legislators also receive a steady stream of proposals from such nongovernmental bodies as the National Conference of Commissioners on Uniform State Laws, the Council of State Governments, the American Law Institute, and the American Bar Association. Other sources of new laws are various departments and agencies of the government, the special-interest lobbies, and in some states the state-sponsored law revision commission.

■ Now and again laws originate with the legislators themselves or with the citizens. For example, the no-fault system in auto accident insurance litigation used in several states was first adopted in Massachusetts as a result of studies and recommendations made over a 40-year period by academics outside the legislative process.

■ A common state constitutional provision is that a bill should deal with only one subject. This is not a requirement for the U.S. Congress.

■ Legislatures often need to drop regular procedure to get things done— this is called a rules suspension and may be allowed only by a two-thirds vote of the legislature.

■ A bill is introduced by a member who acts as its sponsor and steers it through the legislature.

■ The first step is to steer the bill into the appropriate committee and get the committee to place it on the agenda.

■ Once the bill has obtained a favorable committee report, it is placed on the agenda for floor action. At this stage, it may be re-referred to committee—the classic method of killing a bill without anyone's going on record against it on a final vote.

■ In most states, bills are considered by all members of the house sitting as a committee of the whole—in deliberations with no limit on the duration or number of times a member may speak. This time-consuming procedure is on the decline today. Increasingly, bills are debated and voted on the first time they come to the floor rather than being delayed for consideration by a committee of the whole.

■ After the final affirmative vote in the first house, the bill is transmitted to the other house, and if the second house accepts, it returns the bill with a message to that effect. The bill is then sent to the executive for signature. When signed, the bill is filed with the secretary of state and becomes an act, or written law.

■ If the executive vetoes a bill, the legislature may override the veto by a two-thirds majority. In some states, the governor can veto individual items in an appropriations bill—a power known as the *item veto*. If the legislature adjourns before the governor's time for signing runs out, the governor may kill the bill by not acting on it. This is called the *pocket veto*.

A lobbyist occasionally suggests a bill when it is favorable to his client. This complements his usual service of blocking undesired legislation. Elected officials often win their positions by promising new programs during their campaigns, and are then under special pressure to propose legislation because public opinion is focused on them. Information and support for new legislation also comes from nonelected government officials who head the various departments and agencies.

Traditionally, legislatures themselves have not been good sources of proposed legislation, but recent expansions of staff services have increased their capacity to generate their own bills. A few states have now institutionalized independent study by *law revision commissions,* which work outside legislatures but under their sponsorship. These commissions create proposed laws concerning matters such as divorce and contract law, while the legislature deals with taxes, appropriations, and government organization.

Legislation sometimes develops from citizens outside the legislative process whose first thought may have been only: "There ought to be a law." Bridging the gap between the idea and a law by providing a draft of the bill is sometimes an absolute necessity, as the case below dramatically illustrates.

EXAMPLE When Professors Robert Keeton and Jeffrey O'Connell conducted a study of auto accident compensation, their findings led them in 1965 to publish a book in which they recommended a no-fault system over one based on litigation. Their plan was similar to one proposed 39 years earlier in a study done at Columbia University. The difference was that Keeton and O'Connell included a draft no-fault bill in their book. The report on the Columbia study did not. In less than a year no-fault auto insurance moved through the Massachusetts general assembly and eventually became law.

■ **Procedure in a legislature** Although the procedure by which legislation is enacted varies from state to state, some generalizations can be made.

Constitutional requirements A constitution is the basic charter for all levels of government. Constitutions typically specify that some kinds of legislation, like a capital expenditure, require an extraordinary vote, such as passage by two-thirds, rather than by a simple majority. Three separate *readings,* or announcements of a bill to the full house, are commonly required before a vote can be taken. Some constitutions call for a detailed reading each time, but in practice this can be avoided.

In order for a bill to pass, constitutions often require an affirmative vote by a majority of all the members of a house—not just those present. They can also demand that the names of members voting "aye" and "nay" be recorded in the house journal. A constitution can authorize the executive—the governor or mayor, for example—to veto legislation. When the veto power is given, there must also be a procedure established for the legislature to override the veto.

Sometimes a specific period of time is constitutionally prescribed for the legislative session or term, and all work must be completed before the final hour. Legislators have been known to stop the clock on the floor at the 11th hour in order to finish voting on important bills.

Constitutions frequently establish certain officers for the legislature, such as a speaker of the house or president *pro tem (pro tempore,* or "for the time being") detailing how they are to be chosen and what powers they have to assign legislative tasks.

A common state constitutional provision is that a bill deal with only one subject and that it be expressed in the title. For example, "An Act to increase the state sales tax from 3 percent to 4 percent" is a proper title for a bill that does just that and no more. This is not a requirement for the U.S. Congress.

Rules Each legislature adopts its own rules concerning its organization and procedures. The rules are usually the result of the legislature's experience when normal parliamentary procedure did not work well. When, as often happens, legislatures need to depart from regular procedure to get things done, they pass special rules to suspend normal procedure. A rules suspension is allowed only by a two-thirds vote of the legislature. A bicameral legislature may have special procedures for adopting joint rules applicable to both houses or each house may pass separate rules independently.

Resolutions Some of the work of a legislature can be done by *resolution* rather than by a bill. A resolution takes care of an administrative matter or makes a public pronouncement without enacting a law. Resolutions are used, for example, to adopt the rules of the house, to establish committees, to initiate investigations, and to hire legislative employees. Even more simple day-to-day work can be accomplished by a *motion* on the floor. A motion lacks the formality of a resolution because it is not announced or printed in the record of the legislative session. It is a proposal that informally guides the legislators.

A resolution may be adopted by one house, or by both houses. A *joint resolution* originates and is adopted in one house and then is approved in the other house. This is the usual way state constitutional amendments are proposed and amendments to the U.S. Constitution are ratified. In some states, a joint resolution can substitute for a bill if it is submitted to the governor and he signs it.

A *concurrent resolution* also starts in one house and is approved by the other, but it does not have as much legal impact as a formally adopted joint resolution because a formally adopted joint resolution requires the approval of the President or the governor while a concurrent one does not. Concurrent resolutions are commonly used to express opinions, as in petitions from state legislatures to the President or to the U.S. Congress and in commendations to statesmen and winning athletic teams.

■ **From a bill to an act** A bill is introduced into the legislative process by an elected member who serves as its *sponsor.* Some rules allow an unlimited number of sponsors' names on a single bill. The chief sponsor, who may or may not be the author of the bill, is the legislator who steers it through the legislature. He makes tactical decisions and has the responsibility of explaining the bill to everyone and advocating it in committee and on the floor of the house. Choosing cosponsors from the same committee marshals support for the bill from the time it is first considered.

Introducing the bill can be a routine matter or it may require some tactical decisions. For example, a bill can be introduced on a slow day accompanied by a flurry of press releases to attract news coverage. After the bill is introduced, it is referred to a standing (permanent) committee. The subject of a bill often qualifies it for consideration by any of several committees. Wherever possible, sponsors try to steer the bill into a receptive committee, and in most legislatures there is room for such discretion. Major legislation may have to be referred to several committees; in such a case, the issue may be who receives it first.

Placing the bill on the agenda The next step is to convince the committee to give the bill a place on the agenda. Only then can the bill be considered and passed. According to popular opinion, a powerful chairman personally decides which bills will be shelved and which discussed. This view is not entirely untrue, but much of a committee's work is done by group consensus. A committee chairman cannot lead effectively if he totally disregards committee opinions. The competition for committee time is intense. If a spot cannot be won on the committee's agenda, a sponsor can seek subcommittee consideration. In subcommittee, a rough proposal can be polished and expanded into a more solid draft that will appeal to the full committee.

Legislative procedure is designed so that a bill will be considered when a need for it is demonstrated. That need can be created by public demand, skillful lobbying, or a persuasive sponsor. Once a bill starts moving through the committee system, legislators usually allow it to continue. Unless someone steps forward with an amendment, the proposal may get passed just as it is because of legislative momentum. As a bill gets closer to passage, it becomes more difficult to amend or kill.

If a committee decides to table a bill, the bill is stopped for that session of the legislature. If the committee recommends that the bill be indefinitely postponed, the recommendation is reported to the floor as a committee report to be confirmed by a house vote. Adoption of the committee report officially kills the bill. However, if the committee advises passage of the bill, then it is sent to the floor with a favorable report.

After a legislative body adopts an affirmative committee report, the bill is placed on the agenda for floor action. The agenda can be long. While a bill waits, it is subject to a motion to re-refer it back to the same committee or any other committee. This is the classic soft method of quashing a bill without going on record against it on a final vote. The argument that a bill deserves more consideration can always be justifiably made.

Consideration by a committee of the whole In most state legislatures, a bill is first considered on the floor in a *committee of the whole*. This means that all members of the house sit as a committee to debate the bill before votes are recorded. Procedurally, it allows more informal debate—without limits on the duration or number of times a member may speak. Consideration by the committee of the whole also provides an interval between the first formal floor consideration and final passage of the bill. This gives more time for deliberation.

Use of the committee-of-the-whole procedure is declining. Increasingly, bills are debated and voted on the first time they come to the floor.

Almost every legislature has a *consent calendar* for bills that have been identified by committee reports as noncontroversial. Each bill is read at the appointed time, briefly explained, and voted on. If even a few votes dissent, the bill is sent back to the regular calendar for more examination.

Orchestrating debate and passage The legislative leadership usually likes to process major bills in a carefully controlled procedure, using a *special order* to schedule debate, amendment, and passage at a single session. A bill can be designated for special order by a vote of two-thirds or, more commonly, through selection by a priority-setting or policy committee. Appropriations and tax bills can get special-order privileges automatically because it is absolutely necessary that they pass in some form during the legislative session.

Some constitutions, including that of the United States, permit a vote on *final passage* to be oral and unrecorded unless a member calls for the "ayes" and "nays." Immediately after a vote on final passage, a *motion to reconsider* can be made. This is a request for a revote. Although the number of successful reconsiderations is small, the device serves to open the door for additional compromise on an act. After a motion to reconsider has passed (the rules generally permit only one reconsideration of any vote), both sides try to collect switch votes. The winning side usually wants to have the vote on the reconsideration immediately so that the losers do not have time to marshal additional strength. In the U.S. Congress, a motion to reconsider is routinely made after every vote. In this way, the vote becomes final—it precludes a motion to reconsider at any later time.

A bill must be passed by both houses of a bicameral legislature. Once a bill is passed in one house, it usually has a good chance for success in the other because it is by then a product of polishing and compromise. If the houses pass identical but separate bills, their action is ineffective. One house must approve the bill from the other house.

Enrolling the bill After the final affirmative vote for passage in the first house, the bill is put into an official *engrossment,* a formal final copy, and transmitted to the other house for consideration. If the second house accepts the version adopted in the first house, it returns the bill with a message to that effect. The first house then *enrolls* the bill—that is, transcribes and registers it on a roll (record) of bills—and sends it over to the executive for his signature.

If the second house has amended the bill, the bill is sent to the first house with a message asking for agreement on the changes. If the amendments are acceptable, a motion is made to concur and to place the bill on repassage. After the motion passes, all the formalities of a final vote are repeated for the amended bill. Once repassed, the bill is enrolled in its amended form, signed by the legislative officers, and sent off to the executive for his signature. When the two houses cannot agree on a final form for a bill, a compromise can be reached in a *conference committee,* usually composed of three to five members from each house.

The final step in the legislative process is the signing of an enrolled bill by the executive and its filing with the secretary of state. The bill is then an *act,* a written law.

Executive action An executive can refuse to sign a bill. He can return it to the legislature with a veto message explaining why he disapproves. Then the legislature may attempt, first in the house where the bill originated, to override the veto by an extraordinary vote, usually a two-thirds majority. Some state constitutions give the governor authority to pick particular items out of an appropriations bill and veto them individually. This power is called the *item veto*. In these cases, the legislature can try to override each individual veto.

If a governor neither signs a bill nor returns it to his state legislature, the bill becomes law within a certain number of days anyway. The governor then turns the bill over to the secretary of state's office, which records the fact that it became law without the governor's signature. If the legislature adjourns before the governor's time for signing runs out, however, the bill cannot become a law without his signature. In such cases, a governor can kill a bill by doing nothing. This is called the *pocket veto*.

The executive runs a great political risk any time he decides to veto legislation, however, especially if a legislature draws up laws that reflect popular opinion and if the legislative leaders are favored by the voters. Therefore, most executives exercise the veto power cautiously.

legislative Describing the branch of government concerned with enacting laws. The other two branches are the executive and the judicial. See CONSTITUTIONAL LAW.

legislative court Any COURT established by Congress that was not originally provided for in the Constitution. The U.S. Court of Claims and the U.S. Court of Customs and Patent Appeals are examples of legislative courts. States may also create legislative courts.

legislative fact A matter of such general knowledge that it need not be proved to an administrative agency deciding a question of policy. For instance, the terrain of the property would not have to be proven to a local zoning board before it decides whether or not a ski lift can be built on the town's highest slope.

legislative history Background documents and records of hearings on the draft version of a proposed law before it becomes effective. See LEGISLATION.

legislative intent What the lawmakers meant or hoped to accomplish when they enacted a law. The Legislative Intent Rule directs anyone seeking to interpret a law to examine its legislative history.

legitimation See ILLEGITIMACY.

lessee A person who rents property from another. A lessee of land is a tenant. See LANDLORD AND TENANT.

lesser included offense A crime that is part of a more serious crime. It is also called a lesser offense. For example, manslaughter is a lesser crime included in the description of MURDER. See CRIMINAL LAW.

lessor A person who rents property to another. A lessor of land is a landlord. See LANDLORD AND TENANT.

let 1 Award a CONTRACT (as for a construction project) to one of several bidders. 2 Lease.

letter 1 The literal meaning of a document or a law; the exact language—as in "the letter of the law"—rather than the spirit or broad purpose. 2 A formal document, such as a letter of credit.

letter of credit A written statement issued by a bank that it will back up or pay the financial obligations of a merchant in his business transactions elsewhere (usually in another country). See COMMERCIAL PAPER.

letters of administration or letters testamentary Documents issued by a court to permit an individual to take charge of a decedent's property in order to distribute it. If the deceased person made a WILL, it is called a letter testamentary. If there is no will, it is a letter of administration. See EXECUTORS AND ADMINISTRATORS.

levee An embankment built on the edge of a body of water to prevent the flooding of adjacent lands. States usually construct and maintain levees, but the federal government also has power to prevent flooding. Because flood control improves the navigability of a river, the federal government acts under its authority to regulate interstate commerce. See COMMERCE CLAUSE.

The power to construct levees is usually vested in public authorities and not in individuals. Levee districts, created by state legislatures, are the public agencies most frequently involved in building and maintaining flood-control projects. A state legislature may tax directly or delegate the power to local levee districts. Generally, only property that receives benefits from a flood-control project can be taxed for this purpose.

levy 1 Assess, raise, or collect. For example, to levy a tax is to enact it in the legislature or to collect it. 2 Seize and sell property by court order to obtain money—for payment of a money JUDGMENT, for example. See EXECUTION.

lewdness Moral impurity in a sexual sense; illicit sexual intercourse, as at a house of prostitution; open and public indecency. Lewdness is open when committed in a place subject to public view. For example, removing a bathing suit on your own private beach is not lewdness, but doing so at a public beach is.

lex (Latin) "Law"; a collection or body of laws, such as of a particular state or nation.

liability A comprehensive legal term that includes almost every aspect of responsibility; a legal obligation, duty, or debt. For example, a driver has a liability for accidents that he may cause. A homeowner has a liability for unpaid taxes on his property. See NEGLIGENCE; TORT.

liable 1 Responsible, such as for harm done to another person. John is liable for the injuries Larry received when he pushed Larry through a glass door. 2 Having a duty or obligation to another person that is enforceable in court. A citizen is liable for paying federal INCOME TAX. A parent is liable for the support of his minor children. See PARENT AND CHILD.

libel

1 An untrue defamatory (slanderous) statement in a concrete form—such as a writing, cartoon, or film—that injures a person's reputation. See LIBEL AND SLANDER. **2** The name given to a specialized complaint in certain lawsuits. Libels are used primarily in ADMIRALTY (maritime) cases, corresponding to the COMPLAINT of an ordinary civil lawsuit.

libel and slander

Two methods of defamation. This entry discusses the essential elements of libel and slander, defenses that may permit a person to escape part or all liability, and the type of DAMAGES that may be awarded. Because of the development of the mass media over the past 30 years and the expansion of the Constitution's protection of freedom of expression, possible conflicts between the traditional law of libel and slander and constitutional guarantees are included. See SPEECH AND PRESS, FREEDOM OF.

■ **What is defamation?** A defamation is an untrue communication about a person that injures his good name or reputation so that he is subjected to the hatred, abuse, contempt, or ridicule of others. Because it deprives an individual of his right to acquire and enjoy a good reputation, he is entitled to be compensated for this loss.

Libel Libel is defamation if it is in the form of a writing, a printing, an effigy, a motion picture, or a statue that by its physical form has some permanence. If the gossip column in your local newspaper printed an item about your neighbor that was untrue, for instance, the newspaper has committed libel. In a movie, the spoken words are considered part of the picture and are therefore part of the libel. Some courts consider a defamatory statement made on television or radio a libel, even though it is not a writing; other courts consider it slander.

In all libel that is defamatory on its face, *libel per se*, injury to the person is conclusively presumed. A jury can award nominal or substantial damages without the plaintiff's having to plead or prove actual monetary loss. See "Awards for damages" below. If your neighbor is falsely named in a local newspaper as a major supplier of drugs to children, for example, that is libel on its face and he will be entitled to recover for the defamation.

An alleged libel that is not defamatory on its face may require extrinsic (external) facts to explain the defamatory meaning of the words. This is called *libel per quod*.

EXAMPLE Say the town newspaper runs a false story that O——＊ Mary Doe of 1234 Shady Lane has just given birth to twins at a local hospital. The story is libelous because Mrs. Doe has only recently been married and almost everyone in town reading the story knows this fact. The newspaper has committed a classic example of libel per quod.

Slander Slander is defamation that is spoken and heard. For example, the owner of the store next to yours tells his customers that you are a crook. Certain categories of words are *slanderous per se*, which means they prove slander without the plaintiff's having to show actual damages. When the words accuse the plaintiff of conduct that

involves moral turpitude (unjust, dishonest, or immoral acts), they are slanderous per se. Making an untrue statement to a third party that Mary embezzled from her employer is an example of slander per se. Stating publicly that Mary parked on the wrong side of the street or drove without a license would not be included in this category.

Words that impute to the plaintiff a loathsome and communicable disease that banishes him from society are slanderous per se. Today, these words are usually limited to venereal disease.

There is no need to show actual damages when slanderous words affect a plaintiff in his trade, calling, business, profession, or office. Branding a doctor a molester, a lawyer a shyster, a merchant a cheat, or an assemblyman a taker of bribes entitles the victim to money damages for injury to his reputation—if these words were said to or heard by a third person. For example, calling an architect an alcoholic is defamation, while saying he did second-rate work for you is criticism. The statement that "people cannot get money out of him because he is threatening bankruptcy" was considered slanderous per se by a court because the words hurt the victim's business and good reputation.

Criticism v. defamation There is a distinction between criticism and defamation. Criticism is an expression of opinion on facts about which different views may arise. It does not attack the individual's private or personal affairs but deals only with his work or public conduct. Slander and libel, in contrast, attack the personal qualities of the character of an individual with untrue statements that hurt his reputation.

Suing for defamation Libel and slander are TORTS—civil wrongs done to a person by another. State law governs tort actions, and a person who has been defamed is entitled to bring a civil lawsuit for money damages to compensate him for injury to his reputation. In the past, defamation actions could be criminal or civil in nature, but the criminal action has fallen into disuse in recent years.

■ **Elements that constitute defamation and slander** The essential elements common to both libel and slander actions are (1) the making of a defamatory statement by the defendant, (2) the publication (communication) of that statement to someone other than the plaintiff, (3) the identification in some way of the plaintiff as the person defamed, and (4) injury to the plaintiff's reputation.

Defamatory words The words must injure the reputation of a living person or an existing organization because only the injured party may sue for defamation. Some words—such as thief, cheat, liar, murderer, whore, bastard—are usually considered defamatory per se (in and of themselves). Other words may become defamatory in relation to time, place, and historical context. For instance, falsely labeling a person a Communist during the World War II period of U.S.-Soviet cooperation was not a cause for legal action. The same false label was considered defamatory, however, once the Cold War began.

An individual's position in life may give a damaging effect to otherwise innocent words.

EXAMPLE Selling pork is a respectable occupation. But O——＊ when Max suggests that Aaron, a kosher butcher, sells bacon, he has made a defamatory statement. The charge rests on the fact that Aaron's religious customers would disapprove of his having bacon in his store and they would take their business elsewhere.

Those hearing or seeing the statement must take it to be defamatory, regardless of whether they personally believe it to be true. When language is not defamatory per se, then the plaintiff must prove the facts that make it defamatory. He must explain the defamatory meaning of the communication by setting forth the statement word for word.

EXAMPLE A remark that John burned down his own barn is not defamatory per se because John has a right to do so. When, however, it is shown that John had insured his barn and that the words were understood to mean that he was defrauding the insurance company, a charge of arson is implied, which is defamatory.

The plaintiff must establish that someone other than himself understood the words (or image, as in a movie or drawing) to be an attack on his reputation. The defendant, on the other hand, may try to show that the communication was made in jest and could not be taken seriously. If just one person other than the plaintiff understood the communication to be defamatory, however, it is so considered.

Publication Publication means the communication of the defamatory matter to someone other than the one defamed. Printing and distributing printed matter is not required. Publication occurs when, for example, a patient in a crowded waiting room states in a loud voice that the doctor is a drug addict. In this situation, the communicator either intends others to overhear his accusation or is so uncaring that his conduct is considered reckless. When, however, a person does not intend the communication to be conveyed to third persons and takes normal precautions against its being seen or heard, there is no publication.

WHEN SOMEBODY DAMAGES YOUR GOOD NAME

■ What is the difference between libel and slander? Basically, they are the same thing—defamation—an untrue statement that injures your good name and standing, an injury for which you are entitled to compensation. Whereas *libel* is put forth in a way that has some permanence—writing, printing, an effigy, movie, cartoon, or the like—*slander* is just a nasty oral statement that a third person heard and believed. However, to be either libel or slander, the words must falsely accuse you of unjust, dishonest, or immoral acts.

■ If someone defames you on television or radio, the defamation may be considered libel depending on the state where it occurs. In some states, however, such a defamation would be considered slander.

■ If someone spreads the word that you have a loathsome communicable disease, you can sue and get damages. By the same token, people who call a doctor a molester, a lawyer a shyster, a merchant a cheat, a politician a taker of bribes do so at their own peril.

■ If your good name has been defamed and you are considering legal action, check whether these four indispensable elements are present in your case: (1) Was the statement truly defamatory? (2) Did the statement reach someone besides yourself? (3) Were you identified in the statement as its target? (4) Did your reputation really suffer as a result of the statement?

■ A statement that might apply in an innocent way to one person could defame another—for example, suggesting that a kosher butcher sells bacon.

■ When you sue, you must establish that someone other than yourself took the words or image as an attack on your reputation.

■ The technical term for communicating a defamatory statement to third persons is *publication*. Publication occurs, for example, when a patient in a crowded waiting room shouts that the doctor is a drug addict.

■ Courts differ as to whether defamation by radio or TV is slander or libel. This is an important distinction, because in libel actions it is not necessary to prove actual monetary loss, whereas in slander actions there has been this requirement. In many states, however, monetary loss has to be proved in certain kinds of libel.

■ In most states, monetary damages do not have to be proved in either libel or slander if the defamation affects you in your trade, profession, or business or imputes a crime, a loathsome disease, or a woman's unchastity.

■ If you are accused of libel or slander, your possible defenses include truth, consent, and privilege.

■ If what you said was true, it was not defamatory.

■ You can also defend yourself by showing that publication was accidental, without either negligence or intent on your part.

■ Sometimes it is possible to publish defamatory words and not get sued for it—this is what the law calls *privilege*.

■ Statements or arguments that are made during a judicial proceeding are absolutely privileged, even if the statements are known to be false.

■ A legislator is also free to defame anyone as long as the words are used in his or her role as legislator and concern legislative business. Similarly, the state governor has the right to make public accusations and "name names" without risking a libel action—but most state courts refuse to extend this privilege to subordinate state officers, such as mayors, school superintendents, and the like.

■ A slander or libel action brought by one spouse against the other will be unsuccessful because there is absolute immunity for communications between a husband and wife.

■ Public figures—persons occupying a place in the limelight—get less protection against defamation as long as the statement is published without actual malice.

■ If a defamer promptly publishes a retraction with essentially the same prominence that was given the false statement, damages will be reduced. The retraction has got to be complete and unequivocal—anything less will not mitigate damages but may even increase them.

■ Another way to mitigate damages is to allow the victim to use the defamer's facilities to reply to the attack.

■ If a jury decides that a plaintiff did not suffer general damages because his reputation was unimpaired by the defamation (or was not worth much to start with), nominal damages, such as one dollar, may be awarded.

EXAMPLE Suppose Andrews writes Baker, his former business partner, a letter in which he accuses Baker of causing the downfall of their business by "stealing the company blind." Andrews places the letter in a sealed envelope, marks it "personal," addresses it to Baker, and mails it to his house. Baker's son, curious about the letter from his father's former associate, opens and reads the letter before his father sees it and without his authority. There is no publication here and, therefore, no libel.

In another situation Thomas, a store owner, accused Peter of stealing an expensive camera. The charge was false, but no one else was present. Later, the charge was repeated in Greek in the presence of others, but no one except Peter understood Greek. Because no one but Peter heard and understood the statement, there was no publication and, therefore, no slander.

If Steve sends Don a defamatory message by telegram, the reading by telegraph company employees during its transmission does not constitute publication. But most courts hold that dictation of defamatory matter to a secretary is publication.

There is no libel or slander if the victim himself publicizes the communication to others, because it is the defamer who must promote the publication. In the example of the business partners, if Baker opened the letter and then showed it to his son, there would be no publication.

When there is publication, repetition of the original defamation by persons other than the victim constitutes republication. The original communicator as well as the one who repeats the defamation will be held liable for this—provided the republication is foreseeable.

EXAMPLE A defamatory writing, written by an unknown person, was left on the wall in the men's room of Brown's tavern. Jones learned of the writing, which concerned his wife, and asked Brown to remove it. Brown's failure to remove the libel, after he was given a reasonable opportunity to do so, constituted a republication of the defamation that made him liable for damages.

For the newspaper and magazine industry the courts had to decide whether the distribution of each copy of a press-run was a separate publication providing the basis for multiple defamation suits, or whether the whole pressrun was treated as one publication so that the plaintiff could recover only once for libelous statements. The courts arrived at the single-publication rule, which provides that only one suit for defamation arises.

A vendor of newspapers and magazines is not liable if a publication he sells contains libelous matter, if he had no knowledge of the libel. He is not expected to read everything for libelous material before he sells it.

Identification A person cannot sue for libel or slander unless he can establish that he was the one defamed. Often, the target of a defamatory communication is not clearly named, as in a "blind item" in a Hollywood gossip column. Identification of the victim then becomes a problem of analyzing extrinsic (outside) circumstances.

EXAMPLE In *New York Times Co.* v. *Sullivan,* the defendants had published a paid advertisement that alleged, among other things, that the police of Montgomery, Alabama, had improperly "ringed" (encircled) a black college campus to put down a peaceful civil rights demonstration. The ad also charged that certain unnamed "southern violators" had bombed the home of Martin Luther King, Jr.; physically assaulted him; arrested him seven times for "speeding," "loitering," and similar offenses; and had charged him with "perjury."

Some of these statements were erroneous in whole or in part. Although no "southern violator" was named in the ad, L. B. Sullivan, the Commissioner of Public Affairs for Montgomery, filed suit for libel. Sullivan persuaded the jury that he had been referred to in the advertisement because he was the city's police commissioner and would therefore have been responsible for the "ringing" of the campus and the arrests of Dr. King. Sullivan also claimed that being identified as a "southern violator" in conjunction with the arrests had resulted in his identification in the public mind with the other lawless acts listed.

The U.S. Supreme Court reversed a judgment for Sullivan, holding that the identification of Sullivan with the advertisement was inadequate.

Groups Identification may be difficult when a group is defamed. Generally, the courts will not consider a suit when the complainant is a member of a large group that has been defamed, such as by the statement that "all lawyers are shysters." When it is a small homogeneous group, however, the courts will allow a suit by an individual member, sometimes even when the defamation is aimed at only a segment of the group. The plaintiff, however, must convince the court or jury that he was a member of the segment attacked.

EXAMPLE In one famous case, decided in 1952, Jack Lait and Lee Mortimer, the defendants, had written the book *U.S.A. Confidential.* In referring to Neiman-Marcus department store employees, the book said, "Some Neiman models are call girls . . . the salesgirls are good, too—pretty and often much cheaper—twenty bucks on the average . . . most of the male sales staff are fairies." The store employed 9 models, 382 saleswomen, and 25 salesmen. The store and individual employees sued for libel. The court decided that an accusation of gross immorality to some of a small group casts suspicion on all, but when the libeled group is large, no one can sue. The 9 models were a small class and had a cause of action, as did the 25 salesmen. The class of saleswomen, however, was large and thus they were denied recovery.

Injury Because a defamatory statement tarnishes the victim's reputation, he has a right to be compensated by money damages for the injury. In slander cases he must plead and prove he is entitled to compensatory damages if he has suffered actual financial loss.

Actual Losses When words are not slanderous per se, the plaintiff must prove that injury has been caused by the alleged slander. The words "You are drunk," or "You are a [expletive deleted] son of a bitch," will not entitle the victim to damages unless other facts show that the words have an additional meaning.

EXAMPLE Marlene applies to a finance company for a $4,000 car loan and lists Vivian as a personal reference. During the credit investigation, Vivian is interviewed and tells the investigator that Marlene never pays her debts. This false statement is the basis of the company's refusal to authorize the loan. By establishing these facts, Marlene has pleaded and proved actual losses, which she is entitled to recover in the form of damages.

Whether damages need to be proved in cases of defamation by radio or television depends on whether the court considers it slander or libel. Some courts treat defamation by the electronic media as slander, particularly when the statements are ad-libbed or spontaneous. Other courts view it as libel, especially when a written script is involved, based on the belief that the spoken word is only fleeting and temporary while written words and pictures are permanent. In a libel suit there has traditionally been no need to prove actual monetary loss as is necessary in slander cases. Many states now require, however, that such losses be proved in certain kinds of libel.

The use of a gesture as a substitute for spoken words, such as a nod of the head or a wave of the hand or sign language, may be slanderous if its defamatory nature is understood by a person other than the defamed.

Most states require proof of actual damages unless the libel or slander imputes a crime, a loathsome disease, or a woman's unchastity or unless it affects the plaintiff in his trade, profession, or business. A major reason for this rule is that the courts are reluctant to hold newspapers and other media liable for all communications even when they are not aware of their defamatory character.

■ **Defenses** Defenses to a libel or slander suit are truth, consent, privilege, and fair comment. As in other civil actions, the statute of limitations (the time within which a lawsuit must be started) may also be a defense. See Chart 4.

Truth Truth is an absolute and complete defense to charges of libel or slander in all states. The rationale behind this rule is that a person is not entitled to a greater reputation than he deserves and that the public should know as much as possible about those with whom it deals.

The defendant must be able to prove the truth of his entire statement in court. If only part of the communication is verified, the defense will be unsuccessful.

EXAMPLE A newspaper charge that Sam Smith is a habitual vice-law offender is not justified by the paper's proving that he was once convicted of illegal gambling. A statement that a reliable source has informed the communicator that Jane Brown is guilty of tax evasion is not justified by proving that the informer is a reliable source.

The truth of the charge itself must be established even though the defendant was not the originator of the story. This, however, does not mean that the defendant must verify every detail of his communication as long as its substance can be proved. An individual who publicly accuses the treasurer of the local homeowner's association of embezzling $1,500 from the group will escape liability by proving that the treasurer embezzled only $150.

Consent When the person charging libel or slander consented to the publication of the defamatory material, the defendant may use this consent as a defense.

EXAMPLE When the two of them were alone, Don said to Paul, "Paul, you are a perjurer." A friend of the two, Marie, then appeared and Paul said to Don, "I wish you'd tell Marie what you just told me." Don addressed Marie, "I told Paul he was a perjurer." If Paul sues Don he will be unsuccessful because he consented to the publication of the slanderous statement.

Accident It is a defense that the publication of the defamation was made by accident and without either NEGLIGENCE or intent to publish.

EXAMPLE Thinking that no one could overhear him, Jerry told Burt, "Burt, you are a thief and a robber." The words were heard by Joyce, however, who was hidden in a closet. Jerry is not liable for slander because he did not intend publication. If the same words were spoken while Jerry and Burt attended a wedding reception and it could be expected that the statement would be overheard by others, Jerry would be liable.

Privilege A privilege to publish defamatory words arises from the circumstances in which they are published. Despite the fact that the plaintiff suffers harm to his reputation, the defamer may be shielded from liability because the law gives prime importance to the free expression of matters of general concern. The defense of privilege is divided into two categories: absolute privilege and qualified privilege.

Absolute privilege An absolute privilege to defame makes a person completely immune from liability for his statements. It is conferred almost exclusively on those directly involved in furthering the public's business.

Statements or arguments made during a judicial proceeding by the attorneys, judge, jurors, or witnesses are absolutely privileged on the grounds of public policy, even though the statements are known to be false and motivated by personal ill will toward the plaintiff. Judicial proceedings include lunacy, bankruptcy, or naturalization proceedings as well as election contests, such as court-supervised recounts of ballots. This privilege also extends to commissions and boards that have a quasi-judicial character, such as a commission to investigate state nursing homes.

A legislator has complete immunity for defaming anyone as long as the words concern legislative business. If, however, a congressman uses defamatory language on an occasion not connected with any legislative function, he is liable just as is any other citizen. The immunity extends to all phases of the legislative process, including committee meetings, reports, arguments, and voting. Depending on the state, it may not extend to statements made during town meetings and city councils.

Certain executive officers of the government may be protected by absolute privilege in discharging their duties.

EXAMPLE Governor Keen is required to report to the legislature on conditions in the state. In a report that he reads to the legislature, Governor Keen charges Messrs. Hill, Stowe, and Carson, large taxpayers, of evading the tax laws (a criminal offense). In his executive capacity he then releases a copy of his report to the newspapers, explaining why it was made. Hill, Stowe, and Carson would lose a libel action brought against the governor. Both publications were part of his executive function and have absolute immunity. Most courts refuse to extend this absolute privilege to subordinate state officers, such as mayors, aldermen, or school superintendents.

There are a few instances aside from governmental activity in which absolute privilege is available. A slander or libel case brought by one spouse against the other will be unsuccessful because there is absolute immunity for communications between a husband and wife. A radio or television station that is required by the Federal Communications Act to provide equal time for speeches by political candidates is also protected, because it is barred by law from controlling the content of the speeches.

Qualified privilege   A qualified privilege defeats a suit for libel or slander when the publication has been made without malice. Malice, such as hatred for the plaintiff, is an improper motive. The privilege is lost when wanton or reckless conduct causes the defamation, except when it is caused by a mistake due to inexperience.

EXAMPLE A slander action was brought against a telephone ○←※ company and an operator. During a police investigation, the operator had mistakenly identified the plaintiff as the person who had telephoned a false bomb warning. The court decided that police investigations are protected by a qualified privilege because every citizen has the duty and right to communicate information about a crime without fear of civil liability. Here, the defendant, who did not know the plaintiff or his family, had made the identification solely at the request of the police. Because there was no malice, the privilege was upheld. To determine whether the charge was made recklessly or wantonly, the court examined the circumstances of the case. The defendant was helping the police trap a criminal—a situation in which she was totally inexperienced. Her conduct could not be considered reckless because she had told the police only the facts that she knew.

Private interests   There is no specific test for determining when a situation will offer the protection of qualified privilege. Generally, the publication must have been for a proper purpose—such as to protect an important private or public interest—and made in a reasonable manner.

To protect a private interest, there must be some legal or moral duty that justifies the publication of the defamatory communication. The privilege clearly exists when there is a definite legal relationship between the defendant and the person on whose behalf he intervenes. For example, a parent may tell his child not to marry someone because he is a thief. Courts usually treat this kind of defamatory communication as privileged because a reasonable parent feels compelled to speak.

When a matter is none of a person's business, however, and a defamation is published, the privilege may be lost. If an outsider meddles in family matters—telling a husband about his wife's conduct, for example—he has no privilege and may be liable for slander if the information is untrue.

Public interest   The interest of the public has resulted in two qualified privileges. One is a public-interest privilege that protects people who have made defamatory communications to officials expected to act to protect a public interest. For example, communications from public officers and private citizens to the proper authorities in order to prevent or detect a crime or to complain about the conduct of certain officials are protected by the qualified privilege. But unless the statements are made in good faith, without improper motives, the privilege is lost.

The other public-interest privilege is given to the media—with certain limitations—for reporting to the public on official or public proceedings. The reporting must be fair, accurate, and motivated by a sense of duty to those receiving the report. The report must accurately and fairly reflect

what occurred. An incorrect detail that does not affect its essential accuracy or fairness will not destroy the privilege.

If, however, the defamatory report is not made for a proper purpose, the publication will be considered malicious and the privilege will be destroyed. There will also be no privilege if a communication is motivated mainly by some selfish objective of the person making the report, such as enhancing his business interests at the expense of a competitor who is unfavorably referred to in the public proceeding reported.

Fair comment and public officials   Under the common law, fair comment involved the honest expression of the communicator's opinion on all matters of public interest—not just proceedings of a public nature—as long as the opinion was based on facts that were correctly stated. This allows political and artistic criticism by the media. The courts have given broad meaning to fair comment. Commentaries containing exaggeration, sarcasm, ridicule, and even viciousness are protected if at all justified by the underlying facts. The classic example is the criticism leveled at the Cherry Sisters' vaudeville act by a newspaper drama critic:

EXAMPLE "Effie is an old jade of 50 summers, Jessie is a ○←※ frisky filly of 40, and Addie, the flower of the family, a capering monstrosity of 35. Their long skinny arms, equipped with talons at the extremities, swung mechanically. . . . The mouths of their rancid features opened like caverns, and sounds like the wailings of damned souls issued therefrom . . ." When the sisters sued the critic for libel, the court decided that the editor of the newspaper had the right to publish, without malice, fair and reasonable comments, however severe, upon anything that is a subject of public interest.

Malice can negate the defense of fair comment but malice can only be established by examining the motives of the communicator and not by inferring it from the words that are published.

The majority of states limit the common-law fair-comment privilege to opinion and criticism and do not extend it to false statements of facts. While persons holding public office must expect to be subjected to public comment and opinion, they are not to be made victims of misrepresentation without redress. A few states treat false statements of facts as privileged, if they are made for the public benefit with an honest belief in their truth. The public interest demands that those who have information about public servants should not be deterred by fear of suit and having to prove the truth of what they say in court.

In 1964 the qualified privilege of fair comment received constitutional recognition when the U.S. Supreme Court decided in *New York Times Co.* v. *Sullivan* that defamatory communications about the official conduct of a public officer were privileged under the First Amendment's guarantee of freedom of the press. As described earlier in this article (see "Identification"), the *New York Times* ad would have been libelous if it could be satisfactorily identified with the officer, Sullivan, and would not have been protected by the fair-comment privilege because Alabama limited the privilege to opinion only. Because there were misstatements of fact in the ad, the state court found it libelous and awarded Sullivan $500,000 in damages.

The U.S. Supreme Court, however, reversed the judgment of the state court because there was no adequate proof that the ad sufficiently identified Sullivan. More important, the Court established the rule that a public official may not recover damages for a defamatory falsehood relating to his official conduct unless he proves with "convincing clarity" that the statement is made with actual malice. Actual malice is publication with knowledge that the statement is false or with reckless disregard of whether or not it is false. Sullivan could not prove such malice.

The *New York Times Co.* v. *Sullivan* case extended the privilege of fair comment to include facts and to permit the communication of erroneous facts. Fair comment is now a constitutional privilege when it concerns the conduct of public officials in their office.

In proving actual malice, a plaintiff has the right to probe a media defendant's state of mind. He seeks to determine whether the reporter believed the truthfulness of the defamatory material.

EXAMPLE The case of *Herbert* v. *Lando* involved a retired O———* Army colonel who became the subject of national attention in 1969–1970 after he had accused his superior officers of concealing reports of war crimes committed during the Vietnam conflict. The colonel claimed that, in a subsequent television program and a magazine article by the program's producer, the officer was "falsely and maliciously portrayed as a liar and a person who had made war-crimes charges to explain his relief from command." The colonel sued the television network, the show's producer and its reporter, and the magazine for defamation.

Because the colonel was a public figure, he had to prove that the program and article were published with actual malice. In preparing his case, the colonel questioned the producer under oath outside court in an effort to find out the producer's state of mind at the time he organized the program and subsequent article. Refusing to answer some questions, the producer claimed the First Amendment protection of free speech.

At the colonel's request, a court ordered the producer to answer on the ground that such questioning was essential to prove actual malice. However, a federal court of appeals reversed this decision, ruling that the editorial process was protected by the First Amendment and that the producer was within his rights in refusing to answer the questions.

The case reached the Supreme Court, where the defendants argued that inquiry into a reporter's beliefs about the truthfulness of the material he gathered as well as disclosure of editorial conversations would have "an intolerable chilling effect on the editorial process and editorial decision making." The Court held that if the editorial process of a media defendant in a libel case were privileged, it would be extremely difficult for a plaintiff to establish actual malice. It would also undermine the purpose of discovery proceedings, which is to adequately inform the parties in a civil lawsuit of material relevant to their case.

Celebrities and fair comment Subsequent decisions have applied the public-official rule to cases dealing with public figures. A public figure is a person who, by his accomplishments, fame, mode of living, or profession, gives the public a legitimate interest in his life. He is a celebrity, such as an actor, boxer, or baseball player. This category also includes public officers, famous inventors and explorers, war heroes, and child prodigies. Anyone who has arrived at a position where public attention is focused upon him as a person is a public figure. As long as the defamatory material about the public figure is published without actual malice, the qualified privilege of fair comment defeats liability.

Private citizens and fair comment If the person defamed is neither a public figure nor a public official, the qualified privilege of fair comment does not shield the publisher of the defamatory communication from liability.

EXAMPLE The family of a youth killed by a police officer O———* hired a reputable attorney, not generally known to the public, to sue the officer. The publisher of a magazine commissioned a writer to do an article on the case. The article made false statements about the attorney, identifying him with various Communist causes and implying that he had a criminal record. There was no effort made by the magazine publisher to verify the author's charges. When the attorney brought a libel action, the U.S. District Court decided that although the attorney was neither a public official nor a public figure, the privilege of fair comment extended to cover discussion of any public issue regardless of the status of the person defamed. This decision was affirmed by the U.S. Court of Appeals, and the attorney appealed to the U.S. Supreme Court, which reversed the lower courts' judgments.

The Supreme Court reasoned that a private person is more in need of judicial redress because he has not voluntarily invited public comment nor chosen to put his reputation at risk. In addition, he normally has less access to the media to correct the record than a public person. The attorney was permitted to recover compensatory damages for the actual injuries he suffered as a result of the libel.

■ **Awards for damages** The major remedy for injury to reputation is the award of monetary damages. Compensatory damages that reimburse the plaintiff for the actual injury a plaintiff suffers as the result of libel or slander are awarded as discussed earlier. Special damages are a type of compensatory damages whereby the plaintiff is compensated for actual losses that clearly resulted from the defamation. If a lawyer can prove that two businesses have refused to hire him as their counsel because the local newspaper has called him a shyster, he has established special damages. If he can also show that he had to have psychiatric treatment to rebuild his self-esteem after the defamation, he will be entitled to general compensatory damages. He is also entitled to damages awarded for actual and presumed losses to the plaintiff from the defamation, such as hurt feelings, embarrassment, mental and emotional distress, and physical consequences.

In determining an award for damages, the jury may consider various factors, such as the nature of the defamation (irrational name-calling or insinuation of serious wrongdoing), the form and permanency of the publication (conversation or printed article), and the nature of the plaintiff's reputation. When a jury decides that a plaintiff's reputation was unimpaired by the defamation or his reputation was worth little or nothing to begin with, nominal damages, such as one dollar, may be given.

Punitive damages to penalize the defamer for his conduct result only when the defamation was motivated by malice. There may, however, be problems involved in awarding punitive damages against the news media because of the possible chilling effect upon the right to freedom of the press guaranteed by the First Amendment. See SPEECH AND PRESS, FREEDOM OF.

■ **Mitigating damages** Certain defenses, called incomplete defenses, do not bar liability but they do mitigate, or reduce, the amount of damages recoverable by the plaintiff.

Retraction If the defamer promptly publishes a retraction of the defamatory material with essentially the same prominence as he gave the false statement, the likelihood of punitive damages will be decreased. A true retraction shows the good faith of the communicator, rebutting the existence of actual malice and probably reducing the actual harm done to the plaintiff's reputation. It cannot completely erase the defamation, however, and the plaintiff will be entitled to at least token damages.

Retraction, however, must be unequivocal. Less than a full retraction or a veiled continuance of the defamation will not mitigate damages, but may in fact increase them. For example, to say "John Doe hasn't the morals of a tomcat" and then be willing to retract by saying "John Doe does have the morals of a tomcat" will not mitigate damages. A number of states have laws that specify the effects of retraction.

Right of reply Another method of mitigating damages is to allow the victim to use the defamer's facilities, such as a newspaper, to reply to the attack. This does not necessarily establish the defamer's good faith, and he may still have to pay damages. The actual injury to the defamed party may be reduced, however, because of the opportunity to reach and favorably influence those whose good opinion of him have been affected. The government may not require that the print media give the right of reply to victims of its defamatory statement because of conflict with the First Amendment's guarantee of freedom of the press. However, the Supreme Court has decided that broadcasters may be compelled to extend the right to reply, in certain circumstances, to those who have been personally attacked over their facilities. See FEDERAL COMMUNICATIONS COMMISSION.

liberty Freedom from illegal personal restraint; personal freedom under the law.

license 1 A right or permission granted by a government authority, such as the state or one of its political subdivisions, to carry on a business or to do an act that would be illegal without this right or permission. 2 The written document that confers the right or permission, such as a restaurant's liquor license. See Chart 29 for requirements for a driver's license in the 50 states, Chart 24 for auto registration and license plates, and Chart 20 for marriage license requirements. 3 The permission a person may grant to others to make use of his real estate or of a work on which he holds a COPYRIGHT or PATENT.

■ **Government licenses** Licensing is a government's means of taxing and regulating certain businesses, such as banks, airlines, employment agencies, restaurants, and theaters. Only a person, partnership, or corporation having the qualifications set by law and complying with the legal conditions is entitled to a license. There may be a *license fee,* or tax, for the privilege of having the license.

EXAMPLE Unemployed individuals often use employment agencies for help in finding jobs. These agencies are licensed by the state to protect a vulnerable segment of the population from being taken advantage of by unscrupulous persons. In order to be licensed, the owner of an employment agency must be of good character. A state may refuse to grant a license to someone who has been under investigation for or convicted of fraud in the operation of employment agencies in other states. People should deal only with licensed employment agencies because they have met certain standards set by the state.

The authority to license occupations and collect fees usually is included in the state's power to tax for revenue or in its POLICE POWER—its right to make laws that protect the public welfare. For instance, a state requires that medical doctors be licensed to protect its residents against incompetent medical treatment. Similarly, a driver who is unlicensed because he has failed the state's driving test poses a danger on the roads.

A license may be terminated by the expiration of the term for which it was granted, by voluntary abandonment or surrender, or by the death of the licensee (the person who holds the license). Suspension of a license is justified when the licensee violates a law, ignores the regulations of the licensing board, or engages in unprofessional conduct or deceptive advertising. A license may be revoked if it was obtained by fraud. A person whose license is suspended or revoked may appeal for review by a court.

Generally, violations of the license laws are criminal offenses but they may also create civil liabilities. For example, in almost every state the sale of securities is regulated by BLUE-SKY LAWS, under which the state protects the public from fraudulent stock deals. Dealers, brokers, and salesmen of securities must be licensed and bonded. Violations of these laws may result in civil liability, such as requiring the unlicensed broker to return all the purchaser's money, as well as criminal penalties—a fine or prison term.

■ **Private licenses** A landowner and the owner of a copyright or a patent may give other persons license (permission) to use his property in a specific way.

Real estate When real property (real estate) is involved, a license is the permission granted by the landowner (the licensor) to a person (the licensee) to engage in a specified activity on the land. For example, the owner of an apple orchard may give you a license to pick the fruit from his trees in the fall. No formal language or writing is necessary, unless required by law. A license may be implied from the words and acts of the parties and the relation between them. If, for instance, your father owned the orchard and it was a family tradition to pick apples every fall, your license to do so may be implied.

A license that is not based on a consideration (something given or done in exchange for the license), such as paying a fee, may be revoked by the licensor at any time. If a fee was paid, however, a license can be revoked only upon showing reasonable cause.

EXAMPLE Suppose you paid the owner of the orchard $3.00 ⊙——✳ for a license to pick apples. He tells you that no alcohol is allowed in the orchard, but you bring a six-pack of beer with you anyway. The owner of the orchard now has reasonable cause to revoke your license. He may, instead, choose to suspend your license, which means that until you are ready to comply with the conditions of the license, you do not have any legal right to remain on the property. Once you obey the terms of your license—by getting rid of the beer—you will be given the right to stay on the property.

An owner or occupier of the land has a duty to warn a licensee about any known hidden dangers, such as abandoned mine shafts or patches of thin ice on a skating pond. The licensee, however, must assume the risk of visible dangers, such as a large "Keep out!" sign and a barbed wire enclosure around a quicksand pit.

Copyrights and patents   A person who has the copyright on a literary or artistic work or the patent on an invention may grant a license to another—usually for a fee—to reproduce or copy that work or invention. A playwright, for example, may grant a license to a public television station to produce his play.

licensee   1 A person who holds a LICENSE.   2 Someone who is on another's property with permission, but without any invitation by the owner and with no financial gain to him—for example, an invited personal guest. In the law of NEGLIGENCE, the difference between a licensee and an INVITEE is an important one.

lien   A claim or a charge on PROPERTY as security for the payment of a debt. It gives the person to whom the debt is owed, the *lienholder*, or *lienor*, a right to have the property sold to pay the debt. In most states a MORTGAGE is a lien.

Some liens, called statutory liens, are created by law, such as a tax lien that attaches to the property of a person who has failed to pay his real estate tax. Others, called equitable liens, are created under equity—agreements or court judgments prompted by fairness rather than a particular law.

■ **Equitable liens**   An equitable lien may be either express or implied. An *express equitable lien* is one that arises from a written contract that shows an intention to charge some property with a debt. For example, if you pay for a television set with a personal check and the contract of sale expressly (specifically) states that the store owner will have a lien against your car if the check is no good, that lien against your car is an express lien.

An express equitable lien may be governed by the laws of SECURED TRANSACTIONS if it is recognized as a secured transaction by Article 9 of the Uniform Commercial Code (UCC). For example, if you buy a television set on an installment plan and use the set as collateral for the unpaid amount, the lien on the television set creates a secured transaction. Not all liens are secured transactions, however. A landlord's lien to collect rent and an artisan's lien (discussed below) are specifically excluded from the definition of a secured transaction under Article 9 of the UCC.

An *implied equitable lien* is one declared by a court from general considerations of right and justice based on the conduct and dealings of the parties. When a lien is an equitable one, the property in question remains in the possession of the debtor.

■ **Statutory liens**   Various types of liens are created by statute. For most statutory liens the property is in the hands of the lienholder. If you are in possession of someone else's property and you have improved that property or have performed some services for the owner in the ordinary course of business, you may have a lien on the property if the owner refuses to pay you for your improvements or services. Such liens are either specific or general. In one type of statutory lien, a mechanic's lien (discussed later in this entry), the property remains in the hands of the debtor.

Specific lien   A specific statutory lien arises when services are performed that add to the value of personal property (any property that is not real estate), creating a debt. The property remains in the possession of the lienholder until the debt is paid, but the debtor still owns the property. Most cases involving specific liens concern BAILMENT—the handing over of personal property to someone else for a particular purpose, such as giving an item to an artisan so that he can perform some work on it.

EXAMPLE If you take your watch to a jeweler for repair, you ⊙——✳ are giving the jeweler the right to keep the watch in his possession until it can be fixed. This is a bailment. The jeweler has a specific lien, called an *artisan's lien*, on the watch he has repaired until you pay for the services performed. If you fail to pay for the repairs, the jeweler can keep the watch and may be permitted to sell it to pay your debt. Any excess over the repair bill must be returned to you. If you had also taken a bracelet to be fixed, the jeweler would not have a lien against the bracelet based on the watch repairs. A specific lien attaches to the particular item that has been serviced.

A specific lien is dependent on the fact that the lienholder has continuous possession of the property in question. If he gives up possession, he loses his lien and will have to sue for his payment.

The right to keep the property ends when the debt has been paid or if there has been substantial misuse by the lienholder. If the jeweler who repaired your watch allowed his five-year-old daughter to wear it to school, for instance, this might be considered sufficient misuse for him to lose his lien. If the lienholder refuses to give up the property, he may be liable for CONVERSION (wrongful possession or use of someone else's property).

At common law, specific liens include those involving artisans, INNKEEPERS, WAREHOUSEMEN, and common CARRIERS. Today, these businessmen are often given statutory liens. An innkeeper has a lien on the baggage of a guest to secure charges for his lodgings. Under both common law and statutory law, a common carrier is given a lien to the extent of his charges for the transportation of goods and any reasonable expenses incurred in protecting them.

General lien   A general lien arises out of a series of transactions in the general course of business rather than a single specific transaction such as the repair of a watch. Attorneys, bankers, and FACTORS usually have general liens. (A *factor* is an agent who sells goods that the owner has entrusted to him.) To insure that his client will pay him for services already performed, an attorney may retain possession of the papers and personal property of his client that fall into his hands in his professional capacity. He also has a charging lien on any judgment he has obtained for his client for the value of his services. See ATTORNEY AND CLIENT.

A banker may retain stocks, bonds, or other papers that come into his hands from his customer for any general balance owed by the customer. A factor or commission merchant may hold onto all goods entrusted to him for sale by the owner of the goods for any balance due. The merchant may sell the goods to satisfy his lien, but he must account to the owner for any excess realized from the sale. General liens occur less frequently than specific liens.

■ **Mechanic's lien** A type of statutory lien, a mechanic's lien applies to a contractor, subcontractor, laborer, or building supplier who worked or furnished material for building construction or improvement. Suppose your neighbor hires a contractor to add an extra room to his house. After the work is completed, your neighbor loses his job and cannot afford to pay the bill. The contractor will have a mechanic's lien on the house. By law, the "owner" of a building subject to a mechanic's lien can be the actual owner, a lessee, or anyone else who has a legally protected interest in the property. Generally, property devoted to public use is not subject to a mechanic's lien.

To establish a mechanic's lien, you must usually show that the materials furnished or labor performed went into something that became part of the real estate. Whether the value of the real estate must have been increased depends on the statute under which the lien is claimed. Many laws allow a lien for interior improvements and FIXTURES—goods that are attached to real estate but that can be removed, such as stoves, heaters, and furnaces. A mechanic's lien can also attach for window frames, glass, and window and door screens, but not for window shades. A lien may exist for mirrors or mirror cases set in a wall but not for mirrors in removable frames—because a mechanic's lien is on the entire property, not on the specific improvement made to it.

A mechanic's lien usually must be recorded with the county clerk's office or in the registry of deeds. This gives notice of a lien on real estate to persons who are interested in buying it. Generally, any valid lien is enforceable against anyone who purchases that property. The filing requirement, therefore, is an important protection for potential buyers of real estate.

When there is a MORTGAGE as well as a mechanic's lien against property, the one recorded first will be paid off first in states where these obligations must be filed. Otherwise, the first debt created will be paid first. After a recorded mechanic's lien has been paid or settled, the owner of the property should make sure the cancellation is filed.

■ **Assignment of liens** Traditionally, liens were personal and could not be assigned (transferred)—that is, someone with a lien against your property could not sell or otherwise transfer that lien to a second party. Today some states permit assignment of liens by a specific contract but the debt that the lien secures must also be transferred. Usually, statutory liens are not considered assignable.

■ **Enforcement of liens** Liens may be enforced by an action to foreclose. An action to foreclose is a lawsuit brought by the lienholder in which the court decides whether or not the property should be sold. If the court decides for the lienholder, it will issue an order for the sale. The proceeds from the sale are used to pay off the debt and any court costs. The excess will be returned to the debtor. If he has the property in his possession, a lienholder often has the right by law to sell it to satisfy his lien without going to court, once he has given proper notice to the debtor.

■ **Discharge** A lien may be discharged, or ended, when the debtor pays the debt or when the lienholder agrees to waive it. A lien may be lost by the destruction of the property on which the lien exists. It may also be lost when the lien is created by operation of law. For example, by law a creditor has a lien against the estate of a debtor who dies, but he loses the lien if the estate is insolvent, that is, if there are more debts against it than it is worth. Under some laws, a lien is discharged when proceedings to enforce it are not begun within the time limit set by law.

life estate A right to use property only during the lifetime of a particular person. For example, if you have an estate in land for your own lifetime, you may use the land as long as you live, but you cannot pass it on to your heirs. For a full discussion of life estates, see ESTATE.

life in being See RULE AGAINST PERPETUITIES.

LIFO Last in, first out. A method of business inventory accounting. It assumes that the last goods purchased are the first ones sold. Thus, the goods left in the inventory at the end of the year are those that were purchased first. See FIFO.

lift Raise, take up. To lift a promissory note (a written promise to pay a sum of money on a given date) is to end the obligation by paying its amount. To lift the bar of the statute of limitations is to remove the barrier imposed by law by an act or acknowledgment.

EXAMPLE Some states will not allow a lawsuit to be brought
O←─✳ on a debt owed 20 years after it was incurred. This is a 20-year statute of limitations. If, during the 20-year period, the debtor acknowledges in writing that he owes the money and will repay it, the statute of limitations will be lifted; that is, it will begin to run anew from the date of the acknowledgment, thereby extending the time period in which the suit must be started. For example, Mark borrows $6,000 from Steve and promises to repay on August 15, 1981. Mark fails to repay. Steve will have 20 years—until August 15, 2001—to sue Mark. If Mark, on March 10, 1991, sends Steve a note acknowledging the debt, the statute of limitations begins to run anew from the date of the acknowledgment, March 10, 1991. Steve, therefore, has until March 10, 2011 to sue Mark. The written acknowledgment lifts the bar of the statute of limitations that would have been imposed on August 15, 2001.

limitation A restriction or qualification. A limitation on an ESTATE is a restriction on its duration or quality. For example, "Blackacre shall go to John until Mary reaches the age of 21" is a limitation on an estate because John has an interest in Blackacre only for a specified period of time.

limitations of actions

limitations of actions Set periods of time during which civil or criminal legal actions must be started and after which they cannot be brought. These time limits are set by legislation known as statutes of limitations.

A *statute of limitations* is a state or federal law restricting the time within which a legal action can be started. Statutes of limitations are enacted to prevent fraudulent and stale claims from springing up after all the evidence has been lost or the facts have become obscure because of memory loss or the death or disappearance of witnesses. However, the time limit specified must be reasonable in order to give a plaintiff a fair chance to seek relief—otherwise it is unconstitutional. The statute of limitations is a defense usually claimed by a defendant to defeat a criminal prosecution or a civil lawsuit that is brought against him after the appropriate time limit, but it may also be used by a plaintiff in a civil case as a defense against a COUNTERCLAIM.

The legislature that enacts the laws also has the power either to extend or to shorten their time limits by legislation, subject to certain restrictions. In a civil case, the parties themselves may by agreement, such as a provision in a contract, either lessen or lengthen the time period. A statute of limitations cannot be extended by the courts unless the law provides for extension.

■ **Civil actions** In civil cases, the cause of action (facts sufficient to support a valid lawsuit) generally determines what law of limitations shall apply. For example, some states require a person to bring a lawsuit for damages from an assault within one year from the date of the attack.

Figuring the time period Limitations generally begin to run when a valid cause of action arises. In many states, a breach of contract action must be started within six years from the date the contract is violated. The time limit within which to bring an action for fraud, on the other hand, does not commence until the fraud has been discovered. See Chart 4 for the statutes of limitations for starting various types of lawsuits in the 50 states. For limitations of suits for breach of contract, see Chart 7.

EXAMPLE Suppose Sam opens his safe and finds a worthless O——* stock he purchased 20 years ago. He decides to sue the stockbroker who tricked him into buying it. The statute of limitations for fraud is three years from the date of discovery. If Sam could not have learned that he was defrauded from the time he purchased the stock until the day he opened his safe, the statute would not expire until three years after he opened the safe. If, however, Sam could have known of the fraud earlier by being diligent, the three years will be computed from the time he could have known. Such a situation might have arisen if Sam's stockbroker had a much-publicized reputation for fraudulent activities, which Sam disregarded, and Sam failed to check the validity of the stock.

Suspending a time limitation A statute of limitations can be tolled (suspended) by certain acts. This means that although the time limit within which to bring an action is counted from a certain date, its running is postponed until the occurrence of some event specified by law. Tolling provisions benefit a plaintiff because they extend the time within which he is allowed to bring his suit.

Disabilities Although the statute of limitations runs against all people, it will be tolled when one of the parties is under a legal disability at the time the cause of action arises. A legal disability is the lack of legal capacity to do an act. For example, a minor or mentally incompetent person is considered incapable of starting a lawsuit on his own behalf. Imprisonment is also occasionally regarded as a disability. The law specifies which disabilities result in tolling the statute of limitations. The statute begins to run, however, as soon as the disability is removed.

A disability that postpones the operation of the statute against a person may be asserted only by that person.

EXAMPLE Jim, age 15, and John, age 19, sue Don for false O——* imprisonment because he intentionally locked them into an abandoned garage. The statute of limitations for false imprisonment is one year in their state. Being 15, Jim is considered a minor in that state, where the legal age is 18. The statute of limitations on Jim's lawsuit is tolled or suspended for three years until Jim reaches age 18. Once Jim is 18, he will have one year from that date to start his lawsuit against Don for false imprisonment. On the other hand, John, age 19, is treated as an adult and the statute of limitations is not tolled for his action. He must start his action against Don within one year from the date of the false imprisonment.

Once the statute of limitations begins to run, it will not be tolled by the subsequent disability of any of the parties unless stated by law. Suppose John in the example above is arrested for stealing cars and is jailed during the year in which he must begin his false imprisonment suit against Don. Even if being in jail is considered a personal disability, it will not postpone the running of the statute of limitations if it occurs after the cause of action arises—say, for failure to complete a contract.

If a party is under more than one disability at the time a cause of action arises, the statute of limitations does not begin to run until all the disabilities are removed. For example, suppose an insane minor is hit by a car. The statute of limitations on his lawsuit to recover personal injury damages will not begin to run until he reaches his legal age (usually 18 or 21) *and* he is no longer considered insane by law. See INSANE PERSONS.

Death When a suit was barred by the statute of limitations during a person's lifetime, his personal representative cannot start one after the person dies. Many statutes allow a personal representative extra time, however, if the time to bring the action was nearly over when the person died. This is because the appointment of a personal representative sometimes takes a few months, and the right to file a lawsuit should not be lost because of court delays. When there is still a substantial period of time to run, however, no extension will be granted.

When a situation that is the basis for a lawsuit against the estate of a person occurs after his death the statute usually will not start running until a personal representative has been appointed, because until then, there is no one to sue. When the cause of action accrues before the death of the defendant, the running of limitations is usually not suspended.

EXAMPLE Len is killed in a motorcycle accident he caused O——* because he was driving while drunk. Sam, a pedestrian, was hit by Len and received various injuries, including a broken leg. Sam has a cause of action against Len's estate for his injuries. The statute of limitations for

HOW DO STATUTES OF LIMITATIONS WORK?

■ A statute of limitations is a rule of state or federal law limiting the time within which a lawsuit or criminal prosecution for a particular wrongdoing—for example, fraud or larceny—can be brought.

■ The statute of limitations may be used as a defense, but the defendant must plead it when answering the complaint.

■ In civil cases, the cause of action (reason for the lawsuit) determines which statute of limitations applies. In many states, for example, a breach of contract action must be started within six years from the date of breach. The time limit for suing for fraud does not begin to run until the fraud has been discovered.

■ Most of the states have a statute of limitations for all crimes except murder. The statute of limitations on crimes begins to run (the time period

starts being counted) when the crime is committed.

■ Limitations on civil suits begin to run when the cause of the lawsuit arises. The statute of limitations can be tolled (suspended) by certain acts or circumstances. For example, it will be tolled if one of the parties is under a legal disability when the cause of action arises. Let us say a 10-year-old boy is hit by a car. Being a minor is a disability that prevents a person from starting a lawsuit. The statute of limitations on his lawsuit to recover damages for his injuries will not begin to run until he reaches legal age, which is usually 18 or 21.

■ Unexcused failure to begin a lawsuit within the statutory period bars the action. Ignorance of the existence of a cause of action does not suspend the statute, particularly when the facts could have been learned by diligence.

If a cause of action has been fraudulently concealed or could not be discovered by reasonable diligence, the limitations will be tolled until the action is or could have been discovered.

■ Under certain circumstances a party can be barred from using the limitations defense—this is called *estoppel*. To be estopped, the party must have done something that would induce the plaintiff to delay bringing the action. Merely attempting to discourage him is not enough—the plaintiff must have been deliberately hoodwinked into neglecting his own best interests. For example, an insurance company would be barred from using the statute of limitations to defend against a lawsuit brought by a patient when the company intentionally misled the patient and induced him not to file his lawsuit within the limitations period.

Sam's lawsuit does not start until a personal representative is appointed for Len's estate. If Len had lingered for three months before his death, the statute would start running as of the date of the accident.

Other suspensions Limitations are ordinarily tolled on a suit if other pending proceedings prevent enforcement of the remedy that the lawsuit could provide. For instance, a creditor is usually prevented from starting a lawsuit for a debt during the debtor's bankruptcy proceedings. Usually a court order suspending or staying the proceedings tolls the statutory period for the particular lawsuit.

Unexcused failure to begin a suit within the statutory period bars the action. Ignorance of the existence of a cause of action ordinarily does not toll the statute of limitations, when the facts could have been learned by inquiry or diligence. If a cause of action has been fraudulently concealed or could not be discovered by reasonable diligence, the limitations will be suspended until the cause of action is or could have been discovered.

EXAMPLE Janice buys a print from a local art gallery for 0—* $1,000. Its actual value is $50. Over the next two years, people connected with the gallery offer her $1,500 for the print as part of a scheme to have her buy more prints, which she does. When Janice learns she has been cheated, she starts a lawsuit for fraud based on *all* the prints she bought even though the statute of limitations has expired on the first print. The court will allow her to bring an action on *all* the prints because the cause of action on the first was fraudulently concealed.

Mere silence or failure to disclose the existence of a cause of action does not toll the statute, nor does the absence of the plaintiff or defendant from the state unless that exception is a rule of the statute.

The statute of limitations for a debt or obligation is tolled by either an unconditional promise to pay the debt or an acknowledgment of the obligation. This means that the time limitation on bringing a lawsuit to enforce payment of the debt or performance of the obligation will be suspended until the time for payment or performance has become due under the new promise or acknowledgment. As of that due date, the period of limitations will begin to run again. The part payment of the interest or principal on a debt may be sufficient to interrupt or suspend the statute of limitations, depending on state law.

■ **Criminal cases** Most states have statutes of limitations for all crimes except murder. After the statute expires, the court does not have the authority to try or punish a defendant.

EXAMPLE On November 3, 1977, a defendant was charged 0—* with a rape that had occurred March 20, 1973. The defendant appeared without a lawyer, pleaded guilty, and was sentenced to imprisonment. Subsequently, he requested to have the judgment invalidated because there was a three-year statute of limitations for rape. He won. The judgment was set aside.

The statute of limitations usually starts to run when the crime is committed, regardless of when it is discovered. The running of the statute may be tolled (suspended) for the period that the accused party is out of the state.

■ **Pleading** Because the statute of limitations is a defense, in either a civil or criminal case, the defendant must plead, or assert, it before the court when he answers the complaint. If he fails to do so, he has waived it and cannot employ it in any subsequent proceedings. A party against whom the statute is used as a defense should state the facts necessary to qualify his case as an exception. For example, if he was a minor when the action arose, the statute of limitations would not take effect until he reached the legal age of adulthood.

■ **Waiver** The statute of limitations may be waived as a defense by a person who is entitled to use it. The law cannot force anyone to use a statute of limitations as a defense, even though it may be in his best legal interest to do so.

■ **Barring the defense** A defendant may be prevented from using the limitations defense by his agreement, representations, or conduct. Unless required by statute, however, a written statement is not necessary. A defendant can be estopped from using the limitations defense if he did something that induced the plaintiff to delay bringing the action. Statements that only try to discourage a person from beginning a suit, such as "Why tie this up in long and costly court battles?" or negotiations toward an amicable settlement are insufficient.

> EXAMPLE Suppose a malpractice insurance company falsely O——* promises a patient that it will settle his claim against Dr. X for $150,000. The company tells the patient that it will take some time to process the settlement. In the meantime, the statute of limitations on the patient's malpractice suit expires. The insurance company cannot use the statute to defend against a subsequent suit brought by the patient. The defense is invalid because the company intentionally misled the patient and induced him not to file his lawsuit within the limitations period.

limited 1 Partial; restricted. Limited liability is the legal rule that the owners or shareholders of a corporation cannot usually be sued for corporate actions unless they are involved in fraud or a crime. The most they can lose, therefore, is the value of their investment. 2 The British and Canadian word for incorporated, abbreviated "Ltd."

Lindbergh Act The Lindbergh Act, also known as the Federal Kidnapping Act, is a federal law prohibiting the transportation of a kidnapped person across state lines. The law was enacted by Congress in 1932 in response to the overwhelming public concern over the kidnapping and murder of the infant son of Charles A. Lindbergh, who had become a national hero five years earlier when he became the first man to fly solo across the Atlantic Ocean.

Violation of the Lindbergh Act is a FELONY, and a person found guilty of violating it may be sentenced by the jury to imprisonment for any term up to life. Anyone who receives or disposes of ransom money collected in connection with KIDNAPPING across state lines—although he may not have done the actual kidnapping—may be fined up to $10,000 or imprisoned for up to 10 years, or both.

lineal That which comes in a line. A lineal relationship, for example, exists between a parent and child and a grandparent and grandchildren.

line of credit The maximum amount of CREDIT a merchant or bank will extend to a customer.

liquid asset An asset that can be easily converted into cash, such as stocks, life insurance policies with cash surrender values, or U.S. Savings Bonds. A house or land is not a liquid asset because it generally takes a few months before a person has the cash from its sale.

liquidate Pay and settle a debt; settle affairs and distribute assets, such as the money left by a dead person or by a company that goes out of business. To liquidate a business, the owner sells all assets and pays all debtors.

liquidated Ascertained; discharged. A liquidated claim is a claim for a definite amount of money, fixed either by agreement or by court action. A liquidated debt is an obligation that has been paid. Liquidated DAMAGES is a set amount of money, agreed upon by the parties to a CONTRACT, to be awarded to one party should the other violate the contract.

lis pendens (Latin) A "pending lawsuit"; a warning that ownership of real property (real estate) is being contested in court and that anyone who buys it becomes subject to the claims made in the suit. A notice of *lis pendens* is generally published in a paper of general circulation.

listing A contract representing a real estate broker's right to sell property and receive a commission. An *open listing*, or a *general listing*, is a sales right given to more than one agent at a time. An *exclusive agency listing* restricts the right to sell to the owner and one agency for a certain period of time. An *exclusive-authorization-to-sell listing* gives one agency the sole right to sell the property during a fixed time period. This means that, even if the owner finds the buyer, the agency will receive a sales commission. *Multiple listing* occurs when an agent with an exclusive listing shares information about the property with members of a real estate association and divides the commission with the agent who finds a buyer. A *net listing* is an arrangement in which the seller sets a minimum price that he will take for the property, and the agent's commission is the amount of the sale over that figure.

litigant A party to a lawsuit—a plaintiff or a defendant.

litigation A lawsuit, or ACTION; a contest in a court of justice to enforce a right. If one neighbor sues another for trespassing, they are engaged in litigation.

litigious Fond of litigation; prone to engage in lawsuits. If a person sues his neighbor for any and every minor encroachment, he could be described as litigious.

littoral Belonging to the shore, as of seas and lakes. A person whose lands border on a lake or a sea is a littoral owner. See RIPARIAN.

living trust A TRUST that takes effect during the creator's lifetime and is therefore in existence at his or her death. Also called an *inter vivos* trust, a living trust is different from one created by a will (testamentary trust).

LL.B. *Legum baccalaureus*, or Bachelor of Laws; the basic law degree until the late 1960's, when it was replaced by the J.D.—JURIS DOCTOR, or Doctor of Jurisprudence.

LL.M. and LL.D. *Legum magister,* or Master of Laws, and *legum doctor,* or Doctor of Laws. Both are advanced law degrees.

loan shark A person who lends money at an interest rate that is higher than the legal maximum. Charging an illegal rate of interest is a violation of the USURY laws, which in many jurisdictions is a criminal offense.

lobbying Attempting to persuade a legislator, such as a Congressman or state senator, to vote a certain way on a proposed law or to introduce a new bill. Lobbying is not illegal, but it has become subject to increasing state and federal regulation. In Washington, D.C., paid lobbyists must register with the Clerk of the House of Representatives and the Secretary of the Senate. Every three months, a registered lobbyist must file a detailed report stating what money he received and spent, and for what purposes. All this information is made public. Under federal law, a charitable organization can lose its tax-exempt status if it engages in substantial lobbying. What is substantial is determined just as a question of fact by the Internal Revenue Service but ultimately by the federal court.

local action A lawsuit that can arise only in one place. A suit to recover possession of land is a local action.

lockout The refusal by an employer to furnish work for employees in an effort to obtain more desirable terms in a labor dispute. The lockout is an employer's weapon, just as the STRIKE is a union's weapon.

loco parentis See IN LOCO PARENTIS.

locus (Latin) "Place." For example, *locus contractus* is the place where a contract is made.

lodger A person who lives in a part of a building run by another and who does not have control over the rooms in it. Examples of lodgers are residents of boardinghouses. See LANDLORD AND TENANT.

lost instrument A document (such as a deed) that cannot be found in spite of a thorough and diligent search.

In some states a stolen document is a lost instrument. On the other hand, a document deliberately destroyed by the owner, with the intention of canceling it, or one that is mutilated (torn up or inked out), is not a lost instrument.

The loss of a written document has no effect on the validity of the transaction that it represents. A copy can be established in court by starting a suit to restore the lost instrument, which can be done immediately after the loss. All interested persons should be made parties to, and should be given notice of, such proceedings.

A suit to establish a lost instrument showing ownership of land (a deed) can be started by anyone having an interest in the property, such as an heir of a deceased owner. This kind of case is the same as one QUIETING TITLE.

lot **1** A number of associated objects or things taken collectively, such as shipment of dresses to a retailer. **2** A share; portion. **3** A piece or parcel into which land is divided; a small tract or parcel of land in a village, town, or city, suitable for building.

lottery A method for the distribution of prizes by chance among persons who pay for the opportunity to win. A lottery is one form of GAMING, or gambling. The three necessary elements for a lottery are (1) the offering of a prize, (2) the payment of money or something else of value for the opportunity to win the prize, and (3) the awarding of the prize by a system of chance or a drawing. Selling tickets for a new car to be raffled off is a form of lottery. Conducting a lottery that is not permitted by law is usually considered a crime. Many states now sponsor lotteries as a way of increasing government revenues.

L.S. Abbreviation for *locus sigilli,* Latin for "the place of the seal," meaning the place where a seal is to be affixed in order to make a contract binding or a document official. Because the use of SEALS is dying out, these initials are used less than they were formerly.

LSAT Law School Admission Test; the so-called Law Boards, the test used by most American law schools to determine whether an applicant has the educational background and potential needed to complete the studies leading to a law degree.

magistrate A public civil officer; a minor judicial officer, such as a justice of the peace. In some areas, a magistrate has the power to issue a warrant for arrest. Depending on the locale, a magistrate may not exercise any judicial functions, but he might have other responsibilities, such as those of notary or commissioner of deeds.

magistrate's court A state court with limited jurisdiction (authority) to try minor offenses, such as traffic violations, and handle preliminary hearings. See CRIMINAL LAW. Its authority varies from state to state. Magistrates' courts may be divisions of courts of general jurisdiction, sharing jurisdiction with other courts. See Chart 1.

Magna Charta (Latin) "Great Charter"; the constitution granted by King John of England to the barons at Runnymede on June 15, 1215, and afterward confirmed in Parliament by Henry III and Edward I. The Magna Charta is regarded as the foundation of Anglo-American constitutional liberty. Among its 38 chapters are provisions for administering justice, securing personal liberties and property rights, limiting taxation, and preserving church liberties and privileges.

maintenance Unauthorized interference in someone else's lawsuit, usually by furnishing financial support or unsolicited advice. If done by an attorney, it can be a ground for disbarment. See CHAMPERTY AND MAINTENANCE.

majority The age at which a person is entitled, by law, to manage his or her own affairs; the opposite of minority. Anyone who has not yet received his majority is called an INFANT by the law. The age of majority (often 18 or 21) varies with the state and with the type of activity, such as marrying, signing a contract, or driving an automobile.

maker The person who initially signs a negotiable instrument, such as a promissory note, and by doing so promises to pay it. See COMMERCIAL PAPER.

malfeasance Wrongdoing; especially any wrongful conduct that affects, interrupts, or interferes with the performance of duties of a government official. A zoning commissioner who solicits a bribe is committing malfeasance in office as well as committing a crime.

malice The intention or desire to injure someone by deliberately doing some wrongful act without legal excuse or justification. For example, intentionally throwing acid in someone's face is malice.

malice aforethought The predetermination (deciding beforehand) to commit an unlawful act, especially the intention to kill or seriously injure someone; the intent to commit a serious crime.

An essential element of MURDER, malice aforethought exists when the attacker intends to cause death or grievous bodily harm (whether or not the victim is actually killed) or when a person intends to commit any felony whatever with the knowledge that the act will probably cause death or grievous bodily harm.

malicious mischief Willful destruction of personal property because of ill will or resentment toward its owner or possessor. It is a crime. See VANDALISM.

malicious prosecution A lawsuit begun solely to injure the defendant and without good reason to think the case can be won. If the action based on obviously flimsy or nonexistent evidence is decided in favor of the defendant, he can turn around and sue the person who started the case for malicious prosecution.

EXAMPLE Paul sued Rita for the tort of conversion for refusing to return a diamond bracelet that he claimed he loaned her to wear to a dinner dance. In fact, Paul had given Rita the bracelet as an engagement present, and when she broke the engagement, he decided to humiliate her by taking her to court. Rita established that Paul gave her the bracelet, by introducing testimony from the jeweler that she was present when Paul bought the bracelet and that Paul called it his engagement present to her as he slipped it on her wrist. Paul lost his case. Rita could then sue Paul for malicious prosecution to recover compensatory (actual) damages—the money she spent to defend herself, such as attorney's fees, and the salary lost when she took vacation time to attend the trial. She might also be awarded punitive damages if the jury decided that she was entitled to them because Paul's behavior was so spiteful that he should be punished.

malpractice   Any professional misconduct, particularly an unreasonable lack of skill in professional duties; illegal or immoral conduct. When applied to PHYSICIANS AND SURGEONS, malpractice is usually professional misconduct toward a patient, reprehensible either because it is immoral or because it is contrary to law. For example, a New York State court has held that a psychotherapist who had given professional care to a husband and wife, and later married the husband, could be sued for malpractice by the former wife. When applied to lawyers, malpractice refers to any unethical or illegal act committed in a professional capacity. See ATTORNEY AND CLIENT.

malum in se   (Latin) An "offense in itself"; an act inherently illegal according to the principles of natural, moral, and public law. Under the COMMON LAW such offenses as murder and larceny were *malum in se.*

malum prohibitum   (Latin) A "prohibited offense"; an act that is wrong because it is prohibited by law, not because it is inherently immoral. Speeding on a lonely desert highway is *malum prohibitum.*

manager   1 One who controls the business of a corporation or one of its branches and exercises discretion and independent judgment.   2 An individual chosen to administer the affairs of another person or a company.   3 A person appointed on behalf of the House of Representatives to prosecute impeachments before the Senate.

mandamus   (Latin) "We order"; an order issued from a court of superior jurisdiction (authority) to an inferior (lower) court, board, corporation, or person, commanding it or him to do or not to do an act as the law requires. A writ of mandamus is an extraordinary legal remedy not often granted. A court could issue the writ to require the appointment of a person to fill a vacated public office, for example.

mandate   A command, order, or direction—written or oral—that a court is authorized to give and a person is bound to obey.

mandatory   Required; obliged to be followed or obeyed. Some states have a mandatory law that no proposed bill can take effect unless it has been enacted by both houses of the state legislature.

mandatory authority   See BINDING AUTHORITY.

man-in-the-house rule   A former rule in some states that poor families could not receive welfare payments if a man lived with them. See WELFARE PROGRAMS.

Mann Act   The original federal law prohibiting transportation of females across state lines for immoral purposes, such as prostitution.

manslaughter   The unlawful killing of one person by another without MALICE, premeditation, or deliberation. Manslaughter is ordinarily divided into two classes: voluntary and involuntary. Voluntary manslaughter is intentional; involuntary manslaughter is not. Manslaughter is not a lesser degree of murder but a separate crime entirely. Malice aforethought—a determination to kill formed in the mind before the act—is an element of the crime of MURDER but not of manslaughter. Both voluntary and involuntary manslaughter are felonies punishable by prison terms.

■ **Voluntary manslaughter**   Voluntary manslaughter is intentionally killing someone in the heat of passion following adequate provocation. The passion must be strong enough to cause an ordinary person to act on impulse, rather than from reason and premeditation. The provocation and passion, both essential, must occur at the same time. If the killing is done after the time it would take an ordinary man to cool down, the crime is murder.

Provocation sufficient to reduce the crime from murder to manslaughter includes (1) mutual combat, provided the fighting causes great heat of passion; (2) injury to one of the accused person's relatives (wife, mother, brother, child), committed in his presence; (3) a legal arrest attempted in an unlawful manner with unnecessary violence, such as an officer's shooting at a person suspected of a misdemeanor and arousing his passions to the point where he kills the officer; (4) discovering one's husband or wife in the act of adultery and reacting in the heat of passion.

In general, words or gestures alone—however offensive, insulting, abusive, or threatening—are not sufficient provocation to reduce a murder to manslaughter.

■ **Involuntary manslaughter**   Involuntary manslaughter is the unintentional killing of a human being that results from (1) an unlawful act not amounting to a felony, (2) a lawful act done in a criminally negligent manner, or (3) a failing to perform a legal duty under circumstances amounting to criminal negligence. *Criminal negligence* is conduct that shows a reckless disregard for human life or safety and a willful indifference to the injury that is likely to follow.

An unlawful act not a felony   Generally, a person is guilty of involuntary manslaughter if he commits a misdemeanor or lesser offense that, without his intending it, causes the death of another person. (If, during the attempted commission or commission of a felony, a person unintentionally causes the death of another, such as running someone down with a getaway car during a robbery, he will be charged with felony murder, not involuntary manslaughter.) Some states distinguish between an act that is *malum in se* (bad in itself), such as assault, and one that is *malum prohibitum* (bad because prohibited), such as gambling. In some of these states manslaughter is committed only when the unlawful act that causes death is *malum in se* and not a felony. Other states hold that manslaughter may be committed even though the act was merely *malum prohibitum* and not a felony, particularly when the act violated a law intended to prevent injury to others.

EXAMPLE A man named Sampson leased an entire rooming house for three years. According to the terms of the lease, Sampson was to take possession of the building "as is." He was to make all necessary repairs and improvements so that the building would be safe for use as a tenement. Sampson did some interior plastering and painting and then rented the rooms. He did not make any structural repairs and the building remained unsafe. To obtain the license required to run the tenement, Sampson had to have the building inspected and approved by the health authorities. But Sampson knew that the building would not pass, so he did not apply for the license.

One month after the tenants moved into the building, a fire broke out, the four walls collapsed, and seven persons lost their lives. Sampson was charged with involuntary manslaughter. At his trial, he argued that his failure to obtain a license was merely *malum prohibitum,* and that there was no causal connection between his failure to obtain a license and the deaths. The court disagreed and convicted Sampson of involuntary manslaughter. The court held that if an act violates a law intended to prevent injuries to people and death results, the person violating the law is guilty of manslaughter, even though the act may only be *malum prohibitum.*

A lawful act in an unlawful manner   In some states, a person commits only involuntary manslaughter when he does a lawful act in an unlawful or negligent manner, as long as the negligence does not indicate a disregard for human life.

EXAMPLE A man driving an automobile sees a school bus O—＊ discharging passengers about 400 yards ahead. The driver knows that state law requires him to stop, but he is in a hurry, so he slows his automobile to 10 miles an hour and begins to pass the bus. A child darts out from behind the bus, is struck by the automobile, fractures his skull, and dies two days later. The driver is charged with involuntary manslaughter. He was performing the lawful act of driving his automobile, but since he failed to stop for the school bus, he was driving in an unlawful manner. Because he reduced the speed of his automobile to 10 miles per hour, his conduct did not show a reckless disregard for human life. Thus he can be convicted of involuntary manslaughter.

Failure to perform a duty   A death that results from the negligent failure to perform a legal duty can be involuntary manslaughter.

EXAMPLE Parsons and his teenage son Bobby went deer O—＊ hunting. After arriving at their destination in the family truck, Bobby went off on his own. Thinking he saw a deer, he fired his high-powered hunting rifle. A few minutes later, Bobby returned to his father's truck and announced that he had killed a deer. After about 10 minutes, the father agreed to look for the deer. Parsons went in one direction while Bobby went the other way. Instead of a deer, the boy found a large man about 140 yards from the spot where Bobby had fired his rifle. The victim, a man named Sharp, had his left hip almost blown off. He was conscious, however, and he asked the boy to help him. Bobby was an expert in first aid, but he did nothing to stop the flow of blood. He ran to a nearby residence owned by Sharp's elderly father, who returned with him to the scene of the accident. Parsons had arrived there also. Parsons and the boy promised Sharp Senior that they would call an ambulance but made no offer to help him move his son.

Parsons and Bobby then left in the truck. They knew of the seriousness of the victim's injury, but they did not stop to use the telephone at a café only 2.3 miles from where Sharp lay. When they arrived home—14 miles from the accident—they substituted a shotgun for the rifle and then called an ambulance to meet them at the café, where it arrived 25 minutes later. The father and son went back to the scene of the accident, where they found Sharp Senior loading his son into his truck. The victim died just after being transferred to the ambulance.

Bobby and his father were charged with involuntary manslaughter and found guilty.

manufactures   Articles of trade that have been transformed by labor, art, skill, or machine from raw materials into a finished product. The finished product has new forms, qualities, or properties. Fresh tomatoes are not manufactures but canned tomatoes are. Whether or not an item falls into this category is important when considering taxes and other regulations imposed on manufactures.

Mapp v. Ohio   A 1961 U.S. Supreme Court case that established the rule that illegally obtained evidence may not be used to prove guilt at a criminal trial in state courts.

In this case, three Cleveland police officers went to the home of Dollree Mapp after they had received a tip that someone wanted for questioning about a recent bombing was hiding out there and that gambling materials were hidden in the house. Miss Mapp and her daughter lived on the top floor of a two-family house. When the officers demanded entrance, Miss Mapp called her attorney and refused to let them in without a search warrant. About three hours later, more officers arrived and broke down the door to get in. When Miss Mapp's attorney appeared, the police would not let him see his client or enter the house. Miss Mapp again demanded to see a search warrant. One of the men waved a paper (which was not, in fact, a search warrant) and she grabbed it, stuffing it down the top of her dress. A policeman seized her, wrestled the paper away, slapped handcuffs on her, and arrested her for being "belligerent" and resisting his "official rescue of the 'warrant.' " The police searched everything, including personal papers and even a photo album. Finally, they found some obscene books, pictures, and photographs, and Miss Mapp was convicted of possessing them.

The Supreme Court condemned the policemen's actions, calling them "high-handed" and "roughshod," and held that Miss Mapp's privacy had been unconstitutionally invaded. The Court compared the police tactics to a confession forced out of a fearful prisoner and ruled that the only way to compel respect for the constitutional "right of the people to be secure in their persons, houses, papers, and effects against unreasonable searches and seizures" is to exclude illegally obtained evidence from the trial court. Miss Mapp's conviction was reversed because it rested on the illegally obtained evidence.

Protection from illegal searches is guaranteed by the Fourth Amendment to the Constitution. As early as 1886, the Supreme Court had ruled that illegally obtained evidence could not be introduced in federal courts. It was with the Mapp decision in 1961 that the Court finally applied the same principle, called the *exclusionary rule,* to the states. The Court noted that various states had tried to prevent illegal police searches by other means, but the exclusionary rule proved to be the only effective protection for citizens. See also SEARCH AND SEIZURE.

Marbury v. Madison

The 1803 case in which the Supreme Court established its authority to declare unconstitutional a law enacted by Congress.

Just days before Federalist John Adams was succeeded as President by Anti-Federalist (Republican) Thomas Jefferson in 1801, Adams rushed two laws through Congress that doubled the number of federal judges and authorized 42 new justices of the peace in the District of Columbia. Adams signed the commissions (the written authority to take the posts) for the appointees, most of them Federalists, but there was not time to deliver all of them before Jefferson took office. Jefferson ordered his Secretary of State, James Madison, to withhold delivery. Several justices of the peace who did not receive their commissions—one of them William Marbury—sued to get an order compelling Madison to deliver the commissions. Such an order is called a writ of MANDAMUS.

Chief Justice John Marshall, himself a Federalist appointed by Adams one month before the end of his Presidency, delivered the Court's opinion in 1803. The Court held that under a law passed by Congress the Supreme Court was authorized to issue the required writ of mandamus. Marshall, speaking for the court, found, however, that the law in question conflicted with the section of the Constitution that describes the limits of the Supreme Court's authority. Marshall wrote that any law that is in conflict with the Constitution is void; therefore, the Supreme Court had no power to issue a writ of mandamus. Marbury did not get his commission. The Constitution, Marshall wrote, is the supreme law of the land.

The decision firmly fixed the rule that the authority of both Congress and the Supreme Court is strictly limited by the Constitution, but it did so by insisting that the Supreme Court has the power to declare an act of Congress in violation of the Constitution and therefore completely void.

margin

1 Edge or border. When describing the boundary lines of a piece of land, margin may mean the center of a river, creek, or other watercourse, if that is where the boundary falls. The margin of a body of water is the point where the water meets land. **2** A sum of money paid to one's stockbroker after the broker has allowed him to purchase shares of stock on credit. The amount paid is usually a certain percentage of the purchase price set by the federal Securities and Exchange Commission. Margin requirements are designed to protect the national economy from excessive fluctuations of the stock market by reducing the amount of credit available for stock speculation while at the same time protecting the unsophisticated individual investor against improvident speculation on credit.

marital

Having to do with MARRIAGE or the relationship of HUSBAND AND WIFE.

marital deduction

See ESTATE AND GIFT TAX.

maritime law

The law of ships, ocean commerce, and sailors. See ADMIRALTY.

maritime lien

A person's right to force the sale of a ship because he has not been paid money owed to him for services or goods provided for the ship. A maritime lien is usually created by contract. The law gives this kind of security to a creditor so that a ship can obtain repairs and supplies even if it is in a distant port and its officers are without enough money to pay for goods and services. It is not necessary for the creditor to keep possession of the ship in order to assert his claim. A watch repairman, for example, can get the repair bill paid by having the watch sold, but only if he has kept it in his possession while waiting for his money. The holder of a maritime lien can sue to have a vessel sold wherever he finds it.

To enforce a maritime lien, the lienholder must sue in a federal court. Anyone else who has a lien against the ship can intervene in the lawsuit; the court may order the ship and its cargo sold and the proceeds distributed to everyone who proves a valid claim against the ship. When there is not enough money to satisfy every claim, the court can determine which liens have priority and the percentage of full recovery that each claimant is entitled to collect.

The amount of the lien is equal to the reasonable value of services performed in caring for the vessel and of supplies furnished plus interest and minus any setoff (see COUNTERCLAIM) for claims the ship has against the lienholder. The amount usually arises from a contract, but a maritime lien can also be created for money DAMAGES from injuries caused by the ship.

A maritime lien can exist on any movable objects that have something to do with navigation or commerce on navigable waters. That includes every part of a vessel, such as the hull, engine, and tackle. It also includes flatboats, lighters, scows, and dredges used to deepen harbors and channels. There is some disagreement about whether a maritime lien can attach to a raft. Courts have not recognized maritime liens for bridges, dry docks, wharves, or floating structures permanently moored to shore, such as barges used for dancing pavilions.

A person entitled to a maritime lien may lose his right if he delays in enforcing it. Permitting the vessel to depart does not affect the lien, but the total destruction of the vessel abolishes it. When the government seizes a ship because of an illegality, such as smuggling, the lien is still valid, unless the lienholder was involved in the illegality.

marketable title

See VENDOR-PURCHASER RELATIONSHIP.

market price or value

1 The price at which one person is ready and willing to sell and another is ready and willing to buy in the ordinary course of trade. **2** The price given in current transactions on the open market when the sale is not forced. **3** The actual price currently or recently paid for a certain commodity, not including customs duties, sales taxes, or similar charges.

marque and reprisal

A commission granted from the head of a government to a private ship giving it marriage644

authority to capture enemy vessels. The authority is granted in *letters of marque and reprisal*. A letter of marque is permission to cross the frontier into enemy waters, and a letter of reprisal authorizes retaliation, or a "taking in return."

Because letters of marque and reprisal permitted privately owned and operated vessels to carry out acts of war, the practice was also called *privateering*. Privateers operated in addition to regular navies. The primary goal was to harass the enemy, but an enemy's merchant vessels were frequently seized in retaliation for some act of hostility. Privateering was encouraged from about 1692 to 1814, when weak countries used privateers to hurt stronger countries.

Privateering was greatly abused. Without proper letters, a privateer was a pirate and piracy was severely punished throughout the world. Privateers claimed to operate only to defend their sovereigns, but they also made themselves rich. Because they were not subject to naval laws, they frequently seized ships beyond their authority. During the American Revolution and the War of 1812, American privateers captured hundreds of prizes, amassing great wealth for themselves because they were permitted to keep a portion of their booty. See PRIZE.

Privateering was abolished in 1856 by international agreement. But a country may still organize a volunteer navy of private vessels under its control and direction, such as the one that was used for the evacuation of Dunkirk in World War II. The U.S. Constitution grants the federal government, but not the states, the power to issue letters of marque and reprisal.

marriage The civil status and relationship of one man and one woman united in law for life; the wedding ceremony.

A *ceremonial marriage* is one solemnized by a wedding ceremony that conforms to the law of the state where it is performed.

A *common-law marriage* is one entered into by agreement of the parties without a ceremony or an exchange of vows. Most states do not consider such marriages valid. In those that do, the parties are legally married when they agree to it and then live together, publicly recognized as husband and wife, sometimes for a specified length of time.

A *consensual marriage* is one created by words of consent by each party. It is sometimes valid where common-law marriage is recognized, but unlike common-law marriage, it is valid from the time the words of marriage are spoken—even before the parties live together.

This article discusses the nature of marriage under the law, the requisites for a legally valid marriage, the alternatives to customary ceremonial marriage—common-law marriage and cohabitation—and legal agreements made between partners before or during their marriage. For a discussion of the relationship between a husband and wife and the legal rights that grow out of it, including those related to the ownership or property and the rights of inheritance, see HUSBAND AND WIFE. For a discussion of the relationship between a married couple and their children, see PARENT AND CHILD. For a discussion of legal matters involved in the ending of a marriage, see ANNULMENT; CUSTODY; DIVORCE.

■ **Regulation by law** It has been said that marriage does more than any other institution to uphold the morals and security of civilization, and for that reason society has a strong interest in regulating the relationship through law.

The Supreme Court has held that states have the right to regulate marriage. They may by law prescribe who can marry (as discussed in this article), what obligations are created by marriage (as discussed in HUSBAND AND WIFE), and how marriage can be dissolved (as discussed in ANNULMENT and DIVORCE). States cannot, however, absolutely prohibit marriage for any healthy adult without a good reason. In 1978 the Supreme Court threw out a Wisconsin law that prohibited anyone who had been ordered to pay support for a child not in his custody from getting a marriage license without first obtaining a court order, which would not be issued if support payments were overdue or if the child was likely to become a public charge.

EXAMPLE A young man had admitted in court that he became the father of an illegitimate baby girl while he was in high school. The court had ordered him to pay $109 a month for her support until her 18th birthday, but he was unemployed, indigent, and unable to pay. Two and a half years later, the man applied for a marriage license, but his application was denied. In another case, decided along with this one, a man who had fully paid up support for his four children was denied a marriage license because the children were nevertheless on welfare.

The Supreme Court held that banning subsequent marriages was not an appropriate way to enforce support obligations. As Justice John Paul Stevens wrote, "[T]his clumsy and deliberate legislative discrimination between the rich and the poor is irrational in so many ways that it cannot withstand scrutiny under the Equal Protection Clause of the Fourteenth Amendment."

In 1967 the Supreme Court held that the 16 states that still had antimiscegenation statutes (those prohibiting marriages between persons of difference races) were violating the rights of citizens: such laws illegally interfered with marriage, which the Court called a basic civil right.

EXAMPLE A white man and a black woman from Virginia were legally married in Washington, D.C. When they returned to Virginia to live as husband and wife, they were indicted by a grand jury for violating Virginia's ban on interracial marriages and sentenced to one year in jail. The trial judge suspended the sentence for 25 years on condition that they leave Virginia and not return together for that period. The couple moved to Washington, D.C., but sued to have the conviction and sentence set aside. It was overturned by the Supreme Court.

States may not intrude into the privacy of the marriage relationship unless absolutely necessary—to prevent incest, for example. The state's interest in spelling out family obligations clashes with the individual's liberty and happiness, and the latter must be protected.

■ **The nature of marriage** Marriage is both a status and a contract. Marriage is a legal status because the law confers a set of rights and obligations on each partner to it and also gives a separate legal existence to the marriage itself. Marriage is a contract in the sense that the husband and wife agree between themselves how to share responsibilities as they work toward common goals.

For the most part, the law follows a hands-off policy as long as the marriage is ongoing. Judges will not, for example, order a working spouse to give a sum of spending money to a dependent spouse each week or meddle in arguments about balancing the budget. If the marriage begins to break up, however, the law will step in to settle disputes.

Male and female   Marriage is the union of one male and one female. The idea is so basic that laws generally do not express it. But in recent challenges homosexuals have sought to legalize their relationships for a variety of practical reasons, such as to insure economic security for a nonworking "spouse," to secure inheritance rights given to couples, and to qualify for some important tax benefits enjoyed by married couples.

EXAMPLE In 1971 Richard John Baker and James Michael O⊶⚹ McConnell applied for a marriage license in Hennepin County, Minnesota. The county clerk refused to issue one because both applicants were male. They sued the clerk, asking the court to direct him to give them a license. The court denied their petition, pointing out that the law did not necessarily permit what it did not specifically prohibit. The court noted that the marriage law is filled with heterosexual terms such as "husband and wife" and "bride and groom" and traced back to the book of Genesis the concept that the union of man and woman was for the unique purpose of procreating and rearing children. The court found that no constitutional rights were violated when the state continued to preserve the ancient notion that marriage is a relationship between a man and a woman.

The legal questions become complicated when the sex of one marital partner is not clear. If a person undergoes a sex-change operation before marriage and both parties are aware of it, the question arises as to whether an operation can in the eyes of the law change a person's sex.

EXAMPLE In New Jersey, a man and a transsexual, who O⊶⚹ were both aware of the "woman's" sex-change operation, were married after the operation and lived as husband and wife. The husband deserted his wife when he found that he would be disinherited if he did not leave her. She began receiving welfare but asked the court to order him to contribute to her support.

The court stated that, according to law, everyone is either male or female and that this classification depends on anatomy. Doctors recognize that some human beings are not completely male or female. In this case, the judge found that the plaintiff was enough of a woman to have been validly married, and he awarded her $50 per week for support. In his decision, the judge wrote, "The entire area of transsexualism is repugnant to the nature of many persons within our society. However, this should not govern the legal acceptance of a fact."

Two people   The requirement that marriage involve one man and one woman outlawed polygamy—having more than one husband or wife at a time. Once someone is married, he or she must be legally freed by death, divorce, annulment, or dissolution before lawfully marrying again. No state will issue a marriage license to anyone who has a living spouse. Additional marriages are invalid, and most states will prosecute the offender as a criminal.

EXAMPLE The Supreme Court ruled in 1878 that a state O⊶⚹ may prohibit polygamy. The case was brought by a Mormon man who claimed that his church encouraged men to have more than one wife at a time. He said that if Utah were permitted to fine him or imprison him under its bigamy law, his constitutional right to freedom of religion would be denied.

The Court held that he could believe anything he wanted, but he could not put into practice a belief that society condemns. One group of people cannot claim immunity from punishment on the ground that its acts are based on a religious belief contrary to the law. No one would assume, for example, that human sacrifice could be justified as a religious practice. The Mormon Church has now repudiated polygamy and excommunicates members who espouse it, whether or not they practice it.

■ **Requirements for marriage**   A man and woman must meet several other requirements (which vary among the states) before they may be married.

Genetic characteristics   In the early 1900's many states enacted laws that prohibited marriage by criminals, alcoholics, imbeciles, the feebleminded, and INSANE PERSONS, in the belief that the harm done by misfits could be controlled if they were not allowed to marry and reproduce. Some states still prohibit marriage for the insane, imbeciles, or idiots. The theory today is not so much that these people can be prevented from bearing defective children but that they do not have the mental capacity to understand marriage.

Family relationships   Every state prohibits marriage between close relatives. Which relationships are prohibited depends on the law in each state. Every state prohibits marriage to a child or grandchild, parent or grandparent, brother or sister, uncle or aunt, and niece or nephew. This includes illegitimate relatives and relatives of the half blood, such as a half brother who has the same father but a different mother. Many states also prohibit marriage to a first cousin, and some forbid marriage with a more distant relative, such as an in-law and stepparent or stepchild. See Chart 20. See also INCEST.

Age   Another requirement in every state is that the parties be old enough to marry. Usually, females may marry at 16 and males at 18. Some states permit a lower age with written parental consent, and many allow marriage below the minimum age if the female is pregnant and a judge gives permission. See Chart 20.

Formal requirements   Certain formalities are required of a couple before they can be married. These formalities help insure that people do not marry accidentally, unwillingly, in jest, or under the influence of drugs or alcohol. Although the requirements vary from state to state, they generally include blood tests, a marriage license, and a waiting period.

Blood test   Almost every state requires a blood test before marriage. See Chart 20. Some states also require a physical examination. The purpose of the tests is to detect a venereal disease. Sometimes other health problems are revealed, such as the absence of immunity to rubella (German measles) in women of childbearing age, Rh blood factor incompatibility, tuberculosis, or drug addiction. If tests reveal communicable venereal disease, the clerk can refuse to issue the marriage license. A medical examination makes the parties aware of any existing physical problems that may cause them to decide against marriage.

There are different ways of enforcing the health test requirement. For instance, in some states the clerk may not issue a marriage license until the parties produce the results of the tests. In others, the parties risk criminal penalties for giving the clerk false information. Failure to comply with a health test regulation usually does not make the marriage invalid. However, if one party hides the fact of venereal disease or some other affliction, this might give the other person grounds for ANNULMENT of the marriage.

License and banns   It has always been customary to make marriage a public event. The old form of notice was called publication of the banns. The impending marriage was announced in each partner's church on the three consecutive Sundays before the ceremony. This alerted the community to the intended marriage and gave anyone who knew of a reason the two should not be married an opportunity to object.

Modern-day marriage licenses serve as both a public announcement and a public record. Every state issues licenses before marriages can take place. Clerks who issue licenses to unqualified persons and applicants who give false information can face criminal charges, although they seldom do because the law is intended more to prohibit marriages that violate the requirements than to punish offenders.

Waiting period   Most states have a waiting period between the application for a license and its issuance. The time is usually three days, but in some states it is five. In some states there is a waiting period between the time the license is issued and the time the marriage ceremony can take place. Sometimes the requirements are different for those who are under the age of consent or those who are residents of a different state. Usually, the marriage license is valid only for a certain period, but a new license can be obtained if the marriage ceremony does not take place within the time set by the license. See Chart 20.

■ **Ceremonial and common-law marriage**   As indicated above, there are two kinds of marriage in the United States, those marriages that start with a ceremony and those that do not.

Ceremonial marriage   Every state recognizes marriages that start with a wedding ceremony, and many states permit no other kind. The ceremony may be either civil or religious. In some states, all that is required is a declaration by each party, before an authorized person and in the presence of one additional witness, that he or she takes the other in marriage. Some states specifically authorize variations—for Indian tribal customs, for example, or for Quakers, who do not recognize any one person as an authorized minister.

The requirement of an authorized person to perform the marriage ceremony is very flexible. All states recognize the validity of a marriage celebrated by an ordained minister, priest, rabbi, or licensed preacher. Depending on the law of the state, a public official, such as a mayor or a judge, may also perform marriages. States do have an interest, however, in suppressing marriage mills run by quacks who will marry anyone, no questions asked.

EXAMPLE A New York court agreed to annul a marriage on
O←→* the ground that the person who performed the ceremony was not a minister. He was a guitarist and folksinger who had received his "credentials of ministry" by sending money to the Universal Life Church in California. Although the court conceded that everyone is entitled to be married by a minister of his own faith, it found that the Universal Life Church espoused no faith.
In many places, ministers must secure a license before they can perform marriages.

Proxy marriage   Many states relaxed their marital requirements during wartime, permitting the ceremony to be performed even though one person (or sometimes both) could not be present—a proxy stood in and spoke the vows for the absent person with his or her voluntary consent. A typical case might involve a woman who discovered that she was pregnant after the Army had sent her fiancé overseas. Where proxy marriages were legal, a friend could stand in for the groom, and the ceremony could take place before the child was born. Most states no longer permit proxy marriages.

Common-law marriage   Common-law marriages are informal marriages that do not begin with a wedding ceremony. In its "pure" form, common-law marriage is entered into in the same way that a contract is. The parties promise to fulfill the usual duties of husband and wife and agree from that time forward to be married. In states where common-law marriage is valid, it creates the same obligations for husband and wife. The only legal ways out of a valid common-law marriage are death and divorce.

About one-third of the states recognize common-law marriage (see Chart 20), and they do not require it to be in its "pure" form. Instead of asking for proof that the parties privately exchanged marriage vows at the beginning of their relationship, courts will assume that they intended a common-law marriage if they have cohabited for a long time and presented themselves as husband and wife in the community.

The reason for recognizing common-law marriage is to protect the people involved; it seems fair that their children should be legitimate, that widows should receive Social Security, and that families should inherit property in spite of a technical requirement—the ceremony—that was not met many years before.

Unlike a ceremonial marriage, a common-law marriage lacks official documentation, but the question usually does not arise until one party dies or abandons the other. By that time, it is more important to protect the security of family members than to insist on formalities.

■ **Agreements that affect marriage**   Parties who want to alter the rights and obligations of marriage may do so only within the limits set by law, through three kinds of agreements: (1) *antenuptial agreements,* which are entered into before marriage and in anticipation of the marriage relationship; (2) *reconciliation agreements,* which are entered into during marriage and concern continuation of the relationship, usually after some dispute; and (3) *separation agreements,* which are entered into during marriage and anticipate a separation or divorce. The regulations for each type of agreement are different. Although the law seeks to protect every marriage, whether the parties desire it or not, the law encourages people to resolve their own difficulties rather than to place every problem before the courts.

Agreements made before marriage   An *antenuptial agreement* is a contract between two people who plan to marry, in which one or both give up rights or take on obligations that are not provided for in marriage law. The classic agreement is one in which a woman of modest means gives up any rights to inherit the property of a rich man if he marries her. The law scrutinizes such agreements very carefully for two reasons. First, determining the financial consequences of marriage for oneself is against the public policy of the state because the laws that exist are meant to give financial protection to marriage partners. Second, if one partner has greater wealth or business experience, it is easy for him (or her) to take advantage of the other because of the close relationship and the differences in bargaining power.

The courts closely guard the legal rights of the weaker party to an antenuptial agreement. The one who limits his obligations must fully disclose his financial circumstances or make provision for the spouse's future. A husband, for example, might agree to give a dependent wife a specific amount of money at the time the agreement is made if she agrees not to claim anything from his estate when he dies. In a case like this, a court is more likely to hold the agreement valid if the wife has been represented by an attorney. Almost every state requires that an antenuptial agreement be in writing and signed by both parties.

The antenuptial agreement must not degrade the status of marriage.

EXAMPLE   A wealthy man and his intended wife agreed in 0——* writing that the marriage should continue only as long as they were satisfied and happy. If anything should disturb this bliss, she was to leave their home within 24 hours, taking only her personal belongings, and he would give her $100 for each year they had lived together. The parties separated after less than a year. The husband gave the wife a check for $100, and in return she signed a receipt relinquishing all claims for support. The husband died a couple of years later without a will, and the woman submitted a claim to inherit as his widow. The court declared the antenuptial agreement void, saying: "The antenuptial contract was a wicked device to evade the laws applicable to marriage relations, property rights, and divorces, and nothing more . . . than an attempt, on the part of the deceased . . . to legalize prostitution, under the name of marriage, at the price of $100 per year." The court awarded the woman the widow's share of the estate. (See DESCENT AND DISTRIBUTION for a discussion of a widow's right to her husband's estate.)

Premarital agreements can cover everything from the number of children the couple will have and the names in which the couple will own property, to who will wash the dishes and how often the in-laws will visit. Such agreements are not enforceable, however, in the way a contract normally is. The usual legal remedies—money damages, an injunction, even divorce—cannot be used, because the state, not the parties, determines the legal rights that result from marriage. Courts will usually throw out antenuptial agreements as invalid when one spouse has unfairly been taken advantage of by the other or when important facts that

would significantly influence a spouse's decision to sign the agreement have been concealed. When such agreements are void, courts will apply the law instead.

Antenuptial agreements can be of practical use for couples who have been married before, not only because divorced people may be cautious the second time around but also because they may need to plan for children or property they already have. Antenuptial agreements regulating inheritance rights are regularly enforced in court and can be useful in estate planning. If the parties share similar or comparable backgrounds and experiences and it can be established that both knew the legal consequences of the agreement and it was fairly negotiated, an antenuptial agreement will be enforceable.

EXAMPLE   Nancy, a real estate agent, and Don, an advertis-
0——* ing executive, decide to marry, although both have had previous unsuccessful marriages. They sign an antenuptial agreement whereby both promise to waive any inheritance rights to the other's estate. Each wants the children of his or her prior marriage to be the sole heirs of the estate. After Nancy's death, Don seeks to have the antenuptial agreement declared void so that he will be entitled to a share of his wife's estate. A court will hold the agreement enforceable if it can be shown that Don understood the legal consequences of the agreement and that no important facts were concealed from him to trick him into signing the agreement.

Agreements made during marriage   Any agreement that a husband and wife sign *during* a marriage is likely to be given less legal effect than an antenuptial agreement, unless the marriage is faltering. The parties may negotiate details of their financial, sexual, or social relationship, but compliance must usually be voluntary, and courts have refused to enforce agreements to raise children in a particular religion, to pay a wife wages for extra household chores, or to share an "open" marriage with each partner free to seek sexual gratification outside the marriage.

When a marriage has reached the breaking point, the parties may be reconciled if one agrees to forgive the other's misconduct in exchange for something of value. This is a *reconciliation agreement,* which the courts traditionally recognize. For example, many a husband who has been discovered committing adultery has saved his marriage by promising to put title to the house in his wife's name.

Agreements contemplating an end to marriage
The most common agreement between husband and wife is the *separation agreement,* which may be entered into when the marriage breaks up. The parties frequently negotiate terms of separation with the expectation that they will apply to an eventual DIVORCE. But it is usually illegal to include any term in the separation agreement that encourages divorce (because it is against the state's interest to promote divorce); therefore, any agreement in which one party seems to be buying consent to divorce from the other will be held void by the courts. For example, many states will not permit a husband to agree that he will pay his wife's legal expenses if she seeks a divorce (even though a court might order him to do that anyway), because the husband is thereby promoting divorce.

Most states also require the parties to be on the verge of separation or already living apart when the agreement is signed. Otherwise, the agreement might encourage the separation, and the court would disregard its terms.

Generally, courts will accept separation agreements as the parties have negotiated them, incorporate them into judgments of legal separation or divorce, and let either party sue the other to enforce the agreements. The parties may resolve questions of child custody, visitation, child support or alimony payments, and ownership of property in a separation agreement. A court will scrutinize any agreement that comes before it to be sure each party has been honest and that the settlement is not clearly unfair.

Neither party is likely to get everything he or she wants—separation agreements require compromises. Attorneys are virtually a requirement, because the legal issues are so complex that it is extremely unwise to attempt to negotiate an agreement without one. A separated husband who has been harassed by public accusations and endless phone calls from his wife may want nothing more than a "nonmolestation clause" in which the wife agrees to leave him alone, and he may agree to almost anything to obtain such an agreement from her. His attorney, however, will be able to see that the wife's behavior is probably temporary and that the tax, alimony, and child-support problems are far more important and long term.

Once a separation agreement is signed, the parties are both entitled and required to live apart unless both agree to resume marital relations. They may live separated indefinitely, but they are still married and their conduct can still be legal grounds for a DIVORCE. For that reason, many people prefer to go ahead with the divorce. Sometimes the terms of a separation agreement are incorporated into a JUDGMENT of divorce, and remain enforceable as part of that judgment.

If the parties decide to live again as husband and wife, the legal effect of the separation agreement usually ends. Another separation would require a new agreement.

When a marriage falls apart and the parties cannot come to terms on a separation agreement, many states will permit one person to sue in court for a legal separation. The grounds for such a decree depend on the law of the particular state. If a court grants a legal separation—sometimes called a *limited divorce* or a *divorce a mensa et thoro* (divorce from bed and board), the court can dictate the terms. People who are given a separation decree by a court are still married until divorced in court.

■ **Cohabitation** When a man and woman live together without being married, the relationship is called *unwed cohabitation*. It is different from a common-law marriage, which is created by the intention of the parties to be married. The intention of cohabitants is *not* to be married. They do not become married just because time has passed. The law has traditionally condemned unmarried relationships as being akin to prostitution, and has disapproved attempts to avoid marriage laws by cohabiting outside matrimony. Nevertheless, cohabitation is an important legal relationship because so many people now choose it instead of marriage.

There is, strictly speaking, no law governing cohabitation, and cohabitants have none of the legal protections given to married couples. Although some couples may choose cohabitation for exactly that reason—no strings—they often discover that with no plan for ending the relationship the law may settle their property disputes according to common contract principles. If they were married, the laws of divorce or inheritance would prevail.

Property disputes Cohabitation for a brief period generally raises few legal questions. Some couples say they can get a $4 "divorce" at the local small-claims court. If their property is less than the jurisdictional limit for that court, the two parties allow the hearing officer to divide the property that accumulated during their cohabitation.

Longer relationships, however, usually have more complicated problems.

EXAMPLE In 1973 a California court had to decide how to treat the breakup of two people who had lived as though they were married for eight years. Family and friends had believed they were married. Four children had been born, and their birth certificates and school registrations listed both parents with the same last name. The man had supported the family and the woman had cared for the home and children. They had purchased a home, borrowed money, filed joint tax returns, and to all the world appeared to be man and wife.

When the couple ended their relationship, the man asserted the traditional rule that cohabitation does not create any legal rights and claimed all of the property for himself. (They did not have a common-law marriage because California does not recognize such unions.) Had the couple been married, the woman would have been entitled to half the property. The court pointed out that the intention of California's community-property law is to provide security to a spouse who contributes to the marital partnership without earning wages. Because the man had accepted the woman's efforts for their family, he could not now walk off with everything.

EXAMPLE In a later California case, Michelle Triola sought half the property that she and actor Lee Marvin had acquired during the six years they had lived together, while Marvin was still married to someone else. Triola said that she and Marvin had agreed to combine their efforts and earnings and to share equally. She said she performed services as companion, housekeeper, and cook and gave up her career as a singer, and that Marvin had agreed to support her financially for life. When Marvin forced her to move out, she sued. Marvin's defense was that because Triola knew he was married, enforcing her claim would be legalizing prostitution. The court did not find that Marvin had agreed to support Triola for life. It did award her $104,000, however, "so that she may return from her status as a companion of a motion picture star to a separate, independent but perhaps more prosaic existence." This amount was intended to help rehabilitate Triola because it was unlikely that she could return to her career as a singer.

In some states an innocent person who mistakenly thinks he or she is married is protected by the *putative spouse doctrine*. This doctrine says that the law will give a married person's share of property to someone who had honestly believed there was a valid marriage and there was not—because of bigamy, for example.

Other problems Legal problems of cohabitants other than property rights can be even more troublesome. Courts routinely deny CUSTODY of children to a parent who cohabits with anyone but a lawful spouse, and sometimes a divorced person can lose financial support from an ex-spouse if she or he cohabits.

EXAMPLE A financially comfortable physician divorced his 0——* wife and was ordered to pay $200 a month *alimony*. When she moved into another man's house, he stopped paying, claiming that the other man should support her. The man she lived with was unemployed and testified that he could not support her—he had taken her in because she was ill. Although the court admitted that a woman "owes no duty of sexual fidelity to her former husband," it terminated her alimony just the same. Moreover, there was no legal way to order the other man to continue to help her financially.

marshal 1 An officer employed by federal courts to keep the peace, deliver legal orders, and perform duties such as those of a state sheriff. See UNITED STATES MARSHAL. 2 In some cities or towns, the local sheriff or constable.

marshaling assets and securities Arranging, ranking, or distributing assets in a way that best satisfies creditors' claims. The goal is a distribution based on justice and EQUITY rather than on conformity to strict rules of LAW. Sometimes the *two-fund doctrine* is used to make possible fair distribution. It is applied when a debtor has two funds or properties available, and one of his creditors has the right to collect his debt from only one fund while another creditor can collect his debt from either fund.

EXAMPLE Donaldson is unable to pay his bills. He owes 0——* National Bank $4,000 on the mortgage he used to buy a small cabin and $1,000 more on a personal loan the bank gave him to buy an expensive car. He also owes Farmer's Savings and Loan $5,000, for which he pledged the cabin as security. The court orders that the assets be sold to pay the creditors, and the cabin and the car bring in $6,000 apiece. The court then orders National Bank to collect all it is owed from the proceeds of the car sale because Farmer's Savings and Loan can collect only from the sale of the cabin.

martial law Government by the military; temporary rule by military force and authority when the civil government is unable to preserve order. Martial law might properly be called martial rule because it displaces the law of the land with control by force. It rules military and nonmilitary alike, friends and enemies, citizens and aliens. The military commander wields absolute power to restore order; although he cannot be arbitrary, he has the authority to kill someone who resists his orders and detain anyone who stands in his way. That amounts to suspending the writ of HABEAS CORPUS (the right to challenge the legality of an arrest or detention). Consequently, the U.S. Constitution prohibits the government from proclaiming martial law except to put down armed conflicts and then only when the public safety requires it. Martial law must end as soon as the emergency passes.

The authority to declare martial law rests with Congress and the state legislatures, although both may pass laws authorizing executive officers, such as the President or governor, to exercise this power. Martial law must still function with respect to the Constitution, however—military courts cannot try civilians for nonmilitary offenses if the civil courts are able to function. For example, many civilians convicted by military courts in Hawaii after Pearl Harbor were ordered released by the Supreme Court on the ground that the civilian courts could have continued operating and the military should have permitted them to do so.

A governor may declare martial law when storms and flooding cause such serious damage that keeping order is beyond the capabilities of local police departments. Guardsmen may be called up to assist in rescues, deliver food and medical supplies, and prevent looting. See MILITIA. As soon as practicable, however, the military must withdraw and let the civil government resume operation.

A military commander must exercise his authority responsibly; otherwise, he can be sued by those harmed by his actions or be held to answer criminal charges. A commander who fails to control his troops, for instance, can be charged as a war criminal.

A military commander may not attempt to control territory beyond the danger area. In general, he need not wait for the President or governor to revoke the order declaring martial law when the emergency passes.

International law recognizes a military commander's authority to proclaim martial law in a conquered territory, because the defeated land has no legal government until the victors recognize a new civilian government.

EXAMPLE In 1879 a Louisiana plantation owner sued the 0——* U.S. brigadier-general who, during the Civil War, was in charge of an area south of New Orleans. The owner demanded payment for 25 hogsheads of sugar and other property appropriated by Union troops under the officer's leadership. When the officer failed to appear for trial, the local court granted the owner a default judgment, and after the war he went to the general's home state of Maine to enforce the judgment against the general. The general took the case to the Supreme Court, which ruled that the Louisiana court had no authority over a Union general because Louisiana had been occupied enemy territory under martial law—the general represented the only legal government at the time.

Martindale-Hubbell Law Directory A set of reference books used by attorneys. More than 400,000 attorneys in the United States and foreign countries are listed with the following information: address; law firm; date of birth; dates of admission to college, law school and the bar; and whether he or she is a member of the American Bar Association. The biographical section summarizes the careers of attorneys who have earned recommendations from other attorneys and judges. Another volume contains digests of the law in each state, U.S. possessions, Canada, and other foreign countries. This volume provides a quick and easy reference for attorneys to check laws outside their own states.

Massachusetts Trust See BUSINESS TRUST.

mass communications   See COPYRIGHT; FEDER-AL COMMUNICATIONS COMMISSION; FEDERAL TRADE COMMIS-SION; LIBEL AND SLANDER; OBSCENITY; SPEECH AND PRESS, FREEDOM OF.

master   **1** Someone who employs another person to perform services and who exercises authority over how this work is done. See MASTER AND SERVANT.   **2** One having authority; a ruler, superintendent, head, chief, or instructor.   **3** An officer of the court, appointed by the judge to assist him by examining witnesses, computing DAMAGES, or taking testimony, accounts, oaths, affidavits, or acknowledgments of deeds. These duties may be performed by a court clerk, commissioner, auditor, or referee.

master and servant   An employer and his employee. It may seem quaint to describe an employment relationship today in such terms, but the words are still used by lawyers and no insult to the employee is intended.

■ **Employer-employee relationship**   An *employee* is generally anyone who works for another with that person's knowledge and consent. He may be paid or unpaid, but he must be subject to the control of the employer. An employee is different from an *agent* because, unlike the agent, the employee has no authority to act in the place of his employer. See AGENCY. An employee also differs from an independent contractor, who agrees to do a piece of work by his own methods and is answerable to the person who hires him only for the final result. There is no contract of employment unless both employer and employee consent to it.

The employer-employee relationship arises out of a contract, either express or implied. An express contract occurs when an employer and employee specifically agree that the employee accepts a particular position at a certain salary. The responsibilities of the job, the existence of a probationary period during which a person may be fired, vacation and sick days, and grounds for a discharge are usually mentioned as part of the contract. Various fringe benefits such as health, dental, and life insurance coverage; free checking privileges at a local bank; and membership in a credit union can also be included in the contract. Such a contract may be in writing, but it is usually verbal.

In contrast, an implied contract of employment is found when, as a result of the conduct of the parties, it is reasonable to conclude that they have agreed to an employer-employee relationship.

EXAMPLE Jack accepts Jane's offer to do gardening for him. O—➤ He tells her what he wants done and she does it. Although Jack has not told Jane that he has hired her, a court would imply that an employer-employee relationship exists as a result of their conduct toward each other. If Jack refuses to pay Jane after she has finished gardening, she can successfully sue Jack for the reasonable value of her services, usually the going rate in the community for the type of job done. Had Jack told Jane that he would accept her free services, Jane would lose in a lawsuit against Jack because that statement would clearly negate an employer-employee relationship.

The contract may contain whatever terms and conditions the parties see fit to make, as long as they are legal, but the terms must be definite enough that a court can enforce them. For example, an agreement to give a salesman not less than $180 a month and commissions might be too indefinite to enforce.

It is sometimes possible to measure the duration of an employment contract by the length of someone's life—for example, an agreement to nurse a sick person for as long as she lives in return for the deed to her farm. This kind of contract can be enforced by a lawsuit for money DAMAGES against either one who breaks it. But no employment contract can be enforced by making the employee work. That is involuntary servitude, forbidden by the Constitution.

■ **Laws binding the employer**   Federal and state laws regulate some of the conditions of employment—minimum wages, for example, and maximum hours, overtime pay, time off for the Sabbath, collective bargaining with labor union representatives, and cleanliness and safety of machinery, appliances, and the workplace. See LABOR RELATIONS; SUNDAY LAW; Chart 31.

An employer must pay the same amount as the employee does to the employee's SOCIAL SECURITY account, to finance the employee's old-age and disability insurance and Medicare health insurance. Employers must also pay taxes to their states to provide UNEMPLOYMENT COMPENSATION for employees who lose their jobs through no fault of their own. An employer need not offer a PENSION plan to his employees, but if he does so, the plan must be available to all qualified employees and must adhere to government regulations. An employer may also provide group health and life INSURANCE for his employees if it is part of the employment contract.

Generally, laws severely restrict the employment of children, setting the minimum wages they can be paid, limiting the hours they can work, or prohibiting their employment in certain types of jobs. See INFANT and Chart 31. Federal CIVIL RIGHTS laws forbid employers to discriminate on the basis of race, color, religion, sex, age, or national origin.

■ **Hiring and firing**   Although the employer has a right to hire and fire his employees, that right is limited. Some employers are bound by union contracts that contain union security clauses. These clauses prohibit the employer from hiring any worker who is not or will not soon be a member of the union. Some states, however, have RIGHT-TO-WORK LAWS, which make such clauses illegal. See Chart 30. In those states, the employer is free to hire nonunion workers as well as union workers.

Once an employer and employee have a contract, each is bound to honor its terms. The employee cannot refuse to work the hours to which he agreed nor can the employer demand that the employee work double shifts. Should either an employee or employer violate the terms of their agreement, the injured party can sue for breach of contract.

In most cases, when a person is hired for a job, no time limit is specified for the length of his employment. An employee cannot be fired for a reason not permitted by his employment contract or the collective-bargaining agreement that covers his work. Nor can he be discharged because of age, race, color, religion, sex, or national origin under federal law and various state laws known as Fair Employment Practices Act or Human Rights Acts. An employer cannot fire an employee who is exercising certain rights, such as filing a discrimination or job-safety com-

THE LAW AND YOUR JOB

WILLIAM P. MURPHY
Professor of Law,
The University of North Carolina

S orry, you're too old for this job."
"Get paid extra for working on Christmas? Bah, humbug!"

"We don't hire union members. . . ."

Without laws to restrain them, unscrupulous employers have workers at their mercy and can play the tyrant. At one time, not too many years ago, comments like the ones above were not uncommon because the terms and conditions of employment were dictated solely by the employer. As long as workers were plentiful—and they generally were—an employer could demand what he wanted of them. Although not all employers abused their employees, many did, and even men of conscience saw no need to pay their workers more than a bare living wage in return for their hard labor. Personal communications between employer and employee were generally civil, but the employer-employee relationship on the whole was always obviously that of *master and servant*—the legal term for employer and employee.

Development of labor laws

Until this century the law did little to help the struggling worker. In Colonial times the laws were actually on the side of the employer instead of the employee—for example, there were no minimum-wage laws, but maximum-wage laws prohibited a worker from receiving more than a set amount for a particular job. Later, during the 19th and early 20th centuries, some laws—mainly state laws—were passed to prohibit women and very young children from

being worked unendurably long hours, but most workers still had to labor long hours for little pay—the 10-hour day and a decent wage were only dreams.

The first labor unions were organized in the early years of the republic, but they were generally small, ineffective, and short-lived. Unions did not gain strength until the late 19th and early 20th centuries. Then, with their power to organize workers and engage in collective bargaining with employers, they became the sole hope of the laborer. But the unions were strongly opposed by employers, and union activities were frequently enjoined (halted) by the courts. With few laws to help them or the workers they represented, union leaders often resorted to criminal, strong-arm tactics in dealing with both employers and nonunion workers. In many cases, factory yards became bloody battlefields as unions fought to win workers to their side or persuade employers to accept their terms.

In response to the turmoil created by desperate workers, determined union leaders, and obstinate employers, the government began to act. First, many state governments passed laws to help the worker. The federal government had no authority to pass laws regulating the employer-employee relationship unless the employment had some connection with interstate commerce, which Congress under the Constitution did have power to regulate. Consequently, Congress passed laws to regulate employment in companies engaged in interstate commerce. These laws protect workers from unscrupulous employers, guarantee workers fair pay, assure them safe and healthy working conditions, and keep them from being discriminated against because of color, creed, sex, age, or physical handicaps. They also protect employers and employees from the misdeeds of corrupt union officials.

The federal labor laws are our most important, but they apply only when the employer and his employees are connected in some way with interstate commerce. The wording of the particular statute determines exactly how close that connection must be. For example, a statute may apply only to employees actually engaged in interstate commerce, such as workers who package goods that will later be shipped across state lines. Because not all of the federal labor statutes are written alike, it is possible for an employer and his employees to be covered by one or more of them, but not by all. Consequently, the first thing to be determined in any case is whether or not the statute in question applies to the particular individual or activity.

Federal minimum wage laws

Low pay for long hours has always been the chief complaint of the worker, and the federal government has taken steps to prevent the most serious abuses in this area. The Fair Labor Standards Act, popularly known as the wage and hour law, was enacted in 1938 and has been amended many times since then. It applies to employees who are engaged in producing goods for interstate commerce (for example, producing leather goods in Wyoming that are to be sold in New York) or who are employed by an enterprise that is engaged in interstate commerce, such as a trucker or air freight company. The principal requirements of the statute are the payment of a minimum hourly wage plus time and a half for overtime for all hours worked in excess of 40 a week.

In 1938 the minimum wage was 25 cents an hour. By 1981 it was $3.35 an hour. The overtime pay must be based on the employee's actual hourly rate and not on the minimum rate, because in most cases the employee's actual pay rate will be higher than the statutory minimum. Thus, if you are covered by this law and you work for $6 an hour, you should be paid $285 for a 45-hour week—$240 for 40 hours at $6 an hour plus $45 for 5 hours at $9 an hour.

Payment must be made for all compensable time, which may include time for cleaning up and changing clothes, time spent on call, travel time, and similar periods during which the employee is not actually engaged in productive work.

More than 30 kinds of employees, such as farm workers, are exempt from the minimum wage and overtime requirements. Executive, administrative, and professional employees are exempt from the overtime provisions if they receive salaries equal to or above an amount set by the U.S. Secretary of Labor.

The Fair Labor Standards Act has special provisions for dealing with learners, apprentices, students, and the handicapped. It also prohibits the employment of children below certain ages in various kinds of hazardous work.

The U.S. Department of Labor is responsible for enforcing the Fair Labor Standards Act. If you believe that you fall under this law and that you have been underpaid, you may obtain assistance from a regional or subregional office of the Department of Labor. You may also sue your employer in order to recover any amounts he should have paid you under the provisions of the statute.

Other federal laws—the Bacon-Davis Act of 1931, the Walsh-Healy Act of 1936, and the Service Contract Act of 1945—prescribe the labor standards that must be observed in work performed by private concerns that have contracts with the federal government to provide it with goods or services or to perform government construction work. These statutes differ from the Fair Labor Standards Act in two major ways:

(1) The wages paid to employees working on government contract jobs must be at least as high as the wages generally paid to workers engaged in similar work in the same geographic area. In other words, if a private construction company contracts with the federal government to build an office complex in Des Moines, the contractor would be bound to pay all the employees who worked on the project at least as much as employees generally get for working on the construction of other office complexes in that area. The Secretary of Labor is authorized to determine what the prevailing wages in a particular area may be.

(2) Employees may be entitled to overtime pay if they work more than 8 hours a day. Thus an employee who works four 10-hour days may be entitled to 8 hours of overtime (2 hours for each day), even though he worked only 40 hours during the entire week.

Federal safety and health standards

Unsafe and unhealthy working conditions have also plagued many workers. In 1970 Congress considered reports that every year some 15,000 deaths and millions of disabling injuries are job-related. In order to protect employees from needless hazards, Congress passed the Occupational Safety and Health Act, which requires employers to meet specified safety and health standards. The law applies to all employers whose business affects interstate commerce.

Under the Occupational Safety and Health Act, an employer has two duties: (1) the specific duty to conform to any safety and health standard issued by the U.S. Department of Labor that applies to his business and (2) the general duty to furnish his employees with a workplace free of hazards that could cause death or serious physical harm. Thus an employer may violate his general duty to provide a safe workplace even if no specific requirements have been issued for his business.

An employee who believes that his employer is violating a safety or health standard or that a danger exists at the workplace may request an inspection of the workplace by giving notice to one of the regional offices of the Department of Labor. The notice must be in writing, must set forth with reasonable particularity the grounds for the complaint, and must be signed by the employee. The name of the employee will be kept confidential.

After receiving the notice, the Department of Labor will send someone to make a walk-around inspection of the workplace, accompanied by representatives of the employer and the employees. If violations of safety and health standards are found, citations will be issued and fines may be imposed. Fines for willful or repeated violations may be higher than those for first violations caused by negligence or ignorance. Penalties for willful violations that result in the death of an employee may include imprisonment.

Citations and the resulting penalties may be challenged by employers or enforced by the Department of Labor through hearings before an administrative law judge appointed by an agency called the Occupational Safety and Health Review Commission, before the agency itself, and ultimately the federal courts. The federal courts are authorized to issue injunctions against the maintenance of conditions that create imminent danger of death or of serious physical harm.

The Occupational Safety and Health Act is enforced solely by the Department of Labor. There is no provision for suits by employees against employers. The Department of Labor may delegate to a state agency the enforcement of safety and health standards within the state, but only if the state law is as protective of employees and as legally enforceable as the federal law is.

Federal antidiscrimination laws

Among the most recent and most controversial of the federal laws that regulate the employer-employee relationship are the equal employment opportunity laws. These laws are all based on the belief that a person's employment opportunities should be determined by his or her ability and work performance and not by such factors as race, sex, or religion, which in almost all cases have no bearing on a person's ability or performance. Not until the 1960's did this belief become widely enough accepted in the United States to make possible the numerous laws Congress has enacted in an effort to make the belief a reality.

Equal Employment Opportunity Act of 1972

The major federal statute in this area originated as Title VII of the Civil Rights Act of 1964, which was amended in 1972 as the Equal Employment Opportunity Act. This law applies to employers of 15 or more employees, to labor unions with 15 or more members, and to all employment agencies—provided their activities affect interstate commerce. Any act, practice, or decision relating to the employment of job applicants or status of employees is unlawful if it is based on race, color, religion, sex, or national origin. Hiring practices, wages, promotions, transfers, training programs, job referrals, and union membership are only some of the specific areas that are included.

The statute has numerous exceptions. The most important are (1) differential treatment that results from a bona fide seniority plan in a collective bargaining agreement between an employer and a labor union; (2) cases in which religion, sex, or national origin is a bona fide occupational qualification for a particular job, as, for example, a woman to play a woman's role in a movie; and (3) employees of religious associations and institutions (although many people believe this exemption from the law to be an unconstitutional governmental aid to religion).

Employers who intentionally discriminate against job applicants or employees—that is, treat them differently because of their race, color, sex, religion, or national origin—are clearly in violation of the statute. It is also a violation if any employer's practice, even though not discriminatory on its face, adversely affects members of a minority more than other persons and is not necessary to the efficiency or safety of the business. Thus, an employer may not generally use a test or qualification for hiring or promotion that disqualifies more blacks than whites or more females than males. For example, an employee could not require all job applicants to lift a 50-pound weight with arms fully extended unless the job called for heavy lifting, because such a test would undoubtedly disqualify more women than men and has nothing to do with the job.

The Equal Employment Opportunity Act is principally enforced by the Equal Employment Opportunity Commission, a federal agency created for that purpose. If you believe that you have been the victim of job discrimination, you may file a complaint with one of the commission's offices. The commission will investigate the circumstances. If it agrees that the employer in question has treated you in a discriminatory manner, it will try to find a remedy—if necessary, by suing the employer in federal court. If the Equal Employment Opportunity Commission does not pursue the matter, you yourself may sue the employer in federal court. If you are only one of a group of job applicants or employees who have been discriminated against in the same way by the same employer, you may probably bring a class action suit against the employer—that is, sue him on behalf of all the members of that group.

The federal courts may require employers and labor unions not only to stop engaging in discriminatory practices but also to take affirmative action to undo the discrimination—for example, by rehiring discharged employees, offering promotions, or paying back wages. In one leading case, an employer who refused to hire truck drivers because they were black was required to offer them jobs, pay them back wages, and credit them with seniority from the date he had first refused to hire them. In other cases, the courts have ordered employers to adopt preferential hiring practices to remedy past discrimination because of race and sex.

Equal pay for women Another statute, the Equal Pay Act, was passed in 1963 as an amendment to the Fair Labor Standards Act and covers the same employers—those who engage in or produce goods to be sold in interstate commerce. The law prohibits covered employers from discriminating between employees on the basis of sex. Specifically, an employer may not pay employees of one sex lower wages than employees of the other sex for jobs performed under similar working conditions and requiring equal skill,

effort, and responsibility. The purpose of the Equal Pay Act is to eliminate wage discrimination against women, who have generally been paid less than men for the same or similar work.

Under the Equal Pay Act it is not necessary for the female employee to be doing the same job as the male. It is enough that the job be similar and the duties substantially equal. Thus female nurses would generally be entitled to be paid as much as male orderlies. In order to justify a pay differential, the duties performed by men and women must be significantly different and require different physical working conditions.

The Equal Pay Act is enforced by the Equal Employment Opportunity Commission. If you feel you are being paid lower wages because of your sex, you may file a complaint with the commission. You may also sue your employer if the commission does not.

Age discrimination In 1967 Congress passed the Age Discrimination in Employment Act, which prohibits employers and labor unions whose activities affect interstate commerce from discriminating because of age. The law binds private employers of 20 or more workers; federal, state, and local governments; employment agencies serving covered employers; and most labor unions of 25 or more members. It protects employees and job applicants between the ages of 40 and 70. A 1978 amendment prohibits mandatory retirement for employees under the age of 70.

The Age Discrimination in Employment Act has been enforced by the Equal Employment Opportunity Commission since 1979. If you believe that your rights have been violated under this law, you may file charges with the commission, which will investigate the charges and attempt to find a remedy if it agrees that you have been a victim of discrimination. The commission may bring enforcement actions in federal court, but you have the right to bring suit yourself if the commission does not.

Handicapped persons The most recent effort by Congress to provide equal employment opportunities deals with handicapped persons. Under the Vocational Rehabilitation Act of 1973, contractors who provide goods and services to the federal government are required to take affirmative action to employ handicapped persons. This requirement is enforced by the U.S. Department of Health and Human Services.

Handicaps include both physical and mental impairments that substantially limit one or more of a person's major life activities. The statute protects not only persons who actually have a handicap but persons who have recovered from a handicap and persons who do not have a handicap but who are believed by an employer to have one. Employers are required to make reasonable accommodations in their working facilities to enable handicapped persons to perform a particular job.

Labor unions and collective bargaining agreements

The terms and conditions of employment in many businesses are established by collective bargaining agreements between employers and the unions that represent their employees. The broad area of unionization and collective bargaining is regulated by the National Labor Relations Act (NLRA), enacted by Congress in 1935 and amended extensively in 1947 and 1959.

The NLRA applies to virtually all private employment that affects interstate commerce, with certain exclusions, such as agricultural work. Railroad and airline employees are covered under the Railway Labor Act, which was first passed in 1926, but in most respects their rights under that act are the same as they would be under the NLRA.

Right to unionize   Under the NLRA, employees have the right to join unions and to try to organize a union at their place of employment. They have the right to engage in organizational activity at their place of work except during actual working hours. These rights are protected by prohibiting the employer from engaging in certain unfair labor practices. Thus it is unlawful for an employer to discharge or discipline an employee for joining a union or engaging in union activity or for an employer to take any other action that would interfere with, restrain, or coerce the employees in the exercise of their rights. Employers who discharge employees because of their union activity may be required to rehire them and pay them back wages.

Employees must be allowed to decide for themselves whether or not to be represented by a union. Employers are free to try to persuade their employees not to join a union, but it is unlawful for employers to threaten employees or promise them benefits in order to influence their choice. Similarly, it is unlawful for a union to use coercive measures—violence, threats of violence, or threats of economic reprisal—to gain support from employees. Employees usually make their choice in representation elections conducted by the National Labor Relations Board. Elections may be set aside and new elections held if either side used improper tactics before the election.

Collective bargaining   If a majority of the employees voting in the election choose union representation, then the employer is under a legal duty to bargain with the union over the employees' wages, hours, and other terms and conditions of employment. The employer and the union must bargain with each other in good faith and within certain limits prescribed by the law. If the bargaining, after a time, fails to produce an agreement, the parties may resort to economic pressure. This is usually a strike by the employees. The right to strike is protected by the statute, and an employee does not terminate his employment status by striking. It is unlawful for an employer to penalize his employees for striking, but he is free to hire replacements for the strikers if he wishes to operate his business during the strike. Employees may be lawfully discharged if they engage in misconduct during the strike.

Good-faith bargaining will usually produce a written agreement, or contract, that is normally distributed to employees. The contract is usually for a fixed term, such as two or three years, and is legally binding upon the employer, the union, and all employees who are employed during the term of the agreement. Typically, the contract covers a wide variety of subjects, such as hourly rates, overtime, piece rates, shift differentials, shift schedules, meal and rest periods, seniority provisions, vacations, pensions, insurance, holidays, discipline, work rules, safety, and leave.

One important part of the contract is the grievance procedure, through which disputes over the application or interpretation of the contract may be protested and settled or perhaps taken to an impartial arbitrator for a binding decision. The contract may also contain a union security clause under which employees must become members of the union, but such clauses may be prohibited by a state right-to-work law. The contract may also contain a no-strike clause committing the union and the employees not to strike or engage in any work stoppage during the term of the contract.

Fair representation   A union chosen by employees to represent them has the exclusive power of representation. This means that there can be no separate or individual bargaining between the employer and any employee or group of employees. The union, on the other hand, has a duty to represent all the employees fairly, both in the negotiation and administration of the contract. This means that the union may not treat employees differently for such reasons as race, sex, religion, nonmembership in the union, or personal hostility.

Employees who have selected a union to represent them may, if they become dissatisfied, petition for an election to decertify the union. Any employee may sue his union if it unfairly represents him or if it mistreats him.

Running a union   Employees who are members of labor unions enjoy many legal rights within their union. Under the Labor Management Reporting and Disclosure Act of 1959, unions must be run in a democratic manner. Elections must be held at stated intervals, and employees have the right both to nominate and to run for union office themselves. Union dues and dues increases are subject to membership approval. Members have the right of free speech and political activity within the union. Although unions may adopt reasonable rules and regulations and discipline members who violate them, such discipline can only be imposed after a hearing within the union at which the member has the opportunity to present his side of the case. Misuse of union funds by union officers is prohibited.

State labor laws

In addition to federal law, there are many state laws that regulate the employer-employee relationship. Some of these laws overlap the federal laws, either giving added protection to workers and employers or offering protection to employer and employees who are not covered by the federal laws. Thus many states have their own health and safety laws, equal employment opportunity laws, and labor relations laws. Other state laws deal with the terms and conditions of employment and offer compensation for unemployment and for job-related injuries or death.

State laws may deal with the terms and conditions of employment in various ways. In some states an employer is required to pay his employees at stated intervals—for example, at least every two weeks. In other states an employer may be required to give notice of one pay period (or wages for that period) before discharging an employee. As a general rule,

however, if there is no applicable statute and no collective bargaining agreement, all terms and conditions of employment are established by the employer.

In the important area of compensation for work-related injury or death, state law is the source of relief for most Americans. All 50 states have workmen's compensation laws that require employers to pay specific amounts of money to employees or their beneficiaries in the event of certain job-related injuries or death. The injury or death need not have resulted from the employer's negligence, as long as it arose from and occurred in the course of employment. Many state laws also provide payment for occupational diseases. If an employee's disability claim is contested by his employer, it can be brought before an examiner, or referee, for a hearing. The examiner's decision may be appealed to a workmen's compensation commission and the state courts.

Through a cooperative arrangement with the national government, all 50 states have enacted unemployment compensation laws. These laws are meant to provide enough income to sustain an employee who loses his job because of economic conditions. They do not apply to an employee who is discharged for misconduct, and in most states unemployment compensation is not payable to employees who are on strike. Each state decides for itself how many weeks of compensation, and the weekly amount of compensation, that an unemployed person may receive. Normally, payments are made out of funds accumulated through special taxes on employers, but in times of high unemployment Congress has appropriated money directly from general revenues.

Employees of the federal government

Generally speaking, employees of the federal government enjoy the same rights and protections as employees in private employment, although the source of such rights and protections may be a separate act of Congress similar to those discussed above. Agencies of the federal government are thus prohibited from discriminating against employees because of race, creed, color, sex, religion, age, or handicapped status. Since 1978 there is no maximum-age limit in federal employment. For most federal employees, rates of pay, tenure, and many other terms and conditions of employment are established by statute or regulation. Until 1978 these provisions were administered by the U.S. Civil Service Commission. In that year Congress enacted legislation that replaced the Civil Service Commission with two separate agencies—the Office of Personnel Management (OPM) and the Merit Systems Protection Board (MSPB).

The OPM is charged with planning and administering an effective government-wide program of personnel management. The MSPB has primary responsibility for safeguarding merit principles and employees' rights. Individual personnel actions are normally handled by the various departments and agencies. Veterans of the U.S. armed forces enjoy a preference in applications for federal employment.

Under an Executive Order originally issued by President John F. Kennedy and amended by later Presidents, federal employees may choose to be represented by unions for the purpose of collective bargaining with their particular departments or agencies. The collective bargaining agreements cannot conflict with federal law and regulations, and federal employees have no right to strike. Work-related injuries and deaths are covered by the Federal Employees Compensation Act.

Employees of state and local governments

Some of the laws passed by Congress apply to employees of state and local governments as well as to employees of private employers. These include the Equal Employment Opportunity Act of 1972, the Age Discrimination Act, and the Equal Pay Act. In 1972 Congress extended the Fair Labor Standards Act (wage and hour law) to state and local employees, but in 1976 this was held unconstitutional by the U.S. Supreme Court. In certain limited respects, the U.S. Constitution restricts the state and local governments in their employment practices. Thus, for example, aliens may not lawfully be denied most kinds of public employment.

Except for the few limits imposed by the Constitution or federal laws, each state is free to decide for itself what the wages, hours, and terms and conditions of employment shall be for its own employees. As a general rule, local governments have the same power with respect to their employees. State and local laws and regulations dealing with employment status are usually administered by a civil service commission, personnel board, or similar agency. Special kinds of employees—for example, teachers, policemen, and firemen—are frequently governed by separate laws and agencies.

State and local governments are excluded from the National Labor Relations Act. Unionization and collective bargaining by state and local employees therefore depend upon state law, and about three-quarters of the states have enacted laws providing for collective bargaining. Generally speaking, these state laws provide for representation elections among employees and require public employers to bargain with unions chosen by a majority of the employees. The subjects of bargaining are frequently specified in the state law, and the terms of the collective bargaining agreements may not conflict with state laws and regulations. Except in limited situations in a few states, state and local employees are forbidden by law from engaging in strikes. Instead, such techniques as mediation and arbitration are widely used to resolve bargaining disputes.

plaint with a governmental agency or requesting workmen's compensation benefits. Also, an employee cannot be released for insubordination if he refuses to follow illegal instructions from his employer. He cannot be compelled to make false entries in business records, commit perjury, or handle stolen property, for example. An employer who wrongfully discharges an employee may be sued for money damages. An employee can be let go, however, for being unfaithful to his employer's interest, refusing to perform his job, or for being habitually late or frequently absent.

■ **Obligations of the employee** An employee is required to be honest and faithful in his employer's service. An employee who accepts bribes from a vendor to buy equipment for his employer is exposing himself to criminal charges and a lawsuit by the employer for money damages. Usually, the employee cannot compete with his employer, and in some cases the employment contract prohibits competition with the employer even after the employee leaves his job. When an employee learns trade secrets in the course of his work, he is obligated not to divulge them to others either during or after employment. Sometimes an employment contract specifies that the employer owns any new ideas or inventions created by the employee during the period of employment. In that case, the employee has no rights nor any legal ground to ask for extra compensation.

■ **Compensation** An employee can agree to work for nothing, but otherwise an employer is required to pay at the agreed rate. The employer has no right to delay payment of wages or to substitute something other than money unless the employee agrees. The employee is entitled to his wages as long as he completes the work agreed upon. He cannot commit himself to work for three months, quit after one month, and demand one-third of the wages, unless there is an agreement or a law providing otherwise.

If an employee is wrongfully fired, he may collect all the money the employer had agreed to pay him.

EXAMPLE A young man was hired to dance in a summer theater production of *Oklahoma*. He was to work for eight weeks at $150 a week. After two weeks, the producer fired him to make room in the show for her nephew. The dancer sued for six weeks' wages. The producer answered that she should have to pay him only $50 for each of the six weeks because he could have worked as a painter on the set and earned $100 a week but refused to do so. The court found that a dancer does not have to accept work as a painter in order to save an employer who wrongfully discharges him. He must look for other work, but he is entitled to keep looking until he finds a job in his field. The producer had to pay the $900.

While the amount and kind of compensation is generally fixed by agreement, it is affected by a number of laws. Employers must pay a certain minimum wage under most state laws, unless the type of employment is excluded from regulation—for example, certain farm work. The minimum wage laws may permit lower wages for minors, however. See Chart 31. Employers involved in any way with interstate commerce must also meet federal minimum wage standards. Other state and federal laws require employers to allow for paid sick time and extra wages for overtime or holiday work. It is a violation of federal law to pay men and women different wages for similar work. See CIVIL RIGHTS.

■ **Liability of the employer and employee** Under the principle of RESPONDEAT SUPERIOR (Latin for "Let the master answer") an employer is responsible for anything his employee does in the course of employment. Thus an employer can be sued for damages if his employee injures someone while working. The employer is generally not responsible, however, for injuries to one of his employees that are caused by the negligence of another of his employees. This exception, called the FELLOW SERVANT RULE, applies only when the employer has hired enough competent help to make the job reasonably safe. The employer is, of course, liable for any injuries to his employees or others that are caused by his own negligence. Today, however, most jobs are covered by WORKMEN'S COMPENSATION programs, which compensate employees for injuries sustained during the course of employment regardless of fault. Federal employees, seamen, longshoremen, and harbor workers are protected by various federal laws.

material 1 Important; having an influence or effect on the matter at hand; pertinent. For example, testimony that a robber was about 6 feet tall and weighed around 200 pounds is *material evidence*—it will help the jury decide whether the accused is the person guilty of the crime charged. 2 A physical substance; a word often used in law to describe the things needed by an artist or a workman to do his work. For example, a homeowner may hire a carpenter to put paneling into his den and agree that he (the homeowner) will furnish all the necessary materials. Under such a contract, the homeowner will be obligated to pay for the paneling, wood trim, glue, and nails, but not for any new tools the carpenter needs.

material fact 1 An occurrence, event, or bit of information that is important enough to influence someone to enter into a contract. For example, a buyer may find a used car acceptable because the seller tells him that the transmission was recently overhauled. Because this is one reason the buyer agrees to purchase the car, it is a material fact. He will be able to back out of the sales contract if it is not true. With respect to an INSURANCE policy, a material fact is anything that affects the insurance company's decision to write the policy or to charge a certain price for it. For example, heart disease in a person applying for a life insurance policy is a material fact. An arrest for drunken driving is a material fact for a person who wants to buy auto insurance. These facts would have an important influence on the risk an insurance company agrees to take. A person who lies about a material fact when he applies for insurance may not be able to collect benefits later.

2 In formal court precedures—such as DISCOVERY, PLEADING, or DEFENSE—an act or event that is necessary to prove one party's case or that tends to establish a point essential to his position.

material issue A question that is formally in dispute between persons in a lawsuit; a question that must be answered in order to solve the conflict of the suit.

material witness A witness whose testimony is necessary in a civil or criminal trial. A material witness can be compelled to appear and give testimony. If his safety is endangered by this, he may be given legal protection.

matter of fact   Something that can be perceived by the human senses and has an objective reality, as opposed to an opinion, which is subjective. Questions of fact in a courtroom are answered by WITNESSES who give testimony concerning what they have seen, smelled, tasted, touched, or heard. For example, whether a driver stopped at a stop sign is a matter of fact—either he did or he did not. For a detailed discussion, see EVIDENCE.

matter of law   Any legal principle that may be determined from the interpretation of statutes, rules, and court decisions. Questions of law are answered in a lawsuit by referring to sources of law that apply to the particular case.Whether the storage of explosives in a residential neighborhood is a violation of ZONING laws is a question of law that can be determined by reference to the locality's zoning laws.

matter of record   1 Anything entered in the records, the formal written accounts, of a court; something that can be proved by producing a court record.   2 Sometimes, a matter written in any official record.

maturity   The time when a debt becomes due or any legal obligation is enforceable.

maxim   A general statement of the law that sums up a principle. Such a statement is too general to be considered law in itself, but it does express a time-honored principle or common-sense rule. Legal maxims are often written in Latin and sometimes in French. For example, *"Ubi jus ibi remedium"* is a Latin phrase that means "Where there is a right, there is a remedy." See EQUITY.

mayhem   The crime of permanently disfiguring a victim or depriving him of the use of a body part; maiming. Under the common law, mayhem was a crime if it left a man less able to fight for the king. It was a breach of the king's peace.

Today, criminal laws that punish mayhem are more concerned with protecting the individual himself. They generally prohibit unlawfully depriving any person of any body part, rendering it useless, or disfiguring the victim. Some states punish mayhem as a form of aggravated assault, but most prohibit it specifically. Many statutes expressly prohibit slitting the tongue, nose, or an ear, because an injury of this kind is an insult to humanity.

EXAMPLE   In one case, the defendant threw lye into his
O——*   victim's face. The victim's eyesight was somewhat injured and he bore scars all over his face, neck, and shoulders, but he was not blinded. The court held that it is no longer necessary to put out a person's eye to be guilty of mayhem. The cosmetic effects of the scarring brought the case within the kind of permanent disfigurement prohibited by mayhem today.

A victim of castration can sue the offender for money damages, and the offender can also be prosecuted for committing a crime against society.

It is no defense the offender did not intend to deprive the victim of a body part. Nor is it a defense that the victim consents to the maiming. Anyone who maims or assists in mayhem is equally guilty of the crime.

EXAMPLE   In North Carolina, a doctor was convicted of
O——*   mayhem because he injected a drug to numb four fingers on a man's left hand. The man's friend then cut off the fingers with a power saw, and the man turned in a claim for insurance benefits. Since anyone who assists in mayhem is guilty of the crime, the doctor was convicted even though he himself did not remove the fingers.

In another case, every person in a mob was found guilty of mayhem because a policeman lost the use of an eye.

McCulloch v. Maryland   A landmark case decided by the Supreme Court in 1819. It established the principle that the federal government has broad powers to pass many kinds of laws and that the states cannot interfere with any federal agency by taxing it directly.

The case was part of an ongoing debate among the founders of our constitutional government over the balance of powers between the states and the federal government. The Federalists favored a strong central government and the Republicans wanted to leave most powers to the states. The men who wrote and ratified the Constitution finally agreed to grant the federal government certain specific powers, called the *enumerated powers,* and to list them in the Constitution, ending with a general provision that Congress may

"make all Laws which shall be necessary and proper for carrying into Execution the foregoing Powers, and all other Powers vested by this Constitution in the Government of the United States, or in any Department or Officer thereof."

This is called the necessary and proper clause of the Constitution. Some people feared that this provision could become a blanket authorization for the federal government to ride roughshod over the states, but a series of anonymous articles published in New York newspapers in late 1787 and early 1788 defended the clause. These essays came to be called *The Federalist* papers, and eventually it was learned that they had been written by Alexander Hamilton, James Madison, and John Jay. *The Federalist* papers argued that any power is only the ability to do something and that the power to do something necessitates the power to use a means of accomplishing it. A legislature must have the power to make laws, so the proper means of exercising that power is by making "necessary and proper" laws. Thus the Constitution was ratified in 1789 with the necessary and proper clause.

Using the power conferred by that clause, the first Congress passed a law in 1791 incorporating a national bank called the Bank of the United States. The bank operated as a private institution, taking deposits of private funds, making private loans, and issuing bank notes, which could be used like money. It also operated as a place for the federal government to deposit its funds wherever branches were established.

That bank charter was allowed to expire in 1811, but a second Bank of the United States was incorporated in 1816 with one-fifth of its stock owned by the U.S. government. The bank made itself extremely unpopular when it over-expanded credits and then drastically curtailed them, thus contributing to the failure of many state-chartered banks. As a result, a number of states tried to keep out branches of the national bank by passing laws prohibiting any bank not chartered by the state or by imposing heavy taxes on them. This head-on collision of federal and state governments had to be resolved by the Supreme Court.

Maryland actually had one of the milder laws against the bank. It required any bank or branch not established under the authority of the state to use special "stamped paper" for its bank notes, in effect paying two percent of the value of the notes as a tax, or to pay a tax of $15,000 a year. Maryland sued McCulloch, the bank's cashier, for not paying the tax and won. McCulloch appealed to the Supreme Court.

Chief Justice John Marshall wrote the opinion of the Court reversing the Maryland judgment. The Court held that the federal government has the power to do what is "necessary and proper," which includes the authority to establish a national bank. A state cannot under the Constitution destroy—or tax—any agency properly set up by the federal government. The law passed by the Maryland legislature imposing a tax on the Bank of the United States was held to be unconstitutional and void.

mechanic's lien   See LIEN.

mediation   Setting up an independent person between two parties to a dispute in order to help them settle their disagreement. In international law, the friendly interference of one state in the controversies of nations is recognized as a proper act in promoting peace.

meeting of the minds   The time and terms that mark the point at which a CONTRACT is made. There is a meeting of the minds when the purposes and intentions that are known—or should be known—by all the parties reach a point of agreement. No one can claim that there was no meeting of the minds simply because he had a mental reservation that he did not bring to the attention of others.

membership corporation   A company or association formed for purposes other than making a profit, such as a CEMETERY corporation or a RELIGIOUS SOCIETY.

memorandum   1 A brief written note or outline of a transaction or legal document. A memorandum may be accepted in court to show that a contract was actually made. In the sale of real estate, for example, a memorandum can indicate that the parties agreed to the sale of a parcel at a stated price, plus other details. This type of memorandum is sometimes called a *binder*. A binder may be given to someone who is purchasing an INSURANCE policy to insure him until the policy itself can be put into effect.   2 An explanation and summary of a point of law prepared by an attorney for a judge or another attorney.

memorandum decision   A written decision from a court that reports the *ruling*—what the court decides and orders to be done—but does not include an *opinion*—an explanation of the reasons for the decision.

mental anguish   1 The emotional pain and feelings of fright, distress, and anxiety that accompany a physical injury.   2 The emotional suffering that results from strong and painful feelings, such as grief, severe disappointment, indignation, wounded pride, despair, shame, or public humiliation. Mental anguish or suffering may be considered when the amount of money DAMAGES due an injured plaintiff is calculated.

mental cruelty   A course of conduct indulged in by a husband or wife that endangers the well-being of the spouse to a point that the marital relationship becomes intolerable. See DIVORCE.

mercantile agency   A person or business that collects details about the financial standing, ability, and credit of those engaged in business and sells this information to customers, called subscribers. Today these agencies are usually called CREDIT bureaus.

merchantable   Fit to be sold; of the quality and kind generally acceptable among buyers and sellers. See CONSUMER PROTECTION; WARRANTY. A product is merchantable if it is fit for the general purpose for which it is manufactured and sold. A manufacturer or seller can usually be sued by someone who is injured if his product is not merchantable.

merger   The blending or uniting of two things, usually so that the smaller is swallowed up in the larger, losing its individuality and separate identity. Crimes, rights, precontractual agreements, and corporations are subject to merger.

■ **Mergers of crimes**   Under the common law, if two crimes are committed by the same person at the same time, the lesser crime can be merged into the greater one so that only the greater crime is punished. Some states have altered or abolished this rule.

■ **Mergers of rights**   Two rights can be merged. For example, a tenant has the right to live in the house he rents. If he buys the house while he is a tenant, the right of occupancy (leasehold estate) merges with the right of outright ownership (fee simple estate). This is known as a merger of estates.

■ **Mergers of agreements**   The small agreements leading up to a contract become merged in the final agreement.
   EXAMPLE   A buyer will agree to many different provisions
   O▪━✳   while he is negotiating to purchase a new car. First, he will agree to buy a certain model for a particular price. Then, he may agree to one option after another, perhaps changing his mind on one or two as talks progress. Finally, he will agree to a final price for a car with specified equipment. These preliminary agreements are merged in the sales contract. If a dispute over the deal comes to court, neither party can contradict the final written expression of the sales agreement by talking about the preliminary agreements, because they are merged into the contract.

■ **Corporate mergers**   In corporation law a merger is a combination of two companies in which one corporation is absorbed by the other and completely disappears. This is different from a *consolidation*, in which two different corporations lose their separate identities and unite to form one totally new corporation.

State laws establish the precedure to be followed to accomplish corporate mergers. Typically, the board of directors for each corporation must first pass a resolution adopting a plan of merger that specifies the names of the firms involved, the name of the new corporation or the surviving corporation, the terms and conditions of the proposed merger, the manner of converting shares of the old corporations into shares of the new corporation or into some other kind of property, and any other legal provisions agreed to.

Once all the terms of the merger have been settled, each corporation must notify its shareholders that a meeting will be held to approve the merger. When the proper number of shareholders ratifies the plan, the directors must sign the papers and file them with the state. The secretary of state then issues a certificate of merger, which authorizes the new corporation. Usually the statute permits the directors to abandon the plan at any point up to the filing of the final papers. (The same procedure is followed in the consolidation of two companies.)

A merger brings the merged corporation to a complete end. The surviving corporation assumes all the rights and privileges of the merged one and is responsible for all its obligations.

Statutes usually provide that each of two merging corporations formed in different states must follow the rule in its own state in order to merge. Statutes may also provide a way out for shareholders in the disappearing corporation who have voted against the merger plan. In most instances the surviving corporation must buy their shares at fair value.

In additition to the corporation laws of each state, mergers are also strictly regulated by laws affecting particular industries and by federal tax provisions, securities regulation, and antitrust laws.

merits   The rights of the parties in a lawsuit that are the substance of a dispute without regard to the legal technicalities that may affect these rights. A *judgment on the merits* is a final resolution of a particular dispute.

> EXAMPLE Jane, a waitress, sues Leo, a restaurant owner, for paying her less than Al, a waiter who was hired when she was and who does the same job. The merits of the case are Jane's right to equal pay for equal work. If a court decides that Jane does the same work as the waiter and therefore should be paid the same, there has been a judgment on the merits.

merit system   A plan of appointing employees in civil service and promoting them only on the basis of their job performance. It is considered a reform and an improvement over political patronage, or the "spoils system." The federal government first began making merit appointments for certain government jobs around 1886.

mesne   Middle; intermediate; intervening. *Mesne process* is any legal paper or court order issued while a lawsuit is going on. It does not include the papers that start the action, such as a libel or complaint, or those that end one, such as a judgment.

metes and bounds   Literally, measurement and boundary; the boundary lines of land, with their terminal points and angles. A surveyor would be sure to give the metes and bounds of land he has measured.

military law   A system of regulations for governing the armed forces and enforcing internal military discipline. Military law applies only to persons in the ARMED SERVICES of the country, while MARTIAL LAW displaces normal civil government and regulates soldiers and civilians alike. See also UNIFORM CODE OF MILITARY JUSTICE.

militia   A body of citizen soldiers organized and trained for call to temporary duty in time of emergency. The function and importance of a militia are recognized in the Constitution, Article 1, Section 8, which lists the powers of Congress, granting it authority

> " To provide for calling forth the Militia to execute the Laws of the Union, suppress Insurrections and repel Invasions; To provide for organizing, arming, and disciplining, the Militia, and for governing such Part of them as may be employed in the Service of the United States, reserving to the States respectively, the Appointment of the Officers, and the Authority of training the Militia according to the discipline prescribed by Congress."

And the Second Amendment in the Bill of Rights begins:

> " A well regulated Militia, being necessary to the security of a free State . . ."

Under today's laws, every citizen of sufficient age and capacity to bear arms is under an obligation to serve in the militia when called. Statutes exclude certain classes of persons—in general, women, certain professionals or public officials, disabled persons, and those holding a religious belief opposed to war or bearing arms. Sometimes the laws grant certain legal privileges to members of the militia while they are on active duty or traveling to or from a duty assignment. These privileges may include immunity from arrest and exemption from jury duty and from being served with legal papers.

The idea that a militia should be an organized force, capable of being smoothly absorbed into the regular military of the United States, is a fairly modern one. From the days of the Revolutionary War's Minutemen, who considered themselves a militia, until just before World War I, the various militias lacked the training and equipment necessary to make them useful as a reserve force of the Army. Then, in 1916, Congress created the National Guard, uniformed, equipped, and trained the same as the regular army and capable of being "federalized" as a unit so that individual soldiers did not always have to be drafted. In return for placing its militia in readiness for the federal government, each state receives from Congress an allocation of federal equipment and money to supplement the compensation paid to each soldier by the state. Each governor remains in charge of his state's unit of the National Guard except when it is called into active federal service.

Individual guardsmen who are acting within the limits of their authority may, by statute, be granted immunity from liability for harm they cause in the performance of their military duty. This does not mean, however, that they are safe from lawsuits if they violate the law.

EXAMPLE In 1970, college students attempting to demonstrate their opposition to American military involvement in Vietnam gathered in large numbers on the campus of Kent State University in Ohio. The Governor of Ohio called in the National Guard to preserve order and protect public property. During a confrontation between students and the Guard, shots were fired into the crowd. Lawsuits were brought on behalf of four persons killed and nine others injured. The Supreme Court has heard a couple of appeals arising out of this case. In one decision, the Court held that persons who are denied their civil rights are entitled to sue National Guard officers and enlisted members who misuse their power under state law. The case was sent back to the state courts to determine whether the Guardsmen did misuse their authority. Finally, after almost nine years of legal proceedings, the case was settled out of court for $675,000 to be paid by Ohio authorities to the wounded students and the parents of those who had been killed.

mineral rights Ownership of minerals in the ground and the right to remove them. This right can be sold. See MINES AND MINERALS.

mines and minerals Excavations in the earth from which useful substances are taken and the substances that are taken from them. The law of mines and minerals regulates the ownership, sale, and operation of mines, quarries, wells, and rights in natural resources found in the ground. Under the law of most states, the term *minerals* includes such substances as coal, silver, gold, uranium, oil, gas, and petroleum. Stone, rock, and water are also generally covered by mining and mineral law. *Ore* is a rock compound containing some kind of metal that can be mined.

The operation of mines, quarries, and wells is highly regulated by federal and state law. The purposes behind these laws are to protect the health and safety of workers, to safeguard other persons and property in the vicinity of the operations, to encourage the efficient use of natural resources, and to raise tax revenues without discouraging capital investment. The revolution in ENVIRONMENTAL LAW has produced many lawsuits and a great deal of legislation affecting the development of minerals, oil, and gas.

■ **Mineral rights** Mineral rights is a legal term for all the ways one can own minerals in the ground, including the right to enter the land in order to remove them. It is possible to lease the mineral rights without buying the land. Mineral leases can be very complicated because of the large number of rights involved for each party and the great amount of money risked to develop these resources. The landowner may want a percentage of the minerals taken or a percentage of their value. This is the landowner's *right to royalty*.

■ **Minerals on public lands** The United States retains ownership of minerals under public lands. The Supreme Court settled a dispute over minerals under the sea in the *United States* v. *Florida*. That case established that the state of Florida is generally entitled to the lands, minerals, and natural resources under the Atlantic Ocean and the Gulf of Mexico for at least three miles out from its coastline. The United States is entitled to all the lands, minerals, and other natural resources beyond those limits, subject to treaties with other nations. The federal government may arrange to lease the right to remove certain minerals from U.S. lands without transferring ownership of the land. At one time, it was possible to get a prospecting permit from the federal government and to stake out a "location" on approved mineral land. When a prospector made a discovery, he was entitled to claim both the land and the minerals. Today the Secretary of the Department of Energy has the right to issue prospecting permits for public lands and, in the event of a discovery, to lease the right to extract the mineral without passing on ownership of the territory.

ministerial As a legal term, done under the supervision of another; not involving judgment, discretion, or policymaking.

A county clerk's job is ministerial because he must receive documents for recording if they conform to the law. He does not exercise his own judgment about the truth of statements made in them. The validity of these same documents can be questioned by a judge in a lawsuit, however, because the judge's function is not ministerial but judicial.

minor A person who has not yet reached the legal age of an adult. That age may vary for different purposes. For example, a person can vote at age 18, but his state might not permit him to buy intoxicating liquors until he is 21. In law a minor is generally referred to as an INFANT.

minority That period in each person's life before he legally becomes an adult. The time when a person reaches adulthood is called the *age of majority,* and the period after that is called his *majority.* See INFANT.

Miranda v. Arizona A case decided by the Supreme Court in 1966 establishing the rule that any person taken into custody by law-enforcement officials must be told that he has certain rights. The person must also be warned that if he decides to waive these rights, anything he says can be used against him in court.

■ **Miranda's arrest and trial** On March 13, 1963, Ernesto Miranda was arrested in his home on suspicion of kidnapping and rape and taken to a police station in Phoenix, Arizona. There he was identified by the person who had filed a complaint. The police took him to an interrogation room, and two police officers began questioning him. No one told Miranda that he had the right to have an attorney present. Two hours later, the officers emerged from the interrogation room with a written confession signed by Miranda. At the top of that statement was a typewritten paragraph. It said that the confession was made voluntarily, without threats or promises of immunity and "with full knowledge of my legal rights, understanding any statement I make may be used against me."

At the trial, before a jury, the written confession was admitted into evidence over the objection of Miranda's attorney, and the police officers told about the spoken confession he had made before signing the written one. Miranda was found guilty of kidnapping and rape and was sentenced to 20 to 30 years in prison. The Supreme Court of Arizona affirmed his conviction, emphasizing that Miranda had not asked for an attorney.

■ **Miranda's conviction overturned**   The U.S. Supreme Court reversed the conviction. It held that it was impossible to suppose that Miranda had given up his right to have an attorney present without proof that he knew he was entitled to demand counsel. A typed-in clause that he had "full knowledge" of his "legal rights" was no proof at all. Constitutional rights can be relinquished only by a "knowing and intelligent waiver."

In this case, the Court was concerned with protecting the constitutional rights that are fundamental to lawful police practices. It sought to keep coerced confessions out of the legal system by guaranteeing the right to refuse to talk and the right to have an attorney present during questioning. The Court noted that, without these rights, it was too easy to make the questioning inquisitional in character and too easy to browbeat the timid, to push the prisoner into a corner and entrap him.

■ **Rules for a legal confession**   The Court decided to set down clear rules to insure that a confession, when given, is voluntary. These rules must be followed unless the legislature sets up "other procedures which are at least as effective in apprising accused persons of their right of silence and in assuring a continuous opportunity to exercise it." The rules are as follows:

(1) Every person must be told that he has certain constitutional rights whenever he is "first subjected to police interrogation while in custody at the station or otherwise deprived of his freedom of action in any significant way." The rules do not apply when someone volunteers information or statements of any kind after the rules have been read to him, nor must they be followed for "general on-the-scene questioning as to facts surrounding a crime or other general questioning of citizens in the fact-finding process."

(2) Regardless of whether the person in custody may already know his legal rights, "he must be informed in clear and unequivocal terms that he has the right to remain silent." This will guarantee that the ignorant are informed of the right to remain silent and that the pressures of interrogation do not make others forget it.

(3) That warning "must be accompanied by the explanation that anything said can and will be used against the individual in court." This will impress the suspect with the consequences of giving up his privilege to remain silent.

(4) The individual also "must be clearly informed that he has the right to consult with a lawyer and to have the lawyer with him during interrogation." He must be told this whether he already knows it or not, because having his own attorney is the only sure way to protect his privilege against self-incrimination.

(5) The individual must be informed "that if he is indigent a lawyer will be appointed to represent him." The right to call in a lawyer is meaningless to someone with no money.

(6) The individual is always free to exercise his privilege to remain silent. If he "indicates in any manner at any time prior to or during questioning, that he wishes to remain silent, the interrogation must cease." Likewise, if he "states that he wants an attorney, the interrogation must cease until an attorney is present."

(7) If a statement is obtained without the presence of an attorney, "a heavy burden rests on the Government to demonstrate that the defendant knowingly and intelligently waived his privilege against self-incrimination, and his right to retained or appointed counsel." It cannot be assumed that the defendant gave up his privilege just because he sat silently after the warnings were given or because a confession was eventually obtained.

(8) If these rules are not followed, no statement the defendant makes can be used against him in court. Neither a full confession nor the admission of a part of the offense can be used, whether it tends to show guilt or innocence.

(9) No one can be penalized for exercising his privilege to remain silent. For example, the prosecutor cannot "use at trial the fact that [the defendant] stood mute or claimed his privilege in the face of accusation."

These are the rules that grew out of the *Miranda* case. They are now summarized in the famous MIRANDA WARNINGS recited to anyone taken into police custody. Not unexpectedly, this decision was highly controversial. Many people felt that occasional police abuses did not justify such a far-reaching decision, and law enforcement officials feared they would never be able to obtain confessions under the new rule. Recent studies indicate, however, that suspects are talking about as much as they ever did and that police are still getting about as many confessions as they did before *Miranda*.

Miranda Warnings
The simple instructions that must be given to any person after he has been taken into custody and before a law enforcement officer may ask him any questions. Every person must be warned

(1) That he has the right to remain silent.

(2) That any statement he does make may be used as evidence against him.

(3) That he has the right to have an attorney present.

(4) That, if he cannot afford to hire an attorney, one will be appointed for him, if he so desires, before any questioning takes place.

These are called the Miranda Warnings because the Supreme Court first announced that they were required in the case MIRANDA V. ARIZONA.

miscarriage of justice
A legal proceeding or other official action that unfairly harms someone.

miscegenation
Mixture of races; MARRIAGE or sexual intercourse between two persons of different races. Some states punished miscegenation as a crime until the Supreme Court issued a ruling in 1967 making such laws unconstitutional.

misdemeanor
A crime that is less serious than a *felony* and is usually punishable by a fine or less than a year in jail. See CRIMINAL LAW.

misfeasance
Doing something that is wrong or improper but that is legal. It differs from *malfeasance,* which is doing something that is both improper and illegal. For example, the acceptance of a bribe by a judge is malfeasance because it is both improper and illegal, while a judge's derogatory comments about a defense attorney during the course of a trial is misfeasance because the judge has acted improperly but has not broken the law.

misjoinder 1 The improper inclusion of certain persons as plaintiffs or defendants in a lawsuit. 2 The joining of two or more claims, demands, or causes of ACTION in a lawsuit that should be tried separately. See JOINDER.

misrepresentation A false or incorrect statement or account. An *innocent misrepresentation* is made by someone who does not know it is untrue. A *negligent misrepresentation* is one made by someone who should have known better. A *fraudulent misrepresentation* is a deliberate false statement made by someone who intends to mislead.

mistake Unintentional error or act. A *mistake of fact* is made by one who believes that something has happened or exists when that is not the case. A *mistake of law* is made by one who knows the facts but is wrong about the legal effect of an act or event. A *mutual mistake* occurs when both parties to a contract make an incorrect assumption and neither intentionally misleads the other.

mistrial A courtroom trial that is given no legal effect because some mistake has been made that would cause a serious injustice.

EXAMPLE Two women in New York were accused of murder, criminal solicitation, and conspiracy in the fatal shooting of the husband of one of them. The police said to one woman's sister: "Try to talk to her. She won't talk with us." The sister did, and the woman confessed the crime. The judge had to declare a mistrial because the police request made the sister "a willing agent of the police." The law requires any police officer or person acting as an agent for the police to give a suspect the Miranda Warnings before obtaining a confession, and the woman's sister had not done that.
See MIRANDA WARNINGS.

mitigating circumstances Facts or events that do not justify or excuse bad conduct but can reduce the amount of blame. They warrant a reduced penalty, sentence, fine, or amount of money damages assessed.

mitigation of damages Reducing the amount of money DAMAGES sought in a lawsuit by showing that the plaintiff failed to take reasonable steps to minimize his injuries and, therefore, it would be unfair to award him the full amount of damages he has sought.

mittimus A court order sending a convicted person to prison or transferring records from one court to another.

M'Naghten's rule The rule that a person is not guilty because of insanity if, at the time he committed the offense, he could not know the nature of his act or understand right from wrong owing to some defect or disease of the mind. See CRIMINAL LAW.

model act One of a number of proposed laws drawn up by the National Conference of Commissioners on Uniform State Laws. State legislators use them as samples when they write their own laws. The model acts may include variations with explanations for each point. Model acts are different from UNIFORM ACTS, which are also proposed by the commissioners. The uniform laws usually are enacted in exactly the same form in each state, while the model acts are offered as guides.

modus (Latin) "Manner"; means; way. In a criminal indictment, the modus is the statement of how the crime was committed.

moiety Half of anything. For example, joint owners hold their property by the moiety.

monopoly An advantage that exists when a person or company holds the exclusive power to conduct a business or trade, manufacture an article, or control the sale of the whole supply of specific items. Monopolies have always been considered harmful to the general welfare and therefore against PUBLIC POLICY. They are unlawful because they tend to prevent competition and increase the price while lowering the quality of the commodity or service monopolized.

■ **Lawful monopolies** When the safety or interest of the public is involved, a state legislature can grant exclusive FRANCHISES without violating the law against monopolies. The franchise is void, however, if there is no benefit to the public. A municipality or other subordinate government body can also grant exclusive franchises under its powers to pass ordinances for public health and safety. For example, a town may award a contract to one person or corporation for the removal of garbage or approve a franchise to one publisher to supply all the textbooks in a school district without violating the antimonopoly law.

Public service franchises are customarily given to operate toll bridges, turnpikes, and wharves. An exclusive right for a certain number of years to supply gas, water, or electricity to a municipality is often awarded by the town government or state legislature.

The federal government creates lawful monopolies when it gives PATENTS to inventors for their inventions. These monopolies are limited, usually for a period of 17 years.

■ **Restraint of trade** All combinations, contracts, or agreements creating or tending to create a monopoly are in restraint of trade and contrary to public policy. A *combination* is any group of persons or corporations working together to interfere with the normal course of trade. No intent to violate the law is necessary if it appears that a monopoly will result from the combination.

Every agreement restrains trade in some way, however, and not every combination or agreement that limits competition is illegal. Such a strict rule would invalidate many ordinary, necessary business transactions. Only combinations or agreements that injure the public are illegal. If the restraint of trade gives the parties fair protection and does not interfere with public interest, it is not unlawful.

EXAMPLE The Ace Steel Corporation owned a large factory that produced rolled steel, the raw material for fabricated steel products. The Diamond Steel Corporation had facilities for fabricating rolled steel into plates, sheets, and bars used in heavy construction.

The Ace Corporation, finding that the cost of shipping its rolled steel to another area of the country for fabricating had become too expensive, sought to purchase the Diamond Corporation to obtain its facilities, thereby eliminating the cost of shipping. The directors of the Diamond Corporation believed that the sale would be beneficial to its stockholders.

Contending that the proposed sale would create a monopoly and restrain trade, the federal government brought suit to prevent it. The evidence showed that Ace employed almost 6,000 workers in its steel manufacturing plant and that its employees would be seriously affected if it were unable to acquire the fabricating facilities. The court found that there had been no preexisting competition between Ace and Diamond. Other steel firms operating within the territory provided, and would continue to provide, ample competition. Moreover, because the sale would be beneficial to the public in relation to the 6,000 employees at Ace's manufacturing plant, the court approved it.

■ **Federal legislation** Two acts of Congress—the Sherman Antitrust Act and the Clayton Act—form the federal law on unlawful restraint of trade and monopolies.

The Sherman Antitrust Act Passed in 1890, the Sherman Antitrust Act both imposes criminal responsibility and provides a remedy for injuries incurred. Its purpose is to preserve the free enterprise system and to protect the public against monopolies and contracts or combinations that restrict interstate trade or commerce.

All contracts, combinations, and conspiracies that monopolize or otherwise hold back the free flow of trade between states or commerce with foreign nations are forbidden. Contracts aimed at eliminating existing competition or preventing future competition are in violation of the act. Similarly, combinations are prohibited that attempt to exclude outsiders from a business or market or that directly restrain not only the manufacture but also the purchase, sale, or exchange of the article among the states.

Unless protected by a lawfully granted patent monopoly, an agreement to fix the price of an article involved in interstate commerce is, per se, illegal. A fixed price is one that is agreed upon. It is unimportant whether the price is set at a maximum or minimum or whether a formula is used for arriving at the price. Even fixing a price at the current fair market price is illegal. The Sherman Act prohibits any agreement to pay or charge uniform prices, to establish a price range, or to raise or lower prices.

How the act is violated The union of two or more persons or corporations intending to control a particular trade or industry must exist in order for a conspiracy or a combination that breaks the law to be established. If persons in the same trade, after exchanging information, act in the same way but independently of each other in buying, selling, or setting prices, they have done nothing illegal.

A conspiracy may be formed expressly by a verbal agreement or tacitly from the conduct of the parties. For example, if the manufacturers of a particular type of bedding agree that such bedding must sell for one set price, they have conspired to illegally restrain trade. If such manufacturers meet at a bedding convention and, after such meetings, all set the same price at which the bedding is to be sold, it can be inferred that they have agreed to fix prices. As long as restraint or monopoly is the direct result of a combination,

the act has been violated. It is presumed that the combining parties intended the consequences of their acts and agreements. Good motive or good intent is irrelevant.

When a combination or conspiracy to monopolize is found, no overt act by those prosecuted has to be shown. The restraint or monopoly need not have harmed anyone.

Where the act applies The Sherman Antitrust Act does not condemn all combinations or afford remedies for all TORTS (injuries to person or property) committed by or against persons engaged in interstate commerce. It applies only to the deeds that have an effect on market prices by depriving consumers of the benefits of free competition.

For example, luggage manufacturers agree to set the price for overnight bags at $20 more than had been the average market price last year. The manufacturers begin to produce a bag of inferior quality since they know that they will not be undersold by their competitors. This type of price-fixing denies consumers the right to buy the best quality goods for their money and puts them at the mercy of unscrupulous manufacturers.

Size Under the act, a corporation is not objectionable merely because of its size, capital, or production capacity or because it has the power to restrict competition. Size does not in itself deter trade or harm the public. On the contrary, it may increase trade and bring many benefits to consumers. But size carries with it an opportunity for abuse that cannot be ignored. If the power that results from the size of a particular business is improperly used or can be used to harm either a competitor or the public, or if a combination of corporations merely controls all or virtually all of an industry, without any unlawful trade practice, the Sherman Act has been violated.

Persons liable Liability under the act extends to all who violate its provisions. Corporations and unincorporated companies may break this law. Corporate officers can be liable. Corporate officers who are in one department—for example, the manufacturing department—and have nothing to do with the company's competitors, are not liable when other officers conspire to destroy the interstate trade of its competitors. Similarly, a minority stockholder who takes no part in management cannot be held accountable.

The Clayton Act Passed by Congress in 1914, the Clayton Act supplements the Sherman Antitrust Act by prohibiting restraints on interstate commerce not prohibited by the Sherman Act. The Clayton Act makes it unlawful for any person to lease or sell goods and machinery on the condition that his customers will not deal with his competitors, thus limiting competition or creating a monopoly.

■ **State legislation** Monopolies and combinations or contracts in restraint of trade are prohibited by most states. State antitrust laws have generally been upheld as constitutional. Their purpose is the same as the federal law.

moot A subject for argument; undecided. A *moot point* is one not as yet settled by judicial decisions. A *moot case* seeks to answer a question that is theoretical and not based on existing facts or rights. Law schools have moot courts where students practice arguing cases.

moral turpitude Conduct contrary to justice, honesty, modesty, or good morals. It signifies an inherent quality of baseness, vileness, depravity. Examples of crimes involving moral turpitude include RAPE, soliciting for prostitutes, FORGERY, and ROBBERY. See CRIMINAL LAW.

moratorium A temporary suspension of legal remedies against debtors, sometimes authorized by law during times of financial distress. For example, the Secretary of Agriculture can call a moratorium on the payment of principal and interest on federal loans made to farmers to construct or repair farm buildings when the borrower shows that he cannot make the payment without lowering his standard of living. A moratorium also temporarily suspends the performance of a legal obligation.

mortality table A chart used to determine the probable number of years a man or woman of a given age and ordinary health will live. INSURANCE companies use mortality tables as a basis for deciding what premium to charge for insurance coverage, and the courts consult them in awarding money DAMAGES in lawsuits.

mortgage A pledge of property for the payment of a debt or the performance of some other obligation. The *mortgagor* is a property owner who, by a written document, pledges his property as security for a loan. He is the debtor. A *mortgagee*—the lender—is the person who receives the mortgage. Two separate documents are involved in a mortgage agreement—a bond and a mortgage. The bond says the lender will give a particular amount of money to the borrower to be repaid monthly at a certain yearly interest rate for a fixed number of years. In the mortgage document, the borrower gives the lender an interest in the property as security for the loan.

■ **Getting a mortgage** Not many people can afford to buy a house or real estate without some mortgage financing. The usual procedure when buying real estate is for the buyer and seller to sign a CONTRACT of sale that describes the property and states the names of the parties to the deal, the price, the method of payment, and the date when the transfer of ownership will occur. The contract is usually contingent on the buyer being able to obtain a mortgage for a fixed amount within a certain period of time from the date of the contract or else the contract becomes void. For a discussion of the relationship between the buyer and the seller from the signing of the contract to the closing, see VENDOR-PURCHASER RELATIONSHIP.

The prospective buyer then submits a mortgage application with a small fee to various financial institutions such as savings banks, savings and loan institutions, and mortgage companies. The application requires information about the size of the mortgage and the length of time for which it is sought, the applicant's credit history, including his salary, outstanding debts and assets as well as his job history, the location of the property, a survey of the boundary lines of the property, the contract of sale for the property, and the amount of taxes on the property. The lending institution reviews the application and sends an appraiser to assess the value of the property. If the institution is satisfied that the applicant is a good risk—that is, financially stable—it will approve him for a mortgage. The prospective buyer will then receive a letter of commitment from the lender stating

that it will give him the mortgage. The buyer then schedules a date for the closing—the session at which ownership is transferred from seller to buyer. The closing is often held at the lending institution.

Most mortgage payments are made monthly in a set figure that consists of part of the principal of the loan plus interest. Sometimes, the monthly payment includes a fractional portion of real estate tax or mortgage or fire insurance. These monthly payments last the term of the mortgage, usually 20 to 30 years. The repayment of a mortgage in which the periodic payment equals the current interest charge and part of the principal is known as *amortization*.

Redlining The reason the lending institution sends an appraiser to assess the property is to verify that its value is comparable to the amount of the mortgage. This makes sense since the lending institution would have to sell the property to pay the mortgage should the owner default or fall into bankruptcy. To determine the value of the property, the appraiser considers the value of similar property in the area. In the past, if the area was poor and run down, many lending institutions would deny an applicant a mortgage even though the value of the individual property was on a par with the amount of the mortgage and the applicant was a good risk. This discriminatory conduct was called redlining because certain neighborhoods were outlined in red pencil on city maps as being undesirable areas in which to invest funds in the form of home mortgages. Redlining has been outlawed by federal law.

■ **Types of mortgages** There are various types of mortgages available to prospective homeowners.

A *conventional home mortgage* is the most common mortgage for a person who cannot afford to pay the purchase price of a home in cash. Instead, he pays a percentage of the purchase price (usually a 20-30 percent down payment) and gives the seller a check for the balance of the price from his mortgagee. In exchange for the check, the buyer gives the lending institution a security interest in (or, in a few states, legal title to) the property as collateral for the loan. This type of mortgage is called conventional because the lender depends only on the credit of the borrower and the security in the property, not on the additional backing of the government, such as a mortgage that is insured by the Federal Housing Administration (FHA). If the borrower fails to repay his mortgage, his property will be sold and its proceeds used to repay his debt.

In recent years, alternatives to the conventional home mortgage have been devised that make it easier for a person to finance his first home but that may cost more in the end. With a *graduated payment mortgage*, the mortgagor pays smaller monthly payments at the beginning of the mortgage than he would under a traditional mortgage. These payments gradually increase over a number of years as the anticipated income of the mortgagor also increases. The interest rate does not change and the term of the mortgage is the usual 20 to 30 years.

A *variable rate mortgage* is a type of conventional mortgage that stipulates that the lender can adjust the interest rate upward or downward every certain number of years over the term of the mortgage. Such changes are made in response to fluctuations in interest rates and the demand

BUYING YOUR OWN HOME

MANOUEL MANOS
Member, New York Bar

The great American dream is to own your home. Often the dream turns into a nightmare. Purchasers have lost their savings, moved into a home beyond repair, spent years and vast sums of money to perfect their title (right of ownership), and suffered innumerable other disasters. Much of this trouble can be avoided by using a little precaution, by making some minimal investments, and by properly understanding the basics of a property transaction.

Since a new home will cost tens of thousands of dollars over the next 20 or 30 years, you should not enter into any agreement without proper guidance and advice. The costs of the services of an engineer, a lawyer, and a title insurance company, all of whom can help you through the major steps of the transactions, are insignificant when compared with the total cost of the property. The engineer and lawyer will advise you before you sign a contract, and the title insurance company will represent you and act on your behalf from the signing of the contract to the date of the closing (the completion of the contract) and after that as long as you own the home.

Before signing a contract

Do you want to buy a home with a cracked foundation, sagging beams, or a leaky roof? Of course not. That is why you should have a professional engineer, who is trained to spot these conditions, thoroughly inspect the house you are considering. His report will be complete and ought to be heeded. Do not buy an unsound house unless you are willing to spend the time and money to make the necessary repairs or unless you can convince the seller that he should make such repairs before the closing.

A word of caution. It is best not to sign a contract before the engineer's inspection, because you may be incurring unnecessary costs. A contract that provides for the sale to take place only on the condition of a favorable report from the engineer can be canceled if the report is unfavorable. If the contract is canceled, the lawyers who spent time on its preparation are still entitled to a fee. As experience has shown, both seller and purchaser resent paying for the fee for the contract under such circumstances. Nevertheless, you will be responsible for paying your lawyer.

In addition, it is also wise to have a lawyer check the real estate binder before you sign it. Binders, also called *offers to buy* or *deposit receipts,* are frequently used by real estate brokers to acknowledge that a deal has been struck between a buyer and seller and to require the buyer to place a deposit on the property. The purpose of the binder is to hold the buyer and seller to the deal until a contract is drawn up.

Signing a contract

When you are satisfied with the engineer's report, you are ready to go to contract. Now you must have a lawyer. No contract should ever be signed without your lawyer's approval. He will protect your interests from the moment of signing until the date you close title. Never forget that a written contract of sale is a binding instrument that can burden you with heavy expenses and even losses if you are not adequately represented and protected.

Most states have a standard contract for the sale of realty in that particular state. Any knowledgeable person can prepare the basic contract, and many real estate brokers have been known to do so. It is not difficult to type onto the printed contract form the names and addresses of the seller and the purchaser, the consideration (purchase price) to be paid, the manner of payment (normally 10 percent upon execution of the contract and the balance at the closing), the legal description of the property, and the date and place of closing.

Preparing a standard contract is simple, but these standard contracts will not fully protect your interests. Innumerable problems may arise before the sale is completed that may cause you to lose large sums of money or the property itself. But a lawyer can anticipate these problems and have clauses inserted in the contract that will protect you.

The following is a discussion of some of the clauses that a lawyer may have added to the contract to combat the more frequent problems that arise in a real estate transaction.

Mortgage clause   If you are like most people and cannot pay the full price of the house in cash, you must secure financing. Your lawyer will insist that a mortgage clause be inserted in the contract. This clause will permit you to apply to a lending institution for a mortgage loan for a specific amount, payable over a specified term of years at a specified rate of interest (normally the interest rate prevailing at the time of closing). A period of time will be granted to secure such a loan.

If the loan is approved, at the time of closing you will execute a mortgage on the property in favor of the lending institution, which will then pay over to you the proceeds of the loan. If your financial position or income does not satisfy the lending institution's loan requirements and your application for a loan is denied, the mortgage clause will have protected you by requiring, under these circumstances, a refund of your down payment and a cancellation of the contract without further liability of either party to the other.

Two-family residence clause   You are purchasing a two-family home because the rental income will help to pay your real estate taxes, mortgage, and other expenses. Your lawyer will insist on inserting a clause stating that the premises may be lawfully occupied as a two-family residence. In some areas, the law may

require a certificate of occupancy for a two-family dwelling to be issued by the appropriate governmental agency; if that is the case in your area, your lawyer will insert a clause to protect you if no certificate has been issued. If the seller cannot meet the conditions, you can cancel the contract and receive a refund of your down payment.

Maintenance clause   You have paid for an engineer's report and are satisfied with the condition of the home you are purchasing. Remember, however, that the closing normally will not be held for at least six to eight weeks from the date of the contract. Many things can happen during this period, and the contract refers to the condition of the premises as of the date of the contract. For example, the seller may neglect to make essential repairs.

Suppose the boiler cracks, the roof starts leaking, and the dishwasher breaks down prior to the closing. Or suppose the seller moves out and the house is without heat. In the wintertime, water in the pipes can freeze and cause extensive damage to the plumbing and bathroom fixtures.

Experience has taught your lawyer to insist on including a clause in which the seller will guarantee that all plumbing, heating and electrical systems, and appliances will be in good working order and the roof will be free of leaks at the time of closing. Such a clause gives you a remedy for any damage to the premises subsequent to the date of contract.

Refund clause   At the time of the signing of the contract, you will make a down payment of 10 percent of the purchase price. This down payment will be accepted by the seller subject to the conditions in the contract: his ability to deliver a marketable title, free and clear of any liens or other encumbrances, and your ability to secure a mortgage loan. Suppose that he cannot deliver a good title or that you cannot secure the mortgage loan. The contract is specific and you are entitled to a refund of your down payment, which you now request. The seller tells you, "I'm sorry, but I used the down payment you gave me to buy my new house. I will give you your money when I find another buyer."

It is true that you have a lien (a legal claim) on the property but that is not necessarily worth much. The property may be heavily encumbered with prior mortgages, court judgments, or liens. If you sue to collect on your lien, you may not receive anything because the prior mortgages, judgments, or liens will take precedence over yours. You may indeed be compelled to wait for the subsequent sale to recover your down payment.

A lawyer would have avoided such a situation. He would have insisted on a provision in the contract requiring that the down payment paid to the seller be turned over by the seller to his attorney and be held by the attorney until the closing. Then, if for some reason title cannot close, your money would be secure and a refund made promptly.

Settlement clause   You may also include in the contract a clause that states which settlement costs you will pay, which the seller will pay, and which will be negotiated at the time of closing. There are no laws governing who pays what; agreement is usually reached by negotiations between you and the seller or by following local custom. For example, you may offer to assume the responsibility of all settlement costs if you think another buyer is interested in the house and if you think your offer to pay these costs will give you a competitive edge. On the other hand, if the house has been on the market for a long time and the seller is eager to complete the deal with you, he may be willing to pay the settlement costs.

Settlement costs include the loan origination fee (cost of processing the mortgage), loan discount (or "points," usually paid by the buyer to the lending institution as an additional charge on the mortgage—one point is 1 percent of the loan), appraisal fee, credit report fee, pest-inspection fee, mortgage insurance, prepayments of insurance premiums, notary fees, survey fee, local fees and taxes on the sale of property, and other items.

You will know what amounts are involved in the settlement because the lending institution to which you applied for your mortgage is obligated by law to send you a good-faith estimate of the settlement costs and a copy of the booklet *Settlement Costs and You*, published by the U.S. Department of Housing and Urban Development. This booklet describes the settlement process in detail and contains important information on your rights and remedies.

Examination of the title

When you have received approval of your mortgage loan application, the examination of the title begins. In some states, the title is still examined by attorneys who look at prior abstracts of title and who search the records of various government departments and agencies. When these attorneys are satisfied that the seller possesses a marketable title—free and clear of liens, encroachments, and other encumbrances—they certify the title and you can close.

But suppose a defect in the title does not show up until much later when you are selling the property? What if the lawyer who certified the title is dead? Who will then perfect your title? You may be forced to hire a lawyer, at great expense, to commence legal proceedings to clear the title. Your awkward position may be no fault of the lawyer who examined the title, because most of the defects in title that create problems are hidden. For this reason, title examination, traditionally made by your lawyer, is now being done in many states by title insurance companies.

Title insurance protects you for as long as you own the property against unforeseen title problems that may arise. In the event of any problems, the title company will defend your title or take appropriate legal steps to clear it. Should the company fail to clear your title, it will pay you for any losses you sustain.

The premium for title insurance is paid only once, at the time of closing, and is relatively cheap—about 1 percent of the purchase price of the property. It is well worth the price, for the consequences of not having it can be extremely costly.

In one case, a homeowner purchased his property from the heirs of an estate. The title company examined the title and checked all court proceedings. Papers filed in court showed that three brothers and a sister survived the decedent, and based on these records, the title company insured the title upon acceptance of a deed from the brothers and the sister. Many years later, a sister who had been living in South America returned and claimed her rightful share. The papers that had been filed in the court proceedings were fraudulent, because they did not include her as an heir. Since the new homeowner had title insurance, he simply notified the company of the sister's claim and the company satisfactorily cleared the title by securing a deed from her to the homeowner at no added expense to the homeowner. If the homeowner had not had title insurance to protect his ownership, he would have had to pay the sister for her interest in the property and then tried to find those who had sold him the property to recover his loss.

In another case, a person listed his home for sale with a real estate office. He showed the home to the broker and delivered keys to him so that the broker would have access to the house to show it to prospective purchasers. A buyer was found, a contract entered into, and the title closed, with the seller and his wife in attendance. The buyer moved into the home. A few months later the real owner of the premises returned from a lengthy sojourn in Europe and was surprised to find another family living in his home. The purchaser's title was based on fraudulent representation and a forged deed. He could have lost his mortgage if he had not had the foresight to procure title insurance.

The closing

Once you have had the title examined and found it to be clear, you are ready to close. The closing is the important event that makes you a homeowner. If you buy a home, the steps discussed below will probably be followed at your closing.

Adjustment to the final price The first step in the closing procedure will be the computation of the adjustment to the final price, which will be figured by your lawyer and the seller's lawyer. Taxes, water charges, insurance premiums, and fuel oil will be apportioned as of the date of closing. In other words, the seller is responsible for all these charges until the date of closing, and you will reimburse him for any that he may have prepaid. If he has not paid the taxes or water charges, he will give you a credit for his share of the unpaid amount. When the adjustments have been completed, the lawyers will arrive at a balance, which will be an amount due the seller.

Mortgage documents The second step at the closing will be your lawyer's examination of the mortgage documents. These documents are prepared by the lending institution's lawyer and are rarely changed. You will sign a mortgage, which will be a lien against your home until it is paid in full. Should you default in making payments called for in the mortgage, or in any of the other conditions in the mortgage, the lending institution can foreclose its mortgage and dispossess you from your home. Many lending institutions put a clause in the mortgage that permits you to prepay the mortgage, in whole or in part; others put this clause only in the mortgage bond or note, but where it appears is unimportant. The effect will be the same.

The next document to be executed will be the mortgage bond or note. This document is your personal guaranty to the lender that you will pay the loan. In the event you default in making payments on the mortgage and your home is sold at a foreclosure sale for less than the amount due the lender, the lender can look to you for a deficiency judgment under the bond or note—that is, you will have to pay him the difference in the price he got for the house and the amount due on the mortgage.

Disclosure and closing statements After execution of the bond or note, you will be given the disclosure statements required by the Federal Real Property Settlement Procedures Act. These statements record all payments made by the seller and the purchaser to complete the sale, as well as the disposition of the funds advanced by the lending institution.

A final statement of closing costs (also called settlement costs) prepared by the lending institution's lawyer will be given to you for your approval. This shows you the actual amount of the settlement charges for which you previously had a good-faith estimate. If the bank or lending institution required escrow payments for the payment of future taxes, water charges, and fire insurance premiums, they will also appear on this closing statement.

The deed and final payments Upon execution of all the documents for the lender, the lender's lawyer will ask how you want the proceeds of the mortgage loan paid. The lawyer for the seller, who will receive most of the funds, may use them to pay off the seller's mortgage on the property (if he has one) and any brokerage commissions. The balance will then be paid to the seller.

While the checks are being drawn, your lawyer will examine the new deed from the seller to you. The description of the premises in the deed will be compared with the certified description in the title report. If the deed is properly prepared, it will be signed by the seller and witnessed by his lawyer. The title company representative will take the deed to record it.

When the lender's lawyer returns with the checks, you will pay the seller the balance due him, either with cash or by a cashier's or certified check. Most lawyers will not accept a personal check for more than a few hundred dollars at a closing. When the seller has received his money, he will give you the keys to the premises.

Finally, you will pay the title representative both the premium for your title insurance and the fee for recording the deed. You can then look forward to many years of contented living in your new home.

for mortgages. For example, a savings bank advertises that it is offering 30-year mortgages at 11½ percent interest for five years. At the end of the five years, the bank can increase the interest rate to 15 percent, keep it at 11½ percent, or decrease it to 10 percent, depending on the state of the economy. Such mortgages are offered at lower interest rates than conventional mortgages during the same period. The flexible nature of the interest rates protects the lending institutions against being committed to an inadequate return on their investment for long periods of time.

An *FHA mortgage* differs from a conventional mortgage in that it is insured by the Federal Housing Administration, a division of the Department of Housing and Urban Development. An applicant for this type of mortgage follows the same procedure as an applicant for a conventional mortgage since lending institutions grant FHA mortgages. Because of the additional backing of the federal government, however, lenders are often not as strict as in reviewing conventional mortgage applications. People with low incomes find FHA mortgages a more available source of mortgage financing, especially since it allows a buyer to put down a minimal amount (sometimes as low as 5 percent) on a house. See Chart 8.

A *VA* (Veterans Administration) *mortgage* is similar to an FHA mortgage but differs in two ways: (1) only veterans of the armed services are eligible and (2) a purchaser who obtains a VA mortgage is not required to make a down payment. See Chart 8.

A *purchase money mortgage* differs from both conventional and government-insured home mortgages in that the seller lends the purchaser the balance of the purchase price after the down payment has been made. The seller has the same type of security interest in the land (as collateral for the loan) as a bank would have and the purchaser makes monthly payments to the seller just as he would to a bank. Unlike a bank, however, the seller does not give the purchaser a check for the amount of the mortgage, because the purchaser would just have to turn around and pay the seller with the same money. The seller, in effect, would be paying himself. The seller does, however, transfer ownership of the property to the purchaser.

■ **First and second mortgages**   When a borrower has used his property as security to obtain two or more mortgages, the mortgages are classified as either first (senior) mortgages or second (junior) mortgages. A *first mortgage* gives the lender, in case of default, the right to sell the borrower's property to pay off his mortgage without using any of the proceeds to repay anyone else until the first mortgagee's debt is satisfied. A *second mortgage* is satisfied only after the proceeds of the sale of the property are used to pay the first mortgage. The second mortgage is paid before any LIENS or other charges against the property are paid, such as a mechanic's lien. A mortgage is classified as first or second according to the earliest date on which it is recorded in the county clerk's office. (See "Recording and priority," below.)

EXAMPLE   John wants to buy a farm that is selling for $100,000. He has $20,000, or 20 percent of the price for a down payment. His savings bank approves him for a $70,000 mortgage but he still needs $10,000. He obtains a $10,000 mortgage from a mortgage company. If the mortgage company records its mortgage first, it will be the first, or senior, mortgage. It does not matter that it is for a smaller amount than the bank's mortgage or that it was approved after the bank had already given John the $70,000 mortgage. Should John default, the mortgage company has a greater right to the proceeds from the sale of the property than does the savings bank. The bank will be next in line for payment since it was "second in time" in recording its mortgage.

■ **Transferring mortgaged property**   A buyer may often take over a seller's mortgage because its interest rate is lower than the current rate (although this may not be true in the future) or because the seller cannot prepay the mortgage without a penalty fee. There are two ways to take over a mortgage: the purchaser may take the property subject to the seller's mortgage, or he may assume the mortgage.

When property is bought *subject to a mortgage,* the buyer is liable only for the remaining payments on the mortgage, not for the value of the property. This is important should the buyer default on his mortgage payments and the property be sold to pay the mortgage debt. If the sale is for less than what is due, the seller will still be liable for the property.

EXAMPLE   Suppose Owen takes over a $55,000 mortgage on property that is valued at $70,000. After five years and $2,000 of payments, he defaults on the mortgage, causing the property to be sold. The property brings in only $45,000, however, because the neighborhood has deteriorated in the five years. The former owner of the property from whom Owen took the mortgage will be liable for the $8,000 difference.

Taking property subject to a mortgage is clearly not a benefit to the seller, but this type of arrangement may enable a homeowner to sell his house faster during an unfavorable economic market.

When a buyer *assumes the seller's mortgage,* however, he assumes the liability for both the mortgage debt and the value of the property. Should he default, he will be fully responsible.

■ **Essentials of a mortgage**   A mortgage must be in writing, but generally no particular form or words are prescribed by statute.

The parties to the mortgage should be clearly named. When a wife joins in a mortgage with her husband, only her first name is needed as long as she is described as the wife of the mortgagor. When a married woman takes out a mortgage, the mortgage is not invalid if it is made out to her maiden name.

Description of property   A mortgage must describe the land so that it can be identified. For example, a plot located in a city is adequately described by reference to lot and block numbers that correspond to recorded maps of the city. The mortgaged premises may also be identified by its boundary lines. While the description should not be ambiguous, it does not have to be exact. The question is one of identification, not of mathematical precision.

If a piece of land is known by a popular name, such as "C. A. Ingram Farm," it may be described by that name in a mortgage. This rule holds, however, only when the exact size and location of the property can be verified by evidence such as surveys or by reference to recorded documents, such as the title deed.

■ **Amount of mortgage** The mortgage must state the amount of the debt secured by it. It should also state the interest rate and the terms of repayment. However, the omission of this information will not invalidate the mortgage as long as it is contained in the bond. As with any *contract,* there must be valid consideration—any amount of money will do.

Execution and delivery A mortgage must be duly executed—that is, signed by the mortgagor or his agent— someone in his behalf with his consent. If a mortgage of property owned by several persons is not executed by all of them, it is not binding on those who do not sign and acknowledge it. It can, however, be held valid against those who did execute the mortgage and if the other owners join in the execution at a later date, it will bind them also as of that time.

A mortgage must be delivered by the mortgagor (borrower) to the mortgagee (lender). Without delivery, a mortgage cannot take effect as a transfer of title or as a security. However, it is not necessary for the mortgagor to hand over the document to the mortgagee in person. For a discussion of delivery, see CONTRACTS.

Recording and priority A mortgage should be recorded in the county clerk's office. If a lending institution does not record the mortgage on your house, it may have lesser rights to the proceeds from the sale of the house if you default on payment than another mortgagee who has recorded his mortgage.

Usually the date on which a mortgage is recorded determines whether it takes priority over other mortgages and liens on the same property. The one recorded first has priority over the second, the second over the third, and so on. However, a statute may modify the rule. For example, a statute may give priority to payment for water supplied by a city over payment of existing mortgages.

Mortgages that are filed at the same time are equal. If the mortgaged property is sold because of default, the mortgagees (lenders) will share in the proceeds according to the proportionate amount of their mortgages.

EXAMPLE Neighborhood Bank holds a $40,000 mortgage on Tony's house while Merry Mortgage Company holds a $10,000 mortgage. Both mortgages are recorded at the same time. Tony defaults on both mortgages and the house is sold for $50,000. The bank will be entitled to $40,000 while the company will receive $10,000. If the house sold for only $40,000, the bank would receive $32,000 (80 percent of the proceeds since its mortgage was 80 percent of the $50,000 debt) while the mortgage company would receive $8,000 (20 percent of the proceeds since it lent 20 percent of the $50,000).

IF YOU ARE THINKING OF TAKING OUT A MORTGAGE

■ A mortgage is a pledge of a house or land for the payment of a debt (or, in some cases, the performance of some nonmonetary obligation). The *mortgagor* is the borrower, or debtor. A *mortgagee* is the lender, usually a bank or other lending institution.

■ Two separate documents make up a mortgage—a *bond* that says the lender will give the borrower a certain sum of money to be repaid monthly at an annual interest rate for a fixed number of years and a *mortgage* that says the borrower gives the lender a security interest (collateral) in the property being mortgaged.

■ *Amortization* is the repayment of a mortgage in which the periodic payment equals the interest and part of the principal.

■ There are various types of mortgages. The most common is called a *conventional home mortgage,* in which the lender depends only on the credit of the borrower and the collateral of the property. In contrast, a mortgage that is insured by the Federal Housing Administration is backed by the federal government. In a *graduated payment mortgage,* the mortgage payments are lower at the start and gradually get larger over time. The interest rate is constant. In a *variable rate mortgage,* the interest rate can be changed every set number of years according to the economic conditions at that time. A *purchase money mortgage* is when the seller offers to finance the buyer and give him a mortgage. Thus the seller becomes the buyer's "banker."

■ In case of default, a first or senior mortgage is always paid before a second or junior mortgage is paid.

■ A mortgage must be in writing but no particular form is necessary. The parties to a mortgage should be named, the land described, and the amount of the debt, the interest rate, and the terms of repayment should be included.

■ The date on which a mortgage is recorded in the county clerk's office determines whether it takes priority over liens on the same property.

■ When a mortgage is for something other than the payment of a debt, performing the condition will satisfy the mortgage. For example, an elderly couple transfer title to their property to their oldest son upon his promise of lifetime support; they take a mortgage as security, he keeps his promise, and the mortgage is discharged upon the death of the parents.

■ Foreclosure is the sale of the mortgaged property in order to pay the debt the mortgagor has failed to repay according to the terms of his mortgage.

■ Almost every home mortgage has a grace period for late monthly payments—usually 10 to 15 days.

■ You will not be foreclosed for being delinquent on just one monthly payment unless your mortgage contains an acceleration clause. An *acceleration clause* causes the entire debt to become due should one installment payment be late. However, if you pay before a foreclosure complaint is filed, you can have your mortgage reinstated.

■ Foreclosure may result if you default on interest, taxes, or insurance.

■ All states allow a mortgagor to redeem his property in the time between default and foreclosure by paying the debt due.

■ Many states permit a mortgagor to redeem his property after a foreclosure sale—up to a limited time, usually one year—if he pays the sale price, the mortgage debt plus interest, and foreclosure costs.

■ **Discharge of the mortgage** Because the payment of a debt is the condition in almost every mortgage, payment in full discharges the mortgage. Payment may be made by the mortgagor himself, by any joint mortgagors, or by any person on behalf of the mortgagor or succeeding to his rights, such as his widow, the executor of his estate, or his guardian, if he is incapacitated. It should be made directly to the mortgagee or someone authorized to receive payment in his behalf.

Ordinarily, the mortgagor will not be compelled to make, nor the mortgagee forced to accept, payment before the due date. But the time is sometimes extended by agreement between the parties.

Unless the parties agree otherwise, the payment of a mortgage is made in money. The mortgagee may, however, agree to accept merchandise or any other form of personal property in satisfaction of the mortgage debt. For example, the mortgage may be discharged by allowing the mortgagor credit for labor or services performed for the mortgagee. Taking a note or bond for the amount due on the mortgage is not considered payment unless the parties intend it to be.

When a mortgagee gives a mortgage, he has agreed to accept interest over the specified term of the mortgage that gives him an increasing return on his investment the longer the mortgagor takes to repay. If the mortgagor wants to prepay the debt within the first few years after receiving the mortgage, the lending institution loses a certain amount of profit. Thus, a mortgagor has no right to prepay unless the mortgage or local law so provides.

This right to prepay in the first years of a mortgage is embodied in a *prepayment clause*. If the mortgagor exercises this right, he must pay a prepayment penalty, which is usually a percentage of the remaining balance on the loan. Some states have passed laws restricting the amount of the prepayment penalty.

Performance of other conditions A mortgage is sometimes satisfied when a condition other than the payment of a debt is performed, if the terms of the mortgage so provide. Thus, the completion of the condition discharges the obligation. This is the case with a mortgage conditioned on the support and maintenance of the mortgagee.

EXAMPLE Two elderly parents transferred title to their
O——* property to their son in return for his promise to support them for the rest of their lives. The parents took back a mortgage as security for their son's obligation. The son kept his promise and the mortgage was satisfied upon the death of his parents.

A mortgage can also be conditioned on the remarriage of the parties.

EXAMPLE A divorced woman decided that she still loved her
O——* former husband and had made a mistake in divorcing him. She requested the ex-husband to remarry her, and he agreed to do so provided she would give him title to a particular lot that he wanted. To be sure that she did not lose both the husband and the property—the woman agreed to present him with the lot, provided he give her his mortgage and a promissory note for the value of the land. The mortgage was to be satisfied and canceled when the couple remarried.

■ **Foreclosure** The means by which the mortgagor loses his right to redeem the mortgaged property is known as foreclosure. Foreclosure results in the sale of the property for the payment of the debt.

Generally, the right to foreclose arises when the mortgagor fails to pay his debt on the date it is due. If the mortgage is based on performing a condition other than paying money, then nonperformance or other breach of the condition will give rise to foreclosure. Almost every home mortgage provides for a *grace period*—usually 10 to 15 days from the date payment is due—within which the mortgage must be paid. If a mortgagor is late in making a monthly payment, he will be required to pay a late charge. Being delinquent in one monthly payment will not bring about a foreclosure proceeding unless the mortgage contains an acceleration clause.

An *acceleration clause* states that a default in paying an installment accelerates the maturity of the debt and warrants foreclosure. Thus, if the mortgage contains an acceleration clause, the entire debt may become due whenever an installment payment is neglected. The right to foreclose may also arise when the mortgagor defaults on the payment of interest on the principal, taxes, or insurance.

It is the mortgagee's choice whether or not to enforce the acceleration clause by treating the entire debt as due. If the mortgagor makes up his late payment before the mortgagee files a foreclosure complaint to accelerate the debt, the mortgagor reinstates the mortgage so that the mortgage relationship continues. Once the mortgagee decides to accelerate, the mortgagor must repay the entire debt or face foreclosure.

Proceedings Foreclosure proceedings are almost entirely regulated by statute. So the law in your state determines the exact procedure.

A *foreclosure by judicial sale* is the most common type of foreclosure. Since it is court supervised, it is considered the best protection of the rights of all the parties involved. The mortgagee submits copies of a foreclosure complaint to the court and the mortgagor. The mortgagee must then establish that the mortgagor has defaulted on his obligation so that the court will order the sale of the mortgaged property. Once this is done the sheriff or a court-appointed official conducts a public sale of the property. The sale must be confirmed by the court in order to be considered final. See EXECUTION.

A *foreclosure by power of sale* is not conducted under court supervision because a provision of the mortgage has authorized such a sale. The procedure for foreclosure by power of sale is governed by state law. The sale is a public AUCTION that is advertised in local newspapers to give notice to all interested buyers. Since the sale is not confirmed by a court, the purchaser at a foreclosure by power of sale is more likely to be involved in future lawsuits.

In both foreclosure by judicial sale and by power of sale, the proceeds of the sale of the property are used to pay off the mortgage. However, the proceeds must first be used to pay the expenses of foreclosure before the mortgage debt is paid. If any money remains, it will go to the mortgagor after the payment of any other liens on the property. If the proceeds are less than the amount necessary to pay the debt, the mortgagee can sue the mortgagor in court for the difference. The court's decision, called a *deficiency* JUDG-MENT, orders the homeowner to pay the difference. If the homeowner fails to pay, the mortgagee may seek the garnishment of his wages or the attachment of his property. See ATTACHMENT AND GARNISHMENT.

In those few states where a mortgage vests legal title in the mortgagee—which reverts to the mortgagor when the debt is repaid—the mortgagor's default extinguishes his right to regain legal title to his property. The mortgagee then has absolute title to the property and can do whatever he wants with it.

Right of redemption   Many states have laws that permit a mortgagor to redeem (buy back) his property after a foreclosure sale—up to a limited period of time, usually one year—by paying the foreclosure sale price, the mortgage debt plus interest, and the costs of foreclosure. This is known as the *statutory right of redemption*. These laws protect a mortgagor from being victimized by the sale of his property at a price far below its real value. See Chart 13.

The statutory right of redemption is not the same as his right to buy back his property under common law. This privilege, the *equity of redemption,* which exists in all states, permits a mortgagor to redeem his property after default but before foreclosure by paying what he owes the mortgagee—the unpaid balance of the mortgage. Once foreclosure proceedings begin, a mortgagor's equity of redemption ends. Depending on state law, his statutory right of redemption then begins.

most-favored-nation clause   A clause in treaties providing that the citizens of the contracting nations will enjoy the broadest reciprocal rights and privileges possible. The primary effect of such a clause is a lower rate of import taxes. For example, glass Christmas ornaments imported from a most-favored nation might be taxed at 40 percent of their value, while those from a nation that is not in this category might be taxed at 60 percent.

motions and orders   A motion is an application made to a court, or judge, for the purpose of obtaining a mandate directing some act to be done in favor of the applicant. When the court grants a motion, its mandate is called an order. An order must be consistent with the relief sought by the applicant in his motion.

Many different types of motions can be granted depending upon the situation of the applicant. For example, a defendant in a criminal prosecution may make a *motion to suppress* evidence from being used against him if it has been seized illegally. See SEARCH AND SEIZURE. A woman can make a motion in a DIVORCE action for a protective order to prevent her husband from harassing or physically harming her. A motion is one of the basic means by which a person seeks a court's help in obtaining relief from a wrong committed against him.

■ **Making a motion**   Motions are made in civil and criminal actions in federal and state courts. The form and method of making a motion are governed by the Federal Rules of Civil Procedure and the Federal Rules of Criminal Procedure in federal actions. State laws dictate the manner of making a motion in state court.

There is a basic method of making a motion. Anyone whose legal rights have been violated may direct his attorney to apply to the court or a judge for a command that some act be done in favor of him. The motion may be in writing or, if made during the course of a trial, it may be done orally in the presence of the court. A motion is usually made within the framework of an existing lawsuit or proceeding.

EXAMPLE   Jack serves a complaint on Marv to start a lawsuit for assault. He claims that Marv assaulted him with a baseball bat during a barroom brawl one year ago. Marv's attorney submits a motion to the court requesting that the court dismiss the case. The alleged assault took place over two years ago and the time period allowed by law under the statute of limitations for bringing a lawsuit on an assault action is one year. If Marv's motion presents sufficient evidence that proves that the incident was, in fact, committed two years ago, the court will grant his motion and order that Jack's lawsuit be dismissed. This order of dismissal is the result of the court's granting Marv's motion to dismiss.

A motion is usually made with notice being given to the party against whom the order, if granted, will be directed. In the hypothetical example above, when Marv's attorney submits his motion to the court, he sends a copy to Jack so that Jack can present evidence to show that Marv should not be given the relief he seeks.

Sometimes, a motion may be granted without notice to the opposing party but only in emergencies. For example, a motion to stay (postpone) a court decision that allows a construction company to bulldoze a forest pending the outcome of an appeal of the decision by an environmental group could be granted without notice to the construction company if the destruction of the forest is scheduled for two hours from the time the motion is made. Such motions are called *ex parte motions.*

A motion can be made before a trial begins, during a trial, or after a trial.

EXAMPLE   Marv's motion to dismiss Jack's lawsuit is made before the trial begins, to save the time and expense of needless litigation. Suppose the court denies Marv's motion to dismiss because Jack's evidence establishes that the alleged assault occurred 11 months ago and therefore his action is being started within the time specified by law. The trial begins. Jack presents overwhelming evidence that Marv assaulted him with the baseball bat for no reason at all. Marv presents no evidence to the contrary. No reasonable person could find that Marv did not commit the assault. Jack submits a *motion for a directed verdict,* asking the court to decide the issue of Marv's fault without submitting it to the jury. The court will order a directed verdict if, from the evidence presented by both sides, only one verdict is possible.

If the court does not grant the motion for a directed verdict, the jury will be given the case to reach a verdict as to Marv's liability. Suppose the jury returns a verdict of not guilty. Jack is astounded but he learns that two jury members belong to the same social club as Marv and share the ownership of a summer home with him. Even though the trial is over, Jack can file a *motion for a new trial* on the ground that the case was not tried by an impartial jury. If the court agrees, it will issue an order to set aside the judgment and to grant Jack a new trial.

■ **The entry of an order**   Once an order is granted in response to a motion, it must be entered as part of the record of the case. The order must state the relief to be given in explicit enough terms to enable the party to whom it is directed to give the requested relief.

motive An inducement, reason, or incentive for doing an act. In MURDER, motive is what induces a person to kill someone—for example, to obtain his money. Contrary to popular belief, the motive of a murderer is not an element of the crime and need not be proved in order to convict him.

motor vehicle A self-propelled vehicle that runs on the ground without rails or tracks and is used to carry passengers or materials. All types of automobiles, motorcycles, campers, trucks, and buses are considered motor vehicles. See also CARRIER.

In order to provide for the safety and protection of the general public, the federal government controls and regulates the operation of motor vehicles engaged in interstate commerce. Under its POLICE POWER, each state also has the right to govern the use and operation of motor vehicles on the state's public ways. A state may delegate to a municipality the power to regulate motor vehicles within its limits.

■ **Registration of vehicles** Statutes providing for licensing and registration of motor vehicles are primarily regulatory measures, although an incidental purpose is to raise revenue. Registration is required in order for the state to exercise control over the use of highways. It identifies a vehicle and its owner and places them on public records, thereby protecting buyers and persons injured through the operation of vehicles and hindering the sale of stolen vehicles. A certificate of registration gives the owner the privilege of operating his motor vehicle. It relates only to the vehicle and not to the business for which it might be used. A certificate of registration is not the same as a certificate of title. The former is required if a vehicle is to be operated on the roads; the latter is necessary only if a vehicle is to be sold to someone. A certificate of title is a written document that states that a seller of a motor vehicle transferred title to (ownership of) a vehicle to the person named therein as buyer. This is evidence of ownership and required by many states to protect the public from unknowingly buying stolen vehicles. See Chart 24.

Many statutes require that you register a vehicle in your name. When this is the law, a registration made in any other name is invalid. A motor vehicle owned by a corporation should be registered in the name of the corporation. Similarly, one belonging to a partnership should be registered in the partnership name and not in that of an individual partner. Registration is often granted to multiple owners. In the case of a conditional sale—when the seller holds title to the vehicle until it is fully paid for—registration may be in the name of either the seller or the buyer.

As the owner of a motor vehicle, you are generally required to obtain a registration certificate and a set of license plates bearing the numbers (or numbers and letters) that have been assigned to your vehicle. The possession of these articles by anyone driving the vehicle shows that the owner has complied with the law and that the driver has the right to operate that vehicle. For this reason, the law requires you to have the registration with you to show when requested by a police officer.

License plates should be displayed in the required place. They identify the vehicle and its owner. It is usually unlawful to operate a vehicle without proper plates or a permit authorizing temporary plates or to operate it with plates issued to a former owner.

■ **Accident insurance** If you own a car or some other type of motor vehicle, you must usually either take out accident insurance on it or deposit a bond as security to provide compensation to innocent victims of any accidents you may have with your vehicle. If owners of motor vehicles are not forced to take some measures to protect themselves and others against injury and loss resulting from motor accidents involving financially irresponsible drivers, the state would ultimately be liable for such damages by the increased burden on its public hospitals and public assistance programs.

Financial responsibility, or security, laws Many states require that the motorist have some kind of insurance in order to be issued a certificate of registration to operate a vehicle on the road. But a number of states require nothing of the motorist until he has been in an accident. When he is involved in an accident with his vehicle, the motorist must prove either that he has insurance to pay any damages a court may order him to pay if he is found responsible for the accident or post a bond with the court for a particular amount. Depending on the outcome of the trial, the motorist may be held responsible for an amount greater than his bond or insurance coverage, however.

In states that require a motorist to be insured before a certificate of registration will be issued, proof of payment of a policy must be presented. Otherwise, the motorist cannot legally operate his vehicle on state roads.

Future-proof laws Some states have future-proof statutes that require a motorist who has been in an accident to give enough security in the form of bond to cover the damages for personal injuries or damage to property the motorist may cause in a future accident.

Theories of liability There are two basic types of accident insurance—liability and no-fault. With liability insurance, the insurance company of the motorist who was at fault for the accident will reimburse innocent persons for their injuries and property losses. In states that have no-fault accident insurance, each motorist's insurance company will reimburse the policyholder for his own injury and loss up to a certain limit, regardless of whose fault the accident was. For a full discussion of no-fault insurance, see INSURANCE. Chart 26 summarizes state laws concerning insurance and proof of financial responsibility.

Unless he is covered by no-fault insurance, a person may be liable for damages caused by his motor vehicle even if he was not in the car at the time of the accident. When he lends the vehicle to someone else to drive, the owner will be liable for any injuries to people or property caused by the driver's negligence. If, however, the driver has hired or rented the owner's vehicle, he may be solely liable for any damages he causes depending upon the terms of his rental contract with the owner. Under the FAMILY CAR DOCTRINE, the owner of a car is responsible for an accident caused by the negligent driving of any family member who is permitted to drive the vehicle and was driving for a family purpose, such as grocery shopping, taking the children to school, or pleasure.

SOME POINTS ABOUT DRIVER'S LICENSES

■ Remember, driving on a street or highway is not a right but a privilege. In order to exercise this privilege you must obtain a driver's license.

■ In some states, an unlicensed person may drive if accompanied by a licensed driver—elsewhere he needs a learner's permit.

■ A nonresident driver may have to get a license to drive within a state, but most states have reciprocal-benefit statutes.

■ Qualifications for a driver's license vary from state to state but generally include knowledge of traffic laws, the ability to understand highway signs, and the ability to drive safely. Phys-ical and mental disabilities or a past criminal record may disqualify candidates under some regulations, and a license issued to a minor who has lied about his age in order to get the license is absolutely void.

■ You can get a duplicate license if your original is lost, destroyed, or stolen, but not if it is suspended or revoked. The license may be revoked or suspended for any number of reasons, including speeding, reckless driving, involvement in a fatal accident where you were responsible, failure to pay a fine, and drunken driving.

■ Under laws that are known as im-plied-consent statutes, a driver oper-ating within a state is deemed to have given his consent to a chemical test of breath, blood, urine, or saliva to see if he has been drinking more than the legal limit for drivers. You can have your license suspended for refusing to submit to such a test in states that have implied-consent laws.

■ Some states suspend or revoke a driver's license when he has been convicted of a specified number of named offenses, such as speeding. In some instances, point systems are used in conjunction with these laws; when you accumulate the stated number of points within a prescribed period, you can no longer legally drive.

A car owner who is involved in an accident when he has a passenger in the vehicle may be liable for any losses or injuries incurred by the guest. Some states have enacted guest statutes that limit the liability of drivers for the damages suffered by their guests. A guest is present in the vehicle because of the hospitality of the driver. Therefore, an operator should be liable to the guests only if the accident resulted from extreme carelessness, such as excessive speeding or driving while intoxicated. Chart 28 gives state laws affecting liability and damage claims. See also NEGLIGENCE.

State funds States have their own insurance funds. These are designed to provide limited relief to innocent victims of careless uninsured motorists, unidentifiable motorists, or motorists involved in a hit-and-run accident. State insurance funds may be financed through mandatory minimal contributions of all state insurance companies and imposts on the owners of uninsured vehicles when they can be identified.

■ **Reporting an accident** All states require that a motorist file an accident report if he is involved in any accident with his vehicle that results in injury or death to anyone involved. If there is no injury or death, accident reports are required only if the property damage caused by the accident exceeds a certain fixed amount, which varies from state to state. Accident reports should be filed immediately after the accident, but some states permit a motorist to wait several days or even several weeks before reporting a minor accident. The reports should be filed with local or state police, the motor vehicle department, the Department of Transportation, or any other office designated by state or local law. Chart 27 covers state laws that govern the reporting of accidents.

■ **Safety and inspection laws** The National Highway Traffic Safety Administration issues safety standards that apply to new vehicles. See HIGHWAY. More than half the states require that motor vehicles, once they are in use, be inspected regularly (usually every 6 to 12 months) to protect the public from the dangers of the operation of unsafe or defective vehicles. For an outline of the various state laws in this area, see Chart 25.

■ **Licensing and regulation of drivers** The state legislature has full authority under its police power to control and regulate the licensing of drivers. This insures that drivers are competent, regulates transit on the highways in the interest of public safety, and furnishes a further guaranty that proper and lawful use will be made of the vehicle.

Qualifications A state may set qualifications for a driver's license to operate motor vehicles. Such qualifications often include a knowledge of the traffic laws, the ability to read and understand highway signs, and, of course, the capacity to drive. See Chart 29. Licenses are sometimes denied to persons who in the opinion of the authorities should not be granted them, such as those with epilepsy or some other physical or mental disability. A licensing officer may not impose qualifications not contained in the licensing regulation, but he may consider an applicant's history of traffic violations or criminal record. In some places, he is allowed to deny a license to a person who has been convicted of a felony.

Most statutes set a minimum age for obtaining a driver's license. A license issued to a person below that age is void. Some laws require a minor's parent or guardian cosign the application before the license is issued. In addition, the minor, his parent, or spouse may have to take out liability insurance or post a bond as security.

Nonresidents If you drive in a state other than the one that issued your license, you are a nonresident driver. If you move to another state, you may have to obtain a license from your new state after a specified period of time, but most states have reciprocal-benefit statutes. Under these laws, a valid license from your previous state is good in your current state. When, however, a motorist who has his license suspended or revoked in state A moves to state B and obtains a valid license there, the benefits granted him by state B do not apply if he drives back into state A.

Unlicensed operator An unlicensed person may usually operate a motor vehicle if he is accompanied by a licensed operator. This gives a beginner a chance to learn to drive. If you are the licensed operator giving instructions, you must be seated near enough to give prompt advice and assistance to your student if he has trouble with the car.

Duplicate license, reexamination, and renewal You may be issued a duplicate license when your original is lost, destroyed, or stolen. The words "lost or destroyed" mean that you no longer have your license because perhaps you mislaid it—not because it was suspended or revoked.

If you hold a valid license, you cannot ordinarily be required to take a reexamination, but a statute may authorize a special examination to determine if you have some disability that might prevent you from driving safely—deteriorating vision, for example. Similarly, a regulation permitting reexamination of drivers over a certain age—say, 65—who have been involved in an accident is legal and nondiscriminatory.

Your original operator's license can be extended from time to time by an application for a renewal. If the application is not filed before the license expires, you must obtain a new license.

Revocation or suspension There are many reasons why your license could be revoked or suspended. Commonly, drivers have their licenses taken away when they operate a vehicle with a flagrant disregard for the safety of persons or property.

A person may lose his license if he fails to disclose on the application any physical incapacity that makes his driving a menace to the public safety. Being under age will cause him to lose it without any evidence of mental or physical disability and so will the inability to understand English signs and warnings.

A driver's license may be revoked or suspended for exceeding speed limits, driving too fast for road conditions, racing on the public highways, reckless driving, involvement in a fatal accident in which the license holder is shown to have been negligent, not paying a fine imposed by a competent court, or failure to attend a hearing for a violation of the motor-vehicle law.

Under laws known as implied-consent statutes, a motorist automatically consents to a chemical test of his breath, blood, urine, or saliva to discover the amount of alcohol he has consumed. Refusal to submit to a test for intoxication can lead to the suspension or revocation of an operator's license, whatever the reason for refusing. Lawful arrest and a belief that the motorist is intoxicated are prerequisites to asking him to submit to a chemical test. The fact that the driver is found not guilty of driving while intoxicated does not mean that his arrest was unlawful; therefore, it does not rule out the revocation of his license for failure to consent to the test. Nor does it necessarily exonerate him from his refusal to take the test.

In some states, a suspension or revocation must take place when a driver has been convicted of a specified number of named offenses—such as drunken driving and speeding—within a certain period of time. Point systems are also used in conjunction with these statutes—when the driver accumulates the stated number of points within the prescribed period, his license is taken away.

move Bring a motion. See MOTIONS AND ORDERS.

multilevel distributorship A sales scheme by which a person who buys an article from a company is promised payment for each additional buyer he finds for the item. See CONSUMER PROTECTION.

multiplicity of actions or suits A number of unnecessary attempts to litigate the same right or issue. Courts usually do not permit this practice. See ACTION.

municipal Relating to a local governmental unit, such as a city or a town. For instance, *municipal bonds* are BONDS issued by a local government to raise money. A *municipal ordinance* is a local law or regulation.

municipal corporation An incorporated local government that performs some functions of the state government on a local level. It is a political subdivision of the state. Cities, villages, boroughs, and towns are municipal corporations. The term "municipality" is often used instead of municipal corporation.

■ **Local power** The powers of a municipality are conferred by the state's constitution, a state statute, or by the legislature's grant of a municipal charter. A charter defines the rights, powers, and obligations of the municipality. Usually the municipality is free from the control of the state legislature in local matters. This is known as *home rule* and is provided for by the state constitution or statute.

Every municipality has a legislative and administrative body—called a city, common, or village council or board of commissioners—that carries out the sovereign powers of local government by enacting local ordinances. A municipal council holds regular meetings to handle business matters and public meetings to give residents an opportunity to air their views on the way local affairs are being managed.

Many municipalities elect a mayor or municipal manager to serve as the chief administrative and executive officer. His powers are set by law and include presiding over the local council and approving or vetoing their actions. He may convene special sessions of the council for certain circumstances, such as determining how the municipality will rebuild itself after being hit by a tornado. Other officers and members of the council are usually elected but in some places the law allows them to be appointed by the chief executive of the municipality.

In addition to its governing body, a municipality usually has specialized departments such as fire, police, health, parks, water, and building departments. The powers exercised by the departments depend on the state's statute, charter, or constitution.

■ **Public welfare** A municipality has the POLICE POWER to regulate all matters harmful to the safety and general welfare of the public. Since safeguarding the PUBLIC HEALTH is an important function, a municipality has the right to provide for sanitary garbage disposal. It may enact regulations to prevent animals, such as dogs, from running at large. It may also make rules to preserve the public peace, particularly on its streets. The police power also protects public and private property—for example, almost all municipalities have fire-safety regulations.

Restricting private property The owner of private property is entitled to his enjoyment of it, but a municipality may restrict the use of his property for the common good—for example, ZONING property into residential and commercial districts. When necessary, a municipality may destroy private property. For instance, it may order the demolition of buildings unsafe for human use. Monetary compensation for the owner is often provided by statute. Generally, a municipality may not cut down a tree on private property near which it is making street improvements without paying the owner.

Other municipal regulations Suppression of the business of prostitution has traditionally been a subject of municipal regulation. But a municipality may not prohibit a prostitute from living in the community.

Municipalities may ban the use of major thoroughfares by cars with one occupant during rush hours and prohibit the transportation of radioactive or explosive materials through its streets. Bus and other public transportation routes may be restricted. The size and number of billboards displayed may be limited.

Blasting at construction sites may be restricted to hours when there is minimal public use of the surrounding neighborhood. A building permit may be required to construct or renovate any buildings. The permit may require that a certain quality of materials be used and that the building be inspected regularly in the interest of public safety. The construction and maintenance of elevators, escalators, and stairways as well as heating and cooling systems in such buildings are commonly the subjects of ordinances. The construction and operation of garages and automobile service stations are under municipal regulation.

Restaurants, hospitals, hotels, and grocery stores must comply with the requirements of ordinances that are designed to safeguard public health. The services provided by barbers and beauticians, health clubs, dry cleaners, carpet cleaners, laundries, junk dealers, storage and moving companies, plumbers, electricians, building contractors, and employment agencies may be subject to municipal regulations to protect the consumer against defective workmanship or fraudulent practices. See CONSUMER PROTECTION. Smoking may be prohibited in public places. The opening and closing hours of restaurants, bars, discotheques, and nightclubs may be set by ordinance. In times of epidemic, the municipality may enact quarantine ordinances and it may require certain segments of the population to be vaccinated when deemed necessary. Undertakers may also be subject to municipal regulation.

■ **Education** Although education is a function that belongs to the state, a municipality may establish a public school system within its borders as long as the requirements set by state law are met. Such a SCHOOL system is supported by local tax revenues as well as state and federal revenues.

■ **Contracts** Municipalities usually enter into CONTRACTS with other corporations to furnish its citizens with utilities necessary for daily living—gas or electricity, for example—and with private individuals to construct new housing. The power to make municipal contracts usually resides solely in the council.

A municipality about to enter into a contract must publish a notice of its intention. On construction contracts, for example, it should invite competing proposals and

award the contract to the most qualified bidder. A contract in which an officer of the municipality has a personal interest—usually as a member, stockholder, or employee of a firm contracting with the municipality—is void and unenforceable.

■ **Taxation** A municipality has the power to tax its residents for public purposes as authorized by state law. Money raised from taxes is used for constructing, operating, and maintaining municipal buildings, roads, sidewalks, schools, hospitals, and sewers; the salaries of municipal employees, including teachers, fire and police officers, sanitation workers, and clerical and management personnel; and the payment of municipal bonds that have been previously issued to finance public works projects.

Depending on the authority given to it by the state, a municipality may tax any person or corporation within its territorial limits. The tax may be on income, sales, or real estate, for example.

When real estate is taxed, all property that lies within the limits of a municipality and is not exempt by law is subject to assessment (deciding the value of the property for tax purposes). See also TAXATION. Once a tax is levied by a municipality, the inhabitants must pay the appropriate officer, usually the tax collector. If you feel that your property has been wrongly assessed, you can challenge the assessment by following the procedure that has been established in your municipality.

In some instances, you will have to pay the tax "under protest" while pursuing your case. To pay "under protest," you simply write these words on the back of your tax check, followed by your signature. You must pay your taxes even though you question the assessment, because if you do not municipalities will be entitled to place a LIEN on the property. This means that you cannot sell your property until you have paid your taxes, and after a number of years set by law have passed in which you have not paid your property taxes, the municipality can have your property sold to pay the overdue taxes plus any accrued interests and costs. Any money left over will be returned to you. See TAX SALE.

■ **Taxpayer's suit** Every taxpayer of a municipality has a vital interest in, and a right to, the preservation of an orderly and lawful government whether or not his wallet is immediately touched. Because of this, many statutes give the individual taxpayer the right to bring a lawsuit against officers, boards, or commissions of a municipal corporation to recover money that has been wrongfully spent. This type of lawsuit is known as a taxpayer's suit.

EXAMPLE A lighting company submitted the lowest bid for
○—★ a public contract for the installation of street-
lights in town and was awarded the contract. Subsequently, the company violated the bidding requirements by unjustly increasing the price. Taxpayer Jones brought a lawsuit against the town board to set aside the contract with the lighting company. Jones won.

■ **Liability for torts** A municipality may be liable (financially responsible) for the injuries it causes to persons or property through its NEGLIGENCE. For example, if your car is damaged by a city snowplow, you are entitled to collect damages from the city only if the city was negligent in some way—for example, if the snowplow's brakes were in disrepair and faulty.

If the municipality exercises ordinary and reasonable care, however, it will not be held liable for negligence in performing its functions. Examples of common tort suits against municipalities are personal injuries caused by defects in public streets, sidewalks, drains, and sewers.

A municipality may also be liable for the job-related intentional torts of its employees during working hours, depending on the facts of the particular case. For example, if a police officer severely beats a suspect who has been held for interrogation during a criminal investigation, the municipality may be liable under a theory of RESPONDEAT SUPERIOR. A municipality may be sued for the injuries and damages caused when one of its bus drivers injures his passengers when he goes through a red light and crashes into a truck.

In the past, municipalities had SOVEREIGN IMMUNITY against lawsuits for injuries and damages they caused in carrying out their government duties. Consequently a citizen could not sue city hall. This municipal immunity, however, was slowly eroded by court decisions. Some states now have statutes that limit immunity to particular cases, such as when slander is committed during a judicial proceeding.

Claims against a municipality   If you bring a claim against a municipality, you probably will be required to file a notice or statement of it. This is legally known as a *notice of claim*. The notice should enable the municipality to investigate the situation thoroughly and decide whether it will settle the claim in or out of court. For example, if you break your ankle after falling into a pothole, you would file a notice of claim against the municipality. The notice should state the time, place, cause, and nature of the injury alleged. If you fail to comply with the proper requirements, your claim may be rejected.

Your claim must be presented within the time required by statute or charter or else your lawsuit cannot be started—even if the statute of limitations has not run out. This special time requirement applies only to lawsuits against municipalities.

In some states, a suit against a municipality must be started in the county in which it is situated. If the suit is not filed there, the municipality is entitled to have it transferred. A *process* (a WRIT, SUMMONS, or court order) must be served on the mayor or other executive head of the municipality.

The decisions of councils or boards allowing or disallowing claims against municipal corporations are subject to judicial review. Claims against the municipality may be settled or submitted to arbitration at the direction of selectmen or municipal supervisors or after a vote at a town meeting.

EXAMPLE The town of Highland maintained an area of a
O—* park for ice skating. As soon as ice appeared on the pond each year, a guard was assigned to test the ice daily, to post signs indicating whether or not it was safe, and to supervise people gathered in the area. One mild winter day, no one showed up to skate, so the guard left his post and spent the afternoon drinking coffee in a diner. While he was gone, a young man ventured out on the ice because the signs said that the ice was still safe. He fell through a weak spot and drowned. Later the young

man's family sued the town, claiming that it was responsible for the guard's negligence. The town selectmen met to discuss the case. It was clear that the town was going to have to pay damages, so the selectmen voted for a settlement out of court rather than risk an even higher jury verdict against the town.

Civil rights violations   In 1978, the U.S. Supreme Court ruled that local governments are "persons" under the federal statute that imposes liability on persons who commit civil rights violations. This decision opened up an extensive new area of litigation in which municipalities are now becoming embroiled.

In 1980, the Supreme Court decided that when local governments are sued for federal civil rights violations committed by their employees, they are liable whether or not the employee acted in good faith and unintentionally violated the law. When sued as individuals, employees can still claim that they cannot be held liable because they acted in good faith. However, to allow a municipality to make the same claim would deprive an injured person of any remedy for the infringement of his rights.

muniment   A document that is evidence of TITLE to (ownership of) real estate or personal property, such as a DEED to land or a stock certificate.

murder   The unlawful killing of one human being by another with malice aforethought. Murder is a form of HOMICIDE and a felony. It is punishable by long-term imprisonment or, in some states, by death. Murder is to be distinguished from MANSLAUGHTER, which is the unlawful killing of a human being without malice.

■ **Malice aforethought**   In order to commit murder a killer must act with malice. The malice may be either express or implied. *Express malice* is an actual intent to kill someone. Whether the intention was to kill the person killed or someone else is immaterial. Consequently, if Sam shoots at Maurice to kill him, but misses Maurice and accidentally kills Adam instead, Sam is guilty of murder because he killed with malice aforethought even though he hit the wrong victim. *Implied malice* exists when there is no actual intent to kill, but death is caused by an act that discloses in the person who commits it an abandoned (immoral or irresponsible) state of mind that is equivalent to an actual intent to kill. In other words, any wantonly irresponsible and dangerous action establishes implied malice. For instance, Bob shoots into a crowd, saying, "I hope I don't kill anyone," when the probability is that the act will result in a death. There is no difference in legal effect between express and implied malice. The result of either can be murder.

Malice may be established by the presumption that a person intends the natural and probable consequences of his act—the use of a deadly weapon may establish malice. If there is an intent to cause serious bodily injury, and death results, the act is murder, even though there is no specific intent to kill.

EXAMPLE Yvonne, who was drunk, fell asleep. Dave cov-
O—* ered her with straw and threw hot cinders on the straw. It ignited, and Yvonne was burned to death. Dave was charged with murder. The judge properly instructed

the jury that if Dave did not intend to kill Yvonne, but did intend to cause her serious injury, the offense was nevertheless murder.

If a person's conduct creates such a high degree of risk that death will result, it may be presumed that the person acted with malice even though he had no specific intent to kill. This concept is sometimes expressed in the rule that there is murder when the killing takes place under circumstances that show "a heart devoid of social duty and fatally bent on mischief."

EXAMPLE Dick had a revolver with one cartridge in the O—* chamber. He put the cartridge in, so that it would not go off until the sixth time the trigger was pulled—so he thought. He played Russian roulette with his friend, Xavier, playfully putting the revolver against Xavier's side. On the third pull of the trigger, the gun went off, killing Xavier. Dick was convicted of murder. He appealed on the ground that no malice aforethought was shown. The appellate court stated that there had been implied malice and upheld the conviction. Dick's act was intentional. When one commits an intentional and reckless act with a deadly weapon, in total disregard for the safety of others, he acts with malice aforethought. Dick was held to have intended the natural and probable results of his act.

■ **Degrees of murder** Under modern statutes, the crime is usually divided into murder in the first degree and murder in the second degree. More severe penalties are allowed for first-degree than for second-degree murder.

First degree First-degree murder usually involves (1) an intent to kill with deliberation and premeditation, or (2) felony murder, which is a killing that results—intentionally or not—from the commission of a felony, (usually rape, robbery, arson, or burglary). See FELONY-MURDER RULE. Deliberation and premeditation need not be for a long period of time in order to contribute to first-degree murder.

EXAMPLE A man met a woman in a bar. They went outside O—* together and an argument developed. The man took out his penknife, opened it, cut the woman's voice box, so that she could not cry out, and then hacked her until she was dead. The man's actions showed an intent to kill with malice aforethought, deliberation, and premeditation. He was convicted of first-degree murder.

Second degree Second-degree murder results from a killing that includes malice aforethought but is not the product of deliberation and premeditation and is not other-

wise regarded as first-degree murder. Evidence of intoxication or diminished mental ability, even though the accused is not legally insane, may be introduced into court to show a lack of the capacity for deliberation and premeditation. This evidence can reduce the crime from first- to second-degree murder.

EXAMPLE Darwin was romantically involved with Winona, O—* until she told him that she and her husband were reconciling. Upon hearing this news, Darwin began a three-day period of heavy drinking during which he purchased a rifle, went to Winona's home, and killed her and her husband. At Darwin's murder trial, he testified that he had not intended to kill Winona or her husband and that he did not remember doing it. The court refused to give the jury instructions on first-degree murder. Darwin was convicted of murder in the second degree. Although his conduct exhibited malice aforethought, the intoxication obliterated his mind's capacity for deliberation and premeditation.

mutilation 1 Cutting off a part of the body or making it useless. See MAYHEM. 2 Making a legal document imperfect without destroying it. Mutilation of a will, for example, means eliminating from it some essential part through cutting, tearing, burning, erasing, or otherwise making changes. See also SPOLIATION.

mutiny In criminal law, an insurrection of soldiers or seamen against their commanders; any rising against lawful authority. See SEDITION.

mutual Common to both parties; interchangeable; reciprocal; given and received (when duties and obligations are exchanged, such as in the marital relation). Mutual WILLS are often made out by a husband and wife. Usually, each one leaves everything to the other.

mutual fund An investment company that pools investors' money for the purpose of buying shares of stock in many corporations. Shares of mutual funds are bought and sold by the public just like shares of other companies.

mutuality of contract The principle that each side must take some action or make some promise in order to create a binding CONTRACT. Because the parties have reciprocal obligations, neither is bound unless both are.

naked Bare; lacking necessary conditions. For example, a *naked contract* is an incomplete contract.

names Words that identify a person. An individual's full name consists of a given name or names bestowed at birth and a surname (or last name) derived from his or her parents. Generally, a person is not properly identified unless both his given name and surname are used. The rule applies, for example, to the designation of students in school records and to parties in lawsuits. When identity is certain, however, a slight variation in the spelling of a name is immaterial.

Statutes often prescribe ways by which a person may change his name. The usual method is by applying to a court. Granting the name change is usually a matter of judicial discretion. A Minnesota district court judge refused to permit an applicant to change his name legally to the numerals 1069, which, the man said, "describe what is inherent in me."

National Guard See MILITIA.

nationality Citizenship of a particular country, acquired either by birth or by naturalization. See CITIZEN.

National Labor Relations Board A PUBLIC ADMINISTRATIVE AGENCY of the federal government that regulates labor-management activities, such as union elections. See LABOR RELATIONS.

National Reporter System The method for grouping in sets of books all cases from state supreme courts according to regions of the country. The system also contains sets of books for all federal cases. See AMERICAN DIGEST SYSTEM.

native A natural-born subject or CITIZEN; one whose residence or citizenship is determined by birth within a country's borders. The term also includes someone born outside the United States, if his parents were then U.S. citizens and not permanently residing in a foreign land.

naturalization See ALIEN.

natural law Rules of conduct thought to be the same everywhere because they are fundamental to human behavior; basic moral law. The unprovoked killing of another person is contrary to natural law.

navigable waters Waters that provide a channel for commerce. Whether or not waters are navigable is important in determining if federal interstate commerce regulations apply. See ADMIRALTY; SHIPPING.

necessaries Articles that a person actually needs to sustain human life; things essential, proper, or useful in one's life. Food, clothing, and shelter are always regarded as necessaries.

A man is legally responsible for providing necessaries for his wife and children, and in some states a woman is liable for the basic needs of her husband and children. At the basic minimum, this means supplying food, clothing, medical attention, and a suitable residence. It may also mean payment of insurance premiums, legal services, and funeral expenses.

In addition, many states include as necessaries items required to maintain a previously established standard of living, such as articles that reflect the rank, position, fortune, earning capacity, and way of life of the husband or father. Under the laws of these states, the word "necessaries" has no specific meaning but varies with the accustomed manner of living of the parties. In some divorce cases, husbands have to pay for champagne, fur coats, or luxury cars even though such items are not basic needs. See HUSBAND AND WIFE.

A merchant who has supplied goods on credit to a wife or child can sue the man who is legally responsible for that person. If the goods were necessaries that the man had not already provided, the merchant is entitled to collect his money. For further discussion, see CONTRACTS.

A person who has not paid a JUDGMENT made against him in a lawsuit may keep a certain amount of necessaries for himself and his family. See EXECUTION; ATTACHMENT AND GARNISHMENT. When protected in this manner, necessaries are called EXEMPTIONS. The monetary value of necessaries that are exempt from being used to repay a person's debt varies from state to state.

ne exeat (Latin) "Let him not leave." A writ (written order) prohibiting a person from leaving the country, the state, or the jurisdiction (area of authority) of the court.

negligence Conduct that falls below the standard set by law for protecting others against risk or harm. It is an unintentional TORT. A tort is a civil (as opposed to criminal) wrong, other than a breach of contract, that harms another person or his property. Anyone who is injured, or whose property is damaged, as a result of someone else's negligence is entitled to bring a civil lawsuit against the wrongdoer.

To the average person, negligence is a state of mind involving carelessness, forgetfulness, or inattentiveness. In law, negligence is conduct. A person is negligent if he fails to act with a reasonable amount of care and as a result injures another person or thing. Negligence can involve doing something carelessly, such as throwing a lighted match under a fuel truck, or failing to do something that should have been done, such as removing a garden hose from a public sidewalk at night. The law expects people to act carefully so as not to endanger others. Conduct can be negligent even when a person is anxiously concerned for the general safety; a person's state of mind is important only in determining whether his conduct was reasonable in light of what he actually knew. Whether a person's acts *were* reasonable—not whether he *believed* them to be reasonable—determines the issue of negligence. If A's conduct did not pose an unreasonable threat of harm to B, A is not negligent, even if A acted with total indifference to the safety of others.

Negligence is different from an accident. An accident occurs despite the exercise of due care. Negligence causes harm because of a lack of care.

EXAMPLE A driver who suddenly loses control of his car
O⊶✳ because he has a heart attack, stroke, fainting spell, or epileptic seizure is not liable for negligence, because the accident was unavoidable. If, however, he knew that he was likely to suffer such an attack, he may be negligent in driving the car at all.

■ **Winning a negligence suit** In order to sue someone for damages resulting from negligence, you must establish (1) that the defendant owed you a duty to use due (reasonable) care not to injure you or damage your property; (2) that the defendant violated that duty by failing to act according to the required standard of care; (3) that you were injured or that your property was damaged as the result of the defendant's negligent conduct—in other words, his conduct caused your damage.

Duty to use due care In negligence law, a person has an obligation to exercise reasonable care for the physical safety and property of other people. On the other hand, if you are driving your car in an area where there is a risk of accident, say when approaching an intersection, you have a duty to moderate your speed, keep a proper lookout, or blow your horn. You are not, however, under a duty to take precautions against an unexpected explosion that causes a manhole cover to fly up in front of you. If you have a collision because you suddenly swerved to avoid a flying manhole cover, you have had an accident and are not guilty of negligence. The broad concept of duty is limited according to whether a person's conduct would create a foreseeable risk of harm to another. The extent of a person's legal duty is a question of law to be decided by the court and never by the jury. At the same time, certain persons and activities are subject to greater or lesser standards of liability. A manufacturer, for instance, is strictly liable for the physical harm caused by defects in his products—even if he was not negligent—because the consumer relied on his advertised skill. See PRODUCT LIABILITY.

There must be a sufficient relationship between the defendant and his victim in order for the court to find that the defendant had the duty to exercise reasonable care to protect that person. There is no standard, except the judge's conscience, for determining whether a duty exists, but judges usually find that it does.

Misfeasance and nonfeasance Negligence makes a distinction between *misfeasance*, the improper doing of an act, and *nonfeasance*, the failure to perform a required duty. A person is usually liable for his misfeasance because his negligent action may have directly created a risk of harm to another person. But it may be difficult to decide whether the relationship between a person who failed to act and the one injured imposes a liability. This depends on how involved the defendant is with the plaintiff. If his actions affect the plaintiff's interests adversely, in contrast to merely failing to help him, he will be liable. An expert swimmer with a boat and a rope at hand is not legally required to try to save a drowning person, for instance, unless he is a lifeguard hired for that purpose. Many courts find a duty to act if there is any preexisting relationship between the parties so that the victim would reasonably expect aid, such as carrier-passenger, innkeeper-guest, employer-employee, jailer-prisoner, school-pupil, parent-child, husband-wife, merchant-customer, host-guest.

Anyone who voluntarily helps another must act with reasonable care and cannot escape responsibility for not doing so by walking away from the duty he assumed. Liability is usually justified on the ground that the defendant has increased the danger, misled the plaintiff into a false sense of security, or deprived him of possible help from others.

EXAMPLE Although under no legal obligation to do so, a
O⊶✳ salesperson gave medical aid to a customer who became sick in a department store. He brought the customer to the store's infirmary but then kept him there for six hours without any further medical care. The salesperson acted negligently. The court felt that if he had initially done nothing, someone else would have called for an ambulance.

This concept of misfeasance has often led to lawsuits against doctors who stopped on highways to give medical assistance at the scene of accidents. To encourage doctors to continue to help victims of emergencies, Good Samaritan acts were passed in many states to relieve doctors who give emergency treatment from liability for negligence.

Imputed negligence When two persons have some legal relationship to each other, the first may have a duty to see that the second exercises care in regard to any third person, and the negligence of the second may be charged to the first even though the first had nothing to do with the negligence. This is called imputed negligence, or *vicarious*

HOW TO KNOW WHEN YOU MAY SUE FOR NEGLIGENCE

■ In law, negligence is an unreasonable action (or failure to act) that injures another person or damages his property. You can be negligent without meaning to be. If your conduct poses an unreasonable risk of harm, and harm is suffered, then you are negligent in the eyes of the law, regardless of your good intentions. Negligence differs from an accident in that an accident occurs despite the exercise of reasonable care, while negligence causes harm because of the failure to exercise due care.

■ If you suffer harm because of someone else's negligence, you can sue the negligent person and make him pay for the harm he has caused. In order to win a negligence suit, you must establish three things at the trial: (1) that the defendant (the party you are suing) owed you a duty to use care, (2) that he violated that duty by failing to act according to the required standard of care, and (3) that you were injured or that your property was damaged as the result of the defendant's negligence.

■ If a person's conduct can create a reasonable risk to others, he has a duty to use care to avoid harming them. For example, a motorist has a duty to drive carefully, slow down at intersections, and watch for children playing in the streets near schools. If he fails to do so and injures someone as a result, he is negligent in his duty to use care. On the other hand, he does not have a duty to anticipate an underground explosion. If an explosion causes a manhole cover to fly up in front of him and he swerves to avoid it and runs into a parked car, he is not guilty of negligence but has merely had an accident.

■ A manufacturer has a greater duty to use care than the average person and is strictly liable for any damage caused by his product if it was used according to the instructions that came with it—even if he was not negligent.

■ You have no duty to act to help a person unless you have some relationship to him that requires you to act. For example, you have no duty to save a child from drowning, even if you are an excellent swimmer, unless you are on duty as the lifeguard. However, if you do voluntarily try to help someone and then revoke your help before the person has no further need of it, you may be liable. For example, if you helped an injured person and promised to call an ambulance and then failed to do so, you would be liable—if you had done nothing in the first place, someone else might have called an ambulance.

■ An employer has a duty to see that his employees exercise care for the safety of others. If an employee is negligent while doing his job, the employer is liable for any resulting injuries to persons or property.

■ The owner of an automobile may be liable for the damage caused by someone else who is driving his car. On the other hand, automobile guest statutes lessen the duty a driver has to care for the safety of his nonpaying passengers (his guests). He is liable for injuries sustained by his guests only if he was intoxicated, intentionally reckless, or grossly negligent.

■ You may prove that someone violated his duty to use care for your safety by showing that he did not act reasonably under the circumstances. A person is guilty of negligence if he knows or should know of the risk created by his unreasonable conduct. If he knows his dog can be vicious but does not keep it under control, he is liable for your injuries if the dog bites you. He is also liable if he failed to use common sense. He cannot claim that he did not know basic things, such as that gasoline is combustible.

■ Drunkenness does not excuse negligent conduct.

■ Children are responsible for their conduct, but the standard of reasonable behavior is not as stringent as that applied to adults.

■ Standards of conduct in individual special areas are sometimes established by laws. If you are injured because someone else was breaking such a law, that law may be used to set the required standard of conduct.

■ To win a negligence suit, you must establish that the defendant's negligence caused you some harm. The cause may be proximate (direct) or intervening (indirect). If you place another person in danger by your negligence, you are responsible for injuries suffered by the victim's rescuer even though your negligence was only an intervening cause and not the proximate cause of the rescuer's injuries. Similarly, if you spill a large quantity of gasoline and do not clean it up, you are negligent because of the risk that it will be ignited; you are not relieved of liability just because somebody else lights the gasoline.

■ If you are charged with negligence, your defenses may be contributory negligence and assumption of the risk.

■ *Contributory negligence* means that the person suing you (the plaintiff) failed to take reasonable care of himself or his property. In some states, you will win your case if you can prove the plaintiff's contributory negligence.

■ The *last-clear-chance doctrine* remedies the harshness of contributory negligence and excuses the helpless plaintiff who has negligently placed himself in a perilous position from which there is no escape. A classic example is that of the person who has imprudently started driving across railroad tracks without first looking and then gets stalled in front of an oncoming train; although the engineer of the train had a "last clear chance" to prevent an accident, he could not do so because his brakes were not working properly. In such a case, the victim (or the victim's estate) could sue the railroad company.

■ *Comparative negligence* is a concept for determining the degree of the plaintiff's negligence vis-à-vis the defendant's negligence and thereby allotting damages based on the relative fault of each of the parties.

■ *Assumption of the risk* is a defense that says that the injured person voluntarily undertook a known risk. If he does that, he cannot recover damages should he come to grief. If XYZ has a contract with an armored car company limiting the company to $30,000 liability, XYZ cannot sue for more than that amount when the company's car is robbed of $165,450 belonging to XYZ.

liability. For example, an employer is liable for the negligence of his employees. See RESPONDEAT SUPERIOR.

> EXAMPLE A serviceman for Karpet Klean works on a cus-
> O——* tomer's oriental rug while drunk. He uses the wrong cleaning fluid on the rug, and leaves it on too long, and as a result the rug is ruined. The serviceman's negligence will be imputed to the owner of Karpet Klean because the serviceman was acting within the scope of his employment when he ruined the rug. Karpet Klean will be liable for the price of the rug.

In some states, when the owner of a car gives another driver his permission to operate it and that person's negligent driving causes injury to others, the negligence of the driver is imputed to the owner. This means that the owner will be financially responsible for the plaintiff's injury, even if he was not in the car at the time of the accident. If the owner is himself injured and sues the driver, he may lose his suit because the negligence of the driver may be imputed to him because he contributed to the negligence. This is known as imputed contributory negligence.

Automobile guest statutes In some states a driver's duty to care for the safety of his passengers is mitigated by automobile guest statutes. Under these laws, the driver of a car is liable to anyone riding in his car as a nonpaying guest only for some form of aggravated misconduct. These statutes basically make the driver liable to his guest only for gross (extreme) negligence, intoxication, or intentional or reckless misconduct. Their purpose is to avoid collusion (secret and unlawful agreement) between the injured guest and the driver, such as planning to divide insurance proceeds between themselves. Theoretically, a person who receives a free ride has no right to demand that his host exercise ordinary care to prevent injury to him.

> EXAMPLE A driver offers his friend a lift to the office. The
> O——* driver then causes a collision and serious injury to both himself and his friend. Depending on the particular state law, the guest would probably have to pay the costs of his own injuries because they were caused by ordinary negligence, not extreme or intentional behavior.

Automobile guest statutes have created much litigation. Is a person who shares expenses for tolls and gas a guest? Can the owner of the car be a guest when someone else is driving? What is gross negligence or intentional or reckless misconduct? The law of your state must be consulted for the answers because there are so many different guest statutes. For a listing of states that have an automobile guest statute, see Chart 28.

Family car doctrine Another area of negligence law that affects automobiles is the family car doctrine, which makes the owner of an automobile, in most cases, liable for injuries or damage caused by a member of the family while driving the car for family purposes, such as grocery shopping or even taking a ride in the country. Only some states have such laws. See Chart 28. In those that do, the law applies only if the automobile is a family car used for pleasure, although it may be used for business as well. Under the family car doctrine, the automobile is considered to be furnished by the head of the family for family use, and the operator is regarded as the owner's agent—for example, a wife is her husband's agent when she drives the children to school. If an accident occurs while the agent is acting for the owner (a member of the family is driving the car), the owner is responsible for damages that result.

Standard of care In order to sue someone for negligence you must demonstrate that the person violated his duty to use care not to injure you or damage your property. You can best do so by showing that he did not act reasonably under the circumstances. The law of negligence is based on a determination of whether or not conduct was reasonable. All persons are expected to act in a reasonable manner, even those who are hotheaded and quick to react or extremely clumsy. Conduct is usually measured against what a reasonably prudent person would have done under similar circumstances. But who is this reasonably prudent person? In law, he is a composite of the community's judgment on how a fellow member of the community ought to behave in situations that pose a threat of harm to others. It does not matter what the typical citizen or the majority of the community actually does. Common conduct—for example, jaywalking—may fall below the community's standards of safety.

A reasonably prudent person is not expected to be perfect. He may make mistakes of judgment or perception or be momentarily distracted. These errors are usually excusable as long as they are reasonable under the circumstances.

What the person knows Behavior is always judged in terms of what a person knows. Thus, you are responsible for physical harm to another if you knew, or should have known, of the risk created by your unreasonable conduct. If you know your dog or any of your other ANIMALS can be vicious, you are negligent if you do not keep it under control. If you accidentally discover that a product has a hidden defect or if you see another car approaching without lights, you must act reasonably—even though you would not be negligent if you failed to realize these things.

In addition to his actual knowledge, a person is considered to have common sense. He cannot claim that he did not know basic things, such as that live electrical wires are dangerous, gasoline is combustible, or alcohol reduces driving ability. Unless there are extenuating circumstances, a person must see the clearly visible and hear the clearly audible. A driver approaching a railroad crossing where the view is unobstructed cannot say that he did not see the approaching train or hear its whistle. A person must also realize his lack of knowledge—such as when he is walking in a strange, dark hallway or using an unfamiliar product—and use appropriate caution.

Anyone who engages in a particular activity is considered to possess the knowledge common to those who regularly participate in that activity. For instance, a hunter is assumed to know the rules of the forest. This knowledge must be kept reasonably current.

The role of special skills If a person decides to engage in an activity requiring special skills, education, training, or experience, his conduct will be evaluated against the standard of a competent and experienced person engaged in that field. Certain of these activities are licensed—barbering, driving, flying, and practicing medicine or law, for example. Because the general public depends on the expertise of persons engaged in these activities, anyone who performs them (even without payment) is judged by the standards of conduct of those who are properly qualified—

regardless of whether the person is a recognized member of the group. For example, a druggist who diagnoses and prescribes medication for an illness described by a customer will be judged by the standards applicable to a physician.

If a profession, such as medicine or dentistry, recognizes specialists, a certified specialist must act according to the higher standards of his field. The law has generally refused to allow a different standard of care to be applied to the conduct of novices in specialized activities. The learner, the beginner, the trainee—all must conduct themselves in the same manner as those who are skilled and experienced. The public cannot assume the risk of a beginner's lack of competence; it is usually defenseless against such risks. Therefore, the beginner must take into account his lack of skill and experience and act with greater care. For a discussion of malpractice or negligent conduct of a professional, see ATTORNEY AND CLIENT; PHYSICIANS AND SURGEONS.

Physical abilities The reasonableness of conduct depends on a person's physical characteristics or abilities. Conduct is reasonable only if it is physically possible for the person in question to behave in the manner deemed reasonable. Thus, an individual who has a physical impairment must act reasonably in light of his condition. In spite of his handicap, he will be considered negligent if he takes a risk that is unreasonable in view of his known physical limitations. For example, a person whose leg is in a plaster cast up to his thigh is negligent if he takes a crowded department store escalator and knocks down another store customer and injures him. The person in the cast has acted unreasonably in light of his physical condition by taking the crowded escalator in the first place.

Mental capacity Generally, a person's mental capacity does not excuse him from behaving according to the standard of the reasonable person. The fact that a person is deficient in intelligence, judgment, memory, or emotional stability, is voluntarily intoxicated, or even insane, has no bearing on his failure to act as a reasonably sane and sober person would have under the circumstances. Although this imposes a standard that some persons cannot possibly meet, their mental condition may increase the risk of unreasonably dangerous conduct that could injure innocent victims. Therefore, they must be held accountable. On the other hand, an injured person who lacked the mental capacity to recognize or avoid the risk may be allowed to recover damages for his injury, as in cases involving the elderly who are senile.

Drunkenness by itself is not negligence but it does not excuse negligent conduct. Intoxication usually aggravates the wrong. When certain activities, such as operating a bulldozer, are undertaken by a person who is intoxicated, the resulting conduct is negligent.

Children Children are responsible for their conduct. Because they usually cannot meet adult standards of behavior, however, their actions are judged by a lower standard. The test of reasonable behavior for a child depends on his age, intelligence, and experience. There is one major exception to this rule: If a child undertakes an adult activity—such as driving a car or flying an airplane—he will be held to an adult standard of conduct.

Some states apply varying age ranges within which children are legally incapable of negligence. Usually children below the age of seven are not liable for negligence. Between 7 and 18 years, children may be legally negligent depending on the circumstances of the case and the child.

EXAMPLE A 13-year-old student leaves his skateboard on the steps of the public library while he talks to his friends 10 feet away. A woman coming down the steps trips on it and breaks her hip. The student may be found negligent because it is reasonable to expect someone of his age to know the consequences of his carelessness.

A child is usually considered capable of negligence, but it is measured by what is reasonable conduct for a child of that age, intelligence, and experience. Once a child reaches the age of majority (usually 18), he will be held to adult standards of conduct.

Reactions to emergencies The law recognizes that even a reasonable person may make errors of judgment in emergency situations. A person's conduct during an emergency is evaluated as to whether it was a reasonable response under the circumstances, even though in retrospect another course of action might have avoided the injury.

EXAMPLE Suppose two people are dining alone in a hotel room. One person begins to choke on a piece of food lodged in his throat. Instead of seeking help, his companion uses a well-known medical technique to dislodge the food so that the victim may breathe freely. Unfortunately, the technique does not work and the victim dies. Given the emergency, his companion has not acted negligently although, in retrospect, it might have been better if he had sought help.

Failing to anticipate an emergency may be negligence. For example, a theater owner must expect the possibility of fire, and a driver of a car has to be aware that an accident could happen. Sometimes an individual may be held negligent for creating the emergency, even though he acted bravely during it. For instance, a nightclub owner who has disregarded fire-code provisions will be liable for injuries from a blaze caused by these code violations, even though he saved lives during the fire.

Anticipating the conduct of others As a reasonable person, you must anticipate not only the prudent conduct of others, but their foreseeable negligence or unlawful conduct. For example, leaving the keys in the ignition of your unlocked auto in a high-crime neighborhood is negligent because it is foreseeable that the car may be stolen; your insurance company can refuse to pay your claim if the car is stolen. Failing to reduce the car's speed while passing a schoolyard during recess may be negligent because of the possibility of children darting into the street.

An unreasonable risk of harm Negligence occurs when a person by his action creates an unreasonable risk of harm that injures someone else. A risk is unreasonable when the foreseeable probability of harm is greater than the burden to the defendant to act in a way that would have prevented it.

EXAMPLE Bob owns a two-family house. His tenants, Nick and Doris, tell him that one of the wooden stairs leading to their apartment is defective and should be replaced. Bob keeps putting off this simple repair job. One morning, the step splits in half, hurling Doris down the flight of stairs and breaking her arm. Bob's failure to fix the step was negligence.

The likelihood of harm together with its potential seriousness determines the magnitude of the risk.

Statutes that establish standards of conduct A federal, state, or local law may provide that an injured person can sue for negligence if the person who injured him failed to obey the law. Such a statute establishes a standard of conduct that all should observe. A state dramshop (barroom) act is a statute of this kind. It gives someone who has been injured by an intoxicated person the right to bring a civil lawsuit against the bar owner if he supplied the alcoholic beverages to the wrongdoer when the latter was already drunk. See INTOXICATING LIQUOR.

Before a statute may be used to set the required standard of conduct in a negligence case, the court must decide that the statute was designed to protect persons against the particular kind of harm that resulted. For example, violation of a speed limit enacted solely to conserve gasoline cannot be used to determine whether or not the speed was unreasonably dangerous. On the other hand, statutes regulating the sale of firearms, gasoline, explosives, intoxicants, and poisons protect all persons likely to be injured by any violations.

Licensing statutes, such as those for doctors, lawyers, and automobile drivers, present a special problem. Most courts refuse to admit as evidence in a negligence suit the fact that the defendant failed to comply with a licensing statute. Showing that a person was negligent in obtaining a required license does not prove that he was negligent on the occasion in question. Failure to complete procedural requirements in obtaining a license does not establish that the professional acted negligently in the particular case. He may face criminal charges for practicing a profession without a license but his conduct may not be negligent. This conflicts with the intent of licensing statutes to protect the public against those who lack skill and competence in specialized activities.

Violation of a statute may be considered negligence per se (by itself). Unless there is evidence excusing the violation, negligence is conclusively established. In some jurisdictions, however, the violation is only evidence of negligence. A plaintiff must still establish that the breaking of the statute was the direct cause of his injuries.

A violation of a statute may be excused in any of three types of circumstances: (1) when there are physical circumstances beyond a person's control, as when a driver's car lights suddenly go out on a highway at night; (2) when the circumstances pertaining to the statute are unknown, as when a driver is not aware that he is approaching an intersection because it is unlit and unmarked; and (3) when sudden emergencies not of the person's making occur, as when a driver veers his car to one side because a child dashes into the street. In some cases, it may be more dangerous to comply with the statute than to break it—for example, by suddenly braking for a red light and causing a rear-end collision. A defendant needs only to show reasonable care in attempting to comply with the law or that he did obey it. Of course, the defendant can show that he obeyed a statute as proof of his reasonable conduct.

Obedience of the law is considered only along with other evidence, however. A statute usually requires only minimum standards of conduct. Such a law is not necessarily conclusive in establishing whether or not a person has acted reasonably.

EXAMPLE A state law requires that a nightclub must have a minimum number of fire exits. A nightclub owner will not be absolved from liability for negligence in case of fire if access to the fire exits is blocked by heavy storage cabinets, thereby preventing their use by many people. Although he has obeyed the law, his failure to take the reasonable added precaution of free access to the exits makes him negligent.

Cause of the injury or damage To win a negligence suit you must prove that your injuries or the damage to your property was caused by the defendant's negligence. A cause may be proximate or intervening.

Proximate cause In the law of torts, proximate cause refers to the policy of limiting a defendant's liability to consequences that are related to the wrongful conduct. Proximate cause is found if there is a reasonable, causal relationship between the defendant's unreasonable conduct and the plaintiff's injury or damage.

EXAMPLE Suppose Ron is driving at 80 miles an hour and smashes his car into another car, forcing it off the road where it knocks down an electrical utility pole. A blackout occurs in the area, and the county suffers $1 million in damages as a result of widespread looting. Ron's negligence is the ultimate cause of any harm that results from the electrical failure. Under rules of proximate cause, Ron will be liable to the occupants of the car with which he collided for their injuries as well as for property damage to their car. He will, however, be excused from liability for the $1 million in looting damages. Fairness indicates that the looting is too far removed from the consequences of negligent driving.

A defendant is usually not liable for the unforeseen consequences of his negligent conduct, but he is liable for harm that was foreseeable.

EXAMPLE Ned, driving his car with one arm around Barbara and pecking her cheek every few seconds, collided with a truck. He did not know, nor had he any reason to suspect, that the truck was carrying dynamite. The resulting explosion injured Emily, who was two blocks away. To a reasonable man the risk of negligent driving would not include injury to someone who was two blocks away; therefore, Ned would not be liable.

A few courts consider a consequence proximate to a cause if it occurs as a direct result of the wrongful act, whether it was foreseeable or not. In these jurisdictions, Ned, in the example above, would be liable to Emily.

Harm is foreseeable if it may be expected to occur as a result of the defendant's acts. The exact manner in which the harm happens does not have to be foreseeable. For example, injury to pedestrians is a foreseeable risk of negligent driving, whether a driver hits a pedestrian or a utility pole that falls on a passerby.

A defendant is liable for all physical consequences of a plaintiff's injuries, however unusual or unforeseeable. This is sometimes referred to as the "thin-skulled" or "eggshell" plaintiff rule. If, for example, a plaintiff has hemophilia and dies from what would have been a minor injury to almost anyone else, the defendant is nevertheless liable for his death.

If a person places another in danger by his negligence, he is responsible for injuries suffered by a rescuer of the victim. Rescuers are protected as a matter of public policy (policy for the public good).

Intervening cause   Frequently in negligence cases, a plaintiff receives his injury from two or more causes. One is the defendant's negligent conduct, such as hitting the plaintiff with his car. The other is a subsequent act or event that increases the injury, such as the negligent treatment of the plaintiff by an emergency-room doctor. Under some circumstances, the intervening cause will supersede the defendant's wrongful conduct and excuse his liability. A defendant will be liable for the intervening cause only if he should have anticipated it and acted accordingly. If the intervening cause was in effect at the time of the defendant's conduct, it will not excuse the defendant's liability.

EXAMPLE Suppose your next-door neighbor decides to burn 0—* leaves on a very windy day. Instead of putting the leaves in a wire basket with a wire cover, he piles them up in the middle of his yard and drops a lighted match on top. The gusty winds carry the burning leaves to your property, ruining your recently sodded lawn. Your neighbor claims that the winds were the intervening cause of your property damage and, therefore, he is not liable. Since the winds were gusting at the time he began the fire without taking the usual precaution of placing the leaves in a wire basket, he will be liable.

Sometimes the risk of the intervening cause is what makes a defendant's conduct negligent. For example, a person is negligent in spilling a large quantity of gasoline because of the risk that it will be ignited. He is not relieved of liability just because another person lights the gasoline. He remains liable even if a foreseeable intervening act changed the effects of the harm he caused. Thus, the risk of negligently starting a fire also includes the liability of delay by others in notifying the fire department and of foreseeable changes of wind direction and velocity.

Courts often use hindsight in deciding that an intervening cause was foreseeable, even though most people would never anticipate such occurrences. A hit-and-run driver usually does not consider in advance the fact that the victim may be left unconscious on the road to be run over by another car or suffer negligent treatment by a physician, but these events are not so improbable as to be superseding causes, which can relieve the defendant of liability.

Superseding causes are intervening causes that are unforeseeable and produce unforeseeable results. A defendant whose negligence requires a plaintiff to make a detour is not liable for the plaintiff's injury caused by an airplane falling on him or by an unexpected flash flood.

If the result is foreseeably within the risk created by the defendant's negligence, but is brought about by an unforeseeable intervening cause, the defendant remains liable.

EXAMPLE Suppose the XYZ Company is negligent in maintaining its rotting telephone pole, creating a risk that it will topple by itself and injure a pedestrian. If, instead of falling by itself, it is struck by a negligent driver and falls on the plaintiff, the XYZ Company is still liable. The result—injury to the pedestrian when the rotting pole fell—was foreseeable, although the intervening cause, a negligent driver, was not.

When the intervening cause is intentional or criminal, however, the negligent party may be excused from liability. If someone intentionally pushed XYZ's rotting pole over on the plaintiff, the third person would be responsible.

A third person who discovers a danger created by someone else has a duty to act.

EXAMPLE Val stores fireworks in his unlocked toolshed. 0—* One day, Hans, a six-year-old boy who lives next door to him, goes into Val's shed and picks up a firecracker. Later that day Hans's mother sees her son with the firecracker and takes it away from him, but she says nothing to Val and does nothing to keep the child from going back to Val's shed and getting more firecrackers. The next day, Hans does go back to Val's shed and takes a number of large firecrackers. He proceeds to light them all at once. The resulting explosion severely burns Hans. Hans's mother is liable for the injuries suffered by her child because she had a duty to do something that would have prevented Hans from getting more firecrackers.

A third person who deliberately ignores a known danger, thereby exposing others to its risks, is also liable. For example, a retailer discovers that certain bottles of a defendant manufacturer's product marked "kerosene" actually contain dangerous amounts of gasoline, but he continues to sell them without any warning. He is liable for any injuries or damages that occur because his customers did not know they had gasoline. In all of these cases, the intervening cause is considered sufficiently strong and independent to shift liability from the defendant to the intervening third person. The defendant is then excused from liability.

■ **Admissible evidence**   In order to win a negligence case, the plaintiff must produce sufficient evidence that the defendant's conduct under the circumstances was unreasonable and created a foreseeable risk of danger that resulted in the plaintiff's injuries.

Experts   Expert witnesses are frequently introduced to provide jurors with facts beyond their common knowledge—such as scientific data, computations, tests, and experiments. They are also relied on in professional negligence cases to establish the standard of care.

Custom and habit   To define the proper standard of reasonable conduct, evidence of the customary conduct of others under similar circumstances is normally admissible. Frequently, this evidence is applied in cases of alleged negligence in some business activity that is beyond the common knowledge of the jurors. The evidence may be introduced by disinterested witnesses who have experience in the same type of business. Evidence showing that a person followed the usual practice should indicate that his conduct was reasonable. The jury must decide whether a reasonably prudent person would have done more or less than was customary.

EXAMPLE In one instance, the owner of a tugboat sunk in a 0—* storm with two barges was liable for the barges' cargo because the tug was not equipped with a radio, which would have warned of the storm and prevented any loss. Even though evidence had been introduced to show that it was not the usual practice to have radios on ocean tugs, the jury felt that the tugboat owner was negligent because a reasonably prudent man would have carried a radio on an oceangoing tug.

Evidence of habit (that a person customarily behaves in a certain way) generally cannot be used to show that he probably behaved the same way on the occasion in question. Occasionally, it may be admissible to show that a person knew of a condition, custom, or some other fact in issue.

EXAMPLE Jack bragged that in bad weather he always drove O⊶∗ slowly around Deadman's Curve because he knew how quickly it became slippery in the rain. One rainy night, his car crashed on the curve, and he received numerous injuries. In his negligence action against the county highway department, his statement about his cautious driving cannot be admitted as evidence to show that he probably drove slowly on the night of the accident. It may, however, be used to show that Jack knew the dangerous condition on that stretch of road, a fact disputed by the county highway department.

Rules set by organizations Standards for the conduct of an activity are often available from trade associations, safety organizations such as the National Safety Council or Underwriters' Laboratories, federal and state agencies, and even from the rules and bylaws of a defendant company's charter. These may be used as supportive evidence of the proper standard of conduct.

Res ipsa loquitur Because it is generally difficult to prove negligence, the courts usually accept a certain type of circumstantial evidence, not allowed in other cases, when direct evidence is insufficient to prove a case. This type of evidence is called *res ipsa loquitur* (Latin for "the thing speaks for itself"). For example, if a can of food explodes an hour after being delivered to a supermarket and injures the stockboy, the canner may be found negligent in canning the product according to the doctrine of *res ipsa loquitur*.

Three conditions must be met before the courts will allow *res ipsa* evidence: (1) negligence must be inferred; (2) the plaintiff's injury must have been caused by a condition that was within the exclusive control of the defendant; and (3) the plaintiff must have done nothing that contributed to his injury. Thus, in the case of the exploding can, the attorney for the injured boy would argue during the trial that: (1) the can would not have exploded but for the canner's negligence, since cans normally do not explode; (2) the negligence that resulted in the explosion occurred during the canning process, when the can was in the exclusive control of the canner; and (3) the boy did nothing to the can, such as shaking or heating it, that would have caused it to explode. If the canner cannot present evidence that makes it more likely that someone else, other than the canner, was negligent, the injured boy would win his case.

■ **Defenses** The basic defenses to negligence include contributory negligence and assumption of the risk.

Contributory negligence The failure of a person to use the care of a reasonable, prudent man in protecting himself or his property is contributory negligence if the failure contributes to the injury or damage he suffers. Contributory negligence is a complete defense, and a plaintiff will lose his lawsuit if it can be proved.

EXAMPLE John negligently skateboards across a busy intersection against the light. Art is speeding through the intersection when he hits John. If John sues Art, the negligence suit will be defeated in some states because John's own careless conduct was a cause of his injuries.

Last clear chance In certain situations, the effect of a plaintiff's contributory negligence will be excused or negated and he will be allowed to recover damages, despite his own lack of ordinary care, if the defendant had a chance—"the last clear chance"—to avoid causing the injury or damage but failed to do so because of negligence on his part. This last-clear-chance doctrine was created to avoid the harshness of contributory negligence as a complete defense. The classic example involves a helpless plaintiff who has negligently placed himself in a perilous position from which he cannot escape.

EXAMPLE Suppose Jane drives her car across some railroad O⊶∗ tracks without looking for oncoming trains. Her car stalls. The engineer of an approaching train sees Jane and could have stopped if the brakes had not been defective. Although the engineer had "the last clear chance" to avoid the accident, he did not stop in time and the train hit Jane. Under this doctrine, Jane's estate would be entitled to recover from the railroad because the accident resulted from the railroad's negligence in not maintaining adequate brakes.

Comparative negligence Another rule that was developed to soften the harsh effects of contributory negligence is that of comparative negligence. States with comparative negligence laws allot damages in relationship to the relative fault of each of the parties. If, for example, the defendant's fault is determined to be twice that of the plaintiff, then the plaintiff will recover only two-thirds of his damages.

There are two basic kinds of comparative negligence. One allows a plaintiff to recover no matter how great his fault in comparison to that of the defendant. If the plaintiff was 80 percent at fault and the defendant only 20 percent, the plaintiff can recover 20 percent of his damages. Most statutes, however, contain a 50 percent rule by which the plaintiff recovers nothing if his negligence was equal to 50 percent or greater than that of the defendant.

EXAMPLE Dave crosses the street from between double-O⊶∗ parked trucks rather than at the intersection. Steve is driving down the street at 55 miles per hour in a 20-mile-per-hour zone with his view obstructed by the double-parked vehicles. Steve hits Dave. In states with comparative negligence statutes, a jury will decide the degree of fault of Dave's negligent crossing and Steve's negligent driving before determining the amount of damages to be awarded.

Assumption of the risk Assumption of the risk is voluntarily undertaking a known risk. When a person agrees to assume the risk of injury from a hazard, it may completely defeat his lawsuit against the defendant for negligence. A person may take on the risk by an agreement.

EXAMPLE First Bank contracted with the Locktite Armored O⊶∗ Car Service to transport the bank's money. The contract limited Locktite's liability to $30,000 per shipment. Locktite lost a shipment of $165,450 owing to its negligence. The bank sued for that amount. Locktite claimed that its liability was limited by the contract and the court agreed. First Bank and Locktite were in business and made the contract with full knowledge of the risks involved. The bank specifically assumed the risk that the contract limit on liability would not be enough.

Assumption of the risk may be implied from the facts. For example, if a caddy is hurt by a flying golf ball, he cannot hold the golfer liable because, as an experienced caddy, he was aware of the risk of being hit and chose to continue in his job.

EXAMPLE Lou, a former baseball player, was sitting in the grandstand at a baseball game and was injured when a foul ball hit him. He sued the owner of the ball club for damages, charging that the owner was negligent for not maintaining a screen to protect the fans. The owner showed that there was an area protected by a screen near where Lou sat. The court decided that Lou could have sat behind the screen but he chose to sit somewhere else. Because he was familiar with baseball, knew the risk involved, and chose the more dangerous seat, he was not entitled to recover.

In contrast, Jake was hit by a puck at a hockey game, while sitting in unscreened stands. The court permitted Jake to recover damages because the puck does not usually leave the playing area and, therefore, this was not a risk assumed by a spectator.

■ **Degrees of negligence** Negligence is sometimes classified in three degrees—slight negligence, ordinary negligence, and gross negligence. It is generally broken down into these degrees in cases involving the violation of a duty that arose out of a BAILMENT—that is, when the plaintiff's property was in the possession of the defendant for some purpose, such as cleaning or repair—or in which a person is to be held liable for criminally negligent HOMICIDE.

When the degrees of negligence are distinguished, the failure to exercise great or extraordinary care is considered slight negligence.

EXAMPLE Jim lends his lawnmower to his friend Tom because Tom's mower is broken. This is a bailment for the sole benefit of the bailee (Tom). When Tom returns the mower, Jim notices some small nicks on the blades, caused by Tom's running the mower over some rocks he was too lazy to pick up. This is slight negligence, for which Tom is liable to Jim. Since the loan benefited only Tom, Tom was under a duty to take great care of the mower. He is responsible for his slight negligence.

The lack of ordinary care that a reasonable person would exercise under given circumstances constitutes ordinary negligence. John's leaving a roller skate on a heavily traveled stairway, causing Cindy to trip and break her leg, is an example of ordinary negligence because a reasonable person would realize the danger to others created by this conduct. Ordinary negligence is what is meant by the unmodified term "negligence."

The failure to exercise even the slightest care under the circumstances, such as leaving a loaded shotgun in a children's playroom, is gross negligence.

negotiable instrument A signed writing that contains a promise or order to pay a sum of money. Checks, bank drafts, and promissory notes are all negotiable instruments. For a comprehensive discussion of negotiable instruments, see COMMERCIAL PAPER.

negotiate 1 Transact business; deal with another person regarding a purchase and sale; bargain or trade; conclude by bargain, agreement, or treaty. 2 Transfer a negotiable instrument, such as a check or promissory note. See COMMERCIAL PAPER.

neighbors See ADJOINING LANDOWNERS.

net The amount left after all proper deductions have been made, such as charges, expenses, commissions, and taxes. For example, *net worth,* or *net assets,* is what is left after subtracting what one owes from what one has.

neutrality laws Laws of a nation that forbid its citizens to participate in a war between other countries.

Originally, international law recognized no relations between nations except war and peace. Once conflict broke out between two nations, every other country became either a friend or a foe. Eventually, international law recognized not only the right but the duty of other nations to remain neutral. To insure its position of neutrality, a nation passes laws punishing any of its citizens who engage in hostile acts on behalf of a foreign nation at war.

new trial A retrial or reexamination of issues after an earlier trial in the same court. Its purpose is to prevent a miscarriage of justice by correcting obvious errors in the conduct of the first trial without the delay, expense, or inconvenience of an appeal to a higher court. See APPEAL AND ERROR.

A party cannot claim a new trial as a right. Courts generally have the inherent power to authorize a new trial. Frequently, the grounds for granting a new trial are listed in a state law. Among the grounds are empanelment of an unqualified or biased juror; bribery of a juror; introduction of inadmissible evidence; the jury's return of a verdict that is contrary to law or against the weight of the evidence; failure by either side to produce a necessary witness; and discovery of new evidence too late for introduction during the first trial.

A new trial may be granted on the motion of an attorney appearing for a party or by the court itself without an attorney's motion. A new trial may reconsider only specific issues, such as the amount of damages.

next friend One who is acting on behalf of another person who lacks the legal capacity to act for himself; one who represents the interests of a child in court; the person in whose name a child's lawsuit is brought.

next of kin Closest blood relatives. Blood relatives are entitled by law to inherit the property of a person who dies without a valid will. See DESCENT AND DISTRIBUTION.

nihil (Latin) "Nothing." For example, *nihil est* means there is nothing.

nil (Latin) "Nothing." A contracted form of *nihil.*

nisi Latin) "Unless." A *decree nisi* is an interim court decision that will become a final decree unless something changes, or some event takes place. For example, in some states there is a waiting period from the time that a divorce decree is rendered until the divorce becomes final. Until the time expires, the divorce decree is a decree nisi.

nisi prius (Latin) "Unless before." In the English legal system, *nisi prius* formerly described controversies involving issues of fact, which, being brought in the courts of Westminster, were appointed to be tried there by a jury from the county in which the controversy arose, unless before *(nisi prius)* the date of trial, the judges of assize came into the county in question and tried the case before a local jury. In England today, the trial is held in the county.

In America, a *nisi prius court* generally refers to a trial-level court, where a jury hears the case, rather than a higher court that hears appeals without a jury.

NLRB See NATIONAL LABOR RELATIONS BOARD.

no contest See NOLO CONTENDERE.

no fault 1 The popular name for a law that permits DIVORCE without either party having to prove that his or her spouse is guilty of misconduct. 2 A type of automobile INSURANCE required in some states, which provides that each driver may collect insurance money from his own company after an accident regardless of whose fault the accident is.

nolle prosequi (Latin) "To be unwilling to pursue." The position that a plaintiff in a civil lawsuit or a prosecutor in a criminal action may take when he decides or agrees not to continue the case—either against some or all of the defendants or on some or all of the issues. To do this, the plaintiff or prosecutor formally enters his intention in the court record and is thereafter bound by it.

nolo contendere (Latin) "I do not wish to contest it"; a defendant's plea of "no contest" sometimes permitted in criminal cases. The plea means that the defendant is not willing to admit guilt but does submit himself to the court for sentencing or other punishment. See CRIMINAL LAW.

nonage Not yet of legal age; still an INFANT, or minor.

non compos mentis (Latin) "Not having mastery of one's mind," i.e., not of sound mind. See INSANE PERSONS.

nonconforming use A legal exception to ZONING laws. In some cases, the law may allow property to be used in a way that does not conform to zoning laws. For example, a farm stand that has been operated at one location in a residential neighborhood for 40 years may be permitted to continue operating as a *nonconforming use* when zoning laws no longer permit farm stands in the neighborhood.

nonfeasance The failure to perform a required duty, especially by a public official. It is the opposite of *feasance,* which is the performance of an act.

non obstante veredicto (Latin) "Notwithstanding the verdict." A judgment entered for the plaintiff in a civil lawsuit even though the jury decided in favor of the defendant, because the court recognized that legally the defendant admitted something that made him liable. Today the phrase is loosely used when the judge must set aside a jury's verdict in a civil case.

nonprofit organization See CHARITY.

non prosequitur (Latin) "He does not prosecute." If the plaintiff delays unnecessarily in prosecuting his lawsuit or fails to take steps when they are due, the defendant may ask the court to enter a judgment of *non prosequitur.* Then the plaintiff cannot obtain a judgment against the defendant because he has failed to pursue his lawsuit properly.

nonsuit Any one of a variety of ways to end a lawsuit without settling the dispute on the MERITS of the case. For example, a *judgment of nonsuit* may be granted against a plaintiff who abandons his case or neglects to pursue it. See DISMISSAL.

nonsupport Failure to provide financial support for another person despite a legal obligation to do so. Nonsupport of a child, a wife or, sometimes, a husband, may be a crime or can be grounds for a DIVORCE in some states. See HUSBAND AND WIFE; PARENT AND CHILD.

non vult contendere (Latin) "He does not wish to contest it." Sometimes abbreviated *non vult;* this is a variation of NOLO CONTENDERE.

Norris-LaGuardia Act One of the first federal labor laws favoring organized labor. Enacted in 1932, the Norris-LaGuardia Act says that contracts restricting the right of an employee to join a labor union are illegal. These contracts are called *yellow-dog contracts.* The law was originally known as the Anti-Injunction Act because its many restrictions had the practical effect of preventing any federal court from issuing an injunction (a written order) to stop a labor dispute. One section of the act, for example, states that an injunction prohibiting a STRIKE cannot be issued unless the local police are unable or unwilling to prevent damage or violence. Because law-enforcement officials are not likely to admit to that, the law made injunctions in a labor strike rare. For information about how the law has developed since the Norris-LaGuardia Act, see LABOR RELATIONS.

notary A person authorized to certify documents, take oaths, and perform certain other official acts in connection with business matters. The office of notary, or notary public, is MINISTERIAL (administrative) and not judicial.

■ **How to become a notary** State law determines who is eligible to be a notary. Generally, an applicant must be an adult of good character. Laws making aliens ineligible to be notaries have been declared unconstitutional.

To become a notary an eligible person must follow the steps prescribed by state law. He must file an application and may have to pass a test concerning some rules of law and the responsibilities of a notary. If approved, the applicant must take an oath of office and may have to give a BOND for the faithful performance of his duty. The term of office and suspension or removal for misconduct are regulated by state law.

■ **Powers and duties** Originally, a notary's powers were limited to commercial matters. Today, a notary can also stamp documents as official copies to certify that they are genuine, sign papers to show that the person before him has sworn to them (thus making them acceptable as evidence), and administer oaths to witnesses or people taking public office. See OATHS AND AFFIRMATIONS.

A notary does not assume responsibility for the truth of statements made in the documents or testimony. He only certifies that the person presenting them has sworn to their truth or to his own identity. If a notary exercises his duties carelessly, he may be liable for money DAMAGES to anyone who had to rely on his notarization. He may also be criminally responsible for abusing his authority.

A notary may work only within a designated geographical area and up to the expiration of his commission, which he may then renew. He may not act in any matter in which he has a personal interest. A notary is entitled to a fee for his services, but it must not exceed the limit set by law.

note A written, absolute promise to pay, generally called a promissory note. See COMMERCIAL PAPER.

notes of decisions References to the printed decisions of cases that are intended to explain rules of law or parts of statutes; ANNOTATION.

notice Knowledge of certain facts; the formal receipt of papers giving specific information. Notice must be given to the parties involved before certain legal proceedings or transactions can be valid.

■ **When notice is required** Notice is an essential element of the DUE PROCESS OF LAW guaranteed by the U.S. Constitution. No legal action can be taken against someone unless the requirements of notice and an opportunity for a hearing are observed. In this sense, notice has a special meaning that has been developed through statutes and case decisions.

Legal proceedings are started by giving notice to the persons affected. If a person is accused of a crime, he is entitled to notice of the charges against him. In this case, notice means that the law the person is accused of violating must be specific and understandable enough so that he could judge whether or not his conduct was illegal. It also means that formal papers must be drawn up to give the accused person notice of the charges, such as in an INDICTMENT, COMPLAINT, WARRANT, or PRESENTMENT.

If a person is being sued, he must be given notice of the nature of the civil action and what he may lose if he does not defend himself. The procedure for presenting this notice is spelled out in statutes. Courts require strict compliance with these laws. It is generally necessary for the plaintiff to put this information into a formal paper called a COMPLAINT or PLEADING. This formal paper must then be communicated to the defendant in a legal way. It may, for example, be *personally served*—that is, an authorized person hand-delivers it to the defendant, as in a subpoena—

or it may be *served by mail*—registered, certified, or regular mail—depending on the statute. There are also instances in which a court permits or requires *service by posting*—physically attaching the papers to the defendant's last known place of address or to a public place where he is likely to see them—or *service by publication* in a local newspaper.

Notice may also be required at other stages of legal proceedings. For example, the winning party in a civil lawsuit may have to give notice of the final judgment before he can enforce it against the losing party.

Kinds of notice There are different kinds of notice with different legal results for each. The major kinds are actual and constructive (or legal) notice.

The law considers that you have been given *actual notice* when you either have the information or are aware that you can have it. If actual notice is given to you in writing or orally it is called *express notice*. But if, given the facts of the case, you should have been aware of the information, the law presumes that actual notice was given. This is called *implied notice*.

EXAMPLE Mr. Boyle sued a power company for money
0——* damages after he had been injured by an electrical current from overhead wires. He had been installing a CB antenna on his van when it brushed against wires over his driveway. He told the court that he had not realized the wires were there, and that he had never even thought about any possible danger. The court held, however, that it could be assumed that Mr. Boyle had knowledge of the hazard. And if he had not known about the hazard he certainly should have.

Constructive notice, or *legal notice*, is also a type of information that the court will rule "he knew or should have known." It is based on a rule of law, not on the facts of the case. The court presumes receipt of the information because the law requires it. If one partner is cheating the customers, for example, the court assumes that the other partner has knowledge of the dishonest transactions because the law says that a partner has a duty to keep track of all the business affairs of the partnership. If the innocent partner claims, "I didn't know," the court's answer to him will be: "You should have known. A partner has constructive notice of all the partnership business."

notice to quit Written notification given by a landlord, telling the tenant to move from the rented premises. The phrase is sometimes used for notice given by a tenant to his landlord that he intends to vacate the rented premises.

n.o.v. An abbreviation for NON OBSTANTE VEREDICTO.

novation The substitution of a new CONTRACT for an old one, with the new one canceling the rights and obligations that existed under the previous agreement. Usually, a novation occurs when a new person takes over an obligation to pay the debt of an original party to the contract—here, the agreement remains the same but one of the parties changes and the original party is no longer liable for the debt. Another type of novation occurs when a new agreement is substituted for the old one but the original contracting parties remain the same.

nuisance   An act, object, or event that disturbs your peaceful enjoyment of your property. This article explains what kind of conduct can be considered a nuisance, when a person can be held legally liable for creating or maintaining a nuisance, what legal remedies may be granted for a person harmed by a nuisance, and when a nuisance can be legally excused.

■ **Determining when a nuisance occurs**   Legal experts say that it is virtually impossible to define nuisance specifically so that you can be sure when legal action will be permitted. The principle must remain flexible in order to protect the interests of individual parties and the public as a whole. Each case stands on its own merits.

Relationship to trespass   A nuisance is similar to *trespass* in some respects, but trespass is restricted to a direct infringement of your property rights. For example, if someone drives his car across your front lawn, he has trespassed against you. That act clearly intrudes on your property rights. A nuisance is not created unless you are personally disturbed or injured. A driver who left his refrigerated truck running all night beside your bedroom window caused a nuisance because the noisy truck kept you awake and therefore disturbed your peaceful enjoyment of your property (your home). Sometimes a *continuing trespass* becomes a nuisance because the accumulated effect is disturbing.

> EXAMPLE   Andy, an amiable man, was willing to overlook the trespass when his neighbor dumped a tub of soapy wash water over the fence onto his lawn. But when the neighbor continuously drained his washing machine through a hose draped over the fence, the persisting trespass may become a nuisance that Andy found intolerable.

Attractive nuisance   The theory of attractive nuisance is that any landowner who keeps something dangerous that is likely to attract children onto his land will have to pay money damages if a child is hurt. Swimming pools are considered attractive nuisances. You should install a high fence around your pool to avoid liability for injuries to a child who trespasses on your property.

Nuisance per se   A nuisance per se is something that is bound to be annoying, inconvenient, or disturbing per se (in itself). For example, a house of prostitution is generally considered a nuisance per se because it draws together idle and dissolute persons for immoral and unlawful practices, thereby threatening the peace. In a lawsuit against a brothel, you do not have to show that the house is disorderly or annoying. Proof that it exists is sufficient.

Public nuisances   A public nuisance is an act or a failure to act that inconveniences or harms the public at large. It interferes with the reasonable exercise of rights that are common to all, including impairing the public health or morals or the public peace or convenience. Examples of public nuisances are storing explosives; exploding fireworks in the streets; failing to control mosquitoes on a pond; or running a house of prostitution.

A public nuisance is a criminal offense, punishable by fine or imprisonment. No individual who has suffered from a public nuisance can sue for money damages simply on the ground that he is a member of the public at large. If, however, he can show that he has suffered particular damage not suffered by the rest of the community, he can sue the offender.

Private nuisances   A private nuisance is an act or occurrence that interferes with your use and enjoyment of your own land. The possibilities for a private nuisance are almost infinite. It may affect the land itself, such as vibrations, objects hurled upon it, destruction of crops or timber, flooding or pollution of the soil or water. Or it may disturb your comfort, convenience, or health in occupying the land. Foul odors, smoke, dust, insects, noxious gases, excessive light, loud noises, high temperatures, and even repeated telephone calls are private nuisances.

You can settle a private nuisance problem by a civil lawsuit, directing the wrongdoer to pay for the damage and to discontinue the nuisance.

> EXAMPLE   The owner of a second-floor bingo parlor sued the proprietor of a first-floor grocery store over the use of a bell. The store had wired its bell to ring continuously whenever the back door was open. But the ringing of the bell drove the bingo players away and began to force the owner out of business. There was not much point in complaining to the landlord because he owned the grocery store. So the bingo parlor sued him on the ground that the bell was a nuisance. The action was settled when the grocer agreed to reduce the volume of the bell and to stop it from ringing continuously.

A "spite fence" is a common example of a private nuisance. If, without good reason, your neighbor builds a high fence on his property that adjoins yours, thus blocking out your sunlight and air, the interference may be a nuisance for which you can sue him.

Sometimes a nuisance may be both private and public—if a private individual is harmed by it in a way that is different from the harm suffered by the public in general.

> EXAMPLE   A construction company that leaves a large boulder on the shoulder of a public highway after dynamiting may be prosecuted by the state for creating a public nuisance. Individual members of the public cannot sue the company for the inconvenience—not even drivers who daily use the highway. That same boulder can be considered a private nuisance if it blocks the driveway of a homeowner because he suffers a harm different from that affecting the general public. He, and only he, can sue the construction company.

■ **Legal responsibility for a nuisance**   A private nuisance is a type of TORT—a legal wrong suffered by a person because of an act or a failure to act by another. Special rules determine who is legally responsible for a nuisance and under what conditions he is held accountable. Whether a person is legally responsible depends on the elements of (1) fault or intention, (2) whether or not he created substantial interference, and (3) the reasonableness of his actions.

Fault or intention   Nuisance liability is not absolute. This means that the person who creates a situation that disturbs you does not always risk legal penalties. The interference with your legitimate interest must be intentional, reckless, or the result of some extremely dangerous activity.

> EXAMPLE   Zachary has a handsome old oak tree in his yard with one dead limb hanging over his neighbor Joshua's house. He knows the limb must be cut down or it is likely to fall in the next storm. He ties up the limb before sawing, thinking that he can control its fall, but in

spite of the care he takes, it crashes into the giant skylight in Joshua's art studio. Unless there is a specific law in Zachary's state setting a different standard, Zachary is not legally responsible for the damage caused by the nuisance. He did, after all, take reasonable precautions.

To prove fault, it must be shown that the defendant intentionally created a condition or continued his conduct knowing that there was harm, or a risk of harm, to the plaintiff. This is not always the same as proving that the defendant was negligent. See NEGLIGENCE. Sometimes fault exists because the defendant has violated a law, such as one requiring the destruction of diseased crops or plants. Fault in nuisance cases is not just an intention to harm or annoy, but intentionally creating or maintaining the condition complained of.

Substantial interference   Another element that must be proved in a nuisance case is substantial interference with the plaintiff's interest. *Substantial* means that the distur-

bance must be much more than a petty, temporary discomfort. For example, a court is not likely to do anything about your neighbors in the next apartment who have peppers and onions at dinner, even if the smell is a little annoying. A lawnmower can be quite noisy, but you really cannot complain if your neighbor cuts the grass once a week.

Determining what is substantial is not difficult when there is property damage. If your neighbor floods your garden with chlorinated water from a swimming pool, substantial and permanent damage will result. But when the problem is inconvenience, discomfort, or annoyance to a person—which is what helps determine the existence of a nuisance—it is more difficult to determine. Generally, a court will not be overly concerned about complaints from temperamental neighbors. Although it is true that children can occasionally be disruptive, for example, a court will not find your backyard swing to be a nuisance even if your children annoy a cranky neighbor when they use it.

WHEN TO BLOW THE WHISTLE ON A NUISANCE

■ In law, a nuisance is an act, object, or condition that is bound to be harmful, annoying, inconvenient, or disturbing. It is impossible to define nuisance specifically. Because the principle must remain flexible in order to protect individuals and the public, each case stands on its own merits.

■ A *public nuisance* is something that inconveniences or harms the public at large—for example, storing explosives in a residential neighborhood or running an illegal after-hours club in your apartment. A person convicted of creating or maintaining any public nuisance must usually pay a fine or go to jail.

■ A *private nuisance* is an activity that interferes with an individual's use and enjoyment of his land or home. Private nuisance problems can be settled by civil lawsuits directing the wrongdoer to pay for the damage and discontinue the nuisance. A "spite fence" is an example of a private nuisance. If your neighbor builds a high fence alongside your property without good reason, thus blocking out your sunlight and air, you may be able to sue.

■ In order to sue someone for creating a nuisance, you must show that the nuisance was intentional, reckless, or the result of some extremely dangerous activity.

■ A nuisance must also be a substantial interference with your interest. In other words, if your next-door neighbors regularly cook peppers, onions,

and other smelly fare, the court is unlikely to sympathize with your complaint, but if they constantly flood your garden with chlorinated water from their swimming pool, you will have a case against them in court.

■ A neighbor is not guilty of creating a nuisance because of temporary annoyances while he improves his premises for some lawful purpose.

■ A nursing home is not a nuisance just because some people do not want one in their neighborhood. On the other hand, an addict rehabilitation center whose patients have a bad influence on the neighborhood children and rob local merchants may well get closed by court order as a public nuisance.

■ In considering a nuisance action, the court must determine if the defendant is being reasonable. If he is, the court may tell the plaintiff to learn to live with the situation, either with or without recovering money damages. The question of reasonableness may be answered by a statute. For example, a law limiting the noise that jet planes may make establishes that a certain decibel level creates a public nuisance.

■ The courts may issue injunctions against either public or private nuisances. The defendant can be told to do something, such as enclosing a junkyard with a solid fence, or he can be directed *not* to do something, such as idling train engines near homes.

■ If an injunction will cause serious harm or inconvenience to the defendant while benefiting the plaintiff only a little, it will be denied. For example, the court would not order your neighbor to chop down his apple tree just because once a year you have to gather up the fruit that falls in your yard.

■ In some cases, money damages may be awarded to compensate a plaintiff whether or not an injunction is issued. For instance, if a construction company has been blasting near your home, you can sue the company for an amount sufficient to repair cracks the blasting caused in your house.

■ It is no defense for a person accused of creating a nuisance to show that others are equally guilty. Defendants often claim the plaintiff has no right to complain because he "came to the nuisance" by purchasing and moving into a property next to an existing source of interference. The argument usually does not excuse a defendant. A new neighbor is entitled to the reasonable use and peaceful enjoyment of his land as much as anyone else.

■ "Coming to the nuisance" may be considered, however, if it shows the plaintiff has not in fact suffered loss because of the nuisance. For instance, a person who buys a house next to one of the main runways of an international airport cannot claim that jet noises affect the value of his house if he paid less for it than he would have paid for a similar house in a different location.

The question is whether the annoyance substantially interferes with the ordinary comfort of human existence. The law will not deal with something just because one person finds it unsightly or unpleasant or a violation of the rules of convention or good taste. For instance, a person can paint his house any color he wants, even if it annoys everyone else in the neighborhood, unless there is an agreement among landowners or a local law preventing it. A neighbor is not guilty of creating a nuisance because of temporary annoyances while he improves his premises for some lawful purpose. A nursing home or a group home for mentally retarded persons is not a nuisance just because some people would like all others who are different or special to stay away from their neighborhood. On the other hand, residents of a fashionable section of New York City won a court order that closed a drug-addict rehabilitation center in their area. They claimed that the center had a bad effect on school children and that merchants were being robbed and their customers harassed.

Reasonableness   A court must also determine if the person accused of creating a nuisance was acting reasonably. If he was, the court may tell you to learn to live with the situation—either with or without recovering money damages. This requires a balancing process, sometimes taking into account not only your interests and the defendant's rights, but also the public good. The rule is that there are times when a defendant may cause substantial harm or inconvenience to the plaintiff because his conduct is reasonable under all the circumstances—when, for example, closing a street for repairs causes shops located there to lose business.

Proof of reasonableness is important in nuisance cases, because socially useful activities must be encouraged, especially those related to industry, commerce, and trade, even though they may disrupt tranquillity. Courts may require persons engaged in these activities to bear the cost of the harm they cause or to limit the activities as much as possible. But courts need not prohibit them altogether.

EXAMPLE During World War II a large factory was disturbing its neighbors with noise. The neighbors complained, but the factory owners had nearly eliminated the noise at night and had reduced it as much as possible during the day. The court refused to issue an injunction prohibiting noise from the factory. It held that operation of the plant was essential to the war effort and the noise was reasonable under the circumstances.

EXAMPLE In a similar case, a court ordered a cement factory to pay a sum of money to neighbors for the discomfort and inconvenience caused by noise, traffic, and dust. But the factory was allowed to continue operating as long as it controlled the problems as carefully as technology allowed.

An ANIMAL may be a nuisance depending on how it is kept. A rooster, for example, is a nuisance if he crows at dawn in the apartment next door but not if he is kept on the farm down the road. Bees can be a nuisance if hives are tended for honey on a city lot but are not necessarily a problem in rural areas.

Buildings and structures can be nuisances if their use or condition is unreasonable. A brightly lit billboard may be deemed a nuisance in a residential area. A warehouse can be a nuisance if it is used to store large quantities of explosives near homes or businesses. A garage can be a nuisance if it is built right up against a neighbor's driveway. Any structure is a nuisance if it is constructed or maintained so poorly that it is a threat to persons passing by on the street.

In evaluating reasonableness, the kind and seriousness of the nuisance must be balanced against the burden of preventing it and the usefulness of the activity that creates it. There are several specific factors likely to be important in this evaluation: (1) the extent and duration of the interference; (2) the character of the harm; (3) the social value of the complaining party's property or interest; (4) the burden that protecting himself from the harm would place on the plaintiff; (5) the social value of the defendant's conduct, either within the community or for the public as a whole; (6) the cost—or even the possibility—of the defendant's preventing or lessening the harm; and (7) the character of the neighborhood or locality and the suitability of the uses made of it by both defendant and plaintiff.

The legal remedies for nuisances are INJUNCTIONS, DAMAGES, summary abatements, and criminal penalties.

Injunctions   Courts may issue INJUNCTIONS against nuisances, ordering that they be stopped, removed, limited, or restrained. A defendant can be ordered not to continue an existing nuisance or not to proceed with a threatened one. He can be told to do something, such as not to enclose a junkyard with a solid fence, or he can be directed not to do something, such as not to idle train engines on sidings near homes.

Injunctions are drastic remedies granted when the threat or harm is serious and there is a likelihood that it will reoccur if not stopped. Injunctions may give a defendant a choice. For example, an injunction may order the defendant either to provide health and sanitation facilities or to refrain from producing a rock concert in the park. If an injunction will cause serious harm or inconvenience to the defendant while benefiting the plaintiff only a little, it will be denied. The court would not order your neighbor to cut down his apple tree because once a year you have to gather up the fruit that falls in your yard. If an injunction is disobeyed, the court will punish the violator for CONTEMPT of court.

Damages   In some cases, it is appropriate to award money DAMAGES in a private nuisance case to compensate the plaintiff for the harm he has suffered—whether or not an injunction is issued.

EXAMPLE Suppose the Langdons' next-door neighbors begin sponsoring community garage sales every Saturday. Droves of bargain hunters from miles around crowd into the usually quiet, tree-lined street, blocking the Langdons' driveway with their cars, littering their front lawn with newspapers, soda bottles, and beer cans, and trampling their carefully tended shrubs and flower beds. A rented calliope adds to the carnival atmosphere. Langdon's wife, Rose, is recuperating from an operation and is supposed to rest quietly and take frequent naps, which is now impossible. Both Langdons have become so distraught and anxious about this continuing disruption in their lives that they require medication to calm them.

Sam Langdon has spoken to his neighbors about this, suggesting they relocate the sales to the community church, but to no avail. So Langdon brings suit against his neighbors for creating a nuisance. The court orders the neighbors to stop holding the sales and to pay money damages to the Langdons for their lawn, shrubs, medical expenses, and their mental anguish.

Summary abatements   Summary abatement is stopping a nuisance without resorting to legal action. It has been permitted in specific cases, such as when a defendant killed a vicious dog; cut branches from a tree that extended over a property line; sawed off the eaves of a building that hung dangerously over his property. You must give proper notice to the person responsible for the nuisance before trying to stop it of your own accord, except when there is an immediate threat to health, life, or property. For example, an electric company was sued for cutting down a shade tree without first giving notice to the homeowner, but the court found the company not liable because an emergency situation required the tree's immediate removal.

Anyone who tries to abate a nuisance summarily must not unnecessarily damage property, cause personal injuries, or disturb the peace. A neighbor cannot, for example, burn down a house just because it is being used for prostitution. A person who violates a law in the course of summarily abating a nuisance can be prosecuted. If he removes something that is not legally a nuisance, he may have to pay damages or even restore the property. Public officials may abate a public nuisance, but they must follow the procedural steps required by law. Any person responsible for a nuisance may have to pay for the expense of removing it if the abatement was proper.

Criminal penalties   Creating a public nuisance is usually a crime punishable by a jail sentence, a fine, or both. The defendant may also have to remove the nuisance or pay to have it taken away.

■ **Defenses**   Someone who is charged with creating or maintaining a nuisance may offer certain facts in defense, even though the plaintiff proves that the nuisance exists. Generally, courts will take zoning laws into account in deciding whether a use is appropriate. If you build a house in an industrial section of town, you have no right to complain of factory noises. The authority of a zoning law, however, is limited. It does not, for example, justify excessive pollution in an industrial area.

It is no defense to establish that the harm would be insignificant without someone else's additional actions.

EXAMPLE   A stream may be able to absorb a small amount of
○←—✳ pollution from one factory, but it can become contaminated if several factories add their waste. Each factory is then responsible for the harm it causes, but none should have to pay for the total damage.

Defendants in nuisance cases frequently claim that the plaintiff has no right to complain because he "came to the nuisance" by purchasing and moving next to an existing and operating source of interference. These cases do not automatically protect a defendant. A new landowner is entitled to the reasonable use and peaceful enjoyment of his land as much as anyone else. "Coming to the nuisance" may be a factor, however, in showing that the plaintiff has not suffered loss because of the nuisance. For instance, a person who buys a house right next to Runway 31 cannot claim that jet noises have affected the value of his house if he paid less than he would have paid for the same house in a different location.

Most cases have followed the rule that the plaintiff's conduct in regard to the nuisance is an important factor. Usually, however, this will not entirely excuse the defendant for creating or maintaining the nuisance.

null   Nothing; having no legal force.

nunc pro tunc   (Latin) "Now for then." The phrase is used when a thing done now is given the legal consequences it would have had if it had been done at an earlier time. For example, a child born of unmarried parents is illegitimate. Many state laws provide, however, that the child will become legitimate if the parents marry each other. *Nunc pro tunc* means that, instead of being illegitimate up to the time of their marriage and legitimate after that, the child is considered completely legitimate for every legal purpose from the time of his birth.

nuncupative will   An oral will; one not written down but remembered by persons who heard the provisions spoken. Nuncupative wills are not valid in all states and where they are, they are valid only under certain circumstances. For a discussion of oral wills, see WILL.

oaths and affirmations Solemn declarations of truth or obligation; all forms of attestation; declarations by which a person attests to his moral duty; admissions that one is bound by his conscience to perform an act faithfully and truly.

An *oath* is someone's appeal to God to witness the truth of what he is saying or a pledge to do something that is enforced by his responsibility to answer to God. An *affirmation* is a solemn and formal declaration that a statement is true without referring to God. An affirmation can be made by someone who does not believe in God or by someone who does not wish to swear to God.

Under the common law there was no provision for making affirmations. A person who did not believe in the existence of a God who punishes those who swear falsely could not take a valid oath. Thus, only people who believed in God could give sworn testimony. Laws now generally allow affirmations to be made as an alternative to oaths. If no particular form is required for an oath, the words may vary to satisfy each person's conscience, but if a form is prescribed by law, it should be followed exactly. The most famous oath prescribed by law in the United States is the one repeated by the President when he takes his office. The Constitution says that the Chief Executive

"shall take the following Oath or Affirmation: I do solemnly swear (or affirm) that I will faithfully execute the office of President of the United States, and will to the best of my ability, preserve, protect, and defend the Constitution of the United States."

The Constitution also requires every Senator, Representative, state legislator, governor, and state or federal judge to swear or affirm his loyalty to the Constitution, but it specifically forbids any requirement that a federal official swear that he has any religious belief.

To be effective, an oath must be administered by a public official. The law that creates and describes each public office generally specifies who is authorized to administer the oath of office. A spoken oath is usually sufficient, but a written and signed oath can be required by law.

obiter dictum (Latin) "Something said in passing"; opinions expressed in a judge's written decision that are related but are not essential to resolving the issues of the case. Under the common-law system, cases must follow principles established in earlier cases. See STARE DECISIS. This doctrine, which develops and protects established legal principles, is limited to questions actively litigated and answered in a case. See HOLDING. It does not preserve the opinions expressed in obiter dicta. Sometimes lawyers say "dictum" or "dicta" (the plural of dictum) to mean "obiter dictum" or "obiter dicta."

objection A formal statement of disapproval regarding some point of law or procedure during a trial; an assertion of disagreement with a judge's ruling. An appeal to a higher court is usually based on errors objected to during the course of the trial in a lower court. An error that slips by without objection cannot later be put forth as a reason for the appeals court to overturn the original decision. See APPEAL AND ERROR.

obligation Any duty or legal liability. Originally, obligation was a technical term for the responsibility to pay money owed on certain CONTRACTS that were signed under SEAL. Today, an obligation is anything someone is bound to do as the result of a vow, promise, oath, contract, or law. It is a legal duty that one can be forced to do or punished for neglecting.

obligee The person to whom a duty or obligation is owed. The obligation may be to pay money or to do or not to do something. Obligee is frequently used as a synonym for creditor.

obligor The person who owes another person a duty. Obligor is often used instead of the word "debtor."

obliteration The erasure or blotting out of written words. Lines drawn through the signatures of witnesses to a WILL, for example, are an obliteration even if the names can still be read. Obliteration is a way of revoking a will.

obscenity Anything that is designed to stimulate an obsessive interest in nudity, sex, or excretion and which substantially exceeds the usual limits of candor in describing or illustrating such matters. Although freedom of speech and the press have always been guaranteed by the First Amendment to the U.S. Constitution, the federal and state governments have the power to prohibit the use and transmittal of obscene speech and ideas. A precise legal definition of obscenity, however, has eluded the U.S. Supreme Court, which over the years has established and modified various standards to determine what is obscene. The principal problem is that what is obscene to one person may be a work of art to another. Perhaps the most honest test of obscenity was once stated by Supreme Court Justice Potter Stewart: "I know it when I see it."

Broadly defined, obscenity is any kind of matter that—to the average person applying the standards of the local community—appeals to a prurient (lustful) interest in sex in a clearly offensive way without having any serious literary, artistic, political, or scientific value.

A medical textbook on anatomy is not obscene because of its scientific value. But a magazine filled only with pornographic articles and photographs of nude males and females engaging in sex acts may be obscene, depending on the standards of the local community in which the material is circulated.

■ **Tests for obscenity** The Comstock laws, criminal statutes enacted by Congress in the late 1800's, prohibited importing or mailing obscene materials, and many states passed similar criminal obscenity statutes. At that time material thought to be obscene was judged by the effect of isolated passages on persons particularly susceptible to prurient appeal or lustful thoughts. Since the 1950's a succession of Supreme Court decisions has set new standards for obscenity.

Average person test In 1957 the Supreme Court separated protected expression from unprotected obscene expression. Samuel Roth, a New York publisher, was convicted for mailing obscene advertising and an obscene book in violation of the federal obscenity statute. He claimed that the law not only violated his constitutional right to freedom of expression but was also vague about what conduct was prohibited. The Supreme Court affirmed the conviction but rejected the traditional definition of obscenity, which was based on the effect of isolated passages on particularly susceptible individuals. Instead, the Court adopted the following test to determine if a work should be protected by the Constitution: If an average person applying contemporary community standards to the work could decide that its dominant theme, taken as a whole, would appeal to a prurient interest in sex, then the work would be declared obscene. This test acknowledged that there could be a serious expression of sexual matters that was not obscene. "Sex and obscenity are not synonymous. . . . The portrayal of sex . . . in art, literature and scientific works is not itself reason to deny material the constitutional protection of freedom of speech and press." Censorship was still permitted, however, as long as the work met the Court's standard of obscenity.

This test was difficult to apply. The Supreme Court could not definitively measure either the effect of material on "average" persons or how dominant particular obscene themes were in books, motion pictures, or magazines. Nor could the Court decide which community (local, state, or national) should judge the questionable material.

Social value test In 1966, when the Supreme Court decided that the novel *Fanny Hill,* written in 1750 and containing vividly described sex scenes, was not obscene, it added a new dimension to its test for obscenity. A work could only be found obscene if it met these three requirements: "[1] the dominant theme of the material taken as a whole appeals to a prurient interest in sex, [2] the material is patently offensive because it affronts contemporary community standards, and [3] the material is utterly without redeeming social value." A censor or prosecutor had to establish that the challenged expression met all three requirements. The lack of redeeming social value was particularly difficult to prove, because a defendant could almost always produce expert testimony to show that his material had some redeeming social value.

After the *Fanny Hill* decision, prosecutions and censorship attempts dwindled while the flow of pornographic materials increased. As long as the pornographer did not pander to the public, encourage the belief that his product was obscene, or do business with minors, he had little to worry about. In 1973, however, a federal district court declared the film *Deep Throat* to be obscene for its graphic scenes of explicit heterosexual intercourse, group sex, FELLATIO, and SODOMY, and all attempts to show that the film had some redeeming social value—for example, that it was a source of sex education for young adults—were unsuccessful.

Local standards test Later in 1973, in *Miller* v. *California,* the Supreme Court set down new and tougher legal standards for obscenity. Marvin Miller had been tried for mailing unsolicited sexually explicit material to persons in Orange County, California, in violation of a state law that used the three obscenity tests from the *Fanny Hill* decision. The trial judge gave these tests to the jury and instructed them to evaluate the materials in the light of the contemporary community standards in California. The jury convicted Miller and the decision was upheld by the Supreme Court. Although it reaffirmed that obscenity is not protected by the 1st and 14th Amendments, the Court rejected important aspects of the *Fanny Hill* tests. Instead, a new threefold test to guide juries and judges was substituted: (1) whether the average person, applying contemporary community standards, would find that the material, taken as a whole, appeals to prurient interest; (2) whether the work depicts or describes, in a patently offensive way, sexual conduct specifically defined by the applicable state law; and (3) whether the work, taken as a whole, lacks serious literary, artistic, political, or scientific value. The Court indicated that these tests would be applied only to "hardcore" pornography—clearly offensive descriptions or representations (actual or simulated) of normal or perverted sex acts and patently offensive representations or descriptions of masturbation, excretory functions, and lewd exhibition of the genitals. Such pornography was to be determined by reference to local or state community standards and not national standards.

In another 1973 case, *Paris Adult Theatre I* v. *Slaton,* decided on the same day as the Miller case, the Court made it clear that even "consenting adults" should not be exposed to hard-core pornography. It upheld the right of states to bar the exhibition of hard-core pornographic films

SOME WAYS OF THROTTLING OBSCENITY

■ Obscenity may be defined as any kind of material that appeals to a person's prurient interest in sex in a clearly offensive way without having any serious literary, artistic, political, or scientific value.

■ Through the years, the U.S. Supreme Court has applied a number of different tests to material to determine whether or not it is obscene, including the *average person test* (Would an average person consider it obscene?) and the *social value test* (Did it have any redeeming social value?).

■ In the 1970's the Supreme Court applied a threefold test: (1) Would the average person, applying contemporary community standards, find that the material, taken as a whole, appeals to prurient interest? (2) Does the work depict or describe, in a patently offensive way, sexual conduct specifically defined and outlawed by the applicable state law? (3) Does the work, taken as a whole, lack serious

literary, artistic, political, or scientific value? The Court indicated that these tests were to be applied to hard-core pornography, as determined by reference to local or state community standards, not national standards.

■ The Supreme Court has also upheld the right of states to bar hard-core films, even when the exhibitor tries to limit the audience to "consenting adults." In this matter, the Court reasoned that government has a legitimate interest in the community's quality of life and environment, the tone of commerce, and public safety.

■ Other tests have been developed to prevent the pandering of borderline smut as "the real thing," to suppress hard-core filth aimed at deviant adults, and to shield minors from all of these.

■ When a merchant's sole emphasis is on the sexually provocative aspects of his publications, that is enough to get the material banned as obscene.

■ The state's power to regulate obscene materials does not extend to the privacy of an individual's home.

■ When a censor tries to ban a motion picture under local licensing laws, he must seek a court order to prevent the film from being shown, and the court, in turn, must come to a speedy decision as to whether or not the film is obscene.

■ Federal law prohibits broadcasting stations from presenting obscene or indecent material. On the other hand, programs in which sex is openly discussed have been approved for nighttime programming, while prohibition of such programs during the daytime hours, when children might be listening, has been upheld.

■ Under present federal law, anyone who receives "pandering advertisements" for materials that he considers to be prurient may request the Postmaster General to order the sender to stop further mailings to him.

under the standards set in the Miller decision, even when the exhibitor makes every effort to limit the audience to consenting adults. The government has a legitimate interest in shielding not only the young and the unwilling from obscenity but the consenting adult as well. This legitimate interest is concerned with the quality of life in the community, the tone of commerce in the cities, and the public safety. Although the Court recognized that an individual has a constitutional right of privacy with respect to personal intimacies in the home, it refused to extend that right to include viewing pornography in a public place.

The *Paris Adult Theatre* case was also important in establishing that a censor or prosecutor need not produce expert evidence on the obscene nature of the questionable materials placed in evidence. This substantially lightened the burden on the antiobscenity forces and encouraged attempts at censorship and criminal prosecutions.

In 1974, however, the Supreme Court was faced with the problem of balancing differing community standards with the protection afforded a literary work by the Constitution. The Court substituted its own judgment for that of a local jury on the ground that it was the only court that could ultimately decide the scope of the 1st and 14th Amendments. What happened was that a manager of a movie theater in Albany, Georgia, had been convicted for exhibiting the film *Carnal Knowledge,* produced by a recognized group of serious moviemakers, including director Mike Nichols and actor Jack Nicholson. The conviction was affirmed by a divided Georgia Supreme Court, which concluded that the judgment was consistent with the standards set by the U.S. Supreme Court for judging obscenity.

But the U.S. Supreme Court reversed the conviction and held the film not to be obscene.

Adult standards   In 1978 the U.S. Supreme Court reversed a conviction under federal obscenity laws because the jury had been instructed to include children as part of the community by whose standards materials were to be judged obscene. The Court found that only adults, regardless of their differing attitudes toward sex, are to make up the community whose standards are to decide whether a matter is obscene.

Subjectivity   Problems still remain with the Court's approach to obscenity. Beyond recognizing obscenity when confronted with it, as Justice Stewart did, the Court asserts that it can define obscenity with sufficient precision to give fair advance warning as to what is forbidden. Yet the "serious value" test remains highly subjective, because five justices (a majority of the Court) are permitted to decide what is a serious expression and what is not. Even the application of the 1973 test solely to patently offensive hard-core pornography allows for subjectivity because here, too (as in the *Carnal Knowledge* case), in the final analysis, it is the Court that decides whether the application of local community standards by juries is constitutional.

Other standards   The Supreme Court has developed other standards that permit suppression and punishment of expression that falls short of the basic obscenity test. These tests are designed (1) to prevent pandering of borderline material as the "real thing," (2) to suppress expression directed to the prurient interest of sexually deviant adults, and (3) to shield minors from such adult materials as "girlie" magazines.

EXAMPLE The defendant-publisher of a purported sexual autobiography, a hard-core sex magazine, and a sex newsletter was convicted of sending obscene matter through the mail. His conviction was affirmed by the Supreme Court partly because of his own advertising claims and other suggestions that the materials would appeal to the "leer of the sensualist." A majority of the Court ruled that when a merchant's sole emphasis is on the sexually provocative aspects of his publications, that fact may determine that the material is obscene.

Because audiences vary as to age and sexual preference, the Court has held that the standard for suppression may also vary according to these audiences.

EXAMPLE The Court rejected the argument of a publisher and seller of sex books for sadists, masochists, fetishists, and homosexuals that his materials were not obscene because they would not appeal to the prurient interest of average persons but rather would disgust and sicken them. The rule is that when material is designed for, and primarily circulated to, a clearly defined deviant group, it is obscene if its dominant theme, taken as a whole, appeals to the prurient interest in sex of members of that group.

EXAMPLE In another case, the defendant, an operator of a stationery store and luncheonette, was convicted of violating a New York criminal law that prohibits the knowing sale to minors under the age of 17 of any picture that shows uncovered female buttocks and breasts. The defendant had sold two "girlie" magazines to a 16-year-old male. While acknowledging that the magazines were not obscene for adults, the Court affirmed the conviction because of its belief that obscenity varies with the age of the audience. Therefore, states may greatly restrict the access of minors to sex materials.

■ **Home privacy** The power of a state to regulate obscene materials does not extend to mere possession of obscene material by the individual in the privacy of his own home. See PRIVACY, RIGHT OF. Any such law is unconstitutional under the 1st and 14th Amendments.

■ **Prior restraint** Prior restraint is the suppression of material in advance. Licensing laws constitute prior restraint if they require certain types of materials to be submitted to a review board before their release to the public, or if they require the confiscation of disapproved materials or the use of preliminary injunctions to postpone the publication or distribution of such materials before a court can decide whether or not they are obscene. Generally, the Supreme Court has held that prior restraint violates the First Amendment guarantee of freedom of speech and of the press. When permitted at all, it has been severely limited. See SPEECH AND PRESS, FREEDOM OF.

Although all forms of expression can be protected from prior restraint, the majority of lawsuits challenging prior-restraint statutes have involved films. A film exhibitor challenged a state law authorizing certain procedures of the Maryland Board of Censors, including a lengthy appeal process. The Supreme Court struck down the law as violating freedom of expression and established the following safeguards for regulating censorship procedures: (1) Prior restraint, or licensing laws, must place on the censor the burden of proving that the film in question meets the constitutional standards for obscenity. (2) The censor must, within a specified and brief time period, such as two days, either issue a license for exhibition or seek in court to restrain exhibition. (3) The court must assure a prompt and final decision in order to minimize the deterrent effect on an interim refusal to license. (4) Prior-restraint legislation, whether it involves outright censorship or mandatory film classification for the protection of minors, must be precisely written. Nonobservance of these safeguards is considered an infringement on protected expression and a violation of the 1st and 14th Amendments.

Before a film can be seized, a court warrant must be obtained. See SEARCH AND SEIZURE. The seizure of a copy of the film under a valid warrant is only for the purpose of preserving it as evidence in a subsequent trial. It cannot prevent continued showings of the film until the film is determined to be obscene. If there is only one copy available, the film seized must be made available to the exhibitor for copying so that he may continue its exhibition.

Broadcast censorship Federal law prohibits radio and television broadcast stations from presenting any material that is obscene or indecent. Problems arise, however, in determining whether the material is obscene under constitutional standards or is only vulgar and improper. The courts have approved prohibition of explicitly sexual programs—such as radio programs in which listeners freely discuss their sexual practices in a "call-in, disc-jockey" format—during daytime hours when children may be listening. Profanity (such as slang words for sexual organs, excrement, or sexual intercourse) is not by itself obscene because it does not appeal to a prurient interest. For discussion of what may be done to prevent the use of profanity in mass communication, see SPEECH AND PRESS, FREEDOM OF. See also THEATERS AND SHOWS.

■ **Mail censorship** Under present federal law, anyone who receives "pandering advertisements" for materials that he considers erotically arousing or sexually provocative may request the Postmaster General to order the sender to stop further mailings to him. If, after notice and hearing, the Postmaster General determines that the order has been violated, he may request that the Attorney General seek a federal court order directing compliance with the Postmaster's order. Violations of the court order subject the sender to sanctions for CONTEMPT of court.

obstructing justice Interfering by words or actions with the proper workings of courts or court officers. It is a criminal offense under both state and federal law. For example, a person who resists or obstructs an authorized person from serving him with a summons to appear in court may be prosecuted for obstructing justice. Trying to keep a witness from appearing in court, attempting to bribe a juror or a witness, offering false or forged evidence, and suppressing or concealing evidence are other ways of obstructing justice. Under federal law, it is also a crime to obstruct criminal investigations as well as proceedings before departments, agencies, or committees.

occupancy 1 The physical possession of land or buildings with or without legal right. 2 In a fire insurance policy, the purpose for which the property is used.

of counsel A phrase commonly applied to the attorney employed by a person in a lawsuit, particularly to an attorney who is hired to help prepare and manage the case but is not the principal attorney in the matter. For example, when Abe Smith sued ABC Realty for breach of contract, Smith's lawyer, Robert Fisk, asked Mary Davis, a realty lawyer, to act in the case of counsel.

of course As a matter of right; describing actions that a person may take in a lawsuit either without asking the judge's permission or by requesting and getting automatic approval.

offense A crime or misdemeanor; a violation of CRIMINAL LAW.

offer See CONTRACTS.

officer A person who performs the duties and functions of an office. A *public officer* is someone elected or appointed to exercise the functions of an office created by law for the public benefit. The commissioner of your state's department of motor vehicles is a public officer.

A public officer is distinguished from an employee by the requirement of an oath of office, a specified term of office, and the fact that his eligibility, duties, and compensation are prescribed by law. He can be removed from office before the end of his term by a superior officer acting according to law. There must be sufficient cause to justify the removal, such as accepting bribes. If a person is wrongfully removed from his office, he may seek reinstatement.

A *military officer* is an individual who holds a position of authority in the armed services. An *officer of a corporation* is an individual—such as the president, vice president, treasurer, or secretary—whose chief duties are to oversee the operation of the business.

officer of the court A court employee, such as a judge, clerk, sheriff, marshal, bailiff, or constable. A lawyer is also an officer of the court and must obey court rules.

offset See COUNTERCLAIM.

of record Entered on the proper formal records. For example, the attorney of record is the one whose name appears on the court's records as the principal lawyer in the case. A MORTGAGE is of record when entered in the proper records of the clerk of the county in which the mortgaged property is located.

ombudsman A person who acts as a government's complaint bureau and has the power to investigate official misconduct, help fix wrongs committed by the government, and, sometimes, prosecute the wrongdoers.

omnibus Containing two or more separate and independent things. An omnibus bill is a piece of LEGISLATION concerning two or more entirely different subjects.

on demand Immediately. A promissory note payable on demand, for example, means that it is to be paid as soon as payment is requested by the person who has legal possession of the note. See COMMERCIAL PAPER.

on or about Approximately; a legal phrase used to avoid being bound to a more precise statement than the law requires. For example, when you buy a house, the date of the closing—when legal title and possession of the house are transferred from the seller to the buyer—is usually scheduled "on or about" a certain date. This phrase indicates that the parties realize the exact date might not be mutually convenient but that the transfer should be completed as closely as practicable to that date.

open As a legal term, make accessible or available. For example, to open a judgment is to prevent it from being final in order to reexamine the case in which it was handed down. The court officer or bailiff formally opens the court by announcing that its session has begun.

open-end credit A revolving account that allows a person to pay each month only part of the total amount that he owes. This type of credit is often used with bank and department store credit cards.

open-end mortgage A MORTGAGE agreement in which additional amounts of money may be borrowed under the same agreement.

opening statement The statement made by the attorney for each side at the start of a trial. Its purpose is to advise the jury of the issues involved and to give a general picture of the facts so that the jury will be able to understand the evidence.

open shop A shop where both union and nonunion workers are employed. See LABOR RELATIONS.

operation of law The manner in which a person acquires rights, and sometimes liabilities, without any act of his own. For example, when a person dies without a will, his heirs inherit the property by operation of the laws of DESCENT AND DISTRIBUTION.

opinion 1 A judge's statement of the decision he has reached regarding a case tried before him, setting forth the law and the reasons upon which he based the judgment. 2 A document prepared by an attorney for his client, containing the attorney's understanding of the law as it applies to the facts submitted to him. 3 Testimony that discloses what a witness in a lawsuit believes or concludes about the facts in dispute, rather than his objective personal knowledge of the facts themselves. See EVIDENCE.

option A form of CONTRACT that is an offer to enter into a future contract, coupled with the promise to hold the offer open for a given period of time. It is distinct from the future contract.

EXAMPLE A land speculator learns that a corporation is thinking of relocating on a particular 20-acre parcel of land, which it does not yet own. Knowing that if the corporation decides to relocate it will pay a high price for the land, the speculator tells the landowner that he is interested in purchasing the land at $5,000 per acre but that he will need six months to raise the purchase money. The speculator suggests that he and the landowner enter into an option agreement in which he will pay the landowner $10,000 to keep open for six months an offer to sell him the 20 acres at $5,000 per acre. If the landowner agrees, then he and the speculator have entered into an option contract. During the six-month period the landowner cannot sell the property to another buyer. If within the six-month period the speculator notifies the landowner that he accepts his offer and agrees to purchase the 20 acres, a second contract is formed. If the speculator does not pick up his option to buy the land within the six-month period, he forfeits his $10,000 and the landowner can sell to anyone. Another name for an option contract is an irrevocable offer.

oral contract   See CONTRACTS.

order   See MOTIONS AND ORDERS.

ordinance   A rule or regulation enacted by a municipal legislative body, such as a city council. Examples include regulations relating to snow removal, parking, and littering.

organic   Relating to the fundamental law or constitution of a state or nation, written or unwritten, that defines and establishes the organization of its government.

original jurisdiction   The power of a court to take a new lawsuit, try it, and hand down a judgment on the law and the facts. It is distinguished from appellate jurisdiction, the power to hear and judge an appeal. See COURTS.

origination fee   A charge imposed by a bank or some other lending institution for the processing of a loan.

For example, you apply for a mortgage loan of $40,000. The bank agrees to the loan and charges you an origination fee of 1 percent, or $400, in addition to the applicable interest on the loan.

orphan   Any person, particularly a minor, who has lost both parents. See GUARDIAN AND WARD.

overdraft   The drawing out by check of more money than one has on deposit in a bank account. See BANKS AND BANKING.

overrule   Supersede, make void, or reject by a later action or decision. A judicial decision is overruled when the same court or a higher court in the same system hands down a later judgment directly opposite to the earlier decision on the same question of law. The later decision deprives the earlier decision of all authority as precedent. See APPEAL AND ERROR. A judge overrules an objection made by an attorney during the course of a trial when, for example, he rejects his objection to the introduction of particular evidence.

overt   Open; manifest; public. In CRIMINAL LAW, an overt act is one that directly moves a person closer to the commission of a crime than an act of preparation or planning. For example, breaking a window in order to enter and burglarize a building is an overt act in the advancement of that crime.

oyer and terminer   An Anglo-French phrase meaning to hear and determine. The name "court of oyer and terminer" is often used as the title, or part of the title, of a state court with criminal jurisdiction over felonies.

oyez   (Anglo-French) "Hear ye." Cried out three times in some courtrooms to command attention at the start of a session. The word is pronounced "Oh, yes!"

pander **1** Pimp; cater to the gratification of another's lust. **2** Entice or induce a female—by promises, threats, fraud, or trick—to enter into the practice of prostitution. **3** Detain a female, for the purpose of sexual intercourse, on pretense of marriage. **4** As a noun, the person who caters to the lust of others, such as a PIMP or procurer.

panel **1** A jury list including either all persons summoned as jurors for the entire term of court or all those selected for a particular case. **2** A group of judges (less than the entire court) who decide a case.

paper A written or printed document, or instrument; a document filed or introduced in evidence in court, as in the phrases "papers in the case" and "papers on appeal." Letters, memoranda, books of account, and promissory notes are also papers.

par Face value. If, for example, a $2,000 municipal bond sells on the market for exactly $2,000 (and not for more or less), it is said to be going "at par."

paralegal A person who is not a lawyer but who needs some legal skills to do his job. Many people who work for attorneys, such as legal secretaries or assistants, are paralegals, as are many who do legally related work for government agencies.

parcener A joint heir; a person who, together with one or more other individuals, inherits property. Collectively, the joint heirs are called *coparceners*.

pardon An act of grace from the U.S. President or a state governor saving an individual from punishment that the law prescribes for a crime he has committed. It is the private, although official, act of the chief executive of the nation or of a state. There is no right to a pardon.

A pardon may be full or partial, absolute or conditional. It is *full* when it freely and unconditionally absolves the person from all legal consequences of his conviction for a crime. A pardon is *partial* when it absolves the person from only a portion of the legal consequences of his crime. It is *absolute* if it frees the criminal without any condition what-

soever. A pardon is *conditional* if it is effective only when one or more requirements are met.

Amnesty is a general pardon of people charged with some, usually political, offense. It is most often issued on behalf of a group of people who are subject to trial but not yet convicted. Following the end of American hostilities in Vietnam, a Presidential Proclamation of Amnesty relating to draft evaders was declared.

■ **Nature of the power to pardon** The power to pardon is a sovereign one, which is inherent in the state. Most states have constitutional provisions permitting the governor to exercise this power. Under Article 2 of the U.S. Constitution, the President is given power to grant pardons for offenses against the United States, except in cases of impeachment.

The pardoning power cannot be exercised by, or delegated to, a person other than the possessor of the power. Thus, a pardoning board has only advisory power.

Except when constitutional provisions exclude treason or impeachment, the pardoning power extends to almost all criminal offenses. Although the governor's power does not extend to violations of city ordinances, the constitution may confer the authority on a mayor to pardon persons convicted of such violations. The power to pardon does not include the authority to prevent sentencing or to grant relief against an order or judgment in a civil proceeding.

The power to pardon is exercised on the ground that the public welfare will be promoted just as well by lifting the sentence as by carrying it out. The power may also be used to correct an injustice, as when facts are discovered after a case has been decided that convince the pardoning authority that the convicted person is not guilty. Pardons have been granted, for instance, in cases in which it appeared that the person had been judged on the color of his skin, rather than on his conduct.

■ **Essentials** A written document, signed by the chief executive and authenticated by the seal of his office, is the usual form in which a pardon is granted. No particular wording is necessary. Delivery and acceptance are essential. Delivery is often made directly to the person pardoned, but it can also be made to his attorney or to someone else acting for him. Sometimes a pardon is delivered to the officer having custody of the prisoner.

■ **Effect** Because the essence of a pardon is forgiveness, a pardon implies guilt. It has no retroactive operation. It offers no relief from the injury suffered from imprisonment.

Recital of a specific offense in a pardon limits its operation to that one offense. Other violations of law, for which separate penalties are prescribed, remain unaffected.

In general, a pardoned individual is relieved of all legal disabilities based on his conviction. A full pardon restores to the offender the civil rights that customarily belong to a citizen, including the right to vote, the right to serve on a jury, and the right to be a witness. In cases where a public office has been forfeited because of a criminal conviction, a subsequent pardon does not automatically restore the individual to office, although it has been held that a pardon does restore the offender's eligibility to hold public office.

EXAMPLE In 1974 President Gerald Ford pardoned former
O⊷✳ President Richard M. Nixon for his alleged role in the Watergate scandal and its subsequent cover-up. Much controversy surrounded this pardon because Nixon had not even been indicted for a crime. The Constitution gives the President the power to pardon only for "Offences against the United States, except in Cases of Impeachment." It was argued that President Ford did not have the authority to grant the pardon, but no serious challenge was made to it in the interests of public welfare.

If the privilege of practicing a profession has been lost owing to a criminal conviction, a pardon does not restore that privilege. Eligibility to resume practicing a profession must be ruled on by state licensing authorities, such as a state's bar association in the case of attorneys.

■ **Conditions** Pardons are often granted with conditions. The objective of issuing a pardon with attached conditions is to aid in reforming the individual. The conditions are essential parts of the pardon and, to be operative, must be clearly stated in the document.

Various conditions have been held proper, including those requiring that the person pardoned leave the state or be deported from the United States and not return. A pardon may be granted on condition that the person pay a specified sum of money to reimburse the state for expenses incurred in his trial. Other proper conditions include that the pardoned person remain a law-abiding citizen, that he shall not again be convicted for violation of the penal laws, or that he shall be continuously confined to an institution for the care of the insane.

In most states, a pardon is not illegal because its conditions must be observed beyond the time in which the sentence would have been served. But in some, no conditions can extend beyond the term of the sentence. A conditional pardon can be rejected, but once a prisoner accepts it, he is bound by its conditions or risks having it declared void.

■ **Time of granting** When there are no constitutional restrictions, the power to pardon may be exercised at any time after the offense is committed—before or during legal proceedings, after conviction, and even after the offender has suffered the punishment for his crime. In a number of states, however, the governor may grant a pardon only after conviction.

■ **Procedures** Most jurisdictions have laws that state the proper time to apply for a pardon and require notice of the application to be published. A request for pardon should contain only the facts and arguments that would influence a person of ordinary mind and judgment. For example, the question of whether a convict is insane in a degree that would make the death penalty unjust or inexpedient will merit consideration.

■ **Proof** Proof of a pardon can be shown in court by producing the document itself or a certified copy. In some jurisdictions a certified copy can be used only on proof of loss of the original. A pardon can be proved by oral testimony only if it is shown that the original was lost and a certified copy cannot be produced. See COMMUTATION; PAROLE; REPRIEVE.

parens patriae (Latin) "Parent of the country"; referring to the state's sovereign power of guardianship over persons legally unable to act for themselves, such as INFANTS (minors), INSANE PERSONS, or citizens without the power to sue the state. See SOVEREIGN IMMUNITY.

The concept of *parens patriae* comes from the English legal system. Certain duties and powers were retained by the king in his capacity as "father of the country" and were known as the royal prerogative. Traditionally, this meant the king's power as guardian of persons who were legally unable to act. In America, the royal prerogative of the king passed to the states, where it has been greatly expanded. For example, early in the century, the Supreme Court held that the state of Missouri could sue the state of Illinois, as well as a Chicago sanitation district, on behalf of Missouri citizens to protect them from the discharge of sewage into the Mississippi River.

parent and child A father or mother and his or her offspring. The relationship of parent and child is entitled to special legal consideration because it fulfills the important need of protecting and nurturing dependent persons. This article discusses (1) the legal relationship of the parent and the child, (2) constitutional protections, (3) the rights and obligations concerning custody of a minor child, (4) support obligations of either parent or child, (5) the child's earnings and services, (6) wrongful death and wrongful life actions (lawsuit), (7) parental authority, (8) the liability of the parent for the injuries or property damage caused by the child, (9) emancipation of the child, and (10) the parental responsibilities of other persons or institutions *(in loco parentis)*. For other information, see ADOPTION OF PERSONS; DIVORCE; FAMILY; GUARDIAN AND WARD.

■ **Parent and child relationship** A parent, in the narrowest sense, can be only a natural mother or father, whether the child is legitimate or not. Statutes now generally give as many rights and responsibilities to adoptive parents as to natural parents, but not usually to stepmothers or stepfathers or anyone else taking the place of a natural parent. A foster parent or foster-care agency has the legal responsibility to care for and supervise a child, but neither enjoys the full legal status of a parent.

A child is one's offspring, or issue. A *posthumous child* is one born after his father's death. He can inherit from his father as if he had been alive at the time of his father's death. For other purposes, a child is not entitled to his full legal rights unless and until he is born alive. In law, a fetus is not considered a child.

A legitimate child is one whose parents are married to each other, and an illegitimate child is one whose parents are not. In the past the legal term "bastard" was used for an illegitimate child, but it is now being replaced by the term "nonmarital child." A reference to one's "children" in a legal document may or may not be interpreted to include illegitimate and adopted children, depending on the law of the particular state.

The word "child" may be used in the more limited sense of a person below the legal age of majority, but for that purpose the law usually uses the more precise term "infant" or "minor." See INFANT. A judge may call a very young child a child of tender years, meaning that he is most in need of a mother's care. This is called the tender-years doctrine, a principle used in some states to help resolve custody battles between parents.

The law presumes that the relationship of parent and child exists when a parent acknowledges it or lives with and rears the child. It continues as long as both live, unless extraordinary circumstances require that the law intervene. The relationship cannot be destroyed by an outsider unless circumstances require it and proper legal procedures are followed. A parent and child cannot change or dissolve their relationship either individually or by agreement.

As a general rule, a parent has the right to have custody of his child and to control and direct him, and is obligated to nurture and care for him. The child has the right to receive from a parent the care necessary for his well-being, and must submit to reasonable supervision. In addition, the state has an obligation to protect the stability of families and to make sure that children are properly cared for. The extent to which a state may regulate the parent-child relationship is limited by the family's right to be left alone.

The obligations of a parent go beyond merely furnishing daily necessities. A court may reasonably expect a parent to share mutual love and affection with the child and to provide not only for his maintenance but also for his education, social and religious training, and medical care. A parent must discipline his child when necessary, and the child must obey his parent. The parental duty requires an active effort to demonstrate love and concern for the child and not just a passive acceptance of a financial obligation.

■ **Constitutional protections** The laws regulating the relationship of parent and child are primarily state laws, limited by the requirements of both federal and state constitutions. The Supreme Court has held that a number of U.S. constitutional provisions safeguard the integrity of the parental relationship and the rights of parent and child.

HOW THE LAW PROTECTS THE PARENT-CHILD RELATIONSHIP

■ A parent has a right to the custody and control of his child—and the obligation to nurture and rear the child. If parents do not live together, the custodial parent supervises daily care, but the noncustodial parent is usually entitled to be informed about major events in the child's life. In case of a dispute on custody arrangements, the courts have the power to rule. The mother of an illegitimate child has a primary right to custody of her child.

■ The mother's duty to support her child was secondary to that of the father under the common law and arose only if the father was dead, missing, or incapable of supporting the child. This is still the law in many states. In other states, mothers and fathers are equally liable.

■ The father of an illegitimate child must contribute support even if he has never lived with the child.

■ All states require divorced fathers to support children not in their custody, and some states impose the same obligation on noncustodial mothers.

■ Many states require a stepfather to support his wife's children if they live with him.

■ In some states, parents must support a mentally or physically impaired child who is incapable of earning a living, no matter what the child's age.

■ In some states, a child must support a parent who otherwise would be on welfare—unless it is clear that the parent did not take care of the child when he was underage.

■ Many states hold a parent, child, or other relative liable for the cost of keeping a person in a state institution or mental hospital, but the amount ordered is usually based on the person's ability to pay rather than on the actual cost of the care provided.

■ Under the common law, a father is entitled to his child's earnings. Some states have changed this law by giving the primary right to a parent who has custody or by giving both parents an equal right to the child's wages.

■ The services a parent may claim from a child range from making tea to working in the family business.

■ Parents are free to make their own decisions regarding a child's welfare as long as they do not violate minimal standards concerning compulsory school attendance, child abuse, neglect, or dependency.

■ A child has no right to resist moderate punishment, whether it is a tongue-lashing or physical blows—but

the right to use corporal punishment is limited, and the law will step in if parents abuse their children.

■ Under the common law, a parent is not liable for personal injuries or property damage caused by his child unless he encourages the child to cause the harm. If a child beats up another child at his father's suggestion, for example, the father is liable.

■ Nearly all of the states have enacted laws holding parents liable for harm caused by their children up to amounts ranging from $250 to $3,000, depending on the state. Some of these laws cover property damage but not personal injuries and apply only to children between certain ages, such as 12 to 18.

■ Emancipation is the legal event by which the child gains the independence of adulthood. A child may not emancipate himself by running away or defying discipline, but parent and child can agree that it is time for the young one to depart and make his way in the world. From that point on, the parent surrenders his right to custody and control, and the child is on his own. Emancipation can also happen as a result of joining the military, getting married, or taking a full-time job.

Several constitutional rights protect the privacy of a person's decision about bearing a child. Both married and unmarried individuals are entitled to learn about methods of contraception and to obtain birth-control devices. A woman of any age has the right to seek an ABORTION in the first three months of pregnancy, free from interference by the government, her husband, or her parents. Between the third and the seventh month the state may control access to abortions, but may not prohibit them entirely.

The Supreme Court has handled the question of sexual sterilization with great care because it can rarely be undone. The right to bear children is so fundamental that the state cannot force a person to submit to a sterilization operation unless the reasons are compelling and then only if a fair procedure is followed. For example, a state may order involuntary sterilization of criminals or INSANE PERSONS if the law is administered equally and with DUE PROCESS OF LAW. It is not fair to force a welfare applicant to submit to sterilization in order to qualify for relief, because the capacity to become a parent cannot be made to depend on one's wealth. The personal and private character of the decision to become or not to become a parent gives individuals the right to seek voluntary sexual sterilization if they want. A state cannot make sterilization illegal.

■ **Custody of a minor child**   Ordinarily, parents have a natural and legal right to the custody of their minor children. The Supreme Court has declared this a constitutionally protected right. It means that a parent cannot be brought into court without cause and forced to justify his notions of child rearing. A parent does not have to be perfect. Courts generally presume that the welfare of a child is best served by preserving the natural ties of mother or father and child. The state must not interfere with a parent's judgment unless it is clear that a child is in danger.

If two parents do not live together, there is a question of where their children will live. One parent may agree to give up custody to the other without forfeiting any other parental rights. The custodial parent supervises the daily care of the children, but the noncustodial parent is usually entitled to be informed about major events in a child's life, to see the child regularly, and to seek a change in the custody arrangements if circumstances warrant it.

Parental custody disputes   If two separated or divorced parents cannot agree to custody arrangements, a court will resolve the dispute. Some states provide by law that neither parent is entitled to be preferred, and custody must be given to whichever parent is more suitable. Many states still follow the "tender years" rule, which places custody of young children with their mother unless she is proved to be unfit. A few states give preference to the father when children reach their teens. Most courts, however, will inquire into the actual circumstances of the case and decide accordingly. See CUSTODY.

Nonparental custody disputes   A custody dispute does not always involve two parents. It may involve one parent and someone who is not a parent. The nonparent challenging a parent's claim for custody is frequently a grandparent, uncle, foster parent, stepparent, or person seeking to adopt the child. The question may arise when a custodial parent dies, abandons the child, or becomes unable to care for him.

The rule is that a parent has more right to custody than a nonparent. He does not have to prove that he is fit, but the person disputing the parent's right to custody must make a substantial case against him. A parent may even surrender custody without losing his right to reclaim it. For example, a widower left his daughters with their grandparents while he went to Alaska to look for work, but he did not forfeit his right to recover custody when he was able to make a home for them. However, a parent can forfeit his right to custody by leaving his child in someone else's care and failing to maintain parental ties.

Abandonment   An abandonment must be almost total for it to overcome the parent's natural right to custody. Different states have different rules for determining when an abandonment is serious enough to cut off the parent's natural right to have custody. Some states will not interfere until the abandonment has persisted for a specified period of time. Some states follow the *flicker of interest rule,* which holds that a parent has not abandoned his child as long as he shows even a flicker of interest in his welfare. A more moderate approach is to find that a parent has abandoned his child when he demonstrates a desire to be rid of all the obligations of a parent. A state that uses this standard permits its courts to find a case of abandonment even when the parent shows fleeting interest in the child.

Custody of illegitimate children   Custody rights are not the same for parents of children born out of wedlock. See ILLEGITIMACY. The unwed mother of an illegitimate child has a primary right to custody of her child. The father cannot defeat this right because he has not married the mother. In 1972, however, the U.S. Supreme Court held that the father of an illegitimate child is not entirely without rights.

EXAMPLE   A man and a woman had been living together in Illinois for 18 years without being married. When the woman died, the couple's three children were made wards of the state. The Supreme Court held that the man who had sired and raised the children was entitled to a hearing before custody of his children was taken away. This case dealt only with the right of an illegitimate father against a nonparent.

■ **Support obligations**   A parent is generally obligated to pay for the support of a minor child. This obligation covers not only the minimum essentials of food, clothing, and shelter, but also education and medical and dental care. A parent who cannot support his child is excused, but he must show sincere efforts to obtain employment.

A parent who lives with his child will not be told what to buy the child as long as he provides necessary items and maintains a standard of living above the level set by neglect and dependency laws. Courts are traditionally reluctant to interfere in family matters, so a parent may rear his child as he sees fit. He does not necessarily owe the child the best life-style he can afford.

Under the common law, the father had a duty to support his child. A poor father had to devote whatever funds were available to the support of his children and had to actively seek and accept employment. The father had to maintain his children even if the mother or the child himself had more than enough resources of her or his own. If the parents separated, the father's obligation continued unless the mother took the child and left without a good legal cause. As long as he was ready to take back the child and support him under his own roof, the father could not be compelled to pay support money to the mother. The same principle applied to a child who abandoned his father's home. A mother's duty to support her child was secondary to that of the father under the common law. It arose only if the father was dead, incapable of furnishing support, or missing.

This is still the law in many states. In other states, a statute makes the mother and father equally liable. Equally does not mean that each must supply the same dollar amount. It means that each must provide according to his or her own ability under all the circumstances of the case and with consideration of the noneconomic contributions to the care of the child.

A parent may be forced to repay someone who has provided essential things for the support of his child. For example, the father of a severely handicapped girl was required to send regular support payments to the state institution that cared for her. Fathers generally must repay money advanced by social welfare agencies for the support of their children.

Use of the child's funds   Because the primary duty to support a child rests on the parents, they have no right to use money that belongs to their child (except for wages, as explained below), even for the child's support. For example, an inheritance a child receives or money damages he recovers in a personal injury lawsuit may have to be set aside in a special bank account and held for him until he reaches the legal age of majority. A parent may petition the court to release a certain sum of money occasionally to help with the child's expenses, but courts are extremely reluctant to approve these requests. As one court has said, the child is entitled to have his property handed over to him when he reaches the age of majority and not to receive "a bundle of court orders" instead. A fund can be used when circumstances demand it, however. If the fund is large enough and the requested amount too small to make much difference or if the need is very great—life-saving surgery for the child, for example—then it is appropriate for the court to release funds. It is also proper to release money for the support of a child who otherwise would be drawing public money from a welfare program.

Child living apart   A parent does not escape his obligation to support his child just because the child does not live with him. The identified father of an illegitimate child must contribute to the child's support even if he has never lived with the child. All states require divorced fathers to support a child not in their custody, and some states impose the same obligation on noncustodial mothers. The level of support usually depends on the parent's ability to pay and the amount necessary to cover the child's needs. In some cases this formula produces a greater obligation than the law fixes on a parent in an intact family, but it is intended to protect the child from the financial burdens of his parents' divorce. In fact, children of divorced parents generally do not fare as well financially as the children of parents who stay married.

Child who has a child   The parent's obligation to support a minor child may continue even if that child has his or her own illegitimate child.

EXAMPLE   A 17-year-old daughter lived with her parents after she had an illegitimate child. Since the daughter was not yet an adult, her parents had to continue supporting her. She was able to collect welfare payments on behalf of her baby, however, because her parents were not legally obligated to support their grandchild.

On the other hand, parents are not responsible for the support of a married child, whatever the age, because marriage makes a child a legal adult.

Support by stepfathers   Ordinarily, no one is required to support a child not related to him, but in many states a stepfather must support his wife's children if they live with him. In other states, if the children's natural father is not contributing to their support and if the stepfather does not adopt them, they might be entitled to receive welfare benefits. Laws making stepfathers responsible recognize that the family is functioning as a regular family unit that cannot get welfare, and thus remove a reason not to adopt the children.

Adult child   Under the common law, a parent is not required to support an adult child, nor does an adult child have to support his parent or grandparent. This means, for example, that a hospital or nursing home cannot sue the child for payment when care is given to an aging or infirm parent. The parent is relieved of responsibility for a handicapped child when he reaches the age of majority, and a noncustodial parent can stop making child-support payments when the child reaches legal adulthood—even if the child is still in high school. A parent or child who does more than the law requires under these circumstances is considered a volunteer. Therefore, a child who pays expenses for the parent cannot insist on a contribution from brothers or sisters, and a custodial parent who continues to support an adult child who is in school cannot force a noncustodial parent to help.

These circumstances can be changed by an agreement that will be enforced as a contract. For example, a divorced parent may have obligated himself by signing a separation agreement to pay the expenses of a college education or to support a child until his full-time education ceases. A parent may leave the family home to the one child who cares for him rather than dividing his estate among all his children. As long as these agreements are legally sufficient—in writing whenever necessary, clear in their terms, and not the product of fraud or duress—they are binding. The agreement does not have to be between parent and child. A child, for example, may sign a hospital form agreeing to be legally responsible for his parent's expenses, and the hospital can enforce this agreement. Most families, however, give care and attention to aging parents or adult children without involving legal processes.

Relatives   A number of states have changed the common-law rule by enacting statutes making people financially responsible for poor relatives. Some statutes require a parent to support a mentally or physically impaired child who is incapable of earning a livelihood—no matter what the child's age. Some statutes require a child to support a parent who otherwise would be able to collect welfare benefits unless it is clear that the parent did not care for the child when he was below the age of majority. States frequently go to great lengths to find a relative who is liable for a deceased person's funeral expenses. In one case, a court ordered funeral expenses for a parent paid from a fund held for a minor child when there was no one other than the child who could pay. This is an unusual departure from the strong policy of preserving a child's property for him until he grows up. Many states will hold a parent, child, or other relative liable for the cost of keeping a person in a state institution or mental hospital, but the amount of support ordered is usually based on the relative's ability to pay rather than the actual cost of care provided.

These statutes putting financial responsibility on a relative differ widely from state to state, and they are quite controversial. A frequent case under one of these laws involves a destitute parent or child who collects welfare payments. The social services agency locates a relative who is legally responsible for the recipient's support and sues the relative for reimbursement of the public funds paid out. The theory is that needy persons ought to burden their families instead of society. As appealing as this is to taxpayers, it has been strongly criticized because it usually affects poor people, embarrassing the dependent and straining family ties.

■ **Earnings and services of a child** Under the common law a father is entitled to his child's earnings. The mother cannot claim them unless the father is dead or has abandoned the child. Some states have changed this law by giving the primary right to a parent who has custody or by giving both parents an equal right to the child's wages.

Because this right grows out of the parent's duty to support and care for the child, it can be forfeited by a parent who neglects or abandons the child. The child may only keep wages the parent wants him to keep. An employer may be required to pay a child's earnings directly to the parent, but most states require a parent to notify the employer that this is what he wants done. Under such a statute, an employer is protected from having to pay twice if he has already given the money to the child because the parent failed to notify him.

The services a parent may claim from a child range from preparing a cup of tea to working in the family business. The issue generally arises when the parent sues someone who has injured the child and claims money damages for medical expenses and "loss of services." Many courts assume that a parent has been deprived of the child's services when the child is injured; so the parent does not have to prove each chore the child performs, how often he performs it, or what it is worth to the parent. This makes it proper for a parent to recover for loss of services even when a baby has been injured.

■ **Wrongful death and wrongful life** A child has the right to sue anyone who causes the death of his parent. This kind of lawsuit is a WRONGFUL-DEATH ACTION. Courts have had difficulty calculating the financial loss to a parent as the result of the death of a child. Since minors generally do not contribute substantially to the family income, their economic value to the family is questionable. Usually, the parent cannot recover for the emotional harm caused by the loss of a child.

In 1963 an illegitimate child sued his father for the harm caused by being born to parents not married to each other. The Illinois Appellate Court decided against allowing the lawsuit, speculating that it might encourage actions for other causes, such as being born into a poor family, being a certain color, or being born with a hereditary disease. Recently, plaintiffs objecting to the birth of a child have been suing physicians who mishandled an abortion or sterilization operation and pharmacists who dispensed the wrong pills. Many people are starting to call these *wrongful-life* actions. Some courts refuse to hear these suits on the ground that being born must be considered better than not being born, but a growing number of courts have begun to weigh the pleasure a child gives his parents against the cost of raising him. They take into account the degree of negligence on the defendant's part, and Michigan has refused to accept as a defense a defendant's claim that an unwilling mother should have had an abortion or given up her child for adoption.

■ **Parental authority** Historically, the authority of a parent—or, more accurately, of the father—over a child was absolute. Ancient Roman law even gave the father the power of life and death over his children. Today parents are free to make their own decisions regarding a child's welfare as long as they do not violate the minimal standards of law concerning compulsory school attendance, child abuse, neglect, or dependency. Because the parent is obligated to provide a home for the child, the parent is entitled to select a suitable one and the child must move when required to do so. A child has no right to resist moderate punishment, whether it consists of a tongue-lashing or physical blows, but the right to use corporal punishment does not include malicious abuse. A parent may neither force a minor daughter to have an abortion nor prevent her from having it.

Medical care The parent's authority over the child gives him the right and the duty to supervise medical care.
EXAMPLE In one case, a court refused to overturn the decision of parents of seven-year-old twins to allow a kidney to be transplanted from one child to the other. The court noted that a kidney from a twin was more physiologically compatible than a transplant from any other donor and that the outlook for good health and long life for both children after the operation was excellent. In a less compelling case, another court would not allow a mother to consent to the sexual sterilization of her 15-year-old son who suffered "borderline" mental retardation.

A parent who callously ignores a child's health is very likely guilty of criminal neglect. Where essential medical care is not obtained, authorities will begin proceedings to insure care for the child and suitable disciplining of the parent. It is troublesome to decide what to do for a child whose parent is concerned with his health but refuses treatment on religious grounds. In a life-threatening emergency, a court may give permission for doctors to treat a child without a parent's consent, but a far more difficult legal problem occurs when a parent refuses important but not really life-saving medical treatment.

EXAMPLE In one case, a sharply divided New York appeals court refused to order corrective surgery for a 14-year-old boy with a harelip. Doctors testified that while there was little risk in performing the operation, chances for satisfactory results diminished as the child grew older. The boy's father refused to consent, not for religious reasons but because he believed that natural forces had a healing power and should be allowed to take their course. The majority of the judges decided not to interfere because the boy did not want the treatment and he was old enough to have his opinion considered. Moreover, his cooperation in speech therapy after surgery would be essential. The strong dissent argued that a child should not make a decision that would seriously affect his social and working life in the future, especially a child overly influenced by a strong-willed father.

Education   Parental authority includes a wide discretion to supervise the education of the child, but the freedom is not absolute. The right of the state to require education of the child is firmly established. Most states require school attendance for children between 7 and 16 years of age, and some states require attendance for 6-year-olds, 17-year-olds, and 18-year-olds as well.

Two landmark Supreme Court decisions have set constitutional limits to the state's power to compel school attendance. In 1925 the court held that a state may insist on adequate education, but it must permit parents to send their children to private schools if they choose.

ᒪᒪ The fundamental theory of liberty upon which all governments in this union repose excludes any general power of the state to standardize its children by forcing them to accept instruction from public teachers only."

In 1972 the Supreme Court ruled that Wisconsin's compulsory school attendance law cannot be applied to Amish parents who refused to send their children to school after the eighth grade. Expert testimony showed that the Amish religion would not survive if these children were forced to go to school beyond the eighth grade. Chief Justice Warren Burger compared the parents' interest in supervising their children's religious training with the state's interest in making sure everyone receives an education. He found that the harm to the state's interest in this case was so insignificant that the law should step aside for these parents.

Violations   A parent who fails to fulfill his responsibilities or who abuses his authority is committing a crime. A parent who fails to make sure that his child attends school regularly can be convicted for violating the compulsory attendance law. Criminal nonsupport or abandonment laws in many states make it illegal for a parent to fail to provide for his child. In addition, the person or agency that has provided necessary support can sue the parent to recover the cost of services and supplies. A person who has custody or guardianship of the child can start an action asking the court to set a suitable amount of support for the child and require the noncustodial parent to pay regularly.

■ **Parental liability**   Under the common law, a parent is not responsible for injuries caused by his minor child, whether accidental or intentional, unless the parent himself is somehow to blame. The general rule is that a parent must take extra precautions if there is reason to believe that the child has vicious propensities (attacking another without provocation). A parent should never trust such a child with a dangerous article. Under this rule, a parent is not obliged to supervise a child constantly or to guarantee that the child will never cause trouble. Whether the child has shown himself to be dangerous enough to warrant extraordinary care depends on the facts of the case. For example, parents

were not held responsible when their three-year-old struck a pedestrian with his tricycle because there was no evidence that the child habitually used his tricycle in an unusual, intentionally harmful, or other wrongful manner. In another case, a court found that it was inconceivable that parents could "vacuum-pack" their 20-year-old daughter and absolutely prevent her from breaking up another woman's marriage.

Certainly parents are responsible if they aid or encourage the harm caused by a child. A father who armed his son with a baseball bat and told him to go out and "teach that kid a lesson" was liable for the injuries caused, as was another father who stood close by and told his child how to thrash another boy and when to quit. In a different case, a father was not held responsible for a rape attempted by his 15-year-old son even though he had on several occasions in front of witnesses told the boy "how to be a man."

Arming a child with anything that is normally considered dangerous makes the parent liable under the common law to other people if injuries result. For example, a mother who gave her 10-year-old son an air gun, a father who permitted his 11-year-old son to operate a forklift, and a mother who gave her son candles to use in a tent could all be responsible for injuries caused to their children's playmates.

Limited-liability statutes   The common-law rule, by generally exempting parents from liability for injuries caused by their children, has created a situation in which the full burden of juvenile carelessness or mischief falls on the victim. The parent is not responsible and the child is not likely to have any money of his own to pay for damages. The unfairness of this situation has prompted nearly all of the states to enact laws holding parents liable for harm caused by their children up to a certain dollar limit, ranging from $200 to $5,000, depending on the state. The statutes vary from state to state. Some cover property damage but not personal injuries and apply only to children between certain ages, such as 12 to 18. See Chart 5.

Child as an agent   A special rule makes a parent liable for injuries caused by his child when the child acts as an agent for the parent—that is, a person authorized to represent him. A mother was held liable, for example, when she authorized her son to represent her in a business deal and he made fraudulent misrepresentations. About half the states have applied this principle to automobile accidents involving the family car.

This rule, called the FAMILY CAR DOCTRINE, makes the owner of an automobile responsible for any injuries caused by any driver in his family. If the car is generally made available to household members, then they are considered authorized representatives of the owner and he must pay for damages they cause. This doctrine has also been applied to a child's use of the family boat. See Chart 28.

In order to preserve family harmony many states have always refused to allow lawsuits between parents and children for injuries caused by carelessness. A growing minority of states, however, have abandoned this doctrine, especially in automobile accident cases where it seems unfair to let total strangers, but not close family members, collect from an insurance policy.

Other situations   Most states still consider a parent immune from lawsuits for acts involving an exercise of parental authority, especially where food, clothing, housing, medical treatment, or other care is concerned. As a rule, parents cannot be held liable to a child for injuries resulting from the parents' negligent supervision. The truth is that any parent can be made to feel he should have been more careful if his child is injured. It would then be a rare parent indeed who could not be brought into court if such lawsuits were allowed. This rule, though, has numerous exceptions, such as when the child is entrusted with a dangerous instrumentality—such as a car—or when the parent is actively negligent—for example, by letting a four-year-old play in a parking lot.

■ **Emancipation**   The legal event by which a child gains the independence of adulthood is known as emancipation. A child may not emancipate himself by running away from home or by defying parental discipline, but a parent and child can agree that the child may leave the parent's home and make his own way in the world. From that point on, the parent surrenders his right to the custody and control of the child, and the child assumes responsibility for his own support. Even if no words of agreement are spoken, the law will assume that the parent has emancipated his child when all the acts of the parent and child indicate that he has.

Certain events are often considered to constitute emancipation, such as joining the armed services, getting married, or taking a full-time job. A parent may be deemed to have emancipated his child by throwing him out of the house, refusing to establish and maintain a home for the child, or failing to provide money for his support. Even when factors like these are present, however, a parent cannot emancipate a minor child who is unable to support himself. An exception is made for the parent of a child who stubbornly refuses to live at home and submit to reasonable supervision. In that case, the minor usually forfeits his right to receive financial support from the parent.

EXAMPLE A drug-using daughter had borne the illegitimate O⊷⊶ child of a convicted criminal. She refused to return to her family home and chose to live on her own with the help of public assistance. A court refused to make the father reimburse social services for support given to the 20-year-old daughter, finding it "incomprehensible that a parent should be required to contribute toward support of a child where the child commits acts in total derogation of the relationship of parent and child."

Questions of emancipation frequently arise in cases where a child sues his parent for injuries caused by the parent's negligence. Many states follow the rule that parent and child are each immune from lawsuits brought by the other for personal injuries, but the rule does not apply to emancipated minors. After an accident, a family must prove to the insurance company that the child is emancipated even though he has not reached the age of majority. Children, even if they are living away from home, often try to prove that they are not emancipated when they want to collect support payments from a noncustodial divorced parent. Emancipation also may affect the validity of contracts or leases entered into by a minor.

■ **In loco parentis**   People other than natural parents may have some of the rights and responsibilities of a parent in certain circumstances. It is said that they stand *in loco parentis,* a Latin phrase meaning "in the place of a parent."

The general rule is that no one is responsible for a child's supervision or support except the natural or adoptive parent or someone who has contracted to care for the child. Whether the responsibilities of one who stands in the shoes of a parent exist depends on whether or not these obligations were intentionally undertaken. When they are, the role may be filled by an individual, a state agency, or a charitable institution. It is not necessary for the person or group to be given parental responsibilities by a court order in order to stand *in loco parentis.* A foster parent is usually *in loco parentis*—but not always, because he does not assume full legal responsibility for the child. Neither does a college stand *in loco parentis,* even if it does make and enforce certain rules of conduct for students.

parent corporation   A company that controls the policies of another through ownership of a majority of its shares of stock. See CORPORATION.

parol   Oral; expressed only by speech and not in writing. *Parol evidence,* for example, is verbal evidence—testimony given by witnesses before a court. Under the *parol evidence rule,* when parties put an agreement in writing, all previous oral agreements merge in the writing. This written CONTRACT cannot be modified by claims that before or at the signing of the contract different terms were orally agreed upon—unless fraud was used or a mistake was made in preparation of the written contract.

parole   The conditional release of a convict before his term in prison expires, subject to supervision during the remainder of the term and to a return to prison if he violates the conditions imposed. Parole is a correctional procedure authorizing a sentence to be served outside of prison.

Its purpose is to reform rather than to punish. It is intended as a means of restoring to society an offender who is a good social risk and to give him an opportunity to reform under the guidance of a parole officer. An additional purpose is to facilitate the offender's reintegration into society by the time his sentence has expired. The decision to grant parole in a particular case is based on a determination that the prisoner can live in society without violating the law.

States are not required by the U.S. Constitution to provide for the parole of prisoners, but they do have the power to grant parole and can stipulate the terms and conditions of parole. Parole may be granted only by the group or individual, such as a parole board or the governor, on whom the state has conferred the authority.

■ **Parole boards**   A parole board is an independent agency to which broad discretionary powers have been delegated in all matters relating to parole. It cannot, however, change a sentence imposed by a court unless, as sometimes happens, the paroling authority has been given the right to determine the original sentence. While a prisoner is incarcerated, the parole board generally has no jurisdiction (authority) over him, and it may not attempt to devise a treatment program.

If a prisoner is serving concurrent sentences that were imposed by different states, the rules of the parole authorities of the state in which he is serving the longer sentence govern. A state prisoner serving a state sentence is subject to state rather than federal parole authorities, even if he is incarcerated in a federal institution.

A parole board makes rules and regulations governing its procedures, within the limits of its statutory authority. Boards generally adopt and publish standards and guidelines for granting or denying parole based on the severity of the offense, characteristics of the offender, and other similar criteria. Guidelines, however, are only a statement of how the paroling authority generally exercises its discretion and are not the final word on parole eligibility.

■ **Eligibility for parole** Paroles may be granted only to those prisoners who are eligible under the applicable statute. Parole legislation may properly exclude particular classes of persons, such as multiple offenders, narcotics offenders, persons serving a life sentence, or persons condemned to death.

Under various statutes, a prisoner given a specific sentence can become eligible for parole after serving one-fourth, one-third, or one-half of his sentence, or a specific period of time, such as one year. A prisoner given an indeterminate sentence (a sentence for "not less than" so many years and "nor more than" so many years) must usually serve the minimum term of the sentence. Under some statutes, however, the prisoner may become eligible after serving a specified proportion of the minimum sentence, such as one-third.

Deductions from a prisoner's sentence fixed by statute for good behavior may be used in considering parole. Time spent awaiting trial or sentence may or may not be credited against a prisoner's sentence. It is constitutionally permissible for a prisoner in a county jail not to be given credit for presentence jail time, even though such credits are awarded to inmates of other correctional institutions. Under some statutes, the time of parole eligibility is included in the sentencing provisions made by the judge.

■ **Appropriateness for parole** A parole is a privilege, not a right. Therefore, the question of whether a prisoner shall be paroled is a matter for the discretion of the paroling authority, subject to the limitations imposed by law. The paroling authority does not have to grant parole simply because the prisoner has served enough time to be eligible.

The paroling authority must be guided in its decision by two basic considerations: Is there a basic reasonable possibility that the parolee will remain at liberty without violating the law, and is release compatible with the welfare of society? Particular factors considered are the prisoner's life history, habits, and traits; his physical, educational, vocational, and marital status; his mental condition; his age; the number of years of the term he has served; and his progress toward law-abiding conduct. Of course, the prisoner's criminal record, the nature and severity of the offense for which he is incarcerated, any escape or attempted escape, and any crime committed during his escape are also important factors in the decision.

■ **Proceedings** The proceedings to grant or withhold parole are usually informal and are not conducted like a trial, but they must be orderly and fair.

Application and notice Under some statutes the prisoner must apply for parole, but under others the parole board or officer must make a parole investigation when a prisoner has completed a prescribed portion of his sentence, with or without application.

Hearing A prisoner is entitled to a hearing on the question of his right to release on parole. A personal interview with the prisoner satisfies this requirement. A member of the parole board does not have to conduct the hearing—it may be held before a hearing examiner.

Although the federal Constitution's guarantee of DUE PROCESS OF LAW entitles a prisoner to a hearing, due process applies only to a limited extent. A potential parolee does not have the right to representation by a lawyer at the parole-release hearing. According to some state court decisions, the prisoner is not entitled (1) to present witnesses and documentary evidence in support of his release, (2) to confront and cross-examine witnesses or persons who have provided the paroling authority with adverse information, (3) to question the members of the paroling authority, or (4) to rebut information that weighs against his parole. Other decisions state that the applicant must be informed of the parole authority's reliance upon particular information and given an opportunity to dispute its accuracy.

A comprehensive and adequate record of the parole hearing should be kept for the purpose of judicial review—a review in court. When there is no statute requiring a transcript of a hearing with a copy for the prisoner, however, a court cannot order such a transcript.

Under parole regulations, a case may be reviewed in another hearing when new and significant information relating to the possibility of parole is received. In addition, the parole potential of a prisoner may be reconsidered periodically.

Reasons for denial In some states, a prisoner must be told why he was denied parole so that he can appropriately adjust his future conduct. A statement of the reasons must refer to parole eligibility criteria, precisely pinpoint the areas of concern that led to denial, and contain the essential facts the board used to reach its decision. The statement should enable the reviewing body to determine whether or not the paroling authority abused its discretion.

■ **Judicial review** Because the parole board has absolute discretion in determining whether to grant or deny parole, its decisions are not ordinarily subject to review by the courts. Due process of law does not require judicial review of a denial of parole when sufficient facts and reasons for the denial have been given to the prisoner. The purpose of a judicial review is only to determine whether the board abused its discretion, acted arbitrarily or capriciously, acted beyond the scope of its statutory authority, violated its own regulations, or denied constitutional rights. It is up to the prisoner to demonstrate that the parole board failed to follow the law in its consideration of parole.

■ **Parole conditions** In its discretion, the paroling authority can impose conditions on a parole as long as they are not unlawful, immoral, or impossible to perform. A parole does not become effective until it has been accepted by the prisoner, who has a right to accept it with its conditions or reject it. Ordinarily, the conditions should be established and communicated to the inmate at the time of parole so that he may accept or reject them. The trial court can recommend conditions, which may be accepted or rejected by the paroling authority.

Conditions must be reasonable, comprehensible, and not too broad. Generally, a parolee may be restricted to a particular community, job, or home at the discretion of his parole officer. He may also be restricted in his general lifestyle, such as his friendships or associations, or where he can travel. Leaving a particular state or even deportation is a proper condition. The paroling authority may require the parolee to have psychiatric treatment. A condition requiring that the time on parole be forfeited if parole is violated and the parolee is reincarcerated is valid.

■ **Operation and effect** Although a parole grants a convict partial liberty and freedom of movement, it does not change his status as a convict, and it does not operate as a discharge. A paroled prisoner, even though conditionally released from physical custody, remains in legal custody until the maximum term of his sentence expires. The paroling state does not lose jurisdiction by allowing a parolee to go to another state. He is still subject to the terms of his parole. A parole does not set aside, terminate, modify, or shorten the term imposed, and it does not restore the convict's civil rights.

Supervision and searches By accepting the privilege of parole, the prisoner in effect consents to the supervision that his parole officer must exercise over his person and property. Under the parole officer's authority to supervise and investigate, parolees are subject to searches that would not be permitted in ordinary situations, such as a search without a warrant or a search without probable cause. See SEARCH AND SEIZURE. Before he enters the parolee's home, however, the parole officer must make a demand for admittance, when the law so requires, and explain why he wishes to be admitted. A parolee's privacy may be invaded by his parole officer only to carry out the officer's supervising duties. A police officer cannot assume the function of parole supervision and interfere with the parolee's personal liberty, but a policeman may accompany a parole officer and help him search the parolee's person or property.

■ **Cancellation of authorized parole** A parole authority may reconsider and rescind (cancel) a grant of parole either before it becomes effective or before the actual release of the prisoner. According to some court decisions, a parole may be rescinded without a showing of cause on the ground that it has never become effective. Conversely, it has also been held that liberty cannot be denied without showing good cause, and that a prisoner whose parole date has been approved but who has not yet been released is entitled to notice and a hearing concerning the reasons for rescission. When compelling reasons are presented for it, a parolee should be granted the assistance of a lawyer at the parole-rescission hearing. For example, the fact that a prisoner is "dull-normal" in intelligence and has only a fourth-grade education entitles him to counsel because a low intelligence would prevent him from effectively developing his case.

■ **Discharge** A parolee must be discharged from parole when the time he has served in prison and on parole equals the time fixed by the sentence. Although a parolee has no right to be discharged from parole before the specified period expires, the paroling authority may grant him a final discharge from the conditions of his parole when it is believed the rehabilitation process is complete. In some cases the paroling authority may grant a parolee a discharge from parole itself before the end of the parole period.

Under some statutes, a discharge from parole before the entire sentence is served is a recognition of the full atonement for the crime. It terminates the sentence and is a remission of the remaining portion. Under other statutes, however, a discharge from parole does not terminate the sentence, and the former parolee remains under the jurisdiction of the paroling authority until the term of the original sentence has expired.

■ **Revocation of parole** Generally, parole may be revoked for a violation of one of the conditions imposed on the parolee. It may also be revoked if the parolee's continued presence in the community becomes dangerous to the public and incompatible with the welfare of society.

Specific grounds for revocation A parole may be revoked for acts committed by the parolee if he becomes insane. Parole is frequently revocable when the parolee is found with weapons in his possession or when he uses intoxicating liquors or narcotics, conceals his whereabouts, fails to report to the parole authority as required, associates with persons with criminal records, leaves a place where he has been ordered to remain, or goes where he has been ordered not to go. Parole may also be revoked when a parolee is arrested and convicted of another offense or pleads guilty to it. Revocation may be sought even when the parolee has not been convicted of the new criminal charges brought against him. The parole authority may decide not to await the outcome of the criminal charges before issuing or executing a parole-violation warrant. But the court may suspend execution of the warrant to keep the paroling authority from interfering with the trial and the court's authority in the case.

Time of revocation Generally a parole is revocable at any time before the expiration of the parolee's sentence. A parole violation warrant, however, must be acted on within a reasonable time after having been issued. An unreasonable delay can be a denial of due process of law and make the warrant invalid. What a "reasonable time" consists of depends on the circumstances of the particular case. A claim of unreasonable delay may have to show that the parolee was disadvantaged by it, such as showing that evidence has been lost or that witnesses are no longer available.

Arrest of parolee A parolee suspected of having violated his parole may be arrested and returned to custody. The arrest may be made under a warrant issued by the paroling authority, but some courts have held that no warrant is necessary. The arrest of a parolee is not the same as an arrest of a private individual by a police officer. It is rather a transfer of the prisoner from CONSTRUCTIVE (implied) custody to physical custody. Thus, the requirement that an arrested person must be taken before a magistrate without delay does not apply to a parolee arrested for a parole violation. The requirement does apply, however, to a parolee arrested for committing a crime.

A parolee who is arrested should be held in a suitable place that is as near as possible to the place where the parole violation occurred. The parolee may be detained for a reasonable time until the parole authority has an opportunity to act.

Ordinarily parolees are not entitled to bail, but the facts and circumstances of each case must be considered, and in some cases bail may be granted when it appears that the parolee will not flee.

Preliminary revocation hearing   In order to properly revoke a parole, the parolee must be given two hearings, a preliminary hearing and a final one. The purpose of the preliminary hearing is to decide whether there is probable cause to believe the parolee has committed a parole violation that justifies keeping him in custody until a final decision is made about revoking his parole. A preliminary hearing is not required when the parolee admits that he has violated his parole or when he knowingly waives his right to the hearing.

The preliminary hearing should be held at or reasonably near the place where the alleged violation or arrest occurred. It must also be held as soon as convenient after arrest while information is fresh and sources are available.

A denial of a prompt preliminary hearing does not automatically entitle the parolee to return to parole status or prevent the parole authority from revoking parole. The failure to hold the required hearing is immaterial if it does not harm the parolee. It does not harm him, for example, if he admits his violation at the final hearing, if he is found in violation, or if his violation has been established by a conviction or by a plea of guilty.

The parolee must be given notice of the hearing, and the notice must state the violation that is being alleged. The parolee should be asked if he wishes to call any witnesses, and a reasonable effort must be made to locate and interview them or to obtain statements from them by mail. The parolee can appear and speak in his own behalf. He must be informed of his rights, and he is entitled to have the evidence against him disclosed. He also has the right to present evidence, and he can bring letters, documents, or persons who can give relevant information.

Persons presenting adverse information are to be made available for questioning in the presence of the parolee. The parolee's right to confront adverse witnesses is, however, a conditional one, and an informant does not have to be subjected to confrontation and cross-examination if the hearing officer decides that the informant might be harmed if his identity were known.

A parolee is entitled to be represented by counsel, subject to the parole authority's discretion. The authority may deny a request for counsel when the parolee will not be harmed by the denial. A parolee has a constitutional right to be informed that he may request counsel at the preliminary revocation hearing, but he may waive counsel.

Final hearing   A parolee has a constitutional right to a prompt final hearing to evaluate the facts and to determine whether they warrant revocation. Usually, a hearing must be held even when the parolee admits the violation or when he has been convicted of a crime, but some statutes provide for automatic revocation of parole without a hearing when there is a new conviction. These statutes do not violate the parolee's constitutional right to due process of the law because the trial resulting in the conviction has substantiated the parole violation. A failure to hold a prompt hearing can waive a violation claim and result in the restoration of parole and the release of the parolee.

The purpose of the final hearing is to enable the parole authority to reach a final decision as to whether or not the parolee has violated his parole, whether or not he is still a good risk, and whether or not a revocation of his parole is warranted.

The final hearing does not have to be limited to a consideration of the violations charged at the preliminary hearing, nor to the evidence substantiating those violations. The parolee must be given an opportunity to show that he did not violate the conditions of his parole or that there are circumstances that suggest his parole should not be revoked, even though he did violate a parole condition. If the parolee offers a defense to his violation, the parole authority must consider it.

Requisites for the final hearing   Although the final hearing is not required to be as formal as a courtroom trial, the hearing must be based on verified facts. A fair hearing also requires the parolee to be given written notice of the alleged violation. The parolee is also entitled to disclosure of the evidence against him, and he should have access to parole records. The hearing must be conducted by a neutral group, such as the parole board.

At the hearing, the parolee must have the opportunity to be heard in person and to rebut the allegations against him by introducing arguments in his behalf. He has the right to present voluntary witnesses with relevant testimony.

The parolee also has the right to confront and cross-examine adverse witnesses, unless the paroling authority finds good cause for not allowing it, such as probable future harm to an informant. The paroling authority is not required to produce adverse witnesses, however, unless the parolee requests it.

Right to counsel   Unless the parolee's right to counsel at his revocation hearing is provided by state law, the need for counsel must be decided on a case-by-case basis. In every case, however, a parolee must be advised that he has the right to request counsel and that if the request is granted and he does not have the money to hire an attorney, one will be appointed to assist him. Counsel may be granted on such claims as that the parolee did not violate the conditions of his parole or that the reasons for the violation are complex and difficult to develop or present. In every case in which a request for counsel is refused, the grounds for refusal should be stated in the record. Unless the record shows that a parolee's rights were not harmed by the refusal of counsel, failure to offer a lawyer when required may invalidate the revocation proceeding and may entitle the parolee to a new hearing with counsel.

Evidence and findings   The rules of evidence that apply to a judicial CRIMINAL LAW proceeding do not have to be used at a revocation hearing. It is permissible to admit and consider evidence, such as hearsay, that would not be admissible in a criminal prosecution. Illegally obtained evidence may also be used.

EXAMPLE Winston, a parolee, is picked up and accused of committing armed robbery and shooting a man. A parole officer questions Winston about the crime but neglects to inform him of his right to remain silent and consult a lawyer. Winston is frightened into telling the parole officer that he was involved in the robbery but that he did not shoot anyone. Winston's admission that he had participated in the robbery would not be admissible as evidence in his trial for robbery because it is illegally obtained, but the admission would be admissible in a hearing to revoke Winston's parole.

Once the parolee denies the violation of which he is accused, the parole authority has the burden of proving that there has been a violation. Proof that would not be sufficient to support a criminal conviction may be sufficient to support a revocation of parole, because a parole violation does not have to be established by proof beyond a reasonable doubt. A written statement of the evidence and the reasons for parole revocation must be issued and a copy given to the parolee. A parolee who is found guilty of violating his parole may be required to return to prison and serve the unexpired balance of the maximum term to which he was originally sentenced.

Judicial review   The decision handed down at a revocation hearing is subject to limited judicial review (review by a court). The court can consider only whether or not the authority abused its discretion and whether or not the revocation proceedings conformed to the requirements of due process of law and any applicable statutes.

particulars   The details of a claim, or the separate items of an account. See BILL OF PARTICULARS.

partition   Any division of property between co-owners, such as joint tenants or tenants-in-common, so that each may possess and enjoy his share individually. Partition is either voluntary or compulsory. Voluntary partition is a division of the property by the co-tenants (owners) themselves. Compulsory partition is accomplished by judicial proceedings brought by one or more of the co-tenants regardless of the wishes of the other co-tenants.

Voluntary partition is generally effected in one of three ways: (1) The co-owners may mutually exchange individual deeds that each give a specific part of the commonly owned land to only one party. Once the deeds have been exchanged, each co-owner owns a part of the property and ceases to have an undivided interest in the whole. (2) The co-owners may provide for the sale of the property and divide the proceeds among themselves. (3) The co-owners may rely on another method of partition, the selection of disinterested third persons, such as arbitrators or appraisers, to divide the property and to allot shares.

Lawsuits to compel partition may be brought to sever property interests. When that happens, a co-tenant's right to his property is absolute and not up to the discretion of the court. The court's only function is to determine the method of partition.

Every type of property can be the subject of compulsory partition, and the fact that the property is owned in unequal shares does not affect the right to partition. In regard to real estate, partition can be made of a building, such as a house, a story of a building, the land on which a building rests, or the surface of land on which there is an oil and gas lease. The right to compulsory partition of personal property (property other than real estate) has been enforced in cases of a cashier's check payable jointly to tenants-in-common, promissory notes, shares of stock in a corporation, and stocks of merchandise.

partnership   An association of two or more persons who, as co-owners, carry on a business for profit. The word "persons" includes individuals, other partnerships, and corporations. The capacity of a CORPORATION to enter a partnership, however, depends on its charter and on the laws regulating corporations. Unlike the stockholders of a corporation, who risk losing only the amount of money they put into the business by buying stocks, the members of a partnership are personally liable for their business debts, and each partner is responsibile for what the other partners do. See also SMALL BUSINESS.

The law relating to partnerships is codified in the Uniform Partnership Act, adopted, with minor variations, by all the states. Each partner is a co-owner with the power of control over the business but each partner is also an agent of the partnership as a whole.

■ **Existence**   A partnership is ordinarily formed by an agreement, which functions as a contract between the parties who are to become the partners. The contract may be oral or written, express or implied from the conduct of the parties. The fact that two persons co-own property—a house, let us say—as joint tenants or tenants-in-common does not mean they are partners, even though they may share profits when they rent the house to a tenant. On the other hand, the fact that a person receives a share of the profits from a business is *prima facie* evidence (absolute proof if not disproved) that he is acting as a partner. This rule does not apply, however, if the profits the person receives are (1) in payment of a debt owed to him, (2) his wages as an employee, (3) the interest on a loan, (4) in payment for GOOD WILL or other business assets, or (5) an annuity to the widow of a dead partner.

■ **Relationship of partners to each other**   The powers, duties, and liabilities of the partners depend upon and are governed by the provisions of their agreement. Subject to any agreement, the following general rules apply to the rights and duties of the partners: (1) New members of a partnership must be known and approved by all the existing partners, not just by a majority of them. (2) Each partner is entitled to equal participation in the management of the firm's business, although the partners may agree that one or more of them shall have exclusive control. (3) When all liabilities are satisfied, each partner is entitled to be repaid for his capital contributions to the partnership and to share in any profits or surplus that may be left. If a partner has advanced more capital than he originally agreed upon, he is entitled to interest on it from the date it goes into the partnership. When a partner contributes capital that is to be repaid on a certain date and it is not repaid, thereafter he is entitled to interest. A partner is not entitled to any further compensation for his services to the partnership, but a surviving partner has a right to a reasonable sum for his work in winding up the affairs of the business. (4) Every partner is entitled to reimbursement for any of his own money that he has spent and for any personal liability he has incurred in conducting the firm's business or preserving its property. (5) When the partners cannot agree on how to handle some usual matter connected with the firm's business, the decision reached by the majority prevails.

Books   Unless the partners agree to some other arrangement, the firm's account books must be kept at its principal place of business and must be open for inspection by any of the partners. The partners also have the right to copy the entries made in the books.

Fiduciary character   A partnership relation is fiduciary in character (based on trust), and it imposes a duty on each member to deal with the other partners in utmost good faith. Each partner has a duty to account to the firm for any benefit he gains from business connected with the firm but conducted without the agreement of his partners. If he makes a profit, he holds it as a trustee for the firm.

EXAMPLE Smith, Brown, and Jones are partners. Brown O⟶✳ makes $2,000 by using the firm's bulldozer without the consent of Smith and Jones. Brown must disclose the profit to Smith and Jones. If Brown were insolvent, the partnership would be entitled to the $2,000 over Brown's other creditors because he held the money in trust for the partnership.

Accounting   When the partnership is running smoothly, a partner ordinarily is not entitled to a formal accounting of finances, but he is entitled to one when the partnership agreement provides for it. He also has that right when (1) he is excluded from the firm's business or prevented from using its property, (2) when one of the partners makes a profit from business connected with the firm without the consent of all the partners, and (3) whenever it is reasonable under the particular circumstances.

Partnership property   Any property contributed to the firm by the partners when the partnership is formed becomes partnership property. Similarly, property purchased with partnership assets is ordinarily regarded as the firm's property. Real estate can be taken in the partnership name, and when it is, it can be sold or otherwise disposed of only in the name of the partnership.

Partners are co-owners of the partnership property as tenants-in-partnership. As long as the property is used for business purposes, each partner has the right to possess it.

No partner may assign (transfer use or ownership of) partnership property unless he does so together with all the other partners. See ASSIGNMENT. A partner's interest in the partnership property cannot be attached (taken into custody by the court), nor is it subject to execution (forced sale to pay creditors) unless the claim is brought against the partnership as a whole.

When a partner dies, his interest in the partnership property passes to the remaining partners but only for use in the partnership business and not for the surviving partners' personal use (unless the partnership agreement says otherwise). Ultimately, upon the death of the final partner, his interest in the partnership property goes to his estate.

Assignment of interest   Although a partner cannot assign (transfer or sell) his interest in partnership property, he can assign his partnership interest—his share of the

---

THE INS AND OUTS OF PARTNERSHIP

■ A partnership is an association of two or more persons who carry on a business for profit. Each partner is personally liable for the debts and obligations of the partnership. If the business does not have enough money to pay its debts, the partners will have to pay them out of their own pockets.

■ A partnership is usually formed by an agreement between the partners. The specific powers, duties, and liabilities of the partners depend on the provisions of their agreement.

■ New members of a partnership must be approved by all existing partners. Each partner is entitled to an equal participation in the management of the firm's business.

■ Every partner is entitled to reimbursement for any of his own money that he has spent and for any personal liability he has incurred in conducting the firm's business.

■ When all liabilities are satisfied, each partner is entitled to be repaid for his capital contributions to the partnership and to share in any profits or surplus. A partner is generally not entitled to any further compensation for services to the partnership.

■ When partners cannot agree on how some usual matter is to be accomplished, the decision reached by the majority prevails.

■ A partner cannot sell his interest in partnership property, but he can sell his share of the profits and surplus.

■ The partnership is bound by the acts of each member unless a partner lacks the authority to act in a matter and the third person he is dealing with knows it. For example, a partner who notified the bank to stop further overdrafts by his copartner on the firm account was not liable for the amount when the bank permitted another overdraft.

■ Each partner is a general agent of the partnership as a whole. It is assumed that what is known by one partner is known by all.

■ The partnership is liable for any harm done by a partner while he is carrying on company business. For example, if a partner causes an injury by his negligent operation of the firm's automobile while going to see a client, the partnership is liable.

■ Dissolution takes place when the partners stop doing business. It does

not end the partnership, however. The partnership continues until all its affairs, such as the completion of existing contracts, are finished.

■ A partnership may be dissolved by the express will of one partner or all the partners. No person can be forced to continue as a partner against his will. But if he withdraws in breach of the partnership agreement, he may be liable for any damages resulting from his breach.

■ Dissolution can also be accomplished by a court decree. Any of the partners may apply for such a decree when another partner is declared insane or is unable to fulfill his duties.

■ Dissolution ends the authority of the partners to represent the firm except for winding up and completing the firm's transactions.

■ Any partnership may include limited partners as well as general partners. Limited partners are persons who invest money in the partnership but who take no part in the management or operation of the partnership's business. Limited partners are not liable to the business's creditors to the same extent as are general partners.

profits and surplus. Such an assignment does not cause a dissolution of the partnership. The person to whom the interest is assigned does not become a partner. He has no right to become involved in running the partnership or to examine its books of account but only to the profits due to the assigning partner.

■ **Partners and third persons** Each partner is an agent for the partnership as a whole, and the partnership is bound by anything any of the partners does in the ordinary course of the firm's business unless the partner lacks the authority to act in a matter and the third person with whom he is dealing knows it. For example, a partner who notified the bank to stop further overdrafts by his co-partner on the firm account was not liable for the amount when the bank permitted another overdraft.

Without the consent of all the partners, one or more partners cannot sell or otherwise dispose of partnership property, sell or give away its good will, confess to a judgment against it, submit partnership matters to arbitration, or do anything that would prevent the partnership from carrying on its business.

Admissions When a partner who is acting within the scope of his authority makes an admission that is against the interest of partnership business, the admission can be used in court as evidence against the partnership. For an extended discussion of admissions, see EVIDENCE.

Notice Notice to one partner is notice to all. Because each partner is a general agent of the partnership, it is assumed that what is known by one is known by all. Thus, a partner in charge of constructing a dwelling was charged with knowing that a porch railing was defective, even though he did not personally install it, because his partner knew the railing was defective.

Wrongful acts The partnership is liable for the wrongful acts or omissions of a partner who is acting in the course of the partnership's business. It is not responsible for the acts of a partner done after dissolution or those unconnected with partnership business.

Although partners may act for one another in civil matters, they cannot do so in criminal matters. Criminal liability is personal, and in criminal cases a partner is not chargeable with the acts of his co-partners unless he had knowledge of them.

Generally, all the partners are liable for TORTS (injuries to persons or damage to property) committed by one of the members acting in the scope of the firm's business, even though they did not participate in, or know of, the torts.

EXAMPLE Suppose that Sid and Eddie are co-owners of O——* Dainty Dinettes, a partnership. While driving the company station wagon on his way to investigate a complaint about a table, Sid runs a red light and hits and injures a lady who is walking her dog. If the lady sues, the partnership itself is liable and not just Sid. On the other hand, suppose that Eddie uses the company station wagon to drive his family around in the evenings and on Sundays. One Sunday he takes his family to a wedding in the station wagon. When he leaves the reception, he is a bit inebriated and starts the station wagon in reverse, running down and injuring one of the bridesmaids. Eddie is fully responsible for the injuries he has caused, and the partnership cannot be made to pay damages.

In some states, all the partners are jointly and individually liable for the wrongful acts or omissions of one of the partners. This means that the partners can be sued as a group, with each partner paying a share of the damages, or individually, with one partner liable for all the damages. In other states, however, joint liability is the rule. In any state, all the partners are jointly liable for debts and obligations that are not the result of wrongful acts or omissions. If debts cannot be paid from partnership funds, the individual partners must pay them from their personal funds.

■ **Dissolution** Dissolution takes place when the partners stop carrying on the business. It does not end the partnership, however. The partnership continues until all its affairs, such as the completion of existing contracts, are finished.

Grounds for dissolution If there is no time set by agreement for the term of the partnership, it may be dissolved by the express will of any one partner or by all of them. Even when the partnership agreement provides that it is to continue for a certain period of time, a partner who wishes to end the relationship may do so. No person can be forced to continue as a partner against his will. His action, however, is a breach of the partnership agreement, and he may be liable for any damages resulting from his breach. If the remaining partners wish to continue the business, they must form a new partnership.

The expulsion of a partner from the firm for reasons set forth in the partnership agreement is another cause for dissolution. For example, the partnership agreement might provide that any partner who forms or joins a competing organization is to be expelled from the partnership.

Other grounds include the death or BANKRUPTCY of a partner and any circumstance that would make it unlawful to continue the business. For example, if the partnership were operating a barroom, the failure to obtain a renewal of a liquor license would make the sale of liquor illegal and result in the dissolution of the partnership.

Dissolution can also be accomplished by a court decree. Any of the partners is entitled to apply for such a decree when another partner is judicially declared insane, shown to be mentally unsound, or becomes incapacitated in a manner that prevents him from fulfilling his duties. The courts will dissolve a partnership when it is shown that it can only lose money or when a partner persistently breaches the partnership contract. The courts will not dissolve a partnership merely because of friction among the partners. Discord should be settled by the partners themselves.

Effect of dissolution Dissolution ends the authority of the partners to represent the firm except for winding up and completing the firm's transactions. Generally, dissolution applies only to future transactions, and the partnership continues until all past matters are terminated.

Dissolution does not mean that each partner is discharged from his existing liabilities. His discharge is usually accomplished by an agreement with the firm's creditors and the remaining partners that his liabilities have ended.

■ **Winding up** Winding up means the administration of assets for the purpose of terminating the business and discharging the obligations of the partnership to its members and creditors. Ordinarily, those members who have not acted in some wrongful manner leading to the dissolution are entitled to wind up the business, as is the executor or administrator of the final surviving partner.

Distribution The firm's liabilities may be paid from the partnership's assets, including its existing property and any additional property contributed by the partners. The firm's creditors who are not partners must be paid first. Next come partners who have lent money or other property to the partnership, and then partners who contributed capital to the business. Lastly, if there is any surplus remaining it must be distributed to the partners as profits, either in an agreed-upon ratio or equally. If there are not enough funds to pay the firm's outside creditors, the individual partners will be liable for paying these debts from their own personal assets.

■ **Limited partnerships** A limited partnership is a firm composed of one or more general partners and one or several special partners, with the liability of the special partners limited to the amount of capital they have actually contributed to the firm. The purpose of permitting limited partnerships is to encourage persons with capital to become partners with those having business skills. The law concerning these relationships is found in the Uniform Limited Partnership Act in force in all the states.

All partners must file a sworn certificate containing the partnership name, the nature of the partnership business, its location, and the names and addresses of the partners. The certificate must also include the expected duration of the firm, the amount of money or other property contributed by the limited partners, and the compensation each limited partner is to receive in return for his contribution. The certificate must be filed in the place designated by law, such as the county clerk's office in the county where the firm is located.

Any type of business that can be conducted by a general partnership can be conducted by a limited partnership. A limited partner may not, however, contribute his services or participate in the management of the firm's business. His name may not appear as part of the firm's name. His contribution to the firm is restricted to the money or other property he has provided, and he is not personally liable to creditors as is a general partner.

A limited partner has the right to examine and copy the partnership's books and to be informed of all business matters relating to the firm. He also has the right to share in the profits or to receive income according to the provisions of the certificate.

party A person concerned with or taking part in any transaction, proceeding, or other matter; either of the two opposing sides in a judicial proceeding—the plaintiff (or plaintiffs) or the defendant (or defendants).

party wall A wall that is built on the land of each of TWO ADJOINING LANDOWNERS and supports two attached buildings, one on each lot. A party wall gives each owner an EASEMENT, which is the right of a nonowner to use a specific part of another person's property for a specific purpose. Each owner of the party wall owns as much of the wall as stands on his land, and he has the right to use the other's portion of the wall as support for his own building. Town houses, for example, usually have party walls.

■ **Creation** A party wall is ordinarily created by a contract between the adjoining landowners, by statute, by PRESCRIPTION, or by sale.

By contract The parties to a contract to build a party wall may agree that the wall is to be located on land owned entirely by one of them or standing partly, usually equally, on each other's land. Under the most common arrangement, one party builds the wall and the other contributes to its construction. The parties may also agree that an existing dividing wall is to become a party wall.

By statute Statutes permitting the construction of a party wall by one of two adjoining owners, if the line between the properties is unoccupied, have been upheld as a constitutionally valid exercise of a state's POLICE POWER.

By prescription When a wall between adjoining buildings has been continuously and uninterruptedly used as a party wall by the respective owners for a period of time set forth by statute, a *prescription right* to use the wall arises. The wall becomes a party wall, or at least a right to use it as one arises.

By sale A party wall may also be created when the owner of attached buildings with a common wall as part of each building transfers or sells the lots the buildings occupy to different persons. Each owner acquires title to one half the wall and an easement for its support as a party wall in the other half. This rule holds true even though the deeds do not mention the rights of the parties in the wall. The result is the same when one of the lots is retained by the original owner.

■ **Manner of use** A party wall is for the mutual benefit and convenience of the owners. Each adjoining owner has the right to its full use as a party wall in the improvement and enjoyment of his property, but neither may use the wall in a way that impairs the other's easement or interferes with his property rights. One owner may not, for example, extend the front wall, rear wall, or beams of his building beyond his part of the party wall.

■ **Destruction and rebuilding** Ordinarily, neither of the adjoining owners of a party wall has the right to destroy or remove it. On the other hand, if a fire or other occurrence causes the wall to become useless, then either may remove it.

In a number of states, either of the adjoining owners may take down the party wall to replace it with a new wall strong enough to support a new structure requiring greater support. He must replace the wall within a reasonable time and without injuring the adjoining owner's property.

Either party may take down and replace a party wall that is dangerous to life or property or insufficient for the support of existing buildings. Neither owner has any right to have a dangerous wall propped up or sustained by the timbers, walls, or parts of the other's building.

When the adjoining buildings are destroyed and the party wall is left standing, neither adjoining owner is obliged to rebuild his building as it existed.

■ **Addition, alteration, and repair** Unless restricted by title, deed, or agreement, either owner may usually add to, alter, or repair the wall. But he must not damage the adjoining property or impair the easement to which the owner is entitled. Either party, for example, may increase the height of the wall, provided the increase does not weaken the strength of the wall, underpin the wall and sink the foundation deeper, or increase its thickness.

pass **1** To utter or pronounce, as when a court *passes* sentence upon a prisoner. **2** To be rendered or given, as when a judgment is said to *pass* for a plaintiff in a suit. **3** In regard to legislation, a bill or resolution is said to *pass* when it is agreed to or enacted by the legislature. **4** When an auditor appointed to examine accounts certifies to their correctness, he is said to *pass* them; this means that the accounts move through the examination without being stopped or sent back for inaccuracy. **5** In regard to real estate, *pass* means to be transferred from one person to another. When a seller deeds his real estate, it *passes* to the buyer. **6** To examine something and to decide on the disputed questions that it involves. In this sense a jury is said to *pass upon* the issues in litigation.

passport A document addressed to foreign governments that certifies that the person described in it is a citizen of, say, the United States and requests that he be given permission to come and go as well as legal protection.

patent An exclusive right granted by the federal government to an inventor to make, use, and sell his invention for a definite or limited period of time. The U.S. Constitution gave Congress the exclusive power to deal with all matters relating to the issuance of patents.

The law recognizes that an inventor has a natural right to make, use, and sell his invention or discovery. After an invention has been known to the public for a year, however, it becomes public property unless the inventor has obtained a patent from the U.S. Patent and Trademark Office in Washington, D.C. Federal law gives an inventor who holds a patent (the patentee) the right to sue for money damages anyone who has made use of his patent without his permission and without compensating him.

An inventor may freely transfer and assign his property rights in an invention. He may also grant a license to use the invention in exchange for payment, called a royalty.

■ **Nature of right** A patent right gives the inventor the right of a limited monopoly to exclude others from making, using, and selling what he has patented without his permission. The term of a patent is 17 years. Design patents, however, are issued for terms of 3½, 7, or 14 years. Once the term expires, the invention becomes public property, freely available to anyone to use, reproduce, or sell.

A patent is a contract between the inventor and the government under which the public, through the government, agrees that in exchange for the inventor's disclosing how his invention works and granting the public the right to use it after the patent expires, he shall be protected in his exclusive use during the life of the patent. The document containing the grant of a patent right is called the *letters patent*. A patent is considered to be the personal property of the inventor.

■ **What is patentable** A patent may be obtained for certain specified classes of inventions or discoveries not known or used by others in this country and not patented or described in any printed publication in this or any foreign country before the applicant's invention or discovery.

Proper subject matter The classes of patentable subject matter include "any new and useful art, machine, manufacture, or composition of matter or any new and useful improvements" and "any new, original and ornamental design for an article of manufacture."

An *art* is a process for or method of treating certain materials in order to produce a physical change in the character or quality of some material object. Processes that produce their results by chemical reaction, such as the mixing and heating of two chemicals together for oxidation, are included within the term "art."

A *machine* is a device that uses energy in order to get work done—an electric saw, for example.

A *manufacture* is an article made by man.

A *composition of matter* is a compound produced from the combination of two or more specific ingredients, which has properties different from or in addition to those of each ingredient.

An *improvement* is an addition to, or change in, a known art, machine, manufacture, or composition that produces a useful result. The right to a patent is limited to the improvement and does not include the art, machine, or article improved. An invention is an independent invention and not a mere improvement of an existing one, if its essential characteristics are different.

A *design* is an arrangement of lines or images that gives a peculiar and distinctive appearance to an article, such as furniture, jewelry, or machinery. Appearance is the essential consideration. The mechanical usefulness of the design, the manner in which it is made, and its size are not important.

Anything that does not fit into one of these classes will not be patented. A patent is granted for the discovery or invention of some practicable method of producing a beneficial result or effect, not for the result itself. The first person who invented a can opener received a patent only for the way his particular device opened cans. He did not receive a patent for all can openers, because this would extend the exclusive rights of a patent beyond discovery and discourage invention.

A method that uses a principle or law of nature in a new way may be the subject of a patent—for example, a process that uses ultraviolet light in a new way for a beneficial use to society. On the other hand, the discovery of an abstract principle or a law or phenomenon of nature is not patentable, nor are ideas, theories, or plans of action, without concrete means to carry them out, regardless of how revolutionary and useful to mankind they may be.

Requirements for patentability An object that falls into one of the specified classes of patentable subjects must have three characteristics before it may be patented. They are invention, novelty, and utility.

Invention Invention is the development of a new idea and the means for putting it into practice and producing the desired result. An idea is not a completed invention until it is put into a physical form demonstrating its practical efficiency and utility.

Merely changing the form, proportions, size, or degree of an object or process is usually not an invention if it involves doing substantially the same thing by the same means. Invention requires something more than achieving an improved result, or a better way of doing what has already been done, or an extended application of the original idea. For instance, an improvement in an old machine is not patentable if all it does is permit the product to be produced more cheaply.

If a person skilled in the particular subject matter of the invention or discovery would have been able to find the process or device in question from information disclosed prior to the invention, a patent will not be granted, because no substantial innovation was involved. Conversely, an inventor's right to a patent is not affected by the fact that his invention is small and simple, requiring no high degree of imagination—as long as a distinct and innovative advance is achieved. Something as simple as an ironing board with legs connected to form an X-shaped support structure so that the user can iron more comfortably while seated was sufficiently inventive to be patentable because it was not an obvious change.

Novelty In order to be patentable, an invention or discovery must have novelty. This means that the thing or process must not have been known to anyone before the inventor exercised his inventiveness and originality. An invention lacks novelty when it has been anticipated—that is, when it has already been disclosed by someone else.

An invention may be denied a patent if it has been anticipated. Anticipation may occur when substantially similar elements that produce or are capable of producing the same results are found in machines already commercially used. If, however, two similar inventions achieve different results or perform different functions, the earlier one does not anticipate the later one. The later invention will be entitled to a patent even though its structure is virtually identical to the earlier one.

A process or instrument used for one purpose may anticipate an invention that uses substantially the same method for a new but similar use that would be obvious to a person experienced in the field. For example, the invention of bathroom scales would be anticipated by scales used to weigh animals, because the uses are so similar that it would be obvious to anyone in the measurement-data field.

An invention is not anticipated when it has been accidentally produced previously but cannot be repeated, but if the results could be reproduced, the invention may be considered anticipated. Earlier experimental efforts that are abandoned because they failed are not anticipations of an invention. If an experiment is successful, however, the invention is anticipated.

Prior patents No valid patent can be obtained by an inventor if his invention was patented before he made his invention or discovery or if it was patented more than one year before he filed his application. For a prior patent to anticipate disclosure, it must describe the invention in such full, clear, and exact terms that a skilled person would be able to use the invention without exercising any inventive skill of his own.

Prior publications An inventor may not obtain a patent if his invention has been described in a book, catalog, magazine article, thesis, or trade publication, in this or any other country, before he invented it or more than a year before filing his patent application. Descriptions contained in other patents or applications may be sufficient to anticipate an invention.

Utility An invention or discovery must also have utility in order to be patentable. Utility exists if the invention can perform some practical and beneficial function. For instance, a process for producing chemical compounds that inhibits tumor growth in rats or mice has utility. Patents are not granted for trivial or useless devices. Imperfections or drawbacks not affecting the substance of an invention do not make it useless. Designs do not have to meet the standard of utility.

■ **Persons entitled to patents** A person must be the first and original inventor in order to be entitled to a patent. Joint inventors may obtain a patent for a joint invention, but neither one can obtain a patent as the sole inventor. Employers are usually entitled to the patent rights on inventions or discoveries made by their employees during the course of their employment. Employment contracts ordinarily specify that the employee will assign his exclusive rights under any patent to the employer. Frequently, the employee is given a certain percentage of the profits earned by his invention.

Priority of invention When two or more inventors discover or invent the same thing and each of them would appear entitled to a patent if it were not for the other's application, the Patent Office will determine who gets the patent in what is called an interference proceeding. The proceeding determines the *date of conception*. The date of conception is the date on which the idea, including all the essential attributes of the invention, became so clearly defined in the mind of the inventor that he was capable of expressing it physically—he was able to make a drawing of it. The proceeding also determines the *date of reduction to practice*—the date when the workability of the invention could be demonstrated. Usually, an inventor who is the first to conceive of an invention and reduce it to practice will be awarded the patent. However, if an inventor who first conceives of an invention uses reasonable diligence in reducing it to practice, he will be entitled to the patent even though the second inventor may have been the first to reduce it to practice.

Loss of patent right A person who would otherwise be eligible to receive a patent might lose the right to his patent under certain circumstances.

(1) If an inventor lets his invention be put on sale more than one year before filing his patent application, he loses his right to a patent. This insures that an inventor will not enjoy patent protection for the commercial exploitation of his monopoly for longer than the term of his patent.

(2) An inventor loses his patent right if he abandons his invention. An invention is abandoned when it is dedicated to the free and unlimited use of the public. A delay in applying for a patent is not abandonment if the inventor can show he did not intend abandonment.

(3) An inventor forfeits his right to a patent when he delays in making a claim or conceals his invention for too long, because this postpones the time that the public would be entitled to the free use of the invention.

■ **How to obtain a patent** A person must apply to the Patent and Trademark Office in order to obtain a patent. The application must include a specification, a drawing, and an oath by the applicant, and it must be signed by the applicant and accompanied by a fee.

Specification The specification is a written description of the invention, including the manner and process of making, compounding, and using it. The practical limits of the invention must be described in clear, concise, and exact terms. This protects the inventor, informs members of the public of what is still open to them, and enables them to use the invention after the patent has expired. The specification concludes with the *claims*, which explicitly spell out the structure of the invention, not only what it does. The claims enable the Patent Office and the courts to determine whether a patent should be issued or whether the invention has been anticipated by an earlier one. A claim may be rejected by the Patent Office or held invalid if it is vague, indefinite, or incomplete. When a claim is so broad that it includes what is old as well as new, it may be rejected. Only the inventor's actual invention should be covered by the claim, and only one single and distinct invention may be included in each claim. More than one claim may, however, be included in a single application.

Drawings Drawings must accompany a patent application only when they are needed to understand the invention. If they are omitted and deemed necessary, the Commissioner of Patents and Trademarks may require them to be submitted within two months after the inventor has been notified to do so. The Commissioner may require the inventor to provide a model of convenient size to exhibit his invention. When the invention involves a composition of matter, the applicant may have to furnish a specimen for inspection or experiment.

Oath and fee The application for a patent contains an oath, which must be signed by the inventor, stating that he believes himself to be the first and original inventor. A fee of $65 must be submitted with the application. The filing fee for design patents is $20. When a patent is issued, the patentee must then pay $100 more. Fees for issuing design patents are $10 for a 3½-year term, $20 for a 7-year term, and $30 for a 14-year term.

■ **Patent Office proceedings** When an application for a patent is received, the Commissioner examines it to determine whether the applicant is entitled to a patent. If the application is approved, the Commissioner will assign a patent number to the invention. If the application fails to meet the requirements, the Commissioner must notify the applicant of the rejection and its grounds. An applicant may request a reexamination of his application and submit evidence to overcome the reasons for rejection. Failure to do so will be considered a waiver of the right to challenge the rejection.

An application may be amended until the matter is finally decided by the Patent Office, either by the issuance of a patent or by a final order of rejection. An amendment may describe the invention more clearly and accurately, but new and enlarged claims may be added only when they are within the scope of the original disclosure. If the amendment involves a substantial departure from the original specification or goes beyond the scope of the original application, it is invalid. When amendments are made within a reasonable time, they are treated as part of the original application. This is important when two inventors claim virtually the same invention, because time determines who is entitled to the patent.

Appeals Applicants for a patent whose claims have been rejected twice may appeal the final decision of the primary examiner to the Board of Appeals. An applicant dissatisfied with its decision may make a further appeal to the U.S. Court of Customs and Patent Appeals. Or he may bring a civil action against the Commissioner in U.S. District Court for the District of Columbia, if it is started at least 60 days from the date of the board's decision. He may not, however, start both an appeal to the Court of Customs and Patent Appeals and a civil lawsuit.

Reissue and disclaimer Once an inventor has been granted a patent he may apply for a reissue or file a disclaimer if circumstances warrant either action. Reissue is the act by the Commissioner of granting a new patent, which protects the addition of new elements to the original invention. A reissued patent is, in effect, an amendment of the original patent made to correct some defect or insufficiency in the original. If a claim for a reissue is rejected twice, the applicant may appeal the decision in the same way he would appeal the rejection of an original patent.

A disclaimer is the voluntary abandonment of some part of a patent claim that makes it invalid because of a lack of novelty. It confines the claim to what is new, thereby eliminating the part that is invalid. Once an inventor knows that his patent contains invalid claims, he should promptly file a disclaimer. Failure to do so may make the whole patent invalid.

■ **Assignment and license** If an inventor does not have the money to manufacture and market his invention himself, he can assign his patent to another person or to a company or he can give someone a license to use it.

An assignment is a permanent transfer of the patent, consisting of the exclusive right to make, use, and sell the invention throughout, or in a specified part of, the United States. The inventor gives up all of his rights to his invention. The assignment must be in writing and should be recorded in the Patent Office. If not recorded, another purchaser can subsequently take the patent as if there were no assignment at all.

A license, on the other hand, only gives the recipient (the *licensee*) a temporary right to use the patent as agreed. A license does not have to be in writing, and it cannot be transferred unless specified by the agreement. The *licensor* (inventor) usually requires the payment of a royalty for the use of the patent.

■ **Regulation of patented articles** A patentee or any authorized person making or selling any patented article must notify the public that the article is patented by fixing the word "patent" and the number of the patent on the article. If the nature of the article prevents this, a label containing the same information should be enclosed in, or marked on, its package. This marking requirement does not apply to a patent for a process.

In order to recover damages in a suit for infringement when the patentee has failed to obey the marking requirement, it is essential that the infringer was notified of his infringement and that he continued, after the notice, to make, use, or sell the patented article without permission.

Federal law imposes a special penalty for various forms of false marking with the intent to deceive the public, including marking an unpatented article with the word "patent" or any word that implies that the article is patented. State laws about the manufacture and sale of patented articles may also apply.

■ **Infringement** Infringement is the unauthorized making, using, or selling for practical use or for profit of a patented invention. There can be no infringement of a patent before it is issued. Generally, the motive or intent of an alleged infringement is immaterial. A person may infringe a patent without having any actual knowledge of its existence. Contributory infringement occurs when one person intentionally helps another to make, use, or sell a patented invention illegally.

The owner of a patent has a right to bring suit for the unlawful invasion of his patent rights any time within six years after the date the infringement took place. Courts often grant INJUNCTIONS to protect property rights in patents. In this case, the injunction would be a court decree ordering an infringer to stop illegally making, using, or selling the patented article. It is granted only when an award of money damages will not sufficiently remedy the situation, such as when an infringer plans to continue copying and selling an invention as his own. If a person disobeys an injunction, he will be guilty of CONTEMPT and subject to a fine or imprisonment or both.

In a suit for infringement of a patent, compensation may be awarded (but not for using the invention before the patent was issued). The court will award the patentee actual DAMAGES in an amount at least equal to a reasonable royalty for the use made by the infringer, along with any interest or costs fixed by the court. If a jury does not determine the amount of damages, the judge will. In either case, the judge may increase the damages up to three times the amount determined. These treble damages are awarded only in certain cases, such as when the person deliberately and in bad faith infringed the patent. If the defendant unintentionally infringed the patent, as when he honestly but mistakenly believed the invention to be public property, punitive damages will not be awarded.

paternity suit See ILLEGITIMACY.

patients' rights The legal rights of persons who present themselves for medical treatment or care. Patients do not lose their legal rights just because of their physical or mental infirmity. Although there is no set of laws that give special rights to patients, a number of existing rules of law have been applied to patients and these laws are loosely called patients' rights. In addition, some recent statutes have extended special protections to patients. Other entries that discuss patients' rights are INSANE PERSONS; PHYSICIANS AND SURGEONS; PRIVACY, RIGHT OF; WELFARE PROGRAMS.

■ **Consent** An individual has the right to prevent unauthorized interference with the functions of his own body. A doctor who treats a person without first obtaining his consent may be sued for committing a battery. See ASSAULT AND BATTERY.

A patient may give his consent verbally, by signing a written statement, or by submitting himself to a specific procedure, such as being vaccinated. The consent must cover the specific medical procedure contemplated, but it does not have to mention each step in the procedure.

A consent is not valid if the patient has been misled or if he is incapable of understanding what he is consenting to. The scribbled or half-muttered consent of a patient in a semiconscious state is not acceptable.

Minors Generally, minors are legally incapable of giving consent to medical treatment. Usually a minor's parent or guardian must consent to medical treatment for him unless emergency treatment is necessary to prevent death or serious bodily harm. A minor who is married or emancipated should be able to give consent for himself. *Emancipated* means that the child lives apart from his parents and supports himself, and his parents have relinquished all control of him. Minors in the armed services are usually considered emancipated regardless of their parents' attitudes toward them. See INFANT.

Many states have laws permitting minors to give valid consent to medical treatment under certain circumstances (including examination and treatment for venereal disease, pregnancy, and drug and alcohol abuse) and to give consent to treatment of the minor's own children. Some states also permit young people to be examined after a rape, to donate blood, and to obtain birth-control pills. One state allows anyone 14 years old or older to give consent to any lawful kind of medical treatment. In 1976 the U.S. Supreme Court ruled that a minor girl should not be forced by the law to obtain the consent of her parents in order to obtain a legal ABORTION.

Courts can also be asked to give permission for physicians to treat children when their parents refuse to give consent. Many of these cases have involved parents whose religious beliefs do not allow blood transfusions, and some have involved parents who wanted to treat serious illnesses with only health food and an exercise regimen. Generally, courts will intervene if there is a life-threatening situation, but they have been inconsistent when the medical condition was less critical.

EXAMPLE A New York court authorized surgery, over a
O—* mother's religious objections, to repair a serious facial deformity in order to improve a child's appearance, but a Pennsylvania court refused to override parental refusal to permit spinal-fusion surgery.

A court's decision may depend on the child's age and whether or not he agrees with his parents' decision. See also RELIGION, FREEDOM OF.

Incompetents When an adult has been legally judged incompetent, consent must come from his guardian. When there has been no judicial determination of incompetency but it is apparent that the patient cannot decide for himself, a spouse or parent should be able to give consent for him. Sometimes an adult who is otherwise competent cannot give consent for himself because of special circumstances.

EXAMPLE One man who had a sixth-grade education and
O—* whose native language was French was awakened after being given a sedative and handed a consent form for an operation. He signed, but a court later found that this was not a valid consent because earlier the man had refused to consent to that same surgical procedure.

Difficult problems arise when a patient is not competent to give his own consent and the medical procedures proposed are not primarily for his benefit—for example, when the patient is asked to donate an organ for transplant to

YOUR RIGHTS AS A PATIENT

■ You have the right to prevent unauthorized interference with the functions of your own body. You may sue a doctor who treats you without first obtaining your consent.

■ You may give your consent verbally, by signing a written statement, or by submitting yourself to a specific procedure, such as being vaccinated. The consent is not valid if you have been misled or are incapable of understanding what you are consenting to. If you have dependent children, you must give consent for their medical treatment because they are generally considered legally incapable of giving consent themselves.

■ Although you have the right to decline medical treatment for yourself or your child, in certain circumstances courts have authorized compulsory vaccinations and lifesaving transfusions. On the other hand, courts usually do not force a terminally ill person to undergo chemotherapy, surgery, or radiological treatments. "Pulling the plug" on life-support systems in hopeless cases has been the subject of heated controversy. Recent rulings have come round to the view that withdrawal from life-support systems is permissible when the attending doctors conclude that there is no hope, the hospital ethics committee agrees, the attending doctors think the apparatus ought to be turned off, and—lastly—the guardian or family of the patient consent.

■ Some states require your doctor to inform you about all the risks associated with a particular procedure, but other states require him to disclose only those risks that are likely to affect your decision to grant or withhold consent. But your doctor may be exempted from this procedure in an emergency—for example, he is not obliged to sit down and outline the different medical procedures to you while snake venom is coursing through your veins.

■ In some cases, your physician may withhold information from you, but he must disclose details of the risks to your spouse or to another close relative. You need not be informed about anything you make clear that you do not want to know.

■ When a hospital is negligent in protecting your safety and comfort, you may sue it for damages.

■ Your doctor has no right to allow someone unrelated to your case to observe a medical procedure performed on you without first obtaining your consent, especially if the treatment involves substantial physical exposure or significant contact or association with that person.

---

another. It may be possible to petition a court for permission, but courts differ widely in these matters.

EXAMPLE A court in Kentucky held that it had the authority to give consent for a kidney to be removed from a retarded patient and transplanted in his brother, but a court in Louisiana held that neither a court nor the parents could authorize surgery on a retarded boy in order to remove a kidney to be donated to his sister.

Inferred consent   In some cases, a court will infer consent because of an emergency or unanticipated circumstances. A typical example is the case of a child who is found unconscious.

Although a surgeon generally has no right to go beyond an authorized procedure to which the patient has consented before an operation, a court will find implied consent for immediate action if something unforeseen develops during surgery. When a consent is for the result to be achieved, a physician has implied consent to use any medical technique that is necessary and appropriate.

Consent given by the court   Generally, an adult has the right to decline medical treatment for himself, but occasionally a court will order treatment or appoint a guardian to give the necessary consent. For example, courts have authorized compulsory vaccinations and lifesaving blood transfusions in order to save the sole surviving parent of small children. When death is inevitable, courts will usually not force a person to undergo heroic chemotherapy, surgery, or radiological treatments.

Life-support systems   One of the most controversial issues relating to patients' rights is the question of how long a patient must be sustained by artificial life-support systems when there is no hope of his recovery. In the *Matter of Quinlan*, the New Jersey court held that a life-support system could be withdrawn without legal liability, even for a patient whose condition is stable, when (1) the attending physicians conclude that there is no reasonable possibility that the patient will emerge from the present comatose condition, (2) the hospital ethics committee agrees with this opinion, (3) the attending physicians believe that the life-support apparatus should be turned off, and (4) the guardian and the family of the patient agree with this decision. See DEATH. The full implications of this decision are not yet clear, but the principle that seems to be emerging is that patients who cannot give their own consent to end artificial life support may yet have a right to die.

Informed consent   To give his valid consent to medical treatment, a patient must generally be an adult, be able to understand the kind of treatment offered and the risks involved, and be conscious enough to express assent. But consent alone does not authorize a physician to proceed. The patient must be given information about the nature of the treatment, the risks involved, and the alternatives. This is the *doctrine of informed consent*, a legal theory that has been developing only since the 1960's. It recognizes the patient's right of self-determination, preserves human integrity, encourages care by the physician, and involves the public in medical decisions.

Some states require a physician to tell a patient about all the risks associated with a particular procedure, but other states require a physician to disclose only those risks that are likely to affect a patient's decision to grant or withhold consent. Physicians are privileged not to discuss risks in emergency cases when there is no reasonable way to get consent. A New Mexico court held, for example, that a doctor did not have to analyze various methods of treatment and the possible consequences of each one while venom was spreading through the body of a snake-bite victim. Courts may also excuse a doctor whose patient was likely to be so disturbed by the truth that it would render him incapable of making a rational decision, would complicate the needed treatment, or would be likely to result in psychological damage.

EXAMPLE In one case, a court in Hawaii dismissed a complaint against a physician who performed a thoracic aortogram (a diagnostic procedure) on a patient with a suspected aneurysm without discussing the possibility of paraplegia. The court recognized that reasonable persons would not disagree with the physician's decision because the patient was already extremely apprehensive and also suffered from coronary and kidney disease.

Sometimes, in cases like the above, the physician can withhold information from the patient but give it to the patient's spouse or another close relative. A patient does not have to be informed when he makes it clear that he does not want to hear the truth about his condition.

■ **Hospital patients** The hospital is obliged to exercise reasonable care in providing proper medical attention, equipment, supplies, medication, and food for patients. It must be reasonably careful to provide safe physical premises and should have administrative policies and procedures designed to protect the safety and comfort of patients. It has a duty to employ reasonable care in selecting and retaining hospital employees and in granting staff privileges. A hospital that is negligent in performing any of these duties may be sued to compensate a patient who is harmed. The liability of a hospital that is not negligent but that causes harm to a patient by using defective materials, equipment, or drugs is discussed in PRODUCT LIABILITY.

Specifically, hospitals have been responsible for protecting patients from contagious diseases or from other patients who are violent, for properly storing food and drugs, for observing the special dietary needs of individual patients, for discharging incompetent staff members, and for reviewing the courses of treatment given by attending physicians. A hospital also must take reasonable steps to prevent a patient's suicide or to prevent the escape of a violently insane patient. Dangerous conditions in the hospital building or on the grounds must be discovered and corrected, including those conditions that are threatening only because of patients' infirmities.

■ **Human research subjects** In 1974 Congress passed the National Research Act, the first federal legislation to protect the rights of human beings who are the subjects of medical research. The new law came about as a reaction to abuses of unregulated research, including a U.S. Public Health Service study begun in the 1930's to determine the long-term effects of syphilis on men.

EXAMPLE Two groups of black men from the area of Tuskegee, Alabama, were chosen. One group had syphilis and the other was used as a control. The men were given health care for life for everything except syphilis. The study lasted well into the 1960's, but no penicillin was ever given to any of the subjects even after it was known to be a cure for syphilis. In the 1970's a lawsuit was started on behalf of the survivors and the families of the men who had died. The case was settled out of court. Survivors who had syphilis recovered as

much as $37,000, and at least $5,000 went to the estates of deceased participants who had not had syphilis. The Tuskegee syphilis study was widely criticized because none of the participants had given informed consent, and standardized evaluation procedures had not been used.

The National Research Act requires any person or institution that applies for a federal grant or contract to do biomedical or behavioral research using human subjects to show how the work will be reviewed by a board. The board must determine whether the human subjects would be taking risks greater than any likely benefit to them or greater than the comparative value of any new knowledge likely to be acquired. Before any person can be used as the subject of an experiment, he must give his informed consent without undue influence, force, or deceit. The experimenter must give a fair explanation of the procedures and their purposes, a description of the risks or discomforts he expects, any benefits that can reasonably be anticipated, and a description of any alternative forms of treatment that might be good for the subject. The experimenter must give his subject a chance to ask questions and tell him that he can withdraw his consent and quit the project at any time without detriment to himself.

States have begun to enact laws to protect human subjects of medical experimentation. New York has a comprehensive law that permits only authorized researchers to conduct experiments and requires written informed consent from their subjects. A few other states have laws that punish the researcher if he fails to obtain the subject's consent, that restrict the use of psychosurgery, and that prohibit research on human fetuses.

■ **The patient's privacy** The practice of medicine must be done carefully in order to avoid invasions of privacy. For example, a treating physician has no right to allow someone unrelated to the case to observe a medical procedure without first obtaining the patient's consent, especially if the treatment involves substantial physical exposure or significant contact or association with the person accompanying the doctor.

Patients also are entitled to keep their condition and their personal life out of the public view. Medical personnel cannot make public records, movies, photographs, or X-rays of a patient. This right of the patient is balanced with the physician's right of free speech. Disclosures that are likely to offend any reasonable person and do not legitimately concern the public are prohibited. For example, a patient might not be able to sue a doctor who gave a film to a television news team in order to arouse the public to protest inhumane conditions in a hospital, especially if the patient was fully dressed, not identified, and was shown only for a second. On the other hand, a psychiatrist who wrote an embarrassing book about one of his patients, with enough detail to make the subject easily identifiable, might be held liable for invasion of privacy if his only interest was in making a profit.

pawn Deliver personal property, such as a camera, to another (a pawnbroker or any creditor) as security for money that is borrowed. A pawned item is held for a certain period of time. If the money and interest on it are not paid back within that time, the item is sold. See PLEDGE.

pawnbroker A person who makes a business or occupation of lending money at interest on the security of personal property left with him. See PLEDGE.

payable Justly and legally due for payment; a sum of money is said to be payable when a person is under an obligation to pay it. Payable may signify an obligation to pay at a future time, but when used without qualification, it generally means that the debt can be settled at once.

payee The person to whom a negotiable instrument, such as a check, is made out; the person who cashes a check. See COMMERCIAL PAPER.

P.C. Abbreviation for Professional Corporation; a special corporation established in some states by physicians, lawyers, or other professionals who practice together.

peace bond Money posted in court to secure the good behavior of an individual who has been convicted of a BREACH OF THE PEACE. It is another name for a bail bond. See BAIL.

peace officers Sheriffs, constables, marshals, city policemen, and other public officers, whose duty is to enforce and preserve the public peace. See POLICE; SHERIFFS AND CONSTABLES.

peculation 1 Unlawful appropriation, by a depositary of public funds, of governmental property entrusted to his care. 2 Fraudulent misappropriation of money or goods left in one's care. See EMBEZZLEMENT.

pederasty In criminal law, unnatural carnal copulation of a male with a male; a form of SODOMY.

penal damages Punitive DAMAGES.

penalty In general, a punishment, either corporal or pecuniary (financial), for a crime or a civil wrong; usually a sum of money, the payment of which the law demands as punishment for doing a prohibited act or for failing to do a required act. Penalties can be imposed by law or be agreed to in private contracts.

pendente lite (Latin) "Pending the suit"; during the progress of a suit; during litigation.

pendent jurisdiction The power of a federal court to decide all relevant questions in a case, provided a substantial federal issue is involved at some point.

penology The study of prisons and punishment. See PRISONERS' RIGHTS; SENTENCE.

pension A periodic installment of a preestablished amount of money to an individual or his family, paid because of work that has been performed, when conditions such as age and length of employment have been fulfilled. The federal SOCIAL SECURITY program incorporates a public pension plan that covers most of the workers in this country. Private pension plans are set up by individual employers to supply retirement benefits to their employees that will supplement the benefits employees receive from Social Security.

A private pension plan is a program established by an employer, sometimes in conjunction with his employees' union, to provide retirement benefits for his employees. Such a plan is usually put into effect by administrators and protected by trustees of the funds earmarked for the payment of benefits. Each year the employer pays a preestablished amount of money into a fund for each working member of the plan. Depending upon the terms of the plan, the employer may contribute all the money for the annual deposits, or he may deduct part of it from the employees' paychecks. Such money is invested by the trustees of the funds in various income-producing transactions, such as securities, municipal bonds, and interest-bearing accounts, so that it will grow over the years and be adequate to finance the payment of retirement benefits.

An employee who does not have some type of group pension plan (other than Social Security) can open his own Individual Retirement Account (IRA). A self-employed individual can set up a different individual plan, called a Keogh Plan, to supplement his Social Security benefits.

■ **Company plans** The company pension system in the United States developed in response to the change of the American life-style from its rural agrarian beginnings into its present urbanized, wage-earner society. The system has grown slowly. In the 1940's, 4 million employees were protected by private pension plans. By 1950, almost 10 million workers had some sort of pension coverage. Today, more than 40 million employees participate in various company pension plans to provide future financial security for themselves and their dependents.

Types of company plans Although terms may vary, there are two basic types of company plans: defined benefit plans and defined contribution plans.

Defined benefit plans In a defined benefit plan, the benefits, or the formula for arriving at the benefits to be received once a person retires, are fixed. Because the pension payment can be determined in advance, the employer must see that sufficient money is set aside in the pension fund. The contributions made to the fund are not definite because they are determined actuarially (statistically calculated) on the basis of the benefits expected to be paid. Such contributions may vary over the years as a result of inflation, changes in the mortality rates among employees, and other factors.

Under a defined benefit plan, benefits may be distributed in any one of three ways: as a flat benefit, a fixed benefit, or a unit benefit.

A *flat benefit* means that any retiree covered by this plan will receive a specific amount per month, such as $400, once he has retired.

A *fixed benefit* is a payment that is a definite percentage of the retiree's salary for a certain period.

EXAMPLE The terms of Hal's pension plan entitle him to receive a pension equal to 20 percent of his average earnings during the last five years he worked. If he earns an average of $25,000 a year in that period, he will receive monthly payments totaling $5,000 a year.

HOW FEDERAL LAW REGULATES COMPANY PENSION PLANS

■ Most pension plans are sponsored by employers, sometimes in conjunction with their employees' union. There are various types of company pension plans, all of which are regulated by the Employee Retirement Income Security Act (ERISA), which was enacted in 1974.

■ The pension payments you receive after you retire are financed by contributions made to the plan by your employer and perhaps by you too. If you leave your job before retiring, you are always entitled to recover any contributions you made to the plan, plus interest. Your accumulated benefits based on the contributions made by your employer must be irreversibly vested (protected) after you have been in the plan for a specified period of time. This means that you are entitled to receive these benefits even if you leave the company before you retire. ERISA requires that you be at least

50 percent vested (entitled to at least half of your benefits) after you have worked for the company for 10 years and be 100 percent vested (entitled to all your benefits) after you have worked for 15 years.

■ Once your benefits are fully vested, you have a nonforfeitable right to receive them when you retire.

■ Under most company plans, if you retire and die before your spouse, your spouse will continue to receive at least half of your pension benefit until he or she dies unless you had rejected this provision (called a *joint and survivor annuity*) in writing. The only reason for rejecting this annuity is that it reduces the amount of benefits you yourself receive during retirement.

■ Employers need not set up pension plans for employees, but if they do, they must treat all employees equally.

■ All employees 25 years of age or older must be included in the plan

once they have worked for the company for one year (or three years if the plan calls for immediate vesting). A plan may not exclude employees because they are too old. (However, if the plan pays the same flat amount in benefits to all retirees, employees who begin working within five years of retirement may be excluded.)

■ The federal government sets minimum funding requirements for various pension plans. It also requires all plans that provide retirement benefits of set amounts or percentages of employees' salaries to buy termination insurance provided by the Pension Benefit Guaranty Corporation, a federal agency.

■ If there is a pension plan where you work, you should be give a concise description of it written in plain language. You should also be given an annual statement detailing the financial status of the plan.

A *unit benefit* is the payment of a set amount (the unit) multiplied by the number of years of the employee's service. The unit can be a fixed dollar amount that is the same for all plan members or it can be a set percentage of the employee's compensation—generally of his last year's salary or an average of his salary over the last so many years.

EXAMPLE Mary's pension plan with Withers Plumbing Supplies provided that she receive the fixed amount of $25 a month (the unit) times the number of years she worked for the company. Since she had worked for Withers for 30 years when she finally retired, she received a pension of $750 a month.

Andrew's pension plan with Acme Cement Works provided that he receive 1 percent of his last month's salary (the unit) for each year he worked. Andrew worked for Acme for 25 years and his last month's salary was $2,000. Consequently the unit was $20 (1 percent of $2,000) and his monthly pension benefits were $500 (25 times $20).

Defined contribution plans A defined contribution plan is one in which the size of the contributions is fixed rather than the amount of benefits a retired employee will receive. The size of the contributions for each employee may be a certain amount for each hour he worked or a set percentage of his salary.

The most common types of defined contribution plans are target benefit plans, money purchase plans, and profit-sharing plans.

In a *target benefit plan*, contributions are based upon actuarial valuations intended to provide "target" benefits to each plan participant upon retirement. The amount of the benefit depends on various factors—for example, whether

the rate of employee turnover differs significantly from the figure used to determine the size of the contribution.

EXAMPLE Deco Company provides its employees with a target benefit plan. To decide how much money must be contributed to the retirement account of each employee for a monthly target benefit of $1,000, Deco consults mortality tables to determine that its employees have an average life expectancy of 72.1 years and anticipates that 10 percent of its employees will quit before their pension rights vest. If Deco's assumptions about the character of its work force are correct, a fixed monthly contribution of $75 should finance the target benefits. Suppose the life span of its employees is 76.6 years, an increase of 5.5 years in which to collect more pension benefits, and the turnover rate is only 5 percent, so that more employees stay to collect their pensions. Deco's target benefits will be less than $1,000 because of the greater unanticipated burden on its pension system. In contrast, suppose the life span is 70.0 years and the turnover rate is 25 percent. The target benefits drawn by the employees would be more than $1,000, since there is less of a burden on the system than Deco planned for when it determined its defined contribution.

Under a *money purchase plan,* an employer's contribution to the plan has been determined for specific employees and allocated with respect to them. The size of such a contribution is usually a percentage of an individual's salary. The amount of benefits an employee receives under a money purchase plan depends upon how much the employer has actually deposited for the employee's benefit.

A *profit-sharing plan* is one in which the pension benefits to be paid are financed by contributions made by the employer from the yearly profits earned by the company. The employer pays a proportionate share of money into an individual account for each employee. This type of plan is considered a defined contribution plan because each year when contributions are made from profits the amount is a fixed percentage of the salary of each employee.

EXAMPLE If AB Company is having a highly profitable year, Ira, its owner, may choose to contribute 20 percent of each employee's salary. The next year, Ira's profits may drop, so he may decide to contribute only 2 percent of each employee's salary. In a year when AB Company loses money, no contributions will be made to the accounts of Ira's employees.

Unless the terms of the plan require it, an employer does not have to contribute to a profit-sharing plan every year, but he must make regular and significant contributions to the plan in order to enjoy the tax advantages of setting up such a program for his employees.

Under a profit-sharing plan, there must be a formula that shows how contributions made to the plan will be allocated among its members and how the funds accumulated will be distributed after a certain number of years. What an employee will receive once he retires depends upon the contributions made by the employer over the years. It also depends upon other payments from the forfeited accounts of employees who have left before they have become legally entitled to their benefits (vested) and upon gains and losses resulting from the investment of the money set aside for the plan. This means that retiring employees would receive larger pension checks if their employer's business is extremely profitable and he makes large contributions to the plan (rather than reinvesting the profits in expansion or modernization); if numbers of employees quit before they have any rights to the money earmarked for them; and if the plan's funds are wisely invested.

As a general rule, employees are not required to make contributions to profit-sharing plans, but many companies permit them to make contributions, if they wish. This type of plan is known as a *thrift plan*, or *savings plan*. These voluntary contributions may consist of up to 10 percent of an employee's income. Such plans are used frequently in addition to a company's regular pension plan to give employees an opportunity to use their own savings to increase their future retirement income.

Receiving benefits Any company pension plan is a contract between an employer and his employees, whether it is a defined benefit plan or a defined contribution plan. As a result, if you compare the terms of your pension plan with that of your neighbor who works for a different company, you will most likely find that some of the provisions of his plan differ from yours. But even though pensions may provide different benefits, any plan must tell you how you will be paid once you retire.

Generally, your company will pay you in one of three ways: (1) it will send you monthly benefits; (2) it will give you your benefits in a lump sum; or (3) it will take the money you have coming to you and buy you a commercial annuity—a contract that pays you income for a certain number of years or for the rest of your life. Your company may also let you choose among these three methods of receiving your benefits.

Federal regulation Because pension plans directly affect the financial security of millions of Americans, the federal government has enacted laws to assure that such plans are administered fairly. In the past, many employees with long years of service lost anticipated retirement benefits because they were fired before they could retire or because pension funds were mismanaged. Today, all pension plans, except government plans and certain church plans, are regulated by the 1974 Employee Retirement Income Security Act (ERISA), which was designed to protect an employee's rights to his pension.

Vesting When an employee joins a pension plan, he starts to earn (accrue) benefits (credits) based on his employer's contributions to the plan, as well as those based on his own contributions through payroll deductions, if any. If the employee is covered by a defined benefit plan, he may have to work two years in a row before this occurs. ERISA safeguards an individual's right to receive his accrued benefits after he has participated in a plan for a specified period of time. This right is considered *vested* (absolutely owned) by the employee, giving him the legal right to receive payment according to the terms of the pension. Thus, a vested employee who leaves his job anytime before normal retirement age (usually 65) will not lose the benefits that he has accrued up to that time.

Vesting may occur in any one of three ways: (1) An employee's right to his pension may be fully vested at the end of 10 years of service. This is known as *cliff vesting*. Until those 10 years of service have expired, an employee has no vested rights and will lose all his benefits if he leaves the company. (2) An employee's right to his pension may vest gradually over a 15-year period. After 5 years of service, he is entitled to 25 percent vesting, with an additional 5 percent for each year thereafter up to 10 years of service (a total of 50 percent after 10 years) with another 10 percent per year for each remaining year leading up to 100 percent vesting after 15 years of service. This is called *graded vesting*. If an employee leaves the company before he is 100 percent vested, he will receive a percentage of his accrued benefits equal to the amount he is vested. For example, if he leaves when he is 50 percent vested, he will receive half of his accrued benefits. (3) An employee with at least five years of service at the time when his age and years of service add up to 45 has 50 percent vesting of his accrued benefits, with 10 percent more each year thereafter until he is fully vested. This type of vesting is known as the Rule of 45 because the employee's age plus his years of service must equal 45 before vesting will take place.

EXAMPLE A computer programmer who begins a new job when she is 27 years old will have no vested rights in any benefits she has accrued until she has worked with the company for nine years. After that time, her age (which will then be 36) and her years of service (9 years) will add up to 45. She will then be entitled to 50 percent of her accrued benefits once she retires. Vesting will increase 10 percent a year for the next five years so that by the time she is 41 her right to accrued benefits will be fully (or 100 percent) vested.

Regardless of the way vesting occurs, an employee's right to his pension must be at least 50 percent vested after 10 years of service and 100 percent vested after 15 years.

EXAMPLE If Jack started working at age 20 as an account representative for an advertising firm, his right to accrued benefits under his pension plan would be 50 percent vested at age 30 and 100 percent vested when he reached 35.

Any amounts contributed to a pension fund by an employee are always 100 percent vested. ERISA provides a procedure for plans that are funded by both employer and employee contributions so that the size of employee contributions plus interest can be determined.

If an employee with vested benefits decides to leave his employer before retirement age, the terms of the plan may provide him with the option of how he is to receive his benefits. He may elect to receive them in the form of a regular pension based on his number of years of service when he reaches retirement age. He may take them in a lump sum when he leaves his job to use as he sees fit. This lump sum distribution qualifies for favorable income tax treatment if it is made after the employee reaches the age of 59½. The portion of the amount that can be traced to active participation in a plan before 1974 is considered a long-term capital gain, while the part attributable to active participation after 1973 is taxed as ordinary income. Finally, the amount of vested benefits may be used by the employer to buy the employee an annuity. If someone works for different employers at different times and pension rights at both jobs vest, he will be entitled to collect two pensions along with Social Security upon retirement or he may select other pension payments options that both plans provide.

Survivor's benefits Once his benefits are vested, an employee has a nonforfeitable right to receive them upon retirement. But what happens when a retiree dies? Before ERISA was enacted, many employees were unaware that certain steps had to be taken before their retirement to insure that their surviving spouses would receive some pension benefits. Today, in most cases, the spouse of a deceased retiree will continue to receive his pension. This extension of benefits is a result of joint and survivor annuity provisions. A *joint and survivor annuity* is a contract that provides that the employee and his spouse will receive his pension until he dies, at which time the surviving spouse will receive benefits until his or her own death. The payments made to the survivor must be at least one-half but no more than the amount received during the retiree's life.

EXAMPLE Nat, a telephone repairman, will be entitled to $700 a month under his pension without a survivor annuity. If he chooses a joint and survivor annuity, he will receive payments of only $450 a month, but after his death, Alice, his widow, will receive one-half that amount, or $225 per month.

Joint and survivor annuities are automatic features in most company pension plans unless the employee rejects them in writing. ERISA mandates that any pension plan that provides an annuity for the duration of the employee's life must give the employee the opportunity to decide whether or not he wants to protect his surviving spouse by selecting a joint and survivor annuity. Some joint and survivor annuities include payments for minor children.

Under some plans, if a participant dies while he is still working, but after he has reached a specified early retirement age, his vested benefits may die with him unless he has acted to prevent this by taking out an *early survivor annuity*. The terms of an early survivor annuity—which, unlike a joint and survivor annuity, must be elected in writing—provide that if an employee dies before retiring, his surviving spouse will be entitled to a certain percentage of his vested rights. If an early survivor annuity has not been elected, only the accrued benefits derived from the employee's own pocket (through paycheck deductions) will be paid to the employee's survivors.

EXAMPLE Teleco's pension plan, which sets 65 as the normal retirement age, provides early retirement benefits for an employee, if he wishes, at age 55. Bob, an account executive, turns 55 but continues working. His plan requires that an early survivor annuity be elected in writing in order to entitle the surviving spouse to his benefits should the employee die between the ages of 55 and 65. If Bob died at 57, before he retired, Nancy, his wife, would receive part of his pension only if Bob had elected the annuity in writing. If he had not, Nancy would collect only those benefits that had accumulated from pension deductions made from Bob's paycheck over the years.

On the other hand, suppose Bob had retired at age 57 and then died. The joint and survivor annuity would be automatic at the time he retired, and Nancy would be protected unless Bob had specifically put in writing that he did not want the survivor annuity. If Bob had lived and continued working until he was 66, the joint and survivor annuity would be automatic when he reached 65, the normal retirement age, unless he had rejected it in writing.

Both a joint and survivor annuity and an early survivor annuity, which extend the scope of an individual's vested rights, are financed by either a premium paid by the employee or a reduction in the pension benefits to be paid.

Right to participation An employer cannot be forced to establish a pension plan for his employees but, once he does, he must treat all employees fairly. A person can be required to be a certain age and work a number of years before he is allowed to join a plan. ERISA mandates, however, that no one can be prevented from participation once an employee reaches age 25 and completes one year of service or reaches age 25 and completes three years of service if the plan provides for immediate vesting. An employee cannot be excluded from a plan because he works part-time or seasonally if he has a "year of service," usually defined as 1,000 hours of service during a 12-month period. Participation in defined contribution plans cannot be denied because an individual starts working late in life. But defined benefit plans can exclude anyone who starts work within five years of the plan's normal retirement age.

Funding To insure that sufficient funds will be on hand to pay promised benefits once an employee retires, ERISA sets minimum funding requirements for various pension plans. In the case of defined benefit plans, for example, employees must deposit into the fund each year the *normal cost*—that is, the amount of pension benefits earned that year by the employees. Formulas based upon actuarial assumptions, such as the rate of mortality and the ages of plan members, have also been established so that financing will meet the obligations of the plan. Funding is reviewed and adjusted every three years by actuaries to assure the soundness of plans.

Minimum funding rules do not apply to some defined contribution plans, such as target benefit plans or profit-sharing plans, because the size of the benefits is not fixed. They apply to money purchase plans, but only to the extent that the employer is required to contribute the amount specified by the plan formula.

ERISA also requires that certain defined benefit plans be insured in case the plan is terminated. The Pension Benefit Guaranty Corporation (PBGC), a federal agency, was created by ERISA to administer this federally chartered insurance. All covered plans pay premiums to PBGC. The vested pension benefits of employees and retirees are insured up to a certain limit set by law. If a covered plan terminates without enough money to satisfy the benefits that have vested (for example, when a company goes out of business), the PBGC will pay as much of the accrued benefits to retirees and employees as is permitted by law.

Federal tax laws also provide some relief to employees whose retirement plans are being terminated. All accrued benefits to the extent funded will vest completely and immediately upon complete or partial termination. A partial termination occurs, for example, when a corporation shuts down a particular plant and lays off its employees. All accrued benefits of those employees, regardless of whether they have vested, become vested because of the termination. ERISA sets the order in which assets are to be distributed to retirees and plan members.

Reporting and disclosures Federal law requires the pension plan administrators—the people who invest the funds set aside for retirement—to disclose important facts about the plan. The employee must be given a summary plan description, which outlines, in easy-to-understand terms, how the pension plan works, what benefits the plan provides, and how such benefits may be obtained.

An individual is entitled to read the entire pension plan document and must be notified if any significant changes are made. Each year, the employer must send his employee an annual statement detailing the financial position of the plan. A statement of the total benefits accrued, which benefits have been vested, if any, or the earliest date on which the earned benefits will vest must also be furnished upon written request.

■ **Individual Retirement Accounts (IRA's)** An IRA is a retirement plan that allows an employee not covered by a governmental or company plan to invest or deposit 15 percent of his salary annually up to $1,500. Neither the amount set aside nor the interest or profits that accumulate are taxed until the funds are withdrawn after retirement. Then it is taxed as ordinary income, but since most people have smaller incomes after retirement, the tax will be less. Because of this feature, IRA's are considered tax shelters.

IRA's were created by the Employee Retirement Income Security Act (ERISA) of 1974. Each year, the money set aside can be invested in flexible annuity contracts sold by insurance companies; savings accounts and certificates of deposit sold by banks and savings and loan associations; or credit union shares, which operate just like savings accounts. Mutual funds, shares, stocks, or a special type of U.S. Treasury bonds, which can be obtained from Federal Reserve Banks and pay 6 percent interest, can also be bought with such funds.

Eligibility Any employee who is not already an active participant in a company pension plan, a government retirement plan, or a Keogh Plan (discussed later in this article) is eligible to start an IRA. If a husband and wife both work and both are eligible to start IRA's, each may set up his or her own IRA within the limitations of 15 percent of his or her salary or $1,500, giving the couple an annual family tax deduction of as much as $3,000. The Tax Reform Act of 1976 allows an employee who qualifies for an IRA to set aside a benefit for his or her spouse if the spouse does not work. The limit on their joint account is $1,700—that is, $850 for each spouse.

If a person with an IRA becomes a participant in a company pension plan, he must stop making contributions to his IRA; but the contributions already made may remain in the account and continue to accumulate earnings without being taxed until they are withdrawn. If the person later leaves the company and is no longer an active participant in a retirement plan, he may resume making contributions to his IRA. After retirement he will be able to receive the benefits of both plans. If the pension plan he left pays him his vested interest in the plan in the lump sum upon termination, he may, without paying taxes on it, transfer it (roll it over) to the IRA he already has or into a new IRA. A person may have several IRA's, but the total contributions to all of them must not exceed the limit set for one.

Collecting benefits A person may not withdraw funds from an IRA until he reaches the age of 59½ (unless he has become disabled), but he must begin by the time he reaches the age of 70½. The benefits may be collected in any one of three ways: (1) They may be withdrawn as a lump sum, in which case the portion of the amount derived from contributions made after 1973 is taxed as ordinary income, while the portion derived from contributions made up through 1973 is taxed as capital gains. (2) They may be taken in installments over a fixed term of either 10 years or the life expectancy of the individual (as determined by actuarial tables), in which case only the amount withdrawn each year is taxed. (3) They can be used to purchase a commercial annuity, the payments of which are taxed as ordinary income.

Withdrawals made from an IRA account before the participant is 59½—for reasons other than death or disability—invalidate the plan, and all funds in the plan are then subject to income tax plus a 10 percent penalty. If the participant becomes disabled or dies, the funds may be withdrawn without any penalties to him or his heir and will be taxed as ordinary income.

After a participant is 70½, he must take out the amount of money required by the schedule, which is based on his life expectancy. If he takes out less, he is charged a tax of 50 percent of the amount he failed to take out. However, the Internal Revenue Service may waive the 50 percent tax if the taxpayer can show he made a reasonable error and has corrected it or is in the process of doing so.

Employer-sponsored IRA's Employers who do not have company pension plans for their employees may set up IRA's for them and deduct contributions for the accounts from their paychecks. Employers are permitted to contribute up to $7,500 or 15 percent of an employee's salary, whichever is less. This means that the maximum contribution for an employer-sponsored IRA is $6,000 a year more than an employee can contribute to an IRA he started for himself. Employer-sponsored IRA's appeal to employers who have only a few employees and cannot afford the time and expense required to implement a regular company pension plan. They also appeal to the employee, who otherwise would not have a pension plan or would have an IRA to which he could contribute a maximum of $1,500 a year.

To safeguard the interests of the employee, more rigid restrictions have been put on these plans than on regular IRA's. The plan must cover all employees 25 years of age or older who have been with the company for at least three of the preceeding five years. A detailed written description of the plan must be available to the employees. Contributions must be calculated in the same way for all and cannot favor executives or other employees with high salaries. For example, if the employer contributes 10 percent of his own salary to the IRA plan, he must contribute 10 percent of the salaries of all employees.

■ **Keogh Plans** The Self-Employed Individuals Tax Retirement Act of 1962 established tax-deferred retirement plans, commonly known as Keogh Plans, after New York Congressman Eugene Keogh, who sponsored the bill. Keogh Plans are similar to IRA's but are designed for self-employed individuals and their employees, if any. Modifications in the regulations of Keogh Plans were made in 1974 by ERISA.

Eligibility Any self-employed person or group of persons may begin a Keogh Plan. Ordinarily, anyone who pays his own Social Security taxes is considered self-employed. Eligible individuals include free-lance workers, owners of unincorporated businesses, members of a partnership, lawyers, doctors, shop owners, and employees who own more than 10 percent of the business they are working for.

In addition, persons who supplement their regular incomes by doing work on the side can open a Keogh Plan with money they earn from these extra activities, even though they work full time for a firm that has them enrolled in a company pension plan.

If a self-employed person who establishes a Keogh Plan for himself has full-time employees working for him, he must include in the plan all employees who have worked for him for at least three years. A full-time employee is one who works 1,000 hours or more per year. If a partnership is involved, a partner with at least 10 percent interest may elect not to be included in the plan, but as long as one partner sets up a plan, he must include all his full-time employees with three years of service.

Contributions A self-employed person may contribute up to 15 percent of his annual earnings or $7,500 per year, whichever is less. If he earns less than $15,000 a year, he may contribute as much as 100 percent of his earnings up to $750 without regard to the 15 percent limitation. If he has employees, he must contribute to the fund the same percentage of their annual earnings as he is contributing for himself. All of these contributions are tax deductible, as are the earnings they accrue while still in the fund, but retirement benefits taken out of the plan are subject to tax as regular income. The size of the contributions to the fund may vary from year to year, depending on profits.

If a Keogh Plan includes at least one employee, all participants in the plan may make additional voluntary contributions, which are not exempt from income taxes when they are made, in their own behalf of up to 10 percent of their annual earnings. The employer is limited to $2,500 in additional contributions, but the employees can contribute as much as they like as long as it does not exceed 10 percent of their total yearly earnings. These additional contributions are taxed as regular income, but the earnings they accrue while in the fund are not taxed until they are withdrawn. The voluntary contributions, but not their earnings, may be withdrawn at any time without being subject to taxation or tax penalties.

Benefits of all employees are fully vested and cannot be forfeited. An employer can never take back any contributions that have been made for an employee.

Collecting benefits Benefits are paid to an employee when his employment is terminated or when he retires. If he dies before receiving the benefits he is entitled to, the benefits are paid to his beneficiary, if he has named one, or to his estate.

A participant may not begin to receive benefits from a Keogh Plan before he reaches the age of 59½, but he must begin taking them by the time he is 70½, even if he has not retired. If he wishes, however, he may continue to make contributions after this time, but he should first consult a tax lawyer as to the advantages of doing so.

Early or late withdrawals of benefits are subject to tax penalties. Like IRA benefits, Keogh retirement benefits may be taken as a lump sum or in installments over a fixed period of time, or they may be used to purchase a commercial annuity.

per capita (Latin) "By the heads"; by the number of individual persons, each to share equally. When per capita is used to describe the method of dividing the estate of someone who has died, it means that an equal share is given to each of a number of persons, all of whom stand in an equal degree of relationship to the decedent. See DESCENT AND DISTRIBUTION; PER STIRPES.

per curiam (Latin) "By the court"; a phrase used in case reports to distinguish an opinion of the whole court from an opinion written by any one judge.

peremptory challenge Right of the plaintiff or defendant in a TRIAL to object to a specified number of persons called as possible jurors, without having to give any reason for his objection.

peremptory ruling In trial practice, the court's absolute decision on some point, without consideration of any alternatives. The court's instruction to the jury to return a verdict for the defendant, for instance, is a peremptory instruction.

perjury The crime of making a false statement under oath or affirmation in a judicial proceeding. Under many statutes, perjury also includes false swearing in depositions or affidavits, such as those required for tax returns, as well as false swearing in other proceedings.

perpetuating evidence   Assuring that EVIDENCE will be available for possible use at a later trial. The police, for example, may wish to deposit a murder weapon with the court before the trial of the accused.

perpetuating testimony   Taking and preserving a witness's testimony before the trial in which it is intended to be used, lest it be lost. It is usually allowed for witnesses who are old, ill, or about to leave the state. The usual method of perpetuating testimony is by DEPOSITION. See EVIDENCE.

personal injury   Any violation of an individual's rights, other than property rights. The term is not limited to physical injuries but includes such violations as invasion of privacy and LIBEL AND SLANDER. See PRIVACY, RIGHT OF.

personalty   Personal PROPERTY; movable property, as distinguished from real property (real estate).

per stirpes   (Latin) "By roots," or "by stocks"; by representation; a method of dividing a dead person's estate by distributing shares by representation (according to family relationship). See DESCENT AND DISTRIBUTION; PER CAPITA; and Chart 16.

> EXAMPLE   John dies, leaving a $3,000 estate. He is survived only by his sister, Sue, and the two children of his deceased sister, Mary. A *per stirpes* division of his estate would allow $1,500 to Sue and $750 (a division of their mother's share) to each of the deceased sister's children. In contrast, a *per capita* division would allow $1,000 to each of the three survivors.

persuasive authority   Sources of law that a judge might use in deciding a case, such as legal encyclopedias or related cases. A related case may be strongly persuasive if it was decided by a high court or a prominent judge.

petition   A written request to a court that it take a particular action, such as putting a candidate's name on the ballot for an election. In some jurisdictions, the word is used only when there is no opposition. In certain states, the word "petition" is used instead of COMPLAINT to designate the first pleading filed with the court in a lawsuit. In a broader sense of the term, a petition is a request made to a public official.

petition in bankruptcy   A paper filed in a court of BANKRUPTCY by a debtor, requesting relief from his debts. It can also be filed by the creditors, asking that the debtor be put into bankruptcy involuntarily.

petit jury   An ordinary JURY called for a civil or criminal trial. It is also called a petty jury.

Philadelphia lawyer   A phrase once used to praise a lawyer's skill but now used to indicate someone who is sly or tricky.

physicians and surgeons   Persons engaged in the practice of medicine. Medicine is the science and profession of treating disease and injuries to the human mind and body. A physician is a person who is authorized or licensed to practice medicine. A surgeon is a physician who performs operations on the human body. Osteopaths may or may not have the same legal status as physicians, depending on state law. Fields that are related to medicine include dentistry, the treatment of the mouth and teeth; chiropractic, the treatment of diseases by manipulation of the spinal column; and optometry, the use of any means, other than the prescription of drugs, to determine and correct vision. The laws relating to physicians and surgeons usually apply to these other health-care professionals; therefore, the term "physicians and surgeons" is also used here to include these practitioners, unless otherwise noted.

This article covers the licensing requirements for practicing medicine and working in related health fields and the nature of the doctor-patient relationship, including a discussion of malpractice. The rights of a patient are covered in PATIENTS' RIGHTS.

■ **State regulations**   The right to practice medicine or the related health professions is not an absolute or unqualified right but is controlled by the POLICE POWER of the state.

Occupation tax   The state legislature—or a municipality authorized by it—may impose an occupation tax on physicians and surgeons. If it does, however, it must treat all practitioners equally, with no unlawful discrimination.

State license   The state legislature can require a person to obtain a license or certificate from an authorized state board of examiners in order to practice medicine within the state, and it may also require him to register or record his license in a specified public office in the county in which he intends to practice. Failure to do so may result in criminal penalties. The refusal of a license or certificate by the board of examiners may be subject to judicial review, depending on state law.

The state dictates the qualifications for obtaining a license. First of all, an applicant must be honest and of good moral character, and in many states must meet certain health and physical standards. He must also have the necessary knowledge and skill. After graduating from an accredited medical school, the applicant must pass the state licensing examination. If he wants to practice in a specialized field, he usually will have to take additional examinations to obtain a license to practice in that field. A person who fails the test may take it again if the law permits. If it does not, he will not be granted a license to practice in the state. The number of examinations that may be taken by an applicant is usually limited. Some states exempt persons who have been licensed in another state from taking the examination if they meet all the other requirements.

Statutes make it a criminal offense to practice medicine without a license. The statutory term "practice of medicine" usually means the diagnosis and treatment of illness and injury as well as the prescription of drugs. Certain classes of persons, such as commissioned medical officers in the armed services, may be exempt from licensing statutes when performing official medical service in the state. Practitioners of such related health fields as chiropractors, dentists, and optometrists are also exempt from licensing statutes regulating physicians and surgeons because their specialities are strictly regulated by other laws.

Regulation of professional conduct The professional conduct of physicians and surgeons may be reasonably regulated by the state or its supervisory board. For example, the use of the letters "M.D." following the name of an optometrist or anyone else not licensed to practice medicine or surgery is prohibited.

In the past, statutes forbade physicians and surgeons to solicit patients through advertisements. The Supreme Court declared these laws unconstitutional in 1977.

A license may be suspended or revoked if there are sufficient grounds to believe that a physician or surgeon is adversely affecting the health, morals, or safety of the community. The most common reasons for taking away a license are malpractice (discussed below) and unprofessional, dishonorable, or immoral conduct. For example, a dentist who sexually abuses an anesthetized patient is acting unprofessionally and may be subject to suspension or revocation of his license.

A license can be suspended or revoked only by proper proceedings. A person must have notice of the proceedings and a full opportunity to be heard. The decision to suspend or revoke a license may be subject to judicial review.

■ **Relationship to patient** A contract for services exists between a patient and his physician or surgeon. The physician agrees to treat the patient but rarely does he absolutely promise to cure him. In most situations, a physician is not liable for breach of contract if his treatment of the patient is not completely successful. Only when a physician or surgeon makes a special agreement to obtain a particular result and fails will he be liable for breach of contract. For instance, a dental surgeon who agrees to extract four teeth is liable for breach of contract if he removes only three. A physician or surgeon may be liable for malpractice, however, if his conduct is below the standard of his profession.

Malpractice Malpractice is bad, unskilled, or negligent treatment of a patient by a physician or surgeon that results in injuries to the patient. The classic example is the surgeon who leaves a sponge in a patient's stomach. Clearly, the surgeon would be liable for malpractice because of NEGLIGENCE. Malpractice may also include prescribing the wrong medication; misdiagnosing a patient and treating him for the wrong illness; or improperly setting a broken bone.

Malpractice is determined by how advanced the particular area of medicine is at the time the incident occurred.

EXAMPLE In the early 1950's, obstetricians prescribed DES O——* to pregnant women to prevent miscarriages. Years later it was discovered that female children of mothers who took DES may develop cancer after they reach adolescence. However, if an adolescent daughter of a mother who was given DES by her obstetrician in the 1950's develops cancer she cannot charge the doctor with malpractice because the dangerous effects of DES were not known in the 1950's. If the obstetrician prescribed the drug today, however, he would be liable for malpractice in light of the new knowledge of its effects.

Standard of care Negligence is conduct that falls below the standard established by law for the protection of others against unreasonable risk of harm. Today most states define the standard of care to be observed by the medical profession as the degree of skill and learning ordinarily possessed and used by other members of the profession. If the doctor has met the standard, which is established by expert testimony at trial, he generally cannot be found negligent.

A specialist is held to a higher standard of care than a general practitioner. Anyone who presents himself as a specialist or who performs procedures normally done by a specialist will be held to the level of performance applied to that speciality, even though he may not be a certified specialist in that field. For example, a dentist who performs orthodontic work on a patient should be held to the standard of an orthodontist.

Other rules Some courts use other rules in evaluating a doctor's conduct. A few states apply the *respectable minority rule,* which excuses a physician from liability when he chooses to follow one of several recognized courses of treatment. Courts in these states have problems, however, in determining what constitutes a respectable minority or acceptable support for a particular technique. Other states use the *error in judgment rule,* which holds that a medical professional who otherwise follows professional standards should not be found negligent just because he commits an error in judgment in choosing among different treatments or diagnoses. In one case, a doctor was not found negligent when two negative pregnancy tests supported the conclusion that the patient was not pregnant—a conclusion that was found to be incorrect only after a hysterectomy had been begun. An obstetrician who chose to deliver a baby in transverse position in the womb with forceps rather than by cesarean section could not be held liable for that decision if either technique was acceptable.

Confidential communications The personal relationship between a physician or surgeon and his patient is one of trust and confidence, based on the belief that the physician has special knowledge and skill in diagnosing and treating diseases and injuries. A doctor who abuses the trust and confidence that a patient has in him may be subject to disciplinary proceedings before the state supervisory board.

EXAMPLE A patient who is a political candidate reveals to O——* his doctor that he has had a number of homosexual encounters within the last six months and his guilt about them has led to severe insomnia for which he is seeking treatment. At a cocktail party the doctor reveals this confidential information to his brother-in-law, a newspaper reporter, who quotes his anonymous source in a story about the candidate. The doctor has committed a serious breach of the confidential relationship with his patient and is subject to disciplinary proceedings. In addition, the patient may be able to sue the doctor for invasion of privacy, infliction of emotional distress, or malpractice, since the doctor has acted negligently in revealing confidential communications.

The communications between a physician and patient during the course of treatment are privileged. This means that a doctor has a legally recognized right to refuse to disclose information he has received from the patient in a civil lawsuit or criminal trial. For a full discussion of privileged communications, see WITNESS.

picketing The gathering of persons outside a place of business for the purpose of disturbing its activities or informing the public of grievances or opinions about the place. It is usually a technique used in labor disputes. Peaceful picketing for a lawful purpose is protected by the First Amendment to the U.S. Constitution. See LABOR RELATIONS; SPEECH AND PRESS, FREEDOM OF; STRIKE.

pilot   A person whose job is to take charge of a ship or vessel at a particular place for the purpose of guiding it through a river or channel or from or into a port. (For a discussion of airplane pilots, see AERONAUTICS AND AEROSPACE.) A pilot is licensed by either the state or federal government, which require pilots to insure that vessels will be properly operated in state and U.S. waters. State law regulates the need for pilots in bays, inlets, rivers, harbors, and ports, while federal law requires that federally registered pilots navigate the vessels on the Great Lakes. Where the waters are the boundary between two states, a pilot who has been licensed by either state is qualified to navigate the vessel from the port.

A pilot may be personally liable (financially responsible) to the owners of the vessel and to anyone who is injured for damages that result from his negligence. If, however, he exercises sound judgment, he is not liable just because the vessel in his charge has an accident. The negligence of a pilot in the performance of his duty is a maritime tort within the ADMIRALTY jurisdiction of the federal courts.

pimp   In feudal England there were various forms of tenure, a method by which a tenant was entitled to use land belonging to a lord in exchange for providing some service. A tenant holding land under pimp tenure was obliged to provide young women for his lord's pleasure. Today this term describes a person who, for a price, supplies another person with a prostitute (male or female) for sexual purposes. See PANDER; PROSTITUTION.

piracy   In ADMIRALTY law, the crime of robbery or rape on the high seas; in COPYRIGHT law, the illegal reproduction of copyrighted material for commercial distribution.
■ **Admiralty law**   Under international law, piracy is a robbery on the high seas—that is, on waters outside the boundaries of the low-water mark of the seacoast. For example, San Francisco harbor is not the high seas but the the Pacific Ocean is. A tug tied to a pier in a harbor is not on the high seas; thus its theft is not an act of piracy.

Piracy may be punished by any nation because pirates are considered enemies who threaten the safety and well-being of all peoples. The U.S. Constitution gives Congress the power to punish acts of piracy committed by or against any U.S. citizen on vessels registered to the United States. Anyone aiding or committing the crime of piracy can be sentenced to life imprisonment under federal law.
■ **Copyright law**   Piracy in copyright law is the illegal reproduction or duplication of copyrighted material for commercial exploitation. Today, the most frequent acts of piracy involve hit records, tapes, and films.

EXAMPLE A pirate with hidden recording equipment attends a rock concert given by a popular group. He illegally records the concert and reproduces it on tape cassettes, counterfeiting the label of the record company that has paid the rock group for the right to sell tape cassettes of their concert. The pirate sells his cassettes at a fraction of the cost of those of the record company and illegally avoids paying royalties to the rock group and all federal and state taxes.

The federal COPYRIGHT law has enacted special provisions to punish record, tape, or film pirates. A maximum fine of $25,000 or a one-year imprisonment will be imposed for a first offense, and a $50,000 maximum fine or two years imprisonment will be imposed for each subsequent act of piracy.

P.J.   Abbreviation for Presiding Judge.

plagiarism   The crime of taking the copyrighted words, writings, language, or ideas of another and passing them off as one's own. To be liable for plagiarism, it is not necessary to copy another's work exactly or entirely as long as a substantial portion is duplicated. See also COPYRIGHT.

plain error rule   The principle by which an appeals court can reverse a judgment and order a new trial because of an error in the proceedings that clearly prejudices (harms) a person's position and prevents justice from being done—even if the error was not objected to at the time it was made. Conflicting and confusing instructions given by the judge to the jury would be an error of this kind. See APPEAL AND ERROR.

plain meaning rule   The principle of CONTRACT law that determines the actual purpose of the contract that the parties made by studying the text of the document. The court looks at the writing and the language of the contract and, if the meaning of the words is plain and clear, that language will control the obligations of the parties under the contract. No other evidence can be used.

EXAMPLE John agrees to sell Ted his dog for $50. If John only has one dog, the language of the contract is clear and so is the duty of John to give Ted his dog when Ted pays $50. On the other hand, if John has three dogs, two of which are about to have puppies, there could be confusion and disagreement as to which dog John meant to sell. The plain meaning rule could not be used in this case to help resolve the legal dispute between John and Ted because the term "my dog" could apply to any one of John's three dogs. Additional information, apart from the contract, is needed to determine the meaning.

plaintiff   The person who brings a lawsuit against another person or corporation, called the defendant.

plat   A map or drawing of a piece of land, subdivided into lots with streets and alleys.

plea   The defendant's formal answer to a criminal charge. His plea can be guilty, not guilty, or *nolo contendere* (no contest). See CRIMINAL LAW. In civil lawsuits, a plea is a PLEADING.

plea bargaining   The process by which a criminal defendant's attorney negotiates with the prosecutor about the charges to which the defendant will plead guilty and other arrangements, such as the prosecutor's recommendation of a sentence to the judge. See CRIMINAL LAW.

pleading   The process by which each side of a lawsuit makes formal written statements in order to define the issues to be presented at the TRIAL. When one person (the plaintiff) decides to sue another (the defendant), he submits a paper, called the COMPLAINT, to the defendant and files a copy of it with the court. The complaint states the plaintiff's version of the facts at issue and the relief to which he claims to be entitled. The defendant's ANSWER is a written statement that responds to the charges in the plaintiff's complaint by stating what the defendant considers to be the facts and may also state his claims against the plaintiff. It is sent to the plaintiff as well as filed with the court. The plaintiff may deny or contradict the facts and claims contained in the defendant's answer in the reply. This process continues until all the issues and questions are clearly spelled out for trial.

Pleading is also the name given to these formal statements. Their purpose is to present, define, and narrow the issues of the lawsuit. They form the foundation of, and limit, the proof that can be submitted in court. Pleadings are designed to advise the court and the opposing party of the issues and the cause of action (ground for the lawsuit) or the defense to the action so that the court may declare the law and the opposing party may be prepared to meet the issues. When certain facts are not the subject of dispute, they should be clearly stated so that it will be unnecessary for the opposite party to prove them. This saves the court's time.

plebiscite   A vote of all the people of a state or nation who are entitled to vote for or against a proposed law that, if adopted, will result in a major change in their constitution. See also REFERENDUM.

pledge   **1** A promise to make a charitable contribution. See SUBSCRIPTION. **2** A type of SECURED TRANSACTION in which the debtor transfers personal property to a creditor to insure the payment of a debt. If the debtor refuses to pay within the time specified, the creditor may sell the property to pay the debt. The specified article delivered to the creditor's possession, such as a diamond ring, is also called a pledge. The debtor who delivers the property as security is called the *pledgor*. The creditor who holds the property to insure that he will be paid is called the *pledgee*. Pawnbrokers are an example of pledgees.

A pledge differs from a sale; in the case of a pledge only possession and not ownership of the property passes to the pledgee, whereas in a sale both ownership and possession pass to the purchaser.

■ **Elements**   In order for a pledge to exist there must be a pledgor and a pledgee, a debt or obligation, and a contract of pledge. A pledge may be made not only to secure debts and obligations at the time they are created but also to insure payment of past debts as well as anticipated future loans. The contract requires that possession of the pledged property must pass from the pledgor to the pledgee. The pledgee then has a LIEN (legal claim) on the property for the payment of the debt by the pledgor. Unless required by law, a contract of pledge does not have to be in writing.

A debtor may pledge any interest that he owns in personal property. Personal property is any property that is not real estate. It may be something tangible, such as a car or radio, or intangible, such as a stock certificate. Property that does not exist at the time cannot be the subject of the pledge. For example, if your aunt tells you that she has left you her $5,000 grandfather clock in her will, you cannot pledge this property to anyone because the clock will not exist as your property until your aunt dies.

A pledge of personal property must be in either the actual (physical) or constructive possession of the pledgee or his representative. It is in constructive possession of the pledgee if he has some control over it. For example, a pledgee has constructive possession of a ring if he has the only set of keys to the safe-deposit box where the ring is kept. The pledged property must remain in the continuous possession and control of the pledgee in order for his lien (claim) against the property to be effective.

EXAMPLE   George owed Patrick $500 and pledged his ste-
O⊷❋ reo. A month later, Patrick returned the stereo to George upon his promise to pay the debt within two weeks. During this time, George had also borrowed $500 from Owen, who accepted the returned stereo as security for payment of the debt to him. When Patrick demanded payment of the $500 and George failed to pay, Patrick could not demand that the stereo then in Owen's possession be sold to pay the debt. Patrick lost his rights in the pledged property once he returned it to George. Owen, a subsequent creditor, had a legally recognized security interest in the pledged property. Patrick's only recourse was to sue George in small claims court for the payment of the debt.

■ **Rights and liabilities of the pledgee**   A pledgee is entitled to keep possession and control of the pledged property only until the debt has been paid in full, but he is usually not entitled to use it, unless he has the pledgor's permission or it is necessary for its preservation, such as exercising a live animal. If he uses the property without consent, he will be liable to the pledgor for CONVERSION (an act that unjustly deprives a person of his property without his permission).

A pledgee is entitled to reimbursement for expenses reasonably incurred by him in keeping, caring for, and protecting the pledged property. He also has a duty to exercise due care in preserving the property. If the pledgee damages the property either intentionally or negligently, the pledgor may sue him for his loss or set off the amount of damages in an action against him by the pledgee. This means that if the pledgor refuses to pay the debt and is sued by the pledgee, the amount of the debt will be reduced by the amount of damages to the property.

■ **Enforcement**   If the pledgor fails to pay his debt, the pledgee may collect the pledge if he had only constructive possession of it and may sell it without judicial process after giving reasonable notice to the debtor to redeem it (pay his debt). Or, depending on state law, he may bring a lawsuit to enforce the lien on the property in a judicial sale of the property. If the proceeds from the sale do not satisfy the debt, the pledgee may sue the pledgor for the balance. If the proceeds more than pay the debt, the excess must be returned to the pledgor.

plenary   Full, absolute, unqualified. For example, the legislature has plenary power to make the laws.

Plessy v. Ferguson   In this 1896 decision, the Supreme Court upheld the constitutionality of an 1890 Louisiana law that required "white" and "colored" persons to be given "separate but equal" accommodations on railway passenger cars. The plaintiff, Plessy, who "was seven-eighths Caucasian and one-eighth African blood" paid for a first-class seat on a Louisiana railroad. He took a seat in the coach that was reserved for white passengers but was told by the conductor, under threat of being thrown off the train and arrested, to leave the "white" car and go to the "colored" coach. When he refused, he was thrown off the train and jailed. He was tried for breaking a law that he claimed was unconstitutional because it violated the 13th Amendment abolishing slavery and the 14th Amendment prohibiting state laws that discriminate unjustly against people.

The Supreme Court reasoned that the 13th Amendment was insufficient to protect black people from certain harsh state laws that treated them unequally. The Court decided that the law establishing separate but equal public accommodations and facilities was a reasonable exercise of a state's POLICE POWER to promote the public good. "If the two races are to meet upon terms of social equality," the Court wrote, "it must be the result of voluntary consent of the individuals"—and not the result of the government's enforcement of the 14th Amendment.

In 1954, nearly 60 years later, the Supreme Court overruled this decision in the case of BROWN V. BOARD OF EDUCATION and recognized that separate but equal educational facilities were inherently unequal. Subsequent Supreme Court decisions prohibited racial segregation in all public facilities and accommodations. See CIVIL RIGHTS; EQUAL PROTECTION OF LAWS.

plurality   In ELECTION law, a plurality of votes is the excess of votes cast for one candidate over those cast for any of the others. When there are only two candidates, the one who receives the greater number of votes has a majority as well as a plurality. When, however, there are more than two candidates, the person who receives the greatest number of votes has a plurality. He does not have a majority unless he receives a greater number of votes than those cast for all his competitors combined, or, in other words, more than one half of the total number of votes cast.

point   1 An individual legal argument or question raised in a lawsuit. *Points and authorities* is the name for a document prepared to substantiate a legal position taken in a case.   2 The initial fee that MORTGAGE companies charge for lending money. It is usually 1 percent of the amount of the mortgage and can vary according to the lending institution and fluctuations of the economy. For instance, the amount of a point for a $40,000 mortgage would be $400.

poison   Any substance dangerous to living organisms; a substance that destroys some vital body function or kills if applied internally or externally. *Economic poisons* are substances used to control insects, weeds, fungus, bacteria, rodents, predatory animals, or other pests.

■ **Kinds of poisons**   The way a poison is controlled depends on its usefulness, the reasons for its use, and its potential for harm. The principle that the law has a right and a duty to control harmful substances is called the state's POLICE POWER. Broadly speaking, this power enables state governments to control the dangerous qualities of cosmetics; spoiled food; dangerous herbs, leaves, berries, and plants; household and industrial chemicals and cleaning supplies; patent medicines, drugs and narcotics, alcoholic beverages, and other regulated substances; herbicides, insecticides, rodenticides, and other pesticides; and carbon dioxide, noxious fumes, and other dangerous gases.

■ **Regulations**   Poisons are regulated by a wide variety of special statutes. Pesticides must be registered with the federal government, and those denied registration cannot be used. The ENVIRONMENTAL PROTECTION AGENCY has issued a number of regulations governing the use of approved pesticides. For example, a certain amount of time must pass after crops are treated before farm workers may reenter the fields. Federal law also prohibits unauthorized mixing of a poisonous substance with any product and requires clear labeling for anything sold with a poisonous ingredient. It may not be enough to list all the chemicals in a container or even to put the word "poison" on the label. The manufacturer should also give warning of what injuries are likely to occur and under what conditions the poison will cause harm. Stricter standards are applied to household products than to poisonous products intended to be used in a factory, on a farm, or by a specially trained person. Poisonous food products are banned, and pesticide residues on foods are prohibited above certain low tolerance levels.

Laws protecting children   Federal laws require special packaging for some household products so that a child will not mistake them for food or will not be able to open containers. Another law makes federal funds available for local programs to reduce or eliminate the danger of lead-based paint poisoning. Under the Hazardous Substances Act, toys containing poisonous substances can be banned or recalled.

Other areas   For information relating to regulation of dangerous drugs and illegal narcotics, see DRUGS AND NARCOTICS; for control of threats to public health, see PUBLIC HEALTH; for the regulation of environmental hazards, see ENVIRONMENTAL LAW; and for the legal responsibilities of manufacturers or sellers of defective or mislabeled drugs, chemicals, or other poisonous compounds, see PRODUCT LIABILITY.

police   1 A division of a state or local government responsible for the protection of public health, safety, and morals and the prevention of crime.   2 Individuals employed by a municipality or state to enforce local ordinances and state criminal laws so that the peace and order of the community may be preserved.

A police officer is a person hired to work for the police department. Although a police officer belongs to the general category of *peace officers* (persons named by a public authority to protect the peace of the community), not all peace officers are police officers. A police officer is different from a sheriff or constable, who is elected to his position and who is authorized to serve, process, and attach a debtor's property in addition to enforcing criminal laws. See SHERIFFS AND CONSTABLES.

■ **Creation and control of a police system** A police system may be created by a state to maintain law and order throughout the state. A city, town, or other municipal corporation is authorized to establish its own police force to enforce local ordinances, as well as state laws, and to preserve public peace and safety within its boundaries if the state has given it the power to do so. State and local police departments cooperate with one another in the prevention and detection of crime.

A state or municipality may establish its own civil service commission to regulate, manage, and exercise authority over the officers and employees of its police department as well as other public employees. Such a commission sets the qualifications for successful job applicants. Qualifications for police officers often include having a high school diploma and passing entrance and physical examinations that are reasonably related to job performance. In addition, the commission may impose conditions that must be fulfilled if a police officer wants to keep his job, such as mandatory target practice and periodic physical examinations. Rules and regulations may prevent police officers from taking additional employment (called moonlighting) or engaging in certain political activities, such as serving on a city council. Vacation and sick time, pension and disability plans, and medical, dental, and life insurance coverage may also fall within the province of the civil service commission.

■ **Duties and powers** The duties of police officers as prescribed by law and the rules of the department commonly include the enforcement of laws, prevention and detection of crime, and the direction and regulation of traffic. Police officers are usually granted wide powers to preserve the peace and safety of the community, but the exercise of these powers must not infringe upon anyone's constitutional rights. A police officer must obtain a warrant from an impartial magistrate to arrest a person suspected of having committed a crime unless circumstances excuse this requirement. For example, if a person commits a felony (a serious crime) in the presence of the officer, the officer does not need a warrant in order to lawfully seize the suspect. When an officer determines that a person or his property or premises must be searched in the investigation of a crime, he must get a search warrant unless circumstances require immediate action—if the officer is in hot pursuit of the suspect, for example, or if there is a serious likelihood that the property in question will be destroyed before a warrant can be obtained. The constitutional safeguards that must be observed in seizing and examining a criminal suspect and his property are extensively discussed in ARREST and SEARCH AND SEIZURE.

Once police have taken an individual into custody as a suspect, they cannot browbeat or otherwise coerce him into admitting his guilt. A suspect who is held in custody for interrogation has certain constitutional rights that the police may not violate. These rights are embodied in the Miranda Warnings that are recited by the police to the suspect once he is held for questioning. If the police fail to administer these warnings, any statements made by the suspect cannot be used against him in a criminal prosecu-

tion because his privilege against self-incrimination has been violated by their conduct. The denial of a suspect's request to talk to an attorney after he has been apprehended violates another of the suspect's constitutional rights, his right to counsel. This denial also makes a suspect's statements inadmissible evidence. For a detailed discussion of a suspect's constitutional rights after being taken into police custody, see COUNSEL, RIGHT TO; MIRANDA WARNINGS; and SELF-INCRIMINATION.

A police officer may use reasonable force in the apprehension, search, or arrest of a suspect only when the circumstances warrant it. For example, if a person suspected of child molesting does not resist arrest, the arresting officer has no justification for hitting or beating the suspect merely because the nature of the alleged act is repugnant to the officer. When the use of force is justified, the degree of force must not be excessive in light of the facts of the case. A police officer who is punched by a man resisting arrest is not justified in killing him. If, however, the man shot at the officer, the officer could return the fire in self-defense. A police officer and his department may be sued for damages that he has caused as a result of violating a suspect's constitutional rights or as a result of police brutality.

police power The inherent right of a state to make and enforce all laws and regulations necessary for the health, morals, safety, good order, and welfare of the state and its citizens. The state's exercise of its police power is superior to all private CONTRACT and PROPERTY rights.

Examples of the state's police power are laws that promote the public safety by (1) limiting the speed of MOTOR VEHICLES traveling on public highways; (2) limiting the weight of loads carried on public highways; (3) requiring LICENSES and liability INSURANCE for drivers on public roads; (4) requiring large gasoline storage tanks to be underground; and (5) requiring explosives to be manufactured at a safe distance from residential areas.

Other examples are statutes that protect the public morals by suppressing gambling (see GAMING), houses of prostitution, and the sale of INTOXICATING LIQUORS. Laws that protect the PUBLIC HEALTH by requiring vaccinations against disease and the sale of only pure drugs or milk and laws establishing pollution-emission standards for automobiles are also valid exercises of the police power.

A state's police power includes preventing a nonresident from voting or holding public office and charging nonresidents a higher fee for the privilege of hunting or fishing within its borders. See CONSTITUTIONAL LAW.

The federal government has no general police power as do the states, but it does have comparable power to protect the health, safety, and general well-being of the public by virtue of its enumerated powers found in Article I of the Constitution and through laws enacted by Congress. For example, under the COMMERCE CLAUSE, which regulates interstate commerce, and federal laws administered by the FOOD AND DRUG ADMINISTRATION, the federal government can ban the sale of meat products treated with carcinogenic chemicals.

policy 1 The general principles by which a government is guided in its management of public affairs. 2 The

THE ROLE OF THE LAYMAN IN LAW ENFORCEMENT

WILLIAM H. WEBSTER

Director, Federal Bureau of Investigation,
United States Department of Justice

Crime is a distressing fact of modern life. Recently, in a single year, more than 12 million crimes were committed in the United States—an average of some 55 crimes for every 1,000 inhabitants. The Federal Bureau of Investigation's Uniform Crime Reports have shown that a violent crime is committed every 27 seconds and a crime against property every 3 seconds—not including the crimes that are never reported.

Admittedly, crime statistics and percentages can sometimes impart a sense of remoteness and impersonality. The full impact of criminality is often minimized unless one is exposed to it firsthand as either a victim or a witness. Yet statistics show that the odds are overwhelming—most American families will at one time or another be exposed to the stark realities of crime.

All citizens, whether victims of, or witnesses to, a crime should know something of their rights, responsibilities, and obligations in such a circumstance. The actions citizens take—or do not take—immediately following a criminal occurrence can significantly influence the success or failure of society's efforts to identify and apprehend those responsible. Cooperative efforts between citizens and the criminal justice system are absolutely essential to the identification, apprehension, and successful prosecution of the offender. It should also be noted that citizen cooperation may not only assist in punishing the offender, but may also serve to exonerate an innocent person erroneously accused. Each citizen thus has imposed upon him a duty to involve himself in society's organized efforts to maintain peace and order.

From hue and cry to police departments

This duty of a private citizen to become involved in peacekeeping efforts is deeply rooted in our cultural and political evolution. The so-called hue and cry of centuries past, which obligated each citizen within sight or earshot to join in the pursuit of a fleeing criminal, was actually mandated by statute in 13th-century England. Failure to respond to the hue and cry was cause for fine or punishment. When the statute was finally abolished early in the 1800's, habitual response to the hue and cry had become part of the Anglo-Saxon sense of citizenship. In fact, some states still have laws in force compelling citizens to render reasonable aid to law enforcement authorities upon demand.

Midway into the last century, however, law enforcement began to evolve into the position it occupies today in our society. Where formerly each citizen was expected to actively and overtly involve himself in the peacekeeping process when the hue and cry was raised, permanent policing bodies came to be vested with more and more primary crime control duties. The burden that once rested heavily upon the individual passed to public agencies mandated to serve the populace as full-time forces for civic order. That trend led steadily to today's fully equipped departments of police, staffed by trained professionals and supported financially by the citizenry through taxes.

The police profession in recent years has made tremendous gains in education, training, the forensic and social sciences, and technology. These factors have combined to produce a police officer infinitely more competent in the discharge of his responsibilities and more attuned to his role as public servant and protector. He is a true professional who fully merits the trust, confidence, and assistance of all law-abiding citizens.

The policeman's skills and resources will, however, be less valuable if the law enforcement officer does not receive the support of and cooperation from the public. Without pertinent information as to the circumstances surrounding criminal activity, the police are severely handicapped. A recognition of the manner in which the police solve crimes will reveal the importance of citizen input.

How the police solve crimes

When a crime has been committed, the overriding objective of law enforcement authorities is to reconstruct what actually occurred. This reconstruction serves a two-fold purpose. First, it yields tactical investigative assistance in the hours following the criminal event to aid in the solution of the crime, the identification of the perpetrator, and the recovery of the crime's proceeds. Second, it facilitates a later accounting of the incident accurately and fairly in a court of law.

Since a witness or bystander is likely to be the primary link between the crime's occurrence and the investigation conducted by the police officer, the observer's account of what actually took place assumes a significant role in the reconstruction process. An alert, observant witness able to provide a detailed and objective narration of what happened is of great help to the investigator.

Obtaining the observations of a witness is, however, only a part of the total evidence-gathering procedure. Crimes like embezzlement or computer theft are often of such a sophisticated nature that even if a witness were present during their commission, he probably would not realize that illegal activity was taking place. Therefore, the full spectrum of evidence sought by the investigator may consist of witnesses, fingerprints, records, documents, material objects—anything that tends to produce conviction in the mind as to existence of a fact.

In this respect, forensic science has made notable strides in recent years in the scientific examination and evaluation of physical evidence. Employing highly sophisticated techniques, including instrumentation for scientific analysis, criminalists are frequently able to elicit vast amounts of pertinent information from seemingly insignificant items of evidence—a strand of hair, a bit of soil, or an unusual stain.

It is important, therefore, that the citizen recognize this often hidden value of physical evidence at a crime scene and that any available physical evidence be preserved in an undisturbed state until the police arrive. In this way, the evidence will not be contaminated and the chain of control necessary at trial to tie the evidence to the criminal offender will be maintained. Thus any action taken by a witness or victim to preserve such evidence will pay off handsomely in terms of a more efficient and accurate reconstruction of the crime. It should also be noted that physical evidence is not only invaluable as an adjunct to the crime's solution, but it often serves to corroborate an eyewitness account.

If you witness a crime or see something suspicious

Given the need for citizen cooperation and participation in law enforcement, the question becomes what each citizen can do to fulfill this duty. It is recognized that many people are hesitant to call the police because they do not know what activities should be considered suspicious. Others are worried about bothering the police or being embarrassed if their suspicions are unfounded. Others do not call because they assume someone else has already called, and some simply just do not want to get involved. However, the police welcome citizen input, and everyone should take upon himself the personal responsibility to respond to suspicious or criminal activity as he would want his neighbor to respond if his own family needed assistance or his property was being threatened.

Whether or not an event is suspicious depends upon what is normal activity under the same circumstances. In many ways, the term "suspicious" is synonymous with "unusual." Depending on the circumstances, the following activities could possibly be considered suspicious:

- Anyone forcibly entering a car or home.
- Someone who runs from a home or business.
- Anyone with a weapon.
- Someone screaming.
- A stranger who is offering young children candy or money.
- Any indication that a home or business has been forcibly entered or telephone wires cut. (In this circumstance, do not enter the premises but call the police from a nearby location and keep the premises under observation in addition to noting any strange persons or vehicles in the area.)
- Someone whose dress or demeanor is not compatible with the neighborhood.
- A person who seems to have no purpose in the neighborhood.
- A stranger carrying what could be burglary loot—a radio, TV, pillowcase, suitcase—in your neighborhood.
- Strangers looking into parked cars or into the windows of homes, garages, or other structures.
- An individual who rings the front doorbell of a home and then walks around to the rear of the house.
- Adults loitering around schools, playgrounds, or secluded areas.
- A car that seems to be cruising an area or moving slowly and without lights.
- A car that speeds through or away from a location.
- Moving, delivery, or maintenance trucks parked at unoccupied homes.
- A car that has been parked at the same location for several days and is strange to the neighborhood, particularly if it has out-of-town license plates.
- Vehicles with trunk or ignition locks punched or wing vent broken.
- Dirty license plates on a clean car.

Any citizen who notices these types of activities should promptly contact his local police to inform them. When exposed to such activity, it is important for the citizen to be observant and to get a good description of the criminal and his mode of transportation. The citizen should try to fix an image of the persons and vehicles in his mind and should try to remember exactly what happened. It is often helpful for the citizen to immediately write down his observations and to compare the offender's characteristics with his own.

Some of the facts about persons that police need are as follows:

Sex	Race	Age
Height	Weight	Build
Hair color and style		Eyes (including glasses)

Clothing—start at the top (hat) and describe to the bottom (shoes), including any jewelry worn

Any physical deformities or unique characteristics, such as scars or tattoos

Speech pattern (including accent and pitch)

Type of weapons and hand in which held

The police also need as much information as can be remembered about the vehicles involved, such as:

License number (usually most important)		
Colors	Make	Year
Body style	Visible damage	

Accessories (luggage rack, CB antenna)

Direction of travel

Number of occupants and their descriptions

In reporting to the police, remember that time is essential. Call the police *immediately*. Remain calm, speak clearly, and give the following information: your name and telephone number, what has been observed, where and when the event occurred, a complete description of persons and vehicles.

While awaiting the police, the citizen should not disturb the crime scene or handle physical evidence since, as previously discussed, such evidence can often complement and supplement the information provided by the eyewitness. The citizen should also jot down on paper what happened but should not compare with others those notes or his impressions of what occurred until after talking to the police.

If you witness a crime or see something suspicious

With respect to assault, robbery, and rape, the citizen must emotionally prepare himself for the fact that he or she might be attacked on some occasion and should prepare a plan of action ahead of time. If he or she is confronted, the objective should be to get away with the least harm and injury.

If assaulted, robbed, or raped, the citizen should tell the first responsible person he or she meets and point out the attacker if he is still in the vicinity. The police should be notified immediately, even if the citizen has managed to escape unharmed. There is a good possibility that the criminal's next victim may not be as fortunate.

With respect to rape, the victim should not change clothes, bathe, or douche, or touch anything the attacker used or touched. By so doing, she will help law enforcement by preserving valuable evidence against the attacker.

The citizen should realize that his duty to cooperate and participate with the criminal justice system does not end with his notifying the police and reporting the details of the crime. He should contact the police if he recalls any further details at a later time. Moreover, the citizen should be available to the police to view photographs, suspects, and other materials that could assist in solving the crime. The citizen should also be willing and prepared to serve as a witness in any prosecution of the offender. Without such continuing cooperation of the citizen, the law enforcement process is truncated prior to its completion.

In conclusion, law enforcement in our society functions as the entry threshold into the entire criminal justice system. Each time a citizen notifies police authorities of a crime he has witnessed, cooperates fully with police investigators by providing a complete account of what was observed, and fulfills his civic duty to testify in court as to his observations when called upon to do so, our commitment as a people to the rule of law is again underscored. And that citizen can pride himself that he has made a significant contribution to the good mankind has sought for centuries— a harmonious and tranquil society of law-abiding people.

manner in which a law or ordinance affects the welfare of the state or community. See PUBLIC POLICY. **3** The name given to a contract of INSURANCE.

political question A kind of question that courts refuse to hear or to decide on because it relates strictly to policymaking and its determination by the judiciary would therefore infringe on executive or legislative powers in violation of the doctrine of separation of powers. See CONSTITUTIONAL LAW. For example, the determination of whether or not a foreign country has become an independent state is a political question. A court decision in the area of foreign affairs would invade the exclusive power of the executive branch. The fact that a lawsuit seeks to protect a POLITICAL RIGHT, however, does not mean that it presents a political question that the courts cannot decide.

political right **1** A right that may be exercised in establishing or administering the government. **2** A citizen's right, recognized by federal and state constitutions, which gives him power to participate in directing the government. For example, voting in ELECTIONS is a political right. See CITIZEN; CIVIL RIGHTS; CONSTITUTIONAL LAW.

polling the jury The method by which jurors are individually asked in the courtroom whether they assented, and still assent, to the verdict. Each juror is called by name and asked to declare his or her verdict before it is recorded. See JURY.

polls **1** The place where voters cast their ballots. See ELECTION. **2** Individuals; persons considered singly. For example, a challenge to the polls is a challenge to the individual jurors making up the jury panel or an objection to one or more particular jurors.

poll tax A tax of a specific sum levied on each person who votes. Federal laws and decisions in the federal courts, including the Supreme Court, have held that a poll tax cannot be a prerequisite to voting. See ELECTION.

polygamy The criminal offense of having several wives or husbands at one time. See BIGAMY.

popular name table A name for reference charts that aid in finding statutes, if their common names are known. For example, one can find the official name and location in the United States Code of the Sherman Antitrust Act from a popular name table.

positive evidence Direct proof of the fact or point at issue; EVIDENCE that, if proved, definitely establishes the truth or falsehood of a point at issue; another word for direct evidence.

positive law A statute that has been enacted by a legislature and that must be obeyed—as opposed to a moral rule or precept, for example, which cannot be enforced by a political authority. In order to emphasize the fact that statutes are authoritatively imposed, they are described as positive law.

posse comitatus (Latin) "Power of a county." Originally, the term meant the entire population of a county above the age of 15, whom the sheriff could summon to his assistance when necessary, such as to pursue criminals. Now the word "posse" is used to refer to a small group of citizens who may be gathered, either by the sheriff or by some other peace officer, to help enforce the law, usually on an emergency basis. Books and movies about the wild West often show the sheriff rounding up a posse.

possession The control of real estate or personal property, whether or not one is the owner. For example, the tenant of a building and the driver of an automobile have possession, whether or not they own the property. Possession of certain property, such as narcotics, can be a crime.

possessory action A lawsuit to gain or regain control of real property (real estate), as distinguished from one seeking to obtain or prove ownership of it. For example, an eviction proceeding is a possessory action taken by a landlord to regain control of property from a tenant. See LANDLORD AND TENANT.

Postal Service The independent government agency, including local branches in cities and towns, whose function is to receive, transmit, and deliver the mail. Establishment, control, and regulation of the postal service is vested in Congress by the Constitution. Postal services must be provided to all communities in the country, including small towns and rural areas.

postdate To date a written document, such as a check, later than the time it is actually signed. The check is not payable until the day it is dated.

postmortem (Latin) "After death"; an autopsy or examination of a body to determine the cause of death. The term is often applied to a coroner's investigation into the cause of death. See CORONER.

pourover A clause in a WILL or TRUST providing that, upon the person's death, his money or property shall be transferred (poured over) into a different existing trust.

power The capability to do something. In law, it is authority delegated from one person to another, enabling him to do something that he could not do otherwise. The word "power" is sometimes used in the same sense as a "right," such as a property owner's power to use and dispose of his property. See POWER OF APPOINTMENT. Power can also be inherent by virtue of the nature of a thing. For example, a government has the inherent power to handle foreign affairs simply by reason of its function as a government.

power of appointment Authorization given by the owner of property to another person to designate (1) persons (appointees) who are to take the property or (2) proportionate shares that appointees are to take in the property. In most cases, the document creating the power is either a DEED or a WILL. When a power of appointment is exercised, TITLE to (ownership of) the property usually passes to the appointees from the property owner, not from his authorized representative.

Powers of appointment can be exercised for both real estate and personal property. For example, William's will could provide that, upon his death, Harry, his friend, shall have the power to decide how William's stocks should be divided among his three children.

power of attorney A document authorizing someone to act as your agent. Before entering a hospital for an operation, for example, you might want to give your power of attorney to a member of your family.

power of sale A clause sometimes inserted in a MORTGAGE, giving the lender the right to foreclose. He may advertise and sell the property, if the borrower fails to make his payments on time, without having to get court authority.

practicable What can be done or accomplished. The law places only practicable requirements on citizens.

practice 1 Repeated performance; succession of similar acts; CUSTOM AND USAGE. 2 Exercise of a profession. Practice of a profession implies a continuing occupation. 3 The method of proceeding in court in order to enforce rights or redress wrongs; the form of starting and conducting a lawsuit or other judicial proceeding according to legal rules and principles and court regulations and precedents.

preamble A statement at the beginning of a constitution or STATUTE explaining its objectives and the reasons for its enactment.

precatory Expressing a desire or request rather than a positive command or instruction. A precatory TRUST is created by certain words, such as "I wish," "I request," and "I heartily beseech," which make a request or give permission rather than issue a command. Precatory words used in a WILL to dispose of property will not be given effect by a court because they do not command the heirs to distribute the property in a certain way.

precedent A court decision on a question of law that serves as authority for deciding similar questions in future cases. See STARE DECISIS.

precept A written command or order from an authority, such as a court. Warrants and processes in criminal and civil cases are called precepts.

precinct 1 A police district. 2 An ELECTION district created for convenient administration of polling places.

preemption The doctrine that whenever a state and the federal government each has the right to enact legislation in a particular field and the federal government enacts legislation covering the entire field, (1) a state has no authority to enact legislation on the same matter, and (2) any laws on the subject that the states have previously

passed are void. For example, when Congress enacted legislation regulating tobacco inspection, it preempted any state legislation on the subject. The preemption doctrine derives from the SUPREMACY CLAUSE of the Constitution.

preemptive right The right granted each stockholder in a CORPORATION to purchase his proportionate share of any new stock being issued to maintain his proportionate share of ownership in the corporation. For example, 1,000 shares were originally issued and stockholder Rose purchased 200 of them. If, at a later date, another 1,000 shares are issued, Rose has the right to purchase an additional 200 shares before they are offered to new or prospective stockholders.

preference 1 The right of one creditor to be paid from a debtor's assets before other creditors are paid. A preference can only occur when there is a provision in a law or some fixed principle of COMMON LAW that creates a special, superior right in certain creditors over others. For example, if a debtor owes back taxes, the Internal Revenue Service is a preferred creditor and entitled to payment before most other creditors.
2 Payment by an impoverished debtor to one or more of his creditors of a larger amount of their claims than they would be entitled to receive on a pro rata distribution. For example, Deland owes Amos, Brown, and Croft $5,000 each. All three are equally entitled to payment, but Deland has only $12,000 in assets. Instead of paying each creditor $4,000, Deland pays Amos and Brown in full, and pays Croft the remaining $2,000. Such payments usually are not legal but state and federal laws must be consulted to determine the legality of the particular case. See ASSIGNMENT FOR BENEFIT OF CREDITORS; BANKRUPTCY.

preferred stock A class of corporate stock that is given priority over COMMON STOCK in paying dividends (profits). See CORPORATION. Holders of preferred stock are entitled to received dividends at a fixed annual rate. If the earnings are more than sufficient, the remainder is usually given to holders of common stock. Sometimes, however, the remainder is distributed pro rata to both classes of stockholders. If the earnings of the company are not sufficient to pay the preferred stockholders' fixed annual dividend, whatever money is available will be used to pay them.

The fixed dividend of preferred stock may be cumulative or noncumulative. If it is cumulative and the dividend is not earned or paid in full in any one year, it becomes a charge against the surplus earnings of the next year and succeeding years. All such accumulated and unpaid dividends on the preferred stock must be paid off before the common stock is entitled to receive dividends. If the preferred stock is noncumulative, its preference in any year terminates by the failure to pay its dividend in that year.

prejudice A bias; a preconceived opinion not based on knowledge or proper investigation.

A judge's prejudice toward a person in a lawsuit (not his views about the matter in litigation) disqualifies him from the case. No judge may sit in a proceeding when it appears probable that a fair trial cannot take place before him. For example, a judge who stated that deaf mutes were imbeciles was guilty of prejudice when he denied an ADOPTION because the prospective parents were deaf mutes.

When a motion is denied or a bill in EQUITY (a petition for relief) is dismissed *without prejudice,* it means that no rights or privileges of the party are waived or lost. See MOTIONS AND ORDERS.

Either a civil or a criminal case may be dismissed with or without prejudice. The result of a *dismissal with prejudice* is that the plaintiff or the prosecutor cannot ever again bring the same case against the same defendant in the future. The effect of a *dismissal without prejudice* is as if the case had never been brought to court at all. Consequently, the plaintiff or prosecutor may bring the same case against the same defendant at some future time. For an explanation of when cases may be dismissed with prejudice and when without prejudice, see DISMISSAL.

A prejudicial error affects the final result of a lawsuit and is harmful to the rights of one of the parties. In such a case, the party is entitled to appeal his case. An example of a prejudicial error is when the court fails to exclude as evidence a confession that was obtained from a defendant in violation of his right against SELF-INCRIMINATION. See APPEAL AND ERROR.

preliminary hearing   The hearing given to a person accused of a crime to decide whether or not he should be charged with a crime and, if charged, either held in custody or released on bail. The purposes of such a hearing are (1) to determine whether a crime has been committed, (2) to decide whether the accused should be tried, and (3) to eliminate unnecessary trials. At a preliminary hearing, a person has the right to have an attorney represent him and to cross-examine any witnesses who are brought to testify. If the court finds there is probable cause to believe that the accused committed the crime, the case will go before a grand jury or directly to trial, depending on state procedure. See CRIMINAL LAW.

premeditation   The act of planning something in advance; thinking about an intended act, such as MURDER.

premium   1 The sum of money paid for INSURANCE coverage.   2 A reward or BOUNTY.

prepaid legal plan   A group insurance plan that provides coverage for legal services, such as divorce actions, bankruptcy proceedings, and evictions.

preponderance of evidence   A measurement of the comparative weight or quality of EVIDENCE. The side in a lawsuit that has the greater weight of evidence in its favor has a preponderance of evidence. In civil cases, an issue of fact is usually not proved unless the plaintiff produces a preponderance of evidence. This applies to civil cases only; in criminal cases, the standard is beyond a reasonable doubt. See CRIMINAL LAW.

prerogative   An exclusive, unquestionable privilege. The special power vested in an official with respect to his position, or in an official body, such as a court or legislature.

prescription   A particular type of EASEMENT (a limited right to use land owned by someone else) created by long, continued use.

present   1 Submit something for consideration or action, as submitting a petition to a court.   2 Demand payment. In the law of negotiable instruments (documents that are payable in money upon demand or at a specific time, such as checks), to present a check for payment means to show it to the bank on which the check was drawn with a demand for payment. See COMMERCIAL PAPER.   3 As a plural noun, the phrase "these presents," when used in any legal document, means the document itself.

presentation   See PRESENTMENT.

presentence investigation   An investigation by PROBATION or PAROLE officers into a defendant's previous criminal record, educational background, and employment history. The report of this investigation is taken into consideration by the trial judge before he passes SENTENCE on a convicted defendant.

presentment   A GRAND JURY's written statement that a criminal offense has been committed that can be tried in the county and that there is probable cause for believing that the person named or described in the statement committed it.

President   Article II of the U.S. Constitution provides that "the executive power shall be vested in a President of the United States of America." This article discusses the office of the President of the United States, his powers and duties, and the qualifications for President.
■ **The office**   The executive branch of the federal government is one of the three equal branches of government (the others are the judicial and legislative branches) and exercises all executive power, or authority to carry out the laws passed by CONGRESS. The Constitution confers on the President the entire executive power, makes him Commander in Chief of the ARMED SERVICES, and imposes on him the duty to report to Congress on the state of the union and to recommend appropriate action. In addition, the President has supreme power over international matters, except for treaties, which must be ratified by the Senate.
■ **Qualifications**   Only a natural born citizen of the United States (born in the U.S. or has at least one parent who is a U.S. citizen) is eligible to be elected President. Naturalized citizens are not eligible. A Presidential candidate must be at least 35 years old and have been a resident of the United States for at least 14 years.
■ **Election**   The President is elected for a term of four years by the ELECTORAL COLLEGE, which is composed of presidential electors selected in each state.
■ **Term**   The 22nd Amendment to the Constitution provides that no person may be elected President for more than two four-year terms. A person who succeeds to the Presidency for more than two years of a term to which another person has been elected is eligible to serve only one four-year term. For example, after Vice President Gerald R. Ford succeeded to the Presidency on August 9, 1974, he

served more than two years of former President Richard M. Nixon's term. In consequence, President Ford was eligible to be elected for only one four-year term.

■ **Commander in Chief of armed forces** The President, as Chief Executive and Commander in Chief of the armed forces and the states' militia (National Guard), has the power to protect the peace of the United States. He can govern any captured territory until Congress establishes a civil government, declare martial law when there is an actual and present danger that civil government may stop functioning, and end a war by treaty or Presidential proclamation. Although he is Commander in Chief, the President may not declare war. This power is given to Congress under Article I of the Constitution.

Congress has attempted to limit the President's power as Commander in Chief when it is used in undeclared wars. During the Vietnam conflict, the question arose as to whether a President has independent power to use military forces not only to protect the nation from attack but also to further the nation's interests as he sees them. Consequently, Congress enacted the War Powers Resolution in 1973—over a Presidential veto. The resolution restricts a President's power to send troops into hostilities to the following circumstances: (1) when there is a declaration of war, (2) when he has specific statutory authorization, or (3) when there is a national emergency created by an attack on the United States, its territories or possessions, or its armed forces. The effect of this statute is as yet unknown because the resolution acknowledges that the President still can, on his own accord, use military forces for a limited period.

EXAMPLE In May 1975 the *Mayaguez*, a U.S. merchant ship carrying both civilian and military cargo, was seized by Cambodia for intruding into its territorial waters. The President, without consulting Congress, immediately sent naval forces to rescue the crew and the ship. In his report to Congress on the incident, the President cited his executive power and authority as Commander in Chief.

The incident illustrated the President's ability to use American power to protect U.S. interests as he perceived them. The War Powers Resolution seemed to have little impact on the President's power to deploy troops in difficult situations.

The President has the power under federal law to dispatch federal troops or the National Guard to a state in which he believes an insurrection exists. An *insurrection* is an uprising against civil or political authority in open and active opposition to the law.

EXAMPLE During the U.S. Civil War, the President, without authorization by Congress, ordered a blockade of Southern ports. Ships of neutral nations were seized and their cargoes confiscated when they tried to run the blockade. The owners of the confiscated property, who resided in the South and in neutral nations, claimed that the seizure was beyond the power of the President. The Supreme Court decided that the President had acted properly.

The President was—and still is—authorized by laws enacted by Congress in 1795 and 1807 to call out the nation's militia, or National Guard, and to use the armed forces without waiting for special legislative authority in cases of insurrection or invasion by a foreign nation. This is considered the President's fulfillment of his duties as Commander in Chief, not an initiation of war. The President determines what degree of force is required. Such a decision is not reviewable by a court.

The President may call on the armed forces or the National Guard when insurrection or domestic violence disrupts state or federal law in such a way that any group of people is deprived of a "right, privilege, immunity, or protection named in the Constitution and secured by law," and the states are unable, refuse, or fail to protect those rights. For example, in 1962, the President sent the National Guard to the University of Mississippi when the university refused to allow a black student to enroll, in violation of the 14th Amendment, and the state refused to enforce federal law. Where, however, no federal law is to be enforced, the President must wait for a request for help from the state legislature or governor.

■ **Domestic affairs** Executive power over domestic matters includes the power to commute (reduce) sentences and pardon offenses; the power to veto bills passed by Congress; the power to appoint and remove executive employees; the power to issue proclamations and orders; and the responsibility for directing the administration of laws.

Pardons The President has the power to commute (reduce) sentences and PARDON offenses against the United States (with the exception of impeachment), but not against the individual states. A pardon releases a criminal from the legal consequences of his offense and is usually granted only after a person has been convicted. Former President Richard M. Nixon was pardoned by President Gerald Ford for his alleged involvement in the Watergate affair even though he was never even indicted for a crime.

The pardoning power permits the President to issue general amnesties by proclamation, by which entire classes or communities are pardoned, such as the draft and military evaders from the Vietnam conflict. See AMNESTY.

Veto power The President may approve and sign a bill passed by Congress, thereby making it law. When, however, he has objections to a bill and vetoes (refuses to sign) it, it is returned "to that House in which it . . . originated" for reevaluation. If both houses of Congress pass the bill again by a two-thirds vote, the bill becomes a law despite the Presidential veto. Any bill that the President refuses to sign must be returned to the House within 10 days (not counting Sundays) or else it becomes a law, just as if the President had signed it. If Congress has adjourned during this time, preventing the return of the bill, it does not become a law. This is called a *pocket veto*.

Presidents often control the content of legislation to some extent by proposing changes and threatening to veto a bill unless it is modified. The President, however, does not have an *item veto*—that is, he cannot veto part of a bill and approve the remainder. Congress often responds to Presidential pressure by placing provisions in some bills that the President for some reason does not want to veto.

Proclamations and orders The President has the power to issue executive proclamations and orders as long as they are based on powers granted in the Constitution or delegated by Congress. A *proclamation* is the President's official announcement of an order. For example, by the

Emancipation Proclamation, Lincoln declared that all slaves would be freed. The President may issue proclamations when he thinks it proper to give notice or information to the public or to declare a national emergency. Congress may end a national emergency by a concurrent resolution (agreement by both houses), and the President may end it by a proclamation. The difference between an EDICT and a proclamation is that an edict enacts a new statute whereas a proclamation is a declaration of intent. Only Congress can enact a law.

An *executive order* interprets or implements a provision of a statute or the Constitution. It has the same effect as a statute and becomes a part of the law of the land. Executive orders that establish regulations for carrying out federal statutes have the same effect as if they had been included in the act itself.

The President may not take legislative power into his own hands in peacetime by issuing an executive order.

EXAMPLE In 1952 the President ordered the Secretary of Commerce to seize and operate most of the steel mills in the United States to prevent a strike that he believed would jeopardize the national defense. Congress had already rejected seizing the mills as a method of settling the labor dispute. The Supreme Court decided that the President's power as Commander in Chief did not include such an action. This situation occurred during the Korean conflict, which was considered a police action (not a war or other national emergency) by both the President and the Court.

Presidential proclamations and executive orders must be published in the FEDERAL REGISTER to notify the public of actions taken by the President.

Appointment and removal Article II, Section 2, of the Constitution provides that the President "shall nominate, and by and with the Advice and Consent of the Senate, shall appoint Ambassadors, other public Ministers and Consuls, Judges of the supreme Court, and all other Officers of the United States . . ." Any vacancies occurring during the recess of the Senate can be filled by the President. Aside from Senate approval (the House need not consent), there are no constitutional restrictions on Presidential appointments. Even if appointments are made solely for political reasons, they are lawful. But Congress may pass laws imposing certain restrictions. For instance, appointments to independent regulatory commissions are limited by statute to a bipartisan selection. As a consequence, membership on the Federal Communications Commission must be divided between Democrats and Republicans.

The President's power to remove or dismiss appointees is implied in his power of appointment. He can remove all appointees of the executive branch at will, even though their appointments required Senate approval. The President cannot remove Supreme Court justices and judges of lower federal courts who are in good standing or officers of administrative agencies that have been created by Congress. Such officers can be removed only for cause as provided by law. A member of the Federal Trade Commission, for example, cannot be removed because of his views on public policy.

■ **International relations** Only the President and his representatives, such as the Secretary of State, have the authority to represent the United States in international relations. Congress cannot receive ambassadors, nor can individual members of Congress lawfully transact government business with other nations. The President has exclusive authority to communicate with other nations, recognize foreign governments, and make executive agreements. Although the President has great power in conducting international relations, congressional cooperation is required because it is Congress that appropriates funds to carry out such commitments as foreign aid and the maintenance of troops and bases in foreign countries.

Treaty-making power The President can negotiate treaties with the advice and consent of the Senate. Every treaty has two distinct aspects: (1) it is a compact (agreement) with a foreign nation, and (2) it is part of the internal law of the United States. Treaties must be approved by two-thirds of the Senate. They are either self-executing or non-self-executing. A self-executing treaty takes effect without congressional legislation. It becomes part of the law of the land just as it is written. A non-self-executing treaty is one that requires some additional law to be passed by Congress before it can take effect. This distinction is important because only self-executing treaties are considered the supreme law of the land.

EXAMPLE In one case, Ware, a British creditor, sued a resident of Virginia named Hylton, based on the 1783 Treaty of Paris. The Supreme Court permitted the suit, although it was contrary to local law, because the self-executing treaty gave Ware a right to sue that was superior to local law. No legislation had been required to make the treaty effective.

The President may make *international compacts,* which are sometimes called *executive agreements,* with foreign nations without Senate approval. If the international compact is made with congressional authorization or if it is ratified afterward, it is equal to a self-executing treaty as supreme law of the land. When the international compact is made by the President based solely on his executive power, it does not have the same status as law of the land as a self-executing treaty does. Such agreement, however, still is superior to state laws.

EXAMPLE A Russian corporation deposited $10,000 with a private bank in New York called August Belmont and Company. The Soviet government liquidated the corporation and appropriated all of its assets in Russia and abroad, including the $10,000 credit in the Belmont bank. Through diplomatic correspondence, the U.S. President and the Russian government agreed to settle their claims against each other by Russia's assignment to the United States of all its claims against American nationals, including the Belmont bank. The bank, however, refused to pay the $10,000 to the United States, claiming that Russia's appropriation of this credit was contrary to the public policy of New York State and the United States. The United States sued for the deposit.

The Supreme Court decided that the U.S. government was entitled to the deposit. The Court reasoned that the executive branch, through the President, has the authority to speak for the government, in this case without the advice and consent of the Senate. This international compact was superior to any state law or policy on the same subject, making New York policy immaterial. The U.S. courts would not rule on the legality of the Russian government's confiscation of the $10,000 because in international agreements, each sovereign nation recognizes the other as independent in its domestic affairs.

The President's exercise of his constitutional power to conduct foreign relations is not subject to judicial review and binds the courts.

■ **Privilege**   A President has a qualified privilege to protect military, diplomatic, and national security secrets. He does not, however, have an absolute privilege to withhold materials that have been properly subpoenaed.

EXAMPLE A federal grand jury in 1974 indicted seven individuals for various offenses, including conspiracy to defraud the United States and to obstruct justice. Richard M. Nixon, then the President of the United States, was named as an unindicted coconspirator. The Special Prosecutor, who was in charge of the investigation and prosecution of "all offenses arising out of the 1972 Presidental election," popularly known as Watergate, obtained a subpoena directing the President to produce certain tape recordings and documents for the pending criminal trial.

The President moved to quash the subpoena based on, among other grounds, the claim of executive privilege. He alleged that the separation of powers doctrine precluded judicial review of a claim of executive privilege. The claim had two aspects in this case: whether there was an absolute privilege, and, if not, whether there was a qualified privilege that prevailed over the subpoena.

The Supreme Court rejected the contention that a President has an absolute privilege to withhold materials. The Court stated that "neither the doctrine of separation of powers, nor the need for confidentiality of high level communications . . . can sustain an absolute, unqualified presidential privilege of immunity from judicial process under all circumstances."

Although the Court rejected an absolute privilege, it did recognize a qualified privilege. "If a President concludes that compliance with a subpoena would be injurious to the public interest, he may properly, as was done here, invoke a claim of privilege." The federal district court must then "require the Special Prosecutor to demonstrate that the presidential material was essential to the justice of the pending criminal case. Here the district court treated the material as presumptively privileged, and proceeded to find that the Special Prosecutor had made a sufficient showing to rebut the presumption and ordered an in camera examination of the subpoenaed material."

The subpoenaed documents were given to the district court, which inspected them in camera (in private quarters). Those materials that met the test of admissibility and relevance were subsequently given to the Special Prosecutor. The denial of the motion to quash the subpoena was affirmed.

■ **State of the union**   The President has the duty to report to Congress on the state of the union and to recommend any measures that he considers appropriate and necessary. This duty has been called the foundation of the President's legislative leadership.

■ **Presidential succession and impeachment**   The 25th Amendment to the Constitution provides for Presidential succession. If the President is removed from office, dies, or resigns, the Vice President becomes the President. If the office of Vice President becomes vacant, the President nominates a Vice President, who must be confirmed by both houses of Congress. If the President sends a declaration to both houses of Congress stating that he is unable to discharge his duties, the Vice President becomes Acting President until the President sends an opposite declaration. If the Vice President and a majority of either the heads of the executive departments or of another body specified by Congress notify the President Pro Tempore of the Senate and the Speaker of the House of Representatives in writing that the President is unable to discharge the powers and duties of his office, the Vice President acts as President. The President resumes his duties after notifying the President Pro Tempore and the Speaker of the House that the disability no longer exists, provided Congress agrees with his evaluation. If Congress disagrees, the Vice President remains Acting President.

The President, Vice President, and all U.S. civil officers may be impeached for "Treason, Bribery or other high Crimes and Misdemeanors." The precise meaning of "high Crimes and Misdemeanors" has not been specifically determined but its application has usually been limited to indictable criminal offenses. The power of IMPEACHMENT lies with the House of Representatives. Impeachment is an indictment, not a conviction. It does not remove a person from office. The Senate has the power to try all impeachments. A two-thirds vote in the Senate is necessary to convict and remove a person from office. When the President of the United States is tried, the Chief Justice of the Supreme Court presides.

press, freedom of   See SPEECH AND PRESS, FREEDOM OF.

presumption   A conclusion relating to the existence or nonexistence of a fact, reached by reasoning from other facts. For a detailed discussion, see EVIDENCE.

presumptive   Created by or arising from a presumption. For example, an heir presumptive is a person, such as a brother or nephew, who would be his relative's closest heir if his relative were to die immediately, but whose right of inheritance might be lost if someone more closely related to the relative were to be born, such as a son or daughter.

pretermitted heir   A child or other descendant omitted by a deceased person from his WILL. When a testator (a deceased person who has left a valid will) unintentionally has failed to mention in his will a child who either is living at the date the will is signed or is born thereafter, a statute may allow the child to share in the decedent's property as though the person had died without leaving a will. See DESCENT AND DISTRIBUTION.

prevailing party   The person in a lawsuit in whose favor the verdict is rendered and JUDGMENT is entered.

prima facie (Latin) "At first sight"; on the face of it. A party has a prima facie case when the EVIDENCE in his favor is strong enough for him to win his case unless it is contradicted and overcome by evidence presented by his opponent. For example, a plaintiff who testifies that he was hit by the defendant's car and who has witnesses to substantiate his claim, has a prima facie case.

primary authority Legal authority that a court must follow in reaching a decision in a lawsuit. Such authority includes all existing laws and all judicial decisions handed down by the same court or a higher court that relate to the subject matter of the lawsuit. Supreme Court decisions that interpret the federal Constitution and federal legislation are primary authority and binding on both federal and state courts.

primary evidence EVIDENCE that provides the greatest certainty of a fact in question. A written document, for example, is the best possible evidence of its own existence and content and therefore is primary evidence.

primogeniture An archaic concept that the firstborn son inherits all the real estate owned by his ancestor upon the ancestor's death. In the United States today, laws of DESCENT AND DISTRIBUTION provide that all children share equally in their ancestor's estate.

principal 1 Chief, most important. 2 In regard to financial matters, a sum of money that produces interest. 3 In the law of AGENCY, the person who employs and gives authority to an agent to act on his behalf. 4 In CRIMINAL LAW, the chief perpetrator of the crime, as distinguished from an accessory.

principal and surety A *principal* is a person who has the primary obligation to pay a debt or perform another obligation and who usually receives the benefit from the obligation. A *surety* is one who becomes responsible for the principal's debt. He binds himself to pay a sum of money or perform some act for the principal if the principal fails to do so. The *creditor,* or *obligee,* is the person who can enforce the payment or performance.

A *surety bond* is a document in which the surety promises the creditor that, if the principal fails to pay or perform his obligation to the creditor, he, the surety, will be liable. *Suretyship* is lending credit to a principal who has insufficient credit of his own. It is a direct CONTRACT to pay the principal's debt or perform his obligation if he defaults.

Although the relationship between principal and surety arises primarily in commercial transactions, it is also common in personal matters. For example, when you cosign a loan for someone, you are the surety; your friend, the principal; and the lending institution, the creditor. Frequently, a person charged with a crime and a BAIL bondsman are, respectively, principal and surety, with the court functioning as creditor. The bail bondsman's fee is a percentage of the amount of the bond that he gives. If the person does not show up in court on the specified date, the surety (bail bondsman) will have to pay the amount of the bond. Another common suretyship situation arises when a contractor

is hired by a property owner to build, say, a shopping center. The owner usually requires the contractor to obtain a bond that he purchases from a surety, such as a bonding company, for a fee, usually a small percentage of the amount of the bond. The contractor is the principal, the owner is the creditor, and the bonding company is the surety. If the contractor fails to complete the job, the bonding company will be liable to the owner for the bond.

■ **Creation of relationship** In order to have a valid contract creating the surety relationship, there must be competent parties (for example, legally of age and of sound mind), an offer and acceptance, and a valid consideration (something of value that is given or done) by both principal and surety. The creditor must be notified of the suretyship. If the suretyship is written into a contract, that is sufficient notice to the creditor.

EXAMPLE Alice, Beatrice, and Carmen take out a joint loan of $300,000 from their bank to start a restaurant. Each of the women is considered a principal for her one-third share ($100,000) and a surety for the other two. This means that if Beatrice runs off and defaults on her loan payments, Alice and Carmen are responsible for paying Beatrice's share. Moreover, if two of the women run off and leave the third holding the bag, she will be responsible to the bank for the whole $300,000.

Of course, the person or persons who pay the entire amount of the debt can then sue the defaulting party for his proportionate share.

Another example of this form of suretyship is when a husband and wife sign a mortgage together. They become jointly and severally liable for the debt. Should one of them die, the other will be held liable for the amount due. See discussion of "Joint and several liability" in CONTRACTS.

By contract An obligation in suretyship arises only by an express (specific) contract. Yet a form of suretyship known as involuntary suretyship can arise from an implied agreement between the parties. Thus, when two or more persons enter into a joint obligation, such as a loan, then between them each is a principal for his proportionate share of the debt and a surety for the shares of the others. In these cases, however, each borrower is considered by the creditor as a principal for the whole debt.

Another common instance of involuntary suretyship occurs when one person to a contract agrees to assume a debt owed by the other to a third person. The person assuming the indebtedness becomes the principal, and the former debtor a surety. Suppose, for example, a partnership dissolves or its members change and the new firm or continuing partners assume the prior firm's debts. Those who assume the debts are the principals and the retiring partners are the sureties.

■ **Scope of liability** The amount of the surety's liability is determined by his contract, but unless the surety has limited the amount of his liability, his liability is equal to that of the principal. A surety cannot be held liable for more than the amount he agreed to in the contract. Sureties are not liable for costs and expenses incurred by the creditor in imposing liability on the principal, including attorney's fees, unless the contract or a statute so provides.

The surety becomes liable when the principal breaches his contract or fails to perform what he has promised. A surety on a building or construction contract, for example, is liable if the principal does not perform his contract in time, fails to furnish or pay for labor and materials, uses improper materials, or damages adjoining property. When however, the contract makes the architect responsible for proper performance, the owner of the building cannot sue the contractor's surety for using inferior materials. The owner must sue the architect.

■ **Termination of liability** Generally, a surety's liability ends when the principal's obligation is extinguished. No matter who pays it, payment of the principal debt discharges the surety. A surety can successfully defend himself against liability by showing that the obligations for which he was bound have been performed.

principle A basic rule of law, such as the rule that all persons are entitled to equal treatment under the law.

prison A place in which people are confined either for safekeeping until they answer a civil or criminal charge or to serve sentences for crimes of which they have been convicted. Penal custody is a major part of corrections, the field of law covering the entire range of treatment and rehabilitation programs for offenders.

■ **Prison organization and management** A prison can be called a jail, penitentiary, work camp, or state farm. Whether a reform school, juvenile home, or halfway house is part of a prison system depends on the law that created it.

Legislatures can enact laws creating prison systems, or they can appoint an official or a board with the power to determine what prisons are needed and to arrange for their construction and repair. Congress has this authority on the federal level. State legislatures generally give local governments some authority to create local facilities. States can temporarily hold prisoners under federal law, but they are not obligated to do so unless they have an agreement with the federal government. In the same way, states, counties, and municipalities can arrange to use each other's prisons occasionally, but statutes often forbid or limit the time a local prisoner can be held in a state prison.

The management of a prison is regulated by statutes. The head of each prison may be a warden, superintendent, police chief, or chief officer who has the authority to use his own judgment in setting up prison rules. He may employ jailers, keepers, guards, matrons, and cooking and housekeeping personnel as employees. It is not necessarily illegal for him to use prison inmates to do some of the jobs associated with running the prison, but using armed "trusty" inmates as guards has been strongly criticized.

Guards and other employees may receive wages, insurance, and pension, disability, and unemployment insurance benefits. Under the statutes of some states, certain jail officials or employees are classified as civil service employees and they are therefore hired and promoted on merit and have a certain amount of job security.

Even when prison employees enjoy the protection of a civil service system, they may be justifiably fired for such violations as falling asleep while on guard duty, trading with the inmates, or showing up for work intoxicated.

■ **Responsibilities of prison officials** Prison officials have the duty to keep securely confined any prisoners entrusted to them for whatever period of time a court may direct. An official who aids an escape may be charged with a crime, and one who allows a prisoner to escape through his negligence may be sued by anyone who suffers harm because of the escape.

A prisoner may be allowed certain liberties, such as a work furlough or a conditional release. Prison officials are not responsible for his acts if it was reasonable to grant privileges to that prisoner.

Prisons must be run in such a way that inmates are not unreasonably exposed to unsanitary conditions, contagious diseases, or a constant threat of violence. Officials must provide medical care for prisoners, adequate food, regular exercise, and clean clothing. Rules of conduct for prisoners and for guards must be written, distributed, and enforced. Officers must not unreasonably interfere with prisoners' mail, access to courts, or use of lawbooks. They must keep accurate records on each inmate, including his sentence, the time he has served, the medical treatment he receives, and the disciplinary action taken against him. Officials who fail to perform their duties adequately may be sued for the harm caused. Prisoners have recovered damages from prison physicians for medical malpractice, from guards who beat them, and from wardens who unconstitutionally tampered with their mail. Prison officials are held to a standard of reasonable care and diligence, but they do not have to guarantee the safety and comfort of every inmate.

As a result of lawsuits brought by prisoners, courts in recent years have generally become more involved in prison problems and have set new minimum standards for prison conditions.

EXAMPLE In one case, the conditions in the Lucas County Jail in Ohio were found to be so intolerable that they were considered cruel and unusual punishment, which is prohibited by the U.S. Consititution. The court ordered the sheriff to increase jail operating expenditures. It ordered improved lighting for the jail as an aid to controlling filth and violent assaults, and insisted that all nonjail activities be moved out of the building to relieve serious overcrowding. The court also held that more of the sheriff's men could be assigned guard duty within the jail rather than engaging in police activities because only 6 percent of the people in the county lived in areas not covered by other police departments. The court issued further detailed orders concerning sanitation, food, medical care, treatment programs, visitors, mail, legal services, discipline, and reading materials.

The message of the above decision and many other recent ones is that all available resources must be directed toward making prisons constitutionally humane. As a federal judge wrote in a 1970 case that found prison conditions in Arkansas unconstitutional:

Let there be no mistake in the matter; the obligation of [prison officials] to eliminate existing unconstitutionalities does not depend on what the Legislature may do, or upon what the Governor may do, or indeed upon what [prison officials] may actually be able to accomplish. If Arkansas is going to operate a Penitentiary System, it is going to have to be a system that is countenanced by the Constitution of the United States.

See also PRISONERS' RIGHTS.

prisoners' rights   The legal rights of persons who are kept in custody or confinement against their will because of any legal action, civil or criminal. Prisoners do not have all the privileges of free citizens but they are assured of certain minimal rights.

■ **Pretrial detainees**   Pretrial detainees are persons kept in prison even though they have not been convicted of a crime because they cannot afford the price of a BAIL bond. Bail was originally intended to give an arrested person a chance to remain free while he awaited trial. Ironically, bail has had the opposite effect for poor people. They sometimes have fewer ties to the community, such as a stable family and employment, which authorities believe help insure that they will appear in court on the trial date. Therefore, higher bail may be imposed because the risk of flight is greater.

Until recently, there was very little law on the rights of prisoners held in pretrial detention. In 1972 a federal district court in California ruled that people who are in jail solely because they are unable to post bail cannot be deprived of as many rights as convicted criminals because they are presumed to be innocent. They must be treated differently from convicted criminals because they are incarcerated for a different reason.

EXAMPLE A federal district court in New York found in 1974 that the appalling conditions at the Manhattan House of Detention (known as the Tombs) constituted cruel treatment of the detainees. The court ordered prison officials not to subject every prisoner to maximum security conditions; to permit contact between visitors and prisoners; to provide opportunities for exercise and recreation; to reduce the intolerable noise and heat; to open windows; to leave inmates alone if they wanted to spend time in their cells; to hire more guards; to set up fair procedures to enforce discipline; and to eliminate restrictions on the prisoners' mail. Because the old concrete building could not be renovated to satisfy these minimal requirements, it was eventually closed.

In 1979 the Supreme Court rejected the theory that pretrial detainees cannot be deprived of any right but the right to come and go as they please. The Court criticized lower federal courts for telling prison administrators how to do their jobs. Specifically, the Court found no constitutional protection from "double-bunking" two prisoners in a cell originally designed for one, a ban on packages sent from outside the prison, a prohibition of hardcover books sent from anyone but a publisher or bookstore, or routine "shakedown" inspections of belongings outside the presence of the inmates. The Court also held that visual inspection of body cavities after contact visits can be conducted routinely and without suspicion that certain individuals have secreted contraband.

■ **Rights of citizenship**   Convicted offenders are deprived of many of their civil rights, both during and after their incarceration. Most states deprive citizens of the right to vote in all state and federal elections once they have been convicted of a serious crime. Even in a state where the offender can vote after his release, he generally cannot get

WHAT RIGHTS DO PRISONERS HAVE?

■ Convicts are deprived of many civil rights both during and after their imprisonment. For example, most states deprive citizens of the right to vote once they have been convicted of a serious crime.

■ Marital rights may also be affected. In many states, long-term imprisonment is a ground for divorce. Prisoners cannot get married without permission from the prison administrator.

■ Prisoners have no right to have sexual relationships. However, several prisons do allow conjugal visits to allow a prisoner to share companionship, love, and sex with his or her spouse.

■ Prisoners have no right to expect privacy in jail. Officials have the right to monitor prisoners' conversations and even record them—except for those between a prisoner and his or her lawyer or spouse.

■ Prisoners have the right to correspond without undue restrictions. Personal correspondence may not be censored unless the censorship is in the interest of security, order, or rehabilitation.

■ Prison officials must provide needed medical care. If they cruelly withhold it or deliberately mismanage it, they violate the constitutional prohibition of cruel and unusual punishment. If medical treatment is inept, resulting in injury to the prisoner, the prisoner may sue the doctor for malpractice.

■ Prisoners have no right to refuse to work or to choose the work they will do. They may be punished for refusing to do work assigned to them.

■ Every prisoner has the right to be given enough clean food to sustain him. Prisoners with special medical or religious dietary needs are generally accommodated.

■ Prisoners must be permitted to practice their religion to the fullest extent possible without endangering the order and security of the prison.

■ Prison rules must be clearly stated and explained. Each prisoner should get a written list of the rules upon entering the prison.

■ A prisoner cannot be kept locked in leg-irons or chained to a wall. Guards may use force to defend themselves, break up fights, compel obedience to lawful orders, and protect state property. If a guard uses force without such justification, the prisoner does not necessarily have the right to resist, but he may sue for violation of his civil rights or for compensation for any injuries he received.

■ Prison officials have the right to punish prisoners by withdrawing privileges. However, most courts have held that prisoners cannot be denied the fundamental things needed by a human being.

■ Courts have held that prisoners should not be locked up in solitary for long periods for minor infractions.

■ Prisoners are entitled to complain in order to protect a constitutional or civil right, and they cannot be harassed or disciplined for doing so. A prisoner must first pursue procedures existing within the prison. If this fails, he must be allowed to reach a court.

an absentee ballot, which would enable him to vote while he is in prison.

Conviction and incarceration for serious crimes can also result in a total or partial loss of the right to bring a lawsuit or to enter into a contract while in prison. Federal courts, however, are especially careful to protect everyone's right to sue for violation of civil rights. In most states, a prisoner can be sued.

■ **Family rights** Family rights can be seriously affected by conviction and imprisonment, although the law is not the same in every state. A New York court refused, in 1966, to allow a father, who was serving a sentence of 30 years to life, to contest his wife's petition to change her and her children's last name. In many states, long-term imprisonment is a ground for divorce. A prisoner cannot get married without permission from the prison administrator, and courts usually will not interfere with the administrator's decision. In 1973 a federal court upheld a New York law that prohibited the marriage of anyone serving a life sentence. Finally, a woman who gives birth to a child in prison generally does not have the right to keep the baby with her unless prison officials decide that it is good for the child and no threat to order in the prison. Usually, no child over one year old can stay with the imprisoned mother.

Prisoners have no right to insist on the opportunity to have a sexual relationship with a visitor. Several lawsuits have been pursued by prisoners claiming a right to have conjugal visits in order to share companionship, love, and sex with a husband or wife. These actions have been uniformly unsuccessful. Conjugal visits are a matter of policy that must come from legislative reform or prison administrators, not from the courts.

■ **Sterilization of prisoners** In 1942 the Supreme Court struck down an Oklahoma statute that authorized sexual sterilization of habitual criminals who had been convicted of crimes involving moral turpitude (immoral or base conduct). The Court found that the statute violated the equal protection clause of the Constitution because it excluded prisoners who had committed other crimes, such as embezzlement. Since that time, more carefully written and fairly applied sterilization statutes have withstood court challenges based on CRUEL AND UNUSUAL PUNISHMENT, EQUAL PROTECTION OF LAWS, and DUE PROCESS OF LAW.

■ **Workmen's compensation, pensions, inheritances** A few states specifically extend workmen's compensation relief to prisoners who are injured while working for the municipality or a private employer. Most states, however, deny these benefits, and a few even cancel benefits for injuries sustained before conviction.

The right of a prisoner to inherit property or receive a pension can be affected by state laws. Most of these legal disabilities have been found valid on the ground that they do not interfere with fundamental human rights.

■ **Personal property** Prisoners have certain rights concerning personal property in their possession in the jail. Recent decisions have established the right to own some personal items, such as cigarettes, stationery, a watch, cosmetics, or snack foods. In some cases, prison officials are justified in forbidding certain items because accumulating possessions may encourage gambling, theft, or buying favors from guards. In some cases, judges have refused to satisfy prisoner demands for the right to own noisy items, such as radios or typewriters.

■ **Right of privacy** Courts have often said that a prisoner has no right to privacy in a jail. Various cases have established that prison officials may monitor a prisoner's conversations and may even record them, although the prisoner and his visitor should be warned if this is going to be done. Prison officials may not, however, intrude on conversations that are legally entitled to remain confidential, such as those with the prisoner's attorney or spouse.

Prisoners do not have ordinary rights to be free of searches or seizure of their property because the constitutional "right of the people to be secure in their persons, houses, papers and effects" does not wholly apply to them. One court wrote that searches conducted by prison officials "are not unreasonable so long as they are not for the purpose of harassing or humiliating the inmate in a cruel or unusual manner." Most courts have followed this general policy. For example, a prisoner accused of stabbing another inmate or found carrying drugs cannot complain when he and his possessions are searched. It is also reasonable for prison officials to conduct more intensive searches of maximum-security cell blocks; of prisoners returning from outside visits, such as to a courtroom or hospital; or of a prisoner who has tried to escape. The scope of the search must depend on the risk in a given situation. A prisoner does not have the right to be present during a routine search of his belongings.

Although strip frisks and searches of body cavities assault the dignity of a human being and can easily intimidate, embarrass, or degrade a prisoner, the Supreme Court has refused to prohibit them. A federal court in New Jersey held that these searches are proper in a maximum-security prison after personal-contact visits, which are conducted in complete privacy. On the other hand, a federal court in New York refused to allow routine strip frisks of a prisoner who was able to show that the searches were conducted when there was no possible reason to believe he was hiding anything and that he was subjected to physical and verbal abuse when he was searched.

■ **Restriction of mail** Historically, prison officials have severely restricted their inmates' mail. Incoming mail was opened to spot escape plans, weapons and instruments, pornography, drugs, and other contraband. Outgoing correspondence was censored to protect the public from insulting, obscene, or threatening letters or plots; to prevent unfavorable or inaccurate publicity concerning the prison; to monitor frustrations and moods of the prison population; and to frustrate escape plans. Recent cases have established the free-speech right of prisoners to correspond without undue restrictions.

EXAMPLE In 1974 the Supreme Court held that the California Department of Corrections could not censor the personal correspondence of prisoners unless the censorship furthered security, order, and rehabilitation. In addition, some procedure had to be set up to insure that the censorship was neither arbitrary nor unduly burdensome. The Court also held that (1) an inmate must be notified when a letter by or to him is intercepted; (2) the writer of the letter must be given a chance to protest that decision; and (3) complaints must be referred to someone other than the prison official who originally disapproved of the correspondence.

Many prison officials have begun to loosen restrictions on mail because of the time and energy required for censorship, its marginal usefulness, and its contribution to increased tensions in the prisons.

Some courts have required prison officials to give good reasons for banning publications that they consider inflammatory, obscene, or racist. A vague allegation that some book or periodical is likely to stir up trouble has been held insufficient to justify broad censorship.

■ **Free speech**   Most courts have rejected the claim that prisoners have the right to speak out freely. A federal court in Maryland upheld the authority of prison officials to discipline a prisoner who distributed circulars calling for a mass protest against the "mistreatment, inequities, and criminal neglect" of the prison administration. The court ruled that it did not matter whether or not the charges were correct because it constituted incitement to insurrection. Other cases have reached the same result. One federal court, however, did refuse to sanction punishment of a prisoner who had his own inflammatory writings in his cell, but the court added that even these writings could be confiscated if they threatened prison security. In 1977, the Supreme Court held that the First Amendment guarantees of free speech and the freedom to associate did not entitle prisoners in North Carolina to form a labor union, because it would be detrimental to prison order and security. Prison newspapers have long been restricted to safe issues that contribute to good morale, encourage normal living conditions, and promote mental health.

■ **Visitation rights**   It has long been recognized that sensible visitation rights are beneficial to prisoners. Many courts have ordered prison officials to permit contact visits so that prisoners can be in the same room with their visitors. Several courts have held that restrictions on visitation must be reasonable and related only to security needs and good order. For example, one court disapproved of a system that limited visits to one-half hour, even though visitors had come long distances. A federal court in Wisconsin held that a father has a constitutional right to see his children, but other courts have considered such visits a privilege that can be withdrawn or denied.

The right to communicate with and see visitors takes on added legal importance when the proposed visitor is a news reporter. When the right of a free press conflicts with the duty of prison officials to maintain order and discipline, the need for security outweighs the need for access to the media. The basic rule is that a reporter has no more right to visit a prisoner than does any other member of the public. But officials must have a good reason for denying access to the media. A reporter cannot be barred from all prison interviews, for example, unless he is a threat to security. Prison officials are justifiably concerned if one inmate assumes a position of authority among the prisoners because a news reporter treats him as a spokesman or leader. Therefore prison officials can require a prisoner or reporter to fill out an application disclosing who and what will be discussed before an individual interview is approved. Or they may permit only random interviews during a tour of the prison rather than prearranged interviews with specific

prisoners. Face-to-face interviews can be prohibited for any prisoner who is held in maximum security.

A prisoner cannot be punished because he allows himself to be interviewed by a reporter or because prison officials disagree with what he has said.

■ **Treatment and training**   Many court decisions have stated that a prisoner does not have the right to refuse medical, psychiatric, or rehabilitative treatment—such as literacy classes, job training, or drug-abuse programs—and that he may be punished for refusing necessary treatment. Psychiatric treatment raises a constitutional question. Because a prisoner could be intimidated and coerced by the threat of painful treatment, or could be mistakenly packed off to a mental institution, or could be excessively drugged to make him passive, many courts have ruled that psychiatric treatment must be supervised by a doctor. In addition, a prisoner must be given notice and an opportunity to protest before he can be transferred to a psychiatric facility.

Prison officials must provide medical care when it is needed. Not to do so may violate the constitutional prohibition of cruel and unusual punishment. When the treatment is not cruelly withheld or deliberately mismanaged but is inept, prisoners may sue doctors in state courts for medical malpractice. One court pointed out that prisoners, like everyone else, risk occasional medical mistakes.

Courts have not always ruled that prisons must provide other kinds of treatment. While courts have held that alcoholics and drug addicts should have professional care and that dangerous psychopaths must be separated from the prison population, they generally have not found that psychiatric or rehabilitation treatment for prisoners is required.

■ **Work and wages**   Whether or not prisoners are entitled to be paid fair wages for work done while they are in prison has been the subject of several lawsuits. Prisoners typically receive token wages, say 25 cents to a dollar a day, but courts have consistently held that they have no right to be paid at all. The 13th Amendment to the Constitution makes a specific exception for convicted criminals:

❝ Neither slavery nor involuntary servitude, except as a punishment for crime whereof the party shall have been duly convicted, shall exist within the United States, or any place subject to their jurisdiction. ❞

It is also well established that prisoners have no right to refuse to work or to choose the work they will do and they may be punished for refusing to do work assigned to them.

Prisons are not obligated to offer programs of work in order to keep prisoners busy or to offer meaningful or educational work. Those policy decisions are made by prison officials. Some administrators have recognized the value of job training and the opportunity to earn decent wages, but courts have not given these goals the stamp of constitutional necessity.

Some prisoners may be required to serve their sentences at hard labor. States may require persons convicted under certain laws to work off fines that they cannot afford to pay. States may also use prisoners to do public works projects, such as repairing bridges or cleaning out drainage ditches. Contractors were once able to lease convict labor, putting prisoners to work for them in exchange for a fee paid to the government unit that owned the prison. These labor contracts are now illegal in many states. A number of state laws further restrict prisoner labor by limiting the sale of convict-made goods so that they do not compete with goods made by free persons.

■ **Segregation of homosexuals** Homosexuals may be kept separate from the general prison population for their own safety or the safety of others. They should be notified of the reasons for their transfer, but they are not necessarily entitled to a formal hearing. In some cases, courts have insisted that homosexuals be segregated in order to stop overt sexual activity or to prevent threatened assaults. The law in one state permits homosexuals to choose between confinement with other homosexuals or with heterosexuals.

■ **Appropriate food** Every prisoner has the right to be given enough clean food to sustain an average man or woman. A federal judge in 1969 found that a diet of "grue"—a baked mixture of meat, potatoes, vegetables, eggs, oleo, syrup, and seasonings—while not appetizing, was wholesome and sufficient. A later decision held that feeding prisoners "grue" was unconstitutionally cruel.

Various groups of prisoners have protested the failure of prisons to furnish special diets. A series of lawsuits have been brought by Black Muslims to compel prison officials to accommodate their religious ban on eating pork. A number of courts have held that Muslim prisoners must be allowed extra portions of other foods when pork is on the menu, but some have insisted that they be served an alternative source of protein. Orthodox Jews require a diet that is much more restrictive than that of the Muslims. Federal courts in New York considered this problem in detail when Jewish Defense League leader Meir Kahane, an Orthodox rabbi, was imprisoned. The courts held that prisons must provide Orthodox Jewish prisoners with a diet sufficient to maintain health without violating the Jewish dietary laws.

■ **Practice of religion** In general, a prisoner must be permitted to practice his religion to the fullest extent possible. He should be permitted to obtain and keep written materials, to see or communicate with a religious leader, and to obey the rules of his religion that do not endanger the order and security of the prison. Formal religious observances for groups of inmates must be permitted on a regular basis when practical. Prisoners can have access to religious programs broadcast on radio or television. Different religions within a prison must be given equal treatment. For example, a Black Muslim minister has to be paid at the same hourly rate as any other prison chaplain. But the prison does not have to hire a chaplain of a particular faith when there are too few prisoners to justify the expense. In the early 1960's courts did not protect Black Muslims in their religious practices because they held that the Black Muslims were not a bona fide religious group, but more recent cases have recognized Black Muslims as such.

■ **Appearance and cleanliness** Prisons have traditionally been rigid in regulating the appearance of prisoners. Some rules, like shaving a prisoner's head when he emerged from solitary confinement, were probably useful to punish and degrade the inmate but they are rarely, if ever, used today. Many other regulations are justified by prison officials as being economical, efficient, or helpful with security.

Rules regulating hair have irritated many prisoners, but as one court said, such regulations do not deprive prisoners of any federal, civil, or constitutional right. Prisons generally prohibit long hair and beards because they create hygiene problems and make it difficult to identify prisoners. Indians and blacks cannot claim a cultural right to wear long hair if a rule banning it is applied to everyone.

In some cases, courts have found rules governing appearance to be too harsh.

EXAMPLE In 1971 black revolutionaries Bobby Seale and Ericka Huggins objected to appearance regulations. The court found Seale should be allowed his beard, which was little more than a fringe around his mouth, but Huggins could not wear all the jewelry she wanted. She had to follow the rule limiting jewelry to a wristwatch, one pair of small earrings, a ring, and a necklace with a religious medal on it. She also had to observe the rules governing the length of skirts and the fabrics permitted for clothing.

When prisoners have complained that they were denied opportunities to shower or shave, courts have insisted on minimum standards of human decency. Even prisoners in punitive segregation must be given showers—according to one case, three times a week—and the chance to shave. Courts have permitted prisons to force inmates to keep themselves clean, if that is necessary.

■ **Prison rules and punishment** The rules concerning conduct of the prisoners must be clearly stated and explained to the prisoners. Each prisoner should be given a written list of the rules when he enters the correctional facility. General notice of changes should be posted on bulletin boards or some other place likely to reach all the prisoners. All the disciplinary rules should be related to the needs of security, order, and administration. A prisoner should be punished only for violation of a known rule.

A prisoner who is accused of breaking rules is not entitled to all the rights of an accused person at a trial because a prison disciplinary proceeding is not the same as a criminal prosecution. Inmates do not have the right to be represented by an attorney at disciplinary proceedings nor to confront and cross-examine witnesses. Prisoners should be notified of the charges against them, the rules they are charged with breaking, and the penalties for breaking them. When an inmate is illiterate or the case is unusually complex, the prisoner should be able to seek aid from another prisoner or a staff member. Punishment should not be ordered until the prisoner is given a chance to present his side, but a hearing can be very informal for slight infractions. The fact finder should write up a statement concerning the evidence and the reasons for any disciplinary action taken. The punishment should be reasonably related to the seriousness of the infraction. For example, a day or two in segregated confinement might be reasonable punishment for a minor infraction, such as throwing food at another prisoner, but six months in solitary confinement would not be.

Physical force A prisoner cannot be kept locked in leg irons or chained to a wall. In 1968 a court ruled that whipping a prisoner with a leather strap is cruel and unusual punishment. In 1973 a federal court in Texas held that beating, slapping, kicking, and otherwise physically abusing juvenile prisoners is also illegal, except in an emergency. In 1974 a federal court in Indiana ruled that giving juvenile prisoners tranquilizing drugs just to keep them quiet is unconstitutional when done without proper medical supervision. The court also prohibited use of a fraternity paddle to spank the children.

Force is properly used by prison personnel in self-defense, in breaking up fights between inmates, in compelling obedience to lawful orders where milder measures fail, and in protecting state property. A prisoner does not necessarily have the right to resist when guards use force without justification.

EXAMPLE In one Arkansas case a jailor and his deputy repeatedly struck a prisoner on the hand until one finger was broken. The guards were trying to put the prisoner down into the "hole," a dark and filthy little cubicle, and he resisted by bracing his hands and feet on the doorway. A federal court found that the beating was entirely unreasonable and grossly excessive, a violation of the constitutional right to be free of cruel and unusual punishment. Although the jailor argued that he was only doing what had always been done in the jail, the court replied that beating prisoners can never be justified as a standard procedure. The court held, however, that no prisoner has the right to resist a guard's order except to keep himself from getting killed or seriously injured. A prisoner's remedy is to sue on the ground of deprivation of his civil rights and to recover money damages to compensate for his injuries. In this case, the prisoner was awarded $1,500 because the jailors were trying to injure him rather than trying to get him into the cell.

Use of Chemical Mace or other tear gas constitutes physical punishment that is justified only when there is an immediate danger of riot or serious disorder.

Loss of privileges Courts generally continue to permit prison officials to punish prisoners by withdrawing certain privileges, such as seeing visitors, buying items from the commissary, or earning wages. Most courts have held that prisoners cannot be denied fundamental benefits, such as food, clothing, exercise, bathing, or library privileges.

Segregation and isolation Segregation is the most frequent punishment used in prisons. Each prison has its own system and names for different degrees of segregation. Separate areas may be set aside for young prisoners, short-timers, repeat offenders, or prisoners sentenced to death. Homosexuals may be segregated to prevent violence and to protect them from sexual abuse. Segregation may not be used to separate races.

Solitary confinement is not itself unconstitutional, but conditions in some prisons have been so barbarous that they constitute cruel and unusual punishment. For example, prisoners have been stripped of their clothes; not given bedding, soap, or toilet paper; or confined in wet, cold, or unlighted cells. Normal privileges concerning exercise, work or recreation programs, visitation, or library use may be severely curtailed for a prisoner being disciplined, but even in isolation prisoners cannot usually be denied basic food, light, ventilation, or sanitation. A 1971 case did, however, approve the practice of putting prisoners in solitary confinement on a diet of water and two slices of bread a day for up to 15 days, with one full meal on every third day of the period.

Courts have held that the effects of solitary confinement are so severe that, even when the prisoner is treated well, he should not be locked up alone for long periods of time or for minor infractions or without constant checks to be sure he is surviving the ordeal.

Unconstitutional prisons Several courts have found entire prisons to be so bad that being confined in them was CRUEL AND UNUSUAL PUNISHMENT.

EXAMPLE The first landmark case in 1971 examined the treatment of prisoners in Arkansas. Among other things, the court found that (1) the nearly 1,000 men were being guarded by only 8 state employees and a large number of armed inmate trusties who ruled by cruelty and hatred; (2) prisoners were not paid for any work and had to sell their blood to a blood bank to get money to buy food, medical care, and "protection"; (3) the large, open barracks where prisoners were confined encouraged physical and sexual assaults; (4) isolation cells were filthy and overcrowded; and (5) there were no training or rehabilitation programs. The federal court held that the entire Arkansas prison system was unconstitutional.

Since the Arkansas case, several other institutions—including the Lucas County Jail in Ohio, the Mississippi State Penitentiary, the St. Louis County Jail, and the Manhattan House of Detention in New York City—were also found to violate the Constitution.

■ **Prisoners' remedies** A prisoner who needs to protect a constitutional or civil right is entitled to complain, and he cannot be harassed or disciplined for pursuing his constitutional rights. He must first pursue whatever procedures exist within the prison and, if this fails, he must be allowed to reach a court.

Access to courts In a series of cases, the Supreme Court invalidated state procedures that interfered with the right of a prisoner to petition a court for relief. A state or prison official cannot review prisoners' applications, for example, or refuse to send them to federal court for any reason. A prisoner must be permitted to get help from a lawyer or a "jailhouse lawyer"—another inmate who has some experience in the prison system. Although very few prisoners can afford to hire an attorney, neither the courts nor the federal or state governments are required to appoint attorneys for prisoners. However, a prisoner who presents a good case may at some point have an attorney appointed for him by a court.

Prison officials must allow reasonable times and places for prisoners to have confidential consultations with their attorneys, and law students and paralegals cannot be prevented from entering prisons to assist lawyers in case investigations.

Most prisoners must pursue their own rights. To facilitate this, prisons must permit prisoners to keep law books and writing materials in their cells and must provide a prison law library. Mail to and from attorneys, public officials, and courts must be sent without censorship by the prison. If a prisoner is poor, the state cannot require him to pay a fee, no matter how small, to file his legal papers with the court, and it must furnish him with a free record of prior legal proceedings. In addition, there must be a reasonable way for prisoners to have their legal papers notarized.

Civil rights lawsuits Most of the litigation attacking prison conditions or treatment of prisoners has been pursued under the Federal Civil Rights Act, popularly called a

"1983 action" because the law is found in Section 1983 of Title 42 in the U.S. Code Annotated. This law says that you can start a suit in federal court if you are deprived of a federally protected or constitutional right by a person who seems to be or is acting under the authority of state law. A prisoner may sue the prison warden or supervisor, a guard, or the local government that owns and runs the prison.

Habeas corpus Another remedy for prisoners is the writ of HABEAS CORPUS (Latin for "you should have the body"). It is a legal paper that orders anyone officially holding the petitioner to bring him into court so that the court can determine whether he is being detained illegally. A federal court can accept an application for a writ of habeas corpus by a state prisoner if he is being held in custody in violation of the Constitution or the laws of the United States. A prisoner is entitled to the writ if the conditions of his confinement violate his constitutional rights, even though he is lawfully in custody. A prisoner must show that he has first tried every procedure available within the prison or through state laws before a federal court will hear his complaint in a habeas corpus proceeding.

Court-ordered relief When prisoners have successfully demonstrated the unconstitutionality of their conditions of confinement, courts have generally ordered one of the following remedies: (1) requiring prison officials to change their policies or prohibiting them from taking certain actions; (2) ordering specific improvements in the prison building or services; (3) closing down all or certain parts of the prison; (4) ordering officials to release all or some prisoners from solitary confinement or to revoke a transfer to a different institution or to restore lost "good time"; (5) awarding money damages for harm done to the prisoner; or (6) ordering defendants to pay attorneys' fees for the prisoners in connection with one of the other remedies. These remedies can generally be enforced by holding the defendants in contempt if they fail to comply with an order or by appointing special judicial officers to supervise compliance.

privacy, right of

The right to be let alone, to be free of unwelcome intrusions or unwarranted publicity. The right of privacy protects individuals from interference in private affairs that are none of the public's business.

Privacy is a difficult right to understand because it cannot be described with exactness. The Constitution does not use the word "privacy" in its list of guaranteed rights, nor are there sweeping statutes that outlaw invasions of privacy. The reason for this is that one person's right to privacy is often another person's right to free speech or freedom of information. Moreover, the rights of an individual may conflict with the needs of the public. These competing interests must be weighed against each other so that a balance can be struck for each set of circumstances.

The right of privacy derives mainly from the Constitution and TORT law. The Constitution puts limits mostly on government activities, whereas tort law deals with wrongs done to individuals and private property as opposed to the state or the public at large. Tort law gives the injured party the right to sue the offender for DAMAGES.

■ **Constitutional bases** Although the Constitution does not specifically guarantee a right of privacy, many of its provisions clearly indicate that people are entitled to be let alone.

Various parts of the Constitution create what the Supreme Court has called "zones of privacy." The First Amendment, for example, protects the freedom to choose the people with whom one associates. See ASSEMBLY, RIGHT OF; SPEECH AND PRESS, FREEDOM OF. The Third Amendment makes the home secure by forbidding the lawless quartering of soldiers in anyone's house. The Fourth Amendment guarantees "the right of the people to be secure in their persons, houses, papers, and effects, against unreasonable searches and seizures." See SEARCH AND SEIZURE. The Fifth Amendment prevents the government from forcing a person to expose facts that could lead to his own criminal conviction. See SELF-INCRIMINATION. And the Ninth Amendment, which states that the enumeration of certain rights in the Constitution does not mean that any rights not listed are thereby denied to the people, has been held to protect certain aspects of privacy.

Interpretations of privacy The first cases that gave a modern constitutional status to privacy were concerned with protecting family life. Later cases sought to safeguard individual life-styles both within and outside the family.

Sex and procreation The first step in protecting family life was to assure privacy in matters of sex and procreation—the most private and personal of all concerns. In 1942 the Supreme Court struck down an Oklahoma statute that authorized sterilization of criminals who were twice convicted of "felonies involving moral turpitude" but that exempted a few crimes, such as embezzlement and political offenses. The Supreme Court did not say that the statute was unconstitutional because of privacy. But it did rule that procreation is such a basic civil right that a government cannot interfere with it for some felons and not others. That would violate the right of everyone to be treated equally by the law. Because of the intimacy and importance of so basic a right, the Court would not let stand government interference unless the state could show that sterilization was necessary.

Contraceptives Recognition of the importance of sex, MARRIAGE, and procreation was expanded in 1965 when the Supreme Court held that Connecticut could not enforce a statute making it a crime to use a contraceptive or to give advice on how to avoid pregnancy. The Court found the law unconstitutional because, in forbidding the *use* of contraceptives rather than just regulating their manufacture or sale, the law did the greatest possible harm to the privacy to which a marriage is entitled. Justice William O. Douglas wrote for the Court:

Would we allow the police to search the sacred precincts of marital bedrooms for telltale signs of the use of contraceptives? The very idea is repulsive to the notions of privacy surrounding the marriage relationship. . . . We deal with a right of privacy older than the Bill of Rights.

In 1972 the Supreme Court found that the distribution of contraceptives to unmarried people was constitutionally protected. The Court reasoned that the right of privacy in question belongs to all individuals, married or unmarried.

Abortions In 1973 the Supreme Court held that a woman's right of privacy entitles her to decide whether or not she will submit to an ABORTION. The Court explained that a constitutional right of privacy extends only to personal rights that can be considered fundamental because they are implied by our concept of liberty, and this certainly includes activities related to marriage or procreation. On the other hand, because of the interest a state may properly take in safeguarding health, maintaining medical standards, and protecting potential life, the law may place limits on the woman's right by regulating abortions for women in the second three months of pregnancy and by prohibiting abortion in the last three months of pregnancy.

Life-styles   How far the right of privacy can be legally extended depends on future decisions in cases affecting home and family life. A number of Supreme Court rulings have already defined certain specific rights of privacy, most notably (1) the right of local zoning boards to set aside neighborhoods for one-family homes in which groups of people not related to one another may not live together; (2) the right of Amish people to take their children out of school at an age lower than state law normally allows; (3) the right of parents to send their children to private schools if they so choose; and (4) the right of schools to teach sex education and evolution—a right that, the Court determined, does not violate the right of a parent to raise his children as he sees fit.

An individual's personal life-style may be protected if a fundamental interest is involved. For example, people claiming that dress codes and grooming standards of schools and employers violate their rights have both succeeded and failed, depending on whether they were able to convince the court that something such as long hair is a basic and fundamental concern for them. For example, a court might uphold the right of an Orthodox Jew to wear a beard because his religion demands it, but it would probably not agree that an employer must allow his salesmen to wear outrageous clothing or hairstyles that might offend his customers.

YOUR RIGHT OF PRIVACY

■ Although the Constitution nowhere mentions the word "privacy," the right is protected by the First Amendment (freedom of assembly, freedom of speech), the Third Amendment (soldiers cannot be quartered in your home), the Fourth Amendment (no unreasonable searches and seizures), and the Fifth Amendment (no self-incrimination).

■ The use of contraceptives and a woman's decision to have an abortion have been held to be protected by the right to privacy. (The state may still place limits on the right to abortion after the third month, however.)

■ The right of privacy may also extend to doing things in the home that might be offensive to public morality. For example, an individual has the right to have obscene books and movies in his home but not to stand in the street and sell tickets to view stag movies in his basement.

■ Public employees, however, can be fired for immoral conduct in their private lives.

■ Some legal processes can require disclosure of personal information that is usually entitled to privacy—your financial records when you are being audited by the Internal Revenue Service, for instance. Likewise, people suing to recover money damages for physical injuries can be required to submit to medical examinations.

■ If you wish to sue for an invasion of your privacy, one of these grounds must be involved: the appropriation of your name or likeness, an intrusion on your private property, public disclosure of private details of your life, or showing you in a false light.

■ The right not to have your likeness appropriated without your permission is a personal right only—a parent cannot recover damages for invasion of his child's privacy, for example. To sue for misappropriation, you must be able to be identified from the use of your name or picture and the use must have been for commercial purposes.

■ Entry without permission or legal authority into your home, office, hotel room, or stateroom on a ship has been judged by the courts as an intrusion that invades your right of privacy.

■ You have the right to sue for unauthorized eavesdropping, spying, wiretaps, or recording of conversations.

■ Public disclosure of the details of one's private life is not libel or slander if the details are true, but it may be an invasion of privacy.

■ Creating an untrue picture of a person is another ground. Examples of placing a person in a false light are putting a person's name on a petition without his authorization and filing a lawsuit in someone's name without his permission.

■ It is a crime in some states to open and read another's letters or personal papers or to disclose the contents of someone else's telegram or telephone conversation.

■ The Fair Credit Reporting Act of 1970 is designed to protect consumers from invasions of their right of privacy by credit agencies. This law specifies when a financial report on a consumer can be used, prohibits inclusion of obsolete data, describes what information must be released to the government, and outlines how a consumer may gain access to his file and challenge information he thinks is incomplete or incorrect.

■ The Freedom of Information Act requires federal agencies to release information they have on file but not information that is properly privileged and confidential, such as personnel and medical files.

■ The Privacy Act of 1974 enables you to insist that the records kept by an agency, department, or bureau be used only for the purpose for which the information was originally collected.

■ Since 1974, you have had the right to inspect scholastic records kept by the schools on your children. If you find inaccurate, misleading, or inappropriate information in your child's records, you may insist that a written correction be inserted in the file.

■ Records kept on juvenile delinquents and on offenders, such as runaways, must be kept confidential under federal law.

■ Information collected by the census bureau, the armed services, and the Internal Revenue Service is likewise strictly regulated.

Protection of personal life-styles may also extend to permitting individuals to do things in the privacy of their homes that might be offensive to public morality in general. In 1969 the U.S. Supreme Court held that an individual has the right to enjoy obscene books and films in the privacy of his own home.

On the other hand, public employees can be fired for immorality in their private lives. Federal courts upheld the dismissal of a schoolteacher who lived with a man without marriage in a small town where such cohabitation was morally censured and of a homosexual teacher who became active in a gay rights organization.

Limitations   To protect the rights of others, the law puts certain limitations on individual privacy. For example, some legal processes can require disclosure of personal information that is usually entitled to privacy. A person whose tax return is being audited must show where he got his figures. Elected officials can be required to file campaign spending statements. People suing to recover money damages for physical injuries can be required to submit to medical examinations. Personal books and records must be produced when a lawful subpoena has been served.

The right of privacy can be claimed only in situations that are actually private. For example, the sexual practices of a married couple cannot usually be questioned, but no protection shields a married couple who give up their privacy by carrying on in a public place. A prostitute who publicly solicits customers cannot claim a right of privacy because the sex act itself will occur in a private place. Although there is a right to possess pornography in one's home, the protection is lost if a homeowner stands in the street and sells tickets to stag movies in his basement.

■ **Development of privacy suits**   Individuals and businesses can be forced to pay money DAMAGES in a tort action, or lawsuit, started by the injured person on the grounds of an invasion of privacy. If the plaintiff can show that the defendant had no right to do what he did, then the defendant may be ordered to compensate the plaintiff for the harm he has caused.

In the 19th century a person could sue for injury to his reputation only if a false or malicious statement was made about him. See LIBEL AND SLANDER. No specific right of privacy was recognized under the law. Toward the end of the century the need for some defense of privacy grew urgent as newspapers entered a period in which they resorted to increasing sensationalism and muckraking.

In 1890 a Boston newspaper published some offensive publicity concerning the social activities of the family of Samuel Warren, a prominent lawyer. In response, Warren and his partner Louis Brandeis, who later became a noted Supreme Court justice, wrote a pathbreaking article for the *Harvard Law Review* pointing out that the excesses of the newspapers were causing great mental distress for the unlucky victims of their idle, prying gossip. Even if the objectionable statements made by the press did not amount to libel or slander, a person had "the right to be let alone"—a right that ought to be protected against invasion unless there was some compelling reason of public welfare.

Finally, in 1902, the right of privacy was tested in a trial court in New York. The picture of a pretty young woman was used without her consent in advertisements of a certain brand of flour. The words "Flour of the Family" were printed above the portrait, and posters were displayed in stores, warehouses, saloons, and other public places. The woman complained that the picture libeled her by making her easily recognizable and subject to people's scoffs and jeers. The trial court admitted that the theory of a right of privacy was new but held that the plaintiff had a right to be let alone.

When the case was appealed, the highest court in New York reversed that decision. A bare majority of the judges denied the existence of this right of privacy. They feared that allowing monetary recovery in that case would encourage a "vast amount of litigation" and unreasonably restrict free speech and a free press. They did note, however, that the "legislative body could very well interfere and arbitrarily provide that no one should be permitted for his own selfish purpose to use the picture or the name of another for advertising purposes without his consent."

Encouraged by the strong public opinion against the outcome of the case, the New York legislature did just that. It enacted a law that subjects a person to both criminal penalties and a civil lawsuit for using another person's name, portrait, or photograph for advertising or trade purposes without first getting written permission.

In 1905 the Supreme Court of Georgia held that, even without a statute, a right of privacy can be found in natural law—within the concepts of personal security and liberty. Since these two cases, most states have recognized a right of privacy that can be enforced by a civil lawsuit. A few states have applied the right only to the commercial use of one's name or picture, but many more states have held that it protects individuals from a wide variety of abuses.

■ **Current grounds for lawsuits**   Today the right of privacy is no longer seen as a single issue but is divided into four major areas, which the law is prepared to defend. If you wish to sue for an invasion of your privacy, at least one of these four grounds must be involved: (1) appropriation of your name or likeness, (2) intrusion on your private property or belongings, (3) public disclosure of private details of your life, or (4) showing you in a false light.

Appropriation   Appropriation of a person's name or likeness for the defendant's profit or advantage was the first invasion of privacy to be covered by the right to sue. Many diverse privacy cases have successfully established this principle. Thomas Edison sued to prevent a company from using his name on a painkiller he had invented after he sold the formula for it.

Sometimes the cases involve profits lost as a result of the appropriation of the name or likeness. Cases of this type involve not only the right of privacy but also the appropriation of TRADEMARKS AND TRADE NAMES and COPYRIGHTS.

EXAMPLE Theodor Seuss Geisel sued a company in 1968 for selling dolls based on his fantastic characters and using his pen name, Dr. Seuss. He lost on the issue of privacy because the dolls were based on cartoon drawings that he had sold in 1932 for $300 a page. The magazine that bought the drawings had copyrighted them and was entitled to use them and the name "Dr. Seuss" in any way it chose. The magazine had granted the toy company permission to make the dolls. The creator did not have an exclusive right to his name as long as it was used along with the copyrighted drawings or anything based on them. He had sold that much of his private right.

Advertisements that merely imitate or suggest the plaintiff are not illegal invasions of privacy.

EXAMPLE In one case, the Adell Chemical Company was charged with advertising its product on television with a cartoon film of a duck that talked like Bert Lahr, the actor who portrayed the Cowardly Lion in *The Wizard of Oz*. The court rejected Lahr's claim that imitation of his distinctive vocal delivery in a television commercial was an invasion of his personal privacy for the advertiser's profit.

In another case, a court refused to compensate the singing group The Fifth Dimension when a Trans World Airlines commercial used the song "Up, Up and Away," which the group had popularized. There was no claim to the public that the well-known stars were associated with the advertising, and their names were not specifically used.

Acts not considered appropriation   The right of privacy that entitles one to sue for using a likeness or the name of the plaintiff without authorization is a personal right only. A parent cannot recover money damages for invasion of his child's privacy, nor can family members sue after the death of the person whose likeness was misappropriated.

A picture of someone's hand, leg, or foot alone, with nothing more to identify him, is not a violation. Publication of pictures of mutilated or decomposed bodies, though tasteless, does not violate a right of privacy because the bodies are not identifiable, and dead people do not have a right of privacy. A picture of part of a home or car, not further identified, is not an invasion of privacy. Courts have said that anyone may take a picture of a dog without the owner's permission and use it for any purpose as long as the owner is not identified. However, a photographer who is hired to take pictures of a dog for the owner and is paid for them cannot then sell prints to someone else to be used for advertising.

Suing for appropriation   In order to sue on the grounds of appropriation, a plaintiff must show that he is identifiable and that the picture or his name is being used for commercial purposes. Any rules that attempt to enlarge the right much more than this would interfere with the constitutional guarantee of freedom of the press.

It is not enough to show that a newspaper, magazine, movie, or radio or television station using the likeness or name is being operated for profit. The defendant's intention must be to gain a benefit from using the likeness or name. Simply publishing a picture right next to advertising or reprinting an entire news article as part of a magazine advertisement is not an unauthorized appropriation of the plaintiff's name or likeness (but it is a violation of copyright), nor is a mention of one's name or an incidental picture in a newscast or photograph.

The right to prevent unauthorized commercial use of a person's identity suggests that the individual has an exclusive right to market his own name and likeness, almost as if they were trademarks. A person may capitalize on this right by selling a "license," or giving formal permission to use the name in publicity, as many sports figures do when they sell the right to use their name or endorsement to manufacturers of sports equipment.

Intrusion   The right of privacy also offers some protection against intrusions into one's solitude or seclusion. Intrusion is an intentional wrong, a willful act that disturbs someone's mental tranquility, equilibrium, or peace of mind or otherwise inflicts emotional distress. This right of privacy gives each person the choice of when and how much he will permit others to know about his personal affairs or to meddle with his mind, body, or private activities.

Intrusion covers a wide range of intentional, unreasonable, and offensive acts that interfere with an individual's privacy. Entry without permission or legal authority into a person's house, apartment, office, hotel room, or stateroom on a ship—even if he is not there at the time—has been judged by courts as an invasion of the right of privacy. Searches without warrants, probable cause, or permission are illegal whether the search involves an individual's home, desk, personal papers or business books, shopping bag, purse, briefcase, or any other place or possession entitled to be kept private.

Courts have permitted lawsuits for persistent and unwanted telephone calls and unauthorized prying into someone's bank account.

An individual also has a right to sue for unauthorized eavesdropping or spying. Wiretaps, hidden microphones, and window peeping violate the right of privacy, even when no one is listening in or when the information obtained is not passed along. Such eavesdropping is sometimes allowed in criminal investigations, but is strictly controlled by laws of search and seizure, because recording a conversation, for example, is considered a seizure of that conversation. For a discussion of the laws governing electronic surveillance, see SEARCH AND SEIZURE.

Without a doubt, everyone must endure the annoyance of some intrusions. Some noises must be tolerated, such as a fire alarm near a church. Mere bad manners, harsh language, or insulting gestures in public will not normally support a lawsuit. The intrusion must be enough to offend a reasonable person, not a hermit or a person who is excessively and irrationally distrustful of others.

Public versus private   There is no invasion of privacy unless the intrusion invades something that is, and is entitled to be, kept private. Testimony during a trial, for example, is considered a matter of public record. Fingerprints, measurements, and photographs in police files do not have to be kept confidential. Business records that a company is required by law to keep are generally open to inspection and public disclosure. A conversation between a husband and wife is usually surrounded by a shield of privacy, but no claim of intrusion can be made for a conversation that takes place in the presence of other people. A personal letter may be entitled to privacy, but not if it is left open on a table. A person may not like having his picture taken, but he cannot complain if the photograph is snapped in a public place. The photographer is doing no more than making a record of a public scene, which anyone is free to view. The same can be said of news accounts that record public events.

Even in a public place, however, some things are occasionally entitled to be kept private. In one case, a woman had her picture snapped just as her dress blew up above her knees. The court ruled against the photographer, finding that the woman was entitled to expect that much privacy even in public.

There are also times when intrusions that are generally necessary reach a point of excess at which the courts protect the individual. Subpoenas for personal financial books and records are perfectly legal; yet they can sometimes be demanded in such excess as to constitute an invasion of privacy. For instance, demands to disclose "all the bank accounts of all the members of the Newark police department and, in some instances, those of their wives," were considered a broad invasion of privacy. Our vast system of consumer CREDIT, for another example, can only function if financial records are kept on individuals and if bill collectors are able to contact debtors. In order to keep intrusions down to a reasonable level, state and federal laws limit the tactics creditors and credit bureaus may use, and consumers are entitled to sue for serious abuses.

Intrusion upon persons under investigation The law permits a reasonable degree of investigation into the truth of a claim preceding a trial.

EXAMPLE A man claimed to have suffered permanent injuries to his back on the job and applied for workmen's compensation benefits. When a detective hired by his employer took films of the man cutting and gathering wood for his fireplace along a state highway, the man claimed a violation of his right of privacy. The court held that an investigation of the claim was perfectly proper and should have been expected.

In other cases, people have been required to submit to physical examinations or to turn over copies of medical records in order to maintain lawsuits claiming compensation for physical injuries.

But if the investigation becomes intolerable or unreasonable, it may be an illegal intrusion.

EXAMPLE In Georgia a woman filed a claim for damages after she was injured in an automobile collision. The other driver's insurance company hired a national detective agency to follow the woman and furnish reports on her. The detectives started shadowing her, stealthily at first and then with increasingly objectionable behavior. They peeped through her hedge, snooped around her home, eavesdropped on her conversations, parked in front of her home day and night, and followed wherever she drove in her car. The woman's doctor and her husband told her she was imagining these things, and she was tormented by the thought that she was losing her mind. She suffered nervous spasms, sleeplessness, nightmares, and a rash, and eventually had to undergo electroconvulsive shock treatments.

Police finally intercepted the detectives when they were following the woman. The woman's attorney contacted the detectives and warned them that they were driving his client crazy, but the surveillance continued.

The conduct of the defendants in this case was described as vicious and malicious, not at all intended to gather information but deliberately calculated to frighten and torment the plaintiff. In testing the reasonableness of the defendants' actions, the court noted that activities that violate criminal laws, such as the Peeping Tom statutes, certainly give grounds for a civil action seeking money damages to compensate for the invasion of privacy.

Intrusion upon the privacy of public figures It is difficult for the law to protect the privacy of well-known people when they appear in public places unless their rights are blatantly abused.

EXAMPLE One of the most striking examples is the case involving Jacqueline Kennedy Onassis and a free-lance photographer named Ronald E. Galella, who specialized in making and selling photographs of famous people. He characterized himself as a *paparazzo,* the Italian term for a photographer who makes himself as visible to the public and as obnoxious to his photographic subjects as possible in order to advertise himself and promote the sale of his works.

The court found that Galella jumped into the path of John Kennedy's bicycle as he was riding in the park, alarming Secret Service agents who were guarding the boy, so that they placed Galella under arrest. At other times the photographer interrupted Caroline Kennedy as she played tennis, and he invaded the children's private schools. Once he maneuvered a powerboat uncomfortably close to Mrs. Onassis as she was swimming, and he often jumped and postured around in order to provoke a reaction, as when she and friends were attending the theater. He made a practice of bribing apartment house, restaurant, and nightclub doormen, even romancing a family servant in order to keep track of the family's movements.

The court granted an injunction ordering the photographer to keep at least 25 feet away from the President's widow, not to touch her, and to keep at least 30 feet away from the children.

Nuisances Our world is full of generalized assaults on peace and solitude. The Supreme Court has upheld the use of piped-in music in public places, saying that people are not entitled to as much privacy in a public place as they are at home. Yet in another case, the Supreme Court permitted local laws to restrict the use of sound trucks.

Laws frequently regulate the activities of door-to-door salesmen because their customers are so easily pressured (see CONSUMER PROTECTION), but laws cannot entirely prohibit door-to-door sales. A famous Supreme Court decision held that a complete ban would unnecessarily interfere with the religious freedom of groups such as the Jehovah's Witnesses; homeowners who do not care to talk can turn away unwanted strangers.

Even more annoying for many consumers is telephone soliciting. Sometimes a prerecorded message, perhaps six minutes long, is delivered and will not disconnect even if the listener hangs up. These calls have interfered when people were trying to use their telephones to summon a doctor, an ambulance, or the fire department.

Machines that dial one telephone number after another in sequence cannot be banned outright because they are also used to relay prerecorded hurricane or flood warnings and to summon emergency crews during blackouts or other disasters. The intrusion is becoming so serious, however, that future legislation is likely to curb these calls.

Public disclosure of private details Public disclosure of the details of one's private life can be very disturbing; yet it cannot be called defamation (LIBEL AND SLANDER) if it is true. Consequently, the only way an individual may be compensated is by suing for invasion of privacy. Many of the lawsuits involving public disclosure have included other elements as well, such as defamation or unauthorized use of the plaintiff's name or likeness.

EXAMPLE An early application of the prohibition against invasion of privacy to punish public disclosure of private facts was made in a Kentucky case in 1927. There the defendant put a sign in his window that said: "Dr. W. R. Morgan owes an account here of $49.67. And if promises would pay an account, this account would have been settled long ago. This account will be advertised as long as it remains unpaid." The court held this to be an unreasonable disclosure of the private facts of Dr. Morgan's personal finances.

In another case, a defendant unlawfully publicized a debt by stripping the tires off the debtor's car in public because they had not been fully paid for. For a discussion of the current methods used in regulating the collection of debts, see CREDIT.

Many people have been chagrined to find lurid details of their past dredged up and publicized. In a California case, a reformed prostitute who had been charged with committing a notorious murder found herself the subject of a motion picture called *The Red Kimono* seven years after she had settled down to a quiet married life. A man who had been convicted of murder and then pardoned found his story in a television show decades later. A man who had been briefly married to actress Janet Leigh when they were both in high school was embarrassed to find a mushy account of the event in a sensational magazine.

Winning a public disclosure case For plaintiffs to win in cases like this, they must generally show that the disclosure was made to the public and that the details disclosed were not rightfully public information. For example, when a 12-year-old married girl in South Carolina gave birth, the resulting publicity was annoying, but birth facts are a matter of public record, as are military records, patents and registered trademarks, deeds, and trial testimony.

If a newsworthy person or event is involved, what is normally considered private becomes a matter of public record. For example, a courtship is personal, but the news media are permitted to report the budding courtship of a senator or governor.

Most courts will not permit a recovery for public disclosure unless the private facts would be objectionable to an average person, because everyone is somewhat exposed to the public gaze. An ordinary person would not take offense, for instance, if a newspaper mentioned that he had returned from a trip or given a party for a local politician.

EXAMPLE A man who had been a child prodigy received national attention for lecturing to a group of Harvard professors at age 11 and graduating from Harvard at age 16. A shy and retiring person, he then tried to live down his fame and succeeded quite well until *The New Yorker* magazine published an article about him entitled "Where Are They Now?" The sketch recounted the man's unusual background, traced his attempts to conceal his identity over the years, described his menial employment far from the field of his earlier studies, and detailed his bizarre conduct, including his collecting old streetcar transfers. The man did not claim that the facts in the article were untrue or malicious—only that they destroyed the obscurity he had so carefully built. He lost his case because the right of the press to print the truth is so extensive that someone who has been a legitimate subject of public interest may not complain in court unless the disclosure contains facts so intimate and objectionable that an ordinary person would be offended.

False light Creating an untrue picture of a person or placing him in a false light is another cause for bringing suit for the invasion of privacy. Recognition of this as a legal injury seems first to have appeared in 1816, when the English poet Lord Byron succeeded in getting a court order prohibiting circulation of a bad poem attributed to him. Over the years a legal approach to the problem developed through a line of cases, which set limits on the freedom of the press by protecting people from the deliberate publication of false or misleading information about them.

Recently "false light" has come to be recognized as an invasion of the right of privacy. Cases have involved wrongly attributing an opinion or statement to someone, putting a person's name on a petition without his authorization, entering the name of an actor in an embarrassing contest without his consent, and filing a lawsuit in someone's name without his permission.

EXAMPLE The photograph of a child hit by a careless motorist on a public street was published in a newspaper because the event was newsworthy. When the same photograph was printed several months later in the *Saturday Evening Post* to illustrate an article called "They Ask to Be Killed," dealing with childhood carelessness, the publisher was held liable for casting the injured child in the false light of a careless pedestrian.

EXAMPLE In another case, a motion picture studio decided to send 1,000 male householders a letter supposedly written by an actress. The letter read:

Dearest: Don't breathe it to a soul, but I'm back in Los Angeles and more curious than ever to see you. Remember how I cut up about a year ago? Well, I'm raring to go again, and believe me I'm in the mood for fun.

Let's renew our acquaintanceship and I promise you an evening you won't forget. Meet me in front of Warner's Downtown Theatre at 7th and Hill on Thursday. Just look for a girl with a gleam in her eye, a smile on her lips and mischief on her mind!

Fondly,
Your ectoplasmic playmate,
M—— K——

The name at the end was the plaintiff's. The court held that the letter placed her in a false light by casting doubt on her character. It was certainly an invasion of privacy merely to satisfy a business desire for publicity.

A plaintiff will win a lawsuit on the ground of being cast in a false light if he can show that the defendant either intentionally or through carelessness disclosed to the public that the plaintiff acted in a way that he did not. Lawsuits occur only when the false light makes the plaintiff appear worse than he is, not when the plaintiff's reputation is enhanced.

Overlapping of areas Although it is easier to understand invasion of privacy by considering each of its four areas, in practice they often overlap and are bound up together in a lawsuit, as the following case illustrates.

EXAMPLE The famous baseball pitcher Warren Spahn sued the author and publisher of an unauthorized biography of him in 1964. The trial judge found that the "fictionalized" version of the ballplayer's life was made up of invented dialogue, imaginary incidents, and thoughts and feelings that were attributed without justification. Many of the falsifications in the book proved embarrassing for the plaintiff and profitable for the defendants. The trial court found that the defendants had violated Spahn's right of privacy in all four areas and were liable for money damages.

■ **Defenses** Defenses to a lawsuit for damages based on invasion of privacy are similar for all four areas. The most obvious defense is *consent*. If the defendant can show that the plaintiff gave him permission to intrude or to make some information public, he should not have to pay compensation to the plaintiff. Rarely, however, has a plaintiff written and signed a clear authorization unless a business contract was involved. Generally, the problem confronting the judge or jury is whether a reasonable person would have assumed from the plaintiff's words or deeds that he consented to the defendant's appropriation, intrusion, disclosure of private information, or false characterization.

Another valid defense is *privilege*. Privilege means that even though there is a violation of the right of privacy, it is legally justified. A witness, for example, can be required to disclose private details about someone without being liable for public disclosure of private facts, and a policeman is privileged to delve into the personal life of a murder suspect. People are privileged to tap their own telephones. Companies have been permitted to spy on an employee who was suspected of stealing or to watch employees closely in order to conduct an efficiency survey. The privilege in each case is the legally valid excuse for infringing on what would otherwise be someone else's right of privacy.

■ **Privacy statutes** It has long been a crime in some states to open or read another's letters or personal papers or to disclose the contents of someone else's telegram or telephone conversation. Rules governing the relationship of ATTORNEY AND CLIENT or doctor and patient (see PHYSICIANS AND SURGEONS) have always prohibited the disclosure of information given in confidence to the professional person. But most of the laws concerning privacy are fairly recent ones. In the 1970's the federal government enacted a number of specific statutes aimed at preserving certain elements of an individual's right of privacy.

Fair Credit Reporting Act The first major federal law designed to protect the privacy of individuals was the Fair Credit Reporting Act of 1970. Recognizing that "an elaborate mechanism has been developed for investigating and evaluating the credit worthiness, credit standing, credit capacity, character, and general reputation of consumers," Congress enacted this law "to insure that consumer reporting agencies exercise their grave responsibilities with fairness, impartiality, and a respect for the consumer's right to privacy." The law specifies when a financial report on a consumer can be used, prohibits inclusion of obsolete data, describes what information must be released to the government, and outlines how a consumer may gain access to his file and challenge information he thinks is incomplete or inaccurate. See CREDIT.

Freedom of Information Act Another important federal law that touches on the right of privacy is the Freedom of Information Act of 1966, which requires federal agencies to release information they have on file. Called a great milestone because it guarantees the right of people to know about the business of their government, the law allows anyone to obtain reasonably identifiable records or other information from federal agencies—except in certain instances, such as information affecting national defense or foreign policy. Decisions by federal officials to withhold information can be challenged in court, and it is the government that must prove why the information should not be released.

In a way, the Freedom of Information Act is opposite to a privacy law, for public disclosure of information about a person or business that is mentioned in a government file can be, in effect, an invasion of privacy. Therefore, the law exempts the need to disclose certain types of information. For example, trade secrets and commercial or financial information that is privileged or confidential, personnel and medical files, and other similar files would cause a clearly unwarranted invasion of privacy if disclosed.

EXAMPLE In a 1974 case, a company that sold amateur wine-making kits had asked the Bureau of Alcohol, Tobacco, and Firearms to give it a list of all the people who had permits to produce wine for family use without paying a tax. The company wanted the names in order to compile a mailing list for advertising purposes. The bureau resisted, and a federal court held that release of the files would result in a clearly unwarranted invasion of privacy. The lists contained information about the individual's family status and position of responsibility in his household, and they disclosed the fact that a private activity was carried on within the home for the benefit of the family. Comparing this to the purely commercial motive of the plaintiff and the annoyance to wine hobbyists of receiving advertisements in the mail, the court decided to protect the privacy of the individuals.

Privacy Act In 1974 the Freedom of Information Act was revised and strengthened, and a companion act was made into law. The Privacy Act of 1974 was enacted because Congress found that (1) the privacy of the people is affected by the collection and use of personal information by federal agencies; (2) the increasing use of computers and sophisticated technology magnify the possibility of harm to individual privacy; (3) the misuse of information can endanger opportunities to secure employment, insurance, and credit; (4) the right of privacy is a personal and fundamental right protected by the Constitution, even though it is not expressly mentioned in the Constitution.

Under the Privacy Act, an individual can decide what records kept by a federal agency, department, or bureau are important to him, and he can insist that they be used only for the purpose for which the information was originally collected. He is entitled to see the information and to have copies of it made, correcting mistakes or adding important details where necessary. Federal agencies have to organize the information to make it readily identifiable, accurate, and up to date, and they may use it only for lawful purposes. If an individual's rights are violated under this law, he may sue in a federal district court for damages and for a court order directing the agency to comply with the terms of the law.

Family Educational Rights and Privacy Act Also in 1974, Congress enacted a law that gives parents the right to inspect scholastic records kept on their children by schools. If parents find information that is inaccurate, misleading, or inappropriate in a child's records, they may challenge the school and insist that a written correction be inserted in the file. The written consent of parents is generally necessary before scholastic records can be released, but directory information—the student's name, address, and birth date—can be disclosed after parents have been notified and given some time to object. Each institution must keep a record of all requests to see a student's file and the reasons for them, and this information, too, should be available for parents.

After a student reaches age 18 or enrolls in an institution above the high school level, only he—and not his parents—may see his records unless he waives that right. Students may also sign waivers so that information can be released for college admissions, employment, or evaluation for honors, but they cannot be *required* to sign waivers in order to get admitted to a school. It is the obligation of schools to inform parents and students of their rights under this law.

A separate federal law that deals with the education of handicapped children provides the same right of privacy for them and for their parents. See HANDICAPPED PERSONS.

Other privacy laws A variety of other laws give special consideration to personal privacy. Records kept on juvenile delinquents and offenders and on young runaways must be kept confidential under federal law. Disclosure of information collected by the Census Bureau, the ARMED SERVICES, or the Internal Revenue Service is strictly regulated.

Congress also enacted the Right to Financial Privacy Act of 1978 to protect the rights of customers of financial institutions by keeping their financial records private and free from unwarranted governmental investigation. No agency of the federal government may be given access to information contained in the financial records of a customer unless certain conditions are met. In all cases, the desired financial records must be reasonably described. The information may be released if the customer signs a statement permitting the disclosure, identifying the records to be disclosed, and specifying that the time of disclosure must not exceed three months. These statements must be given to both the financial institution and the government agency.

The records may be disclosed by the institution in response to a subpoena or summons that was issued because the information is relevant to a legitimate law enforcement inquiry, such as to find out whether a person has been evading taxes. A copy of the subpoena or summons must be served on the customer or mailed to his last known address on or before the date the institution is served.

Information may also be obtained by the government by means of a search warrant or formal written request, as long as the requirements of the statutes are met.

For purposes of this law, financial institutions include banks, SAVINGS AND LOAN ASSOCIATIONS, building and loan associations, CREDIT UNIONS, and TRUST COMPANIES. See also BANKS AND BANKING.

private attorney general A private person who acts as plaintiff and sues to enforce congressional policy, as by starting a civil rights lawsuit against racial discrimination.

private law 1 The law relating to the enforcement of rights and duties in cases where all persons involved are private citizens. For example, CONTRACT law is private law as is DIVORCE law. 2 A statute enacted to affect one person or a group of persons, such as a law passed to change the name of a charitable organization. See PUBLIC LAW.

private road A road established by public authority, primarily to accommodate one person or a group of persons at his or their request and expense. In recent decisions courts have held that a private road, while chiefly benefiting those who paid to have it built and maintained, is actually a public road open to all others who wish to use it.

■ **Establishment** The power to grant a private road derives from the state's right of EMINENT DOMAIN—the right to take private property for public use. The specific power to create a private road, however, must be clearly conferred by statute.

■ **Proceedings** The proceeding for having a private road built is a civil action strictly between the person seeking the road and the owner or owners through whose land the road is to pass. The proceedings are generally started by petition.

Once the petition is filed, the court usually appoints a panel of impartial viewers who must decide whether or not the road is necessary, determine the best possible route for it, and set the amount of DAMAGES that are to be paid to the landowner over whose land the road is to pass. These matters are not subject to review by a trial court unless the viewers are accused of acting dishonestly.

Necessity As a general rule, land can be taken for private roads only in cases of necessity. There is some disagreement, however, about the required degree of necessity. According to some court decisions, a private road may be built only if it is absolutely indispensable to the applicant as a means of reaching his land. According to other decisions, a reasonable or practical necessity is sufficient. Courts generally agree, however, that private roads may not be opened simply because they will be convenient or save expenses. In deciding whether there is sufficient need for the road, the court must also weigh the amount of injury and inconvenience it will cause the owner of the land over which it is to be laid.

The viewers must plan the most practical route that causes the least possible injury to the person over whose land passage is granted.

Some statutes provide for a hearing before the viewers decide on the necessity of the road. Under other statutes, if the owner of the land over which the road is to be built wants to contest the application, he must file exceptions to the hearing's report. The owner of the land may show that the proposed road is not the most convenient route and defeat the establishment of the proposed route.

When no exceptions are filed, the report is binding on the court, and if the court finds that the report also conforms with the law, it will confirm it. Such a confirmation is, in effect, an order that the road be built.

The judgment handed down by the court should state the amount of compensation, as decided by the viewers, to be paid to the owner of the land over which the road will run, and should describe the location of the road and fix both its end points. Some statutes also require that the width of the road be specified.

Under some statutes the duty to maintain and repair a private road rests on the person for whose benefit the road is established. DAMAGES can be recovered for injuries resulting from the failure to make suitable repairs from the party who has the duty to repair the road.

privilege In law, a particular benefit or advantage enjoyed by a person, company, or class beyond the common advantage of other citizens. See AMBASSADORS AND CONSULS; ARREST; CONGRESS; LIBEL AND SLANDER; PRESIDENT; SELF-INCRIMINATION; WITNESS.

privileged communication Certain communications—between persons who are in a confidential or FIDUCIARY (trustee) relationship to each other—that the law does not permit to be disclosed and that are not admissible as EVIDENCE in court during a trial. A common example is the ATTORNEY AND CLIENT privilege. Other areas of privileged communications include HUSBAND AND WIFE; PHYSICIANS AND SURGEONS; WITNESS.

privileges and immunities Certain protections guaranteed to all U.S. citizens by the Constitution. The privileges and immunities clauses of the Constitution are designed to prevent state legislatures from depriving persons of certain basic rights of state and national citizenship. The bases for these protections are found in Article IV of the Constitution and in the 14th Amendment.

Article IV protects the citizens of one state from being unjustly discriminated against by the laws of another state, holding that "The Citizens of each State shall be entitled to all Privileges and Immunities of Citizens in the several States." The purpose of Article IV was to help fuse the independent sovereign states into one nation. It means that persons traveling from one state to another are guaranteed the same treatment as the citizens of the states through which they pass.

The privileges and immunities clause of the 14th Amendment says, "No State shall make or enforce any law which shall abridge the privileges or immunities of citizens of the United States." Its purpose is to prohibit a state from abridging rights that arise from U.S. citizenship, such as the right to vote in national elections.

In practice, the privileges and immunities clauses have rarely been used by the Supreme Court to invalidate state law, out of respect for the sovereignty of states. The Court has instead applied the concepts of DUE PROCESS OF LAW and EQUAL PROTECTION OF LAWS to declare unreasonable or discriminatory state actions unconstitutional.

■ **Article IV** The privileges and immunities protected by Article IV of the U.S. Constitution include the right to protection by the government of a state; the right to acquire and possess all kinds of property; the right to pass through or reside in any state for purposes of trade, agriculture, or professsional pursuits; the right to claim the benefit of the writ of HABEAS CORPUS; the right to sue and defend lawsuits in court; and the right to be exempt from higher taxes than those paid by the citizens of the state. In effect, each state must give citizens of other states the same privileges and immunities enjoyed by its own citizens.

This clause does not require absolute equality for nonresidents in all matters, but does require that there be some legitimate purpose to a state law that treats a nonresident differently from a resident. For example, a nonresident may not vote or hold office in a particular state, while a resident may. This unequal treatment is permissible because a state has a legitimate interest in having its affairs managed by residents rather than by nonresidents. A state may also give preference to its own residents for employment on a public works project without violating the privileges and immunities clause.

Fish and game rights Traditionally, state statutes that limit or prohibit the rights of nonresidents to take GAME or FISH within their boundaries have been upheld by the Supreme Court. Nonresidents, for instance, may be charged a reasonably higher fee than residents for the privilege of hunting or fishing in the state. These laws help to prevent the state's natural resources from being depleted by outsiders. Discrimination may not be permitted when the reasons for it are invalid or unconstitutional.

Business and professional rights A state may impose certain requirements on residents starting a business within its borders with which nonresidents must comply. In order to protect the public from incompetent professionals, the state may also establish qualifications for both resident and nonresident professionals before allowing them to practice their professions.

Taxes A state may not tax a nonresident at a higher rate than a resident simply because he is a nonresident.

EXAMPLE A New Hampshire statute imposed a tax rate of 4
O—* percent on income above $2,000 earned by nonresidents in New Hampshire. The tax would be reduced to the amount imposed by the nonresident's state if that tax was lower than that of New Hampshire. No tax was imposed on income earned in New Hampshire by its residents. The law also, in effect, provided that income earned by New Hampshire residents outside the state be exempt from this tax. Maine residents challenged the law as an unconstitutional violation of the privileges and immunities clause. The Supreme Court agreed. It held that there must be substantial equality of treatment for the residents of the taxing state and nonresident taxpayers.

Medical treatment Unless there is substantial reason for a state law that treats nonresidents differently from residents, it is invalid. A state may not, for example, refuse medical care to a nonresident simply because he is not a resident.

EXAMPLE A Georgia statute permitted abortions (under
O—* certain circumstances) only for residents. The residency requirement was not based on the need to preserve state-supported hospitals, because it also applied to private hospitals. The state did not show that its

hospitals were used to capacity in caring for Georgia residents. The Supreme Court decided that the residency requirement violated the privileges and immunities clause of Article IV. The Court held that the clause protects "persons who enter Georgia seeking the medical services that are available there. A contrary holding would mean that a state could limit to its own residents the general medical care available within its borders. This we could not approve."

■ **14th Amendment** The privileges and immunities clause of the 14th Amendment to the Constitution says that no state law may unreasonably abridge the right to pass from state to state; the right to vote for national officers; the right to enter public lands; the right to petition Congress to redress grievances; the right to inform the United States of a violation of its laws; the right of protection from violence when in the custody of a federal officer; the right of free access to U.S. seaports; the right to transact business with the U.S. government; the right of access to federal courts; the right to federal protection of a citizen's life, liberty, and property when he is on the high seas within the jurisdiction of a foreign power; and the privilege of HABEAS CORPUS.

Slaughterhouse cases This clause has been narrowly interpreted by the Supreme Court ever since an 1873 Court decision, known as the Slaughterhouse cases.

EXAMPLE A Louisiana law granted to the Crescent City
0—— ＊ Live Stock Landing and Slaughterhouse Company the exclusive right and power for 25 years to operate the only place for slaughtering animals in New Orleans and the surrounding area. This was done as a health measure "to remove from the more densely populated part of the city, the noxious slaughterhouses, and large and offensive collections of animals . . . and to locate them where the convenience, health and comfort of the people require they shall be located. . . ." The Crescent City Company was required to permit other butchers to do their slaughtering on its premises but was to receive fees for the use of these premises. It was forbidden to slaughter animals anywhere else in New Orleans and its vicinity. Butchers alleged that the statute was unconstitutional under the 14th Amendment because it abridged "their privileges and immunities as citizens of the United States." The Supreme Court rejected their claim. They viewed the statute as constitutional and enforceable as a health measure.

In reaching its decision, the Court reasoned that the issue involved was whether pursuing the occupation of butcher was a privilege that was intended to be included in the privileges and immunities clause of the 14th Amendment and, if so, whether that right had been abridged by state law. In order to resolve the issue, the Court reviewed the history of the 14th Amendment, which made former slaves national citizens. If a person resided within a particular state he was made a citizen of that state by virtue of his residence. There are two citizenships, one national and the other state. The 14th Amendment deals only with "privileges and immunities of citizens of the United States," but no state can enact or enforce any law that will diminish these basic rights.

If these words were given an expansive meaning, every businessman who was curtailed in his ambitions by a state

law could contend that what he was doing was a privilege attached to his national citizenship. "The state governments . . ." would be degraded ". . . by subjecting them to the control of Congress . . ." The Court decided that the "pervading purpose" of this and other Civil War amendments was "the freedom of the slave race." The Slaughterhouse Act was a valid exercise of state police power, and butchers in Louisiana had to comply with the act.

Later uses of the 14th Amendment The privileges and immunities clause of the 14th Amendment is little used today in invalidating questionable state statutes. When state laws infringe upon fundamental rights of U.S. citizenship, the equal protection clause comes into play. The Supreme Court examines the law to see if it involves a fundamental right and, if it does, asks (1) if the state has a legitimate interest in regulating the right, and (2) if the law is reasonably related to achieving that interest.

privity 1 Mutual interest in the same things, such as between parties to a CONTRACT. 2 Close, direct financial relationship, such as between the maker of a WILL and the person who receives property under it. 3 Connection or bond of union between parties concerning a particular transaction, such as between a buyer and a seller. In the past, the buyer of a defective product could sue only a party with whom he was in privity—a person who was a direct participant in the sales transaction. This meant that he could sue the seller but not the manufacturer of a defective product. For a discussion of the changing rules concerning privity between parties involved in a consumer sales transaction, see PRODUCT LIABILITY.

privy 1 One who is a coparticipant or who has an interest in any matter; a person who is in PRIVITY with another. 2 As an adjective, it means private.

prize The seizure and capture of a vessel at sea, by authority of a hostile country, either to possess the ship or to become master of its cargo. Goods taken on land from a public enemy are called booty. Those taken at sea are prizes. See MARQUE AND REPRISAL.

prizefighting A boxing match between two persons for a stake or reward, usually in a public exhibition. Promotion of and participation in a prizefight are controlled by state law. Engaging in a professional prizefight without following state regulations, including medical and licensing requirements, is a criminal offense.

probable cause Reasonable ground for suspicion, supported by circumstances strong enough to warrant a cautious man's belief that the law has been, or is being, violated. An officer of the law must have probable cause to make an ARREST or search. See SEARCH AND SEIZURE; CRIMINAL LAW.

EXAMPLE A well-maintained police radar unit showing an
0—— ＊ automobile traveling at 90 miles per hour in a school zone at noon on a weekday establishes probable cause for detaining the driver. The police officer's observation of a machine gun and a homemade bomb sitting on

the seat next to the fast driver establishes probable cause for searching the car.

probate

The procedure used by specialized courts to prove that a WILL is valid and genuine before authorizing the distribution of a deceased person's property according to the will's provisions. Probate comes from the Latin word *probatio,* which means "proof." Every will must be admitted to probate before a court will allow a decedent's property to be distributed to his heirs. Because probate is regulated by state law, you should find out precisely what the procedure is in your state. See Chart 14.

■ **Definitions** Probate is the process by which a document is established by a probate or surrogate court as the duly executed last will of a competent testator. A *will* is a legal document in which a person directs how his property should be distributed after his death. A *testator* is a person who has died leaving a will. A testator is *competent* when, at the time of making his will, he understands the effect of making a will, knows that he is making one, knows the extent of his property, and realizes how making the will affects those persons named in it (and relatives who are not) after his death. Understanding these matters is called *testamentary capacity.*

When a person dies without leaving a will *(intestate),* a personal representative will be appointed by the probate court to distribute the decedent's property according to the state's laws of DESCENT AND DISTRIBUTION.

■ **Functions of probate court** In addition to determining the genuineness of a will, a probate court also has jurisdiction over the administration of a decedent's estate including collecting assets, settling creditors' claims, and closing the estate and distributing the assets. For this reason, a discussion of probate proceedings necessarily includes reference to the functions of EXECUTORS AND ADMINISTRATORS who are appointed by the court to administer the decedent's property. After a will has been declared valid and genuine, the probate court sees that the executor or administrator (1) uses the assets of the estate in an orderly way to pay any outstanding debts and (2) hands out the remaining assets to those entitled to receive them either by will or, if certain parts of the will have been declared legally ineffective, by the state laws of descent and distribution.

■ **Necessity** A will has no legal effect until it is probated. The person having possession of a will, usually the person named as executor in the will or the decedent's attorney, is obligated to produce it as soon as he finds out that the person has died. Many states have statutes imposing penalties for concealing or destroying a will or for not producing it within a given time. The criminal sanctions for not filing a will for probate are designed to prevent any wrongdoing, such as the destruction or concealment of a will, by greedy relatives who would inherit more under the laws of descent and distribution than they would under the will.

■ **Practical aspects of probate** In recent years, there has been much public interest in avoiding probate because it is considered a waste of time and money by those it seeks to protect. Although there have been abuses in the probate process, certain misconceptions about it must be corrected.

In order to bring a will to probate, a number of papers must be prepared and filed with the court—a petition for letters testamentary to appoint the executor, a death certificate, the will, a petition for probate that often includes a rough inventory and appraisal of the decedent's property done by the prospective executor, a list of the decedent's creditors, and the names and addresses of the DISTRIBUTEES (people who would inherit under the laws of descent and distribution if the will is denied probate).

Time The probate of a will can be time-consuming, anywhere from a month to a few years, for a variety of reasons. The calendar of the probate court is usually overcrowded so that once all the papers in a particular case are filed, you must wait before the court can review them. When the court begins to review the case, a delay in the proceedings can occur if the witnesses to the will cannot be easily located or are deceased. This problem emphasizes the importance of carefully choosing witnesses to your will who will most likely remain in the state and survive your death. If the will is being contested—that is, if it is alleged to be invalid by persons who would inherit under the laws of descent and distribution should it be declared so—the proceedings will be prolonged because of the litigation involved. The longer the probate proceeding takes, the higher the attorney's fees that will be paid from the decedent's estate once it is distributed. Since attorney's fees for probate are considered a necessary expense of administration of the estate, it is one of the first debts paid by the executor.

Cost In addition to attorney's fees, probate itself costs money. Statutes establish that certain fees based on the value of the decedent's property passing through probate—that is, property disposed of by the decedent's will—be paid to the probate court for its administrative and supervisory services. For this reason, many people seek to have as much of their property as possible pass outside the will. This can be done by the use of *will substitutes,* legal methods of owning property that are used primarily to avoid the expense of probate. For example, the proceeds of a life insurance policy go directly to the beneficiary without passing through probate court.

Another will substitute is a TRUST arrangement whereby money or property (the principal) is set aside by one person (the settlor) for another (the beneficiary) upon the settlor's death, but during his life the settlor is entitled to income (interest) from the principal. Upon the settlor's death, the beneficiary is legally entitled to the principal without any assistance from the probate court. A Totten Trust, another will substitute, is an arrangement by which a bankbook is designated as being in trust for another person while the depositor retains the right to use the funds. Upon the depositor's death, the funds automatically belong to the other person. See the discussion of will substitutes in WILLS.

Property that is owned jointly by two or more persons, such as when a husband and wife own their house together, passes immediately to the survivor upon the co-owner's death. The probate court need not supervise the transfer of its ownership. By using these devices, probate is avoided but if there is other property that passes under the will the value of those items will be used to calculate the probate fees.

Duties of executor Once the will has been admitted to probate, the court will supervise the administration of the estate by the executor. He must collect the decedent's assets, inventory them, and if their value cannot be easily determined—such as the value of a painting, jewelry, or land—he must have them appraised. See EXECUTORS AND ADMINISTRATORS for a detailed discussion of their duties. States frequently require that the appraiser be appointed by the court to prevent an appraiser friendly to the decedent's family from undervaluing the assets in order to escape higher probate and tax expenses. These court-appointed appraisers receive a commission from the estate, which is usually set by statute. Their actual expenses are determined by the court. Since appraisers' commissions are a necessary administration expense, they will be among the first debts paid off by the executor from the assets of the estate.

The executor must see to it that the creditors of the decedent are notified of the decedent's death. The method and manner of notice is usually specified in the state laws governing probate proceedings. One common way is publication in the local newspaper for several weeks of a notice that contains the name of the decedent, the name and address of the probate court where claims should be sent, and the time within which claims must be presented or else be forever barred. The creditor must file his claim in writing to the probate court in order to receive payment.

■ **Family allowance during probate** A decedent's family may encounter financial hardship because there is not enough money to live on from the time of his death to the completion of probate and the distribution of his property. When a person dies, all his assets, such as funds in savings and checking accounts and dividends from stocks and bonds, are *frozen* until probate is completed—that is, no one can use them. The institutions or corporations involved freeze the assets after receiving notice of the death (usually from the obituary page of the local newspaper).

To soften this financial blow for families, many states have laws that provide a family allowance, an amount of money taken from the decedent's assets and paid to the family as a substitute for the support that had been provided by the decedent. This right to an allowance vests immediately upon the decedent's death. The allowance is given to the family as quickly as possible after all the necessary papers for probate and the petition for a family allowance are filed. Until the papers are filed, however, the family is responsible for meeting its own financial obligations. The laws of your state must be consulted concerning family allowances.

■ **Place of probate** Probate proceedings usually take place in the state in which the decedent made his home at the time of death. If, however, he owned real estate in another state, his will disposing of these assets must also be probated in the other state.

■ **Determining validity of the will** Generally, a document must be of testamentary character—written to take effect after the death of the person making it but permitting him to retain the property under his control during his life. It must also comply with all statutory requirements in order to be probated as a will. A valid will that has some provisions that are invalid or obscure or that cannot be carried out is still entitled to be probated. If, however, the will was made as a result of fraud or undue influence, it will be denied probate.

Altered wills A will that has been altered to revoke all its provisions will be denied probate.

EXAMPLE John drew large X's across every page of his will in the presence of his wife, Alice, and his business partner, Fred, and told them he intended to revoke it. He asked Alice to throw it in the garbage but, unknown to John, she kept it. John died shortly thereafter, and Alice tried to have the will admitted to probate. The court refused to admit the will to probate because of its condition, along with Fred's testimony that John intended to revoke its provisions completely.

If the alteration revokes only certain provisions of the will, the remaining ones may be admitted to probate. If, however, a will has been mutilated and forged paragraphs added, the entire document will be denied probate.

Two wills All separate papers, documents, or sheets making up the testator's will may be admitted to probate. When a later will does not revoke all prior wills, two separate and distinct wills may be probated, provided they cover totally different property and the probating of only one would cause part of the estate to be disposed of by the state laws of descent and distribution. Probate courts distribute property according to state law only when there is no reasonable alternative.

A *codicil* (a supplement or addition to a will) is entitled to be probated together with the will it modifies if it was added according to the state's laws. If it is complete in itself and can stand as a separate testamentary document independent of the will, the codicil alone may be admitted to probate. A codicil that has been revoked by another codicil is not entitled to probate.

Original documents As a general rule, the original document is the one that must be presented for probate. Probate of a copy or duplicate of a will usually is not permitted unless the absence of the original is satisfactorily explained and a thorough and diligent search for the original has been conducted.

Language A will written in a foreign language should be admitted to probate if the testator understood what it contained and if it otherwise complies with the law. A translation usually must accompany the will.

■ **Proceedings** Probate proceedings are governed entirely by statute. The only issue that is determined by the probate court is whether the document offered for probate is the genuine last will of the decedent or whether he died intestate. The probate court has no power to consider matters not related to probate, such as whether an heir owed money to the decedent. The meaning and legal effect of ambiguous provisions in the will are determined by other courts after the will has been probated.

There were two kinds of probate in early English law that are still followed today in some states. In *probate in common form,* the person asserting the validity of the will (the proponent) is permitted to prove it by his oath and the testimony of witnesses without giving notice to interested parties who are discussed later in this article. *Probate in solemn form* involves giving the interested parties notice and an opportunity to be heard in court. Although some states still allow probate without notice, the majority require that all interested persons be notified prior to a probate hearing.

Filing The first step in the probate process is filing the required documents with the clerk of the probate court. The documents required are (1) a copy of the death certificate, (2) the will, and (3) a petition to admit the will to probate and to grant letters testamentary (letters authorizing the executor to distribute the estate). Usually, the executor files these documents, but they may be filed by any person who has a financial interest in the will.

Hearing At the probate hearing, the proponent of the will must prove (1) the death of the testator, usually by a copy of the death certificate; (2) the residence of the decedent in the state where the proceedings are being held; (3) the genuineness of the will; (4) compliance with statutory requirements for the execution of wills; and (5) the competence of the testator when he made the will.

The will's genuineness and the mental capacity of the testator at the time the will was made are usually shown by *attesting witnesses*—persons who were present at the time the will was made and who can certify that it was properly executed. The number of attesting witnesses to a will is set by law. In some states, if fewer than the required number of persons witness a will, the will may be declared void and the testator's property disposed of according to state law. In some states, a will can be admitted to probate even if one or more of the witnesses do not testify at the hearings, while other states require all available witnesses to appear in probate proceedings.

Where some or all the witnesses to a will are unavailable, certain procedures are usually followed. If, for instance, the required witnesses are outside the state, a commission may be sent to take their testimony under oath and return it to the court. If they cannot be located, it must be proved that a diligent search was made for them, that their signatures are genuine, and that the will was duly executed. If the required witnesses have died before the testator, proof of that fact must also be offered. If none of the witnesses can be found, the will still may be admitted to probate. To avoid the time and expense of such a search, it is a good idea to check your will periodically and make sure your witnesses have not moved or died. If they have, you should make a new will, specifically keeping the terms of your former will but having new witnesses to its execution.

■ **Uniform probate code** Over the years, the growing dissatisfaction of some states with their probate laws led them to seek the help of the American Bar Association and the National Conference of Commissioners on Uniform State Laws to develop simpler probate procedures. As a result, the Uniform Probate Code was written and has been adopted in whole or in part by about one third of the states. The major aim of the code is to lessen the unnecessary intervention of probate courts in the administration of a decedent's property whenever possible, thus reducing the time and expense of probate. For example, the code simplifies probate procedure for small estates.

■ **Probate made simple** Many states provide for a simplified probate procedure in certain cases, such as when the decedent owned very little property or if he did not own real estate, an automobile, or stocks and bonds. The laws designate a voluntary administrator to handle the estate. He may be the executor named in the will or, if no will was left, the surviving adult spouse, or if none, a person named in the statute. Such a procedure allows for the distribution of the decedent's assets without the need for court supervision and, therefore, without the expenses of probate.

If no objection is made at the hearing, the court will admit the will to probate.

■ **Contesting probate** The probate of a will may be opposed, or contested, on the ground that the document is invalid because of the testator's incapacity when making the will, the nonobservance of formalities required by law, or for some other reason recognized by law.

EXAMPLE Suppose wealthy Uncle Waldo makes it known that he has named Bill the sole beneficiary in his will. Bill's brother Arnold, extremely jealous of this fact, gets his Uncle Waldo intoxicated and, while in a drunken stupor, Waldo executes a codicil revoking his prior will and leaving his entire estate to Arnold. Clearly, Waldo had no idea what he was doing when he executed this codicil. After Waldo's death, Arnold files the codicil and a petition to admit it to probate. Arnold's chauffeur, who was present during the execution of the codicil, notifies Bill of the circumstances and offers to testify to the truth. Bill could oppose the probate of the codicil because Waldo lacked testamentary capacity at the time the codicil was made.

Will contests assert that a will is invalid because of failure of proper execution, fraud, mistake, lack of testamentary capacity, revocation, or lack of intent that the document be a will.

The probate of a will may only be contested by persons having a valid and legal interest in the testator's estate. These may include next of kin who would inherit property if the will were set aside and the laws of descent and distribution were applied instead, beneficiaries under prior wills, purchasers of property from heirs, and the state—if there is a question of ESCHEAT (the government getting the property because no living heirs can be found). Creditors are not generally entitled to contest the will of a debtor. An executor has the obligation to defend the will against attack from other persons who try to contest it.

There is no constitutional right to trial by jury in probate or will contest proceedings, but most states have laws giving the right to trial by jury in a will contest. Statutes usually set time limits for starting a will contest.

■ **Agreement not to contest** A testator may make a contract with his heir not to contest a will—for example, if the testator gave the heir a lump sum during his lifetime. States vary as to the remedies a person to a no-contest agreement may have if the agreement is broken. Remedies include an INJUNCTION against (an order to stop) the prosecution of the contest and a lawsuit for money DAMAGES. Under some statutes, the agreement must be submitted to the probate court for approval.

probation Allowing a person convicted of an offense to go free-at-large, under suspension of a jail SENTENCE during good behavior, with the supervision of a probation officer. See PAROLE.

pro bono publico (Latin) "For the public good"; for the welfare of the whole. In law, the term refers to free legal work done for a charitable or public purpose.

procedural law   Rules prescribing the formal steps that must be taken to bring or defend a civil suit or a criminal prosecution. The date on which to file a paper in court, for example, is a matter of procedural law. See ADJECTIVE LAW; SUBSTANTIVE LAW.

procedure   The formal methods by which a legal right is enforced in a court or other tribunal; the form, manner, and order of conducting a suit. See EVIDENCE; PLEADING; PRACTICE; PROCESS.

proceeding   1 Any ACTION, hearing, investigation, inquest, or inquiry conducted by a court, administrative agency, arbitrator, hearing officer, or legislative body to determine the legal results of a particular course of action.   2 An individual step taken in a case, such as formally filing an ANSWER to a COMPLAINT in a lawsuit.

process   A means of compelling the defendant in an ACTION (a lawsuit) to appear in court; any method by which a court compels compliance with its demands during the course of a legal proceeding. For example, a WRIT, SUMMONS, SUBPOENA, WARRANT, and other court orders are processes issued to acquire jurisdiction of (authority over) a person or property. See MOTIONS AND ORDERS; JUDGMENTS.

proctor   A person, such as a lawyer, appointed to manage the affairs of another, in or out of court. See PROXY.

produce   Bring forward or exhibit, as in offering testimony or documents to a judicial proceeding. A *motion to produce,* or a *motion for production,* is a request that the court order someone to yield specified documents. See MOTIONS AND ORDERS; SUBPOENA DUCES TECUM.

product liability   The responsibility of a manufacturer or seller to pay for harm caused by a defective product. To determine the extent of this responsibility, the law considers three theories of product liability; a defendant can be held responsible because of NEGLIGENCE, breach of warranty, or strict liability.

Negligence is the failure to exercise reasonable or ordinary care. It means that someone who had a legal duty either did something he should not have done or failed to do something he should have done. A manufacturing company can be found negligent if the plaintiff proves that employees did not perform their work properly or that management chose inferior procedures that resulted in an unsafe product.

Breach of warranty is the failure to live up to the terms of a promise or claim concerning the quality or type of product. The law assumes that a seller gives certain general warranties concerning goods he sells, and also requires that he stand behind any specific assertions he makes.

Strict liability means that the defendant is responsible even if he was not directly at fault. For example, a manufacturer may be liable for injuries caused by a defective product even if the plaintiff cannot prove that the manufacturer was careless.

■ **History of product liability laws**   What follows is a brief history of how the courts have applied the theories of negligence and breach of warranty, and how the principle of strict liability revolutionized the law of product liability.

Negligence   During much of the modern industrial age, courts believed that it would be an impossible burden on industry to permit a lawsuit against a manufacturer every time an employee sent out a product with a harmful mistake in it. Thus, negligence liability had to be limited.

Privity   The limitation the courts used was PRIVITY, the rule that an injured person can sue the negligent person only if the latter dealt with the injured person directly. This rule was pronounced in 1842 in the English case of *Winterbottom* v. *Wright.*

EXAMPLE The defendant, Wright, had a contract to keep a O——* mail coach repaired after it was sold. He performed repairs negligently, and a passenger was injured when the coach collapsed. Applying the rule of privity, the court held that the passenger, Winterbottom, had no right to sue because he had no relationship with the defendant, nor did the defendant have a duty to be careful for the plaintiff.

Because it was clear that consumers had to be protected against products inherently or imminently dangerous to life, the requirement of privity between plaintiff and defendant gave way in time to major exceptions. Food was the first product exempted from privity in negligence cases; soon other products with the capacity to endanger life if defective were also exempted. For example, a manufacturer who carelessly mislabeled a poison was deemed liable to anyone harmed as a result, not just to the person to whom he sold the mislabeled poison.

Although tobacco is not a food, a court in Mississippi allowed a plaintiff to sue without being in privity with the defendant when he bit into a plug of chewing tobacco containing "a human toe in a state of putrefaction." Other courts extended the exception beyond food to anything inherently dangerous if defective, such as an improperly constructed scaffold.

Eventually the exceptions swallowed the rule. A New York court ruled in 1916 that an injured person could sue a manufacturer who built a car with a defective steering wheel even though there was no privity at all between the two. The court held that a manufacturer is liable for negligently making any product that could cause injury if it is defective. This rule has been so widely accepted that privity is now virtually a dead letter in negligence cases.

Who is now liable for negligence   Today the duty to avoid negligence and to supply a safe product applies to everyone in the chain of distribution: the manufacturer, the company that uses the product to assemble something else, and the seller. Even a supplier can be liable for providing a defective product—for example, a dealer who rents out a collapsible grandstand or a beautician who applies dangerously stale chemicals to a customer's hair. These people owe the duty of due care to anyone likely to be injured by a defective product, including the buyer, his employees or relatives, a person to whom he gives the product as a gift, a person who leases the product or is permitted by the buyer to use it, or even a passerby at the time of the accident.

Warranties   Warranties—promises or representations (claims) concerning the quality or character of goods—have been very important in product liability law. A warranty

WHEN AN UNSAFE PRODUCT INJURES YOU OR YOUR PROPERTY

■ You can sue a manufacturer for harm done by a defective product on the grounds of negligence, breach of warranty, or strict liability.

■ *Negligence* means that someone with a legal duty did not do something he should have done or did something he should not have done. A company can be found negligent if you can prove that the employees did their work wrong or the management chose inferior procedures that resulted in an unsafe product.

■ In *breach of warranty*, you have to show that the manufacturer failed to live up to the terms of his promise or claim about the quality or type of product.

■ *Strict liability* means that the manufacturer is responsible even if he is not directly at fault. For example, a manufacturer may be liable for injuries caused by a defective product even if you cannot prove that he was careless.

■ Most states currently recognize strict liability on defective products, but a number of state legislatures have enacted statutes to limit liability in some ways.

■ Everyone in the chain of distribution—the manufacturer, the company that uses the product to assemble something else, and the seller—has an obligation to supply a safe product.

■ Under the Uniform Commercial Code, which applies in all states except Louisiana, there are implied warranties in every sale that the goods are merchantable (fit for use) and fit for the particular purposes for which they have been sold.

■ A consumer must promptly notify the seller or manufacturer whenever he thinks one of them is not living up to his end of the contract.

■ A seller may make a disclaimer or specifically notify the buyer that the seller does not intend to be responsible for certain problems. When someone buys the product, he accepts the disclaimer as part of the sale. Courts and consumer protection laws are beginning to override some disclaimers, however, when it is clear that the buyer never understood them or had a chance to negotiate in the first place.

■ Anyone who sells a product in a defective or dangerous condition is le-

gally liable for any physical harm caused to the user or his property.

■ Any product likely to be used near children or by them must be made safer than a product sold for professional or industrial use.

■ A consumer who plainly misuses a product cannot complain when an injury results. For example, a person who disregards a printed warning to use hair spray away from an open flame or to apply paint only in a well-ventilated area cannot blame the manufacturer for making an imperfect product.

■ A consumer who continues to use an obviously defective product may be precluded from complaining. If you find green slime on a package of cold cuts and go right ahead and eat the meat, you can be said to have assumed the risk of getting sick.

■ If you alter or misuse the product, the manufacturer is no longer liable.

■ A statute of limitations—measured from the time a product is manufactured or first sold—sets a limit on the time manufacturers can be held liable for an injury.

may be either *express* (spelled out) or *implied* (inferred indirectly from the circumstances of the transaction).

Implied warranties   The Uniform Commercial Code (UCC), which is the basic law of SALES in every state except Louisiana, says that in every sale of a product, the law will *imply* that the goods are merchantable and fit for the particular purpose for which they have been sold.

The *warranty of merchantability* means that the product and its container meet certain minimum standards of quality and that the item is fit to be sold and used for the ordinary purposes for which products of this type are generally sold. For example, a toaster should toast bread, a vacuum cleaner should clean carpets, and a lawn mower should cut grass. This warranty also includes a standard of reasonable safety. For example, a new electrical appliance must not have any defects, such as a frayed wire, that would give you an electric shock.

Fit for a particular purpose means that the product is suitable for the buyer's needs if the seller knows that the buyer is relying on him to furnish appropriate goods.

EXAMPLE   Eleanor goes into a housewares store and asks the salesman for a machine that will shred cabbage. The salesman sells her an ordinary blender, assuring her that it will shred cabbage. Eleanor buys the blender and takes it home. The next day she discovers that the blender liquifies the cabbage instead of shredding it. The blender is not fit for the particular purpose for which it was sold.

The warranties of merchantability and fitness for a particular purpose are implied, however, only when the seller is a merchant who regularly deals in goods of the kind sold. An inexperienced salesman in a large department store who casually sells something cannot be assumed to have taken on responsibility for the merchantable quality of the product unless he claims some expert knowledge of the product.

Express warranties   In addition to the implied warranties, the buyer is entitled to rely on any express (stated) warranties made by the seller. An express warranty can be oral, such as words spoken during negotiations, or written, such as words in a sales contract, an advertisement, or a tag attached to the product. An express warranty can also be an earlier purchase of the same kind of product or a sample model of the product, such as a sofa in a showroom. A salesman's opinion concerning the value of the product is not an express warranty. A statement such as "the best car on the market today" is only sales talk, called "puffing."

A buyer does have the right to rely on the seller's opinion, however, if the seller offers special expertise. For example, a registered nurse was able to hold a used car salesman to his recommendation in one case because he had been an automobile mechanic for many years. Where the sales pitch or advertising—unless obviously improbable—was itself the reason for the purchase, the claims are likely to be considered express warranties. One man was allowed to recover for injuries when his hand slipped onto the blade of a knife that had no hilt. The knife had been advertised as slip-proof: "No hilt to get in the way of cutting action. Knife is of such perfect design the hand cannot slip."

Warranty as contract Early statutes described a warranty in terms of a contract between two parties, the buyer and the seller. The courts interpreted this similarity to mean that the seller was responsible if the product did not live up to his warranty, whether he knew about the defect or should have known about it. As a consequence, a manufacturer was responsible for a faulty product even if it could not be proved that he was at fault.

Interpreting warranties as contracts, however, also meant that a seller was liable only to his immediate purchaser. If that purchaser was a wholesaler who sold to a retailer who sold to a consumer, the consumer could not reach the manufacturer because the two were not in privity. Consequently, the barrier of privity was used against warranty cases, just as it had been used against early negligence cases.

Strict liability in warranty cases The first recognition of strict liability for implied warranties without regard to privity began around 1905, when there was a prolonged and vigorous national campaign against marketing unsafe food. Because of the severe health danger of unwholesome food, courts began to permit lawsuits against sellers of unwholesome food, whether or not they were negligent, and against original manufacturers, whether or not they were in privity with the consumers. One court said, "A manufacturer of food products under modern conditions impliedly warrants his goods when dispensed in original packages." The fairness of this development was especially plain in the following case.

EXAMPLE A profitable restaurant in Seattle had purchased a sealed package of cooked tongue and served it without further preparation. The meat turned out to be spoiled, and the patron who bit into it jumped up and loudly denounced the food to all the other customers. The court held that the restaurant could recover damages from the original manufacturer for injury to its reputation and loss of business without having to prove that the manufacturer had been negligent or in privity with the restaurant. This result was dictated by "the demands of social justice."

The first recognition of strict liability for an express warranty without regard to privity was enunciated by a Washington court in 1932.

EXAMPLE Ford Motor Company had distributed literature claiming that its automobile had a "shatterproof" windshield—an express warranty. The plaintiff purchased one of the cars, but the windshield shattered when a pebble struck it and he was injured. The dealer who sold the car said that he was not liable because he had not given the warranty, and the manufacturer claimed that it could not be held liable because it made the warranty only to the dealer. The court ruled that even without privity the manufacturer was liable for the misrepresentation, whether it was done innocently or not.

After the courts began permitting lawsuits on breach of warranty without proof of warranty, statutes required plaintiffs to do everything required of a party to a sales contract if they wanted to win their lawsuits under a breach of warranty theory.

Prompt notification Under sales law, a plaintiff is required to give prompt notice to the defendant whenever he thinks the defendant is not living up to his end of the bargain. For example, a seller who ships cases of rancid salad oil to a grocery store should be able to save everyone the expense of a lawsuit by replacing the bad bottles with good ones. To make this possible, the grocer is expected to notify the wholesaler of the defective goods. Consumers have often been turned out of court because they did not remember to give prompt notice to the seller that the product did not live up to its warranties.

Disclaimers Another contract defense is a seller's *disclaimer*—a specific notice to the buyer that the seller will not be responsible for certain problems. If the buyer makes the purchase, he accepts and is bound by the disclaimer. Courts and CONSUMER PROTECTION laws now override some disclaimers when it is clear that the buyer did not understand them or have a chance to negotiate. Nevertheless, disclaimers, too, have successfully blocked many breach of warranty lawsuits.

Strict liability The principle of strict liability developed because the limitations placed on plaintiffs by both negligence and breach of warranty were sometimes used to prevent people who had been injured by defective products from gaining satisfaction in court. Under strict liability, an innocent consumer who knows nothing about disclaimers and the requirement of giving notice to a manufacturer with whom he did not deal cannot be prevented from suing. The rule avoids the technical limit of privity, which can create an expensive chain of lawsuits back to the party that originally put the defective product into the stream of commerce. It takes the burden of the cost of an injury off the innocent consumer and puts it on the manufacturer, who can spread the cost of an occasional injury among all his customers by adding to the price of each product. It places liability on the party who created the risk by introducing the product in the first place. This rule of strict product liability is now recognized as law in almost every state. Anyone who sells a product in a defective or dangerous condition is legally liable for any physical harm caused to the user or his property—if the seller regularly sells such products and the consumer receives the product without any substantial changes having been made in its condition. The seller (whether a salesman or manufacturer) is liable even though he has been careful in handling the product and even if the consumer bought the product somewhere else and did not deal directly with him.

The first case to apply this modern rule was *Greenman* v. *Yuba Power Products, Inc.* in California in 1963.

EXAMPLE Mrs. Greenman had bought her husband a combination power tool and given it to him for Christmas. After two years, Mr. Greenman bought the attachments he needed to use the tool as a lathe in order to turn a large piece of wood into a chalice. He worked on the piece several times without difficulty before the block of wood suddenly flew out of the lathe and struck him on the forehead, inflicting serious injuries. He sued the manufacturer and produced witnesses to prove that the machine was designed with inadequate set screws.

The manufacturer, who had advertised the power tool as having a "rugged construction" and "positive locks that hold adjustments through rough or precision work," claimed that it should not have to pay money damages because the plaintiff had not given it notice of breach of the warranty within a reasonable time as required. Furthermore, a long line of California cases had said that a plaintiff could not sue someone not in privity with him unless the defective product was food.

The California court replied that this was not a warranty case but a *strict liability* case. The court held that any "manufacturer is strictly liable . . . when an article he places on the market, knowing that it is to be used without inspection for defects, proves to have a defect that causes injury to a human being."

Applying the three theories of liability Many states recognize all three theories of product liability—negligence, breach of warranty, and strict liability. Generally a plaintiff can base his claim on all three theories and the court can grant money damages under whichever theory can be proved.

Strict liability is the simplest approach. A strict liability case can be brought by anyone foreseeably affected by the goods. A plaintiff has to prove that (1) the product was defective, (2) the defect existed when the product left the defendant's hands, and (3) the defect caused the harm.

Proving a breach of warranty case is also rather simple, because again the plaintiff does not have to show that the defendant is at fault in causing the defect. He need only show that the defendant made an express warranty that the product did not live up to or that the product was not merchantable or fit for a particular purpose.

A negligence case is much more difficult to prove because a plaintiff must show what the defendant did to make the product unsafe or defective before the plaintiff ever came into contact with it. For example, the plaintiff can show that the defendant's normal testing or inspection routine is haphazard. Although proving negligence can be difficult, plaintiffs often try this approach because juries are more likely to be sympathetic if they can find fault with the defendant. The amount of money recovered is apt to be larger than in the other two types of product liability cases.

■ **Grounds for product liability lawsuits** If you have been harmed by a product that has been (1) made defectively or poorly inspected, (2) improperly or misleadingly labeled or advertised, or (3) lacking appropriate warnings against possible dangers, you may have grounds for a lawsuit. Generally, the courts consider some types of complaints to be reasonable and justified and others to be unreasonable.

A defective product A defect is an imperfection, deficiency, or insufficiency in a product that makes it unsafe. Although the rules are not the same in every state, some defects are generally accepted as such. For example, a hammer that shatters when someone tries to drive a nail with it is defective because the metal was improperly tempered when it was manufactured. An automobile is defective if an essential pin is missing. Products can also be defective because of poor design. This was true in the case of a tractor and transplanter sold to be used as one unit. The seats of the transplanter were right next to the exhaust pipe of the tractor, so that anyone on a seat was exposed to carbon monoxide fumes. Inadequate testing—for example,

of a new drug—may result in the marketing of a defective product. Inadequate inspection can cause a faulty product, such as contaminated canned food, to slip out into the market undetected.

Something other than the product itself can cause a product to be defective. A caustic chemical should not be stored in a container that makes it look like a soft drink, for example, and carbonated beverages must be in containers that will not explode from the pressure.

If the defect is created by someone other than the manufacturer, then the manufacturer is not liable. For example, a manufacturer is not responsible if he makes a machine with all the necessary safety features but the person who assembles the machine leaves the safety shields off.

The original manufacturer is liable if he creates a defect that survives the various stages of production to the end product. For example, the original seller of coffee beans that are contaminated by a pesticide cannot escape liability even though the beans are roasted, ground, brewed into coffee, and then used to flavor ice cream.

Inadequate labeling and false advertising Improper labeling, instructions, or warning on a product or its container can make a product defective, too. A drug or a poison must be labeled with its correct name. Dangerous products should carry warnings that explain how they should be used, under what circumstances they may cause harm, and what steps to take in an emergency. Warnings can give an antidote for accidental poisoning, for example, or tell how to disengage gears on a piece of machinery, or where to find a kill switch for an electrical circuit.

The principle of proper labeling covers claims made in sales brochures, in displays of the product, and in public advertising. A manufacturer who creates the demand for goods through print and broadcast media is strictly liable for making sure his product has the qualities advertised to the general public.

Courts are beginning to let injured consumers sue when a product does not have the qualities claimed on a label or in an advertisement if the injured person bought the product because of the claim or even if he did not read the label or advertisement. If the advertising is directed toward the public at large and makes claims that a normal consumer would take into account when he made his decision to buy, then the manufacturer should stand behind that claim for every member of the public, whether or not he has personally seen or heard the advertisement. However, the consumer will recover only when the labeling is inaccurate.

EXAMPLE Polly purchased a Brand X car because a special series of advertisements claimed that the car had the safest braking system in American-made cars. After driving the car for 500 miles, Polly was injured when the brakes failed to work at a stoplight. Polly learned from her mechanic that the brakes were defective and had not been used in many brands of cars for the last five years. The manufacturer can be held strictly liable for Polly's injury, which resulted from her reliance on their claim even though the QRS advertising agency had published the ads before showing them to the manufacturer.

When an injury has more than one cause, the plaintiff must prove that the defect was a substantial factor in causing the injury.   *(continued)*

DO YOU HAVE A CASE FOR PRODUCT LIABILITY?

AARON D. TWERSKI
Professor of Law, Hofstra University
School of Law

We are smack in the middle of a product liability revolution. For decades Americans were convinced that consumer products could do no wrong. If anyone was injured while using a product, the natural inference was that the user, not the product, was at fault. Indeed, for many years the law fostered this point of view, since the watchword was *caveat emptor* ("let the buyer beware"). But in one of the century's most dramatic legal turnarounds the courts have set themselves the task of redressing legitimate (and some illegitimate) grievances of consumers who suffer injury arising from defective and dangerous products.

Take, for example, the recent Texas case in which a woman who was attending a party walked from her host's living room toward the patio. Unbeknownst to her, a clear glass door separated the living room and the patio. The glass was cleanly polished and the woman mistook it for open space. The result was a plaintiff with a bruised face. In prior years the plaintiff would have gone home, applied a steak to her black eye, and prepared for a barrage of embarrassing questions from her friends. But the case took place in the 1970's, when consumer consciousness had come into its own. So the plaintiff sued the glass company for manufacturing an "unreasonably dangerous" door. The claim, which was seriously considered by the court, required a decision as to whether the value of clear glass doors, which give homeowners a feeling of being outdoors, outweighed the danger level of the

occasional situation in which someone mistakes a door for open space. The court ultimately decided in favor of the manufacturer and held that the plaintiff could not recover compensation for her injury.

Nonetheless, the case was not treated as a joke. The court considered the option of putting decals and markings on the glass doors and decided that, although it would be safer, it would negatively affect the esthetics that such doors are designed to promote. Such judicial attitudes are light-years removed from the old refrain "Let the buyer beware."

How, then, are you to know whether you have a good product liability claim? In such a fast-moving field of the law, it is impossible to give definitive answers. Only the lawyer who reviews the facts of your case in detail can venture an opinion as to whether or not a claim has real merit. You can, however, become sensitive to the various types of product liability claims so that you may sense the possibility of a case that may be successful.

Products that overpromise

Manufacturers are in the business of selling their products. In their zeal to sell, manufacturers, wholesalers, and retailers sometimes get carried away. A product may not live up to its billing. Ofttimes this leads to injury, and a legitimate claim may be established on the ground that the product simply did not perform as expected. The law does not always take cognizance of loose use of language. Some leeway is permitted for puffing (for example, "This car is really a honey"). Gullibility does have its limits. On the other hand, representations about a product may be very explicit and a buyer's reliance on the product's performance entirely justified.

An excellent example of a court's holding a manufacturer to its own rhetoric can be found in the case of *Crocker* v. *Winthrop Laboratories*. Winthrop Laboratories had developed Talwin®, a fairly strong painkiller advertised to the medical profession as nonaddictive. The plaintiff, who had been injured in an industrial accident, took Talwin regularly, as prescribed by his physician to relieve the pain, and became addicted to it. Sometime thereafter the plaintiff died as a result of taking a dose so large that it was toxic. In permitting a recovery to the plaintiff, the court did not hold that Talwin was a defective drug. There was nothing wrong with Talwin per se. There was a great deal wrong with the way Talwin was marketed. Since it was marketed as nonaddictive, the manufacturing company was hung by its own statement. In upholding the claim of the victim's family, the court held that it made no difference that Winthrop Laboratories honestly believed in the truth of its statements at the time they were made. A promise of performance had to be honored. Good faith was not an excuse for a false representation.

Hidden defects

American industry takes justifiable pride in its system of quality control. Most products do indeed come off the assembly line according to specifications. But sometimes they do not, and therein lies the secret behind much product liability litigation. Under the law as it has developed over the past decade, if a product comes off the assembly line in a defective condition, even if there was no way for the most sophisticated quality control techniques to discover that defect, and if as a result the product causes injury, the victim may win his lawsuit. The manufacturer will not be able to contend that "we did our best." Their best may not be good enough.

The exploding-bottle cases are a prime example of situations in which consumers have been victorious even though the product passed quality control inspection. Typically, the consumer buys the bottle off the shelf and takes it home and puts it in the refrigerator. Some hours later, when the consumer takes the bottle out, it explodes in his hands. If the consumer is smart enough to retain the broken pieces, an expert may determine that the bottle failed because of some imperfection in the glass structure. Should quality control have discovered the defect? It makes little difference. If the bottle was defective and caused injury, the victim will prevail.

Obvious defects

One would think that a product that is honestly marketed and does not misrepresent itself cannot be defective. But this is not always so. Such a product may sometimes be defective and sometimes not.

A knife is a dangerous instrument. Yet if you cut yourself with a sharp knife, you have no one to blame but yourself. You cannot sue the manufacturer of the knife—the knife simply is not defective. Dangerous, yes. Defective, no.

On the other hand, courts throughout the country have held that it is not legitimate for a manufacturer to market a product that is "obviously dangerous" if the product could be made safer.

A fascinating case recently arose in New York. Paul Micallef was employed as an operator on a photo-offset printing press. One day, while working on the press, Micallef discovered a foreign object on the plate of the unit. Such a substance, known in the printing trade as a "hickie," causes a blemish or imperfection on the printed page. To correct this situation, the plaintiff informed his superior that he intended to "chase the hickie." The process of chasing hickies consists of very lightly applying a piece of plastic about eight inches wide to the printing plate, which is wrapped around a circular plate cylinder that spins at high speed. The revolving action of the plate against the plastic removes the hickie. While the plaintiff was engaged in this maneuver, the plastic was drawn into the nip point and the plaintiff's hand was caught between the plate cylinder and an ink roller. The photo-offset machine had no safety guards to prevent such an occurrence, and the plaintiff was unable to stop it quickly because the shutoff button was distant from his position at the machine.

Micallef was fully aware of the danger of getting his hand caught in the press while "chasing hickies on the run," but took the risk anyway because once the machine was stopped, it required at least three hours to resume printing. An expert witness testified that good engineering practice would have dictated that a safety guard be placed near the rollers, since the danger of human contact at the point of operation was well known.

The manufacturer contended that the unguarded machine was "openly and obviously" dangerous. It was the equivalent of a knife. The court rejected this argument. A knife cannot be sharp without cutting human flesh, but it was possible for this printing press to have been made safer. The lesson is worth remembering. Merely because the product is as dangerous as it appears does not mean that a meritorious liability case cannot be made.

Product misuse

Often consumers are their own worst enemies. They decide in advance of consulting a lawyer that they have no claim because a product has been misused. Obviously, they conclude, there is no recovery if they are injured. Well, it all depends.

Consider the case of four-year-old Brenda Ritter. An action was brought on behalf of Brenda against American Motors, the manufacturer of a small 30-inch gas range. Brenda was injured when she opened the oven door and used it as a step stool to look into the pot on top of the stove. The stove tipped forward, causing serious injuries to her. An expert witness testified that the stove was defectively designed because the door could not hold a weight of 30 pounds without tipping the stove. The court held that Brenda had a valid case.

The lesson should not be lost on the reader. Even a serious misuse need not necessarily preclude successful recovery if the product was badly designed or manufactured. If an accident results from a misuse of a product, do not blame yourself (or your child) entirely; there may be plenty of blame to go around.

Warnings versus instructions

Most products are sold with instructions that tell the consumer how to use the product effectively. When an injury results from misuse of a product, consumers often blame themselves for not following instructions. Although this is a very human reaction, they ought not to jump to the conclusion that the failure to follow instructions forfeits their right to sue the manufacturer.

It is crucial to distinguish between warnings and instructions. Instructions tell the consumer how to use the product. Warnings alert the consumer to the dangers of improper use and inform him how to guard against those dangers if possible. For example, an instruction on a bottle of cleaning fluid, "Use With Adequate Ventilation," is not the equivalent of a warning that reads: "Danger: Toxic Fumes. Use Only With Adequate Ventilation." The object lesson: You may have been *instructed* by the manufacturer, but you might not have been *warned.* If the product is dangerous, the law may insist on a sharply worded warning. Failure to warn may be grounds for a well-founded lawsuit.

Keep the evidence

If there is one message that every lawyer would want to deliver to his client in a product liability case, it would be: Don't discard the evidence. After an accident has occurred, and a product is implicated, there is often a natural reaction to rid the house of the offending product. It was, after all, the source of the harm. "I don't want to look at it anymore—I can't stand the sight of it," is a typical response. Resist the temptation to discard with all the power you can muster. In many instances, the success or failure of a lawsuit will depend on having the offending product available for examination by experts who can determine what went wrong. In the case of older products, the retention of evidence is crucial. The manufacturer will argue that through age, deterioration and misuse, the product was damaged and the company ought not to be held responsible for the injury. The most telling rebuttal for this argument is the evidence which demonstrates that the defect existed in the product at the time of manufacture. Hold on even to broken pieces of glass and metal—they may be a veritable gold mine.

Consumer rights have come a long way in a short period of time. The courts have begun to hold sellers responsible for defective and dangerous products. However, these newly found rights can only be exercised by an informed laity that will bring its problems to the attention of lawyers who can make a judgment as to whether a valid claim exists. It is to the interest of no one—neither consumer nor manufacturer—to flood the courts with frivolous or phony claims. It is to everyone's interest to make sure that valid claims are seriously addressed. Consumers ought not to conclude cavalierly that their slight indiscretions in using a product that causes injury spells doom for their claims. The law may grant them more protection than they expect, and, it is to be hoped, not less than they deserve.

Courts have traditionally held that an individual is responsible for being reasonably careful. A consumer who plainly misuses a product or ignores commonly understood hazards cannot complain when an injury results. A person who disregards a printed warning to use hair spray away from an open flame or to apply paint only in a well-ventilated area cannot blame the manufacturer for making an imperfect product. A consumer who continues to use an obviously defective or spoiled product may also be precluded from complaining. For example, a person who finds green slime on a package of cold cuts and goes right ahead and eats the meat can be said to have assumed the risk of getting sick.

Nevertheless, a normally careful person may have moments of carelessness that result in injury. Because of this, courts have recognized that products should be designed and labeled to prevent injuries resulting from human carelessness, as distinguished from blatant misuse. For example, the seller of a lawn mower, a machine that obviously can injure people, was held responsible for failing to include safety devices when a child's hand was cut by the blades. In cases where some risk is involved because of the very nature of the product, courts now want to know how grave the risk is and how it could have been avoided by changes in design, testing, production, inspection, packaging, or in printed directions or warnings.

When a product cannot be made entirely safe, manufacturers must warn buyers and users of the dangers that might arise. This obligation applies not only to the specific uses for which the product was intended but for other normally expected uses as well. For example, a furniture manufacturer knows that people are likely to stand on chairs. He must either make his chair strong enough to stand on without collapsing or warn customers not to stand on it at all.

A manufacturer does not have to print warnings against every conceivable use of this product that might be risky— only for expected uses. For example, a strong chemical made for cleaning out vats in a factory does not have to be labeled the same as a household cleaner.

Any product likely to be used around children, or by them, must be made safer than a product sold for professional or industrial use. Baby toys must not have hidden sharp edges or paint that contains lead because young children put toys in their mouths. Still, a manufacturer does not have to guarantee that no one will be hurt by his product, even if it is made for children. Courts have held, for example, that baseball bats can be expected to break and that a manufacturer of a ball is not liable for injuries to a child's mouth when a playmate hits him with it.

The manufacturer's or seller's duty to include safeguards, take precautions, and give instructions and warnings has the effect of making some unavoidably unsafe products marketable. If the risk can be made reasonable by directions and warnings, the seller is not strictly liable, even though some danger is involved. Drugs illustrate this principle because they can be dangerous if their use is uncontrolled. If strict liability were applied, drug manufacturers might take beneficial drugs that are high-risk and/or create serious side effects off the market. The manufacturer must comply with the regulations that control DRUGS AND NAR-

COTICS, and he must avoid negligence and breach of warranties. Beyond that, courts may find that there is no strict liability in cases where the product is incapable of being made safe.

■ **The cause of injuries**   Whether the basis of the lawsuit is negligence, breach of warranty, or strict liability, the plaintiff must prove that the defect was the real cause of his injury. This question is generally decided by the jury.

EXAMPLE   Owen has an automobile accident because he fails to apply his brakes soon enough and has a blowout just as his car comes to rest. Even though the tire is defective, Owen cannot sue the manufacturer of the tire for all the damage to his car because the tire alone did not cause the accident.

The question of causation can be very complicated. If a pencil breaks because the wood is defective and the plaintiff's scratched arm develops an infection, there certainly is a question whether the harm has been caused by the defective pencil or by germs that happened to be on the pencil. Some courts apply what can be called the "but for" rule in a case like this. They say that the manufacturer of a defective product is liable for injuries that would not have occurred but for the defect.

■ **Recent developments**   In 1978 a jury in California brought in an astounding verdict of $125 million in a negligence case against the Ford Motor Company. The verdict rocked industry because of its implications for the future of product liability law.

EXAMPLE   The case grew out of an accident caused when a new 1972 Ford Pinto stalled on a freeway and was hit from behind by another car. The gas tank exploded and the Pinto burned. The driver was killed and her neighbor, 13-year-old Richard Grimshaw, was burned over 90 percent of his body. He lost his nose, his left ear, and part of his left hand, enduring more than 60 operations over the following six years. After a six-month trial, it took the jury only one day and a half to come back with its verdict.

The attorneys for the plaintiff showed that the gas tank was behind the rear axle, only 3¼ inches behind the differential housing in the Pinto. During a crash, the housing would be pushed into the gas tank causing it to rupture. Test films, made just before the Pinto was put on the market, showed fuel spurting out of the gas tank after the car was backed into a wall at only 20 miles per hour. Ford's own records disclosed that the company's engineers had designed a fire safety device that could be added to the model for $11 per vehicle, or a cost of about $137 million for 12.5 million cars. Estimates of the benefits of the safety device were less exact, but they computed how many possible deaths, burn injuries, and burned vehicles might be prevented. Their conclusions were that even after paying damages in resulting suits Ford could save $100 million by not installing the fire safety device. The company felt that the benefit did not justify the cost and decided not to install the safety device.

The jury decided that the cost per vehicle was insignificant compared to the danger and decided to assess punitive damages for willful disregard of safety. The plaintiffs had asked for punitive damages of $100 million, but the jury felt that that was merely the amount that

Ford had saved by not improving the fuel-tank design. "We wanted Ford to take notice," the jury foreman explained, so they added another $25 million to their final award. The $125 million they assessed was the highest product liability verdict ever given. It was about equal to Ford's profits for one month. The judge reduced the verdict to $3.5 million.

Cases like the Pinto one alarmed insurance companies, manufacturers, and other business leaders. There was no way, they argued, for a potential defendant to protect himself against a judgment like that. Consequently, a number of states passed new laws, most of them limiting the open-ended liability of manufacturers.

New defenses for manufacturers Most of these laws permit manufacturers a defense against being held responsible for some accidents. Some of the laws make alteration of the product or misuse of it an absolute defense. For example, if the bumper had been removed from the Pinto Richard Grimshaw was riding in, Ford could have shown that the car had been altered. If the accident had happened after dark and the driver had not put the lights on yet, Ford could have shown that the car was being misused. Critics argue that the fault of the injured person should be compared to the fault of the manufacturer rather than making the fault of the injured person an absolute defense in every case.

Some statutes give manufacturers the right to defend themselves by showing that their product met generally acceptable safety standards when it was made. This is called the "state of the art" defense. It relieves manufacturers of the impossible job of making a perfect product. An injured consumer cannot sue on the theory that the product would have been safe if the manufacturer had incorporated safety features that were developed only after the product was made.

Statutes of limitations The most frequent way that statutes have controlled liability is by limiting the time within which a lawsuit may be started. See Chart 4. This time limit set by statute is called a statute of limitations and has always started to run from the time that an injury occurred. See LIMITATIONS OF ACTIONS. This has caused manufacturers and insurance companies a great deal of anxiety because in theory the manufacturer can be sued for an injury that occurs anytime during the life of the product.

EXAMPLE The manufacturer of an injection molding machine first sold the machine in 1951 for $15,000. The machine was sold and resold to at least three other buyers until 1972. Then an employee of the latest owner, who had paid $750 for the machine, was injured when she tried to help replace a safety gate that had become disengaged on the machine. The employee brought a product liability lawsuit based on defects in the machine, even though it had served satisfactorily for more than 20 years.

Manufacturers feel that lawsuits like this are most likely to hurt companies that make durable goods, eventually affecting the incentive to make products that last. A statute of limitations measured from the time a product is manufactured or first sold at least sets an outer limit to the time when manufacturers can be liable for an injury, and therefore helps them and their insurance companies to calculate risks and budget for them.

However, many consumers oppose the idea of a statute that starts the clock running at the date of the first sale because the right to sue could expire even before an injury occurs. They suggest that juries take into account the time that has actually passed between the first sale of the offending product and the date of the accident. If a jury finds that a product is so old that it is obsolete, they can bring in a verdict for the manufacturer.

Future of the law Product liability has developed so dramatically in such a short period of time that it is not clear yet what directions the law will take. Such uncertainty has burdened some manufacturers, especially small companies, with insurance costs that have doubled and redoubled, and some of these costs are inevitably passed along to the consumer.

profanity Irreverence toward sacred things; irreverent use of the name of God. See BLASPHEMY; OBSCENITY; SPEECH AND PRESS, FREEDOM OF.

profit à prendre (French) "Profit for taking"; the right to take part of the soil or produce from the land of another. The term includes the right to remove gravel, minerals, timber, and crops. See EASEMENT; PROPERTY.

progressive tax A tax that is graduated upward according to certain specified brackets, such as income brackets. The higher the bracket, the higher the rate of TAXATION. For example, federal INCOME TAX is progressive.

prohibition An order to stop certain actions; a warning not to engage in certain conduct in the future. For example, a *writ of prohibition* is an order from a higher court admonishing a lower court to stop proceeding with a lawsuit over which it has no jurisdiction. The writ of prohibition is an extraordinary REMEDY that is seldom used. See EQUITY; INTOXICATING LIQUORS; MANDAMUS.

promissory estoppel The principle that prevents someone who makes a substantial promise to another from going back on his word when the other person has acted in reliance on the promise. See CONTRACTS.

EXAMPLE Margaret promises to pay Jane $1,500 for the damage her son, Ted, caused when he shot a rifle through Jane's picture window. Margaret delays paying Jane until the statute of limitations (the time within which Jane would have to sue Margaret for the damage) expires. Margaret then refuses to pay Jane. If this were permitted, Jane would be deprived of her right to damages because she relied on Margaret's promise. Under the doctrine of promissory estoppel, Margaret would have to keep her promise to pay Jane.

promissory note A signed, unconditional promise to pay a certain sum of money at a specified time. For a full discussion of promissory notes and other negotiable instruments, see COMMERCIAL PAPER.

promoter One who promotes a plan for a business, such as the person who takes the preliminary steps, as by soliciting stock subscriptions, to form a CORPORATION.

promulgate Publish; announce officially; make public an important matter. For example, a court promulgates its required standards of practice by publishing and disseminating the official rules of court.

proof Establishment of a fact by TESTIMONY or other EVIDENCE; anything that serves to convince the mind of the truth or falsehood of a fact or proposition.

property 1 Any tangible thing in which rights or legal interests exist, such as land, a house, an automobile, or a typewriter. 2 An intangible right and interest that is protected by law, such as the ownership of an invention, a formula, a writing, or a musical composition. This article deals with the rights of a person to acquire, own, possess, use, and dispose of tangible property. For information on laws that protect intangible property, see COPYRIGHT; PATENT; TRADEMARKS AND TRADE NAMES. For information on the various crimes against tangible property, see ARSON; BURGLARY; CONVERSION; EMBEZZLEMENT; LARCENY; NEGLIGENCE; NUISANCE; ROBBERY; THEFT; TRESPASS; VANDALISM.

■ **Real and personal property** Property is divided into two categories: real property (or realty, or real estate) and personal property (or personalty). Sometimes the terms "movables" and "immovables" are also used. Personal property is movable; real property is immovable. Property may be further classified as public or private. Public property belongs to a country, a state, or a political subdivision of a state, such as a city or town. Private property belongs to one or more persons. The terms "real property," "real estate," and "realty" mean land. Land includes not only the face of the earth but everything of a permanent nature over or under it, including minerals, oil, and timber. In modern usage, the word "premises" has come to mean the land itself or the land and all the structures attached to it. In everyday conversation, residential buildings and yards are often referred to as premises, as well as real property.

Generally speaking, the terms "personal property" and "personalty" include everything that can be owned except real estate. In law, items of personal property are often called *chattels*. For instance, some automobile loans are called CHATTEL MORTGAGES, to distinguish them from mortgages on real property.

Usually, the difference between real property and personal property is easy to recognize. The character of property can change, however, by an act of the owner or another person. For example, personal property may become part of realty by being annexed to it—as when rails made into a fence become part of the land. On the other hand, property that is annexed may keep its personal character when the parties agree. Thus your landlord may agree that the new chandelier you want to attach to the ceiling of his apartment will remain your personal property and you can take it with you when you leave. See FIXTURE.

■ **Concepts of ownership and possession** Real and personal property may be owned or possessed. The two terms are not synonymous. Ownership is the right of title. Possession is the right to custody and does not necessarily include the right of title.

Title is evidence of the right a person has to possess or enjoy property to the exclusion of all others; it is the means by which a person's right to property is established. In its strictest sense, title also gives a person a right to dispose of property. Once any property, real or personal, has been owned by someone, there is title to it. The shell on the seashore belongs to no one, but once you pick it up for your collection, you have greater rights to it than anyone else.

Possession is a basic legal interest in property, entitling the possessor to certain rights, including the right (1) to continue peaceful possession against everyone but those who have a better right to it, (2) to recover the property if it is wrongfully taken, and (3) to recover money DAMAGES from someone who has misused or harmed the property. To possess property, a person must intend to possess it and have some amount of actual control over it.

A person can possess property without owning it. A tenant in an apartment house and a driver of a rented car, for example, have possession of the apartment and car even though they do not own them.

Conversely, a person may own property without possessing it. For example, a landlord of an apartment building is not in possession of the apartments he has rented out, and a rental agency whose car is being driven by someone else is not in possession of the car until it is returned; yet the landlord and agency retain title to the apartments and car even while their property is in the possession of others.

Concurrent ownership Property can be owned by an individual, a group, a corporation, or the state. Concurrent ownership is ownership by more than one person at the same time. There are two basic types of concurrent ownership: JOINT TENANCY and TENANCY IN COMMON.

Joint tenancy is the single ownership of property by two or more persons whose interests in the property can be divided. When one of the owners dies, the property goes to the surviving owner or owners free from the claims of heirs or creditors of the deceased co-owner. This is known as the *right of survivorship*. Any type of property can be subject to joint tenancy, ranging from land to a bank account. In some states, when a HUSBAND AND WIFE own property jointly, they are said to have *tenancy by the entirety* because each spouse owns the *entire* property (usually real property) in his or her own right. A tenancy by the entirety is essentially the same as joint tenancy except that the owners must be HUSBAND AND WIFE and the tenancy can be ended only by the agreement of both spouses.

Tenancy in common is the ownership of property in which two or more persons have an undivided interest in the entire property. There is no right of survivorship between tenants in common.

Ownership rights of husband and wife The assignment of ownership of property to a husband and wife is a complicated matter and is treated differently in the various states. Generally, there are two systems for establishing ownership of property in marriage, and laws based upon these systems are applied when couples are divorced and their property must be divided.

In 42 of the 50 states, the *separate-property system* is followed. Under this system, each spouse generally owns whatever property is in his or her name, but some forms of property (especially real estate) are owned jointly.

In the remaining eight states (Arizona, California, Idaho, Louisiana, Nevada, New Mexico, Texas, and Washington), the *community-property system* is followed. Under this system, with some variations, each spouse keeps title to whatever he or she owned before the marriage and whatever he or she inherits during the marriage. All other property is considered community property and is divided equally between husband and wife. For a full discussion of property laws involving married couples, see DIVORCE; HUSBAND AND WIFE.

Estates   An *estate* is the degree, quality, and extent of ownership. Real property ESTATES are divided into three major classifications: FEE SIMPLE, FEE TAIL, and life estates.

A property owner with a *fee simple* interest in his land is entitled to all rights available to property owners. Fee simple is the greatest estate possible.

A *fee tail* interest restricts inheritance. It is usually created by DEED or WILL. For example, a piece of land may be willed to a certain individual and "the heirs of his body." Such an estate must pass, by inheritance, from one generation to the next. The holder of a fee tail estate can use the land or lease it during his lifetime, but he may not dispose of it or prevent his children from inheriting it. Since fee tail restricts the free transfer of property, many states have

YOUR PROPERTY AND THE LAW

■ Property is divided into two classes: real property (realty, or real estate) and personal property (personalty, everything that is not real property). Either may be publicly or privately owned.

■ Ownership and possession of property are not the same thing. *Ownership* means the right of title—the evidence of the right you have to possess or enjoy property to the exclusion of all others. *Possession* is the right to custody and does not necessarily include the right of title. For example, a tenant in an apartment house has possession without ownership, while the landlord owns (has title to) the premises but does not have possession.

■ Possession is a basic interest in property, including (1) the right to continue peaceful possession against everyone but those who have a better right to the property, (2) the right to recover the property if it is wrongfully taken, and (3) the right to recover money damages from someone who has misused or harmed the property.

■ You can own property together with one or more persons by *joint tenancy* (with the right of survivorship, the right to leave it to your heirs) or *tenancy in common* (with no right of survivorship). Joint tenancy can apply to any type of property, and when a co-owner dies the surviving owner or owners get the property free from claims by heirs or creditors.

■ In some states, joint ownership by a husband and wife is called *tenancy by the entirety.*

■ In 42 of the 50 states, each spouse owns whatever property is in his or her name. This is called the *separate-property system.*

■ In the remaining eight states (Arizona, California, Idaho, Louisiana, Nevada, New Mexico, Texas, and Washington), the *community-property system* is used: each spouse keeps title to whatever he or she owned before marriage and whatever he or she inherited during the marriage. All other property is divided equally between husband and wife.

■ Lost or mislaid property continues to be owned by the person who lost or mislaid it.

■ The finder of lost property is entitled to possession against everyone but the rightful owner.

■ The finder of mislaid goods obtains a right to possession only if he owns the land on which they are found.

■ If you buy or otherwise acquire stolen property, that property may be taken from you and returned to its rightful owner with no payment to you, even though you had no way of knowing it had been stolen.

■ A *lien* is a claim on personal or real property that is exacted as security for the payment of a debt. A lienholder has a right to keep your property in his possession until you pay him all that you owe him, such as a garage mechanic who holds on to your repaired car until you have paid him. If you do not pay him, he has the right to sell your property to recover the money you owe him.

■ A property owner has the right to the exclusive possession of the space above and below the surface within his boundaries. He is not entitled to possess all the space above his land projected outward to infinity, but he is entitled to have that space free from intrusions on his reasonable enjoyment of the property.

■ You may not use your property in such a way that it harms your next-door neighbor's property. Thus, if you dig up part of your lawn, you must not throw dirt onto your neighbor's place or undermine his foundations.

■ You are responsible for damages caused by your negligence in keeping your property in good repair.

■ Sometimes there are legal restrictions on the use of property, either by contract or by an act of government such as a zoning law.

■ An *easement* is the right of a nonowner of a piece of land to use the land for a specific purpose. For instance, you might give a neighbor an easement to use part of your property as a road to reach his own property. Rights granted by easements generally remain with the land when it is sold.

■ Governments have the right to acquire property for public use by *eminent domain.*

■ There are two theories of property rights relating to lakes and streams: *riparian rights* and *prior appropriations.* Under both theories, lakes and streams belong to the public unless the whole lake or stream is contained within private boundaries.

■ Under the riparian system (predominant in the eastern United States and a few states west of the Mississippi), persons owning land on the banks of a watercourse have the right to make maximum use of the water as long as the quality and quantity of the water and the use by other owners is not substantially affected.

■ Under the prior appropriation doctrine—in effect in arid western states—the first person who appropriates a supply of water for a beneficial use has the first right to it.

■ Common law regards water underground as the landowner's property.

abolished it by transforming it into fee simple for the first heirs or their children.

A *life estate* gives property interest in land only for the lifetime of some particular person or persons—the life tenants—or until some particular event happens or does not happen. For example, a father may grant a piece of land and a house to his daughter to be held for her lifetime. He may also grant his daughter a life estate in the land and house to be held as long as she does not rent out rooms in the house to boarders. Once she begins taking in boarders, her life tenancy may be terminated.

Estates in personal property are governed, for the most part, by the same general principles that govern similar estates in real property. However, the greatest estate in personal property—the equivalent of a fee simple in real property—is called *absolute title*.

■ **Ownership and possession of personal property** There are many laws governing the acquisition, ownership, possession, and use of personal property. There are also laws that protect the rights of persons whose property is temporarily in the hands of others. Although these laws vary from state to state, certain fundamental concepts are common to all.

Acquisition of personal property Personal property can be acquired in a number of ways—it can be bought, inherited, or received as a gift. Wild ANIMALS are in a slightly different category. Traditionally, anyone who tames a wild animal is viewed as its owner, and when a landowner captures or kills a wild animal on his own property, the animal is his.

Buying property Personal property that is bought is subject to the laws relating to commercial SALES. A sale tranfers ownership of property from the seller to the buyer, and the transfer is effected by a CONTRACT. Contracts for sales of less than $500 may be oral; all others must be written. A written contract may be long and detailed or a simple receipt.

When personal property is purchased, the buyer has a right to get what the seller claims he is getting. The claims of the seller may be in the form of specific or implied warranties. If the product does not live up to these warranties, the buyer has a right to compensation. If he is hurt by the product when using it as it is intended to be used, he may have a right to sue for damages under the laws of PRODUCT LIABILITY.

Inheriting property Inherited property is property received from a person who has died. Title to inherited property is transferred by means of a WILL or, when the deceased owner has left no will, under the laws of DESCENT AND DISTRIBUTION. When a person dies without having made a will and has no relatives who are entitled by law to inherit his property, the state may be entitled to take the property by the right of ESCHEAT.

Gifts The law of GIFTS, which varies very little from state to state, determines when and under what circumstances a donee (recipient of a gift) is entitled to keep a gift. There are two kinds of gifts, gifts *inter vivos* ("during one's life") and gifts *causa mortis* ("in contemplation of death").

A gift *inter vivos* is a gift of real or personal property made during the normal course of a donor's life. Three conditions must be fulfilled to make such a gift legal: (1)

The donor must be able to make the gift—that is, he must be of age and mentally competent. (2) The donor must intend to make the gift, and the intent must exist at the time the donee claims the gift was made. (3) The gift must be delivered or handed over in some way, and it must be unconditionally accepted by the donee.

A gift *causa mortis* is one made by someone who thinks he is about to die. Only personal property can be given *causa mortis*. The three conditions required to make a gift *inter vivos* legal are also needed to make a gift *causa mortis* legal. However, if the donor recovers and does not die as expected, the gift becomes invalid.

Lost, mislaid, and abandoned property Property is *lost* when the owner has been parted from it involuntarily and unwittingly, without knowing where it is. Treasure trove—money concealed in the earth or some private place, whose owner is unknown—is treated as lost property. Property is *mislaid* when the owner has put it in a particular place but is unable to remember where he placed it. Property is *abandoned* when its owner has intentionally given up any claim to it.

Abandoned property can be possessed and owned by the first person who exercises dominion over it, with an intent to claim it as his own. See ABANDONMENT.

The laws involving the possession of found property depend on whether the property was lost or mislaid. See FINDING LOST GOODS. Lost or mislaid property continues to be owned by the person who lost or mislaid it. The finder of lost property is entitled to possession against everyone but the owner. The finder of lost articles on someone else's land is entitled to possession against everyone but the true owner unless the finder is a trespasser. But the finder of mislaid goods does not obtain a right to possession unless he owns the land on which they are found. The owner of the place where an article is mislaid has a right to it against everyone but the rightful owner.

In any case, the law applies whatever rule will most likely result in the return of lost or mislaid property to its rightful owner. For example, possession of articles found during employment is generally awarded to the employer and not to the employee-finder. Certain employees, such as hotel maids and porters, are obligated to deliver found articles to their employer.

Stolen or misappropriated property Property that has been stolen or otherwise misappropriated belongs to the owner from whom it was taken. If you buy or otherwise acquire stolen property, that property may be taken from you and returned to its rightful owner with no payment to you, even though you had no way of knowing that it had been stolen. If you accept property that you know has been stolen and you have no intention of returning it to its rightful owner, you are guilty of a crime—usually a felony, depending in some states on the value of the property. See RECEIVING STOLEN GOODS.

Confusion and accession Two interrelated bodies of law govern the acquisition or loss of title to personal property when it is altered by, improved by, or commingled with the property of others. These are the laws of confusion and ACCESSION.

In *confusion*, the personal property of several different owners is commingled so that it cannot be separated and returned to its rightful owners even though it retains its original characteristics. For example, interchangeable goods, such as food, money, or oil, can be the subject of confusion. Usually, if someone fraudulently mixes his goods with another's so that the goods cannot be distinguished, he forfeits all his interest in the mixture to the other person.

In *accession*, the personal property of one owner is physically integrated with the property of another owner in such a way that it loses its separate identity and becomes a part of it. In one kind of accession the personal property of one owner is so altered by the work of another person that it becomes more valuable. This happens, for example, when lumber is made into carved furniture. In another kind of accession, personal property becomes entirely different property, such as when grapes are made into wine.

Ordinarily, the original owner has the right to his property, together with all changes and additions made to it by another person; but when the additions or changes made to the property by the work and skill of another are of greater value than the property itself, or where the change made is so great that the property cannot be restored to its original state, the person who has changed the property may be entitled to it rather than the original owner. In such a case, however, he must reimburse the original owner for the cost of the original property.

Unauthorized accession is a form of CONVERSION.

Under the doctrine of accession, personal property may become so attached to, or so associated with, the land that it is considered a FIXTURE, or part of the real property.

Emblements   The subject of emblements is a part of the general law of CROPS. Crops fall into the following classes: (1) those resulting from the bounty of nature, such as trees, bushes, and their fruits; and (2) those produced by man's labor, such as annual harvests of the orchard, field, or garden. The crops resulting from man's industry—such as from cultivating, fertilizing, and spraying—are called emblements. Crops grown for sale or personal use are personal property.

In most cases, a tenant for a definite term will not be permitted to remove growing crops after his lease has expired. But a tenant for an undetermined length of time may remove growing crops after his term has expired.

Crops that have been harvested, even if left in the field, are the personal property of the tenant. Ownership of these crops is not lost just because the tenancy ends. If, however, the landlord terminates a lease due to the tenant's breach of promise, the right of the tenant to harvest and remove the crops is forfeited.

Bailment   Personal property that is lent to another; rented, leased, or hired out; or delivered to another person for repair or other work, or for storage or transportation to another place is subject to the law of BAILMENT. The word "bailment" is generally defined as a delivery of personal property for a particular purpose on the basis of a contract. Basically, a bailment differs from a sale in that no transfer of ownership is intended and the return of the identical property that was delivered is required.

Liens   In some cases, a claim may be made on property in the form of a LIEN. A lien is a claim on personal or real property that is exacted as security for the payment of a debt. Often the debt is incurred as the result of bailment, as when goods are left at a shop for repair and the repair work is not paid for. A person who holds a lien on your property has a right to keep the property in his possession until you pay him all you owe him in connection with the particular lien. If you do not pay the lienholder in a reasonable amount of time, he has a right to sell the property in question to get the money owed him. If he sells it for more than is owed him, however, he must turn the balance of the money over to you, for even though the lien gave him possession of your property, it did not make him its owner.

■ **Ownership and possession of real property**   As with personal property, there are various laws governing the acquisition and use of real property. Real property can be bought, inherited, leased, or received as a gift. Leased property comes under the laws governing LANDLORD AND TENANT. Real property received as a gift or inheritance generally falls under the laws of gifts and inheritances described above for personal property. Property can also be acquired through adverse possession (see discussion below).

Conveyance   When ownership of real property is transferred from one person to another, as the result of a sale, inheritance, or gift, it is said to be *conveyed.* Every state in the United States has exclusive jurisdiction (authority) over the land within its borders. Each state, therefore, has the power to determine the form and effect of a conveyance of real property within its borders. Usually, a state will require a DEED to convey realty.

In many real property sales, the buyer borrows a large part of the money needed to pay for the property and places the property under a MORTGAGE. A *mortgage* is a pledge or security of the property for the payment of the debt. In the majority of states a mortgage on real property is regarded as a lien, and so title to the property is held by the mortgagor (the buyer). In states in which the common-law doctrine is still in effect, however, a mortgage transfers the entire legal title to the mortgagee (the party holding the mortgage) as a security for the payment of the debt, and when the debt is paid in full, the mortgage becomes void and the title reverts to the buyer.

Adverse possession   Possession of property against the rights of the true owner can result in the acquisition of title to the property by the possessor. This is known as ADVERSE POSSESSION. To claim title under adverse possession, a person must occupy the property openly and continuously for a certain number of years set by law, all the while actively claiming the right to own and occupy the land. The doctrine of adverse possession is based upon statutes limiting the time for the recovery of property. The statutes of limitation bar one's right to recover property that has been held adversely by another for a specified period of time. See LIMITATIONS OF ACTIONS.

Physical extent of property   A property owner has the right to exclusive possession of the ground and the space above and below the surface within his boundaries. A landowner's rights of possession can be simply illustrated.

EXAMPLE Al owns Blackacre and Barbara owns Whiteacre.
○━━✳ The two pieces of property abut each other along a certain boundary line 200 feet long. Al builds a three-story building on Blackacre, one story of which is a basement underground, and two stories of which are above the

surface. In the process of construction, two "I" beams are so placed in the structure that they extend 16 inches across the common boundary line onto Barbara's Whiteacre. One beam is two feet under the surface, and the other is 15 feet above the surface of the ground. This intrusion onto Barbara's property is known as encroachment.

Barbara has the right within the law to do any one of the following: (1) She may resort to "self-help" and cut off the beams at the common boundary line. (2) She may sue Al for money damages, based on his trespass on her property. (3) She may start a lawsuit to eject Al from her property. (4) She may sue to enjoin Al from maintaining these continuing nuisances. (5) Or she may sue to enjoin Al from committing any further trespasses.

A property owner is not entitled to possess all the space above his land projected outward to infinity. He is entitled to have free from intrusions the space that is necessary to occupy and enjoy the surface. Accordingly, a landowner owns as much of the space above the ground as he can effectively possess or use in connection with the land. Rights in airspace and problems associated with flights over private property are discussed in AERONAUTICS AND AEROSPACE.

Adjoining landowners   Just as a landowner may not encroach upon the property of his neighbor, he may not use or misuse his own property in such a way as to cause harm to the property of his next-door neighbors. Under the laws governing ADJOINING LANDOWNERS, a landowner is responsible for damages caused by his negligence in keeping his property in repair. Each landowner is expected to use his property reasonably, while considering the rights of the owners of connecting land. Thus, if a landowner excavates his land, he must take precautions not to throw dirt or debris onto his neighbor's property or undermine its foundation.

Restricted use of property   Certain restrictions may be placed on the use of real property. These restrictions may be initiated by contract or by an act of the government.

A RESTRICTIVE COVENANT is a provision in a deed that restricts the owner's use of the property. A deed may specify, for example, that a lot may be used only for residential purposes.

A local government may restrict the use of private property by instituting ZONING regulations. For example, a municipality may be divided into districts that are limited to residential, commercial, or industrial use. Zoning ordinances are designed to stabilize neighborhoods, preserve the character of the community, and guide the future growth of the municipality.

An EASEMENT is the right of a nonowner of a piece of land to use a specific part of it for a specific purpose. For example, an easement may give an owner of nearby property the right to use a part of a neighbor's property as a road to reach his own property. Easements are usually created by contract, and the rights granted by them generally remain with the land when it is sold. An easement entitles its holder to use someone else's land; it does not give him the right to remove anything. The right to take part of the soil or produce of another's land is called PROFIT À PRENDRE.

Eminent domain   Governments have a right to acquire property for public use by EMINENT DOMAIN. The right may be exercised by the federal or state government or it may be delegated to a municipality or a private corporation engaged in a business affecting the general welfare of the public. If property is taken, the owner must be paid a just compensation.

Lands under or bordering on water   There are three kinds of ownership of land under or bordering on water.

(1) Owners of land bordering on the ocean usually own to the high-water mark—that is, the line to which the high tide comes. Title to land between the high-water mark and the low-water mark (the shore) is usually held by the state.

(2) Title to land under nonnavigable streams and lakes is generally held by the abutting owner. It extends to the center of the stream or lake.

(3) A stream or lake is considered navigable if it can be used for commerce. Lands under navigable streams or lakes are usually owned by the state through which the stream flows or in which the lake is located. All waters navigable as interstate highways are subject to the control of the federal government. See NAVIGABLE WATERS.

Sometimes, when private property extends to the water of an ocean, lake, or stream, new land is slowly formed at the water's edge. The accretion of soil, called alluvion, belongs to the abutting owner.

■ **Rights to use of water**   Water may be placed into several different categories: lakes and streams on the surface; underground water; percolating water (water that seeps into the earth from the surface); and surface water, which comes from rains, springs, and melting snow or ice.

Lakes and streams   In the United States, there are two theories of water rights relating to lakes and streams—*riparian rights* and *prior appropriations*. Under both theories, the waters of lakes and streams belong to the public. Unless the entire lake or stream is contained within the borders of a person's property, its waters are not the subject of private ownership; they can only be used. The various states have based their laws governing the use of waters from lakes and streams on one of these two theories.

Riparian rights   The riparian system is predominant in the eastern United States, and it is in effect, to some extent, in several other states west of the Mississippi River. Under this system, the person who owns lands on the banks of a watercourse is called a riparian owner or proprietor. There are two theories of water rights under the riparian system—natural flow and reasonable use—and most jurisdictions use a combination of the two theories to settle disputes.

Under the *natural flow theory,* each proprietor of land on a stream or lake has a fundamental right to have the water remain substantially in its natural state, free from being unreasonably made smaller and free from being unreasonably polluted. Because the rights of all riparian owners are equal, a lower riparian owner can sue an upper owner whenever the latter's use of the water substantially affects either the quantity or quality of the lake or stream, even though there is no injury or damage to the lower owner.

Under the *reasonable use theory,* each riparian proprietor has the right to make maximum use of water in the stream or lake, provided that use does not unreasonably interfere with similar use of other riparian owners. A lower riparian owner has no right to sue an upper owner until he can show that the use was unreasonable and caused damage to him.

Under the natural flow theory, every riparian owner knows fairly well just how far he can go in his use of the water. The theory is often criticized, however, because it restricts water usage to the point of promoting waste of a natural resource. The reasonable use theory has the merit of giving each riparian owner the right to make maximum beneficial use of the water, but the theory has the disadvantage of being indefinite, because a riparian proprietor cannot easily determine the extent of his rights and those of his fellow owners.

The two theories of riparian rights are fundamentally different, as the following example shows:

EXAMPLE Abe, an upper riparian owner along a stream, diverts water to irrigate his riparian and nonriparian lands. The diversion causes the water to go down six inches below its normal level, but more than enough water is left in the stream to supply all possible and reasonable uses to which the lower riparian owner, Bob, can put it. Still, Bob sues Abe to stop what he considers an unreasonable use of water in the stream. Under the natural flow theory, Bob would prevail, because he has a right to have the natural level of water in the stream maintained. Under the reasonable use theory, Abe would prevail, since Bob can show no injury to himself as a riparian proprietor.

Prior appropriation Because arid western states have found the doctrine of riparian rights inapplicable to their local conditions, many have abolished it and instead have adopted the *prior appropriation doctrine,* which makes possible the maximum beneficial use of a limited supply of water. The theory says that the first person who appropriates a supply of water to a beneficial use has the first right to it. The wisdom of this first-come, first-served policy in a state where there is not enough water to supply all who could use it beneficially is illustrated by the following:

EXAMPLE Amelia and Betty each own 40 acres of arable and irrigable land, and it takes three acre-feet of water to raise a crop during the growing season. (An acre-foot is the volume of water needed to cover an acre to a depth of one foot.) The available supply of water is just enough to cover 40 acres three feet deep during the season. If the available supply is spread over the entire 80 acres, neither Amelia nor Betty will be able to raise a crop, and all the water will have been lost or wasted. On the other hand, if the entire available water supply is used exclusively either on Amelia's 40 acres or on Betty's 40 acres, there will be at least one 40-acre crop raised. Consequently, if Amelia first appropriates the three acre-feet of water and puts it to a beneficial use on her 40 acres of land, Amelia's right to the water will be recognized prior to any right of Betty's. If Betty makes an appropriation first, Amelia will have no right to the water.

Underground and percolating water Three different rules relate to the use of underground, or percolating, waters. The *common-law* rule regards water beneath the surface as property of the landowner. His exclusive ownership is modified, however, in states that (1) require the water to be used for a beneficial purpose, (2) do not protect a use motivated solely by malice toward neighboring landowners, or (3) have a statute prohibiting waste of underground water.

The *reasonable use* rule permits only uses that are reasonable in the light of the circumstances, particularly when the uses affect neighboring landowners.

The *prior appropriation* doctrine recognizes state ownership of percolating waters and protects appropriators (private property owners) in the order of their seniority.

Surface water Similarly, three different rules affect the conduct of a landowner with regard to surface water, such as that which comes from rains or snows. The *common-law* rule permits the landowner unlimited discretion in dealing with surface water, regardless of the effect on others. The *civil-law* rule states that each landowner has a right to the natural flow of surface water, and a corresponding duty not to interfere with that natural flow. Under this rule, each parcel of real estate, in effect, has a burden to receive the natural flow of surface water from above. The rule of *reasonableness* requires that the landowner use surface water reasonably in the light of the circumstances—which means keeping a reasonable balance between the benefit to the owner and the harm that results to others.

property tax A state tax imposed on real or personal PROPERTY. Generally, any person who lives and owns property in a state comes within its taxing power. The right to own property carries with it the responsibility to contribute to government revenue for public purposes such as education, public housing, or utilities, industries, or other business projects that are owned by the state. All state taxation must be based on valid laws, which should specifically designate the types of property subject to tax, prescribe the method of collection, and comply with constitutional requirements such as applying tax rates equally to persons in similar circumstances. Because property taxes are imposed by the state or their political subdivisions, you should consult the tax laws of your state for greater detail.

■ **Taxable property** For purposes of taxation, there are only three classes of property—tangible personal property, intangible personal property, and real property, all of which have a cash value that can be determined.

Tangible personal property Tangible personal property includes objects that are inherently valuable, such as a car, piano, painting, or jewelry. If tangible property has acquired a permanent *situs* (location) in a particular state, then that state and only that state may levy a tax on it, even if the owner's permanent residence is in a different state.

EXAMPLE If you keep a boat registered in a state where you have a vacation home, but you have your permanent residence in another state, you will be liable for any taxes imposed on the boat if it is designated as a taxable item in your vacation state, even though you are a nonresident. This is done because while the boat remains in that state it is protected by its laws. If the boat is stolen or vandalized, for instance, the matter will be handled by the law enforcement officials of that state.

When tangible personal property is not permanently located but is moved from state to state, or is regularly in transit among the several states, any tax must be reasonably apportioned among the states. When railroad cars, riverboats, or airplanes make regular stops or landings in more than one state, each state that affords protection or benefit through its laws to the vehicle may tax it according to its value. This is called an *ad valorem* tax.

Intangible personal property Intangible personal property includes physical objects that in themselves have no intrinsic or marketable value but are merely the symbol or evidence of value, such as stocks, bonds, or promissory notes. Although these items are merely pieces of paper, they stand for a right to be paid money at some date. A state may impose a tax on intangible personal property, and more than one state may tax the same intangible.

EXAMPLE Chris owned stocks and bonds at her domicile in
O—※ Tennessee. She transferred them to the Title Trust Company in Alabama to hold in trust for her, reserving the right to receive income produced by the trust throughout her life and the power to dispose of the securities by her will at her death. When Chris died, her will gave the securities to the Title Trust Company to hold in a similar trust arrangement for her daughters, Jane and Sally. Her estate was probated both in Tennessee and Alabama. Did both states have the right to levy an inheritance tax on the passing of these intangibles? Yes. When exactly such a problem arose before the U.S. Supreme Court, the Court decided that each state did have a right to tax such intangibles.

Real property All real property within the state, except exempt land such as that owned by a religious organization, is subject to taxation. Real property, for tax purposes, includes land itself, all buildings, structures, or other improvements on it, as well as any objects that have become permanently fixed to it. For example, an in-ground swimming pool that you have built is subject to taxation, but a tin storage shed that you can easily take apart is not. Land is taxed by the state in which it is located.

■ **Assessment** An assessment is the process of evaluating and listing the value of real property for purposes of taxing it. The state legislature usually creates local boards of assessors to establish the assessed value of property in a community, and the tax imposed is generally a certain percentage of that assessed value. Property is frequently reassessed to increase taxes when sewers and sidewalks are installed in the community or when significant additions or improvements are made on a person's property. It is important to have your property assessed at as low an accurate figure as possible; otherwise you will be faced with a higher tax bill. A taxpayer has the right to minimize or avoid taxes by any means the law permits.

Methods of assessment The board of assessors may use either the replacement cost or market value of your property to determine the assessment. Market value normally means the price you would receive for your property, house, or other buildings if you decided to sell them. To keep people from fraudulently underestimating the real value of their property, the assessors also consider the market price for comparable property. A person cannot escape high property tax by failing to use his property in a profitable way. For example, a person who owns a lot on the most exclusive block in the city will not have his lot assessed at a significantly lower value than comparable lots simply because he has not developed it. Certain situations, such as a farm that has been and will continue to be in the family for years, may be exempt by statute.

Another method of assessment, used for buildings and homes, is to consider what it would cost you, the owner, to replace the property if it were destroyed. This figure is reduced by any depreciation in the building's value due to deterioration or the passage of time.

A third way to determine the value of property is to consider its income-producing capability, which is usually treated as a certain percent of its original value. This method is used primarily for businesses and industries.

Challenging an assessment Obviously, a certain amount of personal judgment on the assessor's part is involved. If you feel that your property has been assessed at more than its actual worth, you can take certain steps to challenge the assessment. For example, you can compare the assessed value of your property with virtually identical property.

EXAMPLE Suppose your property tax is 5 percent of the
O—※ assessed value of your home. Your home has been assessed at $50,000, which makes your tax bill $2,500. Virtually identical homes in your neighborhood have been assessed for $40,000, resulting in taxes of $2,000 to their owners. You should notify the board of assessors, or the company that was hired to make the assessment, that you disagree with the assessment. Take these steps promptly, or you may lose the right to appeal because deadlines set by statute may have expired.

A meeting with the proper officials to discuss the disagreement will be arranged. If you fail to reach an agreement with the board, your next step depends upon the procedure in your state. Some states have administrative agencies that handle disputes from assessment boards before finally resorting to the courts. In other states, if the dispute is unresolved after meeting with the board, the courts will then decide the matter.

■ **Tax liens** Failure to pay real property taxes will result in the state government's filing a tax lien against your property. This means that you cannot sell your property to anyone without first paying your back taxes. If you fail to pay your taxes for a number of years, the government may sell your property to satisfy your debts, but only after giving you adequate notice and opportunity to present your side of the dispute. See TAX SALE.

pro rata (Latin) "Proportionately"; according to a certain rate, percentage, or share. If a debtor has some money, but not enough to pay all of his creditors, they might agree among themselves to accept a percentage of what is owed to each. The debtor's money would therefore be distributed pro rata among them.

pro se (Latin) "For himself"; in his own behalf; in person. *Pro se* representation means that a person is handling his own case in court, without a lawyer.

prosecute 1 Carry on a lawsuit or administrative proceeding. 2 Proceed against a suspect by charging him with a crime and bringing him to trial. To prosecute is not only to start an action but to follow it through to its end.

prosecutor Someone who initiates a criminal action against another or who charges a person with a crime and brings him to trial. There are two types of prosecutors, public and private. A *public prosecutor* is an officer of the federal, state, or local government, such as a DISTRICT ATTORNEY, whose function is to prosecute criminal actions. A *private prosecutor* is someone who sets in motion the machinery of criminal justice against a person he believes to be guilty of a crime by swearing to a criminal complaint or accusation, but who is not himself a public officer. For example, a person who intervenes and attempts to break up a fistfight and who is injured by one of the combatants might bring a criminal complaint for assault and battery, as a private prosecutor, against the person who injured him.

prostitution   The act whereby a female offers her body for sexual relations in exchange for money. A *prostitute* is a female who engages in sexual activities for a price. A *house of prostitution* is a place where a prostitute works.
■ **State laws**   Restrictive legislation pertaining to prostitution and related offenses is a proper exercise of the POLICE POWER of the state. In a number of states it is a criminal offense to be a common prostitute, to aid and abet prostitution, to operate a house of prostitution, or to reside in any place that is used for prostitution. Such statutes generally apply to married as well as unmarried women.
■ **Federal law**   The federal White Slave Traffic Act, popularly known as the Mann Act—after Illinois Congressman James Robert Mann, who wrote it—pertains to the transportation of women in interstate or foreign commerce for prostitution or other immoral activities. Under the Mann Act, transporting a woman across state borders for immoral purposes and inducing a woman to travel out of the state on a common carrier for immoral purposes are separate offenses. Both offenses can arise from the same transaction, and one person can be guilty of both. It is also a separate offense to induce or coerce a girl under 18 to travel on interstate transportation for immoral purposes.

The woman's previous character is not important in determining whether the Mann Act was violated. Nor is it necessary for the accused to benefit financially from the traffic in women or for the relationship between the accused and the woman to be a commercial one.

pro tanto   (Latin) "For so much." A defendant's counterclaim against the plaintiff for half the amount sued for is a defense *pro tanto*.

protective order   A court order that is used in some states to limit or regulate disclosures. It is sometimes called a protection order. A protective order may be granted to limit the time when and place where a DEPOSITION can be taken, for example, or to limit the inspection of documents belonging to a party to a lawsuit in order to protect business or trade secrets. A protective order may also be used to regulate or modify the enforcement of judgments.
    EXAMPLE An elderly woman who was in poor health and who lived with her aged mother defaulted on her mortgage. The facts disclosed that she intended to make the payments due on her mortgage. In the interest of justice, the court stayed the enforcement of the foreclosure judgment by a protective order to give her the chance to pay.

pro tem   (Latin) Common abbreviation for *pro tempore*, "for the time being"; temporarily; provisionally.

protest   A formal written statement made by a person who is called upon by a public authority, such as a state tax department, to pay a sum of money. In the statement, the person declares that he does not concede the legality or justice of the claim or his duty to pay it, or he says that he disputes the amount demanded. The purpose of the protest is to protect his right to recover, or reclaim, the amount—a right that would be lost if he did not register his objection. Thus, taxes may be paid under protest.

In connection with negotiable instruments (see COMMERCIAL PAPER), a protest is a formal certificate, made by a U.S. consul or a notary public, stating that a negotiable instrument has been presented for payment and dishonored. Protests apply only to negotiable instruments that have been drawn or made payable outside the United States.

prothonotary   The title given to the head clerk of some courts.

provisional remedy   Legal relief for an immediate need, adapted to the circumstances or necessity; especially, a form of temporary relief that protects the interest of the plaintiff in a civil lawsuit while the action is pending. Provisional relief might secure the plaintiff from drastic loss, irreparable injury, or dissipation of disputed property until the case is settled.
■ **Types of provisional remedies**   Each state has laws making different provisional remedies available in particular situations:
    Attachment is the seizure of a defendant's property so that it cannot be used up, destroyed, or taken beyond the reach of the court. Any property the defendant owns can be attached, even if it is in the possession of someone else. See ATTACHMENT AND GARNISHMENT.
    REPLEVIN is a suit you start to recover personal property held by someone who has less right to it. It does not matter if you are not the true owner, because you need prove only that you have a right to possess the property.
    EXAMPLE Sam purchased a pool table on credit from Top Tables, Inc., which gave him immediate possession of the table. Top Tables retained a security interest in the table by stipulating in its contract that should one monthly payment be missed, it would repossess the property. Sam failed to make one payment, claiming that the table was not of the quality that Top Tables had guaranteed. He sued Top Tables for fraud and threatened to destroy the table. Top Tables brought a replevin action to recover the table until the lawsuit against it was resolved. Replevin may be either a provisional or an ultimate remedy.
    Sometimes you may request that the defendant be put into jail in order to make sure he will appear in court. This is a civil ARREST and is generally available only in extreme situations—as when the defendant is about to flee the state and he has no property that the court can attach in order to enforce a judgment for money damages.
    A *lis pendens* is a notice of a pending lawsuit concerning ownership of a particular item of property, generally land. A creditor, for instance, may file a lis pendens to warn

possible purchasers of the debtor's land that they may not get clear title. The warning is considered a sort of provisional remedy.

A preliminary INJUNCTION is an order from the court requiring a party to do or not to do something until the lawsuit is finished.

RECEIVERSHIP is the management of a party's property or business by someone appointed by the court. It is the receiver's job to preserve the property from mismanagement or fraud while the court hears a legal action to determine who is entitled to the property.

■ **Court decisions** In recent years the U.S. Supreme Court has reviewed the way some of these provisional remedies have been used against consumers. In 1969 the Court held that garnishment, or attachment of a wage earner's income, was unconstitutional under a Wisconsin law that permitted a creditor to receive 50 percent of the defendant's wages every week without giving any prior notice to the defendant.

In 1972 the Court concluded that a Florida replevin statute was also unconstitutional because it failed to provide the defendant with a prompt hearing before an impartial official to determine whether the seizure was justified. In that case, too, the Court held that a general statement in the contract that the creditor could retake property was not clear enough to operate as a waiver of the debtor's constitutional right to a hearing.

Then in 1974 the Court ruled that there may be times when a creditor should be able to seize goods without first notifying the debtor and permitting him a hearing. In order to do this, the creditor must seek an order from a judicial officer and submit a sworn statement of facts indicating that quick action is necessary to secure the creditor's rights. After the seizure, the debtor must be given notice and an opportunity to have a prompt hearing.

■ **Future of other provisional remedies** The cases discussed above have considered the balance required by the U.S. Constitution in the debtor-creditor relationship. If the same principles of DUE PROCESS OF LAW are applied to other provisional remedies, more state laws as they are now written may be invalidated.

Civil arrest seems to be on especially shaky ground. It permits a defendant to be deprived of liberty before trial of his case just on the word of the plaintiff. The future of lis pendens is also uncertain. It makes it possible for one party to render the property of another unsalable just by filing a paper that says he is suing the owner. The constitutional requirements of due process are not as strict in civil as they are in criminal cases, but they may well be applied to insure more protection than some state laws now provide.

proviso 1 A condition or qualification inserted in a document, such as a deed, lease, mortgage, or contract. The validity of the document frequently depends on the fulfillment of the proviso. 2 A clause or part of a clause in a statute. Its purpose is either to except something from the statute, to limit the generality of the statute, or to exclude some possible misinterpretation of its scope.

provocation Conduct by one person that arouses anger, rage, or resentment in another, thereby causing the latter to act against the former. Provocation may be a defense against or may lessen the severity of certain charges, such as ASSAULT AND BATTERY and HOMICIDE.

proximate cause In the law of torts, the proximate cause of an injury is the primary cause from which an injury follows as a direct or immediate consequence and without which the injury would not have happened.

Other terms that are used for proximate cause include *dominant, efficient, immediate, legal,* and *next* cause. The proximate cause is not necessarily the closest cause in time or space or the first event that sets in motion a sequence of events leading to an injury. Proximate cause can be illustrated by the following cases:

EXAMPLE A flying instructor's negligence in allowing a trainee to take off in a solo flight while another student was in the air performing dangerous training maneuvers and his failure to inform the trainee of the presence of the other student constituted the proximate cause of a midair collision.

EXAMPLE An automobile driver's failure to steer slightly to the right after seeing another automobile approaching 100 feet away with its left wheels to the left of the center line of the highway was held to be the proximate cause of the collision with the other automobile, even though both drivers were negligent.

EXAMPLE A man hung a sign over a sidewalk in front of his premises. When a schoolboy struck the sign and dislodged it from its hook, the sign fell, hitting a passerby. It appeared from the manner in which the sign was hung that no reasonable man would have anticipated that the sign would be struck by a force strong enough to dislodge it. In a lawsuit brought against the sign owner by the injured passerby, the manner in which the sign was hung and maintained was held to be a "remote cause" of the accident, and not the proximate cause. As a result, the injured person could not recover for the injury.

For a full discussion of how the law determines and weighs the significance of proximate and other types of cause in tort suits, see NEGLIGENCE; TORT.

proxy An agent representing and acting for another person or the document that appoints such an agent. In connection with corporate meetings, a proxy is an authority to vote stock. A stockholder may not vote by proxy unless the right to do so is conferred by the corporation's constitution, a bylaw, or a statute. If such a right is conferred, only the person who owns legal title to stock, as shown by the corporation's transfer books, is authorized to delegate the right to vote. The proxy to whom the right to vote is delegated does not have to be a stockholder.

Unless there is an express (specific) requirement to the contrary, no particular formality is necessary in appointing a proxy so long as there is sufficient written evidence of the grant of authority. As a general rule, a stockholder may give his proxy any power that he himself possesses to act at a corporate meeting and may even give his representative secret instructions on the manner of voting his stock on particular questions. When the proxy acts within the scope of his authority, the stockholder is as much bound as if he had acted in person.

public   1 The whole body politic; all the citizens of a nation, state, county, or municipality.   2 The inhabitants of a particular place; the people of the neighborhood; a particular segment of the people.   3 As an adjective, belonging to the people; open for the use and enjoyment of the people generally, even though a fee is charged, as in a public dance hall.

public administrative agency   Any agency, commission, board, or other body set up by a federal, state, or local law to perform government or public functions. An agency can be created or terminated only by the legislature or by a constitutional provision or amendment.

An administrative agency is charged with administering and implementing particular legislation through the promulgation of rules and regulations that facilitate compliance with the law, and can offer to various branches of the government guidelines to the interpretation of such laws as a result of investigation, research, and study in the areas of their particular expertise.

Although it is neither an executive, judicial, or legislative department, an administrative agency performs some functions of each. For example, the Securities and Exchange Commission makes and issues rules governing the contents of a prospectus. The promulgation of such rules is similar to the lawmaking process of the legislative branch. If a corporation fails to observe the rules, the SEC may begin enforcement proceedings, a power similar to that of an executive branch to enforce the law. By holding hearings to decide whether the violation of the rules can be punished, the SEC exercises powers similar to those exercised by a court, although there are differences in the proceedings.

Examples of U.S. agencies are the Federal Housing Administration, the Federal Reserve System, the Indian Claims Commission, the Internal Revenue Service, the Social Security Administration, the Federal Trade Commission, the United States Civil Service Commission, the Environmental Protection Agency, and the Veterans Administration. State and local agencies include public utilities commissions, tax commissions, workmen's compensation boards, and zoning boards.

■ **Significance of agencies**   Virtually every activity of daily life is influenced by the operation of public administrative agencies. The character of the neighborhood where you live is governed by a local zoning board. The utilities you use—electricity and gas for light, heating, and cooking; water for hygiene and cleaning; and the telephone for communication—are available because of the workings of various public service commissions. The food and beverages you consume and the medicines and drugs you take are approved by various health agencies before distribution and sale to the public. The transportation you use, whether you drive a car or take public transportation, is supervised by administrative agencies, such as your state's motor vehicle bureau, which determines the qualifications for all licensed drivers; various transportation boards, which govern the operation of mass transit. The purity of the air you breathe and the water you drink is determined by federal and state environmental agencies. State insurance commissions govern various features of the insurance you carry on your car, house, personal possessions, health, and life. If you are disabled, injured on the job, unemployed, retired, or poor, there are administrative agencies to assist you.

The regulations and controls exercised by public administrative agencies and officers and the review exercised by the courts over these agencies and officers have assumed such importance that a body of law known as administrative law has come into being. This area of the law stems from the increasing use of administrative agencies to perform governmental functions. It is a response to the need for broad governmental control over administrative activities that are so complex they cannot be dealt with directly or effectively by the legislature or judiciary.

Because every agency is ruled by the legislation that created it, there are no generalities that apply to every agency. However, certain broad observations can be made that will apply to a large number of existing agencies. The following is a discussion of the general restrictions on the powers, jurisdiction, and internal organization of agencies; a look at how agencies conduct investigations, make rules and regulations, and hold hearings; and a discussion of the courts' use of judicial review to keep agencies in check.

■ **Powers**   An agency's powers are wholly derived from and limited by the constitution, statute, or other legislative enactment that created it. In addition to the powers expressly conferred on it, an agency has whatever implied powers are reasonably necessary to make effective the express powers and duties imposed on it.

An administrative agency must keep within the scope of its powers. It may not ignore or violate any statutory requirements or limits on its power even to accomplish what it believes to be praiseworthy ends. Acts, orders, or regulatory rules that do not come clearly within the powers granted are not merely wrong but are void.

EXAMPLE The zoning board in your village has been empowered to determine the character of your village by establishing the acreage necessary for farms and residences and by banning commercial buildings from certain areas within its authority. It has not been given the power to tax the real estate holdings of local inhabitants. That power has been delegated to the local real estate tax commission. Any action taken by the zoning board that deals with real estate taxes is therefore void.

■ **Jurisdiction**   An administrative agency that first acquires jurisdiction (authority) over a particular matter ordinarily has exclusive jurisdiction, and no other body has any right to interfere with it. An agency, however, may cooperate with other public bodies and officials.

When the power and jurisdiction of federal and state agencies conflict or overlap, the federal authority is supreme and will prevail over that of the state agency. Within the federal domain, if Congress has preempted a particular field and has granted exclusive power over it to a federal agency, the states' powers are suspended and no state agency in that area can have jurisdiction. But when a federal statute authorizes a federal agency to act in a certain field, it does not automatically preempt a state from enacting a statute on the same general subject and creating a state agency for enforcing it. For example, Congress enacts legislation dealing with the production and sale of food products in interstate commerce. The U.S. Department of

WHEN A GOVERNMENT AGENCY IS (AND IS NOT) A LAW UNTO ITSELF

■ The Federal Housing Administration, the Environmental Protection Agency, the Social Security Administration, and the Veterans Administration are typical federal administrative agencies. Workmen's compensation boards, public utilities commissions, and zoning boards are representative of state and local agencies.

■ Although an agency is not an executive nor a legislative nor a judicial department, it performs some functions belonging to each branch of the government. For example, it may make and issue rules, similar to Congress's lawmaking; it can enforce the rules as the executive branch of the government enforces laws; and it can hold hearings and punish those who fail to observe the rules, much as the courts hold trials.

■ An agency's powers are wholly derived from and limited by the constitution, statute, or other legislative enactment that created it.

■ An administrative agency that first acquires jurisdiction (authority) over a particular matter ordinarily has exclusive jurisdiction, and no other body has the right to interfere. When federal and state agencies overlap, the federal authority is supreme and prevails over that of the state.

■ Federal agencies are required by law to publish all regulations and notices that they issue in the *Federal Register*, printed daily by the National Archives and Records Service.

■ An agency may have the power to conduct investigations to obtain useful information, but these investigations are not proceedings in which action is taken against anyone. The information they uncover may be used as a basis for new regulations, for example.

■ Investigating boards have the right to issue subpoenas. They are not bound to conduct their investigations under strict rules of evidence, as in a court of law, but some types

of evidence, such as hearsay, are inadmissible.

■ An agency may make its own rules and regulations when empowered to do so by the law that created the agency. Although these rules and regulations are not laws, they have the force and effect of laws and are binding unless thrown out by a court.

■ The agency may also have the power to prescribe penalties for noncompliance with its rules and regulations. An agency with the power to enforce its rules and regulations generally holds a hearing to decide whether or not a person or corporation has violated them.

■ An agency cannot take any action that would result in a loss to a person or corporation unless it first holds a hearing, except in an emergency. It may, for example, order the destruction of property or prohibit the sale of goods it believes harmful to health, provided it holds a hearing later.

Agriculture and the Food and Drug Administration are responsible for enforcing these laws. A state legislature can pass laws dealing with food products moving in intrastate commerce (that never go outside state borders) because the federal government has not taken exclusive control over the production and sale of food.

■ **Internal organization** Usually, regulations that govern the interior workings of a particular agency are delimited in the law that created the body. In this way, each agency is given the limitations and powers that best serve the purpose for which the agency was created. There are, however, some general provisions of administrative law that apply to many of the agencies now operating.

Personnel All persons are equally eligible to hold an administrative office in an agency unless they are excluded by law. The legislature may fix the qualifications for administrative officers, but the qualifications must be reasonable and not arbitrary. The tenure and term of office of administrative officers are set by the law that created the agency. An officer is usually entitled, and may be required, to hold office until his successor is chosen and qualified.

An officer can be removed only according to the law governing the agency. If the officer is an appointee of the agency, rather than a civil servant, he can be removed without notice or hearing.

When acting in good faith within the scope of their authority, the officers of administrative agencies are not personally liable (financially responsible) for the consequences of their acts. Accordingly, an officer is not liable for money damages because he makes a mistake in exercising his discretion or because he misconstrues or misapplies

the law. On the other hand, when an officer acts outside the scope of his jurisdiction and without authorization of law, he is liable for damages suffered as a result. An officer is not liable for the wrongful acts or omissions of his subordinates unless he directed, authorized, or cooperated in them.

Administrative agencies are continuing organizations, unaffected by personnel changes. Final actions of administrative officers are binding on their successors.

Public disclosures In the interests of orderly procedure and public information, administrative bodies should keep minutes or written records of all proceedings before them and of all actions taken by them. Since administrative bodies speak only through their records, the records must be truthful, clear, and definite.

Records should be open for inspection by any persons who have some real or proper interest in them, such as the parties to the proceeding that has been recorded. When the records are public records, no particular reason has to be given for inspecting them, and they may be examined even out of idle curiosity.

Federal agencies are required by law to publish in the FEDERAL REGISTER all regulations and notices they issue, as well as documents having general applicability and legal effect and documents of particular public interest.

■ **Investigations** Investigations held by administrative agencies or officials are informal proceedings to obtain information that can be used to govern future action. They are not proceedings in which action is taken against anyone.

An agency may be authorized to exercise its discretion in determining when an investigation is to be made. It may also be required to make certain investigations. For example, a statute setting up a public service commission may include a provision that requires the commission to investigate public utilities. The purpose of the investigation might be to determine whether or not a utility was being operated in such a way as to serve the best interests of the public. The information discovered during the investigation might be used, for example, to determine whether or not a utility should be allowed to increase its rates.

Usually no notice of an investigation need be given. An agency is not bound to conduct its investigations under the strict rules of evidence required for courts, but some types of evidence, such as hearsay evidence, have been held to be inadmissible. The costs and expenses of an investigation may be assessed against the particular persons or corporations being investigated.

An investigating board has the right to issue subpoenas requiring witnesses to appear and testify. Witnesses may be entitled to the presence and advice of counsel.

Subpoenas may also be issued for official records, including books, papers, and other documents. A subpoena for records must show that the documents requested are relevant to the inquiry. A person should respond to a subpoena even if he cannot produce all the documents requested.

An agency may conduct its inquiry by correspondence and personal investigation. As a general rule a hearing is not a necessary part of an investigation by an administrative agency or official.

■ **Regulatory functions** Public administrative agencies are generally established to perform specific regulatory functions. An agency may carry out these functions in any one of three ways: (1) It may issue guidelines, memoranda, and policy statements as to the meaning of a statute that it is responsible for implementing; (2) it may make recommendations to the executive or legislative branches of the government for regulating the field in question; or (3) it can make and enforce rules and regulations that establish a pattern of conduct to be followed.

Some agencies are empowered only to interpret statutes and make recommendations to the executive or legislative branch, and may not make their own rules and regulations. For example, the Commission on Civil Rights was created to collect and study information related to civil rights issues and make recommendations for statutes to the President and Congress, but it cannot make or enforce rules.

An agency may make rules and regulations when empowered to do so by the legislation that created it. When it has such power, its rules and regulations must be subordinate to the terms of the legislation and must aid in enforcing its provisions. Although these rules and regulations are not laws, they have the force and effect of laws. The Environmental Protection Agency, for example, develops national standards for air and water quality and makes regulations to control water pollution and protect water supplies.

Any rule or regulation made by an agency must be necessary, fair, and reasonable, and it should not alter, amend, or enlarge a statute, nor should it defeat the spirit and purpose of the statute it is intended to implement. It should also be so definite and certain that anyone interested may be able to determine his own rights and duties under it.

An agency that has adopted a rule or regulation usually must give proper notice to the general public. Compliance with notice provisions can be a condition to an administrative regulation's becoming effective.

An administrative agency ordinarily has the authority to enforce its rules and regulations. It may also be empowered to prescribe penalties for noncompliance.

■ **Hearings** An agency with the power to enforce its rules and regulations generally holds a hearing to decide whether or not a person or corporation has violated its rules or regulations.

EXAMPLE A regulation of the state unemployment agency O➤—✱ requires that a recipient of unemployment insurance report any jobs he holds while receiving benefits. Max, an unemployed teacher, has been receiving unemployment for six months. An anonymous tipster notifies the agency that Max has been working regularly as a house painter for three months. The agency cannot automatically terminate Max's benefits on the basis of the tip. It must provide him with a hearing so that he can appear to present his side of the story.

Ordinarily, an agency cannot deprive a person or corporation of property or rights unless it first gives notice and holds a hearing.

EXAMPLE Suppose a local board of public works authorized O➤—✱ the construction of sidewalks in a neighborhood after a majority of homeowners petitioned for their construction. The board assessed each property for the improvements without giving each owner the opportunity to demonstrate the extent to which his property was benefited—a factor that could increase or decrease the size of an individual assessment. Anyone who objected to his assessment could only file a written complaint. He was not permitted to present any evidence to support his claims or contradict the board's evidence. The homeowners could sue in court because this procedure deprived them of their property without an opportunity to be heard, a violation of their constitutional right to due process of law.

However, in an emergency, such as a threat to public health or safety, a public administrative agency may take summary action, subject to later review. It may, for example, order the destruction of property or prohibit the sale of goods it believes poisonous or injurious to the health, provided a hearing is held later.

The manner in which administrative hearings may be started varies from agency to agency. Sometimes an administrative body may act only after a complaint, charge, or petition is brought by a proper person, but often it may begin proceedings on its own initiative.

Parties The general rules as to necessary and proper PARTIES apply in administrative hearings. Persons whose valuable property or contract rights will be adjudicated in the proceeding are necessary parties. Interested persons who are not parties may intervene in a proceeding only at the discretion of the agency holding the hearing.

Conduct Statutory provisions generally name the officer before whom hearings are to be conducted. Under some statutes, the hearing may be held before the administrative agency, a member of the agency, or a hearing officer or examiner appointed by the body. Under other statutes, the hearing must be held before the administrative body or one of its members, and the board may not delegate the duty to a subordinate or appoint an outside officer or examiner.

As in the case of an investigation, an administrative hearing does not have to be conducted with all the formality of a court hearing, but the procedure must be consistent with the essentials of a fair trial. Within reasonable limits, each of the parties should be permitted to prove his own case in his own way by his own counsel. In order to develop the facts fully and clearly, the person conducting the hearing may ask questions, elicit testimony, call witnesses, and introduce evidence. He has some discretion as to the admission of evidence, the scope of cross-examination, and the order of proof.

Findings, conclusions, and decisions In conducting a hearing, an administrative agency or officer must make *findings of fact* on the issues presented in order to aid a court reviewing a decision of the agency in determining (1) whether there is sufficient evidence to support the agency's final decision in the hearing, (2) whether the facts show a reasonable basis for that decision, (3) whether the decision was based on a proper principle, and (4) whether additional proceedings should be started.

The findings made by administrative agencies are just as far-reaching within their fields as are the judgments of courts. When they are supported by competent and substantial evidence, they are conclusive.

The administrative agency must also make and state the *conclusions of law* on which its final decision is based. The conclusions must be definite and certain, and they must conform to the law and to the facts and the findings. A conclusion is of no use without evidence in the record to support it.

The final *decision*, or *order*, in an administrative hearing is equivalent to the judgment of a court. The findings and conclusions are not part of the final decision, or order, even though they may be incorporated in the same document. The decision must be within the authority granted to the agency and must conform to the PLEADINGS (complaints and answers), issues, evidence, and findings.

■ **Judicial review** Public administrative agencies are held in check mainly through judicial review. The purpose of judicial review is to keep the administrative agency within its jurisdiction and protect substantial rights affected by its decisions. It is designed to protect against mistaken or arbitrary orders and to secure a just result with a minimum of technical requirements. A plaintiff cannot request judicial review unless he has exhausted all channels of appeal offered by the agency in question.

EXAMPLE A woman sued a corporation in federal district court for failing to pay her the same wages as a man who did the same work, a violation of federal law. The corporation asked the court to dismiss the complaint because the woman failed to exhaust her administrative remedies as required by law before coming to court. The federal court agreed and dismissed the case.

The woman had originally filed a sex discrimination complaint with the state human rights agency as well as the federal Equal Employment Opportunity Commission. A hearing was held at the state agency during which the woman presented her side of the case. The corporation did not have the opportunity to cross-examine the woman or to present evidence to support its position. The hearing was adjourned and, subsequently, the woman's attorney requested that the hearing be discontinued because she wanted to sue in federal court. The corporation opposed the request, which was denied with the result that the state agency proceeding was stayed. No additional action, outside of filing the complaint, was taken at the federal commission.

The court reasoned that the exhaustion requirement was intended to encourage a conciliatory resolution of the problem in an administrative setting. To allow a person to abandon administrative procedures, which she voluntarily began, and commence a lawsuit would undermine the purpose of such a law.

No rule of constitutional law requires that all administrative acts be subject to judicial review, nor is there any necessity for an appeal on questions of fact. But when a controversy over personal or property rights is involved, then some provision must be made for judicial review, and unless an appeal to the courts is provided, even though the scope of review is limited, the constitutional guarantee of DUE PROCESS OF LAW is not satisfied.

Judicial review of administrative acts and decisions is limited in scope. Ordinarily, the courts will only pass on the questions: (1) Has the agency acted within its constitutional or statutory powers? (2) Is the agency's order or determination supported by substantial evidence? (3) Is the agency's regulation or action reasonable and not arbitrary? The court will not reverse an administrative decision or order unless it is clearly wrong.

For information on specific public administrative agencies, see ENVIRONMENTAL PROTECTION AGENCY; EQUAL EMPLOYMENT OPPORTUNITY COMMISSION; FEDERAL COMMUNICATIONS COMMISSION; FEDERAL TRADE COMMISSION; FOOD AND DRUG ADMINISTRATION; SECURITIES AND EXCHANGE COMMISSION. See also SOCIAL SECURITY.

publication The act of making something known to people in general, of making it accessible to public scrutiny. (1) In COPYRIGHT law, publication is the act of making a book or other work known to the general public by distributing it or offering it for sale. (2) In the law of LIBEL AND SLANDER, publication is the communication of the offending statement at issue to a person other than the one about whom the statement is made. (3) In the law of WILLS, publication is the act of telling the witnesses to the document that you intend it to be your will at the time you sign it. (4) In the procedural rules governing the practice of law, publication of a SUMMONS is having it appear in a newspaper under the conditions set by law, as a means of notifying a defendant of the lawsuit against him.

public contract A contract to which the state is a party and which concerns all the state's taxpayers. Any formal agreement between a private person or company to do work for a government body—federal, state, or local—is a public contract, whether it is to install sewers, construct schools, or repair highways.

Public contracts are governed to a large extent by the general law of CONTRACTS, although private individuals or corporations are held to more strict requirements when dealing with the government than in private contracts. Limitations imposed by state law must be observed. Limitations imposed by federal law must also be observed, since most public projects receive financial assistance from the federal government.

■ **Conflict of interest** A contract in which a public officer or employee has a private interest is void and unenforceable. The interest does not have to be a direct financial one; even the appearance or potential for CONFLICT OF INTEREST should be avoided. These rules rest on the principle that no person can faithfully serve two masters—personal profit and public interest.

■ **Manner of awarding contracts** The manner of letting (awarding) contracts is usually regulated by law and must be followed in order to create a valid contract.

Bidding In the letting of public contracts, the public body usually invites bids or proposals so that it may award the contract to the bidder qualifying under the terms of the governing statute. The submission of a bid in response to an invitation creates no more than an offer, and although it may not be withdrawn prior to acceptance, it does not become a contract until it is accepted by the appropriate public authority.

Government bodies do not have to solicit bids for public contracts unless required by statute. But even when a public body has no duty to require bids in letting public contracts, it must act in the public interest and be fair, honest, and prudent in awarding them.

Laws often require that public contracts be awarded upon competitive bidding. Competitive bidding is meant to protect the taxpayers against the wasting of public funds and to prevent such abuses as fraud, favoritism, improvidence, and extravagance. It also provides bidders a fair chance to be awarded public contracts.

If contracts are required by law to be let upon competitive bidding, they cannot legally be made in any other way.

Plans and specifications In order to give all bidders an opportunity to bid on the same thing, it is essential that the proper public authorities, before soliciting bids, adopt plans and specifications that fix the extent and type of the work to be done or materials to be furnished. This establishes a standard basis for competitive bidding.

Plans and specifications must be prepared by the public department or agency itself and all prospective bidders must be given the same information. Plans and specifications should be as complete and precise as practicable and should include the quantity and quality of materials required. In setting specifications, however, the public authority has broad discretion as to the particular equipment or product it may require as part of the contract. It is free, for example, to designate a specific product, which may be covered by a patent or manufactured only by one bidder. On the other hand, the plans and specifications may not reserve to the public body the power to make substantial exceptions, releases, and modifications in the contract after it is advertised or awarded.

Request for bids Statutes that require competitive bidding frequently require the public authority to give public notice of its intention to receive bids. The notice must usually be given in the English language and in a newspaper printed in that language.

An invitation to bid should state the deadline for bids to be submitted. The deadline should be sufficiently in advance of the projected contract date to give a rejected bidder time for a conference or informal hearing at which to present his protest.

Conditions for bidding Usually bids must be properly signed and accompanied by a financial statement of the bidder. Common additional requirements are a certificate stating that there has been no collusion with others in submitting the bid and a bond or other security for the performance of the work in question if the contract is won. When a contractor posts a bond, he promises to pay a certain amount of money to the public authority if he fails to fulfill certain obligations. The bond contains two obligations, one for the faithful performance of the contract and the other for the protection of the right of laborers and suppliers to be paid. If the contractor refuses to give the required bond, the public body has the authority either to void the contract or to compel the contractor by a civil action to post it. A contractor's bond is governed by the law of the state in which the contract is to be performed. The law usually does not require a bond to be furnished by a subcontractor, but a contractor may protect himself against the shortcomings of the subcontractor by requiring one of the subcontractor.

A bid for the construction of public works must substantially conform to the details enumerated in the specifications and to the terms and conditions stated in the invitation to submit bids. Failure to comply substantially will result in rejection of the bid, and any contract entered into on the basis of a nonconforming bid is invalid.

Minor or immaterial deviations from the specifications do not, however, require that a bid be rejected. The test is whether the bid stifles fair competition by giving the deviating bidder a significant advantage over other bidders.

Change of bids After the time for filing bids has expired, a contractor is bound by the bid as filed and may not change it. A minor, but never a major, defect can be corrected after the bids have been opened. If essential information is missing from a bid, it may not be supplied then or later by a private understanding between the contractor and the public authority.

As a general rule, a person who files a bid has no right to withdraw it. Some statutes, however, allow a bidder to withdraw his bid at any time before it is accepted if the bidder has made an honest mistake of calculation, which materially affects the substance of his contract. The chance to withdraw, however, is usually granted only for clerical or mathematical mistakes, not for errors in judgment, and only when the contractor has given reasonably prompt notice of his error to the public authority.

Award of contract When a bid is accepted, a public contract is formed. The contract is binding from the time the award is made. In general, the award of a public contract under a competitive-bidding statute must be to the lowest responsible bidder—the contractor whose bid substantially conforms to the plans and specifications and who is able to do the work at the lowest cost. The money amount of a contractor's bid is only one factor in determining who the lowest responsible bidder is. The government unit may also consider a bidder's experience, previous dealings with him, his reputation for satisfactory work, and the fact that he intends to employ local labor, especially if one purpose of the public improvement is to afford relief to the unemployed. A low bidder who has been guilty of delays, lack of cooperation, and poor performance on prior contracts may not be found the lowest responsible bidder.

Minority hiring In 1977 Congress enacted the Public Works Employment Act, which imposed certain conditions on public contracts that receive financial assistance from the federal government. One provision of the act prohibits any local public works project from receiving a federal grant unless at least 10 percent of the grant goes to minority business enterprises. A business is a minority business if at least half of its owners belong to a minority group or, if it is a publicly owned business, if at least 51 percent of its stock is owned by minorities. (Blacks, Hispanics, Orientals, Indians, Eskimos, and Aleuts are considered minorities.)

Another provision says that when any bid is submitted, it must be accompanied by a statement that the bidder has taken steps to assure the involvement of minorities in the project. Much litigation has resulted when the lowest bidder has lost a contract award because he has not complied with this requirement. Some federal district courts have declared this requirement unconstitutional—invidious discrimination based solely on race—while others have upheld it as a constitutional way of remedying past discrimination. In 1980 the Supreme Court found the provision requiring that 10 percent of federal public works funds be spent for minority business enterprises was a constitutional means for groups previously discriminated against to achieve equal economic opportunity.

Preferences Competitive bidding laws may require giving preference to bidders who have met certain requirements, such as satisfactory performance of prior public contracts, payment of state and county taxes, payment by the bidder's supplier of certain taxes, or the bidder's commitment to hire unemployed workers from a particular area.

Rejection of bids Unless a low bidder has blatantly failed to comply with a specific contract provision, he is usually entitled to reasonable notice and a hearing before his bid is rejected on grounds that he is not responsible. Unsuccessful bidders may bring legal actions challenging the rejection of their bids and the letting of a public contract to someone else. Because public contracts are matters of public interest, taxpayers may also challenge the award of a contract.

Generally, courts will not interfere with the action of a public officer or body in accepting or rejecting bids and in awarding a contract so long as the award was made fairly and honestly, in good faith, and in the interest of the public. Courts will hear lawsuits in which it is claimed that an award was made arbitrarily, capriciously, or as a result of favoritism or fraud.

■ **Requisites of a contract** The same rules that govern the validity of contracts between individuals generally control contracts with a public entity.

Subcontracting A contractor may hire subcontractors to perform portions of the work. A subcontractor does not merely supply specified materials, but contracts to perform part of the work which the original contractor

himself has agreed to perform. In the subletting of public contracts, contractors may be bound by statutory requirements. For example, contractors may be limited to choosing subcontractors from competitive lists prepared by the awarding authority.

■ **Performance of a contract** Failure to carry out the contract as agreed makes a contractor liable for breach of contract, but he is still entitled to recover payment for work he has fully or substantially performed. When a contractor substantially performs his contract, but uses defective materials or allows faulty workmanship, he must correct the defects if practicable. If the defects cannot be corrected, he will receive the contract price reduced by the difference between the value of the defective work and its value if perfectly completed.

A public contractor's failure to stay within his bid falls on his shoulders. He is not entitled to receive higher payment for the work agreed upon, even if unforeseen events raise his expenses.

A public contractor may be paid for additional work resulting from authorized changes in the plans and specifications. Sometimes public contracts provide for the cost of extra work in the form of "changed conditions" clauses, which recognize that the contractor may encounter unknown and unanticipated physical conditions. For example, additional compensation will be paid when a hidden geological condition is discovered but not when the contractor's additional work results from his failure to reasonably observe physical factors when he made his bid.

■ **Rights of the contractor and subcontractor** Generally, a contractor may hold the public body with whom he has contracted liable (responsible) in money damages for its acts or omissions in violation of the contract. The authority is liable for a misrepresentation that renders the contractor unable to perform according to the contract and he may pursue an appropriate remedy in the courts.

A subcontractor who has performed labor for, furnished material to, or entered into a subcontract with a contractor for a public improvement has no claim against the public contracting body. But where a law provides, the subcontractor has a LIEN against public funds due the contractor if the subcontractor notifies the public authority of his claim before any payment is made to the contractor.

■ **Rights of the public body** A public body may hold the contractor liable for his breaches of contract, for loss of or damage to property for which he is responsible under the contract, and reimbursement to the government of moneys paid to the contractor to which he was not entitled. It may also recover damages suffered because of delays in completion of the contract caused by the contractor. If a contractor is found guilty of fraud or collusion, he may be required to make restitution to the public treasury.

public defender An attorney employed by the state or local government to represent poor persons who are accused of crimes.

public domain 1 Lands that have always been owned by the United States—more commonly called PUBLIC LANDS. 2 In COPYRIGHT law, a creative work is in the public domain if it is not covered by a copyright or if its copyright has expired; it may be freely copied or reproduced by the general public.

public health

In law, *health* means a state of physical well-being, the freedom from sickness or disability. *Public health* covers the concern for providing healthy, sanitary conditions for the general community. Since good health is a national economic asset, the preservation of the public health is one of the first duties of government.

This article discusses the laws, government regulations, and activities of agencies that were created to prevent the spread of diseases; provide for safe building; control nuisances; and regulate businesses and occupations that pose health hazards.

For additional health-related articles, see ABORTION; DRUGS AND NARCOTICS; FOOD; INTOXICATING LIQUOR; PATIENTS' RIGHTS; PHYSICIANS AND SURGEONS; POISON; SOCIAL SECURITY; and WELFARE PROGRAMS.

■ **Protection of law** Congress has enacted federal laws to protect the health of certain classes of persons, such as victims of poverty. In addition, it regulates the transportation, advertising, and sales of goods in interstate commerce that affect the health of the nation. This authority is used to control the advertising of cigarettes and the sale of dangerous toys, for example. Congress has also provided financial aid to state and local governments to support health programs. One of these programs educated parents about the danger of letting children eat chips of lead-based paint.

States, too, have broad powers to establish and enforce health standards. A state may not interfere with federal laws, but state and local action carry much of the burden of protecting public health in this country. The authority to take whatever measures are necessary to promote and preserve the public health is one of the state's POLICE POWERS.

Citizens have no constitutional right to insist that the government solve all public health problems, however. The federal governments and the states may decide which ones are appropriately controlled by law and where tax dollars are best spent.

■ **Sanitary districts and boards of health** One of the ways that a state protects public health is by setting up sanitary districts. A sanitary district is a political subdivision of the state—a corporation organized for a public purpose. Legislatures have created sanitary districts to supply water, waste disposal, drainage, and sewers. Sometimes people can be charged a fee for the services, and usually income is gleaned from taxes assessed in the district. The duties of a sanitary district may be performed by a board or a commissioner and a staff.

A state may also establish public health boards, departments, or officers, or it may authorize local governments to do so. The statute creating a board of health will spell out the qualifications of members, the method of selecting them, their terms of office and salary, and their powers and duties. A board of health is a PUBLIC ADMINISTRATIVE AGENCY. It usually has the power to make rules or regulations and to enforce them. As long as board members follow lawful procedure, observe the rights of individuals, and act with the intention of protecting public health, they generally are not liable for losses or inconveniences that may be suffered by individuals.

A state or local board of health may not restrain the public unreasonably. Its regulatory measures must be linked to a known risk. It may not, for example, quarantine all victims of cancer on the chance that the disease might be catching. Neither can it take over the treatment of all the victims of a particular disease—for example, Legionnaires' disease—or refuse to let a private doctor treat someone who is in quarantine.

■ **Controlling contagious diseases** The government has a special responsibility to prevent the spread of infectious diseases, because individuals cannot protect themselves. Public health authorities can order dangerous articles to be disinfected or destroyed, and they can seize property or take persons into custody when necessary. Some laws allow for compensation to owners whose property is destroyed or to people who must assist government officials in an emergency. Owners generally must bear the expense of having a home disinfected, for example, or of having clothing and bedding burned.

In emergencies, health officials can close public places such as schools and movie theaters and prohibit gatherings of people—at fairs, circuses, and carnivals, for example. Public schools have been shut down when large numbers of children caught head lice or measles, and public gatherings have been banned when an earthquake destroyed local sanitation systems.

A clear example of the power of a board of health is the control of rabies—a deadly disease that is readily transmitted through the bite of an infected animal. Rabies is so dangerous, a board of health may properly order the seizure of a dog or other animal thought to have it. A stray pet picked up by the authorities may be kept in isolation while being tested and watched for signs of rabies, even though this interferes with the owner's right to take it home. If tests reveal the animal is infected, it is destroyed.

Vaccination Health authorities have the right to demand that you be vaccinated to obtain immunity to certain diseases. The U.S. government once demanded that all citizens traveling abroad be immunized against smallpox. State boards of health have long used this power to order diphtheria vaccinations for all children attending public school. Boards of health can also require schoolchildren to be inoculated against other specific diseases.

When vaccination is mandatory, you cannot refuse to comply simply because you think it is not the best way to control disease. In one case, the court would not excuse a chiropractor who claimed that physical ailments are best treated by manipulating the alignment of body parts. However, some mandatory vaccination laws excuse children whose parents object to injections on religious grounds or people whose health would be endangered.

Reports of contagious diseases Various health laws are designed to inform authorities of infectious diseases in the community. Doctors especially—but any citizens under some laws—may be required to report these diseases. This does not mean, however, that the individual's right to be left alone is always subservient to public health concerns.

EXAMPLE A soldier reported that he had contracted gonorrhea from a woman whom he had met on the street when he was drunk. The soldier's commanding officer reported the woman to the department of health, as he was required to do. When a public health doctor told the woman to appear for an examination, she refused. Her attorney said that her own doctor had examined her and had not found evidence of venereal disease. The attorney also said his client would permit another doctor to examine her, but she would not go to the department of health for an examination by a doctor who seemed to be hostile to her. The public health doctor brought charges against the woman on the grounds that she was a threat to the public health and refused to cooperate with authorities.

Dismissing the charges, the court held that emergency measures were not necessary here as they might be if the woman were thought to have smallpox. It said that a woman with no reputation as a common prostitute cannot be hauled into the department of health to prove that she does not have venereal disease—unless there is more evidence than the testimony of a drunken soldier.

In other cases, courts have approved of laws requiring persons arrested for prostitution to take a blood test for venereal disease. But it is illegal to take samples by force.

Quarantine A long-recognized method of guarding the public from the spread of contagious diseases is quarantine, the enforced isolation of victims. Public health authorities often order a person with an infectious disease to stay inside his house and permit no one to enter or leave until the danger passes. A sign posted outside the house warns people away, and guards can be stationed at the door if necessary. Typhoid fever is a deadly contagious disease. Persons discovered to have or to carry (be able to transmit) the disease may be subject to quarantine.

Because a quarantine is a severe restriction of liberty, health officials may order it only for good reasons. Prostitutes are often infected with venereal disease, a recognized menace to public health. When they are arrested, they may be routinely isolated in jail for a period of time to determine

HOW OUR LAWS PROTECT PUBLIC HEALTH

■ Public health is protected by laws at all levels of government—federal, state, and local.

■ Federal laws guard the health of certain classes of persons, such as victims of poverty, and regulate goods moving in interstate commerce that affect the health of the general public. Federal authority also controls cigarette advertising and the sale of dangerous products and provides funding for state and local health programs.

■ State governments protect public health by setting up sanitary districts and boards of health throughout the state, delegating some of the state's authority to local governments.

■ The government has a special responsibility to prevent the spread of infectious diseases, and boards of health or other public health authorities can order dangerous articles to be disinfected or destroyed. They can also seize property or take persons into custody when necessary.

■ Health authorities have the right to demand that you be vaccinated to obtain immunity from certain diseases. State boards of health have long used this power to demand that public school children have diphtheria and other vaccinations. When vaccinations are mandatory, you may not refuse to comply simply because you think they are ineffective.

■ Public health authorities may order a person with an infectious disease to stay in his house and may permit no

one to enter or leave until the danger passes. A sign posted outside warns people away, and guards can be stationed at the door if necessary.

■ States keep records of births and deaths to facilitate public health and welfare programs. Death certificates help medical experts track contagious diseases and compile health statistics for each region.

■ Generally, a permit is required before a body can be buried, and it will not be issued before a death certificate stating the cause of death is presented to health authorities.

■ Collection and disposal of garbage is an important public health responsibility that is controlled by the law. Local health authorities must provide some reasonable program of garbage collection and disposal. The location and operation of dumps and landfills are also regulated, and usually their owners must hold licenses.

■ A municipality may build a sewer system and require every building in the community to connect with it.

■ Laws protecting public water supplies may require purification systems and chemicals—all of which are regulated and supervised by local health authorities.

■ Public health laws often provide a state or local building code, with different provisions for single-family residences, apartment houses, and commercial and industrial buildings. Most building codes require owners

to get a certificate of occupancy for every new or remodeled building.

■ Local authorities can fight dangerous conditions in a building by ordering repairs, closing the building down, or having it destroyed.

■ Building code provisions for dwellings generally require that premises be kept clean to reduce fire hazards and breeding places for vermin. They may also call for bathing and toilet facilities and adequate heat.

■ Local health authorities can order a *nuisance* (annoying condition) that endangers the public health to be abated, or eliminated, by the party responsible for it. If the party does not comply with the order, the health authority may eliminate the nuisance and charge the party for the expenses incurred.

■ A state has the right to govern businesses that affect the public health. For example, beverage manufacturing, blood banks, and junkyards are usually strictly controlled. Restaurants must pass sanitary inspections, and rest rooms in them must be placed away from dining areas.

■ The scope of public health regulation is broad. Health authorities have prohibited rock festivals until sanitation plans were filed; inspected migrant labor camps, nuclear facilities, and food-processing plants; required employees who handle hospital food to have regular physical exams; prohibited pay toilets; and regulated the sale of tobacco and cigarettes.

whether they are infected. But officials cannot assume that any likely person is a prostitute. A woman arrested for assault during a disturbance in a bar may not be quarantined for venereal-disease testing merely because the police believe that prostitutes frequent that bar. There must be some evidence that the woman has veneral disease or that she is a prostitute. Even then, the time and place of her detainment must be reasonable.

The place of confinement may be determined by the health authorities. A quarantine can be placed on the home of an infected person and trap anyone who just happens to be there—including family, visitors, or a delivery boy. Quarantine can also be appropriate in a hospital, clinic, or camp set aside to control a disease, such as tuberculosis.

A quarantine should last no longer than necessary to protect public health. The case of Jennie Barmore shows just how long this may be in some extreme cases.

EXAMPLE Jennie ran a boardinghouse in Chicago. In 1921 the department of health, finding that several of her roomers had come down with typhoid fever, nailed a large placard on the front of the house warning that a typhoid carrier lived there. Jennie was ordered to remain inside and to prepare food only for herself and her husband. No one was allowed to enter the house, as a roomer or otherwise, unless he was immune to typhoid fever. Jennie protested that she had never been sick with typhoid and that she was being unlawfully detained.

The court heard evidence that Jennie carried typhoid bacteria in her body, that she could be a carrier whether or not she had been sick with the disease, and that although her condition could clear up, even for years, it could recur. The court held, therefore, that the threat to public health was great enough to deny Jennie her liberty. It ruled the quarantine could continue as long as the emergency existed—in effect, for the rest of Jennie's life.

Quarantine is not a proved remedy because it is too difficult to enforce. Nevertheless, it is still used whenever there is a major outbreak of a deadly contagious disease, and the courts will uphold quarantines that were imposed reasonably and for good cause.

EXAMPLE In 1964 a man was quarantined in a California hospital for tuberculosis. He ran away and was subsequently arrested and convicted of violation of the quarantine. In 1966 a California appellate court upheld the conviction, finding that the California board of health's authority to impose the quarantine was valid.

■ **Birth and death** States keep records of births and deaths to facilitate public health and welfare programs. A birth certificate provides each of us with legal proof of our age. It affirms that we are old enough to get a job, marry, drive a car, or collect a pension or Social Security benefits. Death certificates help medical experts track contagious diseases and compile health statistics for each region. Usually, a physician who attends a birth or death must file a birth or death certificate with the department of public health, registrar of vital statistics, or county clerk.

The burial and transportation of DEAD BODIES are also circumscribed in the interest of public health. A burial permit is usually required. Generally, it will not be issued until a death certificate stating the cause of death is presented to the health authorities. The shipment of a dead body is often prohibited unless it is accompanied by a person who has a transit permit.

■ **Garbage** The collection and disposal of garbage is an important public health responsibility that is regulated by law whether the collector is a private company or a public employee. Local health authorities must provide some reasonable program of collection and disposal. The work may be done by public employees, by private contractors hired by local officials (usually on the basis of bids submitted), or by anyone who obtains a license or permit. Owners of apartment or office buildings can be ordered to collect garbage from all their tenants and put it out in a sanitary way for normal pickup by the city.

Other garbage rules may control outdoor cooking, refuse burning, burying dead animals, and disposing of decayed organic matter, such as leaves. Laws may also regulate the disposal of fat and bones from a meat-packing plant as well as dangerous industrial chemical wastes. The location and operation of dumps and landfills are regulated, too, and usually the owners must hold licenses.

■ **Sewage** Sewage disposal systems are needed to handle waste in residential areas. An individual home may be permitted to have a cesspool, but often its distance from the house, as well as its size, materials, and method of construction must comply with local law.

A municipality may build a sewer system and require every building in the community to connect with it. The expense to individual landowners is no excuse for failing to hook up, because a comprehensive sewer system protects the public health. Even an entire neighborhood that has a private sewer system can be ordered to abandon it and connect with the system serving the general public. Industrial users that flush huge amounts of waste into a public sewer system can be charged a higher rate than homeowners.

■ **Water** Protecting the common water supply is vital to public health. Local authorities often construct and operate water supply systems and prevent their pollution. Private springs or wells may have to be tested and found safe before they can be approved for use.

Laws protecting public water supplies may require purification systems and chemicals. Boating and swimming in bodies of water that supply water for a community are customarily outlawed, as is any activity that pollutes or gives the water a bad taste or smell, whether it endangers health or not. A law prohibiting swimming can apply to water within private land that flows into the public supply.

Although the primary purpose of regulating the public water supply is to keep water safe for drinking, health officials also use the water supply to combat disease. Because tooth decay is a common affliction of mankind, the prevention of cavities is proper. Therefore, many courts permit the fluoridation of public water supplies to help fight tooth decay.

■ **Building codes** A legislature may enact laws that improve unsafe conditions in buildings, even though these laws restrict the freedom of owners to enjoy their property. The legislature can also empower various administrative agencies to enforce health and safety rules for buildings.

Public health laws often provide a state or local building code. Different provisions may apply to single-family residences, apartment houses, and commercial or industrial buildings. A code generally regulates elevators, stairs, exits, windows, wiring and plumbing, materials and methods of construction, and lot and building size.

Certificate of occupancy Most building codes mandate owners to obtain a certificate of occupancy for every new or remodeled building. Finishing a basement, building a garage or an in-ground swimming pool, adding an extra bedroom, or putting up a fence may all be considered remodeling. Because local laws differ, you should check yours before undertaking any home building improvements.

A certificate of occupancy is proof that building inspectors found that all construction meets legal specifications. A contractor risks not getting paid if his work does not fit the requirements of law. It is important to have a certificate of occupancy if you decide to sell your property—a buyer will want the building to be legal in all respects. You can be ordered to pay a fine if you do not remove anything that violates building regulations.

Fire laws In most places, the building code includes fire safety regulations to protect the public from fire, smoke, and panic and to make fire fighting easier. Fire extinguishers, fire alarms, or sprinkler systems are usually required, the number of persons who can occupy a building may be limited, and the installation of oil burners and oil or gas tanks may have to be supervised by a fire official.

Fireproof materials, design, or construction may be specified in law—multistory buildings may be required to have fire escapes and heavy metal doors at their stairwells, for example. Owners of public buildings often have to post signs explaining how to leave the building in an emergency.

Those who violate fire regulations risk large lawsuits if anyone is injured, as well as criminal prosecutions. Usually the violator is the owner, but it may be a tenant if he has control of the conditions involved. When fire inspectors issue a certificate stating that the building complies with fire laws, it protects an owner if he is sued or charged with a criminal violation.

Local authorities can fight dangerous conditions in a building by ordering repairs, closing the building down, or having it destroyed. Before boarding up or tearing down a building, authorities should give the owner advance notice of their proposed actions and an opportunity to protest unless the condition creates an emergency.

Provisions for dwellings Building code provisions for dwellings generally require that premises be kept clean to reduce fire hazards and breeding places for vermin. They may also call for bathing and toilet facilities and adequate heat. Dilapidated dwellings or outbuildings can be ordered repaired or demolished. State and local authorities frequently enact special regulations for house trailers and trailer camps.

Multiple dwellings are usually covered by a host of special laws in addition to those for dwellings in general. These regulations may set minimum standards for fire protection, sanitation, light, and air. Courts balance the right of a landlord to make a profit on his investment and the need of tenants to be secure in their homes. A proper balance should encourage both LANDLORD AND TENANT to keep the property in good condition.

Multiple-dwelling laws regulate a variety of things that are important to the safety of the tenants. Stairways should be of a certain size and location and equipped with handrails and proper lighting. The door at the main entrance may have to be guarded or locked and equipped with a buzzer system that enables tenants to know who is at the door. Common areas such as halls, stairs, entrances, or garages should be clean and well lighted. A janitor or superintendent may have to live on the premises of a large building. Adequate heat, water, and bathrooms will be necessary for each rental unit.

Regulations for factories Many of the regulations on factory buildings are concerned with fire safety. Generally, a factory is any place where products are manufactured, repaired, or finished. The laws may differ for large and small factories or they may not apply unless more than a certain number of employees work in the building.

There must be enough exits, conspicuously marked and conveniently located. Storage areas must be kept clean and dangerous chemicals properly stored. Fireproof materials are often required by law in the construction of factory buildings. Doors must usually be kept unlocked whenever workers are inside. Under some statutes, buildings can be shut down for violations while owners or tenants can be fined or imprisoned.

■ **Nuisances** When local health authorities eliminate annoying conditions that endanger the public health they employ their power to abate NUISANCES. The courts will not supervise health officials as long as they do not abuse their authority. One limit to their authority is the public's right to a healthful environment. A board cannot, for example, allow a business to manufacture fertilizer from dead animals in a downtown area. The odors and unsanitary waste of such a factory have no place in a heavily populated area.

The owner of premises is responsible for keeping them free of nuisances, including any conditions that injure health. If local authorities discover such a nuisance, they may order its abatement, or removal. An order to abate a nuisance should specify a reasonable period of time for correcting it. If the owner does not comply, health authorities may act and charge him for the expenses incurred.

EXAMPLE In one case, the city itself was held responsible for
O←——* a public nuisance. Washington, D.C., permitted a landlord to operate an apartment complex for nearly 20 years without complying with the laws relating to licenses or public health violations. His low-income tenants had to live with rats, roaches, faulty plumbing, broken windows and locks, and poor service. Finally, the landlord stopped paying utility bills. The court found that the threatened cutoff of water, gas, and electricity endangered public health and ordered the city to pay utility bills until the problems were solved. The court noted that the city had the right to recover expenses from the landlord by way of taxes or fines and urged the city to take prompt legal action.

A person may sometimes argue against an order to abate a nuisance at a hearing. Or a court can issue an order to SHOW CAUSE—that is, the defendant can be ordered to appear in court and give reasons for not obeying an order to abate a nuisance—to remove junk cars from a suburban yard, for example. When a hearing is not available, anyone who wants to protest an order to abate a nuisance can bring a court action to stop health officials from enforcing it.

■ **Businesses and trades affecting health** Businesses, trades, and occupations that can pose a threat to public health are often regulated. Beverage manufacturing, blood banks, ice making, and junkyards are usually strictly controlled. Laundries, laboratories, massage and tattoo parlors, and tourist cottages or camps can be subject to special restrictions. It may be illegal to use certain materials in the manufacture of bedding or to sell unsanitary clothing, bedding, or furniture. These items must have tags disclosing their composition, and they usually have to be treated so that they resist fire or flames.

Plumbers and others involved in home improvement or service may also be regulated. Undertakers, embalmers, and funeral directors have to meet sanitary standards and are usually licensed. Restaurants must pass sanitary inspections and locate public restrooms away from dining areas. Barbers, beauticians, and cosmetologists usually must be licensed and keep their business premises clean.

States control the keeping of animals to insure their health—to control rabies, for example—and to protect the public from filth and odors. A board of health may require a permit to operate a hog farm and could shut down any business that keeps animals in an unsanitary way.

■ **Other public health measures** The authority of public officials should be flexible enough to stop dangerous conditions before they develop, and to supervise situations that are likely to create health problems. In the past, public health officials have

(1) Required licenses for cesspool cleaners.

(2) Prohibited rock music festivals until adequate plans for health, safety, and sanitation are filed.

(3) Inspected migrant labor camps, nuclear power facilities, and food-processing plants.

(4) Required employees who handle food or care for sick people to have regular physical examinations.

(5) Prohibited pay toilets.

(6) Regulated the sale of tobacco and cigarettes.

All public health laws and regulations state how they will be enforced. It may be through lawsuits between the offended and the offending parties; by public lawsuits brought by an attorney general, public health officials, or a government agency; or by the automatic imposition of criminal penalties such as fines or jail sentences for violators.

public interest Anything that can affect the rights of the general public. If, for example, a person or company receives permission from the government to use public property, and he is the only one that the public can deal with concerning the use of that property, his business is affected by a public interest, which requires him to deal with the public on reasonable terms. Public utility companies are invested with public interest, since they are usually the only ones with whom the public can deal to get essential services such as electricity. But a baker's business is not invested with a public interest merely because he makes products for sale to the general public.

public lands Traditionally, lands held by the United States, which could be sold or disposed of under general laws. These lands, frequently called public domain, were acquired in the early days of the country as a result of treaties made with foreign nations. For example, the territory now making up the southwestern portion of the United States was acquired as a result of the treaty ending the Mexican War in 1848. The federal government used public lands to encourage the growth of the country and economic development.

Although Congress had been vested by the Constitution with the power to control the use of public lands, the Department of the Interior was created in 1849 to handle these matters. It granted the states large tracts of lands, which the states in turn offered to qualified persons to encourage settlement west of the Mississippi. See HOMESTEAD. Railroads and industries were given tracts of land to stimulate the economy. Any lands not developed in this way or sold remained in federal ownership as public lands. Lands reserved for special government or public purposes were not considered public lands. The sites of the Capitol and the Executive Mansion in Washington, D.C., for example, were not public lands.

In 1946, the Bureau of Land Management was created as a branch of the Department of the Interior and given total responsibility for the management of public lands. In addition to disposing of parcels of public land under the general laws, it was given the authority to determine claims concerning the use of public lands—such as whether or not a person had the right to homestead, cut timber, mine, or graze cattle on public lands.

In the 1970's, the definition of public lands was revised to include any land held by the United States and administered by the Secretary of the Interior through the Bureau of Land Management. Only the lands on the Outer Continental Shelf and those held for the benefit of the Indians, Aleuts, or Eskimos are excepted. The new definition of public lands, unlike the traditional definition, may include lands that the Bureau of Land Management reacquired from a state or received from another agency, such as the National Forest Service. Not all federal lands, however, are public lands. National parks administered by the National Park Service, for instance, are federal lands that are not public lands.

Most of the nation's 450 million acres of public lands are found in Alaska and in 11 other western states—Arizona, California, Colorado, Idaho, Montana, Nevada, New Mexico, Oregon, Utah, Washington, and Wyoming. As a result of the recent emphasis on environmental protection, the Bureau of Land Management has developed programs designed to protect the ecological, scenic, and historical qualities of the public lands and their resources by applying principles of land-use planning. See ENVIRONMENTAL LAW.

public law 1 Law that is concerned with either the operation of the government and PUBLIC ADMINISTRATIVE AGENCIES (administrative law) or the relationship between the government and the people, such as CONSTITUTIONAL LAW and CRIMINAL LAW. Public law applies generally to the people of the nation or the state adopting it. It is different from PRIVATE LAW, which affects only individuals, groups, or corporations, such as laws governing CONTRACTS. 2 The original form in which certain federal and state laws are issued. For example, the federal Clean Water Act of 1977 was Public Law 95-217 (Pub.L. 95-217).

public policy A principle of law that holds that no person, business, or branch of the government can lawfully do anything that has a tendency to be injurious to the public or against the public good. Certain acts, such as having a court enforce gambling debts, are considered to be against public policy in some states. Public policy is the legal term for the common sense and conscience of the people applied throughout the state to matters of public morals, health, safety, and welfare. Because it is public opinion that has been recognized and applied by the courts, public policy may vary as the attitudes of the community change.

public service commission A board or commission created by the state legislature to supervise and regulate PUBLIC UTILITY companies.

public utility A business organization that regularly supplies the public with some needed commodity, such as ELECTRICITY, GAS, or TELEGRAPH AND TELEPHONE service. A business or enterprise must be invested with a PUBLIC INTEREST before it is considered a public utility. This means that the service it offers must be regarded as so essential to daily life that there is a public need for it and it must be supplied to the public as a whole.

■ **Rights and duties** When private property is devoted to public use in the business of a public utility, certain legal rights and duties arise between the utility and its customers. The utility must give the public reasonable and adequate service at reasonable rates without delay. The public has the right to demand and receive the best available service. On the other hand, the utility is entitled to be paid for its services by its customers. A customer's consistent failure to pay his bills may justify the utility's cutting off his service until all arrears are paid. If he has been constantly late in paying his bills, the utility may demand a deposit of money as security of payment. Service, however, must be provided to the general public without any arbitrary discrimination. A public utility cannot, for example, demand a security deposit from its black customers without requiring the same from its white customers.

■ **Regulation** A state has power, within reasonable and proper limits, to regulate and control public utilities operating within its borders. Public utility or public service commissions are created by state legislatures to regulate and supervise public utilities operating within their jurisdiction. They are PUBLIC ADMINISTRATIVE AGENCIES, which make and enforce rules and regulations. Their powers extend to the protection and enforcement of the rights and obligations both of the utilities and of the public. A commission's power does not, however, extend to the management of the business; it cannot substitute its judgment for that of the directors of the utility.

■ **Rates** A public utility is entitled to charge just rates for its product or service. The manner in which rates are set is specified by law. Usually, the company files a rate schedule with the public utility commission for its approv-

al, and changes of rates are often subject to review by public hearings or investigations.

public welfare 1 The prosperity, well-being, or convenience of the public at large, including the primary social interests of safety, order, morals, and economic interests. In order to promote the public welfare, a state may enact reasonable regulations on certain activities under its POLICE POWER. 2 In popular usage, government programs of financial aid for the needy. See WELFARE PROGRAMS.

puffing An expression of opinion or judgment that is not meant to be a statement of fact. For example, a statement by a real estate agent that a particular piece of property is a good buy at a named price is not a false representation but merely an expression of an opinion, and is nothing more than "puffing," or sales talk.

punitive damages Money awarded to the plaintiff in a lawsuit over and above what will compensate him for his injury or property loss. Such awards are designed to punish the defendant for his bad behavior or to make an example of him. See DAMAGES.

purchase money mortgage A type of MORTGAGE given by the buyer to the seller of land to secure the unpaid balance of the purchase price.

purge Clear a person from some charge or imputation of guilt. For example, "purging contempt" means clearing a person from contempt of court. It is generally done in return for an apology and the payment of a fee.

pursuant Done in accordance with or by reason of something. For example, "Pursuant to the authority vested in me by the state as justice of the peace, I now pronounce you to be husband and wife."

purview The part of a STATUTE that sets out its purpose and scope. It begins with the words "Be it enacted" and continues as far as the clause repealing part or all of an existing law. It is distinguished from the other parts of a statute, such as the title, preamble, and provisos.

putative Supposed or alleged. For example, a putative father is the alleged or reputed father of an illegitimate child. A putative marriage is one that is contracted in good faith but in ignorance (on one or both sides) that impediments, such as one party's being married or underage, exist to make the marriage unlawful.

pyramid sales scheme A popular name for *referral sales,* a scheme (generally frowned upon and illegal in some states) in which a buyer is offered a commission or a rebate on what he has bought in return for referring other buyers to the seller. See CONSUMER PROTECTION.

qua (Latin) "As"; in the character or capacity of. For example, "the trustee qua trustee is not liable" means that a trustee while acting in his capacity as trustee is not liable.

quaere (Latin) "Ask." When used in a reported case decision or elsewhere, *quaere* indicates that what follows poses a question or that the particular decision, rule, or statement is considered open to question.

qualification Some attribute, quality, property, or possession that a person must have in order to be eligible to fill an office or to perform a public duty or function. For example, attaining the age of 18 is a qualification that must be met before a person can vote. The possession of a certain amount of stock in a corporation may be a qualification for serving on its board of directors.

qualified acceptance In the law of CONTRACTS, a conditional or partial acceptance of an offer that proposes to change the terms of the offer in regard to the sum, time, mode, or place of payment. Because acceptance of an offer to contract must be unconditional, a qualified acceptance is not an acceptance at all but a counteroffer.

quash Overthrow; vacate; make void. In criminal law, the term is often used in connection with voiding an IN-DICTMENT. For example, if, after a person has pleaded to an indictment, a second indictment for the same offense is found, the court will ordinarily quash the first indictment.

quasi (Latin) "As if"; analogous to. The word is used in law to indicate that one subject resembles another in certain characteristics, but that there are intrinsic and important differences between them. A quasi contract, for example, is not an agreement between two parties, but because of circumstances the law imposes obligations on the parties as if they did have an agreement. If you go to a hospital for emergency services, and later refuse to pay for your treatment, you will be obligated to pay. Although you did not enter into a contract, the law will treat the situation as if you did in order not to have you get something for nothing.

When a PUBLIC ADMINISTRATIVE AGENCY, such as the National Labor Relations Board, is required to uncover facts, draw conclusions from these facts as a basis for official action, and exercise discretion in a judicial sense, it is said to act in a "quasi-judicial" character. Similarly, when an administrative agency makes rules and regulations it is said to be acting in a "quasi-legislative" capacity.

query See QUAERE.

quia timet (Latin) "Because he or she fears." In EQUITY practice, the technical name of a paper filed by a party seeking the aid of the court "because he fears" some probable future injury to his rights or interests.

quick assets Personal property that can easily be converted to cash, such as diamond or gold jewelry.

quid pro quo (Latin) "Something for something." The phrase means the mutual consideration (one thing in return for another) that passes between the parties to a CONTRACT and makes the contract valid and binding.

quieting title Confirming a person's title to (ownership of) real estate by establishing that other claims to it are invalid. Courts of EQUITY usually have authority over proceedings to quiet title—that is, to remove an existing cloud from title or to prevent a threatened cloud.

In general, a *cloud* is some outstanding claim or encumbrance that, if valid, would affect or impair the owner's title to his land. Because a cloud, even if unfounded, casts a doubt on the validity of the record title, the owner's interest is to have it removed. The purpose of a suit to remove a cloud (quiet title) is to decide the true status of the title and whether the adverse claims to it are valid.

■ **Existence of a cloud** In order to be considered a cloud on title, a claim must be backed by a seemingly valid CONTRACT for the sale of land, a DEED to the land, or some other legal document that appears to be valid. A merely verbal claim of ownership or assertion of rights to real estate does not amount to a cloud on title. The true test in determining whether or not a claim amounts to a cloud on title is: If the adverse party brought a lawsuit against the owner of the property, would the owner need evidence to defeat the adverse claim? If such proof would be necessary, a cloud exists; if proof would be unnecessary, no cloud is cast by the adverse party's claim.

EXAMPLE James Wiley has a document that he says is the deed to a piece of land George Less owns. The document appears to be genuine and George will have to produce evidence to disprove James's claim to ownership (say, by showing the signatures on James's deed are clever forgeries). Therefore there is a cloud on George's title to the land.

But if the deed that James flourishes as evidence of his ownership of George's property describes the land so vaguely that the deed is obviously void, then George does not have to produce evidence to disprove James's claim and there is no cloud on his title.

It does not matter whether the apparent defect in the title is great or small. If the claim is sufficient to cause a reasonable fear that at some time it may be asserted against the owner to his injury, then a court of equity will step in.

quit Leave; surrender possession of, as when a tenant quits the premises or receives a notice to quit his apartment.

quitclaim deed A DEED intended to pass any title, interest, or claim that the grantor may have in the property without professing that the title is valid and without containing any warranty or COVENANTS for title. The purpose of a quitclaim deed is to convey title without guaranteeing that no one else has an interest in the property. It is obviously not advisable to accept a quitclaim deed because your ownership might be doubtful.

quo animo (Latin) "With what intention." The term is sometimes used instead of the single word ANIMUS to mean design or motive. For example, the *quo animo* was the real subject of the investigation.

quorum The number of members who must be present to make valid the actions of a body, such as a court, legislature, or board of directors. The number is frequently a majority (more than half), but a larger or smaller number may be required.

quo warranto (Latin) "With what right"; a legal proceeding that tests someone's right to an office or a governmental privilege. An *information in the nature of a quo warranto*–the full name of the proceeding–is an extraordinary remedy by which a prosecuting attorney, who is a representative of the people, challenges someone who has usurped a public office or has forfeited an office to which he was entitled by neglecting or abusing it. Even though the remedy of *quo warranto* is, in most states, pursued by a prosecuting attorney, it is generally considered a civil rather than a criminal action. *Quo warranto* is usually the only proper legal remedy for testing someone's right to an office or privilege, unless the legislature has passed a law to provide other forms of relief.

Statutes describing *quo warranto* frequently list the situations in which it is the appropriate form of legal proceeding. In some of these situations, the charge is that the position claimed by the defendant does not exist for him.

EXAMPLE In one case, a county prosecutor had the power to appoint an assistant prosecutor, but instead he hired a special prosecutor whose investigations were independent of his office. A *quo warranto* proceeding determined that the special prosecutor had no authority because his appointment was not valid.

Other situations that call for *quo warranto* proceedings include the unauthorized practice of law, medicine, or dentistry or operating a liquor store, tow truck business, or collection agency without a necessary license.

Quo warranto proceedings have also questioned the right of a county commissioner, county treasurer, school board member, district attorney, judge, or tax commissioner to hold or exercise the authority of his office. In some states, *quo warranto* is the proper proceeding for challenging persons acting as officers or directors of business corporations.

Quo warranto cases sometimes question the qualifications of a person holding an office. A proceeding may be brought against an officeholder for accepting another office that is incompatible with the one he already holds or for failing to take an oath, file a required bond, or live within the district. A proceeding may also be brought to require forfeiture of the office for misconduct or because of conviction of a crime.

Generally a prosecuting attorney must institute *quo warranto* proceedings, but a statute may authorize a private person to do so. Unless a statute provides otherwise, a court must give permission to file *an information in the nature of quo warranto.* The court must exercise discretion in making this decision because *quo warranto* is justified only as an extraordinary exercise of power. It is not a right available just because the proper legal papers are filed. Good reason must be shown why the government–through the courts and the prosecutor–should interfere with the person holding the challenged office, privilege, or license.

race statute A law relating to the official recording of deeds, mortgages, liens, and other transactions concerning real PROPERTY, which states that the person who records his transaction first is given legal priority and protection over a person who records his transactions later. In states that have race statutes, if a landowner sells his land first to Adams and then sells it again to Benson, who records his deed before Adams, Benson's deed has legal priority and is good against Adams's deed.

radio See FEDERAL COMMUNICATIONS COMMISSION.

railroad A graded road laid out with parallel rails of iron or steel, along which cars are drawn by locomotives run by diesel, electric, or other power. The term "car" generally refers to a vehicle adapted to running upon the rails. The purpose of a railroad is to transport persons and property for the benefit of the general public. A railroad company is a public utility, which exercises the functions and performs the duties of a common CARRIER.

■ **Regulation** Maintaining and operating a railroad requires legislative permission. All public services performed by a railroad are subject to government regulation. The state or federal government may control the operation of railroads and the furnishing of incidental facilities, by direct exercise of its power, by legislation, or by a delegated board, commission, or municipality. The government may order improvements necessary for public safety, regardless of the railroad's financial condition.

Either a state or a municipality may regulate the speed of trains passing through its jurisdiction.

A train may not obstruct a traffic crossing for a greater period of time than is permitted by state law or local ordinance. However, any regulation about obstructing streets must be reasonable.

EXAMPLE An ordinance in Ohio making it unlawful for a railroad company or its employees to permit a train, locomotive, or car to block a public street for longer than five minutes was struck down as unreasonable because it contained no provision for circumstances beyond the control of the train operators.

■ **Liability** A railroad has a duty to exercise ordinary care to prevent injuries to animals. Ordinary care may require blowing a whistle or ringing a bell as a warning to animals. In some areas, such signals are required by statute. As a general rule, the people in charge of a train are obligated to keep a lookout for stock on or near the tracks. If they fail to do so and injury results, the railroad can be held liable for damages in accordance with the law of the state in which the injury occurs.

At all times, it is the duty of a railroad to exercise proper care in the management of its trains, in order to prevent collisions. A railroad is liable for injuries to passengers caused by an accident, collision, or in some cases malfunctioning equipment.

In general, a railroad must also maintain a crossing in a reasonably safe condition—not one, however, that will be safe under any possible circumstances. Maintenance of automatic signals at crossings is mandated by many statutes, and the public has the right to rely on them. When it is dark, a railroad must give some signal by light so that people at a crossing can see an approaching train. Although a railroad must exercise care commensurate with the hazards involved at a crossing, it does not insure the safety of persons approaching the tracks. Although it must take due care to avoid injury at a crossing, the railroad is usually entitled to the right of way.

The public, too, has a responsibility for its own safety. In going over a railroad crossing, for example, a motorist or pedestrian has a general duty to look and listen for approaching trains, and if his view or hearing is obstructed, to stop before crossing the tracks. Often, weather conditions require a motorist to stop before going onto a railroad crossing. See NEGLIGENCE.

■ **Passenger service** The Rail Passenger Service Act of 1970 was a national attempt to preserve and revitalize intercity railway passenger service as a necessary part of a balanced transportation system. Enacted by Congress because of declining passenger rail service, this legislation authorized the formation of a National Railroad Passenger Corporation, called Amtrak. It directed the Secretary of Transportation to establish a basic system of intercity passenger rail service for the whole country. The legislation permits a railroad to enter into a contract with Amtrak under which Amtrak assumes the entire responsibility for providing intercity passenger service. Most of the financial burden of providing the service is absorbed by the federal government through its financing of Amtrak.

The Regional Rail Reorganization Act—commonly called the Rail Act—was passed in 1973 to provide more efficient rail service in the Midwest and Northeast. The Rail Act authorized the creation of a new company, Conrail, which can take over the ownership and operation of financially troubled railroads. In essence, the Rail Act provides financing for railroads that would otherwise be forced to end their operations for lack of cash.

It is the declared policy of Congress to restore the financial stability of railroads in the United States. Its goal is for the railway system to provide energy-efficient, ecologically compatible transportation with effectiveness and economy. Congress has also established, in the Treasury of the United States, the Railroad Rehabilitation and Improvement Fund for the purpose of providing capital for maintenance, rehabilitation, and improvement of railway systems.

rape The unlawful carnal knowledge of a female by force and against her will or such knowledge of a female child under a specified age either with or without her consent. *Carnal knowledge* means bodily knowledge. It includes not only sexual intercourse but also the slightest penetration of the female's sexual organ by the male's. The *specified age*—the age of consent—varies from state to state but is usually 16 or 18 years. Carnal knowledge of a consenting underage girl is called *statutory rape.*

Ravishment has the same meaning as rape, but *seduction* does not. In rape the sexual act is committed by force and without the woman's consent, while in seduction the female is persuaded to consent—often by promise of marriage. Legally, a married woman can be raped but not seduced.

■ **Grades and degrees** Usually rape is classified as a felony, an offense punishable by imprisonment in a state prison. There are no degrees (of seriousness) of the felony of rape unless a law creates them. In some states laws divide the crime into degrees according to the circumstances under which the rape was committed—such as the age of the female in relation to the male, consent or lack of consent by an underage female, and the force or violence involved.

■ **Distinct offense** Although separate incidents of intercourse may constitute one criminal offense—for instance, an adulterous affair—rape is ordinarily not a continuous offense. Each act of carnally knowing a female under the age of consent, for example, is a new and separate offense, for which a separate indictment may be brought and prosecuted.

■ **Persons liable** Only a male who has sufficient mental capacity to form a criminal intent and is physically capable

and sexually mature can commit the crime. He need not be legally an adult (in most states 18 years old). A woman herself cannot commit rape under the law, but she can be guilty of rape if she is an accessory to a male who commits the act. Generally, a woman is not even guilty of statutory rape if she has sexual intercourse with an underage male. In 1978, however, a New Hampshire statute of this type was declared unconstitutional because it discriminated between the sexes by naming underage girls, but not boys, as potential victims. Soon after, New Hampshire passed a new law under which either a man or a woman could be guilty of statutory rape.

Under the law presently in force in most states, a man cannot rape his wife. A wife consents by marriage to have intercourse with her husband and her consent cannot be withdrawn. Only divorce revokes the wife's consent. Recently, however, a few states have passed laws providing that marriage is not a defense to rape. One husband brought to trial under an Oregon law of this type was acquitted by a jury in 1978.

■ **Victims** Rape can be committed on any female. Even an unchaste woman can be raped; her previous sexual conduct is neither a defense nor a mitigating circumstance.

Some statutes that punish a man who has carnal knowledge of an underage female with her consent also require her to be "of previous chaste character" or "of good repute"—that is, a virgin. Under these laws no conviction can result from sexual intercourse with an underage girl when it is shown that she was of previous unchaste character. A young girl's unchaste conduct after she was debauched by the defendant is immaterial.

The phrase "of previous chaste character" can be applied to a married woman who has never voluntarily had sexual intercourse out of wedlock.

■ **Elements of the crime** In common law and under many statutes, rape of a female above the age of consent requires three elements: carnal knowledge, commission of the act without the woman's consent or against her will, and the use of force by the man (implying a corresponding resistance by the woman). Although a general criminal intent is involved in the crime of rape, all that is required to demonstrate it is the commission of the acts that make up the offense. For example, when the female is below the age of consent, a man who has sexual intercourse with her is held to have had criminal intent to rape by the very fact that he performed the act.

Carnal knowledge The man must have carnal knowledge of the woman for rape to occur. Carnal knowledge means the actual contact of the sexual organs and an actual penetration of the female sexual organ by the male

---

IF YOU ARE A RAPE VICTIM

■ Do not hesitate to report the crime to the police and to press charges against the rapist.

■ Give the police any clothing you may have been wearing, especially if torn or stained.

■ Do not bathe before you have had a physical examination by a doctor, preferably in the presence of a female police officer.

■ Although a physical examination is not necessary, the physician's findings

can provide vital information to prove you were in fact raped.

■ Some states have adopted rape-shield laws that limit questioning in the courtroom about the victim's previous sexual activities.

sexual organ. There can be no carnal knowledge without penetration, but the sexual act need not be completed—the slightest penetration by the male sexual organ is sufficient. Generally, emission is not necessary to constitute rape.

Lack of consent Rape of an adult woman can be committed only without her consent or against her will.

EXAMPLE A young woman started a load of wash in her
○—* basement laundry room. When she went back upstairs, she encountered a wild-eyed man in her kitchen, holding her two-year-old daughter and muffling her cries with his hand over her mouth. The mother forced herself to speak calmly. She said, "Put the baby down. I'll do whatever you want." The man dropped the little girl, pushed the woman into a bedroom, raped her, and then stole money from her purse. Even though the woman cooperated as much as she could, she did not consent to have sexual relations with this man. Consent forced from the victim is no consent at all.

Sexual intercourse without consent also includes the inability of a woman to exercise any judgment about the situation, such as when she is intoxicated, drugged, asleep, or below the legal age of consent.

When the female is underage, the only material elements needed to constitute rape are carnal knowledge and the fact that the girl is under the age of consent. Some courts have held that the age of consent is reached on the day preceding the birthday that marks the statutory age.

Force and resistance The requirement that the carnal knowledge must be obtained without the adult female's consent or against her will leads naturally to the requirement that the intercourse be accomplished by force. The force and violence necessary in rape depend on the age, size, and strength of the parties. All that is necessary for the crime is enough force to overcome the female's resistance. It is not necessary for the force to be so great that it creates a reasonable fear of death or bodily harm.

EXAMPLE Two men picked up a young hitchhiker. They
○—* drove to a remote area in the country, threatened to kill her, and told her to remove all her clothes. Then they took turns ravishing her. The girl weighed only about 105 pounds, and both her attackers were bigger and stronger. Later at the trial, the defendants claimed that they could not be convicted of rape because their victim did not try forcefully to fight them off. The court disagreed. The girl had testified that she repeatedly told them "no" and begged them to let her go. She could hardly be expected to do more under the circumstances, so this was enough to show that she did not consent.

On the other hand, the female must offer some resistance. It must be real and active, not feigned, passive, or perfunctory. But a woman does not have to resist for as long as her strength endures or consciousness continues. The amount of resistance required depends on the circumstances, such as the relative strength of the rapist and his victim, the uselessness of resistance—for instance, if the rapist is armed—and the degree of force being used.

Incapacity of female When the ability to resist is overcome through the administration of drugs or intoxicants, sexual intercourse with the woman is rape, even though she may be conscious. When the drug or intoxicant cannot overcome the woman's power of resistance but is used merely to incite her passions, and the intercourse occurs with her consent, she has not been raped.

EXAMPLE A carload of teen-agers drove down to the river
○—* one night. Talk turned to sex, and one girl admitted that she was a virgin, saying, "I could never do that." The boys told her that if she drank beer with them she would be excited enough to try anything. After a great deal of drinking, the girl found that her restraint was overcome and she was unable to resist further. The next morning she was very upset and told her parents that she had been raped. However, this is not a case of rape even though the girl's determination not to consent was broken by alcohol. She was not forced to drink nor did she succumb because of a genuine fear of violence.

If the sex act involves a woman who is asleep or has fainted, it is rape; but if the woman is awakened by the act and makes no resistance, it is not rape. Sexual intercourse with a woman mentally incapable of consent because of idiocy, imbecility, or insanity is rape, but a woman with a lesser degree of intelligence than that required to make a contract can still legally consent to intercourse if she has sufficient intellect to know the nature of the act.

Threats or fear Usually, overcoming a woman's resistance and persuading her to have intercourse by threatening her is rape. Some courts have held, however, that the threats must create a reasonable apprehension of great bodily harm. For example, threatening to abandon a woman on a lonely road if she refuses intercourse does not constitute rape.

■ **Defenses** Usually, being too young or physically incapable of sexual activity is an effective defense to a rape prosecution. Under the common law, a male under 14 years of age is conclusively presumed to be incapable of committing rape. That rule has been followed in some areas, but elsewhere the rule has been modified by statute, and the fact that the accused is below 14, while raising a *presumption* of incapacity, can still be rebutted by the state. Lack of capacity because of physical impotency is a good defense against rape.

Neither the woman's consent *after* penetration nor her settling with the accused afterward or even marrying him is a good defense unless a statute provides otherwise.

It is not a defense that a man did not know the age of a girl under the age of consent or that he honestly believed she was over such age, nor does it matter if the act took place in a house of prostitution.

■ **Reporting a rape** The crime of rape was long the subject of false preconceptions. Women were thought to provoke rape or to desire it, for example. As a result, rape victims were often regarded as little better than the rapist and were treated badly by the police, in court, and even by their family and friends. But today the true nature of the crime, as well as the plight of the rape victim, is better understood, and law enforcement officers are being trained to handle rape victims with more consideration.

A woman who is raped should not hesitate to report the crime to the police and press charges against the rapist. Most police jurisdictions now have women on their staffs to deal with rape cases. Some states have adopted rape-shield laws that limit questioning in the courtroom about the victim's past sexual experiences.

Any woman who has been raped should take a few basic steps as soon after the rape as possible. First of all, she should report the crime to the police. She should not bathe, shower, or douche, as this may remove pertinent evidence of the crime from her body—such as evidence of the rapist's semen or blood. She should then have a physical examination, preferably in the presence of a female police officer. The examining doctor should take semen smears, record any bruises or other external or internal injuries to the victim's body, and give the victim a test for venereal disease. The physician's findings can provide vital evidence that rape has been committed. If the victim scratched the rapist during the attack, her fingernails should be examined for possible traces of the rapist's skin or blood. Finally, the victim should give the police the underwear she was wearing at the time of the attack and any other clothing she had on if it was torn or stained. The clothing may carry traces of the rapist's semen or blood or show that he used force. This evidence may help convict the rapist.

ratable   Capable of being appraised, assessed, or adjusted by some formula or percentage. *Ratable value* is appraised or assessed value.

rate   A charge, valuation, payment, or price fixed by a mathematical formula or according to a scale or standard. For example, a *rate of interest* is the ratio between the principal and interest. The buildings in a particular area of a city may be *rated* for insurance purposes according to their insurable qualities, such as age, condition, and use. The term is also used as a synonym for "tax."

ratification   The formal adoption or confirmation of something that has already been done by the person himself or by another. For example, a person can *ratify* an act or contract entered in his behalf by another person who at the time acted as his agent, even though he did not have the authority to do so.

Amendments to the U.S. Constitution are also subject to ratification. Whenever amendments are believed to be necessary, they can be proposed by a vote of two-thirds of both houses of Congress or by a convention called by the Congress at the request of two-thirds of the state legislatures. The proposed amendments must then be ratified either by three-fourths of the state legislatures or by conventions in three-fourths of the states.

ratio decidendi   (Latin) "The ground of a decision"; the principle of law on which the decision in a particular case is based.

> EXAMPLE John White and Fred Grey are walking together
> O—✻ when both men see a $100 bill lying on the sidewalk. White reaches the bill first and takes possession of it. Claiming that he saw it first, Grey demands the bill from White. White refuses and Grey sues him for the money. After hearing the facts of the case, the court decides that the money belongs to White. The principle on which the court based its decision—the *ratio decidendi*—is that lost property belongs either to the true owner or to the first person who finds the article and gains actual physical possession of it.

ravishment   See RAPE.

re   (Latin) "In the matter of"; concerning. The term is frequently used in designating judicial proceedings involving only one party. For example, "*re* Vivian" means "in the matter of Vivian" or "in Vivian's case."

real   Relating to (1) a tangible object, such as a document; (2) land and any structures built on it, as distinguished from personal (movable) PROPERTY.

real action   Traditional name for a lawsuit in which ownership or possession of land (real estate) is at issue.

real estate   See PROPERTY.

real evidence   Evidence furnished by things on view, as distinguished from verbal descriptions of them. Examples of real EVIDENCE are a weapon used in a crime and a jury's visit to the scene of a crime.

realized   Actual; cashed-in. Realized profit is a cash-in-hand gain, as distinguished from a paper profit, such as an increase in value of a stock, which could be lost before it is ever sold. See INCOME TAX.

real property   Land and whatever is growing, erected, or fixed on it, such as crops, buildings, and fences. In many areas, what constitutes real property is clearly defined by statute for tax purposes. Real property is also called real estate or realty. See PROPERTY.

reasonable   Just; proper; ordinary; usual; appropriate under the circumstances. A reasonable rate charged by a public service company, for example, is one not so low that it destroys the company's economic security and not so high that it is an unjust exaction from the public. Reasonable care in driving an automobile is the care that a prudent man would ordinarily exercise under the circumstances. See NEGLIGENCE.

rebate   Discount; reduction of interest on money loaned, in consideration of prompt repayment; deduction from a stipulated charge not credited in advance but returned after payment in full.

rebut   Dispute, defeat, or take away the effect of the other side's facts or arguments. In a civil TRIAL, a defendant in a lawsuit rebuts the plaintiff's charges when he proves them untrue.

rebuttable   Disputable; questionable. For instance, a rebuttable presumption is a conclusion that might be drawn by a court, but against which arguments can be raised by the defendant or plaintiff concerned. See EVIDENCE.

recall   Power of the people to remove elected public officials. Ordinarily an official who is not performing his duties to the satisfaction of the people is allowed to remain in office until the expiration of his term, at which time the people can replace him by electing a different candidate.

But in 12 states and a number of cities an elected officer can be removed by a special vote of the electorate before his term has officially ended. These states are Arizona, California, Colorado, Idaho, Kansas, Louisiana, Michigan, Nevada, North Dakota, Oregon, Washington, and Wisconsin. Some state constitutions set forth particular procedures for initiating recall elections, such as requiring signatures on voters' petitions.

recaption   Repossession. Taking back your borrowed lawn mower from your neighbor's yard is recaption of property that was not voluntarily returned to you.

receipt   Written acknowledgment by a person that money or something else of value has been placed in his possession; written confirmation of payment.

receiver   **1** An independent person appointed by a court to manage money or property during a lawsuit or other proceeding. **2** Under the common law, a person who holds and conceals stolen goods for thieves. This entry concerns itself with the first definition. For a discussion of the other, see RECEIVING STOLEN GOODS.

Under the laws of different states, receivers have been appointed in actions to remove a trustee, foreclose a mortgage, or dissolve a corporation, in divorce proceedings, and in creditors' suits. Appointing a receiver was considered justified when a trespasser was about to harvest and market a crop, when property in dispute was allowed to deteriorate to the point where emergency repairs were needed or when there was good reason to suspect that the property was going to be sold, wasted, taken out of state, misused, or destroyed if the court did not act to preserve it. A receiver can also be appointed when it appears that there is no person with a legal right to manage certain property or no mentally competent adult entitled to hold it.

Sometimes a receiver is appointed to preserve property during a lawsuit between two people who seem to have an equal right to use it but are unwilling to respect each other's interest.

EXAMPLE A man died and was survived by his wife and an
O—⋆ adult son from an earlier marriage. While a lawsuit sought to determine who was entitled to inherit what, the court appointed a receiver to supervise management of a small apartment building the man had owned, collecting rents and paying for utilities, repairs, and taxes.

■ **Appointment**   Courts appoint receivers to hold, manage, and preserve money or property subject to litigation so that it is not spent or disposed of before the court renders final judgment. The power to appoint a receiver is used sparingly by the courts, who exercise it only when it is necessary to preserve the property. Receivership is not only an extraordinary remedy, it is also a harsh one, because it ties up someone's property, takes it out of his control, and causes additional legal expenses.

Frequently, a creditor who has not been paid applies to the court for appointment of a receiver. In fact, he might even suggest a person to act as receiver. However, it is not proper to use receivership to coerce a party or to wrest control of a business from someone who has proved his ability to manage it.

EXAMPLE A company that had been manufacturing chil-
O—⋆ dren's playwear for 17 years had made steady profits every season. The owner then decided to start a new line of luxury items, such as genuine fur coats for toddlers. To enter this market, he had to hire a designer and invest in some new equipment and expensive materials. Sales during the first year the new items were offered were encouraging, but the start-up costs forced the owner into a financial bind. One month he had to choose between meeting his payroll and making payments to creditors. He paid his workers. One of his creditors became very nervous and asked the court to appoint a receiver to protect the assets of the business from risky schemes that could destroy it. The court refused, finding that an experienced and successful businessman is entitled to use his own judgment regarding expansion and he must be allowed to steer his company through a temporary period of insolvency.

The method of appointment and the powers and responsibilities of a receiver are generally set out in statutes. Appointment of the receiver is not the ultimate goal of a lawsuit but is only a provisional remedy while the suit is pending. Usually, a receiver can be appointed only after a lawsuit has been initiated.

A judge may appoint a receiver after an application is made or a petition filed with the court. In some cases, all persons interested in a case may join together to petition the court to appoint a receiver.

A receiver ordinarily should not be appointed until all interested parties are notified and a hearing is held at which a judge evaluates each side's case. However, on good evidence that an emergency exists, a judge may grant the petition for a receivership and hold a hearing as soon as the parties can be notified and prepare arguments.

■ **Duties**   A receiver takes control of all the property subject to the receivership, but he does not take title to (own) the property. A receiver cannot exercise control over property that is outside of the court's authority. Any property already transferred in a sham sale in order to cheat creditors is beyond the receiver's reach, but he does have the power to start a lawsuit asking the court to set aside the transfer. Any rights that other people have in the property continue to be valid. For example, if the property has been pledged as security for a loan, as in a mortgage, anyone who possesses the property can be legally compelled to turn it over to the receiver.

Refusal to comply or interference with the receivership may be punished as CONTEMPT of court.

EXAMPLE Judy knows her antique business is in trouble, but
O—⋆ her creditors are as yet unsuspecting. She approaches one of them, Nathan, who is also a friend, and tells him of her predicament. Judy asks Nathan to apply to the court for the appointment of a receiver and to nominate the receiver. Her intention is good—she hopes to have those creditors who are least well off financially get extra consideration. But her and Nathan's action may be collusion or fraud in the eyes of the law, for they are jeopardizing the interests of some of Judy's creditors.

A receiver does not represent the person whose property he administers; he is an officer of the court and must protect the interests of all parties. He must use his judgment, but

WHEN THE COURT APPOINTS A RECEIVER TO MANAGE PROPERTY

■ A receiver is appointed to manage property during a lawsuit—such as a divorce or a dispute over a will—when there is good reason to suppose that the property will be frittered away or otherwise diminished unless the court acts to preserve it. The law considers receivership a harsh remedy; therefore, courts are slow to use it.

■ During a creditor's suit against a small business a receiver may run the business and try to prevent it from going bankrupt.
■ Receivers are usually appointed only after all interested parties are notified and a hearing is held on the need for a receivership.
■ A receiver controls the designated

property but he does not own it. As an officer of the court, he must protect the interests not only of the person whose property he is administering but of all concerned parties.
■ If the receiver fails to obey the court's orders, neglects his duties, or abuses his authority, he may be removed and held financially liable.

---

his decisions must be reasonable. He can ask the court for advice when his duty is not clear, but if he fails to obey the court's orders, neglects his duties, or abuses his authority, he may be removed and held financially responsible.

EXAMPLE In one case a brother and sister inherited equal interests in a restaurant when their father died. The restaurant had been very successful, but it soon began to fail because of their inexperience in running it. The sister wanted to sell it, but the brother did not. While the matter was in the courts, a receiver was appointed. The sister resented her brother's opposition to selling the restaurant, so she began taking several cases of liquor from the restaurant every week and selling them to her friends. Because the receiver failed to discover this and stop it, he was later ordered to cover the loss himself.

A receiver may have to post a bond to insure the faithful performance of his duties. He must account to the court for all the property entrusted to him at regular intervals during his appointment and when his appointment is concluded.

■ **Compensation** A receiver is entitled to be paid for his services and to be reimbursed for his expenses. For example, when he needs an attorney's advice, he should be allowed counsel fees. The amount paid to him is determined from an itemized report of services that he submits to the court. His payment will depend on the nature, extent, and value of the property, the difficulties he has encountered, the time spent, and his skill, experience, diligence, and effectiveness. How and when the receiver will be paid is up to the court, but he cannot on his own take money out of the property he is managing and pay himself.

receivership A court order that places disputed property under the control of an independent person, called a RECEIVER.

receiving stolen goods Accepting and possessing property while knowing that it has been extorted, embezzled, or stolen. The property must have been taken by someone other than the accused. The value of the goods is generally important only in determining whether the offense is a misdemeanor (punishable by a fine or short prison term) or a felony (punishable by a larger fine or longer imprisonment). See CRIMINAL LAW.

The one receiving the stolen goods need not have hoped to benefit from the act. He need only have intended to aid the thief. Even receiving stolen goods while intending to obtain a reward for returning them is a crime. And paying

for goods known to be stolen is no defense to a charge of receiving stolen goods.

A person must have known the property was stolen when he received it in order to be convicted. Whether or not he had the knowledge is a question of fact that is answered according to the circumstances of the case. The jury decides that question. A jury is unlikely to believe a defendant's claim that he did not know the goods were stolen if he bought three televisions in one week from the same teenager for $5 each, for example. A person who answered an advertisement in the small local newspaper and bought a bicycle for $25, on the other hand, may very well convince a jury that he did not know the bike was stolen.

Authorities differ concerning whether a person can be convicted of receiving stolen goods from his or her spouse, but both can usually be convicted as joint receivers if one has not coerced the other. In many states, if a person is unable to explain his possession of stolen goods the presumption is raised that he received them illegally. See BURGLARY; LARCENY; ROBBERY.

recess A short interval during a court procedure in which business is suspended but not adjourned. The recess of a legislature is an interval between sessions of the same continuous group—but not between the final adjournment of one legislative body and the convening of a new one.

recidivist A habitual criminal; an incorrigible offender; one who makes an occupation of committing crimes.

reciprocal Mutual; bilateral; two-sided or two-way. Reciprocal wills are wills in which two people (often husband and wife) leave money or property to each other, usually upon mutual agreement.

reciprocity Mutuality; corresponding relationship. The word is used when two countries or two states give similar privileges to each other's citizens. See FULL FAITH AND CREDIT.

recital Formal preliminary statement, in a deed or other document, that explains the reasons for the transaction. The recital in a deed might state that the owner is selling his property for a specified amount of money.

recognition 1 Confirmation; acknowledgment that an act done by someone else in your name was authorized and done with your permission.   **2** In tax law, the point at which a taxpayer has received some financial gain is the time when the gain is recognized; the gain must be reported on his INCOME TAX forms and taxes paid on it.   **3** In international law, the formal acknowledgment by one nation of the existence of another as a separate and independent government or the formal acknowledgment by a nation of a state of war.

■ **Recognition of a nation**   The decision to recognize a new national government is a political act left to the judgment of the officials who are responsible for foreign policy—in this country the President. The President can recognize a country by making a formal announcement or by having another official—for example, the Secretary of State—make the announcement for him. One country can also recognize another informally by entering into negotiations or exchanging diplomats with it.

Recognition is more than a mere technicality. A state has no status among nations until it is recognized by other states. It may have all of the other attributes of a state—a definable territory and population, a recognizable government, and a certain amount of continuity or stability—but a nation is not really sovereign and independent unless other nations recognize its sovereignty. Recognition of a nation operates from the time it is given as if the state had always existed, and a new government can carry forward international projects started by the old government it replaces.

Several problems arise when a government is not recognized. An unrecognized government is not entitled to have its laws applied in international lawsuits or to participate in diplomatic negotiations. At different times, the United States has been concerned about the participation by North Vietnam, Cuba, East Germany, and mainland China in peace or trade negotiations because we did not recognize them as states.

EXAMPLE In a case decided in 1959, a group of Chinese people subject to deportation argued that the United States must send them to mainland China rather than to Taiwan. The government refused because the mainland was "occupied" by the then-unrecognized Communist regime. Taiwan, however, was a country to which the aliens could be deported under our Immigration and Nationality Act. The decision was consistent with the rule that a court will not make a judgment based on its belief whether or not a government *should* be recognized (that decision belongs to the President)—but only on whether it *has* been recognized.

■ **Recognition of warfare**   When a *state of belligerency* (warfare) is formally recognized, the law of war applies, with specific protections for prisoners and noncombatants. Thus a small group of radicals who blow up some public buildings may be treated like common criminals under the law of the country where the acts take place, whether or not their motives are revolutionary. But if a full rebellion breaks out and becomes recognized as a civil war, the rebels must be treated like prisoners of war.

Recognition of a state of belligerency is generally made by an uninvolved state that declares itself neutral. A neutral country can recognize a state of belligerency and carry on trade and diplomatic relations with nations on both sides of the conflict. See WAR.

recognizance   A recorded obligation, entered into before a court, in which a person promises to perform a certain act or follow a particular course of conduct. For example, a debtor may enter into a recognizance in which he agrees to pay money he owes.

In criminal law, a person found guilty of an offense can be required to enter into a recognizance by which he binds himself to keep the peace in the future. A person accused of a crime may be permitted to go free before trial without posting a BAIL bond if he gives the court a formal written statement declaring that if he fails to appear for trial, he will pay to the court a specified amount of money. This is a release *upon one's own recognizance.*

reconciliation   The renewal of amicable relations between two persons who have previously been at odds. Reconciliation usually implies forgiveness of injuries on one or both sides. If an estranged HUSBAND AND WIFE resume living together, they are said to have accomplished a reconciliation.

reconveyance   A transfer of land that may occur when a MORTGAGE is paid off and the property is returned to the mortgagor (property owner) free from the debt.

record   A written account of some act, transaction, or document drawn up under authority of law by a proper officer that is to remain as permanent evidence of the matters to which it relates.

A public record is a document filed with or issued by a government agency and open to the public for inspection. A deed (also called a title of record to land) and a marriage license are examples of public records. See Chart 3.

A court record is a formal, written account of a case, containing the complete history of all actions taken, papers filed, rulings made, and opinions written. The term "court of record" refers to all courts but those on the lowest level, such as some small claims courts, in which no permanent chronicles of proceedings are kept.

recoupment   Keeping back something that is due because there is a fair, just reason to withhold it; diminishing part of a claim upon which one is sued because of a COUNTERCLAIM arising out of the same transaction. Recoupment is the right of the defendant in a lawsuit to claim damages from the plaintiff because the plaintiff has not complied with some cross obligation of the transaction on which he is suing.

One of the more common examples of recoupment occurs when a railroad or airline sues a customer for unpaid shipping charges and the customer refuses to pay, claiming the shipper damaged his goods. In withholding an amount of money to cover the damage to the goods, the customer asserts his right to recoupment.

In everyday speech, recoupment also means getting back something that was lost, especially money.

recourse   The right of a person who holds COMMERCIAL PAPER, such as a check, to receive payment on it from anyone who endorsed (signed) it, even if the person who made it out in the first place (the maker) refuses or is unable to pay. When a check is *endorsed without recourse,* the endorser will not be liable to pay if the maker refuses payment. An endorsement without recourse is also called a qualified endorsement.

recovery The obtaining of money damages or other property by court order through a lawsuit brought for that purpose. Recovery also describes the amount finally collected or the amount of the judgment. For example, the recovery was $5,000.

recrimination A charge made by an accused person against the accuser. Recrimination is used as a defense in DIVORCE actions. It usually involves a countercharge of adultery or cruelty made by the defendant against the person suing for divorce. Traditionally, successful recrimination defeated a divorce suit. But in some states today, even when both spouses are at fault, the spouse committing the less serious act can be granted the divorce and, depending on the state, the economic benefits that go to the person who wins the divorce.

recusation 1 The process by which a JUDGE is disqualified or disqualifies himself from hearing a case because of interest or prejudice—for example, when his brother-in-law is on trial for stock fraud. 2 In some jurisdictions, recusation is the process by which potential jurors are challenged. See JURY.

redemption The buying back of property that has been mortgaged or pledged. See MORTGAGE.

redress Satisfaction or payment for injuries received. The *right to redress* is the right to go to court to obtain such payment or other reparation for a wrong.

reductio ad absurdum (Latin) "Reduction to the point of absurdity." The method of disproving an argument by showing that it leads to an absurd result.

reentry Resuming possession of real estate by a right that the person kept when he originally left the property. When a person gives, sells, wills, or leases real estate to another (the grantee), he might impose a condition on its use. If that condition is broken, he will be entitled to reenter the property, if so stipulated in the original agreement. Appropriate language in a deed, will, or lease transferring the interest in the land to the grantee establishes the right of reentry. Typical phrases are "provided that," "but if," "subject to the condition that," or "in the event that."

The right of reentry does not take effect automatically once the condition has been violated. The grantor must choose to exercise his right and take steps to enforce it.

EXAMPLE Adam, who owns a commercial building, leases it O⟵—⁕ to Bob for five years provided that if liquor is sold on the premises, he reserves the right to terminate the lease. Bob sells liquor on the premises. This alone does not end the lease. Adam must first decide to terminate it; then he must *act* to terminate it, perhaps by evicting Bob. Failure to act within a reasonable time after the breach may be interpreted as a waiver of the right.

The right of reentry may be exercised by either a grantor or his heirs. In the above example, if Adam died during the term of the lease and his son Carl inherited the property, Carl could enforce the right of reentry once the condition was broken.

The exercise of a right of reentry always results in a forfeiture of the real estate by the grantee. Courts do not favor the forfeiture of estates, so unless the language is so clear that the court cannot do otherwise, the right of reentry will not be recognized or enforced.

referee in bankruptcy Formerly a person appointed by the courts of BANKRUPTCY under federal law. His functions included taking charge of all administrative matters and preparing the questions for the judge to decide in bankruptcy cases. Under the new federal bankruptcy legislation, however, this position in the bankruptcy court has been eliminated.

reference The process in civil lawsuits by which a court appoints an authority to hear a complex question and determine the issue, or to take evidence and report his decision to the court. The case is said to be *referred,* and the person who handles it is called the *referee.* References usually occur when suits involve complex financial matters with intricate details requiring minute examination by someone with special expertise in the area. Frequently, a reference is ordered when the matter is so complicated that the jury cannot reach a fair and just decision until the matter is simplified.

A court has the power to refer a case to a referee when all the parties agree. This is known as a *reference by consent.* A *compulsory reference* can be granted when a party to an action asks the court to refer the matter. The court must be satisfied that the circumstances justify a compulsory reference, because a reference is not a matter of right.

When a referee acts in his judicial capacity, he is immune from civil liability even if he makes a mistake in a ruling, provided the mistake is an honest one.

A trial or hearing before a referee is usually conducted in the same manner as one before a court sitting without a jury. All parties to the action must be given notice of the proceedings and are entitled to attend. A referee has the power to compel witnesses to attend and produce books and papers as evidence. Although he is the exclusive judge of the weight and sufficiency of the evidence, he is always under the supervision and control of the court.

EXAMPLE Grayson rented a building from Lee and used it O⟵—⁕ as a warehouse. After a huge fire damaged the building and everything in it, Grayson sued Lee for the value of the property stored in the building, claiming that unsafe wiring and an inadequate sprinkler system that were Lee's responsibility caused his loss. The judge referred the matter because he knew that a great deal of time would be used taking proof of the items damaged and their value. The referee, however, found that it was Grayson who was responsible for the fire because he had stored barrels of what the referee knew were flammable liquids. The judge refused to accept the referee's report on the grounds that the referee had violated a rule of evidence. He was not entitled to base his findings on his own opinions of how flammable a particular substance is. He should have had the parties offer their own evidence to prove the point.

Following a hearing, the referee is usually required to make a final written report to the court. The report has no legal effect until the court confirms it or bases a judgment on it. If objections to the findings of the report are filed within a reasonable time, usually before the judgment is given, the court may review the report.

referendum

The submission of a proposed law to the voters for ratification. A state constitution may provide for a ratification vote in any of the following ways: (1) A ratification vote may be called for when a given percentage of the registered voters petitions for it. (2) Specific kinds of legislation may be automatically submitted to the vote of the people. (3) Measures proposed to the legislature by the people but not ratified by the legislature can be placed on the ballot and go directly to a vote. (4) The legislature may ask for voter approval or rejection of its actions through a referendum.

A referendum may also be involved in amending state constitutions. Amendments are submitted to the voters for ratification after legislative or convention endorsement.

referral sales scheme

See CONSUMER PROTECTION for a discussion of this shady business practice.

reformation

Reformation is a remedy used by the courts to correct, or *reform,* a written agreement to make it conform with the original intent of the parties to it. Such legal documents as contracts, deeds, mortgages, and trusts may be reformed.

The court will reform a document only if fraud or mutual mistake occurred when it was originally drawn up.

EXAMPLE For a number of years Steve has acted as a trusted financial manager for Bruce, an illiterate rock musician. Steve and Bruce agree to enter a contract increasing Steve's salary. Unknown to Bruce, however, Steve has inserted a clause in fine print by which Bruce gives him power of attorney. Bruce signs the contract. This document may be reformed, since it does not express the understanding between the parties. Steve fraudulently took advantage of Bruce's illiteracy by failing to disclose all the contract terms. Bruce is entitled to have the contract either reformed by the court to conform to the original agreement or rescinded (canceled as if it never occurred).

A mistake in the description of land and its boundaries usually justifies reformation of a contract when both buyer and seller intended that all or part of the seller's land be sold to the buyer. A mistake of law by which both parties to an agreement have misunderstood its legal effect may also result in reformation.

EXAMPLE Suppose Tim agrees to pay off the debt on Kate's mortgage on land she is selling to him. The contract of sale, however, does not cover this agreement, although both Tim and Kate believe it does. This is a mutual mistake of law about the legal effect of the contract. The contract may be reformed to include the originally intended provision that Tim will assume Kate's mortgage.

Reformation is not granted when it would result in an entirely new agreement or would impose unwarranted hardships. Only a person who has acted in good faith can apply to the court to have a document reformed.

reformatory

A state institution for the confinement of delinquents—children under a certain age (usually 16) who have violated the law or failed to obey the reasonable orders of their parents, guardians, custodians, or the court. Reformatories are intended both to punish crime and to rehabilitate delinquents, making them law-abiding citizens through educational and vocational training. Reformatories are also called houses of refuge, state vocational institutions, reform schools, juvenile correction centers, and industrial or training schools.

A state's authority to establish and maintain reformatories rests on the state's sovereign power as PARENS PATRIAE (parent of the country) to protect the welfare of children within its borders by removing them from harmful environments and placing them in institutions where their development will be supervised. Thus, reformatories are usually not considered prisons. Yet in some states they are part of the prison system and facilities are shared with adult inmates. For a discussion of juvenile delinquents, see INFANT.

refreshing memory

The act performed by a WITNESS when he consults documents, memoranda, or books to bring more distinctly to his recollection the details of past events or transactions about which he is testifying. The witness, however, may not rely entirely on such materials or read directly from them while testifying. He must be able to testify to the facts from a present and independent recollection—his "refreshed memory."

EXAMPLE Raymond was called as a witness in a case and asked if he had seen the defendant, Emily, on the 15th of October the year before. Raymond replied that he did not remember, but indicated that he might be able to refresh his memory by consulting his records. He was then allowed to do so, and found an entry in his diary indicating that he was to spend the weekend of October 14 to 16 with Emily at the Ritz Hotel. He also found a canceled check in his records showing that he had paid for a room at the Ritz for that weekend. This served to prod Raymond's memory of his weekend with Emily and helped him fix the dates of that weekend. After consulting his records he was able to testify that he had seen her, based on his own independent memory and not based only on his records. Later he was asked if he had seen Emily the following weekend. Even though he had a letter from her referring to their meeting then, he had no independent recollection of that meeting. His memory was not refreshed and the letter could not be used to make Raymond admit that he met with Emily on the second weekend.

refunding

Returning money in restitution or repayment; also refinancing or borrowing money done by a company, usually through the sale of bonds, in order to pay off an existing loan with the proceeds.

register

1 Record certain information on a list or in the public records as required by statute—for example, register a trademark with the U.S. Patent Office in Washington, D.C., or register to vote.

2 As a noun, the name given to a book of public facts, such as births, deaths, and marriages. *Registry* is another name for a book of public records. Register can also refer to the public official (also called *registrar)* whose job is to maintain these records.

register of deeds   The title given in some states to the officers who record deeds, mortgages, and other documents affecting real estate in the official books kept for that purpose. They are sometimes called the *recorders of deeds.*

registrar   The public officer whose job involves keeping and maintaining public records—for example, the registrar of voters.

registration   **1** Enrollment, such as the registration of voters.   **2** Recording or making entries in an official register, such as the registration of the names of the owners of stock in the official books of a corporation, the registration of the names of weapons owners in a register maintained by the police department, or the registration of motor vehicles with the state motor vehicle department.

registration of land titles   Systems established in some states by laws commonly called Torrens Acts (after Sir Robert Torrens who developed the idea), in which landowners and the lands they own are officially registered so that the ownership of land can always be readily determined by consulting the public records. The reasons for registering land titles are to simplify real estate transactions and to insure that a person buying land actually gets what he paid for—complete ownership of the land.

Registering land does not have the same legal effect as recording a DEED. You cannot buy registered land without following the registration procedure. But you can buy land without recording the deed. It would, however, be unwise to do so. Whoever sold you the property could sell it to someone else the next week. If the second buyer proves that you did not give notice to the world that you were the owner (by recording the deed), he can keep the land.

Once land is registered, it cannot be sold just by transferring ownership by deed; the sale must be registered as well. If the land is not registered, it can be sold by simply transferring ownership by deed.

Unlike the records of DEEDS, which are filed with the county clerk's office, registration of land titles is initiated when an owner files an application in court to have his title to (ownership of) the land registered.

As a general rule, any title that gives a person complete ownership in the land, such as title by ADVERSE POSSESSION or PRESCRIPTION, must be registered. All persons claiming any interest in the land must be notified of the proceedings so they have an opportunity to make their claims.

Anyone seeking to be registered as the owner of the land must show that he has good title "as against the world," but he need not be in actual possession (custody) of the land. For example, Nick owns a 200-acre farm, which he rents to Sam. The registration of the title to the farm will show Nick as owner, even though Sam has actual possession of it.

Once title to land is established to the court's satisfaction, the court will issue a decree to settle and declare title. The decree must be entered in the records of the court and is conclusive regarding the rights of ownership and the area and boundary lines of the land. Once the decree of registration has been entered, a designated officer—usually called the *registrar of titles*—makes and registers the original certificate of title in the proper register. He must make and deliver a duplicate of the certificate to the registered owner. After this procedure has been completed, the land becomes registered land. Any subsequent transfers and dealings regarding it must be made according to statute.

Some states have not substituted the registration for the deed recording system because of the former's restrictions. For example, you cannot sell registered land without giving the buyer your duplicate copy of the original registered certificate of title. If you cannot find it, you must go to court and prove that you are the owner of the land, a time-consuming and costly procedure.

regressive tax   A tax with a rate that decreases as its base (the income of the taxpayer) increases. Generally, a regressive tax charges everyone the same amount regardless of his or her income, and consequently places a heavier burden on low-income groups. For example, if every taxpayer is made to pay a tax of $100 a year, a person with an annual income of $50,000 is paying a tax equal to only .02 percent of his income, while a person with an annual income of $10,000 a year is paying a full 1 percent of his income. The most common type of regressive tax is a sales tax. A regressive tax differs from a *proportional tax,* in which the tax rate increases proportionately with the taxpayer's income, and from a *progressive tax* (such as income tax), in which the tax rate increases with the taxpayer's income, but at a more rapid rate.

regular   **1** Steady; uniform; with no unusual variations.   **2** Lawful; legal; in conformity with usual practice.

regulation   A rule or order enacted by a PUBLIC ADMINISTRATIVE AGENCY to supervise and control the operation of a business that affects the general public. Both federal and state agencies establish regulations and enforce them for the protection of society. For example, the federal Environmental Protection Agency enacts regulations to control the environmental effects of business on life, and the Equal Employment Opportunity Commission develops regulations to prevent discrimination in hiring employees.

rehabilitation   The restoring of former rights, abilities, or authority. Rehabilitating a witness means restoring his or her credibility or believability after the other side has put it in question. Rehabilitating a prisoner means equipping him for an honest, productive life once he is released from prison.

reinstate   Reestablish; place back in a condition that has ended or been lost. To reinstate an insurance policyholder who has allowed his policy to lapse, for example, means not issuing a new policy but restoring to the insured all the benefits accruing to him under the original policy.

reinsurance   A contract by which one INSURANCE company shares the premiums and the losses with other insurance companies in connection with a risk to protect itself against all or part of the risk. Marine insurance is a typical subject for reinsurance; so are the life and health of a major movie star while he or she is filming a multimillion-dollar production.

EXAMPLE On July 19, 1979, the oil tanker *Atlantic Empress* collided with another vessel, and on August 2 it sank with a cargo of 270,000 tons of crude oil, worth some $45 million. The cargo had been insured by its owner, Mobil Oil Company, with Bluefield Insurance Ltd. Because no one company could bear such a loss, Bluefield had assumed part of the risk and had shared the rest with several reinsurance companies throughout the world. When a final settlement is made, costs will therefore be paid by a number of companies.

relation   1 A relative or kinsman.   2 The connection of two persons associated by birth, by law, or by their own agreement in some type of union for purposes of domestic life. Guardian and ward, husband and wife, and parent and child are relations.   3 The legal nai. e given to a retroactive effect, usually applied where several proceedings are essential to complete a particular transaction. For example, the last proceeding that completes a sale of real estate is considered for certain purposes to take effect *by relation* as of the day when the first proceeding took place.   4 The *doctrine of relation* is a legal principle by which an act done at one time is considered to have been done earlier.

EXAMPLE Most states consider a child illegitimate if his parents were not married when he was born, but that same child is considered legitimate if his parents later marry. The doctrine of relation makes the child legitimate from the date of his birth even though the marriage making him legitimate took place after his birth.

release   A contract by which a person, the *releasor*, agrees to give up a claim or right to someone against whom it could legally be enforced. A *general release* covers all claims between the parties that exist or are contemplated at the time the release is executed. A *specific release* is confined to particular claims that are specified in it.

■ **Requirements**   No particular form or set of words is necessary in a release as long as the contract is complete and the intention of the releasor is clear. Releases need not be in written form unless required by statute.

To be effective, a release must be supported by a sufficient consideration—that is, in exchange for giving up a legal right or claim that he has, the releasor must receive something of value.

EXAMPLE Suppose Alice is hit by a speeding car, and the driver jumps out of the car and asks her to sign a release without offering her anything in exchange. The release would be legally ineffective if Alice signs it, because she would be giving up her claim for injuries that she suffered and not receiving anything in return. If, however, Alice received $50 for signing the release and later had to pay $500 worth of medical bills for her injuries, the release would still be valid because she had been given something of value, even though it was not enough to cover the expenses caused by her injuries.

Consideration may take various forms. Payment to an employee for time lost from his job because of an injury for which his employer is liable for damages—such as an injury received while delivering the employer's goods—is valid consideration in exchange for a release of his claim for damages. Repossession of an automobile in exchange for releasing or discharging the buyer from the balance of the debt is also good consideration.

■ **Validity**   The validity of a release is determined in the same way as that of other CONTRACTS. A voluntary release obtained for a consideration from a person capable of understanding its full force and effect is valid. A person signing a release has the duty to read it before signing it, and cannot have it set aside because he failed to do so or because the bargain was unwise or a hard one.

If the two parties who sign a release both mistake certain pertinent facts regarding it, the court may or may not consider it valid, depending on the circumstances. For example, a mistake concerning the probable side effects of an injury, the quickness of recovery, or the permanent nature of a known injury will not in itself cause the release to be voided. To determine whether a release was executed under a mutual mistake—and whether that mistake is ground for invalidating the release—all of the circumstances relating to it must be considered, including the sum paid for the release, whether the question of liability was in dispute at the time of the settlement, and ignorance of crucial facts.

EXAMPLE In one case, Gus, an old man who was unable to
read or write English, was hit by a car and taken
to a hospital. After a brief examination, Gus—confused
and disoriented—left the hospital against the doctor's
wishes, insisting that he could cure himself. Two days
later, an adjuster from the driver's insurance company,
accompanied by Gus's neighbor, who acted as an interpreter, negotiated a release by which the old man accepted $300 in exchange for his signature. Four days later,
Gus was back in the hospital suffering from internal
injuries caused by the accident—injuries that required an
operation. The court set aside the release because it was
based on the mutual mistake of Gus and the insurance
company about the existence of his injuries.

An innocent misrepresentation by the person seeking a
release—but one that the releasor is meant to rely upon—can
cause the release to be set aside.

EXAMPLE Ted slipped on a wet floor in a department store
and injured his foot. The store's physician examined Ted and told him that he had a slight sprain. Relying
on the diagnosis, Ted signed a release with the store in
exchange for $500. But Ted's injury proved more serious
than innocently misrepresented by the physician, who
had no experience dealing with foot injuries. Although
the doctor had no intent to deceive, Ted would not be
held to the release because he signed it on the basis of the
misrepresentation. He could accept the $500 or negotiate
a new release.

When fraudulent representations are made by the person
seeking a release and are relied on by the releasor, who
gives up the claim for his injury, the courts will invalidate
the release. For example, if an insurance adjuster lies about
the cost of damage to your property and persuades you to
sign a release for a fraction of the money it will cost to
repair the damage, the release will be set aside for fraud.

■ **Tort law**   In common law, when a person who has
been injured by two or more persons acting wrongfully
together (called *joint tort-feasors*) signs a release naming
even one of the defendants, he gives up his claim against the
other defendants as well, unless he specifically reserves his
rights against them in the release. This rule unfairly forces
the injured party to give up his entire claim against all tort-
feasors without necessarily being fully compensated.

Very few states still apply this rule. The majority now
allow a plaintiff to continue his lawsuit against the remaining joint tort-feasors after he has released one of them from
liability unless he has intentionally surrendered his claim or
has been completely compensated. An agreement to surrender claims is known as a *covenant not to sue*. When a
plaintiff signs such an agreement, he does not entirely give
up his lawsuit but merely agrees not to enforce his claim
against a particular joint tort-feasor.

relevancy   The applicability of EVIDENCE to an issue
in a civil lawsuit or a criminal case. Evidence is relevant if it
proves or disproves a theory or position that will influence
the outcome. Evidence must be relevant to be admitted
(accepted) by the court.

relief   1 The financial assistance provided to poor people by the government.   2 The help given by a court to a

person who brings a lawsuit. The relief asked for might be
the return of property taken by another or the enforcement
of a contract.

religion, freedom of   A constitutional guarantee
that all Americans are free to follow the religion of their
choice or none at all.

*" Congress shall make no law respecting an establishment
of religion, or prohibiting the free exercise thereof. . . ."*

With these few words, the first in the Bill of Rights, the
Founding Fathers prohibited the U.S. government from
supporting a religion or from establishing a state religion—
that is, from forcing anyone to attend or support any
religious institution or to believe in its teachings—and protected the individual's right to worship as he pleases.

■ **Religion in the Colonies**   Because of the variety of
religions found in America today, freedom of religion is
often taken for granted, but to the founders of our country
it had overwhelming significance. Many early settlers came
here from Europe to escape oppression from laws that
forced them to support and attend government-favored
churches. In the centuries immediately before and during
the colonization of America, turmoil, civil strife, and perse-
cutions prevailed in many countries because established
sects were determined to maintain their absolute political
and religious supremacy. Men and women were fined,
jailed, tortured, and even killed in efforts to force unques-
tioning loyalty to whatever religious group happened to be
in favor with the government at the time. People suffered
severe punishment for failing to attend government-estab-
lished churches, expressing nonbelief in the churches' doctrines, and failing to pay taxes and tithes to support the
churches.

Such Old World practices were transplanted to the
American Colonies. The English crown's land-grant
charters, for example, stipulated that religious establishments be erected, which all people, whether believers or
not, had to support and attend. Dissenters were forced to
contribute to government-sponsored churches whose ministers preached hatred against them. Against this background, colonists who longed for a government guarantee
of religious liberty realized it could only be achieved by a
government stripped of all power to tax, support, or otherwise assist any or all religions, or to interfere with the
beliefs of any religious individual or group.

In the late 1700's, Thomas Jefferson and James Madison
opposed an attempt by the Virginia legislature to renew a
tax levy supporting the established Anglican Church. In
their writings they argued that true religion could survive
without the buttressing of law and that no person should be
taxed to support any religious institution. The best interest
of a society required that the minds of men always be
wholly free. Later, they incorporated those powerful, and
then revolutionary, ideas into the U.S. Constitution.

■ **What constitutes a religion**   Before it can be decided
whether or not an action of the government violates a
person's right to freedom of religion, a very basic question
must be answered: What qualifies as religion or religious
activities? To our forefathers, the answer was simple. The
First Amendment mandate was against an established
church as it had been known in England and most of the

Colonies. The drafters of the Bill of Rights, however, did not restrict the prohibition to any specific form of state-supported religion. The use of the word "religion" without any qualification made the constitutional provision sufficiently flexible to meet the challenges of time and change.

Supreme Court views   The Supreme Court, too, has avoided a pat and precise definition of what constitutes religion. According to the Court, religion is not limited to conventional faiths such as Baptist, Catholic, or Jewish. In determining the religious nature of a belief, the Court has applied a standard that has proved responsive to society's search for new ideas and philosophies: A *religion* is a sincere and meaningful belief occupying, in the life of the person who holds it, a place parallel to that filled by God for adherents to traditional Western religions.

A belief in the existence of God is not necessary in order for the religion or religious concept to be protected by the Constitution. For example, Buddhism, Taoism, Ethical Culture, and Secular Humanism are religions that do not propound a belief in the existence of God, but all are entitled to constitutional protection. What is more, a belief need not be stated in traditional terms. Scientology is a system of belief that holds that man is essentially a free and immortal spirit who merely inhabits a body. It does not propound the existence of a Supreme Being or essence, and it disavows mysticism and supernaturalism. Scientology qualifies as a religion under the broad definition of the term. The belief in an ultimate universal principle, being, essence, entity, or field of life on which the universe is based is sufficiently similar to the belief in God to establish, under the law, the religious nature of the concept.

Religious activities   An activity may be religious even though it neither is a part of nor derives from a sect recognized by society. The Supreme Court has ruled that a nondenominational prayer said daily in a public school classroom is considered a religious activity, even if the prayer is not composed by a religious group.

EXAMPLE The Court labeled as religious a poem that a
O+——* kindergarten teacher had her class recite prior to their morning snack:

> *We thank you for the flowers so sweet:*
> *We thank you for the food we eat;*
> *We thank you for the birds that sing;*
> *We thank you for everthing.*

The Court claimed that the word "you" referred to a deity and that recitation of the poem thus constituted a religious activity.

Sham religions   Although the definition of religion includes many unorthodox and non-Judeo-Christian faiths, it does not encompass shams that clearly lack any religious sincerity and were created to protect illegal or antisocial behavior.

EXAMPLE A defendant was indicted for illegal possession of
O+——* marijuana and possession and sale of LSD. She claimed that she was an ordained minister in the Neo-American Church, which taught that the drugs were the true host and should be taken regularly by its members. The court refused to recognize the Neo-American Church as a religion, since the tenets of the church did not express adherence to ethical standards and a spiritual discipline.

Disruptive antiauthoritarian political movements, which mock established institutions and operate under the guise of religion are not entitled to constitutional protection either. For example, a prisoner who claimed to be "called" to free all prisoners and destroy the prison system could not be granted freedom-of-religion protection for those beliefs because they would not qualify as religious. For a full discussion of freedom of religion in relation to prisoners, see PRISONERS' RIGHTS.

FREEDOM OF RELIGION—RIGHTS AND LIMITATIONS

■ Freedom of religion is guaranteed in our Bill of Rights: "Congress shall make no law respecting an establishment of religion, or prohibiting the free exercise thereof. . . ."

■ No one can require you to take an oath declaring belief in God as a condition for holding public office.

■ States may reimburse parents of children attending parochial schools for the cost of bus transportation and, in some cases, textbooks. But the Supreme Court has ruled against direct aid to parochial schools.

■ Prayers may not be recited in public schools.

■ Released-time programs for classes in religion are constitutional so long as the classes take place outside public school buildings.

■ A school cannot require your child to salute the flag if doing so is contrary to his religious belief.

■ Sunday closing laws have been upheld by the Supreme Court because of the state's need to provide the same day of rest for all workers.

■ If you adhere to a religion whose Sabbath falls on a day other than Sunday, the state cannot deny you unemployment benefits because you refuse to work on your Sabbath day.

■ Even if your religion forbids inoculations, your child may be compelled to take certain ones before attending school—public-health reasons outweigh freedom of religion in this case.

■ The issue of compulsory blood transfusions remains unsettled, but courts may order them because of the state's interest in its people's health and safety.

■ In some cases, when a patient was unmarried, with no minor dependents, and steadfastly refused a transfusion on religious grounds, the court has not forced it on him.

■ In cases where the state shows a compelling reason to establish the true cause of a death, the government may insist on an autopsy even though it violates the religion of the family of the deceased. If there is no compelling reason, the family's religious practices must be respected.

■ The constitutional guarantee of freedom of religion does not protect you from the private influence of individuals. For example, if your aunt's will requires you to give up your church and join hers in order to inherit from her, you must comply or forfeit your status as beneficiary.

Challenging beliefs Once certain beliefs are determined by the courts to be religious, their basis in reality cannot be challenged.

EXAMPLE A defendant was convicted under federal law for
O—➤—✳ using the mails to obtain money by false representation about his religious group. He had solicited funds for the "I Am" movement, asserting that he had been chosen as the divine messenger who had the power to heal incurable diseases. He also claimed to have talked with Jesus and said he would transmit these conversations to mankind.

The Supreme Court reversed the conviction, ruling that the First Amendment of the Constitution barred the prosecutor from submitting to the jury the question of whether these religious beliefs were true. "Men may believe what they cannot prove. . . . Religious experiences which are as real as life to some may be incomprehensible to others. . . . If one could be sent to jail because a jury in a hostile environment found these teachings false, little indeed would be left of religious freedom."

■ **Constitutional provisions** The U.S. Supreme Court has settled cases concerning church and state and freedom of religion through its interpretations of the First Amendment provision that "Congress shall make no law respecting an establishment of religion, or prohibiting the free exercise thereof." The first part of this provision has become known as the *establishment clause,* the second—the *free exercise clause.*

The 14th Amendment has made the 1st Amendment's guarantee of religious freedom binding on state governments as well. The 14th Amendment provides, in part, that no state shall "deprive any person of life, liberty, or property, without due process of law." The Court has interpreted this *due process clause* to mean that the states cannot interfere with the rights and liberties guaranteed by the Bill of Rights, including the right of freedom of religion. Religious freedom is a liberty the states cannot take away without DUE PROCESS OF LAW.

Finally, Article VI, Clause 3, of the Constitution states that "no religious Test shall ever be required as a Qualification to any Office of public Trust under the United States." This provision applies only to the federal government, but state constitutions and statutes, along with the guarantees of the First Amendment, prohibit states from imposing an oath declaring a belief in God as a condition to holding public office.

■ **The establishment clause** The establishment clause absolutely prohibits the government from interfering with the beliefs you hold or forcing you to profess belief in certain ideas. The federal government cannot enact laws aiding one particular religion or all religions or establishing an official government religion, such as the Church of England. Neither may the government show a marked preference for no religion, since that would, in effect, establish nonbelief as the government position.

The meaning of the establishment clause has been enunciated by the Supreme Court in cases dealing with public financial assistance to church-related institutions (mainly parochial schools) and religious practices in the public schools and other arms of the government. The Court has developed a three-prong test to determine whether a statute violates the establishment clause. A statute is constitutional as long as (1) it has a secular purpose, (2) its primary effect neither advances nor inhibits religion, and (3) there is no "excessive entanglement" with religion.

Aid for parochial school buses One of the earliest cases in which the establishment clause was defined came before the Supreme Court in 1947. It involved providing limited financial support to the parents of school-age children for secular expenses related to their education. A New Jersey law authorized reimbursing parents of schoolchildren for the cost of bus transportation to and from schools that were not operated for profit, including private and parochial schools. A taxpayer challenged the law as unconstitutional because it reimbursed parents of children attending parochial schools, where they received religious instruction.

The Supreme Court upheld the law as constitutional.
❝ The Establishment of Religion Clause of the First Amendment means at least this: Neither a state nor the Federal Government can set up a church. Neither can pass laws which aid one religion, aid all religions, or prefer one religion over another. Neither can force nor influence a person to go to or remain away from church against his will or force him to profess a belief in any religion. . . . Measured by these standards, we cannot say that the First Amendment prohibits New Jersey from spending tax-raised funds to pay the bus fares of parochial school pupils as part of a general program under which it pays the fares of pupils attending public and other schools. ❞

States are permitted to provide many services to church schools, such as police and fire protection, connections for sewage disposal, public highways, and sidewalks.

When dealing with issues concerning the religious guarantees of the First Amendment, there is always a matter of degree. There will always be some minimal contact between church and state. Otherwise, the government, by its total isolation from religious institutions, would be in effect establishing its preference of those having no religion. In addition, the free exercise clause, as well, would be violated, since a person could be inhibited from practicing his religious beliefs because of the government preference for atheists. The government must maintain a neutral stance when dealing with matters involving religion.

Textbooks lent to parochial school children More than 20 years after the Supreme Court first ruled on it, the issue of providing public financial aid to parochial schools arose again. This time textbooks were involved.

EXAMPLE A New York law required local public school
O—➤—✳ boards to lend textbooks without charge to all elementary and secondary school pupils, including those in parochial schools. It was challenged as violating the establishment clause on the ground that since the teaching process in a sectarian school is used to advance religion, secular textbooks would be used for that purpose.

The Court rejected the argument and upheld the law as constitutional. It applied the same rule as it had for transportation to school. Lending state-approved textbooks to all children furthered the educational opportunities for all students. The state has a legitimate interest in the secular education provided by religious schools. Since the law had a secular legislative purpose and did not advance or inhibit religion, and since there was no excessive involvement of the state with religious instruction, the law did not violate the establishment clause.

Direct aid to parochial schools   State or federal laws that provide financial assistance directly to the religious institutions or their instructors, rather than directly to the parent or the child, are likely to be challenged as violations of the establishment clause. As a result of such aid, there is a good possibility that the government will become excessively entangled with the religious institution in the administration of the program.

EXAMPLE   A Rhode Island law provided for supplementary 0⊶⁎ pay directly to teachers at private and parochial schools as long as they used only public school materials and taught only courses given in public schools. Other conditions attached to the grant prohibited the teachers from receiving a higher salary than public school teachers, and required that per pupil expenditures on secular education be less than the average in the state's public schools. Eligible schools had to submit financial data and were subject to an audit. Pennsylvania had a similar statute, with the aid given directly to the school rather than the teachers. The Court held both statutes unconstitutional because the state's entanglement with religion was excessive. The Court reasoned that teachers would "find it hard to make a total separation between secular teaching and religious doctrine." In addition, the government would have to regularly inspect and evaluate school records, and such continuing supervision is "pregnant with dangers of excessive government direction of church schools and hence of churches."

The Higher Education Facilities Act   Not all statutes that provide financial assistance to religious institutions are unconstitutional, however.

The Higher Education Facilities Act (1963) was enacted by Congress to provide financial assistance to colleges and universities for the construction of buildings and facilities, such as foreign-language laboratories. These facilities are to be used exclusively for secular educational purposes, and if they are used for religious purposes during the first 20 years after they are built, a proportionate part of the grant has to be returned to the federal government.

Taxpayers challenged the act as unconstitutional since it aids religious institutions.

Although the Supreme Court ruled that the act was constitutional (just because a religious institution may indirectly benefit from a law does not make the law unconstitutional), the Court invalidated the clause that permitted use of the buildings for religious purposes after 20 years. According to the Court, the facilities must never be used for religious purposes in order for the financial assistance to colleges and universities to be constitutional.

Tax exemptions for religious institutions   The "wall of separation between church and state"—as Jefferson thought of the establishment clause—does not prevent federal and state governments from recognizing the role of religion as a stabilizing force in society. On that basis, religious institutions have traditionally been given tax exemptions. In fact, a challenge to a provision of the New York constitution granting a tax exemption to religious organizations for "real or personal property used exclusive-

ly for religious, educational or charitable purposes" failed in 1970 because the state had not singled out one particular church or religious group or even churches as a whole.

The legislative aim of a property-tax exemption is not to advance religion, but to insure that groups that enhance the moral and mental attitudes of the community will not be inhibited in their activities by property taxes. If the exemption were eliminated, the government would become excessively entangled with religious institutions because, according to the Court, "tax valuation of church property, tax liens, tax foreclosures, and the direct confrontations and conflicts that follow . . . those legal processes" would occur. The exemption restricts the fiscal relationship between church and state and brings about the desired separation, insulating each from the other.

❝ *Nothing . . . in two centuries of uninterrupted freedom from taxation has given the remotest sign of leading to an established church or religion . . . it has operated to help guarantee the free exercise of all forms of religious belief.*❞

Released-time programs   The government's interest in religion as a stabilizing force in society is one reason that U.S. currency, the Pledge of Allegiance, and "The Star-Spangled Banner" all contain references to God. Nevertheless, the line between such acknowledgments of religion and direct recognition of religion is a narrow—and very controversial—one.

EXAMPLE   In 1948 the Supreme Court decided that public 0⊶⁎ school buildings could not be used as the location of a released-time program of religious instruction classes. Released-time programs involve allowing a child to leave school early to attend religious classes while other children remain in school. The establishment clause was being violated in two ways by this arrangement: (1) The state's tax-supported public school buildings were being used for the dissemination of religious doctrines, and (2) religious groups were given invaluable help, since pupils for their religious classes were compelled under law to attend school. Children are often motivated by peer pressure, and the presence of such a program on the premises might make a child feel forced to attend, thus depriving him of his right to believe or not to believe in God.

A released-time program that took place outside of public school buildings, however, was found constitutional. The Court said that this "program involves neither religious instruction in public school classrooms nor the expenditure of public funds. All costs, including the application blanks, are paid by the religious organizations."

Prayers in public schools   Although the government must treat all religious groups with neutrality, it may not sanction the recitation of prayers, even though nondenominational, in public schools.

EXAMPLE   A New York law required that a specific prayer, 0⊶⁎ composed by the state Board of Regents, which controlled education, be said daily by public school classes. The Court held that this requirement violated the establishment clause because the prayer aided religion. The state lost its constitutionally required neutrality in religious matters by composing and imposing the prayer. The fact that the recitation was voluntary was not a valid defense because, unlike matters involving the free exercise clause (discussed below), coercion is not necessary to find a violation of the establishment clause.

Government involvement with Christmas There are still some unanswered questions concerning government involvement in activities that recognize the role of religion in life. For example, is the establishment clause violated if a public school choir sings some religious hymns during its winter concert in December? Each year, public school boards and principals receive complaints if traditional Christmas hymns are sung by schoolchildren during the Christmas season. Should the wall separating church and state extend to this? Thus far, the issue has not been resolved by the courts.

EXAMPLE The federal government's participation in the ◐—※ annual Christmas Pageant of Peace, held on federal parklands adjacent to the White House, was challenged as a violation of the establishment clause. The major point of controversy involved the maintenance of a Nativity scene.

The Court of Appeals determined that the purpose behind the pageant was to encourage tourism and the use of federal parks while showing the nation's goal of peace in the world—a clearly secular purpose. The display of the crèche, although obviously a religious symbol, was intended to commemorate one of the ways in which Christmas is traditionally celebrated in the United States. The government participated in the pageant in two ways: government officials were members of a committee to manage and organize the pageant; and the government was involved in the assembly, dismantling, cleaning, and restoration of the crèche area, and also provided various materials and equipment to be used in the pageant. The Christmas Pageant of Peace, Inc., a nonsectarian, nonpartisan, and nonprofit civil organization promoted by the Washington Board of Trade, bore the expenses and sole responsibility for the use of the crèche.

The Court of Appeals nonetheless decided that the government's involvement in the pageant violated the establishment clause. Government officials had been frequently placed in awkward positions because of their conflicting roles as committee members and government representatives. Such conflict suggested the potential for, or the appearance of, government interference with religion. The court decided that the government must end its membership on committees but not its entire role in the pageant. Limited financial aid and technical sponsorship of the aspects of the pageant that did not involve a crèche were still permitted.

Other religious holidays Even the closing of state government offices on religious holidays of a particular faith is, in certain instances, unconstitutional.

EXAMPLE Until 1976 the governor of California traditional-◐—※ ly ordered its state offices closed on Good Friday between the hours of noon and 3 P.M. These hours have special significance in Christian religions. No similar provisions were made on Yom Kippur and other holidays of faiths other than Christian. State employees were paid for the Good Friday hours, while employees who took off on other religious days had to use vacation time.

An action to enjoin the state from closing its offices was brought, and the court decided that the governor's order violated both the establishment clause of the First Amendment of the U.S. Constitution and the state constitution. The only purpose of the Good Friday order was to aid Christians who wished to observe the religious significance of those hours. It benefited Christian institutions in direct conflict with the government's function to deal with all religions in a neutral fashion.

Still, many public schools close for Yom Kippur and Christmas. However, the purpose of such closings is secular—fall and winter vacations.

■ **The free exercise clause** Our right to practice and propagate a religion without hindrance by the government is guaranteed by the free exercise clause of the First Amendment, but it is not an absolute right. A person may be prevented from practicing his beliefs when there is a substantial and compelling state interest to be served. The difference between the freedom to believe and the freedom to practice a belief is important. A law may restrict the practice of a religious belief but not the belief itself.

There is constant interaction between the establishment clause and the free exercise clause, because government actions that interfere with the practice of religious beliefs may, in effect, put the government in the position of supporting a no-religion stance even when there is no compelling interest to be protected. The most common potential conflict of government interference with free exercise of religion occurs when the government issues a regulation that has a nonreligious purpose, but nonetheless makes some religious belief illegal or its practice burdensome, or that specifically promotes conduct forbidden by some religious belief.

Polygamy The first major Supreme Court decision dealing with the free exercise clause was heard in 1879. It involved a federal law that made polygamy illegal.

EXAMPLE A Mormon was charged with violating this law. ◐—※ His defense was that it was his religious duty as a Mormon to practice polygamy. But the Supreme Court, while agreeing that laws may not interfere with religious beliefs or opinions, ruled the state could prohibit religious practices that violate social duties or are subversive of good order. To permit the Mormon's defense would make religious practice superior to law and permit every citizen to become a law unto himself.

Dangerous practices Some religious practices conflict with public interest by posing a direct threat to safety. For example, in some religions the handling of poisonous snakes and deadly poisons is an important ritual. Actions have been brought to prohibit such religious services as public nuisances because of the danger they pose to public health and safety.

EXAMPLE In a Tennessee case, snakes were handled in a ◐—※ crowded church sanctuary while children roamed about unattended. The handlers, usually ministers or elders in the church, were so enraptured and entranced that they were in a virtual state of hysteria and acting under compulsion. A few church members died as a result of snakebites and poisons taken during the services.

Church members argued that their constitutional right to practice their religion would be violated if the snake handling was made illegal, for it was integral to their faith; it was both a test and proof of the sincerity of their belief and a means to "confirm the Word of God." The state court, however, issued an injunction prohibiting the services because the manner of the snake handling, not the snake handling itself, was a public nuisance that endangered lives.

The distinction made by the court is important. The court did not say that the beliefs of the church were illegal, but only that the manner in which they expressed them posed a threat to public safety.

Illegal conduct performed in the name of religion is not exempt from sanctions by society. Each court, when faced with a law that allegedly interferes with religious practice, must balance the competing interests between religious freedom and the preservation of the health, safety, and morals of society.

Illegal practices Although religious practices that violate the law are usually outside the realm of First Amendment protection, there are some instances in which the law itself excuses certain groups from conforming. Such practices have ranged from using illegal drugs to illegal public demonstrations and soliciting subscriptions.

The use of drugs Members of the Native American Church, which is made up of about 225,000 American Indians, are permitted under some state narcotics laws to use peyote, a usually illegal hallucinatory drug. Peyote is the traditional sacrament of that church, similar to bread and wine in some Christian religions. It is treated as an object of worship to which prayers are directed. To use peyote for nonreligious purposes is sacrilegious and illegal.

In order to be granted an exemption from the law for conduct that is usually illegal, the religious group must show a legitimate religious belief behind the illegal act, adherence to ethical standards, and a spiritual discipline before immunity from the law will be granted. Even then immunity will be given only if a substantial state interest will not be significantly frustrated.

Public demonstrations The members of the Hare Krishna religious society are required to perform a religious ritual known as Sankirtan, which consists of religious chants, dancing, playing sacred instruments, shuffling to the beat of chanting, and soliciting and accepting donations while distributing religious literature in public places. This is done to spread beliefs, attract new members, and support the society's activities.

EXAMPLE In Chicago the Hare Krishna Society sought to enjoin (stop) police from enforcing against its members Chicago municipal ordinances that prohibited any game, sport, amusement, performance, or exhibition on any public way in the city. The society claimed that while practicing their religious beliefs on Chicago streets, its members had been subjected to unlawful and unconstitutional actions by the police department.

The federal district court agreed with the society and granted the injunction, ruling that the city ordinances unjustly prevented Krishna members from fulfilling their religious duty. The city failed to show a compelling interest that could justify restricting the society's exercise of its religious beliefs.

Soliciting subscriptions The state may protect the public against frauds perpetrated under the cloak of religion, but its methods must be constitutional.

EXAMPLE In a Connecticut case, a Jehovah's Witness minister solicited subscriptions on the streets from anyone who would listen. He was convicted of violating a law against soliciting subscriptions for religious or charitable purposes without first applying to public authorities for approval. The minister had not applied. He appealed his conviction on the ground, among others, that the law denied him free exercise of his religion. The state claimed that the statute protected against fraudulent solicitation under the cloak of religion.

The Supreme Court agreed with the minister. He was deprived of his liberty without due process of law, a violation of the 14th Amendment. The law in question was unconstitutional because it called for prior restraint, which inhibits free speech. See SPEECH AND PRESS, FREEDOM OF.

Compulsory education Laws cannot be enforced that compel people to do something that is forbidden by their religion unless a compelling state interest demands it.

EXAMPLE Although Wisconsin law required all children to attend school until age 16, members of the Amish Church refused to send their children beyond the eighth grade, for they viewed secondary school education as an impermissible exposure of their children to "worldly" influences, which conflicted with their religious beliefs. The parents appealed a conviction of violating the compulsory education law.

The Supreme Court ruled in 1972 that the Wisconsin law regulating education must not impinge upon religious freedom unless necessary to promote a compelling state interest. The state justified the law by claiming that education is necessary to prepare citizens to participate in the political system and to be self-sufficient participants in society. The Court concluded, however, that those reasons did not justify encroachment upon the religious beliefs of the Amish. The Amish sect has existed for 300 years and has been a successful and self-reliant part of society. Amish children receive vocational training in their own community after the eighth grade, which substantially achieves the state's educational goals. The purpose of the law would not justify the harm it would do to traditional Amish religious values and therefore it was unconstitutional.

Freedom of expression Freedom to express one's religious beliefs is intertwined with the First Amendment guarantee of freedom of expression. A government that forces a person to state something he does not believe violates one of the cornerstones of a democratic society.

Forced acknowledgment of God Maryland's constitution provided for no religious test as a qualification for holding office "other than a declaration of belief in the existence of God."

EXAMPLE One man refused to take the oath and sued to compel the state to issue him a commission as a notary public. He claimed that the requirement violated the 1st and 14th Amendments. The Supreme Court agreed. The establishment clause means that "Neither a state or the federal government can aid those religions based on a belief in the existence of God as against those religions founded on different beliefs." The provision was unconstitutional.

Disqualification of the clergy While the Maryland constitution had challenged a person's right not to express belief in God, a provision of the Tennessee constitution did the opposite: It said that "Ministers of the Gospel, or priests of any denomination whatever" were barred from being constitutional convention delegates and members of the state House of Representatives.

EXAMPLE A candidate for delegate to the constitutional convention brought a lawsuit to declare his opponent, a Baptist minister, disqualified on the basis of this provision. The Supreme Court, however, ruled that the provision violated the free exercise clause. It held that the provision barring religious ministers from public office clearly restricted a person's right to freely exercise his religious beliefs. The Court rejected the argument that if members of the clergy were elected to public office, the interests of one sect would be promoted over those of another sect.

Flag salute A third case linking freedom of expression with religion involved forcing children to salute the American flag in violation of their religious beliefs.

EXAMPLE The West Virginia Board of Education ordered that the salute to the flag and the Pledge of Allegiance be made a "regular part of the program of activities in the public schools." Children were expelled and listed as delinquents for refusing to salute the flag in school, and their parents faced fines and imprisonment.

The children who refused to salute were often Jehovah's Witnesses, who believe that the law of God as set forth in Exodus proclaimed, "Thou shalt not make unto thee any graven image . . . thou shalt not bow down thyself to them nor serve them." The flag was an image within the Biblical command, and to salute it was contrary to their religious beliefs.

The expelled children and their parents sought a court order to prevent enforcement of the order to salute the flag and the Supreme Court granted it, viewing the flag-salute order as an attempt to censor expression of religious beliefs.

The Court reasoned that censorship is tolerated by the Constitution only when the expression of opinion is likely to lead to a dangerous action, which the state is responsible for preventing and punishing. Refusing to salute the flag on religious grounds posed no such threat. The action of local authorities in compelling the flag salute and pledge invaded the sphere of the intellect and spirit, the defense of which is the purpose of the First Amendment.

Religion and employment Legislation with a valid secular purpose may impose some indirect burden on individuals without violating the free exercise clause unless the secular purpose may be accomplished by other means. Many such cases have involved employment.

Sunday closing laws States and localities often have SUNDAY LAWS, which restrict certain activities on Sunday.

EXAMPLE Pennsylvania prohibited the sale of certain goods on Sunday. Orthodox Jews challenged the constitutionality of this law because their faith requires them to close their businesses on Saturday. They open on Sunday to compensate for their Saturday losses. They claimed that being closed on both Saturdays and Sundays caused them economic hardship.

The Supreme Court decided in 1961 that the Sunday closing law was valid, for it placed only an indirect burden on religion in regulating a secular activity, a uniform day of rest. It did not make any religious practice itself unlawful, because not all members of the Orthodox Jewish faith were inconvenienced by it—only those who believed it necessary to work on Sundays.

Working on the Sabbath Sunday closing laws affect only merchants who own their own businesses. Many other persons who celebrate the Sabbath on a day other than Sunday run into problems because they work for others who are not of the same religion.

EXAMPLE A Seventh Day Adventist was fired from a job because she refused to work on Saturday, the Sabbath day of her faith. When she could not find other employment because she would not work on Saturday and applied for unemployment compensation, she was denied it because she "failed, without good cause . . . to accept available work when offered."

The woman sued the state Employment Security Commission challenging the constitutionality of the decision, based on the free exercise clause. The Supreme Court decided in favor of the woman. A law is unconstitutional if it impedes the observance of a religion or if it discriminates between religions. The woman was denied benefits solely because of the practice of her religion. She was forced to choose between following her religion or receiving benefits. There was no compelling state interest that justified the statute requiring a person to accept work on such mandatory religious holidays or lose benefits.

How does this case differ from that of the Orthodox Jews who were not allowed to remain open on Sunday? The Court said the Sunday closing law was based on a "strong state interest in providing one uniform day of rest for all workers. That secular objective could be achieved . . . only by declaring Sunday to be that day of rest. Requiring exemptions for Sabbatarians, while theoretically possible, appeared to present an administrative problem of such magnitude, or afford the exempted class so great a competitive advantage that such a requirement would have rendered the scheme unworkable." In the case of the Seventh Day Adventist, the state did not prove that any compelling interest would be advanced by denying unemployment benefits to persons who refused to work on Saturday, their Sabbath day.

Religion and medicine Members of a number of religious denominations are forbidden to accept some kinds of medical help or any at all, and people have refused to submit to medical exams, inoculations, and blood transfusions on religious grounds. As a result, problems of public assistance and threats to public and personal health have arisen. In some cases people have been forced to submit to inoculations or blood transfusions even though these were forbidden by their religions.

Medical examinations A state may refuse to pay disability benefits to applicants who refuse to submit to medical examinations on religious grounds.

EXAMPLE A woman applied to her county Social Welfare Board to receive benefits under a program of aid to the disabled. Her physical disabilities included deafness, limited capacity to use her hands, failing eyesight, arthritis in her back, and varicose veins. To be eligible for assistance, however, a medical examination to substantiate the disabilities was required. She refused to submit to an exam because one of the tenets of her religion was that God will cure any physical disability. As a result, she was denied benefits. She appealed the board's decision, but it was upheld.

Although the 14th Amendment safeguards religious liberty from state interference, a state acting through its POLICE POWER to safeguard the public interest may reasonably limit the free exercise of religion for the protection of society. The board, through which the state acts, is financed by state tax money and has a duty to make sure that receivers of tax-financed assistance are eligible for it.

Vaccinations   The state, under its police power, may regulate religious practices in order to protect public health. Many states have laws requiring the vaccination of all children before they attend school to prevent epidemics of contagious childhood diseases. This public health reason outweighs any compelling religious interest that opposes any form of medication or immunization.

Blood transfusions   A number of religions forbid their members to receive blood transfusions, either because they oppose all forms of medical help or because they view transfusions as a form of "drinking blood," which is forbidden by the Bible.

In many cases, a person, usually a Jehovah's Witness or Christian Scientist, has refused a blood transfusion necessary to save his life. Typically, the hospital brings an action in court to have a guardian who will consent to the transfusion appointed for the patient. Each case is decided upon its particular facts.

EXAMPLE In one case, the court reasoned that since the patient sought help, she clearly demonstrated that she wanted to live. She was also the mother of a seven-month-old child, and the court ruled: "The state, as *parens patriae,* will not allow a parent to abandon a child." This interest was considered sufficiently compelling to justify the issuance of an order that in effect authorized the administration of a blood transfusion.

The relevant question to be answered in resolving the blood-transfusion cases is whether there is a compelling state interest that justifies the state's refusal to permit such people to say no to lifesaving help on the basis of their religious beliefs.

Some courts have refused to appoint CONSERVATORS (guardians) to authorize transfusions, especially when the patient is unmarried, with no minor dependents, and steadfastly refuses to accept such treatment because of religious beliefs, even though he is aware that the refusal may result in his death.

This issue has not been definitively settled by the Supreme Court, although the trend of the cases has been to authorize the transfusions in recognition of the compelling interest of the state in protecting the health of its people.

Autopsies   At times, the government may insist on an autopsy even though it violates the religion of the family of the deceased party.

EXAMPLE An Orthodox Jew sought to enjoin an autopsy, which was to be performed on the body of his 18-year-old son, who had died suddenly. The father's religious convictions prohibited any molestation of a body after death. But the injunction was denied, and, on ap-

peal, its denial was upheld. The court recognized the competing interests between the tenets of one's religion and the compelling interest of the state to learn the true cause of death, which could only be accomplished by an autopsy. The state's need to know whether a death resulted from a criminal act or was caused by something that could adversely affect the health and well-being of others justified the ordering of the autopsy.

When the need for an autopsy is not sufficiently demonstrated, a person's religious practices will be respected.

EXAMPLE The son of another Orthodox Jew had died from severe multiple injuries received in a car crash, and the coroner wanted to perform an autopsy to pinpoint the injury that caused the death. The court granted an injunction to prevent the autopsy, since there was no evidence or suspicion of criminality or foul play and therefore no compelling reason to infringe upon the exercise of the father's religious beliefs.

Coercive persuasion   The state may interfere with religious practices of an individual when a threat to the public welfare is sufficiently demonstrated. The 1960's and 1970's were decades during which people sought other spiritual comfort than that offered by orthodox religions. Sometimes, these unconventional religions, which established different ethical and spiritual standards for their members, resulted in the alienation of family members from each other.

EXAMPLE One religion that caused such strain on family relationships was espoused by the New Educational Development, an offshoot of the Unification Church led by Sun Yung Moon. Newspapers frequently reported cases in which members were "snatched" by their families to undergo "deprogramming." Families claimed that the "Moonies" were "programmed" into staying with the church by use of brainwashing techniques such as food and sleep deprivation, isolation of the person from his home and friends, fear and guilt tactics, and indoctrination.

Yet five adult members of the religious group won a court order prohibiting their parents from serving as their temporary conservators (guardians) and forcing them to undergo deprogramming.

Deliberating on the evidence showing that the members had radically changed their life-styles, the California court commented: "When the court is asked to determine whether that change was induced by faith or by coercive persuasion, is it not in turn investigating and questioning the validity of that faith? . . . If it be assumed that certain leaders were using psychological methods to proselytize and hold the allegiance of recruits to the church or cult . . . can it be said their actions were not dictated by faith merely because others who engaged in such practices have recanted?" The parents were not able to demonstrate any compelling state interest that would justify their appointment as conservators to infringe on the religious practice of their adult children.

■ **Establishment and free exercise clauses**   As mentioned above, there is constant interaction between the establishment clause and the free exercise clause of the First Amendment. Problems arising from the interaction are not easy to solve, as the following case shows.

EXAMPLE A suit was brought to declare certain New York O—* State provisions unconstitutional because they permitted the biological parents of a child placed for adoption to specify the religion of the adoptive parents. The provisions stated that this would be done only "so far as consistent with the best interest of the child, and where practicable . . . so as to give effect to the religious wishes" of the parents, since a parent generally has the authority to determine the religious upbringing of his child. In addition, the law provided for public funding of foster care provided by foster parents or institutions of the religious background specified by the parent.

There appeared to be a conflict between the establishment clause, which prohibits the state from aiding a religion, and the free exercise clause, under which a parent has the right to see that his child practices his religion. The state had been placed "in loco parentis in respect to abandoned children." It had no alternative but to "wear two hats, one as surrogate parent obligated to enforce the biological parent's individual right to provide religious direction and the other as a government obligated to refrain from use of its powers to further or inhibit religion."

The court reasoned that the state's arrangement for foster care did not favor one religion over the other. The funds it provided were used solely for the child's secular needs, food, clothing, shelter, secular education, and medical care. The state derived many benefits from the system, and any alternative arrangement proposed to replace the religious-affiliated foster institutions would present even more complex constitutional problems.

&& *The state, if it were required in each case to be responsible for such 'custom-tailoring' of each child's religious training, . . . would be hopelessly entangled in religion far beyond its existing simple relationship with foster parents and religious institutions, under which the latter assume all of these responsibilities for the child's religious education. Such entanglement would itself constitute an establishment of religion.*"

■ **Individuals and corporations** The constitutional guarantee of freedom of religion protects a person's rights from the action of the federal or state government but not from the private influence of individuals.

EXAMPLE Your aunt's will contains a provision that you will O—* forfeit your status as sole beneficiary of her $1 million estate unless you renounce your religious beliefs and join the church she attends. Although this requirement reflects religious bigotry and is clearly contrary to our tradition of religious liberty, it is not an infringement of your constitutional right to freedom of religion.

A bigot may safely express himself and demonstrate his intolerance of others' beliefs without fear of legal restraint or punishment. No matter how intolerant, narrow, prejudiced, or dogmatic the arguments of a particular believer may appear to others, his First Amendment guarantee of freedom of speech will be defended and protected to the utmost, unless fanatical and unrestrained enthusiasm results in unlawful acts. See SPEECH AND PRESS, FREEDOM OF.

Finally, a person's religious beliefs are not protected under the Constitution from infringement by the actions of private corporations or businesses. However, any discriminatory treatment by a private employer solely because of a person's religious beliefs is a violation of the federal CIVIL RIGHTS law and is an unlawful employment practice.

religious society An assembly that meets for the worship of God and religious instruction. Deciding which societies qualify as religious under the law is a delicate matter for the courts to decide in light of constitutional guarantees. See RELIGION, FREEDOM OF.

Religious societies are often incorporated or chartered under state law to provide for the orderly administration of property and to establish tax-exempt status. Although the terms "church" and "religious society" are frequently used interchangeably, religious societies may be independent of any church, as is, for example, the Salvation Army.

A church is a body that deals only with matters relating to religious doctrine apart from secular matters, such as the acquisition of property. A religious society may deal with both spiritual and temporal matters. Many organizations are both churches and religious societies—the Roman Catholic Church, for example.

Religious societies are usually classified as either hierarchical or congregational. A hierarchical society, such as the Roman Catholic Church, is one with a common ruling body or ecclesiastical head. A congregational society, such as the Baptist Church, is an independent organization governed solely within itself, either by a majority of its members or by any other local body.

A religious society owes its existence to the constitution written by its members. This constitution is binding on the members unless contrary to law or PUBLIC POLICY.

■ **Membership** The rules, constitution, or bylaws of the society usually state who can belong to the society and the members' rights and obligations. When you join a religious society, you agree by implication to obey its rules and submit to its authority and discipline.

As a member, you are not individually liable for the society's debts unless its charter so provides or unless you authorize or ratify an obligation. But you are liable for your pledges, or SUBSCRIPTIONS, to the society.

Most often membership in a religious society is ended by mutual agreement or the member's withdrawal. However, you may forfeit your right to membership by failing to abide by the society's rules. If the society moves to expel you, it must exercise this power strictly according to its rules on expulsion. It cannot, for example, expel you for failing to give five hours weekly to the society's work, unless the requirement is spelled out in its rules. Once you have left a society, you no longer have any rights or beneficial interest in the property of that society.

EXAMPLE When Anne and Ted joined their religious soci-O—* ety, they transferred to it the ownership of their $175,000 home. After five years, Anne and Ted became dissatisfied with the group's leaders as well as some of its practices. Once they quit, they discovered to their horror that they were no longer entitled to their home, because its transfer was legally valid. Their withdrawal from the society cost them all beneficial interests in the society's property—including their home.

■ **Meetings and elections** The will of a majority of the members of a religious society is valid only when it follows the society's rules, customs, and practices.

EXAMPLE The religious society to which you belong has open business meetings on the first Thursday of every January, April, July, and October. A group of members who want to rent a new meeting place, in a location convenient to them but not to most members, arrange a business meeting for February 15. Notices are mailed out only 3 days before the meeting, even though your bylaws provide for 10 days' notice of a special meeting. Whatever the members who attend the meeting decide—even if they are the majority—you can challenge, because neither the society's customary practice nor its rules were followed.

Similarly, elections must be conducted according to the requirements of the society's constitution. As a rule, every member of a religious society who qualifies is entitled to vote, but this right may be restricted. Generally, the officers and committees appointed or elected by the society are the legal instruments that carry out the will of its members. They are entrusted with the care and management of the nonspiritual business of the society and are usually empowered to manage church property. Anyone in charge of funds is liable to the church if he diverts them to improper purposes—such as buying a $5,000 diamond wristwatch for himself--or refuses to account for the funds.

A religious society may be bound by contracts made by its officers and trustees only when they act within the scope of their authority. An officer may be personally liable if he has acted for his own benefit in breach of his duty toward the society.

■ **Torts** Traditionally, religious societies were treated as charitable organizations that were immune from liability for their TORTS (wrongs or injuries done to others, for which those responsible can be sued for damages). As cases against charitable groups became more complex, however, many states eliminated charitable immunity and allowed religious societies to be sued. In some states, however, a religious society may be sued for damages only when the damages will be paid by the society's liability insurance. A few states still cling to the tradition of exempting religious societies from tort liability.

■ **Property** Unless authorized by statute, an unincorporated religious society cannot take or hold property in the group's name. The property is usually held by a trustee for the use of the society. On the other hand, an incorporated society generally owns property for religious purposes.

Since church property is private property, the state must protect the property rights of religious societies. Control and use of the property depends largely on the form of government adopted by the society as well as on state and local law. Stipulations in a deed or will that transferred ownership of the property to the society may restrict its use. Property held in trust for specified purposes may not be diverted to any other use. Property owned by religious societies is usually exempt from federal income tax as well as state real estate taxes, as long as it is used exclusively for religious purposes.

remainder A remainder is a future interest in land that takes effect only after another interest in the same land ends. For example, Tom gives his farm to Jake for life, remainder to Jake's son, Jim. Thus, Jim's interest in the farm takes effect only upon the death of Jake. Jim is a *remainderman,* a person who is entitled to land once another interest in it has expired. See ESTATE.

In the law of WILLS, a remainder means the assets of an estate left after the distribution of bequests (personal property) and devises (real property).

EXAMPLE In her will, Jane left her house to Nancy, her bank accounts to Mark, her jewelry to Lisa, her car to Bob, and the rest of her estate to George. George's interest in the estate is a remainder since he is entitled to all the property not specifically bequeathed or devised in Jane's will.

remand Send back. A higher court may remand a case to a lower court, for example, with instructions for specific actions. When a prisoner is remanded into custody after a preliminary court hearing, he is sent back to jail until the hearing is resumed or his trial begins.

remedial statute A law passed to correct a defect in a prior law or to provide a remedy where none previously existed—for example, a law that permits placing a LIEN (claim) on property that formerly was exempted by law.

remedy The method by which a right is enforced by a court after a person suffers some harm. The law of remedies deals with the nature of relief to which a person who has brought a lawsuit (the plaintiff) is entitled once he has established that a substantive right (right to life, liberty, property, or reputation) has been violated by the defendant.

■ **Four major types** There are four major categories of judicial remedies, classified according to their purpose: (1) the remedy of damages, (2) the remedy of restitution, (3) coercive remedies, and (4) declaratory remedies.

Damages The remedy of DAMAGES is meant to compensate the plaintiff financially for any injury he has suffered. When this money is a substitute for what the plaintiff has lost, it is called *compensatory damages.* If Mark sets fire to Paul's house the damages remedy would be the cost of repair of the house or the amount its value has decreased.

Not all damages are compensatory. *Nominal damages,* usually a few cents or $1, can be awarded as a symbolic protection of a plaintiff's right even though no actual harm has occurred. If someone slandered you by spreading the word that you are unable to pay your rent every month, the court might order him to pay nominal damages even though you suffered no harm—even to your credit worthiness—as a result. *Punitive damages* can be imposed upon the defendant to punish him rather than compensate the plaintiff—although it is the plaintiff who collects the damages.

Restitution The remedy of RESTITUTION restores the plaintiff to the position he occupied before the defendant violated his rights. Restitution is usually measured by the defendant's gains rather than by the plaintiff's losses. This prevents the defendant from being unjustly enriched by his wrong.

EXAMPLE Harvey steals money that Sam has hidden in a mattress and invests it in a highly speculative stock. Harvey will be liable to make restitution of the stock's cash value, even if it is worth 10 times the amount stolen. It is no defense to claim that Sam would never have invested the money himself. In this instance, the remedy of restitution gives the plaintiff a windfall profit since it "restores" to him more than he lost. And it denies to the defendant any profit he made by his wrong.

Instead of money, sometimes the remedy of restitution entitles the plaintiff to recover the property. Sam, for instance, could claim the shares of stock in which his stolen money was invested.

Coercive remedies Coercive remedies are orders by the court that compel the defendant to do—or not do—something to the plaintiff. An INJUNCTION backed by the CONTEMPT power of the court is one type of coercive remedy. Here is the way it works: The court issues a personal command to the defendant to act in a certain way—produce his tax records for example. If the defendant willfully disobeys, he may be jailed or fined for contempt. Another coercive remedy, a decree for SPECIFIC PERFORMANCE, commands the defendant to carry out his part of a breached contract.

EXAMPLE You gave a used-furniture dealer a down payment O———* on an old oak bedroom set, which you recognized as distinctive and unique. Before you could arrange for its pickup and make the final payment, he sold it to someone else for a higher price. You might be entitled to specific performance of your contract with the dealer—that is, he would have to sell you that set at the price on which you originally agreed. Courts grant specific performance only when the subject of a contract is unique and money damages are inadequate to compensate for the loss.

Declaratory remedies Declaratory remedies are sought by a plaintiff to determine the exact definition of a law and its constitutionality. If a state enacts a law requiring stores to be closed on Sundays, for example, a businessman may wonder if the statute applies to him and whether it is constitutional. One way for him to find out is to violate the law and provoke an arrest and trial. The penalties for guessing wrong are severe, however. A more sensible method is for the businessman to bring an action for a DECLARATORY JUDGMENT by which the court will establish his rights under the law. The main purpose of the decree is to determine a person's rights in a particular situation. In states without declaratory judgment statutes, a plaintiff may be permitted to sue for the enforcement of a law. This will force a court ruling on its constitutionality.

■ **Legal and equitable remedies** Remedies are also classified as legal or equitable. In a legal remedy, the plaintiff is awarded money damages. When money alone does not afford satisfaction to an injured plaintiff, the court may fashion an equitable remedy, usually through injunctions, decrees of specific performance, declaratory judgments, and CONSTRUCTIVE TRUSTS (court orders to convey money or property that is unfairly held to the person to whom it justly belongs).

Both types of remedies can easily be illustrated. Consider first the legal remedy.

EXAMPLE Jack signs a contract with Ted to buy an air O———* conditioner for $250. But Ted then strikes a deal with Leroy, who pays him $275 for the same machine. Furious at this betrayal and forced to buy a more expensive air conditioner from someone else, Jack brings a breach of contract action against Ted. As a legal remedy, Jack is awarded the difference between the higher price he paid for the new machine and the $250 for which he contracted with Ted.

In the above case, restitution could be made in money because Jack was able to buy a similar air conditioner, and the difference in price was the only problem. An equitable remedy is applicable in a slightly different case.

EXAMPLE Jack signs a contract to purchase an antique car O———* from Ted for $15,000. Ted has second thoughts, reneges on the deal, and refuses to deliver the car. Since the antique car is one of a kind and cannot be purchased elsewhere, Jack is entitled to the equitable remedy of specific performance. Through this remedy the court will order Ted to live up to his part of the contract and deliver the car to Jack.

The distinction between legal and equitable remedies arose when there were two types of tribunals—courts of law and courts of equity. (For a discussion of the development of these courts, see EQUITY.) Today, the courts of law and of equity are merged, but the differences between legal and equitable remedies still have importance. In many courts, a person is entitled to a jury trial if he seeks a legal remedy; this is not so if he files for an equitable remedy.

■ **Election of remedies** The selection of the appropriate remedy by the plaintiff is known as the ELECTION OF REMEDIES. The chosen remedy must match the plaintiff's right. For example, the court will not grant a decree of

---

AFTER YOU WIN YOUR SUIT—JUDICIAL REMEDIES

■ Remedies are the form of relief the court awards you after you have established in a lawsuit that the defendant violated one of your rights.

■ The remedy of *damages* compensates you financially for what you have lost.

■ The remedy of *restitution* restores your property to you and any profit the defendant has made from it.

■ *Coercive remedies* are court orders to do or not to do something.

■ A *declaratory remedy* is what you seek when you want to know exactly how a law applies to you or your business—for example, if you think you want to challenge the constitutionality of the law.

■ Remedies are classified as legal or equitable. A *legal remedy* is always a money remedy.

■ An *equitable remedy* applies to cases where you seek a specific action by the defendant. If a man signed a contract

to sell you his one-of-a-kind antique car and reneged on the deal, the court can order him to live up to his part of the contract—an equitable remedy.

■ You may be entitled to a jury trial if you seek a legal remedy, but not if you file for an equitable remedy.

■ *Provisional remedies* protect a plaintiff in a civil action while the suit is pending. For example, an injunction can prevent the sale of disputed property while the case is being heard.

specific performance in a breach of contract action if the subject of the contract can be obtained easily in the open market. Remember, Jack won a remedy of specific performance to buy the antique car only because it was a one-of-a-kind model. Also, the remedy should be selected with a view toward its procedural or tactical advantages. Since equity cases are not tried by juries, a plaintiff's attorney who thinks his client will fare better in a nonjury trial may choose an equitable remedy.

Practical and convenient administration is an important consideration in selecting a remedy. A court will deem the remedy pertinent as long as it can be sensibly applied to the case. For example, courts are often reluctant to award a decree of specific performance in breach of a building or repair contract because enforcing such a decree would take up too much of their time and would exceed their judicial roles.

■ **Provisional remedies** A remedy may also be provisional. A PROVISIONAL REMEDY depends on present need and is adapted to meet a particular emergency. A court may grant a preliminary injunction, for example, to prevent a strike by teachers until it decides whether their contract has been violated by the school board.

In particular, a provisional remedy is the temporary process available to a plaintiff in a civil action. It protects him against loss, irreparable injury, or dissipation of the property while the action is pending. Some kinds of provisional remedies are injunction; RECEIVERSHIP; ARREST; and ATTACHMENT AND GARNISHMENT.

remission 1 A release of a debt. 2 The forgiveness or condonation of an offense or injury; the act by which a forfeiture or penalty is forgiven.

remit 1 Send, transmit, give up, or relinquish, such as remitting money to pay your bills or remitting a fine for illegal parking.

remittance Money sent from one person to another in cash, by check, or otherwise. Statements sent from a creditor to a debtor, for instance, refer to submitting a monthly remittance.

remittitur (Latin) "It is sent back"; a discretionary order of the court to release the defendant from an extravagant amount of money awarded by the jury. A time-saving technique that precludes a new trial or an appeal, remittitur usually occurs when a defendant, shocked by the judgment against him, asks the court for a new trial. The court, also disturbed by the exorbitant award, studies awards in similar cases and then orders a remittitur. See DAMAGES; JURY; REMEDY.

removal The transfer of a person or thing from one place to another.

In law, *removal from the state* often means specifically an absence of such duration that it constitutes a change of residence. See DOMICILE; RESIDENCY LAWS.

Removal of a cause is the transfer of a case (CAUSE) from one court to another. Cases are transferred most frequently from a state trial court to a U.S. District Court. Usually this removal of a cause is to offset local prejudice or influence. Civil rights cases have sometimes been removed from a state to a federal court on the ground that the rights were denied, or were not enforced, at the local level.

A state has no authority to restrict the right of removal granted by federal statutes. But if a case is to be transferred to federal court, it must be one over which the court could have had jurisdiction (authority) in the first place. For example, since federal courts generally have no power over the disposition of a dead person's property, a PROBATE proceeding cannot be removed from state to federal court. Similarly, since the federal COURTS have no jurisdiction over divorce ACTIONS, such suits cannot be transferred to them.

render Give up; yield; return; surrender; pay or perform, such as rents or services. To *render judgment* is to announce the judgment of the court in a given case. To *render a verdict* is to return the jury's written decision to court and hand it to the trial judge.

renewal An act of reviving; substituting a new right or obligation for another of the same nature; extending the time for paying an obligation or debt. Renewal of a bond means an extension of time for maturity.

In real estate, the renewal of a lease requires making an entirely new lease. By contrast, the extension of a lease is the continuation of the existing one.

renounce See RENUNCIATION.

rent strike An organized refusal by tenants to pay the rent due to their landlord. Through strict interpretation of the law, a rent strike is generally unlawful. A tenant who lives in an apartment is legally bound to pay his rent. Even if the landlord fails to make necessary repairs or to furnish essential services, a tenant generally may not be relieved of his obligation to pay rent unless he moves out because the premises were not habitable (called constructive eviction) or unless the landlord was trying to force him out. There is no general right for a tenant to decide on his own that because he has been deprived of repairs or services he can withhold whatever amount he considers fair. See LANDLORD AND TENANT.

Today, courts are beginning to recognize that this basic legal concept, standing alone, can be unjust. A rental involves not only a physical structure with walls, floors, and ceilings but also a package of services that may include heat, light, air conditioning, garbage disposal, and security. Tenants in some apartment buildings may be entitled to usable laundry rooms, a doorman, a swimming pool or recreation center. At the very least, elevators should be in working order. Depriving tenants of repairs or services significantly reduces the value of rented premises to the tenants. Faced with such denials, tenants, particularly those in large urban areas, are more frequently taking the law into their own hands. They reason that a landlord should not profit from the failure to perform his part of the bargain. When tenants become angry and agree to act in concert, their organized refusal to pay the landlord is a rent strike.

Some courts refuse to recognize rent strikes. They contend that any failure to pay rent is a breach of the tenant's obligation and lawfully subjects him to eviction. A rent strike differs from other rent delinquencies, however, because its purpose is to compel the landlord to fulfill his contract with the tenant. Courts are now beginning to recognize this argument. In some states tenants on rent strike can pay their rent to the court or to a court-appointed RECEIVER. Then the money can be released to the landlord when the necessary repairs have been made, or the receiver may use the money to contract for repairs himself.

renunciation Abandoning a right without transferring it to anyone else; making an affirmative declaration of abandonment; repudiation; rejection; divesting one's self of a right, power, or privilege. If an alien becomes a U.S. citizen, for example, he must renounce his allegiance to his former country.

renvoi (French) "Return"; the legal doctrine that a court may follow in order to decide which law applies when a case involves different states or countries, each having a different law. The doctrine comes to our legal system from England but is not often followed in American courts because the doctrine requires circular reasoning. See CONFLICT OF LAWS.

> EXAMPLE A British court will distribute the property left O——* after the death of a British citizen according to British law if he was living in England and according to French law if he was living in France. However, the law in France says that this person's estate must be distributed according to British law because he was a British citizen. The British court in such a case will go over to French law and then turn back at its direction to apply British law.

reorganization The carrying out, by agreements and legal proceedings, of a business plan for winding up the affairs of an insolvent corporation. Reorganization is usually accomplished by the sale, under court supervision, of the corporate property and formation by the purchasers of a new corporation. Under reorganization, all assets of the old corporation are transferred to the new. The shareholders hold the same proportionate number of shares of stock in the new corporation. See BANKRUPTCY; RECEIVERSHIP.

reparable injury A wrong that can be compensated by payment of money. This differs from an irreparable injury, which cannot be compensated through payment of money DAMAGES. See TORT.

> EXAMPLE Lilly wrongfully keeps a portable radio that be-O——* longs to her friend Ursula. This is a reparable injury because it can be compensated by money. But if Lilly wrongfully refuses to return Ursula's ticket for a seat on the 50-yard line at the Super Bowl, the injury is irreparable. A court order to give Ursula money to cover the cost of the ticket would not compensate her because she cannot replace the ticket. Wrongfully taking something unique is an irreparable injury.

reparation Redress of an injury; amends for a wrong. After a war, the victorious nations may arrange for the payment of reparations by the vanquished.

repeal The complete cancellation of an earlier STATUTE by a later one. Repeal happens (1) by specific declaration, or (2) by implication, as when a statute contains provisions so irreconcilable with those of an earlier law that only one statute can remain.

replevin A court action to recover possession of goods unlawfully taken or retained. To return the goods is to replevy the property. Replevin is one of the oldest types of actions known in common law.

> EXAMPLE Suppose a farmer lends his tractor to a neighbor O——* for spring planting. Later, when the farmer asks about the tractor, the neighbor repeatedly promises to return it. But summer passes by and he does not do so. The farmer may sue his neighbor in replevin to recover possession of the tractor.

The cardinal question in an action for replevin is the plaintiff's right to immediate possession of the property. At the start of the suit the plaintiff usually has to post a bond guaranteeing that the defendant will be reimbursed for damages if the court decides that the property rightfully belongs to the defendant.

replevy Return goods that were unlawfully taken or retained. See REPLEVIN.

replication The traditional and common-law term for REPLY.

reply A plaintiff's response to the first PLEADING filed by the defendant. In a court case, the usual order in which pleadings are filed is (1) the plaintiff's petition or complaint, (2) the defendant's answer, and (3) the plaintiff's reply. The point of the reply is to deny the allegations made in the defendant's answer, not to expand upon the plaintiff's complaint by adding new matter to the case.

reporter A person who compiles court decisions. A court reporter records the proceedings of a court case and then transcribes usable copies of them.

reports Volumes of decisions published by a court or private party, usually a publishing company. Often these reports contain decisions from courts of more than one jurisdiction.

repossession Taking back an item sold on credit when the payments are not made. If you fail to make prompt payments on your new car, the finance company may repossess it. See CONSUMER PROTECTION.

represent 1 Stand in the place of another. To represent a person is to act as his substitute or to be his lawyer. 2 Exhibit. To represent an item is to show it publicly.

representation 1 Any conduct capable of being turned into a statement of fact. Displaying a used car with an odometer reading of 20,000 miles is a representation to a prospective buyer that the automobile has not been driven more than 20,000 miles.

2 An express or implied statement, made by one con-

tracting party to the other, concerning facts that are influential in completing the agreement.

3 In the law of DESCENT AND DISTRIBUTION, representation is the principle by which the children of a deceased person inherit the share of an estate that the deceased would have inherited if he had lived. See PER STIRPES.

representative One who stands in the place of another. In U.S. government, a representative is chosen by the people to be their spokesman in a legislative body, such as in a state legislature or in the U.S. Congress. "Representative" usually refers to a member of the lower house. A *personal representative* is a person named in a will or appointed by a probate court to supervise the distribution of property left by a person who has died. See EXECUTORS AND ADMINISTRATORS.

representative action **1** A lawsuit filed by members of a class—those who have suffered the same type of legal wrong—on behalf of the entire class. See CLASS ACTION. **2** A lawsuit brought on behalf of a CORPORATION by the stockholders to enforce a corporate right.

reprieve In criminal law, the suspension for a period of time of any sentence. In its best-known form, a reprieve is the delay of a death sentence execution. This is ordinarily an act of clemency extended to give a prisoner an opportunity to find a way to save his life by lessening the sentence. A reprieve can be granted only after sentencing.

republic **1** A form of government run by officials who are elected by the people as their representatives. **2** A nation, no matter what its form of government.

repudiation The rejection or refusal of a duty, relation, right, or privilege. For example, when a party to a CONTRACT states on the day that the contract is to be performed that he will not carry out his part of the bargain, it is a repudiation of the contract.

repugnancy **1** A disagreement or inconsistency between two or more clauses of the same legal document or between any two writings. **2** A contradiction or inconsistency in two or more allegations of the same PLEADING.

requirements contract A contract in which the seller agrees to supply all the goods or services that the buyer may need at an agreed price. In exchange, the buyer promises to purchase exclusively from the seller. While the buyer is not obligated to buy specific amounts, he surrenders his legal right to acquire the goods and services from anyone but the seller. For example, a gas station owner and a bus company may create a requirements contract that requires the bus company to purchase all of its gasoline, oil, and grease from the station.

requisition **1** A written request from the governor of one state to the governor of another state for the surrender of a fugitive criminal. **2** The taking of property by government. *Requisition* refers to the taking of personal property and *condemnation* to the seizure of real estate.

res (Latin) "A thing"; an object. The term is ordinarily applied to an object, subject matter, or status that may be at issue in a lawsuit. It can be the object against which the proceedings are taken. For example, a ship captured at sea is the *res*. The proceedings toward the disposition of the ship are said to be *in rem*. The word *res*, however, does not in all cases refer to tangible personal property. In matrimonial actions the *res* is the marital status of the parties.

res adjudicata See JUDGMENT.

rescind Abrogate, annul, avoid, or cancel. The act of rescinding is a *rescission*. Rescission of a CONTRACT is its cancellation or annulment by one or both parties. Rescission amounts to completely undoing the contract, not merely ending it. When a contract is rescinded, the parties are restored to their former positions, while termination cancels whatever remains to be carried out.

EXAMPLE Let us say your friend Marian, expecting to redecorate her home, offers her living room furniture for sale. You agree to buy her sofa for $250 and give her a $50 deposit. When Marian discovers that she owes a big tax bill, she asks if you will let her take back her offer. You agree, and she returns your $50. You are both back exactly where you started—your contract with Marian has been rescinded.

EXAMPLE But suppose you advertised your camping equipment for sale. Mr. Pine agrees to buy it for $450, giving you a $75 deposit, but changes his mind and asks for his deposit back. You tell him that you will have to go to the expense and trouble again of advertising, waiting at home for telephone calls, and showing prospective buyers the equipment. You will not return his $75, but you will not force him to take the equipment and pay the remaining $375. He agrees. The contract is terminated. He keeps his $375 and you do not deliver the equipment.

■ **Rescission by agreement** Mutual rescission, or rescission by agreement, releases both parties from the obligations of a contract by a new agreement that is made before performance of the original contract is due. The mutual rescission is itself a contract.

The parties to a contract may rescind it at any time by mutual agreement, even though the contract contains a contrary provision. The right to rescind is limited to the contracting parties or those authorized to act for them.

Assent All the parties to the contract must assent to its rescission. One party cannot rescind a contract simply by informing the other. But if one party breaches a contract the other can treat the breach as an offer to rescind. Acceptance of this offer concludes an contract for rescission.

Form The rescission agreement can be either written or oral. Unless a statute provides otherwise, an oral rescission agreement is valid even though the contract states it can be altered only in writing. Even an implied rescission can be valid when the assent of the parties can be shown by their acts.

EXAMPLE Your son agrees to buy Ted's stereo for $150. When he receives his college tuition bill, he has second thoughts about the deal and lets Ted know. Ted makes an agreement with Jack to sell him the stereo. Your son pays his tuition. This is an implied rescission since your son and Ted have shown by their action that neither intends to be bound by the contract.

Consideration An agreement to rescind a contract must be based on a sufficient CONSIDERATION, or inducement. When neither party has started to perform his part of the bargain, agreement to rescind by one side is sufficient consideration for the other's agreement to do so. If the terms of the contract have been fully carried out by one side, there can be no valid agreement to rescind unless the party who did not carry out his part of the bargain offers new consideration.

Operation and effect The mutual rights of the parties are controlled by the terms of their rescission agreement. Generally, all rights under the rescinded contract are terminated, and the parties are discharged from their obligations. Thereafter neither party can sue for breach of the old contract.

Whether or not rights or obligations already accrued are abandoned when the contract is rescinded depends on the intention of the parties. Ordinarily no claim for abandoned rights may be made unless the right to claim them has been reserved.

EXAMPLE Jack lends $10,000 to Mario for 30 days at 9 percent interest. Two days after he gets the money, Mario wins $20,000 at the blackjack table in Atlantic City. Mario calls Jack with the good news and wants to return the $10,000. He offers Jack two front-row seats to a Broadway play to rescind their contract. If Jack accepts Mario's offer, he will abandon his right to collect whatever interest has accrued on the money for the two days the contract was in effect. On the other hand, Jack may insist that he will cancel the deal only if the money is repaid with two days' interest, in addition to receiving the Broadway tickets.

■ **Rescission by one party** There is no arbitrary right to rescind a contract. But one party may rescind a voidable contract without the other's consent if there are proper grounds, such as fraud or duress by the adverse party, a mistake, the mental incapacity of one of the parties, or nonperformance or breach.

Fraud and duress To rescind a contract unilaterally on the ground of fraud, the defrauded party must show that he was induced to part with some legal right or to assume some legal liability because of fraudulent representations when the contract was made. On discovering that he was fraudulently induced to make a contract, the party has two choices: He can affirm the contract and sue for damages, or he can repudiate it and give back what he has received and recover what he has parted with.

EXAMPLE Max pays Josh $5,000 for an art print. Josh has lied about the print's authenticity. It is, in fact, worth about $150. Max later learns that he has been duped, but he has grown to like the print. In his lawsuit against Josh, Max can either decide to keep the print (thereby affirming the contract) and sue for the difference between what he paid ($5,000) and the print's real value ($150) or he can rescind the contract, return the print, and demand that he be repaid the full amount.

The rules that apply to fraud also apply to rescinding a contract obtained by duress. The disgruntled party must show, however, that the duress or coercion was so compelling that he lost his freedom of will or action.

Mistake A mutual mistake concerning a material (important) fact entitles the party affected by the mistake to rescind a contract, unless it has already been completed and rescission would be unfair to the other party. Rescission may also be allowed for a unilateral (one-sided) mistake in order to prevent an UNJUST ENRICHMENT of the party who was not in error. If one party knows that the other party is acting under an error, this knowledge is considered a mutual mistake and is ground for rescission.

EXAMPLE A school district invited local dairies to submit bids for the contract to supply it with milk during the school year. Finest Dairy won the bidding because its prices were 60 percent lower than its competitors'. It was later learned that Finest's prices were so low because of an arithmetic error in its bid. This mistake would justify rescission of the contract.

Once the contract is rescinded, the injured party can recover any money or property delivered under the contract.

YOUR RIGHTS WHEN YOU WANT TO RESCIND A CONTRACT

■ Parties to a contract may rescind (cancel) it by mutual agreement at any time, either orally or in writing.

■ You cannot rescind simply by informing the other party. If one party breaches a contract by failing to carry out its terms, the other party can treat the breach as an offer to rescind. Acceptance of the offer results in a contract for mutual rescission.

■ If the terms of a contract have been carried out by one party, agreement to rescind must be based on a new consideration (inducement from the other party)—otherwise the agreement will be void.

■ After rescission of a contract, neither party can sue for breach of that contract.

■ You may rescind a contract without the other party's consent if you have proper grounds, such as fraud, mistake, mental incapacity, or nonperformance (breach) of contract.

■ A contract cannot be rescinded because one of the parties was drunk when he agreed to it. But if the sober party took undue advantage of the intoxicated one, the contract can be set aside for reason of fraud.

■ Inadequacy of consideration does not justify rescission. If you sign a contract to sell property at a price much lower than the going price and then find out you should have asked for more, it is too late—you do not have grounds to rescind the contract.

■ If you willfully fail to do your part of a bargain, you cannot sue when the other party rescinds the contract.

■ Not every breach of contract gives you the right to cancel it. You may rescind only when the other party unmistakably refused to perform an important part of the contract.

■ You must exercise your right to cancel promptly after discovering the facts that justify rescission.

Mental incapacity   A contract made by a person of unsound mind may be rescinded, even though the other party to the contract was unaware of the mental condition and the contract was made in good faith for adequate consideration. When one party knows of the other's incapacity, the contract can be rescinded for fraud.

If both parties are mentally competent when the contract is signed, the subsequent incompetence of one of the parties is not a ground for rescission. An exception is when this mental illness affects the substance of the contract.

EXAMPLE   Let us say the student union at your daughter's college has a contract for the personal services of an entertainer. Before the date of his performance, however, the entertainer tries to commit suicide and is subsequently hospitalized. The contract may be rescinded because he can no longer carry out his obligations.

A contract cannot be rescinded because one of the parties was intoxicated at the time it was made. When it appears, however, that the sober party took undue advantage of the condition of the intoxicated person, the contract can be set aside on the ground of fraud. Similarly, habitual drunkenness that impairs a party's mental abilities may be a ground for rescission.

Nonperformance   A contract can be rescinded because of substantial nonperformance of its terms, or breach, by one of the parties. The party who willfully fails to perform cannot complain of injury because the contract was canceled. The right to rescind does not arise from every breach, however. Rescission is permitted only when the other party indicates—by words or action—his unqualified refusal to perform or to be bound by the contract.

When TIME IS OF THE ESSENCE (a provision in a contract making it unenforceable if it is not performed on time), failure to perform within the time stipulated in the contract is a ground for rescission. If time is not a factor, a delay in performance is not considered a substantial breach of contract. When performance is intended within a reasonable time, however, one party may not suddenly rescind the contract while the other party is attempting to fulfill his part of it.

EXAMPLE   Jack orders five vans from a local car dealer to start his delivery business. Payment is due within a reasonable time after the vans are ready. The vans have been in the dealer's lot for two weeks, but clerical errors made by the bank have delayed Jack's loan. He has, however, been assured by the bank's loan officer that he will have the money within 10 days. The car dealer wants to cancel the deal because he has been offered more money for the vans by someone else. Rescission will not be granted because Jack has done everything possible to complete his part of the bargain.

A party to a contract who is himself in default may not rescind because of a breach by the other party.

When one party abandons a contract after partial performance and refuses to complete his part of the deal, the other party may rescind. Similarly, conduct by one party that indicates abandonment of the contract is ground for rescission. A disagreement over the terms or a refusal to perform in a particular manner is not an abandonment.

Inadequacy of consideration   Mere inadequacy of consideration is not a sufficient reason to justify rescission.

EXAMPLE   You have some lakefront property that you have not visited in 10 years. In that time the rural lakeside village has become a popular family vacation spot. When someone offers you $100,000 for your property you accept quickly and sign a contract. Then you learn about the town's rising fortunes and your falling one—your property was actually worth $150,000, at least. The consideration was inadequate, but you cannot rescind the contract.

Time limit   The right to rescind must be exercised promptly or within a reasonable time after the discovery of the facts that may authorize rescission. Any decision about what is a reasonable time is governed by the circumstances.

EXAMPLE   Suppose a builder is awarded a contract by a town on the basis of a bid that he later discovers contains a sizable mathematical error. He must notify the town of the mistake as soon as possible so that the contract can be canceled and the bidding process reopened. If he fails to do so and waits until construction is almost complete to insure getting the price he wants, he loses his right to rescind the contract.

rescue   The crime of freeing a person from arrest and punishment. Under most laws, the rescue must be made forcibly, but some statutes say that a rescue made by threats of bodily harm is a crime.

It is legal to rescue a person unlawfully arrested or imprisoned as long as no violence is used. See FALSE ARREST; FALSE IMPRISONMENT. Rescue is a crime only if the person freed is legally imprisoned. But when a statute makes it illegal to break into jail to rescue a prisoner, it is a crime to do so even though the prisoner was not legally confined. When someone is rescued from the custody of a private person, the rescuers must know that the custody of the prisoner is lawful in order for the rescue to be a crime.

The escape of the prisoner is necessary to complete the crime, except when he is being forcibly removed from an officer's custody. In that situation the prisoner's escape is not necessary. In all other situations, if the prisoner does not escape, the crime is attempted rescue.

reservation   1 A clause in a real estate deed in which the grantor (the party who is transferring ownership of the property to another) reserves for himself some right or interest in the property granted, such as rent or an EASEMENT.   2 A tract of land withdrawn from sale or settlement and appropriated for specific public uses, such as parks, military posts, or Indian lands.   3 A decision by a trial court to set aside a legal question for future consideration so that the trial may proceed as if the question had been settled. This is known as the *reservation of a point of law*. When the court decides the question, the judgment of the case may be changed to be in accord with the answer.

reserve   Keep back; retain; keep in store for a future or special use. A seller is said to reserve title when he retains ownership of an article until the buyer has fully paid for it.

res gestae   (Latin) "Things done"; facts, circumstances, and statements that result from and illustrate the main controversy in a lawsuit. The *res gestae* rule is usually

---

FACTS YOU SHOULD KNOW ABOUT RESIDENCY LAWS

■ You are a bona fide resident of a state or locality if you actually live there. Some states recognize you as a resident if you conduct a substantial amount of business there.

■ Only under special circumstances may a state impose a condition that you be a resident for a certain time period—called a durational residency requirement—in order to qualify locally for a fundamental right. For example, the Supreme Court has rejected residency time requirements for public housing, welfare benefits, and medical treatment.

■ You may be subject to a waiting period, however, to be eligible to vote in local and state elections, to attend a state or community college, and to practice a profession.

■ Residency in a state is one of the conditions that give you the right to use its courts. The Supreme Court has upheld state requirements that a spouse suing for divorce must have been a resident for a specified length of time.

■ Local governments have the right to require that their officials be bona fide residents.

■ States may not restrict your right to vote in Presidential elections as long as you are a bona fide resident.

---

applied to testimony given by a witness in court about statements he heard out of court; the statements, sometimes called excited utterances, must be so spontaneous and contemporaneous with the event they concern that they exclude the idea that the person deliberated about them or made them up. The admission of statements in evidence under the *res gestae* rule is considered an exception to the rule against hearsay evidence. For a full discussion, see EVIDENCE.

EXAMPLE A motorist was killed when his car collided with O•——※ an approaching truck. During the trial concerning the accident, a witness who was in the car at the time of the collision was permitted to testify that another occupant yelled to the motorist moments before the crash, "Look out! He's on your side of the road!" These statements were considered relevant as part of the *res gestae* because they concerned the issue of whether the collision resulted from the truck driver's negligence.

residence The place where a person dwells, either temporarily or permanently. The term has a wide scope of meaning, and in every case the context in which it is used must be considered.

Although your DOMICILE and residence are usually in the same place and the two terms are frequently used interchangeably, they are not identical. You may have more than one place of residence, such as one in the city and one in the country, but only one domicile. Residence means a particular place in which you live, but domicile means a place where you make your permanent home.

residency laws State or local laws that require you to establish that you have lived in the state or one of its subdivisions for a certain period of time before you will be entitled to the legal protection of that particular law. These laws are also called residency requirements.

There are daily situations in which the fact that you are a resident of a particular state, county, or city entitles you to certain rights and gives you certain responsibilities, such as the payment of state and local income taxes. The right to vote in local elections, to run for public office, to have the court in your state protect your legal rights, to send your children to state-supported schools, to be admitted to certain professions, and to be eligible for certain types of employment—these are just a few examples of rights that

states and localities have tried to make conditional on a person's residency.

Not all attempts have been successful, however. In many instances, efforts by the states to make residency a precondition for certain rights have been held by the courts to conflict with the constitutional right to travel freely from one state to another.

■ **Types of residency laws** There are two types of residency laws that have been imposed by states—bona fide and durational. *Bona fide residency laws* require you to establish the fact that you actually live at a certain location. This is usually demonstrated by the address listed on your driver's license, voter registration card, lease, income tax forms, real estate tax bills, or utilities bills. Some states recognize a person as a bona fide (actual) resident if he has conducted a substantial amount of business there, thus entitling him to certain advantages of residency. *Durational residency laws* require you to show that, in addition to being a bona fide resident of the state or its subdivision, you have lived in the location for a certain period of time.

Courts recognize the validity of imposing bona fide residency requirements in order for a person to receive from the states certain rights that are not among the fundamental rights guaranteed to all U.S. citizens—for example the right to run for public office. The states have been less successful, however, when they have attempted to condition receipt of fundamental rights on the durational residency of the person applying for such benefits.

■ **Fundamental rights** A state may impose durational residency requirements as a condition of eligibility for a fundamental right only under certain circumstances. A fundamental right is any right guaranteed either specifically or implicitly under the U.S. Constitution. Freedom of speech is an explicit fundamental right under the First Amendment, while the right to life, liberty, and the pursuit of happiness may be implied from the Constitution as a whole. There must be a compelling state interest, such as election of state officials, before a state can justify restricting a person's basic rights by imposing durational residency requirements. The decision about whether the state has this significant interest is ultimately made when the question comes before the court, which examines and balances the interests of the state against the rights of the person. When durational residency requirements are found not to serve compelling state interests, they are unconstitutional as denying the right to EQUAL PROTECTION OF LAWS.

Welfare benefits In the late 1960's, two state laws that imposed durational residency requirements on persons applying for welfare were challenged as unconstitutional. Each state required a person to have resided within its borders for at least one year before becoming eligible to apply for welfare benefits. The reasons offered by the states for this discriminatory treatment of new arrivals within their borders included their need to preserve "the fiscal integrity" of state public assistance programs, help estimate the amount of the budget to be allocated to welfare costs, provide an objective method of determining residency, prevent the opportunity for fraud by an applicant who might also be receiving welfare from another state, and encourage new residents to enter the labor force. See WELFARE PROGRAMS.

The U.S. Supreme Court rejected these arguments and declared the laws unconstitutional because new residents were denied equal protection of laws. It reasoned that the nature of the federal union and constitutional guarantees of personal liberty gave each citizen the right to travel throughout the United States without unreasonable restrictions. This implied fundamental right, the Court said, could only be interfered with when a state showed its need to protect some compelling interest. Here, the states discriminated against persons who had recently arrived within their borders for reasons that were based primarily on unfounded claims of administrative convenience.

Although the durational residency requirement for welfare benefits was held unconstitutional, the Court stated in a footnote that not all durational residency requirements were necessarily unconstitutional.

“ We imply no view of the validity of a waiting period or residence requirement determining eligibility to vote, eligibility for tuition-free education, to obtain a license to practice a profession, to hunt or fish. . . . Such requirements may promote compelling state interests on the one hand, or, on the other, may not be penalties upon the exercise of the constitutional right of interstate travel.”

Housing Durational residency requirements have been imposed as a condition for admission to low- and moderate-income public housing projects in various cities around the country.

EXAMPLE The city of New Rochelle, New York, imposed O——⋆ one of the longest periods. Before it would accept an application for its public housing program, a person had to establish that he had been a New Rochelle resident for at least five years before the time of his application. Plaintiffs who brought an action against this requirement had lived in the city before applying for public housing, but did not meet the five-year requirement. They challenged it as a violation of the constitutional guarantee of equal protection of laws.

The federal district court agreed and the federal court of appeals affirmed the decision in 1971. New Rochelle's housing authority did not show any compelling governmental interest to be served by the residency requirement. Its only justification was "that each community should take care of its own first." This purpose is not constitutionally permissible, because the equal protection clause of the 14th Amendment in effect prohibits a state

from apportioning its services among its residents. To do so would mean that the state would have to create discriminatory classifications among its citizens.

The court of appeals emphasized that its decision concerned only durational, not bona fide, residency requirements for public housing. It also acknowledged that there could be other durational residency requirements that promote significant state interests. The U.S. Supreme Court denied certiorari (review) in this case.

Medical treatment The right to receive basic medical services cannot be denied to a person simply because he has not met durational residency requirements as long as he is a bona fide resident.

EXAMPLE An Arizona law required a year's residence in a O——⋆ county as a prerequisite to a poor person's receiving nonemergency hospitalization or medical care at the county's expense. The law was challenged as unconstitutional by a person who was denied admittance to the county's public hospital.

The U.S. Supreme Court reversed the decision of the highest state court in Arizona, which had upheld the law's validity. The Supreme Court noted that medical care was "as much 'a basic necessity of life' to an indigent as welfare assistance." The fact that public services would be diluted by allowing new residents the same treatment as old residents does not justify the durational requirement because a state cannot apportion its services among its citizens. In addition, the failure to provide timely medical care could cause a patient's condition to worsen to a point where more expensive emergency hospitalization (for which there is no durational residency requirement) would be needed. As a result, the patient or his family may have to be placed on the state welfare or disability rolls, an increased burden to the taxpayers.

Voting A state has the right to require bona fide residency as a prerequisite to voting in its elections. It may even impose durational residency requirements when there is a compelling interest to be served by such a measure.

EXAMPLE A suit was brought challenging the constitution-O——⋆ ality of Tennessee laws that required a would-be voter to have resided in the state for four years and in the county for 30 days before he could register to vote. The plaintiff, a law professor who had moved to Tennessee and sought to register as a voter for the coming election, was not permitted to register because he did not meet the residency requirements. The federal district court declared the laws unconstitutional and state officials appealed to the U.S. Supreme Court. The Court affirmed the decision that the laws were invalid. The Court recognized that the states do have the power to require bona fide residence as one type of qualification for voting but before the fundamental right to vote in congressional, state, and local elections can be restricted in any way, a significant state interest must be promoted. (The federal Voting Rights Act prohibits durational residency requirements restricting the right to vote in Presidential elections.)

The state had asserted that these laws were necessary to insure against fraud at the ballot box and to guarantee that voters would be knowledgeable members of the community. The Court stated that the first goal was achieved by the existing voter registration system and noted that determining who is a knowledgeable voter is constitutionally impermissible because it could exclude qualified voters who have minority opinions in their community. The fact that there were two waiting periods of different lengths demonstrated that these requirements were not "tailor-made" to the purposes which they were to serve. In summary, Tennessee failed to demonstrate a compelling interest to justify imposing lengthy durational residency requirements for voting.

Shorter periods of durational residency have been permitted for some state and local elections.

EXAMPLE Arizona had a 50-day durational residency requirement for its voters and, moreover, closed its voter registration lists 50 days before the election. A federal district court declared the residency requirement unconstitutional and enjoined its enforcement. The Supreme Court reversed the decision and found the requirement constitutional because it applied to special, primary, or general elections involving state and local officials. "[A] person does not have a federal constitutional right to walk up to a voting place on election day and demand a ballot. States have valid and sufficient interests in providing for some period of time—prior to an election—in order to prepare adequate voter records and protect its electoral processes from possible frauds."

In this case, the durational residency requirement was necessary in order to give election officials the time needed to prepare accurate voter lists. The state interest was sufficiently compelling.

■ **Use of courts** When your legal rights have been violated, you are entitled to use the courts in your state to bring a lawsuit against those who have committed the violation. But you cannot exercise this fundamental right to use the courts of a state (or one of its subdivisions) unless you can establish that you have some relationship with it that justifies the court's exercise of JURISDICTION (authority). This is usually done when you as the plaintiff file your COMPLAINT, the legal means by which you state, among other things, your relationship with the court to which you apply for RELIEF. Residency in the state, the fact that you have an active business there, or the fact that the wrongful act was committed in the state are some conditions that justify the exercise of jurisdiction by the court. Once you establish your right to use the courts, you must establish that the court has power over the defendant to make its decision legally binding on him, too. Residence of the defendant in the state is one of the factors that gives the court the right to exercise its jurisdiction over him.

EXAMPLE In one case, a woman filed for divorce in Iowa after living there one month. The action was dismissed because she failed to fulfill the requirement of Iowa law that a divorce plaintiff be a resident of the state for one year before bringing the action. She then brought a class action (a lawsuit brought for herself and all other plaintiffs in the same situation) in federal district court seeking to have the residency requirement declared unconstitutional because it violated the guarantee of equal protection of laws. The validity of the requirement was upheld and, upon appeal, the Supreme Court affirmed the constitutionality of the requirement. It rejected the plaintiff's argument that Iowa's requirement unfairly discriminated against those who had recently exercised their constitutional right to travel. In this case the plaintiff was not absolutely denied a right. Instead, she was only delayed from obtaining judicial relief until she had established the requisite permanent relationship with the state.

The Court noted that Iowa demonstrated a compelling interest in imposing its durational residency requirement. It pointed out the serious consequences of a divorce decree on both spouses and took special note of custody and support provisions usually included when a divorce decree is granted to a couple with young children. The Court concluded that with such serious consequences at stake, an individual's attachment to the state—demonstrated by satisfying the durational residency requirement—secures the interest of that state in issuing the decree and makes the decree less susceptible to challenge in another state.

■ **Nonfundamental rights** Many other rights not guaranteed by the Constitution also depend on residency.

Schools Depending on state law, the residency of a child or his parents or guardians in a particular school district determines which public elementary and secondary SCHOOLS he will attend. Also, states may validly establish residency requirements to help determine which students are entitled to lower tuition costs at state-operated colleges and universities. Federal courts have traditionally upheld the right of a state to impose more stringent admission standards and higher tuition costs on out-of-state residents seeking to attend its institutions of higher education. This difference in the treatment of out-of-state students does not penalize their constitutional right to travel because they have chosen to attend the out-of-state school. There is a reasonable basis to this classification because a state's universities are created for its citizens and are substantially supported by state taxes.

The guarantee of equal protection of laws only invalidates classifications that are unconstitutionally discriminatory—such as race, creed, or U.S. citizenship—or that affect fundamental rights without being justified by a compelling state interest. All other classifications need only have some rational basis. A right to an education, for instance, although it is given great weight by society, is not a right guaranteed by the Constitution. As long as a state demonstrates that its classifications serve a rational purpose, they will be upheld.

Employment Residency laws bear on several aspects of employment.

Municipal employment Residency requirement laws have been consistently upheld as valid prerequisites for municipal or civil service employment. There is no constitutional right to be employed by a public agency, but any residency requirement must have some rational basis, such as the promotion of the ethnic balance in the community, the reduction of high unemployment rates of inner-city minority groups, the improvement of relations between such groups and city employees, the reduction of absenteeism and lateness among personnel, the ready availability of manpower in emergency situations, and the general economic benefits derived from employees spending their salaries locally. As long as a municipal employee residency requirement is rationally related to one or more of these legitimate governmental purposes, it will be upheld as valid under the equal protection clause of the 14th Amendment.

Professional requirements Under its POLICE POWER, a state has the right to establish qualifications that must be met by a person seeking to practice his profession within its borders. Doctors, lawyers, optometrists, dentists, and architects are subject to state regulations designed to protect the public from the work of unqualified individuals. Residency in the state in which a professional is seeking to practice is one requirement that has been upheld by various courts; it gives state authorities a sufficient opportunity to investigate the character and integrity of the applicant. But if a residency requirement does not accomplish this purpose, it will be invalidated.

EXAMPLE In Hawaii, any law school graduate who wanted to take the state's bar examination was required to have resided in Hawaii for six months anytime after age 15, had to be a registered voter, and had to register for the exam at least 60 days before it was given. A federal district court declared the six-month residency requirement to be arbitrary and unreasonable. Since the requirement did not have to be fulfilled near the time of the exam, it would not furnish the Hawaii Supreme Court, which was in charge of handling admission procedures, with the facts needed to make an informed decision on the applicant's qualifications—this information was to be obtained during the 60-day preregistration period.

Commercial licenses As with the supervision of professionals seeking to practice in a state, the state may require that applicants for various types of commercial licenses—such as barbers, bar owners, restaurateurs, and taxi drivers—meet certain residency requirements. These requirements must help the state accomplish its legitimate goals of protecting the public health and welfare.

EXAMPLE Maine required applicants for a lobster fishing license to remain physically present within the state for at least eight months of each year and also to have resided in Maine for at least three years before submitting license applications. A plaintiff had obtained a temporary license, which was revoked when the Department of Marine Resources discovered he had been a Maine resident for only two years and three months. He challenged the law as a violation of the equal protection clause because it discriminated unjustly against residents of Maine who did not meet the durational residency requirement. The state argued that without such a measure, the natural supplies of lobster would be depleted for those who depended on fishing for their livelihood. The federal district court ruled that the residency requirement was without a rational basis because it excluded bona fide residents of Maine. The state could have taken other reasonable (though nondiscriminatory) methods to preserve the lobster supply, such as limiting the size of the lobster taken, the size of the catch, the season for fishing, the number of licenses, or the number of traps. The federal court of appeals upheld the decision.

Candidacy for public office The right to become a candidate for public office is not a fundamental right guaranteed by the U.S. Constitution. A state has the right to impose certain requirements on those who wish to run for public office within its borders. However, a residency requirement may violate a person's fundamental right to travel if there are other ways to control the qualifications of the office seeker.

EXAMPLE In one case, the charter of a city in Michigan required that, in addition to being a city resident and property owner, a person must have lived in the city for two years to be eligible for public office. A suit was brought by a plaintiff whose petition as a candidate for city commissioner had been rejected by the city clerk because the property and residency requirements were not met. The plaintiff challenged the constitutionality of the equal protection clause of the 14th Amendment and demanded that his name be placed on the ballot. A federal district court ruled that the property and residency requirements were invalid and ordered the plaintiff's name to be placed on the ballot.

The city election commission appealed the decision, but only on the basis of the court's invalidation of the residency requirement. The commission claimed that this provision served to familiarize potential candidates with the workings of the local government and the problems of the community. The federal court of appeals affirmed the decision that the requirement was unconstitutional because it prevented a person from exercising his fundamental right to travel if he wanted to run for public office. The court also reasoned: "Whether a candidate has the ability to carry out the duties of a particular city office, even though he arrived . . . less than two years prior to election day is a matter of consideration by voters in selecting candidates for that office." The court noted, however, that local governments have a right to require their officials to be bona fide residents of the locale.

residuary Pertaining to the remaining part. A *residuary bequest* is a bequest of all of the estate of a testator (a deceased who has left a valid will) that remains after specific bequests (gifts of personal property) and devises (gifts of real estate) are satisfied. A *residuary clause* is the provision in a WILL that disposes of residuary property.

residuum (Latin) "That which remains"; whatever remains after any process of deduction or separation—such as the residue of a dead person's estate after all debts have been paid and legacies deducted.

res ipsa loquitur (Latin) "The thing speaks for itself." A type of circumstantial EVIDENCE in a civil lawsuit that permits a jury to decide that an event was more likely than not caused by the NEGLIGENCE of the defendant. It is commonly called *res ipsa*.

Negligence is conduct that falls below the standard established by law for the protection of others against unreasonable risk of harm. In order to win a negligence action, a plaintiff (the person injured) must establish by a preponderance of evidence that the defendant's conduct was unreasonable in light of the particular situation and that this conduct brought about the injury. The mere fact that an accident or an injury occurred is not evidence of negligence. The required evidence is often presented in the form of direct testimony by eyewitnesses.

EXAMPLE Mark testifies that he saw Nick put his suitcase down in the middle of a busy sidewalk to hail a taxi. A pedestrian tripped over the bag and broke his arm. Mark's testimony is direct evidence that Nick's unreasonable conduct—putting his suitcase on a well-traveled sidewalk—led to an injury.

When there is no direct evidence of the defendant's negligence, negligence may sometimes be established by circumstantial evidence—a set of facts from which a person can infer the existence of other pertinent facts. For example, skid marks at the scene of an accident are circumstantial evidence that a car was driven at an excessive speed. It leads one to believe the car was speeding but it does not prove it. Circumstantial evidence must make negligence appear more likely than not. The mere presence of a banana peel on the floor, for example, does not show it was there long enough to establish negligence. But if it is black, gritty, and flattened out with age, a defendant could be judged negligent in not having removed it long before an accident occurred.

■ **Basic requirements** There are three basic requirements that must be met before a court will submit the question of negligence to the jury under *res ipsa loquitur*. They are (1) the inference of negligence, (2) the defendant's exclusive control over the conditions that caused the injury, and (3) the plaintiff's blameless conduct.

Inference of negligence It must be determined that the plaintiff's injury was caused under circumstances that generally do not occur unless there has been negligence. Under this requirement, *res ipsa* is used in a wide variety of situations—falling elevators, the presence of a dead mouse in a bottle of soda, a 600-pound steer falling through the ceiling and landing on a person seated in a salesroom below, a streetcar careening through a restaurant.

Although many of the cases involve freakish and improbable situations, ordinary events—a taxi making an abrupt stop that injures a passenger who is jolted from the rear seat—will also warrant the application of *res ipsa*. Similarly, commercial air travel is ruled so safe that the crash of a regularly scheduled commercial flight is immediately assumed to be based on someone's negligence. Automobile accidents that could be caused only by a sudden loss of control—a car skidding on a slippery road and crossing into the wrong lane—justify the conclusion of negligence.

A plaintiff using *res ipsa* to bring his case before a jury must show that the defendant's negligence is the most probable cause. The particular nature of the defendant's negligence does not even have to be pinpointed.

EXAMPLE If a bottle of soda explodes in a supermarket two hours after being delivered by the bottler, Arthur K, who was injured by the explosion, does not have to prove that Fizzy Soda, the bottler, failed to notice a defect in the bottle or that the soda was overcarbonated. It is enough to show that this would in all likelihood not have occurred unless Fizzy Soda had been negligent.

Exclusive control of the defendant The plaintiff's injury must be caused by a condition within the exclusive control of the defendant. Some courts have interpreted this requirement to mean that exclusive control must have existed at the *time of the injury*. This has led to harsh results for the plaintiff.

EXAMPLE In one case a customer waiting for a salesperson sat in a chair that collapsed. The injured customer filed a negligence suit against the store. The action was denied, however, because the court found that the customer, not the store, had exclusive control of the chair.

This application of the rule of exclusive control by the defendant so severely restricts the type of case to which *res ipsa* can be applied that many states require that the negligent act (or failure to act) has to occur *while the defendant had control over the object or event* that caused the damage.

EXAMPLE In the example of the exploding soda bottle, the negligence occurred during the bottling process. The fact that the bottle was no longer in Fizzy Soda Bottling Company's immediate possession but was sitting on a supermarket shelf does not absolve the company from legal responsibility. To prove Fizzy Soda's negligence, Arthur must first show that the bottle was not cracked by mishandling after it left the plant. If he can substantiate that the bottle was carefully handled and not tampered with before it reached the display shelves, the task of proving Fizzy Soda at fault is all but accomplished. *Res ipsa loquitur.*

Since there must be exclusive control by a defendant, *res ipsa* cannot be used against two or more defendants who acted separately.

EXAMPLE Suppose a pedestrian is injured when he is hit by a car that had just collided with another vehicle. The pedestrian brings a negligence action against one driver and seeks to have *res ipsa* applied to his case. An inference of negligence does not arise from the mere fact of the collision, because neither driver had exclusive control of the situation. If, however, the fault of one driver can be eliminated by some specific evidence—say a test shows the other driver was intoxicated—the jury may conclude that the injury was the result of one person's negligence.

The requirement of exclusive control by the defendant does not necessarily limit responsibility to a single defendant. When several defendants have acted jointly, the doctrine of *res ipsa* can be used to establish their negligence.

EXAMPLE A woman was injured when an elevator in which she was riding fell very rapidly. She brought a *res ipsa* negligence action against both the owner of the building and the elevator company. The jury found for the plaintiff because a falling elevator is not the type of accident that occurs without negligence, and the service contract between the company and building owner established that they had joint control over the elevator.

Some state courts have departed from the requirement of exclusive control and applied *res ipsa loquitur* against multiple defendants, even those not acting together.

The plaintiff's conduct The plaintiff must have done nothing that contributed to his suffering an injury. Even this simple requirement, however, often becomes complex.

EXAMPLE A water skier about to be picked up by the towboat was injured when the propeller cut his arm. He sued the driver and the owner of the boat for negligence under *res ipsa*. During the trial, it was affirmed that the plaintiff tried to dive underwater when he saw the boat approaching him but could not escape the whirling propeller. The defendants claimed that the dive caused the accident and therefore *res ipsa* was inapplicable. The trial court accepted this argument.

The ruling was subsequently rejected by the appellate court, which said that the question of whether the dive caused the accident should have been presented to the jury under *res ipsa*. A "plaintiff may . . . rely upon res ipsa loquitur even though he has participated in the events leading to the accident if the evidence excludes his conduct as the responsible cause." Eyewitness testimony, in addition to the skier's testimony, established that his action was not a cause of his injury.

■ **Evidence more accessible to the defendant**   In addition to the three basic requirements, a few states apply *res ipsa* in negligence cases where the evidence is more accessible to the defendant than to the plaintiff.

EXAMPLE In Iowa a plaintiff was injured when bleachers in which she was sitting collapsed during a high school basketball game. She sued the high school athletic association for negligence under the doctrine of *res ipsa*. She won and the appellate court upheld her victory. The athletic association should have been able to ascertain that the bleachers were unsafe, but the injured party had no way of finding this out.

■ **Operation of the doctrine**   *Res ipsa loquitur* is used when there is no direct evidence of the defendant's negligence. Once the court decides that the facts warrant the application of *res ipsa*, it instructs the jury on the basic principles. The jury then decides if the defendant was negligent. A dead mouse found in a bottle of soda, for example, clearly calls for an inference of negligence. If the defendant offers no explanation, the court may direct a verdict in favor of the plaintiff and the case is decided without going to the jury. In a case that is deliberated, the jury may decide that the facts do not logically lead to an indication of the defendant's negligence, even if he offers no evidence in defense. If the defendant presents evidence that makes his negligence unlikely, the plaintiff will lose unless he can rebut it. The defendant's hard evidence destroys the inference of negligence created by *res ipsa*.

Res ipsa often places heavy burdens of proof on the defendant. Some courts hold that unless the defendant offers sufficient evidence in his behalf, there must be a verdict in favor of the plaintiff. Other states have shifted the ultimate burden of proof to the defendant. They require him to introduce evidence of greater weight than that of the plaintiff.

res judicata   See JUDGMENT.

resolution   A formal expression of the will or opinion of an official body or a public assembly, adopted by vote. In legislative practice, the term usually refers to the adoption of a motion that expresses an opinion, alters legislative rules, or provides a vote of thanks or of censure. While a LAW prescribes and directs conduct and is meant to be permanent, a resolution merely expresses an opinion concerning some particular matter and is intended to have only a temporary effect on it.

A *joint resolution* is one that is adopted by both houses of Congress or of a state legislature. When such a resolution has been approved by the President or governor or passed with his approval, it has the effect of a law. In some states a joint resolution is treated as a bill—which means it may become a law if properly passed and signed by the chief executive officer—but in others, it has no status other than as a resolution.

resort   A refuge; recourse. A court whose decision in a particular case is final and from which no further appeal can be taken is known as a *court of last resort*.

respondeat superior   (Latin) "Let the master answer"; a principle of law that holds that an employer is responsible for anything that an employee does in the course of employment.

An employee is an agent for his employer. This means that he is authorized to act for the employer and is entrusted, to an extent, with the employer's business. See AGENCY. The employer controls or has a right to control the time, place, and method of doing work. An employer can be held responsible for injuries caused or sustained by his employee in the course of employment. The employer's liability is not exclusive, however, and the employee can also be held personally responsible for harm he has caused. (Injured parties generally sue both the employer and the employee.)

The determination of an employer's responsibility depends on whether an employee was within the scope of his employment at the time the accident or injury occurred. A court may consider the employee's job description or assigned duties; the time, place, and purpose of the employee's act; how much of what he has done is like the work he was hired to do or the work that is commonly done by employees such as he; and whether or not such an occurrence could reasonably have been expected. In general, anything an employee does that bears some kind of relationship to the work will usually be considered within the scope of employment.

A relatively minor deviation from the assigned work usually does not mean that the act is outside the scope of employment. Personal acts, such as going to the bathroom or getting a cup of coffee, are ordinarily within the scope of employment even though they do not directly get the work done. However, when an employee substantially departs from the work routine—takes what one court called a "frolic and detour"—he is not acting within the scope of his employment.

Yet an employee is not necessarily outside the scope of employment just because he does something he should not do. Nor can an employer disclaim liability just by showing that the employee did not obey instructions. The forbidden act is within the scope of employment if it is necessary to accomplish an assigned task or if it might reasonably be expected that an employee would perform the act. For example, a gun salesman was acting within the scope of his employment when he put a live cartridge into a gun he was showing a customer, even though the store owner specifically directed him not to do it. If the store owner was worried about the possibility of the gun firing accidentally and harming someone, he could have, for instance, provided the salesman with blank cartridges.

An employer is responsible for harm done by the employee within the scope of his employment even though the act was accidental or reckless. He is also responsible for intentional wrongs if they are done at least in part on the employer's behalf. For example, a bill collector who commits assault, battery, or false imprisonment or who defames a person in order to extract overdue payments subjects his employer to legal liability.

Courts generally hold that when the employer is someone who legally owes a duty of special care and protection—such as a bus company, a motel owner, or a hospital—then the employer is liable to the customer even if his employee acts for purely personal reasons.

EXAMPLE A bus driver engages his bus in drag races with other vehicles because he enjoys the excitement. If he injures someone or damages property and the company is sued, it cannot claim the driver acted outside the scope of his employment. The courts have reasoned that employers should not hire such dangerous people and expose the public to a risk while the employee is under the employer's supervision.

Besides having to answer for harm done by an employee acting within the scope of employment, an employer is responsible for his own mistakes. For example, a town that hires policemen and trusts them to carry guns must be very careful in selecting officers, because if it were to arm a psychopath, the town would be liable for NEGLIGENCE if an innocent person were shot. Thus, an employer may be liable for his own carelessness as well as his employee's.

respondent The party against whom an appeal is taken or a motion is brought and who is required to answer (respond). See APPEAL AND ERROR.

responsive Answering; comprising a complete answer. A "responsive PLEADING" is one that directly answers the allegations made by the opposing party in a lawsuit.

rest Cessation of motion, exertion, or labor. In a lawsuit a party is said to rest, or rest his case, when he indicates that he has produced all the evidence that he intends to offer at that stage. When a lawyer says he rests his case he may mean he is submitting it finally to the court for decision, or he may simply be waiting for his opponent to introduce evidence so that he can rebut it.

restatement of law A set of books that present the law in a particular subject area, such as the *Restatement of the Law of Torts,* and that are used for research purposes. A restatement, which is written by scholars, states the opinions of the authors on what the law is, how it is changing, and what direction the changes should take.

restitution The act of making good or of giving an equivalent for any loss, damage, or injury. It is an equitable principle founded on the premise that one who seeks EQUITY must do equity.

The objectives of a suit for restitution are to prevent the defendant from enriching himself unjustly and to obtain for the plaintiff what he is entitled to. For example, if a defendant has embezzled $5,000 and invested it in shares of stock now worth $6,000, a court can order him to turn over the shares of stock to the plaintiff even though they are now

worth more than the amount of money originally taken. This is because the defendant's conduct is wrongful.

The party unjustly enriched does not have to be guilty of any wrongful or fraudulent act; when one person bestows a benefit on another through a mistake of fact or law, the other may still be liable to make restitution. For example, a person whose house is painted by mistake does not have to pay what the job would usually cost, because he did not order the work. If the mistake was made because there were no address numbers on the house, however, the painter is no more at fault than the homeowner, and he should be able to recover the cost of his material. The questions are: Did the defendant obtain something of value to which he was not entitled and were the circumstances such that the defendant should restore what he has received (or its equivalent in money) to the plaintiff? See also CONTRACTS; UNJUST ENRICHMENT.

restrain Prohibit from action; restrict; ENJOIN.

restraining order A judicial command in the nature of an INJUNCTION.

restraint of trade Contracts of combinations (individuals or corporations who join together for an unlawful purpose) are in restraint of trade if they tend or are designed to eliminate or stifle competition, create a monopoly, artificially maintain prices, or otherwise affect or alter the course of trade to favor one party over another. See CLAYTON ACT; SHERMAN ACT.

restrictive covenant A binding provision in a real estate deed that limits the use of the property in some way. Restrictive covenants are commonly included in deeds to lots located in residential areas, requiring a new owner to use the lots only for residential purposes. A church might add a restrictive covenant to the deed of a lot it was selling to keep the buyer from building a cocktail lounge on the lot, which is next door to the church. Restrictive covenants are imposed by the owner (or seller) of the property and are not the same as ZONING restrictions, which are imposed by the government.

restrictive endorsement An endorsement, or signing over, of a check, promissory note, draft, or other document with an added note that limits the endorsement in some way. A restrictive endorsement might (1) contain terms, such as "for deposit" or "for collection," indicating an intent to deposit the document or collect on it; (2) state that the document is for the use or benefit of the endorser or some other person, for example, "Pay John Roe as agent for Jim Doe"; (3) prohibit the instrument from being transferred again; or (4) contain some condition, such as "To be paid to Ace Office Equipment Company upon delivery of typewriter." See COMMERCIAL PAPER.

resulting trust See TRUST.

retainer 1 The act by which a client employs an attorney. 2 The fee the client pays when he retains an attorney to act for him. See ATTORNEY AND CLIENT.

retaliatory eviction   A landlord's action to remove a tenant or his refusal to renew a lease because the tenant has engaged in some activity deemed unfriendly by the landlord. For example, the landlord of an apartment house may try to evict a tenant because he formed a tenant's union or complained of violations in the building to the fire or health department. In a number of states and municipalities retaliatory evictions are prohibited by statute.

retirement   1 The time when a bond or promissory note or other document that represents a debt has been paid off. After a debt has become due and has been paid, it is retired—all obligations on it end and it ceases to have legal existence.
   2 The period in a person's life after he ends his active employment. Retirement is the time of life for which you should plan during your working years, so that once you stop receiving income from employment you will have some other sources of income—from SOCIAL SECURITY, PENSION plans, personal investments, or TRUSTS—to provide the means to meet continuing expenses and to maintain your standard of living.
   Most public officials, civil service employees, and military personnel receive government pensions, and their retirement is regulated by federal and state laws. Millions of Americans receive SOCIAL SECURITY benefits during retirement, but they generally need other income to supplement these payments. Many employees are covered by company PENSION plans. Those who are not can set aside money in tax-free accounts called Individual Retirement Accounts (IRA's) or KEOGH PLANS.
   Federal law will not permit an employer to force an employee into early retirement simply because of his age. The law that protects employees is called the Age Discrimination in Employment Act. The purpose of the act is "to promote employment of older persons based on their ability rather than age [and] to prohibit arbitrary age discrimination in employment." The law also makes it illegal for an employer or a labor union to fire or refuse to hire a person, limit his job opportunities, or reduce his wages just because of his age. As originally enacted in 1967, the protection applied to employees between the ages of 40 and 65. In 1978 an amendment raised the upper limit to age 70 for most employees.
   If you believe that you are being illegally forced into early retirement, or you are losing your job because of your age, you should promptly file a complaint with the nearest district or area office of the federal Equal Employment Opportunity Commission (EEOC). The complaint does not have to conform to any strict legal form, but it must contain enough facts to explain the problem and it must identify the persons or companies involved. Complaints are investigated by EEOC employment opportunity specialists, who attempt to resolve age discrimination complaints administratively. When such attempts are not successful, the EEOC may initiate court action. Employers are prohibited from retaliating against any employee who files a complaint or participates in an investigation.
   If the EEOC does not take legal action in your case, you may file a suit on your own behalf. If you do file a private suit, you must first file a charge of unlawful discrimination with the EEOC and—if the state you live in has its own age discrimination law—with your appropriate state agency. The charges must be filed at least 60 days before you take court action and within 180 days of the alleged violation or within 300 days of the violation if your state takes action under its own discrimination law. If, however, your state agency notifies you that it has ended the proceedings dealing with your claim, you must start your lawsuit within 30 days after receiving this notice.
   If you are thinking about filing a private suit, bear in mind that an age discrimination suit can be successful only if the plaintiff can show that age was the reason for his discharge. On the other hand, the employer need not have made an open statement about his discriminatory policies.
   EXAMPLE A company bought out its competitor and merged the staffs of the two companies. Soon after the merger, the company began laying off sales managers. Within 17 months after the merger, the average age of the managers had dropped from 53 to 40. The company was sued for age discrimination and the court found that it was fair to assume that the company was discriminating on the basis of age even though it refused to acknowledge that it had an overall policy of age discrimination.
   If you do win a suit against your employer for age discrimination, you can be reinstated in your job, recover back pay, and have your employee benefits restored, including any credit for lost time in order to qualify for a pension. In some cases, you may also recover compensation for your court costs and attorney's fees.

retirement income credit   See INCOME TAX.

retraction   See LIBEL AND SLANDER.

retroactive   Affecting something in the past; making a statute or document affect acts, rights, or facts occurring before it came into force. For example, a statute increasing the amount of Social Security benefits paid to retired people might be passed in October and be made retroactive to January 1 of the same year.

return   Bring or send back. A sheriff or constable, for example, makes a return when he brings back to a court a writ, notice, or other paper that he was required to serve. A return is also the endorsement made by the officer upon the writ or other paper in which he states what he did with it, such as the time and method of delivery.

return date   1 Generally, the last day on which a suit may be filed during a particular court term, such as the spring term.   2 The last day on which a defendant can file a PLEADING, such as an answer to a declaration, without being in default. It is sometimes called the *return day*.

revenue   1 Return or profit, such as the rents, interests, or income from any type of property.   2 The income of a corporation.   3 All public moneys collected by the state, from whatever source and in whatever manner.

reverse   Overthrow, set aside, annul, repeal, or revoke. When, for example, an appeals court sets aside the judgment, decree, or sentence of a lower court and either substitutes its own decision or sends the decision back to the lower court with instructions for a new trial, the appeals court reverses the decision of the lower court. See APPEAL AND ERROR.

reversion   Any future interest that a person retains in a piece of real estate after he transfers its ownership to another. See ESTATE.

> EXAMPLE Ruth gives 200 acres of her property to the town, O⟵⟶✱ specifying that the property comes back into her ownership if liquor is ever sold on it. Sixty years later, long after Ruth's death, the town builds a sports stadium on the property and signs a contract with a businessman who sells beer to spectators. Ruth's great-grandson sues the town. The court rules that the property reverts to him as Ruth's heir because the town has violated a condition of the gift.

review   Reexamine judicially for the purposes of correction, such as the examination of a case by a court of appeals. See APPEAL AND ERROR.

revised statutes   **1** A body of statutes that has been revised, collected, arranged in the order in which they were enacted, and reenacted as a whole. It is done whenever Congress or a legislature chooses.   **2** The usual title of the collections of compiled laws of several of the states and also of the United States.

revive   Renew; bring back into force. For example, revival is the act of renewing the legal force of a contract or debt (either by acknowledging it or by giving a new promise) when the unfulfilled obligation is no longer a sufficient foundation for a lawsuit because the time for suing prescribed by the statute of limitations has run out. See LIMITATIONS OF ACTIONS.

The term is also used in the law of domestic relations in connection with a matrimonial offense, such as ADULTERY. Once the matrimonial offense is condoned, it is no longer a ground for DIVORCE. If, however, adultery is committed a second time, then the first offense is said to revive as a ground for divorce.

revocation   The recall of some power or authority that has been granted. *Intentional revocation* is the recall of power by the party who granted it, such as when you cancel a power of attorney you have given or a WILL you have written. *Revocation by operation of law,* or *constructive revocation,* occurs without regard to the intention of the parties involved. For example, a power of attorney is ordinarily revoked by operation of law upon the death of the person who granted it.

revolving charge   A CREDIT agreement by which a customer who charges merchandise may pay for it over a period of time. Revolving charge agreements are usually made in connection with the use of a bank or department store credit card. When all outstanding charges are paid before the date of the second billing, there generally is no service or interest charge against the account.

> EXAMPLE A customer charges $200 in merchandise during O⟵⟶✱ the first week in January. He receives the statement of his outstanding balance on February 2. If he pays the $200 balance in full before he receives his next statement on March 2, no service charge or interest is added to his account.

If the customer does not wish to pay his outstanding balance in full, he may make monthly installment payments. The amount of each payment is determined according to a schedule based on a percentage of the outstanding balance of the account. A monthly service charge can be added to the unpaid balance.

reward   A sum of money or other compensation offered to the general public or to a class of persons for the performance of a designated service. When an offer of reward is accepted—by someone's performing the service—the offer becomes a binding contract, based on and governed by the law of CONTRACTS.

■ **Offer**   There must be an actual, valid offer of reward in order to create a contract of reward. The offer may be made to a particular person or by means of an advertisement or public statement. Unless a statute requires the offer to be in writing, the offer of a reward can be made orally. However, an offer to pay a reward is merely a proposal, a conditional promise by the person offering it. It does not become a contract until someone knowingly accepts the offer by performing the requested service.

Except in the case of rewards authorized by law (discussed below), the general rule is that the claimant must know of the offer and must have performed the services for the purpose of collecting the reward. This rule is based on the premise that without such knowledge there can be no meeting of the minds and, consequently, no contract.

> EXAMPLE A sheriff who was especially irked when a prisoner O⟵⟶✱ escaped from his jail distributed flyers offering $500 for the capture of the prisoner. A farmer apprehended the escaped prisoner as he was breaking into his house and brought him to the sheriff. Only then did he find out about the reward. When the sheriff refused to pay, the farmer sued. The court held in favor of the sheriff. It said that the promise of a reward was only an offer. It could become a legally binding contract only after the farmer's acceptance. The farmer did not accept the offer and close the deal because he did not know about it.

The person offering the reward may do so on any terms he wishes, and his terms must be complied with before the reward can be recovered. The offer might be made, for instance, for the discovery of information and evidence leading to the arrest and conviction of a certain person. Or an offer might require the recovery of stolen property and the apprehension of the thief, the return of a lost pet, or the recovery or rescue of a person.

A prize or premium may also be a valid offer of a reward in the specific context of a contest or competition, such as the best performance in a tournament, the best suggestion of a name, or the best time in a race.

> EXAMPLE A weekly newspaper in a small town announced O⟵⟶✱ in late December that it would give a package of prizes to the first baby born in the new year. It published pictures of 22 prizes to be donated by local merchants.

The first baby was born January 13, and the proud parents submitted a copy of the birth certificate to claim their prizes. The newspaper delivered only seven prizes, explaining that the other merchants had backed out because the publicity was not worth much by the end of January. The parents, however, have a legal claim to every prize listed in the announcement because they accepted the offer as made.

Like any other contract, a contract of reward must be supported by CONSIDERATION (something of value given to induce the other party to enter the contract). The reward itself is the consideration given by the promisor. The consideration that supports a person's right to collect a reward is the trouble he has taken when he acts on the promise of a reward or prize.

■ **Offeror** Any person or entity—including individuals, groups, or corporations—capable of making a contract can be bound in making an offer of a reward. Legislatures have the power to offer rewards for acts that will be of public benefit. A legislature may also empower designated officers—the governor, the attorney general, or a marshal—to offer rewards for certain purposes, such as the apprehension of criminals. Ordinarily, it is against state law for municipal corporations (cities, towns) to offer rewards for criminal offenders.

■ **Revocations** Because an unaccepted offer of reward gives no contractual rights, the offer can be revoked at any time before its acceptance by performance of the service. However, an offer cannot be revoked so as to deprive a person of any compensation he has earned by the performance or partial performance of its conditions.

An offer can be revoked only in the manner in which it was made or in some way that gives the revocation the same publicity as the offer. A later offer, made in different terms from the first and presented in another place, will not revoke the first offer.

EXAMPLE On April 20, 1865, Edwin Stanton, the U.S. Secretary of War, issued a proclamation offering $25,000 and "liberal rewards" for information for the apprehension of John H. Surratt, thought to have been an accomplice of John Wilkes Booth in the assassination of President Lincoln. On November 24, 1865, President Andrew Johnson published an order revoking the reward.

Meanwhile, a man serving as a Zouave in the military service of the Papal government reported to the American minister at Rome that Surratt also was a Zouave in the same service and had confessed his participation in the plot against Lincoln. He did not know at the time that the offer of reward had been revoked. Congress voted in 1868 to pay the man $10,000, but he sued for more money. The Supreme Court held that the man had no legal claim at all. Even though he did not know of the revocation, it was published as widely as the offer had been. The government had the right to withdraw its offer at any time before it was accepted and that in fact is what it did. The man was allowed his $10,000 but only because Congress had authorized it.

Generally, an offer of reward that does not state any time limitation is considered to have been withdrawn after a reasonable time. What is a reasonable period of time depends largely on the circumstances under which the offer was made. In some states, a reward for information about criminals who have been offenders in the past continues until the statute of limitations against the crime for which they are sought has run out.

■ **Performance** In order to claim a reward, a person must have fulfilled all of the conditions of the offer.

Information furnished When a reward is offered for information leading to an arrest and conviction, the return of property, or the location of a missing person, a person is entitled to the reward just for giving the information. He does not have to take part in the arrest, for instance, or return the missing pet to its owner. In the event of a trial, he does not have to testify in order to collect the reward.

The information must be timely and adequate. It is too late when given or acted on after the criminal has surrendered or if the information was already known when the informant supplied it. It is inadequate when it does not lead to the desired result, such as an arrest and conviction or the recovery of property.

When the reward is for locating an offender, conviction is not necessary. The information is sufficient if he is found. When a reward is offered for the arrest of a criminal, a personal arrest by the claimant is usually not necessary.

The person who is arrested must be the one described in the offer, and the arrest must be legal. If someone makes an

---

IF YOU ARE THINKING OF OFFERING OR ACCEPTING A REWARD

■ If you make an offer of a reward, you can revoke it at any time before someone performs the service you requested, but not afterward.

■ You must revoke an offer in the same way it was made—as by advertising in the same kind of newspaper—or in some way that gives the revocation the same publicity as the offer.

■ In order to collect a reward—say, for giving information leading to an arrest—the claimant must usually be aware of the offer when he performs

the service. If he gives the information in ignorance of the offer, he is not entitled to collect.

■ A later offer, presented in different terms from the first and in another place, will not revoke the first offer.

■ If the reward is for information leading to a criminal's arrest, you must supply correct and timely information—and it must lead to the desired result, such as an arrest and conviction of the criminal or the recovery of property.

■ You do not have to make the arrest in person; in fact, if you make an illegal arrest, you cannot recover the reward even though you got the right person.

■ Some states provide for automatic rewards for finders of lost property or compensation for the expense of recovering and preserving it.

■ If a specific reward is offered for lost property—say, $50 for returning a pedigreed dog—you as the finder have a legal claim on the dog in the amount of $50 until you are paid the reward.

illegal arrest, he cannot recover the reward even if has the right person.

Generally, when a reward is offered for the arrest *and* conviction of an offender, the claimant must have supplied information, evidence, or other help that caused both the arrest and subsequent conviction. The reward cannot be apportioned between what is due for the arrest and what is due for the conviction.

Return of lost property   Some state laws provide for a reward for the finder of lost property or for compensation for the expense of recovering and preserving it. If only a proportionate part of the lost property is restored to the loser, the finder is entitled to a proportionate part of the reward. If such a statute does not exist, a finder is not entitled to a reward for restoring the property to the owner if none has been offered.

If the offered reward is specific, the finder has a LIEN (legal claim) on the property in the amount of the reward until the reward is paid. But if the amount of the reward is not specific—such as one that states "liberal reward"—the finder does not have a lien.

EXAMPLE   Carolyn loses her dog. She puts an advertisement O⊷—⊷ in the classified section of the newspaper: "Heartbroken. Lost my small white dog in vicinity of Wilson Avenue. $25 reward for her return. Call 785-5084." George finds the dog, calls the number in the ad, and tells Carolyn, "Bring the reward money and you can have the dog." Carolyn rushes to his house for her dog but tells George that he will have to wait until next Friday for the reward. Can George refuse to return Carolyn's dog until she pays the $25? Yes, because he has a legal claim to the specific amount of money promised as a reward for the dog's return.

■ **Persons entitled**   A reward can be claimed only by a person who has complied with the conditions of the offer before it lapses or is revoked. Performance may be completed by a third person, such as an agent or servant, who is acting for the claimant's interest. See AGENCY. Persons who are under a duty to perform the services for which the reward is offered cannot claim it.

Police and other officers   A promise by a private individual to reward a public officer for doing something that it is his duty to do is void. But when the services require the officer to act outside his line of duty, he is entitled to claim the reward. For example, a policeman who looks for and finds a lost painting during his vacation.

The rule forbidding rewards for services that are within the scope of an officer's duties applies to sheriffs, constables, jailers, policemen, and other officials. It may make no difference that the service is performed at a time when the officer is not on duty or that he acts outside his territorial jurisdiction, if the service is within the line and scope of his duty. His rights depend on the terms of the offer and the public policy in his state.

Illegal acts   The maxim that no man shall profit by his own wrong applies to those claiming rewards. A person who aids or abets in committing a crime is not entitled to a reward for the arrest of a fellow perpetrator. Similarly, a person who purchases stolen property and has reasonable grounds for believing it had been stolen is not entitled to the reward offered for its return.

Richard Roe   A fictitious name often used with "John Doe" in examples illustrating hypothetical legal situations.

rider   An addition to a document. In passing bills through a legislature, when a new clause is added after a bill has passed through committee, the new clause is called a rider. In connection with insurance, a rider is an additional paper attached to and forming part of the policy.

right   A power, privilege, demand, or claim, possessed by a particular person by virtue of law.

Every legal right that one person possesses imposes a corresponding legal duty on another. For example, when you own a home you have a right to possess and enjoy it free from the interference of others, who are under a corresponding duty not to interfere with your rights by trespassing on your property or breaking into your home.

In CONSTITUTIONAL LAW, rights are classified as natural, civil, and political. *Natural rights* are those that are considered to grow out of man's nature and that relate to his personal attitudes, such as the rights to life, liberty, privacy, and the pursuit of happiness.

Civil rights are those that belong to every citizen of the state. They include the rights of property ownership, marriage, protection by law, freedom to contract, and trial by jury. These rights can be enforced or redressed in a civil action in a court.

Political rights are those that lie in a person's power to participate directly or indirectly in the establishment or administration of government. Examples of these include the right of citizenship, the right to vote, and the right to hold public office.

right of action   The right to bring a suit. See ACTION.

right-of-way   1 A right to travel over another person's land. 2 A strip of land granted to a railroad for a track bed. See EASEMENT.

right-to-work law   Any state law or constitutional provision that prohibits the practice of requiring membership in a union as a condition of employment. Where right-to-work laws exist, labor contracts that contain a so-called union security clause are illegal. Under this clause, which is quite common, an employer agrees to hire no worker unless he is, or soon will be, a member of the union. Although such agreements are permitted under federal labor statutes, Congress has left intact the power of the states to prohibit them.

Federal policy has consistently sought to avoid interference with state right-to-work laws or to deprive the states of their powers to prevent compulsory unionism. Furthermore, when the National Labor Relations Act was amended in 1947, a section was added to make certain that no provision in the act will be construed to authorize compulsory unionism in a state or territory where such an arrangement is prohibited.

A sizable minority of states have adopted right-to-work provisions. Recognizing the importance of state protection of employment opportunities, Congress has permitted state regulations to be superimposed upon federal labor legislation. See Chart 30 and CLOSED SHOP; LABOR RELATIONS; OPEN SHOP; UNION SHOP; YELLOW-DOG CONTRACT.

riot   A disturbance of the peace by a group of people who act together in a violent and turbulent manner calculated to terrorize others. Riot is an offense against the public peace and order rather than a violation of the rights of any particular person. It is illegal.

■ **Related offenses**   Riot, rout, UNLAWFUL ASSEMBLY, inciting to riot, and conspiracy to riot are related but different offenses. In a *rout*, riotous behavior is approached but never actually achieved. Exactly when a rout turns into a riot is often difficult to determine.

An *unlawful assembly* takes place when people gather with an intent that would make them rioters but separate without carrying out their intent.

EXAMPLE   When a restaurant owner refused to serve four particular customers and barred them from entering, they stood in front of the restaurant's doors, blocking the entrance to all other customers. Although a riot did not result from their actions, the men were arrested and convicted of unlawful assembly.

Inciting to riot is a crime committed when people provoke a BREACH OF THE PEACE, even though they may have at first assembled for an innocent purpose. Inciting to riot means using language, signs, or conduct that leads others to engage in behavior that, if completed, becomes a riot. *Conspiracy to riot* is also a separate offense, distinct from rioting.

EXAMPLE   During the riots in the Harlem area of New York City in 1964, the leader of a small Marxist group took to the streets with others preaching revolution and organized resistance to lawful authority. He cursed the police, spoke to the people in the crowd about how to fight and kill the police, and generally advocated violent means to gain political ends. The court decided that a person who agrees with others to organize a future riot and who acts in keeping with the agreement is guilty, not of riot, but of conspiracy to riot.

■ **The nature of riot**   Riots can arise from any violent and turbulent activity of a group, such as bands of people making an uproar and displaying guns or knives, violently disrupting a public meeting, or marching on a public street with violence—threatening passersby with displays of force, or destroying property along the way.

EXAMPLE   In a California case, striking orange pickers armed with clubs, metal cables, sticks, and other weapons rushed into an orange grove and assaulted nonstriking pickers. After the nonstrikers were driven out of the grove, the strikers overturned the boxes full of picked oranges and threw oranges and boxes at any nonstrikers they could find. The court held this to be riotous conduct.

Duration of offense   Brief disturbances do not usually qualify as riots.

EXAMPLE   A lock company was picketed in a labor dispute in Brooklyn, New York. When police attempted to escort some people through the picket line, there was a brief general commotion, some scuffling, and an exchange of blows. The police testified that the entire commotion lasted about two or three minutes. The court

held that the crime of riot does not apply to brief disturbances, even those involving violence.

Number of persons necessary   Normally, at least three people must be involved for a disturbance to be called a riot. Some statutes fix the minimum number of people at two.

Purpose of original assembly   Statutes differ about whether the original assembly of people has to be an unlawful one to constitute riot. Some laws require premeditation by the rioters. Others hold that riots can be caused by assemblies that were originally lawful or by groups of people who had assembled inadvertently.

Common intent   A previous agreement or conspiracy to riot is not usually a necessary element of a riot. But the common intent of a group to do an act of violence is sometimes an essential.

EXAMPLE   In Pennsylvania, following a high school football game, a group of boys staged a "violent, brutal, and indecent" attack on the visiting color guards and band members. They punched and kicked many of the visiting boys and assaulted the girls by touching them and by pulling at their shorts. When the visitors tried to leave, the attacks were continued. On trial, the attackers claimed that the charge of riot did not apply to them because they had had no common intent. The court held that "an intent is a mental state which can be inferred from conduct." The defendants were found guilty of riot, and the decision was upheld on appeal.

Terror   A riotous act terrorizes someone. When the riot arises from lawful conduct, terror must be proven. Let us say a group of neighbors decides to remove a pile of smelly garbage—a lawful activity. They do so in a violent and tumultuous manner, but their conduct does not terrorize other people. Therefore, a court would not hold their behavior riotous. But if just one person had been alarmed, the requirement of causing terror would be met.

If the riot arises from an unlawful act, terror need not always be proved. For example, if a person of one race is beaten by a group of people of another race, the district attorney does not have to prove that the victim was terrorized in prosecuting the assailants for rioting. In this case, the elements of force and violence are by their very nature terrifying. (Of course, the attackers would also be brought to court for assault and battery.)

■ **Persons liable for riot**   Principal rioters are those who are present and who actively participate in the riot. All persons present who do not assist in suppressing the riot may be considered participants if their presence is intentional and tends to encourage the rioters.

A MUNICIPAL CORPORATION such as a city, town, or village is not liable for injuries caused by mobs or riotous assemblages unless municipal employees are somehow responsible for the riot. Where statutes do impose such liability, the particular law determines what kind of action may be brought against a city, town, or village.

■ **Defenses**   There is never any justification for riot. The only defense that can be claimed is that you were not rioting. For example, a person who joins rioters after the riotous acts have ended cannot be guilty of riot, because participation is an essential element. Showing that your presence at the scene of a riot is accidental or that your intent was harmless and that you had no desire to engage in riotous conduct may prove your innocence of riot.

■ **Suppression of riot** Private persons may, on their own authority, lawfully try to suppress a riot. Courts have decided that people may arm themselves for that purpose. Whatever they reasonably do to suppress a riot will be supported and justified by law. However, it is more prudent to assist civil authorities than to act independently. Generally, every citizen capable of bearing arms must help to suppress a riot if he is called upon by a proper authority.

The state has the primary duty to protect lives and property from the unlawful violence of mobs. If a militia force is requested by civil authorities to help put down a riot, it has the same powers as civil officers but it may use them only to aid the civil authorities.

In an emergency, and in the absence of constitutional restrictions, a governor may direct the use of the militia to suppress a riot without complying with statutory formalities, such as a request for help from local authorities. When troops are ordered to quell a riot, they are in the service of and subject to the state. See AFFRAY.

riparian Belonging to or relating to the bank of a river or smaller stream of water. For example, a riparian proprietor is an owner of land bounded by a river or stream, or land through which a stream flows. In some states, a riparian proprietor is entitled to benefits from the water touching his land (riparian rights).

For a discussion of the privileges and rights attached to riparian ownership of land, see "Rights to use of water" in the article PROPERTY.

ripe Fully developed. A case is ripe for decision by the Supreme Court if the legal issues are distinctly defined and adequately presented so that a clear decision on the issues of the case can be made. Any court or agency that has the power to turn down cases may use ripeness as a criterion for deciding whether or not to take a case.

robbery The taking of goods or money from a person by force or intimidation. It is a felony.

A *holdup* is an assault for the purpose of robbery. The term originated in the western United States when outlaws demanded that travelers hold up their hands. It has come to have the same meaning as "robbery," but strictly speaking, the word "holdup" refers to the assault rather than the robbery. To *roll*, in police parlance, means to rob a person who is asleep or intoxicated by rolling him, or turning him over to go through his pockets.

To *stick up* is a term that originated in the Australian bush country to describe detaining someone by "sticking" (thrusting) out a gun. It has taken on the colloquial meaning of "to rob at gunpoint."

■ **Nature and elements of robbery** Robbery is an offense against both person and property. In general, the elements are (1) the taking of personal property or money from someone's person or presence, (2) the use of force, (3) the lack of consent on the part of the person from whom the property is taken, and (4) the intent to steal on the part of the offender. Neither deliberation nor premeditation is an essential element of the crime, nor is a specific demand for the property that is taken.

Taking from person, presence, or possession Robbery requires a taking from the "person or presence" or from the "person or possession" of the victim. This means that it is not necessary for the property to be taken from the victim's physical person. It need only be taken from his presence or protection. Presence means that a person has control of his property that is so immediate that violence or intimidation is necessary to separate him from his property, such as taking a color television set from a victim's house while holding him at gunpoint. When property is taken

---

IF YOU ARE A ROBBERY VICTIM

■ If property is stolen from you without force or intimidation, the crime is not robbery but larceny; the criminal is a thief, but not a robber.

■ If someone uses force or fear—say, he threatens to hurt your child—in order to make you give him something of value, he is guilty of robbery.

■ The force or intimidation must precede, coincide with, or occur so soon after that it is part of the act. If a man strikes out with a knife against a woman whose money he has just snatched from her hands, he is guilty of robbery even though he used no force when he actually took the money from her.

■ In some states, purse-snatching is robbery, even when there is no violence. In other states, it is not robbery.

■ Picking pockets by stealth is not robbery.

■ A person who takes property by mistake is not a robber. If you take property that you honestly believe is rightfully yours, you are not committing a robbery.

■ Some courts have ruled that using force or intimidation to make someone pay a debt is robbery. If you use force to take property as payment from someone who owes you a debt or money damages, you are likely to be found guilty of robbery.

■ If someone walks into your office, pulls out a knife, and takes the typewriter on the desk, the crime is robbery even though the machine belongs to your company and not to you.

■ A person is guilty of robbery if he

takes property from a person who has himself stolen it.

■ A husband or wife may be found guilty of robbing his or her spouse of property that is separately owned.

■ In some states where gambling is illegal, the loser in a game of chance may use force to take back the money he has lost without being guilty of robbery.

■ Some states hold that a person who loses fairly is guilty of robbery if he forcibly retakes his losses but is not guilty if he retakes property out of which he was cheated.

■ An unarmed participant in a robbery is as guilty as his armed associate.

■ Persons who help those who do the actual taking to escape from the scene may also be liable.

from the possession and control of a person who is so far away that neither force nor intimidation is used, the crime is LARCENY. If a delivery man sees your watch on the table and quietly pockets it, he is a thief but not a robber.

Force or intimidation   Robbery requires that the taking must be accomplished by force or by intimidation; either one is sufficient. The force must be sufficient for the robber to take the property from the victim. It must be actual personal violence.

EXAMPLE   A salesman demonstrating an automobile was tricked into entering a house, where he was threatened with a gun and tied up. The prospective purchasers then made off with the automobile. They were later arrested and tried for robbery. The court reasoned that the salesman was in possession of the automobile until the accused took actual possession of it. The court held that possession was obtained by force, not by trick, and found the defendants guilty of robbery.

The particular degree of force is immaterial. It becomes important only when the grade of the offense or the punishment is being considered. (See "Seriousness of offense," below.) It is not necessary to show that the victim suffered personal injury or that the force the robber used was strong enough to overcome any resistance the victim was capable of offering.

The force may be constructive rather than actual. *Constructive force* includes demonstrations of force, menaces, and other means that prevent the victim from exercising his free will or from resisting the robbery. Administering a drug in order to make the victim incapable of resistance is an example of the use of a constructive force that will support a robbery charge.

Robbery by *intimidation* means making the victim afraid and taking his property. The fear must be intentionally caused by the robber, not by the victim's timid disposition. The intimidation used must cause a reasonable apprehension of danger, but not necessarily great terror, panic, or hysteria. The fear must be strong enough to overcome the victim's resistance and cause him to give up his property. Putting the victim in fear of bodily injury is sufficient intimidation to sustain a charge of robbery. This may be done by a word or by a gesture, as when the victim is threatened with a gun or knife.

In many jurisdictions it is not necessary that the robbery victim is the person threatened. If you threaten a child to force the mother to give you something of value, it is robbery. Robbery may also be committed by threatening to harm the victim's property.

Taking property by means of threats of arrest and criminal prosecution is not usually considered robbery, but simply larceny. An exception to this general rule is the threat of prosecution for SODOMY. Such a threat can be intimidation sufficient to support a charge of robbery, whether the person threatened is guilty or innocent.

Time   The force or intimidation must either precede or coincide with the taking of the property. Violence or intimidation used after the taking and employed only as a means of escape does not make the crime robbery. However, if the force occurs so soon after the taking that it is part of the act, the violence is considered to be legally concurrent with the taking.

EXAMPLE   A woman is counting her money as she leaves a store. A stranger walks up to her and takes the money out of her hand without a word. The woman is so surprised that she does not resist, and the stranger runs off. Recovering her senses within moments, the woman pursues the man who took her money, and the man strikes at her with a knife, forcing her to give up her efforts to recover the money. The crime is robbery.

Snatching, trickery, pocket picking   There are conflicting views about snatching. According to one view, snatching is robbery, even when there is no violence. Other jurisdictions hold that snatching is not robbery, especially when the property is snatched so quickly that the victim has no time to resist. All jurisdictions, however, hold that snatching is robbery when the victim is intimidated, when the force used knocks the victim down, or when a physical struggle or blow accompanies the snatching. Some robbery statutes include a taking by sudden seizure. Under these laws a sudden snatching or carrying away of anything of value without the permission of the owner is robbery, and neither force nor intimidation is necessary. Where snatching is not robbery, it is still classified as a crime.

Taking property from another by trickery may constitute fraud, but it is not robbery.

Picking pockets is not robbery when neither violence nor intimidation is used. The force used in stealthily removing property from a victim's pocket is not characteristic of robbery. Yet if force or intimidation is used in place of stealth, such as shoving a victim who is unaware that his pocket is being picked, the crime is robbery.

Consent of owner   A robbery must be without the victim's consent or against his will. *Consent* means a voluntary yielding. If the victim places his property in the robber's hands because of force or fear, he is not acting voluntarily, but rather at the will of the robber. When the victim consents to his property's being taken in order to catch the perpetrator in the act, the taking is not a robbery.

Intent   Robbery must be committed with criminal intent, unless a statute provides otherwise. There must be a specific intent to rob—to deprive the owner of his property permanently. When there is no such intent, a person is not guilty of robbery. One who takes property by mistake or as a joke, for example, is not a robber.

The accused person's intent is determined from his words and actions. Premeditation is not a necessary element of robbery, but a person must intend to steal at the time he takes property. When the intent is formed after the taking, the offense is usually not robbery.

EXAMPLE   Suppose a man said to a woman who was waiting on a subway platform, "That's a good-looking purse you have there, lady." Although the woman was not threatened by the man, she reacted with great fear. She thrust the purse into his hands exclaiming, "Here, take it. Just don't hurt me," and ran off. If the man kept the purse, it would be considered larceny and not robbery, because he never intended to take the purse from her.

Claim of right   When you take property in good faith under a claim of right or title to it, you are not committing a robbery; you must believe, however, that you are the owner of the property or are entitled to it. The use of force or intimidation to make someone pay a debt has been considered by some courts to be robbery; other courts have ruled it not to be robbery. A person who uses force or intimidation in actually taking property as payment for a debt or money DAMAGES is guilty of robbery.

EXAMPLE The court awarded Chris $300 as a judgment in ○→※ his lawsuit against Joan. Months went by and Chris received no payment. When he went to Joan to ask her for the money, she said she would never pay. Chris grew angry, pushed Joan on the floor, picked up her old portable television set, and ran off with it. Chris was brought to trial and found guilty of robbery.

Motive Just as with any other crime, motive is not an element of robbery. The reason behind the robbery does not matter, even if you steal food at gunpoint to feed a hungry child. The robber's subsequent use of the money or property, even if he gives it to a worthy charity, has no effect on his guilt.

Taking or asportation In order to constitute a robbery, there must be a taking or an asportation ("carrying away"). The goods must be taken from the victim's possession into the possession of the robber. The crime is complete when the robber acquires possession of the property, even for a short time. He does not have to make his escape with the property or even to carry it out of the physical presence of the person he took it from. The slightest change of location, if it puts the property in the possession of the robber, is sufficient to establish asportation.

EXAMPLE Expecting a friend's visit, you open your door to a ○→※ stranger. Talking fast and claiming to sell custom-made jewelry, the stranger heads for your silver coffee set and picks up the pot. When you protest, she pushes it in her shopping bag and as she heads for the door threatens you with a marble ashtray if you try to stop her. Just then your friend walks in and you both overpower the thief. Then you call the police. She is charged with robbery.

Once the robber takes possession of the property, what he then does with it has no importance. The offense is complete even if he later abandons the goods.

Value of property taken The personal property that is taken must have some value, but the amount of its value is immaterial. It can be very small.

Ownership The property does not have to be taken from the owner. A robbery is committed if property is forcibly taken from the care, custody, or management of a person who has more right to it than the robber. If someone walks into your office, pulls a knife, and walks off with the typewriter on your desk, he is guilty of robbery even though the machine belongs not to you but to the company you work for.

Robbery can be committed by taking property from a person who has himself stolen it. Also, a spouse may be found guilty of robbing his or her spouse of separately owned property.

Ownership by the accused Ordinarily, an owner is not guilty of robbery if he retakes his own property. This applies even if he uses violence when he retakes it from a person who has stolen it. But a person can be guilty of robbery if he takes property he owns jointly with others.

Gambling proceeds In some states where gambling is held illegal, the loser in a game of chance may forcibly retake the money or property he has lost without being guilty of robbery. Some states distinguish between fairly conducted and unfairly conducted games. These states hold that a person who loses fairly is guilty of robbery if he retakes his losses by force, but is not guilty if he retakes property out of which he was cheated. A winner is not guilty of robbery if he takes his winnings from the loser or from the banker in the game.

■ **Seriousness of offense** Under some statutes first-degree robbery—the most serious type of robbery—is robbery by a person armed with a dangerous or deadly weapon. *Armed* means equipped with a weapon; the actual display or use of the weapon is unnecessary. A *dangerous or deadly weapon* is any weapon or instrument that is likely to produce death or great bodily injury. Whether or not the weapon is considered dangerous or deadly depends on its possible use. For example, a toy pistol resembling a .32-caliber automatic, made of metal and weighing one-half pound, was used to intimidate a robbery victim. Because it could have been used as a bludgeon, it was judged a dangerous weapon. Similarly, an unloaded gun can be a dangerous weapon.

Other statutes define robbery in the first degree as a taking from another "by violence to his person, or by putting him in fear of some immediate injury to his person." Either violence or fear of immediate injury is sufficient. Assault does not have to be proved. If intimidation is used, it must arouse a fear of immediate injury.

Under some statutes, second-degree robbery is robbery committed without a dangerous or deadly weapon. Other statutes use the element of fear to determine the degree of the offense. Under these statutes, when the robbery is accomplished by putting the victim in fear of immediate injury to his person, it is robbery in the first degree. In all other cases, such as those that put the victim in fear of immediate injury to his property or in fear of future injury to his person, the crime is robbery in the second degree.

Some states have statutes dividing the crime of robbery into more than two degrees. Each state decides for itself the elements that constitute each degree of robbery.

■ **Persons liable for robbery** In a robbery committed with a dangerous weapon, an unarmed participant is guilty of robbery in the same degree as his armed associate. It is not necesssary to prove that there was an agreement to use the dangerous weapon. If several persons band together to commit robbery and they AID AND ABET in committing the crime or are ready to assist, each of them is guilty. A person can be liable for robbery—whether or not he actually takes property, shares in the proceeds, or frightens the victim. Persons waiting near the scene of the robbery in order to aid those who do the actual taking to escape from the scene may also be liable.

A person does not necessarily need to be present when the crime is committed in order to be liable for robbery.

EXAMPLE A fence (a person who receives stolen goods) ○→※ financed jewel thieves by supplying them with money and transportation. The thieves would track down jewelry salesmen and follow them to discover where they kept their merchandise. The thieves would choose a victim, force his car off the road, and rob him. The fence would then dispose of the stolen jewelry. Even though the fence was never present at the scene of any of the crimes, the court found him guilty of robbery. The court reasoned that the fence was so great an aid to the robbers that it was as if he had been a present participant in each crime.

On the other hand, merely receiving stolen merchandise or other proceeds from a robbery does not necessarily make a person liable for robbery. This rule holds even if the receiver knows the property was taken in a robbery. Knowingly RECEIVING STOLEN GOODS is a crime in itself, but it is not robbery.

Defenses   It is no defense to a charge of robbery that the accused was unlawfully arrested or that he returned the property to its owner. Some rulings have held that intoxication so gross that it prevents the accused from forming a criminal intent is a good defense to a charge of robbery. However, other rulings deny that drunkenness can justify, excuse, or lessen the offense.

rogatory letter   A letter sent by a court in one jurisdiction to a court in another, requesting the testimony of a witness in regard to interrogatories (questions) enclosed with the letter. The letter can be sent to a court in a different state or in a foreign country. Compliance with the request rests entirely on the COMITY (courtesy and respect) of courts toward each other.

roll   A record of the proceedings of a court or public office. In taxation, an *assessment roll* is a list of taxable persons and property, completed, verified, and filed by the assessors in the tax office.

royalty   A payment made to an artist or inventor each time his work is sold, copied, or performed. In mining and oil operations, a royalty is a share of the product or profit paid to the owner of the property. Royalties are matters of CONTRACT law. The royalties a composer or writer receives and the basis for computing them are spelled out in the contract between him and his publisher.

rubric of a statute   The title of a statute. It gives the objective of the legislation and thus provides a means of interpreting the act. It is called a rubric because in ancient times it was written in red, and *rubrica* is Latin for "red."

rule   1 Settle or decide a point of law arising during a trial—as when a judge rules that a witness's testimony is inadmissible as hearsay evidence.   2 As a noun, an established standard, guide, or regulation, such as the rules of a legislative body, of the law, or of ethics. It can also mean a regulation made by a court or a public office relating to the conduct of its business.

rule against accumulations   A rule that prohibits adding income or interest earned by a TRUST back into the principal of the fund beyond the time allowed by the RULE AGAINST PERPETUITIES. The purpose of the rule is to prevent persons from removing their money from the economy for unreasonably long periods of time.

rule against perpetuities   A common-law rule developed by the courts during the 17th century in order to limit a person's power to control the ownership and possession of his property for long periods (or perpetuity) after his death, and to insure that property can be transferred. It holds that "No interest is good unless it must vest, if at all, not later than 21 years after some life or lives in being at the creation of the interest." An *interest* is a right to the ownership of property at a particular time, whether in the present or future. An interest in property is *vested* when it is given unconditionally to a specific person. A *life in being at the creation of the interest* is someone who is alive or about to be born when the will or other document takes effect.

■ **Vesting**   A property interest is vested when it is given to a person in being and when the interest is not subject to a condition precedent (a condition that must be fulfilled before the interest is given to the person).

EXAMPLE If John Brown dies and leaves property to his son O——❋ Robert for life and then to Robert's children living at the time of Robert's death, the children's interest is not vested. Their interest is subject to the condition precedent that they survive their father, Robert. On the other hand, if John Brown leaves his property to his son Robert for life, and then to Robert's children, Sid and Mary, the children's interest is vested even though their right to possess the property may be delayed for many years. If Mary dies before her father, her interest in her grandfather's estate could pass to her heirs.

The rule against perpetuities does not relate to the time when the actual possession of the property vests but only to the time when the interest in the property vests. That is, the rule is concerned with when persons gain the right to property, not when they become the owners. The interest that Robert's children possess is known as a *future interest*. See ESTATE.

■ **Measuring lives**   Under the rule, a future interest must vest within a certain period of time. This period is limited to the duration of a life in being at the time the interest in the property is transferred, plus 21 years. The life in being who is named in the transaction is called the *measuring life*. There may be more than one measuring life.

For purposes of the rule against perpetuities, a person is *in being* once he has been conceived, provided he is born thereafter. Thus the measuring life, or lives, may be the life of a person who is conceived at the time document takes effect and who is born afterward.

EXAMPLE John Jones makes a will, leaving his property "to O——❋ the descendants of George Smith who are living 21 years after the death of my last surviving child." Six months after Jones dies, his wife gives birth to their only child, Lucy. Lucy can be used as the measuring life for the rule, and Smith's descendants who are alive 21 years after Lucy's death will take the property.

The period of gestation can also take place at the end of the measuring life or lives. Thus, a person conceived before but born after the death of a measuring life is considered to be in being for purposes of the rule. The period of the rule can be extended by one or more gestation periods.

EXAMPLE Andrew leaves his estate to his grandchildren O——❋ who attain the age of 21. Andrew's only child, John, is born six months after Andrew's death. John himself has only one child, Charles, who is born six months after John's death. The will provisions leaving the property to Charles are valid, and he will inherit his grandfather's estate when he reaches 21.

To determine the limit of the rule against perpetuities, a 21-year period is added on after the deaths of the person or persons used as the measuring lives.

The measuring life, or lives, are usually persons who are named in the document, such as a will or a trust, that creates the future interest. Often, the person whose life is used as the measuring life also has a preceding interest in the property, such as a person who is given a *life estate*—one who is given the property for the duration of his life, but who may not dispose of it. It is valid to use a large number of persons as measuring lives, provided that the time of the last survivor's death can be discovered without too much difficulty. For example, a bequest by a testator (a deceased person who has left a valid will) who used as measuring lives all of Queen Victoria's lineal descendants living at the time of his death was upheld as valid, even though 120 of the Queen's lineal descendants were living when he died.

■ **Violations of the rule**   If the interest will not vest, or if there is a possibility that it will not vest, until after the expiration of the life or lives in being plus 21 years, then the transfer is void. The following is an example of a situation that would violate the rule.

EXAMPLE   Red Ranchman, a successful cattleman, owns a 50,000-acre spread called Purple Sage. Red's son Jack and Jack's wife, Sarah, live on Purple Sage and help Red manage the ranch. Jack and Sarah are childless. Red wants grandchildren. In order to encourage Jack and Sarah to have children, Red promises that he will give Jack a life estate in Purple Sage and leave the remainder to any children Jack and Sarah have. Red knows that his future grandchildren will need time to mature and to learn the cattle business. He executes a will leaving Purple Sage to Jack for life, and then to Jack's children when they reach 25. The future interest is created by Red's will. His will takes effect at the time of his death. Jack is the measuring life, the life in being at the time the interest is created. Since it is possible for the vesting to occur more than 21 years after Jack's death, the willing of the future interest to the grandchildren is void. For instance, one year after Red's death Sarah and Jack have a baby girl. Two years later they have twin boys. Six months after the birth of the twin boys, Jack is killed in an automobile accident. The interest in Purple Sage will not vest in the three children within 21 years after their father's death, and so they cannot inherit the ranch.

■ **Wait-and-see statutes**   Under the common-law rule, if there is a possibility that the future interest will not vest until after the expiration of the life or lives in being plus 21 years, the interest is void (as in the example above) from the start. Whether or not the interest is void depends on when the future interest was created.

In order to avoid the harshness of this rule, some states have enacted statutes providing that the basis for determining the validity of the interest is the time when the interest actually does vest, rather than the time when it is created. Under these statutes, the courts "wait and see" if the interest does in fact vest within the period of the rule. If Sarah had borne Jack a child two years before Jack's death, for instance, the grandchild would have inherited Purple Sage. If the interest does vest within the period of the life or lives in being plus 21 years, then it is valid. Under other more limited wait-and-see statutes, a decision is made at the time of the death of the life tenant or tenants. These statutes are called *second look* statutes.

rule of law   **1** A system of government in which the highest authority is the law, rather than one person (such as a dictator or a king) or a group of persons (such as a military junta).   **2** A legal principle that can be generally applied because it is recognized by legal authorities.

ruling   A decision made by a judge on a legal question raised during a trial.

run   **1** Have legal validity in a prescribed territory, as when a writ *runs* (is valid) throughout the county.   **2** Be applicable or have legal effect during a prescribed period of time. When, for example, the statute of limitations has run against the claim, the prescribed time for taking action on the claim has passed.

running with the land   A covenant (a written promise or restriction) runs with the land when either the right to take advantage of the covenant or the duty of performing it passes to the grantee of the land (the person to whom the property is transferred). A provision in a deed by which the grantee agrees to maintain a fence or PARTY WALL is an example of a covenant that runs with the land.

sabotage **1** The destruction of a nation's property by enemy agents or sympathizers to obstruct its war effort or national defense. **2** The malicious waste or destruction of an employer's property during labor troubles to force employers to give in to demands by employees. It is willful obstruction and interference with the normal processes of industry. Sabotage aims at inconveniencing and tying up all production but stops short of killing or endangering human life. The original act of sabotage is said to have been done when someone slipped a workman's wooden shoe, called a *sabot,* into a loom in order to stop production. Sabotage is a crime.

said Mentioned previously. The word is constantly used in contracts and other legal papers to refer to some previously stated provision, person, or document.

sales A *sale* is a contract in which title to property (ownership) is transferred from a seller to a buyer for a price. The *law of sales,* which is the topic of this article, is the law that governs transactions involving goods between merchants, such as retailers and manufacturers. It is governed by the general principles of CONTRACT law and by the Sales Article of the Uniform Commercial Code (UCC), which standardizes the rules and practices of sales and has been adopted by every state except Louisiana. Although the UCC is not a consumer-protection measure, its principles apply to consumer sales as well as to sales between merchants. For additional discussion of consumer sales, see CONSUMER PROTECTION; for the sale of real property, see DEED and MORTGAGE.

This article discusses the elements of making a sales contract, the obligations of buyer and seller, breach of a sales contract, and remedies available to buyer and seller for breach of contract.

■ **What are goods?** Goods include movable personal property, growing crops, and unborn animals, such as a puppy from an expected litter. Goods do not include investment securities, such as stocks and bonds, or *future goods,* those that do not yet exist, such as a product not yet manufactured.

Goods are *conforming* when they fulfill the terms of the sales contract, as when an order of 19-inch color television sets with matching metal stands is delivered on the date set for delivery and for an agreed-upon price.

■ **Making a sales contract** A contract for the sale of goods can be made in any form, as long as it shows that the parties have agreed. The contract can be oral, written, or partly oral and partly written. The conduct of the parties—such as an agreement reached in a telephone conversation or the sending of a deposit—may be sufficient to show the existence of a contract. The fact that some of the terms of the contract, such as the price or the number of items, are left open does not mean that the contract is too indefinite to take effect. It will take effect if the parties intended to make a contract.

Like other contracts, a sales contract requires an offer and an acceptance.

Offer Offers can be oral or written. A *firm offer* is a written offer to sell something at a certain price, signed by a merchant and stating that the offer will be held open. When no specific time period for holding it open is mentioned, a firm offer must be held open for a reasonable time, but not longer than three months. If CONSIDERATION for the offer is given, such as mutual promises or a money deposit, the offer may be held open for as long as the parties agree.

Acceptance Under the common law of contracts, an acceptance of an offer took place when it was sent—if it was sent by the same method as the offer. For example, if the offer was sent by letter, then the acceptance had to be sent by letter. If another method of acceptance, such as a telephone call, was used, it was considered a *counteroffer.*

Today, under the Uniform Commercial Code, an offer can be accepted by any reasonable method of communication. A written offer can thus be accepted by a letter, a telegram, a telephone call, or in person. The acceptance takes effect at the time it is sent. If, however, the offer specified acceptance by a particular method, then that method must be used. For example, if the offer stated that it could only be accepted by telegram by a certain date, an acceptance by letter will not be effective. Such an acceptance is a counteroffer.

Additional acceptance terms Under the UCC, an acceptance is valid even when it alters the terms of the offer, unless (1) the offeror has stipulated that acceptance is limited to the specific terms of the offer, (2) the additions would substantially change the contract, or (3) the party making the additions has been notified that the additions or changes are objectionable. This flexibility is intended to cover situations in which buyer and seller agree either verbally or by informal writings, but later draw up formal papers that change the terms agreed upon.

EXAMPLE Harry Helms telephones his order for 25 hammers with 10-inch wooden handles to Supply Central, which accepts the order at a price of $6.95 per hammer and promises delivery within two weeks. When Harry receives a copy of the purchase order from Supply Central, he notices that the size of the handles has been changed to 12 inches and the delivery date is now four weeks. The change in the delivery date is not important to Harry. If this were the only change made by Supply Central in its acceptance of Harry's order, then buyer and seller would have a valid contract. Harry considers the change in handle size to be a substantial change in the terms of the contract (he is already well stocked with 12-inch hammers). This change invalidates Supply Central's acceptance of Harry's order and Harry is no longer bound by the contract.

Performance as acceptance   When a buyer sends a seller a purchase order, such as "Ship 500 hammers at once," the seller can accept the offer either by promptly agreeing to ship the goods or by promptly shipping them. If the goods that are shipped conform to the buyer's order, a contract is formed. If the goods do not conform exactly to the buyer's order, the shipment is still considered the seller's acceptance of the order unless the seller notifies the buyer in a reasonable time that the goods were sent only to accommodate him. For example, the seller may have sent only 400 hammers, not the requested 500. When the seller notifies the buyer that the goods are sent as an accommodation, the shipment is considered a counteroffer.

These provisions were designed to prevent what is called the unilateral contract trick.

EXAMPLE A seller accepts a buyer's offer (500 hammers) by shipping goods (400 hammers). (When an offer is accepted by performance, instead of a promise to perform, a unilateral contract is usually formed.) The 400 hammers shipped do not conform to the orders of the buyer, who has based a sales promotion on them, and the buyer sues the seller for breach of contract. The seller claims in

---

MERCHANTS, CONSUMERS, WHAT DO YOU KNOW ABOUT SALES LAW?

- A standard statute, the Uniform Commercial Code (UCC), governs sales transactions in all of the 50 states, except Louisiana.
- The UCC does *not* cover real estate transactions—these are governed by other state and local laws.
- The UCC applies mainly to sales between merchants; but in certain transactions its principles apply to consumer sales too.
- A firm offer—a written and signed offer to sell goods at a certain price—must be held open for a "reasonable" time—not longer than three months. But if mutual promises are made or a money deposit is given, a firm offer may be held open for as long as the parties agree.
- Under the UCC, any sales agreement for $500 or more must be in writing.
- If you have been roped into an installment contract that grossly takes advantage of you, the court can deny enforcement of the contract or alter it.
- *Express warranties* are assurances by the seller that the goods he delivers will be as he describes them to the buyer. If a clothes manufacturer assures a merchant that his goods are made of 100 percent acrylic yarn and that the colors will not run or fade, he is bound by these assurances.

- A dealer who shows a booklet describing a pickup truck to a customer has created an express warranty that if the customer buys that truck it will match the booklet's description.
- There are also warranties, called *implied warranties,* that the buyer can depend on even if the seller does not state them.
- One implied warranty is that the goods be "merchantable"—that they meet ordinary trade standards of quality and safety. Merchantability also means that goods must be fit for the purpose for which they are ordinarily used—toasters should toast bread, drills should drill holes.
- The second implied warranty is that goods should be suitable for the particular purpose for which they are intended. If you ask a dealer for automobile tires suitable for rough terrain, then the tires he sells you should be good for that particular purpose.
- Goods do not have to be perfect in every detail but only reasonably fit for ordinary use. If a new car's brakes squeak, the seller is not liable for replacing them as long as they work.
- All implied warranties can be excluded by saying the product is being sold "as is." If you buy a raincoat marked "as is" without examining it and later find that the sleeve is ripped,

the seller is not obligated to refund your money. But if you inspect and buy a motorbike marked "as is," and later the tires go flat because the tubes are defective, the seller is obligated because there was no reasonable way for you to know of or discover a defect in the tubes.
- If you decide to reject goods delivered to you, you must notify the seller within a reasonable period of time.
- If the rejected goods are perishable and the seller fails to send instructions for disposing of them, the buyer must try to sell them. The buyer is entitled to recover from the seller reasonable expenses in caring for and selling rejected goods.
- The risk of loss is transferred to the buyer when the seller delivers conforming goods to a carrier or to a named destination or when the buyer takes possession of the goods. If the seller has delivered the goods to a trucking company that loses them, the loss must be borne by the buyer. The buyer may, in turn, sue the carrier, because the carrier is ultimately responsible for the loss.
- When the seller breaches the contract, damages amount to the difference between the goods' actual value and the value they would have had if they conformed to the warranty.

defense that his shipment of nonconforming goods (only 400 hammers) was a counteroffer, which was accepted by the buyer when he took the goods. Now, under the UCC, the seller who ships nonconforming goods cannot defend by claiming that his shipment was a counteroffer unless he has notified the buyer that the goods are sent as an accommodation. If he did not notify the buyer, he would be obligated either to ship the remaining 100 hammers or be liable to the buyer for damages.

Statute of frauds Under the UCC the STATUTE OF FRAUDS prevents the enforcement of some oral contracts by requiring that any sales agreement amounting to $500 or more be in writing. In addition, the contract must be signed by the person against whom the suit to enforce the contract is brought. The agreement will be considered sufficient even if terms relating to quality, price, time of delivery, or payment are omitted or misstated. Enforcement is limited, however, to the quantity of goods stated in the writing.

When one merchant writes to another to confirm an oral contract and the merchant receiving the confirmation has reason to expect the terms stated, a contract is formed that satisfies the statute of frauds. The receiving merchant does not have to reconfirm the contract in writing. But if a merchant receives confirmation of an "agreement" about which he has no knowledge, he must send a written notice objecting to the terms of the confirmation within 10 days.

EXAMPLE Suppose Alvin, a grocery-store owner, receives a letter from Cass, his supplier, confirming a purchase of 12 cases of spicy tomato sauce. In his last conversation with Cass, Alvin did in fact order the tomato sauce. Alvin does not have to reconfirm Cass's letter. They have a contract. On the other hand, suppose Alvin receives a letter from Karl confirming a purchase of 10 cases of spaghetti. Alvin remembers that he did talk to Karl about the order but had refused it because he thought the price was too high. Alvin must send a written objection to Karl within 10 days of receiving Karl's letter.

Exceptions A sales agreement that does not satisfy the statute of frauds (such as an oral agreement for an order for $500 or more) but is otherwise valid can be enforced in three situations. The first occurs when the buyer orders goods that are to be specially manufactured by the seller and that usually cannot be sold to other buyers. The seller must have started to manufacture the goods or obligated himself to obtain the necessary materials before the buyer cancels the order.

EXAMPLE Tweeds Brothers, a men's clothing store, orally contracts with Fitters, a garment maker, for 100 men's jackets with Tweeds's logo sewn on the fabric on the outside of the left sleeve. Fitters has tailored the jackets and is sewing the logos when Tweeds cancels the order. If Fitters sues Tweeds and Tweeds defends the suit on the basis of the statute of frauds, Fitters will be able to enforce the contract and collect from Tweeds.

In the second situation, if the party who is sued admits the existence of the oral contract, the contract can be enforced. But the contract cannot be enforced for more than the quantity that is admitted. Using the previous example, if Tweeds testifies that the store ordered only 50 jackets, then the contract could only be enforced up to the value of the 50 jackets.

The third situation in which a valid contract that does not satisfy the statute of frauds can be enforced occurs when payment for the goods has been made and the goods accepted or when the goods have been received and accepted.

Parol evidence When the parties sign a written contract that is intended to be complete and final, neither party can later claim that there was an oral (parol) agreement prior to the signing of the agreement that contradicts the terms of the contract. The purpose of this rule is to prevent false testimony about verbal side agreements.

However, a court may interpret the meaning of the terms in the contract according to the customs and usage of a particular trade. For example, the term "truck measure" as used in a contract for the sale of sand was ambiguous; the court applied the trade usage in interpreting its meaning.

Unconscionable contracts The UCC empowers the courts to relieve a person from an unconscionable contract or an unconscionable clause in a contract. An *unconscionable contract* is one that is so partial or takes such unfair advantage of one of the parties that it shocks the conscience of the court and offends its sense of decency. If a court decides that a contract or a provision is unconscionable—after hearing evidence of the purpose of the contract and the commercial needs of the particular trade or business—it can deny enforcement of the contract. The court can also strike the unconscionable provisions from the contract and enforce the remaining provisions; or it can restrict the use of a provision to avoid an unconscionable result.

EXAMPLE A refrigerator-freezer was sold by a retail installment contract that required payment of $1,229.76 in 36 monthly installments of $34.16. The buyer failed to complete the payment provisions, and a suit was brought for the balance. The court found that the price of the refrigerator-freezer was 2½ times its reasonable retail value and therefore unconscionable. The buyer had made payments totaling $649.04. The court held the $649.04 to be a reasonable price for the refrigerator-freezer and refused to enforce payment of the balance.

■ **Obligations of the parties** The primary obligation of the seller is to transfer ownership of the goods and to deliver them to the buyer. The buyer is obligated to accept the goods and to pay for them according to the terms of the contract.

Price The price for goods can be paid in money, in other goods or real estate, or by performing services. When payment is made by an exchange of goods, each party has the responsibilities that belong to a seller of goods. You should remember, however, that the UCC does not cover any transactions that involve real estate; transfers of real estate are always governed by state and local statutes.

Open terms If the parties wish to, they can enter a contract without settling on the price. If later the parties cannot agree on a price, or if it was to be set by some standard (such as the accepted price in the trade) or by a governmental agency, but it is not set, then the price is usually the fair market value (cash value) of the goods at the time they are delivered. If the agreement calls for one of the parties to fix the price, he must do so in good faith.

If the parties agree that no binding agreement is formed unless the price is later fixed, and then it is not fixed, no contract is formed. If the buyer has received goods, he must return them (or pay a reasonable price for them), and the seller must return any payment that was made.

Delivery When the sales contract does not mention the manner of delivery, the goods must be offered to the buyer as a single unit. Goods are sometimes described as *commercial units*—items that would lose some of their market value or use if divided. A unit may be a single item, such as a refrigerator; or a set of items, such as a set of dining room furniture; or a quantity of items treated as a unit, such as a truckload or boatload. The buyer is expected to pay the full price at the time of delivery. When it is not practical to deliver all the goods at once, then the goods may be delivered in groups, called *lots*. For example, steel girders to be used for the construction of a building located in a city where space is limited can be delivered in truckloads as the builder needs them, rather than all at once. Payment may be made for each lot separately.

Place If the contract does not mention the place where the goods are to be delivered, the buyer must claim the goods at the seller's business location, such as a warehouse or a manufacturing plant. When both parties know that the goods are located elsewhere, such as in a third person's warehouse, then that is where the delivery will take place.

Time Deliveries or shipments must be made within a reasonable time. What is reasonable depends upon the circumstance of each case, including custom and usage in the particular trade.

Shipment contracts When the seller is obligated to ship the goods to the buyer, the seller must deliver the goods to a CARRIER (shipping company) and arrange for transporting them. The seller must also notify the buyer of the shipment and transfer any documents that the buyer will need to take possession of the goods. A *bill of lading* is the receipt given by a carrier to the seller confirming their contract. A copy is sent to the buyer so that he may claim possession of the goods when the shipment arrives.

The seller's shipping contract with the carrier must take into consideration the nature of the goods. If, for example, the goods are perishable and must be kept frozen, then the seller must arrange for shipment under refrigeration. There are various kinds of shipping arrangements, which are described just below. The terms are negotiable between buyer and seller.

COD Although not defined by the UCC, COD means collect on delivery. The buyer pays no money when he orders the goods, and he promises to pay for the goods when they are delivered to him. The buyer must usually pay in cash, although the delivery person is sometimes authorized to accept a check.

FOB and FAS The letters "FOB" and "FAS" are abbreviations for types of delivery arrangements. FOB means free on board. When FOB is followed by the name of a city or town from which the goods are to be shipped, the seller must give possession of the goods to the carrier at that place and arrange for shipment. The seller bears the risk of loss until the goods are in the carrier's hands. The buyer usually pays for loading and shipping the goods. For example, if you buy a car from the factory in Detroit and arrange to have it shipped FOB Detroit, you will have to pay for loading the car onto the carrier (say, a train) and for shipping it to your hometown.

When FOB is followed by the destination point, the seller must arrange to transport the goods to that point and must notify the buyer of their arrival. The seller bears the cost of transporting the goods and the risk of loss to the destination point. For example, if you bought the same car as above, but it is shipped FOB Tulsa, your hometown, the company that sold you the car would have to arrange and pay for shipping the car to Tulsa.

FOB can also be followed by the type of transportation, such as a ship. The buyer usually names the particular ship or vehicle and pays for shipping the goods. The seller bears the risk and cost of loading the goods.

The term "FAS" means free alongside ship. It declares that the seller is not obligated to load the goods, but he must deliver the goods beside a vessel, at a port or on a dock named by the buyer. The buyer pays for loading and shipping the goods and for damage during shipment.

CFI and C&F The term "CFI" (cost, freight, and insurance) means that the total price includes the cost of the goods, and freight (shipment) to a stated destination point, and insurance. Under a CFI contract, the seller gives possession of the goods to the carrier, has the goods loaded onto the carrier, and pays for insuring and shipping the goods. Responsibility for damage to the goods passes to the buyer upon shipment (because the UCC considers delivery to the carrier to be the same as delivery to the buyer).

The term "C&F" (cost and freight) means that the total price includes the cost of the goods and freight to the stated destination point. Under a C&F contract, the seller's risks and duties are the same as those under CFI, except for insuring the goods.

■ **Seller's warranty obligations** Warranties are guarantees by the seller to the buyer about the quality and title to (ownership of) the goods being sold. Warranties may be either express (stated or written) or implied by law. For a more detailed discussion of consumer-product warranties, see PRODUCT LIABILITY.

Express warranties Whenever a seller makes a statement of fact or a promise to a buyer about the goods—either verbally or in writing—it creates an express warranty that the goods will be as stated or promised. The seller does not have to use such formal terms as "warranty" or "guarantee" in order to create a warranty, nor does he have to intend to make a warranty. For example, if a sweater manufacturer assures a buyer that his sweaters are made entirely of acrylic yarn and that the colors will not run or fade, these assurances are express warranties. If the seller simply states his opinion or praises the goods, a warranty is not created. Mere sales talk, or "puffing," does not create a warranty. See CONSUMER PROTECTION.

Express warranties are also created when the goods are to conform to a particular description or sample. For example, a dealer who shows a booklet describing a pickup truck to a customer has created a warranty that if the customer buys that particular truck, it will match the description in the booklet.

Similarly, a product must match the claims made on a tag attached to a sample of the product in a showroom. The buyer must have the opportunity to read the warranty, if he chooses to, before making the purchase. For example, if a tag attached to a typewriter claims that the ribbon that comes with the machine is two-colored, the ribbon must have two colors on it.

Implied warranties   Under any contract of sale, the seller warrants (guarantees) that he is transferring good title (ownership) to the buyer and that the transfer is legitimate. This warranty protects the buyer from having to defend the title in a lawsuit. The seller is also required to deliver the goods free from all legal claims that are not known to the buyer when he entered the contract. These warranties can be excluded or changed only by specific language and mutual agreement in the sales contract.

The implied warranties of merchantability and fitness for a particular purpose (see below) apply in every sale (except when buyer and seller exclude them by mutual agreement). This is true in every state except Louisiana. In order to be held responsible for these implied warranties (concerning the quality of the goods), a seller must regularly deal in the kinds of goods sold.

Warranty of merchantability   A warranty of merchantability provides that the goods must meet minimum standards of quality and safety and be of the same quality as those usually accepted in the trade. The goods must be fit for the purpose for which they are ordinarily used. For example, toaster-ovens should toast bread, and drills should drill holes. This warranty includes the sale of food and drink, whether or not they are consumed at the place of sale. For example, the mothers of students in a high school band who sold sandwiches and lemonade at an annual fund-raising luncheon would not be held responsible for the fitness of the food because they do not regularly deal in selling food. But a caterer whose business is selling food makes an implied warranty that his food is fit for human consumption, and he can be held responsible for any injuries that result if it is not.

The goods are not required to be perfect in every detail, but only reasonably fit for their ordinary use. For example, a new automobile may have a slight but annoying squeak in the brakes, but as long as the brakes work, the seller is not liable. In addition, the goods must meet the requirements in the contract for packaging and labeling. When goods are labeled, they must meet any promises or statements of fact written on the label.

Fitness for a particular purpose   Another type of implied warranty is created when the buyer relies on the seller to give him goods that are suitable for a particular purpose. For this warranty to be effective, the goods must be used for the purpose for which the seller or manufacturer intended them to be used.

EXAMPLE A trucker wishes to take a motor trip over the
O⟷✷ Baja peninsula. Knowing that the Baja is hard on car tires, the man goes to a tire dealer and explains the nature of his trip. The dealer then sells the man a set of five steel-belted radial tires. This creates an implied warranty that the tires are fit for the purpose of motoring through the Baja.

Additional implied warranties can result from the customs peculiar to a trade, unless specifically excluded or modified. In the sale of a purebred dog, for instance, the usage of the trade usually obligates the breeder-seller to give the buyer a four-generation pedigree, showing that the dog conforms to the contract of sale.

Exclusion or modification   The merchantability warranty (acceptable quality) can be modified or excluded either verbally or in writing. If it is in writing, the modification or exclusion must be conspicuous and the language used must specifically mention the term "merchantability."

The warranty of fitness for a particular purpose can also be excluded, but this must be done in writing and be conspicuously and clearly written. For example:

&& There are no representations or warranties express or implied, including any warranties regarding merchantability or fitness for a particular purpose, not specified on the face of this contract. This contract states the entire obligation of the seller in connection with this transaction."

All implied warranties can also be excluded by saying the product is sold "as is" or by using any other language that alerts the buyer to the fact that all implied warranties are excluded. In addition, if the buyer does not closely examine the goods, then there can be no implied warranty about any imperfections that should have been discovered if a proper examination had been made.

EXAMPLE If you buy a raincoat marked "as is" without
O⟷✷ examining it and later discover that the sleeve is ripped, the seller is not obligated to refund your money. However, if you buy a motorbike marked "as is," inspect it, and later the tires go flat because the tubes are defective, the seller is obligated because there was no reasonable way for you to know or discover a defect in the tubes.

■ **Effect of seller's tender**   Once the goods are properly tendered (offered or delivered) by the seller, the buyer must accept and pay for them according to the terms of the contract.

Correcting an improper delivery   If a seller tenders or delivers nonconforming goods (those that do not meet the terms of the contract) that are rejected by the buyer and the time for fulfilling the contract has not expired, the seller may notify the buyer that he intends to correct the situation. The seller may then deliver conforming goods within the time set by the contract.

On the basis of past dealings with the buyer, a seller may deliver nonconforming goods that he reasonably believes will be acceptable to the buyer, with some adjustment in price. If the buyer rejects them, the seller may have an additional period of time to substitute conforming goods, provided he notifies the buyer within a reasonable time that he intends to do so.

Payment   The seller is not obligated to deliver the goods unless the buyer pays for them or the contract provides otherwise. The buyer may pay for goods by any method used in the usual course of business. If the seller insists on payment in cash, however, the buyer must be given a reasonable extension of time to obtain it. Payment can be made by check, but the goods are not considered paid for until the check clears the bank.

Inspection of goods   Before accepting and paying for the goods, the buyer has a right to inspect them. The inspection must be made at a reasonable time and place and by a reasonable method. If the goods are shipped, the buyer may inspect them after they arrive. The buyer must pay any inspection costs, but if the goods do not conform and the buyer rejects them, the buyer may recover the cost of inspection from the seller.

However, when the contract provides that the goods are to be delivered COD (collect on delivery) or the buyer is to pay after he receives the documents of title (the bill of lading), the buyer has no right to inspect the goods before paying for them.

Acceptance of goods A buyer accepts goods when he indicates to the seller that they conform to the sales contract or that he will keep them even though they do not conform. Acceptance can also take place if the buyer fails to reject the goods or if he exercises control over the goods in a way that suggests acceptance.

EXAMPLE Paul agreed to buy some brick, stone, and mill irons from Ralph and hauled them from Ralph's property to a building site. Paul used some of the materials in his construction and sold some of the remaining materials, but he never paid Ralph for the goods. When Ralph sued Paul for the price of the materials, the court held that there had been an acceptance of all of the materials and that a sale had been completed.

A buyer cannot reject goods after having accepted them. An exception occurs when he knew that the goods did not conform to the contract but accepted them with the belief that the irregularity would be corrected.

■ **Breach and rejection** When the goods that are sold do not conform to the requirements of the contract (a breach of contract), the buyer can accept all of the goods, reject all of them, or accept part of them and reject the remainder.

EXAMPLE A buyer ordered metal fittings, valves, and forged-steel flanges. The flanges sent by the seller were made of cast iron rather than forged steel. The buyer had the right to accept the part of the order that conformed to the contract and to reject the flanges, which were nonconforming.

Rejection If the buyer decides to reject the goods, he must notify the seller within a reasonable period of time after the goods have been delivered or the rejection is not valid. A rejection of a mobile home 17 days after its receipt was considered to have been made within a reasonable time—that is, within a few days after the unit had been connected and all equipment tested, but before the buyer moved into it.

A buyer who takes possession of the goods before rejecting them must take reasonable care of the goods and give the seller a reasonable time and place to repossess them. If the buyer rejects the goods, he may not make any act of ownership over the goods (see "Acceptance of goods" above), such as using them. This rule is intended to insure that the seller can repossess and resell the goods.

Buyer's responsibility for rejected goods When a merchant-buyer takes possession of goods and rejects them, and the seller does not have an agent or place of business where the goods can be returned, the buyer must follow any reasonable instructions sent by the seller. If the seller sends no instructions concerning the goods, the buyer can store the goods, ship them back to the seller, or sell them for the seller. A buyer who attempts in good faith to salvage the goods is not considered to be converting the goods to his own use or accepting them. If the rejected goods are perishable and the seller fails to send instructions, the buyer must try to sell the goods. For example, one court held that Christmas trees cut for marketing during the holiday season were perishable goods, and the buyer, after rejecting them, was required to try to sell them on behalf of the seller.

The buyer is entitled to recover from the seller reasonable expenses in caring for and selling the rejected goods. This includes either the usual sales commission or a reasonable fee (not greater than 10 percent of the gross receipts from the sale).

Notice of breach The seller must be notified of a breach of contract within a reasonable time after the buyer has discovered it. If the buyer fails to notify the seller, he loses his remedy (legal means for enforcing his rights) against the seller.

Once the buyer accepts the goods, he has the burden of proving any breach of contract. When, however, the goods are rejected, the burden of proving that the goods conform to the contract remains on the seller.

Revoking acceptance A buyer can revoke his acceptance of nonconforming goods when their value is substantially impaired (lower than it should be) and the buyer believed that the seller would correct the nonconformity within a reasonable time, but the seller did not.

EXAMPLE A transmission fell out of a used car on the day after it was purchased, and a week after the transmission was repaired the brakes failed. The value of the buyer's contract for the car was judged "substantially impaired," and the buyer was entitled to revoke his acceptance of the car and to get his money back.

The buyer can also revoke his acceptance if difficulties in discovering a defect or assurances made by the seller led him to accept nonconforming goods. For example, a buyer who had little training in the cattle business purchased a bull that the sellers claimed was a good breeding bull, but in fact it was not. Because the buyer was not an expert in the cattle business, the court permitted him to cancel the sale.

Time The buyer must revoke his acceptance within a reasonable time after he discovers the nonconformity and before the condition of the goods changes or deteriorates. What is a reasonable time often depends on the circumstances of the case.

EXAMPLE An automobile buyer's revocation 14 months after he had bought the car was judged reasonable because there had been an almost continuous series of negotiations and attempted repairs on the vehicle during the 14-month period.

EXAMPLE In another case, a buyer of an engine was aware that it was defective almost from the day it was put into use. The buyer delayed sending notice of revocation to the seller for almost six months. The court held that the notice of revocation had not been made within a reasonable time.

■ **Risk of loss** The risk of loss is transferred to the buyer when the seller delivers conforming goods to a carrier (ship, truck, or other vehicle) or to a named destination, or when the buyer takes possession of the goods. Until that time the risk of loss remains with the seller because he usually has possession of the goods and insurance to cover their loss. This means that if the seller has delivered the goods to a ship that later sinks in a storm or to a trucking company that loses them, the buyer must bear the loss.

However, the buyer may, in turn, sue the CARRIER, because the carrier is ultimately responsible under common law.

When the goods are in the possession of a bailee (an intermediary, such as a carrier or warehouseman), the risk of loss is transferred to the buyer when he receives the document of title to the goods or when the bailee acknowledges that the buyer is entitled to take possession of the goods. Buyer and seller are, of course, free to make any other agreement about risk of loss.

When the buyer has rejected nonconforming goods (or accepts them and later rejects them because he discovers they are nonconforming), the seller bears the risk of loss until he corrects the situation or the buyer accepts the goods. If the goods are destroyed, any amount not covered by the buyer's insurance is the seller's responsibility.

EXAMPLE Sal sends Bernie nonconforming goods. Bernie, 0—* because of the difficulty in discovering the nonconformity before acceptance, accepts the goods. After discovering the nonconformity, he rejects the goods, but the goods are then destroyed by fire. Bernie's policy covers only 90 percent of the loss. The remaining 10 percent of the loss rests with Sal.

If the buyer unjustifiably rejects the contract, any risk of loss not covered by the seller's insurance remains with the buyer. Thus, if the value of lost goods is $10,000 and the seller's insurance covers only $7,500, the seller may sue the buyer for the difference.

■ **Seller's remedies** When a buyer breaches a sales contract—by not paying for the goods, by wrongfully rejecting or revoking acceptance of the goods, or by repudiating the sale—the seller has several choices. He may, for example, cancel the contract. If he does, he is entitled to enforce any rights (such as payment for goods) that accrued before the breach and to seek a remedy for it. (A remedy is a legal method of enforcing a right or redressing a wrong.) For example, if a buyer accepted 50 percent of the goods he ordered before breaching the contract, the seller must be paid for those goods even if he decides to cancel the rest of the contract.

If the seller is in possession of the goods, he can refrain from delivering them to the buyer. When a large shipment, such as a boatload or railroad carload, is in the hands of a bailee, such as a carrier or warehouseman, the seller can stop delivery if the buyer fails to meet a payment that is due before delivery. Stopping a delivery for this reason is limited to large shipments because of the inconvenience it causes to the carrier. A seller can stop delivery of small shipments in the hands of the bailee only if he learns that the buyer is insolvent (unable to pay his bills on time).

Reselling goods The seller may finish manufacturing goods that were partially completed at the time of the breach and sell them to someone else in order to minimize his loss. He may also halt the manufacturing process and sell the goods for their scrap or salvage value.

Although the seller is entitled to resell the goods, he must act in good faith and the resale must be commercially reasonable. For example, the seller must try to get the best price for the goods.

The seller can recover compensatory DAMAGES from the buyer—the difference between the resale price and the contract price. If, for example, the goods were to be purchased by the original buyer for $10,000, but are resold for $7,500, the seller can recover the $2,500 from the original buyer. The seller is also allowed to recover incidental expenses, such as storage fees.

The resale may be public or private. If it is private, the buyer must be notified of the intent to resell. If it is public (an auction), the buyer must be notified of the time and place. The seller is permitted to bid at the auction, and he may purchase the goods himself. A buyer at the resale takes title to the goods free and clear of any rights or claims by the original buyer. If the seller makes a profit on the resale, he does not have to account for it to the original buyer.

Damages The damages caused to the seller when the buyer does not accept goods or rejects the sale are measured by the difference between the contract price of the goods and the current market price (cash value) at the time and place of delivery under the contract. For example, if the contract is $2,000 but the market price is only $1,500, the seller is entitled to recover $500 in damages from the buyer, plus any incidental expenses caused by the buyer's breach of contract.

Often, this method of measuring damages does not give the seller as large a profit as he would have made if the buyer had performed his obligation. If so, the seller may also recover from the buyer as much as the profit should have been, plus expenses. Using the figures from the previous example, if the standard list price a seller charges for an order of goods is $2,000 and the seller's cost for the goods is $1,400, the seller is entitled to recover his usual profit of $600, rather than the difference between the $2,000 contract price and the $1,500 market price.

The seller may sue the buyer for the price of the goods if the buyer fails to pay for them after he has accepted them or if they have been lost after responsibility for loss has passed to the buyer. The seller may also sue the buyer for the price when the seller attempts to resell the goods but is unable to get a fair price for them. The seller must then hold the goods for the buyer; if, however, he finds he can resell them, he may do so until the time he collects on his judgment from his lawsuit against the buyer. The buyer must be credited with the proceeds when any of the goods are sold. Once he pays the judgment, he is entitled to any remaining unsold goods.

■ **Buyer's remedies** The buyer has the right to cancel the contract when the seller repudiates it, as by failing to deliver the goods. The buyer may also cancel when he rejects nonconforming goods or later revokes his acceptance. After the buyer has rightfully canceled, he may recover any sum that he has paid to the seller for the goods.

Covering a sale The buyer may "cover" the breached contract by purchasing substitute goods from another seller. This must be done in good faith and within a reasonable period of time. What is reasonable depends on each case. The buyer is also entitled to damages. Damages are measured by the difference between the cost of covering the contract and the contract price. For example, if the contract price is $10,000 and the cost of purchasing substitute goods is $15,000, the buyer may recover $5,000 from the seller, plus any other damages that result from the sale. Expenses saved by the seller's breach, such as the cost of shipping the goods, must be subtracted from the damages.

RESCUE AT SEA—FACTS ABOUT SALVAGE AND SALVAGE CLAIMS

■ Every salvage claim must include these three elements: (1) peril to a ship or cargo; (2) a service that is done voluntarily, not under a contract or other duty; and (3) at least partial success. Typical salvage services include giving advice for removing a vessel from a perilous situation; transmitting information about a vessel in distress so that relief can be sent; standing by and giving some service for a ship's protection; furnishing equipment nec-essary for rescue; and supplying officers and crew.

■ To justify a salvage award, the service performed must have contributed immediately to the rescue of the endangered property.

■ A ship's captain can refuse salvage service, but if his refusal jeopardizes the safety or property interests of others, then it is legal to intervene against his will. His refusal will not prevent salvage claims from being awarded.

■ Goods lost at sea from a damaged ship and found floating on the surface or cast on the shore are subject to salvage. So are cargoes on a wrecked or sunken vessel and the derelict vessel itself.

■ Public servants such as naval officers are not entitled to salvage awards for on-duty services.

■ Passengers cannot claim salvage awards unless they perform some extraordinary service.

Damages Damages for repudiation are measured by the difference between the market price (cash value) at the time the buyer discovers the breach and the contract price, plus incidental and consequential damages. The market price is the existing market price at the place where the goods were to be tendered (offered for delivery) to the buyer. For example, if the contract price is $20,000 but the existing market price at the time and place where the goods were to be tendered is $22,000, the buyer is entitled to recover $2,000 from the seller.

Specific performance When the subject of the contract is a one-of-a-kind item, such as an antique, an heirloom, or a work of art, money damages cannot adequately compensate the buyer for nondelivery or repudiation. In this situation the buyer may seek specific performance of the contract—the court can require the seller to deliver the exact goods described in the contract, if it is possible to do so. This remedy also applies when a seller agrees to deliver his entire output to a particular buyer or to supply all of a buyer's needs.

EXAMPLE Butler Oil Company agreed to supply all of Sky Airlines' fuel requirements at certain cities for five years. When Butler failed to deliver the necessary amount of fuel to three of the five cities, Sky brought suit. The court ruled that Sky Airlines was entitled to have specific performance of its contract with Butler—that is, Butler had to deliver whatever amount of fuel Sky required.

Replevin Another remedy granted to the buyer to secure a specific article is REPLEVIN. The article must be specifically identified in the contract, and the buyer must attempt to purchase a cover (substitute) for it.

EXAMPLE Suppose Miller's Department Store buys 2,000 pairs of Signature jeans to be delivered in time for its annual spring fashion show. When the shipment does not arrive at the expected time, Miller's calls Signature only to find out that they had agreed to sell the jeans to another store for a higher price. Miller's tries other jeans manufacturers, but none of them can fill the order in time for the fashion show. Because Miller's is unable to obtain cover (replacement) for its purchase, it is entitled to have the 2,000 pairs of jeans from Signature.

Breach of warranty When the seller breaches the warranty, damages are determined when and where the buyer makes the acceptance. Damages are the difference between the actual value of the goods and the value the goods would have had if they conformed to the warranty.

EXAMPLE A buyer and seller enter into a contract for 100 aluminum window frames at $25 per unit. After the frames arrive and the buyer accepts and pays for them, he discovers that the frames are not as warranted—they are not 100 percent aluminum. The value of the frames is actually $5 each. The buyer is entitled to damages in the amount of $20 per frame, plus any additional damages resulting from the seller's breach of warranty.

salvage The compensation allowed to persons who voluntarily help to save a ship at sea or its cargo; the property recovered from a derelict vessel or a shipwreck, or in the recapture of a ship previously taken by an enemy. Salvage differs from a prize in that salvage is a reward granted for saving the property of the unfortunate, while a prize is a vessel or cargo captured from an enemy at sea.

Three elements must exist to validate a salvage claim: (1) a marine peril, (2) a service voluntarily performed (one not required from an existing duty or contract), and (3) success in whole or in part or some service contributing to success.

EXAMPLE A ship is disabled on the high seas—it is listing, partly flooded, and unable to proceed under its own power. A second ship appears, removes the passengers and cargo from the crippled ship, and tows the damaged vessel into port. All the officers and crew members of the second ship who helped in the rescue of the first are entitled to salvage. The three conditions have been met: (1) the first ship was in peril, (2) the men aboard the second ship voluntarily performed a service to save the ship even though they were not bound by duty or contract to do so, and (3) the service was successful in removing the disabled ship from its peril.

■ **Marine peril** Ordinarily, the danger does not have to be imminent or absolute. If the vessel has encountered some damage or misfortune that might expose it to destruction, marine peril is established. The peril can, for instance, be brought about by an illness of officers or of the crew that leaves no one capable of sailing the vessel safely to port.

■ **Voluntary service** Useful service of any kind rendered to a vessel or cargo exposed to imminent peril can entitle those who give the service to a salvage award. The salvage service can take place on the high seas, on a public navigable river or lake, or even while the ship is in dry dock. Although the difficulty of relieving the ship and the danger to the salvors have no bearing on the usefulness of their service, these factors do affect the degree of service and the amount of any subsequent reward.

Rescuing a stranded or grounded vessel or its cargo or preventing a vessel from becoming stranded is a service. Merely pulling on a stranded ship just as a favorable tide or swell frees it is not enough to support a claim for salvage. Similarly, securing a drifting vessel or its cargo may be a service, but towing drifting property to shore when the property cannot float away does not count.

Rescuing property in danger of damage by fire or explosion is salvage. Extinguishing or helping to extinguish a fire on board a vessel, towing a vessel to a place where a fire aboard may be more readily put out, towing a ship away from a dock where it is in danger of catching fire, and unloading a ship that is on fire at a wharf—are all salvage services.

Other salvage services include giving advice for removing a vessel from a perilous situation; transmitting information about a vessel in distress so that relief can be sent; standing by and giving some service for a ship's protection; convoying; furnishing equipment necessary for rescue; and supplying officers and crew.

■ **The success of service**   The service performed must have immediately contributed to the rescue of the property in peril. No matter how praiseworthy, unsuccessful efforts do not justify an award. The service need not have been entirely successful, however, nor need it have been the sole cause of the rescue. A service performed counts toward a salvage award even though the salvor was forced by prudence or necessity to stop giving his help and leave the final rescue to others.

■ **Acceptance of service**   A ship's master in control of his vessel can refuse salvage service. No volunteer salvor can expect to be rewarded for services that the master forbids. An owner of a vessel can adopt his own measures for preserving his vessel. When, in his judgment, he has provided the means for his ship's rescue, he cannot be forced to accept offers of help. When assistance is being given, the officers of the vessel in distress are free to decide when the help should end.

If a master's refusal of aid jeopardizes the safety of persons or the property interests of others, then legal justification exists for intervening against his will. Under such circumstances, a master's refusal may be immaterial (unimportant) when salvage claims are pressed.

EXAMPLE Suppose a cargo ship, the *Indomitable*, scraped against some rocks in a storm and had a hole torn into its starboard side. Water started pouring into the ship and it began to list to starboard. Another ship, the *Ranger*, sailed by and rushed to aid the *Indomitable*. But the master of the damaged ship, Captain Whitman, was so obsessed with the idea of self-sufficiency that he insisted that he could maneuver his ship into port without danger. The captain of the *Ranger*, a seaman of long experience, could see that the *Indomitable* would surely sink before reaching land, and took aboard the crew and part of the cargo of the *Indomitable* against Captain Whitman's

wishes. The *Indomitable* did sink a few miles outside of port and Whitman had to row ashore in a lifeboat. The captain of the *Ranger* would be entitled to salvage.

Services offered and given in a dangerous situation cannot be repudiated after the danger is past in order to avoid paying a claim for salvage.

Persons who assist a vessel in distress at the request of its master or owner usually must be paid as salvors. When the services of a salvor vessel have been requested and accepted but the vessel is dismissed, the services that have been performed are salvage services.

■ **Views toward property**   Generally, salvage is limited to ships and other vessels, cargoes, and property lost in navigable waters. The terms "ship" and "vessel" include all structures designed for navigation and transportation. The vessel does not even need to have the power of motion, as for example, a floating wharf.

Goods lost at sea from a damaged ship and found floating on the surface or cast on the shore are subject to salvage. So are cargoes on a wrecked or sunken vessel.

Although a derelict vessel or its cargo is subject to salvage, the abandonment by the captain must be final, without hope of recovery or intention to return. When a master and crew leave temporarily with the intent to return, the ship is not derelict.

EXAMPLE The crew of a torpedoed freighter left it, but remained close by, awaiting expected assistance that soon arrived. The vessel was not abandoned and the crewmen were not discharged. When crew members claimed a salvage award for help they gave in towing the vessel into port, their claim was denied.

■ **Persons entitled to salvage**   Any person not bound by a legal duty to perform the service can be a salvor. Ordinarily, public servants or officers are not entitled to be rewarded as salvors when they are acting within the scope of their duties.

EXAMPLE A tanker carrying oil and gasoline for military operations burst into flames and endangered an entire port. A naval officer in charge of a naval repair shop some 200 yards from the tanker directed the firefighting operations that saved both the tanker and port. Because the man acted as a public servant—as a naval officer—he was not entitled to salvage.

Shipowners can claim compensation for salvage services rendered by their vessels. The fact that the owners of an assisting vessel may also be the owners of the salvaged vessel does not preclude them from recovering salvage compensation for the rescued cargo.

Generally, the master of the salvage vessel and all members of the crew who served in the operation are entitled to share in the salvage award. On the other hand, neither the master nor the crew of a vessel in trouble can file claims as salvors for services performed in rescuing their own ship. In case of danger it is the duty of all persons on board a vessel to give assistance to avert loss and injury. Passengers cannot claim salvage unless they perform extraordinary service.

■ **How liability is assessed**   A salvor is entitled to an award from anyone who has benefited by his service, including the owners of the vessel and the cargo. Under federal law, the U.S. government can be liable for salvage services rendered to its vessels or cargo. In addition, the person who wrongfully caused or was responsible for the peril to the government property can be held liable for the amount awarded.

Generally, any property to which a salvage service is given is the basis for an award. The owner of a vessel is not usually liable for the salvage due from the rescue of its cargo, nor is the owner of the cargo liable for salvage due from the rescue of the vessel.

■ **Size of the award** Salvage awards are based on the facts and circumstances of the case and are made within the court's discretion. Such cases are decided by federal district courts with ADMIRALTY jurisdiction. The amount should be fair and generous, but should not impose undue hardship on the owner of the salvaged property. A variety of factors are considered in deciding the amount of the award, including the place where the salvage operation occurred, the number of persons needed to perform the services, the value of the salvaged property, the degree of risk to which the salvaging vessel was exposed, the time involved in the operation, and the degree of success achieved.

sanction 1 Authorize or confirm another person's actions. 2 A penalty or punishment used to enforce obedience to a law. Sanctions that provide redress for civil wrongs, such as a right to sue for money damages, are called *civil sanctions*. Those that punish crimes are called *penal sanctions*.

sanctuary In old English law, a consecrated place, such as a church, that served as a refuge. Offenders against the law could not be arrested there. The privilege of sanctuary was later abolished.

sanity See INSANE PERSONS.

satisfaction 1 The discharge of an obligation by paying what is due on a mortgage, LIEN, contract, or a court-awarded JUDGMENT. Thus, if a defendant loses in a civil suit he may have to satisfy the judgment by paying the amount awarded. 2 The execution of a judgment or an accord. For example, when a defendant pays the plaintiff the money due on a judgment, the plaintiff can write out (execute) a piece of paper called a satisfaction. See ACCORD AND SATISFACTION.

satisfactory Sufficient; adequate for the purpose. For example, when a contract is fulfilled in the prescribed way, it is said to be performed in a satisfactory manner.

save 1 Preserve from injury. 2 Except, reserve, or exempt, as when a statute "saves vested rights." 3 Suspend the running or operation of something, as to "save the statute of limitations." See LIMITATIONS OF ACTIONS.

savings and loan association A financial institution, chartered and regulated by the federal or state government, in which people may invest funds to provide financing for homes. Federal savings and loan associations are chartered and supervised by the Federal Home Loan Bank Board, which was established in 1932. Because the largest single type of investment made by savings and loan

associations is home mortgages, antidiscrimination regulations have been issued by a variety of state and federal agencies to insure that these associations comply with fair housing laws when passing on mortgage applications.

■ **Funding and management** A savings and loan association is formed by charter from a state or federal agency, which allows the association to accept deposits and make loans as investments. Depositors are paid dividends of specified amounts, and their accounts are usually insured by the Federal Savings and Loan Insurance Corporation. Although changes are occurring, savings and loan associations generally have not been authorized to provide checking accounts for their depositors.

A savings and loan association's policy is set by a board of directors, not by its depositors.

■ **Similar institutions** Savings and loan associations differ from commercial banks in that the associations are designed to provide financing for homes, whereas banks are concerned mainly with short-term business loans. See BANKS AND BANKING. State savings banks and state building and loan associations resemble savings and loan associations, but there are some major differences.

State savings banks These are state-chartered institutions owned by the depositors and managed by a board of directors similar to that of a savings and loan association. Also like the associations, savings banks are organized primarily to make real estate loans. They are nonetheless permitted to maintain a variety of other conservative investments. While savings banks have historically been denied authority to institute checking accounts, there has been a recent trend toward granting them this service.

State building and loan associations Building and loan associations, which are sometimes called building associations or homestead associations, function similarly to the savings banks and savings and loan associations. Lending is limited primarily to the real estate MORTGAGE market, and loans are closely regulated. The authority to make loans that do not concern real estate is, however, more restricted than that of savings banks. Building and loan associations raise money through solicitation of deposits and depositors are paid specified dividends.

Unlike savings and loan associations, building and loan associations are controlled and managed by their depositors, who vote on policy matters at an annual meeting. Building and loan associations are also moving toward the providing of checking accounts for depositors.

schedule 1 A written or printed list; a catalog; an inventory. 2 A sheet of paper attached to a statute, deed, answer in EQUITY, or deposition that exhibits in detail the matters mentioned in the principal document.

school An institution devoted to teaching. Schools are generally divided into three major levels: elementary (grammar schools), secondary (high schools), and higher learning (colleges and universities). Sometimes there are intermediate levels, such as junior high schools and junior colleges. There are also vocational and trade schools, and schools that specialize in a certain field. Schools may be public or private. Public schools are supported by PROPERTY TAXES and other taxes. Private schools are owned and operated by individuals, corporations, or private associations. All schools are regulated by state law within limits set by the federal and state constitutions and laws.

States delegate much of their authority to local school districts. These are governed by school boards, whose members are elected or sometimes appointed.

This article discusses the right to go to public schools, the requirement of attending school under compulsory attendance laws, the organization of public elementary and secondary schools, and the functions and powers of the school boards that run them. For information about institutions of higher learning, see COLLEGES AND UNIVERSITIES. For more information about how the law affects schools and the rights of students and their parents, see CIVIL RIGHTS; EQUAL PROTECTION OF LAWS; PARENT AND CHILD; PRIVACY, RIGHT OF; RELIGION, FREEDOM OF; TENURE.

■ **The right to go to school** All states provide free education although they are not compelled to do so. Many states have committed themselves by constitutional provisions to providing public schools. Washington State's constitution, for example, establishes a "general and uniform system of public schools" that gives every child free access to instructional facilities at least through the 12th grade.

Equal opportunity Public schools must be available to everyone regardless of race. This is one of our basic civil rights. Separate schools for boys or girls may be set aside in a district that is otherwise coeducational, but the system must afford both sexes equal educational opportunities. Also, the special needs of mentally retarded or physically HANDICAPPED PERSONS must be accommodated. No child should be denied schooling for reasons unrelated to the educational process.

Residence requirements Only children who are residents of the public school district qualify for the free education it provides. Some nonresidents may be accepted as students, but the school board is within its rights to charge tuition.

EXAMPLE In one unusual case, decided in Ohio in 1971, a
O—✳ school board tried to collect tuition payments from a family that lived both inside and outside the school district. The family had 11 children and owned two houses, one on each side of the road that divided two school districts. They used one house for sleeping and the other for cooking, eating, and living space. The court considered the ways the family lived in each house and then decided that the children lived in both school districts. They were entitled to go to public school free in either one.

The question of paying tuition arises when the child does not live with his parent. The general rule is that a child is a resident of the place where his parents (or father) live. States have modified this rule to recognize a child's resi-

---

SCHOOLS AND THE RIGHTS OF YOUR CHILD

■ Only children who are residents qualify for the free education supplied by a school district; the school board may charge tuition for nonresidents.

■ In some states the general rule has been that a child is a resident of the place where his parents or father lives. Some states say that a child's residence is where his legal custodian lives—for example, the mother who has custody when parents are divorced or separated.

■ School districts can refuse to enroll a child who has not had the required vaccinations.

■ Whether you want your children immunized makes no difference in most cases, although some states permit members of certain religious groups to refuse vaccinations for their children and still send them to school.

■ Attendance laws vary from state to state, but as a rule all children between 7 and 16 must go to school. Failure to send a child to school regularly can subject a parent to fines and minor prison sentences.

■ If a student reaches the local maximum age without graduating from high school, the school district can expel him and let him complete his education in adult classes.

■ Married or pregnant students can usually be expelled only if it can be proved that their presence substantially interferes with school discipline.

■ You cannot be punished for removing your children from a dangerous school, but you must be able to prove that the school poses a substantial threat to their health and welfare.

■ Some states will let you teach your child at home if you are qualified—qualifications vary from state to state.

■ Students have no right to choose the public school they will attend.

■ If the school offers extracurricular activities, they must be equally available to all students.

■ Students can be barred from sports during the year that they transfer to another district. This is to discourage recruiting and to keep the amateur character of high school athletics.

■ If a student completes his work or passes the required exams, he cannot be denied graduation as a punishment for his misbehavior.

■ Under the common law, public school districts cannot be sued for physical injuries. However, many states have softened the rule of immunity to allow suits in which the plaintiff can show that the injury was caused by the intentional or careless conduct of someone representing or employed by the school district.

■ Signing a waiver, release, or permission slip does not necessarily prevent you from suing if your child is injured in sports or on a field trip.

■ Corporal punishment has been allowed by the Supreme Court and is authorized by 21 states.

■ School officials may not punish students for expressing their opinions, however unpopular.

■ Schools may not censor controversial viewpoints or forbid all distribution of underground newspapers.

■ Students cannot be suspended for refusing to salute the flag or recite the Pledge of Allegiance, whether for reasons of religion or conscience.

■ Bible reading and prayers are prohibited, but short periods of silent "meditation or prayer" are allowed.

■ Schools may offer instruction on religion so long as they do not favor one faith over another.

dence as the place where his legal custodian lives—for example, the mother who has custody when the parents are divorced or separated. Sometimes a parent who cannot make a home for his children will board them with another family. If the family lives in a different school district, the parent can be required to pay tuition. Foster-care programs usually provide for tuition payments to be made by the administering agency. The tuition payments are then recovered from the parent—unless the parent is indigent.

EXAMPLE In one New York case, a school district refused to 0—* enroll eight black children who had been placed in a group home presided over by a man and his wife. The children were from two families and were placed in the home as the only practical way to keep brothers and sisters together. The school district claimed that the children were not residents. Furthermore, admitting them would tip the racial balance of its schools, contribute to overcrowding, and cost the district money. The court answered that the school district had no choice in the matter. These children were living in a "family home" as much as any child who resides with his natural mother and father. As to the district's other arguments, the court asserted that a school district cannot solve its money or racial balance problems by arbitrarily excluding eight children from a public school.

Age of students It is entirely proper for a school district to limit enrollment to children of suitable age. This suitable age is usually fixed by state statute; commonly it includes anyone between 4 and 21 years of age who has not yet completed high school. If age requirements are not applied uniformly, pupils are denied their constitutional right of equal treatment.

EXAMPLE A school refused to admit a girl to kindergarten 0—* because the local district had adopted a different age requirement from that of the state. The state said first-grade enrollment was mandatory if the child was six years old by December 1. The district offered kindergarten to any child who was five by September 1. The child in the case was going to be five in November. The court reasoned that the school could not deny her enrollment in the first grade for the following year; therefore, it was unfair to deprive her of kindergarten by applying a different cutoff date. While the state did not insist that every district establish a kindergarten program, those districts that did had to employ a uniform age requirement.

The age at which children first enroll in public school usually depends on the date of their birth. For example, a law may permit children in a district to start school in September if they attain the minimum age by December 1. Some districts let a principal make an exception for a child who is very close to the necessary age, particularly if the child can pass a readiness test or has completed a preschool program during the preceding year.

Because schools are intended for children, maximum-age requirements are deemed legal. Many school districts offer adult education classes for people who have reached the maximum age without finishing high school. Thus, a school district can expel a student when he reaches the maximum age and let him complete his education in adult classes.

Vaccinations State laws often require children to be vaccinated—against measles and poliomyelitis, for exam-

ple. A state does not have to show that an epidemic is threatening in order to enforce a vaccination law. It is enough that legislators think vaccinations will keep disease down to a manageable level. School districts can refuse to enroll a child who has not had his shots.

Whether the parents want their children immunized makes no difference. Some states have laws that permit members of certain religious groups to refuse vaccinations for their children and still send them to public schools. Where there is no such exception in a statute, courts do not believe that compulsory vaccination laws violate anyone's freedom of religion.

Married students and mothers It was once standard procedure to expel a student who got married during the school term. The schools defended this action on the grounds that married students disrupted the school routine, that schools should not appear to be condoning early marriages, and that married students no longer profited from the school experience. The same arguments, plus the issue of morality, have been used to refuse admission of pregnant students and unwed mothers. Court challenges to these rigid policies have been successful.

EXAMPLE When an 18-year-old pregnant girl brought suit 0—* against a Massachusetts high school that had expelled her, the federal court backed her. The court found that the girl got along well with the faculty and students and that her well-being would be enhanced by continued attendance in classes. The school officials could only consider educational policies that were good for the girl and the school, not inflict punishment for her condition.

Some courts have noted that married students or mothers may be adults in many ways, but they cannot qualify for adult education classes until they reach the age of 18. If the public schools bar them, they will be denied an education.

Some schools try to discourage teenage sex or early marriage by separating offending students from the mainstream—for example, by denying them the opportunity to participate in school athletics or extracurricular activities. But if a board shunts pregnant students into a separate program, the alternative must be educationally equal to the normal school program. A pregnant or married student cannot be denied attendance in public schools unless the student's presence substantially interferes with school discipline.

■ **Compulsory attendance** All states require children to go to school. Laws vary from state to state, but usually every child between the ages of 7 and 16 must attend an approved public or private school unless he has already completed the eighth grade or is physically or mentally unable to attend. The regular program of instruction also varies, but a standard minimum term is six hours a day for 180 days a year. The school board may declare a school closed in an emergency. If a school is shut for so long that it fails to meet the state minimum, then the officials are responsible for scheduling makeup days.

Under the compulsory attendance laws of the various states, when a child is absent his principal or a school attendance officer must find out why. If no valid excuse can be found, then this information must be passed along to the parents and sometimes to a court or the police. The primary obligation of insuring regular attendance is placed on the parent or legal guardian. Failure to send a child to school regularly can subject a parent to fines and minor prison sentences. A child who fails to go to school as required by law is a truant. He may have his grades reduced for classes missed, be assigned to a special disciplinary class or school, or be charged as a juvenile delinquent.

Valid excuses for missing school depend on state law and school rules. Laws recognize that children miss school occasionally when they are ill. Some laws do not inflict punishment until a child is habitually absent without reason. In various cases, a parent has been found not guilty of violating a compulsory attendance law when a child stayed home to care for a sick mother, when a pupil was wrongfully suspended for refusing to salute the flag, or when a child was receiving regular religious instruction.

EXAMPLE In a Pennsylvania case, however, Muslim parents were not allowed to keep their children out of school for the entire day on Fridays, the sacred day of their religion. The court felt they could find a private school that would accommodate them while still offering a full-time program of instruction.

Parents cannot be punished for removing their children from a dangerous school where the child's health and welfare is threatened. The school is supposed to be safe for children, but only a substantial risk justifies the refusal to send a child to school.

Some states will permit a parent to teach his children at home if he is qualified, whether licensed or not, but many states require the parent to have teaching credentials. If the parent is not qualified to teach, the courts will probably force him to send his children to school. But if a qualified teacher gives the instructions and the necessary subjects are taught, the state must be satisfied.

EXAMPLE In one California case, a veterinarian and his wife removed their three children from public school because they believed them too intelligent to benefit from a regular education. The father had insisted that the school let the children skip a grade. But when they had difficulty adjusting—one became a discipline problem—the father began instructing them at home. He also enrolled all three children in a high school correspondence course. The court found that this program was not a "private full-time school," which California accepted as an alternative to public school attendance. The father was not a certified teacher, and the children were not receiving instruction in all the required courses. The children were made wards of the juvenile court, and the parents were ordered to post money bonds to insure that the children would attend school regularly from then on.

■ **Administration of public schools** The basic unit of the public school system is the school district, which is generally created and named by an act of the state legislature. A school district is a political subdivision of the state with responsibilities for education. It encompasses a compact geographical area and usually includes both primary and secondary schools. Some states also have established community college districts that maintain public schools for one or two years of education beyond high school.

The governing body of a school district is the school board, which organizes the schools within its district and makes all major decisions concerning their administration.

School board members are elected or appointed and often serve without pay. The board acts on educational matters at regularly scheduled public meetings, for which notice is posted in advance. The number of members who must be present in order for the board to act and the requirements for voting are determined by local law.

The school board is responsible for a host of policymaking decisions relating to structure of the school system, curriculum, integration, extracurricular activities, and school libraries; its employees implement those policies. The board hires, fires, promotes, and disciplines school employees, including school superintendents, principals, teachers, clerks, bus drivers, and custodians. Where there are unions, the board negotiates their work contracts. The board also sets standards by which employees qualify for given positions.

Teachers and administrators In order to work in the schools, states generally require teachers and administrators to obtain licenses, or certificates. To qualify for a license, an applicant must have completed the required educational level and have student-teaching experience. He may also have to pass competency examinations, either written or oral or both. There may be different licenses for teachers of various subjects or grade levels and for principals and other administrators. A license may not be denied on account of race or a physical handicap that does not impair the ability to teach. One court said that the state may not assume that a blind person is necessarily unqualified to teach. A license granted by one state, however, does not automatically entitle a teacher to work in schools of another state. School districts may also set up their own licensing requirements.

Besides licensing, a state or locality may impose other requirements on applicants. Rejected job seekers have challenged a number of these local requirements in court with mixed results. Courts have upheld regulations requiring teachers to be loyal to the Constitution of the United States, for example, but they have not allowed school boards to reject a job seeker because he or she was once a member of a left-wing organization unless that person had supported the forceful overthrow of the U.S. government. Teachers are generally required to pass physical examinations, and this has led to some problems. For example, a person can fail a physical examination merely because he is overweight. A court in New York, however, decided that a teacher who was more than 40 percent over the normal weight for a person of her build should not be rejected for obesity—particularly in light of her successful three-year teaching record. Some courts have upheld school boards that refuse to hire applicants who have a history of mental illness, while other courts insist that boards give fair consideration to teachers who have been treated for mental illness but can offer proof of rehabilitation. School boards customarily reject teaching applicants who abuse drugs or alcohol or who have been convicted of violent crimes.

A teaching license may be revoked for any conduct that shows unfitness to teach. Licenses have often been revoked for homosexual behavior and convictions for drug abuse. One teacher lost her license after she joined a "swingers" club, became publicly promiscuous, and discussed unconventional sex on a television talk show.

Teachers are, however, entitled to privacy, if they keep their personal lives to themselves. Licenses cannot be revoked for conduct that has no effect on the pupils.

EXAMPLE One teacher lost his license because he admitted to an isolated incident of adultery. But the court overturned the revocation because of his otherwise unblemished record.

EXAMPLE Another court would not permit revocation of a teacher's certification after he was convicted for possession of marijuana. The court ruled that there was no evidence that his conduct disrupted his relationship with his students and other teachers.

When a teacher has been issued a temporary license and it expires, he or she has no right to insist that it be renewed or extended. Also, probationary or conditional licenses may be revoked whenever the teacher fails to meet the requirements for a regular certification. If the teacher fails to fulfill a stipulation within the allotted time, the license can be rescinded. Sometimes the effect of this inflexible rule can be harsh.

EXAMPLE One teacher was granted limited certification on the condition that she complete classes in a modern language by a certain date. She fulfilled the requirement, but she was one semester late because of an illness. The court found that her teaching license was properly revoked for failure to meet the condition on time.

School structure School boards set policy about how the schools in their district will be structured, both physically and philosophically. They must decide such issues as the separate housing of intermediate or junior high grades and how much special attention should be given to gifted children.

Grade levels Local school authorities decide how to organize the grade levels in their schools. Such decisions include whether or not to have a kindergarten and how primary, junior high, and high school grades should be housed in different buildings. Some districts, for example, have middle schools for fifth through eighth or sixth through ninth grades.

Children are most often assigned to grade levels on the basis of age; the exceptions are those whose ability is substantially different from that of most others of their age. A school district may also choose to combine children of different ages in a multigrade classroom or establish ungraded or open classroom schools. Unless the school board offers a choice, parents do not have the right to demand one system over another.

Special schools or classes Boards often assign students to certain schools or classes on the basis of their special needs or talents. Federal law makes money available for states to meet the needs of handicapped children. Where possible, these children are educated along with other children, but an individualized educational plan must be developed so that each handicapped child can receive special services and have his progress monitored. Some courts have held that emotionally disturbed children and those with behavioral problems must also be enrolled in the public schools and, when possible, in regular classrooms.

A school board may set aside schools for special students as long as assignments to these schools are not made for some impermissible reason, such as the student's race.

EXAMPLE In one federal case, a high school girl in Philadelphia challenged that city's system of maintaining two high schools for scholastically superior students—one for boys and one for girls. The plaintiff preferred the high school that had been set aside for boys. The court found that both special high schools offered an excellent program, and it refused to order the boys' school to accept the girl. To rule otherwise, the court said, would mean that every public school in the country would have to be coeducational.

The Supreme Court affirmed the ruling in an evenly split decision. When the nine-member Supreme Court splits evenly—a rare occurrence made possible by the absence or abstention of one or more of the justices—the lower court judgment stands. While this settles the case, it does not serve as a precedent. In two earlier cases, federal courts had ruled that San Francisco and Boston could not operate sex-segregated high schools for academically superior students if the entrance requirements were easier for boys than for girls.

School districts also separate children into groups in order to adjust courses of study to students' differing academic abilities. Called *tracking*, this system does not violate the right of equality even though students in one track are treated differently from those in others. Some schools have special tracks for retarded children, very slow learners, or the intellectually gifted, while the main body of students follow a standard curriculum. Other schools, especially those on the high school level, place each student in one of several tracks depending on the individual's future goals and academic performance.

EXAMPLE One high school had a system made up of five tracks: an academic program, which prepared students for entering college; a scientific program, which was designed for students who leaned toward the study of the sciences; an honors program, which emphasized classical languages; a business program, which taught basic office skills, such as typing and stenography; and a trades program, which emphasized mechanical skills. After the first year of general studies, students were placed into one of these five programs. The students were given some choice, but the honors and scientific programs were open only to students whose grades in the first year of study indicated that they could handle the work. If they did well in science and mathematics, they could choose the scientific program if they wished. If they had very high grades in all subjects, they could join the honors program. On the other hand, students who qualified for the honors or scientific program were not required to enter them but could elect one of the other programs instead. Students who could not qualify for either the honors or scientific program could enter one of the other three programs, depending upon their goals in life.

A tracking system is not fair if it serves to perpetuate the inequalities of a formerly segregated system or consistently locks poor or black children into dead-end programs. A school system may not give up on certain children by dumping them into an inflexible or carelessly designed tracking system. Only when students are classified for educational reasons is a tracking system valid. If the system is fair and sensible—and no mistake has been made in placing a child—parents cannot complain about the track to which their children are assigned.

Curriculum School boards also decide curriculum—what will be taught and how much is required of each student. In large school districts, the board may do little more than outline general educational policy. Frequently, a board evaluates proposals that outline methods of instruction submitted by teachers, department chairmen, or principals. The teachers themselves have some freedom to develop their own teaching styles, but they must stay within the standards set by the school board. As part of a board's policy, teachers can be forbidden to discuss a teachers' strike or labor dispute in class or to subject their students to political harangues.

The law is not entirely settled on the question of whether a parent—or a child whose parent is willing to back him—can demand that the child be excused from a class. At one time courts consistently upheld the parent's right to make such decisions.

EXAMPLE In 1891 a father refused to let his daughter study grammar in school because he did not like the way it was taught. The court saw the issue as a question of who should determine what is best for a child, "a teacher who has a mere temporary interest in her welfare, or her father who may reasonably be supposed to be desirous of pursuing such course as will best promote the happiness of his child." The court ruled in favor of the father.

More recently, courts have assumed that a parent may not always know what is best for a child. They often require parents and students to submit to school policy unless a fundamental right is being violated. A Vermont case decided in federal court in 1975 is typical of the preference of courts to leave school management to local officials.

EXAMPLE A seventh-grade girl who decided she wanted to pursue only intellectual subjects refused to attend a required physical education class. In addition, she objected to the lack of privacy in the open showers of the girls' locker room. The school refused to let her substitute an academic subject for the physical education class. Her father permitted her to drop out of school rather than submit to what she considered an arbitrary rule. A federal court found that the school was reasonable in requiring a period of physical activity. The judge would not let a 12-year-old girl second-guess the educators without more substantial proof that they were wrong.

Textbooks A continuing debate between parents and educators concerns the propriety of a school's textbooks. Educators sometimes choose books that do not meet with the approval of parents. But just as parents cannot stop a school from offering sex-education classes, they usually cannot convince a court to keep a board from using particular books.

EXAMPLE In New York City two parents sued to prevent the teaching of William Shakespeare's *The Merchant of Venice* and Charles Dickens's *Oliver Twist* because of their uncomplimentary portrayals of Jews. The court held that such books should be suppressed only if they were "maliciously written for the apparent purpose of promoting and fomenting a bigoted and intolerant hatred against a particular racial or religious group." In this case, the board of education required teachers to instruct their students that the characters were not typical of any nation or race, including persons of the Jewish faith. The portrayals were not to be interpreted as discrediting any group of people.

Lawsuits to discontinue the use of certain books are fairly common. In one case, decided in 1976, the court ruled that a school board cannot censor books on the basis of social or political beliefs.

EXAMPLE A group of students in Ohio sued to force their school district to approve the purchase of books recommended by their English department. The books were *Catch-22*, by Joseph Heller, and *Cat's Cradle* and *God Bless You, Mr. Rosewater*, both by Kurt Vonnegut. The board not only refused to buy the books but also ordered existing copies removed from the library. Some teachers claimed that they were told not to mention the books in their classrooms. The only explanation for the board's action was that some considered the books "garbage" or "completely sick."

The federal appeals court ordered the board to buy the books. It granted that a school district is not constitutionally required to furnish a library for students and that when a library is established, board members are entitled to select the books for the library and to use their judgment in weeding out obsolete books to suit the shelf space available. Board members may not, however, select or reject books solely on the basis of the members' social or political tastes. A school library has a vital role in the educational process, and censorship of its contents puts a serious burden on the free exchange of ideas protected by the First Amendment. Any person going through an amply stocked library is likely to find at least one book objectionable to him.

Extracurricular activities Students have no constitutional right to insist that schools support extracurricular activities. Those activities that do exist, however, must be open to all students. This does not mean that every student who wants to play on the tennis team or be in the honor society must be permitted to do so; but a school must not refuse to let all girls play tennis or close the honor society to blacks, because discrimination on the basis of sex or color is not permitted.

Reasonable rules governing extracurricular activities will be enforced. An unruly student can be barred from basketball games, for example. Students can also be made ineligible for sports during the year that they transfer out of their home districts; the purpose of the rule is to discourage recruiting and to retain the amateur character of high school athletics. Schools have been upheld in decisions to keep deaf students or students with sight in only one eye off certain athletic teams. As long as the rule is based on sound medical opinion and applied fairly to everyone, it is not unreasonable.

Graduation School boards have some discretion in setting standards for graduation and in granting diplomas. Students who have satisfactorily completed courses of instruction are entitled to a diploma or certificate. Many school systems have different types of diplomas, depending on the student's course of study or level of achievement. Some states require students to pass standardized examinations in order to graduate. They often give a certificate of attendance to students unable to pass the exam for a diploma. If a student completes his work or passes the exam, he cannot be denied graduation on account of misbehavior.

Racial integration of schools   School boards may use their own judgment in assigning pupils to schools within a district, and students generally have no right of choice. A board can institute a freedom-of-choice plan, however, if it does not result in a racially segregated school system.

EXAMPLE In one district in Alabama, the board attempted to desegregate the schools by letting pupils choose which school they would attend. Only 6 percent of the rural black children selected an all-white school, and no white child chose an all-black school. The federal court held that this system was not a desegregation plan at all and was therefore illegal. It is against the law for a public school system to permit the races to remain separate.

It is not necessary for a school board to be color blind in drawing lines within a district. In fact, it must take race into account to prevent one-race schools. Although a one-race school is not illegal in every case, courts demand compelling reasons for the existence of such a school. See BROWN V. BOARD OF EDUCATION.

A school board may achieve an integrated school system in a number of ways. Schools in which the students are all, or mostly, of the same race can be paired or grouped, and children from each race assigned to every school. School zones can be shaped to accommodate the goal of racial integration, even by taking in areas that are not contiguous. Where distance or other conditions (such as safety) require, buses may be provided to transport children. A school board does not have to design a system so that every school reflects the precise racial makeup of the community, but its efforts must show an honest attempt at integration.

The courts have the legal authority to design their own plans if a board refuses to desegregate public schools. When necessary, a court may order that some children be bused to achieve racial integration. The Supreme Court has said that busing must be reasonable. It should take into account the age of the children and the distances they must travel.

■ **Educational malpractice**   Some public high school graduates who are unable to read well enough to compete for a job or to cope with modern life have sued their schools and teachers for educational malpractice. The first such case was brought against the San Francisco Unified School District in 1973.

EXAMPLE One young man, who sued anonymously under the name Peter W. Peter, had gone through the public school system and graduated from a high school in the district. Even though he never exceeded an eighth-grade reading or writing level, he claimed his teachers passed him each year until graduation. He based his theory of malpractice on the assertion that the teachers and school district had a duty to educate him. Their mandate was to advise his parents of his true progress and not to advance him automatically into grades and classes he was unprepared to handle.

The court dismissed the suit. It is impossible, the court concluded, for the law to establish exactly what amount of care the school district owes its pupils. Learning to read and write is affected by so many factors that students cannot fix the blame on teachers or on district policy alone. Peter sought money damages to compensate him for the cost of extra tutoring and diminished earning power over his entire lifetime. The court refused to believe that the school district should be liable to all the "disaffected students and parents in countless numbers." Permitting such lawsuits would burden our already strained school system—and society—beyond calculation.

Liability for injuries   Under the common law, public school districts cannot be sued for physical injuries sustained by children, because public schools have the same SOVEREIGN IMMUNITY as does the government. This rule has been justified on the ground that it preserves tax money for the educational purpose for which it was collected. The unfairness of putting the entire burden of an injury on the victim and his family, however, has led many states to soften or abandon the rule of immunity.

Laws permitting suits against school districts usually require that notice of an intent to sue be sent to the school board, its administrator, or its attorney within 60 to 90 days after the injury. To win a case, the plaintiff must show that the injury was caused by the intentional or careless conduct of someone representing or employed by the district. If the injury is caused by a fellow student, the school may be liable if it has failed to properly supervise the children.

The amount of care owed by a school depends on the circumstances. No one suggests that children be subjected to constant supervision, but more care must be taken with very young children and with older students in cooking or machine-shop classes. Equipment in classrooms, gym, cafeteria, and shop must be in good repair, and children using it must be given proper instructions. Schools are not responsible for accidents in sports and games if conditions are as safe as possible.

Parents who sign waivers, releases, or permission slips approving participation by their children in sports or field trips are not later prevented from suing the school. A parent has no right to waive his child's right to sue, and it is against public policy to relieve anyone of responsibility before an injury occurs.

■ **Discipline**   Schools must maintain order if they are to insure the safety of their students and fulfill their educational purpose. Students who refuse to follow reasonable rules can be disciplined.

Suspension   The most common form of punishment is a suspension from school. In 1975, however, the Supreme Court ruled that when public school students are suspended from school, they are entitled to some elements of the DUE PROCESS OF LAW guaranteed to defendants in criminal cases by the U.S. Constitution.

EXAMPLE In Columbus, Ohio, nine junior high and high school students were suspended from school for up to 10 days after a period of widespread student unrest. None of the students were given reasons for their suspensions or given an opportunity to explain their side of the story. The Supreme Court held that Ohio may not require attendance in public schools and then suspend students arbitrarily. The damage done to the student's academic progress, his reputation in the school, and his opportunities for higher education after a suspension is too severe.

In the Ohio case the Supreme Court did not recommend that school disciplinary hearings be turned into elaborate criminal trials with all their safeguards for the defendant. School officials should be free to handle disciplinary problems expeditiously. However, before being suspended, students should be informed of the charges against them and then given an informal hearing. The school disciplinarian may decide whether the accuser should be summoned and questioned. There may be times when the student should be allowed to present witnesses on his behalf. Actions carrying the sentence of suspensions of 10 days or more require formal hearings. In emergency situations, where there is an immediate and substantial danger to persons or property, a student may be suspended on the spot, but a subsequent hearing should be held as soon as possible.

Corporal punishment Although corporal punishment—striking a child—was the most common means of discipline until the early 1900's, it is now considered too harsh by many and is used less often. Nevertheless, the Supreme Court has refused to condemn it as unconstitutional—that is, as cruel and unusual punishment.

EXAMPLE Two junior high school students were injured from harsh spankings in a Florida school and sued their teachers. The Supreme Court ruled that they had the right to sue because their teachers had abused the use of corporal punishment. The Court noted, however, that corporal punishment has been used to discipline schoolchildren since colonial times, and that it could see no definite trend toward the abolishment of spanking.

The prevailing rule governing the use of corporal punishment is that a teacher or administrator can employ such force as is necessary to control, train, or educate the child. If the amount of force is excessive or unreasonable, the educator can be sued for money damages and prosecuted under the criminal law.

Twenty-one states authorize by statute the use of corporal punishment in their schools. Some of these laws describe very carefully what amount of force is reasonable. Many of them require that parents be notified or give their approval in advance for the use of corporal punishment. Without such a provision, parents have no right to forbid school authorities to spank their children. The statutes usually provide that the punishment be inflicted only by the principal or in the presence of another adult. Where there is no statute on the subject, teachers have the common-law right to use reasonable force to discipline their pupils.

■ **Students' First Amendment rights** There are some things for which schools cannot punish students because the conduct is protected by the First Amendment to the Constitution, which guarantees freedom of speech, the press, and religion.

Freedom of speech Students have the right to express opinions, even if they are unpopular ones, and school officials are prohibited by the First Amendment from punishing a student just because they dislike his opinion. The landmark Supreme Court decision defining this right came down in 1969.

EXAMPLE Three students in a Des Moines, Iowa, public school decided to protest American involvement in Vietnam by wearing black armbands. School officials, warned of the plan, adopted a rule forbidding armbands

in school. John Tinker, his sister Mary Beth, and their friend, Christopher Eckhardt, though knowing the rule, wore black armbands. They were suspended. School officials claimed there was a great deal of hostility to the opinion expressed by wearing the armbands, and they feared that school routines would be disrupted.

The Supreme Court announced that "State-operated schools may not be enclaves of totalitarianism." Other students wore political campaign buttons, and some even flaunted the Iron Cross, long associated with Nazism; yet only the black armbands were forbidden. There was no evidence that the children wearing armbands created a disturbance in the school. The Court said, "Students in school as well as out of school are 'persons' under our Constitution. They are possessed of fundamental rights which the State must respect, just as they themselves must respect their obligations to the State. In our system, students . . . may not be confined to the expression of those sentiments that are officially approved."

School officials are under no obligation to permit an outsider to come into a school to address students, but if they do so, they must give opposing viewpoints a chance to be heard. One New Hampshire principal, for example, was prevented from barring a candidate from the Socialist Workers Party after Democratic and Republican candidates spoke at the high school. Similarly, a school official has no right to censor speakers with whom he disagrees.

Freedom of the press The First Amendment applies to student publications. Schools cannot censor controversial viewpoints or forbid distribution of underground newspapers. Students in Texas won this point in federal court in 1972 when they were suspended for distributing their newspaper outside the school. The paper had offended the school authorities because it printed articles on drug laws, drug counseling, birth control, and venereal disease. The court pointed out that "the purpose of education is to spread, not to stifle, ideas and views."

School officials, however, have the authority to regulate the distribution of student publications as long as the rules are reasonable and fair. They can forbid distribution during classes or on crowded stairways, for example.

The constitutional protections for student newspapers—or any publication—do not extend to LIBEL AND SLANDER or OBSCENITY. While school officials can ban legally libelous or obscene publications, federal courts are divided on whether students must submit publications for approval before distribution. The Constitution prohibits restraint of a publication before it is circulated, but some courts have held that public school officials can require a prior review, which must be done promptly. Also, students are entitled to clear rules about what is libelous, obscene, or disruptive and have the right to appeal a negative decision.

Freedom of religion The First Amendment protects freedom of religion. This right has had a special impact on school routine.

EXAMPLE In 1943 a group of Jehovah's Witnesses sued to stop enforcement of a West Virginia statute requiring their children to salute the flag in school. The group maintained that saluting the flag was against God's commandment not to make graven images or bow down to them or serve them. The Supreme Court recognized that schools do a public service in promoting patriotism and national unity, but it held that schools cannot violate a person's religious scruples.

EXAMPLE A federal court in New Jersey went even further in 1977. It judged that a state law requiring students to stand while the Pledge of Allegiance was recited also violated the First Amendment—even if the children refused as a matter of conscience rather than for religious reasons. Any student who refused to salute the flag or recite the Pledge of Allegiance must be left alone because he is entitled to make that decision, but he may not be disruptive or disrespectful of the other students.

The First Amendment's insistence on separation of church and state also prompted the Supreme Court to rule in 1963 that Bible reading and prayers must not be conducted in the public schools. This prohibition applies to voluntary participation and nondenominational exercises. It is based on a judgment that state-supported schools must neither prefer one religion over another nor promote religious over nonreligious viewpoints. In 1976, however, a federal court in Massachusetts held that state law could establish a short period of daily silent "meditation or prayer" in the schools as long as each student could choose whether to meditate or pray.

As part of their academic program, schools can offer instruction on religion as long as they do not favor one faith over another. A Tennessee statute prohibited the use of any textbook covering the origins of man unless the textbook explained that every theory except the Old Testament story in Genesis is merely opinion not supported by scientific fact. The law promoted the strict religious interpretation of man's origin at the expense of other viewpoints, such as the widely accepted views on evolution by Charles Darwin. The law was declared unconstitutional in 1975.

scienter (Latin) "Knowingly"; with guilty knowledge—that is, knowledge that is sufficient to make a person responsible for the consequences of his acts. In CRIMINAL LAW, the term *scienter,* or its English equivalent, *guilty knowledge,* means an allegation that a person who has been accused of a crime was aware of the wrongfulness of what he was doing. Scienter is a necessary element of many crimes. For example, the prosecution may have to prove scienter to convict a person for selling obscene books. This requires proof that the defendant knew the contents of the books, not that he considered them obscene.

scintilla A glimmer; a spark; the slightest particle or trace. A scintilla of evidence is an insignificant or trifling item of evidence. Yet under the common-law scintilla rule, if there is any evidence at all in a case, even a mere scintilla, the case cannot be taken from the jury. It must be left to their decision.

scire facias (Latin) "You should cause to know"; a judicial writ calling on a defendant to show cause in court why an existing JUDGMENT (court-ordered obligation) should not be executed against him. The purpose of *scire facias* is to revive a dormant judgment (one that has been handed down by the court but not acted upon) before the period of limitations has expired.

scope of employment Everything an employee does that is connected with the performance of his work, including such matters of personal convenience and comfort as going to the bathroom or getting a cup of coffee. In the law of TORTS, the phrase is often used in discussing the liability of the employer for his employees' acts. See AGENCY; MASTER AND SERVANT; RESPONDEAT SUPERIOR.

seal A metal plate with a flat surface on which is engraved a design that can make an impression on wax, paper, or parchment. The impression made by the surface of the plate is also called a seal.

The use of seals began in antiquity, before written signatures were common. In the Middle Ages and later every person of means possessed a coat of arms that would identify him. Seals—usually designed like these coats of arms—were pressed into wax, which was applied to documents or property to show that the documents were authorized or the property was owned by the person whose seal it was. Seals were used on documents in the same way we use signatures today, and sometimes they were used along with signatures, giving double assurance to the authenticity of the document. With the growth of education, however, the signature on a document gradually became of paramount importance.

At one time a sealed document set it above an average legal paper. The trend in modern law, however, is to minimize or eliminate the old distinctions between sealed and unsealed documents. A seal may be required, prohibited, or allowed. If it is allowed, it may have some effect on the legal consequences of the document on which it is used or it may have no effect other than looking official to laymen. The seal with some legal effect may, for example, extend the time during which the law allows a lawsuit to be started to enforce the obligations described in the document. In states that still recognize the use of the seal, the letters "L.S."—for *locus sigilli,* "the place of the seal"—can also be substituted for a material seal. So can the word "seal" or a statement to the effect that the document is equal to a sealed document.

Today seals serve to authenticate such documents as birth and marriage records and deeds to real estate. Seals are also used to authenticate signatures witnessed by a notary public and to formalize corporate documents.

sealed verdict The verdict a jury has reached but has not yet delivered. If the court is not in session when the jury reaches a conclusion, the verdict can be placed in a sealed envelope, and the jurors can separate temporarily. When the court reconvenes, the verdict is delivered to the judge, who then reads it. Some courts hold that a sealed verdict does not become final until it is read into the record and the jurors are discharged.

seaman In the broad sense, a sailor or mariner who does any kind of work aboard a ship in navigation. See NAVIGABLE WATERS. A seaman is not necessarily a member of the ship's *crew*—the group of individuals who are on board primarily to aid in the navigation of the ship. A bartender aboard a passenger ship, for example, would be a seaman but not a member of the crew.

■ **Legal protection** Seamen are protected by the law of ADMIRALTY. Every safeguard that the law can provide is given to them by court decisions and legislative enactments. The courts are periodically called on to scrutinize carefully relations between seamen and their employers. An inequality in the terms of an employment contract will prompt the courts to set it aside. Legislation intended to protect the seaman is liberally interpreted in his favor.

A seaman's relation to his ship begins when he signs the shipping articles. A type of employment contract, written shipping articles define the relationship between the ship's owners and the seaman, mutually binding them according to the terms expressed. Completion of the voyage or any other stipulated period of service terminates the employment contract. This results in the discharge of the seaman.

All seamen are entitled to a staunch, watertight ship that is properly equipped and handled by a competent crew. The employer must supply the seamen with wholesome food during the entire voyage.

Under maritime tradition, a seaman who becomes sick or injured while in ship's service must be given food, lodging, and care. This right is not restricted to cases in which the seaman's employment caused his injury or illness. A seaman is in *service of the ship* when he is under the authority of its officers—whether or not he is working.

EXAMPLE While a ship was docked at San Juan, Puerto Rico, one of its seamen returned to the vessel drunk. After the chief officer found him "ranting and raving," the master ordered him handcuffed to a bed in the ship's hospital and told the chief officer to keep him under constant surveillance. However, the chief officer left the seaman alone for periods of 20 or 30 minutes at a time. The next day a doctor discovered that the seaman's wrist had been broken while he was manacled to the bed. When the injury failed to heal properly and the seaman was unable to work, he sued for compensation for his permanent, partial disability. The court held in favor of the seaman because the master should have known he needed care and should have made sure that he received it.

A disabled seaman should be given medical attention at ports the vessel visits in the regular course of its voyage, even if the ship's master (captain) has to deviate from the scheduled voyage to enter a nearby port. A disabled seaman should also be furnished with proper treatment and care at the end of the voyage.

■ **Ratings and rank** Courts have recognized the propriety of a master's promoting a seaman to a higher rank or rating while at sea. Similarly, while at sea the master has power to demote a member of the crew. The master's action, however, is subject to review in the courts. Proof that continuance of a seaman in his rating will endanger the health or safety of the ship's company provides grounds for demoting him. These grounds include dishonesty, incapacity, incompetency, disobedience, and neglect of duty. An officer displaced from his rating becomes a quasipassenger. He may not exercise authority, but neither is he obligated to perform the work of a common sailor.

■ **Wages** Seamen hired for a particular voyage are entitled to payment of wages for services performed during the trip. If a contemplated voyage never takes place, seamen must be paid for services done in port while preparing for departure. If a voyage breaks up through no fault of the owner or master, the seaman's employment contract for wages is dissolved. Such a situation arises, for instance, in time of war or other national emergency.

The general rule is that a seaman who is injured or becomes sick in service of the ship should receive payment of full wages. The employer's liability for wages has been held to exist even when the seaman's injury was incurred while he was on shore leave.

EXAMPLE A ship's cook was suffering from an unsightly skin condition, so the captain ordered him to be examined by a physician when the ship put in at Buenos Aires. The doctor diagnosed the seaman's problem as secondary syphilis. The captain discharged him, put him ashore and, as the law requires, gave him a voucher to present to the paymaster for money to pay for his return to San Francisco. When he returned to the United States, he sued for his wages. The court said that a seaman must be given one-third of his wages when he is discharged so that he can provide himself with food and shelter. Because the shipping company had not done this, it was ordered to pay double wages to the seaman from the time he was put ashore until he was able to claim his earned wages. It did not matter that his illness was not caused by work done on the ship.

Ordinarily, a seaman's wages are paid in money; if the voyage ends at an American port, the wages should be paid in U.S. currency.

Serious insubordination may subject a seaman to forfeiture of his wages, but slight insubordination, such as using insulting language to the master, does not. Other grounds for pay forfeiture are habitual drunkenness that disqualifies a seaman from performing his duties, deliberate and persistent neglect of work, and smuggling.

■ **Discharge** The master of a vessel has the power to discharge members of the crew as he sees fit. Nevertheless, the propriety of discharging a seaman prior to the completion of his contract of service and without his consent depends on the existence of a substantial ground, such as his being unfit or untrustworthy for service. Other grounds include an attempted rape of a passenger, failure to report for duty either at the time stipulated in the ship's articles or when the ship is about to leave port, deliberate and persistent shirking of duty, and habitually stirring up quarrels.

While willful disobedience of orders can be a ground for discharge, a minor breach of discipline is not. Physical conflict with the master can cost a seaman his job unless he acts in self-defense.

The master is not justified in firing a seaman for trivial causes. Nor can he discharge a seaman in a foreign port unless it is imperative for the seaman's own good or for the safety of the vessel. In court, the burden is on the master to prove that a discharge was reasonable and necessary or that he could not safely keep the seaman on board. The station of the seaman as well as the nature of his work are often significant. It has been held that a ship's officer may be let go for a single offense of drunkenness while on duty. On the other hand, merely drinking while on duty without becoming intoxicated is not a ground for firing an ordinary seaman. Drunkenness while off duty should put no crew member's job in jeopardy.

■ **Liability at sea** The responsibility for the injury or death of a seaman is governed by traditional maritime law as supplemented by the federal Jones Act. This act stipulates that a party's right to recover for injuries on death must be based either on negligence of the employer or on the unseaworthiness of the ship. It may be negligence under the act, for example, for the employer to fail to supply a safe place to work, sanitary living quarters, or suitable appliances and equipment. The owner may be held liable for the death of a seaman washed overboard, for example, if such safeguards as adequate railings were not in place. A shipowner can also be held liable if his employees fail to help rescue a man overboard.

The Jones Act applies only to crew members of a vessel operating in NAVIGABLE WATERS. Whether or not a member qualifies for the law's benefits is determined in court. Some crew members who have been ruled eligible are a ship's carpenter, master, officer, steward, and watchman. By contrast, a painter and sheet-iron worker engaged in repair and longshoremen and stevedores working on a ship in port were denied the benefits of the Jones Act. See MARITIME LIEN; SHIPPING.

search and seizure The examination of a person's property or his body in an attempt to find evidence that will incriminate him and the taking of his property without his consent. The right to be free from indiscriminate searches and seizures is protected by the Fourth Amendment to the U.S. Constitution:

❝ The right of the people to be secure in their persons, houses, papers, and effects, against unreasonable searches and seizures, shall not be violated, and no Warrants shall issue, but upon probable cause, supported by Oath or affirmation, and particularly describing the place to be searched, and the persons or things to be seized.❞

The Constitution does not forbid all searches and seizures, but only those that are unreasonable. What constitutes an unreasonable search and seizure must be decided by the court, which considers the facts of the particular case, including the purpose of the search, the existence of probable cause, the manner in which the search and seizure was made, the place or the thing searched, and the nature and importance of the crime suspected. Exploratory searches made merely on a baseless hunch would obviously be unreasonable.

In compliance with the Fourth Amendment, searches and seizures are generally permitted only with a legitimate search warrant. Under certain circumstances, however, a search and seizure by law enforcement officials can be conducted without a warrant.

The guarantees of the 4th Amendment, which prohibit unreasonable actions by the federal government, have been made legally binding on the states through the due process clause of the 14th Amendment. See DUE PROCESS OF LAW. In addition, all the states have incorporated the provisions of the Fourth Amendment into their own constitutions in order to reinforce the protections and security the amendment was intended to achieve.

■ **Definitions** Definitions of the major terms used in the Fourth Amendment are as follows: A *search* is an examination of an individual's personal property, house, or other premises or of his person, aimed at discovering contraband, illicit, or stolen property or some evidence of the commission of a crime that can be used in a criminal prosecution. A *seizure* is the forcible taking of property from the owner. The seizure of a person is an ARREST. A *search warrant* is a written order in the name of the state or federal government, signed by a magistrate and directed to a peace officer, commanding him to search for property believed to be evidence of a crime. *Probable cause* is a fact or facts that permit a reasonable belief that a crime has been committed.

■ **Background** The primary purpose of the Fourth Amendment is to protect the privacy and security of the people against arbitrary invasions by representatives of the government. The Virginia Bill of Rights, which was a forerunner of the federal Bill of Rights, specifically prohibited "general warrants, whereby an officer or messenger may be commanded to search suspected places without evidence of a fact committed."

Before the Revolutionary War, the American Colonies had had a bitter taste of such abuses, including the issuance of general warrants or writs of assistance, which granted sweeping powers to customs officials and other agents of the King to search at large for smuggled goods. Such warrants and writs had particularly enraged merchants whose products and premises were often searched to check whether the businessmen were obeying Parliamentary revenue measures, such as the Stamp Act. These abuses led to the adoption of the Fourth Amendment prohibition against unreasonable searches and seizures and its limitation on the conditions under which search warrants may be issued.

■ **Significance of the amendment** The rights safeguarded by the Fourth Amendment are the foundation of constitutional liberty, for a person's right to privacy in his life is essential to his personal freedom. See PRIVACY, RIGHT OF. But like other rights, this right is not absolute. In deciding whether a particular search and seizure is constitutional, a court must balance the right of an individual to be free from the unwarranted government intrusion against government's right to discover information needed to support criminal prosecutions in order to protect the safety and welfare of its citizens. The individual's right to privacy must yield when the court believes that evidence of a crime may be discovered.

The Fourth Amendment protects a person's right to the sanctity of his home and his body, as well as the privacy of his books, papers, and property. All persons—including the suspected, accused, or guilty—are entitled to this protection. A corporation is also entitled to invoke the guarantees of the Fourth Amendment to protect itself against the unreasonable search and seizure of its books and papers.

■ **Exclusionary rule** Neither the Fourth Amendment nor federal statutes provide for the punishment of law enforcement officials who violate the prohibition against unreasonable searches and seizures, and until 1914 no case ever successfully challenged the use of illegally seized evidence in a trial. In that year the Supreme Court decided that evidence obtained in violation of the Fourth Amendment could not be used in a federal prosecution. This is known as the exclusionary rule. It was designed "to deter— to compel respect for the constitutional guaranty in the only effectively available way—by removing the incentive to disregard it."

Evidence obtained by an illegal search and seizure also cannot be used against a defendant in a state criminal prosecution. This principle was first applied in 1961 in the case of *Mapp* v. *Ohio*.

EXAMPLE Police had received information that a person
O—* wanted for questioning in a recent bombing case was hiding in the Mapp home. Officers sought to question Miss Mapp, but on the advice of her attorney, she refused to let them into her home without a warrant. An officer showed her a paper, which he claimed was a warrant. She grabbed it and placed it in the front of her dress. The officers retrieved the paper by force and entered the apartment. In a thorough search of the premises, they seized lewd books and pictures. Miss Mapp was convicted of possession of obscene literature, a crime under an Ohio statute.

At the trial, the prosecution produced no search warrant and the failure to produce one was not adequately explained. Ohio law permitted illegally obtained evidence to be admitted in a criminal trial for use against the defendant. Although the Ohio Supreme Court affirmed the conviction, the U.S. Supreme Court reversed it.

Exceptions to the rule The exclusionary rule does not prevent the use of illegally seized evidence in all proceedings or against all persons.

Grand jury A grand jury may require a witness to answer questions based on evidence obtained from an unlawful search and seizure. Such questioning is based on the results of a past unconstitutional search but does not in-

HOW MUCH DO YOU KNOW ABOUT SEARCH AND SEIZURE LAWS?

■ The Constitution does not forbid all searches and seizures but only unreasonable ones.

■ A grand jury may question a witness on evidence obtained from an unlawful search and seizure, and it may vote to indict a person on the basis of that evidence.

■ Unlawfully seized evidence may not be used to get a conviction, but it may be used to expose perjured testimony (lying) in a trial.

■ Evidence obtained by a private individual acting on his own may be used in a criminal proceeding.

■ You are protected against unreasonable searches and seizures in any place that you have a reasonable expectation of privacy.

■ Certain groups of people do not have the same expectation of privacy: military personnel, prisoners, parolees, and to some extent students.

■ A search warrant must be specific—it must describe the place to be searched and persons or items to be looked for. The police cannot rummage through your belongings in search of any evidence of any possible crime, but they can seize articles other than those described in a warrant if the items have a reasonable relationship to the purpose of the search.

■ If deception is used to get a suspect's consent to a search, the consent is not valid. If a suspect gives a blood sample because the police tell him it will be tested for alcohol content, when in fact it is matched with blood found at the scene of a crime, that consent is invalid, and the evidence is illegally obtained.

■ Certain persons—such as spouses, relatives, and business partners—may consent to searches for evidence in places or among belongings they share with the defendant. Evidence turned up in the search is legally seized.

■ When a husband and wife jointly occupy a place, either may consent to a search of the premises for items that may incriminate the other. However, neither husband nor wife may consent to the search of an area, such as a personal bureau drawer, kept private by the other.

■ A child may not give valid consent to a search of his parents' home.

■ A landlord or his agents may consent to a search of hallways and other areas of common access but not to a search of rented premises occupied by a tenant.

■ An attendant in a public garage may consent to the opening of a car door for the police to see items on the floor of the car, but he cannot let them search the trunk without the owner's consent.

■ Police may enter a house without a warrant when there is probable cause to believe that a person inside is threatened with injury or death or that evidence is likely to be destroyed.

■ Police may enter premises without a warrant when they are in "hot pursuit" of an offender.

■ In many states police may not break into private premises to make an arrest unless they have been denied entry after stating their office and purpose.

■ A stop-and-frisk is proper when (1) an officer observes conduct that reasonably leads him to believe there may be criminal activity afoot, (2) the officer believes the suspicious person may be armed and dangerous, (3) the officer identifies himself and makes reasonable inquiries, but (4) nothing in the officer's encounter with the person dispels his fear for his own or another's safety. When all of these requirements are met, the officer has the right to pat down the suspect to check for concealed weapons.

■ A full search of a person may be made only when it is incident to a "full custody arrest"—one made for the purpose of taking the person to the police station.

■ Some courts have suppressed evidence when it was obtained by arresting a person for a minor offense simply to justify a search for evidence of more serious offenses. Other courts, however, have overlooked this type of subterfuge.

■ Spot checks of cars might be unconstitutional. The police may stop a car, however, if they have probable cause to believe a law has been violated, and may search it if they have cause to believe it contains contraband.

■ Border searches are considered unique. A person crossing the border may be required to submit to a warrantless search without the slightest suspicion.

■ Electronic eavesdropping and wiretapping are permitted when authorized by a warrant.

volve a new violation. The Supreme Court reasoned that if questioning could not be based on such evidence, the work of the grand jury would be hindered. The purpose of the exclusionary rule is to deter police from obtaining evidence illegally. This is done by refusing to allow such evidence to be used to convict a person, thus nullifying the point of the search. The rule is not designed to prevent the grand jury from hearing all evidence available before deciding whether or not to indict a person. The result is that if the only evidence against a person is illegally seized, the grand jury may vote to indict him for a crime, but because that evidence cannot be used against him in a criminal trial there must be other evidence which can sustain his prosecution.

The exclusionary rule is not waived for evidence obtained by illegal electronic surveillance and wiretapping. A grand jury may not use such evidence.

Discrediting perjured testimony Evidence subject to the exclusionary rule may be used to impeach or discredit the testimony of a witness in a criminal prosecution.

EXAMPLE A man indicted for purchasing and possessing heroin testified on direct examination that he never possessed any narcotics. On cross-examination, he repeated the same statement. The court permitted the prosecution to introduce evidence of illegally seized heroin, although it had been excluded from use in an earlier unsuccessful prosecution for a similar crime in order to attack the credibility of the defendant. The Supreme Court upheld this use of the evidence.

The exclusionary rule is used to prevent unlawful seizures, not to prevent perjured testimony from being exposed.

Search and seizure by private persons The Fourth Amendment was designed to prevent unreasonable searches and seizures by the government. When evidence is illegally obtained by a private individual acting on his own, without the involvement of any government law enforcement official, that evidence may be used in a criminal proceeding. The exclusionary rule does not apply.

EXAMPLE A man was convicted in federal district court of interstate transportation of forged bank checks. The evidence used against him was obtained when the owner of the motel at which he was staying illegally searched the room and a travel case the man had left behind. The motel owner gave the contents of the case to the local police. The man appealed his conviction, claiming that the evidence was seized in violation of the Fourth Amendment. The federal court of appeals affirmed his conviction, because only government action is regulated by the Fourth Amendment. Evidence obtained by a private citizen need not be excluded in a criminal trial.

Evidence seized from a suspected shoplifter by a store detective may be used in a criminal prosecution. Storeowners are usually permitted by state law to detain customers whom they suspect of shoplifting. If a customer is searched by a privately employed store detective, any incriminating evidence may be used in the subsequent prosecution because there is no government participation or cooperation.

Fruit of the poisonous tree In a criminal prosecution, a defendant is entitled to the suppression not only of illegally obtained evidence but of any derivative use of that evidence. The "fruit of the poisonous tree" doctrine pro-

hibits the use of any evidence obtained as a result of an illegal search and seizure, because the "fruit" (evidence) is obtained from the "poisonous tree" (illegal act).

EXAMPLE In one case, the government photographed illegally obtained documents belonging to the defendant, which were returned to him on court order. The photographs were later used to get a subpoena requiring the defendant to produce the same documents at his trial. When he refused to comply, he was found guilty of contempt. He appealed. The Supreme Court held that the subpoena was unenforceable because the government may not benefit from its own wrongdoing.

There is, however, one exception to the fruit of the poisonous tree doctrine, known as the independent source rule. When facts are discovered or statements are made independently of the illegal search and seizure of evidence, those facts or statements may be used against the defendant. If a person willingly volunteers information, for example, in exchange for being charged with a lesser offense, the initial "taint" resulting from an illegal search and seizure of his property may be eliminated so that his statements can be used as evidence. In such a case, the person is making self-incriminating statements because he has been offered the chance to be charged with a lesser offense and not because he knows that the police have less evidence of his crime. His statements are not fruits of the poisonous tree because they do not stem from the illegally seized evidence. They are derived, rather, from an independent source—the offer of a lesser charge.

■ **Civil rights action** In addition to the remedy of excluding illegally obtained evidence from a criminal prosecution, a person whose constitutional rights have been violated can bring a civil lawsuit for damages against the individuals responsible for the violation. This is known under federal law as a civil action for deprivation of rights.

EXAMPLE Six FBI agents, acting under claim of federal authority, entered a man's apartment without a warrant and arrested him on narcotics charges. He was manacled in front of his family, who were also threatened with arrest, and the apartment was completely searched. The man was taken to a federal courthouse where he was questioned, booked, and subjected to a strip search. He sued the six agents in federal district court for $15,000 in damages for humiliation, embarrassment, and mental suffering caused by their conduct. He alleged that the arrest and search were done without a warrant and that unreasonable force was used in his arrest. The district court dismissed his suit on the grounds that it failed to state a cause of action recognized by law. The federal court of appeals affirmed the decision, but the Supreme Court reversed it.

When a person's rights have been invaded, damages have been traditionally awarded to remedy the wrong. The Fourth Amendment, however, does not specifically provide for money damages in cases of its violation. The Supreme Court ruled in the above case, however, that the petitioner was entitled to recover money damages for any injuries he suffered as a result of the agents' violation of the amendment.

■ **Protected areas** The Fourth Amendment specifically protects a person against unreasonable searches and seizures of his "person, houses, papers, and effects." The word "houses" has been interpreted by courts to include a store, business office, hotel room, automobile, and an occupied taxicab.

This property approach has been rejected by the Supreme Court in favor of a privacy approach. In deciding that eavesdropping into a public telephone booth constituted a search, the Court declined to characterize the booth as a "constitutionally protected area."

The Fourth Amendment protects persons, not places. What a person knowingly exposes to the public, even in his own home or office, is not a subject of Fourth Amendment protection. But what he seeks to preserve as private, even in an area accessible to the public, may be constitutionally protected.

Traditionally, Fourth Amendment protection extended only to areas surrounding a dwelling that came within the common law definition of *curtilage*—that is, buildings and enclosed spaces close to a dwelling that are continually used for domestic purposes and places that are necessary and convenient to a dwelling and are habitually used for family purposes. An open field some distance from a home, for example, was not considered to be within the scope of Fourth Amendment protections.

Since 1967, however, an individual has been protected against unreasonable searches and seizures anywhere he has a reasonable expectation of privacy. The court must consider whether a person actually expected privacy and whether his expectation was reasonable.

For example, if you use a department store fitting room and close the door or curtain in order to try on clothes, you are considered to have a reasonable expectation of privacy against unreasonable searches and seizures. A private room in a hospital also gives a reasonable expectation of privacy, as does a motel or hotel room. You may also expect privacy when driving in your car, although not to the same extent as when you are at home. On the other hand, you may not reasonably expect privacy in the public areas of an apartment house, such as its garage, hallways, basement, stairwells, or lobby.

Any property that is seized in a place so exposed as to immediately negate any reasonable expectation of privacy is not protected by the Constitution. For example, items removed from your trash can at the side of your house are not entitled to Fourth Amendment protection because you give up your expectations of privacy to those items. The same is true for abandoned property. If the court determines that the owner no longer has any reasonable expectation of privacy in the property, it can be searched and seized without meeting the requirements of the Fourth Amendment.

Surveillance   Police may observe suspicious activities on private property from a place where they have a right to be. For example, they may observe bookmaking activity in the backroom of a dry-cleaning establishment while standing in the front part of the store that is open to the general public. They can also legally observe the growing of marijuana plants in a suspect's backyard from the property of a cooperative neighbor and use this discovery as probable cause in obtaining a search warrant for the suspect's property. The Fourth Amendment prohibits the recording—

seizure—of an individual's conversations through illegal electronic surveillance, as discussed in detail later in this article.

Searches of your person   Under the Fourth Amendment, your person can be searched under proper authorization. Such searches may be made in the form of a simple frisking, strip search, or body search. In addition, body fluids may be taken from a person to establish evidence, and surgery may sometimes be authorized in order to find evidence, such as a policeman's bullet.

Strip searches   In a strip search, a person is required to removed his clothing so that each article may be checked for illegal items. An individual may be subjected to a strip search, for example, if customs officials have a "real suspicion" that he is trying to smuggle contraband or weapons hidden on his person into the United States. A *real suspicion* is a subjective suspicion supported by objective facts that in this case would lead a reasonably experienced, prudent customs official to suspect that a particular person seeking to enter the United States is concealing contraband on his body for smuggling purposes. A general suspicion of criminal activity is not enough. The fact that a suspect is unusually dressed or appears to be nervous is not in itself sufficient to justify such a search.

EXAMPLE   A woman was subjected to a strip search because both she and her companions appeared nervous, one of her companions was a known associate of a heroin dealer in New Mexico, their New Mexico automobile was without luggage or purchases, and there were fresh needle marks on the arms of her companions. The defendant was searched only after strip searches of her companions for contraband proved unproductive. These facts, coupled with the customs inspector's subjective knowledge that male narcotics users or addicts frequently use a female companion as a carrier, constituted real suspicion that permitted a strip search of the defendant. The police may also use strip searches to detect hidden objects that may be used to inflict bodily harm. This is considered a reasonable precautionary measure as long as it is conducted without abuse and in a professional manner.

Body searches   In a body search the body cavities and hair of a person are examined for concealed contraband and weapons. A person may be subjected to one only if officials have a "clear indication" that contraband or weapons may be hidden on his body. The standard of a clear indication requires more justification than does "a real suspicion" for a strip search.

EXAMPLE   In one case, police officers with a search warrant were conducting a search for stolen merchandise and heroin. The defendant was placed under arrest and, as an officer was preparing to search him, was seen putting something into his mouth. These circumstances constituted a clear indication that the defendant was attempting to conceal or destroy evidence. A body cavity search was justified.

When it is clear from the circumstances that police or government law enforcement agents were not justified in conducting strip or body searches, the victim of the search may ask the court to exclude the evidence from his criminal prosecution. He may also start a civil rights action against the officials responsible for the search.

Body fluids Body fluids may be "seized" (taken) from a person under the Fourth Amendment only under proper circumstances.

> EXAMPLE In an early case, the Supreme Court reversed a 0—⚹ defendant's conviction for possession of morphine based upon evidence obtained when the police pumped his stomach. He had swallowed morphine capsules when state police entered his home without a warrant. The Court decided that the police methods were unlawful and outrageous because "due process of law . . . cannot be brought about by methods that offend a sense of justice."

This case, although decided on due process grounds, set the outside parameters for the types of searches and seizures of an individual's person that will be upheld. Searches and seizures that "shock the conscience" are unconstitutional.

Later, however, the Court upheld the conviction of an automobile driver for manslaughter even though the police had taken a blood sample from him while he was unconscious, to determine if he was intoxicated at the time of the accident. The blood test was not "conduct that shocks the conscience," the Court said, because it was done "under the protective eye of a physician." The reasonableness of such seizures depends upon the facts of each case.

Surgery Surgery performed to recover a bullet from the body of a criminal suspect usually is not per se (in and of itself) a violation of the Fourth Amendment. Although the Supreme Court has not addressed this issue, some states have adopted rules that treat surgery for this purpose as an automatic violation of the Fourth Amendment. In most cases, certain criteria must be met or else such a "search and seizure" will not be upheld as valid: (1) the evidence must be relevant to the prosecution and there can be no other way to obtain it; (2) the police must have probable cause to believe that the operation will produce the bullet; and (3) a skilled surgeon must perform the surgery after the court has decided, based on medical evidence, that the surgery will be a minor intrusion, which can be performed without risk of harm or injury to the suspect. First, however, there must be a court hearing in which the suspect has the opportunity to cross-examine and offer witnesses. Before the operation is performed, the suspect must be given an opportunity to appeal the court's decision to permit the operation. This is usually done by an application for a writ of PROHIBITION.

> EXAMPLE A defendant was convicted of murder and robbery 0—⚹ based on evidence of bullet fragments removed from his buttocks. The state appellate court reversed the conviction because there had been no prior court hearing to give the defendant a chance to question witnesses and no opportunity for him to seek appellate review of the court's decision. The finding that the surgery would be a minor intrusion was made not by the court but by the surgeon selected to operate. Therefore, the admission of the evidence was a sufficient error to require the reversal of the defendant's conviction and the scheduling of a new trial.

■ **Limitations of protection** The Fourth Amendment was designed to safeguard individuals and corporations (a corporation is in some legal respects a "person") against arbitrary and unwarranted government intrusions into private areas and aspects of their lives. However, because of their circumstances, certain groups of people are not granted as much protection as others. Such groups include military personnel, prisoners, parolees and probationers, and to some extent students. The amount of constitutional protection to which a person is entitled depends upon his status at the time of the search.

Military personnel While members of the military are entitled to constitutional protections, the fundamental necessity for obedience and discipline may make permissible certain government actions that would not be legal in the civilian world.

> EXAMPLE In one case, drug inspections conducted without a 0—⚹ warrant or probable cause were part of a drug control program run by the U.S. Army to eliminate drug abuse. The stated aim of such searches was to examine "the clothing, equipment, and arms of a unit to determine its fitness and readiness to perform its mission, or to seek out contraband (e.g., illegal weapons, explosives, drugs)."

On an appeal from a decision that held such inspections unconstitutional, a federal court of appeals concluded that they were not unreasonable. Among the grounds for its decision, the court noted that a "soldier cannot reasonably expect the Army barracks to be a sanctuary like his civilian home."

Prisoners Prisoners in jail do not have the same rights of privacy as do ordinary citizens. See PRISONERS' RIGHTS. Their protection by the Fourth Amendment is restricted for two reasons: (1) the legitimate needs of the correctional institution to be sure that prisoners are obeying its rules and regulations for the protection of both the prison population and the general public and (2) prisoners' diminished expectations of privacy due to the nature of imprisonment. What constitutes a reasonable search and seizure is determined by the circumstances of the case. For example, screening a prisoner's incoming mail for contraband is reasonably related to maintaining the security of the jail. Also, a prisoner's cell may be searched when necessary to protect other prisoners as well as to prevent riot or escape.

Parolees and probationers Probation and parole officers may subject probationers and parolees to searches without warrants and may make arrests upon evidence that falls short of the usual probable-cause requirement. The parolee or probationer cannot have the same reasonable expectations of privacy as an ordinary citizen. The conditional nature of his release back into society is based upon certain restrictions and his supervision by the proper authorities. Even so, a search is unconstitutional if it is for the purpose of harassing or oppressing the probationer or parolee.

Students Students do not lose their constitutional rights just because they are attending school. The law concerning the Fourth Amendment rights of students, however, is neither clear nor uniform because the Supreme Court has refused to rule on the validity of searches and seizures of students made by school officials. Some courts refuse to apply the Fourth Amendment because they consider the school official to be acting *in loco parentis* ("in the place of the parent"), with the result that the search is a private one and thus not constitutionally protected. Others apply partial Fourth Amendment rights to students: if evidence is obtained in violation of the constitutional guarantees, it may still be admissible if the challenged search did not involve law enforcement officials. (See "Exclusionary rule," earlier in this article.) In some jurisdictions, the Fourth Amendment applies, but the doctrine of *in loco parentis* lowers the standard used in determining the reasonableness of the search. Still other courts apply the Fourth Amendment in full, so that probable cause must exist if a search is to be reasonable.

EXAMPLE Children in a fifth-grade class were taken to the school lavatories and ordered to strip down to their underwear so that their clothing could be searched for $3, which a pupil had reported missing from his coat. On the basis of prior complaints of items lost or missing from the class, school officials conducted the strip search only after receiving no response to their request to the class for information, after searching the classroom itself, and after having the children empty their pockets. The $3 were never recovered. The federal court balanced the seriousness of the suspected crime for which the evidence was sought against the students' right of privacy and the need to protect them from the humiliation and psychological harm likely to result from the search. The special duties of school officials to provide a safe atmosphere for students were taken into account, along with the limited disciplinary powers that school officials possess *in loco parentis*.

In light of the slight danger of the conduct involved (compared to drug possession, for example), as well as the extent of the search and the age of the students, the court ruled the search unreasonable. Although the court conceded that there was reasonable suspicion and even probable cause to believe that someone in the classroom had possession of the stolen money, this did not justify searching everyone.

In another case, the Supreme Court refused to hear the appeal of a high school student who was convicted of possession of marijuana based on evidence seized from him by the assistant principal.

EXAMPLE The principal observed the student and his friends acting surreptitiously. As he approached the students, "one of the fellows jumped up and put something down, ran his hand in his pants." When the students were told to empty their pockets, the defendant produced marijuana. His motion to suppress the evidence was denied and he was convicted.

The highest state court affirmed the conviction and found that the search did not violate the Fourth Amendment. The court reasoned that this search was reasonable in light of the responsibilities of school officials to provide a safe and secure learning environment. The exclusionary rule did not apply to enforce the Fourth Amendment rights of students because no law enforcement officers were involved in the search.

Other court decisions have ruled that student lockers may be opened by a master key and searched by school officials. But this has been allowed only when the presence of drugs or weapons was suspected.

■ **Standing** The constitutional guarantee of the Fourth Amendment is a personal right, which means that only the individual whose right of privacy has been infringed by government action can bring an action challenging its unconstitutionality. This right to contest the validity of the search is known as *standing*.

Obviously, a person who owns the property that is subjected to an unreasonable search may attack its validity. In the past, the Supreme Court also permitted anyone who was "legitimately on the premises" where a search occurred to challenge the legality of the search. This meant that a dinner guest could probably challenge a search of the host's house or that a passenger in a car that was searched by the police could challenge the legality of that search. In 1978, however, the Supreme Court retreated from this position.

EXAMPLE While on patrol, police received a robbery report and stopped the suspected getaway car in which the two defendants were riding. The car was searched. A box of rifle shells was found in the glove compartment and a sawed-off rifle was discovered under the front seat. These objects were confiscated by the police. The defendants were arrested and subsequently convicted of armed robbery after the seized objects were admitted into evidence over their objections. Neither defendant owned the car or the seized evidence. On appeal, the state court held that the defendants lacked standing to object to the search and seizure, and refused to suppress the evidence.

The Supreme Court agreed to hear the case, and in a 5–4 decision affirmed the convictions.

The defendants had claimed standing to challenge the legality of the search since it was directed at them and they were legitimately in the car at the time of the search. The Supreme Court rejected both these arguments. Only a person whose Fourth Amendment rights have been allegedly violated may challenge the legality of a search and seizure.

In this case, the person entitled to standing would be the owner of the car or of the items seized. Anyone else against whom the evidence is used in a criminal prosecution cannot protest the lawfulness of the search. The Court abandoned the use of the phrase "legitimately on the premises," which permitted persons to challenge the constitutionality of searches and seizures. It declared that the phrase created "too broad a gauge for measurement of Fourth Amendment rights." The petitioners had no legitimate expectation of privacy in a car in which they were merely passengers. For this reason, the Supreme Court affirmed the legality of the evidence and the convictions.

■ **Search warrants** The Fourth Amendment specifically describes the type of warrant that will authorize a valid search and seizure. It must be based "upon probable cause, supported by Oath or affirmation, and particularly describing the place to be searched, and the persons or things to be seized." This is to prevent arbitrary actions by the government aimed at harassing individuals or groups who hold unpopular views or are critical of the government.

Magistrates The Supreme Court has ruled that a search warrant can be issued only by a neutral magistrate. The purpose is to protect persons whose property is to be searched or seized by placing a neutral and detached magistrate between them and law enforcement officials, who are "engaged in the often competitive enterprise of ferreting out crime." The Federal Rules of Criminal Procedure, which govern the conduct of federal criminal prosecutions, also require that search warrants be issued by an impartial magistrate.

EXAMPLE A state enacted a law that authorized its attorney O—* general to issue warrants. The Supreme Court declared the law unconstitutional because only neutral and detached magistrates are empowered to authorize warrants. The attorney general could not be considered neutral and detached in issuing search warrants, because he was in charge of the criminal investigations for which evidence of crime was sought. The Court reasoned that prosecutors and police cannot be asked to maintain the neutrality needed to determine whether there is probable cause to issue search warrants.

Who qualifies as a magistrate? Federal case law (based on previous case decisions, not on statutes) specifically acknowledges that a magistrate need not be a lawyer. One warrant system permitted municipal court clerks to issue warrants for violation of city ordinances. The Supreme Court upheld the validity of warrants issued by these magistrates because they were sufficiently removed from the prosecutor or police to determine neutrally whether probable cause actually existed to justify the issuance of a search warrant. Recognizing that in some rural or sparsely populated areas there might be a shortage of judges to issue warrants, the Court has allowed states some flexibility in their designation of magistrates.

Probable cause Before a search or a seizure may be made of any person, place, or thing, a magistrate must decide that use of the search warrant will uncover evidence of criminal activity. This decision is based upon a finding of probable cause, which is reasonable belief that a suspect has committed a crime or that evidence of a crime will be discovered upon a search. Probable cause must be demonstrated in the affidavit that accompanies the application by the law enforcement officials for a search warrant.

Probable cause cannot be established by mere suspicion, however strong. It must be based upon known facts and circumstances. The fact that an officer acts in good faith is immaterial. On the other hand, the evidence before the officer does not have to be so strong as to prove that the accused is guilty.

Probable cause does not mean probable guilt; it means that the apparent facts stated in the affidavit would lead a reasonably prudent man to believe that a crime has been committed.

Reliable hearsay (secondhand information) may constitute probable cause. A warrant may be issued on hearsay obtained from an informer, provided that the officer applying for the warrant discloses the circumstances supporting the informant's reliability and the credibility of his information. The informer does not have to be named. His tip must describe the criminal activity "in sufficient detail so that the magistrate may know that he is relying on something more substantial than a casual rumor circulating in the underworld or an accusation based merely on an individual's general reputation."

EXAMPLE Harris was charged with possession of nontaxed O—* liquor and sought to have the evidence suppressed at his trial on the ground that the affidavit upon which the search of his premises was based was insufficient to establish probable cause. The affidavit stated that Harris had a reputation of trafficking in nontaxed liquor based on reports over the years by various persons; that an informant, who had himself bought illegal liquor from Harris, had detailed Harris's activities; and that the informant was afraid of being killed if identified. The motion to suppress the evidence was denied, an appeal was brought, but the Supreme Court upheld Harris's conviction.

Specific description The constitutional requirement that a search warrant state the address of the place to be searched and describe the person or items to be seized defines and limits the scope of the search and seizure. It insures that the government cannot conduct a search indiscriminately, as by rummaging through a person's belongings looking for any evidence of crime. The officer is left with as little discretion as possible and is prevented from searching property he has no authority to enter. If a search warrant fails to describe with sufficient particularity the place and subjects of the search, it violates the Fourth Amendment and any evidence obtained under it is invalid.

Items other than those described in a search warrant may be seized, however, if they have a reasonable relationship to the purpose of the search. This means that the officers must have probable cause to believe that the object will help bring about a conviction of the suspected crime and the seizure of the item is within one of the traditional exceptions to the requirements of a warrant, discussed later in this article.

Conflicts with other rights The right of the government to make reasonable searches and seizures often clashes with other constitutional rights of the individual. In 1978, in a landmark case, the Supreme Court found that the right of the police to search for evidence of a crime on the premises of a newspaper not implicated in the crime outweighed the right of the press to withhold such evidence on grounds of freedom of the press.

EXAMPLE Police armed with a search warrant entered the O—* offices of the Stanford University student newspaper to look for negatives, film, and pictures revealing the identities of demonstrators who assaulted police during a confrontation in which the administrative offices of the university hospital were seized. The newspaper had already published pictures of the clash—an indication that the photographer could have photographed the assault. This reason, the affidavit submitted by the district attorney stated, was considered sufficient probable cause to justify the issuance of a search warrant. There was no allegation that staff members were involved in the unlawful acts at the hospital.

Photography laboratories, filing cabinets, desks, and wastepaper baskets were searched. Alleging that they had been denied various constitutional rights, the newspaper and various staff members brought a civil action against the police who had conducted the search, the district attorney, and the judge who had issued the warrant.

The district court ruled that the Fourth Amendment barred the use of search warrants for evidence in the possession of parties not accused of a crime unless there was probable cause, based on facts presented in a sworn affidavit, that a subpoena of the evidence would be impracticable—the newspaper staff could be expected to ignore the subpoena and a court order not to remove or destroy evidence. The court went on to say that when a newspaper is innocently implicated, First Amendment interests are also involved and such a search is constitutionally permissible only in rare circumstances. The court of appeals affirmed the decision.

The Supreme Court agreed to hear the case. It found that the language of the amendment does not prohibit third-party search warrants. The interest of a state in enforcing its criminal law and recovering evidence is the same whether or not the owner or possessor of the place to be searched is implicated in the criminal act. In this case, the pictures on the premises constituted evidence of a crime. This is sufficient to justify the issuance of a search warrant.

The Court also addressed the argument that "searches of newspaper offices for evidence of crime reasonably believed to be on the premises will seriously threaten the ability of the press to gather, analyze and disseminate news." It noted that the Fourth Amendment developed against the background of clashes between the British Crown and the press, but held that there is no prohibition against search warrants being issued against the press, although in such cases the requirements of the Fourth Amendment must be applied with "scrupulous exactitude."

■ **Warrantless searches and seizures** The Fourth Amendment establishes the principle that a search and seizure is invalid unless conducted under the authority of a properly issued search warrant. There are, however, certain exceptions to this rule recognized by the Supreme Court. A warrantless search and seizure is legal when the subject of the search has consented to it. In all other cases, "exigent," or emergency, circumstances must exist.

Consent A search and seizure is lawful even though there is no warrant if the individual involved has consented to it. The consent must be freely and voluntarily given—a question of fact to be determined from all the circumstances. In deciding the legality of a search by consent, courts weigh both the legitimate need for the search and the evidence that no form of coercion, either by physical force or implied threat, was used. In some cases, a search authorized by consent may be the only means of obtaining important evidence. In other cases, a fruitless search may convince police that an arrest is unnecessary.

Because it is unlikely that a person would consent to the search of a place where he knows incriminating evidence will be found, federal courts are reluctant to infer consent unless the facts of the case clearly demonstrate it. State courts, however, have not been so reluctant to presume lack of consent. A person's knowledge of his right to refuse a search of his property or person without a warrant is considered when determining whether his consent was voluntary.

Assuming that a person has given a valid consent, the police may not search beyond the physical bounds of the area for which consent was given—as by looking through a locked file cabinet in a den when consent to search had been obtained only for the bedroom.

Deception If deception is used to secure consent, the consent is not valid. If, for instance, a suspect gives a blood sample to the police to be tested for alcohol content but it is instead matched with blood found at the scene of a crime, that consent is invalid; therefore, the search and seizure is

unconstitutional and the evidence obtained could not be used against the defendant in a criminal prosecution.

Third-party consent Certain third parties—such as husbands and wives, relatives, and business associates—may consent to searches that may result in the use of legally seized evidence against the defendant.

EXAMPLE During a murder investigation, the police visited a defendant's home and questioned his wife. The defendant was not present, but his wife voluntarily offered the police four guns belonging to her husband and the clothes worn by him on the night of the murder. One of the guns and the clothes were introduced as evidence against the defendant at his trial and he was convicted.

On appeal, the Supreme Court accepted the wife's consent to the search and held that the evidence was lawfully obtained.

EXAMPLE In another case, consent by a defendant's cousin to search a duffel bag jointly used by them was effective against the defendant because he "must be taken to have assumed the risk that [his cousin] would allow someone else to look inside." The Court held that when two or more persons have joint access to or control of premises, any of them has the right to permit a search.

Husband-wife Most third-party consent cases have involved the husband-wife relationship. The prevailing view is that when a husband and wife jointly own or occupy a place, either may consent to a search of those premises for items that may incriminate the other. Recent decisions have also upheld consents given by lovers who share a home. However, one occupant may not consent to the search of areas kept private by the other. One state court decided that a wife could not authorize a search of her husband's personal effects in a bedroom bureau drawer of their home.

Parent-child If a child is living at the home of his parents, a parent or other head of the household may consent to a search of the child's living quarters. A child may not, however, give valid consent to a full search of the parents' home.

Landlord-tenant A landlord or his agents (such as a building custodian) may consent to a search of hallways, basements, and other common areas but may not consent to the search of rented premises occupied by a tenant. This is true even though the landlord may have some limited right of entry to inspect or clean the premises. A person who rents a hotel room is treated as any other tenant, although once the time of occupancy has expired and the guest has checked out, a hotel representative may then consent to a search for anything the guest has left behind.

EXAMPLE A defendant's hotel room was searched without his consent and without a warrant. The hotel clerk consented to the search, and the defendant was subsequently convicted of armed robbery on the basis of incriminating evidence found in his room. The conviction was set aside by the Supreme Court because the search of his room was illegal. "By engaging a hotel room, petitioner had, in effect, given permission to maids, janitors and clerks to enter his room, but only in the performance of their normal duties."

A tenant may not consent to a search of the premises retained by the landlord, but he may consent to a search of the premises rented to him for items the landlord may have hidden there. A person sharing a house or apartment with another may consent to a search of rooms of common use. A person in lawful possession of the premises may permit a search that will be effective against a non-paying guest or a casual visitor.

Employer-employee   Some courts have upheld the validity of searches of an employee's work and storage areas on the employer's premises when authorized by the employer, and some have not.

Whether an employee can give a valid consent to a search of his employer's premises depends upon the scope of his authority. Generally, an average employee, such as a clerk, janitor, driver, or other person temporarily in charge, is not authorized to give consent. A manager or other person of considerable authority who is left in complete charge for a substantial period of time can, however, waive his employer's rights.

Bailor-bailee   Whether a person who does not own the property but has lawful possession of it (a bailee) can consent to a police search of the property that will be effective against the owner (bailor) depends upon the nature of the BAILMENT (the agreement between the bailor and bailee). The extent to which the bailor has surrendered control and the length of the bailment are most important.

EXAMPLE Let us say you gave your sister your business O—* ledgers for the limited purpose of her doing some clerical work on them. Her surrender of the ledgers to the police would not be valid. But if she were storing some boxes for you in her garage for an indefinite period of time and she had the only key, she could validly consent to a search of your boxes.

Frequently, the nature of the bailment is delicately balanced against the extent of the search. An attendant in a public garage may consent to opening a car door for the police to see items on the floor of the car, but to permit them to search the trunk, the attendant must be authorized to open it.

Exigent circumstances   Exigent, or emergency, circumstances for making a valid arrest without a warrant exist when evidence or life may be harmed or destroyed unless there is immediate entry; when there is hot pursuit of a fugitive from justice; when a lawful arrest has been made; when probable cause exists to believe that an automobile contains contraband subject to seizure; and when evidence comes into the plain view of the officer.

Threat to evidence or life   Law enforcement officers are justified in making warrantless searches and seizures of property when there is probable cause to believe evidence or life may be harmed unless there is immediate entry.

EXAMPLE A reliable informer told the police that cocaine O—* was in the defendant's house and provided ample probable cause for them to arrest the defendant outside the house. When the informer told police that someone else was still in the house, they immediately entered it without a warrant in order to prevent possible destruction of the cocaine, a powder that can be easily flushed down the toilet.

A federal court of appeals found that it was reasonable for the police to suspect that anyone inside the house would be aware of the five police cars circling the premises and the arrest of the defendant outside. It was also reasonable for the police to assume that the person in the house might be the defendant's partner in the drug-related activities. Therefore, the warrantless entry was necessary to preserve evidence and was lawful as an exigent circumstance permitting an exception to the Fourth Amendment requirement of a search warrant.

Police may enter a house without a warrant where there is probable cause to believe that a person is threatened with injury or death. The threat must occur at the time of the warrantless entry. A homicide that has already occurred on the premises does not justify a warrantless search.

EXAMPLE A defendant was convicted in state court of murder, O—* der, assault, and narcotics offenses. On appeal, all the convictions were eventually reversed. The evidence had been obtained during an exhaustive four-day warrantless search of the defendant's home immediately after the murder. The police claimed a warrant was not necessary because a homicide had occurred on the premises. The Supreme Court, in considering the narcotics conviction, decided that nothing suggested that the evidence would be lost, destroyed, or removed during the time needed to obtain a search warrant or that a warrant could not be easily and conveniently obtained. The seriousness of the offense under investigation was not in itself an exigency that justified a warrantless search of the premises. Therefore, the evidence used against the defendant was seized in violation of the Fourth Amendment.

Hot pursuit   Police may enter premises without a warrant when a crime has been committed in their presence or when they are in hot pursuit of an offender. This rule was stated by the Supreme Court in 1967.

EXAMPLE Police were informed that an armed robbery had O—* taken place and that the suspect had entered a certain house five minutes before they reached it. Because any delay would have endangered the lives of the police and others, entry without notice was justified. Once inside, the police were further justified in looking everywhere in the house where the suspect might be hiding and also (before his capture) where weapons might be hidden.

Many cases of warrantless police entry concern entry of the home of a person whom they have grounds to arrest. In order for the entry to be valid, there must be no time to obtain a warrant and there must be a reasonable belief that the suspect is home. An arrest warrant differs from a search warrant in that it does not identify any particular premises. If a wanted person is sought in the homes of third parties, however, an additional search warrant is required in many jurisdictions.

Many states have statutes that specifically prohibit an officer from breaking into private premises for an arrest unless he has been denied admittance after giving "notice of his office and purpose." These laws permit breaking doors and windows as well as opening an unlocked door, but not entering by subterfuge.

Courts have excused lack of notice and demand when it reasonably appeared that (1) the occupants were already aware of the presence of the police and their objective, (2) prompt action was required for the protection of the party within, (3) unannounced entry was required for the protection of the officer or to prevent the destruction of evidence, or (4) by unannounced entry actual commission of the offense could be observed or escape of the person to be arrested could be prevented.

Lawful arrest   Courts have long recognized that when an arrest is made it is reasonable for the arresting officer to search the accused, to remove any weapons that might be used to resist arrest or to escape, and to seize any evidence found on the suspect to prevent its destruction or concealment. This is known as a *search incident to a lawful arrest.* There is a problem, however, about the justification of a search when a person is arrested for a lesser offense, such as a minor traffic violation, because this usually is a low-risk situation. A series of decisions has clarified to what extent a person may be searched in different circumstances.

EXAMPLE   In *Terry* v. *Ohio,* a plainclothes police officer 0⟶✳ became suspicious of Terry and his companions. The officer had observed them walk by and stare in the same store window 24 times, then hold a conference. They appeared to be planning a robbery. The officer stopped the men, identified himself, and asked for their names. They mumbled a response. The officer immediately spun Terry around and patted down his clothing. He found a pistol, which he removed. Terry was charged with carrying a concealed weapon. Terry moved to suppress the pistol as evidence on the ground that it was obtained by an illegal search and seizure. When stopped by the officer, Terry had been "seized," and when he was patted down, he was "searched," within the meaning of the Fourth Amendment. The Supreme Court refused to grant Terry's motion.

The Court had to decide whether or not this kind of search and seizure, known as a stop-and-frisk, was reasonable. Balancing the need to search against the invasion of the individual's Fourth Amendment rights, the Court ruled that, because the government has an interest in crime prevention and detection, the officer was performing a legitimate function when he stopped Terry. After the policeman identified himself and spoke to Terry, the officer's initial suspicions were justified, and he had to protect himself and others nearby from assault with a concealed weapon. Terry was subjected to a pat down, designed to discover guns, knives, or other hidden weapons. This limited search, the Court found, was reasonable. The revolver seized from Terry was lawfully taken from him and properly admitted into evidence.

Based on this decision, a stop-and-frisk is proper when (1) a police officer observes conduct that reasonably leads him to believe that criminal activity may be afoot, (2) the officer reasonably believes that the suspicious persons may be armed and may be presently dangerous, (3) the officer properly identifies himself and makes reasonable inquiries, and (4) nothing in the officer's original encounter with the person dispels his reasonable fear for his own or another's safety. The officer may then pat down the suspect to check for concealed weapons even though there is no probable cause to arrest.

The Supreme Court broadened the *Terry* rule in 1972. EXAMPLE   While a police officer was on duty, a person 0⟶✳ known to him as a reliable informant told him that a man in a nearby car, Williams, was wearing a gun at his waist and was carrying narcotics. The officer approached the car to investigate and asked Williams to open the door. Instead, Williams rolled down the window. The officer reached inside and removed a loaded revolver from Williams's waistband, then arrested him for unlawful possession of a handgun. When a search was made, narcotics were found on Williams and in the car. Williams was convicted of unlawful possession of the handgun and of the narcotics. He petitioned for habeas corpus (release from prison), claiming that his conviction was invalid because the evidence used against him at the trial was obtained by a search that violated his rights under the Fourth Amendment.

The Supreme Court denied his petition. Although the informant's tip may not have constituted probable cause for arrest or a search warrant, the information was sufficient to stop Williams. Because the stop was reasonable, the Court ruled that the officer was justified in reaching into the car to locate the gun to insure his own safety. After discovering the concealed weapon, the officer had probable cause to arrest Williams for unlawful possession of the revolver. The narcotics were discovered when the search was made incident to the lawful arrest. The evidence used to convict Williams was obtained lawfully. For this reason, his petition was denied.

This case broadened the stop-and-frisk rule to include investigations of reasonably suspected possession of prohibited articles and investigations based on an informant's tip instead of a police officer's observation. Finally, in 1973, the Supreme Court decided that a full search of a person may be made when it is "incident" (related) to a "full custody arrest"—one made for the purpose of taking a person to the police station.

Items seized   In a lawful arrest, articles other than those originally sought may be seized. For instance, a switchblade knife found during a search of a person arrested for robbery may be legally seized. If there is no probable cause to take the item in question, it cannot later be used in evidence against the defendant.

EXAMPLE   An officer seized an unlabeled bottle of pills from 0⟶✳ the pocket of a defendant arrested for public intoxication. The seizure was improper because the officer acted only upon suspicion that the pills might be narcotics and not upon reasonable grounds for believing that the article he discovered was contraband.

Area of search   When a person is lawfully arrested, a search of the person and of the immediate area may be made. A search of an entire room or house, however, is not permitted without a warrant.

EXAMPLE   The police arrested a man on the front steps of his 0⟶✳ home. Then they went inside and searched it. Narcotics were found in his bedroom and used against him at his trial. When he was convicted, he appealed, contending that the search of the house without a warrant was unlawful. The Supreme Court agreed. The search must be confined to the immediate vicinity of the arrest, and the arrest was made outside the house.

Prior search   Some courts have invalidated searches solely because they took place before the arrest. Most courts, however, hold that when there are grounds to arrest a person, a search before the arrest involves no greater invasion of privacy than a search at the time of the arrest. Moreover, it can be to the advantage of the suspect, for if the search is not productive, the individual may not be arrested at all.

Delayed search Delayed searches of the person arrested—such as those made on the way to the police station or at the station—are usually upheld for two reasons: (1) police control of the person arrested is so substantial that it necessarily carries with it a continuing right of search, and (2) the police are entitled to inventory the property found on a person before placing him in a cell. The Supreme Court has held that such searches are lawful at least where they "are not unreasonable either because of their number or their manner of perpetration."

Subterfuge Problems arise when police arrest a person for a minor offense in order to justify searching him for evidence of more serious offenses for which they lack probable cause. This can happen when a police officer has discretion to decide whether to give a citation or to arrest and whether to search if an arrest is made. Some courts have suppressed evidence when it was shown that the desire to obtain it was the motivation behind an arrest for a minor crime, such as vagrancy or a traffic violation. Other courts, however, have overlooked strong evidence of subterfuge.

EXAMPLE Policy slips were admitted into evidence against a
O——* defendant in a prosecution for gambling after they had been seized incident to a lawful arrest for parking too close to a crosswalk. The officers who arrested the defendant were assigned to the gambling squad and had suspected that the defendant possessed gambling paraphernalia.

Automobiles Courts have traditionally drawn a distinction between automobiles and homes or offices in cases involving Fourth Amendment rights. Warrantless searches of automobiles have been upheld in circumstances in which a search of a home or office would not. The mobility of automobiles creates circumstances requiring such immediate action that rigorous enforcement of the warrant requirement is impossible. The expectation of privacy in a car is significantly less than in one's home or office. Automobiles, unlike homes, are subjected to governmental regulation and controls, including periodic inspection and licensing requirements. Automobiles travel on public thoroughfares, where both the occupants and often the contents are in plain view.

EXAMPLE A man's car was impounded because of repeated
O——* parking violations. In making a routine inventory of the contents of the car, the police discovered marijuana in the glove compartment. The man was arrested and convicted of possession of marijuana. He appealed, contending that the evidence seized in the warrantless inventory should be suppressed because it was obtained in violation of his Fourth Amendment rights. The Court determined that the police had followed standard procedures prevailing throughout the country in making the search. The purpose of the inventory was to guard the contents of the car and protect the police against disputes over lost or stolen property. There was no improper motive on the part of the police. The evidence was lawfully obtained. The conviction was upheld.

Stopping cars without probable cause Police may stop a car if they have probable cause to believe there has been a violation of the law, and they may search it if they have probable cause to believe it contains contraband. A broken taillight or a missing license plate is enough to justify the police stopping a car, but a mere baseless hunch is not.

EXAMPLE Late one night two county police in an unmarked
O——* car noticed a rental van with out-of-state license plates being driven very slowly but lawfully through the area. The police pulled the van over. The reason the officers gave for stopping the van was that they thought the occupants were lost. The driver produced his license, registration, and rental papers all in proper form. A search of the van produced burglar's tools, a revolver, and ammunition. The three van occupants were indicted and convicted of various crimes after pleading guilty to them. On appeal, the indictments and convictions of the defendants were reversed. The state court decided that the police had had no probable cause to believe that there had been any violation of the law, even a minor one. It held that the initial stopping of the van violated the Fourth Amendment and the evidence seized should have been suppressed.

Spot checks The Supreme Court decided in 1979 that spot checks of automobiles are unconstitutional when they are not based on some suspicion of lawbreaking.

EXAMPLE When a police officer stopped a car to check the
O——* driver's license and car registration, he saw some marijuana in plain view on the floor of the car. The driver was charged with illegal possession of marijuana, but was successful in having the marijuana excluded as evidence in his trial. The state asked the Supreme Court to review the decision to determine whether such automobile stops, popularly known as spot checks, were constitutional. The Court decided that in order to stop the car to check a driver's license and car registration, police must have facts to support a reasonable suspicion that a driver is unlicensed or a car unregistered or that the driver or a passenger violated a law. Otherwise, the search and seizure is unreasonable beyond the scope of constitutional protection. The Court noted, however, that this ruling did not mean that all spot checks were illegal. It did not prevent the states "from developing methods for spot checks that involve less intrusion or that do not involve the unconstitutional exercise of discretion. Questioning of all oncoming traffic at roadblock-type stops is one possible alternative."

Aspect of mobility The Fourth Amendment does not require a warrant for a search or a seizure when either is based upon probable cause and where the delay of obtaining a warrant would substantially hinder the capture of the offender or the seizure of any relative evidence. If the articles subject to seizure are in an automobile, wagon, boat, ship, or other vehicle that, because of its mobility, can be easily moved from the jurisdiction, a warrantless search and seizure may be made upon probable cause.

EXAMPLE Witnesses to a robbery gave police descriptions of
O——* the automobile used by the four robbers and told the police that one of the robbers was wearing a green sweater and another a trench coat. Shortly thereafter, police stopped a car answering the description. One of the four occupants was wearing a green sweater, and there was a trench coat in the car. The four men were arrested. Their car was taken to the police station and searched.

Police found two guns, stolen money, and other incriminating evidence. One of the four men was identified by the robbery victim and was brought to trial. The articles found in the car were introduced as evidence, and the defendant was convicted of robbery. He appealed, contending that the search of the car without a warrant was unlawful and that the evidence should not have been used at trial. The Supreme Court affirmed the conviction. The police had probable cause to arrest the occupants of the car based upon the description given them.

Later the Court limited the circumstances under which automobiles may be searched without a warrant to times when the car might be driven away. When it cannot be driven away or evidence taken from it, a warrant must be obtained unless there are exigent circumstances. For example, an automobile parked in a campsite cannot be searched without a warrant when there is no indication that the persons using the car are preparing to leave.

Plain view   The Supreme Court has declared that an object that comes into "plain view" during a valid search incident to an arrest may be seized without a warrant. This is known as the *plain view exception* to the Fourth Amendment warrant requirement.

In "plain view" cases the police officer is legally justified to conduct the search, during which he inadvertently comes across a completely unexpected piece of evidence incriminating the accused. When these factors are present, the article may be seized.

Let us say the police have a warrant to search the suspect's hotel room for a shotgun and, in the course of the search, come across counterfeit money. The money may be legitimately seized even though it was not mentioned in the search warrant. If, however, the police know in advance of the identity and location of an object, they should first obtain a search warrant.

When police pass up an opportunity to arrest a person on the street and time the arrest to occur when the defendant is within the premises so that they can seize evidence in plain view, courts have suppressed the evidence.

Not all objects may be seized under the plain view doctrine. Only incriminating objects can be lawfully seized this way, and the police must have probable cause to believe that the objects are the fruits, instrumentalities, or evidence of crime.

Border searches   Travelers may be stopped when crossing an international boundary for reasons of national self-protection. Border searches are considered unique, and a person crossing the border may be required to submit to a search of his person, baggage, and vehicle without the slightest suspicion. The search may be made without a warrant, and articles that cannot legally be brought into the country may be seized.

However, some evidence, even though it falls short of probable cause, must exist to justify more intrusive and embarrassing searches. A real suspicion (a subjective suspicion backed by objective facts) is required for a strip search, and a clear indication (even stronger grounds for believing illegal goods are being concealed) for examination of body cavities. The special rules for border searches also apply to persons who have already traveled some distance into the country, if circumstances indicate that any contraband that might be found was in the place searched at the time of entry but somehow escaped detection.

A border search must occur at the border or its functional equivalent, such as an airport. A car being driven near the border but not known to have crossed it may not be subjected to a search for illegal aliens when there is no probable cause or voluntary consent. Such a vehicle may be stopped briefly for questioning of the occupants about their citizenship and immigration status if the officer has specific knowledge that reasonably warrants suspicion that the car contains illegal aliens.

Governmental inspections   A governmental inspection to insure compliance with health or safety regulations, building codes, and other laws may not be undertaken without a search warrant unless the occupant consents to the inspection or the inspection is made in an emergency. Because the search is not made to obtain evidence for use in criminal proceedings but to insure that regulations are being obeyed, a lesser degree of probable cause is required. There must be reasonable legislative or administrative standards for conducting such an inspection.

EXAMPLE   New York law required that welfare department caseworkers make personal visits to the homes of those receiving public funds. These visits were made during normal working hours. The refusal to permit the caseworker to enter was grounds for terminating financial assistance. Therefore, in accepting the financial assistance, the recipients in effect consented to the visits, and no search warrant was needed. The Supreme Court upheld this law because the purpose of the visits was not to discover evidence of unlawful conduct. The Court decided that the visits were reasonable, which is all that is required under the Fourth Amendment.

EXAMPLE   When an inspector attempted to enter a home to investigate compliance with housing regulations, the owner refused to let him in without a warrant. The case reached the Supreme Court, which held that a warrant was necessary to inspect a building in nonemergency situations. Building code violations are relatively difficult to conceal or correct in the short time during which a warrant may be obtained.

The Supreme Court recognizes, however, that certain industries, such as those involved with liquor and firearms, have a tradition of government oversight. When a person decides to enter one of these businesses, he knowingly consents to full government regulation, so warrantless searches are permitted.

The warrant requirement also does not apply to inspection of licensed premises, such as state hospitals and nursing homes, where the nature of the business requires frequent unannounced inspections.

■ **Electronic surveillance**   Eavesdropping by use of electronic devices is considered a search and seizure within the Fourth Amendment. Under proper judicial authority, a concealed electronic device may be used to learn the truth of the allegations of a detailed factual affidavit regarding the commission of a specific crime. In one case, when there was evidence that gambling information was being transmitted by telephone, officers were permitted to listen to the conversations of a specified person from a particular telephone. The Supreme Court found that this surveillance was proper because it was properly authorized and was limited in scope and duration.

Katz v. the United States   Originally, an eavesdropper without a warrant had to physically trespass while obtaining evidence by wiretap in order to have the evidence excluded from a criminal prosecution. Tapping a telephone conversation without a warrant, for example, was not illegal as long as the government agent did not trespass to plant the "bug" (recording device).

With the increasing sophistication of electronic devices, however, the interception of private conversations proliferated, and in 1967 the Supreme Court extended Fourth Amendment protection to persons whose conversations have been illegally intercepted, regardless of whether there was a physical trespass.

EXAMPLE   In the case that brought about this change, *Katz v. the United States,* Charles Katz was convicted of transmitting wagering information by telephone across state lines in violation of a federal statute. The evidence used against him—recordings of his side of telephone conversations—was "seized" by FBI agents through use of an electronic device attached to the outside of a public telephone booth from which Katz placed his calls. The agents did not enter the telephone booth. At his trial, Katz unsuccessfully objected to the use of such evidence, which he claimed was obtained in violation of his Fourth Amendment rights. The court of appeals affirmed Katz's conviction because there had been no physical trespass into the area he occupied, namely, the telephone booth.

The Supreme Court reversed the conviction, ruling that physical trespass was not required for unlawful electronic surveillance to exist. "The Fourth Amendment protects people—and not simply areas—against unreasonable searches and seizures . . ."

The *Katz* case established certain criteria for electronic eavesdropping: (1) A warrant must be issued by an authorized magistrate who has been "properly notified of the need for such investigation, specifically informed on the basis on which it is to proceed and clearly apprised of the precise intrusion it would entail." (2) The search must be confined to the limited area prescribed by the judicial process. (3) Once the search has been completed, the agent must inform the magistrate of all that has been seized.

Berger v. New York   In that same year, the Supreme Court struck down a permissive New York State eavesdrop statute in the case of *Berger* v. *New York.*

EXAMPLE   State authorities obtained evidence that in order to obtain or keep liquor licenses in New York, persons had to bribe officials of its Liquor Authority, using a certain man as a "conduit." Based on information the state obtained, authorization was given to eavesdrop on another man, Berger, who was also believed to be involved in the scheme. As a result of these eavesdrops, Berger was indicted and convicted of conspiracy to bribe the chairman of the Liquor Authority. Berger appealed, claiming that the statute authorizing the wiretapping with court approval was unconstitutional. The Supreme Court agreed and reversed Berger's conviction.

In reaching its decision, the Supreme Court reasoned that conversations are protected by the Fourth Amendment and the use of electronic devices to capture conversations is a "search" within the meaning of the amendment. A warrant is constitutionally valid only when there is probable cause supported by oath or affirmation and when the warrant specifically describes the place to be searched and the persons or things to be seized. The New York statute did not include these requirements, which are especially important in the case of eavesdropping because it is a broad intrusion on privacy.

The Court pointed out that the law also permitted long, continuous eavesdropping and did not set a termination date on which the eavesdropping was to stop once the desired conversation had been seized. This meant that probable cause had to be shown only once for numerous searches and seizures to be conducted. The blanket permission granted by the statute to eavesdrop without adequate judicial supervision or protective procedures violated the Fourth Amendment and gave police unbridled power to invade the privacy of persons not implicated in the illegal situation.

Crime Control Act   In 1968 Congress enacted the Omnibus Crime Control and Safe Streets Act to provide, among other things, for the orderly authorization of and procedure for interceptions of wire or oral communications. Under this law, the unauthorized interception by any kind of device of any communication uttered in the expectation of privacy is prohibited, and such conversations cannot be used by any federal or state body.

The procedures set up by the act for obtaining a warrant for electronic surveillance are largely based on the Supreme Court decisions in the *Katz* and *Berger* cases cited above. An application for a warrant must identify the law enforcement officer making the application and include a statement of probable cause, giving details of the offense, the location of the place where the communication is to be intercepted, a description of the type of communication to be intercepted—if known—and the name of the person who is committing the offense and whose communications are to be intercepted. There must also be a complete statement about whether other investigative procedures have been tried and have failed, or why they are not satisfactory, and the period of time for which the interception is to be maintained. Additional facts may be required by the court before a warrant will be authorized.

After a warrant has been secured, any evidence obtained, even if unrelated to the information originally sought, is admissible. Failure to comply with the requirements of the act does not automatically make the evidence obtained inadmissible. The evidence will be excluded only if it was obtained in violation of the Fourth Amendment, if part of the act was deliberately ignored to give some advantage to the government, or if a major safeguard of the statute was violated.

State electronic surveillance laws are still valid if they are more restrictive than the federal law.

Eavesdropping by informants   Informants who electronically transmit their conversations with a suspect do not subvert the suspect's justified expectations of privacy, because the Fourth Amendment does not protect a wrongdoer who mistakenly believes that a person to whom he confides will not reveal the conversation. Evidence obtained in such a manner is therefore valid.

EXAMPLE A government informant gained the confidence of White. He spoke with White on a number of occasions in White's home, in his own car, and in a restaurant. The informant had radio equipment concealed on his person during these conversations, allowing them to be overheard by government agents. No warrant or court order was ever obtained authorizing this conduct. The evidence procured was used to charge White with various narcotics violations. At White's trial, the prosecution was unable to locate the informant. The agents who conducted the electronic surveillance and overheard the conversations testified.

White was convicted and appealed, contending that use of the electronic eavesdropping to overhear his conversations violated his constitutional rights under the Fourth Amendment. The Supreme Court affirmed White's conviction, holding that the seizure of the conversations was reasonable and lawful under the Fourth Amendment. The evidence of the conversation upon which White was convicted was properly admitted.

In its decision, the Supreme Court held that an undercover agent can, without a warrant, write down his conversations with a suspect and later testify about them. He can also legally record the conversations with electronic equipment or transmit them via radio equipment that he has on his person to recording equipment located elsewhere or to other agents monitoring the transmitting frequency.

National security exemption Over the years, federal courts have recognized a narrow exception to the requirement of a search warrant when a foreign relations or national security operation has been authorized by the President of the United States. This exception has been considered as necessary to the President's constitutional power to conduct the country's foreign affairs. The cases usually involve warrantless electronic surveillance of foreign agents or collaborators with a foreign power.

EXAMPLE The New York headquarters of the Jewish Defense League (JDL), an organization of American Jews who protest the Soviet Union's treatment of Jews within its borders, was subjected to warrantless electronic surveillance by the FBI. The league's members brought a civil rights action against the U.S. Attorney General and the FBI for violation of the Fourth Amendment and the Omnibus Crime Control Act. Both defendants claimed that a warrant was not required since the foreign affairs exemption applied. The JDL, they asserted, threatened American-Soviet relations. The court of appeals rejected this claim.

In its 1976 decision the court stated that a warrant "must be obtained before a wiretap is installed on a domestic organization that is neither the agent of nor acting in collaboration with a foreign power, even if the surveillance is installed under Presidential directive in the name of foreign intelligence gathering for the protection of the national security." The national security exemption could not be used by the defendants in this case to justify their entering and searching the office and records without a warrant.

In another famous case, agents of the executive branch of the federal government tried unsuccessfully to claim the national security exemption as a defense in their criminal prosecution for conspiracy to violate the civil rights of a psychiatrist.

EXAMPLE The defendants had participated in the break-in of the psychiatrist's office in order to seize medical records of one of his patients, Daniel Ellsberg. At that time, Ellsberg was under federal indictment for revealing top-secret documents, which became known as the Pentagon Papers. The defendants had not sought a search warrant, even though the search had been planned for at least a month before the break-in. The defendants claimed that the President is authorized to suspend the warrant requirement in light of his special responsibilities over foreign relations and national defense, but they did not show that the President or the Attorney General, his chief legal adviser, authorized the break-in.

Both the federal district court and the court of appeals in 1976 stated that there must be a specific authorization by the President or by the Attorney General before the national security exemption can be invoked to support a warrantless search.

seasonable Within a reasonable time. The term is usually used in connection with contractual obligations, which must be completed *seasonably*. What constitutes a reasonable period of time is decided according to the facts and circumstances of each case.

SEC See SECURITIES AND EXCHANGE COMMISSION.

secondary authority A persuasive authority, such as a legal encyclopedia, law review article, or other scholarly legal writing, which is cited by lawyers to persuade the court to reach a particular decision in a case, but which a court is not obligated to follow. See PRIMARY AUTHORITY.

secondary boycott Coercive pressure applied by a labor organization on an employer's suppliers, servicers, or customers to induce them to stop doing business with the employer until a dispute between the employer and the union is settled. A secondary boycott is usually illegal. It differs from a primary BOYCOTT by a labor organization, which is the refusal of employees represented by the union to buy, use, or work on a certain employer's products until a labor dispute is settled. For example, union members may refuse to work on products that do not bear a union label. In a primary boycott, only two parties are involved—the employees and their employer. In a secondary boycott, three parties are involved—the employees, their employer, and another employer or a customer. The second employer or the customer is a neutral party with whom the union has no argument.

EXAMPLE A union has a dispute with a retail store that employs its members. The union encourages employees of a wholesale firm that supplies the retail store to refuse to deliver goods to the store even though the wholesaler has no dispute with the store. The union's hope is that if the wholesaler stops supplying goods to the store, the retailer will be forced to give in to the demands of his workers. The union is conducting a secondary boycott against the wholesaler.

The laws that govern LABOR RELATIONS permit employees to conduct a primary but not usually a secondary boycott against their employer. One of the main purposes of the federal labor laws is to confine a dispute to the employer with whom the conflict has arisen and to protect neutral employers from any pressures resulting from the dispute. See BLACKLIST.

second-look statute   A statute enacted in some states to avoid the harshness of the RULE AGAINST PERPETUITIES, which limits a person's power to control what happens to his property after his death.

secretary of state   1 In state governments, the head of the department that administers a variety of formal state business, such as the licensing of corporations, the licensing and regulation of real estate brokers, the appointment of notaries public, and the filing and registration of trademarks. 2 The executive officer who heads the U.S. Department of State. Appointed by the President with the advice and consent of the Senate, the Secretary of State is a member of the Cabinet, and is responsible for the general administration of the international and diplomatic affairs of the government.

section   1 The smallest distinct and numbered subdivision in legal codes, statutes, and textbooks. 2 A parcel of land equal in area to one square mile (640 acres).

secure   Guarantee the payment of a debt or the discharge of an obligation. A debtor secures his creditor by giving him a LIEN, MORTGAGE, or other form of guaranty, to be used in case the debtor fails to make payment.

secured creditor   A creditor who holds some security, such as a MORTGAGE or LIEN, as assurance of payment of a debt owed to him.

secured transaction   Any business deal that gives a person (the creditor) a security interest in the property of another (the debtor). A *security interest* is the right the creditor has in the debtor's property to see that it will be used to pay off a debt or to insure that some obligation will be performed. The creditor with the secured interest is called the *secured party* or *secured creditor*. The property in question is known as *collateral*. If the debtor fails to meet his obligations, the secured creditor may sell the collateral and use the proceeds from the sale to pay off the debt or otherwise satisfy the debtor's obligation and return the remainder of the proceeds, if any, to the debtor. In some cases, he may be allowed to keep the collateral without selling it and without paying the debtor any difference between the worth of the collateral and the debt.

Secured transactions deal only with personal property and fixtures. *Personal property* is any property that is not real estate. *Fixtures* are items, such as stoves and furnaces, that are attached to real estate, but that may be removed. Security interests held on real estate, such as MORTGAGES, are not protected by the law of secured transactions.

The law governing secured transactions is found in Article 9 of the Uniform Commercial Code (UCC). The purpose of the UCC, which also covers CONTRACTS and SALES, is to create a precise guide for various commercial dealings so that businessmen can tell what the result of a particular type of transaction will be. In addition, the UCC assures general uniformity in business deals conducted in a state. Although there are some individual variations, Article 9 has been substantially enacted by the vast majority of states, the District of Columbia, and the Virgin Islands. Some provisions of Article 9 have been revised but not all the states have accepted these changes. The principles of secured transactions discussed here emphasize the uniform concepts of Article 9; consult your state's laws for additional information. Although the law of secured transactions applies to a variety of business transactions, this article discusses only those transactions of particular interest to the consumer.

■ **Creating a secured transaction**   There are two basic situations in which secured transactions are created. (1) The repayment of a money loan is secured by personal property belonging to the borrower.

EXAMPLE Jim lends Ted $500. Ted owns stereo equipment worth $600 and agrees with Jim that the loan will be secured by the stereo equipment. This means that if Ted cannot or will not repay Jim on the date on which they agreed, Jim will be entitled, under certain circumstances, to the stereo equipment to insure that the debt will be paid. This deal creates a secured transaction between Jim and Ted.

(2) The buyer of personal property on credit gives a security interest in the purchased property either to the seller or to the person who makes the loan that enables the buyer to purchase the property.

EXAMPLE Sam wants to buy a color television set but he does not have enough money. The owner of the store, Max, agrees to give Sam credit so that he can buy the set. Sam, however, must give Max a security interest in the set. If Sam fails to pay off this debt according to the terms of the credit agreement, Max will be entitled to take action to use the television set to pay off the debt.

■ **Types of transactions**   There are various types of secured transactions, but the most important to consumers are PLEDGES, CHATTEL MORTGAGES, and purchase money security interests.

A *pledge,* one of the oldest forms of secured transactions, is the delivery of personal property as security for a debt or for the performance of an act. To have a pledge there must be an agreement to pledge the property and the property must be delivered to the secured party. If you borrow $250 from your friend and give him your silver wristwatch with the understanding that he is to return it when you repay the debt, this arrangement is a pledge. Your friend has possession of the watch as insurance that you will pay him back.

A *chattel mortgage* is a debt owed to the lender (mortgagee) by the borrower (mortgagor) for which, by agreement, a specified item of personal property serves as security. It is similar to a mortgage in real estate. A chattel mortgage differs from a pledge in that the debtor keeps possession of the collateral. A chattel mortgage agreement must be filed at a specified local public office. It must describe the property covered and the obligation or debt secured by the mortgage. Suppose, instead of taking possession of your watch, the friend who lent you $250 signed an agreement with you stating that if you failed to pay your debt, he would be entitled to your watch. He files this agreement in the appropriate local public office. This is a chattel mortgage.

A *purchase money security interest* is a secured transaction created by a conditional sale. In a *conditional sale* title to (legal ownership of) the property is kept by the seller until the purchase price has been paid in full. A person might sell goods on installment credit and, by agreement, retain title to the goods until all installments are paid by the buyer. The seller is usually allowed to repossess the goods if the buyer should default, as by making a late installment payment.

EXAMPLE   You want to buy a set of bedroom furniture that costs $1,200. The furniture store owner agrees to grant you credit. You sign a contract in which you promise to pay a monthly installment. If you subsequently fail to pay any installment, even the final one, the store owner has the right to repossess the furniture as long as he complies with the provisions of Article 9 of the UCC.

The conditional sale agreement is basically the same as a chattel mortgage. However, a conditional sale agreement can be used only by a seller of goods and not by a person who lends money on the security of goods. A chattel mortgage, on the other hand, can be used for either a sale of goods paid by installments or a loan secured by goods. A purchase money security interest, which a conditional sale creates, is the most important and most common secured transaction under the UCC.

■ **Collateral**   Any type of goods or other property except real estate can be used as collateral in secured transactions: consumer goods, fixtures, business equipment, inventory, automobiles, livestock, timber, minerals. Checks, stock certificates, bonds, certificates of deposit, and accounts receivable (money owed but not yet paid) may also be used as collateral.

Some types of collateral are subject to their own set UCC regulations—most notably, consumer goods, inventory, and automobiles. *Consumer goods* are goods bought primarily

YOUR RIGHTS IN SECURED TRANSACTIONS

■ A secured transaction—a type of loan or a purchase of personal property on credit—is so called because it is *secured* by the debtor's property (collateral). If a debtor defaults, the secured creditor may sell the collateral and use the proceeds to pay the debts, returning any remainder to the debtor.

■ A *pledge* is the simplest form of secured transaction. Your creditor holds something belonging to you as insurance that you will pay him back.

■ A *chattel mortgage* is like a pledge except that the debtor does not turn the collateral over to his creditor and a written agreement describing the pledged property and the obligation is filed at a specified local office.

■ The most important form of secured transaction today is the conditional interest sale, which is secured by a so-called *purchase money security interest.* The typical consumer installment sale is of this type.

■ In installment sales like this, the seller keeps legal ownership of the property until the price is paid in full, and he is allowed to repossess if the buyer should default—for example, by making a late installment payment.

■ In all secured transactions except for the simple pledge transaction, there must be a written agreement.

■ If there is no written agreement, the creditor has no enforceable rights against the collateral in the debtor's possession, even if the debtor has de-

faulted in paying for goods he purchased on an installment plan.

■ An *acceleration clause* in a secured-transaction agreement permits the creditor to demand immediate payment of the unpaid portion of the debt upon default—if the debtor, for instance, fails to make even one payment on time—or in other circumstances, such as the debtor's death.

■ If the creditor takes default action against the debtor when, in fact, no default has occurred, he may be liable to the debtor for injuries suffered by his wrongful action—that is, he can be sued for money damages.

■ A secured creditor has a right to enforce his interest by acting to take possession of the collateral. To do this, he may sue, or he may even act without judicial process if he can do so without violence or a threat of violence. For example, towing a car from a street or parking lot without the debtor's knowledge has been considered peaceable, but breaking into his garage is wrong because it involves breaking and entering—a crime.

■ Instead of selling the repossessed collateral and applying the proceeds to the debt, the secured creditor may keep the collateral. This is called *strict foreclosure* and is usually preferable, because both debtor and creditor are better off not going through a sale and attempting to settle the surplus or deficiency of the proceeds. Strict fore-

closure is not permitted, however, in the case of consumer goods when at least 60 percent of the debt has already been paid.

■ If a debtor has paid at least 60 percent of the cash price of the goods, a properly conducted resale is likely to result in a surplus. If the creditor fails to sell the goods within 90 days after repossession, he may be liable to the debtor for conversion (unlawfully depriving a person of his property).

■ Beware of buying something from a private individual who, unbeknown to you, may have put it up for collateral in a secured transaction. If he defaults, his creditor may have the right to repossess from you. The creditor will certainly have that right if he filed a financing statement before you bought; he will not be able to repossess from you if he did not file or if the good are consumer goods, such as household items.

■ When a secured debt is paid up, the creditor must send the debtor a written statement to that effect, if the debtor demands it in writing. This is called a *termination statement.* If a secured creditor fails to file a termination statement within 10 days after a proper demand has been made, he can be made to pay the debtor $100.

■ Some states require termination statements to be filed without request because many consumers do not realize their importance.

for personal, family, or household purposes, such as furniture. *Inventory* consists of goods held for sale or lease by a business, goods furnished under contracts, or materials used or consumed by a business. The same item can be either consumer goods or inventory depending upon who has it and for what purpose.

EXAMPLE A vacuum cleaner that is one of hundreds of O——* vacuum cleaners held in the warehouse of an appliance store for possible sale is inventory, and if the owner of the store wished to use it as collateral for a loan, it would be treated as inventory. On the other hand, if the store sells the same vacuum to you for cleaning your own home, you may buy it on credit, using the vacuum cleaner as collateral. In that case the collateral would be treated as consumer goods.

■ **Parties** The parties to a secured transaction are the debtor and the secured creditor. The *debtor* is the person who owes payment or other performance of the obligation secured. If the actual debtor does not own the collateral, the word "debtor" usually refers to the person who does own the collateral, since legal steps will be taken against his property if the actual debtor defaults.

The *secured creditor* is the lender or seller (or his representative) who has the security interest. A *seller* is a person who sells goods on credit and takes a purchase money security interest for the unpaid price. A person who takes over the security interest from the original secured party (by assignment) is also considered a secured creditor.

EXAMPLE A jeweler sells a diamond ring on credit to a O——* young man and retains a security interest on the ring. He then assigns (transfers) the security interest on the ring to a bank as collateral for a loan he (the jeweler) is getting. The bank becomes a secured creditor of the original debtor, the young man, and the jeweler becomes a debtor.

■ **Security agreement** A secured transaction is created only when there is an express (specific) agreement between the debtor and the secured creditor. The agreement must be in writing and must meet certain requirements unless the secured creditor has possession of the collateral, as in a pledge transaction. This written agreement is called a *security agreement*. The writing must include the signatures of the parties, a description of the collateral, and a clear statement of the agreement.

If there is no written security agreement, the secured party has no enforceable rights against the collateral in the debtor's possession, even if the debtor defaults in paying for goods purchased on an installment plan.

■ **Default** Generally, a default occurs when the terms of a valid security agreement have been violated. A breach of any of the terms by a debtor is usually considered a default. The most common type of default is the debtor's failure to pay money when it is due. Security agreements often include *acceleration clauses*, which permit the secured creditor to declare that the unpaid portion of the debt is subject to immediate payment upon default or in other circumstances, such as the debtor's death.

Once default occurs, the secured creditor may act to take possession of the collateral or otherwise collect what is owed him. If the secured creditor takes default action against the debtor when, in fact, no default has occurred, he

may be liable to the debtor for injuries suffered by his wrongful action.

EXAMPLE Suppose that Sheldon borrows money from Mark O——* and agrees to pay him back in 24 monthly installments. To secure the loan, Sheldon offers the inventory of his shoe store as collateral. Immediately after making the sixth monthly payment on his loan, Sheldon dies. No payments are in arrears at that time, and no other event of default has occurred. The security agreement does not specify that the debtor's death will trigger default of the loan. Nevertheless, Mark takes immediate action to get possession of the shoes. A court may hold his action improper. Mark may be liable to Sheldon's heirs for losses suffered by the store because Mark has taken over the inventory. Mark may also have to pay punitive damages.

Remedies of a secured creditor When a debtor is in default, the secured creditor has a right to enforce his security interest in the collateral. He may do this by *foreclosing his security interest*—that is, by acting to take possession of the collateral.

The secured creditor may foreclose his security interest by any judicial procedure available under state law. For example, he may sue to foreclose the security agreement, and if he wins the suit he can take possession of the collateral.

He may also take over the collateral without judicial process if this can be done without breach of the peace (violence or a threat of violence). For example, the removal of collateral, such as a car, from a parking lot without the knowledge or objection of the debtor has been considered peaceable. On the other hand, breaking into his garage to take the car is an improper way to get collateral, as it involves criminal acts—breaking and entering.

If the secured creditor prefers not to foreclose, he can try to collect the amount of the debt by attaching a LIEN on other property of the debtor, by having a garnishment attached to a debt due the debtor from a third person, or by some other legal means. See ATTACHMENT AND GARNISHMENT.

Selling the collateral If the secured party chooses foreclosure and takes possession of the collateral, he may sell it and apply the sales proceeds to the debt. The proceeds must first be used to pay the expenses of selling or leasing the collateral. Reasonable attorneys' fees and legal expenses of the secured creditor may also be paid with the proceeds, if not prohibited by law or by the terms of the security agreement.

After these expenses are paid, the proceeds are used to satisfy the debt, including principal, interest, or finance charges, and any other unpaid charges provided for in the security agreement. If any proceeds remain, they are to be used to pay off any other secured interest in the collateral (claimed in writing). The other secured creditor is usually a different creditor but it may be the same creditor who financed a second secured debt.

EXAMPLE Elsie bought a car for $4,000. She paid $1,000 as a O——* down payment on it and signed a monthly installment agreement for the balance, using the car itself as collateral. When her financial future began to look a bit dim, Elsie took out a $500 loan from a finance company and again used the car as collateral. After failing to pay three monthly installments in a row, the car company repossessed the vehicle and sold it. After the expenses involved in selling the car were paid and the balance due on the car taken care of, the rest of the sale money was applied against Elsie's loan from the finance company. If any proceeds remain after all secured interests have been paid off, they go to the debtor. In most cases, however, money is still owed after the collateral has been sold, because forced sales rarely bring favorable prices and because expenses and attorneys' fees are deducted from the money brought by the sale. This remaining debt is called a deficiency.

Generally, when the value of the collateral is less than the amount owed to the secured creditor, he may obtain a deficiency judgment after foreclosure. The debtor is liable for any deficiency after the secured creditor disposes of the collateral unless there is a contrary agreement.

The secured creditor's sale of the collateral may be public or private. A public sale is by auction, usually conducted on the steps of a courthouse. A private sale is held through commercial channels—often by a dealer whose business is selling goods of that kind. Private sales usually result in a higher price paid.

All sales of collateral must be done in a commercially reasonable manner. This basically means that the secured creditor must make reasonable efforts to sell the collateral at the market price and conform to commercial practices among dealers in the type of property involved. The debtor is entitled to reasonable notification of the time and place of the sale. The debtor benefits from knowing about the sale, because he can respond by paying the debt, finding a buyer, or attending the sale to bid on the collateral or have others bid for him, so that the collateral is not sacrificed by sale at less than its true value.

If consumer goods are involved, only the debtor must be notified. In other cases, any other party who has claimed the collateral in writing must also be notified.

Strict foreclosure   Instead of selling the collateral and applying the sales proceeds to the debt, the secured creditor may keep the collateral in satisfaction of the debt. This is known as *strict foreclosure*. Strict foreclosure is usually preferable, because both debtor and creditor are better off not going through a sale and trying to settle the surplus or deficiency of the proceeds. Strict foreclosure is not permitted, however, in the case of consumer goods when at least 60 percent of the debt is already paid.

To obtain strict foreclosure, a secured creditor must send written notice of his proposal to the debtor unless the debtor signed a statement after default renouncing his rights. If the collateral is consumer goods for which less than 60 percent has been paid, no other notice need be given. In other cases, notice must be sent to any other secured creditor who has claimed the collateral in writing.

If the secured creditor seeking strict foreclosure does not receive any written objection within 21 days after the notice was sent, he may keep the collateral. The obligation is discharged, and the secured creditor gives up any claim to a deficiency. On the other hand, if he sells the collateral at a favorable price, he does not have to account to the debtor for any surplus.

If the secured creditor does receive objections to strict foreclosure during the 21-day period, he must dispose of the collateral by selling or leasing it. He must dispose of consumer goods if the debtor has paid 60 percent of the cash price (in the case of a purchase money security interest) or 60 percent of the loan (in the case of a pledge or chattel mortgage). If a debtor has paid at least 60 percent of the cash price of the loan, a properly conducted resale might result in a surplus. (A note of caution: A secured transaction agreement may contain a clause by which the debtor signs away his right to demand a resale after default.) If a secured party fails to dispose of such goods within 90 days after he takes possession, he may be liable to the debtor for conversion (an unauthorized act depriving a person of his property).

Redemption   Unless otherwise agreed in writing after default, the debtor may redeem the collateral before the secured creditor has sold it or contracted for its sale or before strict foreclosure. The debtor redeems the collateral by paying off the amount of the debt still owed, as well as the expenses incurred by the secured creditor in preparing for the sale of the collateral. Legal expenses and reasonable attorneys' fees must also be paid if specified in the security agreement and not prohibited by law. If the agreement contains a clause accelerating the entire balance due upon default on one installment, the entire balance must be paid. However, some courts have decided that under some circumstances justice is best served by payment only of the amount in default, despite an acceleration clause.

Rights of the debtor   After the secured creditor has disposed of the collateral upon default, he may be liable if he failed to comply with default provisions of the UCC. The debtor may sue for violation of security agreement provisions and may recover any loss caused by the secured creditor's failure to follow default provisions—such as those that prescribe proper methods of sale of property. In the case of consumer goods, the debtor is entitled to a minimum recovery, which is usually the value of the collateral minus the debt, or, as sometimes stated, the difference between the actual disposition price and the price the collateral would have brought if disposed of properly.

■ **Protecting the right of the secured creditor**   The law of secured transactions is concerned primarily with protecting the secured creditor's right to the collateral when the debtor defaults. The extent of this protection depends in many instances on when the security interest *attached*—became effective—or whether or not it was *perfected*—made firm against other creditors.

Attachment of a security interest   In all secured transactions, the security interest of the creditor must be attached. A security interest attaches when it becomes enforceable against the debtor. Once his security interest attaches, the secured creditor has the right to use the collateral to settle the outstanding obligation if the debtor defaults and no other creditor has superior rights to the collateral.

In order for a security interest to attach, three requirements must be met: (1) There must be an agreement between the debtor and the secured party. (2) Something of value must be given the debtor in return for the collateral. (3) The debtor must have rights in the collateral he is offering as security. He has rights to property if he owns it or if he is buying it on an installment plan and has it in his possession. He also has rights to property in which he has a secured interest.

EXAMPLE Tim gives Alice a security interest in his expensive camera in exchange for a $300 loan. Alice transfers her security interest to the City Finance Company as collateral for a $250 loan. Although Alice does not legally own the camera, she does have a security interest in it, which enables her to use it as collateral for her loan from the City Finance Company.

The type of secured transaction determines at what point the security interest attaches. When the secured creditor is given possession of the collateral in a pledge, the security interest attaches automatically. If, however, the secured creditor releases the collateral from his possession, he loses his security interest in it.

EXAMPLE Anna May gave Betty her gold bracelet as collateral in a pledge for a loan of $100. Betty's secured interest in the bracelet attached as soon as Anna May handed the bracelet over to her. After Anna May had paid back $75 of the loan, Betty returned the bracelet even though Betty still owed her $25. At that point, Anna May lost her secured interest in the bracelet, and if Betty later failed to pay the remaining $25, Anna May could not claim the bracelet to pay off the remainder of the debt.

A purchase money security interest attaches when the collateral is delivered to the debtor. For example, if you buy an air conditioner from a department store on an installment plan, the store's security interest in the air conditioner attaches as soon as it has been delivered to you.

The security interest in a chattel mortgage attaches when the security agreement is filed with the appropriate government office. If you borrow money from a bank and offer your automobile as collateral, the bank will file the security agreement, and its secured interest will attach as soon as that paper is filed. The filing of a separate paper—a financing statement—is also a step that can be taken in secured transactions. It is known as *perfecting* the interest.

Perfecting a security interest Perfecting a security interest is an additional step that is required when the secured creditor wants to enforce his interest against third persons who may also claim interests in the collateral, such as other creditors of the debtor (who may obtain a LIEN against the collateral) or persons to whom the debtor sells the collateral. If the secured creditor fails to perfect his interest he can be relegated to the status of a general creditor of an insolvent debtor. This means that if the debtor defaults, the so-called secured creditor will have no greater claim than all of the other unsecured creditors of the debtor. He will be entitled only to a proportionate share of the debtor's assets after the debts of the secured creditors have been satisfied. There is a good chance that he will recover only a part of the debt owed.

Perfection takes place either when the secured creditor takes possession of the collateral—for example, as a pledge—or when a financing statement is filed.

Filing a financing statement A financing statement is a paper that briefly describes property held as collateral in a security agreement. It is designed as a quick reference for persons searching through the records for information about a possible security interest in the property. Although a financing statement may be incorporated into the body of a security agreement, it is a separate paper from the agreement. A financing statement by itself does not usually create a security interest.

The financing statement should be signed by the debtor (and, in some states, by the secured creditor). It should have the mailing addresses of the debtor and secured creditor, and a description of the collateral. If the collateral is a fixture or other property related to real estate, a description of the land involved should be included. Any amendments to the financing statement must be signed by both the debtor and the secured creditor. To facilitate filing, standard forms have been developed for use in most counties and states.

The presentation of a proper financing statement and the payment of a filing fee or acceptance of the statement by the proper official constitutes filing. State law specifies the place of filing. It is usually the office of the secretary of state or the office of the clerk in the county or township in which the debtor resides or has a business.

Article 9 of the UCC does not specifically provide a time within which a financing statement must be filed. However, any delay in filing can be disadvantageous because if someone else files a statement on that collateral before the creditor, the other claim will be paid off first. The late filing subordinates the secured party's claim to the person who has filed his statement earlier.

A financing statement may be amended after it has been filed. If, however, the amendment adds collateral, it is effective with respect to the added collateral only from the filing date of the amendment. An amendment must be signed by both the debtor and secured creditor to show that the amendment was made honestly.

Duration of a financing statement A filed financing statement is generally effective for five years from the date of filing. (Depending on the version of Article 9 observed by your state, there may be an additional 60 days after that maturity date.) When the period is about to expire, the secured creditor may extend the time of perfection by filing a continuation statement. This usually must be done within six months before the expiration of the five-year period. After that time, a new financing statement must be filed to revive perfection.

The secured creditor must sign the continuation statement; the debtor's signature is not needed. Succeeding continuation statements may be filed to extend the period for additional five-year periods.

Temporary perfection For certain types of collateral, such as checks, stock certificates, and bank accounts, a security interest is automatically perfected for a period of 21 days (beginning on the day the security interest is attached) even without filing or taking possession. After the 21 days have passed, the security interest is no longer perfected unless a statement has been filed or the collateral has been taken in possession in the meantime.

Exceptions to perfecting In certain instances, it is not necessary to take any steps to perfect (make firm against the creditors) a security interest other than those steps required for attaching interest (making it enforceable). The most significant type of security interest that is automatically perfected upon attachment is a purchase money security interest in consumer goods (with certain exceptions if the consumer goods are fixtures or motor vehicles). The reason behind this rule is that the benefits of public filing are outweighed by the disadvantages of filing large numbers of transactions involving small amounts of credit and collateral of low value.

EXAMPLE Suppose Lou purchases a combination stereo-television set from the Radio Hut on installment credit. The purchase is made under a written security agreement, and the set is delivered to Lou's home. Upon delivery, the security interest attaches and is perfected upon attachment. If the Radio Hut assigns (transfers) the security interest to a financer, the security interest continues to be perfected.

Suppose the Radio Hut had sold the set for cash, which Lou borrowed from the financer. The security interest is perfected in favor of the financer upon attachment, since the financer has a purchase money security interest. Filing all of these transactions would just clutter the files and inconvenience those involved in the filing process, and it could result in filing fees disproportionate to the amount of credit given.

Filing with respect to this type of collateral is permitted and may be desirable. Because unless a financing statement is filed, a third person may buy consumer goods from the consumer-debtor free of the security interest (even if it was automatically perfected) if the third person also uses the goods for consumer purposes.

EXAMPLE Lou buys his stereo-television set from the Radio Hut on an installment plan. The Radio Hut does not file because it knows that its interest is automatically perfected when the set is delivered to Lou. After a few months Lou runs into financial difficulties and sells the set to his neighbor Phil, without telling Phil that the set is collateral in a secured transaction. A few months later Lou defaults on his payments, but the Radio Hut cannot repossess the set because Phil has bought it free of the security interest. On the other hand, if the Radio Hut had filed before Phil bought the set, it would have had a right to repossess the set even though Phil had bought it in good faith from Lou. Of course, Phil could have protected himself by checking to see if a financing statement had been filed before buying the set and refusing to buy it if he discovered a statement.

The message is clear: Beware of buying consumer goods from a private individual who may, without your knowledge, have put it up for collateral in a secured transaction. If he defaults, his creditor may have the right to repossess from you. The creditor will certainly have that right if he filed a financing statement before you bought: he will not be able to repossess from you if he did not file.

If the collateral is a motor vehicle purchased for personal or family use, a security interest may be perfected only by filing or by complying with a state certificate of title law (motor vehicle registration law). If the collateral is a fixture, such as a furnace in a house, a security interest may be perfected by attachment, but filing is necessary to obtain priority over certain real estate interests. Some states that have rejected certain revisions of Article 9 of the Uniform Commercial Code stick to the older requirement of licensing a motor vehicle or filing for a fixture in order to perfect a security interest.

■ **Termination statement** When there is no longer any outstanding secured debt, the secured creditor must, on written demand by the debtor, send him a termination statement to that effect. Copies of the termination statement must be sent to each officer with whom the financing statement was filed.

As mentioned earlier, many purchase money security interests in consumer goods other than motor vehicles or fixtures do not have to be filed. Obviously, no termination statement is necessary in such cases. But if a financing statement was optionally filed a termination statement is needed. Some states require a termination statement to be filed even without a demand by the consumer since many consumers do not realize the importance of clearing the situation on file. (When motor vehicles as consumer goods are involved, a certificate-of-title law may control the filing and release of the security interest.)

If a secured creditor fails to file a termination statement relating to any type of goods within 10 days after a proper demand has been made, he is liable to the debtor for $100. In addition, he will be liable for any loss suffered by the debtor as a result of such a failure.

■ **Assignments** A security interest may be *assigned,* or transferred, to a third person who, as *assignee,* becomes the secured creditor. An assignment is usually made when a seller of goods on credit takes a purchase money security interest in them and then transfers that interest to a bank or finance company.

Rights of the assignee It is a basic principle of the law of assignments that an assignee receives all the rights, title, or interest of the assignor (person who assigns) in the thing assigned. He does not receive any greater rights than the assignor's. This rule applies to security interests. The rights of an assignee are subject to all the terms of the contract between the original debtor (account debtor) and the original secured creditor (assignor). The assignee is subject to any defense or claim arising from that contract.

EXAMPLE Andy contracted with Bob to build a garage on Andy's land. Bob assigned his right of payment for building the garage to Carl (the assignee) as collateral for a loan Carl made to Bob. When Bob failed to finish the construction, Andy withheld the final payment under the contract. Carl, as assignee, had no claim against Andy because Carl was subject to Andy's refusal to pay since Bob breached the contract by failing to finish the garage (Andy's defense).

A debtor may also have claims against the assignor that are independent of the original contract. The assignee is subject to the independent claims that accrued before the debtor was notified of the assignment, but not to claims arising after he received notice of the assignment.

EXAMPLE Suppose on April 1, Ted contracted with Acme Furniture House for delivery of two bookcases on June 1. On May 1 Ted entered into a second contract with Acme for immediate delivery of another three bookcases. Acme assigned the amount due under the second contract to Gold's Bank on May 2, the same day the company delivered the three bookcases to Ted. The bank notified Ted of the assignment of the amount under the second contract. Acme failed to deliver the two bookcases on June 1 under the first contract. Ted asserted a claim against the payment due the bank under the assignment of the second contract for damages arising from Acme's breach of the first contract. The claim could not be made, however, because it accrued on June 1, after the buyer had been notified of the assignment, and arose under a contract independent of the one assigned.

As a general rule, a debtor may agree that he will not assert against an assignee any claim or defense he may have against the assignor, but there are exceptions to this rule in some states—for instance, if consumer goods are involved.

Assignment of a perfected security interest When a perfected security interest is assigned (one for which a financing statement was filed), no additional filing is required to continue its perfected status.

EXAMPLE McDonald, a farmer, buys a threshing machine from Johnson, a farm equipment supplier. Johnson keeps a security interest in the thresher and perfects that interest. Johnson then assigns the perfected security interest to Clark. The security interest is in Clark's hands, and without further steps on his part, it continues to be perfected against McDonald's creditors. But it is not perfected against Johnson's creditors. If Johnson has assigned his interest to Clark as security for a loan, Clark must take the necessary steps to be protected from Johnson's creditors.

Although a secured transaction that has been assigned does not require additional filing, the financing statement may disclose the assignment, and a separate written statement of assignment may be filed. These filings are required when a continuation statement or termination statement is presented for filing by someone other than the secured creditor named in the financing statement on file.

■ **Determining the right to the collateral** Many of the UCC provisions governing secured transactions are devoted to determining when the secured creditor has a right to the collateral against the debtor's creditors and against those who purchase the collateral from the debtor. Conflicts often arise when the collateral is sold or transferred, when there are two secured parties, when there is a lien on the collateral, or when the debtor declares insolvency or bankruptcy.

When collateral is sold or transferred A secured creditor may authorize the debtor's sale of the collateral by signing a statement releasing all or part of the collateral described in the filed financing statement. If he does so, he loses his security interest in the collateral itself but retains it in the proceeds of the sale received by the debtor.

A security interest continues in collateral that is sold without the consent of the secured creditor. It also attaches to the proceeds of the sale of the collateral. The secured creditor may claim both the original collateral and proceeds, but of course he is entitled only to the amount of the debt owed. The debtor is entitled to any excess.

These rules do not mean, however, that the rights of all buyers of collateral that is sold without the consent of the secured party are subject to the security interest. Certain buyers take collateral free of a security interest. Among them are persons who buy goods in the ordinary course of business. Since they do not know that the sale violates another's rights in the goods (because the goods have been used as collateral), the buyers are entitled to take the goods

free of any security interest. For this to hold true, however, the person who sells the collateral must be in the business of selling goods of that kind and cannot be a pawnbroker.

EXAMPLE If you buy a car from an automobile dealer, you are a buyer in the ordinary course of business. This means you take the car free of any security interest in it—for example, an interest given by the dealer to a bank. But if you buy a car from your neighbor or from a company not in the business of selling cars, such as a car-rental agency, you are not considered a buyer in the ordinary course of business and your interest in the car would be subject to a perfected security interest created by the seller of the car.

A consumer who buys consumer goods (for personal, family, or household use) from another consumer may also take collateral free of security interests—unless he knows of the interest or unless the secured creditor filed a financing statement before the purchase.

EXAMPLE Suppose Sally buys a freezer for use in her home from Star Appliance Company and gives Star a purchase money security interest in the deep freeze for the unpaid price. Star does not file a financing statement because it is not required for perfecting a purchase money security interest. Six months later, Sally sells the freezer to her next-door neighbor, Dennis, who wants it for home use. Although Star has a perfected security interest, the sale is free of that interest if Dennis bought it without knowing of the security interest. If Star had filed a financing statement, however, Dennis's purchase would be subject to the security interest.

On the other hand, suppose that six months after buying her freezer from Star, Sally traded it to another dealer, Frosty Appliances, for a new model. Even if Star did not file, it has a security interest in the freezer greater than the rights of Frosty, because Frosty did not buy it for personal, family, or household purposes.

When there are two secured parties When two secured parties claim rights in the same collateral, the dispute is solved by determining who was the first to file or perfect his security interest. This rule recognizes that a financing statement may be filed before a security interest attaches (becomes enforceable) and therefore before it is perfected. If one of the conflicting security interests is filed or perfected and the other is not, the filed or perfected interest has priority. If both of the conflicting security interests are unperfected, the first to attach has priority. If both security interests are perfected by filing, the earlier date of filing determines priority.

A purchase money security interest has priority over a conflicting security interest in the same collateral if it is perfected within 10 days after the debtor receives possession of the collateral—unless the collateral consists of goods from a business's inventory. Purchase money security interests are perfected automatically upon delivery of the collateral if the collateral consists of ordinary consumer goods, but if the collateral is an automobile or fixture it must generally be filed to perfect.

EXAMPLE Mike purchased a dishwasher (consumer goods) on credit from Midcity Department Store and signed a security agreement giving Midcity a security interest in the dishwasher for the unpaid price. Midcity did not file a financing statement. Later, Mike borrowed from a finance company giving it a security interest in the same dishwasher. The finance company promptly filed a financing statement. Midcity's unfiled security interest is superior to that of the finance company, because Midcity has a purchase money security interest in consumer goods—a type of interest that is perfected without the filing of a financing statement. The interest clearly attached, and therefore was perfected, when Mike received possession of the dishwasher.

If a creditor who has a purchase money security interest fails to file or perfect within 10 days after the debtor receives possession of the collateral, his priority is determined by the "first to file or perfect" rule. This applies to cases where there are two conflicting security interests, both of which are purchase money interests.

EXAMPLE Joy buys a new automobile from City Motors. 0⊶⊸✳ She makes a down payment on the car and agrees to pay the dealer the balance in monthly installments, with the car as collateral to secure the transaction. City Motors fails to file a financing statement on the purchase. A few months later Joy loses her job and desperately needs money, so she sells the car to Lemmon's Used Car Lot. Instead of using the money from the sale of her car to pay off City Motors, Joy uses it to pay other bills. Shortly after buying the car, Lemmon sells it to Ted, who makes a down payment and agrees to pay the balance due in monthly installments, with the car as collateral. Lemmon files a financing statement two weeks after the sale.

A month later Joy fails to make a payment on her car. City Motors remembers it has not perfected the transaction and files at that time. A few months later both Joy and Ted default in their payments and both car dealers try to collect the collateral, which is the same car. Even though City Motors had an interest in the collateral first, they failed to file within 10 days after Joy received delivery of the car. Lemmon did not file within 10 days after the car was delivered to Ted, but he filed before City Motors and has priority over the collateral.

When there is a lien on the collateral Priority rights of a secured party to collateral may be threatened if a creditor has a LIEN against the collateral. A *lien* is a claim on property that has been acquired under certain laws or through such legal proceedings as levies and ATTACHMENT AND GARNISHMENT. See also LEVY.

Certain federal and state laws list various types of liens that take priority even over a perfected security interest. For example, most states have artisan's lien statutes, which give a repairman a lien on goods in his possession for the cost of repairs made or materials used in making repairs. Article 9 of the UCC gives a repairman's lien priority over even a perfected security interest unless a statute specifically makes it subordinate. These liens are given priority because the repairman's work has preserved or enhanced the value of the collateral.

EXAMPLE Suppose that John buys a new automobile and 0⊶⊸✳ borrows the money to pay for the car from Gold's Bank, with the car as collateral in a secured transaction. The bank perfects the transaction immediately. After making only three payments on the car, John is involved in an accident and the car is badly dented and scratched.

He takes it to his local garage and arranges to have the dents pounded out and the entire car repainted. The next day, while repairing the roof of his house, John falls and is seriously injured. He has to stay in the hospital for several weeks and is unable to work for several months after his release.

To add to his troubles, John is a salesman and works on commission. As a result of his high hospital bills, which are only partly covered by insurance, and his loss of commissions, he is not able to make the payments on his car or pay the garage for repairing and painting it. Even though the bank has a perfected security interest in the automobile, the garage has priority in claiming the car as collateral to pay for the work it did, because the garage improved the collateral by repairing and painting it and the state John lives in has an artisan's lien statute. The garage has the right to sell the car and take what is owed for the repairs plus any legal fees and any expenses incurred in selling the car.

The bank is entitled to the balance of the sale price plus interest or as much of the balance as is needed to pay off the debt. If there is any money left, John will get it. If the sale price is not enough to cover all the debts and fees, John will still owe the balance to the bank.

When the debtor is bankrupt or insolvent The debtor in a secured transaction may become insolvent—that is, his debts may exceed his assets. In such a case he will usually start insolvency proceedings under either state or federal law to pay off as many of his creditors as possible. Under state law, the debtor can assign his remaining assets for the benefit of his creditors, or the court can appoint a receiver to manage his remaining assets on behalf of his creditors. See ASSIGNMENT FOR BENEFIT OF CREDITORS. Article 9 of the UCC declares that such an assignee or receiver is considered a lien creditor from the time of his assignment or appointment and has the same rights of priority over secured property as any other lien creditor.

EXAMPLE Sarah, a sailing enthusiast, decided to give herself 0⊶⊸✳ a treat and bought a $5,000 boat. To pay for the boat, she entered into a secured transaction with Ed, the seller, agreeing to pay the $5,000 in 36 monthly installments with the boat as collateral. Ed immediately filed his security interest. After the first year of making payments, Sarah had financial problems and found it difficult to keep up her payments on the boat and to pay her other debts. Consequently she borrowed $1,000 from her friend Mary, offering her washing machine and dryer as collateral. Mary did not perfect her security interest. A month later, Sarah lost her job and was unable to make payments on her boat, repay Mary, or pay her other debts. After months of unemployment, even her unemployment insurance ran out and so she started insolvency proceedings.

The court appointed a receiver to manage the remainder of Sarah's assets. The receiver, from the time of his appointment, had all the rights of a lien creditor. He was given priority over Sarah's washing machine and dryer, because Mary had not perfected her interest in them. Consequently the receiver had both machines sold and used the proceeds to pay Sarah's other creditors. The receiver did not have priority to the boat, however, because Ed had filed his interest before the receiver had been appointed. Ed had the boat sold and used the proceeds to pay off the balance due on the boat. The few dollars that remained from the sale of the boat were given to the receiver to be applied against Sarah's other debts.

Under federal law, an insolvent debtor is declared bankrupt when he files a voluntary petition for bankruptcy or when his creditors file an involuntary petition in bankruptcy court. All of the debtor's property (except certain exempt items, such as household furniture) vests in a court-appointed trustee. A secured creditor with a perfected security interest at the time of bankruptcy is usually able to assert his perfected interest in the collateral against the trustee—and ahead of other creditors.

Securities and Exchange Commission

A PUBLIC ADMINISTRATIVE AGENCY of the federal government, commonly called the SEC. The commission's duties include the administration and enforcement of federal securities laws and the protection of investors and the public by regulating the nation's securities markets, brokers, and dealers. It also regulates mutual funds and other investment companies, holding companies that control electric or gas utilities, and investment advisers and counselors. In addition, the SEC supplies the courts and the parties involved with information concerning the practicality of reorganizing and rehabilitating failing corporations.

The commission is composed of five members. A member is appointed for a five-year term by the President of the United States with the advice and consent of the Senate. Only three of the five members can belong to the same political party. Once appointed, the commissioners cannot participate in any other business, accept any other employment, or participate in any stock-market dealings regulated by the commission. See SECURITIES REGULATION.

securities regulation   Federal and state laws governing the buying and selling of securities. A *security* is an investment of a purchaser's funds in a business enterprise that gives him an interest or share in the business. Stock in a CORPORATION is the most common security bought and sold in everyday business transactions.

■ **Federal regulation**   The buying and selling of investment securities has long been the subject of congressional regulation. In the decades following the 1930's Depression, Congress enacted substantial legislation regulating the purchase and sale of securities in order to protect the general investing public from sharp or unlawful business practices. The SECURITIES AND EXCHANGE COMMISSION (SEC) has primary responsibility for protecting the public interest by enforcing federal securities regulatory laws. Investors should note that foreign business transactions are not within the scope of federal securities laws.

Policy   It is the policy of Congress to encourage high standards of ethics in the securities industry. Accordingly, a fundamental goal of securities regulation is to assure that a purchaser is provided with full disclosure of information concerning his investment. Full disclosure requirements are intended to guard against fraud in the sale of securities. Federal law does not follow the philosophy of CAVEAT EMPTOR ("Let the buyer beware").

To protect the national economy from the consequences of excessive investor speculation and to protect individuals from excessive debt, federal law also regulates the amount of credit that can be extended to persons for the purchase of securities. Buying on margin is stock-market language for buying on credit.

Registration   Congress has the power to regulate interstate traffic in securities, including sales made through the U.S. mail and securities traded on a national securities EXCHANGE. Before these securities can be lawfully offered for sale to the public, federal law requires that a statement disclosing all the important facts about the investment be filed with the Securities and Exchange Commission. The registration statement must disclose, for example, the price at which shares will be offered to the public, commissions paid to underwriters of the security, and any options to purchase that have been issued. From time to time, the company issuing the security must file reports to update its registration information.

Prospectus   A security cannot be sold or delivered by mail or other means of interstate commerce unless it is preceded or accompanied by a prospectus that fully discloses all the *material facts* regarding the investment—those that are necessary to enable a purchaser to weigh the advantages and disadvantages of the investment. The prospectus must include a balance sheet that accurately presents the financial status of the issuing corporation and, preferably, classifies its assets and liabilities. All debts must be clearly revealed. Failure to disclose information violates federal law.

Proxy   Federal law mandates that PROXY solicitations for voting in corporate business will not mislead and thus affect a shareholder's vote. (A *proxy* is a person assigned to represent or vote for another at shareholders' meetings. It is also the vote so assigned.) Proxy solicitations should disclose the issues to be voted on at the forthcoming shareholders' meeting, the expenses of proxy solicitation, and any options the corporation wants to give its executives and directors to purchase corporation stock. Proxy materials should give accurate information about candidates for directorships, compensation of officers or directors, and their dealings with the corporation.

EXAMPLE Since the last stockholders' meeting, the board of directors of Zipco Corporation created two more directorships, filling these slots with the sons of the chairman of the board. The proxy materials sent before the next scheduled meeting did not inform the shareholders of their rights to vote on whether those positions should continue and to elect qualified persons as directors. This failure to disclose such important information violated federal law prohibiting the omission of material facts that affect a stockholder's right to cast an informed vote in corporate matters.

Proxy solicitations should also give information concerning the operation and finances of the corporation. Finally, all information regarding a proposed merger between two corporations should also be disclosed.

Manipulation and deceptive devices   It is unlawful for any person selling securities to use any scheme to defraud. Consequently, any manipulation of the prices of securities registered on a national securities exchange is

SECURITIES AND THE LAW

■ A security is a money investment conferring on you a share in a business. The common form of security is corporation stock.

■ If you buy stock in foreign business enterprises, the transaction is outside the scope of U.S. law.

■ Before securities can be sold by mail or traded on a national securities exchange, federal law requires that a detailed statement be filed with the Securities and Exchange Commission (SEC), disclosing the price of shares, commissions paid to underwriters, options to purchase that have already been issued, etc.

■ Securities cannot be sold by mail unless preceded or accompanied by a prospectus fully disclosing all material facts regarding the investment.

■ You cannot trade in a security if you have inside information—for example, a company president is forbidden to sell all of his shares of stock the day before the corporation plans to declare bankruptcy.

■ The Securities Investor Protection Corporation, made up of brokers and dealers who belong to a national securities exchange, protects its members' customers for up to $100,000 in securities and $40,000 in cash, in the event the member brokerage firm fails.

■ Anyone who sells a security in violation of federal law can be held liable to the person purchasing it. If you are injured as a result of fraudulent or deceptive securities transactions, you can sue in federal court.

■ State laws also regulate securities sales and are commonly called blue-sky laws—because they prevent crooks from selling you stock representing nothing but the blue sky.

■ Most states have a state securities commission, with powers of investigation including the power to compel the appearance of witnesses, to examine them under oath, and to require the surrender of books and papers.

■ In most states, a buyer of securities sold in violation of a regulatory statute may cancel the transaction and try to recover the purchase money.

forbidden. This means that an investor may not initiate a large amount of buying and selling of a stock just to cause its price to fluctuate on the market. Only the law of supply and demand is permitted to determine the price of a security traded on a national exchange.

Federal law forbids the use of deceptive devices in connection with any securities transaction—including such activities as issuing a press release that misleads investors by failing to include known facts concerning debts of the corporate business and issuing a misleading prospectus or a misleading annual report. You cannot trade in a security if you have information that is undisclosed outside the corporation. Such activity is forbidden whether it is done by an officer of the corporation, by an investor who receives a tip from a corporate insider, or by a stock BROKER possessing inside information. For example, a company president is forbidden to sell all of his shares of stock the day before the corporation plans to declare bankruptcy.

Securities Investor Protection Act of 1970 In the late 1960's, many Wall Street brokerage firms experienced serious financial difficulties, and numbers of investors were threatened with the loss of cash and securities that they had left for safekeeping with these firms. Cash, usually the proceeds from the sale of securities or dividends paid, was and still is frequently held by brokers for their customers' convenience. This money is used by the firms to finance the margin purchases (stock bought on credit) of other customers and to operate business generally. Securities, too, are held by brokers for safekeeping or, if they are bought on margin, until the customer has completely paid for them. In the past, both cash and securities kept on deposit with a firm were often used by dishonest or careless brokers to pay off their debtors at the expense of their customers. In 1970 Congress passed the Securities Investor Protection Act to protect investors in case their firms should fail.

The Securities Investor Protection Corporation (SIPC), created under this law as a nonprofit, membership corporation, is not an agency of the U.S. government. It has a seven-member board of directors, including two members of the general public selected by the President, one appointee each of the Secretary of the Treasury and the Federal Reserve Board, and three representatives of the securities industry also selected by the President. All brokers and dealers who are members of a national securities exchange—such as the New York Stock Exchange or the American Stock Exchange—except those who deal mainly in mutual funds, insurance or investment advice, are automatically members of the SIPC.

As required by the 1970 law, a fund is maintained from assessments upon SIPC members so that if a member broker should fail, a customer will not lose his entrusted cash or securities. An investor may recover up to $100,000 of his claims for securities from the fund and up to $40,000 of his cash losses. If a person holds securities in two separate capacities, such as John Doe as an individual and John Doe as trustee for Alice Doe, his daughter, he may be entitled to recover more than $100,000. In the early 1980's SIPC funds were valued at above $150 million. Should widespread financial disaster strike, the SIPC can borrow up to $1 billion from the U.S. Treasury, to be repaid by SIPC members.

When a broker has failed or is in danger of failing to meet his debts—such as when he is insolvent or bankrupt—the SIPC will ask the appropriate court to protect the customers of such a broker under this law. After the court does so, it will name a trustee, specified by the SIPC, to liquidate (wind up the affairs of) the firm. Any outstanding securities deals will be completed, and securities registered (or in the process of being registered) in the customers' names will be returned to them. The trustee is empowered to settle any customer claims that fall within the $40,000 and $100,000 limits.

If you are planning to invest in securities, it is advisable to inquire whether the brokerage house that you are dealing with is a member of SIPC.

Enforcement The SEC is authorized to conduct investigations of probable violations of the securities laws. It can subpoena witnesses and require the presentation of relevant books, papers, or documents. Anyone who offers or sells a security in violation of federal law can be held liable to the person purchasing it. A buyer or seller of securities who is injured as a result of fraudulent or deceptive practices can sue for damages in federal court.

EXAMPLE Stan bought 1,000 shares of stock in a nationwide franchise operation after reading its prospectus, which included an impressive balance sheet. The prospectus also stated that its management team had just left a very successful franchise firm and that its current franchises were operating successfully. The balance sheet was a piece of fiction since the franchise was on the brink of bankruptcy. The prospectus failed to disclose that the management's former firm was under investigation by the SEC and that most of the existing franchises were under investigation by various state securities commissions. These facts, had they been disclosed, would have convinced Stan not to invest. Stan can sue the franchise operation in federal court for his out-of-pocket loss.

■ **State regulation** As a proper exercise of its POLICE POWER, a state may regulate securities traffic conducted within its borders. State statutes enacted for this purpose are commonly called *blue-sky laws*. An Oklahoma court stated that blue-sky laws are intended to stop the sale of corporate stock in fly-by-night concerns, visionary oil wells, distant gold mines, and similar fraudulent exploitations. A California court states that the laws are intended to stop the sale of stock that represents nothing but the blue sky. If it were not for such legislation, speculators would sell building lots in the blue sky.

Blue-sky laws are in effect in all the states, and, like the federal regulations, are intended to protect the investing public from fraud. State control of intrastate securities traffic does not conflict with federal regulation of interstate transactions.

Registration Many states require registration of securities before sale to the public. Registration statutes usually require that corporate financial information be filed with a designated regulatory agency. If a business seems likely to defraud prospective purchasers of its securities, state registration will be withheld. Under some statutes, before a dealer or broker starts operating his business, he must file a notice with the agency informing it of the kind of business he plans to conduct and where he will conduct it.

Monitoring of advisers Some states monitor *investment advisers*—persons who inform their clients about the prudence of investing in, purchasing, or selling securities—by providing guidelines and checking their clients' business operations.

Enforcement Under most state blue-sky laws, a supervisory state official or commission is given powers of investigation. They include the power to compel the appearance of witnesses, to examine them under oath, and to require the presentation of books and papers. A typical investigation may attempt to determine whether the sale of particular securities should be permitted, considering the financial structure of the corporation involved. The discretion of the investigating officials or commission is by no means unlimited—they must have reason to believe that fraudulent acts have been committed.

In most states a buyer of securities sold in violation of state law may rescind (cancel) the transaction and try to recover money he paid. If he has suffered damages from misleading or untrue statements made to him in connection with securities transactions, he can sue for fraud.

security 1 A deposit, MORTGAGE, or LIEN voluntarily given by a debtor to his creditor to guarantee payment of his debt. The security can be taken or sold by the creditor if the debtor fails to meet his financial obligation. A business deal that involves a security that is not a mortgage or lien on real property (real estate) is known as a SECURED TRANSACTION. 2 A person who becomes a SURETY or guarantor for another person. See GUARANTY. 3 A share of stock in a corporation or some other type of investment in a business that gives the purchaser an interest in the business. The buying and selling of securities are controlled by federal and state SECURITIES REGULATIONS.

sedition The incitement of discontent against the government and the disturbance of public tranquillity by means of inflammatory speeches or writings. Sedition is a crime. The distribution of literature discussing the merits of the Communist system at a Communist Party rally was once considered seditious behavior. Today, this would not be considered sedition because of the liberal expansion of First Amendment right to freedom of speech.

seduction The act by which a man induces a woman to whom he is not married to have sexual relations with him by means of persuasion, solicitation, promises, or bribes, but not force. See HEART-BALM ACT.

seizure 1 In criminal law, the forcible taking of property by a law enforcement official from a person who is suspected of violating, or is known to have violated, the law. See SEARCH AND SEIZURE. 2 In civil law, seizure is the act performed by an officer of the law when, under court order, he takes into custody property of a person whom a court has ordered to pay a certain amount of money to another. The property is seized so that it may be sold under the authority of the court to satisfy or pay off the court JUDGMENT. Property will also be seized if a defendant is thought to be hiding or removing it from the jurisdiction of the court (for example, to another county or state) so that if a judgment is made against him, his property cannot be used to pay the judgment. By attaching, or seizing, his property, the court prevents the defendant from perpetrating a fraud on the courts and on his creditors. See ATTACHMENT AND GARNISHMENT.

self-dealing Relating to transactions in which a trustee, an attorney, or other fiduciary (person in a position of trust) takes advantage of his position and acts for his own interests rather than for the interests of the beneficiaries of the trust or of his clients. See ATTORNEY AND CLIENT; TRUST.

self-defense Generally, an act done to protect oneself from some injury attempted by another or to protect another person from some injury attempted by a third person. Self-defense is one of the numerous defenses that a person may use when he is on trial for a criminal offense. See CRIMINAL LAW. The person claiming self-defense must have reasonably believed that he needed to act as he did to prevent injury to himself or someone else. His belief is reasonable if it would be shared by most people under the same circumstances.

■ **Force** A person may use whatever force is necessary to prevent immediate harm to himself. The amount of force used must be reasonable and must not amount to deadly force—force that will probably kill or seriously injure another person. See ASSAULT AND BATTERY. Most jurisdictions permit deadly force only if it is to prevent a serious or possibly deadly injury.

EXAMPLE If you are walking down a street and are suddenly O�led—★ kicked by a passing stranger, you may not defend yourself from further injury by shooting or clubbing him, as you have no reason to believe that he will follow the kick with a deadly assault. Your response must be reasonable in relation to his threat.

In most states if you are acting lawfully and have a right to be in the place where you are attacked, you do not have to retreat. You may even take the life of the person attacking you if deadly force is needed to protect yourself. In some states a person under attack must retreat instead of using deadly force to defend himself, but there are generally exceptions, such as defense in your own home.

EXAMPLE A man broke into a woman's apartment in the O—★ middle of the night. While he was going through some drawers, she woke up and heard him. He jumped on her, held a hand over her mouth, and threatened to kill her if she made a sound. He demanded to know where her money was, so she pointed to a jewelry box across the room. When he turned around, she pulled a gun out of her nightstand and shot him. She was justified in using deadly force because she had good reason to fear for her life and could not protect herself with any lesser force. She could not expect to escape or to subdue a larger and stronger man with her bare hands.

■ **Aggressors** An aggressor usually cannot claim self-defense. An aggressor is not necessarily the person who started the altercation. He is the one who causes a reasonable fear of harm in another person. Let us say you are a lumberjack and a little old man standing next to you at the bar punches you in the nose. If you start taking him apart and he shoots you, he can claim self-defense because you were the one who would cause a reasonable fear in him, not he in you. In order for self-defense to justify a homicide, the reasonable fear caused by the aggressor who is killed by the defender must be fear of death or of serious bodily harm. There is, however, an instance when even an aggressor may claim self-defense. This occurs when he has started an attack on another and then stops, retreats, and plainly shows that he no longer presents any threat. If at that time the original victim turns on the original aggressor and tries to injure him, the original aggressor becomes a victim and may defend himself.

■ **Aiding a third person** In most states, you may go to the assistance of another in those instances in which, if you were he, you would be justified in defending yourself.

EXAMPLE A mechanic was walking around to the back of his O—★ garage when he heard angry voices. He stopped and peeked around the corner to see one man holding a gun on another. He sneaked up behind the man with the gun and hit him hard on the head with a wrench. The mechanic was legally justified in coming to the aid of the other person.

But if you are going to the aid of another, be careful. If you go to the aid of a person thinking he is a victim, and he is really the aggressor, you might be held liable for hurting the real victim. Some states are more lenient than others when you are trying to help someone. In those states, if you reasonably believe that you are helping someone who needs and deserves your help, you will not be liable for making a mistake. A few states let you assist only someone related to you, such as a spouse, child, parent, or sibling.

self-executing Taking effect without further legislation or court action. A constitutional provision or statute is self-executing if no further legislation is needed to carry out its purpose. A court JUDGMENT is self-executing if it requires no further action from the court.

EXAMPLE Suppose a state constitution provides that any O—★ municipality, by vote of four-sevenths of its qualified electors, may issue and sell revenue bonds in order to purchase a public utility. Such a provision is self-executing because it is effective without a legislative enactment.

self-help Redressing or preventing wrongs by one's own action without recourse to legal proceedings. For example, a self-help repossession occurs when a creditor takes it upon himself to tow his debtor's car, which is the subject of the credit agreement, from the street because the debtor has defaulted in making payments on it. Self-help remedies are permitted only when specified by law. They are severely limited because, in effect, they allow people to take the law into their own hands.

self-incrimination Giving testimony that would implicate oneself in a crime. The Fifth Amendment to the U.S. Constitution states, in part, that no person "shall be compelled in any criminal case to be a witness against himself." This is known as the privilege against self-incrimination. It was developed in response to certain historical practices, such as ecclesiastical inquisitions and the proceedings of the STAR CHAMBER in England, in which people were compelled to confess their guilt. The self-incrimination clause was included in the Constitution to prevent torture-induced confessions, which would undermine the integrity of the judicial system. The federal government cannot convict a person of a crime "out of his own mouth" on the basis of a statement he made unwillingly and under coercion.

The due process clause of the 14th Amendment to the Constitution extends the prohibition against self-incrimination to the states. No state may force a person to incriminate himself. See DUE PROCESS OF LAW.

■ **Trials and other proceedings** The privilege against self-incrimination permits you to refuse to testify about facts that would support your conviction or that are links in the chain of evidence needed to prosecute you. This privilege applies not only to criminal proceedings in trial courts and before grand juries. It extends also to civil proceedings, including administrative hearings, congressional investigations, and other types of government investigations that may disclose some evidence or a "lead" for a later criminal prosecution.

EXAMPLE A man was questioned by an Internal Revenue
O⊷✱ Service agent about his prior income tax returns. The agent told him that it was just "a routine tax investigation" and did not warn him that he could refuse to answer the questions if he thought they would incriminate him. The man's incriminating statements led to his conviction for filing false claims for income tax refunds. The U.S. Supreme Court reversed his conviction. Although the tax investigation was initiated for the purpose of a civil action, the agent should have warned the man of his privilege against self-incrimination, because there was a possibility that a criminal prosecution would result.

If you apply for a license from a government agency and withhold information that is substantially relevant to the application—claiming the privilege against self-incrimination—the agency is not required to grant the license.

EXAMPLE A person suspected of close ties with illegal orga-
O⊷✱ nized gambling activity applies for a license to operate a liquor store. The state commission that grants such licenses inquires into his alleged involvement with organized crime. The applicant refuses to answer on the grounds that it might incriminate him. This claim of the privilege is valid, but the state is not legally required to grant a license because the information it requested is essential to the state's regulation of the liquor industry.

■ **Persons protected** The privilege against self-incrimination is a personal privilege. This means that a person can refuse to make only those statements that would incriminate himself. You cannot invoke the privilege to refuse to answer questions or give information that would incriminate someone else.

Individuals versus groups The framers of the constitutional privilege against self-incrimination were interested primarily in protecting the individual's civil liberties. Unincorporated associations and corporations are not entitled to claim this privilege.

EXAMPLE A grand jury subpoenaed the financial records of
O⊷✱ a law firm from one of its partners. He refused to comply on the basis of the Fifth Amendment and was found in contempt of court. The Supreme Court reviewed the contempt order and held that the Fifth Amendment privilege against self-incrimination was limited to protecting individual persons from compulsory incrimination through their own testimony or personal records. In this case the records were part of a collective entity and the partner was a representative of that entity. Even if the records might incriminate the partner personally, he could not claim the Fifth Amendment privilege. The fact that the partner, rather than the partnership, was subpoenaed and was the subject of the investigation still did not permit him to assert the privilege against self-incrimination. The contempt conviction was upheld.

Witnesses If you are a defendant in a trial you cannot be forced to take the witness stand. But if you are a witness you can be forced to take the stand. Once on the stand, however, you may claim the privilege of not testifying on the ground that your testimony may tend to incriminate you. The court has no duty to inform you that you may refuse to answer a question if it might incriminate you. You must claim the privilege yourself. This procedure is popularly known as "taking the Fifth."

Taking the Fifth is a witness's personal privilege. If you make self-incriminating statements on the witness stand that also implicate some other person in criminal activity, he cannot claim the privilege against self-incrimination to exclude those statements from his subsequent criminal prosecution.

If you voluntarily and without claiming the Fifth Amendment privilege give testimony of a fact that incriminates you, you thereby waive the privilege and must testify about any other relevant facts.

You cannot claim the privilege against self-incrimination if (1) you have already been acquitted or convicted of the offense for which your testimony incriminates you, (2) the statute of limitations has run out on the right to prosecute for the offense, or (3) you have been granted immunity from prosecution for it. The danger for which the privilege is granted no longer exists in these circumstances.

The claim of the privilege does not give you the right to make a blanket refusal to answer any questions. It must appear to the court that a particular answer might constitute a dangerous disclosure of a link in the chain of evidence that would lead to your prosecution. A flat declaration that you cannot testify at all for fear of self-incrimination is not enough to invoke the privilege. The privilege must be claimed on a question-by-question basis.

■ **Evidence** The Fifth Amendment protects not only witnesses on the stand but persons accused of crimes from the time they are taken into custody. You have a constitutional right to be protected from actions by law enforcement officials that would compel you to incriminate yourself in a crime. Any confession or statement you make, either as an accused or as a witness, cannot be used in a criminal prosecution if it was the product of physical or mental coercion, fear, terror, trickery, or threat.

The self-incrimination clause protects testimonial evidence—given by word, writing, or any other form of communication such as sign language. It does not apply to physical evidence. Any physical characteristic of a person is considered physical evidence and can be used by law enforcement officials in a criminal prosecution. For example, a person can be required to stand in a pretrial lineup, to give a handwriting sample, or to repeat certain words said during the commission of a crime. These acts do not involve any admission of guilt. Nor is fingerprinting, photographing, or measuring a suspect within the scope of the privilege. A person from whom a blood sample is involuntarily taken to determine alcohol content after he has been in an accident is not considered to have been compelled to testify against himself, but his Fourth Amendment rights to be protected from unreasonable searches and seizures must be safeguarded. See SEARCH AND SEIZURE.

■ **Questioning of suspects** When you have been taken into custody by police, or otherwise deprived of your freedom of action in any significant way, you must usually be warned of your privilege not to testify against yourself. If you are not, the information gained will not be admissible against you in a criminal prosecution and if a conviction were to be obtained on the basis of your statements, it could be reversed. If there is sufficient evidence other than these incriminatory statements, a new trial may be ordered.

The landmark case of MIRANDA V. ARIZONA clearly delineated the type of warnings a suspect being held by the police must receive in order to safeguard his privilege against self-incrimination. As a result of this case, a person subjected to interrogation while in custody must be given four warnings, now known as the MIRANDA WARNINGS. They are: (1) You have a right to remain silent, (2) any statement you give may be used as evidence against you, (3) you have a right to counsel during questioning, and (4) an attorney will be appointed for you if you cannot afford one.

Custodial interrogation is considered inherently coercive, justifying these warnings, but whether the warnings are necessary must be decided in each case.

EXAMPLE A suspect was questioned in his bedroom at 4 A.M. by four police officers who failed to give the Miranda Warnings. The Supreme Court found that, even though the questioning took place outside of the police station, the interrogation was "custodial," since the defendant was not free to leave and was thus deprived of his freedom of action in a significant way. Once custody or deprivation of freedom is established, no interrogation, however routine or casual, is permitted unless the defendant waives his stated rights.

Because a person may unwittingly make incriminating statements, if you are a suspect you must be told that you may have an attorney present to advise you during questioning. This right overlaps your Sixth Amendment right to counsel. See COUNSEL, RIGHT TO. Refusing to permit a suspect to confer with his counsel makes a confession inadmissible against a defendant, both because it is not considered voluntary under the Fifth Amendment and because it is a denial of counsel under the Sixth Amendment.

Claiming the privilege There is no magic language or ritualistic formula necessary to invoke the protection of the Fifth Amendment. On the witness stand, you have only to say, "taking the Fifth." When the police are questioning you, as long as it is sufficiently clear from the circumstances that you are attempting to claim the privilege against self-incrimination, they must respect your wishes. Generally, an interrogation must stop if you indicate that you want to remain silent, but the police may continue questioning you in any area that you are willing to discuss.

Waiver The court will accept a suspect's waiver of the privilege against self-incrimination as valid if it was "voluntarily, knowingly and intelligently" made in light of the circumstances of the case. This means that you must understand the legal effects of the waiver and that the court must consider your mental and physical condition and the setting of the pretrial interrogation. The prosecution must prove beyond a reasonable doubt that there was a waiver.

If you indicate that you want to consult with counsel, there can be no questioning. Even if you have already answered some questions, you are not automatically deprived of your right to invoke the privilege against self-incrimination.

Certain statements made immediately after a second set of Miranda Warnings have been given to a defendant may be admissible even though he had initially refused to make a statement.

EXAMPLE Mosley was arrested for robbery. After receiving the Miranda Warnings he refused to answer questions about the robbery. Two hours later, he was again given the Miranda Warnings and asked about a murder unrelated to the robbery. He made some statements about the murder, which were used against him in his trial for murder. Mosley was convicted and appealed the decision. The Supreme Court held that there was no violation of Miranda because questioning about the robbery had ceased when he refused to answer questions, a substantial period of time had elapsed before questioning on the murder began, and the Miranda Warnings had been given once again.

■ **Failure to testify** If you are accused of a crime, you have the privilege not to testify as a witness. It is your decision whether or not to take the witness stand. The Supreme Court has reasoned:

" It is not everyone who can safely venture on the witness stand, though entirely innocent of the charge against him. Excessive timidity, nervousness when facing others and attempting to explain transactions of a suspicious character, and offenses charged against him, will often confuse and embarrass him to such a degree as to increase rather than remove prejudices against him. It is not everyone, however honest, who would therefore willingly be placed on the witness stand."

However, once you, the accused in a criminal case, voluntarily take the witness stand on your own behalf, you waive the privilege against self-incrimination. Like any other witness, you are subject to cross-examination about the crime charged against you and about any other crime.

The government can neither call a person to testify against himself nor penalize him for claiming the privilege against self-incrimination. Neither the prosecuting attorney nor the judge at trial may comment on the decision of a defendant not to testify, and a jury may not draw an adverse inference from the failure of a defendant to testify.

A person's failure to testify in other official proceedings cannot be commented upon later at a trial.

EXAMPLE Eleven high school students faced expulsion proceedings for rioting at the school. Two of them did not testify at the disciplinary proceedings. This fact was commented upon by the attorney for the school district, who argued that guilt could be inferred from this refusal. A federal district court ruled that the students' rights against self-incrimination were violated because "a high school student punished by expulsion might well suffer more injury than one convicted of a criminal offense." This decision was based on a prior decision by a federal court that "one cannot be denied his Fifth Amendment right to remain silent merely because he is a student . . . his silence shall under no circumstances be used against him as an admission of guilt."

■ **Immunity** The Fifth Amendment privilege against self-incrimination is not absolute. You may be required to give incriminating testimony against yourself if you are granted immunity. Immunity means that you will be free from criminal prosecution involving subjects on which you give testimony to a grand jury or a legislature.

Immunity is granted by federal or state prosecutors or by legislative investigating committees to get persons who may be implicated in a crime to testify against the main perpetrators of that crime. It is often used in grand jury investigations. There are two types of immunity: use and transactional. *Use immunity* prohibits the direct or indirect use of the evidence given under it in any subsequent criminal prosecution—either state or federal. However, a person with use immunity can be convicted for a crime discussed under immunity if the prosecutor can prove the defendant's guilt without using the evidence revealed under immunity or if he got it from an independent, legitimate source—a source other than the defendant's testimony under immunity.

EXAMPLE Herman and his associates were running an underground gambling establishment in Georgia, where gambling is illegal. The district attorney was aware of the gambling establishment but did not have enough evidence to prove who was running it. The district attorney consequently called for a grand jury investigation and the grand jury gave use immunity to Lisa, a blackjack dealer who worked in the establishment. Lisa was compelled to appear before the grand jury and testify about what she knew of the establishment, and her testimony helped indict Herman and his cohorts. Because of the use immunity extended to her, Lisa herself could not be prosecuted for her gambling activities because her testimony before the grand jury was the only evidence against her and it was inadmissible. Later, however, three acquaintances of Lisa's came to the D.A. and told him that they knew of her gambling activities. Using their testimony as evidence, and not alluding at all to Lisa's testimony before the grand jury, the D.A. prosecuted her for gambling, and she was indicted and convicted.

The more comprehensive *transactional immunity* is absolute immunity from prosecution for any offense about which testimony is given. Once a person has testified under transactional immunity he cannot be prosecuted for any crime he admits to in that testimony, no matter how much other evidence of his guilt comes to light after his testimony.

EXAMPLE The mayor of a city was suspected of taking bribes, and a grand jury investigation resulted. The grand jury gave the mayor's secretary, Gina, transactional immunity, and the secretary testified before the grand jury that she had received bribe money from several individuals and had passed it on to the mayor, who subsequently gave certain favors to the bribers. Using this evidence, the grand jury indicted the mayor for accepting bribes. Later, Gina's jilted boyfriend came to the district attorney and told him that he knew that Gina had passed bribes on to the mayor. The D.A. could not prosecute Gina because she had received transactional immunity for that crime.

Although a grant of immunity may bar a subsequent criminal prosecution for the crimes covered in the testimony, it does not protect a person from other consequences, such as a loss of a job or public criticism. A government can compel testimony by offering either use immunity or transactional immunity.

If a person who has been given immunity refuses to testify or answer pertinent questions during his testimony, he may be imprisoned for CONTEMPT for the duration of the investigation (or the term of the grand jury) or until he agrees to cooperate. If he gives false testimony, he may be prosecuted for perjury.

EXAMPLE Suppose that Gina in the above example had refused to testify against her employer after being given immunity. She was then found guilty of contempt of the grand jury and sent to prison for the duration of the jury's term. After spending a few days in jail, Gina decided to testify. When she appeared before the grand jury, she answered all the questions asked about her work and her affiliation with the mayor but either refused to say whether or not she had passed bribes to the mayor or outrageously evaded questions on the subject, such as insisting she could not remember passing bribes. Again Gina is charged with contempt. Rather than face prison once more, she agrees to answer the question but denies having passed bribes. Later, the grand jury hears testimony from two of the secretary's co-workers, who swear that Gina had told them she had passed the bribes to the mayor. At the end of their investigation, the grand jury indicts Gina for perjury because, if the testimony of the two witnesses, both reliable, was to be believed, she obviously lied about passing the bribes.

Finally, in some states when a person is given transactional immunity, it applies only to testimony that is in response to questions asked him. If a person with immunity willingly offers information that implicates him in a crime, but was not given as a response to questions asked him, he may be prosecuted for that crime at a later date.

EXAMPLE Tom distracted a policeman while his friends robbed a nearby drugstore and got away. The police realized that Tom must have been connected with the crime and must therefore know who committed the actual robbery. Several suspects were later arrested and brought before a grand jury. The grand jury gave Tom immunity. Under questioning, Tom admitted that he had cooperated in the robbery and he identified the others involved in the crime. But when answering a question about the drugstore robbery, he added—without being asked—that he had performed the same function in a supermarket robbery a week earlier. Tom's immunity did not extend to voluntary comments about his complicity in the supermarket robbery. In fact, Tom had been warned not to say anything that was not in response to questions put to him. As a result, he could be prosecuted for the supermarket robbery but not for the drugstore robbery.

■ **Admissibility** A self-incriminating statement that is obtained in violation of the Fifth Amendment's self-incrimination clause should be excluded as evidence in a subsequent criminal trial. The admissibility of a confession depends on whether it was voluntary or involuntary. A confession obtained by law enforcement officials after beating a suspect is inadmissible. If a person is under the influence of alcohol or drugs and therefore cannot waive his privilege either voluntarily, knowingly, or intelligently, his confession will be inadmissible against him. If such evidence is admitted by the trial judge, any conviction based on it will be reversed and a new trial granted.

A statement that cannot be used to show guilt because the Miranda Warnings were not given may nevertheless be used for impeachment purposes—that is, to question or discredit a statement—if the accused testifies at trial.

EXAMPLE Harris made a pretrial statement that could not be
O—* used to show his guilt because it did not meet the Miranda requirements. At the trial, he testified in his own defense and made statements that contradicted his pretrial statement. The prosecutor used the pretrial statement to impeach (discredit) Harris's testimony. The Supreme Court said that even if the statement was otherwise inadmissible, it could be used for impeachment purposes. No one has a constitutional right to commit perjury; therefore, the inconsistent pretrial statement could be used for this limited purpose.

When a suspect refuses to testify or answer certain questions on the ground of self-incrimination, the court must determine whether he is justified in claiming the privilege. The trial judge will decide whether a question might cause the suspect to implicate himself in a crime.

■ **Laws requiring self-incrimination** The federal government may not impose burdens that violate the Fifth Amendment privilege against self-incrimination. Statutes requiring registration of some activity have been held unconstitutional if they compel a person to give evidence against himself by virtue of the registration process.

EXAMPLE The Supreme Court reversed the conviction of a
O—* person who accepted wagers for failing to register and pay a federal wagering tax. The privilege against self-incrimination was a complete defense to this prosecution. The registration requirement would open the wagerer to state prosecution for the crime of gambling, because the Internal Revenue Service would provide lists of persons who paid the tax to state law enforcement officials.

Neither can the states legislate away a person's privilege against self-incrimination.

EXAMPLE One state's vehicle and traffic law permitted a
O—* person's refusal to submit to a blood-alcohol-content test to be used as evidence against the person in any subsequent trial. A state court determined that this infringed upon the privilege not to testify against oneself, since the refusal to submit to the test was a form of communication within the scope of the Fifth Amendment. This should not be confused with the fact that the results of such tests—whether administered voluntarily or involuntarily—may be used as evidence without violating the privilege, because they deal with physical, not testimonial or communicative, evidence.

On the other hand, states may enact legislation under their POLICE POWER to regulate activities directly relevant to public safety. The privilege against self-incrimination is balanced against the interests of the state to protect its citizens. Therefore, laws that require motor accidents to be reported do not violate the privilege against self-incrimination. The incidental and limited risk of self-incrimination that may be caused by the identification of motor vehicle operators who threaten public safety is far outweighed by the state's desire to protect the public.

Senate The upper house of the U.S. CONGRESS. All legislative powers of government granted by the U.S. Con-

stitution are vested in the Congress, which consists of the Senate and the House of Representatives. See LEGISLATION. The Senate is composed of two Senators from each state, elected by the people of that state for a term of six years. Each Senator has one vote in the Senate. One-third of the Senators are elected every even-numbered year. As ordered in the Constitution: "The Times, Places, and Manner of holding Elections for Senators . . . shall be prescribed in each State by the Legislature thereof; but the Congress may at any time by Law make or alter such Regulations, except as to the Places of choosing Senators." When a vacancy occurs in the Senate, the governor of the state whose Senator has left issues a writ (an order) of election to fill the vacancy. The state legislature may empower the governor to make a temporary appointment until the people elect a new Senator.

A Senator must be at least 30 years old, must have been a U.S. citizen for nine years when he is elected, and must be an inhabitant of the state for which he is chosen.

The Vice President of the United States is president of the Senate, but he has no vote unless the Senators are equally divided on a question. His vote breaks the tie. The Senate chooses its other officers, including a president pro tempore, who acts in the absence of the Vice President or whenever the Vice President must assume the duties of the office of President of the United States. The Senate determines the rules of its own proceedings. It may punish members for disorderly behavior and, with the concurrence of two-thirds, expel a member.

It has sole power to try all impeachments of federal officers. When sitting for that purpose, the Senators are under oath or affirmation.

senior interest A SECURITY interest, such as a MORTGAGE, that attaches (becomes effective) prior to competing (junior, or subordinate) interests. A senior interest is entitled to payment before other interests. For example, a first mortgage is an interest that is senior to a second mortgage and all subsequent mortgages.

sentence A JUDGMENT pronounced by a judge or court after an accused person is found guilty in a criminal prosecution. The sentence formally declares the punishment for the crime of which the accused is convicted.

■ **Kinds of punishment** There are four kinds of punishment that can be given to a convicted criminal. They are the DEATH PENALTY, imprisonment, PROBATION or a SUSPENDED SENTENCE, and a FINE. A sentence may call for any one of these or for a combination. In addition, a criminal stands to lose some of his rights as a citizen—this, too, is a form of punishment. See PRISONERS' RIGHTS.

■ **Authority for sentencing** The authority to sentence comes from the legislature, which sometimes sets criteria that must be used in determining the appropriate sentence in particular cases. Legislatures pass laws delegating the sentencing powers to the courts and to such agencies as the probation and parole departments.

Each state has its own system for determining the lengths of prison sentences and the amounts of fines. Usually, maximum terms or fines are fixed by statute for each crime. Sometimes statutes specify a range between a minimum

FACTS ABOUT SENTENCES AND SENTENCING

■ The authority and general guidelines for sentencing come ultimately from the legislature, but the responsibility for imposing sentences in actual cases belongs to the judge or sometimes the jury.

■ Several states require a presentence report to help the judge determine the most appropriate sentence for the individual offender.

■ In most states, the presentence report is kept confidential; in California, it is a matter of public record.

■ A defendant during sentencing is entitled to the presence of his attorney, to equal protection of the laws, and to the opportunity to request an appeal of the judgment and, on occasion, of the sentence itself.

■ The right to be represented by counsel at a sentencing hearing is a constitutional right, because sentencing is a critical stage in a criminal prosecution.

■ It is not a violation of equal protection for one defendant to receive a longer sentence than another for the same crime.

■ In most states, a sentence within the limits of a statute is left alone. In about 15 states, the law allows review in some cases.

■ Occasionally, a sentence is overturned because the defendant was denied a procedural right during the sentencing process.

■ The state may not retaliate against an offender who appeals a verdict or sentence by giving him a more severe sentence at a retrial or rehearing obtained by appeal. If a judge does impose a heavier sentence, he must have information justifying the increased sentence that was not available the first time around.

---

and a maximum, such as "a term not to exceed seven years," or "a fine not to exceed $50," or "any term between 10 and 20 years." In such cases, a judge must use his discretion in deciding the length of the term or the amount of the fine, but he must keep it within the specified limits. Some statutes require the jury to assess the amount of a fine to be imposed, and some even require the jury to decide when the death penalty shall be imposed.

■ **Types of sentences** For certain types of offenses (such as first-degree murder or large-scale sales of heroin) and for some kinds of offenders (such as habitual criminals or sexual psychopaths) the law may compel a specified sentence, such as life imprisonment. These are called *mandatory sentences.*

In some states, a judge may be permitted or required to impose an *indeterminate sentence* for certain crimes. An indeterminate sentence is one for which no maximum term is established. Other laws permit an *indefinite sentence,* which specify a maximum term but permit correction officials to decide whether or not the prisoner can be released earlier. This kind of sentencing is intended to make the system flexible enough to return an offender to society as soon as he is rehabilitated. The use of indeterminate and indefinite sentences has been criticized for leaving too much to the discretion of correction officials.

Actually, most fixed-term sentences are indefinite in effect because statutes generally allow most prisoners to be considered for PAROLE after they have served a part of their sentences—typically one-third of the maximum. Other statutes permit an early or a conditional release if a prisoner has accumulated *good time credits.* In such cases, the sentence can be reduced by a certain number of days for every month of good behavior, for donations of blood, and so on. The decision to grant parole is left almost entirely to the prison administrators or parole board. Few prisoners actually serve their maximum sentences.

■ **Concurrent and cumulative sentences** Sometimes a person is given sentences for two or more crimes at the same time, such as robbery and murder. Multiple sentences may be served in one of two ways—concurrently or cumulatively. *Concurrent sentences* allow a prisoner to apply the same jail time to more than one sentence. *Cumulative sentences* must be served one at a time.

EXAMPLE Paul was sentenced to serve three years for embezzlement and one year for theft. If the sentencing judge allows him to serve the sentences concurrently, he will be in jail for three years. If the sentences are cumulative, he will be in jail for four years.

■ **Role of the judge** Generally after a defendant in a criminal case has pleaded guilty or been found guilty, the judge presiding over the case must sentence him. The judge must use his discretion in determining an appropriate sentence unless the sentence is mandated by statute.

When determining a sentence, the judge may have several objectives in mind, and in each case he must decide which of these objectives are most important, or even possible. The objectives are (1) prevention, or persuading the criminal to give up committing crimes in the future because the punishment for crime is unpleasant; (2) restraint, or keeping the criminal from committing more crimes by isolating him from society; (3) rehabilitation, or providing the criminal with treatment or training that will make him into a satisfactory citizen; (4) deterrence, or warning others not to commit crimes by making an example of the criminal; (5) education of the public, or making a clear distinction between good and bad conduct by punishing bad conduct; and (6) retribution, or giving the criminal the punishment he deserves and society its revenge.

When the trial judge has the discretion to fix the sentence for a particular crime, he must weigh all the factors in that particular case and not give the same sentence for all cases involving that crime.

EXAMPLE In one federal case, decided in 1971, a young man was sentenced to five years in prison for refusing to obey his draft board's order to be inducted into the armed services. This sentence was reversed on appeal because that trial judge had given the same maximum sentence to every draft evader before him for over 20 years. The appeals court held that "A trial court which fashions an inflexible practice in sentencing contradicts the judicially approved policy in favor of 'individualizing sentences.' "

Presentence reports   A trial judge is usually allowed considerable latitude in imposing sentence. To act wisely, he must have access to as much information about the defendant as possible. During the trial, the judge learns about the nature of the crime and the defendant's role in it. After the trial the judge may receive a presentence report prepared by a probation officer who has investigated the defendant's background. Presentence reports are not constitutionally necessary, but correctional experts recommend them whenever there is the possibility of a jail sentence. Several states require them by law.

A presentence report should set forth the offender's prior arrests and convictions. Ideally, it should also include a complete description of the situations surrounding his criminal activity and summaries of his education and employment history, his home and family life, his medical history, the environment to which he will return, the resources available to assist him, and his motivations and ambitions. In fact, it is a practical impossibility to assemble all of this information on every offender before sentence, but a report should include as much as can be gathered in the time allotted.

Since presentence reports have come into use, there has been considerable controversy over who should be able to look at them. In California, for example, a presentence report is a matter of public record, but in most states it is kept confidential. There are good reasons for not allowing defendants to read the reports: Disclosure is likely to dry up sources of information, delay proceedings, and discourage the defendant's efforts to improve himself. This does not mean that a judge may keep the information in a presentence report secret from everyone.

EXAMPLE In 1977 the Supreme Court reversed a death 0⊷⊸⊷ sentence ordered for a man who had killed his wife in Florida. When the trial judge had imposed the death sentence, he had said that he was relying in part on information in a presentence report. That information was not revealed to the defendant or his counsel. The Supreme Court held that it is a denial of due process to rely on information that could be incorrect and not to give the defendant an opportunity to deny or explain it.

A fundamental right given to a criminal defendant at his trial is the right to confront and cross-examine (through his counsel) witnesses who testify against him. But the type and extent of the information contained in a presentence report make it totally impractical to allow a convicted defendant to cross-examine all who contributed to the report. However, at least one court has held that a defendant is not completely without the right of confrontation. The court said that when the defendant vigorously denies having made a damaging statement to a presentence investigator, the court must either disregard the statement or call in the investigator and question him about it.

Evidence   In sentencing, a judge may also take into account EVIDENCE that was inadmissible in the trial. In some cases, appeals courts have refused to criticize sentencing because judges relied on hearsay information or on conversations obtained by an illegal wiretap. In other cases, judges were not allowed to rely on vague allegations of underworld connections, evidence of crimes that were never charged, or hearsay. See CRIMINAL LAW.

■ **The defendant**   A convicted criminal has few rights in challenging the sentence imposed by the judge. He is, however, entitled to the presence of his attorney, to equal protection of the laws, and to the opportunity to request an appeal of the judgment and, occasionally, of the sentence.

Right to an attorney   In 1967 the Supreme Court held that a defendant has the right to be represented by counsel at a sentencing hearing, because sentencing is a critical stage in a criminal prosecution, and the Constitution assures everyone the right to have an attorney at any critical stage of a prosecution.

During the sentencing process an attorney can challenge and contradict any information that is used against his client, including unreliable hearsay and inaccurate or unsubstantiated statements in presentence reports. He can also find out what sentencing alternatives and community services are available for offenders like his client—for example, probation, work release, or placement in a drug-abuse program. Finally, he can recommend to the court a sentence that best fits the needs of his client, while always arguing for as much freedom as possible.

Equal protection   The 14th Amendment of the Constitution guarantees all U.S. citizens the right to EQUAL PROTECTION OF THE LAWS. Sentences violate this constitutional right if they are affected by arbitrary distinctions based on wealth or gender.

EXAMPLE In Illinois a man was convicted of petty theft and 0⊷⊸⊷ given the maximum sentence: one year in jail and a fine of $500, plus $5 court costs. The court said that if the fine and costs were not paid by the end of the prison sentence, the defendant could work off the obligation by staying in prison for a credit of $5 a day. Since the man was too poor to pay, he was to have been held in jail 101 days longer than the maximum sentence for his crime. The Supreme Court reviewed this case in 1970 and held that the statute under which the sentence was imposed unconstitutionally violated equal protection.

Equal protection arguments have also won offenders the right to credit for time spent in jail before trial toward the term of the sentence finally imposed. Otherwise, a defendant who cannot raise BAIL money must serve much more time in jail than someone who can post bail.

The equal protection clause of the Constitution has also been applied to state laws that discriminate on the basis of sex.

EXAMPLE In 1968 a Pennsylvania court struck down a stat- 0⊷⊸⊷ ute that required indeterminate sentences for women but specific sentences for men who committed the same offenses. The court said that denying the trial judge a chance to give a woman a sentence that would be sure to result in less than the maximum term for the offense was unreasonable and unaccountable by any rational sentencing objective.

Another law in Oklahoma was struck down in 1972 because it extended the benefits of juvenile courts to females up to age 18 but for males only to age 16.

Courts generally have limited their scrutiny to sex discrimination in the statutes themselves and have refused to invalidate sentences just because all men or all women happened to end up with harsher sentences for a given type of crime.

But when a state law, without any justification, imposed great disparity on sentences for juveniles and adults for the same crime the law was struck down.

EXAMPLE In 1974 a federal court in New York held that a state statute discriminated against young people because it specified sentences of up to four years for people aged 16 to 21 for offenses for which an adult could get only one year. The court was not impressed with the state's claim that juveniles should be kept as long as it took to rehabilitate them because it found that the juveniles did not in fact receive treatment.

It is not a violation of equal protection for one defendant to receive a longer sentence than another for the same crime. Individualization of sentences was actually a hard-won advance, accomplished after a battle of more than 50 years. Appeals courts rarely overturn a sentence that is within the range allowed by statute.

Appeals After a verdict and sentence are handed down, an offender may want to ask an appeals court to reconsider the result. However, appeals courts concentrate almost exclusively on the verdict and not the sentence. A verdict can be overturned if certain constitutional rights or procedural requirements have been violated. Once the defendant is found guilty, though, almost any sentence the judge hands down is acceptable to an appeals court.

There are several reasons for refusing to reconsider a sentence. Courts have said that the sentence is discretionary and should suit the offense rather than follow some fixed standard. Sentencing is a matter less of the law than of judgment, and appeals courts are not in a position to assess the individual defendant. There is also a fear that courts will be overwhelmed with even more appeals if offenders are encouraged to challenge their sentences.

For these reasons, in most states a sentence within the limits of a statute is usually left alone. In about 15 states, statutes allow review in some cases. Occasionally a sentence is overturned because the defendant was denied a procedural right during the sentencing process. On rare occasions sentences have been found to violate the constitutional right of equal protection or the prohibition of CRUEL AND UNUSUAL PUNISHMENT.

EXAMPLE In 1909 the Supreme Court overturned a defendant's sentence to 12 to 20 years at hard labor with ankle and wrist chains for the entire period, along with a permanent loss of all civil rights, which was imposed for the crime of being an accessory to the falsification of a public document. The Court held that the sentence was so excessive that it amounted to cruel and unusual punishment.

When a verdict on a sentence is being appealed, the judge is limited in the reasons he can have for imposing a harsher sentence than the original. He cannot, for instance, increase the sentence in order to discourage appeals or to retaliate against offenders by giving them stiffer sentences at retrials obtained by appeal. The Supreme Court has held that the judge must have information justifying the increased sentence that was not available the first time sentence was imposed.

■ **Plea bargaining** Sometimes a person guilty of a crime can receive a lighter sentence by negotiating with the prosecutor, either personally or through his attorney, be-

fore going to court. The process is called plea bargaining. Defendants are encouraged to plead guilty in exchange for favored treatment by the prosecutor. The prosecutor can reduce the charge to a lesser offense, drop some of the charges, agree not to pursue additional charges that could be brought against the defendant or someone else, or agree to recommend a specific sentence to the court. The bargain may look good to a defendant who does not want to risk conviction on more serious charges, who already has a bad record, or who feels that the cost and delay of a long trial are not worth his trouble since he is likely to be convicted.

Critics of the plea bargaining system claim that it can cover up illegal investigative procedures by policemen, that it encourages prosecutors to throw the book at a defendant, because they are confident that the charges will be reduced through negotiation, or—most important—that it encourages innocent people to plead guilty.

Hazards of going to trial Many defendants plead guilty only because they are afraid that if they go to trial they will be found guilty and receive harsher sentences. This fear is bolstered if the prosecutor offers to reduce the offense or recommend a more lenient sentence in return for a guilty plea. The defendants may also feel that the judge will give them a harsher sentence if they put the state to the expense of conducting a long trial to prove their guilt.

EXAMPLE The hazards of going to trial are well illustrated by a federal case in which five codefendants were charged with offenses relating to interstate theft. Four of them, including the ringleader, pleaded guilty and received prison sentences of one to two years. All four had prior criminal records. One man, named Wiley, refused to plead guilty, went to trial, and was convicted. The judge acknowledged that he was a minor participant in the overall criminal scheme but sentenced him to three years. The defendant appealed.

The appeals court took the unusual action of sending the case back to the trial judge for resentencing because, it said, the facts in the record pointed convincingly to the conclusion that the district court had arbitrarily singled out a minor defendant and imposed on him a more severe sentence than it had imposed upon the codefendants.

Validity of a guilty plea The Supreme Court has reviewed many guilty pleas and has decided that to be valid they must be made knowingly and voluntarily.

❝ A plea of guilty entered by one fully aware of the direct consequences, including the actual value of any commitments made to him by the court, prosecutor, or his own counsel, must stand unless induced by threats (or promises to discontinue improper harassment), misrepresentation (including unfulfilled or unfulfillable promises), or perhaps by promises that are by their nature improper as having no proper relationship to the prosecutor's business (e.g. bribes). ❞

In 1970 the Supreme Court considered the propriety of accepting a guilty plea from a defendant who nevertheless insists that he is innocent.

EXAMPLE The defendant pleaded guilty and evidence of his guilt was presented at his sentencing hearing. Then the defendant took the stand and told the court that he was pleading guilty only because he risked the death penalty if he went to trial. The judge sentenced him to 30 years. The Supreme Court sustained the sentence because the record strongly indicated the defendant's guilt. The Court held that "an individual accused of a crime may voluntarily, knowingly and understandingly consent to the imposition of a prison sentence even if he is unwilling or unable to admit his participation in the acts constituting his crime."

This decision leaves other questions unanswered. If a defendant enters a guilty plea, while refusing to acknowledge his participation in the crime, and there is no substantial evidence of guilt, his case will be much more difficult to decide. Yet, if the court ever decides that a guilty plea can be accepted only if the defendant admits guilt, that will mean that he will be forced to go through a trial he does not want and risk a heavier sentence by insisting that he is innocent.

separate but equal   The legal principle that separate facilities for blacks and whites were valid under the equal protection clause of the 14th Amendment to the Constitution as long as the facilities were equal. It was enunciated by the Supreme Court in the 1896 case of PLESSY V. FERGUSON and was used to justify segregated public facilities until the 1954 decision of BROWN V. BOARD OF EDUCATION. In this landmark case, the Supreme Court ruled that separate schools were inherently unequal. Later cases ruled that racial segregation in public facilities, housing, and public accommodations, such as hotels, violates the constitutional guarantee of EQUAL PROTECTION OF LAWS.

separate maintenance   A money allowance from a husband to his wife granted by the court. Its purpose is to support the wife and her children while she lives apart from her husband. See DIVORCE.

separation   The termination of cohabitation between a husband and wife by mutual agreement or by a court decree. See DIVORCE; MARRIAGE.

> EXAMPLE   After discovering that Harvey, her husband, had
> O⊶✳ an affair with Alice, her best friend, Janice asked him to move out of their home. Because of her religious convictions, Janice does not want a divorce, but Harvey has stopped paying all the household bills, leaving her penniless. After consulting a lawyer, Janice decides to sue Harvey for separation and asks the court for separate maintenance. Because adultery is a ground for separation (as well as divorce) in the state in which Janice lives, she can be successful in her lawsuit.

separation of powers   See CONSTITUTIONAL LAW.

sequestration   1 Isolation. Sequestration of members of a jury means isolating them during a trial from the world outside the courtroom.   2 Holding aside, confiscating. In EQUITY proceedings, a writ (order) of sequestration authorizes a sheriff to take possession of the property of a defendant who is in contempt of court. The property is held in the custody of the court until the defendant clears himself of the contempt charge.   3 Depositing with a third person something that is the subject of a controversy or lawsuit between two persons until the controversy or lawsuit is settled.

> EXAMPLE   You and your sister Agnes have been arguing
> O⊶✳ over who is entitled to the china collection of your late Aunt Agatha. Agnes took it from Agatha's house the day of her funeral. Agatha's will says you are to receive the collection, but Agnes has refused to give the collection to the executor of Agatha's estate so that he may deliver it to you. Agnes claims that it belongs to her because Agatha, on her deathbed, promised it to her. You demand that the executor sue Agnes for the return of the collection. The court orders that the china be sequestered with the county clerk until it decides who should receive the collection.

servant   See MASTER AND SERVANT.

service   In legal practice, the act of showing or delivering a legal document—such as an injunction, a NOTICE, a summons, or a writ—to a person, thereby officially notifying him of a legal proceeding that involves him. *Service of process,* as it is called, must be made by a legally authorized person, such as a sheriff or constable. *Personal service* is delivery of the legal notice in person. *Substituted service* or *constructive service* is any form of service other than personal service, such as service by mail or by publication in a newspaper.

servitude   1 The condition of being a slave or servant.   2 A charge or burden imposed upon a person's real estate for the benefit or advantage of another. The land bearing the burden (the servitude) of a restriction is called the servient estate, while the land enjoying the benefit of the restriction is the dominant estate. Easements and covenants create servitudes, and in fact the word "servitude" is used for an EASEMENT in civil law.

The owner of a piece of land may be required by the deed not to build within 1,500 yards of the next house. The land so restricted is the servient estate, the land benefiting from the restriction is the dominant estate, and the restriction itself is the servitude.

session   The sitting of a court, legislature, council, or commission for the transaction of its business. A session can be part of a day or one or more days, weeks, or months. When applied to courts, the word "session" is similar to the word "term." The session of a court is the time during which it actually sits each day for the transaction of judicial business. A term of court is the period fixed by law, usually many days or weeks, during which it is open for judicial business and can hold daily sessions. However, the two words are frequently used interchangeably.

session laws   The name commonly given to the body of laws enacted by a state legislature during one of its annual or biennial sessions. See REVISED STATUTES; STATUTE.

setback   A ZONING provision requiring buildings to be a certain distance away from a curb, highway, or another building.

set down   Enter a case in a court calendar, list, or docket for trial or hearing during a particular court term.

setoff and recoupment   See COUNTERCLAIM.

settle   Approve, arrange, ascertain, liquidate, or reach an agreement. A trust is settled when its terms are established and it goes into effect. Persons and businesses are said to settle an account when they go over items and agree upon the balance due from one to the other. When the person who owed money pays his balance, he is also said to have settled it. *Settlement* means the act of determining and adjusting the dealings or difficulties between persons. A settlement between disputing parties is an agreement of what is due from one to the other, or a full and final payment or discharge of an account. See COMPROMISE AND SETTLEMENT.

Settle up is a popular rather than legal phrase, which is applied to the final collection, adjustment, and distribution of the estate of a deceased person, a bankrupt, or an insolvent corporation. The process includes collecting the property, paying the debts and charges, and turning over the balance to those entitled to receive it. See EXECUTORS AND ADMINISTRATORS.

settlor   A person who establishes a TRUST.

severable   Describing something that can be divided, or cut off, from other things to which it was joined and still maintain a complete and independent existence. A *severable contract,* for example, can be divided into two or more parts that are not necessarily dependent upon each other.

> EXAMPLE A seller accepted a buyer's order for 60 dozen O→✱ caps of different sizes and colors. He shipped all except five dozen to the buyer, who then refused to accept the order, even though the contract did not say that the whole order had to be delivered at one time. The seller sued the buyer for breach of contract. The court held that the buyer could not escape liability just because five dozen caps had not been shipped, since an order for caps of different patterns, sizes, and colors constituted a severable contract.

A *severable statute* can be separately enforced after an invalid portion of it has been stricken.

severally   Distinctly, separately. For example, when a number of parties to a CONTRACT are said to be "severally liable," each one is individually liable.

severalty ownership   Sole ownership of property; individual ownership.

severance   **1** Dividing a lawsuit into two or more independent CAUSES OF ACTION, each of which ends in a separate, final, and enforceable decision or judgment. For example, when there are several defendants in a trial, a severance of the case may mean that each person is tried separately at a different time. **2** In regard to real estate, the cutting and removal of anything attached to the land, such as standing timber or crops.

sewer service   The illegal practice of filing false affidavits with a court, thereby stating that legal process, such as a NOTICE, SUMMONS, or WRIT, has been properly served when in reality the process has been discarded. For example, a process server may throw the papers he is supposed to serve down a sewer and claim he has served them in order to collect his fees without doing his work.

sex offenses   Sexual conduct prohibited by a state's criminal laws. There are two major categories of sexual offenses. One category includes "unnatural" sexual intercourse between two persons—such as SODOMY, FELLATIO, or CUNNILINGUS—or between a person and an animal—BESTIALITY. Such acts were considered at COMMON LAW to be crimes against nature, and they are still illegal today, even when the parties may consent to them. However, there has been social opposition to treating certain sexual acts as sex offenses when two consenting adults are involved.

The second category consists of sexual acts committed by one person against another without the latter's consent. There is lack of consent when physical force or threats of physical harm are used to force a person to engage in sexual conduct, such as in the case of RAPE. Under the law, a person who is under a certain age (frequently 16) or mentally incompetent (unable to understand the nature of the acts) is not capable of consenting to sexual intercourse. Anyone who engages in sexual conduct with such a person does so against her or his will and is guilty of STATUTORY RAPE.

Not all sex offenses fall into these two categories. The crime of INCEST—sexual intercourse with or marriage to a person closely related by blood or marriage—is a sex offense. In some states FORNICATION (generally, sexual intercourse between unmarried persons) and ADULTERY (sexual intercourse between a married person and someone who is not his or her spouse) are also considered sex offenses.

"Sex offenses" is also a catchall phrase to describe various sex-related offenses by which sexual conduct is illicitly offered for a price to the public, either for viewing in pornographic films, plays, or books (OBSCENITY) or for participation (PROSTITUTION). Indecent exposure—the display of a person's genitals in a lewd or offensive manner in a public place—is also a sex offense.

The punishment for conviction of a sex offense is usually a jail sentence or a fine. It is established by a state's criminal law that defines and prohibits the particular conduct.

sham   False. The term is used in connection with legal PLEADINGS (complaint and answer), the written statements made by each party at the start of a lawsuit. A *sham pleading* is one that is in proper form but presents false facts.

> EXAMPLE While riding her bicycle, Mary was hit by a O→✱ delivery van driven by Jack, who was intoxicated. Mary served Jack with a complaint alleging that her injuries were caused by his negligent operation of the delivery van, which bore the name of his flower business. In his answer, Jack completely denied the allegations, going so far as to deny ownership of the delivery van. Jack's answer is a sham pleading since it is false.

share   **1** A portion; a part. A share of a sum of money or some other divisible thing is one of the parts into which it may be divided. **2** A unit of corporate stock. See COMMON STOCK; CORPORATION; PREFERRED STOCK.

Shelley's case   An early English case that set forth the legal principle known as the rule in Shelley's case, which was used in England from 1324 to 1925, when it was barred by statute. It is also part of the COMMON LAW in the United States, but most states have now changed the law by statute. Under this rule, which was still in effect in six states in 1980, when an owner of real estate transfers it to another person and gives a REMAINDER interest to that person's heirs, the heirs receive nothing and the recipient of the property becomes its owner in FEE SIMPLE (absolute ownership). He may therefore dispose of the property without leaving it to his heirs. This contradicts the original owner's wish, since a remainder—when not subject to the rule in Shelley's case—guarantees that the heirs will receive the property upon the death of the owner. See ESTATE.

EXAMPLE Smith owns Farmacres. He deeds Farmacres "to Willis for life, remainder to his heirs." Under the rule in Shelley's case, Willis becomes the absolute owner of Farmacres and Willis's heirs take nothing. In states where the rule has been abolished, Willis would receive only a life estate, which means he could use the property during his lifetime but not dispose of it, and upon his death his heirs would inherit Farmacres.

shepardizing   Using a CITATOR (a set of books that list references to statutes and court cases) to trace the history of a case or a statute to determine if it is still good law or if it has been overruled. Because the most thorough and widely used citator is *Shepard's Citations*, which lists virtually every statute and case printed in the United States, "using a citator" and "shepardizing" have become virtually synonymous.

sheriffs and constables   County and municipal peace officers. A *sheriff* is an executive of the county and an officer of its courts. He is subject to the orders and directions of the courts. A *deputy sheriff* is a sheriff's assistant; he acts for the sheriff and not in his own right. A *constable* is an officer of an incorporated municipality. His function is similar to that of the sheriff, but he has less authority and the area of his jurisdiction (authority) is smaller.

■ **Qualifications**   State constitutions and statutes usually establish prerequisites for holding the office of sheriff or constable. In most cases, a sheriff or constable is required to be a U.S. citizen, a qualified voter, and a resident in the area of his jurisdiction. Also, state constitutions and statutes usually require a sheriff or constable to be free from certain specified disqualifications. For example, a person could be disqualified because he currently practices law, since the two functions might conflict, or because he has been convicted of committing a serious crime.

■ **Election and removal**   Sheriffs and constables are elected by the people they are expected to serve. A sheriff-elect or constable-elect is generally required to post a BOND as security for faithful performance of the duties of his office. The bond protects everyone who might be harmed by his neglect of duty.

EXAMPLE A sheriff is obligated to seize property from a person who has failed to repay a loan and sell it when the creditor (the person to whom the money was owed) gets a court decree authorizing the seizure and sale of the property for the payment of the debt. If the sheriff damages the property by his carelessness, the creditor may sue the sheriff on his bond.

Ordinarily, the term of office of a sheriff or constable is fixed by state law, which also determines when and how he may be removed from office. Usually the governor of the state may remove a sheriff or constable for neglect of duty.

■ **Police duties**   Because sheriffs and constables are peace officers, they often perform the duties of policemen, including the enforcement of criminal laws. If a sheriff believes that local authorities—such as the village or town police—are not enforcing the law properly, he is obligated to undertake the job himself. The authority of a sheriff is superior to that of a constable. In case of a conflict over who has jurisdiction (authority), the constable must yield.

■ **Service of process**   Serving PROCESS—for example, a SUMMONS or writ (court order)—is an important function of a sheriff or constable. The courts, which issue the summonses and writs, do not direct officers how to serve them. The sheriff or constable should serve process on the designated person within a reasonable time after receiving his name. The sheriff or constable should use diligence in serving, but he is not required to make every possible effort.

■ **Attachment**   Another function of a sheriff or constable is to attach (seize) a debtor's property, when asked to do so by a creditor who has received the court's permission. He must take the property into custody, carefully preserving everything. In most cases he is expected to sell the property, collect the purchase money, and then distribute the proceeds from the sale as ordered by the court. See ATTACHMENT AND GARNISHMENT; EXECUTION; LEVY; SHERIFF'S DEED.

■ **Criminal liability**   A sheriff or constable is subject to criminal prosecution for any conduct that the law says is an offense when done by anyone else. For example, sheriffs have been prosecuted for forcibly entering a residence to serve civil process, failing to deliver money collected, and making false written statements about serving process.

sheriff's deed   A document showing that real estate owned by a debtor was seized and sold by the sheriff to pay the money owed to creditors. See ATTACHMENT AND GARNISHMENT; DEED; EXECUTION; LEVY.

Sherman Act   A federal law designed to protect against conspiracies to restrain trade or commerce and MONOPOLIES in trade and commerce.

shifting the burden of proof   Transferring from one party to the other party the duty of proving a disputed fact during a lawsuit. Once the party upon whom the burden of proof originally rested has introduced EVIDENCE tending to prove a fact, it then becomes the duty of the other party to rebut it by contradictory or defensive evidence.

shipping   The transportation of goods. This article discusses the law concerned with the shipment of goods over water by merchant vessels, including ships and barges. For a discussion of the law relating to shipping over land or by air, see CARRIER.

■ **Federal control** A sovereign nation has the power to regulate all vessels flying its flag on the high seas, and under the Constitution, Congress has the power to enact legislation controlling U.S. merchant ships that sail the high seas. It has exercised this power by creating a comprehensive procedure for the inspection of vessels and the licensing of ships' officers, following an examination of their character and experience.

■ **Ownership** Like other personal property, ships can be owned either by one person or by co-owners. Most merchant vessels are held by more than one owner. A bill of sale is the usual evidence of title to (ownership of) a vessel.

Between co-owners, the right to control and use the vessel is usually reserved for the one who has the greatest interest in the vessel. If co-owners cannot absolutely agree on how to use the vessel, it is possible for one or more of them to obtain a court decree for its sale. Ordinarily, however, a part owner shares proportionately in profits and expenses from use of the ship.

■ **Agent** The owners of merchant ships and barges generally hire agents to carry on all business related to the vessels while docked. The owners of a merchant vessel are responsible for the acts of their agents. See AGENCY. They must pay for the supplies, services, and repairs he orders.

A *ship's husband* is the owners' general agent for affairs conducted in the vessel's home port. He is commonly called the *managing owner* and is entitled to be paid for his services and to be reimbursed for his expenditures as a representative of the owners. A ship's husband sees that the ship is ready for navigation and commercial use. Agents are not part of a vessel's officers and crew, who are bound by the laws of ADMIRALTY.

■ **Bill of lading** A BILL OF LADING is an acknowledgment by the captain or owner that he has received the particular goods to be carried aboard the vessel. Every shipper is entitled to receive a bill of lading from the shipowner or his representative.

In everyday transactions, a bill of lading signed by the captain makes the owner of the vessel responsible for the goods listed in it. The bill prevents disputes over whether goods were received and over their condition when placed aboard the vessel.

■ **Liability** Shipowners are responsible for all damage caused by negligent management of their vessel. For instance, they can be held liable for damage done by the vessel to an underwater cable or to a bridge or pier. Shipowners are also liable for personal injuries to their workers, if the injuries are caused by any defective conditions aboard the vessel. Similarly, they are responsible for providing a reasonably safe working area for employees of a stevedoring contractor. When there is no controlling treaty or statute, however, shipowners are not liable to a stranger in peril on the high seas if the ship's captain fails to aid him. See MARITIME LIEN; NAVIGABLE WATERS; PILOT; SALVAGE; SEAMAN; TOWAGE; WHARF.

shop-book rule A doctrine permitting books consisting of original entries made in the usual course of a business to be received by a court as EVIDENCE, once they are authenticated. In the laws governing evidence, the shop-book rule is an exception to the HEARSAY rule.

short cause A lawsuit or other legal matter that is not likely to occupy a great deal of a court's time. It may be entered on the list of short causes upon application of one of the parties to the dispute and will be heard more speedily than it would be in its regular order. The time allowed for the hearing varies in different courts.

short sale A method of profiting from the expected fall in the price of a stock. A person who sells short is one who sells stock or other securities that he does not own and that are not immediately available for delivery. The seller usually borrows from a broker the shares needed to cover the sale, and he delivers these shares to the buyer. The seller deposits with the broker an amount equal to the value of the borrowed shares. This sum remains on deposit with the broker until the stock is returned. The seller's hope is that the stock's value will fall, so that he will be able to buy the replacement stock at a lower price than he received for the borrowed stock he sold.

The seller must eventually return the same number of shares of the same stock to the broker, and the transaction is not complete until the stock is returned. The broker who lends the stock is entitled to all the benefits he would have received if he had not lent the stock. If the dividend is paid, the seller-borrower must pay the broker-lender an amount equal to the dividends.

EXAMPLE On June 28 a stock is selling for $75 per share. Brown wants to buy it because he believes that by June 30 it will sell for $100 per share. His friend, Stein, believes that by June 30 its value will fall to $50 per share. Both Brown and Stein are willing to gamble on the value of the stock. Stein agrees to deliver the 100 shares to Brown at $75 per share and calls Martin, his stockbroker, to borrow the shares. After Stein delivers the stock to Brown, it drops to $40 per share. This means that when Stein buys the stock to return the borrowed stock to Martin he will pay $4,000 for the same 100 shares that sold for $7,500. By selling short, Stein has made a profit of $3,500 on the transaction.

show cause A court order requiring a person or corporation that has already been commanded to do or not to do some act to appear in court to explain why the court should not enforce the original order. The party that is ordered to appear must give a legitimate reason (show cause) why the order should not be obeyed.

sic (Latin) "Thus"; in such manner; so. When "(sic)" follows a word in a quotation, it usually means that there was an error in the original, and that the person transcribing or quoting the word is aware of the error.

sight Presentment; presentation. When a draft or bill of exchange is payable at sight, it is payable on presentation to the drawee (frequently a bank) named in the draft or bill. See COMMERCIAL PAPER.

signature Any mark or sign made on an instrument (a document) as a token of knowledge, approval, acceptance, or obligation. An *instrument* is any formal written document, such as a contract, will, bond, or check. A signature consists of both the act of writing one's name and the intention of authenticating the document signed.

■ **Form** A person can sign his name in any common form. Discrepancies between the signature and the name in the body of the instrument do not necessarily invalidate the instrument. A person may also lawfully use a fictitious name or the name of a business firm if there is no intent to defraud. A person's signature may be sufficient to validate an instrument even if the signature is virtually illegible. The entire name does not have to be written. The inclusion or omission of a middle name does not matter.

When a more complete signature is not required, an instrument can be properly signed (1) with the initial letter or letters of the given name or names and the full surname, (2) with only the full surname, (3) with only the given name, or (4) with only the initials.

Unless a statute provides otherwise, a person may use any character, symbol, figure, or designation he wants as a signature. If he uses it as a substitute for his name, he is bound by it. He may also use a mark.

A *mark* is usually an "X" made as a substitute for a signature by a person who does not know how to write. Unless a statute provides otherwise, a mark may also be used by a person who knows how to write but cannot because of some physical disability or illness. When a signer uses a mark, he is just as bound as he would be if he had written his name.

The name of the person who makes his mark is usually written—next to the mark—by someone else. But when there is no statute stating otherwise, the mark is valid even if no name accompanies it. Nor is the mark necessarily invalid because the person writing the name misspells it or because there are no words stating it is intended to be a mark.

When a mark is used as a signature, it can be placed wherever the customary signature can be placed. When the name must accompany the mark, the mark and the name do not have to be right next to each other.

Some statutes require a signature made by mark to be witnessed. Under these statutes, if the mark is not properly witnessed, the document is not signed no matter how much other evidence can be produced to show that the mark was made by the signer. Under other statutes, if the mark is not properly witnessed, other evidence can be used to prove the mark is a valid signature.

■ **Hand of another** A person can have his signature made by someone he has authorized to sign for him. However, if a statute requires a document to be signed in person, the signature must be made in the person's own hand or by another person at his specific request and in his presence. Previous authority or later ratification is not sufficient under such a statute.

A signature can be made with the help of another person who guides the signer's pen or pencil. When the maker's hand is guided or steadied, the signature is the maker's act and not the act of the person assisting him.

■ **Affixing a signature** A signature can be affixed to a document in many different ways. It can be written by hand, printed, stamped, typewritten, engraved, photographed, or cut from one instrument and attached to another. For example, if you are a businessman who has to sign a lot of papers, you may use a rubber stamp for signing the majority of them. Or if you broke the hand you write with, you might make a photocopy of an old signature, cut it out, and glue it to a document. If you do not write the signature by hand, however, you or anyone else who wants to prove the signature is valid must show that it was affixed with your authority. If you testify that you affixed the signature or authorized someone else to do so, the signature will be considered valid.

■ **Location** The usual place for a signature is at the end of the instrument. It must be at the end when, for example, a statute provides that a writing must be *subscribed*—that is, written at the bottom of the instrument. When there is no statute about the location of a signature, it can be placed in any part of the instrument, such as at the head, in the body, or across the face of the document.

When a person intends to sign as a witness but mistakenly signs the document in the place where the principal is to sign, the fact that he signed as a witness can be indicated on the document. Similarly, when a signer intends to sign as a principal but signs in the place for a witness, that fact can be indicated.

simultaneous death Loss of life by two or more persons at the same time or under circumstances that make it impossible to tell who died first. The question of who died first often comes up in cases determining the inheritance of property when enforcing WILLS or providing for the distribution of property of persons who died without a will. The issue is generally a *matter of fact*, which means that the answer must come from all the surrounding circumstances.

Under the common law, the courts would not step in and assume that one person had died first but would wait for proof, no matter how slight. This posed a problem when there was no satisfactory proof, so over the years various states enacted laws permitting judges to presume that one person survived another under certain circumstances. For example, one state presumed as a *matter of law* that a 17-year-old lived longer than a 25-year-old when both died in an auto accident. Louisiana—following French law—presumed that a man outlived a woman. States generally did not rely on proof that one person was in better health than the other to support a presumption.

Over the years these arbitrary and complicated presumptions proved inconvenient. Now almost every state has enacted an effective uniform law called the Simultaneous Death Act. There are some minor variations from state to state, but the law basically provides that property will be inherited or distributed as if each person had outlived the other. In other words, each person's estate is distributed as if the other person is already dead, with no claims against the estate. This saves the property from passing into and then out of the estate of a second person already deceased—a wasteful procedure that incurs extra legal processes, costs, and estate taxes.

EXAMPLE Sal and Sally Clacker were returning from their second honeymoon in Hawaii when their airplane developed engine trouble and crashed into the sea. The Clackers died in the crash. Rather than passing Sally's property into Sal's estate and then out again to their children, or vice versa, the law permits the Clacker children to inherit directly from each parent.

The Simultaneous Death Act does not apply if there is evidence that one person did live longer than the other. It applies only where it cannot be determined who died first. It is generally not necessary that the persons involved die in the same disaster (they may have died in different places and under different circumstances) as long as it is impossible to prove that one survived the other. See also WILL.

sine die   (Latin) "Without day." For example, a legislature adjourns *sine die* when it adjourns without appointing a day on which it will assemble again. When used in a trial court announcement about the end of a court term, *sine die* means "without assigning a day for the next term."

sine qua non   (Latin) "Without which not"; an indispensable requisite or condition. In the law of TORTS, which governs NEGLIGENCE suits, a PROXIMATE CAUSE (direct cause) exists when it can be said that "but for" the defendant's act the injury to the plaintiff or his property would not have occurred. This test is known as the sine qua non rule or the BUT-FOR RULE.

sit   1 Hold court or do any act of a judicial nature.   2 Hold a session—that is, be formally organized and proceed with the transaction of business, such as a session of a court, grand jury, or legislative body.

situs   (Latin) "Site"; location. For example, personal property usually has its taxable situs in the state where its owner lives. The situs of a TRUST is the place where the trustee performs his duties in managing the trust.

slander   See LIBEL AND SLANDER.

slating   See BOOKING.

slave   A person held as property by another. When slavery was legal, a master absolutely owned his slave and was entitled to command the slave's obedience, to manage his life, and to compel his labor and service for the master's benefit.

White slavery is not really slavery at all. It is a term commonly applied to PROSTITUTION. A federal law called the Mann Act makes it a criminal offense for any person to transport a woman across a state line for immoral purposes or to induce, compel, or entice her into prostitution.

■ **The 13th Amendment**   After the Civil War the Constitution was amended to abolish slavery absolutely. The 13th Amendment says:

❝ Neither slavery nor involuntary servitude, except as a punishment for crime whereof the party shall have been duly convicted, shall exist within the United States, or any place subject to their jurisdiction.❞

This amendment has been applied to every kind of involuntary servitude except work done by prisoners. It prohibits every kind of labor forced against the worker's will for the benefit of someone else. It was enforced against Chinese coolie traders and against the Mexican peonage system of binding a worker to the land while he worked off a debt. It ended the custom among some Indian tribes in Alaska of keeping slaves.

EXAMPLE In an Alaskan case, decided in 1887, Sah Quah, a man suing for his freedom, said that he had been captured and sold into slavery as a boy. He had lost one eye, and both ears were badly mutilated. The court discovered that it was customary to put out an eye, bore the ears, or otherwise mark the flesh of a slave to humiliate him. Moreover a slave could be killed to mark an event, such as the death of his master or the completion of a new house. A person known as the juggler could be called upon to drive a rebellious spirit out of a slave by incantation and exorcisms, and the slave was forced to submit. Sah Quah's master argued that slavery had been customary among isolated Alaskan tribes from time immemorial and that the U.S. government had no right to meddle in internal tribal affairs. The federal judge found that Alaskan Indians were subject to the control of U.S. law and could not be allowed slavery by tribal law. Of Sah Quah the court said, "The crack of the lash, the torture of mutilation, the fear of death, the annoyance of the juggler, the excess of manual labor imposed upon him, the extreme hardships of his life, with the sense of degradation and inferiority constantly before him, have subdued his manhood, and the pitiable spectacle of his once stately form is an evidence of the blighting effect of slavery."

The courts have used the prohibition against involuntary servitude in the 13th Amendment to prevent the enforcement of personal service contracts by SPECIFIC PERFORMANCE—a legal method of forcing a person to carry out his contract as nearly as practicable because nothing else could compensate the other party for the breach of contract. For example, a court may order specific performance of a contract to sell a fan Elvis Presley's guitar because neither money nor another guitar could compensate the buyer for his loss if the seller refused to deliver Presley's guitar. But since the 13th Amendment prohibits involuntary servitude, the court could not order specific performance of a contract that provides for someone to do some work.

EXAMPLE If John and Judy make a contract with the nation's most renowned organist to play at their wedding and the organist later refuses to play, John and Judy could not ask the court to force the organist to play. Even though John and Judy would be losing something they valued highly on the most important day of their lives, forcing the organist to play would amount to forcing him into involuntary servitude.

It is not, however, a violation of the 13th Amendment to assign attorneys to represent indigent clients without compensation or to subject persons to compulsory military service. Nor is a child a slave just because he must submit to reasonable supervision by his parents. Former husbands who must pay alimony are not being subjected to involuntary servitude, nor are conscientious objectors who must perform alternative service in a hospital. Public employees who are not allowed to strike are not enslaved because they can always quit and seek jobs elsewhere. In other words, not every restraint on liberty is a form of slavery. Citizens have always had responsibilities, and the 13th Amendment was never intended to relieve them of their duties.

■ **The 14th Amendment**   The 14th Amendment gives full citizenship rights to everyone who is born or naturalized in the United States. It forces the federal government and each state government to preserve the rights of citizens.

■ **Recent slave cases** Pure slavery cases are very rare today, but they are vigorously prosecuted when they occur. Two cases surfaced in 1978.

EXAMPLE A Pakistani couple was charged with enslaving a
O——※ 10-year-old African girl in their home in Florida. The couple had allegedly found the girl when they were touring Africa. They gave the child's mother $200 and promised to give her the advantage of a comfortable home and an American education. Here, however, they gave the girl only a dress—no shoes, socks, or underwear—and refused to send her to school. They forced her to do household chores for long hours every day.

An FBI agent described this as "the first classic case of slavery in this century," but it was only a few months later that an even more bizarre case came to light.

EXAMPLE A New Jersey woman was arrested for enslaving
O——※ residents of two boardinghouses she ran. The woman was charged with unlawful imprisonment for locking seven residents up in rooms without food or care. The indictment also charged her with forcing one resident to work as a slave in her home and with compelling a young psychiatric patient to do housekeeping chores and to perform sexual acts with men in the boardinghouse.

slip decision A copy of a court decision that is distributed almost immediately after it is handed down by the court. It is also called a *slip opinion* or *slip sheet.*

slip law A copy of a bill passed by Congress and signed by the President, or passed by a state legislature and signed by the governor, and printed and distributed almost immediately.

small business An independently owned and operated business that is usually not dominant in its field of operation. The size of a small business depends on the industry. One person who is a hot dog vendor is a small business, but so is a machine shop with 50 employees and a volume of business of hundreds of thousands of dollars a year. Ranches, farms, meat lockers, mom-and-pop grocery stores, laundries, roller skate rental concessions, importers, florists, plumbers, carpenters, barbers, luncheonettes, and day-care centers—can all be small businesses.

It is the policy of the federal government to encourage, assist, and protect small businesses. Federal law declares that the

❝ *essence of the American economic system of private enterprise is free competition. Only through full and free competition can free markets, free entry into business, and opportunities for the expression and growth of personal initiative and individual judgment be assured. The preservation and expansion of such competition is basic not only to the economic well-being but to the security of this Nation. Such security and well-being cannot be realized unless the actual and potential capacity of small business is encouraged and developed.*❞

To implement this policy, Congress has created the Small Business Administration (SBA). This agency is authorized, among other things, to make loans to small businesses, either directly or in cooperation with banks or other lenders; to make grants for research or counseling on the managing, financing, and operation of small businesses; and to channel extra assistance into areas of high unemployment, disaster areas, and businesses owned by or concerned with minorities or handicapped persons. The SBA helps the small businessman steer his way through new or complicated laws concerning the environment, energy, health and safety, and employee benefits. It also gives the small businessman a voice in Washington.

■ **Financing a small business** Every business requires some capital to get started. Many people first start a small business with an asset they have on hand, but even then more cash and supplies will be needed.

EXAMPLE A woman who owns a sewing machine wants to
O——※ start taking in mending from her local dry cleaner and do alterations for a children's clothing store. She has to purchase a supply of various buttons, zippers, and thread in the most commonly used colors. She needs to keep money on hand to buy an odd color of thread and to pay for gas when she has to pick up or deliver work.

When larger amounts of capital are needed—for example, to lease an office or to buy a truck—people usually have to borrow money. Friends or family members may have enough confidence in the individual and his goals to lend the money. Banks lend money for starting small businesses, but they want to be sure the money will be repaid. A person approaching a bank for a loan to start a small business must show that he has planned carefully and has the skills necessary to run the kind of business he proposes. Usually, the bank requires the borrower to promise personally to repay the loan and to pledge something he owns as security. A young or inexperienced person may be required to have another financially responsible person cosign the loan.

■ **Three basic forms** A person who wants to start a small business must at the outset choose the best form for the business. A small business may basically be run as a SOLE PROPRIETORSHIP, a PARTNERSHIP, or a CORPORATION.

A *sole proprietorship* is owned and managed by one person. The sole proprietor has the right to make all his own business decisions, but he is also personally liable for all the debts incurred by the business.

A *partnership* is owned and operated by two or more persons who are bound by a partnership agreement, which determines each partner's rights and responsibilities in relation to the other partners. All the partners are personally liable for the business's debts, and each is responsible for what the other partners do in the name of the business.

A *corporation* is a business organization chartered by the state. A corporation is generally created by a number of persons, but some states allow an individual to create one all by himself. A corporation is financed by the sale of shares of stock. It is owned by the persons who own its stock, but it is a business entity separate from the shareholders. A corporation pays its own debts and the shareholders are liable only for the amount they invested in the business; they are not personally liable for the debts of the business as are sole proprietors and partners.

■ **Operating a small business** Anyone operating a small business will have to become familiar with the law of BANKS AND BANKING, CREDIT, CONTRACTS, TORTS, and INSURANCE. Anyone who offers a service should find out about LIENS and LICENSES. Anyone who sells goods should check into the law of SALES, SECURED TRANSACTIONS, WARRANTY, and PRODUCT LIABILITY. A small businessman who hires employees should know about the law of AGENCY, MASTER AND SERVANT (employer and employee), and RESPONDEAT SUPERIOR. He must keep careful records for SOCIAL SECURITY, WORKMEN'S COMPENSATION, and INCOME TAX purposes. There may come a time when he needs advice concerning PENSIONS or LABOR RELATIONS. Then there are a host of laws and regulations affecting particular businesses. Finally, even a hardworking businessman may someday have to consider BANKRUPTCY.

■ **Going out of business** The owner of a sole proprietorship can usually decide for himself when he wants to go out of business. He can stop taking in new business and finish performing all of his outstanding obligations.

Whenever any partner chooses to pull out, a partnership ceases to function. Like the sole proprietorship, it must finish performing all of its outstanding obligations before it is dissolved. There is a formal winding-up period during which one partner is designated to wrap up the partnership business. Every partner is then entitled to an accounting, which discloses the financial transactions of the business and the final disposition of its assets.

Shareholders have the legal right to dissolve their corporation, generally by a majority vote. They surrender their charter to the state and pay their final tax bill. The corporate assets may be used to satisfy outstanding debts. States may also provide a mechanism for dissolving corporations involuntarily by court order. This may be done because the corporation is violating the law or, in some states, because it has stopped doing business.

A healthy business does not have to be dismantled—it can be sold. A small business can be sold by a sale of its building, equipment, materials, inventory, and accounts. Even where there are no tangible assets, the company's good name and reputation, called goodwill, or its trade secrets, customer lists, or trademarks may be sold as valuable assets.

The sale of any business that principally sells merchandise from stock, including businesses that manufacture what they sell, is regulated by a Bulk Sales Act in each state. This law does not cover such businesses as farming, contracting, or professional services or such service-performing businesses as dry cleaners, barbershops, pool halls, hotels, and restaurants because they are not primarily engaged in selling merchandise. The law requires advance notice of the sale to be given to creditors of a business covered by the act. The purpose of this requirement is to protect creditors from a merchant who owes debts but sells out his business, pockets the proceeds, and disappears. The advance notice allows the creditors to take legal steps to protect their claims. If the notice requirements are not formally observed, the creditors can ignore the fact of the sale and collect what is owed out of the assets of the business even though they then belong to the purchaser.

small claims Demands for money or property of relatively small value, usually limited by law to no more than $1,000. Almost every state has special courts where small claims can be asserted with minimal formality. These small claims courts are meant to provide a forum for the "little guy" in cases not worth pursuing in higher courts because of the time and costs involved. The types of cases most often heard in small claims courts include collection of unpaid bills, consumer protection cases, suits by tenants to recover security deposits wrongfully withheld by their landlords, and suits for money to cover property damage—especially damage that is sustained in minor automobile accidents.

EXAMPLE Someone breaks your picture window and refuses to pay for the damage. If you want to sue the culprit for the actual cost of the repairs, you can probably start an action against him in small claims court by filing a simple statement of the problem on a form supplied by the court along with a claim for the amount of money involved. The court will send a summons to the window breaker. If he does not decide to settle with you out of court, there will be a simple, informal hearing before a judge or arbitrator, who will decide whether or not you should be paid for the window. If the court does award you payment, it will also decide on the amount of money you should get.

The cases heard in small claims courts are limited to claims for small amounts of money. The maximum claim allowable varies from state to state. Some states limit small claims to controversies involving no more than a few hundred dollars, but others allow cases involving a maximum of $1,000 or more. Because of the small amounts of money involved in the cases, the courts hear them quickly and at little cost to the plaintiff. Most cases are scheduled for a few weeks after the claim is filed by the plaintiff, and the actual hearing generally takes only a few minutes. The court charges the plaintiff only a nominal fee (often less than $5) when he files a claim, but if he wins the case, he may recover that cost from the defendant along with the money awarded. Costs are also kept down by discouraging—and in some places even forbidding—the use of attorneys to represent the parties and by eliminating most of the paperwork required by other courts.

Generally, anyone of full legal age (18 to 21, depending on the state) may sue in a small claims court. Many states will not permit corporations to be plaintiffs, because small claims courts are intended to help consumers stand up to businesses. The courts might become nothing more than collection agencies against consumers if corporations could use them to collect debts. Some states do not prohibit all corporations from suing in small claims courts, however, on the theory that an efficient and speedy legal process for collecting on overdue bills encourages stores to extend credit to consumers. There is generally no restriction regarding the type of person or business that can be sued in small claims court, except that the defendant must live, work, or have an office within the area served by the court.

Some small claims courts hold sessions at night so that people do not have to miss work in order to use them. The cases may be heard by a judge or by an arbitrator, who is not a judge and may not even be an attorney. Often there is no right to appeal the decision, and usually there is no jury. As many as half of the cases filed do not result in a final decision by the judge or arbitrator, because the parties involved agree on a compromise. *(continued)*

IF YOU ARE GOING INTO BUSINESS

DANIEL Q. POSIN
Professor of Law, Hofstra University School of Law

So you would like to go into business for yourself. Perhaps you would like to start a small restaurant or a hardware store or a boutique. Perhaps you would like to buy a house or an apartment building and rent it out. Perhaps you have a patent or know of a secret process that you would like to build a business around. Whatever kind of business you may be considering, one thing is sure: the form of business you select will have an important impact on your chances for success. In making your choice, you should always consult a lawyer, but this article will help to bring out the points that you should discuss with him.

Sole proprietorship

The sole proprietorship is the simplest form of doing business. One person, the sole proprietor, owns and operates the business. The sole proprietor may rent or buy equipment and office space to run his business. He may also employ others to help him. There is no need to prepare a partnership agreement or articles of incorporation. There may, however, be local requirements concerning licenses for a particular type of business or requiring the sole proprietor to register if he does business in any name other than his own. There are also certain other advantages and disadvantages that should be considered.

Control The sole proprietor has complete control over his business. He need consult no one else concerning his business decisions.

Liability for debts The sole proprietor of a business is personally liable for all debts he incurs in the course of his business. Thus, if there is a major setback, a sole proprietor could lose his car, house, or other personal assets.

Raising of additional capital If the sole proprietor wishes to expand his business, he is limited by his own personal credit in raising additional capital.

Federal income taxes The income or loss from the sole proprietorship—determined after deduction for wages, rents, depreciation, and other expenses—belongs only to the sole proprietor. The income or loss appears on his federal income tax return along with any other income or loss he may have from other employment or investments.

Continuity of the business The sole proprietor may will the business to whomever he chooses to receive it upon his death. Since he has probably been the guiding light of the business, however, it is likely the business will come to an end at the time of his death and be sold by the executor or administrator of his estate. Unfortunately, such a sale may be made at a disadvantageous price, because it may be done under the pressure of time.

In short Because of its simplicity, including the relatively modest legal fees required, the sole proprietorship is the choice of millions of small businesses throughout the country.

The partnership

The partnership is a somewhat more complicated form of doing business. It is governed by the state partnership law, which provides that for two or more people to conduct business as a partnership they must enter into a partnership agreement. This agreement can be a simple oral agreement between two people to form a partnership, or it can be an elaborate, written agreement among many partners in a large business. State partnership law establishes rules for how partnerships shall operate when its members have no written agreement, but many of these rules can be changed by a written partnership agreement.

Control   In the most common form of partnership, the *general partnership,* all the partners have the authority to run the business. Each partner can act for and legally bind the partnership. Hence, it is advisable for the partnership agreement to specify what would happen in the event of disagreement among the partners. It is a good idea to provide for a majority vote or some method of arbitration to decide the differences. The alternative is to provide in the agreement some way to allocate management of the business among the partners—for instance, with one partner in charge of manufacturing, one partner in charge of sales, one partner in charge of personnel, and so forth, according to the expertise of each partner.

Liability for debts   Whatever property each partner contributes to the partnership becomes the property of the partnership and is to be used in the conduct of the business. This property can also serve to satisfy debts incurred by the partnership.

One very important characteristic of a partnership is that each partner is personally responsible for the debts of the partnership. If the partnership faces a huge debt (perhaps arising from a lawsuit) that exhausts the assets of a partnership, then the assets of the individual partners may be reached. Because each partner has the power to legally bind the partnership, it is possible that one partner, acting irresponsibly, could commit the partnership to a large obligation—for which the law would hold the other partners personally responsible. The message is clear: you should only go into partnership with people whom you know well and trust.

A variation of the partnership form, the *limited partnership,* offers protection for the partners' personal assets. The limited partner's liability for the debts of the partnership is restricted to the amount of money or property he contributes to the partnership. Thus, if the partnership faces a huge debt, a creditor cannot reach the personal car or house of the limited partner but only the property he has contributed to the partnership.

The limited partner, however, cannot manage the affairs of the partnership. If you wish to have a significant say in running the business, you should be a general partner, not a limited partner. Typically, a limited partner is a wealthy investor in the business who wants to limit his liability and does not wish to take an active role in managing the business.

A limited partnership must have at least one general partner and one or more limited partners. Particularly because of its tax advantages, discussed below, the limited partnership has become a popular form of business enterprise in recent years.

Raising of additional capital   A partnership can raise additional capital by admitting new partners, generally with the consent of the other partners. A limited partnership can be particularly effective in raising new capital because the new limited partners know that their liability will be limited.

Federal income taxes   A partnership does not pay any federal income taxes. Rather, the profit on the business is determined at the end of the year, and each partner is taxed on his own tax return on his share of the partnership profit. This is true whether or not the profits are actually distributed to the partners. Unless the partnership agreement provides otherwise, each partner shares in the partnership profits in proportion to the amount of capital he has contributed to the partnership. Similarly, if the partnership business has shown a loss for the year, each partner takes a deduction on his own tax return for his share of the loss. This deduction cannot exceed the amount the partner has invested in the business.

Partnership income or loss thus "passes through" and is reflected on the tax returns of individual partners. This "pass through" has led to the so-called tax shelter device, using the limited partnership. In the typical tax shelter a number of high-income investors—such as doctors, lawyers, or executives—invest in a business as limited partners. Through various complex arrangements, large tax losses can be passed through to these investors, reducing their taxable income from their professions as doctors, lawyers, or executives. Such arrangements are now generally available only in real estate and should not be entered into without advice from an attorney who is experienced in this field.

Continuity of the business

Under state law, the general rule is that when a partner dies the partnership is dissolved. However, the partnership agreement can provide that the partnership will continue after the death of a partner. It is advisable for the partnership agreement to so stipulate, to insure that the business will continue unimpaired on the death of any partner.

In short

The partnership is a very flexible form of doing business. It can be a small, two-person arrangement, or it can involve many partners in a large, sophisticated business undertaking. The partnership agreement can provide, with great flexibility, how the partners will share the management of the business and how the partnership income and losses will be allocated. The tax treatment of the limited partnership has made it an attractive form for use by investors seeking tax shelter for their high income.

The corporation

The corporation is the most complex form of business organization and requires the most legal advice to set up and maintain. A corporation is formed by the sale of shares of stock to individuals, who become the stockholders. The money raised by the sale of the stock is then used by the corporation to buy property and equipment and to conduct the corporate business. If the corporation makes a profit, it can be paid to the stockholders in the form of dividends on their stock. If the profits are not paid out but are reinvested in the business, this may still benefit the stockholders because the value of their stock will go up, reflecting the increased value of the corporation. Similarly, if the corporation shows a loss in the business, the value of the stock in the stockholder's hands will go down, reflecting the decreased value of the corporation. (The value of the stock will also be affected by other factors, such as changes in the overall economic outlook or new government business policies.)

The corporation is the form of business most widely used by large business enterprises, and the names of the major corporations in this country are household words—General Motors, AT&T, IBM. However, the corporate form can also be very attractive for the small business.

Control

The corporation consists of the stockholders, who own the company; the board of directors, who decide on general business policy; and the officers (president, vice president, secretary, treasurer), who are concerned with the day-to-day operations of the business. The stockholders elect the directors, and the directors select the officers.

In the small, or "closely held," corporation, the stockholders, board of directors, and officers are often the same people. This is a common arrangement for a small business. In such a closely held corporation setting, control among the several people involved is allocated by giving out varying amounts of the common stock of the corporation to the participants, usually in proportion to the money they invest in the corporation. Thus, since each share of stock counts as one vote, a person who owned 60 percent of the common stock of the corporation would control the corporation even though several people owned the other 40 percent.

There is, however, great flexibility in allocating control of a small corporation. For example, one person may wish to contribute a large amount of money to the corporation but not take any active part in managing the business. He might, however, want to be assured that he will be paid dividends on his stock. Such a person could be given preferred stock. Preferred stock must be paid a dividend before a dividend is paid on common stock. The preferred stock holder might not be given voting rights in the corporation. This nonvoting preferred stock might be an attractive investment for the person who wanted to be fairly certain that he would get dividends but who did not want to manage the business.

There are also other varieties of control arrangements in a closely held corporation, such as a requirement that major actions of the corporation may not be taken without a unanimous vote of the shareholders or provisions for arbitration in the event of a disagreement among shareholders.

Another important technique for maintaining control of a closely held corporation is for the stockholders to agree that if one of them wishes to withdraw from the corporation, he will offer his stock to the other stockholders at a prearranged price. The other stockholders will thus have the opportunity to buy out the withdrawing party rather than have that party sell his stock to a stranger, who might disrupt the close working relationship in the business. Similar arrangements can be made for buying back the stock on the death of one of the stockholders.

Liability for debts   One of the outstanding characteristics of the corporation is that the stockholders can lose only the amount they have invested in the corporation. Unlike the case of the sole proprietorship or general partnership, creditors of the corporation cannot go after the personal assets of the stockholders. This so-called limited-liability feature of corporations has some exceptions, however. The major exception is that if the stockholders use the corporate form to defraud creditors, courts will allow the creditors to "pierce the corporate veil" and reach the personal assets of the stockholders.

There is a negative aspect to limited liability, too. If a corporation has few assets, a bank or other creditor may be hesitant to lend it money, because the bank knows that it can only recover against the corporation, not its stockholders. In such a case, if a loan is desired, it may be necessary for the stockholders to personally guarantee the loan.

Raising of additional capital   Upon vote of the board of directors or the stockholders, a corporation can raise additional capital by selling new shares of stock. This can be done by selling shares to a few new investors or by making a large offering of stock to members of the general public. In the case of such a large offering, detailed rules of the Securities and Exchange Commission, which relate to the disclosure of information regarding the business of the corporation, must be followed. Failure to follow these disclosure requirements could result in stringent penalties. Therefore, such a public sale of stock should be undertaken only under the guidance of experienced legal counsel.

The sale of stock of a closely held corporation to the public is a major event in the life of the corporation. It transforms the corporation from a small business to a major enterprise. This process of "going public" is a path often followed by a successful small business that wishes to expand significantly. The ability of the corporation to raise substantial new capital by sales of stock to the general public is one of its outstanding features.

Federal income tax   A corporation must pay federal income taxes on its profits. If what remains after that tax is paid is distributed by the corporation to the shareholders as a dividend on their stock, the shareholders will then pay a tax on that dividend. Thus it is often said that the profits of a corporation are taxed twice—once at the corporate level and once again at the level of the shareholders. This is only true, however, if the corporation distributes a dividend to the shareholders. If, instead of distributing a dividend, the corporation uses its after-tax profits to invest in new plant and equipment, there will of course be no tax on the shareholders.

If the individuals starting a small business have high incomes from salaries or other investments, they may find it attractive to form the new business as a small corporation, because a small corporation may be taxed at a lower rate than the high-income individuals. Overall taxes can thus be saved.

Another tax advantage of corporations is that pension and profit-sharing plans can easily be set up. Such plans, as well as the other matters discussed in this section, should be dealt with on the advice of an experienced attorney.

Finally, it is possible to do business as a "Subchapter S Corporation." This is a special type of corporation, which is taxed, roughly speaking, as a partnership—with income and losses passing through to the stockholders (see the discussion of taxation of partnerships above). However, the Subchapter S Corporation is a complex form and should only be employed by the relatively sophisticated business.

Continuity of the business   The corporation is a legal entity separate from its stockholders. It may contract with third parties, sue, and be sued in its own name. The corporation's life is perpetual (unless its stockholders vote to dissolve). The death or withdrawal of any of its stockholders does not terminate the life of the corporation. Thus the corporate form is an excellent way to insure continuity of the business.

In short   Because of its great flexibility in allocating control of the business, its tremendous potential for raising new capital, and its possible tax advantages, the corporation is an excellent form of doing business, particularly for the well-developed, relatively profitable business.

Making a choice

Part of the genius of the American business system is that there are so many forms from which to choose in setting up a business, and as this brief discussion has indicated, there are many factors to consider when you select what form you will use. Your financial success will depend largely upon your picking the form that is right for you.

■ **Step-by-step procedure** The steps to be followed in a small claims case may vary from state to state, but they are always basically simple. Before starting an action, however, you should take steps to settle your dispute through ordinary means. First, you should politely request a settlement from the offending party by visiting, telephoning, or writing him. If he fails to give you satisfaction, your next request should be in a letter.

After you have written two letters without receiving any indication that the offending party will settle to your satisfaction, go to your local small claims court and file suit against him. Be sure you know the address and exact legal name of the company—you can find it in a business directory at your local library. A company can be sued only in its legal name; short forms of the name are not acceptable.

You will be charged a small fee for filing suit and probably a charge for registered mail postage used to serve a summons on the defendant. If there are any witnesses who can help your case and you are not sure they will be willing to appear at your request, you may be able to have subpoenas served on them at the same time. The court will set a date and time for the hearing.

When he receives the summons, the defendant may offer to settle with you out of court. If he does settle, you can drop the suit. If not, appear promptly for the hearing, armed with all the receipts and correspondence involved in the case and as much other evidence as you can gather. Also bring along any friendly witnesses.

When you come up before the judge (or arbitrator), explain your case simply and clearly without exaggerating or becoming excited. Try to show that your demands are reasonable and that you have tried other means to induce the defendant to settle with you. (Copies of your letters and his answers to your letters, if there are any, can be used as evidence.) Give the judge any papers he asks for, and answer all his questions as best you can. Let the defendant state his side of the case. After the judge has all the information he needs, he will decide whether or not you should receive what you are asking for. If he decides the defendant is in the wrong, he will order him to pay you either the full amount you asked for or a portion of it. The costs of the court case will be taken into consideration by the judge and included in the judgment.

EXAMPLE During a party a guest spilled a glass of red wine O—✸ on Ethel's sofa and stained the velvet upholstery. The next morning Ethel called Smith's Upholstery Renewers and had them come to her home and clean the entire sofa, hoping to get rid of the stain and improve the appearance of the sofa in general. The cleaning got rid of all but a trace of the stain, but the cleaning substance the worker used left the velvet matted and ugly. Ethel complained to the owner of Smith's Upholstery Renewers, and after many delays the owner sent someone to look at the sofa. The serviceman told Ethel that the condition of the upholstery was not caused by the cleaning. He said that she must have washed the sofa in an effort to remove the rest of the stain, and that had caused the matting. Ethel insisted she had not, and even if she had, the matting would then have been only in the area that was stained and not, as was the case, over the entire sofa. The company refused to do anything about it. She wrote the owner, recapitulating all that had happened, and firmly insisted that he pay to have the sofa recovered. The owner wrote back offering to cancel the bill for the cleaning but refusing to pay for the recovering, still insisting that the matting was her fault. Ethel wrote again and sent a copy of her letter to the Better Business Bureau. She received no answer.

At that point Ethel took photographs of the damaged upholstery and had the sofa recovered. She then went to the small claims court to file suit against Smith's.

At the courthouse a clerk had Ethel fill out a form listing her own name and address, the name and address of the offending company, the nature of her complaint, and a statement of the amount of the damages she thought she should be reimbursed for. The clerk charged Ethel a few dollars for filing the suit and postage to send a summons by registered mail. He sent a copy of Ethel's complaint and a summons to appear in court to Smith's Upholstery Renewers.

When the owner of Smith's was served with the summons, he requested and got from the court a continuance (postponement of the hearing). Either party may request a continuance if they are unable to attend or be ready on the scheduled day. Smith's later obtained a second and third continuance in the hope of discouraging Ethel, but she refused to be discouraged.

When her case finally came up, Ethel told the judge exactly what had happened and showed him the photographs of the ruined sofa and the receipt for the recovering. The owner of Smith's insisted that Ethel had washed the sofa and ruined it herself. The judge found for Ethel and awarded her payment of what she had spent for recovering the sofa plus court costs. Smith's was obliged to pay the full amount.

■ **Collecting after a judgment** Plaintiffs who win a judgment often have trouble collecting what is due them. To collect, you may have to send a copy of the judgment to the defendant together with a letter requesting payment, or you may return to the court and request a writ of EXECUTION, commanding a sheriff or other officer to seize the defendant's property in order to satisfy the judgment.

smart money In law, the DAMAGES awarded in a suit that are in excess of the actual loss suffered by the plaintiff. Smart money is another name for punitive or exemplary damages that are awarded when a TORT (harm done to a person or property) is aggravated by actual malice, deliberate violence, or fraud on the part of the person who committed the tort.

smuggling The crime of bringing into or taking out of the country goods that are prohibited or on which CUSTOMS or excise duties have not been paid.

Federal law prohibits the importation of a variety of items that are dangerous to public health or welfare. For example, it is illegal to carry into this country diseased plants or animals, obscene films and magazines, and narcotic drugs that have not been properly prescribed by a physician. Importation of some other articles—such as goods manufactured in some Communist countries—is prohibited for political reasons.

Federal law also prohibits the importation of goods on which required duties have not been paid. In some cases customs or excise duties are imposed on goods in order to raise revenue and to influence commerce. For example, federal customs laws allow the President to adjust tariffs on foreign-made goods so that they do not compete unfairly with American-made products.

Anyone caught smuggling a prohibited item or something on which duties have not been paid risks more than one penalty: the smuggled item can be seized and kept by the government; any vehicle or vessel used for smuggling it is subject to forfeiture; and the smuggler himself can be imprisoned or fined.

All of the following are cases of smuggling:

(1) A young man who brings a new bicycle into Texas by riding it across a dry section of the Rio Grande without paying customs duties.

(2) A farmer who brings new farm machinery across the Canadian border without paying duties.

(3) A trainer who brings a diseased racehorse into New York City from England by filing false papers with the customs officials.

(4) An importer who removes labels from Cuban cigars, repacks them in cartons labeled "Colombia," and brings them into the United States.

(5) A small group of political radicals who ship guns to rebels in another country in boxes marked "hand tools."

■ **Border searches** Travelers at international borders can be stopped and required to identify themselves and to submit to a search. If they are caught carrying anything that they have not declared to customs inspectors or anything that is prohibited, they can be forced to pay the required duties, plus penalties, and can be arrested. Illegal goods can be seized by the customs agents.

Travelers who think they can slip things past customs officials when they return to this country are taking great risks. Anyone crossing the border can expect to be searched. Customs agents have the authority to search a person and his baggage or any packages or containers sent into the country. Ordinary searches within this country cannot be conducted unless the police have a warrant or probable cause to suspect illegality or the consent of the person being searched. These requirements do not necessarily apply to border searches. Customs agents may search anyone at a border for no reason at all, but a person who arouses suspicion is more likely to be searched thoroughly. In one case a person wearing heavy clothes in warm weather and looking bulky around the waist put agents on the alert. Often agents take note of a person who simply looks nervous. Even a baby can be searched because experienced agents know that illegal drugs are often secreted in a diaper.

EXAMPLE A woman returning from Europe feels certain
0⊶—⚹ that she can slip through customs with minimum scrutiny because she is middle-aged and well dressed. She has never committed a crime before, but now she decides to hide under some intimate apparel in her suitcase some jewelry she purchased abroad. She steps confidently into line after leaving the plane but grows more nervous as she approaches the customs inspector. Finally, he asks for her customs declaration. She has listed a few items on which duties were due, but not the jewelry. The customs inspec-

tor examines her suitcase and, without hesitation, removes the apparel the woman had thought would be embarrassing to him. Upon finding the hidden jewelry, he arrests her for smuggling.

■ **Civil and criminal penalties** Under federal law, anyone who intentionally smuggles goods into the country by hiding them from the customs inspector or lying about them on documents can be fined up to $10,000 or imprisoned up to five years or both. In addition, the smuggled goods shall be forfeited to the United States.

Aside from a criminal record and a substantial fine, the woman in the above example also faces a civil penalty. If she offers to pay the duties after the inspector has discovered the jewelry, she will pay a penalty of 100 percent of the duties that she tried to evade. This amount must be paid within 30 days. If she pays immediately, she may keep the jewelry (provided that she has been acquitted of criminal charges). Otherwise, it will be held by the government until the duties and penalty are paid or other security (such as a bond) is deposited to assure that the penalty will be paid. The goods will be forfeited, by means of a civil court action, to the government if the woman fails to pay her penalty on time.

If the woman challenges the civil action, the items may be kept by the government as evidence pending the outcome of the trial. The maximum penalty that the woman would have to pay should she lose her case is the domestic value of the merchandise.

■ **Smuggling by mail** It is as illegal to send prohibited items into the country as it is to carry them, and postal inspectors have the authority to search packages.

EXAMPLE Postal inspectors detected the odor of marijuana
0⊶—⚹ in a package mailed from Mexico to Detroit. They opened the package and found 10 sandwich-sized plastic bags of marijuana wrapped in new towels with a card that said: "Best wishes at your wedding. Love, Luis." The inspectors rewrapped the package and put it back into the mail. Authorities in Detroit were alerted. When a young man picked up the package at the post office in Detroit, he carried it out to his car, opened it up, and drove off. A block away, he was stopped and arrested for smuggling and possession of a controlled substance. Not only did he face a possible fine and jail sentence, but federal officers also seized his car, as any vehicle or vessel used for smuggling is subject to forfeiture.

■ **Forfeiture of vehicles** The forfeiture of vehicles or vessels used in smuggling has become a special worry to boat owners. Sometimes people who are able to use their expensive pleasure craft only a few weeks out of the year keep them in a warm climate and let other parties charter them the rest of the time.

EXAMPLE A man kept his 60-foot sailboat in the Virgin
0⊶—⚹ Islands. Two men chartered it for two weeks in September, telling him that they wanted to do some vacation sailing. Instead, they tried to smuggle heroin into the United States. The Coast Guard caught them, placed them under arrest, and seized the boat. The owner was finally able to prevail in the forfeiture proceedings because he was not involved in the drug-running scheme. However, his boat was in custody for a long time and legal expenses were very high.

■ **Knowledge of the deed**   A person must know that he has the smuggled goods in order to be convicted. If someone secretly plants drugs in your baggage, you are not smuggling—he is. Once you find that you are in possession of smuggled goods, however, you must do something.

EXAMPLE Most foreign films that enter the United States 0←→＊ come into New York. Obscene films are prohibited items, but film importers do not always know when a particular film will turn out to be obscene. Therefore, when a film arrives in New York, it is placed under customs seal and sent to a projection room where a customs inspector reviews it. If he finds that the film is not obscene, it is released to the importer. If he finds that the film is clearly obscene, he sends it to the District Attorney for proceedings to prevent its importation. When the film importer is notified that the film is being detained, he may agree to its forfeiture, send the film back out of the country, or delete the offensive scenes. If he claims that the film is not obscene, then customs officials have to prove that it is obscene at forfeiture proceedings. Anyone who attempts to bring films into the country outside of this type of procedure is smuggling.

■ **Penalties**   Federal law deals harshly with smugglers. A person can be convicted for smuggling merely for having illegal goods in his possession if he fails to explain them satisfactorily to a jury. Anyone who knowingly smuggles any merchandise that is prohibited by law or that should have come through customs, anyone who receives, buys, sells, or transports such merchandise, or anyone who helps to do one of these things can be fined up to $10,000 or sentenced to up to five years in jail or both. He may also be subject to civil penalties. In addition, the merchandise itself and any vessel or vehicle used to transport it can be forfeited to the United States.

Social Security   A U.S. government program designed to protect people from the risk of financial disaster when family earnings are reduced or stopped. The program, which was initiated in 1935, provides Old-Age, Survivors, and Disability Insurance (OASDI) for the nation's workers and their families and a health insurance plan, called Medicare. Complementing OASDI is a special insurance plan for railroad workers. All of these plans are discussed in this article. The Social Security program also helps states set up insurance programs to provide UNEMPLOYMENT COMPENSATION for those who lose their jobs.

In addition to these plans, which are designed chiefly to help people who qualify on the basis of their employment record, the Social Security program also includes plans that help people who qualify simply on the basis of need. These plans include Supplemental Security Income (SSI), which gives help to persons in financial need who are blind, disabled, or at least 65 years old; Aid to Families with Dependent Children (AFDC); and Medicaid, a health assistance program for those in financial need. For a discussion of these programs, SEE WELFARE PROGRAMS.

■ **Concept and development of social security**   As a general term, social security refers to the economic security and social welfare of an individual and his family as well as the consequent economic stability of society as a whole. Although in this country the term is used to refer to a specific federal program, it also describes any plan designed to protect society from the instability that results when families or households suffer such personal catastrophes as unemployment or the death of a wage earner.

In the 19th century, as industrialization took a firm hold on much of the Western world, it became increasingly obvious that something should be done to protect the interests of the workers. Germany was the first industrial country to adopt a public plan of social security. In the 1880's Chancellor Otto von Bismarck instituted a plan of compulsory insurance to protect wage earners and their dependents from the financial consequences of illness and old age. Over the next 50 or so years other European and Latin American countries established programs to benefit different categories of workers.

The United States before 1935   In the United States the pressure to establish a comprehensive scheme of social legislation grew more slowly. In the 19th century the United States was basically an agricultural nation, and Americans who lost jobs when the demands of industry shifted could always go west and work the abundant land. In the cities, as industry grew, workers formed mutual aid societies and fraternal orders, which offered funeral, sickness, and old-age insurance. For many years the federal government encouraged people to set aside money for future emergencies with a popular postal savings plan. People who could not manage were helped, if at all, only by private charity, because it was generally believed that those who wanted to help themselves could. These federal policies and voluntary efforts were the "social security" Americans had up through the first three decades of the 20th century— a time when industry and the economy were expanding rapidly. Then the Great Depression of the 1930's wrought financial havoc over the entire nation. Americans were shocked into realizing that steps had to be taken to restore the country's social security and to make sure that it could not be so shaken again.

The Social Security Act   The first Social Security Act became law in the United States in 1935 as part of President Franklin D. Roosevelt's New Deal of economic and social reforms. As originally enacted, it authorized payment of monthly old-age benefits to qualified wage earners who were at least 65 years old or payment of a lump-sum death benefit to the estate of a wage earner who died before reaching the age of 65.

In 1939 Congress created a separate monthly Social Security benefit for dependent wives, children, widows, and parents of wage earners. It was Congress's intent to soften the economic blow to these people when they lost a wage earner's support. These people are called secondary beneficiaries because they are entitled to their own benefits directly on account of the contributions made to the plan by the wage earner.

Social Security covered only workers in industry and commerce when the program began. Many classes of workers were excluded because the expense and inconvenience of collecting contributions were too great. For example, Congress exempted household workers, farmers, and family businesses because it felt they were not likely to maintain adequate employment records. In the 1950's, however, coverage was extended to include most self-employed indi-

YOUR PROTECTION UNDER SOCIAL SECURITY

■ The Social Security program provides workers and their families with Old-Age, Survivors, and Disability Insurance (OASDI) and Medicare. OASDI provides retirement benefits and monthly checks for disabled persons and for the families of deceased workers. Medicare provides hospital and medical insurance for persons who are 65 or older and some others.

■ Your right to collect Social Security benefits is based on the amount of time you worked under the program and the amount of the wages on which you paid Social Security taxes.

■ You should check your Social Security record every three years to be sure your earnings have been accurately credited.

■ Normal retirement age is 65, but you can retire and start receiving Social Security checks as early as age 62. You can also keep working full time after 65, but if you do and you earn more than a certain minimum amount, you will not get benefits until you retire or reach age 72.

■ If you do not retire at 65, you can get credit toward larger benefits up to age 72.

■ You may also choose to go back to work full time after you start getting Social Security checks. Your retirement benefits will then cease while you are working, but the amount will be refigured automatically when you stop working again.

■ You may work part time after retirement, but if you earn more than a certain amount, your Social Security checks will be reduced or stopped.

■ Income from sources other than work (company retirement benefits, inheritances, investments, insurance, or the like) do not affect your Social Security retirement benefits.

■ When you retire under Social Security, your husband or wife can receive secondary benefits amounting to one-half of yours if he or she applies after reaching 65 or reduced benefits if he or she applies after reaching 62.

■ A divorced man or woman can collect secondary benefits at age 62 or over if he or she was married to the worker for at least 10 years.

■ If you have young unmarried children when you retire, they may receive monthly payments until they are 18 or until they are 22 if they are full-time students. When the law provides benefits for a worker's children, illegitimate, adopted, and stepchildren are usually included.

■ If, when you die, you are survived by a spouse or dependent children, those survivors can receive Social Security benefits whether you had reached retirement age or not.

■ A widow or widower who retires can collect survivors' benefits as early as age 60.

■ A widow or widower may lose the right to receive benefits when she or he remarries.

■ If a worker dies leaving a divorced wife who was married to him for at least 10 years, she can also receive survivors' benefits at age 60 if she retires. (A divorced man cannot receive survivors' benefits based on his former wife's work record.)

■ A worker's family may receive a lump-sum payment of $255 after the worker's death.

■ A parent who has been depending on an adult child for at least half of his or her support is entitled to survivors' benefits.

■ If you suffer from a long-term disability (one that is expected to last more than a year) or a terminal illness, you can receive Social Security checks before retirement age. Payments can begin five months after the onset of the disability.

■ If you die after a long disability without ever having applied for disability benefits, your family may apply for them within three months after your death.

■ All disabling conditions must be proved medically.

■ The final decision to approve or deny disability benefits is made by the Social Security evaluating team. You cannot claim permanent disability if your condition can be substantially improved—benefits can be denied if you refuse reasonable treatment.

■ If you are denied disability benefits, you can ask for a reconsideration, and if the results of that seem incorrect to you, you may get a hearing before an administrative law judge of the Social Security Administration at no cost. If still dissatisfied, you may take your case to the federal courts.

■ If you are injured on the job, you can collect disability payments from Social Security as well as your workmen's compensation benefits.

■ Total family benefits received from both sources cannot be greater than 80 percent of your income before the disability occurred. (This means 80 percent from all sources—not just work that was covered by Social Security.)

■ You may continue to receive retirement checks if you spend time or live outside the United States, except for some restrictions if you are staying in certain Communist countries. But when you return, you will receive any back checks you missed.

■ Persons who are not U.S. citizens who have worked in the United States long enough to qualify for benefits will get benefit checks as long as they stay in the country.

■ Medicare consists of (1) a hospital insurance plan, and (2) an insurance plan for other medical expenses.

■ You can sign up for medical and hospital insurance benefits between January 1 and March 31 of any year, but premiums are increased 10 percent for every year after age 65 you wait to sign up.

■ After enrolling, you can cancel your participation in the medical insurance program, but you can reenroll only once.

■ Hospital benefits come in benefit periods. A benefit period starts when you enter the hospital and ends 60 days after medical services stop. A new benefit period can start with the next hospital stay. There is no limit to the number of benefit periods.

■ Medical insurance pays all or part of medical expenses not covered by the hospital plan. The patient must pay 20 percent of the reasonable charge plus any amount above the reasonable charge on any bill. He must also pay a set amount each year (called the annual deductible) before benefits begin.

viduals and household and farm workers, plus most state and local government employees, members of the armed forces, and clergymen.

Social Security in the 1980's   By 1980 almost all the jobs in the United States were covered by Social Security, and roughly one out of six persons were receiving monthly Social Security checks. Most Americans who were 65 and over and millions of disabled Americans under age 65 had health insurance under Medicare. In addition, millions of workers and their dependents received monthly disability checks from Social Security.

■ **Old-Age, Survivors, and Disability Insurance** When most people talk about their Social Security, they mean the benefits they receive from federal Old-Age, Survivors, and Disability Insurance (OASDI). These are monthly payments sent out to retired people, to families that have lost a wage earner, and to workers who are not able to continue working because of illness or an accident.

OASDI is financed by workers and employers. During their working years, employees and their employers together and self-employed persons alone make contributions to Social Security in the form of contributions based on their income. This money is used only to pay benefits to those who are currently eligible and to defray administrative costs. Since benefits under the program are wage related and not based on need, workers qualify for protection simply by having been employed for at least the minimum amount of time—acquiring sufficient *work credit*—and by making contributions to Social Security. Once a worker qualifies for protection, his family is also covered. The entire program is directed toward helping families as a matter of social policy.

Your Social Security card and record   All contributions made to Social Security in your name are credited to your Social Security account number, and your benefits are based on the record kept under that number. When you begin to earn money, if your employment is covered by Social Security, you should get a Social Security card, which you can easily obtain by applying to your local Social Security office and submitting your birth certificate. The number on your card identifies you for Social Security purposes throughout your lifetime.

It is a good idea to check your Social Security record every three years to be sure your earnings have been accurately reported. This is especially important if you change jobs frequently. Merely write to the Social Security Administration and request a statement of your earnings, giving your name, address, birth date, and Social Security number. Be sure to sign the request personally, as this information is private and cannot be given out without your signature. Postcards for this purpose are available at your local Social Security office. If you do not have a special postcard, address your enquiries to Social Security Administration, P.O. Box 57, Baltimore, Md. 21203.

Contributions   The amount of your contribution to Social Security is fixed by Congress as a percentage of your annual wages up to a certain maximum. Both the percentage and the maximum vary from year to year. For example, you had to pay a 6.05-percent tax on wages up to $17,700 in 1978, a 6.13-percent tax on wages up to $22,900 in 1979, a 6.13-percent tax on wages up to $25,900 in 1980, and a 6.65-percent tax on wages up to $29,700 in 1981. Of this amount 1 percent was set aside for hospital insurance under Medicare in 1978, 1.05 percent in 1979 and 1980, and 1.3 percent in 1981 through 1984. In addition, your employer had to match these amounts with equal contributions.

If you are self-employed—for instance, if you own a business or have your own professional practice—you generally must contribute about 1½ times as much to Social Security as do employees, although you still pay less for yourself than is paid for an employee by the employee and employer together. For example, a self-employed person paid a 9.3-percent tax on income up to $29,700 in 1981, but an employee paid a 6.65-percent tax on the same amount and his employer paid an additional 6.65-percent tax on it, bringing the total paid to 13.3 percent.

If you work for someone else, your employer will automatically deduct your Social Security taxes from your gross wages and send them to the Internal Revenue Service with an equal amount of his own, and your earnings will be credited to your account. If you are self-employed, you must pay your Social Security taxes when you file your income tax. In the event that you work for someone else and also earn money from self-employment, your wages count first for Social Security. If your wages in a given year amount to less than the maximum coverable income for that year, you pay the self-employment contribution only on the difference between the total amount of your wages and the maxiumum covered by Social Security.

EXAMPLE Aloysius is a college professor who during the summer months operates his own bicycle shop in a resort town. In 1981 Aloysius earned $25,000 for teaching and $5,000 from his bicycle business, giving him total earnings of $30,000 for the year. The maximum amount covered by Social Security in 1981 was $29,700. The school Aloysius worked for deducted 6.65 percent of his salary from each of his paychecks (a total of $1,662.50 for the year) and paid it with an equal amount from the school's funds to Social Security to be credited to Aloysius's account. When he sent in his federal income tax for 1981, Aloysius paid Social Security 9.3 percent of $4,700 of his bicycle shop earnings ($437.10). The remaining $300 he had earned from his shop was over the maximum covered by Social Security for that year and was not subject to contributions.

Work credit   You are fully insured for Social Security benefits if you have a record of having worked and contributed to Social Security for at least the minimum number of calendar quarters for your age group. A *calendar quarter* is one-fourth of a year, or three months. Before 1978 the general rule was that you received credit any time you earned at least $50 in a quarter. In 1978 you earned credit for a quarter for each $250 you made in wages at any time during a single year up to a maximum of four quarters a year. Even if you earned the full $1,000 during the first quarter of the year (January through March) and earned no more the rest of the year, you would be credited with four quarters for that year. The $250 figure increases from year to year. In 1981, each $310 in wages gave you one quarter of coverage. The number of quarters you must accumulate in order to qualify for Social Security benefits depends on the type of benefit you are requesting and when you were born.

For old-age benefits In order to qualify for Social Security old-age benefits, you must generally accumulate the equivalent of one calendar quarter of work credit under the plan for each year after 1950 or after the year you reached the age of 21, if that is later, up to the year you reach 61 years of age. However, you never need more than 40 quarters of credit, but you must have at least six.

EXAMPLE John was born in 1918 and his brother Glen was born in 1930. John decided to retire in 1980 when he reached 62 years of age. Since he had been 21 years old before 1950, he needed to have worked and contributed to Social Security one calendar quarter for every year that elapsed after 1950, or 29 quarters, in order to retire. (The year in which a worker retires is not counted.) But Glen was not 21 until 1951. If he wished to retire at the age of 62, in 1992, he would need one quarter of work credit for every year after 1951—the year he reached 21. Consequently, he would need 40 quarters of work credit.

For survivors' benefits If, when you die, you are survived by a spouse or dependent children, those survivors can receive Social Security benefits whether you had reached retirement age or not. For your survivors to qualify, you must have been employed and contributing to Social Security long enough for someone your age to qualify for your own old-age or disability benefits as of the year of your death. Under a special rule, your survivors may receive benefits if you die by age 28 and have worked under Social Security for at least 1½ years out of the last 3 years before you died.

For disability benefits You can qualify for disability benefits before retirement age if you have worked enough calendar quarters under Social Security before the onset of your disability. The number of quarters needed depends upon your age at the time you become disabled. If you are under the age of 24, that time is as little as six quarters in the three years before you become disabled. If you are between the ages of 24 and 30, you must have worked at least half the time between your 21st birthday and the time you became disabled. If you are more than 30 years old, you need to have worked between 20 and 40 quarters, depending on your age, with at least 20 of those quarters occurring in the 10 years before you became disabled (excluding previous periods of disability). Again, you never need more than a total of 40 quarters of work credit to qualify for benefits.

EXAMPLE After leaving college in June 1966, Ed got a job as a researcher for a major corporation. He soon developed emotional problems and found it difficult to concentrate on his work. He quit his job after 2½ years and went for more than a year without working. During the 1970's he held a number of odd jobs, but never for more than a few months at a time. The rest of the time he was not working. Finally, in 1980, when he was 35 years old, Ed had a severe emotional breakdown and his doctors believed he would be incapable of holding any kind of a job for at least a year. By this time Ed had worked a total of 2½ years (10 quarters) in the late 1960's and a total of 18 quarters during the 1970's. To be eligible for disability benefits a 35-year-old worker must have 20 quarters of work credit. But even though Ed had a total of 28 quarters of work credit, he did not qualify. He had

worked only 18 of those quarters in the last 10 years and he would have had to work at least 20 quarters in the last 10 years to qualify.

Collecting old-age benefits When you retire at age 62 or older, you will receive old-age benefits from Social Security if you are eligible. If you work for someone else, you are considered retired when you give up your job, although you may work providing you do not earn more than a certain amount of money, as discussed below. If you are self-employed, you are considered retired for Social Security purposes if you are not performing substantial services for a business. In deciding whether services are substantial, the considerations are whether you are doing highly skilled work, are planning for and managing a business, or are devoting a considerable amount of time to your work. Fewer than 15 hours a month is never considered substantial, but more than 45 hours a month usually is.

Amount of benefits Once you earn work credit for the required number of calendar quarters, you are fully insured for a benefit, and when you retire you will receive benefits based on your actual average covered income during the years you worked. But remember, your covered income is not the same as your full income. You are credited for income only up to the maximum amount of money covered by Social Security for those years. For example, if you had earned $30,000 in 1980, when the maximum was $25,900, you would have received no credit for $4,100, which was over the limit for that year. The actual amount of monthly Social Security benefits varies from person to person. The maximum monthly payment that a person retiring at 65 in 1980 could receive was $572.

Minimum benefit If you worked for very low wages all your life, Social Security provides a special minimum benefit at retirement. The amount of this minimum benefit depends on the number of years you worked and contributed to Social Security, but if you worked the minimum number of years needed to qualify for benefits and you retired in the first half of 1981 at age 65, you qualified for a benefit of at least $153.10 a month. You can figure the number of years you can count toward qualifying for the minimum benefit by adding together all your wages from 1937 to 1950 and dividing that total by 900. Any number up to 14 years count. You can add one to that for every year after 1950 that you earned at least 25 percent of the maximum wages covered by Social Security in that year. Since 1979 the special minimum benefit has been increased to keep pace with the cost of living.

Retirement age The normal retirement age is 65, but you can retire and start receiving Social Security checks as early as age 62. You can also continue working after you are 65, but if you do, and you earn more than a certain amount of money, you will not begin receiving benefits until you retire or until you reach the age of 72.

If you retire before you are 65, your benefits are permanently reduced. You may receive the same total amount over the years, but your monthly checks are smaller to cover the longer period of time you are receiving checks.

EXAMPLE Eloise, an efficiency expert, retired in 1978 at the age of 62 and received monthly Social Security checks of $386.10. Had she retired at 65 she would have received monthly checks for $482.60—an additional

$96.50 per month. However, Eloise was collecting checks for three years longer by retiring early, and if she lived to be 77 years old, she would receive roughly the same total amount of money from Social Security over the years as she would have if she had retired at 65. On the other hand, if Eloise lived to be older than 77, she would receive less money in the long run.

If you do not retire at age 65, you will get special credit toward larger benefits up to age 72. If you reach age 65 by 1981, the credit amounts to an additional 1 percent for each year you work. If you reach age 65 after 1981, the credit will amount to an additional 3 percent. So if you become 65 in 1982 and continue working for five years, when you do retire your Social Security check will be 15 percent higher than it would have been if you had retired when you were 65. In addition, your earnings during that period, if higher than in earlier years, will increase your benefits.

Working after retirement You may also choose to return to work full time after you start receiving Social Security checks. In that case, your retirement benefits may stop while you are working, but the amount will be refigured automatically when you stop working again. You will usually find that the added earnings have earned you higher benefits. If you retire before you are 65 and then return to work, you will also get special credit toward larger benefits for any months before age 65 that you work without collecting Social Security benefits.

You can work part time after you retire and continue to receive full benefits as long as your earnings from employment do not go over a certain amount. In 1981, if you are between 65 and 71, that amount is $5,500. In 1982, if you are between 65 and 69, that amount is $6,000. If your earnings exceed these amounts, $1 of benefits is withheld for every $2 you earn in wages above the exempt amount. The exempt amount is somewhat lower if you are under 65. It was $4,080 in 1981. A special rule applies to the year in which you retire. In that year, benefits are paid for any month in which you earn less than one-twelfth the exempt amount for that year, regardless of your earnings over the entire year. No amount of work affects your retirement benefits if you are 72 or older. Starting in 1982, this age will drop to 70. From those ages on, you receive Social Security checks regardless of how much you earn.

EXAMPLE Gordon, a 65-year-old secretary, retired on June 1, 1979. In September of the same year he did some typing at home for his old firm to help them out in a pinch. In that year a 65-year-old retired person could earn up to $4,500 without its affecting his Social Security benefits. In September Gordon earned $350, which was less than one-twelfth of $4,500, so it did not affect his Social Security check, even though he had earned much more than $4,500 so far that year because of his salary in January through May. In October, however, he earned $500, which was $125 more than the monthly amount allowed him in the year he retired. Consequently, part of his October benefit was withheld since he earned in excess of the amount allowed. Gordon did not work in November or December, and so his later Social Security checks that year were not affected.

In August through December of 1980 Gordon worked as a bookkeeper for his daughter, who ran a greeting card shop. He earned $6,000. Since the amount allowed him in 1980 was only $5,000, Gordon had his Social Security benefits reduced by $500 for that year. Even though he had not worked at all during the first half of the year, the amount of earnings allowed applies to the entire year. Only in the year he retired were his benefits figured month by month.

In 1981 Gordon worked most of the year and earned $18,000. Consequently, his Social Security benefits stopped because he was making $12,500 more than the $5,500 limit for that year, and after deducting $1 for every $2 of the excess, there was nothing left. However, while Gordon was working he was contributing to Social Security again, and when he stopped working his benefits would be refigured and they would probably be increased for future years.

All kinds of earnings count in figuring out whether you have enough income to affect your Social Security benefits, with some minor exceptions. Total wages or, for a self-employed person, net earnings must be counted—not just take-home pay.

Income from sources other than work—such as retirement benefits from company or personal pension plans or income from savings, inheritances, investments, or insurance—do not affect retirement benefits. Rental income from real estate does not count unless you are a real estate dealer or help in the management of a farm you rent out. Royalties from copyrights or patents that were obtained before age 65 do not count as income if they are received when you are 65 or older. Sometimes retirement payments from a partnership, sick pay, trust and annuity payments, moving or travel expenses that are paid by someone else, and payment for jury duty do not count.

Benefits for a spouse When you retire under Social Security, your husband or wife can receive his or her own (secondary) benefits in the amount of one-half of your benefits if applying after he or she reaches 65, or he or she may begin receiving reduced benefits after reaching age 62. If you are entitled to receive both primary benefits based on your own work record and secondary benefits as the spouse of a worker, you can collect whichever benefit is larger but not both. However, you will be paid primarily from your own records. If the benefit due you is larger than your own record permits, the balance will be made up from your spouse's record. Therefore, the check will be issued under your own Social Security number even though it is paid out from both your records.

EXAMPLE Stella, an advertising copywriter, worked most of her life, and when she retired at 65 in 1980, she received monthly Social Security benefits of $482.60. Stella's husband, Henry, had not worked for long periods of time because of health problems, and when he had worked he had earned low salaries. Henry was the same age as Stella, and he also applied for benefits at 65. Based on his work credits and covered earnings he was only eligible for Social Security benefits of $121.80 per month, but he was also potentially eligible for secondary benefits of $241.30 per month as Stella's husband. Since the secondary benefits due him were larger than his own primary benefits, Henry collected his own benefits plus a part of Stella's to bring him up to full secondary benefits.

The wife of a worker who is receiving old-age or disability benefits can collect secondary benefits through her husband's qualifications before she is 62 if she is caring for his or their child who is either under 18 or disabled.

To qualify for secondary benefits as a spouse, you must prove that your marriage is valid. This is usually done by presenting your marriage certificate. It is not enough to show that you lived with the worker—even for a long period of time—and that people thought you were married. Generally, you must have been married to the worker for at least one year before you can apply for secondary retirement benefits. A legitimate common-law spouse may also receive Social Security benefits.

A divorced man or woman can collect secondary benefits at age 62 or over if he or she was married to the worker for at least 10 years before the divorce. Before 1979 the marriage had to have lasted at least 20 years for the former spouse to qualify for benefits.

Benefits for children If you have young unmarried children when you retire, they are entitled to receive monthly payments until they reach the age of 18, or if they are full-time students, they can receive secondary benefits until they are 22. Benefits can also be paid for children of any age who were permanently disabled before the age of 22. A student is attending school full time if he is enrolled in a program which the school considers full time for day students and which is at least 13 weeks long or requires him to attend at least 20 hours a week. Checks continue during regular vacations of no more than four months if the student intends to return to school when the vacation ends.

Benefits continue for a college student who does not yet have a bachelor's degree until the end of the semester or quarter when he turns 22. Benefits continue for a trade or vocational school student until the end of the course or two months after the month in which he reaches the age of 22, whichever comes first.

Benefits stop when any student marries or stops attending school full time. Benefits are reduced or stopped whenever a student earns over a certain amount of money. For example, a student who earned more than $3,720 for the entire year of 1980 had his benefits reduced by $1 for every $2 of income over the limit. However, for the first year in which the student has a month in which he earns less than one-twelfth of the annual amount, he can claim benefits for nonwork months (months in which he earns less than the amount allowed and did not perform substantial services as a self-employed individual) regardless of his total earnings for the year. This exception to the rule is valid only for the first year in which nonwork months occur.

EXAMPLE Kathleen enrolled as a freshman in college in September 1978—six months after her 18th birthday. Her father had retired in June of that year. Although Kathleen had passed her 18th birthday, she was eligible to receive Social Security checks based on her father's retirement as long as she was a full-time student, and she received full benefits through the fall of 1978. Beginning in January 1979 Kathleen took a part-time job on her school campus to help pay her tuition. She earned $400 a month through the entire year, which brought her earnings for 1979 to a total of $4,800. Since that was $1,320 more than $3,480, the amount allowed for 1979, her

Social Security checks were reduced by a total of $660 for the year—$1 for every $2 over the limit.

In 1980 Kathleen still had her job, which paid her $400 a month, but she was asked to work only half her usual time during the summer months for only $200 a month. As this was the first year in which Kathleen had a month in which she earned less than the amount allowed monthly (the amount allowed for 1980 was $310 per month, or one-twelfth of $3,720), she was able to claim full benefits for the summer months as nonwork months even though her total earnings for the year were higher than the amount allowed for 1980. Consequently, her Social Security checks for the summer were not reduced. However, even though the same thing happened in 1981, she was not able to claim her summer months as nonwork months because the rule is that a student is allowed to do so only the first year in which nonwork months occur. Kathleen's benefits would stop completely after the spring 1982 semester even if she had not received her bachelor's degree by then, because she would have had her 22nd birthday during that semester.

Since a student's right to benefits is based on his parent's record, he will not receive checks if the parent loses his right to benefits. This may happen if the parent reenters the work force after having retired.

Children who qualify When the law provides benefits for a worker's children, it means all of his children. A child continues to be eligible for benefits if his parents are divorced. He can receive Social Security based on the work record of either one and does not have to be living with the parent who has established his eligibility for benefits.

If applying on his natural father's record, an illegitimate child is entitled to Social Security benefits even without being financially dependent on the father if (1) the child is entitled to inherit from the father under the law in their state, (2) the child is illegitimate only because of some technical defect in a marriage ceremony the parents went through, or (3) the child is made legitimate by some process under state law. In any case, the child can always receive benefits on the natural mother's record.

Even if the child does not meet one of these conditions, he can still receive Social Security benefits by proving that the wage-earning parent was supporting him or living with him when the parent qualified for benefits or, if the child was born after that time, that the parent supported or lived with the child after he was born. Social Security does not insist that the parent make substantial regular payments to support an illegitimate child. It is enough if the parent was contributing to the child's support in accordance with his financial condition. If the parent was, the child is as much entitled to Social Security benefits as a legitimate child.

Adopted children An adopted child is entitled to benefits if he was adopted within two years after the parent became eligible for Social Security benefits. Sometimes a child is entitled to benefits without final legal adoption if the qualified worker has lived with and supported the child, showed that he wants to adopt the child, and taken steps to secure an adoption. Taking a child into the home and caring for him on a temporary basis or accepting support for the child from another source will generally prevent a court from treating the relationship as an adoption.

Stepchildren   A stepchild is entitled to receive benefits if the stepparent married the child's natural mother or father at least one year before applying for benefits for the child based on the stepparent's own retirement. A child can be considered a stepchild even if the marriage of his natural parent and stepparent was found to be legally invalid after they went through a wedding ceremony.

Collecting survivors' benefits   Survivors' benefits are payments made to members of a worker's family when the worker dies. These benefits can help ease the financial strain caused by loss of the worker's income, allowing the family to stay together and the children to finish their education. It also insures lifetime support for children who were disabled before they were 22 years old and who will never be able to work.

Benefits for a spouse   Benefits can go to a surviving spouse when the worker dies. A widow or widower who retires can generally begin collecting survivors' benefits as early as age 60 but ordinarily loses the right to receive those benefits if he or she remarried before age 60. A widow or widower who remarries after age 60 is able to receive benefits without reduction but may be entitled to a higher benefit based on the new spouse's record.

If a worker dies leaving a divorced wife who was married to him for at least 10 years, she can also receive survivors' benefits at age 60 if she retires. (If the worker had remarried, his new wife would also receive benefits.) However, a divorced wife always loses the right to receive these benefits if she remarries. A divorced man cannot receive survivors' benefits based on his former wife's work record.

A surviving widow, widower, or divorced woman (but not a divorced man) can receive Social Security checks on the deceased worker's record as early as age 50 if he or she becomes disabled. A surviving widow, widower, or divorced woman (but not a divorced man) who is taking care of a deceased worker's child who is receiving Social Security can qualify for his or her own benefits before age 60. These survivors' benefits are reduced if the person works and earns above a certain amount each year. The amount was $4,080 in 1981 but it increases from year to year.

EXAMPLE   Ken and Nancy were divorced after 15 years of marriage, and their son, Burt, went to live with Nancy. A year later Ken died. Nancy had no right to receive survivors' benefits based on Ken's work record until she reached 60 years of age. However, she was taking care of Burt, who was only 12 years old and who was receiving survivors' benefits based on his father's work credits. This entitled Nancy to receive her own secondary benefits until Burt reached the age of 18 (or 22 if he were a full-time student). However, Nancy's benefits were reduced if she earned more than the amount allowed in any year.

On the other hand, if Nancy had died and Ken had lived and taken care of Burt, Ken would not have been eligible for benefits in his own name either while he was caring for Burt or after he was 60 years old. The provision applies only to a divorced *woman.*

When Social Security was set up in the 1930's, its provisions were based upon the economic roles of males and females then prevailing. In recent years these roles have changed dramatically and many Social Security provisions have been changed to extend benefits equally to both men and women. The provision prohibiting the payment of survivors' benefits to divorced men was one of the few discriminatory provisions still in effect in 1980, but like all Social Security benefits it is subject to change at any time.

Benefits for children   Both mothers and fathers earn protection for their children by working and contributing to Social Security. If a wage earner dies, all of his or her unmarried children are entitled to receive benefits until they are 18, or until they are 22 if they are full-time students. This includes posthumous children—those whose fathers died before their birth—and any illegitimate children, adopted children, stepchildren, or dependent grandchildren. Generally, if a child would be eligible for secondary benefits when his worker-parent (or supporting grandparent) retired, he would be eligible for survivors' benefits. In addition, if the deceased worker was in the process of adopting a child when he died, that child will be entitled to benefits if the surviving spouse completes the adoption within two years of the worker's death. A stepchild may receive benefits if his stepparent married his natural parent at least nine months before the stepparent died.

If the child of a deceased wage earner becomes permanently disabled before age 22, he can continue to receive survivors' benefits at any age unless he becomes self-supporting or marries. An exception to this rule provides that a surviving son or daughter who becomes disabled before age 22 and who marries another person who is also entitled to receive secondary benefits, whether under the old-age or the survivors' plan, can continue to draw benefits. This exception was meant to relieve the special hardship for these people.

EXAMPLE   John died when he was 55 years old, after having worked under Social Security all his adult life. He was survived by four unmarried children—John, Jr., who was 21 years old; Jane, who was 20; and Jeff and Jim, who were 19-year-old twins. John, Jr., and Jane, although not married, were working and received no survivors' benefits, but the twins were going to school full time and so received benefits as survivors of their father. A few months before his 22nd birthday, John, Jr., was stricken with a disease that paralyzed him completely and made him unfit for any type of work. He began receiving Social Security benefits based on his deceased father's work credits. A few months later, the other three children were involved in a freak automobile accident. Jane was totally blinded by broken glass from the windshield, the twins were crippled for life, and none of them were able to work or go to school. Consequently, these three children also began collecting benefits on their father's record.

A number of years later John, Jr., sufficiently recovered from his paralysis to be able to work. He got a job and lost his Social Security survivors' benefits but began to earn work credits for himself once again. At about the same time, Jeff married a woman who had also become physically disabled at a young age after her parents' death. Both Jeff and his wife continued to receive their survivors' benefits. A year later Jim married a young woman who was not receiving Social Security benefits and lost his own benefits. Jane remained single until she was 60 years old; then she met and married a man of 66, who was collecting old-age benefits. Jane lost the secondary benefits coming to her on her father's work record but began receiving a wife's benefits based on her retired husband's record.

Grandchildren Sometimes a grandchild can receive Social Security benefits as if he were the worker's child. This is possible when the child's parents are disabled or dead, the working grandparent has been supporting him, and the child was living with the grandparent when he or she died.

Benefits for parents In some cases a parent who has depended on an adult child to provide at least half of his support is entitled to Social Security survivors' benefits after the child's death. A person claiming benefits must be an actual parent, someone who would inherit the child's property if the child left no will. No matter how close the relationship, someone who was "like a mother" does not qualify. To determine whether the child was supporting the parent, Social Security will count cash and purchases made for the parent each year. If the child has paid for some special service or purchase, however—such as having a new water well drilled—the contribution will not all count for one year but will be spread over the years that the item can be expected to be useful. If the parent did not receive support for a substantial period of time before the child's death, or if the parent remarried after the child's death, benefits are not paid. However, if support stopped because the worker was disabled, the one-half support requirement met at the time could qualify the parent for benefits if the child later dies.

Lump-sum payment In addition to monthly checks, the worker's family may receive a lump-sum payment of $255 after the worker's death. This payment goes to the worker's widow or widower if either one was living with the worker at the time of death. Otherwise, it can be used to help pay the worker's burial expenses.

Collecting disability benefits If you become unable to work or to engage in gainful employment and expect to be disabled for at least 12 months or if you are likely to die from your condition, you can receive Social Security checks before retirement age if you have worked long enough under Social Security. If you have dependents, they will probably receive secondary benefits if they would be eligible for them if you retired or died.

Social Security payments can begin five calendar months after the onset of the disability. If you fail to apply for benefits when you are eligible, you can sometimes collect back payments, but not for more than 12 months. Even if you recover from a disability that lasted for more than 12 months, you can apply for back benefits within 14 months of your recovery. If you die after a long period of disability without ever having applied for Social Security, your family may apply for your benefits within three months of your death. Your family would then also be eligible for survivors' benefits effective the month you died.

What constitutes a disability? A disability is any physical or mental condition that prevents you from doing substantial gainful work. The mere existence of an impairment—even a permanent injury like the loss of an arm or a leg—does not necessarily make you unemployable. The question is whether or not you are capable of working to earn a living.

Some examples of disabilities that may be qualifying are brain damage; heart disease; kidney failure; severe arthritis; uncontrolled cancer; digestive diseases resulting in malnutrition, weakness, and anemia; total inability to speak; blindness; the inability to use two or more limbs; and serious mental illness. Pain and discomfort alone can be bad enough to be disabling, and emotional and psychological problems sometimes prevent gainful employment.

A person is considered disabled by blindness if his vision is no better than 20/200 in the better eye while using glasses or if his field of vision is reduced to 20 degrees or less. Like other disabled people, blind workers are entitled to benefits if they are unable to do substantial gainful work. Benefits stop if the blind person is able to resume a substantial amount of work, but they start up again without his filing a new application when he stops working.

A special rule applies to older workers who lose their sight. Blind people between the ages of 55 and 65 are entitled to monthly checks if they cannot do the same kind of work they did before age 55 or before they were blinded. This allows an older person to qualify for benefits while working on a job that is less demanding than previously. But his or her earnings must not exceed a certain maximum amount. The amount was $5,500 per year in 1981.

Evaluating a disability Whatever its character, a disabling condition must be proved medically. This means that a doctor must be able to discover the ailment, or it must be discoverable in laboratory tests. If you claim disability payments, you must submit medical records of your doctor's diagnosis or laboratory reports from a hospital, clinic, or other institution that has been treating you. These records and the application for benefits will be evaluated by a team of specialists, including a doctor. The physician or institution that has been treating you will be asked to give facts concerning your overall health, what your disability is, how it was discovered or diagnosed, how severe it is, how it has been treated, and whether it will improve. If the information supplied is not sufficient, Social Security can require you to undergo further tests at government expense before making a final decision on the application.

The final decision to approve or deny disability benefits will be made by the members of the Social Security evaluating team, who will apply Social Security regulations to the medical facts given to them. They will not determine whether or not you are ill or well but only whether your condition will keep you from working for a year or more. Social Security has its own regulations to follow in making this determination, and they are not necesssarily the same as standards used by other government agencies or by private insurance companies. However, Social Security may use the results of examinations conducted by other agencies or their decisions as evidence in a case. But even though your doctor may tell you that you are disabled, you still may not meet Social Security requirements.

The evaluating team will consider your medical records; the opinions of your examining physicians; your own testimony and testimony from your family and others concerning your pain and your inability to do normal things; and your education, age, and work history. All of these factors will be weighed together to establish exactly what your condition is. You will have to show that your condition prevents you from continuing in your job. Then the evaluating team will have to determine that your condition also prevents you from engaging in any other kind of employment. You will not be considered disabled simply because you cannot find work locally or because you find that employers are reluctant to hire you because you are handicapped. On the other hand, the Social Security Administration commission does not have to find that there are job openings available for you.

You cannot claim to be permanently disabled if your condition can be substantially improved. Social Security will not require you to undergo experimental, risky, and painful treatment, but it can deny you benefits if you refuse to undergo reasonable treatment.

You may ask to have your case reconsidered if you are denied disability benefits. If you believe that the results of the reconsideration are not correct, you may then request a hearing before an administrative law judge of the Social Security Administration at no charge to you—unless you elect to hire an attorney to help you. If you are still dissatisfied with the decision, you may ask for a review by the Appeals Council of the Social Security Administration and—finally—take your case to the federal courts.

Rehabilitation Disabled persons—sometimes even if they do not qualify for disability benefits—are offered a wide range of services designed to retrain and help them to reenter the job market. Rehabilitation services include medical examinations, surgery, and hospitalization; artificial limbs, braces, hearing aids, and eyeglasses; counseling and guidance; job training in a vocational school or college; and job placement. If you are claiming disability, you will not get more favorable action on your application if you accept rehabilitation services while your case is being considered, but benefits can later be stopped if you refuse offers to help you to again become self-supporting.

Return to work If you have a medical condition that clears up completely, you are no longer considered disabled, but you are entitled to receive disability benefits for three months after your recovery to help you adjust to being self-sufficient. If you recover from a disability only partially but are able to resume working, you are also no longer considered disabled and your monthly checks will stop. You are allowed a *trial work period* so that you will not be afraid to try working and risk losing your benefits if you discover that you were not sufficiently recovered. (If your disability clears up completely you are not entitled to a trial work period.) During a trial work period you can take a job and work for nine months, testing your ability to handle the work while receiving full benefits without interruption. The trial work period will allow you to be sure you are able to support yourself before it is decided whether or not you are again employable. At the end of nine months, if it is decided that you are able to do substantial gainful work, you will continue to receive benefits for two months after the month in which the decision is made.

EXAMPLE Agnes, a fashion designer, suffered from a crippling disease that left her with only minimal use of her legs and right arm, and there was no hope of improvement. Totally unable to work, she began collecting disability benefits. Meanwhile she undertook a strenuous program of physical therapy, and a year later she was able to walk with difficulty and regained some use of her arm. Although she was still not able to return to her former line of work, which required free use of her right arm, Agnes took advantage of the trial work period and accepted a job as a receptionist, which required only that she greet people, use the telephone, and do light paperwork. Determined to make a go of it, Agnes stuck out the job for the nine-month period, but at the end of that time her doctors found that even that job was too taxing for her and that her health was deteriorating as a consequence of her work. Throughout the nine-month period, Agnes had been receiving her regular disability checks as well as her salary. When she left the job, she continued to receive her disability checks without interruption.

The trial work period is allowed only for disabled workers and for persons who were disabled in childhood. It is not allowed for disabled widows and widowers, who are discussed later in this article.

To determine whether the job you start is substantial gainful employment, Social Security will look at the skills and experience necessary for your work, your responsibilities in the job, and your hours of labor, productivity, and pay. If you can earn more than a certain maximum amount ($300 a month in 1981), you are ordinarily doing substantial gainful work. If you are self-employed, more attention is given to your skills, experience, hours, responsibility, and productivity and less to your actual earnings, because your income may be affected by economic conditions, help from unpaid family members, and other factors that have nothing to do with your disability. If you are employed for low wages in a special workshop for the handicapped, you are usually not considered to be doing substantial gainful work.

If you recover and begin doing substantial gainful work, you can again start receiving benefits if the disabling condition returns within five years. You do not have to wait five months for monthly payments to begin as you did the first time. Since the amount of disability benefits is about the same as full retirement benefits, if you have taken reduced retirement benefits before age 65, you can switch to higher disability benefits if you later suffer a disabling condition.

Workmen's compensation and disability benefits If you are hurt on the job, you will generally receive WORKMEN'S COMPENSATION benefits, but this does not keep you from collecting disability payments from Social Security as well. The total family benefits received from both sources, however, cannot be greater than 80 percent of your income before the disability occurred. This is 80 percent of the average monthly income from all sources, not just work that was covered by Social Security. If the combination of disability payments and workmen's compensation exceeds the 80-percent limitation, the Social Security check is decreased accordingly. The adjustment is never so large as to result in total Social Security and workmen's compensation benefits that are less than the amount your family would have received from Social Security alone.

Disabled dependents If you are disabled but have not worked under Social Security long enough to qualify for benefits on your own record, you may still be entitled to disability benefits if you are a dependent of a retired, disabled, or deceased worker. For example, if you are a disabled widow or widower of at least 50 years of age, you may qualify for monthly checks if your disability occurred before your spouse's death, within seven years after it, or within seven years after you stop receiving benefits because of caring for a child.

EXAMPLE Soon after Francis married Therese, he was ○—＊ stricken with paralysis and unable to work. Therese worked and supported Francis until she died at 55 years of age, at which time she was fully insured under Social Security. Francis was not yet 60 years old—the age at which he could normally receive survivors' benefits based on Therese's work record, but since he was over 50 and had become disabled before his wife's death, he was entitled to disability benefits.

EXAMPLE Joan became disabled six years after her retired ○—＊ husband's death—at the age of 58—and began receiving disability benefits based on her husband's work record. But her 58-year-old friend Burt, who became disabled eight years after his wife's death, could not receive disability benefits based on his wife's record, because the seven-year limit had expired.

EXAMPLE When he was in his early fifties Alec developed a ○—＊ severe heart condition that kept him from working. He began collecting disability benefits based on his own work record and died of a massive heart attack two years later. He was survived by his 48-year-old wife, Margaret, and their 16-year-old son, Kirk. Margaret supported Kirk until he was 18 and received survivors' benefits during that time. Kirk got married at 19 and Margaret was no longer able to receive survivors' benefits until she reached 60 years of age. But six years after Kirk's marriage Margaret developed a severe case of anemia and was unable to work. She did not have enough work credit of her own under Social Security to qualify for disability benefits, and her husband had died more than seven years before and she was not yet 60 years of age, so she did not qualify for benefits on that score. But it had been less than seven years since she had last received benefits for taking care of Kirk, so she qualified for benefits on her husband's record for that reason.

You can receive benefits at any age if you were disabled before you were 22 years old and are the son or daughter of a worker who has earned old-age, survivors', or disability benefits. In this case, you can receive Social Security payments as soon as your parent qualifies, without the five-month waiting period.

Receiving OASDI checks Once your application for any type of OASDI (Old-Age, Survivors, and Disability Insurance) benefits has been processed and your period of eligibility has begun, you will receive monthly benefit checks. You may receive the checks directly or have them deposited in a bank account. A person who is convicted of spying, sabotage, or treason against the United States may—in addition to other penalties—lose his benefits.

U.S. citizens abroad Many citizens who are collecting Social Security benefits—especially those who are retired—like to travel abroad or even live in a foreign country where the cost of living is low. Ordinarily this does not keep you from receiving Social Security benefit checks.

If you are a U.S. citizen who is due Social Security benefits and you are living in the United States but plan to be out of the country for up to three months, you can arrange for your checks to be kept for you in the United States. "Out of the country" means out of the 50 states, the District of Columbia, Puerto Rico, the U.S. Virgin Islands, Guam, and American Samoa.

If you expect to spend more than three months out of the country, you can have your Social Security checks mailed to your foreign address. It is a good idea, if you are going abroad, to find out about the tax laws from the foreign country's embassy in Washington, D.C. Although Social Security benefits are not taxed in the United States, they often are in foreign countries.

If you are staying in a foreign country for an extended period of time, remember that as long as you stay abroad, the Social Security Administration requires answers on a questionnaire once each year. If this form is not filled out and returned, your checks might stop. Lost or destroyed checks can be replaced, but there may be even more delay than if you were living in the United States.

No one can receive Social Security checks while staying in certain Communist countries. The list of countries may change from time to time, but you can easily find out from your local Social Security office which countries are included. When you leave the countries in question, you can begin receiving your Social Security checks again, and you can also get any back checks you may have missed.

Aliens Persons who are not U.S. citizens but who have worked in the United States long enough to qualify for Social Security benefits will receive benefit checks as long as they remain in the country. If they leave the country, they may or may not receive benefit checks, depending upon what country they are citizens of or what country they are staying in.

The United States has a reciprocal agreement with a number of other countries concerning the payment of Social Security benefits. The United States pays Social Security benefits to eligible citizens of those countries even when they are not living in the United States; in return, those countries pay U.S. citizens any benefits they have earned under that country's social security program even if they have returned to the United States. An up-to-date list of these countries is always available at your local Social Security office.

EXAMPLE Eric, a U.S. citizen, went to work in West Ger-○—＊ many. He worked there long enough to qualify for the West German equivalent of Social Security retirement benefits and then returned home to live. West Germany paid him the benefits he earned because it is one of the countries involved in a reciprocal agreement. Elsa, a West German, moved to the United States and worked long enough to receive U.S. Social Security retirement payments; then she retired and returned to Germany. The United States paid her benefits even though she was not a U.S. citizen and had left the country.

As a rule, a person who is not a citizen of the United States or of one of the countries involved in a reciprocal agreement cannot continue to receive Social Security checks after he has been out of this country for six months. (Again, "out of this country" means out of the 50 states, the District of Columbia, Puerto Rico, the U.S. Virgin Islands, Guam, or American Samoa.) The six months will run out even if the person has a reentry permit and plans to come back to a permanent home in the United States. Once the checks stop, they cannot be started again until the person has been back in the United States for at least a month.

There are some exceptions to the general rule that a person who is not a citizen of the United States or of one of the countries involved in a reciprocal agreement cannot collect benefits for more than six months while absent from the United States. Such a person can still collect benefits after six months abroad (1) if he was eligible for Social Security benefits by December 1956; (2) if he is on active duty with the U.S. armed forces; (3) if the worker on whose record the Social Security benefits are paid died in the U.S. military service; (4) if the worker on whose record the benefits are paid died as a result of a service-connected disability and was not dishonorably discharged; (5) if the worker on whose record benefits are paid lived in the United States for at least 10 years or worked under Social Security for at least 10 years (or 40 calendar quarters); or (6) if he worked for a railroad company under Social Security coverage.

Since June 1968 citizens of certain countries have not been allowed to use the 10 years of residence or 40 quarters of coverage to qualify for benefits after an absence from the United States of more than six months. Those countries have laws that restrict the right of U.S. citizens to receive payments there, so the United States will not allow their citizens to receive U.S. benefits in these countries in every case. Your local Social Security office can always tell you which countries are currently on this list.

No one can receive Social Security benefits while staying in certain Communist countries. If a person who is not a U.S. citizen stays in one of those countries, he loses his benefits for that period. When he leaves that country he can again begin to receive benefits, but he can never recover back checks he missed, as U.S. citizens can.

An alien who is deported from the United States loses his right to collect Social Security benefits under some circumstances until he is able to regain lawful admittance to the United States for permanent residence. A deported alien's dependents do not necessarily lose their rights to secondary benefits based on his work record. They can receive checks if they are U.S. citizens or, if they are not U.S. citizens, they can receive checks for any month when they are within this country for the entire month.

■ **Railroad Retirement Act**   Since 1937 the Railroad Retirement Act has provided a special system of annuities for railroad workers. Like OASDI, the system pays retirement, survivors', and disability benefits. Workers who are eligible for retirement or disability benefits under the Railroad Retirement Act are also eligible for Medicare.

■ **Medicare**   Medicare is a two-part system of health insurance. One part is a hospital insurance plan, and the other part is an insurance plan for other medical expenses.

Medicare hospital insurance is financed by the contributions made to Social Security by employees, their employers, and self-employed people. Most people who are at least 65 years old are eligible for Medicare hospital insurance even if they are not actually retired. If you are 65 but have not worked long enough to be eligible, you may enroll in the hospital insurance plan by paying a monthly premium. The cost of the premium in the 12-month period ending

June 30, 1982, was $89 a month. Even if you are not 65, you are eligible for hospital insurance if you have been entitled to disability benefits for 24 consecutive months or more. Finally, you, your spouse, or your dependent children may be entitled to hospital insurance at any age if in need of kidney dialysis or a kidney transplant whether you are collecting any other benefits or not.

The medical insurance part of Medicare is financed by monthly insurance premiums paid by people who sign up for coverage, along with money contributed by the federal government. Anyone who is at least 65 years old or who is otherwise eligible for hospital insurance can get medical insurance. Everyone who gets medical insurance must pay a monthly premium for it. The monthly premium varies from year to year. For the 12-month period ending June 30, 1982, it was $11. The amount paid by individuals can be raised to cover increasing costs, but federal law limits increases to a percentage no greater than the percentage increase in OASDI cash benefits the year before.

You can sign up for medical and hospital insurance benefits during the three months before or after your birthday or between January 1 and March 31 of any year, but generally premiums are increased by 10 percent for every year after age 65 you wait to sign up. After enrolling, you can cancel your participation in the medical insurance program, but you can reenroll only once, and your premiums will be higher. If you pay for hospital insurance, you cannot cancel your medical insurance without losing both benefits. However, you can cancel your hospital insurance without losing your medical insurance.

Processing claims   The federal government has private insurance companies process Medicare claims. The government supervises the quality of medical care delivered by requiring every person or institution providing services to meet all state and local licensing laws. Federal law requires every institution participating in Medicare to treat patients regardless of race, color, or national origin.

Certain persons and organizations have to meet special standards to receive Medicare payments for their services. These include hospitals, skilled nursing homes, medical laboratories and X-ray services, ambulance companies, chiropractors, speech and physical therapists, and facilities that provide kidney dialysis or transplant services. Medicare generally will not pay for services provided by organizations that are not approved.

Hospital insurance   The purpose of Medicare hospital insurance is to help a patient pay the expenses he incurs while confined in a hospital. Medicare payments are usually made only for services in the 50 states, the District of Columbia, Puerto Rico, Guam, the U.S. Virgin Islands, and American Samoa. However, in some cases Medicare also covers treatment in foreign countries. For example, if you live in the United States and a qualified Canadian or Mexican hospital is closer to your home than the nearest U.S. hospital that can provide the care you require, Medicare hospital insurance will help you pay for the covered services you receive in that Canadian or Mexican hospital.

Benefit periods   Benefits paid under hospital insurance are provided for *benefit periods*. A benefit period starts when the patient enters the hospital and ends 60 days after medical services stop. A new benefit period can start with the next hospital stay; there is no limit to the number of benefit periods a person can have. In any benefit period, Medicare hospital insurance pays for all covered services during the first 60 days except for an initial deductible amount, which must be paid in full by the patient. In 1981 the deductible amount was $204. Then it pays for all covered services above a certain amount ($51 a day in 1981) for the next 30 days. A lifetime total of 60 reserve days can also be used whenever necessary for additional hospital stays. Each reserve day you use in any benefit period permanently reduces the total number of reserve days you have left. For each of the reserve days you use, Medicare hospital insurance pays for all the covered services except for a certain amount ($102 a day in 1981).

EXAMPLE Agnes, who was fully insured under Medicare, 0➞✷ had a severe accident early in 1979. She was brought to the hospital where she lay in a coma for months; then she began to improve and was slowly nursed back to health. She was confined to the hospital for a total of 140 days. Medicare paid most of her hospital expenses. She had to pay only the deductible amount for the first 60 days she spent in the hospital, $40 a day for the next 30 days, and $80 a day for the remaining 50 days. The last 50 days were from her reserve days.

In late 1981 Agnes was stricken with cancer and was hospitalized once again. This, of course, constituted a different benefit period. She was released after 110 days. Again Medicare paid all but the deductible amount for her hospital expenses in the first 60 days of her new confinement. Agnes paid $51 a day for the next 30 days, and $102 a day for the following 10 days. But this ended her reserve days. She was due a lifetime total of 60 reserve days and had used 50 of them during her earlier confinement and 10 during the latter. Consequently, she had to pay all her expenses for the final 10 days in the hospital because none of this time was covered by Medicare. If Agnes were hospitalized a third time, she would be covered as before for the first 90 days—as it would be in a new benefit period—but she would not receive any more reserve days as long as she lived.

Medicare also pays for the first 20 days of care in a skilled nursing home and for expenses above so much a day ($25.50 in 1981) for the next 80 days when such care is necessary. Furthermore, payment may be made for up to 100 home health visits provided by a home health agency for up to 12 months after the patient's discharge from a hospital or nursing home.

Extent of coverage Any reasonable and medically necessary treatment given in a hospital or skilled nursing home is covered by hospital insurance. This includes the cost of a semiprivate room with two to four beds, meals, drugs and supplies ordinarily furnished to inpatients, regular nursing services, and the cost of special care, such as intensive care for a patient who has had a heart attack. It also includes services provided by a home health agency, such as part-time nurses or health aides, physical therapy, occupational therapy, medical social services, and certain medical equipment and supplies.

Hospital insurance does not pay for extra, unnecessary treatment, doctor bills, private nurses, homemaker services, meals delivered to the patient's home, or custodial care—such as help with bathing, dressing, or walking—that can be provided by nonprofessionals or for such items of convenience as a telephone or television set in the hospital room. Furthermore, it does not pay for the first three pints of blood needed in one benefit period, but the blood does not have to be paid for if it is replaced by a donor or through a blood plan.

Medical insurance   Medical insurance generally pays some of the medical expenses not covered by the hospital plan. Bills are paid directly to the doctor, if he consents; otherwise, money is sent to the patient to pay them.

Extent of coverage Medical insurance helps pay for physicians' services, whether given in a hospital, office, or home; diagnosis or treatment in an emergency room or clinic; some ambulance services; chiropractic treatment and physical or speech therapy; and up to 100 home health agency visits each calendar year under certain conditions. The 100 home health visits are in addition to the 100 visits paid for by hospital insurance following a period of confinement in a hospital. It also pays for such diagnostic and treatment services as X-rays and radiation therapy; surgical dressings, casts, splints, and braces; artificial limbs or eyes; certain colostomy supplies; and equipment that must be rented or purchased for use at home, such as a wheelchair or oxygen tank. However, it does not make any payments for routine physical checkups, drugs and medicines, or such items as eyeglasses, hearing aids, dentures, and orthopedic shoes.

Medicare medical insurance pays only a certain amount toward covered medical treatment, generally 80 percent of what is considered to be a reasonable charge for each kind of service. The first $60 of medical expenses is an annual deductible—the amount an individual must pay each year before Medicare medical payments begin.

The reasonable charge for each kind of treatment is determined by the insurance organizations that handle Medicare claims for the federal government. They are based on what doctors and suppliers customarily charge in that part of the country. These amounts are updated every year, but there is no guarantee that a given doctor will not charge more. The patient must pay the remaining 20 percent of the reasonable charge plus any amount above the reasonable charge on every bill, in addition to the first $60 of expenses each year.

There are exceptions to the general rule that medical insurance pays 80 percent of the reasonable charges above $60. For a hospital patient, Medicare pays the entire cost of a radiologist or pathologist, even before the annual deductible amount is reached. After the annual deductible, it pays the entire cost of home health services. Medicare payments for an independent physical therapist are limited to $80 a year, and for psychiatric treatment by a doctor outside a hospital they are limited to $250 a year.

How payments are made Medical insurance payments can be made in one of two ways. The money can be sent directly to the doctor or supplier, or payment can be made to the person receiving care. In either case, a notice is sent to the patient after the doctor or supplier files his medical insurance claim. The notice lists the medical services supplied, explains which services are covered by Medicare and have been approved, how much is credited toward the annual deductible, and how much Medicare has paid. If you find anything on the report that is questionable, you should report it to the insurance company handling the claim or to Social Security. If you disagree with the decision on the claim, you can ask the insurance company to review it. If you are still not satisfied, you can get a formal hearing on claims that, if paid, would total at least $100. All the claims submitted during the six-month period allowed to begin appeals can be combined in order to reach the $100 minimum. Cases that involve $1,000 or more can eventually be appealed to a federal court.

Waiver of beneficiary liability Medicare law includes a special provision that relieves individuals of the responsibility of paying some charges that turn out not to be covered by the insurance. This provision is called a *waiver of beneficiary liability.* It says that any physician or supplier of medical services who turns in a claim for what was later determined to be only custodial care or treatment that was not reasonable and necessary cannot collect from the patient after Medicare disallows the claim if the patient could not have been expected to know that the services were not covered by Medicare. For example, this sometimes happens if a patient is placed in a hospital when all he really needed was someone to help him with bathing, eating, or walking in his home. The waiver provision generally applies to hospital insurance. It does not apply to medical insurance unless arrangements were made for Medicare payments to be sent directly to the doctor or other person who furnished services.

sodomy   The crime of unnatural copulation. From early times, sodomy has been referred to in statutes and court cases as "the crime against nature," by a man with a man, by a man with an animal (bestiality), or, in an unnatural manner, by a man with a woman. In some states sodomy between consenting adults is no longer illegal.

Soldiers' and Sailors' Civil Relief Act   A
federal law designed to insure that persons in the military service are fully informed of any civil legal proceedings against them and that they be given adequate time and opportunity to appear at the proceedings and protect their rights. See ARMED SERVICES.

sole proprietorship   A business owned by one
person. It is one of the three basic forms of business, which also include PARTNERSHIPS and CORPORATIONS. A sole proprietorship is completely owned and run by the proprietor, although he may hire employees to help him or even to run the business for him. The business itself does not pay income taxes, but the owner pays personal income taxes on any profits he derives from the business.

A great many SMALL BUSINESSES are operated as sole proprietorships because they are so simple to start.

EXAMPLE Adam wants to open a bookstore. He applies for a
O——✳ bank loan of $10,000, and when he receives the money he leases a store; installs shelves, counters, and equipment; purchases inventory; and opens his doors to customers.

The legal consequences of operating a sole proprietorship are not simple, however. The owner has the right to make all his business decisions, but he is personally responsible for all the debts of the business.

EXAMPLE Adam is responsible for paying back his bank
O——✳ loan, paying rent on his bookstore, and paying for the inventory and alterations in the store. He must pay these debts whether the business makes money or not. Even if he goes out of business, he is still responsible for them. Whatever he owns, including his home and personal property, can be sold to satisfy the debts of the business. If a customer trips over a carton of books in the store, that customer can sue Adam for the injury.

solicitation   Asking; enticing; urgently requesting. Solicitation of another to commit a crime, such as by a prostitute, is itself a crime.

solicitor   1 Chief law officer of a city, town, or other governmental body or department.   2 A type of lawyer in England. Formerly, a solicitor was a lawyer who was admitted to practice law in a court of EQUITY, and some states in the United States adopted this use of the term to distinguish equity lawyers from the lawyers who practiced in the COMMON LAW courts, who were called barristers in England and counsellors in this country. Since the common-law courts and equity courts have been generally merged in the United States, the distinction is no longer made. In England today, solicitors are still distinguished from barristers, but the major difference is that barristers argue cases in courts and solicitors conduct legal business and give advice out of court, although they are permitted to represent clients in some minor courts.

Solicitor General   An officer of the U.S. Department of Justice, second in rank and authority to the U.S. Attorney General. His chief function is to represent the United States in the Supreme Court and the Court of Claims in all cases in which the federal government is involved. He must also discharge the duties of the Attorney General when the Attorney General is absent or disabled or when the office is vacant.

solvency   The ability to pay debts as they become due in the ordinary course of business; the condition of having property of sufficient value to discharge all of one's debts; the opposite of INSOLVENCY.

sound   1 Have reference to or aim at. A lawsuit is said to *sound in damages* when it is brought only for damages, and not to recover a specific item of property.   2 As an adjective, whole, in good condition, marketable, or free from disease; free from error; free from danger to life, safety, and welfare.

Sound judicial discretion is discretion exercised in full and fair consideration of the facts presented to the judge in the proper mode of procedure.

Sound mind means the normal condition of the human mind, in which its faculties of perception and judgment are developed and unimpaired by insanity.

Regarding the execution of a WILL, *a sound and disposing mind and memory* means the testator knows and understands that he is making his will.

In INSURANCE law, *sound health* means the applicant has no disease or ailment that affects his general health.

sovereign immunity

The principle that the federal and state governments cannot be sued without their consent. Based on the idea that the king can do no wrong, this rule came into the American legal system from English common law. The 11th Amendment to the U.S. Constitution as well as other federal and state laws adopted and preserved this common-law doctrine. Sovereign immunity, also known as governmental immunity, can be waived only by the enactment of a state or federal statute.

The use of sovereign immunity is declining at all levels of government. Every state has enacted statutes waiving sovereign immunity in certain cases. Under the Federal Torts Claims Act, TORT actions (damage suits) can be brought against the United States for personal injuries, death, and property damage or loss resulting from the negligent conduct of a government employee acting within the scope of his employment. On the other hand, the principle of sovereign immunity still applies to intentional torts, such as assault, battery, fraud, libel, and slander. Immunity also covers acts or omissions by a government agency or employee exercising a discretionary function or duty at the planning or policy-making level, as opposed to the operational, or lower, levels of government.

sovereignty

Supreme or absolute power; the source of authority; a political unit that is independent of outside control. A sovereign government is a political authority that makes and applies laws, imposes and collects taxes, makes war and peace, forms alliances and negotiates treaties, and regulates commerce with other sovereignties.

special appearance

Coming into court and submitting to the court's JURISDICTION (authority) for some specific purpose only, not for all of the purposes of the lawsuit being heard. A special appearance is usually entered to test whether the service of PROCESS (for example, a summons) was properly made (according to the rules of civil procedure) or whether the court has jurisdiction to decide the case.

EXAMPLE Jack, a Minnesota resident, ordered a $13,000 sable coat from the Christmas catalog of Max, a Maine furrier. When the coat arrived, it was not what it was advertised to be but a poor imitation. Jack returned the coat to Max, who refused to accept delivery. Max was subsequently served with a summons and complaint notifying him that Jack was suing him for breach of contract in a Minnesota court. Jack claimed that since Max sent his catalog through the Minnesota mail, Max was doing business there. The Minnesota court would therefore have jurisdiction over him. Max agreed to make a special appearance in the Minnesota court to challenge the jurisdiction of the court to hear a lawsuit against him, claiming that his use of the mails in the state did not mean he was doing business there. Max's appearance in the court did not give the court the right to decide the dispute between Jack and Max, because the appearance was specifically intended to settle only whether the court would have the right to exert its power over Max.

special assessment

A real estate tax proportionately imposed on homeowners and landowners to pay for such improvements as sidewalks and sewer connections, which will benefit those who pay the tax. Each pays according to the relative value of the improvement for his property. A homeowner might pay less than a business, for example, if the business profits more from the improvement.

specialty

A CONTRACT under SEAL. A *specialty debt* is a debt that is acknowledged to be due by a deed or a document under seal.

special warranty deed

A transfer or sale of real estate by a DEED containing a special clause in which the grantor (original owner) assures the grantee (new owner) that neither he nor his heirs will do anything to interfere with the grantee's rights to the property. In the clause the grantor promises that he and his heirs will "warrant and forever defend" the right of the grantee and his heirs to own the property against all claims to the property made "by, through, or under" the grantor or his heirs, or against any encumbrances on the property made or permitted by the grantor. If the warranty is against all claims whatsoever, it is called a *general warranty deed*.

The kind of deed a buyer receives is the subject of bargaining. Naturally the buyer will try to get as many assurances as possible against claims on the property.

specific performance

A REMEDY, or legal method for enforcing a right, that compels a party to perform a CONTRACT precisely or substantially according to the terms agreed on, so that justice between the parties to the contract will be done. Specific performance gives the plaintiff what he actually bargained for in the contract rather than granting him money DAMAGES for not receiving it. Specific performance can be granted by a court after it considers the relief being sought and whether there is a valid contract that can be enforced. It is generally applied in breach of contract actions where money damages are inadequate.

EXAMPLE Justin contracted with the Buena Vista Real Estate Company to buy a restaurant on a corner property in Slumville, a run-down area of the city. After signing the contract, but before the sale went through, the company told Justin it had made a mistake in selling the restaurant. Subsequently Buena Vista agreed to sell the business to a corporation for three times the price Justin had agreed to pay. It came to light that Slumville had suddenly become valuable because the county planned to erect an office building in it—right across the street from the restaurant. Justin sued Buena Vista for breach of contract and asked the court for specific performance. Buena Vista offered Justin two lots in another part of the city at the same price as he had contracted for the disputed property, but Justin refused to accept them. The court ruled in Justin's favor because the value of the restaurant could not be adequately measured in light of the county's plans. The company would have to sell the restaurant to Justin at the original price.

If a defendant refuses to obey a court order for specific performance, the court can cite him for CONTEMPT and even send him to jail. If he continues to refuse to obey the order, the court can keep him in jail until he does obey it. In this situation, it is said that the defendant "has the keys to his freedom in his pocket." This means he can have himself released when he decides to obey the court order. This enforcement power of the court is one of the major reasons why plaintiffs seek specific performance of contracts.

■ **Contracts subject to specific performance** Specific performance will be denied if money can compensate the plaintiff for his loss. The court determines whether or not money can compensate the plaintiff after it examines the subject matter of the contract. The fact that the defendant is financially unable to pay damages to the plaintiff has no bearing on whether or not specific performance will be granted. The court determines only whether or not money damages are an adequate remedy; it does not take into consideration the defendant's financial resources to pay the judgment.

Contracts for property Specific performance is often granted for contracts dealing with the sale of property. If the contract is for the purchase of land, an award of money damages is considered inadequate because land is unique—no two pieces of land are exactly alike. An award of money damages will not enable the plaintiff to get the same piece of land anywhere else. Courts, however, frequently award money damages when a contract for the sale of a home is breached. The damages are measured by the difference between the price paid to find a comparable house and the original contract price.

If the contract involves the sale of ordinary personal property—such as furniture, appliances, or machinery— money damages are usually adequate because almost identical items can easily be purchased on the open market, and the buyer can be compensated for the amount he had to spend above the original contract price.

Specific performance will be granted when the contract involves personal property that is unique—that cannot be duplicated. The court determines whether or not property is unique. A rare stamp or a coin collection is considered unique for purposes of specific performance, but stock listed on the New York and American stock exchanges is not. Antiques, heirlooms, and items that are one of a kind are also considered unique; money cannot compensate the plaintiff for their loss. The claim that an object has sentimental value to the plaintiff is not, by itself, sufficient to justify specific performance. But sometimes facts and circumstances endow an item with a special value that make it a family heirloom.

EXAMPLE You learn that your uncle, who has suffered a number of financial setbacks, is considering selling to an antique dealer a rare violin that has been passed down in your family since the 17th century. You offer your uncle a fair price to sell it to you because you value it as a family heirloom. Your uncle agrees but then, in a moment of pique for not being invited to your son's wedding, he sells it to the antique dealer for the same price. You sue him for breach of contract, asking for specific performance, since in your mind the violin is irreplaceable. The court will order that your uncle deliver the violin to you.

On the other hand, suppose the violin was neither rare nor very old, but just happened to be a family possession that you played in your childhood. Your uncle, if he broke his agreement to sell it to you, could be ordered only to pay you money damages, if you lost any money as a result of his change of heart.

Money damages are considered inadequate if the estimate is difficult to make, such as in REQUIREMENTS CONTRACTS, in which a buyer agrees to purchase all the goods he needs from a particular seller and from no one else, but does not agree upon any specific amount of goods he will buy. The same is true if the goods in question are scarce and cannot be readily found on the open market even if they are not unique.

EXAMPLE In one case, specific performance of a contract to purchase tomatoes was granted by a court. There was only a six-week season to can tomatoes, and a limited supply was on the market. The quality of any tomatoes that could have been purchased on the open market might not have been as good as the defendant's, and the success of the plaintiff's business depended on the quality of his purchase.

If there is a combination of unique and ordinary items in the same contract, the entire contract will be specifically enforced.

Service contracts Breaches of personal service contracts are usually compensated by money damages unless the services are unique. In contracts for services that are unique, there is usually a *negative covenant*—a clause that prohibits a person from performing his unique services for anyone else within a certain distance from his former employer for a certain period of time. If the negative covenant is breached, the former employer may seek to specifically enforce it.

EXAMPLE A superstar singer has signed a contract to appear at a nightclub in Las Vegas. Her contract contains a negative covenant by which she agrees not to appear at any other club in Las Vegas until her contract expires. After many disagreements with the club owner, the singer quits and signs to appear at another nightclub. In this situation a court cannot order the singer to appear at the original nightclub, but it can order her not to appear at any other club until her contract ends. Since the singer's talents are considered unique, it would be unfair and harmful to the club owner not to specifically enforce the negative covenant.

Negative covenants are sometimes called *covenants not to compete*. They will be upheld only if they are reasonable in scope. Otherwise money damages will be awarded. A court will never specifically enforce an employment contract by ordering an employee to work for his employer, because this would be considered involuntary servitude, or slavery, which the 13th Amendment to the Constitution prohibits.

Acts the courts cannot supervise As a general rule, courts will not decree acts they cannot supervise. In many instances, specific performance has been denied when courts would be unduly burdened by supervising the performance of the contract.

Supervision is a particular problem in building or repair contracts because the court lacks the technical know-how, means, or agencies to learn exactly what the contractor is doing or if he is doing it well. There are certain exceptions to this rule. If the plans for the building are clearly defined

WHEN YOU SUE FOR SPECIFIC PERFORMANCE

■ Specific performance is granted when money damages are inadequate to compensate for a breach of contract.

■ If a defendant refuses to obey a court order for specific performance, he can go to jail for contempt of court and he can be kept in jail until he does obey the order.

■ If money can compensate you for your loss, the court will not grant you specific performance. If the contract was for the purchase of land, the court may grant you specific performance—that is, the defendant will have to sell to you as agreed in the contract—because no two pieces of land are exactly

alike. However, if your contract was for the sale of a home, the court may award money damages instead of specific performance, and the damages will be measured by the difference between the price for a comparable house and the original contract price.

■ A rare stamp or coin collection is considered unique by the court for purposes of specific performance; so are antiques, heirlooms, and other one-of-a kind items.

■ A personal service contract for a unique service (in the sports or entertainment business, for example) generally contains a negative convenant

prohibiting the person covered from working for someone else for a certain period of time. If this negative covenant is breached, the other party to the contract may seek to specifically enforce it.

■ The court will never specifically enforce an employment contract by ordering an employee to work for his employer, because this would be considered slavery.

■ A plaintiff seeking specific performance must have contracted in good faith. If he acted fraudulently or took unfair advantage, he will not be entitled to specific performance.

or if there has been sufficient partial performance of the contract so that supervision of the remainder is not difficult, the court may grant specific performance for the completion of the building.

Trying to enforce a building repair contract presents more complex problems for the court. It must first determine what repairs are to be made and how soon they must be done. Then it must decide whether there has been substantial performance, and if not, whether the defendant has any excuse for it. Usually there is another adequate remedy—money damages equaling the excess of the construction cost paid over the original contract price. If damages are not adequate the court may order specific performance.

■ **Validity of the contract**   For a court to order specific performance, the contract involved must be valid and it must contain definite terms. A court cannot be expected to enforce either an invalid contract or one that is so vague in its terms that the court cannot determine just what it must order each party to do. It would be unjust for a court to try to interpret and enforce the terms of an ambiguous contract, because the court might erroneously order what the parties never intended or contemplated.

■ **Plaintiff 's conduct**   A plaintiff seeking specific performance of a contract must have contracted in good faith. If he has acted fraudulently or has taken unfair advantage of his superior bargaining power in establishing extremely harsh contract terms against the defendant, he will not be entitled to specific performance. He is then said to have *unclean hands*—that is, he has acted unjustly in the transaction for which he is seeking the court's help.

EXAMPLE A classic example of the clean hands doctrine
O→ * involved Charlie Flowers, an outstanding college football player who was drafted by the New York Giants and the Los Angeles Chargers. In November 1959 Flowers signed to play football with the Giants. College rules made any player who signed a contract to play with a professional team ineligible for further intercollegiate games. Since Flowers wanted to play in the Sugar Bowl on January 1, 1960, both he and the Giants agreed to keep his signing of the contract confidential, deceiving his

college, the opposing team, and the football public in general. One of the terms of the contract provided that it was binding only when approved by the commissioner of football. Part of the plan was that the contract would not be submitted for approval until after January 1.

When Flowers tried to withdraw from the contract a short while later, the Giants promptly filed it with the commissioner, who approved it December 15. Public announcement was withheld, however, until after January 1. On December 29, Flowers negotiated a better contract with the Chargers and signed it after the Sugar Bowl game. He notified the Giants on December 29 that he was withdrawing from his contract with them and returned his uncashed bonus checks.

The Giants sought specific performance of their contract with Flowers. The court denied relief and refused to enforce the contract because the Giants did not have "clean hands." Specific performance will be denied to anyone who has acted inequitably or with bad faith, regardless of how improper the defendant's behavior may have been. The misconduct does not necessarily have to be a crime, nor need it justify legal proceedings. Any intentional act that violates the standards of fairness and justice is sufficient to prohibit the granting of specific performance. In this case the Giants created the situation by their devious conduct, and therefore had no right to ask a court for relief.

At all times, a plaintiff must be willing to *do equity*. This means that he must fulfill whatever equitable obligations the court imposes upon him to do what is just and fair to the defendant. A person will be granted specific performance only if he has done, has offered to do, or is ready and willing to do all that was required of him by the terms of the contract.

■ **Defenses to specific performance**   An oral contract that is unenforceable because it has not complied with the STATUTE OF FRAUDS, which requires that certain types of contracts be written, cannot be enforced under a decree of specific performance. Consequently this fact is a defense against a demand for specific performance.

Laches is also a defense that prevents the enforcement of a contract by specific performance. Laches is an unreasonable delay in asserting a right, so that its enforcement would cause injury, prejudice, or disadvantage to others. It is applied only where enforcement of a right will bring about injustice. See EQUITY; LACHES.

The clean hands doctrine is a defense in an action for specific performance. As explained above in the Charlie Flowers case, if the plaintiff has acted fraudulently, he will be denied specific performance for that action. In addition, a contract may not be specifically enforced if the plaintiff has used superior bargaining power to take unfair advantage of a vulnerable defendant. This situation occurs when the consideration (one party's obligation that induces the other to enter the contract) is so inadequate as to "shock the conscience" and when there have been "sharp dealings."

Failure to disclose material (important) facts to the defendant will also result in the denial of specific performance when a contract is breached.

EXAMPLE Walter was designated executor of John's estate. O—✻ Mary, John's widow, wants to sell John's collection of antique cars because she needs the money for her children's education. The collection is easily worth $150,000, but Mary does not know this. She tells Walter she will take whatever she can get for it. Walter asks his cousin Fred to offer Mary $50,000, with the understanding that they will split the $100,000 profit when they resell the collection. Mary accepts Fred's offer after consulting with Walter. Before giving up the collection, however, she learns that she is being cheated and refuses to deliver it. Fred sues Mary for breaching their contract, asking the court to specifically enforce it because the collection is one of a kind. In this situation, the court will refuse to award specific performance because material facts that would have affected Mary's decision to sell to Fred were concealed from her.

Mistakes and misrepresentations in the terms of a contract may be a basis for defense against specific performance. If they are sufficient to justify rescission (cancellation or annulment) of the contract, they are sufficient to prevent its enforcement. Only a contract with definite and certain terms will be enforced by the court.

speech and press, freedom of

The constitutional rights of Americans to speak freely and of the press to gather and disseminate news without arbitrary interference from the government. These rights are protected by the First Amendment to the U.S. Constitution, which states that "Congress shall make no law . . . abridging the freedom of speech, or of the press." Although the 1st Amendment applies only to the federal government, the 14th Amendment, through its due process clause, extends that protection to the state level. See DUE PROCESS OF LAW.

Our freedom to speak and write extends even to expressing ideas that criticize the government. The U.S. Supreme Court has acknowledged that the 1st and 14th Amendments embody our "profound national commitment to the principle that debate on public issues should be uninhibited, robust, and wide-open and . . . may well include vehement, caustic, and sometimes unpleasantly sharp attacks on government and public officials."

Implicit in the guarantee of free speech is the absolute right to think and believe as we wish. No government can regulate our thoughts and beliefs. What the Constitution does guarantee is the freedom to express our ideas in any form, including verbal statements, writing of any kind, radio broadcasts, telecasts, recordings, and even picketing and symbolic speech—the use of nonverbal symbols to express feelings, such as wearing a black armband to protest the government's involvement in a war. This freedom is not absolute, however, as is the freedom to think and believe as we wish. Although the government cannot constitutionally suppress our freedom of expression, it can regulate it in order to serve a legitimate and compelling governmental interest when the time, place, or circumstances warrant it.

■ **Background** Throughout history free-thinking men have fought for freedom of speech, but usually to no effect. Even in the ancient Greek democracy, the great philosopher Socrates was put to death for corrupting the youth of Athens with his teaching, and through the millennia countless other men have died because they spoke out against their government or church. Freedom of the press fared no better. Men were often put to death or severely punished for what they wrote. After the invention of the printing press, suppression of the written word became even more severe because printing made it available to more people. In England, for example, the government instituted licensing acts, which permitted only a few printers—who were considered "safe" by the ruling authorities—to use the presses, and these acts remained in effect until 1690, when Parliament refused to continue them.

American colonists were particularly vociferous in their demands for freedom of expression, but the British Crown managed to exercise a great deal of control over the colonies by imposing heavy taxes on periodicals, by refusing to permit the introduction of printing presses in many of the American colonies, and most important, by vigorously enforcing the law of seditious libel everywhere. Under this law, anyone who made or printed a statement that offended the government and its ministers could be severely punished—even when the statement was true. Worse yet for the defendant, the Crown's own judges determined whether the utterance or writing was defamatory to the government.

In 1734 the royal governor of New York, William Cosby, prosecuted John Peter Zenger, a New York printer, for publishing articles in his *Weekly Journal* that criticized Cosby's administration of the colony. Although Zenger did not deny publishing the articles, the jury refused to convict him. The case was a first step toward eliminating abuse of licensing and censorship and punishing political expression. See ZENGER CASE.

Freedom of expression finally came to America in 1791 with ratification of the Bill of Rights—the first 10 amendments to the Constitution. But the rivalry between political parties in the early years of our republic gave rise to much vicious criticism of the government in the press. In 1798 Congress passed the Sedition Act (one of the Alien and Sedition Acts), which forbade making any criticism of federal officeholders "with intent to defame" or to bring them "into contempt or disrepute." The conviction and imprisonment of newspaper editors under the Sedition Act caused a furor. The Kentucky and Virginia legislatures declared the act unconstitutional and null and void in their states. The federal government allowed the law to expire after two years without renewing it, and as a result of the strong public opinion against the act, politicians for generations avoided any measures that would restrain the press. Freedom of expression became firmly entrenched in the American system.

■ **Prior restraint** To restrain speech or publication even before it is accomplished is the most serious and least tolerable infringement on the rights guaranteed by the First Amendment. Freedom of speech and freedom of the press have generally been interpreted as placing "a heavy pre-

sumption" against the constitutional validity of prior restraints, or censorship of what *may* be said or printed. Prior restraint is official restriction imposed in advance, as distinct from a subsequent punishment for a communication made in violation of a law forbidding that type of communication.

The most serious problem caused by prior restraint is its chilling effect on freedom of expression. People, fearful of having their expression reviewed beforehand by a government censor or licensing authority, may be intimidated into speaking less freely. Thus, any law that denies you the right to speak, solicit membership in an organization, distribute handbills, solicit orders for the sale of books, pamphlets,

FREEDOM OF SPEECH AND YOU

■ The First Amendment to the Constitution guarantees Americans freedom of speech and of the press.

■ The most serious infringement of free expression is *prior restraint*—the official restriction of a communication before you make it—such as having to submit an article for censorship before you publish it. Prior restraint of communications protected by the First Amendment is unconstitutional.

■ When towns and localities require permits to distribute handbills, use sound trucks, or stage rallies, their restriction must apply only to time and place. They cannot bar such activities altogether.

■ Local laws passed to stop certain unpopular groups from conducting peaceful demonstrations are unconstitutional, even if those groups' views are offensive to most people.

■ Courts sometimes issue orders to prevent distribution of government classified or secret information; such injunctions are often upheld on appeal if justified on grounds of national security, especially in time of war.

■ A court may sometimes issue a *gag order*, a court decree to prevent the circulation of information by the news media that might prejudice a jury. But unless the information to be suppressed is specifically described, the order can be unconstitutional.

■ Certain types of language are not protected by the guarantee of free expression: libel (written lies) and slander (spoken lies)—because they are unjust—and insulting and obscene language.

■ No one has the right to make or publish statements that may harm the

welfare of the nation or to advocate the overthrow of the U.S. government. However, advocating forcible overthrow solely as an abstract revolutionary principle unconnected with any concrete plan may not be prohibited. Teachers are exceptions: they may be held ineligible to teach in a public school if they belong to an organization that advocates the forcible overthrow of the government.

■ Teachers may be forbidden to make statements that interfere with their teaching duties, disrupt the school, violate an express need for confidentiality, or the like. In most cases, however, a teacher may not be fired from public employment for speaking out on issues of public importance.

■ Military personnel and prisoners are subject to having their freedom of expression curtailed. Students' right to freedom of speech is protected, provided they do not substantially disrupt the maintenance of discipline in the schools or infringe upon the rights of others.

■ Some government workers' rights of free speech and press may be regulated in certain situations. For example, a former CIA employee may not disclose classified information obtained while still employed, if the material was not already known to the general public at the time.

■ Picketing may be reasonably regulated but not prohibited. It is legal even when it discourages customers from patronizing a store.

■ First Amendment protection was extended during the 1970's to "commercial speech," or advertising, and it is no longer possible for states or lo-

calities to prohibit or regulate the dissemination of commercial information. For example, abortion clinics may advertise in newspapers, and prescription drug prices may be advertised without hindrance from state or professional authorities.

■ Broadcasters maintain a substantial degree of independence from government regulation, but they are required to encourage presentation of opposing views on controversial issues.

■ A broadcaster does not have to sell editorial time, but if he does he must provide equal time to opposing viewpoints and ideas.

■ Broadcasters must make air time available to all legally qualified candidates who run for political office on the federal level.

■ More than half the states have "shield laws" to protect the confidentiality of news-gathering activities. Even under shield laws, however, a defendant's rights may outweigh the reporter's, and the reporter may be forced to testify.

■ News media do not enjoy any special constitutional right to information. For example, a broadcasting company was successfully sued for trespassing when its employees burst into a restaurant against the owner's wishes in order to gather news.

■ The Constitution does not protect you from the attempts of a private person or corporation to restrict your freedom of speech. When you are on private property, your constitutional right to express ideas and views must usually yield to the owner's right to be protected against trespass or invasion of privacy.

circulars, pictures, merchandise, or other articles—unless you first obtain a license from an official who has discretion to deny you the license or to make you pay a tax for the privilege—is void on its face (automatically illegal) because it abridges freedom of expression.

Near v. Minnesota   In the most important case involving prior restraint, the Supreme Court struck down a state law that prohibited the publication of defamatory articles. By threatening to shut down any publication that printed such articles, the law acted as a censor.

EXAMPLE A Minnesota statute provided that any person O——* who regularly publishes "a malicious, scandalous and defamatory newspaper, magazine or other periodical, is guilty of a nuisance" and could be forced to stop. In 1927 authorities charged a newspaper publisher named J. M. Near with violating the statute when his paper claimed that a gangster was in control of gambling, bootlegging, and racketeering in Minneapolis and that law enforcement officials were not doing their duty. Near was enjoined to stop publishing, and the supreme court of Minnesota upheld the order, saying that the statute was aimed at preventing the circulation of scandalous material that is "detrimental to public morals and to the general welfare."

Near's defense in appealing the decision was that the law was unconstitutional because it deprived him of "liberty" of free press. The Supreme Court agreed, pointing out that the statute compelled every publisher who would expose crime and dishonesty among public officials to run the risk of having his paper abated as a nuisance unless he could prove that the facts were true and "published with good motives and for justifiable ends." The statute subjected every publisher to "effective censorship." It enabled the public officers being investigated to order the publisher to submit his publication to a judge to determine whether the material published was scandalous and defamatory.

"This is the essence of censorship" said the Court, and it is not justified "to prevent the circulation of scandal which tends to disturb the public peace . . . Charges of reprehensible conduct, and in particular of official malfeasance, unquestionably create a public scandal, but the theory of the constitutional guaranty is that even a more serious public evil would be caused by authority to prevent publication." The Court ruled the Minnesota statute invalid as a prior restraint.

Freedom of expression in public places   Towns and localities may require permits to distribute handbills, to use sound trucks for conveying political messages, or to stage rallies or protests in parks, streets, and other public property. However, the official in charge of issuing the permits has no right to prohibit the activity altogether. His discretion is limited to the time when and place where it may take place. The Supreme Court has stated that anyone "who is rightfully on a street carries with him there as elsewhere the constitutional right to express his views in an orderly fashion . . . by handbills and literature as well as by the spoken word."

Handbills   The Supreme Court has consistently upheld the right of persons to distribute handbills without prior restraint from the government.

EXAMPLE A Los Angeles city ordinance provided that no O——* one could distribute handbills that did not carry the names and addresses of their distributors and authors or printers. A man named Talley was convicted of violating this ordinance by distributing a handbill listing no name except "National Consumer Mobilization, Box 65, Los Angeles, California." The handbill urged readers to boycott merchants who sold goods from producers who refused equal employment to blacks, Mexicans, and Orientals.

The Supreme Court reversed Talley's conviction. The ordinance was void on its face, since it violated both freedom of the press and freedom of speech.

The Court also pointed out that anonymous leaflets and other literature have played an important role in the progress of mankind. "Before the Revolutionary War colonial patriots frequently had to conceal their authorship or distribution of literature that easily could have brought down on them prosecutions by English-controlled courts . . . Even the Federalist Papers, written in favor of the adoption of the Constitution, were published under fictitious names. It is plain that anonymity has sometimes been assumed for the most constructive purposes." Identification and fear of reprisals suppress freedom to speak, write, publish, and distribute. For these reasons, the ordinance was declared unconstitutional.

In another case, an ordinance prohibited handbills from being circulated without first obtaining written permission from the city manager. The ordinance was declared invalid because it applied to any distribution of any literature at any time and gave the city manager uncontrolled discretion.

An injunction barring the distribution of a political pamphlet may be unconstitutional even if the pamphlet results in the harassment of the person who is its target.

EXAMPLE The Organization for a Better Austin wanted to O——* distribute pamphlets criticizing a real estate broker named Keefe. The handbills accused Keefe of "blockbusting"—encouraging panic selling to blacks, and thus upsetting the racial balance of neighborhoods. The pamphlet requested readers to telephone Keefe at home and urge him to sign a pledge to stop "panic peddling." Keefe obtained an injunction in state court that prevented the distribution of the leaflets anywhere in the city. The Supreme Court reversed the injunction because it applied prior restraint.

Loudspeakers   Because the noise made by loudspeakers on trucks can disturb the peace, the government may restrict the times at which they may be used. However, the use of a loudspeaker cannot be banned altogether if it is to be used as an instrument of public speech.

In the late 1940's an ordinance in one town banned the use of loudspeakers on trucks except for disseminating news and matters of public concern—and in those cases the police chief's permission had to be obtained first. In 1948 the Supreme Court declared the law unconstitutional because it established a prior restraint on free speech:

❝ Loudspeakers are today indispensable instruments of effective public speech. The sound truck has become an accepted method of political campaigning. It is the way people are reached. [Any] abuses which sound trucks create can be controlled by narrowly drawn statutes. When a city allows

an official to ban them in his uncontrolled discretion, it sanctions a device for suppression of free communication of ideas. In this case a permit is denied because some people find the sound annoying. In the next one a permit may be denied because some people find the ideas annoying. Annoyance at ideas can be cloaked in annoyance at sound. The power of censorship in this type of ordinance reveals its vice."

Another town ordinance banning vehicles with sound amplifiers emitting "loud and raucous noises" was subsequently upheld in 1949. The Supreme Court reasoned that "the unwilling listener is not like the passer-by who may be offered a pamphlet in the street but cannot be made to take it. In his home or on the street he is practically helpless to escape this interference with his privacy by loudspeakers except through the protection of the municipality."

The two decisions may appear contradictory, but the Court found a difference between the cases. The statute in the 1948 case had prevented the use of sound trucks to spread political views unless the police chief's permission was obtained. The statute in the 1949 case was directed solely at preventing the use of sound trucks for any purpose, so that peace on the city's streets would not be disturbed. It did not prevent the use of sound trucks in public parks or other open spaces off the public streets. The Supreme Court stated that "such distractions would be dangerous to traffic at all hours useful for the dissemination of information." Three justices dissented, finding no difference between the 1948 and 1949 cases.

As the law stands today, all sound trucks may or may not be banned, depending on local ordinances. No one official may, however ban such trucks for political activities since such unbridled discretion violates the right of free speech exercised by the operators of such trucks.

Demonstrations Ordinances that prevent groups with unpopular or even offensive viewpoints from conducting peaceful demonstrations are not constitutional.

EXAMPLE In 1978 a Nazi organization planned to hold a O⊶＊ rally in front of a village hall in the predominantly Jewish community of Skokie, Illinois. When the rally was announced, the village immediately enacted three ordinances. The first required groups holding rallies to obtain a permit and to post public liability and property damage insurance; the second prohibited the dissemination of material that intentionally incited racial or religious hatred; the third banned political parties from participating in public demonstrations while wearing military-style uniforms.

The leader of the organization applied for a permit, stating the date of the assembly, its location, the length of time involved, and the fact that traffic would not be disrupted. He also explained that participants, in uniforms with swastikas, would hold placards proclaiming free speech for white persons. Literature would not be distributed. The permit was denied.

The applicant brought an action against the village. The federal district court declared the ordinances void and prohibited the village from enforcing them, and a federal court of appeals affirmed the decision. "There is no room under the First Amendment for the government to protect targeted listeners from offensive speech."

Skokie therefore issued the permit for a demonstration at the town hall, but the group moved the rally to Chicago, where it was held for two days. In an attempt to prevent further problems in Skokie, a county court later issued an injunction against the organization from parading, demonstrating, or distributing literature in the village. The Nazis sought a stay (postponement) of the injunction, pending an appeal, but were denied. The Supreme Court, on hearing the matter, reversed the decision, sending the case back to court. The trial court modified the injunction so that only displaying swastikas during a parade was banned. That injunction, too, was eventually reversed.

The village next appealed the decision that had declared its original three ordinances unconstitutional. The Supreme Court denied the application. The village then petitioned the Supreme Court to hear the case by certiorari—that is, to review the written record of proceedings in the lower court. Certiorari was denied, with two justices dissenting.

Classified information   The courts have occasionally issued injunctions to prevent distribution of certain information, usually classified. Such injunctions are acts of prior restraint, but, depending upon the nature of the information likely to be disclosed, an injunction may be justified. For example, an exception to the prohibition on prior restraint may be allowed for matters of national security or for military secrets in the time of war.

EXAMPLE In one of the few cases based on this exception, O⊶＊ the federal government sought to temporarily enjoin two newspapers from publishing "History of United States Decision-Making Process on Viet Nam Policy," popularly known as the Pentagon Papers. It stated that publication might endanger national security and requested time to study and assess that possibility. The newspapers claimed, however, that to restrain publication violated freedom of the press, and the majority of the Supreme Court agreed.

The case was unusual in that each justice wrote his own opinion of the issue. Two decided that any prior restraint is unconstitutional. Another stated that prior restraint is justified only when the nation is at war and specific, compelling reasons are shown, such as troop movements and their location. Two justices said that publication could be enjoined only upon a showing of "grave and irreparable danger to national security." Another argued that Congress had considered and refused to enact legislation making publication of such top secret documents unlawful and that the Court should not enact law that Congress had refused to pass. The minority consisted of three justices, who argued for a prompt trial and a full record on which they could decide the merits of the case. Another controversial case involved the publication of some government information concerning the H-bomb.

EXAMPLE The federal government sought to prevent *The* O⊶＊ *Progressive* magazine from publishing an article entitled "The H-Bomb Secret—How We Got It, Why We're Telling It." The author claimed he had gathered his information from sources available to the public, including unrestricted material resulting from visits to atomic energy plants. The government disputed the claim, asserting that the nature of the information used in the article brought it within the restricted data provisions of the Atomic Energy Act of 1954. To publish such information would violate the act.

A federal district court judge issued a preliminary injunction to bar publication of the article. "One cannot enjoy freedom of speech . . . or freedom of the press unless one continues to enjoy the right to life."

This case was distinguished from the Pentagon Papers case because here a specific law was allegedly violated. The judge noted that the affidavits of both the Secretary of State and the Secretary of Defense claiming that United States national security could be irreparably harmed if the article was published were significant factors in his decision.

In September 1979 the injunction against the magazine was dissolved (terminated) and the lawsuit dismissed at the government's request. This strange turn of events occurred after the nationwide publication of a letter written by a computer programmer to a U.S. Senator, complaining of security leaks in the government's handling of its thermonuclear projects. The letter revealed as much classified information as the H-bomb story. Efforts by the government to suppress its publication were generally unsuccessful. As a result of the public disclosure of this information, the government decided that its case against *The Progressive* magazine was pointless.

Gag orders A gag order is a court decree imposed by a trial judge on the news media to prevent the circulation of information that might prejudice or inflame a jury. The order might be imposed during pretrial hearings or in the course of a criminal prosecution to protect the constitutional right of the accused to a fair and impartial trial. A gag order is a form of prior restraint. Unless the information to be suppressed is narrowly specified, the order can be judged unconstitutional.

EXAMPLE In Nebraska a case of multiple murders and the O——* subsequent arrest of a suspect received widespread news coverage. At a pretrial hearing, which was open to the press and the public, the prosecutor introduced confessions made by the accused. In the interest of assuring the accused of a fair trial by an unbiased jury, the presiding judge issued a gag order prohibiting the news media from reporting the confession itself, any statements by the accused that had not been made directly to the press, and any other facts that were "strongly implicative" of the accused's role in the murders.

Members of the news media sought to have the order invalidated, but it was upheld by various courts. Only the U.S. Supreme Court found it unconstitutional. The Court reasoned that although the Nebraska judge had concluded that the massive pretrial publicity in the case "could impinge upon the defendant's right to a fair trial [under the Sixth Amendment], this was, at best, speculation." The court that had granted the gag order had failed to consider alternatives—for example, a change of venue, postponement of the trial until the publicity subsided, or sequestration of the jury. Without evidence that such alternatives would fail, the judge was not justified in limiting the freedom of the press. Furthermore, the gag order had forbidden the publication of evidence offered at the pretrial hearing, and that violated the principle that "there is nothing that proscribes the press from reporting events that transpire in the courtroom." Finally, the Supreme Court pointed out that the restraint on "implicative" information was too vague to be constitutional.

■ **Restrictions on freedom of expression** Ideally, there should be no restrictions on any type of expression, but in some cases allowing freedom of expression may do more harm than limiting it. Some forms of expression are prohibited outright, such as obscenity. Individual statements that may endanger the government or the country may also be prohibited, as may statements that infringe on the constitutional rights of others. Finally, some modes of expression, such as broadcasting, pose such unique and special problems that they may be subject to certain government regulations.

Libel, slander, obscenity, insults Libel (written lies) and slander (spoken lies) are not sanctioned under the guarantee of free expression because they are unjust. See LIBEL AND SLANDER. The Supreme Court has held that

&& *The right of a man to the protection of his own reputation from unjustified invasion and wrongful hurt reflects no more than our basic concept of the essential dignity and worth of every human being—a concept at the root of any decent system of ordered liberty."*

Lewd or obscene language is not protected by the First Amendment, although it was not until 1957 that the Supreme Court made that determination. Even today the Court has remained vague in defining obscenity. Basically, it is literature, movies, or live performances that depict sexual conduct in such a way that the average person, applying the contemporary standards of his community, would find that the material appealed to prurient interests. Such displays must have no literary, artistic, or scientific value to be judged obscene. See also OBSCENITY.

Insulting language, or "fighting words," is not protected by the First Amendment.

EXAMPLE The classic example of "fighting words" was O——* given in a 1942 case when a person who called the city marshal a "racketeer" and "a damned Fascist" was convicted under a state law prohibiting a person from calling another an offensive, derisive, or annoying name in a public place. The Supreme Court upheld the statute and the conviction. Since such words have a minimal social value and are not essential for the free exchange of ideas, they may be restricted by the state in the greater social interest of maintaining order and morality. The government cannot, however, punish a person merely for using profanity in public without showing its tendency to bring about an immediate breach of the peace.

■ **Clear and present danger** No one has the right to make or publish statements that may harm the welfare of the nation or advocate the overthrow of the U.S. government. One of the first tests used by the Supreme Court in deciding when freedom of expression could be restricted was the clear-and-present-danger test. This test, proposed in a 1919 case, permitted expression to be punished when "the words used are used in such circumstances and are of such a nature as to create a clear and present danger that they will bring about the substantive evils that Congress has a right to prevent."

EXAMPLE The case in point was that of *Schenck* v. *United* O——* *States.* The defendants were convicted of a conspiracy to violate the federal Espionage Act by trying to cause insubordination in the armed forces and by hindering the recruiting and enlistment process. In 1917, during World War I, they had printed and circulated a document that described conscription as a form of slavery and called it unconstitutional.

The Supreme Court affirmed the convictions unanimously: "We admit that in many places and in ordinary times the defendants in saying all that was said in the circular would have been within their constitutional rights. But the character of every act depends upon the circumstances in which it is done. The most stringent protection of free speech would not protect a man in falsely shouting fire in a theatre and causing a panic.... When a nation is at war many things that might be said in time of peace are such a hindrance to its effort that their utterance will not be endured so long as men fight and no Court could regard them as protected by any constitutional right."

Abstract doctrine and concrete plan   There is a distinction between the expression of an abstract doctrine and the advocacy of a concrete plan. Laws may prohibit the advocacy of a concrete plan to forcibly overthrow the government, but they may not prohibit the advocacy of forcible overthrow solely as an abstract principle that is unconnected with any concrete plan to put that principle into practice.

EXAMPLE The federal Smith Act made it a crime to conspire O——* to advocate the duty and necessity of overthrowing and destroying the federal government by force and violence. Several defendants, all Communists, were convicted under this act. They appealed, claiming that their First Amendment rights were violated. The Supreme Court affirmed the conviction.

The freedom to discuss, teach, and advocate new theories of government, including communism or anarchy, and to induce others to attempt to change the existing government by lawful and constitutional means is protected by the Constitution. But freedom of speech, unlike the freedom to believe or think, must yield to other values, such as protecting organized government, since all freedoms are threatened if the government itself is destroyed. The conspiracy of the defendants constituted a clear and present danger to the U.S. government.

On the other hand, the Supreme Court declared unconstitutional a California law requiring that, in order to be eligible for a veteran's property tax exemption, the applicant had to swear that he did not advocate either the overthrow of the government "by force or violence or other unlawful means" or "the support of a foreign government against the United States in event of hostilities." This law sought to suppress the advocacy of an abstract principle as well as a concrete plan. The Court ruled that when a state seeks to deny a person his constitutional right of free speech through its general taxing program, due process requires that the state offer sufficient proof to justify its action.

Teachers   Despite the abstract-principle doctrine, teachers may be held ineligible to teach in a public school if they are members of any organization that advocates the overthrow of the government by force or unlawful means. The Supreme Court upheld as constitutional a state law to that effect, stating:

"*A teacher works in a sensitive area in the schoolroom. There he shapes the attitude of young minds towards the society in which they live. In this the state has a vital concern. It must preserve the integrity of the schools. That the school authorities have the right and the duty to screen the officials, teachers and employees as to their fitness to maintain the integrity of the schools as part of ordered society cannot be doubted. One's associates, past and present, as well as one's conduct, may properly be considered in determining fitness and loyalty.*"

A person's reputation, as established by the company he keeps and the organizations to which he belongs, is proper consideration in determining fitness for teaching.

On the other hand, teachers are not stripped of all their rights in this area. A Maryland law required teachers to take an oath stating, "I am not engaged in one way or another in the attempt to overthrow the Government of the United States . . . by force or violence." The Supreme Court declared the law unconstitutional because it was so broad as to make possible "oppressive or capricious applications as regimes change."

Other government employees   The exception made for teachers has not been allowed for other government employees or officials. In 1966 the Supreme Court held that the Georgia State House of Representatives violated the rights of expression of a duly elected state legislator by excluding him from membership because he verbally opposed the war in Vietnam. In 1967 the Court invalidated a New York law allowing state employees to be fired and applicants for state jobs to be rejected merely for holding membership in the Communist Party, even though they showed no specific intent to further the unlawful aims of the Communists.

Finally, the Court also struck down the portion of the 1967 Subversive Activities Control Act that provided that any member of a Communist-action organization could not "engage in any employment in any defense facility." Although the Court was "not unmindful of the congressional concern over the danger of sabotage and espionage in national defense industries," it ruled that Congress had to achieve its goals by means that impinged less drastically on First Amendment freedoms.

■ **Regulation and the balancing of interests**   Constitutional rights constantly overlap and interact with each other. Consequently, the Supreme Court attempts to balance competing governmental interests in determining whether or not the regulation of expression is justified. For example, the Court may have to balance the right of the press to report facts about a murder against the defendant's constitutional right to a fair trial.

EXAMPLE The Supreme Court used the balancing test in a O——* 1950 case in which certain labor unions attacked a provision of the Labor Management Relations Act. The provision in dispute barred unions from access to procedures important to the collective-bargaining process unless their officers signed affidavits declaring that they were not affiliated with the Communist Party. The unions said that the provision violated their leaders' First

Amendment right to hold and express whatever political views they chose and to associate with whatever political groups they wished. The Court weighed First Amendment interests against the interest defended by the act—to keep interstate commerce free from the disruption of political strikes—and ruled against the unions.

In 1961 the Supreme Court decided that a state had not violated a person's freedom of expression by denying him admission to the bar because he refused to answer the state bar committee's questions concerning his alleged membership in the Communist Party. The candidate had challenged the state's action as a violation of protected rights of free speech and association, but the Court rejected the argument. It found that the state's interest in safeguarding the bar from possible subversive influence outweighed interests protected by the 1st and 14th Amendments.

Fair trial The classic example of the clash between freedom of the press and the Sixth Amendment right to a fair trial is the case of Dr. Samuel Sheppard.

EXAMPLE Dr. Sheppard was accused of murdering his pregnant wife, Marilyn, in the 1950's. The excessive and abusive pretrial publicity and the media's improper courtroom conduct eventually led the Supreme Court to reverse Sheppard's conviction and order a new trial—after he had served 10 years in an Ohio penitentiary.

Some examples of the pretrial publicity that deprived him of an impartial trial included the extensive coverage by local newspapers of Sheppard's refusal to take a lie detector test; continual front-page editorials claiming that someone was "getting away with murder"; an editorial criticizing the lack of an inquest, which led to one; and an editorial demanding to know why Sheppard was not in jail, which led to his arrest and imprisonment. Thereafter, media publicity intensified.

Once the trial began, abuses continued. The names, addresses, and telephone numbers of the jurors were published, resulting in numerous anonymous letters and telephone calls about the prosecution. The press set up shop inside the bar of the courtroom (where only the parties in the action are permitted to sit), making confidential discussions between Sheppard and his counsel during the trial virtually impossible. Newspapers reported alleged evidence contradicting Sheppard's statements, but it was never introduced at trial. What is more, the jury remained unsequestered until the case was submitted to it for a verdict.

In reviewing the case, the Supreme Court recognized that a responsible press is indispensable to fair and effective judicial administration. But juries exposed to massive publicity and "evidence" not introduced at trial can be improperly influenced in their deliberations and decisions. Since Sheppard's original conviction, the Supreme Court had already ruled a number of times that when pretrial publicity leads to a high probability of prejudice, such prejudice could be presumed to exist. Actual evidence of the exposure to and the effect on individual jurors of such publicity need not be presented. For that reason, among others, Sheppard's conviction was reversed and the case sent back for trial.

In 1979 the U.S. Supreme Court decided that the public and the news media did not have a separate right under the 1st and 14th Amendments to demand access to pretrial hearings when the accused, the prosecution, and the trial judge agreed that the proceeding be closed so that the defendants could receive a fair trial.

Massive publicity does not automatically rule out the chance of a fair trial. Otherwise, the more notorious the crime the less chance would exist of obtaining a conviction in this era of mass media. If the supposed prejudice resulting from widespread publicity is clearly rebutted (shown not to exist) when prospective jurors are examined under oath and when circumstances surrounding the trial do not indicate inflamed community sentiment, the defendant has not been denied a fair trial merely because the case was publicized.

The right to be let alone Frequently, the exercise of one person's freedom of expression clashes with another's right to be let alone—that is, his right of privacy, which has been recognized by the Supreme Court as a constitutional right implied in the Bill of Rights. See PRIVACY, RIGHT OF. For example, a person's freedom to use sound trucks to convey political messages may be regulated by state and local government as to the time, place, and manner in which the trucks are to operate. Thus, the person disseminating the message is permitted expression, and the public is insulated from constant, offensive bombardment of amplified messages—the right to be let alone. In these cases, neither right is absolute, but each must yield to a limited extent to the other.

One of the most common everyday annoyances is junk mail—advertisements for everything from fruit baskets to real estate in Arizona. In soliciting business the advertiser is merely exercising his right of free expression. The recipient of the mail, however, might regard such unsolicited communication as a violation of his right to be let alone. Federal law now protects recipients of at least one type of unrequested advertisements—that dealing with sexually oriented merchandise.

EXAMPLE In 1970 publishers, distributors, owners, and operators of mail-order houses and mail service organizations sought to have a federal law that prohibited "pandering advertisements in the mails" declared unconstitutional. They claimed that it unjustly infringed upon their right to communicate. The law provided that a householder could request the Postmaster General to order an advertiser to stop mailing "matter which the addressee in his sole discretion believes to be erotically arousing or sexually provocative." The purpose of the law was to protect recipients of unsolicited lewd and salacious information.

The Supreme Court upheld the law's constitutionality. After balancing the right of every person to be let alone with the rights of others to communicate, the Court concluded that "a mailer's right to communicate must stop at the mailbox of an unreceptive addressee . . . Nothing in the Constitution compels us to listen to or view any unwanted communication, whatever its merit."

Elections A person has a constitutional right to vote in ELECTIONS, but his right to contribute money to the campaigns of candidates to federal elective office is limited. Federal law was enacted to prevent the corruption and influence buying that frequently occur when individuals make large contributions to political candidates. The restriction limits a contributor's right to express the extent of his support for a candidate. It also limits the financial means by which a candidate may freely express his views.

The Federal Election Campaign Act established financial limits on individual or group contributions to and expenditures for candidates for elective office and restricted overall general election and primary campaign expenditures by candidates. Several political candidates charged that the law violated their First Amendment rights to freedom of expression, since limiting their financial resources would reduce the means and opportunities for them to present their views to the electorate.

The Supreme Court ruled that the limits on individual contributions were constitutional despite First Amendment objections, but it invalidated the restrictions on the amount of money a politician may spend on his campaign. The Court reasoned that a limitation upon the amount that any one person or group may contribute to a candidate or political committee entails only a marginal restriction on the contributor's free expression. But limiting the amount of money that a politician or political group may spend on a campaign "necessarily reduces the quantity of expression by restricting the number of issues discussed, the depth of their exploration, and the size of the audience reached. This is because virtually every means of communicating ideas in today's mass society requires the expenditure of money."

■ **Restrictions for certain persons** Although all of us are guaranteed freedom of expression, this right may be restricted for persons living or working under certain conditions. Members of the military, prisoners, government workers, and even teachers and students may have a more limited right than others to express themselves freely.

The military Because commanders in the armed forces must balance legitimate military needs against individual liberties, military personnel may not be allowed as much freedom as civilians in expressing themselves.

EXAMPLE In one controversial case, an Army captain and physician, Howard Levy, was convicted in 1967 by a general court-martial for violating the Uniform Code of Military Justice (UCMJ). He had made public statements urging black soldiers to disobey orders to go to Vietnam and had characterized Special Forces personnel as "liars and thieves," "killers of peasants," and "murderers of women and children."

According to the UCMJ, which the captain was convicted of violating, a commissioned officer could be punished for "conduct unbecoming an officer and gentleman" which brings "dishonor or disrepute upon the military service." Such conduct included "all disorders and neglects to the prejudice of good order and discipline in the armed forces." The captain claimed, however, that the code deprived him of his freedom of speech and that the language of the UCMJ was too vague to clearly indicate prohibited conduct.

In 1974 the Supreme Court upheld the UCMJ provision as constitutional. Although "members of the military are not excluded from the protection granted by the First Amendment, the different character of the military community and of the military mission requires a different application of those principles."

Prisoners A prisoner has rights under the First Amendment, but restrictions may be imposed when necessary to maintain prison discipline, security, or some other compelling state interest.

EXAMPLE Prisoners' rights were violated when the California Department of Corrections instituted regulations permitting prison officials to read mail sent out by prisoners and to censor statements that "unduly complain" or "magnify grievances"; expressions of "inflammatory political, racial or religious or other views"; and matters deemed "defamatory" or "otherwise inappropriate." In 1974 the Supreme Court found the regulations unconstitutional because they infringed on the freedom of expression of both the prisoners and their correspondents. The regulations, the Court said, "fairly invited prison officials and employees to apply their own personal prejudices and opinions as standards for prisoner mail censorship." The Court acknowledged that prison mail censorship is justified when "substantial governmental interests of security, order and rehabilitation" are furthered, but it insisted that when censorship is imposed, it must be specifically aimed at achieving those interests.

Another California prison regulation prohibited news interviews with individual inmates. The Supreme Court held it constitutional even though it was challenged both by prisoners, who claimed it violated their freedom of expression, and by members of the news media, who said it interfered with their news-gathering activities. The Court said that the entry of people into the prisons for face-to-face communications with inmates must be limited in the face of institutional considerations, such as security and related administrative problems. The press was not suffering discrimination through the regulation, since it merely did away with a special privilege that had formerly been given to it and not to the public in general.

Students The scope of a student's right of freedom of expression is determined in light of the special characteristics of the school environment. The Supreme Court has recognized that students do not "shed their constitutional rights to freedom of speech or expression at the schoolhouse gate." They may exercise their First Amendment rights provided they do not substantially disrupt discipline in the SCHOOLS or infringe upon the rights of others.

EXAMPLE In the 1969 case of *Tinker* v. *Des Moines School District*, the U.S. Supreme Court upheld students' right to protest against the Vietnam War by wearing black armbands to classes. Five students who were suspended until they would agree to return to school without the armbands sought an injunction to prevent the school from disciplining them. A lower federal court upheld the school's action, but the Supreme Court reversed the lower court's decision and sent the case back for trial. The Court reasoned that the school authorities had no reason to anticipate that the wearing of armbands would substantially interfere with the work of the school or impinge upon the rights of other students.

Teachers A school may forbid a teacher to make statements that may impair his ability to carry out his daily duties or disrupt the regular operation of the school. But a person does not relinquish the constitutional right to free speech merely by becoming a schoolteacher.

EXAMPLE School officials fired a public high school teacher 0⊷✸ because he wrote a letter to the local newspaper criticizing the school board's handling of previous school revenue proposals. The Supreme Court held that the dismissal was improper and violated the teacher's right to freedom of expression. While insisting that teachers have the same rights as all citizens to comment on matters of public concern, the Court acknowledged that "The problem in any case is to arrive at a balance between the interests of the teacher, as a citizen, in commenting upon matters of public concern, and the interest of the state, as an employer, in promoting the efficiency of the public services it performs through its employees."

Among the factors to be considered in limiting a teacher's free expression are (1) whether the statements impede the teacher's proper performance of his daily duties in the classroom, (2) whether they substantially disrupt the regular operation of the school, (3) whether they violate an express need for confidentiality, (4) whether, if the statements are a public criticism of a superior by a subordinate, they seriously undermine the effectiveness of their working relationship, and (5) whether the school administration's interest in limiting a teacher's contribution to public debate outweighs the individual teacher's interest in commenting upon matters of public concern.

If the answer to these questions is no, and as long as the statements are not deliberate falsehoods or recklessly made, a teacher may not be fired from public employment for speaking out on issues of public importance.

Government workers The rights of free speech and press of government employees and public officials may be regulated in certain situations. For example, former employees of the Central Intelligence Agency (CIA) have the right to speak and write about the agency and its operation and to criticize it as any other citizen might but they must first receive clearance from the agency before any writing is done. The permission is necessary because before any employee is hired, he must sign a promise that he will never publish anything about the CIA without its approval. CIA employees are not entitled to disclose classified information they obtained during the course of their employment unless the material was already in the public domain.

Corporations Under the laws governing free speech and press, corporations are considered persons. They have the same freedom of expression as do individuals and may not be deprived of their right to make their views known on matters of public concern.

EXAMPLE Massachusetts law made it a crime for business 0⊷✸ corporations to contribute money to influence the outcome of any question submitted to voters other than one materially affecting the property, business, or assets of the corporations. Several banks that wanted to advertise their opposition to a referendum on a graduated personal income tax challenged the constitutionality of the law, claiming it restrained their freedom of speech.

Massachusetts claimed that the law served important governmental interests because it preserved the individual citizen's active role in elections. Because corporations have vast available funds to publicize their views, the state feared that opposing views would be overwhelmed in the wake of corporate publicity.

The Massachusetts courts upheld the statute, stating that corporate speech was protected by the First Amendment only when it directly related to the corporations' business interests. The Supreme Court struck down the law, declaring that the state failed to show that its fears of corporate views overwhelming the opposition were well founded. Furthermore, in areas where free speech is protected, the legislature cannot dictate on what subjects persons—including corporations—may speak.

Picketing Those who convey their ideas by picketing are not afforded the same kind of freedom as those engaged in pure speech. The government may impose reasonable regulations regarding the time, place, and manner of picketing to prevent unreasonable interference with the rights of others to use sidewalks and streets, to have access to store entrances, and to utilize police and fire protection. When used to enlighten the public about a dispute or a grievance with business, picketing is legal even though it may discourage customers from entering or patronizing a store or business.

EXAMPLE A gravel pit owner, who employed 15 to 20 men, 0⊷✸ sued to enjoin picketing by a labor union that had failed in an effort to unionize his employees. Pickets at the entrance of the pit carried signs reading "The men on this job are not 100% affiliated with the A.F.L." As a result, several trucking companies refused to deliver and haul goods to and from the plant, causing substantial damage to the owner.

The state court granted the owner an injunction against the picketers, deciding their purpose was illegal coercion of the employer to persuade his employees to join the union—an unfair labor practice under state law. The Supreme Court upheld the injunction. The mere fact that there is picketing "does not automatically justify its restraint without an investigation into its conduct and purposes," the Court said, but if the purpose of the picketing violates a valid state law, the court is justified in issuing an injunction to restrain the pickets.

■ **Advertising** All forms of advertising are considered *commercial speech,* as distinguished from the speech of individuals and corporations. The Supreme Court has ruled that the states may regulate commercial speech under certain circumstances. Specifically, they may always prohibit deceptive or misleading advertisements, and they can place restrictions on the time, place, and manner of commercial speech. However, the states may not completely suppress any truthful information about lawful activity.

The Supreme Court did not always hold that commercial speech could not be suppressed. In 1942 it ruled that commercial speech was not protected by the First Amendment when it unanimously sustained an ordinance that prohibited the distribution of commercial handbills.

EXAMPLE A distributor of commercial handbills that an- 0⊷✸ nounced the exhibition of a submarine was found guilty of breaking a local ordinance against such advertising. The distributor argued that the ordinance infringed on his freedom of expression, for printed on the reverse side of his handbills was a protest against an official refusal to allow him to use the city pier for the exhibit—a form of political rather than commercial speech. The Supreme Court unanimously ruled that the protest on the back of the handbill was merely a subterfuge to get around the ordinance. The Court stated, "We are equally clear that the Constitution imposes no such [First Amendment] restraint on government as respects purely commercial advertising." Apparently the government could constitutionally regulate advertising without abridging the First Amendment.

Not until 1975 did the Supreme Court reevaluate its position that commercial speech was outside the protection of the First Amendment.

EXAMPLE Jeffrey Bigelow was the managing editor of the *Virginia Weekly,* which ran an advertisement for a referral service for an abortion clinic in New York City. Bigelow was convicted of violating a Virginia statute making it a misdemeanor for any person to encourage or prompt the procuring of abortions by means of an advertisement.

The Supreme Court reversed the conviction, stating that an advertisement is not stripped of all First Amendment safeguards merely because it is commercial speech. It retains some degree of constitutional protection, which must be weighed against the state's interest in regulating the particular advertisement. The abortion-referral ad did more than provide financial profit for the newspaper. It conveyed information of potential interest to *Virginia Weekly* readers who might need the service offered, who were concerned about New York's laws, or who were seeking abortion law reform in Virginia. To prohibit the ad was to regulate without just cause what Virginia citizens heard or read about another state's services.

In 1976 the Supreme Court went even farther in extending First Amendment protection to advertising.

EXAMPLE Consumers of prescription drugs sued the Virginia State Board of Pharmacy for prohibiting the advertisement of prescription drug prices. The plaintiffs argued that the statute that had established the prohibition violated the 1st and 14th Amendments.

The board argued that such price information was not protected by the First Amendment because it was commercial speech. The federal district court declared the law invalid, and the Supreme Court agreed, ruling that commercial speech is protected by the First Amendment, although it can be regulated.

Commercial speech in the form of advertisements may serve the general public interest: "Advertising, however tasteless and excessive it sometimes may seem, is nonetheless dissemination of information as to who is producing and selling what product, for what reason, and at what price. So long as we preserve a predominantly free enterprise economy, the allocation of our resources in large measure will be made through numerous private economic decisions. It is a matter of public interest that those decisions . . . be intelligent and well informed. To this end, the free flow of commercial information is indispensable."

■ **Broadcasting** Since there are only a limited number of radio and television frequencies available, the constitutional right to freely express one's views through those media must necessarily be denied to many. To keep the airwaves from becoming a "cacophony of competing voices," the government has granted the FEDERAL COMMU-

NICATIONS COMMISSION (FCC) the power to license and regulate broadcasting so that it serves the best public interests.

Although the broadcasting media in this country are licensed and regulated by the government, the broadcasters maintain a substantial degree of journalistic independence. On the other hand, broadcast stations must encourage the presentation of opposing opinions on controversial issues so that the public will be able to make an informed decision after hearing all sides.

Editorial commercials Although broadcasters must devote air time to controversial issues, they are not required to do so through the sale of advertising space.

EXAMPLE A broadcaster adopted a general policy of not selling advertising time to individuals or groups wishing to speak out on issues they considered important. Two organizations sought to have the broadcaster's policy declared unconstitutional as a First Amendment violation. The U.S. Supreme Court upheld the broadcaster's policy, ruling that broadcasters are not constitutionally required to accept editorial advertisements.

If a broadcaster does sell editorial advertisement time, however, he is obligated to provide equal time to individuals or groups of opposing viewpoints. In addition, broadcasters must make air time available to all candidates for federal political office, either as part of regular programming or as advertising space.

Regulating offensive material The FCC may to some extent regulate the broadcast of material that is offensive to the majority of the people, but it must use the utmost discretion in doing so, lest it stifle the free expression of ideas as guaranteed by the Constitution.

EXAMPLE As part of an afternoon program, a radio station aired a satirical monologue entitled "Filthy Words," which listed and repeated various colloquial uses of "words you couldn't say on the public airwaves." While driving with his young son that afternoon, a father heard the broadcast and filed a complaint with the FCC. The agency warned the station that further complaints would result in appropriate action, including possible withdrawal of the station's license. According to the FCC, the monologue was "patently offensive" although not necessarily obscene. The broadcaster appealed, claiming that the power of the FCC to restrict such broadcasts violated his First Amendment rights.

The Supreme Court rejected the broadcaster's argument and upheld the FCC decision, but in its opinion it carefully outlined its reasons for doing so. "The fact that society may find speech offensive is not sufficient reason for suppressing it," the Court said. If there were any reason to believe that the monologue in question was offensive because of its political content or because it satirized contemporary attitudes about four-letter words, then it should be given constitutional protection. But the Court found that this was not the case. It found the monologue indisputably "vulgar" and agreed with the FCC that such "obnoxious gutter language . . . has the effect of debasing and brutalizing human beings by reducing them to their mere bodily functions."

In some cases, the Court continued, even the most offensive words are entitled to constitutional protection if the context surrounding them warrants it. Broadcasting, however, has the most limited First Amendment protection because it uniquely pervades American life both in public and in the privacy of our homes, where our right to be let alone plainly outweighs the First Amendment rights of an intruder.

"To say that one may avoid further offense by turning off the radio when he hears indecent language is like saying that the remedy for an assault is to run away after the first blow. One may hang up on an indecent phone call, but that option does not give the caller a constitutional immunity or avoid a harm" that has occurred.

Another reason broadcasting has more limited First Amendment protection is that it is easily accessible to children. The Court decided that the FCC was justified in ruling the monologue indecent at the early hour it was broadcast. That did not mean, however, that the same monologue could not be broadcast at a later hour—such as 2 A.M.—when a different audience would be listening.

■ **News media privileges** More and more often in recent years news reporters have been arguing that the Constitution gives them special privileges in gathering news. The most controversial of these is that a reporter cannot be compelled to testify on his news-gathering activities, whether in a civil lawsuit, a grand jury procedure, or a criminal trial. Reporters argue that forcing them to testify will dry up their access to sensitive and confidential news sources, thus restricting the flow of news to the public in violation of the First Amendment. Some states have special laws—called shield laws—that do allow news reporters to refuse to testify about their news-gathering activities in a criminal trial, but even under these laws a defendant's rights may overbalance the right protected by the shield law, and the reporter may be forced to testify. News reporters have also demanded the right of access to places not open to the general public and have attempted to free themselves from searches by the police even when the police have a legitimate warrant.

Testifying in civil suits The claim of the privilege not to testify in a civil lawsuit was first made in a 1958 suit brought by the singer and movie star Judy Garland.

EXAMPLE Garland charged that the Columbia Broadcasting
O—⭑ System (CBS) had been responsible for false and defamatory published statements about her. Some of the statements appeared in a New York *Herald Tribune* column by Marie Torre and were attributed to an unnamed CBS executive. When Garland's attorney questioned the columnist under oath, she refused to disclose the name of the executive, asserting that to do so would violate a journalistic confidence.

Garland took the columnist to court to compel her to disclose the name. Again she refused. The columnist was held in contempt and sentenced to 10 days' imprisonment. On appeal, she raised the constitutional issue.

While recognizing that compulsory disclosure of a journalist's confidential sources might abridge freedom of the press, the court said that this abridgment had to be balanced against the obvious need in the judicial process to compel testimony in some instances. Since the need for the testimony sought went to the heart of Garland's claim, a federal district court decided that the Constitu-

tion did not give the columnist the right to refuse to answer. The columnist's contempt citation was affirmed.

Testifying before grand juries In 1972, in the case of *Branzburg* v. *Hayes*, the U.S. Supreme Court had to decide whether news reporters could legally refuse to testify before grand juries regarding criminal activities they might have witnessed in the course of their work. A related question was whether they could be compelled to identify those engaged in such activities.

Paul Branzburg, a Louisville, Kentucky, reporter, wrote of seeing two local residents synthesizing hashish from marijuana. He appeared before a local grand jury in response to a summons but refused, despite a trial judge's order, to identify the people he observed. In another article, Branzburg interviewed unnamed drug users. Again he refused to answer any questions concerning drug violations. The Kentucky Court of Claims rejected his claim of a First Amendment privilege.

At about the same time, Paul Pappas, a Massachusetts TV newsman, refused to answer any question put to him by a local grand jury about his visit to a Black Panthers headquarters, and Earl Caldwell, a *New York Times* reporter, refused to reveal certain information to a federal grand jury investigating the possible criminal activities of Black Panthers. Both were denied their claims of First Amendment privilege.

In arguing their cases before the courts, Branzburg, Pappas, and Caldwell recognized the occasional need for disclosure of information to a grand jury. They insisted, however, that a reporter should not be forced to testify before a grand jury unless (1) he possesses information relevant to a crime the grand jury is investigating, (2) he is the only available source of the information, and (3) the need for the information is sufficiently compelling to override the invasion of First Amendment rights caused by the disclosure.

All of the above cases were brought to the Supreme Court. The Court ruled that the public interest in effective grand jury proceedings outweighed "the consequential, but uncertain, burden on news gathering that is said to result from insisting that reporters, like other citizens, respond to relevant questions put to them in the course of a valid grand jury investigation or criminal trial." Branzburg, Pappas, and Caldwell had to appear before grand juries and answer *relevant* questions or be held in contempt.

This decision did not say, however, that a news reporter must answer *all* questions when summoned by a grand jury. In a concurring opinion, Justice Lewis Franklin Powell, Jr., a member of the five-person majority, summarized the Court's decision: "The asserted claim to privilege should be judged on its facts by the striking of a proper balance between freedom of the press and the obligation of all citizens to give relevant testimony with respect to criminal conduct. The balance of these vital constitutional and societal interests on a case by case basis accords with the tried and traditional way of adjudicating such questions."

This balancing test would begin only after the newsperson appears and refuses to answer specific questions on First Amendment grounds.

Shield laws The heated controversy over whether or not a member of the news media can be legally compelled to reveal the identity of his news source or any other aspect of the news-gathering process is complicated by the fact that reporters sometimes claim a common-law privilege, similar to that accorded to the confidential relationships of attorney and client, doctor and patient, and husband and wife. See WITNESS. Although it has been argued that such a privilege would encourage and facilitate a freer flow of news and information to the public, the courts have consistently refused to recognize this privilege, since it would make it more difficult to determine the facts in court cases and to make and enforce laws.

More than half the states, however, have enacted special *shield laws*, which exempt reporters from revealing confidential sources. (Although bills have been introduced in Congress with increasing frequency since 1929, no federal shield laws have been enacted.) But even shield laws, common as they are, at best provide uncertain protection for the news reporters because they must be interpreted and applied by state courts, which have been traditionally hostile to their aim.

EXAMPLE Myron Farber, a reporter for *The New York Times*, refused to obey a court order requiring him to turn over notes he had amassed investigating the Dr. X murders for which Dr. Mario Jascalevich was indicted. Farber's investigation was largely responsible for Jascalevich's indictment and prosecution for the murders of several patients in 1965 and 1966 by injection of the deadly drug curare.

During the course of the murder trial, Farber and the *Times* refused to comply with two subpoenas ordering them to submit material that Farber uncovered but that was not in the prosecutor's file. They claimed immunity under the First Amendment and argued that the shield law in New Jersey, where the trial took place, not only protected sources but also safeguarded a reporter's unpublished materials, such as tape recordings or notes for possible use in future stories.

Farber and the *Times* moved to quash the subpoenas, but the state trial court ordered them to produce the information. Further appeals failed, and ultimately a state judge found both Farber and the *Times* guilty of contempt. Farber was sentenced to six months in the county jail and fined $1,000 for criminal contempt and fined another $1,000 and sentenced to remain in jail until he obeyed the order. The *Times* was fined $100,000 plus $5,000 a day until the materials were produced.

Farber challenged his imprisonment without a hearing, but withdrew the challenge when the court learned that he had agreed to write a book on the case, publicly revealing his material after all. The court asked to see the manuscript, but Farber refused. Meanwhile, after subpoenas to other parties had produced virtually the same information, the *Times* turned over its documents to the court. The *Times* then asked the court to purge it from its contempt (end the daily $5,000 fine), but the court refused to do so until the newspaper ordered Farber to turn over his notes. Both Farber and the *Times* appealed to the Supreme Court, which refused to hear the case.

The case was returned to the New Jersey Supreme Court, which ruled the First Amendment claims unfounded. As to the claims of protection under the shield laws, the New Jersey court found that a provision of the state constitution affording a criminal defendant the right to compel the attendance of witnesses and the production of documents prevails over a shield law.

The New Jersey court did recognize, however, that before a member of the press reveals confidential information from a secret source, he is entitled to a hearing to determine whether the subpoenaed information is relevant and material to the criminal prosecution and unavailable from any other source. Since the material sought in the Farber case was both relevant and otherwise unavailable, the convictions of Farber and the *Times* for contempt because they refused to produce it were justified.

Dr. Mario Jascalevich was eventually acquitted, but Farber never turned over his notes and remained in jail until the Jascalevich trial ended. The remainder of his prison sentence was then suspended and the daily fines against the *Times* ended. By that time the amount of fines paid by the *Times* amounted to $185,000 for civil contempt and $101,000 for criminal contempt.

Right of access   Although the news media serve a vital role in stimulating informed public discussion, they do not enjoy any special constitutional right to access of information.

EXAMPLE In Santa Rita, California, a broadcasting company was refused permission to inspect and photograph part of an Alameda County jail where a prisoner had, according to a psychiatrist, committed suicide because of the condition of his cell. The broadcasting company and the National Association for the Advancement of Colored People sued the county sheriff who was in charge of the jail for depriving them of their First Amendment rights. The Supreme Court ruled that the news media did not have a constitutional right of access to a county jail over and above that of other persons.

In another case, a broadcasting company was successfully sued for trespassing when its employees burst into a restaurant against the owner's wishes for the purpose of gathering news.

Immunity from searches   Finally, the news media have claimed immunity from SEARCH AND SEIZURE that extends beyond the protection against arbitrary searches and seizures guaranteed all persons by the Fourth Amendment. In a controversial case, the Supreme Court decided that the press did not have First Amendment protection from a search of its offices by police seeking photographs that might identify persons who had committed a crime.

EXAMPLE Police entered the office of the Stanford University student newspaper armed with a valid search warrant. They were seeking photographs of people who had taken part in an unruly campus demonstration. The newspaper staff objected, claiming that the First Amendment protected it from such action. Subjecting the press to such searches, they argued, would impede its news-gathering capabilities. Confidential sources would not speak for fear of being identified. If the police wanted certain material, they could subpoena it, without jeopardizing the newspaper's constitutional rights. If the paper failed to comply with a subpoena, then the police could take more drastic steps.

The Supreme Court rejected the argument. Where a search warrant is properly issued, the ability of the press to gather, analyze, and disseminate the news is sufficiently protected from interference. The Court discounted the fear that confidential sources would disappear or that the press would suppress news through fears that authorities under investigation would secure warrants and seize crucial material.

Not everyone was as optimistic as the Court, however. In fact, the decision was considered so startling a threat to freedom of the press that Congress enacted legislation requiring law enforcement officers to subpoena desired material instead of obtaining search warrants.

■ **Symbolic speech** Expression may be symbolic as well as verbal. Symbolic speech, or symbolic conduct, is an action that communicates an idea. The term is often used to express opposition to the government or a government policy. For example, in the case of *Tinker* v. *Des Moines School District,* cited above, the Supreme Court decided that the wearing of black armbands was a form of symbolic speech entitled to constitutional protection. Flag desecration and draft card burning are forms of symbolic expression that were popular in the late 1960's. The Supreme Court recognized that speech may be nonverbal when, in 1931, it struck down on grounds of First Amendment vagueness a law prohibiting the display of a red flag "as a sign, symbol or emblem of opposition to organized government." Symbolic speech is entitled to protection under the 1st and 14th Amendments, but there are restrictions. The act must neither incite others to act illegally nor violate reasonable regulatory laws.

Draft card burning Until the mid-1970's men 18 years of age had to register with their local Selective Service boards to determine their eligibility for induction into the armed services. The board issued each man a selective service registration certificate, popularly known as a draft card, which he was required by federal regulations to keep.

EXAMPLE In 1966, during the time of the Vietnam conflict, O⊷⊷ David O'Brien and three other men burned their draft cards on the steps of the South Boston Courthouse. O'Brien was convicted in federal court of knowingly burning his draft card in violation of federal law. He stated that he did so "to influence others to adopt his antiwar beliefs" and claimed that the law he was accused of breaking deprived him of his constitutional right to freedom of expression by means of symbolic speech.

The Supreme Court disagreed, refusing to "accept the view that an apparently limitless variety of conduct can be labeled 'speech' whenever the person engaging in the conduct intends thereby to express an idea." The Court said that "when 'speech' and 'non-speech' elements are combined in the same course of conduct, a sufficiently important governmental interest in regulating the non-speech element can justify limitations on First Amendment freedoms." The use of draft cards, the Court felt, served as a "legitimate and substantial administrative aid in the functioning of [the Selective Service] system that Congress had established to raise armies." The Court concluded that punishing the intentional destruction or mutilation of draft cards was an appropriately narrow means of protecting this government interest, since only the independent noncommunicative part of the conduct was punished.

Flag desecration The American flag has often been used to express dissatisfaction with conditions in this country, and the Supreme Court has been asked to rule on the use of the flag as symbolic speech.

EXAMPLE A black man named Street publicly burned an O⊷⊷ American flag after he heard on a news broadcast that civil rights leader James Meredith had been shot by a sniper in Mississippi. As the flag burned, Street shouted: "If they did that to Meredith, we don't need an American flag" and "We don't need no damn flag." State law made it a crime to "publicly mutilate, deface, defile, or defy, trample upon or cast contempt upon, either by words or act," any flag of the United States.

Street was convicted but appealed, claiming the law denied him freedom of expression. In a 5-4 decision the Supreme Court reversed Street's conviction because the lower court had used the law to punish him for his words and not for his actions. The part of the law that punished him "merely for speaking defiant or contemptuous words about the American flag" violated the constitutional guarantee of freedom of expression. The conviction was reversed without the Court's dealing with the part of the law pertaining to the act of burning the flag.

EXAMPLE On May 10, 1970, a few days after the United O⊷⊷ States invaded Cambodia and National Guardsmen killed demonstrating students at Kent State University in Ohio, a college student hung a 3-by-5-foot American flag upside down from his apartment window with a black peace symbol attached. The student was convicted of violating a state law that prohibited placing "any word, figure, mark, picture, design, drawing or advertisement of any nature" upon any U.S. flag or exhibiting any such decorated flag.

It was clear that the student's conduct was a protest against the invasion of Cambodia and the Kent State killings. "[I] felt that the flag stood for America and I wanted people to know that I thought America stood for peace," he said. The Supreme Court reversed his conviction, recognizing the act as a form of harmless expression guaranteed by the Constitution.

■ **Nongovernmental suppression** The 1st and 14th Amendments prohibit government suppression of speech and press, but the Constitution does not protect you from the efforts of a private corporation or person to restrict your freedom of expression. On private property used for an owner's private purposes, your constitutional right to disseminate ideas and views must usually yield to the owner's right to be protected against trespass or invasion of his privacy. See PRIVACY, RIGHT OF. In 1968 the question as to whether people have the right to picket and demonstrate in privately owned shopping malls was tested.

EXAMPLE Members of a local union picketed a large shop- O⊷⊷ ping center store that employed a wholly non-union staff. The peaceful picketing took place on the shopping center's property in the immediate vicinity of the store.

A Pennsylvania court issued an injunction that required all picketing to be confined to public areas outside the shopping center. The state supreme court affirmed the order, but the U.S. Supreme Court reversed the decision because the shopping center was "the functional equivalent of the business district" of the town. The Court also pointed out that the picketing was "directly related in its purpose to the use to which the shopping center property was being put."

The Court modified that position in a 1972 case.

EXAMPLE Five people distributed handbills against the war O⊶—⊷ in Vietnam in a shopping center where the owner had established a rule of no handbilling of any kind on the premises. Security guards told the distributors to leave, which they did, to avoid arrest. They later sued for relief in a federal district court.

The court held that distributing handbills on the shopping center's property is protected by the 1st and 14th Amendments and enjoined (ordered) the mall owner to permit handbilling. The Court of Appeals affirmed the ruling, but the Supreme Court reversed it, rejecting the argument that the property of a large shopping center, even though it is privately owned, is "open to the public" and therefore has been dedicated to certain types of public use. The Court distinguished this case from the prior case, in which picketing was directed specifically at one of the tenants of the shopping mall. Since the war did not directly involve the mall and the protesters had other alternatives to express their views, the Court sent the case back to the lower court to vacate the injunction. The mall could enforce its policy of no handbilling.

After this case, the Supreme Court became even stricter in applying First Amendment rights to persons in private shopping malls. In fact, it overturned its 1968 decision permitting the local union to picket a store in a mall.

EXAMPLE A group of labor union members picketed peace- O⊶—⊷ fully in front of their employer's leased store in a privately owned shopping mall in Georgia to protest the company's failure to agree to demands made by their union in contract negotiation. (The protest was by warehouse employees, but the warehouse was not located in the shopping center.) The mall's general manager told them he would have them arrested for criminal trespass if they did not leave. The union then filed with the National Labor Relations Board (NLRB) a charge of unfair labor practice against the owner of the shopping center. The NLRB upheld the charges, and the owner sought review. The Court of Appeals enforced the NLRB cease-and-desist order, which, in effect, ordered the shopping center owner to allow the picketing.

The mall owner finally appealed to the Supreme Court, which ruled that the pickets did not have a First Amendment right to enter the shopping center for the purpose of advertising their strike.

According to the Court, if the anti-Vietnam protesters had no First Amendment rights to demonstrate on privately owned property, the pickets could not be permitted to do so simply because the nature of their protest differed. To make a distinction would allow the government to approve certain expression because of its content while banning other communications—an obvious violation of the 1st and 14th Amendments.

People may reasonably exercise their right to free speech in a privately owned shopping center when a state law or constitutional provision has been interpreted by the state's highest court to permit this.

EXAMPLE High school students had set up a table in a O⊶—⊷ private shopping center in Campbell, California, to distribute pamphlets and solicit signatures for petitions against a United Nations resolution against Zionism. A security guard asked the students to leave because a regulation of the center prohibited "any publicly expressive activity . . . not directly related to its commercial purposes." The students left but sued in state court to enjoin (prevent) the owner from refusing to allow them to circulate their petitions. The court ruled that the students had no right under the federal or state constitution to express themselves on privately owned property when there were other reasonable ways to accomplish their goals, such as by circulating the petitions on the public sidewalks. The highest state court reversed the lower court, ruling that the right of speech and petitioning guaranteed by the state constitution may be exercised on privately owned shopping centers as long as done so reasonably. An injunction was granted.

On appeal to the U.S. Supreme Court, the owner argued that his property was unconstitutionally taken from him without just compensation and that, by being forced to permit others to use his center as a speech forum, he was denied his right to free speech. The Court rejected both arguments. Because the value of the shopping center was not shown to have dropped because of such activity, the owner was not deprived of his property. Regarding his right to free speech, the Court found that since a shopping center is not for the personal use of its owner but is open to the public, the views expressed there would not necessarily be considered those of the owner. In addition, the state only required that access could not be denied to the center but it did not attempt to dictate the type of message to be expressed. Thus, the Court ruled that the owner's right to free speech was not infringed.

This case differed from other cases because the state constitution gave state residents a greater right to free speech than the one given under the federal Constitution.

■ **Freedom of Information Act** The importance of freedom of speech and freedom of the press is to encourage the free exchange of ideas and to expose corruption so that self-government may flourish. The First Amendment would be empty rhetoric if people were unjustly denied access to information on which to base their opinions. Yet for nearly 200 years, from the time of George Washington's Presidency until 1966, both the federal and state governments claimed the right to withhold or restrict in the "public interest" information about their activities and operations.

In 1966, however, Congress enacted the Freedom of Information Act (and many states enacted similar laws) granting to the press and public a "right to know" facts contained in many government documents and records. Even now, not all requested information must be disclosed by the government, since such areas as national security must remain secret. But a great amount of previously classified information is now available, and the act, which has been amended over the years, has done much to encourage confidence in the integrity of a government that freely discloses information to keep its citizens informed.

speedy trial The Sixth Amendment to the Constitution provides, in part, that "In all criminal prosecutions, the accused shall enjoy the right to a speedy and public trial." The guarantee of a speedy trial is an important safeguard against undue and oppressive imprisonment of the accused before he has his day in court. It also minimizes the anxiety generated by public accusations of criminal conduct and reduces the chance that a long delay will impair the accused's ability to defend himself because of loss of evidence or memory lapses on the part of witnesses.

The constitutional requirement of a speedy trial in criminal prosecution has been applied to the states through the due process clause of the 14th Amendment. See DUE PROCESS OF LAW. States also provide for a defendant's right to a speedy trial in their constitutions and laws. See the section on speedy trial in CRIMINAL LAW.

spendthrift **1** In popular usage, a person who spends money profusely or unwisely. **2** Under various statutes, a person who wastes or decreases his estate (money, real estate, and other property) by excessive drinking, gambling, idleness, or debauchery, and thereby causes himself or his family need or suffering. **3** A person who causes a public agency to be charged with his support or the support of his family.

When authorized by law, a spendthrift's creditors or neglected family or an agency charged with his support can ask the court to place the spendthrift's property under guardianship. This means a court can appoint a guardian to protect the spendthrift against his wasteful habits by taking care of his property. Such a guardian can be a relative, a friend, a trust company, or anyone whom the court considers qualified to act in the spendthrift's best interests. Statutes providing for the guardianship of spendthrifts are based on the government's right to protect its citizens' property for the benefit of their families, the community, and themselves. See GUARDIAN AND WARD; TRUST.

spin-off A spin-off occurs when a parent CORPORATION organizes a subsidiary corporation and transfers part of its assets to the subsidiary in exchange for all of the subsidiary's capital stock. The subsidiary's stock is then distributed to the parent corporation's shareholders, who are not required to surrender any of their parent stock in exchange. When the parent company declares the distribution of stock to be a dividend, it is taxable.

If the shareholders *are* required to surrender part of their parent stock in exchange, then the transaction is called a *split-off*.

split-off See SPIN-OFF.

split-up A split-up occurs when a parent corporation transfers all its assets to two or more corporations and then liquidates. The shareholders of the parent corporation surrender all their stock in exchange for stock in the transferee corporations.

spoliation **1** Any erasure, addition, or change in a document, such as a check or promissory note, by someone acting without the consent of the persons who have an interest in the instrument. See ALTERATION OF AN INSTRUMENT. **2** Failure of a person involved in a lawsuit to produce evidence in his possession or under his control—probably because he thinks it would act against him. The person who fails to produce the evidence is called the spoliator. Any inferences against him that result from his failure to produce the evidence are allowed.

EXAMPLE The mayor of your city is accused of accepting bribes from various contractors who have been awarded public contracts. The mayor's secretary testifies at the mayor's trial that the mayor noted every bribe he received in a ledger that he kept in a safe at his home. The mayor refuses to produce the ledger. This spoliation of evidence entitles the jury to infer that the ledger did list the bribes that he had taken.

sports and entertainment Sports events and other forms of public entertainment do not have a special group of laws that regulate them. They are affected by a wide variety of federal, state, and local laws as well as by fundamental principles expressed in the common law. Although the field of entertainment law is relatively new, some lawyers have become specialists in it.

■ **Contracts** A major portion of the sports and entertainment world is regulated by CONTRACT law. Sports leagues, for example, are started when teams agree to form an association to cooperate in scheduling competitions and formulating rules and to designate a person or commission to administer their plan. Their agreement is a contract and must not contain illegal provisions, such as antitrust violations. Some courts have recognized that each team has an interest in the financial health of every other team.

Athletes and entertainers also need contracts of employment that spell out the obligations of each party, the compensation to be paid, and the remedies for violations. One of the most common features of these employment contracts is an acknowledgment that the services of the athlete or entertainer are unique. His special skill makes it impossible to replace him if he fails to perform his obligations. For this reason, if he fails to live up to the terms of his contract a court may not only assess money DAMAGES but also issue an INJUNCTION (court order) forbidding the athlete or entertainer to perform for someone else. For example, while it would be awkward and impractical for a court to try to make an actor play a part as agreed, and do his best, a court can forbid him from working for someone else during the run of the play in the breached contract. See SPECIFIC PERFORMANCE.

Once a performer or athlete achieves public recognition, his name and image become valuable assets. He has what is sometimes called the private and personal right of publicity, which entitles him to sell the right to use his name or image for advertising purposes. See PRIVACY, RIGHT OF. For example, ball players agree to let bubble-gum manufacturers use their names and pictures on trading cards; singers do television commercials for auto companies; and skiers endorse clothing brands and allow their names to be stamped on equipment. These arrangements are also governed by contract law.

■ **Regulation** It is entirely proper for the government to regulate sports and entertainment in the public interest.

Some activities are prohibited because they are dehumanizing, antisocial, and offensive to the community. Cockfighting, bearbaiting and bullfighting are all illegal. Most communities will not allow nude or indecent dancing in nightclubs. Many states prohibit entertainments that are generally associated with gambling and corruption, such as horse racing, dog racing, and prizefighting. Statutes forbidding wrestling matches by women have been upheld in some places, but rules preventing women from working as jockeys have been thrown out in other places.

Violation of some laws regarding sports and entertainment events is a crime. For example, it may be a criminal offense to stage a bullfight for public entertainment even if there is no intention to kill the bull. "Tampering with a sporting event" is criminal. A jockey who uses an electronic prod, a coach who slips drugs into his football team's water, and a race-car driver who uses illegal equipment in his car are guilty of tampering.

■ **Taxing and licenses** Some forms of entertainment are specially taxed or must be licensed. Many forms of amusements are taxed in order to help pay for the cost of regulating them because they have a tendency to become NUISANCES if not strictly supervised. Pinball machines, jukeboxes, poolrooms, and bowling alleys may be taxed for this reason. Golf courses, skating rinks, health spas, and public swimming pools may have to be licensed in order to insure compliance with health and safety regulations. Any event likely to attract crowds, such as a rock concert or a street fair, must be licensed so that authorities can be sure that crowd-control and sanitation plans are adequate. Theaters generally have to be licensed as evidence of compliance with fire and health code requirements and obscenity restrictions. See THEATERS AND SHOWS. Individuals in certain fields of entertainment may have to be licensed to help authorities screen out gamblers, con men, and persons associated with organized crime.

■ **Admission and tickets** A person who seeks admission to a public entertainment or sports event can be excluded for disorderly conduct but not because of his race, color, religion, or national origin. See CIVIL RIGHTS. An admission ticket is evidence that the holder is entitled to enter because a price has been paid. If there are no reserved seats, the ticket holder may sit in any unoccupied seat set aside for the kind of ticket he holds. A reserved seat ticket entitles the holder to the seat shown on the ticket. If a mistake has been made and the seat was already sold, the ticket holder has no right to complain if the management courteously offers to refund his money or give him a different seat of the same price. Persons who buy quantities of tickets for resale may be regulated as agents. Scalping, or reselling tickets at more than their face value, is a crime in some places.

■ **Safety of patrons, spectators, or participants** The owner of a place of public amusement must keep it reasonably safe from the special risks of his business. For example, a nightclub owner who provides a dance band and soft lights must be sure that an employee watches for spilled drinks and promptly cleans up the floor. An amusement-park owner must follow a careful routine of preventive maintenance because of the likelihood of serious injuries if a ride breaks down. The owner of a roller-skating rink must

hire enough people to supervise large crowds of teenagers who frequent the rink on weekend nights.

An owner does not have to insure the safety of patrons, spectators, or participants at his place of amusement.

EXAMPLE (1) A 15-year-old novice skier cannot hold a ski resort liable for injuries he sustains while skiing on a trail that is clearly marked "expert."

(2) A visitor to a drive-through animal park has no legal claim against the owners if he is injured as a result of getting out of his car to feed bear cubs in spite of posted warnings.

(3) A spectator who is hit by a hockey puck cannot sue the owners of the sports arena, the team, or the player because the law says that spectators assume the natural risks to which they voluntarily expose themselves at sports events.

(4) A high school football player who suffers a broken neck has no complaint against his school if his coach has carefully taught safety to the players and if practice sessions and games have always been well supervised.

Injured people can sue owners of places of amusement if the owners are unreasonably careless.

EXAMPLE (1) A bareback rider can recover for injuries from a rodeo producer if he can show that the horse bolted through a gate that should have been kept shut.

(2) Passengers on a bobsled at a winter resort have cause for complaint if the owners allow dangerous slush to accumulate at the bottom of the run.

(3) A second baseman is assumed to accept the risk that he might incur injuries from a baseball or be run over by another player, but the ball park operator is responsible if a spectator hits a player with a beer bottle bought from the ball park concession.

■ **Antitrust laws and sports** The Supreme Court has said that antitrust laws "are as important to the preservation of economic freedom as the Bill of Rights is to the protection of our fundamental personal freedoms." Antitrust laws make it illegal for one person, business, or group to gain so much control of a certain market or commodity that it can restrain free buying, selling, or bargaining; federal antitrust laws make it illegal for MONOPOLIES to engage in interstate commerce. See COMMERCE CLAUSE. Antitrust laws have a unique place in the history of sports in this country.

Baseball During the 1800's, small or regional professional baseball leagues were formed, and often disbanded, all over the country. In 1876 several of these teams started the National League in order to compete against each other. Another association, called the Western League, changed its name to the American League in 1900 and within a few years became the second major league. In 1913 ball teams from Brooklyn, Pittsburgh, Buffalo, Baltimore, St. Louis, Kansas City, Indianapolis, and Chicago founded the Federal League to compete with the National and American Leagues. After two years, however, seven of the Federal League teams signed a "peace agreement" with the National and American Leagues.

This agreement brought the Federal League teams into a system that required every player on the major league teams and on the minor league farm teams associated with them to contract with only one team. The standard player's

---

SPORTS, ENTERTAINMENT, AND THE LAW

■ You can be excluded from admission to a public entertainment or sports event for disorderly conduct but not because of race, color, religion, or national origin.

■ If your reserved seat has been sold to someone else by mistake, you have no right to complain if the management courteously offers to refund your money or give you a different seat worth the same price.

■ Scalping (reselling tickets at more than their face value) is a crime in some places.

■ The owner of a place of public amusement must keep it reasonably safe, but he does not have to insure the safety of patrons. Patrons have some responsibility for their own actions and for assuming the natural risks associated with the particular sport or amusement.

■ Injured people can sue owners of places of amusement if the owners are unreasonably careless.

■ Governments have the right to regulate sports and entertainment in the public interest. They may make certain activities a crime. Cockfighting and bullfighting are criminal offenses, as is tampering with a sporting event—for example, using illegal equipment in race cars.

---

contract contained a reserve clause that allowed a player to negotiate only with the team that held his contract. If a player violated this clause, he was guilty of "contract jumping," and his name was placed on an ineligible list. All the teams agreed not to hire any player who was on this list. The leagues believed that without the reserve system, the most highly skilled players would be absorbed by the wealthier clubs. Some ball clubs would then be so superior to the others that games would be dull and fans would stop attending them. Once an individual player signed a contract with a club, however, he had no say in his career. If he was unhappy with his club he had to stay there until the club sold his contract to another team.

The reserve clause and the ineligible lists kept players from violating their contracts and helped preserve the American and National Leagues. But the Federal Baseball Club of Baltimore said that the reserve clause destroyed them. The control the American and National Leagues had over their ball players prevented them from moving to Federal teams and thus enabled them to force seven of the Federal League teams to disband.

The Federal League case   The Baltimore Club refused to disband and sued the National League and the American League under federal antitrust laws. It claimed that their monopoly had cost the Baltimore Club $80,000, which should be tripled as a penalty. At the trial Baltimore won a verdict of $240,000 plus costs and attorney fees. On appeal the judgment was reversed, and the Supreme Court upheld the reversal in 1922. The Court recognized the value of the reserve clause in bringing order to the sport and in creating a balance among the major league teams. Most importantly, it declared that a major league baseball game is "local in its beginning and in its end." Since the federal law prohibiting monopolies applies only to businesses engaged in interstate commerce, it did not apply to local sports exhibitions, "which are purely state affairs."

The baseball players' case   Thirty years later a group of professional baseball players sued their club owners, charging that the reserve clause violated federal antitrust law; that it exploited the players who attracted profits for the benefit of the clubs and leagues; that the network of agreements among the ball clubs and with the Mexican League deprived players and organizations of the right to bargain freely; and that professional baseball in the United States was operated as a monopoly.

The Supreme Court quickly disposed of the case in 1953. The Court stated that the rule of law had been settled in the Federal Baseball League case and that it was inappropriate for the judges to change the rules after baseball had been allowed to develop for 30 years. The Court believed that any change in the law should be made by Congress because a legislature is more responsive to the people than a court. Two justices dissented, declaring that "it is a contradiction in terms to say that the defendants in the cases before us are not now engaged in interstate commerce." They cited the huge investments of the teams, the constant travel across state lines, large expenditures for accommodations and equipment, interstate advertising, radio and television broadcasts, and the highly organized farm system.

The Curt Flood case   In October of 1969 Curtis Charles Flood was traded to the Philadelphia Phillies in a multiplayer transaction. Flood had been with the St. Louis Cardinals for 12 seasons and as a highly ranked outfielder commanded a $90,000 salary. He had not been consulted and received formal notice only after the deal had been completed. He asked the commissioner of baseball to make him a free agent so that he could negotiate with other major league teams, but his request was refused. He sat out 1970 because of his refusal to play, played briefly in 1971, and thereafter did not play professional baseball again.

In January of 1970 Flood sued the commissioner of baseball, the presidents of the two leagues, and the 24 major-league clubs. His complaint charged, among other things, violations of federal antitrust laws. In this case the Supreme Court did rule that professional baseball was engaged in interstate commerce. However, its reserve system enjoyed an exemption from federal antitrust law that made it an anomaly in law. The Court called this an aberration but still held to the position that Congress, not a court, should change the law. Flood did not win his suit.

Boxing   Perhaps because of the dissent in the baseball players' case, athletes in other sports decided to test the application of federal antitrust laws to the sports and entertainment business.

EXAMPLE   The federal government tried to break up a monopoly of three corporations and two individuals who had promoted and allegedly controlled major prizefights. While the case was in federal court, the Supreme Court reaffirmed its 1922 decision that antitrust laws do not apply to baseball, so the trial judge dismissed the government's case against the boxing promoters. On appeal of this case to the Supreme Court in 1955, the dismissal was reversed. The Supreme Court was persuaded that the boxing matches did amount to interstate commerce because, among other things, they were promoted in several states and produced substantial income from the sale of rights to television and radio broadcasts and motion pictures. The majority of the Court refused to rule that all professional sports were outside the reach of antitrust laws. Again there was strong dissent, with two justices declaring that "It would baffle the subtlest ingenuity to find a single differentiating factor between other sporting exhibitions, whether boxing or football or tennis, and baseball insofar as the conduct of the sport is relevant to the criteria or considerations" that make antitrust law applicable to interstate commerce.

Football and other sports   In 1957 the Supreme Court heard an appeal by a football player who had sued the National Football League for unreasonably restraining free trade. His case had also been dismissed by a lower court because of the baseball cases, but the Supreme Court reversed the decision.

EXAMPLE   The football player, William Radovich, was playing for the Detroit Lions in 1946 when he asked to be transferred to Los Angeles because his father was ill there. The Detroit Lions refused his request. He broke his contract and began playing for the Los Angeles Dons, which belonged to the All-American Conference, a league that disbanded in 1949. In 1948 the San Francisco Clippers, a Pacific Coast League team, offered him a job as player-coach, but the National League gave notice that Radovich was blacklisted and any team that signed him up would suffer severe penalties. This blacklisting prevented Radovich's further employment in professional football. Moreover, Radovich claimed that there was a conspiracy to squeeze out the All-American Conference by boycotting its players, thus strengthening the monopoly of the National Football League.

The National League argued that football and baseball were different from other businesses and needed to be organized as monopolies. The Supreme Court disagreed. The Court said that if it were "considering the question of baseball for the first time upon a clean slate," it would not exempt baseball from antitrust laws. It also reiterated its belief that new legislation was the fairest way to change the long-standing Supreme Court decision as it affected baseball. The Court refused to extend that interpretation of the law to football, however, even though it conceded that the distinction might seem "unrealistic, inconsistent, or illogical."

In various cases, federal courts have ruled that basketball, hockey, and golf are not exempt from antitrust laws.

End of the reserve clause   In 1975 Andy Messersmith of the Los Angeles Dodgers and Dave McNally of the Montreal Expos failed to come to terms with their clubs when their contracts expired. At the end of their option year—the period for which their contracts required them to play at the same salary if a new agreement could not be reached—both men announced that they considered themselves free agents. The dispute went to arbitration. The arbitrator ruled that a player became a free agent after he had played his option year with the team holding his contract. This decision was appealed in federal court and upheld. The old reserve system was legally dead by 1976.

A new system   Both the players and the owners agreed that a new system was needed to forestall chaos and to prevent the wealthier teams from accumulating all the best talent. In 1976 a four-year labor contract was negotiated to organize a reentry draft for players who became eligible to negotiate with other teams. It provided that at the end of the season all the teams would get a list of free agents. Each team could then designate players on the list with whom it wished to deal, and the team with the worst record in the previous season would get to designate players first. Up to 12 teams could negotiate with a player, plus the team for which he had been playing. The number of players a team could choose depended on the number of eligible free agents in the pool. The purpose of this system was to prevent contract negotiations during the baseball season (while players were concentrating on their current team) and to insure that only the teams in the lower half of the rankings for the year could seek available players.

squatter   A person who settles on someone else's land without legal authority or without obtaining a legal title. Most often the word is applied to a person who settles on new public land. The word "squatter" is also synonymous with the words "intruder" and "trespasser." A person who occupies land that does not belong to him for a specified period of time and under certain conditions may eventually receives legal title to it by ADVERSE POSSESSION.

ss.   An abbreviation used in an AFFIDAVIT, PLEADING, or record. It is commonly read as "to wit" or "namely."

stale check   A check that is held too long before an attempt is made to cash it. A check is considered stale when it has not been cashed for a period of six months or longer. A bank is not obligated to pay such a check. See COMMERCIAL PAPER.

stamp tax   A tax imposed by most states on certain transactions, such as the transfer of real property (real estate). The tax is paid by purchasing stamps that are then glued to the deed. Metering machines that imprint stamps on the deed are also used. The tax may be imposed, for example, at the rate of $1 for each $1,000. If a home is sold for $50,000, then $50 worth of tax stamps must be purchased by the seller and attached to the deed. If the stamps are not attached to the deed, it usually cannot be recorded.

stand   1 Appear in court or submit to the court's authority, as "to stand trial."   2 The place in a courtroom where the parties and witnesses give their testimony.

standing   The rule developed by the courts that a person who challenges the constitutionality of a statute or the action of an agency that administers a statute must prove that he is directly affected or injured by it.

Usually a person lacks standing to contest the constitutional rights of another person. For example, a doctor who argued that his state's abortion statutes violated his patient's constitutional rights lacked standing to contest his patient's rights. On the other hand, an association such as the National Association for the Advancement of Colored People has standing to contest the constitutionality of a law that adversely affects the rights of its members.

The party must also show that the interest he is seeking to protect falls "within the zone of interests to be protected by the statute or constitutional guarantee in question." For example, schoolchildren and their parents who were directly affected by state law concerning religious exercises in the schools, such as Bible reading, had standing to complain that these practices were unconstitutional under the First Amendment. The interest they sought to protect—freedom of religion—fell within the "zone of interests" guaranteed by the First Amendment.

stand mute   Refusal by the defendant in a criminal prosecution to plead either "guilty" or "not guilty." When this occurs the court will usually enter a plea of "not guilty" for the defendant. A defendant sometimes stands mute because he is deaf or does not speak English and no interpreter is available. Most often, however, a defendant stands mute out of sheer obstinacy.

Star Chamber   A high court in England from the late 15th century to the middle of the 17th century, named probably for the gilt stars that decorated the ceiling of the room in which the court sat.

In order to deal with the nobles and others of the gentry class (who were above ordinary common law), the King appointed members of his Privy Council to sit with the royal judges in both civil and criminal cases without a jury. This relieved the King from the time-consuming task of hearing cases personally. Subsequently, this group evolved into a court that was called the Star Chamber. However, the Star Chamber eventually became a tool of oppression. It met in secret, extracted evidence by torturing witnesses, and handed out severe punishments—even mutilation. It completely disregarded established law and sometimes acted on mere rumor in order to squelch opposition to the King. Because of these abuses, the Star Chamber was abolished by Parliament in 1641.

In modern usage the term "Star Chamber" is applied to any lawless and oppressive tribunal, especially one that meets in secret.

stare decisis   (Latin) "To stand by decided matters." *Stare decisis* is the policy of courts to adhere to a principle of law that has been laid down in a certain case and to apply it to all future cases in which the facts are substantially the same. The principle of law becomes a binding precedent in that court and in other courts of equal or lower rank.

> EXAMPLE   The U.S. Supreme Court has ruled that saying a nondenominational prayer in public schools violates the clause of the federal Constitution that prohibits the establishment of religion by the government. Any court hearing a case challenging the recitation of prayers in public schools is bound by *stare decisis* to follow the Supreme Court decision.

statement of affairs   Financial form filed in BANKRUPTCY proceedings. It contains information about the debtor's assets and liabilities and the reason for his bankruptcy.

state's evidence   Testimony given on behalf of the prosecution by a person who was a participant or accomplice in a crime. Under an agreement with the prosecutor, the person is granted immunity from prosecution if he freely, fully, and fairly discloses his own guilt as well as that of the other participants. See SELF-INCRIMINATION.

states' rights   The United States is a single, sovereign nation made up of 50 distinct states, each having most of the lawmaking powers of an independent country. The states are bound in an indestructible union with each other and with the national government. See FEDERALISM. This article briefly discusses the various constitutional clauses and amendments that spell out the rights of the individual states in the Union and the rights of the federal government that binds them together as a nation.

■ **Full faith and credit clause**   Article IV, Section 1, of the federal Constitution provides:

> 66 *Full Faith and Credit shall be given in each State to the public Acts, Records, and judicial Proceedings of every other State.*"

This clause requires each state to recognize the governmental and public matters of all the other states. For instance, a marriage that is valid in one state is valid in all the others, and a final JUDGMENT by a court in one state will generally be recognized as binding in another state. The reason for recognizing judgments of different states is to stop endless litigation of an issue. Once a particular issue is settled in one state, it should be regarded as settled in every other state. By adopting the U.S. Constitution, every state became bound by this policy. The FULL FAITH AND CREDIT clause refers only to judgments by courts of states in the United States and not to judgments of courts in foreign nations. See COMITY; CONFLICT OF LAWS.

■ **Privileges and immunities clause**   Article IV, Section 2, Clause 1 of the federal Constitution provides:

> 66 *The Citizens of each State shall be entitled to all Privileges and Immunities of Citizens in the several States.*"

The PRIVILEGES AND IMMUNITIES clause, sometimes called the comity clause, prohibits a state from discriminating against citizens of other states in favor of its own citizens. Although the U.S. Supreme Court has refused to specifically define state privileges and immunities—preferring to decide each case as it arises—the clause does protect the right of all U.S. citizens, without regard to their state citizenship, (1) to be protected by the government in any state; (2) to acquire and possess all kinds of property in any state; (3) to enjoy life, liberty, safety, and happiness in any state; (4) to start and defend lawsuits in court; and (5) to pass through or reside in any state for purposes of trade, agriculture, or professional pursuits.

For example, a Georgia statute that authorized abortions only for state residents came before the Supreme Court. In its decision in 1973 the Court held that a state may not make residency in the state a prerequisite to obtaining medical care within its borders. Just as the privileges and

---

WHAT STATES' RIGHTS MEAN TO YOU

■ A final judgment by a court in one state is binding in other states.

■ A marriage that is valid in one state is valid in all the others.

■ No state may discriminate against citizens of other states in favor of its own citizens.

■ As a U.S. citizen, you have the right, regardless of your state citizenship, to be protected by the government of any state; to acquire and possess all kinds of property; to start and defend lawsuits; and to pass through or reside in any state.

■ A state may not, therefore, make residency in the state a prerequisite for obtaining medical care, for example.

■ Persons accused of crimes who have fled to other states may be extradited if there is a formal criminal charge and a formal demand is made by the governor of the state wanting the fugitive to the governor of the state where the fugitive is located.

■ Each state is immune from being sued in federal courts by its own citizens as well as by citizens of other states or of foreign governments.

■ State officials do not, however, enjoy absolute immunity from being taken to court and sued. If the court rules that an official acted without the proper authority of the state, he may be subject to a lawsuit.

■ The Second Amendment to the U.S. Constitution prevents the federal government from interfering with the people's right to keep and bear arms in maintaining a state militia. The Supreme Court has never precisely defined the scope of this amendment, but a lower federal court has held that "the federal government can limit the keeping and bearing of arms by a single individual."

---

immunities clause protects persons who enter the state to work at their trade, so must it protect those who enter to seek medical services. Otherwise a state would be able to restrict to its own residents the medical care available within its borders. The Court could not approve this.

■ **Extradition clause**   Article IV, Section 2, Clause 2, of the federal Constitution states:

&& *A Person charged in any State with Treason, Felony, or other Crime, who shall flee from Justice, and be found in another State, shall on Demand of the executive Authority of the State from which he fled, be delivered up, to be removed to the State having Jurisdiction of the Crime."*

This clause is called the interstate rendition or extradition clause. It establishes the basis for states to aid each other in bringing to trial persons accused of crimes who have fled to other states. The clause is applicable to persons accused of any crime, whether a felony or misdemeanor.

In 1973 Congress enacted a statute prescribing the procedure for interstate EXTRADITION:

(1) There must be a formal criminal charge against the alleged fugitive from justice.

(2) A formal demand must be made by the governor of the extraditing state to the governor of the state where the fugitive is located.

The governor of the state where the fugitive is located must then have him arrested and delivered to the representative of the governor of the demanding state.

■ **Guaranty clause**   Article IV, Section 4, of the federal Constitution provides:

&& *The United States shall guarantee to every State in this Union a Republican Form of Government, and shall protect each of them against Invasion."*

The federal government used this clause after the Civil War to justify its involvement in setting up new state governments in the South.

■ **Foreign relations**   Article I, Section 10, of the federal Constitution provides:

&& *No state shall enter into any Treaty, Alliance, or Confederation."*

The federal government has exclusive control over all relations between the United States and foreign nations. The states have no power to enter into any agreement with a foreign power, but they may enter into compacts with each other. Formation of a bistate port authority is an example of a permissible agreement. See INTERSTATE COMPACT.

■ **Money**   Article I, Section 10, of the federal Constitution states:

&& *No State shall . . . coin Money; emit Bills of Credit; make any Thing but gold and silver Coin a Tender in Payment of Debts."*

Thus, the U.S. Constitution forbids the states from creating metal or paper money. Only Congress may establish, maintain, and control a uniform national currency.

■ **Federal supremacy**   Article VI of the U.S. Constitution provides:

&& *This Constitution, and the Laws of the United States which shall be made in Pursuance thereof; and all Treaties made, or which shall be made, under the Authority of the United States, shall be the supreme Law of the Land; and the Judges in every State shall be bound thereby, any Thing in the Constitution or Laws of any State to the Contrary notwithstanding."*

The SUPREMACY CLAUSE clearly announces that acts of the federal government in carrying out its constitutional functions are the supreme law of the land. Federal laws are part of the laws of every state. It is the duty of all state judges to recognize and enforce the Constitution, as well as federal laws and treaties. The supremacy clause voids every state law or constitutional provision that conflicts with the U.S. Constitution, or a federal statute or treaty.

EXAMPLE Dick, a Swiss citizen, lived in Virginia for many O——* years. He acquired real estate in Virginia, where he died without a will and without a wife or children. Under a Virginia statute, Dick's land was to be turned over to the state. Peter, Dick's heir who lived in Switzerland, claimed the property. A U.S. treaty with Switzerland gave foreign heirs in Switzerland the right to inherit their ancestor's property or to sell it and take the proceeds from this country. Peter's rights under the treaty will prevail over the state law.

■ **Bearing arms**   The Second Amendment to the federal Constitution provides:

" A well regulated Militia, being necessary to the security of a free State, the right of the people to keep and bear Arms, shall not be infringed. "

The purpose of this amendment is to prevent the federal government from interfering with the right of the people to keep and bear arms in maintaining a state militia.

The Second Amendment does not prohibit all regulation of firearms by the federal government. The Supreme Court has, for example, upheld the National Firearms Act, which prohibits the transportation of unregistered shotguns in interstate commerce. The Court based its decision upon the absence of evidence that possession or use of any prohibited weapon would affect the efficiency of a state MILITIA.

Nevertheless, the Supreme Court has never precisely defined the full scope of the Second Amendment, although a lower federal court has reasoned: "Apparently, then, under the Second Amendment, the federal government can limit the keeping and bearing of arms by a single individual, as well as by a group of individuals, but it cannot prohibit the possession or use of any weapon which has any reasonable relationship to the preservation or efficiency of a well-regulated militia." See ARMS, RIGHT TO BEAR.

■ **Reserved powers**   The 10th Amendment to the federal Constitution provides:

" The powers not delegated to the United States by the Constitution, nor prohibited by it to the States, are reserved to the States respectively, or to the people. "

This amendment confirms the intention of the framers of the Constitution to protect the states' rights to exercise all powers of government that the Constitution does not specifically give to the federal government, such as the power to declare war.

■ **Sovereign immunity**   The 11th Amendment to the federal Constitution states:

" The Judicial power of the United States shall not be construed to extend to any suit in law or equity, commenced or prosecuted against one of the United States by Citizens of another State, or by Citizens or Subjects of any Foreign State. "

This amendment recognizes the sovereignty of each state and its immunity from being sued in the federal courts by citizens of other states or of foreign governments. Although the 11th Amendment is directed toward suits in the federal court system, the concept of SOVEREIGN IMMUNITY means that no government may be sued, without its consent, by its own citizens or by citizens of another state or country. The U.S. Supreme Court has held that this amendment does not grant state officials absolute immunity from suit. Immunity depends on the functions and responsibilities of the official involved.

EXAMPLE A suit was brought against the attorney general of O━━✴ Minnesota to prevent him from enforcing a state law to reduce railroad rates. Because the statute was invalid, the Supreme Court stated that the attorney general, in seeking to enforce it, had proceeded without the authority of the state in its sovereign capacity. He was therefore subject to suit. He did not, however, lose his job.

■ **Police power**   A state's POLICE POWER—the right to establish and enforce laws to protect the safety, health, morals, and general well-being of its people—is a right that is inherent in the nature of government. It is not specifical-

ly granted by the U.S. Constitution but it is implied by the 10th Amendment. For example, it is a valid exercise of its police power for a state, in order to protect its residents against incompetent doctors, to enact laws requiring that physicians be licensed to practice in the state. See also CONSTITUTIONAL LAW.

The federal government has power to protect its citizens' CIVIL RIGHTS, regardless of contrary state laws or customs. The Supreme Court has held that the federal Civil Rights Act of 1964 supersedes state legislation requiring segregation of the races. Thus the Supreme Court upheld a federal statute barring discrimination by interstate carriers and, at the same time, struck down a state statute requiring racial segregation on interstate buses. The federal statute was a valid exercise of Congress's power over interstate COMMERCE. See also COMMERCE CLAUSE; COURTS; DUE PROCESS OF LAW; EQUAL PROTECTION OF LAWS; SEPARATE BUT EQUAL; TAXATION; UNITED STATES.

status   A person's standing, state, or condition, such as being a minor, a married man or woman, or a prisoner.

status quo   (Latin) "State in which." The existing state of things at any given time. For example, when one of the parties to a contract becomes incompetent and the court places the parties in status quo, this means that the court will order that each party return to the other anything they exchanged under the contract.

statute   A particular law by which a legislature declares, commands, or prohibits something in writing. Statutes make up the law along with written court decisions (COMMON LAW) and rules and regulations established by government agencies. For a discussion of how statutes are created, see LEGISLATION.

■ **Statutes in our legal system**   The law of TORTS (individual grievances) and CONTRACT law are primarily based on common law. The more specialized fields of law are dominated by statutes. Workmen's compensation, for example, is created by statute, as are welfare programs, Medicare, and vocational rehabilitation programs. State and federal acts governing administrative procedure set up the systems under which government agencies work. Marriage and divorce law, labor law, consumer protection laws, local government law, business law, patent law, bankruptcy law, criminal law, corporate law, and probate administration are all governed by systems of statutes.

A statute states a general proposition of law, which courts apply to specific situations. An interpretation in one case establishes a precedent of what the statute means and how it will be enforced in the future. An antitrust statute, for example, prohibits businesses from restricting free trade, but a court must determine whether specific acts or agreements between manufacturers violate the law.

The law changes to meet new situations and changing conditions. When a court makes an exception to an established rule, the change is usually small and limited to a certain type of situation. A legislature, on the other hand, can make a dramatic break with tradition. By enacting a single statute, it can allow divorces, for example, to couples who could never be granted them before.

■ **Title and subject of a statute** A common provision in state constitutions is: "Each bill shall have a single subject which shall be expressed in its title." Although the U.S. Congress is under no such constitutional restraint, rules in the House and Senate do set some limits.

Allowing only one subject per statute permits representatives to concentrate on and debate one topic at a time and prevents them from arbitrarily throwing together a lot of unrelated subjects. Combining ideas for political reasons—so that an unpopular provision can pass on the coattails of a popular one—prevents an orderly consideration of the merits of each proposal.

Broad legislation can meet the single-subject rule with a title that identifies a unifying factor in the legislation. For example, a 300-page bill that significantly revises all the commercial law of a state (such as the Uniform Commercial Code) meets this test because there is unity in its broad purposes. The purpose of a title is to notify everyone of the contents of a statute.

■ **Statute books** A bill becomes an act after it is passed by the legislature, and the chief executive (the President or governor) files it with the secretary of state. This filed copy is called an *enrolled bill*. All of the statutes passed in the annual or biennial session of the legislature are published in a book as the *session laws*. Each act is a chapter in the book. Acts are numbered in the order in which they were filed with the secretary of state. These volumes are usually entitled *Laws of [State] 19–*. The session laws of the Congress are called *United States Statutes at Large—Congress, First [or Second] Session*. Laws enacted by cities or towns are called ORDINANCES. They are usually filed with the city or village clerk and published in a legal newspaper or in the legal section of a general newspaper. A copy of a particular statute or ordinance can usually be obtained from any office that handles them.

■ **Statutory compilations** Books of statutory compilation are easier to use than bound volumes of session laws because they organize legislative law by topic. For example, all of a state's traffic laws that are in effect, regardless of when they were passed, would be arranged in a logical order in one chapter. A few states appoint a person called the *Revisor of Statutes*, or *Code Revisor*, to put together an official compilation.

■ **Major legislative revisions** From time to time legislatures undertake comprehensive overhauls of the law called *law revisions*. A law revision is an act that repeals all the law on a particular topic and enacts a new version. A law revision can be limited to editing the style and form of a law, eliminating duplicated or obsolete provisions, and reorganizing sections. Or it can be a whole new approach to the substance of the law.

Legislatures also may codify laws. A *code* is a systematic and comprehensive statement of all the principal rules of law on one subject, as enacted by a legislature. Codification is different from law revision because it always involves a complete reworking of the law. Some of the most significant codifications are the Uniform Commercial Code, probate codes, criminal codes, and motor vehicle codes.

■ **Statutory construction** Figuring out what a statute means is called statutory interpretation or statutory construction (that is, construing the language of the statute).

When the meaning of a statute is questioned in a lawsuit, the court hearing the case must construe the words of the statute. Until the statute is further construed in subsequent decisions, the statute means what the court has said it means. If an appeal is taken to the highest court in the state (or to the Supreme Court), then the interpretation given by that court is binding on every lower court.

To make the law more understandable and predictable, certain rules have developed over the years to standardize statutory interpretation. They are called *canons of construction*, or rules of statutory interpretation. These rules are not usually enacted statutes; they are based on tradition.

Interpretative rules When a court interprets a statute, it will find the statute constitutional if at all possible. It will not rule that the legislature has passed an invalid (unconstitutional) law unless there is no other reasonable interpretation.

Consistent construction It is the duty of the courts to construe all parts of a statute together and to read different statutes on the same subject so that they are consistent. This is known as the rule of *pari materia* ("of the same matter"). For example, it must be assumed that the legislature intended all the laws on corporations to be consistent. If one statute is ambiguous on whether corporate directors have certain powers, then the interpretation of another statute may be used to settle the issue. Helpful guides in interpreting a statute are interpretations of similar statutes in other places and comments by legislators that are made when a statute is passed.

When two different statutes appear to be inconsistent, the more specific one will be read as an exception to the general one. A special law prevails over a general law, and a specific provision prevails over a general provision. When two statutes cannot be reconciled, the later act prevails over the previous one because it is a more recent expression of legislative will. This rule does not apply to a law revision, which is intended to change the form of the law without changing its meaning.

Strict and liberal construction Sometimes a statute specifically states that it should be *liberally construed*, which means that the statute is intended to apply to every situation that seems appropriate. For example, Social Security benefits are usually construed liberally so that everyone arguably qualified to collect a benefit does receive one. Other statutes are given a *strict construction*—that is, the statute can be applied only to situations it specifically covers. Tax and criminal laws are given a strict interpretation because no one should have to pay a tax or go to jail unless it is certain that the statute is applicable to him.

Exclusion rule When a statute mentions a particular circumstance, the assumption is that others were intentionally omitted. This canon is known as *expressio unius est exclusio alterius* ("expressing one thing excludes others"). It determines what a statute does *not* mean. For example, if the law says that robbery means forcibly taking property from a *person*, then stealing a fur coat off a rack in a store is not robbery; it is theft, or larceny.

Language rules The language of a statute may be relied upon. This means that if the statute says that the word "Secretary" means "Secretary of Labor," then that definition applies in every provision of that statute. Words and phrases are interpreted according to dictionary meanings and the usual rules of grammar.

Technical words, legal words, and words with special meanings are given their special meanings according to the context of the statute. Words of any gender refer to both male and female. Singular also means plural, and plural includes singular. Verbs in any tense include present, past, and future tenses. Although statutes are generally written in the masculine gender, singular number, and present tense, they are not usually limited to those meanings.

If a word can have different meanings at different times, its meaning is influenced by the words around it. This rule is called *noscitur a sociis* ("known by its associates"). For example, "doctor" may refer either to a medical doctor or to someone with another advanced degree, such as doctor of philosophy. If a statute says "doctors, chiropractors, podiatrists, and optometrists," then "doctor" is construed to mean "medical doctor."

When a general word or phrase is used in a list, its meaning must fit in with the specific words in the list. This rule is called *ejusdem generis* ("of the same class").

> EXAMPLE A statute that prohibits "all shooting, hunting, fishing, playing, horse racing, gaming, or other public sports, exercises, or shows on Sunday" was held to mean that only those kinds of *outdoor* activities were prohibited. In another case, an ice pick was held to be a dangerous weapon under a statute prohibiting the possession of any "dagger, dirk, dangerous knife, razor, stiletto, or any other dangerous weapon."

Some states have codified terms that have caused much judicial interpretation in the past—that is, they have passed laws that give the words specific meanings. Typical of some common constructions are the terms "civil action," which includes violations of traffic regulations; "day" or "calendar day," which refers to the time from midnight to midnight; "working days," which designates the days as they succeed each other exclusive of Sundays and holidays; and "injury to property," which means a breach of contract or an act that reduces someone else's estate.

statute of frauds

A statute that provides that certain types of CONTRACTS be in writing. See Chart 6. The primary purpose for having contracts in writing is to prevent a nonexistent agreement, alleged to have been made between two parties, from being "proved" by fraud or false testimony. It accomplishes this by enforcing specified types of contracts only if there is a written note or memorandum of the agreement that has been signed by the parties or their authorized representatives. A written contract is an indication that the parties voluntarily entered an agreement that has certain and definite terms.

For a contract to be legally binding under the statute, it must state with reasonable certainty the identity of the parties, the subject matter of the contract, and its terms and conditions. The necessary SIGNATURES may be in the form of initials, a typewritten name, or even a rubber stamp, as long as they are intended to be signatures.

The statute of frauds can be used as a defense in breach of contract lawsuits. If the defendant can establish that the contract he has failed to perform is legally unenforceable because it does not meet the requirements of the statute, he

cannot be liable for its breach. The statute of frauds may not be used as a defense when a written contract has been lost by a fraudulent act, such as one that occurs when a party to the contract takes the document for safekeeping and later denies that he ever took it.

■ **Contracts to be in writing** The original statute of frauds, enacted in England in 1677, specifies certain contracts to which it applies:

(1) A contract in which something of value is given or promised in exchange for marriage (not just the mutual promises of a man and woman to marry). For instance, Aunt Bertha promises to give Ted her 200-acre farm if he marries Barbara. Unless this contract is in writing, Ted cannot enforce it after his marriage.

(2) A contract for a sale of interest in land. This type of contract also includes leases for more than a one-year term and EASEMENTS.

(3) A contract that cannot be performed within one year of its making and that has not been fully performed by one of the parties. If a movie star promises on January 15 to make a one-hour television appearance on June 15 of the following year, this promise must be in writing to be enforceable against her.

(4) A contract for the sale of goods or CHOSE IN ACTION (legal right to money that can be enforced by the courts) that exceeds a certain dollar amount (specified by state law—usually $500). If Charles sells a used car to Amy for $1,375, he will not be able to enforce payment against her unless the sales agreement is in writing.

(5) A contract in which the executor or administrator of an estate promises to be personally liable for the debts of the estate.

> EXAMPLE Suppose Alice, the decedent, owed Pauline $1,000. Donna, Alice's sister and the executrix of her estate, promised to pay Pauline the debt out of her own pocket so that all the money in Alice's estate would go to Alice's children. Donna later reneged on her promise, and Pauline sued her for breach of contract. Because a contract of this type must be in writing under the statute of frauds, Pauline's claim is unenforceable.

(6) Any contract in which a person promises to pay another's creditor that individual's debts when they become due or upon his failure to pay them must be in writing to be enforced. This type of contract to pay debts when they are due is called a *suretyship contract.* The promise to pay the debts upon the debtor's failure to pay is called a contract of GUARANTY. See also PRINCIPAL AND SURETY.

States have extended the application of the statute to other types of contracts, such as a life insurance contract, which cannot be performed within the lifetime of the insured; a contract to transmit property by will; a contract that authorizes an agent to sell real estate for another; a contract for a real estate agent's sales commission; and a contract that may be enforced even though it has been barred by the statute of limitations, such as one that is created when a person acknowledges in writing a 20-year-old unpaid debt. See LIMITATIONS OF ACTIONS.

■ **Part performance** Part performance by one party of a contract that does not comply with the statute of frauds (such as an oral contract) may nevertheless make the contract enforceable. Part performance refers to acts performed by the party because he is relying on the other party to perform his part of the contract. The party's actions must be substantial to show that he believed that there was a contract and that he was actually carrying it out.

For example, taking possession of personal property, such as a car, and making part payment for it under an oral contract clearly shows a buyer-seller relationship. This is usually sufficient to remove a contract from the requirements of the statute of frauds and make the oral contract enforceable. However, payment of all or part of the purchase price of the land under an oral contract will not exempt the contract from the statute of frauds. And, in many jurisdictions, neither will just taking possession of the land make an oral contract enforceable. A few states though, will enforce it.

If services have been performed based on a contract that is unenforceable because of the statute of frauds, the value of those services may nevertheless be recovered on the basis of *quantum meruit*—literally, "as much as he deserves," or the reasonable value of the services. Either a court or a jury can decide under what circumstances recovery is possible and what the amount of recovery will be.

> EXAMPLE You make an oral agreement with Alvin to have O—* him paint your great-aunt's portrait for $650. He is halfway finished with the portrait when you find out that your great-aunt has cut you out of her will. You cancel the order for the portrait and refuse to pay Alvin. Alvin will be able to collect the reasonable value of his services, which includes the cost of his materials (paints and other supplies) and his labor (the amount of time he has spent on the portrait), based on *quantum meruit*.

A person may, however, recover expenses incurred at the other party's request even if they are made in connection with an unenforceable contract.

> EXAMPLE A defendant, Smith, orally agreed to lease certain O—* premises to the plaintiff, White, for a nightclub for three years. At Smith's request, White hired an attorney to draw up the lease, which Smith approved but did not sign. White also hired a watchman, obtained a liquor license, and gave Smith a check for $2,500. Subsequently, Smith refused to sign the lease. White sued for his expenses and for $15,000 in damages for loss of the use of the premises for one year. The court dismissed his breach of contract action because the contract was unenforceable. The statute of frauds required the lease to be in writing since it was for more than one year. Because Smith had not signed the lease, White could not obtain damages for loss of the use of the premises for one year. However, he could recover the expenses he made at Smith's request, on a different basis of liability. The law will enforce a promise by the defendant to pay for expenses incurred at his request. The matter was sent back for trial on the items of damage.

If a person performs services relying on an oral promise that he will inherit certain property, and that promise is not kept, he may sue the decedent's estate on a *quantum meruit* basis for the value of his services. An action for breach of contract will not be permitted.

Some courts will not allow the statute of frauds to be used as a defense if one party has relied on an oral contract and will be irreparably injured if the contract is not enforced. See EQUITABLE; ESTOPPEL.

> EXAMPLE A Michigan farmer sued a corporation for dam- O—* ages he suffered when the corporation breached its oral contract concerning a hog-leasing program. The farmer put up $50,000 and agreed to lease hogs in hopes of developing a reputation as a breeder of good hogs. The corporation agreed to take care of any surplus stock the farmer could not sell and to provide technical assistance in hog breeding. The farmer promised to use only the corporation's products, and the corporation would feature the farmer and this experimental program in its advertisements for its farm products. This arrangement went along smoothly until the corporation reneged on its promise to take and sell the farmer's surplus stock. Thereafter, the corporation refused to carry out any part

---

THINGS TO KNOW ABOUT THE STATUTE OF FRAUDS

■ A statute of frauds provides that certain types of contracts be in writing.

■ The purpose of having written contracts is to prevent someone from alleging that a nonexistent agreement was in fact made and then "proving" it by fraud or false testimony.

■ For a contract to be binding under the statute of frauds, it must state the identity of the parties, the subject matter of the contract, and its terms and conditions.

■ Signatures may be written, typed, or even stamped, as long as they are intended to be signatures.

■ If someone promises to sell you land and then reneges, you are out of luck without a written contract.

■ If you make an oral sales agreement exceeding $500 and the other party reneges, you cannot enforce payment (except, perhaps, in Louisiana).

■ If an estate executor makes an oral promise to be personally liable for the debts of the estate and then goes back on his word, creditors' claims against that executor will be unenforceable.

■ In some cases, partial performance of an oral contract may make the contract enforceable even though it does not comply with the statute of frauds—for example, if you take possession of an automobile and pay for part of it under an oral contract.

■ If you performed services based on an unenforceable oral contract, and the person for whom you performed them refuses to pay, you may still be allowed to recover the reasonable value of your services.

■ If you perform services relying on an oral promise that you will inherit certain property and that promise is not kept, you may sue the deceased person's estate for the value of your services—but you could not sue for breach of contract.

■ If you relied on an oral contract and will be irreparably injured if the contract is not enforced, the other party will not be allowed to use the statute of frauds as a defense. This is not necessarily the case in every state, however, so try to *get it in writing!*

of the agreement. It claimed that the contract was unenforceable because it did not comply with the statute of frauds. The court ruled in favor of the farmer in 1965 because he was encouraged to and did rely on the agreement made with the corporation and invested much money in order to carry it out. To permit the corporation to hide behind the statute of frauds to evade its responsibility to the farmer would be unjust and would ruin the farmer financially. The corporation was liable for the damages caused by its abandonment of its agreement with the farmer.

The crucial question is whether the party has changed his position so much that justice demands that the contract be enforced. If the court decides that the answer is yes, the contract will be enforced even though it fails to comply with the statute of frauds.

statute of limitations   For a discussion of the set periods of time during which civil and criminal legal actions can be brought, see LIMITATIONS OF ACTIONS.

statutes at large   The written laws of the United States collected into bound books in the order in which Congress enacted them. See also STATUTE.

statutory   Relating to a statute; required or defined by a statute. For example, statutory rape is a crime defined and created by statute. Females whom the law deems too young to give consent to sexual intercourse can be the victims of statutory rape even if they willingly took part in the sexual act.

statutory rape   The crime of having sexual intercourse with a female who is under a statutorily prescribed age, and who is therefore considered incapable of giving her consent. See RAPE.

stay   The act of stopping a judicial proceeding by a court order. For example, a court may issue a *stay of proceedings* until one of the persons in a lawsuit performs either some step that has been omitted or some act required by the court, such as giving security for the payment of COSTS. A *stay of execution* of a criminal refers to a court's order postponing or stopping the imposition of the death penalty upon a person convicted of a capital offense.

steam   Because steam boilers may be classified as dangerous, their control is a proper exercise of the state's POLICE POWER. This includes enacting and enforcing reasonable regulations concerning the inspection and operation of boilers and the licensing of persons who manage, own, and operate them.

stenographer   A person who writes in shorthand or uses a mechanical device to record spoken words. A *court stenographer* is usually an officer of the court and considered to be a state or public official.

The appointment and term of court stenographers are usually regulated by statute. The stenographer is usually appointed by the court in an official act that should be made a matter of record.

A court stenographer is an official under the control and direction of the court, not of the attorneys in a case. Under some statutes, the judge who appoints the stenographer also has the power to remove him. Under other statutes that fix the term of office, a judge cannot remove a stenographer at will, even though the judge has the power to appoint him.

It is the stenographer's duty to be present in court or on call throughout a trial. The stenographer must take complete notes of the proceedings before the court; transcribe and file the notes within the time allowed; and prepare and sign a certificate stating that the proceedings were fully and accurately recorded at the trial and that the transcript is a correct translation of the notes.

The compensation of a court stenographer may be in the form of a salary, a per diem allowance, or an allowance for work actually performed. When there is no statute fixing his fees, a stenographer is entitled to reasonable compensation for his services. Liability for a stenographer's compensation is usually defined by law, which may authorize the payment of his fees by the state, by the county, or by the parties to the litigation.

stepparent   A person who "steps into" the place of a parent by marrying a child's mother or father. A stepparent has some rights and obligations regarding a stepchild, but they are not exactly the same as the rights and duties of a natural or adoptive parent. See CUSTODY; PARENT AND CHILD; ILLEGITIMACY; WELFARE PROGRAMS.

stipulation   An agreement between attorneys designed to simplify, shorten, or settle court litigation and to save costs. Courts look with favor on stipulations, but a court cannot require one of the parties in a lawsuit to enter into a stipulation with his adversary.

■ **Content**   Any matter involving the rights or obligations of the parties can be the subject of a stipulation. Ordinarily, courts encourage parties to stipulate (agree) to a statement of facts on which to submit their case.

Parties may also make valid stipulations to dismiss or discontinue an action; to prescribe the issues to be tried; and to admit, exclude, or withdraw evidence. They can stipulate to allow copies of papers, rather than the originals, to be admitted as evidence, agree to use affidavits as evidence, use foreign laws in evidence, waive objections to the competency of witnesses, or agree to the qualifications of a witness. The parties can also agree on what testimony would be given by an absent witness if he were present, and the facts so stipulated can be used in evidence. Stipulations can also concern the appointment of an administrator, attorney's fees, and costs.

The parties to a lawsuit cannot stipulate as to the validity or constitutionality of a statute, or what the law is; these questions must be decided by the court. Other invalid stipulations include those relating to the legal effect of a contract, the evidence necessary to prove a given fact, and the interpretation given to a will.

EXAMPLE   The estate of composer Igor Stravinsky was settled by a stipulation in 1979 after an eight-year dispute between his widow and the children of his first marriage. Stravinsky had left all of his assets in a trust from which his widow was to receive the "entire net income." After her death, the children, a grandchild, and another individual would share in the remainder of the estate. Valued at about $3.5 million, the estate included the handwritten score of "The Rite of Spring," other musical works and recordings, manuscripts, and royalties from around the world. Royalty income from the estate averaged about $500,000 annually.

The children had challenged their stepmother's accounting of the assets of the estate and accused her of misappropriating the assets. For example, Mrs. Stravinsky had sold the original score of "The Rite of Spring" for $220,000, which she said was personal property, a gift from her husband while he was alive. The children claimed that the score belonged to the estate. Mrs. Stravinsky declared that, according to the community property laws of California, 40 percent of Stravinsky's holdings belonged to her. The children claimed that the personal property left by their father, including memorabilia, was worth hundreds of thousands of dollars, not the $250 asserted by Mrs. Stravinsky.

The stipulation, agreed to by everyone involved, gave Mrs. Stravinsky 38.93 percent of the community property rights to almost all of the royalties from Stravinsky's works and 20 percent of the community property interest after her death, which she may bequeath. The children and the grandchild were given the remainder of the royalties and a voice in the administration of the trust, which was placed under court jurisdiction. Two additional trustees were appointed for the trust—one representing Mrs. Stravinsky, the other representing the children. If the lawyers cannot agree on an action connected with the estate, the court will have to resolve the matter. In addition, all objections to the previous administration of the estate were withdrawn.

A valid stipulation is binding only on the parties who agree to it. Courts are usually bound by valid stipulations and must enforce them.

■ **Form**   A stipulation does not have to follow any particular format, but its meaning must be certain. In many jurisdictions, stipulations are required to be in writing in order to prevent claims of fraud and disputes about the terms of an oral stipulation. A stipulation made in the judge's chambers must be in writing. But stipulations made in open court do not have to be written and are as binding as written ones. The writing rule also does not apply to a stipulation made out of court that has been entirely or partially carried out or to one that is admitted by the person against whom it is to be enforced. When the facts are not disputed, there is no reason for a writing.

stock dividend   A corporate dividend that is paid in stock rather than in money. It is an increase in the number of shares declared out of the profits, which is done at the discretion of the directors of the corporation. When a stock dividend is declared, additional surplus (undivided profits) is added to the capital (all the money that is invested in the corporation but that can never be used to pay dividends) to reflect the additional shares being issued by the corporation. The increased number of shares has the same proportionate value as the smaller number of shares originally held by the stockholder, but the cash value of the individual

shares is not reduced. The stockholder owns the same percentage of the corporation as he did before the stock dividend was declared.

EXAMPLE Arthur owns 100 of the 10,000 outstanding shares of BX Company, or 1 percent of the corporation. The directors of BX, which is having an extremely profitable year, decide to declare a stock dividend of 1 share for every 10 held (10 percent dividend): Arthur receives 10 shares as his dividend, giving him a total of 110 shares. Additional surplus has been added to the capital to reflect the additional shares being issued. The total number of outstanding shares of BX after the stock dividend has been declared is 11,000. Arthur still owns 1 percent of BX, his 110 is still 1 percent of its 11,000 shares.

Although the value of the corporation's shares often increases following a stock dividend, this is by no means guaranteed. A stock dividend is really a part of corporation bookkeeping.

A *stock split* is not the same as a stock dividend. In a stock split, no adjustment is made to the capital; there is merely an increase in the number of shares representing the same amount of capital. This means that the cash value of the individual shares decreases in proportion to the size of the stock split.

EXAMPLE A stockholder owns 10 shares of stock worth $100 per share. The company authorizes a stock split of one share for every share he owns. (This is known as a two-for-one split because after the split the stockholder will own two shares, whereas before he had only one.) After the stockholder receives the additional shares, he will have 20 shares valued at $50 per share. The value of his individual shares is reduced because no money has been added to the corporate capital. The stockholder has a greater number of shares, but the stock has the same total cash value as before.

stop order   **1** A notice from a depositor to his bank ordering the bank to refuse payment on a particular check he has drawn. **2** An order by a customer to his stockbroker directing him to buy or sell a stock or commodity when its market value reaches a particular figure.

stoppage in transit   An unpaid seller's right to stop the delivery of goods to a buyer after the goods have been delivered to a common carrier, such as a railroad or a trucking company. See SALES.

straight-line depreciation   A method used to calculate depreciation for income tax purposes. Under this procedure, the annual depreciation charge is figured by dividing the cost of the property, less its expected salvage value (the amount the asset is expected to be worth when it is sold at the end of its useful life) by the number of years of expected service life.

EXAMPLE A small-appliance store purchases a delivery van for $8,000. The van has an expected service life of three years, after which time it is expected to be worth $2,000. The cost of the van ($8,000) less its expected salvage value ($2,000) equals $6,000. The $6,000 is divided by three, the number of years of useful service life. Thus, the van can be depreciated at the rate of $2,000 per year for three years. The $2,000 may be entered as a deductible business expense on the appliance store's tax return.

stranger A third person; a person other than the parties involved. For example, a person who is not party to a contract is a *stranger to the contract.*

straw man **1** A person who acts as a front for those who actually bear the expense and take the profits of a transaction. Sometimes, a straw man is used to circumvent the law. For example, people who have criminal records are usually denied licenses to own liquor stores, bars, and gun shops. Often, a straw man is used as a front in order to get a license when, in reality, a convicted person owns and operates the business. This use of a straw man is illegal, and both the straw man and the actual owner may be prosecuted.

2 In the language of real estate agents, an intermediary or go-between who holds and transfers title to property as a matter of convenience for undisclosed persons.

> EXAMPLE An Arab oil dealer wants to sell property he owns
> 0⟶✱ in the United States. Fearing he will never be able
> to get good value for the property because of anti-Arab
> sentiments in this country, he hires a real estate agent to
> act as his straw man for the sale so that his identity will
> not be disclosed until the deal is completed.

street railroad A RAILROAD constructed on streets or highways that makes frequent stops within a city or town and that transports people or property. A *subway* is a street railroad running under the surface of the street or highway. An *elevated railway* is a street railroad built above the surface of the roadway.

As a general rule, municipalities have the power to regulate the operation of street railroads within their boundaries. A governing board or commission is usually appointed and makes regulations for the protection of people and property. For example, it may prohibit cars from standing idly on the tracks. It may grant the right to carry passengers and, at the same time, deny or limit permission for the operation of freight cars. See CARRIER.

strict Accurate; precise; absolute. For example, *strict construction* (interpretation) of a statute means that everything is excluded that does not clearly come within the scope of the language used.

strict foreclosure A decree that absolutely forecloses a MORTGAGE of real estate. It states the amount due under the mortgage, orders the amount to be paid within a specified time, and provides that if payment is not made, the mortgagor's right to redeem is barred and foreclosed forever. If the mortgagor fails to pay within the time specified, title to the property vests in (passes to) the mortgagee without any sale of the property. Strict foreclosure is a drastic and rarely used measure because it does not allow the defaulting mortgagor a second chance to redeem his property.

Most states use regular foreclosure *(statutory foreclosure)* under which the property is put up for sale and the mortgagor has the chance to pay his debt and buy back his land. This is known as the mortgagor's *right of redemption.*

Strict foreclosure may also be used in situations when a person defaults on a loan for which he has used personal property as collateral. See SECURED TRANSACTION.

strict liability Legal responsibility for harm done even when there is no proof of carelessness or fault on the part of the person or company that caused the injury. The theory of strict liability may be applied to manufactured products. For example, the manufacturer of a drill press may be ordered to pay money damages to a person injured by a defective mechanism in the machine, even though the manufacturer was as careful as could reasonably be expected in making the drill press. See PRODUCT LIABILITY.

strike A work stoppage; the concerted refusal by employees to do the work assigned to them. Its purpose is to pressure the employer to increase wages or improve other conditions of employment.

■ **Constitutional right** The 13th and 14th Amendments to the Constitution abolished slavery and guaranteed to everyone the right to sell or withhold his labor as he sees fit. This means that every American worker has an absolute right to quit his job. When an individual quits his job because of poor working conditions, his employer may suffer a temporary setback while he trains a new worker, but there is little incentive for the employer to improve the conditions. If an employee persuades most of the other employees to join him in withholding labor from the employer, however, his bargaining position is greatly strengthened. An employer who cannot easily find replacement workers suffers economically and may be forced to improve working conditions. American workers have not always had the right to strike. What each could do individually, they could not do together. Until special labor laws were passed, strikes were illegal.

■ **Historical development** One of the first American labor cases arose in the early 1800's when the industrial revolution upset the economic balance of the local marketplace. Journeyman bootmakers in Philadelphia—called cordwainers because they worked with cordovan leather—had agreed to work for lower wages than journeymen elsewhere. (Journeymen are skilled laborers.) In 1805, however, the Philadelphia bootmakers decided to ask for wages equal to those paid in New York and Baltimore. Their masters turned them down, and the journeymen went on strike. The strikers stayed out for several weeks until eight leaders were arrested. The journeymen then returned to work at the old rates, completely defeated.

The eight leaders, in what is now called the Philadelphia cordwainers' case, were charged with criminal conspiracy because, under the common law, it was a crime to combine (join together) and conspire to create higher prices. The judge in the cordwainers' case told the jury that they should consider how a group of workers could injure the public interest and how a demand for artificially high wages from one segment of the population could interfere with the natural balance of supply and demand. Because the masters would probably pass along the increase, the public would surely pay higher prices. Not surprisingly, the jury found that the defendants did combine to raise their wages and the court fined them $8 each.

Strikes become legal It was not until 1842 that a court held that workers who banded together to influence their employers were not committing a crime. The defendants in the case were seven workers who made boots in Boston. They were charged with illegally combining and conspiring to "extort great sums of money" and refusing to work for any master who employed workers who were not members of their society. The seven were found guilty, but the Supreme Judicial Court of Massachusetts overturned the conviction. The court held that it was not necessarily illegal to form an association to achieve a common goal. A conspiracy was criminal only if the people intended to accomplish an unlawful purpose or to accomplish a lawful purpose by unlawful means. Seeking to influence wages or prices was not illegal in itself.

But this did not mean that such associations, or unions, were free to call strikes. After the Massachusetts decision, the legal battle moved from the criminal courts to the civil courts. Employers pleaded that unions restrained trade and inflicted irreparable damage on a company when they went out on strike, and the courts granted INJUNCTIONS (court orders prohibiting specific actions) against further group activities by workers. The injunction proved an effective weapon against strikers. As soon as workers began to strike, BOYCOTT, or PICKET, the affected employer went to court and claimed that violence was imminent and that his business would be irreparably harmed. In the face of such grave dangers, courts frequently granted temporary restraining orders and scheduled the case for trial weeks later. Since a preliminary order halts group activities under the court's threat of CONTEMPT citations and jail, there often was no need for a trial later, because the strike had already been broken. When the case was tried, it was usually decided not by a jury but by a judge, and judges were likely to see strikes as a threat to free enterprise. Most harmful to the cause of unions was the frequency with which violence did occur. Foreclosed from lawful methods, angry workers resorted to rock throwing, sabotage, and threats. Employers responded with strikebreakers, armed guards, and sometimes murder.

Antitrust laws The Sherman Anti-Trust Act of 1890 made illegal "every contract, combination . . . or conspiracy, in restraint of trade or commerce among the several States." Although aimed at halting big-business monopolies, the law was interpreted to apply to labor unions in a number of federal courts, and in 1908 the Supreme Court upheld this application of the law. Under the Sherman Act, the individual employees were ordered to pay treble damages (triple the actual amount of damages). The Clayton Act of 1914 enlarged federal antitrust law but specifically stated that injunctions could not be granted to stop strikes, picketing, and boycotts. A Supreme Court decision in 1921 gave this provision such a narrow interpretation, however, that labor unions were not much helped by it.

Federal labor laws Until the 1930's, labor had to battle management without the protection of law. Unions called strikes, and the employers fired strikers until one side or the other retreated. In 1932 Congress passed the Norris-LaGuardia Act, which established the freedom of employees to organize and bargain collectively with their employers. The act prohibited the issuing of injunctions in most labor disputes and set up strict procedures for the rare cases in which injunctions could be issued. The Supreme Court interpreted this law as drastically limiting the effect of the Sherman Act on labor unions.

In 1935 Congress enacted the first affirmative labor relations law, the National Labor Relations Act, popularly called the Wagner Act. The act set up the National Labor Relations Board to monitor unfair labor practices and to supervise elections so that employees could choose their union. The board was given authority to go to court in order to enforce its orders.

The next few years saw a dramatic increase in the number and size of unions. Many people began to think the National Labor Relations Board was too harsh toward employers and ignored corruption or unfairness within the unions. Congress reacted by passing the Taft-Hartley Act of 1947, which increased the number of members on the board, removed its power to investigate and prosecute unfair labor practices, abolished the closed shop (where the employer agreed to hire only union members), prohibited unfair labor practices by unions as well as by employers, and guaranteed more freedom for workers, whether they joined a union or not.

The Taft-Hartley Act also established a legal procedure for dealing with a strike that poses a national emergency. The President is authorized to appoint a board of inquiry to determine whether a threatened or actual strike or LOCKOUT (shutdown by employer) endangers or will endanger the national health or safety. The board can review disputes that involve an entire industry or a substantial part of an industry that is engaged in interstate commerce. (Railroads and airlines are excepted because they are covered by a different statute.) The board of inquiry conducts hearings to gather information and makes a report (but no recommendations) to the President, who may then ask the Attorney General to seek an injunction in federal court. If the injunction is granted, neither the union nor the employer may take any action for up to 80 days from the day the injunction is granted. This cooling-off period is to encourage a settlement. A strike or lockout may proceed when all the procedures have been exhausted.

In 1959 the Landrum-Griffin Act was passed to protect individual employees and safeguard the public interest in labor disputes. It gave union members a bill of rights and required unions to file reports on their dealings with employers and on their management of welfare and pension funds. It also strengthened the limitations on union boycotts of companies that did business with an employer who was being struck and on a union's refusal to handle the products of any employer involved in a labor dispute.

■ **Right to strike** Since the 1930's, when employees won the right to organize into unions and to bargain collectively, they have also been able to conduct strikes with the protection of the law. Employees have the right to strike for economic reasons, to improve their working conditions, or for the mutual aid and protection of employees in another union. Employees may agree to stop working as a group even if they do not have a union, and they are entitled to all the protections afforded organized strikers.

Federal labor laws provide that there must be a 60-day waiting period before workers can strike to force the termination or modification of an existing collective-bargaining agreement. During this cooling-off period, the terms of the agreement remain in full effect, and any employee who strikes can be fired. The 60-day period begins when the union notifies the employer of the pending strike or when the contract ends. This provision does not affect the right of employees to strike against an unfair labor practice—such as giving financial support to favor one union over another—but it helps to prevent premature strikes.

Public employees   In 1962 President John F. Kennedy issued an executive order that revolutionized labor law for public employees. It authorized a limited form of collective bargaining for federal employees. Since then, state after state has enacted its own plan for collective bargaining for state and local employees. These statutes permit public employees to form unions and negotiate the terms and conditions of their employment. They deny public employees the right to strike and instead set up other procedures for resolving disputes. A federal employee who is convicted of striking against the government can be fined up to $1,000 and sentenced to jail for up to one year and a day. If the striker has civil-service status, it will be forfeited and he will not be eligible to be reemployed by the federal government for three years.

Because a person does not have a constitutional right to strike (only to quit his job), public employees can refuse to work as a group only if a law permits them to do so. It is not unreasonable in the eyes of the law for the government to refuse to extend the right to strike to public employees, because they can paralyze government by striking. A federal court, deciding in 1971 against the postal workers who had struck, pointed out that strikes were permitted for private employees in order to equalize their bargaining position with employers. Unlike private employees who have had to obtain their employment benefits and job security through hard-fought labor disputes, public employees have received their benefits through civil-service laws. Thus, the law considers disputes over working conditions for public employees a political question that should be resolved by political processes. This legal principle has been strongly criticized by public employees, and they have increasingly demanded the right to strike.

■ **Rights of strikers**   There are generally two kinds of strikes. An *economic strike* is called to secure some economic benefit for the workers, such as an improved pension plan, or to force recognition of their union. An *unfair labor practice strike* is called to protest some act of the employer that the workers consider an unfair labor practice—as when

---

YOUR RIGHT TO STRIKE

■ Strictly speaking, a person does not have a constitutional right to strike but only to quit his job.

■ Employees may agree to stop working as a group even if they do not have a union, and they are entitled to all the protections afforded organized strikers under the law.

■ Federal labor laws require a 60-day waiting period before workers in the private sector can strike to change or end an existing agreement.

■ Federal and many state and local government employees may not strike, and if they do they can be fined and jailed. But they may form unions and engage in collective bargaining.

■ If you have been on strike over an unfair labor practice and the dispute is settled in your favor, you are entitled to be reinstated even if your replacement has to be fired. If the dispute is over wages or benefits, your employer may not have to rehire you.

■ You are not entitled to be paid while you are on strike, and you do not have the right to claim unemployment benefits—unless your state has a law allowing them—since you are still legally employed.

■ If you refuse to cross a picket line on principle, you will be treated the same as a striker—even if you are a member of a different union—but if you are kept from your job by fear of violence, you can collect unemployment compensation.

■ You lose your right to keep your job status if the strike you participate in is illegal.

■ Workers lose the protection of federal labor laws if they break a law. Workers who struck on board a ship, for example, lost protection because they violated the laws against mutiny.

■ Picketing is legal when used to inform the public or others about the dispute, but it cannot be used to threaten people or to provoke violence.

■ As a union member, you can be fined or expelled for crossing a picket line; however, before you can be expelled, you are entitled to written notice of the charges, a reasonable time to prepare your defense, and a full and fair hearing by the union.

■ A union cannot expel you for exercising your constitutional rights and campaigning for a political candidate opposed by the union.

■ Technically, federal laws protect any employees who act together to improve their working conditions, but courts have not favored wildcat strikes

(work stoppages not authorized by the union) because they disrupt labor relations. Since a wildcat strike usually violates an existing collective-bargaining agreement, the strikers have no protection unless the whole union joins them and ratifies their protest.

■ Walkouts are illegal if deemed irresponsible or indefensible by the court. A court has upheld the legality of a walkout, however, because it involved workers who did not have a union or any other way to make management listen to their repeated complaints of bad working conditions. And some courts have said that employees have the right to strike whenever they think they have good reason.

■ A surprise lockout by an employer is generally upheld because of the employer's right to protect his property.

■ Slowdowns, when employees stay on the job but deliberately decrease their productivity, are consistently held to be illegal.

■ An employer who does not want to negotiate always has the right to cease operations entirely (just as a worker can always quit his job), but he may not avoid bargaining by moving operations elsewhere or by assigning the same work to one of his other plants.

employees strike because they believe their fellow employees have been unfairly discharged.

An employer has the right to try to keep his business operating when his employees go out on strike, and he can hire replacements for the strikers. The employee's right to return to his job depends on whether the strike was an economic or an unfair labor practice strike. If you have been on strike regarding an unfair labor practice and the dispute is settled, you are entitled to be reinstated as soon as you offer unconditionally to return to work—even if your replacement has to be fired. If the dispute is only for economic reasons, your employer may not have to take you back. You are entitled to reinstatement if a vacancy occurs, but your employer does not have to rehire you if you have found substantially equivalent work somewhere else or if he has a legitimate and substantial business reason for not reinstating you. Often, reinstatement of strikers is negotiated as part of the settlement.

You are not entitled to be paid while you are on strike. You also have no right to claim unemployment compensation benefits unless your state has a law allowing them, because you are still employed in the eyes of the law. If you participate in or are directly interested in the outcome of the dispute, you are disqualified from unemployment compensation. If you refuse to cross a picket line on principle, you will be treated the same as the strikers—even if you are a member of a different union. But if you are kept from your job by the fear of violence, you can collect unemployment compensation. These rules apply to any labor dispute, whether it is a strike or a lockout and regardless of who is right or who started the dispute.

You will lose your right to keep your employment status if the strike you are participating in is illegal. In general, a strike is legal if employees use it to bring economic pressure on the employer in order to improve the conditions of their employment. A strike is illegal if it is for some other purpose or if it is directed at someone other than the employer. An employer has the right to fire employees who call a strike to demonstrate their opposition to proposed labor legislation before Congress, let us say, because the employer does not have the power to decide what laws will be passed. Federal law prohibits most boycotts or picketing directed at a party not involved in the primary dispute. These tactics are called SECONDARY BOYCOTTS or secondary picketing. They are strictly limited so that businesses not directly concerned will not become victims in a labor dispute that they cannot resolve. This helps to keep local disputes from disrupting large, unrelated areas of business and industry.

■ **Illegal tactics** A strike is usually lawful if strikers do not breach the peace, but workers lose the protection of federal labor laws if they break a law.

EXAMPLE In one case, workers who struck on board a ship O•——※ were found to have violated the laws against mutiny even though their conduct did not violate labor laws. In another case, employees who struck for higher wages lost their labor-law protection because they demanded an increase greater than that allowed by an emergency price control law.

Picketing is legal when it is used to inform the public, the employer, or other workers about the dispute, but it cannot be used to threaten people or provoke violence. Under federal law, mass picketing is illegal because large, unruly crowds are usually assembled to intimidate others. A small group can communicate the union's ideas just as effectively as a large crowd without creating the same risk of violence. It is illegal for picketers to block entrances to an employer's premises or to picket in front of an employer's home. States may also regulate picketing by statute.

A strike is never a legal excuse for violence. Workers are entitled to seek higher wages, but they cannot intimidate an employer by acts of violence, such as bombings, burning, looting, shooting, rock throwing, window smashing, or beatings. When there is violence, a union may be fined or found guilty of an unfair labor practice by a state or federal court or the National Labor Relations Board and may be ordered to stop the violence. A state court may issue an injunction to halt the strike or picketing. Individuals may be prosecuted for crimes. Employers who use violence against strikers are subject to the same penalties.

Isolated minor incidents are expected during labor disputes. Mere name-calling, a shove, or, as one judge observed, a single "moment of animal exuberance" should not be enough for a court to halt an otherwise lawful strike.

■ **Disciplining of union members** As a union member, you can be fined or expelled for crossing a picket line, failing to honor a lawful strike, or participating in violence during a strike. You may also be disciplined by the union for conduct that is antagonistic to it. For example, the union may expel you for violating work rules, accepting wages below the union scale, participating in an unauthorized strike, belonging to a rival union, or spying for the company. Before you can be expelled for any reason except for not paying your dues, you are entitled to written notice of the specific charges, a reasonable time to prepare your defense, and a full and fair hearing by the union. A union cannot expel you for exercising your constitutional rights—say, for campaigning for a political candidate whom the union opposes.

■ **Legality of certain kinds of strikes** Unions have no right to use a strike to interfere with company policies that do not directly affect the employment relationship but are management prerogatives. For example, management is usually entitled to determine what hours a store will be open. A union may try to bargain for higher wages for employees who work unpopular hours, but it cannot strike because members are displeased about the hours they work.

Wildcat strike When employees are represented by a union and a minority of them engage in a work stoppage job action not authorized by the union, this is a wildcat strike. Although federal labor laws technically protect any employees who act together to improve their working conditions, the wildcat strike has been disfavored by courts because it disrupts labor relations. Usually, a wildcat strike violates an existing collective-bargaining agreement (agreement between a union and an employer), so the strikers have no protection unless the whole union joins them and ratifies their protest.

Walkout A walkout is an unannounced refusal to work, either as a spontaneous protest or as a secretly planned action. If the court finds the employees' conduct to be an irresponsible or indefensible way of accomplishing their goals, the walkout is illegal. When strikers specifically intend the walkout to cause the employer the most inconvenience possible or to destroy property, they are not protected by labor laws.

EXAMPLE In one case, employees walked out and left molten iron in a position where it could have caused costly damage to plant equipment. In another case, waitresses deliberately chose the middle of a busy dinner hour to stage their walkout because their employer would suffer most from their action at that time. Both groups of strikers were held to have no labor law protection because their actions were unreasonable—the amount of the damage caused was not justified by the situation. The waitresses, for instance, could have pressed their grievance, about the firing of a popular assistant manager, through their union. Both the waitresses and the molten iron workers were fired from their jobs and not reinstated.

In another case, a walkout was deemed justified because the workers did not have a union or any other way to make management listen to their repeated complaints of intolerable working conditions.

Sometimes the court will try to balance the risk of danger or damages with the importance of what the employees are trying to accomplish, but some courts have cautioned that employees have the right to strike whenever they think they have a good reason. For example, employees who walked out of a cold shop on a winter day were protected under the law, even though the strike could be considered unfair in light of the continuing efforts of their employer to repair the furnace.

Although the legality of a walkout is often determined by what the court deems reasonable, a surprise lockout by an employer is generally found to be legal because of the employer's right to protect his property. An automobile dealer is justified in locking out employees who might have damaged cars brought in for repair, for example, and a food manufacturer can use a lockout if he expects a strike that can cause massive spoilage.

Slowdown Intermittent work stoppages, or slowdowns, by employees who remain on the job but deliberately decrease their productivity are consistently held illegal by the courts and the National Labor Relations Board. Slowdowns give employees an unfair bargaining advantage because they make it impossible for the employer to plan for production or the work force. What is perhaps more important is that management is entitled to run the business. Employees who choose to stay on the payroll have no right to pick and choose the work they will do. An employee who thinks he can work only on his own terms can be fired without recourse to the labor laws.

Sit-down strike A sit-down strike occurs when employees not only stop working but also refuse to leave the employer's premises. Friends, fellow employees, and family members may manage to slip food, cigarettes, and blankets to the occupying strikers, and it becomes impossible for the employer to continue his business. Violence has almost always accompanied sit-down strikes because of the tensions created by such confrontations. Sit-down strikes played a major role in unionizing the automobile and rubber industries in the late 1930's. However, the Supreme Court ruled in 1939 that such strikes must be considered illegal under most circumstances because they deprive the employer of his property. Since then, sit-down strikes have been rare.

Other strikes A *sympathy strike* is a work stoppage called to give support to a related union engaged in an employment dispute. It is not illegal in itself, but often a union, in its collective bargaining agreement with the employer, gives up the right to use this tactic. Employees of the same company or other companies who refuse to cross a picket line in sympathy with strikers become strikers in the eyes of the law.

A *jurisdictional strike* occurs when there is a dispute between labor unions over which one is entitled to represent the employees, and one of the unions calls a strike. Jurisdictional strikes are forbidden by federal labor laws because the argument is between unions and not between a union and the employer.

A *whipsaw strike* is a work stoppage against one employer at a time of a bargaining unit to which a number of employers belong—for example, a group formed by eight employers in the linen supply business who hire teamsters. Employers may respond to such a strike by locking employees out of the facilities that belong to all of them.

A *general strike* is a mass refusal of all kinds of workers to do their jobs. General strikes, which are often called only for one or two days, have been used in highly centralized countries like France, but in the United States they have been rare, usually encompassing a single city at a time.

■ **Settling strikes** Strikes are usually settled by negotiation between the employer and the employees or the union that represents them. An employer who does not want to negotiate always has the right to cease operations entirely (just as a worker can always quit his job), but an employer may not avoid bargaining by moving operations elsewhere or assigning the same work to one of his other plants. If the employer and employees bargain in good faith, they usually can settle their differences and sign a collective bargaining agreement. See LABOR RELATIONS. Employers and unions generally submit their differences to binding ARBITRATION if they cannot resolve the problems themselves. After every other grievance procedure has been exhausted, an unsatisfied party may be permitted to take the dispute into court.

string citation A series of references (CITATIONS) to legal authorities and precedents, such as statutes, reported cases, and treatises, added at the end of an asserted point of law or conclusion as authority supporting it.

strong-arm provision The portion of the federal BANKRUPTCY law that gives the trustee who represents the creditors all the rights of the most secure creditor, so that he or she can gather all of the debtor's property for appropriate distribution.

sua sponte (Latin) "Of his own will or motion"; voluntarily. When a court acts on its own motion, and not at the request of one of the parties in a lawsuit or criminal case, the court is said to be acting *sua sponte*.

subcontractor A person who enters into a CONTRACT to do part of a job with a person who has already contracted to do the entire job. For example, a builder who has contracted to erect a house enters into a contract with an electrician who agrees to wire the house; the electrician is a subcontractor.

sublease A lease given by a tenant to another person for the whole or part of the rented premises during a part of the tenant's unexpired term—if the tenant has this right under his lease with the landlord.

EXAMPLE Abbott, a businessman, signs a three-year lease
O—* for an apartment. After living in it for two months, he is transferred to England for one year. Abbott (the original lessee) rents his apartment for the one-year period to Rachel, a teacher (the subtenant), who pays her rent to Abbott. Since Abbott remains responsible to his original lessor (the landlord), he must pay the landlord the rent. Abbott is entitled to possession of his apartment when the sublease with Rachel expires at the end of the one-year period.

A sublease is different from an assignment. In an assignment the original lessee transfers all of his rights and interest in the lease. The assignee (the person to whom the lease is assigned) then becomes responsible for paying the rent to the lessor. If the assignee fails to pay the rent, the lessor can sue him. If a subtenant fails to pay, he can be sued only by the tenant. However, if the landlord in a sublease arrangement is not receiving his rent, he can sue the original tenant in either a sublease or an assignment situation. See LANDLORD AND TENANT.

submission of controversy A procedure in which parties submit a matter of real controversy between them to a court for a final decision. Because the parties submit an agreed-upon statement of facts along with the controversy, this procedure dispenses with the formalities of a summons, complaint, and answer required in civil ACTIONS. A submission of controversy is a consent proceeding and consequently a substitute for a civil action.

The statutes granting the right to submit controversies determine what kind of controversies can be submitted under this procedure. For example, the controversy must affect the private rights of the parties. It must be real and not fictitious—that is, two or more parties must have opposite viewpoints on the issue. It must present a question of law that can be resolved by a court decision. If a question of law does not arise from the case, the court will not decide it. If the question is an abstract or debatable one, presented for the court's advice or opinion, the controversy cannot be submitted. Submission is also denied when the controversy involves a matter of PUBLIC POLICY (protection of the public good) or when the court does not have the jurisdiction (authority) to order relief or a remedy.

EXAMPLE A real estate company challenged the constitu-
O—* tionality of a local law that the defendants, members of a city council, proposed to pass. The ordinance would ban the display of "for sale" signs on property. Both parties agreed on a statement of facts and submitted the controversy to the court. The court dismissed the case because it did not have the jurisdiction to pronounce advisory opinions—courts cannot protect rights that may be violated by a law that has not yet been passed.

If, however, the law had been passed before there was a submission of the controversy, the court could determine the rights of the parties, because there would be a question about the constitutionality of the ordinance.

submit 1 Present for determination; commit to another person's discretion or judgment—as to submit a political issue to the judgment of the voters. 2 Introduce evidence in a court—as to submit a contract of sale for the court's inspection.

subordination 1 The act of classifying in a lower order or category; making subject to or subservient. 2 In law, the establishment of priority between existing LIENS or ENCUMBRANCES on the same parcel of property. Subordination is used almost exclusively in mortgage situations, as discussed below.

A *subordination agreement* is a contract between a debtor and creditor in which a creditor agrees that the claims of a specified senior creditor or creditors must be paid in full before any payment can be made to the subordinate creditor on his debt. Subordination agreements are found in mortgage contracts as subordination clauses. A *subordination clause* in a mortgage is a provision that gives priority to a later mortgage.

EXAMPLE Andy needs a new building to house his growing
O—* toy-manufacturing business. He has $100,000 to use for a down payment. The building he decides to buy is priced at $500,000, and it is mortgaged by the owner to a bank for $350,000, which is due in three years. Glen, the owner of the building, agrees to accept the $100,000 payment and to give a mortgage to Andy for $50,000. Andy agrees to assume Glen's original $350,000 mortgage, knowing that in three years he will need $350,000 to pay it off. Both Andy and Glen know that the new mortgagee, Andy's bank, will give Andy a mortgage only if it can have priority over the $50,000 mortgage Glen holds. This means that, in the event of foreclosure, Andy's bank holding the $350,000 mortgage will be paid before Glen's $50,000 mortgage. Thus Glen agrees to a subordination clause in the $50,000 mortgage he gives to Andy. When Andy obtains financing to pay off the existing $350,000 mortgage, the $50,000 mortgage will be subordinate to the new $350,000 mortgage, and the new mortgage will be recorded as the paramount mortgage.

subornation of perjury The crime of inducing another person to lie under oath. See PERJURY.

subpoena (Latin) "Under penalty." A formal writing issued by a court to a witness ordering him to appear before the court on a certain day and give testimony for one of the parties or to face a penalty for failure to obey. The technical and descriptive name for this common type of subpoena is a *subpoena ad testificandum*.

subpoena duces tecum (Latin) "Under penalty, take with you." A formal writing issued by a court, at the request of a person filing suit, ordering a witness to bring to court some document or paper that is pertinent to the issues in the lawsuit.

subrogation The substitution of another party in place of a creditor, so that the party succeeds to the rights of the creditor concerning the debt. Subrogation is used when one party, under some kind of obligation, pays a debt for which someone else is primarily responsible and which in EQUITY (fairness) and good conscience should have been paid by the second party. The party who paid the debt then becomes the creditor, with the creditor's legal rights.

There are two kinds of subrogation: legal and conventional. *Legal subrogation* takes place with or without a contract. However, the parties may agree in a contract to modify or exclude the right of legal subrogation.

EXAMPLE A married couple sold some out-of-state land O⊷⊶ without revealing that there was an unsatisfied lien against the property. The buyers' attorney failed in his responsibility to discover and tell the buyers about the lien. The buyers sued the attorney for malpractice. His malpractice insurance company settled with them for the amount needed to pay the lien.

The malpractice insurers then sued the sellers for the amount of the unsatisfied lien, claiming subrogation to the buyers' right to sue the sellers for breach of contract. The sellers wanted the case dismissed. They argued that because there was no contract between the insurer and the buyers, the insurer was not entitled to be subrogated to the buyers' claim against the seller.

Although a lower court dismissed the lawsuit, an appellate court agreed with the malpractice insurers. It was only equitable to permit the insurers to sue the sellers. The sellers' breach of contract caused the buyers' loss. The insurance company was liable to the buyers because its insured, the attorney, did not properly perform his job. When, however, the sellers sold the property, they had a duty to pay off the lien with the proceeds. The court decided that the insurance company was legally subrogated to the buyers' claim so that the financial responsibility for the breached contract would fall where it really belonged—on the sellers.

Conventional subrogation can take effect only by a contract, whereby one party pays another's debt as the result of a specific (express) or implied agreement that any claims or liens existing as security for the debt be retained for the benefit of the party who pays the debt.

EXAMPLE Your car is hit by a car driven by a drunk driver. O⊷⊶ You promptly report the accident to your insurance company, and it agrees to pay for the damages. Your policy contains a provision that states that the insurance company will be subrogated to your claims against anyone who has caused you injury in an accident. The company sues the driver of the other car to recover the amount of money it has paid you. This is conventional subrogation. Your insurance policy is the contract, the debt is the damages your insurance company paid, and the claims or liens existing as security for the debt are your right to sue the drunk driver. This right must be retained for the benefit of the insurance company that has paid the debt.

■ **When subrogation applies** The subrogation doctrine is highly favored by the courts and is liberally applied in many different areas. Whether or not subrogation is applicable in a particular situation, however, depends on the facts of the case.

Subrogation is not allowed when another adequate remedy is applicable—for example, when other specific rights are spelled out in a contract, such as liquidated DAMAGES. Nor is it available when another person has equal or superior interests and he is opposed to the person seeking subrogation. The remedy is also forbidden when the person seeking subrogation has interfered with the rights of others or is guilty of fraud or negligence.

EXAMPLE After your automobile accident (in the example O⊷⊶ above), your insurance agent forges your signature on a settlement agreement with the drunken driver and then cashes the check for himself. The insurance company will no longer be subrogated to your right to sue the other driver because it has been negligent in protecting your rights. This negligence gives you an interest superior to that of the insurance company seeking subrogation. You have the greater interest and the right to sue the driver to recover the damages you have suffered. It would be unjust to permit the company to sue for its own benefit when it has not paid you anything. The company cannot expect to recover the money it lost to its dishonest agent by taking your place in your lawsuit.

Estates Generally, when a person, such as an heir or surviving spouse, pays a debt owed by the estate or has an interest in the estate subject to the payment of such a debt, he is subrogated to the claim of any creditor against the estate. Creditors receive payment only after the estate has been administered. For example, subrogation against an estate was allowed to a widow who paid for a monument over her deceased husband's grave before an administrator was appointed for the estate. In other words, the estate "reimbursed" the widow for an expense for which the estate was primarily responsible.

Wrongdoing Generally, a person who has paid for a loss or injury resulting from another person's wrong will be subrogated to the rights of the injured person against the wrongdoer.

EXAMPLE The driver of a company delivery truck causes a O⊷⊶ motor vehicle accident. The company is sued by the injured party and pays him for his damages (under the theory that the employer is responsible for the job-related actions caused by his employees). The company can, in turn, sue the driver to recover moneys it paid out because of his negligence.

subscribe 1 Write underneath; place a signature at the end of a document. A *subscribing witness* is a person who sees a writing executed or hears it acknowledged and who signs his name as a witness at the request of the party who executed the document. 2 Under corporate law, a *subscriber* is a person who agrees to take part of the original issue of corporate stock. See CORPORATION.

subscription A contract by which a person voluntarily promises to contribute for a designated purpose (such as a charity) a sum of money or other property (such as land) or to perform some other act (such as providing the labor required to construct a new building). Subscriptions are popularly known as pledges.

The subscription contract may be in writing (such as a written promise to contribute $500 to a hospital building

WHEN YOU MAKE A PLEDGE (SUBSCRIPTION) TO A CHARITY

■ If you call in a pledge to a charity telethon, bear in mind that you are making an oral contract that may be enforceable under state law, according to where you live.

■ Before a pledge is binding, a letter or receipt must acknowledge it. A pledge, as an offer, may be withdrawn at any time before its acceptance.

■ If the recipient of a pledge has begun work or incurred a liability relying on the subscription, the court will uphold it.

■ If false representations were made to deceive you into making a charitable subscription, you will be justified in canceling your pledge.

■ If the purpose of the subscription is illegal, the pledge is invalid.

■ Contractual rights on a subscription may be transferred, unless the terms of the pledge prohibit this. For instance, an organization promoting the education of disabled children may assign its rights to collect your pledge to a school for disabled chil-

dren, and the school will have a legally enforceable right against you if you fail to pay your pledge.

■ A subscription may be revoked on notice given by the subscriber if it has not yet been accepted or if a condition on which it is based has not been performed.

■ If the subscriber dies or becomes incompetent (senile, for example) before his pledge is accepted or before consideration is given for it, the subscription becomes legally ineffective.

fund) or oral (such as a pledge called in to a charity telethon). The enforceability of subscriptions is determined by state law.

■ **Form** A subscription need not be in any particular form as long as the promisor clearly states his intention to have such an agreement or contract. In states where a writing is required, the subscriber's name may be signed to the contract by the person who solicits the contribution as long as the subscriber authorizes him to do so.

■ **Acceptance** In order to legally bind the subscriber, there must be an acceptance of the offered subscription, such as a letter or receipt acknowledging a pledge. It is important that this be done because the subscription, as an offer, may be withdrawn at any time before its acceptance.

■ **Consideration** As a matter of policy, courts uphold subscriptions if any CONSIDERATION (something of value given to or done by the recipient of the pledge) can be found. Consideration is given for the subscriber's promise if the recipient of the subscription, relying on it, has begun work or incurred a liability—such as when trustees authorize maintenance work on a church in reliance on a pledge. A benefit to the subscriber, which he and other members of the public enjoy, is also consideration for the promise. For example, a subscription to an art museum will be upheld under this principle because the subscriber shares its cultural benefits with other members of the public.

■ **Fraud and misrepresentation** The discovery of any false representations made intentionally to deceive a person making a charitable subscription will justify canceling the subscription. For example, if a person is told that his subscription will go to fund the development of a student library when, in fact, it will be used to finance a meeting place for political extremists, that person is justified in canceling his subscription.

■ **Illegal subscriptions** If the purpose of a subscription is illegal or against PUBLIC POLICY, it is invalid. A pledge to support an organization set up to smuggle heroin into the country, for example, obviously cannot be enforced.

■ **Ambiguous language** When the terms of a subscription are vague or ambiguous, the court will determine its meaning by evaluating the subject matter of the agreement, the inducement that influenced the subscription, and the circumstances under which it was made and its language.

EXAMPLE A subscription contract stated that the subscriber O—* would pay a proportionate share of any deficit resulting from an opera's summer season, which was to continue for two or more weeks "according to the success of the enterprise." The subscriber did not want to pay because the season was not a financial success. The court interpreted this phrase to mean that the continuation of the season was not dependent on financial success, because "success" means attainment of a desired end, which may or may not be financial.

■ **Assignment** The contractual rights against a subscriber may be assigned (transferred) to someone else unless the terms of the subscription specifically prohibit this. The assignment is a right to collect the funds, not to spend them.

EXAMPLE An organization for teaching disabled children O—* may assign its rights to collect $5,000 from Tom Smith's subscription to a new school using experimental techniques to teach disabled children. The school has a legally enforceable right against Smith if he fails to pay his pledge.

■ **Conditions** Any conditions required by a subscription contract must be fulfilled before a court will enforce the contract.

EXAMPLE A charity solicited subscriptions to construct a O—* memorial building, described in its literature as a new three-story brick structure. A subscriber promised to pay a fixed amount when "construction of the building is begun." The charity did not put up a new building but instead repaired an old wooden structure, naming it the memorial building. Because the condition of the subscription was not performed, the subscriber could not be forced to pay.

Conditions of a subscription may include time restrictions or a requirement for a program of matching corporate grants. If a subscription states that any substantial change in the plan or purpose for which the subscription was made cannot be done without the consent of the subscriber, the subscriber will be released from his obligation if such a change is done without his consent.

If an enterprise is abandoned before its purpose is accomplished, the courts will not, as a rule, enforce the subscription. The project must be totally abandoned, however, in order to relieve the subscriber from liability.

■ **Payment** Once the subscriber's liability has become fixed—when the recipient has carried out all his promises—the subscriber must pay the pledge according to its terms. If the promise is to pay as the work progresses, the work need not be completed before payment is due.

■ **Revocation and lapse** A subscription may be revoked on notice given by the subscriber if it has not yet been accepted or if a condition upon which it is based has not been performed. However, a subscriber may be prevented from revoking a subscription when this would be against the interests of justice.

EXAMPLE Jake Whittier, a wealthy cattle rancher, has been solicited by his alma mater, a southern university, to contribute $150,000 so that it can establish a school of engineering within the next two years. He agrees to do so and signs a pledge stating that he will be a founder of such a school. Because of a number of financial setbacks in the cattle business, Whittier has requested and received several extensions of time to pay. In the meantime, the university has bought supplies, hired engineering professors, and offered courses, although no building has been constructed.

On the advice of his accountant, Whittier notifies his alma mater four years from the time he made his pledge that he will not honor it. He claims that the university no longer has a right to the contribution because it did not build a school within two years of the pledge. The university disagrees and sues to enforce the pledge. A court can find Whittier liable for the subscription because it would be against the interests of justice to do otherwise. Clearly, his alma mater has depended on his promise to be a founder when it spent money for a teaching staff and supplies as well as offering courses. Whittier's subscription was not conditioned on the actual construction of a building. In addition, by requesting additional time to pay his pledge, Whittier had encouraged the university to rely on his promise.

Many courts also rule that when subscriptions are made for public or quasi-public enterprises—for example, education or medical care—any doubtful questions, such as the interpretation of ambiguous language, are resolved against the subscriber who is trying to evade his promise. In this example, Whittier's claim that the pledge depended upon the actual construction of a school would be resolved against him.

If the subscriber dies or becomes legally incompetent (senile, for example) before his pledge is accepted or before consideration is given for it, the subscription lapses (becomes legally ineffective).

■ **Lawsuits** Because a subscription is a type of contract, governed by the general rules of contract law, the remedies for its breach are the same as those for breach of CONTRACT.

subsidiary Auxiliary; in an inferior position or capacity. A *subsidiary corporation* is one in which another CORPORATION owns at least a majority of the shares and thus controls the subsidiary. The controlling corporation is called the *parent corporation*.

substantial Of real worth and importance. For example, the right to trial by jury is a substantial right.

substantiate Establish the existence of a fact or the truth of some matter by competent EVIDENCE; verify. For example, a plaintiff who testifies in court that while he was crossing a street he was struck and injured by the defendant's automobile might call upon an eyewitness to substantiate his testimony.

substantive law The part of the law that creates, defines, and regulates rights and duties, such as the law of CONTRACTS, TORTS, or WILLS. It is different from *adjective law*, or *procedural law*, which prescribes the methods of enforcing rights or obtaining redress for wrongs, such as the law relating to JURISDICTION (whether a court has authority to hear a particular type of case), VENUE (where a case can be tried), and PLEADING (the form in which a case is presented to the court).

substituted service The SERVICE of process, such as a WRIT or SUMMONS, upon a defendant in any manner authorized by statute other than personal service within the jurisdiction. For example, substituted service can be by publication in a newspaper circulated in the county where the defendant resides or by mailing a copy of the summons to his last known address.

succession Transfer of title to (ownership of) property under the law of DESCENT AND DISTRIBUTION.

sue 1 Begin or engage in a lawsuit or a legal proceeding for the enforcement of a right or the redress of a wrong. 2 Prosecute; make a legal claim; bring a lawsuit against another party.

suffer Allow or admit an act to be done or a condition to exist. The term conveys passivity, indifference, or abstaining from preventive action, as distinguished from an affirmative act. For example, the tenant of a property uses it to distill liquor unlawfully. The owner *suffers* this unlawful use of his property if he knows of it and fails to take effective measures to stop it.

suffrage The right to cast a vote at public ELECTIONS.

suicide The taking of one's own life. At common law, it was a felony. The offender forfeited all his goods and CHATTELS (personal, movable property), and his body was buried in the highway. Suicide is no longer regarded as a crime. However, aiding, advising, or inciting a person to commit or attempt to commit suicide is a felony in several states. In some states, a person who attempts suicide is required to undergo a period of hospitalization and psychological observation.

sui generis (Latin) "Of its own kind or class," that is, the only one of its kind; unique.

sui juris (Latin) "Of his own right." A legal term applied to a person who possesses full social and civil rights, including the right to sue, and who is not under any disability, such being an INSANE PERSON or a minor (INFANT), that would prevent him from acting for himself.

suit A lawsuit; a civil ACTION or proceeding for the enforcement of a right or for the redress of a wrong. See also DAMAGES.

summary Short and concise; immediate; without a jury trial. A *summary proceeding* is a way of settling a lawsuit promptly. In such a proceeding the regular steps in a lawsuit are shortened and simplified. Depending on state law, a summary proceeding is available for certain types of cases, such as an eviction by a landlord, which require prompt action and involve just a few straightforward issues.

A *summary judgment* is a final decision in a case that does not require a lengthy presentation of evidence. It is considered an extreme remedy and should be granted only when it is clear that there is no material (important) issue of fact. It completely avoids the necessity of a jury trial because the issues are clear as a MATTER OF LAW. For a discussion of how a summary judgment works, see JUDGMENT.

summary process A court order that can be obtained without delay and that takes effect immediately. It is usually an order that compels the defendant in a civil lawsuit or criminal trial to appear in court.

summons A formal document served on a person being sued or directed to a sheriff or other officer requiring him to notify the person named in the document that a lawsuit has been started against him. The summons also states the name of the court, the day, and the time when the person must appear in court to respond to the lawsuit.

UNITED STATES DISTRICT COURT
for the
SOUTHERN DISTRICT OF NEW YORK
Civil Action File Number 0001

x JOHN DOE , *Plaintiff*

v. } Summons

x RICHARD ROE , *Defendant*

To the above-named Defendant:

You are hereby summoned and required to serve upon BARRY BARRISTER , plaintiff's attorney, whose address is 100 Bench Street , an answer to the complaint which is herewith served upon you, within 20 days after service of this summons upon you, exclusive of the day of service. If you fail to do so, judgment by default will be taken against you for the relief demanded in the complaint.

(Seal of the U.S. District Court) (KURT CLARK) *Clerk of Court*
Dated:

Sunday law Sunday is legally a day of rest in most states; however, the purpose of a Sunday law (often called a blue law) is not to impose the observance of Sunday as a religious duty but to enforce a cessation from labor on one day in seven. Except when a statute provides otherwise, Sunday is generally regarded as the natural day of 24 hours between midnight at the end of Saturday and midnight at the beginning of Monday.

Enacting Sunday regulations is a constitutional exercise of a state's POLICE POWER, and municipalities may also have the power to enact Sunday regulations. The words "Sabbath" and "The Lord's Day" are used synonymously with "Sunday" in legislation.

■ **Scope of Sunday laws** Only a law can prohibit persons from doing certain acts on Sunday. All acts that are not otherwise unlawful and not prohibited by statute may lawfully be done.

Labor When a Sunday law prohibits "labor," the word includes every kind of work—mental or physical, in any trade, profession, or business. An activity can be considered labor even if the person who does it receives no compensation. An employer who keeps his employees working on Sunday and who personally oversees and carries on his business is doing labor, even though he does not perform manual tasks.

Business or occupation In many jurisdictions, conducting or transacting business on Sunday is specifically prohibited by statute or by local ordinance. Under some statutes, business includes only those acts that are performed for profit. A person can be found guilty of conducting a business on Sunday when he knows and consents to its operation, even though he does not personally engage in any transaction but merely operates the business through his employees.

Keeping open shop Courts have generally upheld Sunday closing laws. Statutes that simply prohibit "keeping open" are usually interpreted to mean keeping open for business purposes. Whenever an establishment is kept accessible to persons wishing to enter for purposes of trade or employment, it is "open," whether or not a sale is made.

Anyone who controls the opening or closing of an establishment is responsible for violation of closing laws if he keeps the business open. A member of a business partnership is individually liable if he himself opens the partnership's establishment and engages in Sunday trade.

Necessity or charity Acts of necessity or charity that are exempt from the Sunday laws are difficult to classify, and there is no general rule for determining them. However, the necessity for the work must be real and urgent. The test is not whether it must be done sometime, but whether it must be done on Sunday. The fact that Sunday work will lead to an increase in the worker's income does not constitute a case of necessity.

Any work required to secure the public safety, such as a policeman performing his official duties, or to preserve or prevent a serious loss of property is exempt from Sunday laws. This rule is not limited to cases in which the property is of great value.

A work of charity—an act without compensation or private gain—is also exempt.

Persons observing another day Unless there is a statutory exemption in their favor, persons observing a day of rest other than Sunday may not perform acts forbidden by Sunday laws. However, valid exceptions often enable such persons to perform these acts without violating the Sunday laws. For example, some laws specify that anyone who observes a day other than Sunday as the Sabbath may keep his business open on Sundays. Exceptions in favor of persons observing another day do not apply to persons who believe the seventh day is the Sabbath but do not observe it as such or to business corporations, because a corporation is held incapable of having religious beliefs.

■ **Specific acts permitted or prohibited** Under the Sunday laws, some acts have been specifically permitted or prohibited. For example, the purchase of a home (real estate) has been held to be a work of necessity and therefore an exception to laws prohibiting the purchase of other kinds of real estate on Sunday. Drawing up a contract is considered business and therefore prohibited under many Sunday laws. (However, it is permitted under laws that forbid only labor that disturbs others and laws that forbid only menial labor, such as physical labor.) When a plant or factory, such as an ice factory, must operate continuously to be effective, operating it on Sunday is permitted under Sunday laws. Necessary repairs in manufacturing plants or similar industrial establishments may also be permitted on Sunday under these laws.

Selling food or drink, including liquor, in stores is prohibited under many Sunday laws, but selling them for consumption at inns or restaurants is a work of necessity and therefore an exception to the laws. (This exception does not include selling food that is to be consumed off the premises of a restaurant or inn, such as take-out orders.)

A farmer who sells his farm products at his farm on Sunday is not considered a merchant or trader and is permitted to sell his products under Sunday laws forbidding business sales. In cases of necessity or charity, a pharmacist may enter his store to supply the required drugs or medicines, but it is an offense for him to open his store and sell drugs or medicines generally when such sales are forbidden by Sunday laws.

sunset law A statute that puts a time limit on the existence of a government group. The purpose of sunset laws is to force agencies that have outlived their usefulness to disband. If the authority to act automatically expires after a specific period of time, then a legislature must act to renew any committee, commission, or agency that is doing an ongoing job. This insures regular reevaluation of an agency and prevents ineffective groups from continuing to exist.

sunshine law A statute that requires government agencies to open their meetings to the public; also called an open meeting law, open government law, or government in the sunshine law.

■ **Federal law** The federal Sunshine Act applies to about 50 federal agencies. It sets up standards for open meetings whenever a quorum of members gathers to discuss and conduct agency business.

Agency meetings The law requires that every agency meeting be open to the public except during the discussion of a matter that falls into one of 10 exceptions. The exceptions include trade secrets, criminal investigations, properly classified secrets relating to national defense and foreign policy, and internal personnel rules and practices of the agency. Only the part of the meeting where such an excepted topic is discussed can be closed; the rest of the meeting must be open. When there is doubt about whether or not a topic falls into an excepted category, the topic must be discussed in an open meeting.

The Sunshine Act sets a strict procedure for publicizing agency meetings. A public announcement of every meeting—listing time, date, location, and other relevant information—must be made at least a week before the meeting is held unless a majority of agency members agree that business cannot be delayed that long. The meeting must be open to the public unless a majority votes to close it under one of the permitted exceptions. The votes of the agency members are recorded and made available to the public. This informs the public on the attitude of each agency member toward open meetings. When the vote is to close a meeting or a portion of it, a full written explanation of the reasons and a list of persons expected to attend the closed meeting must also be released to the public.

A complete verbatim transcript or electronic recording must be made at closed meetings, which must be released to the public if it is later determined that the matter discussed was not an exception to the open-meeting requirement. (Written minutes must be taken at open meetings, and those, too, must be made available to the public.)

Individual rights The provisions of the Sunshine Act are written to supplement the protection given to personal rights under the Privacy Act of 1974 and the federal Freedom of Information Act. See PRIVACY, RIGHT OF. These laws attempt to balance the competing interests of privacy and open government.

Anyone harmed by an agency's decision to close a meeting may start a legal action in federal court. The court will review the agency's decision to determine whether the meeting was closed for a proper reason. The court can grant any appropriate relief, including releasing the transcript of a meeting that should not have been closed. Costs assessed against an agency are paid by the U.S. government. Reasonable attorney's fees and other litigation costs can be assessed against a plaintiff who loses his case only if the court finds that he started the lawsuit for frivolous or dilatory purposes to harass and delay action by an agency.

■ **State laws** Some states also have sunshine laws. The specific provisions vary from state to state, but their purpose is the same as that of the federal law.

superior Higher; taking precedence.
EXAMPLE When liens (claims against property as security
O►──✳ for a debt) exist against real estate, one may be
superior to another. A lien filed by the federal government against a taxpayer's land because he has failed to pay his income tax for four years is superior to a lien held by a village for property taxes that have not been paid for the past two years. This means that if the property is sold, the debt owed to the federal government must be paid first. Any money remaining will be used to satisfy the village lien.

supersedeas A writ (written order) that contains a command from an appellate court to stay (halt) proceedings in a lower trial court. The writ suspends the power of a trial court to issue an EXECUTION (an order to carry out) of a judgment that has been appealed. The writ of supersedeas can be applied only to the particular judgment being appealed. The term is sometimes used synonymously with "stay of proceedings."

supervening Something additional or unforeseen. For example, a *supervening cause* is a new CAUSE that, operating independently of anything else, becomes the proximate cause (direct cause) of an accident.

supplementary proceeding A proceeding in which a judgment debtor (a debtor who has not satisfied a court's JUDGMENT that was entered against him in a civil suit) is summoned to court for questioning by a judgment creditor (a creditor who has not received payment on his judgment). In questioning the debtor, the judgment creditor tries to discover if the debtor has any money or other property available that can be used to satisfy the judgment. If so, the court can order the debtor to pay the judgment creditor with the specific property that has been disclosed in the proceedings.

support 1 Maintain or provide for. See HUSBAND AND WIFE; PARENT AND CHILD. 2 In regard to real property, the right to have one's ground held up so that it will not cave in when an adjoining landowner makes an excavation. This support is of two kinds, lateral and subjacent. *Lateral support* is the right to have a lot (piece) of land supported by the land that lies next to it. *Subjacent support* is the right to have a piece of land supported by the land that lies directly under it.

sup-pro See SUPPLEMENTARY PROCEEDING.

supremacy clause Name for Article VI, Section 2, of the U.S. Constitution, which establishes the Constitution, all federal laws, and treaties ". . . made under the Authority of the United States [as] . . . the supreme Law of the Land."

The supremacy clause makes it the duty of all state judges to recognize and enforce the Constitution and any laws and treaties made under federal authority. All of these are part of the law of every state as well as part of the national law.

■ **Application to state laws** No action taken by the federal government within the sphere of its constitutional powers can be contradicted or overridden by state laws. For example, a state cannot grant a PATENT to an inventor because the law of patents is governed exclusively by the federal government.

The federal government and its agencies are not subject to state taxation because the supremacy clause makes the federal government supreme.

EXAMPLE This principle was declared by the Supreme Court in 1819 in the historic case of *McCulloch* v. *Maryland.* Congress had established a Bank of the United States, with a branch in Maryland. The Maryland legislature passed a statute ordering a stamp tax on the notes issued by the bank. The Supreme Court declared both the state law and the tax unconstitutional. The federal statute that authorized the creation of the bank was the supreme law of the land; the bank was an instrument of the federal government. If the federal government could be taxed by each state, it could be destroyed. On the other hand, the Constitution does not give the federal government the power to tax an activity or agency

of a state government. This implied right of the states to their existence is based on the 10th Amendment, which reserves to the states (or to the people) powers not delegated to the federal government. See STATES' RIGHTS.

Treaties The supremacy clause also voids every state constitutional provision or state law that conflicts with any TREATY. A treaty is superior to state law even when it affects the use of state lands. However, if a provision of federal law conflicts with a provision of a treaty, then the most recent provision will govern because it is the latest expression of national policy.

Supreme Court 1 The highest federal court in the nation. 2 In most states, a court of high powers and broad authority.

■ **State supreme courts** In some states, the supreme court is the chief court for appeals, the court of last resort. In New York, however, the supreme court is the basic trial-level court authorized to hear appeals from some lower local courts, while the highest appeals court in the state is called the court of appeals. In Connecticut, the supreme court of errors is the highest appeals court. In Maine and Massachusetts, the highest appeals court is called the supreme judicial court.

■ **Composition of U.S. Supreme Court** The judges on the U.S. Supreme Court are called Justices. The number of Justices is set by federal statute and has been changed a few times through the years. Originally, in 1789, the Court had six members. Since 1869 there have been nine Justices.

There is a Chief Justice and eight Associate Justices. Justices are appointed for life terms by the President, but his choices must first be confirmed by the Senate. The Constitution does not set any qualifications, such as age, citizenship, or experience, for Justices. Not even a legal education is required. By custom, however, Justices are usually lawyers and have been judges in other courts.

Justices may be removed from office only if impeached by the House and convicted by the Senate. When the office of Chief Justice is vacant, the President may select from among the Associate Justices or choose an outsider to fill the position. Whenever the Chief Justice is unable to serve or the office is vacant, the Associate Justice who has been on the Supreme Court for the longest time performs his duties. The Court can take official action with as few as six Justices participating in decisions, but it will sometimes postpone extremely important cases until all nine Justices can participate.

The Court sits in Washington, D.C., and begins its term each year on the first Monday in October. The Court decides how long the term will run. It may hold adjourned or special terms (terms outside the regularly scheduled term) whenever necessary. The law allows for appointment of a clerk of the Supreme Court, deputy clerks, a marshal, a court reporter, a librarian, an administrative assistant, and law clerks and secretaries for the Justices.

■ **Background** The Supreme Court was established by Article III, Section 1, of the Constitution, and its organization and functions were defined by the Judiciary Act of 1789. John Jay, the first Chief Justice of the United States, did not believe the Court would ever achieve the power and respect that the highest court in the nation ought to have.

THE HIGHEST COURT IN THE LAND, THE U.S. SUPREME COURT

■ Do not confuse the authority of your state supreme court with that of the U.S. Supreme Court.

■ In some states, the court of last resort is called the supreme court, but in others a different name is given to the highest appeals court.

■ The U.S. Supreme Court can try from the beginning lawsuits involving foreign diplomats, suits between the federal government and a state, suits by a state against an alien or a citizen of another state, and suits between two states (such as a boundary dispute).

■ The Supreme Court may review decisions made by a lower court in cases posing questions of federal law or constitutionality, in controversies between citizens of different states, in admiralty cases, in cases in which the United States is a party, and in suits between a state and a citizen of another state.

■ There is a right to appeal to the Supreme Court when a lower federal court holds a law unconstitutional or when the highest court of a state denies the unconstitutionality of a given state law.

■ Most of the cases reviewed by the Supreme Court are chosen by the Justices themselves on the basis of whether a substantial federal question is involved.

■ The Court decides a case before it by a majority vote. As few as six judges can participate in a decision, but on an important issue the Court prefers to have all nine Justices hear and vote on the case.

■ After a case has been decided, one of the Associate Justices writes the majority opinion.

■ The Supreme Court will accept the trial court's view of the facts unless it is clearly wrong.

■ Decisions of the U.S. Supreme Court cannot be appealed.

Under Chief Justice John Marshall, who served from 1801 to 1835, however, the Court established such great principles of constitutional law that its position as the final arbiter of the Constitution and the laws of the land has since remained unquestioned.

The concerns of the Court and how it interprets the law and the Constitution have changed with the times. For example, in its early days, the Supreme Court was mostly concerned with issues that had to do with the proper division of authority and power between the federal and state governments. Such issues included judicial review, under which the Court has the power to declare an act of Congress unconstitutional (see MARBURY V. MADISON), and the doctrine of implied powers, which gives the federal government powers in addition to those specifically granted by the Constitution (see CONSTITUTIONAL LAW; MCCULLOCH V. MARYLAND). The Court also dealt with contract and commerce issues.

In the late 19th and early 20th centuries, the Court focused on protecting property rights. In modern times, the Supreme Court has been concerned with issues dealing with the rights and liberties of individuals, such as racial discrimination (see BROWN V. BOARD OF EDUCATION), voting rights (see BAKER V. CARR), rights of accused persons (see MIRANDA V. ARIZONA), and the freedoms of speech, religion, and press.

■ **Authority** The Supreme Court does not have jurisdiction (authority) to hear every kind of case. Limitations are imposed because of the division of powers between the federal and state governments and between the legislative, executive, and judicial branches of the federal government. The Supreme Court is empowered to hear some cases from the beginning and other cases only on appeal.

Original jurisdiction The Supreme Court has original jurisdiction (the authority to try a case from the beginning) in lawsuits involving foreign ambassadors, consuls, or members of their staffs, and in certain controversies in which a state is a party to the suit—such as a dispute between the federal government and a state, a suit by a state against a citizen of another state, or a suit by a state against an ALIEN (noncitizen).

Cases between two states—for example, a dispute over boundary lines or water supplies—may be tried only in the Supreme Court. This is called original and exclusive jurisdiction. Such cases between two states must be taken directly to the Supreme Court. These cases are frequently given to special masters (officers of the Court, often retired judges appointed by the Court), who hear the evidence, make findings, and recommend a decision to the Justices of the Court.

Appellate jurisdiction The Supreme Court has appellate jurisdiction, the authority to review a decision made by a lower court (1) in *federal question cases*, which arise under the Constitution, treaties, or federal law; (2) in *diversity cases*, which arise in controversies between citizens of different states; (3) in ADMIRALTY cases; (4) in cases in which the United States is a party; and (5) in suits between a state and a citizen of another state.

Congress has the power to make exceptions to this list and to make rules to keep the number of cases manageable.

Mandatory jurisdiction Originally, the Supreme Court was required to hear every case under its appellate jurisdiction. This is called mandatory jurisdiction. Because of the increasing burden on the Court, Congress has continually reduced the number of cases the Court is required to hear. Some kinds of cases are considered so important, however, that Congress has preserved for them the right of appeal to the Supreme Court. For example, the right to appeal exists when a federal court holds a state law unconstitutional or when the highest court of a state denies the unconstitutionality of a state statute.

Discretionary jurisdiction Most of the cases that come to the Supreme Court fall under its discretionary jurisdiction, under which the Justices choose the cases they want to hear. Usually, they select cases on the basis of whether a substantial federal question is involved.

When a party seeking review petitions the Court for a

writ of certiorari, a document granting the right of review, the Justices deliberate privately to decide whether the issues of a case are important enough to merit review. If any four Justices favor it, CERTIORARI is granted, and the Justices either decide the case on the basis of the papers submitted or may schedule a full-dress argument in court. If certiorari is denied, the matter ends. See APPEAL AND ERROR.

Certified questions The Supreme Court also has special jurisdiction to answer *certified questions,* which are received from a federal court of appeals or from the U.S. Court of Claims. The lower court may certify a question that it cannot answer, and the Supreme Court can either give instructions that the lower court must follow or require the lower court to send over the entire record so that the Supreme Court can make a decision on the entire case.

On a few occasions, the Supreme Court has answered certified questions because they involved an issue identical to a question in a case being considered by it.

EXAMPLE In 1963 eight federal judges for the U.S. Court of Appeals were evenly divided on the question of whether Gov. Ross Barnett and Lt. Gov. Paul Johnson, Jr., of Mississippi were entitled to have a trial by jury. Their trial involved contempt charges for refusing to obey the court's order to permit James Meredith to enroll as a student at the University of Mississippi. The massive resistance to racial integration in Mississippi at the time had led to violence, disorder, and many hotly contested lawsuits. Usually, a court of appeals reviews the decision of a lower federal court. If the vote of the court of appeals is evenly split, the lower court decision stands. In this case, the governor and lieutenant governor were charged with willfully disobeying a direct order from the court of appeals. There was no lower court decision to revert to, so the court of appeals certified the question. The Supreme Court decided the issue, holding that there was no right to have this case heard by a jury.

■ **Decisions** Justices discuss the case in private, and cases are decided by a majority vote.

An Associate Justice who voted with the majority writes the *majority opinion,* also called the *opinion of the court.* A Justice who disagrees with the majority opinion may write a *dissenting opinion.* A Justice who agrees with the result of the majority opinion but wants to express his own reasons for the decision may write a *concurring opinion.* These opinions are later published in the *United States Reports,* the *Supreme Court Reporter,* and elsewhere.

Bases for decisions The Supreme Court will accept the trial court's view of the facts of the case unless it is clearly wrong—for example, if a party had to be 10 feet tall to have bumped his head on a door and suffered brain damage. Only questions that have been raised in the lower court or presented in a petition for certiorari will be weighed. The Court tends to avoid dealing with issues that are not essential to the decision of a case and to ignore constitutional questions when a case can be decided by a statute or on an error that was made in procedure.

EXAMPLE A man claims that his right of equal protection was violated when the city that employed him refused to give him paternity leave to care for his young child while granting such leaves to mothers. If a court discovers that local law required applications for such leaves three months in advance and the man never applied properly, the Court can refuse to consider the larger constitutional issue.

However, if the error was small and legally harmless, the Court will not reverse the decision.

Types of decisions The Supreme Court's final decision may be to dismiss the case (because certiorari should not have been granted) or to affirm, reverse, VACATE (declare void), or modify the trial court's judgment, or to remand (send back) the case to the lower court with directions on how it should be reconsidered.

Effects of decisions A Supreme Court decision cannot be appealed. It stands unless the Constitution is formally amended to change the law or unless the Supreme Court eventually overrules itself because it believes an error was made or because changes in society require a different decision. Usually, however, the Supreme Court follows its earlier decisions for similar cases. Lower courts must follow the decision of the Supreme Court in similar cases. This helps guarantee equal justice to all.

surcharge 1 An additional charge on something that is already charged—for example, interest on interest. 2 In law, the penalty imposed on a fiduciary, such as a trustee, for failing to exercise common prudence, skill, and caution in performing his duties. See EXECUTORS AND ADMINISTRATORS; TRUST.

surety A person who is responsible for a debt or other obligation incurred by someone else. The surety obligates himself to pay the money or perform the duty if the other person (the principal) fails to act. If payment or performance is enforced against the surety, he is entitled to be paid back by the principal. See PRINCIPAL AND SURETY.

In return for a fee based on the amount of the security required, a surety company assumes the responsibility of a surety on bonds that are posted by persons in positions of financial trust, such as trustees and guardians, or by persons who promise to perform work, such as builders, entertainers, and authors of books.

EXAMPLE Church trustees execute a contract with a builder to construct a Sunday school annex for $18,000. The contract requires the builder to post a performance bond to guarantee completion of the work. The builder pays a surety company $575 to cover the cost of a bond. If the builder fails to complete the work, the surety company will pay up to $18,000, the amount of the bond, to have the work done.

surplusage Unnecessary or irrelevant matter. For example, any allegation in the pleadings (COMPLAINT and ANSWER) in a lawsuit that is extraneous to the action is surplusage.

surprise In law, surprise may be one of the grounds for a new trial or for discrediting a witness. When a party to a lawsuit is unexpectedly placed in a situation of surprise, and it is harmful to his case, he may ask for a new trial. The condition or situation must be one that he could not reasonably have anticipated and that he could not have guarded against or prevented. When a party is taken by surprise by the testimony of his own witness, he may be permitted to discredit the witness by showing prior contradictory or inconsistent statements.

EXAMPLE Kevin was on trial for robbery. When he was
O—＊ arrested, his friend Greg had protested: "You got the wrong guy. I was with Kevin that night at a hockey game. I know he didn't rob anybody."

At the trial, Kevin's attorney called Greg as an alibi witness. Once on the stand, Greg refused to swear that he had been with Kevin on the night of the robbery. Because this came as a surprise, Kevin's attorney was permitted to ask questions about Greg's earlier statements that contradicted his present testimony. These questions were allowed to show that the testimony might not be credible.

surrender Give back, yield, or restore. In a landlord-tenant relationship (see LANDLORD AND TENANT), surrender occurs when a tenant, with the landlord's agreement, gives back his leased premises to his landlord before the expiration of the lease and the landlord agrees to accept the return of the premises. Both parties must agree in order for a surrender to take place.

surrogate In some states, the name given to the judge or judicial officer who adjudicates probate matters, such as the administration of estates and guardianships. See EXECUTORS AND ADMINISTRATORS; GUARDIAN AND WARD.

survivorship The state of one person's outliving another person or persons. You have a right of survivorship when you become entitled to property because you have outlived another person who had an interest in the property. The most common example of survivorship occurs when on the death of one of two joint tenants, such as two persons who jointly own a home, all of the property passes to the survivor.

suspended sentence In criminal law, a SENTENCE that is served without imprisonment and without supervision. It is different from a *probated sentence*, which is served under the supervision of a probation officer.

sustain Support, warrant, or uphold. When an attorney objects to the introduction of evidence during a trial and the judge agrees with the objection, the judge "sustains" the objection. Similarly, when the evidence presented during a trial supports the verdict, the evidence is said to sustain the verdict.

syllabus A headnote or summary of a case that has been decided; it contains a brief statement of the court rulings on the various points decided in the case.

symbolic delivery The transfer of an item of sale or gift by delivering some article that represents it, makes it accessible, or serves as evidence of the buyer's or donee's (recipient's) title to (ownership of) it. For example, a gift of the contents of a bank safe-deposit box can be symbolically delivered by transferring the key to the box to the donee.

syndicate An association of persons formed for the purpose of conducting some particular business transaction. The term is synonymous with JOINT ADVENTURE.

synopsis A brief or partial statement or summary of the record of a case.

Taft-Hartley Act   Amendments made in 1947 to the National Labor Relations Act (NLRA) of 1935. The 1947 act was a recognition of the fact that unfair labor practices were committed not only by management but by labor unions and it outlawed unfair union practices. See also LABOR RELATIONS; STRIKE.

tail   Limited; abridged. See FEE TAIL.

talesman   **1** A person summoned to act as a juror from among the bystanders in the court. **2** A person summoned as an additional juror if one is needed on a jury panel. See also JURY.

tangible   Capable of being touched, possessed, or realized. *Tangible personal property* is property that can be seen, weighed, measured, or estimated by the physical senses and that can be possessed, such as an automobile, furniture, or jewelry.

tariff   **1** The schedule, or list, of articles on which a duty is imposed when they are imported into the United States, along with the rates at which the articles are taxed. **2** The CUSTOMS, or duties, payable on such articles.

taxable income   Under federal tax law, the amount of money earned by an individual—such as salary, investment dividends, and bank interest—reduced by personal exemptions and permissible deductions. It is the income against which tax rates are applied to compute the amount of federal INCOME TAX owed. State income tax laws usually compute taxable income by the same general method.

taxation   The process by which the legislative branch of the government raises money for public purposes by placing charges on persons, businesses, and property. Taxes are imposed to support the government in return for the advantages and protection that government provides to the taxpayer and his property. Because government cannot operate without the means to pay its expenses, it has the right to compel all citizens and property within its limits to share its costs. Both the state and federal governments have the power to tax their citizens.

■ **Types of taxes**   There are two basic types of taxes: excise taxes and property taxes.

Excise tax   An EXCISE tax is one imposed directly by a government's lawmaking body on certain products or transactions, such as carrying on a profession or business, getting a license, or transferring property. It is a fixed and absolute charge that does not depend upon the taxpayer's financial status. An *estate tax* is placed on, and paid by, the deceased person's ESTATE for the privilege of transferring property to his or her heirs. Those who inherit property may be required to pay an *inheritance tax* on the value of the particular property they receive. A *gift tax* is often incurred by the giver when he gives another person a valuable gift. See ESTATE AND GIFT TAX.

A *sales tax* is an excise tax placed on certain goods and services. For example, paper products bought at a supermarket may be taxable while food is not, but the same food served to you in a restaurant is taxable. The state legislatures decide what goods and services should be taxed. Sometimes people speak of a *luxury tax*, which is just a sales tax on expensive items considered luxuries, such as a yacht, jewelry, or furs. Taxes on the processing of tobacco, meat, cheese, and sugar are also excise taxes.

A *corporate tax*, measured by the income of corporations, is an excise tax on the privilege of doing business in the corporate capacity, which offers certain advantages to individuals, such as limited liability.

Property tax   A property tax takes into account the taxpayer's wealth represented by his income or the property he owns. Property taxes are imposed on real estate, but INCOME TAXES also fall into this category. The more commonly known PROPERTY TAXES are imposed primarily on real estate.

■ **Direct and indirect taxes**   Sometimes taxes are classified as direct and indirect. A *direct tax* is assessed on the property, business, or income of individuals who are to pay the tax, such as a tax on land and buildings. An *indirect tax* occurs when taxes are levied on and paid by the producers of commodities before they reach the consumer but which are ultimately passed along to the consumer as part of the market price of the commodity. Such tax is considered indirect because the producer shifts his responsibility for the tax to the consumer in the form of higher-priced goods.

■ **Federal taxes** The federal government is authorized by the Constitution and laws passed by Congress to collect various taxes. Article I, Section 8, of the Constitution authorizes Congress "To lay and collect Taxes, Duties, Imposts and Excises, to pay the Debts and provide for the common Defence and general Welfare of the United States." *Duties* are taxes on imports. See CUSTOMS. They can be either AD VALOREM (a percentage of the value of the property) or specific (a fixed amount). All of these taxes are excise taxes. Congress may not tax exports.

The 16th Amendment empowers Congress to impose a federal INCOME TAX. Congress has also enacted laws that permit the federal government to tax estates left after people die and gifts made while people are alive. Such estate and gift taxes are excise taxes.

■ **State taxes** States also have the inherent power to levy both property and excise taxes. The 10th Amendment to the Constitution, which reserves to the states powers that have not been granted to the United States or prohibited to the states by the Constitution, implicitly acknowledges this fundamental right. See STATES' RIGHTS. A state may raise funds by taxation in aid of its own welfare as long as the tax does not unjustly discriminate among those who are to share the tax burden. Property taxes, for instance, may be imposed on the owners of land within the state. The state may also levy income and gift and estate taxes on its residents in addition to their federal tax obligations. Inheritance tax is also frequently imposed.

■ **Principles of taxation** Two fundamental principles of taxation are equality and uniformity. The taxing power of the legislature should always be exercised so that the burdens imposed by taxation are placed as equally as possible on all classes. One way this is done is through a *progressive tax,* which imposes a higher tax rate on people with larger incomes than on people with smaller incomes.

Equality in taxation is also achieved when no higher rate in proportion to value is imposed on one person or his property than on other people or property in similar circumstances. It does not require that the benefits arising from taxation should be enjoyed by all the people in equal degree or that each person should share in each particular benefit. For example, the fact that a married couple have no children or send their children to private school does not mean that they can stop paying local school taxes.

Uniformity of taxation is necessary for equality of taxation because similar items are taxed equally only if the mode of assessment is the same, or uniform. A person in Florida will pay the same amount of federal tax on a gift to his spouse as a person in Alaska, if their financial circumstances are comparable. Similarly, you and your neighbor pay property tax according to the same rate of taxation.

A tax that is levied on property must be set according to its value, usually determined as its fair cash or fair market value. This requirement safeguards equality and uniformity of taxation by preventing arbitrary or inconsistent methods of deciding how much tax is due.

tax avoidance The use of legal tax methods, such as exemptions and deductions, in order to pay lower taxes. Tax avoidance differs from TAX EVASION, which is the use of illegal methods to avoid paying taxes.

EXAMPLE Say you have $10,000. You can avoid paying
O←──➤ federal income taxes by investing the money in municipal bonds because the interest earned on municipal bonds is not included as taxable income. If you take the same amount and instead place it in a savings account, any interest earned on it is taxable as income. Thus, by investing in the municipal bonds, you have legally avoided a certain amount of income tax because your taxable income is lower than if the money had been placed in a savings account.

Not all municipal bonds offer tax-exempt interest for federal income tax purposes, however. Some offer only exemption from state and local taxes, while others offer exemption from all three.

Tax Court The U.S. Tax Court was established under Article I of the Constitution to provide a place for taxpayers to challenge INCOME TAX and ESTATE AND GIFT TAX liability assessed against them without first having to pay the tax and then sue for its return. See also Chart 1.

tax deed A document that serves as proof of ownership of land purchased from the government at a TAX SALE after title to the land has been taken from another person by the government for failure to pay taxes and offered for sale.

tax evasion Illegally paying less in income, gift, or estate taxes than the law requires by committing fraud in filing or paying taxes. Failure to disclose $20,000 worth of prizes on a federal INCOME TAX return is an example of tax evasion because the $20,000 is taxable income. Claiming pets or nonexistent children as dependents in order to take additional personal exemptions on an income tax return is also tax evasion. Tax evasion is a crime under both federal and state laws. A person convicted of any form of tax evasion may be sentenced to jail, fined, or both.

taxing costs The process of determining and charging to the losing party in a lawsuit the amount of COSTS (expenses involved in bringing or defending the action) to which the successful side is legally entitled.

tax sale A sale of land to collect unpaid taxes after the legal time for their payment has expired. As a means of forcing taxpayers unable or unwilling to pay their taxes, or negligent in doing so, states have laws authorizing tax sales to collect taxes long overdue them. A tax sale is a forfeiture of property for failure to fulfill one's legal obligation to pay the taxes on it.

■ **Procedure** Any sale of land for unpaid taxes must comply with the requirements of the law or the sale will be invalidated.

Publication of delinquencies The tax collector is usually required to publish a list of lands on which the taxes are delinquent. State and local statutes may specify the newspapers in which the list is to be published. The list must contain a description of each parcel of land that may be sold, the name of the owner, the amount due, and the period of time for which the taxes are due. The interest allowed by law on the unpaid taxes, penalties for default in payment, and the costs of the sale may also be included in the amount due. In some states, the list must be filed in the office of the county clerk.

The purpose of a notice (list) of a tax sale is to warn the property owner and to provide information to prospective buyers. The owner also receives a separate notice, which is usually sent along with his tax bill, or the notice is printed on the bill to the effect that, because of his failure to pay the tax as requested a certain number of times, his property will be put up for sale on a certain date. Failure to give notice to the owner invalidates any subsequent sale of his property. This rule follows DUE PROCESS OF LAW, which requires that before any person is deprived of his property he must be given notice and opportunity to defend himself or to redeem the property by paying back taxes plus any other legal charges due.

Manner of sale   The manner in which a tax sale is conducted is regulated by state law. As a general rule, the sale is open to the public to insure a fair price for it in the open market. A private sale is valid, however, if it is authorized by statute.

■ **Sale price**   Generally, land offered at a tax sale must bring at least the entire amount of taxes due on it, in addition to the lawful costs and charges of the sale. A sale for a smaller amount is invalid in some states. If the property is sold at a tax sale for more than what is owed, the excess amount must be given to the delinquent taxpayer.

■ **Purchaser**   The land goes to the highest bidder unless he is disqualified by statute—because he has conflict of interest, for example. Once the purchaser has paid the amount of his bid, he is given a TAX DEED, which is proof of his ownership of the property. Some states require that a tax sale be confirmed in a court proceeding before the purchaser actually takes title (ownership).

A state, county, municipal corporation, or other governmental body may purchase land sold at a tax sale only if authorized by statute.

■ **Redemption from tax sale**   The owner of the property has the right by law to redeem it from a tax sale. This means that if, within a specified time, the owner pays the back taxes plus any other legal charges due, he will regain complete ownership of his property free of his prior tax debt. The policy of the law is to give the taxpayer every reasonable opportunity to redeem his property because the law considers forfeiture a drastic remedy. As a general rule, a person who has a legal or equitable interest in the land that will be affected by the sale, such as a person who holds a LIFE ESTATE in the property, is also entitled to redeem it.

EXAMPLE Matt Jones owns a 1,500-acre cattle ranch in
O⊷⊶᎐ Wyoming. He has given his son, Josh, a life estate (use of the ranch until his death) to it, with a remainder to his grandchildren, Betty and Bart, upon Josh's death. Matt has been feuding with the county tax assessor for years, finally refusing to pay his tax bill on the ranch. The ranch is listed for sale by the county for delinquent taxes. Although Josh has a right to use the ranch only during his lifetime, this interest is considered significant enough to entitle him to redeem the ranch.

■ **When a sale is prohibited**   A court may prohibit a tax sale in the following circumstances: (1) The taxes have already been paid. (2) The levy or the assessment of the tax was illegal or fraudulent—if land had been granted tax-exempt status, for example. (3) The valuation was grossly excessive—if, for example, the tax assessor arbitrarily assessed one parcel of land for significantly more taxes than an identical parcel.

The tax sale will not be prevented when there were errors in the tax assessment that could have been corrected if promptly brought to the attention of the proper authorities and the tax is substantially just.

telegraphs and telephones   Telegraph and telephone companies are private CORPORATIONS that are also PUBLIC UTILITIES. The courts consider that they have a duty to serve the best interests of the public. For example, in maintaining their wires and poles, telegraph and telephone companies must be careful not to cause the public needless inconvenience, and they must avoid all unnecessary obstruction of streets and highways. They also have a duty to keep their offices open at times convenient for the general public in the community they serve.

■ **Telephone service**   Upon receiving an application for service, a telephone company is entitled to a reasonable time in which to install its equipment. In most places, the subscriber's name and number is placed in the local directory.

A telephone company may discontinue service to a subscriber for just cause. Just cause has been found when equipment is used for an illegal purpose, such as for conducting an illegitimate betting operation, for failure to make regular payments for service, for continuous interference with the conversations of other patrons sharing a party line, and for failure to comply with reasonable rules of the company. Agreements that the company may stop serving a customer who uses obscene language on its wires have been upheld by the courts. A subscriber is entitled to have his telephone service restored when delinquent amounts have been paid in full. However, restoration of service is subject to the availability of the company's facilities. The subscriber may have to wait a period of time until the telephone company has the equipment and/or labor to restore the line.

■ **Crimes**   Telegraphs and telephones may not be used for illegal purposes. Profane, indecent, vulgar, or obscene language used in telegraph messages or telephone calls, and telephone calls designed solely to harass a person, are criminal offenses under both federal and state law and punishable by fines or imprisonment or both. Abusive "dunning" telephone calls used by a creditor to intimidate and harass a debtor into paying his bills are also prohibited by federal and state consumer protection laws. Unless legally authorized by a federal or state law, wiretapping is considered an illegal SEARCH AND SEIZURE, which violates a person's constitutional rights under the Fourth Amendment. State and federal criminal statutes may make other uses of the telephone a crime, such as when it is used to further illegal gambling activities.

television   For a discussion of government regulation of television, see FEDERAL COMMUNICATIONS COMMISSION.

temporary restraining order   A command from a court ordering someone not to change a situation during the few days that it takes for the court to decide whether or not to issue an INJUNCTION.

EXAMPLE Richards owned a detective agency. He tried to O◄—※ place an advertisement in the classified section of the telephone book, claiming that his company could detect illegal surveillance devices and "debug your home or office." The telephone company refused to accept the advertisement because it believed that readers would assume that the company could be hired to place bugging devices for customers. Richards sued the telephone company, asking for a million dollars to cover his loss of business and for a temporary order restraining publication of the phone book without his advertisement.

The court refused to grant the temporary restraining order. It balanced the financial harm to the phone company against the possibility that Richards would lose business without the advertisement. The court decided that Richards could be adequately compensated with money damages if he ultimately prevailed. A temporary restraining order was too extreme a remedy under the circumstances.

tenancy **1** A situation that exists when one person leases real estate to another, creating the relationship of LANDLORD AND TENANT and giving the tenant the right to possess the property. **2** The relationship of a tenant to the land he holds, such as the extent of his interest (his ESTATE) in the property. Any words that show an owner's intent to transfer some property interest to another person are sufficient to create a tenancy.

tenancy by the entirety A form of ownership shared by HUSBAND AND WIFE in which both spouses own property (usually real estate) together. Neither spouse can sell the property or his or her interest in it alone, and when one spouse dies the other automatically takes over full ownership as the survivor. Tenancy by the entirety—sometimes called tenancy by the entireties or estate in the entireties—is not recognized in all states.

EXAMPLE Oscar owns a 400-acre farm. In his will he writes O◄—※ that his widow shall have the farm to live on and use for the rest of her life and that at her death it passes to their eldest daughter. This provision creates a life tenancy for Oscar's wife.

tenancy in common Concurrent ownership of real property (real estate) or personal property in which two or more persons are entitled to possession at the same time. Each tenant in common owns his share of the property and has an equal right to occupy or possess the whole in common with his cotenants.

A tenancy in common is created automatically when two or more persons own a piece of property without specifying the form of their ownership. A tenancy in common can also be created intentionally, as by a deed or other document.

Tenants in common do not have a right of survivorship. Each tenant's share of the property is taken by his heirs when he dies, not by his cotenants. This means a surviving tenant in common can take the entire property *only* when he or she is the deceased's heir or is named as the recipient in the deceased's will. (This is just the opposite of JOINT TENANCY, where the cotenant automatically inherits the deceased's share of the property.) See ESTATE.

EXAMPLE Alvin and Bill each threw in $500 for a lakeside O◄—※ fishing cabin; the deed merely listed both as owners of the property. Alvin and Bill thus became tenants in common in the cabin. When Bill died, Wilma, his widow, was his only heir. Wilma inherited Bill's interest in the common property and became a tenant in common with Alvin. Alvin's share in the property was unaffected by Bill's death.

Tenants in common share the right and duty to keep their property in good repair; each cotenant is responsible for his respective share of all necessary expenses to maintain the property. A cotenant is not responsible for the cost of unnecessary repairs unless he authorized them.

A limited FIDUCIARY relationship (a relationship of trust and confidence) exists among tenants in common. Cotenants have a duty not to disrupt or compromise their common interest in the property. For example, one tenant should not gain a secret profit to the disadvantage of his cotenants. A tenant in common who *commits waste upon the land*—any action that destroys or permanently injure the land—is liable to his cotenants for the damage he causes. Removing necessary soil, rock, or timber or damaging a house are examples of WASTE.

Tenancy in common terminates whenever the unity of possession (shared ownership) is destroyed—for example, when one cotenant repudiates or abandons his interest in the property. It also ends when all the cotenants agree to partition their respective interests.

EXAMPLE Willy and Chris owned a house that they rented O◄—※ to tenants, sharing the income equally. One year the tenant lost his job and failed to pay the rent for three months. The boiler had to be replaced and the roof repaired. Because of the big expenses and loss of income, Willy and Chris did not pay their taxes or mortgage. Foreclosure was threatened. Although Willy could afford to pay all the bills himself, he told Chris that he was not putting another cent into the venture and that Chris could have the house. This was an abandonment that terminated the tenancy in common.

EXAMPLE Sylvester left his 300-acre farm to his children, O◄—※ Virginia and Donald, in his will. This made them tenants in common, each entitled to possession with the other of the whole farm. They decided to terminate the cotenancy by partition. Virginia took the house and 20 acres and Donald took the remaining 280 acres to farm.

tenant **1** In the broadest sense, a person who holds or possesses lands or buildings by any kind of right or title, whether *in fee* (completely), for life, for a specific number of years, or at the pleasure or sufferance of the owner. **2** In a more restricted sense, a tenant is a person who has the temporary use and occupation of real property (real estate) owned by another person, called the landlord. See LANDLORD AND TENANT.

tender **1** An offer of money or other types of property, such as goods in a SALES transaction. **2** The act by which a person produces and offers to another the amount of money he believes and admits to be due to satisfy the other person's claim or demand, without any condition being attached to the offer.

EXAMPLE Alberta offered her house for sale for $50,000. O——* Frank agreed to buy it at that price, and they entered a contract to close the deal on June 1. Meanwhile, Alberta's deal to buy a condominium fell through. She called Frank and told him the sale was off. Nevertheless, Frank tendered the $50,000 on June 1 in order to show that he was able and willing to buy the house as agreed. Later, when he sued to enforce the contract of sale, it was essential for him to prove the tender of the purchase price at the agreed-upon time. This convinced the judge that Frank had done everything required of him in the agreement and that Alberta had breached the contract.

tender offer An offer made by a group of investors to purchase the stock of a particular company at a fixed price per share, in order to gain control over it. The stock of the company may be purchased for cash or exchanged for some other corporate security, such as shares in the corporation that is making the tender offer.

tenement A building or block of buildings with rooms or apartments that are leased for residential purposes to separate families. The word is often defined by statute, and its meaning varies from state to state.

tenor 1 An exact copy of the wording of a legal document. 2 The general course or drift of a thought or its impact. Thus, for example, the tenor of a will is its meaning and effect, not its exact wording.

tenure 1 The right to hold land. During the Middle Ages in England, possession and ownership of real property (land) were distributed according to an elaborate system in which the king or nobleman owned the land, and tenure—the right to live on and cultivate the land—was granted to peasants.
2 The right to hold an office or position. Supreme Court justices have tenure for life, for example.
Tenure is especially important in the academic world. Systems of tenure protect teachers, after a probationary period, from arbitrary dismissal. The terms under which tenure is granted are usually set by statute, but they may be affected by an employment contract or an agreement with a union. A teacher cannot earn tenure by completing professional requirements. Nor can he or she demand tenure. A teacher can insist, however, that a school board make a decision at the end of the probationary period. A teacher with tenure status can be fired only for incompetence or serious misconduct and is thus protected from unfair firings for personal vengeance or political maneuvering. Granting tenure helps assure the community of the continued services of able and experienced teachers.
Tenure rights of professors in public colleges and universities are generally protected by state statutes, whereas tenure rights of professors in private colleges and universities are generally protected by contract.

term 1 The time set by law during which a court may be in session. The session of the court is the time of its actual sitting, but term and session are often used interchangeably. 2 The period granted in a lease during

which the lessee may occupy the rented premises. It does not include the time between the making of the lease and the tenant's entry. See LANDLORD AND TENANT. 3 The extent of time for which an ESTATE is granted, such as an estate for a certain number of years or a life estate. 4 Term of office is the period during which an elected official or appointee is entitled to hold office, perform its functions, and enjoy its privileges.

termination An ending or conclusion. Termination of a lawsuit is the final determination of the suit. In CONTRACT law, termination or cancellation means not performing whatever remains to be done under the contract. Termination is different from rescission, which is restoration of the parties to the positions that they held before the contract was agreed upon. See RESCIND. When a contract is terminated, there are no further obligations for either party.
EXAMPLE Taylor bought a small racetrack in Iowa. He O——* signed a contract with Vernon allowing Vernon to sell food at the concession stand for the first year. Because the racetrack venture did not earn a profit after six months, Taylor decided to close it down. He and Vernon agreed to terminate their concession contract. This was the same as saying that the contract was cancelled. Taylor does not have to provide a place for the concession stand or to conduct scheduled races. Vernon does not have to pay for his use of the facilities or to serve food on scheduled race days.
Termination of a lease is the conclusion and severance of the relationship of LANDLORD AND TENANT before the expiration of the lease.

territorial courts Courts established by Congress in lands outside the United States that are subject to some U.S. control. An example of such a land is the Virgin Islands. See COURTS; FEDERAL COURTS; TERRITORY.

territory As regulated by U.S. law, a territory is a political subdivision of the outlying dominion of the United States. It is created by Congress and is not located within the boundaries of any state. Guam and the Virgin Islands are such territories. Puerto Rico is a commonwealth, which is more independent than a territory and has fewer powers than a state. It, too, is ultimately under the authority of the United States.
Territorial government is composed of an executive, a legislative, and a judicial branch. Members of the legislature are elected biennially. The executive branch is headed by a governor and a lieutenant governor who are elected to four-year terms. The judicial functions are performed by a district court with an appellate (appeals) division and by other lesser courts established under the laws of the particular territory. The district court has jurisdiction (authority) as a federal district court, and the presiding justice is appointed by the President. See FEDERAL COURTS.
The residents are subject to both local law and to U.S. laws that apply to the particular territory. Residents are also required to pay federal income taxes.

testacy The state or condition of leaving a WILL at

one's death. A person who dies *testate* is one who dies leaving a will.

testament   A WILL.

testator   A person who makes a WILL.

test case   A case brought to establish an important legal principle or right. A test case is selected from a number of suits pending at the same time before the same court, brought by several plaintiffs against the same defendant or by one plaintiff against different defendants. The case must be similar in circumstances to the other cases, embracing the same questions and supported by the same evidence. The case selected goes to trial first, and its decision serves as a test of the rights of others similarly situated. The parties to the other suits are bound by the results of the test case.

testify   Give EVIDENCE, under oath or affirmation, for the purpose of establishing some fact.

testimony   Oral EVIDENCE given by a competent witness under oath or affirmation. It is different from evidence derived from writings and other sources.

theaters and shows   Theaters are places for viewing films, plays, exhibitions, or other presentations broadly called shows. Because such forms of entertainment affect the public interest, it is proper that they be regulated by the government. Regulation must be exercised reasonably, however, because it restrains the free speech rights of those who create, present, and distribute the shows. See SPEECH AND PRESS, FREEDOM OF. A city cannot outlaw all theaters and shows, but it may regulate them in several areas. For example, children may be forbidden to see pornographic shows or to be in a theater after dark unaccompanied by a parent or guardian. Public seances for money-making purposes may be declared illegal because they can be used to cheat weak or bereaved people.

■ **Fire safety and crowd control**   Local regulations may require theater buildings to be constructed with flameproof materials for floors, walls, seats, curtains, and carpeting. Usually, a certain amount of light must be provided even during performances. Exits must be large enough to handle crowds at different sides of the building and must be clearly marked. Theaters are generally required to have ushers on duty to keep order and to supervise the movement of crowds. Anyone who creates a disturbance or becomes a nuisance may be removed from the theater. For example, a person who interferes with a performance, as by heckling the performers or harassing the audience, may be asked to leave the theater. If he refuses to comply, the police may forcibly evict him from the premises. For a discussion of the liability of theater owners, see SPORTS AND ENTERTAINMENT.

Temporary shows that are likely to draw large crowds in a short period of time—such as religious or political rallies or outdoor rock concerts—must be approved in advance by authorities, who must oversee plans for protecting the health and safety of people attending the event and of

residents in the area. For example, public sanitation facilities may have to be installed for use during a concert in a park. Local authorities require the producer or organizer of a show to obtain a permit. The permit insures that local regulations are met.

■ **Tickets**   The sale of tickets is generally governed by the principles of contract law. The sale of a ticket is an agreement between seller and buyer. In exchange for the price of a ticket, the buyer is entitled to admittance to a show, usually at a specified date, time, and place. The seller is bound to offer the show. The seller may prescribe certain conditions for the tickets, but they may be regulated by consumer protection laws, because the purchaser is in no position to negotiate terms. A harsh term, such as "no refunds under any circumstances," will not be enforced unless it is clear that the buyer willingly accepted that term when he bought his ticket. The seller is not permitted to sell tickets for more seats than he has. If he does, the buyer is usually entitled to a refund.

Scalping   Scalping is buying tickets at the usual price and then selling them at outrageously high prices because the show is very popular and tickets are difficult or impossible to obtain. To prevent scalping, a state or local government may make it a crime to sell a ticket for more than the price stamped on it. As with many criminal laws, it generally does the defendant no good to claim that he did not know his act was illegal. But sometimes a court takes a different view.

EXAMPLE   A New York judge refused to convict a British citizen who sold two Metropolitan Opera tickets worth $20 each for $40 a ticket. The woman had bought the tickets hoping for a reconciliation with her estranged husband. When it became clear that she could not use them, she offered to sell them in a newspaper advertisement. An alert policeman answered the ad, negotiated the price, and then arrested her.

The court recognized the valid purpose of the scalping law, but it could not agree that the law was intended to punish every isolated transaction by someone who was not aware of the law or her rights. A conviction not only would stigmatize the defendant but would also jeopardize her temporary visa and perhaps prevent her from ever entering the United States again. The judge said that he could not in good conscience hand down a conviction. He urged that the force of the law be directed at dishonest ticket brokers and hawkers. The woman was not convicted.

Ticket brokers   Where a law forbids resale of tickets for more than the price paid, an exception is generally made to allow a reasonable profit to licensed ticket brokers, people who are in the business of selling tickets for many theaters to the public. Brokers are strictly regulated in order to protect the public from fraud, extortion, and exorbitant rates. For example, a dishonest broker might sell tickets for performances not scheduled, sell seats already sold, or scalp the tickets. A state or city may require anyone reselling tickets to be licensed, and it may revoke the license of any broker who abuses his authority. A law may forbid theaters to sell more than, say, 10 tickets to anyone who does not have a license.

■ **Obscenity**   Communities have a legitimate interest in controlling OBSCENITY, or pornography, in theaters. It is

YOUR PROTECTION WHEN YOU BUY A TICKET TO A THEATER OR A SHOW

■ A theater is usually not permitted to sell more seats than it has available. If you are assigned a nonexistent or occupied seat, you will probably be entitled to a refund.

■ Many state and local governments make it a crime to "scalp," or sell a ticket for more than the price stamped on it. This law does not cover the reasonable profit to which licensed ticket brokers are entitled.

■ Brokers are strictly regulated in order to protect the public from fraud, extortion, and exorbitant rates.

■ A law may forbid theaters to sell more than a certain number of tickets—10 tickets, for example—to anyone who is not a licensed broker.

■ Films and stage shows containing explicit sex scenes can be regulated if they appeal to a prurient interest and portray sex in a patently offensive way and if they lack serious literary, artistic, or scientific value.

■ Communities may apply their own local standards in judging shows—this has led to conflicting decisions in different places.

■ If a film is found obscene, a court may order the exhibitor not to show it; and if he violates the order, he may have committed a crime or he may be guilty of contempt of court, according to state law.

■ If a live performance is banned, the government is using prior restraint—which is generally unconstitutional—and the Supreme Court requires the official who is exercising such restraint to show that there is a "clear and present danger" of great violence and severe injury.

appropriate to protect the sensibilities of unsuspecting or unwilling adults from assaults of indecency and to shield children from pornography. The Supreme Court has interpreted the Constitution to allow individuals to view obscene materials in the privacy of their homes, but theaters are public places. The law may regulate indecent exhibitions in theaters even if everyone present expects to view pornography and enters willingly, although some states decline to prosecute under such circumstances. Exhibitors of lewd films in coin-operated booths in amusement arcades cannot claim any right of privacy even though patrons view the films alone in the booths.

Censorship of obscene shows is legal, but it is not always easy to determine what is obscene. The Supreme Court said in 1973 that works that describe or depict sexual conduct can be regulated if, taken as a whole, (1) they appeal to a prurient interest and portray sexual conduct in a patently offensive way and (2) they lack serious literary, artistic, political, or scientific value. The Supreme Court has also said that communities may apply their own local standards in judging shows, and this has led to conflicting decisions in different courts.

EXAMPLE A federal court in New York found in 1968 that O—* the Swedish film I Am Curious—Yellow was not obscene because the dominant theme of the movie as a whole was not prurient sex. A year later the highest court in Maryland upheld a decision not to license the film in Baltimore. The court held that the explicit sexual sequences in the film were found to be its dominant theme and were intended to appeal to a prurient interest in sex.

Films There are several ways a state can regulate motion picture theaters in order to control pornography. A state may require film distributors or exhibitors to be licensed and then revoke the license of anyone who traffics in obscene films. In the past, some states and municipalities set up a board of censors, which was authorized to preview films before they were shown to the public. This type of censorship, called prior restraint, is in direct conflict with free speech; so the procedures for carrying it out must be strictly controlled. Therefore, very few cities or states still have laws setting up a board of censors that judges the obscenity of films before they are shown to the public.

States and local governments do take strong action, however, after obscene shows are actually exhibited. A number of courts have warned that authorities may not confiscate all copies of a film until a court has found it to be obscene. One copy may be taken pursuant to a court order and held for evidence at a trial. If a film is found to be obscene, a court may order the exhibitor not to show it. If he violates this order, he might have committed a crime or be guilty of CONTEMPT of court, depending on state law.

EXAMPLE The film Deep Throat was found obscene by a O—* court in Texas and all copies of the film were confiscated. The exhibitor paid his $25 fine and then demanded that his film be returned, presumably so that he could show it again. The court refused to return it, saying that there is no right to show a film after a court has specifically found it to be obscene.

Sometimes a court permits an objectionable film to be shown if certain words or scenes are cut out. Some films can be shown only to adult audiences, and they cannot be shown at drive-in theaters where they would be visible to passersby and neighboring homes.

Live performances Live performances are somewhat more difficult to regulate than films because restraint of an anticipated obscenity requires some guesswork about the ultimate content of the show. There is also the chance that a performer will have been deprived of his freedom to speak when it turns out later that his speech was not legally obscene. Under the law, the freedom to speak is given such a high priority that the risk of having improper content in a show must be taken. See SPEECH AND PRESS, FREEDOM OF.

EXAMPLE In 1971 an entertainment promoter sued to force O—* officials in Atlanta, Georgia, to lease the Civic Center for performances of the rock musical Hair. City officials claimed that Hair was obscene and pornographic and that its performance would violate criminal statutes that punish indecent exposure and flag desecration. They felt that the acting part of the play was "nonspeech" and was thus not protected by the First Amendment. Finally, they claimed they had the right to decide what types of shows should be permitted in the Civic Center, and they wanted to limit performances to family entertainment.

The federal court disagreed. Even though the play

included a brief nude scene, it was part of the political and social commentary of the play. This kind of nonverbal speech is protected by the First Amendment. The court ruled that the show did not violate the criminal statutes as claimed and rejected the idea that city officials could exercise unfettered judgment over the content of performances in the Civic Center. The auditorium is a public forum for expression and it must be available for the exercise of First Amendment rights. The court repeated the rule that prior restraint is presumed to be unconstitutional, and anyone who attempts to use it must clearly justify his acts. Not liking a show is not enough. A public official must show that there is a "clear and present danger" of great violence and severe injury if fights break out at the scene of performances.

theft   Colloquial term for LARCENY. The word "theft" has a broader meaning than "larceny" and includes any criminal taking of another person's property, particularly by swindling, FALSE PRETENSES, EMBEZZLEMENT, or any other form of guile. Because of the similarity of embezzlement, false pretenses, larceny, and larceny by trick, several states have grouped these offenses into a single statutory crime designated as "theft."

third degree   **1** A colloquial term for illegal methods of forcing a person to confess to a crime by overpowering his will through psychological or physical violence. Evidence obtained by third-degree means may be considered inadmissible at a trial. See MIRANDA V. ARIZONA; MIRANDA WARNINGS. **2** The least severe level of a crime that may be included in a state statute dividing the severity of a crime into DEGREES.

third party   A person who has no direct connection with a legal transaction, such as a CONTRACT, but who may be affected by it. For example, a third-party beneficiary is a person for whose benefit a contract is created, even though he is not a party to the contract. The beneficiary can sue to enforce the contract or promise made for his benefit.

EXAMPLE Ross buys life insurance from the Heartfelt Insurance Company. The insurance is a contract. Ross agrees to pay annual premiums, and Heartfelt agrees to pay benefits when Ross dies to anyone he has named. Ross names his wife. She is not a party to the contract, but she is a third-party beneficiary. Even though she was not part of the original contract, she can enforce the agreement. If Heartfelt refuses to pay benefits when Ross dies, his wife can sue the company in her capacity as the third-party beneficiary.

threat   A communicated intention to inflict harm. In many jurisdictions, statutes forbid any person to use threats or other unlawful communications. Threats made with an intent to obtain a financial advantage, intimidate a person, compel a person to act against his will, or prevent a person from engaging in a lawful occupation are forbidden. Also forbidden are threats to use a deadly weapon on another person, injure another person or his property, maim or wound another, and injure anyone's creditworthiness or general reputation. Other unlawful communications include letters tending to provoke a breach of the peace and letters to discredit the sexual reputation of a female.

See also BLACKMAIL; CONSUMER PROTECTION; CRIMINAL LAW; EXTORTION; LIBEL AND SLANDER.

time   A measure of duration. Time is the relation that an event has to any other event, past, present, or future. A trial court will accept without proof the fact that time is divided into years, months, weeks, days, hours, minutes, and seconds. See JUDICIAL NOTICE; EVIDENCE.

■ **Zones**   The states followed different standards of time until federal statutes adopted the standard time zone system established by the nation's railroads. Under the system, the United States is divided into different zones. The time of each zone is based on the mean (average) astronomical time of a specific degree of longitude west from Greenwich, England, gaining (or losing) one hour with every 15 degrees. Accordingly, eastern standard time is based on the mean astronomical time of the 75th degree of longitude west from Greenwich, central standard time is based on the 90th degree, mountain time on the 105th degree, and Pacific time on the 120th degree.

Daylight saving time, adopted by a number of states, occurs when a state's usual time system is advanced one hour during the summer months to take advantage of longer periods of daylight. A local government—such as a county or a municipality—must follow the system of time adopted by its state legislature. Several states are in two time zones; they may use standard and daylight saving systems in different regions. If a municipality falls on a time-zone line, it may be allowed by the state to choose which time system it will use. The time kept by a municipality is called civic time.

■ **Computing time**   When computing a specific number of days for an agreement or contract, it is customary to exclude the first day and include the last. Consequently, when a lease states that it will continue for a specified period from a particular day, that day is excluded in computing the term. The same rule is applied when computing time for matters of practice and procedure, such as the time period in which a lawsuit can be started (the day the cause of the suit occurred is excluded) and the period in which an appeal from a judgment may be taken (the date the decision was pronounced is excluded). See LIMITATIONS OF ACTIONS.

As a general rule, when the last day of a time period within which an act is to be done falls on a Sunday or holiday, that day is excluded from the computation. The act may rightfully be done on the following business day. This rule has been applied to deadlines for (1) holding a meeting of corporate shareholders, (2) filing a claim against the estate of a dead person, (3) filing a statement proposing a new ordinance for a municipality, (4) recording a mortgage, (5) redeeming property from a sale foreclosing a mortgage, and (6) filing a tax form.

time draft   A draft (check) that is payable at a certain time in the future. Time drafts are often used by merchants to finance the movement of goods. See COMMERCIAL PAPER.

time is of the essence   A provision in a CONTRACT requiring one of the parties bound by the contract to fulfill his part of it within a specified period of time. If the party fails to act within the time required, he is guilty of a breach of the contract, which makes the contract unenforceable. It is said that *time is not of the essence* if a moderate delay in performance would not be an absolute violation of a contract. If you had a contract to sing at a wedding, time would be of the essence. On the other hand, if you agreed to supply a boutique with 24 hand-knit berets on November 15, for Christmas business, but you delivered them on November 22, time would probably not be of the essence.

timely Being or occurring at the proper time. For example, the filing of a lawsuit is timely when it is brought before it is barred by the statute of limitations—that is, before the time allowed by law for filing that particular type of suit has run out. See LIMITATIONS OF ACTIONS.

In many instances, the meaning of the word must be determined by the facts and circumstances of each case. The courts have a great deal of discretion in deciding whether or not a party has acted in a timely manner in filing papers, serving NOTICES, or litigating MOTIONS AND ORDERS in a lawsuit.

time-price differential The difference between a cash-and-carry price and a credit price. A seller may charge one price for an immediate cash payment for merchandise and a different price when payment is made at a future date or in installments. The former is the *cash price*, and the latter is the *time price*, or *credit price*. The difference in price is the time-price differential.

EXAMPLE A set of dining room furniture can be purchased for a cash price of $2,660. The same set can be purchased by making 60 monthly installment payments for a total time price of $3,703. The $1,043 difference between the cash price and the time price is the time-price differential.

title 1 The legal basis of ownership of any kind of property. In its broadest sense, title includes all the rights to a piece of property that can be enjoyed and secured under the law. The word is often used to mean absolute ownership. Accordingly, when used in reference to real estate, title implies an estate in FEE SIMPLE (full and absolute ownership).

2 A document that serves as evidence of ownership, such as the certificate of title to an automobile.

3 The official name of a court action, petition, or other proceeding. The title of a court proceeding includes the name of the court in which it is pending and the names of the parties.

EXAMPLE *State ex rel. James* v. *O'Brien* means that the state is bringing an action on behalf of, or at the instigation of, James against the defendant, O'Brien. *Ex rel.(ex relatione)* means "in the name of," or "on the relation of." The state prosecutes the action through its attorney general or a prosecutor or some other appropriate official.

4 The heading or preliminary part of a STATUTE. The title of a statute furnishes the name by which the act is individually known. It is usually prefixed to a statute in the form of a brief summary of its contents, such as "An act for the prevention of cruelty to animals."

toll 1 A sum of money paid for the use of a public road, highway, tunnel, or bridge. 2 As a verb, to suspend the running of the time period of a statute of limitations. For example, the period of time within which a person may sue someone for an injury or wrong done him is usually limited by statute. However, if the injured party is not legally an adult when the injury or wrong occurs, the statute of limitations may be tolled until he becomes of age—that is, the time period in which he has a right to sue may begin to run on the day he legally becomes an adult instead of on the date he received the injury.

EXAMPLE When Eric was 17, he was hit by a car as it ran a red light. As a result of the accident, Eric lost partial use of his left arm. The state in which the accident took place had a two-year statute of limitations on suits for personal injuries. If Eric had been an adult legally, he would have had to sue within two years of the accident or not at all. But in that state, a person is not an adult until he is 18. Therefore, the statute of limitations was tolled for Eric until he reached 18, and he could sue any time within the two years after he reached that age.

A statute of limitations may also be tolled if the injured party is insane or in prison. The statute of limitations for suing to collect a debt may be tolled if the debtor promises to repay the debt, but a new period begins to run if the debtor fails to pay on the date promised. See also LIMITATIONS OF ACTIONS.

toll road See TURNPIKE.

tontine 1 An association or partnership of persons who agree to pool certain sums of money or something else of value, allowing the last surviving member of the group to take all. 2 A type of life INSURANCE policy. The holders of tontine life insurance policies agree to pay premiums for a specified number of years, called the tontine years, before they acquire the right to receive dividends—a share of the company's surplus paid out to policyholders each year or part of a year. If a policyholder dies during the tontine years, his beneficiary receives only the benefits provided under the policy but no dividends. The earnings that normally would be used to pay dividends are accumulated during the tontine years and then paid out only to policyholders who are still living at the end of the term. These are sometimes called dividend-preferred policies. They have been widely criticized and are prohibited by many states.

tort A civil (as opposed to criminal) wrong, other than a breach of contract, done to another person. An injured person may sue anyone who commits a tort against him and collect DAMAGES—money to help compensate him for the wrong. The person who is injured and sues for damages as a result of the wrongful conduct is the *plaintiff* in the lawsuit. The person who has acted wrongfully and becomes liable to the plaintiff is the *tortfeasor*, or *defendant*.

The law of torts deals with the allocation of responsibility for loss or harm arising out of human activities. Virtually any type of activity—driving a car, engaging in business, speaking, writing, owning or using property—may be a source of harm and, therefore, of tort liability.

The common thread woven into all torts is unreasonable interference with the interests of others. Liability is based upon conduct that society considers unreasonable. For example, the operation of a house of prostitution in a residential neighborhood provides the basis for a tort action for NUISANCE because it substantially interferes with the adjoining owners' right to enjoy their property. The difficulty in establishing liability often lies in striking a reasonable balance between the plaintiff's (injured party's) claim of protection against damage and the defendant's (tortfeasor's) claim to freedom of action. Each state usually applies its own rules of tort law in the lawsuits presented to its courts unless two or more states are involved in the same case and there is a CONFLICT OF LAWS, when the court applies the law of the appropriate state.

A civil tort action (lawsuit) is brought by the injured person, so that he may be compensated for the damages he suffered at the hands of the defendant. If he wins his case, he will be given a judgment of money that the defendant will have to pay.

■ **Tort versus crime**   A tort is not a crime. A *crime* is an offense against the community, for which the state, as the representative of the public, prosecutes the wrongdoer. Because a tort action and a criminal prosecution have different purposes, a single wrongdoing may result in the wrongdoer's being brought to court as the defendant in

WHEN SOMEBODY HARMS YOU OR INTERFERES WITH YOUR RIGHTS

■ A tort is not a crime but a civil wrongdoing. The one feature all torts have in common is one person's unreasonable interference with the interests of another.
■ Tort law has three basic goals: to compensate the victim for the harm he suffered; to place the burden on the person responsible; and to serve as a deterrent in cases where malice was involved, by awarding money damages not to compensate the victim (whose injury may have been slight) but to punish the offender.
■ Torts are classified as intentional torts, torts resulting from negligence, and torts based on strict liability, without regard to fault.
■ An *intentional tort* arises from any deliberate invasion of another person's rights, causing injury without just cause or excuse. For example, you quarrel with your neighbor and he sprays paint on your new car. You can sue him to pay to have your car repainted. Intentional torts include interference with a person's freedom of movement, defamation (libel and slander), invasion of privacy, interference with property rights, misuse of legal process, fraud, and the intentional infliction of emotional distress.
■ If someone detains you under a false claim of legal authority, he may be guilty of the tort of *false arrest.* If a neighbor spitefully locks you in your garage, he is guilty of *false imprisonment.*
■ *Trespass* is a tort because it interferes with a person's property rights. You are trespassing if you go into a neighbor's yard without permission, build a structure that extends onto his property, or direct a drain so that it empties onto his property.
■ If you refuse to return a lawnmower you borrowed from your neighbor, you are guilty of *conversion.*
■ Intentionally and successfully deceiving a person to induce him to part with his property or give up a right is the tort of fraud. If someone sells you a magazine subscription claiming that half the money will go to the United Way, and it does not, he has committed fraud.
■ If someone uses the courts to prosecute you for a crime he knows you did not commit, for the sole purpose of hurting you, he is guilty of *malicious prosecution,* and you can sue him.
■ *Intentional infliction of emotional distress* is a tort. For example, a baker who wraps a dead rat instead of a loaf of bread to scare a customer would be liable for the customer's injuries.
■ *Negligence* is an unintentional tort. If a drunk driver inadvertently runs over someone, the driver is guilty of negligence. (Negligence is discussed in the entry under that name.)
■ Three groups of persons face *strict liability* (liability without fault): owners of animals, persons engaged in highly dangerous activities, and manufacturers and sellers of products that may injure a buyer.
■ Many states have imposed strict liability for damage done by trespassing dogs.
■ If you are involved in crop-dusting your land and a sudden breeze blows the poison into a neighbor's beehives, killing the bees, you are strictly liable, whether the actual dusting was done by you or by a hired crop duster, since crop-dusting is considered an unusually dangerous activity.
■ If you buy a new hunting gun and the first time you shoot it the gun explodes, both the manufacturer and the dealer can be made to pay damages.
■ Workmen's compensation statutes make an employer strictly liable for injuries an employee gets on the job.
■ Traditionally, charitable, educational, and religious organizations have been immune from tort liability; today, most states reject the concept of charitable immunity. Some states permit a charity to be sued for a tort in certain instances.
■ In many states, husbands and wives and parents and children are immune from tort liability to one another. But other states have abolished this common-law immunity, at least in part.
■ There are three kinds of damages: nominal, compensatory, and punitive. *Nominal damages* (symbolic awards of money, such as $1) are awarded on recognition of the fact that the defendant was in the wrong, even though he did not cause substantial loss or injury. *Compensatory damages* may not exceed the amount lost or suffered. *Punitive damages* may be awarded to punish the defendant for malicious, willful, or wanton acts.
■ Juries render judgment in most tort cases that are not settled out of court. Generally, the jury returns a verdict fixing liability and setting an amount of damages. The judge may accept the amount and enter a judgment in that amount or set it aside.
■ An appeals court can affirm the judgment or remand for a new trial on the issue of liability or the amount.

separate civil and criminal trials. A decision against the defendant in a tort action does not determine the defendant's guilt or innocence in the criminal action. Similarly, a conviction or acquittal in the criminal case may not generally be used as evidence in the tort action.

EXAMPLE Jim hits Jerry over the head with a lamp during O—* an argument. Jerry may bring a civil lawsuit to recover damages against Jim for the tort of assault and battery. He may also swear out a complaint against Jim with the police so that Jim will be prosecuted for the crime of assault and, if convicted, sentenced to jail.

■ **Goals of tort law**   Tort law has three basic goals:

(1) Compensating persons who have suffered a loss or harm from another's conduct. Fundamental to tort law is the idea that the damages a person has received as the result of a tort can be measured in money. The basic tort remedy is to make the tortfeasor pay the victim for the harm suffered—called compensatory damages. For a discussion of how the amount of damages is determined, see DAMAGES.

(2) Making only the person who in justice should shoulder the costs be responsible for them.

(3) Preventing future losses and harms by regulating human behavior. In this respect, tort law serves an educational function. Theoretically, a tortfeasor held liable for damages will himself be more careful in the future. The general threat of tort liability is an incentive to all to regulate their conduct according to established standards. In this way, tort law supplements criminal law and serves as an even greater deterrent. Punitive damages allowed in cases involving malice, for example, reinforce this goal. Punitive damages are money judgments awarded to punish the wrongdoer—not to compensate the person harmed, whose injury may be slight.

■ **Types of tort**   Under the law, torts are classified as intentional torts, resulting from purposeful wrongful conduct; torts resulting from negligence; and torts based on strict liability—that is, liability without regard to fault.

Intentional torts   Any deliberate invasion of or interference with the property rights, personal rights, or personal liberties of another that causes injuries without just cause or excuse is an intentional tort.

EXAMPLE John had a fight with his neighbor Dan. While he O—* was still angry, John sprayed white paint all over Dan's black automobile. John was guilty of an intentional tort because he purposely interfered with Dan's property rights. Dan could sue John for his action and would probably be awarded money damages that would cover the cost of having his car repainted.

As the name suggests, an element common to all intentional torts is the defendant's intent. He must have meant to commit the tort. Intent is usually defined as the desire to cause certain immediate consequences. Although intent is a state of mind and a subjective matter, the law defines it objectively: you are considered to intend the consequences of your act if you know or believe they are substantially certain to result, whether or not you wish them to do so.

EXAMPLE Ted throws a bomb into a room in which Bob and O—* Carl are sitting. Ted wants to kill Bob. He knows that Carl is present but has no desire to hurt him and, indeed, fervently hopes that Carl will not be injured.

Nevertheless, since Ted knew that physical harm to Carl was substantially certain, he is considered to have intended that harm.

A unique concept in the area of intentional torts, encountered almost exclusively in the area of ASSAULT AND BATTERY, is the doctrine of *transferred intent*. Under this doctrine, you can be said to have intended to injure a person if you accidentally harm him while intentionally acting to harm someone else. In other words, if Joe acts with intent to injure Chuck but at the same time, or instead, injures Bert, his intent to injure Chuck transfers to Bert. Joe is deemed to have committed an intentional tort upon Bert, even though he was completely unaware of his existence or of any risk of harm to him.

EXAMPLE Alice shoots at Dave and misses him. The bullet O—* strikes Hal, who was hidden from view and not known to be in the vicinity. Alice is liable to Hal for battery (the intentional use of force against another person). She will also be liable for assault (an act that arouses a reasonable fear of an imminent battery) upon Dave. If she had wounded instead of having missed him, she would have been liable for assault and battery.

Assault and battery are intentional torts against physical safety. Some other intentional torts are interference with a person's freedom of movement, defamation, invasion of privacy, interference with property rights, misuse of legal process, fraud, interference with contracts, and the intentional infliction of emotional distress.

Interference with freedom of movement   If someone interferes with your freedom of movement, he may be liable for the tort of false imprisonment or false arrest. Any unlawful detention or restraint upon a person's liberty and freedom of movement is false imprisonment whether it occurs in a prison or elsewhere. If you are kept in prison without probable cause, you may, of course, sue for false imprisonment. And if a neighbor spitefully locks you in your garage because he is angry with you, he too is guilty of false imprisonment.

If someone restrains or detains you under a false claim of legal authority, he may be guilty of the tort of false arrest. Thus, a police officer who arrests you on false charges and a man who forces you to accompany him somewhere, while pretending to be a policeman with the legal authority to do so, are both guilty of false arrest. For more details, see FALSE ARREST; FALSE IMPRISONMENT.

Defamation   Defamation is an untrue communication about a person that injures his good name or reputation so that he is subjected to the hatred, abuse, contempt, or ridicule of others. It may take the form of either libel or slander. *Libel* is an untrue defamatory statement in a physical form, such as in a letter, newspaper, cartoon, or film. If a newspaper unjustly accused you of offering bribes to a local politician, you could sue the newspaper for libel. *Slander* is a defamatory statement that is spoken and heard. If your neighbor Mrs. Allen told another neighbor that you gave bribes to politicians and the statement was untrue, Mrs. Allen would be guilty of the intentional tort of slander. For a detailed discussion of torts involving defamation, see LIBEL AND SLANDER.

Invasion of privacy   The right of privacy is the right to be let alone and to be free of unwelcome and unwarrant-

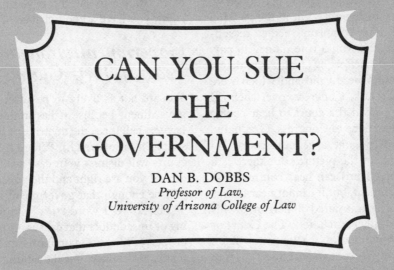

CAN YOU SUE THE GOVERNMENT?

DAN B. DOBBS
Professor of Law,
University of Arizona College of Law

Can you sue the government? Thousands of citizens do so every year. Many of them recover substantial sums, and lawyers are no longer surprised at judgments against the government in the hundreds of thousands of dollars.

But if you ask a lawyer whether you can sue the government, and you should if you are even thinking of it, his answer is likely to be a very firm "Maybe."

In spite of the huge sums paid out by the government in lawsuits, there is a good chance that if you sue the government you will lose. Naturally enough, you will lose if your case is not a good one. But there is also a chance that you will lose even if the government is in the wrong and you are in the right—just because government is government. At best, your suit is likely to be a difficult, technical, and time-consuming enterprise. Probably you will need not only a good lawyer but a specialist.

Government is also empowered to do certain things that private individuals and companies may not do. For example, government levies taxes on most citizens and does so under such complicated laws that unfairness, mistakes, and disputes are inevitable. Government also administers benefits of various kinds, such as Social Security, and when they are reduced or terminated, a dispute is again very likely. The list of governmental actions is practically endless, and disputes with government can arise at almost any point in your daily life. These may range from government's discriminatory application of the law to its failure to protect the environment to its insistence that you pay customs duty on that half-empty bottle of cognac you brought back from France.

The point is that not all disputes with the government are alike, and naturally enough the rules for suing the government vary in different situations. To complicate matters more, state and local governments are governed by their own individual rules that vary from state to state.

Sovereign immunity

Many of the problems of suing the government grow out of old English law. One line of medieval English thought was that "the king can do no wrong." Another line was that you could not sue the king because the courts were the "king's courts" and it would be a contradiction for the king to be sued in his own courts. American lawyers generally followed the English common law even after the American Revolution, and American courts accepted the English ideas. The principle that one could not sue the king became known as sovereign immunity. "Immunity," of course, meant a shield of protection for the government, and it came down to a rule that you could not sue the government unless the government consented to the suit.

Congressional consent—contracts and taxes

The doctrine of sovereign immunity protected the government from suit, but it did not protect Congress from petitions. Aggrieved citizens, unable to get relief against the government in court, petitioned in Congress. In effect, Congress was put in the position of a court: If the citizen's complaint seemed reasonable, Congress could and would vote money to pay. But petitions involved an effort by Congress to determine which complaints were valid and which were not, mainly a court's task. Congress, overwhelmed with claims, finally provided a court to hear claims and make recommendations to Congress. Gradually, this Court of Claims became a genuine court and Congress stepped out of the picture. But there is a catch. The Court of Claims can hear contract disputes with the government, but it cannot hear claims that the government has injured a person or his property. There is another catch, too: The Court of Claims sits in Washington, D.C., a long way from most citizens who might want to take their dispute with government to court.

Another area in which Congress has permitted citizens to sue the government is that of tax dispute. If the Internal Revenue Service notifies you that there is a deficiency in your return (for example, because you claimed a deduction the IRS believes improper), there are ways to fight it. After a certain amount of effort to make the IRS see it your way, you have the right to present your side of the story to the Tax Court, a special administrative court for hearing tax matters.

Like the Court of Claims, the Tax Court sits in Washington, D.C. Both courts, however, have a system of sorts for holding some or all of the trial closer to the citizen's home, and you also have the option of presenting both your contract dispute and your tax dispute to the "local" federal district courts near you. There are federal district courts in every state, often several of them, and none is beyond a reasonable driving distance.

In many ways, bringing suit in the local federal court is preferable for the citizen, but there is—as always—a catch. Only the relatively small contract claim may be brought locally; if it is over $10,000, it must be heard in the Court of Claims in Washington. As for tax disputes, the local federal court is available only if you pay the disputed taxes in advance—the very thing you may be unable to do. The difficulty of using the local federal court is illustrated by the fact that something like 10,000 suits a year are filed in Tax Court but only about 10 percent of that number in the federal District Court.

One thing can be said in favor of the law about contract and tax disputes: You may have to go to

extra trouble to sue the government, but if you are right, you have a good chance of winning.

Government wrongdoing—the Federal Torts Claims Act

You are not as likely to be successful if you sue the government because it has injured you. In the field lawyers call torts, the doctrine of sovereign immunity swings a lot of weight. Where that doctrine applies, courts will dismiss your case against the government even if you are right and the government is wrong; it will be enough that government is government.

The lawyer's word "tort" simply means wrongdoing or misconduct that causes injury to a person or his property. The most common tort is negligent driving that causes injury; but the field includes medical and other professional malpractice, injuries caused by defective products, and such special torts as fraud, invasion of privacy, and libel.

In 1946 Congress passed the statute known as the Federal Torts Claims Act (FTCA). The gist of the statute was a consent to tort suits against the government, which was to be treated like any citizen in similar circumstances. But, once again, there was a catch. Actually there were several.

Limiting tort suits against the government

One catch was that the Congress said in so many words that the government did not consent to certain kinds of tort suits—such as suits for libel, battery, and fraud, to name a few in a long list. This means that if the postman spreads false and nasty stories about you after reading your postcards, or the welfare officer spits in your face, or the Federal Housing Authority inspector fraudulently misrepresents the condition of the house you buy, you cannot sue the government. Although those particular incidents are not likely to happen, government employees have done similar things on occasion. Private companies are responsible for torts committed by their employees while on the job, but the government is protected.

Another catch is that courts often interpret the Federal Torts Claims Act with needle-eyed narrowness. For instance, the FTCA does not permit suit for battery, but it does permit suits for negligence. In a Minnesota case, a patient went into a Veterans Administration hospital for removal of his left leg. He awoke to find the good right leg had been removed instead. Was this negligence? If so, the government would be liable. Or was it "battery"? If it was battery, the FTCA would shield the government no matter how much it was at fault. *Battery* is a legal term that means an intentional touching of another person in a way he does not consent to and in a manner that is harmful or seriously offensive. Usually it is the act of an intentional wrongdoer—it is the sock in the jaw in a bar. The mistaken removal of the patient's good leg hardly sounds like battery, but the court held that it was battery and that the government, although it was clearly at fault, would not be required to pay any damages to the patient.

The Supreme Court itself has invented a few special rules to prevent recovery. When a serviceman was burned to death in a barracks fire negligently caused by the Army, his family brought suit against the government. At about the same time, another serviceman discovered that an Army surgeon had left a towel some 18 inches wide and 30 inches long in his abdomen in the course of surgery. He also sued the government. The two cases went together to the Supreme Court of the United States, which solemnly declared that servicemen could not sue the government—even though the FTCA as passed by Congress had said nothing on the subject of servicemen. This exception to government liability is still the law today.

Discretionary immunity Besides listing a wide range of activities for which the government is not liable, the Federal Torts Claims Act also provides protection for the government whenever it causes injury by carrying out some "discretionary" activity. No one knows exactly what this means. It is one of those legal ideas that are easy to understand in the clear cases but are not helpful in the difficult ones where help is needed.

The general concept behind this protection for discretionary activity seems to be that courts should not too readily condemn the important policy decisions of Congress or the executive branch of the government. After all, the Constitution did not make the courts all-powerful; it gave some powers to the other two branches, too. The courts should not undercut those powers by holding the government liable whenever the courts disagree with Congress or the President.

In an old case from North Carolina, a citizen was injured by fireworks and sued the city council for not making fireworks illegal. He lost. The same rule would apply to suits against the federal government based on congressional acts. If citizens could sue the government every time Congress failed to act for the greatest possible safety, the logic goes, the political questions that the Constitution has given to the legislative branch would soon be tried in the courts and the system of government would no longer resemble the one prescribed by the Constitution. A similar idea applies to actions of the executive department. For instance, someone whose car is stolen might claim that the FBI—which is a part of the executive department—should have given him enough protection to prevent the theft or should have recovered the car when it was taken across state lines. If courts were to pass on this kind of question and hold the government liable, courts would be substituting their own judgment for that of the FBI.

These illustrations suggest part of the meaning of the government's special protection for discretionary activities. But illustrations do not tell you how particular cases should be decided or what your rights are. Some federal courts have found a discretionary function in almost any government activity, and the Supreme Court itself encouraged the view that, despite the FTCA, the government should not be held wholly accountable for its faults. In one case, the government supported a program to export fertilizer to friendly countries. But the government, according to the people injured, failed to control the shipping and labeling of the fertilizer. As a result, a large quantity of fertilizer with explosive qualities was on board a ship in the harbor of Texas City, Texas. It exploded and virtually destroyed the town. Whatever the government did or did not do with the fertilizer was said to be discretionary. The injured citizens once again found the government fully protected by sovereign immunity.

It may well be that courts will not be so protective of the government in the future. The early cases were decided by judges who had never heard of government liability, and their conditioning led them to fear a "raid on the Treasury." Courts today show some signs of willingness to hold government accountable even when some policy judgment is involved.

In a recent case, a government agency approved the release of a large quantity of polio vaccine, even though there were some signs of danger in it. A citizen vaccinated from this batch was injured because of the defective quality. The government argued that in spite of the defects of the vaccine, which would harm a few people, it was beneficial to release the vaccine because without it there might well have been a serious epidemic of polio.

At one time courts might have said this was a discretionary or policy decision. But on this occasion the court did not. Instead it held that the government could be liable if it was negligent in releasing the vaccine. This decision, handed down in 1974, may turn out to be the signal for a more liberal approach to governmental accountability to injured citizens.

Misuse of power—a special case

There are many ways in which the government can abuse its vast powers. Frequently the abuse is a battery (an improper touching) or a false imprisonment (an improper detention, not necessarily in jail). The most publicized cases are those in which government officers break into a citizen's home without warrant or warning. In many instances the officers get the wrong citizen. There are also more subtle abuses of power. For example, the government can discriminate in hiring or in promoting its employees, deny a citizen the right to vote, or refuse a person a fair trial.

When misuses of power such as these occur, what can you do? If a federal officer or employee commits a wrong against you, you may also be able to sue him as an individual if he commits a wrong under state law or if he violates the federal Constitution. But suing a federal officer is not the same as suing the government itself. The main difference is money. If there are heavy money damages at stake, the government is more likely to be able to pay than the officer as an individual. Can you, then, sue the government when its employee abuses governmental power?

Perhaps. Under the peculiar arrangement of the laws, Congress has given consent to some suits against the federal government—but only where state law (not federal) gives the citizen a right. In many instances state tort law does give a citizen a right. For example, if a person's home is entered by an officer (or anyone else) without any right to do so, the officer commits what lawyers call *trespass to land*. If he goes further and touches the citizen without a right to do so, this is called *battery*. If he detains the citizen improperly (even in his own home), this is *false imprisonment*. In each of these cases state laws agree that the citizen could sue and that he has no less right to sue simply because the wrong was done by a government employee.

But has the Congress consented in the Federal Torts Claims Act? The act provides that the government is not usually liable for battery or false imprisonment, but it also provides that if the battery or false imprisonment is committed by an "investigative or law enforcement officer" the government is liable.

In the cases of improper break-ins, therefore, there is a very good chance that a suit against the government would be upheld. Probably it would amount to a trespass, a battery, or false imprisonment, or all three under state law, and the government has consented to suit in such cases if the wrong is done by an "investigative officer." However, if the same wrong is done by a welfare case worker or an OSHA (Occupational Safety and Health Administration) inspector at large in the community, the government will *not* be responsible unless Congress changes the rule to include all federal employees or unless the courts decide that all such government officials are investigative or law enforcement officers.

When it comes to more subtle forms of abusing government power, the legal waters become murkier. As of this writing, you can sue the federal government only if it violates *state* law. Violation of the federal Constitution is ground for suing the federal official as an individual but not ground for suing the government. What this means in practice is that some kinds of rights get very little protection. State laws about wrongdoing grew out of the Middle Ages, when wrongdoing meant rough stuff—trespass, battery, and false imprisonment. State laws in these areas are very good, but those on discrimination, eavesdropping, or due process of law are relatively weak. If a government official uses electronic devices to eavesdrop on your bedroom conversations, this may violate constitutional rights, but it probably will not give you any right to sue the government, only the officer.

Disputes about benefits

Many disputes with the government are not decided by courts but by administrators, who are employees of the executive branch. For instance, administrators will decide whether you are entitled to Social Security, and if so, how much; whether you are entitled to claim deductions on your income taxes; or whether you are eligible for public assistance because of poverty.

If you sue the government in the sense that you make a claim with some federal agency, the main questions may be: Do you get a hearing? How formal is it? What protective procedures exist to make sure the agency does not take arbitrary action?

In many cases the agency in question will provide a formal hearing, similar to the hearing you would get in court, but without a jury and on the whole involving a more casual procedure. For example, John West worked on an assembly line until he was 55 years old. At that point arthritis in his fingers made assembly line work impossible for him and he was not able to find another job. He applied for Social Security disability benefits, to which he was entitled if completely disabled. When the Social Security office notified him that he was not, in their view, disabled, he gave notice of appeal on a form that they provided. A hearing officer, who is called an administrative law judge, then heard Mr. West's side of the story, listened to the doctor and vocational expert, and wrote out his decision on the matter. This kind of hearing had all the elements of a court-type trial. West had an opportunity to be present, to confront witnesses against him, to present his own evidence, and to make his own arguments. It is a fair procedure, even if it does not involve all the customary rules of a court hearing.

Many kinds of administrative decisions, however, are arrived at without a hearing, thus raising the question of constitutionality. The U.S. Constitution states that the government may not take your life, liberty, or property without due process of law. When faced with administrative procedures that did not require a court-type hearing—an opportunity, in effect, to sue the government—some citizens have gone to court to argue that the Constitution requires administrators to hold hearings when serious disputes arise. They have contended that the constitutional guarantee of due process of law means that a court-type hearing is always required before administrative agencies may make decisions directly affecting citizens.

In one case, the Supreme Court agreed. It held that welfare benefits could not be terminated without a hearing, because if welfare benefits were cut off, someone who turned out in the end to be entitled to those benefits would be deprived of the means to live while he waited for the hearing to be scheduled. This meant that the agency in question could not make decisions against providing welfare benefits, even if those decisions were informed and careful, until a hearing was held. But the Court has refused to go so far in other cases. In fact, it has held that the Social Security agencies could terminate benefits without a prior hearing because those benefits were not usually important means of staying alive in the way that welfare benefits are. This does not mean you will not get any hearing at all on such a claim, nor does it mean the agency is entitled to arbitrarily cut off or reduce your benefits. It does mean that the agency can make a decision first, cut off the benefits, and put the burden on you to seek a hearing after the benefits have been terminated.

This may not be as bad as it sounds. Agencies can be and are mistaken in some cases, and sometimes serious harm results from these errors. But it is not possible to hold formal hearings on every issue that may arise. And informal communications are often good enough—a phone call or letter, or both, may suffice to give the agency your side of the dispute. An actual discussion may be more likely to improve understanding than an elaborate hearing of evidence.

Your right to sue a state

The states are also protected by sovereign immunity, but most states now agree that some kinds of suits against them should be permitted. However, as in the case of the federal government, there are many exceptions. And because there are 50 different state governments, each making its own laws on this point, there is no one set of laws to describe the rights of every citizen. Roughly speaking, the states stack up like this:

All of the states retain the discretionary immunity, or basic policy immunity, discussed in connection with the federal government.

Generally, it is possible to sue states in contract disputes.

Most states generally permit tort claims against them, subject to a list of exceptions. Some of these lists are very long and detailed.

One small group of states has established administrative agencies to hear tort claims against the state. These usually limit the amount of dollar recovery one can have.

Another small group of states permits citizens to sue for torts in court, but only in a limited class of cases—for example, when the state agency causing the injury has liability insurance.

State discretionary immunity Aside from the problem of statute interpretation, the chief obstacle is the discretionary immunity. Everyone agrees that the judges should not take over the executive branch, but it is very difficult to know where to draw the line.

There are many cases to illustrate the difficulty. A parole board decides to grant a prisoner parole; the prisoner was in fact dangerous to society, and shortly after parole he killed a man. A juvenile agency places a dangerous child in a foster home without warning the foster parents of his violent tendencies. A dangerous criminal who is free on probation commits a new crime, but his probation is not promptly revoked and he injures or kills those who caused his recent arrest. In all variations of these cases the problem is the same: Would holding the state liable be too great an interference with running another department of the government? These cases sometimes impose liability on the state and sometimes do not. Even in the same state the answers may vary because of small differences in the facts.

In general, state courts are very reluctant to impose liability on the state government when there is room for judgment, even though in the particular case bad judgment was used.

Suing the states in federal court

If states are not willing to impose liability upon themselves under their own laws, it is possible that the federal government might impose liability upon them. Can you sue a state in a federal court? The answer for almost all cases is that you cannot. The 11th Amendment to the U.S. Constitution, as interpreted by the Supreme Court, prevents a citizen's suit against states (and therefore state agencies) in federal court.

There are two special rules that permit suits—in effect—against the state in spite of the 11th Amendment. The first rule permits a citizen to sue a state officer (such as the attorney general or treasurer) in federal court and to get an injunction against him in his official capacity if he is violating federal law. For example, the state attorney general might be enjoined by the federal court from enforcing an unconstitutional state law. This is not really a suit against the state, but it has the effect of one.

The other special rule lets a citizen sue the state itself in one narrow kind of case—when states discriminate against some of their employees, for example, on the basis of sex or race. The reason for this exception is that the 14th Amendment to the Constitution authorized Congress to enforce equal protection of the laws even against the states and the Congress has done so in prohibiting employment discrimination. This rule only works to permit suits against states when Congress has actually used the powers granted to it by the 14th Amendment to make the states liable. Not every kind of civil rights claim is covered.

Suing cities and other local governments

Suing a city is somewhat like suing a state, but there are important differences, mostly derived from historical situations. One striking difference is that cities can be sued under federal law even though states cannot. The 11th Amendment does not prevent suits against local governments, such as cities, but only suits against statewide agencies and suits against states themselves.

If a city violates a federal law, a federal court suit against the city is permitted. But it is necessary for the city to violate federal law before this can be done. The main federal law now being litigated against cities is usually called a 1983 claim—a reference to Section 1983 of Title 42 of the United States Code. This section provides that any person who violates another's constitutional rights may be held liable for damages. It is now held by the Supreme Court that a city is a "person" who may be liable under this statute.

The rule is that the city will be liable under this statute only if the general city policy violates the plaintiff's constitutional rights. The city will not be liable merely because a city employee, not carrying out a city policy, violates someone's rights. Once the city itself violates constitutional rights, however, the fact that it acted in good faith is no defense. One interesting sidelight on these cases is that they may be brought in both federal courts and state courts—even though it is federal law that applies.

Suing cities under state law is a bit more like suing states. Laws differ from state to state on this subject, but many states have abolished the general immunity of cities and permit suits against cities in at least some cases. Here again the discretionary immunity will protect a city, just as it protects the state and federal governments. For example, states often hold that a police decision not to provide protection or make an arrest is discretionary—a citizen injured because the city police failed to act has no claim.

Most states that have not abolished immunity do permit suits against cities when the city acts in a "proprietary" rather than a "governmental" way. A city that operates a city-owned electrical company, for example, is acting as a private business and is liable if it operates that business in a negligent way so as to injure someone.

Special protective procedures

When you are thinking about bringing suit against anybody, it is always better to see a lawyer sooner rather than later. No matter how just your claim is, time for filing it may run out, witnesses may move away, or documents may be lost. In suing the government—local, state, or federal—there are additional reasons for acting promptly.

Many cities are protected by special *notice rules,* which can provide traps even for lawyers. These require notice to the city before a claim is brought in court or, sometimes, within a certain time after the reason for the claim arises. The effect of these statutes or ordinances is sometimes very severe, and more than one person has lost a good claim because he waited too long to get it started.

Special procedures are also commonly required in suits against the states and suits against the federal government. These typically require presentation of the claim to the government department that allegedly caused the injury, and usually also require special procedures for giving notice of the court suit if one is filed.

If your claim is for injury, most lawyers will accept the claim on a contingent fee, charging you a percentage of recovery if you win and only expenses if you lose. In most cases, there would be no charge for a consultation to find out whether your claim should be pursued. A phone call to the lawyer you have in mind will usually suffice to find out whether there is a consultation charge and whether a contingent fee arrangement is possible. One piece of good news: in the case of suing the federal government under the Federal Torts Claims Act, the lawyer's contingent fee is limited by Congress to 25 percent of any recovery and less than that if the recovery is made by agreement with the administrative agency.

ed intrusions. Torts involving invasions of privacy are divided into four major areas:

(1) Appropriation of a person's name or likeness for profit—such as use of your picture without your permission to advertise a product.

(2) Intrusion upon a person's private property, solitude, or seclusion—such as coming into your hotel or motel room while you are out, eavesdropping, wiretapping, reading your personal mail, or persistently making unwanted phone calls to you.

(3) Publicly disclosing details of a person's private life that are of no concern to the public.

(4) Showing someone in a false light even if it does not amount to actual defamation—such as using the picture of an honest policeman to illustrate an article on dishonest cops. For a full discussion of these areas of tort law, see PRIVACY, RIGHT OF.

Interference with property rights   In addition to invasion of privacy, torts that interfere with a person's property rights include TRESPASS, NUISANCE, and CONVERSION. Nuisance and trespass involve real property (real estate), and conversion involves personal property (any property that is not real estate).

Trespass is any unlawful, forcible entry of another's real property. The entry can be made in person or by causing or permitting something to cross the boundary of the premises. You can commit trespass by going into your neighbor's yard without his permission, by building a structure that extends onto his property, or by directing a drain so that it empties onto his property. Trespass also includes any injury to another's property or any interference with his possession of his property. For example, if three hunters are shooting in your woods where you had planned a picnic and prevent your use of the area that afternoon, they are committing a trespass.

Nuisance is an act or occurrence that harms or disturbs someone's peaceful enjoyment of his property. Nuisance is related to trespass, but it goes further. Your neighbor can trespass on your property by simply walking into your backyard against your will. To be guilty of nuisance, however, he must do some damage to your property or disturb you in some way—such as persistently making noise late at night that keeps you from sleeping and therefore from the quiet enjoyment of your property.

Conversion is any act that deprives an owner of his personal property without permission or just cause. If you refuse to return a lawnmower you borrowed from your neighbor, you are guilty of conversion. You may also be guilty of conversion if you misuse someone else's property—for example, if you borrowed your neighbor's lawnmower and broke the blades by using it on a rocky stretch of lawn even though he had asked you not to use it on rocky ground. Finally, a person who changes the nature of another's property is guilty of conversion—for example, if you took your neighbor's lawnmower apart and used the motor along with parts from other tools to build a different type of machine.

Misuse of legal process   If someone uses the courts to prosecute you for a crime he knows you did not commit for the sole purpose of hurting you, he is guilty of the tort of *malicious prosecution* and you can sue him.

EXAMPLE Murray, a salesman, lost an important customer to Lenny and bitterly resented it. In order to get even with Lenny for taking away his customer, Murray went to the police and accused Lenny of molesting a young girl. Lenny was eventually brought to trial as a result of Murray's accusation. At the trial, Murray admitted his great animosity toward Lenny and the jury found Lenny not guilty. Lenny later sued Murray for malicious prosecution and won his suit.

Although suits for malicious prosecution were originally used only as a protection against improper criminal actions, they are also used when civil proceedings are brought for ulterior motives.

EXAMPLE Smith, a candidate for the office of city councilman, bribed several people to testify that his opponent, Jones, was spreading rumors that Smith drank heavily and beat his children when he was drunk. Smith then sued Jones for libel, and a great deal of publicity was given the dispute. Jones won the case but lost the election. Jones sued Smith for malicious prosecution, showing that Smith had prosecuted him for libel merely to make him look bad in the eyes of the voters and cause him to lose the election. Jones won his suit.

A similar tort is the tort of *malicious abuse of process*. Like malicious prosecution, it involves a misuse of the legal process to hurt someone. But abuse of process implies a valid legal proceeding brought for an invalid (unlawful) purpose or for a purpose different from the one usually sought in that type of proceeding. For example, if you get a valid show cause order served on a person, ordering him to appear in court on February 2 at 9:30 A.M., when your only purpose for obtaining the order is to ruin his wedding scheduled for that day and hour, you are guilty of malicious abuse of process because you are using the legal process for an unlawful purpose.

EXAMPLE If your neighbor sues you for trespass simply to force you to sell him a piece of property he has long been trying to buy from you, he is guilty of malicious abuse of process because he is using the legal process for a purpose different from the one usually sought in a trespass proceeding.

Fraud   The tort of fraud is the intentional and successful practice of deception to induce a person to part with property or to surrender some legal right. For example, if a young man knocks at your door and sells you a number of magazine subscriptions based on the fact that half the money paid goes to the United Way and it does not, he has committed fraud. Fraud can be committed in almost any area of human activity. In order to maintain a lawsuit for fraud, the following five elements must be present: (1) A statement of fact must be made. (2) The statement must be false and the person who makes it must know it is false. (3) The person who makes the statement must intend to deceive the person to whom he makes it. (4) The latter must rely on the false statement. (5) The person to whom the statement was made must be wronged as a result. For more details, see FRAUD.

Interference with contracts   The tort of interference with contracts is the wrongful interference by one person with the formation or performance of a contract between two other persons. No unlawful means need be used to accomplish this result, so long as the wrongful act was done intentionally and without justification or excuse.

EXAMPLE The classic case of the tort of interference with O⊶⚹ contract involved Johanna Wagner, an opera singer who was under contract with the plaintiff to sing only in his theater for a certain period of time. The defendant, "knowing the premises, and maliciously intending to injure plaintiff . . . enticed and procured" the singer to refuse to carry out her contract. The court decided that the defendant was liable for the damages suffered by the owner of the theater when the singer breached her contract.

Not all states, however, recognize this tort as stated. Some states require that unlawful means must be used to induce the breach before there will be a cause of action.

Intentional infliction of emotional distress This tort may be committed by intentionally using words or doing something that is meant to cause someone fright, terror, anxiety, or distress of mind. The words or action must actually cause such emotional distress.

EXAMPLE In Iowa, a man committed suicide in a friend's O⊶⚹ kitchen by cutting his throat with a knife. When the woman discovered the corpse in her kitchen she was shocked, became nervous, and had difficulty sleeping thereafter. She sued the man's estate for the injuries she received. Although the trial court directed a verdict for the man's estate, the appellate court reversed the verdict and held that the woman should be paid damages if the jury found that the suicide was willful (intentional or with disregard of the safety of others).

There can be no recovery, however, for emotional distress alone unless the conduct is extreme and outrageous, going beyond all reasonable bounds of decency. A baker who wraps up a gory dead rat instead of a loaf of bread to scare a difficult customer would be held liable for the customer's injuries.

The injury must be real and substantial, and the plaintiff's emotional response to the defendant's conduct must be severe. Mere annoyance or hurt feelings will not support a lawsuit. Nor will losing a few nights sleep or becoming unhappy, humiliated, or mildly despondent for a short time. If the emotional anguish is great, and particularly if it is prolonged, most courts will allow the lawsuit whether or not there is any physical manifestation of the mental suffering or bodily harm (such as a physical illness, heart condition, or miscarriage) caused by it.

The defendant is liable for the plaintiff's emotional response as long as it is within the range of normal human reaction to that conduct. In addition, if the defendant knows that the plaintiff has a special sensitivity, he may be liable for conduct that is extreme and outrageous solely in light of that special vulnerability.

EXAMPLE When Linda was a young girl, her mother was O⊶⚹ killed in a fire and the trauma of the tragedy left Linda with a lifelong abnormal dread of fire. Dan knew this, but as a cruel practical joke he burned some trash outside her window so that the smoke would go into her house, and then ran into the house yelling, "Fire! Fire!" Linda became hysterical and had to be sedated, and she had horrible nightmares about fire for months thereafter. Dan was liable for Linda's emotional distress.

A defendant's acts do not need to be directed at the plaintiff so long as he intentionally or recklessly causes mental anguish to the plaintiff. He will be liable to the plaintiff for shocking conduct directed at some third person, provided the plaintiff's mental harm was also intended or recklessly caused. Because the courts have generally required that the plaintiff witness the conduct and that the defendant know or have reason to know of the plaintiff's presence, these cases usually involve family members. Liability may occur when a pregnant woman witnesses the brutal beating of her husband for refusing to pay his gambling debts.

Negligence The second of the three major categories of tort liability, negligence is conduct that falls below the standard set by the law for protecting others against risk of harm. It is an unintentional tort. A person guilty of negligence does not want to cause the consequences that follow, and he does not know or believe that they are substantially certain to occur. There is, however, a great enough risk of such consequences to lead a reasonable person in his position to anticipate and guard against them.

EXAMPLE If an automobile driver intentionally runs down a O⊶⚹ pedestrian, he commits the intentional tort of battery. On the other hand, if the driver is drunk, fails to notice that the pedestrian is crossing in front of him, and consequently runs him down, the driver is guilty of negligence. Although he had no desire to hurt the victim, he acted unreasonably in failing to guard against a risk that any responsible driver should have anticipated—that driving while drunk impairs a driver's senses.

In order to bring a lawsuit based on negligence, a plaintiff must show (1) that the defendant owed the plaintiff a duty to use due care, (2) that the defendant breached that duty by being negligent, and (3) that the plaintiff was injured and the defendant's negligence caused the injury. For a full discussion of this area of tort law, see NEGLIGENCE.

Strict liability The third basic category of tort liability is strict liability—liability regardless of the defendant's fault, or absolute liability. It is imposed by law on a person even if he has not been guilty of any negligent act or any wanton, willful, or intentional wrongdoing. Generally, three groups of persons face strict liability: owners or possessors of animals (for damage done by the animals); those who either maintain conditions or engage in activities that are highly dangerous and a threat to the general safety; and the manufacturers and sellers of products that injure a buyer of the product.

The concept of "fault" in strict liability carries with it no meaning of moral wrong. The idea is that neither party is really to blame, but in balancing the social equities and determining who can best bear the loss, the loss has been shifted by law from plaintiff to the defendant. The reason for this shift of liability is that the defendant is usually acting for his own purposes, seeking a benefit or profit from his activities, so that it is deemed fair that he, and not the public or the innocent victim, be responsible for any injuries caused by his behavior.

Keeping animals Traditionally, a person who owned animals was liable, without any fault of his own, for any damages done by them. Strict liability for damage caused by animals has survived to this day, but with modifications.

Certain kinds of animals present an obvious danger to the community, even if they are carefully kept. Those who keep them for their own purposes must protect the community against the risk involved and are strictly liable for any harm they do.

Animals are generally classified by law into three groups: (1) those that are considered safe and threaten no harm to human beings, such as rabbits and canaries; (2) domestic animals, which are considered safe in the absence of knowledge or notice of some dangerous propensity for injuring people, such as dogs and cats, cattle, horses, sheep, goats, and hogs; and (3) wild animals, which are considered by nature dangerous to human beings, such as poisonous snakes and spiders, monkeys, wolves, hyenas, lions, tigers, and elephants.

Canaries and rabbits are generally considered harmless. Owners are not liable for injuries they cause unless the owner is negligent.

EXAMPLE Patrick is not liable when his pet canary is startled by an unexpected noise and flies into Stephen's face, injuring his eye. Philip is liable, though, when as a prank he slips his pet rabbit into James's bed and the rabbit scratches James's eye.

The law distinguishes between wild and domestic animals when imposing liability for harm other than trespass. The keeper of animals that are customarily domesticated and kept in a region where the damage occurred—for example, dogs or cattle—is strictly liable for the harm they cause only if he had known or should have known that the animal had a potentially harmful trait, such as viciousness or destructive tendencies that caused the harm.

EXAMPLE Michael's pet dog, Frisky, is huge even though she is still less than a year old. Michael knows that the dog is playful and he has been trying to break her of the habit of jumping on people. Michael was walking outside with Frisky when an elderly neighbor approached. Frisky gave her usual friendly greeting and knocked down the neighbor, whose hipbone was broken in the fall. Michael is liable even though he was neither negligent nor guilty of an intentional wrong because the dog had shown a tendency to do something that is likely to injure someone.

People who keep wild animals are strictly liable for the harm they cause if they escape, regardless of whether the animal is dangerous. Such animals are known to revert to their natural tendencies, so they are considered to be wild no matter how well trained or domesticated.

EXAMPLE Harvey had a tame pet lion that he kept in his apartment in downtown Indianapolis. The neighborhood children all knew and loved the lion. Harvey considered the lion his best friend and told everyone that the animal was safer than many of the people on the streets. One day, as Harvey was walking his pet, the lion went berserk and attacked a man eating a hotdog on the corner. Harvey was liable for the man's injuries because lions are considered wild animals in law no matter how tame they appear to be.

When the injury occurs on the owner's premises while the animal is confined or restrained, however, the courts tend to deny strict liability, usually on the theory that the injured person assumed the risk of injury.

In most states, keepers of all animals, including domesticated ones, are strictly liable for damage resulting from the trespass of their animals on the property of another. There are three main exceptions to this rule, however:

(1) Owners of dogs and cats are not necessarily liable for their trespasses unless there has been negligence. It may be negligence, for example, to allow your fence to deteriorate or to leave your gate open if you have a dog. However, many states or counties have imposed strict liability by statute for damage done by trespassing dogs.

EXAMPLE Gary's county had a local law requiring dog owners to keep their pets leashed whenever the animals were not on their own property. Gary kept his dog inside his backyard fence but the dog was big enough to jump over the fence and often did. Gary's neighbor complained constantly that the dog was damaging her garden by relieving himself on the plants. Gary answered that he was trying to train the dog and was doing the best he could. Finally, the neighbor shot and killed the dog. Gary sued for the value of the dog. He won. The court held that even though Gary should have kept his dog confined, this did not give the neighbor a right to kill the dog. She could have sued Gary and recovered damages to compensate for the harm done to her garden.

(2) Because highways may be used for moving livestock, there is no liability for trespass without negligence for damage caused when they stray from the road.

EXAMPLE Bill is driving his small herd of sheep down the highway when a frisky lamb suddenly bolts. She plunges through the open door of Harriet's roadside antique shop and does considerable damage. Harriet cannot recover money for the damage because owners of domesticated animals being driven along a highway are liable only for their own carelessness. Here, Bill was not negligent.

(3) In some parts of the West, certain farm animals, such as cattle, are permitted by custom or statute to graze at large on the range, and so their owners are not strictly liable for their trespasses. Some states have enacted *fencing-out laws,* which require landowners who want to exclude such animals to build a certain type of fence. Once this is done, the owner of the animals will be strictly liable for any trespasses. Other states have *fencing-in laws,* which relieve the owner of strict liability if he has put up a certain fence to keep his animals on his own property. A different type of fencing-in law requires property owners to fence in their property to keep ranging animals from entering and harming themselves.

EXAMPLE Lee owned land in an area where animals were permitted to roam through the grazing range. Ranchers there were required by law to fence in hay. Lee neglected to fence in his hay lot, however, so he was liable for the value of cows that wandered into the area and ate hay until they foundered (collapsed).

For more details on the owner's liability for damage done by his animals, see ANIMALS.

Abnormally dangerous activities A person will be strictly liable for harm that results from abnormally dangerous conditions and activities, such as storing harmful chemicals or blasting. Such dangerous conditions and activities are not so unreasonable as to be prohibited altogether. In fact, they may be socially useful. But they are dangerous enough to create sufficiently unusual risks that the law requires them to be carried on at the peril of the person who conducts the activity. By making the person who conducts ultrahazardous activities strictly liable, the law attempts to insure that he will act to protect others against the harm that could result from the risk he creates.

Merely requiring that he exercise due care or even the utmost care would not adequately protect the general public from the threat of harm. Moreover, anyone who maintains dangerous conditions on his land or who pursues ultrahazardous activities is considered by society to be in a better position than anyone else to bear the burdens of injury. If he creates an extraordinary threat he should bear the entire burden for the harm done. He can do this either by purchasing insurance or by increasing the price of his product and thereby shifting the loss to the public at large in the event that he must pay damages for an injury resulting from his activities.

Strict liability will be imposed for harm resulting from an activity that, although legal, is unusual, extraordinary, or inappropriate in light of the place and manner in which it is conducted. For example, collecting water or gas in household pipes is appropriate, but collecting water in large tanks dangerously close to someone else's land or storing a large quantity of gas in aboveground tanks in a densely populated area is not.

EXAMPLE Bernard decided to turn several hundred acres of O⟵⟶ swampland he owned to profit. He performed work on the land so that water would collect into a reservoir big enough for him to charge a fee to fishermen who wanted to fish there. The land was unsuitable for the project, however, and water ran off into a mine shaft worked by a neighboring coal company. When the mine shaft became flooded, the company sued Bernard and recovered money damages.

Storing quantities of explosives or flammable liquids, blasting, and accumulating sewage have been considered sufficiently unusual and excessive to justify strict liability. The storage of explosives in quantity and blasting create unusual and unacceptable risks in the midst of a large city and consequently strict liability. Similar activities in remote rural areas would not create strict liability. If the activity is appropriate to the area, there is strict liability only if it is conducted in an unusual or abnormal way.

EXAMPLE Schroeder had a legal right to apply weed killers O⟵⟶ to his seed crops. One year he decided to hire a crop duster to spread the weed killer. An unexpected breeze kicked up and blew the poisonous chemical over a neighbor's beehives, killing all the bees. The neighbor sued Schroeder for the value of 56 hives. Schroeder argued that a good farmer has to apply weed killers. The court ruled that crop dusting is unusually dangerous because the effect of the wind cannot be controlled. Since crop dusting is ultrahazardous in law, Schroeder was held strictly liable for any damage the crop duster caused.

Products that injure buyers Manufacturers and those who make or sell their products have a responsibility to the public to make sure that their products are safe. If a product injures a buyer, the manufacturer and seller of that product may be strictly liable for the injury.

EXAMPLE Suppose that George bought a new hunting gun O⟵⟶ and the first time he shot it the gun exploded in his face and killed him. Both the manufacturer of the gun and the shop that sold the gun could be made to pay money damages to George's heirs under the law of strict liability.

The fact that neither the manufacturer nor the seller is negligent does not relieve him of liability for a product that injures the buyer. By selling the product, each in effect assures the purchaser that the product is safe. For a full discussion of how strict liability applies to products, see PRODUCT LIABILITY.

Strict liability by statute Activities and conditions other than those mentioned above can be made subject to strict liability by specific statutes. For example, WORKMEN'S COMPENSATION statutes make an employer strictly liable for injuries his employee receives on the job. In some states, dramshop (barroom) acts make the seller of intoxicating liquor strictly liable to a person who is injured as a result of his intoxication and to his family if he is killed. Usually the liquor sale must be illegal, such as to a minor or to a person who is already clearly intoxicated, but this is not always the case.

■ **Special rules of liability** A number of special rules govern the liability of persons for torts committed in particular situations. These rules either extend or limit the duty that would otherwise exist in response to considerations of public policy—notions of what is good for society in general.

Employer liability The doctrine of RESPONDEAT SUPERIOR ("let the master answer") makes an employer liable for the torts committed by his employee while performing the employer's business. For example, the driver of a delivery truck for a baking company runs a red light while making deliveries and hits a child. The owner of the company as well as the driver will be liable to the child for his injuries.

The reasoning behind this doctrine is that the employer has the obligation to guarantee the quality of his employee's performance and he is in a better financial position to compensate the injured person for the torts committed by his employees. This is one form of vicarious liability, which is liability imposed on a person who is otherwise free of fault and holds him responsible for the tortious conduct of another.

Automobiles Because automobile accidents are so frequent, special rules govern liability to insure that a financially responsible defendant will compensate the plaintiff's loss. The FAMILY CAR DOCTRINE makes the owner of the automobile liable for its negligent operation while driven by members of his immediate household for their personal use. As a result of *guest statutes,* the auto owner's or driver's duty to guest passengers is limited so that he will be liable in cases only where his conduct was reckless or the injury was caused by his intoxication. (Guest passengers are those who are neither paying for their ride nor carrying on any other form of business with or for the driver.) For a full discussion of guest statutes, see NEGLIGENCE.

The widespread adoption of automobile INSURANCE, particularly no-fault insurance, has limited the financial liability of insured defendants because the losses of plaintiffs who are compensated are in fact already being spread among the motoring public as a group. The impact on the defendant is slight, usually an increase in his insurance rates. The cost of driving assessed to each motorist is not the full cost of his individual fault but merely his proportionate share of the total fault of the entire group of insured motorists.

Torts against civil rights The DUE PROCESS OF LAW clause of the 14th Amendment to the Constitution prohibits the states from abridging any person's constitutional rights. Under the Civil Rights Act of 1871, any state or local government that violates a person's civil rights is liable for the tort. In other words, no rights created by the Constitution or by federal statutes can be denied by state or local officers, employees, or others seeming to act with the authority of the state or local government behind them. If a person's rights are curtailed by a state or local government or government representative, that person may bring an action in tort against the offending party and be awarded damages for the wrong done him.

■ **Immunities** Certain groups or classes of persons or entities (such as a unit of government) are given immunity from tort liability. Because they are given special consideration for reasons of public policy, they are not held responsible for their torts even though this works at the expense of the injured parties. Historically, tort litigation against units of government, public officers, and charities, between spouses, and between parents and children has been limited or prohibited.

The government—sovereign immunity The concept of governmental immunity, or sovereign immunity, means that the government may not be sued for a tort without its consent. This concept was based on the idea that the King can do no wrong. Sovereign immunity of federal, state, and local governments has been eroded over the years by court decisions and the enactment of statutes by which the governments have given consent to be sued in certain instances. For example, under the Federal Tort Claims Act, tort actions can generally be brought against the United States for damages for personal injuries, death, and property damage or loss resulting from most kinds of negligent conduct of a government employee who was acting within the scope of his employment. On the other hand, sovereign immunity is still applied for intentional torts, such as assault and battery, fraud, libel, and slander. In such cases, however, the injured party can sue the employee as an individual. Sovereign immunity is also applied for acts or omissions by an agency or employee performing "a discretionary function or duty" at the planning or policy-making level of the federal government, although what is discretionary (as opposed to mandatory) varies from situation to situation. The states have also waived sovereign immunity to some degree, and the doctrine seems to be declining in force throughout the country.

The liability for the personal torts of government officers and employees is not the same as that for the government itself.

EXAMPLE A U.S. Senator who beats his neighbor with a tire iron during a dispute over a blocked driveway will be liable for the tort of battery. On the other hand, if during the course of a congressional investigation the same Senator slanders a former judge suspected of corruption, he will not be liable for slander. His actions are protected by the free speech and debate clause of the Constitution, which safeguards members of Congress against defamation lawsuits when conducting congressional business.

Charities Traditionally, charitable, educational, religious, and benevolent organizations were immune from tort liability. One of the reasons offered for this immunity was that the use of charitable funds to pay tort claims might discourage donations to charities that do public good. Today, most states reject the concept of charitable immunity. Some states will permit a charity to be sued for a tort only when liability insurance will pay for the damages, so that none of the charity's own funds will be used. In other states, recovery is allowed against charitable hospitals in such suits as malpractice actions, but all other charities remain immune. Almost all states will impose liability in certain situations, such as when fraud is committed during fund-raising activities.

Intrafamily immunities In many states, if the person injured and the tortfeasor are husband and wife or parent and child, the tortfeasor may be immune from liability. Brothers, sisters, and other relatives are not immune from tort liability by reason of their relationship to one another.

Under common law, neither a husband nor a wife could sue the other for torts committed while they were married, because a wife was not considered a legal entity separate from her husband. More recently, however, laws have been passed to recognize that married women are entitled to their own legal rights, and many states have done away with this common-law immunity. Some states allow lawsuits only for intentional torts. About half the states permit lawsuits between spouses for torts caused by negligence. Other states retain husband-wife immunity but recognize certain exceptions to it, such as for torts committed before marriage. For an extended discussion of liability between spouses, see HUSBAND AND WIFE.

Although common law did not recognize the legal unity of a parent and his child, the general rule was that a child could not recover damages from his parents for their personal torts (injuries to his person). This rule was based on the need to protect parental discipline and control as well as to safeguard family unity and tranquillity. Today, more than one-third of the states have ended this immunity. In the remaining states, a number of exceptions have evolved. For example, most states allow a parent to be found liable for bodily harm intentionally or recklessly inflicted on his child. Where the immunity exists, it extends only to unemancipated minor children (minor children who have not left home, married, or become self-supporting). Persons who act in loco parentis ("in the place of a parent") are not given immunity. For additional information on parent-child immunity, see PARENT AND CHILD.

Ordinarily, a parent is liable for his own torts, and a child is liable for his own torts. Sometimes statutes impose liability on a parent up to a certain amount for automobile accidents caused by their children or for specified torts committed by their children. When there is no such statute, a parent is liable only for his own negligence. For example, a parent who gives a gun to a 12-year-old and fails to supervise him may be liable for harm done by the child but only because of the parent's own negligence. See Chart 5.

■ **Statutes of limitations** Although a person may sue anyone who commits a tort against him, he must generally do it within a certain amount of time. Each state has its own laws governing the period of time within which a person may bring suit for a particular tort. These laws are called statutes of limitations. The purpose of these statutes is to prevent fraudulent and stale claims from being made long after the evidence needed for the case has been lost or memory of the facts has become obscure because of the passage of time. For a full discussion of statutes of limitations in both civil and criminal law, see LIMITATIONS OF ACTIONS. See also Chart 4, which lists the time limitations for bringing suit for various torts in each state.

■ **Damages** Damages are money compensation that may be recovered in the courts by one who has suffered loss, detriment, or injury as a result of the defendant's tort. Justice requires that the plaintiff be restored to the condition he was in before his injury as far as it is possible for money to do so. This means he should be reimbursed not only for his money losses but also for his noneconomic damage—that is, his loss of physical and mental well-being. There are three major categories of damages in tort actions—nominal, compensatory, and punitive.

Nominal damages are token, symbolic awards of money, such as $1. They are awarded in recognition of the fact that the defendant violated a legal right of the plaintiff even though he did not cause the plaintiff to suffer any substantial loss or injury.

EXAMPLE During an argument, Ted slapped Debbie in the face and Debbie sued Ted for the intentional tort of battery. During the proceeding it was brought out that even though Ted wrongfully slapped Debbie, she had sustained no injuries and had not had to spend money to go to a doctor or buy medication. The judge awarded Debbie $1 in nominal damages.

Compensatory damages are awards of money to compensate the plaintiff for actual injury or loss suffered as a result of the defendant's failure to act. Compensatory damages should not be in excess of the amount lost or suffered by the defendant. The aim of the law is to make the plaintiff "whole" and not to provide him with a profit. If Ted had broken Debbie's jaw when he slapped her, Debbie would have been entitled to compensatory damages for recovery of her medical and hospital expenses, for any salary lost while recovering from her injury, and for her pain and suffering. A plaintiff may receive either an award of nominal or compensatory damages, but not both.

Punitive damages are amounts of money sometimes awarded to the plaintiff to punish the defendant for malicious, willful, or wanton acts. Punitive damages are not awarded in cases of negligence unless the conduct was so reckless or wanton that it was equal to intentional wrongdoing. Leaving a loaded machine gun in an unlocked storage closet in the recreation room of a day camp may justify the award of punitive damages against the negligent camp owner to the parents of an injured camper. Punitive damages are awarded in addition to nominal or compensatory damages. For further discussion, see DAMAGES.

■ **Roles of judges and juries** The vast majority of tort cases, especially accident cases, are settled before a lawsuit is filed or before the trial begins, largely on the basis of the judgment of the plaintiff's attorney as to what jury verdict would be likely if the case were brought to court. In cases that cannot be settled out of court, a jury trial is usually sought. (Where there is provision for jury trial, usually either party may demand one. See JURY.) During a jury trial, two types of questions arise: questions of fact, which are addressed to the jury, and questions of law, which are addressed to the court (judge).

Questions of fact There are three kinds of jury questions, all relating to the facts of the case:

(1) The jury must determine what really happened—for example, was the light red or green when the defendant drove through it?

(2) In most cases, the jury is required to make one or more decisions as to the legal consequences of these facts—for example, was the plaintiff or the defendant negligent or were the words defamatory? The answers to the questions are usually based on some general legal definition (as of negligence and defamation) given by the court.

(3) The jury must determine whether or not the plaintiff was damaged by the defendant's wrongful conduct, and if he was, it must assign a dollar value to the plaintiff's compensable damages.

Questions of law There are several key issues of law that the judge must decide, such as:

(1) Did the defendant owe the plaintiff any recognized legal duty, or did the plaintiff have a legal right?

(2) What elements of proof (EVIDENCE sufficient to make up a case) are needed to establish liability or nonliability?

(3) How should the damages be measured?

(4) Do the facts show that some particular rule of law imposes or excuses liability as a matter of law? For example, there is a rule that violation of a certain safety statute is negligence in and of itself.

In addition, issues that are normally questions of fact for the jury become questions of law if the judge decides that the evidence on that issue so overwhelmingly favors one conclusion that reasonable people could not reach the opposite conclusion.

Finally, it is the judges who apply the rules of procedure, especially rules concerning the admission and exclusion of evidence and the burden of proof. Generally, the ordinary rules of evidence established for civil trials apply to proceedings involving torts. In cases of negligence, a special rule is also allowed. It is *res ipsa loquitur* ("the thing speaks for itself"). Only the judge can determine when it can be applied. For a full discussion of this rule, see RES IPSA LOQUITUR.

Although judges have the ultimate powers to decide every issue in a case, juries are permitted to render judgment in a substantial proportion of tort cases. Generally, the jury returns a verdict fixing liability and setting an amount of damages. The judge may accept this amount and enter a judgment in that amount or set it aside on the ground that no reasonable interpretation of the facts can justify that amount. An appeals court can affirm the judgment or remand (send back) to a lower court for a new trial on the issue of liability or the amount of damages.

For a discussion of how civil actions, including tort actions, are conducted, see TRIAL.

Totten Trust   A type of bank account in which a person deposits money in his own name but arranges that it be held in trust for another. The bankbook of a Totten Trust may read, for example, "John Smith in trust for Alice Brown." The person for whose benefit the account is established—Alice Brown, the beneficiary—need not know about the arrangement. The depositor, or trustee, John Smith, is entitled to deposit and withdraw funds from the account as he sees fit. He may even close out or revoke the account without obtaining the beneficiary's permission. When the trustee dies, any funds in the account automatically become the property of the beneficiary. They may, however, be subject to the claims of the trustee's creditors.

Totten Trusts are usually established to avoid the trouble of executing a WILL for the funds involved and the consequent expense and delay of PROBATE and administration. Such an arrangement is known as a *testamentary substitute*.

towage   The supplying of power by one vessel (the tug) in order to draw another vessel (the tow). To tow means to drag a vessel forward in the water by using a rope or cable. Various statutes require the placement of bright lights on vessels that are towing and being towed.

The captain of a ship has power to contract for any necessary towage, either in writing or verbally over the ship's radio. Ordinarily, a LIEN (a claim on property) arises against the vessel being towed until payment for the service has been tendered.

In the absence of any agreement to the contrary, the captain of the tug is responsible for control and management of both tug and tow. It is his responsibility to decide when it is safe to proceed with towing. The tow has to follow the guidance of the tug and to conform with its directions. See also SEAMAN; SHIPPING.

to wit   That is to say; namely.

town   A political subdivision of a state, varying in size and importance, but usually one of the subdivisions of a COUNTY. A town can be created by a state legislature after a large number of houses and other buildings, private and public, have been built in a particular locality. The main function of a town is to exercise the power of the state on the local level and to promote greater prosperity, safety, convenience, health, and common good for all people.

Some states use the word "township" instead of "town," and the two words are often used interchangeably. In some parts of the country, however—especially in the Midwest—a township may be made up of several towns. State law determines the precise functions of towns and townships.

In the Middle Atlantic states, as well as other parts of the country, local government is divided between counties and towns. Because the laws differ from state to state, you must check local law to determine what functions will be performed by the county and what by the town.

A town is a municipality. See MUNICIPAL CORPORATION for functions and duties of towns not covered in this article.

■ **Powers**   Generally, towns have only the powers given to them by the state legislature. Usually a town is granted power to raise money by taxation, construct its own public buildings, and lease its property to others.

Towns are commonly granted home rule by the state legislature. This means that a town can govern itself without the continuous supervision of the state. Towns are generally given power to enact ordinances concerned with local matters, but the ordinances must be reasonable and must protect the public in some appreciable manner. For example, many state laws authorize towns to enact ZONING ordinances, which, by placing restrictions on the use of property, protect the health and safety of the public.

Typical town ordinances include (1) banning pinball machines from any place of business, (2) requiring the purchase of a permit for excavating land, (3) prescribing regulations for the construction of new buildings, and (4) restricting the removal of sand and topsoil. As with other legislation, the ordinances a town passes are subject to review by the courts, particularly with respect to reasonableness. For example, a town ordinance requiring billboards to be lighted all night was held unreasonable because there was no proof that the legislation safeguarded life or health.

■ **Government**   Towns govern themselves either by town meetings or by town boards.

Town meetings   In the six New England states the town is the dominant unit of local government. The powers of a town are exercised by vote of a town meeting. Town meetings serve both legislative and executive functions. All the qualified townspeople meet to discuss and, if need be, to vote on matters dealing with their self-government. Payment of town taxes is one way a person qualifies as a voter in town meetings.

Statutes regulate all types of town meetings—annual, regular, or special—as to the business that can be transacted at each type of meeting and the manner in which the meetings are to be conducted.

Town board   A town board (also commonly referred to as a town council) is created by the state legislature to supervise the affairs of the town. Like a town meeting, its duties are legislative and administrative. Some of its powers include appointing police officers and a town attorney, making public improvements, and providing for the audit and payment of claims against the town.

The members of the town boards, sometimes called *selectmen*, are elected by the voters of the town to take care of the town's general business and to exercise certain executive powers. Usually a board can function only when a majority of selectmen are present at a meeting. A selectman is disqualified from voting on propositions in which he has a financial interest if his vote may be decisive.

The meetings of town boards are recorded by the town clerk in a record book. A town clerk keeps the records of the board's activities, issues calls for council meetings, and performs the duties of secretary to the organization.

trademarks and trade names   Two areas of the law that protect a business from having the name or symbol of its products or services or its name unjustly used by a competitor and that shield the public from the possibility of buying products or services that are not what they appear to be. A third, related area of the law, unfair competition, also prohibits other underhanded business practices.

■ **Trademarks** A trademark is a name, sign, symbol, or device that is attached to goods offered for sale to distinguish them from similar goods. It signifies that the goods are made, worked on, imported, selected, certified, or sold by a particular manufacturer or seller. A trademark may cover not only the physical article sold but also the inherent right to receive further service with it.

A *service mark* indicates the type of services rendered. For example, the use of the slogan "We Print-it in a Minit" by a printing business indicates the type of service rendered to its customers. A service mark can be registered and protected in the same way as a trademark.

Rights in trademarks derive from common law, and these rights are protected in all 50 states. Statutes providing for the registration and protection of trademarks have been enacted by the federal and state governments.

Common law A trademark is, in a sense, PROPERTY. Its owner has the right to use it, and he may seek protection from the court if someone else tries to use it. The value of a trademark is that the public sees it as an exclusive sign of a business. It is evidence of the origin and quality of the product to which it is attached.

The protection given by law to trademarks benefits their owners and protects the public from being deceived by manufacturers who use the trademarks of others. Trademarks identify products and services. A trademark assures customers that they are getting what the trademark generally stands for and builds up a relationship of good will between the business and the buyer. When a trademark is used on another company's product, this good will may be lost—for example, if the product is inferior. The business that owns the trademark also loses money because its customers buy its competitor's product without realizing it.

More than one trademark may be acquired for the same goods. For example, different trademarks can indicate different grades of the same product.

EXAMPLE A manufacturer of power hand tools used two different trademarks for his products. His top-of-the-line tools, suitable for heavy use every day by a carpenter, bore the label "First Prize." His second-line tools, more suitable for occasional use by homeowners, were called "Blue Ribbon."

The owner of a trademark has a right to its exclusive use and may stop its unauthorized use to protect his reputation. He does not, however, have the right to prohibit the use of the words of the trademark except if they are used in another trademark and thus likely to confuse buyers. The owner's right of exclusive use of his trademark extends only to other goods that are similar to his. For example, a manufacturer of canned soups cannot lawfully use a trademark owned by a manufacturer of canned peas. The public might conclude that both canned foods had been produced by the same company. But using another's trademark may be lawful if its use is so different from the original owner's that the public is not likely to believe that the two products were produced by the same manufacturer. For example, Esquire is a legal trademark for both a magazine and a shoe polish.

A trademark extends to every market where the trader's goods have become known and identified by his use of the mark. Subject to treaties, it extends even to markets outside the United States.

Requirements for a valid trademark Under the common law, an exclusive trademark must use words in a purely arbitrary or fanciful way. Examples of fanciful terms used as trademarks include Sunkist for fruits, Q-Tips for cotton-tipped medical swabs, and Beautyrest for mattresses. But "Lemon Concentrate" would not qualify as a trademark for a lemon concentrate. A word or a mark that involves substantial untruth, misrepresentation, or bad faith can never be a valid trademark. "P-Nut Butter Sandwiches" cannot be used for cookies that have no peanuts or peanut butter.

As a rule, a trademark cannot contain laudatory or commendatory expressions or words or marks merely indicating superior excellence, popularity, or universal use—for example, "best," "standard," and "favorite." However, similar words—such as "perfection," "ideal," and "champion"—have been upheld as valid.

Descriptive terms are prohibited as trademarks so that anyone can be free to use the necessary or appropriate terms to describe his goods and business. Otherwise, there would be a danger of depleting the general vocabulary for describing merchandise. Phonetic equivalents or misspellings of these words are not allowed.

EXAMPLE Miller Brewing Company began making and selling a reduced calorie, reduced carbohydrate beer under the name "Lite." Later, other companies put out similar low-calorie beers labeled "light." Miller began trademark infringement actions against its competitors to prevent their use of the word "light." The court decided that "light" had long been used in the beer industry to describe a particular kind of beer. Because a term commonly used to name or describe goods can never be a valid trademark, the word "light" and its phonetic equivalent "lite" could not be used exclusively by Miller.

Numbers arbitrarily used to indicate origin or ownership, particularly when used with letters or other devices, or when printed in a distinctive form or color, may be used as trademarks—for example, Union 76 is the trademark for a gasoline. However, the numbers cannot be used as trademarks to indicate grade, class, or quality. The same rules apply to the use of letters.

Neither words representing colors nor the colors themselves can be valid trademarks. But a color impressed in a particular design—such as a circle, square, triangle, cross, or star—or used in connection with other characters may be used as a trademark. The mere size or shape of goods, packages, or labels cannot be exclusively used as a trademark. The substance or any useful part or feature of the article itself or its package cannot be used as a trademark.

EXAMPLE Sylvania Electric Products, Inc., had been selling flashbulbs—with a blue dot on the top of each bulb—to camera users for many years. The company used the words "blue dot" to market the flashbulbs. When another company began to sell flashbulbs with blue dots, Sylvania sued. The court ruled against Sylvania on the ground that the blue dot was an integral and functioning part of the flashbulb. When the flashbulbs were manufactured, a little dot of cobalt was put inside the top of each glass bulb. It was pink when applied but turned blue when all the air inside the bulb was removed. That indicated to the manufacturer that all the bulbs with blue dots were properly made, but those with pink dots were defective. Because the blue dot was functional, it could not be a trademark. The other company thus had a right to make flashbulbs with blue dots on them.

Pictures or characters, such as the Jolly Green Giant and Charlie the Tuna, are trademarks. Symbols, such as the Blue Cross insignia, are also trademarks. Foreign words, phrases, or letters may be valid trademarks if they are not generic or descriptive terms when translated into English.

Labels used on goods are not trademarks, nor are directions, advertisements, or notices used with the goods. However, the name of a game on a box may be a trademark—for example, Monopoly.

Acquisition Any person, PARTNERSHIP, CORPORATION, or unincorporated ASSOCIATION that can own personal property may acquire a right to a trademark for business products. Under the common law, a trademark can be acquired only by using the word or mark in the manner that trademarks are generally used. Merely planning to use the trademark does not give the owner legally enforceable rights. However, the trademark does not have to be used for any definite or considerable length of time.

A person who first uses a trademark in connection with a particular class of goods acquires the prior and exclusive right to use it, even if someone else was the first to register the mark with the U.S. Patent and Trademark Office. This rule of priority does not apply if the trademark has lost its originality and distinctiveness through long general use.

Registration Any valid trademark may be registered. Registration of trademarks is not necessary, but it affords the best legal protection in case of infringement. The federal government and all the states have trademark registration statutes that regulate and protect trademarks. Trademarks for goods that are sold in interstate commerce can be registered with the U.S. Patent and Trademark Office. State registration laws are patterned after the federal statute.

In order to be registered under federal law, a trademark or service mark must be used in interstate commerce and meet the common-law requirements outlined above. Certain things cannot be registered under federal law: flags or insignias of municipalities, states, or nations; geographical names or terms that denote localities, such as the name of a city or country, a subdivision of the country (e.g., "New England," "Southwest"), or a particular section of the globe ("The Horn of Africa"); marks likely to cause confusion; or the name of an individual, firm, corporation, or association.

In one case, for example, Sally Chain Stores sued to prevent another business from using the name "Sally's Fur Studio." The court denied relief because a name is not entitled to any trademark protection at all.

A trademark cannot consist of the name, portrait, or signature of a living person without his written consent, nor can the name, signature, or portrait of a deceased U.S. President be used during the life of his widow without her

---

USING TRADEMARKS AND TRADE NAMES

■ A *trademark* is a name, sign, symbol, or device placed on goods to distinguish them from similar goods. Pictures or characters, such as the Jolly Green Giant or Charlie the Tuna, are trademarks. A trademark is the exclusive property of its owner, and he may stop its unauthorized use to protect his reputation.

■ A *trade name* denotes a manufacturer of or dealer in goods. Unlike a trademark, a trade name is not exclusively affixed to a particular product; for example, R. H. Macy & Co., the name of a New York City department store, is a trade name.

■ A trademark assures customers that they are getting what the trademark represents, and it promotes good will between the business and the buyer. If the trademark is illegally used on another product, this good will may be lost if the other product is inferior.

■ The owner of a trademark can prohibit the use of the words of the trademark by anyone else only if that use might confuse buyers. For example, a manufacturer of canned soups cannot lawfully use a trademark owned by a manufacturer of canned peas, because the public might think that both canned foods had been produced by the same manufacturer.

■ On the other hand, you may use someone else's trademark if your application of it is so different from the original owner's that the public would not be confused. Esquire is a legal trademark for both a magazine and a shoe polish.

■ A trademark must use words in a purely arbitrary or fanciful way. The trademarks Sunkist, Q-Tips, and Beautyrest meet this requirement. The words "Lemon Concentrate" would not qualify as a trademark for a lemon concentrate. Numbers arbitrarily used may qualify as trademarks— Union 76, for example. The same rule applies to the use of letters.

■ A trademark cannot consist of the name, portrait, or signature of a living person without his written consent.

■ Anyone who wants to register a trademark must submit the required forms and a filing fee to the U.S. Patent and Trademark Office in Washington, D.C. Only the owner of a trademark may register it. Registration protects the trademark for 20 years and may be renewed.

■ It is a fraud to pass off your goods under someone else's trademark.

■ If a trademark has been abandoned—because, for example, its owner has not used it for years—the defendant in an infringement of trademark suit may use this fact to escape liability. A trade name does not have to be registered, but it does have to be used in order to establish the owner's rights.

■ The owner of a trade name has the right to collect money damages from someone who wrongfully appropriates his trade name, and the owner can obtain a court order to stop further use of the name.

written consent. It is also unlawful to use the insignia of the Red Cross in a trademark or a picture of a person wearing, displaying, or using the Red Cross insignia in order to prevent the false impression that the goods are the products of the Red Cross or sponsored by it.

Filing an application   Only the owner of a trademark may register it. This means that he must have used it in commerce. Anyone who wants to register a trademark must submit the required forms and a filing fee to the U.S. Patent and Trademark Office in Washington, D.C. Let us say you want to register three balloons as a trademark for a brand of children's vitamins. Besides such basic facts as your residence, you will have to give the dates of the first use of the mark (as on a sample or upon adoption at a corporate meeting) and of its first use in commerce, as well as the duplicate samples of the trademark, such as a tag or label. You must state that you own the mark and that no one else, as far as you can determine, has the right to use it.

Notice of application   Upon receipt of your application, the Commissioner of the Patent and Trademark Office will refer it to an examiner to determine whether the mark is entitled to be registered. If it is, the mark is published in the *Trademark Official Gazette,* which notifies everyone that federal registration is pending for the mark, so that objections to its registration can be filed. If no objections are forthcoming in the next 30 days, the trademark is considered registered.

Rejection of application   If an examiner decides that the symbol is not a valid trademark, he will refuse to register it. You then have up to six months to appeal this decision or to change your mark and resubmit it for consideration. If you fail to do so, the application is considered abandoned unless you can show that the delay was unavoidable. In that case, the time to reply may be extended.

Consequences of registration   Once your trademark is registered, it is placed on the *principal register,* which announces your claim of ownership and right to use it exclusively. Anyone subsequently using the mark is liable for infringement. Registration protects the trademark for 20 years and may be renewed, but after the first 6 years, you must file an affidavit with the Patent Office saying that the mark is still in use.

Notice of trademark   As the owner of a registered trademark, you must display with it the words "Registered in the U.S. Patent Office," "Reg. U.S. Pat. Off.," or the letter "R" enclosed in a circle. Failure to give this notice will prevent you from recovering damages for infringement of your mark, unless the defendant knew the mark was registered.

Interference and opposition   Sometimes an application is made to register a mark that resembles one previously registered by someone else. If your new trademark is likely to cause confusion or to deceive purchasers, the commissioners may declare that an *interference* exists. Similarly, if any other person feels that he would be damaged by the registration of your mark, he may, upon payment of a specified fee, file a notice of *opposition* in the Patent Office, stating his grounds within 30 days after the publication of the mark in the *Trademark Official Gazette.* A member of the public who has no personal interest in your trademark cannot oppose it.

Cancellation   A person who believes that he is or will be damaged by a registered mark may apply for its cancellation. Your trademark may be canceled if it was wrongfully registered, because, for example, it consists of merely descriptive matter; it is similar enough to a previous mark to cause confusion; it is a corporate name; it is deceptive or misleading; or it has been abandoned. The registration of a trademark may also be canceled if at the end of the first six years the owner fails to file an affidavit with the Patent Office saying that the mark is still in use.

Appeals   An appeal of a registration or interference decision may be taken to the Commissioner of Patents. The final decision of the Patent Office may then be appealed to the U.S. Court of Customs and Patent Appeals.

Assignments and licenses   Trademarks can be transferred from one business to another by ASSIGNMENT or LICENSE, provided the transfer is made by the business that has been using it and the assignee uses the trademark in the same sense as originally conveyed by the trademark. An assignment transfers full title to (ownership of) the trademark. A license does not pass title to the licensee, nor does it permit him to assign the trademark to anyone else.

Infringement   Infringement of a trademark means that another person has used the trademark without permission on goods similar to those identified by the mark. It is a FRAUD to pass off your goods under someone else's mark. For example, in recent years, poor-quality denim jeans bearing a famous maker's trademark have been offered for sale in Europe. This actual copying and use of a trademark on the same type of goods is infringement.

Another method of infringement is the unauthorized use of a trademark on dissimilar goods, which reduces the value of the trademark by its extensive use. This is an exception to the general rule that a trademark may be used on dissimilar goods. Let us say a manufacturer of toilet paper used the trademark of a high-fashion line of clothes for his product. This use dilutes or reduces the good will built up for the fashion trademark.

The trademark does not have to be copied exactly; similarity is sufficient. However, the imitation must be so close to the original that a person who usually purchases the original goods would be deceived into mistakenly purchasing the other.

It is not necessary to prove actual deception or confusion of purchasers in order to prove infringement and stop the person from using your trademark—a reasonable probability of confusion is enough. This is established by polling the average purchasers of such a product about the similarity of the marks. To recover money DAMAGES in a lawsuit, however, you must prove actual deception of the public.

Defenses   There are various defenses against a suit for trademark infringement. For example, if the defendant can establish that the trademark he is accused of infringing is invalid, he will escape liability. This defense was used successfully by competitors of the Miller Brewing Company against Miller's trademark infringement lawsuit challenging the use of the word "light" in describing a low-calorie beer. (See "Requirements for a valid trademark," above.)

If the trademark is not federally registered, a person who has innocently used it in another part of the country may not be guilty of infringement. An innocent user of an unregistered mark will not be held liable for damages, but he may be enjoined (prevented) from further use of it. If the trademark is federally registered, innocent use is not a valid defense.

Abandonment of a trademark by its owner may be used as a defense in an infringement suit. There must, however, be clear proof that the owner intended to abandon the mark. Nonuse of a trademark for two consecutive years is evidence of abandonment but may be rebutted by evidence that shows that there was no intent to abandon the trademark. If, for instance, a trademark is temporarily discontinued while its owner experiments with a different color or design, there is no intent to abandon.

■ **Trade names** Trade names are distinctive names used in commerce to designate a particular business (such as the Stork Club), a place where a business is located (such as Napa Valley wines), or a class of goods (such as the Marantz Pro-Line stereo systems). A trade name is really descriptive of the manufacturer or dealer. It is a valuable property right that helps to secure a good reputation for a business and can be sold as part of its good will.

Trade names are different from trademarks because they are not exclusively attached to a particular product in order to identify the source, quality, or nature of that product to the public. They may contain descriptive words or words that are in common use, which would not be allowed registration as trademarks. A name may become a trade name as the result of use by a business or it may be a corporate name, registered with the state and reserved for exclusive use by that corporation. The first business to use a trade name and give it value owns it.

A trade name does not necessarily preserve an exclusive right for its owner. For example, Wm. Smith and Co. may come to be associated with a store that sells fine furniture in Davenport, Iowa. That use makes it a trade name that is valuable to that business. The right to use the name is not exclusive, as a trademark would be, because other people named William Smith have a right to use their names. They do not, however, have the right to open a discount furniture store just outside of Davenport named the William Smith Furniture Company. That would infringe on the trade name already established by the existing store.

Trade names are favored and given broad protection under the law not only because they are valuable to their owners but also because they protect the buying public from fraud and confusion.

EXAMPLE The Aunt Jemima Mills Co. owned the trademark and name "Aunt Jemima's." It had been marketing flour under that trademark for over 20 years when another company, Rigney & Co., began selling maple syrup with "Aunt Jemima" on the label. The Aunt Jemima Mills Co. sued and was granted an order enjoining Rigney & Co. from further use of the trademark and name. The court held that, even though the two companies were marketing different products, the unauthorized use of a name already owned by another was likely to confuse the public. Not only is the real owner wrongfully deprived of profits he is entitled to make, but the public is misled by relying on the established reputation of the known trade name.

A trade name can be—but does not have to be—registered. However, it must be used in order to establish the owner's rights. Some states provide for the registration of a fictitious name under which a business is conducted. For example, Raymond and Kenny Jackson may operate a business that they call Family Drug Store. If they register this fictitious name with the state, that will serve to notify everyone of their use of "Family Drug Store" as a trade name. Registration does not conclusively establish their ownership of the trade name, but it does record when they began using the name in case of any future dispute. This is the type of protection given to a corporate name used as a trade name. In the case of a dispute over rights to the trade name, the corporate records help to establish use of the name in the state where the business was incorporated.

The owner of a trade name has the right to collect damages from anyone who wrongfully appropriates it, and the owner can obtain an INJUNCTION (a court order) against further use of the name. Damages may amount to all the profits the wrongdoer has made by using the name.

EXAMPLE R. H. Macy & Co., a department store in New York City, sells a high volume of women's clothing and accessories every year, shipping items to customers all over the country. When a women's clothing store opened in Oklahoma under the name Macys Inc., R. H. Macy & Co. sued to prevent use of its trade name. The Oklahoma businessman claimed that he used the name Morris but that his given name was Moses, or Moesche in Yiddish, which he pronounced Macy. The court determined, however, that he had intentionally chosen the name to cash in on the popularity of the New York store's name and ordered him to stop using it.

Trade names are also protected by antidilution and unfair competition laws that may provide for punitive damages in addition to court orders prohibiting their further use by the appropriator. An *antidilution statute* forbids any business practice that gradually diminishes the value of a trade name—for example, by using it on inferior goods or goods of a different type. In addition to damages and injunctions, anyone who wrongfully appropriates someone else's trade name may be subject to criminal penalties—a fine or imprisonment.

■ **Unfair competition** Any person who tries to pass off his goods or business as someone else's is engaging in unfair competition. Infringement of trademarks, misappropriation of trade names, wrongful taking of trade secrets, and price-fixing in violation of federal and state laws all constitute unfair competition. The law of unfair competition is designed to protect the honest businessman, to punish the dishonest businessman who is taking his competitor's trade away by unfair means, and to protect the public from the deception (FRAUD) that arises from such unfair practices.

The law of unfair competition extends only to fraudulent practices that cause confusion of goods and deception of the public. It is not aimed at favoring MONOPOLY or preventing competition.

EXAMPLE The earliest manufacturer of watches in Waltham, Massachusetts, was the American Waltham Watch Co. At first, the manufacturer used "Waltham" on the face of its watches in a merely geographical sense.

Long use of the word associated it in the minds of customers with this particular company. People generally referred to its product as "Waltham Watches." A second company then began manufacturing watches in the town, and it was quickly ordered by the court to stop naming its product "Waltham Watches." It continued to put on the plates of its watches the words "Waltham" or "Waltham, Mass." The Supreme Judicial Court of Massachusetts held that even this was unfair competition. The court said that the first in a field has a right to put latecomers to some trouble to distinguish their product from one already established.

Methods by competitors that popularize their products without causing deception or confusion are not prohibited. Actual or probable deception must be shown.

If there is no agreement restricting an employee from engaging in a competitive business, he may leave to carry on a similar business in the same neighborhood. He may even approach the customers of his former employer, provided he does not use trade secrets and confidential information from his former position or diminish his former employer's good will or reputation.

Federal control   The Federal Trade Commission Act states that unfair competition as well as unfair or deceptive acts and practices in commerce is unlawful. The FEDERAL TRADE COMMISSION (FTC) enforces this law in the public interest. The FTC will act only when deception is practiced on the public, such as when false and misleading labels are placed on products. The FTC has the power to suppress unfair methods of competition by issuing a *cease and desist order* (similar to a court's injunction) to stop the unlawful conduct. Violations of such orders and deliberate breaking of FTC rules and regulations can be punished by fine. The FTC can also sue in federal or state court for money damages on behalf of businesses that have been injured by unfair or deceptive acts or practices.

■ **Remedies for the injured business**   Because unfair competition includes trademark infringement as well as the unauthorized use of trade names, there are common remedies available in all three instances.

Injunction   The first thing a plaintiff in an unfair competition action wants is to stop the illegal conduct. If there is clear proof that the value of his trademark or trade name is being irreparably harmed, for example, a court can grant a preliminary INJUNCTION, pending the outcome of the lawsuit. If the plaintiff wins his lawsuit, the court grants a permanent injunction and perhaps damages to permanently prevent the defendant from misusing the plaintiff's mark or name. Failure to obey the injunction is a CONTEMPT of court, punishable by a fine or imprisonment or both. If an injunction is granted to protect the exclusive right to a trademark or trade name, it must be limited to the territory within which the mark or name has a business value. The use of a nationwide trade name or a federally registered trademark is forbidden throughout the country.

EXAMPLE Vacuous Company made the most expensive vacuum cleaners in the country. Every housewife who could afford the $500 price wanted one. Value-Added Company began advertising "rebuilt Vacuous vacuum cleaners" for only $100. Whenever people responded to the advertisement, Value-Added sent salesmen to their homes. The salesmen told prospective customers that the rebuilt Vacuous was not really very good and tried to switch them to a $500 Value-Added machine that was in direct competition with the better-known Vacuous cleaners. Vacuous sued, claiming that this was a bait-and-switch scheme—a form of unfair competition.

The court agreed and entered an injunction prohibiting the practice. Value-Added stopped runnng the offending advertisements, but its door-to-door salesmen continued to use the same tactic. They offered cheaper rebuilt Vacuous cleaners in order to get inside a person's home, and then they tried to switch the customer to an expensive Value-Added machine. Vacuous went back into court seeking to enforce the injunction by way of contempt. The court held that Value-Added was willfully disobeying the court order prohibiting bait-and-switch and found that that was a contempt of court. The company was fined $1,000 and the injunction was continued.

Damages   A plaintiff also wants to be compensated for the financial losses he has suffered by the misappropriation of his trademark or trade name or by the unfair competition. These are known as *compensatory damages.* Among the losses he may recover are the injury to his business standing or good will; the impairment of the good will of his trademark; the loss of business or profits on lost sales; and the loss from the reduction of the price of goods caused by the defendant's wrong. A court determines these DAMAGES by ordering an accounting of the monetary loss suffered by the plaintiff and the profits earned by the defendant.

EXAMPLE A man from Rhode Island sued the Columbia Broadcasting System in what one court called a case of " 'coincidence' run riot . . . more bizarre than most television serial installments." The man charged CBS with unjust enrichment, infringement of his common-law service mark, and unfair competition. He said that he had spent two years as a young man working as a cowboy out West. His fondness for the way of life never diminished, even after he returned to Rhode Island to work as a mechanic. In 1947 he began to participate in rodeos, horse shows, horse auctions, and parades. He developed a distinctive Western character, whom he called Paladin, to play in these shows. He wore a black cowboy suit, a black flat-crowned hat with a St. Mary's medal on it, an old derringer hidden under his arm, and a holster with a chess piece on it. He passed out calling cards featuring a chess piece and the words "Have Gun Will Travel, Wire Paladin, N. Court St., Cranston, R.I." In the late 1950's, CBS began to run a weekly television series *Have Gun Will Travel,* in which Richard Boone played a knight-errant of the Old West who was always on the side of Good—for a fee. The television Paladin and his calling card were virtually identical to the character of the mechanic from Rhode Island. The show was enormously successful for more than eight years, grossing more than $14 million.

The television people testified steadfastly that all similarities between the two characters were purely coincidental. A federal magistrate ordered them to account in detail for all profits from the series in order to fix the amount of damages CBS would have to pay. It held that they were guilty of infringement of the service mark in copying the calling card and of unfair competition.

A U.S. court of appeals reversed the decision. It said, among other things, that there can be no damages except for competing unfairly in business. Because the Rhode Island man played his cowboy character only as a weekend hobby, it was not certain that he had suffered any business injury. Furthermore, there was not enough evidence to show that the public was actually confused by the two characters. Although the court recognized that the plaintiff had lost something of value, it held that the law afforded him no relief in this case.

Punitive damages may be awarded to punish a defendant in cases where there was a willful and deliberate wrongdoing.

Damages for the infringement of trademarks used in interstate or foreign commerce are governed by federal law as are violations of a federal law, such as a Federal Trade Commission rule. Otherwise, state law controls.

Criminal actions Various forms of unfair competition may subject the violator to criminal prosecution under state and federal law. Persons convicted of such actions may be punished by fine or imprisonment or both. A manufacturer of work clothes in Pennsylvania was convicted of sewing counterfeit union labels into garments. A gasoline dealer in Arkansas was convicted of filling his tanks with a brand of gasoline different from that named on his sign and pumps. A dairy owner in New York was convicted of refilling bottles from another dairy and then selling them. All of these criminal practices constituted unfair competition.

trade union A group of workers of the same trade or several related trades who unite to obtain favorable wages, hours, working conditions, and benefits. The International Brotherhood of Electrical Workers is a trade union. The United Auto Workers is an INDUSTRIAL UNION. See LABOR RELATIONS.

trading coupon A ticket, certificate, or order blank that can be exchanged for something of value, such as money or a discount on a purchase. Trading coupons can be distributed with the product; in advertising circulars, newspapers, or magazines; or by themselves. A coupon creates legal obligations based on the terms written on it. Generally, the coupon is proof of a promise by a manufacturer to give something of value to a person who buys his product and presents the coupon for redemption.

A trading coupon may be in the form of a rebate mailed to the purchaser from the manufacturer. To get a rebate the purchaser must send in the rebate coupon and a sales slip to prove that he bought the product. Many coupons, however, offer a discount that is granted at the time of purchase.

EXAMPLE The manufacturer of a new dessert topping wants O→* to create interest in its product, so it buys advertising space in all the women's magazines and includes a 10-cents-off coupon. The coupon says that anyone who purchases the new dessert topping can pay 10 cents less than the price marked on the product if he presents the coupon at the time of purchase. The small print on the coupon also informs retail merchants that the manufac-

turer promises to pay back 10 cents plus a small service charge for each coupon returned by a merchant.

This promise on the coupon is a CONTRACT that is enforceable as soon as the retail merchant takes the manufacturer up on his offer. The merchant must submit proof that he bought enough stock to have made the sales he claims.

The obligations created by coupons may also be enforceable by criminal penalties. In many places it is a FRAUD to misuse coupons. For example, a merchant who returns coupons to a manufacturer and claims a refund without ever having sold the product may be guilty of a crime.

EXAMPLE A district attorney discovered widespread fraud O→* by a coupon-clipping ring that was collecting thousands of dollars a week by falsifying purchase orders. The scheme was uncovered when a large manufacturer, cooperating with the police, accepted coupons for a product that never existed. Several retailers were arrested after they mailed coupons and false records to the manufacturer, claiming that they had bought and sold quantities of the nonexistent product.

trading stamps Printed stamps that can be accumulated and pasted into booklets and then exchanged for merchandise. Three parties are involved in a trading stamp transaction: a trading stamp company, a retail merchant, and a customer of the merchant. A trading stamp company prints up its own stamps in a distinctive design. Then it negotiates agreements permitting, or licensing, retail merchants to give stamps to customers according to the amount of money they spend at the merchant's store. The retailer pays the company for the stamps he distributes.

The customer saves stamps he accumulates from different purchases and pastes them into a booklet provided by the trading stamp company. When filled, these books can be exchanged for merchandise offered by the trading stamp company through a catalog or at a redemption center.

The entire trading stamp plan is based on the consumer's quest for stamps. Consumers will generally patronize the stores that offer the stamps they collect.

■ **Trading stamp exchanges** In the 1960's there were some half dozen major distributors of trading stamps. A family primarily interested in S & H green stamps (distributed by the Sperry and Hutchinson Company) would occasionally receive another brand of trading stamps. Most people simply traded among friends to acquire the brand of trading stamps they were collecting. But this informal exchange did not always meet customers' need for additional stamps. To fill the need, some individuals and retailers began to set up trading stamp exchanges. For a fee of 25 or 50 cents, the service would exchange one kind of stamp for the same number of another.

The trading stamp companies were opposed to these exchanges because a customer who could get the stamps he or she needed from an exchange had no incentive to patronize the stores that had purchased the stamps. The stamp company's system of promoting business was therefore seriously undercut.

EXAMPLE Sperry and Hutchinson, the largest trading stamp O→* company, vigorously prosecuted lawsuits against the trading stamp exchanges. Between 1964 and 1966 it was involved in 43 actions in 19 states. In every one of those lawsuits an injunction (a court order) was granted against the exchange.

Then the Federal Trade Commission began investigating Sperry and Hutchinson to determine whether the company was engaged in unfair methods of competition and violating federal trade laws prohibiting unfair business practices. It issued a cease and desist order prohibiting Sperry and Hutchinson from interfering with persons trafficking in its trading stamps.

A federal court reversed this order, and the Supreme Court let the decision stand. Trading stamp companies were once again allowed to sue stamp exchanges.

■ **Current legal status of stamps** As long as the trading stamp company honors its contract to provide stamps and publicity for its licensed retailers and to offer normal quality merchandise for consumers, the business is lawful.

Although trading stamps are still in some use, their popularity dropped dramatically in the 1960's as customers began to realize that stores issuing stamps had to pass along their cost to the customers.

transcript A copy, particularly an official or certified copy, of the record of what took place in a court during a trial or other legal proceeding.

transfer tax **1** A tax imposed on the passing of TITLE to (ownership of) property from the estate of a deceased person by INHERITANCE, DEVISE, or BEQUEST or a tax on a transfer of an interest (such as a life ESTATE) in such property. **2** A tax on the transfer of INCORPOREAL property, such as stocks and bonds, between living persons. See also ESTATE AND GIFT TAX. **3** A tax imposed by some states on the seller of real property (real estate) when he transfers the deed to the property to the buyer.

transitory action A lawsuit that can be tried in whatever place the defendant can be found and served with a SUMMONS. A transitory action differs from a *local action*, which can be tried only in the place where the reason for the lawsuit arose. Suits to recover DAMAGES for breach of CONTRACT or for injuries caused by NEGLIGENCE are transitory actions.

> EXAMPLE Linda took a bus from her home in Detroit to her grandmother's home in Fort Wayne, Indiana. A Chicago company owned the bus. There was an accident near Fort Wayne, and Linda was injured. She had a right to sue the bus company in Michigan, Indiana, or Illinois because her personal injury suit was a transitory action.

A suit involving the ownership of property is a local action and ordinarily must be tried in the county where the property is located.

> EXAMPLE Jake wanted permission from his zoning board to build a barn at the back of his suburban property and keep a horse for his daughter, even though such a barn would violate the zoning regulations in his neighborhood. The zoning board refused, and Jake wanted to sue. He had to bring his action against the zoning board in that county because his suit was a local action.

treason A breach of allegiance to a government by a person who owes allegiance to it. *Misprision of treason* is the crime of knowing about an act of treason or a treasonable plot and failing to report it to the proper authorities.

■ **Essential elements** Treason is regarded as the highest crime known to the law. According to the Constitution, "Treason against the United States, shall consist only in levying War against them, or in adhering to their Enemies, giving them Aid and Comfort." Treason is the only crime defined by the Constitution. There are no DEGREES of the crime of treason (such as in first or second degree MURDER), and the specific definition given in the Constitution leaves Congress no power to enlarge or restrict the offense.

Intent An intent to give aid and comfort to the enemy is an essential element of treason, and without it the crime is not committed. In treason the character of the act is not as significant as whether or not the act is done with an intent to betray.

Overt act A CONSPIRACY to overthrow the government or an intention to commit treason is not sufficient to constitute treason. There must be some overt act to carry out the traitorous intention. Although the crime of treason is not committed by expressions of opinion or criticism, words may be an element of the crime. For instance, statements made on a radio broadcast can amount to treason. Thus, during World War II, a U.S. citizen who had broadcast speeches, comments, and other propaganda from Germany to the United States in an effort to undermine the morale of American citizens was guilty of treason.

Aid and comfort to enemies Treason consists of "adhering" to the enemy and giving him "Aid and Comfort." The aid and comfort must be given during time of war. The courts have held that "adhering to their Enemies, giving them Aid and Comfort" includes such acts as furnishing the enemy with arms, troops, information, shelter, means of transportation, or any act indicating disloyalty to the United States and sympathy with the enemy.

Merely to favor the enemy is not sufficient, however. A person may favor the enemy and harbor sympathies or convictions disloyal to his country's policy or interest. But if he does not commit an act that aids or comforts the enemy, he has not committed treason.

An act that intentionally strengthens the government's enemies or that weakens the U.S. government's power to attack or resist its enemies amounts to aid and comfort.

> EXAMPLE A U.S. citizen of Japanese ancestry was attending a university in Japan at the outbreak of World War II. He completed his studies in 1943 and then went to work in Japan as an interpreter for a mining company that used American prisoners of war. His acts of cruelty to American prisoners working in the mines helped make them fearful, docile, and subservient. They tended to strengthen the Japanese war effort and therefore gave aid and comfort to the enemy.

■ **Persons liable** Treason can be committed by any person who owes allegiance to the government. ALIENS living in this country can commit treason because they owe allegiance to the United States while they stay here.

Treason differs from other crimes in that there are no ACCESSORIES. Persons who would be accessories in a felony, such as those who are present at the treasonable act and AID AND ABET or counsel the person who actually does it are all regarded as principals to treason.

■ **Defenses** A person will not be found guilty of treason if his treasonable acts were performed under coercion or compulsion rather than willingly or voluntarily. The defense of duress or compulsion is allowed only if the defendant feared immediate injury or death.

■ **Evidence** The Constitution stipulates that a conviction for treason requires the testimony of two witnesses to the same overt act or a confession made in open court. The purpose of this constitutional provision is to minimize the danger of convicting an innocent person. Although two witnesses must testify about the same act, their testimony does not have to be identical.

Treasury, Department of the
The department of the federal government that prints the currency and mints coins, acts as the government's financial agency, and recommends financial and tax policies. The Department of the Treasury includes the Bureau of Alcohol, Tobacco and Firearms; the Office of the Comptroller of the Currency; the United States Customs Service; the Bureau of Engraving and Printing; the Bureau of Government Financial Operations; the Internal Revenue Service; the Bureau of the Mint; the Bureau of the Public Debt; the United States Savings Bonds Division; and the United States Secret Service. The Secretary of the Treasury, who heads the department, is appointed by the President with the advice and consent of the Senate.

treasury stock
Shares of stock in a CORPORATION that the corporation has issued (sold or distributed to shareholders) and then reacquired. The corporation might reacquire the stock when someone sells it back to the corporation. The shares of stock then become an asset of the corporation. The corporation may want to hold treasury stock, for example, in order to sell it when cash is needed, thus saving the cost of borrowing money to raise the cash.

Shares of stock that the corporation has authority to issue but has not issued are usually not considered treasury shares. They are simply unissued shares.

treaty
A formal international agreement between two or more nations expressing in writing their agreement to be bound on some point negotiated by their representatives. Treaties extend to every concern that affects foreign relations under INTERNATIONAL LAW. For example, treaties fix boundary lines; they regulate commerce, smuggling, extradition, immigration, citizenship, war, and use of the sea.

■ **Negotiating a treaty** In order to negotiate a treaty or be a party to one, a government must have SOVEREIGNTY, or political independence. The United States is a sovereign power capable of making treaties, but the individual states of the Union are not. The states surrendered this power to the federal government so that the nation could speak on the subject of international affairs with one voice.

Traditionally, treaties were negotiated at high-level conferences by authorized diplomats who carried identification documents from their governments called "full powers." Thus the representatives themselves were often called *plenipotentiaries,* which means "those with full powers." Treaties, especially those of great economic or political importance, are still negotiated at high-level diplomatic conferences today. However, nations now conclude routine agreements by an informal exchange of diplomatic notes.

■ **Ratifying a treaty** Once a treaty has been negotiated, it must be formally ratified by each party according to the procedure of that country. The U.S. Constitution gives the PRESIDENT power to make treaties with the advice and consent of the Senate. After the President negotiates a treaty with another country, he submits it to the Senate for consideration. If at least two-thirds of the Senators voting on the treaty support it, it is ratified and becomes law in the United States.

The Constitution establishes that treaties, along with constitutional provisions and federal law, constitute "the supreme Law of the Land." This means that state laws cannot be enforced if they violate a U.S. treaty obligation, and court decisions must be consistent with treaties.

If there are questions about the validity and interpretation of a treaty, they must be answered by the branch of government or the leaders who formulate policy in a country. Such questions are political, not legal questions.

■ **Enforcing a treaty** Treaties are enforced by the pressure of international opinion and the necessity of order. Nations use economic and political pressure to force countries to honor treaties.

Ordinarily, a treaty remains in effect even though there is a change in the political status of one party. A new government that takes over an old government simply takes its place as a party to the existing treaty. The new government may, of course, choose to withdraw from a treaty, but the treaty remains valid until it does. If a party to a treaty is split into two new nations, other parties to the treaty may assume that both new nations remain bound to the treaty. If a party to a treaty is invaded and taken over by another country, its treaties become invalid because it no longer has sovereign political independence.

All the parties to a treaty can agree at any time to modify or abandon it. If one or more parties do not agree to modify a treaty, the remaining parties may still modify it if the treaty specifically allows such a change or if the change does not affect the parties who do not consent to it. In the end, however, a treaty cannot remain in effect if one party refuses to remain bound by it. If a nation violates a treaty, the other parties may try to negotiate a change that will preserve as much as possible of the treaty, they may choose to realign themselves against the violator, or they may give up the entire treaty as void. The original treaty is not valid after one party abandons it.

A violation of a treaty does not necessarily mean that a country wishes to abandon it. The parties may be able to obtain assurances that the violator—in spite of the violation—will henceforth honor its obligations. Even an act of WAR is not always a violation of a treaty, because some treaties—such as the Geneva Convention for the Amelioration of the Wounded and Sick of the Armies of the Field—are designed to regulate the conduct of war. These treaties usually deal with such problems as the treatment of noncombatants or prisoners of war or outlaw the use of certain types of weapons or methods of warfare.

treble damages
A tripling by the court of the amount of DAMAGES awarded by a jury to a plaintiff in a

lawsuit. Designed to discourage certain kinds of wrongful conduct, treble damages can be awarded only when allowed by statute.

trespass   An unlawful intrusion that interferes with someone else's possession of his PROPERTY. A trespass gives the property owner a right to bring a civil lawsuit and collect money DAMAGES for the interference and for any harm caused. Usually a trespass is considered an intentional TORT (a civil wrongdoing), but some states have laws that make trespass a crime and provide punishment by fines and imprisonment. Generally, a trespass is committed on real property (real estate or land and everything that is attached to it), but a trespass can also be to personal property (all other forms of property) as well.

■ **Trespass on land**   The owner of real property or anyone who has a lawful right to occupy the property—for example, the owner of an apartment building, a tenant, or a member of the tenant's family—can sue anyone who interferes with the right of ownership or possession. It does not matter whether the invasion is by the trespasser himself or something that he has put into motion. A hunter who enters a field where hunting is forbidden is a trespasser as is a demolition company that throws rocks onto neighboring land when it is blasting.

Every unlawful entry on another's property is trespass, even if no harm is done. A person who has a right to come onto the land may become a trespasser by committing wrongful acts after his entry. For example, the mailman has a right to come up the sidewalk at a private home, but he is not entitled to go through the front door and walk from room to room. It is also a trespass for a person who has permission to enter the property to stay after he has been told to leave. An intruder cannot defend himself in a trespass lawsuit by showing that the plaintiff did not have a completely valid legal right to the property. For example, the intruder cannot use as a defense the fact that a tenant's lease was not properly signed or that a purchaser had not yet received his DEED to the house.

To win his case, the plaintiff does not have to prove that the defendant intended to trespass but only that he intended to do the act that caused the trespass. Thus it does not matter that the trespasser does not understand the wrong or mistakenly believes that he is doing no wrong. For example, a child who swims in a neighbor's pond can be a trespasser, as can a hunter who thought he was shooting on his own land.

To be guilty of trespass, a person does not have to do injury to the property, although the amount of damages awarded in a suit for trespass will generally reflect the extent of any harm done.

EXAMPLE   Ebenezer, a crabby old recluse who never wanted O⊶⊷ people near him, sued a group of picnickers who ate lunch under a tree on the grounds surrounding his house. Because the picnickers had not harmed the property in any way, the court awarded Ebenezer only $5 in nominal damages. At another time, however, Ebenezer came upon four people camping out on his land and cutting down trees for firewood. He sued the campers and recovered a much more substantial amount in damages to pay for the lost trees.

Trespassers are responsible for most of the consequences of their unlawful entry, even those that probably could not have been anticipated or those that are not the result of anything wrongful beyond the trespass itself. For example, if a trespasser carefully lights a fire in the stove of a mountain cabin and a fault in the stove causes the cabin to burn down, the trespasser can be held liable. In a New York case, a balloonist was held responsible for all the damage done when he landed on the plaintiff's property and crowds rushed in, trampling the plaintiff's garden.

Trespass above and below land   Courts have had to consider how far up and how far down the right to possession of property extends. Although there is a public right to travel in the airspace over the United States, it is a trespass to infringe on a landowner's right to use and enjoy his property. Some cases have involved airplanes flying at low altitudes.

EXAMPLE   In a famous 1946 case, the U.S. Supreme Court O⊶⊷ held the U.S. government liable for harm caused to a poultry business by low-altitude military flights. The government was held responsible because its activity was deemed a "taking" of private property for which the Fifth Amendment requires just compensation. This type of taking has been considered by legal authorities as trespass of airspace over the plaintiff's property that interfered with his use of it.

It may be a trespass to tunnel or mine under another person's property, to force water or soil under his property, or to build a foundation that crosses under his boundary line. How far down the property owner's rights extend has not really been answered. Underground encroachments are usually an exception to the rule that no harm has to be shown in order to prove a trespass. Although there have been few cases to the contrary, trespass suits are generally permitted only where there is some damage to the land's surface or some interference with the owner's right to use his property.

EXAMPLE   A person in Yonkers, New York, sold property O⊶⊷ subject to two mortgages, the right of some monthly tenants, and the zoning ordinances of the city. The seller warranted that the property was free from any other legal encumbrances. Later, the buyer discovered that the Bronx Valley sewer commission had the right to build a sewer line 150 feet below the surface of the property. The buyer claimed that the seller had breached his warranty because this sewer line was another encumbrance. The court disagreed. It held that the sewer line was not an encumbrance because it did not interfere in any way with the buyer's use or possession of the property. The buyer would be entitled only to nominal damages because the sewer commission had no right of access to the sewer line from the surface of the purchaser's property and did not interfere with his use of the land.

Continuing trespass   A trespass is continuing when the offending object remains on someone else's property. A building or fence that encroaches on a neighbor's property creates a continuing trespass, as does a tree that falls across a boundary line or a parked car left long past the time when it should have been removed. Some courts have allowed a series of lawsuits for a continuing trespass, but the prevailing view is that the dispute should be settled entirely in one

ARE YOU TRESPASSING?

■ Trespass means not only unlawful entry of another's property but also any interference with the owner's possession and enjoyment of it.

■ You can trespass on someone's property without setting foot on it simply by causing something to cross the boundary lines—say, by throwing rocks on your neighbor's land.

■ You can be a trespasser even if you do not understand you committed a wrong or if you made a mistake. For example, a child who swims in a neighbor's pond can be a trespasser, as can a hunter who thought he was shooting on his own land.

■ Even if you have permission to go onto someone's land, you may be trespassing if you commit a wrongful act

after you enter. For example, if you are allowed to enter your neighbor's front yard to check his mail and while there you destroy his rosebush, you are guilty of trespass.

■ It is also a trespass if you allow an offending object to remain on someone else's property—for example, a tree that has fallen into your neighbor's yard or a parked car left for an unreasonable length of time.

■ Trespass to protect life or property may be justifiable in an emergency.

■ You cannot use force against a trespasser or intentionally injure him except when trying to prevent a violent crime, such as murder or robbery.

■ Although you are not ordinarily liable for the injuries suffered acci-

dentally by trespassers on your property, you may be responsible in some cases—such as in certain instances when trespassing children are injured.

■ A trespasser may not only be sued in civil court for the damage he has done but may also be prosecuted by the state for the crime of trespass.

■ Any unlawful entry on another's land that involves violence or injury to a person or property is criminal trespass. In some states, a trespass is criminal if the person entered the property for an unlawful purpose, such as robbery. In other states, trespass is not criminal unless a warning has first been given to the trespasser.

■ Criminal trespass is punishable by fine or imprisonment or both.

---

action. The remedies can be tailored to the particular kind of harm done. The defendant may be enjoined from (ordered to stop) carrying on an offensive activity, he may have to pay money damages to repair the plaintiff's property, or he may have to compensate the plaintiff for diminishing the value of his property. If a trespassing structure or object is on the plaintiff's property, the defendant may be ordered to remove it. If no physical object actually trespasses onto the plaintiff's property, he may instead be able to sue the defendant for NUISANCE if the peaceful enjoyment of his property is disturbed—for example, by noise or noxious odors.

Consent and license A person entering someone else's property with consent or LICENSE is not guilty of trespass unless he exceeds the bounds that are set by the consent or license.

Consent means that the owner allows someone on his land. A mother who lets the neighbor's children play in her yard has given consent. Consent does not have to be given expressly in every situation. It can be implied from the circumstances.

EXAMPLE If Pete calls a painter and asks for an estimate for painting the outside of his house, he cannot later complain that the painter trespassed when he came into the yard to get a good look at the house. But if the painter goes inside Pete's house and searches through his closets and drawers, Pete can sue him for trespass.

Sometimes consent to enter on another's land is called license, which is simply a legal term for permission. A license is usually a written agreement.

EXAMPLE The local electric company has a license to enter Lavinia's property for the purpose of maintaining electrical lines over her property. The employees of the electric company cannot act unreasonably, as by coming onto the property in the middle of the night and making excessive noise when there is no emergency, and they are liable for any damage they cause, such as breaking Lavin-

ia's picture window by backing their truck into it. Their license to enter is a defense to any claim of trespass.

The electric company did not get its license directly from Lavinia. It had first approached an earlier owner of the property 60 years ago and paid him a price for a license to enter and maintain the lines. Thereafter, the property had been sold to Lavinia, and she took it subject to the electric company's right, which was noted in the deed.

If a license to enter property is for a certain period, the holder of the license is guilty of trespass if he enters the property after the license expires. In the above example, if the electric company's license is for 60 years, it cannot come onto Lavinia's property after 60 years unless Lavinia renews the license. If its workers do so, they are trespassing.

Other justifications for entering In some cases, a defendant is not liable for trespass even though he has intruded on another's property without the owner's consent or license—for example, a police officer with a search warrant. See SEARCH AND SEIZURE. A policeman may also lawfully pursue a criminal across private property.

A person may not be guilty of trespass if he goes onto another's property in an emergency to protect life or property. For example, a passerby who sees a man pointing a gun at a woman may cross onto the property and jump him from behind, or someone at the scene of a traffic accident may go onto private property to pull a victim from a car.

A hotel employee who enters a guest's room in order to perform maid services is not a trespasser, because it is customary to assume that guests want their hotel rooms cleaned. A landlord, on the other hand, does not have the right to enter a tenant's apartment whenever he wants. See LANDLORD AND TENANT.

Trespass by one entitled to possession Confusing decisions have long come down in the courts when the person entitled to possession of real property tries to enter and recover it by force. In nearly all of the states, a person who forcibly enters land is guilty of a crime. The states provide legal procedures for a rightful owner to recover his land and seek in this way to discourage people from taking action that may lead to violence. Few things are more likely to lead to a brawl than a landlord trying to toss out a tenant on his own. In some states, an illegal occupant cannot sue the rightful owner for his forcible entry, but he can sue for ASSAULT AND BATTERY or damage to his personal property resulting from the forcible entry.

Duty to trespassers   There are limits to what a home-owner can do to protect his family and property from trespassers. Obviously he cannot shoot children who keep cutting through his yard, no matter how rude and annoying they are. Nor can he set deadly traps to kill anyone who dares trespass on his property. Deadly force in any manner is generally not justifiable except to prevent a violent fel-ony such as MURDER, RAPE, ROBBERY, ARSON, or BURGLARY. Mere trespass is not a felony.

The owner or person in possession of real property can be held liable if guests are injured on his property because of his NEGLIGENCE. A property owner does not have that same duty to make his premises safe for a trespasser. A trespasser assumes the risk that he might be injured by an unguarded excavation, a fence accidentally electrified by a fallen wire, or a broken stair. The occupier of real property has a duty only to refrain from intentionally injuring a trespasser after he discovers his presence on the premises. Reckless or wanton conduct is the same as an intentional act—for example, telling the trespasser to run and then turning loose vicious dogs. If a property owner knows that people frequently trespass at a particular place on his land, he must act affirmatively to keep them out or exercise more care to prevent injury to them.

EXAMPLE Jason has a mile-long driveway leading to his secluded mansion on the coast. Ordinarily, Jason can drive as he pleases on the driveway. But he knows that during the summer neighbors use the driveway as a shortcut to the beach on the other side. Consequently, during the summer months he must drive carefully and look out for them on the driveway.

Children who trespass   Most but not all states require the occupier of land to be more careful if the trespasser is a child. This is because a child cannot always be expected to understand and appreciate the dangers he may encounter and to weigh the risks of trespassing. Although it is true that parents and guardians are responsible for supervising children, the law does not require a child to be kept on a leash. The law recognizes that the property owner may be in the best position to prevent injury to a child he finds trespassing. There is no hard-and-fast rule, but generally the occupier of real property must refrain from hurting the child intentionally, as with any trespasser. In addition, he must pay money damages to any trespassing child who is injured as a result of the following four conditions:

(1) There is reason to know or expect that children will trespass there; for example, if the property is near the street or close to a playground.

(2) Whatever caused the injury could be expected to cause injury, such as an unfenced swimming pool or a tractor left running.

(3) It is likely that a child would not discover or appreci-ate the danger. For example, a three-year-old leaning

against a weak screen in a third-floor apartment window cannot understand the risk.

(4) The danger to a trespassing child outweighs the burden of correcting the dangerous condition or protecting children from it. For example, a homeowner whose cess-pool collapses can cover the hole and rope it off until repairs are made. A builder can close a door behind him and lock it before he leaves an unfinished house. It is not too much to expect precautions like these. If they are not taken, an owner or occupier of land can be held liable for injuries to children even if the children are trespassing.

■ **Trespass to personal property**   Long ago, the kinds of acts that made up trespass to land were also illegal if directed at another person's *chattels*—goods or personal property. A suit for trespass to chattels could be brought against someone for shooting a dog, frightening and stam-peding horses, rummaging through a purse, or cutting fishing nets. Like a trespass to land, these acts intruded and interfered with another person's rightful ownership or pos-session. Some cases allowed a lawsuit merely for the tres-pass without any showing of damage to the property, but others required proof of some injury resulting from the trespass. Of course, taking goods or depriving the plaintiff of the rightful possession of his chattels—even for a brief moment—was always a wrong, and that act could satisfy the requirement of actual injury.

Today laws and court decisions are more likely to men-tion damage or injury to personal property instead of using the older phrase, "trespass to chattels," but the same kinds of acts are still wrongful. Recent cases have concerned claims against defendants who moved into a new house and took furniture that the seller was going to remove a few days later and others who conducted a sit-in at a superin-tendent's office and soiled and damaged his furnishings.

■ **Criminal trespass**   In some states, a trespass is not criminal unless it is accomplished by violence or tends to be a BREACH OF THE PEACE. Some statutes make any unlawful entry on another's real property criminal. When the tres-pass involves violence or injury to a person or property, it is always considered criminal, and penalties may be increased for more serious or malicious acts. Criminal intent may have to be proved in order to convict a trespasser under some statutes, but in some states it is an offense to trespass regardless of intent. Some statutes consider a trespass criminal only if the intruder has an unlawful purpose in entering or remaining in the place where he has no lawful right to be. The unlawful purpose may be theft, arson, or an attempt to disrupt a government office, for example. Stat-utes in some states specify that a trespass is not criminal until after a warning has been given to the trespasser, either spoken or posted on signs. Criminal trespass is punishable by fine or imprisonment or both.

trial   A judicial examination of the issues raised in a civil or criminal action. This article briefly outlines the way a trial is conducted for a civil action. Criminal trials are discussed under CRIMINAL LAW.

A civil action (lawsuit) is a proceeding in a court of justice in which a decision is requested. Its purpose is to permit one party to sue another in order to redress a legal wrong or to enforce a legal right. For example, you may sue your neighbor for cutting down a tree on your property (a legal wrong, or TORT) or you may sue a mechanic to make him complete the repairs on your car for which he signed a CONTRACT with you, thereby enforcing a legal right. The complaining party in a civil suit is called the *plaintiff*. The party being sued is the *defendant*.

An action must be started and carried forward, or *maintained*, in the name of the party who has an interest in it. For example, a person can sue for himself, a parent can sue as a representative of his child or an executor in the interest of the estate he represents, but a person with no interest in the action cannot sue. If your neighbor throws a stone and breaks your picture window, you yourself can sue him, but your friend down the block cannot sue him in your name.

■ **Issues** A civil lawsuit starts when the first pleadings are filed. Pleadings are formal written statements that outline the issues of the case. The plaintiff usually begins by preparing his first pleading, called a complaint or petition, and having it served on the defendant. The *complaint* gives the plaintiff's version of the wrong he believes has been done him or the right he feels he has been deprived of and states the relief (money, services, or property) he claims to be due him. After the plaintiff's complaint has been served, the defendant serves his first pleading, usually called an *answer,* which responds to the claims and demands of the plaintiff by denying the plaintiff's version of the facts in the case and sometimes asserting the defendant's counterclaims against the plaintiff.

The plaintiff may then respond with a second pleading if he wishes to refute the facts and claims contained in the defendant's answer, and the defendant may respond with a second pleading. The pleadings are all filed with the appropriate court, and the case is scheduled for a courtroom trial before a judge and perhaps a JURY.

Generally, either the plaintiff or defendant may demand a jury, although a jury may not be allowed for disputes involving less than a specified amount or in courts with authority to hear cases involving only a small amount of money—small claims court, for example. Sometimes neither party wants a jury trial, either because it is slower and more costly or because the issues are complex.

At the trial, all questions in the case involving law (matters of law) are decided by the judge. Questions concerned with the facts of the case (matters of fact) are decided by the jury if there is a jury and otherwise by the judge. In other words, the jury decides what actually happened and the judge decides how the law should be applied to what happened.

■ **Selecting a jury** Names of jurors are drawn at random from a list of prospective jurors for each term of court. Such a *jury list* may be compiled from lists of voters, taxpayers, property owners, motor vehicle drivers, or from whatever else the state's law may direct. Before any trial can begin, the prospective jurors are questioned by the court (presiding judge) and sometimes by attorneys for the plaintiff and defendant. Prospective jurors may be challenged on the ground that they could not make an impartial decision. Attorneys for the plaintiff and defendant may object to jurors who seem unfavorable to each side's position on the issues. Other grounds for challenging jurors include (1) conviction of a serious crime, (2) financial

interest in the outcome of the litigation, (3) another proceeding pending between the prospective juror and a party to the trial, and (4) business, professional, or family relationship to a party. These are called *challenges for cause.* In addition, each party may challenge a specified number of jurors without stating a particular reason. Those are called *peremptory challenges.*

■ **Sequence of events** After the jury has been chosen and sworn, the trial proceeds in a particular order. First, in an opening statement the lawyer for the plaintiff (or the plaintiff himself if he appears PRO SE) concisely states his claim and the EVIDENCE by which he plans to prove it. Next, the defendant's lawyer briefly states his defense. Following these opening statements, the plaintiff produces his evidence in order to prove his case. He does this by presenting WITNESSES, documents, and exhibits. The defendant then offers his evidence in opposition. Rules concerning the offering of documents and exhibits and the examination and cross-examination of witnesses vary in different states and different courts. For the remainder of the trial, the parties are limited to presenting evidence rebutting each other's allegations, unless the court, in its discretion, permits further introduction of new material.

After the evidence has been presented, the parties present their closing arguments to the jury—first the plaintiff and then the defendant who tries to rebut the plaintiff's argument. Some jurisdictions permit the plaintiff to make a final argument after the defendant's rebuttal. When the arguments are concluded, the judge gives his final instructions, or charge, to the jury, stating the law applicable to the case and explaining what the jurors must decide. Either party may offer written instructions to the judge on matters of law and ask him to give them to the jury.

The jury retires to deliberate on the case in private, taking any written instructions into the deliberation room. When the jury has agreed upon a VERDICT, either for the plaintiff or for the defendant, it returns to the courtroom, and the foreman (the jury's presiding member and spokesman) announces the verdict. Based on the verdict, the court renders its JUDGMENT—the final determination of all the issues in the case. If the verdict given by the jury was for the plaintiff, the judgment would order the defendant to pay the plaintiff DAMAGES or provide other appropriate relief. Once the judgment has been given the trial ends.

tribunal A general term for a COURT.

trover The technical name for a lawsuit to recover DAMAGES for a wrongdoer's CONVERSION (wrongful taking or misuse) of personal property belonging to someone else. In trover actions, the measure of damages is normally the value of the property at the time of the conversion. Examples of actions in trover include conversion of corporate stock certificates, business account books, and animals. So long as you can identify your personal property, you can sue for its conversion, even though the physical form has changed considerably—for example, if someone has traded stock certificates you own for an automobile.

true bill The term written on an INDICTMENT for a crime, to show that the majority of the members of a GRAND

THE CIVIL TRIAL: FROM PLEADINGS TO VERDICT

HON. JOSEPH R. NOLAN
Associate Justice,
Massachusetts Appeals Court

If an examination of court records reveals anything, it is the fact that Americans are litigious people. "Pay me or I'll sue" is the battle cry. In increasing numbers, people are "going to law" to settle disputes. They complain because their cases are stalled in the judicial gristmill, which grinds so slowly partly because of the nature of the process but more especially because of the sheer volume of business. While a better substitute for going to law may someday be found, for most disputes there is no other satisfactory remedy on the horizon.

When two opposing parties go to law, their dispute is settled in a civil trial, which differs from a criminal trial. In a criminal trial, the government seeks to prove that a person is guilty of some crime, with the view of punishing him if he is guilty. A civil trial is a court proceeding in which a decision is requested. To whom does a certain piece of property belong? Should A be made to pay B the money B claims A owes him? Is a divorce to be granted? Were someone's civil rights curtailed? Can a landlord evict a tenant? Did one person cause the injury another is suffering, and if so, should he pay him money to help compensate for the injury? Did C breach his contract with D, as D claims? During a civil trial, each party, usually represented by a lawyer, battles with the other in the presence of a judge and often of a jury.

A civil trial is an adversary proceeding—a contest between two opposing parties theoretically equal because each is represented by a qualified lawyer.

The adversary process has evolved as the best system for resolving disputes when settlement is im-possible. Strife is at its very heart. Trial lawyers are the modern-day gladiators in the juridical forum. They are featured on TV as modern-day heroes. The lawyer stars never lose a case. Justice always appears to triumph, and the loser always appears to have deserved to lose.

Commencement of the action

A civil trial is commenced when a party with a grievance files with the court a document called a pleading, declaration, or complaint, which sets forth the facts that constitute the grievance. It may be as simple as "Plaintiff says that the defendant owes him the sum of $10,000 for money lent by the plaintiff to the defendant on March 17, 1981."

The plaintiff is the party with the grievance who is seeking redress. The defendant is the party against whom he is seeking redress. A civil case, or lawsuit, may be cited in the lawbooks as "Peter Moran, Plain-tiff, *v.* Sylvester Magruder, Defendant."

If the plaintiff wants to hold some of the defendant's property as security for payment if he wins the case, he can ask the court to *attach* (hold in custody) the defendant's real estate or other property—that is, he can get a court order to prevent the defendant from selling or otherwise transferring the property to someone else until the lawsuit is ended. However, the defendant has a constitutional right to appear before the court and be heard before his property can be attached, unless the plaintiff can convince the court (lawyers use the word "court" for "judge") that immediate action is required to prevent the defendant from disposing of the property before a hearing can be scheduled. Even if this request is granted, the defendant has the right to present to the court reasons why the attachment should be lifted or reduced in amount. A plaintiff who abuses this power of attachment runs the risk of being sued for malicious abuse of process.

The next step requires the defendant to file an answer to the plaintiff's pleading. He may deny that he owes anything. He may admit that he owes money but plead that the statute of limitations has run out and that the plaintiff's claim is barred because he did not bring the action within the period prescribed by law. A host of answers are available to the defendant under appropriate circumstances. A defendant may even become a plaintiff in a sense by asserting his own claim against the plaintiff. This device is known as a counterclaim.

The plaintiff must decide at the outset whether he wishes to try his case before a jury or before a judge sitting without a jury. In some states, the amount in controversy governs whether a jury is available in the first instance. If a plaintiff is permitted to avail himself of a jury, he must decide whether it is the kind of controversy that he wants decided by a jury. A complicated fact and law problem may better be decided by a judge, although the jury system has much to recommend it. A plaintiff may decide not to claim a jury, but the defendant may exercise his right for one. If either party requests a jury, and a jury is permitted for the controversy involved, then the trial will be heard by a jury even if it is against the wishes of the other party.

Pretrial discovery

Both plaintiff and defendant have a right to discover facts the other may be holding in his hand. Liberal discovery rules permit each party to compel answers to *interrogatories*—questions propounded by one side to the other, which require answers under oath. These questions and answers may be used at trial. Fuller statements of a party's case are available through depositions, which can require one party to submit to questioning under oath by counsel for the other party. Even prospective witnesses may be deposed. A court has power to prevent oppressive and unreasonable discovery.

Discovery is important. It shortens the time required for trial. It gives to each party a clearer picture of the "cards" held in his opponent's hand. It permits a party to take a second look at his case. It results in settlements when the weaker side is faced with overwhelming odds against victory.

Many lawyers believe that every case can be settled. Although it is true that too many cases that should be settled are being tried, there is a hard core of cases that just do not lend themselves to settlement short of a verdict or a finding by a judge. The chemistry of the litigants plays a large part in settlement. There are some people who "stand on principle." They picture a settlement as a compromise of their principles. They seek vindication without much thought as to the money involved. Some are looking for "blood." To these people, settlement is abhorrent. To another type of person, a bird in the hand is the goal. The vagaries of a trial, particularly a jury trial, are problems to avoid. Personal aversion to the strife engendered in a lawsuit forces many settlements. If the case cannot be settled, a trial follows.

Jury selection

On a jury list (venire), jurors are merely names, addresses, and occupations. But jurors are really people, human beings with emotions, prejudices, virtues, and vices. The ideal jury is composed of 12 or 6 persons who pay strict attention to all the evidence and do not permit their prejudices to interfere with a true verdict based on evidence. Their verdict is not based on a hunch, a "sneaky feeling," a whim, or a good guess. It is based on the evidence.

When the jury is impaneled, the judge is required to ask each prospective juror certain questions to determine whether or not he or she meets the minimum standards of fairness and whether or not he or she is related to or familiar with the parties, attorneys, and witnesses in the case. If the judge finds a juror with a bias or interest in the case, he excuses that person. The judge declares the balance of the panel "indifferent."

At this point the attorneys for the plaintiff and defendant may examine the prospective jurors and exercise their right to challenge them.

Each side to the case has a certain number of challenges, called peremptory challenges, that may be exercised without giving any reason for the challenge. If the defendant is a taxi driver, the plaintiff may challenge all taxi drivers on the panel. Most jurors never know the real reason why they have been challenged. One old lawyer who represented plaintiffs in personal injury actions routinely challenged druggists because, as he was wont to say, "They think small because they are always working with small items like pills." The logic may be weak, but the pharmacists on his jury list were challenged.

In addition to peremptory challenges, for which no reason need be given, a party may challenge a prospective juror "for cause." The judge must pass upon these challenges. A challenge for cause may be made because of an apparent friendship between the juror and the opponent or because of a similarity between the juror's occupation and that of a party to the trial.

Opening statement to jury

The plaintiff has the privilege of opening and closing the case. He is the first to address the jury and the last. In his opening, counsel (attorney) for the plaintiff outlines the case. A well-prepared opening argument or statement enables the jury to follow the scenario of the case, but it is not evidence on which the jury may base a verdict.

The defendant's attorney may make an opening immediately after the plaintiff's, or he may wait until the plaintiff's case is completed. This timing depends upon defense strategy. A defendant's lawyer may wish to blunt a particularly effective opening before it can take its effect on the jury. On the other hand, defense counsel may prefer to wait until all the plaintiff's evidence has been presented and then to launch an attack before presenting his own evidence. Generally, the defendant's approach is to remind the jury that there are two sides to every controversy and that fairness demands they give the defendant the opportunity to present the other side of the case.

Presentation of evidence

After the opening statement or statements, the plaintiff is ready to call his first witness. Strategy differs from lawyer to lawyer and from case to case. In some instances, the first witness will be the most important, while in other cases counsel will build up to a climax, saving his best ammunition until the end.

The witness is sworn by the clerk of court, and the plaintiff begins his examination of the witness. Such examination is called direct examination, and the rules of evidence must be observed. A witness must not be led by questions that suggest the answer, because leading questions are not proper except in unusual circumstances.

The following is a leading question: "When you approached the taxi and saw the defendant thrashing the plaintiff, what did you do?" What is wrong with this question is that it assumes the truth of the statement that the defendant was thrashing the plaintiff. If opposing counsel thinks that a question is improper, he must immediately object. On the other hand, the question may be proper, but the answer may violate a rule of evidence—as, for example, an answer that is not responsive to the question. If the witness is asked, "What did you say to the defendant at this time?" his answer is unresponsive if he says, "I went to New York City." If this occurs, defense counsel moves to strike the answer from the record. And so it goes—question and answer.

When the direct examination of the witness has been completed, counsel for the defendant takes the witness on cross-examination. It has been said that cross-examination of a witness is the gristmill for truth. The goal of the cross-examiner may be to reveal to the jury a weakness in the witness's direct testimony that did not become apparent under the friendly questions of the direct examiner. The cross-examiner may impeach the witness's testimony—that is, challenge its credibility—by eliciting bias, prejudice, or inability to know the facts that he testified to and that are crucial to the other party's case. A good cross-examiner will never permit the witness to buttress his direct testimony.

Unless a witness has hurt a party's case, it is good practice not to cross-examine. It may boomerang. There is an art in knowing when not to cross-examine.

If the witness has been called by the plaintiff, the next examination after cross-examination of this witness is called redirect. Often its purpose is to rehabilitate a witness whose testimony has been shredded by a zealous cross-examination. There may then follow recross-examination if necessary.

In addition to the testimonial evidence obtained from witnesses, there is also real evidence (objects), including documentary evidence, which a jury may consider. In a contract case, a copy of the contract is evidence just as truly as the testimony of a witness. A viewing by the jury may be evidence in the case of a taking of real estate by eminent domain (by the government). In this instance the judge and jury travel to the property that was taken and examine it along with counsel for both parties—the state and the owner. The impressions of the jury at the scene constitute evidence, which the jury may consider in rendering their verdict. Photographs are also competent evidence if they fairly represent a matter relevant and important to the case and if they are not so inflammatory as to prejudice the jury.

The jury is permitted to draw all reasonable inferences from the evidence presented. It is in connection with inferences that mention should be made of circumstantial evidence. For example, if one issue in a case is whether the newsboy has delivered the morning paper, evidence tending to show that the paper has been delivered every morning by the newsboy is admissible. When the owner testifies that he opened his front door and found the newspaper, the jury may infer that it was delivered by the newsboy. Nobody has seen the newsboy nor heard him. It is possible that a neighbor on this particular morning, knowing the newsboy was ill, left the paper. However, the jury may infer that it was the newsboy. On the other hand, in the absence of eyewitness testimony, the jury may not infer that the newsboy wore a red sweater, because such an inference is unreasonable, even though it is possible that he did.

Rules of evidence

Baseball requires the presence of an umpire and certain rules. A trial requires a judge to make rulings of law and to enforce the rules of evidence. These rules are necessary if the ultimate goal—a just verdict—is to be achieved. In the ordinary civil case, the plaintiff has the burden of proving his case by a fair preponderance of the evidence. This concept has been described as greater likelihood than not. Using the analogy of a scale, the plaintiff must demonstrate by the evidence that the scale is tilted in his favor. He is not required to prove his case overwhelmingly, nor is he required to eliminate all causes of his harm except the defendant's wrongdoing. This is seldom possible. It would impose an impossible burden. However, the jury is not permitted to guess or to play hunches as to the defendant's liability.

It is the judge's function, when an objection to evidence is raised, to rule whether the evidence is admissible or not. Herein lies the importance of the rules of the game—the rules of evidence. If the judge errs in administering these rules an appellate court may reverse his ruling. These are questions of law and they concern only the judge. They are distinguished from questions of fact (what actually happened), which are reserved for the jury.

A common example of inadmissible evidence is hearsay. While everybody relies on hearsay evidence

in his daily life, such evidence is not the most reliable for searching out the truth in the judicial forum. What somebody has said out of court, while he is not under oath and at a time when he is not confronted by the person against whom his statement is offered, is hearsay, and unless qualified under one of the exceptions, it is not admissible evidence. It is essential that counsel object to inadmissible evidence because without an objection the judge will not rule and the evidence will remain in the case for the jury's consideration.

A plaintiff is required to introduce some competent evidence on every component of his case. If he fails, the judge, if requested by the defendant, is required to direct a verdict for the defendant. In this instance, the jury never takes the case for deliberation because there is but one verdict that can be rendered and this is for the defendant. The plaintiff in this instance has failed, not because the jury does not believe him but because he has not presented a case for their consideration.

Closing arguments

After the plaintiff has introduced all the evidence that he has, he rests. It is time for the defendant's case to be presented. The same order of witness examination follows—direct, cross, redirect, and perhaps recross. When the defendant has rested, the time has arrived for the final arguments. The defendant argues to the jury first. The plaintiff then addresses the jury.

Closing arguments are not evidence, but they represent an important part of the trial. Each attorney contends for his position. The defendant's lawyer may adopt the role of the spoiler. He may appeal to the jury's sense of fairness and urge the jurors not to succumb to the anticipated arguments of the plaintiff's lawyer. He will strive to point out inconsistencies in the plaintiff's case. He will try to persuade the jury that justice can be accomplished only by a verdict for the defendant. He will expose whatever gaping holes there might be in the plaintiff's case and try to persuade the jury that the plaintiff has not met his burden of persuasion.

The plaintiff has the last word with the jury. This is a distinct advantage. He is able to answer the defendant's arguments as well as promote his own case. He will generally acknowledge that he has the burden but will hasten to point out that he has met that burden. While sympathy should play no part in a juror's consideration, a plaintiff commonly insinuates sympathy.

Judge's instructions, jury's verdict

It is then time for the judge to instruct the jurors as to their obligations. In many states, the judge is forbidden to comment on the weight or persuasive power of the evidence. This element is exclusively the jury's province. However, a judge may refer to the evidence for the purpose of instructing the jury in the law.

Although the jurors are the sole arbiters of the facts, they are not free to apply law to these facts. They are required to take the law from the judge. They may not like the law as it stands but apply it they must. It is the judge's function to teach the jury about the burden of proof, the applicability of inferences, the effect of legal documents, and the elements of the plaintiff's case. The jury is routinely told that it must decide whether a witness is to be believed in whole or in part. Credibility of witnesses is the exclusive domain of the jury. Before proceeding to decide the amount of damages to be awarded the plaintiff, jurors are told to decide whether or not the defendant is liable (financially responsible). It is only after this adjudication of liability that the jury should concern itself with the question of how much to award the plaintiff. A unanimous vote is not required to decide civil cases in most states.

The jury system is not perfect. Although cautioned against permitting bias, sympathy, and prejudice to infect their verdict, jurors are human beings. They bring into the jury box all their virtues and vices. All that can be expected is that they will do their best to give a verdict unaffected by their prejudices, because the prejudices do not vanish when the juror's oath is taken. Americans boast of their sense of fair play. They are capable of returning just verdicts. They do so every day.

JURY found the evidence presented to them sufficient to warrant a prosecution.

trust   A relationship in which someone holds property for the benefit of another. The person who creates the trust is the *settlor;* the person who holds the property for another's benefit is the *trustee;* the person who benefits from the trust is the *beneficiary;* and the property that makes up the trust is the *trust property.*

> EXAMPLE Rose's mother signs over certain stock to a bank O──✳ with instructions to give Rose the dividend checks each year until she turns 30, when she is to get all the stock. Rose's mother is the settlor of the trust, the bank is the trustee, the stock is the trust property, and Rose is the beneficiary.

A settlor of a trust may designate that he is to be sole beneficiary of a trust, with another person acting as trustee. This type of trust is known as a *self-settled* trust, because the settlor is taking care of himself. Rose's mother could have told the bank that only she was to receive the dividend checks until she died.

A person may keep the right to revoke the trust at any time and have the trust property returned to him. This is known as a *revocable trust,* and keeping the right to revoke the arrangement must be clearly stated at the time the trust is created. Otherwise, a trust is irrevocable. The person who sets up an *irrevocable trust* cannot demand that the trust be ended or that the property be returned to him. In the above example, Rose's mother created an irrevocable trust because she did not state that she intended to keep the right to revoke the arrangement.

A trust is a FIDUCIARY relationship between the settlor and the trustee in which the settlor places a special confidence in the trustee. As a result of this confidence, the trustee must act in good faith with strict honesty and due regard to protect and serve the interests of the beneficiaries. The trustee also has a fiduciary relationship with the beneficiaries of the trust.

A trustee takes *legal title* to the trust property. This means that his interest in the property appears to be one of full and complete ownership and possession, but he does not have the right to receive any benefits from the property. The right to benefit from the property, known as *equitable title,* belongs to the beneficiary. In the example cited, the bank, which serves as trustee, has legal title to the stock and must carry out all the legal obligations and duties connected with the possession of the stock. Rose, as beneficiary, has equitable title and receives all the benefits from the stock. When Rose becomes 30 and is given all the stock, the trust ends. Rose then has the legal title to the stock as well as the equitable title. She has outright ownership of the stock, including the right to receive all the benefits from her ownership.

The *terms of the trust* state the duties and powers of the trustee and the rights of the beneficiary that are determined by the settlor when the trust is created. In the above example, the instructions to the bank to pay the dividends from the stock to Rose until she reaches 30 and then to give her the stock are the terms of the trust created by Rose's mother. The bank has the duty to pay the dividends to Rose, who has an enforceable right to them.

The terms of the trust will usually specify what is to happen to the trust property when the trust is ended. If the terms do not do so, the ownership of the trust property will ultimately revert to the settlor, if he is alive, or to his heirs at the termination of the trust. The trustee will hold the property in a resulting trust for the settlor or his estate (see "Implied Trusts" later in this article).

■ **Law governing trusts**   Trusts are governed by state law. A trust of real property (real estate) is governed by the law of its *situs*—that is, the state in which the property is located. A trust of personal property (any property except real estate) is frequently governed by the law of the state of the settlor's domicile (residence). In determining which state has the greatest interest in regulating the trust property, courts consider a number of factors, such as the intention of the settlor, the state where he lives, the state where the trustee lives, and the location of the trust property.

■ **Reasons for trusts**   Trusts are established for two main reasons—to take advantage of the tax benefits they offer and to provide a way to take care of other people.

Tax benefits   One of the most important reasons for setting up a trust is the favorable tax treatment that results from its use. Trusts are usually created by persons in high income tax brackets who want to reduce their taxable incomes without giving up ownership of income-producing assets. This is done by naming beneficiaries who are in lower income tax brackets than are the settlors of the trust, such as children and grandchildren. The yearly income that is paid out from the trust to the beneficiaries is included in their taxable income.

A trust may be taxed as a separate entity, apart from the individual taxpayer, if, under special limited circumstances, the yearly income earned by the trust is not distributed to the beneficiaries. When this occurs, rather than having this excess income taxed directly to the person who set up the trust, placing him in a higher tax bracket, the income will be included in the taxable income of the trust, which has a lower tax bracket than does the settlor.

If you have property that will be subject to estate taxes when you die, you may use a trust as a way of reducing the size of your estate and subsequently reducing the amount of tax that will have to be paid out of your estate upon your death. There are various ways to accomplish this goal.

You may, for example, set aside during your lifetime a certain sum, say $100,000, the income of which is to be paid to your heirs. This is an *inter vivos trust.* The trust must be irrevocable in order for it to reduce the size of your taxable estate. Your heirs will have the use of the income or benefits from the trust property, and your estate will be taxed at a lower rate than it would have been if you had left the property in the estate to be inherited by your heirs.

A *testamentary trust,* created as a result of provisions in your will, can serve to reduce the taxable estate of your surviving spouse. If you set aside $500,000 in trust, the income can be paid to your wife and, upon her death, to your children. This arrangement gives your wife the benefit of using the income of such money without increasing the size of the estate she will leave upon her death.

The area of law involving trusts and taxes is very complicated. You should consult an attorney who specializes in this area to find what type of trust arrangements will give you the greatest tax benefits. For a more detailed explanation, see ESTATE AND GIFT TAX.

Caring for others People who want to take care of their family, friends, or even unfortunate strangers often use trusts to achieve these goals. For example, a husband may create an *insurance trust* to take care of his wife and children if he should die. To do this he takes out a life insurance policy and pays the premiums on it. The insurance company, in return, promises to pay the proceeds of the policy to the person named by the insured to act as trustee. The trustee is given the duty to support the beneficiaries—usually the insured's spouse and children—until the proceeds of the policy are depleted.

A *spendthrift trust* is one by which the settlor or the law specifically prohibits the beneficiary from signing away his right to future income from the trust. This arrangement is used primarily to support beneficiaries who are careless in handling financial matters.

Charitable trusts are usually created to benefit a certain segment of society. For example, a trust fund established for the education and support of children born with Down's syndrome in New York State is a charitable trust.

■ **Express trusts** Generally when people speak of a trust, they mean an express trust. An *express trust* is created when the settlor states his intention to create a trust, usually in writing, and goes through the required formalities to establish the trust. For example, if Adam executes a document making Joe the trustee of the profits of his factory, which are to go to Adam's niece Beth, an express trust has been created. Express trusts are to be distinguished from *implied trusts,* which are created by the courts. Implied trusts are discussed near the end of this article.

As a general rule, personal property may be held in a trust that is created verbally, but in most states trusts of real estate must be in writing to be enforceable, as required by the STATUTE OF FRAUDS.

An express trust of real estate or personal property created by a will (a testamentary trust) is effective only upon the death of the settlor.

EXAMPLE In his will, Jim provides that $1 million is to be left in trust and the income it produces is to be paid for the care of his 29-year-old mentally retarded son, Bruce. Jim stipulates that when Bruce dies, whatever money remains in the trust is to be given to the Association to Help Retarded Children. These provisions do not take effect until Jim's death. If Bruce dies before Jim, the $1 million will pass directly to Jim's estate, because the purpose of the trust no longer exists.

Express trusts include both private trusts, the beneficiary of which is a private person or group of persons, and charitable trusts, the beneficiary of which is generally a charitable organization serving a particular group of persons, such as Cambodian refugees.

Private trusts Every private trust has four elements: (1) an intention of the settlor to create a trust, (2) trust property, (3) a trustee, and (4) a beneficiary. Unless these elements are present, a court cannot enforce an arrangement as a trust.

Intention The settlor must intend to create a trust and to impose duties on a trustee to deal with the property for the benefit of another.

EXAMPLE Max died leaving a will in which he specified that the income derived from his shopping center was to be divided equally among five of his children. He instructed the executor of his estate to rent the shopping center and divide this income among the children. By the language of Max's will, there is a trust created for the benefit of the named children. Clearly, an outright gift of the shopping center was not intended. It is immaterial that the word "trust" was not used.

Precatory words Sometimes it is not clear whether a person intended to create a trust, even though he expresses a wish, hope, or recommendation that certain property be used for the benefit of another. For example, Ruth, instead of giving property to Alice "in trust for Betty," gives it to Alice "with a desire that Alice care for Betty from the income of such property." The word "desire," as well as the terms "request," "wish," "hope," "recommend," "in confidence that," or "rely," are called precatory words. Courts generally treat these words as a moral obligation, not a legal one. Giving a person who holds property an option to use it for the benefit of another usually is not sufficient intent to create a trust.

When weighing the effect of precatory expressions, courts consider the entire document and the circumstances of the person who attempted to create the trust, his family, and other interested parties. In a few special cases, courts will consider precatory words sufficient to establish a trust. Their decisions may be influenced by whether a hardship or inequity would result from finding either a trust or no trust. If, for example, Betty were old and crippled and had no other income, the court might find that Ruth intended to create a trust for her.

Present trust The settlor must intend to create a trust in the present. Demonstrating an intent to create a trust in the future is not sufficient.

EXAMPLE Steve, the owner of bonds, tells Jim that he plans to transfer the bonds to him in trust for Randy the day after tomorrow. No trust is created until the transfer is made to Jim.

If Steve tells Jim that he intends to purchase 1,000 shares of ABC stock and, when he does, will hold them in trust for Jim, no trust arises until he declares himself trustee for Jim.

When a settlor does not immediately designate the beneficiary and trust property, a trust will not be created until he does so. Let us say Alex delivers to Marcia bonds to be held in trust for someone whom, he tells Marcia, he will designate in a few days. Alex dies before he names anyone. No trust has been created.

However, a trust is created if the settlor intends, when he creates the trust, that the interest of the beneficiary will take effect at a future date.

EXAMPLE Fred appoints Ellen trustee of 1,000 shares of stock, the dividends of which are to be paid to his daughter Stacey when she turns 16 next month, and when she turns 30 she is to be given outright ownership of the 1,000 shares. Although Stacey does not have an immediate right to receive the dividends but must wait a month, a present trust is created.

Illusory trust Occasionally, a person will name himself trustee of property or transfer trust property to someone else as trustee, but he keeps so much control over it that it is clear he did not intend to give up any of his rights in it. This is an *illusory trust,* which courts refuse to enforce. An illusory trust is not a real trust because the settlor has no intention of giving up his control over the trust property.

EXAMPLE Anna signed a trust agreement transferring all her property to her sister Teresa as trustee. Anna kept the right to the property during her lifetime plus the right to revoke the trust and to change the beneficiary. She also retained the power to tell the trustee how to manage the trust. Upon Anna's death, Teresa was to give the trust property to Anna's niece, Norma. Anna set up the trust to deprive her husband, Nick, of any rights he could claim to her property once she died. The state in which she lived had a law that gave a surviving spouse a one-third share in property owned by the deceased spouse.

Upon Anna's death, Nick sued for his legal share of the property that Anna allegedly left in trust. The court agreed that Nick was entitled to it. When Anna transferred the property to Teresa, she really gave up no control over it because she kept so many rights of ownership, including the power to manage the property. Her arrangement only created the *illusion* of a trust. It was clear from the circumstances that Anna never intended to part with the ownership of her property until her death.

An illusory trust is most often used by a person who wants to deprive his spouse from getting his rightful share (elective share) of the deceased spouse's property. In the above case, the fact that Anna created the trust to deprive Nick of his rights in her estate did not make the trust invalid. If she had given up control of the trust property, which would have created a valid trust, the trust would have been upheld despite Anna's motive to deprive Nick of his legal share of her estate. This is not the case everywhere, however. In some states, the fact that a trust was created with the intent to deprive a spouse of his lawful share will invalidate the trust. For a discussion of a spouse's elective share, see WILLS and DESCENT AND DISTRIBUTION.

Often an illusory trust is created by someone who wants to evade taxes.

Trust property An essential element of every trust is the trust property—sometimes called the subject matter, principal, body, corpus (Latin for "body"), or trust *res* (Latin for "thing"). Property must exist and be definite when the trust is created and must remain so as long as the trust continues to exist. Although bonds, stocks, and deeds are the most common types of trust property, any property interest that can be freely transferred by the owner may be held in trust, such as interest in a patent, trademark, or copyright.

A mere expectation, such as the interest of a person who expects to inherit property under a will, cannot be held in trust for another, because that property interest does not yet exist. In contrast, a VESTED interest (a right that cannot be forfeited) in an insurance policy can be held in trust because it is a contract right that will be realized, not merely an expectation.

If the trust property is totally destroyed, the trust ends. For example, if the trust property consists of uninsured lumber that is destroyed by fire, the trust comes to an end.

SOME BASIC FACTS ABOUT THE LAW OF TRUSTS

■ A trust is a legal arrangement by which one person holds property for the benefit of another. The person who makes the arrangement is the *settlor,* the person who holds the property is the *trustee,* and the person for whom the property is held is the *beneficiary.*

■ While a trust lasts, the trustee (a bank, for example) has legal title to the trust property; the beneficiary has the right to benefit from the property, called *equitable title.*

■ The most common types of trust property are bonds, stocks, and deeds. Interest in a patent, trademark, or copyright may also be held in trust.

■ Money to be received under a will cannot be held in trust for someone else, because it is only an expectation and does not yet exist.

■ If the trust property is totally destroyed, as by fire, the trust comes to an end, but the beneficiary may be able to sue the trustee for negligence.

■ Anyone who is legally of age and legally competent may serve as a trustee. Some states give the courts discretion to exclude nonresidents from serving; likewise, whether a noncitizen may act as a trustee is determined by state law.

■ A trustee can be removed by the court for habitual drunkenness, dishonesty, incompetence, or wasting trust's assets. Mere friction between trustee and beneficiary is not enough to justify removal of the trustee.

■ A *spendthrift trust* is one in which the beneficiary's creditors are unable to force the trustee to pay the beneficiary's debts directly. However, the creditors can claim their money from the beneficiary once the money from the trust has been paid to him.

■ Certain creditors are exempt from this rule. Those who may tap a spendthrift trust's resources include the beneficiary's spouse, children, physician, or lawyer.

■ Under a *discretionary trust,* the trustee pays the beneficiary only as much as the trustee sees fit.

■ In a *support trust,* the trustee pays the beneficiary only as much as is needed to educate and support him.

■ Some trusts contain a *forfeiture provision,* which immediately cancels the beneficiary's interest in the trust if he tries to assign his interest to someone else (a creditor, for example) or if creditors try to reach his interest in the trust. The trust property is then given as a gift to someone else, as designated in the trust document.

■ If you do not specifically reserve the power to revoke or modify a trust when you create it, you ordinarily cannot do so later on. For example, unless you kept the power to revoke the trust you set up for your spouse, you cannot terminate it when you and your spouse later become estranged.

■ The length of time a trust is to continue is usually stated in the trust document. If it is not definitely fixed, the period lasts no longer than necessary to accomplish the purpose for which the trust was created.

The beneficiary might have a claim against the trustee for negligence, however, if he failed to insure the lumber.

Often, the beneficiary receives only the income from the trust property, such as the dividends on stocks or the rent on land. In such a case, the settlor may stipulate that the principal will go to the beneficiary or his heirs after a certain time or that the trust is to pass to a different beneficiary. When there is no such provision, however, the principal will revert to the settlor or, if the settlor is dead, to his heirs once the purpose of the trust has been accomplished or the beneficiary dies. If the principal is being paid to the beneficiary and there is property left in the trust when the beneficiary dies, it will revert back to the settlor or his heirs unless the settlor has made different provisions.

Trustee Any person who has the capacity to take, hold, and administer property for his own use may take, hold, and administer property in trust. Persons who are not legally of age (at least 18 or 21, depending on the state) and INSANE PERSONS will usually be removed as trustees if they have been named, because they cannot properly administer a trust. In such a case, the court will appoint a new trustee.

Nonresidents of the state in which the trust is to be administered may be trustees. In some states, however, courts can refuse to confirm the appointment of a nonresident as a testamentary trustee. Whether an alien may act as a trustee is determined by state law.

Corporations and partnerships can sometimes act as trustees, depending upon state laws. Banks are often named as trustees.

The United States, a state, or a municipality (such as a city or town) may hold property as a trustee. This usually happens when a settlor creates a trust for the benefit of a state college or when he sets aside property to serve as a public park. There are problems in designating governmental bodies as trustees, because under the doctrine of SOVEREIGN IMMUNITY they cannot be sued without their consent. Courts of claims have been set up by Congress and by many states to hear claims against the government concerning the enforcement of trusts.

An unincorporated association—such as a labor union, social club, or lodge—usually cannot serve as a trustee.

A trust will not be declared void if a settlor fails to designate a trustee—the court will appoint one. In some rare situations, a settlor may create a trust on the condition that only a particular person serve as trustee. If that person cannot serve, or refuses to, the trust will not be formed.

A sole beneficiary cannot also be the sole trustee of a trust but two or more beneficiaries can be trustees.

Death of a trustee If there is only one trustee for a trust, the trust does not terminate upon his death; a court will appoint a successor.

When there are two or more trustees, they always hold title to (ownership of) the trust property in joint tenancy with the right of survivorship. This means that if one or more of the trustees dies, the surviving trustee inherits the entire interest.

Resignation or removal of a trustee A trustee cannot resign without the permission of the court unless the trust document provides for it or the beneficiaries consent to it. The court will usually permit the trustee to resign if his resignation will not cause great harm to the trust.

A trustee may be removed by the court for habitual drunkenness, dishonesty, incompetence in handling the trust property, or wasting the trust's assets. Incompatibility between the trustee and beneficiary will justify the court's removal of the trustee only if the friction endangers the trust property or makes the accomplishment of the trust impossible.

The powers and duties of a trustee are discussed later in this article.

Beneficiary In every private trust, a beneficiary must be specifically named or described so that his identity can be learned within the time limit of the RULE AGAINST PERPETUITIES—a limit usually measured by the life of a person living or conceived at the time the trust is created plus 21 years. This rule prevents a person from tying up his property in a trust for an unlimited number of years.

If the identity of the beneficiary cannot be determined with reasonable certainty, the trust fails (is not formed) and the property is held in trust for the settlor or his heirs. Such a trust is a *resulting trust*—a kind of implied trust, discussed near the end of this article.

A person or corporation that is legally capable of taking and holding legal title to property can be a beneficiary of a trust. Partnerships and unincorporated associations may be beneficiaries and unless restricted by state law, aliens may also be beneficiaries.

Multiple beneficiaries Two or more beneficiaries may be named in a trust. Multiple beneficiaries of a trust are tenants in common (no right of survivorship, so property goes to heirs or creditors of the deceased beneficiary) unless the trust specifically provides that they shall hold as joint tenants (right of survivorship, so property goes to the other beneficiaries).

EXAMPLE Susan transfers property to Ted in trust for Adrian, Buck, and Charley. These beneficiaries each own an undivided one-third of the trust property. If they take the property as tenants in common, upon each of their deaths the heirs of Adrian, Buck, and Charley will inherit their proportionate shares. If, however, Susan specified in the trust document that they were to take the property as joint tenants, then upon Adrian's death Buck and Charley would split his share, and on Buck's death Charley would have the complete benefits of the trust.

Classes of persons A class of persons may be named beneficiaries of a trust if the class is definite or can be determined. If property is left in trust for "my children," the class is definite and the trust is valid. If a trust is designated for "my family," the validity of the trust depends upon the interpretation of the court. If it construes the term to mean immediate family, the class is sufficiently definite to make the trust valid. If it is construed to mean all relations, the trust would fail because the class is indefinite. A trust for "my relatives" is usually interpreted to mean NEXT OF KIN so that the class is sufficiently definite.

Giving a trustee the power to select from a class of beneficiaries does not affect the validity of a trust as long as the beneficiaries are selected from that class.

EXAMPLE Bob sets up a trust fund naming his attorney, Joanne, as trustee. The income of the trust is to be paid "to the most deserving" of Bob's three children—Ed, Kathy, and Ray. Joanne's power to select the recipient of the income from the three definite choices does not make the trust invalid.

When a trust is created for the benefit of *any* person or persons whom the trustee selects, the trustee is considered to have an unrestricted power of disposition. He himself can take the settlor's property as an absolute gift. This situation differs from one in which a settlor fails to name a beneficiary but has said or implied that the trustee cannot dispose of property for his own benefit. In that case the trust fails and the trustee holds a resulting trust for the settlor's heirs.

Unborn beneficiaries Unborn children may be beneficiaries of a trust if there is another beneficiary living when the trust is created who can enforce the trust.

EXAMPLE Sharon died leaving a will in which she left her
O⊷＊ Arizona ranch to "Kent in trust for the children of my son, Ray, during the life of Ray and at his death then the property to be distributed to Ray's children, share and share alike." At the time of Sharon's death, her son, Ray, was still unmarried. This will creates a trust even though not all the beneficiaries are alive at the time that the trust is created. Ray's children can and will qualify as beneficiaries. If Ray has no children at the time of his death, the trust will fail. To qualify for a share of the trust, any other children of Ray's must be born not later than nine months after Ray's death.

Kent will manage the land and accumulate the net profits from it for Ray's children, who will become beneficiaries as they are born. If no children have been born or conceived at Ray's death, the trustee will hold the property in trust for Sharon's heirs.

Charitable trust A charitable trust consists of (1) an intention of the settlor to create this type of trust, (2) a trust property, (3) a trustee, (4) a definite class of persons composed of indefinite beneficiaries (not specifically designated individuals), and (5) an expressly designated charitable purpose. The requirements of intention, trust property, and trustee are the same as those of a private trust.

Beneficiary The class to be benefited in a charitable trust must be a definite segment of the public. The class must be large enough so that the community is affected; yet it must not include the entire human race. Within the class, however, the specific persons to benefit must be indefinite. A trust "for the benefit of the orphans of veterans of the Vietnam conflict" is charitable. The class is definite—the orphans of Vietnam veterans. The indefinite persons within the class are the ones who are ultimately selected by the trustee to be paid benefits. The class is large enough so that the community is interested in the enforcement of the trust. A trust for named persons cannot be a charitable trust.

Charitable purpose Because charitable trusts are aimed at social benefits, the law gives them certain privileges, such as an advantageous tax status. Consequently, before a court will enforce a charitable trust it will give it close scrutiny.

A charitable purpose is one designed to benefit mankind. The relief of poverty, the improvement of government, and the advancement of religion, education, and health are some examples of charitable purposes. Trusts "to build a monument to Abraham Lincoln," "to prevent cruelty to animals," or "to beautify Northtown" are charitable pur-

poses aimed at fostering patriotism, kindness to animals, and community happiness.

A trust that serves both charitable and noncharitable purposes will fail if the two are inseparable.

EXAMPLE Hodge bequeaths $100,000 to Thomson "to hold
O⊷＊ in trust for the benefit of all the schools in Norrisville." Hodge's son, Paul, will inherit whatever money remains in the estate once all the dispositions of the will are satisfied. Some schools in Norrisville are public and charitable institutions, while others are private and operated for profit. Hodge has not indicated how much of the $100,000 may be used for the public schools and how much may be used for the private schools.

The valid part—to be given to public schools and charitable institutions—cannot be separated from the invalid part—to be given to the private and profit-making institutions. For this reason, the trust fails as a charitable trust. It also fails as a private trust because no definite beneficiary is stated.

Consequently, Thomson, the trustee, holds the sum of $100,000 in trust for Paul's benefit.

As a general rule, a charitable trust may last forever, unlike a private trust, which must comply with the RULE AGAINST PERPETUITIES or be declared illegal.

Enforcement The beneficiary is the proper person to enforce a private trust, while the attorney general of the state, who represents the public, enforces a charitable one. The settlor, his heirs, or personal representatives (such as EXECUTORS AND ADMINISTRATORS); the members of the general public; and possible beneficiaries cannot sue to enforce a charitable trust. Some states, however, have expanded the group that may enforce the trust.

Cy pres The doctrine of cy pres is taken from the Anglo-French phrase *cy pres comme possible,* or "as near as possible." It refers to a court's power to change administrative provisions in charitable trusts if the settlor's directions hinder the trustee in accomplishing the trust purpose.

EXAMPLE A settlor directed that his property be used as a
O⊷＊ home for retired clergymen, but he prohibited the wives of the residents from living there with them. This trust provision greatly reduced the number of applicants to the home. A court ordered the trustee to ignore this provision under the doctrine of cy pres.

Under the cy pres doctrine, if a settlor has left funds for a charitable purpose that has become impractical or impossible to accomplish, a court can direct the funds to a different charitable purpose. Because a charitable trust may last forever, it may become obsolete because of changing economic, social, political, or other conditions. For example, a trust set up in 1790 to combat yellow fever would be of little practical value today since that disease has been virtually eliminated by modern medicine. When cy pres is applied, the court reasons that the settlor would have wanted his general charitable purposes carried out despite the changing conditions.

The cy pres doctrine can be applied only by a court. Some states allow a living settlor to veto a court's application of cy pres.

Cy pres is not used if a settlor is concerned with only one specific charitable objective, which fails, or if the settlor provides that another gift is to be made upon failure of the charitable gift. When cy pres is not applied, and the trust fails and no alternative gift has been specified, the trust property is held in trust for the settlor or his successors.

■ **Creating an express trust** In order to create an express trust, the settlor must own the trust property or have power over it or power to create it. A settlor must be legally competent to create a trust. If he is bankrupt or not legally of age or if he lacks mental capacity, it may be impossible for him to create a trust, or if he does so, he may be able to cancel the trust if he wishes.

A trust may not be created for an illegal purpose, such as to cheat creditors or to deprive a spouse of his lawful share. The purpose of a trust is considered illegal when its objectives are contrary to public policy. For example, if a trust provision encourages a divorce or violates the RULE AGAINST PERPETUITIES it will not be enforced.

If the illegal provision involves the whole trust, the trust is void. If it does not affect the whole trust, only the illegal provision is stricken, and the trust is given effect without it.

The law provides five methods for creating an express trust: (1) an express declaration of trust, (2) a transfer in trust made either during a settlor's lifetime or under his will, (3) an exercise of the power of appointment, (4) a contract, or (5) a statute.

Declaration of trust A trust is created by a declaration of trust when the owner of property declares that he holds it as a trustee for the benefit of another.

EXAMPLE Sherman is the owner of 100 shares of stock. He declares himself trustee of the shares for the benefit of his sons, Bobby and Buddy. There is no need for a transfer of the stock to the trustee because the trustee is Sherman, who already has legal title to the stock.

An oral declaration is usually enough to transfer title to personal property. This is not usually true for land.

When an owner of property writes a document transferring property to himself as trustee, the document has the same effect as if he had declared himself trustee. Clint, who owns a vacation home in the mountains, executes, acknowledges, and records a DEED transferring the property to himself as trustee for Ray. The trust is effective.

Transfer in trust A trust is created when property is transferred in trust to a trustee for the benefit of another or even for the benefit of the settlor himself.

A transfer in trust may be by deed or some other arrangement made during the settlor's lifetime. This is known as an *inter vivos* (or *living*) *trust*, in contrast to a trust created by will, which is called a *testamentary trust*. Both inter vivos and testamentary trusts are created by transfer.

Powers of appointment A power of appointment is the right that one person (the donor) gives in a deed or a will to another (the donee) to select the person (the appointee) who should receive the benefits from the donor's will, deed, or trust.

Depending upon the donor's directions, the person with a *general* power of appointment can give the property outright to anyone he wishes or he can set up the trust and select anyone, even himself, to be a beneficiary of the trust.

EXAMPLE In his will, Jack, a bachelor, gave his brother, Al, the right to create a trust using $250,000 of Jack's estate to benefit any members of the family who were still living at the time of his death. Since Al fits this descrip-

tion, he may appoint himself as beneficiary of the trust he has created at Jack's testamentary direction.

A person holding a *special* power of appointment can appoint only among particular persons, and he cannot create a trust for his own benefit.

EXAMPLE Lee leaves real estate to Doug for life, with a testamentary power of appointment in Doug to appoint the remainder among Arthur, Bert, and Charles in such shares and interests as are determined by Doug. This means that Doug inherits the right to use the property from Lee and may keep it as long as he lives, but when he dies he must leave the property (the remainder of the estate) only to Arthur, Bert, and Charles. Doug can use his own discretion in determining how to divide up the property among them, but he cannot leave it to anyone other than these three.

Contract Trusts may be created by various kinds of contractual arrangements. Common types of contractual trusts are INSURANCE trusts. A person may take out a life insurance policy on his own life and pay the premiums on the policy. In return, the company promises to pay the proceeds of the policy to an individual who is to act as a trustee for a beneficiary named by the insured person. The trustee is given the duty to support the beneficiary of this trust from the proceeds. This is the creation of a trust by the insured (as settlor) by entering a contract with the insurance company in favor of a trustee. The trust is created when the insurance company issues its policy.

Statute Statutes may provide for the creation of trusts in various instances. For example, in cases in which someone wrongfully causes the death of another, statutes often provide that the deceased person's surviving spouse or his executor or administrator has a right to sue the person or persons responsible. Any money awarded in the suit is to be held in trust for designated beneficiaries.

■ **Protection from creditors' claims** A beneficiary may freely transfer his interest in a trust unless he is restricted from doing so by the trust agreement. When a beneficiary decides to transfer his interest, he does not have to notify the trustee. When there are no restrictions on transfers, creditors of the beneficiary can force the beneficiary to transfer his interest in the trust to them in payment of his debts—for example, by garnishment of the income from the trust. See ATTACHMENT AND GARNISHMENT.

Various devices have been developed to protect a beneficiary's interest from his creditors. The most common are spendthrift trusts, discretionary trusts, and support trusts. In addition, some trusts contain forfeiture provisions. These devices are designed to safeguard the trust interest while it is still in the hands of the trustee but have no effect once funds have been paid over to the beneficiary.

Spendthrift trusts A spendthrift trust is created to provide a fund for the support of a person known to be a *spendthrift*—a person who by excessive drinking, gambling, or debauchery is considered to be capable of wasting his assets to such an extent as to become a *public charge* if something is not done to preserve his assets. A spendthrift trust is set up either because of a settlor's instructions or because state law has ruled the beneficiary to be a spendthrift. You are not permitted to establish a spendthrift trust for yourself.

EXAMPLE Oliver, an oil tycoon, sets up a spendthrift trust for his 20-year-old alcoholic son, Brad, who spends money wildly and with no thought for the future. Under the terms of the $500,000 trust, which is to be administered by the family's lawyer, the son is to receive $20,000 a year.

The beneficiary of a spendthrift trust is unable to transfer his right to income or capital, and his creditors are unable to force the trustee to pay the beneficiary's debts directly. However, his creditors can claim their money from the beneficiary once the money from the trust has been disbursed to him. This means, in the above example, that any of Brad's creditors can make claim to the money he has already received. A creditor's claims to future payments under the trust, however, are restrained. Brad's creditors cannot get at the $20,000 that he is to be paid in a subsequent year until it is actually paid out to him.

Doctrine of surplus income   In some states, under the doctrine of surplus income, creditors can claim any spendthrift trust income that exceeds the amount necessary to support and educate the beneficiary. The court decides the amount needed to support the beneficiary in the manner to which he has been accustomed. A few states have statutes that fix the percentage of trust income that is exempt from a creditor's claims.

Exceptions   Certain individuals who are not ordinary creditors are allowed to reach the beneficiary's interest in a spendthrift trust in many states. Examples are persons whom the beneficiary is legally bound to support, such as a spouse and children; persons who perform necessary personal services to the beneficiary, such as a physician; and persons whose services preserve the beneficiary's interest in the trust.

EXAMPLE Vincent leaves property to Eileen to hold for Ned. Under the trust terms, Ned is not permitted to transfer income from the property, so that it is not subject to the claims of his creditors. Ned's wife and young children, who are entitled to support from him, may reach the income. They are not ordinary creditors— Ned is bound by law to support them. Ned's physician, who treated him after he was injured in a car crash, and his lawyer, who saved the trust income for him in court, also may reach the trust income.

Claims against the beneficiary resulting from lawsuits for wrongdoing or negligence and claims by a state or the United States, such as for income tax, are also exceptions to spendthrift provisions and can be paid from the trust.

In some states, when a beneficiary and spouse are divorced and the spouse has been awarded alimony, the trustee cannot be compelled to pay the full amount of alimony until the court that has jurisdiction over the trust deems it to be fair. Only then will the trustee be permitted to pay it.

Most states authorize spendthrift trusts; those that do not will void spendthrift provisions.

Discretionary trusts   Sometimes a settlor specifies that the trustee shall pay the beneficiary only as much of the income or capital of the trust as the trustee sees fit, with the remaining income or capital to be used for another purpose. This is a *discretionary trust*—the trustee has discretion to give the beneficiary as much of the benefits as he chooses, or none at all. The beneficiary cannot force the trustee to use any of the trust property for his benefit.

Creditors cannot reach the interest from a discretionary trust until the trustee has decided to pay or apply some of the trust property to the beneficiary. The beneficiary's creditors may then reach it unless it is additionally protected by a spendthrift trust clause. A person who has been assigned an interest in the trust by the beneficiary may hold the trustee liable for any future payment to the beneficiary by notifying him of the assignment.

EXAMPLE Sally gives $5,000 to Stan in discretionary trust for Elaine. Before Stan has decided to make any payment to Elaine, she assigns to Todd a right to $25 of any payment Stan elects to make to her. Todd notifies Stan of the assignment and demands that, if he decides to pay Elaine any amount up to $25, Stan must pay it to him and not Elaine. If Stan decides not to pay Elaine, Todd has no right. If Stan does decide to pay Elaine $25, he is liable to Todd for it.

You may create a discretionary trust for your own benefit. If you do, however, your creditors can reach the maximum amount that the trustee can pay to you.

Support trusts   A trust directing a trustee to pay or apply only as much of the income and principal as is necessary to educate and support a beneficiary is a *support trust*. Support trusts are generally used in states that prohibit spendthrift trusts. A typical support trust clause would read: "I hereby transfer $100,000 to the trustee, Jane Doe, in trust to pay or apply so much of the income as is necessary for the education and reasonable support of Tom Brown during his life." The interest of the beneficiary cannot be transferred because paying money to a creditor or assignee of the beneficiary would not achieve the education or support of the beneficiary.

A person can create a support trust for his own benefit— for example, if he considers himself a spendthrift. However, his creditors can reach the maximum amount that the trustee could apply for or pay to him under the trust terms.

A settlor can express support and education as the motive for a trust without creating a support trust. In this case, the beneficiary is entitled to the stated amount of the trust property or income from it, whether it is more or less than the sum needed to support and educate him. His rights may be transferred to others or reached by creditors unless protected by a spendthrift clause.

EXAMPLE Allan transfers property to Ernie to pay the annual income it earns to Bart for his comfort and support. Bart is entitled to the entire income, which he can assign and which can be sought by his creditors for payment of his debts. The words for "his comfort and support" merely described Allan's motive for making the trust; it does not create a support trust.

Forfeiture provision   A forfeiture provision in a trust provides that the interest of the beneficiary immediately ceases if he attempts to assign his interest to someone else or if his creditors try to reach his interest. The property that is thus forfeited is given as a gift to another person.

EXAMPLE Duane transfers property to First National Trust Company in trust to pay the income to Hilda during her life and then to give the property to Cathy. The trust document states that if Hilda tries for any reason to assign her interest, if she goes bankrupt, or if a creditor tries to claim the interest, then Hilda's interest will end and the property will be given to Cathy.

■ **Management of a trust** The trustee of an express trust is given certain powers and duties, which he is expected to exercise as any reasonable and prudent person would. Generally, only one trustee is named for each trust, whether it is an individual, a partnership (such as a small law firm), or a corporation (such as a bank). Often, however, more than one trustee is named. When a settlor names two or more trustees of a private trust, the trustees hold and exercise their powers and duties jointly unless the trust provides otherwise. The courts consider that the settlor intended the beneficiaries to benefit from the judgment of all the trustees. Any attempt by one cotrustee to act for the trust independently in an important matter will usually be legally ineffective unless he acts in an emergency to prevent a loss of the trust property.

Powers of a trustee A trustee has different types of powers in managing a trust. These powers may be expressed in the trust agreement or implied in it. They may also be either *mandatory*, requiring the trustee to use them exactly as specified, or *discretionary*, permitting the trustee to use them according to his own judgment.

Express and implied powers The terms of a written trust document (or the statements of a settlor when he creates an oral trust) set out the specific powers of a trustee. These *express powers* are often the power to sell the original trust property, to invest the proceeds of any property sold, and to collect the income of the trust property and pay it to the beneficiaries.

The trustee also has a number of *implied powers*. These are assumed to have been intended by the settlor because they are needed to accomplish the purposes of the trust.

EXAMPLE Fred leaves an apartment building in a trust for the benefit of his children and designates Francis as trustee. The trust document directs Francis to collect the income derived from the apartment building and pay it to Fred's children for their support. The trust document says nothing about giving Francis the right to rent the apartments, but Francis has the implied power to do so because that is the customary way of getting income from apartment buildings.

Mandatory powers A settlor may direct the trustee to perform a certain act during the administration of the trust, such as selling trust realty as soon as possible and investing the proceeds in bonds. This direction creates a *mandatory power*, or *imperative power*—in this case to sell and invest the proceeds. If the trustee fails to carry it out, he is guilty of a breach of trust. The beneficiary may obtain a court order compelling the trustee to perform the mandatory act, or the court may order the trustee to pay damages for delaying or failing to use the power. The trustee may also be removed and replaced by the court with someone else.

Discretionary powers A trustee may be authorized by the settlor to use his discretion in deciding whether or not a certain act should be done in order to carry out trust purposes. If a settlor creates a trust for his widow and directs that the trustee should pay the widow as much money as he decides is necessary for her comfortable support, the trustee has been given a *discretionary power*.

Courts usually will not upset the decision of a trustee provided that it was made in good faith after considering the intent of the settlor. This is so even if the court would have taken different action or even if it believes that a reasonable man would have acted differently.

EXAMPLE A trustee was given discretionary power to deliver all or part of the principal of a trust fund to the settlor's daughter when he thought it was necessary to do so. The daughter had a history of mental illness but recovered her health and demanded that the trustee deliver the trust property to her. The trustee refused. The court declined to interfere with the trustee's decision, because he was honestly exercising his discretion and there was no evidence of bad faith.

On the other hand, if a trustee acts in bad faith or arbitrarily (an *abuse of discretion*), a beneficiary may seek court intervention.

EXAMPLE A trustee has discretionary power to pay the widow of the settlor as much of a $15,000 annual trust income as he thinks necessary for her support. The widow is an invalid needing special medical care and hospitalization. The trustee refuses to pay for this care and pays her only $5,000 a year. A court would almost certainly find an abuse of discretion and order a larger payment to be made.

When the trustee is directed to do something if and when a certain event occurs, and that event can be determined by objective standards, the trustee is given mandatory, not discretionary, power.

EXAMPLE Green, a trustee, is instructed to pay over the principal of the trust created by Brown to the beneficiary, Brown's son Bob, if the son is ever judicially declared to be sane. Green has the duty to find out whether that event has happened, and if it has, he is obligated to pay the principal to Bob.

Duties of a trustee A trustee must manage the trust with the skill and prudence that he would use in his own affairs. A trustee's duties are based upon the fiduciary relationship he shares both with the settlor of the trust at the time of its creation and with the beneficiaries. The settlor selected the trustee because of his confidence and trust in him. It is this trust that must guide the trustee's conduct in administering the trust.

The trustee must be loyal to the beneficiaries, protect the trust property, foster the growth of income from the trust property, and make payments to the beneficiaries. Failure to perform these duties will make a trustee liable for breach of trust. However, if a trustee invests income from trust property when economic conditions make it prudent to do so, he will not be held liable if the investment fails.

Loyalty to beneficiaries A trustee must administer the trust solely for the benefit of the beneficiaries. He must exclude any considerations of personal profit or advantage. If a trustee acts otherwise, the beneficiary may apply to the court to have the actions of the trustee set aside, or the beneficiary may treat the actions as legally binding if it is in his interest to do so.

EXAMPLE Raymond leaves real estate in trust to support his adult daughter, Rosalie, naming Vincent as trustee. Vincent sells the real estate to himself, putting himself in a position where his own interest to get the property at the lowest price conflicts with his interest as trustee to sell for the highest price. Vincent has involved himself in a conflict of interest.

Rosalie may do one of three things. She may affirm (accept) the transaction, treating the price Vincent paid for the real estate as trust property and allowing Vincent to keep the real estate as his own. She may have the sale set aside and get a court decree that the property be restored to the trust on the return of the purchase price. Or she may take from Vincent any profit he might have made on a resale of the property. It is immaterial whether or not Vincent acted in good faith and with honest intentions or whether or not he made a profit.

A newly appointed trustee should learn who the beneficiaries are and notify them of their interests. He must take possession of the trust property as soon as possible. If he fails to do so, he might be held liable for any resulting loss.

A trustee has a duty to defend the trust and the interests of its beneficiaries against any baseless claims that the trust is invalid. A failure to do so makes the trustee liable for any damages that result. If the claim is well founded and it would be useless to defend against such an attack, the trustee should accede to the claim to avoid unnecessarily wasting the trust property in legal battles.

Protecting the trust property Trust property must be earmarked and kept separate from a trustee's individual property and from property he holds for others.

The law says that the trustee must take whatever steps "a reasonable and prudent person" would deem necessary to protect and preserve the trust property from loss or damage. Taking out fire and liability insurance on property, making repairs on real estate to prevent deterioration, cultivating and fertilizing farmland, and paying property taxes and assessments are just a few of the ways a trustee must act to protect the trust property.

Fostering the growth of income Generally, a trustee is directed to collect and distribute income; therefore he has a duty to invest the trust property to produce income as soon as he can. This duty of investment may be regulated by the directions of the settlor in the trust document, by court orders, by the consent of the beneficiaries, or by statute. When a trustee follows the settlor's directions, he is protected from liability unless there is clear evidence that such action would be harmful. When a trustee has been given discretion to make investments, he must use reasonable skill and judgment.

A number of states have statutes listing various types of investments in which a trustee may invest (a *permissive list*) or must invest (a *mandatory list*). These are known as *legal list statutes*. If a trustee follows a list, he may be protected from liability, depending upon whether the statute says he may or must use the list. A permissive list allows a trustee to invest in any assets on the lists. He may also invest in other types of securities not on the list, provided he uses reasonable care and skill. If the list is mandatory, an investment outside the list is considered a breach of trust, no matter how great the care and judgment used. Only a few states have mandatory lists.

The trustee must also periodically review the investments of the trusts to see if they should be kept or sold. If they are sold, the proceeds should be reinvested.

Making payments to the beneficiaries A trustee must make payments of income to the beneficiaries and distribute the trust principal according to the terms of the trust, unless otherwise directed by a court. He must take care to make the proper payment to the right persons. A trustee will not be excused for making an improper payment or a payment to the wrong person even though he shows that he acted honestly and used what he thought was reasonable care or even if his mistake was based on ignorance, mistake, forgery, or fraud.

A settlor cannot change payment provisions unless he expressly reserves that power when he creates the trust. He must also obtain the approval of all the beneficiaries.

Courts can permit the trustee to deviate from the trust terms for the time and the form of payment, but the relative size of the beneficiaries' interests cannot be changed.

EXAMPLE Ezra set up a testamentary trust to benefit his young son, Thomas. The trust document directed the trustee to accumulate the income derived from the trust property until Thomas reached the age of 21 and then to pay Thomas the accumulated income and the trust principal. When Ezra died, Thomas was only 7 years old. By the time Thomas was 17, the cost of living and the price of tuition had risen so high that it was impossible for Thomas to live comfortably and go to college (as his father had wished) on the income he had at his disposal. Convinced that Thomas was in great need of the funds for his education and support, the court ordered that the accumulation provision of the trust be disobeyed and that the trustee pay the necessary income to Thomas.

This is called *hastening the enjoyment of the trust fund*. Courts justify such deviations from payment directions on the ground that the fundamental objectives of the trust are being carried out.

■ **Termination of a trust** The length of time a trust is to continue is usually established in the trust document. For example, a settlor may state that the trust shall last until the beneficiary reaches the age of 21 or 35, or until he marries. When this period ends, the trust ends.

When the duration of a trust is not definitely fixed, the basic rule is that a trust will last no longer than necessary to accomplish its purpose. A trust to educate your grandchildren would end when their education is completed.

A trust is also ended when its purposes become impossible or illegal. For example, if Steve sets up a trust fund for his alma mater but the school closes because of declining enrollment, the trust will terminate.

If both the beneficiaries and the settlor of a trust ask the court to have the trust terminated, it will be ended, even though the trust purposes have not been accomplished. If the settlor does not join in the request and if one or more of the purposes of the trust can still be accomplished, the courts generally will not terminate the trust. On the other hand, if the purposes have been accomplished, the beneficiaries alone can end the trust. Testamentary trusts created by the will of the settlor to take effect upon his death cannot be terminated.

EXAMPLE A testamentary trust directed the trustee to pay the settlor's son $10,000 when he reached 21; $10,000 when he became 25; and the balance of the trust principal when he became 30. When the son reached 21, he applied for the remainder of the principal. The court refused to permit payment, reasoning that it was clearly the will of the settlor that "neither the income nor any part of the principal should now be paid to the plaintiff.... The restriction upon the plaintiff's possession and control is, we think, one that the testator had a right to make."

If all of the beneficiaries do not or cannot consent to the termination of a trust, it will not be ended. As a general rule, a legally incompetent beneficiary, such as a young child or someone recognized as legally insane, cannot consent to the termination of a trust. Even if all the living beneficiaries and the settlor agree that a trust should be terminated, there still might be problems if there is the possibility of unborn beneficiaries.

EXAMPLE Francis sets up a trust of stocks and bonds held by O⟶✴ Leroy "in trust for my grandchildren." After 25 years, Francis agrees with his two grandchildren that the trust should be terminated. However, there is the possibility that more grandchildren might be born in the future. In some states the trust may be terminated if Francis and his grandchildren consent. Other states might require that a guardian be appointed by the court to represent unborn heirs. Such a guardian might protect the rights of the unborn heirs by objecting to the proceedings or by asking that certain amounts be set aside for their benefit.

■ **Implied trust** An implied trust is a trust that is presumed by a court to exist or that is imposed by a court in the name of justice. It is created even when the people who stand to be benefited and the person who is financially responsible have not explicitly expressed an intent to create a trust. There are two types of implied trusts, resulting and constructive.

Resulting trust A resulting trust is created by a court when the court presumes from certain acts that a person intended a trust to exist even though he made no explicit written or oral statement of such an intent. Resulting trusts often arise when an explicit trust cannot run its course because it has failed—because one of the requirements for setting up an express trust was omitted, for example—or because of unforeseen circumstances. In such cases, the court decrees a resulting trust in an attempt to do with the property what the settlor of the express trust would have wanted. Generally, the court will decree that the trustee of the express trust hold the property in trust for the original settlor (or for his heirs if he is dead). The ownership of the property ultimately reverts to the settlor or his legal heirs.

EXAMPLE John gives his farm to Ted to hold in trust for his O⟶✴ newly born grandniece, Ann. Unknown to John, Ann had died before he created the trust. The express trust fails because the beneficiary is dead. The court will order Ted to hold the farm in resulting trust for John. When an express trust does not use or exhaust all the trust property, a resulting trust arises.

EXAMPLE Maurice transfers $100,000 in trust to pay Bonnie O⟶✴ $1,000 a month during her life. No other disposition is specified. Bonnie dies after having received $25,000. The trustee will hold the remaining $75,000 in a resulting trust for Maurice.

Constructive trust A constructive trust is a trust imposed by a court to compel someone who unfairly holds property to transfer it to the person to whom it more justly belongs. It is a device aimed at achieving justice. A constructive trust may be imposed by a court when one person holds legal title to property that should, in fairness, belong to another because the title was gained by fraud.

EXAMPLE Upon his death, Ted's will gave his younger O⟶✴ sister, Beth, the title to his 1,000-acre farm. Beth's older brother, Ben, who managed the finances of his own farm as well as Ted's, convinced Beth to put only his name on the deed for the farm. He told her that in order to get federal government farm subsidies for both farms, he needed to show that he alone had title to them.

Beth, who was naive and inexperienced in business, trusted Ben's statements and did what she was told. Once his name was on the deed, Ben tried to sell Beth's farm. A lawyer friend of Beth's persuaded her to ask a court to help her get the deed to her farm returned to her. A court would impose a constructive trust upon the farm since Ben took unfair advantage of his trusted relationship with Beth to cheat her of her farm.

■ **Honorary trust** A trust for specific noncharitable purposes with no definite beneficiary is not an enforceable trust. Such distributions are known as *honorary trusts*. Trusts for the erection of monuments, the care of graves, the saying of masses, or the care of specific animals—such as your cat, dog, or horse—are examples of honorary trusts. In many jurisdictions, however, special provisions for the upkeep of graves and monuments are valid. And trusts for the saying of masses are often upheld as charitable trusts. Honorary trusts for the benefit of specific animals are considered different from charitable trusts for the benefit of animals in general.

As a general rule, the purported trustee may carry out the intent of the settlor if he chooses to do so. Because there is no beneficiary who could enforce the trust, however, the carrying out of the trust purposes is dependent on the honor of the trustee. If he does not carry out the trust duties, he will be holding the property for the settlor or the settlor's heirs as a resulting trust.

The extent to which honorary trusts will be recognized differs from state to state. Honorary trusts are usually limited by considerations of public policy. For example, they may not exist beyond the period of the RULE AGAINST PERPETUITIES, nor can their amounts be unreasonably large for their purposes. The purpose must not be capricious.

trust company A CORPORATION, usually a bank, that manages TRUSTS for persons and organizations. The person who sets up the trust (the settlor) appoints the trust company to see that the property is handled according to his wishes as expressed in the terms of the trust.

Sometimes trust companies act as fiscal agents for corporations, attending to the registration and transfer of their stocks and bonds, dealing with their bond and mortgage creditors, and transacting general banking and loan business on behalf of the corporation.

trust deed See DEED OF TRUST.

trustee 1 An individual or a corporation, such as a TRUST COMPANY, named by a settlor—a person who establishes a TRUST—to manage the trust according to the terms of the document that created it. A trustee is entitled to remuneration for his expenses and to a fee or commission as set by the laws of the state. **2** An individual appointed by the federal BANKRUPTCY court to handle the property of a bankrupt person.

trust receipt A written document by which one person lends money to someone to buy something and the borrower promises to hold what is bought in trust for the lender until the debt is paid off.

> EXAMPLE A banker lends money to a car dealer to buy a 0⊶⊷ fleet of automobiles. The banker takes title to the cars in his own name—that is, the rights of ownership to the cars are in the banker's name. The banker has the cars delivered to the dealer, who has agreed to hold the fleet in trust for the banker until the loan is paid. The banker is given a trust receipt for the fleet as evidence of this agreement. In other words, the banker is legally the owner of the cars and any income derived from their sale must go to the banker until the amount of the debt is fully repaid. As soon as the debt is paid, full title to the cars is given to the dealer.

Trust receipts are used primarily in business transactions and are governed by the complex law of SECURED TRANSACTIONS.

try **1** Argue a civil or criminal case in court as an attorney. **2** Sit as a judge in a civil or criminal case. See ACTION; CRIMINAL LAW; TRIAL.

turnpike Any road maintained with the money people pay to use it; also called a *toll road.* Payment is enforced by gates or bars preventing entry or exit until the *toll,* or charge for the privilege of passage, is paid. The distinguishing feature of turnpikes is the management's right to turn back anyone who refuses to pay the toll.

Turnpikes can be constructed only with legislative approval, and the legislature can prohibit a turnpike that will pose competition for one already authorized. A local government may have the authority to build a turnpike without state permission provided the road does not compete with an existing turnpike.

A turnpike wholly within a state may be built without the approval of municipalities through which it will pass.

The powers of a state turnpike commission are limited to those specified in the law that created it. So long as it operates within the scope of its authority, the courts will not interfere with the way it exercises its power.

tying arrangement An agreement by which a seller offers two separate items for sale but will not sell the first item, or *tying item,* unless the buyer agrees to purchase the second item, or *tied item.* Such agreements are common in FRANCHISE licensing. For example, the tying arrangement in one franchise licensing fast-food stores that specialized in chicken was that the franchisees must buy from the franchiser essential cooking equipment, batter mixes, and packaging bearing the franchiser's trademark.

When a seller has a MONOPOLY on a product; the tying arrangement may violate antitrust acts.

UCC   See UNIFORM COMMERCIAL CODE.

UCCC   See UNIFORM CONSUMER CREDIT CODE.

UCMJ   See UNIFORM CODE OF MILITARY JUSTICE; ARMED SERVICES.

ultra vires   (Latin) "Beyond the powers." In CORPORATION law, an act of a corporation is *ultra vires* when it is beyond the scope of the powers granted to the corporation in its charter.

unauthorized practice   The act of performing legal services without being licensed as an attorney. Such conduct is prohibited and punishable under state criminal laws. For example, a layman who prepared a CONTRACT for a real estate sale and received a fee for the work from both the buyer and seller was convicted of unauthorized practice of law. He was ordered to cease the activity and was fined.

unconscionable   Conduct that is monstrously harsh and shocking to the conscience. An unconscionable CONTRACT is one that no sensible person would make and that no honest and fair person would accept. Courts will not enforce unconscionable contracts.

> EXAMPLE A sale of a refrigerator-freezer under a retail
> 0⟶✳ installment contract required the buyer to make
> 36 monthly payments totaling 2½ times the item's value.
> The buyer made only 12 payments and was sued for the
> balance of the purchase price. A state law authorized the
> courts to limit any contract clause that would produce an
> unconscionable result. The court held that, in this case,
> the 12 payments received by the plaintiff were reasonable
> payment for the merchandise and refused to enforce
> payment of the balance.

understanding   An informal agreement; a valid CONTRACT of an informal nature.

undertaker   The common name for a person whose business is arranging funerals and burials. Undertakers, embalmers, and funeral directors are subject to state regulation to protect the public health. Reasonable regulations may govern the location of undertaking and embalming establishments, the methods of their operation, and the qualifications of applicants for undertaking licenses. Regulations may also prohibit solicitation and contracts for prearranged funeral services and may require itemized funeral charges. For a discussion of burial and funeral regulations, see DEAD BODY.

undertaking   1 A promise by one party to a contract to the other party.   2 A promise or agreement regarding business before the court. See also STIPULATION. For example, an undertaking of BAIL in a criminal case is money presented as security to guarantee the defendant's appearance. It is forfeited if the defendant fails to appear for trial.   3 A written promise given as security for the performance of an act ordered by the court.

> EXAMPLE Monica and Pierre are divorced. Pierre wants to
> 0⟶✳ take their two children to visit his family in
> France, but Monica refuses to give him their passports
> because she is afraid that he will keep the children there.
> Pierre seeks a court order requiring her to turn over the
> passports. The court grants the order but requires Pierre
> to file an undertaking in the amount of $10,000 to guarantee the return of the children to their mother. If Pierre
> fails to bring the children back, he will have to pay the
> court $10,000.

underwrite   1 Insure payment of a sum upon loss of life or property. An *underwriter,* or insurer, is the person who insures another's life or property in an INSURANCE policy.   2 A person or company that agrees to assume the risk of offering a company's corporate SHARES or BONDS to the public; in the event the public does not buy all the shares mentioned in the agreement, the underwriter will take the remaining shares.

undue   More than necessary; not proper; illegal. For example, *undue influence* is any wrongful constraint or persuasion that overpowers a person's will and induces him to do something against his own free will. Undue influence can be used as a ground for canceling a CONTRACT, WILL, or real estate DEED. In order to justify a cancellation on the ground of undue influence, three things must be shown: (1)

the person concerned must have been capable of being unduly influenced, (2) improper influence must have been exerted against him, and (3) he must have submitted to the overpowering effect of the influence.

> **EXAMPLE** Helen's father had cancer. Just before he died, she
> O➞✸ persuaded him to change his will, making her sole beneficiary because, she said, her brother had been cheating their father in the family business during his illness. After their father's death, her brother challenged the will because it replaced one that divided the property equally between him and Helen. The court found that the will was invalid because it was the product of undue influence. It was not true that the brother had been cheating, but the father had trusted Helen.

unemployment compensation

An insurance program for the benefit of employees who lose their jobs through no fault of their own. The program was established by the federal Social Security Act of 1935 but is administered by the individual states. It is supported by federal and state taxes paid exclusively by employers. It entitles employees who lose their jobs to collect a certain amount of money for every week they are unemployed for a certain maximum period of time.

■ **State laws** Every state plus the District of Columbia and Puerto Rico has its own unemployment compensation program. As long as a state's program complies with federal law, the state receives federal money to help pay the benefits to unemployed workers. The federal money can also be used for administrative costs and to set up unemployment offices that help workers find new jobs.

Who must pay Usually every employer who has at least a specified number of employees (often four) must pay the tax. There is a basic or standard rate that each employer must pay. Often the basic rate is a percentage of the total payroll paid. Sometimes employers do not pay the standard rate. They may pay more if they fired a lot of people one year or less if they fired fewer people than could be expected. Employers are given an experience rating that reflects their record for firing people. The amount of tax an individual employer pays is affected by his experience rating.

One other factor affects the amount of tax an employer pays in some states. An employer might be able to choose to make extra contributions to the unemployment system in order to lower the tax he has to pay some other year. He might do this for tax reasons. For instance, if he had to lay off half of his work force in 1979 but had made extra contributions in 1977 and 1978, he has spread out the cost of his unemployment tax by paying extra in the prior years. Some states will not allow an employer to lower the amount of his tax through either of these two provisions if the amount of money in the state's fund falls below a specified level. The federal Internal Revenue Code requires employers also to pay a federal unemployment tax. If the employer pays an unemployment tax through an approved state unemployment compensation plan, he is entitled to certain credits that reduce his liability for the federal unemployment tax.

Exemptions Certain kinds of employment are excluded from unemployment coverage. These include some agricultural labor, some exclusively charitable or nonprofit

work, and some government jobs. People who work for themselves—such as independent insurance agents, musicians, salesmen, and taxi drivers—are not covered by unemployment compensation laws.

Who may collect Any person who qualifies under the state unemployment compensation law has a right to collect benefits. The payments are not charity. They are insurance benefits that are available to everyone in order to insure the economic stability of the country. To be eligible, a person must be unemployed for a reason that is acceptable under state law, and he must be willing and able to work. He must also have worked for a certain number of weeks and earned at least the minimum amount specified by state law during the period before he became unemployed. To collect benefits he must in fact be unemployed, although some states will pay reduced benefits if part-time work is providing only a small amount of money.

A worker does not have to prove that he needs money or has no other means of support to collect benefits. Payments are intended to replace part of the wages lost during temporary periods of unemployment. Severance pay does not necessarily prevent payment of benefits, but some laws treat it as earnings, and unemployment benefits can be paid only after the time that the severance pay covers has ended. Accumulated vacation time, vacation pay, or a leave of absence will also postpone or prevent payment of benefits until the employment relationship officially ends.

> **EXAMPLE** Jeannette's employer had to let her go because
> O➞✸ business was falling off. Because she was entitled to two weeks' vacation that she had not yet taken that year, her employer gave her two weeks' pay to cover it. He also gave her two weeks' severance pay. When she applied for unemployment compensation, she was told that she would be considered unemployed starting four weeks after her last day of work because the extra pay covered those four weeks.

A person cannot be denied benefits because he refuses to accept a new job under any of the following conditions: (1) the position offered is vacant because of a strike, lockout, or other labor dispute; (2) the wages, hours, or other conditions of work are substantially less favorable than those prevailing for similar work in the area; or (3) the individual is required to join a company union or to resign from or refrain from joining any labor organization.

Furthermore, benefits cannot be denied solely because of pregnancy or because an application for benefits has been made in another state. Of course, benefits cannot be collected from two states at the same time.

Acceptable reasons for unemployment Once an employee is fired, he is entitled to compensation unless the reason for his discharge is listed in the law as a ground for denying benefits.

A person who is fired for good cause—such as misconduct—can be denied benefits. Misconduct in his private life or during off-duty hours may be good cause for firing an employee if it has a bad effect on his work.

A single minor incident may not be good cause for discharging an employee, but a series of such incidents can be. Carelessness, disregard for the employer's interest, intoxication, illegal work slowdowns, and use of abusive language may be good reasons for a discharge and denial of unemployment benefits. Absenteeism and habitual lateness are also good reasons.

An employer may not provoke an employee into quitting or allow his supervisors to do so, but this does not prevent an employer from taking disciplinary measures. If an employee quits his job because such disciplinary measures were taken, he will not be entitled to receive unemployment compensation.

EXAMPLE Barney offered to sell confidential information O╼╼* from his employer's files to a competitor. When the employer found out, he demoted Barney from his high-paying sales job and assigned him routine paperwork to be done in the office. He also took Barney's office keys and told him to stay out of the office after hours. Barney quit, claiming that he could not tolerate the new working conditions. The state unemployment compensation board denied him unemployment compensation benefits.

Willing and able to work   An unemployed worker must actively seek a new job while he is collecting benefits. If it appears that he is not actually willing and able to work, he is not entitled to unemployment compensation. A person who is too ill to work, has no means of transportation, or refuses to accept more than a small amount of work so that he will not lose retirement benefits is not considered available for work and therefore is not eligible for benefits. Employees who are on strike usually cannot collect unemployment compensation, although a few states do provide some benefits.

A state may not assume that an unemployed worker is unable to work because of some condition, such as pregnancy or motherhood. For example, a pregnant woman is entitled to work as long as her health permits. If she is willing but unable to find work, she is entitled to unemployment compensation until there is medical proof that she is no longer available for work. Similarly, a state cannot assume that a parent who is responsible for the care of small children is unavailable for work. When a claim for unemployment compensation is made, the decision must depend only on whether the applicant is actually willing and able to work but involuntarily unemployed.

There is no guarantee that an out-of-work individual will find a job that is attractive and convenient. If jobs are available, even outside his local area, he must find one. A person is not disqualified from receiving unemployment compensation just because he has recently moved, unless he moves to one of the geographical areas that are considered to have an unemployment problem that is especially serious or persistent. A person cannot move to one of these areas, add to an already serious unemployment problem, and collect compensation when he does not find a job. If you move to a state that is not a hard-core pocket of unemployment, you can collect unemployment compensation from your former state through an interstate claim.

EXAMPLE Lillian had worked for many years in a candy O╼╼* factory when the industry began to suffer from declining sales. She was laid off and began receiving unemployment compensation benefits. The unemployment compensation office gave her a booklet that described benefits and warned that she could not continue receiving benefits if she moved to an area of persistent

high unemployment. Because the candy factory was the biggest employer in Lillian's small town, her area was now considered one of persistent high unemployment.

Lillian did not have to move elsewhere to look for work, but anyone who moved into her town now would not be able to collect unemployment compensation because he would not expect to find work in an area of persistent high unemployment. Lillian could continue to collect benefits if she moved to another town to look for work—unless that town was also in an area of persistent high unemployment.

An unemployed worker cannot refuse to accept a new job just because he does not like the wages or working hours. If he is offered a job that is reasonable and suited to his skills, he is no longer eligible for unemployment compensation.

Hearing for denials   Federal law specifies that every state must provide an "opportunity for a fair hearing before an impartial tribunal, for all individuals whose claims for unemployment compensation are denied." The procedure in every state is different. A fair hearing means a hearing before an impartial person at the administrative level. A decision at that level can sometimes be appealed in court.

■ **Tax on benefits**   The amount you receive as unemployment compensation may have to be included as income on your federal tax return. For example, if you were single or separated from your spouse for the entire year and not filing a joint return, part or all of your benefits were includable in your taxable income only if the benefits and your other income totaled $20,000 or more. Married people filing joint returns could have a total of $25,000 in benefits and other income before the benefits were included as income in 1980.

EXAMPLE Willard had income of $10,000 and collected O╼╼* $5,000 in unemployment compensation benefits in 1980. His wife had no income that year, but they filed a joint return. Since their total for the year was less than $25,000, the amount of the benefits was not included as taxable income for them that year.

EXAMPLE Florence and her husband had an income of O╼╼* $30,000 in 1980. In addition, she collected $2,000 in unemployment compensation benefits. When they filed their joint return, they reported a total of $32,000 in income and benefits, or $7,000 more than $25,000. Half of that excess is $3,500. They were required to add to their taxable income half of the excess ($3,500) or the total amount of unemployment compensation ($2,000), whichever was less. Therefore, they paid taxes on income and benefits of $32,000.

If, however, you were married and living with your spouse but did not file a joint return with your spouse for that year, one-half of the amount of benefits received were taxable.

unethical conduct   Conduct that falls below the standards of practice in a particular profession, such as law or medicine. See CODE OF PROFESSIONAL RESPONSIBILITY.

unfair competition   See FEDERAL TRADE COMMISSION; TRADEMARKS AND TRADE NAMES.

unfair labor practice   See LABOR RELATIONS.

uniform Conforming to a single rule or unchanging standard; regular. A statute is said to be uniform when it applies equally to all persons within its scope. A tax is uniform when it is the same on all those who must pay it—a sales tax, for example.

uniform act A law intended for general adoption by all the states. Uniform acts, or uniform laws, are prepared and sponsored by the National Conference of Commissioners on Uniform State Laws. The commissioners are experienced lawyers, judges, and law professors, usually appointed by their state governors. The UNIFORM COMMERCIAL CODE is an example of a uniform act that has been adopted, at least in part, by all 50 states. Its purpose is to promote uniformity and fairness in commercial transactions.

Uniform Code of Military Justice
The collection of federal laws that constitutes a justice system that applies to the United States ARMED SERVICES.

The rights of people serving in the armed forces are not as extensive as civilian rights because the military is subject to the overriding demands of discipline and duty. The Constitution expressly gave to Congress the task of setting up a system of military justice and courts.

After World War II, Congress reformed and modernized the Articles of War and Articles for the Government of the Navy that had been in effect. The Uniform Code of Military Justice (UCMJ) was enacted in 1950.

The comprehensive system is applicable to all members of the military establishment—not only men and women on active duty but also retired and reserve personnel, students at military academies, and prisoners of war. Crimes committed by military personnel as well as violations that threaten military discipline are covered in the UCMJ. The laws also set up the system of courts-martial that administers military justice. The highest court in this system is the U.S. Court of Military Appeals.

Uniform Commercial Code
A comprehensive body of laws adopted at least in part by all the states to promote uniformity and fair dealing in commercial transactions. The Code includes provisions relating to SALES, COMMERCIAL PAPER, bank deposits and collections, letters of CREDIT, bulk transfers, warehouse receipts, investment securities, and SECURED TRANSACTIONS.

Uniform Consumer Credit Code
A comprehensive body of laws on retail installment sales, consumer CREDIT, small loans, disclosure of terms to the consumer, advertising, and home solicitation sales. The Code, generally referred to as the UCCC, has been adopted by only a few states. See also CONSUMER PROTECTION.

unilateral One-sided; relating to only one of two or more persons or things. For example, under a unilateral CONTRACT only one of the parties makes a specific promise or performs some act without receiving, as is usual in contracts, a return promise of performance from the other party to the contract.

union See LABOR RELATIONS.

union shop A business in which the employer is permitted to hire a nonunion worker, with the understanding that the worker is later required to join the union in order to keep the job. In contrast, a *closed shop* may offer jobs only to those who are already union members.

United States The separate states formed by the U.S. Constitution into a union known as the United States of America. In international affairs the United States is a single sovereign nation. See SOVEREIGNTY.

The federal government gains its power from the U.S. Constitution, whose framers started with the premise that all powers of government reside in the people (not in the state). Through the Constitution, the people delegate certain powers to the federal government, reserve others to the states, and still others to the people.

To prevent excessive concentration of power in any part of the government, the authors of the Constitution created a system of checks and balances by establishing legislative, executive, and judicial branches with distinct and separate powers. CONGRESS, with its two chambers—the SENATE and the HOUSE OF REPRESENTATIVES—exercises the legislative powers. The PRESIDENT exercises the executive or administrative powers. The judicial branch is made up of all FEDERAL COURTS, including the SUPREME COURT.

The separation of powers guarantees that each of the three branches of government is coequal with the other two. The tripartite system of checks and balances permits each department to check on the others and to have its own power balanced by that of the others. For example, Congress has the power of the purse—it appropriates and authorizes spending money; the President has the power to veto bills; and the Supreme Court rules on the constitutionality of legislation.

United States Code The STATUTE books containing the laws of the United States.

United States Code Annotated The statutory law of the United States arranged by subject matter under 50 titles—among them *Public Health and Welfare; Foods and Drugs;* and *Crimes and Criminal Procedure.* These lawbooks contain ANNOTATIONS of federal and state court decisions that interpret and apply the federal statutes. The Code includes various additional research aids, such as historical notes and library references, and regulations promulgated by certain federal agencies.

United States courts See FEDERAL COURTS; SUPREME COURT.

United States magistrate A federal officer who functions as an assistant judge. Until 1968, U.S. magistrates were called United States commissioners.

The office of federal magistrate was created in order to relieve overburdened federal judges of certain routine matters. For instance, federal magistrates can receive affidavits and fees for the court, and they can issue search warrants. The decisions and orders of magistrates must be reviewed and approved by the federal judges for whom they work before they can be considered final and compulsory.

U.S. magistrates are appointed by district court judges as they are needed. They must be licensed attorneys in good standing unless there are no qualified members of the bar available in the area. They may work either full time or part time. Full-time magistrates may not practice law independently or engage in any other business that conflicts with their duties. Part-time magistrates may have a law practice, but not one that conflicts with their position.

United States marshal

United States marshals are the chief law enforcement officers for the federal courts. They keep the peace, serve legal papers, and enforce court orders. The President appoints a U.S. marshal for a four-year term, and although the Senate must confirm the appointments, the President has the power to remove a marshal at any time.

One marshal is appointed for each judicial district in the United States. For a discussion of judicial districts, see FEDERAL COURTS. The U.S. Attorney General decides where in each district the marshal's office shall be located, but each marshal can appoint his own deputies and clerical assistants, with salaries determined by federal law.

A U.S. marshal is obligated to enforce the orders of federal courts. He must arrest people, care for property in the custody of the court, and deliver legal papers as directed.

unjust enrichment

The principle that a person is not permitted to profit (enrich himself) at another's expense, as when he gains money or property that in fairness and good conscience belongs to some other person.

In order to prevent unjust enrichment, the law applies the concept of a *contract implied in law,* or quasi CONTRACT (not a true contract). A contract implied in law is actually a duty imposed by law and is considered a contract only to remedy an unfair situation.

If you feel that someone has unjustly enriched himself at your expense, you must first establish that he requested, by words or implication, that you provide a benefit for which you expected compensation. You must also show that it would be unjust for the other person to retain or profit from the benefit without paying for it.

EXAMPLE Erica, after receiving emergency medical treatment for an eye injury at a hospital, refused to pay the bill. The hospital could sue Erica in quasi contract to get the money for its services. Erica, by asking the hospital to help her, had created a quasi contract. By not paying the bill, she was unjustly enriching herself from the treatment.

unlawful assembly

An assembly of usually three or more persons who gather to commit a crime or to carry out a lawful purpose in a manner that is likely to endanger the peace. If those who assemble take steps to accomplish their purpose and disrupt the peace, the actions are termed a *rout;* if the persons actually carry out their purpose, the rout becomes a RIOT.

EXAMPLE An angry crowd tried to take a prisoner from a sheriff's custody in order to whip him. The people in the crowd were guilty of unlawful assembly because their purpose was illegal. On the other hand, a group of machinists peacefully picketing outside their employer's shop are not guilty of unlawful assembly because their purpose is legal. If they begin throwing rocks and threatening people who pass their picket line, they are guilty of unlawful assembly because they are pursuing their lawful purpose in an illegal way.

At COMMON LAW, the assembly of three or more persons for an unlawful purpose constituted a crime. Today, however, some statutes require both the assembly and an actual attempt to commit a forbidden act. Ordinarily, an unlawful assembly is a MISDEMEANOR.

The essence of unlawful assembly is the intent of the persons assembled. They must hold a fixed purpose to do an unlawful act or disrupt the peace. It does not matter when the intent is formed.

Persons who assemble to carry on their ordinary business are not unlawfully assembled. They are, however, when three or more act together in committing an ASSAULT AND BATTERY, for example, or in preventing a court from sitting. Strikers who occupy the premises of a company to prevent its employees from performing their duties are unlawfully assembled. See STRIKE. Blocking traffic, which may be an illegal act in itself, can amount to an unlawful assembly if the act is violent and terrorizes others.

All who join in unlawful assemblies are criminally responsible for the acts of their associates done to further their common goal. If the assembly is unlawful, a person's presence is sufficient to charge him with participation.

unlawful detainer

The ground for a lawsuit to remove a tenant who originally occupied a landlord's premises legally but who refuses to leave when his right to possession has ended. The tenant's lease may have expired or been terminated. See LANDLORD AND TENANT.

unliquidated

Uncertain in amount; remaining unassessed or unsettled. For example, a debt is unliquidated when the exact amount that is owed cannot be decided from the terms of a contract or some other standard. Under the law relating to ACCORD AND SATISFACTION, a claim or debt is unliquidated if the amount is in dispute.

use and occupation

A court ACTION brought by a landlord against a tenant for rent when no valid lease exists that can be enforced. For example, when land is occupied under a lease that is not valid because of some technicality, the landlord can still bring a use and occupation lawsuit to get a fair rent for the use of his property.

usufruct

The right to use and enjoy another person's property, provided it is not impaired or altered. For example, the right to use water from a stream in order to generate power, as opposed to a claim of legal ownership of the water itself, is a *usufructuary right.*

usury

Charging more interest on a loan than the law allows. Usury may be a crime, or the lender may be prevented from collecting the money owed on a usurious loan.

Each state permits interest charges within the limits of its particular usury laws. Different limits are set for different kinds of loans, the rate for home MORTGAGES usually being lower than that for other types of loans. Because lenders cannot afford to make many small loans at the same rate, consumer loans–such as personal loans or automobile loans–can usually be made at higher interest rates.

All lenders–including banks, credit card companies, and finance companies–are required under the federal Truth-in-Lending law to give you a disclosure statement that explains exactly what your loan is going to cost. For example, if your interest rate is 1½ percent per month, the disclosure statement must tell you that the effective annual interest rate is 18 percent. In addition, the disclosure statement must explain how penalties will be computed, such as for late payments, and how any discounts can be earned, such as for early payments. For a more detailed discussion of consumer loans, see CREDIT and CONSUMER PROTECTION.

Some laws set no limit on the amount of interest a large CORPORATION can agree to pay, because it is assumed that corporations have enough bargaining power to negotiate a fair rate of interest for themselves.

"Loan sharks" (usurers) can go to jail, or can be prohibited from collecting the excess interest or any interest at all, or can be prohibited from recovering the *principal* (the original amount that was loaned out).

utter   Declare or assert; put a document, such as a NEGOTIABLE INSTRUMENT, into circulation. For example, it is a crime to utter a forged check. See FORGERY.

V

vacate 1 Annul, set aside, or render void a court JUDG-MENT or order. 2 Surrender possession or occupancy of real estate and leave the premises empty of all contents.

vagrancy The state of being a vagrant. State laws and municipal ordinances generally define a vagrant as an able-bodied person who habitually loafs, loiters, and idles in a public place for the larger portion of his time without regular employment and without any visible means of support. Vagrancy is a public offense that is punishable by imprisonment or a fine. However, vagrancy laws are strict-ly construed in favor of the citizen's liberty. Vagrancy statutes are meant to prevent crimes, such as theft, that are likely to result from a vagrant's idle way of life.

A vagrancy statute must be precise and clear enough so that a person of ordinary intelligence cannot break the law without realizing it. It cannot prohibit a person from sim-ply being out late at night with no obvious or lawful purpose. Neither can a statute prohibit just "being some-thing," such as a "suspicious person." The conduct cannot be criminal without some observable act.

> **EXAMPLE** A young man was charged with vagrancy after he was arrested for "loitering in a public place for the purpose of engaging in sexual relations for a price." He claimed that this was an illegal statute because it accused him simply of "being something." The court disagreed. It held that he not only had been loitering on the street but had also stopped passersby and made sug-gestive remarks to them. The overt acts in addition to the loitering were enough to convict him.

vague Indefinite; uncertain. A STATUTE is said to be vague when it is written in such imprecise terms that persons of ordinary intelligence must guess at its meaning and differ as to how the statute will be applied. A vague statute is unenforceable.

valid Legally sufficient; binding. For example, a valid CONTRACT is one that complies with all the necessary legal formalities and is binding and enforceable.

valuable consideration A term used synony-mously with CONSIDERATION—something, such as money, that the law regards as legally sufficient exchange for property or service that is received as part of the bargain in a CONTRACT. Valuable consideration is distinguished from *good consideration,* which is based on a blood relationship or love and affection and occurs when a person gives property or grants an estate through generosity and natural duty.

> **EXAMPLE** After John had spent the whole day helping his neighbor Harold put a new roof on Harold's house, John asked if he could buy Harold's old car. Harold said that he would be glad to be rid of it and, since John had helped him that day, John could just take it. John said that he would pick it up on Monday.
>
> Sunday afternoon a woman knocked on Harold's door and asked if the old car he had outside was for sale. When he told her that he had just given it away, she became very excited. "You're crazy," she said, "that car is worth at least $2,000 as an antique. I'll give you $1,500 cash right now." Harold agreed and took the money. When the woman sent her truck to pick up the car, John had already taken it. She sued to recover the car and won.
>
> The court held that her agreement was supported by valuable consideration—the $1,500. Even though John's agreement was made before her agreement, his was not enforceable. Harold had agreed to give John the car in consideration of the help he had already given, but this is not sufficient in law. At the time Harold had said he would give John the car, there was nothing that John was obligated to do or to pay. In other words, John's bargain was not supported by valuable consideration.

value The estimated or appraised worth in money of personal property or real estate. The market value of an item is the price that a willing purchaser will pay for it under ordinary market conditions.

vandalism The crime of damaging or destroying objects that are treasured for their literary or artistic value; the crime of willfully destroying someone else's property. Many of the statutes that prohibit intentional destruction of public or private property use the term *criminal mischief* or *malicious mischief* rather than vandalism.

In order to convict someone of vandalism, it is generally necessary to prove three things: (1) that the defendant damaged or destroyed some property, (2) that the property did not belong to him, and (3) that he acted intentionally and with MALICE.

Without proof that damage was done to the property, the defendant might be found guilty of a TRESPASS but not of vandalism. Without proof that the damage was done intentionally, the defendant can be sued by the owner of the property and made to pay money DAMAGES to repair or replace the property, but he cannot be convicted of the crime of vandalism. *Malice* means that the defendant acted even though he knew or should have known that what he was doing was wrong or illegal. Malice can be willful or it can be a reckless disregard of the fact that damage is likely to occur. Courts will occasionally accept ill will against the owner of the property as evidence of malice, but more often the strict legal meaning of malice is used.

Because destruction of private and public property threatens the security of society as a whole, modern laws make vandalism a crime. The penalties may be a fine, a jail sentence, an order to pay for repairs or replacement, or all of these.

A group of people can be convicted for conspiring or acting together to commit vandalism. Usually an unsuccessful attempt to commit vandalism is also an offense, but penalties are less than for the completed crime. Penalties may also depend on the value of the property destroyed or the cost to repair it.

■ **Federal laws** One federal law prohibits plundering or damaging any property owned by the United States government or manufactured or built for it. Recent cases have involved defendants who poured blood on draft records at a Selective Service office, defendants who broke into a post office, and a person who vandalized a nuclear-armed B-52 bomber. One man was prosecuted under this law for attempting to blow off the head and one arm of the Statue of Liberty with 30 sticks of dynamite.

Offenders can be imprisoned for up to a year and fined as much as $1,000 for causing up to $100 worth of damage; they can be imprisoned for up to 10 years and fined as much as $10,000 for causing more than $100 of damage.

Another federal law punishes any amount of damage to communications lines owned by the United States or used in the national defense with fines up to $10,000 and imprisonment up to 10 years. There are also federal laws that specifically prohibit violent interference with military installations or supplies and foreign commerce.

■ **State laws** State vandalism or malicious mischief laws punish many kinds of destructive conduct. One state outlawed the use of EXPLOSIVES to damage property belonging to someone else, but in one case a judge refused to apply that statute to a man who had put a firecracker into the coin-return slot of a pay telephone for the reason that a firecracker was not an explosive under the statute. Under more general statutes, however, many people have been convicted for taking revenge on coin-operated machines.

Feuds between neighbors have sometimes led to criminal vandalism.

EXAMPLE If a man builds his fence too close to his neighbor's driveway, the neighbor is correct in complaining that the fence is illegal. The neighbor is wrong, however, if he goes out and chops down the fence—he can

be prosecuted for malicious destruction of property belonging to another.

People have been convicted of vandalism for acts prompted by a wide variety of motives. For example, two men who burned a cross on the lawn of a black family new in the neighborhood were convicted of malicious mischief. A man who cut firewood on someone else's farm was found guilty of vandalism. A man who fired a pellet gun through the windows of his estranged wife's apartment was prosecuted for vandalism. Another man was convicted for kicking the window out of a police car after he was arrested. People have been convicted of vandalism or malicious mischief for cutting telephone wires, spray-painting graffiti on the sides of bridges, and slashing tires on school buses.

Some states make parents liable for acts of vandalism committed by their minor children, up to specified limits. These statutes are intended to encourage parental supervision and to shift part of the cost of vandalism from the public to the individuals. See PARENT AND CHILD and Chart 5.

■ **Penalties** Persons convicted of breaking federal vandalism laws can be punished by fines or imprisonment as mentioned above. States also impose fines and imprisonment for acts of vandalism, but they may also impose other penalties.

Judges have been imaginative in fixing penalties for vandalism, ordering some defendants to repair the damage and others to work on public improvement projects. In addition, judges have required vandals to make restitution when convicted in a criminal proceeding without the victim's having to bring a civil suit for money damages.

Sometimes state laws provide harsher penalties for destruction of certain types of property. Desecration of a church or synagogue may be punished more severely because a special harm is done to the community if bigotry is not firmly controlled. Destruction of prison property may incur harsher penalties because order and discipline are essential in prisons. Intentional destruction of property belonging to a public utility may merit special treatment because of the potential for harm to so many people. For example, damage in one small spot can interrupt water, electricity, or telephone service for thousands of homes. The danger of widespread looting during blackouts has made it especially important to protect power stations and generators.

■ **Defenses** It generally is no defense to a charge of vandalism that the defendant lost his temper. Criminal laws are meant to discourage hotheaded confrontations. It also is no excuse that the defendant had in mind what he thought was a noble purpose for the destruction. People who admitted destroying draft records in order to register opposition to the Vietnam conflict had to accept the penalties for their conduct. Others have been convicted when they tore down fences and barricades surrounding nuclear power plants and interfered with their construction. Courts have often imposed maximum sentences on protestors who declare that they will continue to commit acts of vandalism in order to publicize their political positions.

variance 1 The difference between what a party to a lawsuit says he will prove in his PLEADINGS (documents summarizing the arguments to be presented in a civil lawsuit) and what he actually does prove during the trial. In a criminal case, a variance is the gap between accusation and proof—for example, when a prosecutor alleges the defendant committed ROBBERY but instead proves the crime was BURGLARY.

2 In ZONING laws, a variance is an official permit to use land or property in a way that does not conform to zoning regulations applying to other land or property in the same neighborhood. For example, a doctor or lawyer wishing to practice his profession in a neighborhood that is zoned for residential use might be required to obtain a variance in order to open an office in such a neighborhood.

vendee In law, a person who purchases property. See VENDOR-PURCHASER RELATIONSHIP.

vendor In law, a person who sells property. See VENDOR-PURCHASER RELATIONSHIP.

vendor-purchaser relationship
The relationship between the seller and buyer of real property (real estate) during the time lag between the execution of the contract and the date of its consummation. A land sales contract is *executed* when the seller (vendor) and buyer (purchaser or vendee) sign a sales contract, but the contract is not *consummated* until the seller delivers the DEED to the buyer and the buyer pays the seller his price for the land. The consummation is also referred to as the closing of ESCROW, the date of closing, or merely a CLOSING.

■ **Marketable title** The vendor-purchaser relationship begins when the parties enter into a written contract for the sale of real estate. One assumption of that relationship is that the vendor has a marketable TITLE to the land—that he does, in fact, own the land and can legally sell it and that the purchaser will have the same right once the sale is completed. Because clearing a title to land is a complex process, most purchasers offer to buy land before making any investigation of the title. At first glance, that practice may appear foolhardy, but it is not because the law permits the buyer to withdraw from the sales contract if the title turns out to be unmarketable.

A marketable title must be (1) a title that the vendor does in fact have; (2) a title that is not subject to any encumbrances—interest in the property held by someone other than the vendor or purchaser; and (3) a title that is, therefore, not subject to doubt regarding its validity.

An *encumbrance* that makes a title unmarketable may take any of several forms—an outstanding MORTGAGE, for example, or a tenant's lease that will continue in force after the sale (whether or not it is financially advantageous to the new owner of the property). The mere existence of an encumbrance will not cause the title to be unmarketable, if the parties have provided for it in their contract.

EXAMPLE Vickie and Marie signed a contract in which
O—* Marie agreed to buy 40 acres of land belonging to Vickie. The next day, Marie discovered that Vickie had title to only 25 acres. Since Vickie lacked a marketable title to the 40 acres, she was not able to enforce the contract on the closing day. If Vickie had actually had title to all 40 acres but that title had been subject to an encumbrance in the form of an outstanding mortgage, she still would not

have been able to enforce the contract because her title would have been unmarketable. On the other hand, if the only encumbrance on the title was a continuing lease that Marie had agreed to honor, Vickie would have been able to enforce the contract.

Unless the agreement indicates otherwise, the purchaser is entitled to an absolutely undivided interest in all the property he has contracted to buy. If the seller does not have such an interest, the purchaser may withdraw from the contract, on the ground that the vendor cannot produce a marketable title. Let us say, for example, that Gail signs a contract with Margie to buy Margie's land but discovers before the closing that Margie does not own the land by herself but owns it in JOINT TENANCY with Norman. Gail is not obligated to complete the purchase.

Many real estate sales contracts today call for an insurable title to the property. When a recognized insurance company is willing to insure a title without making exceptions to the coverage, the purchaser must then accept it as marketable.

■ **Risk of loss** There are three ways to treat accidental losses that occur during the contract period between vendor and purchaser—equitable conversion, the so-called Massachusetts rule, and the Uniform Vendor and Purchaser Risk Act.

Equitable conversion Most states hold strictly to the doctrine of equitable conversion. As soon as the sales contract is signed, the purchaser is regarded as the real (equitable) owner of the property. Even though the seller keeps legal title, he does so only as security (collateral) for the purchase price. If the seller tries to back out of the deal, the sales contract can usually be enforced against him.

Because the purchaser is now the owner, he is required to bear the risk of loss during the contract period and cannot withdraw from the agreement if the property is damaged prior to the closing.

EXAMPLE On January 1 Albert and Louis contracted for the
O—* sale of Albert's apartment building, with the escrow closing set for March 1. On February 1 a fire, caused by neither party, virtually destroyed the premises. Under the doctrine of equitable conversion, Louis is still obligated to complete the contract and pay the purchase price to Albert.

Equitable conversion is a harsh rule because the buyer must cover losses even though the seller has possession of the property and is in a better position to prevent them. Although the purchaser can buy insurance to cover the risk of loss, a better solution is to provide in the contract of sale (1) that the seller is liable for all risk of loss until the deed is delivered to the buyer and (2) that the seller will carry insurance to cover that risk.

Massachusetts rule A number of states follow the so-called Massachusetts rule, which holds that the contract of sale cannot be enforced if the seller cannot deliver the premises on the day of closing. Under this rule, the purchaser is entitled to withdraw from the contract if the property is damaged during the escrow period.

EXAMPLE On January 1 Albert and Louis contract for the
O—* sale of Albert's apartment building, with the closing date set for March 1. On February 1 a fire of unknown origin causes $3,000 worth of damage to the paint

on the side of the building. On March 1 Louis has the right to call off the deal. If Louis wants to go through with the deal, he can have Albert burdened with the $3,000 cost of repairing the damage or have the original purchase price reduced by the $3,000 that it will cost Louis to fix the damage. It is up to Louis and Albert to reach an agreement if Louis wants the deal honored.

Uniform Act   Several states have adopted the Uniform Vendor and Purchaser Risk Act, which allocates innocent losses occurring during the contract period to the vendor—unless the purchaser has taken possession of the property, in which case the loss is the purchaser's responsibility. In other words, the Uniform Act places the risk of losses on the person in possession because he is in the best position to take care of the PROPERTY.

venire facias   (Latin) "That you should cause to come." A judicial WRIT (order) directing the sheriff of a county to have a JURY assemble.

venireman   A member of a JURY panel; a juror summoned by a writ of VENIRE FACIAS.

venue   The particular county or territory in which a civil lawsuit or a criminal prosecution may or must be brought for TRIAL; the place where an injury or a crime occurred and where a court having JURISDICTION (authority) can properly hear and decide the case.

verdict   The formal decision or finding of a JURY regarding the issues submitted to it during a trial. The verdict must be reported to the court, which may enter a JUDGMENT based on it.

verify   **1** Confirm the truth or authenticity of a statement, fact, or document. **2** Confirm by making a formal OATH. The law may require verification for certain types of papers in some cases—for example, a BILL OF PARTICULARS, a statement of account, or a COMPLAINT. Verification is made by attaching a sworn statement to the paper that it is true.

versus   (Latin) "Facing." In the title of a case, the plaintiff's name is put first, followed by the word "versus," then the defendant's name: *"Fletcher* versus *Peck."* The word is also commonly abbreviated *v.* or *vs.*

vested   Fixed; absolute; not conditional; not subject to being lost if some particular event occurs. In PROPERTY law, vested signifies a person's fixed present right to either the immediate or the future enjoyment of property. For example, a man who, in his WILL, leaves land to his widow for the remainder of her life and directs that at her death his grandson shall receive the property is giving the grandson a vested interest in the property, even though the grandson's enjoyment of it is postponed until after his grandmother's death. See ESTATE.

veteran   See ARMED SERVICES; INSURANCE.

Veterans Administration   The federal agency that administers many benefits and programs for veterans

of the U.S. ARMED SERVICES and their dependents, including medical care, education and rehabilitation programs, disability compensation, and insurance benefits.

veterinarian   A person who practices veterinary medicine. Veterinary medicine includes diagnosing, treating, operating on, or prescribing for any animal because of disease, pain, injury, deformity, or other physical condition. At least one state (New York) authorizes veterinarians to treat every kind of living creature except human beings.

In order to practice veterinary medicine, a person must obtain a LICENSE from the state. License requirements vary, but an applicant must generally have good character and a specified amount of education and experience. The state may also require him to pass a written examination. He will probably have to be over a specified minimum age and a citizen of the state and may also have to be a citizen of the United States.

The practice of veterinary medicine is considered a profession. Because CORPORATIONS are generally not allowed to practice a profession, a businessman usually cannot form a corporation and hire veterinarians to treat his customers' pets. Some states do allow professional persons to form a special kind of professional corporation for tax and PENSION benefits, but this way of doing business is not allowed everywhere. Where professional corporations are allowed, a professional person is still held to high standards in dealing with his clients. His liability cannot be limited by the corporate form of doing business.

EXAMPLE Curtis, a businessman, forms a corporation to operate a feed store. The corporation owns all the assets of the business and pays all the bills. Curtis owns all the shares of stock in the business, but the corporation is actually the business. When Curtis carelessly mixes an insecticide with oats and a customer loses four racehorses that eat the contaminated feed, the customer can sue the corporation but not Curtis.

A veterinarian cannot insulate himself from liability this way. If he carelessly gives poisonous food to an animal, all of his personal property can be taken to pay off a money judgment against him because he is a professional person.

Veterinarians may practice as business partners, but they generally may not form PARTNERSHIPS with anyone except other licensed veterinarians.

■ **Public health**   Many veterinarians work for the government to help safeguard PUBLIC HEALTH. It was veterinarians who first proposed that laws require the inspection of meat and milk to prevent the spread of tuberculosis. Today they help develop and enforce regulations that control disease, maintain the purity of food products for both humans and animals, supervise the slaughtering of animals and disposal of animal carcasses, and prevent cruelty to animals. Veterinarians are considered so important to public health that their education is subsidized by the federal government.

Federal law requires that most dogs, cats, and certain other animals offered for sale have a veterinarian's certificate not more than 10 days old that certifies the animal's good health. Federal law also provides that dealers and exhibitors of animals and research facilities that use animals must maintain humane standards of treatment for the animals, including adequate veterinary care.

■ **Rights and responsibilities**   In the eyes of the law, the animal a veterinarian treats is the owner's personal property. While the animal is in the veterinarian's custody, he must be sure it is fed, exercised, kept in a clean place, protected from harsh weather or extreme temperatures, and separated from other animals that might injure it or spread disease to it. Any medical care or treatment he administers must be given carefully.

A veterinarian who fails to furnish adequate food and drink for an animal entrusted to him may be subject to criminal penalties for violating a law that prohibits cruelty to animals. It is no excuse that the owner has failed or refused to pay the veterinarian for boarding or treating the animal. In such a case, the veterinarian may have the right to turn the animal over to a pound or private organization— even if that means that the animal may ultimately be destroyed. Before he does this, however, the veterinarian should give the owner clear notice of what he intends to do and what may happen to the animal. If an owner abandons an animal left with a veterinarian, the veterinarian may dispose of the animal in the same way. But again the veterinarian must provide adequate care as long as he has possession of the animal.

No one has to take a lost animal or stray to a veterinarian, but anyone who does so is obligated to pay the veterinarian's bill the same as he would for his own pet.

■ **Liability of veterinarians**   A veterinarian who treats animals is not subject to all the laws of medical malpractice that apply to physicians. See PHYSICIANS AND SURGEONS. On the other hand, he is generally liable for harm he causes to someone's animal. For example, an owner who leaves healthy puppies overnight with a veterinarian for routine shots can reasonably expect to pick them up in good condition. If the puppies are dead the next day, the law will presume that the veterinarian was negligent. The owner should be able to recover the value of the puppies.

Generally, an owner cannot recover more than the value of the animal no matter how close his emotional ties with it, but there have been exceptions.

EXAMPLE   A woman's dog had been shot and she could not O——* afford surgery for it. Because the dog was in pain, she paid the veterinarian $10 and agreed to let him destroy it. The doctor, however, allowed two of his helpers to try to nurse the dog back to health. When the dog recovered, they gave it to a friend, who happened to live in the original owner's neighborhood. When she saw the dog alive, she was terribly upset. She testified that she had had nightmares when she thought her dog had been destroyed and had suffered months of anguish. The jury awarded her damages, totaling $5,200.

■ **Expert opinions**   A veterinarian can testify as an expert WITNESS. In one case, a veterinarian was able to identify a valuable show dog that had run away and was claimed by two persons. Among other things, the veterinarian pointed out to the jury the distinctive way the animal's ears had been clipped.

Veterinarians also give opinions on the soundness of animals that are about to be sold. They might, for example, certify that a mare or a cow is pregnant.

EXAMPLE   A buyer agreed to take and pay for a horse on the O——* condition that it was found to be sound by a veterinarian. The veterinarian checked the horse and found that it was healthy but blind in one eye. The contract of sale was canceled, and the buyer recovered all the money he had paid to the seller.

If a veterinarian mistakenly certifies the soundness of an unhealthy animal, he can be held liable for losses suffered by someone who relies on his incorrect opinion.

veto   A refusal by the PRESIDENT or governor to sign into law a bill that has been passed by a legislature. A veto is also the President's or governor's message to the legislature stating his refusal to sign and his reasons for it.

Under the federal Constitution the President has 10 days, excluding Sundays, to sign or veto a bill and return it to Congress. If he does not return the bill within that time, the bill automatically becomes law, unless the Congress adjourns, preventing the bill from being returned. When that adjournment takes place before the 10 days expire, and the President has neither returned the bill nor signed it, it is called a pocket veto, which has the same effect as a regular veto. A two-thirds vote in both houses of the U.S. Congress can override a Presidential veto. States follow this procedure for the veto of legislation by governors. For a detailed explanation of how a bill does or does not become a law, see LEGISLATION.

vexatious litigation   A lawsuit brought by a person who is not acting in good faith but seeks merely to annoy or embarrass his opponent. A court sometimes considers vexatious litigation to be a malicious abuse of the legal process. See CONTEMPT; TORT.

vicarious liability   Legal responsibility imposed on one person for another's acts, such as an employer's responsibility for an employee's negligent conduct during the course of employment. See NEGLIGENCE; RESPONDEAT SUPERIOR; TORT.

vice   1 A fault, defect, or imperfection; such illegal activities as the sale of drugs, gambling, and prostitution.   2 (Latin) "In the place or stead." For example, a *vice consul* is second in rank to a consul; he may act in the place of the consul, or he may have charge of a portion of his territory. See AMBASSADORS AND CONSULS.

Vice President   The second-highest officer in the executive branch of the United States government. The primary function of the Vice President is to preside over the SENATE. He has no vote, however, unless the Senators are equally divided on a particular issue.

Like the PRESIDENT and all civil officers of the United States, he can be removed from office upon IMPEACHMENT (indictment) and conviction for "treason, bribery, or other HIGH CRIMES AND MISDEMEANORS." The Constitution states these as grounds for impeachment, but the Supreme Court has not yet defined "high crimes and misdemeanors."

If the Vice President leaves office for any reason, the President nominates a successor, who takes office upon confirmation by a majority vote of both houses of CONGRESS.

A Vice President of the United States must be a native-born citizen, must be at least 35 years old, and must have resided in the United States for no less than 14 years. Like the President, the Vice President holds office for a term of four years and is chosen by the ELECTORAL COLLEGE unless appointed by the President to fill a vacant office.

If the President-elect should die before taking office, the Vice President-elect becomes President of the United States. If at any time during his term, the President is removed from office, dies, or resigns, the Vice President becomes President of the United States. If the President notifies both houses of Congress in writing that he is unable to discharge the powers and duties of his office, the Vice President will assume the responsibilities as Acting President until the President declares in writing that he is able to take over again.

The Vice President can also become Acting President against the President's wishes if the Vice President and a majority of either the executive department (the Cabinet) or another body that Congress specifies declares to both houses in writing that the President is unable to discharge the powers and duties of his office. The President may resume his duties after (1) notifying the President pro tempore of the Senate and the Speaker of the HOUSE OF REPRESENTATIVES that the disability no longer exists and (2) Congress votes its agreement with him. Otherwise, the Vice President continues as Acting President. See CONSTITUTIONAL LAW; ELECTION.

victim of crime

A person who suffers direct harm from a crime, such as a woman who is robbed or a murdered man and his dependents. Victims of crimes have been virtually forgotten or ignored by the criminal justice system. As New Jersey Congressman Peter Rodino said in the House of Representatives:

“ Millions of taxpayer dollars are spent to rehabilitate offenders in an attempt to ensure that they do not reenter society embittered and angry; yet little has been done to counter those same feelings in innocent victims.”

A man who shot and killed a jeweler while robbing his store was caught, tried, and convicted. Altogether, the state spent more than $250,000 to apprehend, house, feed, clothe, counsel, and rehabilitate the criminal, even enabling him to finish work for his master's degree in psychological counseling while he was in prison. Yet not a cent went to compensate the victim's family for their loss.

Some attempts are now being made to change these priorities and put the crime victim first. This article discusses some of the laws that can aid crime victims.

■ **The right to sue** Anyone who suffers injury or loss of property because of another's intentional act, whether a crime or not, generally has the right to sue the wrongdoer. If the victim proves his case, a jury can award him money DAMAGES to compensate for what he has lost.

Suing the criminal is often impossible or impractical, however. First, the criminal is not always caught. Second, even if the criminal is caught, the victim may be too poor to pay for a lawsuit. Third, the criminal may be too poor to pay damages.

As an alternative, a few crime victims have successfully sued local governments that failed to protect them from the criminal. Usually a municipality is not legally liable for an individual's crime-related injuries, because it has only a general duty to provide police protection for the public at large. Occasionally, however, a police department has a special duty to protect a certain individual or a certain group of people.

EXAMPLE In 1958 a New York court upheld the right of an informer to sue New York City for failing to provide adequate police protection. A young man who had identified the nationally known criminal Willie Sutton from a wanted poster contacted the police and cooperated until Sutton's arrest. After the ensuing publicity, the young man reported that threats had been made on his life, and three weeks later he was shot and killed on his way home.

When the victim's family sued, the court held that there was a special relationship between the victim and the police department that obligated the city to protect him from the threat of death. Moreover, the police knew that the danger existed and yet failed to provide police protection. In such a case, the municipality or county or state that maintains the police force can be held liable.

EXAMPLE In another case, in the late 1970's a young man sued the city of Yonkers, New York, claiming that its police department had bungled a murder investigation. A police search for the Son of Sam (also known as the .44-caliber killer), who had been shooting young girls and couples in parked cars, led to a man named David Berkowitz. The police did not at first have enough evidence to make an arrest, however, and before Berkowitz was apprehended, he shot this young man and his companion, blinding him in one eye and killing her.

In his suit, the victim claimed that the police had a special duty to find such a dangerous, psychotic killer and that Berkowitz should have been investigated more thoroughly and rapidly, thereby preventing the crime that blinded the victim and killed his companion. The judge disagreed, holding that this victim was no more than a member of the general public, with no right to sue the police simply because it takes a certain amount of time to locate a criminal, even a notorious killer.

■ **Victims as witnesses** Some states provide special support for crime victims in order to encourage cooperation with prosecutors. Crime victims have generally been reluctant to report crimes or testify in court, where they must face the criminal who attacked or robbed them.

To help relieve some of the pressure on victims, victim witness bureaus have been established in some large cities such as Chicago and New Orleans and in some smaller places such as Covington, Kentucky, and Boulder, Colorado. Bureau counselors help to calm victims, arrange for the return of property held as evidence, and keep victims informed about changed court dates or the final outcome of a case. District attorneys report that programs like these drastically reduce the number of cases dismissed because of the victim's refusal to cooperate at trial.

■ **Crime victim compensation plans** In 1979, 25 states had some kind of plan to provide direct compensation to crime victims. Crime victim compensation laws pay money from the public treasury to the victim or his family for lost earnings, medical expenses, or missing property.

Most plans are not so generous as to replace every dollar lost, but they do help soften the blow.

Most plans are limited to victims who are left destitute by their misfortune. Other plans pay benefits only to victims who are physically injured or, if they are killed, to their families. Certain plans compensate for missing or damaged property, but this benefit may be limited to particular victims, such as elderly people or those who also suffered physical injury.

Some plans provide benefits for any "innocent victim." An innocent victim is someone who did not contribute to the cause of his injuries—say, by pulling out a gun when it was not necessary.

Usually a victim can apply for compensation by filling out a form provided by the proper state office. A parent, guardian, or other legal representative can file an application for children or anyone else incapable of managing his own affairs. Anyone applying for crime victim compensation must do so promptly because states generally have a limited period in which applications may be filed.

According to some compensation laws, any money paid to a convicted criminal for selling his story to a writer or filmmaker or for a book, story, or dramatization of the crime must be turned over to the state. The money is then held in a special escrow account to pay any victim who successfully sues the criminal. These laws generally extend the time limit in which a victim must start a lawsuit, since victims usually have no reason to sue poor criminals until after lucrative book or movie deals are made.

EXAMPLE When John Wojtowicz and a companion bungled a bank robbery and were surrounded by police, they grabbed several bank employees as hostages and barricaded themselves inside the bank. Finally, police coaxed Wojtowicz out of the bank and rescued the hostages. Only after the tense scenes were dramatically portrayed in the movie *Dog Day Afternoon* did the hostages have any hope of being compensated for their suffering, and that is when they sued.

vide (Latin) "See." A word used to refer the reader to something else. For example, *vide ante* ("see [what came] before") or *vide supra* ("see above") refers to a previous passage or section in a book, while *vide post* ("see [what comes] after" or "see what follows") or *vide infra* ("see below") refers to a subsequent passage or section.

vi et armis (Latin) "With force and arms." A common-law TRESPASS action for damages caused by a defendant who used direct force or violence against the plaintiff or his property. Modern laws relating to liability for NEGLIGENCE and battery (see ASSAULT AND BATTERY) developed from the common-law action *vi et armis*.

virtue Authority; force—generally preceded by "in" or "by" and followed by "of." For example, money paid to a sheriff to redeem land from a FORECLOSURE sale is money he receives "by virtue of his office."

vis (Latin) "Force," "violence." The word is used in many legal phrases and maxims—for example, *Vis legibus est inimica* ("Violence is inimical to the laws").

visa An endorsement by one country on a PASSPORT issued by another, signifying that the passport has been examined by the proper authorities and that the bearer is permitted to travel in the particular country. The visa may be written, printed, or stamped on a separate paper rather than stamped or written into the actual passport.

viva voce (Latin) "With the living voice"; by word of mouth. Viva voce voting is oral—saying "aye" or "nay," for example—rather than a written ballot.

viz. An abbreviation of the Latin word *videlicet*, meaning "to wit," "namely," or "that is to say." It is used to point out or make more specific something previously stated only in general language. For example, a court decision may say, "This action may not be maintained because it was begun after the time allowed for such actions in Section 203 of the Code of Civil Procedure; viz. two years. The defendant's motion to dismiss is granted."

void Null; having no legal force or binding effect. For example, a void CONTRACT has no legal existence or effect and cannot be made legal by confirmation or RATIFICATION. Since the contract lacks some essential element, either party may therefore ignore it at his pleasure.

voidable Something that can be declared VOID but that is not absolutely void in itself. For example, a CONTRACT induced by FRAUD is not void but is voidable at the option of the person who was defrauded. However, the defrauded party must take positive action to relieve himself of the contractual obligation. Until then, the contract is treated as valid.

voir dire (French) "To speak the truth." A voir dire describes a court's preliminary examination of a prospective juror or WITNESS whose competency or qualifications have been challenged. See JURY.

Volstead Act A statute also known as the National Prohibition Act that enforced the 18th Amendment to the U.S. Constitution and prevented the manufacture and sale of INTOXICATING LIQUORS. It was abrogated by the 21st Amendment, which repealed Prohibition.

voting rights See ELECTION; Chart 34.

voting trust An agreement in which two or more owners of corporate stock that carries voting rights with it transfer the stock to a trustee so the trustee can vote and manage corporate affairs in place of the stockholders. The agreement may or may not specify that the stockholders can direct the trustee how to vote. See PROXY.

wage assignment See ATTACHMENT AND GARNISHMENT; Chart 9.

Wagner Act The National Labor Relations Act of 1935. It gave employees the right to organize unions and to bargain collectively for wages, hours, and working conditions. See LABOR RELATIONS.

wait and see statute A statute some states have enacted to avoid the harshness resulting from the RULE AGAINST PERPETUITIES.

waiver The voluntary relinquishment of a known right; conduct implying that a right has been relinquished. For example, a landlord who accepts late rental payments for several months has waived his rights under the lease to receive payment on the first day of those months. Another example is an accused person in a criminal case who voluntarily becomes a WITNESS in his own behalf; he thus waives his privilege against SELF-INCRIMINATION and can be cross-examined.

wanton Reckless; malicious. A wanton act is a reckless disregard for and indifference to the life, safety, health, reputation, or property rights of another person. Such an act is more than NEGLIGENCE—even gross negligence—since its results are the same as those of willful misconduct.
> EXAMPLE Driving along a two-lane highway, Frank turned 0⟶✳ into the left lane to pass the automobile ahead. Even though he discovered that a vehicle was approaching rapidly from the opposite direction, he persisted in attempting to pass. Frank was guilty of wanton conduct.

war A conflict between the armed forces of two or more nations under the authority of their respective governments. When a country is at war, it has certain added powers and obligations, which are granted it or imposed on it by national and INTERNATIONAL LAW. These powers and obligations are the subject of this article. For a discussion of the law of war (controls set on nations at war by treaty or custom), see WAR CRIME.
■ **Declaration** In the United States the power to declare war resides with the federal government only—and specifically with the CONGRESS. The PRESIDENT, although unable to declare war unless Congress gives him that power, does have the authority to turn back invasions without a declaration of war. In repelling an attack, the President can even order the immediate invasion of another country; without the potential for rapid military response, the country could be defeated or badly crippled before Congress could act.

War can exist with or without a formal declaration. The start of a war is more a question of fact and history than of law. For example, the Vietnam conflict was never declared a war by Congress.
■ **Enemy** In international law, the word "belligerents" means nations that are actually at war and those that actively cooperate as allies. Enemy territory includes both the land in the enemy's possession in time of war and all territory within the boundaries of the enemy country even though it might be military forces of another belligerent.
■ **Status and rights of citizens** In time of war a nation has the power to compel all its citizens and subjects to serve the common cause. Citizens who are abroad are not automatically obligated to return simply because war has been declared, but if they are recalled they can be penalized for failure to obey. Private rights and duties are affected by war only when they are incompatible with the rights of war.

The word "enemy" includes all the citizens of the enemy state, wherever they might be, and a nation at war can take any steps against enemy ALIENS (those who are not citizens) that it believes necessary for national security. An enemy alien has no rights other than those the nation chooses to grant him. Aliens who are within enemy country at the outbreak of war or who enter it during the war are subject to arrest, detention, internment, or deportation.
> EXAMPLE A young man was a U.S. citizen because he was 0⟶✳ born in West Virginia. Both his parents were Italian, and they took him back to Italy to live when he was still a child. During World War II he served in the Italian army and was taken prisoner by the Allies. He was sent to the United States and held in a prisoner-of-war camp. He sued for his freedom, claiming that his American citizenship prevented his detention as a prisoner of war. The court rejected his claim, holding that he was an enemy because he had remained in Italy and supported it during the war.

According to the laws of war, an individual is considered neutral or belligerent according to the position taken by his country; a resident of a neutral country is a neutral and as such can enter into or continue a contract with a citizen of a warring country. If the neutral citizen later becomes a belligerent because his nation becomes involved in the war, the contract would then involve commerce with the enemy, and the contract would be void.

■ **Intercourse with the enemy**   Generally, in time of war all intercourse, correspondence, and traffic between citizens of opposing belligerent states that might give aid or comfort to the enemy are absolutely forbidden. For example, sending money across enemy lines is against the laws of war.

All trading with the enemy and other commercial relations are forbidden while a state of war exists. After a declaration of war, a citizen of a belligerent state living in the enemy country ordinarily cannot remove his property from there. If he is only temporarily within the enemy's country at the outbreak of war, however, he is entitled to a reasonable time to collect his belongings or convert them into available funds and withdraw them.

■ **Martial law**   Martial rule, or MARTIAL LAW, exists when military authorities exercise control over civilians. It is enforced in a territory where, because of war or public commotion, the civil government is unable to preserve order and enforce the law.

■ **Acts in exercise of war power**   The federal government's power to wage war is not restricted to winning victories in the field and repulsing enemy forces. It extends to every matter and activity that affects its conduct and progress, including the mobilization and use of all the country's resources and the protection of war matériel, price controls, and rationing.

Requisition of private property   Generally, the power to requisition private property for the good of the nation belongs to Congress. As Commander in Chief of the armed forces, the President also has the power to requisition private property needed to prosecute a war. A military commander can also seize a citizen's private property, either for public use or to prevent it from falling into enemy hands, but only in cases of immediate and impending danger or necessity.

Statutes, orders, and proclamations specify the extent of a particular officer's or agency's power to requisition property. The entire facilities and functions of some businesses, such as steel manufacturing and shipping companies, can be requisitioned. The government can also requisition patent rights.

An owner whose property is requisitioned by the government is entitled to just compensation. It does not have to be paid in advance, however, or even when the property is taken; but when he is paid, the owner is entitled to receive the fair MARKET PRICE OR VALUE of the property—not the amount it will cost him to replace the property or the property's special value to the government.

EXAMPLE An oil company owned storage tanks on an island in the Pacific. The military commander requisitioned the contents of one tank for use by his troops during the war. He gave the oil company a receipt but did not pay for the oil. A month later, intelligence reports warned the commander that the enemy was about to launch a massive invasion that would surely enable it to capture the island. The commander ordered his troops to destroy everything that could be used by the enemy, including the remaining oil in storage. After the war, the oil company sued the government and recovered a fair price for the oil requisitioned but nothing for the oil destroyed. The government was liable only for what it used.

War matériel   Congress can and must stimulate production of necessary war equipment and supplies by all proper means, including paying subsidies, restricting profits, and seizing or controlling private businesses.

Congress is also responsible for taking steps under its war powers to guarantee sufficient food for civilian and military needs, although it can delegate authority to an administrative agency to run a food program. Such a program may allocate food and prescribe sanitary regulations.

Price and rent control   Congress can regulate and control prices, as a war emergency measure and as part of a wartime anti-inflation program, in order to stabilize economic conditions, prevent speculative and abnormal increases in prices, increase production, and assure an adequate supply of goods at fair prices.

Rent control is a proper exercise of the government's war power because it helps to prevent inflation and rent gouging and to utilize all available housing accommodations. Rent control provisions do not change the terms of an existing lease or prevent landlords and tenants from bargaining and entering into new leases so long as the established rent ceilings are not exceeded.

Allocating and rationing commodities   Congress may allocate and ration materials and facilities necessary to national defense, or it may delegate that power to the President. He and his agencies can issue binding regulations. Some items that have been rationed in wartime include gasoline, meat, and sugar.

war crime   A violation of the law of war. The law of war is enforced by military law and discipline within armies. Persons who commit war crimes may be tried and punished by their own countrymen or by international tribunals. War crimes are punished because a war without rules is a war that nobody wins.

■ **The law of war**   The law of war is not enacted by a legislature the way a criminal statute is. It results primarily from custom or from TREATIES. Nations recognize that there must be a limit to what can be done even during armed conflict. Just as murder is intolerable within a country, war crimes among nations are unacceptable in INTERNATIONAL LAW. The economic, political, and humanitarian interests of each nation dictate that it should observe the same law of war that it wishes its enemies to recognize.

Traditionally, the law of war has prohibited

(1) Attacking another country without declaring war.

(2) Violating treaties.

(3) Attacking for reasons of personal vengeance.

(4) Firing on passenger ships without rescuing the passengers.

(5) Firing on hospitals or medical personnel.

(6) Using forced labor or slavery.

(7) Killing or mistreating prisoners of war.

(8) Failing to wear the uniform of one's country.

(9) Mistreating dead bodies.

(10) Poisoning water supplies.

(11) Using chemical or biological weapons.

(12) Terrorizing noncombatant civilians or forcing them from their homes.

Although most of the rules are unwritten and have evolved by custom, nations agree from time to time to specific rules and write them down in treaties, which bind the nations that are parties to them. For example, the Geneva Conventions are international treaties that were signed in 1864, 1906, and 1929 and revised and expanded in 1949. The 1949 Geneva Conventions provide rules for the humanitarian treatment of civilians, prisoners of war, and of the sick and wounded during war. Most nations in the world have formally accepted them. Other rules of conduct are included in codes of military law and enforced within a nation's own ARMED SERVICES. See also UNIFORM CODE OF MILITARY JUSTICE.

■ **Enforcing the law of war** Although there are no international policemen to arrest war criminals and bring them to trial, most nations follow the rules most of the time and insist that their soldiers do so, because the costs of doing otherwise would outweigh the benefits. The International Red Cross, military law, and war crimes trials in national or international courts all help to encourage respect for the rules of war.

The Red Cross A Swiss citizen, Henri Dunant, appalled at the neglect and ill treatment given the wounded in the Battle of Solferino in 1859, convinced the Swiss government to call an international conference to negotiate the first treaty to protect such persons. The outcome was the first of the Geneva Conventions. Later, Dunant organized the International Committee of the Red Cross to oversee the conduct of nations at war. The Red Cross now oversees the needs of prisoners of war during armed conflicts whenever the warring nations so request. It handles communications between prisoners and their families, ships provisions to prisoners, and visits prison camps. It reports to each nation how the enemy is treating its prisoners, and this helps insure that they receive food, clothing, and medical attention. Because the Red Cross can tell the world if a country is mistreating or killing prisoners of war, its presence helps to prevent such crimes.

Military law In the United States all soldiers are taught the Geneva Conventions rules of warfare, and those who violate them can be court-martialed and punished under military law.

EXAMPLE One of the most widely publicized cases of an American soldier convicted of war crimes was that of Lt. William Calley. The U.S. Court of Military Appeals found Calley guilty of murder for shooting unarmed civilians in 1968 at Son My village, also called My Lai, in Vietnam. Calley claimed that he had been ordered to kill everything that breathed in the village, but the court ruled that killing people who are not fighting is so clearly illegal that such an order—even if it had been given, as Calley claimed—should not be obeyed.

War crimes trials A war criminal—for example, an occupying soldier who committed atrocities on the civilian population—may also be treated as a common criminal by local police and courts. If the area is under MARTIAL LAW, military tribunals may sit instead of civilian courts.

After World War II, thousands of war criminals were tried by military tribunals set up in individual countries. They handled criminals who were caught where the crimes had been committed, and they applied both local law and the international law of war. Some countries also passed laws making officers responsible for crimes committed by their soldiers.

Two international courts—the Nuremberg and the Far East military tribunals—tried war criminals whose crimes went beyond a single geographical location. The defendants—civilians as well as military men—were provided with defense attorneys and given trials according to recognized fair procedures.

EXAMPLE At Nuremberg, Germany, the defendants explained first that in committing the crimes they had merely followed orders and that to do otherwise was to risk execution. The prosecution argued that anyone who obeys an illegal order must answer for it under international law; what is more, the defendants were themselves architects of criminal policies, not innocent victims. The next defense was that the Nazis were being tried only because they had lost the war, for the Allies, too, had committed war crimes—such as the firebombing of Dresden,which killed 150,000 civilians. The prosecution countered that two wrongs do not make a right. The final defense was that the court was creating new laws at Nuremberg and applying them to the defendants' past activities. The prosecution responded by citing established traditions of war and listing all the customs and treaties the Nazis had broken. Even though the defendants had not expected an international court to try them for war crimes, they should have known that their crimes would outrage the world. All but 3 of the 22 defendants were found guilty and sentenced to imprisonment or death.

The International Military Tribunal for the Far East was convened by Gen. Douglas MacArthur in January 1946. Eleven judges from various countries found 23 Japanese military and political leaders guilty of war crimes.

EXAMPLE The most controversial of these men was Gen. Tomojuki Yamashita, the "Tiger of Singapore." In the last desperate days of the war, his troops had ransacked the Philippines, committing terrible atrocities with which he, as their leader, was charged. Seven American military officers defended General Yamashita, arguing that he was cultured and intelligent and neither knew about nor condoned the brutality of his troops. Furthermore, his army had become so disordered that he could not have stopped them anyway. Nevertheless, Yamashita was found guilty of the crimes committed by his troops. He appealed to the U.S. Supreme Court, but it affirmed his conviction and General MacArthur immediately carried out the order of execution.

ward 1 A territorial division in most American cities into which the municipalities are separated for purposes of elections, police and sanitary regulations, and fire prevention. They are also called precincts and districts. 2 A person, usually a child, who cannot manage his own affairs and is placed by a court under the care and supervision of a guardian. See GUARDIAN AND WARD.

warehouse receipt

A receipt given by a warehouseman for goods he receives for storage. The receipt serves as evidence of ownership of the stored goods. Many warehouse receipts are NEGOTIABLE INSTRUMENTS.

EXAMPLE Lounger Company makes furniture in North Carolina and ships it all over the country. Much of its furniture is sold to retailers in the Midwest. Lounger sends regular shipments of various pieces of furniture to a warehouseman in Chicago. The warehouseman gives Lounger a receipt for each truckload. Because the receipt is negotiable, Lounger can transfer ownership of the furniture by transferring the warehouse receipt. It does this by ordering the warehouseman to deliver the furniture to the retailer who bought it or to deliver it to his order. The retailer can pick up the furniture himself with the properly made-out receipt or he can direct the warehouseman to give it to the trucker he sends for the furniture ("to his order").

The law relating to warehouse receipts is found in Article 7 of the uniform commercial code and has been adopted by all 50 states. See SALES.

Ordinarily, a warehouse receipt should contain the following: (1) the location of the warehouse, (2) the date of issue, (3) its consecutive number, (4) a statement specifying the person to whom the goods are to be delivered, (5) the storage rate and handling charges, (6) a statement describing the goods or their packaging, (7) the signature of the warehouseman or his agent, and (8) the amount of advance payment. When a warehouse receipt does not contain these provisions, the warehouseman can be liable to a person who is financially harmed by the omission of these terms. The warehouseman is a bailee and is subject to the law of BAILMENTS.

warrant

1 Promise that a fact stated in a CONTRACT is as it is claimed to be. See WARRANTY.

2 Assure by a promise spelled out in a real estate DEED that the TITLE to (ownership of) the property shall be good and the buyer's ownership will be undisturbed.

3 As a noun, written authorization. An *arrest warrant* is a writ (order), issued by a judge or a magistrate, addressed to a peace officer, requiring him to arrest and bring before the court the person named in the document. See SEARCH AND SEIZURE. A *tax warrant* is written authority issued to a tax collector empowering him to collect the taxes listed on the assessment roll or to place a tax LIEN (claim) on the goods and lands of those persons who fail to pay. A *stock warrant* is an option to purchase corporate stock.

warranty

A promise that a particular statement of fact is true. A valid warranty is a legally binding promise. If the promise is broken, the person to whom it was made can go to court to seek compensation for any harm he suffered as a result. Such court action must be started within a limited period of time after the warranty is breached. See Chart 4. The law of SALES, for example, specifies that buyers have the legal right to assume that the merchandise they buy lives up to promises made by the seller. See

CONSUMER PROTECTION; PRODUCT LIABILITY. A purchaser of real estate can rely on promises concerning ownership of the property. See DEED.

wash sale

A fictitious sale of stock. A broker receives an order from one person to buy a certain quantity of a given stock or commodity at a certain price and a second order from another client to sell the same stock at a specified price. The broker simply transfers the stock from one person to the other and pockets the difference between the selling and buying prices, along with his fees. The practice is prohibited on the various stock exchanges. The orders to sell and to buy should be executed separately so that both customers can take advantage of the competitive prices on the open markets.

waste

An unlawful act or omission by a tenant that causes permanent damage to the land, houses, gardens, trees, or some other part of the property. *Voluntary waste* is an aggressive act of destruction, such as pulling down a house or removing a large part of it. *Permissive waste* is waste allowed by the tenant through neglect or by giving someone else permission to harm the property—for example, by permitting a building to decay or to be destroyed by fire. The owner of the property can start a lawsuit against the tenant and recover damages for the waste. See LANDLORD AND TENANT.

water right

A legal right to use the water of a natural stream, a ditch, or a canal for such purposes as irrigation, mining, power, and domestic use, so long as the rights of other users of the same waters are not injured. It includes the right to change the place of diversion and the right of storage. A *water right claim* is a declaration of intention to create a water right, usually filed with a state water department or engineer. For a discussion of water as property, see PROPERTY.

weapon

An instrument of offensive or defensive combat, including anything used to injure an enemy. Depending on its use, even a toothpick might be a weapon.

■ **Types of weapons** There are various types of weapons. A *firearm* is any weapon that discharges a shot by means of an explosive force, but the term is usually applied only to small firearms, such as a pistol, revolver, rifle, or shotgun. *Gun* is a general term that in popular usage means any portable firearm.

According to the law, a *dangerous weapon*, or *deadly weapon*, is one likely to produce death or great bodily harm. A weapon that is capable of producing death but not likely to do so, such as an ordinary penknife, is therefore not necessarily a deadly weapon under the law.

■ **Right to bear arms** The right to bear arms is said to be an inherent and inalienable right. While the U.S. Constitution does not confer this right on the people, it safeguards it, as do state constitutions. Although laws may regulate the bearing of arms by individuals, they cannot interfere with the people's right to maintain a militia. See ARMS, RIGHT TO BEAR; Chart 32.

■ **Criminal responsibility** Generally, neither carrying nor possessing a weapon is a criminal offense, nor does it constitute a BREACH OF THE PEACE. However, some states have laws that prohibit the carrying or concealment of various kinds of weapons in some places or in all places, except by certain persons, such as policemen. Under such laws an offender must intend to carry or conceal a weapon.

Intent Intent is an essential element of the crime of carrying or possessing a weapon. It is proved simply by the fact that the person knows he is carrying or has the weapon.

The word "carry" means to have the weapon "on or about the person," not necessarily to be moving it somewhere. A weapon is carried on or about the person when he has it in his hand, in the clothes he is wearing, or in a garment, such as a coat, that he is carrying over his arm. A weapon is also generally considered on or about the person when it is in a receptacle attached to, or carried by, a person as he moves—for example, in a handbag or knapsack.

When the state says carrying a concealed weapon is unlawful, the weapon must not only be intentionally carried but also intentionally concealed to constitute an offense. According to the law, *concealed* means that the weapon is hidden from the general view of persons near enough otherwise to see it. The fact that a weapon's outlines are distinguishable and that it is recognizable as a weapon does not rule out concealment if it is covered from view. The courts have held that the law is violated if a weapon is concealed carelessly—that is, without the specific purpose of hiding it.

Under some statutes any person who has or carries a prohibited or concealed weapon is acting unlawfully, even though his purpose is merely to exhibit the weapon as a curiosity or to try to sell it or return it to its owner after repairing it. Under other statutes, however, it is not unlawful to have or to carry a prohibited weapon for a harmless or legitimate purpose. Under these laws, carrying a weapon to its owner or to any other person entitled to have it is not an offense. Similarly, an owner of a weapon has the right to take the weapon to his new residence when he moves. A person who finds a weapon can pick it up and take it with him to his destination and then take it home with him.

Anyone who carries a prohibited weapon with the intention of surrendering it to the police is not breaking the carrying and possession laws unless he fails to turn over the weapon within a reasonable time.

Weapons prohibited Carrying or possessing a particular weapon is not unlawful unless the weapon falls into a category prohibited by statute. For example, many weapons are prohibited under such broad terms as "arms," "firearms," and "weapons." Some statutes name the weapons that cannot be possessed or carried, such as billies, blackjacks, bowie knives, brass knuckles, daggers, dirks, razors, machine guns, and sawed-off shotguns.

Other laws both list certain prohibited weapons and use an umbrella term, such as "other dangerous weapons," which, in particular cases, has included a butcher knife, a bayonet, an iron bar, and a piece of rubber hose.

Places prohibited Under some statutes that prohibit carrying or possessing a weapon, a person can legally carry or possess a forbidden weapon in his own home or place of business or on his own land. If a weapons statute makes no exception as to locality, it is unlawful to possess the prohibited weapon anywhere, even in one's own home. Under some statutes, carrying a weapon in certain public places, assemblies, or gatherings is a separate offense. A public assembly can include a courtroom during a trial, a parade, or even a public barbecue.

Weber case *(United Steelworkers of America* v. *Weber)* A historic Supreme Court case involving CIVIL RIGHTS, in which a white worker lost his lawsuit for reverse discrimination when a less qualified black worker was preferred over him for a promotion. Brian F. Weber was a white unskilled production worker at Kaiser Aluminum and Chemical Corporation's Gramercy, Louisiana, plant when, in 1974, the company agreed in the course of collective bargaining with the union, the United Steelworkers of America (USWA), to set up an affirmative action plan "to eliminate conspicuous racial imbalances in Kaiser's then almost exclusively white craft forces."

Prior to 1974, Kaiser had hired only experienced men to be craft workers. Because blacks had traditionally been excluded from craft unions, few had qualified for the jobs. Although the labor force around Gramercy was 39 percent black, the minority held only 1.83 percent—5 out of 273—of the skilled jobs at the plant. To correct the imbalance, Kaiser established on-the-job training programs, with admission to the program based on seniority. One-half of the openings, however, were reserved for black employees.

Seven black and six white employees were selected for the first training program. Weber applied but was rejected in favor of a black employee with less seniority. Weber brought a class action against Kaiser and the United Steelworkers, claiming that the preference given to black workers over white ones with more seniority discriminated against him and other whites in violation of federal law.

Weber's argument was based on Title VII of the Civil Rights Act of 1964, which made it "an unlawful employment practice" to hire or fire a person or deprive him of employment opportunities because of his "race, color, religion, sex, or national origin." A federal district court agreed that the Kaiser plan violated Title VII and issued an INJUNCTION prohibiting the company and USWA from preventing Weber and other workers access to the program because of their race. A federal court of appeals affirmed the decision.

The U.S. Supreme Court agreed to consider just one issue in the case: "Whether Title VII forbids private employers and unions from agreeing upon bona fide affirmative action plans that accord racial preferences in the manner and for the purpose provided in the Kaiser-USWA plan." (Unlike the BAKKE CASE, this case did not present the problem of whether Weber was denied his constitutional right to EQUAL PROTECTION OF LAWS because no state or federal government participated in the program.)

Weber argued that the Court had only to look to the very words of Title VII to determine that the Kaiser plan was illegal. Title VII reads:

❝ *It shall be an unlawful employment practice for any employer, labor organization, or joint labor-management committee controlling apprenticeship or other training or retraining, including on-the-job training programs, to discriminate against any individual because of his race, color, religion, sex, or national origin in admission to, or employ-*

ment in, any program established to provide apprenticeship or other training."

This language, coupled with an earlier Supreme Court decision that whites as well as blacks were entitled to Title VII protection from certain forms of racial discrimination, was cited as support for Weber's claim that the Kaiser-USWA plan violated Title VII.

The Court disagreed, however. While admitting that Weber's arguments were "not without force," the Supreme Court refused to apply Title VII literally, saying that such an interpretation would "bring about an end completely at variance with the purpose of the statute." The act was passed in 1964 because of congressional concern with the plight of black people. Unless they were given job opportunities that had been closed to them in the past, because of their race, integration would never be accomplished.

weight of evidence

The effect and influence of EVIDENCE presented during a trial. The jury or judge listens to the testimony of both sides and *weighs* the evidence. A judge or jury usually must give greater weight, for example, to direct and unimpeached evidence than to evidence that is vague, indefinite, or improbable. Evidence given by a WITNESS who is testifying from personal observation (direct evidence) is of greater weight than that of a witness who is testifying merely from general knowledge. The decision or verdict in a case is based on the effectiveness with which one side or the other has proved the facts and circumstances it sets forth. The weight of the evidence may be said to lie with the side whose arguments are more persuasive. If the jury or judge refuses to believe uncontradicted evidence and finds against the weight of the evidence, there may be an appeal.

weights and measures

Fixed standards that are used to determine the heaviness, amount, volume, or dimensions of an object or a material or to determine the distance between points. The regulation of weights and measures is a proper and necessary subject of legislative action. Under the federal Constitution, Congress is given the power to establish uniform weights and measures. The states can also regulate weights and measures as long as their regulations are not in conflict with federal law. Legislation adopting a uniform system of weights and measures and requiring its use is a valid exercise of the government's POLICE POWER.

In 1975 Congress enacted a national policy of voluntary conversion to the metric system, which is used in most parts of the world. In order to implement this policy, Congress authorized establishment of a United States Metric Board to create and put into effect a plan to educate the public in the metric system. The goal is that the system will be in general but not exclusive use in the United States by 1985.

welfare programs

Welfare is a general term referring to well-being. An individual's welfare has to do with his health, happiness, and prosperity. Government welfare programs are systems designed to maintain a minimum standard of well-being for everyone. This is accomplished by providing benefits to the poor to bring their standard of living up to the level of that minimum. Various kinds of welfare programs exist at different levels of government (federal, state, and local), but all are designed to help people who qualify for aid on the basis of need. Technically, this is what distinguishes welfare programs from other government benefits for which people qualify on some other basis—by being, for example, veterans, senior citizens, employees injured on the job, owners of small businesses, unemployed workers, or victims of a disaster.

Welfare programs discussed in this article provide public assistance for eligible people in the form of cash benefits, medical care, and housing.

■ **Federal Social Security programs** The federal government funds the largest welfare programs in the country under the provisions of the Social Security Act. These welfare programs are distinct from the SOCIAL SECURITY benefits paid to aged, disabled, and unemployed workers and their dependents, based on the employment record of a worker. The programs include Supplemental Security Income, Aid to Families with Dependent Children, and Medicaid—the programs that most people are referring to when they say "welfare."

Supplemental Security Income The federal Supplemental Security Income program (SSI) provides money for needy aged, blind, and disabled persons. In 1974 it replaced separate state-administered plans for these three categories of people. The federal program makes money available from the general treasury of the United States to provide monthly benefits at a standard rate all over the country. States already providing these benefits have added their benefits to those provided by the federal government.

Eligibility By enacting a federal plan of welfare for the aged, blind, and disabled, Congress created uniform standards of eligibility in every state. Applications for SSI are handled by local Social Security offices. An applicant must be a resident in the United States and a citizen or one of a few classes of ALIENS (noncitizens). No one can collect benefits for any month during all of which he is outside the 50 states and the District of Columbia. After a person has been out of the country for 30 days, he must return and remain at least 30 days before he is again eligible for SSI. A person generally cannot collect SSI for months that he is an inmate in a public institution, unless it is a community-run group home with no more than 16 residents.

A person is considered eligible because of *age* if he is 65 or older. He is considered *blind* if the visual acuity in his better eye is $^{20}/_{200}$ or less with the use of a corrective lens. A *disability* is defined as a physical or mental condition that can be expected to cause death or to prevent substantial gainful employment for 12 months or more. The disability must be diagnosable by medical tests or examination. Blind or disabled persons can qualify for SSI at any age, but the income and resources of a child's parents with whom he lives are used to determine whether the child is needy.

Income limitations Besides being aged, blind, or disabled, a person must show that he has income below the level set by federal law and does not own property that could be used for his support. In general, income includes all wages and earnings from employment plus support received from another person and benefits from an ANNUITY, PENSION, WORKMEN'S COMPENSATION program, or

Social Security. Gifts, prizes, awards, life INSURANCE proceeds, inheritances, ALIMONY, interest, dividends, rental income, and royalties must all be counted as income.

Certain amounts may be subtracted from the total: for example, the earned income of a child in school, the first $240 of income in a year, money received irregularly and infrequently, and certain amounts exempted for aged or blind people. One-third of any child-support payment made by an absent parent does not affect eligibility, nor does any amount received for a foster child placed in the applicant's home by an agency.

In determining how much the applicant owns in resources, his home, household goods, personal effects, and an automobile of reasonable value are excluded. Tools or equipment used for self-support also do not count. Other than these items, an applicant generally may not own assets worth more than $1,500.

The purpose of the SSI plan is to guarantee that qualified recipients have at least a minimum amount of cash to live on. The federal statute says $1,752 per year for an eligible individual, $2,628 if he has an eligible spouse. This is reduced by the amount of income he has. State benefits may be added.

If a recipient's monthly earnings are greater than the monthly benefits available, the first $65 of income a month will not count and only $1 will be lost for every $2 earned over the level of benefits. This encourages people to work if they can.

Aid to Families with Dependent Children   The primary concern of Congress in establishing the Aid to Families with Dependent Children program (AFDC) was the welfare and protection of needy, dependent children. The plan is aimed at providing basic necessities for the children while preserving the family unit. The program makes regular cash benefits available to the relative taking care of the child so that the family can stay in its own home.

Administration   AFDC is based on *cooperative federalism.* This is a system that allows each state to set up its own welfare system within the broad scheme established by Congress. Any state that participates—and all do—can get funding from the federal government. A system like this attacks problems that are national in scope but leaves room for each state to modify solutions in accordance with local conditions. Policy is set on the national level, but the state can experiment in implementing the program on the local level. The state submits a plan for approval by the Secretary of Health and Human Services. The program must allow anyone who wants to apply for aid to do so, it must be uniformly applied throughout the state, and assistance must be promptly furnished to all eligible individuals. Any delay by a state in providing aid to a qualified family must be explained by the agency responsible.

Eligibility   AFDC benefits are money payments furnished for the support of a needy, dependent child and a relative with whom he is living. The relative may be a parent, grandparent, brother, sister, stepparent, stepbrother, stepsister, uncle, aunt, first cousin, nephew, or niece of the child. The child must be unmarried and must be under the age of 18, or under 21 and regularly attending school. Some states cover unborn children so that mothers can begin to receive aid while they are pregnant. A child is

considered dependent if he has been deprived of parental support or care because a parent has died, has left the home, or is physically or mentally unable to fulfill his responsibilities to the child. Application for AFDC is made at the local office of the state's welfare agency.

Once a child is determined to be dependent, the state agency will calculate whether he is needy. Each state sets a minimum income level that is considered necessary to keep someone from being needy. If a child and his family have income below this level, they are considered needy. All income is considered, and the value of the family's assets is taken into account. Some income, of certain types and up to certain amounts, does not count in the total because the government wants the family to be better off when, for example, child-support payments are fully paid by a divorced parent or when the relative caring for the child is employed. Some assets are allowed for every family because they are basic needs. State law determines which assets are allowed (exempt).

Each state makes various allowances for special circumstances. For example, a state may allow some of the money received from Social Security because of the death of a parent to be set aside and saved for a child's future education. Then that portion does not count as income for the child. Some states require money recovered in a lawsuit because of injuries a child received to be counted as a resource to be used for the child's support. Other states allow money recoveries like this to be saved for the child's future expenses. In no event may a state count as income or resources any money not actually received by the family—for example, child support that an absent father is ordered to pay but does not pay in full.

EXAMPLE   One woman applied for AFDC benefits for herself and her two children after she and her husband separated. A family of three living in their own house in that state ordinarily qualified for benefits of $217.60 a month, which included $103 as their basic shelter allowance. The monthly mortgage payment on the house, owned jointly by the woman and her husband, was $184. The woman knew that the welfare department would not pay over its maximum of $103, but she asked for $84 because her husband was paying $100 a month on the mortgage directly to the bank. The welfare department determined that she was entitled to only $3 a month for shelter, and a court upheld this decision. Even though the husband made mortgage payments directly to the bank, this money had to be considered income for the woman and her children. AFDC, therefore, had to pay only the difference between that income and the maximum allowable shelter allowance.

Income limitations   Once the state agency determines the income of a family, it compares the income to the state's standard of need. The standard of need is based on the number of people in the family, sometimes up to a specified maximum. If there is too little income to meet what the state considers a minimum amount for its needs, based on the family's size, sometimes up to a specified maximum, then an AFDC check can make up the difference each month.

Family responsibilities   Every individual, as a condition to receiving AFDC, can be required to work or to register for employment or training except (1) a child who is under age 16 or attending school full time, (2) someone who is too old or too ill to work, (3) a person who lives too far away from a federal or state work-incentive project, (4) someone who has to stay home and care for another family member, or (5) a mother or other relative caring for a child under the age of six. Anyone else who refuses to work or to register for employment or training cannot be counted among family members when family aid is calculated.

Family members who do work have an extra economic incentive to be employed. At least some of their job-related expenses—such as transportation, lunches, and tools—are subtracted from what is calculated to be the family's income. In figuring the family's income, the welfare agency also disregards all the income of a dependent child who is a full-time student and the first $30 plus one third of any more money earned by any other family member.

Responsibilities of the state agency All AFDC payments must be used by the relative caring for qualified children in ways that benefit the children. If a state agency has reason to believe that payments are not being used in the best interests of the children, it must attempt to correct the situation. It may provide counseling to the adult, warn him or her that the money can be turned over to someone else on the children's behalf, try to have a guardian appointed for the children, or seek criminal penalties. The state cannot simply cut off aid to the family. It has a duty to make sure that AFDC children do not starve because of a parent's mismanagement.

An adult applying for AFDC has a duty to supply accurate information. The agency must rely on the applicant as its principal source of information, and the applicant's answers must be accepted unless they appear untrue because of inconsistency, lack of clarity, or incompleteness. If more information is necessary, the agency may make inquiries elsewhere, but it may not explore eligibility in any way that the applicant refuses to allow. An applicant who refuses to cooperate, however, might not receive aid.

The agency must decide promptly on eligibility and send the applicant written notice of the decision. If the application is rejected the agency must inform the applicant of his right to request a fair hearing, at which he can present his side of the story to an impartial hearing officer who is not from the welfare office.

The agency may reinvestigate a family periodically in order to affirm its continued eligibility.

Protection of privacy Welfare departments sometimes compile extensive records on the private lives of recipients. AFDC law requires the state welfare agencies to "provide safeguards which restrict the use or disclosure of information concerning applicants and recipients to purposes directly connected with the administration of aid to families with dependent children."

The Health, Education and Welfare Department (predecessor of the Health and Human Services Department) ruled that agencies generally should not divulge any information from a welfare file without first notifying the recipient and obtaining his or her permission whenever possible. Information can be released immediately in an emergency, but the recipient must be promptly notified.

A different question arises when welfare recipients ask to see their own case files. Because there may be persons mentioned whose identities should not be disclosed and comments made by agency personnel that may cause bad feelings, the agency does not have to open its files to recipients. However, every applicant is entitled to find out the source and content of any information that leads to a decision against him, and any information used in a fair hearing must be disclosed.

Medicaid The largest government welfare program that provides something other than money for poor people is Medicaid. Medicaid should not be confused with Medicare, which is a program of hospitalization and medical insurance for persons who qualify for SOCIAL SECURITY benefits or who are over 65 and pay the premiums.

Medicaid, like AFDC and SSI, is a joint federal-state effort. Federal money is provided to a state on condition that it furnish additional financing and administer a medical program for the needy that meets federal standards.

Eligibility The purpose of Medicaid is to make private medical care available to the poor. States can establish their own methods of determining qualifications for Medicaid as long as their procedures are reasonable. Application for Medicaid can be made at the local welfare office.

States may not reduce any other welfare benefits that applicants are receiving when they become eligible for Medicaid. States can require that an applicant be a state resident, but they cannot set any requirement regarding the length of his residency. See RESIDENCY LAWS. Nor can states exclude anyone who is a citizen of the United States. There can be no minimum or maximum age requirement. Medicaid must be available for everyone receiving benefits under one of the following programs: Old-Age Assistance (Social Security), AFDC, Aid to the Blind, Aid to the Disabled, and SSI (with some exceptions to SSI—check your state's laws).

Medicaid may also be extended to people who are "medically needy" because they are unable to cover costs for their medical care, even though their incomes or resources are above the level that would qualify them for other forms of welfare.

Required services Medicaid law specifies the kinds of medical services that must be furnished for eligible poor people. Some of the general categories of treatment included are: (1) inpatient hospital services; (2) outpatient hospital services; (3) other laboratory and X-ray services; (4) skilled nursing facility services; (5) screening for early discovery of physical and mental defects or chronic conditions in children under 21, diagnosis of children, and family-planning services; and (6) physicians' services. A state has some options in deciding what services to provide for people who are medically needy.

Generally, each of these services deals with conditions that cause acute suffering, endanger life, result in illness or infirmity, interfere with the capacity for normal activity, or threaten some kind of significant handicap. Assistance can usually be provided for mental problems, too.

Persons who use Medicaid have the right to select their own doctor, hospital, or other medical facility and to have their religious beliefs honored. No one can be discriminated against because of race, religion, or national origin.

Payment of fees Medicaid is called a *vendor plan* because payment is made directly to the "vendor"—the physician, nurse, technician, hospital, clinic, or other person or institution—who furnishes the services and not to the patient who receives them.

Nursing homes, doctors, and other providers of medical care must be approved before they are allowed to receive Medicaid payments for their services. Once authorized, their participation in the program cannot be arbitrarily terminated, but they can lose their certification for failing to provide good care or for submitting improper claims.

Criminal penalties for Medicaid fraud may be imposed upon anyone who files false statements; misrepresents services; or solicits, offers, or receives bribes or kickbacks. In addition, states are authorized to recover payments that were improperly obtained.

■ **Food plans** Food is another basic need that the government has tried to supply for the poor. The federal government oversees several different programs, including the distribution of surplus farm commodities, nutrition programs, and food stamp programs.

Surplus farm commodities Under the Commodities Distribution Act, the U.S. Secretary of Agriculture has the authority to distribute surplus agricultural commodities to needy families, Indian tribes, qualified summer camps for children, and school lunch and breakfast programs. The basic commodities that can be distributed under the law are hogs, cattle, wheat, rye, flax, barley, cotton, field corn, grain sorghums, rice, potatoes, tobacco, peanuts, sugar beets, sugarcane, and milk and milk products. Whenever the Secretary of Agriculture determines that an excess of one of these commodities has caused the market price to fall below a fair level, he can purchase the product for processing and distribution, thus helping to stabilize food supplies while feeding the poor.

Nutrition programs Child nutrition programs provide federal donations of cash and food to public and private nonprofit schools, summer recreation programs, day care centers, and institutions for runaway, abused, or neglected children and chronically ill or delinquent children. The donations are made so that milk and well-balanced meals, usually lunches and breakfasts, can be served to the children at moderate cost. Additional money is provided so that free or reduced-price food can be given to children of needy families. Approved state and federal agencies distribute the foods.

A special program provides food supplements for pregnant and nursing mothers and their children up to age four in areas that have large numbers of people who are considered nutritional risks. The program concentrates on providing nutrients that are generally lacking in the diets of these people, especially high-quality proteins, iron, calcium, vitamin A, and vitamin C. The Department of Agriculture recommends that nursing mothers and children from one to four years receive a quart of milk a day plus eggs, cereal, and fruit juice. Monthly food packages for infants up to 12 months old include an iron-fortified formula, cereal, and fruit juice.

Food stamps The most important food plan in the country is the food stamp program, inaugurated by the Food Stamp Act of 1964. This law allows needy individuals or households to obtain official stamps, or coupons of various denominations, that can be exchanged like money for food at an authorized store. After a store accepts food stamps, it redeems them for money through an authorized bank or food wholesaler, who then forwards them to the state. The state, in turn, is reimbursed by the federal government. Each state must account to the federal government for the value of the food stamps it has distributed. The state pays the costs of determining who is eligible to receive food stamps and of distributing the stamps.

Enough stamps are issued to each qualified household to cover the cost of a nutritionally adequate diet. The household pays an amount for the stamps that ranges from no cost to a maximum of 30 percent of its monthly income.

Eligibility Federal law allows food stamps for persons whose income is below a certain level (determined and revised periodically by the federal government) unless they are otherwise disqualified. In figuring a household's income, certain kinds of income are not counted. For example, there is usually a standard deduction of $60 a month. In addition, irregular and infrequent sources of money, foster care payments, some student loans, and income earned by students under 18 do not count. Households that have low incomes but own substantial assets do not qualify.

States are not required to participate in the federal food stamp plan, and even within a state some localities may offer the coupons while others do not.

A college student is not qualified to receive food stamps if he is over 18 and actually dependent on a taxpayer who could claim him as a dependent. Nor is he eligible if he refuses to work, as demonstrated by his failure to register with a state or federal employment office or his refusal to accept a job that pays the state or federal minimum wage.

Food stamps can be denied to anyone who refuses to register for or accept employment, anyone who fails to provide necessary information for the application, aliens not lawfully admitted to the United States, persons who give away property in order to prove their poverty, and those found to have fraudulently used food stamps or authorization cards for them.

Sales regulation The use of food stamps is ordinarily limited to the purchase of food at retail grocery stores, but there are exceptions. For example, elderly persons who are unable to prepare their meals may use food stamps to purchase prepared meals distributed by authorized delivery services or served at authorized communal dining facilities, such as senior citizen centers. The food stamps of alcoholics or drug addicts who are regularly participating in a treatment and rehabilitation program may be pooled by the treatment center to buy food for them. Alaskans who live in areas far from retail food stores and rely principally on hunting and fishing for their subsistence can use food stamps to buy equipment such as harpoons, spears, and fishing tackle but not firearms, ammunition, and other explosives.

Purchases made with food stamps in retail stores are limited to food or food products considered fit for human consumption. Tobacco, alcoholic beverages, and imported foods are not included, nor are soaps, paper products, and other nonfood items. The law does allow the purchase of seeds and plants to grow food for the personal consumption of the eligible household, however.

Retail grocers who accept food stamps must be approved by the Department of Agriculture. Approval depends on the store's offering a variety of low-cost staples. For example, a store that sold mostly exotic teas and coffees was turned down, as was one that sold mostly high-priced prepared and convenience foods. Stores can lose the privilege of selling for food stamps if they accept coupons for prohibited items or if they give change in cash for an amount larger than the smallest denomination of food stamp.

■ **Public housing**   Public housing was established in 1937 with a federal program intended to clear up slums and stimulate employment. In the Housing Act of 1949 the government declared a national policy of providing a "decent home and a suitable living environment for every American family." In its efforts to reach this goal, the federal government has become heavily involved in public housing programs.

Various programs are available for building public housing projects that make possible private involvement in construction and management, site selection, and use of existing housing. The common thread in almost all these programs is a reliance on local public housing agencies. These agencies are created by state laws or by local government units that are authorized by the state. Federal assistance is channeled through the state and local agencies by the U.S. Department of Housing and Urban Development. Federal funds cover the capital costs, and the local agency sets rents that will cover operating costs. The participation of the federal government makes possible lower rents than those for comparable private housing.

To obtain space in a public housing project, an individual or household must have an income below a specified limit. However, once admitted, tenants are usually permitted to continue living in public housing if their income rises above the level that allowed them to get into a project. As the tenant's income rises, he may be charged a higher rent so that rents can be kept lower for tenants in greater need. Federal law, however, limits the percentage of a tenant's income that can be charged for rent in low-income housing.

The federal government also encourages construction of low-rent housing by guaranteeing MORTGAGES for individuals and companies. This makes it easier for a builder to borrow money at a lower interest rate.

Eligibility   The public housing agency must follow the same procedure in evaluating each application, and it must tell applicants how claims are processed. Applications must be processed promptly. If many people qualify—as generally happens—a waiting list must be prepared in a fair manner—for example, by drawing names or by listing persons in order of the date of their applications. Anyone who is turned down must be given the reasons in writing and the opportunity for an interview with an agency staff member.

Housing agencies may screen out applicants who make more than the maximum allowable income, who owe back rent from an earlier tenancy in public housing, or who pose a threat to the project community. People have been excluded, for example, for a history of drug use, gambling activities, prostitution, or violent crimes. A parent's application can be denied if a child who lives with him is found to be dangerous and antisocial. Housing agencies are not allowed to insist that a person live in the area for a certain period of time before he can apply for a housing unit. See RESIDENCY LAWS.

Protection against eviction   For a long time, courts took the position that a public housing agency was the same as a private landlord. By giving only month-to-month leases, the local agency could get rid of a tenant it considered troublesome simply by refusing to renew his lease at the end of any month. However, federal courts have ruled that arbitrary actions by such agencies may result in violations of the constitutional right of DUE PROCESS OF LAW.

EXAMPLE   In 1955 a federal court held that an agency could not terminate a monthly lease because a tenant refused to swear that he was not a member of a subversive organization. The court said: "The government as landlord is still the government. It must not act arbitrarily for, unlike private landlords, it is subject to the requirements of due process of law. Arbitrary action is not due process."

Under the public housing laws tenants must be notified before they are evicted and given substantial reasons, which they have an opportunity to refute at a hearing.

EXAMPLE   A woman received an eviction notice stating that she was losing her apartment because her children disrupted the peace in the building. At a hearing the judge found that her three children liked to play loud disco music after school. When the woman got home from work about an hour after the children, she always quieted things down, but one neighbor refused to be satisfied. It was not the volume of the music that upset him as much as the kind of music being played. He hated disco music.

The judge extracted a promise from the children to turn down their music and cautioned the neighbor to be more neighborly. He recognized that the woman was a tenant in a public housing project because she would never be able to afford suitable quarters for her family elsewhere. He would not allow the city housing agency to evict her unless there was a compelling reason to do so, and this he did not find.

■ **Rights of welfare recipients**   The Constitution does not specifically protect welfare recipients as a class, but various provisions of the Constitution have been invoked to protect the poor from arbitrary governmental actions. Many welfare regulations have been found unconstitutional because they make assumptions that are invalid or not reasonably related to what they are intended to accomplish, thereby subverting the purpose of relief.

For a long time, poverty was considered an affront to American society. The law dealt with the poor by making their families—even remote relatives—liable for their support. Anyone who had nowhere else to go was sent to a poorhouse or poor farm, where conditions were intentionally bad in order to discourage people from taking refuge there at the taxpayers' expense.

The attitude that poor people were to blame for their poverty was embodied in a legal principle that government benefits were a privilege and not a right. Calling welfare a privilege meant that there were no constitutional rights for recipients. State and local governments were able to impose all kinds of conditions on public assistance, many of them arbitrary and selectively applied. Since the late 1960's these have been struck down one by one and replaced with the principle that the government must be fair to all people.

Equal protection of the law A number of welfare laws have been struck down because they violate the recipients' constitutional right to EQUAL PROTECTION OF LAWS. These laws discriminated against new residents, college students, and foster children.

Historically, communities had always limited relief to local residents in order to keep the number of welfare cases as small as possible. Many states passed legislation restricting relief to poor people who had a *legal settlement* in the town or district where they applied for aid. Depending on the statute, someone's legal settlement might be the place where he was born or where he had lived for a specified number of years. More recently, these laws have been called durational RESIDENCY LAWS because they require an applicant to have been a resident for a certain period of time before he can qualify for assistance.

EXAMPLE In 1969 the Supreme Court held that a Connecticut law requiring applicants for public assistance to have been residents of the state for at least one year was unconstitutional. The Court specifically said that a state cannot escape the duty to treat citizens equally under the law by calling welfare benefits a privilege. The Constitution guarantees a right to travel freely from state to state. A law that puts welfare applicants into two classes, depending on whether they have lived in the state more or less than the required time, violates everyone's right of equal protection and penalizes those who have exercised their right to travel.

In 1978 the Supreme Court refined its holding that a person's right to travel may not be violated by welfare laws by restricting it to mean travel within the United States.

In 1971 the Supreme Court held that needy 18- to 20-year-olds cannot be denied AFDC benefits just because they are in college.

EXAMPLE An Illinois law provided that mothers and 18- to 20-year-old dependent children qualified for benefits if the child was in vocational training, but not if he attended a college or university. The Supreme Court found that classifying welfare applicants according to the type of education they were getting was improper and that all should be treated equally.

In one case in 1971, however, the Supreme Court recognized that welfare benefits must be limited realistically.

EXAMPLE A Maryland statute set an upper limit to the amount of welfare money a family could receive. Each family's need was computed according to the number of people in the household, but the limit prevented large families from receiving the same amount per person as smaller families. No matter how many members, a family's benefits could not go over $250 a month in Baltimore and in certain counties or over $240 a month elsewhere in the state. The Court found that states might reasonably figure that large families could economize in ways that smaller households could not. It decided that the statute was reasonably related to the goal of the welfare program and free of unjustified discrimination.

Invasion of privacy When welfare was regarded as a privilege and not a right, recipients had little hope of making the government leave them alone.

Chaste mother During the first third of the 20th century, some states that were giving small pensions to widowed mothers withdrew benefits whenever there was evidence that they were having sexual relations. The reason given was a fear that more illegitimate children would be born in poor families. An additional reason, however, was that the authorities were trying to impose strict moral values on the welfare recipients. Racial antagonism was also often involved.

After the federal government began funding AFDC in 1955, some states continued to require welfare mothers to be chaste, despite criticism from the federal level.

EXAMPLE In 1960 Louisiana enacted a law that said that any mother who had an illegitimate child after receiving public assistance was not maintaining a suitable home and thus would lose her welfare aid. Secretary of Health, Education, and Welfare Arthur Sherwood Flemming issued the Flemming Ruling, which stated that the federal government would not continue to fund any state welfare plan that cut off welfare benefits for a needy child because his home conditions were found unsuitable. If a home is not suitable for a child, the state must follow a strict process for removing the child from his home and then place him somewhere that provides suitable care. Cutting off his only source of support is not permissible.

Man-in-the-house rule The chaste-mother rule was not the only provision under which welfare officials attempted to supervise the life of recipients. The traditional notion that a family was self-supporting as long as it had a man was embodied in the man-in-the-house rule.

EXAMPLE An Alabama law followed the tradition by denying AFDC benefits whenever the mother lived with a man, even if she was not married to him. Alabama argued that the law was intended to discourage immorality in the home and to keep down the number of illegitimate births, but the Supreme Court held in 1968 that it is not permissible to put the burden of this goal on needy children and held the rule to be illegal.

EXAMPLE A California law held an unmarried man in the house responsible for supporting the children and said whatever financial resources he had were assumed to be resources available for this purpose. A woman who lived with him therefore could not receive AFDC. Thus the children were treated as though they were not needy even if they were in fact. The Supreme Court in 1970 found this approach unconstitutional. It concluded that the likelihood that a man living with a poor mother would contribute "his income to the children—even if legally obligated to do so—is sufficiently uncertain . . . to prevent viewing him as a 'breadwinner' unless the bread is actually set on the table."

This same principle has been applied to men who marry the mother of children receiving AFDC. If a stepfather is not legally obligated to support children or if he is obligated but the obligation is not enforced, the children cannot be denied welfare. In calculating whether a family is poor enough to qualify for AFDC, a state can count only income that is actually received for the family's support.

Father's responsibility In some cases welfare officials do have a right to pry into an applicant's private life. A parent has the primary obligation to support his or her child. If the child is on welfare because a parent is absent from the home, then public officials have the right to locate that parent and enforce his or her obligation to support. A vigorous national plan of helping local governments track down delinquent parents has been successful in recovering millions of dollars paid out as AFDC.

A father is responsible for supporting his child whether or not the child is legitimate. When the parents of the child have not been married, welfare officials must establish legally who the father is before they can enforce his obligation to support, even though this requires inquiry into the mother's private life. The state is responsible for enforcing a father's obligation and preserving tax money insofar as possible.

It is illegal to cut off AFDC benefits in whole or in part if a mother refuses to identify the father of her illegitimate child or to cooperate in a lawsuit to establish the father's identity or to force the father to contribute to the child's support. A state can, however, punish an uncooperative mother for CONTEMPT even though that may involve imprisonment. Before finding a mother in contempt the court must be satisfied that she does not have a good reason to refuse to answer questions. Whether or not a reason is good must be measured by the best interests of the child.

Home visits   The privacy of welfare recipients may be interrupted by home visits. A social worker can call on a family receiving AFDC in order to make sure that the child lives there and is benefiting from the aid given in his behalf.

wharf   A structure built along the shores of NAVIGABLE WATERS, where vessels can be brought for loading and unloading. A *public wharf* is one that can be used by the general public, either with or without payment of a fee. Generally, the wharf belongs to a city, town, or other government organization. A *private wharf* is owned or leased by a person for his own use. When a private wharf is open for public use on payment of wharfage rates, it becomes a *quasi-public wharf* available to all who can pay. Whether a wharf is public or private depends primarily on the use made of it rather than its ownership.

Wharfage usually refers to the use of a wharf, such as in loading and unloading goods and passengers, storing goods there, or keeping a ship alongside the wharf for protection from the weather. Wharfage also means the charge for the use of a wharf. A *wharfinger* is a person who is paid to receive merchandise on his wharf for forwarding or delivery.

■ **Government regulation**   Because wharves are essential to the public welfare, governments regulate their use, usually through state laws establishing supervisory boards or commissions. Such agencies regulate the construction of wharves, their use and maintenance, the depth of waters surrounding them, and their lighting and policing.

■ **Rates**   Wharfage rates for the use of public wharves may be governed by local laws and can be adjusted to encourage or discourage commerce in a port. The rates must be reasonable, however.

Generally, using a wharf for even a short time requires payment of wharfage charges. The amount may be graduated according to the gross tonnage of the vessel using the wharf. When the dock is private, owner and user are usually free to bargain over the rates and the rule that wharfage rates must be reasonable does not apply.

■ **Liability for damages**   The proprietor of a wharf must use reasonable care to keep it in a safe condition. He must exercise reasonable diligence to discover defects, obstructions, and other hazards that would make the wharf unsafe to vessels, such as a submerged rock, and he is liable for the damage done to any vessel resulting from neglect of that duty.

whereas   When in fact; because; by reason of. A *whereas clause* in a CONTRACT is an introductory statement that explains the reasons for the contract and may also describe its purposes. Although the whereas clause may be used in interpreting the contract, it is not a legally essential part of it.

When used at the beginning of a legislative bill, "whereas" is followed by an explanation of the reasons for enacting the LEGISLATION.

whereby   By or through which; in accordance with which. For example: "An emergency might someday occur whereby the United States would be unable to secure enough oil to meet its needs."

wherefore   For which reason. The word is often used in an *averment*, a positive statement of fact in the PLEADINGS (formal papers) that must be filed with the court in a lawsuit. "Wherefore the defendant says that said promissory note was and is void" is an example of an averment.

wildcat strike   A STRIKE that is not authorized by the labor organization to which the striking workers belong.

will   An expression of a person's intention as to the distribution of his property after his death. A person's right to own and use property as he pleases is one of the most important rights protected by our legal system. This right of ownership includes the power to decide how the property a person owned during his lifetime should be treated upon his death. The law of wills implements this right.

■ **Why a will is important**   It is important to make a will for several reasons: (1) It enables you to select the people to whom you wish to leave your possessions rather than allowing state laws to choose your heirs—the law may select blood relatives but they may be people you dislike or distant relatives you never met. (2) It allows you to decide who is best qualified to serve as executor of your estate, fairly distributing your property to your beneficiaries while protecting their interests—otherwise the law would appoint a stranger as administrator. See EXECUTORS AND ADMINISTRATORS. (3) It gives you the right to handpick a guardian to continue raising your young children, if you have any when you die. See GUARDIAN AND WARD. (4) Not having a will might ultimately reduce the size of your estate, since additional legal fees and time delays always result when a court must appoint an administrator or guardian or deal with any other matter that could have been disposed of by a will.

This entry discusses, among other things, the requirements for a valid will, the various types of wills that can be made, and the rights of certain people, such as the surviving spouse and children, to inherit property regardless of the provisions of a will.

■ **Basic terms** There are several terms that are commonly used in speaking or writing about the law of wills. To begin with, there is the word *will* itself. A will is a document in which a person states how he wants his property handled and distributed after his death. All property is either real property or personal property. *Real property* is real estate—that is, land and anything of a permanent nature under or over the land, including houses and other structures. *Personal property* is any other kind of property, including money. A person's real and personal property make up his ESTATE.

In the past under the common law, a document disposing of personal property was called a *testament;* a will disposed of only real property. Over the years, this distinction has been eliminated so that a will, sometimes called a *last will and testament,* disposes of both real and personal property. A will is *executed,* or made, when it is in writing and complies with state requirements.

A *decedent* is a person who has died. A *testator* or *testatrix* is a man or woman who has died *testate*—that is, leaving a will. If a person dies without leaving a will or if his will is invalidated because it was not properly made, he is called an *intestate.* The estate of an intestate will be distributed according to the laws of the state, known as the statutes of *descent and distribution,* or *intestacy.* For a full discussion of the distribution of the property of a person who dies without a will, see DESCENT AND DISTRIBUTION and Chart 16.

A person who receives real property under the provisions of a will is a *devisee,* and the property itself is a *devise.* Real property is *devised* by will.

A *legacy* is money that passes under a will to a *legatee,* the individual who receives it.

A *bequest* is a gift of personal property, such as furniture, jewelry, or stock. Sometimes the terms "legacy" and "bequest" are used interchangeably because money is a type of personal property. Personal property is *bequeathed* to an heir by will.

The *residue* of an estate, which is given to persons named in the *residuary clause,* is any property belonging to the decedent that was not specifically given to others as a bequest, devise, or legacy.

The typical will names an *executor* (male) or *executrix* (female) to carry out the provisions of the will and to distribute the estate after estate taxes and debts are paid. An *administrator* is a person appointed by the court to distribute the estate of a person who has died intestate, either by

WHEN YOU ARE MAKING A WILL

■ To make a valid will, a person must be "of sound mind." This means he understands the nature and extent of his property, recognizes and remembers family members to whom he would normally leave his estate, and knows he is making a document that tells how his property will be distributed when he dies.

■ A person who uses drugs or alcohol may validly execute a will as long as he was not under the influence at the time he made the will. Illiteracy, deafness, muteness, severe illness, or extreme old age does not deprive a person of *testamentary* capacity—the ability to make a valid will.

■ A will must be signed by its maker. Some states permit another to sign a will at the testator's (maker's) direction or request or with his consent.

■ In many states, the signature must be affixed to the end of the will; if it is not, the property will pass according to state laws of descent and distribution.

■ Two or three witnesses are required for a will, depending on the state. Witnesses should not have a financial interest in the will.

■ In some states, an oral will, made on the testator's deathbed or in expectation of imminent death, may be valid; but only personal property, not real property (real estate), can be disposed of by such a will.

■ Many states do not recognize a will that is entirely written and signed in the testator's handwriting, called a *holographic will.*

■ If you make more than one will disposing of the same property, the later will is valid. If the wills were executed at the same time and are contradictory, they are all invalid.

■ A *codicil* is a separate document attached to a will that adds or changes provisions to it or revokes all of it.

■ In most states, a widow or widower is legally entitled to a one-half or one-third lifetime ownership in the property owned by the deceased spouse, no matter what the deceased spouse's will provides. When applied to a widow, this is called *dower;* when applied to a widower, it is called *curtesy.* The spouse can use the property during his or her lifetime but may not sell it or pass it to heirs.

■ In states that have elective-share statutes, the surviving spouse may choose between his or her share under the will or either (1) one-third of the estate if there are children or one-half if no children, or (2) what he or she would get under state law if the spouse had died without a will. An elective share gives the spouse the right to sell the property or will it to heirs.

■ You can revoke your will whenever you like; for revocation to be effective, you must perform some act to indicate your intent. If, for example, you intentionally tear up your will or burn it, revocation is effective.

■ Many states provide that divorce automatically revokes a provision in your will for your ex-spouse, unless you update your will to include your former spouse.

■ When a will cannot be found but was known to be in the testator's possession at the time of death, it is often presumed that he revoked it. If it was last known to be in someone else's possession, however, there is no such presumption.

■ If you own land in one state and personal property in another, you must make sure your will complies with the laws of both states.

■ You can disinherit your heirs only by leaving the property to others.

■ If you are deprived of your rightful share under a will because the deceased was subject to fraud or undue influence, a court will impose a trust on the property and compel the wrongdoer to turn the property over to you, the intended beneficiary.

not leaving a will or leaving one that is not valid. If a valid will fails to name an executor or if the designated person is dead or unable or unwilling to assume the responsibility, the probate court will appoint an *administrator c.t.a.* to distribute the estate according to the terms of the will—*c.t.a.* is an abbreviation of the Latin *cum testamento annexo* ("with the will annexed").

A *codicil* is a document that changes, revokes, or amends part or all of a validly executed will. In order for it to be effective, it must conform to the same formalities as a will.

Probate is the legal process that establishes a will as being valid and genuine. Courts that have the power to determine PROBATE matters are known as *probate courts* or *surrogate's courts.* They are usually county courts, whose jurisdiction is defined by state law.

■ **Law governing wills** The right to dispose of property by a will is governed by statute. When a person dies, the laws of the state where his primary home is located regulate how his personal property—such as money, stock, or automobiles—will be distributed. The disposition of his real property—a house, a farm, a ranch, or vacant acreage—will pass to his intended heirs within limitations prescribed by the law of the state in which the property is located. A person who owns personal property in one state and real property in another must make sure that his will is properly executed according to the laws of both states or else his property may be distributed according to the laws of descent and distribution.

■ **Requirements for a valid will** A will is not valid unless certain essential elements are present: (1) The person making the will must be a competent testator. (2) The document must fulfill the statutory requirements dealing with writing, signing, witnessing, attesting, and acknowledging the will. Often called the statutes of wills, these requirements insure that the will is not a fraud. (3) It must be clear that the testator intended the document to be a will. See Chart 14.

If a will does not satisfy these requirements, any person having a financial interest in the estate under the laws of descent and distribution may, through the probate or surrogate's court, challenge the validity of the will. The people who benefit from the will are its *proponents* and will defend it against such an attack. This proceeding is known as a *will contest.* If those who oppose a will are successful, the testator's estate will be distributed according to the laws of descent and distribution.

Competent testator To be a competent testator a person must be over a minimum age, usually 18, at the time the will is made. A person under the minimum age will die intestate and his property will be distributed according to the laws of descent and distribution.

An individual must have testamentary capacity (be of "sound mind") to make a valid will. This means he must be able to understand the nature and extent of his property, to recognize and remember the "natural objects of his bounty" (family members to whom he would normally leave his estate even if he decides not to do so), and to understand the nature of the testamentary act (that is, know that he is making a document that tells how his property will be distributed when he dies). He must also understand how these elements are related so that he may express how he

wants his property disposed. No particular degree of mental competence is required, however.

A testator is considered mentally incompetent and therefore incapable of making a will if he has some recognized mental deficiency or suffers from some form of mental derangement. *Mental deficiency* means a lack of the intelligence and memory that are important in making a will. A person whom the law considers *mentally deranged* (such as one suffering from paranoia or senility) usually has *insane delusions*—beliefs for which there is no supporting evidence but much contradictory evidence. He may be unable to form a rational testamentary plan. However, a will made by someone suffering from an insane delusion is not automatically void.

EXAMPLE Arthur believes that Martians are spying on him and plan to kill him on the vernal equinox. He decides to make a will, to take care of his family in light of his imminent death. His will complies with all the statutory requirements. It will be upheld even though it was made as a result of an irrational belief. The delusion did not influence the way in which the will was made.

For an insane delusion to invalidate a will, it must substantially affect the way the testator disposes of his property. If a person has insane delusions about his property or his family, his will will not be valid even though he was rational on other subjects.

EXAMPLE Fred became obsessed with an irrational belief that his paralyzed wife, Martha, had been repeatedly unfaithful to him, sneaking out at night to meet a variety of young men. In fact, it was physically impossible for her to do so. Fred's will, which deliberately excluded her in retaliation for her alleged conduct, would be invalidated because it was the result of an insane delusion.

A will made during a lucid interval by a person whom the courts have determined is insane might be valid. See INSANE PERSONS. A lucid interval occurs when a person has regained, although momentarily, his ability to understand the nature of his intended actions, the extent of his property, and whom he wants to inherit his property.

EXAMPLE In an Oregon case, a 68-year-old widow suffered from a persecution complex and heard voices. Although she had suffered from mental illness for some time, she was not sent to the state hospital until the day after she executed her will. There she was diagnosed as "schizophrenic . . . with marked paranoid trends." After her death, her nephew challenged the will, claiming that she had lacked testamentary capacity. The court found that the will was executed during a lucid interval of the woman's illness. She had given her attorney the names of her intended beneficiaries, their relationship to her, and their addresses. She also indicated the names of various relatives and explained why she had made no provision for them, indicating that they were not close to her or they had not been nice to her and consequently she did not want to leave them any of her property. She also made provisions specifying the type of funeral she wanted. Thereafter, she executed the will according to the formalities required by law.

The adjudication of a person as insane and his confinement to a mental institution or the appointment of a guardian to handle his affairs do not always mean that he is incompetent to make a will. A person may need help in managing his daily affairs and still have testamentary capacity.

Mere eccentricities, such as a refusal to bathe, are not considered insane delusions, nor are mistaken beliefs or prejudices regarding family members.

EXAMPLE Anne's father-in-law, Sam, developed a violent ○← ✳ dislike and distrust of her, suddenly and for no apparent reason. He refused to see her and sent back gifts of his favorite foods that Anne had George, her husband, take to him. In Sam's will he left all his other daughters-in-law a sum of money and a piece of jewelry. He stated that he had left Anne out intentionally. Anne contested the will, but the court upheld it.

A person who uses drugs or alcohol may validly execute a will as long as he is not under their influence at the time. Illiteracy, old age, deafness, muteness, or severe physical illness do not automatically deprive a person of testamentary capacity, although they are factors to be considered in addition to the other facts of the case.

Testator's intent In order for a will to be admitted to probate and given legal effect, it must be clear that the testator acted freely in making it. A will drawn up as a result of undue influence, FRAUD, or mistake may be declared completely or partially void in a probate proceeding, depending upon state law.

Undue influence Undue influence is pressure that causes a person to yield his free will to make decisions in favor of the will of the influencer. In order to find out if a testator was subject to undue influence at the time his will was executed, certain elements must be present: (1) The testator must be susceptible (that is, he must be capable of being influenced); (2) there must be an opportunity and an attempt to improperly influence him; and (3) the provisions of the will must show the effect of such influence. Mere advice, persuasion, affection, or kindness alone does not constitute undue influence.

EXAMPLE A will was made by a 76-year-old testator who ○← ✳ was known to trust everyone who was friendly to him. After his death, it was discovered that his will did not conform to the intentions he had expressed both before and after it was made. He left his entire estate to two nephews he hardly knew, while excluding his sister with whom he had a long, close relationship. The sister challenged the will on the ground of undue influence.

The nephew who was the chief beneficiary not only had an opportunity to improperly influence the testator through his father, the testator's brother, but actively helped do so. Both men convinced the testator that his sister had tried to cheat him out of his share of another relative's estate. The nephew and his family then influenced the testator to omit the sister as his beneficiary.

After executing his will contrary to his previously expressed intent, the testator realized that his nephew's concern was based solely on greed and repeated his desire to take care of his sister under his will. Unfortunately he died before he could change the document, but his intention indicated to the court that the will was the result of undue influence.

Frequently, a confidential relationship between a testator and a beneficiary raises the possibility of undue influ-

ence. Suspicion of undue influence arises, for example, when a will seems to deal unjustly with persons believed to be the natural beneficiaries.

EXAMPLE Geoffrey, an attorney, drafts a will for an old ○← ✳ Army buddy José, who gives him the entire estate while excluding his eight children. In a proceeding to challenge the will, it may be presumed from their confidential relationship that Geoffrey exerted undue influence on José as well as from the fact that it is unusual for a person to exclude all his children from his will.

A confidential relationship, however, is not in itself cause to invalidate a will for undue influence. After considering other evidence, the court may call for evidence to show that there was not undue influence. Similarly, the mere inequality of the provisions of a will does not establish undue influence, because that would interfere with the right of a testator to dispose of his property as he pleases.

EXAMPLE If José gives a good share of his property to ○← ✳ Geoffrey, who saved his life during the Korean War, and only a pittance to three of his children who never visit or write to him, the court may uphold José's right to so dispose of his property.

A testator acting under undue influence executes the will and realizes what he is doing but does so out of fear, desire for peace, or some other feeling that overcomes his true wishes. Threats of violence, criminal prosecution of the testator, abandonment of him when he is ill, even excessive flattery and affection may be undue influence.

A will made under undue influence does not become valid just because the testator allowed it to stand after the pressure was removed. If, however, the testator added a codicil to such a will, it must be proved that undue influence continued to be exerted on the testator at the time the codicil was made. Otherwise, the court will declare the original will valid because it will presume that the testator had an opportunity to change the will while free of undue influence but did not choose to do so.

EXAMPLE Ten years after he last saw Geoffrey, José used ○← ✳ another lawyer to draft a codicil to his will. The new codicil did not change the provisions of his will that left José's entire estate to Geoffrey. Under these circumstances, Geoffrey would be entitled to everything. The codicil was not written as a result of Geoffrey's undue influence. Since José, acting this time without any pressures, still chose to leave all to Geoffrey, his intention would be enforced by the court.

Fraud Fraud is different from undue influence in that it involves lying or misrepresenting essential facts to the testator in order to get him to make and sign a will that will benefit the deceiver. The testator acts freely. There are two types of fraud—fraud in the execution and fraud in the inducement.

Fraud in the execution If you are deceived by another person regarding the character of the document you are signing, you are the victim of fraud in the execution. The document may be properly executed as a will but you have no intention that it is your will.

EXAMPLE Maurice, an elderly man who does not speak ○← ✳ English, is brought by his son to an attorney's office on the pretext of signing a building permit so that he may construct a barn on his property. Maurice relies

MAKING YOUR WILL CLAUSE BY CLAUSE

E. LISK WYCKOFF, JR., Consultant
Member, New York Bar

"I JOHN DOE, residing at Seaside, North Carolina, do hereby make, publish, and declare this to be my Last Will and Testament, hereby revoking any wills and codicils heretofore made by me." These are the opening words of a typical will. If you are making your will—and you should be, if you have not already done so—you ought to begin in a similar way. But what should follow?

Making a will can be a complicated matter. Many people assume that they need only a simple will, but actually no will is ever simple because it must deal with complex human relationships and frequently a complicated set of assets and circumstances. While many kinds of printed forms for wills are available, you should not use them without legal advice because too many factual and legal complexities are involved. In many cases, wills made without a lawyer's help have been invalidated or have contained mistakes or ambiguities that required extensive litigation to resolve. If you are to make your will properly, you must do so with the advice of your lawyer and other family advisers, including your tax adviser, who will know the ins and outs of federal and state tax laws that must be considered when making a will.

In order to help your lawyer prepare your will, you should give him a list of the names, addresses, and ages of all the people you intend to leave something to (your beneficiaries). You should also let him know of any previous marriages or any separation agreements and provide him with statements of your assets, the assets of your spouse, and the assets of other intended beneficiaries, when appropriate (for example, if your children already have substantial assets). Your lawyer will ask you for further information if it is needed.

Wills can take many different forms depending upon who writes them. The following is a general outline of the provisions you may expect to include in your will. Bear in mind, however, that the order in which these provisions are set forth is not a legal requirement. The order may vary according to the format used by the lawyer preparing your will.

Introductory clause

The opening sentence should make clear that the document is your will. It should also give your name and current place of residence. Finally, it should make clear that the document revokes any former wills you may have made and any codicils to former wills. A codicil is an amendment to an existing will and forms a part of the will. (Generally speaking, it is inadvisable to use a codicil because of the potential legal problems involved.)

Funeral arrangements and the payment of debts

Following the introductory clause, you may want to add a provision directing that your funeral expenses and debts be paid as shortly after your death as practicable. Although this kind of direction is not necessary, it is customarily placed in most wills. Be careful, however, because an unqualified direction to pay your debts could result in accelerating the mortgage debt on your house or any loan you may have on your insurance policy. It could also prejudice a court against your estate if a creditor brings suit against it. For example, if a creditor sues for payment of a bill and the estate claims that payment is not due, a court may decide for the creditor if the evidence presented by both sides is equal and you have directed that all your debts be paid.

You may wish to have a particular kind of funeral service or to have your remains disposed of in a certain way. Although there is no harm in having such directions placed in your will, remember that your will may not be reviewed until after your family has made final arrangements, and these arrangements may conflict with what you wanted. Consequently, it is more advisable to have such directions contained in a letter and kept apart from your will. In some states, they must actually be lodged with a funeral parlor or crematorium so that your wishes will be carried out.

If you wish to make anatomical gifts of your eyes, kidneys, or other organs, or of your entire body, you may have a direction added to your will disposing of the organs or body to particular organ banks or hospitals. Again, time is of the essence, and so it is usually better to use instead one of the forms that have been authorized in many states for the disposition of bodies or organs. If you fill out such a form, you will be given a donor card indicating what is to be done upon your death. You should always carry this card. If you do, it is more likely that your wishes as to the disposition of your remains will be carried out. You should also apprise your lawyer and family advisers of your action so that they too can help carry out your wishes when the time comes.

Legacies—dispositions of money

The next step is to provide for gifts to specific beneficiaries of money in its various forms—that is, cash, stocks, or bonds. Such gifts are technically known as legacies. You should also consider making legacies to charities in order to reduce possible estate taxes. In making cash or other legacies, be sure to identify the beneficiaries properly.

If you are making a general legacy, such as "all of my General Motors stock," you must decide whether or not you want all stock splits or other capital changes occurring after the date of your will to be included as part of the legacy. For example, if you own 300 shares of common stock of General Motors, it might end up, owing to capital changes, as 1,000 shares by the time of your death. Consequently, you must decide when you are making your will whether to make the legacy for the stock in the amount it is now (300 shares) or the amount it will be when you die (1,000 shares)—and so indicate in your will.

Bequests—dispositions of tangible personal property

Personal property is any property that is not real estate. Tangible personal property includes such property as automobiles, boats, furniture, jewelry, books, art works, stamp and coin collections, and (in some states) cash. Gifts of tangible personal property, technically known as bequests, are generally provided for following the clause on legacies.

A special exception under the federal income tax law eliminates tax on the distribution of much inherited personal property. Consequently, it is usually desirable to make specific bequests of tangible personal property rather than have it pass as part of the residuary estate. The residuary estate is all the property not specifically mentioned in the will—that is, the property covered by a phrase such as "all the rest of my property." By providing for specific bequests of tangible personal property you may avoid federal income taxes on the distribution of the property to your beneficiaries.

If you do bequeath specific items to your beneficiaries, be sure to describe each item with some particularity so that it can be readily identified. For example, a bequest of "my diamond ring in a gold setting to my daughter, Jean" is not sufficient if the estate contains two or more diamond rings that are set in gold.

The law in many states differentiates between specific bequests and general bequests. A *specific bequest* is one that names a particular item, such as "my three-carat diamond pendant on the gold chain." A *general bequest* is one that is more vague, such as "half the furniture in the summer house." If you live in a state that distinguishes between specific and general bequests, be sure to qualify any specific bequests you make with a word such as "my" or whatever your state law requires (your lawyer will know). The use of such a qualifying term will assure that the bequest will be deemed a specific one under the law. This is important because a specific bequest of property that is no longer owned at the time of his death by the person who made the will is deemed to have expired, and the beneficiary is not entitled to anything in its place. A general bequest, on the other hand, may require the executor of the estate to go out and purchase a similar item to fulfill the bequest if the item is no longer in the estate. Thus, if you bequeathed "a diamond ring in a gold setting to my beloved niece Ruth" and you sold the ring and had no such ring in your estate when you died, the executor of your estate might have to buy a diamond ring in a gold setting with funds from the estate and give it to Ruth. This is a result that you would obviously want to avoid.

When you make bequests of household furnishings and furniture, be careful to specify the appropriate beneficiary—for example, "my said wife, if she shall survive me, or if she shall not survive me, then to such of my children as shall survive me, in shares that are as nearly equal as practical." If you bequeath personal property to more than one beneficiary, you should provide for its equitable division. You can do this by leaving the division to the discretion of the administrator of your estate (provided he is not a beneficiary of such property) or by arranging that the beneficiaries draw lots to see who will take any particular item in the event of a dispute. Unfortunately, disputes frequently arise among relatives over items that have more sentimental value than intrinsic worth, and it is best to establish a method for settling such disputes before they occur.

Devises—dispositions of real estate

The third, and often most important, type of property to be disposed of in your will is real property, or real estate. Dispositions of real estate are technically known as devises. Real estate is devised to beneficiaries.

It is important at the outset to determine how you hold your real estate. You may own it outright with no strings attached (in *fee simple)*, in which case you may dispose of it in your will as you wish, or you may own it together with one or more persons, in which case you may be somewhat more restricted.

Frequently, real estate is held by husband and wife (in states that do not have community-property laws) as *tenants by the entirety*. This means that when one spouse dies, the surviving spouse takes the property by operation of law outside the will.

In cases not involving husband and wife, real estate may be owned by more than one person as *joint tenants with right of survivorship*. In such cases, when one owner dies, the property passes to the surviving owner by operation of law outside the will. Thus, if you and your cousin Beatrice own a cabin in the mountains in joint tenancy with right of survivorship, Beatrice will automatically get full ownership of the cabin when you die (provided she outlives you), without your providing for it in your will. She may then pass it on to her own heirs as she sees fit, without any regard to what you might have wanted.

If you hold property as a *tenant in common*, you do so as a co-owner with one or more persons, but the other owner or owners do not automatically take over your interest in the property when you die, as there is no right of survivorship. You can will your interest in the property to someone else, but that beneficiary would own the property only to the extent that you owned it, as a tenant in common. Thus, if you and your cousin Beatrice each own half of a cabin in the mountains as tenants in common, you can leave your half interest in the cabin to anyone you wish by providing for it in your will. Beatrice will not inherit your part of the cabin unless you will it to her, and whoever you name to receive your interest in the cabin will own only half of it, as you did. Beatrice will retain her half interest until she sells it, gives it away, or dies and leaves it to someone else.

Tenancies in common can be troublesome if they are held by a number of persons, some of whom (such as minors) are legally unable to make a contract, thus restricting the ability to sell the property. Consequently, you should give careful consideration to the manner in which you own your real estate and to whom you intend to leave it when you die.

In your will you must deal with all the real estate you own—either as full or part owner—except for the property that will pass by operation of law through a tenancy by the entirety or a joint tenancy with the right of survivorship. You may devise your real estate separately, or you may let it pass as part of your residuary estate (all of your property not specifically mentioned in your will).

Carefully choose the method you will use, as it may affect the ability of your beneficiaries to use or dispose of the property as suits your aims or their desires. For example, suppose Constance, a widow, owns both a home in the city and a small country home that is worth half as much as the city place. Constance has three children. Her oldest child, Cecilia, loves the country home and spends most of her summers there with her mother. The other two children, Bob and Barbara, do not care for the country home. If Constance wants Cecilia to have the country home, she should devise it to her in her will. If Constance lets the two houses pass as part of the residuary estate together with other real estate to her three children and her invalid sister, the country house might have to be sold in order to distribute the property evenly among the four beneficiaries.

Other dispositions

At this point you may want to include other bequests and devises, such as gifts to your employees, if you have any, and gifts of condominiums or cooperatives. You may also provide for the forgiveness of debts owed to you by others. If you have not already made any specific dispositions to your spouse, you should do so here to qualify him or her for the estate tax marital deduction. You can use one of two different formulas to arrange a disposition to your spouse—the pecuniary formula (which should be included here or earlier in the will) or the fractional formula (which should be included in the residuary clause). This area of wills can be complicated and you should ask your lawyer to discuss which formula is better for you. The results of using the different formulas will have different consequences on the amount your husband or wife receives and on the amount of income taxes he or she will have to pay.

Residuary clause

The next clause disposes of all the property not covered earlier. As mentioned above, it is frequently called the residuary clause, although it is sometimes called the residual bequest and devise. The property covered by this clause is called the residuary estate. Normally, the bulk of a person's property is disposed of by the residuary clause.

You can use the residuary clause to pass property to a beneficiary or beneficiaries in any of several ways. You may pass all of the property covered by the clause outright. You may pass part of the property outright and part of it in trust. You may specify that all of the residuary estate be placed in trust. You may also provide that the property be *poured over* into a trust that was established during your lifetime or (if the laws of your state permit it) into a trust created under someone else's will. Finally, you can leave the distribution of the residual estate to the discretion of the executor or of someone else you appoint.

It is most important that the residuary clause contain an ultimate disposition of your property. For example, it is possible that your immediate family may die before you do, leaving you with no immediate family beneficiaries. Consequently, your will should always provide for alternative beneficiaries in the event of such an unfortunate occurrence—whether the ultimate takers of the property be other relatives or friends or charities.

Simultaneous death clause

There is always a possibility that you and your spouse or some other beneficiary may die under circumstances in which it is impossible to determine who died first. For example, two people may be killed in an automobile accident or a plane crash—frequently referrred to as a common accident or disaster. To cover such an unfortunate turn of events, your will should contain a simultaneous death clause, leaving the property to someone else should you and your beneficiary die at the same time. The utilization of such a clause will permit you to pass property to the desired beneficiaries rather than to unintended beneficiaries. Under certain circumstances it will also keep the government from levying unnecessary estate or inheritance taxes upon the estate of the person you named to receive the property should you and that person die at the same time.

Property passing to minors

Under the law, a minor is considered incapable of handling his own affairs. If he inherits or is given property, that property must be held in trust or managed by a guardian. If no such arrangements are made for a minor who receives property under a will, the court will appoint a guardian to handle the property for him. Consequently, your will should contain a provision that permits the executor or a trustee to hold property that may pass to persons who may still be minors at the time of your death. Such a provision will avoid the necessity for appointing guardians for such minors.

You may provide that property that may pass to a minor be put into a minority trust for him—an arrangement by which the property will be managed for him until he comes of age. If you provide for a form of minority trust, it may be possible to minimize taxes on the minor's estate should the minor die before reaching the age of majority. With respect to minority trusts, the laws of many states define the age of minority as 18 rather than 21. If you wish, however, you may continue the trust until the beneficiary is 21, thus allowing the property that is held in trust to be further used for his maintenance and education.

If the minor is your child and your spouse dies before you, the child will probably be eligible for a federal estate-tax deduction under the *orphan's exclusion*—made available by the 1976 Tax Reform Act. Ask your lawyer how you can word your will so that your child might be able to take advantage of this tax break if you and your spouse should die before he is 21 years old.

Your will may also provide for the appointment of a guardian of the persons and the property of minors. Frequently, the decision as to who should be appointed guardian of their children is a difficult one that is vigorously discussed between the parents. In any event, if you have minor children, it is important that you designate a guardian of both their property and their persons in order to minimize the possibility of a court appointment. Otherwise, the court may appoint a guardian who would have been unacceptable to you.

Executors and trustees

It is also advisable to appoint an executor for your estate and a trustee for any trusts you set up in your will. The selection of the executor and trustee should be carefully considered. The duties of an executor require an ability to deal with the administration of the estate, including the management of assets, payment of taxes, and ultimate distribution of property to beneficiaries either outright or in trust. Consequently, you should not consider the designation of an executor an honorary appointment but a very serious responsibility. People often think they are being nice when they name a friend or relative their executor or trustee, but they are often placing a burden on their shoulders. Always keep in mind that the job of both an executor and a trustee involves very serious responsibilities affecting the lives of the beneficiaries and the proper carrying out of your aims.

In order for the executor or trustee to function properly, you must provide him or her with adequate powers over your property after your death. These powers include the authorization to make investments, sell property, and distribute property to your beneficiaries. State laws often provide lists of powers that may be exercised by the executor or trustee. However, the statutory powers may not provide all the powers that should be given; ask your lawyer to draw up a comprehensive list.

Once you have chosen the persons who can be expected to act properly as executor or trustee, you ought to give them broad powers over investments and the property of the estate or trust generally, so as to permit flexibility and appropriate management of the property during the administration of the estate or during the continuance of any trust that is created under the will. The powers of the executor or trustee

are often referred to as standard, but such powers are extremely important. Consider them carefully.

Frequently, special kinds of powers should be expressly included in the will. For example, in many states, if the executor is not authorized to continue a family business or a sole proprietorship (a business owned entirely by one person), that business must be liquidated when the owner dies and the assets must be distributed promptly unless the local court authorizes the continuance of the business. Giving the executor the power to continue such a business is most important for the family or other beneficiaries of the deceased owner.

Estate and inheritance taxes

State and federal estate or inheritance taxes will be levied on your estate or beneficiaries when you die. Unless you provide for the way in which these taxes will be paid, they may be levied on beneficiaries whom you do not want to bear the burden.

In most states, if a will does not direct otherwise, the estate taxes will be levied proportionately on all of the property in your estate. Thus, if you do not include a tax apportionment provision in your will, beneficiaries who receive your household furniture will be responsible for paying estate taxes on it.

A common way of avoiding this problem is to add a clause to your will providing that all the taxes be levied on your residuary estate. In this way, all the property disposed of in other parts of your will—bequests of jewelry and furniture, for example—will pass tax-free to your beneficiaries. In particular circumstances, however, arranging for all taxes to be levied on your residuary estate may be undesirable or impossible. For example, if you specifically devise all your real estate (that is, name each piece of real estate and say who should receive it instead of letting it pass under the residuary clause as part of the rest of your estate), you may prefer to arrange that the beneficiaries who receive the real estate pay a large part of the estate taxes.

Treatment of spouses and grandchildren

In many states, a surviving spouse is given the right, as a matter of law, to choose (elect) to receive the property he or she was left under the will or an elective share. Depending on the state, an elective share is either a forced share (one third or one half of the estate) or what he or she would have received if there had been no will. If your state has such a law, you must give careful thought to how much you leave your spouse. If you leave less than the elective share, he or she may take property you intended for others.

You may also have to consider certain of your grandchildren. In some states, if your child is deceased but has a living child (your grandchild), that grandchild may successfully claim against your will if it failed to mention either him or his deceased parent. Again, you must carefully consider such provisions—commonly known as the *pretermitted heir statute*—in order to insure that your will properly carries out your intentions.

Testamonium clause

Although not required as part of the document, most wills usually include a testamonium clause that states, in effect, that the person making the will has set his hand and seal to the will as of that date (which is given). There then follows a signature line for the person who is making the will to sign. Although most states do not require a will to be dated, you should date your will in order to fix the date it was signed.

Attestation clause

An attestation clause is a statement that the witnesses who signed the will actually saw the person who made the will sign it. Although an attestation clause is not necessary to make a will valid, in cases in which a will is challenged it can provide some evidence that the witnesses observed the signing of the will by the person who made it and that they themselves signed the will after he did. Many lawyers read the attestation clause to the witnesses at the time the will is signed by its maker in order to fix in the witnesses' minds the solemnity of the occasion.

Signing the will

Unlike other kinds of legal documents, a will must be signed in a prescribed manner if it is to be valid. This signing procedure—commonly called an *execution ceremony*—should be done under the supervision of a lawyer. Unless the will is signed in the presence of two (or in some states, three) witnesses, all of whom are present when the will is signed and who also sign it in each other's presence, the will is not validly signed, or *executed*, and it will not be valid.

Certain variations in this signing procedure are permitted—usually to fit special circumstances. For example, in some states a person may make a valid holographic will—a document that is written in the maker's own hand and signed by him without any witnesses being present. Special kinds of signing ceremonies are also available to servicemen on active military duty and to seamen at sea. You should never use these procedures, however, unless absolutely necessary, and then—if possible—only after you have consulted a lawyer.

Finally, unlike other documents, a will is signed only once. When you make your will, you should not sign a number of copies of it and have them witnessed in the belief that the first copy signed and witnessed is the original will and that the copies that were subsequently signed and witnessed are merely copies. On a proper copy of a will the names of the persons who signed the original should be typed or printed exactly as they were signed on the original.

After the signing

Once your will has been properly executed, you should either give the original to your lawyer or place it in your safe-deposit box for safekeeping. But before you put it there, check your state law. Many states require a special court procedure to open a deceased person's safe-deposit box to get his will for probate. While such a court procedure is simple, it may take time to complete. If your state has such a law, it may be advisable for you to leave your will with your lawyer or another family adviser. Many states also provide a system in the local probate court that allows you to place your will in the court, on file for safekeeping.

Once you have made your will, executed it, and placed it somewhere for safekeeping, you may relax with the knowledge that if you die suddenly and unexpectedly, your money and other property will go to those you would most like to have them. Although making a will can be an arduous, complicated task, it is a task you should undertake at once.

completely on his son to tell him what he is signing. The alleged building permit is actually a will that makes the son sole beneficiary of his father's estate, deliberately omitting a daughter. The father signs the will based on his son's representations. It can be invalidated for fraud in the execution, since the father was intentionally misled regarding the nature of the document he was signing.

Fraud in the inducement   Fraud in the inducement occurs when you know you are making your will but its terms are based on misrepresentations of important facts made to you by someone who will benefit from your belief in his lies. The liar must know that his statements are false—unintentional or innocent misrepresentations will not invalidate a will. Misrepresentations also occur when facts are concealed that, if revealed, would cause the testator to distribute his property differently in his will.

EXAMPLE   Mildred, an 86-year-old woman, left a will by which she gave $35,000 in legacies to various relatives and the rest of her estate—more than $100,000—to John, her beloved 22-year-old husband of two months. The will was challenged by Mildred's relatives on the ground of fraud in the inducement: John already had a wife from whom he had not been divorced when he married Mildred and had, in fact, continued to see her secretly during his bigamous marriage to Mildred, who never knew the truth. John's deliberate concealment of his marital status justified the court's voiding the section of Mildred's will that provided for John.

A misrepresentation after a will has been executed does not affect its validity.

Constructive trust   Persons deprived of benefiting under a will because of fraud or undue influence can obtain relief only if the will is invalidated. If a testator has been prevented from making or revoking a will by fraud or undue influence, the courts often impose a constructive TRUST against the wrongdoer in favor of the person who otherwise would have benefited. In a constructive trust, the will remains in force as written and the estate is passed to the person indicated in the will. The court immediately imposes a trust on the property, however, compelling the person to turn the property over to the intended beneficiary.

EXAMPLE   A testatrix—let's call her Mary—died leaving a will giving her whole estate to the leader of a religious cult and to one of his followers. After making this will, she often expressed the determination to execute a new will in favor of her niece. Before her death, her attorney drafted a new will to this effect. Using false representation, undue influence, and physical force, however, the beneficiaries under the first will prevented Mary from executing the second. The surrogate's court ruled that the niece was entitled to a constructive trust, which was then imposed on the estate.

Mistake   A mistake may invalidate a will, even though the intention of the testator is clear. If you think you are executing your will, but by mistake you sign the wrong one, that mistakenly signed document will not be given legal effect by the courts.

EXAMPLE   Marge and Ann, twin sisters, go to their attorney's office to have their individual wills prepared. By mistake, they sign each other's wills instead of their own. Only after Ann's death is the error realized.

Although completely unintentional, it will prevent Ann's property from being distributed according to the terms of her will that was erroneously signed by Marge. Such *mistakes in execution* often occur when husband and wife draft mutual wills.

If a provision of your will is somehow omitted when it is drawn up, nothing can be done after your death to reinstate it. The fact that the will was properly executed creates a presumption that it contained all the provisions you intended.

Some states permit a provision mistakenly *included* in a will to be omitted by the probate court providing, of course, that the persons contesting the will can prove the provision was included by mistake. Permission also depends on whether the deletion will substantially alter other provisions in the will and, if so, whether the intention of the testator will be best accomplished by probating the will as written or by deleting the materials mistakenly included.

The lesson is obvious—read your will carefully just before you sign.

Wrong descriptions of persons or things in a will sometimes occur even though you had the proper designation in mind when you drew up the will but a typist made an error in the description so that it does not appear in the final document as you intended. If the mistake is merely a wrong description, and nothing more, the will probably will be admitted to probate as it was written.

EXAMPLE   Let us say you describe the car that you are leaving to your niece Joan as a blue 1979 Fuel Saver, but the typist types "blue 1977." If the only other car you have is a white 1980 Gas Guzzler, which you leave to your wife, your niece would probably get the 1979 Fuel Saver car upon your death.

You might also have intended that your will should read as it does, but you designated the property or beneficiary incorrectly. This is not a mistake in content that requires the will to be voided. The court will determine whether a certain person is entitled to particular property by CONSTRUCTION of the will—it will study ambiguities and uncertainties to determine your intention.

EXAMPLE   A provision of John's will left his treasured hunting rifle to his cousin Randy, an avid hunter. Before signing the will, John read it over and found it to be fine. When the will was presented to probate after John's death, the court discovered that John had two cousins named Randy. One was a three-year-old preschooler, while the other was a member of a nationwide rifle organization and had a reputation in the community as an excellent hunter. The court recognized that John had had the older Randy in mind when he made the will.

When there is no mistake as to what the will contains but you merely misunderstood the legal effect of the language used, your will should not be rejected. This is true even if incorrect advice from an attorney caused the error.

An error regarding facts outside the document itself is called a *mistake in the inducement*. Some examples of mistakes in inducement that you might make in drawing up your will are the misconceptions you might have about the nature, condition, or extent of your property or about the conduct or status of the "natural objects of your bounty" or of other beneficiaries. Courts generally will not invalidate a will because of a mistake in inducement where there is no fraud, because almost every testator is mistaken about some of the facts that go into making a will—such as mistakes about the amount of loans and advancements (money or property given by a person during his lifetime to an heir that is intended to be deducted from the heir's eventual share of the estate), the value of his property, and errors in believing that a beneficiary is living or dead. These are not grounds for refusing probate. A few states provide that children erroneously believed to be dead and therefore not provided for in a parent's will may take the same share as they would have received if the testator had died intestate.

Writing A will must usually be in writing, but it may be in any language and inscribed with any material or device on any substance that produces a readable and fairly permanent record. A writing on the sand of the seashore would not be sufficient, but an inscription on a slate or on paper with lead pencil, pen and ink, or typewriter would be.

Although you are not legally bound to do so, it is a good idea to type your will to avoid the risk of illegibility. Typing the document also discourages you from making additions after the will is executed—changes that later could lead to long and expensive court battles.

To be sure that the will presented for probate will be the very document that you executed, avoid making erasures, changes, or corrections on the face of the will whenever humanly possible. If an error in language occurs, the entire page should be retyped; if that is not possible, you should sign the margin opposite the change, indicating your approval of it. In addition, the witnesses should sign at these places to indicate that the alteration was made before the will was signed.

The pages of the will should be numbered and fastened together in some permanent form—by staples, for example—at the time of execution. This insures that no additional pages will be fraudulently inserted into the will.

Signing A will must be signed by the testator. Any mark—such as an *X*, a zero, check mark, or other mark that a competent testator makes to authenticate his will—is a valid signing. Some states permit another person to sign a will for a testator at the testator's direction or request or with his consent.

The location of the signature on the will is significant in many states. Usually the law in those states requires that the signature be at the end of the will, and if it is not, the entire will can be invalidated. The testator's property will then be divided according to the state's laws of descent and distribution.

The testator should sign the will before the witnesses do, but the reverse order is usually permissible.

Witnessing Statutes require a certain number of witnesses to a will. Most require two, although some mandate three. The witnesses serve two functions: signing the will and attesting (certifying) that the testator was competent at the time he made it. The only qualifications for a witness are that he be credible (trustworthy) and competent—able to understand and remember what he witnessed in case he is called to testify in a proceeding for the probate of the will. A minor may be a witness if state law permits.

Although most states require only two witnesses for the execution of a will, it is a good idea to have three. Perhaps another state in which you buy property will require three

witnesses at the time of your death. Or perhaps one of the witnesses cannot be located or has predeceased you. Probate will be permitted on the testimony of the extra witness—called a *supernumerary witness* because he is more than the number legally required.

The witnesses need not know you, but they must be capable of observing your mental capacity at the time you make the will. It may be better to use close acquaintances, however, especially if you are elderly or infirm or if there is any other reason that your testamentary capacity may be challenged in a probate proceeding. It is also a good idea to have witnesses who are younger than you and likely to outlive you. In addition, you should choose witnesses who are permanent residents of the locality so that they can be reached when needed.

When seeking witnesses for your will, it is important to choose people who do not have any financial interest in it. If a witness has an interest, his testimony regarding the circumstances under which the will was made will be suspect, since he will profit by its admission to probate. In most states, such a witness must either *purge* his interest under the will—that is, forfeit his rights under the will—or be barred from testifying. Without the witness, the will may be ruled invalid and the property distributed according to state law.

Purging statutes have been enacted by many states to eliminate the interests of witness-beneficiaries in order that they may testify honestly regarding the making of the will.

EXAMPLE Jane left $1,000 to Tom in her will, to which he was a witness. Under a purging statute, Tom would have to forfeit his interest under the will in order to testify about its execution. If, however, Tom would inherit from Jane under the state's laws of descent and distribution should the will be invalidated, generally only his interest in excess of the amount he would receive if the will was voided would be purged.

A purging statute does not affect indirect interests. If a testator leaves $100,000 to his church and one of the witnesses to the will is a church member, the gift to the church is not voided.

Interests of creditors, attorneys, and executors of the deceased's estate do not disqualify them from benefiting from the will. When the spouse of a witness is a beneficiary, some states allow the witness to testify and the spouse to take the interest. Other states purge the spouse's interest.

EXAMPLE Emily was one of the witnesses to John's will. In the will, John left Emily's husband, Bertrand, $5,000 to pursue his work as a botanist. The applicable state law allowed the spouses of witnesses to benefit under a will, and so Emily was able to testify as a witness to the will without affecting her husband's right to the $5,000. Had the parties lived in a state that requires the spouse to purge his interest, things might have been different. If Emily had testified as a witness, Bertrand might not have received his $5,000. But even in such a state, if Emily was one of three witnesses and that state required only two witnesses for probate, Emily could have refrained from testifying and let the other two witnesses testify. Then Bertrand could have received his $5,000.

In most states with purging statutes, the law provides that if a will is witnessed by more than the required number of witnesses, those disinterested witnesses will be called to testify in probate proceedings. This allows those witnesses who would benefit under the will to keep their rights.

An attestation clause is a certificate signed by witnesses to a will verifying that they observed formalities of execution being performed. It usually is not required to establish validity of the will, but in some states it is PRIMA FACIE evidence (evidence sufficient to establish a fact unless it is contradicted) of the truth of the testator's statements that he is of sound mind and that this is his last will and testament.

Acknowledgment   A testator is usually required to "publish" his will—that is, to declare to the witnesses that the document is his will. Such a declaration is called an acknowledgment. No state requires that the witnesses know the contents of the will, however. Although some states insist that a testator sign his will in the presence of witnesses, most states require only that he acknowledge the signature as his to the witnesses.

■ **Rules of construction**   A will should be interpreted in light of the general circumstances surrounding the testator at the time of the will's execution. But when a testator's intention is not clear, either in the language of the will or from the surrounding circumstances, the court applies statutory and case-made rules of construction. For a discussion of the rules of construction see STATUTE.

In some states, probate includes construction of will provisions, while in other states, probate only determines whether a will is valid and construction proceedings immediately follow to interpret ambiguous provisions.

To begin, a will is always construed to pass all the property that the testator owns at his death, including property he acquired after he made the will.

EXAMPLE Peter's only property at the time he executed his will was his Wisconsin farm. In his will he provided, "I give and devise all of my property to Lucy." Later he bought a Chicago condominium. On his death, he owned both the farm and the condominium. Lucy took both properties.

If—as sometimes happens—a description in a will applies equally to two or more persons or objects, the court receives evidence as to which person or object was intended by the testator, and allows people to testify regarding his statements of intention.

EXAMPLE In her will Rose stated simply that she was leaving "$1,000 to my nephew John with whom I shared many happy times," although she has two nephews of that name. In taking evidence during probate, the court learned that one nephew, John S., lived near Rose and invited her regularly to his home. Rose was a godmother to one of his daughters. The other nephew, John K., lived across the country and Rose never saw him and wrote to him only at Christmas. It was clear to the court that Rose meant to leave the $1,000 to John S.

Problems also arise when the testator fails to use precise language. Suppose Jack stated in his will, "It is my wish that Jane, my faithful secretary, share my estate with my wife, Ann." This is not clear and definite. It is *precatory language*—expressing a wish, hope, or desire. Precatory language has not been recognized as legally binding in most situations because it is merely advisory, not mandatory. In the above example, the court would not interpret Jack's wish to be legally binding and it would allow the estate to pass only to his wife, Ann. Jane could not enforce her claim against the estate.

You should note that every time a will goes before a court to have a matter determined, such as the construction of a provision, the value of the estate is reduced by the additional legal fees and costs. In addition, extensive time delays are involved, which postpone the distribution of the estate to the beneficiaries.

■ **Custody of completed wills**   After all the formalities are completed in executing your will, it will be given to you. Now you must decide where to keep it. Some people keep their wills in safe-deposit boxes along with their valuables. Statutes in some jurisdictions permit the will to be delivered to the probate office for safekeeping. Some testators have their attorneys keep their wills in their office files or safes. Sometimes, to reduce the risk of loss, two or more identical copies of a will are each completely executed, but, since there is only one will according to law, only one copy is probated. Such duplicate wills are generally inadvisable, however, because the probate court might conclude that the testator revoked the will and destroyed his copy if all of the duplicates are not accounted for. In whatever safe place you decide to keep your will, be sure to let someone know of it—your lawyer, your wife or children, or some trusted person who will be likely to survive you.

■ **Special types of wills**   Some states have laws that recognize certain kinds of wills that are executed with less formality than ordinary wills. The theory is that such wills are made under circumstances that mitigate against fraud.

Holographic wills   Unlike most wills, a holographic will is completely written and signed in the handwriting of the testator, such as a letter specifically discussing his intended distribution of his estate after his death. Many states refuse to recognize such a will. However, a holographic will may be admitted to probate in a state that does not allow such wills if it was executed in a state where holographic wills are valid. See Chart 14. In states that do recognize such wills, the general rules regarding testamentary capacity and intent apply. Some jurisdictions require that holographic wills be dated by the testator's hand. The will must usually observe the formalities of execution unless exempted by statute. For example, holographic wills usually do not need to be witnessed.

The reason for having the will entirely in the testator's handwriting is that it guarantees its genuineness. When the document contains any printed or typed matter or words in another's handwriting, some courts will not include the added material as part of the will, and will declare the will valid without it. Where, however, those words can be proved to have been intended as part of the will, the entire document becomes invalid.

EXAMPLE In one case, a testator had written "my country place Cragthorn." The entire will was in the testator's own hand except that the name Cragthorn was inserted with a rubber stamp. The will was invalidated because it was not written entirely in the testator's hand.

This theory is applied by only a few states because of its harsh results. The presence of certain nonholographic writing on the paper—for example, a printed heading—will not invalidate the document in any state. Some states require only that the signature and important provisions of the will be in the testator's handwriting.

Oral wills   Oral wills are technically known as *nuncupative wills*. Not all states recognize the validity of such wills because of the possibility of fraud, and those that do recognize them impose certain requirements. See Chart 14.

(1) A nuncupative will must be made during the testator's last sickness or in expectation of imminent death.

(2) The testator must intend that what he has said operate as his will. The words themselves must be definite. They must clearly show that his intention is to create a will and that he is indicating what he wants done with his property upon his death. Giving instructions for a written will or giving checks and notes to another person with directions for their use does not amount to a nuncupative will, since there is no testamentary intent.

(3) The testator must indicate to the required number of witnesses that he wishes them to witness his oral will.

(4) Only personal property, not real estate, can be disposed by a nuncupative will. Where an oral will attempts to dispose of both real estate and personal property, the personal property will go according to the will but the real estate will pass according to the statutes of descent and distribution of the state in which the property is located.

(5) An oral will usually cannot be probated more than six months after the time the words were spoken unless they were written down within a certain number of days, specified by law, after the oral will was made.

Soldiers' and sailors' wills   Several states have laws that relax the requirements for the wills that members of the armed forces make while on actual military duty or at sea. This privilege is based on English law, which adopted the practice of Julius Caesar, who allowed his soldiers to make wills without the formalities required of other persons.

The verbal or handwritten will of someone on military duty can pass personal property only, and some states impose financial limits on the amount of personal property that can be passed. Most states do not permit real estate to be passed by soldiers' and sailors' wills.

Whether these testamentary dispositions must be witnessed depends on state law. Statutes also often stipulate that the wills are valid for only a certain period of time after the testator has left the service. In other states, however, the will remains valid.

Joint wills   An ordinary will written and executed by two testators, usually husband and wife, is a *joint will*. When one dies it is probated as his will, and when the other dies it is probated again. A joint will is rarely used because in order to revise or update it both persons must go through all the statutory formalities again.

Whether a joint will can be revoked after one person's death depends on state law and the language used in the will. If the will clearly states that it cannot be revoked, then it cannot be revoked. On the other hand, if the will is silent as to revocability but contains language to the effect "we declare this and none other to be the testators' will," some courts infer that the parties have agreed prior to its execution that the will cannot be revoked. Other courts will not arrive at such a presumption. There is no clear rule on the revocation of joint wills.

Mutual wills   A joint will differs from a *mutual will,* which is really two separate wills containing identical or reciprocal provisions that each testator will give some or all of his or her property to the other. After the property of the one who dies first is distributed to the other, the living person's will then has no practical value. A mutual will is more flexible than a joint will because one of the testators can revoke it without the other's consent. Otherwise, it has no advantage over a joint will.

Revoking mutual wills   Either party to mutual wills may revoke his will at any time, except when they have made a CONTRACT not to revoke them. If one will is thus revoked, most courts will treat it as a breach of contract when asked to do so by the person who has been hurt by the revocation. In some cases, courts may impose a constructive trust for the benefit of the injured party.

EXAMPLE   Ed and Nancy made mutual wills with reciprocal provisions that each was to get the other's property. In a contract signed at the time they made their wills they stipulated that these provisions were not revocable. Ed later revoked his will and executed another will giving his property to Carol. When Ed's last will was probated and the property distributed to Carol, Nancy had two legal alternatives: she could have asked the court to compel Carol to hold the property in constructive trust for her or she could have made a claim against Ed's estate for breach of contract damages.

Simultaneous death   Problems arise in distributing property according to the reciprocal provisions of mutual wills when two people, usually spouses, are killed at the same time in the same circumstance and it is impossible to determine who died first, and when their wills make no provisions regarding how their estates should be handled in case this situation occurs. Typical examples of such a situation, called a *common disaster* or *simultaneous death,* are the deaths of a husband and wife in an automobile accident or a plane crash.

Usually, when one spouse dies before the other, his property is distributed to the surviving spouse according to the reciprocal provisions, after deductions have been made for legal fees, probate expenses, and taxes. When the surviving spouse subsequently dies, her estate, including whatever remains of what she had inherited from her spouse, is again probated, with another series of fees, expenses, and estate taxes. Meanwhile, of course, she had the use of the property left her by her husband for as long as she lived.

When both spouses die at the same time, however, there is no practical point to having the estate of one pass to the estate of the other and then to the surviving beneficiaries. Such a system merely harms the beneficiaries, usually the children, because it virtually doubles the legal expenses, probate costs, estate taxes, and the time involved because both wills have to be probated.

In order to be fairer to the beneficiaries, many states have enacted *simultaneous death acts.* Although these laws vary from state to state, they generally provide that unless there is sufficient evidence that one person died before another, a court will presume that they died at the same time. The property of each spouse is then distributed according to the terms of his own will as if he were the only survivor of the common disaster. This means that his estate is directly distributed to his surviving beneficiaries without his property passing unnecessarily in and out of his dead spouse's estate.

EXAMPLE Janice and Chuck are killed in a car crash. Two children, Lisa and Mark, survive. In their mutual wills, Janice and Chuck provided that upon one's death, the survivor would get everything. As a result of this unforeseen disaster, the court must distribute their estate, consisting of a jointly owned home worth $80,000, joint bank accounts totaling $30,000, and $10,000 worth of antiques owned by Janice and $75,000 worth of stock Chuck owned. The court will treat the couple's individually held assets as if each had died before the other. Any property jointly held would, however, be equally divided between the couple (once the court is satisfied that each person contributed equally to acquiring the asset).

Normally, if Janice had survived Chuck, she would completely own the jointly held property. Since this is not the case, only the actual interest held by each co-owner during the time both are alive will be included in the individual estates. Chuck's estate would then include his one-half interest in their home, or $40,000, his half interest in the bank accounts, or $15,000, and the $75,000 worth of stock, which only he owned. The value of his total estate would be $130,000. Janice's estate would be worth $65,000: her half interests in the home, $40,000, and in the bank accounts, $15,000, and her antiques valued at $10,000.

By having two separate estates, Lisa and Mark will inherit more of Chuck and Janice's property than if their estates were combined before being distributed. Estate taxes, legal fees, and other expenses are usually a percentage of the value of the estate—the larger the estate, the greater the percentage charged. The use of two smaller estates reduces these costs.

■ **Contracts to devise or bequeath property** A contract may be made to leave a certain person some particular property in a will. For example, a bakery shop owner may make a contract with a barber to leave the shop to him when he dies in return for which the barber agrees to help by working in the shop. A contract to make a will is regulated by the law of CONTRACTS.

A will must be probated whether or not it is the same as a previously made contract. When probating the will results in a breach of contract, the usual remedy is to impose a constructive trust on the property.

EXAMPLE In one case, an elderly man had no relatives except for a niece. He made an agreement with her that if she took care of him for the rest of his days, he would make a will giving her all his property. She agreed and he moved into her house, living there until his death. She performed her part of the contract completely. After he died, his niece discovered that he had made a will in favor of another person, revoking the will under which she was the sole beneficiary.

The niece sued in surrogate's court to get the property that was supposed to be left to her. The court decided that the contract between the testator and his niece was valid. But the subsequent will that the testator made was also valid even though it violated the testator's contract with his niece. The beneficiary of the second will received legal title to the property, which equitably (justly) belonged to the niece. The court therefore declared the beneficiary to be the trustee of the property he had received from the testator and ordered him to convey the property to her according to the contract.

■ **Determining what constitutes the will** One of the duties of a probate court is to establish *integration* of a will—that is, to determine what constitutes the will. In some cases more than one will may have been executed by the testator. In other cases outside documents, trusts, and persons not known at the time the will is executed—such as a future spouse or an employee yet to be hired—may be included in the will. The court must decide which of these are valid so as to judge their effect on the will.

Multiple wills If you make two or more wills disposing of the same property, the latest will is valid. If they were executed at the same time and contradict one another, they are all invalid. However, there may be more than one will devising different property admitted to probate.

EXAMPLE Nick made a first will giving his Manhattan townhouse to his brother, Joe. He made a second will devising his house in Beverly Hills, California, to his faithful secretary, Becky. In a third will, he left his Aspen, Colorado, condominium to his old Army buddy Harvey. Nick's fourth will gave his summer house in Seal Harbor, Maine, to his business partner, Helen. After Nick died, all the wills were offered for probate, and all were admitted, because the four were wholly compatible with each other and none contained provisions revoking the others.

In this case, each will had to be properly executed according to the laws of the state where the real estate was located and probated in that state. If any of these wills had been executed at the same time and had been inconsistent with each other—for example, if Nick had given his Manhattan townhouse to Joe in one will and to Becky in another—the conflicting wills would have been denied probate. Such property then would be distributed to Nick's heirs as determined by the laws of descent and distribution in the state where the property was located.

Incorporation by reference Sometimes a person will refer in his will to a letter or list that describes additional property he wants to pass under the will. This will be done only if the state has a statute permitting incorporation by reference—making outside material such as that contained in a book, record, or memorandum referred to in a provision of a will a valid part of that will. For this doctrine to be applied by a court, the will must refer to such material as being in existence at the time the will was made and must show intention to incorporate it. The extraneous material itself must also be precisely that referred to or described in the will.

Generally, documents not in existence at the time a will is executed cannot be incorporated by reference.

EXAMPLE On January 2, 1977, Paul executed his will, which provided, "I give the property which I have described on the flyleaf of my Bible to the person whose name I have written on the flyleaf of my Bible." Evidence showed that Paul had written on the flyleaf of the Bible on December 26, 1976, "my piano to Harriet Brown, my friend." The residuary clause of Paul's will (the clause that said who should receive any property Paul did not specifically dispose of in his will) named Pat Smith.

When Paul died, both Harriet and Pat claimed the piano. In order to determine who was entitled to the piano, the doctrine of incorporation by reference was applied, and since the reference was to a source existing when the will was executed, Harriet received the piano.

If this situation had occurred in a state that refused to apply the doctrine, the piano would have gone to Pat as part of the property passing under the residuary clause. If Paul had written what he did on the flyleaf of the Bible after he had executed his will, the piano would have gone to Pat whether or not the state law permitted incorporation by reference because to be valid the reference must be to something already existing when the will was made.

Certain documents cannot be incorporated, including those that are not clearly or properly referred to in a valid will and those that seem to be part of a will but that are disconnected and not consecutive.

EXAMPLE After Jack died, a sealed envelope was found O—* containing four pieces of paper apparently cut from the provisions of a completed will. On one piece, a paragraph stated an intention to make a will; on another, labeled "First," the writer directed certain debts to be paid; on yet another, marked "Eighth," was a residuary clause. Jack's signature, an attestation clause, and signatures of witnesses appeared on a separate sheet.

Because there was no relationship between the pieces of paper and no internal coherence in sense, the papers could not be integrated as Jack's will. To do so would open the door to fraud. A court dealing with an identical situation reasoned that "Any evil-minded person might, with comparative ease, take a will, and, by cutting from it sections or paragraphs, entirely defeat the object of the testator."

On the other hand, suppose Jack died leaving four sheets of paper on which he had written his will. If one page is signed and placed under the other three, there is continuous literary sense from beginning to end, especially when the middle of a sentence falls on the last line of a page and is continued at the top of the next page. These four sheets, being obviously connected as a single document, should be admitted to probate as Jack's will.

Independent significance You may leave property in your will to people who accomplish certain acts or take part in some event—even if you do not know who they are when you execute your will. Such acts or events have *independent significance*—that is, they have importance apart from the will.

EXAMPLE Mark died leaving a will that stated, "I give the O—* rest, residue, and remainder of my property to the persons who have been in my employ not less than 10 years at the date of my death." The will was made in 1965 and Mark died in 1981. At that time, there were five people who answered the description in the will, all of whom had been hired by Mark between 1966 and 1970—after the will had been made. They are all entitled to take the remaining property. The five beneficiaries were designated by an act that had significance apart from their becoming beneficiaries under a will; they were hired primarily to get a job done.

An act of the beneficiary may be the reference by which a will disposes of property. If Anselm provides in his will that the family's antique jewelry be left to "the woman whom my son John marries," and Judy marries John, Judy's act of marrying John makes her a beneficiary under Anselm's will.

Pourovers into trusts Sometimes a person (a settlor) sets up a TRUST during his lifetime for the benefit of a spouse, a child, or another dear one or for charitable purposes. The terms of such an arrangement are expressed in a document creating the trust. The settlor then provides in his will for additional gifts to be made to the trust upon his death. This is known as a *pourover provision*.

EXAMPLE Laura, a successful artist, set aside $200,000 in O—* trust for her twin five-year-old sons, Max and Sam. She drew up a document in February 1980 naming First Bank as trustee. In the will Laura drafts in May 1980, she provides that in the event she dies before either son reaches 25, 60 percent of her estate, not including the family home, is to be added (poured over) to the trust fund created in February 1980, which is administered by First Bank. This direction is called a pourover provision.

Upon Laura's death in June 1982, 60 percent of her estate will equal $300,000. This money will be poured over to the $200,000 that makes up the trust established while Laura is alive. Since the trust exists at the time Laura makes her will and is specifically referred to in it, the court will treat the original trust as part of Laura's will. A testamentary trust will be created combining the original $200,000 with the $300,000 left by Laura.

If the trust document is not in existence when the will is drawn or if it can be amended or revoked, some courts hold that it cannot be incorporated by reference. What happens in such a case depends on the law in the state. In some states the testamentary gift to the trust will be invalid, in others it will be valid.

■ **Revocation of a will** A will is *ambulatory*—that is, you may change or revoke it any time so long as you are competent. You can revoke your will by an action that indicates that you no longer want it to be binding. The law will abide by your decision.

Act of revocation For revocation to be effective, your intent, whether expressed or implied, must be clear and there must be some act of revocation consistent with this intent. When you execute a codicil (discussed below) that revokes some provisions of a previous will or when you execute a new will that completely revokes an earlier one, this act indicates your intent to revoke your will.

Statements you make at or near the time you intentionally destroy your will by burning, mutilating, or tearing it demonstrate your intent to revoke it. State laws usually designate which acts constitute revocation and require that the actions be done by the testator himself or by someone else at his direction and in his presence.

Revocation by act of law Sometimes revocation of a will occurs by OPERATION OF LAW. The law recognizes that significant events in your life—such as a marriage, divorce, the birth of a child, or the sale of property that you disposed of in the will—automatically change your legal duties. The will is sometimes considered by law to be revised to reflect those changes.

Many states, for example, provide that when a testator and spouse have been divorced but the will has not been revised or updated to reflect this change, any disposition to the former spouse is revoked. This does not mean, however, that you cannot provide for a former husband or wife under your will. It does mean that if you want to do so, you must revise the will so that it incorporates your changed marital status. Otherwise, the disposition you made while you were still married to your former spouse may be voided by state law.

Lost wills When a will cannot be found at the testator's death but was known to be in his possession, it is often presumed that he revoked it. If, however, it was last known to be in someone else's possession, there is no such presumption. The contents of a lost and unrevoked will may be proved by oral evidence.

■ **Codicils** A codicil is a separate document that adds things to an existing will or that revokes parts of or all of an existing will. A codicil is usually executed to make a change in the will without drawing up an entirely new will. The will remains the same except for the modifications made by the codicil.

A codicil must be executed with the same formalities as a will. It should refer to the will by identifying its date of execution and then state the changes to be made.

EXAMPLE In her will, made on July 3, 1980, Jane leaves the furnishings of her house to her daughter, Sally, but provides that her neighbor Molly receive her valuable Oriental rug. Six months later, Molly moves to Rome and Jane changes her mind about her bequest to Molly. She decides that she would like Sally to have the rug. Jane draws up a codicil that states that the provisions of her July 3, 1980, will are to remain in force except for the bequest to Molly. That provision is to be revoked and replaced with the provision that the Oriental rug is to be given to Jane's daughter, Sally.

A codicil can also be used to *republish* (acknowledge) an existing will. Republication is the validating of an existing will that is for some reason not valid.

EXAMPLE On March 1, 1977, Jim, with only one witness, executed his will naming Adam as sole beneficiary. In 1980 Jim executed a holographic (handwritten) codicil specifically affirming the provisions of his will of March 1, 1977. When Jim died, his nephew, Bruce, was his sole heir under the laws of intestacy—that is, if Jim died without leaving a valid will, Bruce would inherit his property. Both Adam and Bruce claimed Jim's property.

The statute of wills in the state required two witnesses to an ordinary will. Holographic wills, on the other hand, were valid if completely written, signed, and dated in the testator's handwriting. Although the 1977 will was invalid because it did not comply with the formalities of execution required by law, Adam was still entitled to be the sole beneficiary of Jim's estate. When Jim executed a valid holographic codicil referring to his earlier invalid will and reaffirmed its provisions, the will was considered republished as of the date of the codicil. Jim's last will was actually the 1977 will plus the 1980 codicil.

If Jim had not properly executed the holographic codicil, his estate would have passed to Bruce under the laws of intestacy.

Republication is also a means of affirming an earlier will by a more recent one or by a codicil, making the earlier will apply as of the date of the reaffirming document. The existing will is said to be *revived*—that is, it becomes legally effective. In a few states, if a first will is revoked by a second will that is subsequently revoked, the first will is automatically revived by the revocation of the second will. In most states, once a will has been revoked, it can be revived only by repeating the formalities of its execution, which includes republishing (reacknowledging) it, or by making a codicil that reacknowledges it.

■ **Protection of the family** Protecting the spouse and children of a decedent from economic failure is one reason the government regulates the disposition of property by will. Statutes focus on three basic issues: (1) the portion of the decedent's estate to which a surviving spouse is entitled, (2) the extent to which the spouse's rights to inherit may be defeated, and (3) the extent to which a spouse may take priority over a creditor's claims.

Types of laws that have been passed to protect the surviving spouse against disinheritance include those of community property, dower or curtesy, and the elective share. Children may be disinherited but may be given the benefit of the doubt in ambiguous cases. Families may also be protected by limitations on deathbed gifts to charities and laws governing incompleted or lapsed gifts and changes in willed property. Inheritances can be protected from creditors or unnecessary fees and taxes through laws of abatement, homestead, family allowance, and exempted property.

Community property A community-property system generally treats the HUSBAND AND WIFE as co-owners of property acquired by either husband or wife during their marriage. On the death of one spouse, the survivor is entitled to keep his or her one-half share of the community property. The remaining one-half of the community property plus the deceased spouse's noncommunity property is passed according to the deceased's will or the laws of descent and distribution if he dies intestate. Property received as a gift or through a will or inheritance and property acquired before the marriage are not community property. The community property system is used in eight states—Arizona, California, Idaho, Louisiana, Nevada, New Mexico, Texas, and Washington.

Dower or curtesy At common law, a wife was entitled to *dower*—a life interest in one-third of the land owned by her husband during the marriage. *Curtesy* was the right of the husband to a life interest in all of his wife's lands. A life interest is the right to occupy and benefit from property throughout your lifetime without having the power to sell it or give it away or pass it to the heirs of your choice. In other words, under the common-law dower system, a widow who was entitled to receive life interest in one-third of her husband's lands could live on those lands or collect rent from them, but she could not sell them. When the widow died, the lands would go to her former husband's heirs, and she would have no say in the matter—if she had remarried and had children from her new marriage, for example, she would not be able to leave the lands to those children.

Most states have abolished common-law dower and curtesy, which treat men and women differently. Many states have replaced them with their own dower and curtesy laws, which treat husband and wife identically—each receiving a life estate in one-third or one-half of the deceased spouse's property, depending on the state law. Some states include personal property as well as real estate under dower or curtesy. Some states allow creditors to take what is owed them from dower or curtesy. Certain states allow dower or curtesy in addition to provisions in a will, but others allow dower or curtesy only in place of testamentary provisions.

EXAMPLE Tom's will provided that his wife, Colleen, was to receive only $80,000 of his $400,000 estate. The law in the state where Tom and Colleen lived entitled a widow to dower, a life interest in one-half of all her husband's real and personal property, and allowed her to take either her dower share or what she had been given in the will. Colleen may take the $80,000 outright or a life interest in one-half of the $400,000 estate, depending on her financial situation. Half the estate would give her the use of her four-family house, its furniture, and one of the family cars. She could live in one of the apartments in the house and rent the other three. The rents would give her enough money to live in reasonable comfort but would leave her with little extra cash.

If Colleen had been an older woman who was content to live quietly, she would have taken the dower share. But Colleen was a young woman and desperately needed cash to finish law school. Since she would not be able to sell any of her inherited property to get cash if she chose her dower share, she took the $80,000 to pay her tuition and living expenses for her last two years in school and to help support her in her first year or two of law practice.

Elective share The states that have not passed community-property laws or dower or curtesy laws have passed statutes giving a surviving spouse the right to an elective share that gives her an alternative to what has been provided for her in the will. A few states have both dower and curtesy and elective share statutes, and the surviving spouse must choose one of them or what she or he is entitled to under the will. See Chart 17.

Under an elective share statute, a surviving spouse may choose (elect) to receive the property he or she received under the will or an elective share. An elective share is either a forced share (usually one-third of the estate if there are surviving children or one-half if there are not) or what he or she would have received under intestacy, depending on the state. (In some states, the elective share is the same as the dower or curtesy share.) While dower or curtesy entitles a widow or widower only to lifetime use of property, an elective share gives her or him ownership of both real estate and personal property.

EXAMPLE Tim expressly provides in his will that his wife, Karen, is to receive $15,000 of his $3 million estate after taxes, debts, and other expenses have been paid. Tim and Karen have no children. The bulk of his estate is to go to his faithful assistant, Elaine. Karen, however, is legally entitled to take either her testamentary share (the $15,000) or her forced share, $1.5 million (assuming that state law permits the surviving spouse, with no children surviving, to take one-half of the estate). This election must be exercised in the manner and within the time set by statute. If the law also gives Kathy the

right of dower, she could choose to have lifetime use of $1.5 million. The choice is hers.

Election provisions are subject to creditors' claims—that is, the creditors take what is owed them before the estate can be distributed.

Reducing an elective share Sometimes because of bitterness, hard feelings, and jealousy one spouse will try to reduce the amount of the elective share that the other would be legally entitled to by making gifts to someone else while alive, thus reducing the size of the estate. Not all gifts are made for that reason, however. When a testator's lifetime gifts are challenged, the surrogate's court must determine whether the gift was made with the intent to reduce the spouse's elective share.

United States Savings Bonds can be used to defeat a surviving spouse's elective share.

EXAMPLE Although Donna and Dave have been married more than 30 years, they have been separated by mutual agreement for more than 20 years. Religious convictions prohibit them from getting a divorce. Donna inherits $25,000 from her mother and is determined that Dave never set a finger on it. She purchases U.S. Savings Bonds with it, designating them payable to herself and, on her death, to various nephews and nieces. After Donna dies, Dave, who has been intentionally omitted from her will, tries to claim his elective share from the $25,000 in Savings Bonds. He is unsuccessful, however, because federal law provides that the bonds automatically become the property of the named beneficiaries rather than of the decedent's estate.

Prohibited spouses As a general rule, surviving spouses are prohibited from taking their elective share under certain circumstances. For example, a surviving spouse who unjustly deserted the testator for years before and up to his death might be barred from her elective share. The same might be true of an adulterous or bigamous spouse. For example, a fashion model who leaves her photographer husband to live with her stockbroker will not be entitled to her elective share when her husband dies if state law bars it to spouses guilty of misconduct.

Obviously, you would not qualify as a surviving spouse if you have been divorced from the testator or your marriage has been annulled. But when a husband and wife are merely separated, even if there is a separation agreement, neither spouse loses his statutory rights as surviving spouse unless the agreement expressly contains a release of their rights in each other's estates.

Making and retracting an election The right of election must usually be exercised personally by the spouse. When the spouse is not legally of age (18 or 21, depending on the state) or is legally incompetent, a guardian or committee may make the election if authorized by law. An election must be made within the time specified by statute, usually six months from the date that the letters testamentary are issued. (The letters testamentary are papers issued by the surrogate's court permitting the executor to distribute the decedent's property.) The election is made by written notice to the executor of the will—the person named in the will to see that its provisions are carried out.

Once an election is made, it is final and may not be retracted unless it resulted from fraud or misunderstanding.

EXAMPLE An elderly widow was badgered by her children into signing an election to take the property left her in her husband's will, which gave her only a small fraction of her statutory right to one-third of his estate. At the time she made the election, four weeks after her husband's death, she was still extremely distraught and depressed. She was told by one child, "If you don't take what is under the will, we will sell the farm and everything will be thrown in the road." Other misrepresentations were made to her about what would happen if she decided to take her statutory share.

After she signed the election, she talked things over with her banker, who explained the legal consequences of her conduct and urged her to promptly retract her election. She did so, and her children sued, challenging the legality of her retraction. A court upheld her retraction and awarded her one-third of the estate. It was clear from the circumstances that the widow signed the election while in a confused mental condition and under extremely high pressure. To give effect to such an election would be unfair and unjust.

Waiving a spouse's rights A spouse may usually waive, release, or contract away his statutory rights to an elective share or to dower or curtesy by either an antenuptial or a postnuptial agreement if the agreement is fair and made with knowledge of all the relevant facts. As a general rule, such agreements must be in writing. The fact that a spouse releases such statutory rights does not prevent the spouse from taking property left to him or her in the deceased spouse's will.

Children Generally, a testator may completely disinherit his own child—he may even disinherit a young child to the extent that he does not provide for raising it even though he is financially able to do so. It is usually better for a testator to specifically mention in his will that he is intentionally disinheriting certain named children. Otherwise, the disinherited child can challenge in court the testator's mental capacity, particularly in recognizing the "natural objects of his bounty." The cost of litigation will be deducted from the estate's assets. The states have different variations on this law, however. Some permit children known to be alive when the will was made to inherit their intestate share as *pretermitted* (omitted) heirs unless it was clear that they were meant to be disinherited. A nominal testamentary provision for a child is usually enough to prevent him from taking more as a pretermitted heir under the statute.

When a pretermitted heir takes his intestate share, and he is not the only heir to the estate, the statutes provide how his share is to be made up. A typical plan is that all other beneficiaries must contribute proportionately out of the parts willed to them. The omitted child does not assert his rights by contesting the will. He is not claiming that the will is invalid but he is taking independently of will provisions. He brings suit to get his share after the will has been admitted to probate.

Many states allow children who are born or adopted after the execution of a will and who are not mentioned in it to receive an intestate share unless the omission was intentional. See ADOPTION OF PERSONS. These provisions may also extend to children thought dead when the will was executed.

Charitable gifts At one time, various statutes restricted or forbade charitable and religious organizations from owning property. These laws, known as statutes of mortmain (literally "dead hand"), were intended to prevent land from becoming perpetually controlled by one dead hand, that of the charitable organization.

Today, anyone is entitled to receive property by will. Many states, however, have mortmain-type statutes that limit the testator's power to make charitable gifts. These laws are meant to protect the testator's family from being disinherited by gifts he makes to charity. Such limitations are in effect only when near relatives (usually children, grandchildren, parents, or spouse) survive. The amount of the charitable gift may be restricted to a certain proportion of the estate, usually 50 percent. Some states do not consider charitable gifts valid if they are made within a specified period—for example, six months—before death.

As a general rule, gifts made in excess of these limitations can be challenged only by those near relatives who stand to gain financially if the gifts are declared illegal. If successful, such relatives will receive only the amounts they would have received if all eligible persons contested the validity of the gift, and never more than they would have received if the testator had died without leaving a will and his property were distributed according to the state's law of intestacy.

EXAMPLE One month before her death, Clara made a will leaving all of her property to various charities. A provision in the will stated: "I have knowingly and intentionally failed to make any provision herein for my granddaughter, Susan, who has shown me no affection over the years, and it is my express desire that she in no way share in my estate." The will contained no other clause that would dispose of the estate if the gifts to the charities failed because they did not comply with the law. The state where Clara lived had a mortmain statute that voided charitable gifts made less than six months before a person's death if they exceeded 25 percent of the testator's net probate estate. Under the laws of descent and distribution, Susan was the only legal heir. Even though Clara intentionally disinherited Susan, Susan was entitled to inherit 75 percent of the estate.

You can disinherit your heirs and next of kin only by leaving the property to others. Mere words of disinheritance are not enough if you do not dispose of property by will. It descends and is distributed under the state's statute of intestacy.

Under some statutes, if a person who is legally entitled to challenge a charitable gift fails to do so, the share he would have received remains with the original charity. In such cases, the charity will receive more than the statutory limit.

There are ways in which you can get around limitations on charitable gifts. For example, you may provide in your will that if a charitable gift should fail (by being larger than the law permits), then the gift (or the residuary estate) should go to a nonrelative. This arrangement prevents a contest of the gift, because the law says that only a relative may contest the gift, and no relative would stand to benefit financially if the gift was declared illegal.

Lapse and antilapse statutes A gift in a will is said to *lapse* if the beneficiary is living when the will is executed but dies before the testator. A gift by will to a person already deceased at the time the will is made is void. Both void and lapsed gifts become part of the residuary estate. When the beneficiaries of a residuary estate die and it lapses, the property passes according to the laws of intestacy.

Many states have enacted antilapse statutes, however. Such statutes usually provide that the surviving issue (children or grandchildren) of the deceased beneficiary (if he was a relative of the testator) take the gift in his place.

Ademption Ademption is, in effect, a way you can renege on a declaration in your will by either changing the property (say, by selling it) or removing it from your estate.

The gift a person is to receive under a will is usually classified according to the type of gift it is. A *specific bequest* is a gift of a particular identifiable item of personal property, such as Dick's baby grand piano, whereas *a specific devise* is an identifiable gift of real property (land), such as Dave's ranch in Wyoming.

A *demonstrative bequest* is a gift of a certain amount of property out of a specific fund or source of property. When Gail provides that John be given $1,000 out of her bank account at Third National Bank, she has made a demonstrative bequest.

A *general bequest* is a gift of property payable from the general assets of the testator's estate. Gail simply leaves John $1,000, not specifying its source.

Ademption by extinction When specific devises and bequests are no longer in your estate or have been substantially changed in character at the time of your death (regardless of your intention), this is called ademption by extinction. The beneficiary of an adeemed legacy or devise gets nothing because the specific legacy or devise no longer exists.

EXAMPLE In his will Ted gave his beach house in Cape Cod O⊶✳ to Arthur and his diamond ring to Beth. Before he died, Ted sold the beach house and lost the ring. He placed the money he received for the real estate in one of his bank accounts, which Ted left to his wife. After Ted died, Arthur claimed the proceeds from the sale of the house and Beth claimed that the executor of Ted's estate should pay her the value of the diamond ring.

Both claims were rejected by the probate court. When Ted sold his house, that specific devise to Arthur was adeemed—it was removed from and extinguished as part of Ted's property. Neither it nor the money received for it could be claimed under the devise. When Ted died, the diamond ring no longer existed as part of his property and, therefore, its bequest was also adeemed.

Ademption by satisfaction Ademption by satisfaction occurs when during your lifetime, you give to your intended beneficiary all or part of a gift you had intended to give by will. Here your intention is crucial. Ademption by satisfaction applies to general legacies as well as to specific ones. If the gift made during your lifetime is identical with the gift made in your will, it is presumed that the gift is in place of the will's provision, if the gift is made to a parent, child, grandparent, or grandchild. In other instances, however, the presumption is against ademption by satisfaction unless it can be established by proof.

■ **Abatement** Abatement is the process of determining the order in which property in the estate will be applied to the payment of debts, taxes, and expenses. If the intention of the testator is expressed in the will, it will govern the order in which the property will abate. When the will is silent, the following order is usually applied: intestate property (property owned by the testator but not covered in the will), residuary gifts, general bequests, demonstrative bequests (if the fund exists at the time of death; if not, they will be treated as general bequests), and specific bequests and devises.

Within the same classification, gifts abate pro rata (proportionately).

EXAMPLE In his will, Fred leaves $1,000 to each of his O⊶✳ nephews, Alan, Bob, and Carl; his 1979 Mercedes-Benz sports car to Harry; $1,000 on deposit at Second County Bank to Ed; $1,000 on deposit at Third National Bank to Frank; and his residuary estate to Greg. Fred does not indicate which property should be used to pay debts, taxes, and expenses of his estate. By virtue of abatement, the residuary gift is used first to satisfy the creditors so Greg will receive nothing. Then the general legacies to Alan, Bob, and Carl are tapped, so they, too, get no inheritance. Finally, the demonstrative bequests to Ed and Frank are abated pro rata—each receives $750. Harry receives his specific bequest because the debts and expenses have been paid in full by that point.

Homestead, family allowance, and exemptions Statutes providing for HOMESTEAD, family allowance, and exempt properties are intended to help protect the family at the time of death. These provisions vary from state to state.

Homestead allows the family to continue living in the family home free from creditors' claims, usually until the children reach adulthood or the widow or widower dies. See Chart 10. The *family allowance* (usually not available to a widower) allows a certain amount for the support of the widow and the children while the estate is being administered. A probate court has the discretion to fix the amount of the allowance after considering such factors as the solvency and net worth of the estate and the age, health, and earning capacity of the family members. *Exempt property* usually allows specified personal property, such as wearing apparel, furniture, and personal effects to pass to the family of the decedent not subject to the claims of general creditors. See EXEMPTION.

■ **Will substitutes** You may control the distribution of your property after your death without resorting to a will by using such will substitutes as TOTTEN TRUSTS, life INSURANCE policies, or living TRUSTS. You may use these devices to avoid the problems, expenses, and time delays involved with the probate of a will. However, they all make up part of your estate and will be subject to state and federal estate tax when you die. See ESTATE AND GIFT TAX.

A *Totten Trust* is a bank account into which you may deposit a sum of money in your own name in trust for another, but still retain your right to add or withdraw money from the account. The money remaining in the account at the time of your death will pass automatically to your beneficiary without going through the probate process. This arrangement reduces the size of the portion of your estate that will be subject to administration, which reduces the costs of probate and fees to be paid to executors and attorneys. If, however, your will specifies that the account is to go to someone other than the beneficiary designated on the passbook, the rightful beneficiary will be determined by the probate court.

A life insurance policy is another will substitute you can use to avoid probate. The beneficiary you name in the policy will be legally entitled to the proceeds upon your death without having to go to probate court. By investing in life insurance policies, you can reduce but not completely eliminate the costs of administration of your estate, as a person's entire wealth usually cannot be reduced to insurance or any other form of will substitute.

If you prefer to create a living trust, you (the settlor) may transfer real estate or personal property to another person (the trustee) to hold and manage for the benefit of a third person (a beneficiary) once you have died. During your lifetime, however, you may keep the right to receive income from the property and the right to revoke or cancel the arrangement or change the beneficiaries. Upon your death, your beneficiary will be legally entitled to his rights under the trust without being subject to the probate process.

To determine what are viable will substitutes for you, you must consult the laws and court decisions in your state.

willful   Voluntary; intentional. In law, a *willful act* is one that is done intentionally, knowingly, and purposely; it is distinguished from an act done carelessly, thoughtlessly, or inadvertently.

The precise meaning of the word depends, however, upon the context in which it is used. In criminal statutes, *willfully* usually means with an evil purpose or criminal intent, especially if the forbidden act is one that is wrong in itself or involves MORAL TURPITUDE (depravity). For example, *willful murder* is the unlawful killing of another person without excuse or mitigating circumstances. If the forbidden act is not wrong in itself or does not involve moral turpitude, willfully means intentionally, purposefully, or knowingly. See CRIMINAL LAW.

> **EXAMPLE** A motorist intended to use a toll-free bridge, but O→＊ because of detours she became confused and drove onto the approach to a toll bridge. The approach was designed for one-way traffic, and she was unable either to turn off or to turn back. When she reached the tollbooth she refused to pay the toll, because she claimed that it was not her intention to use the toll bridge. A complaint was issued against the motorist, and the court held that she willfully evaded payment of the toll in violation of law.

Under the UNEMPLOYMENT COMPENSATION laws, an employee who is discharged from his job on the ground of *willful misconduct* is not entitled to recover unemployment compensation benefits. Common examples of such willful misconduct include excessive absenteeism, habitual lateness, deliberate violations of an employer's rules and regulations, reporting for work drunk, or drinking alcoholic beverages on the job.

Under WORKMEN'S COMPENSATION acts, willful misconduct by an employee means intentionally performing an act with the knowledge that it is likely to result in serious injuries or with reckless disregard of its probable consequences. A finding of willful misconduct bars an employee from receiving compensation.

> **EXAMPLE** An employer instructed one of his truck drivers O→＊ not to permit anyone else to drive the truck or to take on passengers, especially those who were drinking beer or hard liquor. The employee permitted his brother to drive the truck down a dangerous mountain road under hazardous weather conditions. The brother had no previous experience in driving the particular truck, and he had also been drinking. The truck, containing 9,000 gallons of gasoline, slid off the highway, plunged into a canyon and exploded. When the employee tried to recover workmen's compensation for injuries received in the accident, the court found that his misconduct was willful and barred his recovery of compensation.

wind up   Settle the accounts and liquidate the assets of a PARTNERSHIP or CORPORATION, for the purpose of making distribution and dissolving the concern.

withholding tax   Taxes that an employer must deduct from the wages of his employees and pay to the federal, state, and, where required, municipal governments in prepayment of the employee's INCOME TAXES.

without recourse   A type of qualified endorsement on a negotiable instrument, such as a check or a promissory note. The phrase means that the endorser intends to save himself from liability to subsequent holders of the instrument. It notifies them that if the parties who are primarily liable on the instrument default, there can be no recourse to the endorser. See COMMERCIAL PAPER.

witness   A person who gives EVIDENCE in a proceeding before a court or legislative body; a person who testifies about a fact or event because he has sufficient knowledge of it, based on what he has seen, heard, or observed. An *eyewitness* is a person who saw the object or event about which he is testifying.

■ **Attendance**   Persons called as witnesses have a public duty to attend the court or legislative body to which they are summoned and to give testimony.

Process   A person accused of a crime has the right to compulsory PROCESS for obtaining witnesses in his behalf—that is, he may have the witnesses served with SUBPOENAS, which legally bind them to appear and testify. The accused cannot be deprived of this right by the court, jury, or legislature. Parties to a civil lawsuit (the plaintiff and defendant) also have a right to compulsory process for obtaining the attendance of essential witnesses. Similarly, the state is entitled to compulsory process in any proceeding to which it is a party. Administrative agencies also have the right to compel the attendance of witnesses to testify about matters under investigation by those bodies. The right of a party to enforce the attendance of a witness cannot be denied by the court's prejudging the relevance of the testimony that the witness might give.

A subpoena is an order from a court commanding a person to appear and testify. The recipient is bound to obey it. An individual who is present in the courtroom can be required to testify without a subpoena.

As a general rule, witnesses can be compelled to attend court until dismissed by the court or the party who sum-

---

IF YOU ARE ASKED TO APPEAR AS A WITNESS IN COURT

■ A person accused of a crime has the right to have witnesses served with subpoenas, which legally bind them to appear and testify.

■ An individual who happens to be present in the courtroom can be required to testify without a subpoena.

■ A witness who is subpoenaed is entitled to travel expenses and fees as compensation for his time and expenses. A witness who fails to appear and testify in obedience to a lawful subpoena is liable for contempt.

■ In some states, expert witnesses who testify as to matters of opinion requiring special scientific or professional knowledge are allowed extra compensation in addition to the ordinary witness's fee. An expert can refuse to testify until his extra compensation is paid.

■ A very young child can be a competent witness.

■ In most states, spouses can testify for or against each other in civil cases. In criminal cases, one spouse can ordinarily testify in behalf of the other.

■ In most states, the prosecution in a criminal case can call the spouse of the accused to the stand only if the accused consents. In a few states, however, the husband or wife of the accused can be called to testify against his or her spouse regardless of the spouse's objections. But when a crime is committed by one spouse against the other, the victim can testify against the accused.

■ In most states communications made by a client to his attorney and a patient to a physician advising or treating him are privileged.

■ A physician cannot disclose the advice he gave to his patient, or any details about the treatment or operation, when he testifies in a civil case. The privilege does not extend to testimony in criminal trials.

■ Members of the clergy cannot disclose confessions or admissions made to them if the confiding party objects.

---

moned them. If he is wanted, a witness must remain after the day cited in the subpoena without being served a new subpoena.

Refusal to appear or testify A witness who fails to appear and testify in obedience to a lawful subpoena or who fails to remain as long as is required, is liable for CONTEMPT. A person cannot be punished for contempt if he is unable to obey a subpoena.

EXAMPLE Katherine was amazed to receive two subpoenas O——* in one week. The first called her to testify in a federal court in Brooklyn on March 16 at 9:30 in the morning about an auto accident she had witnessed. The other ordered her to be present with employment records for a lawsuit charging her company with discrimination in a state court in Manhattan on March 16 at 9:30. There was no way that she could be in both courts at the same time, so neither court would punish her for contempt if she notified them immediately of the conflict.

Similarly, a witness who is ill or physically unable to attend court cannot be punished for contempt. Finally, a witness cannot be punished for not appearing when the subpoena is served so late that he does not have enough time to comply.

A witness who refuses to testify or to answer proper questions when under examination before a court is also liable for contempt. An evasive or noncommittal answer is not considered a refusal to answer, unless the court directs the witness to be more specific. A witness cannot be punished for contempt for refusing to answer questions when his answers would incriminate him. See SELF-INCRIMINATION.

Damages When a witness refuses to obey a subpoena, he may be liable to the party who summoned him for any DAMAGES that result from his failure to testify.

EXAMPLE Tina and Patty were in a car that collided with O——* Bill's car. Bill sued Tina as owner and operator of that car, and he subpoenaed Patty as a witness because he could remember nothing about the accident. When Patty failed to show up at the trial, Bill lost his lawsuit. After that, he sued Patty for her failure to obey the subpoena, and he recovered money damages. He proved that he would have won his lawsuit if Patty had appeared and testified that Tina had taken a cold capsule that caused her to fall asleep at the wheel. He recovered from Patty an amount equal to what probably would have been awarded as damages in the lawsuit against Tina.

When the facts can be determined by some means other than the testimony of the defaulting witness, there is no right to recover damages from him.

Damages resulting from a postponement of the trial because of a witness's failure to attend, such as the extra court costs and legal fees, can be assessed against the party who insists on a delay in order to produce the witness.

In some states, a witness who fails to obey a subpoena has to pay a penalty set by statute to the party harmed by his default. The right to the penalty can be asserted as soon as the disobedience occurs without awaiting the outcome of the proceeding in which the witness is subpoenaed. In order to receive the penalty the harmed party must show that the witness was subpoenaed in the proper way and at the proper time, and that the witness's fees and expenses (discussed below) were paid or offered to him.

■ **Compensation** A witness who is subpoenaed is entitled to travel expenses and to fees to help compensate him for his time and expenses, but only if there is a state law to that effect. A party to a lawsuit is entitled to have a person who is already in court sworn as a witness without paying his expenses.

To be entitled to compensation, a witness must be in actual attendance in the courtroom. If he is in court he will be entitled to compensation even though he is not called on to testify or even though he is disqualified as a witness.

Who must pay In civil suits, a witness is ordinarily entitled to recover fees and travel expenses from the person or that person's attorney who subpoenaed him. Who is responsible for paying the fees for witnesses called by the prosecuting attorney and by the defendant in a criminal proceeding is a matter of the relevant state or federal law.

Amount recoverable The sums allowed for time spent in attendance and for mileage for travel between the witness's home and the court are fixed by law. The daily allowance of a subpoenaed witness is computed according to the time during which he is in attendance, not the time during which he testifies.

Experts Under some statutes, witnesses who testify as to matters of opinion requiring special or scientific or professional knowledge are allowed extra compensation in addition to the ordinary witness's fee.

EXAMPLE Wanda ate some potato salad at a restaurant and
O—* then became violently ill. She was rushed to a large hospital, which called in its gastroenterologist (specialist in digestive disorders). When Wanda sued the restaurant, she called this doctor as a witness. He testified not only about her condition and his treatment but also about the characteristics of food poisoning. The court ruled that he was entitled to extra compensation for his expert opinions on that particular medical problem.

But a professional who testifies as an ordinary witness—say, an accountant who witnessed a train derailment—is entitled only to ordinary witness's fees.

An expert can refuse to testify until his extra compensation is paid, and he is not liable for contempt by his refusal.

If a specialist signs a contract offering testimony in the area of his expertise in return for a certain fee, he can sue for breach of contract if he testifies and does not receive the fee. This rule holds true for the attending physician of a patient who is the subject of the testimony, provided the testimony extends to technical inferences and conclusions.

■ **Competency** As a general rule, in order to be considered competent as a witness a person must be able to perceive, remember, and communicate. He must also believe he is morally obligated to tell the truth. The legislature has the power to prescribe a standard of competency for witnesses, and the uniform tendency is to remove restrictions on competency rather than to tighten them. The reasons for disqualifying a witness must be found in specific provisions of law. A witness is not to be disqualified by implication, and if there is a reasonable doubt the witness should be held competent.

Knowledge of facts A competent witness is properly allowed to testify to any relevant fact within his personal knowledge. He can also testify as to the nonexistence of facts when he would probably have known of such facts if they had existed. On the other hand, a witness is not allowed to testify regarding a fact of which he has no personal knowledge.

The witness does not have to obtain his knowledge in any particular manner. He can testify as to what he hears, feels, tastes, and smells, as well as to what he sees. A witness who saw goods being sold can testify to the sale. He can testify whether or not a photograph is a likeness of its purported subject, even though he neither made the photograph nor saw it made. A witness can testify as to records made under his supervision. A wife who has seen her husband's monthly paychecks is competent to testify to his earning capacity.

Memory of facts All testimony is given and received on the theory that it is given according to the witness's best memory. Accordingly, a witness can testify as to facts within his knowledge, even though his recollection of them may be vague or imperfect. He can testify only to facts within his recollection, but it does not matter how long before the trial they occurred. A witness cannot, however, testify about things that occurred when he was so young that he could not personally remember them, but may "recollect" them from having heard others talk about them in later years. The fact that a witness had refreshed his memory as to particular matters in preparation to testify does not make him incompetent to testify on those matters. See REFRESHING MEMORY.

EXAMPLE This exchange could take place during a breach
O—* of contract trial:
ATTORNEY: What day did you warn the buyers that you could not fill their order?
WITNESS: I don't know, but I sent them a telegram that same afternoon.
ATTORNEY: Is this the telegram?
WITNESS: Yes. The date is right. I remember now. It was the Friday before the three-day weekend.

Mental capacity One of the tests of a witness's competency is his intelligence and understanding. The law does not fix any standard of intelligence, but leaves the determination of that capacity almost wholly to the court's discretion. The test is whether the witness has sufficient capacity to observe and describe correctly the facts about which he is called to testify. A witness should not be barred from testifying on the ground of mental incapacity unless the proof is clear and conclusive.

Unsoundness of mind does not per se make a witness incompetent. Even someone who has been judged an INSANE PERSON can act as a witness if he can understand his obligation to tell the truth and can give a correct account of those matters he has seen or heard that relate to the issues in the lawsuit. This determination is within the discretion of the court. A like rule also applies in the case of witnesses who may be slow-witted, feebleminded, or otherwise mentally deficient.

EXAMPLE Stanley was confined to a hospital for the crimi-
O—* nally insane after he killed his mother and dismembered the body. Nevertheless, he had periods of lucidity. After he saw a guard at the hospital attack one of the patients, he was called as a witness. The court questioned him and ruled that he was competent to testify even though still medically insane.

Children Unless there is a statute that declares children under a certain age incompetent or that raises a presumption of incompetency (that says that the person who calls the child has the burden of proving he is competent to testify), a witness is not disqualified because of his youth. No precise age determines the question of competency. A very young child can be a competent witness when he understands his obligation to tell the truth, has sufficient intelligence to receive correct impressions from his senses, and can recollect and relate them correctly. This determination rests with the court's discretion. A child is competent to testify to events he remembers, even if they happened at a time when he was too immature to testify.

Intoxication and drugs A witness is not automatically considered incompetent because he was drunk on the occasion to which his testimony relates. Nor does the fact that he is drunk at the time of giving his testimony or the fact that he has been drinking heavily on the day he testifies make him incompetent as a witness, so long as he is able to narrate the facts and events reliably. The trial court must decide whether or not his testimony should be received.

Similarly, a witness is not automatically considered incompetent because he was under the influence of a drug on the occasion to which his testimony relates or at the time when he is giving his testimony. A drug addict can be a competent witness.

Illness, character, and conduct A witness is not regarded as incompetent merely because he is ill, physically disabled, of bad character, or because of past conduct.

At one time the law looked upon deaf-mutes as idiots and held them incompetent as witnesses. Today deaf-mutes are competent as witnesses, so long as they can communicate the facts by some method.

A person is not considered incompetent as a witness because he has committed UNCONSCIONABLE, immoral, or fraudulent acts; has been charged with a crime; or has been found guilty of a crime. Government spies ("stool pigeons"), members of the Nazi party, and self-confessed criminals have all been held to be competent witnesses, even though their character or conduct may affect their credibility.

Parties to the trial Parties and other persons who have an INTEREST (stake) in the outcome of a civil suit are competent as witnesses. Their interests may affect their total credibility as witnesses and the weight given to their testimony, but not their competency.

Relationship to a party Ordinarily a witness is not disqualified by the fact that he is related to one of the parties by blood or MARRIAGE, although such a relationship may affect his credibility.

Under the common law neither spouse could act as a witness for or against the other in a civil or criminal proceeding because the law presumed that he or she was too strongly interested in the outcome of the proceeding. Today this rule has been modified by statute in most states so that either spouse can testify for or against the other in civil cases. See HUSBAND AND WIFE.

In a prosecution of a person for committing a crime against someone other than his spouse, one spouse can ordinarily testify in behalf of the other. In most states, the prosecution can call the spouse to the stand to testify against his or her mate only if the accused consents. Some states allow the spouse to refuse to testify. In other states, the husband or wife of the accused can be called to testify against his or her spouse regardless of the spouse's objections.

Ordinarily, when a crime is committed by one spouse against the other, the spouse against whom the crime is committed can testify against the accused even in states that do not otherwise permit anyone to testify against his or her spouse in criminal cases.

■ **Privileged relationships and communications** The law holds certain relationships to be confidential and certain communications to be privileged against disclosure by a witness. This rule of privilege, which is based on PUBLIC POLICY, is an exception to the general rule that the public has a right to every man's evidence. The fact that the parties believe a communication to be confidential does not make it privileged in a legal sense, nor can a witness be exempted from testifying about some matter just because it was told to him in confidence and with a promise of secrecy. The rule of privilege applies only to certain types of communication—between husband and wife, attorney and client, and physician and patient—and is often extended to confidential communications made to the clergy.

Husband and wife Communications between husband and wife, made during their marriage, out of the presence or hearing of third persons, are generally privileged. The privilege ordinarily belongs to the spouse who made the communication, and it cannot be disclosed unless he waives the privilege and consents to disclosure. In some states, however, both spouses hold the privilege.

Generally, the privilege applies only to communications that are specially intended to be private. The term "communications" is given a broad interpretation. It is not confined, for example, to conversations between spouses, but includes all facts that come to a spouse's knowledge by reason of the confidence of the marital relationship. Although all communications between husband and wife are presumed to be confidential, the presumption can be overcome by proof that the communications were not intended to be private.

Third persons A communication between a husband and wife in the presence or hearing of someone else is generally not a privileged communication. This rule holds true whether the communication was overheard accidentally or intentionally, but the spouses must know that the third person is either present or within hearing distance. This exception to privilege usually occurs when the husband and wife join in conversation with the third person, and any one of the three can give testimony about the conversation.

EXAMPLE Jeff and Charles ran into Jeff's house, and Jeff O—* told his wife not to tell anyone, but they had just robbed a gas station and hidden the money under the front porch. Jeff and Charles were later arrested. At the trial, the prosecutor called Jeff's wife and asked her where the money was hidden. She refused to testify, but the court ordered her to answer. Since Jeff had told her where the money was hidden while another person was present, the statement could not be considered a private conversation between husband and wife.

Subject matter Generally, the privilege for confidential marital communications extends only to utterances. Some statutes, however, have the effect of extending the privilege to acts and transactions.

When the rule of privilege applies, a witness cannot testify about his or her spouse's threats to kill a third person or about statements concerning the state of his or her health made before buying life INSURANCE. Testimony relating to a spouse's property is also privileged.

The rule does not prohibit testimony about the act of communicating even though it does prohibit testimony about the contents of the communication. Thus a husband may testify that he discussed a certain subject with his wife without telling the court what was said during that conversation. A witness may testify that a document is written in his spouse's handwriting, or he may acknowledge the receipt of a gift from his spouse or the existence of a WILL.

Business communications or transactions between husband and wife are usually not privileged on the ground that business matters are not private. Similarly, when one spouse has acted as agent for the other, no privilege exists as to communications concerning the subject of the AGENCY, because such communications are not necessarily private.

A private letter sent by one spouse to the other is a privileged communication, even though the spouse who wrote the letter admits writing it and identifies the letter. Neither the writer of the letter nor the spouse who received it can be required to produce it in evidence or to testify concerning it or its contents.

The privileged communication rule does not apply when the letter relates purely to business or contains nothing confidential. The rule also does not apply to a threatening letter from the husband to his wife (or vice versa) while they are living apart awaiting a divorce or to a letter that was never received by the spouse to whom it was addressed.

In most states, a confidential communication loses its privileged character when it comes into the hands of a third person, and it can be introduced as evidence unless the third person obtained it through force or some other form of coercion. A third person who is voluntarily shown the contents of a letter by its writer can also testify as to its contents, even though the letter is addressed to the spouse of the writer.

Attorney and client   For a discussion of the attorney-client privilege, see ATTORNEY AND CLIENT.

Physician and patient   Most states have laws providing that communications made by a patient to a physician who is acting in his professional capacity are privileged. This privilege is for the protection of the patient and not the physician or other persons.

EXAMPLE A doctor gave Susan an injection of a drug without warning her that many people suffer serious reactions to the drug. Susan lost consciousness and was in a coma for a week. It was months before she fully recovered. She sued the doctor for medical malpractice because he failed to obtain her informed consent. The doctor refused to testify about his conversation with Susan before the injection. The court ordered him to answer because the privilege was Susan's, not his. If she did not want to protect the confidentiality of their conversation, he had to testify.

The privilege is ordinarily granted in civil cases of all kinds, including legislative investigations. However, it is not extended to criminal proceedings. The rule applies even though the patient is not a party to the proceeding and is not present to object to the testimony.

When a relationship is privileged   The relationship of physician and patient must have existed at the time when the physician acquired the information that he is called on to disclose. A physician can testify about what he observed or learned of a person's condition before the physician-patient relationship was established.

The confidential relationship does not exist when a physician is hired by an insurance company to examine a prospective policyholder who knows the physician will report to the company, or when a physician is employed to examine a person charged with a crime in order to pass on his mental or physical condition.

On the other hand, when a person or corporation responsible for an accident employs a physician to treat someone who was injured in that accident, the physician cannot testify regarding what he learned from his patient. The privilege can also exist between a physician and a patient he is treating in a publicly financed hospital or clinic.

The rule against disclosure by a physician does not depend upon his receiving any compensation for his services.

Third persons   When a conversation between a physician and his patient takes place in the presence and hearing of a third person, the third person can ordinarily testify as to what was said, except when the third person is the physician's assistant or is there to aid the patient. A physician cannot disclose information received from the patient to a third person and thereby enable the third person to testify in court.

Subject matter   The privilege against a physician testifying applies only to matters that relate to his professional relationship with a patient he is treating. It does not prohibit disclosure of facts that any lay person could observe without professional knowledge.

A physician is free to testify about the fact that he was consulted by a certain patient, the fact that the patient was ill, the place of the treatments, the number and dates of his visits, and similar facts. A physician cannot disclose the advice he gave to his patient, the particulars of the treatment administered, or the operation he performed. Nor can he disclose even whether or not he advised the patient of the nature of his illness.

Clergy   Statutes in a number of states provide that communications made to a spiritual adviser are privileged. A statute granting the privilege to the clergy cannot limit the privilege to the clergy of any one denomination; it must include all denominations.

Members of the clergy cannot disclose confessions or admissions made to them in the course of their religious duties if the confiding party objects. To be privileged the communication must be made to a spiritual adviser in his or her professional capacity by a person seeking religious or spiritual advice, aid, or comfort. The communication must also have been made and received in confidence, although no specific promise of secrecy is necessary.

If a court believes that a witness is not entitled to remain silent in his capacity as a spiritual adviser, it may direct the witness to answer the questions put to him. A witness is not required to disclose the communication for the purpose of enabling the court to determine whether or not it is privileged. Before directing a witness to answer, the court should be satisfied from the facts and circumstances leading up to the communication that the witness is mistaken in claiming the privilege.

Claiming or waiving a privilege   A person who wants to exclude a witness's testimony on the ground of a privileged communication must object to the testimony. The proper time for an objection is when a question calling for disclosure of privileged matter is asked and before the witness answers. If the affected person fails to object, the privilege is regarded as waived, and the testimony is properly admitted. A court should exclude testimony by an attorney or physician as to confidential matters when the client or patient involved is not a party to the proceeding and not in a position to assert or waive his privilege.

The privilege belongs to the person making the communication, such as the client or patient, husband or wife, or other person to whom the statute extends the privilege. No other person has the right to object to testimony concerning a privileged communication. When a person refuses to permit the disclosure of confidential communications, no unfavorable presumption arises and no unfavorable inference can be drawn by the court or jury. In addition, the admissibility of evidence is often determined when the jury is not present.

EXAMPLE A trucking company was suing its former bookkeeper to recover $10,000 that she had embezzled. Officials of the company wanted the bookkeeper's husband to testify about how she explained the extra money she brought home. The bookkeeper refused to let her husband testify. The trucking company's attorney could not comment on the husband's failure to testify, and the jury was not allowed to consider his failure to testify as evidence of her guilt.

The privilege with respect to confidential communications can be waived only by the person who holds it.

■ **Credibility and impeachment** Courts and juries can accept all of a witness's testimony, reject it all, or accept part and reject part. Full faith is ordinarily given a witness's statements unless his testimony has been impeached (discredited). Courts are slow to impute PERJURY (lying under oath) to an apparently credible witness; a witness is usually presumed to speak the truth.

A *credible witness* is one who is legally competent to testify and whose statements are reasonable and believable. Anything that will shed light on the accuracy, truthfulness, and sincerity of a witness can be considered in determining the credit to be given his testimony. Therefore, either party can prove facts tending to show what weight should be given to testimony.

Factors affecting credibility A witness's knowledge and recollection are basic to his credibility. A person who lacks knowledge about the subject under investigation is not a credible witness. It is proper to inquire about the source of the witness's information, his opportunity for accurate observation, his understanding of the facts about which he is testifying, his ability to recollect the facts and his reason for remembering them, and his general understanding of the subject to which his testimony relates.

Demeanor In deciding on a witness's credibility it is proper to consider his appearance and demeanor, his manner of testifying (such as the frankness or evasiveness of his testimony), and even the intonation of his voice. His positiveness as well as his uncertainty as to the facts can be considered. The mere fact, however, that a witness hesitates and reflects before answering a question should not be taken to indicate that his answer is untrue.

Right to discredit witnesses A party in any proceeding has the right to introduce evidence directly attacking the credibility of a witness. To *impeach a witness* means to call into question his truthfulness by offering evidence showing that he should not be believed. Every witness is subject to impeachment, including a defendant who takes the stand in his own behalf.

As a general rule, a party—plaintiff or defendant—cannot impeach a witness that he himself has called and examined on an issue. In the interests of justice, however, this rule is subject to a number of exceptions. A plaintiff or defendant's own witness may be the subject of impeachment if he turns out to be hostile during the examination, if he gives surprise testimony resulting from the plaintiff's or defendant's being misled by the witness, or if his testimony prejudices the plaintiff's or defendant's case.

EXAMPLE The prosecution in a murder case called as a witness a woman who had seen the fight outside a bar. The woman had told police at the scene that she had seen a blackjack in the defendant's hand. The prosecutor asked her about the blackjack at the trial in order to overcome the defendant's claim that the victim had accidentally hurt his head when he tripped and fell. The woman testified that she did not know what a blackjack was and that she had seen nothing in the defendant's hand. This testimony not only surprised the prosecutor but also substantially harmed his case against the defendant. Because of the surprise, the court allowed the defendant to impeach the witness by proving that she had made an inconsistent statement to the police and by proving that she wanted to protect the defendant because they were lovers.

A witness called to the stand by the court is not a witness of either party, and either can impeach him. A party can also impeach a witness whom he is compelled to call, such as a witness to a will that is in contention in the case.

Generally, a witness can be impeached only by a direct attack on his testimony or character. The impeachment can be accomplished by other witnesses, by documentary evidence affecting his or her credibility, or by demonstrating that the witness made contradictory statements.

Character or reputation It is permissible to impeach or discredit a witness by an attack on his "character" or "reputation," which in law are synonymous words.

Generally, either party can impeach the character of a witness who has testified adversely to him (including an expert witness) or of a witness called to impeach another witness. A party who calls the opposite party as a witness cannot attack his character.

A person accused in a criminal prosecution who becomes a witness in his own behalf can be impeached by an attack on his character or reputation. The state, however, cannot impeach its own witness.

It is usually permissible to impeach a witness on the ground that his general moral character is bad. In some states, however, the impeachment cannot go beyond an attack on the witness's reputation for truth.

Proof of a witness's reputation should be confined to the community or neighborhood where he lives at the time or where he has lived recently. The inquiry concerning reputation can extend, however, to any community where he has an established reputation, such as the place where he conducts his business or maintains a summer home.

Criminal conduct In general, a witness can be impeached and his credibility attacked by proof of his conviction of a serious crime or one that involves MORAL TURPITUDE, such as fraud or soliciting for prostitutes, but not by conviction of a minor offense, such as drunkenness, disorderly conduct, or gambling. Not surprisingly, a conviction for perjury weighs the heaviest against the credibility of a witness.

The impeaching evidence is usually restricted to the fact of conviction. A jury's verdict of guilty or even a defendant's plea of guilty is not of itself sufficient to amount to a conviction. There must also be a JUDGMENT of guilty or a sentence imposed by the court. It is not permissible to show the details of the crime or to identify the person against whom the crime was committed. The name and nature of the crime, however, and the number of convictions can all be shown.

A conviction cannot be shown when it took place so long ago that it has no bearing on the witness's present character. Whether or not a conviction is too remote is usually a matter for the court to decide in the light of all the facts. In some states, however, the period of time that must have elapsed since a conviction is determined by statute.

women's rights   See ABORTION; ANNULMENT; DIVORCE; EQUAL PROTECTION OF LAWS; HUSBAND AND WIFE; MARRIAGE.

Words and Phrases   The name of a set of lawbooks containing all the judicial definitions and constructions (interpretations) given by federal and state courts to words and phrases found in STATUTES, court rules, administrative regulations, CONTRACTS, and other documents. *Words and Phrases* is a legal research tool, which can lead attorneys to a PRIMARY AUTHORITY (a case, statute, or constitutional provision).

words of limitation   In connection with a transfer of real PROPERTY (real estate) by a DEED or a WILL, words that indicate the duration of a person's legal INTEREST in the property. See ESTATE.

EXAMPLE In his will, Harry provided that his wife, Gertrude, be left all his land as long as she does not remarry. The words "as long as she does not remarry" limit the duration of Gertrude's estate. If she does remarry at any time after Harry's death, she loses the land.

words of purchase   In connection with a transfer of real PROPERTY (real estate) by a DEED or a WILL, words indicating who the property owner will be.

EXAMPLE Brown deeds land to Black for 21 years, at the end of which time it will go to Black's children. The word "children" denotes the persons who will take the property when Black's term expires, and so is called a word of purchase.

workmen's compensation   A system designed to relieve the financial distress caused by a worker's injury or death on the job. All 50 states have workmen's compensation laws, but some states now call their plans workers' compensation in recognition of the fact that not all working people are men.

The purpose of workmen's compensation is to take the burden of an employment-related injury or death off the individual worker and his family and to place it on the employer. The employer is expected to add the cost of

compensation to his business expenses and pass it along to consumers. This spreads the cost over many people, so that no one family is devastated by an accident. There are two different systems for providing money to pay workmen's compensation benefits. State law may require employers to contribute to a fund held by the state or it may require them to buy insurance to cover the risks.

An employee who is injured must promptly notify his employer of his accident. Then, within a certain period of time, the employee must formally apply for workmen's compensation benefits. If benefits are denied, the worker can demand a hearing before the workmen's compensation commission or board. If the worker is not satisfied with the decision, he may be able to appeal to a court. In some states, a worker who wins in court will also be awarded the money to pay his legal costs.

■ **Employer's liability**   Workmen's compensation is based on a theory of STRICT LIABILITY, which says that the employer is liable for injuries that his employees sustain during the course of his business without any question of fault. An injured employee must be compensated if the employer was negligent, the employee himself was careless, or the accident was completely unavoidable. Contributory NEGLIGENCE (the rule that an employee is responsible for his injury if he could have done anything to prevent it), ASSUMPTION OF RISK (the rule that by taking on a job the employee assumed all risks connected with it), and the FELLOW SERVANT RULE (the rule that an employer is not responsible to an employee for an accident caused by another worker's carelessness) are abolished as defenses by a workmen's compensation law. This is strict liability.

The only questions in a workmen's compensation case are whether the person claiming benefits was an employee acting within the scope of his employment at the time of his injury and, if so, how much compensation should be paid.

These questions must be answered in terms of the particular law that creates the injured worker's right to compensation. Each state has its own laws and some employees are also covered by federal laws—for example, employees of businesses that engage in interstate commerce. If there is a federal law covering the employment that led to the injury, the federal law is applied instead of the state law.

Sometimes an injury involves more than one state law—such as when a worker is hurt in a state different from the one in which he was hired or in which he generally works. In such cases it is not always easy to tell which law applies, but it may be important because the amount of the benefits allowed for a particular injury may be different in the two states. The final decision depends on a number of factors, such as where the worker was hired, where he worked, and where the injury occurred. When appropriate, the state concerned with settling a case will apply the compensation formula of another state.

■ **Employment and employees covered**   Not every kind of employment is covered by workmen's compensation—what is covered depends on state and federal law. Under statutes that cover some kinds of work but not others, an employer might have to provide compensation for employees in some departments but not in others. Generally, if a statute can be read to include an employee in workmen's compensation, he should be included.

WHO IS ELIGIBLE FOR WORKMEN'S COMPENSATION?

■ Workmen's compensation laws are based on the concept that employers are strictly liable for their employees' on-the-job injuries. An employee must be compensated whether the employer was negligent, the employee himself was careless, or the accident was purely unavoidable.

■ In some states, employers must contribute to a fund held by the state, and in others they must buy insurance to cover the risks. The kinds of employment covered depend on the applicable state or federal law.

■ Employers with fewer than a minimum number of employees may be exempt from providing coverage.

■ Federal, state, and local governments are responsible for compensating their employees. Some high-income employees may be excluded from workmen's compensation.

■ If you are covered, you are entitled to benefits even if your boss has not paid Social Security for you or withheld income for your taxes. Independent contractors are not entitled to compensation.

■ Ordinarily, no benefits are paid to an employee for illness, even if its source can be traced to the job—unless the employee was unexpectedly exposed to an unusual danger.

Particular employment may be listed in a statute as exempt from workmen's compensation coverage. It is not unusual for household and domestic workers and farm laborers to be excluded, for example. Some statutes limit coverage to trades or businesses operated for a profit.

The following are some rules regarding coverage that apply in many states:

(1) A permanently employed worker is usually entitled to coverage from the time he begins working.

(2) Temporary employees may not be covered.

(3) Usually only employers with a minimum number of employees, such as four or five, are required to provide coverage.

(4) An individual employer, a PARTNERSHIP, and a CORPORATION are each responsible for providing workmen's compensation.

(5) An ASSOCIATION, such as a labor union, is responsible to workers hired by it.

(6) An injured employee is entitled to compensation even if the employer is a relative of his.

(7) Federal, state, and local governments are responsible for compensating their employees. Whether a charitable institution must compensate injured employees depends on the state's law.

(8) Sometimes employees who earn more than a certain amount in wages are excluded from a workmen's compensation plan.

(9) A covered employee is entitled to benefits even though the employer has not paid SOCIAL SECURITY for him or withheld income for his taxes.

(10) Casual (not regular) employees usually are not covered by workmen's compensation statutes because their work is not regular, periodic, or recurring. The exclusion exists because it is difficult to provide in advance for employment that lasts only a day or so. A workmen's compensation statute, however, can require coverage even for casual employees if the legislature chooses.

(11) A volunteer worker is usually not entitled to workmen's compensation, but an ALIEN (not a U.S. citizen), a nonresident, or a substitute worker is, because these factors do not change the employment relationship.

(12) Independent contractors also are not covered by workmen's compensation, because they undertake to do a certain piece of work by their own methods and without close supervision.

EXAMPLE A builder who is putting up houses in a new development might hire a plumber to do all the plumbing in the houses. The plumber works for himself, not for the builder. He is an independent contractor. Both the builder and the plumber are likely to have their own employees, who might be entitled to workmen's compensation if they are injured on the job.

■ **The right to sue** Some states allow employers or employees to choose whether or not they want to participate in a workmen's compensation plan. Under such a statute the decision must be in writing and made before an accident occurs. If there is no coverage, the employee may be entitled to sue the employer in the event the employee is injured on the job.

Most states simply specify which employers and employees will be covered by workmen's compensation and require participation for them. Participation for an employee means that he must accept workmen's compensation benefits after an injury, and he cannot sue his employer for NEGLIGENCE. Participation for the employer means making required payments to the state fund or purchasing insurance in the required amount. An employer who fails to maintain workmen's compensation might be subject to criminal penalties or to a negligence lawsuit by an employee and unlimited money damages.

■ **Kinds of injuries covered** A law may provide workmen's compensation coverage for some types of injuries, but not others. If there is doubt about whether a particular injury was meant to be included, the injured employee generally receives his benefits.

Statutes ordinarily expressly cover "injuries," "injuries by accident," or "accidents." Unless the injury is caused by something unforeseen—sudden, and accompanied by force, for example—it may not qualify as an accident for which benefits can be paid. In one case a bookkeeper who hurt her back when she bent over to pick up a piece of paper was found not to have suffered an accident because her movement was routine. When an accident does occur, benefits are paid without any question about fault or negligence.

Work related The basic requirement is that the injury must be work related.

Some statutes say that the injury, to be work related, must have occurred in the *course of employment*—that is, it must have happened within the time and place that the employee was expected to perform his duties. The question of whether an injury took place in the course of employment has been argued in a great many cases. One court said that a factory worker's employment began when he arrived at the plant and ended when he left it.

EXAMPLE A police officer has been said to be outside the
0←—※ course of his employment when he leaves the boundaries of his jurisdiction without legal authority. An officer who could legally cross a county line in hot pursuit would be within the course of his employment in chasing a crook outside his jurisdiction without first obtaining the authority. But he would need authority to leave his jurisdiction if he were not in hot pursuit.

Usually an employee is considered outside the course of his employment when he leaves his office at lunchtime, but a salesman in one case was covered by workmen's compensation when he choked on a piece of meat at a business lunch. On the other hand, simply being on the employer's premises does not always mean that what the employee is doing is within the course of his employment. For example, a mechanic who uses his employer's tools after hours is not within the course of his employment.

Many states require not only that the injury occur within the course of employment but also that it arise *out of the employment*—that is, the accident must be related to the work itself. For example, a night watchman at a warehouse who is shot by a burglar has an injury that arises out of his employment.

Fewer injuries, of course, will be compensated under a law that requires an injury to occur in both the course of employment and as a result of it. The standards applied in each state depend on the words of the workmen's compensation statute and the ways it has been applied in actual cases.

Illness The laws usually compensate only physical harm to the employee. Ordinarily, no benefits are paid for illness, even if its source can be traced to working conditions, unless the employee was unexpectedly exposed to an unusual danger.

EXAMPLE One court refused to grant workmen's compensa-
0←—※ tion benefits to the family of a man who died of pneumonia after working for eight days cleaning mud off machinery that had been covered by floodwaters. Another court granted benefits to a nurse who contracted poliomyelitis after someone infected with the disease sneezed in her face while they were on a hospital elevator.

Some occupational diseases, caused by years of exposure to hazardous substances, are covered by industrial disease compensation laws that are separate from workmen's compensation.

Injuries caused by a fellow worker or employer
Injuries caused by a fellow employee are compensable, even if the fellow employee was acting intentionally—for example, horsing around or playing a joke. When a fight breaks out among employees, the worker claiming benefits cannot collect if he was the aggressor or, under some statutes, if the argument had nothing to do with the work. Some laws allow an employee to collect workmen's compensation benefits if his employer attacks him, and some deny benefits but leave the employee the right to sue the employer for money damages.

Misconduct Employers generally are not held liable for injuries caused by an employee's serious and WILLFUL

misconduct, but a mistake or carelessness alone will not keep an employee from receiving benefits.

EXAMPLE An employer had fumigated a grain bin with a
0←—※ lethal gas in order to kill vermin. All employees were told to stay away that day, and signs warned of the danger. Nevertheless, one employee went into the grain bin to take a sample that he had been told to take the day before. The gas killed him. His family was denied workmen's compensation benefits because his conduct constituted serious and willful misconduct.

Employers usually do not have to compensate employees who are reckless or who are violating laws or the employer's rules or orders when they are injured. Employees may not receive compensation if they fail to use safety equipment furnished by the employer or show up at work drunk and then sustain injuries.

■ **Benefits** The amount of benefits paid to an injured worker is usually determined by a schedule enacted as law. The laws generally allow for four different kinds of compensation: (1) for death; (2) for disability, either total or partial and either permanent or temporary; (3) for loss of a bodily function or body part, such as loss of hearing, loss of an eye, or loss of two fingers; and (4) for bodily disfigurement, such as an embarrassing scar or loss of teeth or hair.

Compensation laws list all the kinds of harm that can be done to the human body and fix a dollar amount of benefits for each. The total compensation for one accident may include amounts for more than one type of injury. A blow to the head, for example, may entitle the victim to compensation for the permanent partial loss of sight in one eye plus an amount for a permanent disfigurement resulting from a broken nose.

If the employee has died, his family is entitled to receive the compensation. Generally, the recovery is divided among relatives who were dependent on the worker for support. In some cases the amount of the recovery depends on the wages that the employee was receiving at the time of his death, and in others it is calculated on the future earning potential of the deceased worker.

Most often compensation is paid as a weekly or monthly benefit. Payment in one lump sum may be illegal or allowed only in special circumstances. Lump-sum payments are disfavored because they do not insure regular support for the injured worker or his surviving family and because large settlements can deplete the fund of money available to pay out benefits to other workers.

■ **Compromise on amount of claim** A worker may compromise on the amount of his workmen's compensation claim, but such an agreement must comply with the statute. Some, but not all, states allow a worker to settle for less than the scheduled amount for his injury in cases that are not clear-cut. There might be a dispute between the employer and perhaps his insurer and the worker about whether the injury occurred during the course of employment, for example, or over the nature or extent of injuries. The state's workmen's compensation board might then agree to compensate the worker provided he takes less than the usual amount of the claim. This avoids costly litigation.

For a settlement to be valid, the worker must clearly understand his rights and the effect of the agreement on them. There must be no doubt that a compromise was reached. Simply because a worker accepts reduced payments for a number of weeks, for example, does not prove that he agreed to settle for less. If there is fraud, duress, or misrepresentation by one party, the settlement is not binding. A worker who is not mentally capable of making decisions at the time of settlement cannot be held to the agreement. In some states, an agreement must be drawn up in an official form or approved by a court or workmen's compensation board or filed with the board or clerk of the court. See also COMPROMISE AND SETTLEMENT.

work-product rule   The rule that certain materials prepared by an attorney in preparation for litigation for his client are privileged from DISCOVERY by the attorney for the opposing party. The rule applies when the opposing side attempts to compel the attorney who holds the privilege to produce his *work product*. An attorney's work product includes information from interviews, statements, memoranda, correspondence, briefs, mental impressions, and theories and strategies he will use in conducting his litigation. See ATTORNEY AND CLIENT.

writ   A written order or direction issued by a court and addressed to a sheriff, a constable, or some other appropriate officer or a person whom the court wants to act. When the writ relates to the commencement of a lawsuit or to a matter incidental to a lawsuit already in progress—as it usually does— it notifies the person named in the writ that he is a defendant in the lawsuit and orders him to appear in court on a certain day or suffer the legal consequences of a DEFAULT. See JUDGMENT.

wrong   A violation of another person's legal rights; a TORT. The word usually signifies a personal injury or an injury to property, but not a violation of a contractual right.

wrongful-death action   A lawsuit by survivors seeking compensation in money DAMAGES for a DEATH caused by another person's wrongful act. The right to sue for wrongful death belongs to people who suffer financial loss because of the decedent's death.

■ **Type of loss**   The financial loss suffered as a result of the injury caused by the wrongdoer may be a direct loss of support from the family wage earner, or it may be indirect, as when the services of a mother who has died must be replaced by a paid housekeeper. It may be a loss likely to be realized in the future, as when a parent loses a child who would otherwise be available to support him in his old age.

Wrongful-death suits cannot be started for the death of an unborn fetus, because a child does not have separate legal status until he is born alive. If a mother is injured during pregnancy and thereby loses the child, she may sue only for her personal injuries and plead the loss of the child as an extra element in her case. If the infant is born alive, however, and then dies of the injuries, the relatives do have the right to sue for his wrongful death.

A wrongful-death action is independent of criminal charges. If a defendant is charged in both criminal and civil proceedings, neither controls the other.

■ **Grounds for wrongful-death action**   A wrongful-death action may be brought for an act that intentionally or unintentionally caused death or an injury resulting in death or for a failure to act when action was required by law. The injury received by a person who is stabbed in a barroom brawl is intentionally caused, for example. A broken back received in an automobile accident is unintentionally caused; nevertheless, the driver or the owner of the car who is at fault is liable for his NEGLIGENCE.

EXAMPLE Townsend built a swimming pool in his backyard
O← * the summer after his grandchildren came to live with him. Although local law required him to build a six-foot fence enclosing the backyard (to prevent a child from wandering into the pool and drowning), Townsend did not want to cut off the scenic view from his backyard. When a neighborhood child, attracted by the splashing and laughter from the pool, fell into the pool and drowned, Townsend was held liable for the death for not having built the fence as required by law.

■ **Who may sue**   The persons entitled to sue for wrongful death are designated by state law. Many of these laws provide for recovery by a widow or widower, next of kin, children, or distributees (people who would inherit the deceased person's property if he died without a WILL). In some states, a surviving spouse may sue if the couple was separated but not if the survivor had deserted or failed to provide support to the deceased. A divorced husband or wife is not a surviving spouse. Wrongful death as a CAUSE OF ACTION exists only for surviving beneficiaries and a lawsuit cannot be brought if there are none.

A lawsuit for wrongful death must be started sometime within six years from the date of death, depending on state law. To find out the time limit in your state, see Chart 4.

Parent or child   The beneficiaries may not have to prove that they were dependent on the decedent for their support; they must prove only that they have suffered some financial loss. For example, a husband could sue on account of his wife's wrongful death because replacing her services to the family would cause financial loss. Many states have held, however, that a parent may recover for the wrongful death of a child even though the parent does not suffer financial loss.

Generally, a child may sue for the wrongful death of a parent, and a parent may bring suit for the death of a child. But some states permit only minor children (usually those under 18 or 21) to sue for the death of a parent, and some do not allow a parent to recover for the death of a child who was married. Usually, the parent must be the legal parent, whether natural or adoptive. A foster parent or someone who occasionally acts in the place of a parent cannot recover damages, even if the child was supporting him. A parent who has neglected or failed to support a child generally cannot sue for wrongful death.

The Supreme Court has said that a state may not deny an illegitimate child who was dependent on his father the right to sue for his father's wrongful death if it permits a legitimate child to do so.

■ **Who may be sued**   The surviving beneficiaries may sue the person who committed the injuries that caused death, unless the law rules otherwise.

Family immunity   One exception to the rule is the principle of family immunity, which means that a person cannot be sued by a member of his family. The rule was developed to promote family harmony, to prevent family members from plotting together to defraud an INSURANCE company, and to keep a person from profiting by his own wrongful act. Sometimes, however, the principle can cause hardship and injustice.

EXAMPLE A man is driving with his wife in the car. He takes O⊷✳ his eyes off the road for a second while he lights a cigarette; the car veers off the road and strikes a tree. Both people are killed. If the state in which the accident occurred has a strict rule of family immunity, the couple's two young children would not be able to sue their father's estate to compensate them for the loss of their mother, whose death was caused by the father's negligence. Moreover, because they are related to the driver, the children would not be able to collect from their father's automobile insurance company.

Many states no longer apply the rule of family immunity strictly. For example, a woman in one case recovered proceeds from her husband's insurance policy when their child was killed in an automobile accident caused by the father's drunken driving. In another case, children were able to sue their father after he had killed their mother with a shotgun.

Sovereign immunity A government is said to be sovereign, that is, supreme and independent, and SOVEREIGN IMMUNITY is the government's privilege to be free from lawsuits. The government cannot be sued for causing a death unless it waives that immunity.

Sovereign immunity developed on the theory that since government functions for the good of all, its treasury should not be wiped out because of an injury resulting from the negligence of one of its servants. Like family immunity, however, sovereign immunity was found to cause undue hardship. It was unfair that one injured person should suffer all the consequences of his injuries, which he did not cause, when the expense could be divided among taxpayers or covered by insurance purchased by the government.

Today the majority of states have given up the right to claim sovereign immunity in many cases. Many state and local governments can now be sued for wrongful deaths caused, for example, by their badly maintained roads or by policemen or bus drivers.

States that permit actions against government agencies typically require the plaintiff to warn the government promptly that a lawsuit is contemplated. The time within which a *notice of claim* must be filed is usually very short, perhaps only 30, 60, or 90 days after the injury occurred. Without the notice, no suit is possible.

Suing the defendant's employer When a death occurs, it may be possible to sue someone who did not cause the accident. The MASTER AND SERVANT rule says that an employer is responsible for injuries his employee causes while working for him. See RESPONDEAT SUPERIOR.

EXAMPLE If the driver of a bread truck runs over and kills a O⊷✳ child, the parents may sue the bakery. The theory is that employers should hire responsible people and make sure they are trained to carry out their duties safely. Because the employer receives the benefit of the employee's work, the victim's family should not be penalized for the employee's negligence. The family of the child can also sue the driver, but the employer is far more likely to be able to pay damages if a jury awards them.

More than one defendant Someone who starts a wrongful-death action may sue any individual or corporation responsible; in practice, he should sue everyone involved and let the court decide who is responsible. Anyone who is liable to the deceased for his injuries is also liable to the decedent's survivors for wrongful death. For example, a passenger injured in a collision of two cars can sue both drivers. The court will decide how much each driver is liable. If the passenger dies, his beneficiaries can sue both drivers for wrongful death.

■ **Proving the defendant's responsibility** Anyone suing for wrongful death must be prepared to prove that the defendant's actions were the PROXIMATE CAUSE of the deceased person's death. This means that the defendant's wrongful act must have set up a natural, unbroken sequence of events that led to the harm.

YOUR RIGHT TO COMPENSATION IF A FAMILY MEMBER IS KILLED

■ In many states, wrongful-death laws permit the dependents of a person who has been killed as a result of someone else's action, through negligence or by intention, to sue the wrongdoer for money damages.

■ State laws designate the persons entitled to sue for wrongful death—usually a surviving spouse, next of kin, children, or others who would inherit the deceased person's property if he dies without a will. A divorced husband or wife is not a surviving spouse.

■ The Supreme Court has ruled that a state may not refuse to let an illegitimate child who was financially dependent on his father sue for his father's wrongful death and then permit a legitimate child to do so.

■ A person usually cannot be sued by any member of his immediate family for wrongful death—this rule is called *family immunity*. Many states, however, have relaxed this rule when its strict application would cause hardship and injustice. For example, a woman recovered the proceeds from her husband's insurance policy when their child was killed in an accident caused by the father's drunken driving.

■ Under sovereign immunity, the government cannot be sued for causing a death unless it waives immunity.

■ Nowadays most states have given up sovereign immunity in many cases and can be sued for wrongful deaths caused, for example, by their badly maintained roads. In such cases, however, the notice of claim against the government must be filed soon after the injury occurred—sometimes within 30 days. If the notice is not filed on time, you cannot sue.

■ A successful plaintiff generally recovers the costs of the decedent's medical or funeral expenses, plus the amount of financial support he would have been entitled to if the decedent had not been injured, and possibly an amount representing the loss of personal services or companionship.

EXAMPLE A defendant left his car parked on a hill. The car rolled downhill and crashed into a drugstore killing two female employees. The judge held that there could be no question that the defendant caused the accident, either by parking his car improperly or by failing to set the brake or both.

A defendant may be acquitted of wrongful death by showing that the deceased person was not blameless. One rule is that there can be no recovery if the dead person was negligent (CONTRIBUTORY NEGLIGENCE) or, in most states, if the dead person was *more* negligent than the defendant (COMPARATIVE NEGLIGENCE). Another rule is that an injured person (and hence his survivors) cannot recover if he could have saved himself, even though the defendant was at fault. This is the *last clear chance* rule.

EXAMPLE A man driving a car went through a stop signal, parked his car on the railroad tracks, and was then struck by a train. His family cannot recover for wrongful death because the deceased person was to blame for the accident. If the accident was not the driver's fault—if his car stalled on the tracks, for instance—recovery for wrongful death might still be blocked if he had had plenty of time to get out of his car before the train hit it. The last clear chance rule requires people to avoid disaster whenever possible.

■ **Amount of damages awarded** The amount of DAMAGES recoverable by beneficiaries depends on the law of each state. Most states consider damages to be *compensation* for the expenses incurred as a result of the injury and death and sometimes also for the loss of the decedent's companionship and financial support. Some states consider the damages to be *punishment* of a wrongdoer. In these states, the amount of such damages—called *punitive damages*—depends on how much the defendant can be blamed. For example, damages would be low if the defendant's car skidded on wet pavement, striking the decedent as he walked along the road. Damages would be very high, however, if the defendant got drunk, stole a car, and was speeding away from police when he hit his victim.

Compensatory damages Compensatory damages are much more common than punitive damages. A plaintiff who wins his suit generally recovers the costs of the decedent's medical or funeral expenses. He may also receive the amount of financial support he would have been entitled to if the victim had not died. In addition, he could win a sum of money that represents his loss of personal services or companionship from the decedent. See CONSORTIUM.

While the law makes no attempt to place a dollar value on a human life, it must still settle the amount of damages in a wrongful-death action. One method is to multiply the salary the decedent could have earned by the number of years he probably would have worked had he lived to the age projected by life-expectancy tables. A jury can take into account the mental condition and health of the person as well as the kind of work he did. Someone who died when he was just starting in a profession might have been making less money than a laborer but could reasonably be expected to have earned much more during his lifetime.

Since not everyone is employed, it is unrealistic to consider only possible earnings when calculating damages for a wrongful-death action. The personal services of a housewife and mother have been figured to be worth as much as $15,000 a year and more. Furthermore, the nonfinancial value of a spouse or parent may sometimes justify an additional recovery.

Any amount recovered is distributed among survivors according to the law of each state. Courts often apportion an award according to the extent of loss to each survivor. For example, in the death of a parent, a 7-year-old child might receive a larger share than a 17-year-old.

Amount recoverable Only Colorado and New Hampshire specify the amount recoverable in wrongful-death actions, and some states have constitutional provisions prohibiting the state legislature from passing a law specifying the amount recoverable. The reason is to prevent people from trying to sue in the state that has the highest limit. This would unfairly make the defendant's liability depend on where the plaintiff could succeed in dragging him into court.

Special statutes limit the liability of a defendant for death caused in certain situations. International treaties among nations, for example, limit the amount of money that can be recovered for the death of international-airline passengers. And in every state, WORKMEN'S COMPENSATION acts limit an employer's liability for injuries or death suffered by workers on the job.

X In law, a cross made as a substitute for a SIGNATURE by a person who is unable to write, either because he has never learned or because he is physically unable to do so.

yellow-dog contract An agreement in which an employee promises his employer that he will not join or remain in a labor union. Before passage of the National Labor Relations Act of 1935, employees often had to make such promises in writing or be left without a job. The legislation outlawed the controversial agreements once and for all. See LABOR RELATIONS.

yield The proportionate rate that the income from an investment bears to the total cost of the investment. For example, a profit of $100 on an investment of $1,000 equals a 10-percent yield.

Z **1** A regulation published by the Federal Reserve Board to carry out the purposes of the Truth in Lending Law. The regulation prescribes precisely what information a lender must disclose to a borrower in a consumer CREDIT transaction and also the manner in which it must be disclosed. **2** A mark to fill in unused spaces on a legal document, such as a CONTRACT, in order to prevent the spaces from being filled in at a later time.

Zenger case A colonial case that established the principle that truth is a defense to libel. John Peter Zenger immigrated to America from Germany in 1710 and was trained as a printer by William Bradford. In 1733 he started publishing his own newspaper, the *New-York Weekly Journal*, in competition with Bradford's *New York Gazette*. Articles in the *Weekly Journal* bitterly attacked New York's governor, William Cosby, and Zenger was imprisoned for seditious libel. See LIBEL AND SLANDER. Under the British law of seditious libel, which was in effect in the Colonies at that time, a person could be punished for printing any statement criticizing the government whether the statement was true or not. At the trial, Zenger's lawyer, Andrew Hamilton, admitted that Zenger had published the articles in question but denied that they contained any false allegations and defended Zenger's right to publish matters "supported with truth." The judge instructed the jury to determine only whether or not Zenger had published the articles and let the court (the judge) decide the question of libel. Hamilton convinced the jury to ignore the judge's instructions and to find Zenger not guilty.

Zenger's case is a very important foundation for freedom of speech and press. Since the decision in 1735, anyone accused of libel has been able to defend himself by showing that his statements are true, and juries decide that question. See SPEECH AND PRESS, FREEDOM OF.

zero-bracket amount See INCOME TAX.

zoning Regulation and restriction of PROPERTY by a local government. The essence of zoning is division of territory according to the character of lands and structures and their suitability for particular uses, such as residential, commercial, or industrial.

Zoning laws are intended to promote the health, safety, welfare, convenience, morals, and prosperity of people in the community. Ideally, they aim to promote the welfare of the community as a whole, rather than to further the economic interests of any particular property owners. Zoning ordinances are designed to preserve the character of the community and guide its growth.

■ **Districts** The basic purpose of most municipal zoning ordinances is to separate residential, commercial, and industrial districts from one another. Use of property within a particular district is generally uniform. For example, if an area is zoned for residences, no industry is permitted there. A shopping area is built only in a locality zoned for commercial use, probably not far from the residential zone that it supports. Industry is permitted in a zone adjacent to the commercial district, but usually a considerable distance away from the residential district. Most zoning ordinances do permit limited use of land in a residential district for necessary nonresidential purposes, such as schools, churches, hospitals, and philanthropic institutions.

Municipalities have exercised wide discretion in fixing the boundaries of commercial and industrial districts. Many ordinances have been enacted with the objective of protecting residential zones from encroachment by gas stations, public parking garages or lots, liquor stores and bars, and smoke- or odor-producing factories.

Anyone thinking of purchasing real estate should be certain that it can be put to the use he has in mind. He should also find out what uses can be made of neighboring property. He may want to bargain for a provision that lets him out of the contract to buy the property if the zoning laws will prevent his use and enjoyment of the property.

■ **Police power** The power of a municipality to enact zoning regulations is derived from the state. Local zoning regulations are an exercise of the POLICE POWER of the state. Authority to impose zoning restrictions is conferred on a municipality by a state's enabling statute, the objectives of which generally include (1) lessening congestion in the streets; (2) securing safety from fire, panic, and similar dangers; (3) providing adequate light and air; (4) preventing overcrowding of lands; (5) avoiding undue concentration of population; and (6) assuring adequate provision of transportation, water, sewerage, schools, and parks.

■ **Comprehensive plan** Zoning regulations must be enacted in accordance with a well-considered, comprehensive plan in order to avoid arbitrary exercise of governmental power. A comprehensive plan is a general plan to control the use of properties in the entire municipality, or at least in a large part of it. Individual pieces of property should not be singled out for special treatment. One or two lots may not be placed in a separate zone and subjected to restrictions not applicable to similar adjoining lands.

■ **Exclusionary zoning** In recent years, zoning has been used to advance certain interests of the municipality at the expense of surrounding regions in order to establish or perpetuate social and economic segregation. Such discriminatory zoning—most often described as exclusionary zoning—is often put into effect in affluent suburban areas and new communities in order to keep out persons with low—or even moderate—incomes. As a consequence, those who are excluded are left housed inadequately in the cities and older suburbs, far from new sources of employment. The use of exclusionary zoning has been strongly condemned in the courts because it violates the principle that municipal zoning ordinances should further the general welfare.

Exclusionary zoning can assume many different forms. Some of the more sophisticated techniques are requiring minimum house sizes, lot sizes, and lot frontages, and prohibiting multifamily housing and mobile homes. A municipality has a legitimate interest, however, in assuring that residential development proceeds in an orderly and planned fashion, that the burdens upon municipal services do not increase faster than their ability to expand, and that exceptional environmental and historical features are not demolished. As the Pennsylvania Supreme Court stated in 1965: "Zoning is a means by which a governmental body can plan for the future—it may not be used as a means to deny the future."

See also CIVIL RIGHTS; DEED; EMINENT DOMAIN; PUBLIC HEALTH; LANDMARK; MUNICIPAL CORPORATION; NONCONFORMING USE; NUISANCE; PROPERTY; RESTRICTIVE COVENANT; TAXATION; VARIANCE.

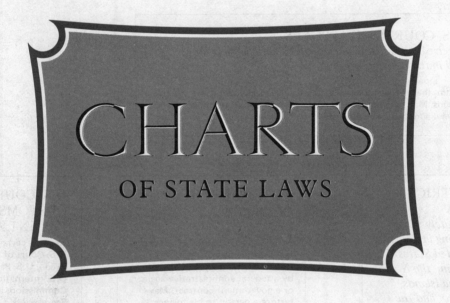

CHARTS
OF STATE LAWS

Chart 1   **1076**

FEDERAL AND STATE COURT SYSTEMS

SUPREME COURT OF THE UNITED STATES
Washington, D.C.

Tries lawsuits between the states and those involving an ambassador or consul from a foreign nation. May review decisions made in U.S. Courts of Appeals or in the specialized federal courts. May review a decision by the highest court of a state if a constitutional question or federal law is involved

DECISIONS OF HIGHEST STATE COURTS

U.S. COURTS OF APPEALS
Twelve courts sitting in each of 11 judicial circuits and in the District of Columbia

Hear appeals from federal District Courts in the United States and Guam, the Northern Mariana Islands, Puerto Rico, and the Virgin Islands. May hear appeals from decisions of bankruptcy courts and federal administrative agencies

U.S. DISTRICT COURTS
Approximately 90 courts sitting in all parts of the United States and in Guam, the Northern Mariana Islands, Puerto Rico, and the Virgin Islands

Try both criminal and civil cases, including patent and admiralty cases. May review decisions of federal administrative agencies and bankruptcy courts

U.S. COURT OF CLAIMS
Washington, D.C.

Hears suits against the U.S. government arising out of the Constitution, a federal law, any regulation by a federal administrative agency, or a government contract. May restore a person to his former position, order that records be corrected, or award money damages

U.S. COURT OF CUSTOMS AND PATENT APPEALS

Reviews certain decisions of U.S. Court of International Trade, U.S. Patent Office, U.S. International Trade Commission, and U.S. Secretary of Commerce

U.S. COURT OF INTERNATIONAL TRADE
New York, N.Y.

Hears cases involving persons who protest the amount of customs duties they must pay under federal tariff laws

U.S. TAX COURT

Hears cases involving disputes over whether taxpayers (including individuals, private foundations, public charities, and qualified pension plans) owe additional taxes

BANKRUPTCY COURTS
Associated with District Courts throughout the country

Hear all bankruptcy cases. Beginning in 1984 will be reorganized with some new powers and duties

APPEALS FROM MILITARY TRIBUNALS

U.S. COURT OF MILITARY APPEALS

Hears appeals from court-martial convictions. There is no further appeal from the decisions of this court

The federal and state court systems are the two separate systems functioning in the United States. The Supreme Court of the United States was established by the U.S. Constitution, which also gave Congress the authority to create lower federal courts. Each state has designed its own court system, and these vary from state to state. The diagram below shows a typical state court system. In both systems, the courts are organized in layers, and appeals flow from the lower courts to the higher ones. See APPEAL AND ERROR. *For a more detailed description of how the federal and state courts function, see* COURTS, FEDERAL COURTS, *and* SUPREME COURT.

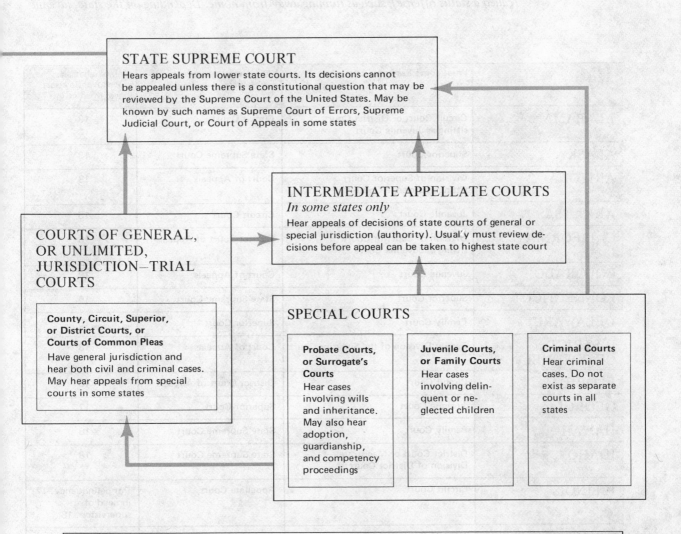

STATE SUPREME COURT
Hears appeals from lower state courts. Its decisions cannot be appealed unless there is a constitutional question that may be reviewed by the Supreme Court of the United States. May be known by such names as Supreme Court of Errors, Supreme Judicial Court, or Court of Appeals in some states

INTERMEDIATE APPELLATE COURTS
In some states only
Hear appeals of decisions of state courts of general or special jurisdiction (authority). Usual'y must review decisions before appeal can be taken to highest state court

COURTS OF GENERAL, OR UNLIMITED, JURISDICTION—TRIAL COURTS

County, Circuit, Superior, or District Courts, or Courts of Common Pleas
Have general jurisdiction and hear both civil and criminal cases. May hear appeals from special courts in some states

SPECIAL COURTS

Probate Courts, or Surrogate's Courts
Hear cases involving wills and inheritance. May also hear adoption, guardianship, and competency proceedings

Juvenile Courts, or Family Courts
Hear cases involving delinquent or neglected children

Criminal Courts
Hear criminal cases. Do not exist as separate courts in all states

COURTS OF LIMITED JURISDICTION—LOCAL COURTS
Hear cases involving lesser amounts of money or property of limited value or less severe violations of law than do courts of general jurisdiction. Usually do not keep records of proceedings

Traffic Courts

Magistrate's Courts

Justice Courts, or Justice of the Peace Courts

City Courts, or Municipal Courts

Police Courts

Small Claims Courts

Chart 2   **1078**

JUVENILE COURTS

Cases involving juvenile delinquents and offenders are usually heard in a court or division of a court separate from the adult criminal system. These juvenile courts generally have authority (jurisdiction) only when children are below an age specified by state law. They hear cases in which the child is charged with a criminal act or with noncriminal misbehavior (called a status offense), such as running away from home. Depending on the state, juvenile

	What court has jurisdiction?	Where may appeals be heard?[1]	Below what age does juvenile court have jurisdiction?[2]
ALABAMA	Circuit Court or District Court sitting as Juvenile Court	Circuit Court	18
ALASKA	Superior Court	State Supreme Court	18
ARIZONA	Division of Superior Court sitting as Juvenile Court	Court of Appeals	18
ARKANSAS	Juvenile Court	Circuit Court	18
CALIFORNIA	Division of Superior Court sitting as Juvenile Court	District Court of Appeals	18
COLORADO	Juvenile Court	Court of Appeals	18
CONNECTICUT	Superior Court	State Supreme Court	16
DELAWARE	Family Court	Superior Court	18
DISTRICT OF COLUMBIA	Family Division of the Superior Court	Court of Appeals	18
FLORIDA	Circuit Court	District Court of Appeals	18
GEORGIA	Juvenile Court	Superior Court	17
HAWAII	Family Court	State Supreme Court	18
IDAHO	District Court or Magistrate Division of District Court	State Supreme Court	18
ILLINOIS	Circuit Court	Appellate Court	For delinquency, 17; in need of supervision, 18
INDIANA	Juvenile Court	Court of Appeals	18
IOWA	Juvenile Court	Court of Appeals	18; if regularly attending high school or vocational school, 21
KANSAS	District Court or District Magistrate's Court	Court of Appeals or District Court	18

[1] These are the courts that review decisions and final orders of the trial-level juvenile courts. Some states have intermediate appellate courts, whose decisions may be appealed to a higher court, perhaps the state's highest court. Sometimes appeals may eventually go to the Supreme Court of the United States.

*courts may also hear cases involving adoption, abuse or neglect of a child, failure to support
a child, or contributing to the delinquency of a child. In some states, a juvenile accused
of a serious or violent crime, such as murder, is tried in an adult criminal court, and a local
court may have authority when a juvenile violates a local ordinance, such as loitering. For
a more detailed description of how juvenile courts function, see INFANT.*

	What court has jurisdiction?	Where may appeals be heard?[1]	Below what age does juvenile court have jurisdiction?[2]
KENTUCKY	Juvenile Session of District Court	Circuit Court	18
LOUISIANA	Juvenile Court or City, Parish, District, or Family Court exercising juvenile jurisdiction	Court of Appeals	17
MAINE	District Court sitting as Juvenile Court	Superior Court	18
MARYLAND	Circuit Court sitting as Juvenile Court (in Montgomery County, District Court sitting as Juvenile Court)	Court of Appeals	18
MASSACHUSETTS	Juvenile Court or District Court	Juvenile Appeals Session of the District Court	17
MICHIGAN	Juvenile Division of Probate Court	Circuit Court	18
MINNESOTA	Juvenile Court	State Supreme Court	18
MISSISSIPPI	Family Court or Youth Court	State Supreme Court or Chancery Court	18
MISSOURI	Juvenile Division of Circuit Court	Court of Appeals	16
MONTANA	Youth Court of the District Court	State Supreme Court	18
NEBRASKA	County Court or District Court; separate Juvenile Court established in counties over 50,000	From separate juvenile courts to State Supreme Court; from county courts to district courts	18
NEVADA	District Court sitting as Juvenile Court	State Supreme Court	18
NEW HAMPSHIRE	District Court or Municipal Court	Superior Court	18
NEW JERSEY	Juvenile and Domestic Relations Court	Appellate Division of Superior Court	18
NEW MEXICO	Division of District Court sitting as Children's Court or Family Court	Court of Appeals	18
NEW YORK	Family Court	Appellate Division of State Supreme Court	16
NORTH CAROLINA	District Court	Court of Appeals	18

[2] These ages apply to the age of the child when he committed the act that put him under the juvenile court's authority. In certain instances, trials may be held or courts may continue to supervise a juvenile on probation beyond the specified age. A different age may apply to cases involving adoption or failure to support a child.

Chart 2   1080

JUVENILE COURTS *(continued)*

	What court has jurisdiction?	Where may appeals be heard?[1]	Below what age does juvenile court have jurisdiction?[2]
NORTH DAKOTA	Division of District Court sitting as Juvenile Court	State Supreme Court	18
OHIO	Juvenile Court	Court of Appeals	18
OKLAHOMA	District Court	Court of Criminal Appeals or State Supreme Court	18
OREGON	Juvenile Court	County Court to Circuit Court; Circuit Court to Court of Appeals	18
PENNSYLVANIA	Court of Common Pleas	Superior Court	18
RHODE ISLAND	Family Court	State Supreme Court	18
SOUTH CAROLINA	Family Court	State Supreme Court	17
SOUTH DAKOTA	Circuit Court	State Supreme Court	18
TENNESSEE	Juvenile Court	Circuit Court	18
TEXAS	Juvenile Court	Court of Civil Appeals	17
UTAH	Juvenile Court or District Juvenile Court	State Supreme Court	18
VERMONT	District Court sitting as Juvenile Court	State Supreme Court	18
VIRGINIA	Juvenile and Domestic Relations Court	Circuit Court	18
WASHINGTON	Division of Superior Court sitting as Juvenile Court	State Supreme Court	18
WEST VIRGINIA	Circuit Court	Circuit Court or Supreme Court of Appeals	18
WISCONSIN	County judge has jurisdiction in each county	Court of Appeals	18
WYOMING	Juvenile Court; concurrent jursidiction in some cases in Municipal Court or District Court	State Supreme Court	19

WHERE RECORDS ARE KEPT

Many occasions arise when you need copies of birth, death, marriage, or divorce records. This chart shows where to write in your state for information or copies of these records. The fee for a certified copy of a record must be paid in advance.

	Birth and death records	Marriage records	Divorce records
ALABAMA	*Since 1908:* Division of Vital Statistics State Department of Health Montgomery 36130	*Since Aug. 1936:* Division of Vital Statistics State Department of Health Montgomery 36130 *Before Aug. 1936:* Probate judge, county where license was issued	*Since 1950:* Division of Vital Statistics State Department of Health Montgomery 36130 *Before 1950:* Court of Equity clerk or registrar, county where divorce was granted
ALASKA	Vital Statistics Bureau Room 115 Alaska Office Building Pouch H-03 Juneau 99811	Vital Statistics Bureau Room 115 Alaska Office Building Pouch H-03 Juneau 99811	*Since 1950:* Vital Statistics Bureau Room 115 Alaska Office Building Pouch H-03 Juneau 99811 *Before 1950:* Superior Court clerk, judicial district where divorce was granted: Juneau and Ketchikan (1st district), Nome (2nd), Anchorage (3rd), Fairbanks (4th)
ARIZONA	Vital Records Section Department of Health Services P. O. Box 3887 Phoenix 85030	Superior Court clerk, county where license was issued	Superior Court clerk, county where divorce was granted
ARKANSAS	*Since Feb. 1914:* Division of Vital Records Arkansas Department of Health Little Rock 72201 *Before Feb. 1914:* Arkansas Historical Commission State Capitol Mall Little Rock 72201	*Since 1917:* Division of Vital Records Arkansas Department of Health Little Rock 72201 *Before 1917:* County clerk, county where license was issued	*Since 1923:* Division of Vital Records Arkansas Department of Health Little Rock 72201 *Before 1923:* County or Chancery Court clerk, county where divorce was granted
CALIFORNIA	*Since July 1905:* Vital Statistics Branch Department of Health Services 410 N Street Sacramento 95814 *Before July 1905:* County recorder or city health office, county or city where event occurred	Vital Statistics Branch Department of Health Services 410 N Street Sacramento 95814	*Since 1962:* Vital Statistics Branch Department of Health Services 410 N Street Sacramento 95814 *Before 1962:* Superior Court clerk, county where divorce was granted

Chart 3   1082

WHERE RECORDS ARE KEPT *(continued)*

	Birth and death records	Marriage records	Divorce records

COLORADO	Records and Statistics Section
	Department of Health
	4210 East 11th Avenue
	Denver 80220
		Records and Statistics Section
		Department of Health
		4210 East 11th Avenue
		Denver 80220
		Or county clerk, county
		  where license was issued
			1940-67:
			District or County Court
			  clerk, county where divorce
			  was granted
			Before 1940 and since 1967:
			Records and Statistics Section
			Department of Health
			4210 East 11th Avenue
			Denver 80220

CONNECTICUT	*Since July 1897:*
	Public Health Statistics
	  Section
	State Department of Health
	79 Elm Street
	Hartford 06115
	Before July 1897:
	Registrar of vital statistics,
	  town where event occurred
		Since July 1897:
		Public Health Statistics
		  Section
		State Department of Health
		79 Elm Street
		Hartford 06115
		Before July 1897:
		Registrar of vital statistics,
		  town where license
		  was issued
			Since 1935:
			Superior Court where
			  divorce was granted
			Before 1935:
			Head clerk of court,
			  courthouse where
			  divorce was granted

DELAWARE	Bureau of Vital Statistics
	Division of Public Health
	Department of Health and
	  Social Services
	Jesse S. Cooper
	  Memorial Building
	Dover 19901
		Bureau of Vital Statistics
		Division of Public Health
		Department of Health and
		  Social Services
		Jesse S. Cooper
		  Memorial Building
		Dover 19901
			Since 1970:
			Family Court, county where
			  divorce was granted.
			  Family Court addresses:
			  Wilmington 19801;
			  Dover 19901;
			  Georgetown 19947
			Before 1970:
			Head clerk of court, county
			  where divorce was granted

DISTRICT
OF COLUMBIA
	Bureau of Vital Statistics
	300 Indiana Avenue NW
	Washington, D.C. 20001
		Clerk of Superior Court
		Building A, Room 111
		505 Fifth Street NW
		Washington, D.C. 20001
			Since Sept. 16, 1956:
			Clerk, Superior Court for
			  the District of Columbia
			Family Division
			500 Indiana Avenue NW
			Washington, D.C. 20001
			Before Sept. 16, 1956:
			Clerk, U.S. District Court for
			  the District of Columbia
			Washington, D.C. 20001

FLORIDA	Department of Health and
	  Rehabilitative Services
	P.O. Box 210
	Jacksonville 32231
		Since June 6, 1927:
		Bureau of Vital Statistics
		P.O. Box 210
		Jacksonville 32231
		Before June 6, 1927:
		Circuit Court clerk, county
		  where license was issued
			Since June 6, 1927:
			Bureau of Vital Statistics
			P.O. Box 210
			Jacksonville 32231
			Before June 6, 1927:
			Circuit Court clerk, county
			  where divorce was granted

GEORGIA	Vital Records Service
	State Department of Human
	  Resources
	47 Trinity Avenue SW
	Atlanta 30334
		Since June 9, 1952:
		Vital Records Service
		State Department of Human
		  Resources
		47 Trinity Avenue SW
		Atlanta 30334
		Before June 9, 1952:
		County ordinary (county
		  financial officer), county
		  where license was issued
			Since 1952:
			Vital Records Service
			State Department of Human
			  Resources
			47 Trinity Avenue SW
			Atlanta 30334
			Before 1952:
			Superior Court clerk, county
			  where divorce was granted

	Birth and death records	Marriage records	Divorce records
HAWAII	Research and Statistics Office State Department of Health P.O. Box 3378 Honolulu 96801	Research and Statistics Office State Department of Health P.O. Box 3378 Honolulu 96801	*Since July 1951:* Research and Statistics Office State Department of Health P.O. Box 3378 Honolulu 96801 *Before July 1951:* Circuit Court, county where divorce was granted

IDAHO	Bureau of Vital Statistics
	State Department of Health
	  and Welfare
	Statehouse
	Boise 83720
		Since 1947:
		Bureau of Vital Statistics
		State Department of Health
		  and Welfare
		Statehouse
		Boise 83720
		Before 1947:
		County recorder, county
		  where license was issued
			Since 1947:
			Bureau of Vital Statistics
			State Department of Health
			  and Welfare
			Statehouse
			Boise 83720
			Before 1947:
			County recorder, county
			  where divorce was granted

ILLINOIS	*Since 1916:*
	Office of Vital Records
	State Department of Public
	  Health
	535 West Jefferson Street
	Springfield 62761
	Before 1916:
	County clerk, county where
	  event occurred
		Since 1962:
		Office of Vital Records
		State Department of Public
		  Health
		535 West Jefferson Street
		Springfield 62761
		Before 1962:
		County clerk, county where
		  license was issued
			Since 1962:
			Office of Vital Records
			State Department of Public
			  Health
			535 West Jefferson Street
			Springfield 62761
			Before 1962:
			Circuit Court clerk, county
			  where divorce was granted

INDIANA	*Births since Oct. 1907 and
	  deaths since 1900:*
	Division of Vital Records
	State Board of Health
	1330 West Michigan Street
	Indianapolis 46202
	*Births before Oct. 1907 and
	  deaths before 1900:*
	Health officer, city or county
	  where event occurred
		Since 1958:
		Division of Vital Records
		State Board of Health
		1330 West Michigan Street
		Indianapolis 46202
		Before 1958:
		Circuit or Superior Court
		  clerk, county where
		  license was issued
			County clerk, county where
			  divorce was granted

IOWA	Vital Records Section State Department of Health Lucas Building Des Moines 50319	Vital Records Section State Department of Health Lucas Building Des Moines 50319	*Since 1906:* Vital Records Section State Department of Health Lucas Building Des Moines 50319 *Before 1906:* County clerk, county where divorce was granted

KANSAS	*Since July 1911:*
	Department of Health and
	  Environment
	Vital Statistics
	Topeka 66620
	Before July 1911:
	County clerk, county where
	  event occurred
		Since May 1913:
		Department of Health and
		  Environment
		Vital Statistics
		Topeka 66620
		Before May 1913:
		District Court marriage
		  license clerk, county where
		  license was obtained
			Since July 1951:
			Department of Health and
			  Environment
			Vital Statistics
			Topeka 66620
			Before July 1951:
			Clerk of District Court where
			  divorce was granted

Chart 3   1084

WHERE RECORDS ARE KEPT *(continued)*

	Birth and death records	Marriage records	Divorce records
KENTUCKY	*Since Jan. 1911:* Office of Vital Statistics 275 East Main Street Frankfort 40621 *Before Jan. 1911:* Historical Society 3016 P.O. Box H Frankfort 40621	*Since July 1958:* Office of Vital Statistics 275 East Main Street Frankfort 40621 *Before July 1958:* County Court clerk, county where license was issued	*Since July 1958:* Office of Vital Statistics 275 East Main Street Frankfort 40621 *Before July 1958:* Circuit Court clerk, county where divorce was granted
LOUISIANA	*Since July 1914:* Office of Vital Records P.O. Box 60630 New Orleans 70160 *Before July 1914:* Parish clerk, parish where event occurred NEW ORLEANS *Since 1790:* Office of Vital Records P.O. Box 60630 New Orleans 70160	*Since 1946:* Office of Vital Records P.O. Box 60630 New Orleans 70160 *Before 1946:* Court clerk, parish where license was issued NEW ORLEANS *Since 1831:* Office of Vital Records P.O. Box 60630 New Orleans 70160	*Since 1946:* Office of Vital Records P.O. Box 60630 New Orleans 70160 *Before 1946:* Court clerk, parish where divorce was granted NEW ORLEANS Civil District Court 421 Loyola Avenue New Orleans 70112
MAINE	*Since 1892:* Office of Vital Statistics State Department of Human Services State House Augusta 04333 *Before 1892:* Town clerk, town where event occurred	Office of Vital Statistics Department of Human Services State House Augusta 04333 Or local office where intentions were filed	*Since 1892:* Office of Vital Statistics State Department of Human Services State House Augusta 04333 Or court where divorce was granted *Before 1892:* Superior Court clerk, county where divorce was granted; or District Court clerk, judicial division where divorce was granted
MARYLAND	Division of Vital Records Department of Health and Mental Hygiene Herbert R. O'Conor Building 201 West Preston Street Baltimore 21201	*Since June 1951:* Division of Vital Records Department of Health and Mental Hygiene Herbert R. O'Conor Building 201 West Preston Street Baltimore 21201 *Before June 1951:* Clerk of Circuit Court, county where marriage occurred	*Since June 1961:* Division of Vital Records P.O. Box 18146 Baltimore 21203 *Before June 1961:* Clerk of Circuit Court, county where divorce was granted
MASSACHUSETTS	*Since 1841:* Registrar of Vital Statistics McCormack Building 1 Ashburton Place Boston 02108 *Before 1841:* Clerk, city or town where event occurred	Registrar of Vital Statistics McCormack Building 1 Ashburton Place Boston 02108	Superior Court clerk or registrar of probate, county where divorce was granted

	Birth and death records	Marriage records	Divorce records
MASSACHUSETTS *(continued)*	BOSTON City Registrar Registry Division Health Department Room 705 1 City Hall Square Boston 02201	BOSTON City Registrar Registry Division Health Department Room 705 1 City Hall Square Boston 02201	BOSTON City Registrar Registry Division Health Department Room 705 1 City Hall Square Boston 02201

MICHIGAN	Office of Vital and Health
	  Statistics
	Department of Public Health
	3500 North Logan Street
	P.O. Box 30035
	Lansing 48909
	Or county clerk, county
	  where event occurred
		Office of Vital and Health
		  Statistics
		Department of Public Health
		3500 North Logan Street
		P.O. Box 30035
		Lansing 48909
		Or county clerk, county
		  where license was issued
			Office of Vital and Health
			  Statistics
			Department of Public Health
			3500 North Logan Street
			P.O. Box 30035
			Lansing 48909
			Or county clerk, county
			  where divorce was granted

MINNESOTA	*Since 1908:*
	Minnesota Department of
	  Health
	Section of Vital Statistics
	717 Delaware Street SE
	Minneapolis 55440
	Before 1908:
	District Court clerk, county
	  where event occurred
	MINNEAPOLIS and ST. PAUL
	City Health Departments
		Since 1958:
		Minnesota Department of
		  Health
		Section of Vital Statistics
		717 Delaware Street SE
		Minneapolis 55440
		Before 1958:
		District Court Clerk, county
		  where license was issued
			Since 1970:
			Minnesota Department of
			  Health
			Section of Vital Statistics
			717 Delaware Street SE
			Minneapolis 55440
			Before 1970:
			District Court clerk, county
			  where divorce was granted

MISSISSIPPI	Vital Records
	  Registration Unit
	State Board of Health
	P.O. Box 1700
	Jackson 39205
		*Since 1926 (excluding period
		  July 1, 1938-Dec. 31, 1941):*
		Vital Records
		  Registration Unit
		State Board of Health
		P.O. Box 1700
		Jackson 39205
		*Before 1926 and for period
		  July 1, 1938-Dec. 31, 1941:*
		Circuit clerk, county where
		  license was issued
			Chancery clerk, county
			  where divorce was granted

MISSOURI	*Since Jan. 1, 1910:*
	Vital Records
	Division of Health
	P.O. Box 570
	Jefferson City 65101
		Since July 1948:
		Vital Records
		Division of Health
		P.O. Box 570
		Jefferson City 65101
		Before July 1948:
		Recorder of deeds, county
		  where license was issued
			Since July 1948:
			Vital Records
			Division of Health
			P.O. Box 570
			Jefferson City 65101
			Before July 1948:
			Circuit Court clerk, county
			  where divorce was granted

MONTANA	Bureau of Records and
	  Statistics
	State Department of Health
	  and Environmental Sciences
	Helena 59601
		Since 1943:
		Bureau of Records and
		  Statistics
		State Department of Health
		  and Environmental Services
		Helena 59601
		Before 1943:
		District Court clerk, county
		  where license was issued
			Since 1943:
			Bureau of Records and
			  Statistics
			State Department of Health
			  and Environmental Services
			Helena 59601
			Before 1943:
			District Court clerk, county
			  where divorce was granted

Chart 3 1086

WHERE RECORDS ARE KEPT *(continued)*

	Birth and death records	Marriage records	Divorce records

NEBRASKA	*Since 1904:*
	Bureau of Vital Statistics
	State Department of Health
	301 Centennial Mall South
	P.O. Box 95007
	Lincoln 68509
	Before 1904:
	Division of Vital Statistics
	Omaha/Douglas County
	  Health Department
	Civic Center
	1819 Farnam
	Omaha 68102
		Since 1909:
		Bureau of Vital Statistics
		State Department of Health
		301 Centennial Mall South
		P.O. Box 95007
		Lincoln 68509
		Before 1909:
		County court, county where
		  license was issued
			Since 1909:
			Bureau of Vital Statistics
			State Department of Health
			301 Centennial Mall South
			P.O. Box 95007
			Lincoln 68509
			Before 1909:
			Clerk of District Court
			  where divorce was granted

NEVADA	*Since July 1911:*
	Department of Human
	  Resources
	Division of Health
	Section of Vital Statistics
	Capitol Complex
	Carson City 89710
	Before July 1911:
	County recorder, county
	  where event occurred
		Since Jan. 1968:
		Department of Human
		  Resources
		Division of Health
		Section of Vital Statistics
		Capitol Complex
		Carson City 89710
		Before Jan. 1968:
		County recorder, county
		  where license was issued
			Since Jan. 1968:
			Department of Human
			  Resources
			Division of Health
			Section of Vital Statistics
			Capitol Complex
			Carson City 89710
			Before Jan. 1968:
			County clerk, county where
			  divorce was granted

NEW HAMPSHIRE	Division of Public
	  Health Services
	Bureau of Vital Records and
	  Health Statistics
	Health and Welfare Building
	Hazen Drive
	Concord 03301
		Division of Public
		  Health Services
		Bureau of Vital Records and
		  Health Statistics
		Health and Welfare Building
		Hazen Drive
		Concord 03301
			Division of Public
			  Health Services
			Bureau of Vital Records and
			  Health Statistics
			Health and Welfare Building
			Hazen Drive
			Or clerk of Superior Court
			  where decree was issued

NEW JERSEY	*Since June 1878:* State Department of Health Bureau of Vital Statistics P.O. Box 1540 Trenton 08625 *1848-May 1878:* State Archives	State Department of Health Bureau of Vital Statistics P.O. Box 1540 Trenton 08625	Clerk, Superior Court State House Annex P.O. Box 1300 Trenton 08625 Att: Matrimonial Unit

NEW MEXICO	Vital Statistics Bureau
	Health and Environmental
	  Department
	P.O. Box 968
	PERA Building, Room 118
	Santa Fe 87503
		County clerk, county where
		  marriage was performed
			District Court clerk, county
			  where divorce was granted

NEW YORK	Bureau of Vital Records
	State Department of Health
	Albany 12237
		1880-1907 and since
		  May 1915:
		Bureau of Vital Records
		State Department of Health
		Albany 12237
		1908-Apr. 1915:
		County clerk, county
		  where license was issued
			Since 1963:
			Bureau of Vital Records
			State Department of Health
			Albany 12237
			Before 1963:
			County clerk, county
			  where divorce was granted

	Birth and death records	Marriage records	Divorce records
NEW YORK *(continued)*	NEW YORK CITY Bureau of Records and Statistics, borough where event occurred	NEW YORK CITY *Since May 13, 1943:* City clerk's office where license was obtained *1908-May 12, 1943:* City clerk's office in borough of bride; nonresidents, city clerk's office where license was obtained	NEW YORK CITY Borough of court where divorce was granted
NORTH CAROLINA	*Since Oct. 1, 1913:* Vital Records Branch Division of Health Services P.O. Box 2091 Raleigh 27602	*Since 1962:* Vital Records Branch Division of Health Services P.O. Box 2091 Raleigh 27602 *Before 1962:* Register of deeds, county where marriage was performed	*Since 1958:* Vital Records Branch Division of Health Services P.O. Box 2091 Raleigh 27602 *Before 1958:* Superior Court clerk, county where divorce was granted
NORTH DAKOTA	Division of Vital Records State Department of Health State Capitol Bismarck 58505	*Since July 1925:* Division of Vital Records State Department of Health State Capitol Bismarck 58505 *Before July 1925:* County judge, county where license was issued	*Since July 1949:* Division of Vital Records State Department of Health State Capitol Bismarck 58505 *Before July 1949:* District Court Clerk, county where divorce was granted
OHIO	*Since Dec. 20, 1908:* Division of Vital Statistics State Department of Health G-20 State Departments Building 65 South Front Street Columbus 43215 *Before Dec. 20, 1908:* Probate Court, county where event occurred	*Since 1948:* Division of Vital Statistics State Department of Health G-20 State Departments Building 65 South Front Street Columbus 43215 *Before 1948:* Probate judge, county where license was issued	*Since 1948:* Division of Vital Statistics State Department of Health G-20 State Departments Building 65 South Front Street Columbus 43215 *Before 1948:* Court of Common Pleas clerk, county where divorce was granted
OKLAHOMA	Vital Records Division Oklahoma State Department of Health 1000 NE 10th Street P.O. Box 53551 Oklahoma City 73152	Court clerk, county where license was issued	Court clerk, county where divorce was granted
OREGON	Vital Statistics Section Oregon State Health Division P.O. Box 231 Portland 97207	*Since 1906:* Vital Statistics Section Oregon State Health Division P.O. Box 231 Portland 97207 *Before 1906:* County clerk, county where license was issued	*Since 1925:* Vital Statistics Section Oregon State Health Division P.O. Box 231 Portland 97207 *Before 1925:* County clerk, county where divorce was granted
PENNSYLVANIA	*Since 1906:* Division of Vital Statistics P.O. Box 1528 New Castle 16103 *Before 1906:* Register of wills, Orphan's Court, county where event occurred	Marriage license clerk, county courthouse, county seat where license was issued	Head clerk of court, county courthouse, county seat where divorce was granted

Chart 3 1088

WHERE RECORDS ARE KEPT *(continued)*

	Birth and death records	Marriage records	Divorce records
RHODE ISLAND	*Since 1853:* Division of Vital Statistics State Department of Health Room 101, Health Building Davis Street Providence 02908 *Before 1853:* Town clerk, town where event occurred	*Since 1636:* Division of Vital Statistics State Department of Health Room 101, Health Building Davis Street Providence 02908 *Before 1636:* Rhode Island Historical Society 110 Benevolent Street Providence 02906	Family Court of Rhode Island 22 Hayes Street Providence 02908 Or Family Court clerk, county where divorce was granted
SOUTH CAROLINA	Office of Vital Records South Carolina Department of Health and Environmental Control Sims Building Columbia 29201 *Before 1915:* County Health Department, county where event occurred	*Since July 1950:* Office of Vital Records South Carolina Department of Health and Environmental Control Sims Building Columbia 29201 *July 1911-June 1950:* Probate judge, county where license was issued	*Since July 1962:* Office of Vital Records South Carolina Department of Health and Environmental Control Sims Building Columbia 29201 *Apr. 1949-June 1962:* County clerk, county where petition was filed
SOUTH DAKOTA	Public Health Statistics State Department of Health Joe Foss Building Pierre 57501	*Since 1905:* Public Health Statistics State Department of Health Joe Foss Building Pierre 57501 *Before 1905:* County treasurer, county where license was issued	*Since 1905:* Public Health Statistics State Department of Health Joe Foss Building Pierre 57501 *Before 1905:* Court clerk, county where divorce was granted
TENNESSEE	Vital Records State Department of Public Health C3-324 Cordell Hull Building Nashville 37219	*Since July 1945:* Vital Records State Department of Public Health C3-324 Cordell Hull Building Nashville 37219 *Before July 1945:* County Court clerk, county where license was issued	*Since July 1945:* Vital Records State Department of Public Health C3-324 Cordell Hull Building Nashville 37219 *Before July 1945:* Clerk of court where divorce was granted
TEXAS	Bureau of Vital Statistics Texas Department of Health 1100 West 49th Street Austin 78756	*Since Jan. 1966:* Bureau of Vital Statistics 1100 West 49th Street Austin 78756 *Before Jan. 1966:* County clerk, county where license was issued	*Since Jan. 1968:* Bureau of Vital Statistics 1100 West 49th Street Austin 78756 *Before Jan. 1968:* District Court clerk, county where divorce was granted
UTAH	*Since 1905:* Utah State Division of Health Bureau of Health Statistics 150 West North Temple P.O. Box 2500 Salt Lake City 84110 *Before 1905:* County clerk, county where event occurred SALT LAKE CITY and OGDEN City Boards of Health	County clerk, county where license was issued	District Court clerk, county where divorce was granted

	Birth and death records	Marriage records	Divorce records

VERMONT	*Since 1955:*
	Public Health Statistics
	Vermont Department of
	  Health
	115 Colchester Avenue
	Burlington 05401
	Before 1955:
	Public Records Division
	Administration Department
	133 State Street
	Montpelier 05602
		Since 1955:
		Public Health Statistics
		Vermont Department of
		  Health
		115 Colchester Avenue
		Burlington 05401
		1857-1954:
		Public Records Division
		Administration Department
		133 State Street
		Montpelier 05602
		Before 1857:
		Town clerk, town where
		  license was issued
			Since 1968:
			Public Health Statistics
			Vermont Department of
			  Health
			115 Colchester Avenue
			Burlington 05401
			1860-1967:
			Public Records Division
			Administration Department
			133 State Street
			Montpelier 05602
			Before 1860:
			County Court, county where
			  divorce was granted

VIRGINIA	*1853-96 and since*
	* June 14, 1912:*
	Bureau of Vital Records and
	  Health Statistics
	State Department of Health
	Madison Building
	P.O. Box 1000
	Richmond 23208
	1897-June 13, 1912:
	Health Department, city where
	  birth or death occurred
		Since 1853:
		Bureau of Vital Records and
		  Health Statistics
		State Department of Health
		Madison Building
		P.O. Box 1000
		Richmond 23208
		Before 1853:
		Court clerk, county or city
		  where license was issued
			Since 1918:
			Bureau of Vital Records and
			  Health Statistics
			State Department of Health
			Madison Building
			P.O. Box 1000
			Richmond 23208
			Before 1918:
			Court clerk, county or city
			  where divorce was granted

WASHINGTON	*Since July 1907:*
	Vital Records
	P.O. Box 9709
	Olympia 98504
	Before July 1907:
	Auditor, county where
	  event occurred
		Since 1968:
		Vital Records
		P.O. Box 9709
		Olympia 98504
		Before 1968:
		County auditor, county
		  where license was issued
			Since 1968:
			Vital Records
			P.O. Box 9709
			Olympia 98504
			Before 1968:
			County clerk, county where
			  divorce was granted

WEST VIRGINIA	*Since 1917:*
	State Registrar of Vital
	  Statistics
	State Capitol Building
	Charleston 25305
	Before 1917:
	County Court clerk, county
	  where event occurred
		Since 1921:
		State Registrar of Vital
		  Statistics
		State Capitol Building
		Charleston 25305
		Before 1921:
		County clerk, county where
		  license was issued
			Circuit Court clerk,
			  Chancery Side, county
			  where divorce was granted

WISCONSIN	Section of Vital Records Division of Health P.O. Box 309 Madison 53701	Section of Vital Records Division of Health P.O. Box 309 Madison 53701	Section of Vital Records Division of Health P.O. Box 309 Madison 53701

WYOMING	*Since 1909:*
	Vital Records Services
	Division of Health and
	  Medical Services
	Hathaway Building
	Cheyenne 82002
	Before 1909:
	State Archives
		Since May 1941:
		Vital Records Services
		Division of Health and
		  Medical Services
		Hathaway Building
		Cheyenne 82002
		Before May 1941:
		County clerk, county where
		  license was issued
			Since May 1941:
			Vital Records Services
			Division of Health and
			  Medical Services
			Hathaway Building
			Cheyenne 82002
			Before May 1941:
			District Court clerk, county
			  where divorce was granted

Chart 4   **1090**

STATUTES OF LIMITATIONS FOR STARTING A CIVIL ACTION

Limitation in years

	Assault and battery	Fraud	Libel	Slander	Personal injury	Wrongful death	Trespass	Damage to personal property	Conversion	Medical malpractice	False imprisonment	Malicious prosecution	Breach of warranty
ALABAMA	6	1	1	1	1	2	6	1	6	2^1	6	1	4
ALASKA	2	2	2	2	2	2	6	6	6	2	2	2	4
ARIZONA	2	3	1	1	2	2	2	2	2	3^2	1	1	4
ARKANSAS	1	5	3	1	5^3	5^3	3	5^3	3	2	1	5	4
CALIFORNIA	1	3	1	1	1	1	3	3	3	1^1	1	1	4
COLORADO	1	3	1	1	6	2^4	6	6	6	2	1	6	4
CONNECTICUT	3	3	2	2	2	2	3	2	3	3	2	3	4
DELAWARE	2	3	2	2	2	2	3	2	3	2^1	2	2	4
D.C.	1	3	1	1	3	1	3	3	3	3^1	1	1	4
FLORIDA	4	4	4	4	4	2	4	4	4	2^1	4	4	4
GEORGIA	2	4	1	1	2	2	4	4	4	$2^{1,5}$	2	2	4
HAWAII	2	6	2	2	2	2	2	2	6	2^1	6	6	4
IDAHO	2	3	2	2	2	2	3	3	3	2	2	4	4
ILLINOIS	2	5	1	1	2	2	5	5	5	2	2	2	4
INDIANA	2	6	2	2	2	2	6	2	6	2	2	2	4
IOWA	2	5	2	2	2	2	5	5	5	2	2	2	5
KANSAS	1	2	1	1	2	2	2	2	2	2	1	1	4
KENTUCKY	1	5	1	1	1	1	5	5	5	1	1	1	4
LOUISIANA	1	1	1	1	1	1	1	1	1	1	1	1	1
MAINE	2	6	2	2	6	2	6	6	6	2	2	6	4
MARYLAND	1	3	1	1	3	3	3	3	3	3	3	3	4
MASSACHUSETTS	3	3	3	3	3	3	3	3	3	3	3	3	4
MICHIGAN	2	6	1	1	3	3	3	3	3	2	2	2	4
MINNESOTA	2	6	2	2	6	3^4	6	6	6	2	2	2	4
MISSISSIPPI	1	6	1	1	6	6	1	6	6	6	1	1	4
MISSOURI	2	5	2	2	5	3	5	5	5	2	2	5	4

[1] But action must be brought no later than a specified number of years from the date of injury. This time limit varies from 2-8 years.

[2] Limit runs from injury date with exceptions.

[3] Limit is 4 years in certain cases involving construction or improvement to real estate.

Statutes of limitations specify the period of time within which you may start a lawsuit (civil action) to redress a harm done to you or your property by someone else's NEGLIGENCE *or deliberate intention. These time limits vary from state to state and according to the type of harm you suffered. Unless otherwise specified, the time limit for fraud, personal injury, and medical malpractice runs from the date of discovery; for wrongful death, from the time of death. See* ACTION, LIMITATIONS OF ACTIONS, *and* TORT, *as well as such entries as* ASSAULT AND BATTERY, FRAUD, *and* LIBEL AND SLANDER. *Statutes of limitations for breach of contract can be found in Chart 7.*

Limitation in years

	Assault and battery	Fraud	Libel	Slander	Personal injury	Wrongful death	Trespass	Damage to personal property	Conversion	Medical malpractice	False imprisonment	Malicious prosecution	Breach of warranty
MONTANA	2	2	2	2	5	3	2	2	2	3	2	5	4
NEBRASKA	1	4	1	1	4	2	4	4	4	2	1	1	4
NEVADA	2	3	2	2	2	2	3	3	3	2	2	2	4
NEW HAMPSHIRE	6	6	6	6	6[6]	2	6	6	6	6	6	6	4
NEW JERSEY	2	6	1	1	2	2	6	6	6	2	2	6	4
NEW MEXICO	3	4	3	3	3	3	4	4	4	3	3	3	4
NEW YORK	1	6	1	1	3	2	3	3	3	2½	1	1	4
NORTH CAROLINA	1	3	1	1	3	2	3	3	3	3	1	3	4
NORTH DAKOTA	2	6	2	2	6	2	6	6	6	2	2	6	4
OHIO	1	4	1	1	2	2	4	2	4	1	1	1	4
OKLAHOMA	1	2	1	1	2	2	2	2	2	2	1	1	5
OREGON	2	2	1	1	2	3[4]	6	6	6	2	2	2	4
PENNSYLVANIA	2	6	1	1	2	1	2	2	2	2	2	2	4
RHODE ISLAND	10	10	10	1	3	2	10	10	10	2	10	10	10
SOUTH CAROLINA	2	6	2	2	6	6	6	6	6	3[1]	2	6	6
SOUTH DAKOTA	2	6	2	2	3	3	6	6	6	2	2	6	4
TENNESSEE	1	3	1	½	1	1	3	3	3	1	1	1	4
TEXAS	2	2	1	1	2	2	2	2	2	2	2	1	4
UTAH	1	3	1	1	4	2	3	3	3	2	1	1	4
VERMONT	3	6	3	3	3[6]	2	6	3	6	2[1]	3	3	4
VIRGINIA	2	3	2	2	2	2	5	5	5	2	2	1	4
WASHINGTON	2	3	2	2	3	3	3	3	3	1[1]	2	3	4
WEST VIRGINIA	2	2	1	1	2	2	2	2	2	2	1	1	4
WISCONSIN	2	6	2	2	3	3	6	6	6	3	2	2	6
WYOMING	1	4	1	1	4	2	4	4	4	2	1	1	4

[4] Limit runs from the time the injury causing death occurred.

[5] But only 1 year from the date of discovery of a foreign object in the body.

[6] For skiing injuries, the limit is shorter.

Chart 5   **1092**

PARENTAL LIABILITY LAWS

	Are parents liable for torts of children?	If so, until child reaches what age?	What is limit of parental liability for each tort?	To what kinds of torts does liability extend?
ALABAMA	Yes	18	$500[1]	Intentional, malicious, or willful acts
ALASKA	Yes	18	$2,000[1]	Malicious or willful destruction of property
ARIZONA	Yes	18	$500	Malicious or willful misconduct
ARKANSAS	Yes	18	$2,000	Malicious or willful destruction of property
CALIFORNIA	Yes	18	$2,000	Willful misconduct
COLORADO	Yes	18	$1,500[2]	Malicious or willful destruction of property
CONNECTICUT	Yes	18	$3,000	Malicious or willful destruction of property
DELAWARE	Yes	18	$1,000	Malicious or willful destruction of property
D.C.	No	——	——	——
FLORIDA	Yes	18	$2,500[1]	Malicious or willful destruction or theft of property
GEORGIA	Yes	18	$500	Willful and malicious damage to property
HAWAII	Yes	18	No stated limit	All torts
IDAHO	Yes	18	$1,500	Malicious or willful destruction of property
ILLINOIS	Yes	19	$500[1]	Malicious or willful acts (no liability for child under 12)
INDIANA	Yes	18	$750[1]	Intentional and knowing damage to property
IOWA	Yes	18	$1,000[3]	Unlawful acts injuring person or property
KANSAS	Yes	18	$1,000[1,4]	Willful or malicious destruction of property
KENTUCKY	Yes	18	$2,500[5]	Willful defacement or damage of property
LOUISIANA	Yes	18	No stated limit	All torts
MAINE	Yes	18	$800	Willful and malicious injury to person or property (no liability for child under 7)
MARYLAND	Yes	18	$5,000	Willful or malicious destruction or theft of property; injury to person
MASSACHUSETTS	Yes	17	$500[6]	Willful injury to person or property (no liability for child under 8)
MICHIGAN	Yes	18	$2,500	Willful or malicious destruction of property; injury to person
MINNESOTA	No	——	——	——
MISSISSIPPI	Yes	18	$1,000	Malicious and willful destruction of property (no liability for child under 11)
MISSOURI	Yes	21	$300	Marking, defacing, or damaging property
MONTANA	Yes	18	$1,500[2]	Willful or malicious destruction of property

[1] Plus court costs.
[2] Plus court costs and attorney's fee.

[3] Or $2,000 to the same plaintiff damaged for 2 or more acts.
[4] No limit if act is result of parental neglect.

[5] For 1 act, $2,500 limit; for more than 1 act, cumulative total of $10,000.

Under the common law, a parent is not liable for his child's TORTS *(injuries to person or property) unless the parent is at fault in some way—for example, if he gave the child a dangerous article, such as an air gun. The victim has to absorb his losses. This unfairness led many states to pass laws making parents liable in some cases. If a child causes an auto accident, the parent may be liable under the family car doctrine (see Chart 28). See also* INFANT; PARENT AND CHILD.

	Are parents liable for torts of children?	If so, until child reaches what age?	What is limit of parental liability for each tort?	To what kinds of torts does liability extend?
NEBRASKA	Yes	19	No stated limit	Willful or intentional injury to person or property
NEVADA	Yes	18	$3,000	Willful misconduct resulting in injury to person or property
NEW HAMPSHIRE	No	——	——	——
NEW JERSEY	Yes	18	No stated limit[7]	Willful, malicious, or unlawful destruction of property
NEW MEXICO	Yes	18	$1,000[2]	Malicious or willful injury to person or property
NEW YORK	Yes	18	$1,000	Willful, malicious, or unlawful destruction of property (no liability for child under 11)
NORTH CAROLINA	Yes	18	$500	Willful or malicious destruction of property
NORTH DAKOTA	Yes	18	No stated limit	No statutory provision
OHIO	Yes	18	$2,000[8]	Willful destruction or theft of property or malicious assault of person
OKLAHOMA	Yes	18	$1,500	Violent or delinquent act causing injury to person or property
OREGON	Yes	18	$1,500	Intentional torts
PENNSYLVANIA	Yes	18	$300[9]	Willful, tortious act resulting in injury to person; theft or destruction of property
RHODE ISLAND	Yes	18	$500	Willful or malicious injury to person or property
SOUTH CAROLINA	Yes	17	$1,000	Malicious destruction, damage, or theft of property
SOUTH DAKOTA	Yes	18	$300[1]	Willful or malicious acts
TENNESSEE	Yes	18	$5,000	Willful or malicious destruction of property
TEXAS	Yes	18	$5,000[2]	Willful or malicious conduct resulting from parental neglect (no liability for child under 13)
UTAH	No	——	——	——
VERMONT	Yes	17	$250	Willful or malicious destruction of property
VIRGINIA	Yes	18	$200	Willful or malicious destruction of property
WASHINGTON	Yes	18	$3,000	Willful or malicious injury to person or property
WEST VIRGINIA	Yes	18	$300[1]	Willful or malicious destruction of property
WISCONSIN	Yes	18	$500[1]	Willful, malicious, or wanton acts
WYOMING	Yes	17	$300[1]	Willful or malicious destruction of property (no liability for child under 10)

[6] Or $1,000 for damage to cemetery property.
[7] For damage to public railroad or bus property, $1,000 plus court costs.
[8] For injury to person, $2,000 plus court costs; for damage to property, $3,000 plus court costs.
[9] For 1 act, $300; if more than 1 person is damaged by 1 act, $1,000 maximum.

Chart 6   **1094**

CONTRACTS THAT MUST BE IN WRITING

Some agreements must be in the form of a written CONTRACT if they are to be enforced in a court of law according to the STATUTE OF FRAUDS. All agreements to sell real estate must be in writing, as must all contracts for the sale of goods worth more than $500.[1] Contracts that are not to be performed within a stated period of time and leases that will run longer than a stipulated period must also be in writing. These time periods are given below for each state.

	Contracts not to be performed within	Leases for a period of more than		Contracts not to be performed within	Leases for a period of more than
ALABAMA	1 year	1 year	MONTANA	1 year	1 year
ALASKA	1 year	1 year	NEBRASKA	1 year	1 year
ARIZONA	1 year	1 year	NEVADA	1 year	1 year
ARKANSAS	1 year	1 year	NEW HAMPSHIRE	1 year	NSP*
CALIFORNIA	1 year	1 year	NEW JERSEY	1 year	3 years
COLORADO	1 year	1 year	NEW MEXICO	1 year	3 years
CONNECTICUT	1 year	1 year	NEW YORK	1 year	1 year
DELAWARE	1 year	1 year	NORTH CAROLINA	NSP*	3 years
D.C.	1 year	1 year	NORTH DAKOTA	1 year	1 year
FLORIDA	1 year	1 year	OHIO	1 year	___[2]
GEORGIA	1 year	1 year	OKLAHOMA	1 year	1 year
HAWAII	1 year	1 year	OREGON	1 year	1 year
IDAHO	1 year	1 year	PENNSYLVANIA	NSP*	3 years
ILLINOIS	1 year	1 year	RHODE ISLAND	1 year	1 year
INDIANA	1 year	3 years	SOUTH CAROLINA	1 year	1 year
IOWA	1 year	1 year	SOUTH DAKOTA	1 year	1 year
KANSAS	1 year	1 year	TENNESSEE	1 year	1 year
KENTUCKY	1 year	1 year	TEXAS	1 year	1 year
LOUISIANA	NSP*	NSP*	UTAH	1 year	1 year
MAINE	1 year	NSP*	VERMONT	1 year	NSP*
MARYLAND	1 year	1 year	VIRGINIA	1 year	1 year
MASSACHUSETTS	1 year	NSP*	WASHINGTON	1 year	1 year
MICHIGAN	1 year	1 year	WEST VIRGINIA	1 year	1 year
MINNESOTA	1 year	1 year	WISCONSIN	1 year	1 year
MISSISSIPPI	15 months	1 year	WYOMING	1 year	1 year
MISSOURI	1 year	1 year			

*No statutory provision.   [1] In Louisiana, a contract for the sale of goods worth $500 or more must be in writing unless it can be proved by 2 witnesses.   [2] All leases must be in writing.

LIMITATIONS OF SUITS FOR BREACH OF CONTRACT

Statutes of limitations specify the time within which you may start certain types of lawsuits, including those for breach of contract (see LIMITATIONS OF ACTIONS). This chart gives the time limits allowed by each state for oral, written, and sealed CONTRACTS. A sealed contract, which may be impressed with a SEAL, is considered more formal than an ordinary written contract. Limitations for breach of SALES contracts, also given below, often differ from those for other types of contracts.

Limitation in years

	Oral contract	Written contract	Sealed contract	Sales contract
ALABAMA	6	6	10	4
ALASKA	6	6	10	4
ARIZONA	3	6[1]	6[1]	4
ARKANSAS	3	5	5	4
CALIFORNIA	2	4	4	4
COLORADO	3-6[2]	3-6[2]	3-6[2]	4
CONNECTICUT	3	6	6	4
DELAWARE	3	3	3	4
D.C.	3	3	12	4
FLORIDA	4	5	5	4
GEORGIA	4	6	20	4
HAWAII	6	6	6	4
IDAHO	4	5	5	4
ILLINOIS	5	10	10	4
INDIANA	6	10	10	4
IOWA	5	10	10	5
KANSAS	3	5	5	4
KENTUCKY	5	15	15	4
LOUISIANA	10	10	10	1
MAINE	6	6	20	4
MARYLAND	3	3	12	4
MASSACHUSETTS	6	6	20	4
MICHIGAN	6	6	6	4
MINNESOTA	6	6	6	4
MISSISSIPPI	3	6	6	4
MISSOURI	5	10	10	4

Limitation in years

	Oral contract	Written contract	Sealed contract	Sales contract
MONTANA	5	8	8	4
NEBRASKA	4	5	5	4
NEVADA	4	6	6	4
NEW HAMPSHIRE	6	6	20	4
NEW JERSEY	6	6	16	4
NEW MEXICO	4	6	6	4
NEW YORK	6	6	6	4
NORTH CAROLINA	3	3	10	4
NORTH DAKOTA	6	6	6	4
OHIO	6	15	15	4
OKLAHOMA	3	5	5	5
OREGON	6	6	6	4
PENNSYLVANIA	6	6	20	4
RHODE ISLAND	10	10	20	4
SOUTH CAROLINA	6	6	20	6
SOUTH DAKOTA	6	6	20	4
TENNESSEE	6	6	6	4
TEXAS	2	4	4	4
UTAH	4	6	6	4
VERMONT	6	6	8	4
VIRGINIA	3	5	5	4
WASHINGTON	3	6	6	4
WEST VIRGINIA	5	10	10	4
WISCONSIN	6	6	20	6
WYOMING	8	10	10	4

[1] The limit is 4 years on written contracts executed outside the state.

[2] Depending on the terms of the contract.

Chart 8   1096

FHA AND VA MORTGAGES

The Federal Housing Administration of the Department of Housing and Urban Development and the Veterans Administration guarantee MORTGAGE *loans for the purchase of mobile homes and single-family homes (defined by the agencies as homes for one to four families in which the owner occupies one apartment) under the terms shown below. Eligibility does not expire.*

	FHA mortgages	VA mortgages
Who is eligible?	(1) Persons who have satisfactory credit records, the cash needed at closing of the mortgage, and enough steady income to make monthly mortgage payments without difficulty (2) Service personnel who have been on active duty for at least 2 years (3) Veterans who were on active duty for at least 90 days and who received honorable discharges	(1) Veterans who served between September 16, 1940, and the present and were discharged under conditions other than dishonorable after at least 90 days active service[1] (2) Service personnel who have served more than 180 days (3) Unremarried surviving spouses of veterans whose deaths were service connected and spouses of service personnel officially listed as missing in action or captured for more than 90 days (4) Certain U.S. citizens who served in the armed forces of a U.S. ally
What is the maximum loan?	97% of first $25,000 of appraised value and closing costs; 95% of balance over $25,000. For servicemen and veterans, 100% of first $25,000; 95% of balance over $25,000. Maximum loan is $60,000 on a house for 1 family; $65,000 for 2 and 3 families; $75,000 for 4 families[2]	No maximum loan, but the loan may not exceed the reasonable value of the property as determined by the VA. VA guarantees 60% of the loan up to $25,000. Closing costs may not be included in the loan
What is the down payment?	Difference between sale price and insured mortgage as described above	There is no VA requirement for a down payment if the purchase price does not exceed the reasonable value of the property, but the lender may require one
What is the allowable interest rate?	Prevailing rate at time of closing	Rate changes in accordance with market conditions and VA regulations
What is the maximum term?	30 years	30 years, 32 days
What is the maximum service charge for loan?	1% of the amount of loan	There is no VA charge for securing a loan, but the lender may charge reasonable closing costs, which are usually paid by a borrower,[3] and also a flat charge of up to 1% of the mortgage loan amount for other origination costs
Is there a prepayment penalty?	No	No

[1] Or who served a lesser period and were discharged for a service-connected disability.

[2] If mortgage covers a home approved for FHA mortgage after building begins and before the home is a year old, mortgage limit is 90% of value and closing costs.

[3] Closing costs generally include VA appraisal, credit report, survey, title evidence, and recording fees.

GARNISHMENT OF WAGES

If necessary, a creditor may go to court to collect an overdue debt, and the court may issue a writ of garnishment—an order that the debtor's wages be garnisheed (paid by his employer to his creditor). But a court cannot generally order all a debtor's earnings to be garnisheed. The Federal Consumer Credit Protection Act prohibits garnishment of more than 25 percent of a debtor's disposable earnings (the part of his pay remaining after taxes and other deductions required by law). It also requires that the debtor be left with a weekly disposable income that is at least as much as the federal minimum hourly wage times 30. See ATTACHMENT AND GARNISHMENT. State laws further limit the amount that wages may be garnisheed, as shown in this chart. All earnings are subject to garnishment under court orders for support, BANKRUPTCY, or payment of state or federal taxes.

	How much of your wages is exempt from garnishment?
ALABAMA	For consumer debts, 80% or 50 times federal minimum hourly wage, whichever is greater; for nonconsumer debts, 75%
ALASKA	75% of disposable earnings or $114 per week, whichever is greater
ARIZONA	50% of money earned within 30 days preceding writ of garnishment; after writ, 75% of disposable earnings or 30% of federal minimum hourly wage, whichever is greater
ARKANSAS	$500 ($200 if unmarried) of money earned within 60 days preceding writ of garnishment or 60 days' wages, whichever is less; $25 per week after issuance of writ of garnishment
CALIFORNIA	75% of disposable earnings or 30 times federal minimum hourly wage, whichever is greater
COLORADO	75% of disposable earnings or 30 times federal minimum hourly wage, whichever is greater
CONNECTICUT	75% of disposable earnings or 40 times federal minimum hourly wage, whichever is greater
DELAWARE	85% of earnings (except when garnishment is for debts to state)
DISTRICT OF COLUMBIA	75% of disposable earnings or 30 times federal minimum hourly wage, whichever is greater
FLORIDA	75% of disposable earnings or 30 times federal minimum hourly wage, whichever is greater
GEORGIA	75% of disposable earnings or 30 times federal minimum hourly wage, whichever is greater
HAWAII	95% of the first $100 of monthly earnings; 90% of the next $100; 80% of monthly earnings over $200 (50% in some cases)
IDAHO	75% of disposable earnings or 30 times federal minimum hourly wage, whichever is greater
ILLINOIS	85% of gross earnings or 30 times federal minimum hourly wage, whichever is greater

Chart 9 1098

GARNISHMENT OF WAGES *(continued)*

	How much of your wages is exempt from garnishment?
INDIANA	75% of disposable earnings or 30 times federal minimum hourly wage, whichever is greater (resident householders may qualify for higher exemptions)
IOWA	75% of disposable earnings or 30 times federal minimum hourly wage, whichever is greater (no single garnishment may exceed $250 a year)
KANSAS	75% of disposable earnings or 30 times federal minimum hourly wage, whichever is greater
KENTUCKY	75% of disposable earnings or 30 times federal minimum hourly wage, whichever is greater
LOUISIANA	75% of disposable earnings or 30 times federal minimum hourly wage, whichever is greater
MAINE	100%
MARYLAND	$120 per week or 75% of earnings, whichever is greater; in Caroline, Kent, Queen Anne's, and Worcester counties, 75% of earnings or 30 times federal minimum hourly wage, whichever is greater
MASSACHUSETTS	$125 per week
MICHIGAN	No specific provision
MINNESOTA	75% of disposable earnings or 40 times federal minimum hourly wage, whichever is greater (plus 100% of earnings within 30 days preceding writ of garnishment if necessary for family support)
MISSISSIPPI	75% of earnings
MISSOURI	75% of earnings or 30 times federal minimum hourly wage, whichever is greater; 90% of earnings for resident head of household
MONTANA	100% of wages earned by head of household or a person over 60 within 45 days preceding writ of garnishment; after issuance of writ of garnishment, 50% for gasoline debts incurred by head of household or his family
NEBRASKA	75% of disposable earnings or 30 times federal minimum hourly wage, whichever is greater; 85% of disposable earnings for head of household
NEVADA	75% of disposable weekly earnings or all disposable weekly earnings in excess of 30 times federal minimum hourly wage, whichever is greater
NEW HAMPSHIRE	50 times federal minimum hourly wage earned before issuance of writ of garnishment (except in suit on a debt on a New Hampshire judgment); all wages earned after issuance of writ of garnishment
NEW JERSEY	$48 per week plus 90% of excess; the court may fix a larger percentage if annual income exceeds $7,500

	How much of your wages is exempt from garnishment?
NEW MEXICO	75% of disposable earnings or 40 times federal minimum hourly wage, whichever is greater
NEW YORK	90% of earnings; but if earnings are less than $85 per week, garnishment is not permitted
NORTH CAROLINA	100% of wages earned 60 days preceding order to satisfy judgment debt if wages are necessary for family support
NORTH DAKOTA	75% of disposable earnings or 40 times federal minimum hourly wage, whichever is greater
OHIO	75% of disposable earnings or 30 times federal minimum hourly wage, whichever is greater, within 30 days preceding writ
OKLAHOMA	Before judgment, 75% of all earnings in last 90 days and 100% of earnings for personal services; after judgment, 75% of all earnings and 100% of earnings for 90 days if necessary for family support
OREGON	75% of disposable earnings or 40 times federal minimum hourly wage, whichever is greater
PENNSYLVANIA	100%, but no exemption is given if suit is for support or for board for 4 weeks or less
RHODE ISLAND	$50 per week
SOUTH CAROLINA	100%
SOUTH DAKOTA	No specific provision
TENNESSEE	75% of disposable earnings or 30 times federal minimum hourly wage, whichever is greater
TEXAS	100%
UTAH	75% of disposable earnings or 40 times federal minimum hourly wage, whichever is greater
VERMONT	No specific provision
VIRGINIA	75% of disposable earnings or 30 times federal minimum hourly wage, whichever is greater
WASHINGTON	75% of disposable earnings or 40 times state minimum hourly wage, whichever is greater
WEST VIRGINIA	80% of disposable earnings or 30 times federal minimum hourly wage, whichever is greater
WISCONSIN	75% of disposable earnings or 30 times federal minimum hourly wage, whichever is greater
WYOMING	75% of disposable earnings or 30 times federal minimum hourly wage, whichever is greater

Chart 10   **1100**

HOMESTEAD EXEMPTION LAWS

	How much is protected from creditors?	Is exemption continued for surviving spouse or children?
ALABAMA	Up to 160 acres, value not over $2,000	Yes
ALASKA	Up to 160 acres outside town or 1/4 acre in town, value not over $12,000; $8,000 for mobile home	No
ARIZONA	Value not over $20,000; $10,000 for mobile home	No
ARKANSAS	Up to 160 acres outside town or 1 acre in town, value not over $2,500; up to 80 acres outside town or 1/4 acre in town regardless of value	Yes
CALIFORNIA	Value not over $40,000 for head of household or person age 65 or older; $25,000 for all others	Yes
COLORADO	Value not over $7,500	Yes
CONNECTICUT	Homestead not specifically protected from creditors	——
DELAWARE	Homestead not specifically protected from creditors	——
DISTRICT OF COLUMBIA	Homestead not specifically protected from creditors	——
FLORIDA	Up to 160 acres outside town or 1/2 acre in town	Yes
GEORGIA	Value not over $5,000 combined real and personal property, or up to 50 acres plus 5 acres for each child under 16 outside town, value not over $200, or land in town worth up to $500	Yes
HAWAII	Up to 1 acre, value not over $30,000 for head of household or person age 65 or older; $20,000 for others	Yes, but only for value up to $5,000
IDAHO	Value not over $10,000 for head of household; $4,000 for others	Yes
ILLINOIS	Value not over $10,000	Yes
INDIANA	Homestead not specifically protected from creditors	——
IOWA	Up to 40 acres outside town or 1/2 acre in town, but value at least $500	Yes
KANSAS	Up to 160 acres outside town or 1 acre in town	Yes
KENTUCKY	Value not over $1,000	Yes
LOUISIANA	Up to 160 acres, value not over $15,000	Yes
MAINE	Value not over $5,000	No
MARYLAND	Homestead not specifically protected from creditors	——
MASSACHUSETTS	Value not over $40,000	Yes
MICHIGAN	Up to 40 acres outside town or 1 lot in town, value not over $3,500	Yes
MINNESOTA	Up to 80 acres outside town or 1/2 acre in town	Yes
MISSISSIPPI	Up to 160 acres, value not over $15,000	Yes
MISSOURI	Value not over $10,000	No

If necessary, a creditor may go to court to collect an overdue debt, and the court may order that the debtor's property be sold to satisfy the debt. But there are laws limiting the property that can be sold. Many state laws allow the head of a household to keep the homestead (family residence) free of creditors' claims, but only up to a specified value and sometimes size. Certain states extend this EXEMPTION *for a surviving spouse or children if the debtor dies.*

	How much is protected from creditors?	Is exemption continued for surviving spouse or children?
MONTANA	Up to 320 acres outside town or 1/4 acre in town, value not over $20,000	Yes
NEBRASKA	Up to 160 acres outside town or 2 city blocks, value not over $4,000	Yes
NEVADA	Value not over $25,000	Yes
NEW HAMPSHIRE	Value not over $2,500	Yes
NEW JERSEY	Homestead not specifically protected from creditors	——
NEW MEXICO	Value not over $10,000	Yes
NEW YORK	Value not over $10,000	Yes
NORTH CAROLINA	Value not over $1,000	Yes
NORTH DAKOTA	Value not over $60,000	No
OHIO	Value not over $1,000	Yes
OKLAHOMA	Up to 160 acres outside town or 1 acre in town, value not over $5,000; 1/4 acre in town regardless of value	No
OREGON	Up to 160 acres outside town or 1 block in town, value not over $12,000	No
PENNSYLVANIA	Homestead not specifically protected from creditors	——
RHODE ISLAND	Homestead not specifically protected from creditors	——
SOUTH CAROLINA	Value not over $1,000	Yes
SOUTH DAKOTA	Up to 160 acres outside town or 1 acre in town, value not over $30,000; but land acquired under U.S. mining law is limited to 40 acres outside town or 1 acre in town	Yes
TENNESSEE	Value not over $1,000	Yes
TEXAS	Up to 200 acres outside town or 1 or more lots in town, value up to $10,000	Yes
UTAH	Value not over $6,000 for head of household plus $2,000 for spouse and $800 for each additional family member	Yes, but only for value up to $4,000 plus $600 for each minor and dependent child
VERMONT	Value not over $5,000	Yes
VIRGINIA	Value not over $5,000	Yes
WASHINGTON	Value not over $20,000	Yes
WEST VIRGINIA	Value not over $5,000	Yes
WISCONSIN	Value not over $25,000	Yes
WYOMING	Value not over $6,000	Yes

Chart 11 1102

TIME LIMITS FOR PRESENTING CLAIMS AGAINST AN ESTATE

ALABAMA	6 months after the grant of letters testamentary or letters of administration
ALASKA	4 months after first publication of notice to creditors; if no publication, 3 years after decedent's death[1]
ARIZONA	4 months after first publication of notice to creditors; if no publication, 3 years after decedent's death[1]
ARKANSAS	6 months after first publication of notice to creditors
CALIFORNIA	4 months after first publication of notice to creditors[2]
COLORADO	4 months after first publication of notice to creditors; if no publication, 1 year after decedent's death[1]
CONNECTICUT	Not more than 12 months nor less than 3 months from the date creditors are ordered by Probate Court to present their claims[3,4]
DELAWARE	6 months after issuance of letters testamentary or letters of administration
DISTRICT OF COLUMBIA	No statutory provision, but distribution begins 13 months after issuance of letters; time limit may be extended 4 months
FLORIDA	3 months after first publication of notice to creditors
GEORGIA	3 months after publication of last notice to creditors
HAWAII	4 months after first publication of notice to creditors; if no publication, 3 years after decedent's death[1]
IDAHO	4 months after first publication of notice to creditors; if no publication, 3 years after decedent's death[1]
ILLINOIS	6 months after issuance of letters testamentary or letters of administration
INDIANA	5 months after first publication of notice to creditors
IOWA	6 months after second publication of notice to creditors
KANSAS	6 months after first publication of notice to creditors
KENTUCKY	1 year after appointment of executor or administrator; if none appointed, 3 years after decedent's death

[1] The time limit does not apply to certain insurance claims or the foreclosure of lien claims.

[2] If claimant was out of state at time of notice, he may present his claim within 1 year of such time limit and before petition for final distribution of the estate has been filed.

Creditors' claims against the estate of a deceased person must be filed with the executor or administrator within the time allowed by law. A person is an executor if he is distributing the deceased's property in accordance with a will. An administrator is appointed by the court to distribute the property of someone who died without a will in accordance with the state's laws of DESCENT AND DISTRIBUTION. *See also* EXECUTORS AND ADMINISTRATORS.

LOUISIANA	No statutory limit
MAINE	6 months after appointment of executor or administrator
MARYLAND	6 months after appointment of administrator[1]
MASSACHUSETTS	Within 2 months of notice to creditors or within 9 months of giving bond, whichever is later. The Probate Court may extend the time limit
MICHIGAN	4 months after first publication of notice to creditors or after claim is due, whichever is later; if no notice, 3 years after decedent's death
MINNESOTA	4 months after clerk's notice to creditors; if no publication, within 3 years of decedent's death[1]
MISSISSIPPI	3 months after first publication of notice to creditors
MISSOURI	6 months after first publication of notice of administration
MONTANA	4 months after first publication of notice to creditors; if no publication, within 3 years of decedent's death[1]
NEBRASKA	2 months after first publication of notice to creditors; if no notice, within 3 years after decedent's death[1]
NEVADA	3 months after first publication of notice to creditors
NEW HAMPSHIRE	6 months after issuance of letters testamentary or letters of administration
NEW JERSEY	6 months after court order to publish notice to creditors
NEW MEXICO	2 months after first publication of notice to creditors; if no notice, within 3 years of decedent's death[1]
NEW YORK	Date specified in public notice to creditors or, if none is published, 7 months after issuance of letters testamentary or letters of administration
NORTH CAROLINA	6 months after first publication of notice to creditors
NORTH DAKOTA	3 months after first publication of notice to creditors; if no publication, within 3 years of decedent's death
OHIO	3 months after appointment of executor or administrator

[3] Time limit may be extended if merited.

[4] Probate Court sets the exact time limit.

Chart 11

1104

TIME LIMITS FOR PRESENTING CLAIMS
AGAINST AN ESTATE *(continued)*

OKLAHOMA	2 months after first publication of notice to creditors. But if the claimant was out of state at time of notice, he may present his claim anytime before final distribution of the estate
OREGON	4 months after first publication of notice to creditors; if no publication, within 3 years after decedent's death[5]
PENNSYLVANIA	No statutory time limit, but all claims must be presented in court at the audit of the executor's or administrator's account
RHODE ISLAND	6 months after first publication of notice to creditors
SOUTH CAROLINA	5 months after first publication of notice to creditors. Mortgages and judgments that were liens at the time of decedent's death are not subject to the time limit
SOUTH DAKOTA	2 months after first publication of notice to creditors. But if the claimant was out of state at time of notice, he may present his claim anytime before final distribution of the estate
TENNESSEE	6 months after first publication of notice to creditors
TEXAS	6 months after issuance of letters testamentary or letters of administration[5]
UTAH	3 months after first publication of notice to creditors; if no notice, within 3 years after decedent's death[1]
VERMONT	4 months after publication of notice to creditors; if no publication, within 3 years of decedent's death[1]
VIRGINIA	No statutory limit
WASHINGTON	4 months after first publication of notice to creditors. Certain liability or casualty insurance claims are not subject to the time limit
WEST VIRGINIA	Not less than 4 months nor more than 6 months after first publication of notice to creditors; time limit specified in notice
WISCONSIN	3 months from date of court order for publication of notice to creditors[4]
WYOMING	3 months after first publication of notice to creditors. But if the claimant was out of state at time of notice, he may present his claim anytime before final distribution of the estate

[5] Claims presented after that date will be honored only if there is money remaining after payment of claims presented before that date.

ADVERSE POSSESSION: WHEN OTHERS OCCUPY YOUR LAND

Under the laws of ADVERSE POSSESSION, *others who use or occupy your land openly and unchallenged may claim ownership of it after a certain period of time has passed. See* LIMITATIONS OF ACTIONS. *This chart shows the statutory period in each state. The period of time is shorter in some states if the land is occupied under color of title—that is, if the person occupying the land appears to be the owner because he has a document saying that he is, but that document has not given him valid legal title.*

Number of years after which original owner cannot claim his property

ALABAMA	10^1	KENTUCKY	15	NORTH DAKOTA	20^{11}
ALASKA	10^2	LOUISIANA	30^6	OHIO	21
ARIZONA	10^3	MAINE	20	OKLAHOMA	15
ARKANSAS	7	MARYLAND	20	OREGON	10
CALIFORNIA	5	MASSACHUSETTS	20^7	PENNSYLVANIA	21
COLORADO	18^4	MICHIGAN	15	RHODE ISLAND	10
CONNECTICUT	15	MINNESOTA	15	SOUTH CAROLINA	10
DELAWARE	20	MISSISSIPPI	10	SOUTH DAKOTA	20
D.C.	15	MISSOURI	10	TENNESSEE	20^2
FLORIDA	7	MONTANA	5	TEXAS	25^{12}
GEORGIA	20^5	NEBRASKA	10	UTAH	7
HAWAII	20	NEVADA	5^8	VERMONT	15
IDAHO	5	NEW HAMPSHIRE	20	VIRGINIA	15
ILLINOIS	20	NEW JERSEY	30^9	WASHINGTON	10
INDIANA	10	NEW MEXICO	10	WEST VIRGINIA	10
IOWA	10	NEW YORK	10	WISCONSIN	20^{13}
KANSAS	15	NORTH CAROLINA	20^{10}	WYOMING	10

[1] 20 years in some cases.

[2] Under color of title, 7 years.

[3] For up to 160 acres if the land is enclosed or described in some recorded memorandum; 5 years if the land is a city lot or held under a recorded deed and the person possessing it has used it and paid taxes on it; or 3 years under color of title.

[4] Or 7 years under color of title, all taxes having been paid.

[5] Or 7 years under color of title.

[6] Or 10 years under color of title and in good faith.

[7] Title to registered land cannot be acquired by adverse possession.

[8] Or 2 years for recovery of mining claims.

[9] Or 60 years for woodlands and uncultivated tracts.

[10] Or 7 years for property with known, visible boundaries held under color of title.

[11] Or 10 years if all taxes and assessments have been paid.

[12] Or fewer years if held under color of title or some other claim.

[13] Or 10 years under color of title based on a written document or a judgment.

Chart 13   1106

REDEEMING PROPERTY AFTER FORECLOSURE

The person who holds a MORTGAGE *on your real estate has the right to start a foreclosure suit to take over your property whenever you miss a payment. Eventually, the property can be sold to pay off the balance of the mortgage. Before the sale, you ordinarily have the right to redeem the*

	Time allowed for redemption			Time allowed for redemption
ALABAMA	1 year		ILLINOIS	1 year
ALASKA	1 year		INDIANA	No statutory right to redeem after sale
ARIZONA	6 months		IOWA	1 year
ARKANSAS	1 year		KANSAS	1 year[3]
CALIFORNIA	1 year		KENTUCKY	1 year[4]
COLORADO	75 days[1]		LOUISIANA	No statutory right to redeem after sale
CONNECTICUT	No statutory right to redeem after sale		MAINE	90 days[5]
DELAWARE	No statutory right to redeem after sale		MARYLAND	No statutory right to redeem after sale
DISTRICT OF COLUMBIA	No statutory right to redeem after sale		MASSACHUSETTS	3 years
FLORIDA	No statutory right to redeem after sale		MICHIGAN	6 months
GEORGIA	No statutory right to redeem after sale		MINNESOTA	6 months
HAWAII	No statutory right to redeem after sale		MISSISSIPPI	No statutory right to redeem after sale
IDAHO	6 months[2]		MISSOURI	1 year

[1] Or 6 months for agricultural real estate.

[2] Or 1 year if over 20 acres.

[3] Or 6 months where court finds that owner abandoned land.

[4] Applies only if property is sold for less than 2/3 its appraised value.

[5] Or 1 year for mortgages executed before Oct. 1, 1975.

[6] After a judgment for the balance due on the debt.

[7] 1 year for mortgages executed before Apr. 1, 1968.

[8] But the foreclosure court may allow up to 6 months after the sale.

property by paying everything that is owed on the mortgage plus costs and interest. In addition, many states have a law that allows you to redeem your property even after the foreclosure sale. The chart below shows how much time you have after the sale to redeem your property in those states.

	Time allowed for redemption
MONTANA	1 year
NEBRASKA	Until confirmation of sale
NEVADA	1 year
NEW HAMPSHIRE	1 year
NEW JERSEY	6 months[6]
NEW MEXICO	9 months
NEW YORK	No statutory right to redeem after sale
NORTH CAROLINA	No statutory right to redeem after sale
NORTH DAKOTA	1 year
OHIO	Until confirmation of sale
OKLAHOMA	No statutory right to redeem after sale
OREGON	1 year
PENNSYLVANIA	No statutory right to redeem after sale

	Time allowed for redemption
RHODE ISLAND	No statutory right to redeem after sale
SOUTH CAROLINA	No statutory right to redeem after sale
SOUTH DAKOTA	1 year
TENNESSEE	2 years
TEXAS	No statutory right to redeem after sale
UTAH	6 months
VERMONT	6 months[7]
VIRGINIA	No statutory right to redeem after sale[8]
WASHINGTON	1 year[9]
WEST VIRGINIA	No statutory right to redeem after sale
WISCONSIN	No statutory right to redeem after sale
WYOMING	3 months[10]

[9] Or 8 months for mortgages executed after June 30, 1961, on nonagricultural property where creditor waived right to a deficiency judgment; no right to redeem improved agricultural land abandoned at least 6 months before foreclosure.

[10] For agricultural property, 9 months after sale or until Nov. 1 of that year, whichever is later.

Chart 14   1108

REQUIREMENTS FOR A VALID WILL

In order to be valid, your WILL must meet certain legal requirements, which vary from state to state, as shown in this chart. First, your will cannot be accepted if you are not legally old enough to make it. Second, the will must generally be witnessed by a minimum number of persons. Some states, however, recognize a holographic will—one written entirely in the hand of the person making it. A holographic will does not usually have to be witnessed.

	At what age may you make a will?	How many witnesses are needed?	Are holographic wills recognized?		At what age may you make a will?	How many witnesses are needed?	Are holographic wills recognized?
ALABAMA	19	2	No	MONTANA	18	2	Yes
ALASKA	19	2	Yes	NEBRASKA	18	2	Yes
ARIZONA	18	2	Yes	NEVADA	18	2	Yes
ARKANSAS	18	2	Yes	NEW HAMPSHIRE	18	3	No
CALIFORNIA	18	2	Yes	NEW JERSEY	18	2	Yes
COLORADO	18	2	Yes	NEW MEXICO	18	2	No
CONNECTICUT	18	2	No	NEW YORK	18	2	Yes[4]
DELAWARE	18	2	No	NORTH CAROLINA	18	2	Yes
D.C.	18	2	No	NORTH DAKOTA	18	2	Yes
FLORIDA	18	2	No	OHIO	18	2	No
GEORGIA	14	2	No	OKLAHOMA	18	2	Yes
HAWAII	18	2	No	OREGON	18[2]	2	No
IDAHO	18	2	Yes	PENNSYLVANIA	18	2	Yes
ILLINOIS	18	2	No	RHODE ISLAND	18	2	Yes[5]
INDIANA	18[1]	2	No	SOUTH CAROLINA	18	3	Yes[5]
IOWA	18	2	No	SOUTH DAKOTA	18	2	Yes
KANSAS	18	2	No	TENNESSEE	18	2	Yes
KENTUCKY	18	2	Yes	TEXAS	18[2]	2	Yes
LOUISIANA	16	2	Yes	UTAH	18	2	Yes
MAINE	18[2]	3	No	VERMONT	18	3	No
MARYLAND	18	2	Yes[3]	VIRGINIA	18	2	Yes
MASSACHUSETTS	18	2	No	WASHINGTON	18	2	No
MICHIGAN	18	2	Yes	WEST VIRGINIA	18	2	Yes
MINNESOTA	18	2	No	WISCONSIN	18	2	No
MISSISSIPPI	18	2	Yes	WYOMING	19	2	Yes
MISSOURI	18	2	No				

[1] Younger if a serviceman or a merchant marine.

[2] Younger if married or widowed.

[3] But only if made by a serviceman on duty outside U.S. territory.

[4] But only if made by a serviceman during armed conflict or by a merchant marine.

[5] But only if made by a serviceman on active duty or by a merchant marine and for personal property, not real estate.

WHEN YOUR SPOUSE MAY LEGALLY BE PRESUMED DEAD

Laws in each state provide that a person missing for the number of years shown here may legally be presumed dead and that his or her estate may then be distributed according to a WILL or the state laws of DESCENT AND DISTRIBUTION. See also DEATH. These laws do not apply to the number of years a person must be missing before his or her spouse can get a DIVORCE, although in some states a divorce can be obtained after a spouse has been missing without explanation for five successive years.

ALABAMA	7 years	MONTANA	7 years
ALASKA	5 years	NEBRASKA	5 years
ARIZONA	5 years	NEVADA	7 years
ARKANSAS	5 years	NEW HAMPSHIRE	6 years[5]
CALIFORNIA	7 years	NEW JERSEY	5 years
COLORADO	7 years[1]	NEW MEXICO	5 years
CONNECTICUT	7 years[2]	NEW YORK	5 years
DELAWARE	7 years	NORTH CAROLINA	7 years[6]
D.C.	7 years	NORTH DAKOTA	7 years
FLORIDA	5 years[1]	OHIO	5 years
GEORGIA	7 years	OKLAHOMA	7 years
HAWAII	5 years	OREGON	7 years
IDAHO	5 years	PENNSYLVANIA	7 years
ILLINOIS	7 years	RHODE ISLAND	7 years[4]
INDIANA	5 years	SOUTH CAROLINA	7 years[4]
IOWA	5 years	SOUTH DAKOTA	7 years
KANSAS	7 years[1]	TENNESSEE	7 years[6]
KENTUCKY	7 years	TEXAS	7 years
LOUISIANA	10 years	UTAH	7 years[4]
MAINE	7 years	VERMONT	5 years[7]
MARYLAND	No statutory provision[3]	VIRGINIA	7 years
MASSACHUSETTS	7 years[4]	WASHINGTON	7 years
MICHIGAN	7 years	WEST VIRGINIA	7 years
MINNESOTA	4 years[1]	WISCONSIN	7 years[4]
MISSISSIPPI	7 years	WYOMING	7 years
MISSOURI	7 years		

[1] A diligent search for the missing person must be made before he or she is presumed dead.

[2] A person's estate will be distributed after 7 years if a bond is posted; otherwise, 12 years after disappearance.

[3] The court may make the presumption if the evidence warrants it.

[4] Common-law presumption.

[5] The court may appoint an administrator of the missing person's estate after 1 year of absence, but the estate may not be distributed until 5 years after appointment of administrator.

[6] The presumption is not mandatory, but the court may decide if such presumption is justified.

[7] Court will permit administration of missing person's estate after 5 years but will only distribute property 5 years from date of administration if a bond is posted. If no bond is posted, distribution is 7 years after administration.

Chart 16 1110

WHAT HAPPENS TO YOUR PROPERTY IF YOU DIE

Should you die without a valid will, your property will be distributed according to the laws of DESCENT AND DISTRIBUTION in your state, which are outlined in this chart. If you have a life ESTATE in real property (real estate), you have the right to use the property during your lifetime but not the right to sell it or pass it on to an heir. After the holder of a life estate dies, the real property (called the remainder) passes on to the person or persons designated by law. Some states have life estate provisions; others do not. If you are

	WHEN YOUR CLOSEST SURVIVING RELATIVE IS		
	Your wife or husband and children or their issue:		Your wife or husband and no children or their issue survive:
	What share of your real property (real estate) does each receive?	What share of your personal property does each receive?	What must your spouse share with your surviving parent(s)?
ALABAMA	If husband survives, life estate; if wife survives, life estate in 1/3; children, remainder	If husband survives, 1/2; children, 1/2. If wife survives with (1) 1 child: wife, 1/2; child, 1/2. (2) With 2-4 children: wife and children share equally. (3) With more than 4 children: wife, 1/5; children, 4/5	If husband survives, life estate plus 1/2 personal property; parents, remainder of real estate and rest of personal property. If wife survives, life estate in 1/3 plus all personal property; parent(s), remainder
ALASKA	Spouse, $50,000 plus 1/2 balance; children, residue	Same as real estate	Spouse, first $50,000 plus 1/2 balance of property; parent(s), residue
ARIZONA	Spouse, all	Same as real estate	Nothing
ARKANSAS	Spouse, life estate in 1/3; children, remainder	Spouse, 1/3; children, 2/3	If married less than 3 years, spouse, 1/2; parent(s), 1/2. If married 3 years or more, nothing
CALIFORNIA	Separate property: (1) with 1 child: spouse, 1/2; child, 1/2. (2) With more than 1 child: spouse, 1/3; children, 2/3. Community property: all to spouse	Same as real estate	Spouse, all community property plus 1/2 separately owned property; parent(s), balance
COLORADO	Spouse, $25,000 plus 1/2 balance; children, residue[1]	Same as real estate	Nothing
CONNECTICUT	Spouse, $50,000 plus 1/2 balance; children, residue[1]	Same as real estate	Spouse, $5,000 plus 3/4 residue; parent(s), 1/4
DELAWARE	Spouse, life estate; children, remainder	Spouse, $50,000 plus 1/2 balance; children, residue[1]	Spouse, life estate and $50,000 plus 1/2 balance; parent(s), remainder and balance

[1] If surviving children are not the issue of the surviving spouse: spouse, 1/2 estate; decedent's issue, residue.

WITHOUT A WILL

survived only by your children, your property will be equally divided among them; if one or more of your children are deceased, their issue (children, grandchildren, etc.) will inherit their deceased parent's share and divide it equally among themselves. This is called inheriting per stirpes. Per stirpes distribution is also made when a person dies leaving only brothers and sisters or their issue. Residue, in this chart, means what remains of an estate after prior claims have been paid.

WHEN YOUR CLOSEST SURVIVING RELATIVE IS		
Your wife or husband and no children or their issue survive:	Your parent(s) (neither wife nor husband nor children nor their issue survive):	Your brother(s) and sister(s) or their issue (neither parents nor wife nor husband nor children nor their issue survive):
What must your spouse share with your brother(s) and sister(s) or their issue if your parents are not alive?	What share does each receive?	What share does each receive?
If husband survives, life estate plus 1/2 personal property; brothers and sisters, remainder of real estate and balance of personal property. If wife survives, life estate in 1/3 plus all personal property; brothers and sisters, remainder	(1) If both parents survive, 1/2 to each. (2) If 1 parent, 1/2 to parent; 1/2 to brothers and sisters or their issue *per stirpes*. (3) If 1 parent and no brothers and sisters or their issue *per stirpes*, all to parent	Equal shares to brothers and sisters or their issue *per stirpes*
Nothing	1/2 to each parent or all to surviving parent	Equal shares to brothers and sisters or their issue *per stirpes*
Nothing	1/2 to each parent or all to surviving parent	Equal shares to brothers and sisters or their issue *per stirpes*
If married less than 3 years, spouse, 1/2; brothers and sisters, 1/2	1/2 to each parent or all to surviving parent	None; equal shares to heirs of deceased spouse
Spouse, 1/2 separately owned property; brothers and sisters, 1/2	1/2 to each parent or all to surviving parent	Equal shares to brothers and sisters or their issue *per stirpes*
Nothing	1/2 to each parent or all to surviving parent	Equal shares to brothers and sisters or their issue *per stirpes*
Nothing	1/2 to each parent or all to surviving parent	(1) Equal shares to brothers and sisters or their issue *per stirpes*. (2) Equal shares to half-brothers and half-sisters or their issue *per stirpes*
Nothing	1/2 to each parent or all to surviving parent	Equal shares to brothers and sisters or their issue *per stirpes*

Chart 16 1112

WHAT HAPPENS TO YOUR PROPERTY IF YOU DIE WITHOUT A WILL (continued)

	WHEN YOUR CLOSEST SURVIVING RELATIVE IS		
	Your wife or husband and children or their issue:		Your wife or husband and no children or their issue survive:
	What share of your real property (real estate) does each receive?	What share of your personal property does each receive?	What must your spouse share with your surviving parent(s)?
DISTRICT OF COLUMBIA	Spouse, life estate in 1/3; children, remainder	Spouse, 1/3; children, 2/3	Spouse, 1/2; parent(s), 1/2
FLORIDA	Spouse, $20,000 plus 1/2 balance; children, residue[1]	Same as real estate	Nothing
GEORGIA	Wife, equal shares with children but never less than 1/5; husband, equal shares with children regardless of number of children	Same as real estate	Nothing
HAWAII	Spouse, 1/2; children, 1/2	Same as real estate	Spouse, 1/2; parent(s), 1/2
IDAHO	Separate property: spouse, $50,000 plus 1/2 balance; children, residue.[1] Community property: all to spouse	Same as real estate	Spouse, all community property, 1/2 separate property; parent(s), 1/2 separate property
ILLINOIS	Spouse, 1/3; children, 2/3	Same as real estate	Nothing
INDIANA	(1) With 1 child: spouse, 1/2; child, 1/2. (2) With more than 1 child: spouse, 1/3; children, 2/3	Same as real estate	Spouse, 3/4; parent(s), 1/4
IOWA	Spouse, 1/3;[2] children, 2/3	Same as real estate	Spouse, $25,000 of nonexempt property plus 1/2 balance; parent(s), other 1/2 residue
KANSAS	Spouse, 1/2; children, 1/2	Same as real estate	Nothing
KENTUCKY	Spouse, dower or curtesy; children, remainder	Spouse 1/2; children, 1/2	Spouse, dower or curtesy plus 1/2 personal property; parent(s), remainder of real estate and residue of personal property
LOUISIANA	Spouse, life estate; children, remainder	Same as real estate	Spouse, 1/2; parent(s), 1/2
MAINE	Spouse, 1/3; children, 2/3	Same as real estate	Spouse, $10,000 plus 1/2 personal property and 2/3 real estate; parent(s), residue
MARYLAND	Spouse, 1/2; children, 1/2	Same as real estate	Spouse, 1/2; parent(s), 1/2
MASSACHUSETTS	Spouse, 1/2; children, 1/2	Same as real estate	Spouse, $50,000 plus 1/2 balance; parent(s), residue
MICHIGAN	Spouse, $60,000 plus 1/2 balance; children, residue[1]	Same as real estate	Spouse, $60,000 plus 1/2 balance; parent(s), residue

[2] If 1/3 does not equal $25,000, then spouse takes first $25,000.

WHEN YOUR CLOSEST SURVIVING RELATIVE IS		
Your wife or husband and no children or their issue survive:	Your parent(s) (neither wife nor husband nor children nor their issue survive):	Your brother(s) and sister(s) or their issue (neither parents nor wife nor husband nor children nor their issue survive):
What must your spouse share with your brother(s) and sister(s) or their issue if your parents are not alive?	What share does each receive?	What share does each receive?
Spouse, 1/2; brothers and sisters, 1/2	1/2 to each parent or all to surviving parent	Equal shares to brothers and sisters or their issue *per stirpes*
Nothing	1/2 to each parent or all to surviving parent	Equal shares to brothers and sisters or their issue *per stirpes*
Nothing	Equal shares to parents, brothers, and sisters or their issue *per stirpes*	Equal shares to brothers and sisters or their issue *per stirpes*
Nothing	1/2 to each parent or all to surviving parent	Equal shares to brothers and sisters or their issue *per stirpes*
Nothing	1/2 to each parent or all to surviving parent	Equal shares to brothers and sisters or their issue *per stirpes*
Nothing	Equal shares to parents, brothers, and sisters or their issue *per stirpes*, but if one parent is dead, surviving parent takes a double share	Equal shares to brothers and sisters or their issue *per stirpes*
Nothing	1/4 to each surviving parent and the rest equally to brothers and sisters or their issue *per stirpes*	Equal shares to brothers and sisters or their issue *per stirpes*
Spouse, first $25,000 of nonexempt property plus 1/2 balance; brothers and sisters, residue	1/2 to each parent or all to surviving parent	Equal shares to brothers and sisters or their issue *per stirpes*
Nothing	1/2 to each parent or all to surviving parent	Equal shares to brothers and sisters or their issue *per stirpes*
Spouse, dower or curtesy plus 1/2 personal property; brothers and sisters, remainder and balance of personal property	1/2 to each parent or all to surviving parent	Equal shares to brothers and sisters or their issue *per stirpes*
Nothing	1/4 to each parent and the rest in equal shares to brothers and sisters or their issue *per stirpes*	Equal shares to brothers and sisters or their issue *per stirpes*
Spouse, $10,000 plus 1/2 personal property and 2/3 real estate; brothers and sisters, balance	1/2 to each parent or all to surviving parent	Equal shares to brothers and sisters or their issue *per stirpes*
Nothing	1/2 to each parent or all to surviving parent	Equal shares to brothers and sisters or their issue *per stirpes*
Spouse, $50,000 plus 1/2 balance; brothers and sisters, residue	1/2 to each parent or all to surviving parent	Equal shares to brothers and sisters or their issue *per stirpes*
Nothing	1/2 to each parent or all to surviving parent	Equal shares to brothers and sisters or their issue *per stirpes*

Chart 16
1114

WHAT HAPPENS TO YOUR PROPERTY IF YOU DIE WITHOUT A WILL *(continued)*

	WHEN YOUR CLOSEST SURVIVING RELATIVE IS		
	Your wife or husband and children or their issue:		Your wife or husband and no children or their issue survive:
	What share of your real property (real estate) does each receive?	What share of your personal property does each receive?	What must your spouse share with your surviving parent(s)?
MINNESOTA	(1) With 1 child: spouse, 1/2; child, 1/2. (2) With more than 1 child: spouse, 1/3; children, 2/3	Same as real estate	Nothing
MISSISSIPPI	Equal shares to spouse and children	Same as real estate	Nothing
MISSOURI	Spouse, 1/2; children, 1/2	Same as real estate	Spouse, 1/2; 1/2 divided equally among parent(s), brothers, and sisters
MONTANA	If children are issue of surviving spouse, spouse, all[3]	Same as real estate	Nothing
NEBRASKA	Spouse, $35,000 plus 1/2 balance; children, residue[1]	Same as real estate	Spouse, $35,000 plus 1/2 balance; parent(s), residue
NEVADA	Separate property: (1) with 1 child: spouse, 1/2; child, 1/2. (2) With more than 1 child: spouse, 1/3; children, 2/3. Community property: all to spouse	Same as real estate	Spouse, all community property, 1/2 separately owned property; parent(s), other 1/2
NEW HAMPSHIRE	Spouse, $50,000 plus 1/2 balance; children, residue[1]	Same as real estate	Spouse, $50,000 plus 1/2 balance; parent(s), residue
NEW JERSEY	Spouse, $50,000 plus 1/2 balance; children, residue[1]	Same as real estate	Spouse, $50,000 plus 1/2 balance; parent(s), residue
NEW MEXICO	Separate property: spouse, 1/4; children, 3/4. Community property: all to spouse	Same as real estate	Nothing
NEW YORK	(1) With 1 child: spouse $4,000 plus 1/2 balance; child, residue. (2) With more than 1 child: spouse, $4,000 plus 1/3 balance; children, residue	Same as real estate	Spouse, $25,000 plus 1/2 balance; parent(s), residue
NORTH CAROLINA	(1) With 1 child: spouse, 1/2; child, 1/2. (2) With more than 1 child: spouse, 1/3; children, 2/3	Same as real estate	Spouse, 1/2 real estate plus $10,000 personal property and 1/2 balance; parent(s), residue
NORTH DAKOTA	Spouse, $50,000 plus 1/2 balance; children, residue[1]	Same as real estate	Spouse, $50,000 plus 1/2 balance; parent(s), residue
OHIO	(1) With 1 child: spouse, $30,000 plus 1/2 balance; child, residue.[4] (2) With more than 1 child: spouse, $30,000 plus 1/3 balance; children, residue[5]	Same as real estate	Nothing
OKLAHOMA	(1) With 1 child: spouse, 1/2; child, 1/2. (2) With more than 1 child: spouse, 1/3; children, 2/3	Same as real estate	Spouse, 1/2; parent(s), 1/2

[3] If surviving children are not the issue of the surviving spouse: with 1 child, spouse, 1/2; child, 1/2. With more than 1 child: spouse, 1/3; children, 2/3.

[4] If surviving child is not the natural or adopted child of the surviving spouse: spouse, $10,000 plus 1/2 balance; child, residue.

WHEN YOUR CLOSEST SURVIVING RELATIVE IS		
Your wife or husband and no children or their issue survive:	**Your parent(s) (neither wife nor husband nor children nor their issue survive):**	**Your brother(s) and sister(s) or their issue (neither parents nor wife nor husband nor children nor their issue survive):**
What must your spouse share with your brother(s) and sister(s) or their issue if your parents are not alive?	**What share does each receive?**	**What share does each receive?**
Nothing	1/2 to each parent or all to surviving parent	Equal shares to brothers and sisters or their issue *per stirpes*
Nothing	Equal shares to parents, brothers, and sisters or their issue *per stirpes*	Equal shares to brothers and sisters or their issue *per stirpes*
Spouse, 1/2; 1/2 divided equally among brothers and sisters	Equal shares to parents, brothers, and sisters or their issue *per stirpes*	Equal shares to brothers and sisters or their issue *per stirpes*
Nothing	1/2 to each parent or all to surviving parent	Equal shares to brothers and sisters or their issue *per stirpes*
Nothing	1/2 to each parent or all to surviving parent	Equal shares to brothers and sisters or their issue *per stirpes*
Spouse, 1/2 separately owned property; brothers and sisters, 1/2	1/2 to each parent or all to surviving parent	Equal shares to brothers and sisters or their issue *per stirpes*
Nothing	1/2 to each parent or all to surviving parent	Equal shares to brothers and sisters or their issue *per stirpes*
Nothing	1/2 to each parent or all to surviving parent	Equal shares to brothers and sisters or to their issue *per stirpes*
Nothing	1/2 to each parent or all to surviving parent	Equal shares to brothers and sisters or their issue *per stirpes*
Nothing	1/2 to each parent or all to surviving parent	Equal shares to brothers and sisters or their issue *per stirpes*
Nothing	1/2 to each parent or all to surviving parent	Equal shares to brothers and sisters or their issue *per stirpes*
Nothing	1/2 to each parent or all to surviving parent	Equal shares to brothers and sisters or their issue *per stirpes*
Nothing	1/2 to each parent or all to surviving parent	Equal shares to brothers and sisters or their issue *per stirpes*
Spouse, 1/2; brothers and sisters, 1/2	1/2 to each parent or all to surviving parent	Equal shares to brothers and sisters or their issue *per stirpes*

[5] If the surviving children are not the natural or adopted children of surviving spouse: spouse, $10,000 plus 1/3 balance; children, residue.

Chart 16   1116

WHAT HAPPENS TO YOUR PROPERTY IF YOU DIE WITHOUT A WILL *(continued)*

| | WHEN YOUR CLOSEST SURVIVING RELATIVE IS | | |
| | Your wife or husband and children or their issue: | | Your wife or husband and no children or their issue survive: |
	What share of your real property (real estate) does each receive?	What share of your personal property does each receive?	What must your spouse share with your surviving parent(s)?
OREGON	Spouse, 1/2; children, 1/2	Same as real estate	Nothing
PENNSYLVANIA	(1) With 1 child: spouse, 1/2; child, 1/2. (2) With more than 1 child: spouse, 1/3; children, 2/3	Same as real estate	Spouse, $20,000 plus 1/2 balance; parent(s), residue
RHODE ISLAND	Spouse, life estate; children, remainder	Spouse, 1/2; children, 1/2	Spouse, life estate plus $50,000 personal property and 1/2 balance; parent(s), residue
SOUTH CAROLINA	(1) With 1 child: spouse, 1/2; child, 1/2. (2) With more than 1 child: spouse, 1/3; children, 2/3	Same as real estate	Spouse, 1/2; 1/2 divided equally among parent(s), brothers, and sisters
SOUTH DAKOTA	(1) With 1 child: spouse, 1/2; child, 1/2. (2) With more than 1 child: spouse, 1/3; children, 2/3	Same as real estate	Spouse, $100,000 plus 1/2 balance; parent(s), residue
TENNESSEE	Equal shares to spouse and children, but spouse must get at least 1/3 share	Same as real estate	Nothing
TEXAS	Separate property: spouse, life estate in 1/3; children, remainder. Community property: spouse, 1/2; children, 1/2	Separate property: spouse, 1/3; children, 2/3. Community property: spouse, 1/2; children, 1/2	Spouse, all community property and personal property plus 1/2 separately owned real estate; parents, brothers, and sisters, residue in equal shares
UTAH	Spouse, $50,000 plus 1/2 balance; children, residue[1]	Same as real estate	Spouse, $100,000 plus 1/2 balance; parent(s), residue
VERMONT	(1) With 1 child: spouse, 1/2; child, 1/2. (2) With more than 1 child: spouse, 1/3; children, 2/3	Spouse, all clothing and ornaments plus 1/3 balance; children, residue	Spouse, $25,000 plus 1/2 balance; parent(s), residue
VIRGINIA	Spouse, life estate in 1/3; children, remainder	Spouse, 1/3; children, 2/3	Nothing
WASHINGTON	Spouse, all community property, 1/2 other property; children, residue	Same as real estate	Spouse, all community property plus 3/4 balance; parent(s), residue
WEST VIRGINIA	Spouse, life estate in 1/3; children, remainder	Spouse, 1/3; children, 2/3	Nothing
WISCONSIN	(1) With 1 child: spouse, $25,000 plus 1/2 balance; child, residue. (2) With more than 1 child: spouse, 1/3; children, residue	Same as real estate	Nothing
WYOMING	Spouse, 1/2; children, 1/2	Same as real estate	Spouse, $20,000 plus 3/4 balance; parent(s), residue

WHEN YOUR CLOSEST SURVIVING RELATIVE IS		
Your wife or husband and no children or their issue survive:	Your parent(s) (neither wife nor husband nor children nor their issue survive):	Your brother(s) and sister(s) or their issue (neither parents nor wife nor husband nor children nor their issue survive):
What must your spouse share with your brother(s) and sister(s) or their issue if your parents are not alive?	What share does each receive?	What share does each receive?
Nothing	1/2 to each parent or all to surviving parent	Equal shares to brothers and sisters or their issue *per stirpes*
Spouse, $20,000 plus 1/2 balance; brothers and sisters, residue	1/2 to each parent or all to surviving parent	Equal shares to brothers and sisters or their issue *per stirpes*
Spouse, life estate in all real property plus 1/2 balance; brothers and sisters, residue	1/2 to each parent or all to surviving parent	Equal shares to brothers and sisters or their issue *per stirpes*
Spouse, 1/2; 1/2 divided equally among brothers and sisters	Equal shares to parents, brothers, and sisters or their issue *per stirpes*	Equal shares to brothers and sisters or their issue *per stirpes*
Spouse, $100,000 plus 1/2 balance; brothers and sisters, residue	1/2 to each parent or all to surviving parent	Equal shares to brothers and sisters or their issue *per stirpes*
Nothing	1/2 to each parent or all to surviving parent	Equal shares to brothers and sisters or their issue *per stirpes*
Spouse, all personal property plus 1/2 separately owned real estate; brothers and sisters, residue	1/2 to each parent; but if only 1 parent survives, 1/2 to parent and 1/2 to brothers and sisters or their issue *per stirpes*	Equal shares to brothers and sisters or their issue *per stirpes*
Nothing	1/2 to each parent or all to surviving parent	Equal shares to brothers and sisters or their issue *per stirpes*
Spouse, $25,000 plus 1/2 residue; brothers and sisters, balance	1/2 to each parent or all to surviving parent	Equal shares to brothers and sisters or their issue *per stirpes*
Nothing	1/2 to each parent or all to surviving parent	Equal shares to brothers and sisters or their issue *per stirpes*
Spouse, all community property plus 3/4 balance; brothers and sisters, residue	1/2 to each parent or all to surviving parent	Equal shares to brothers and sisters or their issue *per stirpes*
Nothing	1/2 to each parent or all to surviving parent	Equal shares to brothers and sisters or their issue *per stirpes*
Nothing	1/2 to each parent or all to surviving parent	Equal shares to brothers and sisters or their issue *per stirpes*
Spouse, $20,000 plus 3/4 balance; brothers and sisters, residue	Equal shares to parent(s), brothers, and sisters or their issue *per stirpes*	Equal shares to brothers and sisters or their issue *per stirpes*

Chart 17   **1118**

WHAT YOUR RIGHTS ARE IF YOU DO NOT LIKE YOU

Curtesy rights for a husband and dower rights for a wife entitle a spouse to use for life 1/2 or 1/3 of the land owned by the deceased spouse. In states that have dower or curtesy rights, the spouse may choose between what he or she would receive under the deceased spouse's WILL or by dower or curtesy. In states that have a right of election, a spouse may choose between the share left in the will or an elective share. An elective share may be any amount that has been set by state law and, as

	Does husband have curtesy right?	Does wife have dower right?	Does husband have right of election?	Does wife have right of election?
ALABAMA	No	Yes	No	Yes
ALASKA	No	No	Yes	Yes
ARIZONA	No	No	No	No
ARKANSAS	Yes	Yes	Yes	Yes, but only if the will was executed prior to her marriage
CALIFORNIA	No	No	No	No
COLORADO	No	No	Yes	Yes
CONNECTICUT	No	No	Yes	Yes
DELAWARE	No	No	Yes	Yes
DISTRICT OF COLUMBIA	Yes	Yes	Yes	Yes
FLORIDA	No	No	Yes	Yes
GEORGIA	No	No	No	No, but widow may seek 1 year's support from husband's estate unless will negates it
HAWAII	No	No	Yes	Yes
IDAHO	No	No	Yes	Yes

[1] Where there are no children or other issue and personal estate exceeds $50,000, widow may elect to receive the first $50,000 of personal estate, and balance will be distributed according to will.

SPOUSE'S WILL

shown in this chart, is sometimes the share set by dower or curtesy or an intestate share, which is what you would receive if your spouse died without a will. The size of the intestate share is governed by state laws of DESCENT AND DISTRIBUTION. *See Chart 16. In states that have both dower or curtesy rights and a right of election, a spouse may usually choose between the deceased spouse's will, the elective share, or the dower or curtesy share.*

If spouse has right of election, what share is he or she entitled to?	Where is election filed?	What is the time limit for filing election?
Dower plus intestate share of personal property[1]	Probate Office	Within 6 months of probate of will (or where litigation concerning wife's title to property is pending, 15 months from probate of will)
1/3 of augmented estate[2]	Superior Court	Within 6 months of notice to creditors
Spouse cannot choose between the terms of the will and the share allowed under state intestacy laws, but the will does not affect the right to community property		
Intestate share	Office of clerk of Probate Court	Within 1 month of expiration of time for filing claims
Spouse may not will away more than 1/2 of community property. Unless the will shows contrary intent, surviving spouse can take community share as well as property given under will		
1/2 of augmented estate[2]	District Court; in Denver, Probate Court	Within 6 months of notice to creditors or 1 year of death, whichever is first
Life estate in 1/3 of entire estate	Probate Court	Within 2 months of expiration of time for filing claims
$20,000 or 1/3 of estate, whichever is less	Court of Chancery	Within 6 months of grant of letters testamentary or letters of administration
Dower plus either 1/2 of net personal estate or intestate share of net personal estate	Probate Court	Within 6 months of admission of will to probate
30% of net estate	Court where estate is administered	Within 4 months of the date of notice of administration
——	——	——
1/3 of net estate	Probate Court	Within 9 months of death or 6 months of probate of will, whichever is later
1/2 of augmented estate[2]	District Court	Within 6 months of notice to decedent's creditors

[2] Augmented estate is similar to net estate.

Chart 17   1120

WHAT YOUR RIGHTS ARE IF YOU DO NOT LIKE YOUR SPOUSE'S WILL *(continued)*

	Does husband have curtesy right?	Does wife have dower right?	Does husband have right of election?	Does wife have right of election?
ILLINOIS	No	No	No	No
INDIANA	No	No	Yes	Yes
IOWA	No	No	Yes	Yes
KANSAS	Yes	Yes	Yes	Yes
KENTUCKY	Yes	Yes	Yes	Yes
LOUISIANA	No	No	No	No
MAINE	No	No	Yes	Yes
MARYLAND	No	No	Yes	Yes
MASSACHUSETTS	Yes, spouse entitled to lifetime use of all real estate		Yes	Yes
MICHIGAN	No	Yes	Yes	Yes
MINNESOTA	No	No	Yes	Yes
MISSISSIPPI	No	No	Yes, but no right of election if surviving spouse has separate property equal in value to his or her intestate share. If separate property is less than intestate share, spouse may elect to make up the difference. If separate property equals 1/5 or less of intestate share, spouse may take entire estate share	
MISSOURI	No	No	Yes	Yes
MONTANA	No	No	Yes	Yes
NEBRASKA	No	No	Yes	Yes
NEVADA	No	No	No	No
NEW HAMPSHIRE	No	No	Yes	Yes
NEW JERSEY	Yes	Yes	Yes	Yes

If spouse has right of election, what share is he or she entitled to?	Where is election filed?	What is the time limit for filing election?
——	——	——
1/3 of net estate	Office of clerk of court where will is probated	Within 10 days of expiration of time for filing claims or within 30 days of the termination of pending litigation
1/3 of net estate	Office of clerk of District Court	Within 6 months of second publication of notice of admission of will to probate
Intestate share	District Court	Within 4 months of admission of will to probate
Dower or curtesy plus intestate share of personal property	Office of clerk of County Court where will is probated	Within 6 months of admission of will to probate
Spouse may not will away more than 1/2 of community property		
Intestate share	Registry of Probate Court	Within 6 months of admission of will to probate
Intestate share limited to 1/3 of net estate if surviving issue; otherwise, 1/2	Orphan's Court	Within 30 days of expiration of time for filing claims, unless extended by court order
Intestate share limited to $25,000 plus income from balance for life[3]	Registry of Probate Court	Within 6 months of admission of will to probate
1/2 intestate share subject to statutory limitations	Probate Court	Within 60 days of date for presenting claim or of filing inventory, whichever is later
Intestate share limited to 1/2 of entire estate if decedent left no issue	Probate Court	Within 9 months of death or within 6 months of admission of will to probate, whichever is later
Intestate share limited to 1/2 entire estate	Office of Chancery Court	Within 3 months of admission of will to probate
If issue survive, 1/3 of estate; otherwise, 1/2	Probate Court	Within 10 days of expiration of time for contesting will or 90 days of final determination of litigation
1/3 of augmented estate[2]	District Court	Within 6 months of notice to creditors or 1 year of death, whichever is first
1/3 of augmented estate[2]	County Court	Within 6 months of notice to creditors or 1 year of death, whichever is first
Spouse may not will away more than 1/2 of community property		
Intestate share	Probate Office	Within 6 months of appointment of executor or administrator
Dower or curtesy	Surrogate or Superior Court	Within 6 months of admission of will to probate

[3] The size of the share varies if there are children or other kin.

Chart 17   1122

WHAT YOUR RIGHTS ARE IF YOU DO NOT LIKE YOUR SPOUSE'S WILL *(continued)*

	Does husband have curtesy right?	Does wife have dower right?	Does husband have right of election?	Does wife have right of election?
NEW MEXICO	No	No	No	No
NEW YORK	No	No	Yes, but certain provisions in will can defeat right of election	
NORTH CAROLINA	No	No	Yes	Yes
NORTH DAKOTA	No	No	Yes	Yes
OHIO	Yes	Yes	Yes	Yes
OKLAHOMA	No	No	Yes	Yes
OREGON	No	No	Yes	Yes
PENNSYLVANIA	No	No	Yes	Yes
RHODE ISLAND	No, but a statute allows the use for life of all lands owned by deceased spouse		Yes	Yes
SOUTH CAROLINA	No	Yes	No	Yes
SOUTH DAKOTA	No	No	No	No
TENNESSEE	No	No	Yes	Yes
TEXAS	No	No	No	No
UTAH	No	No	Yes	Yes
VERMONT	Yes	Yes	Yes	Yes
VIRGINIA	Yes	Yes	Yes	Yes
WASHINGTON	No	No	No	No
WEST VIRGINIA	Yes	Yes	Yes	Yes
WISCONSIN	Yes	Yes	Yes	Yes
WYOMING	No	No	Yes	Yes

If spouse has right of election, what share is he or she entitled to?	Where is election filed?	What is the time limit for filing election?
——	——	——
If issue survive, 1/3 of net estate; otherwise, 1/2	Surrogate Court	Within 6 months of issuance of letters testamentary
Intestate share limited to 1/2 estate	Superior Court	Within 6 months of issuance of letters testamentary
1/3 of augmented estate[2]	County Court	Within 9 months of death or 6 months of admission of will to probate, whichever is later
Intestate share limited to 1/2 estate	Probate Court	Within 1 month of date of notice from court to elect
Intestate share	District Court	Within 6 months of the final distribution or settlement of the estate
1/4 of net estate	Probate Court	Within 90 days of admission of will to probate or 30 days after filing of inventory, whichever is later
If issue survive, 1/3 of estate; otherwise, 1/2	Orphan's Court	Within 6 months of admission of will to probate
Lifetime use of real estate plus intestate share of personal property	Probate Court	Within 6 months of admission of will to probate
Dower	Probate Court	At time of or before distribution of estate
——	——	——
Intestate share	Probate Court or County Court	Within 6 months of admission of will to probate
——	——	——
1/3 of augmented estate times fraction set by statute[2]	District Court	Within 1 year of death or 6 months of probate of will, whichever is later
Dower or curtesy	Probate Court	Within 3 months of admission of will to probate
Dower or curtesy plus either 1/3 of personal property if issue survive or 1/2 of personal property if not	Court with probate jurisdiction	Within 1 year of admission of will to probate[4]
——	——	——
Intestate share as if decedent died leaving children	Office of clerk of County Court	Within 8 months of admission of will to probate
1/3 of net estate	Probate Court	Within 6 months of death, unless extended by court order
Intestate share of estate limited to 1/4 of estate if issue survive and 1/2 if not	Office of clerk of District Court	Within 3 months of admission of will to probate

[4] May be extended 6 months from outcome of lawsuit on the validity of will provision.

COMMISSIONS FOR EXECUTORS AND ADMINISTRATORS

ALABAMA	Such commission as the court may deem just and fair, not to exceed 2½% of moneys received plus 2½% of moneys paid out (plus expenses)[1]
ALASKA	No statutory rate. A reasonable commission is permitted
ARIZONA	No statutory rate. A reasonable commission is permitted
ARKANSAS	10% on first $1,000 of personal property; 5% on next $4,000; 3% on balance over $5,000. Probate Court may permit additional compensation for extraordinary services or for services in connection with real estate
CALIFORNIA	4% on first $15,000 of estate value; 3% on next $85,000; 2% on next $900,000; 1% on balance over $1 million. Probate Court may permit additional compensation for extraordinary service
COLORADO	No statutory rate. A reasonable commission is permitted
CONNECTICUT	No statutory rate. Commission is set by the Probate Court
DELAWARE	No statutory rate. A reasonable commission is permitted
DISTRICT OF COLUMBIA	1%-10% of the appraised value of the estate; exact commission is set by the Probate Court
FLORIDA	No statutory rate. A reasonable commission is permitted
GEORGIA	2½% on moneys received plus 2½% on moneys paid out (plus expenses). Probate Court may permit additional compensation for extraordinary services or for services in connection with real estate
HAWAII	No statutory rate. A reasonable commission is permitted. No commission is permitted on real estate sold during administration of estate
IDAHO	No statutory rate. A reasonable commission is permitted
ILLINOIS	No statutory rate. Commission is set by the Probate Court
INDIANA	No statutory rate. Commission is set by the Probate Court
IOWA	6% on first $1,000 of estate value; 4% on next $4,000; 2% on balance over $5,000. Probate Court may permit additional compensation for extraordinary services
KANSAS	No statutory rate. A reasonable commission is permitted

[1] For real estate, 2½% of value of lands sold for division but no more than $100 unless sold under terms of a will.

[2] If there is more than 1 executor or administrator, 1 commission is divided equally among them.

[3] If there is more than 1 executor or administrator, commission may be increased by no more than 1% for each additional executor or administrator. If administration of the estate lasts more than 25 years, additional compensation may be granted up to 1/5 of 1% for each additional year.

The executor you appoint in your will or the court-appointed administrator of your estate
if you do not leave a valid will is entitled to the fees set forth by state law as shown below.
See EXECUTORS AND ADMINISTRATORS.

KENTUCKY	5% of value of personal property plus 5% of income received thereon. Probate Court may permit additional compensation for extraordinary services or for services in connection with real estate
LOUISIANA	2½% of appraised value of estate. If there is more than 1 executor or administrator, total compensation is set by the Probate Court[1]
MAINE	No statutory rate. Commission is set by court, not to exceed 5% of estate value (plus expenses)[1]
MARYLAND	Such commission as the court may deem appropriate, not to exceed 10% on first $20,000 of personal property and 4% on balance unless the will provides for a larger commission. No commission on real estate or income from real estate
MASSACHUSETTS	No statutory rate, but 2½%-3½% on personal property up to $500,000 and 1% on balance is usually not considered unreasonable
MICHIGAN	No statutory rate. A reasonable commission is permitted
MINNESOTA	No statutory rate. A reasonable commission is permitted
MISSISSIPPI	Commission is set by the Probate Court, but in no case may it exceed 7% of value of entire estate
MISSOURI	5% on first $5,000 of estate value; 4% on next $20,000; 3% on next $75,000; 2¼% on next $300,000; 2½% on next $600,000; 2% on balance over $1 million
MONTANA	A reasonable commission is permitted, not to exceed 3% on first $40,000 of estate value; 2% on balance. Probate Court may permit additional compensation for extraordinary service
NEBRASKA	No statutory rate. A reasonable commission is permitted
NEVADA	6% on first $1,000 of estate value; 4% on next $4,000; 2% on balance over $5,000. Probate Court may permit additional compensation for extraordinary service[2]
NEW HAMPSHIRE	No statutory rate. If claim for compensation is deemed reasonable, the court directs payment from the estate
NEW JERSEY	Principal of estate: 5% on first $100,000 and on the balance such percentage as set by Probate Court, but in no case more than 5%. Income from estate: 6%[3]
NEW MEXICO	No statutory rate. A reasonable commission is permitted. Probate Court sets the commission on real estate

[4] If there is more than 1 executor or administrator, commission is divided among them as follows: (1) if the value of the estate is $100,000 or less, the commission is divided equally among them; (2) if the estate is over $100,000 but less than $200,000, each gets a full commission unless there are more than 2 representatives; in the latter case, the total of 2 full commissions is divided equally among them; (3) if the estate is $200,000 or more, each representative gets a full commission unless there are more than 3 representatives. In such a case, 3 full commissions are divided equally among them.

Chart 18   1126

COMMISSIONS FOR EXECUTORS
AND ADMINISTRATORS *(continued)*

NEW YORK	For receiving and paying, 4% on first $25,000; 3½% on next $125,000; 3% on next $150,000; 2% on sums over $300,000[4]
NORTH CAROLINA	Commission is within discretion of clerk of court and may not exceed 5% on moneys received and paid out
NORTH DAKOTA	No statutory rate. A reasonable commission is permitted
OHIO	6% on first $1,000 of estate value; 4% on next $4,000; 2% on balance over $5,000. Probate Court may permit additional compensation for extraordinary services or for services in connection with real estate
OKLAHOMA	5% on first $1,000 of estate value; 4% on next $4,000; 2½% on balance over $5,000. Probate Court may permit additional compensation for extraordinary service
OREGON	7% on first $1,000 of estate value; 4% on next $9,000; 3% on next $40,000; 2% on balance over $50,000. Probate Court may permit additional compensation for extraordinary service
PENNSYLVANIA	No statutory rate but usually 5% of principal and income on small estates; 3% of principal and income on large estates
RHODE ISLAND	No statutory rate. Commission is set by Probate Court
SOUTH CAROLINA	2½% on appraised value of personal assets received and 2½% on personal assets paid out plus 10% of interest on money loaned. Probate Court may permit additional compensation for extraordinary service
SOUTH DAKOTA	5% on first $1,000 of personal property; 4% on next $4,000; 2½% on balance over $5,000. Probate Court sets commission on real estate
TENNESSEE	No statutory rate. A reasonable commission is set by the Probate Court
TEXAS	5% of all moneys received in cash plus 5% of all moneys paid out in cash. Total commission can never be more than 5% of the gross fair market value of the estate
UTAH	Commission may not exceed 5% on first $1,000 of estate value; 4% on next $4,000; 3% on next $5,000; 2% on next $40,000; 1½% on next $50,000; 1% on excess over $100,000. Probate Court may permit additional compensation for extraordinary services or for services in connection with real estate
VERMONT	$4 a day. Probate Court may permit additional compensation for extraordinary service
VIRGINIA	No statutory rate. A reasonable commission is permitted, usually 5% of estate value
WASHINGTON	No statutory rate. Commission is set by Probate Court
WEST VIRGINIA	No statutory rate. A reasonable commission is permitted, usually 5% on moneys received
WISCONSIN	2% of inventory value of property. Probate Court may permit additional compensation for extraordinary service
WYOMING	10% on first $1,000 of estate value; 5% on next $4,000; 3% on next $15,000; 2% on balance over $20,000. Probate Court may permit additional compensation for extraordinary service

Chart 19

ADOPTION LAWS

Generally, a child must consent to his own adoption after he reaches a certain age—even though he is still a minor. Most states will not grant an adoption immediately but require a period of probation during which the child lives with the adoptive family. An adopted child usually loses his right to inherit from his natural parents and gains the right to inherit from his adoptive parents. He does not lose his parental relationship with a natural parent, however, when he is adopted by a stepparent who is married to that natural parent. See ADOPTION OF PERSONS.

	At what age is child's consent to adoption needed?	How long is the period of probation before adoption order becomes final?	Which court has jurisdiction?	May the child inherit from his or her adoptive parents if they die without a will?	Does adopted child retain the right to inherit from his or her natural parents if they die without a will?
ALABAMA	Over 14	6 months	Probate Court	Yes	No[1]
ALASKA	Over 10	There is none[2]	Superior Court	Yes	No
ARIZONA	12 or over	6 months	Juvenile Division of Superior Court	Yes	No
ARKANSAS	Over 10	6 months	Probate Court	Yes	No
CALIFORNIA	Over 12	No statutory provision	Superior Court	Yes	No
COLORADO	12 or over	6 months	Juvenile Court	Yes	No
CONNECTICUT	14 or over	There is none	Court of Probate	Yes	No
DELAWARE	14 or over	1 year[3]	Superior Court	Yes	No
DISTRICT OF COLUMBIA	Over 14	6 months	Superior Court	Yes	No
FLORIDA	Over 12	90 days	Circuit Court	Yes	No
GEORGIA	14 or over	60 days	Superior Court	Yes	No
HAWAII	Over 10	There is none[4]	Family Court	Yes	No
IDAHO	Over 12	There is none	District Court	Yes	No
ILLINOIS	14 or over	6 months	Circuit Court	Yes	No
INDIANA	Over 14	Left to discretion of judge	Court with probate jurisdiction	Yes	No

[1] Unless final order of adoption provides otherwise.

[2] But child must have lived in the adoptive home and a qualified person or agency must have investigated.

[3] Or 6 months if recommended by an authorized agency.

[4] But adoption order can be set aside any time within 1 year of the time it is granted.

Chart 19

1128

ADOPTION LAWS (continued)

	At what age is child's consent to adoption needed?	How long is the period of probation before adoption order becomes final?	Which court has jurisdiction?	May the child inherit from his or her adoptive parents if they die without a will?	Does adopted child retain the right to inherit from his or her natural parents if they die without a will?
IOWA	14 or over	180 days	District Court	Yes	No
KANSAS	Over 14	There is none	District Court	Yes	No
KENTUCKY	12 or over	There is none	Circuit Court	Yes	No
LOUISIANA	No statutory provision	6 months[5]	Juvenile Court	Yes	Yes
MAINE	14 or over	1 year	Probate Court	Yes[6]	Yes
MARYLAND	10 or over	Not more than 1 year	Circuit Court	Yes	No
MASSACHUSETTS	Over 12	6 months if under 14	Probate Court	Yes	No
MICHIGAN	Over 10	1 year	Probate Court	Yes	No
MINNESOTA	Over 14	6 months	Juvenile Court	Yes	No
MISSISSIPPI	Over 14	6 months	Chancery Court	Yes	No
MISSOURI	14 or over	9 months	Juvenile Division of Circuit Court	Yes	No
MONTANA	12 or over	6 months	District Court	Yes	No
NEBRASKA	Over 14	6 months	County Court	Yes	No
NEVADA	Over 14	6 months	District Court	Yes	No
NEW HAMPSHIRE	12 or over	6 months	Probate Court	Yes	No
NEW JERSEY	10 or over	6 months	County Court or Superior Court where parents were divorced	Yes	No
NEW MEXICO	Over 10	6 months	District Court	Yes	No
NEW YORK	Over 14	6 months[7]	Family Court or Surrogate Court	Yes	No

[5] But child must have lived with adoptive parents at least 1 year.

[6] But adopted child cannot inherit property that has been limited by statute to be passed on only to natural-born children of the parents.

	At what age is child's consent to adoption needed?	How long is the period of probation before adoption order becomes final?	Which court has jurisdiction?	May the child inherit from his or her adoptive parents if they die without a will?	Does adopted child retain the right to inherit from his or her natural parents if they die without a will?
NORTH CAROLINA	12 or over	1 year	Superior Court	Yes	No
NORTH DAKOTA	Over 10	6 months	District Court	Yes	No
OHIO	Over 10	6 months	Probate Court	Yes	No
OKLAHOMA	12 or over	6 months	County Court	Yes	No
OREGON	14 or over	There is none	Court with probate jurisdiction or Circuit Court	Yes	No
PENNSYLVANIA	Over 12	6 months	Court of Common Pleas	Yes	No
RHODE ISLAND	14 or over	6 months	Family Court	Yes	Yes
SOUTH CAROLINA	No statutory provision	6 months	Court of Common Pleas	Yes	No
SOUTH DAKOTA	Over 12	6 months	Circuit Court	Yes	No
TENNESSEE	14 or over	1 year	Chancery or Circuit Court	Yes	No
TEXAS	12 or over	6 months	Family District Court	Yes	Yes
UTAH	Over 12	6 months	District Court	Yes	No
VERMONT	14 or over	6 months	Probate Court	Yes	Yes
VIRGINIA	14 or over	6 months	Court of Record having chancery jurisdiction	Yes	No
WASHINGTON	14 or over	6 months	Superior Court	Yes	No
WEST VIRGINIA	12 or over	6 months	Circuit Court or Juvenile Court	Yes	No
WISCONSIN	14 or over	6 months[8]	Circuit Court	Yes	No
WYOMING	Over 14	6 months	District Court	Yes	No

[7] Or 1 year for private placement of child brought into state.

[8] There is none if adopting parent is related to child by blood or is his stepparent or if child's previous guardian has given written approval.

Chart 20   1130

MARRIAGE LAWS

All states require that persons be at least a certain minimum age in order to obtain a marriage license. Persons below that age—18 in most states—must usually have the consent of their parents under oath before a judge or a witness. Court approval may also be required. In all states, it is illegal for a man to marry his sister, half-sister, mother, daughter, granddaughter, grandmother, great-grandmother,

	At what age may you legally be married?				What other relatives are you prohibited from marrying?[1]
	With parental consent		Without parental consent		
	Male	Female	Male	Female	
ALABAMA	14	14	18	18	Stepparent, stepchild, son-in-law, daughter-in-law
ALASKA	16	16	18	18	——
ARIZONA	16	16	18	18	First cousin
ARKANSAS	17	16	21	18	First cousin
CALIFORNIA	No statutory provision	No statutory provision	18	18	——
COLORADO	16	16	18	18	——
CONNECTICUT	16	16	18	18	Stepparent, stepchild
DELAWARE	18	16	18	18	First cousin
DISTRICT OF COLUMBIA	16	16	18	18	Stepparent, stepchild, stepgrandparent, father-in-law, mother-in-law, son-in-law, daughter-in-law, spouse's grandparent or grandchild, spouse of grandparent or grandchild
FLORIDA	16	16	18	18	——
GEORGIA	Under 16	Under 16	16	16	Stepparent, stepchild, stepgrandparent, stepgrandchild, father-in-law, mother-in-law, son-in-law, daughter-in-law
HAWAII	16	16	18	18	——
IDAHO	16	16	18	18	First cousin
ILLINOIS	16	16	18	18	First cousin
INDIANA	17	17	18	18	First cousin
IOWA	16	16	18	18	First cousin, stepparent, stepchild, father-in-law, mother-in-law, son-in-law, daughter-in-law, spouse of grandchild

[1] Besides siblings, parents, children, grandchildren, grandparents, great-grandparents, uncles, aunts, nieces, and nephews.

aunt, or niece. A woman may not marry her brother, half-brother, father, son, grandson, grandfather, great-grandfather, uncle, or nephew. Many states also prohibit marriages between more distant relatives. Every state must recognize a common-law marriage that has been entered into in another state and is considered valid in that state. These and other state laws regulating marriage are summarized below.

Is a blood test required to obtain a license?	What is the waiting period between application and issue of a license?	How soon after issue of license may you marry?	How long is license valid after issuance?	Are common-law marriages recognized?
Yes	None	Immediately	30 days	Yes
Yes	3 days	Immediately	90 days	No
Yes	None	Immediately	No statutory provision	No
Yes	3 days	Immediately	No statutory provision	No
Yes	None	Immediately	90 days	No
Yes	None	Immediately	30 days	Yes
Yes	4 days	Immediately	65 days	No
Yes	None	1 day [2]	30 days	No
Yes	3 days	Immediately	No statutory provision	Yes
Yes	3 days	Immediately	30 days	No, unless entered into before Jan. 1, 1968
Yes	3 days	Immediately	30 days	Yes
Yes	None	Immediately	30 days	No
Yes	3 days if either is under 18; otherwise, none	Immediately	No statutory provision	Yes
Yes	None	3 days	60 days	No, unless entered into before June 30, 1905
Yes	3 days	Immediately	60 days	No, unless entered into before 1958
Yes	3 days	Immediately	20 days	Yes

[2] But there is a 4-day waiting period if both parties are nonresidents.

Chart 20   1132

MARRIAGE LAWS *(continued)*

	At what age may you legally be married?				What other relatives are you prohibited from marrying?[1]
	With parental consent		Without parental consent		
	Male	Female	Male	Female	
KANSAS	Under 18	Under 18	18	18	First cousin
KENTUCKY	No statutory provision	No statutory provision	18	18	First cousin, first cousin once removed
LOUISIANA	18	16	18	18	First cousin
MAINE	16	16	18	18	Stepparent, stepchild, father-in-law, mother-in-law, son-in-law, daughter-in-law, spouse's grandparent or grandchild, spouse of grandparent or grandchild
MARYLAND	16	16	18	18	Stepparent, stepchild, father-in-law, mother-in-law, son-in-law, daughter-in-law, spouse's grandparent or grandchild, spouse of grandparent or grandchild
MASSACHUSETTS	No statutory provision	No statutory provision	18	18	Stepparent, stepchild, stepgrandparent, father-in-law, mother-in-law, son-in-law, daughter-in-law
MICHIGAN	18	16	18	18	First cousin
MINNESOTA	No statutory provision	16	18	18	First cousin
MISSISSIPPI	——[3]	——[3]	17	15	First cousin, stepparent, stepchild, father-in-law, mother-in-law, son-in-law, daughter-in-law
MISSOURI	15	15	18	18	First cousin
MONTANA	16	16	18	18	First cousin
NEBRASKA	17	17	19	19	First cousin
NEVADA	16	16	18	18	First cousin
NEW HAMPSHIRE	14	13	18	18	First cousin, stepparent, son-in-law, daughter-in-law
NEW JERSEY	16	16	18	18	——
NEW MEXICO	16	16	18	18	——
NEW YORK	16	16	18	18	——

[3] There is no statutory minimum age limit; both parental consent and court order are required.

Is a blood test required to obtain a license?	What is the waiting period between application and issue of a license?	How soon after issue of license may you marry?	How long is license valid after issuance?	Are common-law marriages recognized?
Yes	3 days	Immediately	No statutory provision	Yes, but parties guilty of misdemeanor
Yes	3 days	Immediately	30 days	No
Yes	None	3 days	30 days	No
Yes	5 days	Immediately	60 days	No
No	2 days	Immediately	6 months	No
Yes	3 days	Immediately	60 days	No
Yes	3 days	Immediately	33 days	No, unless entered into before Jan. 1, 1957
No	5 days	Immediately	6 months	No, unless entered into before Apr. 16, 1941
Yes	3 days if 1 person is under 21	Immediately	No statutory provision	No, unless entered into before Apr. 5, 1956
Yes	3 days	Immediately	No statutory provision	No, unless entered into before Mar. 31, 1921
Yes	None	3 days	180 days	Yes
Yes	2 days	Immediately	No statutory provision	No, unless entered into before 1923
No	None	Immediately	No statutory provision	No, unless entered into before Mar. 29, 1943
Yes	5 days	Immediately	90 days	No
Yes	3 days	Immediately	30 days	No, unless entered into before Dec. 1, 1939
Yes	None	Immediately	No statutory provision	No
Yes	None	1 day	60 days	No, unless entered into before Apr. 29, 1933

Chart 20

1134

MARRIAGE LAWS *(continued)*

	At what age may you legally be married?				What other relatives are you prohibited from marrying?[1]
	With parental consent		Without parental consent		
	Male	Female	Male	Female	
NORTH CAROLINA	16	16	18	18	Double first cousin
NORTH DAKOTA	16	16	18	18	First cousin
OHIO	18	16	18	18	First cousin
OKLAHOMA	16	16	18	18	First cousin
OREGON	17	17	18	18	First cousin
PENNSYLVANIA	16	16	18	18	First cousin, stepparent, stepchild, son-in-law, daughter-in-law
RHODE ISLAND	18	16	18	18	Stepchild, father-in-law, mother-in-law, spouse's grandparent or grandchild
SOUTH CAROLINA	16	14	18	18	Stepparent, stepchild, father-in-law, mother-in-law, son-in-law, daughter-in-law, spouse's grandparent or grandchild, spouse of grandparent or grandchild
SOUTH DAKOTA	16	16	18	18	First cousin, stepparent, stepchild
TENNESSEE	16	16	18	18	Stepparent, stepchild, stepgrandchild, grandnephew, grandniece
TEXAS	14	14	18	18	——
UTAH	14	14	18	18	First cousin
VERMONT	16	16	18	18	——
VIRGINIA	16	16	18	18	——
WASHINGTON	17	17	18	18	First cousin
WEST VIRGINIA	18	16	18	18	First cousin, double cousin
WISCONSIN	16	16	18	18	First cousin, unless female 55 years or older
WYOMING	16	16	18	18	First cousin

[4] A physical examination showing freedom from uncontrolled epilepsy, tuberculosis, idiocy, and insanity is also required.

Is a blood test required to obtain a license?	What is the waiting period between application and issue of a license?	How soon after issue of license may you marry?	How long is license valid after issuance?	Are common-law marriages recognized?
Yes[4]	None	Immediately	No statutory provision	No
Yes	None	Immediately	60 days	No
Yes	5 days	Immediately	60 days	Yes
Yes	3 days if either is under 18	Immediately	30 days	Yes
Yes	7 days	Immediately	30 days after blood test	No
Yes	3 days	Immediately	60 days	Yes
Yes	None[5]	Immediately	3 months	Yes
No	Yes	Immediately	No statutory provision	Yes
Yes	None	Immediately	20 days	No, unless entered into before July 1, 1959
Yes	3 days if either is under 18	Immediately	30 days	No
Yes[6]	None	Immediately	21 days after medical examination	Yes
Yes	None	Immediately	30 days	No
Yes	None	5 days from application of license	60 days	No
Yes	None	Immediately	60 days	No
No	3 days	Immediately	30 days	No
Yes	3 days	Immediately	60 days	No
Yes[4]	5 days	Immediately	30 days	No, unless entered into before 1917
Yes	None	Immediately	No statutory provision	No

[5] But there is a 5-day waiting period for female nonresidents.
[6] A physical examination is also required.

WHEN A MARRIAGE IS VOID OR MAY BE ANNULLED

Under certain circumstances, a marriage may be annulled or declared void. An ANNULMENT declares that what seems to be a marriage is not one. Annulments may be granted when a marriage is void—never legally existed. For example, the marriage of a person under a certain age or of persons who are too closely related (an incestuous marriage) is void (see Chart 20). Annulments may also be granted for a marriage that is voidable—that is, can be declared void but is effective if no

	Underage at time of marriage	Bigamous marriage	Incestuous marriage	Consent obtained by fraud	Consent obtained under duress
ALABAMA	Yes	Yes	Yes	Yes	No
ALASKA	Yes	Yes	Yes	Yes	Yes
ARIZONA	Yes	Yes	Yes	Yes	Yes
ARKANSAS	Yes	Yes	Yes	Yes	Yes
CALIFORNIA	Yes	Yes	Yes	Yes	Yes
COLORADO	Yes	Yes	Yes	Yes	Yes
CONNECTICUT	An incestuous marriage is void. Where a married person is convicted of a sex offense, an annulment may be granted. In other cases, the common law determines whether or not a marriage is voidable				
DELAWARE	Yes	Yes	Yes	Yes	Yes
DISTRICT OF COLUMBIA	Yes	Yes	Yes	Yes	Yes
FLORIDA	No statutory grounds; courts can annul on common-law grounds. Incestuous marriages are void				
GEORGIA[1]	Yes	Yes	Yes	Yes	Yes
HAWAII	Yes	Yes	Yes	Yes	Yes

[1] An annulment will not be granted if children have been born or are about to be born, nor will it be granted for any ground that is also a ground for divorce.

one challenges it in court. For instance, a marriage may be voidable if one of the persons lacked an understanding of what was going on—perhaps he was too drunk—or was forced into marriage (under duress), as in a shotgun wedding. Most states have statutes that provide for annulment. A few states have no specific annulment statutes but permit the courts to declare certain marriages void. This chart gives the grounds for which a marriage may be declared void or annulled in the various states.

Lack of understanding	Inability to consummate marriage	Other grounds	Time limit for bringing suit to annul
No	No	Insanity at time of marriage	No statutory provision
Yes	Yes	———	No statutory provision
Yes	No	———	No statutory provision
Yes	Yes	———	For age, up to age of consent; otherwise, no statutory provision
Yes	Yes	———	For age, within 4 years of reaching age of consent; for bigamy or lack of understanding, during lifetime of either party; for fraud, within 4 years of discovery; for duress or inability to consummate, within 4 years of marriage
Yes	Yes	Marriage entered into while intoxicated or as a jest or dare	For age, within 2 years of marriage; for bigamy or incestuous marriage, during lifetime of either party; for fraud, duress, lack of understanding, or marriage entered into as a jest or dare, within 6 months of discovery; for inability to consummate, within 1 year of discovery
			For sex offense, within 4 months of conviction
Yes	Yes	Marriage entered into as a jest or dare. Party has a venereal disease, is a habitual drunk, is a confirmed narcotic user, is a patient in an insane asylum, is on probation or parole and fails to get consent to marry, or is divorced without certificate to that effect at time of marriage	For age, within 1 year of marriage; for bigamy or incestuous marriage, during lifetime of either party; for fraud, duress, lack of understanding, or marriage entered into as a jest or dare, within 90 days of discovery; for inability to consummate, within 1 year of discovery
Yes	Yes	———	No statutory provision
			No statutory provision
No	No	———	No statutory provision
Yes	Yes	Concealment of a venereal disease	For bigamy, during lifetime of either party; for inability to consummate, within 2 years of marriage; otherwise, no statutory provision

Chart 21 1138

WHEN A MARRIAGE IS VOID OR MAY BE ANNULLED *(continued)*

	Underage at time of marriage	Bigamous marriage	Incestuous marriage	Consent obtained by fraud	Consent obtained under duress
IDAHO	Yes	Yes	Yes	Yes	Yes
ILLINOIS	Yes	Yes	Yes	Yes	Yes
INDIANA	Yes	Yes	Yes	Yes	No
IOWA	No	Yes	Yes	No	No
KANSAS	No statutory provision	Yes	Yes	Yes	No
KENTUCKY	Yes	Yes	Yes	Yes	Yes
LOUISIANA	No	Yes	No	Yes	Yes
MAINE	Yes	Yes	Yes	No	No
MARYLAND	No	Yes	Yes	No	No
MASSACHUSETTS	Yes	Yes	Yes	Yes	Yes
MICHIGAN	Yes	Yes	Yes	Yes	Yes
MINNESOTA	Yes	Yes	Yes	Yes	Yes
MISSISSIPPI	Yes	Yes	Yes	Yes	Yes
MISSOURI	No	Yes	Yes	Yes	Yes
MONTANA	Yes	Yes	Yes	Yes	Yes
NEBRASKA	Yes	Yes	Yes	Yes	Yes
NEVADA	Yes	Yes	Yes	Yes	No
NEW HAMPSHIRE	Yes	Yes	Yes	No	No
NEW JERSEY	Yes	Yes	Yes	Yes	Yes
NEW MEXICO	Yes	No	Yes	No	No
NEW YORK	Yes	Yes	Yes	Yes	Yes

Lack of understanding	Inability to consummate marriage	Other grounds	Time limit for bringing suit to annul
Yes	Yes	———	For age, within 4 years of reaching age of consent; for bigamy or lack of understanding, during lifetime of either party; for fraud, within 4 years of discovery; for duress or inability to consummate, within 4 years of marriage
Yes	Yes	———	For age, up to age of consent; for incestuous marriage, during lifetime of either party; for inability to consummate, within 1 year of discovery
Yes	No	———	No statutory provision
Yes	Yes	———	No statutory provision
No statutory provision	Yes	Marriage entered into less than 30 days after entry of divorce decree from a previous marriage	No statutory provision
Yes	Yes	Marriage not solemnized or contracted in the presence of authorized person or society	For age, up to age of consent; for incestuous marriage, within 1 year of discovery; for other grounds, within 90 days
Yes	No	Mistake as to other person	No statutory provision
Yes	Yes	———	No statutory provision
No	No	———	No statutory provision
Yes	Yes	Insanity or idiocy	No statutory provision
Yes	No	———	For age, up to age of consent; otherwise, no statutory provision
Yes	Yes	———	For age, up to age of consent; for incestuous marriage, within 1 year of discovery; for other grounds, within 90 days
Yes	Yes	Failure to procure license unless followed by cohabitation; husband did not know about pregnancy of wife by another at time of marriage; insanity or idiocy	For age, fraud, duress, lack of understanding, inability to consummate, or pregnancy by another, within 6 months of discovery; for insanity or idiocy, within 6 months of marriage
No	Yes	Insanity	No statutory provision
Yes	Yes	———	For age, up to age of consent; for bigamy or incestuous marriage, during lifetime of either party; for fraud or duress, within 2 years of discovery; for lack of understanding, within 1 year of discovery; for inability to consummate, within 4 years of discovery
Yes	Yes	———	No statutory provision
Yes	No	———	For age, within 1 year of reaching age of consent; otherwise, no statutory provision
No	No	———	No statutory provision
Yes	Yes	———	No statutory provision
No	No	———	No statutory provision
Yes	Yes	Either party has been incurably insane for 5 years	Generally 5 years or during lifetime of either party, depending on ground

Chart 21   1140

WHEN A MARRIAGE IS VOID OR MAY BE ANNULLED *(continued)*

	Underage at time of marriage	Bigamous marriage	Incestuous marriage	Consent obtained by fraud	Consent obtained under duress
NORTH CAROLINA	Yes	Yes	Yes	Yes	Yes
NORTH DAKOTA	Yes	Yes	Yes	Yes	Yes
OHIO	Yes	Yes	No statutory provision	Yes	Yes
OKLAHOMA	Yes	Yes	Yes	No	No
OREGON	Yes	Yes	Yes	Yes	Yes
PENNSYLVANIA	No	Yes	No	No	No
RHODE ISLAND	Yes	No, but ground for divorce	No, but ground for divorce	No	No
SOUTH CAROLINA	No	Yes	Yes	No statutory provision	No statutory provision
SOUTH DAKOTA	Yes	Yes	Yes	Yes	Yes
TENNESSEE	Yes	Yes	Yes	No	No
TEXAS	Yes	Yes	Yes	Yes	Yes
UTAH	Yes	Yes	Yes	Yes	Yes
VERMONT	Yes	Yes	Yes	Yes	Yes
VIRGINIA	Yes	Yes	Yes	Yes	Yes
WASHINGTON	Yes	Yes	Yes	Yes	Yes
WEST VIRGINIA	Yes	Yes	Yes	No	No
WISCONSIN	Yes	Yes	Yes	Yes	Yes
WYOMING	Yes	Yes	Yes	Yes	Yes

Lack of understanding	Inability to consummate marriage	Other grounds	Time limit for bringing suit to annul
Yes	Yes	_____	No statutory provision
Yes	Yes	_____	For age, within 4 years of reaching age of consent; for fraud, duress, inability to consummate, within 4 years of marriage; for other grounds, during lifetime of either party
Yes	Yes	_____	No statutory provision
Yes	No	Remarriage within 6 months of divorce	No statutory provision
Yes	No	_____	No statutory provision
No	No	_____	No statutory provision
No	No	_____	No statutory provision
No statutory provision	No statutory provision	Lack of consent or other cause showing that no real marriage contract was entered into if there was no cohabitation	No statutory provision
Yes	Yes	_____	For age, within 4 years of reaching age of consent; for fraud, within 4 years of discovery; for inability to consummate, within 4 years of marriage; otherwise, no statutory provision
Yes	Yes	Any ground for which divorce may be granted or where court finds plaintiff is entitled to relief	No statutory provision
Yes	Yes	Either party concealed a prior divorce	For age, within 90 days of marriage; otherwise, no statutory provision
Yes	Yes	Either party has a venereal disease; lack of legal marriage ceremony	No statutory provision
Yes	Yes	_____	For inability to consummate, within 2 years of marriage; otherwise, no statutory provision
Yes	Yes	Wife was a prostitute or pregnant by another at marriage; husband fathered child of another within 10 months of marriage; premarriage felony conviction unknown to other party	No statutory provision
Yes	No	_____	No statutory provision
Yes	Yes	Either party has a venereal disease; wife did not know husband was licentious person; wife was a prostitute or pregnant by another at marriage; premarriage felony conviction unknown to other party	No statutory provision
Yes	Yes	_____	For age, within 1 year of marriage; for incestuous marriage, within 10 years of marriage; for other grounds, within 1 year of marriage
Yes	Yes	_____	For inability to consummate, within 2 years of marriage; otherwise, no statutory provision

Chart 22 1142

RESIDENCE REQUIREMENTS AND GROUNDS FOR

All states grant DIVORCES *on various grounds and most, but not all, grant legal separations. See* MARRIAGE. *Generally, you must have been a resident of the state for a certain period of time before you can sue for a divorce or separation. The grounds for divorce and separation vary widely. Often, the spouse who sues must show that the other spouse is at fault—that is, guilty of some wrong, such as adultery or desertion. In some states, however, a couple may get a no-fault divorce or separation*

	Residence requirement before commencing action	No-fault (irretrievable breakdown)	Adultery	Desertion	Mental or extreme cruelty	Physical cruelty	Impotence
ALABAMA	6 months for plaintiff if defendant is non-resident; otherwise, none	D	D/S	D/S 1 year	S	D/S	D/S
ALASKA	None	D	D	D 1 year	D	D	D
ARIZONA	90 days	D/S	No	No	No	No	No
ARKANSAS	60 days	No	D/S	D/S 1 year	D/S	D/S	D/S
CALIFORNIA	6 months in state; 3 months in county	D/S	No	No	No	No	No
COLORADO	90 days	D/S	No	No	No	No	No
CONNECTICUT	None if plaintiff was married in state or if cause of divorce arose in state; otherwise, 1 year	D/S	D/S	D/S 1 year	D/S	D/S	No
DELAWARE	6 months	D	No	No	No	No	No
DISTRICT OF COLUMBIA	6 months	No	S	D/S 1 year	S	S	No
FLORIDA	6 months	D	No	No	No	No	No
GEORGIA	6 months	D	D	D 1 year	D	D	D
HAWAII	6 months in state; 3 months in circuit	D	No	No	No	No	No

[1] Or 1 year if for a crime that violates conjugal duty.

DIVORCE AND SEPARATION

by showing that their marriage is irretrievably broken down without proving that either party is at fault. A few states allow couples to choose between fault and no-fault divorce and separation. This chart lists the residence requirements and grounds in each state. D indicates a ground for divorce, S a ground for separation. The time periods given indicate the length of time the condition must last before it becomes a ground for divorce or separation. See also ANNULMENT.

Nonsupport (willful neglect)	Insanity (length of commitment)	Alcoholism	Drug addiction	Conviction of a felony (length of sentence)	Living apart	Other grounds
D/S 2 years	D/S 5 years	D/S No time specified	D/S No time specified	D/S 7 years	No	Husband did not know that wife was pregnant by another man at time of marriage; crime against nature (D/S); living under decree of separation for 2 years (D)
D 1 year	D 18 months	D 1 year	D No time specified	D No time specified	No	——
No	No	No	No	No	No	Decree of separation may be converted into decree of dissolution of marriage (divorce)
D/S No time specified	D 3 years	D/S 1 year	No	D/S No time specified	D 3 years	Spouse from undissolved former marriage still living (D/S)
No	D/S Must be incurable	No	No	No	No	——
No	No	No	No	No	No	Decree of separation may be converted into decree of dissolution of marriage (divorce) after 6 months
No	D/S 5 years	D/S No time specified	No	D/S Life[1]	D/S 18 months	Marriage entered into as a result of fraud; spouse is absent for 7 years without being heard from (D/S)
No	No	No	No	No	No	——
No	No	No	No	No	D 6 months S No time specified	——
No	No	No	No	No	No	Mental incompetence for at least 3 years (D)
No	D 2 years	D No time specified	D No time specified	D 2 years	No	Mental incapacity at time of marriage; husband did not know that wife was pregnant by another man at time of marriage (D)
No	No	No	No	No	D 2 years	Decree of separation for 2 years or less may be granted if court finds that marriage is temporarily disrupted; divorce may be granted after decree of separation has expired

Chart 22

1144

RESIDENCE REQUIREMENTS AND GROUNDS FOR DIVORCE AND SEPARATION *(continued)*

	Residence requirement before commencing action	No-fault (irretrievable breakdown)	Adultery	Desertion	Mental or extreme cruelty	Physical cruelty	Impotence
IDAHO	6 weeks	D	D	D 1 year	D	D	No
ILLINOIS	90 days	No	D/S	D 1 year S No time specified	D/S	D/S	D/S
INDIANA	6 months in state; 3 months in county	D	No	No	No	No	D
IOWA	1 year	D/S	No	No	No	No	No
KANSAS	60 days	D/S	D/S	D/S 1 year	D/S	D/S	No
KENTUCKY	180 days	D/S	No	No	No	No	No
LOUISIANA	1 year	No	D/S	S No time specified	S	S	No
MAINE	6 months	D[4]	D	D 3 years S 1 year	D	D	D
MARYLAND	If ground is insanity, 2 years; otherwise, 1 year	No	D	D/S 1 year	S	S	D
MASSACHUSETTS	None if cause of divorce arose in state and plaintiff resided in state when he or she filed for divorce; otherwise, 1 year	D	D	D 1 year	D	D	D
MICHIGAN	6 months in state; 10 days in county	D/S	No	No	No	No	No
MINNESOTA	6 months	D/S	No	No	No	No	No
MISSISSIPPI	6 months	D	D	D 1 year	D	D	D
MISSOURI	90 days	D/S	D/S	D/S 6 months	D/S	D/S	No

[2] Confinement need not be continuous.

[3] Or 6 months if both spouses sign an affidavit stating that they have lived apart for 6 months and irreconcilable differences make their living together impossible.

Nonsupport (willful neglect)	Insanity (length of commitment)	Alcoholism	Drug addiction	Conviction of a felony (length of sentence)	Living apart	Other grounds
D No time specified	D 3 years	D 1 year	No	D No time specified	D 5 years	——
No	No	D 2 years S No time specified	D 2 years S No time specified	D/S No time specified	No	Spouse from undissolved former marriage still living; attempt on spouse's life; communication of a venereal disease (D/S)
No	D 2 years	No	No	D No time specified	No	——
No	No	No	No	No	No	——
D/S No time specified	D/S 3 years[2]	D/S No time specified	No	D/S No time specified	No	——
No	No	No	No	No	No	——
S No time specified	No	S No time specified	No	D/S No time specified	S 1 year[3]	Public defamation; attempt on spouse's life; spouse is guilty of a felony but has fled from justice (S); decree of separation may be converted into decree of divorce after 1 year
D No time specified	D 7 years S 1 year	D No time specified	D No time specified	No	S 1 year	——
No	D 3 years	No	No	D 3 years	D/S 3 years[5]	Spouse from undissolved former marriage still living; couple related within prohibited degree of relationship (marriage is legally incestuous) (D)
D No time specified	No	D No time specified	D No time specified	D 5 years	No	Any justifiable reason for living apart (S); spouse continuously absent so that presumption of death is raised (D)
No	No	No	No	No	No	——
No	No	No	No	No	No	——
No	——	D No time specified	D No time specified	D No time specified	No	Spouse from undissolved former marriage still living; couple related within prohibited degree of relationship (marriage is legally incestuous); insanity or idiocy at time of marriage unknown to other spouse; husband did not know that wife was pregnant by another man at time of marriage (D)
No	No	No	No	No	D/S 2 years[5]	——

[4] But only if parties have received counseling.   [5] But 1 year if by mutual consent.

Chart 22   1146

RESIDENCE REQUIREMENTS AND GROUNDS FOR DIVORCE AND SEPARATION *(continued)*

	Residence requirement before commencing action	No-fault (irretrievable breakdown)	Adultery	Desertion	Mental or extreme cruelty	Physical cruelty	Impotence
MONTANA	90 days	D/S	No	No	No	No	No
NEBRASKA	None if plaintiff was married in state and has resided in state since then; otherwise, 1 year	D	No	No	No	No	No
NEVADA	6 weeks	D/S	No	S 90 days	No	No	No
NEW HAMPSHIRE	None if both parties were residents of state when cause of divorce arose; otherwise, 1 year	D	D/S	D/S 2 years	D/S	D/S	D/S
NEW JERSEY	None if ground is adultery and either party resided in state when adultery was committed; otherwise, 1 year	No	D/S	D/S 1 year	D/S	D/S	No
NEW MEXICO	6 months	D	D	D	D	D	No
NEW YORK	2 years if only one party resides in state; otherwise, 1 year	No	D/S	D 1 year S No time specified	D/S	D/S	No
NORTH CAROLINA	6 months	No	D	S No time specified	S	S	D
NORTH DAKOTA	If ground is insanity and insane party is confined outside of state, 5 years; otherwise, 1 year	D	D/S	D/S 1 year	D/S	D/S	No
OHIO	6 months	No	D	D 1 year	D	No	D
OKLAHOMA	6 months in state; 30 days in county	D/S	D/S	D/S 1 year	D/S	D/S	D/S

Nonsupport (willful neglect)	Insanity (length of commitment)	Alcoholism	Drug addiction	Conviction of a felony (length of sentence)	Living apart	Other grounds
No	No	No	No	No	No	Decree of separation may be converted into a decree of dissolution of marriage (divorce) after 6 months
No	No	No	No	No	No	Any grounds the court deems sufficient (S)
No	D/S 2 years	No	No	No	D/S 1 year	——
D/S 2 years	No	D/S 2 years	No	D/S 1 year	No	Spouse is a member of a religious sect that professes that the conjugal relation is unlawful and spouse refuses to cohabit for 6 months (D/S)
No	D/S 2 years	D/S 1 year	D/S 1 year	D/S 18 months	D/S 18 months	Deviant sexual conduct without consent of spouse (D/S)
No	No	No	No	No	S No time specified	——
S No time specified	No	No	No	D/S 3 years	D 1 year	——
No	D 3 years	S No time specified	S No time specified	D 1 year	D 1 year	Maliciously turning spouse out-of-doors (S); husband did not know that wife was pregnant by another man at time of marriage; crime against nature or bestiality (D)
D/S 1 year	D 5 years	D/S 1 year	D/S No time specified	D/S No time specified	No	——
D No time specified	D 4 years	D No time specified	No	D No time specified	D 2 years	Spouse from former undissolved marriage still living; marriage entered into as a result of fraud; out-of-state divorce that did not release spouse in Ohio from marital obligations (D)
D/S No time specified	D/S 5 years	D/S No time specified	No	D/S No time specified	No	Marriage entered into as a result of fraud; husband did not know that wife was pregnant by another man at time of marriage; gross neglect of duty; out-of-state divorce that did not release spouse in Oklahoma from marital obligations (D/S)

Chart 22   **1148**

RESIDENCE REQUIREMENTS AND GROUNDS FOR DIVORCE AND SEPARATION *(continued)*

	Residence requirement before commencing action	No-fault (irretrievable breakdown)	Adultery	Desertion	Mental or extreme cruelty	Physical cruelty	Impotence
OREGON	6 months	D/S	No	No	No	No	No
PENNSYLVANIA	1 year	No	D	D 2 years	D	D	D
RHODE ISLAND	1 year	D/S	D/S	D/S 5 years	D/S	No	D/S
SOUTH CAROLINA	If both parties are state residents, 3 months; otherwise, 1 year	No	D	D 1 year	No	D	No
SOUTH DAKOTA	None	No	D/S	D/S 1 year	D/S	D/S	No
TENNESSEE	For members of armed forces, 1 year; for all others, 6 months	No	D	D 1 year	D/S	D/S	D
TEXAS	6 months in state; 90 days in county	D	D	D 1 year	D	D	No
UTAH	3 months	No	D	D/S 1 year	D	D	D
VERMONT	6 months	No	D/S	D/S No time specified	D/S	D/S	No
VIRGINIA	6 months	No	D	D/S 1 year	D/S	D/S	No
WASHINGTON	Plaintiff must be state resident or stationed in state in armed forces (no duration is specified in statute)	D/S	No	No	No	No	No
WEST VIRGINIA	1 year	D	D	D 6 months	D	D	No
WISCONSIN	6 months in state; 30 days in county	D/S	No	No	No	No	No
WYOMING	60 days	D/S	No	No	No	No	No

Nonsupport (willful neglect)	Insanity (length of commitment)	Alcoholism	Drug addiction	Conviction of a felony (length of sentence)	Living apart	Other grounds
No	No	No	No	No	No	_____
No	D No time specified	No	No	D 2 years	No	Spouse from former undissolved marriage still living; couple related within prohibited degree of relationship (marriage is legally incestuous); marriage entered into as a result of fraud, duress, or coercion (D)
D/S 1 year	No	D/S No time specified	D/S No time specified	D/S Life	D/S 3 years	Gross misbehavior and wickedness; marriage is legally void or voidable; spouse is presumed dead (D/S); any other grounds at court's discretion (S)
No	No	D No time specified	D No time specified	No	D 3 years	_____
D/S 1 year	D/S 5 years	D/S 1 year	No	D/S No time specified	No	_____
No	No	D No time specified	D No time specified	D No time specified	No	Spouse from former undissolved marriage still living; husband did not know that wife was pregnant by another man at time of marriage; attempt on spouse's life; indignities by husband; wife's refusal to move to Tennessee and her absence for 2 years; any other grounds at court's discretion (D)
No	D 3 years	No	No	D 1 year	D 3 years	_____
D/S No time specified	D No time specified	D No time specified	No	D/S No time specified	D 3 years	_____
D/S No time specified	D/S 5 years	No	No	D/S 3 years	D/S 6 months	Unexplained absence of spouse for 7 years (D)
No	No	No	No	D 1 year	D 1 year	Sodomy or buggery outside the marriage (D)
No	No	No	No	No	No	_____
No	D 3 years	D No time specified	D No time specified	D No time specified	D 1 year	Abuse or neglect of a child (D)
No	No	No	No	No	No	_____
No	D/S 2 years	No	No	No	No	_____

Chart 23   1150

WAITING PERIODS BETWEEN DIVORCE AND REMARRIAGE

	Time required between filing of suit and final decree	Time required between interlocutory and final decrees	Time that must elapse after final decree before plaintiff or defendant may remarry
ALABAMA	None	None	60 days
ALASKA	30 days	None	None
ARIZONA	60 days	None	None
ARKANSAS	30 days[1]	None	None
CALIFORNIA	6 months	None	None
COLORADO	90 days	None	None
CONNECTICUT	90 days	None	None
DELAWARE	None	None	None
DISTRICT OF COLUMBIA	After expiration of time for appealing	None	None
FLORIDA	20 days	None	None
GEORGIA	30 days[2]	None	At discretion of court
HAWAII	None	None	None
IDAHO	None	None	None
ILLINOIS	None	None	None
INDIANA	60 days	None	None
IOWA	90 days	None	None
KANSAS	60 days	None	30 days
KENTUCKY	None[3]	None	None
LOUISIANA	None	None	None
MAINE	60 days	None	None
MARYLAND	None	None	None
MASSACHUSETTS	18 months[2]	6 months	None
MICHIGAN	60 days[4]	None	None
MINNESOTA	30 days	None	None
MISSISSIPPI	60 days[2]	None	None[5]
MISSOURI	30 days	None	None

[1] But no waiting period is required if ground for divorce is willful desertion for 1 year or continuous separation for 3 years without cohabitation.

[2] When divorce was granted upon no-fault ground; otherwise, no waiting period.

[3] But when there are children from the marriage or when divorce was granted upon no-fault ground, 60 days.

[4] But when there are dependent children under 18, 6 months.

[5] But if ground is adultery, court may prohibit remarriage for defendant.

Most states require a minimum waiting period between the filing of a suit for DIVORCE and the issuance of the final divorce decree. A few states require a waiting period between the interlocutory and final decrees. (An interlocutory decree is a preliminary decree that is issued pending the final one.) Finally, some states have waiting periods between divorce and remarriage.

	Time required between filing of suit and final decree	Time required between interlocutory and final decrees	Time that must elapse after final decree before plaintiff or defendant may remarry
MONTANA	20 days	None	None
NEBRASKA	60 days	6 months	None
NEVADA	None	None	None
NEW HAMPSHIRE	None	None	None
NEW JERSEY	None	None	None
NEW MEXICO	None	None	None
NEW YORK	None	None	None
NORTH CAROLINA	None	None	None
NORTH DAKOTA	None	None	At discretion of court
OHIO	None[6]	None	None
OKLAHOMA	None	6 months	6 months
OREGON	90 days	60 days or until appeal settled	60 days or until appeal settled
PENNSYLVANIA	None	None	None[7]
RHODE ISLAND	60 days	3 months	None
SOUTH CAROLINA	3 months	None	None
SOUTH DAKOTA	60 days	None	None
TENNESSEE	None	None	None
TEXAS	60 days	None	30 days
UTAH	90 days	3-6 months	None, but no remarriage pending appeal
VERMONT	None	3 months	None
VIRGINIA	None	None	None, but no remarriage pending appeal
WASHINGTON	90 days	None	None
WEST VIRGINIA	None	None	None
WISCONSIN	120 days[8]	None	6 months after final decree
WYOMING	20 days	None	None

[6] But proceedings may be held up by court for 90 days after ground has been established if court feels parties should attempt reconciliation.

[7] But if ground is adultery, defendant may not marry corespondent during lifetime of plaintiff.

[8] Unless court orders an immediate hearing to protect a party or a child.

Chart 24   **1152**

OWNERSHIP AND REGISTRATION OF YOUR AUTOMOBILE

State laws provide for the licensing and registration of MOTOR VEHICLES. *The length of time you may use your car in another state without obtaining a new registration varies from state to state, frequently depending on reciprocity agreements between states. In a reciprocity registration agreement, State A will allow a motorist with a State B auto registration to operate his car in State A for a specified period of time, and State B will extend a similar courtesy to State A. A certificate of title is a written*

	Is certificate of title required?	Who issues certificate of title?	How long is out-of-state registration valid?	Who gets license plates when car is sold?
ALABAMA	Yes	Motor Vehicle Division Alabama Revenue Department Montgomery 36116	30 days	Buyer
ALASKA	Yes	Department of Public Safety P.O. Box 960 Anchorage 99501	90 days or 15 days after employment	Buyer
ARIZONA	Yes	Motor Vehicle Division Department of Transportation Phoenix 85007	6 months or until employment or school enrollment	Buyer
ARKANSAS	Yes	Motor Vehicle Division P.O. Box 1272 Little Rock 72203	10 days after employment. Tourists are allowed 90 days if they obtain a visitor's permit after 30 days	Seller
CALIFORNIA	Yes	Department of Motor Vehicles Sacramento 95806	Until expiration, but no more than 1 year	Buyer
COLORADO	Yes	County clerk For Denver, Motor Vehicle Department	30 days after employment or 90 days after establishing residence	Seller
CONNECTICUT	Yes	Commissioner of Motor Vehicles Wethersfield 06109	60 days after establishing residence	Department of Motor Vehicles
DELAWARE	Yes	Motor Vehicle Division Dover 19901	90 days after establishing residence or until employment or school enrollment	Buyer
DISTRICT OF COLUMBIA	Yes	Bureau of Motor Vehicle Services Washington, D.C. 20001	Until expiration of reciprocity agreement	Seller
FLORIDA	Yes	Division of Motor Vehicles Tallahassee 32304	Until 10 days after establishing residence or 10 days after school enrollment	Seller
GEORGIA	Yes[1]	Motor Vehicle Division State Department of Revenue Atlanta 30334	30 days after establishing residence	Buyer

[1] For 1963 and later model vehicles.

*document that is evidence of ownership of a vehicle and is required if the vehicle is to be sold. It is
also necessary to have a set of license plates for your car. When you sell the car you may have to pass
the plates on to the buyer or keep them yourself, depending on the law in your state. This chart
shows the laws for automobile ownership and registration in the various states. For more detail, contact
your state department of motor vehicles.*

	Is certificate of title required?	Who issues certificate of title?	How long is out-of-state registration valid?	Who gets license plates when car is sold?
HAWAII	Yes	County treasurer or director of finance	10 days, but a non-resident may obtain a permit to operate his vehicle with his out-of-state registration until it expires	Buyer
IDAHO	Yes	Motor Vehicle Division Department of Law Enforcement Boise 83703 Or county assessor	Until employment or 90 days after establishing employment	Seller
ILLINOIS	Yes	Secretary of State Vehicle Services Department Springfield 62756	Until expiration of reciprocity agreement or establishing residence	Seller
INDIANA	Yes	Bureau of Motor Vehicles 401 State Office Building Indianapolis 46204	60 days	Seller
IOWA	Yes	County treasurer	Until establishing residence or employment, but seasonal or temporary employment of less than 90 days excluded	Buyer
KANSAS	Yes	County treasurer	Until expiration of reciprocity agreement	Seller
KENTUCKY	Yes	County clerk	Until expiration of reciprocity agreement or establishing residence	Buyer
LOUISIANA	Yes	Department of Public Safety Motor Vehicle Division Baton Rouge 70896	Until expiration of reciprocity agreement or employment	Seller
MAINE	Yes[2]	Motor Vehicle Division Child Street Augusta 04333	30 days after establishing residence	Seller
MARYLAND	Yes	Motor Vehicle Administration Glen Burnie 21061	A nonresident's permit may be obtained in lieu of registration if living in the state temporarily for 60 days	Seller

[2] For 1975 and later model vehicles.

Chart 24   **1154**

OWNERSHIP AND REGISTRATION OF YOUR AUTOMOBILE *(continued)*

	Is certificate of title required?	Who issues certificate of title?	How long is out-of-state registration valid?	Who gets license plates when car is sold?
MASSACHUSETTS	Yes[3]	Registry of Motor Vehicles Boston 02114	Until expiration of reciprocity agreement	Seller
MICHIGAN	Yes	Secretary of State Lansing 48918	Until establishing residence or 90 days, whichever is less	Seller
MINNESOTA	Yes	Commissioner of Public Safety Motor Vehicle Division St. Paul 55155	Until expiration of reciprocity agreement or 60 days after establishing residence	Buyer
MISSISSIPPI	Yes	Motor Vehicle Comptroller P.O. Box 1140 Jackson 39205	Until expiration of reciprocity agreement	Buyer
MISSOURI	Yes	Motor Vehicle Registration Unit Jefferson City 65101	Until establishing residence	Seller
MONTANA	Yes	Registrar of Motor Vehicles Deer Lodge 59722	Until employment, establishing residence, or school enrollment	Seller
NEBRASKA	Yes	County clerk	Until expiration of reciprocity agreement or establishing residence	Seller
NEVADA	Yes	Department of Motor Vehicles Registration Division Carson City 89711	45 days after establishing residence	Seller
NEW HAMPSHIRE	Yes[3]	Director of Motor Vehicles Concord 03301	60 days after establishing residence	Seller
NEW JERSEY	Yes	Motor Vehicles Director Trenton 08625	60 days after establishing residence	Seller
NEW MEXICO	Yes	Department of Motor Vehicles Santa Fe 87503	180 days or 30 days after establishing residence	Buyer
NEW YORK	Yes[4]	Department of Motor Vehicles Empire State Plaza Albany 12228	30 days after establishing residence	Seller
NORTH CAROLINA	Yes	Commissioner of Motor Vehicles Raleigh 27602	Until expiration of reciprocity agreement or employment	Seller
NORTH DAKOTA	Yes[3]	Registrar of Motor Vehicles Bismarck 58505	Until employment or establishing residence	Buyer
OHIO	Yes	Clerk of county court	Until expiration of reciprocity agreement or 30 days after establishing residence	Seller
OKLAHOMA	Yes	Oklahoma Tax Commission Oklahoma City 73194	60 days	Buyer

[3] For vehicles less than 10 years old.   [4] For 1973 and later model vehicles.

	Is certificate of title required?	Who issues certificate of title?	How long is out-of-state registration valid?	Who gets license plates when car is sold?
OREGON	Yes	Motor Vehicles Division Department of Transportation Salem 97310	Until establishing residence	Buyer
PENNSYLVANIA	Yes	Department of Transportation Harrisburg 17122	Nonresident may operate vehicle for non-commercial uses until establishing residence or employment	Seller
RHODE ISLAND	Yes	Registry of Motor Vehicles Providence 02903	30 days	Seller
SOUTH CAROLINA	Yes	Motor Vehicle Division Department of Highways and Public Transportation Columbia 29216	10 days after establishing residence	Buyer
SOUTH DAKOTA	Yes	Department of Public Safety Public Safety Building Pierre 57501	60 days or until employment or school enrollment	Buyer
TENNESSEE	Yes	Motor Vehicle Division Department of Revenue Nashville 37219	Until expiration of reciprocity agreement, establishing residence, or employment	Seller
TEXAS	Yes	Department of Highways and Public Transportation Motor Vehicle Division Austin 78779	Until establishing residence or employment	Buyer
UTAH	Yes	Department of Motor Vehicles Salt Lake City 84116	Until establishing residence or employment	Seller
VERMONT	Yes[5]	Department of Motor Vehicles Montpelier 05602	Until establishing residence or 6 months after employment	Seller
VIRGINIA	Yes	Division of Motor Vehicles Richmond 23261	6 months	Seller
WASHINGTON	Yes	Department of Licensing Olympia 98504 Or county auditor	60 days	Buyer
WEST VIRGINIA	Yes	Department of Motor Vehicles Charleston 25305	30 days	Seller
WISCONSIN	Yes	Vehicle Registration Department of Transportation P.O. Box 7909 Madison 53707	Until expiration of reciprocity agreement or establishing residence	Seller
WYOMING	Yes	County clerk	30 days	Seller

[5] For 1972 and later model vehicles.

Chart 25   1156

AUTOMOBILE INSPECTION LAWS

	Does state require inspections and, if so, how frequently?
ALABAMA	No, but cities have the authority to maintain inspection stations and enact local inspection laws
ALASKA	No, but police may inspect any vehicle at the roadside if there is a reasonable cause to believe it is unsafe
ARIZONA	No, but annual inspections of engine exhaust emissions are required in Maricopa and Pima counties
ARKANSAS	Yes, annually
CALIFORNIA	No, but police may inspect any vehicle at the roadside if there is reasonable cause to believe vehicle is unsafe
COLORADO	Yes, annually
CONNECTICUT	Only for used out-of-state vehicles being registered in Connecticut and Connecticut cars more than 10 years old before resale or transfer. There are also provisions for voluntary inspections
DELAWARE	Yes, annually
DISTRICT OF COLUMBIA	Yes, annually
FLORIDA	Yes, annually
GEORGIA	Yes, annually. Newly registered vehicles must be inspected within 5 days of registration unless displaying valid out-of-state inspection stickers
HAWAII	Yes, vehicles 10 years or older and rented vehicles, semiannually; others, annually
IDAHO	No
ILLINOIS	Only for trucks, semiannually
INDIANA	Yes, annually. Vehicles must be reinspected if sold or transferred or if police consider an inspection warranted following an accident
IOWA	Yes, prior to first registration in Iowa and on all transfers
KANSAS	Yes, prior to resale. Police may stop a vehicle for inspection if there is reasonable cause to believe it is unsafe
KENTUCKY	No, but vehicles not previously registered in state (except new vehicles from licensed Kentucky dealers) must be inspected before registration
LOUISIANA	Yes, annually or semiannually at the discretion of the director of public safety
MAINE	Yes, semiannually
MARYLAND	Only for used passenger cars upon resale or transfer or when moving to Maryland from another state
MASSACHUSETTS	Yes, twice a year, Apr. 1-May 15 and Sept. 1-Oct. 15. A vehicle registered between inspection periods must be inspected within 7 days of registration
MICHIGAN	No, but there are provisions for random inspections and for individual inspections when there is reasonable cause to believe vehicles are unsafe

Well over half the states require regular inspections of automobiles and other MOTOR VEHICLES, as shown below. These inspections—generally for brakes, lights, and the like—are designed to protect the public from the dangers of the operation of unsafe or defective vehicles. Some states require inspections only of newly registered vehicles. Others require no regular inspections but allow state police to conduct random roadside inspections.

	Does state require inspections and, if so, how frequently?
MINNESOTA	No, but municipalities may provide for inspections and police may conduct spot inspections
MISSISSIPPI	Yes, annually
MISSOURI	Yes, annually, no more than 60 days prior to renewal of registration
MONTANA	No
NEBRASKA	Yes, annually
NEVADA	No
NEW HAMPSHIRE	Yes, semiannually; first inspection during month of birth date of owner and then every 6 months. Newly registered vehicles must be inspected within 10 days of registration
NEW JERSEY	Yes, annually during the month of renewal of registration
NEW MEXICO	Yes, semiannually
NEW YORK	Yes, annually
NORTH CAROLINA	Yes, annually. All vehicles purchased outside state or brought into state for registration must be inspected and must display certificate within 10 days
NORTH DAKOTA	No, but police may conduct roadside inspections
OHIO	No, but police may conduct roadside inspections
OKLAHOMA	Yes, annually
OREGON	No, but police may conduct roadside inspections
PENNSYLVANIA	Yes, semiannually
RHODE ISLAND	Yes, at least once a year but no more than twice a year
SOUTH CAROLINA	Yes, annually
SOUTH DAKOTA	No
TENNESSEE	No, but state law permits inspections by cities
TEXAS	Yes, annually and after an accident
UTAH	Yes, at least once a year
VERMONT	Yes, semiannually
VIRGINIA	Yes, immediately after first registration, then 12 months later and semiannually thereafter
WASHINGTON	No, except as result of citation for defective equipment or spot check by police
WEST VIRGINIA	Yes, annually. New vehicles purchased in state must be inspected within 3 days; vehicles purchased out of state, within 10 days after entry into state
WISCONSIN	No, but spot checks are conducted by police for defective or missing equipment
WYOMING	No

Chart 26   1158

AUTOMOBILE INSURANCE OR PROOF OF FINANCIAL

All states require motorists to buy insurance or show that they are financially able to pay for damages they cause in accidents. There are several types of laws. Security laws, which some states call financial responsibility laws, require a motorist to do nothing unless he has an accident. However, when he has his first accident, he either must show that he has insurance to pay court-ordered damages for that accident if he is found responsible or must post a bond with the court for a particular amount. Future proof laws go one step further. Once the motorist has been judged responsible for an accident or has been convicted of vehicular homicide, drunken driving, or some

	Type of law	What results of accidents are covered?	Minimum liability for property damage	Minimum liability for injury or death
ALABAMA	Security	Injury, death, over $50 damage	$5,000	$10,000/$20,000
ALASKA	Security	Injury, death, over $500 damage	$10,000	$25,000/$50,000
ARIZONA	Security	Injury, death, over $300 damage	$5,000	$15,000/$30,000
ARKANSAS	No-fault or security	Injury, death, over $250 damage	$5,000	$10,000/$20,000
CALIFORNIA	Financial responsibility	Injury, death, over $350 damage	$5,000	$15,000/$30,000
COLORADO	No-fault	——	——	——
CONNECTICUT	No-fault	——	——	——
DELAWARE	No-fault	——	——	——
DISTRICT OF COLUMBIA	Security	Injury, death, over $100 damage	$5,000	$10,000/$20,000
FLORIDA	No-fault	——	——	——
GEORGIA	No-fault	——	——	——
HAWAII	No-fault	——	——	——
IDAHO	Security	Injury, death, over $100 damage	$5,000	$10,000/$20,000
ILLINOIS	Security	Injury, death, over $250 damage	$5,000	$10,000/$20,000
INDIANA	Security	Injury, death, over $200 damage	$10,000	$15,000/$30,000
IOWA	Security	Injury, death, over $250 damage	$5,000	$10,000/$20,000

RESPONSIBILITY

other such crime, he either must show that he has insurance to cover future accidents or must post a bond to cover them. Some states require all vehicles to be covered by no-fault insurance—a type of insurance that pays damages caused by accidents no matter who was to blame—before being registered. This chart shows what is required by each state, including—where no-fault insurance is not compulsory—the amount of insurance or bond required. In the case of liability for injury or death, the first figure given is the minimum amount for accidents that cause the injury or death of one person; the second is the minimum for accidents that cause injury or death to more than one person. See also INSURANCE.

	Type of law	What results of accidents are covered?	Minimum liability for property damage	Minimum liability for injury or death
KANSAS	No-fault	——	——	——
KENTUCKY	No-fault	——	——	——
LOUISIANA	Security	Injury, death, over $200 damage	$1,000	$5,000/$10,000
MAINE	Security	Injury, death, over $200 damage	$10,000	$20,000/$40,000
MARYLAND	No-fault	——	——	——
MASSACHUSETTS	No-fault	——	——	——
MICHIGAN	No-fault	——	——	——
MINNESOTA	No-fault	——	——	——
MISSISSIPPI	Security and future proof	Injury, death, over $100 damage	$5,000	$10,000/$20,000
MISSOURI	Security	Injury, death, over $100 damage	$2,000	$10,000/$20,000
MONTANA	Security and future proof	Injury, death, over $250 damage	$5,000	$10,000/$20,000
NEBRASKA	Security	Injury, death, over $250 damage	$10,000	$15,000/$30,000
NEVADA	Security	Injury, death, over $250 damage	$5,000	$20,000/$40,000
NEW HAMPSHIRE	Security	Injury, death, over $300 damage	$5,000	$20,000/$40,000
NEW JERSEY	No-fault	——	——	——
NEW MEXICO	Future proof	Injury, death, over $100 damage	$5,000	$15,000/$30,000

Chart 26

1160

AUTOMOBILE INSURANCE OR PROOF OF
FINANCIAL RESPONSIBILITY *(continued)*

	Type of law	What results of accidents are covered?	Minimum liability for property damage	Minimum liability for injury or death
NEW YORK	No-fault	———	———	———
NORTH CAROLINA	Security	Injury, death, over $200 damage	$5,000	$15,000/$30,000
NORTH DAKOTA	Security	Injury, death, over $200 damage	$5,000	$10,000/$20,000
OHIO	Security	Injury, death, over $100 damage	$7,500	$12,500/$25,000
OKLAHOMA	Security	Injury, death, over $100 damage	$5,000	$5,000/$10,000
OREGON	No-fault	———	———	———
PENNSYLVANIA	No-fault	———	———	———
RHODE ISLAND	Security	Injury, death, over $200 damage	$10,000	$25,000/$50,000
SOUTH CAROLINA	No-fault or security	Injury, death, over $200 damage	$5,000	$15,000/$30,000
SOUTH DAKOTA	No-fault or future proof	Injury, death, over $400 damage	$10,000	$15,000/$30,000
TENNESSEE	Security and future proof	Injury, death, over $200 damage, or payment of moving traffic violation	$5,000	$10,000/$20,000
TEXAS	Security	Injury, death, over $250 damage	$5,000	$10,000/$20,000
UTAH	No-fault	———	———	———
VERMONT	Security and future proof	Injury, death, over $200 damage	$5,000	$10,000/$20,000
VIRGINIA	No-fault or security and future proof	Injury, death, over $250 damage	$10,000	$25,000/$50,000
WASHINGTON	Security and future proof	Injury, death, over $300 damage	$5,000	$15,000/$30,000
WEST VIRGINIA	Security and future proof	Injury, death, over $300 damage	$10,000	$20,000/$40,000
WISCONSIN	Security	Injury, death, over $200 damage	$10,000	$15,000/$30,000
WYOMING	Security	Injury, death, over $250 damage	$5,000	$10,000/$20,000

HOW TO REPORT
AN AUTOMOBILE ACCIDENT

Laws in all states require that automobile accidents involving any personal injury or death and more than a specified amount of property damage be reported.

	Property damage in excess of	Time limit (in days) for filing report	Where to file
ALABAMA	$50	10	Local police
ALASKA	$500	10	Department of Public Safety Motor Vehicle Division P.O. Box 960 Anchorage 99510
ARIZONA	$300	5	Motor Vehicle Division Department of Transportation 1801 West Jefferson Street Phoenix 85007
ARKANSAS	$250	30	State police
CALIFORNIA	$350	15	Local police or highway patrol
COLORADO	$250	10	Motor Vehicle Department 140 West Sixth Avenue Denver 80204
CONNECTICUT	$400	5	Commissioner of Motor Vehicles Department of Motor Vehicles 60 State Street Wethersfield 06109
DELAWARE	$250	Immediately	Local police
DISTRICT OF COLUMBIA	$100	5	Bureau of Motor Vehicle Services 301 C Street NW Washington 20001
FLORIDA	$100	5	Department of Highway Safety and Motor Vehicles Kirkman Building Tallahassee 32301
GEORGIA	$100	10	Bureau of Safety Responsibility Department of Public Safety P.O. Box 1456 Atlanta 30301
HAWAII	$300	1	Local police
IDAHO	$250	Immediately	Motor Vehicle Division Department of Law Enforcement P.O. Box 34 Boise 83731
ILLINOIS	$250	10	Director Department of Transportation Springfield 62756
INDIANA	$100	5	State police
IOWA	$250	3	Peace officer as near as practicable to place of accident

HOW TO REPORT AN AUTOMOBILE ACCIDENT *(continued)*

	Property damage in excess of	Time limit (in days) for filing report	Where to file
KANSAS	$200	10	Motor Vehicle Department State Office Building Topeka 66626
KENTUCKY	$200	10	Department of Justice Frankfort 40601
LOUISIANA	$100	1	Division of state police or local police
MAINE	$300	Immediately	State or local police
MARYLAND	$100	15	Motor Vehicle Administration 6601 Ritchie Highway NE Glen Burnie 21062
MASSACHUSETTS	$200	5	Local police and Registrar of Motor Vehicles 100 Nashua Street Boston 02114
MICHIGAN	$200	Immediately	Local police
MINNESOTA	$300	10	Commissioner of Public Safety State Highway Building St. Paul 55155
MISSISSIPPI	$250	10	Department of Public Safety Jackson 39205
MISSOURI	$100	60	Director of Internal Revenue State Office Building Jefferson City 65101
MONTANA	$250	10	Local police, sheriff, or highway patrol
NEBRASKA	$250	10	Department of Motor Vehicles State Capitol Building Lincoln 68509
NEVADA	$250	10	Department of Motor Vehicles Driver's License Division Safety Responsibility Section Carson City 89711
NEW HAMPSHIRE	$100	5	Director of Motor Vehicles Department of Safety Loudon Road Concord 03301
NEW JERSEY	$200	5	Director Division of Motor Vehicles Trenton 08625
NEW MEXICO	$100	5	Division of Motor Vehicles Santa Fe 87501
NEW YORK	$150	10	Commissioner of Motor Vehicles Department of Motor Vehicles Empire State Plaza Albany 12228
NORTH CAROLINA	$200	Immediately; within 48 hours if collision with unattended vehicle	Local police or state highway patrol

	Property damage in excess of	Time limit (in days) for filing report	Where to file
NORTH DAKOTA	$300	10	Highway Commissioner Bismarck 58501
OHIO	$100	30	Local police or county sheriff
OKLAHOMA	$100	10	Commissioner of Public Safety 3600 North Eastern Avenue Oklahoma City 73111
OREGON	$200	3	Local police or sheriff
PENNSYLVANIA	When car is so damaged that it cannot be driven safely or requires towing	5	Bureau of Motor Vehicles Department of Transportation Harrisburg 17122
RHODE ISLAND	$200	10	Division of Motor Vehicles State Office Building Providence 02903
SOUTH CAROLINA	$200	15	State Department of Highways and Public Transportation Drawer 1458 Columbia 29250
SOUTH DAKOTA	$400	Immediately	Local police and Director of Division of Highway Patrol Public Safety Building Pierre 57501
TENNESSEE	$200	20	Department of Safety P.O. Box 945 Nashville 37202
TEXAS	$100	10	Statistical Services Texas Department of Public Safety P.O. Box 4087 Austin 78773
UTAH	$400	5	Department of Public Safety Salt Lake City 84114
VERMONT	$100	3	Commissioner of Motor Vehicles Montpelier 05602
VIRGINIA	$350	5	Division of Motor Vehicles 2220 West Broad Street Richmond 23220
WASHINGTON	$300	1	Local police
WEST VIRGINIA	$250	5	Department of Motor Vehicles State Capitol Building Charleston 25305
WISCONSIN	$200	10	Department of Motor Vehicles 4802 Sheboygan Avenue Madison 53702
WYOMING	$250	5	State Highway Department State Board of Equalization Cheyenne 82001

Chart 28   **1164**

LIABILITY FOR AUTOMOBILE ACCIDENTS

The states have various types of liability laws for automobile accidents. Guest statutes prohibit a guest in an automobile or other MOTOR VEHICLE *from suing the driver for injuries suffered in an accident unless it was caused by the driver's extreme* NEGLIGENCE. *The family car doctrine makes the car owner liable if his automobile was negligently driven by a family member. Comparative negligence*

	Guest statute?	Family car doctrine?	Comparative or contributory negligence?	Within how many years must you sue:		
				For property damage?	For personal injury?	For wrongful death?
ALABAMA	Yes	No	Contributory	1	1	2 years of death
ALASKA	No	No	Comparative	6	2	2 years of death
ARIZONA	No	Yes	Contributory	2	2	2 years of death
ARKANSAS	Yes[1]	No	Comparative	3	5	3 years of death
CALIFORNIA	No	No	Comparative	3	1	1 year of death
COLORADO	No	Yes	Comparative	6	6	2 years of accident
CONNECTICUT	No	Yes	Comparative	2	2	2 years of accident
DELAWARE	Yes	No	Contributory	2	2	2 years of death
D.C.	No	Yes	Contributory	3	3	1 year of death
FLORIDA	No	No[2]	Comparative	4	4	2 years of death
GEORGIA	Yes	Yes	Comparative	4	2	2 years of death
HAWAII	No	No	Comparative	2	2	2 years of death
IDAHO	Yes	Yes[3]	Comparative	3	2	2 years of death
ILLINOIS	Yes	No	Contributory	5	2	2 years of death
INDIANA	Yes	No	Contributory	2	2	2 years of death
IOWA	Yes	Yes[3]	Contributory	5	2	2 years of death
KANSAS	No	No[4]	Comparative	2	2	2 years of death
KENTUCKY	No	Yes	Contributory	5	1	1 year of death
LOUISIANA	No	No[5]	Contributory	1	1	1 year of death
MAINE	No	No	Comparative	6	6	2 years of death
MARYLAND	No	No	Contributory	3	3	3 years of death
MASSACHUSETTS	Yes	No[2]	Comparative	3	3	3 years of death
MICHIGAN	No	Yes	Contributory	3	3	3 years of death
MINNESOTA	No	Yes[3]	Comparative	6	6	3 years of accident
MISSISSIPPI	No	No	Comparative	6	6	6 years of death
MISSOURI	No	No	Contributory	5	5	3 years of death

[1] But only for guests related by blood or marriage.

[2] But owner is liable when anyone, not just a family member, uses his car.

[3] And owner is liable when anyone, not just a family member, uses his car with specific or implied consent.

laws reduce a driver's liability in proportion to the victim's negligence. Contributory negligence laws completely absolve a driver of liability if he can show that the victim's negligence contributed to the accident. Statutes of limitations specify the time within which you may sue for property damage, personal injuries, or WRONGFUL DEATH *(death caused by another's negligence or wrongful act).*

	Guest statute?	Family car doctrine?	Comparative or contributory negligence?	Within how many years must you sue:		
				For property damage?	For personal injury?	For wrongful death?
MONTANA	No	No	Comparative	2	2	3 years of death
NEBRASKA	Yes	Yes	Comparative	4	4	2 years of death
NEVADA	No	Yes	Comparative	3	2	2 years of death
NEW HAMPSHIRE	No	No	Comparative	6	2	2 years of death
NEW JERSEY	No	Yes	Comparative	6	2	2 years of death
NEW MEXICO	No	No	Contributory	4	3	3 years of death
NEW YORK	No	Yes[3]	Comparative	3	3	2 years of death
NORTH CAROLINA	No	Yes	Contributory	3	3	2 years of death
NORTH DAKOTA	No	Yes	Comparative	6	6	2 years of death
OHIO	No	No	Contributory	2	2	2 years of death
OKLAHOMA	No	No	Comparative	2	2	2 years of death
OREGON	Yes	Yes	Comparative	6	2	3 years of accident
PENNSYLVANIA	No	No	Comparative	2	2	1 year of death
RHODE ISLAND	No	No	Comparative	10	3	2 years of death
SOUTH CAROLINA	Yes	Yes	Contributory	6	6	6 years of death
SOUTH DAKOTA	No	No	Comparative	6	3	3 years of death
TENNESSEE	No	Yes	Contributory	3	1	1 year of death
TEXAS	Yes[6]	No	Comparative	2	2	2 years of death
UTAH	Yes	No	Comparative	3	4	2 years of death
VERMONT	No	No	Comparative	3	3	2 years of death
VIRGINIA	Yes	No	Contributory	5	2	2 years of death
WASHINGTON	No	Yes	Comparative	3	3	3 years of death
WEST VIRGINIA	No	Yes	Contributory	2	2	2 years of death
WISCONSIN	No	No	Comparative	6	3	3 years of death
WYOMING	Yes	No	Comparative	4	4	2 years of death

[4] But owner is liable when anyone under 16, not just a family member, uses his car with his consent.

[5] But father is liable when a minor child living at home uses his car.

[6] But only for guests that are at least as closely related to the owner as his grandparents or grandchildren either by blood or marriage.

Chart 29   1166

REQUIREMENTS FOR A DRIVER'S LICENSE

Every state requires that you carry a driver's license if you want to operate a car or other MOTOR VEHICLE *on public streets or highways. In some states, you must get a learner's permit in order to practice while learning to drive, and you may drive with it only when you are accompanied by a licensed driver. Teenagers who are not old enough to get a regular license may get a junior license. To get a junior license the applicant has to pass the same tests that are required for a regular license, and a driver education course may have to be completed as well. A junior*

	What is minimum age for license?	Does state issue junior license and, if so, at what age?	Is learner's permit required?	What tests are required for original license?
ALABAMA	16	Yes: at 14, for light-weight motorcycles only	Yes	Written, driving, and eye
ALASKA	18; 16 with written parental consent	No	Yes	Written, driving, and eye
ARIZONA	18; 16 with notarized parental consent	No	No	Written, oral, driving, and eye
ARKANSAS	18; 16 if parent signs application	Yes: at 14, but driver under 16 must be accompanied by licensed adult	Yes	Written, oral, driving, and eye
CALIFORNIA	18; 16 if applicant has completed a driver education course	Yes: at 15	Yes	Written, road sign, driving, and eye
COLORADO	21	Yes: at 16, but it must be renewed annually	Yes	Written, driving, and eye
CONNECTICUT	18; 16 if applicant has completed a driver education course	No	For motorcycles only	Written, oral, driving, and eye
DELAWARE	18; 16 if applicant has completed a driver education course	No	Yes	Written, driving, and eye
DISTRICT OF COLUMBIA	18; 16 with written parental consent	No	Yes	Written, oral, driving, and eye
FLORIDA	16 with notarized parental consent	Yes: at 15	Yes	Written, road sign, driving, eye, and hearing
GEORGIA	16	No	Yes	Written, driving, and eye
HAWAII	18; 15 with parental consent	No	Yes	Written, driving, and eye

license permits the operator to drive only under certain conditions, such as during daylight hours or just to and from school. In some states, a junior license is called a minor's license, a probationary license, a restricted license, or a provisional license. Generally, if you move to another state, you must get a new license in that state within a specified period of time. Some states base this time limit on reciprocal agreements with other states. This means that certain states will mutually agree to recognize the validity of the others' licenses until they expire.

Is licensee's photograph required?	How long is license valid?	What tests are required for renewal?	How long is a nonresident license valid?
Yes	4 years; it expires on anniversary of date of issue	None	30 days
Yes, on license	5 years; it expires on driver's birthday	Eye	90 days
Yes, on license	3 years; it expires on driver's birthday	Written and eye	Until employment; visitors need permit after 10 days
Yes, on license	2 or 4 years at driver's option; it expires on last day of driver's month of birth	None	90 days; visitors must register after 30 days
Yes, in color, on license	4 years; it expires on driver's birthday	Written and eye	10 days after establishing residence
Yes, in color, on license	4 years; it expires on driver's birthday	Eye and in some cases written	30 days after establishing residence or being employed
Yes, on licenses issued after July 1, 1977	4 years; it expires on driver's birthday	None	60 days after establishing residence
Yes, in color, and new photograph every 4 years	4 years; it expires on driver's birthday	Eye	90 days after establishing residence
Yes, in color	4 years; it expires on driver's birthday	Eye plus special tests for drivers 70 and over	Reciprocal basis; visitors need permit after 14 days
Yes, in color	4 years; it expires on driver's birthday	Road sign, eye, and hearing	Until establishing residence or being employed
Yes, in color, on license	4 years; it expires on driver's birthday	Eye	30 days or until being employed
Yes, in color, on license	4 years, but 2 years if driver is 15-24 or over 65; it expires on driver's birthday	Written and eye	Until it expires

Chart 29   1168

REQUIREMENTS FOR A DRIVER'S LICENSE *(continued)*

	What is minimum age for license?	Does state issue junior license and, if so, at what age?	Is learner's permit required?	What tests are required for original license?
IDAHO	16 with parental consent	Yes: at 14 if applicant has completed a driver education course	No	Written, driving, and eye
ILLINOIS	18; 16 if parent signs application and applicant has completed a driver education course	No	Yes	Written, driving, and eye
INDIANA	18	Yes: at 16 years and 6 months with parental consent or at 16 years and 1 month if applicant has completed a driver education course	Yes	Written, driving, and eye
IOWA	18; 16 if applicant has completed a driver education course	Yes: at 14, but it is valid only for driving to and from school	No	Written, driving, and eye
KANSAS	16	Yes: at 14	Yes	Written, driving, and eye
KENTUCKY	18; 16 with written parental consent	No	Yes	Written, driving, eye, hearing, and physical disability
LOUISIANA	17	Yes: at 15 with parental consent, but it is valid only during certain hours	No	Written, driving, and eye
MAINE	18; 17 with parental consent	Yes: at 15 if applicant has completed a driver education course, but it is valid only for driving to and from school	Yes	Written, oral, driving, and eye
MARYLAND	18; 16 if parent signs application and applicant has completed a driver education course	No	Yes	Written, driving, and eye
MASSACHUSETTS	18	Yes: at 17, or at 16 years and 6 months if applicant has completed a driver education course, but it is valid only during certain hours unless driver is accompanied by parent	Yes	Written, driving, and eye
MICHIGAN	18; 16 if parent signs application and applicant has completed a driver education course	Yes: at 14 with parental consent, but it must be renewed annually	Yes	Written, oral, driving, and eye

Is licensee's photograph required?	How long is license valid?	What tests are required for renewal?	How long is a nonresident license valid?
Yes, taken at sheriff's office at no charge	3 years; it expires on driver's birthday	Eye	90 days or until establishing residence or being employed
Yes	3 years; it expires on driver's birthday	Written and eye every 9 years; every 3 years if driver is over 69	90 days after establishing residence
Yes	4 years, but 2 years if driver is over 75; it expires on last day of driver's month of birth	Written and eye; for drivers over 75, driving	60 days or until establishing residence
Yes	4 years, but 2 years if driver is 16-18 or over 64; it expires on driver's birthday	Eye	Until establishing residence
Yes	4 years; it expires on driver's birthday	Written and eye	Reciprocal basis
Yes	2 years; it expires on last day of driver's month of birth	None	Reciprocal basis
Yes, in color, on license	4 years, but 2 years if driver is 70 or over; it expires on driver's birthday	Eye and every 4 years written	Until establishing residence
No	4 years, but 2 years if driver is over 75; it expires on driver's birthday	Eye when driver is 40, 52, or over 65	30 days after establishing residence
No	4 years; it expires on driver's birthday	None	Until establishing residence
Yes, in color	4 years; it expires on driver's birthday	Eye	Reciprocal basis
Yes, in color, on license	4 years, but 2 years for problem drivers; it expires on driver's birthday	Written and eye	Until establishing residence

Chart 29

1170

REQUIREMENTS FOR A DRIVER'S LICENSE *(continued)*

	What is minimum age for license?	Does state issue junior license and, if so, at what age?	Is learner's permit required?	What tests are required for original license?
MINNESOTA	18	Yes: at 16	Yes	Written, driving, and eye
MISSISSIPPI	15	No	Yes	Written, road sign, driving, and eye
MISSOURI	16	No	No	Written, road sign, driving, and eye
MONTANA	18	Yes: at 15 if applicant has completed a driver education course; at 16 with parental consent	Yes	Written, driving, and eye
NEBRASKA	16	No	Yes	Written, driving, and eye
NEVADA	18; 16 with parental consent	No	Yes	Written, driving, and eye
NEW HAMPSHIRE	18; 16 if applicant has completed a driver education course	No	No	Written, oral, driving, and eye
NEW JERSEY	17	Yes: at 16, but only for agricultural work	Yes	Written, driving, and eye
NEW MEXICO	16; 15 if applicant has completed a driver education course	No	Yes	Written, driving, and eye
NEW YORK	18; 17 if applicant has completed a driver education course	Yes: at 16, but it is valid only during certain hours unless driver is accompanied by parent, and it is not valid in New York City	Yes	Written, road sign, driving, eye, and driver training
NORTH CAROLINA	18; 16 if parent signs application and applicant has completed a driver education course	No	Only for drivers 16-18	Written, road sign, driving, and eye
NORTH DAKOTA	16	Yes: at 14	Yes	Written, driving, and eye
OHIO	18; 16 if applicant has completed a driver education course	Yes: at 14 in hardship cases	Yes	Written, driving, and eye
OKLAHOMA	16	No	Yes	Written, driving, and eye
OREGON	16	Yes: at 14, but it is valid only for driving to and from school	Yes	Written, driving, and eye

Is licensee's photograph required?	How long is license valid?	What tests are required for renewal?	How long is a nonresident license valid?
Yes, in color	4 years; it expires on driver's birthday	Eye	60 days after establishing residence
No	2 years; it expires on last day of driver's month of birth	None	60 days
Yes, in color, on license	3 years; it expires on driver's birthday	Eye	Reciprocal basis
Yes	4 years; it expires on driver's birthday	None	90 days
No	4 years; it expires on driver's birthday	Written and eye	30 days after establishing residence
No	4 years, but 2 years if driver is over 70; it expires on driver's birthday	Driving and eye for drivers over 70	45 days after establishing residence
Yes, in color, on license	4 years; it expires on driver's birthday	Eye	60 days after establishing residence
No	2 years; it expires on anniversary of date of issue	Eye every 10 years	Reciprocal basis
No	4 years; it expires on last day of driver's month of birth	Written and eye	30 days after establishing residence or 180 days
Yes	4 years; expiration dates are staggered	Eye	30 days after establishing residence
Yes	4 years; it expires on driver's birthday	Written, road sign, driving, and eye, but written and driving tests are waived if driver committed no traffic offense in last 4 years	30 days after establishing residence
Yes, in color, on license	4 years; expiration dates are staggered	Eye for drivers under 21 or over 70	60 days after establishing residence
Yes, in color, on license	4 years; it expires on driver's birthday	None	Until establishing residence
Yes, in color, on license	2 years; it expires on last day of driver's month of birth	None	Until establishing residence
Yes, in color, on license	2 years; it expires on driver's birthday	None	Until establishing residence

Chart 29
1172

REQUIREMENTS FOR A DRIVER'S LICENSE (continued)

	What is minimum age for license?	Does state issue junior license and, if so, at what age?	Is learner's permit required?	What tests are required for original license?
PENNSYLVANIA	18; 17 if applicant has completed a driver education course	Yes: at 16 with parental consent, but it is valid only during certain hours unless driver is accompanied by parent	Yes	Written, driving, eye, and physical
RHODE ISLAND	18; 16 if parent signs application and applicant has completed a driver education course	No	Yes	Written, driving, and eye
SOUTH CAROLINA	16	Yes: at 15	Yes	Written, driving, and eye
SOUTH DAKOTA	16	Yes: at 14, but it is valid only during certain hours	No	Written, driving, and eye
TENNESSEE	16	Yes: at 14, but it is valid only for daylight driving to or from school, grocery store, church, doctor's office, or farm	Yes	Written, driving, and eye
TEXAS	18; 16 if applicant has completed a driver education course	Yes: at 15 if applicant is taking a driver education course	No	Written, driving, and eye
UTAH	16, but applicant must have completed a driver education course	No	Yes	Written, driving, and eye
VERMONT	18	Yes: at 16	Yes	Written, driving, and eye
VIRGINIA	18; 16 if parent signs application and applicant has completed a driver education course	No	Yes	Written, oral, driving, and eye
WASHINGTON	18; 16 if applicant has completed a driver education course	No	Yes	Written, driving, and eye
WEST VIRGINIA	18	Yes: at 16 with written parental consent	Yes	Written, driving, and eye
WISCONSIN	18; 16 if applicant has completed a driver education course	No	Yes	Written, driving, and eye
WYOMING	18; 16 with parental consent	No	No	Written, driving, and eye

Is licensee's photograph required?	How long is license valid?	What tests are required for renewal?	How long is a nonresident license valid?
Yes, in color, on license	4 years; it expires on last day of driver's month of birth	Eye or physical or both at department's discretion	Until establishing residence
Yes	2 years; it expires on driver's birthday	None	90 days or until establishing residence
Yes, in color, on license	4 years; it expires on driver's birthday	Eye	90 days after establishing residence
Yes	4 years; it expires on driver's birthday	Written, driving, and eye, but written and driving tests are waived if driver committed no traffic offense in last 4 years	90 days after establishing residence
No	2 years; it expires on driver's birthday	None	90 days after establishing residence
Yes	4 years; it expires on driver's birthday	Eye	30 days after establishing residence
Yes, in color, on license	4 years; it expires on driver's birthday	Written, driving, and eye	60 days after establishing residence
Optional	2 years; it expires on driver's birthday	None	Until establishing residence
Yes, in color, on license	4 years; it expires on last day of driver's month of birth	Written and eye	30 days
Yes	2 years; it expires on driver's birthday	Eye	1 year or until establishing residence
No	4 years; it expires on driver's birthday	None	30 days
No	2 years; it expires on driver's birthday	Eye every 4 years	Reciprocal basis until establishing residence
Yes	4 years; it expires on driver's birthday	Written and eye	30 days after establishing residence or being employed

Chart 30   **1174**

STATE LABOR LAWS

	Fair employment practices act	Civil or human rights commission[1]	Right-to-work law	Workmen's compensation
ALABAMA	No	No	Yes	Yes
ALASKA	Yes	Yes	No	Yes
ARIZONA	Yes	Yes	Yes	Yes
ARKANSAS	Yes	Yes	Yes	Yes
CALIFORNIA	Yes	Yes	No	Yes
COLORADO	Yes	Yes	No	Yes
CONNECTICUT	Yes	Yes	No	Yes
DELAWARE	Yes	Yes	No	Yes
DISTRICT OF COLUMBIA	Yes	Yes	No	Yes
FLORIDA	No	Yes	Yes	Yes
GEORGIA	Yes	No	Yes	Yes
HAWAII	Yes	No	No	Yes
IDAHO	Yes	Yes	No	Yes
ILLINOIS	Yes	Yes	No	Yes
INDIANA	Yes	Yes	No	Yes
IOWA	Yes	Yes	Yes	Yes
KANSAS	Yes	Yes	Yes	Yes
KENTUCKY	Yes	Yes	No	Yes
LOUISIANA	No	No	Yes	Yes[2]
MAINE	Yes	Yes	No	Yes
MARYLAND	Yes	Yes	No	Yes
MASSACHUSETTS	Yes	Yes	No	Yes
MICHIGAN	Yes	Yes	No	Yes
MINNESOTA	Yes	Yes	No	Yes
MISSISSIPPI	No	No	Yes	Yes

[1] Equal opportunity commissions and human relations councils are included in this category.

[2] But not compulsory, employers and employees may elect to be covered.

[3] But only prevents union interference in the case of a sole proprietor or a partnership of 2 persons engaged in a retail business or an amusement activity.

[4] The Commission of the Bureau of Labor hears discrimination complaints.

[5] But only applies to state employees.

[6] But only hears complaints of discrimination against state employees.

This chart shows which states have fair employment practices acts prohibiting discrimination in employment; civil or human rights commissions that deal with violations of such laws; RIGHT-TO-WORK LAWS protecting a person's right to work regardless of his membership or nonmembership in a union; and WORKMEN'S COMPENSATION acts that provide financial protection for a worker who is injured on the job. See also CIVIL RIGHTS; MASTER AND SERVANT.

	Fair employment practices act	Civil or human rights commission[1]	Right-to-work law	Workmen's compensation
MISSOURI	Yes	Yes	No	Yes
MONTANA	Yes	Yes	Yes[3]	Yes
NEBRASKA	Yes	Yes	Yes	Yes
NEVADA	Yes	Yes	Yes	Yes
NEW HAMPSHIRE	Yes	Yes	No	Yes
NEW JERSEY	Yes	Yes	No	Yes
NEW MEXICO	Yes	Yes	No	Yes
NEW YORK	Yes	Yes	No	Yes
NORTH CAROLINA	Yes	Yes	Yes	Yes
NORTH DAKOTA	Yes	No	Yes	Yes
OHIO	Yes	Yes	No	Yes
OKLAHOMA	Yes	Yes	No	Yes
OREGON	Yes	No[4]	No	Yes
PENNSYLVANIA	Yes	Yes	No	Yes
RHODE ISLAND	Yes	Yes	No	Yes
SOUTH CAROLINA	Yes[5]	Yes[6]	Yes	Yes
SOUTH DAKOTA	Yes	Yes	Yes	Yes
TENNESSEE	Yes	Yes	Yes	Yes
TEXAS	Yes[5]	Yes	Yes	Yes
UTAH	Yes	No[7]	Yes	Yes
VERMONT	Yes	Yes	No	Yes
VIRGINIA	Yes	No[8]	Yes	Yes
WASHINGTON	Yes	Yes	No[9]	Yes
WEST VIRGINIA	Yes	Yes	No	Yes
WISCONSIN	Yes	Yes	No	Yes
WYOMING	Yes	Yes	Yes	Yes[10]

[7] The Industrial Commission hears discrimination complaints.

[8] The Commission of Labor and Industry hears discrimination complaints.

[9] But under state statute, an agricultural laborer may not be denied work because of his membership or nonmembership in a labor union.

[10] But only for workers in extra-hazardous industries.

Chart 31   **1176**

MINIMUM WAGES AND MAXIMUM HOURS OF LABOR

	Basic hourly minimum wage		Overtime pay required
	Adults	**Minors**	
ALABAMA	No statutory provision	No statutory provision	No statutory provision
ALASKA	$3.85	$3.85	1½ times regular pay rate after 40 hours per week
ARIZONA	No statutory provision	No statutory provision	No statutory provision
ARKANSAS	$2.70	$2.40	1½ times regular pay rate after 40 hours per week
CALIFORNIA	$3.35	$2.85	1½ times regular pay rate after 8 hours in a 24-hour period
COLORADO	$1.90	$1.65 for workers under 18	1½ times regular pay rate after 40 hours per week or, if worker is under 18, after 24 hours per week
CONNECTICUT	$3.37	$3.37	1½ times regular pay rate after 40 hours per week
DELAWARE	$2.00	$2.00	No statutory provision
DISTRICT OF COLUMBIA	$2.50–$3.75, depending on occupation	$1.93–$2.48, depending on occupation, for workers under 18	1½ times regular pay rate after 40 hours per week
FLORIDA	No statutory provision	No statutory provision	No statutory provision
GEORGIA	$1.25	$1.25	No statutory provision
HAWAII	$3.35	$3.35	1½ times regular pay rate after 40 hours per week
IDAHO	$2.30	$2.30	No statutory provision
ILLINOIS	$2.30	$1.95 for workers under 18	1½ times regular pay rate after 40 hours per week
INDIANA	$2.00	No minimum for workers under 17	No statutory provision

Both federal and state laws set minimum wages and overtime pay rates. Federal law requires that all employees covered by the law (generally those in some way engaged in interstate commerce) be paid at least $3.35 per hour and that they be paid 1½ times their regular pay rate for work they do in excess of 40 hours per week. State wage laws, which apply to employees not covered by the federal law, are outlined in this chart. Other laws limit the amount of time an employee may work. Generally, these laws apply to adults only if they work in certain dangerous or unhealthy jobs, such as underground mining. Most of the states, however, have laws that limit the amount of time a minor may work in a day or week, as shown in this chart. See INFANT; LABOR RELATIONS; MASTER AND SERVANT.

Maximum number of hours a minor may work per day	Maximum number of hours a minor may work per week
If under 16: 4 hours on school days; 8 hours on vacation days	*If under 16:* 28 hours during school weeks; 40 hours during vacation
If under 16: 9 hours minus hours spent in school	*If under 16:* 23 hours during school weeks
If under 16: 3 hours on school days; 8 hours on vacation days	*If under 16:* 18 hours during school weeks; 40 hours during vacation
If under 16: 8 hours *If 16 or 17:* 10 hours	*If under 16:* 48 hours *If 16 or 17:* 54 hours
If under 18: 4 hours on school days; 8 hours on vacation days	*If under 18:* 24 hours during school weeks; 48 hours during vacation
If under 16: 6 hours on school days; 8 hours on vacation days *If 16 or 17:* 8 hours	*If under 18:* 40 hours
If under 18: 9 hours	*If under 18:* 48 hours
If under 16: 8 hours	*If under 16:* 48 hours
If under 18: 8 hours	*If under 18:* 48 hours
If under 16: 4 hours on school days; 10 hours on vacation days	*If under 16:* 40 hours
If under 16: 4 hours on school days; 8 hours on vacation days	*If under 16:* 40 hours
If under 16: 10 hours minus hours spent in school	*If under 16:* 40 hours
If under 16: 9 hours	*If under 16:* 54 hours
If under 16: 3 hours on school days; 8 hours on vacation days	*If under 16:* 23 hours during school weeks; 48 hours during vacation
If under 16: 3 hours on school days; 8 hours on vacation days *If 16:* 5 hours on school days; 8 hours on vacation days	*If under 16:* 23 hours during school weeks; 40 hours during vacation *If 16:* 40 hours during school weeks; 48 hours during vacation

Chart 31   1178

MINIMUM WAGES AND MAXIMUM HOURS OF LABOR *(continued)*

	Basic hourly minimum wage		Overtime pay required
	Adults	**Minors**	
IOWA	No statutory provision	No statutory provision	No statutory provision
KANSAS	$1.60	$1.60	1½ times regular pay rate after 46 hours per week; no overtime required for workers under 18
KENTUCKY	$2.15	$2.15	1½ times regular pay rate after 40 hours per week
LOUISIANA	No statutory provision	No statutory provision	No statutory provision
MAINE	$3.35	$3.35	1½ times regular pay rate after 40 hours per week
MARYLAND	$3.35	$3.35	1½ times regular pay rate after 40 hours per week
MASSACHUSETTS	$3.35	$3.35	1½ times regular pay rate after 40 hours per week
MICHIGAN	$3.35	No minimum for workers under 18	1½ times regular pay rate after 40 hours per week
MINNESOTA	$3.10	$2.79 for workers under 18	1½ times regular pay rate after 48 hours per week
MISSISSIPPI	No statutory provision	No statutory provision	No statutory provision
MISSOURI	No statutory provision	No statutory provision	No statutory provision
MONTANA	$2.00	$2.00	1½ times regular pay rate after 40 hours per week
NEBRASKA	$1.60	$1.60	No statutory provision
NEVADA	$2.75	$2.34 for workers under 18	1½ times regular pay rate after 8 hours per day or 40 hours per week
NEW HAMPSHIRE	$3.35	$2.51 for workers under 18	No statutory provision
NEW JERSEY	$3.10	$1.00–$1.50, depending on occupation, for workers under 18	1½ times regular pay rate after 40 hours per week
NEW MEXICO	$3.35	No minimum for workers under 19	1½ times regular pay rate after 48 hours per week
NEW YORK	$3.35	$2.80 for workers under 18	1½ times minimum pay rate after 40 hours per week

Maximum number of hours a minor may work per day	Maximum number of hours a minor may work per week
If under 16: 4 hours on school days; 8 hours on vacation days	*If under 16:* 28 hours during school weeks; 40 hours during vacation
If under 16: 8 hours	*If under 16:* 40 hours
If under 16: 3 hours on school days; 8 hours on vacation days *If 16 or 17:* If a student, 8 hours; if not a student, 10 hours	*If under 16:* 18 hours during school weeks; 40 hours during vacation *If 16 or 17:* If a student, 48 hours; if not a student, 60 hours
If under 16: 3 hours on school days; 8 hours on vacation days	*If under 16:* 44 hours
If under 16: 4 hours on school days; 8 hours on vacation days	*If under 16:* 28 hours during school weeks; 48 hours during vacation
If under 16: 4 hours on school days; 8 hours on vacation days *If 17:* 12 hours minus hours spent in school	*If under 16:* 23 hours during school weeks; 40 hours during vacation
If under 16: 8 hours *If 16 or 17:* 9 hours	*If under 18:* 48 hours
If under 18: 10 hours	*If under 18:* 48 hours minus hours spent in school
If under 16: 8 hours	*If under 16:* 40 hours
If under 16: 8 hours	*If under 16:* 44 hours
If under 16: 8 hours	*If under 16:* 40 hours
No statutory provision	No statutory provision
If under 16: 8 hours	*If under 16:* 48 hours
If under 16: 8 hours	*If under 16:* 48 hours
If under 16: 3 hours on school days; 8 hours on vacation days	*If under 16:* 23 hours during school weeks; 48 hours during vacation
If under 16: 8 hours minus hours spent in school *If 16 or 17:* 8 hours	*If under 18:* 40 hours
If under 14: 8 hours	*If under 14:* 44 hours
If under 16: 3 hours on school days; 8 hours on vacation days *If 16 or 17:* 4 hours on school days; 8 hours on vacation days	*If under 16:* 23 hours during school weeks; 40 hours during vacation *If 16 or 17:* 28 hours during school weeks; 48 hours during vacation

Chart 31   **1180**

MINIMUM WAGES AND MAXIMUM HOURS OF LABOR *(continued)*

	Basic hourly minimum wage		Overtime pay required
	Adults	**Minors**	
NORTH CAROLINA	$2.90	$2.90	1½ times regular pay rate after 45 hours per week
NORTH DAKOTA	$2.80–$3.10, depending on occupation	$2.80–$3.10, depending on occupation	1½ times regular pay rate after 40 hours per week
OHIO	$2.30	$2.30	1½ times regular pay rate after 40 hours per week
OKLAHOMA	$3.10	No minimum for workers under 18	No statutory provision
OREGON	$3.10	$3.10	1½ times regular pay rate after 40 hours per week
PENNSYLVANIA	$3.35	$3.35	1½ times regular pay rate after 40 hours per week
RHODE ISLAND	$3.10	$3.10	1½ times regular pay rate after 40 hours per week
SOUTH CAROLINA	No statutory provision	No statutory provision	No statutory provision
SOUTH DAKOTA	$2.30	No minimum for workers under 18	No statutory provision
TENNESSEE	No statutory provision	No statutory provision	No statutory provision
TEXAS	$1.40	No minimum for workers under 18	No statutory provision
UTAH	$2.75	$2.75	No statutory provision
VERMONT	$3.35	$3.35	1½ times regular pay rate after 40 hours per week
VIRGINIA	$2.65	No minimum for workers under 16	No statutory provision
WASHINGTON	$2.30	$2.30	1½ times regular pay rate after 40 hours per week
WEST VIRGINIA	$2.75	$2.75	1½ times regular pay rate after 40 hours per week
WISCONSIN	$3.25	$2.90 for workers under 18	1½ times regular pay rate after 40 hours per week
WYOMING	$1.60	No minimum for workers under 18	No statutory provision

Maximum number of hours a minor may work per day	Maximum number of hours a minor may work per week
If under 16: 3 hours on school days; 8 hours on vacation days	*If under 16:* 18 hours during school weeks; 40 hours during vacation
If under 16: 3 hours on school days; 8 hours on vacation days	*If under 16:* 24 hours during school weeks; 48 hours during vacation
If under 16: 3 hours on school days; 8 hours on vacation days	*If under 16:* 18 hours during school weeks; 40 hours during vacation
If under 16: 8 hours	*If under 16:* 48 hours
If under 16: 10 hours	*If under 18:* 44 hours
If under 16: 4 hours on school days; 8 hours on vacation days *If 16 or 17:* 8 hours	*If under 16:* 18 hours during school weeks; 44 hours during vacation *If 16 or 17:* 26 hours during school weeks; 44 hours during vacation
If under 16: 8 hours *If 16 or 17:* 9 hours	*If under 16:* 40 hours *If 16 or 17:* 48 hours
No statutory provision	No statutory provision
If under 16: 8 hours	*If under 16:* 40 hours
If under 16: 3 hours on school days; 8 hours on vacation days	*If under 16:* 18 hours during school weeks; 40 hours during vacation
If under 15: 8 hours	*If under 15:* 48 hours
If under 16: 4 hours on school days; 8 hours on vacation days	*If under 16:* 40 hours
If under 16: 8 hours *If 16 or 17:* 9 hours	*If under 16:* 48 hours *If 16 or 17:* 50 hours
If under 16: 8 hours	*If under 16:* 40 hours
If under 16: 3 hours on school days; 8 hours on vacation days *If 16 or 17:* 8 hours	*If under 16:* 18 hours during school weeks; 40 hours during vacation *If 16 or 17:* 40 hours
If under 16: 8 hours	*If under 16:* 40 hours
If under 18: 8 hours	*If under 16:* 24 hours during school weeks; 40 hours during vacation *If 16 or 17:* 40 hours during school weeks; 48 hours during vacation
If under 16: 8 hours	No statutory provision

YOUR RIGHT TO OWN AND CARRY FIREARMS

	Before buying a handgun, must you file an application or get a license or permit?	Waiting period between purchase and delivery	Are handgun sales reported?	Who may not buy a handgun?
ALABAMA	No	48 hours	Yes	Persons under 18; persons convicted of a violent crime; drug addicts; alcoholics; persons of unsound mind
ALASKA	No	None	No	No statutory provision
ARIZONA	No	None	No	Persons under 18 without written parental consent
ARKANSAS	No	None	No	No statutory provision
CALIFORNIA	No	15 days	No, but dealer must keep a record	Persons under 16; persons under 18 without parental consent
COLORADO	No	None	No, but dealer must keep a record	No statutory provision
CONNECTICUT	Yes	2 weeks	No, but dealer must keep a record	Persons under 18; persons convicted of a felony; aliens
DELAWARE	No	None	No, but dealer must keep a record	Minors; persons convicted of a felony, violent crime, or drug offense; intoxicated persons; mental incompetents
DISTRICT OF COLUMBIA	Yes	48 hours	Yes	Persons under 18; persons 18-20 without parental consent; persons indicted for or convicted of a violent crime or weapons offense persons who within the past 5 years were indicted for or convicted of a drug offense or were adjudicated insane or alcoholic (unless there is proof of recovery); persons adjudicated negligent in an injurious firearms mishap; persons with physical handicaps that make use of firearms unsafe; persons who have failed the visual test for a District of Columbia driver's license

[1] But it is illegal to carry a loaded gun in a vehicle.

Citizens have a constitutional right to keep and bear arms (see ARMS, RIGHT TO BEAR), but the use and ownership of firearms is regulated by state law. Federal law requires licenses for certain importers, manufacturers, and dealers; prohibits the selling of firearms to young people, criminals, and mental incompetents; controls the carrying of firearms on public transportation; and outlaws traffic in stolen WEAPONS and in guns that have had their identification numbers altered or removed. In Illinois, Massachusetts, and the District of Columbia, you must have a license to buy ammunition.

Must you have a license or permit to carry a handgun?	Who may not use or possess a handgun?	Is possession of a rifle or shotgun regulated?	Do dealers need a license to sell firearms?
Yes, if concealed, except at home, in your place of business, on your own property, or in a motor vehicle	Persons convicted of attempting or committing a violent crime; drug addicts; alcoholics	No	Only for handguns
No, but it is illegal to carry one concealed	Persons under 16 without parental consent; convicted felons; persons under the influence of drugs or alcohol	No	No
No, but it is illegal to carry one concealed	Persons under 18 without written parental consent; persons convicted of a violent crime or serving a term of imprisonment; adjudicated mental incompetents or patients	No	No
It is illegal to carry one except at home, in your place of business, or on your own property	Persons under 18; persons convicted of a felony; adjudicated mental incompetents; involuntary mental patients	No	No
Yes, if concealed	Minors, unless accompanied by a parent or with written parental consent; convicted felons; drug addicts	No	Only for handguns
Yes, if concealed, except at home, in your place of business, on your own property, or in a motor vehicle	Persons convicted of attempting, conspiring to commit, or committing a violent crime for 10 years after release or escape from prison	No	No
Yes	Persons under 18; convicted felons; aliens	No[1]	Only for handguns
Yes, if concealed	Persons under 16; anyone who may not buy a handgun	No	Yes
Yes	Anyone who may not buy a handgun	Yes	Yes

Chart 32   **1184**

YOUR RIGHT TO OWN AND CARRY FIREARMS *(continued)*

	Before buying a handgun, must you file an application or get a license or permit?	Waiting period between purchase and delivery	Are handgun sales reported?	Who may not buy a handgun?
FLORIDA	No	None	No	Persons under 18
GEORGIA	No	None	No	Persons under 21
HAWAII	Yes	None	Yes	Persons under 18; persons convicted of a felony or drug offense; fugitives from justice; aliens
IDAHO	No	None	No	Persons under 16 without parental consent
ILLINOIS	Yes, firearm owner's identification card needed	72 hours	No, but dealer must keep a record	Persons under 18; delinquents under 21; felons convicted or having served a sentence within the past 5 years; drug addicts; persons who were mental patients within the past 5 years; mentally retarded persons
INDIANA	Yes	7 days	Yes	Persons under 18; persons convicted of a violent crime; drug addicts; alcoholics; intoxicated persons; persons of unsound mind
IOWA	Yes	None	Yes	Persons under 21; persons convicted of a felony or of harassment or assault; drug addicts; alcoholics; persons who are mentally defective or have a history of repeated acts of violence
KANSAS	No	None	No	Persons under 18; persons convicted of a felony within the past 5 years; drug addicts; alcoholics
KENTUCKY	No	None	No	No statutory provision
LOUISIANA	Yes	None	Yes	Persons under 18; enemy aliens
MAINE	No	None	No, but dealer must keep a record	Persons under 16

[2] But all firearms must be registered with chief of police within 48 hours of arrival in state.

Must you have a license or permit to carry a handgun?	Who may not use or possess a handgun?	Is possession of a rifle or shotgun regulated?	Do dealers need a license to sell firearms?
Yes	Persons under 16 unless supervised by an adult; 16- or 17-year-olds without parental consent; convicted felons unless civil rights have been restored; persons of unsound mind	Yes	No
Yes, if concealed, except at home, in your place of business, or on your own property	Persons under 21; persons with charges pending for a felony, misdemeanor involving force, or weapons offense; persons convicted of a felony involving force and not free of imprisonment or parole for 10 years; persons convicted of a felony not involving force or of a misdemeanor involving force and not free of imprisonment or parole for 5 years; persons convicted of a weapons offense and not free for 3 years; fugitives from justice; drug addicts; alcoholics; mental patients	No	Only for handguns
Yes	Persons convicted of a felony or drug offense; fugitives from justice	No[2]	Yes
Yes, if concealed	Persons under 12 while in a vehicle, tent, camp, field, or forest	No	No
Yes, but it is illegal to carry one concealed except at home, in your place of business, or on your own property	Persons who are hooded, robed, or masked; anyone who may not buy a handgun	Yes	No
Yes, except at home, in your place of business, or on your own property	No statutory provision	No	Only for handguns
Yes, except at home, in your place of business, or on your own property	Persons 14-21 without supervision of a parent or spouse; anyone who may not buy a handgun	No	No
No, but it is illegal to carry one concealed except at home, in your place of business, or on your own property	Anyone who may not buy a handgun	No	No
No, but it is illegal to carry one concealed except in the glove compartment of a motor vehicle	Convicted felons	No	No
No, but it is illegal to carry one concealed	Persons convicted of a violent felony within the past 10 years unless granted a special permit; enemy aliens	Yes	Yes
Yes, if concealed	Persons under 16; convicted felons for 5 years after release from prison	No	No

Chart 32   **1186**

YOUR RIGHT TO OWN AND CARRY FIREARMS *(continued)*

	Before buying a handgun, must you file an application or get a license or permit?	Waiting period between purchase and delivery	Are handgun sales reported?	Who may not buy a handgun?
MARYLAND	Yes	7 days	Yes	Persons under 21; persons convicted of a violent crime; fugitives from justice; drug addicts; alcoholics; persons who have spent more than 30 consecutive days in a mental hospital
MASSACHUSETTS	Yes, firearm owner's identification card needed	None	No, but dealer must keep a record and purchaser must report any resale within 7 days	Persons under 15; persons 15-18 without parental consent; persons convicted of a felony or drug offense who served a sentence within the past 5 years; persons who have been alcoholics within the past 5 years; mentally unfit persons
MICHIGAN	Yes	None	Yes	Persons under 18; persons convicted of a felony within the past 8 years; persons not residents of the state for 6 months; insane persons
MINNESOTA	Yes	7 days	Yes	Persons under 14 unless supervised by a parent; persons 14-17 in any municipality without the consent of a parent, the police, or a magistrate; persons convicted of a violent crime for 10 years after end of sentence; drug addicts; alcoholics; persons confined for mental illness
MISSISSIPPI	No	None	No, but dealer must keep a record and purchaser must register gun within 10 days	Minors; intoxicated persons
MISSOURI	Yes	None	Yes	Minors; persons who are not of good moral character or who sheriff feels might endanger the public safety
MONTANA	No	None	No	No statutory provision
NEBRASKA	No	None	No	No statutory provision
NEVADA	No	None	No	Persons under 18
NEW HAMPSHIRE	No	None	Yes	Minors
NEW JERSEY	Yes	7 days	Yes	Persons under 18; persons convicted of a crime; drug addicts; alcoholics; mental incompetents

[3] If firearm is up to 30 inches in length.

Must you have a license or permit to carry a handgun?	Who may not use or possess a handgun?	Is possession of a rifle or shotgun regulated?	Do dealers need a license to sell firearms?
Yes	Persons under 18 without parental consent; persons convicted of a violent crime or weapons offense; fugitives from justice; drug addicts; alcoholics	No	Only for handguns
Yes	Persons under 18; persons convicted of a felony or drug offense; aliens	Yes	Yes
Yes, if you carry one in a motor vehicle or concealed, except at home, in your place of business, or on your own property	Anyone who may not buy a handgun	Yes[3]	No
Yes, except at home, in your place of business, or on your own property	Anyone who may not buy a handgun	No	No
No, but handgun must be registered, and it is illegal to carry one concealed	Persons under 16; convicted felons; intoxicated persons	No[4]	No
No, but it is illegal to carry one concealed	Minors without parental consent; anyone at a public assembly; intoxicated persons	No	No
Yes, except at home, in your place of business, or on your own property	Persons under 14 unless supervised by an instructor or other authorized adult	No	No
No, but it is illegal to carry one concealed except while on lawful business or for defense where justified	Persons under 18; convicted felons; fugitives from justice	No	No
No, but it is illegal to carry one concealed	Persons under 14 unless supervised by an adult; convicted felons; aliens	No	No
Yes, unless handgun is unloaded and carried openly at home, in your place of business, or on your own property	Convicted felons without a permit; nonresidents unless qualified to carry one in home state or holding a permit from the police	No	Only for handguns
Yes	Persons under 18 unless holding a valid limited license for minors and either supervised by an adult or hunting legally; anyone without a permit	Yes	Yes

[4] But high-powered rifles must be registered, as must machine guns and submachine guns.

Chart 32   **1188**

YOUR RIGHT TO OWN AND CARRY FIREARMS *(continued)*

	Before buying a handgun, must you file an application or get a license or permit?	Waiting period between purchase and delivery	Are handgun sales reported?	Who may not buy a handgun?
NEW MEXICO	No	None	No	No statutory provision
NEW YORK	Yes	None	No, but dealer must keep a record	Persons under 16
NORTH CAROLINA	Yes	None	No, but dealer must keep a record	Minors; convicted felons
NORTH DAKOTA	Yes	None	Yes	Persons under 17; persons convicted of a violent crime or weapons crime within the past 10 years; drug addicts; alcoholics; emotionally unstable persons
OHIO	No	None	No	Persons under 21; persons indicted or convicted of a violent felony or drug offense; fugitives from justice; drug addicts; alcoholics; persons under the influence of drugs or alcohol; mental incompetents
OKLAHOMA	No	None	No	Minors; convicted felons; persons under the influence of drugs or alcohol; mentally incompetent or disturbed persons
OREGON	No	120 hours	Yes	Persons under 18; persons convicted of a felony other than a marijuana offense unless sentence completed more than 15 years ago; inmates of a penal institution; persons who have committed murder or manslaughter or have recklessly killed or injured someone
PENNSYLVANIA	No	48 hours	Yes	Persons under 18; persons convicted of a violent crime; drug addicts; alcoholics; persons of unsound mind
RHODE ISLAND	Yes	72 hours	Yes	Persons under 21; drug addicts; adjudicated alcoholics; mental incompetents; aliens in the United States less than 10 years
SOUTH CAROLINA	No	None	No	Persons convicted of a violent crime; fugitives from justice; drug addicts; alcoholics; adjudicated mental incompetents; members of a subversive organization; persons adjudicated unfit to carry a handgun

[5] Unless it is to be carried in a motor vehicle in Philadelphia.

Must you have a license or permit to carry a handgun?	Who may not use or possess a handgun?	Is possession of a rifle or shotgun regulated?	Do dealers need a license to sell firearms?
No, but it is illegal to carry one loaded except at home, in your place of business, or on your own property	Persons under 18 unless a hunter safety course has been completed or unless supervised by an adult; prisoners; persons under the influence of drugs or alcohol in a hunting area or boat	No	No
Yes, if concealed, but it is illegal to carry one loaded	Persons under 16; persons convicted of a crime; mental incompetents; aliens	No	Yes
No, but it is illegal to carry one concealed	Persons under 12 unless supervised by a parent; convicted felons	No	No
Yes, unless you carry one openly at home, in your place of business, or on your own property	Persons under 17; persons convicted of a violent crime or a weapons crime within the past 10 years; drug addicts; alcoholics; emotionally unstable persons	No	Only for handguns in some cities
No, but it is illegal to carry a handgun concealed or to carry one loaded in a motor vehicle	Persons under 18 except for hunting, instruction, or marksmanship under the supervision of an adult; persons indicted for or convicted of a violent felony or drug offense; fugitives from justice; drug addicts; alcoholics; persons under the influence of drugs or alcohol; mental incompetents	No	No
No, but it is illegal to carry one concealed	Convicted felons; persons under the influence of drugs or alcohol	No[1]	No
Yes, if concealed or in a motor vehicle	Persons convicted of a felony other than a marijuana offense unless sentence completed more than 15 years ago; inmates of a penal institution; persons who have committed murder or have recklessly killed or injured someone	No	Yes
Yes, if concealed or in a motor vehicle	Persons convicted of a violent crime	No[5]	Yes
Yes, except at home, in your place of business, or on your own property	Persons under 21; persons convicted of a violent crime; fugitives from justice; persons under the influence of drugs or alcohol; aliens in the United States less than 10 years	No[1]	Yes
It is illegal to carry one except at home, in your place of business, closed in the trunk or glove compartment of a car, for hunting, or for military or civil parades	Anyone who may not buy a handgun	No	Only for handguns

Chart 32

1190

YOUR RIGHT TO OWN AND CARRY FIREARMS *(continued)*

	Before buying a handgun, must you file an application or get a license or permit?	Waiting period between purchase and delivery	Are handgun sales reported?	Who may not buy a handgun?
SOUTH DAKOTA	No	48 hours	Yes	Persons convicted of a violent crime within the past 15 years
TENNESSEE	No	15 days	Yes	Minors; persons convicted of a violent crime; fugitives from justice; drug addicts; alcoholics; persons convicted of an illegal sale of alcoholic beverages; persons of unsound mind
TEXAS	No	None	No	Persons under 18 without parental consent; intoxicated persons; persons who intend to use handgun unlawfully
UTAH	No	None	No	No statutory provision
VERMONT	No	None	No, but dealer must keep a record	No statutory provision
VIRGINIA	No	None	No	No statutory provision
WASHINGTON	Yes	72 hours	Yes	Persons under 21; persons convicted of a violent crime; drug addicts; alcoholics; persons of unsound mind
WEST VIRGINIA	No	None	Yes	No statutory provision
WISCONSIN	No	48 hours	No	Minors
WYOMING	No	None	No, but dealer must keep a record	No statutory provision

Must you have a license or permit to carry a handgun?	Who may not use or possess a handgun?	Is possession of a rifle or shotgun regulated?	Do dealers need a license to sell firearms?
Yes, in a motor vehicle or if concealed, except at home, in your place of business, or on your own property	Persons under 15 without parental consent or within 1 mile of a city or town; persons convicted of a violent crime within the past 15 years; intoxicated persons	No	No
No, but it is illegal to carry a handgun "with intent to go armed"	Convicted felons	No	Yes
It is illegal to carry one except at home, in your place of business, on your own property, when traveling, or for hunting, fishing, or other sport	Persons convicted of a violent felony	No	No
Yes, if concealed, except at home, in your place of business, or on your own property; it is illegal to carry a loaded handgun in a vehicle	Persons under 14 unless accompanied by a parent; persons 14-17 without parental consent; persons convicted of a violent crime; state prisoners; persons on parole for a felony; drug addicts; mental incompetents; aliens	No	No
No, but it is illegal to carry one on the grounds of a public institution or with intent to injure	Persons under 16 without parental consent; children at school	No	No
Yes, if concealed	Minors; persons convicted of a felony involving the use of firearms; hunters under the influence of drugs or alcohol	No	Only for handguns
Yes, if concealed, except at home, in your place of business, on your own property, or in a motor vehicle if loaded	Persons under 14 unless supervised by an adult; persons convicted of a violent crime; drug addicts; alcoholics; persons confined to a mental institution	No	Only for handguns
Yes, except at home, in your place of business, or on your own property	Persons under 18; persons not residents of state for 1 year and of county for 60 days; persons not gainfully employed for 5 years; drug addicts; alcoholics; patients at a state hospital; youths at a youth facility; aliens	Yes	Only for handguns
No, but it is illegal to carry one concealed	Persons under 14 unless accompanied by a parent; persons 14-16 unless accompanied by a parent or unless they have a certificate for training in safe use of firearms; persons under the influence of an intoxicant	No	No
Yes, if concealed	Persons convicted of a violent crime; persons who intend to use handgun unlawfully; aliens	No	Only for rifles or shotguns

Chart 33   1192

STATE ENVIRONMENTAL AGENCIES

	Air pollution agencies	Water pollution agencies
ALABAMA	Air Pollution Control Commission 645 South McDonough Street Montgomery 36130	Water Improvement Commission Perry Hill Office Park 3815 Interstate Court Montgomery 36109

ALASKA	Division of Environmental Quality
	  Operations
	Department of Environmental Conservation
	Pouch O
	Juneau 99811
		Division of Environmental Quality
		  Operations
		Department of Environmental Conservation
		Pouch O
		Juneau 99811

ARIZONA	Air Quality Control Department of Health Services 1740 West Adams Phoenix 85007	Water Quality Control Department of Health Services 1740 West Adams Phoenix 85007

ARKANSAS	Department of Pollution Control
	  and Ecology
	P.O. Box 9583
	Little Rock 72219
		Department of Pollution Control
		  and Ecology
		P.O. Box 9583
		Little Rock 72219

CALIFORNIA	Air Resources Board P.O. Box 2815 Sacramento 95812	Water Resources Control Board P.O. Box 100 Sacramento 95801
COLORADO	Office of Health Protection Department of Health 4210 East 11th Avenue Denver 80220	Office of Health Protection Department of Health 4210 East 11th Avenue Denver 80220
CONNECTICUT	Department of Environmental Protection 165 Capitol Avenue State Office Building Hartford 06115	Department of Environmental Protection 165 Capitol Avenue State Office Building Hartford 06115

DELAWARE	Division of Environmental Control
	Department of Natural Resources
	  and Environmental Control
	P.O. Box 1401
	Dover 19901
		Division of Environmental Control
		Department of Natural Resources
		  and Environmental Control
		P.O. Box 1401
		Dover 19901

DISTRICT OF COLUMBIA	Bureau of Air and Water Quality 5010 Overlook Avenue SW Washington 20032	Bureau of Air and Water Quality 5010 Overlook Avenue SW Washington 20032
FLORIDA	Department of Environmental Regulation 2600 Blair Stone Road Tallahassee 32301	Department of Environmental Regulation 2600 Blair Stone Road Tallahassee 32301

If you have a question or a complaint about air or water pollution, you may write to the appropriate agency in your state. In some cases, one agency handles both air and water pollution. See ENVIRONMENTAL LAW.

	Air pollution agencies	Water pollution agencies
GEORGIA	Environmental Protection Division Department of Natural Resources 270 Washington Street Atlanta 30334	Environmental Protection Division Department of Natural Resources 270 Washington Street Atlanta 30334

HAWAII	Environmental Protection and Health
	  Service Division
	Department of Health
	P.O. Box 3378
	Honolulu 96801
		Environmental Protection and Health
		  Service Division
		Department of Health
		P.O. Box 3378
		Honolulu 96801

IDAHO	Bureau of Air Quality Department of Health and Welfare 450 West State Street Boise 83720	Bureau of Water Quality Department of Health and Welfare 450 West State Street Boise 83720
ILLINOIS	Division of Air Pollution Control Environmental Protection Agency 2200 Churchill Road Springfield 62706	Division of Water Pollution Control Environmental Protection Agency 2200 Churchill Road Springfield 62706
INDIANA	Bureau of Engineering Board of Health 1330 West Michigan Street Indianapolis 46206	Bureau of Engineering Board of Health 1330 West Michigan Street Indianapolis 46206
IOWA	Air and Land Quality Division Department of Environmental Quality Henry A. Wallace Building 900 East Grand Avenue Des Moines 50319	Chemicals and Water Quality Division Department of Environmental Quality Henry A. Wallace Building 900 East Grand Avenue Des Moines 50319
KANSAS	Bureau of Air Quality Department of Health Topeka 66620	Division of Environment Department of Health Topeka 66620
KENTUCKY	Division of Air Pollution Control Department of Natural Resources U.S. 127 South West Frankfort Complex Frankfort 40601	Division of Water Quality Department of Natural Resources U.S. 127 South West Frankfort Complex Frankfort 40601

LOUISIANA	Office of Health Services and
	  Environmental Quality
	Department of Health
	P.O. Box 60630
	New Orleans 70160
		Office of Health Services and
		  Environmental Quality
		Department of Health
		P.O. Box 60630
		New Orleans 70160

Chart 33   **1194**

STATE ENVIRONMENTAL AGENCIES   *(continued)*

	Air pollution agencies	Water pollution agencies
MAINE	Bureau of Air Quality Department of Environmental Protection State House Station 17 Augusta 04330	Bureau of Water Quality Department of Environmental Protection State House Station 17 Augusta 04330
MARYLAND	Environmental Health Administration Department of Health 301 West Preston Street Baltimore 21201	Water Resources Administration Department of Natural Resources Tawes State Office Building Annapolis 21401
MASSACHUSETTS	Division of Air and Hazardous Materials 600 Washington Street Boston 02116	Division of Water Pollution Control 110 Tremont Street Boston 02108
MICHIGAN	Air Quality Division Department of Natural Resources Third Floor General Office Building Secondary Complex P.O. Box 30028 Lansing 48909	Water Quality Division Department of Natural Resources Eighth Floor Mason Building P.O. Box 30028 Lansing 48909
MINNESOTA	Air Quality Division Pollution Control Agency 1935 West County Road, B2 Roseville 55113	Water Quality Division Pollution Control Agency 1935 West County Road, B2 Roseville 55113
MISSISSIPPI	Bureau of Pollution Control P.O. Box 827 Jackson 39205	Bureau of Pollution Control P.O. Box 827 Jackson 39205
MISSOURI	Clean Air Commission Department of Natural Resources 2010 Missouri Boulevard Jefferson City 65101	Clean Water Commission Department of Natural Resources 2010 Missouri Boulevard Jefferson City 65101

MONTANA	Department of Health and
	  Environmental Sciences
	Cogswell Building
	Helena 59601
		Department of Health and
		  Environmental Sciences
		Cogswell Building
		Helena 59601

NEBRASKA	Air Pollution Control Division Department of Environmental Control P.O. Box 94877 Lincoln 68509	Water Pollution Control Division Department of Environmental Control P.O. Box 94877 Lincoln 68509

NEVADA	Division of Environmental Protection
	Department of Conservation and
	  Natural Resources
	201 South Fall Street
	Capitol Complex
	Carson City 89710
		Division of Environmental Protection
		Department of Conservation and
		  Natural Resources
		201 South Fall Street
		Capitol Complex
		Carson City 89710

NEW HAMPSHIRE	Air Resources Agency Hazen Drive Concord 03301	Water Supply and Pollution Control Hazen Drive Concord 03301

	Air pollution agencies	Water pollution agencies
NEW JERSEY	Division of Environmental Quality Department of Environmental Protection P.O. Box CNO 29 Trenton 08625	Division of Water Resources Department of Environmental Protection P.O. Box CNO 28 Trenton 08625
NEW MEXICO	Air Quality Section Health and Environment Department P.O. Box 968 Crown Building Santa Fe 87503	Water Pollution Control Section Health and Environment Department P.O. Box 968 Crown Building Santa Fe 87503
NEW YORK	Division of Air Resources Department of Environmental Conservation 50 Wolf Road Albany 12233	Division of Pure Waters Department of Environmental Conservation 50 Wolf Road Albany 12233

NORTH CAROLINA	Air Planning and Environmental
	  Standards Branch
	Department of Natural Resources
	P.O. Box 27687
	Raleigh 27611
		Air Planning and Environmental
		  Standards Branch
		Department of Natural Resources
		P.O. Box 27687
		Raleigh 27611

NORTH DAKOTA	Division of Environmental Engineering Department of Health Missouri Office Building 1200 Missouri Avenue Bismarck 58505	Division of Water Supply and Pollution Control Department of Health Missouri Office Building 1200 Missouri Avenue Bismarck 58505
OHIO	Office of Air Pollution Control Environmental Protection Agency 361 East Broad Street Columbus 43215	Office of Water Pollution Control Environmental Protection Agency 361 East Broad Street Columbus 43215
OKLAHOMA	Air Quality Service Department of Health P.O. Box 53551 Oklahoma City 73152	Water Quality Service Department of Health P.O. Box 53551 Oklahoma City 73152
OREGON	Department of Environmental Quality P.O. Box 1760 Portland 97207	Department of Environmental Quality P.O. Box 1760 Portland 97207
PENNSYLVANIA	Bureau of Air Quality Control Department of Environmental Resources P.O. Box 2063 Fulton Building 200 North Third Street Harrisburg 17120	Bureau of Water Quality Control Department of Environmental Resources P.O. Box 2063 Fulton Building 200 North Third Street Harrisburg 17120
RHODE ISLAND	Division of Air Resources Department of Environmental Management Room 204 Cannon Building 75 Davis Street Providence 02908	Division of Water Resources Department of Environmental Management Room 209 Cannon Building 75 Davis Street Providence 02908

Chart 33 1196

STATE ENVIRONMENTAL AGENCIES *(continued)*

	Air pollution agencies	Water pollution agencies
SOUTH CAROLINA	Division of Environmental Quality Control Department of Health 2600 Bull Street Columbia 29201	Division of Environmental Quality Control Department of Health 2600 Bull Street Columbia 29201
SOUTH DAKOTA	Division of Air Quality Department of Health Foss Building Pierre 57501	Division of Water Quality Department of Water and Natural Resources Foss Building Pierre 57501
TENNESSEE	Division of Air Pollution Control Department of Public Health 256 Capitol Hill Building Nashville 37219	Division of Water Quality Control Department of Public Health 602 Cordell Hull Building Nashville 37219
TEXAS	Air Control Board 8520 Shoal Creek Boulevard Austin 78758	Department of Water Resources Stephen F. Austin Building 1700 North Congress Avenue Austin 78701
UTAH	Department of Health 150 West North Temple P.O. Box 2500 Salt Lake City 84110	Department of Health 150 West North Temple P.O. Box 2500 Salt Lake City 84110
VERMONT	Air Pollution Control Division Agency of Environmental Conservation State Office Building Montpelier 05602	Water Resources Department State Office Building Montpelier 05602
VIRGINIA	Air Pollution Control Board Room 1106 Ninth Street Office Building Richmond 23219	Water Control Board Public Information Office P.O. Box 11143 Richmond 23230
WASHINGTON	Office of Air Programs Department of Ecology Olympia 98504	Office of Water Programs Department of Ecology Olympia 98504
WEST VIRGINIA	Air Pollution Control Commission 1558 Washington Street East Charleston 25311	Division of Water Resources Department of Natural Resources 1201 Greenbrier Street Charleston 25301
WISCONSIN	Bureau of Air Management Department of Natural Resources P.O. Box 7921 Madison 53707	Bureau of Water Quality Department of Natural Resources P.O. Box 7921 Madison 53707
WYOMING	Department of Environmental Quality Hathaway Building Cheyenne 82001	Department of Environmental Quality Hathaway Building Cheyenne 82001

HOW YOU QUALIFY TO VOTE

Generally, every U.S. citizen who is at least 18 years old has a right to vote, but the states have the right to set qualifications for voters as long as those qualifications do not discriminate against any citizen. See ELECTION. *States may require prospective voters to register to vote – either in person or by mail. Many states require a voter to have been a resident of the locality for a certain period of time, but under federal law no residence requirement of more than 30 days may be imposed for federal elections. Some states have no residence requirement but require a voter to register to vote within a certain number of days before the election. Although this has the same effect as a residence requirement, as a voter must live in a locality in order to register to vote there, it is usually not intended as such. Rather it is imposed to give the state time to prepare its registration records for the election. This chart gives the residence and registration requirements for all the states and the District of Columbia.*

	Residence requirement			Registration		Where to register
	State	County	Precinct	In person	By mail	
ALABAMA	None	None	10 days[1]	Yes	No	County Board of Registrars
ALASKA	30 days	None	30 days	Yes	Yes	State Election Office, city or borough clerk, or precinct registrar if in person; if by mail: Lieutenant Governor Pouch AA Juneau 99811
ARIZONA	50 days	None	None	Yes	No	County recorder, justice of the peace, or deputy registrar
ARKANSAS	None	None	20 days[1]	Yes	No	Permanent registrar or his deputy
CALIFORNIA	None	None	29 days[1]	Yes	Yes	County clerk or registrar of voters
COLORADO	32 days	None	32 days	Yes	No	County clerk and recorder
CONNECTICUT	None	None	None	Yes	No	Town clerk or registrar of voters
DELAWARE	None	None	None	Yes	Yes	County Department of Elections
DISTRICT OF COLUMBIA	None	None	30 days[1]	Yes	Yes	District Board of Elections, public libraries, or other designated places
FLORIDA	30 days	30 days	None	Yes	No	County supervisor of elections
GEORGIA	None	30 days	30 days	Yes	No	County registrar
HAWAII	None	None	30 days[1]	Yes	No	County clerk (city clerk in Honolulu)
IDAHO	None	5 days[1]	10 days[1]	Yes	No	County clerk

[1] A registration requirement, not a residence requirement.

Chart 34   1198

HOW YOU QUALIFY TO VOTE (continued)

	Residence requirement			Registration		Where to register
	State	County	Precinct	In person	By mail	
ILLINOIS	30 days	30 days	30 days	Yes	No	County clerk or Board of Election Commissioners
INDIANA	None	None	30 days	Yes	No	County clerk or Board of Registration
IOWA	None	None	10 days[1]	Yes	Yes	City or town clerk, commissioner of registration, or mobile registrar
KANSAS	None	None	20 days[1]	Yes	Yes	County clerk or election commissioner
KENTUCKY	30 days	None	30 days	Yes	Yes	County clerk
LOUISIANA	None	None	30 days[1]	Yes	No	Registrar of voters of parish
MAINE	None	None	None	Yes	No	Registrar of voters in towns; Board of Registration in cities
MARYLAND	30 days	None	None	Yes	Yes	Board of Supervisors of Election[2]
MASSACHUSETTS	None	None	None	Yes	No	City or town clerk[3]
MICHIGAN	30 days	30 days	30 days	Yes	No	Township, city, and village clerks
MINNESOTA	20 days	None	None	Yes	Yes	City clerk, county auditor, or at polls election day
MISSISSIPPI	30 days	30 days	30 days	Yes	No	County registrar
MISSOURI	None	None	None	Yes	No	County clerk or Board of Election Commissioners[4]
MONTANA	30 days	30 days	None	Yes	Yes	County clerk and recorder and deputy registrars in each precinct
NEBRASKA	None	None	None	Yes	No	County clerk or election commissioner
NEVADA	30 days	30 days	10 days	Yes	No	County clerk and deputy registrar
NEW HAMPSHIRE	None	None	10 days[1]	Yes	No	Board of Supervisors of Checklist of city or town, city or town clerk
NEW JERSEY	30 days	30 days	29 days[1]	Yes	Yes	County Board of Elections, commissioner of registration, or municipal clerk
NEW MEXICO	None	None	42 days[1]	Yes	No	County clerk

[2] Registration closes on fifth Monday before election.

[3] Registration closes 30 days before election for state and 20 days before election for city.

[4] Registration closes at 5 P.M. on fourth Wednesday before election.

	Residence requirement			Registration		Where to register
	State	County	Precinct	In person	By mail	
NEW YORK	30 days	30 days	10 days[1]	Yes	Yes	County Board of Elections
NORTH CAROLINA	30 days	None	30 days	Yes	No	County Board of Elections or local registrars
NORTH DAKOTA	None	None	30 days	Not required	Not required	———
OHIO	30 days	None	30 days[1]	Yes	Yes	County Elections Board, registrar, or deputy registrar of motor vehicles
OKLAHOMA	None	None	30 days	Yes	No	County Elections Board
OREGON	20 days	None	None	Yes	Yes	County clerk, motor vehicle offices, banks, and post offices
PENNSYLVANIA	30 days	None	30 days	Yes	Yes	County Board of Elections (Registration Division in Philadelphia)
RHODE ISLAND	None	None	30 days[1]	Yes	No	Local Board of Canvassers and Registration
SOUTH CAROLINA	None	None	30 days[1]	Yes	No	County Registration Board
SOUTH DAKOTA	None	None	15 days[1]	Yes	Yes	County or city auditor, town clerk, or municipal finance officer
TENNESSEE	20 days	None	29 days[1]	Yes	Yes	County Election Commission
TEXAS	None	None	None	Yes	Yes	County tax assessor-collector or county clerk
UTAH	30 days	None	10 days[1]	Yes	Yes	County clerk
VERMONT	None	None	None	Yes	Yes	Board of Civil Authority of town or city[5]
VIRGINIA	None	None	30 days[1]	Yes	No	General registrar of county or city
WASHINGTON	None	None	30 days[1]	Yes	No	County auditor or city clerk
WEST VIRGINIA	None	None	30 days[1]	Yes	No	Clerk of county commission
WISCONSIN	None	None	10 days	Yes	Yes	City, town, or village clerk (Board of Election Commissioners in Milwaukee)[6]
WYOMING	None	None	30 days[1]	Yes	No	Registry agent (county or city clerk)

[5] Registration closes at noon on third Saturday before election.

[6] Registration in person closes at 5 P.M. on second Wednesday before election; registration by mail must be postmarked by second Wednesday before election.

INDEX

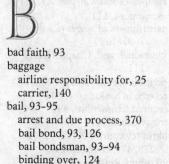

market price or value, 643, 1023

marque and reprisal, 643–644

marriage, 644–649
  abduction for purposes of, 3
  adultery and, 18, 19
  affinity, relationship by marriage, 25
  agreements affecting, 646–648
  alienation of affection, 33
  a mensa et thoro, 36
  annulment, grounds for (Chart 21), 1136–1141
  antenuptial settlement, 46
  bigamy, 123
  breach of marriage promise, 127
  cohabitation, 648
  common-law marriage, 178
  divorce and separation, residence requirements and grounds for (Chart 22), 1142–1149
  engagement ring returned, 183
  equal protection clause, license requirements, 400
  incest and, 42, 542–543, 645, 1130–1135 (Chart 20), 1136–1141 (Chart 21), 1142–1149 (Chart 22)
  income tax exemption, 548, 553
  laws, 645–646, 1130–1135 (Chart 20)
  license, 646
  miscegenation, 396–397, 663
  property ownership and, 774–775
  records (Chart 3), 1081–1089
  requirements for, 645–646
  separation, 893
  voidable marriage, bigamous, 123
  waiting periods between divorce and remarriage (Chart 23), 1150–1151
  ward, end of status, 512
  wills and, 1045, 1047, 1048
  See also annulment; divorce; husband and wife.

marriage of relatives
  as grounds for annulment (Chart 21), 1136–1141
  as grounds for divorce and separation (Chart 22), 1142–1149
  marriage laws (Chart 20), 1130–1135

marriage records
  where records are kept (Chart 3), 1081–1089

marshal, 649, 1020

marshaling assets and securities, 649

martial law, 649
  military law compared with, 661

Martindale-Hubbell Law Directory, 649

Massachusetts rule and risk of loss, 1025

Massachusetts Trust, 134

mass communications   *See* copyright; Federal Communications Commission; Federal Trade Commission; libel and slander; obscenity; speech and press, freedom of.

master, 650

master and servant   *See* employer and employee.

material, 658
  alteration of an instrument (document), 34

material fact, 435, 658

material issue, 435, 658

material witness, 658–659

matter of fact, 659

matter of law, 659

matter of record, 659

maturity, 659

maxim, 659

maximum hours of labor
  state and federal laws, 608, 650, 1176–1181 (Chart 31)

Mayflower Compact, 178

mayhem, 659

McCulloch v. *Maryland*, 659–660

measuring lives, 839–840

mechanic's lien, 635

mediation, 660

Medicaid, 1037–1038

medical attention
  consent by minor, 563
  Good Samaritan acts limiting liability for, 682
  misfeasance and, 682
  necessaries, 681
  parent and child, 707
  patients' rights, 720–722
  prisoners' rights, 749
  seamen, 859
  state laws and, 760–761
  trustee and abuse of discretion, 1013
  unjust enrichment and patient's responsibility, 1020

medical malpractice   *See* malpractice.

medical treatment and residency laws, 825

Medicare, 650, 917–919

medicines, 354

meeting of the minds, 660

membership corporation, 660

memorandum, 660

memorandum decision, 660

memory, refreshing, 805

mental anguish, 660
  See also emotional distress.

mental cruelty, 343–344, 660
  as grounds for divorce and separation (Chart 22), 1142–1149

mercantile agency, 660

merchant
  duty to assist customer, 682
  infliction of emotional distress by, 983
  trading stamps, 994

merchantable, 660
  warranty of merchantability, 766

merger, 416, 660–661
  agreements, 660
  corporate, 660–661
  lease and transfer of landlord's right, 617

merits, 661
  decision on the merits, 313

merit system, 661

mesne, 661

metes and bounds, 661

methadone maintenance program, 361

military law, 661, 1032
  armed services, 55–58
  Uniform Code of Military Justice, 58, 1020

militia, 661–662

mineral rights, 662

mines and minerals, 662
  commerce clause, 168
  flooding in mine by careless neighbor, 985
  mineral rights, 662
  profit à prendre, 773
  property, 774
  trespass, tunnel or mine under another person's property, 997

minimum wage, 650, 658
  minimum wages and maximum hours of labor (Chart 31), 1176–1181
  state and federal laws, 608

ministerial, 662

minor, 662
  abatement of lawsuit and, 2
  abduction of female, 3
  adoption laws (Chart 19), 1127–1129

P

painting, property tax on, 779
pander, 702
panel, 702
paper, 702
  See also commercial paper.
par, 702
paralegal, 702
parcener, 702
pardon, 702–703
  amnesty and, 37
  habeas corpus, 518
  Presidential power, 742
parens patriae, 703
  reformatory and, 805
parental consent for marriage
  marriage laws (Chart 20),
    1130–1135
parental liability laws (Chart 5),
  1092–1093
parent and child, 703–709
  abandonment, 705
  abortion, requirement of consent
    by parent, 5
  adoption, and abandonment of
    children, 15
  adoption laws (Chart 19),
    1127–1129
  adult child, 706
  apprenticeship contract, signature,
    45
  authority of parent, 707–708
  chastity of mother receiving
    welfare aid, 1040–1041
  concealment of birth or death of
    newborn child, 182
  custody of children, 288–294, 705
  duty of parent to assist child, 682
  education, 708
  emancipation, 709
  father's responsibility and welfare
    aid, 1040
  gift to child, delivery
    requirements, 508
  guardianship of child, 512–514
  inheritance of property if owner
    dies without a will (Chart
    16), 1110–1117
  injuries to child, lawsuits
    surviving death of party, 2
  in loco parentis, 567, 709
  intrafamily immunities from tort
    liability, 986–987
  lawsuit brought by parent as
    representative of child, 1000

parent and child (continued)
  liability of parent, 708–709
  medical care, 707–708
  necessaries, 681
  parental authority, 707
  parental liability laws (Chart 5),
    1092–1093
  right to use force in defense of,
    885
  search and seizure, 867
  spendthrift trusts and, 1012
  stepparent, 706, 947
  support, 705–706
  unemployment compensation for
    mother, 1019
  vandalism by child, 1024
  See also adoption of persons;
    illegitimacy.
parent corporation, 709
parish court
  juvenile courts (Chart 2), 1079
parol, 709
  evidence rule, 436
parole, 372, 709–713
  boards, 709–710
  cancellation, 711
  conditions, 710–711
  discharge, 711
  eligibility for, 710
  habeas corpus, 518
  limited protection from search
    and, 864
  proceedings, 710
  review by courts, 710
  revocation, 711–713
  See also probation.
parol evidence, sales and, 843
particulars, 713
partition, 713
partnership, 713–716
  accounting, 714
  acknowledgment of document by
    partner, 8
  affidavit, power of partner to
    make, 25
  architects and nonarchitects, 54
  assignment of interest, 714–715
  books, 713–714
  business trust compared to, 134
  dissolution of, 715–716
  fiduciary character, 714
  income tax, 548, 902–903
  limited partnerships, 716
  relationship of partners, 713–714
  self-incrimination and, 886
  small business, 899–900, 902–903
  third persons and, 715
  trademarks, 990

partnership (continued)
  trustee, partnership may be
    named as, 1009, 1013
party, 716
  abatement of lawsuit, 2
  aggrieved, 28
  amicus curiae, 36
  arbitration, 52–53
  joinder, 590
  lawsuit, 1000
  misjoinder of parties, 664
  prevailing, 744
  third, 971
  unilateral contract, 1020
party wall, 716–717
pass, 717
passenger
  automobile guest statute, 684,
    1164–1165 (Chart 28)
  duty of carrier to assist, 682
passport, 397, 717
patent, 717–720
  lawful monopolies, 664
  license, 634
Patent and Trademark Office, U.S.,
  990
patent medicines, 354
paternity suit, 538–539
  filiation proceedings, 484
patients' rights, 720–722
pawn, 722
pawnbroker, 723
payable, 723
payee, 723
  checks, 114
  fictitious, 116
payment, days of grace and, 307
P.C., 723
peace
  breach of, 129
  unlawful assembly and disturbance
    of the, 1020–1021
peace bond, 723
peace officers, 723
  police, 733–734
  sheriffs and constables, 895
peculation, 723
pederasty, 723
  homosexuals, rights of, 527
penal damages See damages.
penal sanctions, 850
penalty, 723
pendente lite, 723
pendent jurisdiction, 723
penology, 723
pension, 723–728
  employer providing, 650
  estate planning, 426